Dear Reader

The present volume is the 21st edition

G

D0835575

The unb ... *election*

is the resu_ _f ___ __ nquiries
by our inspectors.
In addition we receive considerable help
from our readers' invaluable letters
and comments.

It is our purpose
to provide up-to-date information
and thus render a service to our readers.
The next edition is already in preparation.

Therefore, only the guide of the year
merits your complete confidence,
so please remember to use the latest edition

Bon voyage

Contents

Choosing
a hotel or restaurant

This guide offers a selection of hotels and restaurants to help the motorist on his travels. In each category establishments are listed in order of preference according to the degree of comfort they offer.

CATEGORIES

🏨	Luxury in the traditional style	XXXXX
🏨	Top class comfort	XXXX
🏨	Very comfortable	XXX
🏨	Comfortable	XX
🏨	Quite comfortable	X
↑	Simple comfort	
↑	Other recommended accommodation, at moderate prices	
without rest.	The hotel has no restaurant	
	The restaurant also offers accommodation	with rm

PEACEFUL ATMOSPHERE AND SETTING

Certain establishments are distinguished in the guide by the red symbols shown below.
Your stay in such hotels will be particularly pleasant or restful, owing to the character of the building, its decor, the setting, the welcome and services offered, or simply the peace and quiet to be enjoyed there.

🏨 to ↑	Pleasant hotels
XXXXX to X	Pleasant restaurants
« Park »	Particularly attractive feature
🦢	Very quiet or quiet, secluded hotel
🦢	Quiet hotel
≤ sea	Exceptional view
≤	Interesting or extensive view

The maps located at the beginning of each regional section in the guide indicate places with such peaceful, pleasant hotels and restaurants.

By consulting them before setting out and sending us your comments on your return you can help us with our enquiries.

Hotel facilities

In general the hotels we recommend have full bathroom and toilet facilities in each room. However, this may not be the case for certain rooms in categories 🏨, 🏠, 🏫 and 🏠.

30 rm	Number of rooms
🛗	Lift (elevator)
🗔	Air conditioning
📺	Television in room
🚭	Establishment either partly or wholly reserved for non-smokers
☏	Telephone in room: outside calls connected by the operator
☎	Telephone in room: direct dialling for outside calls
⚹	Rooms accessible to disabled people
🏊 🏊	Outdoor or indoor swimming pool
🏋 🧖	Exercise room – Sauna
🌳	Garden
🎾 ⛳	Hotel tennis court – Golf course and number of holes
🎣	Fishing available to hotel guests. A charge may be made
🏛 150	Equipped conference hall: maximum capacity
🚗	Hotel garage (additional charge in most cases)
🅿	Car park for customers only
🐕‍🦺	Dogs are not allowed in all or part of the hotel
Fax	Telephone document transmission
May-October	Dates when open, as indicated by the hotelier
season	Probably open for the season – precise dates not available Where no date or season is shown, establishments are open all year round
LL35 OSB	Postal code
(Forte)	Hotel Group (See list at end of the Guide)

Animals

It is forbidden to bring domestic animals (dogs, cats...) into Great Britain and Ireland.

Cuisine

Certain establishments deserve to be brought to your attention for the particularly fine quality of their cooking. **Michelin stars** are awarded for the standard of meals served. For each of these restaurants we indicate three culinary specialities typical of their style of cooking to assist you in your choice.

ⓈⓈⓈ | **Exceptional cuisine, worth a special journey**
Superb food, fine wines, faultless service, elegant surroundings. One will pay accordingly !

ⓈⓈ | **Excellent cooking, worth a detour**
Specialities and wines of first class quality. This will be reflected in the price.

Ⓢ | **A very good restaurant in its category**
The star indicates a good place to stop on your journey.
But beware of comparing the star given to an expensive « de luxe » establishment to that of a simple restaurant where you can appreciate fine cooking at a reasonable price.

THE RED « Meals »

Whilst appreciating the quality of the cooking in restaurants with a star, you may, however, wish to find some serving a perhaps less elaborate but nonetheless always carefully prepared meal.
Certain restaurants seem to us to answer this requirement. We bring them to your attention by marking them with a red « Meals » in the text of the Guide.

Please refer to the map of Ⓢ *and* Meals *rated restaurants located at the beginning of each regional section in the guide.*

Alcoholic beverages-conditions of sale

The sale of alcoholic drinks is governed in Great Britain and Ireland by licensing laws which vary greatly from country to country.
Allowing for local variations, restaurants may stay open and serve alcohol with a bona fide meal during the afternoon. Hotel bars and public houses are generally open between 11am and 11pm at the discretion of the licensee. Hotel residents, however, may buy drinks outside the permitted hours at the discretion of the hotelier.
Children under the age of 14 are not allowed in bars.

Prices

Prices quoted are valid for autumn 1993. Changes may arise if goods and service costs are revised.

Your recommendation is self-evident if you always walk into a hotel guide in hand.

Hotels and restaurants in bold type have supplied details of all their rates and have assumed responsibility for maintaining them for all travellers in possession of this guide.

Prices are given in £ sterling, except for the Republic of Ireland (Punts). Where no mention **s., t.,** or **st.** is shown, prices may be subject to the addition of service charge, V.A.T., or both (V.A.T. does not apply in the Channel Islands).

MEALS

M 13.00/24.00	**Set meals** – Lunch 13.00, dinner 24.00 – including cover charge, where applicable
Meals 15.00/25.00	See page 7
s.	Service only included
t.	V.A.T. only included
st.	Service and V.A.T. included
🍷 6.00	Price of 1/2 bottle or carafe of house wine
M a la carte 20.00/25.00	**A la carte meals** – The prices represent the range of charges from a simple to an elaborate 3 course meal and include a cover charge where applicable
🍽 8.50	Charge for full cooked breakfast (i.e. not included in the room rate) Continental breakfast may be available at a lower rate

🏠 : Dinner in this category of establishment will generally be offered from a fixed price menu of limited choice, served at a set time to residents only. Lunch is rarely offered. Many will not be licensed to sell alcohol.

ROOMS

rm 50.00/80.00	Lowest price 50.00 per room for a comfortable single and highest price 80.00 per room for the best double
rm 🍽 55.00/75.00	Full cooked breakfast (whether taken or not) is included in the price of the room

SHORT BREAKS

Many hotels now offer a special rate for a stay of two nights which comprises dinner, room and breakfast usually for a minimum of two people.

SB 70.00/90.00	Prices indicated are lowest and highest per person for two nights.

DEPOSITS – CREDIT CARDS

Some hotels will require a deposit, which confirms the commitment of customer and hotelier alike. Make sure the terms of the agreement are clear.

	Credit cards accepted by the establishment: Access (MasterCard, Eurocard) – American Express – Diners Club – Visa – Japan Card Bank

Towns

✉ York	Postal address
☎ 0225 Bath	STD dialling code (name of exchange indicated only when different from name of the town). Omit 0 when dialling from abroad
401 M 27, ⑩	Michelin map and co-ordinates or fold
West Country G.	See the Michelin Green Guide England : The West Country
pop. 1057	Population
ECD : Wednesday	Early closing day (shops close at midday)
BX **A**	Letters giving the location of a place on the town map
⛳₁₈	Golf course and number of holes (handicap usually required, telephone reservation strongly advised)
⁂, ≼	Panoramic view, viewpoint
✈	Airport
🚗 ✆ 261 1234	Place with a motorail connection; further information from telephone number listed
⛴	Shipping line
⇐	Passenger transport only *see list of companies at the end of the Guide*
🛈	Tourist Information Centre

Standard Time

In winter standard time throughout the British Isles is Greenwich Mean Time (G.M.T.). In summer British clocks are advanced by one hour to give British Summer Time (B.S.T.). The actual dates are announced annually but always occur over weekends in March and October.

Sights

STAR-RATING

★★★	Worth a journey
★★	Worth a detour
★	Interesting
AC	Admission charge

LOCATION

See	Sights in town
Envir.	On the outskirts
Exc.	In the surrounding area
N, S, E, W	The sight lies north, south, east or west of the town
A 22	Take road A 22, indicated by the same symbol on the Guide map
2 m.	Mileage

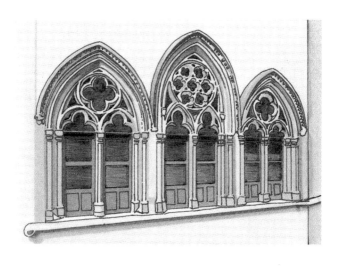

Town plans

ⓐ   **Hotels – Restaurants**

Sights

Place of interest and its main entrance
Interesting place of worship

Roads

Motorway
   Interchanges : complete, limited
Dual carriageway with motorway characteristics
Main traffic artery
Primary route
   (network currently being reclassified)
One-way street – Unsuitable for traffic
Pedestrian street
Piccadilly   Shopping street – Car park
Gateway – Street passing under arch – Tunnel
Low headroom (16'6" max.) on major through routes
Station and railway
Funicular – Cable-car
Lever bridge – Car ferry

Various signs

Tourist information Centre
Mosque – Synagogue
Communications tower or mast – Ruins
Garden, park, wood – Cemetery
Stadium – Racecourse – Golf course
Golf course (with restrictions for visitors)
View – Panorama
Monument – Fountain – Hospital
Pleasure boat harbour – Lighthouse
Airport – Underground station
Ferry services :
   passengers and cars
Main post office with poste restante, telephone
Public buildings located by letter :
C   County Council Offices
H   M   T   Town Hall – Museum – Theatre
U   University, College
POL   Police (in large towns police headquarters)

London

BRENT SOHO   Borough – Area
Borough boundary – Area boundary

Car, tyres

The wearing of seat belts in Great Britain is obligatory for drivers, front seat passengers and rear seat passengers where seat belts are fitted. It is illegal for front seat passengers to carry children on their lap.

In the Republic of Ireland seat belts are compulsory, if fitted, for drivers and front seat passengers. Children under 12 are not allowed in front seats unless in a suitable safety restraint.

CAR MANUFACTURERS AND MICHELIN TYRE SUPPLIERS

A list of the main car manufacturers head offices is contained at the end of the guide.

In the event of a breakdown the location of your nearest dealer can be obtained by calling the telephone number listed between 9am – 5pm.

ATS Tyre dealers

The address of the nearest ATS tyre dealer can be obtained by contacting the address below between 9am and 5pm.

ATS HOUSE   180-188 Northolt Rd.
Harrow,
Middlesex HA2 OED
(081) 423 2000

MOTORING ORGANISATIONS

The major motoring organisations in Great Britain are the Automobile Association and the Royal Automobile Club. Each provides services in varying degrees for non-resident members of affiliated clubs.

AUTOMOBILE ASSOCIATION
Fanum House
BASINGSTOKE, Hants., RG21 2EA
℘ (0256) 20123

ROYAL AUTOMOBILE CLUB
RAC House, Lansdowne Rd.
CROYDON, Surrey CR9 2JA
℘ (081) 686 2525

Ami lecteur

*Le présent volume représente la 21ᵉ édition
du Guide Michelin
Great Britain and Ireland.*

*Réalisée en toute indépendance,
sa sélection d'hôtels et de restaurants
est le fruit des recherches
de ses inspecteurs,
que complètent
vos précieux courriers et commentaires.*

*Soucieux d'actualité et de service,
le Guide prépare déjà sa prochaine édition.*

*Seul le Guide de l'année
mérite ainsi votre confiance.*

Pensez à le renouveler...

Bon voyage avec Michelin

Sommaire

Le choix
d'un hôtel, d'un restaurant

Ce guide vous propose une sélection d'hôtels et restaurants établie à l'usage de l'automobiliste de passage. Les établissements, classés selon leur confort, sont cités par ordre de préférence dans chaque catégorie.

CATÉGORIES

命命命	Grand luxe et tradition	XXXXX
命命	Grand confort	XXXX
命命	Très confortable	XXX
命	De bon confort	XX
命	Assez confortable	X
⌂	Simple mais convenable	
↑	Autre ressource hôtelière conseillée, à prix modérés	
Without rest.	L'hôtel n'a pas de restaurant	
	Le restaurant possède des chambres	with rm

AGRÉMENT ET TRANQUILLITÉ

Certains établissements se distinguent dans le guide par les symboles rouges indiqués ci-après. Le séjour dans ces hôtels se révèle particulièrement agréable ou reposant.
Cela peut tenir d'une part au caractère de l'édifice, au décor original, au site, à l'accueil et aux services qui sont proposés, d'autre part à la tranquillité des lieux.

命命 à ↑	Hôtels agréables
XXXXX à X	Restaurants agréables
« Park »	Élément particulièrement agréable
⑤	Hôtel très tranquille ou isolé et tranquille
⑤	Hôtel tranquille
≤ sea	Vue exceptionnelle
≤	Vue intéressante ou étendue.

Les localités possédant des établissements agréables ou tranquilles sont repérées sur les cartes placées au début de chacune des régions traitées dans ce guide.
Consultez-les pour la préparation de vos voyages et donnez-nous vos appréciations à votre retour, vous faciliterez ainsi nos enquêtes.

L'installation

Les chambres des hôtels que nous recommandons possèdent, en général, des installations sanitaires complètes. Il est toutefois possible que dans les catégories 🏨, 🏠, ☆ et ⌂, certaines chambres en soient dépourvues.

30 ch	Nombre de chambres
🛗	Ascenseur
▤	Air conditionné
TV	Télévision dans la chambre
✗	Établissement entièrement ou en partie réservé aux non-fumeurs
☎	Téléphone dans la chambre relié par standard
☎	Téléphone dans la chambre, direct avec l'extérieur
♿	Chambres accessibles aux handicapés physiques
🏊 🏊	Piscine : de plein air ou couverte
🏋 ⚖s	Salle de remise en forme – Sauna
🌳	Jardin de repos
✂ 🏌	Tennis à l'hôtel – Golf et nombre de trous
🎣	Pêche ouverte aux clients de l'hôtel (éventuellement payant)
🎪 150	Salles de conférences : capacité maximum
🚗	Garage dans l'hôtel (généralement payant)
🅿	Parking réservé à la clientèle
🐕	Accès interdit aux chiens (dans tout ou partie de l'établissement)
Fax	Transmission de documents par télécopie
May-October	Période d'ouverture, communiquée par l'hôtelier
season	Ouverture probable en saison mais dates non précisées. En l'absence de mention, l'établissement est ouvert toute l'année.
LL35 OSB	Code postal de l'établissement
(Forte)	Chaîne hôtelière (voir liste en fin de guide)

Animaux

L'introduction d'animaux domestiques (chiens, chats...) est interdite en Grande-Bretagne et en Irlande.

La table

LES ÉTOILES

Certains établissements méritent d'être signalés à votre attention pour la qualité de leur cuisine. Nous les distinguons par **les étoiles de bonne table.**
Nous indiquons, pour ces établissements, trois spécialités culinaires qui pourront orienter votre choix.

✿✿✿	**Une des meilleures tables, vaut le voyage** Table merveilleuse, grands vins, service impeccable, cadre élégant... Prix en conséquence.
✿✿	**Table excellente, mérite un détour** Spécialités et vins de choix... Attendez-vous à une dépense en rapport.
✿	**Une très bonne table dans sa catégorie** L'étoile marque une bonne étape sur votre itinéraire. Mais ne comparez pas l'étoile d'un établissement de luxe à prix élevés avec celle d'une petite maison où à prix raisonnables, on sert également une cuisine de qualité.

« Meals »

Tout en appréciant les tables à « étoiles », on peut souhaiter trouver sur sa route un repas plus simple mais toujours de préparation soignée. Certaines maisons nous ont paru répondre à cette préoccupation.
Le mot « Meals » rouge les signale à votre attention dans le texte de ce guide.
Consultez les cartes des localités (étoiles de bonne table et Meals) *placées au début de chacune des régions traitées dans ce guide.*

La vente de boissons alcoolisées

En Grande-Bretagne et en Irlande, la vente de boissons alcoolisées est soumise à des lois pouvant varier d'une région à l'autre.
D'une façon générale, les hôtels, les restaurants et les pubs peuvent demeurer ouverts l'après-midi et servir des boissons alcoolisées dans la mesure où elles accompagnent un repas suffisamment consistant. Les bars ferment après 23 heures.
Néanmoins, l'hôtelier a toujours la possibilité de servir, à sa clientèle, des boissons alcoolisées en dehors des heures légales.
Les enfants au-dessous de 14 ans n'ont pas accès aux bars.

Les prix

Les prix que nous indiquons dans ce guide ont été établis en automne 1993. Ils sont susceptibles de modifications, notamment en cas de variations des prix des biens et services.

Entrez à l'hôtel le guide à la main, vous montrerez ainsi qu'il vous conduit là en confiance.

Les prix sont indiqués en livres sterling (1 £ = 100 pence), sauf en République d'Irlande (Punts).

Lorsque les mentions **s.**, **t.**, ou **st.** ne figurent pas, les prix indiqués peuvent être majorés d'un pourcentage pour le service, la T.V.A., ou les deux. (La T.V.A. n'est pas appliquée dans les Channel Islands.)

Les hôtels et restaurants figurent en gros caractères lorsque les hôteliers nous ont donné tous leurs prix et se sont engagés, sous leur propre responsabilité, à les appliquer aux touristes de passage porteurs de notre guide.

REPAS

M 13.00/24.00	**Repas à prix fixe** – Déjeuner 13.00, diner 24.00. Ces prix s'entendent couvert compris
Meals 15.00/25.00	Voir page 17
s.	Service compris
t.	T.V.A. comprise
st.	Service et T.V.A. compris (prix nets)
🍷 6.00	Prix de la 1/2 bouteille ou carafe de vin ordinaire
M à la carte 20.00/25.00	**Repas à la carte** – Le 1er prix correspond à un repas simple mais soigné, comprenant : petite entrée, plat du jour garni, dessert. Le 2e prix concerne un repas plus complet, comprenant : hors-d'œuvre, plat principal, fromage ou dessert. Ces prix s'entendent couvert compris
🍵 8.50	Prix du petit déjeuner à l'anglaise, s'il n'est pas compris dans celui de la chambre. Un petit déjeuner continental peut être obtenu à moindre prix

🏠: Dans les établissements de cette catégorie, le dîner est servi à heure fixe exclusivement aux personnes ayant une chambre. Le menu, à prix unique, offre un choix limité de plats. Le déjeuner est rarement proposé. Beaucoup de ces établissements ne sont pas autorisés à vendre des boissons alcoolisées.

CHAMBRES

rm 50.00/80.00	Prix minimum 50.00 d'une chambre pour une personne et prix maximum 80.00 de la plus belle chambre occupée par deux personnes
rm 🍵 55.00/75.00	Le prix du petit déjeuner à l'anglaise est inclus dans le prix de la chambre, même s'il n'est pas consommé

« SHORT BREAKS »

SB 70.00/90.00 | Prix minimum et maximum par personne pour un séjour de deux nuits en conditions avantageuses ou « Short Break ». Ce forfait comprend la chambre, le dîner et le petit déjeuner, en général pour un minimum de deux personnes.

LES ARRHES – CARTES DE CRÉDIT

Certains hôteliers demandent le versement d'arrhes. Il s'agit d'un dépôt-garantie qui engage l'hôtelier comme le client. Bien faire préciser les dispositions de cette garantie.

🆑 🆎 ⓪ *VISA* JCB | Cartes de crédit acceptées par l'établissement : Access (Eurocard) – American Express – Diners Club – Visa – Japan Card Bank

Les villes

✉ York	Bureau de poste desservant la localité
☎ 0225 Bath	Indicatif téléphonique interurbain suivi, si nécessaire, de la localité de rattachement (De l'étranger, ne pas composer le 0)
🟦401 M 27 ⑩	Numéro des cartes Michelin et carroyage ou numéro du pli
West Country G.	Voir le guide vert Michelin England : The West Country
pop. 1057	Population
ECD : Wednesday	Jour de fermeture des magasins (après-midi seulement)
BX **A**	Lettres repérant un emplacement sur le plan
🏌18	Golf et nombre de trous (Handicap généralement demandé, réservation par téléphone vivement recommandée)
⁂, ≼	Panorama, point de vue
✈	Aéroport
🚗 ℰ 261 1234	Localité desservie par train-auto. Renseignements au numéro de téléphone indiqué
🚢	Transports maritimes
🚤	Transports maritimes (pour passagers seulement) *Voir liste des compagnies en fin de guide*
🛈	Information touristique

Heure légale

Les visiteurs devront tenir compte de l'heure officielle en Grande Bretagne : une heure de retard sur l'heure française.

Les curiosités

INTÉRÊT

★★★	Vaut le voyage
★★	Mérite un détour
★	Intéressant
AC	Entrée payante

SITUATION

See	Dans la ville
Envir.	Aux environs de la ville
Exc.	Excursions dans la région
N, S, E, W	La curiosité est située : au Nord, au Sud, à l'Est, à l'Ouest
A 22	On s'y rend par la route A 22, repérée par le même signe sur le plan du Guide
2 m.	Distance en miles

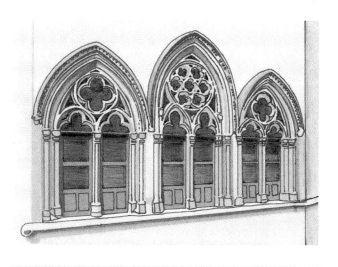

Les plans

@   Hôtels – Restaurants

Curiosités

Bâtiment intéressant et entrée principale
Édifice religieux intéressant

Voirie

Autoroute
    échangeurs : complet, partiel
Route à chaussées séparées de type autoroutier
Grand axe de circulation
Itinéraire principal (Primary route)
    réseau en cours de révision
Sens unique – Rue impraticable
Rue piétonne
Rue commerçante – Parc de stationnement
Porte – Passage sous voûte – Tunnel
Passage bas (inférieur à 16′6″) sur les grandes voies de circulation
Gare et voie ferrée
Funiculaire – Téléphérique, télécabine
Pont mobile – Bac pour autos

Signes divers

Information touristique
Mosquée – Synagogue
Tour ou pylône de télécommunication – Ruines
Jardin, parc, bois – Cimetière
Stade – Hippodrome – Golf
Golf (réservé)
Vue – Panorama
Monument – Fontaine – Hôpital
Port de plaisance – Phare
Aéroport – Station de métro
Transport par bateau :
    passagers et voitures
Bureau principal de poste restante, téléphone
Bâtiment public repéré par une lettre :
    C   Bureau de l'Administration du Comté
H   M   T   Hôtel de ville – Musée – Théâtre
    U   Université, grande école
    POL.   Police (commissariat central)

Londres

BRENT   SOHO   Nom d'arrondissement (borough) – de quartier (area)
Limite de « borough » – d'« area »

La voiture, les pneus

En Grande-Bretagne, le port de la ceinture de sécurité est obligatoire pour le conducteur et le passager avant ainsi qu'à l'arrière, si le véhicule en est équipé. La loi interdit au passager avant de prendre un enfant sur ses genoux.

En République d'Irlande, le port de la ceinture de sécurité est obligatoire pour le conducteur et le passager avant, si le véhicule en est équipé. Les enfants de moins de 12 ans ne sont pas autorisés à s'asseoir à l'avant, sauf si le véhicule est muni d'un système d'attache approprié.

MARQUES AUTOMOBILES ET FOURNISSEURS DE PNEUS MICHELIN

Une liste des principales marques automobiles figure en fin de guide.
En cas de panne, l'adresse du plus proche agent de la marque vous sera communiquée en appelant le numéro de téléphone indiqué, entre 9 h et 17 h.

ATS Spécialistes du pneu

Des renseignements sur le plus proche point de vente de pneus ATS pourront être obtenus en s'informant entre 9 h et 17 h à l'adresse indiquée ci-dessous.

ATS HOUSE   180-188 Northolt Rd.
Harrow,
Middlesex HA2 OED
(081) 423 2000

Dans nos agences, nous nous faisons un plaisir de donner à nos clients tous conseils pour la meilleure utilisation de leurs pneus.

AUTOMOBILE CLUBS

Les principales organisations de secours automobile dans le pays sont l'Automobile Association et le Royal Automobile Club, toutes deux offrant certains de leurs services aux membres de clubs affilés.

AUTOMOBILE ASSOCIATION
Fanum House
BASINGSTOKE, Hants., RG21 2EA
☎ (0256) 20123

ROYAL AUTOMOBILE CLUB
RAC House, Lansdowne Rd,
CROYDON, Surrey CR9 2JA
☎ (081) 686 2525

Amico Lettore

*Questo volume rappresenta
la 21^{esima} edizione
della Guida Michelin
Great Britain and Ireland.*

*La sua selezione di alberghi
e ristoranti, realizzata in assoluta
indipendenza, è il risultato
delle indagini dei suoi ispettori,
che completano
le vostre preziose informazioni
e giudizi.*

*Desiderosa di mantenersi sempre
aggiornata per fornire un buon
servizio, la Guida sta già
preparando la sua prossima edizione.*

*Soltanto la Guida dell'anno
merita perciò la vostra fiducia.
Pensate a rinnovarla...*

Buon viaggio con Michelin

Sommario

La scelta
di un albergo, di un ristorante

Questa guida Vi propone una selezione di alberghi e ristoranti stabilita ad uso dell'automobilista di passaggio. Gli esercizi, classificati in base al confort che offrono, vengono citati in ordine di preferenza per ogni categoria.

CATEGORIE

	Gran lusso e tradizione	XXXXX
	Gran confort	XXXX
	Molto confortevole	XXX
	Di buon confort	XX
	Abbastanza confortevole	X
	Semplice, ma conveniente	
	Altra risorsa, consigliata per prezzi contenuti	
without rest.	L'albergo non ha ristorante	
	Il ristorante dispone di camere	with rm

AMENITÀ E TRANQUILLITÀ

Alcuni esercizi sono evidenziati nella guida dai simboli rossi indicati qui di seguito. Il soggiorno in questi alberghi dovrebbe rivelarsi particolarmente ameno o riposante.
Ciò può dipendere sia dalle caratteristiche dell'edifico, dalle decorazioni non comuni, dalla sua posizione e dal servizio offerto, sia dalla tranquillità dei luoghi.

a	Alberghi ameni
XXXXX a X	Ristoranti ameni
« Park »	Un particolare piacevole
	Albergo molto tranquillo o isolato e tranquillo
	Albergo tranquillo
⩽ sea	Vista eccezionale
⩽	Vista interessante o estesa

Le località che possiedono degli esercizi ameni o tranquilli sono riportate sulle carte che precedono ciascuna delle regioni trattate nella guida.

Consultatele per la preparazione dei Vostri viaggi e, al ritorno, inviateci i Vostri pareri ; in tal modo agevolerete le nostre inchieste.

Installazioni

Le camere degli alberghi che raccomandiamo possiedono, generalmente, delle installazioni sanitarie complete. È possibile tuttavia che nelle categorie 🏨, 🏬, 🛖 e 🏠 alcune camere ne siano sprovviste.

30 rm	Numero di camere
🛗	Ascensore
▤	Aria condizionata
TV	Televisione in camera
⤬	Esercizio riservato completamente o in parte ai non fumatori
☏	Telefono in camera collegato con il centralino
☎	Telefono in camera comunicante direttamente con l'esterno
🕭	Camere di agevole accesso per i minorati fisici
🏊 🏊	Piscina : all'aperto, coperta
🛌 🛋	Palestra – Sauna
🌿	Giardino da riposo
🎾 🏌	Tennis appartenente all'albergo – Golf e numero di buche
🎣	Pesca aperta ai clienti dell' albergo (eventualmente a pagamento)
🛦 150	Sale per conferenze : capienza massima
🚘	Garage nell'albergo (generalmente a pagamento)
Ⓟ	Parcheggio riservato alla clientela
🐕	Accesso vietato ai cani (in tutto o in parte dell'esercizio)
Fax	Trasmissione telefonica di documenti
May-October	Periodo di apertura, comunicato dall'albergatore
season	Probabile apertura in stagione, ma periodo non precisato. Gli esercizi senza tali menzioni sono aperti tutto l'anno.
LL35 OSB	Codice postale dell' esercizio
(Forte)	Catena alberghiera (Vedere la lista alla fine della Guida)

Animali

L'introduzione di animali domestici (cani, gatti...), in Gran Bretagna e in Irlanda, è vietata.

La tavola

Alcuni esercizi meritano di essere segnalati alla Vostra attenzione per la qualità tutta particolare della loro cucina. Noi li evidenziamo con le « **stelle di ottima tavola** ». Per questi ristoranti indichiamo tre specialità culinarie e alcuni vini locali che potranno aiutarVi nella scelta.

✿✿✿	**Una delle migliori tavole, vale il viaggio** Tavola meravigliosa, grandi vini, servizio impeccabile, ambienta-zione accurata... Prezzi conformi.
✿✿	**Tavola eccellente, merita una deviazione** Specialità e vini scelti... AspettateVi una spesa in proporzione.
✿	**Un'ottima tavola nella sua categoria** La stella indica una tappa gastronomica sul Vostro itinerario. Non mettete però a confronto la stella di un esercizio di lusso, dai prezzi elevati, con quella di un piccolo esercizio dove, a prezzi ragionevoli, viene offerta una cucina di qualità.

« Meals »

Pur apprezzando le tavole a « stella », si desidera alle volte consumare un pasto più semplice ma sempre accuratamente preparato.

Alcuni esercizi ci son parsi rispondenti a tale esigenza e sono contraddistinti nella guida con « Meals » in rosso.

Consultate le carte delle località con stelle e con Meals *che precedono ciascuna delle regioni trattate nella guida.*

La vendita di bevande alcoliche

In Gran Bretagna e Irlanda la vendita di bevande alcoliche è soggetta a leggi che possono variare da una regione all'altra. In generale gli alberghi, i ristoranti e i pubs possono restare aperti il pomeriggio e servire bevande alcoliche nella misura in cui queste accompagnano un pasto abbastanza consistente. I bars chiudono dopo le ore 23.00.

L'albergatore ha tuttavia la possibilità di servire alla clientela bevande alcoliche anche oltre le ore legali.

Ai ragazzi inferiori ai 14 anni è vietato l'accesso ai bar.

I prezzi

I prezzi che indichiamo in questa guida sono stati stabiliti nel l'autunno 1993. Potranno pertanto subire delle variazioni in relazione ai cambiamenti dei prezzi di beni e servizi.

Entrate nell'albergo o nel ristorante con la guida alla mano, dimostrando in tal modo la fiducia in chi vi ha indirizzato.

Gli alberghi e i ristoranti vengono menzionati in carattere grassetto quando gli albergatori ci hanno comunicato tutti i loro prezzi e si sono impegnati, sotto la propria responsabilità, ad applicarli ai turisti di passaggio, in possesso della nostra guida.

I prezzi sono indicati in lire sterline (1 £ = 100 pence) ad eccezione per la Repubblica d'Irlanda (Punts).

Quando non figurano le lettere **s.**, **t.**, o **st.** i prezzi indicati possono essere maggiorati per il servizio o per l'I.V.A. o per entrambi. (L'I.V.A. non viene applicata nelle Channel Islands).

PASTI

M 13.00/24.00	**Prezzo fisso** – Pranzo 13.00, cena 24.00. Questi prezzi comprendono il coperto
Meals 15.00/25.00	Vedere p. 27
s.	Servizio compreso
t.	I.V.A. compresa
st.	Servizio ed I.V.A. compresi (prezzi netti)
🍾 6.00	Prezzo della mezza bottiglia o di una caraffa di vino
M a la carte 20.00/25.00	**Alla carta** – Il 1° prezzo corrisponde ad un pasto semplice comprendente : primo piatto, piatto del giorno con contorno, dessert. Il 2° prezzo corrisponde ad un pasto più completo comprendente : antipasto, piatto principale, formaggio e dessert Questi prezzi comprendono il coperto
🍵 8.50	Prezzo della prima colazione inglese se non è compreso nel prezzo della camera. Una prima colazione continentale può essere ottenuta a minor prezzo

↑ : Negli alberghi di questa categoria, la cena viene servita, ad un'ora stabilita, esclusivamente a chi vi alloggia. Il menu, a prezzo fisso, offre una scelta limitata di piatti. Raramente viene servito anche il pranzo. Molti di questi esercizi non hanno l'autorizzazione a vendere alcolici.

CAMERE

rm 50.00/80.00	Prezzo minimo 50.00 per una camera singola e prezzo massimo 80.00 per la camera più bella per due persone
rm 🍵 55.00/75.00	Il prezzo della prima colazione inglese è compreso nel prezzo della camera anche se non viene consumata

SB 70.00/90.00 | Prezzo minimo e massimo per persona per un soggiorno di due notti a condizioni vantaggiose o « Short Break ». Questo forfait comprende la camera, la cena e la colazione del mattino generalmente per un minimo di due persone.

LA CAPARRA – CARTE DI CREDITO

Alcuni albergatori chiedono il versamento di una caparra. Si tratta di un deposito-garanzia che impegna tanto l'albergatore che il cliente. Vi raccomandiamo di farVi precisare le norme riguardanti la reciproca garanzia di tale caparra.

🂠 AE Ⓞ VISA JCB | Carte di credito accettate dall'esercizio Access (Eurocard) – American Express – Diners Club – Visa – Japan Card Bank

Le città

✉ York	Sede dell'ufficio postale
☎ 0225 Bath	Prefisso telefonico interurbano (nome del centralino indicato solo quando differisce dal nome della località). Dall'estero non formare lo 0
401 M 27 ⑩	Numero della carta Michelin e del riquadro o numero della piega
West Country G.	Vedere la Guida Verde Michelin England : The West Country
pop. 1057	Popolazione
ECD : Wednesday	Giorno di chiusura settimanale dei negozi (solo pomeriggio)
BX **A**	Lettere indicanti l'ubicazione sulla pianta
⛳18	Golf e numero di buche (handicap generalmente richiesto, prenotazione telefonica vivamente consigliata)
❊, ≤	Panorama, punto di vista
✈	Aeroporto
🚗 ☎ 261 1234	Località con servizio auto su treno. Informarsi al numero di telefono indicato
⛴	Trasporti marittimi
⛴	Trasporti marittimi (solo passeggeri) *Vedere la lista delle compagnie alla fine della Guida*
🛈	Ufficio informazioni turistiche

Ora legale

I visitatori dovranno tenere in considerazione l'ora ufficiale in Gran Bretagna : un'ora di ritardo sull'ora italiana.

Le curiosità

GRADO DI INTERESSE

★★★	Vale il viaggio
★★	Merita una deviazione
★	Interessante
AC	Entrata a pagamento

UBICAZIONE

See	Nella città
Envir.	Nei dintorni della città
Exc.	Nella regione
N, S, E, W	La curiosità è situata : a Nord, a Sud, a Est, a Ovest
A 22	Ci si va per la strada A 22 indicata con lo stesso segno sulla pianta
2 m.	Distanza in miglia

Le piante

@   **Alberghi – Ristoranti**

Curiosità

Edificio interessante ed entrata principale
Costruzione religiosa interessante

Viabilità

Autostrada
   svincoli : completo, parziale,
Strada a carreggiate separate di tipo autostradale
Asse principale di circolazione
Itinerario principale
   (« Primary route », rete stradale in corso di revisione)
Senso unico – Via impraticabile
Via pedonale
Via commerciale – Parcheggio
Porta – Sottopassaggio – Galleria
Sottopassaggio (altezza inferiore a 16′6″) sulle grandi
vie di circolazione
Stazione e ferrovia
Funicolare – Funivia, Cabinovia
Ponte mobile – Battello per auto

Simboli vari

Ufficio informazioni turistiche
Moschea – Sinagoga
Torre o pilone per telecomunicazioni – Ruderi
Giardino, parco, bosco – Cimitero
Stadio – Ippodromo – Golf
Golf riservato
Vista – Panorama
Monumento – Fontana – Ospedale
Porto per imbarcazioni da diporto – Faro
Aeroporto – Stazione della Metropolitana
Trasporto con traghetto :
   passeggeri ed autovetture
Ufficio centrale di fermo posta, telefono
Edificio pubblico indicato con lettera :
   Sede dell'Amministrazione di Contea
   Municipio – Museo – Teatro
   Università, grande scuola
   Polizia (Questura, nelle grandi città)

C

H M T

U

POL.

Londra

BRENT   SOHO   Nome del distretto amministrativo (borough) –
del quartiere (area)
Limite del « borough » – di « area »

L'automobile, I pneumatici

In Gran Bretagna, l'uso delle cinture di sicurezza è obbligatorio per il conducente e il passeggero del sedile anteriore, nonchè per i sedili posteriori, se ne sono equipaggiati. La legge non consente al passaggero d'avanti di tenere un bambino sulle ginocchia.

Nella Repubblica d'Irlanda, l'uso delle cinture di sicurezza è obligatorio per il conducente e il passeggero d'avanti, se il veicolo ne è equipaggiato. I bambini di meno di 12 anni non sono autorizzati a viaggiare sul sedile anteriore, a meno che questo non sia fornito di un sistema di ritenuta espressamente concepito per loro.

MARCHE AUTOMOBILISTICHE, RIVENDITORI DI PNEUMATICI MICHELIN

L'elenco delle principali case automobilistiche si trova alla fine della guida.
In caso di necessità l'indirizzo della più vicina officina autorizzata, vi sarà communicato chiamando, dalle 9 alle 17, il numero telefonico indicato.

ATS Specialista in pneumatici

Potrete avere delle informazioni sul più vicino punto vendita di pneumatici ATS, rivolgendovi, tra le 9 e le 17, all'indirizzo indicato qui di seguito :

ATS HOUSE	180-188 Northolt Rd.
	Harrow,
	Middlesex HA2 OED
	(081) 423 2000

Le nostre Succursali sono in grado di dare ai nostri clienti tutti i consigli relativi alla migliore utilizzazione dei pneumatici.

AUTOMOBILE CLUBS

Le principali organizzazioni di soccorso automobilistico sono l'Automobile Association ed il Royal Automobile Club : entrambe offrono alcuni loro servizi ai membri dei club affiliati.

AUTOMOBILE ASSOCIATION
Fanum House
BASINGSTOKE, Hants., RG21 2EA
℘ (0256) 20123

ROYAL AUTOMOBILE CLUB
RAC House, Lansdowne Rd,
CROYDON, Surrey CR9 2JA
℘ (081) 686 2525

Lieber Leser

Der Rote Michelin-Führer
Great Britain and Ireland
liegt nun schon in der 21. Ausgabe vor.
Er bringt eine
in voller Unabhängigkeit getroffene,
bewußt begrenzte Auswahl
an Hotels und Restaurants.
Sie basiert auf den regelmäßigen
Überprüfungen durch unsere Inspektoren,
komplettiert durch die zahlreichen
Zuschriften und Erfahrungsberichte
unserer Leser.

Wir sind stets um die Aktualität
unserer Informationen bemüht
und bereiten schon jetzt
den Führer des nächsten Jahres vor.
Nur die neueste Ausgabe
ist wirklich zuverlässig –
denken Sie bitte daran,
wenn der nächste
Rote Michelin-Führer erscheint.

Gute Reise mit Michelin !

Inhaltsverzeichnis

Wahl
eines Hotels, eines Restaurants

Die Auswahl der in diesem Führer aufgeführten Hotels und Restaurants ist für Durchreisende gedacht. In jeder Kategorie drückt die Reihenfolge der Betriebe (sie sind nach ihrem Komfort klassifiziert) eine weitere Rangordnung aus.

KATEGORIEN

🏰	Großer Luxus und Tradition	XXXXX
🏨	Großer Komfort	XXXX
🏨	Sehr komfortabel	XXX
🏨	Mit gutem Komfort	XX
🏛	Mit ausreichendem Komfort	X
⚘	Bürgerlich	
⌂	Preiswerte, empfehlenswerte Gasthäuser und Pensionen	
without rest.	Hotel ohne Restaurant	
	Restaurant vermietet auch Zimmer	with rm

ANNEHMLICHKEITEN

Manche Häuser sind im Führer durch rote Symbole gekennzeichnet (s. unten). Der Aufenthalt in diesen Hotels ist wegen der schönen, ruhigen Lage, der nicht alltäglichen Einrichtung und Atmosphäre und dem gebotenen Service besonders angenehm und erholsam.

🏰 bis ⌂	Angenehme Hotels
XXXXX bis X	Angenehme Restaurants
« Park »	Besondere Annehmlichkeit
🦢	Sehr ruhiges, oder abgelegenes und ruhiges Hotel
🦢	Ruhiges Hotel
⩽ sea	Reizvolle Aussicht
⩽	Interessante oder weite Sicht

Die den einzelnen Regionen vorangestellten Übersichtskarten, auf denen die Orte mit besonders angenehmen oder ruhigen Häusern eingezeichnet sind, helfen Ihnen bei der Reisevorbereitung. Teilen Sie uns bitte nach der Reise Ihre Erfahrungen und Meinungen mit. Sie helfen uns damit, den Führer weiter zu verbessern.

Einrichtung

Die meisten der empfohlenen Hotels verfügen über Zimmer, die alle oder doch zum größten Teil mit einer Naßzelle ausgestattet sind. In den Häusern der Kategorien 🏨, 🏠, ☆ und ⌂ kann diese jedoch in einigen Zimmern fehlen.

30 rm	Anzahl der Zimmer
⇕	Fahrstuhl
▤	Klimaanlage
TV	Fernsehen im Zimmer
⤬	Hotel ganz oder teilweise reserviert für Nichtraucher
☏	Zimmertelefon mit Außenverbindung über Telefonzentrale
☎	Zimmertelefon mit direkter Außenverbindung
&	Für Körperbehinderte leicht zugängliche Zimmer
⚓ 🏊	Freibad, Hallenbad
⚐ ⬚	Fitneßcenter – Sauna
🛋	Liegewiese, Garten
✖ 🏌	Hoteleigener Tennisplatz – Golfplatz und Lochzahl
⚲	Angelmöglichkeit für Hotelgäste, evtl. gegen Gebühr
🅰 150	Konferenzräume : Höchstkapazität
🚗	Hotelgarage (wird gewöhnlich berechnet)
℗	Parkplatz reserviert für Gäste
🐕	Hunde sind unerwünscht (im ganzen Haus bzw. in den Zimmern oder im Restaurant)
Fax	Telefonische Dokumentenübermittlung
May-October	Öffnungszeit, vom Hotelier mitgeteilt
season	Unbestimmte Öffnungszeit eines Saisonhotels. Die Häuser, für die wir keine Schließungszeiten angeben, sind im allgemeinen ganzjährig geöffnet
LL35 OSB	Angabe des Postbezirks (hinter der Hoteladresse)
(Forte)	Hotelkette (Liste am Ende des Führers)

Tiere

Das Mitführen von Haustieren (Hunde, Katzen u. dgl.) bei der Einreise in Großbritannien und Irland ist untersagt.

Küche

DIE STERNE

Einige Häuser verdienen wegen ihrer überdurchschnittlich guten Küche Ihre besondere Beachtung. Auf diese Häuser weisen die Sterne hin.

Bei den mit « **Stern** » ausgezeichneten Betrieben nennen wir drei kulinarische Spezialitäten, die Sie probieren sollten.

❀❀❀ | **Eine der besten Küchen : eine Reise wert**
Ein denkwürdiges Essen, edle Weine, tadelloser Service, gepflegte Atmosphäre ... entsprechende Preise.

❀❀ | **Eine hervorragende Küche : verdient einen Umweg**
Ausgesuchte Menus und Weine ... angemessene Preise.

❀ | **Eine sehr gute Küche : verdient Ihre besondere Beachtung**
Der Stern bedeutet eine angenehme Unterbrechung Ihrer Reise. Vergleichen Sie aber bitte nicht den Stern eines sehr teuren Luxusrestaurants mit dem Stern eines kleineren oder mittleren Hauses, wo man Ihnen zu einem annehmbaren Preis eine ebenfalls vorzügliche Mahlzeit reicht.

« Meals »

Wir glauben, daß Sie neben den Häusen mit « Stern » auch solche Adressen interessieren werden, die einfache, aber sorgfältig zubereitete Mahlzeiten anbieten.

« Meals » im Text weist auf solche Haüser hin.

Siehe Karten der Orte mit « Stern » und « Meals », die den einzelnen im Führer behandelten Regionen vorangestellt sind.

Ausschank alkoholischer Getränke

In Großbritannien und Irland unterliegt der Ausschank alkoholischer Getränke gesetzlichen Bestimmungen, die in den einzelnen Gegenden verschieden sind.

Generell können Hotels, Restaurants und Pubs nachmittags geöffnet sein und alkoholische Getränke ausschenken, wenn diese zu einer entsprechend gehaltvollen Mahlzeit genossen werden. Die Bars schließen nach 23 Uhr.

Hotelgästen können alkoholische Getränke jedoch auch außerhalb der Ausschankzeiten serviert werden.

Kindern unter 14 Jahren ist der Zutritt zu den Bars untersagt.

Preise

Die in diesem Führer genannten Preise wurden uns im Herbst 1993 angegeben. Sie können sich mit den Preisen von Waren und Dienstleistungen ändern.

Halten Sie beim Betreten des Hotels den Führer in der Hand. Sie zeigen damit, daß Sie aufgrund dieser Empfehlung gekommen sind.

Die Preise sind in Pfund Sterling angegeben (1 £ = 100 pence) mit Ausnahme der Republik Irland (Punts).

Wenn die Buchstaben **s., t.**, oder **st.** nicht hinter den angegebenen Preisen aufgeführt sind, können sich diese um den Zuschlag für Bedienung und/oder MWSt erhöhen (keine MWSt auf den Channel Islands).

Die Namen der Hotels und Restaurants, die ihre Preise genannt haben, sind fett gedruckt. Gleichzeitig haben sich diese Häuser verpflichtet, die von den Hoteliers selbst angegebenen Preise den Benutzern des Michelin-Führers zu berechnen.

MAHLZEITEN

M 13.00/24.00	**Feste Menupreise** – Mittagessen 13.00, Abendessen 24.00 (inkl. Couvert)
Meals 15.00/25.00	Siehe Seite 37
s.	Bedienung inkl.
t.	MWSt inkl.
st.	Bedienung und MWSt inkl.
⌻ 6.00	Preis für 1/2 Flasche oder eine Karaffe Tafelwein
M a la carte 20.00/25.00	**Mahlzeiten « à la carte »** – Der erste Preis entspricht einer einfachen aber sorgfältig zubereiteten Mahlzeit, bestehend aus kleiner Vorspeise, Tagesgericht mit Beilage und Nachtisch. Der zweite Preis entspricht einer reichlicheren Mahlzeit mit Vorspeise, Hauptgericht, Käse oder Nachtisch (inkl. Couvert)
⌸ 8.50	Preis des englischen Frühstücks, wenn dieser nicht im Übernachtungspreis enthalten ist. Einfaches, billigeres Frühstück (Continental breakfast) erhältlich

↑ : In dieser Hotelkategorie wird ein Abendessen normalerweise nur zu bestimmten Zeiten für Hotelgäste angeboten. Es besteht aus einem Menu mit begrenzter Auswahl zu festgesetztem Preis. Mittagessen wird selten angeboten. Viele dieser Hotels sind nicht berechtigt, alkoholische Getränke auszuschenken.

ZIMMER

rm 50.00/80.00	Mindestpreis 50.00 für ein Einzelzimmer und Höchstpreis 80.00 für das schönste Doppelzimmer
rm ⌸ 55.00/75.00	Übernachtung mit englischem Frühstück, selbst wenn dieses nicht eingenommen wird

« SHORT BREAKS »

SB 70.00/90.00 | Mindest- und Höchstpreis pro Person bei einem Aufenthalt von 2 Nächten (« Short Break »). Diese Pauschalpreise (für mindestens 2 Personen) umfassen Zimmer, Abendessen und Frühstück.

ANZAHLUNG – KREDITKARTEN

Einige Hoteliers verlangen eine Anzahlung. Diese ist als Garantie sowohl für den Hotelier als auch für den Gast anzusehen.

🔲 AE ⓪ VISA JCB | Vom Haus akzeptierte Kreditkarten :
Access (Eurocard) – American Express – Diners Club – Visa (Carte Bleue) – Japan Card Bank

Städte

⊠ York | Zuständiges Postamt
✆ 0225 Bath | Vorwahlnummer und evtl. zuständiges Fernsprechamt (bei Gesprächen vom Ausland aus wird die erste Null weggelassen)
401 M 27 ⑩ | Nummer der Michelin-Karte und Koordinaten des Planfeldes oder Faltseite
West Country G. | Siehe auch den grünen Michelinführer « England : The West Country »
pop. 1057 | Einwohnerzahl
ECD : Wednesday | Tag, an dem die Läden nachmittags geschlossen sind
BX **A** | Markierung auf dem Stadtplan
🏌18 | Öffentlicher Golfplatz und Lochzahl (Handicap erforderlich, telefonische Reservierung empfehlenswert)
✳, ≼ | Rundblick, Aussichtspunkt
✈ | Flughafen
🚗 ✆ 261 1234 | Ladestelle für Autoreisezüge – Nähere Auskünfte unter der angegebenen Telefonnummer
⛴ | Autofähre
⛴ | Personenfähre
Liste der Schiffahrtsgesellschaften am Ende des Führers
🛈 | Informationsstelle

Uhrzeit

In Großbritannien ist eine Zeitverschiebung zu beachten und die Uhr gegenüber der deutschen Zeit um 1 Stunde zurückzustellen.

Sehenswürdigkeiten

BEWERTUNG

★★★	Eine Reise wert
★★	Verdient einen Umweg
★	Sehenswert
AC	Eintritt (gegen Gebühr)

LAGE

See	In der Stadt
Envir.	In der Umgebung der Stadt
Exc.	Ausflugsziele
N, S, E, W	Im Norden (N), Süden (S), Osten (E), Westen (W) der Stadt
A 22	Zu erreichen über die Straße A 22
2 m.	Entfernung in Meilen

Stadtpläne

◎　　**Hotels – Restaurants**

Sehenswürdigkeiten
Sehenswertes Gebäude mit Haupteingang
Sehenswerter Sakralbau

Straßen
M 1 Autobahn
　　Anschlußstellen : Autobahneinfahrt und/oder-ausfahrt,
Schnellstraße mit getrennten Fahrbahnen
Hauptverkehrsstraße
A 2 Fernverkehrsstraße (Primary route)
　　Netz wird z.z. neu eingestuft
Einbahnstraße – nicht befahrbare Straße
Fußgängerzone
Piccadilly P Einkaufsstraße – Parkplatz
Tor – Passage – Tunnel
15.6 Unterführung (Höhe angegeben bis 16′6″) auf
Hauptverkehrsstraßen
Bahnhof und Bahnlinie
Standseilbahn – Seilschwebebahn
B Bewegliche Brücke – Autofähre

Sonstige Zeichen
Informationsstelle
Moschee – Synagoge
Funk-, Fernsehturm – Ruine
Garten, Park, Wäldchen – Friedhof
Stadion – Pferderennbahn – Golfplatz
Golfplatz (Zutritt bedingt erlaubt)
Aussicht – Rundblick
Denkmal – Brunnen – Krankenhaus
Jachthafen – Leuchtturm
Flughafen – U-Bahnstation
Schiffsverbindungen :
　　Autofähre
Hauptpostamt (postlagernde Sendungen), Telefon
Öffentliches Gebäude, durch einen Buchstaben
gekennzeichnet :
C　　　　Sitz der Grafschaftsverwaltung
H M T Rathaus – Museum – Theater
U　　　　Universität, Hochschule
POL.　　Polizei (in größeren Städten Polizeipräsidium)

London
BRENT SOHO Name des Verwaltungsbezirks (borough) – des Stadtteils
(area)
Grenze des « borough » – des « area »

Das Auto, die Reifen

In Großbritannien herrscht Anschnallpflicht für Fahrer, Beifahrer und auf dem Rücksitz, wenn Gurte vorhanden sind. Es ist verboten, Kinder auf den Vordersitzen auf dem Schoß zu befördern. In Irland besteht für den Fahrer und den Beifahrer Anschnallpflicht, wenn Gurte vorhanden sind. Kinder unter 12 Jahren dürfen allerdings nicht auf den Vordersitzen befördert werden, es sei denn es existiert ein entsprechender Kindersitz.

AUTOMOBILFIRMEN
LIEFERANTEN VON MICHELIN-REIFEN

Eine Liste der wichtigsten Automobilhersteller finden Sie am Ende des Führers.
Im Pannenfall erfahren Sie zwischen 9^{00} und 17^{00} die Adresse der nächstgelegenen Vertrags werkstatt, wenn Sie die angegebene Rufnummer wählen.

ATS Reifenhändler

Die Anschrift der nächstgelegenen ATS-Verkaufsstelle erhalten Sie auf Anfrage (9-17 Uhr) bei

ATS HOUSE 180-188 Northolt Rd.
Harrow,
Middlesex HA2 OED
(081) 423 2000

AUTOMOBILCLUBS

Die wichtigsten Automobilclubs des Landes sind die Automobile Association und der Royal Automobile Club, die den Mitgliedern der der FIA angeschlossenen Automobilclubs Pannenhilfe leisten und einige ihrer Dienstleistungen anbieten.

AUTOMOBILE ASSOCIATION
Fanum House
BASINGSTOKE, Hants., RG21 2EA
℘ (0256) 20123

ROYAL AUTOMOBILE CLUB
RAC House, Lansdowne Rd
CROYDON, Surrey CR9 2JA
℘ (081) 686 2525

County abbreviations
Abréviations des comtés
Abbreviazioni delle contee
Abkürzungen der Grafschaften

England

Avon .... Avon	Kent .... Kent
Bedfordshire .... Beds.	Lancashire .... Lancs.
Berkshire .... Berks.	Leicestershire .... Leics.
Buckinghamshire .... Bucks.	Lincolnshire .... Lincs.
Cambridgeshire .... Cambs.	Merseyside .... Mersey.
Cheshire .... Ches.	Norfolk .... Norfolk
Cleveland .... Cleveland	Northamptonshire .... Northants.
Cornwall .... Cornwall	Northumberland .... Northd
Cumbria .... Cumbria	North Yorkshire .... N. Yorks.
Derbyshire .... Derbs.	Nottinghamshire .... Notts.
Devon .... Devon	Oxfordshire .... Oxon.
Dorset .... Dorset	Shropshire .... Shrops.
Durham .... Durham	Somerset .... Somerset
East Sussex .... E. Sussex	South Yorkshire .... S. Yorks.
Essex .... Essex	Staffordshire .... Staffs.
Gloucestershire .... Glos.	Suffolk .... Suffolk
Greater Manchester Gtr. Manchester	Surrey .... Surrey
Hampshire .... Hants.	Tyne and Wear ...... Tyne and Wear
Hereford	Warwickshire .... Warks.
and Worcester ... Heref. & Worcs.	West Midlands .... W. Mids.
Hertfordshire .... Herts.	West Sussex .... W. Sussex
Humberside .... Humbs.	West Yorkshire .... W. Yorks.
Isle of Wight .... I.O.W.	Wiltshire .... Wilts.

Wales

Clwyd .... Clwyd	Mid Glamorgan .... M. Glam.
Dyfed .... Dyfed	Powys .... Powys
Gwent .... Gwent	South Glamorgan .... S. Glam.
Gwynedd .... Gwynedd	West Glamorgan .... W. Glam.

Starred establishments
Les établissements à étoiles
Gli esercizi con stelle
Die Stern-Restaurants

England

Bray-on-Thames	Waterside Inn
London	La Tante Claire

England

Bristol	Lettonie
London	Le Gavroche
–	Chez Nico at Ninety Park Lane
	(at Grosvenor House H.)
–	The Restaurant (at Hyde Park H.)

Longridge	Paul Heathcote's
Oxford	Le Manoir aux Quat' Saisons
Reading	L'Ortolan

Scotland

Ullapool	Altnaharrie Inn

England

Baslow	Fischer's at Baslow Hall
Bath	Lucknam Park
Bourton-on-the-Water	Lords of the Manor
Bradford	Restaurant Nineteen
Bristol	Harvey's
Broadway	Buckland Manor
Chagford	Gidleigh Park
Cheltenham	Epicurean
Chester	Arkle
	(at Chester Grosvenor H.)
Earl Stonham	Mr. Underhill's
Faversham	Read's
Grantham	Harry's Place
Great Malvern	Croque-en-Bouche
London	The Canteen
–	Capital
–	Connaught
–	Four Seasons (at Four Seasons H.)
–	Grill Room at the Café Royal
–	Leith's
–	Oak Room (at Le Meridien London H.)
–	Oriental (at Dorchester H.)
–	Pied à Terre
–	Les Saveurs
–	The Square
–	Suntory
Newcastle upon Tyne	21 Queen St.
Oakham	Hambleton Hall
Plymouth	Chez Nous
Pool in Wharfedale	Pool Court
Royal Leamington Spa	Mallory Court

Storrington	Manley's
Stroud	Oakes
Taplow	Waldo's (at Cliveden)
Taunton	Castle
Tetbury	Calcot Manor
Truro	Pennypots
Waterhouses	Old Beams
Winteringham	Winteringham Fields

Wales

Pwllheli	Plas Bodegroes

Scotland

Aberfoyle	Braeval Old Mill
Dunkeld	Kinnaird
Fort William	Inverlochy Castle
Gullane	La Potinière
Port Appin	Airds
Portpatrick	Knockinaam Lodge

Northern Ireland

Belfast	Roscoff

Channel Islands

St. Saviour (Jersey)	Longueville Manor

Republic of Ireland

Dublin	The Commons
–	Patrick Guilbaud
Kenmare	Park
–	Sheen Falls Lodge
Straffan	Byerley Turk
	(at Kildare H. & Country Club)

Autres tables qui méritent votre attention
Altre tavole particolarmente interessanti
Weitere empfehlenswerte Häuser

Meals

England

Barnsley	Peano
Blackpool	River House
Brimfield	Poppies
Brockenhurst	Le Poussin
Calstock	Danescombe Valley
Dorking	Partners West Street
Drewsteignton	Hunts Tor House
Eastbourne	Hungry Monk
Fowey	Food for Thought
Frampton-on-Severn	Savery's
Goring	Leatheme Bottel
Hastings	Röser's
King's Lynn	Congham Hall
Leeds	Leodis Brasserie
Liskeard	Well House
London	Alastair Little
–	Al Bustan
–	Bibendum
–	Bistrot Bruno
–	Le Caprice
–	Chutney Mary
–	Clarke's
–	Fifth Floor (at Harvey Nichols)
–	Greenhouse
–	Hilaire
–	Kensington Place
–	Malabar
–	Nico Central
–	Percy's
–	Pont de la Tour
–	Quaglino's
–	Simply Nico
–	Zen Central
Maiden Newton	Le Petit Canard
Midhurst	Angel
Milford-on-Sea	Rocher's
Moulsford	Beetle & Wedge
Newcastle upon Tyne	Horton Grange
Old Burghclere	Dew Pond
Padstow	Seafood
Pateley Bridge	Dusty Miller

Portsmouth	Bistro Montparnasse
Royal Tunbridge Wells	Cheevers
Rushlake Green	Stone House
Salisbury	Howard's House
Storrington	Old Forge
Torquay	Table
Totnes	Floyd's Inn (sometimes)
Towcester	Vine House
Ullswater	Sharrow Bay Country House
Wiveliscombe	Langley House
Worcester	Brown's

Wales

Llansanffraid Glan Conwy	Old Rectory

Scotland

Achiltibuie	Summer Isles
Gullane	Greywalls
Kingussie	The Cross
Mull (Isle of)	Tiroran House
Newtonmore	Ard-na-Coille

Northern Ireland

Portrush	Ramore

Channel Islands

Gorey (Jersey)	Jersey Pottery (Garden Rest.)

Republic of Ireland

Adare	Mustard Seed
Ahakista	Shiro
Bunratty	MacCloskey's
Castlebaldwin	Cromleach Lodge
Cork	Cliffords
Dingle	Doyle's Seafood Bar
Dublin	Clarets
–	Ernie's
Gorey	Marlefield House
Moycullen	Drimcong House
Shanagarry	Ballymaloe House

England

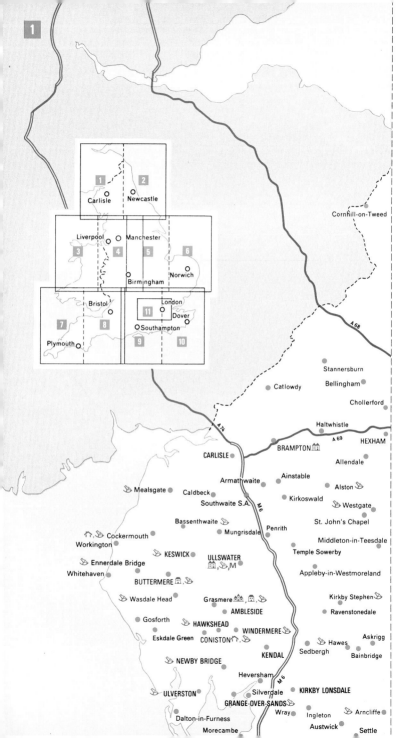

1

Carlisle
Newcastle

1 **2**

Liverpool
Manchester

3 **4** **5** **6**

Birmingham
Norwich

Bristol

London
Dover

11

7 **8**
Southampton

9 **10**

Plymouth

Cornhill-on-Tweed

Stannersburn
Catlowdy
Bellingham
Chollerford
Haltwhistle
A 69
HEXHAM
BRAMPTON
Allendale
CARLISLE
Ainstable
Armathwaite
Alston
Mealsgate
Caldbeck
Kirkoswald
A 74
Southwaite S.A.
Westgate
Bassenthwaite
St. John's Chapel
Cockermouth
Mungrisdale
Penrith
Middleton-in-Teesdale
Workington
KESWICK
Temple Sowerby
Ennerdale Bridge
ULLSWATER
Whitehaven
Appleby-in-Westmoreland
BUTTERMERE
Wasdale Head
Grasmere
Kirkby Stephen
Gosforth
AMBLESIDE
Ravenstonedale
HAWKSHEAD
Eskdale Green
WINDERMERE
CONISTON
Askrigg
Hawes
NEWBY BRIDGE
KENDAL
Sedbergh
Bainbridge
Heversham
ULVERSTON
Silverdale
KIRKBY LONSDALE
GRANGE-OVER-SANDS
Dalton-in-Furness
Wray
Arncliffe
Ingleton
Morecambe
Austwick
Settle
M 6
A 68

Place with at least :

one hotel or restaurant .... ● Ripon
a pleasant hotel or restaurant .... 🏰🏰🏰, 🏠, ✗
one quiet, secluded hotel .... ॐ
one restaurant with .... ⚑, ⚑⚑, ⚑⚑⚑, Meals (M)
See this town for establishments
  located in its vicinity .... LEICESTER

Localité offrant au moins :

une ressource hôtelière .... ● Ripon
un hôtel ou restaurant agréable .... 🏰🏰🏰, 🏠, ✗
un hôtel très tranquille, isolé .... ॐ
une bonne table à .... ⚑, ⚑⚑, ⚑⚑⚑, Meals (M)
Localité groupant dans le texte
  les ressources de ses environs .... LEICESTER

La località possiede come minimo :

una risorsa alberghiera .... ● Ripon
Albergo o ristorante ameno .... 🏰🏰🏰, 🏠, ✗
un albergo molto tranquillo, isolato .... ॐ
un'ottima tavola con .... ⚑, ⚑⚑, ⚑⚑⚑, Meals (M)
La località raggruppa nel suo testo
  le risorse dei dintorni .... LEICESTER

Ort mit mindestens :

einem Hotel oder Restaurant .... ● Ripon
ein angenehmes Hotel oder Restaurant .... 🏰🏰🏰, 🏠, ✗
einem sehr ruhigen und abgelegenen Hotel .... ॐ
einem Restaurant mit .... ⚑, ⚑⚑, ⚑⚑⚑, Meals (M)
Ort mit Angaben über Hotels und Restaurants
  in seiner Umgebung .... LEICESTER

Berwick-upon-Tweed

Belford
BAMBURGH
Seahouses

Powburn ॐ
ALNWICK
Alnmouth

Rothbury

Kirkwhelpington
Ashington
Morpeth
A 696
Whitley Bay
Tynemouth
Corbridge
Wylam
❀NEWCASTLE-UPON-TYNE GATESHEAD South Shields
M ✗✗ with rm.
Ebchester
Burnopfield
Sunderland
Carterway Heads
Washington
Blanchland
Chester-le-Street

DURHAM
Crook
Bowburn
HARTLEPOOL
Hamsterley ॐ
A1
Bishop Auckland

BARNARD CASTLE
STOCKTON-ON-TEES
Redcar
Thornaby-on-Tees
Greta Bridge
Middlesbrough
Loftus ॐ
DARLINGTON
Yarm
Great Ayton ॐ
WHITBY
Scotch Corner
Stokesley
Reeth
Moulton
ॐ GREAT BROUGTON
ॐ RICHMOND
GOATHLAND
Rosedale Abbey
Patrick Brompton
NORTHALLERTON ॐ
Thoralby ॐ
W. Witton
Bedale
Leeming Bar
LASTINGHAM ॐ
SCARBOROUGH ॐ
ॐ MIDDLEHAM
E. Witton
Pickhill
Kirkbymoorside
MASHAM
THIRSK
HELMSLEY
PICKERING
Brompton by Sawdon
KETTLEWELL
Hunmanby
Hovingham
Ripon
EASINGWOLD
MALTON
M PATELEY BRIDGE
Sherriff Hutton ॐ
Bridlington

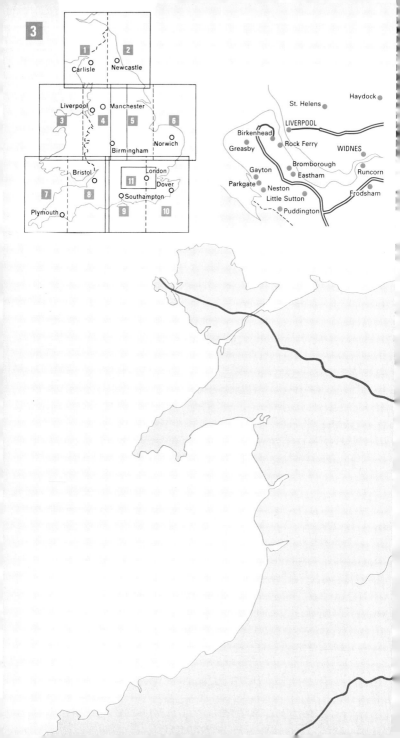

3

1 Carlisle 2 Newcastle

3 Liverpool 4 Manchester 5 6
Birmingham Norwich

7 8 Bristol London 11 Dover
Plymouth 9 Southampton 10

St. Helens Haydock

LIVERPOOL
Birkenhead Rock Ferry
Greasby WIDNES
Gayton Bromborough Runcorn
Parkgate Eastham
Neston Frodsham
Little Sutton
Puddington

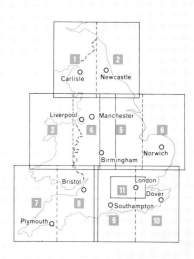

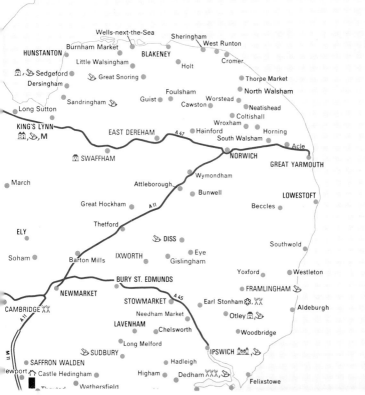

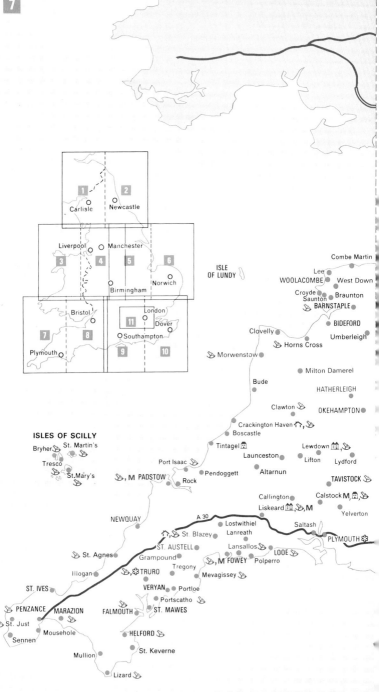

7

Combe Martin
Lee
WOOLACOMBE ● West Down
ISLE
OF LUNDY
Croyde ● Braunton
Saunton
BARNSTAPLE ●
BIDEFORD
Clovelly ● Umberleigh
Horns Cross
Morwenstow ●
● Milton Damerel

Bude ●
HATHERLEIGH
Clawton ● OKEHAMPTON ●
Crackington Haven
Boscastle
Tintagel ● Lewdown ●
Launceston ● Lifton
Port Isaac ● Altarnun Lydford
PADSTOW ● Pendoggett ● TAVISTOCK
Rock
Callington ● Calstock M,
Liskeard ●, M
Yelverton
NEWQUAY A 30 Lostwithiel Saltash
St. Blazey ● Lanreath
St. Agnes ● ST. AUSTELL ● Lansallos PLYMOUTH
Grampound ● M FOWEY LOOE
Illogan ● Tregony ● Polperro
TRURO ● Mevagissey
VERYAN ● Portloe
ST. IVES ● Portscatho
PENZANCE MARAZION FALMOUTH ST. MAWES
St. Just
Mousehole HELFORD
Sennen
St. Keverne
Mullion
Lizard

ISLES OF SCILLY
Bryher ● St. Martin's
Tresco
St. Mary's

Map index:
1 Carlisle
2 Newcastle
3 Liverpool
4 Manchester
5 Birmingham
6 Norwich
Bristol
7 8 London
11 Dover
Southampton
9 10
Plymouth

SAFFRON WALDEN
Newport ⌂ Castle Hedingham
Hadleigh
Higham ● Dedham △△△, ⛵
Felixstowe
Baldock
Clavering
Thaxted
Wethersfield
Manningtree
Harwich and Dovercourt
Stanstead Airport
Braintree
Earls Colne
Coggeshall
COLCHESTER
Standon
WARE
Great Dunmow
BISHOP'S STORTFORD
Hertford ⛵
Witham
Frinton-on-Sea

CHELMSFORD

Maldon
South Woodham Ferrers
Burnham-on-Crouch

West Mersea

Basildon

Southend-on-Sea

North Stifford
Gravesend
Rochester
Farthing Corner S.A.
Newington
Sittingbourne M 2 FAVERSHAM ❀
Selling
CANTERBURY
Wingham

Birchington
Broadstairs
Herne Bay
RAMSGATE
Sandwich
DEAL ⛵

LONDON ❀❀❀

A 2

Cobham

WEST MALLING

MAIDSTONE ⛵
Warren Street
⌂, ⛵

DOVER

Edenbridge
Horley⌂
Turners Hill ⛵
Penshurst ⛵
Brenchley
Pluckley ⛵
Frittenden
ASHFORD ⛵
Bethersden ⌂
Folkestone
Hythe
ROYAL TUNBRIDGE WELLS
M
Goudhurst
Biddenden
EAST GRINSTEAD
CRAWLEY ♨, ⛵
Hartfield
Wadhurst
CRANBROOK ⛵
Tenterden
FOREST ROW
Ardingly
Crowborough
Hawkhurst
Benenden ⌂
Cuckfield
MAYFIELD
Ticehurst
Haywards Heath
Uckfield ♨
Heathfield
Sedlescombe
RYE ⛵
Lewes A 27
Halland
Rushlake Green ⌂, M
Herstmonceux
Battle
Winchelsea
A 259
Bexhill
BRIGHTON AND HOVE
HAILSHAM
Hastings and St. Leonards M
Alfriston
Rottingdean
SEAFORD ⛵
EASTBOURNE ⛺△△, M

10

1 Carlisle
2 Newcastle

3 Liverpool
4 Manchester
5
6 Norwich

Birmingham

7
8 Bristol
11 London
Dover
9 Southampton
10 Plymouth

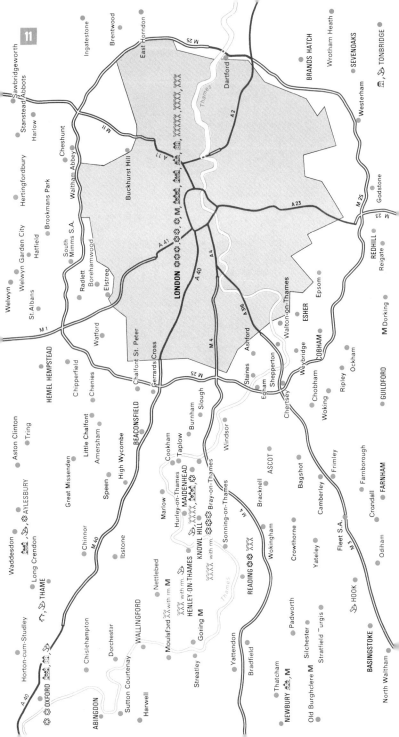

ABBERLEY Heref. and Worcs. 🔲403 404 M 27 – pop. 604 – ECD : Wednesday – ✉ Worcester – ✆ 0299 Great Witley.

◆London 137 – ◆Birmingham 27 – Worcester 13.

🏠 **The Elms** (Q.M.H.) ⬛, WR6 6AT, W : 2 m. on A 443 ✆896666, Telex 337105, Fax 896804, ≤, « Queen Anne mansion », ☞, park, ✂ – 🔲 ☎ ❷ – 🔬 40. 🔳 🅰🅴 🔲 ₪️
✎
M (bar lunch Monday to Saturday)/dinner 22.00 **st**. and a la carte 15.25/32.95 **st**. ▮ 6.25 –
24 rm ⊏⊐ 82.00/150.00 **st**., 1 suite – SB (except Christmas and New Year) 130.00/180.00 **st**.

🏠 **Manor Arms** ⬛, Abberley Village, WR6 6BN, ✆896507, ☞ – 🔲 ☎ ❷. 🔳 🔲
M (closed Sunday dinner to non-residents) 10.95/12.95 **t**. and a la carte ▮ 4.50 – **10 rm** ⊏⊐ 30.00/40.00 **t**. – SB 63.00/86.00 **st**.

ABBOTSBURY Dorset 🔲403 404 M 32 The West Country G. – pop. 401 – ✆ 0305.

See : Town★★ – Chesil Beach★★ – Swannery★ AC – Sub-Tropical Gardens★ AC.

Envir. : St. Catherine's Chapel★, ½ m. uphill (30 mn rtn on foot).

Exc. : Maiden Castle★★ (≤★) NE : 7½ m.

◆London 146 – Exeter 50 – Bournemouth 44 – Weymouth 10.

🏠 **Ilchester Arms**, 9 Market St., DT3 4JR, ✆871243 – ≤ rest 🔲 ☎ ❷. 🔳 🔲
M a la carte 9.05/15.70 **t**. – **10 rm** ⊏⊐ 40.00/60.00 **t**.

ABBOT'S SALFORD Warks. 🔲403 404 O 27 – see Evesham (Heref. and Worcs.).

ABINGDON Oxon. 🔲403 404 Q 28 Great Britain G. – pop. 29130 – ECD : Thursday – ✆ 0235.

See : Town★ – County Hall★.

🏌 Drayton Park, Steventon Rd, Drayton, Abingdon ✆550607.

🚤 to Oxford via Sandford and Iffley Locks (Salter Bros Ltd) (summer only).

🇮 Abbey House, Abbey Close, OX14 3JD ✆522711.

◆London 64 – ◆Oxford 6 – Reading 25.

🏨 **Upper Reaches** (Forte), Thames St., OX14 3JA, ✆522311, Fax 555182 – ≤ 🔲 ☎ ❷ –
🔬 60. 🔳 🅰🅴 ⓞ 🔲 🅹🅲🅱
M (bar lunch Monday to Saturday)/dinner 17.95 **st**. and a la carte ▮ 5.25 – ⊏⊐ 8.50 – **25 rm** 78.00/89.00 **st**. – SB (except Bank Holidays) 116.00 **st**.

🏨 **Abingdon Lodge**, Marcham Rd, OX14 1TZ, W : 1 m. on A 415 ✆553456, Fax 554117 –
≤ rm 🔲 ☎ ❷ – 🔬 140. 🔳 🅰🅴 ⓞ 🔲 ✎
M (carving lunch) 8.95/10.95 **st**. and dinner a la carte – ⊏⊐ 4.00 – **63 rm** 40.00/80.00 **st**. –
SB (July-August and weekends only) 54.00/84.00 **st**.

🏠 **Crown and Thistle** (Chef & Brewer), Bridge St., OX14 3HS, ✆522556, Fax 553281 – 🔲
☎ ❷. 🔳 🔲 ✎
M 15.00/20.00 **t**. and a la carte – **21 rm** ⊏⊐ 34.95/38.45 **t**.

⌂ **Thame Lane House**, 1 Thame Lane, Culham, OX14 3DS, SE : 1 ¾ m. on A 415
✆524177, ☞ – ≤ 🔲 ❷. 🔳 🔲 ✎
M - French (closed Monday lunch and Sunday dinner) (booking essential) 16.50/26.00 **st**.
▮ 5.00 – **5 rm** ⊏⊐ 29.00/54.00 **st**. – SB (weekends only) 71.00/99.00 **st**.

at Clifton Hampden SE : 3¾ m. on A 415 – ✉ ✆ 0867 Abingdon :

🏮 **Barley Mow** (Chef & Brewer), OX14 3EH, on Long Wittenham Rd ✆307847, ☞ – 🔲 ☎
❷. 🔳 🅰🅴 🔲 ✎
M 15.00/20.00 **t**. and a la carte – **4 rm** ⊏⊐ 29.95/33.45 **t**.

at Frilford W : 3¾ m. on A 415 – ✉ ✆ 0865 Abingdon :

🏠 **Dog House**, Frilford Heath, OX13 6QJ, NE : 1¼ m. by A 338 on Cothill rd ✆390830,
Fax 390860, ☞ – ≤ rm 🔲 ☎ ❷. 🔳 🅰🅴 ⓞ 🔲
M (bar lunch)/dinner a la carte approx. 10.00 **t**. ▮ 3.40 – **19 rm** ⊏⊐ 60.00/69.00 **st**.

ACLE Norfolk 404 Y 26 Great Britain G. – pop. 2 025 – ✆ 0493 Great Yarmouth.

Envir. : The Broads★.

◆London 118 – Great Yarmouth 8 – ◆Norwich 11.

🏠 **Forte Travelodge** without rest., Acle by Pass, NR1 3BE, on A 47 at junction with B 1140
✆751970, Reservations (Freephone) 0800 850950 – 🔲 🔬 ❷. 🔳 🅰🅴 🔲 ✎
40 rm 31.95 **t**.

ADDERBURY Oxon. 🔲403 404 Q 27 – see Banbury.

ADLINGTON Ches. – see Macclesfield.

ADLINGTON Lancs. 🔲402 404 M 23 – pop. 5 619 – ECD : Wednesday – ✆ 0257.

◆London 217 – ◆Liverpool 35 – ◆Manchester 21 – Preston 16.

🏠 **Gladmar**, Railway Rd, PR6 9RG, ✆480398, Fax 482681, ☞ – 🔲 🔲 ☎ ❷. 🔳 🅰🅴 ⓞ 🔲 ✎
closed 25 December-1 January – **M** (bar lunch)/dinner a la carte 10.00/14.80 **st**. – **20 rm**
⊏⊐ 26.00/58.00 **st**.

AFFPUDDLE Dorset 🗺️ **408** **404** N 31 The West Country G. – pop. 425 – ✉ Dorchester – ☎ 0305 Puddletown.

Envir. : Moreton Church★★, S : 2½ m. by B 3390.

Exc. : Bere Regis (St. John the Baptist Church★★) NE : 3½ m. by B 3390 and A 35.

◆London 121 – Bournemouth 19 – Exeter 60 – ◆Southampton 47 – Weymouth 14.

   ⌂ **Old Vicarage** 🐾 without rest., DT2 7HH, ☎ 848315, « Tastefully furnished Georgian house », 🚗 – 📺 🅿. 🦢
      closed Christmas-New Year – **3 rm** ☟ 20.00/40.00 **s.**

AIGBURTH Mersey. – see Liverpool.

AINSTABLE Cumbria **401** **402** L 19 – ✉ Carlisle – ☎ 0768 Penrith.

◆London 304 – ◆Carlisle 19 – Kendal 45 – Lancaster 62.

   🏠 **New Crown Inn,** CA4 9QQ, ☎ 896273 – 📺 🅿
      M *(closed Monday lunch except Bank Holidays)* (in bar) a la carte 8.50/15.50 **t.** 🍷 4.00 –
      3 rm ☟ 27.50/50.00 **t.**

AISLABY N. Yorks. – see Pickering.

ALBERBURY Shrops. **402** **403** L 25 – see Shrewsbury.

ALBRIGHTON Shrops. **402** **403** L 25 – see Shrewsbury.

ALBURY Surrey – see Guildford.

   Great Britain and Ireland is now covered
   by an Atlas at a scale of 1 inch to 4.75 miles.

   Three easy to use versions: Paperback, Spiralbound and Hardback.

ALDBOURNE Wilts. **403** **404** P 29 – pop. 1 479 – ☎ 0672 Marlborough.

◆London 77 – ◆Oxford 36 – ◆Southampton 53 – Swindon 9.

   XX **Raffles,** 1 The Green, SN8 2BW, ☎ 40700, Fax 40038 – 🔊 🅰🅴 ⓞ 𝗩𝗜𝗦𝗔
      closed lunch Monday and Saturday. Sunday dinner and 25 to 30 December – **M** (restricted menu Friday dinner) a la carte 12.65/21.45 **t.** 🍷 6.95.

ALDEBURGH Suffolk **404** Y 27 – pop. 2 711 – ECD : Wednesday – ☎ 0728.

🏌️ Thorpeness Golf Hotel, Thorpeness ☎ 452176, N : 2 m.

🎭 The Cinema, High St., IP15 5AU ☎ 453637 (summer only).

◆London 97 – ◆Ipswich 24 – ◆Norwich 41.

   🏨 **Wentworth,** Wentworth Rd, IP15 5BD, ☎ 452312, Fax 454343, ≤ – 📺 ☎ 🅿. 🔊 🅰🅴 ⓞ
      𝗩𝗜𝗦𝗔
      closed 27 December-10 January – **M** 13.50/17.50 **t.** and dinner a la carte 🍷 4.00 – **31 rm** ☟ 50.50/100.00 **t.** – SB 92.00/131.00 **t.**

   🏨 **White Lion** (Best Western), Market Cross Pl., IP15 5BJ, ☎ 452720, Fax 452986, ≤ – 📺 ☎
      🅿 – 🔬 100. 🔊 🅰🅴 ⓞ 𝗩𝗜𝗦𝗔
      M (bar lunch Monday to Saturday)/dinner 16.95 **st.** and a la carte 🍷 6.00 – **38 rm** ☟ 57.50/80.00 **st.** – SB 99.00/156.00 **st.**

   🏨 **Brudenell** (Forte), The Parade, IP15 5BU, ☎ 452071, Fax 454082, ≤ – 🛗 🔜 📺 ☎ 🅿 –
      🔬 45. 🔊 🅰🅴 ⓞ 𝗩𝗜𝗦𝗔 𝗝𝗖𝗕
      M *(closed lunch Monday to Thursday November-March)* 11.95/17.50 **st.** and dinner a la carte 🍷 5.75 – ☟ 8.95 – **47 rm** 75.00/95.00 **st.** – SB (except 24 to 26 December) 114.00/129.00 **st.**

   🏠 **Uplands,** Victoria Rd, IP15 5DX, ☎ 452420, 🚗 – 🔜 rest 📺 ☎ 🅿. 🔊 🅰🅴 ⓞ 𝗩𝗜𝗦𝗔. 🦢
      closed 23 December-4 January – **M** *(closed Sunday in winter)* (dinner only) 20.00 **t.** 🍷 3.95 –
      20 rm ☟ 43.00/65.00 **t.** – SB (October-May) 70.00/100.00 **st.**

   XX **Austins** with rm, 243 High St., IP15 5DN, ☎ 453932, Fax 453668 – 📺 ☎. 🔊 𝗩𝗜𝗦𝗔
      M *(closed Sunday dinner and Monday)* (dinner only and Sunday lunch)/dinner 21.00 **t.** 🍷 4.00 – **7 rm** ☟ 47.75/75.00 **t.**

   X **New Regatta,** 171-173 High St., IP15 5AN, ☎ 452011, Fax 452011 – 🔊 🅰🅴 𝗩𝗜𝗦𝗔
      April-October and Christmas – **M** a la carte 12.85/16.40 **t.** 🍷 3.50.

ALDERHOLT Hants. – see Fordingbridge.

ALDERLEY EDGE Ches. **402** **403** **404** N 24 – pop. 4 272 – ECD : Wednesday – ☎ 0625.

🏌️ Wilmslow, Great Warford, Mobberley ☎ 0565 (Knutsford) 872148, SW : 3 m. – 🏌️ Brook Lane ☎ 585583.

◆London 187 – Chester 34 – ◆Manchester 14 – ◆Stoke-on-Trent 25.

   🏨 **Alderley Edge,** Macclesfield Rd, SK9 7BJ, ☎ 583033, Fax 586343, 🚗 – 📺 ☎ 🅿 –
      🔬 120. 🔊 🅰🅴 ⓞ 𝗩𝗜𝗦𝗔. 🦢
      M 17.50/23.00 **t.** and a la carte 🍷 6.50 – ☟ 8.50 – **32 rm** 87.00/125.00 **st.**

   🏨 De Trafford Arms, London Rd, SK9 7AA, ☎ 583881, Fax 586625 – 🛗 📺 ☎ 🅿. 🦢
      37 rm.

ALDRIDGE W. Mids. 402 403 404 O 26 – pop. 17 549 – ECD : Thursday – ✉ Walsall – ☎ 0922.
◆London 130 – ◆Birmingham 12 – Derby 32 – ◆Leicester 40 – ◆Stoke-on-Trent 38.

🏨 **Fairlawns,** 178 Little Aston Rd, WS9 0NU, E : 1 m. on A 454 ℰ 55122, Fax 743210 –
▤ rest ☑ ☎ ❷ – 🔬 80. 🔼 🝙 🝙 🚾
M *(closed Saturday lunch and Sunday dinner to non-residents)* 15.75/
19.75 **st.** and a la carte ⓘ 4.80 – **35 rm** ☲ 45.00/77.50 **st.** – SB (weekends only) 70.00 **st.**

◎ ATS 106 Leighswood Rd ℰ 51968/53970

ALDWINCLE Northants. 402 404 S 26 – pop. 302 – ✉ Kettering – ☎ 0832 Clopton.
◆London 84 – ◆Cambridge 40 – ◆Leicester 40 – Northampton 26 – Peterborough 18.

↑ **The Maltings** ❧ without rest., NN14 3EP, ℰ 720233, Fax 720326, ☞ – ⅏ ☑ ❷. 🔼 🚾.
❈
3 rm ☲ 30.00/41.00 **st.**

ALFRETON Derbs 402 403 404 P 24 – pop. 21 117 – ECD : Wednesday – ☎ 0773.
🝙 Shirland, Lower Delves ℰ 834935, N : 1 m. by A 61 – 🝙 Ormonde Fields, Nottingham Rd,
Codnor, Ripley ℰ 742987, S : 6 m.
◆London 134 – Derby 13 – ◆Nottingham 19 – ◆Sheffield 27.

🏨 Granada, DE55 1HJ, S : ¾ m. by A 61 at junction with A 38 ℰ 520040, Fax 521087 –
⅏ rm ☑ ☎ ⅋ ❷ – 🔬 50. ❈
M (grill rest.) – **61 rm.**

ALFRISTON E. Sussex 404 U 31 – pop. 811 – ECD : Wednesday – ✉ Polegate – ☎ 0323.
◆London 66 – Eastbourne 9 – Lewes 10 – Newhaven 8.

🏨 **Deans Place,** BN26 5TW, ℰ 870248, Fax 870918, ⅏ heated, ☞ – ☑ ☎ ❷ – 🔬 150. 🔼
🝙 🚾 🝙
M 12.95/18.95 **t.** ⓘ 6.50 – **36 rm** ☲ 65.00/85.00 **t.** – SB 85.00/99.00 **st.**

🏨 **Star Inn** (Forte), High St., BN26 5TA, ℰ 870495, Fax 870922 – ⅏ rm ☑ ☎ ❷. 🔼 🝙 🝙
🚾 🝙
M (bar lunch Monday to Saturday)/dinner 17.95 **st.** and a la carte ⓘ 6.45 – ☲ 8.50 – **34 rm**
84.00/99.00 **st.** – SB (except Christmas and New Year) 124.00 **st.**

ALLENDALE Northd. 401 402 N 19 – pop. 1 604 – ✉ ☎ 0434 Hexham.
🝙 High Studdon, Allenheads Rd ℰ 091 (Tyneside) 267 5875, S : 1½ m. by B 6295.
◆London 314 – ◆Carlisle 39 – ◆Newcastle upon Tyne 33.

🏠 **Bishop Field Country House** ❧, NE47 9EJ, W : 1 m. on Whitfield rd ℰ 683248,
Fax 683830, ☞ – ⅏ rest ☑ ☎ ❷. 🔼 🚾
closed February-March and Christmas-New Year – **M** (residents only) (dinner only) 16.00 **st.** ⓘ 4.30 – **6 rm** ☲ 48.00/76.00 **st.** – SB 88.00/128.00 **st.**

↑ **Thornley House,** NE47 9NH, W : ¾ m. on Whitfield rd ℰ 683255, ☞ – ❷
M 8.50 **st.** – **3 rm** ☲ 21.00/35.00 **st.**

ALLESLEY W. Mids. 403 404 P 26 – see Coventry.

ALMONDSBURY Avon 403 404 M 29 – see Bristol.

ALNE N. Yorks. – see Easingwold.

ALNMOUTH Northd. 401 402 P 17 Great Britain G. – pop. 605 – ECD : Wednesday – ☎ 0665.
Envir. : Warkworth Castle★ *AC,* S : 4 m. by B 1338 and A 1068.
🝙 Alnmouth Village, Marine Rd ℰ 830370.
◆London 314 – ◆Edinburgh 90 – ◆Newcastle upon Tyne 37.

↑ **Marine House,** 1 Marine Rd, NE66 2RW, ℰ 830349, ≤, ☞ – ⅏ ☑ ❷. 🔼 🚾
10 rm ☲ (dinner included) 78.00 **t.**

↑ **The Grange** without rest., NE66 2RJ, ℰ 830401, ≤, ☞ – ⅏ ☑ ❷. ❈
5 rm ☲ 18.00/36.00 **st.**

ALNWICK Northd. 401 402 O 17 Great Britain G. – pop. 6 972 – ECD : Wednesday – ☎ 0665.
See : Town★ – Castle★★ *AC.*
Exc. : Dunstanburgh Castle★ *AC,* NE : 8 m. by B 1340 and Dunstan rd (last 2½ m. on foot).
🝙 Swansfield Park ℰ 602632.
🄱 The Shambles, NE66 1TN ℰ 510665.
◆London 320 – ◆Edinburgh 86 – ◆Newcastle upon Tyne 34.

🏨 **White Swan,** Bondgate Within, NE66 1TD, ℰ 602109, Fax 510400 – ☑ ☎ ❷ – 🔬 100.
🔼 🝙 🚾
closed 3 to 17 January – **M** 12.30/17.00 **t.** and a la carte ⓘ 4.65 – **43 rm** ☲ 49.50/68.00 **t.** –
SB 95.00/120.00 **st.**

🏠 **Oaks,** South Rd, NE66 2PN, SE : ½ m. ℰ 510014, Fax 603219 – ☑ ☎ ❷. 🔼 🝙 🚾 🝙
M 10.50/18.50 **st.** and a la carte ⓘ 4.75 – **13 rm** ☲ 40.00/65.00 **st.** – SB 82.00/135.00 **st.**

↑ **Bondgate House,** 20 Bondgate Without, NE66 1PN, ☞ 602025, Fax 602554 – ≒ rest 🖵
🅿 . ❀
M (by arrangement) 10.00 ⅊ 3.80 – **8 rm** ⊑ 22.00/36.00 **st.**

XX **John Blackmore's,** 1 Dorothy Forster Court, Narrowgate, NE66 1NL, ☞ 604465 – ≒.
🖪 AE ⓞ VISA
closed Sunday, Monday and January – **M** (dinner only) 16.50 **t.** and a la carte.

at Eglingham NW : 7 m. on B 6346 – ⊠ 🏀 0665 Alnwick :

↑ **Ogle House,** NE66 2TZ, ☞ 578264, ≈ – ≒ 🖵 🅿
closed 21 December-1 February – **M** 10.95 **st.** – **3 rm** ⊑ 22.50/37.00 **st.**

ALPORT Derbs. – see Bakewell.

ALSAGER Ches. 402 403 404 N 24 Great Britain G. – pop. 12 944 – ⊠ Stoke-on-Trent –
🏀 0270.
Envir. : Little Moreton Hall★★ *AC,* NE : 4 m. by A 50 and A 34.
◆London 180 – Chester 36 – ◆ Liverpool 49 – ◆ Manchester 32 – ◆ Stoke-on-Trent 11.

🏨 **Manor House,** Audley Rd, ST7 2QQ, SE : ½ m. ☞ 884000, Fax 882483, 🖳 – 📺 ☎ & 🅿 –
🔬 200. 🖪 AE VISA
M 10.50/16.95 **st.** and a la carte ⅊ 4.50 – **57 rm** ⊑ 74.50/84.50 **st.**

ALSTON Cumbria 401 402 M 19 – pop. 1 968 – ECD : Tuesday – 🏀 0434.
🔭 Alston Moor, The Hermitage ☞ʰ 381675, S : 2 m. on B 0277.
🅱 The Railway Station, CA9 3JB ☞ 381696.
◆London 309 – ◆Carlisle 28 – ◆Newcastle upon Tyne 45.

🏨 **Lovelady Shield Country House** ⌕, Nenthead Rd, CA9 3LF, E : 2 ½ m. on A 689
☞ 381203, Fax 381515, ≼, ⌖, ❀ – ≒ rest 📺 🖵 🅿 . 🖪 AE ⓞ VISA
closed 4 January-12 February – **M** (bar lunch)/dinner 23.50 **t.** ⅊ 4.95 – **12 rm** ⊑ 42.00/
98.00 **t.** – SB (October-May) 125.00/161.00 **t.**

🏨 **Nent Hall Country House,** CA9 3LQ, E : 2½ m. on A 689 ☞ 381584, Fax 382668, ≈ –
📺 🖵 🅿 . 🖪 AE VISA
M (bar lunch)/dinner 19.50 **st.** ⅊ 4.40 – **18 rm** ⊑ 44.00/79.00 **st.** – SB 95.00/163.00 **st.**

ALTARNUN Cornwall 403 G 32 – ⊠ 🏀 0566 Launceston.
◆London 279 – Exeter 56 – ◆Plymouth 36 – Truro 39.

🏨 **Penhallow Manor** ⌕, PL15 7SJ, ☞ 86206, Fax 86179, ≈ – 📺 ☎ 🅿 . 🖪 VISA . ❀
M (bar lunch Monday to Saturday)/dinner 19.95 **t.** and a la carte – **7 rm** ⊑ 37.50/74.00 **t.** –
SB 94.00/98.00 **st.**

ALTON Hants. 404 R 30 – pop. 14 163 – ECD : Wednesday – 🏀 0420.
🔭 Old Odiham Rd ☞ 82042, N : 2 m.
🅱 7 Cross and Pillory Lane, GU34 1HL ☞ 88448.
◆London 53 – Reading 24 – ◆Southampton 29 – Winchester 18.

🏨 **Swan** (Forte), High St., GU34 1AT, ☞ 83777, Fax 87975 – ≒ 📺 ☎ 🅿 – 🔬 50. 🖪 AE ⓞ
VISA
M (closed Saturday lunch) 12.95/17.95 **st.** and a la carte ⅊ 4.95 – ⊑ 8.95 – **36 rm**
65.00/95.00 **st.** – SB 80.00 **st.**

🏨 **Grange,** London Rd, GU34 4EG, NE : 1 m. on A 339 ☞ 86565, Fax 541346, ≈ – ≒ 📺 ☎
🅿 . 🖪 AE ⓞ VISA . ❀
M (bar lunch Saturday) 9.95/19.50 **t.** and a la carte ⅊ 4.95 – **30 rm** ⊑ 49.50/125.00 **t.** –
SB (except Christmas and New Year) (weekends only) 70.00/90.00 **t.**

🏨 **Alton House,** Normandy St., GU34 1DW, ☞ 80033, Fax 89222, 🏊 heated, ≈, ❀ – 📺 ☎
🅿 – 🔬 130. 🖪 AE VISA . ❀
closed 26 December – **M** 12.95 **t.** (dinner) and a la carte – **38 rm** ⊑ 45.00/63.00 **t.** –
SB (weekends only) 69.00/79.00 **t.**

ALTRINCHAM Gtr. Manchester 402 403 404 N 23 – pop. 39 528 – ECD : Wednesday –
🏀 061 Manchester.
🔭 Altrincham Municipal, Stockport Rd, Timperley ☞ 928 0761 – 🔭 Ringway, Hale Mount, Hale
Barns ☞ 904 9609.
🅱 Stamford New Road, WA14 1EJ ☞ 941 7337.
◆London 191 – Chester 30 – ◆Liverpool 30 – ◆Manchester 8.

🏨 **Cresta Court,** Church St., WA14 4DP, on A 56 ☞ 927 7272, Telex 667242, Fax 926 9194 –
|🛏| 📺 ☎ 🅿 – 🔬 300. 🖪 AE ⓞ VISA
M 7.75/9.25 **st.** and a la carte ⅊ 4.00 – **139 rm** ⊑ 30.00/72.00 **st.** – SB (weekends only)
60.00/70.00 **st.**

🏨 **Woodland Park,** Wellington Rd, WA15 7RG, off A 560 ☞ 928 8631, Fax 941 2821 – 📺 ☎
🅿 – 🔬 100. 🖪 AE ⓞ VISA . ❀
M (closed Sunday lunch) 8.95/15.50 **t.** and a la carte – **45 rm** ⊑ 60.00/90.00 **t.**

🏨 **Pelican County Inn,** Manchester Rd, West Timperley, WA14 5NH, N : 2 m. on A 56
☞ 962 7414, Fax 962 3456 – ≒ rm 📺 ☎ 🅿 . 🖪 AE VISA . ❀
M (closed Saturday lunch) 9.95/12.50 ⅊ 3.60 – ⊑ 3.50 – **48 rm** 39.50 **t.** – SB 68.00/99.00 **st.**

at Hale SE : 1 m. on B 5163 – ⊠ Altrincham – ✆ 061 Manchester :

🏛 **Ashley** (De Vere), Ashley Rd, WA15 9SF, ✆ 928 3794, Fax 926 9046 – 📱 📺 ☎ – 🅰 200. ⚠ 🆔 ⑩ 𝑽𝑰𝑺𝑨
M *(closed Sunday lunch) (light lunch)/dinner* 11.50 **st.** ⅄ 4.50 – **47 rm** ⊑ 50.00/60.00 **st.** – SB (weekends only) 70.00/120.00 **st.**

✗ **Est, Est, Est!**, 183 Ashley Rd, WA15 9SD, ✆ 928 1811
closed 25-26 December and 1 January – **M** - Italian (dinner only) 12.95 **t.** and a la carte ⅄ 4.75.

at Halebarns SE : 3 m. on A 538 – ⊠ Altrincham – ✆ 061 Manchester :

🏛 **Four Seasons**, Manchester Airport, Hale Rd, WA15 8XW, ✆ 904 0301, Telex 665492, Fax 980 1787, – 📱 ▤ rest 📺 ☎ ❷ – 🅰 150. ⚠ 🆔 ⑩ 𝑽𝑰𝑺𝑨 ✨
M 15.95/16.95 **st.** and a la carte ⅄ 6.25 – ⊑ 9.50 – **90 rm** 92.50/113.50 **st.**, 4 suites.

at Bowdon SW : 1 m. – ⊠ Altrincham – ✆ 061 Manchester :

🏛 **Bowdon Croft** ⦿, Green Walk, WA14 2SN, ✆ 928 1718, Fax 928 1718, ≤, « Tastefully furnished 19C house », ☞ – 📺 ☎ ❷. ⚠ 🆔 𝑽𝑰𝑺𝑨 ✨
M (booking essential) 9.50/19.50 **st.** – **9 rm** ⊑ 55.00/85.00 **st.**

🏛 **Bowdon**, Langham Rd, WA14 2HT, ✆ 928 7121, Fax 927 7560 – 📺 ☎ ❷ – 🅰 130. ⚠ 🆔 ⑩ 𝑽𝑰𝑺𝑨
M (bar lunch)/dinner 15.95 **t.** and a la carte ⅄ 5.95 – **82 rm** ⊑ 58.00/79.00 **t.** – SB 73.00/98.00 **st.**

🌀 ATS 74 Oakfield Rd ✆ 928 7024

ALVELEY Shrops. – see Bridgnorth.

ALVERSTONE I.O.W. 403 404 Q 32 – see Wight (Isle of).

ALVESTON Avon 403 404 M 29 – pop. 3 154 – ECD : Wednesday – ⊠ Bristol – ✆ 0454 Thornbury.
♦London 127 – ♦Bristol 11 – Gloucester 23 – Swindon 42.

🏛 **Alveston House**, BS12 2LJ, on A 38 ✆ 415050, Fax 415425, ☞ – 📺 ☎ ❷ – 🅰 80. ⚠ 🆔 ⑩ 𝑽𝑰𝑺𝑨
M 10.75/17.00 **st.** and a la carte ⅄ 5.20 – **30 rm** ⊑ 65.50/85.50 **st.** – SB (weekends only) 81.00/89.00 **st.**

🏛 **Forte Posthouse**, Thornbury Rd, BS12 2LL, on A 38 ✆ 412521, Fax 413920, ⊒ heated, ☞ – ✠ rm 📺 ☎ ❷ – 🅰 100. ⚠ 🆔 ⑩ 𝑽𝑰𝑺𝑨
M a la carte approx. 17.50 **t.** ⅄ 4.65 – ⊑ 6.95 – **74 rm** 53.50/69.50 **st.** – SB (except Christmas) 90.00 **st.**

ALWALTON Cambs. 402 404 T 26 – see Peterborough.

AMBERLEY Glos. 403 404 N 28 – see Stroud.

AMBERLEY W. Sussex 404 S 31 Great Britain G. – pop. 516 – ⊠ Arundel – ✆ 0798 Bury.
Envir. : Bignor Roman Villa (mosaics★) *AC*, NW : 3½ m. by B 2139 via Bury.
♦London 56 – ♦Brighton 24 – ♦Portsmouth 31.

🏛 **Amberley Castle** ⦿, BN18 9ND, SW : ½ m. on B 2139 ✆ 831992, Fax 831998, « 14C castle, 12C origins », ☞, park – 📺 ☎ ❷ – 🅰 40. ⚠ 🆔 ⑩ 𝑽𝑰𝑺𝑨 ✨
M 21.50/40.00 **st.** and dinner a la carte ⅄ 9.00 – **14 rm** ⊑ 85.00/225.00 **st.** – SB 150.00/395.00 **st.**

AMBLESIDE Cumbria 402 L 20 Great Britain G. – pop. 2 689 – ECD : Thursday – ✆ 053 94.
Envir. : Lake Windermere★★ – Dove Cottage, Grasmere★ *AC* AY **A** – Brockhole National Park Centre★ *AC*, SE : 3 m. by A 591 AZ.
Exc. : Wrynose Pass★★, W : 7½ m. by A 593 AY – Hard Knott Pass★★, W : 10 m. by A 593 AY.
🅱 Old Courthouse, Church St., LA22 0BT ✆ 32582 (summer only) AZ – Main Car Park, Waterhead, LA22 0EN ✆ 32729 (summer only) BY.
♦London 278 – ♦Carlisle 47 – Kendal 14.

Plan on next page

🏛 **Rothay Manor**, Rothay, LA22 0EH, S : ½ m. on A 593 ✆ 33605, Fax 33607, ≤, « Regency style country house », ☞ – ✠ rest 📺 ☎ ❷. ⚠ 🆔 ⑩ 𝑽𝑰𝑺𝑨 ✨ BY **r**
closed 2 January-12 February – **M** (buffet lunch Monday to Saturday)/dinner 27.00 **t.** ⅄ 5.00 – **15 rm** ⊑ 69.00/120.00 **t.**, 3 suites – SB (November-March except Christmas and New Year) 105.00/180.00 **t.**

🏛 **Kirkstone Foot Country House**, Kirkstone Pass Rd, LA22 9EH, NE : ¼ m. ✆ 32232, ☞ – ✠ rest 📺 ☎ ❷. ⚠ 𝑽𝑰𝑺𝑨 ✨ AZ **c**
closed January – **M** (dinner only) 19.50 **t.** ⅄ 4.25 – **15 rm** ⊑ (dinner included) 39.50/116.00 **t.** – SB (November-March except Christmas-New Year) 79.00/116.00 **st.**

🏛 **Salutation**, Lake Rd, LA22 9BX, ✆ 32244, Fax 34157 – ✠ rest 📺 ☎ ❷. ⚠ 𝑽𝑰𝑺𝑨 AZ **r**
M (bar lunch)/dinner 18.00 **st.** and a la carte ⅄ 5.50 – **29 rm** ⊑ 49.50/79.00 **st.**

AMBLESIDE
GRASMERE

Town plans: *roads most used by traffic and those on which guide listed hotels and restaurants stand are fully drawn; the beginning only of lesser roads is indicated.*

Borrans Park, Borrans Rd, LA22 0EN, ℘ 33454, 🌳 – 🚭 [TV] ☎ ♿ [P]. [AE] [VISA]. 🐕 BY **a**
closed 20 to 28 December – **M** (dinner only) 16.00 **st.** 🍷 4.25 – **12 rm** ☐ 27.50/75.00 **st.** – SB 80.00/100.00 **st.**

Laurel Villa, Lake Rd, LA22 0DB, ℘ 33240 – 🚭 rest [TV] [P]. [AE] [VISA] AZ **s**
closed Christmas – **M** *(closed Sunday)* (dinner only) 25.00 **t.** – **7 rm** ☐ 50.00/80.00 **t.**

Elder Grove, Lake Rd, LA22 0DB, ℘ 32504 – 🚭 rest [TV] ☎ [P]. [AE] [VISA] AZ **a**
mid February-mid November – **M** (bar lunch)/dinner 15.50 **t.** and a la carte 🍷 4.25 – **12 rm** ☐ 25.50/51.00 **t.** – SB (except July-September) 69.00/82.00 **t.**

Riverside 🐦, Under Loughrigg, LA22 9LJ, ℘ 32395, 🌳 – 🚭 rest [TV] ☎ [P]. [AE] [VISA]. 🐕 BY **s**
March-November – **M** (bar lunch)/dinner 18.00 **t.** and a la carte 🍷 4.50 – **10 rm** ☐ (dinner included) 62.50/100.00 **t.**

Rothay Garth, Rothay Rd, LA22 0EE, ℘ 32217, Fax 34400, 🌳 – 🚭 rest [TV] ☎ [P]. [AE] [AE] [DC] [VISA] [JCB]. 🐕 AZ **e**
M (bar lunch Monday to Saturday)/dinner 19.50 **st.** 🍷 4.80 – **15 rm** ☐ 44.00/88.00 **st.**, 1 suite – SB (except Bank Holidays) 64.00/102.00 **st.**

Drunken Duck Inn, Barngates, LA22 0NG, SW : 3 m. by A 593 off B 5286 ℘ 36347 – [TV] ☎ [P]. [AE] [VISA] BY
M (in bar) approx. 11.00 🍷 3.25 – **9 rm** ☐ 45.00/74.00 **st.**

Crow How 🐦, Rydal Rd, LA22 9PN, NW : ½ m. on A 591 ℘ 32193, ≤, 🌳 – [TV] [P]. [AE] [VISA] BY **x**
closed December and January – **M** 11.00 **st.** 🍷 4.10 – **9 rm** ☐ 24.50/58.00 **st.** – SB (winter only) (weekends only) 56.00/74.00 **st.**

Chapel House, Kirkstone Rd, LA22 9DZ, ℘ 33143 – 🚭. 🐕 AZ **n**
closed January-February (restricted service November and December) – **M** 15.00 **st.** 🍷 5.00 – **10 rm** ☐ (dinner included) 37.00/79.50 **st.**

at Waterhead S : 1 m. on A 591 – BY – ✉ ☎ 053 94 Ambleside :

Low Wood, LA23 1LP, SE : ½ m. on A 591 ℘ 33338, Fax 34072, ≤, 🏋, 🧖, 🏊, squash – 🛗 🚭 rest [TV] ☎ [P] – 🎤 300. [AE] [AE] [DC] [VISA] [JCB]
M (bar lunch)/dinner 17.50 **st.** and a la carte – **99 rm** ☐ 60.00/98.00 **st.** – SB (except Bank Holidays) 138.00/200.00 **st.**

Wateredge, Borrans Rd, LA22 0EP, ℘ 32332, Fax 32332, ≤, « Part 17C fishermen's cottages, lakeside setting », 🌳 – 🚭 rest [TV] ☎ [P]. [AE] [AE] [VISA]. 🐕 BY **o**
closed 4 December-4 February – **M** (light lunch)/dinner 24.90 **t.** – **23 rm** ☐ (dinner included) 68.00/156.00 **t.** – SB (November-April except Easter) 94.00/140.00 **st.**

Regent, Borrans Rd, LA22 0ES, ℘ 32254, Fax 31474, 🏊 – 🚭 rest [TV] ☎ [P]. [AE] [VISA]
M (bar lunch)/dinner 24.00 **t.** 🍷 6.50 – **21 rm** ☐ 49.50/109.00 **t.** – SB (except Bank Holidays) 70.00/150.00 **st.** BY **e**

at Clappersgate W : 1 m. on A 593 – BY – ✉ ☎ 053 94 Ambleside :

Nanny Brow Country House 🐦, LA22 9NF, ℘ 32036, Fax 32450, ≤, « Landscaped gardens », 🎣 – 🚭 rest [TV] ☎ [P]. [AE] [AE] [DC] [VISA] BY **u**
closed 3 to 28 January – **M** (dinner only) 24.50 **t.** and a la carte 🍷 6.50 – **15 rm** ☐ 45.00/110.00 **t.**, 3 suites – SB 110.00/160.00 **st.**

Grey Friar Lodge, LA22 9NE, ℘ 33158, ≤, 🌳 – 🚭 [TV] [P]. 🐕 BY **n**
March-October – **M** (residents only) (dinner only) 15.50 **st.** – **8 rm** ☐ 29.00/60.00 **st.** – SB (March and April) (weekends only) 65.00/79.00 **st.**

at Skelwith Bridge W : 2½ m. on A 593 – AY – ✉ ☎ 053 94 Ambleside :

Skelwith Bridge, LA22 9NJ, ℘ 32115, Fax 34254 – 🚭 rest [TV] ☎ [P]. [AE] [VISA] AY **v**
M (bar lunch Monday to Saturday)/dinner 17.75 **st.** 🍷 4.85 – **29 rm** ☐ 40.00/90.00 **st.** – SB (except September-October and Bank Holidays) 56.00/90.00 **st.**

at Little Langdale W : 4½ m. by A 593 – ✉ Langdale – ☎ 053 94 Ambleside :

Three Shires Inn 🐦, LA22 9NZ, ℘ 37215, ≤, 🌳 – 🚭 rest [P]. 🐕 AY **z**
closed January and weekdays November-Christmas – **M** (bar lunch)/dinner 17.00 🍷 4.85 – **11 rm** ☐ 30.00/66.00 **t.**

at Elterwater W : 4½ m. by A 593 off B 5343 – AY – ✉ ☎ 053 94 Ambleside :

Langdale H. & Country Club, Great Langdale, LA22 9JD, NW : 1¼ m. on B 5343 ℘ 37302, Fax 37694, 🏋, 🧖, 🏊, park, squash – 🚭 rest [TV] ☎ [P] – 🎤 90. [AE] [AE] [DC] [VISA]. 🐕 AY **c**
M (buffet lunch)/dinner 26.95 **t.** and a la carte 🍷 4.75 – **65 rm** ☐ 81.00/162.00 **t.** – SB 154.00/202.00 **st.**

Eltermere Country House 🐦, LA22 9HY, ℘ 37207, ≤, 🌳 – [TV] [P]. 🐕 AY **i**
M (dinner only) 17.00 **t.** 🍷 4.85 – **18 rm** ☐ 27.00/75.00 **st.** – SB (except Bank Holidays) 64.00/98.00 **st.**

at Great Langdale W : 6 m. by A 593 on B 5343 – AY – ✉ ☎ 053 94 Ambleside :

Long House 🐦, LA22 9JS, ℘ 37222, ≤ Langdale valley, 🌳 – 🚭 [P]. [AE] [VISA]. 🐕
closed December and January – **M** (by arrangement) 14.00 **st.** – **3 rm** ☐ 44.00/50.00 **st.**

♦London 29 – Aylesbury 16 – ♦Oxford 33.

🏨 **Crown** (Forte), 16 High St., HP7 0DH, ℰ 721541, Fax 431283, « Former coaching inn », 🞈 – 🞈 rest 📺 ☎ 🅿 – 🔬 30. 🔼 🕮 ⑩ 𝕍𝕀𝕊𝔸 ᴶᶜᴮ. ⬚
M (bar lunch Monday to Saturday)/dinner 17.95 **st.** and a la carte ⅋ 4.85 – � 8.50 – **22 rm** 95.00/105.00 **st.**, 1 suite – SB (except Christmas) (weekends only) 108.00 **st.**

🍴🍴 **King's Arms**, High St., HP7 0DJ, ℰ 726333, Fax 433480 – 🅿. 🔼 🕮 ⑩ 𝕍𝕀𝕊𝔸
closed Sunday dinner and Monday – **M** 11.50/17.00 **t.** and a la carte ⅋ 4.00.

🍴 **Romna**, 20-22 The Broadway, HP7 0HP, ℰ 433732 – 🔲. 🔼 🕮 ⑩ 𝕍𝕀𝕊𝔸
M - Indian (buffet lunch Sunday) 13.00/20.00 **t.** and a la carte.

Envir. : Stonehenge★★★ *AC*, W : 2 m. by A 303.
Exc. : Wilton (Wilton House★★★ *AC*, Royal Wilton Carpet Factory★ *AC*) SW : 13 m. by A 303, B 3083 and A 36.

🏢 Redworth House, Flower Lane, SP4 7HG ℰ 622833/623255.

♦London 87 – ♦Bristol 52 – Taunton 66.

🏠 **Forte Travelodge** without rest., SP4 7AS, N : ¼ m. at junction of A 303 with A 345 ℰ 624966, Reservations (Freephone) 0800 850950 📺 🔬 🅿. 🔼 🕮 𝕍𝕀𝕊𝔸. ⬚
32 rm 31.95 **t.**

🏌 Ampfield Par Three, Winchester Rd ℰ 68480.

♦London 79 – Bournemouth 31 – Salisbury 19 – ♦Southampton 11 – Winchester 7.

🏨 **Potters Heron** (Lansbury), Winchester Rd, SO51 9ZF, on A 31 ℰ 0703 (Southampton) 266611, Fax 251359, ⅃ₐ, 🞈 – 🞈 🞈 rm 📺 ☎ 🔬 🅿 – 🔬 120. 🔼 🕮 ⑩ 𝕍𝕀𝕊𝔸
M 13.95/15.95 **st.** and a la carte ⅋ 5.75 – **54 rm** ⊊ 75.50/97.00 **st.** – SB (weekends only) 49.00/98.00 **st.**

🍴🍴 **Keats**, Winchester Rd, SO51 9BQ, on A 31 ℰ 68252 – 🅿. 🔼 🕮 ⑩ 𝕍𝕀𝕊𝔸 ᴶᶜᴮ
closed Sunday and Monday – **M** - Italian 9.00/27.00 **t.** and a la carte ⅋ 5.40.

🏌 51 Winchester Rd ℰ 323980, S : ½ m. on A 3057.
🏢 Town Mill House, Bridge St., SP10 1BL ℰ 324320.

♦London 74 – Bath 53 – Salisbury 17 – Winchester 11.

🏨 **Ashley Court**, Micheldever Rd, SP11 6LA, via London Street and Wolversdene Rd ℰ 357344, Fax 356755, ⅃ₐ, 🞈 – 📺 ☎ 🅿 – 🔬 120. 🔼 🕮 𝕍𝕀𝕊𝔸
M (bar lunch Saturday) 14.50 **st.** and a la carte ⅋ 4.15 – **35 rm** ⊊ 55.00/80.00 **st.**

🏨 **White Hart** (Forte), Bridge St., SP10 1BH, ℰ 352266, Fax 323767 – 🞈 rm 📺 ☎ 🅿 – 🔬 65. 🔼 🕮 ⑩ 𝕍𝕀𝕊𝔸 ᴶᶜᴮ
M (bar lunch)/dinner a la carte 10.50/15.00 **t.** ⅋ 4.95 – ⊊ 8.50 – **20 rm** 55.00/65.00 **t.** – SB (weekends only) 70.00 **st.**

at Barton Stacey SE : 5½ m. by A 303 – ✉ ☎ 0264 Andover :

🏠 **Forte Travelodge** without rest., SO21 3NP, on A 303 ℰ 72260, Reservations (Freephone) 0800 850950 – 📺 🔬 🅿. 🔼 🕮 𝕍𝕀𝕊𝔸. ⬚
20 rm 31.95 **t.**

🔧 ATS 51a New St. ℰ 323606/7

🏌 Appleby, Brackenber Moor ℰ 51432, SE : 2 m.
🏢 Moot Hall, Boroughgate, CA16 6XD ℰ 51177.

♦London 285 – ♦Carlisle 33 – Kendal 24 – ♦Middlesbrough 58.

🏨 **Appleby Manor** (Best Western) ⤳, Roman Rd, CA16 6JB, E : 1 m. by B 6542 via Station Rd ℰ 51571, Fax 52888, ≤, 🞈, ⅃ₐ – 📺 ☎ 🅿 – 🔬 25. 🔼 🕮 ⑩ 𝕍𝕀𝕊𝔸
M – Oak Room 18.95/25.95 **st.** and a la carte ⅋ 5.75 – **30 rm** ⊊ 64.00/98.00 **st.** – SB 98.00/156.00 **st.**

🏨 **Tufton Arms**, Market Sq., CA16 6XA, ℰ 51593, Fax 52761, ⤳ – 📺 ☎ 🅿 – 🔬 120. 🔼 🕮 ⑩ 𝕍𝕀𝕊𝔸
M 8.40/15.50 **t.** and a la carte ⅋ 3.75 – **17 rm** ⊊ 37.50/110.00 **t.**, 2 suites – SB (November-April) 80.00/150.00 **st.**

🏠 **Royal Oak Inn**, Bongate, CA16 6UN, SE : ½ m. on B 6542 ℰ 51463, Fax 52300 – 🞈 rest 📺 ☎ 🅿. 🔼 🕮 ⑩ 𝕍𝕀𝕊𝔸
accommodation closed 24 and 25 December – **M** (closed 24 December) a la carte approx. 13.00 **t.** ⅋ 3.95 – **9 rm** ⊊ 25.50/68.50 **t.** – SB 80.00/90.00 **st.**

◆London 37 – ◆Brighton 20 – Crawley 11.

🏠 **Ardingly Inn,** Street Lane, RH17 6UA, 🖉 892214, Fax 892635, 🍽 – 📺 **P**. 🔄 **VISA**
M *(closed dinner Sunday and Monday to non-residents)* (in bar) à la carte 8.95/
15.95 **t.** and à la carte 🕯 3.50 – **5 rm** 🖃 28.00/44.00 **t.** – SB 48.00/70.00 **st.**

ARMATHWAITE Cumbria 401 402 L 19 – ✉ Carlisle – ✪ 069 74.
◆London 302 – ◆Carlisle 17 – Kendal 46 – Lancaster 60.

🏠 **Dukes Head,** Front St., CA4 9PB, 🖉 72226, 🍽 – 📺 **P**
M (bar lunch Monday to Saturday)/dinner à la carte approx. 13.00 **t.** 🕯 3.95 – **5 rm** 🖃 25.00/
50.00 **t.**

ARMITAGE Staffs. 402 403 404 O 25 – pop. 4 155 – ✉ Rugeley – ✪ 0543.
◆London 135 – ◆Birmingham 25 – Derby 26 – ◆Stoke-on-Trent 25.

XX **Old Farmhouse,** Armitage Rd, WS15 4AT, on A 513 🖉 490353 – **P**. 🔄 🖭 ① **VISA**
closed Saturday lunch, Sunday dinner, Monday and 14 to 31 August – **M** 7.95 **t.** (lunch) and
à la carte 20.00/23.00 **t.** 🕯 4.90.

ARNCLIFFE N. Yorks. 402 N 21 – pop. 67 – ✉ Skipton – ✪ 0756.
◆London 232 – Kendal 41 – ◆Leeds 41 – ◆Preston 50 – York 52.

🏠 **Amerdale House** 🌭, BD23 5QE, 🖉 770250, ≤, 🍽 – ⧖ rest 📺 **P**. 🔄 **VISA**. �&
mid March-mid November – **M** (dinner only) 18.00 **t.** 🕯 4.35 – **11 rm** 🖃 (dinner included) 59.50/109.00 **st.**

ARUNDEL W. Sussex 404 S 31 Great Britain G. – pop. 2 595 – ECD : Wednesday – ✪ 0903.
See : Castle★ *AC.*
🛈 61 High St., BN18 9AJ 🖉 882268.
◆London 58 – ◆Brighton 21 – ◆Southampton 41 – Worthing 9.

🏨 **Norfolk Arms,** 22 High St., BN18 9AD, 🖉 882101, Fax 884275 – ⧖ rm 📺 ☎ **P**. 🔄 🖭
① **VISA**
M 10.95/16.50 **t.** and à la carte 🕯 4.00 – **34 rm** 🖃 44.95/69.90 **t.** – SB 105.90/135.90 **st.**

🏨 **Arundel Resort,** 16 Chichester Rd, BN18 0AD, W : 1 m. on A 27 🖉 882677, Fax 884154 –
⧖ rm 📺 ☎ **P** – 🔬 140. 🔄 🖭 ① **VISA**
M 8.25 **t.** and à la carte – 🖃 7.50 – **27 rm** 55.00/65.00 **t.** – SB 80.00/90.00 **st.**

🏠 **Arundel Park,** Station Rd, BN18 9JL, E : ½ m. on A 27 🖉 882588, Fax 883808 – 📺 **P**. 🔄
VISA. �&
M à la carte 10.70/17.70 **t.** 🕯 5.00 – **12 rm** 🖃 29.50/39.50 **t.**

🏠 **Howards,** Crossbush, BN18 9PQ, E : 1 m. on A 27 at junction with A 284 🖉 882655,
Fax 883384 – 📺 ☎ **P**. 🔄 🖭 ① **VISA**. �&
M (carving rest.) 15.70 **t.** and à la carte 🕯 3.75 – 🖃 7.50 – **9 rm** 37.50/50.00 **t.** – SB 70.00/
110.00 **st.**

🏠 **St. Mary's Gate,** London Rd, BN18 9BA, 🖉 883145 – 📺 ☎ **P**. 🔄 🖭 ① **VISA**
M 10.00 **t.** – 🖃 6.00 – **7 rm** 25.00/50.00 **t.**

🏠 **Portreeves Acre** without rest., The Causeway, BN18 9JL, 🖉 883277, 🍽 – 📺 **P**
3 rm 🖃 30.00/40.00 **st.**

at Burpham NE : 3 m. by A 27 – ✉ ✪ 0903 Arundel :

🏠 **Burpham Country** 🌭, Old Down, BN18 9RJ, 🖉 882160, ≤, 🍽 – ⧖ rest 📺 **P**. 🔄 **VISA**.
�&
M (dinner only) 16.50 **t.** 🕯 4.00 – **10 rm** 🖃 40.00/68.00 **t.** – SB (except Bank Holidays)
79.00/87.00 **st.**

at Walberton W : 3 m. by A 27 off B 2132 – ✉ Arundel – ✪ 0243 Yapton :

🏨 **Avisford Park,** Yapton Lane, BN18 0LS, on B 2132 🖉 551215, Fax 552485, ≤, 🍽,
🏊 heated, 🔲, 🖫, 🍽, park, 🌂, squash – ⧖ rest ▦ rest 📺 ☎ 🕭 **P** – 🔬 300. 🔄 🖭 ①
VISA. �&
M *(closed Saturday lunch)* (buffet lunch Monday to Friday)/dinner 25.00 **st.** and à la carte –
121 rm 🖃 70.00/120.00 **st.**, 5 suites – SB (except Easter, Christmas and Bank Holidays)
(weekends only) 130.00/195.00 **st.**

ASCOT Berks. 404 R 29 – pop. 17 930 (inc Sunningdale) – ECD : Wednesday – ✪ 0344.
🖫 Mill Ride, North Ascot 🖉 886777, W : 2 m.
◆London 36 – Reading 15.

🏨 **Royal Berkshire** (Hilton) 🌭, London Rd, Sunninghill, SL5 OPP, E : 2 m. on A 329
🖉 23322, Telex 847280, Fax 27100, « Queen Anne mansion », 🍽, 🔲, 🍽, park, 🌂,
squash – 📺 ☎ **P** – 🔬 70. 🔄 🖭 ① **VISA**
M (see Stateroom below) – 🖃 11.50 – **60 rm** 105.00/145.00 **t.**, 3 suites.

🏨 **Berystede** (Forte), Bagshot Rd, Sunninghill, SL5 9JH, S : 1 ½ m. on A 330 🖉 23311,
Fax 872301, 🏊 heated, 🍽, park – 🏗 rm 📺 ☎ **P** – 🔬 120. 🔄 🖭 ① **VISA** **JCB**
M *(closed Saturday lunch)* 17.50/20.00 **st.** and à la carte 🕯 6.95 – 🖃 10.50 – **90 rm**
95.00/120.00 **st.**, 1 suite – SB 148.00 **st.**

☆ **Royal Foresters,** London Rd, SL5 8DR, W : 1 ½ m. on A 329 – ✆ 884747, Fax 884115 – ▥
☎ ℗. ☒ AE ◎ VISA ⬩
M (Beeefeater grill) a la carte approx. 16.00 **t.** – ☲ 4.95 – **33 rm** 35.50 **t.**

XXX **Stateroom** (at Royal Berkshire H.), London Rd, Sunninghill, SL5 0PP, E : 2 m. on A 329
– ✆ 23322, Telex 847280, Fax 27100, ⇄ – ℗. ☒ AE ◎ VISA
M 19.50/28.00 ⬩ 8.50.

XX **Ciao Ninety,** 6 Hermitage Par., High St., SL5 7TE, ✆ 22285 – 🍽. ☒ AE ◎ VISA
closed Saturday lunch and Sunday – **M** - **Italian** 11.00/18.00 **t.** and a la carte ⬩ 4.00.

at Sunninghill S : 1 ½ m. by A 329 on B 3020 – ✉ ✿ 0344 Ascot :

🏠 Highclere, Kings Rd, SL5 9AD, ✆ 25220, Fax 872528 – ▥ ☎ ℗. ⬩⬩
11 rm.

XX **Jade Fountain,** 38 High St., SL5 9NE, ✆ 27070 – 🍽. ☒ AE ◎ VISA
– **Chinese** (Canton, Peking) 12.50/25.00 **t.** and a la carte ⬩ 4.00.

ASENBY N. Yorks. – see Thirsk.

ASHBOURNE Derbs. 402 403 404 O 24 *Great Britain G.* – pop. 5 909 – ✿ 0335.

Envir. : Dovedale★★ (Ilam Rock★) NW : 6 m. by A 515.

▜ Clifton ✆ 42078, W : 2 m. on A 515.

🅱 13 Market Pl., DE6 1EU ✆ 43666.

⬩London 146 – Derby 14 – ⬩Manchester 48 – ⬩Nottingham 33 – ⬩Sheffield 44.

🏨 **Callow Hall** ⬙, Mappleton Rd, DE6 2AA, W : ¾ m. (via Union St.) ✆ 343403,
Fax 343624, ⬃, ⟲, park – ⬅⬆ rest ▥ ☎ ℗. ☒ AE ◎ VISA ⬩⬩
closed 25 and 26 December – **M** *(closed Sunday dinner to non-residents)* (lunch by
arrangement)/dinner 28.00 **t.** and a la carte ⬩ 4.50 – **12 rm** ☲ 65.00/120.00 **t.** – SB 120.00/
190.00 **st.**

🏨 **Ashbourne Lodge,** Derby Rd, DE6 1XH, SE : 1 m. on A 52 ✆ 346666, Fax 346549 – |⧝|
⬅⬆ rm ▥ ☎ ⅋ ℗ ⬩⬩ 170. ☒ AE ◎ VISA
M (bar lunch Monday to Saturday)/dinner 15.95 **st.** and a la carte ⬩ 6.50 – **47 rm** ☲ 59.00/
69.00 **st.**, 2 suites – SB (weekends only) 77.00/97.00 **st.**

◍ ATS Blenheim Rd, Airfield Ind. Est. ✆ 344644

Great Britain and Ireland are covered entirely

at a scale of 16 miles to 1 inch by our map *« Main roads »* 986.

ASHBURTON Devon 403 I 32 *The West Country G.* – pop. 3 610 – ECD : Wednesday – ✿ 0364.

Envir. : Dartmoor National Park★★ (Brent Tor ⩻★★, Haytor Rocks ⩻★).

⬩London 220 – Exeter 20 – ⬩Plymouth 23.

🏨 **Holne Chase** ⬙, TQ13 7NS, W : 3 m. on Two Bridges rd ✆ 036 43 (Poundsgate) 471,
Fax 453, ⩻, ⬃, ⟲, park – ⬅⬆ rest ▥ ☎ ℗ – ⬩⬩ 30. ☒ AE ◎ VISA
M 14.75/19.50 **st.** ⬩ 4.25 – **14 rm** ☲ 47.50/125.00 **st.** – SB (except Christmas and New Year)
105.00/130.00 **st.**

🏠 **Ashburton,** 79 East St., TQ13 7AL, ✆ 652784, Fax 652784, ⇄ – ▥ ☎. ☒ ◎ VISA
M 7.50/12.00 **t.** and a la carte ⬩ 5.00 – ☲ 3.50 – **4 rm** 29.50/50.00 **st.**

🏠 **Gages Mill,** Buckfastleigh Rd, TQ13 7JW, SW : 1 m. on old A 38 ✆ 652391, ⇄ – ⬅⬆ rest
℗. ⬩⬩
closed December – **M** (by arrangement) 9.50 **t.** ⬩ 3.50 – **8 rm** ☲ 18.50/43.00 **t.**

at Holne W : 4 ½ m. by Two Bridges rd – ✉ Ashburton – ✿ 036 43 Poundsgate :

🏠 **Wellpritton Farm** ⬙, TQ13 7RX, E : 1 m. ✆ 273 – ⬅⬆ rm ℗. ⬩⬩
closed 25 and 26 December – **M** (by arrangement) 8.00 – **4 rm** ☲ (dinner included)
21.00/50.00.

ASHBY DE LA ZOUCH Leics. 402 403 404 P 25 – pop. 9 987 – ECD : Wednesday – ✿ 0530.

▜ Willesley Park, Measham Rd ✆ 411532, S : 2 m. by B 5006.

🅱 North St., LE65 1HU ✆ 411767.

⬩London 119 – ⬩Birmingham 29 – ⬩Leicester 18 – ⬩Nottingham 22.

🏨 **Fallen Knight,** Kilwardby St., LE65 2FQ, ✆ 412230, Fax 417596 – |⧝| ▥ ☎ ℗ – ⬩⬩ 50. ☒
AE ◎ VISA ⬩⬩
M 9.95/15.95 **t.** and a la carte ⬩ 4.00 – **24 rm** ☲ 50.00/112.00 **st.**

XX **Rajni,** 48 Tamworth Rd, LE65 2PR, S : ½ m. on B 5006 ✆ 560349 – 🍽 ℗. ☒ AE ◎ VISA
closed 25 December – **M** - **Indian** a la carte 7.00/15.55 **st.**

◍ ATS Kilwardby St. ✆ 412791

ASHFORD Kent 404 W 30 – pop. 45 198 – ECD : Wednesday – ✿ 0233.

▜ Ashford Manor, Fordbridge Rd ✆ 252049, off A 308.

✈ Lydd - Ashford Airport, Romney Marsh, TN29 9QL ✆ 0679 (Lydd) 20401, Fax 21516.

🅱 18 The Churchyard, TN23 1QG ✆ 629165.

⬩London 56 – Canterbury 14 – ⬩Dover 24 – Hastings 30 – Maidstone 19.

Eastwell Manor (Q.M.H.) ⑤, Eastwell Park, Boughton Lees, TN25 4HR, N : 3 m. by A 28 on A 251 ℘ 635751, Telex 966281, Fax 635530, ≤, « Reconstructed period mansion in formal gardens », park, ✂ – |‡| TV ☎ P – 🏛 70. AE ⓓ VISA
M 14.50/35.00 **t.** 6.75 – **20 rm** ☐ 100.00/150.00 **t.**, 3 suites – SB (except Christmas and New Year) (weekends only) 160.00/260.00 **st.**

Ashford International (Q.M.H.), Simone Weil Av., TN24 8UX, ℘ 611444, Group Telex 96498, Fax 627708, Fб, ≘s, 🏊 – |‡| ⇔ rm ▤ rest TV ☎ ♿ P – 🏛 400. AE ⓓ VISA
M *(in bar Saturday lunch and Sunday)* 13.00/17.00 **st.** 5.25 – **198 rm** ☐ 100.00/118.00 **st.**, 2 suites – SB (weekends only) 104.00 **st.**

Forte Posthouse, Canterbury Rd, TN24 8QQ, ℘ 625790, Fax 643176, ⚘ – ⇔ rm TV ☎ ♿ P – 🏛 70. AE ⓓ VISA JCB. ✂
M a la carte approx. 17.50 **t.** 4.65 – ☐ 6.95 – **60 rm** 53.50 **st.** – SB (weekends only) 90.00 **st.**

Master Spearpoint (Best Western), Canterbury Rd, Kennington, TN24 9QR, NE : 2 m. on A 28 ℘ 636863, Fax 610119, ⚘ – TV ☎ P – 🏛 60. AE ⓓ VISA
M (carving lunch)/dinner a la carte 10.40/13.60 **st.** 4.85 – **35 rm** ☐ 46.00/53.00 **st.**

at Hothfield NW : 3 ½ m. by A 20 – ✉ ☎ 0233 Ashford :

Holiday Inn Garden Court, Maidstone Rd, TN26 1AR, N : 1 m. on A 20 ℘ 713333, Fax 712082, Fб, ⚘ – |‡| ⇔ rm ▤ rest TV ☎ ♿ P – 🏛 25. AE ⓓ VISA JCB
M (dinner only) 12.95 **t.** and a la carte – ☐ 7.00 – **104 rm** 58.00 **t.**

Travel Inn, Maidstone Rd, Hothfield Common, TN26 1AP, on A 20 ℘ 712571, Fax 713945 – ⇔ rm TV ♿ P. AE ⓓ VISA. ✂
M (Beefeater grill) a la carte approx. 16.00 **t.** – ☐ 4.95 – **40 rm** 33.50 **t.**

ATS Hythe Rd, Henwood Ind. Est. ℘ 622450/624891

ASHFORD Surrey 404 S 29 – ECD : Wednesday – ☎ 0784.

♦London 21 – Reading 27.

XX **Terrazza,** 45 Church Rd, TW15 2TY, ℘ 244887 – ▤. AE ⓓ VISA
closed Saturday lunch, Sunday and Bank Holidays – **M** - **Italian** 19.50 **st.** and a la carte.

ASHFORD-IN-THE-WATER Derbs. 402 403 404 O 24 – see Bakewell.

ASHINGTON W. Sussex 404 S 31 – pop. 1 728 – ECD : Wednesday – ✉ Pulborough – ☎ 0903.

♦London 50 – ♦Brighton 20 – Worthing 9.

Mill House ⑤, Mill Lane, RH20 3BZ, ℘ 892426, Fax 892855, ⚘ – TV ☎ P – 🏛 40. AE ⓓ VISA
M 9.95/13.95 **t.** and a la carte 4.55 – **10 rm** ☐ 40.60/87.00 **t.** – SB (except Christmas-New Year) 89.60 **t.**

XX **Willows,** London Rd, RH20 3JR, on A 24 ℘ 892575 – P. AE VISA
closed Saturday lunch, Sunday dinner and Monday – **M** (lunch by arrangement)/dinner 17.65 **t.** 3.95.

ATS Lintonville Terr. ℘ 817013/817038

ASHINGTON Northd. 401 402 P 18 – pop. 27 665 – ☎ 0670.

♦London 303 – ♦Edinburgh 102 – ♦Newcastle upon Tyne 17.

Lakeside, Queen Elizabeth II Country Park, Woodhorn, NE63 9AT, N : 2½ m. by A 197 on A 189 ℘ 862001, Fax 860986, ≘s, 🏊 – TV ☎ ♿ P – 🏛 100. AE ⓓ VISA. ✂
M (dinner only and Sunday lunch)/dinner 14.95 **t.** 4.75 – **20 rm** ☐ 55.00/70.00 **t.** – SB (weekends only) 65.00 **st.**

ASHPRINGTON Devon 403 I 32 – see Totnes.

ASHTON KEYNES Wilts. 403 404 O 29 – pop. 1 275 – ☎ 0285 Cirencester.

♦London 98 – ♦Bristol 40 – Gloucester 27 – ♦Oxford 42 – Swindon 14.

2 Cove House, SN6 6NS, (behind White Hart Inn) ℘ 861221, ⚘ – P. ✂
closed 20 December-1 January – **M** (by arrangement) (communal dining) 16.50 **st.** – **3 rm** ☐ 28.00/50.00 **st.** – SB 69.00/97.00 **st.**

ASHTON-UNDER-LYNE Gtr. Manchester 402 403 404 N 23 – pop. 43 605 – ECD : Tuesday – ☎ 061 Manchester.

♦London 209 – ♦Leeds 40 – ♦Manchester 7 – ♦Sheffield 34.

York House, York Pl., off Richmond St., OL6 7TT, ℘ 330 5899, Fax 343 1613 – TV ☎ P – 🏛 30. AE ⓓ VISA JCB
M *(closed Saturday lunch and Sunday)* 9.50/15.00 **st.** and a la carte 4.25 – **34 rm** ☐ 46.00/71.00 **st.**

XX **Woodlands** with rm, 33 Shepley Rd, Audenshaw, M34 5DL, S : 2 m. by A 635, Audenshaw Rd and Guide Lane (A 6017) on B 6169 ℘ 336 4241 – TV ☎ P. VISA
closed Saturday lunch, Sunday, Monday, 1 week Easter, 2 weeks August and first week January – **M** 15.65 **t.** and a la carte – ☐ 6.50 – **3 rm** 40.00/60.00.

ASKRIGG N. Yorks. [402] N 21 – pop. 404 – ✉ Leyburn – 📞 0969 Wensleydale.
◆London 251 – Kendal 32 – ◆Leeds 70 – York 63.

🏨 **King's Arms,** Market Sq., DL8 3HQ, ✆ 50258, Fax 50635 – [TV] ☎ [P]. [Access] [AE] [VISA] [JCB]
M 12.50/30.00 **t.** and a la carte 🍷 4.00 – **9 rm** ☕ 45.00/95.00 **t.** – SB (except Bank Holidays) 110.00/150.00 **st.**

🏨 **Winville,** Main St., DL8 3HG, ✆ 50515, Fax 50594, 🌳 – [TV] ☎ [P]. [Access] [DC] [VISA]
M 16.95 **st.** (dinner) and lunch a la carte approx. 12.25 **st.** 🍷 3.50 – **10 rm** ☕ 42.00/68.00 **st.** – SB (except Christmas-New Year) 86.00/110.00 **st.**

ASPLEY GUISE Beds. [404] S 27 – pop. 2 314 – 📞 0908 Milton Keynes.
⛳18 Woburn Sands, West Hill ✆ 582264, W : 2 m. by M 1 (junction 13) – ⛳18 Millbrook, Ampthill ✆ 0525 (Ampthill) 404683, W : 5 m. by A 1 junction 13 and A 507.
◆London 52 – Bedford 13 – Luton 16 – ◆Northampton 22.

🏨🏨 **Moore Place,** The Square, MK17 8DW, ✆ 282000, Fax 281888, 🌳 – [TV] ☎ [P] – 👥 50. [Access] [AE] [DC] [VISA]. 🚫🐕
M *(closed Saturday lunch)* a la carte 24.05/29.45 **st.** – **53 rm** ☕ 59.50/75.00 **st.**, 1 suite – SB (weekends only) 95.00 **st.**

ASTON S. Yorks. [402] [403] [404] Q 23 – pop. 13 864 – ✉ 📞 0742 Sheffield.
◆London 161 – Lincoln 39 – ◆Sheffield 8.

🏨🏨 Aston Hall, Worksop Rd, S31 0EE, ✆ 872309, Fax 873228, 🌳, park – [TV] ☎ [P] – 👥 400. 🚫🐕
22 rm.

ASTON CLINTON Bucks. [404] R 28 – pop. 3 671 – ECD : Wednesday – ✉ 📞 0296 Aylesbury.
◆London 42 – Aylesbury 4 – ◆Oxford 26.

🏨🏨 **Bell Inn,** London Rd, HP22 5HP, ✆ 630252, Fax 631250, « Courtyard and gardens » – [TV] ☎ [P] – 👥 150. [Access] [AE] [VISA]
M 25.00/36.00 **t.** and a la carte 🍷 6.50 – ☕ 12.50 – **15 rm** 92.00/107.00 **t.**, 6 suites – SB (except Christmas and New Year) 125.00/200.00 **t.**

ATHERSTONE Warks. [403] [404] P 26 – pop. 9 959 📞 0827.
◆London 120 – ◆Birmingham 22 – ◆Coventry 15 – ◆Leicester 30.

🍴🍴 **Chapel House** with rm, Friars Gate, CV9 1EY, ✆ 718949, Fax 717702, « Part Georgian former dower house », 🌳 – [TV] ☎. [Access] [AE] [DC] [VISA]. 🚫🐕
closed 25 and 26 December – **M** *(closed Sunday)* (dinner only) 18.95/21.95 **t.** – **12 rm** ☕ 37.50/60.00 **st.** – SB (weekends only) 52.45/89.90 **st.**

ATTLEBOROUGH Norfolk [404] X 26 – pop. 6 322 – ECD : Wednesday – 📞 0953.
◆London 94 – ◆Cambridge 47 – ◆Norwich 15.

🏨 **Sherbourne House,** Norwich Rd, NR17 2JX, NE : ½ m. ✆ 454363, Fax 453509, 🌳 – [TV] ☎ [P]. [Access] [VISA]
M *(closed Sunday to Thursday to non-residents)* (dinner only) 20.00 **t.** – **8 rm** ☕ 25.00/70.00 **st.** – SB (October-April except Christmas) (weekends only) 76.00/90.00 **st.**

🛞 ATS London Rd ✆ 453883

AUST SERVICE AREA Avon – ✉ Bristol – 📞 0454 Pilning

🏨 **Pavilion Lodge** without rest., BS12 3BJ, M 4 junction 21 ✆ 633313, Fax 633819 – [TV] ♿ [P]. [Access] [AE] [DC] [VISA]
☕ 4.00 – **51 rm** 31.95/35.95 **st.**

AUSTWICK N. Yorks. [402] M 21 – ✉ Lancaster – 📞 052 42 Clapham.
◆London 259 – Kendal 28 – Lancaster 20 – ◆Leeds 46.

🏨 **The Traddock,** LA2 8BY, ✆ 51224, Fax 51224, 🌳 – 🚭 rest [TV] ☎ [P]. [Access] [VISA]. 🚫🐕
M 7.00/18.00 **st.** and a la carte 🍷 3.50 – **11 rm** ☕ 30.00/60.00 **st.** – SB 80.00/110.00 **st.**

AVON Hants. – see Ringwood.

AXMINSTER Devon [403] L 31 The West Country G. – pop. 4 457 – ECD : Wednesday – 📞 0297.
Envir. : Lyme Regis★ – The Cobb★, SE : 5½ m. by A 35 and A 3070.
[i] The Old Courthouse, Church St., EX13 5AQ ✆ 34386 (summer only).
◆London 156 – Exeter 27 – Lyme Regis 5.5 – Taunton 22 – Yeovil 24.

🏨🏨 **Fairwater Head** 🐦, Hawkchurch, EX13 5TX, NE : 3 ¾ m. by A 35 off B 3165 ✆ 0297 (Hawkchurch) 678349, < Axe Vale, 🌳 – 🚭 rest [TV] ☎ [P]. [Access] [AE] [DC] [VISA]. 🚫🐕
closed January and February – **M** (bar lunch Monday to Saturday)/dinner 20.50 **t.** and a la carte – **21 rm** ☕ (dinner included) 59.00/144.00 **t.**

AYLESBURY Bucks. [404] R 28 Great Britain G. – pop. 51 999 – ECD : Thursday – 📞 0296.
Envir. : Waddesdon Manor (Collection★★) NW : 5½ m. by A 41.
⛳18 Weston Turville, New Rd ✆ 24084, SE : 1½ m. – ⛳9 Hulcott Lane, Bierton ✆ 399644, NE : 3 m.
[i] County Hall, Walton St., HP20 1UA ✆ 382308/383095.
◆London 46 – ◆Birmingham 72 – Northampton 37 – ◆Oxford 22.

⌂⌂⌂⌂ **Hartwell House** ☾, Oxford Rd, HP17 8NL, SW : 2 m. on A 418 ☏ 747444, Fax 747450, ≤, « Part Jacobean, part Georgian house, former residence of Louis XVIII », 🏋, ♨, 🏊, 🎣, 🌳, park, 🎾 – ⇕ 🚭 rest 📺 ☎ Ⓟ – 👥 80. ▣ AE ⓓ VISA. 🚫🐕
M 16.50/38.00 **st.** and a la carte – ☕ 10.75 – **34 rm** 90.00/135.00 **st.**, 13 suites – SB 184.00/258.00 **st.**

⌂⌂⌂ **Forte Posthouse,** Aston Clinton Rd, HP22 5AA, SE : 2 m. on A 41 ☏ 393388, Fax 392211, 🏋, ♨, 🏊, 🌳 – 🚭 rm ▤ rest 📺 ☎ ♿ Ⓟ – 👥 100. ▣ AE ⓓ VISA
M (bar lunch Saturday) a la carte approx. 17.50 **t.** 🍷 4.65 – ☕ 6.95 – **92 rm** 53.50/69.50 **st.**, 2 suites – SB (except Christmas) 90.00 **st.**

⌂⌂ **Watermead** without rest., Buckingham Rd, HP19 3FY, N : 1 m. on A 413 ☏ 398839, Fax 394108 – 🚭 📺 ☎ ♿ Ⓟ – 👥 40. ▣ AE ⓓ VISA. 🚫🐕
40 rm 55.00/60.00 **st.**

⌂ **Horse and Jockey,** Buckingham Rd, HP19 3QL, ☏ 23803, Fax 395142 – 📺 ☎ Ⓟ. ▣ AE ⓓ VISA. 🚫🐕
M (in bar) approx. 10.95 **t.** – **24 rm** ☕ 43.00/55.00 **st.**

⊙ ATS Gatehouse Way ☏ 433177

BABBACOMBE Devon 403 J 32 – see Torquay.

BADBY Northants. – see Daventry.

BADMINTON Avon 403 404 N 29 – pop. 283 – ⊛ 0454 Chipping Sodbury.
♦London 114 – ♦Bristol 19 – Gloucester 26 – Swindon 33.

⌂⌂ **Petty France,** Dunkirk, GL9 1AF, NW : 3 m. on A 46 ☏ 238361, Fax 238768, 🌳 – 🚭 rest 📺 ☎ Ⓟ – 👥 25. ▣ AE ⓓ VISA
M 19.00 **t.** and a la carte 🍷 5.50 – ☕ 8.50 – **20 rm** 65.00/110.00 **t.** – SB 96.00/130.00 **t.**

⌂ **Bodkin House,** Dunkirk, GL9 1AF, NW : 3 m. on A 46 ☏ 238310, Fax 238422 – 📺 ☎ Ⓟ. ▣ AE ⓓ VISA JCB. 🚫🐕
M *(closed Sunday dinner)* 8.95/13.95 **t.** and a la carte 🍷 3.75 – **8 rm** ☕ 40.00/70.00 **t.** – SB 75.00/125.90 **st.**

BAGINTON Warks 403 404 P 26 – see Coventry.

BAGSHOT Surrey 404 R 29 – pop. 4 239 – ECD : Wednesday – ⊛ 0276.
♦London 37 – Reading 17 – ♦Southampton 49.

⌂⌂⌂ **Pennyhill Park,** London Rd, GU19 5ET, SW : 1 m. on A 30 ☏ 471774, Fax 473217, ≤, ♨, 🏊 heated, ⛳9, 🎣, 🌳, park, 🎾 – 🚭 rm 📺 ☎ Ⓟ – 👥 50. ▣ AE ⓓ VISA JCB. 🚫🐕
M 16.95/28.00 **st.** and dinner a la carte 🍷 6.60 – ☕ 13.00 – **70 rm** 120.00/184.00 **st.**, 6 suites – SB (weekends only) 170.00 **st.**

⌂ **Cricketers,** London Rd, GU19 5HR, N : ½ m. on A 30 ☏ 473196, Fax 451357, 🌳 – 📺 ☎ Ⓟ. ▣ AE ⓓ VISA. 🚫🐕
M (Beefeater grill) a la carte 10.80/16.70 **t.** 🍷 5.00 – ☕ 4.95 – **27 rm** 39.50 **st.**

BAINBRIDGE N. Yorks. 402 N 21 – pop. 474 – ECD : Wednesday – ✉ ⊛ 0969 Wensleydale.
♦London 249 – Kendal 31 – ♦Leeds 68 – York 61.

⌂ **Rose and Crown,** DL8 3EE, ☏ 50225, Fax 50735 – 📺 Ⓟ. ▣ VISA
M (bar lunch Monday to Saturday)/dinner a la carte 13.25/18.25 **t.** – **12 rm** ☕ 34.00/68.00 **t.** – SB 72.00/96.00 **st.**

BAKEWELL Derbs. 402 403 404 O 24 **Great Britain G.** – pop. 3 839 – ECD : Thursday – ⊛ 0629.
Envir. : Chatsworth★★★ (Park and Garden★★★) *AC*, NE : 2½ m. by A 619 – Haddon Hall★★ *AC*, SE : 2 m. by A 6.
ℹ Old Market Hall, Bridge St., DE4 1DS ☏ 813227.
♦London 160 – Derby 26 – ♦Manchester 37 – ♦Nottingham 33 – ♦Sheffield 17.

⌂⌂ **Rutland Arms** (Best Western), The Square, DE4 1BT, ☏ 812812, Fax 812309 – 🚭 rest 📺 ☎ Ⓟ – 👥 80. ▣ AE ⓓ VISA JCB
M 10.95/18.50 **st.** and a la carte 🍷 5.25 – **35 rm** ☕ 42.00/85.00 **st.** – SB 92.00/120.00 **st.**

⋀ **Milford House,** Mill St., DE45 1DA, ☏ 812130, 🌳 – 📺 Ⓟ. 🚫🐕
April-October – **M** (by arrangement) 15.25 **t.** 🍷 4.00 – **12 rm** ☕ 33.00/70.00 **t.** – SB 89.00/100.00 **st.**

at Hassop N : 3½ m. by A 619 on B 6001 – ✉ Bakewell – ⊛ 062 987 (3 fig.) and 0629 (6 fig.) Great Longstone :

⌂⌂⌂ **Hassop Hall** ☾, DE45 1NS, ☏ 640488, Fax 640577, ≤, « Part 16C hall », 🌳, park, 🎾 – ⇕ 📺 ☎ Ⓟ. ▣ AE ⓓ VISA JCB
accommodation closed 3 days at Christmas – **M** *(closed Monday lunch and Sunday dinner)* approx. 17.00/28.00 **t.** – ☕ 9.95 – **13 rm** 70.00/120.00 **t.**

at Great Longstone N : 4 m. by A 619 off B 6001 – ✉ Bakewell – ⊛ 062 987 (3 fig.) and 0629 (6 fig.) Great Longstone :

⌂ **Croft** ☾, DE45 1TF, ☏ 640278, 🌳 – 🚭 rest 📺 Ⓟ. ▣ VISA. 🚫🐕
closed 3 January-3 February – **M** (dinner only) 20.50 **t.** 🍷 4.00 – **9 rm** ☕ 58.00/90.00 **t.** – SB 98.00/108.00 **t.**

at Alport S : 4 m. by A 6 off B 5056 – ⊠ Bakewell – 🕓 0629 Youlgreave :

⌂ **Rock House** without rest., DE45 1LG, ℰ 636736, 🐎 – ⇥ 🅿. 🛠
3 rm 19.00/38.00 **s.**

at Ashford-in-the-Water NW : 1¾ m. by A 6 and A 6020 on B 6465 – ⊠ 🕓 0629 Bakewell :

🏦 **Riverside Country House,** Fennel St., DE45 1QF, ℰ 814275, Fax 812873, 🐎 – ⇥ 📺
☎ 🅿. 🔦 🆎 VISA. 🛠
M 13.95/29.00 **t.** and lunch a la carte 🍴 5.75 – 🖃 5.00 – **15 rm** 75.00/99.00 **t.** – SB (except Christmas)144.00/150.00 **st.**

BALDOCK Herts. ████ T 28 – pop. 6 703 – ECD : Thursday – 🕓 0462.

◆London 42 – Bedford 20 – ◆Cambridge 21 – Luton 15.

🏠 **Forte Travelodge** without rest., A 1 Great North Road, Hinxworth (southbound carriageway), SG7 5EX, NW : 3 m. by A 507 on A 1 ℰ 835329, Reservations (Freephone) 0800 850950 – 🔟 🕭 🅿. 🔦 🆎 VISA. 🛠
40 rm 31.95 **t.**

BALSALL COMMON W. Mids. – see Coventry.

BAMBER BRIDGE Lancs. ████ M 22 – see Preston.

BAMBURGH Northd. ████ ████ O 17 Great Britain G. – pop. 567 – ECD : Wednesday – 🕓 066 84 (3 fig.) and 0668 (6 fig.).

See : Castle★ AC.

◆London 337 – ◆Edinburgh 77 – ◆Newcastle upon Tyne 51.

🏠 **Lord Crewe Arms,** Front St., NE69 7BL, ℰ 243 – 📺 🅿. 🔦 VISA
April–October – **M** (bar lunch)/dinner 18.50 🍴 3.50 – **25 rm** 🖃 35.00/64.00 **t.** – SB 80.00/118.00 **st.**

at Waren Mill W : 2¾ m. on B 1342 – ⊠ Belford – 🕓 0668 Bamburgh :

🏦 **Waren House** 🐾, NE70 7EE, ℰ 214581, Fax 214484, ←, 🐎, 🛠 – ⇥ 📺 ☎ 🅿. 🔦 🆎 ⓞ VISA. 🛠
Easter–October – **M** (dinner only) 22.50 **st.** 🍴 5.75 – **5 rm** 🖃 72.00/104.00 **st.**, 2 suites – SB 136.00/186.00 **st.**

BAMPTON Devon ████ J 31 – ⊠ Tiverton – 🕓 0398.

◆Lancaster 192 – Exeter 23 – Minehead 21 – Taunton 21.

⌂ **Bark House,** Oakfordbridge, EX16 9HZ, W : 3 m. by B 3227 on A 396 ℰ 039 85 (Oakford) 236, 🐎 – 📺 ☎ 🅿. 🔦 VISA
March–November – **M** (residents only) (dinner only) 14.50 **st.** 🍴 4.50 – 🖃 6.00 – **6 rm** 19.00/56.00 **st.**

BANBURY Oxon. ████ ████ P 27 Great Britain G. – pop. 37 463 – ECD : Tuesday – 🕓 0295.

Exc. : Upton House★ AC, NW : 7 m. by A 422.

🏌 Cherwell Edge, Chacombe ℰ 711591, NE : 4 m.

🎫 Banbury Museum, 8 Horsefair, OX16 0AA ℰ 259855.

◆London 76 – ◆Birmingham 40 – ◆Coventry 25 – ◆Oxford 23.

🏨 **Whately Hall** (Forte), Horsefair, by Banbury Cross, OX16 0AN, ℰ 263451, Fax 271736, « Part 17C hall », 🐎 – 🛌 ⇥ rm 📺 ☎ 🅿 – 🔬 80. 🔦 🆎 ⓞ VISA JCB
M 9.95/16.95 **t.** and a la carte 🍴 5.25 – 🖃 8.50 – **72 rm** 78.00/88.00 **st.**, 2 suites – SB (except Easter and Christmas) 108.00/123.00 **st.**

🏦 **Banbury Moat House** (Q.M.H) 27-29 Oxford Rd, OX16 9AH, ℰ 259361, Telex 838967, Fax 270954 – ⇥ rm 📺 ☎ 🅿 – 🔬 80. 🔦 🆎 ⓞ VISA 🛠
M (bar lunch Saturday) 13.50/14.50 **st.** and a la carte 🍴 4.50 – **48 rm** 🖃 69.00/99.00 **st.** – SB (weekends only) 78.00 **st.**

🏠 **Easington House,** 50 Oxford Rd, OX16 9AN, ℰ 270181, Fax 269527, 🐎 – 📺 ☎ 🅿. 🔦 🆎 ⓞ VISA
M *(closed Sunday and Bank Holiday Mondays)* (dinner only) 9.50 **st.** and a la carte 🍴 4.50 – **12 rm** 🖃 31.00/70.00 **st.** – SB (except Bank Holidays) (weekends only) 49.00/100.00 **st.**

⌂ **Prospect** without rest., 70 Oxford Rd, OX16 9AN, ℰ 268749, 🐎 – 📺 🅿. 🔦 🆎 VISA. 🛠
8 rm 🖃 34.00/48.00 **t.**

at Adderbury S : 3 m. on A 423 – ⊠ 🕓 0295 Banbury :

🏠 Red Lion, The Green, OX17 3LU, ℰ 810269, Fax 811906, « Part 16C inn » – ⇥ rest 📺 ☎ 🅿
8 rm.

at North Newington W : 2¼ m. by B 4035 – ⊠ 🕓 0295 Banbury :

🏠 **La Madonette Country** 🐾 without rest., OX15 6AA, ℰ 730212, ⬛ heated, 🐎 – 📺 ☎ 🅿. 🔦 VISA. 🛠
5 rm 🖃 32.00/55.00 **st.**

at Wroxton NW : 3 m. by A 41 on A 422 – ⊠ ⊕ 0295 Banbury :

🏨 **Wroxton House** (Best Western), Silver St., OX15 6QB, ℰ 730777, Fax 730800 – ⊱⊷ rest
📺 ☎ 🅿 – 🔬 60. 🔼 ᴀᴇ ⓞ 𝑽𝑰𝑺𝑨
M (bar lunch Saturday) 17.50/25.00 **t.** and a la carte ⏐ 6.50 – **32 rm** ⊊ 79.00/120.00 **t.** –
SB (except Christmas and 8 to 11 July) (weekends only) 115.00/130.00 **st.**

at Shenington NW : 6 m. by A 41 off A 422 – ⊠ Banbury – ⊕ 0295 Tysoe :

⋔ **Sugarswell Farm** ⑊, OX15 6HW, NW : 2¼ m. on Edge Hill rd ℰ 680512, ≼, ⫰ – ⊱⊷
🅿 ⫰
M (by arrangement) 20.00 **st.** – **3 rm** ⊊ 29.00/50.00 **st.**

🔘 ATS Beaumont Ind. Est., Beaumont Close ℰ 253525

BANTHAM Devon – see Kingsbridge.

BARFORD Warks. 🄐🄑 P 27 – see Warwick.

BAR HILL Cambs. 🄓 U 27 – see Cambridge.

BARKWITH Lincs. 🄒🄓 T 24 – see East Barkwith.

BARMBY MOOR Humbs. 🄑 R 22 – see Pocklington.

BARNARD CASTLE Durham 🄑 O 20 Great Britain G. – pop. 6 075 – ECD : Thursday –
⊕ 0833 Teesdale.
See : Bowes Museum⋆ *AC.*
Exc. : Raby Castle⋆ *AC*, NE : 6½ m. by A 688.
🄸 Harmire Rd ℰ 37237.
🄱 43 Galgate, DL12 8EL ℰ 690909.

◆London 258 – ◆Carlisle 63 – ◆Leeds 68 – ◆Middlesbrough 31 – ◆Newcastle upon Tyne 39.

🏠 **Jersey Farm** ⑊, Darlington Rd, DL12 8TA, E : 1½ m. on A 67 ℰ 38223, Fax 31988,
« Working farm », park – 📺 ☎ 🅿 – 🔬 150. 🔼 𝑽𝑰𝑺𝑨
M (dinner only and Sunday lunch)/dinner 15.60 **t.** ⏐ 4.50 – **16 rm** ⊊ 41.00/50.00 **t.**, 3 suites
– SB (except Bank Holidays) 60.00/80.00 **st.**

at Romaldkirk NW : 6 m. by A 67 on B 6277 – ⊠ Barnard Castle – ⊕ 0833 Teesdale :

🏨 **Rose and Crown**, DL12 9EB, ℰ 50213, Fax 50828 – 📺 ☎ 🅿. 🔼 𝑽𝑰𝑺𝑨
closed 25 and 26 December – **M** *(closed Sunday dinner)* (bar lunch Monday to Saturday)/
dinner 24.00 **st.** ⏐ 5.30 – **9 rm** ⊊ 52.00/74.00 **st.**, 2 suites – SB (October-May) (weekends
only) 98.00 **st.**

BARNARD GATE Oxon. 🄐🄓 P 28 – see Witney.

BARNSDALE BAR W. Yorks. 🄒🄓 Q 23 – ⊠ ⊕ 0977 Pontefract.
◆London 181 – ◆Leeds 22 – ◆Nottingham 53 – ◆Sheffield 26.

🏠 **Forte Travelodge** without rest., WF8 3JB, on A 1 ℰ 620711, Reservations (Freephone)
0800 850950 – 📺 ♿ 🅿. 🔼 ᴀᴇ 𝑽𝑰𝑺𝑨. ⫰
56 rm 31.95 **t.**

BARNSLEY Glos. 🄐🄓 028 – see Cirencester.

BARNSLEY S. Yorks. 🄒🄓 P 23 – pop. 76 783 – ECD : Thursday – ⊕ 0226.
🄸 Wakefield Rd, Staincross ℰ 382856, N : 4 m. on A 61 – 🄸 Silkstone, Field Head, Elmhirst
Lane ℰ 790328, W : 1 m. by A 628 – 🄵 Wombwell Hillies, Wentworth View, Wombwell
ℰ 754433, SE : 4 m.
🄱 56 Eldon St., S70 2JL ℰ 206757.
◆London 177 – ◆Leeds 21 – ◆Manchester 36 – ◆Sheffield 15.

🏨 **Ardsley Moat House** (Q.M.H.), Doncaster Rd, Ardsley, S71 5EH, E : 2½ m. on A 635
ℰ 289401, Telex 547762, Fax 205374, ⫰ – 📺 ☎ 🅿 – 🔬 250. 🔼 ᴀᴇ ⓞ 𝑽𝑰𝑺𝑨
accommodation closed 25 to 27 December – **M** (bar lunch Saturday) 14.50 **st.** and a la carte
⏐ 5.00 – ⊊ 8.00 – **73 rm** 50.00/75.00 **st.** – SB (weekends only) 82.00/92.00 **st.**

🏠 **Forte Travelodge** without rest., Doncaster Rd, S70 3PE, E : 2½ m. on A 635 ℰ 298799,
Reservations (Freephone) 0800 850950 – 📺 ♿ 🅿. 🔼 ᴀᴇ 𝑽𝑰𝑺𝑨. ⫰
32 rm 31.95 **t.**

🏠 Periquito, Regent St., S70 2HQ, ℰ 731010, Fax 248719 – ⊱⊷ rm 📺 ☎ 🅿 – 🔬 150
51 rm.

XX **Restaurant Peano**, 102 Dodworth Rd, S70 6HL, on A 628 ℰ 244990 – 🅿. 🔼 ᴀᴇ 𝑽𝑰𝑺𝑨
closed Saturday lunch, Sunday, Monday, 1 week September and 26 to 31 December –
Meals (lunch by arrangement)/dinner 14.50 **st.** and a la carte ⏐ 5.00.

🔘 ATS Huddersfield Rd ℰ 281888/287406   ATS Wombwell Lane, Aldham Bridge, Wombwell
                                                                                    ℰ 753511

BARNSTAPLE Devon 403 H 30 The West Country G. – pop. 24 490 – ECD : Wednesday –
✆ 0271 – See : Town★ – Long Bridge★.

Envir. : Arlington Court★★ (Carriage Collection★) *AC*, NE : 6 m. by A 39.

🟦, ⛳ Chulmleigh, Leigh Rd ✆ 0769 (Chulmleigh) 80519, N : 1 m.

🚢 to the Isles of Lundy (Lundy Co.) (2 h 15 mn) (summer only).

🏢 North Devon Library, Tuly St., EX31 1TY ✆ 388583/388584.

◆London 222 – Exeter 40 – Taunton 51.

🏨 **Park,** Taw Vale, EX32 8NJ, ✆ 72166, Fax 78558 – 📺 ☎ 🅿 – 🔬 100. 🔄 AE ⓞ VISA
M 7.50/12.50 **st.** and a la carte ⅓ 4.25 – **41 rm** ⌸ 37.00/55.00 **st.** – SB (weekends only)
80.00/99.00 **st.**

🍴🍴 **Lynwood House** with rm, Bishops Tawton Rd, EX32 9DZ, S : 1 ½ m. by A 361 and
Newport rd ✆ 43695, Fax 79340 – ⟲ rest 📺 ☎ 🅿. 🔄 AE VISA. 🛇
M *(closed Sunday to non-residents)* 13.95 **t.** (lunch) and a la carte 21.25/38.40 **t.** ⅓ 4.95 –
5 rm ⌸ 40.50/60.50 **st.** – SB 97.50/100.00 **st.**

at Bishop's Tawton S : 2¾ m. by A 39 on A 377 – ⊠ ✆ 0271 Barnstaple :

🏨 **Downrew House** ⤢, EX32 0DY, SE : 1 ½ m. on Chittlehampton rd ✆ 42497, Fax 23947,
⪕, ⤢ heated, ⪕, park, ⚒ – ⟲ rest 📺 ☎ 🅿 – 🔬 50. 🔄 VISA
closed January – **M** (bar lunch Monday to Saturday)/dinner 18.50 **st.** and a la carte ⅓ 4.40 –
12 rm ⌸ 51.50/97.00 **st.** – SB (except July-August and Christmas) 85.00/130.00 **st.**

🏛 **Halmpstone Manor** ⤢, EX32 0EA, SE : 3 m. by Chittlehampton rd ✆ 830321,
Fax 830826, ⪕, ⪕, park – ⟲ rest 📺 ☎ 🅿. 🔄 AE ⓞ VISA
closed December except Christmas and January – **M** (lunch by arrangement)/din-
ner 27.50 **t.** – **5 rm** ⌸ 70.00/130.00 **t.** – SB 124.00/195.00 **st.**

🔘 ATS Pottington Ind. Est., Braunton Rd ✆ 42294/5

BARROW-IN-FURNESS Cumbria 402 K 21 – pop. 50 174 – ✆ 0229.

🟦 Rakesmoore Lane, Hawcoat ✆ 825444 – 🟦 Furness, Walney Island ✆ 471232.

🏢 Forum 28, Duke St., LA14 1HU ✆ 870156.

◆London 295 – Kendal 34 – Lancaster 47.

🏨 **Abbey House,** Abbey Rd, LA13 0PA, NE : 2 m. on A 590 ✆ 838282, Telex 65357,
Fax 820403, « Lutyens house », ⪕, park – 🔲 📺 ☎ 🅿 – 🔬 100. 🔄 AE ⓞ VISA
M (bar lunch Saturday) 10.95/17.50 **t.** and a la carte ⅓ 4.75 – ⌸ 7.25 – **28 rm** 42.00/
104.50 **t.** – SB 82.50/113.00 **st.**

🏛 **Arlington House,** 200/202 Abbey Rd, LA14 5LD, ✆ 831976 – 📺 ☎ 🅿. 🔄 VISA. ⪕
M *(closed Sunday)* (dinner only) 15.00/20.00 **t.** ⅓ 4.75 – **8 rm** ⌸ 49.00/70.00 **t.**

🔘 ATS 149-151 Ainslie St. ✆ 828513/828663

BARTHOMLEY Ches. – see Crewe.

BARTON MILLS Suffolk. 404 V 26 – pop. 866 – ✆ 0638 Mildenhall.

◆London 72 – Cambridge 21 – ◆Ipswich 37 – ◆Norwich 40.

🏛 **Forte Travelodge** without rest., Fiveways Roundabout, IP28 6AE, on A 11 ✆ 717675,
Reservations (Freephone) 0800 850950 – 📺 ⚒ 🅿. 🔄 AE VISA. ⪕
32 rm 31.95 **t.**

BARTON STACEY Hants. 403 404 P 30 – see Andover.

BARTON UNDER NEEDWOOD Staffs. – see Burton-upon-Trent.

BARWICK Somerset 403 404 M 31 – see Yeovil.

BASFORD Staffs. – see Stoke-on-Trent.

BASILDON Essex 404 V 29 – pop. 94 800 – ECD : Wednesday – ✆ 0268.

🟦 Clayhill Lane, Sparrow's Hearne, Kingswood ✆ 533297, S : 1 m. by A 176 – 🟦, ⛳ Langdon
Hills, Lower Dunton Rd, Bulphan ✆ 548444, SW : 2 m. by B 164 and A 176 – ⛳ Pipps Hill,
Cranes Farm Rd ✆ 23456, N : 1 m. on A 1235.

◆London 30 – Chelmsford 17 – Southend-on-Sea 13.

🏨 **Forte Posthouse,** Cranes Farm Rd, SS14 3DG, NW : 2 ¼ m. by A 176 off A 1235
✆ 533955, Fax 530119, ⪕ – ⟲ ⟲ rm 📺 ☎ 🅿 – 🔬 250. 🔄 AE ⓞ VISA
M a la carte approx. 17.50 **t.** ⅓ 4.65 – ⌸ 6.95 – **110 rm** 53.50 **st.** – SB (weekends only)
90.00 **st.**

🏛 **Travel Inn,** Felmores, East Mayne, SS13 1BW, N : 1½ m. on A 132 ✆ 522227, Fax 530092
– ⟲ rm 📺 ⚒ 🅿. 🔄 AE ⓞ VISA. ⪕
closed Christmas – **M** (Beefeater grill) a la carte approx. 16.00 **t.** – ⌸ 4.95 – **32 rm** 33.50 **t.**

🏛 **Campanile,** A 127 Southend Arterial Rd, Pipp's Hill, SS14 3AE, NW : 1 m. on A 176
✆ 530810, Fax 286710 – 📺 ☎ ⚒ 🅿 – 🔬 30. 🔄 AE VISA
M a la carte approx. 9.95 **t.** ⅓ 2.95 – ⌸ 4.25 – **97 rm** 35.75 **t.**

MICHELIN Distribution Centre, Bramston Link, Southfields Industrial Area, Laindon,
SS15 6TX, ✆ 491150, Fax 491163.

🔘 ATS Archers Field ✆ 525177

BASINGSTOKE Hants. [403] [404] Q 30 – pop. 73 027 – ☎ 0256.

⛳18 Test Valley, Micheldever Rd, Overton ☎ 771737, S : 2 m. (M 3 junction 8) Z – ⛳9 Basingstoke Hospitals, Aldermaston Rd ☎ 20347, N : 1 ½ m. Z.

[i] Willis Museum, Old Town Hall, Market Pl., RG21 1QD ☎ 817618.

♦London 55 – Reading 17 – ♦Southampton 31 – Winchester 18.

BASINGSTOKE

London Street .... Y 19
Upper Church Street .... Y 24
Winchester Street .... Y 27

Aldermaston Road .... Z 2
Beaconsfield Road .... Y 3
Buckland Avenue .... Z 5
Chequers Road .... Y 6
Church Street .... Y 7
Churchill Way East .... Z 9
Churchill Way West .... Z 10
Council Road .... Y 12
Cross Street .... Y 13
Fairfields Road .... Y 14
Houndmills Road .... Z 17
New Road .... Y 20
Reading Road .... Z 22
Southern Ringway .... Z 23
Victoria Street .... Y 25
Wote Street .... Y 28

North is at the top on all town plans.

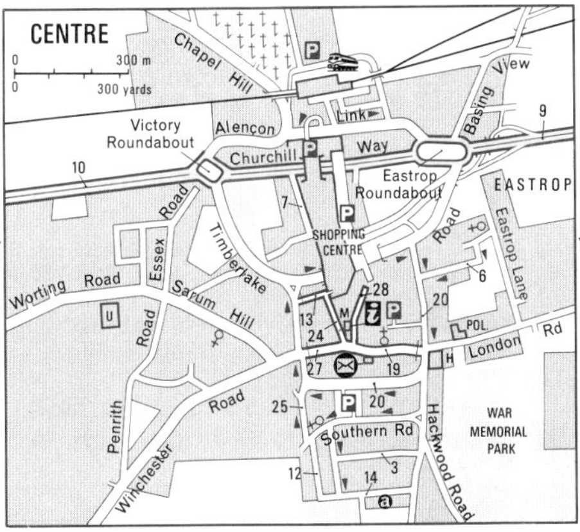

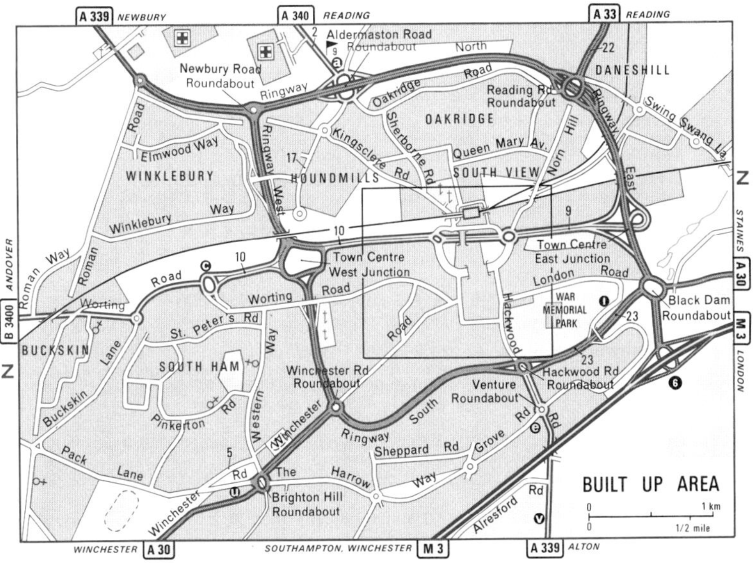

🏨 **Audleys Wood** (Mt. Charlotte Thistle) 🐴, Alton Rd, RG25 2JT, S : 1 ½ m. on A 339 ☎ 817555, Fax 817500, « Gothic Renaissance mansion », park – 🚭 rm [TV] ☎ ♿ [P] – 🎤 40. [AE] [O] [VISA] [JCB]. ✈ Z **v**
M *(closed lunch Saturday and Bank Holidays except 25 and 26 December)* 20.00/29.00 **st.** and a la carte 🍷 6.00 – ☕ 8.75 – **69 rm** 85.00/105.00 **st.**, 2 suites – SB (weekends only) 124.00/130.00 **st.**

🏨 Centre Court H. & Tennis Centre, Centre Drive, Chineham, RG24 0FY, NE : 2½ m. by A 33 and Great Binfields Rd ☎ 816664, Fax 816727, 🏋, [S], 🏊, 🎾 – 🛗 🚭 rm [TV] ☎ [P] – 🎤 90. ✈ Z
50 rm.

🏨 **Hilton National,** Old Common Rd, Black Dam, RG21 3PR, 𝒫 460460, Telex 859038, Fax 840441, 𝄃₆, ≘ﬆ – ≒⊁ rm ▤ rest 📺 🕿 🛋 ℗ – 🔏 150. ◪ ஊ ⑩ 𝗩𝗜𝗦𝗔 𝗝𝗖𝗕   Z i
M (carving rest.) a la carte approx. 15.50 **st.** ⅄ 5.50 – ⊑ 9.50 – **137 rm** 59.50/76.50 **st.** – SB (except summer) (weekends only) 88.00 **st.**

🏨 **Forte Posthouse,** Grove Rd, RG21 3EE, S : 1 m. junction A 339 and A 30 𝒫 468181, Fax 840081 – ≒⊁ rm 📺 🕿 ℗ – 🔏 150. ◪ ஊ ⑩ 𝗩𝗜𝗦𝗔 𝗝𝗖𝗕   Z e
M a la carte approx. 17.50 **t.** ⅄ 4.65 – ⊑ 6.95 – **84 rm** 53.50 **st.** – SB (except Christmas) 90.00 **st.**

🏨 **Ringway** (Hilton), Poplar Way, Aldermaston Roundabout, Ringway North, RG24 9NV, N : 2 m. junction A 339 and A 340 𝒫 20212, Telex 858223, Fax 842835, 𝄃₆, ≘ﬆ, ◪, –   Z a
≒⊁ rm 📺 🕿 ℗ – 🔏 150. ◪ ஊ ⑩ 𝗩𝗜𝗦𝗔
M (dancing Friday and Saturday) (carving rest.) (bar lunch)/dinner approx. 17.00 **t.** – ⊑ 4.75 – **134 rm** 40.00/60.00 **t.** – SB 70.00/140.00 **st.**

🏨 **Travel Inn,** Worting Rd, RG22 6PG, 𝒫 811477, Fax 819329 – ≒⊁ rm 📺 🛋 ℗. ◪ ஊ ⑩   Z c
𝗩𝗜𝗦𝗔 ⌖
M (Beefeater grill) a la carte approx. 16.00 **t.** – ⊑ 4.95 – **49 rm** 33.50 **t.**

🏨 **Forte Travelodge,** Stag & Hounds, Winchester Road, RG22 6HN, 𝒫 843566, Reserva-   Z u
tions (Freephone) 0800 850950 – 📺 🛋 ℗. ◪ ஊ 𝗩𝗜𝗦𝗔 ⌖
M (Harvester grill) a la carte approx. 16.00 **t.** – ⊑ 5.50 – **32 rm** 31.95 **t.**

🏠 **Fernbank** without rest., 4 Fairfields Rd, RG21 3DR, 𝒫 21191, Fax 21191 – ≒⊁ 📺 ℗. ◪   Y a
𝗩𝗜𝗦𝗔 ⌖
18 rm ⊑ 25.00/44.00 **st.**

at Oakley W : 4 ¾ m. on B 3400 – Z – ✉ Oakley – ☎ 0256 Basingstoke :

🏨 **Beech Arms,** RG23 7EP, on B 3400 𝒫 780210, Fax 780557, ☞ – 📺 🕿 🛋 ℗ – 🔏 25. ◪ ஊ ⑩ 𝗩𝗜𝗦𝗔 ⌖
closed 25 and 26 December – **M** (bar lunch Monday to Saturday)/dinner a la carte 13.00/ 21.50 **t.** ⅄ 6.50 – **32 rm** ⊑ 55.00/75.00 **st.**

🅰 ATS Moniton Trading Est., West Ham Lane   ATS Armstrong Rd, Daneshill East 𝒫 462448 𝒫 51431/2

BASLOW Derbs. 🅐🅑🅒 P 24 Great Britain G. – pop. 1 205 – ECD : Wednesday – ✉ Bake-well – ☎ 0246.

See : Chatsworth★★★ (Park and Garden★★★) *AC.*

◆London 161 – Derby 27 – ◆Manchester 35 – ◆Sheffield 13.

🏨 **Cavendish,** DE45 1SP, on A 619 𝒫 582311, Fax 582312, ⩽ Chatsworth Park, ✎, ☞ – ≒⊁ rest 📺 🕿 ℗. ◪ ஊ ⑩ 𝗩𝗜𝗦𝗔 ⌖
M 24.75 **t.** and a la carte – ⊑ 8.65 – **23 rm** 83.00/125.00 **t.**

XXX ❀ **Fischer's at Baslow Hall** (Fischer) with rm, Calver Rd, DE45 1RR, on A 623 𝒫 583259, Fax 583818, « Edwardian manor house », ☞ – ≒⊁ rest 📺 🕿 ℗. ◪ ஊ 𝗩𝗜𝗦𝗔 ⌖
closed 26 and 26 December – **M** *(closed Sunday dinner to non-residents)* 20.00/34.00 **t.** ⅄ 5.25 – ⊑ 4.50 – **5 rm** 70.00/120.00 **t.** 1 suite – SB 143.00/228.00 **st.**
Spec. Sea bream in puff pastry with beluga caviar, Saddle of venison with game sauce, Gratin of exotic fruits, Kirsch and pineapple sorbet.

BASSENTHWAITE Cumbria 🅐🅑 K 19 – pop. 533 – ✉ ☎ 076 87 Bassenthwaite Lake.

◆London 300 – ◆Carlisle 24 – Keswick 7.

🏨 **Armathwaite Hall** ⌖, CA12 4RE, W : 1 ½ m. on B 5291, ✉ Keswick 𝒫 76551, Fax 76220, ⩽ Bassenthwaite Lake, « Part 18C mansion in extensive grounds », 𝄃₆, ≘ﬆ, ◪, ✎, ☞, park, % – ⋮⊁ rest 📺 🕿 ℗ – 🔏 100. ◪ ஊ ⑩ 𝗩𝗜𝗦𝗔
M 14.95/27.95 **t.** and a la carte ⅄ 5.00 – **42 rm** ⊑ 50.00/184.00 **t.** – SB (except August-October) 140.00/217.00 **t.**

🏨 **Overwater Hall** ⌖, CA5 1HH, NE : 2¼ m. on Uldale rd, ✉ Ireby 𝒫 76566, ⩽, ☞, park – 📺 ℗ 𝗩𝗜𝗦𝗔
M (dinner only and Sunday lunch)/dinner 22.95 **st.** – **13 rm** ⊑ 34.00/68.00 **st.** – SB 65.00/ 112.00 **st.**

🏠 **Pheasant Inn,** CA13 9YE, SW : 3 ¼ m. by B 5291 off A 66, ✉ Cockermouth 𝒫 76234, Fax 76002, « 16C inn », ☞ – ≒⊁ rest ℗. ⌖
closed 24 and 25 December – **M** 12.00/22.00 **st.** and lunch a la carte ⅄ 4.20 – **20 rm** ⊑ 55.00/94.00 **st.** – SB (November-March) 96.00/110.00 **st.**

When visiting the West Country,

use the Michelin Green Guide **"England: The West Country".**

– *Detailed descriptions of places of interest*
– *Touring programmes by county*
– *Maps and street plans*
– *The history of the region*
– *Photographs and drawings of monuments, beauty spots, houses*

BATH Avon **403 404** M 29 The West Country G. – pop. 84 283 – ECD : Monday and Thursday – ☎ 0225.

See : City★★★ – Royal Crescent★★★ AV (No 1 Royal Crescent★★ *AC* AV **D**) – The Circus★★★ AV – Museum of Costume★★★ *AC* AV **M2** – Royal Photographic Society National Centre of Photography★★ *AC* BV **M3** – Roman Baths★★ *AC* BX **B** – Holburne Museum and Crafts Study Centre★★ *AC* Y **M1** – Pump Room★ BX **A** – Assembly Rooms★ AV – Bath Abbey★ BX – Pulteney Bridge★ BV – Bath Industrial Heritage Centre★ *AC* AV **M4**.

Envir. : Lansdown Crescent★★ (Somerset Place★) Y – Claverton (American Museum★★ *AC*, Claverton Pumping Station★ *AC*) E : 3 m. by A 36 Y – Camden Crescent★ Y – Beckford Tower and Museum *AC* (prospect★) Y **M6**.

Exc. : Corsham Court★★ *AC*, NE : 8½ m. by A 4 – Dyrham Park★ *AC*, N : 6½ m. by A 4 and A 46 – Norton St. Philip (George Inn★) S : 7¼ m. by A 367 – Z - and B 3110.

☖, ☖ Tracy Park, Bath Rd, Wick ℘ 027 582 (Abson) 2251, N : 5 m. by Lansdown Rd Y – ☖ Lansdown ℘ 425007, NW : 2 m. by Lansdown Rd Y – ☖ Sham Castle, North Rd ℘ 425182, E : 1½ m. by A 36 Y – ☖ Entry Hill ℘ 834248, S : 1 m. by A 3062 Z.

🛈 The Colonnades, 11-13 Bath St., BA1 1SW ℘ 462831.

♦London 119 – ♦Bristol 13 – ♦Southampton 63 – Taunton 49.

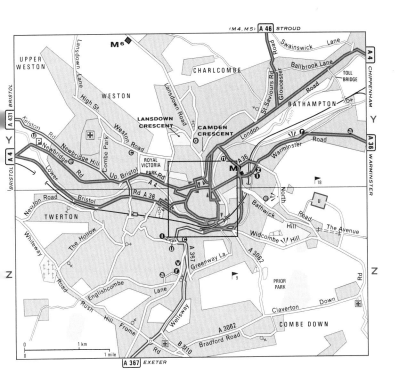

Bath Spa (Forte) ⌖ Sydney Rd, BA2 6JF, ℘ 444424, Telex 449729, Fax 444006, « Part 19C mansion in landscaped gardens », 🛋, ☎s, 🏊, ⚒ – 🛗 ⇔ rm 🍽 rest 📺 ☎ ♿ 🅿 – 🔑 80. ⚫ 🅰🅴 ◉ 𝘝𝘐𝘚𝘈 𝘑𝘊𝘉 Y z
M – **Vellore** 18.00/34.00 **st.** and a la carte ▮ 8.50 – **Alfresco Colonnade** (closed Sunday) a la carte 14.85/24.65 **t.** ▮ 8.50 – ☐ 11.75 – **91 rm** 125.00/160.00 **st.**, 7 suites – SB (except Christmas and New Year) 198.00/218.00 **st.**

Royal Crescent (Q.M.H.), 16 Royal Cres., BA1 2LS, ℘ 319090, Telex 444251, Fax 339401, ≼, « Tastefully restored Georgian town houses », ⌖ – 🛗 🍽 rest 📺 ☎ ⇔ – 🔑 35. ⚫ 🅰🅴 ◉ 𝘝𝘐𝘚𝘈 ⚒ AV a
M 19.95/30.00 **st.** and dinner a la carte ▮ 8.00 – ☐ 5.00 – **34 rm** 98.00/195.00 **st.**, 8 suites – SB 170.00/268.00 **st.**

🏨🏨 **The Priory,** Weston Rd, BA1 2XT, ℰ 331922, Fax 448276, ≼, ⅏ heated, 🌴 – ✘ rest 📺 ☎ ℗. 🔄 🆎 ⓪ 𝑽𝑰𝑺𝑨
Y **c**
M 23.00/38.00 **st.** and dinner a la carte 🍷 8.00 – ⊑ 12.00 – **21 rm** 85.00/195.00 **st.** – SB 190.00/280.00 **st.**

🏨🏨 **Queensberry,** Russell St., BA1 2QF, ℰ 447928, Telex 445628, Fax 446065, « Georgian town houses » – 🔺 📺 ☎. 🔄 🆎 𝑽𝑰𝑺𝑨.
AV **x**
closed 24 to 31 December – **M** (see *Olive Tree* below) – ⊑ 7.50 – **22 rm** 84.00/149.00 **st.** – SB (November-March) 120.00 **st.**

🏨🏨 **Fountain House** without rest., 9-11 Fountain Buildings, Lansdown Rd, BA1 5DV, ℰ 338622, Fax 445855 – 🔺 📺 ☎. 🔄 🆎 ⓪ 𝑽𝑰𝑺𝑨
BV **e**
13 suites 92.00/168.00 **st.**

🏨🏨 **Hilton National,** Walcot St., BA1 5BJ, ℰ 463411, Telex 449519, Fax 464393, 🏋, ≘, 🔲 – 🔺 ✘ rm 📺 ☎ – 🔼 240. 🔄 🆎 ⓪ 𝑽𝑰𝑺𝑨 𝑱𝑪𝑩
BV **i**
M *(closed Saturday lunch)* 11.50/17.50 **st.** and a la carte 🍷 5.50 – ⊑ 10.25 – **150 rm** 84.00/160.00 **st.** – SB 174.00 **st.**

🏨🏨 **Francis** (Forte), Queen Sq., BA1 2HH, ℰ 424257, Telex 424257, Fax 319715 – 🔺 ✘ rm 📺 ☎ ℗ – 🔼 80. 🔄 🆎 ⓪ 𝑽𝑰𝑺𝑨 𝑱𝑪𝑩
AV **i**
M *(closed Saturday lunch)* 9.95/17.95 **t.** and a la carte 🍷 6.45 – ⊑ 8.50 – **92 rm** 88.00/108.00 **st.**, 1 suite – SB (except Christmas) 128.00 **st.**

🏨 **Lansdown Grove** (Best Western), Lansdown Rd, BA1 5EH, ℰ 315891, Fax 448092, 🌴 – 🔺 📺 ☎ ℗ – 🔼 100. 🔄 🆎 ⓪ 𝑽𝑰𝑺𝑨
Y **o**
M 9.75/17.50 **t.** and a la carte – **45 rm** ⊑ 65.00/115.00 **t.** – SB 102.00/110.00 **st.**

🏨 **Compass Abbey,** North Par., BA1 1LG, ℰ 461603, Telex 44812, Fax 447758 – 🔺 📺 ☎ – 🔼 35. 🔄 🆎 ⓪ 𝑽𝑰𝑺𝑨
BX **e**
M 8.00/15.20 **st.** 🍷 4.20 – **54 rm** ⊑ 55.00/72.50 **st.** – SB 82.50/112.00 **st.**

🏨 **Pratt's,** South Par., BA2 4AB, ℰ 460441, Fax 448807 – 🔺 📺 ☎ – 🔼 50. 🔄 🆎 ⓪ 𝑽𝑰𝑺𝑨
BX **c**
M (bar lunch Monday to Saturday)/dinner 18.50 **st.** and a la carte 🍷 6.00 – **46 rm** ⊑ 39.95/85.00 **st.** – SB (except Christmas and Bank Holidays) 85.90/115.90 **st.**

🏨 **Apsley House,** 141 Newbridge Hill, BA1 3PT, ℰ 336966, Fax 425462, 🌴 – ✘ rest 📺 ☎ ℗. 🔄 🆎 𝑽𝑰𝑺𝑨 𝑱𝑪𝑩. ✘
Y **e**
M (dinner only) 18.50 **st.** 🍷 4.50 – ⊑ 5.00 – **7 rm** 60.00/110.00 **st.** – SB 90.00/200.00 **st.**

🏨 **Bath** (Best Western), Widcombe Basin, BA2 4JP, ℰ 338855, Fax 428941 – 🔺 📺 ☎ ℗ – 🔼 80. 🔄 🆎 ⓪ 𝑽𝑰𝑺𝑨
BX **a**
M 13.50/17.50 **st.** and a la carte 🍷 5.25 – ⊑ 8.50 – **93 rm** 65.00/70.00 **t.** – SB (except Christmas and New Year) 92.00/120.00 **st.**

🏨 **Dukes,** Great Pulteney St., BA2 4DN, ℰ 463512, Telex 449227, Fax 483733 – ✘ rest 📺 ☎. 🔄 🆎 ⓪ 𝑽𝑰𝑺𝑨
BV **s**
M (dinner only) 15.50 **t.** 🍷 5.50 – **22 rm** 45.00/70.00 **t.** – SB (except Bank Holidays) 80.00/130.00 **st.**

🏠 **Paradise House** ☜ without rest., 86-88 Holloway, BA2 4PX, ℰ 317723, Fax 482005, ≼, 🌴 – 📺 ☎. 🔄 🆎 𝑽𝑰𝑺𝑨. ✘
Z **c**
closed 20 to 27 December – **9 rm** ⊑ 35.00/68.00 **st.**

🏠 **Sydney Gardens** without rest., Sydney Rd, BA2 6NT, ℰ 464818, ≼, 🌴 – ✘ 📺 ☎ ℗. 🔄 𝑽𝑰𝑺𝑨
Y **i**
closed Christmas and 3 weeks January – **6 rm** ⊑ 59.00/69.00 **st.**

🏠 **Bloomfield House** without rest., 146 Bloomfield Rd, BA2 2AS, ℰ 420105, Fax 481958, ≼, 🌴 – ✘ 📺 ☎ ℗. 🔄 𝑽𝑰𝑺𝑨
Z **r**
8 rm ⊑ 30.00/75.00 **st.**

🏠 **Newbridge House,** 35 Kelston Rd, BA1 3QH, ℰ 446676, Fax 447541, ≼, « Georgian house », – ✘ 📺 ☎ ℗. 🔄 🆎 ⓪ 𝑽𝑰𝑺𝑨 𝑱𝑪𝑩. ✘
Y **u**
M 10.95/30.00 **t.** and a la carte 🍷 5.50 – **9 rm** ⊑ 65.00/160.00 **t.** – SB 160.00/190.00 **st.**

🏠 **Holly Lodge** without rest., 8 Upper Oldfield Park, BA2 3JZ, ℰ 424042, Fax 481138, ≼, 🌴 – ✘ 📺 ☎ ℗. 🔄 🆎 ⓪ 𝑽𝑰𝑺𝑨. ✘
Z **i**
6 rm ⊑ 46.00/85.00 **st.**

🏠 **Arden** without rest., 73 Great Pulteney St., BA2 4DL, ℰ 466601, Fax 465548 – 📺 ☎. 🔄 𝑽𝑰𝑺𝑨 𝑱𝑪𝑩. ✘
BV **c**
10 rm ⊑ 39.00/74.00 **t.**

🏠 **Somerset House,** 35 Bathwick Hill, BA2 6LD, ℰ 466451, ≼, 🌴 – ✘ ☎ ℗. 🔄 🆎 𝑽𝑰𝑺𝑨
Z **e**
M *(closed Sunday dinner)* (dinner only and Sunday lunch November-May)/dinner 17.80 **st.** 🍷 3.75 – **10 rm** ⊑ 30.20/60.40 **st.** – SB (except May, June and September) (weekdays only) 75.60/80.60 **st.**

🏠 **North Parade,** 10 North Par., BA2 4AL, ℰ 463384, Fax 442322 – 📺 ☎. 🔄 🆎 ⓪ 𝑽𝑰𝑺𝑨. ✘
M (dinner only) 12.00 **t.** and a la carte 🍷 4.55 – **16 rm** ⊑ 26.75/70.00 **t.**, 2 suites – SB (except Bank Holidays) 64.00/92.00 **st.**
BX **i**

BATH

BATH

- 🏠 **Orchard House,** Warminster Rd, Bathampton, BA2 6XG, ℰ 466115, Fax 406050, ⬱s – ⠦ rest 📺 ☎ 🅿. 🔼 🆎 ⓞ 𝘝𝘐𝘚𝘈 — Y **a**
  M (dinner only and Sunday lunch)/dinner 20.00 **t.** – **14 rm** ⊠ 45.00/59.00 **t.**

- 🏠 **Villa Magdala** without rest., Henrietta Rd, BA2 6LX, ℰ 466329, 🌳 – 📺 ☎ 🅿. 🔼 𝘝𝘐𝘚𝘈. ⋇
  closed Christmas – **17 rm** ⊠ 40.00/70.00 **st.** BV **r**

- 🏠 **Haydon House** without rest., 9 Bloomfield Park, off Bloomfield Rd, BA2 2BY, ℰ 427351, Fax 427351, 🌳 – ⠦ 📺 ☎. 🔼 🆎 𝘝𝘐𝘚𝘈. ⋇ Z **a**
  4 rm ⊠ 40.00/65.00.

- 🏠 **Bath Tasburgh** without rest., Warminster Rd, Bathampton, BA2 6SH, ℰ 425096, Fax 463842, ⩺, 🌳 – 📺 ☎ 🅿. 🔼 🆎 ⓞ 𝘝𝘐𝘚𝘈. ⋇ Y **r**
  13 rm ⊠ 34.00/70.00 **st.**

- 🏠 **Brompton House** without rest., St. John's Rd, Bathwick, BA2 6PT, ℰ 420972, 🌳 – ⠦ 📺 ☎ 🅿. 🔼 𝘝𝘐𝘚𝘈. ⋇ Y **n**
  closed Christmas and New Year – **18 rm** ⊠ 32.00/65.00 **st.**

⌂ **Leighton House** without rest., 139 Wells Rd, BA2 3AL, ℘ 314769 – 📺 ☎ 🅿. 🔜 𝖵𝖨𝖲𝖠. ⚄
7 rm ⊇ 42.00/64.00 st.
AX **e**

⌂ **Cheriton House** without rest., 9 Upper Oldfield Park, BA2 3JX, ℘ 429862, Fax 428403, ✍ – 📺 🅿. 🔜 𝖵𝖨𝖲𝖠. ⚄
closed Christmas and New Year – **9 rm** ⊇ 32.00/58.00 st.
Z **u**

⌂ **Laura Place** without rest., 3 Laura Pl., Great Pulteney St., BA2 4BH, ℘ 463815, Fax 310222 – 📺 ☎. 🔜 ᴀᴇ 𝖵𝖨𝖲𝖠. ⚄
closed Christmas-February – **8 rm** ⊇ 50.00/80.00 st.
BV **v**

⌂ **Oakleigh** without rest., 19 Upper Oldfield Park, BA2 3JX, ℘ 315698 – 📺 🅿. 🔜 𝖵𝖨𝖲𝖠. ⚄
4 rm ⊇ 35.00/60.00 st.
Z **i**

⌂ **Dorian House** without rest., 1 Upper Oldfield Park, BA2 3JX, ℘ 426336, Fax 444699, ⚄ – 📺 ☎ 🅿. 🔜 ᴀᴇ 🅞 𝖵𝖨𝖲𝖠. ⚄
7 rm ⊇ 37.00/69.00 st.
Z **u**

⌂ **Wentworth House,** 106 Bloomfield Rd, BA2 2AP, ℘ 339193, ⌑, ✍ – ⇔ rest 📺 ☎ 🅿.
closed Christmas – **M** (by arrangement) 12.50 – **20 rm** ⊇ 25.00/60.00 st.
Z **v**

⌂ **Kennard** without rest., 11 Henrietta St., BA2 6LL, ℘ 310472, Fax 442456 – 📺 ☎. 🔜 ᴀᴇ
12 rm ⊇ 30.00/55.00 st.
BV **u**

⌂ **Brocks** without rest., 32 Brook St., BA1 2LN, ℘ 338374, Fax 338374 – 📺. 🔜. ⚄ AV **c**
closed 2 weeks January – **8 rm** ⊇ 21.00/52.00 t.

⌂ **Oldfields** without rest., 102 Wells Rd, BA2 3AL, ℘ 317984, Fax 444471, ✍ – 📺 🅿. 🔜 𝖵𝖨𝖲𝖠. ⚄
14 rm ⊇ 30.00/60.00 st.
AX **n**

✕✕ **Pino's Hole in the Wall,** 16 George St., BA1 2EH, ℘ 425242 – 🔜 ᴀᴇ 🅞 𝖵𝖨𝖲𝖠 AV **u**
closed Sunday and Christmas – **M** - Italian 9.50/20.00 t. and a la carte.

✕✕ **Garlands,** 7 Edgar Buildings, George St., BA1 2EE, ℘ 442283 – 🔜 ᴀᴇ 🅞 𝖵𝖨𝖲𝖠 AV **c**
closed Sunday lunch and 26 December – **M** 14.95/18.50 t.

✕✕ **Clos du Roy,** 1 Seven Dials, Saw Close, BA1 1EN, ℘ 444450, Fax 460218 – 🔜 ᴀᴇ 🅞 𝖵𝖨𝖲𝖠
closed Bank Holidays – **M** 11.50/22.00 st. and dinner a la carte ⒜ 14.25.
AX **r**

✕ **Olive Tree** (at Queensberry H.), Russell St., BA1 2QF, ℘ 447928, Telex 445628, Fax 446065 – ⇔ ⚄ 🔜 ᴀᴇ 𝖵𝖨𝖲𝖠
closed Monday lunch and Sunday – **M** 12.50/19.50 t. and a la carte ⒜ 5.50.
AV **x**

✕ **Woods,** 9-13 Alfred St., BA1 2QX, ℘ 314812, Fax 443146 – 🔜 ᴀᴇ 𝖵𝖨𝖲𝖠 AV **v**
closed Sunday – **M** 9.50 t. (lunch) and a la carte 9.50/17.50 t. ⒜ 4.20.

✕ **Moon and Sixpence,** 6a Broad St., BA1 5LJ, ℘ 460962 – 🔜 ᴀᴇ 𝖵𝖨𝖲𝖠 BV **z**
M 13.95 t. (lunch) and a la carte 15.20/20.10 t. ⒜ 6.00.

✕ **Clarets,** 7a Kingsmead Sq., BA1 2AB, ℘ 466688 – 🔜 𝖵𝖨𝖲𝖠 AX **v**
closed Sunday dinner in summer and Bank Holidays – **M** 12.50 t. (lunch) and a la carte 15.40/20.60 t. ⒜ 5.00.

✕ **New Moon,** Seven Dials, Sawclose, BA1 1EN, ℘ 444407 – 🔜 ᴀᴇ 𝖵𝖨𝖲𝖠 AX **r**
M a la carte 11.75/18.50 t. ⒜ 5.50.

✕ **Beaujolais,** 5 Chapel Row, BA1 1HN, ℘ 423417 – 🔜 ᴀᴇ 𝖵𝖨𝖲𝖠 AX **x**
closed Sunday lunch and 1 to 16 January – **M** - French 17.50/20.00 t. and a la carte ⒜ 4.50.

✕ Peking, 1-2 New St., BA1 2AF, ℘ 466377, Fax 482232 – ▦ AX **u**
M - Chinese.

✕ **Sukhothai,** 90a Walcot St., BA1 5BG, ℘ 462463, Fax 462463 – 🔜 ᴀᴇ 𝖵𝖨𝖲𝖠 BV **a**
M - Thai 10.00/20.00 t. and a la carte.

at Colerne (Wilts.) NE : 6½ m. by A 4 – Y – and Bannerdown rd – ⊠ ☙ 0225 Bath :

🏯 ☙ **Lucknam Park** ⚜, SN14 8AZ, N : ½ m. on Marshfield rd ℘ 742777, Fax 743536, ⩽, « Early 18C country house in park », ℔, ⩌s, ⌑, ✍, ✕ – 📺 ☎ 🅿 – ⚄ 25. 🔜 ᴀᴇ 🅞 𝖵𝖨𝖲𝖠 ᴊᴄʙ. ⚄
M 22.50/37.50 t. ⒜ 8.00 – ⊇ 5.50 – **38 rm** 95.00/155.00 t.. 4 suites – SB 241.00/276.00 st.
Spec. Medallions of monkfish coated with sesame seeds, soya and ginger sauce, Roast loin of lamb wrapped in Parma ham on a bed of ratatouille (May-Oct.). Exotic fruits with a nest of vanilla ice cream.

at Bathford E : 3½ m. by A 4 – Y – off A 363 – ⊠ ☙ 0225 Bath :

🏠 **Eagle House** ⚜ without rest., Church St., BA1 7RS, ℘ 859946, Fax 859601, ⩽, « Georgian house », ✍ – 📺 ☎ 🅿
closed 23 December-3 January – ⊇ 2.50 – **8 rm** 33.00/89.00 st.

🏠 **Orchard** ⚜ without rest., 80 High St., BA1 7TG, ℘ 858765, « Georgian house », ✍ – ⇔ 📺 🅿. ⚄
closed December and January – **4 rm** ⊇ 55.00 st.

⌂ **Old School House,** Church St., BA1 7RR, ℘ 859593, Fax 859590, ✍ – ⇔ 📺 🅿. 🔜 𝖵𝖨𝖲𝖠. ⚄
M (by arrangement) 19.50 st. ⒜ 5.50 – **4 rm** ⊇ 45.00/65.00 st. – SB (November-March) 92.50/120.00 st.

at Limpley Stoke (Lower) SE : 5½ m. by A 36 – Y – and B 3108 – ✉ ☎ 0225 Bath :

Cliffe ≫, Cliffe Drive, Crowe Hill, BA3 6HY, ☎ 723226, Fax 723871, ≤, heated, 🌳 – [TV] ☎ [P]. [AE] [VISA] [JCB]
M 15.00 **t.** (lunch) and dinner a la carte 14.85/18.65 **t.** 🍷 5.10 – **11 rm** ☕ 66.50/105.00 **t.** – SB (except Christmas-New Year) 109.00/170.00 **st.**

at Winsley (Wilts) SE : 6½ m. by A 36 – Y – on B 3108 – ✉ Bradford-on-Avon – ☎ 0225 Bath :

Burghope Manor ≫, BA15 2LA, on B 3108 ☎ 723557, Fax 723113, « 13C manor house, country house atmosphere », 🌳 – 🚭 rm [TV] [P]. [AE] [VISA]. ✗
closed Christmas – **M** (booking essential) (communal dining) 29.50 **t.** – **5 rm** ☕ 45.00/65.00 **t.**

at Hinton Charterhouse S : 5¾ m. by A 367 – Z – on B 3110 – ✉ ☎ 0225 Bath :

Homewood Park ≫, BA3 6BB, E : 1¼ m. on A 36 (North) ☎ 723731, Fax 723820, ≤, « Part Georgian country house », 🌳, park, 🎾 – 🚭 rest [TV] ☎ [P]. [AE] [VISA]. ✗
M 18.50/32.00 **t.** – **15 rm** ☕ 90.00/130.00 **st.** – SB (November-Easter) 145.00/165.00 **st.**

Green Lane House without rest., Green Lane, BA3 6BL, ☎ 723631 – [P]. [AE] [VISA]. ✗
4 rm ☕ 37.00/49.00.

at Norton St. Philip (Somerset) S : 7¼ m. by A 367 – Z – on B 3110 – ✉ Bath (Avon) – ☎ 0225 Limpley Stoke :

The Plaine without rest., BA3 6LE, ☎ 0373 (Frome) 834723, « 16C cottages » – 🚭 [TV] [P]. [AE] [VISA]. ✗
3 rm ☕ 30.00/55.00 **s.**

Monmouth Lodge without rest., BA3 6LH, ☎ 0373 (Frome) 834367, 🌳 – 🚭 [TV] [P]. [VISA]. ✗ by A 367
closed 18 to 27 December – **3 rm** ☕ 35.00/46.00 **st.**

at Hunstrete W : 8½ m. by A 4 – Y – and A 39 off A 368 – ✉ Bristol – ☎ 0761 Mendip :.

Hunstrete House ≫, BS18 4NS, ☎ 490490, Fax 490732, ≤, « 18C country house, gardens and deer park », heated, 🎾 – 🚭 rest [TV] ☎ [P]. [VISA]. ✗
M 30.00/38.00 **t.** and a la carte 🍷 6.25 – **23 rm** ☕ 95.00/175.00 **t.**, 1 suite – SB (except Bank Holidays) 175.00/225.00 **st.**

ATS London Rd ☎ 338899/338924

Great Britain and *Ireland* is now covered
by an *Atlas* at a scale of 1 inch to 4.75 miles.

Three easy to use versions: Paperback, Spiralbound and Hardback.

BATHFORD Avon [403] [404] M 29 – see Bath.

BATTLE E. Sussex [404] V 31 Great Britain G. – pop. 4 662 – ☎ 042 46 (4 fig.) and 0424 (6 fig.).
See : Town★ – Abbey and Site of the Battle of Hastings★ *AC*.
[i] 88 High St., TN33 0AQ ☎ 773721.
◆London 55 – ◆Brighton 34 – Folkestone 43 – Maidstone 30.

Netherfield Place ≫, TN33 9PP, NW : 2 m. by A 2100 on Netherfield rd ☎ 774455, Fax 774024, ≤, « Georgian style country house », 🌳, park, 🎾 – [TV] ☎ [P] – 🏛 50. [AE] [VISA]. ✗
closed last week December and first 2 weeks January – **M** 14.95/22.50 **t.** and a la carte 🍷 5.50 – **14 rm** ☕ 60.00/125.00 **t.** – SB 95.00/170.00 **st.**

Powdermills ≫, Powdermill Lane, TN33 0SP, S : 1½ m. by A 2100 on B 2095 ☎ 775511, Fax 774540, ≤, « Part Georgian gunpowdermill, antiques », 🏊, 🎣, 🌳, park – [TV] ☎ [P]. [AE] [VISA]
M – **Orangery** *(closed Sunday dinner in winter)* 14.50/18.00 **st.** and dinner a la carte – **16 rm** ☕ 45.00/105.00 **st.** – SB 90.00/140.00 **st.**

George (Resort), 23 High St., TN33 0EA, ☎ 774466, Fax 774853 – [TV] ☎ [P] – 🏛 40. [AE] [VISA]
M 14.50 **t.** and a la carte 🍷 3.95 – **22 rm** ☕ 24.00/60.00 **t.** – SB (except Bank Holidays) 68.00/88.00 **st.**

Little Hemingfold ≫, Telham, TN33 0TT, SE : 1¾ m. on A 2100 ☎ 774338, ≤, « Lakeside setting », 🎣, 🌳, park, 🎾 – [TV] ☎ [P]. [AE] [VISA]
M 18.50 **st.** 🍷 4.75 – **12 rm** ☕ 45.00/70.00 **st.** – SB (except Christmas-New Year) 96.00/134.00 **st.**

BAWTRY S. Yorks [402] [403] [404] Q 23 – ✉ ☎ 0302 Doncaster.
⛳18 Austerfield Park, Cross Lane ☎ 710841, NE : 2 m. by A 614.
◆London 157 – ◆Leeds 37 – Lincoln 30 – ◆Nottingham 36 – ◆Sheffield 20.

Crown (Forte), High St., DN10 6JW, ☎ 710341, Fax 711798 – 🚭 rm [TV] ☎ [P] – 🏛 100. [AE] [VISA]. ✗
M (bar lunch Monday to Saturday)/dinner 15.95 **st.** and a la carte 🍷 6.45 – ☕ 8.50 – **57 rm** 50.00/70.00 **st.** – SB 86.00 **st.**

♦London 26 – Aylesbury 19 – ♦Oxford 32.

🏨 **Bellhouse** (De Vere), Oxford Rd, HP9 2XE, E : 1 ¾ m. on A 40 🖉 0753 (Gerrards Cross) 887211, Fax 888231, *🛋*, ≋s, 🔲, 🖾, squash – 🔄 🏿 rm 🔟 ☎ 🅿 – 🔬 450. 🔂 🄰🄴 ⓞ 🗷🗷🗷
M *(closed Saturday lunch)* 16.50/18.50 **st.** and a la carte – **133 rm** 🗕 90.00/115.00 **st.**, 3 suites – SB 104.00/124.00 **st.**

🍴🍴 **Leigh House,** 53 Wycombe End, HP9 1LX, 🖉 676348 – 🄴, 🔂 🄰🄴 ⓞ 🗷🗷🗷
M - Chinese (Peking) 9.50/24.00 **t.** and a la carte.

🍴🍴 **La Lanterna,** 57 Wycombe End, HP9 1LX, 🖉 675210 – 🄴, 🔂 🄰🄴 ⓞ 🗷🗷🗷
closed Sunday – **M** - Italian 12.50/19.75 **t.** and a la carte.

🍴🍴 **China Diner,** 7 The Highway, Station Rd, Beaconsfield New Town, HP9 1QD, 🖉 678346 – 🔂 🄰🄴 ⓞ 🗷🗷🗷
closed 25 to 27 December – **M** - Chinese 7.50/20.00 **t.** and a la carte 🍷 4.00.

at Wooburn Common SW : 3 ½ m. by A 40 – ✉ Beaconsfield – 🟤 062 85 (5 fig.) and 0628 (6 fig.) Bourne End :

🏠 **Chequers Inn** 🐾, Kiln Lane, HP10 0JQ, SW : 1 m. on Bourne End rd 🖉 529575, Fax 850124 – 🔟 ☎ 🅿 – 🔬 30. 🔂 🄰🄴 🗷🗷🗷 🗷🗷🗷
M 14.95/17.95 **t.** and a la carte – **17 rm** 🗕 72.50/77.50 **t.** – SB (weekends only) 84.50 **st.**

Envir. : Parnham House★★ *AC*, S : ¾ m. by A 3066.

♦London 149 – Dorchester 19 – Exeter 40 – Taunton 31.

🏠 **Hams Plot** without rest., 6 Bridport Rd., DT8 3LU, on A 3066 🖉 862979, 🔲, 🖾, 🍴🍴 – 🅿
🖾🖾
April-September – **3 rm** 🗕 36.00/55.00 **st.**

Plans de ville : Les rues sont sélectionnées en fonction de leur importance
pour la circulation et le repérage des établissements cités.

Les rues secondaires ne sont qu'amorcées.

See : Town★★ - National Motor Museum★★ *AC*.

Envir. : Buckler's Hard★ (Maritime Museum★ *AC*) SE : 2 m.

♦London 102 – Bournemouth 24 – ♦Southampton 13 – Winchester 23.

🏨 **Montagu Arms,** Palace Lane, SO42 7ZL, 🖉 612324, Fax 612188, « Part 18C inn, gardens » – 🔟 ☎ 🅿. 🔂 🄰🄴 ⓞ 🗷🗷🗷
M 14.95/23.90 **t.** – **22 rm** 🗕 67.90/129.90 **t.**, 2 suites – SB (except Easter, Christmas and New Year) 119.00/189.00 **st.**

at Bucklers Hard S : 2 ½ m. – ✉ Brockenhurst – 🟤 0590 Bucklers Hard :

🏨 **Master Builder's House,** SO42 7XB, 🖉 616253, Fax 616297, 🖾 – 🔟 ☎ 🅿 – 🔬 40. 🔂
🄰🄴 ⓞ 🗷🗷🗷
M 13.95/15.45 **t.** – **23 rm** 🗕 50.00/95.00 **st.** – SB 108.00/123.00 **st.**

Envir. : The Broads★.

🛋 The Common 🖉 712244.

🅱 The Quay, Fen Lane, NR34 9BH 🖉 713196 (summer only).

♦London 113 – Great Yarmouth 15 – ♦Ipswich 40 – ♦Norwich 18.

🏠 **Riverview House** without rest., 29 Ballygate, NR34 9ND, 🖉 713519, 🖾 – 🔟
closed 20 December-2 January – **10 rm** 🗕 17.50/39.00 **st.**

🔘 ATS Waveney Garage, Ravensmere 🖉 713222/715570

♦London 124 – Leicester 43 – Lincoln 20 – ♦Nottingham 28 – ♦Sheffield 46.

🍴🍴 **Black Swan,** Hillside, LN5 0RF, 🖉 626474, 🖾 – 🏿 🅿. 🔂 🗷🗷🗷
closed Sunday dinner and Monday – **M** (booking essential) (lunch by arrangement)/dinner 16.00 **t.** and a la carte 🍷 4.20.

🍴 **Woolpack** with rm, BA3 6SP, 🖉 831244, Fax 831223, « Part 16C inn » – 🏿 rest 🔟 ☎ 🅿.
🔂 🗷🗷🗷 🔲🔲🔲
M a la carte 14.45/24.00 **t.** 🍷 5.50 – **10 rm** 🗕 44.50/69.50 **t.** – SB (weekends only) 74.50/ 84.50 **st.**

BEDALE N. Yorks. 402 P 21 – pop. 2 158 – ECD : Thursday – ✉ Darlington – ☎ 0677.

🛆 Leyburn Rd ℰ 422568.

🖪 Bedale Hall, DL8 1AA ℰ 424604 (summer only).

◆London 225 – ◆Leeds 45 – ◆Newcastle 30 – York 38.

↑ **Hyperion House** without rest., 88 South End, DL8 2DS, ℰ 422334, ⊸ – ⇔ ➋
closed Christmas and New Year – **3 rm** ⊐ 18.00/33.00 **st.**

%% **Plummer's,** 7-10 North End, DL8 1AF, ℰ 423432 – ◫ VISA
M a la carte 12.60/17.95 **t.** ⏶ 5.50.

BEDFORD Beds. 404 S 27 – pop. 75 632 – ECD : Thursday – ☎ 0234.

🛆 Bedfordshire, Bromham Rd, Biddenham ℰ 53241, NW : 1 ½ m. on A 428 – 🛆 Mowsbury, Kimbolton Rd ℰ 216374, N : 3 m. on B 660.

🖪 10 St. Paul's Sq., MK40 1SL ℰ 215226.

◆London 59 – ◆Cambridge 31 – Colchester 70 – ◆Leicester 51 – Lincoln 95 – Luton 20 – ◆Oxford 52 – Southend-on-Sea 85.

🏨 **Barns** (Lansbury), Cardington Rd, MK44 3SA, E : 2 m. on A 603 ℰ 270044, Fax 273102,
≋, ⊸ – ⇔ rm ◫ ☎ & ➋ – 🔼 90. ◫ 瓯 ◑ VISA 🛠
M *(closed lunch Saturday and Bank Holidays)* 11.50/15.75 **t.** and a la carte ⏶ 4.50 – **49 rm**
⊐ 69.50/110.00 **t.** – SB (weekends only) 110.00/171.50 **st.**

🏨 **Bedford Swan,** The Embankment, MK40 1RW, ℰ 346565, Telex 827779, Fax 212009, ◫
– ⌷ ◫ ☎ ➋ – 🔼 300. ◫ 瓯 ◑ VISA
M 12.50 **st.** and a la carte ⏶ 4.75 – **114 rm** ⊐ 66.00/76.00 **st.**, 1 suite – SB (weekends only)
72.00 **st.**

🏨 De Parys, 41-45 De Parys Av., MK40 2UA, ℰ 352121, Fax 353889, ⊸ – ◫ ☎ ➋ – 🔼 80
25 rm.

🏨 **Wayfarer,** 403 Goldington Rd, Goldington, MK40 0DS, E : 2 m. on A 428 ℰ 272707,
Fax 272707, ⊸ – ◫ ☎ & ➋ – 🔼 30. ◫ 瓯 ◑ VISA 🛠
M a la carte 5.85/15.15 **st.** – **29 rm** ⊐ 40.00/65.00 **st.**

🏨 **Edwardian House,** 15 Shakespeare Rd, MK40 2DZ, ℰ 211156 – ◫ ☎ ➋. ◫ 瓯 ◑ VISA 🛠
M *(closed Saturday and Sunday)* (lunch by arrangement)/dinner 15.00 **st.** and a la carte
⏶ 4.95 – **19 rm** ⊐ 29.50/38.00 **st.**

↑ **Hertford House** without rest., 57 de Parys Av., MK40 2TP, ℰ 350007, Fax 353468, ⊸ –
◫ ➋. ◫ VISA. 🛠
16 rm ⊐ 25.00/55.00 **st.**

at Houghton Conquest S : 6½ m. by A 6 – ✉ ☎ 0234 Bedford :

%% **Knife and Cleaver** with rm, MK45 3LA, ℰ 740387, Fax 740900, ⊸ – ◫ ☎ ➋. ◫ 瓯 VISA
closed 27 to 30 December – **M** *(closed Saturday lunch and Sunday dinner)* 13.50/19.25 **t.**
and a la carte ⏶ 5.00 – **9 rm** ⊐ 41.00/66.00 **t.** – SB (weekends only) 86.00/140.00 **st.**

at Marston Moretaine SW : 6¼ m. by A 6 off A 421 – ✉ ☎ 0234 Bedford :

🏨 **Forte Travelodge** without rest., Beancroft Rd junction, MK43 0PZ, on A 421 ℰ 766755,
Reservations (Freephone) 0800 850950 – ◫ & ➋. ◫ 瓯 VISA. 🛠
32 rm 31.95 **t.**

%% **Moreteyne Manor,** Woburn Rd, MK43 0NG, ℰ 767003, Fax 765382, « 15C moated
manor house », ☞ – ➋. ◫ 瓯 VISA
closed Sunday dinner and Monday – **M** (booking essential) 18.50/22.50 **t.** ⏶ 6.50.

at Clapham NW : 2 m. on A 6 – ✉ ☎ 0234 Bedford :

🏨 **Woodlands Manor** ☞, Green Lane, MK41 6EP, ℰ 363281, Fax 272390, ⊸ – ◫ ☎ ➋ –
🔼 30. ◫ 瓯 ◑ VISA. 🛠
M *(closed lunch Bank Holidays)* 14.00/28.95 **st.** ⏶ 6.95 – **24 rm** ⊐ 65.00/90.00 **st.**, 1 suite –
SB (except Christmas) (weekends only) 92.00 **st.**

MICHELIN Distribution Centre, H.T. Centre, Hammond Rd, Elms Farm Industrial Estate,
MK41 0LG, ℰ 271100, Fax 269453

◍ ATS 3 London Rd ℰ 358838

BEER Devon 403 K 31 The West Country G. – pop. 1 328 – ✉ ☎ 0297 Seaton.

Envir. : Seaton (≤★★) N :¾ m.

🛆 Axe Cliff, Squires Lane, Axmouth, Seaton ℰ 24371, E : 2 m.

◆London 170 – Exeter 22 – Taunton 28.

⚲ **Anchor Inn,** Fore St., EX12 3ET, ℰ 20386, ≤ – ◫. ◫ VISA. 🛠
closed 24 to 28 December – **M** a la carte 10.70/20.15 **t.** – **8 rm** ⊐ 34.00/56.00 **t.** – SB (October-March) 69.00/84.00.

*Great Britain and Ireland are covered entirely
at a scale of 16 miles to 1 inch by our map « Main roads » 986.*

BEESTON Ches. 402 403 404 L 24 – pop. 221 – ⊠ Tarporley – ☎ 0829 Bunbury.
◆London 186 – Chester 15 – ◆Liverpool 40 – Shrewsbury 32.

　🏨 **Wild Boar,** Whitchurch Rd, Bunbury, CW6 9NW, on A 49 ℰ 260309, Fax 261081 – 🖥 rest
　📺 ☎ ♿ 🅿 – 🔬 50. 🖭 🖭 ⑩ 𝗩𝗜𝗦𝗔
　M 14.25/18.50 **st.** and a la carte ⌀ 5.25 – **37 rm** ⲻ 62.50/97.00 **st.** – SB (weekends only)
　86.00/106.00 **st.**

BELCHAMP WALTER Essex 404 W 27 – see Sudbury.

BELFORD Northd. 401 402 O 17 – pop. 943 – ECD : Thursday – ☎ 0668.
◆London 335 – ◆Edinburgh 71 – ◆Newcastle upon Tyne 49.

　🏨 **Blue Bell,** Market Pl., NE70 7NE, ℰ 213543, Fax 213787, 🚗 – ⓧ rest 📺 ☎ ♿ 🅿. 🖭 🖭
　𝗩𝗜𝗦𝗔
　M (bar lunch Monday to Saturday)/dinner 18.00 **t.** and a la carte ⌀ 4.95 – **17 rm** ⲻ 38.00/
　96.00 **t.** – SB (except Christmas-New Year) 90.00/110.00 **st.**

BELLINGHAM Northd. 401 402 N 18 – ⊠ ☎ 0434 Hexham.
🏌 Bellingham ℰ 220530.
🏛 Main St., NE48 2BQ. ℰ 220616.
◆London 315 – Carlisle 48 – ◆Newcastle upon Tyne 33.

　🏛 **Riverdale Hall** ⌘, NE48 2JT, E : ½ m. ℰ 220254, Fax 220457, ≼, 🏊, 🔲, ⬟ – 📺 ☎ 🅿.
　🖭 🖭 ⑩ 𝗩𝗜𝗦𝗔
　M (bar lunch Monday to Saturday)/dinner 17.50 **t.** and a la carte ⌀ 4.95 – **22 rm** ⲻ 39.00/
　78.00 **t.** – SB 84.00/99.00 **st.**

BELPER Derbs. 402 403 404 P 24 – pop. 17 164 – ☎ 0773.
◆London 141 – Derby 8 – ◆Manchester 55 – ◆Nottingham 17.

　🏨 **Makeney Hall Country House** ⌘, Makeney, Milford, DE56 0RU, S : 2 m. by A 6
　ℰ 842999, Fax 842777, 🚗 – 🗐 ⓧ rm 📺 ☎ 🅿 – 🔬 180. 🖭 🖭 ⑩ 𝗩𝗜𝗦𝗔
　closed 26 to 30 December – **M** (closed Saturday lunch) 14.50/18.50 **t.** and a la carte ⌀ 6.50 –
　ⲻ 5.50 – **44 rm** 65.00/125.00 **t.**, 1 suite – SB 90.00/120.00 **st.**

BENENDEN Kent 404 V 30 – ⊠ Cranbrook – ☎ 0580.
◆London 50 – Hastings 20 – Maidstone 20.

　🏠 **Crit Hall,** Cranbrook Rd, TN17 4EU, W : 1 m. on B 2086 ℰ 240609, Fax 241743, 🚗 – ⓧ
　📺 🅿. 🛇
　closed mid December-mid January – **M** (communal dining) 15.00 – **3 rm** ⲻ 28.00/45.00.

BEPTON W. Sussex – see Midhurst.

BERKELEY Glos. 403 404 M 28 Great Britain G. – pop. 1 498 – ECD : Wednesday – ☎ 0453
Dursley – See : Berkeley Castle★★ AC.
Exc. : Wildfowl and Wetlands Trust, Slimbridge★ AC, NE : 6 ½ m. by B 4066 and A 38.
◆London 129 – ◆Bristol 20 – ◆Cardiff 50 – Gloucester 18.

　🏛 **Old School House,** Canonbury St., GL13 9BG, ℰ 811711 – 📺 ☎ 🅿. 🖭 𝗩𝗜𝗦𝗔. 🛇
　closed 24 December-3 January – **M** (closed Sunday and Monday lunch) 15.75 **t.** (dinner)
　and a la carte 12.05/15.00 **t.** ⌀ 3.75 – **7 rm** ⲻ 40.00/55.00 **t.** – SB 77.50 **st.**

BERKSWELL W. Mids. 403 404 P 26 – see Coventry.

BERWICK-UPON-TWEED Northd. 401 402 O 16 Great Britain and Scotland G. – pop. 12 772 –
ECD : Thursday – ☎ 0289.
See : Town★ - Walls★.
Envir. : Foulden★, NW : 5 m. – Paxton House (Chippendale furniture★) AC, W : 5 m. by A 6105,
A 1 and B 6461.
Exc. : SW : Tweed Valley★★ – Eyemouth Museum★ AC, N : 7 ½ m. by a 1 and A 1107 – Holy
Island★ (Priory ruins★ AC, Lindisfarne Castle★ AC) SE : 9 m. by A 1167 and A 1.
🏌 Goswick Beal ℰ 87256, S : 5 m. by A 1 – 🏌 Magdalene Fields ℰ 306384.
🏛 Castlegate Car Park, TD15 1JS. ℰ 330733.
◆London 349 – ◆Edinburgh 57 – ◆Newcastle upon Tyne 63.

　🏠 **Harberton,** 181 Main St., Spittal, TD15 1RP, SE : 2 ¼ m. by A 1167 ℰ 308813, ≼, 🚗 – 📺
　🅿
　closed Christmas – **M** 11.50 – **5 rm** ⲻ 17.50/42.00.

🔧 ATS 78-80 Church St. ℰ 305720/308222

BETHERSDEN Kent 404 W 30 – pop. 1 273 – ⊠ ☎ 023 382 (3 fig.) or 0233 (6 fig.).
◆London 63 – Folkestone 20 – Maidstone 27.

　🏠 **Little Hodgeham** ⌘, Smarden Rd ⊠ Ashford, TN26 3HE, W : 2 m., ⊠ Ashford
　ℰ 850323, « 15C cottage, antique furniture », 🌊, 🚗 – 🅿. 🛇
　mid March-August – **M** (by arrangement) (communal dining) – **3 rm** ⲻ (dinner included)
　58.00/99.00 **s.**

Humbs. 402 S 22 Great Britain G. – pop. 19 368 – ECD : Thursday – ✉ 🕿 0482 Kingston-upon-Hull.

See : Town★ - Minster★★ – St. Mary's Church★.

🔞 The Westwood 🖉 867190.

🏛 Guildhall, Register Sq., HU17 9AU 🖉 867430/883898.

◆London 188 – ◆Kingston-upon-Hull 8 – ◆Leeds 52 – York 29.

🏨 **Beverley Arms** (Forte), North Bar Within, HU17 8DD, 🖉 869241, Fax 870907 – 📳 ⠴ 📺
🕿 🅿 – 🔬 60. 🖪 🕮 🕮 ⓞ 𝖵𝖨𝖲𝖠 𝖩𝖢𝖡
M 11.95/16.95 **t.** and a la carte ⚱ 4.75 – ⊆ 8.95 – **57 rm** 75.00/110.00 **t.** – SB 116.00/
140.00 **st.**

🏨 **Kings Head,** 38 Market Pl., HU17 9AH, 🖉 868103, Fax 871201 – 📺 🕿 🅿. 🖪 🕮 ⓞ 𝖵𝖨𝖲𝖠
M 21.00 **st.** and a la carte ⚱ 3.95 – **12 rm** ⊆ 30.00/49.50 – SB 60.00/110.00 **st.**

🏨 **Lairgate,** 30 Lairgate, HU17 8EP, 🖉 882141, Fax 861067 – 📺 🕿 🅿. 🖪 𝖵𝖨𝖲𝖠
M 12.00/18.00 **st.** and dinner a la carte ⚱ 5.00 – **23 rm** ⊆ 40.00/65.00 **st.** – SB (weekends
only) 68.00/110.00 **st.**

🍴🍴 **Cerutti 2,** Beverley Station, Station Sq., HU17 0AS, 🖉 866700, Fax 587597 – 🅿. 🖪 𝖵𝖨𝖲𝖠
closed Sunday and Bank Holidays – **M** a la carte 12.25/19.50 **t.** ⚱ 4.50.

at Tickton NE : 3½ m. by A 1035 – ✉ Kingston-upon-Hull – 🕿 0964 Hornsea :

🏨 **Tickton Grange,** HU17 9SH, on A 1035 🖉 543666, Fax 542556, ☞ – 📺 🕿 🅿 – 🔬 60. 🖪
🕮 ⓞ 𝖵𝖨𝖲𝖠
M (closed Sunday dinner) 12.95/23.75 **t.** and a la carte ⚱ 5.95 – ⊆ 6.45 – **18 rm** 43.50 **t.** –
SB (weekends only) 64.90/86.30 **st.**

at Walkington SW : 3½ m. by A 164 – ✉ Beverley – 🕿 0482 Kingston-upon-Hull :

🍴🍴🍴 **Manor House** 🐾 with rm, Northlands, Newbald Rd, HU17 8RT, NE : 1 m. via Northgate
🖉 881645, Fax 866501, « Late 19C house, conservatory », ☞ – 📺 🕿 🅿. 🖪 𝖵𝖨𝖲𝖠 🍴
M (closed Sunday) (dinner only and lunch Wednesday and Friday)/dinner 15.00/27.50 **t.** –
⊆ 6.50 – **7 rm** 65.00/100.00 **t.** – SB (weekends only) 125.00 **st.**

at South Dalton NW : 6¼ m. by A 164 off B 1248 – ✉ 🕿 0430 Howden :

🍴🍴 Pipe and Glass, West End, HU17 7PN, 🖉 810246, ☞ – 🅿.

🅰 ATS 379 Grovehill Rd 🖉 868655/882644

E. Sussex 404 V 31 – pop. 34 625 – ECD : Wednesday – 🕿 0424.

🔞 Cooden Beach 🖉 842040 – 🔞 Ellerslie Lane 🖉 212625, N : 2 m.

🏛 De La Warr Pavilion, Marina, TN40 1DP 🖉 212023.

◆London 66 – ◆ Brighton 32 – Folkestone 42.

🏨 **Cooden Resort,** Cooden Sea Rd, Cooden Beach, TN39 4TT, W : 2 m. on B 2182
🖉 842281, Fax 846142, ⇆🇸, ⊒ heated, 🖂, ☞ – 📺 🕿 🅿 – 🔬 140. 🖪 🕮 ⓞ 𝖵𝖨𝖲𝖠
M 13.00/17.25 **t.** and a la carte – ⊆ 7.50 – **41 rm** 65.00/90.00 **t.** – SB 96.00/126.00 **st.**

🍴 **Lychgates,** 5a Church St., Old Town, TN40 2HE, 🖉 212193 – 🖪 𝖵𝖨𝖲𝖠
closed Tuesday lunch, Sunday, Monday, 2 weeks July, 25 December and Bank Holidays –
M 12.95/21.95 **t.** ⚱ 5.50.

Glos. 403 404 O 28 Great Britain G. – pop. 603 – ECD : Wednesday – ✉ 🕿 0285
Cirencester.

See : Village★.

◆London 86 – Gloucester 26 – ◆Oxford 30.

🏨 **Swan,** GL7 5NW, 🖉 740695, Fax 740473, « Attractively furnished inn with gardens and
trout stream », ☜ – 📳 📺 🕿. 🖪 🕮 𝖵𝖨𝖲𝖠 𝖩𝖢𝖡 🍴
closed 29 December-11 January – **M** 23.00/40.00 **st.** and dinner a la carte ⚱ 8.00 – **18 rm**
⊆ 90.00/220.00 **st.** – SB (except Christmas) 180.00/240.00 **st.**

🏠 **Cotteswold House** without rest., Arlington, GL7 5ND, on B 4425 🖉 740609 – ⠴ 📺 🅿.
🍴
3 rm ⊆ 22.00/38.00 **s.**

Devon 403 J 31 The West Country G. – pop. 205 – ECD : Tuesday – ✉ Tiverton –
🕿 0884.

See : Village★★ - Bickleigh Mill Craft Centre and Farms★★ AC – Bickleigh Castle★ AC.

Envir. : Tiverton : Museum★ AC, N : 2½ m. by A 396 – Knightshayes Court★ AC, N : 4 m. by
A 396.

Exc. : Uffculme (Coldharbour Mill★★ AC) NE : 7½ m.

🔞 Post Hill 🖉 252114, N : 2½ m. by A 396.

◆London 195 – Exeter 9 – Taunton 31.

🏨 **Bickleigh Cottage Country,** Bickleigh Bridge, EX16 8RJ, on A 396 🖉 855230, « Part
17C thatched cottage, riverside setting », ☞ – 🅿. 🖪 𝖵𝖨𝖲𝖠 🍴
April-October – **M** (residents only) (dinner only) 12.50 **t.** – **9 rm** ⊆ 21.50/45.00 **t.**

🏨 **Fisherman's Cot,** EX16 8RW, on A 396 🖉 855237, Fax 855241, ☜, ☞ – ⠴ rm 📺 🕿 🅿.
🖪 𝖵𝖨𝖲𝖠
M (carving lunch Sunday) 10.95/15.95 **t.** and a la carte ⚱ 5.35 – **20 rm** ⊆ 46.00/66.00 **t.**

BIDDENDEN Kent 404 V 30 Great Britain G. – pop. 2 229 – ⊠ Ashford – ✆ 0580.
Envir. : Sissinghurst Castle★ *AC*, W : 3 m. by A 262.
◆London 51 – Folkestone 29 – Hastings 23 – Maidstone 14.

> ✗ **West House,** 28 High St., TN27 8AH, ℰ 291341 – ✆, ⚑ VISA
> *closed Sunday dinner, Monday, 1 week January, 1 week April and 1 week August-September* – **M** – **Italian** 12.50 **st.** and a la carte ⚑ 4.90.

BIDEFORD Devon 403 H 30 The West Country G. – pop. 13 826 – ECD : Wednesday – ✆ 0237.
See : Bridge★★ – Burton Art Gallery★ *AC* – Envir. : Appledore★, N : 2 m.
Exc. : Clovelly★★, W : 11 m. by A 39 and B 3237 – Lundy Island★★, NW : by ferry – Great Torrington (Dartington Crystal★ *AC*) SE : 7 ½ m. by A 386.
⛳ Royal North Devon, Golf Links Rd, Westward Ho ℰ 473824, N : 2 m. by A 39 – ⛳ Torrington, Weare Trees ℰ 0805 (Torrington) 22229, S : 6 m. by A 386.
⛴ to the Isle of Lundy (Lundy Co.) (2 h 15 mn).
🛈 Victoria Park, The Quay, EX39 2QQ ℰ 477676/421853.
◆London 231 – Exeter 43 – ◆Plymouth 58 – Taunton 60.

> 🏨 **Durrant House,** Heywood Rd, Northam, EX39 3QB, N : 1 m. on A 386 ℰ 472361, Fax 421709, ⚐, ⚑ – 🛗 📺 ☎ ✆ – 🔬 300. ⚑ ⚑ 🕐 VISA
> *closed 2 to 9 January* – **M** 7.50/15.00 **t.** and a la carte – **118 rm** ⊇ 46.75/81.00 **t.**, 2 suites – SB 82.50/127.50 **st.**

> 🏨 **New Bridge,** Northam, EX39 3QA, N : 1 m. on A 386 ℰ 474989, Fax 474989 – ⚐ rest 📺 ☎ ✆, ⚑ VISA ⚐
> **M** *(closed Sunday dinner and Monday)* (dinner only and Sunday lunch)/dinner approx. 12.00 **st.** ⚑ 5.00 – **10 rm** ⊇ 25.00/50.00 **st.**

> 🏨 **Orchard Hill,** Orchard Hill, Northam, EX39 2QY, N : ¾ m. by A 386 ℰ 472872, Fax 424926, ⚐ – 📺 ✆ ⚑ VISA ⚐.
> **M** (dinner only) a la carte 12.50/17.50 **t.** ⚑ 5.00 – **9 rm** ⊇ 35.00/50.00 **t.**

> *at Instow* N : 3 m. on A 39 – ⊠ Bideford – ✆ 0271 Instow :

> 🏨 **Commodore,** Marine Par., EX39 4JN, ℰ 860347, Fax 861233, ≼ Taw and Torridge estuaries, ⚐ – 📺 ☎ ✆ ⚑ ⚑ VISA ⚐
> **M** 10.00/20.00 **st.** and a la carte ⚑ 4.75 – **20 rm** ⊇ (dinner included) 50.00/120.00 **st.**

> *at Eastleigh* NE : 2 ½ m. by A 386 (via Old Barnstaple Rd) – ⊠ Bideford – ✆ 0271 Instow :

> 🏠 **Pines,** EX39 4PA, ℰ 860561, Fax 861166, ≼, ⚐ – 📺 ☎ ✆. ⚑ VISA
> **M** 12.95 **st.** ⚑ 3.00 – **11 rm** ⊇ 23.00/50.00 **st.** – SB (October-March) 54.00/67.00 **st.**

⚙ ATS New Rd ℰ 472451

BIGBURY-ON-SEA Devon 403 I 33 – pop. 559 – ECD : Thursday – ⊠ Kingsbridge – ✆ 0548.
◆London 196 – Exeter 42 – ◆Plymouth 17.

> 🏨 **Burgh Island** ⚐, TQ7 4AU, S : ½ m. by sea tractor ℰ 810514, Fax 810243, ≼ Bigbury Bay, « Island setting, Art Deco », ⚐, park, ⚐ – 🛗 📺 ☎ ⚐. ⚑ ⚑ 🕐 VISA ⚐
> *closed Sunday to Thursday January-February* – **M** (booking essential) 9.00/28.00 **t.** and lunch a la carte ⚑ 6.00 – **14 suites** ⊇ (dinner included) 83.00/200.00 **t.**

> 🏠 **Henley** ⚐, Folly Hill, TQ7 4AR, ℰ 810240, Fax 810020, ≼ Bigbury Bay and Bolt Tail, ⚐ – ⚐ ⚐ ✆. ⚑ VISA
> **M** 14.50 **st.** ⚑ 3.75 – **8 rm** ⊇ 25.00/85.00 **st.** – SB 75.00/90.00 **st.**

BILBROOK Somerset 403 J 30 – ⊠ Minehead – ✆ 0984 Washford.
◆London 179 – ◆Bristol 56 – Minehead 7 – Taunton 17.

> 🏨 **Dragon House,** TA24 6HQ, on A 39 ℰ 40215, Fax 41340, ⚐ – 📺 ☎ ✆. ⚑ ⚑ VISA
> **M** (bar lunch Monday to Saturday)/dinner 9.50 **st.** and a la carte ⚑ 3.20 – **9 rm** ⊇ 18.00/46.00 **st.** – SB 43.00/60.00 **st.**

BILBROUGH N. Yorks. 402 Q 22 – see York.

BILLESLEY Warks. – see Stratford-upon-Avon.

BILLINGSHURST W. Sussex 404 S 30 – pop. 5 301 – ECD : Wednesday – ✆ 0403.
◆London 44 – ◆Brighton 24 – Guildford 25 – ◆Portsmouth 40.

> 🏨 **Forte Travelodge** without rest., Five Oaks, Stane St., RH14 9AE, N : 1 m. on A 29 ℰ 782711, Reservations (Freephone) 0800 850950 – 📺 ⚐ ✆. ⚑ ⚑ VISA ⚐
> **26 rm** 31.95 **t.**

> 🏠 **Old Wharf** ⚐ without rest., Wharf Farm, Newbridge, RH14 OJG, W : 1 ¾ m. on A 272 ℰ 784096, ≼, « Restored canalside warehouse », ⚐, ⚐, park – ⚐ 📺 ☎ ✆. ⚑ ⚑ 🕐 VISA ⚐
> *closed 2 weeks Christmas-New Year* – ⊇ 5.00 – **4 rm** 40.00/60.00 **st.**

86

BINBROOK Lincs. 🔲🔲 T 23 – ✪ 0472 Grimsby.

◆London 162 – Great Grimsby 10 – Lincoln 26 – Scunthorpe 32.

♤ **Hoe Hill,** Swinhope, LN3 6HX, NE : 1 m. on B 1203 ℰ 398206, ☞ – ✇ **P**. ⛊
  M (by arrangement) (communal dining) 10.00 – **3 rm** ⊑ 12.00/30.00 **s.**

BINGHAM Notts. 🔲🔲 R 25 – ✪ 0949.

◆London 125 – Lincoln 28 – ◆Nottingham 11 – ◆Sheffield 35.

🏨 **Bingham Court,** Ming House, Market St., NG13 8AB, ℰ 831831, Fax 838833 – |❄| ▤ rest
  📺 ☎ **P**. 🔲 *VISA*. ⛊
  M – Yeung Sing - Chinese (Canton) (dinner only and Sunday lunch)/dinner
  16.50 **t.** and a la carte ⒜ 5.00 – **13 rm** ⊑ 38.50/48.00 **t.**

◍ ATS 1 Moorbridge Rd ℰ 837717

BINGLEY W. Yorks. 🔲🔲 O 22 – pop. 18 954 – ECD : Tuesday – ✉ ✪ 0274 Bradford.

🏌 St. Ives Est. ℰ 562436.

◆London 204 – Bradford 6 – Skipton 13.

🏨 **Bankfield** (Jarvis), Bradford Rd, BD16 1TU, SE : 1½ m. on A 650 ℰ 567123, Fax 551331,
  ☞ – |❄| ▤ rest 📺 ☎ ⅋ ☜ ☞ **P** – 🔏 200. 🔲 🔲 🔲 *VISA*
  M (carving rest.) (bar lunch Saturday and Bank Holidays) 9.95/25.00 **t.** and a la carte ⒜ 6.00
  – ⊑ 8.50 – **103 rm** 79.00/99.00 **t.**

♤ **Hallbank,** Beck Lane, BD16 4DD, ℰ 565296 – ✇ rest 📺 ☎ **P**. ⛊
  closed Christmas – **M** 10.00 **st.** ⒜ 4.00 – **9 rm** ⊑ 40.00/50.00 **st.** – SB (weekends only)
  60.00/70.00 **st.**

Prices	For full details of the prices quoted in the guide,
	consult the introduction.

BIRCHINGTON Kent 🔲🔲 X 29 – ✪ 0843 Thanet.

◆London 71 – ◆Dover 20 – Maidstone 40 – Margate 5.

☝ Crown Inn (Cherry Brandy House), Ramsgate Rd, Sarre, CT7 OLF, SW : 4 m. on A 28
  ℰ 47808, Fax 47914 – 📺 ☎ ⅋ **P**
  12 rm.

BIRCH SERVICE AREA Gtr. Manchester 🔲🔲 ㉒ 🔲🔲 ③ 🔲🔲 ⑩ – ✉ Heywood (Lancs.) –
✪ 061 Manchester

🏨 **Granada Lodge** without rest., OL10 2QH, on M 62, between junctions 18 and 19
  ℰ 655 3403, Fax 655 3358, Reservations (Freephone) 0800 555300 – ✇ 📺 ⅋ **P**. 🔲 🔲
  VISA. ⛊
  ⊑ 4.00 – **40 rm** 34.95/37.95 **st.**

BIRDLIP Glos. 🔲🔲 N 28 Great Britain G. – ECD : Saturday – ✉ ✪ 0452 Gloucester.

Envir. : Crickley Hill Country Park (⭍*) N : 1½ m. by B 4070 and A 417.

◆London 107 – ◆Bristol 51 – Gloucester 9 – ◆Oxford 44 – Swindon 24.

🏨 **Royal George,** GL4 8JH, ℰ 862506, Fax 862277, ☎s, ☞ – ✇ rm 📺 ☎ **P** – 🔏 100. 🔲
  🔲 🔲 *VISA*. ⛊
  M 9.95/18.50 **t.** and a la carte ⒜ 6.45 – **35 rm** ⊑ 59.50/71.00 **st.**, 1 suite – SB 86.00/94.00 **st.**

✗ **Kingshead House,** GL4 8JH, ℰ 862299 – **P**. 🔲 🔲 🔲 *VISA*. ⛊
  *closed Saturday lunch, Sunday dinner, Monday, 10 days July-August, 26-27 December and
  1-2 January* – **M** 23.50 **t.** (dinner) and lunch a la carte 15.00/21.00 **t.**

BIRKENHEAD Mersey. 🔲🔲 K 23 – pop. 99 075 – ECD : Thursday – ✪ 051 Liverpool.

🏌 Arrowe Park, Woodchurch ℰ 677 1527, S : 3 m. by A 552 – 🏌 Prenton, Golf Links Rd, Prenton
ℰ 608 1461.

⛴ to Liverpool and Wallasey (Mersey Ferries) (except Saturday and Sunday in summer).

🅱 Woodside Visitors Centre, Woodside Ferry Terminal, L41 6DU ℰ 647 6780.

◆London 222 – ◆Liverpool 2.

Plan : see Liverpool p. 3

🏨 **Bowler Hat,** 2 Talbot Rd, Oxton, L43 2HH, ℰ 652 4931, Fax 653 8127, ☞ – 📺 ☎ **P** –
  🔏 100. 🔲 🔲 🔲 *VISA*. ⛊   AZ
  M *(closed Saturday lunch)* 12.95/16.95 **t.** and a la carte ⒜ 4.95 – **28 rm** ⊑ 39.50/69.50 **st.**,
  1 suite – SB 86.90/88.20 **st.**

🏨 **Riverhill,** Talbot Rd, Oxton, L43 2HJ, ℰ 653 3773, Fax 653 7162, ☞ – 📺 ☎ **P**. 🔲 🔲 🔲
  VISA. ⛊   AZ
  M 8.95/13.75 **t.** and a la carte ⒜ 4.95 – **16 rm** ⊑ 29.95/65.00 **t.**

✗ **Beadles,** 15 Rosemount, Oxton, L43 5SG, ℰ 653 9010 – 🔲 *VISA*   AZ
  closed Sunday, Monday and 2 weeks August-September – **M** (dinner only) a la carte
  approx. 17.00 **t.** ⒜ 3.50.

◍ ATS 40 Mill Lane, Wallasey, Wirral ℰ 638 1949/8606

BIRMINGHAM W. Mids. 403 404 O 26 Great Britain G. – pop. 1 013 995 – ECD : Wednesday – ✪ 021.

See : City★ – Museum and Art Gallery★★ JZ **M2** – Barber Institute of Fine Arts★★ (at Birmingham University) EX – Museum of Science and Industry★ JY **M3** – Cathedral of St. Philip (stained glass portrayals★) KYZ.

Envir. : Aston Hall★★ FV **M**.

🅱 Edgbaston, Church Rd ℰ 454 1736, S : 1½ m. by A 38 FX – 🅱 Hilltop, Park Lane, Handsworth ℰ 554 4463, NW : 4½ m. by A 41 CU – 🅱 Hatchford Brook, Coventry Rd, Sheldon ℰ 743 9821, SE : 8½ m. by A 45 HX – 🅱 Brand Hall, Heron Rd, Oldbury ℰ 552 7475 by B 4171 BU – 🅱 Harborne Church Farm, Vicarage Rd, Harborne ℰ 427 1204, SW : 3½ m. EX.

✈ Birmingham Airport : ℰ 767 5511, Telex 335582, Fax 782 8802, E : 6½ m. by A 45 DU.

🅱 Convention & Visitor Bureau, 2 City Arcade, B2 4TX ℰ 643 2514 – Convention & Visitor Bureau, National Exhibition Centre, B40 1NT ℰ 780 4321 – Birmingham Airport, Information Desk, B26 3QJ ℰ 767 7145/7146.

◆London 122 – ◆Bristol 91 – ◆Liverpool 103 – ◆Manchester 86 – ◆Nottingham 50.

Town plans : Birmingham pp. 2-7
Except where otherwise stated see pp. 6 and 7

🏨 **Hyatt Regency,** 2 Bridge St., B1 2JZ, ℰ 643 1234, Telex 335097, Fax 616 2323, ≤, ſ₅, ≦s, ⬜ – |₤| ⇆ rm 🔟 ☎ ⇔ – 🔬 180. 🕾 🝙 ⓪ 𝘝𝘐𝘚𝘈 ✼ JZ **a**
M 12.76 **t.** (lunch) and a la carte 17.25/28.50 **t.** ᵻ 6.50 – ⬜ 11.00 – **315 rm** 118.00/140.00 **st.**, 4 suites.

🏨 **Swallow,** 12 Hagley Rd, B16 8SJ, ℰ 452 1144, Fax 456 3442, ſ₅, ⬜ – |₤| ⇆ rm 🔳 🔟 🔲 👍 🄿 – 🔬 30. 🕾 🝙 ⓪ 𝘝𝘐𝘚𝘈 p. 4 FX **c**
M – Langtrys a la carte 18.95/28.90 **st.** ᵻ 8.00 – (see also **Sir Edward Elgar's** below) – **94 rm** ⬜ 115.00/140.00 **st.**, 4 suites – SB (weekends only) 145.00 **st.**

🏨 **Forte Crest,** Smallbrook Queensway, B5 4EW, ℰ 643 8171, Fax 631 2528, ſ₅, ≦s, ⬜, squash – |₤| ⇆ rm 🔳 🔟 ☎ 🄿 – 🔬 630. 🕾 🝙 ⓪ 𝘝𝘐𝘚𝘈 KZ **o**
M 14.95/16.95 **st.** and a la carte ᵻ 6.10 – ⬜ 9.95 – **252 rm** 80.00/90.00 **st.**, 1 suite – SB (weekends only) 99.00/105.00 **st.**

🏨 Midland, 128 New St., B2 4JT, ℰ 643 2601, Telex 338419, Fax 643 5075 – |₤| 🔟 ☎ – 🔬 200 KZ **r**
109 rm, 2 suites.

🏨 **Copthorne,** Paradise Circus, B3 3HJ, ℰ 200 2727, Telex 339026, Fax 200 1197, ſ₅, ≦s, ⬜ – |₤| ⇆ rm 🔳 rest 🔟 ☎ 🄿 – 🔬 150. 🕾 🝙 ⓪ 𝘝𝘐𝘚𝘈 𝘑𝘊𝘉. 3 suites – SB (weekends only) JZ **e**
M 16.95 **st.** ᵻ 6.95 – ⬜ 9.75 – **209 rm** 99.00/120.00 **st.**, 3 suites – SB (weekends only) 98.40/167.90 **st.**

🏨 **Holiday Inn,** Central Sq., Holliday St., B1 1HH, ℰ 631 2000, Telex 337272, Fax 643 9018, ſ₅, ≦s, ⬜ – |₤| ⇆ rm 🔳 🔟 ☎ 👍 🄿 – 🔬 150. 🕾 🝙 ⓪ 𝘝𝘐𝘚𝘈 JZ **z**
M 14.50/16.95 **t.** and a la carte ᵻ 6.50 – ⬜ 9.95 – **284 rm** 99.00/108.00 **t.**, 4 suites.

🏨 **Plough and Harrow** (Forte), 135 Hagley Rd, Edgbaston, B16 8LS, ℰ 454 4111, Fax 454 1868, ☞ – |₤| ⇆ rm 🔟 ☎ 🄿 – 🔬 60. 🕾 🝙 ⓪ 𝘝𝘐𝘚𝘈 𝘑𝘊𝘉 p. 4 EX **x**
M (closed Saturday lunch) 11.25/15.95 **t.** and a la carte – ⬜ 8.50 – **42 rm** 80.00/90.00 **st.**, 2 suites – SB 98.00 **st.**

🏨 **Jonathan's,** 16-24 Wolverhampton Rd, B68 0LH, W : 4 m. by A 456 ℰ 429 3757, Fax 434 3107, « Authentic Victorian furnishings and memorabilia » – 🔟 ☎ 🄿. 🕾 🝙 ⓪ 𝘝𝘐𝘚𝘈 p. 2 BU **e**
M - English (closed Sunday dinner) 18.50 **t.** (dinner) and a la carte 16.20/35.50 ᵻ 5.50 – **19 rm** ⬜ 69.00/80.00 **st.** 11 suites – SB (weekends only) 95.00/107.50 **st.**

🏨 **Grand** (Q.M.H.), Colmore Row, B3 2DA, ℰ 236 7951, Telex 338174, Fax 233 1465 – |₤| 🔳 rest 🔟 ☎ – 🔬 450. 🕾 🝙 ⓪ 𝘝𝘐𝘚𝘈 JKY **c**
closed 24 to 30 December – **M** 12.95 **st.** and a la carte ᵻ 4.00 – **171 rm** ⬜ 80.00/95.00 **st.**, 2 suites – SB (weekends only) 80.00 **st.**

🏨 **Royal Angus Thistle** (Mt. Charlotte Thistle), St. Chad's, Queensway, B4 6HY, ℰ 236 4211, Telex 336889, Fax 233 2195 – |₤| ⇆ rm 🔟 ☎ 🄿 – 🔬 140. 🕾 🝙 ⓪ 𝘝𝘐𝘚𝘈 𝘑𝘊𝘉. ✼ KY **s**
M (closed Saturday lunch) 11.95/16.95 **t.** and a la carte ᵻ 6.10 – ⬜ 8.50 – **131 rm** 75.00/95.00 **st.**, 2 suites – SB (weekends only) 96.00/136.00 **st.**

🏨 **Strathallan Thistle** (Mt. Charlotte Thistle), 225 Hagley Rd, Edgbaston, B16 9RY, ℰ 455 9777, Telex 336680, Fax 454 9432 – |₤| ⇆ rm 🔳 rest 🔟 ☎ 🄿 – 🔬 170. 🕾 🝙 ⓪ 𝘝𝘐𝘚𝘈 𝘑𝘊𝘉 p. 4 EX **i**
M (closed Saturday lunch) 12.25/17.25 **t.** and a la carte ᵻ 5.25 – ⬜ 8.95 – **163 rm** 75.00/85.00 **t.**, 4 suites.

🏨 **Novotel,** 70 Broad St., B1 2HT, ℰ 643 2000, Telex 335556, Fax 643 9796, ſ₅, ≦s – |₤| ⇆ rm 🔳 rest 🔟 ☎ 👍 🄿 – 🔬 220. 🕾 🝙 ⓪ 𝘝𝘐𝘚𝘈 p. 4 FV **a**
M a la carte 8.55/20.40 **st.** ᵻ 5.95 – ⬜ 7.50 – **148 rm** 67.00/77.00 **st.**

🏨 **Apollo** (Mt. Charlotte Thistle), 243 Hagley Rd, Edgbaston, B16 9RA, ℰ 455 0271, Telex 336759, Fax 456 2394 – |₤| ⇆ rm 🔳 rest 🔟 ☎ 🄿 – 🔬 150. 🕾 🝙 ⓪ 𝘝𝘐𝘚𝘈
M 14.50/16.95 **st.** ᵻ 4.50 – ⬜ 8.50 – **124 rm** 70.00/75.00 **st.**, 2 suites – SB (weekends only) 66.00/72.00 **st.** p. 4 EX **o**

🏠 **Asquith House,** 19 Portland Rd, off Hagley Rd, Edgbaston, B16 9HN, ℰ 454 5282, Fax 456 4668, « Attractive furnishings », ☞ – 📺 ☎. 🔼 ☒ 𝐕𝐈𝐒𝐀 p. 4 EX **c**
M (by arrangement Sunday dinner and Bank Holidays) 16.00/18.10 **t.** and a la carte ⅛ 3.75 –
10 rm ⊇ 50.60/61.80 **st.** – SB (weekends only) 108.50/128.50 **st.**

🏠 **Westbourne Lodge,** 27-29 Fountain Rd, Edgbaston, B17 8NJ, ℰ 429 1003, Fax 429 7436, ☞ – 📺 ☎ ℗. 🔼 ☒ 𝐕𝐈𝐒𝐀 p. 4 EV **x**
M (bar lunch)/dinner 15.50 **t.** ⅛ 4.80 – **17 rm** ⊇ 30.00/56.00 **t.**

🏠 **Copperfield House,** 60 Upland Rd, Selly Park, B29 7JS, ℰ 472 8344, Fax 472 8344, ☞ –
⅜❤ rest 📺 ☎ ℗. 🔼 ☒ 𝐕𝐈𝐒𝐀 p. 4 FX **a**
M 16.00/19.00 **st.** ⅛ 3.75 – **18 rm** ⊇ 47.50/59.50 **st.** – SB (weekends only) 105.00/149.00 **st.**

🏠 **Fountain Court,** 339-343 Hagley Rd, Edgbaston, B17 8NH, ℰ 429 1754, Fax 429 1209, ☞ – 🔼 📺 ☎ ℗. 🔼 ☒ 𝐕𝐈𝐒𝐀 p. 4 EX **u**
M (closed Saturday and Sunday) (dinner only) 13.50 **st.** ⅛ 4.95 – **25 rm** ⊇ 30.00/55.00 **st.**

🏠 **Portland,** 313 Hagley Rd, Edgbaston, B16 9LQ, ℰ 455 0535, Fax 456 1841 – 📳 🔼 rest 📺 ☎ ℗ – ⅜ 80. 🔼 ☒ 𝐕𝐈𝐒𝐀 p. 4 EX **r**
M (closed Saturday lunch, Sunday and Bank Holidays) 10.95/13.95 **t.** and a la carte ⅛ 3.95 –
62 rm ⊇ 31.95/52.95 **t.** – SB (weekends only) 62.40/99.90 **st.**

🏠 **Hagley Court,** 229 Hagley Rd, Edgbaston, B16 9RP, ℰ 454 6514, Fax 456 2722 – 📺 ☎
℗. 🔼 ☒ 𝐕𝐈𝐒𝐀 p. 4 EX **s**
closed 23 December-1 January – **M** (closed Friday to Sunday and Bank Holidays) (dinner only) 13.50 **st.** and a la carte ⅛ 4.50 – **27 rm** ⊇ 37.00/65.00 **st.**

🏠 **Friendly New Cobden,** 166-174 Hagley Rd, Edgbaston, B16 9NZ, ℰ 454 6621, Fax 356 2935, 𝟏₆, ⊜, 🔼, ☞ – 📳 ⅜❤ rm 📺 ☎ ℗ – ⅜ 75. 🔼 ☒ ⑩ 𝐕𝐈𝐒𝐀 𝐉𝐂𝐁. ⅜❤
M 10.00/12.50 **st.** and a la carte – ⊇ 6.75 – **230 rm** 54.00/73.00 **st.** – SB (weekends only) 77.00/84.00 **st.** p. 4 EX **e**

🏠 **The Wharf,** 20-22 Bridge St., B1 2JH, ℰ 633 4820, Fax 633 4779 – 📳 ⅜❤ rm 📺 ☎ & ℗ – ⅜ 40. 🔼 ☒ ⑩ 𝐕𝐈𝐒𝐀. ⅜❤ JZ **c**
M (Beefeater grill) a la carte approx. 16.00 **t.** – ⊇ 4.95 – **52 rm** 33.50 **t.**

🏠 **Campanile,** 55 Irving St., B1 1DH, ℰ 622 4925, Telex 333701, Fax 622 4195 – 📺 ☎ & ℗. 🔼 ☒ 𝐕𝐈𝐒𝐀 p. 4 FX **e**
M (grill rest.) 9.45 **t.** ⅛ 4.65 – ⊇ 4.25 – **47 rm** 35.75 **t.**

🏵🏵🏵🏵 **Sir Edward Elgar's** (at Swallow H.), 12 Hagley Rd, B16 8SJ, ℰ 452 1144, Fax 456 3442 –
🗐 ℗. 🔼 ☒ ⑩ 𝐕𝐈𝐒𝐀 p. 4 FX **c**
closed Saturday lunch – **M** 23.50/30.00 **st.** and a la carte ⅛ 8.00.

🏵🏵🏵 **Sloans,** 27-29 Chad Sq., Hawthorne Rd, Edgbaston, B15 3TQ, ℰ 455 6697, Fax 454 4335 – 🔼 ☒ 𝐕𝐈𝐒𝐀 p. 4 EX **v**
closed Saturday lunch, Sunday and 1 week Christmas-New Year – **M** 12.00 **t.** (lunch) and a la carte 18.00/32.25 **t.**

🏵🏵 **Maharaja,** 23-25 Hurst St., B5 4AS, ℰ 622 2641 – 🗐. 🔼 ☒ ⑩ 𝐕𝐈𝐒𝐀 KZ **i**
closed Sunday and Bank Holidays – **M** - North Indian 10.70/15.25 **t.** and a la carte.

🏵🏵 **Purple Rooms,** 1076 Stratford Rd, Hall Green, B28 8AD, SE : 4¼ m. by A 41 on A 34 ℰ 702 2193, Fax 702 2520 – 🔼 ☒ ⑩ 𝐕𝐈𝐒𝐀 GX **a**
closed lunch Monday to Thursday – **M** - Indian 12.00/18.60 **t.** and a la carte.

🏵🏵 **Henry's,** 27 St. Paul's Sq., B3 1RB, ℰ 200 1136 – 🗐. 🔼 ☒ ⑩ 𝐕𝐈𝐒𝐀 JY **a**
closed Sunday and Bank Holidays – **M** - Chinese (Canton) 13.00 **t.** and a la carte ⅛ 5.80.

🏵🏵 **Henry Wong,** 283 High St., Harborne, B17 9QH, W : 3¾ m. by A 456 ℰ 427 9799 – 🗐. 🔼 ☒ ⑩ 𝐕𝐈𝐒𝐀 p. 4 EX **n**
closed Sunday and Bank Holidays – **M** - Chinese (Canton) 15.00 **t.** and a la carte.

🏵🏵 **Days of the Raj,** 51 Dale End, B4 7LS, ℰ 236 0445 – 🗐. 🔼 ☒ ⑩ 𝐕𝐈𝐒𝐀 KY **n**
closed lunch Saturday and Sunday and 25-26 December – **M** - Indian (buffet lunch)/dinner a la carte 11.35/25.25 **t.** ⅛ 3.50.

🏵🏵 **Dynasty,** 93-103 Hurst St., B5 4TE, ℰ 622 1410 – 🔼 ☒ ⑩ 𝐕𝐈𝐒𝐀 KZ **e**
closed Sunday lunch, 25-26 December and 1 January – **M** - Chinese a la carte 12.70/18.80 **t.**

🏵 **Franzl's,** 151 Milcote Rd, Bearwood, Smethwick, B67 5BN, ℰ 429 7920, Fax 429 1615 –
🔼 ☒ 𝐕𝐈𝐒𝐀 p. 4 EV **a**
closed Sunday, Monday and first 3 weeks August – **M** - Austrian (dinner only) 19.95 **t.** ⅛ 4.50.

at Erdington NE : 5 m. by A 5127 – ✉ ✪ 021 Birmingham :

🏠 **Willow Tree,** 759 Chester Rd, B24 0BY, on A 452 ℰ 373 6388, ☞ – ⅜❤ rest 📺 ☎ ℗. 🔼 𝐕𝐈𝐒𝐀. ⅜❤ DT **e**
M (by arrangement) 10.00 – **7 rm** ⊇ 25.00/44.00 **st.** – SB (weekends only) 49.00/78.00 **st.**

at Birmingham Airport SE : 9 m. by A 45 – DU – ✉ ✪ 021 Birmingham :

🏨 **Novotel,** Passenger Terminal, B26 3QL, ℰ 782 7000, Telex 338158, Fax 782 0445 – 📳 ⅜❤ rm 🗐 rest 📺 ☎ & – ⅜ 30. 🔼 ☒ ⑩ 𝐕𝐈𝐒𝐀
M 12.50 **st.** and a la carte – ⊇ 7.50 – **195 rm** 67.00/77.00 **st.** – SB (weekends only) 82.00/102.00 **st.**

🏨 **Forte Posthouse,** Coventry Rd, B26 3QW, on A 45 ℰ 782 8141, Fax 782 2476 – ⅜❤ rm 📺 ☎ ℗ – ⅜ 150. 🔼 ☒ ⑩ 𝐕𝐈𝐒𝐀 𝐉𝐂𝐁
M a la carte approx. 17.50 **t.** ⅛ 4.65 – ⊇ 6.95 – **136 rm** 53.50/69.50 **st.** – SB (weekends only) 90.00 **st.**

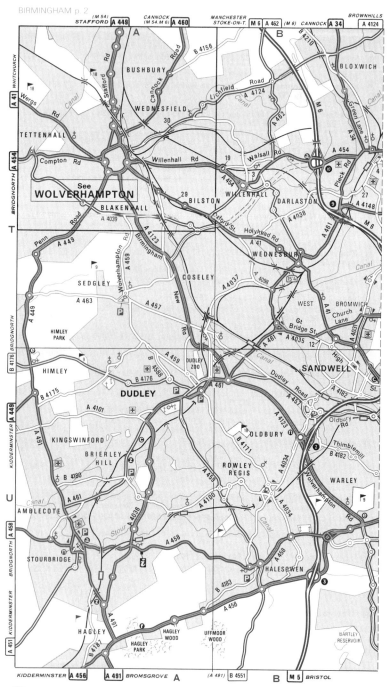

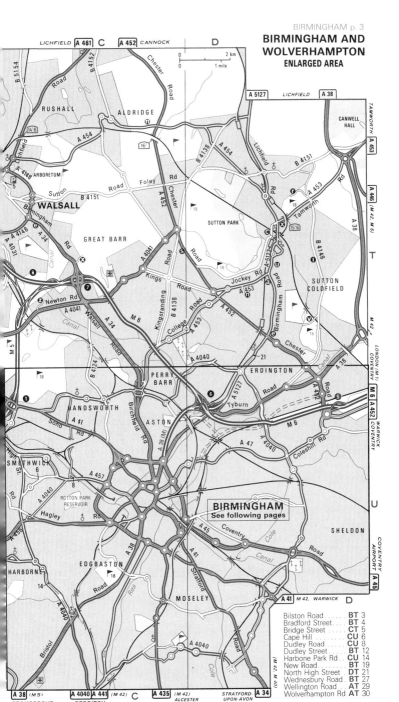

BIRMINGHAM AND WOLVERHAMPTON
ENLARGED AREA

LICHFIELD A 461 C A 452 CANNOCK D

A 5127 LICHFIELD A 38

TAMWORTH A 453

RUSHALL

ALDRIDGE

CANWELL HALL

A 446 (M 42, M 6)

Chester Road

B 4152

B 5154

A 4148 ARBORETUM

A 454

B 4138 A 454

Lichfield

B 4151

A 4148

WALSALL

Sutton Road

Foley Rd

Chester

A 452

B 4151

A 453

B 4148

A 38

SUTTON PARK

Tamworth

GREAT BARR

A 4041

A 4041

Kings Road

Jockey Rd

A 453

SUTTON COLDFIELD

A 4148

A 34

A 4031

Newton Rd

M 6

Walsall Road

A 34

Kingstanding

B 4138

College

A 453

A 452

Birmingham

Chester

M 42

Canal

A 4040

B 4124

PERRY BARR

A 4127

ERDINGTON

Tyburn Road

A 38

LONDON (M 1) COVENTRY

HANDSWORTH

Soho

A 41

Birchfield Rd

ASTON

A 38 (M)

M 6

M 6, A 452 COVENTRY

WARWICK COVENTRY

SMETHWICK

High St.

A 4040

A 457

A 47

A 4040

Coleshill Rd

ROTTON PARK RESERVOIR

BIRMINGHAM
See following pages

SHELDON

COVENTRY AIRPORT

Hagley Rd

A 38

A 45

Coventry

Cole

Canal

U

HARBORNE

EDGBASTON

Rea

A 4040

A 41

Stratford Road

A 45

MOSELEY

A 41 M 42, WARWICK D

Bristol

A 4040

A 4040

Cole

Road

A 38 (M 5) A 4040 A 441 (M 42) A 435 (M 42) STRATFORD- A 34
BROMSGROVE REDDITCH ALCESTER UPON-AVON

(M 42, M 40)

Bilston Road	BT	3
Bradford Street	BT	4
Bridge Street	CT	5
Cape Hill	CU	6
Dudley Road	CU	8
Dudley Street	BT	12
Harborne Park Rd.	BT	14
New Road	BT	19
North High Street	DT	21
Wednesbury Road	BT	27
Wellington Road	AT	29
Wolverhampton Rd	AT	30

91

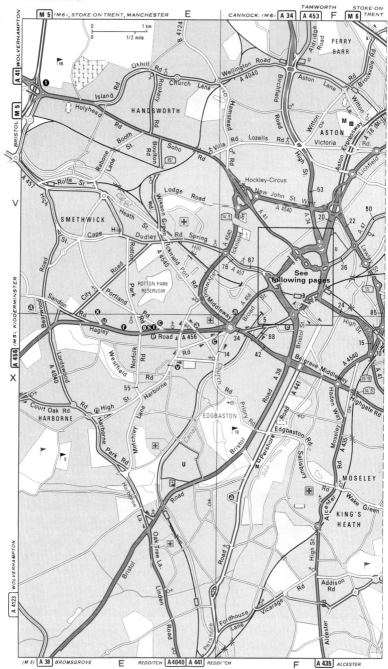

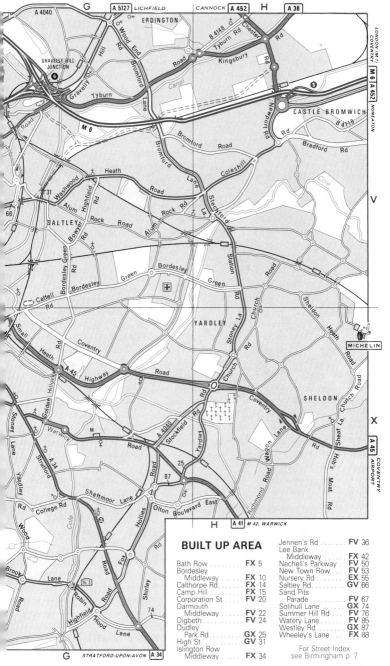

BUILT UP AREA

For Street Index
see Birmingham p. 7

CENTRE

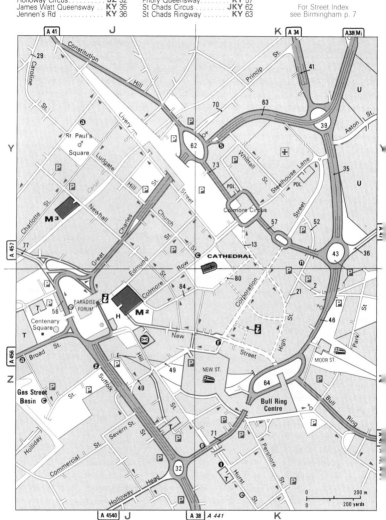

« **Short Breaks** »

Many hotels now offer a special rate for a stay of 2 nights
which includes dinner, bed and breakfast.

STREET INDEX TO BIRMINGHAM TOWN PLANS

« Short Breaks » (SB)

De nombreux hôtels proposent des conditions avantageuses
pour un séjour de deux nuits comprenant la chambre, le dîner et le petit déjeuner.

at National Exhibition Centre SE : 9 ½ m. on A 45 –DU – ✉ ⊕ 021 Birmingham :

🏨 **Birmingham Metropole**, Bickenhill, B40 1PP, ℰ 780 4242, Telex 336129, Fax 780 3923, squash – 🛗 ↔ rm 🖵 📺 ☎ 👌 🅿 – 🔬 2 000. 🔼 ⒶⒺ ⓞ 𝗩𝗜𝗦𝗔
M 21.75 **st.** and a la carte ¼ 7.50 – **787 rm** ⊑ 118.00/186.00 **t.**, 15 suites – SB 110.00/126.00 **st.**

🏨 **Arden**, Coventry Rd, B92 0EH, ℰ 0675 (Hampton-in-Arden) 443221, Fax 443221, 𝑓ₛ, 🈺, 🖵 – 🔼 ↔ rm 📺 ☎ 👌 🅿 – 🔬 130. 🔼 ⒶⒺ ⓞ 𝗩𝗜𝗦𝗔
M (bar lunch Saturday) 13.50 **t.** and a la carte ¼ 4.15 – ⊑ 7.00 – **146 rm** 65.00/89.50 **t.**

at Northfield SW : 6 m. by A 38 – CU – ✉ ⊕ 021 Birmingham :

🏨 **Norwood**, 87-89 Bunbury Rd, B31 2ET, ℰ 411 2202, Fax 411 2202, 𝒜 – 📺 ☎ 🅿 🔼 𝗩𝗜𝗦𝗔
closed 24 to 27 December – **M** *(closed Sunday)* (dinner only) 14.95 **st.** ¼ 4.75 – **15 rm** ⊑ 40.00/59.75 **st.**

at Oldbury W : 7 ¾ m. by A 456 on A 4123 – ✉ ⊕ 021 Birmingham :

🏨 **Forte Travelodge** without rest., Wolverhampton Rd, B69 2BH, on A 4123 ℰ 552 2967, Reservations (Freephone) 0800 850950 – 📺 👌 🅿. 🔼 ⒶⒺ 𝗩𝗜𝗦𝗔 ✄ p. 2 BU **n**
33 rm 31.95 **t.**

at Great Barr NW : 6 m. on A 34 – ✉ ⊕ 021 Birmingham :

🏨 **Forte Posthouse**, Chapel Lane, B43 7BG, ℰ 357 7444, Fax 357 7503, 𝑓ₛ, 🈺, 🔼 – ↔ rm CT **x**
📺 ☎ 🅿 – 🔬 120. 🔼 ⒶⒺ ⓞ 𝗩𝗜𝗦𝗔 𝗝𝗖𝗕 ✄
M a la carte approx. 17.50 **t.** ¼ 4.65 – ⊑ 6.95 – **192 rm** 53.50 **st.** – SB (weekends only) 90.00 **st.**

🏨 **Great Barr**, Pear Tree Drive, Newton Rd, B43 6HS, W : 1 m. by A 4041 ℰ 357 1141, Fax 357 7557, 𝒜 – 📺 ☎ 🅿 – 🔬 120. 🔼 ⒶⒺ ⓞ 𝗩𝗜𝗦𝗔 ✄ CT **z**
M *(closed Bank Holidays)* 14.00/18.00 **st.** and a la carte ¼ 6.00 – ⊑ 7.00 – **110 rm** 55.00/75.00 **st.**

at West Bromwich NW : 6 m. on A 41 – ✉ ⊕ 021 Birmingham :

🏨 **West Bromwich Moat House** (Q.M.H.) Birmingham Rd, B70 6RS, ℰ 553 6111, Telex 336232, Fax 525 7403 – 🛗 ↔ rm ▤ rest 📺 ☎ 🅿 – 🔬 180. 🔼 ⒶⒺ ⓞ 𝗩𝗜𝗦𝗔 BU **c**
closed 24 to 30 December and 1-2 January – **M** *(bar lunch Saturday)* 12.95/14.50 **t.** and a la carte ¼ 4.25 – ⊑ 5.95 – **170 rm** 69.50/79.50 **t.** – SB (weekends only) 66.80/107.80 **st.**

MICHELIN Distribution Centre, Valepits Rd, Garrett's Green, B33 0YD, ℰ 789 7100, Fax 789 7323 p. 5 HX

📶 ATS 1558 Pershore Rd., Stirchley ℰ 458 2951
ATS 158 Slade Rd. Erdington ℰ 327 2783
ATS 1189 Chester Rd, Erdington ℰ 373 6104/382 7533
ATS 94 Aldrige Rd, Perry Barr ℰ 356 5925/6632
ATS 314 Bearwood Rd. Bearwood ℰ 420 2000
ATS 427 Bordesley Green, Bordesley Green ℰ 772 6514
ATS 43 Whitmore Rd. Small Heath ℰ 772 2571

ATS 341 Dudley Rd, Winson Green ℰ 454 2588/2536
ATS Dudley Rd. Halesowen ℰ 550 2464
ATS 947 Bristol Rd South, Northfield ℰ 475 1244
ATS Bromford Rd, Oldbury, West Bromwich ℰ 552 6131
ATS 87 Old Meeting St., West Bromwich ℰ 553 3495

BISHOP AUCKLAND Durham 🄰🄾🄸 🄰🄾🄶 P 20 – pop. 23 560 – ECD : Wednesday – ⊕ 0388.

🝙 High Plains, Durham Rd ℰ 602198, NE : ½ m. – 🝘 Aycliffe, School Aycliffe Lane, Newton Aycliffe ℰ 0325 (Aycliffe) 310820, SE : 5 m. – 🝘 Woodham G. & C.C., Burnhill Way, Newton Aycliffe ℰ 0325 (Aycliffe) 318346, SE : 4 m.

♦London 253 – ♦Carlisle 73 – ♦Middlesbrough 24 – ♦Newcastle upon Tyne 28 – Sunderland 25.

🏨 **Park Head**, New Coundon, DL14 8QB, NE : 1 ¾ m. by A 689 on A 688 ℰ 661727, Fax 661727 – 📺 ☎ 🅿. 🔼 ⓞ 𝗩𝗜𝗦𝗔
M 9.95/14.95 **st.** and a la carte ¼ 3.75 – **31 rm** ⊑ 35.00/75.00 **st.**

📶 ATS Cockton Hill ℰ 603681

BISHOP'S HULL Somerset – see Taunton.

BISHOP'S STORTFORD Herts. 🄰🄾🄸 U 28 – pop. 22 535 – ECD : Wednesday – ⊕ 0279.

✈ Stansted Airport : ℰ 680500, Telex 818708, Fax 662066, NE : 3 ½ m.

🆔 2 The Causeway, CM22 2EJ ℰ 655261 ext : 251.

♦London 34 – ♦Cambridge 27 – Chelmsford 19 – Colchester 33.

↑ **The Cottage** 🈺, 71 Birchanger Lane, CM23 5QA, NE : 2 ¼ m. by B 1383 on Birchanger rd ℰ 812349, « Part 17C and 18C cottages », 𝒜 – ↔ 📺 🅿. 🔼 𝗩𝗜𝗦𝗔 ✄
closed 24 to 28 December – **M** (by arrangement) 11.00 ¼ 4.00 – **10 rm** ⊑ 28.00/44.00 **st.**

at Hatfield Heath SE : 6 m. on A 1060 – ⊠ ✆ 0279 Bishop's Stortford :

🏨 **Down Hall Country House** ⌕, CM22 7AS, S : 1½ m. ✆ 731441, Fax 730416, ≤, « 19C Italianate mansion », ⇌, 🏊, 🐎, park, ✗ – 🛗 📺 ☎ ❷ – 🕍 200. 🖭 🖭 ⑩ 𝘝𝘐𝘚𝘈. ✗
M 17.00/19.00 **st.** and a la carte ╏ 6.00 – ⌂ 9.25 – **103 rm** 80.00/135.00 **st.** – SB (weekends only) 155.00/175.00 **st.**

⑩ ATS 14 Burnt Mill, Harlow ✆ 421965

BISHOP'S TAWTON Devon **403** H 30 – see Barnstaple.

BLABY Leics. **402 403 404** Q 26 – pop. 7 030 – ✆ 0533.

◆London 100 – ◆Coventry 10 – ◆Leicester 4 – Northampton 38.

🏨 **Time Out,** 15 Enderby Rd, LE8 3GD, ✆ 787898, Fax 787898, 𝓕6, ⇌, 🏊, 🐎 – 📺 ☎ ⅙ ❷ – 🕍 40. 🖭 🖭 ⑩ 𝘝𝘐𝘚𝘈. ✗
M (closed Saturday lunch, Sunday dinner and Bank Holidays) 12.50/16.95 **t.** ╏ 5.50 – **24 rm** ⌂ 45.00/75.00 **t.** – SB (except Christmas) (weekends only) 83.90/143.90 **st.**

BLACKBURN Lancs. **402** M 22 – pop. 109 564 – ECD : Thursday – ✆ 0254.

🏌 Pleasington ✆ 202177, SW : 3 m. – 🏌 Wilpshire, 72 Whalley Rd ✆ 248260/249691, NE : 3 m. by A 666 – 🏌 Great Harwood, Harwood Bar ✆ 884391, NE : 5 m.

🎏 King George's Hall, Northgate, BB2 1AA ✆ 53277.

◆London 228 – ◆Leeds 47 – ◆Liverpool 39 – ◆Manchester 24 – Preston 11.

🏨 Blackburn Moat House (Q.M.H.), Yew Tree Drive, Preston New Rd, BB2 7BE, NW : 2 m. at junction A 677 and A 6119 ✆ 264441, Telex 63271, Fax 682435 – 🛗 ⅞ rm 📺 ☎ ❷ – 🕍 350
96 rm, 2 suites.

at Mellor NW : 4 m. by A 677 – ⊠ ✆ 0254 Blackburn :

🏨 **Millstone,** Church Lane, BB2 7JR, ✆ 813333, Fax 812628 – ⅞ rm 📺 ☎ ❷. 🖭 🖭 ⑩ 𝘝𝘐𝘚𝘈
M (closed Saturday lunch) 11.50/18.00 **st.** and a la carte ╏ 6.45 – **20 rm** ⌂ 56.00/84.00 **st.**, 1 suite – SB 78.00/98.00 **st.**

⑩ ATS Pendle St., Copy Nook ✆ 55963/59272/665115

BLACKPOOL Lancs. **402** K 22 Great Britain G. – pop. 146 297 – ECD : Wednesday – ✆ 0253.

See : Tower★ *AC* AY **A.**

🏌 Blackpool Park, North Park Drive ✆ 393960, E : 1½ m. BY – 🏌 Poulton-le-Fylde, Myrtle Farm, Breck Rd ✆ 0253 (Poulton) 892444, NE : 3 m. by A 586 BY.

✈ Blackpool Airport : ✆ 343061, Fax 405009, S : 3 m. by A 584.

🎏 1 Clifton St., FY1 1LY ✆ 321623/325212 – 87a Coronation St., FY1 4PD ✆ 321891 – Pleasure Beach, 525 Ocean Boulevard, South Promenade, FY4 1PL ✆ 403223 (summer only).

◆London 246 – ◆Leeds 88 – ◆Liverpool 56 – ◆Manchester 51 – ◆Middlesbrough 123.

Plan on next page

🏨 **Imperial** (Forte), North Promenade, FY1 2HB, ✆ 323971, Telex 677376, Fax 751784, ≤, 𝓕6, ⇌, 🏊 – 🛗 ⅞ rm 📺 ☎ ❷ – 🕍 400. 🖭 🖭 ⑩ 𝘝𝘐𝘚𝘈   AY **c**
M 16.50 **st.** (dinner) and a la carte 17.00/32.50 **st.** – ⌂ 9.50 – **175 rm** 85.00/95.00 **st.**, 8 suites – SB (except Christmas and New Year) 98.00/138.00 **st.**

🏨 **Pembroke,** North Promenade, FY1 2JQ, ✆ 323434, Telex 677469, Fax 327864, ≤, 🏊 – 🛗 ⅞ rm 🖹 rest 📺 ☎ ❷ – 🕍 500. 🖭 🖭 ⑩ 𝘝𝘐𝘚𝘈 𝘑𝘊𝘉   AY **x**
M (carving lunch) 13.50/15.50 **st.** and dinner a la carte ╏ 8.00 – **268 rm** ⌂ 99.00/125.00 **st.**, 6 suites – SB 118.00/185.00 **st.**

🏨 **Savoy,** Queens Promenade, FY2 9SJ, ✆ 352561, Fax 500735 – 🛗 📺 ☎ ❷ – 🕍 300. 🖭 🖭 ⑩ 𝘝𝘐𝘚𝘈   AY **a**
M (bar lunch)/dinner 14.50 **t.** and a la carte ╏ 5.25 – **142 rm** ⌂ 32.50/105.00 **st.**, 6 suites.

🏨 **Clifton,** Talbot Sq., FY1 1ND, ✆ 321481, Fax 327345 – 🛗 📺 ☎ – 🕍 80. 🖭 🖭 ⑩ 𝘝𝘐𝘚𝘈   AY **v**
M a la carte 9.95/11.95 **st.** ╏ 4.00 – **75 rm** ⌂ 40.00/95.00 **st.**, 2 suites.

🏨 **Warwick** (Best Western), 603-609 New South Promenade, FY4 1NG, ✆ 342192, Fax 405776, 🏊 – 🛗 📺 ☎ ❷ – 🕍 50. 🖭 🖭 ⑩ 𝘝𝘐𝘚𝘈 𝘑𝘊𝘉   BZ **u**
M (bar lunch)/dinner 12.95 **st.** ╏ 4.50 – **52 rm** ⌂ 38.00/78.00 **st.** – SB 78.00/81.90 **st.**

🏨 **Shellard,** 18-20 Dean St., South Shore, FY4 1AU, ✆ 342679 – 🛗 📺 ☎ ⅙ ❷. 🖭 𝘝𝘐𝘚𝘈. ✗
M (dinner only) 15.00 **t.** ╏ 2.55 – **20 rm** ⌂ 27.00/54.00 **t.**   AZ **a**

🏨 **Brabyns,** 1-3 Shaftesbury Av., North Shore, FY2 9QQ, ✆ 354263, Fax 352915 – 📺 ☎ ❷. 🖭 🖭 ⑩ 𝘝𝘐𝘚𝘈 𝘑𝘊𝘉   BY **i**
M 7.00/11.00 **t.** ╏ 4.50 – **25 rm** ⌂ 25.00/52.00 **t.** – SB (November-Easter) 50.00/75.00 **st.**

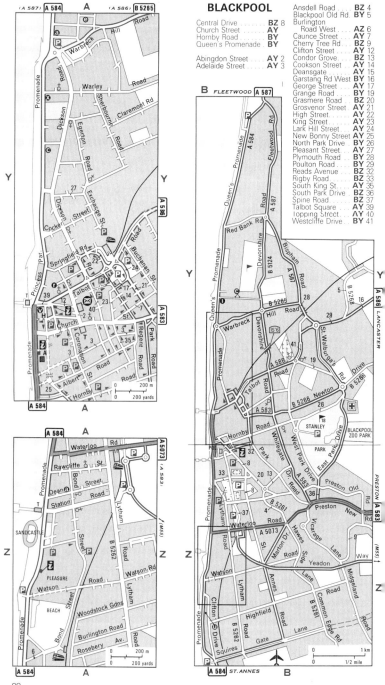

BLACKPOOL

⚅ **Sunray,** 42 Knowle Av., off Queens Promenade, FY2 9TQ, ℰ 351937 – 📺 ☎ 🅿 🔼 VISA
closed mid December-mid January – **M** 10.00 **st.** – **9 rm** ⊐ 27.00/54.00 **st.** – SB 60.00/
70.00 **st.**   BY **c**

⚅ **Burlees,** 40 Knowle Av., off Queen's Promenade, FY2 9TQ, ℰ 354535 – � rest 📺 🅿 🔼
VISA ⌘   BY **c**
closed mid November-February – **M** 9.00 **st.** ░ 4.00 – **9 rm** ⊐ 19.55/46.00 **st.**

⚅ **Denely** without rest., 15 King Edward Av., FY2 9TA, ℰ 352757 – 🅿 ⌘   AY **e**
9 rm ⊐ 15.00/32.00 **s.**

✗ **September Brasserie,** 15-17 Queen St., FY1 1PU, ℰ 323282. 🔼 🌊 ⓞ VISA   AY **r**
closed Sunday, Monday, 2 weeks summer and 2 weeks winter – **M** 15.50 **t.** (dinner) and a la
carte 16.50/24.40 t. ░ 4.50.

at Little Thornton NE : 5 m. by A 586 – BY – off A 588 – ⊠ Blackpool – ☎ 0253
Thornton :

✗✗ **River House** ⌘ with rm, Skippool Creek, Wyre Rd, FY5 5LF, ℰ 883497, Fax 892083, ≼,
⌘ – 🌊 🅿. 🔼 VISA
Meals *(closed Sunday dinner)* (booking essential) 18.50 **t.** and a la carte 25.00/36.50 **t.** ░ 7.50
– **4 rm** ⊐ 50.00/100.00 **t.**

at Little Singleton NE : 6 m. by A 586 – BY – on A 585 – ⊠ ☎ 0253 Blackpool :

⌂ **Mains Hall,** 86 Mains Lane, FY6 7LE, ℰ 885130, Fax 894132, ⌘ – ⇒px rm 📺 ☎ 🅿. 🔼 🔼
VISA
M 18.50/25.00 **st.** and dinner a la carte Tuesday to Saturday ░ 7.50 – ⊐ 5.00 – **9 rm**
55.00/125.00 **st.**

⌂ **Singleton Lodge** ⌘, Lodge Lane, FY6 8LT, S : ½ m. on B 5260 ℰ 883854, Fax 894432,
⌘ – 📺 ☎ 🅿. 🔼 🔼 VISA
closed 25 to 28 December – **M** (dinner only and Sunday lunch)/dinner 16.00 **t.** ░ 4.50 –
10 rm ⊐ 50.00/65.00 **t.**

◍ ATS Clifton Rd, Marton ℰ 695033/4

Prices   For full details of the prices quoted in the guide,
consult the introduction.

BLACKROD Lancs. 402 404 M 23 – ☎ 0942 Wigan.
◆London 220 – Burnley 25 – ◆Liverpool 31 – ◆Manchester 16 – Preston 18.

🏨 **Georgian House,** Manchester Rd, BL6 5RU, SE : 1 ½ m. by B 5408 on A 6 ℰ 814598,
Fax 813427, ℉, ≤s, 🔼 – 📺 📺 ☎ ♿ 🅿 – 🔼 200. 🔼 🔼 ⓞ VISA
M 11.00/18.00 **st.** and a la carte ░ 4.60 – **101 rm** ⊐ 54.00/112.25 **st.** – SB (weekends only)
89.00 **st.**

BLACKWATER Cornwall 403 E 33 – see Truro.

BLAKENEY Norfolk 404 X 25 – pop. 1 559 – ECD : Wednesday – ⊠ Holt – ☎ 0263 Cley.
◆London 127 – King's Lynn 37 – ◆Norwich 28.

🏨 **Blakeney,** The Quay, NR25 7NE, ℰ 740797, Fax 740795, ≼, ≤s, 🔼, ⌘ – ⇒px rest 📺 ☎ ♿
🅿 – 🔼 150. 🔼 🔼 VISA
M (light lunch Monday to Saturday)/dinner 15.75 **t.** and a la carte ░ 4.50 – **60 rm** ⊐ 63.00/
152.00 **t.** – SB (except Christmas, New Year and Bank Holidays) 110.00/146.00 **st.**

⌂ **Manor,** The Quay, NR25 7ND, ℰ 740376, Fax 741116, ≼, ⌘ – ⇒px rest 📺 ☎ 🅿
M (bar lunch)/dinner 14.50 **st.** and a la carte ░ 4.00 – **37 rm** ⊐ 25.00/78.00 **st.** – SB (mid
October-mid June) 72.00/120.00 **st.**

⚏ **White Horse,** 4 High St., NR25 7AL, ℰ 740574 – 📺 🅿. 🔼 🔼 VISA ⌘
M (bar lunch Monday to Saturday)/dinner a la carte 12.75/18.00 **t.** – **9 rm** ⊐ 30.00/70.00 **t.**
– SB (October-May except Christmas) 75.00 **st.**

at Cley next the Sea E : 1½ m. on A 149 – ⊠ Holt – ☎ 0263 Cley :

⚏ **George & Dragon,** NR25 7RN, ℰ 740652, Fax 741275 – 📺 🅿
M a la carte 7.30/16.45 **t.** – **9 rm** ⊐ 30.00/70.00 **t.**

⚅ **Cley Mill** ⌘, NR25 7NN, ℰ 740209, ≼, « 18C redbrick windmill on saltmarshes » – 🅿
closed 15 January-end February – **M** (by arrangement) 15.50 **st.** – **6 rm** ⊐ 29.00/59.00 **st.**

at Morston N : 2 m. on A 149 – ⊠ Holt – ☎ 0263 Cley :

✗✗ **Morston Hall** with rm, NR25 7AA, ℰ 741041, Fax 741041, ⌘ – 📺 🅿. 🔼 🔼 VISA
closed January-late February – **M** (dinner only and Sunday lunch)/dinner 21.00 **st.** ░ 4.00 –
4 rm ⊐ (dinner included) 75.00/130.00 **st.**

BLANCHLAND Northd. 401 402 N 19 – pop. 178 – ECD : Monday and Tuesday – ⊠ Consett
(Durham) – ☎ 0434 Hexham.
◆London 298 – ◆Carlisle 47 – ◆Newcastle upon Tyne 24.

⌂ **Lord Crewe Arms** ⌘, DH8 9SP, ℰ 675251, Fax 675337, « Part 13C abbey », ⌘ – 📺
☎. 🔼 🔼 VISA
M (bar lunch Monday to Saturday)/dinner 28.00 **t.** ░ 6.50 – **18 rm** ⊐ 65.00/105.00 **t.** –
SB 110.00/170.00 **t.**

BLANDFORD FORUM Dorset 403 404 N 31 The West Country G. – pop. 7 249 – ECD : Wednesday – ✆ 0258 Blandford.

See : Town★ – Envir. : Kingston Lacy★★ *AC*, SE : 5 ½ m. by B 3082 – Royal Signals Museum★, NE : 2 m. by B 3082.

Exc. : Milton Abbas★, SW : 8 m. by A 354.

☞ Ashley Wood, Tarrant Rawston ✆ 452253, SE : 1 ½ m. – ☞ The Mid Dorset, Belchalwell ✆ 861386, Fax 860656.

🅿 Marsh and Ham Car Park, West St., DT11 7AW ✆ 454770.

◆London 124 – Bournemouth 17 – Dorchester 17 – Salisbury 24.

   🏨 **Crown,** West St., DT11 7AJ, ✆ 456626, Fax 451084, ⇘, ⟍ – TV ☎ 🄿 – 🛋 100. 🔼 🄰🄴 ⓞ *VISA*
   M (bar lunch Saturday) 11.75 **t.** and a la carte – **31 rm** ⊠ 64.00/74.00 **t.**, 1 suite – SB (weekends only) 84.00 **st.**

   XX **La Belle Alliance** with rm, Portman Lodge, White Cliff Mill St., DT11 7BP, ✆ 452842, Fax 480053 – TV ☎ 🄿. 🔼 🄰🄴 *VISA*
   closed first 3 weeks January – **M** *(closed Sunday and Monday)* (dinner only) 21.00 **st.** ⅃ 4.95
   – **6 rm** ⊠ 40.00/66.00 **st.** – SB 89.00/119.00 **st.**

   at Pimperne NE : 2 ½ m. on A 354 – ✉ ✆ 0258 Blandford Forum :

   🏠 **Anvil,** Salisbury Rd, DT11 8UQ, ✆ 453431 – TV ☎ 🄿. 🔼 🄰🄴 ⓞ *VISA*
   M a la carte 13.80/21.15 **t.** ⅃ 5.00 – **9 rm** ⊠ 40.00/65.00 **t.**

   at Farnham NE : 7 ½ m. by A 354 – ✉ Blandford Forum – ✆ 0725 Tollard Royal :

   🏠 **Museum,** DT11 8DE, ✆ 516261, ⟍ – TV ☎ 🄿. 🔼 *VISA*. ⌇
   closed 25 December – **M** (booking essential) 20.00. **st.** and a la carte ⅃ 5.50 – **4 rm** ⊠ 35.00/50.00 **st.**

BLAWITH Cumbria 402 K 21 – see Coniston.

BLEDINGTON Glos. 403 404 P 28 – see Stow-on-the-Wold.

BLOCKLEY Glos. 403 404 O 27 – pop. 1 729 – ECD : Thursday – ✉ Moreton-in-Marsh – ✆ 0386.

◆London 89 – ◆Birmingham 40 – Gloucester 29 – ◆Oxford 33.

   🏨 **Crown Inn,** High St., GL56 9EX, ✆ 700245, Fax 700247, « Converted 17C coach house and cottages » – TV ☎ 🄿. 🔼 🄰🄴 ⓞ *VISA*
   M 13.95/19.95 **t.** and a la carte – **21 rm** ⊠ 53.00/114.00 **t.** – SB (except Christmas-New Year) 104.00/138.00 **st.**

   ⋔ **Lower Brook House** without rest., Lower St., GL56 9DS, ✆ 700286, « Part 17C cottages », ⟍ – 🄿
   3 rm ⊠ 28.00/45.00 **s.**

BLUNDELLSANDS Mersey. 402 403 K 23 – see Liverpool.

BLUNSDON Wilts. 403 404 O 29 – see Swindon.

BLYTH Notts. 402 403 404 Q 23 – pop. 1 179 – ✉ Worksop – ✆ 0909.

◆London 166 – Doncaster 13 – Lincoln 30 – ◆Nottingham 32 – ◆Sheffield 20.

   🏠 **Granada Lodge** without rest., Hilltop roundabout, S81 8HG, N : ¾ m. by B 6045 at junction A 1 (M) and A 614 ✆ 591836, Fax 591831, Reservations (Freephone) 0800 555300 – ⅙↔ TV & 🄿. 🔼 🄰🄴 *VISA*. ⌇
   ⊠ 4.00 – **39 rm** 34.95/37.95 **st.**

   🏠 **Forte Travelodge** without rest., A 1 southbound, S81 8EZ, SE : 1 m. by A 634 on A 1 ✆ 591775, Reservations (Freephone) 0800 850950 – TV & 🄿. 🔼 🄰🄴 *VISA*. ⌇
   32 rm 31.95 **t.**

BODINNICK-BY-FOWEY Cornwall – see Fowey.

BODYMOOR HEATH Staffs. 402 403 404 O 26 – see Tamworth.

BOLDON Tyne and Wear 401 402 O 19 – see Newcastle upon Tyne.

BOLLINGTON Ches. 402 403 404 N 24 – see Macclesfield.

BOLTON Gtr. Manchester 402 404 M 23 – pop. 143 960 – ECD : Wednesday – ✆ 0204.

☞ Bolton Municipal, Links Rd, Chorley New Road ✆ 42336, W : 3 m. by A 673 – ☞ Lostock Park ✆ 43278, W : 3 m. – ☞ Bolton, Old Links, Chorley Old Rd, Monserrat ✆ 840050, NW : 3 m. on B 6226.

🅿 Town Hall, Victoria Sq, BL1 1RU ✆ 364333.

◆London 214 – Burnley 19 – ◆Liverpool 32 – ◆Manchester 11 – Preston 23.

   🏨🏨 **Bolton Moat House** (Q.M.H.), 1 Higher Bridge St., BL1 2EW, ✆ 383338, Fax 380777, « Cloisters restaurant in 19C church », ⅃₆, ≦ₛ, 🔲 – 🕃 ⅙↔ rm ≣ rest TV ☎ 🄿 – 🛋 300. 🔼 🄰🄴 ⓞ *VISA*. ⌇
   M *(closed Saturday lunch)* 10.50/14.25 **st.** and a la carte – **126 rm** ⊠ 65.00/99.00 **st.**, 2 suites – SB (weekends only) 86.00 **st.**

🏨 **Forte Posthouse,** Beaumont Rd, BL3 4TA, SW : 2½ m. on A 58 – 𝒫 651511, Fax 61064 –
🍴 rm 📺 ☎ 🅿 – 🔏 80. ◪ 🆎 ⓪ 𝓥𝓘𝓢𝓐 ⚘
M a la carte approx. 17.50 **t.** ↓ 4.65 – � 6.95 – **96 rm** 53.50 **st.** – SB 90.00 **st.**

🏨 **Pack Horse** (De Vere), Nelson Sq., Bradshawgate, BL1 1DP, 𝒫 27261, Fax 364352 – 🛗
🍴 rm 📺 ☎ 🅿 – 🔏 250. ◪ 🆎 ⓪ 𝓥𝓘𝓢𝓐
M (lunch by arrangement)/dinner 16.50 **st.** ↓ 6.00 – **72 rm** ⊆ 50.00/90.00 **st.** – SB (weekends only) 70.00 **st.**

🏠 **Broomfield,** 33-35 Wigan Rd, Deane, BL3 5PX, SW : 1 ½ m. on A 6140 𝒫 61570,
Fax 650932 – 📺 🅿. ◪ 𝓥𝓘𝓢𝓐
M (lunch by arrangement)/dinner 15.00 **st.** and a la carte ↓ 4.50 – **15 rm** ⊆ 24.50/36.00 **st.**
– SB (weekends only) 55.00/76.00 **st.**

at Egerton N : 3½ m. on A 666 – ✉ 🕿 0204 Bolton :

🏨 **Egerton House** ⌂, Blackburn Rd, BL7 9PL, 𝒫 307171, Fax 593030, ☞ – 📺 ☎ 🅿 –
🔏 150. ◪ 🆎 ⓪ 𝓥𝓘𝓢𝓐 ⚘
M *(closed Saturday lunch)* 9.95/12.95 **t.** and a la carte ↓ 4.95 – **32 rm** ⊆ 49.50/84.50 **t.** –
SB 86.00 **st.**

at Bromley Cross N : 4 m. by A 666 on B 6472 – ✉ 🕿 0204 Bolton :

🏨 **Last Drop Village,** Hospital Rd, BL7 9PZ, 𝒫 591131, Fax 304122, « Village created from
restored farm buildings », 𝐼₆, ≦s, 🔲, ☞, squash – 📺 ☎ 🅿 – 🔏 180. ◪ 🆎 ⓪ 𝓥𝓘𝓢𝓐 𝓙𝓒𝓑
M *(closed Saturday lunch)* 12.50/16.50 **st.** and a la carte ↓ 4.10 – **80 rm** ⊆ 72.50/94.50 **st.**,
3 suites – SB (except Christmas-New Year) (weekends only) 192.00/215.00 **st.**

◍ ATS Foundry St. 𝒫 22144/27841/388681   ATS Chorley Rd, Fourgates, Westhoughton
ATS Moss Bank Way, Astley Bridge, Bolton (ASDA   𝒫 813024
car park) 𝒫 300057

Prices	For full details of the prices quoted in the guide,
	consult the introduction.

BOLTON ABBEY N. Yorks. 🗺️ O 22 Great Britain G. – pop. 122 – ✉ – 🕿 0756 Skipton.
See : Bolton Priory★ *AC.*

♦London 216 – Harrogate 18 – ♦Leeds 23 – Skipton 6.

🏨 **Devonshire Arms Country House** ⌂, BD23 6AJ, 𝒫 710441, Telex 51218, Fax 710564,
≤, « Part 17C restored coaching inn », 𝐼₆, ≦s, 🔲, ☜, park, ⚘ – 🍴 📺 ☎ & 🅿 –
🔏 150. ◪ 🆎 ⓪ 𝓥𝓘𝓢𝓐
M - Burlington 21.00/35.00 **st.** and a la carte ↓ 7.95 – **40 rm** ⊆ 85.00/125.00 **st.** –
SB 125.00/175.00 **st.**

BONCHURCH I.O.W. 🗺️ 🗺️ Q 32 – see Wight (Isle of).

BOOTLE Mersey. 🗺️ ㉘ 🗺️ ② – see Liverpool.

BOREHAMWOOD Herts. 🗺️ T 29 – pop. 28 298 – 🕿 081.
🅱 Civic Offices, Elstree Way, WD6 1WA 𝒫 207 2277/7496.

♦London 10 – Luton 20.

Plan : see Greater London (North West)

🏨 **Elstree Moat House** (Q.M.H.), Barnet By-Pass, WD6 5PU, at junction of A 5135 with
A 1 𝒫 953 1622, Telex 928581, Fax 207 3194, 𝐼₆, ≦s, 🔲 – 🛗 🍴 rm 🍽️ rest 📺 ☎ & 🅿 –
🔏 100. ◪ 🆎 ⓪ 𝓥𝓘𝓢𝓐 ⚘   CT **s**
M (bar lunch Saturday and Bank Holidays) 12.00/17.00 **t.** and a la carte – ⊆ 8.95 – **131 rm**
85.00/125.00 **st.** – SB (weekends only) 56.00/76.00 **st.**

🏠 **Oaklands** (Toby), Studio Way, WD6 5JY, off Elstree Way (A 5135) 𝒫 905 1455,
Fax 905 1370 – 🍴 rm 📺 ☎ & 🅿 – 🔏 35. ◪ 🆎 ⓪ 𝓥𝓘𝓢𝓐   CT **i**
M (grill rest.) 7.50 **t.** and a la carte ↓ 4.55 – **38 rm** ⊆ 63.00/73.00 **t.**

BORROWDALE Cumbria 🗺️ K 20 – see Keswick.

BOSCASTLE Cornwall 🗺️ F 31 The West Country G. – 🕿 0840.
See : Village★.

♦London 260 – Bude 14 – Exeter 59 – ♦Plymouth 43.

↑ **St. Christopher's Country House,** High St., PL35 0BD, S :½ m. by B 3266 𝒫 250412 –
🍴 rest 📺 🅿. ◪ 𝓥𝓘𝓢𝓐
March-October – **M** 10.50 **t.** ↓ 2.80 – **9 rm** ⊆ 16.00/32.00 **t.**

↑ **Old Coach House** without rest., Tintagel Rd, PL35 0AS, S :¾ m. on B 3263 𝒫 250398 –
📺 🅿. ◪ 𝓥𝓘𝓢𝓐 ⚘
March-October – **6 rm** ⊆ 22.50/45.00 **s.**

BOSHAM W. Sussex 🗺️ R 31 – see Chichester.

BOSTON Lincs. 402 404 T 25 Great Britain G. – pop. 33 908 – ECD : Thursday – ✆ 0205.

See : St. Botolph's Church⋆.

🔃 Cowbridge, Horncastle Rd 🖉 362306, N : 2 m. by B 1183.

🅱 Blackfriars Arts Centre, Spain Lane, PE21 6HP 🖉 356656.

◆London 122 – Lincoln 35 – ◆Nottingham 55.

🏨 **White Hart,** Bridge Foot, PE21 8SH, 🖉 364877, Fax 355974 – 📺 ☎ ⓟ – 🛦 80. 🖎 ⌸ 𝚅𝙸𝚂𝙰. ⌸
M (closed Sunday dinner) (grill rest.) a la carte 4.90/12.90 **t.** ⓘ 4.45 – **22 rm** ⌷ 29.95/33.45 **t.**

🏠 **Friendly Stop Inn,** Bicker Bar Roundabout, PE20 3AN, SW : 8 m. at junction of A 17 and A 52 🖉 820118, Fax 820228, 🛌 – ⌻ rm 🖀 rest 📺 ☎ ⓖ ⓟ – 🛦 70. 🖎 ⌸ ◑ 𝚅𝙸𝚂𝙰
M 6.95 **st.** and a la carte ⓘ 4.95 – ⌷ 5.50 – **55 rm** 34.75 **t.**

⓪ ATS London Rd 🖉 362854

BOSTON SPA W. Yorks. 402 P 22 – pop. 6 022 – ⌷ Wetherby – ✆ 0937.

◆London 205 – Harrogate 11 – ◆Leeds 12 – ◆Middlesbrough 52 – York 14.

✕✕ **La Jardinière,** 174 High St., LS23 6BW, 🖉 845625 – 🖎 𝚅𝙸𝚂𝙰
closed Sunday and 25-26 December – **M** (lunch by arrangement)/dinner 22.00 **t.** ⓘ 4.95.

BOTLEY Hants. 403 404 Q 31 – pop. 2 156 – ECD : Thursday – ⌷ Southampton – ✆ 0489.

🔃 Botley Park H. & C.C., Winchester Rd 🖉 780888 ext : 444.

◆London 83 – ◆Portsmouth 17 – ◆Southampton 6 – Winchester 11.

🏯 **Botley Park,** Winchester Rd, Boorley Green, SO3 2UA, NW : 1 ½ m. on B 3354 🖉 780888, Fax 789242, 🛌, ⌸s, ⛝, 🔃, park, ✕✕, squash – ⌻ rm 🖀 rest 📺 ☎ ⓖ ⓟ – 🛦 200. 🖎 ⌸ ◑ 𝚅𝙸𝚂𝙰
M (closed Saturday lunch) 13.25/17.95 **t.** and a la carte ⓘ 7.50 – **100 rm** ⌷ 79.50/177.00 **t.** – SB 116.00 **st.**

✕✕ **Cobbett's,** 15 The Square, SO3 2EA, 🖉 782068, Fax 799641 – ⓟ. 🖎 𝚅𝙸𝚂𝙰
closed lunch Monday and Saturday, Sunday, 2 weeks summer and 2 weeks winter – **M** - **French** 15.50 **t.** (lunch) and a la carte 18.80/24.75 **t.** ⓘ 6.60.

BOUGHTON Kent – see Faversham.

BOUGHTON MONCHELSEA Kent – see Maidstone.

BOURNE Lincs. 402 404 S 25 – pop. 7 672 – ECD : Wednesday – ✆ 0778.

◆London 101 – ◆Leicester 42 – Lincoln 35 – ◆Nottingham 42.

🏠 **Bourne Eau House,** 30 South St., PE10 9LY, on A 15 🖉 423621, « Part Elizabethan and Georgian house », ⌲ – ⌻ rm 📺 ⓟ. ⌸
M (closed Sunday) (residents only) (communal dining) (dinner only) 18.00 **st.** – **3 rm** ⌷ 35.00/60.00 **st.**

🏠 **Toft House,** Main Rd, Toft, PE10 0JT, SW : 3 m. by A 151 on A 6121 🖉 077 833 (Witham-on-the-Hill) 614, Fax 264, 🔃, ⌲ – 📺 ☎ ⓟ – 🛦 80. 🖎 𝚅𝙸𝚂𝙰. ⌸
M (closed Sunday dinner) 8.00/14.50 **t.** ⓘ 3.80 – **22 rm** ⌷ 30.00/60.00 **t.**

⓪ ATS 18 Abbey Rd 🖉 422811

BOURNE END Herts. 404 S 28 – see Hemel Hempstead.

BOURNEMOUTH Dorset 403 404 O 31 The West Country G. – pop. 142 829 – ECD : Wednesday and Saturday – ✆ 0202.

See : Compton Acres⋆⋆ (English Garden ≤⋆⋆⋆) AC AX – Bournemouth Museums⋆ (Russell-Cotes Art Gallery and Museum AC DZ - Shelley Rooms AC EX).

🔃 Queens Park, Queens Park West Drive 🖉 396198, NE : 2 m. DV – 🔃 Meyrick Park 🖉 290871 CY.

✈ Bournemouth (Hurn) Airport : 🖉 593939, Fax 570266, N : 5 m. by Hurn – DV.

🅱 Westover Rd, BH1 2BU 🖉 789789.

◆London 114 – ◆Bristol 76 – ◆Southampton 34.

Plans on following pages

🏩 **Carlton,** Meyrick Rd, East Overcliff, BH1 3DN, 🖉 552011, Fax 299573, ≤, 🛌, ⌸s, ⛝ heated, ⌲ – 🛗 🖀 rest 📺 ☎ ⓟ – 🛦 160. 🖎 ⌸ ◑ 𝚅𝙸𝚂𝙰
EZ **a**
M 17.50/23.50 **t.** and a la carte ⓘ 6.25 – **64 rm** ⌷ 69.00/150.00 **st.**, 6 suites – SB 138.00/158.00 **st.**

🏩 **Royal Bath** (De Vere), Bath Rd, BH1 2EW, 🖉 555555, Fax 554158, ≤, 🛌, ⌸s, ⛝, ⌲ – 🛗 📺 🖎 ⌸ ◑ 𝚅𝙸𝚂𝙰 – 🛦 500. ⌸
DZ **a**
M 16.50/25.00 **st.** and a la carte – (see also **Oscars** below) – **124 rm** ⌷ 91.00/220.00 **st.**, 7 suites – SB 120.00/270.00 **st.**

🏩 **Norfolk Royale,** Richmond Hill, BH2 6EN, 🖉 551521, Fax 299729, ⌸s, ⛝ – 🛗 ⌻ rm 🖀 rest 📺 ☎ ⓖ – 🛦 80. 🖎 ⌸ ◑ 𝚅𝙸𝚂𝙰 ⌸
CY **u**
M 9.95/18.00 **st.** and lunch a la carte ⓘ 5.00 – ⌷ 8.75 – **90 rm** 90.00/130.00 **st.**, 5 suites – SB (weekends only) 126.00/186.00 **st.**

🏨🏨 **Swallow Highcliff,** 105 St. Michael's Rd, West Cliff, BH2 5DU, 📞 557702, Fax 292734, ≼, ≊, ⊥ heated, ◿, ✗ – 🛗 📺 ☎ 🅿 – 🚗 450. 🅿 🆎 ⓪ 𝗩𝗜𝗦𝗔 𝗝𝗖𝗕   CZ **z**
M 12.50/17.50 **st.** and a la carte ⌕ 4.75 – **154 rm** ⌑ 85.00/130.00 **st.**, 3 suites – SB 130.00/185.00 **st.**

🏨🏨 **Palace Court,** Westover Rd, BH1 2BZ, 📞 557681, Fax 554918, ≼, ƒₛ, ≊, 🔲 – 🛗 📺 ☎ 🅿 – 🚗 250. 🅿 🆎 ⓪ 𝗩𝗜𝗦𝗔. ✗   DZ **n**
M 12.50/18.50 **st.** and dinner a la carte ⌕ 6.65 – **104 rm** ⌑ 65.00/150.00 **st.**, 6 suites – SB 99.00/110.00 **st.**

🏨 **East Cliff Court,** East Overcliff Drive, BH1 3AN, 📞 554545, Fax 557456, ≼, ≊, ⊥ heated – 🛗 📺 ☎ 🅿. 🅿 🆎   EZ **v**
M *(closed Saturday lunch)* 7.50/16.50 **st.** ⌕ 4.25 – **68 rm** ⌑ (dinner included) 60.00/120.00 **st.** – SB (September-May) 95.00 **st.**

🏨 **Marsham Court,** Russell-Cotes Rd, East Cliff, BH1 3AB, 📞 552111, Fax 294744, ≼, ⊥ heated – 🛗 📺 ☎ 🅿 – 🚗 200. 🅿 🆎 ⓪ 𝗩𝗜𝗦𝗔   DZ **e**
M (bar lunch)/dinner 16.00 **st.** and a la carte – **85 rm** ⌑ 49.00/78.00 **st.**, 1 suite – SB 98.00/118.00 **st.**

🏨 **Forte Posthouse,** Meyrick Rd, The Lansdowne, BH1 2PR, 📞 553262, Fax 557698 – 🛗 ⤢ rm 📺 ☎ 🅿 – 🚗 100. 🅿 🆎 ⓪ 𝗩𝗜𝗦𝗔   DY **a**
M a la carte approx. 17.50 **t.** ⌕ 4.65 – ⌑ 6.95 – **98 rm** 53.50 **st.** – SB (except Christmas and New Year) (weekends only) 90.00 **st.**

🏨 **Chesterwood,** East Overcliff Drive, BH1 3AR, 📞 558057, Fax 556285, ≼, ⊥ heated – 🛗 ⤢ rest 📺 ☎ 🅿. 🅿 🆎 ⓪ 𝗩𝗜𝗦𝗔   EZ **i**
M (bar lunch)/dinner 19.50 **t.** and a la carte ⌕ 5.00 – **51 rm** ⌑ 32.00/180.00 **st.** – SB (October-May) (weekends only) 57.00/64.00 **st.**

🏨 **Courtlands** (Best Western), 16 Boscombe Spa Rd, East Cliff, BH5 1BB, 📞 302442, Fax 309880, ≊, ⊥ heated – 🛗 ⤢ rest 📺 ☎ 🅿 – 🚗 45. 🅿 🆎 ⓪ 𝗩𝗜𝗦𝗔   DX **o**
M (bar lunch Monday to Saturday)/dinner 21.00 **t.** and a la carte – **58 rm** ⌑ 44.90/82.00 **t.** – SB 79.00/116.00 **st.**

🏨 **Collingwood,** 11 Priory Rd, BH2 5DF, 📞 557575, ≊, 🔲 – 🛗 📺 ☎. 🅿 𝗩𝗜𝗦𝗔. ✗ CZ **n**
M (bar lunch Monday to Saturday)/dinner 12.95 **t.** ⌕ 3.45 – **54 rm** ⌑ (dinner included) 42.00/96.00 **t.**

🏨 **Connaught,** West Hill Rd, West Cliff, BH2 5PH, 📞 298020, Fax 298028, ƒₛ, ≊, 🔲 – 🛗 ⤢ rm 📺 ☎ 🕭 🅿. 🅿 𝗩𝗜𝗦𝗔   CZ **s**
M (bar lunch Monday to Saturday)/dinner 18.50 **st.** and a la carte ⌕ 4.95 – **59 rm** ⌑ 38.00/96.00 **st.**, 1 suite – SB 80.00/105.00 **st.**

🏨 **Bournemouth Heathlands,** 12 Grove Rd, East Cliff, BH1 3AY, 📞 553336, Fax 555937, ƒₛ, ≊, ⊥ heated – 🛗 📺 ☎ 🅿 – 🚗 250. 🅿 🆎 ⓪ 𝗩𝗜𝗦𝗔   EZ **c**
M (bar lunch)/dinner 15.00 **st.** ⌕ 5.00 – **113 rm** ⌑ 52.00/84.00 **st.**, 2 suites – SB (except Easter, Christmas and New Year) 78.00/96.00 **st.**

🏨 **Anglo-Swiss,** 16 Gervis Rd, East Cliff, BH1 3EQ, 📞 554794, Fax 299615, ƒₛ, ≊, 🔲 – 🛗 📺 ☎ 🅿 – 🚗 70. 🅿 𝗩𝗜𝗦𝗔   EY **e**
M (bar lunch)/dinner 14.00 **t.** – **68 rm** ⌑ 43.00/90.00 **t.** – SB (weekdays only) 56.00/80.00 **st.**

🏨 **Queens,** Meyrick Rd, East Cliff, BH1 3DL, 📞 554415, Fax 294810, ƒₛ, ≊, 🔲 – 🛗 🖺 ▭ rest 📺 ☎ 🅿 – 🚗 200. 🅿 𝗩𝗜𝗦𝗔   EYZ **r**
M 9.25/18.95 **t.** and dinner a la carte ⌕ 4.50 – **114 rm** ⌑ 40.00/110.00 **t.** – SB (April-October) (weekends only) 84.50/87.50 **st.**

🏨 **New Durley Dean,** 28 Westcliff Rd, BH2 5HE, 📞 557711, Fax 292815, ƒₛ, ≊ – 🛗 ⤢ rest 📺 ☎ 🅿 – 🚗 80. 🅿 🆎 𝗩𝗜𝗦𝗔. ✗   CZ **a**
M (bar lunch Monday to Saturday)/dinner 13.95 **st.** and a la carte ⌕ 4.95 – **111 rm** ⌑ 28.00/105.00 **st.** – SB (except Bank Holidays) 59.50/89.50 **st.**

🏨 **Royal Exeter** (Chef & Brewer), Exeter Rd, BH2 5AG, 📞 290566, Fax 297963 – 🛗 📺 ☎ 🅿. 🅿 🆎 𝗩𝗜𝗦𝗔   CZ **e**
M 15.00/20.00 **t.** and a la carte – **36 rm** ⌑ 34.95/38.45 **t.**

🏨 **Belvedere,** 14 Bath Rd, BH1 2EU, 📞 297556, Fax 294699 – 🛗 📺 ☎ 🅿. 🅿 🆎 ⓪ 𝗩𝗜𝗦𝗔. ✗   DYZ **c**
M (bar lunch Monday, Tuesday and Saturday) 9.50/13.50 **st.** and a la carte ⌕ 5.50 – **62 rm** ⌑ 39.50/79.00 **st.** – SB (except Bank Holidays) 99.00 **st.**

🏨 **Hinton Firs,** 9 Manor Rd, East Cliff, BH1 3HB, 📞 555409, Fax 299607, ≊, ⊥ heated – 🛗 ⤢ rest 📺 ☎ 🅿. 🅿 𝗩𝗜𝗦𝗔. ✗   EY **n**
M (dinner only and Sunday lunch October-May)/dinner 12.50 **st.** and a la carte ⌕ 3.80 – **52 rm** ⌑ 35.00/76.00 **st.** – SB (October-May except Easter and Christmas-New Year) 67.00/79.00 **st.**

🏨 **Porter's,** 18 Herbert Rd, Westbourne, BH4 8HD, 📞 763825 – ⤢ rest 🅿. ✗   CX **a**
M (dinner only) 12.50 **st.** ⌕ 6.00 – **8 rm** ⌑ 22.50/45.00 **st.** – SB (except July-September and Bank Holidays) 55.00/60.00 **st.**

🏨 **Cliff House,** 113 Alumhurst Rd, Alum Chine, BH4 8HS, 📞 763003, ≼ – 🛗 📺 🅿. ✗ *March-October and Christmas* – **M** (dinner only) 11.00 **st.** ⌕ 2.50 – **11 rm** ⌑ 25.00/60.00 **st.** – SB (except June-September) 60.00/72.00 **st.**   CX **s**

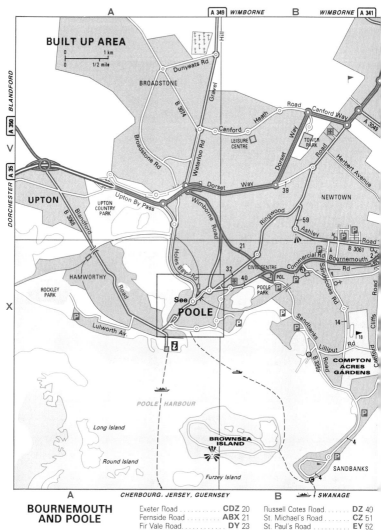

A 349 WIMBORNE · WIMBORNE A 341

BUILT UP AREA

BLANDFORD A 350 · DORCHESTER A 35

BROADSTONE

Dunyeats Rd

B 3074 · Gravel Hill

Canford Heath · Road · Canford Way A 3049

Broadstone Rd · Waterloo Rd

LEISURE CENTRE

TOWER PARK · Herbert Avenue

Dorset Way · Way

UPTON

Blandford B 3068

UPTON COUNTRY PARK

Upton By Pass · Wimborne Road

Dorset Way · 39 · NEWTOWN

Ringwood · 59 · Ashley · B 3061

HAMWORTHY

Road

Holes Bay Rd · 21 · 32 · CIVIC CENTRE · Commercial Rd · Bournemouth Rd · Sandbanks Rd

ROCKLEY PARK

See POOLE

40 · POLE · POOLE PARK

Lulworth Av.

Sandbanks Rd · Cliffs · Catford Road

14 · 18

COMPTON ACRES GARDENS

B 3369 · Lilliput Rd

POOLE HARBOUR

Long Island

BROWNSEA ISLAND

Round Island

Furzey Island

SANDBANKS

4

A · CHERBOURG, JERSEY, GUERNSEY · B · SWANAGE

104

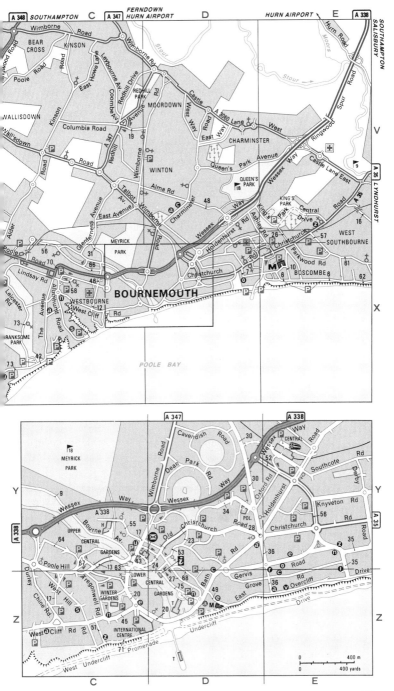

🏠 **Chinehead,** 31 Alumhurst Rd, BH4 8EN, ✗ 752777, Fax 752778 – 📺 ☎ 🅿. ◪ 𝗩𝗜𝗦𝗔
◪
closed January – **M** (dinner only and Sunday lunch)/dinner 12.95 **st.** and a la carte ≬ 4.80 –
21 rm ⊇ 35.00/50.00 **st.** – SB (except December and Bank Holidays) 70.00 **st.**

🏠 **Tudor Grange,** 31 Gervis Rd, East Cliff, BH1 3EE, ✗ 291472, ⇌ – 📺 ☎ 🅿. ◪ 𝗩𝗜𝗦𝗔
M (residents only) (dinner only) 9.00 **st.** ≬ 4.00 – **12 rm** ⊇ 20.00/60.00 **st.** – SB (except
July-September and Bank Holidays) 44.00/56.00 **st.**

🏠 **Wood Lodge,** 10 Manor Rd, East Cliff, BH1 3EY, ✗ 290891, ⇌ – 📺 🅿. ◪ 𝗩𝗜𝗦𝗔 ◪
April-October – **M** 9.00 **st.** ≬ 2.75 – **15 rm** ⊇ 24.00/48.00 **t.**

𝕏𝕏𝕏 **Oscars** (De Vere) (at Royal Bath H.), Bath Rd, BH1 2EW, ✗ 555555, Fax 554158 – ⬅. ◪
𝗔𝗘 ⓞ 𝗩𝗜𝗦𝗔
M a la carte 26.00/45.00.

𝕏𝕏 **Salathai,** 1066 Christchurch Rd, Boscombe East, BH7 6DS, ✗ 420772 – ▤. ◪ 𝗔𝗘 𝗩𝗜𝗦𝗔
closed Sunday and 25-26 December – **M** - **Thai** 7.95/12.95 **t.** and a la carte.

𝕏 **Sophisticats,** 43 Charminster Rd, BH8 8UE, ✗ 291019
closed Sunday, Monday, 2 weeks February, 1 week July and 2 weeks November –
M (dinner only) a la carte 18.25/21.60 **t.** ≬ 4.00.

𝕏 **Helvetia,** 61 Charminster Rd, Charminster, BH8 8UE, ✗ 555447 – ▤. ◪ 𝗔𝗘 ⓞ
𝗩𝗜𝗦𝗔
closed Sunday lunch – **M** - **Swiss** 8.50 **t.** (lunch) and a la carte 14.50/22.35 **t.** ≬ 5.30.

🔘 ATS 892 Christchurch Rd, Boscombe ✗ 424457   ATS 1 Fernside Rd, Poole ✗ 733301/733326

☞ Inclusion in the **Michelin Guide** *cannot be achieved by
pulling strings or by offering favours.*

BOURTON-ON-THE-WATER Glos. ⁴⁰³ ⁴⁰⁴ O 28 Great Britain G. – pop. 2 538 – ECD : Saturday
– ⊙ 0451 Cotswold.
See : Town★.
◆London 91 – ◆Birmingham 47 – Gloucester 24 – ◆Oxford 36.

🏠 **Dial House,** The Chestnuts, High St., GL54 2AN, ✗ 822244, Fax 822244, ⇌ – ✂ 📺 ☎
🅿. ◪ 𝗔𝗘 𝗩𝗜𝗦𝗔
M 9.95/16.00 **t.** and a la carte ≬ 6.00 – **10 rm** ⊇ 35.75/99.00 **t.** – SB 98.00/120.00 **st.**

🏠 **Lansdowne Villa,** Lansdowne, GL54 2AT, ✗ 820673 – ✂ rest 📺 🅿. ⊠
closed January – **M** 12.00 **t.** – **12 rm** ⊇ 22.00/38.50 **t.**

🏠 **Coombe House** without rest., Rissington Rd, GL54 2DT, ✗ 821966, ⇌ – ✂ 📺 🅿. ◪
𝗔𝗘 𝗩𝗜𝗦𝗔 ⊠
7 rm ⊇ 35.00/62.00 **st.**

🏠 **Broadlands,** Clapton Row, GL54 2DN, ✗ 822002 – ✂ rest 📺 🅿. ⊠
closed January – **M** 10.00 **st.** – **11 rm** ⊇ 30.00/55.00 **st.**

🏠 **Triangle** without rest., Station Rd, GL54 2ER, ✗ 821037, ⇌ – ✂ 🅿. ⊠
mid March-October – **3 rm** ⊇ 30.00/42.00 **s.**

at Little Rissington E : 1 ¾ m. on Little Rissington rd – ✉ Bourton-on-the-Water –
⊙ 0451 Cotswold :

🏠 **Touchstone** without rest., GL54 2ND, ✗ 822481, ⇌ – 📺 🅿
closed 15 December-15 February – **3 rm** ⊇ 25.00/38.00 **st.**

at Great Rissington SE : 3¼ m. – ✉ Cheltenham – ⊙ 0451 Cotswold :

🐾 **Lamb Inn,** GL54 2LP, ✗ 820388, « Part 17C Cotswold stone inn », ⇌ – 🅿. ◪ 𝗔𝗘 𝗩𝗜𝗦𝗔
closed 25 and 26 December – **M** (bar lunch)/dinner a la carte 11.25/18.15 **t.** ≬ 5.25 – **13 rm**
⊇ 30.00/72.00 **t.** – SB (November-March) 55.00/85.00 **st.**

at Lower Slaughter NW : 1 ¾ m. by A 429 – ✉ Cheltenham – ⊙ 0451 Cotswold :

🏛 **Lower Slaughter Manor** ⌂, GL54 2HP, ✗ 820456, Fax 822150, ≼, « 17C manor house,
gardens », ⇌s, ◪, ✂ – ✂ rest 📺 ☎ 🅿. ◪ 𝗔𝗘 𝗩𝗜𝗦𝗔
closed 2 weeks January – **M** 17.95/29.50 **t.** ≬ 8.00 – **15 rm** ⊇ 120.00/200.00 **t.** – SB (winter
only except Christmas-New Year) 145.00/300.00 **st.**

🏛 **Washbourne Court,** GL54 2HS, ✗ 822143, Fax 821045, « Part 17C house in picturesque
village », ⇌ – ✂ rest 📺 ☎ 🅿. ◪ 𝗔𝗘 𝗩𝗜𝗦𝗔
M 15.00/19.50 **t.** and dinner a la carte – **12 rm** ⊇ 65.00/110.00 **t.**, 6 suites – SB (except
Easter and Christmas-New Year) 110.00/190.00 **st.**

at Upper Slaughter NW : 2¾ m. by A 429 – ✉ Cheltenham – ⊙ 0451 Costwold :

🏛 ❄ **Lords of the Manor** ⌂, GL54 2JD, ✗ 820243, Fax 820696, ≼, « Part 17C manor
house », ⬉, ⇌, park – 📺 ☎ 🅿 – ⏢ 30. ◪ 𝗔𝗘 ⓞ 𝗩𝗜𝗦𝗔 ⊠
M 24.50 **t.** (dinner) and a la carte approx. 33.50 **t.** ≬ 6.95 – **29 rm** ⊇ 80.00/185.00 **st.** –
SB (except Easter, Christmas and New Year) 150.00/240.00 **st.**
Spec. Terrine of salmon and brill with salad niçoise, Grilled sirloin of Aberdeen Angus, celeriac purée and onion sauce,
Apple tart on a caramel sauce with sultana and Calvados ice cream.

See : St. Peter, St. Paul and St. Thomas of Canterbury Church★.

Envir. : Dartmoor National Park★★ (Brent Tor ≤★★, Haytor Rocks ≤★).

🖼 Newton Abbot 🖉 52460, S : 4 m. by A 382.

♦London 214 – Exeter 14 – ♦Plymouth 32.

🏨 **Edgemoor,** Haytor Rd, TQ13 9LE, W : 1 m. on B 3387 🖉 832466, Fax 834760, 🌿 – 🐾 rest 📺 ☎ 🅿 – 🔼 50. 🔼 🖭 🕦 𝗩𝗜𝗦𝗔
M (booking essential) 19.85 **t.** and lunch a la carte ≬ 4.15 – **12 rm** ⚏ 44.75/82.50 **t.** – SB (except Christmas) 80.00/104.50 **st.**

🏠 **Coombe Cross,** Coombe Cross, TQ13 9EY, E : ½ m. on B 3344 🖉 832476, Fax 835298, 🌿, ☎, 🔲, 🌿 – 🐾 rest 📺 ☎ 🅿. 🔼 🖭 𝗩𝗜𝗦𝗔
M (bar lunch)/dinner 18.95 **t.** ≬ 5.45 – **24 rm** ⚏ 35.00/60.00 **t.** – SB 66.00/98.00 **st.**

↑ **Willmead Farm** 🐾 without rest., TQ13 9NP, NW : 2 ¾ m. by A 382 🖉 064 77 (Lustleigh) 214, ≤, « Part 14C thatched farmhouse », 🌿, park – 🐾 🅿. 🌿 closed Christmas and New Year – **3 rm** ⚏ 30.00/46.00 **st.**

↑ **Front House Lodge,** East St., TQ13 9EL, 🖉 832202, Fax 834931, 🌿 – 🐾 📺 🅿. 🔼 🖭 𝗩𝗜𝗦𝗔
M (by arrangement) 14.00 **s.** – **6 rm** ⚏ 20.00/38.00.

at Haytor W : 2½ m. on B 3387 – ✉ Bovey Tracey – ☎ 0364 Haytor :

🏨 **Bel Alp House** 🐾, TQ13 9XX, on B 3387 🖉 661217, Fax 661292, ≤ countryside, « Country house atmosphere », 🌿 – ▮◗ 🐾 rest 📺 ☎ 🕭 🅿. 🔼 𝗩𝗜𝗦𝗔
M (booking essential) (dinner only) 33.00 **t.** ≬ 5.00 – **9 rm** ⚏ 72.00/150.00 **t.** – SB 162.00/240.00 **st.**

at Haytor Vale W : 3½ m. by B 3387 – ✉ Newton Abbot – ☎ 0364 Haytor :

🏠 **Rock Inn,** TQ13 9XP, 🖉 661305, Fax 661242, « 18C inn », 🌿 – 🐾 📺 ☎ 🅿. 🔼 🖭 𝗩𝗜𝗦𝗔. 🌿
M a la carte 11.00/19.00 **t.** ≬ 5.95 – **9 rm** ⚏ 39.95/75.00 **t.** – SB (except Bank Holidays) 100.90/112.00 **st.**

♦London 265 – Durham 3 – ♦Middlesbrough 20.

🏠 **Bowburn Hall,** DH6 5NH, E : 1 m. 🖉 377 0311, Fax 377 3459, 🌿 – 📺 ☎ 🅿. 🔼 🖭 🕦 𝗩𝗜𝗦𝗔 𝗝𝗖𝗕
M 14.95 **st.** (dinner) and a la carte ≬ 3.75 – **19 rm** ⚏ 40.00/65.00 **st.** – SB (weekends only) 75.00/87.00 **st.**

🅱 2 Bridge St., NN13 5EP 🖉 700111.

♦London 67 – ♦Birmingham 53 – Northampton 21 – ♦Oxford 21.

🏠 **Crown** (Resort), 20 Market Pl., NN13 5DP, 🖉 702210, Fax 701840 – 📺 ☎ – 🔼 60. 🔼 🖭 🕦 𝗩𝗜𝗦𝗔. 🌿
M a la carte approx. 7.95 **t.** ≬ 3.00 – **19 rm** ⚏ 45.00/60.00 **t.** – SB (weekends only) 58.00/100.00 **st.**

⊚ ATS Station Building, Northampton Rd 🖉 702000/703188

🖼 Downshire Easthampstead Park, Wokingham 🖉 424066, SW : 3 m.

🅱 The Look Out, Nine Mile Ride, RG12 4QW 🖉 868196.

♦London 35 – Reading 11.

🏨 **Coppid Beech,** John Nike Way, RG12 8TF, NW : 3 m. by A 329 on B 3408 🖉 303333, Fax 301200, 🐾, ≘, 🔲, 🌿 – 🐾 rm 🖀 rest 📺 ☎ 🕭 🅿 – 🔼 350. 🔼 🖭 🕦 𝗩𝗜𝗦𝗔. 🌿
M – Rowans (closed Saturday lunch) 18.50/24.50 **st.** and a la carte ≬ 7.85 – **205 rm** ⚏ 100.00/295.00 **st.** – SB (weekends only) 95.00/125.00 **st.**

🏨 **Hilton National,** Bagshot Rd, RG12 3QJ, S : 2 m. on A 322 🖉 424801, Telex 848058, Fax 487454, ≘, – ▮◗ 🐾 rm 🖀 rest 📺 ☎ 🅿 – 🔼 200. 🔼 🖭 🕦 𝗩𝗜𝗦𝗔 𝗝𝗖𝗕
M 15.00/23.00 **st.** and a la carte – ⚏ 10.25 – **167 rm** 92.00/105.00 **st.** – SB (weekends only) 139.00/144.00 **st.**

BRADFIELD Berks. 403 404 Q 29 – pop. 1 416 – ⊠ ✪ 0734 Reading.

◆London 56 – ◆Oxford 28 – Reading 7.

⌂ **Boot Farm** without rest., Southend Rd., Southend Bradfield, RG7 6ES, SW : 2 m. ℰ 744298, ☞ – ᚼ – 🆃🆅 ℗. ⌀
4 rm ⫞ 17.00/38.00 **st.**

BRADFIELD COMBUST Suffolk – see Bury St. Edmunds.

We suggest :

For a successful tour, that you prepare it in advance.
Michelin maps and guides will give you much useful information on route planning,
places of interest, accommodation, prices etc.

BRADFORD W. Yorks. 402 O 22 Great Britain G. – pop. 293 336 – ECD : Wednesday – ✪ 0274.

See : City★.

ᚽ West Bowling, Newall Hall, Rooley Lane ℰ 724449 BY – ᚽ Chellow Grange, Haworth Rd ℰ 542767, W : 3 m. by B 6144 AX - ᚽ Woodhall Hills, Pudsey ℰ 564771/554594, E : 4 m. by A 647 BX – ᚽ Bradford Moor, Scarr Hall, Pollard Lane ℰ 638313 BX – ᚽ East Bierley, South View Rd ℰ 681023, SE : 4 m. BX on Leeds town plan – ᚽ Queensbury ℰ 882155, SW : 4 m. by A 647 AY.

✈ Leeds and Bradford Airport : ℰ 0532 (Rawdon) 509696, Telex 557868, Fax 505426 NE : 6 m. by A 658 BX.

🄱 National Museum of Photography, Film & TV, Pictureville, BD1 1NQ ℰ 753678.

◆London 212 – ◆Leeds 9 – ◆Manchester 39 – ◆Middlesbrough 75 – ◆Sheffield 45.

Plan on next page
Plan of Enlarged Area : see Leeds

🏨 **Stakis Norfolk Gardens,** Hall Ings, BD1 5SH, ℰ 734734, Telex 517573, Fax 306146 – 🛗 ⇘ rm 🍽 rest 🆃🆅 ☎ – 🔬 700. 🄰 🄰🄴 ⓪ 𝘝𝘐𝘚𝘈 𝐉𝐂𝐁   BZ **e**
M (carving lunch) 8.50/16.95 **st.** and a la carte – ⫞ 8.95 – **116 rm** 82.00/102.00 **st.**, 4 suites – SB 78.00/108.00 **st.**

🏨 **Tong Village** (Lansbury), The Pastures, Tong Lane, BD4 0RP, SE : 4¾ m. by A 650 - BY – on Tong Lane ℰ 854646, Fax 853661, 𝑓ₛ, ⥲ – 🛗 ⇘ rm 🆃🆅 ☎ ℗ – 🔬 250. 🄰 🄰🄴 ⓪ 𝘝𝘐𝘚𝘈
closed 26 December and 1 January – **M** 15.50 **t.** and a la carte ⫟ 6.25 – **58 rm** ⫞ 69.50/ 81.00 **t.**, 2 suites – SB (weekends only) 92.00 **st.**

🏨 **Guide Post,** Common Rd, Low Moor, BD12 OST, S : 3 m. by A 641 off A 638 ℰ 607866, Fax 671085 – 🆃🆅 ☎ ℗ – 🔬 100. 🄰 🄰🄴 ⓪ 𝘝𝘐𝘚𝘈 ⌀   on plan of Leeds   AX **c**
M *(closed Saturday lunch)* 9.95/10.95 **t.** and dinner a la carte ⫟ 3.35 – **43 rm** ⫞ 30.00/ 85.00 **t.**

🏨 **Novotel Bradford,** Euroway Trading Estate, Merrydale Rd, BD4 6SA, S : 3 ½ m. by A 641 and A 6117 off M 606 ℰ 683683, Telex 517312, Fax 651342, ⤤ heated – 🛗 ⇘ rm 🆃🆅 ☎ ♿ ℗ – 🔬 200. 🄰 🄰🄴 ⓪ 𝘝𝘐𝘚𝘈   on plan of Leeds   AX **a**
M 15.00 **st.** (dinner) and a la carte 7.05/21.85 **st.** ⫟ 5.95 – ⫞ 7.50 – **131 rm** 49.50/85.00 **st.** – SB (weekends only) 67.00/89.00 **st.**

🏨 **Park Drive,** 12 Park Drive, Heaton, BD9 4DR, ℰ 480194, Fax 484869, ☞ – 🆃🆅 ☎ ℗. 🄰 🄰🄴 𝘝𝘐𝘚𝘈 ⌀   AX **e**
M (bar lunch)/dinner 12.50 **st.** – **11 rm** ⫞ 47.00/58.00 **st.** – SB 67.00/107.00 **st.**

⌂ **Norland House,** 695 Great Horton Rd, BD7 4DU, ℰ 571698, Fax 503290 – 🆃🆅 ℗   AY **i**
M (by arrangement) 6.00 **s.** – **8 rm** ⫞ 19.50/37.00 **s.**

XXX ✪ **Restaurant Nineteen** (Smith) with rm, 19 North Park Rd, Heaton, BD9 4NT, ℰ 492559, Fax 483827 – 🆃🆅 ☎ ℗. 🄰 🄰🄴 𝘝𝘐𝘚𝘈 ⌀   AX **n**
closed Sunday, 2 weeks August-September and 1 week Christmas – **M** (dinner only) 26.00 **t.** ⫟ 7.50 – **4 rm** ⫞ 60.00/70.00 **t.** – SB (except December and New Year) 100.00/ 160.00 **st.**
Spec. Salad of wood pigeon with vegetables and honey dressing. Rack of lamb with grilled aubergines, mint and pistachio salsa. Hazelnut parfait with caramelised apricot sauce.

XXX **Bombay Brasserie,** Simes St., Westgate, BD1 3RB, ℰ 737564, « Former Baptist church » – ℗. 🄰 🄰🄴 ⓪ 𝘝𝘐𝘚𝘈   AZ **a**
M - Indian 7.75/15.00 **t.** and a la carte ⫟ 4.00.

at Gomersal SE : 7 m. by A 650 on A 651 – BY – ⊠ ✪ 0274 Bradford :

🏨 **Gomersal Park,** Moor Lane, BD19 4LJ, NW : 1 ½ m. by A 651 off A 652 ℰ 869386, Fax 861042, 𝑓ₛ, ⥲, ☒ – 🆃🆅 ☎ ℗ – 🔬 80. 🄰 🄰🄴 ⓪ 𝘝𝘐𝘚𝘈
M 9.50/15.95 **st.** and a la carte ⫟ 5.95 – ⫞ 7.25 – **49 rm** 70.00/80.00 **st.**, 1 suite – SB (week-ends only) 78.00 **st.**

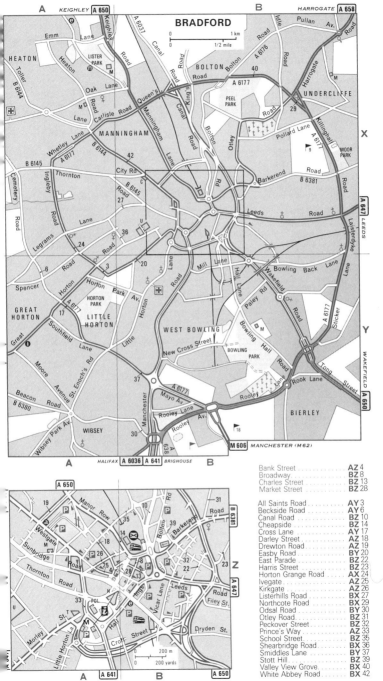

BRADFORD

109

See : Town★★ - Saxon Church of St. Lawrence★★ – Bridge★.

Envir. : Great Chalfield Manor★ (All Saints★) *AC*, NE : 3 m. by B 3109 – Westwood Manor★ *AC*, S : 1 ½ m. by B 3109 – Top Rank Tory (≼★).

Exc. : Bath★★★, NW : 7½ m. by A 363 and A 4 – Corsham Court★★ *AC*, NE : 6½ m. by B 3109 and A 4.

🛏 The Library, Bridge St., BA15 1BY ☞ 865797.

◆London 118 – ◆ Bristol 24 – Salisbury 35 – Swindon 33.

🏨 **Woolley Grange** ⊜, Woolley Green, BA15 1TX, NE : ¾ m. by B 3107 on Woolley St. ☞ 864705, Fax 864059, ≼, « 17C manor house », 🔲 heated, 🌳, ✸ – 🔟 ☎ 🅿. ⚠ ⓞ **VISA JCB**
M 28.00 **st.** (dinner) and a la carte 11.00/25.00 **st.** ♦ 4.95 – **18 rm** ☞ 80.00/175.00 **st.**, 2 suites.

🏠 **Widbrook Grange,** Trowbridge Rd, Widbrook, BA15 1UH, SE : 1 m. on A 363 ☞ 864750, Fax 862890, ≼, 🔲, 🌳, park – ⋈ rest 🔟 ☎ 🅿 – 🔬 25. ⚠ ⚠ ⓞ **VISA** ✸
M (closed Sunday) (by arrangement) (residents only) (dinner only) 22.00 **t.** ♦ 6.50 – **17 rm** ☞ 30.00/75.00 **t.**, 1 suite.

🏠 **Georgian Lodge,** 25 Bridge St., BA15 1BY, ☞ 862268 – 🔟 ☎. ⚠ ⚠. ✸
M (closed Monday lunch) a la carte 13.50/17.00 **st.** ♦ 3.75 – **10 rm** 30.00/75.00 **st.**

⚕ **Bradford Old Windmill,** 4 Masons Lane, BA15 1QN, on A 363 ☞ 866842, 🌳 – ⋈ 🔟 🅿. ⚠ **VISA**
M - Vegetarian (by arrangement) 18.00 **st.** – **4 rm** ☞ 45.00/69.00 **st.**

⚕ **Priory Steps,** Newtown, off Market St., BA15 1NQ, ☞ 862230, Fax 866248, ≼, « 17C weavers cottages », 🌳 – 🔟 🅿. ⚠ **VISA** ✸
M (by arrangement) 15.00 **st.** ♦ 3.25 – **5 rm** ☞ 42.00/56.00 **st.**

🅛 Kings Lane, Stisted ☞ 346079, E : 1 m. by A 120 – 🅛 Towerlands, Panfield Rd ☞ 552487/326802, NW : 1 m.

🛏 Town Hall Centre, Market Sq., CM7 6YG ☞ 550066.

◆London 45 – ◆Cambridge 38 – Chelmsford 12 – Colchester 15.

🏨 **White Hart,** Bocking End, CM7 6AB, ☞ 321401, Fax 552628, ≋s – ⋈ rm 🔟 ☎ 🅿 – 🔬 40. ⚠ ⚠ ⓞ **VISA** ✸
M (grill rest.) a la carte 6.35/19.30 **st.** – **31 rm** ☞ 59.50/71.00 **st.** – SB (weekends only) 76.00/158.00 **st.**

◎ ATS 271-275 Rayne Rd ☞ 323306

◆London 190 – Chesterfield 35 – ◆Manchester 11.

🏨 **Bramhall Moat House** (Q.M.H.), Bramhall Lane South, SK7 2EB, on A 5102 ☞ 439 8116, Telex 668464, Fax 440 8071, ≋s – ⫿ 🔟 ☎ ♿ 🅿 – 🔬 110. ⚠ ⚠ ⓞ **VISA** ✸
closed 25 to 30 December – **M** (bar lunch Monday to Saturday)/dinner 13.50 **st.** and a la carte ♦ 5.90 – **65 rm** ☞ 65.00/75.00 **st.** – SB (weekends only) 77.00 **st.**

Envir. : Hadrian's Wall★★, NW : by A 6077.

🅛 Talkin Tarn ☞ 2255, SE : 1 m. on B 6413.

🛏 Moot Hall, Market Pl., CA8 1RA ☞ 3433 (summer only).

◆London 317 – ◆Carlisle 9 – ◆Newcastle upon Tyne 49.

🏨 **Farlam Hall** ⊜, CA8 2NG, SE : 2¾ m. on A 689 ☞ 46234, Fax 46683, ≼, « Gardens » – 🔟 ☎ 🅿. ⚠ ⚠ **VISA**
closed 26 to 30 December – **M** (dinner only) 29.50 **t.** ♦ 5.25 – **13 rm** ☞ (dinner included) 80.00/196.00 **t.** – SB (November-April except Bank Holidays) 130.00/171.00 **st.**

🏠 **Kirby Moor,** Longtown Rd, CA8 2AB, N : ½ m. on A 6071 ☞ 3893, Fax 41847, 🌳 – 🔟 ☎ 🅿. ⚠ ⚠ **VISA**
M 11.95 **t.** and a la carte ♦ 4.15 – **6 rm** ☞ 35.00/45.00 **t.** – SB 70.00/90.00 **st.**

at Kirkcambeck N : 7¾ m. by A 6071 and Walton rd – ✉ Brampton – ☎ 069 77 Roadhead :

⚕ **Cracrop Farm** ⊜, CA8 2BW, W : 1 m. by B 6318 on Stapleton rd ☞ 48245, « Working farm », ≋s, – ⋈ 🅿. ⚠ **VISA**
closed Christmas – **M** (by arrangement) (communal dining) 12.00 – **4 rm** 18.00/40.00 **s.**

at Lanercost NE : 2 m. by A 689 – ⊠ 🏢 069 77 Brampton :

🛦 **Abbey Bridge Inn,** CA8 2HG, 𝒫 2224 – ⅍ rm 🅿. 🖾
M a la carte 9.35/18.45 **st.** 🍴 3.95 – **7 rm** ⇌ 20.00/50.00 **st.** – SB (except June-September and Easter) 60.00 **st.**

at Talkin S : 2 ¾ m. by B 6413 – ⊠ Brampton – 🏢 069 77 Hallbankgate :

🛏 **Hullerbank** ⤜, CA8 1LB, NW : ½ m. by Hallbankgate rd 𝒫 46668, « Working farm », ⍗ – ⅍ 🅿
M (by arrangement) (communal dining) 11.50 **st.** – **3 rm** ⇌ 26.00/36.00 **st.**

BRANDON Warks. 403 404 P 26 – see Coventry (W. Mids.).

BRANDS HATCH Kent – ⊠ Dartford – 🏢 0474 Ash Green.

⌃₉ Corinthian, Gay Dawn Farm 𝒫 707559.

◆London 22 – Maidstone 18.

🏨 **Brands Hatch Thistle** (Mt. Charlotte Thistle), DA3 8PE, on A 20 𝒫 854900, Telex 966449, Fax 853220 – ⅍ rm 🔳 rest 🅣 ☎ & 🅿 – 🔏 300. 🖾 🖾 ⓞ 🆅🆂🅰 🄹🄲🄱
M 14.95/19.95 **t.** and a la carte 🍴 5.00 – ⇌ 8.75 – **135 rm** 70.00/80.00 **t.**, 2 suites – SB (weekends only) 100.00/130.00 **st.**

at Fawkham E : 1 ½ m. by A 20 – ⊠ 🏢 0474 Ash Geen :

🏨 **Brands Hatch Place,** DA3 8NQ, 𝒫 872239, Fax 879652, 𝟦, ⩲s, 🔳, ⍗, ❨, squash – 🅣
☎ 🅿 – 🔏 120. 🖾 🖾 ⓞ 🆅🆂🅰 ❩
M (closed Saturday lunch) 17.50/18.50 **t.** and a la carte – **29 rm** ⇌ 75.00/120.00 **t.**

BRANSCOMBE Devon 403 K 32 The West Country G. – pop. 506 – ECD : Thursday – ⊠ Seaton – 🏢 029 780 (3 fig.) and 0297 (5 fig.).

See : Village★.

Envir. : Seaton (⩠★★) NW : 3 m.

◆London 167 – Exeter 20 – Lyme Regis 11.

🏠 **The Look Out** ⤜, EX12 3DP, S : ¾ m. by Beach rd 𝒫 262, Fax 272, ⩠ cliffs and Beer Head, « Tastefully converted coastguards cottages », ⍗ – ⅍ rest 🅣 🅿
closed 1 week Christmas – **M** (closed Monday) (dinner only) 19.50 **t.** 🍴 5.25 – **5 rm** ⇌ 49.00/85.00 **t.** – SB (November-March) (weekdays only) 112.00/139.00 **st.**

BRANSTON Lincs. 402 404 S 24 – see Lincoln.

BRANSTON Staffs. – see Burton-upon-Trent.

BRATTON FLEMING Devon 403 I 30 – ⊠ Barnstaple – 🏢 0598 Brayford.

◆London 228 – Barnstaple 6 – Exeter 46 – Taunton 36.

🏠 **Bracken House** ⤜, EX31 4TG, 𝒫 710320, ⩠, ⍗ – ⅍ rest 🅣 🅿. 🖾 🆅🆂🅰
late February-late November – **M** (dinner only) 13.00 **t.** 🍴 3.75 – **8 rm** ⇌ 43.00/66.00 **t.** – SB 70.00/92.00 **st.**

BRAUNSTONE Leics. 402 403 404 Q 26 – see Leicester.

BRAUNTON Devon 403 H 30 The West Country G. – pop. 9 004 – ECD : Wednesday – 🏢 0271.

See : Town★ - St. Brannock's Church★.

Envir. : Braunton Burrows★, W : 3 m. by B 3231.

ⅠB, ⍗B Saunton 𝒫 812436.

◆London 226 – Exeter 47 – Taunton 58.

❨❨ **Grays Country,** Knowle, EX33 2NA, N : 1 ¼ m. on A 361 𝒫 812809, ⍗ – 🅿. 🖾 🆅🆂🅰
closed Sunday and Monday – **M** (dinner only) a la carte 15.90/22.65 **st.** 🍴 5.50.

BRAY-ON-THAMES Berks. 404 R 29 – pop. 9 427 – ⊠ 🏢 0628 Maidenhead.

◆London 34 – Reading 13.

Plan : see Maidenhead

❨❨❨❨ ✿✿✿ **Waterside Inn** (Roux) with rm, Ferry Rd, SL6 2AT, 𝒫 20691, Fax 784710, « ⩠ Thames-side setting », ⍗ – 🔳 rest 🅣 ☎ 🅿. 🖾 🆅🆂🅰 🄹🄲🄱 ❩ X **s**
closed 26 December-5 February – **M** - French (closed Tuesday lunch, Sunday dinner from 3rd weekend October-2nd weekend April, Monday and Bank Holidays) 29.00/58.00 **st.** and a la carte 52.00/73.50 **st.** 🍴 11.50 – **6 rm** 115.00/150.00 **st.**
Spec. Tronçonnettes de homard poêlées minute au porto blanc, Filets de lapereau grillés aux marrons glacés, Soufflé chaud aux framboises (summer).

🏨 **Monkey Island,** SL6 2EE, SE : ¾ m. by Old Mill Lane 𝒫 23400, Fax 784732, ⩠, « Island on River Thames », ❨, ⍗ – ⅍ rm 🅣 ☎ 🅿 – 🔏 120. 🖾 🖾 ⓞ 🆅🆂🅰 ❩ X
closed 26 December-mid January – **M** (bar lunch Saturday) 17.00/22.50 **t.** and a la carte – ⇌ 8.50 – **23 rm** 85.00/120.00 **t.**, 2 suites – SB (weekends only) 130.00 **st.**

BREADSALL Derbs. – see Derby.

BREDONS NORTON `403` `404` N 28 – see Tewkesbury.

BRENCHLEY Kent `404` V 30 – pop. 2 582 – ⊠ Tonbridge – ☎ 089 272 (4 fig.) or 0892 (6 fig.).

🏞, 🏞 Moatlands, Watermans Lane ⚲ 724400.

♦London 44 – ♦Brighton 41 – Hastings 28 – Maidstone 15.

  ⚘ **Bull Inn**, High St., TN12 7NQ, ⚲ 722701 – 📺 🅿 ⚘
    M 12.50/15.95 **t.** and a la carte 🍷 3.25 – **4 rm** ⊒ 24.00/50.00 **t.** – SB (except Christmas and Bank Holidays) 60.00/100.00 **st.**

BRENT ELEIGH Suffolk – see Lavenham.

BRENT KNOLL Somerset `403` L 30 – pop. 1 092 – ECD : Wednesday and Saturday – ⊠ Highbridge – ☎ 0278.

🏞 Brean, Coast Rd, Burnham-on-Sea ⚲ 751595, NW : 4 m. by B 3140.

♦London 151 – ♦Bristol 33 – Taunton 21.

  ⌂ **Battleborough Grange,** Bristol Rd, TA9 4HJ, E : 2 m. on A 38 ⚲ 760208, Fax 760208, ≪ – 📺 ☎ 🅿 – 🔬 90. 🖭 🖭 ⑩ 💳 ⚘
    M *(closed Sunday dinner)* 13.95 **t.** (dinner) and a la carte 8.65/17.55 **t.** 🍷 4.10 – **18 rm** ⊒ 30.00/65.00 **st.** – SB (except Bank Holidays) 67.00 **st.**

BRENTWOOD Essex `404` V 29 – pop. 51 212 – ECD : Thursday – ☎ 0277.

🏞 King George's Playing Fields ⚲ 218714 – 🏞 Bentley, Ongar Road ⚲ 373179 – 🏞 Warley Park, Magpie Lane, Little Warley ⚲ 224891, S : 2 m.

🛈 Old House, 5 Shenfield Rd, CM15 8AG ⚲ 200300.

♦London 22 – Chelmsford 11 – Southend-on-Sea 21.

  🏩 **Brentwood Moat House** (Q.M.H.), London Rd, CM14 4NR, SW : 1 ¼ m. on A 1023 ⚲ 225252, Telex 995182, Fax 262809, ≪ – 📺 ☎ ċ 🅿 – 🔬 55. 🖭 🖭 ⑩ 💳 💳 ⚘
    M 19.50/25.00 **t.** and a la carte 🍷 4.90 – ⊒ 8.00 – **32 rm** 85.00/97.00 **st.**, 1 suite – SB (weekends only) 103.00/143.00 **st.**

  🏨 **Forte Posthouse,** Brook St., CM14 5NF, SW : 1 ¾ m. on A 1023 ⚲ 260260, Fax 264264, 🍴, ⌂, 🖳 – 📵 ⊁ rm 📺 ☎ 🅿 – 🔬 100. 🖭 🖭 ⑩ 💳 ⚘
    M a la carte approx. 17.50 **t.** 🍷 4.65 – ⊒ 6.95 – **111 rm** 53.50/69.50 **st.** – SB 90.00 **st.**

◎ ATS Fairfield Rd ⚲ 211079   ATS Unit 30, Wash Rd, Hutton Ind. Est. ⚲ 262877

BRERETON Cheshire – see Holmes Chapel.

BRIDGNORTH Shropshire `403` `404` M 26 Great Britain G. – pop. 10 332 – ECD : Thursday – ☎ 0746.

Exc. : Ironbridge Gorge Museum★★ *AC* (The Iron Bridge★★ - Coalport China Museum★★ - Blists Hill Open Air Museum★★ - Museum of the River and Visitor Centre★) NW : 8 m. by B 4373.

🏞 Stanley Lane ⚲ 763315, N : 1 m.

🛈 The Library, Listley St., WV16 4AW ⚲ 763358.

♦London 146 – ♦Birmingham 26 – Shrewsbury 20 – Worcester 29.

  ⌂ **Croft**, 11 St. Mary's St., WV16 4DW, ⚲ 762416 – ⊁ rest 📺 ☎. 🖭 🖭 💳
    M (by arrangement) 12.95 **st.** 🍷 4.50 – **12 rm** ⊒ 30.50/48.00 **st.** – SB 61.00/71.00 **st.**

  at Worfield NE : 4 m. by A 454 – ⊠ Bridgnorth – ☎ 074 64 (3 fig.) and 0746 (6 fig.) Worfield :

  🏚 **Old Vicarage** ⚲, WV15 5JZ, ⚲ 497, Fax 552, ≪ – ⊁ 📺 ☎ ċ 🅿. 🖭 🖭 ⑩ 💳
    M *(closed Saturday lunch)* 16.50/31.50 **t.** 🍷 7.50 – **13 rm** ⊒ 63.50/100.00 **t.**, 1 suite – SB 119.00/159.00 **st.**

  at Alveley SE : 7 m. by A 442 – ⊠ Bridgnorth – ☎ 0746 Quatt :

  🏩 **Mill,** Birdsgreen, WV15 6HL, NE : ¾ m. ⚲ 780437, Fax 780850, ≪, park – 📵 ▤ rest 📺 ☎ 🅿 – 🔬 200. 🖭 🖭 ⑩ 💳 ⚘
    M 7.70/15.75 **t.** and a la carte 🍷 4.50 – ⊒ 3.50 – **21 rm** 39.00/186.00 **t.** – SB 85.00/127.50 **st.**

  at Middleton Priors W : 7½ m. by B 4364 – ⊠ Bridgnorth – ☎ 0746 34 Ditton Priors :

  ⌂ **Middleton Lodge** ⚲ without rest., WV16 6UR, ⚲ 228, « Part 17C hunting lodge », ≪ – ⊁ 📺 🅿. 🖭 ⚘
    closed Christmas – **3 rm** ⊒ 25.00/45.00 **st.**

BRIDGWATER Somerset `403` L 30 The West Country G. – pop. 30 782 – ECD : Thursday – ☎ 0278.

See : Town★ – Castle Street★ – St. Mary's★ – Admiral Blake Museum★ *AC*.

Envir. : Westonzoyland (St. Mary's Church★★) SE : 4 m. by A 372 – North Petherton (Church Tower★★) S : 3½ m. by A 38.

Exc. : Stogursey Priory Church★★, NW : 14 m. by A 39.

🏞 Enmore Park ⚲ 671244, W : 3 m.

🛈 50 High St., TA6 3BL ⚲ 427652 (summer only).

♦London 160 – ♦Bristol 39 – Taunton 11.

🏠 **Friarn Court,** 37 St. Mary St., TA6 3LX, 𝒫 452859, Fax 452988 – 📺 ☎ 🅟. ⊠ 🆑 ⑩ 𝓥𝓘𝓢𝓐. ※
M (bar lunch)/dinner 15.50 **st.** and a la carte ⫴ 3.50 – ⊑ 2.00 – **12 rm** 35.00/59.90 **st.** – SB (weekends only) 60.00/100.00 **st.**

🏠 **Old Vicarage,** 45-51 St. Mary St., TA6 3EQ, 𝒫 458891, Fax 445297 – 📺 ☎ 🅟. ⊠ 🆑 𝓥𝓘𝓢𝓐
M a la carte 10.50/18.50 **t.** – **16 rm** ⊑ 39.50/69.50 **t.** – SB (weekends only) 95.00/135.00 **st.**

🏠 **Watergate,** 10-11 West Quay, TA6 3DB, 𝒫 423847 – 📺 ☎. ⊠ 🆑 ⑩ 𝓥𝓘𝓢𝓐. ※
M (closed Sunday) 14.50/16.50 **t.** and a la carte ⫴ 4.00 – **8 rm** ⊑ 37.00/47.00 **t.**

at West Huntspill N : 6 m. on A 38 – ⊠ Highbridge – ☎ 0278 Burnham-on-Sea :

🏠 **Sundowner,** 74 Main Rd, TA9 3QU, on A 38 𝒫 784766, Fax 784766 – 📺 ☎ 🅟. ⊠ 🆑 𝓥𝓘𝓢𝓐
M (closed Sunday dinner except Bank Holidays) 8.95/10.45 **t.** and a la carte ⫴ 3.75 – **8 rm** ⊑ 32.00/48.00 **t.** – SB (October-April) (weekends only) 60.00/80.00 **st.**

at North Petherton S : 3 m. on A 38 – ⊠ ☎ 0278 Bridgwater :

🏦 **Walnut Tree Inn** (Best Western), TA6 6QA, 𝒫 662255, Fax 663946 – 📺 ☎ 🅟 – 🏛 60. 🆑 🆎 ⑩ 𝓥𝓘𝓢𝓐 𝙅𝘾𝘽. ※
M a la carte 12.85/17.90 **t.** – **27 rm** ⊑ 49.00/64.00 **t.**, 1 suite – SB (weekends only) 86.00 **st.**

at Cannington NW : 3½ m. on A 39 – ⊠ ☎ 0278 Bridgwater :

🏠 **Priory** without rest., Fore St., TA5 2HQ, on A 39 𝒫 652079, ⌇ – 📺 🅟. 🆑 𝓥𝓘𝓢𝓐
4 rm ⊑ 25.00/40.00 **s.**

🔘 ATS Friarn St. 𝒫 455891/455795

BRIDLINGTON Humbs. 402 T 21 Great Britain G. – pop. 28 426 – ECD : Thursday – ☎ 0262.
Envir. : Flamborough Head★, NE : 5½ m. by B 1255 and B 1259 – Burton Agnes Hall★ *AC*, SW : 6 m. by A 166.

📌 Belvedere Rd 𝒫 672092/606367, S : 1½ m. – 📌 Flamborough Head, Lighthouse Rd 𝒫 850333, NE : 5 m.

🗓 25 Prince St., YO15 2NP 𝒫 673474/606383.

◆ London 236 – ◆Kingston-upon-Hull 29 – York 41.

🏦 **Expanse,** North Marine Drive, YO15 2LS, 𝒫 675347, Fax 604928, ≤ – ⫴👤⫴ 📺 ☎ 🅟. 🆑 🆎 ⑩ 𝓥𝓘𝓢𝓐. ※
M 9.25/14.50 **st.** and dinner a la carte – **48 rm** ⊑ 42.50/68.00 **st.** – SB 64.00/99.00 **st.**

🏠 **Monarch,** South Marine Drive, YO15 3JJ, 𝒫 674447, Fax 604928, ≤ – ⫴👤⫴ 📺 ☎ 🅟. 🆑 🆎 ⑩ 𝓥𝓘𝓢𝓐. ※
Easter-September – **M** (bar lunch Monday to Saturday)/dinner 14.00 **t.** ⫴ 4.20 – **40 rm** ⊑ 29.50/65.00 **t.** – SB 80.00/90.00 **st.**

🔘 ATS Springfield Av. 𝒫 675571

BRIDPORT Dorset 403 L 31 The West Country G. – pop. 10 615 – ECD : Thursday – ☎ 0308.
Exc. : Parnham House★★ *AC*, N : 6 m. by A 3066 – Lyme Regis★ - The Cobb★, W : 11 m. by A 35 and A 3052.

📌 Bridport and West Dorset, East Cliff, West Bay 𝒫 422597, S : 1½ m.

🗓 32 South St., DT6 3NQ 𝒫 424901.

◆London 150 – Exeter 38 – Taunton 33 – Weymouth 19.

🏠 **Roundham House,** Roundham Gdns, West Bay Rd, DT6 4BD, S : 1 m. by B 3157 𝒫 422753, Fax 421145, ≤, ⌇ – ⫴⊱ rest 📺 ☎ 🅟. 🆑 ⑩ 𝓥𝓘𝓢𝓐. ※
February-October – **M** (bar lunch)/dinner 13.50 **t.** ⫴ 3.50 – **8 rm** ⊑ 35.00/57.50 **st.**

🏠 **Britmead House,** 154 West Bay Rd, DT6 4EG, S : 1 m. on B 3157 𝒫 422941, ⌇ – ⫴⊱ rest 📺 🅟. 🆑 🆎 ⑩ 𝓥𝓘𝓢𝓐 𝙅𝘾𝘽. ※
M 11.50 **st.** ⫴ 3.90 – **7 rm** ⊑ 28.00/50.00 **st.** – SB (except Bank Holidays) 58.00/83.00 **st.**

at Powerstock NE : 4 m. by A 3066 – ⊠ Bridport – ☎ 0308 Powerstock :

🎋 **Three Horseshoes Inn,** DT6 3TF, 𝒫 485328 – 📺 🅟. 🆑 🆎 𝓥𝓘𝓢𝓐
M 12.50/16.50 **t.** and a la carte ⫴ 4.50 – **4 rm** ⊑ 24.00/45.00 **t.**

at Shipton Gorge SE : 3 m. by A 35 – ⊠ ☎ 0308 Bridport :

🎋🎋 **Innsacre** ⌑ with rm, Shipton Lane, DT6 4LJ, N : 1 m. 𝒫 56137, Fax 27277, ⌇ – 📺 🅟. 🆑 𝓥𝓘𝓢𝓐
closed 2 weeks November and 25-26 December – **M** (closed to non-residents Sunday and Monday except Bank Holidays) (dinner only) 21.50/26.00 **t.** ⫴ 6.00 – **6 rm** ⊑ 45.00/66.00 **t.** – SB (except Bank Holidays) 90.00/140.00 **st.**

🔘 ATS Victoria Grove 𝒫 23661/2

BRIGHOUSE W. Yorks. 402 O 22 – pop. 32 597 – ☎ 0484.
◆London 213 – Bradford 12 – Burnley 28 – ◆Manchester 35 – ◆Sheffield 39.

🏨 **Forte Crest,** Clifton Village, HD6 4HW, SE : 1 m. on A 644 𝒫 400400, Fax 400068, 🛁, ≘s, ⊠, ◻ – ⫴⊱ rm 📺 ☎ 🅖 🅟 – 🏛 200. 🆑 🆎 ⑩ 𝓥𝓘𝓢𝓐 𝙅𝘾𝘽
M 12.00/18.50 **t.** and a la carte ⫴ 6.60 – ⊑ 9.95 – **92 rm** 89.00 **t.**, 2 suites – SB (weekends only) 98.00 **st.**

BRIGHTON AND HOVE

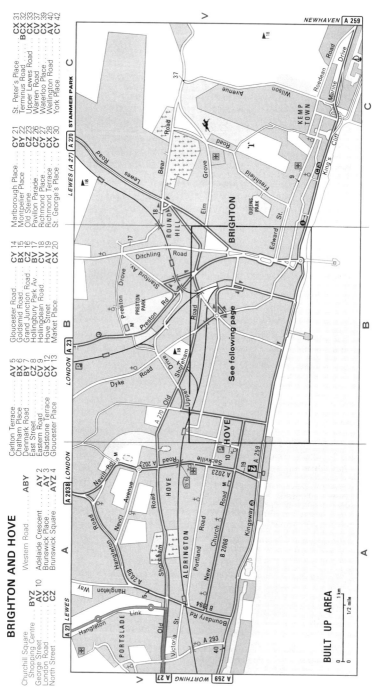

BUILT UP AREA

114

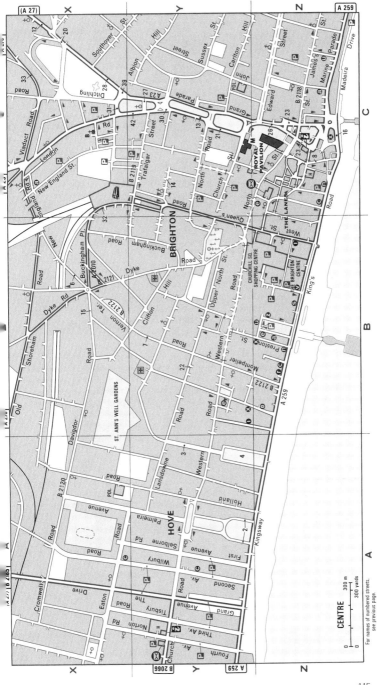

CENTRE

0 _____ 300 m
0 _____ 300 yards

For names of numbered streets,
see previous page.

115

BRIGHTON AND HOVE E. Sussex **404** T 31 Great Britain G. – pop. 200 168 (inc. Hove) – ✆ 0273.

See : Town★★ – Royal Pavilion★★★ AC CZ – Seafront★★ – The Lanes★ BCZ – St. Bartholo-mew's★ AC CX **B** – Art Gallery and Museum (20C decorative arts★) CY **M**.

Envir. : Devil's Dyke (≤★) NW : 5 m. by Dyke Rd (B 2121) BY.

🏌 East Brighton, Roedean Rd ✆ 604838 CV – 🏌 The Dyke, Dyke Rd ✆ 857296, N : 4 m. BV – 🏌 Hollingbury Park, Ditchling Rd ✆ 552010, NE : 1 m. CV – 🏌 Waterhall, Devils Dyke Rd ✆ 508658, N : 3 m. AV – 🏌 Pyecombe ✆ 845372, N : 5 m. by A 272 BV.

✈ Shoreham Airport : ✆ 452304, Fax 440146, W : 8 m. by A 27 AV.

🛈 10 Bartholomew Sq., BN1 1JS ✆ 323755 at Hove : Norton Rd, BN3 4AH ✆ 778087.

King Alfred Leisure Centre, Kingsway, BN3 2WW ✆ 746100.

◆London 53 – ◆Portsmouth 48 – ◆Southampton 61.

Plans on preceding pages

Grand (De Vere), King's Rd, BN1 2FW, ✆ 321188, Fax 202694, ≤, ⒑, ≋, ⬚ – ⧉ 🖵 ☎ ৬ – 🚗 800. ◫ ⬛ ⑩ *VISA*   BZ **v**
M 16.50/32.00 **t.** and a la carte ⒑ 5.75 – **195 rm** ⊒ 125.00/225.00 **t.**, 5 suites – SB (except Christmas-New Year) 160.00 **st.**

Brighton Thistle (Mt. Charlotte Thistle), King's Rd, BN1 2GS, ✆ 206700, Telex 878555, Fax 820692, ≤, ⒑, ≋, ⬚ – ⧉ 🗏 rm 🖃 🖵 ☎ ৬ ⇔ – 🚗 350. ◫ ⬛ ⑩ *VISA* *JCB* CZ **n**
M 9.75/14.75 **st.** and a la carte ⒑ 6.00 – (see also **La Noblesse** below) – ⊒ 9.75 – **200 rm** 115.00/159.00 **st.**, 4 suites.

Brighton Metropole, King's Rd, BN1 2FU, ✆ 775432, Telex 877000, Fax 207764, ≤, ⒑, ≋, ⬚ – ⧉ 🗏 rm 🖃 rest 🖵 ☎ – 🚗 1200. ◫ ⬛ ⑩ *VISA*   BZ **s**
M 17.50 **t.** and a la carte ⒑ 8.20 – **312 rm** ⊒ 104.00/160.00 **t.**, 16 suites – SB 130.00/ 160.00 **st.**

Bedford, King's Rd, BN1 2JF, ✆ 329744, Fax 775877, ≤ – ⧉ 🖃 rest 🖵 ☎ ⇔ – 🚗 300. ◫ ⬛ ⑩ *VISA*   BZ **c**
M 24.00/30.00 **st.** and a la carte ⒑ 5.95 – **125 rm** ⊒ 90.00/128.00 **st.**, 4 suites – SB (week-ends only) 102.00/244.00 **st.**

Topps, 17 Regency Sq., BN1 2FG, ✆ 729334, Fax 203679 – ⧉ 🖵 ☎. ◫ ⬛ ⑩ *VISA*. ⌾
M (closed Sunday and Wednesday) (dinner only) 22.95 **st.** ⒑ 3.95 – **14 rm** ⊒ 45.00/ 79.00 **st.** – SB 104.00/170.00 **st.**   BZ **a**

Preston Resort, 216 Preston Rd, BN1 6UU, N : 1 ½ m. on A 23 ✆ 507853, Fax 540039, ≋, ⬚ – ⧉ 🗏 rm 🖵 ☎ ℗ ⇔ – 🚗 60. ◫ ⬛ ⑩ *VISA*   BV **e**
M (bar lunch Monday to Saturday)/dinner 12.95 **t.** and a la carte – **34 rm** ⊒ 62.50/80.00 **t.** – SB 80.00/145.00 **st.**

Brighton Oak, West St., BN1 2RQ, ✆ 220033, Fax 778000 – ⧉ 🖵 ☎ ৬ – 🚗 120. ◫ ⬛ ⑩ *VISA* *JCB*   BZ **i**
M 11.95 **st.** (dinner) and a la carte 11.85/19.50 **st.** – ⊒ 6.25 – **136 rm** 42.00/80.00 **st.**, 2 suites – SB 79.00/119.00 **st.**

Old Ship, Kings Rd, BN1 1NR, ✆ 329001, Telex 877101, Fax 820718 – ⧉ 🖵 ☎ ⇔ – 🚗 300. ◫ ⬛ ⑩ *VISA*   CZ **c**
M (dancing Saturday evening) 14.50/20.00 **st.** and a la carte – **149 rm** ⊒ 60.00/105.00 **st.**, 3 suites – SB (except Easter, Christmas and New Year) (weekends only) 98.00/138.00 **st.**

West Beach, 135 King's Rd, BN1 2HX, ✆ 323161, Fax 776982 – ⧉ 🖵 ☎ – 🚗 50. ◫ ⬛ ⑩ *VISA*. ⌾
M (dinner only and Sunday lunch)/dinner 13.50 **st.** ⒑ 6.25 – **41 rm** ⊒ 75.00/95.00 **st.**, 2 suites – SB 79.00/95.00 **st.**   BZ **n**

Adelaide, 51 Regency Sq., BN1 2FF, ✆ 205286, Fax 220904 – ⌿ rest 🖵 ☎. ◫ ⬛ ⑩ *VISA* ⌾   BZ **z**
M (closed Sunday and Wednesday) (dinner only) 14.75 **st.** ⒑ 4.00 – **12 rm** ⊒ 38.00/ 75.00 **st.** – SB (except Bank Holidays) 74.00/141.00 **st.**

Dove, 18 Regency Sq., BN1 2FG, ✆ 779222, Fax 746912 – ⌿ rest 🖵 ☎. ◫ ⬛ ⑩ *VISA* *JCB*. ⌾   BZ **e**
M (by arrangement) (residents only) (dinner only) 13.50 **st.** ⒑ 4.00 – **9 rm** ⊒ 32.00/78.00 **st.**

Twenty One, 21 Charlotte St., BN2 1AG, ✆ 686450, Fax 607711 – 🖵 ☎. ◫ ⬛ *VISA* *JCB* ⌾   CV **i**
M (closed Sunday and Monday) (dinner only) 21.50 **st.** ⒑ 4.10 – **6 rm** ⊒ 40.00/68.00 **st.** – SB (November-March except Bank Holidays) (weekdays only) 69.00/110.00 **st.**

Allendale, 3 New Steine, BN2 1PB, ✆ 675436, Fax 602603 – 🖵 ☎. ◫ ⬛ ⑩ *VISA*. ⌾   CZ **u**
M (by arrangement) 13.00 **st.** – **13 rm** ⊒ 27.00/66.00 **st.**

Prince Regent without rest., 29 Regency Sq., BN1 2FH, ✆ 329962, Fax 748162 – 🖵 ☎. ◫ ⬛ *VISA* *JCB*. ⌾   BZ **u**
20 rm ⊒ 30.00/50.00 **t.**

Dudley House without rest., 10 Madeira Pl., BN2 1TN, ✆ 676794 – ⌿ 🖵. ⌾   CZ **a**
6 rm ⊒ 28.00/55.00 **st.**

XXX **La Noblesse** (at Brighton Thistle H.), King's Rd, BN1 2GS, ℘ 206700, Telex 878555, Fax 820692 – ▤ ⇔, 🔳 AE ⓞ VISA JCB   CZ **n**
closed Saturday lunch, Sunday and Bank Holidays – **M** 14.95/18.95 **st.**

XX Langan's Bistro, 1 Paston Pl., Kemp Town, BN2 1HA, ℘ 606933   CV **a**

XX **La Marinade,** 77 St. Georges Rd, Kemp Town, BN2 1EF, ℘ 600992 – ▤. 🔳 AE ⓞ   CV **c**
VISA
closed Saturday lunch, Sunday dinner and Monday – **M** 12.50/25.00 **t.** and a la carte ¶ 5.35.

XX **New Dynasty,** 33 Preston St., BN1 2HP, ℘ 202708, Fax 822716 – ▤. 🔳 AE ⓞ VISA   BZ **x**
M - **Chinese** 15.00/25.00 **t.** and a la carte ¶ 5.00.

X **Whytes,** 33 Western St., BN1 2PG, ℘ 776618 – 🔳 AE VISA   BZ **o**
closed Sunday – **M** (dinner only) 17.95 **t.** ¶ 3.50.

X **Le Grandgousier,** 15 Western St., BN1 2PG, ℘ 772005 – 🔳 AE VISA   BY **x**
closed Saturday lunch and 23 December-3 January – **M** - **French** 5.00/11.00 **t.**

X **Black Chapati,** 12 Circus Par., off New England Rd, BN1 4GW, ℘ 699011 – 🔳 AE   CX **a**
VISA
closed Sunday dinner, Monday, 1 week June and 1 week Christmas – **M** - **Indian** (booking essential) (lunch by arrangement Monday to Saturday) a la carte 15.50/20.50 **t.**

X **Foggs,** 5 Little Western St., BN1 2PU, ℘ 735907 – 🔳 AE ⓞ VISA JCB   BY **e**
closed 26 to 31 December – **M** (dinner only) a la carte 14.30/20.50 **t.** ¶ 3.50.

at Hove – ✉ Hove – 🕿 0273 Brighton :

🏨 **Whitehaven,** 34 Wilbury Rd, BN3 3JP, ℘ 778355, Fax 731177, ☞ – 📺 🕿. 🔳 AE ⓞ VISA   AX **c**
⚘
M *(closed lunch Saturday and Sunday and to non-residents Sunday dinner)* 13.50/19.50 **st.**
¶ 4.00 – **17 rm** ⊡ 55.00/80.00 **st.** – SB (except Christmas and New Year) 60.00/70.00 **st.**

🏨 **Claremont House,** Second Av., BN3 2LL, ℘ 735161, Fax 324764, ☞ – 📺 🕿. 🔳 AE ⓞ   AY **c**
VISA JCB
M 12.50/14.50 **st.** and a la carte ¶ 3.25 – **12 rm** ⊡ 33.00/68.00 **st.** – SB (weekends only) 59.00/110.00 **st.**

X **Le Classique,** 37 Waterloo St., BN3 1AY, ℘ 734140 – 🔳 AE ⓞ VISA   BY **i**
closed Sunday – **M** - **French** (dinner only) 15.00 **t.** and a la carte ¶ 4.00.

⊚ ATS 40 Bristol Gdns ℘ 680150/686344   ATS Franklin Rd, Portslade ℘ 415327/414488

BRIMFIELD Heref. and Worcs. 403 404 L 27 Great Britain G. – pop. 490 – ✉ Ludlow (Shrops.) – 🕿 0584.

Envir. : Berrington Hall★ *AC*, S : 3 m. by A 49.

◆London 149 – ◆Birmingham 41 – Hereford 21 – Shrewsbury 32 – Worcester 39.

🏨 **Forte Travelodge** without rest., Woofferton, SY8 4AL, N : ½ m. on A 49 ℘ 711695, Reservations (Freephone) 0800 850950 – 📺 ௧ 🅿. 🔳 AE VISA. ⚘
32 rm 31.95 **t.**

XX **Poppies** (at The Roebuck) with rm, SY8 4NE, ℘ 711230, Fax 711654 – 📺 🕿 🅿. 🔳 AE VISA
⚘
closed 2 weeks February and 1 week October – **Meals** *(closed Sunday and Monday)* 18.50 **t.** (lunch) and a la carte 27.00/33.50 **t.** – **3 rm** ⊡ 45.00/60.00 **t.**

BRIMSCOMBE Glos. 403 404 N 28 – see Stroud.

BRISTOL Avon 403 404 M 29 The West Country G. – pop. 413 861 – 🕿 0272.

See : City★★ – St. Mary Redcliffe★★ DZ – The Georgian House★★ AX **A** – Industrial Museum★★ CZ **M2** – SS Great Britain★★ *AC* AX **B** – The Old City★ CYZ : Theatre Royal★★ CZ **T** – Merchant Seamen's Almshouses★ **K** – St. Stephen's City★ CY **F** – St. John the Baptist★ CY – St. Nicholas Church Museum★ CDY **M3** – Cathedral District★ CYZ (Bristol Cathedral★, Lord Mayor's Chapel★) – Bristol "Exploratory"★ DZ – John Wesley's New Room★ DY **E** – Quakers Friars★ DY – City Museum and Art Gallery★ AX **M** – Red Lodge★ CY.

Envir. : Clifton★ AX (Suspension Bridge★★★, R.C. Cathedral of SS. Peter and Paul★★ **F**, Bristol Zoological Gardens★★ *AC*, Village★) – Blaise Hamlet★★ – Blaise Castle House Museum★, NW : 5 m. by A 4018 and B 4057 AV.

Exc. : Bath★★★, SE : 13 m. by A 4 BX – Chew Magna★ (Stanton Drew Stone Circles★ *AC*) S : 8 m. by A 37 – BX - and B 3130 – Clevedon★ (Clevedon Court★ *AC*, ≤★) W : 11½ m. by A 370, B 3128 – AX - and B 3130.

🏌 Mangotsfield, Carsons Rd ℘ 565501, NE : 6 m. by B 4465 BV – 🏌 Beggar Bush Lane, Failand ℘ 0275 (Lulsgate) 393117/393474, W : 2 m. off Clifton suspension Bridge AX – 🏌 Knowle, Fairway, Brislington ℘ 776341, S : 3 m. by A 4 BX – 🏌 Long Ashton ℘ 0275 (Lulsgate) 392229, S : 3 m., by B 3128 AX – 🏌 Stockwood Vale, Stockwood Lane, Keynsham ℘ 866505, SE : 10 m. by A 431 BX.

✈ Bristol Airport : ℘ 0275 (Lulsgate) 474444, Fax 474800, SW : 7 m. by A 38 AX.

🚗 ℘ 0345 090700.

🛈 14 Narrow Quay, BS1 4QA ℘ 260767 – Bristol Airport, BS19 3DY ℘ 0275 (Lulsgate) 474444.

◆London 121 – ◆Birmingham 91.

Plans on following pages

117

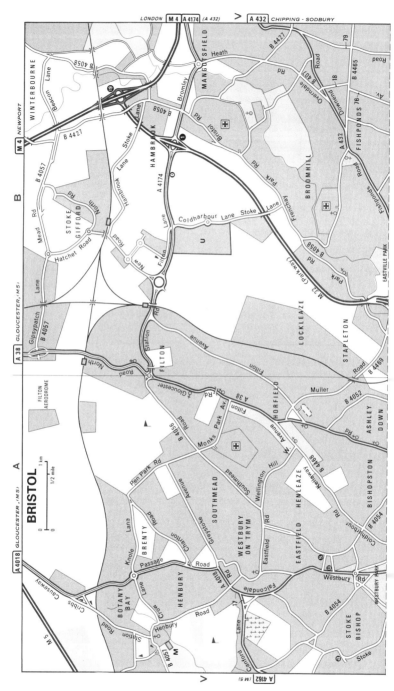

BRISTOL

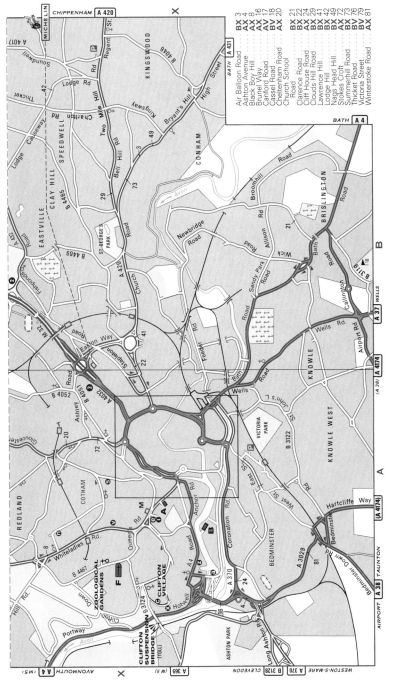

CHIPPENHAM **A 420**

MICHELIN

A 431 BATH

		BX	3
Air Balloon Road		BX	3
Ashton Avenue		AX	4
Black Boy Hill		AX	16
Brunel Way		AX	17
Canford Road		AV	18
Cassel Road		BV	20
Cheltenham Road		AX	20
Church School			
Road		BX	21
Clarence Road		BX	22
Cliff House Road		AX	24
Clouds Hill Road		BX	29
Lawrence Hill		BX	41
Lodge Hill		BX	42
Nags Head Hill		BX	49
Stokes Croft		AX	72
Summerhill Road		BX	73
Thicket Road		BV	76
Victoria Street		BV	79
Winterstoke Road		AX	81

A 4 BATH

A 37 WELLS

A 4174 (A 38)

A 38 TAUNTON AIRPORT

A 4174

BEDMINSTER

KNOWLE WEST

KNOWLE

BRISLINGTON

CONHAM

KINGSWOOD

SPEEDWELL

EASTVILLE

CLAY HILL

REDLAND

COTHAM

CLIFTON VILLAGE

ZOOLOGICAL GARDENS

CLIFTON SUSPENSION BRIDGE

VICTORIA PARK

ASHTON PARK

BEDMINSTER

A 369 AVONMOUTH (M 5)

A 370 / B 3128 CLEVEDON WESTON-S-MARE

A 4 (M 5) AVONMOUTH

A 4017

119

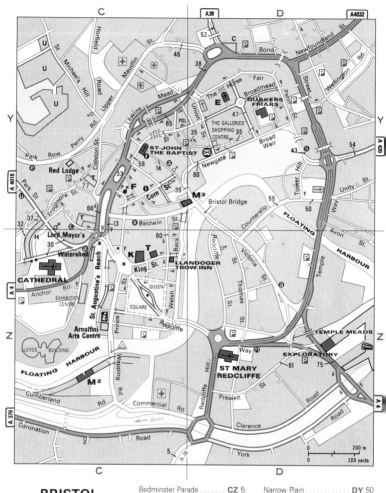

BRISTOL
CENTRE

Swallow Royal, College Green, BS1 5TA, ℰ 255100, Fax 251515, ℎ₅, ⇖, ▨ – ◧ ⤢ rm
▤ ▥ ☎ & ℗ – 🖦 250. ◭ ▥ ⓘ 𝙑𝙄𝙎𝘼
CZ **a**
M 15.00/19.00 **st.** and a la carte ⓘ 6.00 – **227 rm** 🛏 99.50/119.00 **st.**, 15 suites – SB (except Christmas and New Year) (July-August and weekends only) 140.00 **st.**

Bristol Marriott, 2 Lower Castle St., Old Market, BS1 3AD, ℰ 294281, Fax 225838, ⇖,
ℎ₅, ⇖, ▨ – ◧ ⤢ rm ▥ ☎ & ℗ – 🖦 600. ◭ ▥ ⓘ 𝙑𝙄𝙎𝘼 ◦
DY **s**
M – Le Chateau (closed Sunday) 14.95 **st.** and a la carte – **The Brasserie** (dinner only) –
🛏 10.25 – **282 rm** 105.00/115.00 **st.**, 7 suites – SB (weekends only) 128.00 **st.**

Holiday Inn Crown Plaza (Q.M.H.), Victoria St., BS1 6HY, ℰ 255010, Fax 255040, ℎ₅ –
◧ ⤢ rm ▤ rest ▥ ☎ & ℗ – 🖦 200. ◭ ▥ ⓘ 𝙑𝙄𝙎𝘼
DZ **a**
closed 26 to 31 December – **M** – **Spires** 14.50/17.50 **st.** and a la carte – **128 rm** 🛏 95.00/
105.00 **t.**, 4 suites – SB (weekends only) 86.00 **st.**

Bristol Hilton, Redcliffe Way, BS1 6NJ, ℰ 260041, Telex 449240, Fax 230089, ℎ₅, ⇖, ▨
– ◧ ⤢ rm ▤ rest ▥ ☎ ℗ – 🖦 300. ◭ ▥ ⓘ 𝙑𝙄𝙎𝘼 𝙅𝘾𝘽
DZ **n**
M (closed Saturday lunch) 16.50/19.50 **t.** and a la carte ⓘ 7.00 – 🛏 10.50 – **200 rm** 80.00 **st.**,
1 suite – SB (weekends only) 152.00 **st.**

Grand (Mt. Charlotte Thistle), Broad St., BS1 2EL, ℰ 291645, Telex 449889, Fax 227619 –
◧ ▥ – 🖦 600. ◭ ▥ ⓘ 𝙑𝙄𝙎𝘼 𝙅𝘾𝘽
CY **a**
M (closed Saturday lunch) 12.50/16.50 **st.** and a la carte ⓘ 5.20 – 🛏 8.00 – **175 rm** 70.00/
90.00 **st.**, 3 suites – SB 86.00/88.00 **st.**

Avon Gorge (Mt. Charlotte Thistle), Sion Hill, Clifton, BS8 4LD, ℰ 738955, Telex 444237,
Fax 238125, ⇗ – ◧ ▥ ☎ – 🖦 100. ◭ ▥ ⓘ 𝙑𝙄𝙎𝘼 𝙅𝘾𝘽
AX **x**
M 10.75/14.25 **st.** and a la carte ⓘ 5.10 – 🛏 6.75 – **74 rm** 70.00/85.00 **st.**, 2 suites –
SB 150.00/170.00 **st.**

St. Vincent Rocks (Forte), Sion Hill, Clifton, BS8 4BB, ℰ 739251, Fax 238139, ⇗ –
⤢ rm ▥ ☎ ℗ – 🖦 35. ◭ ▥ ⓘ 𝙑𝙄𝙎𝘼
AX **c**
M 19.95/21.95 **t.** and a la carte ⓘ 5.60 – 🛏 8.50 – **46 rm** 80.00/100.00 **st.** – SB 108.00/
120.00 **st.**

Berkeley Square, 15 Berkeley Sq., BS8 1HB, ℰ 254000, Fax 252970 – ◧ ⤢ rm ▥ ☎
⇗, ◭ ▥ ⓘ 𝙑𝙄𝙎𝘼 ⇗
AX **i**
M (closed Saturday lunch and Sunday dinner) 16.00 **t.** and a la carte ⓘ 5.90 – 🛏 8.50 –
42 rm 72.50/95.00 **st.**, 1 suite – SB (weekends only) 108.00/158.00 **st.**

Westbury Park, 37 Westbury Rd, BS9 3AU, ℰ 620465, Fax 628607 – ▥ ☎. ◭
𝙑𝙄𝙎𝘼
AV **u**
M (closed Saturday and Sunday) (dinner only) 10.50 **st.** ⓘ 3.50 – **9 rm** 🛏 25.00/48.50 **st.**

Lawns without rest., 91 Hampton Rd, Redland, BS6 6JG, ℰ 738459, ⇗ – ▥ ℗. ⇗
closed Christmas and New Year – **4 rm** 🛏 23.00/42.00 **s.**
AX **n**

Downlands without rest., 33 Henleaze Gdns, BS9 4HH, ℰ 621639 – ▥. ◭ 𝙑𝙄𝙎𝘼 AV **s**
10 rm 🛏 23.00/46.00 **st.**

XXX ❀ **Harveys**, 12 Denmark St., BS1 5DQ, ℰ 277665, Fax 253378, « Medieval cellars and
wine museum » – ▤. ◭ ▥ ⓘ 𝙑𝙄𝙎𝘼
CY **c**
closed Saturday lunch, Sunday and Bank Holidays – **M** 16.50/29.00 **st.** and dinner a la
carte 26.00/36.15 **st.** ⓘ 7.50
Spec. Bresaola of beef accompanied by a niçoise salad with balsamic dressing, Breasts of pigeon on a potato and
parsnip rösti with roasted goose liver, Harveys speciality British dessert.

XX ❀❀ **Lettonie** (Blunos), 9 Druid Hill, Stoke Bishop, BS9 1EW, ℰ 686456 – ◭ ▥ 𝙑𝙄𝙎𝘼
closed Sunday, Monday, 2 weeks August, 2 weeks Christmas and Bank Holidays –
M - French (booking essential) 15.95/29.95 **t.**
AV **a**
Spec. Scrambled duck egg with sevruga caviar, blinis and a glass of vodka, Roasted, spiced rump of lamb with garlic
fritters, olive oil mashed potatoes and a cream sauce, Apricot "5" ways.

XX **Markwicks**, 43 Corn St., BS1 1HT, ℰ 262658, Fax 262658 – ◭ ▥ 𝙑𝙄𝙎𝘼
CY **i**
closed Saturday lunch, Sunday, 1 week Easter, last 2 weeks August, 1 week Christmas and
Bank Holiday Mondays – **M** 13.00/19.50 **t.** and a la carte ⓘ 5.00.

XX **Hunt's**, 26 Broad St., BS1 2HG, ℰ 265580 – ◭ 𝙑𝙄𝙎𝘼
CY **r**
closed Saturday lunch, Sunday, Monday, 1 week Easter, 1 week July and 1 week Christmas
– **M** 11.95 **st.** (lunch) and a la carte 20.90/24.50 **st.** ⓘ 6.35.

XX **Du Gourmet**, 43 Whiteladies Rd, BS8 2LS, ℰ 736230, Fax 237394 – ◭ ▥ ⓘ 𝙑𝙄𝙎𝘼
closed Saturday lunch, Sunday, 24 December-1 January and Bank Holidays – **M** a la
carte 14.35/20.75 **t.** ⓘ 4.45.
AX **v**

XX **China Palace**, 18a Baldwin St., BS1 1SE, ℰ 262719, Fax 256168 – ▤. ◭ ▥ 𝙑𝙄𝙎𝘼 𝙅𝘾𝘽
M - Chinese 11.50/25.00 **t.** and a la carte ⓘ 4.50.
CY **x**

XX **Thai House**, 52 Park Row, BS1 5LH, ℰ 253079 – ▤. ◭ ▥ ⓘ 𝙑𝙄𝙎𝘼 𝙅𝘾𝘽
CY **a**
closed Sunday and Christmas – **M** - Thai 16.00/26.00 **st.** and a la carte.

XX **Rajdoot**, 83 Park St., BS1 5PJ, ℰ 268033 – ◭ ▥ ⓘ 𝙑𝙄𝙎𝘼
CY **u**
closed lunch Sunday and Bank Holidays and 25-26 December – **M** - Indian 8.00/
18.50 **t.** and a la carte.

XX **Michaels**, 129 Hotwell Rd, BS8 4RU, ℰ 276190, Fax 253629 ⤢. ◭ ▥ ⓘ 𝙑𝙄𝙎𝘼 AX **z**
closed Saturday lunch, Sunday, Monday, 26 December and 1 January – **M** 12.50/22.50 **t.**
ⓘ 4.35.

✗ **Bistro Twenty One**, 21 Cotham Road South, Kingsdown, BS6 5TZ, ✑ 421744 – 🔺 ⒶⒺ
 𝗩𝗜𝗦𝗔 JCB   AX s
 closed Saturday lunch, Sunday and Bank Holidays – **M** 12.50/14.75 **t.** and a la carte.

✗ **Howards**, 1a/2a Avon Crescent, Hotwells, BS1 6XQ, ✑ 262921 – 🔺 ⒶⒺ 𝗩𝗜𝗦𝗔   AX a
 closed Saturday lunch and Sunday – **M** 13.00/15.00 **t.** and a la carte ⑂ 3.95.

✗ **Danton**, 2 Upper Byron Pl., The Triangle, BS8 1JY, ✑ 268314 – 🔺 ⒶⒺ ⓄD 𝗩𝗜𝗦𝗔   AX e
 closed Saturday lunch, Sunday, 1 week Christmas and Bank Holidays – **M** 15.75 **t.** (lunch)
 and a la carte 16.95/21.95 **t.** ⑂ 5.25.

 at Patchway N : 6 ½ m. on A 38 – BV – ✉ Bristol – ✆ 0454 Almondsbury :

🏨 **Stakis Bristol**, Woodlands Lane, BS12 4JF, off A 38 ✑ 201144, Telex 445741,
 Fax 612022, ⇌ₛ, 🔳 – ✄rm ⊟ rest 📺 ☎ & Ⓟ – 🔏 80. 🔺 ⒶⒺ ⓄD 𝗩𝗜𝗦𝗔 JCB
 M (carving lunch) 12.50/16.50 **t.** and a la carte – 🗔 8.50 – **108 rm** 82.00/102.00 **st.**, 2 suites
 – SB 84.00/114.00 **st.**

 at Almondsbury N : 7 ½ m. on A 38 – BV – ✉ Bristol – ✆ 0454 Almondsbury :

🏨 **Aztec**, Aztec West Business Park, BS12 4T5, S : 1 m. on a 38 ✑ 201090, Fax 201593, 🛋,
 ⇌ₛ, 🔳, squash – 🛗 ✄rm ⊟ rest 📺 ☎ & Ⓟ – 🔏 200. 🔺 ⒶⒺ ⓄD 𝗩𝗜𝗦𝗔
 M *(closed Saturday lunch)* 12.95/18.00 **st.** and a la carte ⑂ 6.45 – **87 rm** 🗔 79.00/98.00 **st.**,
 1 suite – SB (except Bank Holidays) 98.00/118.00 **st.**

 at Hambrook NE : 5 ½ m. by M 32 on A 4174 – ✉ ✆ 0272 Bristol :

🏨 **Forte Crest**, Filton Rd, BS16 1QX, ✑ 564242, Fax 569735, 🛋, ⇌ₛ, 🔳, ➳, park – 🛗
 ✄rm ⊟ rest 📺 ☎ Ⓟ – 🔏 300. 🔺 ⒶⒺ ⓄD 𝗩𝗜𝗦𝗔   BV o
 M *(closed Saturday lunch)* 17.95 **t.** and a la carte ⑂ 6.60 – 🗔 9.95 – **193 rm** 89.00 **st.**, 4 suites
 – SB (weekends only) 108.00 **st.**

 at Winterbourne NE : 7 ½ m. by M 32 and A 4174 on B 4058 – BV – ✉ Bristol –
 ✆ 0454 Winterbourne :

🏨 **Grange Resort** ⬙, Northwood, BS17 1RP, NW : 2 m. by B 4057 on B 4427 ✑ 777333,
 Fax 777447, ⇌ₛ, 🔳, park – ✄rm 📺 ☎ Ⓟ – 🔏 100. 🔺 ⒶⒺ ⓄD 𝗩𝗜𝗦𝗔
 M *(closed Saturday lunch)* 14.25/17.55 **t.** and a la carte – 🗔 7.95 – **52 rm** 80.00/90.00 **st.** –
 SB (weekends only) 100.00 **st.**

 at Saltford SE : 7 ½ m. on A 4 – BX – ✉ Bristol – ✆ 0225 Bath :

↑ **Brunel's Tunnel House**, High St., BS18 3BQ, off Beech Rd ✑ 873873, Fax 874875, ➳ –
 📺 ☎ Ⓟ. 🔺 ⒶⒺ 𝗩𝗜𝗦𝗔
 closed 24 to 26 December – **M** (by arrangement) 13.50 **st.** ⑂ 5.50 – **7 rm** 🗔 46.00/55.00 **st.**
 – SB (except Bank Holidays) (weekends only) 74.00/118.00 **st.**

 at Chelwood S : 8½ m. by A 37 – BX – on A 368 – ✉ Bristol – ✆ 0761 Compton Dando :

🏠 **Chelwood House**, BS18 4NH, SW : ¾ m. on A 37 ✑ 490730, Fax 490730 (ext. 504), ⬅,
 ➳ – ✄rest 📺 ☎ Ⓟ. 🔺 ⒶⒺ ⓄD 𝗩𝗜𝗦𝗔
 closed 24 December-10 January – **M** *(closed lunch Monday to Friday and Sunday dinner to*
 non-residents) dinner a la carte 14.40/24.90 **st.** ⑂ 4.95 – **11 rm** 🗔 49.00/85.00 **st.** –
 SB 99.00/130.00 **st.**

 at Stanton Wick S : 9 m. by A 37 and A 368 on Stanton Wick rd – BX – ✉ Bristol –
 ✆ 0761 Compton Dando :

🏠 **Carpenters Arms**, BS18 4BX, ✑ 490202, Fax 490763 – 📺 ☎ Ⓟ. 🔺 ⒶⒺ 𝗩𝗜𝗦𝗔 ✑
 M 7.50/15.00 **st.** and a la carte ⑂ 3.50 – **12 rm** 🗔 45.50/52.50 **st.** – SB 70.00/80.00 **st.**

MICHELIN Distribution Centre, Pennywell Rd, BS5 0UB, ✑ 414415, Fax 553820 BX

🅐 ATS 68-72 Avon St. ✑ 711269   ATS 34-38 St. Johns Lane, Bedminster ✑ 776418/
 ATS 551 Gloucester Rd, Horfield ✑ 514525   770674
 ATS 58-60 Broad St., Staple Hill ✑ 564741/565396/
 564594/571483

BRIXHAM Devon 𝟰𝟬𝟯 J 32 The West Country G. – pop. 15 171 – ECD : Wednesday –
 ✆ 080 45 (4 & 5 fig.) and 0803 (6 fig.).
 Envir. : Berry Head★ (≼★★★) NE : 1½ m.
 🅩 The Old Market House, The Quay, TQ5 8TB ✑ 852861.
 ◆London 230 – Exeter 30 – ◆Plymouth 32 – Torquay 8.

✗ **Lobster Pot**, 13a The Quay, TQ5 8AW, ✑ 853131 – 🔺 ⒶⒺ ⓄD 𝗩𝗜𝗦𝗔
 closed lunch Saturday and Sunday and 24 to 26 December – **M** - **Seafood** (live music most
 evenings) a la carte 20.15/38.40 **t.** ⑂ 4.95.

BROAD CAMPDEN Glos. – see Chipping Campden.

BROAD CHALKE Wilts. 𝟰𝟬𝟯 𝟰𝟬𝟰 O 30 – see Salisbury.

BROADHEMBURY Devon 𝟰𝟬𝟯 K 31 – ✉ ✆ 0404 Honiton.
 ◆London 191 – Exeter 17 – Honiton 5 – Taunton 23.

✗ **Drewe Arms**, EX14 0NF, ✑ 841267, « Part 13C thatched inn », ➳ – Ⓟ
 closed Sunday dinner – **M** - **Seafood** 16.95 **st.** and a la carte ⑂ 6.00.

BROADSTAIRS Kent **404** Y 29 – pop. 21 551 (inc. St. Peter's) – ECD : Wednesday – ❺ 0843 Thanet.

🔼, 🔼 North Foreland, Kingsgate, Broadstairs ℰ 862140.

🅱 67 High St., CT10 1JH ℰ 862242.

◆London 78 – ◆Dover 21 – Maidstone 47.

🏨 **Castlemere**, 15 Western Esplanade, CT10 1TD, ℰ 861566, Fax 866379, ≤, 🚲 – 📺 ☎ ❷. 🔼 💳
    M (bar lunch)/dinner 15.00 **st.** ⒜ 4.35 – **36 rm** ⊆ 37.50/72.00 **st.** – SB (except Christmas and Bank Holidays) (weekdays only) 87.00/95.00 **st.**

🍴 **Marchesi**, 18 Albion St., CT10 1LU, ℰ 862481, Fax 861509, ≤ – ❷. 🔼 AE ⓞ 💳
    closed Monday lunch and 26 to 30 December – **M** 8.50/17.50 **st.** and a la carte ⒜ 4.75.

BROADWATER Herts. – see Stevenage.

BROADWAY Heref. and Worcs. **403** **404** O 27 Great Britain G. – pop. 1 931 – ECD : Thursday – ❺ 0386.

See : Town★.

Envir. : Country Park (Broadway Tower ✳★★), SE : 2 m. by A 44 – Snowshill Manor★ (Terrace Garden★) *AC*, S : 2½ m.

🔼 Willersey Hill ℰ 858997, E : 1½ m.

🅱 1 Cotswold Court, WR12 7AA ℰ 852937 (summer only).

◆London 93 – ◆Birmingham 36 – Cheltenham 15 – Worcester 22.

🏨 **Lygon Arms**, High St., WR12 7DU, ℰ 852255, Telex 338260, Fax 858611, « Part 16C inn », 🔽, ≋, 🔲, 🚲, ✳ – 📺 ☎ ❷ – ⒜ 80. 🔼 AE ⓞ 💳 🔲
    M 19.50/29.75 **t.** and a la carte 28.00/39.00 **t.** – ⊆ 8.25 – **60 rm** 92.40/144.90, 5 suites – SB 195.00/270.00 **st.**

🏨 **Broadway**, The Green, WR12 7AA, ℰ 852401, Fax 853879, 🚲 – ⇥ rm 📺 ☎ ❷. 🔼 AE ⓞ 💳. ✳
    M (bar lunch Monday to Saturday)/dinner 21.00 **t.** and a la carte ⒜ 4.25 – **20 rm** ⊆ 52.50/92.00 **t.** – SB 105.00/119.00 **st.**

🏨 **Collin House** 🈯, Collin Lane, WR12 7PB, NW : 1¼ m. by A 44 ℰ 858354, 🔻, 🚲 – ❷. 🔼 💳. ✳
    closed 24 to 29 December – **M** 15.00/23.00 **st.** ⒜ 4.80 – **7 rm** ⊆ 45.00/86.00 **st.** – SB (except Bank Holidays) 110.00/114.00 **st.**

🏠 **Small Talk Lodge**, Keil Close, 32 High St., WR12 7DP, ℰ 858953 – ⇥ rest 📺 ❷. 🔼 💳. ✳
    closed February – **M** (by arrangement) 15.00 **st.** ⒜ 4.50 – **8 rm** ⊆ 20.00/48.00 **st.** – SB (except Bank Holidays) 70.00/90.00 **st.**

🏠 **Windrush House** without rest., Station Rd, WR12 7DE, ℰ 853577, 🚲 – ⇥ 📺 ❷
    5 rm ⊆ 25.00/42.00.

🏠 **Whiteacres** without rest., Station Rd, WR12 7DE, ℰ 852320, 🚲 – ⇥ 📺 ❷. ✳
    March-October – **6 rm** ⊆ 36.00/42.00 **st.**

🍴 **Hunters Lodge**, High St., WR12 7DT, ℰ 853247, 🚲 – ❷. 🔼 AE ⓞ 💳
    closed Sunday dinner, Monday and Tuesday – **M** (dinner only and lunch Wednesday, Saturday and Sunday) 13.50/17.50 **t.** and a la carte ⒜ 4.40.

    at Willersey (Glos.) N : 2 m. on B 4632 – ✉ ❺ 0386 Broadway :

🏠 **Old Rectory** 🈯 without rest., Church St., WR12 7PN, ℰ 853729, 🚲 – ⇥ 📺 ☎ ❷. 🔼 💳. ✳
    closed Christmas – **8 rm** ⊆ 50.00/95.00 **t.**

    at Willersey Hill (Glos.) E : 2 m. by A 44 – ✉ ❺ 0386 Broadway :

🏨 **Dormy House**, WR12 7LF, ℰ 852711, Telex 338275, Fax 858636, 🚲 – ⇥ rest 📺 ☎ ❷ – ⒜ 200. 🔼 AE ⓞ 💳
    closed 25 and 26 December – **M** (bar lunch Saturday) 17.00/26.50 **t.** and a la carte – **46 rm** ⊆ 58.00/116.00 **t.**, 3 suites – SB 142.00 **st.**

    at Buckland (Glos.) SW : 2¼ m. by B 4632 – ✉ ❺ 0386 Broadway :

🏨 ⚅ **Buckland Manor** 🈯, WR12 7LY, ℰ 852626, Fax 853557, ≤, « Part 13C manor », 🔻 heated, 🚲, park, ❷ – ⇥ rest 📺 ☎ ❷. 🔼 AE 💳. ✳
    M a la carte 26.50/40.00 **t.** ⒜ 5.50 – **12 rm** ⊆ 135.00/270.00 **t.**
    Spec. Pithivier of Cornish scallops with caviar and chives, Garlic and herb coated rack of lamb, roasted with a rosemary jus. Glazed summer berries with a basket of homemade cinnamon ice cream.

    at Wormington (Glos.) SW : 4¼ m. by B 4632 on Wormington rd – ✉ ❺ 0386 Broadway :

🏠 **Leasow House** 🈯 without rest., Laverton Meadows, WR12 7NA, E : 1¼ m. ℰ 584526, Fax 584596, ≤, 🚲 – ⇥ 📺 ☎ ⓖ ❷. 🔼 AE 💳
    7 rm ⊆ 35.00/48.00 **t.**

BROADWELL Glos. **403** **404** O 28 – see Stow-on-the-Wold.

Hants. 408 404 P 31 Great Britain G. – pop. 2 939 – ECD : Wednesday – ✆ 0590 Lymington.

Envir. : New Forest★★ (Rhinefield Ornamental Drive★★, Bolderwood Ornamental Drive★★).

🚇 Brockenhurst Manor, Sway Rd ✆ 23332, SW : 1 m. by B 3055.

♦London 99 – Bournemouth 17 – ♦Southampton 14 – Winchester 27.

🏨 **Rhinefield House** ⬧, Rhinefield Rd, SO42 7QB, NW : 3 m. ✆ 22922, Fax 22800, « Victorian country mansion, formal gardens », 🛁, 🚭, 🛆 heated, park, ※ – 🔄 rm 🔲 ☎ 🄿 – 🔏 80. 🔼 🄰🄴 ⓞ 🆅🆂🅰
M *(closed Saturday lunch)* 14.00/19.95 **t.** and a la carte – **34 rm** ⌷ 75.00/165.00 **t.** – SB (except Christmas) 125.00/144.00 **st.**

🏨 **Careys Manor,** Lyndhurst Rd, SO42 7RH, on A 337 ✆ 23551, Fax 22799, 🛁, 🚭, 🛆, 🖉 – 🔄 🔲 ☎ 🄿 – 🔏 100. 🔼 🄰🄴 ⓞ 🆅🆂🅰
M (dancing Saturday evening) 13.75/19.95 **t.** and a la carte – (see also **Le Blaireau** below) – **79 rm** ⌷ 59.00/149.00 **t.** – SB 99.00/109.00 **st.**

🏨 **Balmer Lawn** (Hilton), Lyndhurst Rd, on A 337, SO42 7ZB, ✆ 23116, Telex 477649, Fax 23864, ≼, 🛁, 🚭, 🛆 heated, 🔲, 🖉, ※, squash – |ф| 🔄 rm 🔲 ☎ ⅙ 🄿 – 🔏 90. 🔼 🄰🄴 ⓞ 🆅🆂🅰
M *(bar lunch Saturday)* 8.95/14.50 **t.** and dinner a la carte ⎧ 4.25 – **58 rm** ⌷ 52.50/85.00 **t.** – SB 95.00/120.00 **st.**

🏨 **Whitley Ridge** ⬧, Beaulieu Rd, SO42 7QL, E : 1 m. on B 3055 ✆ 22354, Fax 22856, 🖉, ※ – 🔲 ☎ 🄿. 🔼 🄰🄴 ⓞ 🆅🆂🅰 🄹🄲🄱
M (dinner only and Sunday lunch)/dinner 18.00 **st.** and a la carte ⎧ 4.50 – **13 rm** ⌷ 46.00/ 82.00 **st.** – SB 94.00/126.00 **st.**

🏠 **Cottage,** Sway Rd, S042 7SH, ✆ 22296, 🖉 – 🔄 rest 🔲 🄿. 🔼 🆅🆂🅰 ※
M *(bar lunch)* (dinner by arrangement Monday to Thursday)/dinner a la carte 12.45/ 16.40 **st.** ⎧ 4.25 – **6 rm** ⌷ 32.00/64.00 **st.** – SB (winter only) 76.00/80.00 **st.**

🍴🍴🍴 **Le Poussin,** The Courtyard, rear of 49-55 Brookley Rd, SO42 7RB, ✆ 23063, Fax 22912 – 🔄. 🔼 🆅🆂🅰
closed Sunday dinner, Monday and Tuesday – **Meals** (booking essential) 13.00/25.00 **t.**

🍴 **Le Blaireau** (at Carey's Manor H.), SO42 7RH, ✆ 23032 – 🄿. 🔼 🄰🄴 ⓞ 🆅🆂🅰
M - French 7.95/15.95 **t.** and a la carte ⎧ 5.95.

at Sway SW : 3 m. by B 3055 – ⊠ Lymington – ✆ 0590.

🏠 **Sway Tower** ⬧, Barrows Lane, SO41 6DE, ✆682117, Fax 683785, ≼, « Converted Victorian folly », 🔼, 🖉 – 🔄 rm 🔲 ☎ 🄿. 🔼 🄰🄴 ⓞ 🆅🆂🅰 ※
M *(closed Monday)* (booking essential) (dinner only) 28.00 **st.** ⎧ 7.50 – **4 rm** ⌷ 98.00/ 125.00 **st.** – SB (winter only) (weekdays only) 115.00/196.00 **st.**

Mersey. 402 408 L 24 – pop. 14 901 – ⊠ Wirral – ✆ 051 Liverpool.

🚇 Raby Hall Rd ✆ 334 2155 – 🚇 Ellesmere Port, Chester Rd, Hooton, South Wirral, Ches. ✆ 339 7689, SE : 3 m.

♦London 210 – Chester 14 – ♦Liverpool 6.5 – ♦Manchester 46.

🏨 Cromwell, High St., L62 7HZ, ✆ 334 2917, Telex 628225, Fax 346 1175, 🚭 – 🔲 ☎ ⅙ 🄿 – 🔏 130. ※
31 rm.

🏨 **The Village H. & Leisure Club,** Pool Lane, L62 4UE, on A 41 ✆ 643 1616, Fax 643 1420, 🛁, 🚭, 🔲, ※, squash – |ф| 🔄 rest 🔲 ☎ ⅙ 🄿 – 🔏 200. 🔼 🄰🄴 ⓞ 🆅🆂🅰 ※
M *(closed Saturday lunch)* 11.00 **st.** and a la carte – **89 rm** ⌷ 73.50/94.00 **st.**

Suffolk 404 X 26 – see Diss (Norfolk).

Gtr. Manchester 402 404 M 23 – see Bolton.

N. Yorks. 402 S 21 – pop. 1 827 – ⊠ ✆ 0723 Scarborough.

♦London 242 – ♦Kingston-upon-Hull 44 – Scarborough 8 – York 31.

🍴🍴 Brompton Forge, YO13 9DP, ✆ 859409 – 🄿.

Heref. and Worcs. 408 404 N 26 – pop. 24 576 – ECD : Thursday – ✆ 0527.

🚩 Bromsgrove Golf Centre, Stratford Rd ✆ 570505.

🏛 Bromsgrove Museum, 26 Birmingham Rd ✆ 31809.

♦London 117 – ♦Birmingham 14 – ♦Bristol 71 – Worcester 13.

🏨 **Stakis Country Court,** Birmingham Rd, B61 0JB, N : 2 ½ m. on A 38 ✆ 021 (Birmingham) 447 7888, Telex 336976, Fax 447 7273, 🛁, 🚭, 🔲, 🖉 – 🔄 rm 🔳 rest 🔲 ☎ ⅙ 🄿 – 🔏 80. 🔼 🄰🄴 ⓞ 🆅🆂🅰 🄹🄲🄱
M 12.50/17.95 **st.** and a la carte – ⎧ 8.95 – **130 rm** 88.00/108.00 **st.**, 10 suites – SB 94.00/ 154.00 **st.**

🏨 **Pine Lodge,** 85 Kidderminster Rd, B61 9AB, W : 1 m. on A 448 𝒫 576600, Fax 78981, ↳,
⇌s, 🔲 – 🔯 ⇔ rm 🔳 rest 🆀 🖙 ♿ 🄿 – 🔬 200. 🄰 🄰🄴 🄾 📶
M (light lunch Saturday) 12.95/15.50 **st.** and a la carte – **112 rm** ⊑ 83.00/95.00 **st.**, 2 suites
– SB (weekends only) 75.00/85.00 **st.**

🏨 **Perry Hall** (Jarvis), 13 Kidderminster Rd, B61 7JN, 𝒫 579976, Fax 575998, ⇌ – 🆀 🖙 🄿
– 🔬 60. 🄰 🄰🄴 📶 ⇌
M (bar lunch Saturday) 10.95/14.95 **t.** and a la carte – ⊑ 8.00 – **58 rm** 69.00/87.00 **t.** –
SB (weekends only) 79.00/99.00 **st.**

🏠 **Bromsgrove Country,** 249 Worcester Rd, Stoke Heath, B61 7JA, SW : 2 m. 𝒫 35522,
Fax 71257, ⇌ – ⇔ rm 🆀 🄿. 🄰 📶 ⇌
closed Christmas-New Year – **M** *(closed Saturday and Sunday)* (residents only) (dinner
only) 12.00 **st.** ♟ 4.50 – ⊑ 5.00 – **10 rm** 31.00/49.00 **st.**

🏯🏯🏯 **Grafton Manor** with rm, Grafton Lane, B61 7HA, SW : 1 ¾ m. by Worcester Rd
𝒫 579007, Fax 575221, « 16C and 18C manor », ⇌, park – 🆀 🖙 🄿. 🄰 🄰🄴 🄾 📶 ⇌
M *(closed Saturday lunch)* 20.50/29.50 **st.** ♟ 4.95 – **7 rm** ⊑ 85.00/125.00 **st.**, 2 suites.

BROMYARD Heref. and Worcs. 🛆🛆🛆 M 27 – pop. 2 760 – 🕳 0885.

🄸 T.I.C. & Heritage Centre, 1 Rowberry St., HR7 4DX 𝒫 482038.

♦London 138 – Hereford 15 – Leominster 13 – Worcester 14.

🏠 **Falcon,** Broad St., HR7 4BT, 𝒫 483034, Fax 488818 – 🆀 🖙 🄿. 🄰 📶
M (bar lunch)/dinner 15.95 **st.** ♟ 4.25 – **7 rm** ⊑ 39.50/49.50 **st.** – SB 98.00 **st.**

BROOK Hants. 🛆🛆🛆 P 31 – ECD : Tuesday – ⊠ Lyndhurst – 🕳 0703 Southampton.

♦London 92 – Bournemouth 24 – ♦Southampton 14.

🏨 **Bell,** SO43 7HE, 𝒫 812214, Fax 813958, ↳ – 🆀 🖙 🄿. 🄰 🄰🄴 📶
M *(closed Sunday lunch)* 9.50/30.00 **st.** and dinner a la carte ♟ 3.15 – **25 rm** ⊑ 60.00/
90.00 **st.** – SB (weekdays only) 120.00 **st.**

┌─────────────┐
│ Die Preise │ Einzelheiten über die in diesem Führer angegebenen Preise
└─────────────┘ finden Sie in der Einleitung.

BROOKMANS PARK Herts. 🛆🛆 T 28 – pop. 4 020 – 🕳 0707 Potters Bar.

♦London 21 – Luton 21.

🏯🏯 **Villa Rosa,** 3 Great North Rd, AL9 6LB, SE : 1 ¾ m. on A 1000 𝒫 651444 – 🄿. 🄰 🄰🄴 🄾
📶
M - Italian a la carte 14.05/22.90 **t.** ♟ 4.25.

BROUGHTON Lancs. 🛆🛆🛆 L 22 – see Preston.

BROXTED Essex 🛆🛆🛆 U 28 – see Stansted Airport.

BROXTON Ches. 🛆🛆🛆 🛆🛆🛆 L 24 – pop. 384 – 🕳 0829.

♦London 197 – ♦Birmingham 68 – Chester 12 – ♦Manchester 44 – Stoke-on-Trent 29.

🏨 **Frogg Manor,** Barn Hill, Nantwich Rd, CH3 9JH, on A 534 𝒫 782629, Fax 782238, ⇌, ⚒
– ⇔ rm 🆀 🖙 🄿. 🄰 🄰🄴 🄾 📶
M 14.10/17.65 **st.** and a la carte ♟ 4.25 – ⊑ 7.50 – **6 rm** 40.00/95.50 **st.** – SB (except Christmas and New Year) 90.00/130.00 **st.**

🏠 **Broxton Hall Country House** Whitchurch Rd, CH3 9JS, at junction A 41 with A 534
𝒫 782321, Fax 782330, ⇌ – 🆀 🄿. 🄰 🄰🄴 🄾 📶
closed 25 and 26 December – **M** 24.00 **t.** (dinner) and lunch a la carte 10.00/18.50 **t.** ♟ 5.00 –
11 rm ⊑ 55.00/95.00 **t.** – SB (weekends only) 110.00/160.00 **st.**

BRUSHFORD Somerset 🛆🛆🛆 J 30 – see Dulverton.

BRUTON Somerset 🛆🛆🛆 🛆🛆🛆 M 30 The West Country G. – pop. 1 759 – 🕳 0749.

Exc. : Stourhead★★★ *AC,* W : 8 m. by B 3081.

♦London 118 – ♦Bristol 27 – Bournemouth 44 – Salisbury 35 – Taunton 36.

🏵 **Claire de Lune** with rm, 2-4 High St., BA10 0EQ, 𝒫 813395 – 🆀. 🄰 🄰🄴 📶 ⇌
closed 2 to 14 January – **M** *(closed Sunday and Monday)* (booking essential) (dinner
only) 16.95 **t.** and a la carte ♟ 4.50 – ⊑ 2.50 – **2 rm** 27.50/35.00 **t.**

🏵 **Truffles,** 95 High St., BA10 0AR, 𝒫 812255
closed Sunday dinner and Monday except Bank Holidays – **M** (booking essential) 13.95/
20.50 **st.** ♟ 4.50.

BRYHER Cornwall 🛆🛆🛆 ㉟ – see Scilly (Isles of).

BUCKDEN Cambs. 🛆🛆🛆 T 27 – pop. 2 605 – ⊠ 🕳 0480 Huntingdon.

♦London 65 – Bedford 15 – ♦Cambridge 20 – Northampton 31.

🏠 **Lion,** High St., PE18 9XA, 𝒫 810313, Fax 811070, « Part 15C inn » – 🆀 🖙 🄿. 🄰 🄰🄴 🄾
📶
M 7.90/15.00 **t.** and a la carte ♟ 4.50 – **15 rm** ⊑ 52.00/68.00 **t.** – SB (weekends only)
75.00/110.00 **st.**

BUCKHURST HILL Essex 404 ㊸ – pop. 11 147 – ECD : Wednesday – ⚙ 081 London.
♦London 13 – Chelmsford 25.

Plan : see Greater London (North-East)

🏨 **Roebuck** (Forte), North End, IG9 5QY, ✆ 505 4636, Fax 504 7826 – ⊁ 📺 ☎ Ⓟ – 🎤 200. ▣ AE ⓓ VISA JCB HT **u**
M 9.95/20.00 **st.** and a la carte 🌢 5.25 – ☕ 8.50 – **29 rm** 60.00/70.00 **st.** – SB 86.00 **st.**

BUCKINGHAM Bucks. 403 404 Q 27 **Great Britain G.** – pop. 6 439 – ECD : Thursday – ⚙ 0280.
Exc. : Claydon House★ *AC*, S : 8 m. by A 413.
⛳18 Silverstone, Silverstone Rd, Stowe ✆ 850005.
♦London 64 – ♦Birmingham 61 – Northampton 20 – ♦Oxford 25.

🏨 **Villiers,** 5 Castle St., MK18 1BP, ✆ 822444, Fax 822113 – 🛗 ▤ rest 📺 ☎ Ⓟ. ▣ AE ⓓ VISA. ✂
M (bar lunch Monday to Saturday)/dinner 15.00 **t.** and a la carte 🌢 5.00 – **34 rm** ☕ 60.00/75.00 **st.**, 1 suite – SB 90.00/110.00 **st.**

🏨 **Buckingham Lodge** (Best Western), Buckingham Ring Rd, MK18 1RY, W : 1 ¼ m. by A 413 on A 421 ✆ 822622, Fax 823074, 🏋, ♨, 🏊 – ⊁ rm ▤ rest 📺 ☎ ♿ Ⓟ – 🎤 160. ▣ AE VISA. ✂
M 8.75/11.50 **st.** and a la carte – **70 rm** 49.00/79.00 **st.** – SB (except Easter, Christmas and New Year) 69.00/108.00 **st.**

BUCKLAND Glos. 403 404 O 27 – see Broadway (Heref. and Worc.).

BUCKLERS HARD Hants. 403 404 P 31 – see Beaulieu.

We suggest :

For a successful tour, that you prepare it in advance.
Michelin maps and guides will give you much useful information on route planning, places of interest, accommodation, prices etc.

BUCKLOW HILL Ches. 402 403 404 M 24 – see Knutsford.

BUCKNELL Shrops. 403 L 26 – pop. 496 – ⚙ 05474.
♦London 158 – ♦Birmingham 55 – Hereford 29 – Shrewsbury 31.

⌂ **Bucknell House** 🐌 without rest., SY7 0AD, on B 4367 ✆ 248, 🎣, 🌳, park, 🎾 – 📺 Ⓟ
closed December and January – **3 rm** ☕ 22.00/35.00 **st.**

BUDE Cornwall 403 G 31 **The West Country G.** – pop. 2 679 – ECD : Thursday – ⚙ 0288.
See : The Breakwater★★ – Compass Point (≤★).
Envir. : Poughill★★ (Church★★) N : 2 ½ m. - E : Tamar River★★ – Kilkhampton (Church★) NE : 5 ½ m. by A 39 – Stratton (Church★) E : 1 ½ m. – Launcells (Church★) E : 3 m. by A 3072 – Marhamchurch (St. Morwenne's Church★) SE : 2 ½ m. by A 39 – Poundstock★ (≤★★, church★, guildhouse★) S : 4 ½ m. by A 39.
Exc. : Jacobstow (Church★) S : 7 m. by A 39 – ⛳18 Burn View ✆ 352006.
ℹ The Crescent Car Park, EX23 8LE ✆ 354240.
♦London 252 – Exeter 51 – ♦Plymouth 44 – Truro 53.

🏨 **Hartland,** EX23 8JY, ✆ 355661, Fax 355664, ≤, 🏊 heated – 🛗 📺 ☎ Ⓟ
Easter-early November – **M** 16.45/19.50 **t.** 🌢 4.60 – **29 rm** ☕ 38.00/72.00 **t.**

🏨 **Camelot,** Downs View, EX23 8RE, ✆ 352361, Fax 355470, 🌳 – ⊁ rest 📺 ☎ Ⓟ. ▣ VISA. ✂
March-October – **M** (dinner only) 14.00 **st.** and a la carte 🌢 4.50 – **21 rm** ☕ 25.00/50.00 **st.** – SB 60.00/76.00 **st.**

🏨 **Bude Haven,** Flexbury Av., EX23 8NS, ✆ 352305, 🌳 – ⊁ rest 📺 Ⓟ. ▣ AE VISA. ✂
closed November and Christmas – **M** (bar lunch)/dinner 8.50 **st.** 🌢 3.50 – **12 rm** ☕ 21.00/38.00 **st.**

⌂ **Meva Gwin,** Upton, EX23 0LY, S : 1 ¼ m. on coast rd ✆ 352347, ≤ – ⊁ rest 📺 Ⓟ. ✂
April-8 October – **M** 8.50 **st.** 🌢 3.50 – **12 rm** ☕ 16.00/44.00 **st.**

BUDLEIGH SALTERTON Devon 403 K 32 **The West Country G.** – pop. 4 456 – ⚙ 0395.
Envir. : East Budleigh (Church★) N : 2 ½ m. by A 376 – Bicton★ (garden★) *AC*, N : 3 m. by A 376.
⛳18 East Devon, North View Rd ✆ 442018.
ℹ Fore St., EX9 6NG ✆ 445275.
♦London 215 – Exeter 16 – ♦Plymouth 55.

⌂ **Long Range,** Vales Rd, EX9 6HS, by Raleigh Rd ✆ 443321, 🌳 – ⊁ rest 📺. ✂
April-October – **M** 10.00 **st.** 🌢 2.50 – **7 rm** ☕ 21.00/42.00 **st.**

BUDOCK WATER Cornwall – see Falmouth.

BULKINGTON Warks. 403 404 P 26 – see Nuneaton.

BUNWELL Norfolk **404** X 26 – pop. 797 – ECD : Monday and Wednesday – ☎ 095 389 (3 and 4 fig.) and 0953 (6 fig.).

◆London 102 – ◆Cambridge 51 – ◆Norwich 16.

  🏠 **Bunwell Manor** ⤳, Bunwell St., NR16 1QU, NW : 1 m. ℰ 788304, ⚞ – 📺 ☎ ℗, ◪ AE
  VISA
  M 12.75 **t.** and a la carte ⓘ 3.90 – **10 rm** � 40.00/65.00 **t.** – SB (except Christmas and New Year) 70.00/100.00 **st.**

BURBAGE Wilts. **403 404** O 29 – see Marlborough.

BURFORD Oxon. **403 404** P 28 – pop. 1 371 – ECD : Wednesday – ☎ 0993.

🏌 ℰ 822149, S : ½ m. on A 361.
🏢 The Brewery, Sheep St., OX18 4LP ℰ 823558.

◆London 76 – ◆Birmingham 55 – Gloucester 32 – ◆Oxford 20.

  🏛 **Bay Tree,** 12-14 Sheep St., OX18 4LW, ℰ 822791, Fax 823008, « 16C house, antique furnishings », ⚞ – 📺 ☎ ℗, ◪ AE ◑ VISA
  M (see below) – **20 rm** ⊔ 70.00/105.00 **t.**, 2 suites – SB 125.00/210.00 **st.**

  🏛 **Golden Pheasant,** 91 High St., OX18 4QA, ℰ 823223, Fax 822621 – ⚔ rest 📺 ☎ ℗, ◪
  AE VISA
  M a la carte 11.60/19.00 **t.** ⓘ 4.50 – **12 rm** ⊔ 48.00/85.00 **t.** – SB (except Bank Holidays) 98.00/134.00 **st.**

  🏠 **Lamb Inn,** Sheep St., OX18 4LR, ℰ 823155, Fax 822228, « Part 14C inn, antique furnishings », ⚞ – ⚔ rest 📺, ◪ VISA
  closed 25 and 26 December – **M** (bar lunch Monday to Saturday)/dinner 18.50 **t.** ⓘ 4.50 – **15 rm** ⊔ 35.00/80.00 **t.** – SB (except Easter and Christmas) 100.00/110.00 **t.**

  🏠 **Andrews** without rest., 99 High St., OX18 4QA, ℰ 823151, Fax 823240, ⚞ – 📺, ◪ ◑
  VISA, ⚘
  closed 25 and 26 December – **9 rm** ⊔ 45.00/80.00 **t.**

  🏠 **Inn For All Seasons,** The Barringtons, OX18 4TN, W : 3 ¼ m. on A 40 ℰ 0451 (Cotswold) 844324, Fax 844375, ⚞ – 📺 ☎ ℗, ◪ AE VISA, ⚘
  M 15.75 **st.** (dinner) and a la carte 10.75/17.50 **st.** ⓘ 4.25 – **9 rm** ⊔ 45.00/70.00 **st.** – SB 80.00/120.00 **st.**

  ✕✕ **Bay Tree,** 12-14 Sheep St., OX18 4LW, ℰ 822791, Fax 823008, ⚞ – ⚔ ℗, ◪ AE ◑ VISA
  M 9.95/19.95 **t.** and a la carte ⓘ 4.95.

  at Fulbrook NE : ¾ m. on A 361 – ✉ ☎ 0993 Burford :

  ↰ **Elm Farm House** ⤳, Meadow Lane, OX18 4BW, ℰ 823611, Fax 873937, ⚞ – ⚔ 📺 ☎
  ℗, ◪ VISA, ⚘
  closed 20 December-20 January – **M** 15.00 **st.** – **7 rm** ⊔ 29.50/55.00 **st.** – SB (October-March) 65.00/99.00 **st.**

BURLAND Ches. – see Nantwich.

BURLEY Hants. **403 404** O 31 *Great Britain G.* – pop. 1 492 – ECD : Wednesday – ✉ Ringwood – ☎ 042 53 (4 fig.) and 0425 (6 fig.).

Envir. : New Forest★★ (Rhinefield Ornamental Drive★★, Bolderwood Ornamental Drive★★).

🏌 Burley, Ringwood ℰ 402431.

◆London 102 – Bournemouth 17 – ◆Southampton 17 – Winchester 30.

  🏛 **Burley Manor,** Ringwood Rd, BH24 4BS, ℰ 403522, Fax 403227, ⤬ heated, ⚞ – 📺 ☎
  ℗ – 🖋 80, ◪ AE ◑ VISA
  M *(closed Saturday lunch)* 16.50/25.00 **t.** and dinner a la carte ⓘ 5.25 – **30 rm** ⊔ 49.95/89.90 **t.**

  🏠 **Toad Hall,** The Cross, BH24 4AB, ℰ 403448, Fax 402505 – 📺 ☎ ℗, ◪ AE ◑ VISA
  M *(closed Sunday dinner and Monday to non-residents)* 10.95/15.45 **t.** and dinner a la carte ⓘ 4.95 – **8 rm** ⊔ 35.00/65.00 – SB 85.00/105.00 **st.**

BURNHAM Bucks. **404** S 29 – pop. 11 199 – ECD : Thursday – ☎ 0628.

◆London 33 – ◆Oxford 37 – Reading 17.

  🏛🏛 **Burnham Beeches Moat House** (Q.M.H.) ⤳, Grove Rd, SL1 8DP, NW : 1 m. by Britwell Rd ℰ 603333, Fax 603994, ℔, ≘, ◪, ⚞, park, ✕ – ⫿ ⚔ rm 📺 ☎ 🕭 ℗ – 🖋 180, ◪ AE ◑ VISA
  closed 25 to 29 December – **M** *(closed Saturday lunch)* 16.00/19.00 **t.** and a la carte – **73 rm** ⊔ 49.50/110.00 **t.**, 2 suites – SB (August and weekends only) 110.00 **st.**

BURNHAM MARKET Norfolk **404** W 25 *Great Britain G.* – pop. 943 – ☎ 0328 Fakenham.

Envir. : Holkham Hall★★ *AC*, E : 3 m. by B 1155.

◆London 128 – ◆Cambridge 71 – ◆Norwich 36.

  🏠 **Hoste Arms,** The Green, PE31 8HD, ℰ 738257, Fax 730103, ⚞ – ⚔ rest 📺 ☎ ℗, ◪
  VISA
  M (bar lunch)/dinner a la carte 10.00/15.25 **t.** ⓘ 3.25 – **12 rm** ⊔ 32.00/76.00 **t.** – SB (except Bank Holidays) (weekdays only) 82.00/86.00 **st.**

BURNHAM-ON-CROUCH Essex 404 W 29 – pop. 6 268 – ECD : Wednesday – ✆ 0621 Maldon.

◆London 52 – Chelmsford 19 – Colchester 32 – Southend-on-Sea 25.

- XX **Contented Sole**, 80 High St., CM0 8AA, ℰ 782139. ☒ ☒
  closed Sunday dinner, Monday, 4 weeks January and last 2 weeks July – **M** 11.00/16.50 **t.** and a la carte § 5.00.

BURNLEY Lancs. 402 N 22 – pop. 76 365 – ✆ 0282.

☖ Towneley, Towneley Park, Todmorden Rd ℰ 51636, E : 1½ m. – ☖ Glen View ℰ 21045.

🛈 Burnley Mechanics, Manchester Rd, BB11 1JA ℰ 455485.

◆London 236 – Bradford 32 – ◆Leeds 37 – ◆Liverpool 55 – ◆Manchester 25 – ◆Middlesbrough 104 – Preston 22 – ◆Sheffield 68.

- 🏨 **Oaks**, Colne Rd, Reedley, BB10 2LF, NE : 2½ m. on A 56 ℰ 414141, Fax 33401, ₤₅, ≘s, ⬛, ☞ – ⬚ rm ⊡ ☎ ℗ – 🕭 120. ☒ ☒ ⑩ ☒
  M *(closed Saturday lunch)* (bar lunch)/dinner 18.00 **st.** and a la carte § 6.45 – **58 rm** ⊂ 69.00/88.00 **st.** – SB (except Bank Holidays) 98.00/118.00 **st.**

- 🏠 **Rosehill House**, Rosehill Av., Manchester Rd, BB11 2PW, ℰ 453931, Fax 455628, ☞ – ⊡ ☎ ℗. ☒ ☒ ⑩ ☒
  M (lunch by arrangement)/dinner 12.50 **t.** and a la carte § 4.50 – **20 rm** ⊂ 29.50/56.00 **t.**

- 🏠 **Forte Travelodge** without rest., Cavalry Barracks, Barracks Rd, BB11 4AS, W : ½ m. at junction of A 671 and A 679 ℰ 416039, Reservations (Freephone) 0800 850950 – ⊡ & ⬚ st. ☒ ☒ ⬚ st.
  32 rm 31.95 **t.**

🛈 ATS Healey Wood Rd ℰ 22409/38423/51624

La guida cambia, cambiate la guida ogni anno.

BURNOPFIELD Durham 401 402 O 19 – ✆ 0207.

☖ Beamish Park, Beamish, Stanley ℰ 091 (Newcastle upon Tyne) 370 1133, SE : 5 m. – ☖ Hobson Municipal, Hobson ℰ 71605, by A 692.

◆London 287 – ◆Middlesbrough 48 – ◆Newcastle upon Tyne 13.

- 🏠 **Burnbrae**, Leazes Villas, NE16 6HN, ℰ 70432, ☞ – ⬚ ⊡ ℗. ☒ ☒ ⬚ st.
  M 12.50 – **6 rm** ⊂ 22.00/40.00 **st.**

BURNSALL N. Yorks. 402 O 21 – pop. 116 – ECD : Monday and Thursday – ✉ Skipton – ✆ 0756.

◆London 223 – Bradford 26 – ◆Leeds 29.

- 🏠 **Red Lion**, BD23 6BU, ℰ 720204, Fax 720204 – ⊡ ℗. ☒ ☒ ⬚ st.
  M (bar lunch Monday to Saturday)/dinner 19.00 **t.** § 4.40 – **11 rm** ⊂ 32.00/64.00 **t.** – SB (November-Easter) (weekdays only) 85.00/99.00 **st.**

BURPHAM W. Sussex 404 S 30 – see Arundel.

BURRINGTON Devon 403 I 31 – pop. 482 – ECD : Saturday – ✆ 0769 High Bickington.

◆London 260 – Barnstaple 14 – Exeter 28 – Taunton 50.

- 🏨 **Northcote Manor** (Best Western) ⮑, EX37 9LZ, NW : 1½ m. by Barnstaple rd ℰ 60501, Fax 60770, ⬚, ⬛, park, ⮑ – ⬚ rest ⊡ ☎ ℗. ☒ ☒ ⑩ ☒ ☒
  March-October – **M** (booking essential) (dinner only) 20.00 **t.** § 4.80 – **11 rm** ⊂ 51.00/104.00 **t.** – SB 118.00/128.00 **st.**

BURSTALL Suffolk – see Ipswich.

BURTON-UPON-TRENT Staffs. 402 403 404 O 25 – pop. 59 040 – ECD : Wednesday – ✆ 0283.

☖ Branston, Burton Rd ℰ 43207, S : ½ m. by A 38 – ☖, ☖ Craythorne Road, Stretton ℰ 64329, N : 1½ m.

🛈 Unit 40, Octagon Centre, New St., DE14 3TN ℰ 516609.

◆London 128 – ◆Birmingham 29 – ◆Leicester 27 – ◆Nottingham 27 – Stafford 27.

- 🏨 Stanhope, Ashby Rd East, DE15 0PU, SE : 2½ m. on A 50 ℰ 217954, Fax 226199, ≘s – ⊡ ☎ ℗ – 🕭 150. ☒
  29 rm.

- 🏨 **Queens**, 2-5 Bridge St., DE14 1SY, ℰ 64993, Fax 517556 – ⊡ ☎ ℗ – 🕭 80. ☒ ☒ ☒ ☒
  M (bar lunch Saturday) 9.95 **t.** (lunch) and a la carte 10.65/18.85 **t.** § 3.90 – **24 rm** ⊂ 59.50/69.50 **st.**, 3 suites.

at Stretton N : 3½ m. by A 50 off A 5121 – ✉ ✆ 0283 Burton-upon-Trent :

- XXX **Dovecliff Hall** ⮑ with rm, Dovecliff Rd, DE13 0DJ, ℰ 31818, Fax 516546, ⬚, « Carefully restored Georgian house », ☞, park – ⊡ ☎ ℗. ☒ ☒ ⬚ st.
  closed 1 week January and 2 weeks summer – **M** *(closed Saturday lunch, Sunday dinner and Bank Holidays)* 10.50/19.50 **t.** and dinner a la carte § 8.50 – **7 rm** ⊂ 55.00/95.00 **t.** – SB (weekends only) 103.00/147.00 **st.**

at Rolleston-on-Dove N : 3 ¾ m. by A 50 on Rolleston Rd – ⊠ ☺ 0283 Burton-upon-Trent :

🏨 **Brookhouse Inn,** Brookside, DE13 9AA, ℰ 814188, Fax 813644, « Part 17C house, antiques », ☞ – 🖵 ☎ 🅿. ↖ 🆎 ⓪ 𝗩𝗜𝗦𝗔 ⚘
M *(closed Saturday lunch and Sunday dinner)* 9.25 **st.** (lunch) and a la carte 16.00/31.00 **st.**
🛢 4.50 – **19 rm** ⊆ 65.00/85.00 **st.** – SB (weekends only) 72.00/86.00 **st.**

at Newton Solney NE : 3 m. by A 50 on B 5008 – ⊠ ☺ 0283 Burton-upon-Trent :

🏨 **Newton Park** (Jarvis), DE15 0SS, ℰ 703568, Fax 703214, ☞ – 🛗 ⥼ rm 🖵 ☎ ☉ 🅿 –
🏧 100. ↖ 🆎 𝗩𝗜𝗦𝗔
closed 27 to 30 December – **M** *(closed Saturday lunch)* 11.50/27.50 **t.** 🛢 7.85 – ⊆ 8.00 –
51 rm 85.00/95.00 **t.** – SB (weekends only) 76.00/80.00 **st.**

at Branston SW : 1 ½ m. on A 5121 – ⊠ ☺ 0283 Burton-upon-Trent :

🏨 **Riverside** ⤋, Riverside Drive, off Warren Lane, DE14 3EP, ℰ 511234, Fax 511441, ⅂ₐ,
☞ – 🖵 ☎ 🅿 – 🏧 150. ↖ 🆎 𝗩𝗜𝗦𝗔
M *(closed Saturday lunch)* 11.75/15.95 **t.** and a la carte 🛢 4.95 – **22 rm** ⊆ 55.00/65.00 **t.** –
SB (weekends only) 86.90/93.90 **st.**

✗✗ **Old Vicarage,** 2 Main St., DE14 3EX, ℰ 33222 – 🅿. ↖ 🆎 𝗩𝗜𝗦𝗔
closed Sunday dinner, first 2 weeks August and 27 to 31 December – **M** 12.00/19.95 **st.**
🛢 5.00.

at Barton-under-Needwood SW : 5 m. by A 5121 on A 38 – ⊠ ☺ 0283 Burton-upon-Trent :

🏠 **Forte Travelodge** without rest., Lichfield Rd, DE13 0ED, on A 38 (northbound carriageway) ℰ 716343, Reservations (Freephone) 0800 850950 – 🖵 ☒ 🅿. ↖ 🆎 𝗩𝗜𝗦𝗔 ⚘
20 rm 31.95 **t.**

🏠 **Forte Travelodge** without rest., DE13 8EJ, on A 38 (southbound carriageway) ℰ 716784, Reservations (Freephone) 0800 850950 – 🖵 ☒ 🅿. ↖ 🆎 𝗩𝗜𝗦𝗔 ⚘
40 rm 31.95 **t.**

◍ ATS All Saints Rd ℰ 65994/63170

BURTONWOOD SERVICE AREA Ches. 402 M 23 – ⊠ ☺ 0925 Warrington

🏠 **Forte Travelodge** without rest., WA5 3AY, M 62 (westbound carriageway) ℰ 710376, Reservations (Freephone) 0800 850950 – 🖵 ☒ 🅿. ↖ 🆎 𝗩𝗜𝗦𝗔 ⚘
40 rm 31.95 **t.**

BURY Gtr. Manchester 402 N 23 403 ② 404 N 23 – pop. 61 785 – ECD : Tuesday – ☺ 061 Manchester.

⅂ₐ Unsworth Hall, Blackford Bridge ℰ 766 4897 – ⅂₉ Lowes Park, Hill Top, Walmersley ℰ 764 1231, NE : 2 m. by A 56.

🖪 Derby Hall, Market St., BL9 0BN ℰ 705 5111.

◆London 211 – ◆Leeds 45 – ◆Liverpool 35 – ◆Manchester 9.

🏨 **Normandie** ⤋, Elbut Lane, Birtle, BL9 6UT, NE : 3 m. by B 6222 ℰ 764 1170, Fax 764 4866, ⤋ – 🛗 ⥼ rm 🖵 ☎ 🅿. ↖ 🆎 𝗩𝗜𝗦𝗔 ⚘
closed 26 December-9 January, 30 March-5 April and Bank Holidays – **M** (see below) –
⊆ 6.95 – **23 rm** 49.00/79.00 **t.**

✗✗✗ **Normandie,** Elbut Lane, Birtle, BL9 6UT, NE : 3 m. by B 6222 ℰ 764 1170, Fax 764 4866 –
🅿. ↖ 🆎 ⓪ 𝗩𝗜𝗦𝗔
closed 26 December-9 January, 30 March-5 April and Bank Holidays – **M** - **French** (closed Monday and Saturday lunch and Sunday) (booking essential) 15.00/18.95 **t.** and a la carte
🛢 6.10.

✗ **Est, Est, Est!,** 703 Manchester Rd, BL9 9SS, ℰ 766 4869 – 🗐 🅿. ↖ 🆎 𝗩𝗜𝗦𝗔
closed Saturday and Sunday lunch, 25-26 December and 1 January – **M** - **Italian** 12.95 **t.** and a la carte 🛢 4.75.

at Walmersley N : 1 ¾ m. on A 56 – ⊠ Walmersley – ☺ 0706 Ramsbottom :

🏠 **Red Hall,** Manchester rd, BL9 5NA, N : 1 ¼ m. on A 56 ℰ 822476, Fax 828086 – ⥼ rest
🖵 ☎ 🅿. ↖ 🆎 ⓪ 𝗩𝗜𝗦𝗔 ⚘
closed 23 December-2 January – **M** *(closed lunch Monday and Saturday)* 9.50/11.50 **t.** and a la carte 🛢 5.00 – **20 rm** ⊆ 36.00/62.00 **t.**

◍ ATS John St. ℰ 764 2830/6860

BURY ST. EDMUNDS Suffolk 404 W 27 Great Britain G. – pop. 30 563 – ECD : Thursday – ☺ 0284.

See : Town★ - Abbey and Cathedral★★.

Envir. : Ickworth House★ *AC*, SW : 3 m. by A 143.

⅂ₐ Fornham Park, St. John's Hill Plantation, The Street ℰ 706777, NW : 2 m. off A 1101.

🖪 6 Angel Hill, IP33 1UZ ℰ 764667.

◆London 79 – ◆Cambridge 27 – ◆Ipswich 26 – ◆Norwich 41.

🏨 **Angel,** 3 Angel Hill, IP33 1LT, ℰ 753926, Fax 750092 – ⊱∞ rest 📺 ☎ ℗ – 🅰 140. ⚠ AE
⓪ VISA
  M 13.95/19.75 **st.** and a la carte 🍴 4.25 – ⊒ 2.50 – **41 rm** 65.00/115.00 **st.**, 1 suite – SB
(except Christmas) (weekends only) 118.00/138.00 **st.**

🏨 **Butterfly,** Symonds Rd, IP32 7BW, SE : 1½ m. by A 1302 and A 134 at junction with A 45
  ℰ 760884, Fax 755476 – 📺 ☎ ℗ – 🅰 40. ⚠ AE ⓪ VISA
  M 8.75/11.50 **st.** and a la carte 🍴 4.50 – ⊒ 6.00 – **65 rm** 39.00/49.00 **st.** – SB (weekends
only) 75.00/113.00 **st.**

🏨 **Suffolk** (Forte), 38 The Buttermarket, IP33 1DL, ℰ 753995, Fax 750973 – ⊱∞ 📺 ☎ ⇔ ℗
  – 🅰 25. ⚠ AE ⓪ VISA JCB
  M (bar lunch Monday to Saturday)/dinner 17.95 **t.** and a la carte 🍴 5.95 – ⊒ 9.00 – **33 rm**
65.00/75.00 **t.** – SB (except Christmas and New Year) 86.00/120.00 **st.**

🏨 **Ounce House,** 13 Northgate St., IP33 1HP, ℰ 761779, Fax 768315, ☞ – ⊱∞ 📺 ☎ ℗. ⚠
  VISA
  M (by arrangement) (communal dining) 22.00 **st.** 🍴 3.50 – **3 rm** ⊒ 35.00/70.00 **st.**

🏠 **Olde White Hart** without rest., 35 Southgate St., IP33 2AZ, ℰ 755547, Fax 724770 – ⊱∞
  📺 ☎ ℗. ⚠ AE VISA. ✼
  10 rm ⊒ 35.00/59.50 **st.**

🍴 **Mortimer's,** 31 Churchgate St., IP33 1RG, ℰ 760623, Fax 752561. ⚠ AE ⓪ VISA
  closed 2 weeks August-September, 24 December-6 January and Bank Holidays – **M** –
  Seafood (closed Saturday lunch, Sunday and Bank Holiday Monday and Tuesday) a la
  carte 13.85/23.20 **t.** 🍴 5.20.

  at Rougham Green SE : 4 m. by A 1302 and A 134 off A 45 – ✉ Bury St. Edmunds –
  ✆ 0359 Beyton :

🏨 **Ravenwood Hall,** IP30 9JA, ℰ 70345, Fax 70788, ⤴ heated, ☞, park, ✼ – 📺 ☎ ℗ –
  🅰 120. ⚠ AE ⓪ VISA
  M 16.95 **t.** and a la carte – **14 rm** ⊒ 59.00/97.00 **t.** – SB 110.90/187.90 **t.**

  at Bradfield Combust SE : 4½ m. on A 134 – ✉ ✆ 0284 Bury St. Edmunds :

🍴🍴 **Bradfield House** with rm, Sudbury Rd, IP30 0LR, ℰ 386301, Fax 386301, ☞ – 📺 ☎ ℗.
  ⚠ VISA ✼
  closed 1 week Christmas-New Year – **M** *(closed Sunday)* (dinner only) 16.50 **st.** and a la
  carte 🍴 4.00 – **4 rm** ⊒ 50.00/85.00 **st.** – SB 100.00/113.00 **st.**

🛆 ATS Unit 1 and 3, Ailwin Rd, Moreton Hall Ind. Est. ℰ 705610

BUTTERMERE Cumbria 402 K 20 – pop. 194 – ✉ Cockermouth – ✆ 076 87.

◆London 306 – ◆Carlisle 35 – Kendal 43.

🏠 **Bridge,** CA13 9UZ, ℰ 70252, Fax 70252, ⇐ – ⊱∞ rest ☎ ℗. ⚠ VISA. ✼
  M (bar lunch)/dinner 16.50 **t.** and a la carte 🍴 4.90 – **22 rm** ⊒ 46.50/99.00 **t.** – SB (except
Bank Holidays) (weekdays only) 70.00/85.00 **st.**

  at Brackenthwaite Fell NW : 4 m. on B 5289 – ✉ ✆ 0900 Cockermouth :

🏠 **Pickett Howe** ⤴, CA13 9UY, ℰ 85444, ⇐, « Part 17C longhouse », ☞ – ⊱∞ 📺 ☎ ℗.
  ⚠ VISA. ✼
  April-mid November – **M** (residents only) (communal dining) (dinner only) 18.00 **st.** 🍴 3.55 –
  4 rm ⊒ 60.00/68.00 **st.**

BUXTON Derbs. 402 403 404 O 24 – pop. 19 502 – ECD : Wednesday – ✆ 0298.

🏌 Buxton and High Peak, Townend ℰ 23453, NE : by A 6.

🎫 The Cresent, SK17 6BQ ℰ 25106.

◆London 172 – Derby 38 – ◆Manchester 25 – ◆Stoke-on-Trent 24.

🏨 **Lee Wood** (Best Western), 13 Manchester Rd, SK17 6TQ, on A 5004 ℰ 23002, Fax 23228,
  ☞ – 🛏 ✼ – rm 📺 ☎ ℗ – 🅰 100. ⚠ AE ⓪ VISA. ✼
  M 10.75/17.95 **t.** and a la carte 🍴 4.50 – **36 rm** ⊒ 64.00/84.00 **t.** – SB 92.00/128.00 **st.**

🏠 **Brookfield Hall** ⤸, Long Hill, SK17 6SU, NW : 1¾ m. on A 5004 ℰ 24151, Fax 24151, ⇐,
  « Victorian country house », ☞ – 📺 ☎ ℗. ⚠ VISA. ✼
  M (dinner only and Sunday lunch) 13.50/17.50 **t.** and a la carte 🍴 4.00 – **6 rm** ⊒ 47.50/
70.00 **t.**

🏠 **Coningsby,** 6 Macclesfield Rd, SK17 9AH, ℰ 26735, ☞ – ⊱∞ 📺 ℗. ✼
  closed December and January – **M** (communal dining) 12.50 **s.** 🍴 3.75 – **3 rm** ⊒ 30.00/
40.00 **s.**

🏠 **Hartington,** 18 Broad Walk, SK17 6JR, ℰ 22638 – ⊱∞ rest 📺 🅶. ⚠ AE VISA ✼
  closed 6 to 16 July and Christmas-New Year – **M** (by arrangement) 9.90 **t.** 🍴 3.20 – **17 rm**
⊒ 20.00/52.00 **t.** – SB 50.00/90.00 **st.**

🛆 ATS Staden Lane, off Ashbourne Rd ℰ 25608/25655

During the season, particularly in resorts, it is wise to book in advance.

CADNAM Hants. [403] [404] P 31 – pop. 1 882 – ECD : Wednesday – ☏ 0703 Southampton.

♦London 91 – Salisbury 16 – ♦Southampton 8 – Winchester 19.

- 🏠 **Walnut Cottage** without rest., Old Romsey Rd, SO4 2NP, off A 31 ☎ 812275, 🌳 – [TV] [P]. 🐕
  closed 24 to 26 December – **3 rm** ☕ 25.00/42.00 **s.**

CALCOT Glos. – see Tetbury.

CALDBECK Cumbria [401] [402] K 19 – pop. 606 – ✉ Wigton – ☏ 069 74.

♦London 308 – ♦Carlisle 13 – Keswick 16 – Workington 23.

- 🏠 **Parkend** 🐦, Park End, CA7 8HH, SW : 1 ½ m. on B 5299 ☎ 78494, « Converted 17C farmhouse », 🌳 – 🚭 rest [TV] [P]. [CB] [AE] [DC] [VISA]
  closed 9 January-1 February – **M** 14.95 **t.** 🍷 3.95 – **3 rm** ☕ 30.00/45.00 **t.**

CALLINGTON Cornwall [403] H 32 The West Country G. – pop. 2 579 – ECD : Wednesday – ☏ 0579 Liskeard.

Exc. : Launceston★ - Castle★ (≤★) St. Mary Magdalene★, South Gate★, N : 11 ½ m. by A 388.

♦London 252 – Exeter 51 – Penzance 67 – ♦Plymouth 14.

- 🍺 **Coachmakers Arms,** Newport Sq., PL17 7AS, ☎ 82567 – [TV] [P]. [CB] [DC] [VISA]. 🐕
  closed 22 to 27 December – **M** a la carte 10.50/13.75 **st.** 🍷 3.00 – **4 rm** ☕ 25.00/38.00 **st.**

CALNE Wilts. [403] [404] O 29 The West Country G. – pop. 10 235 – ECD : Wednesday – ☏ 0249.

Envir. : Bowood House★ *AC*, (Library ≤★) SW : 2 m. by A 4 – Avebury★★ (The Stones★, Church★) E : 6 m. by A 4.

⛳18 Bowood G. & C.C., Derry Hill ☎ 822228.

♦London 91 – ♦Bristol 33 – Swindon 17.

- 🏨 **Chilvester Hill House,** SN11 OLP, W : ¾ m. by A 4 on Bremhill rd ☎ 813981, Fax 814217, 🏊 heated, 🌳 – 🚭 rest [TV] [P]. [CB] [AE] [DC] [VISA]. 🐕
  M (booking essential) (residents only) (communal dining) (dinner only) 22.00 **st.** 🍷 4.35 – **3 rm** ☕ 50.00/75.00 **st.**

🔧 ATS Unit 4, Maundrell Rd., Portmarsh Ind. Est. ☎ 821622

CALSTOCK Cornwall [403] H 32 The West Country G. – pop. 4 079 – ✉ – ☏ 0822 Tavistock.

Envir. : Tamar River★★ – Cotehele★ *AC*, SW : 1 m. - Morwellham★ *AC*, NE : 1 ½ m.

♦London 246 – Exeter 48 – ♦Plymouth 22.

- 🏨 **Danescombe Valley** 🐦, Lower Kelly, PL18 9RY, W : ½ m. ☎ 832414, Fax 832414, ≤ Viaduct and Tamar Valley, « Country house atmosphere » – 🚭 rest [P]. [CB] [AE] [DC] [VISA]. 🐕
  closed Wednesday, Thursday and November to March except Christmas – **Meals** (dinner only) 30.00 **st.** 🍷 3.85 – **5 rm** ☕ 72.50/125.00 **st.**

CAMBERLEY Surrey [404] R 29 – pop. 45 108 – ECD : Wednesday – ☏ 0276.

♦London 40 – Reading 13 – ♦Southampton 48.

- 🏨 **Frimley Hall** (Forte) 🐦, Lime Av. via Conifer Drive, GU15 2BG, E : ¾ m. off Portsmouth Rd (A 325) ☎ 28321, Fax 691253, 🌳 – 🚭 rm [TV] ☎ [P] – 🎤 65. [CB] [AE] [DC] [VISA] [JCB]
  M 15.75/21.75 **st.** and a la carte 🍷 6.05 – ☕ 8.95 – **66 rm** 95.00/110.00 **st.** – SB (weekends only) 108.00 **st.**

CAMBRIDGE Cambs. [404] U 27 Great Britain G. – pop. 87 111 – ECD : Thursday – ☏ 0223.

See : Town★★★ – St. John's College★★★ *AC* Y – King's College★★ (King's College Chapel★★★) Z The Backs★★ YZ – Fitzwilliam Museum★★ Z **M1** – Trinity College★★ Y – Clare College★ Z **B** – Kettle's Yard★ Y **M2** – Queen's College★ *AC* Z.

⛳18 Cambridgeshire Moat House Hotel, Bar Hill ☎ 0954 (Bar Hill) 780555, NW : 5 ½ m. by A 1307 X.

✈ Cambridge Airport : ☎ 61133, Fax 321032, E : 2 m. on A 1303 X.

[i] Wheeler St., CB2 3QB ☎ 322640.

♦London 55 – ♦Coventry 88 – ♦Kingston-upon-Hull 137 – ♦Ipswich 54 – ♦Leicester 74 – ♦Norwich 61 – ♦Nottingham 88 – ♦Oxford 100.

Plan on next page

- 🏨 **Garden House** (Q.M.H.), Granta Pl., off Mill Lane, CB2 1RT, ☎ 63421, Fax 316605, ≤, 🌳 – [lift] 🚭 rm [TV] ☎ [P] – 🎤 250. [CB] [AE] [DC] [VISA]. 🐕 — Z **n**
  M 18.95/22.50 **t.** and a la carte – ☕ 7.50 – **118 rm** 90.00/170.00 **t.**
- 🏨 **University Arms** (De Vere), Regent St., CB2 1AD, ☎ 351241, Fax 315256 – [lift] 🚭 rm [TV] ☎ ♿ [P] – 🎤 200. [CB] [AE] [DC] [VISA] — Z **e**
  M (light lunch Saturday) 11.00/16.00 **st.** and a la carte 🍷 5.00 – **114 rm** ☕ 81.00/110.00 **st.**, 1 suite – SB 110.00/120.00 **st.**
- 🏨 **Holiday Inn,** Downing St., CB2 3DT, ☎ 464466, Fax 464440, 🏊 – [lift] 🚭 rm ▤ [TV] ☎ ♿ [P] – 🎤 150. [CB] [AE] [DC] [VISA] [JCB]. 🐕 — Z **a**
  M 12.95/18.50 **st.** and a la carte 🍷 6.95 – ☕ 10.50 – **197 rm** 95.00/120.00 **t.**, 2 suites – SB (July, August, December and weekends only) 96.00 **st.**

CAMBRIDGE

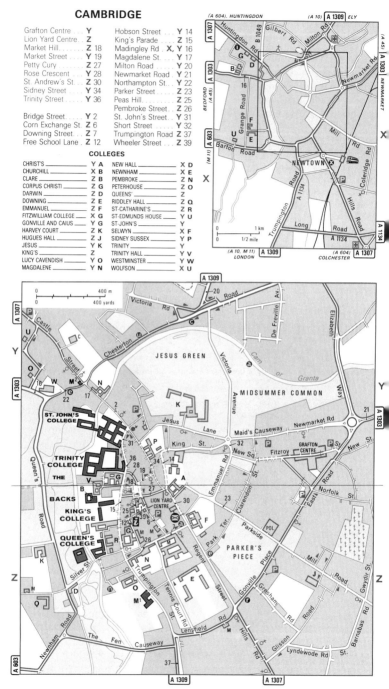

🏨 **Arundel House,** 53 Chesterton Rd, CB4 3AN, ℰ 67701, Fax 67721 – ▤ rest 📺 ☎ 🄿 –
🔼 35. 🔼 🄰🄴 🄾 𝗩𝗜𝗦𝗔
closed 25 and 26 December – **M** 9.75/13.95 **t.** and a la carte ⅄ 3.95 – � 2.25 – **105 rm**
28.00/75.00 **t.** – SB (weekends only) 82.50/103.00 **st.**

🏨 **Gonville,** Gonville Pl., CB1 1LY, ℰ 66611, Fax 315470 – ▤ ▤ rest 📺 ☎ 🄿 – 🔼 200. 🔼 🄰🄴
🄾 𝗩𝗜𝗦𝗔
M 12.50/14.50 **t.** and a la carte ⅄ 5.00 – **64 rm** ⊠ 68.00/85.00 **t.** – SB 90.00/119.00 **st.**

🏨 **Centennial,** 63-71 Hills Rd, CB2 1PG, ℰ 314652, Fax 315443 – ⇥x⇤ rm 📺 ☎ 🄿. 🔼 🄰🄴 🄾
𝗩𝗜𝗦𝗔 ✺
closed 23 December-2 January – **M** (lunch by arrangement) 15.00/17.00 **t.** and a la carte
⅄ 4.00 – **39 rm** ⊠ 55.00/75.00 **t.** – SB (mid October-mid March) (weekends only) 80.00/
140.00 **st.**

🏨 **Cambridge Lodge,** 139 Huntingdon Rd, CB3 0DQ, ℰ 352833, Fax 355166, ⨶ – 📺 ☎ 🄿.
🔼 🄰🄴 🄾 𝗩𝗜𝗦𝗔
M *(closed Saturday lunch)* 14.95/19.95 **t.** and a la carte ⅄ 4.25 – **11 rm** ⊠ 60.00/65.00 **st.**

🍴🍴 **Midsummer House,** Midsummer Common, CB4 1HA, ℰ 69299, ⨶ – 🔼 🄰🄴 🄾 𝗩𝗜𝗦𝗔
closed Saturday lunch, Sunday dinner and Monday – **M** 13.95/38.00 **st.** ⅄ 5.50.

🍴🍴 **22 Chesterton Road,** 22 Chesterton Rd, CB4 3AX, ℰ 351880 – 🔼 🄴
closed Sunday, Monday and 1 week Christmas – **M** (dinner only) 23.00 **t.**

🍴 **Michel's Brasserie,** 21-24 Northampton St., CB3 0AD, ℰ 353110 – 🔼 🄰🄴 🄾 𝗩𝗜𝗦𝗔
M 14.95 **t.** and a la carte.

at Impington N : 2 m. on B 1049 at junction with A 45 – X – ⊠ ✪ 0223 Cambridge :

🏨 **Forte Posthouse,** Lakeview, Bridge Rd, CB4 4PH, ℰ 237000, Fax 233426, 🛌, ⇌, 🔽, ⨶
– ⇥x⇤ rm 📺 ☎ 🄿 – 🔼 60. 🔼 🄰🄴 🄾 𝗩𝗜𝗦𝗔
M a la carte approx. 17.50 ⅄ 4.65 – ⊠ 6.95 – **118 rm** 53.50/69.50 **st.** – SB (weekends only)
90.00 **st.**

at Fowlmere S : 8 ¾ m. by A 1309 – X – and A 10 on B 1368 – ⊠ Royston (Herts.) –
✪ 0763 Fowlmere :

🍴🍴 **Chequers,** High St., SG8 7SR, ℰ 208369 – 🄿. 🔼 🄰🄴 🄾 𝗩𝗜𝗦𝗔
closed Christmas Day – **M** 14.25 **t.** (lunch) and dinner a la carte 15.50/25.60 **t.** ⅄ 3.60.

🍴 **Maguire's,** High St., SG8 7SR, ℰ 208444 – 🄿. 🔼 🄰🄴 🄾
closed Sunday dinner and 25-26 December – **M** 16.50/19.75 **t.** and a la carte ⅄ 4.65.

at Duxford S : 9 ½ m. by A 1309– X – A 1301 and A 505 on B 1379 – ⊠ ✪ 0223
Cambridge :

🏨 **Duxford Lodge,** Ickleton Rd, CB2 4RU, ℰ 836444, Fax 832271, ⨶ – 📺 ☎ 🄿 – 🔼 30. 🔼
🄰🄴 🄾 𝗩𝗜𝗦𝗔
closed 27 to 30 December – **M** *(closed Saturday lunch)* 13.00 **st.** and a la carte ⅄ 4.25 –
15 rm ⊠ 58.50/87.50 **st.** – SB (weekends only) 95.50/98.00 **st.**

at Bar Hill NW : 5 ½ m. by A 1307 – X – off A 604 – ⊠ Bar Hill – ✪ 0954 Crafts Hill :

🏨 **Cambridgeshire Moat House** *(C.M.H.)*, CB3 8EU, ℰ 780555, Telex 817141,
Fax 780010, 🛌, ⇌, 🔽, 🛌, ⨶, ✎, squash – 📺 ☎ 🄿 – 🔼 180. 🔼 🄰🄴 🄾 𝗩𝗜𝗦𝗔
closed 25 and 26 December – **M** *(closed Saturday lunch)* 15.50/16.75 **st.** and a la carte
⅄ 5.50 – **99 rm** ⊠ 53.50/78.00 **st.** – SB 92.00/99.00 **st.**

at Lolworth Service Area NW : 6 m. by A 1307 – X – on A 604 – ⊠ Cambridge –
✪ 0954 Crafts Hill :

🏨 **Forte Travelodge** without rest., CB3 8DR, (northbound carriageway) ℰ 781335, Reservations (Freephone) 0800 850950 – 📺 ⅋ 🄿. 🔼 🄰🄴 𝗩𝗜𝗦𝗔. ✺
20 rm 31.95 **t.**

at Swavesey Service Area NW : 8 m. by A 1307 on A 604 – X – ⊠ Cambridge –
✪ 0954 Crafts Hill :

🏨 **Forte Travelodge** without rest., CB4 5QR, (southbound carriageway) ℰ 789113, Reservations (Freephone) 0800 850950 – 📺 🄿. 🔼 🄰🄴 𝗩𝗜𝗦𝗔. ✺
36 rm 31.95 **t.**

🔘 ATS 143 Histon Rd ℰ 61695

▭ **CANNINGTON** Somerset 🄰🄾🄳 K 30 – see Bridgewater.

▭ **CANNOCK** Staffs. 🄰🄾🄸 🄰🄾🄳 🄰🄾🄴 N 25 Great Britain G. – pop. 54 503 – ECD : Thursday – ✪ 0543.
Exc. : Weston Park★★ *AC*, W : 11 m. by A 5.
🏌 Cannock Park Municipal, Stafford Rd ℰ 578850, N : ½ m. on A 34.
◆London 135 – ◆Birmingham 20 – Derby 36 – ◆Leicester 51 – Shrewsbury 32 – ◆Stoke-on-Trent 28.

🏨 **Roman Way,** Watling St., Hatherton, WS11 1SH, SW : 1 ¼ m. by A 460 on A 5
ℰ 572121, Fax 502749 – ⇥x⇤ rm 📺 ☎ ⅋ 🄿 – 🔼 120. 🔼 🄰🄴 𝗩𝗜𝗦𝗔
M (bar lunch Saturday) 6.95 **st.** (lunch) and a la carte 11.85/21.95 **st.** ⅄ 5.25 – **56 rm**
⊠ 59.50 **t.** – SB (weekends only) 75.00/103.00 **st.**

🏨 **Travel Inn,** Watling St., WS11 1SJ, SW : 1 m. at junction of A 460 with A 5 ℘ 572721, Fax 466130 – ⇔ rm 📺 ٤ ٤. 🅿 🆎 ① 🆅🅸🆂🅰. ✇
M (Beefeater grill) a la carte approx. 16.00 **t.** – ☲ 4.95 – **38 rm** 33.50 **st.**

🔧 ATS Cannock Rd, Chadsmoor ℘ 574580/504985   ATS Cannock Rd, Heath Hayes ℘ 274200

CANON PYON Heref. and Worcs. 🔢 L 27 – see Hereford.

"Short Breaks"

Many hotels now offer a special rate for a stay of 2 nights which includes dinner, bed and breakfast.

CANTERBURY Kent 🔢 X 30 Great Britain G. – pop. 34 546 – ECD : Thursday – ☎ 0227.

See : City★★★ – Cathedral★★★ Y – St. Augustine's Abbey★★ *AC* YZ **K** – King's School★ Y **B** – Mercery Lane★ Y **12** – Christ Church Gate★ Y **A** – Weavers★ Y **D** – Hospital of St. Thomas the Martyr, Eastbridge★ Y **E** – Poor Priests Hospital★ *AC* Y **M1** – St. Martin's Church★ Y **N** – West Gate★ *AC* Y **R.**

🛈 34 St. Margaret's St., CT1 2TG ℘ 766567.

◆London 59 – ◆Brighton 76 – ◆Dover 15 – Maidstone 28 – Margate 17.

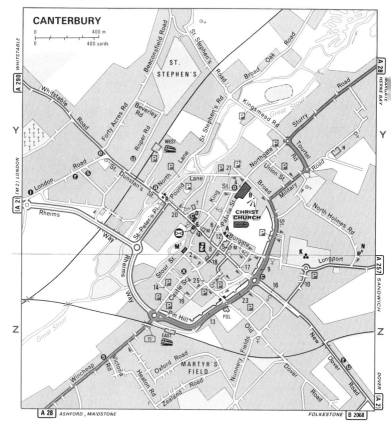

CANTERBURY

County, High St., CT1 2RX, ℘ 766266, Fax 451512 – |♦| TV ☎ ⇔ P – 🏛 180. EN AE ◑ VISA JCB. ✗ Y n
M (see **Sullys** below) – ☐ 8.50 – **72 rm** 69.00/93.00 **t.**, 1 suite.

Chaucer (Forte), 63 Ivy Lane, CT1 1TU, ℘ 464427, Fax 450397 – ⊁ TV ☎ P – 🏛 80. EN AE ◑ VISA JCB Z c
M (bar lunch Monday to Saturday)/dinner 18.95 **st.** and a la carte ⅰ 6.45 – ☐ 8.50 – **42 rm** 75.00/85.00 **st.** – SB 116.00/136.00 **st.**

Falstaff (Lansbury), 8-12 St. Dunstan's St., CT2 8AF, ℘ 462138, Fax 463525 – ⊁ rm TV ☎ P – 🏛 40. EN AE ◑ VISA Y a
M 9.95/13.95 **t.** and a la carte ⅰ 5.75 – **23 rm** ☐ 69.50/91.00 **t.** – SB (weekends only) 106.00/126.00 **st.**

Thanington without rest., 140 Wincheap, CT1 3RY, ℘ 453227, Fax 453225, ⊡, ⚘ – ⊁ TV ☎ P. EN AE ◑ VISA JCB Z s
10 rm ☐ 38.00/62.00 **t.**

Victoria (Chef & Brewer), 59 London Rd, CT2 8JY, ℘ 459333, Fax 781552 – TV ☎ P. EN AE VISA. ✗ Y i
M 15.00/20.00 **t.** and a la carte – **34 rm** ☐ 34.95/38.45 **t.**

Pilgrims, 15 The Friars, CT1 2AS, ℘ 464531, Fax 762514 – TV ☎. EN AE VISA Y c
M (carving lunch)/dinner a la carte 12.95/16.00 **t.** ⅰ 3.75 – **15 rm** ☐ 45.00/75.00 **t.** – SB 70.00/120.00 **st.**

Canterbury, 71 New Dover Rd, CT1 3DZ, ℘ 450551, Fax 780145 – |♦| TV ☎ P – 🏛 40. EN AE ◑ VISA Z u
closed January and February – **M** (lunch by arrangement)/dinner 11.50 **st.** and a la carte ⅰ 5.25 – **27 rm** ☐ 40.00/50.00 **st.** – SB 65.00/80.00 **t.**

Ebury, 65-67 New Dover Rd, CT1 3DX, ℘ 768433, Fax 459187, ⊡, ⚘ – ⊁ rest TV ☎ P. EN AE VISA. ✗ Z r
closed 15 December-15 January – **M** (dinner only) (light dinner Sunday) a la carte 10.80/13.20 **t.** ⅰ 5.20 – **15 rm** ☐ 41.00/62.00 **t.** – SB (except Sunday) 71.00/92.00 **st.**

Pointers, 1 London Rd, CT2 8LR, ℘ 456846, Fax 831131 – TV ☎ P. EN AE ◑ VISA JCB Y e
closed 23 December-15 January – **M** (dinner only) 13.50 **t.** ⅰ 4.00 – **14 rm** ☐ 35.00/56.00 **t.** – SB 72.00/100.00 **st.**

Ann's House without rest., 63 London Rd, CT2 8JZ, ℘ 768767, Fax 768172, ⚘ – TV P. EN AE VISA. ✗ Y r
18 rm ☐ 18.00/45.00 **st.**

Magnolia House without rest., 36 St. Dunstan's Terr., CT2 8AX, ℘ 765121, Fax 765121, ⚘ – ⊁ TV P. EN AE VISA. ✗ Y s
6 rm ☐ 35.00/80.00 **t.**

Alexandra House without rest., 1 Roper Rd, CT2 7EH, ℘ 767011, ⚘ – TV P. ✗ Y u
7 rm ☐ 18.00/45.00 **st.**

Highfield without rest., Summer Hill, Harbledown, CT2 8NH, ℘ 462772, ⚘ – P. EN VISA. ✗ by Rheims way Y
closed Christmas-New Year – **8 rm** ☐ 27.00/52.00 **st.**

Sullys, (at County H.) High St., CT1 2RX, ℘ 766266, Fax 451512 – ▤ P. EN AE ◑ VISA JCB Y n
M 15.00/19.00 **t.** and a la carte.

Tuo e Mio, 16 The Borough, CT1 2DR, ℘ 761471 – EN AE ◑ VISA Y o
closed Tuesday lunch, Monday, last 2 weeks February and last 2 weeks August – **M** - **Italian** a la carte 14.25/22.00 **t.** ⅰ 3.50.

George's Brasserie, 71-72 Castle St., CT1 2QD, ℘ 765658 – EN AE ◑ VISA JCB Z x
closed Sunday – **M** 7.00/30.00 **st.** and a la carte ⅰ 4.00.

at Chartham SW : 3 ¼ m. by A 28 – Z – ✉ ☎ 0227 Canterbury :

Thruxted Oast ⚘ without rest., Mystole, CT4 7BX, SW : 1 ¼ m. by Rattington St. and Cockering Rd on Mystole Lane ℘ 730080, ≤, ⚘ – ⊁ TV P. EN AE ◑ VISA. ✗
closed Christmas – **3 rm** ☐ 63.00/73.00 **s.**

at Chartham Hatch W : 3 ¼ m. by A 28 – Z – ✉ ☎ 0227 Canterbury :

Howfield Manor, Howfield Lane, CT4 7HQ, SE : 1 m. ℘ 738294, Fax 731535, ⚘ – TV ☎ P – 🏛 80. EN AE VISA. ✗
M (see **Old Well** below) – **13 rm** ☐ 62.50/90.00 **st.** – SB 97.50/117.50 **st.**

Old Well (at Howfield Manor H.), Howfield Lane, CT4 7HQ, SE : 1 m. ℘ 738294, Fax 731535, ⚘ – P. EN AE VISA
M 13.95/18.95 **st.** and a la carte ⅰ 5.00.

ATS 29 Sturry Rd ℘ 464867/765021

CARBIS BAY Cornwall 403 D 33 – see St. Ives.

CARCROFT S. Yorks. 402 403 404 Q 23 – see Doncaster.

See : Town★ - Cathedral★ (Painted Ceiling★) AY E – Tithe Barn★ BY A.

Envir. : Hadrian's Wall★★, N : by A 7 AY.

🏌 Aglionby ℰ 513303, E : by A 69 BY – 🏌 Stoneyholme ℰ 34856, E : 1 m. by St. Aidan's Rd BY – 🏌 Dalston Hall, Dalston ℰ 710165, SW : 5 m. by A 595 and B 5299 AZ.

✈ Carlisle Airport ℰ 573641, Telex 64476 , Fax 573310, NW : 5½ m. by A 7 BY and B 6264 – **Terminal** : Bus Station, Lowther Street.

🚗 ℰ 0345 090700.

🛈 Carlisle Visitor Centre, Old Town Hall, Green Market, CA3 8JH ℰ 512444.

◆London 317 – ◆Blackpool 95 – ◆Edinburgh 101 – ◆Glasgow 100 – ◆Leeds 124 – ◆Liverpool 127 – ◆Manchester 122 – ◆Newcastle upon Tyne 59.

CARLISLE

Botchergate	**BZ**	Annetwell Street	**AY** 2	Lowther Street	**BY** 15
Castle Street	**BY** 6	Bridge Street	**AY** 3	Port Road	**AY** 16
English Street	**BY** 13	Brunswick Street	**BZ** 4	St. Marys Gate	**BY** 17
Scotch Street	**BY** 19	Caldcotes	**AY** 5	Spencer Street	**BY** 20
The Lanes		Charlotte Street	**AZ** 7	Tait Street	**BZ** 21
Shopping Centre	**BY**	Chiswick Street	**BY** 8	Victoria Viaduct	**ABZ** 24
		Church Street	**AY** 10	West Tower Street	**BY** 26
		Eden Bridge	**BY** 12	West Walls	**ABY** 27
		Lonsdale Street	**BY** 14	Wigton Road	**AZ** 29

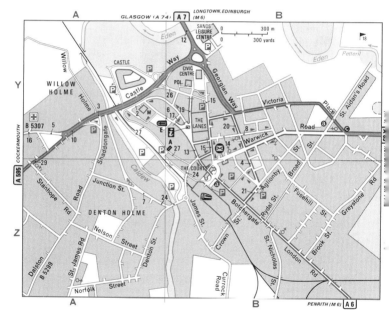

🏨 **Cumbrian,** Court Sq., CA1 1QY, ℰ 31951, Telex 64287, Fax 47799 – 🛗 ↔ rm 📺 ☎ ⚹
⇔ 🅿 – 🔬 300. 🔼 🆎 ⓪ 𝒱𝐼𝒮𝒜
                                                       BZ **a**
   M (closed lunch Saturday and Sunday) 9.50/14.95 **st.** and a la carte ⅋ 4.95 – **70 rm**
   ⚏ 30.00/95.00 **st.** – SB 90.00 **st.**

🏨 **Cumbria Park,** 32 Scotland Rd, CA3 9DG, N : 1 m. on A 7 ℰ 22887, Fax 514796 – 🛗 📺
   ☎ 🅿 – 🔬 100. 🔼 𝒱𝐼𝒮𝒜 ❦
                                                          BY
   closed 25 and 26 December – **M** (bar lunch Sunday) 13.50/16.50 **t.** and a la carte – **49 rm**
   ⚏ 53.00/64.00 **t.** – SB (October-April) (weekends only) 83.00/118.00 **st.**

🏨 **Swallow Hilltop,** London Rd, CA1 2PQ, SE : 1 m. on A 6 ℰ 29255, Fax 25238, 🏋, ≘,
   🔲 – 🛗 📺 ☎ 🅿 – 🔬 500. 🔼 🆎 ⓪ 𝒱𝐼𝒮𝒜
                                                           BZ
   M (bar lunch Monday to Saturday)/dinner 30.00 **st.** and a la carte ⅋ 4.50 – **90 rm** ⚏ 59.50/
   85.00 **st.** – SB 75.00/120.00 **st.**

🏨 **Gosling Bridge,** Kingstown Rd, CA3 0AT, N : 1 ¾ m. on A 7 ℰ 515294, Fax 515220 – 📺
   ☎ ⚹ 🅿. 🔼 🆎 ⓪ 𝒱𝐼𝒮𝒜 ❦
                                                           BY
   M 15.00 **st.** and a la carte ⅋ 3.75 – **30 rm** ⚏ 42.95/47.95 **t.** – SB (weekends only) 59.95/
   93.90 **st.**

⌂ **Beeches** without rest., Wood St., CA1 2SF, E : 1 ½ m. by A 69 off Victoria Rd ℰ 511962 –
BY
📺 ℗. ✖
3 rm ☑ 25.00/35.00 **st.**

⌂ **Avondale,** 3 St. Aidan's Rd, CA1 1LT, ℰ 23012 – 📺 — BY **a**
M (by arrangement) (communal dining) 8.00 – **3 rm** ☑ 30.00/36.00 **st.**

⌂ **Courtfield House,** 169 Warwick Rd, CA1 1LP, ℰ 22767 – 📺 — BY **c**
M (by arrangement) 7.50 **s.** – **4 rm** ☑ 25.00/35.00 **s.**

at Kingstown N : 3 m. by A 7 at junction 44 – BY – off M 6 – ⊠ 🌣 0228 Carlisle :

🏨 **Forte Posthouse,** Park House Rd, Kingstown, CA3 0HR, on A 7 ℰ 31201, Fax 43178, 𝐽ₛ,
⇌, 🏊 – ⅙ rm 📺 ☎ ℗ – 🔬 60. 🆔 ⁄ AE ⁄ ⓞ ⁄ VISA ⁄ JCB
M a la carte approx. 17.50 **t.** ⅄ 4.65 – ☑ 6.95 – **93 rm** 53.50 **st.** – SB (weekends only)
90.00 **st.**

at Crosby-on-Eden NE : 4 ½ m. by A 7 and A 689 – BY – on B 6264 – ⊠ Carlisle –
🌣 0228 Crosby-on-Eden :

XX **Crosby Lodge** with rm, High Crosby, CA6 4QZ, ℰ 573618, Fax 573428, ≼, « 18C
country mansion », ≂ – ⅙ rest 📺 ☎ ℗. 🆔 ⁄ AE ⁄ VISA. ✖
closed 24 December-mid January – **M** *(closed Sunday dinner to non-residents)* 18.50/
29.00 **t.** and a la carte ⅄ 6.25 – **11 rm** ☑ 65.00/88.00 **t.** – SB (except Bank Holidays) (winter
only) (weekends only) 115.00 **st.**

at Faugh E : 8 ¼ m. by A 69 – BY – ⊠ 🌣 0228 Carlisle :

🏨 **String of Horses Inn,** Heads Nook, CA4 9EG, ℰ 70297, Fax 70675, « Elaborately
furnished 17C inn », ⇌, 🏊 heated – 🍴 rest 📺 ☎ ℗. 🆔 ⁄ AE ⁄ ⓞ ⁄ VISA. ✖
M 10.95/16.95 **t.** and a la carte ⅄ 4.00 – **14 rm** ☑ 58.00/95.00 **t.** – SB (except Bank Holidays) 84.00/128.00 **st.**

at Wetheral SE : 6 ¼ m. by A 6 – BZ – ⊠ 🌣 0228 Carlisle :

🏨 **Crown,** CA4 8ES, on B 6263 ℰ 561888, Fax 561637, 𝐽ₛ, ⇌, 🏊, ≂, squash – ⅙ rm 📺
☎ ♿ ℗ – 🔬 175. 🆔 ⁄ AE ⁄ ⓞ ⁄ VISA
M *(bar lunch Saturday)* 12.95/18.00 **st.** and a la carte ⅄ 6.45 – **50 rm** ☑ 68.00/108.00 **st.**,
1 suite – SB (weekends only) 114.00/124.00 **st.**

🛞 ATS Rosehill Ind. Est., Montgomery Way ℰ 25277

▐CARLTON▐ N. Yorks. 402 O 21 – see Middleham.

▐CARLYON BAY▐ Cornwall 403 F 33 – see St. Austell.

▐CARNFORTH▐ Lancs. 402 L 21 – see Lancaster.

▐CARTERWAY HEADS▐ Northd 401 402 O 19 – ⊠ Shotley Bridge – 🌣 0207 Consett.
♦London 272 – ♦Carlisle 59 – ♦Newcastle upon Tyne 21.

XX **Manor House Inn,** DH8 9LX, on A 68 ℰ 55268 – ℗. 🆔 VISA
closed Christmas Day – **M** 15.00 **st.** and a la carte ⅄ 3.50.

▐CARTMEL▐ Cumbria 402 L 21 – see Grange-over-Sands.

▐CARTMELL FELL▐ Cumbria 402 L 21 – see Newby Bridge.

▐CASTLE ASHBY▐ Northants. 404 R 27 – pop. 142 – ⊠ Northampton – 🌣 060 129 (3 fig.) and
0604 (6 fig.) Yardley Hastings.
♦London 76 – Bedford 15 – Northampton 11.

🏨 **Falcon** (Best Western) ✖, NN7 1LF, ℰ 696200, Fax 696673, ≂ – 📺 ☎ ℗. 🆔 ⁄ AE ⁄ VISA ⁄ JCB
M 18.50 **t.** and a la carte ⅄ 4.60 – **14 rm** ☑ 58.50/73.00 **st.** – SB (weekends only) 88.00 **st.**

▐CASTLE CARY▐ Somerset 403 404 M 30 – pop. 2 599 – ECD : Thursday – 🌣 0963.
♦London 125 – ♦Bristol 28 – Taunton 31 – Yeovil 13.

🏨 **George,** Market Pl., BA7 7AH, ℰ 350761, Fax 350035 – 📺 ☎ ℗. 🆔 VISA
M *(closed Sunday dinner)* (bar lunch Monday to Saturday)/dinner a la carte 11.35/16.25 **t.**
⅄ 3.70 – **15 rm** ☑ 40.00/65.00 **t.** – SB (except Bank Holidays) 80.00/120.00 **st.**

XX **Bond's** with rm, Ansford Hill, Ansford, BA7 7JP, N : ¾ m. on A 371 ℰ 350464, ≂ – 📺 ☎
℗. 🆔 VISA. ✖
closed 1 week Christmas – **M** (dinner only) 16.50 **st.** and a la carte ⅄ 4.00 – **7 rm** ☑ 38.00/
80.00 **st.** – SB 90.00/132.00 **st.**

▐CASTLE COMBE▐ Wilts. 403 404 N 29 The West Country G. – pop. 347 – ⊠ Chippenham –
🌣 0249.
See : Village★★.
♦London 110 – ♦Bristol 23 – Chippenham 6.

🏨 **Manor House** ✖, SN14 7HR, ℰ 782206, Telex 449931, Fax 782159, « Part 14C manor
house in park », 🏊 heated, ⥲, ≂, ✖ – 📺 ☎ ℗. 🆔 ⁄ AE ⁄ ⓞ ⁄ VISA
M 16.95/32.00 **t.** and a la carte – ☑ 10.00 – **34 rm** 95.00/295.00 **t.**, 2 suites – SB (except
Easter, May and Christmas-New Year) 140.00/180.00 **st.**

137

at Ford S : 1 ¾ m. on A 420 – ⊠ Chippenham – ☺ 0249 Castle Combe :

🏠 **White Hart Inn,** SN14 8RP, ℰ 782213, Fax 783075 – 📺 ☎ 🅿. 🕿 🖭 𝒱𝐼𝒮𝒜
M a la carte approx. 17.00 **st.** 🍴 4.00 – **11 rm** ⯐ 43.00/59.00 **st.** – SB 83.00/100.00 **st.**

at Nettleton Shrub W : 2 m. by B 4039 on Nettleton rd (Fosse Way) – ⊠ Chippenham – ☺ 0249 Castle Combe :

🏠 **Fosse Farmhouse,** SN14 7NJ, ℰ 782286, Fax 783066, ⇜ – ⑭ rest 📺 🅿. 🕿 🖭 𝒱𝐼𝒮𝒜
M 25.00 **t.** and a la carte 🍴 6.00 – **6 rm** ⯐ 45.00/110.00 **st.** – SB (except May, Christmas-New Year and Bank Holidays) 120.00/150.00 **st.**

CASTLE DONINGTON Leics. 402 403 404 P 25 – pop. 5 854 – ⊠ ☺ 0332 Derby.

🛫 East Midlands, ℰ 810621, Fax 850393, S : by B 6540 and A 453.

◆London 123 – ◆Birmingham 38 – ◆Leicester 23 – ◆Nottingham 13.

🏨 **Hilton National,** East Midlands Airport, Derby Rd, Lockington, DE7 2RH, E : 3 ¼ m. by B 6540 on A 453 at junction of A 6 and M 1 ℰ 0509 (Loughborough) 674000, Fax 672412, 🖪, ⇌, 🏊 – 🖏 – 🍴 ⑭ rm 🗐 🅿 – 🔬 250. 🕿 🖭 🕥 𝒱𝐼𝒮𝒜
M (bar lunch Saturday) 12.95/16.95 **t.** and a la carte 🍴 6.95 – **Zen** - **Japanese** (Teppan Yaki) (closed Saturday lunch) a la carte 12.00/30.00 **t.** 🍴 6.00 – ⯐ 10.25 – **151 rm** 89.00 **st.**, 1 suite – SB 72.00/160.00 **st.**

🏨 **Donington Thistle** (Mt. Charlotte Thistle), East Midlands Airport, DE74 2SH, SE : 3 ¼ m. by B 6540 on A 453 ℰ 850700, Telex 377632, Fax 850823, 🖪, ⇌, 🏊 – ⑭ rm 🗐 rest 📺 ☎ 🅿 – 🔬 220. 🕿 🖭 🕥 𝒱𝐼𝒮𝒜
M (bar lunch Saturday and Bank Holidays) 14.00/19.95 **st.** and a la carte 🍴 5.25 – ⯐ 8.95 – **108 rm** 85.00/140.00 **st.**, 2 suites – SB 108.00 **st.**

🏨 **Priest House** 🏊, Kings Mills, DE74 2RR, W : 1 ¾ m. by Park Lane ℰ 810649, Fax 811141, ≤, « Riverside setting », 🏊, park – 📺 🕿 🅿 – 🔬 150. 🕿 🖭 🕥 𝒱𝐼𝒮𝒜
M 10.95/16.50 **t.** and a la carte 🍴 5.25 – **43 rm** ⯐ 72.00/102.00 **t.**, 2 suites – SB (weekends only) 78.00/158.00 **st.**

🏨 **Donington Manor,** High St., DE74 2PP, ℰ 810253, Fax 850330 – 📺 ☎ 🅿 – 🔬 80. 🕿 🖭 🕥 𝒱𝐼𝒮𝒜 𝐉𝐂𝐁. ⑭
closed 26 to 31 December – **M** 7.75/9.60 **st.** and a la carte – **36 rm** ⯐ 54.00/72.50 **st.**

at Isley Walton SW : 1 ¾ m. by B 6540 on A 453 – ⊠ ☺ 0332 Derby :

🏠 **Park Farmhouse,** Melbourne Rd, DE74 2RN, W : ¾ m. ℰ 862409, Fax 862364, ≤ – 📺 ☎ 🅿. 🕿 🖭 🕥 𝒱𝐼𝒮𝒜 𝐉𝐂𝐁
closed Christmas – **M** (residents only) (dinner only) approx. 14.00 **t.** 🍴 4.00 – **9 rm** ⯐ 35.00/55.00 **t.** – SB (winter only) (weekends only) 59.50/119.00 **st.**

CASTLE HEDINGHAM Essex 404 V 28 – pop. 1 193 – ⊠ ☺ 0787 Halstead.

◆London 53 – ◆Cambridge 30 – Chelmsford 20 – Colchester 18.

🏠 **Old School House,** St. James St., CO9 3EW, ℰ 61370, Fax 61605, « Cottage garden » – ⑭. ⑭
M (by arrangement) (communal dining) 16.00 **st.** – **3 rm** ⯐ 25.00/49.00 **st.**

✕✕ **Rumbles Castle,** 4 St. James St., CO9 3EJ, ℰ 461490 – ⑭. 🕿 𝒱𝐼𝒮𝒜
closed Saturday lunch, Sunday dinner, Monday and Tuesday – **M** (lunch by arrangement)/dinner 13.00 **t.** and a la carte 🍴 4.00.

CASTLETON Derbs. 402 403 404 O 23 Great Britain G. – pop. 881 – ECD : Wednesday – ⊠ Sheffield (South Yorks.) – ☺ 0433 Hope Valley.

Envir. : Blue John Caverns★ *AC*, W : 1 m.

◆London 181 – Derby 49 – ◆Manchester 30 – ◆Sheffield 16 – ◆Stoke-on-Trent 39.

🏠 **Ye Olde Nags Head,** S30 2WH, ℰ 620248, Fax 621604 – 📺 ☎ 🅿. 🕿 🖭 🕥 𝒱𝐼𝒮𝒜. ⑭
M 11.95/16.95 **t.** and a la carte – **8 rm** ⯐ 39.50/84.00 **st.** – SB (except December and Bank Holidays) 62.45 **st.**

CATLOWDY Cumbria 401 402 L 18 – ⊠ Carlisle – ☺ 0228 Nicholforest.

◆London 333 – ◆Carlisle 16 – ◆Dumfries 36 – Hawick 31 – ◆Newcastle upon Tyne 65.

🏠 **Bessiestown Farm** 🏊, CA6 5QP, ℰ 577219, 🖎, ⑭, park – ⑭ 🅿. 🕿 🖭 𝒱𝐼𝒮𝒜. ⑭
M (by arrangement) 10.00 **st.** 🍴 3.00 – **4 rm** ⯐ 24.00/38.00 **st.**

CAWSTON Norfolk 404 X 25 Great Britain G. – pop. 1 218 – ⊠ ☺ 0603 Norwich.

Envir. : Blicking Hall★★ *AC*, NE : 5 m. by B 1145 and B 1354.

◆London 122 – Cromer 15 – King's Lynn 42 – ◆Norwich 13.

🏠 **Grey Gables** 🏊, Norwich Rd, NR10 4EY, S : 1 m. ℰ 871259, ⇜, ⑭ – ⑭ rest 📺 ☎ 🅿. 🕿 𝒱𝐼𝒮𝒜
M (lunch by arrangement)/dinner 21.50 **st.** 🍴 5.50 – **8 rm** ⯐ 19.00/58.00 **t.** – SB (except Bank Holidays) 64.00/100.00 **st.**

CHADDESLEY CORBETT Heref. and Worcs. 403 404 N 26 – see Kidderminster.

En haute saison, et surtout dans les stations, il est prudent de retenir à l'avance.

◆London 74 – Cheltenham 32 – ◆Oxford 18 – Stratford-upon-Avon 25.

🏨 **Manor** ≫, OX7 3LX, ℰ 711 (676711 from April 94), ≤, ☞, park – ⇤⇥ rest 📺 ☎ 🅿. 🅿.
🆅🅸🆂🅰. ⚞
M (dinner only) 25.50 **st.** ⋔ 4.00 – **7 rm** ⊐ 60.00/120.00 **st.** – SB (except Bank Holidays)
(weekdays only) 110.00/140.00 **st.**

🏠 **Chadlington House**, OX7 3LZ, ℰ 437 (676437 from April 94), Fax 503 (676503 from
April 94), ☞ – ⇤⇥ rest 📺 ☎ 🅿. 🅿. 🆅🅸🆂🅰. ⚞
closed January and February – **M** (residents only) (dinner only) 18.00 **st.** and a la carte
⋔ 4.50 – **10 rm** ⊐ 30.00/70.00 **st.** – SB (except Bank Holidays) 65.00/110.00 **st.**

Envir. : Dartmoor National Park★★ (Brent Tor ≤★★, Haytor Rocks ≤★).

◆London 218 – Exeter 17 – ◆Plymouth 28.

🏨 ❀ **Gidleigh Park** ≫, TQ13 8HH, NW : 2 m. by Gidleigh Rd ℰ 432367, Fax 432574, ≤,
Teign Valley, woodland and Meldon Hill, « Timbered country house, water garden »,
park, ⚒ – ⇤⇥ rest 📺 ☎ 🅿. 🅿. 🆅🅸🆂🅰. 🅰🅴 ⏹ 🆅🅸🆂🅰
M (booking essential) 50.00/55.00 **st.** ⋔ 8.75 – **13 rm** ⊐ (dinner included) 190.00/360.00 **st.**,
2 suites – SB (December-February) (except 23 December-2 January) 207.00/576.00 **st.**
Spec. Terrine of duck foie gras, Steamed turbot with crab raviolo and broad bean sauce, Noisettes of English lamb with
aubergine and tomato.

🏠 **Thornworthy House** ≫, Thornworthy, TQ13 8EY, SW : 3 m. by Fernworthy rd on
Thornworthy rd ℰ 433297, ≤, « Country house atmosphere », ☞, park, ⚒ – ⚒
M *(closed Monday and Tuesday)* (by arrangement) (dinner only) 17.50 **st.** – **6 rm** ⊐ 32.50/
70.00 **st.**

🏠 **Bly House** ≫ without rest., Nattadon Hill, TQ13 8BW, E :¼ m. ℰ 432404, ☞, ⚒ – 📺 🅿
6 rm ⊐ 30.00/50.00 **s.**

at Sandy Park NE : 2¼ m. on A 382 – ✉ ☺ 0647 Chagford :

🏨 **Mill End**, TQ13 8JN, on A 382 ℰ 432282, Fax 433106, « Country house with water mill »,
⚒, ☞ – 📺 ☎ ⟵ 🅿. 🅿. 🆅🅸🆂🅰. 🅰🅴 ⏹ 🆅🅸🆂🅰
closed 10 to 20 December and 10 to 20 January – **M** (lunch by arrangement)/dinner 26.50 **t.**
⋔ 5.25 – **17 rm** 35.00/90.00 **t.** – SB (except Christmas and New Year) 120.00/150.00 **t.**

🏨 **Great Tree** ≫, TQ13 8JS, on A 382 ℰ 432491, Fax 432562, ≤, « Country house atmosphere », ⚒, ☞, park – ⇤⇥ rest 📺 ☎ 🅿. 🅿. 🆅🅸🆂🅰. 🅰🅴 ⏹ 🆅🅸🆂🅰
M (lunch by arrangement)/dinner 19.50 **t.** ⋔ 5.15 – **12 rm** ⊐ 49.00/97.00 **t.** – SB 103.00/
136.00 **st.**

at Easton Cross NE : 1 ½ m. on A 382 – ✉ ☺ 0647 Chagford :

🏠 **Easton Court**, TQ13 8JL, ℰ 433469, « Part 15C thatched house », ☞ – ⇤⇥ rest 📺 ☎.
🆅🅸🆂🅰. 🅰🅴 🆅🅸🆂🅰
closed January – **M** (dinner only) 22.00 **st.** ⋔ 3.75 – **7 rm** ⊐ 42.00/76.00 **st.** – SB 80.00/
120.00 **st.**

🏌 Harewood Downs, Cokes Lane, Chalfont St. Giles ℰ 762308.

◆London 24 – ◆Oxford 43.

🍴 **Water Hall**, Amersham Rd, SL9 0PA, N : ½ m. on A 413 ℰ 873430 – 🅿. 🆅🅸🆂🅰. 🅰🅴 🆅🅸🆂🅰
closed Sunday dinner and Bank Holidays except Christmas – **M** - French 16.50/
19.50 **st.** and a la carte ⋔ 5.00.

Envir. : Chard (Museum★) *AC*, N : 3 m. by A 358.

◆London 160 – Exeter 31 – Lyme Regis 9.5 – Taunton 20 – Yeovil 21.

🏨 **Tytherleigh Cot**, EX13 7BN, ℰ 21170, Fax 21291, ⚞, ⚒ heated, ☞ – 📺 ☎ 🅿. 🆅🅸🆂🅰. 🆅🅸🆂🅰
M (dinner only) 21.00 **t.** ⋔ 6.75 – **19 rm** ⊐ 55.00/98.00 **t.** – SB 123.50/148.50 **st.**

◆London 72 – ◆Birmingham 50 – ◆Oxford 15.

🏠 **Bell** (Best Western), Church St., OX7 3PP, ℰ 810278, Fax 811447 – 📺 ☎ 🅿 – 🔒 50. 🆅🅸🆂🅰.
🅰🅴 ⏹ 🆅🅸🆂🅰 🅹🅲🅱
M 15.00 **t.** and a la carte ⋔ 4.75 – **14 rm** ⊐ 50.00/75.00 – SB 98.00 **st.**

🏠 **Bull at Charlbury,** Sheep St., OX7 3RR, ℰ 810689 – 📺 🅿. 🆅🅸🆂🅰. 🆅🅸🆂🅰. ⚒
M *(closed Sunday dinner and Monday to non-residents)* (bar lunch)/dinner a la carte
approx. 19.95 **st.** – **5 rm** ⊐ 40.00/50.00 **st.**

CHARLECOTE Warks. 403 404 P 27 – see Stratford-upon-Avon.

CHARLESTOWN Cornwall 403 F 32 – see St. Austell.

CHARLTON W. Sussex 404 R 31 – see Chichester.

CHARMOUTH Dorset 403 L 31 – pop. 1 121 – ECD : Thursday – ⊠ Bridport – ☎ 0297.
♦London 157 – Dorchester 22 – Exeter 31 – Taunton 27.

🏠 **White House,** 2 Hillside, The Street, DT6 6PJ, ℰ 60411, Fax 60702 – 📺 ☎ 🄿. 🗚 🗚 ⓞ
  VISA ⚘
  March-October – **M** (dinner only) 18.50 **st.** ⅄ 5.50 – **10 rm** ⌖ 30.00/92.00 **st.** – SB (except
  Bank Holidays) 90.00/126.00 **st.**

↑ **Newlands House,** Stonebarrow Lane, DT6 6RA, ℰ 60212, ⚘ – ⥱ 📺 🄿
  March-October – **M** (by arrangement) 11.30 **st.** – **12 rm** ⌖ 24.50/49.00 **st.**

↑ **Hensleigh,** Lower Sea Lane, DT6 6LW, ℰ 60830 – ⥱ rest 📺 🄿
  March-October – **M** 10.50 **t.** ⅄ 3.50 – **10 rm** ⌖ 21.75/43.50 **t.**

CHARTHAM Kent 404 X 30 – see Canterbury.

CHARTHAM HATCH Kent 404 X 30 – see Canterbury.

CHATTERIS Cambs. 402 404 U 26 – pop. 3 127 – ☎ 0345 March.
♦London 85 – ♦Cambridge 26 – ♦Norwich 71.

🏠 **Cross Keys,** 16 Market Hill, PE16 6BA, ℰ 693036 – 📺 ☎ 🄿. 🗚 🗚 ⓞ *VISA*
  M a la carte 10.20/17.20 **st.** ⅄ 3.50 – **7 rm** ⌖ 21.00/45.00 **st.**

CHEDDLETON Staffs. 402 403 404 N 24 – pop. 1 321 – ⊠ Leek – ☎ 0538 Churnet Side.
♦London 125 – ♦Birmingham 48 – Derby 33 – ♦Manchester 42 – ♦Stoke-on-Trent 11.

↑ **Choir Cottage** without rest., Ostlers Lane, via Hollows Lane, ST13 7HS, ℰ 360561 – ⥱
  📺 ⚘ 🄿
  closed Christmas and New Year – **3 rm** ⌖ 35.00/50.00 **st.**

CHEDINGTON Dorset 403 L 31 – pop. 96 – ⊠ Beaminster – ☎ 093 589 (3 fig.) and 0935
(5 fig.) Corscombe.
🏌 Halstock, Common Lane ℰ 891689, NE : 4 m. – 🏌 Chedington Court, South Perrott
ℰ 891413.
♦ London 148 – Dorchester 17 – Taunton 25.

🏰 **Chedington Court** ⚘, DT8 3HY, ℰ 891265, Fax 891442, ≼ countryside, « Country
  house in landscaped gardens », 🏌, park – 📺 ☎ 🄿. 🗚 🗚 *VISA*
  closed 3 January-3 February – **M** (dinner only) 27.50 **st.** ⅄ 5.00 – **10 rm** ⌖ 50.50/121.00 **st.** –
  SB 136.00/196.00 **st.**

🏰 **Hazel Barton** ⚘ without rest., DT8 3HY, ℰ 891613, Fax 891370, ≼, ⚘ – 📺 ☎ 🄿. ⚘
  4 rm ⌖ 75.00/95.00 **st.**

CHELMSFORD Essex 404 V 28 – pop. 91 109 – ECD : Wednesday – ☎ 0245.
🅱 E Block, County Hall, Market Rd, CM1 1GG ℰ 283400.
♦London 33 – ♦Cambridge 46 – ♦Ipswich 40 – Southend-on-Sea 19.

🏰 **South Lodge,** 196 New London Rd, CM2 0AR, ℰ 264564, Fax 492827 – ⥱ rm 📺 ☎ 🄿 –
  🛏 35. 🗚 🗚 ⓞ *VISA* ⚘
  M 12.50 **st.** and a la carte ⅄ 5.00 – ⌖ 3.50 – **41 rm** 55.00/77.50 **t.**

🏨 **County,** 29 Rainsford Rd, CM1 2QA, ℰ 491911, Fax 492762 – 📺 ☎ 🄿 – 🛏 150. 🗚 🗚 ⓞ
  VISA
  closed 27 to 31 December – **M** 10.95/13.50 **st.** and a la carte – **35 rm** ⌖ 58.50/79.50 **st.** –
  SB (weekends only) 71.90/79.90 **st.**

at Great Baddow SE : 3 m. by A 130 – ⊠ ☎ 0245 Chelmsford :

🏨 **Pontlands Park** ⚘, West Hanningfield Rd, CM2 8HR, ℰ 476444, Fax 478393, ≼, ≋,
  🛆 heated, 🗔, ⚘, park – 📺 ☎ 🄿 – 🛏 40. 🗚 🗚 ⓞ *VISA* ⚘
  closed first week January – **M** *(closed lunch Monday and Saturday and Sunday dinner to
  non-residents)* 20.00 **t.** and a la carte ⅄ 7.15 – ⌖ 9.90 – **16 rm** 75.00/110.00 **t.**, 1 suite.

🛞 ATS 375 Springfield Rd ℰ 257795   ATS Town Centre, Inchbonnie Rd, South Woodham
ATS Chelmer Village Centre, Springfield (ASDA car   Ferrers (ASDA car park) ℰ 324999
park) ℰ 465676

CHELSWORTH Suffolk 404 W 27 – pop. 133 – ⊠ Ipswich – ☎ 0449 Bildeston.
♦London 68 – Colchester 21 – ♦Ipswich 16.

🏠 **Peacock Inn,** The Street, IP7 7HU, ℰ 740758, ⚘ – 📺 🄿. 🗚 *VISA*. ⚘
  M a la carte 8.75/19.25 **t.** ⅄ 3.00 – **5 rm** ⌖ 20.00/40.00 **t.**

☞ *When in a hurry use the Michelin Main Road Maps :*
  970 Europe, 980 Greece, 984 Germany, 985 Scandinavia-Finland,
  986 Great Britain and Ireland, 987 Germany-Austria-Benelux, 988 Italy,
  989 France, 990 Spain-Portugal *and* 991 Yugoslavia.

See : Town★ – Pitville Pump Room★ *AC* A **A.**

Exc. : Sudeley Castle★ (Paintings★) *AC*, NE : 7 m. by B 4632 A.

🏌 Cleeve Hill ✆ (024 267) 2025, NE : 3 m. by B 4632 A – 🏌 Cotswold Hills, Ullenwood ✆ 522421, S : 3 m. by B 4070 A.

🛈 77 Promenade, GL50 1PP ✆ 522878.

◆London 99 – ◆Birmingham 48 – ◆Bristol 40 – Gloucester 9 – ◆Oxford 43.

Plan on next page

🏨 **Queen's** (Forte), Promenade, GL50 1NN, ✆ 514724, Fax 224145, ☞ – 🛗 ⇔ rm 📺 ☎ 🅿 – 🔬 200. 🖎 🝙 ⑩ **VISA** **JCB**.   B **n**
M 16.00/21.00 **st.** ♨ 6.50 – ☐ 9.50 – **74 rm** 85.00/140.00 **st.** – SB (weekends only) 158.00 **st.**

🏨 **Cheltenham Park,** Cirencester Rd, Charlton Kings, GL53 8EA, ✆ 222021, Fax 226935, ☞, park – ⇔ rm 🔲 rest 📺 ☎ 🕭 🅿 – 🔬 300. 🖎 🝙 ⑩ **VISA** **JCB**. ✎   A **e**
M 18.50 **st.** (dinner) and a la carte – ☐ 8.50 – **149 rm** 78.00/98.00 **st.**, 1 suite – SB (except New Year) (weekends only) 79.00/99.00 **st.**

🏨 **On the Park,** 38 Evesham Rd, GL52 2AH, ✆ 518898, Fax 511526 – 📺 ☎. 🖎 🝙 ⑩ **VISA**. ✎   C **r**
closed 1 week January – **M** – (see **Epicurean** below) – ☐ 4.50 – **9 rm** 70.00/80.00 **t.**, 2 suites – SB (except Christmas and New Year) 117.00/170.00 **st.**

🏨 **Golden Valley Thistle** (Mt. Charlotte Thistle), Gloucester Rd, GL51 0TS, W : 2 m. on A 40 ✆ 232691, Telex 43410, Fax 221846, ♨, ☎, ▨, ☞, ✗ – 🛗 ⇔ rm 🔲 rest 📺 ☎ 🅿 – 🔬 220. 🖎 🝙 ⑩ **VISA** **JCB**. ✎   A
M 15.00/22.00 **st.** and a la carte – ☐ 8.95 – **120 rm** 80.00 **st.**, 4 suites – SB (except Easter and Christmas) (weekends only) 90.00 **st.**

🏨 **Prestbury House,** The Burgage, GL52 3DN, NE : 1 ½ m. by Prestbury Rd (B 4632) off New Barn Lane ✆ 529533, Fax 227076, ☞ – 📺 ☎ 🅿 – 🔬 30. 🖎 🝙 ⑩ **VISA**   A **r**
M 19.50 **st.** and a la carte ♨ 4.50 – **17 rm** ☐ 63.00/78.00 **st.** – SB 86.00/140.00 **st.**

🏠 **Charlton Kings,** London Rd, Charlton Kings, GL52 6UU, ✆ 231061, Fax 241900, ☞ – ⇔ 📺 ☎ 🅿. 🖎 🝙 **VISA**. ✎   A **c**
M (dinner only and Sunday lunch)/dinner 14.95 **t.** and a la carte – **14 rm** ☐ 49.00/84.00 **t.** – SB 106.00/180.00 **st.**

🏠 **Lypiatt House** without rest., Lypiatt Rd, GL50 2QW, ✆ 224994, Fax 224996 – 📺 ☎ 🅿. 🖎 **VISA**   B **c**
10 rm ☐ 44.00/65.00 **t.**

🏠 **Milton House,** 12 Royal Parade, Bayshill Rd, GL50 3AY, ✆ 582601, Fax 222326 – ⇔ 📺 ☎ 🅿. 🖎 🝙 **VISA**. ✎   B **e**
M (by arrangement) (dinner only) 16.00 **t.** – **8 rm** ☐ 30.00/60.00 **t.**

🏠 **Regency House,** 50 Clarence Sq., GL50 4JR, ✆ 582718, Fax 262697, ☞ – ⇔ 📺 ☎. 🖎 **VISA**   C **c**
closed Christmas and New Year – **M** (by arrangement) (dinner only) 15.00 **t.** ♨ 3.00 – **8 rm** ☐ 25.00/48.00 **t.**

🏠 **Stretton Lodge,** Western Rd, GL50 3RN, ✆ 528724, Fax 570771, ☞ – ⇔ 📺 ☎. 🖎 🝙 **VISA**. ✎   B **v**
M (by arrangement) (dinner only) 12.50 **st.** – **9 rm** ☐ 37.50/65.00 **st.**

🏠 **Travel Inn,** Tewkesbury Rd, Uckington, GL51 9SL, NW : 1 ¾ m. on A 4019 at junction with B 4634 ✆ 233847, Fax 244887 – ⇔ rm 📺 ♨ 🅿. 🖎 🝙 **VISA**. ✎   A **a**
M (Beefeater grill) a la carte approx. 16.00 **t.** – ☐ 4.95 – **40 rm** 33.50 **t.**

🏡 **Hannaford's,** 20 Evesham Rd, GL52 2AB, ✆ 515181, Fax 515181 – 📺 ☎. 🖎 🝙 **VISA**. ✎
closed 23 to 29 December – **M** (by arrangement) 15.00 **t.** ♨ 4.50 – **8 rm** ☐ 29.00/58.00 **t.** – SB (except Bank Holidays) (weekends only) 70.00/100.00 **st.**   C **u**

🏡 **Hunting Butts Farm,** Swindon Lane, GL50 4NZ, N : 1 ½ m. by A 435 ✆ 524982, « Working farm », ☞ – ⇔ rm 📺 🅿   A **n**
M (by arrangement) 9.00 **st.** – **7 rm** ☐ 20.00/35.00 **st.**

🏡 **Abbey,** 16 Bath Par., GL53 7HN, ✆ 516053, Fax 513034, ☞ – 📺 ☎. 🖎 🝙 **VISA**   C **e**
M 15.00 **st.** ♨ 3.50 – **11 rm** ☐ 28.00/58.00 **st.**

🏡 **Hollington House,** 115 Hales Rd, GL52 6ST, ✆ 519718, Fax 570280, ☞ – ⇔ 📺 🅿. 🖎 🝙 **VISA**. ✎   A **s**
M (by arrangement) approx. 15.00 **t.** ♨ 4.50 – **9 rm** ☐ 28.00/56.00 **t.** – SB (except Bank Holidays) 70.00/90.00 **st.**

🏡 **Abbots Lee** without rest., Priory Walk, GL52 6DU, ✆ 515255 – ⇔ 🅿. 🖎 🝙 **VISA**. ✎   C **a**
3 rm ☐ 21.00/35.00 **st.**

🏡 **Beaumont House,** 56 Shurdington Rd, GL53 0JE, ✆ 245986, Fax 245986, ☞ – ⇔ rest 📺 ☎ 🅿. 🖎 🝙 **VISA**   A **u**
M (by arrangement) 15.95 **t.** ♨ 3.95 – **18 rm** ☐ 22.00/60.00 **st.** – SB (weekends only) 67.90/85.90 **st.**

🏡 **Battledown,** 125 Hales Rd, GL52 6ST, ✆ 233881, ☞ – ⇔ rest 📺 🅿. ✎   A **x**
M 12.00 **st.** – **6 rm** ☐ 16.00/44.00 **st.**

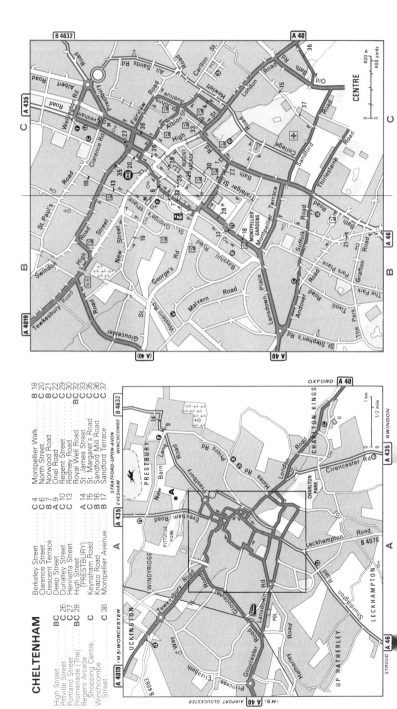

CHELTENHAM

XXX ✿ **Epicurean** (McDonald), (at On The Park H.) 38 Evesham Rd, GL52 2AH, ✆ 222466 – 🔼
🟦 🔹 **VISA**   C   r
M *(closed Sunday dinner, Monday and 3 weeks January)* 15.00/45.00 **st.** and a la carte
25.00/45.00 **st.** ₪ 6.75
Spec. Salad of roast sweetbreads, Stuffed trotter, sage, onion and truffle, Peach soufflé.

XX **Le Champignon Sauvage,** 24-26 Suffolk Rd, GL50 2AQ, ✆ 573449 – 🔼 🟦 🔹 **VISA** B **a**
closed Saturday lunch, Sunday, 2 weeks June, 2 weeks Christmas and Bank Holidays –
M 17.50/27.00 **t.** ₪ 3.95.

XX **Bonnets Bistro at Staithes,** 12 Suffolk Rd, GL50 2AQ, ✆ 260666, Fax 261427 – ✺. 🔼
🟦 🔹 **VISA**   B **a**
closed Saturday lunch, Sunday and 12 to 29 June – **M** a la carte 15.40/22.50 **t.**

XX **Mayflower,** 32-34 Clarence St., GL50 3NX, ✆ 522426, Fax 251667 – 📠. 🔼 🟦 🔹
VISA   B **r**
closed Sunday lunch and 25 to 27 December – **M** - Chinese 6.50/18.50 **t.** and a la carte.

at Woolstone N : 6¼ m. by A 435 – A – ✉ ✿ 0242 Cheltenham :

↑ **Old Rectory** ⌖ without rest., GL52 4RG, ✆ 673766, ✿ – ✺ 📺 🅿. ✾
mid March-October – **3 rm** 🖙 23.00/38.00 **st.**

at Cleeve Hill NE : 4 m. on B 4632 – A – ✉ ✿ 0242 Cheltenham :

🏨 **Rising Sun,** GL52 3PX, ✆ 676281, Fax 673069, ≤, ⬱, ✿ – ✺ rm 📺 ☎ 🅿. 🔼 75. 🔼
🟦 🔹 **VISA** ✾
M 11.50/16.00 **t.** and a la carte – **24 rm** 🖙 54.50/71.00 **t.** – SB (weekends only) 90.00 **st.**

🏨 **Cleeve Hill** without rest., GL52 3PR, ✆ 672052, ≤, ✿ – ✺ 📺 ☎ 🅿. 🔼 🟦 **VISA**.
✾
10 rm 🖙 40.00/65.00 **st.**

at Colesbourne SE : 7 m. on A 435 – A – ✉ ✿ 0242 Cheltenham :

🏨 **Colesbourne Inn,** GL53 9NP, ✆ 870376, Fax 870397, ✿ – 📺 ☎ 🅿. 🔼 🟦 🔹
VISA
M 11.95 **t.** (dinner) and a la carte 10.70/20.70 **t.** ₪ 4.25 – **9 rm** 🖙 35.00/50.00 **t.** – SB (except
Christmas-New Year) 63.00/85.00 **t.**

at Shurdington SW : 3¾ m. on A 46 – A – ✉ ✿ 0242 Cheltenham :

🏨 **Greenway** ⌖, GL51 5UG, ✆ 862352, Fax 862780, ≤, « Part 17C Cotswold country
house, gardens » – 📺 ☎ 🅿 – 🔼 30. 🔼 🟦 🔹 ✾
closed 3 to 7 January – **M** *(closed lunch Saturday and Bank Holidays)* 17.00/
25.00 **t.** and a la carte ₪ 5.50 – **19 rm** 🖙 85.00/175.00 **t.** – SB (except Christmas-New Year)
160.00/200.00 **st.**

🏨 **Allards,** Shurdington Rd, GL51 5XA, ✆ 862498, Fax 863017, ✿ – 📺 ☎ 🅿. 🔼 🟦 **VISA**
🏧. ✾
M 10.75/13.95 **t.** ₪ 3.95 – **12 rm** 🖙 35.00/60.00 **t.**

at Staverton W : 4¼ m. by A 40 on Staverton rd – A – ✉ Cheltenham – ✿ 0452
Gloucester :

🏨 **White House** (Best Western), Gloucester Rd, GL51 0ST, ✆ 713226, Fax 857590 – 📺 ☎
🅿 – 🔼 180. 🔼 🟦 🔹 **VISA**
M 15.80 **st.** and a la carte ₪ 6.00 – **48 rm** 🖙 42.00/97.00 **st.**, 1 suite – SB (weekends only)
70.00/90.00 **st.**

🔧 ATS Chosen View Rd ✆ 521288   ATS 99-101 London Rd ✆ 519814

CHELWOOD Avon – see Bristol.

CHENIES Bucks. 404 S 28 – pop. 2 240 – ECD : Thursday – ✉ ✿ 0923 Rickmansworth
(Herts.).

♦London 30 – Aylesbury 18 – Watford 7.

🏨 **Bedford Arms Thistle** (Mt. Charlotte Thistle), WD3 6EQ, ✆ 283301, Fax 284825, « 16C
inn », ✿ – ✺ rm 📺 ☎ 🅿. 🔼 🟦 🔹 **VISA** 🏧
M (bar lunch Saturday) 15.00/18.50 **t.** and a la carte ₪ 6.50 – 🖙 8.75 – **10 rm** 75.00/
100.00 **st.** – SB (weekends only) 117.00 **st.**

CHERITON BISHOP Devon 403 I 31 The West Country G. – pop. 587 – ECD : Wednesday –
✉ Exeter – ✿ 0647.

Exc. : Crediton (Holy Cross Church★) NE : 6½ m. by A 30.

♦London 211 – Exeter 10 – ♦Plymouth 51.

🏠 **Old Thatch Inn,** EX6 6HJ, ✆ 24204 – 📺 🅿. 🔼 **VISA** ✾
closed first 2 weeks November – **M** a la carte 7.00/12.80 **st.** ₪ 3.95 – **3 rm** 🖙 34.00/45.00 **st.**

CHERTSEY Surrey **404** S 29 ② – ✿ 0932.

🏌, 🏌 Foxhills, Stonehill Rd, Ottershaw 🖉 093 287 (Ottershaw) 2050.

♦London 28.

🏨 **Crown,** 7 London St., KT16 8AP, 🖉 564657, Fax 570839 – ✂ rm 📺 ☎ ⅋ 🅿 – 🔬 100. 🖾
🖾 ⓞ 𝐕𝐈𝐒𝐀
M *(closed Saturday lunch)* (carving rest.) 7.95/15.95 **st.** and a la carte ⱡ 5.00 – **30 rm**
� 80.00/120.00 **st.** – SB (weekends only) 88.00/190.00 **st.**

CHESHUNT Herts. **404** T 28 – pop. 49 525 – ✉ Broxbourne – ✿ 0992.

🏌 Cheshunt Park, Park Lane 🖉 29777.

♦London 22 – ♦Cambridge 40 – ♦Ipswich 70 – Luton 34 – Southend-on-Sea 39.

🏨 **Cheshunt Marriott,** Halfhide Lane, Turnford, EN10 6NG, NW : 1 ¼ m. on B 176
🖉 451245, Fax 440120, 🖪, 🖾 – 🛗 ✂ rm ▤ 📺 ☎ ⅋ 🅿 – 🔬 220. 🖾 🖾 ⓞ 𝐕𝐈𝐒𝐀
M *(closed Saturday lunch)* 9.95/15.95 **st.** and a la carte ⱡ 5.95 – ⊒ 8.95 – **127 rm** 75.00 **st.**,
12 suites.

CHESTER Ches. **402** **403** L 24 Great Britain G. – pop. 80 154 – ECD : Wednesday – ✿ 0244.

See : City★★ – The Rows★★ – Cathedral★ – City Walls★.

Envir. : Chester Zoo★ *AC*, N : 3 m. by A 5116.

🏌 Upton-by-Chester, Upton Lane 🖉 381183, N : by A 5116 – 🏌 Curzon Park 🖉 675130.

🅷 Town Hall, Northgate St., CH1 2HJ 🖉 317962 – Chester Visitor Centre, Vicars Lane, CH1 1QX
🖉 351609/318916.

♦London 207 – Birkenhead 7 – ♦Birmingham 91 – ♦Liverpool 19 – ♦Manchester 40 – Preston 52 – ♦Sheffield 76 –
♦Stoke-on-Trent 38.

Plan on next page

🏨 **Chester Grosvenor,** Eastgate St., CH1 1LT, 🖉 324024, Fax 313246, 🖪, ⥥ – 🛗 ▤ 📺 ☎
⅋ 🅿 – 🔬 250. 🖾 🖾 🖾 𝐕𝐈𝐒𝐀 🍴 𝐉𝐂𝐁. ﹪   **a**
closed 25 and 26 December – **M** – **La Brasserie** a la carte 13.00/27.00 **t.** – (see also **Arkle**
below) – ⊒ 9.95 – **83 rm** 103.00/178.00, 3 suites – SB (weekends only) 160.00/220.00 **st.**

🏨 **Moat House International** (Q.M.H.), Trinity St., CH1 2BD, 🖉 322330, Fax 316118, 🖪,
⥥ – 🛗 ✂ rm ▤ rest 📺 ☎ ⅋ 🅿 – 🔬 500. 🖾 🖾 ⓞ 𝐕𝐈𝐒𝐀   **r**
closed 25 to 28 December – **M** *(closed lunch Saturday, Wednesday in August and Bank
Holidays)* 13.50/17.00 **st.** and a la carte ⱡ 4.50 – **146 rm** ⊒ 99.75/145.00 **st.**, 6 suites –
SB (weekends only) 120.00 **st.**

🏨 **Crabwall Manor** ⌖, Parkgate Rd, Mollington, CH1 6NE, NW : 2 ¼ m. on A 540
🖉 851666, Telex 61220, Fax 851400, « Part 16C manor », ✍ – 🛗 rest 📺 ☎ ⅋ 🅿 – 🔬 80.
🖾 🖾 ⓞ 𝐕𝐈𝐒𝐀 ﹪
M a la carte 17.00/34.25 **t.** – ⊒ 7.70 – **42 rm** 98.50/125.00 **t.**, 6 suites – SB (except Christmas and New Year) (weekends only) 150.00/190.00 **st.**

🏨 **Mollington Banastre** (Best Western), Parkgate Rd, Mollington, CH1 6NN, NW : 2 ¼ m.
on A 540 🖉 851471, Telex 61686, Fax 851165, 🖪, ⥥, 🖾, ✍, ✍, squash – 🛗 ✂ rm 📺 ☎ 🅿
– 🔬 250. 🖾 🖾
M 10.55/19.50 **st.** and a la carte – **64 rm** ⊒ 77.00/125.00 **st.** – SB 108.00/116.00 **st.**

🏨 **Hoole Hall,** Warrington Rd, Hoole, CH2 3PD, NE : 2 m. on A 56 🖉 350011 – 🛗 ✂ rm 📺
☎ ⅋ 🅿 – 🔬 100. 🖾 🖾 𝐕𝐈𝐒𝐀
M (bar lunch Saturday) 8.95/16.50 **t.** and a la carte ⱡ 4.95 – **99 rm** ⊒ 59.95/85.00 **t.** –
SB 85.00/130.00 **st.**

🏨 **Redland** without rest., 64 Hough Green, CH4 8JY, SW : 1 m. by A 483 on A 5104
🖉 671024, Fax 681309, « Victorian town house », ⥥ – 📺 ☎ 🅿. ﹪
12 rm ⊒ 40.00/65.00 **st.**

🏨 **Forte Posthouse,** Wrexham Rd, CH4 9DL, S : 2 m. on A 483 🖉 680111, Fax 674100, 🖪,
⥥, 🖾, ✍ – ✂ rm ▤ rest 📺 ☎ 🅿 – 🔬 100. 🖾 🖾 🖾 𝐕𝐈𝐒𝐀
M a la carte approx. 17.50 **t.** ⱡ 4.65 – ⊒ 6.95 – **105 rm** 53.50 **st.** – SB (except Christmas and
New Year) (weekends only) 90.00 **st.**

🏨 **Blossoms** (Forte), St. John St., CH1 1HL, 🖉 323186, Fax 346433 – 🛗 ✂ 📺 ☎ – 🔬 100.
🖾 🖾 ⓞ 𝐕𝐈𝐒𝐀 𝐉𝐂𝐁   **e**
M 9.95/16.95 **st.** and a la carte ⱡ 5.50 – ⊒ 8.50 – **63 rm** 80.00/90.00 **st.**, 1 suite – SB (except
Christmas-New Year) 108.00/123.00 **st.**

🏨 **Cavendish,** 42-44 Hough Green, CH4 8JQ, SW : 1 m. by A 483 on A 5104 🖉 675100,
Fax 682946, ✍ – ⅋ 📺 ☎ ⅋ 🅿. 🖾 🖾 𝐕𝐈𝐒𝐀
M 12.50/17.50 **t.** ⱡ 4.50 – **18 rm** ⊒ 41.00/65.00 **t.** – SB (except Christmas and New Year)
75.00/110.00 **st.**

🏨 **Alton Lodge,** 78 Hoole Rd, CH2 3NT, 🖉 310213, Fax 319206 – 📺 ☎ 🅿. 🖾 𝐕𝐈𝐒𝐀 ﹪
M (by arrangement) (dinner only) 10.50 **st.** – ⊒ 5.50 – **13 rm** 32.50/35.00 **st.**
                                                                              by Hoole Way and Hoole Rd

🏨 **Green Bough,** 60 Hoole Rd, CH2 3NL, on A 56 🖉 326241, Fax 326265 – 📺 ☎ 🅿. 🖾 🖾
𝐕𝐈𝐒𝐀
                                                                              by Hoole Way and Hoole Rd
closed Christmas and New Year – **M** (lunch by arrangement)/dinner 11.75 **t.** ⱡ 3.75 – **19 rm**
⊒ 38.00/58.00 **t.** – SB 63.00/70.50 **st.**

CHESTER

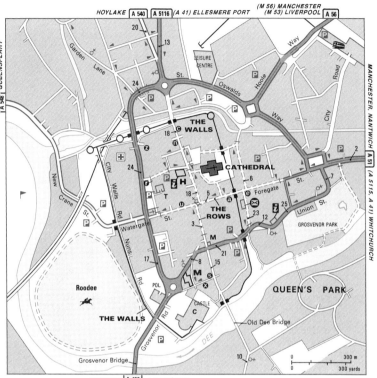

HOYLAKE [A 540] [A 5116] *(A 41) ELLESMERE PORT* — *(M 56) MANCHESTER* — *(M 53) LIVERPOOL* [A 56]

WREXHAM [A 483] *A 55: CONWY*

Pied Bull, Upper Northgate St., CH1 2HQ, ℰ 325829, Fax 350322 – 📺 ☎ ℗. 🔼 🅰🅴 *VISA*. ⊛
M (in bar) a la carte 7.45/12.85 **st.** – **12 rm** ⊡ 42.95/60.00 **st.** – SB (winter only) 55.00/90.00 **st.**
n

Gloster Lodge, 44 Hoole Rd, CH2 3NL, on A 56 ℰ 348410 – 📺 ☎ ℗. 🔼 🅰🅴 *VISA*. ⊛
closed 24 December-2 January – **M** *(closed Sunday)* (dinner only) 8.00 **st.** – **8 rm** ⊡ 25.00/36.50 **st.**
by Hoole Way and Hoole Rd

Chester Court, 48 Hoole Rd, CH2 3NL, on A 56 ℰ 320779, Fax 344795 – 📺 ☎ ℗
20 rm.
by Hoole Way and Hoole Rd

Ye Olde King's Head, 48/50 Lower Bridge St., CH1 1RS, ℰ 324855, Fax 315693, « 16C inn » – 📺 ☎ ⇦. 🔼 🅰🅴 ⓪ *VISA*
M a la carte 8.95/18.00 **st.** ⅃ 3.95 – **8 rm** ⊡ 46.95/51.95 **st.**
s

Chester Town House without rest., 23 King St., CH1 2AH, ℰ 350021 – 📺 ℗. 🔼 *VISA*
4 rm ⊡ 32.00/50.00 **st.**
z

Edwards House, 61-63 Hoole Rd, CH2 3NJ, ℰ 318055 – ⇝ rm 📺 ☎ ℗. 🔼 *VISA*. ⊛
M 12.50 **st.** ⅃ 2.95 – **8 rm** ⊡ 24.00/42.00 **st.**
by Hoole Way and Hoole Rd

Castle House without rest., 23 Castle St., CH1 2DS, ℰ 350354, « Part Elizabethan town house » – 📺. 🔼 🅰🅴 *VISA*
5 rm ⊡ 22.00/44.00 **s.**
x

Stone Villa without rest., 3 Stone Pl., CH2 3NR, ℰ 345014 – ⇝ 📺 ℗. ⊛
6 rm ⊡ 22.00/38.00 **s.**
by Hoole Way and Hoole Rd

XXXX ❀ **Arkle** (at Chester Grosvenor H.), Eastgate St., CH1 1LT, ✆ 324024, Fax 313246 – ✿✖ ▤
ⓟ. 🔄 ᴀᴇ ⓞ *VISA* ᴊᴄʙ   **a**
closed Monday lunch, Sunday, 24 to 30 December, 1 to 6 January – **M** (booking essential)
22.50/37.00 **t.** and a la carte 28.85/46.00 **t.** ⌾ 7.75
Spec. Daube de Lapin, pomme de terre fondante, Frivolité d'abats, Gaufrette de chocolat au praliné.

XX **Chester Rows,** 24 Watergate Row, CH1 2LD, ✆ 316003, « Part 15C and 17C town
house » – 🔄 *VISA*   **u**
M 6.50/12.95 **t.** and a la carte ⌾ 4.50.

XX **Garden House,** 1 Rufus Court, off Northgate St., CH1 2JH, ✆ 320004, Fax 327604 – 🔄
VISA   **c**
M *(closed Sunday)* 19.50 **t.** and lunch a la carte ⌾ 4.25.

at Mickle Trafford NE : 2½ m. by A 56 – ⊠ Chester – ❀ 0244 Mickle Trafford :

🏠 Royal Oak (Toby), Warrington Rd, CH2 4EX, on A 56 ✆ 301391, Fax 301948 – ✿✖ 📺 ☎ ⓟ
36 rm.

at Rowton SE : 3 m. by A 41 – ⊠ ❀ 0244 Chester :

🏠 **Rowton Hall,** Rowton Lane, CH3 6AD, ✆ 335262, Telex 61172, Fax 335464, ⌿⊿, ⌾⌾s, 🔄,
⚗ – 📺 ☎ ⛆ ⓟ – ⚖ 200. 🔄 ᴀᴇ ⓞ *VISA*
closed 25 to 27 December – **M** 12.50/16.50 **t.** and a la carte ⌾ 8.50 – **42 rm** ⌥ 72.00/
128.00 **t.** – SB 116.00/156.00 **st.**

at Two Mills NW : 5¾ m. on A 540 at junction with A 550 – ⊠ Ledsham – ❀ 051
Liverpool :

🏠 Tudor Rose Lodge, Parkgate Rd, L66 9PD, ✆ 339 2399, Fax 347 1725 – 📺 ☎ ⛆ ⓟ. ⚗
31 rm.

MICHELIN Distribution Centre, Sandycroft Industrial Estate, Glendale Av., Sandycroft,
Deeside, CH5 2QP, ✆ 537373, Fax 537453 by A 548

⓪ ATS 7 Bumpers Lane, Sealand Trading Est. ✆ 375154

▦ **CHESTERFIELD** Derbs. 402 403 404 P 24 – pop. 73 352 – ECD : Wednesday – ❀ 0246.
🏌 Chesterfield Municipal, Murray House, Crow Lane ✆ 273887 – 🏌 Grassmoor, North Wing-
field Rd ✆ 856044, S : 2 m. on B 6038.
🅱 Peacock Information Centre, Low Pavement, S40 1PB ✆ 207777.
♦London 152 – Derby 24 – ♦Nottingham 25 – ♦Sheffield 12.

🏠 **Forte Travelodge** without rest., Birmington Rd North, Wittington Moor, S41 9BE, N :
2 m. on A 61 ✆ 455411, Reservations (Freephone) 0800 850950 – 📺 ⛆ ⓟ. 🔄 ᴀᴇ *VISA*
20 rm 31.95 **t.**

⓪ ATS 512 Sheffield Rd ✆ 452281

▦ **CHESTER-LE-STREET** Durham 401 402 P 19 – pop. 34 776 – ECD : Wednesday – ❀ 091
Tyneside.
🏌 Lumley Park ✆ 388 3218 – 🏌 Roseberry Grange ✆ 370 0670, W : 3 m. on A 693.
♦London 275 – Durham 7 – ♦Newcastle upon Tyne 8.

🏠 **Lumley Castle,** DH3 4NX, E : 1 m. on B 1284 ✆ 389 1111, Fax 387 1437, « 13C castle »,
⚗ – ✿✖ rm 📺 ☎ ⓟ – ⚖ 150. 🔄 ᴀᴇ ⓞ *VISA*. ⚗
closed 25-26 December and 1 January – **M** (bar lunch Saturday) 13.50/19.75 **st.** and dinner
a la carte – **65 rm** ⌥ 79.50/98.00 **st.**, 1 suite – SB (weekends only) 129.00/200.00 **st.**

MICHELIN Distribution Centre, Drum Rd Industrial Estate, Drum Rd, DH3 2AF, ✆ 410 7762,
Fax 492 0717

▦ **CHESTERTON** Cambs. – see Peterborough.

▦ **CHESTERTON** Oxon. 404 Q 28 – ⊠ Bicester – ❀ 0869.
🏌 Chesterton ✆ 241204.
♦London 69 – ♦Birmingham 65 – Northampton 36 – ♦Oxford 15.

XX **Bignell Park** with rm, OX6 8UE, on A 4095 ✆ 241444, Fax 241444, ⚗ – 📺 ☎ ⓟ. 🔄 ᴀᴇ
ⓞ *VISA*. ⚗
M *(closed Sunday dinner and Bank Holidays)* 10.50/17.50 **t.** and a la carte ⌾ 5.00 – **5 rm**
⌥ 65.00/85.00 **t.** – SB (except Christmas and Bank Holidays) 100.00/170.00 **st.**

Pleasant hotels and restaurants
are shown in the Guide by a red sign.

Please send us the names
of anywhere you have enjoyed your stay.

Your Michelin Guide will be even better.

🏨 ... ⌂

XXXXX ... X

See : City★ – Cathedral★ BZ **A** – St. Mary's Hospital★ BY **D** – Pallant House★ *AC* BZ **M**.

Envir. : Fishbourne Roman Palace (mosaics★) *AC* AZ **R**.

Exc. : Weald and Downland Open Air Museum★ *AC*, N : 6 m. by A 286 AY.

📷 Goodwood 🏌 785012, NE : 3 m. by A 27 AY – 🏌, 🏌 Chichester Golf Centre, Hoe Farm, Hunston 🏌 533833, S : 3 m. by B 2145 AZ.

🏢 St. Peter's Market, West St., PO19 1AH 🏌 775888.

◆London 69 – ◆Brighton 31 – ◆Portsmouth 18 – ◆Southampton 30.

CHICHESTER

East Street	**BZ**	Chichester Arundel Road	**AY** 7	St. John's Street .... **BZ** 23
North Street	**BYZ**	East Pallant .... **BZ** 9	St. Martin's Square ..... **BY** 24
South Street	**BZ**	Florence Road .... **AZ** 10	St. Pancras .... **BY** 25
		Hornet (The) .... **BZ** 12	St. Paul's Road .... **BY** 27
Birdham Road	**AZ** 2	Kingsham Road .... **BZ** 13	Sherborne Road .... **AZ** 28
Bognor Road	**AZ** 3	Lavant Road .... **AY** 14	Southgate .... **BZ** 29
Cathedral Way	**AZ** 4	Little London .... **BY** 15	South Pallant .... **BZ** 31
Chapel Street	**BY** 6	Market Road .... **BZ** 16	Spitalfield Lane .... **BY** 32
		Northgate .... **BY** 17	Stockbridge Road ..... **AZ** 33
		North Pallant .... **BZ** 19	Tower Street .... **BY** 35
		St. James's .... **AZ** 21	Westhampnett Road ... **AYZ** 36

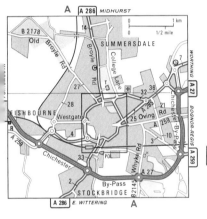

🏨 **Dolphin and Anchor** (Forte), West St., PO19 1QE, 🏌 785121, Fax 533408 – 🛏 📺 ☎ – 🔥 180. ⚞ 🅰🅴 ⑩ 💳 BZ **a**
M 12.95/16.95 **st.** and a la carte ⚞ 5.25 – ☐ 8.50 – **49 rm** 75.00/120.00 **st.** – SB (except 26 to 30 July and Christmas-New Year) 116.00/131.00 **st.**

🏨 **Chichester Resort**, Westhampnett, PO19 4UL, 🏌 786351, Fax 782371, ☐, 🔲 – 🛏 rm AY **e**
📺 ☎ ⭤ 🅿 – 🔥 300. ⚞ 🅰🅴 ⑩ 💳
M *(closed Saturday lunch)* 13.50/17.50 **st.** and a la carte ⚞ 5.00 – ☐ 7.50 – **76 rm** 65.00/85.00 **st.**, 1 suite – SB (except Christmas and New Year) 96.00/146.00 **st.**

🏨 **Crouchers Bottom**, Birdham Rd, Apuldram, PO20 7EH, SW : 2 ½ m. on A 286 🏌 784995, Fax 539797, ≤, ☞ – 🛏 📺 ⭤ 🅿. ⚞ 🅰🅴 💳 ⚞ AZ
closed 1 week Christmas – **M** (residents only) (dinner only) 19.75 **t.** – **6 rm** ☐ 54.00/80.00 **t.** – SB 98.00/140.00 **st.**

🏨 **Suffolk House**, 3 East Row, PO19 1PD, 🏌 778899, Fax 787282, ☞ – 📺 ☎. ⚞ 🅰🅴 ⑩ 💳
M (dinner only) 12.50 **st.** and a la carte ⚞ 3.60 – **10 rm** ☐ 43.50/95.00 **st.** – SB (winter only) 75.00/144.00 **st.** BY **a**

🍴🍴 **Cafe de Chine**, 117 St. Pancras, PO19 4LH, E : ¼ m. on A 285 🏌 784232 – ⬛. ⚞ 🅰🅴 ⑩ 💳 BY
closed Tuesday – **M** - **Chinese** (lunch by arrangement Saturday and Sunday) 8.50/ 15.00 **t.** and a la carte ⚞ 5.50.

🍴🍴 **Comme ça**, 67 Broyle Rd, PO19 4BD, on A 286 🏌 788724, Fax 530052, ☞ – 🅿. ⚞ 🅰🅴 💳
closed Sunday dinner, Monday and Bank Holidays – **M** - **French** 15.50/16.50 **st.** and a la carte ⚞ 4.80. AY **c**

at Charlton N : 6¼ m. by A 286 – AY – ✉ Chichester – ❄ 0243 Singleton :

🏨 **Woodstock House**, PO18 0HU, 🏌 811666, Fax 811666, ☞ – 📺 ☎ 🅿. ⚞ 💳 ⚞
M (dinner only) a la carte approx. 17.50 **t.** ⚞ 4.00 – **11 rm** ☐ 38.50/66.00 **t.** – SB 77.00/ 90.00 **st.**

at Halnaker NE : 3 ¼ m. on A 285 – BY – ⊠ ☎ 0243 Chichester :

⋔ **Old Store** without rest., Stane St., PO18 0QL, on A 285 ℰ 531977, ☞ – 📺 🅿 ◪ ⑩ 𝗩𝗜𝗦𝗔 ❀
7 rm ⊂⊃ 25.00/50.00 st.

at Chilgrove N : 6 ½ m. by A 286 – AY – on B 2141 – ⊠ ☎ 0243 East Marden :

✗✗ **White Horse Inn,** 1 High St., PO18 9HX, ℰ 535219, Fax 535301 – 🅿 ◪ ⑩ 𝗩𝗜𝗦𝗔
closed Sunday dinner, Monday, February and last week October – **M** - **English** 17.50/23.00 **t.** and a la carte ⓛ 4.75.

at Goodwood NE : 3 ½ m. by A 27 – AY – on East Dean Rd – ⊠ ☎ 0243 Chichester :

🏨 **Goodwood Park,** PO18 0QB, ℰ 775537, Fax 533802, *Ƒ₆,* ⋐, ◪, ⒩₈, ☞, ✗, squash – ↫ rest 📺 ☎ & 🅿 – ⅋ 120. ◪ ⒜⒠ ⑩ 𝗩𝗜𝗦𝗔 ❀
M 12.95/22.25 **t.** and a la carte ⓛ 5.25 – **88 rm** ⊂⊃ 79.00/144.00 **st.** – SB 90.00/160.00 **st.**

at Bosham W : 4 m. by A 259 – AZ – ⊠ ☎ 0243 Chichester :

🏨 **Millstream** (Best Western), Bosham Lane, PO18 8HL, ℰ 573234, Fax 573459, ☞ – 📺 ☎ 🅿 – ⅋ 30. ◪ ◪ ⑩ 𝗩𝗜𝗦𝗔
M 10.50/17.95 **t.** – **29 rm** ⊂⊃ 59.00/109.00 **t.** – SB 110.00/160.00 **st.**

⋔ **Hatpins** without rest., Bosham Lane, PO18 8HG, ℰ 572644, ⋐, ☞ – ↫ 📺 🅿 ❀
3 rm ⊂⊃ 25.00/50.00.

✗✗ **Wishing Well Tandoori,** Bosham Roundabout, PO18 8PG, N : ¾ m. on A 259 ℰ 572234 – 🅿 ◪ ⒜⒠ 𝗩𝗜𝗦𝗔
closed Christmas Day – **M** - Indian a la carte 12.80/18.60 **t.** ⓛ 3.95.

at Chidham W : 6 m. by A 259 – AZ – ⊠ ☎ 0243 Chichester :

⋔ **Old Rectory** ⤬ without rest., Cot Lane, West Chidham, PO18 8TA, ℰ 572088, 🏊, ☞ – ↫ 📺 🅿
4 rm ⊂⊃ 16.00/46.00 st.

🔧 ATS Terminus Rd Ind Est. ℰ 773100

CHIDHAM W. Sussex – see Chichester.

CHILGROVE W. Sussex 𝟦𝟢𝟦 R 31 – see Chichester.

CHILLINGTON Devon 𝟦𝟢𝟥 I 33 – see Kingsbridge.

CHINNOR Oxon. 𝟦𝟢𝟦 R 28 The West Country G. – pop. 5 432 – ☎ 0494 High Wycombe.
Exc. : Ridgeway Path★★.
◆London 45 – ◆Oxford 19.

✗ **Sir Charles Napier Inn,** Sprigg's Alley, by Bledlow Ridge rd, OX9 4BX, SE : 2 ½ m. ℰ 483011, Fax 484929, ☞ – 🅿 ◪ 𝗩𝗜𝗦𝗔
closed Sunday dinner and Monday – **M** 14.00 **t.** and a la carte ⓛ 5.00.

CHIPPENHAM Wilts. 𝟦𝟢𝟥 𝟦𝟢𝟦 N 29 The West Country G. – pop. 21 325 – ECD : Wednesday – ☎ 0249.
See : Yelde Hall★.
Envir. : Corsham Court★★ *AC,* SW : 3 ½ m. by A 4 – Sheldon Manor★ *AC,* W : 1 ½ m. by A 420 – Biddestone★, W : 4 ½ m. – Bowood House★ *AC* (Library ⇐★) SE : 5 m. by A 4 and A 342.
Exc. : Castle Combe★★, NW : 6 m. by A 420 and B 4039.
⌐₅ Monkton Park Par Three ℰ 653928.
🇮 The Neeld Hall, High St., SN15 3ER ℰ 657733.
◆London 106 – ◆Bristol 27 – ◆Southampton 64 – Swindon 21.

🏨 **Stanton Manor** ⤬, Stanton St. Quinton, SN14 6DQ, N : 5 m. by A 429 ℰ 0666 (Malmesbury) 837552, Fax 837022, ☞ – 📺 ☎ 🅿 ◪ ⒜⒠ 𝗩𝗜𝗦𝗔 ❀
closed 2 weeks August and 1 week Christmas-New Year – **M** *(closed Sunday to non-residents)* a la carte 16.15/24.95 **st.** – **10 rm** ⊂⊃ 68.00/82.00 **st.** – SB (weekends only) 105.00/160.00 **st.**

🔧 ATS Cocklebury Rd ℰ 653541

CHIPPERFIELD Herts. 𝟦𝟢𝟦 ⓐ – pop. 1 764 – ECD : Wednesday – ⊠ ☎ 0923 Kings Langley.
◆London 27 – Hemel Hempstead 5 – Watford 6.

🏨 Two Brewers Inn (Forte), The Common, WD4 9BS, ℰ 265266, Fax 261884 – ↫ 📺 ☎ 🅿 – ⅋ 25
20 rm.

CHIPPING Lancs. 𝟦𝟢𝟤 M 22 – pop. 1 376 – ⊠ Preston – ☎ 0995.
◆London 233 – Lancaster 30 – ◆Leeds 54 – ◆Manchester 40 – Preston 12.

🏨 **Gibbon Bridge Country House** ⤬, PR3 2TQ, E : 1 m. on Clitheroe rd ℰ 61456, Fax 61277, ⇐, *Ƒ₆,* ☞, ✗ – ↫ 📺 ☎ & 🅿 ◪ ⑩ 𝗩𝗜𝗦𝗔 ❀
M 11.00/20.00 **t.** and dinner a la carte ⓛ 4.25 – **15 rm** ⊂⊃ 60.00/80.00 **t.**, **15 suites** 100.00/150.00 **t.** – SB (except Bank Holidays) 90.00/120.00 **st.**

See : Town★.

Envir. : Hidcote Manor Garden★★ *AC*, NE : 2½ m.

🏛️ Woolstaplers Hall Museum, High St., GL55 6HB ℘ 840101 (summer only).

♦London 93 – Cheltenham 21 – ♦Oxford 37 – Stratford-upon-Avon 12.

🏨 **Cotswold House,** The Square, GL55 6AN, ℘ 840330, Fax 840310, « Attractively converted Regency town house », ☞ – ⇔ rest 📺 ☎ ℗. 🖎 🆎 ⓞ 𝒱𝒾𝒮𝒜. ✻
closed 24 to 27 December – **M** (light lunch Monday to Saturday)/dinner 24.50 **t.** – **15 rm** ⊑ 65.00/120.00 **t.** – SB 117.00/158.00 **st.**

🏨 **Seymour House,** High St., GL55 6AH, ℘ 840429, Fax 840369, « Mature grapevine in restaurant », ☞ – 📺 ☎ ℗. 🖎 🆎 𝒱𝒾𝒮𝒜. ✻
M 12.50/22.00 **t.** and lunch a la carte ♦ 5.00 – ⊑ 7.15 – **13 rm** 45.00/76.50 **t.**, 3 suites – SB (except Christmas-New Year) 84.00/192.00 **st.**

🏨 **Noel Arms** (Best Western), High St., GL55 6AT, ℘ 840317, Fax 841136 – 📺 ☎ ℗. 🖎 🆎 𝒱𝒾𝒮𝒜. ✻
🛎️ 35. 🖎 🆎 𝒱𝒾𝒮𝒜. ✻
M (bar lunch Monday to Saturday)/dinner 15.75 **st.** and a la carte – **26 rm** ⊑ 58.00/78.00 **st.** – SB 80.00/132.00 **st.**

🍴 **Caminetto,** Old Kings Arms Pantry, High St., GL55 6HB, ℘ 840934 – 🖎 𝒱𝒾𝒮𝒜
closed Monday lunch, Sunday and 3 weeks Easter – **M** - **Italian** a la carte 9.55/24.30 **t.** ♦ 4.85.

at Mickleton N : 3¼ m. by B 4035 and B 4081 on B 4632 – ⊠ Chipping Campden – ✆ 0386 Mickleton :

🏨 **Three Ways,** GL55 6SB, ℘ 438429, Fax 438118, ☞ – 📺 ☎ ℗ – 🛎️ 75. 🖎 🆎 ⓞ 𝒱𝒾𝒮𝒜
M (bar lunch Monday to Saturday)/dinner 16.50 **st.** – **40 rm** ⊑ 44.00/68.00 **st.** – SB (except Bank Holidays) 90.00/110.00 **st.**

🏠 **Holly Mount** without rest., High St., GL55 6SL, ℘ 438243, Fax 438858, ☞ – 📺 ℗
3 rm ⊑ 33.00/40.00 **s.**

at Charingworth E : 3 m. by B 4035 – ⊠ Chipping Campden – ✆ 0386 78 (3 fig.) and 0386 (6 fig.) Paxford :

🏨 **Charingworth Manor** ⬙, GL55 6NS, on B 4035 ℘ 555, Telex 333444, Fax 353, ≼, « Early 14C manor house with Jacobean additions », ⓢ, 🖎, ☞, park, ✻ – 📺 ☎ ℗ –
🛎️ 30. 🖎 🆎 ⓞ 𝒱𝒾𝒮𝒜
M 15.50/27.50 **st.** ♦ 6.00 – **24 rm** ⊑ 85.00/210.00 **t.** – SB 145.00/254.00 **st.**

at Broad Campden S : 1¼ m. by B 4081 – ⊠ Chipping Campden – ✆ 0386 Evesham :

🏠 **Malt House** ⬙, GL55 6UU, ℘ 840295, Fax 841334, « 17C house », ☞ – ⇔ rest 📺 ℗.
🖎 𝒱𝒾𝒮𝒜
closed 23 December-1 January – **M** *(closed Monday)* (residents only) (communal dining) (dinner only) 19.50/22.50 **st.** ♦ 6.00 – **5 rm** ⊑ 37.50/87.50 **st.** – SB (April-October) (except Bank Holidays) 70.00/80.00 **st.**

Envir. : Chastleton House★★, NW : 4 m. by A 44.

🛫 Lyneham ℘ 0993 (Shipton-under-Wychwood) 831841, W : 4 m. by A 361.

♦London 77 – ♦Birmingham 44 – Gloucester 36 – ♦Oxford 21.

🏨 **White Hart** (Resort), High St., OX7 5AD, ℘ 642572, Fax 644143 – 📺 ☎ ℗ – 🛎️ 55. 🖎 🆎 ⓞ 𝒱𝒾𝒮𝒜
M a la carte 8.95/13.15 **t.** – **20 rm** ⊑ 45.00/75.00 **st.**

♦London 55 – ♦Oxford 7.

🏠 **Coach and Horses,** OX44 7UX, ℘ 890255, Fax 891995 – 📺 ☎ ℗. 🖎 🆎 ⓞ 𝒱𝒾𝒮𝒜. ✻
M *(closed Sunday dinner)* 11.75/25.00 **t.** and a la carte ♦ 3.75 – **9 rm** ⊑ 35.00/45.00 **st.** – SB (weekends only) 70.00/90.00 **st.**

♦London 216 – Barnstaple 14 – Exeter 28 – Taunton 45.

🏨 **Highbullen** ⬙, EX37 9HD, ℘ 540561, Fax 540492, ≼, ⓢ, 🖎 heated, 🖎, 🛶, ⬙, ☞, park, ✻, squash – ⇔ rest 📺 ☎ ℗ – 🛎️ 25. ✻
M (bar lunch)/dinner 17.50 **st.** ♦ 4.75 – ⊑ 2.50 – **37 rm** (dinner included) 60.00/140.00 **st.**

♦London 35 – Reading 21 – ♦Southampton 53.

🍴 **Quails,** 1 Bagshot Rd, GU24 8BP, ℘ 858491 – 🖎. 🖎 🆎 ⓞ 𝒱𝒾𝒮𝒜
closed Saturday lunch, Sunday dinner and Monday – **M** 15.95 **t.** and a la carte.

CHOLLERFORD Northd. 401 402 N 18 Great Britain G. – pop. 813 – ⊠ ☻ 0434 Hexham.

Envir. : Hadrian's Wall★★ – Chesters★ (Bath House★) *AC*, W : ½ m. by B 6318.

◆London 303 – ◆Carlisle 36 – ◆Newcastle upon Tyne 21.

🏨 **George** (Swallow), NE46 4EW, ℰ 681611, Fax 681727, ≤, « Riverside gardens », �, 🖾, ➡ – ☒⇔ rm ⊡ ☎ & ℗ – 🔬 60. 🖾 🖭 ⑩ 𝚅𝙸𝚂𝙰
M 14.50/22.00 **st.** and a la carte ↕ 5.00 – **50 rm** ⊏ 78.50/98.50 **st.** – SB (except Christmas-New Year) 130.00 **st.**

CHORLEY Lancs. 402 404 M 23 – pop. 33 465 – ECD : Wednesday – ☻ 025 72 (5 fig.) and 0257 (6 fig.).

🏌 Duxbury Park, Duxbury Hall Rd ℰ 265380, S : 1 ½ m. – 🏌 Shaw Hill Hotel G. & C.C., Preston Rd, Whittle-le-Woods ℰ 269221, N : 1 ½ m. by A 6.

◆London 222 – ◆Blackpool 30 – ◆Liverpool 32 – ◆Manchester 26.

🏨 **Hartwood Hall**, Preston Rd, PR6 7AX, N : 1 m. on A 6 ℰ 269966, Fax 241678 – ⊡ ☎ ℗ – 🔬 100. 🖾 🖭 ⑩ 𝚅𝙸𝚂𝙰 𝙹𝙲𝙱
closed 25 to 30 December and 1 January – **M** (bar lunch Saturday) 6.75/15.50 **st.** and a la carte ↕ 5.50 – **22 rm** ⊏ 32.80/62.00 **st.** – SB 68.00/120.00 **st.**

at Whittle-le-Woods N : 2 m. on A 6 – ⊠ ☻ 0257 Chorley :

🏨🏨 **Shaw Hill H. Golf & Country Club** ⟋, Preston Rd, PR6 7PP, ℰ 269221, Fax 261223, ≤, 🏌 – ⊡ ☎ ℗ – 🔬 60. 🖾 🖭 𝚅𝙸𝚂𝙰
M (bar lunch Saturday) 10.95/17.95 **st.** and a la carte – **22 rm** ⊏ 65.00/110.00 **st.** – SB 87.50/165.00 **st.**

🏠 **Parkville**, 174 Preston Rd, PR6 7HE, ℰ 261881, Fax 273171, ☞ – ⊡ ☎ ℗. 🖾 🖭 ⑩ 𝚅𝙸𝚂𝙰 𝙹𝙲𝙱 ✻
M *(closed Sunday to non-residents)* (dinner only) 15.00 **t.** and a la carte ↕ 4.50 – **13 rm** ⊏ 40.00/80.00 **st.** – SB 80.00/160.00 **st.**

🔘 ATS 18 Westminster Rd ℰ 62000/65472

CHORLTON CUM HARDY Gtr. Manchester 402 403 404 N 23 – see Manchester.

CHRISTCHURCH Dorset 403 404 O 31 The West Country G. – pop. 32 854 – ECD : Wednesday – ☻ 0202.

See : Town★ – Priory★.

Envir. : Hengistbury Head★ (≤★★) SW : 4 ½ m. by A 35 and B 3059.

🏌 Highcliffe Castle, 107 Lymington Rd, Highcliffe-on-Sea ℰ 0425 (Highcliffe) 272953, W : 2 m. – 🏌 Iford Bridge, Barrack Rd, Iford ℰ 473817.

🛈 23 High St., BH23 1AB ℰ 471780.

◆London 111 – Bournemouth 6 – Salisbury 26 – ◆Southampton 24 – Winchester 39.

🏠 **Travel Inn**, Somerford Rd, BH23 3QG, E : 2 m. by A 35 on B 3059 ℰ 485376, Fax 474939 – ☒⇔ rm ⊡ & ℗ – 🔬 60. 🖾 🖭 𝚅𝙸𝚂𝙰 ✻
M (Beefeater grill) a la carte approx. 16.00 **t.** ↕ 5.60 – ⊏ 4.95 – **38 rm** 33.50 **t.**

🍴 **Splinters Brasserie**, 12 Church St., BH23 1BW, ℰ 483454, Fax 483454 – 🖾 🖭 ⑩ 𝚅𝙸𝚂𝙰
closed Monday lunch, Sunday and 9 to 24 January – **M** 8.60 **t.** (lunch) and a la carte 12.50/25.30 **t.** ↕ 4.70.

at Mudeford SE : 2 m. – ⊠ ☻ 0202 Christchurch :

🏨🏨 **Avonmouth** (Forte), 95 Mudeford, BH23 3NT, ℰ 483434, Fax 479004, ≤, 🔥 heated, ☞ – ☒⇔ ⊡ ☎ ℗ – 🔬 60. 🖾 🖭 ⑩ 𝚅𝙸𝚂𝙰
M (bar lunch Monday to Saturday)/dinner 15.95 **st.** and a la carte – ⊏ 8.95 – **41 rm** 75.00/90.00 **st.** – SB 128.00/144.00 **st.**

🏨🏨 **Waterford Lodge** (Best Western), 87 Bure Lane, Friars Cliff, BH23 4DN, ℰ 0425 (Highcliffe) 272948, Fax 279130, ☞ – ⊡ ☎ ℗. 🖾 🖭 𝚅𝙸𝚂𝙰 𝙹𝙲𝙱
M 15.00 **st.** (lunch) and a la carte 17.90/27.50 **st.** ↕ 4.80 – **17 rm** ⊏ 66.00/103.00 **st.** – SB (except Christmas) 104.00/180.00 **st.**

CHURCHILL Oxon. 403 404 P 28 – pop. 421 – ⊠ Chipping Norton – ☻ 060 871 (3 and 4 fig.) and 0608 (6 fig.) Kingham.

◆London 79 – ◆Birmingham 46 – Cheltenham 29 – ◆Oxford 23 – Swindon 31.

🏠 **Forge House** without rest., OX7 6NJ, ℰ 658173 – ⊡ ℗. ✻
4 rm ⊏ 30.00/50.00 **st.**

CHURCH STRETTON Shrops. 403 L 26 Great Britain G. – pop. 2 932 – ECD : Wednesday – ☻ 0694.

Envir. : Wenlock Edge★, E : by B 4371.

🏌 Trevor Hill ℰ 722281, W : ½ m. by A 49.

◆London 166 – ◆Birmingham 46 – Hereford 39 – Shrewsbury 14.

🏠 **Mynd House**, Ludlow Rd, Little Stretton, SY6 6RB, SW : 1 m. on B 4370 ℰ 722212, Fax 724180, ☞ – ⊡ ☎ ℗. 🖾 🖭 𝚅𝙸𝚂𝙰
closed January and 1 week summer – **M** (bar lunch)/dinner 25.00 **st.** and a la carte ↕ 4.40 – **7 rm** ⊏ 40.00/75.00 **st.**, 1 suite – SB (except Bank Holidays) 90.00/110.00 **st.**

🔘 ATS Crossways ℰ 722526/722112

Glos. **403 404** O 28 Great Britain G. – pop. 13 491 – ECD : Thursday – ✆ 0285.

See : Town★ – Church of St. John the Baptist★ – Corinium Museum★ (Mosaic pavements★)
AC.

Envir. : Fairford : Church of St. Mary★ (stained glass windows★★) E : 7 m. by A 417.

🚉 Cheltenham Rd ✆ 653939, N : 1½ m. on A 435.

🏢 Corn Hall, Market Pl., GL7 2NW ✆ 654180.

◆London 97 – ◆Bristol 37 – Gloucester 19 – ◆Oxford 37.

🏨 **Fleece** (Resort), Market Pl., GL7 2NZ, ✆ 658507, Fax 651017 – 📺 ☎ **❷** – 🛄 30. 🅰 🅰🅴 🅾
VISA
M (bar lunch Monday to Saturday) 9.95/12.95 **st.** and dinner a la carte – ⬜ 7.50 – **30 rm**
55.00/75.00 **st.** – SB 80.00/120.00 **st.**

↑ **Wimborne House,** 91 Victoria Rd, GL7 1ES, ✆ 653890, ☞ – ⇄ 📺 **❷**. ❀
closed Christmas-New Year – **M** (by arrangement) 6.50 **st.** – **5 rm** ⬜ 28.00/45.00 **st.**

✗ **Harry Hare's,** 3 Gosditch St., GL7 2AG, ✆ 652375, ☞ – 🅰 🅰🅴 **VISA**
M a la carte 14.40/20.95 **t.** ▮ 3.95.

at Rendcomb N : 6¼ m. by A 417 and A 435 – ✉ ✆ 0285 Cirencester :

↑ **Shawswell Country House** ⍋, GL7 7HD, N : 1½ m. on No Through Rd ✆ 831779, ≤,
« Part 17C and 18C house », ☞, park – ⇄ 📺 **❷**. ❀
closed December and January – **M** *(by arrangement)* 16.00 **st.** ▮ 7.25 – **5 rm** ⬜ 35.00/
55.00 **st.** – SB (except Bank Holidays) 74.50/97.00 **st.**

at Barnsley NE : 4 m. by A 429 on B 4425 – ✉ ✆ 0285 Cirencester :

🛏 **Village Pub,** GL7 5EF, ✆ 740421 – 📺 ☎ **❷**. 🅰 🅰🅴 **VISA**
closed 25 December – **M** a la carte 8.50/13.65 **t.** ▮ 3.60 – **5 rm** ⬜ 29.00/44.00 **st.**

at Ampney Crucis E : 2¾ m. by A 417 – ✉ ✆ 0285 Cirencester :

🏨 **Crown of Crucis,** GL7 5RS, ✆ 851806, Fax 851735, ☞ – ⇄ 📺 ☎ **❷** – 🛄 80. 🅰 🅰🅴 🅾
VISA
M (bar lunch Monday to Saturday)/dinner 15.00 **t.** and a la carte ▮ 4.80 – **25 rm** ⬜ 49.00/
60.00 **t.** – SB (weekends only) 86.00/124.00 **st.**

↑ **Waterton Garden Cottage** ⍋, GL7 5RX, S : ½ m. by Driffield rd turning right into
unmarked driveway ✆ 851303, « Converted Victorian stables, walled garden », 🏊 heated – ⇄ rm **❷**
(booking essential) closed 2 weeks Christmas – **M** (by arrangement) 20.00 – **3 rm** ⬜ 25.00/
45.00 **s.**

at Ewen SW : 3¼ m. by A 429 – ✉ ✆ 0285 Cirencester :

🛏 **Wild Duck Inn,** Drake's Island, GL7 6BY, ✆ 770310, Fax 770310, « Part 16C former farm
buildings », ☞ – 📺 ☎ **❷**. 🅰 🅰🅴 **VISA**
M a la carte 10.45/18.40 **t.** – **9 rm** ⬜ 48.00/75.00 **st.** – SB 80.00/110.00 **st.**

at Kemble SW : 4 m. by A 433 on A 429 – ✉ ✆ 0285 Cirencester:

↑ **Smerrill Barns** without rest., GL7 6BW, on A 429 ✆ 770907, Fax 770907 – ⇄ 📺 **❷**. 🅰
VISA. ❀
7 rm ⬜ 20.00/65.00 **t.**

at Stratton NW : 1¼ m. on A 417 – ✉ ✆ 0285 Cirencester :

🏨 **Stratton House,** Gloucester Rd, GL7 2LE, ✆ 651761, Fax 640024, ☞ – 📺 ☎ **❷** –
🛄 150. 🅰 🅰🅴 🅾 **VISA**
M (bar lunch Monday to Saturday)/dinner 16.95 **st.** and a la carte – **41 rm** ⬜ 55.00/
90.00 **st.** – SB (except Christmas and New Year) 85.90/135.90 **st.**

◍ ATS 1 Mercian Close, Watermoor End ✆ 657761

Oxon. **403 404** P 28 – pop. 822 – ECD : Wednesday and Saturday – ✆ 036 781.

◆London 76 – ◆Oxford 20 – Swindon 17.

✗✗✗ **Plough at Clanfield** with rm, Bourton Rd, OX18 2RB, on A 4095 ✆ 222, Fax 596, « Small
Elizabethan manor house », ☞ – ⇄ rest 📺 ☎ **❷**. 🅰 🅰🅴 🅾 **VISA** **JCB**. ❀
M 14.95/32.95 **t.** – **6 rm** ⬜ 60.00/95.00 **t.** – SB 110.00/140.00 **st.**

Beds. **404** S 27 – see Bedford.

Cumbria – see Ambleside.

Lancs. **402** M 21 – see Lancaster.

Essex **404** U 28 – pop. 1 076 – ✉ ✆ 0799 Saffron Walden.

◆London 44 – ◆Cambridge 25 – Colchester 44 – Luton 29.

✗ **Cricketers,** CB11 4QT, ✆ 550442, Fax 550882 – **❷**. 🅰 **VISA**
closed 25 and 26 December – **M** (bar lunch Monday to Saturday)/dinner 18.50 **t.** ▮ 6.50.

Ganz EUROPA auf einer Karte (mit Ortsregister) :
Michelin-Karte Nr. **970**

CLAWTON Devon `403` H 31 The West Country G. – pop. 300 – ✉ Holsworthy – ☎ 040 927 (3 fig.) and 0409 (6 fig.) North Tamerton.

Envir. : W : Tamar River★★.

◆London 240 – Exeter 39 – ◆Plymouth 36.

🏠 **Court Barn** ⏴, EX22 6PS, W : ½ m. ℰ 219, ⌁, ✂ – ⫣ rm 📺 ☎ 🅿. ⌂ 🆎 ⓪ *VISA*
M 11.00/19.50 **t.** 🍷 3.95 – **8 rm** ⊏ 35.00/86.00 **t.** – SB (except Bank Holidays) 84.00/100.00 **st.**

CLAYGATE Surrey `404` @ – see Esher.

CLAYTON-LE-MOORS Lancs `402` M 22 – pop. 5 484 – ECD : Wednesday – ✉ ☎ 0254 Accrington.

◆London 232 – Blackburn 3.5 – Lancaster 37 – ◆Leeds 44 – Preston 14.

🏨 Dunkenhalgh, Blackburn Rd, BB5 5JP, W : 1 ½ m. on A 678 ℰ 398021, Telex 63282, Fax 872230, 🛵, ☎ˢ, ⬛, ⌁ – 📺 ☎ 🅿 – 🏌 400
79 rm, 1 suite.

🏠 **Sparth House**, Whalley Rd, BB5 5RP, ℰ 872263, Fax 872263, ⌁ – ⫣ rest 📺 ☎ 🅿. ✂
M *(closed Sunday dinner)* 9.50/13.95 **t.** and a la carte 🍷 4.50 – **15 rm** ⊏ 56.25/95.00 **t.** – SB (weekends only) 68.25/140.40 **st.**

CLAYTON-LE-WOODS Lancs. – pop. 8 002 (inc. Cuerden) – ✉ Chorley – ☎ 0772 Leyland.

◆London 220 – ◆Liverpool 31 – ◆Manchester 26 – Preston 5.5.

🏨 **Pines**, Preston Rd, PR6 7ED, on A 6 ℰ 38551, Fax 629002, ⌁ – ⫣ rm 📺 ☎ 🅿. ⌂ 🆎 *VISA* *JCB* ✂
closed 25 and 26 December – **M** 10.50/18.50 **t.** and a la carte – **39 rm** ⊏ 50.00/85.00 **t.** – SB (weekends only) 90.00/140.00 **st.**

Europe If the name of the hotel
is not in bold type,
on arrival ask the hotelier his prices.

CLEARWELL Glos. – see Coleford.

CLEETHORPES Humbs. `402` `404` U 23 – pop. 33 238 – ECD : Thursday – ☎ 0472.
🛈 42-43 Alexandra Rd, DN35 8LE ℰ 200220.

◆London 171 – Boston 49 – Lincoln 38 – ◆Sheffield 77.

Plan : see Great Grimsby

🏨 **Kingsway**, Kingsway, DN35 0AE, ℰ 601122, Fax 601381, ≤ – |🛗 📺 ☎ ⊜ 🅿. ⌂ 🆎 ⓪ *VISA* ✂
BZ **a**
closed 25 and 26 December – **M** 11.50/15.25 **t.** and a la carte 🍷 4.60 – **50 rm** ⊏ 54.00/80.00 **t.** – SB (weekends only) 82.00 **st.**

CLEEVE HILL Glos. `403` `404` N 28 – see Cheltenham.

CLEY NEXT THE SEA Norfolk `404` X 25 – see Blakeney.

CLIFTON HAMPDEN Oxon. `403` `404` Q 29 – see Abingdon.

CLITHEROE Lancs `402` M 22 – pop. 13 729 – ☎ 0200.
🛈 Whalley Rd ℰ 22618, S : 2 m.
🛈 12-14 Market Pl., BB7 2DA ℰ 25566.

◆London 64 – ◆Blackpool 35 – ◆Manchester 31.

✗ **Auctioneer**, New Market St., BB7 2JW, ℰ 27153 – ⌂ *VISA*
closed Monday and 1 week January – **M** 12.75/19.75 **t.** and lunch a la carte 🍷 4.75.

🔧 ATS Salthill Rd ℰ 23011

CLOVELLY Devon `403` G 31 The West Country G. – ✉ ☎ 0237 Bideford.

See : Village★★.

Exc. : Hartland : Hartland Church★ – Hartland Quay★ (viewpoint★★) – Hartland Point ≤★★★, W : 6 ½ m. by B 3237 and B 3248.

🏠 **Red Lion**, The Quay, EX39 5TF, ℰ 431237, Fax 431044, ≤ – 📺 🅿. ⌂ *VISA* ✂
M 9.50/19.50 **st.** 🍷 5.00 – **12 rm** ⊏ 37.50/59.00 **st.** – SB (October-March) 69.00 **st.**

CLOWNE Derbs. `402` `403` `404` Q 24 Great Britain G. – pop. 6 846 – ECD : Wednesday – ☎ 0246 Chesterfield.

Exc. : Bolsover Castle★ *AC*, S : 6 m. by B 6417 and A 632.

◆London 156 – Derby 40 – Lincoln 35 – ◆Nottingham 30 – ◆Sheffield 12.

🏨 **Van Dyk**, Worksop Rd, S43 4TD, N : ¾ m. by A 618 on A 619 ℰ 810219, Fax 819566 – 📺 ☎ 🅿 – 🏌 80. ⌂ 🆎 *VISA*
M *(closed Sunday dinner)* 16.95 **st.** and a la carte – **16 rm** ⊏ 40.00/50.00 **st.**

CLYST ST. GEORGE Devon – see Exeter.

COALVILLE Leics. 402 403 404 P 25 – pop. 28 772 – 🕓 0530.

🔲 Snibston Discovery Park, Ashby Rd, LE6 2LN ✆ 813608.

◆London 115 – ◆Birmingham 32 – ◆Leicester 15 – ◆Nottingham 25.

🏨 **Hermitage Park**, Whitwick Rd, LE67 3FA, off High St. ✆ 814814, Fax 814202, 🕿 –
🔲 rest 📺 ☎ 🅿 – 🔬 30. 🔃 🆎 *VISA* 🛇
M a la carte approx. 10.00 – **24 rm** ⊑ 35.00/59.50 t., 1 suite – SB (weekends only) 45.00/
80.00 **st.**

COATHAM MUNDEVILLE Durham 402 P 20 – see Darlington.

COBHAM Kent 404 V 29 – pop. 13 795 (inc. Oxshott) – ✉ 🕓 0474 Gravesend.

🝙 Silvermere, Redhill Rd ✆ 867275.

◆London 27 – Maidstone 13 – Rochester 6.

🝣 **Ye Olde Leather Bottle** (Chef & Brewer), The Street, DA12 3BZ, ✆ 814327, 🏜 – 📺 ☎
🅿. 🔃 🆎 *VISA* 🛇
M 15.00/20.00 **t.** and a la carte – ⊑ 3.50 – **7 rm** 34.95/38.45 **t.**

COBHAM Surrey 404 S 30 – pop. 13 920 – ECD : Wednesday – 🕓 0932.

◆London 24 – Guildford 10.

Plan : see Greater London (South-West)

🏨 **Hilton National**, Seven Hills Rd South, KT11 1EW, W : 1 ½ m. by A 245 ✆ 864471, Telex
929196, Fax 868017, 🕿, 🔲, 🏜, park, 🎾, squash – 📳 ⇔ rm 📺 ☎ 🅿 – 🔬 250. 🔃 🆎 ⓞ
VISA *JCB*   by A 3   AZ
M (closed Saturday lunch) (dancing Friday and Saturday evenings) 12.50/25.00 **st.** and a la
carte 🍴 6.75 – ⊑ 10.25 – **149 rm** 99.00/124.00 **st.**, 3 suites.

🏠 **Cedar House**, Mill Rd, KT11 3AN, ✆ 863424, Fax 862023, 🏜 – 📺 ☎ 🅿. 🔃 🆎 *VISA*.
🛇
closed 25 to 31 December – **M** (closed Sunday and Monday) (dinner only)
19.95 **t.** and a la carte 🍴 5.25 – **6 rm** ⊑ 40.00/75.00 **t.**   by A 307   AZ

at Stoke D'Abernon SE : 1 ½ m. on A 245 – AZ – ✉ Cobham – 🕓 0372 Oxshott :

🏨 **Woodlands Park**, Woodlands Lane, KT11 3QB, on A 245 ✆ 843933, Fax 842704, 🏜,
park, 🎾 – 📳 ⇔ rm 📺 ☎ 🅿 – 🔬 200. 🔃 🆎 ⓞ *VISA* 🛇
M (closed Saturday lunch) 12.75/15.75 **st.** and a la carte 🍴 4.00 – ⊑ 8.50 – **57 rm** 100.00/
130.00 **st.**, 1 suite – SB (weekends only) 120.00/160.00 **st.**

COCKERMOUTH Cumbria 401 402 J 20 – pop. 7 074 – ECD : Thursday – 🕓 0900.

🝙 Embleton ✆ 076 87 (Bassenthwaite) 76223, E : 4 m.

🔲 Town Hall, Market St., CA13 9NP ✆ 822634.

◆London 306 – ◆Carlisle 25 – Keswick 13.

🏨 **Trout**, Crown St., CA13 0EJ, ✆ 823591, Fax 827514, 🔍, 🏜 – 📺 ☎ 🅿 – 🔬 50. 🔃
VISA
M 9.95/17.95 **t.** and a la carte 🍴 4.95 – **23 rm** ⊑ 35.00/69.95 **t.** – SB (except Bank Holidays)
69.00/87.80 **st.**

🏠 **Low Hall** 🌥, Brandlingill, CA13 0RE, S : 3¼ m. by A 5086 on Lorton rd ✆ 826654, ≼, 🏜
– ⇔ 🅿. 🔃 *VISA* 🛇
March-October – **M** 15.00 **st.** 🍴 4.25 – **6 rm** ⊑ 30.00/56.00 **st.**

COGGESHALL Essex 404 W 28 – pop. 3 505 – ECD : Wednesday – ✉ Colchester – 🕓 0376.

🝙, 🝙 Earls Colne ✆ 0787 (Halstead) 224466, N : 2 m. by A 120 and B 1024.

◆London 49 – Braintree 6 – Chelmsford 16 – Colchester 9.

🏨 **White Hart**, Market End, CO6 1NH, ✆ 561654, Fax 561789, « Part 15C guildhall », 🏜 –
📺 ☎ 🅿. 🔃 🆎 ⓞ *VISA* 🛇
M - Italian (closed Sunday dinner) 13.95/14.95 **t.** and a la carte 🍴 4.99 – **18 rm** ⊑ 55.35/
97.00 **t.** – SB (weekends only) 95.50/136.30 **st.**

🍴🍴 **Baumann's Brasserie**, 4-6 Stoneham St., CO6 1TT, ✆ 561453 – 🔃 🆎 *VISA*
closed Saturday lunch, Sunday dinner, Monday and first 2 weeks January – **M** 24.50 **t.** and a
la carte 🍴 4.25.

GRÜNE REISEFÜHRER

Landschaften, Baudenkmäler
Sehenswürdigkeiten
Fremdenverkehrsstraßen
Tourenvorschläge
Stadtpläne und Übersichtskarten

COLCHESTER Essex 404 W 28 **Great Britain G.** – pop. 87 476 – ECD : Thursday – ☏ 0206.

See : Castle and Museum★ *AC* – ⛳ Birch Grove, Layer Rd ✆ 734276, S : 3 m. by B 1026.

ℹ 1 Queen St., CO1 2PJ ✆ 712920.

◆London 52 – ◆Cambridge 48 – ◆Ipswich 18 – Luton 76 – Southend-on-Sea 41.

- **Red Lion** (Best Western), 43 High St., CO1 1DJ, ✆ 577986, Fax 578207, « Part 15C inn » – TV ☎ – 40. AE VISA
  M *(closed Sunday lunch)* 13.85 **st.** and a la carte – **24 rm** 35.00/55.00 **st.** – SB (weekends only) 80.00/130.00 **st.**
- **George** (Q.M.H.), 116 High St., CO1 1TD, ✆ 578494, Fax 761732, – TV ☎ – 90. AE VISA
  M (bar lunch Monday to Friday)/dinner 10.25 **st.** and a la carte 4.60 – **47 rm** 59.00/83.00 **st.** – SB (weekends only) 80.00 **st.**
- **Butterfly,** Old Ipswich Rd, CO7 7QY, NE : 4¼ m. by A 1232 at junction of A 12 and A 120 ✆ 230900, Fax 231095 – TV ☎ – 80. AE VISA
  M 8.75/11.50 **st.** and a la carte 4.50 – 6.00 – **50 rm** 49.00/80.00 **st.** – SB (weekends only) 67.50/86.00 **st.**
- **Rose and Crown,** East St., Eastgates, CO1 2TZ, ✆ 866677, Fax 866616 – TV ☎ – 100. AE VISA
  M 13.95 **t.** and a la carte 3.85 – **31 rm** 55.00 **t.** – SB 79.00/118.00 **st.**
- **Warehouse Brasserie,** 12a Chapel St. North, CO2 7AT, ✆ 765656 – VISA
  closed Good Friday lunch and 25-26 December – **M** a la carte 12.70/16.40 **t.** 3.75.

at Nayland N : 6½ m. by A 134 – ✉ ☏ 0206 Colchester :

- **Martha's Vineyard,** 18 High St., CO6 4JF, ✆ 262888 – VISA
  closed Sunday, Monday, 2 weeks summer and and 3 weeks winter – **M** (dinner only) a la carte 14.70/18.95 **t.**

at Stoke by Nayland N : 8½ m. by A 134 on B 1087 – ✉ ☏ 0206 Colchester :

- **Angel Inn** with rm, Polstead St., CO6 4SA, ✆ 263245, Fax 37324, « Part timbered 17C inn » – TV ☎. AE VISA JCB
  closed 25-26 December and 1 January – **M** a la carte 11.10/15.50 **t.** 3.50 – **6 rm** 43.50/57.50 **st.**

at Eight Ash Green W : 4 m. by A 604 and A 12 – ✉ ☏ 0206 Colchester :

- **Forte Posthouse,** Abbotts Lane, CO6 3QL, at junction of A 604 with A 12 ✆ 767740, Fax 766577, – rm TV ☎ – 50. AE VISA JCB
  M a la carte approx. 17.50 **t.** 4.65 – 6.95 – **110 rm** 53.50 **st.** – SB (weekends only) 90.00 **st.**

at Marks Tey W : 5 m. by A 12 at junction with A 120 – ✉ ☏ 0206 Colchester :

- **Marks Tey,** London Rd, CO6 1DU, on B 1408 ✆ 210001, Fax 212167, – rm TV ☎ – 200. AE VISA
  closed 24 December-4 January – **M** 10.50/13.50 **t.** and a la carte 4.80 – 6.00 – **109 rm** 53.50/56.50 **t.**, 1 suite – SB (weekends only) 79.00 **st.**

ATS East Hill ✆ 866484/867471
ATS 451 Ipswich Rd ✆ 841404
ATS Telford Way, Severalls Park Ind. Est. ✆ 845641

COLEBROOK Devon 403 H 32 – see Plymouth.

COLEFORD Devon 403 I 31 – ✉ Crediton – ☏ 0363 Copplestone.

◆London 214 – Barnstaple 29 – Exeter 14 – Taunton 42.

- **New Inn,** EX17 5BZ, ✆ 84242, Fax 85044, « Part 13C thatched inn » – rm TV. AE VISA
  M (in bar) a la carte 8.75/14.25 **t.** 4.50 – **3 rm** 33.00/52.00 **st.**

COLEFORD Glos. 403 404 M 28 **Great Britain G.** – pop. 8 246 – ECD : Thursday – ☏ 0594 Dean.

Envir. : W : Wye Valley★.

⛳ Forest of Dean, Lords Hills ✆ 832583, SE : ½ m. on Parkend Rd – ⛳ Forest Hills, Mile End Rd ✆ 810620, W : 1 m. on Gloucester Rd.

ℹ Woolstaplers Hall Museum, High St., GL55 6HB ✆ 840101.

◆London 143 – ◆ Bristol 28 – Gloucester 19 – Newport 29.

- **Speech House** (Forte), Forest of Dean, GL16 7EL, NE : 3 m. by B 4028 on B 4226 ✆ 822607, Fax 823658, – TV ☎. AE VISA
  M (bar lunch Monday to Saturday)/dinner 17.95 **t.** and a la carte 6.45 – 8.50 – **14 rm** 70.00/110.00 **t.** – SB 138.00 **st.**

at Clearwell S : 2 m. by B 4228 – ✉ Coleford – ☏ 0594 Dean :

- **Wyndham Arms,** GL16 8JT, ✆ 833666, Fax 836450 – TV ☎. AE VISA JCB
  M 12.75/15.25 **t.** and a la carte 3.75 – **17 rm** 35.00/60.00 **t.**
- **Tudor Farmhouse,** GL16 8JS, ✆ 833046, Fax 837093 – rm TV ☎. AE VISA JCB. – **M** *(closed Sunday except Bank Holidays)* (dinner only) 15.00 **t.** – **8 rm** 42.50/59.00 **t.**, 1 suite – SB (except Bank Holidays) 65.00/115.00 **st.**

COLERNE Wilts. 408 404 M 29 – see Bath (Avon).

COLESBOURNE Glos. 408 404 N 28 – see Cheltenham.

COLESHILL Warks. 408 404 O 26 – pop. 6 038 – ECD : Monday and Thursday – ⊠ Birmingham – 🕿 0675.

◆London 113 – ◆Birmingham 8 – ◆Coventry 11.

  🏨 Coleshill, 152 High St., B46 3BG, 𝒫 465527, Fax 464013 – ⫤ rm 📺 🕿 🅟 – 🔬 150. ⋘
    23 rm.

COLLYWESTON Northants. 402 404 S 26 – see Stamford (Lincs.).

COLNE Lancs. 402 N 22 – pop. 19 094 – 🕿 0282.

🚗 Law Farm, Skipton Old Rd 𝒫 863391, N : 1 ½ m. – 🚗 Ghyll Brow, Barnoldswick 𝒫 842466.

◆London 234 – ◆Manchester 29 – Preston 26.

  🏠 **West Lynn Country House,** Barrowford Rd, BB8 9QW, W : ½ m. on B 6247 𝒫 869199,
    Fax 869199, ☞ – 📺 🕿 🅟. 🗚 🖭 ⋘
    M *(closed Sunday dinner)* (dinner only and Sunday lunch)/dinner 13.95 **st.** and a la carte
    ⅛ 3.95 – **12 rm** � 42.50/60.00 **st.** – SB 72.90/97.90 **st.**

  🏠 **Higher Slipper Hill Farm** ⏤, Foulridge, BB8 7LY, NW : 3 ¾ m. by A 56 and B 6251 on
    Barrowford rd 𝒫 863602, ≼, ☞ – 📺 🅟. 🗚 🖭 🖭 ⋘
    M *(closed Saturday and Sunday)* (residents only) (dinner only) a la carte 12.15/18.00 **st.** –
    9 rm ⊒ 38.80/50.55 **st.**

  🏠 Old Stone Trough, Kelbrook, BB8 6XY, N : 3 m. on A 56 𝒫 844844, Fax 844428 – 📺 🕿 &
    🅟 – 🔬 40
    M (carving rest.) – **37 rm.**

⑩ ATS Corporation St. (ASDA) 𝒫 864616

    Great Britain and Ireland are covered entirely
    at a scale of 16 miles to 1 inch by our map « Main roads » 986.

COLN ST. ALDWYNS Glos. – ⊠ 🕿 0285 Cirencester.

◆London 101 – ◆Bristol 53 – Gloucester 20 – Swindon 15.

  🏠 **New Inn,** GL7 5AN, 𝒫 750651, Fax 750657, « 16C inn » – 📺 🕿 🅟. 🗚 🖭 🖭 ⋘
    M (bar lunch)/dinner 15.50/21.50 **t.** and a la carte ⅛ 4.00 – ⊒ 3.00 – **10 rm** 45.00/80.00 **st.** –
    SB (except Bank Holidays) 77.00/138.00 **st.**

COLSTERWORTH Lincs. 402 404 S 25 – pop. 1 107 – 🕿 0476 Grantham.

◆London 105 – Granthan 8 – ◆Leicester 29 – ◆Nottingham 32 – Peterborough 14.

  🏠 **Granada Lodge** without rest., Granada Service Area, NG33 5JR, (southbound carriage-
    way) 𝒫 860686, Fax 861078, Reservations (Freephone) 0800 555300 – ⫤ 📺 🕿 & 🅟 –
    🔬 30. 🗚 🖭 🖭 ⋘
    ⊒ 4.00 – **36 rm** 34.95/37.95 **st.**

  🏠 **Forte Travelodge** without rest., NG33 5JJ, E : ½ m. by B 6403 on A 1 (southbound
    carriageway) 𝒫 861181, Reservations (Freephone) 0800 850950 – 📺 & 🅟. 🗚 🖭
    🖭
    32 rm 31.95 **t.**

  🏠 **Forte Travelodge** without rest., New Fox, South Witham, LE15 8AU, S : 3 m. by B 6403
    on A 1 (northbound carriageway) 𝒫 0572 (South Witham) 767586, Reservations (Free
    phone) 0800 850950 – 📺 & 🅟. 🗚 🖭 🖭
    32 rm 31.95 **t.**

COLTISHALL Norfolk 404 Y 25 Great Britain G. – pop. 1 314 – ⊠ 🕿 0603 Norwich.

Envir. : The Broads★.

◆London 133 – ◆Norwich 8.

  🏨 **Norfolk Mead** ⏤, Church St., NR12 7DN, 𝒫 737531, Fax 737521, 🔱 heated, ⏛, ☞,
    park – ⫤ 🅟. 🗚 🖭 ⑩ 🖭 ⋘
    closed 25 to 30 December – **M** *(closed Sunday dinner and Bank Holidays)* (dinner only and
    Sunday lunch)/dinner a la carte 17.00/26.00 **t.** – **10 rm** ⊒ 55.00/85.00 **t.** – SB (except New
    Year) 80.00/138.00 **st.**

COLYTON Devon 408 K 31 The West Country G. – pop. 2 435 – 🕿 0297.

See : Town★ - Church★.

Envir. : Axmouth (≼★) SE : 3 m. by B 3161, A 3052 and B 3172.

◆London 160 – Exeter 23 – Lyme Regis 7.

  🏠 **Old Bakehouse,** Lower Church St., EX13 6ND, 𝒫 552518 – 📺 🅟. 🗚 🖭
    M a la carte 13.70/19.75 **t.** ⅛ 4.00 – **10 rm** ⊒ 18.00/44.00 **t.** – SB 55.00/64.00 **st.**

  🏠 **Swallows Eaves,** Colyford, EX13 6QJ, SE : 1 ¼ m. on A 3052 𝒫 553184, ☞ – ⫤ 📺 🅟.
    ⋘
    M (dinner only) 16.50 **st.** – **8 rm** ⊒ 35.00/59.00 **st.** – SB (October-April) 74.00/101.00 **st.**

COMBE MARTIN Devon **403** H 30 − pop. 2 279 − ECD : Wednesday − ✉ Ilfracombe − ☎ 0271.

See : Ilfracombe : Hillsborough (≤★★) *AC*, Capstone Hill★ (≤★), St. Nicholas' Chapel (≤★) *AC*.

🛈 Cross St., EX34 0DN 🖉 883319 (summer only).

◆London 218 − Exeter 56 − Taunton 58.

🏠 **Coulsworthy Country House** ⬲, EX34 0PD, SE : 2½ m. by A 399 and Hunters Inn rd 🖉 882463, ≤, « Country house atmosphere », ⬳ heated, 🐎, ❀ − ⤞ rest 📺 🅿. ⬛ 𝗩𝗜𝗦𝗔
closed 8 December-8 February − **M** *(closed Sunday dinner to non residents)* (dinner only and Sunday lunch)/dinner 25.00 **st.** − **9 rm** ⌑ 26.00/74.00 **st.** − SB 96.00/180.00 **st.**

🏠 **Rone House,** King St., EX34 0AD, 🖉 883428, ⬳ heated, 🐎 − 📺 🅿. ⬛ 𝗩𝗜𝗦𝗔
March-October − **M** (dinner only) 11.00 **t.** and a la carte 🛦 3.50 − **11 rm** ⌑ 16.00/44.00 **st.**

🍴 **Just Johnsons,** King St., EX34 0BS, 🖉 883568 − ⬛ 𝗩𝗜𝗦𝗔
closed Monday and Tuesday in winter, Sunday and last 2 weeks May − **M** (dinner only) a la carte 14.00/18.90 **s.** 🛦 3.60.

CONGLETON Ches. **402** **403** **404** N 24 Great Britain G. − pop. 23 482 − ECD : Wednesday − ☎ 0260.

Envir. : Little Moreton Hall★★ *AC*, SW : 3 m. by A 34.

🛅 Biddulph Rd 🖉 273540, E : 1½ m. by A 527.

🛈 Town Hall, High St., CW12 1BN 🖉 271095.

◆London 183 − ◆Liverpool 50 − ◆Manchester 25 − ◆Sheffield 46 − ◆Stoke-on-Trent 13.

🏨 **Lion and Swan,** Swan Bank, CW12 1JR, 🖉 273115, Fax 299270, « 16C inn » − 📺 ☎ 🅿 −
🛦 80. ⬛ 🆎 ⓞ 𝗩𝗜𝗦𝗔 𝗝𝗖𝗕. ❀
M 15.95/19.95 **st.** and a la carte 🛦 5.95 − **21 rm** ⌑ 58.00/100.00 **st.**

⬙ ATS Brookside 🖉 273720

CONISTON Cumbria **402** K 20 Great Britain G. − pop. 1 713 − ☎ 053 94.

Envir. : Coniston Water★ − Brantwood★ *AC*, SE : 2 m. on east side of Coniston Water.

🛈 16 Yewdale Rd, LA21 8DU 🖉 41533 (summer only).

◆London 285 − ◆Carlisle 55 − Kendal 22 − Lancaster 42.

🏠 **Coniston Lodge,** Sunny Brow, LA21 8HH, 🖉 41201 − ⤞ 📺 ☎ 🅿. ⬛ 🆎 𝗩𝗜𝗦𝗔. ❀
M *(closed Sunday and Monday)* (dinner only) 17.50 **t.** 🛦 6.75 − **6 rm** ⌑ 35.00/70.00 **t.** −
SB (November-March except Christmas and New Year) 79.00/112.00 **st.**

🏠 **Sun,** LA21 8HQ, 🖉 41248, ≤, 🐎 − ⤞ rest 📺 ☎ 🅿
closed weekdays January − **M** (bar lunch)/dinner a la carte 10.15/17.35 **t.** − **11 rm** ⌑ 35.00/
70.00 **t.** − SB (except Bank Holidays) (weekdays only) 80.00/101.00 **st.**

at Torver SW : 2¼ m. on A 593 − ✉ ☎ 053 94 Coniston :

🏠 **Wheelgate Country House,** Little Arrow, LA21 8AU, NE : ¾ m. on A 593 🖉 41418,
« Part 17C farmhouse », 🐎 − ⤞ 📺 🅿. ❀
February-November − **M** (dinner only) 19.50 **t.** 🛦 3.75 − **8 rm** ⌑ 30.00/65.00 **t.**

🏠 **Old Rectory,** LA21 8AX, 🖉 41353, Fax 41156, ≤, 🐎 − ⤞ rest 📺 🅿
M *(closed Sunday)* (residents only) (dinner only) 15.00 **t.** 🛦 4.50 − **7 rm** ⌑ 35.00/66.00 **t.** −
SB (winter only) (weekends only) 51.00/90.00 **st.**

⬥ **Arrowfield,** Little Arrow, LA21 8AU, NE : ¾ m. on A 593 🖉 41741, ≤, 🐎 − ⤞ 📺 🅿. ❀
March-November − **M** (by arrangement) 13.00 **st.** 🛦 3.00 − **5 rm** ⌑ 17.00/42.00 **st.** −
SB 54.00/64.00 **st.**

at Water Yeat S : 6½ m. by A 593 on A 5084 − ✉ Ulverston − ☎ 0229 Lowick Bridge :

⬥ **Water Yeat,** LA12 8DJ, 🖉 885306, 🐎 − ⤞ rm 🅿. ❀
mid February-mid December − **M** (by arrangement) 16.00 **t.** − **7 rm** ⌑ 20.00/54.00 **t.**

at Blawith S : 7¼ m. by A 593 on A 5084 − ✉ Ulverston − ☎ 0229 Lowick Bridge

⬥ **Appletree Holme** ⬲, LA12 8EL, W : 1 m. taking unmarked road opposite church and
then right hand fork 🖉 885618, ≤, 🐎 − ⤞ 📺 🅿. ⬛ 🆎 𝗩𝗜𝗦𝗔. ❀
M 23.00 **st.** 🛦 3.25 − **4 rm** ⌑ (dinner included) 61.00/120.00 **st.**

CONSTANTINE BAY Cornwall **403** E 32 − see Padstow.

COOKHAM Berks. **404** R 29 Great Britain G. − pop. 5 865 − ECD : Wednesday and Thursday −
✉ Maidenhead − ☎ 062 85 (5 fig.) and 0628 (6 fig.) Bourne End.

See : Stanley Spencer Gallery★ *AC*.

◆London 32 − High Wycombe 7 − Reading 16.

🍴 **Alfonso's,** 19 Station Hill Par., SL6 9BR, 🖉 525775 − ⬛ 🆎 ⓞ 𝗩𝗜𝗦𝗔
closed Saturday lunch, Sunday, 2 weeks August and Bank Holidays − **M** 12.50 **t.** (lunch) and
a la carte 16.50/25.30 **t.**

🍴 **Peking Inn,** 49 High St., SL6 9SL, 🖉 520900 − ▤. ⬛ 🆎 ⓞ 𝗩𝗜𝗦𝗔
M - Chinese (Peking) 15.00/25.00 **st.** and a la carte.

COPDOCK Suffolk **404** X 27 − see Ipswich.

COPTHORNE W. Sussex **404** T 30 − see Crawley.

156

CORBRIDGE Northd. **401** **402** N 19 Great Britain G. – pop. 2 757 – ECD : Thursday – 🅰 0434 Hexham.

Envir. : Hadrian's Wall★★, N : 3 m. by A 68 – Corstopitum★ *AC*, NW : ½ m.

🛈 Hill St., NE45 5AA 🏃 632815 (summer only).

◆London 300 – Hexham 3 – ◆Newcastle upon Tyne 18.

- 🏠 **Riverside** without rest., Main St., NE45 5LE, 🏃 632942 – 📺 🅿. 🖭 *VISA*
  closed December and January – **10 rm** ⊑ 25.00/48.00 **t.**

- 🏠 **Lion of Corbridge,** Bridge End, NE45 5AX, 🏃 632504, Fax 632571 – 📺 ☎ ⅙ 🅿. 🖭 ⒶⒺ ⑩
  VISA *JCB*. 🖭
  M (dinner only and Sunday lunch)/dinner 17.00 **t.** and a la carte 🍴 4.45 – **14 rm** ⊑ 46.00/
  53.50 **st.** – SB (weekends only) 130.00 **st.**

- 🏠 **Wheatsheaf,** St. Helens St., NE45 5HE, 🏃 632020, Fax 632801, 🌂 – 📺 ☎ 🅿. 🖭 ⒶⒺ *VISA*
  🖭
  M (bar lunch)/dinner 9.95 **st.** and a la carte 🍴 3.25 – **6 rm** ⊑ 37.50/49.50 **st.** – SB (October-
  May) (weekends only) 52.50/85.00 **st.**

- 🏠 **Low Barns,** Thornbrough, NE45 5LX, E : 1¼ m. on B 6530 🏃 632408, 🌂 – ⅙ rest 📺 🅿.
  🖭 *VISA*
  M (by arrangement) 14.00 **s.** – **3 rm** ⊑ 30.00/42.00 **s.**

- 🍴🍴🍴 **Ramblers Country House,** Farnley, NE45 5RN, S : 1 m. on Riding Mill Rd 🏃 632424 –
  🅿. 🖭 ⒶⒺ ⑩ *VISA*
  closed Sunday dinner and Monday – **M** - **German** (lunch by arrangement)/dinner 15.75 **t.**
  and a la carte 🍴 3.85.

- 🍴🍴 **Valley,** The Old Station House, Station Rd, NE45 5AY, S : ½ m. by Riding Mill Rd
  🏃 633434, Fax 633923 – 🖭 ⒶⒺ ⑩ *VISA*
  M - **Indian** (closed Sunday) (dinner only) 20.00 **st.** and a la carte.

CORBY Northants. **404** R 26 Great Britain G. – pop. 48 471 – ✉ 🅰 0536.

Envir. : Boughton House★★ *AC*, S : 5½ m. by A 6116 and A 43.

🛈 Priors Hall, Stamford Rd, Weldon 🏃 60756, E : 4 m. by A 43.

🛈 Civic Centre, George St., NN17 1QB 🏃 407507.

◆London 100 – ◆Leicester 26 – Northampton 22 – Peterborough 24.

- 🏨 **Carlton Manor,** Geddington Rd, NN18 8ET, SE : 1¾ m. on A 6116 🏃 401020,
  Fax 400767, 🍴, ☎, 🖾 – 🖞 📺 ☎ 🅿 – 🕍 190. 🖭 ⒶⒺ ⑩ *VISA*
  M 12.75/14.75 **st.** and a la carte 🍴 5.90 – ⊑ 6.50 – **72 rm** 62.00/72.00 **st.**, 2 suites – SB
  (except Christmas) (weekends only) 78.00 **st.**

- 🏨 **Forte Posthouse,** Rockingham Rd, NN17 1AE, 🏃 401348, Fax 66383 – ⅙ rm 📺 ☎ 🅿 –
  🕍 400. 🖭 🖭 ⑩ *VISA* *JCB*
  M a la carte approx. 17.50 **t.** 🍴 4.65 – ⊑ 6.95 – **68 rm** 53.50 **st.** – SB (weekends only)
  90.00 **st.**

🅾 ATS St. James Rd 🏃 69519

CORFE CASTLE Dorset **403** **404** N 32 The West Country G. – pop. 1 338 – ✉ Wareham –
🅰 0929 – See : Castle★★ (≤★★) *AC*.

◆London 129 – Bournemouth 18 – Weymouth 23.

- 🏨 **Mortons House,** 45 East St., BH20 5EE, 🏃 480988, Fax 480820, « Elizabethan manor »,
  🌂 – ⅙ rest 📺 ☎ 🅿. 🖭 ⒶⒺ *VISA*
  M 15.00/22.50 **t.** – **16 rm** ⊑ 55.00/96.00 **t.**, 1 suite.

CORNHILL-ON-TWEED Northd. **401** **402** N 17 – pop. 312 – ECD : Thursday – 🅰 0890
Coldstream.

◆London 345 – ◆Edinburgh 49 – ◆Newcastle upon Tyne 59.

- 🏠 **Coach House,** Crookham, TD12 4TD, E : 4 m. on A 697 🏃 820293, 🌂 – ⅙ rest ⅙ 🅿. 🖭
  VISA
  March-October – **M** 14.50 **t.** 🍴 5.50 – **9 rm** ⊑ 21.00/62.00 **t.**

CORSE LAWN Heref. and Worcs. – see Tewkesbury (Glos.).

CORSHAM Wilts. **403** **404** N 29 The West Country G. – pop. 11 259 – ECD : Wednesday –
🅰 0249 – See : Corsham Court★★ *AC* – Envir. : Castle Combe★★, N : 5½ m. - Biddestone★,
N : 2 m. – Exc. : Bath★★★, SW : 9 m. by A 4.

◆London 110 – ◆Bristol 22 – Swindon 25.

- 🏨 **Rudloe Park,** Leafy Lane, SN13 0PA, W : 2 m. by B 3353 on A 4 🏃 0225 (Bath) 810555,
  Fax 811412, ≤, 🌂 – ⅙ rest 📺 ☎ 🅿 – 🕍 80. 🖭 🖭 ⑩ *VISA*
  M 15.95/20.95 **st.** 🍴 5.50 – **11 rm** ⊑ 55.00/90.00 **st.** – SB 70.00/90.00 **st.**

- 🏠 **Methuen Arms,** 2 High St., SN13 0HB, 🏃 714867, Fax 712004, 🌂 – 📺 ☎ 🅿. 🖭 *VISA*. 🖭
  closed 25 to 27 December – **M** (closed Sunday dinner and Bank Holidays) 15.00/17.50 **t.**
  and a la carte – **25 rm** ⊑ 41.00/65.00 **st.** – SB (weekends only) 79.00/129.00 **st.**

COSGROVE Northants. **404** R 27 – see Stony Stratford.

COSHAM Hants. **403** **404** Q 31 – see Portsmouth and Southsea.

157

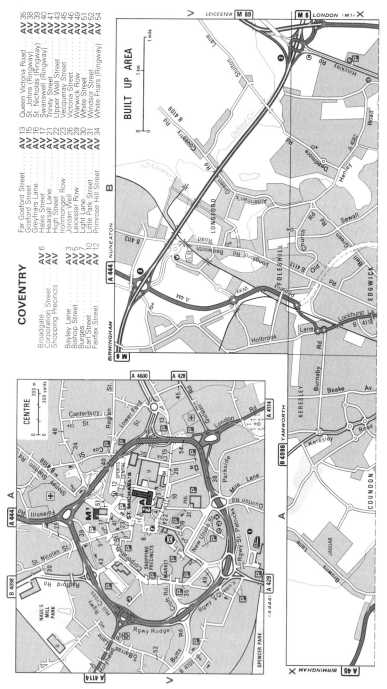

COVENTRY

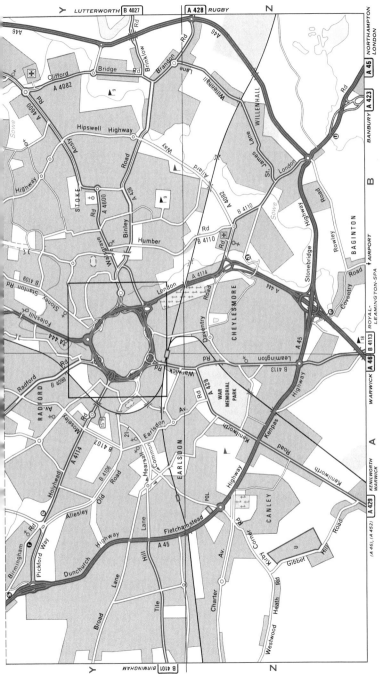

See : City★ – New St. Michael's Cathedral★★★ *AC* AV – Old St. Michael's Cathedral★ AV **A** – Museum of British Road Transport★ *AC* AV **M1**.

🏌 Finham Park 𝒫 411123, S : 2 m. on A 444 BZ – 🏌 Windmill Village, Birmingham Rd, Allesley 𝒫 407241, W : 3½ m. by A 45 AY – 🏌 Sphinx, Siddeley Av., Stoke 𝒫 451361, E : by A 428 BY.

✈ Coventry Airport : 𝒫 301717, Telex 31646, Fax 306000, S : 3½ m. by Coventry Rd BZ.

🅱 Bayley Lane, CV1 5RN 𝒫 832303/832304,.

♦London 100 – ♦Birmingham 18 – ♦Bristol 96 – ♦Nottingham 52.

Plans on preceding pages

🏨 **De Vere,** Cathedral Sq., CV1 5RP, 𝒫 633733, Fax 225299 – |🛗| 🖵 rest 📺 ☎ ❷ – 🕍 400. ◫ ⅋ ⓞ 𝐕𝐈𝐒𝐀
AV **n**
M 12.50/22.50 **st.** and a la carte – **180 rm** ⚏ 75.00/85.00 **st.**, 10 suites – SB (September-May) (weekends only) 80.00/176.00 **st.**

🏨 **Brooklands Grange,** Holyhead Rd, CV5 8HX, 𝒫 601601, Fax 601277 – 📺 ☎ ❷. ◫ ⅋ ⓞ 𝐕𝐈𝐒𝐀 ❀
AY **e**
M *(closed Saturday lunch)* 10.95/13.95 **st.** and a la carte – **30 rm** ⚏ 50.00/90.00 **st.** – SB (weekends only) 81.90/117.90 **st.**

🏨 **Leofric,** Broadgate, CV1 1LZ, 𝒫 221371, Fax 551352 – |🛗| 🖵 rest 📺 ☎ ❷ – 🕍 450. ◫ ⅋ ⓞ 𝐕𝐈𝐒𝐀 ❀
AV **r**
closed 24 December-1 January – **M** 8.95/15.00 **t.** and a la carte – ⚏ 7.50 – **89 rm** 79.50/94.50 **t.**, 5 suites – SB (except Christmas) (weekends only) 85.00 **st.**

🏨 **Campanile,** Abbey Rd, Whitley, CV2 2SD, SE : 2½ m. by A 4114 off A 444 𝒫 622311, Fax 602362 – 📺 ☎ ⅋ ❷. ◫ ⅋ 𝐕𝐈𝐒𝐀
BZ **a**
M 9.45 **t.** and a la carte ⅋ 2.65 – ⚏ 4.25 – **47 rm** 35.75 **t.**

🏠 **Crest** without rest., 39 Friars Rd, CV1 2LJ, 𝒫 227822, Fax 227244 – ⅋ 📺 ❀
AV **e**
closed 25 December-2 January – **4 rm** ⚏ 20.00/40.00 **s.**

🏠 **Baccara** without rest., 20 Park Rd, CV1 2LD, 𝒫 226530 – 📺 ❷ ❀
AV **i**
7 rm ⚏ 15.00/30.00 **st.**

🏠 **Ashbourne** without rest., 33 St. Patricks Rd, CV1 2LP, 𝒫 229518 – 📺 ❀
AV **a**
closed Christmas and New Year – **5 rm** ⚏ 25.00/35.00 **st.**

🏠 **Abigail** without rest., 39 St. Patricks Rd, CV1 2LP, 𝒫 221378 – 📺
AV **x**
closed 2 weeks Christmas-New Year – **5 rm** ⚏ 16.00/30.00 **s.**

at Longford N : 4 m. on A 444 – ✉ ✆ 0203 Coventry :

🏨 **Novotel,** Wilsons Lane, CV6 6HL, 𝒫 365000, Fax 362422, ⌇ heated – |🛗| ⅋ rm 🖵 rest 📺 ☎ ⅋ ⅋ ❷ – 🕍 150. ◫ ⅋ ⓞ 𝐕𝐈𝐒𝐀 𝐉𝐂𝐁
BV **v**
M 11.00/13.00 **st.** and a la carte ⅋ 5.95 – ⚏ 7.50 – **100 rm** 53.00/63.00 **st.** – SB (July-August and weekends only) 68.00/96.00 **st.**

at Walsgrave NE : 3 m. on A 4600 – ✉ ✆ 0203 Coventry :

🏨 **Hilton National,** Paradise Way, The Triangle, CV2 2ST, NE : 1 m. by A 4600 𝒫 603000, Telex 311333, Fax 603011, ⅃₅, ≘s, ⬛ – |🛗| ⅋ rm 🖵 📺 ☎ ⅋ ❷ – 🕍 600. ◫ ⅋ ⓞ 𝐕𝐈𝐒𝐀 𝐉𝐂𝐁
BX **c**
M (bar lunch Saturday) 14.00/17.50 **t.** and a la carte ⅋ 5.00 – ⚏ 10.25 – **169 rm** 85.00/105.00 **st.**, 3 suites.

🏨 **Forte Crest,** Hinckley Rd, CV2 2HP, NE : ½ m. on A 4600 𝒫 613261, Fax 621736, ⅃₅, ≘s, ⬛ – |🛗| ⅋ rm 🖵 rest 📺 ☎ ⅋ ❷ – 🕍 425. ◫ ⅋ ⓞ 𝐕𝐈𝐒𝐀
BX **e**
M (bar lunch Saturday) 12.25/16.95 **t.** and a la carte ⅋ 6.60 – ⚏ 9.95 – **145 rm** 80.00 **st.**, 2 suites – SB 98.00 **st.**

🏠 **Campanile,** Wigston Rd off Hinckley Rd, CV2 2SD, NE : ½ m. by A 4600 𝒫 622311, Telex 317454, Fax 602362 – 📺 ☎ ⅋ ❷. ◫ ⅋ 𝐕𝐈𝐒𝐀
BX **a**
M 9.45 **t.** and a la carte ⅋ 4.65 – ⚏ 4.25 – **47 rm** 35.75 **t.**

at Ansty (Warks.) NE : 5¾ m. by A 4600 – BY – on B 4065 – ✉ ✆ 0203 Coventry :

🏨 **Ansty Hall,** CV7 9HZ, 𝒫 612222, Fax 602155, « 17C mansion », ⅌, park – 📺 ☎ ❷ – 🕍 80. ◫ ⅋ ⓞ 𝐕𝐈𝐒𝐀
M 18.00 **st.** and a la carte – ⚏ 7.50 – **31 rm** 70.00/90.00 **st.** – SB (except Christmas) (weekends only) 90.00/115.00 **st.**

at Brandon (Warks.) E : 6 m. on A 428 – BZ – ✉ ✆ 0203 Coventry :

🏨 **Brandon Hall** (Forte), Main St., CV8 3FW, 𝒫 542571, Fax 544909, ⅌, park, squash – ⅋ 📺 ☎ ❷ – 🕍 90. ◫ ⅋ ⓞ 𝐕𝐈𝐒𝐀 𝐉𝐂𝐁
M (bar lunch Saturday) 12.00/23.50 **st.** and a la carte ⅋ 5.95 – ⚏ 8.50 – **60 rm** 70.00/105.00 **st.** – SB (except Christmas) (weekends only) 98.00/113.00 **st.**

at Ryton on Dunsmore SE : 4¾ m. by A 45 – ✉ ✆ 0203 Coventry :

🏨 **Coventry Knight,** London Rd, CV8 3DY, on A 45 (northbound carriageway) 𝒫 301585, Fax 301610 – ⅋ rm 🖵 rest 📺 ☎ ⅋ ❷ – 🕍 300. ◫ ⅋ ⓞ 𝐕𝐈𝐒𝐀
BZ **u**
M *(closed Saturday lunch)* 9.95/15.25 **t.** and a la carte ⅋ 5.75 – **47 rm** ⚏ 65.50/77.00 **st.**, 2 suites – SB (weekends only) 75.90 **st.**

at Baginton (Warks.) S : 3 m. by A 4114 and A 444 off A 45 (off westbound carriageway and Howes Lane turning) – ⊠ 🅐 0203 Coventry :

🏨 **Old Mill** (Chef & Brewer), Mill Hill, CV8 2BS, ℰ 303588, Fax 307070, « Converted corn mill », ☞ – 🔟 🅿. 🔄 🝐 ☑ 🅥🅘🅢🅐. BZ **e**
M (grill rest.) 15.00/20.00 **t.** and a la carte – **20 rm** ⊊ 44.95/48.45 **t.**

at Berkswell W : 6 ½ m. by B 4101 – AY – ⊠ 🅐 0203 Coventry :

🏨 **Nailcote Hall** ⤢, Nailcote Lane, CV7 7DE, S : 1 ½ m. on B 4101 ℰ 466174, Fax 470720, « Part 17C timbered house », ☞, ⤢ – 🔟 🝐 ☑ 🅥🅘🅢🅐. 🅐 65. 🔄 🝐 ☑ 🅥🅘🅢🅐.
M *(closed Saturday lunch)* (booking essential) 29.50/31.00 **t.** and a la carte 🍴 4.75 – **20 rm** ⊊ 95.00/200.00 **st.** – SB (July-September) 140.00/300.00 **st.**

at Balsall Common W : 6 ¾ m. by B 4101 – AY – ⊠ Coventry – 🅐 0676 Berkswell :

🏨 **Haigs**, 273 Kenilworth Rd, CV7 7EL, on A 452 ℰ 533004, Fax 534572, ☞ – 🔟 🝐 🝐. 🔄 🅥🅘🅢🅐
closed 24 December-5 January – **M** *(closed Sunday dinner)* (dinner only and Sunday lunch)/dinner 16.75 **st.** and a la carte 🍴 5.80 – **13 rm** ⊊ 49.95/59.95 **st.**

at Allesley NW : 3 m. on A 4114 – ⊠ 🅐 0203 Coventry :

🏨 **Forte Posthouse**, Rye Hill, CV5 9PH, ℰ 402151, Fax 402235 – 🛗 ⤢ rm 🔟 🝐 🝐 – 🅐 110. 🔄 🝐 ☑ 🅥🅘🅢🅐. AXY **s**
M a la carte approx. 17.50 **t.** 🍴 4.65 – ⊊ 6.95 – **184 rm** 53.50 **st.** – SB (weekends only) 90.00 **st.**

🏨 **Allesley**, Birmingham Rd, CV5 9GT, ℰ 403272, Fax 405190 – 🛗 🖳 rest 🔟 🝐 🝐 – 🅐 400. 🔄 🝐 ☑ 🅥🅘🅢🅐. AY **r**
M (bar lunch Saturday) 12.75/13.75 **st.** and a la carte 🍴 3.25 – **90 rm** ⊊ 65.00/90.00 **st.** – SB (weekends only) 90.00/180.00 **st.**

at Meriden NW : 6 m. by A 45 on B 4102 – AX – ⊠ Coventry – 🅐 0676 Meriden :

🏨 **Forest of Arden H. Golf & Country Club,** Maxstoke Lane, CV7 7HR, NW : 2 ¾ m. by Maxstoke rd ℰ 22335, Fax 22711, ≼, ⊠, ▣, ⩗, ◩, park, ⚒, squash – 🛗 ⤢ rm 🖳 rest 🔟 🝐 🝐 🝐 – 🅐 150. 🔄 🝐 ☑ 🅥🅘🅢🅐. ⤢
M *(closed Saturday lunch)* a la carte 8.90/27.00 **st.** 🍴 4.90 – **150 rm** ⊊ 110.00/135.00 **t.**, 2 suites – SB (weekends only) 124.00/178.00 **st.**

🏨 **Manor** (De Vere), Main Rd, CV7 7NH, ℰ 22735, Fax 22186, ☞ – ⤢ rm 🔟 🝐 🝐 🝐 – 🅐 275. 🔄 🝐 ☑ 🅥🅘🅢🅐.
M *(closed Saturday lunch)* 11.75/15.75 **st.** and a la carte 🍴 4.25 – **74 rm** ⊊ 75.00/95.00 **st.** – SB 64.00/84.00 **st.**

🝐 ATS Ashmore Lake Way, Willenhall ℰ 602555/ 605098

ATS Kingswood Close, off Holbrook Lane, Holbrooks ℰ 638554

COWAN BRIDGE Cumbria 🔲 M 21 – see Kirkby Lonsdale.

COWES I.O.W. 🔲 🔲 P 31 – see Wight (Isle of).

CRACKINGTON HAVEN Cornwall 🔲 G 31 The West Country G. – ECD : Tuesday – ⊠ Bude – 🅐 0840 St. Gennys.
Envir. : Poundstock★ (≼★★, church★, guildhouse★) NE : 5 ½ m. by A 39 – Jacobstow (Church★) E : 3 ½ m.
◆London 262 – Bude 11 – Truro 42.

🕭 **Manor Farm** ⤢, EX23 0JW, SE : 1 ¼ m. by Boscastle rd and Church park Rd, then take first right ℰ 230304, « Part 11C manor », ☞, park – ⤢ 🝐. ⤢
M (communal dining) (dinner only) 15.00 🍴 5.00 – **5 rm** ⊊ 30.00/60.00 **s.**

🕭 **Trevigue** ⤢, EX23 0LQ, SE : 1 ¼ m. on High Cliff rd ℰ 230418, « 16C farmhouse » – ⤢ rest 🝐. ⤢
closed December and January – **M** 14.00 **t.** 🍴 3.50 – **4 rm** ⊊ 30.00/50.00 **t.**

CRANBORNE Dorset 🔲 🔲 O 31 – pop. 596 – 🅐 0725.
▣, ◩ Crane Valley, West Arm, Romford, Verwood ℰ 0202 (Verwood) 814088, SE : 5 ½ m. by B 3078 and B 3081.
◆London 107 – Bournemouth 21 – Salisbury 18 – ◆Southampton 30.

🕥 **Fleur De Lys,** Wimborne St., BH21 5PP, on B 3078 ℰ 517282, Fax 517765 – 🔟 🝐. 🔄 🅥🅘🅢🅐. ⤢
closed 24 and 25 December – **M** 11.95 **t.** and a la carte 🍴 4.95 – **8 rm** ⊊ 25.00/50.00 **t.** – SB (except Bank Holidays) 55.00/73.00 **st.**

🍴🍴 **La Fosse** with rm, London House, The Square, BH21 5PR, ℰ 517604 – 🔟 🔄 🅥🅘🅢🅐. ⤢
M *(closed Saturday lunch and Sunday dinner)* 17.00/27.00 and a la carte 🍴 4.50 – **4 rm** ⊊ 22.50/45.00 **t.** – SB (except Christmas, New Year and Bank Holidays) 55.00/62.50 **st.**

CRANBROOK Kent `404` V 30 Great Britain G. – pop. 3 593 – ECD : Wednesday – ✆ 0580.

Envir. : Sissinghurst Castle★ *AC*, NE : 2½ m. by A 229 and A 262.

🏢 Vestry Hall, Stone St., TN17 3HA ✆ 712538 (summer only).

◆London 53 – Hastings 19 – Maidstone 15.

🏠 **Hartley Mount,** TN17 3QX, S : ½ m. on A 229 ✆ 712230, Fax 715733, ⚞, ※ – ⇥ 📺 ☎ ⟺ **ⓟ**, 🅽 AE VISA ※
M (lunch by arrangement)/dinner 15.50 **st.** and a la carte ⅄ 4.50 – **5 rm** ⟷ 55.00/98.00 **st.** – SB (September-April except Bank Holidays) 92.00 **st.**

🏠 **Old Cloth Hall** ⤸, TN17 3NR, E : 1 m. by Tenterden Rd ✆ 712220, ⚞, « Tudor manor house, gardens », ⤳, park, ※ – 📺 **ⓟ**. ※
closed Christmas – **M** *(unlicensed)* (residents only) (dinner only) 25.00 – **3 rm** ⟷ 45.00/95.00.

at Sissinghurst NE : 1¾ m. by B 2189 on A 262 – ✉ ✆ 0580 Cranbrook :

✕ **Rankins,** The Street, TN17 2JH, ✆ 713964 – 🅽 VISA
closed Sunday dinner, Monday, Tuesday, 1 week May and 1 week October – **M** 19.50/22.50 **t.**

CRANLEIGH Surrey `404` S 30 – pop. 10 967 – ECD : Wednesday – ✆ 0483.

🏌 Fernfell G. & C.C., Barhatch Lane ✆ 268855, 1 m. by A 281.

◆London 42 – ◆Brighton 36 – Reading 36 – ◆Southampton 58.

✕✕ **La Barbe Encore,** High St., GU6 8AE, ✆ 273889 – 🅽 AE VISA
closed Saturday lunch, Sunday dinner, Monday and 25 to 29 December – **M** - French 14.95/17.95 **st.** ⅄ 4.50.

CRANTOCK Cornwall `403` E 32 – see Newquay.

CRAVEN ARMS Shrops. `403` L 26 Great Britain G. – ✆ 0588.

Envir. : Wenlock Edge★, NE : by B 4368.

◆London 170 – ◆Birmingham 47 – Hereford 32 – Shrewsbury 21.

🏠 **Old Rectory** ⤸, Hopesay, SY7 8HD, W : 3¾ m. by B 4368 ✆ 058 87 (Little Brampton) 245, ⚞, « Part 17C », – ⇥ **ⓟ** ※
M (by arrangement) (communal dining) 17.00 – **3 rm** ⟷ 28.00/60.00.

CRAWLEY W. Sussex `404` T 30 – pop. 80 113 – ECD : Wednesday – ✆ 0293.

🏌 Cottesmore, Buchan Hill ✆ 528256, S : 4 m. by A 264 on plan of Gatwick Z – 🏌, 🏌 Tilgate Forest, Titmus Drive, Tilgate ✆ 530103, SE : 1½ m. by M 23 on plan of Gatwick Z – 🏌 Gatwick Manor, London Rd ✆ 538587, SW : 1 m. from Gatwick Airport by A 23 on plan of Gatwick Y – 🏌 Horsham Rd, Pease Pottage ✆ 521706, S : by A 23 on plan of Gatwick Z.

◆London 33 – ◆Brighton 21 – Lewes 23 – Royal Tunbridge Wells 23.

Plan on next page
Plan of enlarged Area : see Gatwick

🏨 **Holiday Inn London Gatwick,** Langley Drive, Tushmore Roundabout, RH11 7SX, ✆ 529991, Telex 877311, Fax 515913, ⅃⅄, ≋, 🄻 – ⅃ ⇥ rm ▤ rest 📺 ☎ ⅃ **ⓟ** – 🔔 200. 🅽 AE ⓞ VISA JCB. ※
BY **n**
M 12.95/19.50 **st.** and a la carte ⅄ 4.50 – ⟷ 9.95 – **221 rm** 68.50 **st.**, 2 suites.

🏨 **George** (Forte), High St., RH10 1BS, ✆ 524215, Fax 548565 – ⇥ rm 📺 ☎ **ⓟ** – 🔔 35. 🅽 AE ⓞ VISA JCB. ※
BY **o**
M (dinner only and Sunday lunch)/dinner 16.95 **t.** and a la carte ⅄ 5.25 – ⟷ 8.50 – **81 rm** 55.00/59.00 **st.** – SB (weekends only) 80.00/140.00 **st.**

🏨 **Goffs Park,** 45 Goffs Park Rd, Southgate, RH11 8AX, ✆ 535447, Fax 542050, ⚞, ⤳ – **ⓟ** – 🔔 120. 🅽 AE ⓞ VISA ※
AZ **s**
M (dancing Friday and Saturday evenings) 10.95/13.00 **st.** and a la carte ⅄ 5.25 – ⟷ 7.75 – **64 rm** 35.00/70.00 **st.**

at Copthorne NE : 4½ m. on A 264 – BY – ✉ Crawley – ✆ 0342 Copthorne :

🏨 **Copthorne London Gatwick,** Copthorne Way, RH10 3PG, ✆ 714971, Telex 95500, Fax 717375, ⅃⅄, ≋, ⤳, park, squash – ⇥ rm ▤ rest 📺 ☎ **ⓟ** – 🔔 110. 🅽 AE ⓞ VISA JCB
M (in bar Saturday lunch, Sunday and Bank Holidays) 19.75/22.00 **st.** and a la carte ⅄ 5.00 – ⟷ 9.95 – **222 rm** 98.00/128.00 **st.**, 5 suites – SB (weekends only) 189.00/199.00 **st.**

🏨 **Copthorne Effingham Park,** West Park Rd, RH10 3EU, on B 2028 ✆ 714994, Telex 95649, Fax 716039, ⚞, ⅃⅄, 🄻, 🏌, ⤳, park – ⇥ rm ▤ rest 📺 ☎ **ⓟ** – 🔔 500. 🅽 AE ⓞ VISA ※
M 15.50/20.00 **st.** and a la carte – ⟷ 9.95 – **119 rm** 98.00/128.00 **st.**, 3 suites.

at Three Bridges E : 1 m. on Haslett Av. – BY – ✉ ✆ 0293 Crawley :

🏨 **Scandic Crown,** 18-23 Tinsley Lane South, RH11 1NP, N : ½ m. by Hazelwick Av. ✆ 561186, Telex 87485, Fax 561169, ⅃⅄, ≋, 🄻, ※ – ⅃ ⇥ rm ▤ rest 📺 ☎ & **ⓟ** – 🔔 200. 🅽 AE ⓞ VISA ※
plan of Gatwick Y **n**
M *(closed Saturday lunch)* 9.95/16.50 **st.** and dinner a la carte ⅄ 3.65 – ⟷ 9.50 – **149 rm** 90.00 **st.**, 2 suites.

162

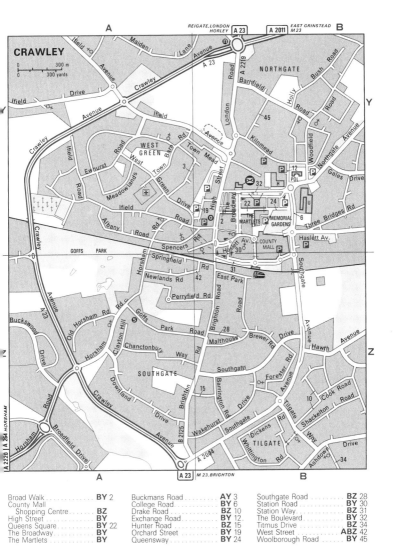

CRAWLEY

at *Maidenbower* E : 2 ½ m. by Haslett Av. and Worth Rd on B 2036 – BY – ⊠ ✆ 0293 Crawley :

🏨 **Europa Gatwick**, Balcombe Rd, RH10 4ZR, on B 2036 ✆ 886666, Fax 886680, ℱ₅, ≋s, ⊠, ☞ – 🕼 ⇆ rm 🗏 📺 ☎ & 🅿 – 🔬 150. 🅰 🆎 ① 𝘝𝘐𝘚𝘈. 🛠
M – **Mediteranee** *(closed Saturday lunch)* 12.50/20.00 **t.** and dinner a la carte ♪ 5.00 – (see also **Silk Trader** below) – ☷ 8.50 – **174 rm** 100.00/120.00 **st.**, 4 suites – SB (weekends only) 140.00 **st.**   plan of Gatwick   Z **a**

🍴🍴 **Silk Trader** (at Europa Gatwick H.), Balcombe Rd, RH10 4ZR, on B 2036 ✆ 886666, Fax 886680, ☞ – 🗏 🅿. 🅰 🆎 ① 𝘝𝘐𝘚𝘈   plan of Gatwick   Z **e**
closed Sunday – **M** - **Chinese** 13.00/35.00 **st.** and a la carte ♪ 5.50.

🔧 ATS Reynolds Rd, West Green ✆ 533151/2

Your recommendation is self-evident if you always walk into a
hotel Guide in hand.

CREDITON Devon **403** J 31 – ⊙ 0363.

◆London 209 – Barnstaple 40 – Exeter 8 – Taunton 49.

↑ **Thatched Cottage,** Barnstaple Cross, EX17 2EW, W : 1 ¾ m. on A 377 ✎ 773115, ≼, « Part 17C thatched cottage », ☞ – ⇆ 📺 ℗
closed December – **M** (by arrangement) (communal dining) 17.00 **s.** – **3 rm** ⊐ 27.50/42.00 **st.**

CREWE Ches. **402 403 404** M 24 – pop. 59 097 – ECD : Wednesday – ⊙ 0270.

⌷₉ Queen's Park Gardens ✎ 666724, 1 ½ m. off Victoria Av.

◆London 174 – Chester 24 – ◆Liverpool 49 – ◆Manchester 36 – ◆Stoke-on-Trent 15.

🏨 **Crewe Arms** (Jarvis), Nantwich Rd, CW1 1DW, ✎ 213204, Fax 588615 – ⇆ rm 📺 ☎ ℗ – 🔏 80. 🄽 🄰🄴 ⓞ 🆅🅸🆂🅰
M 13.95 **t.** and a la carte – ⊐ 8.00 – **53 rm** 26.00/82.00 **t.** – SB (except Christmas and New Year) 65.00/73.00 **st.**

at Barthomley SE : 5 ½ m. by A 5020 on A 500 – ✉ ⊙ 0270 Crewe :

🏛 **Forte Travelodge** without rest., Alsager Rd, CW2 5PT, at junction with M 6 ✎ 883157, Reservations (Freephone) 0800 850950 – 📺 ♿ ℗. 🄽 🄰🄴 🆅🅸🆂🅰. 🇸
42 rm 31.95 **t.**

◎ ATS Gresty Rd ✎ 256285

CREWKERNE Somerset **403** L 31 The West Country G. – pop. 6 018 – ECD : Thursday – ⊙ 0460.

Envir. : Forde Abbey★ *AC*, SW : 8 m. by B 3165 and B 3162 – Clapton Court Gardens★ *AC*, S : 3 ½ m. by B 3165.

Exc. : Montacute House★★ *AC*, NE : 7 m. by A 30 – Parnham House★★ *AC*, SE : 7 ½ m. by A 356 and A 3066.

⌷₁₈ Windwhistle G. & C.C., Cricket St. Thomas, Chard ✎ 0460 (Chard) 30231, W : 4 ½ m. by A 30.

◆London 145 – Exeter 38 – ◆Southampton 81 – Taunton 20.

↑ **Broadview,** 43 East St., TA18 7AG, ✎ 73424, ☞ – ⇆ rest 📺 ℗. 🇸
M (by arrangement) 10.00 – **3 rm** ⊐ 25.00/40.00.

at Haselbury Plucknett NE : 2 ¾ m. by A 30 on A 3066 – ✉ ⊙ 0460 Crewkerne :

↑ **Oak House,** North St., TA18 7RB, ✎ 73625, « 16C thatched cottage », ☞ – ⇆ rest ℗
Easter-October – **M** (by arrangement) 10.00 **st.** – **8 rm** ⊐ 20.00/46.00 **st.**

at North Perrot E : 3 ½ m. by A 30 on A 3066 – ✉ ⊙ 0460 Crewkerne :

⌂ **Manor Arms,** TA18 7SG, ✎ 72901, « 16C inn » – ⇆ ℗. 🄽 🆅🅸🆂🅰 🇸
M (in bar Sunday dinner and Monday) a la carte 7.45/13.55 **t.** ⏐ 4.30 – ⊐ 3.50 – **5 rm** 26.00/39.00 **t.** – SB 70.00/89.00 **st.**

CRICK Northants. **403 404** Q 26 – see Rugby.

CRICKLADE Wilts **403** ⬜ **404** O 29 – pop. 3 574 – ECD : Wednesday and Saturday – ⊙ 0793 Swindon.

⌷₉ Cricklade Hotel, Common Hill ✎ 570751, SW : 1 m. by B 4040.

◆London 90 – ◆Bristol 45 – Gloucester 27 – ◆Oxford 34 – Swindon 6.

🏨 **Cricklade H. & Country Club,** Common Hill, SN6 6HA, SW : 1 m. on B 4040 ✎ 750751, Fax 751767, ≼, ⌿, ⌑, 🎏, ⌷₉, park, 🏊 – 📺 ☎ ℗ – 🔏 120. 🄽 🄰🄴 🆅🅸🆂🅰 🇸
M 15.00/19.00 **st.** and a la carte ⏐ 5.75 – **46 rm** ⊐ 70.00/95.00 **st.** – SB 104.00/136.00 **st.**

CROCKERTON Wilts. – see Warminster.

CROFT-ON-TEES Durham **402** P 20 – see Darlington.

CROMER Norfolk **404** X 25 – pop. 5 934 – ECD : Wednesday – ⊙ 0263.

⌷₁₀ Royal Cromer, Overstrand Rd ✎ 512884, E : 1 m.

🅱 Bus Station, Prince of Wales Rd, NR27 9HS ✎ 512497 (summer only).

◆London 132 – ◆Norwich 23.

↑ **Morden House,** 20 Cliff Av., NR27 0AN, ✎ 513396 – ⇆ rest
M 11.50 – **6 rm** ⊐ 19.50/42.00.

↑ **Birch House,** 34 Cabbell Rd, NR27 9HX, ✎ 512521 – ⇆ 📺
M 7.00 **st.** – **8 rm** ⊐ 16.00/38.00 **st.**

CRONDALL Hants. **404** R 30 – pop. 4 133 – ⊙ 0252 Farnham.

⌷₁₈ Oak Park, Heath Lane ✎ 850880.

◆London 56 – Reading 21 – Winchester 30.

XX **Chesa,** Bowling Alley, GU10 5RJ, N : 1 m. ✎ 850328, Fax 850328 – ℗. 🄽 🄰🄴 ⓞ 🆅🅸🆂🅰
closed Sunday dinner and Monday – **M** (lunch by arrangement)/dinner 40.00 **t.**

CRONTON Ches. **402 403 404** L 23 – see Widnes.

☞ *Michelin puts no plaque or sign on the hotels and restaurants mentioned in this Guide.*

[CROOK] Durham [401] [402] O 19 – pop. 8 414 – ✉ ☏ 0388 Bishop Auckland.

⛳18 Low Job's Hill ☎ 762429, E : 1/2 m. by A 689.

♦London 261 – ♦Carlisle 65 – ♦Middlesbrough 34 – ♦Newcastle upon Tyne 27.

🏠 Helme Park Hall 🌿, DL13 4NW, NW : 3 1/4 m. by A 689 on A 68 ☎ 730970, Fax 730970, ≤, 🌳 – [TV] ☎ [P]. 🚫🐕
13 rm.

⌂ **Greenhead** without rest., Fir Tree, Bishop Auckland Rd, DL15 8BL, SW : 3 1/2 m. by A 689 off A 68 ☎ 763143, 🌳 – [TV] [P]. [S] [VISA]. 🚫🐕
6 rm ☕ 30.00/45.00 **s.**

[CROSBY-ON-EDEN] Cumbria [401] [402] L 29 – see Carlisle.

[CROSCOMBE] Somerset [403] [404] M 30 – see Wells.

[CROWBOROUGH] E. Sussex [404] U 30 – pop. 17 008 – ECD : Wednesday – ☏ 0892.

♦London 45 – ♦Brighton 25 – Maidstone 26.

🏨 **Winston Manor,** Beacon Rd, TN6 1AD, on A 26 ☎ 652772, Fax 665537, 🏋, ≘s, 🏊 – 🛗 [TV] ☎ [P] – 🪑 250. [S] [AE] [O] [VISA] [JCB]
M (light meals Monday to Saturday lunch and Sunday dinner)/dinner 16.95 **t.** and a la carte 🍷 4.95 – **50 rm** ☕ 50.00/90.00 **t.** – SB (except Christmas and New Year) 90.00 **st.**

Ⓐ ATS Church Rd ☎ 662100

[CROWTHORNE] Berks. [404] R 29 – pop. 19 166 – ECD : Wednesday – ☏ 0344.

♦London 42 – Reading 15.

🏨 **Waterloo** (Forte), Dukes Ride, RG11 7NW, on B 3348 ☎ 777711, Fax 778913 – 🚭 rm [TV] ☎ [P] – 🪑 40. [S] [AE] [O] [VISA] [JCB]. 🚫🐕
M (dinner only and Sunday lunch)/dinner 15.95 **st.** and a la carte 🍷 4.95 – ☕ 8.50 – **58 rm** 90.00/110.00 **st.** – SB (except Christmas) (weekends only) 86.00 **st.**

🍴🍴 **Beijing,** 103 Old Wokingham Rd, RG11 6LH, NE : 3/4 m. by A 3095 ☎ 778802 – ▤ [P]. [S] [AE] [O] [VISA]
closed Sunday lunch – **M** - **Chinese** 15.50/18.50 **t.**

We suggest :

For a successful tour, that you prepare it in advance.
Michelin maps and guides will give you much useful information on route planning, places of interest, accommodation, prices etc.

[CROXDALE] Durham – see Durham.

[CROYDE] Devon [403] H 30 **The West Country G.** – ✉ Braunton – ☏ 0271.

♦London 232 – Barnstaple 10 – Exeter 50 – Taunton 61.

🏠 **Kittiwell House,** St. Mary's Rd, EX33 1PG, ☎ 890247, Fax 890469, « 16C thatched Devon longhouse » – 🚭 rm [TV] ☎ [P]. [S] [VISA]
closed 12 January-12 February – **M** (dinner only and Sunday lunch)/dinner 21.00 **st.** and a la carte 🍷 4.00 – **12 rm** ☕ 44.00/74.00 **st.** – SB 90.00/116.00 **st.**

🏠 **Croyde Bay House** 🌿, Moor Lane, Croyde Bay, EX33 1PA, NW : 1 m. by Baggy Point rd ☎ 890270, ≤ Croyde Bay, 🌳 – 🚭 rest [TV] [P]. [S] [VISA]
March-mid November – **M** (dinner only) 17.75 **t.** 🍷 3.90 – **7 rm** ☕ 39.50/79.00 **t.**

🏠 **Whiteleaf,** Hobbs Hill, EX33 1PN, ☎ 890266, 🌳 – 🚭 rest [TV] ☎ [P]. [S] [VISA]
closed January, 2 weeks April, 2 weeks July and 2 weeks October – **M** (dinner only) 21.75 **s.** 🍷 4.00 – **3 rm** ☕ 34.50/54.00 **s.**

[CRUDWELL] Wilts. [403] [404] N 29 – see Malmesbury.

[CUCKFIELD] W. Sussex [404] T 30 – pop. 2 650 – ECD : Wednesday – ☏ 0444 Haywards Heath.

♦London 40 – ♦Brighton 15.

🏨 **Ockenden Manor** 🌿, Ockenden Lane, RH17 5LD, ☎ 416111, Fax 415549, « Part 16C manor », 🌳 – [TV] ☎ [P] – 🪑 30. [S] [AE] [O] [VISA]. 🚫🐕
M 18.50/29.50 **t.** and a la carte 🍷 5.75 – ☕ 3.75 – **20 rm** 70.00/155.00 **t.**, 2 suites – SB 156.00/200.00 **st.**

[CULLOMPTON] Devon [403] J 31 **The West Country G.** – pop. 5 044 – ☏ 0884.

See : Town★ – St. Andrew's Church★.

Envir. : Uffculme (Coldharbour Mill★★ *AC*) NE : 5 1/2 m. by B 3181 and B 3391.

Exc. : Killerton★★, SW : 6 1/2 m. by B 3181 and B 3185.

⛳9 Padbrook Park ☎ 38286.

♦London 197 – Exeter 15 – Taunton 29.

⌂ **Lower Beers** 🌿, Brithem Bottom, EX15 1NB, NW : 2 3/4 m. by B 3181 ☎ 32257, « 16C farmhouse », 🌳 – 🚭 [P]. 🚫🐕
closed 15 December-15 January – **M** (by arrangement) (communal dining) 22.00 **st.** 🍷 5.00 – **3 rm** ☕ 25.00/55.00 **st.**

CULWORTH Oxon. ₄₀₄ Q 27 – ⊠ Banbury – ✆ 0295 Sulgrave.

♦London 84 – ♦Birmingham 48 – ♦Coventry 23 – ♦Oxford 31.

↑ **Fulford House** ⤴, The Green, OX17 2BB, ℰ 760355, Fax 768304, « 17C house », 🐎 – ⇔ rm 📺 **📞**. ❀
closed mid December-mid February – **M** (by arrangement) (communal dining) 18.00 **st.**
🍷 4.50 – **3 rm** �??? 30.00/57.00 **st.**

DALTON-IN-FURNESS Cumbria ₄₀₂ K 21 – pop. 7 427 – ✆ 0229.

🏌 The Dunnerholme, Askham-in-Furness ℰ 62675, NW : 4 m. by A 595.

♦London 283 – Barrow-in-Furness 3.5 – Kendal 30 – Lancaster 41.

▥ **Clarence House,** Skelgate, LA15 8BQ, N : ¼ m. on A 595 ℰ 62508, Fax 467177, 🐎 – 📺 **📞**. **🔂** 🅰🅴 _VISA_
M (dinner only and Sunday lunch)/dinner 25.00 **t.** and a la carte 🍷 7.50 – **16 rm** �??? 55.00/75.00 **t.**

DARESBURY Ches. ₄₀₂ ₄₀₃ ₄₀₄ M 23 – pop. 353 – ⊠ ✆ 0925 Warrington.

♦London 197 – Chester 16 – ♦Liverpool 22 – ♦Manchester 25.

▥ **Lord Daresbury** (De Vere), Chester Rd, WA4 4BB, on A 56 ℰ 267331, Fax 265615, 🏊, ⇌, 🅽, squash – 🔖 ⇔ rm 📺 ☎ **📞** – 🔏 400. 🔂 🅰🅴 ⓪ _VISA_
M 12.50/20.00 **st.** and dinner a la carte 🍷 6.00 – **139 rm** �??? 85.00/95.00 **st.**, 2 suites –
SB 106.00 **st.**

DARLEY ABBEY Derbs. ₄₀₂ ₄₀₃ ₄₀₄ P 25 – see Derby.

DARLINGTON Durham ₄₀₂ P 20 – pop. 85 519 – ECD : Wednesday – ✆ 0325.

🏌 Blackwell Grange, Briar Close ℰ 464464, S : 1 m. on A 66 – 🏌 Stressholme, Snipe Lane ℰ 363928, S : 2 m. on A 167.

✈ Teesside Airport : ℰ 332811, E : 6 m. by A 67.

🄸 4 West Row, DL1 5PL ℰ 382698.

♦London 251 – ♦Leeds 61 – ♦Middlesbrough 14 – ♦Newcastle upon Tyne 35.

▥ **Blackwell Grange Moat House** (Q.M.H.), Blackwell Grange, DL3 8QH, SW : 1¾ m. on A 66 ℰ 380888, Fax 380899, 🏊, ⇌, 🅽, 🏌, park – 🔖 ⇔ rm 📺 ☎ **📞** – 🔏 300. 🔂 🅰🅴 ⓪ _VISA_. ❀
M 11.50/19.95 **st.** and a la carte – **96 rm** �??? 80.00/98.00 **st.**, 3 suites – SB 102.00/184.00 **st.**

▥ **Swallow King's Head,** Priestgate, DL1 1NW, ℰ 380222, Fax 382006 – 🔖 ⇔ rm 📺 ☎ **📞** – 🔏 200. 🔂 🅰🅴 ⓪ _VISA_
M 14.50 **st.** (dinner) and a la carte 15.75/33.75 **st.** – **85 rm** �??? 78.00/94.00 **st.** – SB 90.00 **st.**

🏠 **Cricketers,** 53-55 Parkgate, DL1 1RR, ℰ 384444 – 📺 ☎ **📞**. 🔂 🅰🅴. ❀
M (Sunday dinner residents only) 8.50/15.00 **st.** and a la carte 🍷 3.50 – **15 rm** �??? 45.00/60.00 **st.**

↑ **Woodland** without rest., 63 Woodland Rd, DL3 7BQ, ℰ 461908 – 📺
8 rm �??? 19.00/39.00 **st.**

XX **Sardis,** 196 Northgate, DL1 1QU, ℰ 461222 – 🔂 _VISA_
closed Sunday and Bank Holidays – **M** 10.50/16.00 **t.** and a la carte.

XX Sitar, 204 Northgate, DL1 1RB, ℰ 360787.

X **Victor's,** 84 Victoria Rd., DL1 5JW, ℰ 480818 – 🔂 🅰🅴 ⓪ _VISA_
closed Sunday, Monday and 1 week Christmas-New Year – **M** 8.50/20.00 **t.** 🍷 3.95.

at Coatham Mundeville N : 4 m. by A 167 – ⊠ ✆ 0325 Darlington :

▥ Hall Garth Country House, DL1 3LU, N : 4 m. on A 167 ℰ 300400, Fax 310083, 🏊, ⤫ heated, 🐎, park, ❅ – 📺 ☎ **📞** – 🔏 300. ❀
39 rm, 1 suite.

at Teesside Airport E : 5½ m. by A 67 – ⊠ ✆ 0325 Darlington :

▥ **St. George** (Mt. Charlotte Thistle), DL2 1RH, ℰ 332631, Telex 587623, Fax 333851, ⇌, squash – 📺 ☎ **📞** – 🔏 150. 🔂 🅰🅴 ⓪ _VISA_
M (closed Monday and Saturday lunch and Sunday dinner) 9.00/14.50 **t.** and a la carte 🍷 4.75 – **58 rm** �??? 74.00/84.00 **st.**, 1 suite – SB (weekends only) 80.00/104.00 **st.**

at Neasham SE : 6½ m. by A 66 off A 167 – ⊠ ✆ 0325 Darlington :

▥ Newbus Arms (Best Western) ⤴, Hurworth Rd, DL2 1PE, W : ½ m. ℰ 721071, Fax 721770, 🐎, squash – 📺 **📞** – 🔏 60. ❀
15 rm.

at Croft-on-Tees S : 3½ m. on A 167 – ⊠ ✆ 0325 Darlington :

↑ **Clow Beck House** ⤴ without rest., Monk End Farm, DL2 2SW, W : ½ m. via South Parade ℰ 721075, ≤, « Working farm », 🐎, 🐎, park – 📺 **📞**. ❀
3 rm �??? 25.00/47.00 **s.**

166

at Headlam NW : 6 m. by A 67 – ✉ Gainford – ☎ 0325 Darlington :

Headlam Hall 🌿, DL2 3HA, ☎ 730238, Fax 730790, ≤, « Part Jacobean mansion », ≘, 🏊, 🌳, park, 🎾 – TV ☎ P – 🏛 30. [AE] VISA ✗
closed 25 and 26 December – **M** (dinner only and Sunday lunch)/dinner 15.00 **st.** and a la carte 🍷 3.50 – **24 rm** ☕ 55.00/75.00 **st.**, 2 suites – SB (except Christmas) (weekends only) 88.00/130.00 **st.**

at Redworth NW : 7 m. by A 68 on A 6072 – ✉ ☎ 0388 Bishop Auckland :

Redworth Hall, DL5 6NL, on A 6072 ☎ 772442, Fax 775112, « Part 18C and 19C manor house », Lб, ≘, 🏊, 🌳, park, 🎾, squash – |$| ⇔ rm ▤ rest TV ☎ ♿ P – 🏛 300. [AE] VISA
M 11.50/24.95 **t.** and a la carte – **86 rm** ☕ 89.00/105.00 **st.**, 14 suites – SB (weekends only) 129.00/169.00 **st.**

ATS Albert St., off Neasham Rd ☎ 469271/469693

DARTFORD Kent 404 U 29 – ☎ 0322.

The Clocktower, Suffolk Rd, DA1 1EJ ☎ 343243.

♦London 20 – Hastings 51 – Maidstone 22.

Stakis Country Court, Masthead Close, Crossways Business Park, DA2 6QF, NE : 2 ½ m. by A 226, Cotton Lane and Crossways Boulevard ☎ 284444, Telex 911038, Fax 288225, Lб, ≘, 🏊 – |$| ⇔ rm ▤ TV ☎ ♿ P – 🏛 210. [AE] VISA JCB ✗
M 15.20/17.50 **t.** and a la carte 🍷 7.70 – ☕ 7.95 – **172 rm** 59.00/89.00 **st.**, 4 suites – SB 68.00/118.00 **st.**

If you find you cannot take up a hotel booking you have made, please let the hotel know immediately.

DARTMOUTH Devon 403 J 32 The West Country G. – pop. 5 282 – ECD : Wednesday and Saturday – ☎ 0803.

See : Town★★ – Dartmouth Castle (≤★★★) *AC*.

Exc. : Start Point (≤★) S : 13 m. (including 1 m. on foot).

11 Duke St., TQ6 9PY ☎ 834224.

♦London 236 – Exeter 36 – ♦Plymouth 35.

Royal Castle, 11 The Quay, TQ6 9PS, ☎ 833033, Fax 835445, ≤ – TV ☎. VISA
M (bar lunch Monday to Saturday)/dinner 24.50 **st.** 🍷 4.95 – **25 rm** ☕ 48.00/104.00 **st.** – SB (except Bank Holidays) 79.50/128.00 **st.**

Dart Marina (Forte), Sandquay, TQ6 9PH, ☎ 832580, Fax 835040, ≤ – ⇔ TV ☎ P. [AE] VISA JCB
M (bar lunch Monday to Saturday)/dinner 16.95 **t.** 🍷 5.25 – **35 rm.**

Ford House, 44 Victoria Rd, TQ6 9DX, ☎ 834047, 🌳 – TV ☎ P. VISA
closed January and February – **M** *(residents only) (communal dining) (unlicensed)* (dinner only and Sunday lunch)/dinner 25.00 **st.** – **3 rm** ☕ 35.00/60.00 **st.**

Wavenden House 🌿, Compass Cove, TQ6 0JN, S : 1 ¼ m. via Warfleet by Newcomen Rd, off Castle Rd ☎ 833979, ≤ River Dart and sea, 🌳 – ⇔ rm P. ✗
closed Christmas-New Year (booking essential) – **M** (by arrangement) (communal dining) 15.00 **st.** – **3 rm** ☕ 22.00/36.00 **st.**

Wadstray House 🌿 without rest., Blackawton, TQ9 7DE, W : 4 ½ m. on A 3122 ☎ 712539, 🌳 – TV P
3 rm ☕ 25.00/45.00 **st.**

Three Feathers without rest., 51 Victoria Rd, TQ6 9RT, ☎ 834694 – TV. ✗
5 rm ☕ 35.00 **s.**

Carved Angel, 2 South Embankment, TQ6 9BH, ☎ 832465, ≤ Dart Estuary
closed Sunday dinner, Monday, 3 January-mid February and 24 to 26 December – **M** 27.50/42.50 **st.** and lunch a la carte 🍷 7.00.

Exchange II Brasserie, 5 Higher St., TQ6 9RB, ☎ 832022, « 13C town house » – [AE] VISA
closed Sunday, Monday and mid January-February – **M** a la carte 9.75/21.75 **t.**

Billy Budd's, 7 Foss St., TQ6 9DW, ☎ 834842 – VISA
closed Sunday, Monday except Bank Holidays and 4 weeks late February-March – **M** (booking essential) (light lunch)/dinner a la carte 16.85/20.70 **t.**

at Stoke Fleming SW : 3 m. on A 379 – ✉ Dartmouth – ☎ 0803 Stoke Fleming :

Stoke Lodge, Cinders Lane, TQ6 0RA, ☎ 770523, Fax 770851, ≤, Lб, ≘, 🏊 heated, 🏊, 🌳, 🎾 – TV ☎ P. [AE] VISA
M 9.75/16.95 **t.** and a la carte 🍷 5.25 – **24 rm** ☕ 37.50/74.00 **t.** – SB (except Easter, Christmas and New Year) 77.00/107.00 **st.**

New Endsleigh, New Rd, TQ6 0NR, ☎ 770381 – ⇔ TV ☎ P. VISA ✗
M (bar lunch Monday to Saturday in summer)/dinner 9.50/14.00 **t.** 🍷 4.50 – **12 rm** ☕ 31.00/64.00 **t.** – SB (mid September-mid July except Bank Holidays) 60.00/70.00 **st.**

DAVENTRY Northants 404 Q 27 – pop. 15 934 – ECD : Thursday – ✆ 0327.

☒ Norton Rd ℰ 702829, E : 2 m. – ☒ Hellidon Lakes Hotel & C.C., Hellidon, Daventry ℰ 62550, SW : 7 m. via A 361 – ☒ Staverton Park Hotel, Staverton ℰ 311428, SW : 1 m. off A 425.

🏛 Moot Hall, Market Sq., NN11 4BH ℰ 300277.

♦London 79 – ♦Coventry 23 – Northampton 13 – ♦Oxford 46.

🏨🏨 **Daventry Resort,** Ashby Rd, NN11 5SG, N : 2¼ m. on A 361 ℰ 301777, Telex 312513, Fax 706313, *Ls*, ≘s, ◻, ◻ – ⚞ rm ▤ rest 📺 ☎ ⟨ ☺ 🅟 – 𝐀 600. 🆗 🆎 ⓞ 𝗩𝗜𝗦𝗔
M (closed Saturday lunch) 16.50 **t.** (dinner) and a la carte 16.85/24.45 **t.** – ⌑ 7.50 – **136 rm** 75.00/95.00 **t.**, 2 suites – SB 96.00/116.00 **st.**

🏨 **Britannia,** London Rd, NN11 4EN, SE : ¾ m. on A 45 ℰ 77333, Fax 300420 – ⟨⟩ ⚞ rm 📺 ☎ 🅟 – 𝐀 300. 🆗 🆎 𝗩𝗜𝗦𝗔
M (carving rest.) 10.95/15.00 **st.** ↟ 8.45 – ⌑ 6.75 – **144 rm** 55.75/83.25 **st.**, 4 suites – SB (weekends only) 75.00 **st.**

at Badby S : 3½ m. by A 45 on A 361 – ⊠ ✆ 0327 Daventry :

🏠 **Windmill Inn,** Main St., NN11 6AN, ℰ 702363, Fax 311521 – 📺 ☎ 🅟. 🆗 🆎 ⓞ 𝗩𝗜𝗦𝗔
M a la carte 9.70/15.70 **t.** – **8 rm** ⌑ 35.00/54.00 **t.** – SB (weekends only except Bank Holidays) 55.00/78.00 **st.**

at Hellidon SW : 9½ m. by A 45 and A 361 on Hellidon rd – ⊠ ✆ 0327 Daventry :

🏨🏨 **Hellidon Lakes** ⟨⟩, NN11 6LN, SW : ¼ m. ℰ 62550, Fax 62559, ≼, *Ls*, ≘s, ◻, ⟨, park, ⟨⟩ – 📺 ☎ ⟨ ☺ 🅟 – 𝐀 50. 🆗 🆎 ⓞ 𝗩𝗜𝗦𝗔
M 15.95/17.50 **t.** and a la carte ↟ 5.00 – **23 rm** ⌑ 85.00/115.00 **t.**, 2 suites – SB (except Christmas and New Year) 110.00/185.00 **st.**

DAWLISH Devon 403 J 32 – pop. 8 030 – ECD : Thursday and Saturday – ✆ 0626.

☒ Warren ℰ 862255, E : 1½ m.

🏛 The Lawn, EX7 9PW ℰ 863589.

♦London 215 – Exeter 13 – ♦Plymouth 40 – Torquay 11.

🏨 **Langstone Cliff,** Dawlish Warren, EX7 0NA, N : 2 m. by A 379 ℰ 865155, Fax 867166, ⟨ heated, ◻, ☞, ⟨⟩ – ⟨⟩ 📺 ☎ 🅟 – 𝐀 400. 🆗 🆎 ⓞ 𝗩𝗜𝗦𝗔
M 9.50/14.50 ↟ 4.20 – **68 rm** ⌑ 45.00/80.00 **st.** – SB (except Easter, Christmas and New Year) 90.00/100.00 **st.**

DEAL Kent 404 Y 30 – pop. 26 548 – ECD : Thursday – ✆ 0304.

☒ Walmer & Kingsdown, The Leas, Kingsdown ℰ 373256, S : 2½ m.

🏛 Town Hall, High St., CT14 6BB ℰ 369576.

♦London 78 – Canterbury 19 – Dover 8.5 – Margate 16.

at Kingsdown S : 2¾ m. by A 258 on B 2057 – ⊠ ✆ 0304 Deal :

↷ **Blencathra Country,** Kingsdown Hill, CT14 8EA, off Upper St. ℰ 373725, ☞ – 📺 🅟. ⟨⟩
M (by arrangement) 8.00 **st.** – **7 rm** ⌑ 17.00/36.00 **st.**

at Finglesham NW : 3½ m. by A 258 and Burgess Green on The Street – ⊠ ✆ 0304 Deal :

↷ **Finglesham Grange** ⟨⟩, without rest., CT14 0NQ, NW : ¾ m. on Eastry rd ℰ 611314, ☞ – 🅟
3 rm ⌑ 22.50/45.00 **s.**

⊚ ATS 40 Gilford Rd ℰ 361543

DEANSHANGER Bucks. 404 R 27 – see Stony Stratford.

DEDDINGTON Oxon. 403 404 Q 28 – pop. 1 617 – ✆ 0869.

♦London 72 – ♦Birmingham 46 – ♦Coventry 33 – ♦Oxford 18.

🏨 **Holcombe** (Best Western), High St., OX15 0SL, ℰ 38274, Fax 37167, ☞ – ⚞ rm 📺 ☎ 🅟. 🆗 🆎 𝗩𝗜𝗦𝗔
closed 2 to 12 January – **M** 19.95/26.25 **st.** and a la carte ↟ 4.25 – **17 rm** ⌑ 55.00/105.00 **st.** – SB 98.00/174.00 **st.**

✗ **Tiffany's,** Market Pl., OX15 0SE, ℰ 38813 – 🆗 ⓞ 𝗩𝗜𝗦𝗔
closed Sunday, Monday, 1 week early May and 2 weeks September – **M** (dinner only) a la carte approx. 17.20 **t.** ↟ 4.25.

DEDHAM Essex 404 W 28 Great Britain G. – pop. 1 905 – ECD : Wednesday – ⊠ ✆ 0206 Colchester.

Envir. : Stour Valley★ – Flatford Mill★, E : 6 m. by B 1029, A 12 and B 1070.

♦London 63 – Chelmsford 30 – Colchester 8 – ♦Ipswich 12.

🏨🏨 **Maison Talbooth** ⟨⟩, Stratford Rd, CO7 6HN, W : ½ m. ℰ 322367, Fax 322752, ≼, ☞ – 📺 📺 🅟 🆗 𝗩𝗜𝗦𝗔 ⟨⟩
M – (see **Le Talbooth** below) – ⌑ 7.50 – **9 rm** 82.50/137.50 **st.**, 1 suite – SB (October-April) 145.00/165.00 **st.**

🏨 **Dedham Vale,** Stratford Rd, CO7 6HW, W : ¾ m. 𝒫 322273, Fax 322752, ≤, ☞ – TV ☎
🅿. 🄽 AE VISA ⋙
   M – (see **Le Talbooth** below) – ⟷ 6.00 – **6 rm** 55.00/79.50 **st.** – SB (October-April except
   Bank Holidays) 115.00/130.00 **st.**

XXX **Le Talbooth,** Gun Hill, CO7 6HP, W : 1 m. 𝒫 323150, Fax 322752, « Part Tudor house in
   attractive riverside setting », ☞ – 🅿. 🄽 🄽 VISA
   M 19.50 **t.** and a la carte 19.75/36.00 **t.** ▮ 5.50.

XX **Fountain House & Dedham Hall** ⌂ with rm, Brook St., CO7 6AD, 𝒫 323027, ☞ –
   ⋟⋛ rest TV 🅿. 🄽 VISA ⋙
   M (closed Sunday dinner, Monday and Bank Holidays) (dinner only and Sunday lunch)/
   dinner 17.50 **t.** ▮ 6.00 – **6 rm** ⟷ 38.00/57.00 **t.**

DENTON Gtr. Manchester 402 404 N 23 – pop. 37 227 – 😊 061 Manchester.

🏠 Denton, Manchester Rd 𝒫 336 3218.

◆London 196 – Chesterfield 41 – ◆Manchester 6.

🏨 **Old Rectory,** Meadow Lane, Haughton Green, M34 1GD, S : 2 m. by A 6017 𝒫 336 7516,
   Fax 320 3212 – TV ☎ 🅿 – ⋔ 100. 🄽 AE ⓞ VISA ⋙
   M (closed Saturday lunch) 11.00/26.00 **t.** and a la carte ▮ 4.95 – **35 rm** ⟷ 35.00/59.50 **st.**,
   1 suite – SB (except Christmas) (weekends only) 80.00/130.00 **st.**

DERBY Derbs. 402 403 404 P 25 Great Britain G. – pop. 218 026 – ECD : Wednesday – 😊 0332.

See : City★ – Museum and Art Gallery★ (Collection of Derby Porcelain★) YZ **M1** – Royal Crown
Derby Museum★ AC Z **M2.**

Envir. : Kedleston Hall★★ AC, NW : 4½ m. by Kedleston Rd X.

🏠 Wilmore Rd, Sinfin 𝒫 766323, S : 2 ¼ m. by Sinfin Lane X – 🏠 Mickleover, Uttoxeter Rd
𝒫 513339, W : 3 m. by A 516 and A 38 X – 🏠 Kedleston Park 𝒫 840035, NW : 5½ m. by A 52 X –
🏠, 🏠 Breadsall Priory Hotel G. & C.C., Moor Rd, Morley 𝒫 832235, NE : 4 m. by A 52 off A 61 via
Rectory Lane X – 🏠 Allestree Park, Allestree Hall 𝒫 550616, N : 2 m. by A 6 X.

✈ East Midlands, Castle Donington 𝒫 810621, Fax 850393, SE : 12 m. by A 6 X.

🅱 Assembly Rooms, Market Pl., DE1 3AH 𝒫 255802.

◆London 132 – ◆Birmingham 40 – ◆Coventry 49 – ◆Leicester 29 – ◆Manchester 62 – ◆Nottingham 16 – ◆Sheffield 47 –
◆Stoke-on-Trent 35.

Plan on next page

🏨 **Midland** (Best Western), Midland Rd, DE1 2SQ, 𝒫 45894, Telex 378373, Fax 293522, ☞ –   Z i
   ⋟⋛ rm TV ☎ 🅿 – ⋔ 150. 🄽 AE ⓞ VISA
   closed 24 to 26 December and 1 January – **M** (closed lunch Saturday and Bank Holidays) 12.50/15.25 **t.** – ⟷ 7.00 – **100 rm** 68.00/114.00 **t.** – SB (weekends only) 88.00 **st.**

🏨 **La Gondola,** 220 Osmaston Rd, DE23 8JX, 𝒫 32895, Fax 384512 – TV ☎ 🅿 – ⋔ 70. 🄽   X c
   AE ⓞ VISA ⋙
   M (closed Sunday) (dancing Saturday) 7.25/11.50 **t.** and a la carte ▮ 5.50 – ⟷ 4.50 – **19 rm**
   45.00/56.00 **t.**, 1 suite.

🏨 Oast House Country Inn, Foresters Leisure Park, 220 Osmaston Park Rd, DE3 8AG,   X e
   𝒫 270027, Fax 270528 – TV ☎ & 🅿 – ⋔ 40. ⋙
   25 rm.

🏨 **Periquito,** 119 London Rd, DE1 2QR, 𝒫 40633, Fax 293502 – ⋟⋛ rm TV ☎ 🅿 – ⋔ 150. 🄽   Z o
   AE VISA ⋙
   closed Christmas-New Year – **M** (closed lunch Bank Holidays) 8.95/12.85 **st.** and a la carte
   ▮ 5.00 – ⟷ 5.50 – **101 rm** 49.00/58.00 **st.**

XX **New Water Margin,** 72-74 Burton Rd, DE1 1TG, 𝒫 364754, Fax 364754 – 🔲 🅿. 🄽 AE   Z e
   ⓞ VISA
   M - Chinese (Canton) 14.50 **t.** and a la carte ▮ 3.50.

X **G.C's,** 22 Iron Gate, DE1 3GP, 𝒫 368732 – ⋟⋛. 🄽 AE ⓞ VISA   Y a
   closed Sunday and Monday – **M** 6.95/12.95 **t.** and a la carte ▮ 5.10.

   at Darley Abbey N : 1¾ m. on A 6 (Duffield Rd) – X – ✉ 😊 0332 Derby :

XX **Darleys on the River,** Darley Abbey Mills, DE22 1DZ, E : ½ m. via Mileash Lane and Old
   Lane 𝒫 364987, Fax 364987, ≤ – ▤. 🄽 AE ⓞ VISA
   closed Sunday dinner – **M** 11.95 **t.** (lunch) and a la carte 19.40/27.80 **t.**

   at Breadsall NE : 4 m. by A 52 off A 61 – X – ✉ 😊 0332 Derby :

🏨 **Breadsall Priory H. Golf & Country Club,** Moor Rd, Morley, DE7 6DL, NE : 1¼ m. via
   Rectory Lane 𝒫 832235, Fax 833509, ⌖, ≦s, 🄽, 🏠, ☞, ⋙, squash – 🈯 ⋟⋛ rm TV ☎ &.
   🅿 – ⋔ 90. 🄽 AE ⓞ VISA ⋙
   M (carving lunch) 12.85/18.50 **t.** – **91 rm** ⟷ 93.00/150.00 **t.** – SB (except Christmas and
   New Year) (weekends only) 110.00/140.00 **st.**

   at Littleover SW : 2½ m. on A 5250 – ✉ 😊 0332 Derby :

🏨 **Forte Posthouse,** Pastures Hill, DE3 7BA, 𝒫 514933, Fax 518668, ☞ – ⋟⋛ rm TV ☎ &.   X a
   🅿 – ⋔ 60. 🄽 AE ⓞ VISA
   M a la carte approx. 17.50 **t.** ▮ 4.65 – ⟷ 6.95 – **60 rm** 53.50 **st.**, 2 suites – SB 90.00 **st.**

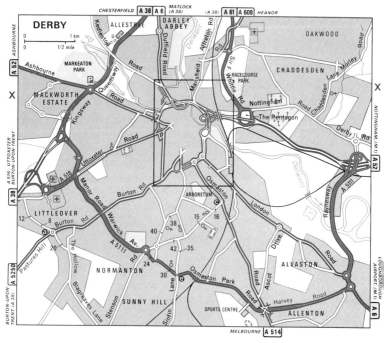

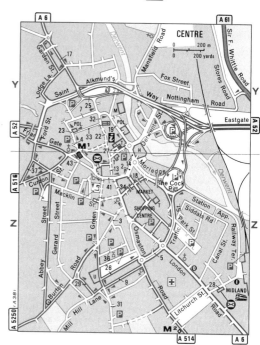

170

at Mackworth NW : 2 ¾ m. by A 52 – X – ⊠ ☻ 0332 Derby :

🏠 **Mackworth,** Ashbourne Rd, DE22 4LY, on A 52 ℰ 824324, Fax 824692, ⊠ – 📺 ☎ 🅿. 🔼
🅰🅴 𝑽𝑰𝑺𝑨
M (carving rest.) 7.95 **t.** (dinner) and a la carte 11.40/20.55 **t.** ⅃ 4.95 – **14 rm** ⊑ 42.00/
55.00 **t.**

at Kedleston NW : 4 m. by Kedleston Rd – X – ⊠ ☻ 0332 Derby :

🏠 Kedleston Country House, Kedleston Rd, DE6 4JD, E : 2 m. ℰ 559202, Fax 558822 – 📺 ☎
🕭 🅿
14 rm.

🔧 ATS Gosforth Rd, off Ascot Drive ℰ 40854   ATS 67 Bridge St. ℰ 47327

DERSINGHAM Norfolk 402 404 V 25 – pop. 3 263 – ☻ 0485.
♦London 110 – ♦Cambridge 53 – ♦Norwich 46.

🏠 **Westdene House,** 60 Hunstanton Rd, PE31 6HQ, ℰ 540395, ⊠ – 📺 🅿. 🔼 𝑽𝑰𝑺𝑨. ✎
M 7.95 **s.** ⅃ 3.00 – **5 rm** ⊑ 15.00/30.00 **s.**

DESBOROUGH Northants. 404 R 26 – pop. 6 404 – ☻ 0536 Kettering.
♦London 83 – ♦Birmingham 52 – ♦Leicester 20 – Northampton 20.

🏠 **Forte Travelodge** without rest., Harborough Rd, NN14 2UG, N : 1 ½ m. on A 6 ℰ 762034,
Reservations (Freephone) 0800 850950 – 📺 🕭 🅿. 🔼 🅰🅴 𝑽𝑰𝑺𝑨. ✎
32 rm 31.95 **t.**

I prezzi	Per ogni chiarimento sui prezzi qui riportati,
	consultate le spiegazioni alle pagine dell'introduzione.

DETHICK Derbs. – see Matlock.

DEVIZES Wilts. 403 404 O 29 The West Country G. – pop. 12 430 – ECD : Wednesday – ☻ 0380.
See : St. John's Church★★ – Market Place★ – Devizes Museum★ *AC.*
Envir. : Potterne (Porch House★★) S : 2 ½ m. by A 360 – E : Vale of Pewsey★.
Exc. : Stonehenge★★★ *AC,* SE : 16 m. by A 360 and A 344 – Avebury★★ (The Stones★,
Church★) NE : 7 m. by A 361.
🔟₈ Erlestoke Sands, Erlestoke ℰ 831027, S : 8 m. by B 3098.
🅱 39 St. John's St., SN10 1BN ℰ 729408.
♦London 98 – ♦Bristol 38 – Salisbury 25 – Swindon 19.

🏠 **Rathlin,** Wick Lane, SN10 5DP, S : ¾ m. by A 360 ℰ 721999, ⊠ – 📺 🅿. ✎
closed 25 and 26 December – **M** 8.00 **s.** – **4 rm** ⊑ 25.00/38.00 **s.**

at Rowde NW : 2 m. by A 361 on A 342 – ⊠ ☻ 0380 Devizes

🍴 **George & Dragon,** SN10 2PN, on A 342 ℰ 723053, ⊠ – 🅿. 🔼 𝑽𝑰𝑺𝑨
closed Sunday, Monday and 2 weeks Christmas-New Year – **M** (booking essential) 10.00 **t.**
(lunch) and a la carte 12.75/26.25 **t.** ⅃ 3.75.

at Westbrook NW : 6 m. by A 361 and A 342 on B 3102 – ⊠ Chippenham – ☻ 0380
Devizes :

🏠 **Cottage** without rest., SN15 2EE, on A 3102 ℰ 850255, « Gardens » – 📺 🅿. ✎
3 rm ⊑ 25.00/40.00.

DIDDLEBURY Shrops. 403 L 26 Great Britain G. – pop. 526 – ⊠ Craven Arms – ☻ 058 476
(3 fig.) and 0584 (6 fig.) Munslow.
Envir. : NW : Wenlock Edge★.
♦London 169 – ♦Birmingham 46.

🏠 **Glebe Farm** ⦉ without rest., SY7 9DH, ℰ 221, « Part Elizabethan house », ⊠ – 📺 🅿.
✎
March-November – **6 rm** ⊑ 22.00/50.00 **s.**

DIDSBURY Gtr. Manchester 402 403 404 N 23 – see Manchester.

DINNINGTON S. Yorks. 402 403 404 Q 23 – pop. 1 870 – ⊠ Sheffield – ☻ 0909.
♦London 166 – Lincoln 37 – ♦Sheffield 12.

🏨 Dinnington Hall ⦉, Falcon Way, S31 7NY, off B 6060 ℰ 569661, Fax 569661, ⊠ – 📺 ☎
🅿
10 rm.

DISLEY Ches. 402 403 404 N 23 – pop. 3 425 – ECD : Wednesday – ⊠ Stockport – ☻ 0663.
♦London 187 – Chesterfield 35 – ♦Manchester 12.

🏨 **Moorside,** Mudhurst Lane, Higher Disley, SK12 2AP, SE : 2 m. by Buxton Old Rd
ℰ 764151, Fax 762794, ≼, ⅃₄, 😴, 🔲, 🔟, ✎, squash – 📺 ☎ 🅿 – 🔬 250. 🔼 🅰🅴 ⓓ 𝑽𝑰𝑺𝑨
M 12.50/25.00 **st.** and a la carte ⅃ 5.95 – **91 rm** ⊑ 73.00/88.00 **st.,** 2 suites.

DISS Norfolk ████ X 26 – pop. 5 463 – ECD : Tuesday – ✆ 0379.

🚇 Stuston Common ✆ 642847, SE : 1 m.

🎫 Meres Mouth, Mere St., IP22 3AG ✆ 650523 (summer only).

♦London 98 – ♦Ipswich 25 – ♦Norwich 21 – Thetford 17.

XX **Salisbury House** with rm, 84 Victoria Rd, IP22 3JG, ✆ 644738, « Attractively decorated Victorian house », ☞ – 📺 🄿. ◪ 🆅🆂🄰 ⁂
closed 2 weeks August and 1 week Christmas – **M** *(closed Saturday lunch, Sunday and Monday)* (lunch by arrangement)/dinner 22.00 **t.** ⱡ 3.70 – ⌷ 3.50 – **3 rm** 39.00/70.00 **t.** – SB (weekends only) 97.00/107.00 **st.**

X **Weavers,** Market Hill, IP22 3JZ, ✆ 642411 – ◪ ⑩ 🆅🆂🄰
closed Saturday lunch, Sunday, 10 days August-September, 1 week Christmas and Bank Holidays – **M** 12.50 **t.** (lunch) and a la carte 13.65/17.45 **t.**

at Gissing NE : 5 m. via Burston rd – ✉ Diss – ✆ 037 977 Tivetshall :

⌂ **Old Rectory** ⌕, Rectory Rd, IP22 3XB, ✆ 575, Fax 4427, ≼, ◪, ☞ – ⤙ 📺 🄿. ◪ 🆅🆂🄰 ⁂
M (by arrangement) 20.00 **st.** – **3 rm** ⌷ 34.00/56.00 **st.** – SB (weekdays only) 82.00/120.00 **st.**

at Scole E : 2½ m. by A 1066 on A 143 – ✉ ✆ 0379 Diss :

🏛 Scole Inn (Best Western), Main St., IP21 4DR, ✆ 740481, Fax 740762, « 17C inn » – ▦ rest 📺 ☎ 🄿 – 🄰 40
23 rm.

at Brome (Suffolk) SE : 2¾ m. by A 143 on B 1077 – ✉ ✆ 0379 Eye :

🏛 **Oaksmere** ⌕, IP23 8AJ, ✆ 870326, Fax 870051, « Part 16C house, topiary gardens », park – 🄿 🄰 40. ◪ ⑩ 🆅🆂🄰
M 15.90/23.50 **st.** and a la carte ⱡ 6.00 – **11 rm** ⌷ 59.50/85.00 **st.** – SB (except Christmas and New Year) 115.00 **st.**

at South Lopham W : 5½ m. on A 1066 – ✉ Diss – ✆ 037 988 (3 and 4 fig.) and 0379 (6 fig.) Bressingham :

⌂ **Malting Farm** ⌕ without rest., Blo' Norton Rd, IP22 2HT, ✆ 201, ≼, « Working farm » – ⤙ 🄿. ⁂
closed Christmas and New Year – **3 rm** ⌷ 25.00/38.00 **s.**

at Fersfield NW : 7. m. by A 1066 – ✉ Diss – ✆ 037 988 (3 and 4 fig.) and 0379 (6 fig.) Bressingham :

⌂ **Strenneth Farmhouse** ⌕, Old Airfield Rd, IP22 2BP, ✆ 8182, Fax 8260, ☞ – 📺 🄿. ◪ 🆅🆂🄰
M (by arrangement) 13.00 **st.** – **9 rm** ⌷ 21.00/56.00 **st.** – SB 56.00/76.00 **st.**

◎ ATS Shelfanger Rd ✆ 642861

GREEN TOURIST GUIDES

Picturesque scenery, buildings

Attractive routes

Touring programmes

Plans of towns and buildings.

DITTON PRIORS Shrops. ████ ████ M 26 – pop. 550 – ✉ Bridgnorth – ✆ 074 634 (3 fig.) and 0746 (6 fig.).

♦London 154 – ♦Birmingham 34 – Ludlow 13 – Shrewsbury 21.

⌂ Court House ⌕, South Rd, WV16 6SJ, ✆ 554, ☞ – ⤙ 📺 🄿
M (by arrangement) – **3 rm.**

XX **Howard Arms,** WV16 6SQ, ✆ 200, ☞ – 🄿. ◪ 🆅🆂🄰
closed Sunday dinner, Monday and 2 weeks September – **M** (dinner only and Sunday lunch)/dinner 29.00 **t.** ⱡ 4.60.

DODDISCOMBSLEIGH Devon – see Exeter.

DONCASTER S. Yorks. ████ ████ ████ Q 23 – pop. 74 727 – ECD : Thursday – ✆ 0302.

🚇 Doncaster Town Moor, The Belle Vue Club ✆ 535286 – 🚇 Crookhill Park, Conisborough ✆ 0709 (Rotherham) 862979, W : 3 m. by A 630 – 🚇 Wheatley, Armthorpe Rd ✆ 831655, E : 3 m. by A 18 – 🚇 Owston Park, Owston ✆ 330821, N : 5 m. by A 19.

🎫 Central Library, Waterdale, DN1 3JE ✆ 734309.

♦London 173 – ♦Kingston-upon-Hull 46 – ♦Leeds 30 – ♦Nottingham 46 – ♦Sheffield 19.

🏨 **Doncaster Moat House** (Q.M.H.), Warmsworth, DN4 9UX, SW : 2¾ m. on A 630 ✆ 310331, Telex 547963, Fax 310197, ⌗, ≋, ◪ – ⧈ ⤙ rm 📺 ☎ 🄿 – 🄰 350. ◪ 🄰🄴 ⑩ 🆅🆂🄰 ⁂
M *(closed lunch Saturday)* 11.95/14.50 **st.** and a la carte ⱡ 4.95 – **98 rm** ⌷ 73.00/88.00 **st.**, 2 suites – SB (weekends only) 88.00/106.00 **st.**

172

🏨 **Danum Swallow,** High St., DN1 1DN, ✆ 342261, Fax 329034 – 📱 ⤫ rm 📺 ☎ 🄿 –
🛦 280. 🔼 🄰🄴 🄻🄴 *VISA* ⅏
M *(closed Saturday lunch)* 8.95/15.50 **st.** and a la carte – ☲ 5.00 – **62 rm** 72.00/86.00 **st.**,
2 suites – SB (except Christmas and New Year) 90.00 **st.**

🏨 **Punch's** (Toby), Bawtry Rd, Bessacarr, DN4 7BS, SE : 3 m. on A 638 ✆ 370037,
Fax 532281 – ⤫ rm 📺 ☎ ⅙ 🄿 – 🛦 40. 🔼 🄰🄴 ⅏
M 10.50 **st.** and a la carte ⅋ 3.50 – **24 rm** ☲ 39.95/69.95 **st.**

🏨 **Grand St. Leger** (Best Western), Racecourse Roundabout, Bennetthorpe, DN2 6AX,
SE : 1½ m. on A 638 ✆ 364111, Fax 329865 – 📺 ☎ 🄿 🔼 🄰🄴 🄻🄴 ⓪ *VISA*. ⅏
M 12.50/15.95 **st.** and a la carte – **20 rm** ☲ 66.00/80.00 **st.** – SB (weekends only) 50.00/
132.00 **st.**

🏨 **Campanile,** Doncaster Leisure Park, Bawtry Rd, DN4 7PD, SE : 2 m. on A 638 ✆ 370770,
Telex 547942, Fax 370813 – 📺 ☎ ⅙ 🄿 – 🛦 30. 🔼 🄰🄴 *VISA*
M 9.45 **t.** and a la carte ⅋ 4.65 – ☲ 4.25 – **51 rm** 35.75 **t.**

🏠 **Ashlea** without rest., 81 Thorne Rd, DN1 2ES, ✆ 363374, Fax 760215 – 📺 ☎ 🄿. 🔼 *VISA*.
12 rm ☲ 22.00/40.00 **st.**

at Rossington SE : 6 m. on A 638 – ⊠ ⚙ 0302 Doncaster :

🏨 **Mount Pleasant,** Great North Rd, DN11 0HP, on A 638 ✆ 868219, Fax 865130, ⪯ – 📺
☎ ⅙ 🄿 – 🛦 60. 🔼 🄰🄴 ⓪ *VISA*. ⅏
M 10.95/14.95 **t.** and a la carte – **32 rm** ☲ 42.00/70.00 **t.** – SB (weekends only) 59.95/
97.90 **st.**

at Carcroft NW : 6½ m. on A 1 – ⊠ ⚙ 0302 Doncaster :

🏠 **Forte Travelodge** without rest., Great North Rd, (northbound carriageway) ✆ 330841,
Reservations (Freephone) 0800 850950 – 📺 ⅙ 🄿. 🔼 🄰🄴 *VISA*. ⅏
40 rm 31.95 **t.**

🔘 ATS Carr Hill, Balby ✆ 367337/366997

DORCHESTER Dorset **403 404** M 31 The West Country G. – pop. 13 734 – ECD : Thursday –
⚙ 0305.

See : Town★ – Dorset County Museum★ *AC.*

Envir. : Maiden Castle★★ (≼★) SW : 2½ m. – Puddletown Church★, NE : 5½ m. by A 35.

Exc. : Moreton Church★★, E : 7½ m. – Bere Regis (St. John the Baptist Church★★) NE : 11 m.
by A 35 – Athelhampton★ *AC*, NE : 6½ m. by A 35 – Cerne Abbas★, N : 7 m. by A 352.

🏌 Came Down ✆ 812531, S : 2 m.

🄱 1 Acland Rd, DT1 1JW ✆ 267992.

♦London 135 – Bournemouth 27 – Exeter 53 – ♦Southampton 53.

🏨 **King's Arms,** 30 High East St., DT1 1HF, ✆ 265353, Fax 260269 – 📱 📺 ☎ 🄿 – 🛦 80. 🔼
🄰🄴 *VISA*
M a la carte 13.70/19.65 **st.** ⅋ 5.95 – **33 rm** ☲ 55.50/79.00 **st.** – SB (weekends only) 65.00/
128.00 **st.**

🏨 **Wessex Royale,** 32 High West St., DT1 1UP, ✆ 262660, Fax 251941 – 📺 ☎ – 🛦 80. 🔼
🄰🄴 ⓪ *VISA*
M 10.00 **st.** and a la carte ⅋ 3.95 – **23 rm** ☲ 30.00/59.95 **st.**

🏠 **Casterbridge** without rest., 49 High East St., DT1 1HU, ✆ 264043, Fax 260884,
« Georgian town house » – 📺 ☎. 🔼 🄰🄴 ⅏
closed 25 and 26 December – **14 rm** ☲ 28.00/60.00 **st.**

🏠 **Yalbury Cottage** ⌂, Lower Bockhampton, DT2 8PZ, E : 2¼ m. by B 3150 and
Bockhampton rd ✆ 262382, Fax 266412, ⪯ – 📺 ☎ 🄿. 🔼 🄰🄴 *VISA*. ⅏
closed 3 weeks January – **M** (booking essential) (dinner only) 22.50 **st.** and a la carte 14.85/
23.75 **st.** – **8 rm** ☲ 61.50/95.00 **st.** – SB (except Christmas and New Year) 115.00/159.00 **st.**

🏠 **Junction,** 42 Great Western Rd, DT1 1UF, ✆ 268826 – 📺 🄿. 🔼 *VISA*. ⅏
M *(closed dinner Friday to Saturday and Sunday)* (in bar) 12.00 **t.** ⅋ 3.95 – ☲ 4.50 – **6 rm**
29.50/38.00 **t.**

🏠 **Westwood House** without rest., 29 High West St., DT1 1UP, ✆ 268018, Fax 250282 – 📺
☎. 🔼 *VISA*. ⅏
7 rm ☲ 29.50/58.00 **st.**

⤫⤫ **Shapla Tandoori,** 14 High East St., DT1 1HH, ✆ 269202 – 🖩. 🔼 🄰🄴 ⓪ *VISA*
M - Indian a la carte approx. 11.15 **t.**

⤫ **Mock Turtle,** 34 High West St., DT1 1UP, ✆ 264011 – 🔼 *VISA*
closed lunch Monday and Saturday, Sunday and 26 to 28 December – **M** 12.50/19.95 **t.**
⅋ 5.35.

at Frampton NW : 6 m. by B 3147 and A 37 on A 356 – ⊠ Dorchester – ⚙ 0300 Maiden
Newton :

🏠 **Hyde Farm House** ⌂, DT2 9NG, NW : ½ m. on A 356 ✆ 20272, ≼, « Part 18C and 19C
house », ⪯ – 🄿. ⅏
M (by arrangement) (unlicensed) 12.00 **st.** – **3 rm** ☲ 22.50/45.00 **st.**

🔘 ATS Unit 4, Great Western Ind. Centre ✆ 264756

DORCHESTER Oxon. 📖🄳🄴 Q 29 Great Britain G. – pop. 1 045 – ☎ 0865 Oxford.

See : Town★.

Exc. : Ridgeway Path★★.

◆London 51 – Abingdon 6 – ◆Oxford 8 – Reading 17.

🏨 **White Hart**, 26 High St., OX10 7HN, ℰ 340074, Fax 341082, « 17C coaching inn » – 📺
☎ ℗, 🄲 🄰🄴 ⓞ 𝓥𝓘𝓢𝓐, 🕸
closed 24 and 25 December – **M** (bar lunch Monday to Saturday)/dinner 13.50/
19.50 **t.** and a la carte ⅄ 4.50 – **15 rm** ⊑ 66.50/87.00 **st.**, 4 suites – SB 85.00/135.00 **st.**

🏨 **George**, 23 High St., OX10 7HH, ℰ 340404, Fax 341620, 🛋 – 📺 ☎ ℗ – 🏛 40
18 rm.

DORKING Surrey 🄴 T 30 – pop. 14 602 – ECD : Wednesday – ☎ 0306.

◆London 26 – ◆Brighton 39 – Guildford 12 – Worthing 33.

🏨🏨 **Burford Bridge** (Forte), Box Hill, RH5 6BX, N : 1½ m. on A 24 ℰ 884561, Fax 880386,
🛋, heated, 🖉 – 🕸 rm 📺 ☎ ℗ – 🏛 300. 🄲 🄰🄴 ⓞ 𝓥𝓘𝓢𝓐 🄹🄲🄱
M 15.35/20.95 **t.** and a la carte ⅄ 6.10 – ⊑ 8.50 – **48 rm** 85.00 **st.** – SB (weekends only)
116.00 **st.**

🏨 **White Horse** (Forte), High St., RH4 1BE, ℰ 881138, Fax 887241, 🛋 heated – 🕸 rm 📺 ☎
℗ – 🏛 50. 🄲 🄰🄴 ⓞ 𝓥𝓘𝓢𝓐
M 13.95/17.95 **st.** and a la carte ⅄ 5.00 – ⊑ 8.95 – **68 rm** 70.00 **st.** – SB (weekends only)
98.00 **st.**

🏨 **Forte Travelodge** without rest., Reigate Rd, RH4 1QB, E : ½ m. on A 25 ℰ 740361,
Reservations (Freephone) 0800 850950 – 📺 🕭 ℗, 🄲 🄰🄴 𝓥𝓘𝓢𝓐, 🕸
29 rm 31.95 **t.**

XX **Partners West Street**, 2-4 West St., RH4 1BL, ℰ 882826 – 🕸, 🄲 🄰🄴 ⓞ 𝓥𝓘𝓢𝓐
closed Saturday lunch, Sunday dinner and Monday – **Meals** 9.95/19.95 **st.** and a la
carte 14.95/32.85 **st.** ⅄ 4.50.

X **Fountain Garden**, 16 West St., RH4 1BL, ℰ 876678 – 🗏, 🄲 🄰🄴 𝓥𝓘𝓢𝓐
closed Sunday lunch – **M** - Chinese 7.00/12.00 **t.** and a la carte.

📛 *Michelin hangt keine Schilder an die empfohlenen Hotels und Restaurants.*

DORMINGTON Heref. and Worcs. – see Hereford.

DORRINGTON Shrops. 🄴🄰🄴 🄴🄰🄴 L 26 – see Shrewsbury.

DOULTING 🄴🄰🄴 🄴🄰🄴 M 30 – see Shepton Mallet.

DOVER Kent 🄴🄰🄴 Y 30 Great Britain G. – pop. 33 461 – ECD : Wednesday – ☎ 0304.

See : Castle★★ AC Y.

🚢 to France : Boulogne and Calais (P & O European Ferries) (1 h 15) – Calais (Hoverspeed)
(35 mn) (frequent services) – to France : Calais (Stena Sealink Line) (1 h 30 mn) (frequent
services) – to Belgium : Ostend (Dover-Ostend Line) (4 h) – To France : Ouistreham (Brittany
Ferries).

🄴 Townwall St., CT16 1JR ℰ 205108.

◆London 76 – ◆Brighton 84.

Plan on next page

🏨🏨 **Forte Posthouse**, Singledge Lane, Whitfield, CT16 3LF, NW : 3½ m. by A 256 on A 2
ℰ 821222, Fax 825576 – 🕸 rm 🗏 rest 📺 ☎ ℗ – 🏛 40. 🄲 🄰🄴 ⓞ 𝓥𝓘𝓢𝓐, 🕸   Z o
M a la carte approx. 17.50 **t.** ⅄ 4.65 – ⊑ 6.95 – **67 rm** 53.50 **st.** – SB 90.00 **st.**

🏨🏨 **Dover Moat House** (Q.M.H.), Townwall St., CT16 1SZ, ℰ 203270, Telex 96458,
Fax 213230, 🛋 – 📳 – 🕸 rm 📺 🕭 – 🏛 80. 🄲 🄰🄴 ⓞ 𝓥𝓘𝓢𝓐   Y z
M 16.25 **st.** and a la carte – ⊑ 8.70 – **79 rm** 60.00/92.00 **st.** – SB (weekends only)
100.00/104.00 **st.**

🏨 **Travel Inn**, Folkestone Rd (A 20), CT15 7AB, SW : 2½ m. on A 20 ℰ 213339, Fax 214504
– 🕸 rm 📺 ⅄ ℗, 🄲 🄰🄴 ⓞ 𝓥𝓘𝓢𝓐, 🕸   Z
closed 24 and 25 December – **M** (Beefeater grill) a la carte approx. 16.00 **t.** – ⊑ 4.95 –
30 rm 33.50 **st.**

🏨 **Mildmay**, 78 Folkestone Rd, CT17 9SF, ℰ 204278, Fax 215342 – 📺 🕭 ℗, 🄲 𝓥𝓘𝓢𝓐, 🕸
closed 15 December-10 January – **M** (lunch by arrangement)/dinner a la carte 9.95/
23.00 **st.** ⅄ 4.50 – ⊑ 3.50 – **21 rm** 35.00/50.00 **st.**   Y n

⌂ **East Lee** without rest., 108 Maison Dieu Rd, CT16 1RT, ℰ 210176, Fax 210176 – 🕸 📺
🕭, 🄲 𝓥𝓘𝓢𝓐, 🕸   Y o
4 rm ⊑ 28.00/38.00 **st.**

⌂ **Penny Farthing** without rest., 109 Maison Dieu Rd, CT16 1RT, ℰ 205563 – 📺 ℗, 🕸
6 rm ⊑ 20.00/38.00 **s.**   Y i

⌂ **Number One** without rest., 1 Castle St., CT16 1QH, ℰ 202007, 🖉 – 📺 ⇦, 🕸   Y u
5 rm ⊑ 38.00.

⌂ **St. Martins and Ardmore** without rest., 17-18 Castle Hill Rd, CT16 1QW, ℰ 205938,
Fax 208229 – 📺, 🕸   Y r
12 rm ⊑ 25.00/45.00 **st.**

174

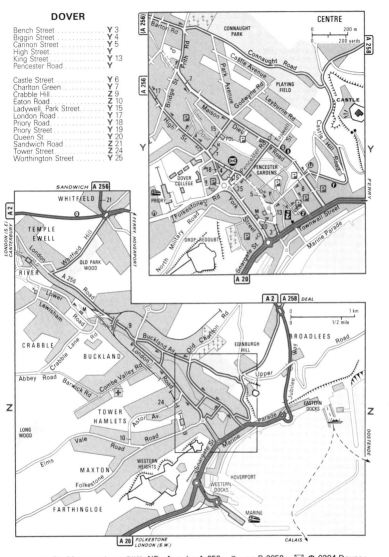

DOVER

at St. Margaret's at Cliffe NE : 4 m. by A 258 – Z – on B 2058 – ✉ ☎ 0304 Dover :

XX **Wallett's Court** 🏡 with rm, West Cliffe, CT15 6EW, NW : ¾ m. on B 2058 ℰ 852424, Fax 853430, « Part 17C manor house, 13C cellars », ⟿, ⬭ – 📺 ☎ ℗. 🄰 VISA ⬭ *closed 5 days at Christmas –* **M** *(closed Sunday)* (dinner only) 25.00 t. ↓ 5.50 – **7 rm** ⬭ 30.00/70.00 **st.** – SB (October-March) 100.00/130.00 **st.**

DOWN HATHERLEY Glos. – see Gloucester.

DOWNTON Wilts. 408 404 O 31 – see Salisbury.

L'EUROPE en une seule feuille
Carte Michelin n° 970.

DREWSTEIGNTON Devon 403 I 31 The West Country G. – pop. 557 – ✆ 0647.

Envir. : Dartmoor National Park★★ (Brent Tor ⇐★★, Haytor Rocks ⇐★).

◆London 216 – Exeter 15 – ◆Plymouth 46

⌂ **Hunts Tor,** EX6 6QW, ℰ 21228 – ⇔ rest
closed December and January – **Meals** (booking essential) 17.00 **st.** ▮ 4.30 – **4 rm** ⌧ 25.00/50.00 **st.**

DRIFFIELD Humbs. 402 S 21 – see Great Driffield.

DRIFT Cornwall – see Penzance.

DROITWICH Heref. and Worcs. 403 404 N 27 – pop. 18 025 – ECD : Thursday – ✆ 0905.

🖭 Ombersley, Bishopswood Rd ℰ 620747.

🖪 St. Richard's House, Victoria Sq., WR9 8DS ℰ 774312.

◆London 129 – ◆Birmingham 20 – ◆Bristol 66 – Worcester 6.

🏨 **Raven,** St. Andrews St., WR9 8DU, ℰ 772224, Fax 772371, ☞ – ▮≑▮ 🖵 ☎ ❶ – 🔬 150. ◪ 🖭 ⑩ 𝘝𝘐𝘚𝘈 ⚘
closed Christmas – **M** *(closed Saturday lunch and Sunday dinner)* 11.00/16.00 **st.** and a la carte – ⌧ 9.95 – **71 rm** 49.95/119.95 **st.**, 1 suite.

🏠 **St. Andrews House,** Worcester Rd, WR9 8AL, S : ¼ m. by A 38 ℰ 779677, Fax 779752, ☞ – 🖵 ☎ ❶ – 🔬 80. ◪ ◪ 🖭 ⑩ 𝘝𝘐𝘚𝘈 ⚘
M (grill rest.) (bar lunch Monday to Saturday)/dinner a la carte 15.00/20.00 **t.** ▮ 3.00 – ⌧ 5.00 – **29 rm** 35.00/60.00 **t.**

🏠 **Forte Travelodge** without rest., Rashwood Hill, WR9 8DA, NE : 1 ½ m. on A 38 ℰ 052 786 (Wychbold) 1545, Reservations (Freephone) 0800 850950 – 🖵 ⅀ ❶. ◪ ◪ 𝘝𝘐𝘚𝘈 ⚘
32 rm 31.95 **t.**

☞ *Michelin non applica targhe pubblicitarie agli alberghi e ristoranti segnalati in Guida.*

DRONFIELD Derbs 402 403 404 P 24 – pop. 22 641 – ECD : Wednesday – ✉ Sheffield (S. Yorks.) – ✆ 0246.

◆ London 158 – Derby 30 – ◆ Nottingham 31 – ◆ Sheffield 6.

🏠 **Manor House,** 10-15 High St., S18 6PY, ℰ 413971 – ⇔ rest 🖵 ❶. ◪ ◪ 🖭 ⑩ 𝘝𝘐𝘚𝘈 ⚘
M *(closed Sunday and Monday)* 20.00/22.50 **t.** and a la carte ▮ 4.00 – **10 rm** ⌧ 35.00/60.00 **st.** – SB 90.00 **st.**

DUDDENHOE END Essex 404 U 27 – see Saffron Walden.

DUDLEY W. Mids. 402 403 404 N 26 – pop. 185 721 – ECD : Wednesday ✆ 0384.

🖭₈, 🖙 Swindon, Bridgnorth Rd ℰ 0902 (Wombourne) 897031, W : 6 m. by B 4176 AU – 🖙 Sedgley, Sandyfields Rd ℰ 0902 (Sedgley) 880503, N : 4½ m. by A 459 AT.

🖪 39 Churchill Precinct, DY2 7BL ℰ 250333.

◆London 132 – ◆Birmingham 10 – Wolverhampton 6.

Plan : see Birmingham p. 2

🏨 **Copthorne Merry Hill,** The Waterfront, Level St., Brierley Hill, DY5 1UR, SW : 2 ¼ m. by A 461 ℰ 482882, Fax 482773, ▮₆, ☲s, ◪ – ▮≑▮ ⇔ rm ▮ rest 🖵 ☎ ⅀ ❶ – 🔬 250. ◪ ◪ ⑩ 𝘝𝘐𝘚𝘈 𝘑𝘊𝘉   AU **z**
M a la carte 10.25/24.15 **st.** ▮ 6.95 – ⌧ 9.25 – **129 rm** 89.50/99.00 **st.**, 9 suites.

🏠 Himley House, Himley, DY3 4LD, W : 4 m. by B 4176 on A 449 ℰ 0902 (Wolverhampton) 892468, Fax 892604, ☞ – 🖵 ☎ ❶   AU **e**
M (grill rest.) – **24 rm.**

🏠 **Forte Travelodge** without rest., Dudley Rd, Brierley Hill, DY5 1LQ, SW : 2 m. on A 461 ℰ 481579, Reservations (Freephone) 0800 850950 – 🖵 ⅀ ❶. ◪ ◪ 𝘝𝘐𝘚𝘈 ⚘   AU **c**
32 rm 31.95 **t.**

🅐 ATS Oakeywell St. ℰ 238047

DULVERTON Somerset 403 J 30 The West Country G. – pop. 1 301 – ECD : Thursday – ✆ 0398.

See : Village★.

Envir. : Tarr Steps★★, NW : 6 m. by B 3223.

◆London 198 – Barnstaple 27 – Exeter 26 – Minehead 18 – Taunton 27.

🏠 **Ashwick House** ⅏, TA22 9QD, NW : 4 ¼ m. by B 3223 ℰ 23868, ⇐, « Country house atmosphere », ☞ – ⇔ rest 🖵 ☎ ❶. ⚘
M (dinner only and Sunday lunch)/dinner 22.50 **t.** ▮ 5.60 – **6 rm** ⌧ 49.00/80.00 **t.** – SB 98.00/146.00 **st.**

at Brushford SW : 1 ¾ m. on B 3223 – ✉ ✆ 0398 Dulverton :

🏨 **Carnarvon Arms,** TA22 9AE, ℰ 23302, Fax 24022, ⅃ heated, ⩘, ☞, park, ✾ – 🖵 ☎ ❶ – 🔬 100. ◪ 𝘝𝘐𝘚𝘈
M 19.75/30.75 **t.** and a la carte ▮ 4.00 – **22 rm** ⌧ 35.00/70.00 **t.**, 1 suite – SB 114.00/140.00 **st.**

DUNCHURCH Warks. 403 404 O 26 – pop. 2 409 – ⊠ ✪ 0788 Rugby.

◆London 90 – ◆Coventry 12 – ◆Leicester 24 – Northampton 26.

🏨 **Forte Travelodge** without rest., London Rd, Thurlaston, CV23 9LG, NW : 2½ m. on A 45 ✆ 521538, Reservations (Freephone) 0800 850950 – 📺 ﯼ **ᴘ**. 🔼 🆎 VISA. ⬚ **40 rm** 31.95 **t.**

DUNSFORD Devon 403 I 31 – pop. 637 – ✪ 0647.

◆London 206 – Exeter 6 – ◆Plymouth 35.

🏨 **Dunsford Mills,** EX6 7EF, SW : ½ m. on B 3212 (Moretonhampton rd) ✆ 52011, Fax 52988, « Converted 18C water mill », ☞, park – 📺 **ᴘ**. 🔼 🆎 VISA. ⬚ **M** 10.00/14.95 **t.** and dinner a la carte ⅄ 4.50 – **10 rm** ⊇ 90.00 **t.**

DUNSLEY N. Yorks. – see Whitby.

DUNSTABLE Beds. 404 S 28 – pop. 48 436 – ECD : Thursday – ✪ 0582.

🏌 Tilsworth, Dunstable Rd ✆ 0525 (Leighton Buzzard) 210721/210722, N : 2 m. on A 5.

🅱 The Library, Vernon Pl., LU5 4HA ✆ 471012.

◆London 40 – Bedford 24 – Luton 4.5 – Northampton 35.

🏨 **Old Palace Lodge,** Church St., LU5 4RT, ✆ 662201, Fax 696422 – 📳 ⬚ rm 🖿 rest 📺 ☎ **ᴘ** – ⚞ 35. 🔼 🆎 VISA JCB
closed 26 to 30 December – **M** *(closed Saturday lunch)* 16.95 **st.** and a la carte – ⊇ 7.95 – **49 rm** 43.00/120.00 **st.**

🏨 **Highwayman,** London Rd, LU6 3DX, SE : 1 m. on A 5 ✆ 661999, Fax 603812 – 📺 ☎ **ᴘ** – ⚞ 40. 🔼 🆎 ① VISA. ⬚ **M** (bar lunch Monday to Saturday)/dinner 12.50 **st.** and a la carte ⅄ 3.75 – **53 rm** ⊇ 47.00/ 56.00 **st.** – SB (weekends only) 72.50/125.50 **st.**

at Hockliffe NW : 3¼ m. on A 5 – ⊠ Dunstable – ✪ 0525 Leighton Buzzard :

🏨 **Forte Travelodge** without rest., LU7 9NB, ✆ 211177, Reservations (Freephone) 0800 850950 – 📺 ﯼ **ᴘ**. 🔼 🆎 VISA. ⬚ **28 rm** 31.95 **t.**

DUNSTER Somerset 403 J 30 The West Country G. – pop. 793 – ECD : Wednesday – ⊠ Minehead – ✪ 0643.

See : Town★★ – Castle★★ *AC* (Upper rooms ≤★) – Dunster Water Mill★ *AC* – St. Georges Church★ – Dovecote★.

Envir. : Exmoor National Park★★ (Dunkery Beacon★★★, Watersmeet★, Valley of the Rocks★, Vantage Point★) – Cleeve Abbey★★ *AC*, SE : 5 m. by A 39 – Timbercombe (Church★) SW : 3½ m. by A 396.

◆London 184 – ◆Bristol 61 – Exeter 40 – Taunton 22.

🏨 **Luttrell Arms** (Forte), 36 High St., TA24 6SG, ✆ 821555, Fax 821567, « Part 15C inn », ☞ – ⬚ 📺 ☎. 🔼 🆎 ① VISA JCB
M (bar lunch Monday to Saturday)/dinner 16.95 **t.** and a la carte ⅄ 6.45 – ⊇ 8.50 – **27 rm** 75.00/95.00 **t.** – SB 128.00 **st.**

🏨 **Exmoor House,** 12 West St., TA24 6SN, ✆ 821268, ☞ – ⬚ 📺. 🔼 🆎 ① VISA
February-November – **M** (dinner only) 14.50 **st.** ⅄ 3.90 – **7 rm** ⊇ 27.50/55.00 **st.** – SB 70.00/ 91.00 **st.**

DURHAM Durham 401 402 P 19 Great Britain G. – pop. 38 105 – ECD : Wednesday – ✪ 091.

See : City★★★ – Cathedral★★★ (Nave★★★, Chapel of the Nine Altars★★★, Sanctuary Knocker★) B – Oriental Museum★★ *AC* (at Durham University by A 167) B – City and Riverside (Prebends' Bridge ≤★★★ A , Framwellgate Bridge ≤★★ B) – Monastic Buildings (Cathedral Treasury★, Central Tower≤★) B – Castle★ (Norman chapel★) *AC* B.

🏌 Mount Oswald, South Rd ✆ 386 7527, SW : by A 177 B.

🅱 Market Pl., DH1 3NJ ✆ 384 3720.

◆London 267 – ◆Leeds 77 – ◆Middlesbrough 23 – Sunderland 12.

Plan on next page

🏨 **Royal County** (Swallow), Old Elvet, DH1 3JN, ✆ 386 6821, Fax 386 0704, ℄, ≘s, 🔲 – 📳 ⬚ rm 🖿 rest 📺 ☎ **ᴘ** – ⚞ 120. 🔼 🆎 ① VISA B a
M 13.50/19.50 **st.** and a la carte ⅄ 6.00 – **149 rm** ⊇ 94.00/115.00 **st.**, 1 suite – SB (December-January, July-August and weekends only) 100.00/120.00 **st.**

🏨 **Three Tuns Swallow,** New Elvet, DH1 3AQ, ✆ 386 4326, Fax 386 1406 – ⬚ rm 📺 ☎ **ᴘ** – ⚞ 250. 🔼 🆎 ① VISA B e
M *(closed Saturday lunch)* 9.95/16.25 **st.** and a la carte – **47 rm** ⊇ 80.00/125.00 **st.** – SB (July-August and weekends only) 100.00/110.00 **st.**

at Croxdale S : 3 m. by A 1050 on A 167 – B – ⊠ ✪ 091 Tyneside :

🏨 **Bridge Toby,** DH1 3SP, ✆ 378 0524, Fax 378 9981 – ⬚ rm 📺 ☎ **ᴘ** – ⚞ 50. 🔼 🆎 ① VISA
M (grill rest.) 7.50 **st.** and a la carte – **46 rm** ⊇ 49.95/59.95 **st.** – SB (weekends only) 59.00/63.00 **st.**

🔧 ATS Finchale Rd, Newton Hall ✆ 3841810   ATS Mill Rd, Langley Moor ✆ 3780262

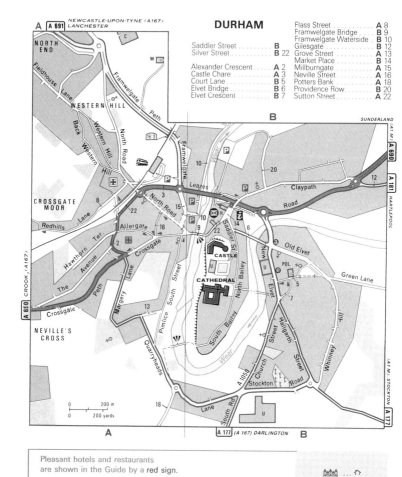

DURHAM

Saddler Street . . . . **B**
Silver Street . . . . **B** 22

Alexander Crescent . . . . . **A** 2
Castle Chare . . . . **A** 3
Court Lane . . . . **B** 5
Elvet Bridge . . . . **B** 6
Elvet Crescent . . . . **B** 7

Flass Street . . . . **A** 8
Framwelgate Bridge . . . . **B** 9
Framwelgate Waterside . . **B** 10
Gilesgate . . . . **B** 12
Grove Street . . . . **A** 13
Market Place . . . . **B**
Millburngate . . . . **A** 15
Neville Street . . . . **A** 16
Potters Bank . . . . **A** 18
Providence Row . . . . . . **B** 20
Sutton Street . . . . **A** 22

Pleasant hotels and restaurants
are shown in the Guide by a red sign.

Please send us the names
of anywhere you have enjoyed your stay.

Your Michelin Guide will be even better.

DUXFORD Cambs. 404 U 27 – see Cambridge.

EAGLESCLIFFE Cleveland 402 P 20 – see Stockton-on-Tees.

EARL'S COLNE Essex 404 W 28 – ⊠ Colchester – 🕾 0787.

♦London 55 – ♦Cambridge 33 – Chelmsford 22 – Colchester 10.

⌂ **Elm House,** 14 Upper Holt St., CO6 2PG, on A 604 ℰ 222197, ☞
M (by arrangement) (communal dining) 12.00 **s.** – **3 rm** ⊇ 19.00/50.00 **s.**

EARL SHILTON Leics. 403 404 Q 26 – pop. 16 484 – ECD : Wednesday – ⊠ Leicester – 🕾 0455.

♦London 107 – ♦Birmingham 35 – ♦Coventry 16 – ♦Leicester 9 – ♦Nottingham 35.

🏨 **Mill on the Soar,** Coventry Rd, Sutton in the Elms, LE9 6QD, SE : 4 ½ m. by B 581 on
A 4114 ℰ 282419, Fax 285937 – 📺 🕾 🅿 – 🔏 40. 🔼 🆎 ⓪ 𝘝𝘐𝘚𝘈. 🛇
M (closed Sunday dinner) (bar lunch Monday to Saturday)/dinner a la carte 11.55/15.74 **t.**
↑ 5.95 – ⊇ 4.95 – **20 rm** 28.50/39.50 **st.**

EARL SOHAM Suffolk 404 X 27 – see Framlingham.

EARL STONHAM Suffolk 404 X 27 – ⊠ 🕲 0449 Stowmarket.

♦London 81 – ♦Cambridge 47 – ♦Ipswich 10 – ♦Norwich 33.

XX 🕲 **Mr. Underhill's** (Bradley), IP14 5DW, Junction of A 140 and A 1120 𝒫 711206 – 🅿. 🖂 🆔 𝗩𝗜𝗦𝗔
   closed Saturday lunch, Sunday dinner and Monday – **M** (lunch by arrangement Tuesday to Friday) (booking essential)/dinner 35.00 **t.** 🍷 5.75
   Spec. Ceviche of salmon with lime, Confit of Barbary duck, Poached pear with a sorbet of the poaching juices.

EASINGWOLD N. Yorks. 402 Q 21 – pop. 3 468 – ⊠ York – 🕲 0347.

🄱 Stillington Rd 𝒫 21486.
🄱 Chapel Lane, YO6 3AE 𝒫 21530 (summer only).

♦London 217 – ♦Middlesbrough 37 – York 14.

⌂ **Old Vicarage** without rest., Market Pl., YO6 3AL, 𝒫 821015, 🌤 – 📺 🅿
   March-October – **5 rm** ⊔ 20.00/40.00 **st.**

at Alne SW : 4 m. on Alne Rd – ⊠ Aldwark – 🕲 0347 Tollerton :

🏨 **Aldwark Manor** 🦆, YO6 2NF, SW : 3½ m. by Aldwark Bridge rd 𝒫 838146, Fax 838867,
   ≤, 🄱, 🌤, park – 📺 ☎ 🅿 – 🕍 100. 🖂 ⒶⒺ ⓞ 𝗩𝗜𝗦𝗔 𝗝𝗖𝗕
   M 8.50/16.50 **st.** and a la carte 🍷 6.00 – **20 rm** ⊔ 65.00/85.00 **st.**

at Raskelf W : 2¾ m. – ⊠ York – 🕲 0347 Easingwold :

🏠 **Old Farmhouse**, YO6 3LF, 𝒫 821971 – 🅿
   closed 23 December-31 January – **M** *(closed Sunday and Monday to non-residents)*
   (dinner only) 16.00 **t.** 🍷 4.00 – **10 rm** ⊔ 28.00/46.00 **t.** – SB (November-April) 70.00/80.00 **st.**

☞ *There is no paid publicity in this Guide.*

EAST BARKWITH Lincs. 402 404 T 24 – ⊠ Lincoln – 🕲 0673 Wragby.

♦London 152 – Boston 30 – Great Grimsby 28 – Lincoln 13.

⌂ **Grange,** Torrington Lane, LN3 5RY, 𝒫 858249, « Working farm », 🌤, 🍴 – 🖂 📺 🅿. 🍴
   closed Christmas and New Year – **M** (communal dining) 12.00 **s.** – **3 rm** ⊔ 25.00/40.00 **s.**

EASTBOURNE E. Sussex 404 U 31 Great Britain G. – pop. 86 715 – ECD : Wednesday – 🕲 0323.

See : Seafront★.
Envir. : Beachy Head★★★, SW : 3 m. by B 2103 Z.

🄱, 🄱 Royal Eastbourne, Paradise Drive 𝒫 29738 Z – 🄱 Eastbourne Downs, East Dean Rd
𝒫 20827, W : 1 m. by A 259 Z – 🄱 Eastbourne Golfing Park, Lottbridge Drove 𝒫 520400, N :
½ m. of Hampden Park Y.

🄱 Cornfield Rd, BN21 4QL 𝒫 411400.

♦London 68 – ♦Brighton 25 – ♦Dover 61 – Maidstone 49.

Plan on next page

🏨 **Grand** (De Vere), King Edward's Par., BN21 4EQ, 𝒫 412345, Fax 412233, ≤, 🄱, ≘s,
   🏊 heated, 🖂, 🌤 – rm 📺 ☎ 🅿 – 🕍 350. 🖂 🅿   Z   x
   M 14.00/25.00 **st.** and a la carte 🍷 5.50 – (see also **Mirabelle** below) – **146 rm** ⊔ 90.00/
   150.00 **st.**, 15 suites – SB 100.00/200.00 **st.**

🏨 **Cavendish** (De Vere), 37-40 Grand Par., BN21 4DH, 𝒫 410222, Fax 410941, ≤ – 🛗 📺 ☎
   🅿 – 🕍 200. 🖂 ⒶⒺ ⓞ 𝗩𝗜𝗦𝗔   X   r
   M 7.95/25.00 **st.** and a la carte – **108 rm** ⊔ 65.00/75.00 **st.**, 4 suites – SB 104.00/200.00 **st.**

🏨 **Queen's** (De Vere), Marine Par., BN21 3DY, 𝒫 722822, Fax 731056, ≤ – 🛗 📺 ☎ 🅿 –
   🕍 160. 🖂 ⒶⒺ ⓞ 𝗩𝗜𝗦𝗔   V   e
   M 11.25/15.50 **t.** and a la carte – **106 rm** ⊔ 60.00/80.00 **st.**, 2 suites – SB 94.00/106.00 **st.**

🏨 **Wish Tower,** King Edward's Par., BN21 4EB, 𝒫 722676, Fax 721474, ≤ – 🛗 🖂 rest 📺 ☎
   – 🕍 40. 🖂 ⒶⒺ ⓞ 𝗩𝗜𝗦𝗔 🍴   Z   r
   M (bar lunch Monday to Saturday)/dinner 12.95 **t.** 🍷 6.00 – **65 rm** ⊔ 45.00/90.00 **t.** –
   SB (except Christmas and New Year) 80.00/120.00 **st.**

🏨 **Lansdowne** (Best Western), King Edward's Par., BN21 4EE, 𝒫 725174, Fax 739721, ≤ –
   🛗 📺 ☎ 🚗 – 🕍 130. 🖂 ⒶⒺ ⓞ 𝗩𝗜𝗦𝗔 𝗝𝗖𝗕   Z   z
   closed 1 to 15 January – **M** 15.00 **st.** (dinner) and lunch a la carte 7.00/10.50 **st.** 🍷 4.95 –
   127 rm ⊔ 49.00/94.00 **st.** – SB (16 January-8 May and 30 October-23 December) 83.00/
   96.00 **st.**

🏨 **Sussex Toby,** 25-26 Cornfield Terr., BN21 4NS, 𝒫 727681, Fax 646077 – 🛗 🖂 rm 📺 ☎ 🅿
   27 rm.   V   c

🏠 **Brownings,** 28 Upperton Rd, BN21 1JS, 𝒫 724358, Fax 731288, 🏊 heated – 📺 ☎ 🅿. 🖂
   ⒶⒺ ⓞ 𝗩𝗜𝗦𝗔. 🍴   Z   a
   M *(closed Sunday dinner)* (dinner only and Sunday lunch)/dinner 15.95 **t.** 🍷 4.50 – **11 rm**
   ⊔ 35.00/65.00 **st.**

🏠 Mandalay, 16 Trinity Trees, BN21 3LE, 𝒫 729222, 🌤 – 🖂 rest 📺 🅿. 🍴   V   v
   14 rm.

🏠 **Oban,** King Edward's Par., BN21 4DS, 𝒫 731581, Fax 731581 – 🛗 📺 ☎   X   a
   closed January-March – **M** (bar lunch)/dinner 10.00 **t.** 🍷 3.50 – **30 rm** ⊔ 22.00/60.00 **t.** –
   SB 50.00/88.00 **st.**

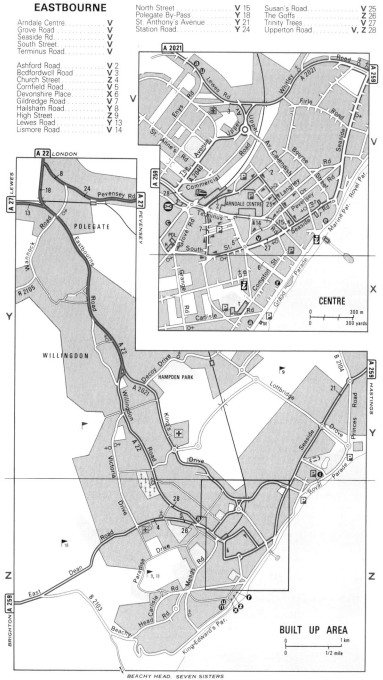

EASTBOURNE

CENTRE

0   300 m
0   300 yards

BUILT UP AREA

0   1 km
0   1/2 mile

BEACHY HEAD. SEVEN SISTERS

↟ **Far End,** 139 Royal Par., BN22 7LH, ☎ 725666 – ⅏ rest 📺 ℗.   Y – **i**
May-September – **M** (by arrangement) 7.00 **st.** – **10 rm** ⊑ 17.00/44.00 **st.**

↟ **Cherry Tree,** 15 Silverdale Rd, BN20 7AJ, ☎ 722406 – ⅏ rest 📺 ☎. 🔼 VISA. ⅏   Z – **u**
M (by arrangement) 9.50 **t.** ⋕ 3.00 – **10 rm** ⊑ 22.00/54.00 **t.** – SB (October-May) 53.00/
58.00.

↟ **Southcroft,** 15 South Cliff Av., BN20 7AH, ☎ 729071 – ⅏   Z – **n**
closed Christmas – **M** (by arrangement) 7.00 **st.** ⋕ 2.50 – **6 rm** ⊑ 21.00/42.00 **st.**

↟ **Camelot Lodge,** 35 Lewes Rd, BN21 2BU, ☎ 725207 – ⅏ rest 📺 ℗. 🔼 VISA. ⅏ V – **a**
April-October – **M** (by arrangement) 8.00 **st.** – **9 rm** ⊑ 24.00/48.00 **st.**

XXXX **Mirabelle,** (at Grand H.), King Edward's Par., BN21 4EQ, ☎ 410771, Fax 412233 – ▤ ℗.
🔼 AE ① VISA
closed Sunday and Monday – **M** (booking essential) 15.00/28.00 **st.** and a la carte ⋕ 5.50.

XX **Downland** with rm, 37 Lewes Rd, BN21 2BU, ☎ 732689 – 📺 ☎ ℗. 🔼 AE ① VISA JCB   Z – **u**
closed 19 December-27 January except Christmas – **M** (dinner only) 17.50 **t.** and a la carte
⋕ 4.50 – **14 rm** ⊑ 29.50/75.00 **t.** – SB 70.00/80.00 **t.**

at Jevington NW : 6 m. by A 259 – Z – on B 2105 – ✉ ☎ 032 12 (4 fig.) and 0323
(6 fig.) Polegate :

XX **Hungry Monk,** The Street, BN26 5QF, ☎ 482178, Fax 483989, « Part Elizabethan cottages », ⅏ – ℗. 🔼
closed 24 and 26 December and Bank Holidays – **Meals** (booking essential) (dinner only and
Sunday lunch)/dinner 23.00 **t.**

at Wilmington NW : 6 ½ m. by A 22 on A 27 – Y – ✉ ☎ 032 12 (4 fig.) and 0323
(6 fig.) Eastbourne :

X **Crossways** with rm, Lewes Rd, BN26 5SG, ☎ 482455, Fax 487811, ⅏ – 📺 ☎ ℗. 🔼 AE
① VISA JCB. ⅏
closed 22 December-22 January – **M** *(closed Sunday and Monday)* (dinner only) 22.95 **t.**
⋕ 5.25 – **7 rm** ⊑ 34.00/65.00 **st.** – SB (except Bank Holidays) 85.00/110.00 **st.**

⑩ ATS Langney Rise ☎ 761971

Great Britain and Ireland is now covered
by an Atlas at a scale of 1 inch to 4.75 miles.

Three easy to use versions: Paperback, Spiralbound and Hardback.

EAST BUCKLAND Devon 🔳 I 30 – see South Molton.

EAST DEREHAM Norfolk 🔳 W 25 – pop. 11 798 – ☎ 0362 Dereham.
◆London 109 – ◆Cambridge 57 – King's Lynn 27 – ◆Norwich 16.

🏠 George, Swaffham Rd, NR19 2AZ, ☎ 696801, Fax 695711 – 📺 ☎ ℗. ⅏
8 rm.

↟ **King's Head,** 42 Norwich St., NR19 1AD, ☎ 693842, Fax 693776, ⅏, ⅏ – 📺 ☎ ℗. 🔼
AE ① VISA
M 9.50/14.95 **t.** and a la carte – **15 rm** ⊑ 36.00/50.00 **t.** – SB (except Christmas) 66.00/
110.00 **st.**

at Wendling W : 5½ m. by A 47 – ✉ ☎ 0362 Wendling :

↟ **Greenbanks,** Swaffham Rd, NR19 2AR, ☎ 687742, ⅏ – 📺 ℗. 🔼 VISA. ⅏
M 22.00 **st.** ⋕ 4.50 – **4 rm** ⊑ 32.00/48.00 **st.** – SB 58.50/102.00 **st.**

EAST GRINSTEAD W. Sussex 🔳 T 30 – pop. 23 867 – ECD : Wednesday – ☎ 0342.
🏠₁₈ Copthorne, Borers Arm Rd ☎ 712508.
◆London 32 – ◆Brighton 29 – Eastbourne 33 – Lewes 21 – Maidstone 32.

🏠 **Woodbury House,** Lewes Rd, RH19 3UD, SE :½ m. on A 22 ☎ 313657, Fax 314801, ⅏ –
📺 ☎ ℗. 🔼 AE ① VISA JCB. ⅏
closed 26 and 27 December – **M** 13.50/17.50 **st.** ⋕ 4.25 – **14 rm** ⊑ 55.00/75.00 **st.** –
SB (weekends only) 53.50/105.00 **st.**

at Gravetye SW : 4 ½ m. by B 2110 taking second turn left towards West Hoathly –
✉ East Grinstead – ☎ 0342 Sharpthorne :

🏠 **Gravetye Manor** ⅏, Vowels Lane, RH19 4LJ, ☎ 810567, Fax 810080, ≼, « 16C manor
house with gardens and grounds by William Robinson », ⅏, park – ⅏ rest 📺 ☎ ℗. 🔼
VISA. ⅏
M (booking essential) 20.00/26.00 **s.** and a la carte 25.30/41.70 **s.** ⋕ 10.50 – ⊑ 8.10 – **18 rm**
85.00/190.00 **s.**

⑩ ATS London Rd, North End ☎ 410740

EASTHAM Mersey. 🔳 L 24 – pop. 16 228 – ✉ Wirral – ☎ 051 Liverpool.
◆London 209 – ◆Birmingham 45 – Chester 13 – ◆Liverpool 7.5 – ◆Manchester 45.

🏠 **Forte Travelodge** without rest., New Chester Rd, L62 9AQ, junction of M 53 with A 41
☎ 327 2489, Reservations (Freephone) 0800 850950 – 📺 ♿ ℗. 🔼 AE VISA. ⅏
31 rm 31.95 **t.**

♦London 21 – Chelmsford 13 – Southend-on-Sea 17.

  ⌂ **Forte Travelodge** without rest., CM13 3LL, on A 127 (eastbound carriageway) *&* 810819, Reservations (Freephone) 0800 850950 – 📺 & 🅿. 🔼 🗛 ᴠɪsᴀ. ⛶
    22 rm 31.95 **t.**

EASTLEIGH Devon 📠 H 30 – see Bideford.

EASTLEIGH Hants. 📠 P 31 – pop. 58 585 – ECD : Wednesday – ✿ 0703.

🇮🇸 Fleming Park *&* 612797.

✈ Southampton/Eastleigh Airport *&* 629600, Fax 629300.

🅱 Town Hall Centre, Leigh Rd, SO5 4DE *&* 641261.

♦London 74 – Winchester 8 – ♦Southampton 4.

  ⚑ **Forte Crest**, Leigh Rd, SO5 5PG, *&* 619700, Fax 643945, 🏋, ≋, 🔲 – 🛗 ᶑ᷂ rm 🍽 rest 📺 ☎ & 🅿 – 🔏 250. 🔼 🗛 ᴠɪsᴀ
    M *(closed Saturday lunch)* 13.95/17.95 **t.** and a la carte 🍴 6.60 – 🖵 9.95 – **117 rm** 75.00 **t.**,
    3 suites – SB (weekends only) 98.00 **st.**

  ⌂ **Forte Travelodge**, Twyford Rd, SO5 4LF, N : 1m. on A 335 *&* 616813, Reservations (Freephone) 0800 850950 – 📺 & 🅿. 🔼 🗛 ᴠɪsᴀ. ⛶
    M (Harvester grill) a la carte approx. 16.00 **t.** – (🖵 not served) – **32 rm** 31.95 **t.**

  🅾 ATS Dutton Lane, Bishopstoke Rd *&* 613027/613393

EAST MOLESEY Surrey 📠 ⑫ – see Esher.

EASTON CROSS Devon 📠 I 31 – see Chagford.

EAST RETFORD Notts. 📠 📠 R 24 – pop. 19 133 – ✿ 0777 Retford.

🅱 Amcott House Annexe, 40 Grove St., DN22 6JU *&* 860780.

♦London 148 – Lincoln 23 – ♦Nottingham 31 – ♦Sheffield 27.

  ⌂ **Old Plough** ⌕, Top Street, North Wheatley, DN22 9DB, NE : 5 m. by A 620 *&* 0427 (Gainsborough) 880916, ≤, ᵚ – ᶑ᷂ rm 📺 🅿. ⛶
    M (by arrangement) (communal dining) 12.50 **s.** – **3 rm** 🖵 25.00/50.00 **s.**

  🅾 ATS Babworth Rd *&* 706501

EAST WITTON N. Yorks. 📠 O 21 – ✉ Leyburn – ✿ 0969 Wensleydale.

♦London 238 – ♦Leeds 45 – ♦Middlesbrough 30 – York 39.

  ✕✕ **Blue Lion** with rm, DL8 4SN, *&* 24273, ᵚ – 📺 🅿. 🔼 ᴠɪsᴀ. ⛶
    M (in bar Tuesday to Saturday lunch, Sunday dinner and Monday) dinner a la carte 16.95/
    26.45 **t.** – **9 rm** 🖵 35.00/60.00 **t.** – SB (except Bank Holidays) 80.00/90.00 **st.**

EAST WITTERING W. Sussex 📠 R 31 – pop. 3 503 – ✿ 0243 Chichester.

♦London 74 – ♦Brighton 37 – ♦Portsmouth 25.

  ✕ **Clifford's Cottage**, Bracklesham Lane, Bracklesham Bay, PO20 8JA, E : 1 m. by B 2179
    on B 2198 *&* 670250, ᵚ – 🅿. 🔼 🗛 ⓐ ᴠɪsᴀ
    closed Sunday dinner, first week February and first 2 weeks November – **M** (dinner only
    and Sunday lunch)/dinner 17.50 **st.** and a la carte 🍴 3.95.

EBCHESTER Durham 📠 📠 O 19 – ✉ Consett – ✿ 0207.

🇮🇸 Consett and District, Elmfield Rd, Consett *&* 502186, S : 2 m.

♦London 275 – ♦Carlisle 64 – ♦Newcastle upon Tyne 16.

  ⚑ Raven, Broomhill, DH8 6RY, SE : ¾ m. on B 6309 *&* 560367, Fax 560262, ≤ – 📺 ☎ & 🅿.
    ⛶
    28 rm.

ECCLESHALL Staffs. 📠 📠 📠 N 25 – pop. 5 481 – ECD : Wednesday – ✿ 0785.

♦London 149 – ♦Birmingham 33 – Derby 40 – Shrewsbury 26 – ♦Stoke-on-Trent 12.

  ⌂ **St. George**, Castle St., ST21 6DF, *&* 850300, Fax 851452 – 📺 ☎ 🅿. 🔼 🗛 ⓐ ᴠɪsᴀ
    M 10.95/18.95 **t.** and dinner a la carte 🍴 3.95 – **10 rm** 🖵 39.00/55.00 **st.** – SB (weekends
    only) 70.00/98.00 **st.**

EDENBRIDGE Kent 📠 U 30 Great Britain G. – pop. 7 674 – ✉ ✿ 0732.

Envir. : Hever Castle★ *AC*, E : 2½ m. – Chartwell★ *AC*, N : 3 m. by B 2026.

🇮🇸 Crouch House Rd *&* 867381, W : 2 m.

♦London 35 – ♦Brighton 36 – Maidstone 29.

  ✕✕✕ **Honours Mill**, 87 High St., TN8 5AU, *&* 866757, « Carefully renovated 18C mill » – 🔼 🗛
    ᴠɪsᴀ
    closed Saturday lunch, Sunday dinner, Monday, 10 days after Christmas and Bank Holidays
    – **M** 14.50/31.75 **st.** 🍴 5.50.

EGERTON Gtr. Manchester 📠 ㉑ 📠 ② 📠 ⑨ – see Bolton.

EGHAM Surrey 404 S 29 – pop. 21 337 – ECD : Thursday – ☎ 0784.

◆London 29 – Reading 21.

🏨 **Runnymede,** Windsor Rd, TW20 0AG, on A 308 ℰ 436171, Telex 934900, Fax 436340, ≼, ₤₅, ≘s, 🔲, ✍ – ₿ ⅙₊ rm 🔟 ☎ ❷ – 🔏 350. 🖾 🖽 ⑩ 𝘝𝘐𝘚𝘈
M *(closed Saturday lunch and Sunday dinner)* 16.95/19.95 **st.** – ☲ 9.95 – **171 rm** 110.00/ 145.00 **st.** – SB (weekends only) 118.00 **st.**

🏨 **Great Fosters,** Stroude Rd, TW20 9UR, S : 1 ¼ m. by B 388 ℰ 433822, Fax 472455, « Elizabethan mansion, gardens », ≘s, 🔲 heated, park, ✍ – 🔟 ☎ ❷ – 🔏 80. 🖾 🖽 ⑩ 𝘝𝘐𝘚𝘈
M 10.50/22.50 **st.** and a la carte ₤ 5.00 – **42 rm** ☲ 71.00/105.00 **st.**, 2 suites.

❌❌ La Bonne Franquette, 5 High St., TW20 9EA, ℰ 439494 – ❷.

EGLINGHAM Northd. 401 402 O 17 – see Alnwick.

EGTON BRIDGE N. Yorks. – see Goathland.

EIGHT ASH GREEN Essex 404 W 28 – see Colchester.

ELLAND W. Yorks. 402 O 22 – see Halifax.

ELSLACK N. Yorks. 402 N 22 – see Skipton.

ELSTREE Herts. 404 T 29 – ☎ 081 London.

🏌 Watling St. ℰ 953 6115, N : 1 m. on A 5183.

◆London 10 – Luton 22.

Plan : see Greater London (North West)

🏨 Edgwarebury, Barnet Lane, WD6 3RE, ℰ 953 8227, Fax 207 3668, ✍, park, ✍ – ⅙₊ rm 🔟 ☎ ❷ – 🔏 80. ✍
50 rm.
CT **e**

ELTERWATER Cumbria – see Ambleside.

Plans de ville : Les rues sont sélectionnées en fonction de leur importance
pour la circulation et le repérage des établissements cités.

Les rues secondaires ne sont qu'amorcées.

ELY Cambs. 404 U 26 Great Britain G. – pop. 9 006 – ECD : Tuesday – ☎ 0353.

See : Cathedral★★ *AC.*

🏌 Cambridge Rd ℰ 2751.

🅱 Oliver Cromwells House, 29 St. Mary's St., CB7 4HF ℰ 662062.

◆London 74 – ◆Cambridge 16 – ◆Norwich 60.

🏨 **Lamb** (Q.M.H.), 2 Lynn Rd, CB7 4EJ, ℰ 663574, Fax 666350 – 🔟 ☎ ❷ – 🔏 40. 🖾 🖽 ⑩ 𝘝𝘐𝘚𝘈
M 11.00/15.00 **st.** and a la carte – **32 rm** ☲ 58.00/63.00 **st.** – SB 80.00/100.00 **st.**

🏨 **Forte Travelodge** without rest., A 10/A 142 roundabout, Ely by pass, ℰ 668499, Reservations (Freephone) 0800 850950 – 🔟 ₤ ❷. 🖾 🖽 𝘝𝘐𝘚𝘈. ✍
39 rm 31.95 **t.**

❌ **Old Fire Engine House,** 25 St. Mary's St., CB7 4ER, ℰ 662582, ✍ – ❷. 🖾 𝘝𝘐𝘚𝘈
closed Sunday dinner, 2 weeks Christmas-New Year and Bank Holidays – **M** - English (booking essential) a la carte 16.75/23.00 **t.**

❌ **Peking Duck,** 26 Fore Hill, CB7 4AF, ℰ 662948 – 🖾 🖽 𝘝𝘐𝘚𝘈
closed Tuesday lunch, Monday and 25-26 December – **M** - Chinese 9.00/16.00 **t.** and a la carte ₤ 4.00.

at Littleport N : 5¾ m. on A 10 – ✉ ☎ 0353 Ely :

❌❌ **Fen House,** 2 Lynn Rd, CB6 1QG, ℰ 860645 – 🖾 ⑩ 𝘝𝘐𝘚𝘈
closed Sunday and Monday – **M** (dinner only) a la carte 18.50/25.25 **st.** ₤ 6.00.

◉ ATS 11 Broad St. ℰ 662758/662801

EMPINGHAM Leics. 402 404 S 26 – see Stamford (Lincs.).

EMSWORTH Hants. 404 R 31 – pop. 17 604 (inc. Southbourne) – ECD : Wednesday – ☎ 0243.

◆London 75 – ◆Brighton 37 – ◆Portsmouth 10.

🏨 **Brookfield,** 93-95 Havant Rd, PO10 7LF, ℰ 373363, Fax 376342, ✍ – ▤ rest 🔟 ☎ ❷ – 🔏 50. 🖾 🖽 𝘝𝘐𝘚𝘈. ✍
closed 24 December-2 January – **M** 12.95 **t.** and a la carte ₤ 4.50 – **41 rm** ☲ 49.00/63.50 **t.** – SB (weekends only) 75.00 **st.**

❌❌❌ 36 on the Quay, 47 South St., The Quay, PO10 7EG, ℰ 375592 – 🖾 🖽 ⑩ 𝘝𝘐𝘚𝘈
closed Saturday lunch, Sunday dinner, Tuesday, 2 weeks October and Bank Holidays – **M** 19.50/30.00 **t.** and dinner a la carte ₤ 6.50.

❌❌ **Spencer's,** 36 North St., PO10 7DG, ℰ 372744 – ▤. 🖾 🖽 𝘝𝘐𝘚𝘈
closed Saturday lunch, Sunday, Monday and 25-26 December – **M** 22.00 **t.** (dinner) and lunch a la carte 9.95/11.75 **t.**

183

ENNERDALE BRIDGE Cumbria [402] J 20 – ✉ Cleator – ☎ 0946 Whitehaven.

◆London 315 – ◆Carlisle 35 – Keswick 25 – Whitehaven 7.

🏠 **Routen Llama Farm** 🐦, Roughton, CA23 3AU, NE : 3½ m. on Croasdale rd ☎ 861270, < Ennerdale Water, « Working farm », 🌳, park – 🚭 [TV] [P]. [S] [VISA]. 🚫🐕
M (by arrangement) (communal dining) 14.00 **st.** 🍷 3.50 – **3 rm** ☕ 21.00/46.00 **st.** – SB (except Bank Holidays) 68.00/72.00 **st.**

ENSTONE Oxon. [403] [404] P 28 – pop. 1 022 – ✉ Chipping Norton – ☎ 0608.

◆London 73 – ◆Birmingham 48 – Gloucester 32 – ◆Oxford 18.

🏠 **Swan Lodge,** Oxford Rd, OX7 4NE, on A 44 ☎ 678736, 🌳 – [TV] [P]. [S] [VISA]
closed 20 December-1 January – **M** (by arrangement) 15.00 **st.** – **3 rm** ☕ 30.00/45.00 **st.**

EPSOM Surrey [404] ㉚ – pop. 65 830 (inc. Ewell) – ECD : Wednesday – ☎ 0372.

⛳18 Longdown Lane South, Epsom Downs ☎ 721666 – ⛳18 Horton Park C.C., Hook Rd, Ewell ☎ 081 (London) 393 8400.

◆London 17 – Guildford 16.

Plan : see Greater London (South-West)

XX **Le Raj,** 211 Fir Tree Rd, Epsom Downs, KT19 3LB, SE : 2¼ m. by B 289 and B 284 on B 291 ☎ 0737 (Burgh Heath) 371371 – ▤. [S] [AE] [D] [VISA] CZ
closed 25 and 26 December – **M** - **Indian** 15.00/20.00 **t.** and a la carte.

X **River Kwai,** 4 East St., KT17 1HH, ☎ 741475 – [S] [AE] [D] [VISA] CZ **a**
closed Sunday lunch and 25-26 December – **M** - **Thai** 8.00/15.00 **st.** and a la carte 🍷 3.75.

ERDINGTON W. Mids. [403] [404] O 26 – see Birmingham.

Prices For full details of the prices quoted in the guide, consult the introduction.

ESCRICK N. Yorks. [402] Q 22 – see York.

ESHER Surrey [404] S 29 – pop. 46 688 (inc. Molesey) – ECD : Wednesday – ☎ 0372.

⛳9 Thames Ditton & Esher, Portsmouth Rd ☎ 081 (London) 398 1551 BZ – ⛳9 Moore Place, Portsmouth Rd ☎ 463533 BZ – ⛳9, ⛳9 Sandown Park, More Lane ☎ 463340 BZ.

◆London 20 – ◆Portsmouth 58.

Plan : see Greater London (South-West)

XX **Good Earth,** 14-18 High St., KT10 9RT, ☎ 462489 – ▤. [S] [AE] [D] [VISA] BZ **e**
closed 24 to 27 December – **M** - **Chinese** 12.00/24.00 **t.** and a la carte 🍷 3.60.

X La Orient, 63 High St., KT10 9RQ, ☎ 466628 – ▤ BZ **a**
M - **South East Asian.**

at East Molesey N : 2 m. by A 309 – ✉ East Molesey – ☎ 081 London

XX **Le Chien Qui Fume,** 107 Walton Rd, KT8 0DR, ☎ 979 7150, Fax 941 5317 – [S] [AE] [D] [VISA] BY **c**
closed Sunday dinner and Monday – **M** - **French** 14.95/29.50 **t.** and a la carte 🍷 4.25.

at Claygate SE : 1 m. by A 244 – ✉ ☎ 0372 Esher :

XXX **Les Alouettes,** 7 High St., KT10 0JW, ☎ 464882, Fax 465337 – ▤. [S] [AE] [VISA] BZ **n**
closed Saturday lunch, Sunday dinner and 26 to 30 December – **M** - **French** 17.95/20.00 **st.** and a la carte 🍷 5.50.

X **Le Petit Pierrot,** 4 The Parade, KT10 0NU, ☎ 465105 – [S] [AE] [D] [VISA] BZ **r**
closed Saturday lunch, Sunday and Bank Holidays – **M** - **French** 16.85/18.95 **t.** 🍷 4.25.

ESKDALE GREEN Cumbria [402] K 20 **Great Britain G.** – pop. 457 – ECD : Wednesday and Saturday – ✉ Holmrook – ☎ 094 67 Eskdale.

Exc. : Hard Knott Pass★★, E : 6 m. – Wrynose Pass★★, E : 8 m.

◆London 312 – ◆Carlisle 59 – Kendal 60.

🏨 Bower House Inn 🐦, CA19 1TD, W : ¾ m. ☎ 23244, Fax 23308, 🌳 – [TV] ☎ [P]. 🚫🐕
24 rm.

ETTINGTON Warks. [403] [404] P 27 – see Stratford-upon-Avon.

EVERCREECH Somerset [403] [404] M 30 – see Shepton Mallet.

EVERSHOT Dorset [403] [404] M 31 – pop. 224 – ✉ Dorchester – ☎ 0935.

◆London 149 – Bournemouth 39 – Dorchester 12 – Salisbury 53 – Taunton 30 – Yeovil 10.

🏨 **Summer Lodge** 🐦, Summer Lane, DT2 0JR, ☎ 83424, Fax 83005, « Part Georgian dower house, country house atmosphere », 🏊 heated, 🌳, 🎾 – [TV] ☎ [P]. [S] [AE] [VISA]
M 19.50/25.00 **t.** and dinner a la carte 🍷 5.00 – **17 rm** ☕ 100.00/185.00 **t.** – SB (October-Easter except Bank Holidays) 147.50/195.00 **st.**

🏠 **Rectory House,** Fore St., DT2 0JW, ☎ 83273, 🌳 – [TV] [P]. [S]. 🚫🐕
closed December – **M** (by arrangement) 16.00 **st.** 🍷 3.50 – **6 rm** ☕ 35.00/60.00 **st.** – SB 76.00/88.00 **st.**

🖼 Almonry Museum, Abbey Gate, WR11 4BG ✆ 446944.

◆London 99 – ◆Birmingham 30 – Cheltenham 16 – ◆Coventry 32.

🏨 **Evesham,** Coopers Lane, off Waterside, WR11 6DA, ✆ 765566, Fax 765443, ⊠, 🛲 – 📺
🕾 **🅿**, **🔄** **AE** ① **VISA**
closed 25 and 26 December – **M** a la carte 10.65/18.25 **st.** ⬩ 6.20 – **40 rm** ⊑ 60.00/94.00 **st.**
– SB 86.00/122.00 **st.**

🏠 **Waterside,** 56-59 Waterside, WR11 6JZ, ✆ 442420, 🛲 – ⅛ rest 📺 🕾 **🅿**, **🔄** **AE** **VISA**
M 7.85 **t.** and a la carte – **14 rm** ⊑ 34.00/70.00 **t.** – SB (weekends only) 69.90/74.60 **st.**

at Harvington N : 3¾ m. by A 4184 and A 435 off A 439 – ⊠ ✪ 0386 Evesham :

🏨 **Mill at Harvington** ⤳, Anchor Lane, WR11 5NR, SE : 1 ½ m. by A 439 ✆ 870688,
Fax 870688, ≼, « 18C mill with riverside garden », ⊒, heated, ⌖, ⁎ – 📺 🕾 **🅿**, **🔄** **AE** ①
VISA, ⁎
closed 24 to 27 December – **M** 14.50/23.00 **st.** ⬩ 4.50 – **15 rm** ⊑ 54.00/85.00 **st.** – SB
(except New Year) 95.00/132.00 **st.**

at Abbot's Salford N : 4¾ m. by A 4184 and A 435 on A 439 – ⊠ ✪ 0386 Evesham :

🏨 **Salford Hall,** WR11 5UT, ✆ 871300, Fax 871301, « Tudor mansion with early 17C extension and gatehouse », 🚬, 🛲, ⁎ – ⅛ rest 📺 🕾 **🅿** – 🔬 25. **🔄** **AE** ① **VISA** **JCB**, ⁎
closed Christmas – **M** 14.95/30.00 **t.** – **34 rm** ⊑ 75.00/120.00 **t.** – SB 115.00/140.00 **st.**

⚙ ATS Worcester Road ✆ 765313

◆London 194 – Exeter 23 – Minehead 19 – Taunton 23.

🏠 **Anchor Inn,** TA22 9AZ, ✆ 23433, « Riverside setting », ⌖, 🛲 – 📺 🕾 **🅿**, **🔄** **VISA**
M (bar lunch Monday to Saturday)/dinner 18.95 **st.** and a la carte ⬩ 4.50 – **6 rm** ⊑ 37.00/
76.00 **st.** – SB (October-March) (weekdays only) 90.00/110.00 **st.**

See : City★★ – Cathedral★★ Z – Maritime Museum★★ AC Z – Royal Albert Memorial Museum★
Y **M2**.

Exc. : Killerton★★ AC, NE : 7 m. by B 3181 V – Ottery St. Mary★ (St. Mary's★★) E : 12 m. by
B 3183 – Y - A 30 and B 3174.

🏌 Downes Crediton, Hookway ✆ 0363 (Crediton) 773991, NW : 6 m. by A 377 V.

✈ Exeter Airport : ✆ 367433, Telex 42648, Fax 364593, E : 5 m. by A 30 V – **Terminal** : St.
David's and Central Stations.

🖼 Civic Centre, Paris St., EX1 1JJ ✆ 265700 – Exeter Services, Sandygate (M 5), EX2 7NJ
✆ 437581/79088.

◆London 201 – Bournemouth 83 – ◆Bristol 83 – ◆Plymouth 46 – ◆Southampton 110.

Plans on following pages

🏨🏨 **Forte Crest,** Southernhay East, EX1 1QF, ✆ 412812, Telex 42717, Fax 413549, *f*₆, 🚬, ⊠
– ⅄ ⅛ rm 📺 🕾 **🅿** – 🔬 150. **🔄** **AE** ① **VISA** **JCB**   Z **a**
M (bar lunch Saturday) 12.95/17.95 **st.** and a la carte ⬩ 6.60 – ⊑ 9.95 – **109 rm** 80.00 **st.**,
1 suite – SB 110.00 **st.**

🏨🏨 **Royal Clarence** (Q.M.H.), Cathedral Yard, EX1 1HB, ✆ 58464, Fax 439423 – ⅄ 📺 🕾 –
🔬 100. **🔄** **AE** ① **VISA**, ⁎   Y **z**
M 17.00/21.00 **t.** and a la carte – **55 rm** ⊑ 60.00/80.00 **t.**, 1 suite – SB (weekends only)
110.00 **st.**

🏨 **Buckerell Lodge,** Topsham Rd, EX2 4SQ, SE : 1 m. on B 3182 ✆ 52451, Fax 412114, 🛲
– ⅛ rm 📺 🕾 **🅿** ♿ 🅿 – 🔬 60. **🔄** **AE** ① **VISA**   X **a**
M 10.50/16.50 **st.** and a la carte ⬩ 5.95 – **54 rm** ⊑ 50.00/85.00 **st.** – SB 82.00/140.00 **st.**

🏨 **St. Olaves Court,** Mary Arches St., EX4 3AZ, ✆ 217736, Fax 413054, 🛲 – 📺 🕾 **🅿**, **🔄**
AE ① **VISA**, ⁎   Z **e**
M (closed Saturday lunch and Sunday) 12.50/20.50 **t.** and dinner a la carte ⬩ 6.00 – **15 rm**
⊑ 40.00/95.00 **t.** – SB 85.00/95.00 **st.**

🏨 **Rougemont** (Mt. Charlotte Thistle), Queen St., EX4 3SP, ✆54982, Telex 42455,
Fax 420928 – ⅄ ⅛ rest 📺 🕾 **🅿** – 🔬 300. **🔄** **AE** ① **VISA**   Y **x**
M 9.50/15.95 **st.** and a la carte ⬩ 4.60 – **88 rm** ⊑ 69.00/79.00 **st.**, 2 suites – SB 88.00 **st.**

🏨 **Exeter Arms Toby,** Rydon Lane, Middlemoor, EX2 7HL, E : 3 m. on B 3181 ✆ 435353,
Fax 420826 – ⅛ rm 📺 🕾 **🅿**, **🔄** **AE** ① **VISA**, ⁎   X **e**
M (grill rest.) 7.50 **st.** and a la carte ⬩ 3.50 – **37 rm** ⊑ 48.00/58.00 **st.** – SB (weekends only)
73.00/131.30 **st.**

🏨 **Countess Wear Lodge** (Q.M.H.), 398 Topsham Rd, EX2 6HE, S : 2 ½ m. at junction of
A 379 and B 3182 ✆ 875441, Fax 876174 – ⅛ rm 📺 🕾 **🅿** – 🔬 185. **🔄** **AE** ① **VISA**, ⁎
M (bar lunch) 11.00/19.00 **st.** ⬩ 4.95 – **44 rm** ⊑ 59.00/89.00 **st.** – SB (except Christmas)
86.00/150.00 **st.**   X **o**

🏨 **Devon Motel,** Matford, EX2 8XU, S : 3 m. by A 377 on A 379 ✆ 59268, Fax 413142, 🛲 –
📺 🕾 **🅿** – 🔬 80. **🔄** **AE** ① **VISA**, ⁎   X
M (carving lunch Monday to Saturday)/dinner 12.50 **t.** and a la carte ⬩ 4.50 – **41 rm** 42.00/
75.00 **st.**

EXETER
BUILT UP AREA

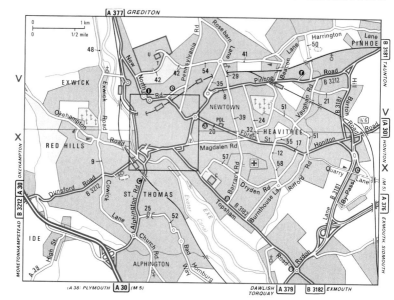

🏠 **St. Andrews,** 28 Alphington Rd, EX2 8HN, ℰ 76784, Fax 50249 – 📺 ☎ 🕭 🅿. 🖾 🆎 ⓞ
🆅🅸🆂🅰. 🛇   X c
closed Christmas-New Year – **M** (bar lunch)/dinner a la carte approx. 14.50 **t.** ⦚ 4.40 – **16 rm**
⇌ 35.00/51.00 **t.**

🏠 **Edwardian** without rest., 30-32 Heavitree Rd, EX1 2LQ, ℰ 76102 – 📺 ☎. 🖾 🆎 ⓞ 🆅🅸🆂🅰
closed Christmas and New Year – **14 rm** ⇌ 20.00/44.00 **st.**   V a

🏠 **Red House,** 2 Whipton Village Rd, EX4 8AR, ℰ 56104, Fax 435708 – 📺 ☎ 🅿. 🖾 🆎
🆅🅸🆂🅰   V r
M (in bar) 10.50 **st.** and a la carte ⦚ 3.95 – **12 rm** ⇌ 30.00/50.00 **st.** – SB 50.00/80.00 **st.**

⭡ **The Grange** 🦢 without rest., Stoke Hill, EX4 7JH, N : 1 ¾ m. by Old Tiverton Rd.
ℰ 59723, ≤, 🏊 heated, ☞ – 📺 🅿. 🛇   V
4 rm ⇌ 17.00/32.00 **st.**

⭡ **Raffles,** 11 Blackall Rd, EX4 4HD, ℰ 70200 – 📺 🖾 🆎 🆅🅸🆂🅰   V e
M 11.50 **st.** – **7 rm** ⇌ 26.00/40.00 **st.** – SB (October-May) 55.00/72.00 **st.**

⭡ **Park View** without rest., 8 Howell Rd, EX4 4LG, ℰ 71772 – 📺 ☎ 🅿. 🖾 🆅🅸🆂🅰   V i
closed Christmas – **15 rm** ⇌ 18.00/45.00 **t.**

✗ **Lamb's,** 15 Lower North St., EX4 3ET, ℰ 54269, Fax 431145 – 🍴. 🖾 🆎 🆅🅸🆂🅰   Y c
M (closed Saturday lunch) 8.00 **st.** and a la carte ⦚ 4.00.

at Pinhoe NE : 2 m. by A 30– V – ✉ 🕿 0392 Exeter :

🏨 **Gipsy Hill** 🦢, Gipsy Hill Lane, via Pinn Lane, EX1 3RN, ℰ 465252, Fax 464302, ☞ – 📺
☎ 🅿 – 🔏 120. 🖾 🆎 🆅🅸🆂🅰
closed 24 to 30 December – **M** 8.50/15.00 **t.** and a la carte ⦚ 4.50 – ⇌ 7.50 – **37 rm**
52.50/85.00 **t.** – SB (weekends only) 142.00/160.00 **st.**

at Huxham N : 5 m. by A 377 off A 396 – V – ✉ 🕿 0392 Exeter :

✗✗ **Barton Cross** 🦢 with rm, Stoke Canon, EX5 4EJ, ℰ 841245, Fax 841942, « Part 17C
thatched cottages », ☞ – 📺 ☎ 🅿. 🖾 🆎 ⓞ 🆅🅸🆂🅰
M (closed Sunday to non-residents) 14.50/25.00 **st.** – **6 rm** ⇌ 63.50/85.00 **st.** – SB 110.00/
135.00 **st.**

at Whimple NE : 9 m. by A 30 – V – ⊠ Exeter – ✆ 0404 Whimple :

🏠 **Woodhayes** ⊱, EX5 2TD, ✆ 822237, « Georgian country house », ⚘, ✵ – ⇆ rest 📺
☎ 🅿. 🔼 🅰🅴 ⓞ 𝗩𝗜𝗦𝗔. ✵
M (booking essential) (dinner only) 25.00 **st.** – **6 rm** ⊇ 70.00/90.00 **st.** – SB 130.00/
170.00 **st.**

at Clyst St. George SE : 5 m. on A 376 – X – ⊠ ✆ 0392 Exeter :

🏠 **St. George and Dragon Toby**, EX3 0QJ, ✆ 876121, Fax 876121, ⚘ – 📺 ☎ 🅿 – 🔏 80.
🔼 🅰🅴 ⓞ 𝗩𝗜𝗦𝗔. ✵
M (grill rest.) a la carte 8.65/17.15 **st.** 🍷 4.85 – **13 rm** 48.00/58.00 **st.**

at Kennford S : 5 m. on A 38 – X – ⊠ ✆ 0392 Exeter :

🏠 **Fairwinds**, EX6 7UD, ✆ 832911 – ⇆ 📺 ☎ 🅿. 🔼 𝗩𝗜𝗦𝗔. ✵
closed 5 to 31 December – **M** (dinner only) 14.95 **t.** 🍷 3.95 – **8 rm** ⊇ 25.00/48.00 **t.** –
SB 60.00/90.00 **st.**

✧ **Gissons Arms**, EX6 7UX, ✆ 832444 – 📺 ☎ 🅿. 🔼 𝗩𝗜𝗦𝗔
M (in bar) a la carte 9.25/17.00 **t.** 🍷 4.00 – **6 rm** ⊇ 30.00/40.00 **t.** – SB 50.00/80.00 **st.**

187

at Doddiscombsleigh SW : 10. m. by B 3212 off B 3193 – X – ⊠ Exeter – ⚙ 0647 Christow :

⚘ **Nobody Inn** ⌂, EX6 7PS, ℰ 52394, Fax 52978, ≼, « Part 16C inn », ☞ – 📺 ☎ 🅿. 🅐. VISA. ⌂

accommodation closed 25 December – **M** *(closed Sunday and Monday)* (bar lunch)/dinner a la carte 12.30/18.20 **t.** ⏐ 3.50 – **7 rm** ⊑ 23.00/53.00 **t.**

at Ide SW : 3 m. by A 377 – X – ⊠ ⚙ 0392 Exeter :

XX **Old Mill**, 20 High St., EX2 9RN, ℰ 59480 – 🅿. 🅐. AE VISA

closed Saturday lunch, Sunday and 26 to 28 December – **M** 9.95/14.00 **t.** and a la carte ⏐ 3.50.

◉ ATS 276/280 Pinhoe Road, Polsloe Bridge ℰ 55465

EXETER SERVICE AREA Devon **403** J 31 – ⊠ ⚙ 0392 Exeter

🏨 Granada, Moor Lane, Sandygate, EX2 4AR, M 5 Junction 30 ℰ 74044, Fax 410406 – ⛓ rm 📺 ☎ ⅋ 🅿 – 🅐 70. ⌇
M (grill rest.) – **76 rm.**

LES GUIDES VERTS MICHELIN

Paysages, monuments
Routes touristiques
Géographie
Histoire, Art
Itinéraires de visite
Plans de villes et de monuments

EXMOUTH Devon **403** J 32 The West Country G. – pop. 28 037 – ECD : Wednesday – ⚙ 0395.
Envir. : A la Ronde★ *AC*, N : 2 m. by B 3180.
🛈 Alexandra Terr., EX8 1NZ ℰ 263744.
♦London 210 – Exeter 11.

🏨 **Imperial** (Forte), The Esplanade, EX8 2SW, ℰ 274761, Fax 265161, ≼, ⌇ heated, ☞, ✳
– ⎸⎹ ⛓ 📺 ☎ ⅋. 🅐. AE ⓞ VISA JCB
M (bar lunch Monday to Saturday)/dinner 16.95 **st.** and a la carte ⏐ 6.45 – ⊑ 8.50 – **57 rm** 70.00/85.00 **st.** – SB 116.00/131.00 **st.**

🏨 **Royal Beacon** (Best Western), The Beacon, EX8 2AF, ℰ 264886, Fax 268890, ≼, ☞ – ⎸⎹
📺 ☎ ⤳ 🅿 – 🅐 70. 🅐. AE ⓞ VISA JCB
M 7.45/17.00 **t.** and a la carte ⏐ 4.50 – **30 rm** ⊑ 45.70/78.40 **t.** – SB (September-April) 60.00/72.00 **st.**

🏠 **Barn** ⌂, Foxholes Hill, EX8 2DF, E : 1 m. ℰ 224411, Fax 224411, ≼, ☞ – 📺 ☎ 🅿 –
🅐 50. 🅐. VISA. ⌇
closed 20 December-10 January – **M** (bar lunch Monday to Saturday)/dinner 13.50 **t.** ⏐ 5.25
– **11 rm** ⊑ 32.00/64.00 **t.**

XX **Temple Winds** with rm, The Beacon, EX8 1PB, ℰ 222201, Fax 225913 – 📺. 🅐
M - **Seafood** (closed Sunday dinner and Monday) 13.00/24.00 **st.** ⏐ 6.50 – **4 rm** ⊑ 35.00/55.00 **st.**

at Lympstone N : 3 m. by A 376 – ⊠ ⚙ 0395 Exmouth :

XX **River House** with rm, The Strand, EX8 5EY, ℰ 265147, ≼ Exe Estuary – 📺. 🅐. AE VISA. ⌇
M *(closed Sunday dinner and Monday to non-residents)* 18.50/28.00 **t.** and a la carte ⏐ 6.00
– ⊑ 6.50 – **2 rm** 55.00/74.00 **t.**

EYAM Derbs. **402** **403** **404** O 24 – ⊠ Sheffield – ⚙ 0433 Hope Valley.
♦London 163 – Derby 29 – ♦Manchester 32 – ♦Sheffield 12.

⚘ **Miners Arms**, Water Lane, S30 1RG, ℰ 630853 – 📺 🅿. ⌇
M *(closed Sunday dinner and Monday)* (bar lunch Tuesday to Saturday)/dinner a la carte 12.25/16.50 **t.** ⏐ 4.50 – **6 rm** ⊑ 25.00/45.00 **t.**

EYE Suffolk **404** X 27 – pop. 1 782 – ⊠ ⚙ 0379.
♦London 94 – ♦Ipswich 19 – Thetford 23.

⚘ **Four Horseshoes**, Thornham Magna, IP23 7HD, SW : 5 m. by B 1117 off A 140
ℰ 0379 71 (Occold) 777, Fax 8134, ☞ – 📺 🅿. 🅐. AE ⓞ VISA
M 9.95/16.00 **st.** and a la carte – **10 rm** ⊑ 37.00/55.00 **st.** – SB 70.00/90.00 **st.**

EYTON Heref. and Worcs. – see Leominster.

FACCOMBE Hants. – see Hurstbourne Tarrant.

See : Town★ – Pendennis Castle★ (≤★★) *AC* B.

Envir. : Glendurgan Garden★★ *AC*, SW : 4½ m. by Swanpool Rd A – Mawnan Parish Church★
(≤★★) S : 4 m. by Swanpool Rd A – Cruise to Truro★ – Cruise along Helford River★.

Exc. : Trelissick Garden★★ (≤★★) NW : 13 m. by A 39 and B 3289 A – Carn Brea (≤★★) NW :
10 m. by A 393 A – Gweek (Setting★, Seal Sanctuary★) SW : 8 m. by A 39 and Treverva rd –
Wendron (Poldark Mine★) *AC*, SW : 12½ m. by A 39 – A – and A 394.

🆃₁₈ Swanpool Rd ✆ 311262 A – 🆃₉ Budock Vean Hotel ✆ 250288, SW : 5 m. by Trescobeas Rd A.

🅱 28 Killigrew St., TR11 3PN ✆ 312300.

◆London 308 – Penzance 26 – ◆Plymouth 65 – Truro 11.

Plan on next page

🏨 **Greenbank,** Harbourside, TR11 2SR, ✆ 312440, Fax 211362, ≤ harbour, 🏖, ⇌s – 🛗
⚄ rm 📺 ☎ ⇔ ℗ – 🔬 30. 🔼 🆬 ⑩ 𝚅𝙸𝚂𝙰   A   a
closed 24 December-15 January – **M** – **Nightingales** 10.00/25.00 **t.** and a la carte 🍴 6.00 –
61 rm ⊑ 60.00/144.00 **t.** – SB (weekends only) 111.00/118.00 **st.**

🏨 **Royal Duchy,** Cliff Rd, TR11 4NX, ✆ 313042, Fax 319420, ≤, ⇌s, 🔲, 🛬 – 🛗 📺 ☎ ℗. 🔼
🆬 ⑩ 𝚅𝙸𝚂𝙰 ✂   B   a
M 8.00/14.25 **t.** and a la carte 🍴 6.75 – **45 rm** ⊑ 44.00/140.00 **t.**, 2 suites – SB (except
August, Christmas and New Year) 82.00/140.00 **st.**

🏨 **St. Michael's of Falmouth,** Gyllyngvase Beach, Seafront, TR11 4NB, ✆ 312707,
Fax 211772, ≤, 🏖, ⇌s, 🔲, 🛬 – 📺 ☎ ℗ – 🔬 70. 🔼 🆬 ⑩ 𝚅𝙸𝚂𝙰   A   z
M (bar lunch Monday to Saturday)/dinner 16.00 **st.** and a la carte 🍴 4.25 – **66 rm** ⊑ 55.00/
150.00 **st.** – SB (except Bank Holidays) 118.00/136.00 **st.**

🏨 **Penmere Manor** (Best Western) ⚘, Mongleath Rd, TR11 4PN, ✆ 211411, Fax 317588,
🏖, ⇌s, 🔲 heated, 🔲, 🛬 – ⇌ rest 📺 ☎ ℗ – 🔬 60. 🔼 🆬 ⑩ 𝚅𝙸𝚂𝙰   A   e
closed 23 to 26 December – **M** (bar lunch Monday to Saturday)/dinner 18.00 **st.** and a la
carte 🍴 3.75 – **39 rm** ⊑ 57.00/112.00 **st.** – SB 108.00/144.00 **st.**

🏠 **Broadmead,** 66-68 Kimberley Park Rd, TR11 2DD, ✆ 315704, Fax 311048 – ⇌ rest 📺 ☎
℗. 🔼 𝚅𝙸𝚂𝙰   A   u
closed Christmas-New Year – **M** (dinner only) 18.95 **t.** 🍴 4.50 – **12 rm** ⊑ 21.00/52.00 **t.** –
SB (September-May) 60.00/69.00 **st.**

🏠 **Carthion,** Cliff Rd, TR11 4AP, ✆ 313669, ≤, 🛬 – ⇌ rest 📺 ℗. 🔼 🆬 ⑩ 𝚅𝙸𝚂𝙰   B   v
Easter-October – **M** (dinner only) 12.50 **t.** 🍴 4.00 – **18 rm** ⊑ 29.35/65.00 **t.**

🏠 **Gyllyngvase House,** Gyllyngvase Rd, TR11 4DJ, ✆ 312956, 🛬 – ⇌ rest 📺 ☎ ℗.
                                                                                       B   s
April-October – **M** 8.00 **st.** 🍴 4.80 – **15 rm** ⊑ 18.00/40.00 **st.**

🏠 **Trevaylor,** 8 Pennance Rd, TR11 4EA, ✆ 313041, ≤ – ⇌ rest 📺 ℗. ✂   A   r
May-September – **M** 6.00 **s.** – **7 rm** ⊑ 20.00/32.00 **s.**

🏠 **Tresillian House,** 3 Stracey Rd, TR11 4DW, ✆ 312425, 🛬 – ⇌ rest 📺 ☎ ℗. 🔼 𝚅𝙸𝚂𝙰
✂   A   n
March-October – **M** 11.50 **st.** 🍴 3.50 – **12 rm** ⊑ 21.00/42.00 **st.** – SB 49.00/56.00 **st.**

🏠 **Rosemullion,** Gyllyngvase Hill, TR11 4DF, ✆ 314690 – ⇌ 📺 ℗. ✂   B   c
May-September – **M** 7.50 **st.** – **13 rm** ⊑ 16.50/33.00 **st.**

🏠 **Melvill House,** 52 Melvill Rd, TR11 4DQ, ✆ 316645 – ⇌ 📺 ℗   B   o
closed Christmas and New Year – **M** (by arrangement) 7.00 – **7 rm** ⊑ 18.50/36.00.

🏠 **Esmond,** 5 Emslie Rd, TR11 4BG, ✆ 313214 – ⇌ 📺. ✂   B   e
April-October – **M** (by arrangement) 7.00 **s.** 🍴 2.25 – **7 rm** ⊑ 16.00/32.00 **s.**

at Mawnan Smith SW : 5 m. by Trescobeas Rd – A – ✉ ✆ 0326 Falmouth :

🏨 **Meudon** ⚘, TR11 5HT, E :½ m. via Carwinion Rd ✆ 250541, Fax 250543, « ≤ Terraced
gardens landscaped by Capability Brown », park – 📺 ☎ ℗. 🔼 🆬 𝚅𝙸𝚂𝙰
closed December and January – **M** (lunch by arrangement Monday to Friday)/din-
ner 19.50 **t.** 🍴 4.50 – **30 rm** ⊑ 65.00/150.00 **t.**, 2 suites – SB (except May, June and September) 120.00/170.00 **st.**

🏨 **Nansidwell Country House** ⚘, TR11 5HU, SE : ¼ m. via Carwinion Rd ✆ 250340,
Fax 250460, ≤, « Country house atmosphere, gardens », park, ✎ – 📺 ☎ ℗. 🔼 𝚅𝙸𝚂𝙰
closed January – **M** 14.75/23.00 **t.** and dinner a la carte 🍴 5.00 – ⊑ 4.00 – **12 rm** (dinner
included) 95.00/186.00 **t.**

🏠 **Trelawne** ⚘, Maenporth Rd, TR11 5HS, E : ¾ m. via Carwinion Rd ✆ 250226,
Fax 250909, ≤, 🔲, 🛬 – ⇌ rest 📺 ☎ ℗. 🔼 🆬 ⑩ 𝚅𝙸𝚂𝙰
closed 28 December-11 February – **M** (bar lunch Monday to Saturday)/dinner 22.50 **st.**
🍴 4.90 – **14 rm** ⊑ 44.00/78.00 **st.** – SB (except May-September) 78.00/84.00 **st.**

at Budock Water W : 2¼ m. by Trescobeas Rd - A – ✉ ✆ 0326 Falmouth :

🏠 **Penmorvah Manor** ⚘, TR11 5ED, S :¾ m. ✆ 250277, Fax 250509, 🛬 – ⇌ rm 📺 ☎ ℗.
🔼 🆬 𝚅𝙸𝚂𝙰 𝙹𝙲𝙱. ✂
M (bar lunch Monday to Saturday)/dinner 13.50 **st.** 🍴 4.10 – **27 rm** ⊑ 40.00/80.00 **st.** –
SB (except Bank Holidays) 88.50/107.00 **st.**

🅰 ATS Dracaena Av. ✆ 319233

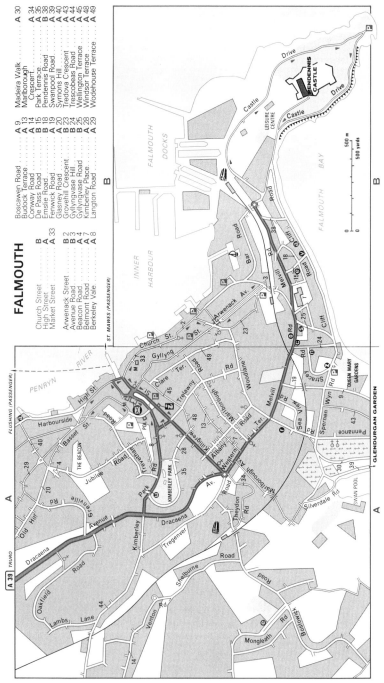

FALMOUTH

Hants. **403** **404** Q 31 Great Britain G. – pop. 55 563 (inc. Portchester) – ECD : Wednesday – ☎ 0329.

Envir. : Portchester castle★ *AC*, SE : 2½ m. by A 27.

🏛 Westbury Manor, West St., PO16 0JJ ✆ 221342/824896.

◆London 77 – ◆Portsmouth 9 – ◆Southampton 13 – Winchester 19.

🏨🏨 **Solent,** Solent Business Park, Whiteley, PO15 7AJ, NW : 5 ¼ m. by A 27 ✆ 0489 (Locks Heath) 880000, Fax 880007, *f₆*, ≘s, 🏊, park, ※, squash – 📶 ⃰⃰ rm ⛖ rest ⛖ ☎ & ℗ – 🔬 250. 🔼 🝱 🝫 **VISA**
M *(closed Saturday lunch)* 13.95/19.50 **st.** and a la carte ⅃ 5.50 – **83 rm** ⇌ 79.00/112.00 **st.**, 7 suites – SB 118.00/190.00 **st.**

🏨🏨 **Forte Posthouse,** Cartwright Drive, Titchfield, PO15 5RS, W : 4½ m. on A 27 ✆ 844644, Fax 844666, *f₆*, ≘s, 🏊 – ⃰⃰ rm ⛖ ☎ & ℗ – 🔬 140. 🔼 🝱 🝫 **VISA**
M a la carte approx. 17.50 **t.** ⅃ 4.65 – ⇌ 6.95 – **126 rm** 53.50 **t.** – SB (weekends only) 90.00 **st.**

🏨 Red Lion, East St., PO16 0BP, ✆ 822640, Telex 86204, Fax 823579, ≘s – ⛖ ☎ & ℗ – 🔬 80. ❀
44 rm.

🏨 **Lysses House,** 51 High St., PO16 7BQ, ✆ 822622, Fax 822762, ☞ – 📶 ⛖ ☎ ℗ – 🔬 100. 🔼 🝱 🝫 **VISA**. ❀
closed 24 December-2 January and Bank Holidays – **M** *(closed Saturday lunch and Sunday)* 11.75/17.95 **st.** and a la carte ⅃ 5.00 – **21 rm** ⇌ 35.00/69.00 **st.**

🏠 **Avenue House** without rest., 22 The Avenue (A 27), PO14 1NS, ✆ 232175, Fax 232196, ☞ – ⛖ ☎ & ℗ – 🔬 🔼 🝱 **VISA**
13 rm ⇌ 29.50/54.00 **st.**

◍ ATS Queens Rd ✆ 234941/280032

Avon **403** M 29 The West Country G. – pop. 1 131 – ✉ Bath – ☎ 0761 Compton Dando.

Exc. : Bath★★★, NE : 7½ m. by A 39 and A 4.

◆London 137 – Bath 7.5 – ◆Bristol 12 – Wells 13.

🏠 **Streets,** The Street, BA3 1AR, ✆ 471452, Fax 471452, 🏊 heated, ☞ – ⛖ ☎ ℗. 🔼 🝱 **VISA** ❀
closed 22 December-2 January – **M** (residents only) (dinner only) 14.00 **st.** ⅃ 4.50 – **8 rm** ⇌ 42.00/65.00 **st.** – SB (except Bank Holidays) 80.00/130.00 **st.**

Hants. **404** R 30 – pop. 48 063 – ECD : Wednesday – ☎ 0252.

🏌 Southwood, Ively Rd ✆ 548700, W : ¾ m. by A 325.

◆London 41 – Reading 17 – ◆Southampton 44 – Winchester 33.

🏨🏨 **Forte Crest Farnborough,** Lynchford Rd, GU14 6AZ, S : 1 ½ m. on Farnborough Rd (A 325) ✆ 545051, Group Telex 859637, Fax 377210, *f₆*, ≘s, 🏊 – ⃰⃰ rm ⛖ ☎ ℗ – 🔬 120. 🔼 🝱 🝫 **VISA** **JCB**
M (bar lunch Saturday) 13.00/16.95 **st.** and a la carte ⅃ 7.00 – ⇌ 9.95 – **110 rm** 99.00/ 110.00 **st.** – SB (weekends only) 110.00/130.00 **st.**

🏠 **Falcon,** 68 Farnborough Rd, GU14 6TH, S :¾ m. on A 325 ✆ 545378, Fax 522539 – ⃰⃰ rm ⛖ ☎ ℗. 🔼 🝱 🝫 **VISA**. ❀
M *(closed lunch Saturday and Bank Holidays)* 12.50/15.50 **st.** ⅃ 4.50 – **30 rm** ⇌ 65.00/ 75.00 **st.** – SB (weekends only) 55.00/90.00 **st.**

🍴🍴 **Wings Cottage,** 32 Alexandra Rd, GU14 6DA, S : 1 ¼ m. by A 325 off Boundary Rd ✆ 544141, Fax 549361 – 🗐. 🔼 🝱 🝫 **VISA**
M - **Chinese** 12.50/24.50 **st.** and a la carte ⅃ 4.50.

Dorset **403** **404** N 31 – see Blandford Forum.

Surrey **404** R 30 – pop. 34 541 – ECD : Wednesday – ☎ 0252.

🏌 Farnham Park, Par Three ✆ 715216.

🏛 Vernon House, 28 West St., GU9 7DR ✆ 715109.

◆London 45 – Reading 22 – ◆Southampton 39 – Winchester 28.

🏨 **Bush** (Forte), The Borough, GU9 7NN, ✆ 715237, Fax 733530, ☞ – ⃰⃰ rm ⛖ ☎ ℗ – 🔬 60. 🔼 🝱 🝫 **VISA**
M *(closed Saturday lunch)* 10.25/17.95 **t.** and a la carte ⅃ 5.00 – ⇌ 8.50 – **66 rm** 65.00/ 80.00 **t.** – SB 98.00 **st.**

🏨 **Bishop's Table** (Best Western), 27 West St., GU9 7DR, ✆ 710222, Telex 94016743, Fax 733494, ☞ – ⛖ ☎ & ℗. 🔼 🝱 🝫 **VISA**. ❀
closed 31 August-14 September and 24 December-4 January – **M** *(closed lunch Saturday and Bank Holidays)* 16.50/25.00 **t.** ⅃ 5.75 – **18 rm** ⇌ 70.00/85.00 **t.** – SB (weekends only) 100.00/126.00 **st.**

🍴🍴 **Banaras,** 40 Downing St., GU9 7PH, ✆ 734081 – 🔼 🝱 🝫 **VISA**
closed 25 and 26 December – **M** - **Indian** 12.50/14.50 **t.** and a la carte ⅃ 3.95.

at Seale E : 4 m. by A 31 – ✉ Farnham – ☎ 0252 Runfold :

🏨 **Hog's Back** (Jarvis), GU10 1EX, on A 31 ✆ 782345, Fax 783113, ≤, *f₆*, ≘s, 🏊, ☞ – ⛖ ☎ & ℗ – 🔬 120. 🔼 🝱 🝫 **VISA**
M *(closed Saturday lunch)* 15.50 **t.** and a la carte ⅃ 6.25 – ⇌ 8.00 – **89 rm** 82.00/102.00 **t.** – SB 92.00/139.00 **st.**

at Frensham S : 3 m. by A 287 – ⊠ ✆ 0252 Farnham :

🏨 **Frensham Pond,** GU10 2QB, SW : 1 ¼ m. by A 287 ℘ 795161, Fax 792631, « Lakeside setting », ƒ₅, ☎, ◰, squash – ⌷ rest ⌷ ☎ Ⓟ – 🏛 120. ◪ 🄰🄴 ⑩ 𝗩𝗜𝗦𝗔
M 12.75/16.95 **t.** and a la carte ¼ 6.00 – **53 rm** ⥮ 50.00/125.00 **st.** – SB (except Christmas and New Year) (weekends only) 78.00/186.00 **st.**

FARRINGTON GURNEY Avon 🗚🗚🗚 🗚🗚🗚 M 30 The West Country G. – pop. 587 – ⊠ Bristol – ✆ 0761 Temple Cloud.

Envir. : Downside Abbey★ (Abbey Church★) SE : 5 m. by A 37 and B 3139.

Exc. : Wells★★ – Cathedral★★★, Vicars' Close★, Bishop's Palace★ *AC* (≤★★) SW : 8 m. by A 39 – Chew Magna★ (Stanton Drew Stone Circles★ *AC*) NW : 9½ m. by A 37 and B 3130.

♦London 132 – Bath 13 – ♦Bristol 12 – Wells 8.

🏠 **Country Ways,** Marsh Lane, BS18 5TT, ℘ 452449, Fax 453360, ☞ – ⌷ ☎ Ⓟ. ◪ 🄰🄴 ⑩ 𝗩𝗜𝗦𝗔 ✼
closed 1 week Christmas – **M** *(closed Sunday)* a la carte 18.60/22.95 **t.** ¼ 4.25 – **6 rm** ⥮ 50.00/65.00 **t.** – SB 85.00/130.00 **st.**

FAR SAWREY Cumbria 🗚🗚🗚 L 20 – see Hawkshead.

FARTHING CORNER SERVICE AREA Kent – ⊠ Gillingham – ✆ 0634 Medway.

🄴 Pavilion Farthing Corner, Services (M 2) Motorway, Gillingham, ME8 8PG ℘ 360323.

♦London 39 – Canterbury 22 – Maidstone 11.

🏠 **Pavilion Lodge** without rest., ME8 8PW, on M 2 ℘ 377337, Fax 360848 – ☞ ⌷ ᵹ. Ⓟ. ◪ 🄰🄴 ⑩ 𝗩𝗜𝗦𝗔 𝗝𝗖𝗕
⥮ 4.00 – **58 rm** 31.95/35.95 **st.**

FAUGH Cumbria – see Carlisle.

FAVERSHAM Kent 🗚🗚🗚 W 30 – pop. 15 914 – ECD : Thursday – ✆ 0795.

🄴 Fleur de Lis Heritage Centre, 13 Preston St., ME13 8NS ℘ 534542.

♦London 52 – ♦Dover 26 – Maidstone 21 – Margate 25.

🍴🍴 ✿ **Read's** (Pitchford), Painter's Forstal, ME13 0EE, SW : 2 ¼ m. by A 2 ℘ 535344, Fax 591200 – Ⓟ. ◪ 🄰🄴 ⑩ 𝗩𝗜𝗦𝗔 𝗝𝗖𝗕
closed Sunday, Monday and last 2 weeks August – **M** 14.50/29.00 **t.** ¼ 6.50
Spec. A hot soufflé of Montgomery cheddar, New season Romney Marsh lamb, Provence vegetables and garlic potatoes, An 'image' of Read's sweets.

at Boughton SE : 3 m. by A 2 – ⊠ Faversham – ✆ 0227 Canterbury :

🍴 **White Horse Inn,** The Street, ME13 9AX, ℘ 751343, Fax 751090 – ⌷ ☎ Ⓟ. ◪ 𝗩𝗜𝗦𝗔
M a la carte 15.40/20.50 ¼ 2.95 – **11 rm** ⥮ 35.00/45.00 **st.** – SB 75.00/95.00 **st.**

🍴🍴 **Garden** with rm, 167-169 The Street, ME13 9BH, ℘ 751411, Fax 751801 – ⌷ rest ⌷ ☎ Ⓟ. ◪ 🄰🄴 𝗩𝗜𝗦𝗔. ✼
M *(closed Sunday dinner)* 10.50/16.95 **t.** and a la carte ¼ 4.25 – **10 rm** ⥮ 55.00/75.00 **st.** – SB (weekends only) 75.40/147.90 **st.**

◍ ATS 20 North Lane ℘ 534039

FAWKHAM Kent – see Brands Hatch.

FELIXSTOWE Suffolk 🗚🗚🗚 Y 28 – pop. 24 207 – ECD : Wednesday – ✆ 0394.

🗚₈ Felixstowe Ferry, Ferry Rd ℘ 286834, NE : 2 m.

⛴ to Belgium : Zeebrugge (P & O European Ferries) (5 h 45 mn) – to France : Boulogne (Hoverspeed) (55 mn).

⛴ to Harwich (Orwell & Harwich Navigation Co. Ltd) 5 daily (15 mn).

🄴 Leisure Centre, Undercliff Road West, IP11 8AB ℘ 276770.

♦London 84 – ♦Ipswich 11.

🏨 **Orwell Moat House** (Q.M.H.), Hamilton Rd, IP11 7DX, ℘ 285511, Fax 670687, ☞ – |♯|
⌷ ☎ Ⓟ – 🏛 200. ◪ 🄰🄴 ⑩ 𝗩𝗜𝗦𝗔
M 14.50/18.50 **st.** and a la carte ¼ 7.50 – ⥮ 7.50 – **56 rm** 60.00/75.00 **st.**, 1 suite – SB (except Christmas and New Year) 70.00/100.00 **st.**

🏠 **Waverley,** Wolsey Gdns, IP11 7DF, ℘ 282811, Fax 670185, ≤ – ⌷ ☎ Ⓟ – 🏛 70. ◪ 🄰🄴 ⑩ 𝗩𝗜𝗦𝗔
M 11.50/14.95 **t.** and a la carte ¼ 4.25 – ⥮ 6.50 – **19 rm** 46.50/64.25 **t.** – SB (except Christmas) 86.75/95.00 **st.**

🏠 **Marlborough,** Sea Rd, IP11 8BJ, ℘ 285621, Fax 670724, ≤ – |♯| ⌷ ☎ Ⓟ – 🏛 100. ◪ 🄰🄴 ⑩ 𝗩𝗜𝗦𝗔
M (bar lunch Saturday) 10.95/12.50 **t.** and a la carte – **47 rm** ⥮ 42.00/65.00 **st.** – SB (except Easter, Christmas and New Year) (weekends only) 70.00 **t.**

◍ ATS 4-8 Sunderland Rd, Carr Rd Ind. Est.   ATS Crescent Rd ℘ 277596/277888
℘ 675604

FELSTED Essex 👁️👁️ V 28 – pop. 2 509 – ⊠ ☻ 0371 Great Dunmow.

◆London 39 – ◆Cambridge 31 – Chelmsford 9 – Colchester 24.

※ **Rumbles Cottage,** Braintree Rd, CM6 3DJ, ℰ 820996 – 🖴 𝐕𝐈𝐒𝐀
closed Saturday lunch, Sunday dinner and Monday – **M** (lunch by arrangement)/dinner 13.00 **t.** and a la carte ¦ 4.00.

FENNY BRIDGES Devon 👁️👁️ K 31 – ⊠ ☻ 0404 Honiton.

◆London 166 – Exeter 12.

※ **Greyhound Inn** (Chef & Brewer), EX14 0BJ, on A 30 ℰ 850380, « 17C thatched inn », �─ – 🖵 ☎ 𝐏. 🖴 𝐀𝐄 𝐕𝐈𝐒𝐀. ﹪
M (carving rest.) 9.95 **t.** and a la carte ¦ 4.65 – **10 rm** ⊆ 29.95/33.45 **t.**

FERNDOWN Dorset 👁️👁️ 👁️👁️ O 31 – pop. 23 921 – ECD : Wednesday – ☻ 0202.

◆London 108 – Bournemouth 6 – Dorchester 27 – Salisbury 23.

🏨 **Dormy** (De Vere), New Rd, BH22 8ES, on A 347 ℰ 872121, Fax 895388, 𝄃₆, ☎s, 🖾, �─, ﹪, squash – 🔋 🖵 ☎ 𝐏 – ⚓ 230. 🖴 𝐀𝐄 ⓞ 𝐕𝐈𝐒𝐀
M *(closed Saturday lunch)* 13.95/22.00 **st.** and a la carte – **123 rm** ⊆ 62.50/105.00 **st.**, 5 suites – SB (except Bank Holidays) 134.00 **st.**

🏠 **Travel Inn,** Ringwood Rd, Tricketts Cross, BH22 9BB, NE : 1 m. on A 348 ℰ 874210 – ﹩﹢ rm 🖵 & 𝐏. 🖴 𝐀𝐄 𝐕𝐈𝐒𝐀. ﹪
M (Beefeater grill) a la carte approx. 16.00 **t.** – ⊆ 4.95 – **32 rm** 33.50 **t.**

FERRYBRIDGE SERVICE AREA W. Yorks. – ⊠ Leeds – ☻ 0977 Pontefract.

◆London 178 – ◆Leeds 14 – Doncaster 14 – Rotherham 28 – York 28.

🏠 **Granada Lodge** without rest., Ferrybridge Services, WF11 0AF, E : ½ m. at junction 33 of M 62 with A 1 ℰ 670488, Reservations (Freephone) 0800 555300 – ﹩﹢ 🖵 ☎ & 𝐏. 🖴 𝐀𝐄 𝐕𝐈𝐒𝐀. ﹪
⊆ 4.00 – **35 rm** 34.95/37.95 **st.**

FERSFIELD Norfolk – see Diss.

FINGLESHAM Kent – see Deal.

FIVE ASHES E. Sussex. – see Mayfield.

FLAMSTEAD Herts. 👁️👁️ S 28 – pop. 1 407 – ⊠ St. Albans – ☻ 0582 Luton.

◆London 32 – Luton 5.

🏨 **Hertfordshire Moat House** (Q.M.H.), London Rd, AL3 8HH, on A 5 ℰ 840840, Fax 842282, 𝄃₆ – 🖵 ☎ 𝐏 – ⚓ 350. 🖴 𝐀𝐄 ⓞ 𝐕𝐈𝐒𝐀
M *(closed Saturday lunch)* 16.95 **st.** and a la carte ¦ 4.95 – ⊆ 7.95 – **89 rm** 50.00/89.00 **st.** – SB 78.00/92.00 **st.**

FLEET SERVICE AREA Hants. – ⊠ Basingstoke – ☻ 0252 Farnborough

🏠 **Forte Travelodge** without rest., Hartley Witney, RG27 8BN, M3 between junctions 4a and 5 (southbound carriageway) ℰ 815587, Reservations (Freephone) 0800 850950 – 🖵 & 𝐏. 🖴 𝐕𝐈𝐒𝐀. ﹪
40 rm 31.95 **t.**

FLEETWOOD Lancs. 👁️👁️ K 22 – pop. 27 899 – ECD : Wednesday – ☻ 0253.

🇶 Fleetwood, Golf House, Princes Way ℰ 873114, W : 1 m.

⛴ to the Isle of Man : Douglas (Isle of Man Steam Packet Co.) (summer only) (3 h 20 mn).

🅱 Ferry Office, Ferry Dock, The Esplanade ℰ 773953.

◆London 245 – ◆Blackpool 10 – Lancaster 28 – ◆Manchester 53.

🏨 **North Euston,** The Esplanade, FY7 6BN, ℰ 876525, Fax 777842, ﹤ – 🔋 🖵 ☎ 𝐏 – ⚓ 180. 🖴 𝐀𝐄 ⓞ 𝐕𝐈𝐒𝐀. ﹪
M *(closed Saturday lunch)* 9.50/15.50 **st.** and a la carte ¦ 4.75 – **55 rm** ⊆ 46.00/65.00 **st.** – SB (except September, October and Bank Holidays) (weekends only) 80.00/86.00 **st.**

🔘 ATS 238 Dock St. ℰ 771211

FLITWICK Beds. 👁️👁️ S 27 – pop. 8 421 – ☻ 0525.

◆London 45 – Bedford 13 – Luton 12 – Northampton 28.

🏨 **Flitwick Manor** 🌿, Church Rd, MK45 1AE, off Dunstable Rd ℰ 712242, Fax 718753, ﹤, « 18C manor house », �─, park, ﹪ – ﹩﹢ rest 🖵 ☎ 𝐏. 🖴 𝐀𝐄 𝐕𝐈𝐒𝐀
M 21.50/33.50 **t.** and dinner a la carte ¦ 5.25 – **15 rm** ⊆ 88.00/190.00 **t.** – SB (except Bank Holidays) (weekends only) 170.00 **t.**

See : The Leas★ (⩽★) Z.

⇌ to France : Boulogne (Hoverspeed) (55 mn) (4-6 daily).

🛈 Harbour St., CT20 1QN ✆ 258594 – Eurotunnel Exhibition Centre, St. Martins Plain, Cheriton
High St., CT19 4QD ✆ 270547.

◆London 76 – ◆Brighton 76 – ◆Dover 8 – Maidstone 33.

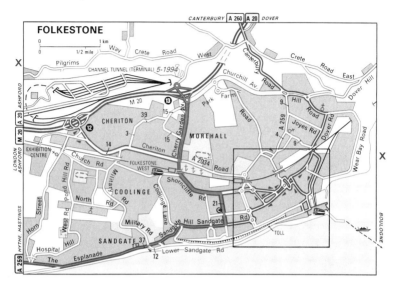

Guildhall Street	**YZ** 23
Rendezvous Street	**YZ** 35
Sandgate Road	**Z**
Tontine Street	**Y**
Ashley Avenue	**X** 3
Black Bull Road	**X, Y** 4
Bouverie Place	**Z** 6
Bouverie Road East	**Z** 7
Bradstone Road	**Y** 8
Canterbury Road	**X** 9
Castle Road	**Z** 12
Cheriton Place	**Z** 13
Cheriton High Street	**X** 14
Cherry Garden Lane	**X** 15
Clifton Crescent	**Z** 16
Clifton Road	**Z** 17
Durlocks (The)	**Y** 20
Earl's Av.	**Z** 21
Grace Hill	**Y** 22
Harbour Street	**Y** 24
Harbour App. Road	**Z** 25
Langhorne Gardens	**Z** 27
Manor Road	**Z** 28
Marine Terrace	**Y** 29
Morrison Road	**Y** 31
North Street	**Y** 32
Radnor Bridge Road	**Y** 33
Remembrance (Rd of)	**Z** 34
Ryland Place	**Y** 36
Sandgate High Street	**X** 37
Shorncliffe Road	**X** 38
Tilekiln Lane	**X** 39
Trinity Gardens	**Z** 41
Victoria Grove	**Y** 43
Wear Bay Road	**X** 44
West Terrace	**Z** 45

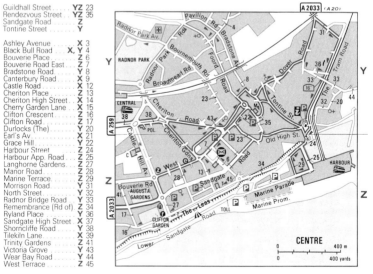

🏛 **Clifton**, The Leas, CT20 2EB, ✆ 851231, Fax 851231, ⩽, 🍴 – 🛗 📺 ☎ – 🔬 100. 🅰 🅰🅴 ⓪
🆅🅸🆂🅰 🅹🅲🅱
Z r
M 10.25/17.00 **st.** and a la carte ↕ 7.75 – 🖵 8.50 – **80 rm** 57.50/80.00 **st.** – SB (weekends
only) 85.00/106.00 **st.**

⌂ **Wards,** 39 Earls Av., CT20 2HB, ℰ 245166, Fax 254480 – 📺 ☎ 🅿 – 🅰 50. 🅰 🅰🅴 ⓘ 𝗩𝗜𝗦𝗔
⅍   X c
M a la carte 10.00/22.85 **t.** ⵢ 3.75 – **10 rm** ⊆ 45.00/85.00 **t.** – SB (weekends only) 84.00/
144.00 **st.**

⌂ **Banque** without rest., 4 Castle Hill Av., CT20 2QT, ℰ 253797 – 📺 ☎. 🅰 🅰🅴 ⓘ 𝗩𝗜𝗦𝗔
12 rm ⊆ 30.00/50.00 **st.**   Z z

%% **La Tavernetta,** Leaside Court, Clifton Gdns, CT20 2AF, ℰ 254955 – 🅰 🅰🅴 ⓘ 𝗩𝗜𝗦𝗔   n
closed Sunday and Bank Holidays – **M** - **Italian** 9.40 **t.** (lunch) and a la carte approx. 13.85 **t.**
ⵢ 3.95.

% **Paul's,** 2a Bouverie Rd West, CT20 2RX, ℰ 259697 – 🅰 𝗩𝗜𝗦𝗔   Z e
closed 1 week Christmas – **M** 16.85 **t.** ⵢ 4.25.

◎ ATS 318/324 Cheriton Rd ℰ 275198/275121

FONTWELL W. Sussex – ✉ Arundel – ✿ 0243 Eastergate.

🅿 Little Chef Complex, BN18 0SD ℰ 543269.

◆London 60 – Chichester 6 – Worthing 15.

⌂ **Forte Travelodge** without rest., BN18 0SB, at A 27/A 29 roundabout ℰ 543973, Reservations (Freephone) 0800 850950 – 📺 ⅋ 🅿. 🅰 🅰🅴 𝗩𝗜𝗦𝗔 ⅍
32 rm 31.95 **t.**

FORD Wilts. – see Castle Combe.

FORDINGBRIDGE Hants. **403 404** 0 31 – pop. 3 026 – ECD : Thursday – ✿ 0425.

🅿 Salisbury St., SP6 1AB ℰ 654560 (summer only).

◆London 101 – Bournemouth 17 – Salisbury 11 – Winchester 30.

%% **Hour Glass,** Salisbury Rd, Burgate, SP6 1LX, N : 1 m. on A 338 ℰ 652348, « 14C
thatched cottage » – 🅿. 🅰 ⓘ 𝗩𝗜𝗦𝗔
closed Sunday dinner, Monday and 2 weeks November – **M** 10.95/17.95 **t.** ⵢ 4.50.

at Woodgreen NE : 4 m. by B 3078 – ✉ Fordingbridge – ✿ 0725 Downton :

⌃ **Cottage Crest** without rest., Castle Hill, SP6 2AX, ℰ 512009, ≒ – 📺 🅿. ⅍
3 rm ⊆ 19.00/38.00 **st.**

at Stuckton SE : 1 m. by B 3078 – ✉ ✿ 0425 Fordingbridge :

% **Three Lions,** Stuckton Rd, SP6 2HF, ℰ 652489, Fax 656144 – 🅿. 🅰 𝗩𝗜𝗦𝗔
closed Sunday, Monday, 6 February-15 March and 10 days Christmas-New Year –
M (booking essential) a la carte 13.65/29.55 **t.** ⵢ 5.50.

at Alderholt SW : 2 m. – ✉ ✿ 0425 Fordingbridge :

%% **Moonacre,** SP6 3BB, ℰ 653142 – 🅿. 🅰 𝗩𝗜𝗦𝗔
closed Sunday dinner, Monday and last week January-first week February – **M** (dinner only
and Sunday lunch)/dinner 11.00 **st.** and a la carte ⵢ 3.25.

at Rockbourne NW : 4 m. by B 3078 – ✉ Fordingbridge – ✿ 072 53 (3 fig.) and 0725
(6 fig.) Rockbourne :

⌃ **Shearings** ⌕, SP6 3NA, ℰ 256, Fax 256, « Picturesque 16C thatched cottage », ≒ –
🅿. ⅍
closed mid December-mid February – **M** (by arrangement) 19.00 **st.** – **3 rm** ⊆ 22.00/
46.00 **st.**

FOREST ROW E. Sussex **404** U 30 – pop. 3 842 – ECD : Wednesday – ✿ 0342 82 (4 fig.) and
0342 (6 fig.).

🖥, 🖥 Royal Ashdown Forest, Chapel Lane ℰ 822018.

◆London 35 – ◆Brighton 26 – Eastbourne 30 – Maidstone 32.

⌂ **Brambletye,** The Square, RH18 5EZ, ℰ 824144, Fax 824833 – 📺 ☎ 🅿. 🅰 🅰🅴 𝗩𝗜𝗦𝗔
M (carving lunch)/dinner 13.95 **st.** and a la carte ⵢ 4.50 – **22 rm** ⊆ 54.00/75.00 **st.** –
SB 85.00/140.00 **st.**

⌂ **Chequers Inn,** The Square, RH18 5ES, ℰ 824394, Fax 825454 – 📺 ☎ ⇔ 🅿. 🅰 🅰🅴 ⓘ
𝗩𝗜𝗦𝗔 𝗝𝗖𝗕 ⅍
closed 26 December – **M** 10.95/25.00 **st.** and a la carte ⵢ 3.00 – **25 rm** ⊆ 36.50/80.00 **st.** –
SB (weekends only) 60.00/90.00 **st.**

at Wych Cross S : 2½ m. on A 22 – ✉ ✿ 034 282 (4 fig.) and 0342 (6 fig.) Forest Row :

🏨 **Roebuck** (Jarvis), RH18 5JL, ℰ 823811, Fax 824790, ≒ – 📺 ☎ 🅿 – 🅰 110. 🅰 🅰🅴 ⓘ
𝗩𝗜𝗦𝗔
M 15.95 **t.** and a la carte ⵢ 5.95 – **30 rm** ⊆ 70.00/80.00 **t.** – SB (weekends only) 79.00 **st.**

FORTON SERVICE AREA Lancs. – ECD : Wednesday – ✉ ✿ 0524 Forton.

🅿 (M 6) Forton, Bay Horse, LA2 9DU ℰ 792181.

⌂ **Pavilion Lodge** without rest., LA2 9DU, on M 6 ℰ 792227, Fax 792241 – ≒ 📺 ⅋ 🅿. 🅰
🅰🅴 ⓘ 𝗩𝗜𝗦𝗔 𝗝𝗖𝗕
⊆ 4.00 – **41 rm** 31.95/35.95 **st.**

FOTHERINGHAY Northants. 404 S 26 – see Oundle.

FOULSHAM Norfolk – pop. 688 – ⊠ East Dereham – 🖏 036 284.

◆London 121 – ◆Cambridge 69 – King's Lynn 31 – ◆Norwich 18.

  ✗ **The Gamp,** Claypit Lane, NR20 5RW, 🏠 4114 – ⇔ 😊, 🄰 *VISA*
    closed Sunday dinner, Monday and first 2 weeks January – **M** 9.95 **st.** (lunch) and a la
    carte 14.75/18.60 **st.** ♦ 3.60

FOUR MARKS Hants. 403 404 Q 30 – pop. 2 429 – ⊠ 🖏 0420 Alton.

◆London 58 – Guildford 24 – Reading 29 – ◆Southampton 24.

  🏠 **Forte Travelodge** without rest., 156 Winchester Rd, GU34 5HZ, on A 31 🏠 562659,
    Reservations (Freephone) 0800 850950 – 📺 ৬ 😊, 🄰 🄰🄴 *VISA*. ⍉⍉
    31 rm 31.95 **t.**

FOWEY Cornwall 403 G 32 The West Country G. – pop. 2 092 – ECD : Wednesday – 🖏 0726.

See : Town★★.

Envir. : Gribbin Head★★ (≼★★) 6 m. rtn on foot – Bodinnick (≼★★) - Lanteglos Church★, E :
5 m. by ferry – Polruan (≼★★) SE : 6 m. by ferry – Polkerris★, W : 2 m. by A 3082.

🛈 The Post Office, 4 Custom House Hill, PL23 1AA 🏠 833616.

◆London 277 – Newquay 24 – ◆Plymouth 34 – Truro 22.

  🏠 **Marina,** 17 The Esplanade, PL23 1HY, 🏠 833315, ≼ Fowey river and harbour, ☞ –
    ⇔ rest 📺 ☎, 🄰 *VISA*
    March-October – **M** (bar lunch)/dinner 16.00 **t.** and a la carte ♦ 3.75 – **11 rm** ⊇ 40.50/
    80.00 **t.** – SB 80.00/124.00 **st.**

  🏠 **Carnethic House** ⍦, Lambs Barn, PL23 1HQ, NW : ¾ m. on A 3082 🏠 833336,
    ζ heated, ☞, ⍉⍉ – ⇔ rest 📺 😊, 🄰 🄰🄴 🄾🄳 *VISA*. ⍉⍉
    closed December and January – **M** (bar lunch)/dinner 13.00 **st.** ♦ 3.50 – **8 rm** ⊇ 30.00/
    55.00 **st.** – SB (except July and August) 76.00/106.00 **st.**

  ↑ **Ocean View** without rest., 24 Tower Park, PL23 1JB, 🏠 832283, ≼, ☞ – ⇔. ⍉⍉
    Easter-September – **4 rm** ⊇ 18.00/36.00 **s.**

  ✗✗ **Food for Thought,** 4 Town Quay, PL23 1AT, 🏠 832221, Fax 832221, « Converted coast-
    guard's cottage on quayside » – 🄰 *VISA*
    closed Sunday, January, February and Christmas – **Meals** (dinner only) 19.95 **t.** and a la
    carte 21.85/33.85 **t.** ♦ 3.95.

    at Golant N : 3 m. by B 3269 – ⊠ 🖏 0726 Fowey :

  🏠 **Cormorant** ⍦, PL23 1LL, 🏠 833426, Fax 833426, ≼ River Fowey, 🌊, ☞ – ⇔ 📺 ☎ 😊,
    🄰 🄰🄴 *VISA*
    closed 4 to 21 January – **M** – **Riverside** (light lunch)/dinner 26.00 **t.** and a la carte ♦ 4.50 –
    11 rm ⊇ 61.00/92.00 **t.** – SB (except Christmas and New Year) 100.00/140.00 **st.**

    at Bodinnick-by-Fowey E : ¼ m. via car ferry – ⊠ Fowey – 🖏 072 687 (3 fig.) and 0726
    (6 fig.) Polruan :

  🏠 **Old Ferry Inn,** PL23 1LX, 🏠 870237, ≼ Fowey Estuary and town, « Part 16C inn » – 📺
    😊, 🄰 *VISA*
    April-October – **M** (bar lunch)/dinner 25.00 **t.** and a la carte – **12 rm** ⊇ 35.00/80.00 **t.**

FOWLMERE Cambs. 404 U 27 – see Cambridge.

FOWNHOPE Heref. and Worcs. 403 404 M 27 – pop. 1 362 – ⊠ Hereford – 🖏 043 277 (3 fig.)
and 0432 (6 fig.).

◆London 132 – ◆Cardiff 46 – Hereford 6 – Gloucester 27.

  🏠 **Green Man Inn,** HR1 4PE, 🏠 860243, Fax 860207, ☞ – 📺 ☎ 😊, 🄰 🄰🄴 *VISA*. ⍉⍉
    M (bar lunch Monday to Saturday)/dinner a la carte 12.10/16.45 **t.** ♦ 4.25 – **20 rm** ⊇ 31.00/
    49.00 **t.** – SB (except Bank Holidays) 69.00/74.00 **t.**

  ↑ **Bowens Country House,** HR1 4PS, on B 4224 🏠 860430, ☞, ⍉⍉ – ⇔ rest 📺 😊, 🄰
    VISA. ⍉⍉
    M (by arrangement) 16.00 **t.** ♦ 3.50 – **12 rm** ⊇ 19.50/49.00 **t.** – SB (except Easter, Christ-
    mas and Bank Holidays) 39.00/62.00 **st.**

When travelling for business or pleasure
in England, Wales, Scotland and Ireland :

  – use the series of five maps
    (nos 401, 402, 403, 404 and 405) at a scale of 1:400 000

  – they are the perfect complement to this Guide

FRAMLINGHAM Suffolk **404** Y 27 – pop. 1 830 – ECD : Wednesday – ⊠ Woodbridge – ☎ 0728.

◆London 92 – ◆Ipswich 19 – ◆Norwich 42.

🏨 **Crown** (Forte), Market Hill, IP13 9AN, ℰ 723521, Fax 724274, « 16C inn » – ⇖ 🖵 ☎ 🅿. ⚠ 🖭 ⑩ 𝘝𝘐𝘚𝘈
M (bar lunch Monday to Saturday)/dinner 18.95 **t.** and a la carte ₰ 6.45 – ⚌ 8.50 – **14 rm** 70.00/85.00 **t.** – SB 108.00 **st.**

at Earl Soham W : 3½ m. by B 1119 on A 1120 – ⊠ Woodbridge – ☎ 0728.

⋔ **Abbey House** ॐ, Monk Soham, IP13 7EN, NW : 2½ m. by Kenton rd ℰ 685225, 🖉 – 🅿.
March-October – **M** (by arrangement) (communal dining) 12.00 **st.** – **3 rm** ⚌ 21.00/42.00 **st.**

FRAMPTON Dorset **403 404** M 31 – see Dorchester.

FRAMPTON-ON-SEVERN Glos. **403 404** M 28 – pop. 1 208 – ☎ 0452 Gloucester.

◆London 121 – ◆Bristol 48 – Gloucester 14.

XX **Savery's,** The Green, GL2 7EA, ℰ 740077 – ⚠ 𝘝𝘐𝘚𝘈
closed Sunday, Monday and 2 weeks February – Meals (dinner only) 21.95 **st.**

FRANKLEY SERVICE AREA W. Mids. **403 404** ⑲ – ⊠ ☎ 021 Birmingham

🏨 **Granada Lodge** without rest., B32 4AR, M5, between junctions 3 and 4 ℰ 550 3261, Fax 501 2880, Reservations (Freephone) 0800 555300 – ⇖ 🖵 & 🅿. ⚠ 🖭 𝘝𝘐𝘚𝘈. ⅋
⚌ 4.00 – **60 rm** 34.95/37.95 **st.**

"Short Breaks" (SB)

Zahlreiche Hotels bieten Vorzugspreise bei einem Aufenthalt

von zwei Nächten.

Diese Preise umfassen Zimmer, Abendessen und Frühstück.

FRANT Kent **404** U 30 – see Royal Tunbridge Wells.

FRENSHAM Surrey **404** R 30 – see Farnham.

FRESHWATER BAY I.O.W. **403 404** P 31 – see Wight (Isle of).

FRIETH Bucks. – see Henley-on-Thames (Oxon.).

FRILFORD Oxon. **403 404** P 28-29 – see Abingdon.

FRIMLEY Surrey **404** R 30 – pop. 44 674 (inc. Camberley) – ⊠ ☎ 0276 Camberley.

◆London 39 – Reading 17 – ◆Southampton 47.

🏨 **One Oak Toby,** 114 Portsmouth Rd, GU15 1HS, NE : 1 m. on A 325 ℰ 691939, Fax 676088 – ⇖ rm 🖵 ☎ 🅿 – ₰ 25. ⚠ 🖭 ⑩ 𝘝𝘐𝘚𝘈 𝘑𝘊𝘉. ⅋
M (grill rest.) 5.95/15.00 **t.** and a la carte – **40 rm** ⚌ 69.50/79.50 **t.** – SB (weekends only) 63.00/93.30 **st.**

FRINTON-ON-SEA Essex **404** X 28 – pop. 12 507 (inc. Walton) – ECD : Wednesday – ☎ 0255.

🖻₁₈, 🖻₉ 1 The Esplanade ℰ 674618.

◆London 72 – Chelmsford 39 – Colchester 17.

⋔ **Uplands,** 41 Hadleigh Rd, CO13 9HQ, ℰ 674889, 🖉 – ⇖ rm 🅿. ⅋
M (by arrangement) 11.50 – **8 rm** ⚌ 20.50/52.50.

FRITTENDEN Kent **404** V 30 – pop. 1 938 (inc. Sissinghurst) – ☎ 0580 80.

◆London 50 – Folkestone 34 – Hastings 23 – Maidstone 13.

⋔ **Maplehurst** ॐ, Mill Lane, TN17 2DT, NW : 1 m. ℰ 203, « Converted water mill », 🖉 – ⇖ 🖵 🅿. ⚠ 𝘝𝘐𝘚𝘈. ⅋
closed June – **M** 16.00 **s.** ₰ 4.00 – **3 rm** ⚌ 37.00/54.00 **s.**

FRODSHAM Ches. **402 403 404** L 24 – pop. 9 143 – ⊠ Warrington – ☎ 0928.

◆London 203 – Chester 11 – ◆Liverpool 21 – ◆Manchester 29 – ◆Stoke-on-Trent 42.

🏨 **Heathercliffe Country House** ॐ, Manley Rd, WA6 6HB, S : 1½ m. by B 5152 ℰ 733722, Fax 735667, ≼, 🖉, park – ⇖ rest 🖵 ☎ 🅿. ⚠ 𝘝𝘐𝘚𝘈
M (closed Sunday dinner) 12.95/17.95 **t.** and a la carte ₰ 3.75 – **9 rm** ⚌ 38.00/75.00 **st.** – SB (weekends only) 74.00 **st.**

🏨 **Old Hall,** Main St., WA6 7AB, ℰ 732052, Fax 739046, 🖉 – 🖵 ☎ 🅿. ⚠ 🖭 ⑩ 𝘝𝘐𝘚𝘈
M 10.75/13.50 **t.** and a la carte ₰ 4.25 – **20 rm** ⚌ 35.00/69.00 **st.**, 1 suite – SB (weekends only) 60.00/100.00 **st.**

🕮 ATS Brooklyn Garage, Chester Rd ℰ 33555

FULBROOK Oxon. **403 404** P 28 – see Burford.

FULWOOD Lancs. **402** L M 22 – see Preston.

GALMPTON Devon – ✉ ☎ 0803 Brixham.

◆London 229 – ◆Plymouth 32 – Torquay 6.

  🏠 **Lost and Found** ⌾, Maypool, TQ5 0ET, by Greenway Rd 𝒫 842442, Fax 845782, ⪦, ☞
    – ⥺ 🅃🅅 ☎ 🄿. 🄰 🄰🄴 𝘝𝘐𝘚𝘈. ⌾
    M (closed Sunday dinner to non-residents) (bar lunch Monday to Saturday)/dinner
    18.50 **t.** and a la carte ⓐ 4.50 – **16 rm** ⥶ 35.00/71.00 **t.** – SB (weekends only) 97.00 **st.**

GARFORTH W. Yorks. 402 P 22 – see Leeds.

GARSTANG Lancs. 402 L 22 – pop. 3 576 – ☎ 0995.

🇪 Discovery Centre Council Offices, High St., PR3 1FU 𝒫 602125.

◆London 233 – ◆Blackpool 13 – Manchester 41.

  🏠 **Pickerings,** Garstang Rd, Catterall, PR3 OHD, S : 1 ½ m. on B 6430 𝒫 602133,
    Fax 602100, ☞ – 🅃🅅 ☎ 🄿. 🄰 🄰🄴 ⓞ 𝘝𝘐𝘚𝘈
    M (closed Bank Holidays) 12.50/28.50 **st.** ⓐ 4.80 – **16 rm** ⥶ 40.00/70.00 **st.** – SB 92.00/
    120.00 **st.**

GATESHEAD Tyne and Wear 401 402 P 19 Great Britain G. – pop. 91 429 – ECD : Wednesday –
☎ 091 Tyneside.

Exc. : Beamish : North of England Open Air Museum★★ AC, SW : 6 m. by A 692 and A 6076
BX.

🏔 Ravensworth, Moss Heaps, Wrekenton 𝒫 487 6014/487 2843, S : 3 m. by B 1296 BX – 🏔 Heworth, Gingling Gate 𝒫 469 2137 BX.

🇪 Central Library, Prince Consort Rd, NE8 4LN 𝒫 477 3478 BX – Gateshead Metro Centre
Portcullis, 74 Russell Way, NE11 7XX 𝒫 460 6345 AX.

◆London 282 – Durham 16 – ◆Middlesbrough 38 – ◆Newcastle upon Tyne 1 – Sunderland 11.

Plan : see Newcastle upon Tyne

  🏨 **Newcastle Marriott,** Metro Centre, NE11 9XF, 𝒫 493 2233, Fax 493 2030, 𝑓ₛ, ⪦, ▤ –
    🛏 ⥺ rm ▤ 🅃🅅 ☎ & 🄿 – 🔬 400. 🄰 🄰🄴 ⓞ 𝘝𝘐𝘚𝘈   AX **e**
    M 14.95/16.50 **st.** and dinner a la carte ⓐ 7.95 – ⥶ 10.75 – **150 rm** 92.00 **st.** – SB (weekends
    only) 115.00/150.00 **st.**

  🏨 **Springfield** (Jarvis), Durham Rd, NE9 5BT, S : ½ m. on A 167 𝒫 477 4121, Fax 477 7213 –
    🛏 🅃🅅 ☎ & 🄿 – 🔬 100. 🄰 🄰🄴 ⓞ 𝘝𝘐𝘚𝘈   BX **s**
    M (bar lunch Monday to Saturday)/dinner a la carte 10.60/14.95 **t.** ⓐ 5.50 – ⥶ 8.00 – **60 rm**
    47.50/80.00 **t.** – SB (except Christmas and New Year) 80.00 **st.**

  🏨 **Swallow,** High West St., NE8 1PE, 𝒫 477 1105, Fax 478 7214, 𝑓ₛ, ⪦, ▤ – 🛏 ⥺ rm 🅃🅅
    ☎ 🄿 – 🔬 300. 🄰 🄰🄴 ⓞ 𝘝𝘐𝘚𝘈   BX **r**
    M (closed Saturday lunch) 11.45/19.50 **st.** and a la carte ⓐ 4.15 – **99 rm** ⥶ 78.00/89.50 **st.**,
    4 suites – SB (June-September and weekends only) 85.00/95.00 **st.**

  at Low Fell S : 2 m. by A 167 and Belle Vue Bank – BX – ✉ Gateshead – ☎ 091 Tyneside :

  🏠 **Eslington Villa,** 8 Station Road, NE9 6DR, 𝒫 487 6017, Fax 482 2359, ☞ – ⥺ rest 🅃🅅 ☎
    🄿. 🄰 🄰🄴 ⓞ 𝘝𝘐𝘚𝘈. ⌾
    closed 25 to 31 December – **M** (closed Sunday and Bank Holidays) 13.95/22.95 **t.** and a la
    carte ⓐ 5.50 – **12 rm** ⥶ 30.00/69.00 **t.**

🔘 ATS Earlsway, First Av., Team Valley Trading Est. 𝒫 4910081

GATWICK AIRPORT W. Sussex 404 T 30 – ✉ Crawley – ☎ 0293 Gatwick.

✈ Gatwick Airport : 𝒫 0293 (Crawley) 535353 and 𝒫 081 (London) 763 2020.

🇪 International Arrivals, Concourse, South Terminal, RH6 0NP 𝒫 560108.

◆London 29 – ◆Brighton 28.

Plan on next page

  🏨 **London Gatwick Airport Hilton,** Gatwick Airport, (South Terminal), RH6 0LL,
    𝒫 518080, Telex 877021, Fax 528980, 𝑓ₛ, ⪦, ▤ – 🛏 ⥺ rm ▤ 🅃🅅 ☎ & – 🔬 360. 🄰 🄰🄴
    ⓞ 𝘝𝘐𝘚𝘈   Y **u**
    M 14.95/23.50 **st.** and a la carte ⓐ 5.50 – ⥶ 12.95 – **547 rm** 125.00/135.00 **st.**, 3 suites –
    SB (weekends only) 170.00/212.00 **st.**

  🏨 **Ramada H. Gatwick,** Povey Cross Rd, ✉ Horley (Surrey), RH6 0BE, 𝒫 820169, Telex
    87440, Fax 820259, 𝑓ₛ, ⪦, ▤, squash – 🛏 ⥺ rm ▤ 🅃🅅 ☎ 🄿 – 🔬 150. 🄰 🄰🄴 ⓞ 𝘝𝘐𝘚𝘈 𝘑𝘊𝘉
    M (closed Saturday lunch) 12.95/17.75 **st.** and a la carte ⓐ 5.50 – ⥶ 8.50 – **255 rm** 95.00 **st.**,
    5 suites.   Y **a**

  🏨 **Forte Crest,** Gatwick Airport (North Terminal), RH6 0PH, 𝒫 567070, Telex 87202,
    Fax 567739, 𝑓ₛ, ⪦, ▤ – 🛏 ⥺ rm ▤ 🅃🅅 ☎ & – 🔬 300. 🄰 🄰🄴 ⓞ 𝘝𝘐𝘚𝘈 𝘑𝘊𝘉   Y **e**
    M 12.95/14.95 **st.** and dinner a la carte ⓐ 5.90 – ⥶ 9.95 – **451 rm** 89.00 **st.**, 13 suites –
    SB (weekends only) 116.00 **st.**

  🏨 **Forte Posthouse,** Povey Cross Rd, ✉ Horley (Surrey), RH6 0BA, 𝒫 771621, Fax 771054,
    ⤴ – 🛏 ⥺ rm ▤ rest 🅃🅅 ☎ 🄿 – 🔬 120. 🄰 🄰🄴 ⓞ 𝘝𝘐𝘚𝘈 𝘑𝘊𝘉   Y **c**
    M a la carte approx. 17.50 **t.** ⓐ 4.65 – ⥶ 6.95 – **210 rm** 53.50 **st.** – SB (weekends only)
    90.00 **st.**

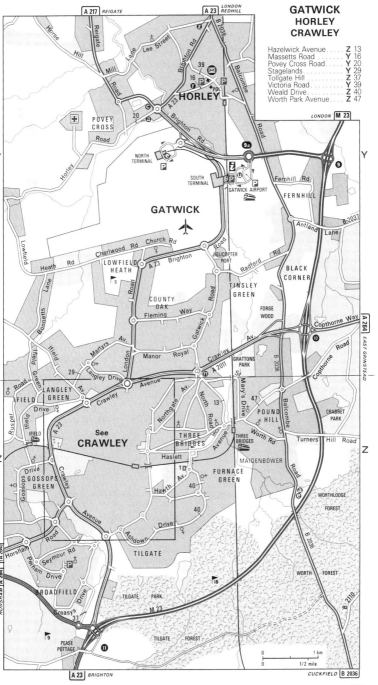

GATWICK
HORLEY
CRAWLEY

199

GAYTON Mersey. – ⊠ Wirral – ✪ 051 Liverpool.

♦London 206 – Birkenhead 12 – Chester 13 – ♦Liverpool 10.

🏠 **Travel Inn,** Chester Rd, L60 3FD, on A 540 at junction with A 551 ℰ 342 1982, Fax 342 8983 – ❧ rm 📺 ৬ **𝐏**. 🔼 🄰🄴 ① 🆅🅸🆂🄰 . ❀
M (Beefeater grill) a la carte approx. 16.00 **t.** 🍷 5.60 – ⊠ 4.95 – **37 rm** 33.50 **t.**

GERRARDS CROSS Bucks. 404 S 29 – pop. 19 447 (inc. Chalfont St Peter) – ECD : Wednesday – ✪ 0753.

🏠 Denham Court, Denham Court Drive, Denham ℰ 0895 (Denham) 835777, S : 4 m.

♦London 22 – Aylesbury 22 – ♦Oxford 36.

🏨 **Bull** (De Vere), Oxford Rd, SL9 7PA, on A 40 ℰ 885995, Fax 885504, ☞ – ⧮ ❧ rm 📺 ☎ **𝐏** – 🛦 200. 🔼 🄰🄴 ① 🆅🅸🆂🄰. ❀
M (bar lunch Saturday) 19.50/25.75 **st.** and dinner a la carte 🍷 8.50 – **93 rm** ⊠ 105.00/ 125.00 **st.**, 2 suites – SB 80.00/98.00 **st.**

GILLAN Cornwall 403 E 33 – see Helford.

When visiting the West Country,

use the Michelin Green Guide **"England: The West Country".**

  – Detailed descriptions of places of interest

  – Touring programmes by county

  – Maps and street plans

  – The history of the region

  – Photographs and drawings of monuments, beauty spots, houses...

GILLINGHAM Dorset 403 404 N 30 The West Country G. – pop. 5 379 – ✪ 0747.

Exc. : Stourhead★★★ AC, N : 9 m. by B 3092, B 3095 and B 3092.

♦London 116 – Bournemouth 34 – ♦Bristol 46 – ♦Southampton 52.

🏨 **Stock Hill Country House** ❧, Wyke, SP8 5NR, W : 1 ½ m. on B 3081 ℰ 823626, Fax 825628, « Victorian country house, antiques », ☞, park, ❀ – ❧ rest 📺 ☎ **𝐏**. 🔼 ① 🆅🅸🆂🄰 ❀
M (booking essential) (lunch by arrangement)/dinner 26.50 **t.** 🍷 5.95 – **7 rm** ⊠ (dinner included) 85.00/190.00 **t.**, 1 suite – SB (November-March except Christmas) (weekdays only) 160.00 **st.**

GISBURN Lancs. 402 N 22 – pop. 435 – ECD : Wednesday – ⊠ Clitheroe ✪ 0200.

♦London 243 – ♦Manchester 37 – Preston 25.

🏠 Stirk House, BB7 4LJ, SW : 1 m. on A 59 ℰ 445581, Fax 445744, 𝐼₆, ♨s, 🔼, ☞, squash – ❧ rest 📺 ☎ **𝐏** – 🛦 250. ❀
46 rm.

GISLINGHAM Suffolk 404 X 27 – pop. 589 – ⊠ Eye – ✪ 0379 Mellis.

♦London 93 – ♦Cambridge 45 – ♦Ipswich 20 – ♦Norwich 30.

↥ **Old Guildhall,** Mill St., IP23 8JT, ℰ 783361, ☞ – ❧ 📺 **𝐏**
closed January – **M** (by arrangement) 10.00 **t.** 🍷 3.25 – **3 rm** ⊠ 35.00/50.00 **t.** – SB 70.00/ 90.00 **st.**

GISSING Norfolk – see Diss.

GITTISHAM Devon 403 K 31 – pop. 233 – ECD : Thursday – ⊠ ✪ 0404 Honiton.

♦London 164 – Exeter 14 – Sidmouth 9 – Taunton 21.

🏨 **Combe House** ❧, EX14 0AD, ℰ 42756, Fax 46004, ≼, « Elizabethan mansion, country house atmosphere », ↖, ☞, park – 📺 ☎ **𝐏**. 🔼 🄰🄴 ① 🆅🅸🆂🄰
closed Monday January-February – **M** (dinner only) a la carte 23.75/30.75 **st.** – **14 rm** ⊠ 63.00/125.00 **st.**, 1 suite.

GLASTONBURY Somerset 403 L 30 The West Country G. – pop. 6 751 – ECD : Wednesday – ✪ 0458.

See : Town★★ – Abbey★★★ (Abbots Kitchen★) AC – St. John the Baptist Church★★ – Somerset Rural Life Museum★ AC – Glastonbury Tor★ (≼★★★).

Envir. : Wells★★ - Cathedral★★★, Vicars' Close★, Bishop's Palace★ AC (≼★★) NE : 5 ½ m. by A 39.

Exc. : Wookey Hole★★ (Caves★ AC, Papermill★, Fairground Collection★) NE : 8 m. by A 39.

🗋 The Tribunal, 9 High St., BA6 9DP ℰ 832954.

♦London 136 – ♦Bristol 26 – Taunton 22.

🏠 **George and Pilgrims** (Resort), 1 High St., BA6 9DP, ℰ 831146, Fax 832252, « Part 15C Inn » – 📺 ☎. 🔼 🄰🄴 ① 🆅🅸🆂🄰
M a la carte approx. 7.95 **t.** 🍷 3.50 – **13 rm** ⊠ 45.00/75.00 **t.**

XX **Number Three** with rm, 3 Magdalene St., BA6 9EW, ✆ 832129, « Georgian house », – ⊁ rest [TV] ☎ [P]. [S] [VISA]. ⊁
closed December and January – **M** *(closed Sunday and Monday)* (booking essential) (dinner only) 26.00 **t.** 5.00 – 5.50 – **6 rm** 50.00/75.00 **st.**

at West Pennard E : 3 ½ m. on A 361 – ✉ ☎ 0458 Glastonbury :

Red Lion, BA6 8NN, ✆ 832941, Fax 832941 – [TV] ☎ [P]. [S] [AE] [O] [VISA]. ⊁
M a la carte 10.45/15.95 **st.** 3.50 – **7 rm** 30.00/45.00 **st.**

GLEWSTONE Heref. and Worcs. – see Ross-on-Wye.

GLOOSTON Leics. – see Market Harborough.

GLOSSOP Derbs. [402] [403] [404] O 23 – pop. 29 923 – ECD : Tuesday – ☎ 0457.

Sheffield Rd ✆ 865247, E : 1 m. by A 57.

[i] The Gatehouse, Victoria St., SK13 8HT ✆ 855920.

♦London 194 – ♦Manchester 18 – ♦Sheffield 25.

Wind in the Willows ⊁, Hurst Rd, Derbyshire Level, SK13 9PT, E : 1 m. by A 57 ✆ 868001, Fax 853354, – [TV] ☎ [P]. [S] [AE] [O] [VISA]. ⊁
M (dinner only) 17.50 **st.** 5.00 – **11 rm** 52.00/90.00 **st.**

GLOUCESTER Glos. [403] [404] N 28 **Great Britain G.** – pop. 106 526 – ECD : Thursday – ☎ 0452.

See : City★ – Cathedral★★ Y – The Docks★ Y – Bishop Hooper's Lodging★ *AC* Y **M.**

18, 9 Gloucestershire Hotel, Matson Lane ✆ 525653, S : 3 m. by B 4073 Z.

[i] St Michael's Tower, The Cross, GL1 1PD ✆ 421188.

♦London 106 – ♦Birmingham 52 – ♦Bristol 38 – ♦Cardiff 66 – ♦Coventry 57 – Northampton 83 – ♦Oxford 48 – ♦Southampton 98 – ♦Swansea 92 – Swindon 35.

Plan on next page

Forte Crest, Crest Way, Barnwood, GL4 7RX, E : 3 m. off A 417 ✆ 613311, Fax 371036, ⊁, – ⊁ rm [TV] ☎ ♿ [P] – 100. [S] [AE] [O] [VISA] [JCB]. ⊁ Z
M (bar lunch Saturday) 12.95/21.00 **st.** and a la carte 5.50 – 9.95 – **122 rm** 89.00 **st.**, 1 suite – SB (except Christmas) (weekends only) 108.00/118.00 **st.**

Gloucester H. & Country Club (Jarvis), Robinswood Hill, Matson Lane, GL4 9EA, SE : 3 m. by B 4073 ✆ 525653, Fax 307212, 18, 9, squash – ⊁ rm [TV] ☎ [P] – 180. [S] [AE] [O] [VISA] Z c
closed 24 to 26 December – **M** (bar lunch Saturday and Sunday) 12.50/14.50 **t.** 4.65 – 8.50 – **102 rm** 60.00/95.00 **st.**, 5 suites – SB (except 31 December) 88.00/110.00 **st.**

Travel Inn, Tewkesbury Rd, Longford, GL2 9BE, N : 1 ¾ m. on A 38 – ✆ 523519, Fax 300924 – ⊁ rm [TV] ♿ [P]. [S] [AE] [O] [VISA]. ⊁ Z
M (Beefeater grill) a la carte approx. 16.00 **t.** – 4.95 – **40 rm** 33.50 **t.**

XX **Yeungs,** St. Oswald's Rd, Cattle Market, GL1 2SR, ✆ 309957 – Z e
closed Monday lunch and Sunday – **M** - **Chinese** 12.00/22.50 **t.** and a la carte.

at Down Hatherley NE : 3 ¼ m. by A 38 – Z – ✉ ☎ 0452 Gloucester :

Hatherley Manor, Down Hatherley Lane, GL2 9QA, ✆ 730217, Fax 731032, – ⊁ rest [TV] ☎ ♿ [P] – 250. [S] [AE] [O] [VISA]
M 10.50/13.50 **st.** 4.25 – **56 rm** 55.00/72.00 **st.** – SB (weekends only) 90.00 **st.**

at Upton St. Leonards SE : 3 ½ m. by B 4073 – Z – ✉ ☎ 0452 Gloucester :

Hatton Court, Upton Hill, GL4 8DE, S : ¾ m. on B 4073 ✆ 617412, Fax 612945, ≤, heated, – [TV] ☎ [P] – 60. [S] [AE] [O] [VISA] [JCB]. ⊁
M – **Carringtons** 14.00/19.75 **t.** and a la carte – **45 rm** 75.00/99.00 **t.** – SB (except Christmas and New Year) 110.00/130.00 **st.**

Bowden Hall Resort, Bondend Lane, GL4 8ED, E : 1 m. by Bondend rd ✆ 614121, Fax 611885, ≤, park – ⊁ rm [TV] ☎ [P] – 80. [S] [AE] [O] [VISA]
M (bar lunch Saturday) (carving lunch Sunday) 10.00/14.95 **t.** and a la carte 5.00 – 7.50 – **72 rm** 75.00/100.00 **st.** – SB (weekends only) 96.00 **st.**

Bullens Manor Farm without rest., High St., GL4 8DL, SE : ½ m. ✆ 616463, Fax 371695, « Working farm », park – ⊁ [TV] [P]. ⊁
3 rm 20.00/35.00 **s.**

at Witcombe SE : 7 m. by A 40 on A 417 – Z – ✉ ☎ 0452 Gloucester :

Travel Inn, GL3 4SS, on A 417 ✆ 862521, Fax 864926 – ⊁ rm [TV] ♿ [P]. [S] [AE] [O] [VISA]. ⊁
closed 24 to 27 December – **M** (Beefeater grill) a la carte approx. 16.00 **t.** – 4.95 – **39 rm** 33.50 **t.**

ATS St. Oswalds Rd ✆ 527329

GLOUCESTER

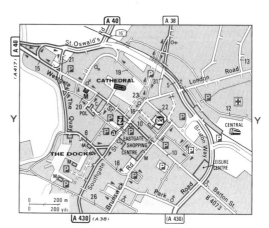

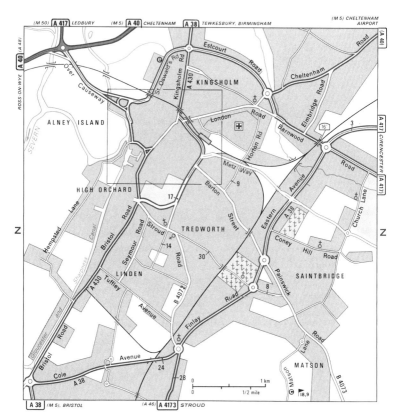

202

GOATHLAND N. Yorks. 402 R 20 – pop. 442 – ECD : Wednesday and Saturday – ✉ 0947 Whitby.

◆London 248 – ◆Middlesbrough 36 – York 38.

⌂ **Mallyan Spout** ⌖, The Common, YO22 5AN, ℘ 86486, Fax 86327, ≼, ≼ – 📺 ☎ 🅿. 🖼 ⓞ VISA
M (bar lunch Monday to Saturday)/dinner 18.00 **t.** and a la carte ⌀ 5.85 – **24 rm** ⊂⊃ 50.00/100.00 – SB (except Bank Holidays) 50.00/135.00 **st.**

⌂ **Whitfield House** ⌖, Darnholm, YO22 5LA, NW : ¾ m. ℘ 86215, ≼ – ⊱⊰ rest 📺 ☎ 🅿. 🖼 VISA
closed December and January – **M** 13.75 **st.** ⌀ 3.00 – **8 rm** ⊂⊃ 26.00/50.00 **st.** – SB (October-April) 66.00/80.00 **st.**

⌂ **Heatherdene** ⌖, The Common, YO22 5AN, ℘ 86334, ≼, ≼ – ⊱⊰ rest 📺 🅿. ⌖
May-October – **M** 10.00 – **6 rm** ⊂⊃ 16.00/36.50.

⌂ **Prudom House** ⌖, The Common, YO22 5AN, ℘ 86368, ≼ – ⊱⊰ rest. ⌖
closed November and December – **M** 8.50 **st.** – **7 rm** ⊂⊃ 21.50/39.00 **st.**

at Egton Bridge NW : 4¾ m. – ✉ 🕾 0947 Whitby :

⌖ **Horseshoe** ⌖, YO21 1XE, ℘ 85245, ≼ – 📺 🅿. 🖼 🆃 VISA. ⌖
closed 25 December – **M** 12.00/20.00 **st.** and a la carte ⌀ 4.60 – **6 rm** ⊂⊃ 24.00/46.00 **st.**

*The names of main shopping streets are indicated in red
at the beginning of the list of streets.*

GODALMING Surrey 404 S 30 – pop. 18 758 – ECD : Wednesday – 🕾 0483.

☖ West Surrey, Enton Green ℘ 421275 – ☖ Shillinglee Park, Chiddingfold ℘ 0428 (Chiddingfold) 653237.

◆London 38 – Guildford 5 – ◆Southampton 51.

🏨 **Inn on the Lake,** Ockford Rd, GU7 1RH, ℘ 415575, Fax 860445, ≼ – 📺 ☎ 🅿. 🖼 🆃 ⓞ VISA
M 9.95/16.50 **t.** – **17 rm** ⊂⊃ 75.00/85.00 **t.** – SB (weekends only) 81.00/143.00 **st.**

⌂ **Kings Arms and Royal,** High St., GU7 1EB, ℘ 421545, Fax 415403 – 📺 ☎ 🅿. 🖼 🆃 VISA. ⌖
closed 25 December – **M** (in bar Sunday)/dinner a la carte approx. 12.00 **t.** – **16 rm** ⊂⊃ 50.00/60.00 **t.** – SB (weekends only) 60.00/120.00 **st.**

⌂ **Meads,** 65 Meadrow, GU7 3HS, N : ½ m. on A 3100 ℘ 421800 – 📺 🅿. 🖼 🆃 VISA
closed 25 December-2 January – **M** (by arrangement) 10.00 **t.** – **15 rm** ⊂⊃ 23.00/42.00 **t.**

at Hascombe SE : 3½ m. on B 2130 – ✉ Godalming – 🕾 048 632 Hascombe :

✗ **White Horse,** GU8 4JA, ℘ 258, ≼ – 🅿. 🖼 🆃 VISA
closed Sunday dinner and 25 December – **M** a la carte 21.50/24.50 **t.** ⌀ 7.50.

⚙ ATS Meadrow ℘ 421845/422219

GODSTONE Surrey 404 T 30 – pop. 2 567 – 🕾 0342 South Godstone.

◆London 22 – ◆Brighton 36 – Maidstone 28.

✗✗✗ **La Bonne Auberge,** Tilburstow Hill, South Godstone, RH9 8JY, S : 2¼ m. ℘ 892318, Fax 893435, ≼ – 🅿. 🖼 🆃 ⓞ VISA
closed Sunday dinner, Monday and 26 to 30 December – **M** - French 14.50/24.50 **st.** and a la carte ⌀ 4.90.

GOLANT Cornwall 403 G 32 – see Fowey.

GOLCAR W. Yorks. – see Huddersfield.

GOLDEN GREEN Kent 404 U 30 – see Tonbridge.

GOMERSAL W. Yorks. 402 O 22 – see Bradford.

GOODWOOD W. Sussex 404 R 31 – see Chichester.

GORDANO SERVICE AREA Avon – ✉ Bristol – 🕾 027 581 (4 fig.) 0275 (6 fig.) Pill.

⌂ **Forte Travelodge** without rest., BS20 9XG, M 5 : junction 19 ℘ 373709, Reservations (Freephone) 0800 850950 – 📺 ♿ 🅿. 🖼 🆃 ⓞ VISA
40 rm 31.95 **t.**

GORING Berks. 403 404 Q 29 The West Country G. – pop. 4 257 – 🕾 0491.

Exc. : Ridgeway Path★★.

◆London 56 – ◆Oxford 16 – Reading 12.

✗✗ **Leatherne Bottel,** RG8 0HS, N : 1½ m. by B 4009 ℘ 872667, ≼, « Thames-side setting » – 🅿. 🖼 🆃 VISA
closed Christmas Day – **Meals** a la carte 20.50/31.40 **t.**

GORLESTON-ON-SEA Norfolk 404 Z 26 – see Great Yarmouth.

GOSFORTH Cumbria 402 J 20 – pop. 1 272 – ⊠ Seascale – ✆ 094 67.

☂ Seascale, The Banks ✆ 28202/28800, SW : 3 m.

◆London 317 – Kendal 55 – Workington 21.

🏠 **Westlakes,** Gosforth Rd, CA20 1HP, on A 595 ✆ 25221, ☞ – TV ☎ P. ↗ AE VISA. ✦
  M (closed Sunday lunch) a la carte 13.00/19.50 **st.** ↥ 4.00 – **6 rm** ⊑ 45.00/56.00 **st.**

GOSFORTH Tyne and Wear 401 402 P 18 – see Newcastle upon Tyne.

GOUDHURST Kent 404 V 30 Great Britain G. – pop. 2 673 – ECD : Wednesday – ⊠ Cranbrook – ✆ 0580.

Envir. : Sissinghurst Castle★ AC, E : 5½ m. by A 262.

◆London 45 – Hastings 22 – Maidstone 13.

🏠 **Star and Eagle,** High St., TN17 1AL, ✆ 211512, « 14C inn » – TV ☞ P. ↗ AE VISA
  M a la carte 7.60/14.30 **t.** ↥ 3.90 – **11 rm** ⊑ 30.00/55.00 **t.**

GOVETON Devon 403 I 33 – see Kingsbridge.

GRAMPOUND Cornwall 403 F 33 The West Country G. – pop. 435 – ⊠ Truro – ✆ 0726 St. Austell.

Envir. : Trewithen★★★ AC, W : 2 m. by A 390 – Probus★ (tower★, Country Demonstration Garden★ AC) W : 2½ m. by A 390.

◆London 287 – Newquay 16 – ◆Plymouth 44 – Truro 8.

XX **Eastern Promise,** 1 Moor View, TR2 4RT, ✆ 883033 – ↤ P. ↗ AE ⓞ VISA JCB
  closed Wednesday – **M** - **Chinese** (booking essential) (dinner only) 17.50 **st.** and a la carte ↥ 3.50.

Great Britain and Ireland is now covered
by an Atlas at a scale of 1 inch to 4.75 miles.

Three easy to use versions: Paperback, Spiralbound and Hardback.

GRANGE-IN-BORROWDALE Cumbria 402 K 20 – see Keswick.

GRANGE-OVER-SANDS Cumbria 402 L 21 Great Britain G. – pop. 3 864 – ECD : Thursday – ✆ 053 95.

Envir. : Cartmel Priory★, NW : 3 m.

☂ Meathop Rd ✆ 33180, E : off B 5277 – ☂ Grange Fell, Fell Rd ✆ 32536.

🏛 Victoria Hall, Main St., LA11 6PT ✆ 34026 (summer only).

◆London 268 – Kendal 13 – Lancaster 24.

🏠 **Netherwood,** Lindale Rd, LA11 6ET, ✆ 32552, Fax 34121, ≤ Morecambe Bay, ↗, ☞, park – 🛗 ↤ ☰ rest TV ☎ & P – ⚠ 150. ↗ VISA
  M 13.50/23.00 **t.** and lunch a la carte ↥ 4.75 – **29 rm** ⊑ 41.75/101.00 **t.** – SB (November-March) 95.00/105.00 **st.**

🏠 **Graythwaite Manor** ⚘, Fernhill Rd, LA11 7JE, ✆ 32001, Fax 35549, ≤ gardens and Morecambe Bay, « Extensive flowered gardens », park, ✕ – ↤ rest TV ☎ ⇌ P. ↗ VISA. ✦
  closed January – **M** 13.50/25.00 ↥ 3.75 – **22 rm** ⊑ 37.50/80.00 **t.** – SB (except Bank Holidays) 90.00/114.00 **st.**

🏠 **Hampsfell House** ⚘, Hampsfell Rd, LA11 6BG, ✆ 32567, ☞ – ↤ rest TV P. ↗ VISA
  M (bar lunch)/dinner 16.00 **t.** ↥ 4.75 – **8 rm** ⊑ 27.50/50.00 **t.** – SB (except Bank Holidays) 66.00/82.00 **st.**

at Lindale NE : 2 m. on B 5277 – ⊠ ✆ 053 95 Grange-over-Sands :

⌂ **Greenacres,** LA11 6LP, ✆ 34578 – ↤ TV P. ✦
  closed December – **M** (by arrangement) 13.50 **s.** – **5 rm** ⊑ 30.00/57.00 **s.** – SB (except Bank Holidays) 75.00/96.00 **st.**

at Witherslack NE : 5 m. by B 5277 off A 590 – ⊠ ✆ 053 95 Witherslack :

🏛 **Old Vicarage** ⚘, Church Rd, LA11 6RS, ✆ 52381, Fax 52373, « Part Georgian country house », ☞, ✕ – ↤ rest TV ☎ P. ↗ AE ⓞ VISA JCB
  M (booking essential) (dinner only and Sunday lunch)/dinner 27.50 **t.** ↥ 6.00 – **15 rm** ⊑ 59.00/138.00 **t.** – SB (except Bank Holidays) 97.00/183.00 **st.**

at Cartmel NW : 3 m. – ⊠ Cartmel – ✆ 053 95 Grange-over-Sands :

🏛 **Aynsome Manor** ⚘, LA11 6HH, NE : ¾ m. by Newby Bridge rd and Wood Broughton rd ✆ 36653, Fax 36016, ☞ – ↤ rest TV ☎ P. ↗ AE VISA
  closed 2 to 26 January – **M** (closed Sunday dinner to non-residents) (dinner only and Sunday lunch)/dinner 18.50 **t.** ↥ 4.75 – **13 rm** ⊑ (dinner included) 51.00/102.00 **t.** – SB (except Bank Holidays) 77.00/90.00 **st.**

XX **Uplands** ⚘ with rm, Haggs Lane, LA11 6HD, E : 1 m. ✆ 36248, ≤, ☞ – ↤ rest TV ☞ P. ↗ AE VISA
  closed 1 January-23 February – **M** (closed Monday) (booking essential) 14.00/26.00 **st.** ↥ 3.70 – **5 rm** ⊑ (dinner included) 75.00/130.00 **t.** – SB (November-April) 104.00/150.00 **st.**

GRANTHAM Lincs. 402 404 S 25 Great Britain G. – pop. 30 700 – ECD : Wednesday – ☎ 0476.

See : St. Wulfram's Church★.

Envir. : Belton House★ *AC*, N : 2½ m. by A 607.

Exc. : Belvoir Castle★★ *AC*, W : 6 m. by A 607.

18, 9 Belton Park, Belton Lane, Londonthorpe Rd ✆ 67399, N : 2 m. – 18, 9 Belton Woods ✆ 593200, N : 2 m. by A 607.

ℹ The Guildhall Centre, St. Peters Hill, NG31 6PZ ✆ 66444.

◆London 113 – ◆Leicester 31 – Lincoln 29 – ◆Nottingham 24.

Swallow, Swingbridge Rd, NG31 7XT, S : 1 ¼ m. at junction of A 607 with A 1 southbound sliproad ✆ 593000, Fax 592592, Lö, ≘s, 🏊 – ⇔ TV ☎ ♿ P – 🏛 200. AE ⓓ VISA
M 17.50 **st.** and a la carte – **88 rm** ☐ 80.00/95.00 **st.**, 1 suite – SB 105.00 **st.**

Belton Woods H. & Country Club, Belton, NG32 2LN, N : 2 m. on A 607 ✆ 593200, Fax 74547, Lö, ≘s, 🏊, 18, 9, 🌳, park, 🎾, squash – |⇕| ⇔ rm TV ☎ ♿ P – 🏛 275. AE ⓓ VISA. ✂
M 13.50/22.50 **st.** and a la carte 🍷 8.00 – **92 rm** ☐ 95.00/140.00 **st.**, 4 suites – SB 160.00 **st.**

Angel and Royal (Forte), High St., NG31 6PN, ✆ 65816, Fax 67149, « Part 13C » – ⇔ TV ☎ P – 🏛 25. AE ⓓ VISA JCB. ✂
M (bar lunch Monday to Saturday)/dinner 16.95 **t.** and a la carte 🍷 6.45 – ☐ 8.50 – **29 rm** 70.00/80.00 **st.**, 1 suite – SB (except Bank Holidays) 98.00 **st.**

at Great Gonerby NW : 2 m. on B 1174 – ✉ ☎ 0476 Grantham :

XX ✿ **Harry's Place** (Hallam), 17 High St., NG31 8JS, ✆ 61780 – ⇔. VISA
closed Sunday, Monday and 25-26 December – **M** (booking essential) a la carte 27.50/38.00 **t.** 🍷 9.00
Spec. Smoked haddock soufflé in pastry with shiitaki mushrooms, Breast of free-range cornfed chicken with red wine and bacon, Pithivier of almonds and mincemeat.

at Grantham Service Area NW : 3 m on B 1174 at junction with A 1 – ✉ ☎ 0476 Grantham :

Forte Travelodge without rest., NG32 2AB, ✆ 77500, Reservations (Freephone) 0800 850950 – TV ♿ P. AE VISA. ✂
40 rm 31.95 **t.**

ATS East St. ✆ 590222 ATS Elmer St. South ✆ 590444

For maximum information from town plans: consult the conventional signs key.

GRASMERE Cumbria 402 K 20 Great Britain G. – ECD : Thursday – ☎ 053 94 Ambleside.

See : Dove Cottage★ *AC* AY **A**.

Envir. : Lake Windermere★★, SE : by A 591 AZ.

ℹ Redbank Rd, LA22 9SW ✆ 35245 (summer only) – BZ.

◆London 282 – ◆Carlisle 43 – Kendal 18.

Plans : see Ambleside

Michaels Nook Country House 🐦, LA22 9RP, NE : ½ m. off A 591, turning by Swan H. ✆ 35496, Fax 35765, ≤ mountains and countryside, « Antiques and gardens » – ⇔ rest TV ☎ P. AE ⓓ VISA. ✂ AY **n**
M (booking essential) 27.50/47.00 **t.** 🍷 6.00 – **12 rm** ☐ (dinner included) 108.00/290.00 **t.**, 2 suites – SB (November-March) 170.00/290.00 **st.**

Wordsworth, Stock Lane, LA22 9SW, ✆ 35592, Fax 35765, ≘s, 🏊, 🌳 – |⇕| ⇔ rest ▤ rest TV ☎ P – 🏛 100. AE ⓓ VISA. ✂ BZ **s**
M – **Prelude** 17.50/29.50 **t.** and a la carte 🍷 6.50 – **35 rm** ☐ 58.50/140.00 **t.**, 2 suites.

Swan (Forte), LA22 9RF, on A 591 ✆ 35551, Fax 35741, ≤, 🌳 – ⇔ TV ☎ P. AE ⓓ VISA JCB AY **r**
M 10.95/20.50 **t.** and a la carte 🍷 6.00 – ☐ 8.50 – **36 rm** 80.00/110.00 **st.** – SB 118.00/170.00 **st.**

White Moss House, Rydal Water, LA22 9SE, S : 1 ½ m. on A 591 ✆ 35295, ≤, 🌳 – ⇔ rest TV ☎ P. VISA. ✂ BY **v**
March-November – **M** *(closed Sunday)* (booking essential) (dinner only) 26.00 **st.** 🍷 4.50 – **6 rm** ☐ 54.00/120.00 **st.**

Rothay Garden, Broadgate, LA22 9RJ, ✆ 35334, Fax 35723, 🌳 – ⇔ rest TV ☎ P. VISA AY **e**
M (bar lunch Monday to Saturday)/dinner 16.95 **t.** 🍷 4.50 – **24 rm** ☐ 30.00/91.00 **t.** – SB (winter only) 74.00/85.00 **st.**

Oak Bank, Broadgate, LA22 9TA, ✆ 35217, 🌳 – ⇔ rest TV ☎ P. VISA JCB BZ **e**
closed January – **M** (bar lunch)/dinner a la carte approx. 15.50 **t.** – **16 rm** ☐ 45.00/120.00 **st.**

Grasmere, Broadgate, LA22 9TA, ✆ 35277, Fax 35277, 🌳 – ⇔ rest TV ☎ P. VISA JCB BZ **r**
closed January – **M** (dinner only) 18.50 **t.** 🍷 5.50 – **12 rm** ☐ 30.00/84.00 **t.** – SB (November-April except Easter) 70.00/104.00 **st.**

⌂ **Lancrigg Vegetarian Country House** ≫, Easedale Rd, LA22 9QN, W : ½ m. on Easedale Rd ℰ 35317, ← Easedale Valley, ☞, park – ✤ rest 📺 **℗**. 🖪 💳 AY **u**
M (light lunch)/dinner 18.50 **t**. – **13 rm** 🖙 (dinner included) 43.00/140.00 **t**.

⌂ **Bridge House,** Stock Lane, LA22 9SN, ℰ 35425, ☞ – ✤ rest 📺 **℗**. 🖪 💳 JCB. ✼
early March-early November – **M** (dinner only) 13.50 **t**. ≬ 4.50 – **12 rm** 🖙 30.00/60.00 **t**. –
SB 78.00/82.00 **st**.
BZ **n**

⌂ **Rothay Lodge** ≫ without rest., White Bridge, LA22 9RH, ℰ 35341, ☞ – ✤ 📺 **℗**.
March-October – **5 rm** 🖙 22.00/44.00 **st**.
AY **o**

⌂ **Banerigg** without rest., Lake Rd, LA22 9PW, S : ¾ m. on A 591 ℰ 35204, ←, ☞ – ✤ **℗**
closed January and February – **6 rm** 🖙 18.00/43.00 **st**.
AY **a**

GRASSINGTON N. Yorks. 402 O 21 – pop. 1 220 – ECD : Thursday – ✉ Skipton – 🕿 0756.

🖪 National Park Centre, Hebden Rd, BD23 5LB ℰ 752774 (summer only).

◆London 240 – Bradford 30 – Burnley 28 – ◆Leeds 37.

⌂ **Ashfield House,** BD23 5AE, ℰ 752584, ☞ – ✤ 📺 **℗**. 🖪 💳. ✼
mid February-October – **M** (by arrangement) 12.50 **st**. ≬ 4.50 – **7 rm** 🖙 25.50/55.50 **st**. –
SB (mid February-April) (weekdays only) 58.00/64.00 **st**.

⌂ **Lodge,** 8 Wood Lane, BD23 5LU, ℰ 752518 – ✤ rest **℗**
March-October and weekends in December – **M** 10.00 **st**. – **7 rm** 🖙 22.00/56.00 **st**. –
SB 60.00/64.00 **st**.

at Threshfield SW : ½ m. on B 6265 – ✉ Skipton – 🕿 0756 Grassington :

⌂ **Greenways** ≫, Wharfeside Av., BD23 5BS, ℰ 752598, ←, ☞ – ✤ rest 📺 **℗**
March-October – **M** (by arrangement) 12.50 **st**. ≬ 4.00 – **4 rm** 🖙 24.00/50.00 **st**.

GRAVESEND Kent 404 V 29 – pop. 53 450 – ECD : Wednesday – 🕿 0474.

🛳 to Tilbury (White Horse Ferries Ltd) frequent services daily (5 mn).

🖪 10 Parrock St., DA12 1EL ℰ 337600.

◆London 25 – ◆Dover 54 – Maidstone 16 – Margate 53.

🖭 **Overcliffe,** 15-16 Overcliffe, DA11 0EF, ℰ 322131, Fax 536737 – 📺 🕿 **℗**. 🖪 🆎 ⓞ 💳
M a la carte 15.50/18.50 **st**. ≬ 4.00 – **29 rm** 🖙 50.00/70.00 **st**.

GRAVETYE E. Sussex – see East Grinstead.

GRAYSHOTT Hants. 404 R 30 – ✉ Hindhead (Surrey) – 🕿 0428.

◆London 46 – ◆Portsmouth 31.

✗ **Woods Place,** Headley Rd, GU26 6LB, ℰ 605555, Fax 605555 – 🖪 🆎 ⓞ 💳
closed Sunday and Monday – **M** a la carte 16.00/20.20 ≬ 3.90.

GREASBY Mersey. 402 ② 403 ⑫ – pop. 44 272 – ✉ Wirral – 🕿 051 Liverpool.

◆London 220 – ◆Liverpool 9.

🖭 **Twelfth Man Lodge,** Greasby Rd, L49 2PP, ℰ 677 5445, Fax 678 5085 – 📺 🕿 ♿ **℗**. 🖪
🆎 ⓞ 💳
M 10.00 **st**. and a la carte ≬ 4.50 – 🖙 4.95 – **30 rm** 39.00 **st**.

GREAT AYTON N. Yorks. 402 Q 20 Great Britain G. – pop. 4 690 – ✉ 🕿 0642 Middlesbrough
(Cleveland).

See : Captain Cook Birthplace Museum ★ *AC*.

🖪 High Green Car Park, TS9 6BJ ℰ 722835 (summer only).

◆London 245 – ◆Leeds 63 – ◆Middlesbrough 7 – York 48.

🏨 **Ayton Hall** ≫, Low Green, TS9 6BW, ℰ 723595, Fax 722149, « Tasteful decor », ☞ –
📺 🕿 **℗**. 🖪 🆎 ⓞ 💳. ✼
M 11.95/25.00 **t**. and a la carte ≬ 8.95 – **12 rm** 🖙 35.00/125.00 **t**. – SB (weekends only)
160.00/180.00 **st**.

GREAT BADDOW Essex 404 V 28 – see Chelmsford.

GREAT BARR W. Mids. 403 404 O 26 – see Birmingham.

When visiting Great Britain,
use the Michelin Green Guide "Great Britain".
– *Detailed descriptions of places of interest*
– *Touring programmes*
– *Maps and street plans*
– *The history of the country*
– *Photographs and drawings of monuments, beauty spots, houses...*

N. Yorks. 402 Q 20 – pop. 909 – ⊠ ⊛ 0642 Middlesborough.

◆London 241 – ◆Leeds 61 – ◆Middlesborough 10 – York 54.

⌂ **Wainstones,** 31 High St., TS9 7EW, ℘ 712268, Fax 711560 – 📺 ☎ 🅿. 🖭 🆎 𝘝𝘐𝘚𝘈. ⁒
    M a la carte 13.45/17.85 **t.** ⁑ 3.95 – **23 rm** ⊏ 40.00/59.50 **t.** – SB (weekends only) 75.00/
    130.00 **st.**

    at Ingleby Greenhow E : 2½ m. on Ingleby Greenhow rd – ⊠ ⊛ 0642 Great Ayton :

⌂ **Manor House Farm** ⤸, TS9 6RB, SE : 4¼ m. by B 1257 ℘ 722384, ≤, ⇗ – ⥱⟵ 🅿. ⁒
    closed 19 to 29 December – **M** (by arrangement) ⁑ 3.70 – **3 rm** ⊏ (dinner included)
    37.00/74.00 **st.** – SB 63.00/68.00 **st.**

Humbs. 402 S 21 Great Britain G. – pop. 8 970 – ECD : Wednesday –
⊠ York – ⊛ 0377 Driffield.

Exc. : Burton Agnes Hall★ *AC*, NE : 6 m. by A 166 – Sledmere House★ *AC*, NW : 8 m. by A 166
and B 1252.

🛏 Driffield, Sunderlandwick ℘ 253116 – 🛏 Hainsworth Park, Brandesburton ℘ 0964 (Hornby)
2362.

◆London 201 – ◆Kingston-upon-Hull 21 – Scarborough 22 – York 29.

🏨 **Bell** (Best Western), 46 Market Pl., YO25 7AP, ℘ 256661, Fax 253228, ℟₆, ≘s, 🔲, squash
    – ⥱⟵ rest 📺 ☎ 🕭 🅿 – 🔬 250. 🖭 🆎 ⑩ 𝘝𝘐𝘚𝘈. ⁒
    M (dinner only and Sunday lunch)/dinner a la carte 12.00/20.00 **st.** ⁑ 4.00 – **11 rm** ⊏ 65.00/
    91.00 **st.**, 3 suites – SB (weekends only) 100.00 **st.**

    at North Dalton SW : 7 m. by A 164 and A 163 on B 1246 – ⊠ York – ⊛ 0377 Middleton-
    on-the-Wolds :

🏠 **Star Inn,** Warter Rd, YO25 9UX, ℘ 217688 – 📺 ☎ 🅿. 🖭 𝘝𝘐𝘚𝘈. ⁒
    M 9.95 **t.** and a la carte ⁑ 3.30 – **7 rm** ⊏ 29.90/39.90 **t.**

⊚ ATS 14 Westgate ℘ 252386/253628

LES GUIDES VERTS MICHELIN

Paysages, monuments
Routes touristiques
Géographie
Histoire, Art
Itinéraires de visite
Plans de villes et de monuments

Essex 404 V 28 – pop. 4 026 – ECD : Wednesday – ⊛ 0371.

◆London 42 – ◆Cambridge 27 – Chelmsford 13 – Colchester 24.

🏨 **Saracen's Head** (Forte), High St., CM6 1AG, ℘ 873901, Fax 875743 – ⥱⟵ rest 📺 ☎ 🅿 –
    🔬 40. 🖭 🆎 ⑩ 𝘝𝘐𝘚𝘈. ⁒
    M (bar lunch Monday to Saturday)/dinner 15.95 **st.** and a la carte ⁑ 5.00 – ⊏ 8.50 – **24 rm**
    70.00/90.00 **st.** – SB (except Christmas) 86.00/116.00 **st.**

%%% **Starr** with rm, Market Pl., CM6 1AX, ℘ 874321, Fax 876337 – ⥱⟵ 📺 ☎ 🅿. 🖭 🆎 𝘝𝘐𝘚𝘈.
    closed first week January – **M** (closed Saturday lunch and Sunday dinner) 12.00/
    22.50 **t.** and lunch a la carte ⁑ 5.50 – **8 rm** ⊏ 52.00/80.00 **st.** – SB (weekends only) 112.00/
    137.00 **st.**

Lincs. 402 404 S 25 – see Grantham.

Humbs. 402 404 T 23 – pop. 91 532 – ECD : Thursday – ⊛ 0472 Grimsby.

🛏 Littlecoates Rd ℘ 342823 Y.

✈ Humberside Airport : ℘ 0652 (Barnetby) 688456, Fax 680524, W : 13 m. by A 46 and A 18 Y.

🚩 The National Fishing Heritage, Alexandra Dock, DN31 1UF ℘ 342422 BZ.

◆London 172 – Boston 50 – Lincoln 36 – ◆Sheffield 75.

Plan on next page

🏨 **Forte Posthouse,** Littlecoates Rd, DN34 4LX, ℘ 350295, Telex 527776, Fax 241354, ≤,
    ⇗ – ⫼ ⥱⟵ rm 📺 ☎ 🅿 – 🔬 150. 🖭 🆎 ⑩ 𝘝𝘐𝘚𝘈   Y **c**
    M a la carte approx. 17.50 **t.** ⁑ 4.65 – ⊏ 6.95 – **52 rm** 53.50 **st.** – SB (weekends only)
    90.00 **st.**

🏨 **St. James** (Forte), St. James Sq., DN31 1EP, ℘ 359771, Telex 527741, Fax 241427, ≘s –
    ⫼ ⥱⟵ rm 📺 ☎ 🅿 – 🔬 65. 🖭 🆎 ⑩ 𝘝𝘐𝘚𝘈 𝘑𝘊𝘉   AZ **n**
    M a la carte 12.95/22.65 **st.** ⁑ 5.50 – ⊏ 9.50 – **125 rm** 50.00 **st.**

⊚ ATS 2 Abbey Rd ℘ 358151

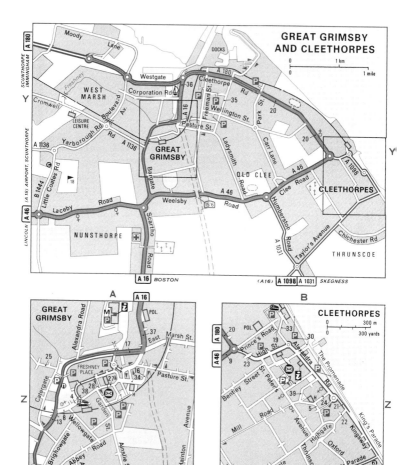

GREAT GRIMSBY AND CLEETHORPES

GREAT GRIMSBY

CLEETHORPES

Do not mix up:

Comfort of hotels	🏨🏨🏨🏨 ... 🏠, 🛏, ⌂
Comfort of restaurants	XXXXX ... X
Quality of the cuisine	✿✿✿, ✿✿, ✿, **Meals**

♦London 86 – ♦Cambridge 41 – ♦Norwich 23.

↑ **Church Cottage** without rest., Breckles, NR17 1EW, N : 1 ½ m. by A 1075 ✆ 498286, Fax 498320, ☖, 🗱 – ℗, 🗱
closed Christmas and New Year – **3 rm** ⚏ 16.00/32.00 **s.**

GREAT LANGDALE Cumbria – see Ambleside.

GREAT LONGSTONE Derbs. O 24 – see Bakewell.

When visiting Scotland,
use the Michelin Green Guide "Scotland".
– *Detailed descriptions of places of interest*
– *Touring programmes*
– *Maps and street plans*
– *The history of the country*
– *Photographs and drawings of monuments, beauty spots, houses...*

GREAT MALVERN Heref. and Worcs. ⚏ ⚏ N 27 – pop. 30 153 – ECD : Wednesday – ☺ 0684 Malvern.

🏰 Wood Farm, Malvern Wells ✆ 573905, S : 2 m. by A 449 A.

🎪 Winter Gdns Complex, Grange Rd, WR14 3HB ✆ 892289 B.

♦London 127 – ♦Birmingham 34 – ♦Cardiff 66 – Gloucester 24.

Plan on next page

🏠 **Priory Park,** 4 Avenue Rd, WR14 3AG, ✆ 565194, Fax 893603, 🗱 – 📺 ☎ ℗. 🖿 *VISA*. 🗱   **B x**
M (booking essential) 14.00/20.00 **st.** – **6 rm** ⚏ 38.00/68.00 **st.** – SB 58.00/76.00 **st.**

🏠 **Cotford,** 51 Graham Rd, WR14 2HU, ✆ 574680, 🗱 – 📺 ☎ ℗. 🖿 *VISA*   **B o**
M (dinner only) 16.00 ♷ 3.50 – **16 rm** ⚏ 33.00/58.00 **st.** – SB (weekends only) 76.00/84.00 **st.**

↑ **Sidney House,** 40 Worcester Rd, WR14 4AA, ✆ 574994, ⇐ – ⇙ rest 📺 ℗. 🖿 *AE* *VISA*.   **B s**
🗱
closed Christmas and New Year – **M** (by arrangement) 15.00 **st.** – **8 rm** ⚏ 20.00/59.00 **st.**

↑ **Red Gate,** 32 Avenue Rd, WR14 3BJ, ✆ 565013, Fax 565013, 🗱 – ⇙ 📺 ℗. 🖿 *VISA*   **B r**
🗱
closed 2 weeks April and Christmas – **M** (by arrangement) 14.00 **st.** ♷ 3.75 – **7 rm** ⚏ 28.00/54.00 **st.** – SB 78.00/92.00 **st.**

at Welland SE : 4 ½ m. by A 449 on A 4104 – A – ⊠ Great Malvern – ☺ 0684 Hanley Swan :

🏠 **Holdfast Cottage** ⌖, Marlbank Rd, WR13 6NA, W : ¾ m. on A 4104 ✆ 310288, « 17C country cottage », 🗱 – ⇙ 📺 ℗. 🖿 *VISA*
M (dinner only) 16.00 **st.** ♷ 4.95 – **8 rm** ⚏ 40.00/76.00 **st.** – SB 98.00/116.00 **st.**

at Malvern Wells S : 2 m. on A 449 – ⊠ ☺ 0684 Malvern :

🏨 **Cottage in the Wood** ⌖, Holywell Rd, WR14 4LG, ✆ 573487, Fax 560662, ⇐ Severn and Evesham Vales, 🗱 – ⇙ rest 📺 ☎ ℗. 🖿 *VISA*   **A z**
M 9.95/26.00 **st.** and a la carte ♷ 7.50 – **20 rm** ⚏ 58.00/130.00 **st.** – SB (except Christmas and New Year) 96.00/150.00 **st.**

🏠 **Essington** ⌖, Holywell Rd, WR14 4LQ, ✆ 561177, ⇐, 🗱 – 📺 ℗. 🖿 *VISA*   **A e**
M (booking essential) (dinner only) 14.00 **st.** ♷ 5.75 – **9 rm** ⚏ 31.00/60.00 **t.** – SB 80.00/84.00 **st.**

↑ **Old Vicarage,** Hanley Rd, WR14 4PH, ✆ 572585, ⇐, 🗱 – 📺 ℗   **A c**
M (by arrangement) 15.00 **st.** ♷ 5.50 – **6 rm** ⚏ 30.00/48.00 **st.** – SB (winter only) 69.00/94.00 **st.**

XX ☺ **Croque-en-Bouche** (Marion Jones), 221 Wells Rd, WR14 4HF, ✆ 565612 – ⇙. 🖿 *VISA*   **A u**
closed Sunday to Tuesday, 2 weeks May, 2 weeks September and Christmas-New Year –
M (booking essential) (dinner only) 33.50 **st.** ♷ 4.80
Spec. Sushi selections, Roast leg of lamb with couscous, preserved lemon and pimiento, Salads and herbs from the garden.

at Wynds Point S : 4 m. on A 449 – ⊠ Great Malvern – ☺ 0684 Colwall :

🏠 **Malvern Hills,** Jubilee Drive, British Camp, WR13 6DW, ✆ 40237, Fax 40327, 🗱 – 📺 ☎ ℗. 🖿 *VISA*   **A s**
M *(closed Sunday dinner to non-residents)* (bar lunch Monday to Saturday)/dinner 15.00 **st.** ♷ 4.50 – **16 rm** ⚏ 30.00/65.00 **st.** – SB (except Bank Holidays) 70.00/100.00 **st.**

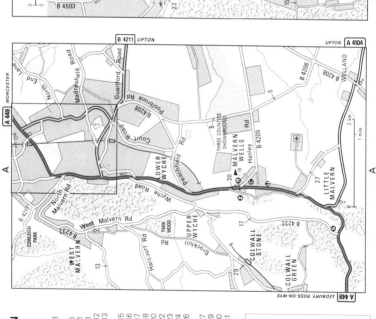

GREAT MALVERN

210

Town plans
roads most used
by traffic and those
on which guide listed
hotels and restaurants
stand are fully drawn;
the beginning only
of lesser roads
is indicated.

GREAT MILTON Oxon. 408 404 Q 28 – see Oxford.

GREAT MISSENDEN Bucks. 404 R 28 – pop. 7 429 (inc. Prestwood) – ECD : Thursday – ✪ 0494.

•London 34 – Aylesbury 10 – Maidenhead 19 – ♦Oxford 35.

XX **La Petite Auberge,** 107 High St., HP16 0BB, ℰ 865370 – ⟐ 𝑽𝑰𝑺𝑨
closed Sunday and 3 weeks Christmas – **M** - French (dinner only) a la carte 22.80/25.70 **t.**

GREAT OFFLEY Herts. 404 S 28 – pop. 1 365 – ✉ Hitchin – ✪ 0462 Offley.

•London 40 – Bedford 14 – ♦Cambridge 29 – Luton 6.

⌂ Red Lion, Kings Walden Rd, SG5 3DZ, ℰ 768281, Fax 768281, ☞ – 𝐓𝐕 ☎ 🅿. ⋙
5 rm.

GREAT RISSINGTON Glos. – see Bourton-on-the-Water.

GREAT SNORING Norfolk 404 W 25 – pop. 180 – ✉ ✪ 0328 Fakenham.

•London 115 – ♦Cambridge 68 – ♦Norwich 28.

▥ **Old Rectory** ⟿, Barsham Rd, NR21 0HP, ℰ 820597, Fax 820048, « Country house atmosphere », ☞ – ✦⟿ rest 𝐓𝐕 ☎ 🅿. ⟐ ⓞ. ⋙
closed 24 to 27 December – **M** (booking essential) (dinner only) 22.50 **t.** – **6 rm** ⊂ 68.00/ 87.50 **t.** – SB (November-March except Bank Holidays) 120.00/159.00 **st.**

GREAT TEW Oxon. 408 404 P 28 – pop. 157 – ✪ 060 883.

•London 75 – ♦Birmingham 50 – Gloucester 42 – ♦Oxford 21.

⌂ **Falkland Arms,** OX7 4DB, ℰ 653, Fax 656, « 17C inn in picturesque village », ☞ – 𝐓𝐕. ⋙
M *(closed Sunday and Monday)* (in bar) (lunch only) approx. 9.25 **st.** – **4 rm** ⊂ 30.00/ 48.00 **st.**

Pour un bon usage des plans de ville, voir les signes conventionnels.

GREAT YARMOUTH Norfolk 404 Z 26 Great Britain G. – pop. 54 777 – ECD : Thursday – ✪ 0493.

Envir. : The Broads★.

🏌 Gorleston, Warren Rd ℰ 661911, S : by A 12 – 🏌 Beach House, Caister-on-Sea ℰ 720421.

🛈 Town Hall, Hall Quay, NR30 2PX ℰ 846345 – Marine Parade, NR30 2EJ ℰ 842195 (summer only).

•London 126 – ♦Cambridge 81 – ♦Ipswich 53 – ♦Norwich 20.

🏨 **Carlton,** 1-5 Kimberley Terr., Marine Par., NR30 3JE, ℰ 855234, Fax 852220 – ▯ 𝐓𝐕 ☎ ♿
⟸ – ⚖ 150. ⟐ ⟐ ⓞ 𝑽𝑰𝑺𝑨
M *(closed Saturday lunch)* 6.95/28.50 **st.** and dinner a la carte ⓘ 6.95 – **88 rm** ⊂ 56.00/ 88.50 **st.**, 2 suites – SB 79.00/90.00 **st.**

🏨 **Dolphin,** 14-15 Albert Sq., NR30 3JH, ℰ 855070, Fax 853798, ℐ₆, ⇌, ♨ heated, ☞ – 𝐓𝐕 ☎ 🅿. ⚖ 130. ⟐ ⟐ ⓞ 𝑽𝑰𝑺𝑨
M 13.50/20.00 **st.** and a la carte ⓘ 5.00 – **49 rm** ⊂ 55.00/85.00 **st.** – SB (winter and spring only) 65.00/100.00 **st.**

🏨 **Embassy,** Camperdown, NR30 3JB, ℰ 843135, Fax 331064 – ▯ 𝐓𝐕 ☎. ⟐ 𝑽𝑰𝑺𝑨
M (dinner only and Sunday lunch)/dinner 15.00 ⓘ 3.00 – **24 rm** ⊂ 27.50/65.00 **t.** – SB 54.00/68.00 **st.**

at Gorleston-on-Sea S : 3 m. on A 12 – ✉ ✪ 0493 Great Yarmouth :

🏨 **Cliff** (Best Western), Cliff Hill, NR31 6DH, ℰ 662179, Fax 653617, ☞ – 𝐓𝐕 ☎ 🅿 – ⚖ 120. ⟐ ⟐ ⓞ 𝑽𝑰𝑺𝑨. ⋙
M 15.50/18.50 **t.** and a la carte ⓘ 6.00 – **38 rm** ⊂ 62.00/110.00 **t.**, 1 suite – SB (weekends only) 90.00/120.00 **st.**

◍ ATS Suffling Rd ℰ 858211

GRENOSIDE S. Yorks. 402 408 404 P 23 – see Sheffield.

GRETA BRIDGE Durham 402 O 20 – ✪ 0833 Teesdale.

•London 253 – ♦Carlisle 63 – ♦Leeds 63 – ♦Middlesbrough 32.

▥ **Morritt Arms,** DL12 9SE, ℰ 27232, Fax 27392, ⟍, ☞ – 𝐓𝐕 ☎ ⟸ 🅿. ⟐ ⟐ 𝑽𝑰𝑺𝑨
M (bar lunch Monday to Saturday)/dinner 22.00 **st.** ⓘ 4.50 – **16 rm** ⊂ 50.00/68.00 **st.** – SB (except Christmas-New Year) 88.00/124.00 **st.**

GRIMSBY Humbs. 402 404 T 23 – see Great Grimsby.

GRIMSTON Norfolk – see King's Lynn.

GRINDLEFORD Derbs. 402 408 404 P 24 – ✉ Sheffield (S. Yorks) – ✪ 0433 Hope Valley.

•London 165 – Derby 31 – ♦Manchester 34 – ♦Sheffield 10.

🏨 Maynard Arms, Main Rd, S30 1HP, ℰ 630321, Fax 630445, ≤, ☞ – 𝐓𝐕 ☎ 🅿 – ⚖ 120
13 rm.

GRINDLETON Lancs. [402] M 22 – pop. 1 451 (inc. West Bradford) – ✉ ✆ 0200 Bolton-by-Bowland.

◆London 241 – ◆Blackpool 38 – Lancaster 25 – ◆Leeds 45 – ◆Manchester 33.

⌂ **Harrop Fold Country Farmhouse** 🐑, Harrop Fold, BB7 4PJ, N : 2 ¾ m. by Slaidburn Rd ☎ 447600, ≤, « 17C longhouse », 🌳 – [TV] ☎ [P]. [AE] [VISA]. ✖
M (residents only) (dinner only) 18.00 **st.** 🍷 3.50 – **8 rm** ☕ 40.50/61.50 **st.** – SB (weekdays only) 89.00/114.00 **st.**

GRINDON Staffs. – see Leek.

GRIZEDALE Cumbria [402] K 20 – see Hawkshead.

☞ *Michelin puts no plaque or sign on the hotels and restaurants mentioned in this Guide.*

GUILDFORD

Friary Centre . . . . Y
High Street . . . . Y
Market Street . . . . Y 18
North Street . . . . Y
Tungsgate Shopping Centre . . . . . Y

Bedford Road . . . . Y 2
Bridge Street . . . . Y 3
Castle Street . . . . Y 5
Chertsey Street . . . . Y 6
Commercial Road . . . . Y 8
Eastgate Gardens . . . . Y 9
Friary Bridge . . . . Y 12
Ladymead . . . . Z 13
Leapale Lane . . . . Y 15
Leapale Road . . . . Y 16
Leas Road . . . . Y 17
Mary Road . . . . Y 19
Midleton Road . . . . Z 20
Millbrook . . . . Y 21
New Inn Lane . . . . Z 22
One Tree Hill Road . . . . Z 24
Onslow Street . . . . Y 25
Park Street . . . . Y 27
Quarry Street . . . . Y 28
Stoughton Road . . . . Z 30
Trood's Lane . . . . Z 31
Tungsgate . . . . Y 33
Warwick's Bench . . . . Y 34
Woodbridge Road . . . . Z 37

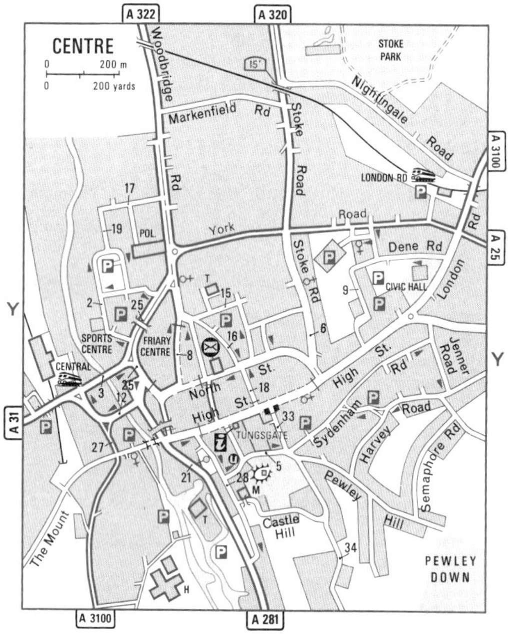

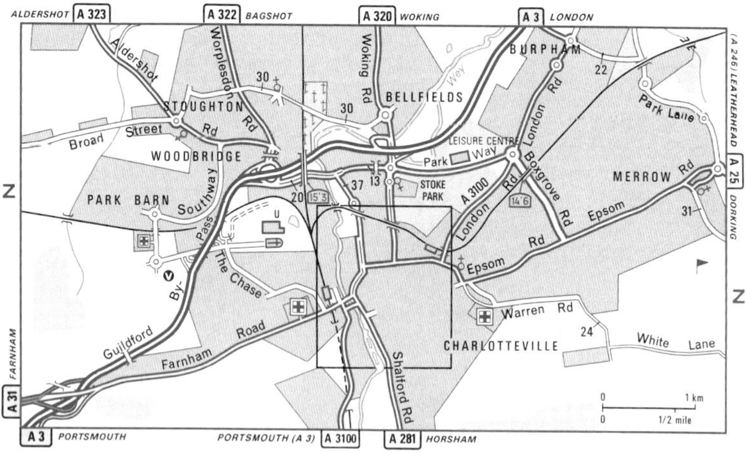

🛃 The Undercroft, 72 High St., GU1 3HE ℰ 444007 Y.

◆London 33 – ◆Brighton 43 – Reading 27 – ◆Southampton 49.

Plans on preceding page

🏨 **Forte Crest,** Egerton Rd, GU2 5XZ, ℰ 574444, Fax 302960, *Ᏺ*, ☎, 🔲, *⊶* – ⇔ rm 📺 ☎   Z   v
  & 🄿 – 🔬 100. 🄰 🄰🄴 🅅🅸🅂🄰 🄹🄲🄱
  M 16.95 **st.** and a la carte 🍴 6.60 – ☑ 9.95 – **109 rm** 99.00 **st.**, 2 suites – SB (weekends only)
104.00 **st.**

XX **Rumwong,** 16-18 London Rd, GU1 2AF, ℰ 36092 – 🔲. 🄰 🅅🅸🅂🄰   Z
closed Monday and last 2 weeks July – **M** Thai 15.00/17.50 **t.** and a la carte 🍴 4.75.

XX **Café de Paris,** 35 Castle St., GU1 3UQ, ℰ 34896 – 🄰 🄰🄴 🄾 🅅🅸🅂🄰   Y   u
closed Saturday lunch, Sunday and Bank Holidays – **M** - French 11.80 **t.** and a la carte
🍴 4.30.

at Albury E : 6¾ m. by A 25 – Z – on A 248 – ⊠ Guildford – ✆ 0483 Shere

🏠 **Drummond Arms,** GU5 9AG, ℰ 202039 – 📺 🄿. 🄰 🅅🅸🅂🄰 . *⊶*
M (in bar Sunday dinner and Monday) 14.95 **t.** and a la carte 🍴 5.35 – ☑ 6.00 – **7 rm**
38.00/50.00 **st.**

at Bramley S : 3 m. on A 281 – Z – ⊠ ✆ 0483 Guildford :

🏨 **Bramley Grange** (Best Western), Horsham Rd, GU5 0BL, ℰ 893434, Fax 893835, *⊶* –
  📺 ☎ 🄿 – 🔬 70. 🄰 🄰🄴 🅅🅸🅂🄰
  M (closed lunch Saturday) 12.50/25.00 **st.** and a la carte 🍴 5.75 – **45 rm** ☑ 65.00/105.00 **st.**
– SB 60.00/165.00 **st.**

XX **Le Berger,** 4a High St., GU5 0HB, ℰ 894037, *⊶* – ⇔. 🄰 🄰🄴 🄾 🅅🅸🅂🄰
closed Sunday, Monday and 2 weeks January – **M** 16.50 **t.** and a la carte 🍴 4.25.

Zum besseren Verständnis der Stadtpläne lesen Sie bitte die Zeichenerklärung.

🛃 Fountain St., TS14 6QF ℰ 633801.

◆London 250 – ◆Leeds 68 – Middlesbrough 8 – Scarborough 42.

XX Hideaway, 61b Westgate (1st floor), TS14 6AF, ℰ 635453, Fax 630076.

◆London 119 – ◆Cambridge 67 – King's Lynn 29 – ◆Norwich 20.

XX **Tollbridge,** Dereham Rd, NR20 5NU, S : ½ m. on B 1110 ℰ 359, ≤, « Attractive setting
on banks of River Wensum », *⊶* – 🄿. 🄰 🅅🅸🅂🄰
closed Sunday dinner and Monday – **M** (booking essential) (dinner only and Sunday
lunch)/dinner a la carte 16.85/23.20 🍴 4.25.

◆London 95 – ◆Birmingham 47 – Gloucester 30 – ◆Oxford 39.

🏠 **Guiting Guest House,** Post Office Lane, GL54 5TZ, ℰ 850470, « 16C farmhouse » –
  ⇔ rm 📺 🄿
  M (by arrangement) 12.50 **st.** – **3 rm** ☑ 17.50/45.00 **st.**

◆London 132 – Lincoln 32 – ◆Nottingham 12 – ◆Sheffield 40.

🏨 **Unicorn,** Gunthorpe Bridge, NG14 7FB, SE : 1½ m. ℰ 663612, Fax 664801 – 📺 ☎ 🄿. 🄰
  🄰🄴 🅅🅸🅂🄰
  M (grill rest.) a la carte 7.55/15.45 **st.** 🍴 3.75 – **16 rm** ☑ 37.50/57.50 **st.** – SB 47.50/95.00 **st.**

🛃 Toppesfield Hall, IP7 5DN ℰ 822922.

◆London 72 – ◆Cambridge 49 – Colchester 17 – ◆Ipswich 10.

🏠 **Edgehill,** 2 High St., IP7 5AP, ℰ 822458, *⊶* – ⇔ 📺 ☎ 🄿
closed 24 December-1 January – **M** (by arrangement) 15.00 **st.** 🍴 4.50 – **9 rm** ☑ 35.00/
65.00 **st.** – SB (except Bank Holidays) 55.00/100.00 **st.**

🏠 **Gables,** 63-67 Angel St., IP7 5EY, ℰ 827169, *⊶* – 📺 ☎ 🄿
closed 25-26 December and 31 December-1 January – **M** (by arrangement) 16.00 **st.** 🍴 4.00
– **4 rm** ☑ 22.00/64.00 **st.**

🏠 Odds and Ends House, 131 High St., IP7 5EG, ℰ 822032, *⊶* – ⇔ rest 📺 & 🄿
9 rm.

🛆 Wellhurst G. & C.C., North St., Hellingly ✍ 042 53 (Fordingbridge) 3636, N : 2 m. by A 267.

🛈 The Library, Western Rd, BN27 3DN ✍ 840604.

◆London 57 – ◆Brighton 23 – Eastbourne 7 – Hastings 20.

🏨 Boship Farm, Lower Dicker, BN27 4AT, NW : 3 m. by A 295 on A 22 ✍ 844826, Fax 843945, ⛳, 🐝, ⬛ heated, 🌳, ℀ – ✎ rm 📺 ☎ ❶ – 🛦 120
44 rm, 2 suites.

🏨 **Forte Travelodge** without rest., Boship Roundabout, Lower Dicker, BN27 4DT, NW : 3 m. by A 295 on A 22 ✍ 844556, Reservations (Freephone) 0800 850950 – ✎ 📺 ♿ ❶.
🈁 🈁 🈁 ℀
40 rm 31.95 t.

at Magham Down NE : 2 m. by A 295 on A 271 – ⊠ Hailsham – ✆ 0323 Eastbourne :

🏨 **Olde Forge**, BN27 1PN, ✍ 842893 – 📺 ☎ ❶. 🈁 🈁 ⓞ 🈁
closed 24 December-7 January – **M** (lunch residents only)/dinner 11.50 **t**. and a la carte
🍴 3.95 – **8 rm** ⊡ 32.00/50.00 **st**. – SB (except Bank Holidays) 65.00/96.00 **st**.

℀℀ **Sykes House,** CV36 5BT, ✍ 740976, « 16C house », 🌳 – ❶. 🈁
closed Sunday to Tuesday and 24 to 30 December – **M** (booking essential) (dinner only) 32.50 **t**. 🍴 4.25.

*En saison, surtout dans les stations fréquentées, il est prudent de retenir à l'avance.
Cependant, si vous ne pouvez pas occuper la chambre que vous avez retenue,
prévenez immédiatement l'hôtelier.*

*Si vous écrivez à un hôtel à l'étranger, joignez à votre lettre
un coupon-réponse international (disponible dans les bureaux de poste).*

🛆 Halifax Bradley Hall, Holywell Green ✍ 374108, S : by A 6112 – 🛆 West End, Highroad Well ✍ 353608, NW : 3 m. – 🛆 Union Lane, Ogden ✍ 244171, N : 4 m. on A 629 – 🛆 Ryburn, Norland, Sowerby Bridge ✍ 831355, S : 3 m. – 🛆 Elland, Hammerstones Leach Lane, Hullen Edge ✍ 372505, S : 4 m. by A 629 – 🛆 Lightcliffe, Knowle Top Rd ✍ 202459, E : 3 m. by A 649.

🛈 Piece Hall, HX1 1RE ✍ 368725.

◆London 205 – Bradford 8 – Burnley 21 – ◆Leeds 15 – ◆Manchester 28.

🏨 **Holdsworth House,** Holmfield, HX2 9TG, N : 3 m. by A 629 on Holdsworth Rd ✍ 240024, Fax 245174, « Part 17C house », 🌳 – ✎ 📺 ☎ ♿ ❶ – 🛦 80. 🈁 🈁 ⓞ
🈁
closed 24 to 30 December – **M** (closed Saturday lunch) 12.50/19.50 **st**. and a la carte –
⊡ 5.00 – **36 rm** 69.90/86.50 **st**., 4 suites – SB (weekends only) 90.00/115.00 **st**.

🏨 **Imperial Crown,** 42-46 Horton St., HX1 1BR, ✍ 342342, Fax 349866, park – 📺 ☎ ❶ –
🛦 130. 🈁 🈁 ⓞ 🈁 ℀
M (closed Sunday dinner) (dinner only and Sunday lunch)/dinner 13.75 **t**. and a la carte –
39 rm ⊡ 63.50/74.50 **st**., 2 suites – SB (weekends only) 112.00/150.00 **st**.

at Luddenden Foot W : 4¼ m. on A 646 – ⊠ ✆ 0422 Halifax :

🏨 **Collyers,** Burnley Rd, HX2 6AH, on A 646 ✍ 882624, Fax 883897 ✎ rm 📺 ☎ ❶. 🈁 🈁
ⓞ 🈁
closed first week January – **M** a la carte 13.65/16.20 **st**. 🍴 4.65 – **6 rm** ⊡ 23.00/55.00 **st**. –
SB (except Christmas) (weekends only) 70.00/90.00 **st**.

at Elland S : 3½ m. by A 629 – ⊠ ✆ 0422 Halifax :

℀ **Berties Bistro,** 7-10 Town Hall Buildings, HX5 0EU, ✍ 371724, Fax 372830 – ☰. 🈁 🈁
🈁
closed Monday, 26 December and 1 January – **M** (dinner only) a la carte 9.40/18.40 **t**.
🍴 3.50.

🛞 ATS Hope St. ✍ 365892/360819

◆London 48 – ◆Brighton 16 – Eastbourne 16 – Royal Tunbridge Wells 19.

🏨 **Halland Forge,** BN8 6PW, on A 22 ✍ 840456, Fax 840773, 🌳, park – 📺 ☎ ❶. 🈁 🈁 ⓞ
🈁 ℀
M 16.95/21.50 **t**. and a la carte 🍴 5.30 – ⊡ 8.00 – **20 rm** 46.00/58.00 **t**. – SB 106.00/
141.10 **st**.

HALTWHISTLE Northd 401 402 M 19 Great Britain G. – pop. 3 522 – ✆ 0434.

Envir. : Hadrian's Wall★★, N : 4½ m. by A 6079 – Housesteads★★ *AC*, NE : 6 m. by B 6318 – Roman Army Museum★ *AC*, NW : 5 m. by A 69 and B 6318 – Vindolanda (Museum★) *AC*, NE : 5 m. by A 69 – Steel Rig (≼★) NE : 5½ m. by B 6318.

⛳ Greenhead ✆ (06977) 47367, W : 3 m. by A 69.

🏛 Church Hall, Main St., NE49 0BE ✆ 322002.

◆London 335 – ◆Carlisle 22 – ◆Newcastle upon Tyne 37.

⌂ **Ashcroft** without rest., Lantys Lonnen, NE49 0DA, ✆ 320213, « Gardens » – ⌿⇌ 🅿. ✻ closed 20 December-5 January – **8 rm** ⟂ 15.00/32.00.

HAMBLETON Leics. – see Oakham.

HAMBROOK Avon 403 404 M 29 – see Bristol.

HAMSTEAD MARSHALL Berks. 403 404 P29 – see Newbury.

HAMSTERLEY Durham 401 402 O 19 – pop. 384 – ✉ ✆ 0388 Bishop Auckland.

◆London 260 – ◆Carlisle 75 – ◆Middlesbrough 30 – ◆Newcastle upon Tyne 22.

⌂ **Grove House** ⤳, Hamsterley Forest, DL13 3NL, W : 3¾ m. via Bedburn ✆ 88203, ☞ – ⌿⇌ 🅿. ✻
M 12.00 – **3 rm** ⟂ 19.00/40.00 st.

HANDFORTH Ches. 402 403 404 N 23 – see Wilmslow.

HANSLOPE Bucks. 404 R 27 – see Milton Keynes.

HANWOOD Shrops. 402 403 L 25 – see Shrewsbury.

HAREWOOD W. Yorks. 402 P 22 – pop. 3 429 – ✉ ✆ 0532 Leeds.

◆London 214 – Harrogate 9 – ◆Leeds 10 – York 20.

🏨 **Harewood Arms,** Harrogate Rd, LS17 9LH, on A 61 ✆ 886566, Fax 886064, ☞ – 📺 ☎
🅿. ◪ ⒶⒺ ⓞ *VISA* ✻
M 10.50/16.00 **t.** and dinner a la carte – **24 rm** ⟂ 65.00/78.00 **t.** – SB (except Christmas) (weekends only) 90.00/110.00 **st.**

HARBERTONFORD Devon 403 I 32 – pop. 970 – ECD : Saturday – ✉ ✆ 0803 Totnes.

◆London 228 – Exeter 28 – ◆Plymouth 24 – Torquay 13.

🏛 **Old Mill Country House** ⤳, TQ9 7SS, NW : 1¼ m. by Woodland Rd ✆ 732349, ⌦, ☞
– 📺 ☎ 🅿. ◪ *VISA*
M (bar lunch Monday to Saturday)/dinner 14.00 **t.** and a la carte ▲ 4.00 – **8 rm** ⟂ 34.50/
65.00 **t.**

HARLOW Essex 404 U 28 – pop. 79 150 – ECD : Wednesday – ✆ 0279.

🏛 Nazeing, Middle St. ✆ 0992 (Nazeing) 893798, SW : 3 m.

◆London 22 – ◆Cambridge 37 – ◆Ipswich 60.

🏨 **Churchgate Manor** (Best Western), Churchgate St., Old Harlow, CM17 OJT, E : 3¼ m. by A 414 and B 183 ✆ 420246, Fax 437720, Ⓕ₄, ⓢ, ◪, ☞ – 📺 ☎ 🅿 – ▲ 170. ◪ ⒶⒺ ⓞ *VISA* ⎰ᴄʙ
M (closed Saturday lunch) 11.95/16.25 **t.** and a la carte ▲ 5.30 – ⟂ 7.95 – **82 rm** 53.50/
82.00 **t.**, 3 suites.

🏨 **Harlow Moat House** (Q.M.H.), Southern Way, CM18 7BA, SE : 2¼ m. by A 1025 on
A 414 ✆ 422441, Telex 81658, Fax 635094 – ⌿⇌ rm 📺 ☎ 🅿 – ▲ 150. ◪ ⒶⒺ ⓞ *VISA* ✻
closed 24 December-2 January – **M** (bar lunch Saturday and Bank Holidays) 16.50 **st.**
and a la carte ▲ 5.00 – **120 rm** ⟂ 40.00/72.00 **st.** – SB (weekends only) 76.00/84.00 **st.**

🏨 **Green Man** (Forte), Mulberry Green, Old Harlow, CM17 0ET, E : 2¼ m. by A 414 and
B 183 ✆ 442521, Fax 626113 – ⌿⇌ rm 📺 ☎ 🅿 – ▲ 60. ◪ ⒶⒺ ⓞ *VISA* ⎰ᴄʙ
M (closed Saturday lunch) 9.95/15.95 **st.** and a la carte ▲ 5.25 – ⟂ 8.50 – **55 rm** 75.00/
85.00 **st.** – SB 86.00 **st.**

🏠 **Travel Inn,** Cambridge Rd, Old Harlow, CM20 2EP, NE : 3¼ m. by A 414 on A 1184
✆ 442545, Fax 452169 – ⌿⇌ rm 📺 ⅄ 🅿. ◪ ⒶⒺ ⓞ *VISA* ✻
M (Beefeater grill) a la carte approx. 16.00 **t.** – ⟂ 4.95 – **38 rm** 33.50 **t.**

🚗 ATS 14 Burnt Mill ✆ 421965

HARNHAM Wilts. 403 404 O 30 – see Salisbury.

HAROME N. Yorks. – see Helmsley.

HARPENDEN Herts. 404 S 28 – pop. 28 589 – ECD : Wednesday – ✆ 0582.

◆London 32 – Luton 6.

🏨 **Harpenden Moat House** (Q.M.H.), 18 Southdown Rd, AL5 1PE, ✆ 764111, Telex
826938, Fax 769858, ☞ – ⌿⇌ rm 📺 ☎ 🅿 – ▲ 100. ◪ ⒶⒺ ⓞ *VISA*
M (closed lunch Saturday and Bank Holidays) 14.95/18.95 **t.** – **51 rm** ⟂ 42.00/120.00 **st.**.
2 suites – SB (July-September) (weekends only) 104.00/124.00 **st.**

🏛 **Glen Eagle,** 1 Luton Rd, AL5 2PX, ✆ 760271, Fax 460819, 🌫 – ⌗ ▤ rest 📺 ☎ 🅿 – 🕰 35. 🖭 AE ⓞ VISA ✀
closed 26 to 30 December – **M** *(closed Sunday dinner)* 11.50/20.00 **st.** and a la carte ⌗ 4.75 – ☑ 7.95 – **49 rm** 69.50/79.50 **st.**

XX **Chef Peking,** 5-6 Church Green, AL5 2TP, ✆ 769358 – ▤. 🖭 AE ⓞ VISA
M - Chinese (Peking. Szechuan) a la carte 14.00/19.80 **t.** ⌗ 4.00.

HARROGATE N. Yorks. 402 P 22 Great Britain G. – pop. 63 637 – ECD : Wednesday – ✆ 0423.

See : Town★.

Exc. : Fountains Abbey★★★ *AC* – Studley Royal★★ *AC* (⇐★ from Anne Boleyn's Seat) – Fountains Hall (Façade★), N : 13 m. by A 61 and B 6265 AY – Harewood House★★ (The Gallery★) *AC*, S : 7½ m. by A 61 BZ.

🖸 Forest Lane Head, ✆ 863158, E : 2 m. by A 59 CY – 🖸 Follifoot Rd, Pannal ✆ 871641, S : 2½ m. by A 61 BZ – 🖸 Oakdale ✆ 567162, NW : ½ m. by A 61 AY – 🖸 Crimple Valley, Hookstone Wood Rd ✆ 883485, SE : 1½ m. by A 61 CZ.

🖸 Royal Baths Assembly Rooms, Crescent Rd, HG1 2RR ✆ 525666.

♦London 211 – Bradford 18 – ♦Leeds 15 – ♦Newcastle Upon Tyne 76 – York 22.

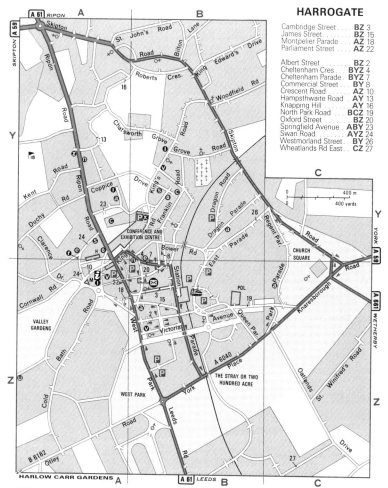

HARROGATE

Cambridge Street	**BZ** 3
James Street	**BZ** 15
Montpelier Parade	**AZ** 18
Parliament Street	**AZ** 22
Albert Street	**BZ** 2
Cheltenham Cres.	**BYZ** 4
Cheltenham Parade	**BYZ** 7
Commercial Street	**BY** 8
Crescent Road	**AZ** 10
Hampsthwaite Road	**AY** 13
Knapping Hill	**AY** 16
North Park Road	**BCZ** 19
Oxford Street	**BZ** 20
Springfield Avenue	**ABY** 23
Swan Road	**AYZ** 24
Westmorland Street	**BY** 26
Wheatlands Rd East	**CZ** 27

🏨 **Nidd Hall** 🐾, Nidd, HG3 3BN, N : 4¼ m. by A 61 on B 6165 ⌂ 771598, Fax 770931, ≼, « 19C manor house », ₤₅, ⌘, ⌂, ⌂, park, ⌘, squash – ▯ ⬚ 🆚 ☎ 🅿 – 🚗 100. 🅰 🅰🅴
AY
⑩ 𝗩𝗜𝗦𝗔 𝗝𝗖𝗕
M – Garden (closed Saturday lunch) 15.95/25.00 **t.** and dinner a la carte ⌂ 7.80 – ⌂ 5.50 –
56 rm 95.00/150.00 **st.**, 3 suites – SB (weekends only) 130.00/190.00 **st.**

🏨 **Old Swan,** Swan Rd, HG1 2SR, ⌂ 500055, Fax 501154, ⌂, park – ▯ 🆚 ☎ 🅿 – 🚗 350.
AY **e**
🅰 🅰🅴 ⑩ 𝗩𝗜𝗦𝗔
M 13.50/20.00 **t.** and a la carte – **125 rm** ⌂ 70.00/100.00 **st.**, 10 suites – SB 99.00/120.00 **st.**

🏨 **Majestic** (Forte), Ripon Rd, HG1 2HU, ⌂ 568972, Fax 502283, ₤₅, ⬚₅, 🔲, ⌂, ⌘, squash
– ▯ 🆚 rm 🆚 ☎ 🅿 – 🚗 300. 🅰 🅰🅴 ⑩ 𝗩𝗜𝗦𝗔 𝗝𝗖𝗕 AY **c**
M (bar lunch Monday to Saturday)/dinner 23.95 **st.** and a la carte ⌂ 9.00 – ⌂ 9.95 – **146 rm**
90.00/110.00 **st.**, 10 suites – SB 138.00/158.00 **st.**

🏨 **Moat House International** (Q.M.H.), Kings Rd, HG1 1XX, ⌂ 500000, Telex 57575,
Fax 524435, ≼ – ▯ 🆚 rm ▤ rest 🆚 ☎ 🅿 – 🚗 350. 🅰 🅰🅴 ⑩ 𝗩𝗜𝗦𝗔 BY **x**
M – Abbey (carving rest.) 12.00/14.95 **st.** ⌂ 5.60 – Boulevard (closed Sunday dinner and
Monday) 14.00/26.00 **st.** and a la carte ⌂ 5.60 – **205 rm** ⌂ 99.00/129.00 **st.**, 9 suites.

🏨 **Crown** (Forte), Crown Pl., HG1 2RZ, ⌂ 567755, Fax 502284 – ▯ 🆚 rm 🆚 ☎ 🅿 – 🚗 300.
AZ **i**
🅰 🅰🅴 ⑩ 𝗩𝗜𝗦𝗔
M (bar lunch)/dinner 16.95 **t.** and a la carte ⌂ 6.45 – ⌂ 8.50 – **116 rm** 60.00/70.00 **st.**,
5 suites – SB 85.45/120.00 **st.**

🏨 **Imperial,** Prospect Pl., HG1 1LA, ⌂ 565071, Fax 500082 – ▯ 🆚 ☎ 🅿 – 🚗 200. 🅰 🅰🅴 ⑩
𝗩𝗜𝗦𝗔 𝗝𝗖𝗕. ⌘ BZ **z**
M (buffet lunch Monday to Saturday)/dinner 16.50 **t.** and a la carte ⌂ 4.75 – **84 rm**
⌂ 80.00/95.00 **st.**, 1 suite – SB 80.00/96.00 **st.**

🏨 **St. George** (Swallow), 1 Ripon Rd, HG1 2SY, ⌂ 561431, Telex 57995, Fax 530037, ⬚₅, 🔲
– ▯ 🆚 🆚 ☎ 🅿 – 🚗 150. 🅰 🅰🅴 ⑩ 𝗩𝗜𝗦𝗔 AY **o**
M (buffet lunch)/dinner 16.95 **st.** and a la carte – **92 rm** ⌂ 85.00/100.00 **st.**, 1 suite –
SB 101.95/133.90 **st.**

🏨 **Studley,** 28 Swan Rd, HG1 2SE, ⌂ 560425, Telex 57506, Fax 530967 – ▯ ▤ rest 🆚 ☎ 🅿.
AZ **x**
🅰 🅰🅴 ⑩ 𝗩𝗜𝗦𝗔. ⌘
closed 25 and 26 December – **M** 15.50 **t.** (dinner) and a la carte 16.25/20.90 **t.** ⌂ 4.20 –
34 rm ⌂ 77.00/95.00 **st.**, 2 suites – SB (weekends only) 100.00 **st.**

🏨 **Balmoral,** 16-18 Franklin Mount, HG1 5EJ, ⌂ 508208, Fax 530652, « Antique furnishings » – 🆚 ☎. 🅰 🅰🅴 𝗩𝗜𝗦𝗔 BY **v**
M (dinner only) 23.50 **st.** ⌂ 4.15 – ⌂ 7.50 – **19 rm** 65.00/90.00 **st.**, 1 suite – SB (weekends
only) 94.00/148.00 **st.**

🏨 **Grants,** Swan Rd, HG1 2SS, ⌂ 560666, Fax 502550 – ▯ ▤ rest 🆚 ☎ 🅿 – 🚗 70. 🅰 🅰🅴
⑩ 𝗩𝗜𝗦𝗔. ⌘ AY **s**
M (bar lunch Monday to Saturday) 14.95 **t.** ⌂ 4.50 – **41 rm** ⌂ 81.50/128.00 **t.**, 1 suite
– SB 65.00/100.00 **st.**

🏨 **Hospitality Inn** (Mt. Charlotte Thistle), Prospect Pl., West Park, HG1 1LB, ⌂ 564601,
Telex 57530, Fax 507508 – ▯ 🆚 ☎ 🅿 – 🚗 150. 🅰 🅰🅴 ⑩ 𝗩𝗜𝗦𝗔. ⌘ BZ **v**
M 8.50/23.50 **st.** and dinner a la carte ⌂ 5.10 – ⌂ 7.50 – **66 rm** 69.00/85.00 **st.**, 5 suites –
SB (weekends only) 80.00/88.00 **st.**

🏨 **Alexandra Court** without rest., 8 Alexandra Rd, HG1 5JS, ⌂ 502764, Fax 523151 – 🆚
🆚 ☎ 🅿. 🅰 𝗩𝗜𝗦𝗔. ⌘ BY **o**
closed 31 December – **14 rm** ⌂ 38.00/55.00 **st.**

🏨 **White House,** 10 Park Par., HG1 5AH, ⌂ 501388, Fax 527973, ⌂ – 🆚 ☎ 🅿. 🅰 🅰🅴 ⑩
𝗩𝗜𝗦𝗔. ⌘ CZ **a**
M 14.95 **t.** and a la carte ⌂ 4.85 – **10 rm** ⌂ 72.50/105.00 **t.** – SB 105.00/200.00 **st.**

🏨 **Gables,** 2 West Grove Rd, HG1 2AD, ⌂ 505625, Fax 561312 – 🆚 ☎ 🅿. 🅰 𝗩𝗜𝗦𝗔 BY **i**
M (lunch by arrangement)/dinner a la carte 14.00 **t.** ⌂ 5.55 – **9 rm** ⌂ 31.00/62.00 **t.** –
SB 78.00/90.00 **st.**

🏨 **Britannia Lodge,** 16 Swan Rd, HG1 2SA, ⌂ 508482, Fax 508482 (ext. 223) – 🆚 rest 🆚
☎ 🅿. 🅰 🅰🅴 ⑩ 𝗩𝗜𝗦𝗔. ⌘ AYZ **r**
M 6.50/12.50 **t.** ⌂ 3.50 – **12 rm** ⌂ 35.00/60.00 **st.** – SB 69.00/84.00 **st.**

🏨 **Alexa House,** 26 Ripon Rd, HG1 2JJ, ⌂ 501988, Fax 504086 – 🆚 rest 🆚 ☎ 🅿. 🅰 ⑩
𝗩𝗜𝗦𝗔. ⌘ AY **n**
M (dinner only) 10.00 **st.** ⌂ 4.50 – **13 rm** ⌂ 30.00/52.00 **st.**

🏨 **Arden House,** 69-71 Franklin Rd, HG1 5EH, ⌂ 509224 – 🆚 ☎ 🅿. 🅰 𝗩𝗜𝗦𝗔 BY **c**
M (dinner only) 13.00 **st.** – **14 rm** ⌂ 23.50/54.00 **st.**

🏨 **Stoney Lea** without rest., 13 Spring Grove, HG1 2HS, ⌂ 501524 – 🆚. ⌘ AY **i**
closed Christmas-New Year – **7 rm** ⌂ 25.00/38.00.

🏨 **Garden House,** 14 Harlow Moor Drive, HG2 0JX, ⌂ 503059 – 🆚 rest 🆚. 🅰 🅰🅴 𝗩𝗜𝗦𝗔. ⌘
M (by arrangement) 10.00 **st.** ⌂ 3.50 – **7 rm** ⌂ 21.00/44.00 **st.** AZ **u**

🏨 **Ashwood House** without rest., 7 Spring Grove, HG1 2HS, ⌂ 560081 – 🆚 🆚. ⌘
closed 24 December-1 January – **10 rm** ⌂ 19.00/48.00 **st.** AY **a**

🏨 **Brookfield House,** 5 Alexandra Rd, HG1 5JS, ⌂ 506646 – 🆚 rest 🆚 🅿. ⌘ BY **s**
M (by arrangement) 12.00 **t.** – **6 rm** ⌂ 35.00/55.00 **st.**

↑ **Abbey Lodge,** 29-31 Ripon Rd, HG1 2JL, ✆ 569712, Fax 530570 – 📺 ☎ 🅿 ⛔ 𝚅𝙸𝚂𝙰
closed 25 to 30 December – **M** 12.95 **t.** ⫿ 5.20 – **19 rm** ⌑ 25.50/55.00 **t.** – SB (October-
April) 65.00 **t.**   AY **z**

↑ **Daryl House,** 42 Dragon Par., HG1 5DA, ✆ 502775 – 📺. ⪩   BY **a**
M (by arrangement) 7.00 **st.** – **6 rm** ⌑ 14.00/30.00 **st.**

↑ **Knox Mill House** ⪩ without rest., Knox Mill Lane, HG3 2AE, N · 1 ½ m. by A 61 AY
✆ 560650, ⪡ – 🅿 ⪩
3 rm ⌑ 38.00 **s.**

XX **Grundy's,** 21 Cheltenham Cres., HG1 1DH, ✆ 502610 – ⛔ 𝔸𝔼 𝚅𝙸𝚂𝙰   BYZ **n**
closed Sunday, 2 weeks January-February, 2 weeks July-August and Bank Holidays – **M**
(dinner only) 13.95 **t.** and a la carte.

XX **Harrogate Brasserie** with rm, 28-30 Cheltenham Par., HG1 1DB, ✆ 505041, Fax 530920
– 📺 ☎ 🅿 ⛔ 𝚅𝙸𝚂𝙰   BY **e**
M 10.00/15.00 **t.** and a la carte ⫿ 4.95 – **13 rm** ⌑ 35.00/65.00 **st.** – SB 70.00/100.00 **st.**

XX **Millers,** 1 Montpellier Mews, HG1 2TG, ✆ 530708 – ⛔ 𝔸𝔼 𝚅𝙸𝚂𝙰   AZ **v**
M a la carte 16.00/29.75 **t.**

X **Drum and Monkey,** 5 Montpellier Gdns, HG1 2TF, ✆ 502650 – ⛔ 𝚅𝙸𝚂𝙰   AZ **v**
closed Sunday and 24 December-2 January – **M** - **Seafood** (booking essential) a la
carte 10.15/21.70 **t.** ⫿ 3.30.

at Markington NW : 8 ¾ m. by A 61 – AY – ✉ ✆ 0423 Harrogate :

🏨 **Hob Green** ⪩, HG3 3PJ, SW : ½ m. ✆ 770031, Fax 771589, ⪡, « Country house in
extensive parkland », ⪩ – 📺 ☎ 🅿 ⛔ 𝔸𝔼 ⓞ 𝚅𝙸𝚂𝙰 𝙹𝙲𝙱
M (bar lunch Monday to Saturday)/dinner a la carte 17.85/26.85 **st.** ⫿ 4.95 – **11 rm**
⌑ 70.00/97.50 **st.**, 1 suite – SB (except Christmas and New Year) 113.00/160.00 **st.**

⬡ ATS Leeds Rd, Pannal ✆ 879194

HARTFIELD E. Sussex **404** U 30 – pop. 2 179 – ✆ 0892 Tunbridge Wells.
♦London 47 – ♦Brighton 28 – Maidstone 25.

↑ **Bolebroke Mill** ⪩, Edenbridge Rd, TN7 4JP, N : 1 ¼ m. by B 2026 on unmarked rd
✆ 770425, « Part early 17C cornmill, original features », ⪩ – ⪧ 📺 🅿 ⛔ 𝔸𝔼 𝚅𝙸𝚂𝙰 . ⪩
March-November – **M** (by arrangement) 16.00 **s.** – **4 rm** ⌑ 43.00/63.00 **s.**

HARTFORD Ches. **402 403 404** M 24 – pop. 4 000 – ✆ 0606 Northwich.
♦London 188 – Chester 15 – ♦Liverpool 31 – ♦Manchester 25.

🏨 Hartford Hall, 81 School Lane, CW8 1PW, ✆ 75711, Fax 782211, ⪩ – 📺 ☎ 🅿 – ⪦ 35
20 rm, 1 suite.

HARTINGTON Derbs. **402 403 404** O 24 – pop. 1 143 – ✉ ✆ 0298 Buxton.
♦London 168 – Derby 36 – ♦Manchester 40 – ♦Sheffield 34 – Stoke-on-Trent 22.

↑ **Biggin Hall** ⪩, Biggin, SK17 ODH, SE : 2 m. by B 5054 ✆ 84451, Fax 84681, ⪡, « 17C
hall », ⪩ – ⪧ rest 📺 🅿 ⛔ 𝔸𝔼 𝚅𝙸𝚂𝙰 . ⪩
M 14.50 **st.** ⫿ 4.50 – ⫿ 3.50 – **14 rm** 27.50/80.00 **st.** – SB (except Christmas-New Year)
59.00/105.00 **st.**

HARTLEBURY Heref. and Worcs. **403** N 26 – pop. 2 491 – ✆ 0299.
♦London 135 – ♦Birmingham 20 – Worcester 11.

🏨 **Forte Travelodge** without rest., Crossway Green, DX11 6DR, S : 2 ½ m. by B 4193
on A 449 (southbound carriageway) ✆ 250553, Reservations (Freephone) 0800 850950 –
📺 ⪤ 🅿 ⛔ 𝚅𝙸𝚂𝙰 . ⪩
32 rm 31.95 **t.**

HARTLEPOOL Cleveland **402** Q 19 – pop. 91 749 – ECD : Wednesday – ✆ 0429.
🏌 Seaton Carew, Tees Rd ✆ 266249 – 🏌 Castle Eden and Peterlee ✆ 836220 – 🏌 Hart Warren
✆ 274398.

✈ Teesside Airport ✆ 0325 (Darlington) 332811, SW : 20 m. by A 689, A 1027, A 135 and
A 67.

🚏 Dept. of Economic Developments & Leisure, Civic Centre, Victoria Rd, TS24 8AY ✆ 266522
ext : 2408.

♦London 263 – Durham 19 – ♦Middlesbrough 9 – Sunderland 21.

🏨 **Grand,** Swainson St., TS24 8AA, ✆ 266345, Fax 265217 – |⫶| 📺 ☎ – ⪦ 150. ⛔ 𝔸𝔼 ⓞ 𝚅𝙸𝚂𝙰
M 6.50/8.50 **st.** and a la carte ⫿ 4.95 – **47 rm** ⌑ 44.95/90.00 **st.**

🏨 **York,** 185-187 York Rd, TS26 9EE, ✆ 867373, Fax 867220 – 📺 ☎. ⛔ 𝔸𝔼 ⓞ 𝚅𝙸𝚂𝙰 . ⪩
M (dinner only) 12.00 **st.** and a la carte ⫿ 4.00 – **14 rm** ⌑ 18.00/48.00 **st.**

at Seaton Carew SE : 2 m. on A 178 – ✆ 0429 Hartlepool :

X **Krimo's,** 8 The Front, TS25 1BS, ✆ 266120 – ⛔ 𝚅𝙸𝚂𝙰
closed Saturday lunch, Sunday, Monday, first 2 weeks August, 25-26 December and
1 January – **M** 9.00 **st.** (lunch) and a la carte 11.80/20.15 **st.** ⫿ 3.70.

⬡ ATS York Rd ✆ 275552

HARVINGTON Heref. and Worcs. **403 404** O27 – see Evesham.

218

Oxon. **403 404** Q 29 – ۞ 0235.

◆London 64 – ◆Oxford 16 – Reading 18 – Swindon 22.

🏨 **Kingswell,** Reading Rd, OX11 0LZ, S : ¾ m. on A 417 ℰ 833043, Telex 83173, Fax 833193
– 📺 ☎ 🄿 – 🔬 30. 🖭 🖭 ⑩ 𝑉𝐼𝑆𝐴 . ⚘
M 11.50/17.50 **t.** and a la carte 🍴 4.95 – **22 rm** ⌫ 60.00/90.00 **st.** – SB (weekends only)
75.00/145.00 **st.**

Essex **404** X 28 – pop. 17 245 – ECD : Wednesday – ۞ 0255.

🚢 Station Rd, Parkeston ℰ 503616.

⛴ to Germany : Hamburg (Scandinavian Seaways) (18 h 30 mn) (summer only) – to
Denmark : Esbjerg (Scandinavian Seaways) (19 h) – to The Netherlands : Hook of Holland
(Stena Sealink Line) – to Sweden : Gothenburg (Scandinavian Seaways) (24 h).

⛴ to Felixstowe (Orwell & Harwich Navigation Co. Ltd) 5 daily (15 mn).

🛈 Essex County Council, Parkeston Quay, CO12 4SP ℰ 506139.

◆London 78 – Chelmsford 41 – Colchester 20 – ◆Ipswich 23.

🏨 **Cliff,** Marine Par., Dovercourt, CO12 3RE, ℰ 503345, Fax 240358, ← – 📺 ☎ 🄿 – 🔬 220.
🖭 🖭 ⑩ 𝑉𝐼𝑆𝐴 ⚘
M 9.25/10.75 **t.** and a la carte 🍴 3.75 – **26 rm** ⌫ 50.00/60.00 **t.**, 1 suite – SB (except
Christmas and New Year) (weekends only) 123.00 **st.**

🍴🍴 **Pier at Harwich** with rm, The Quay, CO12 3HH, ℰ 241212, Fax 322752, ← – 📺 ☎ 🄿. 🖭
🖭 ⑩ 𝑉𝐼𝑆𝐴 ⚘
M - Seafood 11.75/16.00 **t.** and a la carte 🍴 4.95 – ⌫ 4.00 – **6 rm** 45.00/72.50 **st.** –
SB (weekends only) 95.00/160.00 **st.**

🛢 ATS 723 Main Rd, Dovercourt ℰ 508314

*Great Britain and Ireland is now covered
by an Atlas at a scale of 1 inch to 4.75 miles.*

Three easy to use versions: Paperback, Spiralbound and Hardback.

Surrey – see Godalming.

Somerset **403** L 31 – see Crewkerne.

Surrey **404** R 30 – pop. 10 544 – ECD : Wednesday – ۞ 0428.

◆London 47 – ◆Brighton 46 – ◆Southampton 44.

🏨 **Lythe Hill,** Petworth Rd, GU27 3BQ, E : 1 ½ m. on B 2131 ℰ 651251, Fax 644131, ←, ⚘,
park, ⚘ – 📺 ☎ 🄿 – 🔬 60. 🖭 🖭 𝑉𝐼𝑆𝐴
M 17.50 **st.** and a la carte 🍴 6.00 – **Auberge de France - French** (closed Monday) (dinner only
and Sunday lunch)/dinner a la carte 26.50/35.50 **st.** 🍴 6.00 – ⌫ 8.00 – **29 rm** 76.00/95.00 **st.**,
11 suites – SB (except Christmas-New Year) (weekends only) 109.00 **st.**

🏨 **Georgian,** High St., GU27 2JY, ℰ 651555, Fax 661304, ⚘ – 📺 ☎ 🄿 – 🔬 80. 🖭 🖭 ⑩
𝑉𝐼𝑆𝐴
M 15.95 **t.** and a la carte 🍴 4.95 – **23 rm** ⌫ 55.00/70.00 **t.**, 1 suite – SB 89.00/96.00 **st.**

🍴🍴🍴 Morels, 23-27 Lower St., GU27 2NY, ℰ 651462
M - French rest.

Derbs. – see Bakewell.

E. Sussex **404** V 31 – pop. 74 979 – ۞ 0424.

🚢 Beauport Park, Battle Rd, St. Leonards, ℰ 852977, NW : 4 m. by B 2159 AY.

🛈 4 Robertson Terr., TN34 1EZ ℰ 718888 – Fishmarket, The Stade (summer only)

◆London 65 – ◆Brighton 37 – Folkestone 37 – Maidstone 34.

Plan on next page

🏨 **Royal Victoria,** Marina, TN38 0BD, ℰ 445544, Fax 721995, ← – 🛗 ⇔ rm 📺 ☎ – 🔬 70.
🖭 🖭 ⑩ 𝑉𝐼𝑆𝐴   AY **e**
M 12.00/16.00 **t.** and dinner a la carte 🍴 4.50 – **50 rm** ⌫ 33.00/110.00 **t.** – SB 96.00/
110.00 **st.**

🏨 **Beauport Park** (Best Western) ⚘, Battle Rd, TN38 8EA, NW : 3 ½ m. at junction of
A 2100 with B 2159 ℰ 851222, Fax 852465, ←, « Formal garden », ⚏ heated, 🚢, park, ⚘
– 📺 rest 📺 ☎ 🄿 – 🔬 60. 🖭 🖭 ⑩ 𝑉𝐼𝑆𝐴 𝐽𝐶𝐵   AY
M 13.50/15.50 **st.** and a la carte 🍴 4.50 – **23 rm** ⌫ 62.00/95.00 **st.** – SB 110.00 **st.**

🏨 **Cinque Ports,** Summerfields, Bohemia Rd, TN34 1ET, ℰ 439222, Fax 437277 – 📺 ☎ 🄿
– 🔬 250. 🖭 🖭 ⑩ 𝑉𝐼𝑆𝐴   AZ **a**
M 10.50/18.50 **st.** and a la carte 🍴 4.50 – **40 rm** ⌫ 44.00/76.00 **st.** – SB 88.00/122.00 **st.**

🏠 **Parkside House,** 59 Lower Park Rd, TN34 2LD, ℰ 433096, ⚘ – ⇔ 📺 ⚘   BY **e**
M 10.00 **s.** – **5 rm** ⌫ 25.00/48.00 **s.** – SB 56.00/86.00 **st.**

🏠 **Norton Villa** without rest., Hill St., Old Town, TN34 3HU, ℰ 428168, ←, ⚘ – ⇔ 📺 🄿.
⚘   BY **n**
4 rm ⌫ 22.00/40.00 **s.**

HASTINGS
AND ST. LEONARDS

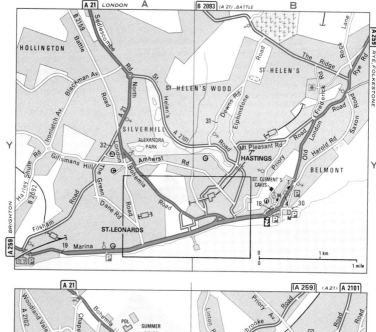

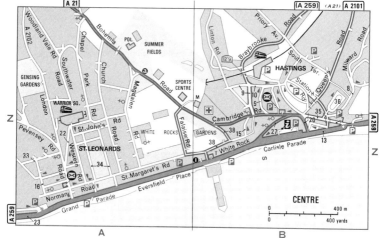

⋔ **Chimes,** 1 St. Matthews Gdns, Silverhill, TN38 0TS, 𝒸 434041, ≈ – 📺 ⌕ AY **a**
M (by arrangement) 10.00 – **9 rm** ⇆ 18.00/38.00 – SB (except July, August and Bank Holidays) (weekends only) 51.00/60.00 **st.**

⋔ **Tower House,** 28 Tower Rd West, TN38 0RG, 𝒸 427217, ≈ – ⇚ rest 📺. 🅰 🅰🅴 ① 𝗩𝗜𝗦𝗔 ⌕
M 10.00 **st.** ⧍ 5.00 – **12 rm** ⇆ 30.00/47.50 **st.** – SB 62.00/77.00 **st.** AY **c**

XX **Röser's**, 64 Eversfield Pl., TN37 6DB, ℰ 712218 – ▣ ▣ ⓞ ▣   BZ   **i**
closed Saturday lunch, Sunday, Monday, first week January and 1 week August – **Meals**
15.95 **st.** (lunch) and a la carte 20.85/30.40 **st.** ⋔ 4.95.

◍ ATS Pondswood Ind. Est., Menzies Rd. St. Leonards ℰ 427780/424567

▣▣▣▣ **HATCH BEAUCHAMP** Somerset ▣▣▣ K 30 – see Taunton.

▣▣▣▣ **HATFIELD** Herts. ▣▣▣ T 28 Great Britain G. – pop. 33 174 – ECD : Monday and Thursday –
● 0707.

See : Hatfield House** *AC.*

▣ Hatfield London, Bedwell Park, Essendon ℰ 42624.

♦London 27 – Bedford 38 – ♦Cambridge 39.

🏨 Hazel Grove (Best Western), Roehyde Way, AL10 9AF, S : 2 m. by B 6426 on A 1001
ℰ 275701, Fax 266033 – ⛶ rm ▣ ☎ & ❷ – 🔬 140. ⌀
76 rm.

🏨 **Comet** (Jarvis), 301 St. Albans Rd West, AL10 9RH, W : 1 m. by B 6426 on A 1057 at
junction with A 1001 ℰ 265411, Fax 264019 – ⛶ rm ▣ ☎ ❷ – 🔬 100. ▣ ▣ ⓞ ▣. ⌀
M (carving rest.) (bar lunch Saturday) 18.95 **st.** ⋔ 6.25 – ⌷ 8.00 – **55 rm** 70.00/110.00 **st.** –
SB (weekends only) 75.00/119.00 **st.**

▣▣▣▣ **HATFIELD HEATH** Essex. ▣▣▣ U 28 – see Bishop's Stortford (Herts.).

▣▣▣▣ **HATHERLEIGH** Devon ▣▣▣ H 31 – pop. 1 355 – ECD : Wednesday – ✉ ● 0837 Okehampton.

♦London 230 – Exeter 29 – ♦Plymouth 38.

🏠 **The Tally Ho**, 14 Market St., EX20 3JN, ℰ 810306, « Part 16C inn », ⤳ – ⛶ rm ▣. ▣
▣ ▣
M *(in bar Sunday, Wednesday and Thursday)* (bar lunch)/dinner 18.00 **st.** and a la carte
⋔ 4.00 – ⌷ 2.75 – **3 rm** 30.00/45.00 **st.**

at Sheepwash NW : 5 ½ m. by A 3072 – ✉ Beaworthy – ● 040 923 (3 fig.) and 0409
(6 fig.) Black Torrington :

🏨 **Half Moon Inn**, The Square, EX21 5NE, ℰ 376, « 17C inn », ⤳ – ▣ ☎ ❷. ▣ ▣
M (bar lunch)/dinner 17.50 **t.** ⋔ 4.25 – **14 rm** ⌷ 25.00/70.00 **t.**

En saison, surtout dans les stations fréquentées, il est prudent de retenir à l'avance.
Cependant, si vous ne pouvez pas occuper la chambre que vous avez retenue,
prévenez immédiatement l'hôtelier.

Si vous écrivez à un hôtel à l'étranger, joignez à votre lettre
un coupon-réponse international (disponible dans les bureaux de poste).

▣▣▣▣ **HATHERSAGE** Derbs. ▣▣▣ ▣▣▣ ▣▣▣ P 24 – pop. 1 966 – ECD : Wednesday – ✉ Sheffield
(s. Yorks.) – ● 0433 Hope Valley.

▣ Sickleholme, Bamford ℰ 651306, NW : 2 m. by A 625.

♦London 165 – ♦Manchester 33 – ♦Sheffield 10.

🏨 **George**, Main Rd, S30 1BB, ℰ 650436, Telex 547196, Fax 650099 – ⛶ ▣ ☎ ❷ – 🔬 30.
▣ ▣ ⓞ ▣. ⌀
M 8.75/21.35 **t.** and a la carte ⋔ 5.25 – **18 rm** ⌷ 59.50/71.00 **t.** – SB (except Christmas)
(weekends only) 70.00/118.00 **st.**

🏠 **Highlow Hall** ⤳ without rest., S30 1AX, S : 1 ½ m. by B 6001 on Abney rd ℰ 650393, ≤,
🌳, park – ❷
M (by arrangement) 12.95 **st.** ⋔ 4.50 – **6 rm** ⌷ 18.00/46.00 **st.**

▣▣▣▣ **HATTON** Warks. – see Warwick.

▣▣▣▣ **HAVANT** Hants. ▣▣▣ R 31 – pop. 50 098 – ECD : Wednesday – ● 0705.

▣ 1 Park Rd South, PO9 1HA ℰ 480024.

♦London 70 – ♦Brighton 39 – ♦Portsmouth 9 – ♦Southampton 22.

🏨 **Bear**, 15 East St., PO9 1AA, ℰ 486501, Fax 470551 – ⛶ rm ▣ ☎ ❷ – 🔬 100. ▣ ▣ ⓞ
▣.
M 8.95/12.95 **t.** and a la carte ⋔ 6.50 – **42 rm** ⌷ 55.50/67.50 **t.** – SB (weekends only)
93.40/135.90 **st.**

◍ ATS 60-62 Bedhampton Rd ℰ 483018/451570

▣▣▣▣ **HAWES** N. Yorks. ▣▣▣ N 21 – pop. 1 177 – ● 0969 Wensleydale.

▣ Dales Countryside Museum, Station Yard, DL8 3NT ℰ 667450 (summer only).

♦London 253 – Kendal 27 – ♦Leeds 72 – ♦York 65.

🏨 **Simonstone Hall** ⤳, Simonstone, DL8 3LY, N : 1 ½ m. on Muker rd ℰ 667255,
Fax 667741, ≤, 🌳 – ⛶ rest ▣ ❷. ▣ ▣
closed 9 to 27 January – **M** (bar lunch Monday to Saturday)/dinner 21.50 **t.** ⋔ 4.75 – **10 rm**
⌷ 65.00/135.00 **t.** – SB (except Easter, Christmas and New Year) 110.00/170.00 **st.**

🏨 **Stone House** ⚿, Sedbusk, DL8 3PT, N : 1 m. by Muker rd on Askrigg rd ℰ 667571, Fax 667720, « Collections of ornaments and curios », ☞ – ⇔ rest 📺 ☎ 🅿. ⚠ 💳
closed January and weekdays in December – **M** (dinner only) 14.95 **t.** ⓵ 3.75 – **18 rm** ⚏ 30.00/72.00 **t.** – SB (October-April except Christmas and Easter) 71.00/110.00 **st.**

🏨 **Rookhurst Georgian Country House** ⚿, Gayle, DL8 3RT, S : ½ m. by Gayle rd ℰ 667454, ☞ – ⇔ 📺 💳 ⚠ 🌿
closed January – **M** (booking essential) (residents only) (dinner only) 22.00 **t.** ⓵ 4.95 – **5 rm** ⚏ (dinner included) 45.00/112.00 **t.** – SB (February, March and November-19 December) 84.00/120.00 **st.**

🏨 **Cockett's**, Market Pl., DL8 3RD, ℰ 667312, Fax 667162, ☞ – ⇔ 📺 ☎. ⚠ 💳 🌿
closed 30 November-27 December – **M** (light lunch March to October)/dinner 15.95 **st.** and a la carte ⓵ 4.95 – **8 rm** ⚏ 35.00/64.00 **st.**

🏨 **Herriot's**, Main St., DL8 3QU, ℰ 667536 – 📺. ⚠ 💳
March-October – **M** (bar lunch)/dinner a la carte 11.80/13.65 **t.** ⓵ 3.80 – **6 rm** ⚏ 28.50/46.00 **t.** – SB (March-May except Bank Holidays) (weekdays only) 68.00/79.00 **st.**

⌂ **Brandymires**, Muker rd, DL8 3PR, ℰ 667482 – ⇔ 🅿
February-October – **M** (by arrangement) 10.00 **st.** ⓵ 3.75 – **4 rm** ⚏ 25.50/35.00 **st.**

HAWKHURST Kent 404 V 30 Great Britain G. – pop. 3 192 – ECD : Wednesday – 🕿 0580.

Envir. : Bodiam Castle★★ *AC*, SE : 3 ½ m. by B 2244.

◆London 47 – Folkestone 34 – Hastings 14 – Maidstone 19.

🏨 **Tudor Court** (Best Western), Rye Rd, TN18 5DA, E : ¾ m. on A 268 ℰ 752312, Telex 957565, Fax 753966, ⇐, « Gardens », 🎾 – 📺 ☎ 🅿 – ⚖ 40. ⚠ 🆎 ⓞ 💳 🄹🄲🄱
M 12.95/14.95 **st.** and dinner a la carte ⓵ 4.50 – **18 rm** ⚏ 49.00/78.00 **st.** – SB 84.00/96.00 **st.**

HAWKRIDGE Somerset 403 J 30 The West Country G. – ✉ Dulverton – 🕿 064 385 (3 fig.) and 0643 (6 fig.) Winsford.

Envir. : Tarr Steps★★, NE : 2 ½ m.

Exc. : Exmoor National Park★★.

◆London 203 – Exeter 32 – Minehead 17 – Taunton 32.

🏨 **Tarr Steps** ⚿, TA22 9PY, NE : 1 ½ m. ℰ 293, ⇐, 🐎, ☞, park – 🅿. ⚠ 💳
closed February and first 2 weeks March – **M** (bar lunch Monday to Saturday)/dinner 21.50 **t.** ⓵ 3.70 – **13 rm** ⚏ 38.00/76.00 **t.** – SB (except Christmas-New Year) 115.00 **st.**

HAWKSHEAD Cumbria 402 L 20 Great Britain G. – pop. 660 – ECD : Thursday – ✉ Ambleside – 🕿 053 94.

See : Village★.

Envir. : Lake Windermere★★ – Coniston Water★ (Brantwood★, on east side), SW : by B 5285.

🛈 Main Car Park, LA22 0NT ℰ 36525 (summer only).

◆London 283 – Carlisle 52 – Kendal 19.

🏨 **Highfield House** ⚿, Hawkshead Hill, LA22 0PN, W : ½ m. on B 5285 (Coniston rd) ℰ 36344, ⇐ Kirkstone Pass and Fells, ☞ – ⇔ rest 📺 🅿. ⚠ 💳
closed 24 to 26 December – **M** (light lunch)/dinner 16.00 **st.** ⓵ 3.50 – **11 rm** ⚏ 32.00/66.00 **st.** – SB (mid November-March except New Year) 80.00/87.00 **st.**

🍽 **Queen's Head**, Main St., LA22 0NS, ℰ 36271, Fax 36722 – 📺 ☎. ⚠ 💳 🌿
M (bar lunch)/dinner a la carte 10.50/21.25 **t.** ⓵ 4.95 – **12 rm** ⚏ 32.00/66.00 **t.**

⌂ **Rough Close** ⚿, LA22 0QF, S : 1 ½ m. on Newby Bridge rd ℰ 36370, ☞ – ⇔ 🅿. ⚠ 💳 🌿
April-October – **M** 11.00 **t.** ⓵ 4.00 – **5 rm** ⚏ 29.00/48.00 **t.**

🅿 **Ivy House**, Main St., LA22 0NS, ℰ 36204 – ⇔ rest 📺 💳 🄹🄲🄱
March-November – **M** 10.00 ⓵ 3.10 – **11 rm** ⚏ 25.25/54.50 **t.**

at Near Sawrey SE : 2 m. on B 5285 – ✉ Ambleside – 🕿 053 94 Hawkshead :

🏨 **Ees Wyke** ⚿, LA22 0JZ, ℰ 36393, ⇐ Esthwaite water and Grizedale Forest, ☞ – ⇔ rest 📺 🅿. ⚠
March-December – **M** (booking essential) (dinner only) 17.00 **t.** ⓵ 4.00 – **8 rm** ⚏ 36.00/72.00 **t.**

⌂ **Garth Country House** ⚿, LA22 0JZ, ℰ 36373, ⇐, ☞ – 📺 🅿
closed December and January – **M** 10.00 **st.** – **7 rm** ⚏ 28.00/46.00 **st.**

at Far Sawrey SE : 2 ½ m. on B 5285 – ✉ Ambleside – 🕿 053 94 Windermere :

⌂ **West Vale**, LA22 0LQ, ℰ 42817, ⇐ – ⇔ rest 🅿 🌿
March-October – **M** 10.00 **st.** ⓵ 3.75 – **8 rm** ⚏ 20.50/41.00 **st.**

at Grizedale SW : 2 ¾ m. – ✉ Ambleside – 🕿 053 94 Hawkshead :

🏨 **Grizedale Lodge** ⚿, LA22 0QL, ℰ 36532 – ⇔ 📺 🅿. ⚠ 💳 🌿
closed 2 January-11 February – **M** (bar lunch)/dinner 17.95 **t.** ⓵ 4.00 – **9 rm** ⚏ 43.00/70.00 **t.** – SB (November-March) 75.00/101.00 **st.**

HAWNBY N. Yorks 402 Q 21 – see Helmsley.

HAWORTH W. Yorks. 🗺️ 402 O 22 Great Britain G. – pop. 5 041 – ECD : Tuesday – ✉ Keighley – 📞 0535.

See : Haworth Parsonage and the Brontës★ *AC*.

🛈 2-4 West Lane, BD22 8EF ℰ 642329.

◆London 213 – Burnley 22 – ◆Leeds 22 – ◆Manchester 34.

🏠 **Old White Lion,** 6 West Lane, BD22 8DU, ℰ 642313, Fax 646222 – 📺 ☎ 🅿. 🔦 AE ⓪ VISA 🦷
M (bar lunch Monday to Saturday)/dinner 12.00 **t.** and a la carte 🍴 4.00 – **14 rm** ⛳ 35.00/45.00 **t.** – SB (except Bank Holidays) 67.00/100.00 **st.**

🏠 **Ferncliffe,** Hebden Rd, BD22 8RS, on A 6033 ℰ 643405, ≤, – 📺 🅿. 🔦 VISA
M (by arrangement) 9.75 **st.** 🍴 4.50 – **6 rm** ⛳ 21.00/39.00 **st.** – SB (winter only) (weekends only) 58.00/77.50 **st.**

XX **Weaver's** with rm, 15 West Lane, BD22 8DU, ℰ 643822, « Converted weavers cottages » – 📺 ☎. 🔦 AE ⓪ VISA 🦷
closed 2 weeks July-August and 2 weeks Christmas-New Year – **M** (closed Sunday and Monday) (dinner only) 13.50 **t.** and a la carte 🍴 4.25 – **4 rm** ⛳ 45.00/65.00 **t.**

HAYDOCK Mersey. 🗺️ 402 403 404 M 23 – pop. 17 372 – ✉ Newton-le-Willows – 📞 0942 Ashton-in-Makerfield.

◆London 198 – ◆Liverpool 17 – ◆Manchester 18.

🏨 **Haydock Thistle** (Mt. Charlotte Thistle), Penny Lane, WA11 9SG, NE : ½ m. on A 599 ℰ 272000, Fax 711092, ℱ₅, ⚓, 🔲, ⚘ – ⇔ rm 🔳 rest 📺 ☎ 🕭 🅿 – 🔬 250. 🔦 AE ⓪ VISA JCB
M (closed Saturday lunch) 10.00/17.50 **st.** and dinner a la carte 🍴 5.00 – ⛳ 8.95 – **135 rm** 79.00/89.00 **st.**, 4 suites – SB (weekends only) 84.00/133.00 **st.**

🏨 **Forte Posthouse,** Lodge Lane, WA12 0JG, NE : 1 m. on A 49 ℰ 717878, Fax 718419, ℱ₅, ⚓, 🔲 – 🛏 ⇔ rm 🔳 rest 📺 ☎ 🅿 – 🔬 160. 🔦 AE ⓪ VISA
M a la carte approx. 16.00 **t.** 🍴 4.65 – ⛳ 6.95 – **136 rm** 53.50/69.50 **st.** – SB (weekends only) 90.00 **st.**

🏠 **Forte Travelodge** without rest., Piele Rd, WA11 9TL, on A 580 ℰ 272055, Reservations (Freephone) 0800 850950 – 📺 🕭 🅿. 🔦 AE VISA
40 rm 31.95 **t.**

🛞 ATS Legh Rd, St. Helens ℰ 50551

HAYFIELD Derbs. 🗺️ 402 403 404 O 23 – ✉ Stockport (Ches.) – 📞 0663 New Mills.

◆London 191 – ◆Manchester 22 – ◆Sheffield 29.

X **Bridge End** with rm, 7 Church St., SK12 5JE, ℰ 747321, Fax 742121 – 📺 🅿. 🔦 AE ⓪ VISA 🦷
closed Sunday dinner and Monday – **M** (dinner only and Sunday lunch)/dinner 15.00 **t.** and a la carte 🍴 4.00 – **4 rm** ⛳ 33.00/45.00 **t.**

HAYLING ISLAND Hants. 🗺️ 404 R 31 – pop. 12 410 – ECD : Wednesday – 📞 0705.

🛝 Links Lane ℰ 463712/463777.

🛈 Beachlands Seafront, PO11 0AG ℰ 467111 (summer only).

◆London 77 – ◆Brighton 45 – ◆Southampton 28.

🏠 **Cockle Warren Cottage,** 36 Seafront, PO11 9HL, ℰ 464961, 🔲 heated – ⇔ 📺 ☎ 🅿. 🔦 VISA 🦷
closed 1 week June and 1 week October – **M** (by arrangement) 23.50 **st.** 🍴 4.00 – **5 rm** ⛳ 45.00/84.00 **st.**

HAYTOR Devon – see Bovey Tracey.

HAYTOR VALE Devon – see Bovey Tracey.

HAYWARDS HEATH W. Sussex 🗺️ 404 T 31 – 📞 0444.

🛝 Paxhill Park, Lindfield ℰ 484467, NE : 4 m.

◆London 41 – ◆Brighton 16.

🏨 **Birch,** Lewes Rd, RH17 7SF, E : ¾ m. on A 272 ℰ 451565, Fax 440109 – ⇔ rm 📺 ☎ 🕭 🅿 – 🔬 60. 🔦 AE ⓪ VISA
M (buffet dinner Sunday) 10.95/15.95 **st.** and a la carte 🍴 4.95 – **53 rm** ⛳ 25.00/66.00 **st.** – SB 70.00/144.90 **st.**

🛞 ATS Gower Rd ℰ 412640/454189

HEACHAM Norfolk 🗺️ 402 404 V 25 – see Hunstanton.

HEADLAM Durham – see Darlington.

HEALEY N. Yorks. 🗺️ 402 O 21 – see Masham.

HEATHFIELD E. Sussex 🗺️ 404 U 31 – pop. 4 848 – ✉ 📞 0435.

◆London 51 – ◆Brighton 23 – Eastbourne 16.

🏠 **Risingholme** without rest., 38 High St., TN21 8LS, ℰ 864645, ⚘ – ⇔ 📺 🅿. 🦷
4 rm ⛳ 25.00/40.00 **s.**

HEATHROW AIRPORT Middx. – see Hillingdon (Greater London).

HEBDEN BRIDGE W. Yorks. 402 N 22 – pop. 4 167 – ECD : Tuesday – ⊠ Halifax ☎ 0422.
⌂ Hebden Bridge, Wadsworth ℰ 842896, N : 1 m.
🛈 1 Bridge Gate, HX7 8EX ℰ 843831.
◆London 223 – Burnley 13 – ◆Leeds 24 – ◆Manchester 25.

🏨 **Carlton,** Albert St., HX7 8ES, ℰ 844400, Fax 843117 – |🛗| 📺 ☎ – 🏄 100. 🔼 AE VISA
M 9.95/17.50 **t.** ⌀ 5.20 – **18 rm** ⊑ 49.00/79.00 **t.** – SB (except Christmas-New Year) 85.00/90.00 **st.**

HEDON Humbs. 402 T 22 – see Kingston-upon-Hull.

HELFORD Cornwall 403 E 33 The West Country G. – ⊠ Helston – ☎ 0326 Manaccan.
Envir. : Lizard Peninsula★.
Exc. : Helston (Flora Day Furry Dance★★) (May) W : 11 m.
◆London 324 – Falmouth 15 – Penzance 22 – Truro 27.

XX **Riverside** ⌂ with rm, TR12 6JU, ℰ 231443, Fax 231103, ≼, « Converted cottages in picturesque setting », ⌖ – 📺 🅿. 🍴
mid February-early November – **M** (dinner only) 28.00 **st.** ⌀ 4.50 – ⊑ 4.50 – **6 rm** 60.00/120.00 **st.**

at Gillan SE : 3 m. – ⊠ Helston – ☎ 0326 Manaccan :

🏨 **Tregildry** ⌂, TR12 6HG, ℰ 231378, Fax 231561, ≼ Gillan Creek, sea, ⌖ – 🐾 📺 🅿. 🔼
VISA
March-October – **M** (bar lunch)/dinner 17.00 **t.** – **10 rm** ⊑ 40.00/60.00 **t.**

"Short Breaks" (SB)

De nombreux hôtels proposent des conditions avantageuses
pour un séjour de deux nuits
comprenant la chambre, le dîner et le petit déjeuner.

HELLIDON Northants. 404 Q 27 – see Daventry.

HELMSLEY N. Yorks. 402 Q 21 Great Britain G. – pop. 1 399 – ECD : Wednesday – ☎ 0439.
Envir. : Rievaulx Abbey★★ *AC*, NW : 2½ m. by B 1257.
⌂ Ampleforth College, 56 High St. ℰ 770678.
🛈 Town Hall, Market Pl., YO6 5BL ℰ 770173 (summer only).
◆London 234 – ◆Middlesbrough 29 – York 24.

🏨 **Black Swan** (Forte), Market Pl., YO6 5BJ, ℰ 770466, Fax 770174, « 16C inn », ⌖ – 🐾
📺 ☎ 🅿. 🔼 AE ① VISA JCB
M 15.00/25.00 **st.** and dinner a la carte ⌀ 7.50 – ⊑ 8.50 – **44 rm** 85.00/180.00 **st.** – SB
(except Christmas and New Year) 128.00/148.00 **st.**

🏨 **Feversham Arms** (Best Western), 1 High St., YO6 5AG, ℰ 770766, Fax 770346, ⌷ heated, ⌖, ※ – 📺 ☎ 🅿 – 🏄 30. 🔼 AE ① VISA
M 20.00/25.00 **t.** and a la carte ⌀ 4.00 – **18 rm** ⊑ 55.00/80.00 **t.** – SB (except Bank Holidays) 98.00 **st.**

⌂ **Feathers,** Market Pl., YO6 5BH, ℰ 770275, Fax 771101, ⌖ – 📺 🅿. 🔼 AE ① VISA. ※
closed 23 December-2 January and last 2 weeks January – **M** (bar lunch Monday to
Saturday)/dinner 16.50 ⌀ 3.50 – **18 rm** ⊑ 16.00/53.00 **t.** – SB 68.00/84.00 **st.**

⌂ **Laskill Farm,** NW : 6¼ m. on B 1257 ℰ 798, « Working farm », ⌖ – 📺 🅿
M (by arrangement) (communal dining) 11.00 **st.** ⌀ 4.50 – **6 rm** ⊑ 16.50/40.00 **st.**

at Harome E : 2¾ m. by A 170 – ⊠ York – ☎ 0439 Helmsley :

🏨 **Pheasant,** YO6 5JG, ℰ 771241, ⌖ – 🐾 rest 📺 ☎ 🅿
closed January, February and Christmas – **M** (bar lunch)/dinner 19.50 **t.** ⌀ 2.60 – **12 rm**
⊑ (dinner included) 49.00/118.00 **t.**, 2 suites – SB (November-mid May) 98.00/110.00 **st.**

at Nawton E : 3¼ m. on A 170 – ⊠ York – ☎ 0439 Helmsley :

⌂ **Plumpton Court,** High St., YO6 5TT, ℰ 771223, ⌖ – 🅿. ※
March-October – **M** 10.00 **st.** ⌀ 3.10 – **8 rm** ⊑ 30.00/46.00 **st.**

at Nunnington SE : 6¼ m. by A 170 off B 1257 – ⊠ York – ☎ 0439 Nunnington :

XX **Ryedale Lodge** ⌂ with rm, YO6 5XB, W : 1 m. ℰ 748246, ≼, « Converted railway
station », 🐾, ⌖ – 🐾 rest 📺 ☎ 🅿. 🔼 VISA
M (dinner only) 26.75 **t.** ⌀ 5.00 – **7 rm** ⊑ 51.50/83.00 **t.** – SB (except Bank Holidays)
118.00/156.50 **st.**

at Hawnby NW : 6¼ m. by B 1257 – ⊠ Helmsley – ☎ 0439 Bilsdale :

🏨 **Hawnby** ⌂, YO6 5QS, ℰ 748202, Fax 748417, 🐾, ⌖ – 📺 ☎ 🅿. 🔼 VISA. ※
closed February – **M** (dinner only and Sunday lunch)/dinner 14.00 **t.** ⌀ 3.75 – **6 rm** ⊑ 50.00/70.00 **t.**

🚌 Little Hay, Box Lane, Bovington 🖉 833798, W : 2 m. by B 4505 – 🚌 Boxmoor, 18 Box Lane 🖉 242434, W : 1 m. on B 4505.

🖪 Pavilion Box Office, Marlowes, HP1 1HA 🖉 64451.

◆London 30 – Aylesbury 16 – Luton 10 – Northampton 46.

🏨 **Forte Posthouse**, Breakspear Way, HP2 4UA, E : 2 ½ m. on A 414 🖉 251122, Fax 211812, 𝄢, 🛋, 🖎 – 🛌 ⇆ rm 📺 🅿 🔥 🅰 🔵 – 🔬 60. 🖎 🕰 ⓞ 𝘝𝘐𝘚𝘈 𝘑𝘊𝘉
M a la carte approx. 17.50 **t.** 🍷 4.65 – ⊐ 6.95 – **146 rm** 53.50/69.50 **st.** – SB 90.00 **st.**

🏨 **Boxmoor Lodge**, London Rd, HP1 2RA, W : 1 m. on A 41 🖉 230770, Fax 252230 – 📺 ☎ 🅿, 🖎 🕰 ⓞ 𝘝𝘐𝘚𝘈 𝘑𝘊𝘉
closed 26 December-3 January – **M** *(closed Monday lunch and Sunday)* 9.95/ 15.75 **t.** and a la carte 🍷 4.45 – **18 rm** ⊐ 48.00/65.00 **t.**

at Bourne End W : 2¼ m. on A 41 – ⊠ Hemel Hempstead – 🕿 0442 Berkhamsted :

🏨 **Hemel Hempstead Moat House** (Q.M.H.), London Rd, HP1 2RJ, 🖉 871241, Fax 866130 – ⇆ rm 📺 ☎ 🅿 – 🔬 100. 🖎 🕰 ⓞ 𝘝𝘐𝘚𝘈
M *(closed Saturday lunch)* 13.75 **st.** and a la carte – **61 rm** ⊐ 55.00/74.50 **st.** – SB (weekends only) 75.00 **st.**

◆London 47 – ◆Brighton 10 – Worthing 11.

🏩 **Tottington Manor**, Edburton, BN5 9LJ, SE : 3½ m. by A 2037 on Fulking rd 🖉 815757, Fax 879331, ≼, 🖄 – 📺 ☎ 🅿. 🖎 🕰 ⓞ 𝘝𝘐𝘚𝘈
closed first week January – **M** 18.00 **t.** (dinner) and a la carte 17.40/24.05 **t.** 🍷 4.00 – **6 rm** ⊐ 30.00/50.00 **t.**

at Wineham NE : 3 ½ m. by A 281, B 2116 and Wineham Lane – ⊠ Henfield – 🕿 0403 Partridge Green :

↑ **Frylands** 🖄, BN5 9BP, W : ¼ m. taking left turn at telephone box 🖉 710214, Fax 711449, ≼, « Part Elizabethan farmhouse », 🗋 heated, 🌿 – 📺 🅿. 🛝
closed 23 December-2 January – **M** (by arrangement) 8.50 **s.** – **3 rm** ⊐ 16.00/35.00 **s.**

"Short Breaks"

Many hotels now offer a special rate for a stay of 2 nights which includes dinner, bed and breakfast.

◆London 104 – ◆Birmingham 15 – Stratford-upon-Avon 8 – Warwick 8.5.

🏩 **Ashleigh House**, Whitley Hill, B95 5DL, E : 1¾ m. on B 4095 🖉 792315, Fax 794133, 🌿 – 📺 ☎ 🅿. 🖎 𝘝𝘐𝘚𝘈. 🛝
M (by arrangement) 10.50 **st.** 🍷 4.00 – **10 rm** ⊐ 40.00/55.00 **st.**

XX **Le Filbert Cottage**, 64 High St., B95 5BX, 🖉 792700 – 🖎 🕰 ⓞ 𝘝𝘐𝘚𝘈
closed Sunday, Monday and Bank Holidays – **M** - French 20.00 **t.** and a la carte 🍷 4.00.

🚌 Huntercombe, Nuffield 🖉 641207, W : 6 m. by A 423.

🚢 to Reading via Shiplake, Sonning and Caversham Locks (Salter Bros Ltd) (summer only) – to Marlow via Hambleden Lock and Hurley Locks (Salter Bros Ltd) (summer only).

🖪 Town Hall, Market Place, RG9 2AQ 🖉 578034.

◆London 40 – ◆Oxford 23 – Reading 9.

↑ **Shepherds** 🖄 without rest., Rotherfield Greys, RG9 4QL, W : 3½ m. by Peppard rd on Shepherds Green rd 🖉 628413, 🌿 – ⇆ 📺 🅿. 🛝
closed Christmas – **4 rm** ⊐ 22.00/46.00 **s.**

XX **Villa Marina**, 18 Thameside, RG9 1BH, 🖉 575262, Fax 411394 – 🖎 🕰 ⓞ 𝘝𝘐𝘚𝘈
M - Italian 11.00/18.00 **t.** and a la carte 🍷 4.00.

XX **Slow Boat**, 25 Duke St., RG9 1UR, 🖉 410001 – 🖎 🕰 ⓞ 𝘝𝘐𝘚𝘈
closed 25 to 27 December – **M** - Chinese (Peking) (buffet lunch Sunday) 5.50/ 13.00 **t.** and a la carte.

at Stonor N : 4 m. by A 423 on B 480 – ⊠ Henley-on-Thames – 🕿 0491 Turville Heath :

XXX **Stonor Arms** with rm, RG9 6HE, 🖉 638345, Fax 638863, 🌿 – 📺 ☎ 🅿. 🖎 🕰 𝘝𝘐𝘚𝘈. 🛝
M - Stonor *(closed Sunday)* (dinner only) 27.50/31.50 **t.** – **8 rm** ⊐ 82.50/92.50 **t.**, 1 suite.

XX **Blades** - **M** a la carte 15.05/25.30 **t.**

at Frieth (Bucks.) NE : 7 ½ m. by A 4155 – ⊠ Henley-on-Thames – 🕿 0494 High Wycombe :

X **Yew Tree**, RG9 6RJ, 🖉 882330 – 🅿. 🖎 🕰 𝘝𝘐𝘚𝘈
M 12.95/18.95 **t.** and a la carte 🍷 5.95.

HEREFORD Heref. and Worcs. 408 L 27 Great Britain G. – pop. 48 277 – ECD : Thursday – ✆ 0432.

See : City★ – Cathedral★★ (Mappa Mundi★) A **A** – Old House★ A **B**.

Exc. : Kilpeck (Church of SS. Mary and David★★) SW : 8 m. by A 465 B.

⌕ Ravens Causeway, Wormsley ℰ 71219, NW : 7 m. by A 438 – B – and A 480 – ⌕ Belmont House, Belmont ℰ 352666, SE : 2 m. by A 465 B – ⌕, ⌕ Holmer Rd ℰ 271639 B.

🛈 Town Hall Annexe, St. Owens St., HR1 2PJ ℰ 268430.

♦London 133 – ♦Birmingham 51 – ♦Cardiff 56.

HEREFORD

Broad Street . . . . **A** 7
Commercial Street . . . **A** 13
High Street . . . . **A** 19
High Town . . . . **A** 20
Maylord Orchards
    Shopping Centre . . . **A**

Aubrey St. . . . . **A** 3
Berrington St. . . . . . . **A** 5

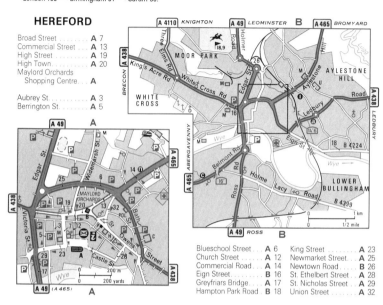

Blueschool Street . . . **A** 6
Church Street . . . . . . **A** 12
Commercial Road . . . **A** 14
Eign Street . . . . **B** 16
Greyfriars Bridge . . . **A** 17
Hampton Park Road . **B** 18

King Street . . . . **A** 23
Newmarket Street . . . **A** 25
Newtown Road . . . . . **B** 26
St. Ethelbert Street . . **A** 28
St. Nicholas Street . . **A** 29
Union Street . . . . **A** 32

🏨 **Hereford Moat House** (Q.M.H.), Belmont Rd, HR2 7BP, SW : 1 ½ m. on A 465 ℰ 354301, Fax 275114 – 📺 ☎ & ❷ – 🔄 300. 🄰🄴 ① 𝚅𝙸𝚂𝙰 B **c**
M (bar lunch Monday to Saturday)/dinner 15.95 **st.** and a la carte ▯ 5.25 – **60 rm** ⬚ 73.00/90.00 **st.** – SB (weekends only) 96.00 **st.**

🏨 **Merton**, 28 Commercial Rd, HR1 2BD, ℰ 265925, Fax 354983, ☞ – 📺 ☎. 🄰🄴 ① 𝚅𝙸𝚂𝙰. ⌘ A **n**
M 20.00/25.00 **st.** and a la carte ▯ 5.00 – **19 rm** ⬚ 45.00/70.00 **st.** – SB 65.00/95.00 **st.**

🏨 **Travel Inn**, Holmer Rd, Holmer, HR4 9RS, N : 1 ¾ m. on A 49 ℰ 274853, Fax 343003 – ⌘ rm 📺 & ❷. 🄰🄴 ① 𝚅𝙸𝚂𝙰. ⌘ B
M (Beefeater grill) a la carte approx. 16.00 **t.** – ⬚ 4.95 – **39 rm** 33.50 **st.**

🏠 **Somerville**, 12 Bodenham Rd, HR1 2TS, ℰ 273991, Fax 265862, ☞ – 📺 ☎ ❷. 🄰🄴 𝚅𝙸𝚂𝙰 B **i**
closed 23 December-7 January – **M** 18.00 **t.** ▯ 4.40 – **10 rm** ⬚ 27.00/53.00 **t.** – SB 63.00/81.00 **st.**

🏠 **Ferncroft**, 144 Ledbury Rd, HR1 2TB, ℰ 265538, ☞ – 📺 ❷. 🄰🄴 𝚅𝙸𝚂𝙰. ⌘ B **a**
closed 2 weeks December-January – **M** (by arrangement) 15.00 **st.** ▯ 3.50 – **11 rm** ⬚ 21.00/45.00 **st.**

at Marden N : 5¾ m. by A 49 – B – ✉ Hereford – ✆ 056 884 Bodenham :

🏠 **The Vauld Farm** ⤵, HR1 3HA, NE : 1 ½ m. by Urdimarsh rd ℰ 898, « 16C timbered farmhouse », ☞ – ❷. ⌘
M (by arrangement) (communal dining) 15.00 **s.** – **5 rm** ⬚ 18.00/60.00 **s.**

at Canon Pyon N : 7 m. on A 4110 – B – ✉ Hereford – ✆ 043 271 Canon Pyon :

🏠 **Hermitage Manor** ⤵ without rest., HR4 8NR, S : 1 m. on A 4110 ℰ 0432 (Hereford) 760317, ≤ Vale of Hereford, ☞ – ⌘ 📺 ❷. ⌘
Easter-November – **3 rm** ⬚ 30.00/50.00 **s.**

at Dormington E : 5¼ m. on A 438 – B – ✉ ✆ 0432 Hereford :

🏨 **Dormington Court**, HR1 4DA, ℰ 850370, Fax 850370, ☞ – 📺 ❷. 🄰🄴 𝚅𝙸𝚂𝙰
M 12.00/16.50 **t.** ▯ 4.50 – **9 rm** ⬚ 30.00/60.00 **t.** – SB 80.00/90.00 **st.**

at Much Birch S : 5½ m. on A 49 – B – ⊠ Hereford – ✆ 0981 Golden Valley :

🏨 **Pilgrim,** Ross Rd, HR2 8HJ, on A 49 ✆ 540742, Fax 540620, ≤, 🐎 – ⇘ 📺 ☎ Ⓟ – 🏄 45. 🖪 🖽 ⓞ 𝗩𝗜𝗦𝗔
M (bar lunch)/dinner 19.50 **st.** and a la carte ₰ 4.95 – **20 rm** ⊇ 39.50/59.50 **st.** – SB 84.00/138.00 **st.**

at Ruckhall W : 5 m. by A 49 off A 465 – B – ⊠ Eaton Bishop – ✆ 0981 Golden Valley :

🔆 **Ancient Camp Inn** 🤏, HR2 9QX, ✆ 250449, ≤ River Wye and countryside, « Tastefully renovated inn » – 📺 ☎ Ⓟ. 🖪 𝗩𝗜𝗦𝗔. 🎁
M *(closed Sunday dinner and Monday)* (bar lunch)/dinner a la carte 11.50/16.25 **t.** ₰ 5.00 –
5 rm ⊇ 35.00/58.00 **t.**

◉ ATS 6 Kyrle St. ✆ 265491

HERNE BAY Kent 404 X 29 – pop. 26 523 – ECD : Thursday – ✆ 0227.

🚉 Herne Bay, Eddington ✆ 374097.

🛈 Central Bandstand, Central Par., CT6 5JJ ✆ 361911.

◆London 63 – ◆Dover 24 – Maidstone 32 – Margate 13.

🔆 **Northdown** without rest., 14 Cecil Park, CT6 6DL, ✆ 372051, Fax 372051, 🐎 – 📺 ☎ Ⓟ. 🖪 🖽 𝗩𝗜𝗦𝗔. 🎁
5 rm ⊇ 20.00/44.00 **st.**

HERSTMONCEUX E. Sussex 404 U 31 – pop. 2 246 – ✆ 0323.

◆London 63 – Eastbourne 12 – Hastings 14 – Lewes 16.

✕✕ **Sundial,** Gardner St., BN27 4LA, ✆ 832217, « Converted 16C cottage », 🐎 – Ⓟ. 🖪 🖽 ⓞ 𝗩𝗜𝗦𝗔
closed Sunday dinner, Monday, 9 August-5 September and Christmas-20 January –
M - French 15.50/24.50 **t.** and a la carte ₰ 5.50.

HERTFORD Herts. 404 T 28 – pop. 21 630 – ✆ 0992.

🛈 The Castle, SG14 1HR ✆ 584322.

◆London 24 – ◆Cambridge 35 – Luton 26.

🏨 **Hall House** 🤏, Broad Oak End, SG14 2JA, NW : 1 ¾ m. by A 119 and Bramfield Rd ✆ 582807, 🤏, heated, 🐎 – ⇘ 📺 Ⓟ. 🖪 𝗩𝗜𝗦𝗔. 🎁
closed Christmas – **M** (by arrangement) 20.00 **s.** – **3 rm** ⊇ 45.00/60.00 **s.**

HERTINGFORDBURY Herts. 404 T 28 – pop. 658 – ⊠ ✆ 0992 Hertford.

◆London 26 – Luton 18.

🏨 **White Horse** (Forte), Hertingfordbury Rd, SG14 2LB, ✆ 586791, Fax 550809, 🐎 – ⇘ 📺 ☎ Ⓟ – 🏄 60. 🖪 🖽 ⓞ 𝗩𝗜𝗦𝗔 𝗝𝗖𝗕
M (bar lunch Saturday) 11.25/18.95 **st.** and a la carte – ⊇ 8.95 – **42 rm** 75.00/90.00 **st.** –
SB (weekends only) 98.00 **st.**

HETHERSETT Norfolk 404 X 26 – see Norwich.

HETTON N. Yorks. 402 N 21 – pop. 115 – ⊠ Skipton – ✆ 075 673 (3 fig.) and 0756 (6 fig.) Cracoe.

◆London 237 – Burnley 25 – ◆Leeds 33.

✕✕ **Angel Inn,** BD23 6LT, ✆ 730263, Fax 730363, « Attractive 18C inn » – Ⓟ. 🖪 𝗩𝗜𝗦𝗔
closed Sunday dinner, 25 December, 1 January and third week January – **M** (dinner only and Sunday lunch)/dinner 21.95 **t.**

HEVERSHAM Cumbria 402 L 21 – ⊠ Milnthorpe – ✆ 053 95.

◆London 270 – Kendal 7 – Lancaster 18 – ◆Leeds 72.

🏨 **Blue Bell,** Princes Way, LA7 7EE, on A 6 ✆ 62018, 🐎 – 📺 ☎ Ⓟ. 🖪 🖽 𝗩𝗜𝗦𝗔
M 10.50/15.95 **t.** and a la carte ₰ 4.95 – **21 rm** ⊇ 34.50/65.00 **t.** – SB (except Christmas, New Year and Bank Holidays) 86.00/90.00 **st.**

HEXHAM Northd 401 402 N 19 Great Britain G. – pop. 8 914 – ECD : Thursday – ✆ 0434.

See : Abbey★ (Saxon Crypt★★, Leschman chantry★).

Envir. : Hadrian's Wall★★, N : 4½ m. by A 6079.

Exc. : Housesteads★★, NW : 12½ m. by A 6079 and B 6318.

🚉 Spital Park ✆ 602057 – 🚉 Slaley Hall ✆ 673350 – 🚉 Tynedale, Tyne Green ✆ 608154.

🛈 The Manor Office, Hallgate, NE46 1XD ✆ 605225.

◆London 304 – ◆Carlisle 37 – ◆Newcastle upon Tyne 21.

🏨 **Beaumont,** Beaumont St., NE46 3LT, ✆ 602331, Fax 602331 – ⇘ rm 📺 ☎ – 🏄 80. 🖪 🖽 ⓞ 𝗩𝗜𝗦𝗔
closed 25 and 26 December – **M** 12.50 **t.** (dinner) and a la carte 13.00/24.10 **t.** ₰ 3.50 –
23 rm ⊇ 50.00/80.00 **t.** – SB (weekends only) 80.00/100.00 **st.**

🏨 **County,** Priestpopple, NE46 1PS, ✆ 602030 – 📺 ☎. 🖪 🖽 𝗩𝗜𝗦𝗔
M a la carte 6.60/21.50 **t.** ₰ 4.00 – **9 rm** ⊇ 45.00/58.00 **t.** – SB (October-May) 70.00 **st.**

⌂ **Middlemarch** without rest., Hencotes, NE46 2EB, ℰ 605003 – ⇤ ⊡ Ⓟ. ✵
3 rm ⊒ 25.00/48.00 **s.**

⌂ **West Close House** without rest., Hextol Terr., NE46 2AD, by Allendale Rd ℰ 603307, ⇡
– ⇤ Ⓟ
4 rm ⊒ 17.50/46.00 **st.**

XX **Black House,** Dipton Mill Rd, NE46 1RZ, S : 1 ¼ m. by B 6306 and Whitley Chapel rd
ℰ 604744 – ⇤ Ⓟ. ⊠ VISA
closed Sunday and Monday – **M** (dinner only) a la carte 17.90/28.10 **t.** ⓖ 5.00.

at Wall N : 4 m. on A 6079 – ✪ 0434 Hexham :

⌂ **Hadrian,** NE46 4EE, ℰ 681232, ⇡ – ⊡ ☎ Ⓟ. ⊠ AE ⓞ VISA JCB. ✵
M 15.00 **st.** and a la carte ⓖ 3.50 – **7 rm** ⊒ 35.00/49.00 **st.**

at Slaley SE : 5 ½ m. by B 6306 – ⊠ ✪ 0434 Hexham :

⌂ **Rye Hill Farm** ⑇, NE47 0AN, NW : 1 m. ℰ 673259, « Working farm » – ⇤ rm ⊡ Ⓟ
M 10.00 **st.** – **6 rm** ⊒ 20.00/36.00 **st.**

◍ ATS Haugh Lane ℰ 602394

HIGHAM Suffolk 🄳🄳🄳 W 28 – pop. 142 – ⊠ Colchester – ✪ 020 637 (3 fig.) and 0206 (6 fig.).
♦London 55 – Colchester 10 – ♦Ipswich 11.

⌂ **Old Vicarage** ⑇ without rest., CO7 6JY, ℰ 248, ≼, « 16C former vicarage », ⎏ heated,
⬥, ⇡, ✵ – Ⓟ
3 rm ⊒ 25.00/52.00 **st.**

HIGHER BURWARDSLEY Ches. – see Tattenhall.

HIGH WYCOMBE Bucks. 🄳🄳🄳 R 29 – pop. 69 575 – ECD : Wednesday – ✪ 0494.
🛧 Penn Rd, Hazlemere ℰ 714722, NE : 3 m. on B 474 – 🛧, 🛧 Wycombe Heights, Rayners Av.,
Loudwater ℰ 816686, ½ m. from M 40 junction 3 on A 40 to Wycombe.
🄱 6 Cornmarket, HP11 2BW ℰ 421892.
♦London 34 – Aylesbury 17 – ♦Oxford 26 – Reading 18.

🏨 **Forte Posthouse,** Handy Cross, HP11 1TL, SW : 1 ½ m. by A 404 ℰ 442100, Fax 439071
– ⇤ rm ⊟ rest ⊡ ☎ ⑃ Ⓟ – ⚿ 100. ⊠ AE ⓞ VISA
M a la carte approx. 17.50 **t.** ⓖ 4.65 – ⊒ 6.95 – **106 rm** 53.50 **st.** – SB (weekends only)
90.00 **st.**

🏨 **Alexandra,** Queen Alexandra Rd, HP11 2JX, ℰ 463494, Fax 463560 – ⊡ ☎ ⑃ Ⓟ. ⊠ AE
VISA
closed 24 to 29 December – **M** *(closed Saturday and Sunday)* 8.95/15.00 **st.** and dinner a la
carte ⓖ 4.25 – ⊒ 7.90 – **28 rm** 54.00/120.00 **st.,** 1 suite.

◍ ATS Copyground Lane ℰ 525101/438019

HILLSFORD BRIDGE Devon – see Lynton.

HILMARTON Wilts. 🄳🄳🄳 🄳🄳🄳 O 29 – ⊠ Calne – ✪ 0249.
♦London 94 – ♦Bristol 36 – Salisbury 39 – Swindon 14.

⌂ **Burfoots,** 1 The Close, SN11 8TQ, ℰ 760492, Fax 760609, ⎏ heated, ⇡ – ⇤ ⊡
M (by arrangement) 10.00 **st.** – **3 rm** ⊒ 22.50/45.00 **st.**

HILTON PARK SERVICE AREA W. Mids. – ⊠ Wolverhampton – ✪ 0922 Cheslyn Hay

🏠 **Pavilion Lodge** without rest., WV11 2DR, M 6 between junctions 10 A and 11 ℰ 414100,
Fax 418762 – ⇤ ⊡ ⑃ Ⓟ. ⊠ AE ⓞ VISA JCB
⊒ 4.00 – **64 rm** 31.95/35.95 **st.**

HINCKLEY Leics. 🄳🄳🄳 🄳🄳🄳 🄳🄳🄳 P 26 – pop. 35 510 – ECD : Thursday – ✪ 0455.
🄱 Hinckley Library, Lancaster Rd, LE10 0AT ℰ 635106.
♦London 103 – ♦Birmingham 31 – ♦Coventry 12 – ♦Leicester 14.

🏨 **Sketchley Grange** (Best Western), Sketchley Lane, LE10 3HU, S : 1 ½ m. by B 4109
(Rugby Rd) ℰ 251133, Fax 631384, ⇡ – ⊡ ☎ ⑃ Ⓟ – ⚿ 300. ⊠ AE ⓞ VISA
M *(closed Saturday lunch and Sunday dinner)* 11.50/17.50 **st.** and a la carte ⓖ 6.25 – **38 rm**
⊒ 73.00/89.00 **st.** – SB (weekends only) 90.00/100.00 **st.**

◍ ATS 5 Leicester Rd ℰ 632022/635835

HINDON Wilts. 🄳🄳🄳 🄳🄳🄳 N 30 – pop. 489 – ECD : Saturday – ⊠ Salisbury – ✪ 0747.
♦London 107 – Bath 28 – Bournemouth 40 – Salisbury 15.

🏨 **Lamb at Hindon,** SP3 6DP, ℰ 820573, Fax 820605 – ⇤ rest ⊡ ☎ Ⓟ. ⊠ AE VISA. ✵
M 19.95 **t.** (dinner) and lunch a la carte 13.50/20.00 **t.** ⓖ 4.95 – **13 rm** ⊒ 38.00/60.00 **t.** –
SB (October-April) 86.00/126.00 **st.**

HINTLESHAM Suffolk 🄳🄳🄳 X 27 – see Ipswich.

HINTON CHARTERHOUSE Avon – see Bath.

Herts. 404 T 28 – pop. 33 480 – ECD : Wednesday – ✆ 0462.
🔼 Hitchin Library, Paynes Park, SG1 1EW ✆ 434738/450133.
◆London 40 – Bedford 14 – ◆Cambridge 26 – Luton 9.

🛎 **Lord Lister,** Park St., SG4 9AH, ✆ 432712, Fax 438506 – 📺 ☎ 🅿. ◪ 🆀 ⓪ 𝗩𝗜𝗦𝗔. ✦
   M (dinner only) 10.95 **st.** and a la carte ♨ 3.75 – **20 rm** ⊡ 36.00/60.00 **st.** – SB (weekends
   only) 70.00/120.00 **st.**

   at Little Wymondley SE : 2½ m. by A 602 – ⊠ Hitchin – ✆ 0438 Stevenage :

🏨 **Blakemore Thistle** (Mt. Charlotte Thistle), Blakemore End Rd, SG4 7JJ, ✆ 355821,
   Fax 742114, ♨ heated, ☞ – ▥ ⇆ rm 📺 ☎ 🅿 – 🔏 150. ◪ 🆀 ⓪ 𝗩𝗜𝗦𝗔
   M (bar lunch Saturday) 14.25/17.25 **st.** and a la carte ♨ 4.75 – ⊡ 8.25 – **79 rm** 75.00/
   85.00 **st.**, 3 suites – SB (weekends only) 98.00 **st.**

XX **Redcoats Farmhouse** with rm, Redcoats Green, SG4 7JR, S : ½ m. by A 602 ✆ 729500,
   Fax 723322, « Part 15C farmhouse », ☞ – 📺 ☎ 🅿. ◪ 🆀 ⓪ 𝗩𝗜𝗦𝗔. ✦
   closed Christmas-New Year – **M** (closed Saturday lunch, Sunday dinner and Bank Holiday
   Mondays) 13.50/20.00 **t.** and a la carte ♨ 5.00 – **14 rm** ⊡ 50.00/91.00 **st.** – SB (weekends
   only) 79.00/134.00 **st.**

Warks. 403 404 O 26 – pop. 3 507 – ⊠ Solihull – ✆ 0564 Lapworth.
◆London 117 – ◆Birmingham 11 – ◆Coventry 17.

XXX **Nuthurst Grange** with rm, Nuthurst Grange Lane, B94 5NL, S : ¾ m. by A 3400
   ✆ 783972, Fax 783919, ☞ – 📺 ☎ 🅿 – 🔏 100. ◪ 🆀 ⓪ 𝗩𝗜𝗦𝗔. ✦
   M (closed Saturday lunch) 14.95/19.95 **t.** and a la carte ♨ 5.50 – ⊡ 8.90 – **15 rm** 89.00/
   135.00 **t.** – SB (weekends only) 125.00/180.00 **st.**

Beds. 404 S 28 – see Dunstable.

Shrops. 402 403 404 M 25 – pop. 1 343 – ✆ 0630.
◆London 166 – ◆Birmingham 50 – Chester 32 – ◆Stoke-on-Trent 22 – Shrewsbury 14.

🏠 **Bear,** Shrewsbury St., TF9 3NH, ✆ 84214, Fax 84787 – 📺 ☎ 🅿. ◪ 𝗩𝗜𝗦𝗔. ✦
   M a la carte 10.25/17.00 **t.** ♨ 4.00 – **6 rm** ⊡ 30.00/55.00 **t.** – SB (except Christmas) 75.00/
   80.00 **st.**

Devon 403 I 32 – pop. 588 – ✆ 075 530.
◆London 236 – Exeter 40 – ◆Plymouth 10 – Torquay 26.

🏨 **Alston Hall** ⅏, Alston, PL8 1HN, SW : 2½ m. ✆ 555, Fax 494, ≤, ⇌s, ♨, ◪, ☞, ✖ –
   ⇆ rm 🔏 75. ◪ 🆀 𝗩𝗜𝗦𝗔
   M (bar lunch Monday to Saturday)/dinner 22.00 **t.** and a la carte ♨ 5.00 – **20 rm** ⊡ 65.00/
   130.00 **t.** – SB (except Bank Holidays) 119.00 **st.**

Northants. – ⊠ ✆ 0604 Northampton.
◆London 77 – ◆Birmingham 58 – ◆Leicester 26 – Northampton 6.

XXX **Lynton House** ⅏ with rm, NN6 8DJ, SE : ¼ m. ✆ 770777, ☞ – 📺 ☎ 🅿. ◪ 🆀 𝗩𝗜𝗦𝗔. ✦
   closed 1 week spring, 2 weeks summer and Christmas – **M** - Italian (closed Sunday and
   lunch Monday and Saturday) 13.75 **t.** (lunch) and dinner a la carte 17.00/23.00 **t.** ♨ 6.95 –
   5 rm ⊡ 49.00/55.00 **t.**

Somerset 403 K 30 Great Britain G. – pop. 266 – ⊠ Bridgwater – ✆ 027 874 (3 fig.)
and 0278 (6 fig.).
Envir. : Stogursey Priory Church★★, W : 4½ m.
◆London 171 – ◆Bristol 48 – Minehead 15 – Taunton 22.

🏠 **Combe House** ⅏, Holford Combe, TA5 1RZ, S : 1 m. ✆ 741382, « Country house
   atmosphere », ⇌s, ◪, ☞, ✖ – ⇆ rest 📺 ☎ 🅿. ◪ 🆀 𝗩𝗜𝗦𝗔
   mid March-October – **M** (bar lunch)/dinner 15.50 **st.** ♨ 3.75 – **20 rm** ⊡ 34.00/90.00 **st.** –
   SB 80.00/86.00 **st.**

W. Yorks. – see Holmfirth.

Ches. 402 403 404 M 24 – pop. 4 672 – ✆ 0477.
◆London 181 – Chester 25 – ◆Liverpool 41 – ◆Manchester 24 – ◆Stoke-on-Trent 20.

🏨 **Old Vicarage,** Knutsford Rd, Cranage, CW4 8EF, NW : ½ m. on A 50 ✆ 532041,
   Fax 535728 – 📺 ☎ ♿ 🅿 – 🔏 30. ◪ 🆀 𝗩𝗜𝗦𝗔. ✦
   M a la carte 13.30/17.00 **t.** ♨ 4.95 – **25 rm** ⊡ 62.00/74.00 **st.** – SB (weekends only) 80.00/
   84.00 **st.**

🏨 **Holly Lodge,** 70 London Rd, CW4 7AS, on A 50 ✆ 537033, Fax 535823 – ⇆ rm 📺 ☎ 🅿
   – 🔏 120. ◪ 🆀 𝗩𝗜𝗦𝗔
   M (closed Bank Holidays) 8.00/12.70 **st.** and a la carte – **33 rm** ⊡ 31.00/94.00 **st.**

🏠 Oak Cottage Motel, London Rd, Allostock, WA16 9LU, N : 3 m. on A 50 ✆ 0565 (Knutsford) 722470, Fax 722749 – 📺 ☎ 🅿. ✦
   12 rm.

   at Brereton SE : 2 m. on A 50 – ⊠ Sandbach – ✆ 0477 Holmes Chapel :

🏨 **Bear's Head,** Newcastle Rd, CW11 9RS, ✆ 535251, Fax 535888, ☞, ✖ – 📺 ☎ 🅿. ◪ 🆀
   𝗩𝗜𝗦𝗔. ✦
   M (closed Sunday dinner) 10.95 **t.** (lunch) and a la carte 12.95/26.15 **t.** ♨ 4.75 – ⊡ 4.50 –
   22 rm 25.00/65.00 **st.**

HOLMFIRTH W. Yorks. [402] [404] O 23 – pop. 21 148 – ECD : Tuesday – ✉ Huddersfield – ☏ 0484.

ℹ 49-51 Huddersfield Rd, HD7 1JP ✆ 687603.

♦London 195 – ♦Leeds 23 – ♦Manchester 25 – ♦Sheffield 22.

🏨 **Old Bridge**, HD7 1DA, ✆ 681212, Fax 687978 – [TV] ☎ [P]. 💳 [AE] ⓓ VISA
accommodation closed 25 December – **M** 9.95/15.00 **t.** and a la carte 🍷 4.50 – **20 rm** 🛏 40.00/110.00 **t.** – SB (except Christmas) (weekends only) 85.00/120.00 **st.**

at Holme SW : 2½ m. on A 6024 – ✉ Huddersfield – ☏ 0484 Holmfirth :

⌂ **Holme Castle**, HD7 1QG, ✆ 686764, Fax 687775, ≤ – 🚭 [TV] [P]. 💳 [AE] VISA JCB. 🐕
M (by arrangement) 19.00 **t.** 🍷 3.75 – **8 rm** 🛏 20.00/65.00 **t.**

HOLNE Devon [403] I 32 – see Ashburton.

HOLT Norfolk [404] X 25 – pop. 2 502 – ECD : Thursday – ☏ 0263.

♦London 124 – King's Lynn 34 – ♦Norwich 22.

🍴🍴 **Yetman's**, 37 Norwich Rd, NR25 6SA, ✆ 713320 – 🚭
closed Monday and Tuesday – **M** (dinner only and lunch Saturday and Sunday) a la carte 22.25/25.90 **t.**

⊛ ATS Hempstead Rd Ind. Est. ✆ 712015

HOLYWELL Cambs. [404] T 27 – see St. Ives (Cambs.).

HONILEY Warks. – see Warwick

HONITON Devon [403] K 31 The West Country G. – pop. 6 490 – ECD : Thursday – ☏ 0404.

See : All Hallows Museum★ *AC*.

Envir. : Ottery St. Mary★ (St. Mary's★) SW : 5 m. by A 30 and B 3177.

Exc. : Faraway Countryside Park (≤★) *AC*, SE : 6½ m. by A 375 and B 3174.

ℹ Dowell Street, East Car Park, EX14 8LT ✆ 43716 (summer only).

♦London 186 – Exeter 17 – ♦Southampton 93 – Taunton 18.

🏨🏨 **Deer Park** 🌿, Buckerell Village, Weston, EX14 0PG, W : 2½ m. by A 30 ✆ 41266, Fax 46598, ≤, ♨, 🏊 heated, 🎣, 🌳, park, 🎾, squash – [TV] ☎ [P] – 🧑‍🏫 50. 💳 [AE] ⓓ VISA. 🐕
M 13.50/30.00 **st.** and a la carte 🍷 4.00 – **30 rm** 🛏 35.00/130.00 **st.** – SB (except Bank Holidays) 80.00/170.00 **st.**

at Wilmington E : 3 m. on A 35 – ✉ Honiton – ☏ 040 483 (3 fig.) and 0404 (6 fig.) Wilmington :

🏨 **Home Farm**, EX14 9JR, on A 35 ✆ 831278, « Part 16C thatched farm », 🌳 – [TV] ☎ [P]. 💳 [AE] VISA
M (bar lunch Monday to Saturday)/dinner 12.00 **t.** and a la carte 🍷 6.50 – **13 rm** 🛏 24.00/56.00 **t.** – SB 76.00 **st.**

at Payhembury NW : 7½ m. by A 30 – ✉ Honiton – ☏ 040 484 Broadhembury :

⌂ **Cokesputt House** 🌿, EX14 0HD, ✆ 289, ≤, « Part 17C and 18C house », 🌳 – 🚭 [P]. 💳 [AE] VISA. 🐕
closed Christmas – **M** (booking essential) (communal dining) 16.00 **st.** – **3 rm** 🛏 30.00/56.00 **st.**

HOOK Hants. [404] R 30 – pop. 2 562 – ECD : Thursday – ✉ Basingstoke – ☏ 0256.

♦London 47 – Reading 13 – ♦Southampton 35.

🏨🏨🏨 **Basingstoke Country**, London Rd, Nately Scures, RG27 9JS, W : 1 m. on A 30 ✆ 764161, Telex 859981, Fax 768341, 🏋, ♨, 🏊, 🌳 – |🛗| ▤ rest [TV] ☎ ♿ [P] – 🧑‍🏫 125. 💳 [AE] ⓓ VISA JCB. 🐕
M *(closed Saturday lunch)* 14.50/19.50 **st.** and a la carte 🍷 5.00 – 🛏 9.00 – **69 rm** 69.50/82.50 **st.**, 1 suite – SB (weekends only) 100.00 **st.**

🏨🏨 **Raven**, Station Rd, RG27 9HS, ✆ 762541, Fax 768677, ♨ – 🚭 rm [TV] ☎ [P] – 🧑‍🏫 90. 💳 [AE] ⓓ VISA
M *(closed Saturday lunch)* 10.50 **t.** and a la carte 🍷 3.85 – **38 rm** 🛏 55.00/71.00 **t.**

🏨 Hook House, London Rd, RL27 9EQ, ✆ 762630, Fax 760232, « Part Georgian house », ♨, 🏊, 🌳 – 🚭 [TV] ☎ [P]. 🐕
6 rm.

🏨 **White Hart**, London Rd, RG27 9DZ, on A 30 ✆ 762462, Fax 768351, 🌳 – [TV] ☎ [P]. 💳 [AE] VISA
M a la carte 8.50/21.00 **t.** – **22 rm** 🛏 57.00/64.00 **st.**

at Rotherwick N : 2 m. by A 30 and B 3349 on Rotherwick rd – ✉ ☏ 0256 Basingstoke :

🏨🏨🏨🏨 **Tylney Hall** 🌿, RG27 9AJ, S : 1½ m. by Newnham rd on Ridge Lane ✆ 764881, Fax 768141, « 19C mansion in extensive gardens », 🏋, ♨, 🏊 heated, 🏊, park, 🎾 – [TV] ☎ [P] – 🧑‍🏫 50. 💳 [AE] ⓓ VISA. 🐕
M 19.00/27.00 **st.** and a la carte 🍷 5.20 – **82 rm** 🛏 94.00/160.00 **st.**, 9 suites – SB 147.00/290.00 **st.**

HOOK Wilts. – see Swindon.

HOPE Derbs. 402 403 404 O 23 – ✉ Sheffield – ✪ 0433 Hope Valley.

◆London 180 – Derby 50 – ◆Manchester 31 – ◆Sheffield 15 – ◆Stoke-on-Trent 40.

🏠 **Rising Sun,** Castleton Rd, S30 2AL, E : 1½ m. on A 625 ℰ 651323, Fax 651601 – 📺 ☎ 🅿.
 🔼 𝑉𝐼𝑆𝐴 ✆
 M (grill rest.) 15.95/24.95 **t.** ♦ 3.95 – **11 rm** ⊑ 30.00/60.00 **t.** – SB 60.00/90.00 **st.**

⌂ **Underleigh** ⬙, S30 2RG, N : 1 m. by Edale rd ℰ 621372, ≤, ☞ – ⇖ rest 📺 🅿. 🔼 𝑉𝐼𝑆𝐴.
 ✆
 M (communal dining) 14.50 **st.** ♦ 3.50 – **7 rm** ⊑ 32.00/46.00 **st.** – SB 67.00/90.00 **st.**

HOPE COVE Devon 403 I 33 – see Salcombe.

HOPTON WAFERS Shrops. 403 404 M 26 – pop. 948 – ✉ Kidderminster – ✪ 0299 Cleobury
Mortimer.

◆London 150 – ◆Birmingham 32 – Shrewsbury 38.

🏠 **Crown Inn,** DY14 0NB, on A 4117 ℰ 270372, Fax 271127 – 📺 ☎ 🅿. 🔼 𝑉𝐼𝑆𝐴
 M (closed Sunday dinner and Monday) (bar lunch Monday to Saturday)/dinner 21.00 **st.**
 ♦ 4.25 – **8 rm** ⊑ 37.50/60.00 **st.** – SB 95.00/105.00 **st.**

HOPWOOD W. Mids. – ✉ ✪ 021 Birmingham.

◆London 131 – ◆Birmingham 8.

🏨 **Westmead** (Lansbury), Redditch Rd, B48 7AL, on A 441 ℰ 445 1202, Fax 445 6163, ≦s –
 ⇖ rm 🍽 rest 📺 ☎ 🅿 – 🔬 250. 🔼 🅰🅴 ⓪ 𝑉𝐼𝑆𝐴 ✆
 M 9.95/14.95 **st.** and a la carte – **58 rm** ⊑ 59.50/85.00 **st.** – SB (except Christmas and New
 Year) (weekends only) 78.00 **st.**

HORLEY Surrey 404 T 30 – pop. 17 700 – ECD : Wednesday – ✪ 0293.

◆London 27 – ◆Brighton 26 – Royal Tunbridge Wells 22.

Plan : see Gatwick

🏨 **Chequers Thistle** (Mt. Charlotte Thistle), Brighton Rd, RH6 8PH, on A 23 ℰ 786992,
 Telex 877550, Fax 820625, ⬙, ⇖ rm 📺 ☎ 🅿 – 🔬 60. 🔼 🅰🅴 ⓪ 𝑉𝐼𝑆𝐴 𝐽𝐶𝐵. ✆   Y z
 M (closed Saturday lunch) 11.50/17.00 **st.** – ⊑ 8.50 – **78 rm** 79.00/89.00 **st.**

🏠 **Langshott Manor,** Langshott, RH6 9LN, via Ladbroke Rd ℰ 786680, Fax 783905, « Part
 Elizabethan manor house », ☞ – 📺 ☎ 🅿. 🔼 🅰🅴 ⓪ 𝑉𝐼𝑆𝐴   Y
 closed 24 to 30 December – **M** (closed lunch Saturday and Sunday) (booking essential) 15.00/25.00 **st.** ♦ 6.00 – ⊑ 8.00 – **5 rm** 78.00/128.00 **st.** – SB (October-April) 118.00/
 182.00 **st.**

⌂ **Lawn** without rest., 30 Massetts Rd, RH6 7DE, ℰ 775751, Fax 821803, ☞ – ⇖ 📺 🅿. 🔼
 🅰🅴 ⓪ 𝑉𝐼𝑆𝐴   Y r
 closed Christmas and New Year – **7 rm** ⊑ 24.00/42.00 **st.**

HORNCASTLE Lincs. 402 404 T 24 – ✪ 0507.

◆London 140 – Boston 19 – Great Grimsby 31 – Lincoln 21.

🏨 **Admiral Rodney,** North St., LN9 5DX, ℰ 523131, Fax 523104 – 📳 ⇖ rm 📺 ☎ 🅿 –
 🔬 100. 🔼 🅰🅴 ⓪ 𝑉𝐼𝑆𝐴 ✆
 M (in bar) 8.40/11.05 **st.** – **32 rm** ⊑ 37.50/75.00 **st.** – SB (except Christmas and New Year)
 65.00/110.00 **st.**

HORNING Norfolk 404 Y 25 Great Britain G. – pop. 1 033 – ECD : Wednesday – ✉ Norwich –
✪ 0692.

Envir. : The Broads★.

◆London 122 – Great Yarmouth 17 – ◆Norwich 11.

🏨 **Petersfield House** ⬙, Lower St., NR12 8PF, ℰ 630741, Fax 630745, ☞ – 📺 ☎ 🅿. 🔼
 🅰🅴 ⓪ 𝑉𝐼𝑆𝐴
 M (dancing Saturday evening) 14.00/16.00 **t.** and a la carte ♦ 4.75 – **18 rm** ⊑ 58.00/85.00 **t.**
 – SB (except Bank Holidays) 96.00/146.00 **st.**

HORNINGSHAM Wilts. 403 404 N 30 – see Warminster.

HORNS CROSS Devon 403 H 31 The West Country G. – ECD : Wednesday – ✉ Bideford –
✪ 0237.

Exc. : Clovelly★★, NW : 7 m. by A 39 and B 3237.

◆London 237 – Barnstaple 15 – Exeter 48.

🏨 **Foxdown Manor** ⬙, Foxdown, EX39 5PJ, S : 1 m. ℰ 451325, Fax 451525, ≤, ≦s,
 ⬙ heated, ☞, park – ⇖ rest 📺 ☎ 🅿. 🔼 𝑉𝐼𝑆𝐴 ✆
 M (bar lunch Monday to Saturday)/dinner 16.95/28.00 **st.** ♦ 6.80 – **6 rm** ⊑ 45.00/140.00 **st.**,
 1 suite.

🏠 **Penhaven Country** ⬙, Parkham, EX39 5PL, S : 2 m. ℰ 451711, Fax 451878, ☞, park –
 ⇖ rest 📺 ☎ 🅿. 🔼 🅰🅴 ⓪ 𝑉𝐼𝑆𝐴
 M (dinner only and Sunday lunch)/dinner 13.50 **st.** and a la carte ♦ 4.75 – **12 rm** ⊑ 43.95/
 90.00 **st.** – SB (October-May except Christmas-New Year) 99.00/109.00 **st.**

↑ **Old Rectory** ⚓, Parkham, EX39 5PL, S : 2 m. ℰ 451443, ⚐ – ⇔ 🅿 ✖
M 18.00 **s.** ≬ 4.00 – **3 rm** ⊑ 49.00/78.00 **s.** – SB (January-February and November) 90.00/110.00 **st.**

HORSFORTH W. Yorks. 402 P 22 – see Leeds.

HORSHAM W. Sussex 404 T 30 – pop. 38 356 – ECD : Monday and Thursday – ✆ 0403.
🏠 Mannings Heath, Goldings Lane ℰ 210168, SE : 3 m. by A 281.
🗐 9 Causeway, RH12 1HE ℰ 211661.
♦London 39 – ♦Brighton 23 – Guildford 20 – Lewes 25 – Worthing 20.

🏨 **South Lodge** ⚓, Brighton Rd, Lower Beeding, RH13 6PS, SE : 5 m. on A 281 ℰ 891711, Fax 891766, ≤, « Victorian mansion, gardens », ⚘, park, ✖ – ⇔ rest 📺 ☎ 🅿 – 🔥 80.
🖎 AE ⓞ VISA JCB ✖
M 15.00/32.00 **t.** and a la carte ≬ 8.50 – ⊑ 10.00 – **37 rm** 90.00/175.00 **t.**, 2 suites – SB 147.50/170.00 **st.**

🏨 **Cisswood House,** Sandygate Lane, Lower Beeding, RH13 6NF, SE : 3 ¾ m. on A 281 ℰ 891216, Fax 891621, 🔲, ⚐ – 📺 🅿 – 🔥 120. 🖎 AE VISA ✖
closed 3 March-6 April, 19 to 30 August and Christmas-New Year – **M** *(closed Sunday)* 17.75/19.75 **t.** ≬ 5.50 – ⊑ 4.50 – **30 rm** 65.00/87.50 **st.**, 2 suites.

🏠 **Travel Inn,** The Station, 57 North St., RH12 1RB, ℰ 250141, Fax 270797 – ⇔ rm 📺 🕭
🅿 . 🖎 AE ⓞ VISA
M (Beefeater grill) a la carte approx. 16.00 **t.** ≬ 4.95 – **40 rm** 33.50 **t.**

✗ **Jeremy's** (at the Crabtree), Brighton Rd, Lower Beeding, RH13 6PT, SE : 5¼ m. on A 281 ℰ 891257 – 🅿 . 🖎 VISA
M *(closed Sunday dinner and 25 December)* (bar lunch Monday to Saturday)/dinner 18.95 **t.** ≬ 6.50.

at Slinfold W : 4 m. by A 281 off A 264 – ⊠ ✆ 0403 Horsham :

🏠 **Random Hall,** Stane St., RH13 7QX, W : ½ m. on A 29 ℰ 790558, Fax 791046, « Part 16C farmhouse » – 📺 🅿 . 🖎 AE VISA ✖
M 15.95 **st.** ≬ 5.50 – ⊑ 7.50 – **15 rm** 65.00/90.00 **st.** – SB (except Christmas) (weekends only) 96.70/143.70 **st.**

◍ ATS Rear of Brighton Rd Filling Station ℰ 67491/51736

HORSHAM ST. FAITH Norfolk 404 X 25 – see Norwich.

HORTON Dorset 403 404 O 31 – see Wimborne Minster.

HORTON Northants. 404 R 27 – pop. 500 – ⊠ ✆ 0604 Northampton.
♦London 66 – Bedford 18 – Northampton 6.

✗✗ **French Partridge,** Newport Pagnell Rd, NN7 2AP, ℰ 870033, Fax 870032 – 🅿
closed Sunday, Monday, 2 weeks Easter, 3 weeks August and 2 weeks Christmas – **M** (booking essential) (dinner only) 22.00 **st.** ≬ 5.50.

HORTON-CUM-STUDLEY Oxon. 403 404 Q 28 – pop. 500 – ECD : Wednesday – ⊠ Oxford – ✆ 0865 Stanton St. John.
♦London 57 – Aylesbury 23 – ♦Oxford 7.

🏨 **Studley Priory** ⚓, OX33 1AZ, ℰ 351203, Fax 351613, ≤, « Elizabethan manor house in park », ⚐, ✖ – 📺 ☎ 🅿 – 🔥 25. 🖎 AE ⓞ VISA JCB ✖
M 18.50/25.00 **st.** and a la carte ≬ 6.00 – **18 rm** ⊑ 88.00/150.00 **st.**, 1 suite – SB (except Christmas) 120.00/150.00 **st.**

HORWICH Lancs. 402 404 M 23 – pop. 16 656 – ⊠ ✆ 0204 Bolton.
♦London 214 – Liverpool 32 – ♦Manchester 18 – Preston 19.

🏠 **Swallowfield,** Chorley New Rd, BL6 6HN, SE : ¾ m. on A 673 ℰ 697914, Fax 68900 – 📺
☎ 🅿 . 🖎 AE VISA
closed 2 weeks Christmas-New Year – **M** (dinner only) 14.50 **st.** and a la carte ≬ 4.00 –
32 rm ⊑ 39.00/55.00 **st.**

HOTHFIELD Kent 404 W 30 – see Ashford.

HOUGHTON CONQUEST Beds. 404 S 27 – see Bedford.

HOVE E. Sussex 404 T 31 – see Brighton and Hove.

HOVINGHAM N. Yorks. 402 R 21 – pop. 310 – ECD : Thursday – ⊠ York – ✆ 0653.
♦London 235 – ♦Middlesbrough 36 – York 25.

🏨 **Worsley Arms,** YO6 4LA, ℰ 628234, Fax 628130, ⚐ – 📺 ☎ ⇔ 🅿 . 🖎 AE VISA
M 12.50/18.50 **t.** and lunch a la carte ≬ 4.50 – **22 rm** ⊑ 65.00/84.00 **t.** – SB (except Christmas and last week May) 98.00/118.00 **st.**

HOWTOWN Cumbria – see Ullswater.

☖, ☖ Bradley Park, Bradley Rd ℘ 539988 – ☖ Woodsome Hall, Fenay Bridge ℘ 602971, SE : 6 m. – ☖ Outlane, Slack Lane ℘ 0422 (Ryburn) 374762, W : 4 m. – ☖ Meltham, Thick Hellins Hall ℘ 850227, W : 5 m. – ☖ Fixby Hall. Lightbridge Rd ℘ 420110, N : 2 m. by A 6170 – ☖ Crosland Heath ℘ 653216, W : 3 m.

🛈 3-5 Albion St., HD1 2NW ℘ 430808.

◆London 191 – Bradford 11 – ◆Leeds 15 – ◆Manchester 25 – ◆Sheffield 26.

🏨 **Pennine Hilton,** Ainley Top, HD3 3RH, NW : 2 ½ m. at junction A 629 and A 643 ℘ 0422 (Elland) 375431, Telex 517346, Fax 310067, ₤₅, ≘s, ⬛ – ▯ – ⧖ rm ▤ rest 📺 ☎ 🅿 – 🚗 300. ☒ 厓 ⓪ 𝘝𝘐𝘚𝘈 𝘑𝘊𝘉 M (bar lunch Saturday) (carving lunch) 12.95/17.95 **st.** and a la carte ₰ 5.50 – ⚌ 10.25 – **117 rm** 65.00/75.00 **st.**, 1 suite.

🏨 **George,** St. George's Sq., HD1 1JA, ℘ 515444, Fax 435056 – ▯ ⧖ rm 📺 ☎ & 🅿 – 🚗 150. ☒ 厓 ⓪ 𝘝𝘐𝘚𝘈 ⅏ M (bar lunch Saturday) 9.25/15.95 **st.** and a la carte ₰ 6.00 – **59 rm** ⚌ 49.50/85.00 **st.**, 1 suite.

🏨 **Lodge,** 48 Birkby Lodge Rd, Birkby, HD2 2BG, N : 1 ½ m. by A 629 and Blacker Rd ℘ 431001, Fax 421590, ⩩ – ⧖ rm 📺 ☎ 🅿 – 🚗 35. ☒ 厓 ⅏ closed 26 and 27 December – **M** (closed Sunday dinner to non-residents) (restricted lunch Saturday) 14.75/20.50 **t.** ₰ 4.85 – **11 rm** ⚌ 50.00/70.00 **t.** – SB (weekends only) 101.00/141.00 **st.**

🏩 **Briar Court,** Halifax Rd, Birchencliffe, HD3 3NT, NW : 2 m. on A 629 ℘ 519902, Fax 431812 – 📺 ☎ 🅿 – 🚗 80. ☒ 厓 ⓪ 𝘝𝘐𝘚𝘈 𝘑𝘊𝘉 ⅏ M 10.95 **t.** (dinner) and a la carte 7.85/21.70 **t.** ₰ 3.90 – **44 rm** ⚌ 31.00/73.00 **st.**, 3 suites.

🏩 **Cote Royd,** 7 Halifax Rd, HD3 3AN, NW : 1½ m. on A 629 ℘ 547588, Fax 547588, ≘s, ⩩ – 📺 ☎ 🅿. ☒ 厓 ⓪ 𝘝𝘐𝘚𝘈 𝘑𝘊𝘉 ⅏ M (closed Sunday dinner and Bank Holidays except Christmas Day) (dinner only and Sunday lunch)/dinner 13.25 **t.** – **21 rm** ⚌ 39.50/50.00 **t.**

🏩 **Huddersfield,** 37-47 Kirkgate, HD1 1QT, ℘ 512111, Fax 435262, ≘s – ▯ 📺 ☎ 🅿. ☒ 厓 ⓪ 𝘝𝘐𝘚𝘈 M (closed Sunday dinner) 6.50/15.50 **st.** and a la carte ₰ 5.00 – **46 rm** ⚌ 46.00/68.00 **st.** – SB (weekends only) 79.00/141.00 **st.**

🏩 **Wellfield House,** 33 New Hey Rd, Marsh, HD3 4AL, W : 1 ½ m. on A 640 ℘ 425776, Fax 532122, « Victorian house », ⩩ – ⧖ rest 📺 ☎ 🅿. ☒ 厓 𝘝𝘐𝘚𝘈 ⅏ closed 24 December-2 January – **M** (residents only) (dinner only) 15.50 **st.** ₰ 3.95 – **5 rm** ⚌ 40.00/55.00 **st.** – SB (weekends only) 81.00/108.00 **st.**

⌂ **Elm Crest,** 2 Queens Rd., off Edgerton Rd (A 629), HD2 2AG, ℘ 530990, Fax 516227 – ⧖ 📺 ☎ 🅿. ☒ 厓 𝘝𝘐𝘚𝘈 ⅏ M (by arrangement) 18.00 **st.** ₰ 4.00 – **8 rm** ⚌ 22.00/58.00 **st.** – SB (except Bank Holidays) (weekends only) 62.00/100.00 **st.**

at Golcar W : 3½ m. by A 62 on B 6111 – ✉ ✆ 0484 Huddersfield :

✗✗ **Weaver's Shed,** Knowl Rd, via Scar Lane, HD7 4AN, ℘ 654284, « Converted 18C woollen mill » – 🅿. ☒ 厓 𝘝𝘐𝘚𝘈 closed Saturday lunch, Sunday, Monday, first 2 weeks January and last 2 weeks July – **M** 10.95 **t.** (lunch) and a la carte 11.40/23.15 **t.**

at Outlane NW : 4 m. on A 640 – ✉ Huddersfield – ✆ 0422 Halifax :

🏨 **Old Golf House** (Lansbury), New Hey Rd, HD3 3YP, ℘ 379311, Fax 372694 – ⧖ rm 📺 ☎ 🅿 – 🚗 70. ☒ 厓 ⓪ 𝘝𝘐𝘚𝘈 ⅏ M (closed Saturday lunch) 12.50/18.50 **t.** and a la carte – **50 rm** ⚌ 45.00/87.00 **st.** – SB (weekends only) 87.00/136.00 **st.**

⑩ ATS Leeds Rd ℘ 534441

HULL Humbs. 402 S 22 – see Kingston-upon-Hull.

Envir. : Littlecote★★ (arms and armour★, Roman mosaic floor★) AC, NW : 2 m. by A 4 and B 4192.

Exc. : Savernake Forest★★ (Grand Avenue★★★) W : 7 m. by A 4.

◆London 74 – ◆Bristol 57 – ◆Oxford 28 – Reading 26 – ◆Southampton 46.

🏨 **Bear** (Resort), 17 Charnham St., RG17 0EL, on A 4 ℘ 682512, Fax 684357 – ⧖ rm 📺 ☎ 🅿 – 🚗 80. ☒ 厓 ⓪ 𝘝𝘐𝘚𝘈 𝘑𝘊𝘉 M 8.75/12.75 **st.** and a la carte – ⚌ 7.50 – **41 rm** 65.00/85.00 **st.** – SB (weekends only) 96.00/112.00 **st.**

🏩 **Three Swans** (Resort), High St., RG17 0DL, ℘ 682721, Fax 681708 – ⧖ rm 📺 ☎ 🅿 – 🚗 60. ☒ 厓 ⓪ 𝘝𝘐𝘚𝘈 M a la carte 6.45/10.90 **t.** ₰ 4.00 – **15 rm** ⚌ 50.00/65.00 **t.** – SB 80.00 **st.**

⋔ **Marshgate Cottage** without rest., Marsh Lane, RG17 0QX, W : ¾ m. by Church St. ✍ 682307, Fax 685475, ≼, ☞ – ⇆ 📺 ☎ ℗, 🅰 🆎 *VISA* 🛠.
closed 24 December-15 January – **9 rm** ⟺ 25.50/48.50 **st.**

✗ **Just William's,** 50 Church St., RG17 0JH, ✍ 681199 – 🅰 *VISA*
closed Monday dinner and Sunday – **M** a la carte 13.75/16.95 **t.**

HUNMANBY N. Yorks. 402 T 21 – pop. 2 623 – ⊠ Filey – ✆ 0723 Scarborough.
◆London 198 – ◆Kingston-upon-Hull 40 – Scarborough 9 – York 41.

🏠 **Wrangham House,** 10 Stonegate, YO14 0NS, ✍ 891333, ☞ – ⇆ rm 📺 ℗.
VISA
M (dinner only) 13.00 **st.** and a la carte ⬧ 3.50 – **13 rm** ⟺ 25.00/78.00 **st.** – SB (except Bank Holidays) 76.00/100.00 **st.**

HUNSTANTON Norfolk 402 404 V 25 – pop. 3 990 – ECD : Thursday – ✆ 0485.
🏌 Hunstanton ✍ 532811, NE : ½ m.
🛈 The Green, PE36 5AH ✍ 532610.
◆London 120 – ◆Cambridge 60 – ◆Norwich 45.

🏨 **Le Strange Arms,** Golf Course Rd, PE36 6JJ, N : 1 m. by A 149 ✍ 534411, Fax 534724, ≼, – 📺 ☎ ℗ – 🔬 120. 🅰 🆎 ⓘ *VISA*
M (bar lunch Monday to Saturday)/dinner 20.00 **st.** and a la carte – **38 rm** ⟺ 45.00/75.00 **st.** – SB (except Christmas-New Year) 90.00/120.00 **st.**

⋔ **Claremont** without rest., 35 Greevegate, PE36 6AF, ✍ 533171 – ⇆ 📺 🅰 *VISA*
7 rm ⟺ 23.00/46.00 **s.**

⋔ **Fieldsend** without rest., 26 Homefields Rd, PE36 5HL, ✍ 532593 – 📺 ℗. 🛠
3 rm ⟺ 20.00/38.00 **st.**

⋔ **Pinewood,** 26 Northgate, PE36 6AP, ✍ 533068 – ⇆ rest 📺 ℗. 🅰 🆎 *VISA*
closed Christmas-New Year and January – **M** (by arrangement) 12.95 **t.** ⬧ 4.95 – **8 rm** ⟺ 35.00/50.00 **st.** – SB (except July-August and Bank Holidays) 55.00/59.00 **st.**

at Heacham S : 3 m. by A 149 – ⊠ King's Lynn – ✆ 0485 Heacham :

🏠 **Holly Lodge,** Lynn Rd, PE31 7HY, ✍ 70790, « Country house atmosphere », ☞ – ⇆ ℗. 🅰 *VISA* 🛠
closed January and February – **M** (closed Sunday) (dinner only) 25.00 **t.** and a la carte ⬧ 4.00 – **6 rm** ⟺ 60.00/85.00 **st.** – SB (except Bank Holidays) 112.50 **st.**

HUNSTRETE Avon 403 404 M 29 – see Bath.

HUNTINGDON Cambs. 404 T 26 – pop. 14 395 – ECD : Wednesday – ✆ 0480.
🏌 Brampton Park, Buckden Rd ✍ 434700, W : 3 m. by A 1 and A 604 – 🏌 Hemingford Abbots, New Farm Lodge, Cambridge Rd ✍ 495000.
🛈 The Library, Princes St., PE18 6PH ✍ 425831.
◆London 69 – Bedford 21 – ◆Cambridge 16.

🏨 **Old Bridge,** 1 High St., PE18 6TQ, ✍ 52681, Fax 411017 – 📺 ☎ ℗ – 🔬 40. 🅰 🆎 ⓘ *VISA*
M a la carte 20.00/29.00 **st.** ⬧ 4.25 – **26 rm** ⟺ 69.50/120.00 **st.** – SB (weekends only) 135.00/155.00 **st.**

🏨 **George** (Forte), George St., PE18 6AB, ✍ 432444, Fax 453130 – ⇆ 📺 ☎ ℗ – 🔬 150. 🅰 🆎 ⓘ *VISA* ᴊᴄʙ
M (bar lunch Monday to Saturday)/dinner 16.95 **t.** and a la carte ⬧ 6.45 – ⟺ 8.50 – **24 rm** 75.00/85.00 **st.**

🏠 **Forte Travelodge** without rest., SE : 5 ½ m. on A 604 (eastbound carriageway) ✍ 0954 (Swavesey) 30919, Reservations (Freephone) 0800 850950 – 📺 ♿ ℗. 🅰 🆎 *VISA* 🛠
40 rm 31.95 **t.**

◎ ATS Nursery Rd ✍ 451031/451515

HURLEY-ON-THAMES Berks. 404 R 29 – pop. 2 068 – ECD : Wednesday – ⊠ Maidenhead – ✆ 0628 Littlewick Green.
◆London 38 – ◆Oxford 26 – Reading 12.

🏨 **Ye Olde Bell** (Resort), High St., SL6 5LX, ✍ 825881, Fax 825939, « Part 12C inn », ☞ – 📺 ☎ ℗ – 🔬 140. 🅰 🆎 ⓘ *VISA* ᴊᴄʙ
M 14.95/18.95 **t.** and a la carte ⬧ 4.75 – ⟺ 7.50 – **35 rm** 75.00/95.00 **st.**. 1 suite – SB (except 29 June-3 July and Christmas-New Year) 105.00/170.00 **st.**

HURSTBOURNE TARRANT Hants. 403 404 P 30 – pop. 709 – ⊠ Andover – ✆ 0264.
◆London 77 – ◆Bristol 77 – ◆Oxford 38 – ◆Southampton 33.

🏨 **Esseborne Manor** ⌕, SP11 0ER, NE : 1½ m. on A 343 ✍ 76444, Fax 76473, ☞, ✗ – 📺 ☎ ℗. 🅰 🆎 ⓘ *VISA* 🛠
M 19.50/38.00 **t.** and dinner a la carte ⬧ 6.00 – **12 rm** ⟺ 84.00/125.00 **t.** – SB (except Easter and Christmas) 150.00/185.00 **st.**

at Faccombe N : 3½ m. by A 343 – ⊠ Andover – ✆ 026 487 Linkenholt :

⋔ Jack Russell, SP11 0DS, ✍ 315 – 📺 ℗. 🛠
3 rm.

234

HURST GREEN Lancs. 402 M 22 – ⊠ Whalley – ✪ 0254 Stonyhurst.

◆London 236 – Blackburn 12 – Burnley 13 – Preston 12.

血 **Shireburn Arms,** Whalley Rd, BB6 9QJ, ℰ 826518, Fax 826208, 🐖 – 🗺 ☎ 🅿. 🖪 🖭 ⑩ *VISA*
M 7.50/10.00 **t.** and dinner a la carte ⌁ 5.00 – **15 rm** ⎓ 29.00/49.00 **t.**

HUSBANDS BOSWORTH Leics. 403 404 Q 26 – pop. 889 – ⊠ Lutterworth – ✪ 0858 Market Harborough.

◆London 88 – ◆Birmingham 40 – ◆Leicester 14 – Northampton 17.

血 **Fernie Lodge,** Berridges Lane, LE17 6LE, by Bell Lane ℰ 880551, Fax 880014 – 🙌 rest
🗏 rest 🗺 ☎ 🅿 – 🔬 50. 🖪 🖭 *VISA*
M 11.95/17.95 **st.** ⌁ 2.90 – **17 rm** ⎓ 20.00/67.00 **st.**, 1 suite – SB (weekends only) 51.00/
105.00 **st.**

HUTTON-LE-HOLE N. Yorks. 402 R 21 – see Lastingham.

HUXHAM Devon – see Exeter.

HUYTON Mersey. 402 403 L 23 – see Liverpool.

☛ *When in a hurry use the Michelin Main Road Maps :*
970 Europe, 980 Greece, 984 Germany, 985 Scandinavia-Finland,
986 Great Britain and Ireland, 987 Germany-Austria-Benelux, 988 Italy,
989 France, 990 Spain-Portugal and 991 Yugoslavia.

HYTHE Kent 404 X 30 – pop. 13 118 – ECD : Wednesday – ✪ 0303.
🏌 Sene Valley, Sene ℰ 268513, N : 2 m.
🖪 Prospect Rd Car Park, CT21 5NH ℰ 267799 (summer only).

◆London 68 – Folkestone 6 – Hastings 33 – Maidstone 31.

血血 **Hythe Imperial** (Best Western) ⚲, Prince's Par., CT21 6AE, ℰ 267441, Fax 264610, ≼,
🏌, 🛥, 🔲, 🖾, 🐖, ✋, ✋, squash – 🗃 🗺 ☎ & 🅿 – 🔬 220. 🖪 🖭 ⑩ *VISA*. ✀
M 15.00/22.00 **t.** and a la carte ⌁ 6.10 – **98 rm** ⎓ 85.00/120.00 **t.**, 2 suites – SB (except
Bank Holidays) 125.00/157.00 **st.**

血 **Stade Court** (Best Western), West Par., CT21 6DT, ℰ 268263, Fax 261803, ≼ – 🗃 🗺 ☎
🅿 – 🔬 35. 🖪 🖭 ⑩ *VISA*
M 10.00/14.95 **t.** and a la carte ⌁ 6.00 – **42 rm** ⎓ 55.00/75.00 **t.** – SB (except Christmas and
New Year) 90.00/140.00 **st.**

IBSTONE Bucks – pop. 224 – ⊠ High Wycombe – ✪ 0491 Turville Heath.

◆London 39 – ◆Oxford 20 – Reading 19.

血 **Fox of Ibstone Country,** HP14 3GG, ℰ 638722, Fax 638873, 🐖 – 🗺 ☎ 🅿. 🖪 🖭 ⑩
VISA. ✀
M 10.00/20.00 **t.** and a la carte ⌁ 4.00 – **9 rm** ⎓ 58.00/71.00 **st.** – SB (weekends only)
50.00/92.00 **st.**

IDE Devon 403 J 31 – see Exeter.

IFFLEY Oxon – see Oxford.

ILKLEY W. Yorks. 402 O 22 – pop. 13 060 – ECD : Wednesday – ✪ 0943.
🏌 Myddleton ℰ 607277.
🖪 Station Rd, LS29 8HA ℰ 602319.

◆London 210 – Bradford 13 – Harrogate 17 – ◆Leeds 16 – Preston 46.

血 **Rombalds,** 11 West View, Wells Rd, LS29 9JG, ℰ 603201, Fax 816586 – 🗺 ☎ 🅿 –
🔬 50. 🖪 🖭 ⑩ *VISA*
closed 27 to 31 December – M 10.75/14.95 **t.** and a la carte ⌁ 5.00 – **11 rm** ⎓ 72.00/
100.00 **t.**, 4 suites – SB (except Christmas and New Year) 110.00/172.00 **st.**

血 **Grove,** 66 The Grove, LS29 9PA, ℰ 600298 – 🗺 ☎ 🅿. 🖪 *VISA*. ✀
closed 20 December-3 January – M (bar lunch)/dinner 15.00 **st.** ⌁ 3.50 – **6 rm** ⎓ 38.00/
52.00 **st.**

血 **Cow and Calf,** Moor Top, LS29 8BT, SE : 1 ¼ m. ℰ 607335, Fax 816022, ≼, 🐖 – 🗺 ☎
🅿. 🖪 🖭 ⑩ *VISA*
M 7.95/13.75 **st.** and a la carte ⌁ 4.50 – **17 rm** ⎓ 45.00/75.00 – SB 75.00/90.00 **st.**

⌂ **Moorview House,** 104 Skipton Rd, LS29 9HE, W : ¼ m. on A 65 ℰ 600156, ≼, 🐖 – 🗺
🅿.
closed 24 December-2 January – M (by arrangement) 12.95 **st.** – **12 rm** ⎓ 30.00/50.00 **st.**

XXX **Box Tree,** 29 Church St., LS29 9DR, ℰ 608484, Fax 607186 – 🖪 *VISA*
closed Saturday lunch, Sunday dinner, Monday, 27 to 30 December and 21 to 31 January –
M 22.50/29.50 **st.** ⌁ 6.95.

235

ILLOGAN Cornwall 403 E 33 The West Country G. – pop. 11 782 – ⊠ ⊕ 0209 Redruth.
Envir. : Portreath★, NW : 2 m. by B 3300 – Hell's Mouth★, SW : 5 m. by B 3301.
☐ Tehidy Park, Camborne ℘ 0209 (Redruth) 842208.
◆London 305 – Falmouth 14 – Penzance 17 – Truro 11.

⌂ **Aviary Court** ⌂, Mary's Well, TR16 4QZ, NW : ¾ m. by Alexandra Rd ℘ 842256, ☞ –
◻ ☎ 🅿. ⬛ AE ⓿ 𝚅𝙸𝚂𝙰 ⌦
M (dinner only and Sunday lunch)/dinner 11.50 **t.** and a la carte ⌁ 5.00 – **6 rm** ⌸ 40.00/
58.00 **t.**

ILMINSTER Somerset 403 L 31 The West Country G. – pop. 3 722 – ⊕ 0460.
See : Town★ - St. Mary's★★.
Envir. : Barrington Court Gardens★ AC, NE : 3½ m. by B 3168.
◆London 145 – Taunton 12 – Yeovil 17.

⌂ **Forte Travelodge** without rest., Southfield Roundabout, Horton Cross, TA19 9PT, NW :
1½ m. at junction of A 303 and A 358 ℘ 53748, Reservations (Freephone) 0800 850950 –
◻ ⅋ 🅿. ⬛ AE 𝚅𝙸𝚂𝙰. ⌦
32 rm 31.95 **t.**

IMPINGTON Cambs. – see Cambridge.

INGATESTONE Essex 404 V 28 – pop. 6 150 – ECD : Wednesday – ⊠ Chelmsford –
⊕ 0277 Brentwood.
◆London 27 – Chelmsford 6.

🏠 **Ivy Hill**, Writtle Rd, Margaretting, CM4 0EW, NE : 2¼ m. by A 12 ℘ 353040, Fax 355038,
⌂ heated, ☞, ⌘ – ◻ ☎ 🅿. ⬛ AE ⓿ 𝚅𝙸𝚂𝙰. ⌦
M (closed Monday lunch and dinner Saturday and Sunday) (bar dinner) a la carte 12.50/
20.50 **st.** ⌁ 4.75 – ⌸ 6.95 – **18 rm** 40.00/90.00 **st.**

I prezzi	Per ogni chiarimento sui prezzi qui riportati,
	consultate le spiegazioni alle pagine dell'introduzione.

INGHAM Lincs. 404 S 23 – pop. 671 – ⊠ ⊕ 0522 Lincoln.
◆London 147 – Lincoln 7 – ◆Sheffield 55.

XX **Moulin Maison**, The Mill House, Clifftop, LN1 2YQ, E : 1¼ m. on B 1398 ℘ 730130, ☞ –
🅿. ⬛ 𝚅𝙸𝚂𝙰
closed Sunday to Wednesday – **M** (dinner only) 22.00 **t.** ⌁ 4.25.

INGLEBY GREENHOW N. Yorks. 402 Q 20 – see Great Broughton.

INGLETON N. Yorks. 402 M 21 – pop. 1 769 – ⊠ Carnforth – ⊕ 052 42.
🄳 Community Centre Car Park, LA6 3HJ ℘ 41049 (summer only).
◆London 266 – Kendal 21 – Lancaster 18 – ◆Leeds 53.

⌂ **Moorgarth Hall Country House**, New Rd, LA6 3HL, SE : ¼ m. on A 65 ℘ 41946,
Fax 42252, ☞ – rest ◻ 🅿. ⬛ 𝚅𝙸𝚂𝙰 ⌦
closed January – **M** (closed Thursday) (dinner only) 14.50 **st.** and a la carte ⌁ 3.80 – **8 rm**
⌸ 33.00/61.00 **st.** – SB 70.00/90.00 **st.**

⌂ **Pines Country House**, New Rd, LA6 3HN, NW : ¼ m. on A 65 ℘ 41252, ☞ – ⌦ ◻ 🅿.
𝚅𝙸𝚂𝙰
M (by arrangement) 10.50 **t.** – **5 rm** ⌸ 20.00/36.00 **st.** – SB 53.00/69.00 **st.**

INSTOW Devon 403 H 30 – see Bideford.

IPSWICH Suffolk 404 X 27 Great Britain G. – pop. 129 661 – ECD : Monday and Wednesday –
⊕ 0473.
See : Christchurch Mansion (collection of paintings★) X B.
☐ Rushmere Heath ℘ 727109, E : 3 m. by A 1214 Y – ☐, ☐ Purdis Heath, Bucklesham Rd
℘ 727474, E : 3 m. by A 1156 Z – ☐ Fynn Valley, Witnesham ℘ 785463, N : 2 m. by B 1077 Y.
✈ Ipswich Airport ℘ 720111, Fax 710055 Z.
🄳 Town Hall, Princes St., IP1 1BZ ℘ 258070.
◆London 76 – ◆Norwich 43.

Plan on next page

🏨 **Belstead Brook**, Belstead Rd, IP2 9HB, SW : 2½ m. ℘ 684241, Fax 681249, ☞ – ⌷
⌦ rm ◻ ☎ ⅋ 🅿 – ⌸ 50. ⬛ AE ⓿ 𝚅𝙸𝚂𝙰 ⌦ Z u
M (bar lunch Saturday) 14.00 **st.** and a la carte ⌁ 5.00 – ⌸ 7.00 – **89 rm** 49.50/59.50 **st.**,
2 suites – SB (weekends only) 90.00/100.00 **st.**

🏨 **Suffolk Grange** (Lansbury), The Havens, Ransomes Europark, IP3 9SJ, SE : 3½ m. by
A 1156 and Nacton Rd at junction with A 45 ℘ 272244, Fax 272484, ⌨, ⌖ – ⌷ ⌦ rm
▦ rest ◻ ☎ ⅋ 🅿 – ⌸ 180. ⬛ AE ⓿ 𝚅𝙸𝚂𝙰 Y
M (bar lunch Saturday and Bank Holidays) 11.50/15.50 **st.** and a la carte – **60 rm** ⌸ 65.50/
77.00 **st.** – SB (weekends only) 94.00 **st.**

IPSWICH

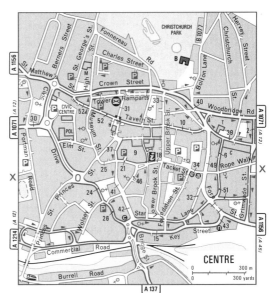

CENTRE

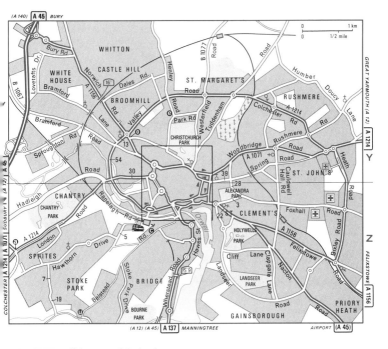

Europe

If the name of the hotel
is not in bold type,
on arrival ask the hotelier his prices.

🏨 **Marlborough** (Best Western), Henley Rd, IP1 3SP, ℰ 257677, Fax 226927, ☞ – ✦✕ 📺 ☎
🅿 – 🕮 60. 🔼 🄰🄴 ⓞ 𝗩𝗜𝗦𝗔   Y **e**
M 15.00/22.50 **t.** 🍴 4.50 – **21 rm** ⊠ 55.00/75.00 **t.**, 1 suite – SB 95.00 **st.**

🏨 **Novotel,** Greyfriars Rd, IP1 1UP, ℰ 232400, Telex 987684, Fax 232414 – |🛗| ✦✕ rm 📺 📞
🔥 🅿 – 🕮 160. 🔼 🄰🄴 ⓞ 𝗩𝗜𝗦𝗔 🄹🄲🄱   X **c**
M 12.00 **st.** and a la carte 🍴 4.50 – ⊠ 7.50 – **100 rm** 57.50/62.50 **st.** – SB (weekends only)
70.00/90.00 **st.**

🏨 **Forte Posthouse,** London Rd, IP2 0UA, SW : 2 ¼ m. on A 1214 ℰ 690313, Fax 680412,
🔲 heated – ✦✕ rm 📺 ☎ 🅿 – 🕮 110. 🔼 🄰🄴 ⓞ 𝗩𝗜𝗦𝗔 🄹🄲🄱. ☞   Z **a**
M a la carte approx. 17.50 **t.** 🍴 4.65 – ⊠ 6.95 – **112 rm** 53.50 **st.** – SB (weekends only)
90.00 **st.**

♧ **Bentley Tower,** 172 Norwich Rd, IP1 2PY, ℰ 212142, Fax 212142 – 📺 🅿. 🔼 𝗩𝗜𝗦𝗔
☞   Y **o**
closed 25 December-2 January – **M** (bar lunch)/dinner 15.50 **st.** and a la carte 🍴 3.00 –
10 rm ⊠ 38.00/48.00 **st.** – SB 55.00/96.00 **st.**

↑ **Highview House,** 56 Belstead Rd, IP2 8BE, ℰ 688659, ☞ – 📺 ☎ 🅿. 🔼 𝗩𝗜𝗦𝗔
☞   Z **c**
closed 25 and 26 December – **M** (by arrangement) 12.70 **st.** 🍴 3.20 – **11 rm** ⊠ 40.00/
50.00 **st.**

🍴🍴 **Orwell House,** 4 Orwell Pl., IP4 1BB, ℰ 230254 – 🔼 🄰🄴 ⓞ 𝗩𝗜𝗦𝗔   X **e**
closed Sunday and Monday – **M** 8.95/15.00 **t.** and a la carte 🍴 4.00.

🍴🍴 **Bombay,** 6 Orwell Pl., IP4 1BB, ℰ 251397   X **a**
M - **Indian** 6.50/7.50 **t.** and a la carte 🍴 3.50.

🍴 **Mortimer's on the Quay,** Wherry Quay, IP4 1AS, ℰ 230225 – 🔼 🄰🄴 ⓞ 𝗩𝗜𝗦𝗔   X **n**
*closed Saturday lunch, Sunday, 2 weeks August-September, 24 December-6 January and
Bank Holidays* – **M** - **Seafood** a la carte 12.95/21.95 **t.** 🍴 5.20.

at Copdock SW : 4 m. by A 1214 off A 1071 – Z – ✉ ✪ 0473 Ipswich :

🏨 **Ipswich Moat House** (Q.M.H.), Old London Rd, IP8 3JD, ℰ 730444, Fax 730801, 𝄢, ≋
– |🛗| 📺 ☎ 🔥 🅿 – 🕮 350. 🔼 🄰🄴 ⓞ 𝗩𝗜𝗦𝗔
M (carving lunch)/dinner 14.95 **st.** and a la carte 🍴 4.50 – **74 rm** ⊠ 45.00/70.00 **st.** –
SB (weekends only) 64.00/114.00 **st.**

at Burstall W : 4 ½ m. by A 1214 off A 1071 – Y – ✉ ✪ 0473 Ipswich :

↑ **Mulberry Hall** ☜, IP8 3DP, ℰ 652348, ☞, ☜ – ✦✕ 🅿. ☞
M (by arrangement) (communal dining) 13.50 **s.** – **3 rm** ⊠ 17.50/35.00 **s.**

at Hintlesham W : 5 m. by A 1214 on A 1071 – Y – ✉ ✪ 0473 Ipswich :

🏰 **Hintlesham Hall** ☜, IP8 3NS, ℰ 652334, Fax 652463, ≤, « Georgian country house
of 16C origins », ≋, 🅵, 🐾, ☞, park, ☜ – ✦✕ rest 📺 ☎ 🅿 – 🕮 30. 🔼 🄰🄴 ⓞ
𝗩𝗜𝗦𝗔
M (closed Saturday lunch) 18.50/22.00 **st.** and a la carte 26.00/44.00 **st.** – ⊠ 12.50 – **29 rm**
85.00/160.00 **st.**, 4 suites – SB (except Bank Holidays) 140.00/295.00 **st.**

◎ ATS White Elm St. ℰ 217157

IRONBRIDGE Shrops. 🄢🄞🄓 🄢🄞🄓 M 26 – pop. 1 456 – ✪ 0952.

🅱 The Wharfage, TF8 7AW ℰ 432166.

◆London 135 – ◆Birmingham 36 – Shrewsbury 18.

🏨 **Valley,** Buildwas Rd, TF8 7DW, on B 4380 ℰ 432247, Fax 432308, ☞ – 📺 ☎ 🅿 – 🕮 250.
🔼 🄰🄴 𝗩𝗜𝗦𝗔
M (closed Sunday lunch) 30.00 **st.** and a la carte 🍴 3.95 – **34 rm** ⊠ 43.00/72.00 **st.** –
SB 90.00/120.00 **st.**

↑ **Bridge House** without rest., Buildwas, TF8 7BN, W : 2 m. on B 4380 ℰ 432105, ☞ – 🅿.
closed 3 weeks Christmas – **4 rm** ⊠ 25.00/46.00 **s.**

ISLEY WALTON Leics. – see Castle Donington.

IVINGHOE Bucks. 🄢🄞🄓 S 28 – pop. 2 517 (inc. Pitstone) – ✉ Leighton Buzzard –
✪ 0296 Cheddington.

🅵₉ Wellcroft ℰ 668696.

◆London 42 – Aylesbury 9 – Luton 11.

🍴🍴 **King's Head,** Station Rd, LU7 9EB, ℰ 668388, Fax 668107 – ▤ 🅿. 🔼 🄰🄴 ⓞ 𝗩𝗜𝗦𝗔
M 19.95 **st.** and a la carte 🍴 6.75.

IVY HATCH Kent – see Sevenoaks.

IXWORTH Suffolk 404 W 27 – pop. 2 121 – ⊠ Bury St. Edmunds – ☎ 0359 Pakenham.

◆London 85 – ◆Cambridge 35 – ◆Ipswich 25 – ◆Norwich 36.

XX **Theobalds,** 68 High St., IP31 2HJ, ℰ 31707 – 🔄 VISA
closed Saturday lunch, Sunday dinner, Monday and Bank Holidays – **M** 15.95 **t.** (lunch) and a la carte 22.50/26.50 **t.**

at Pakenham S : 3¼ m. by A 1088 – ⊠ Bury St. Edmunds – ☎ 0359 Pakenham :

🏠 **Hamling House** ⤸, Bull Rd, IP31 2LW, ℰ 30934, Fax 32298, ☞ – ⚶ rest 📺 ☎ 🅿. 🔄 AE ① VISA
M 10.50/16.50 **st.** ⌀ 2.80 – **6 rm** ⊵ 48.00/60.00 **st.** – SB 84.00/96.00 **st.**

JERVAULX ABBEY N. Yorks. – see Masham.

JEVINGTON E. Sussex 404 U 31 – see Eastbourne.

KEDLESTON Derbs. 402 403 404 P 25 – see Derby.

KEIGHLEY W. Yorks. 402 O 22 – ☎ 0535.

🛝 Branshaw, Branshaw Moor, Oakworth ℰ 643235, SE : 2 m. by B 6143 – 🛝 Riddlesden, Howden Rough ℰ 602148, N : 3 m.

◆London 200 – Bradford 10 – Burnley 20.

🏨 **Beeches** (Toby), Bradford Rd, BD21 4BB, ℰ 610611, Fax 610037 – ⚶ rm 📺 ☎ ⌂ 🅿 – 🔬 35. 🔄 AE ① VISA 🕸
closed 1 week Christmas – **M** (grill rest.) a la carte 8.30/17.65 **t.** – **43 rm** ⊵ 60.00/70.00 **st.**

🏠 **Dalesgate,** 406 Skipton Rd, Utley, BD20 6HP, ℰ 664930, Fax 611253 – 📺 ☎ 🅿. 🔄 AE ① VISA 🕸
M *(closed Sunday)* (dinner only) 15.50 **t.** and a la carte ⌀ 3.65 – **21 rm** ⊵ 29.00/52.00 **t.** – SB (weekends only) 68.00/115.80 **st.**

⑩ ATS 69-73 Bradford Rd, Riddlesden ℰ 607533/607933

KEMBLE Glos. 403 404 N 28 – see Cirencester.

KENDAL Cumbria 402 L 21 Great Britain G. – pop. 23 710 – ECD : Thursday – ☎ 0539.

Envir. : Levens Hall and Garden★ AC, S : 4½ m. by A 591, A 590 and A 6.

Exc. : Lake Windermere★★, NW : 8 m. by A 5284 and A 591.

🛝 The Heights ℰ 724079.

🛈 Town Hall, Highgate, LA9 4DL ℰ 725758.

◆London 270 – Bradford 64 – Burnley 63 – ◆Carlisle 49 – Lancaster 22 – ◆Leeds 72 – ◆Middlesbrough 77 – ◆Newcastle upon Tyne 104 – Preston 44 – Sunderland 88.

🏨 Woolpack, Stricklandgate, LA9 4ND, ℰ 723852, Fax 728608 – ⚶ rm 📺 ☎ 🅿 – 🔬 100
54 rm.

🏠 **Garden House,** Fowl-Ing Lane, LA9 6PH, NE : ½ m. by A 685 ℰ 731131, Fax 740064, ☞ – ⚶ 📺 ☎ 🅿. 🔄 AE ① VISA JCB
closed 25 December-9 January – **M** (bar lunch Monday to Saturday)/dinner 18.50 **st.** and a la carte ⌀ 5.00 – **10 rm** ⊵ 50.00/70.00 **st.** – SB 80.00/116.00 **st.**

🏠 **Lane Head House** ⤸, Helsington, LA9 5RJ, S : 1¾ m. on A 6 ℰ 731283, ≤, ☞ – ⚶ rest 📺 ☎ 🅿. 🔄 JCB. 🕸
closed November – **M** *(closed Sunday)* (dinner only) 17.50 **st.** – **7 rm** ⊵ 40.00/60.00 **st.** – SB (except July-September and Bank Holidays) 70.00/80.00 **st.**

at Selside N : 6 m. on A 6 – ⊠ Kendal – ☎ 0539 Selside :

↑ **Low Jock Scar** ⤸, LA8 9LE, off A 6 ℰ 823259, ☞ – ⚶ 🅿
March-November – **M** (by arrangement) 13.00 **st.** ⌀ 3.00 – **5 rm** ⊵ 23.50/45.00 **st.**

⑩ ATS Mintsfeet Est. ℰ 721559/723802

KENILWORTH Warks. 403 404 P 26 Great Britain G. – pop. 18 782 – ☎ 0926.

See : Castle★ AC.

🛈 The Library, 11 Smalley Pl., CV8 1QG ℰ 52595/50708.

◆London 102 – ◆Birmingham 19 – ◆Coventry 5 – Warwick 5.

🏨 **De Montfort** (De Vere), The Square, CV8 1ED, ℰ 55944, Fax 57830 – 🛗 ⚶ rm 📺 ☎ 🅿 – 🔬 250. 🔄 AE ① VISA
M 12.00/15.75 **st.** and dinner a la carte – **94 rm** ⊵ 70.00/80.00 **st.**, 1 suite.

🏨 **Periquito Chesford Grange,** Chesford Bridge, CV8 2LD, SE : 1¾ m. on A 452 ℰ 59331, Fax 59075, ⒡₆, ☞, park – ⚶ rm 📺 ☎ 🅿 – 🔬 800. 🔄 AE ① VISA
M (bar lunch Saturday) 16.00 **t.** and a la carte ⌀ 6.00 – ⊵ 6.50 – **129 rm** 37.50/70.00 **st.**, 1 suite – SB (weekdays only) 67.00/154.50 **st.**

🏠 **Victoria Lodge,** 180 Warwick Rd, CV8 1HU, 🖉 512020, Fax 58703, 🦐 – ⤢ 📺 ☎ 🄿. 🔼 🖭 🚗
  M *(closed Sunday)* (residents only) (lunch by arrangement) a la carte 8.00/14.75 **st.** – **6 rm**
  ⌴ 31.00/51.00 **st.**

🏠 **Castle Laurels,** 22 Castle Rd, CV8 1NG, 🖉 56179, Fax 54954 – ⤢ 📺 ☎ 🄿. 🔼 🖭 🚗
  closed 23 December-2 January – **M** (dinner only) a la carte 8.00/15.00 **st.** ▯ 3.95 – **12 rm**
  ⌴ 31.50/49.00 **st.**

↱ **Abbey** without rest., 41 Station Rd, CV8 5JD, 🖉 512707 – 📺. 🚗
  7 rm ⌴ 18.00/40.00 **s.**

XX **Bosquet,** 97a Warwick Rd, CV8 1HP, 🖉 52463 – 🔼 🖭 🚗
  closed Sunday, Monday, 3 weeks August and 1 week Christmas – **M** - **French** (lunch by
  arrangement)/dinner 28.00 **t.** and a la carte ▯ 6.00.

XX **Diment,** 121-123 Warwick Rd, CV8 1HP, 🖉 53763 – 🄿. 🔼 🖭 ⑩ 🚗
  closed Saturday lunch, Sunday, Monday, 1 week Easter, first 3 weeks August and Bank
  Holidays – **M** 10.75 **t.** (lunch) and a la carte 17.65/24.15 **t.** ▯ 4.75.

KENNFORD Devon 408 J 32 – see Exeter.

KESWICK Cumbria 402 K 20 Great Britain G. – pop. 4 777 – ECD : Wednesday – ✿ 076 87.

Envir. : Derwentwater★ Y – Thirlmere (Castlerigg Stone Circle★), E : 1½ m. Y A.

🔳 Threlkeld Hall 🖉 79324, E : 4 m. by A 66 Y

🄱 Moot Hall, Market Sq., CA12 4JR 🖉 72645 – at Seatoller, Seatoller Barn, Borrowdale
Keswick, CA12 5XN 🖉 77294 (summer only).

◆London 294 – ◆Carlisle 31 – Kendal 30.

Plan on next page

🏨 **Underscar Manor** ⌯, Applethwaite, CA12 4PH, N : 1¾ m. by A 591 on Underscar rd
  🖉 75000, Fax 74904, ≼ Derwent Water, « Italianate Victorian country house », 🦐, park –
  ⤢ rest 📺 ☎ 🄿. 🔼 🖭 🚗
  M 18.50/25.00 **t.** and a la carte ▯ 7.00 – **11 rm** ⌴ (dinner included) 90.00/250.00 **t.**

🏨 **Brundholme Country House** ⌯, Brundholme Rd, CA12 4NL, 🖉 74495, Fax 73536, ≼,   Y **e**
  🦐 – ⤢ rest 📺 ☎ 🄿. 🔼 🖭
  closed December to mid February – **M** (dinner only) 25.00 **t.** and a la carte ▯ 4.95 – **11 rm**
  ⌴ 40.00/120.00 **t.** – SB (except Bank Holidays) 100.00/140.00 **st.**

🏨 **Lyzzick Hall** ⌯, Underskiddaw, CA12 4PY, NW : 2½ m. on A 591 🖉 72277, Fax 72278,
  ≼, ♨ heated, 🦐 – ⤢ rest 📺 ☎ 🄿. 🔼 🖭 ⑩ 🚗 🚗   Y
  closed 24 to 26 December and February – **M** 18.00/20.00 **t.** and a la carte – **25 rm** ⌴ 32.00/
  72.00.

🏠 **Grange Country House** ⌯, Manor Brow, Ambleside Rd, CA12 4BA, 🖉 72500, ≼, 🦐 –
  ⤢ rest 📺 ☎ 🄿. 🔼 🚗. 🚗   Y **u**
  4 March-5 November – **M** (light lunch)/dinner 17.75 **st.** ▯ 4.50 – **10 rm** ⌴ 47.00/79.00 **st.** –
  SB 87.00/94.00 **st.**

🏠 **Dale Head Hall** ⌯, Thirlmere, CA12 4TN, SE : 5¾ m. by A 591 🖉 72478, ≼ Lake
  Thirlmere, 🐟, 🦐, 🎾 – ⤢ ☎ 🄿. 🔼 🖭 🚗. 🚗   Y
  M (dinner only) 20.00 **st.** ▯ 5.00 – **9 rm** ⌴ (dinner included) 69.00/130.00 **st.** – SB (Novem-
  ber-April) 89.90/99.00 **st.**

🏠 **Applethwaite Country House** ⌯, Underskiddaw, CA12 4PL, NW : 1¾ m. on Ormath-
  waite rd 🖉 72413, ≼, 🦐 – ⤢ rest 📺 🄿. 🔼 ⑩ 🖭. 🚗   Y
  M (dinner only) 14.50 **t.** ▯ 3.75 – **12 rm** ⌴ 28.00/56.00 **t.**

🏠 **Chaucer House,** Ambleside Rd, CA12 4DR, 🖉 72318, Fax 72318 – 📳 ⤢ rest 📺 🄿. 🔼
  🖭 ⑩ 🚗 🚗   Z **a**
  closed December and January – **M** (lunch by arrangement)/dinner 14.00 **st.** and a la carte
  ▯ 4.00 – **35 rm** ⌴ 22.50/64.00 **st.** – SB (except April-September) (weekdays only) 58.75/
  74.00 **st.**

🏠 **Crow Park,** The Heads, CA12 5ER, 🖉 72208, Fax 74776, ≼ – ⤢ 📺 ☎ 🄿. 🔼 🖭 🚗
    Z **e**
  M (dinner only) 13.00 **st.** ▯ 3.00 – **27 rm** ⌴ 26.50/53.00 **st.** – SB (November-March)
  59.00 **st.**

🏠 **Lairbeck** ⌯, Vicarage Hill, CA12 5QB, 🖉 73373, 🦐 – ⤢ 📺 ☎ 🄿. 🔼 🖭. 🚗
  M (dinner only) 13.00 **st.** ▯ 3.50 – **14 rm** ⌴ 29.00/58.00 **st.** – SB (November-May) 70.00/   Y **a**
  84.00 **st.**

↱ **Acorn House** without rest., Ambleside Rd, CA12 4DL, 🖉 72553 – ⤢ 📺 🄿. 🔼 🖭. 🚗   Z **s**
  mid February-mid November – **10 rm** ⌴ 30.00/50.00 **st.**

↱ **Brackenrigg Country House,** Thirlmere, CA12 4TF, SE : 3 m. on A 591 🖉 72258, 🦐,
  🦐 – ⤢ 🚗   Y
  Easter-October – **M** (by arrangement) 14.50 – **6 rm** ⌴ 21.50/47.00 – SB 76.00.

↱ **Claremont House,** Chestnut Hill, CA12 4LT, 🖉 72089, ≼, 🦐 – ⤢ 🄿. 🚗   Y **r**
  M (by arrangement) 14.95 **t.** ▯ 3.50 – **5 rm** ⌴ 20.00/48.00 **s.** – SB (except Bank Holidays)
  70.00/73.90 **st.**

KESWICK

*North is at the top
on all town plans.*

*Les plans de villes
sont disposés
le Nord en haut.*

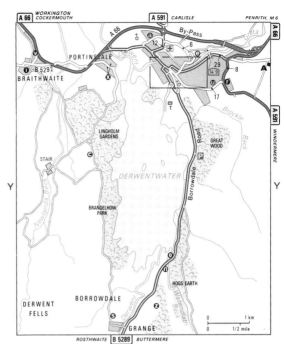

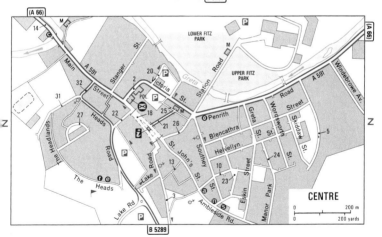

↟ **Greystones,** Ambleside Rd, CA12 4DP, ℰ 73108 – ⇌ TV ℗. ⚗   **Z n**
  closed December and January – **M** (by arrangement) 12.50 **st.** ⏐ 3.75 – **8 rm** ⚏ 22.50/
  41.00 **st.** – SB 64.00/70.00 **st.**

↟ **Linnett Hill,** 4 Penrith Rd, CA12 4HF, ℰ 73109 – ⇌ TV ℗. ◪ VISA JCB. ⚗   **Z o**
  M 11.25 **t.** ⏐ 4.50 – **10 rm** ⚏ 23.50/45.00 **t.** – SB (November-May except Bank Holidays)
  59.00/73.00 **st.**

↟ **Highfield,** The Heads, CA12 5ER, ℰ 72508, ≼ – ⇌ rest TV ℗   **Z r**
  April-October – **M** (by arrangement) 12.00 **t.** ⏐ 4.50 – **19 rm** ⚏ 17.00/55.00 **t.**

XX **La Primavera,** Greta Bridge, High Hill, CA12 5NX, ℰ 74621 – ℗. ◪ AE VISA   **Z c**
  M - Italian (closed Monday except Bank Holidays, Bank Holiday Tuesdays and 9 January-
  3 March) (bar lunch) 17.90 **t.** and a la carte ⏐ 4.10.

at Threlkeld E : 4 m. by A 591 off A 66 – Y – ⊠ ● 076 87 Keswick :

↟ **Scales Farm,** CA12 4SY, NE : 1 ¾ m. on A 66 *℘* 79660, *☞* – ⅍ rest ☑ ●
M (by arrangement) 12.00 **s.** – **5 rm** ⊡ 25.00/40.00 **s.**

at Borrowdale S : 3 ¼ m. on B 5289 – ⊠ Keswick – ● 076 87 Borrowdale :

🏨 **Stakis Lodore Swiss,** CA12 5UX, *℘* 77285, Telex 64305, Fax 77343, ≼, *ⅈⅆ*, ⅀ⅇ, ⅀
heated, *☞*, park, ✼, squash – 🚶 ☑ ☎ ⟺ ● – 🅰 80. 🄰 🄰🄴 ⊙ *VISA* *JCB* ✼   Y   **n**
M *(bar lunch Monday to Saturday)/dinner* 19.50 **t.** and a la carte – ⊡ 8.50 – **67 rm**
65.00/125.00 **st.**, 1 suite – SB 120.00/150.00 **st.**

🏨 **Mary Mount,** CA12 5UU, *℘* 77223, ≼, *☞* – ☑ ●, 🄰 *VISA*   Y   **o**
M (bar lunch Monday to Saturday)/dinner a la carte 9.75/13.25 **t.** ⅃ 3.75 – **14 rm** ⊡ 25.00/
50.00 **t.**

🏨 **Greenbank** ⅍, CA12 5UY, *℘* 77215, ≼, *☞* – ⅍ ● ✼   Y   **z**
closed December and January – **M** (dinner only) 12.00 **st.** ⅃ 3.00 – **10 rm** ⊡ 24.00/48.00 **st.**
– SB (February-March) 55.00/61.00 **st.**

at Grange-in-Borrowdale S : 4 ¾ m. by B 5289 – Y – ⊠ ● 076 87 Keswick :

🏨 **Borrowdale Gates Country House** ⅍, CA12 5UQ, *℘* 77204, Fax 77254, ≼, *☞* –
⅍ rest ☑ ☎ ●, 🄰 *VISA* ✼   Y   **s**
closed first 3 weeks January – **M** (bar lunch Monday to Saturday)/dinner 19.75 **t.** ⅃ 4.75 –
23 rm ⊡ (dinner included) 67.25/127.00 **t.**

at Rosthwaite S : 6 m. on B 5289 – Y – ⊠ ● 076 87 Keswick :

🏨 **Hazel Bank** ⅍, CA12 5XB, *℘* 77248, ≼, *☞* – ⅍ ● ●, 🄰 *VISA*
March-October – **M** (dinner only) – **6 rm** ⊡ (dinner included) 42.00/84.00 **st.**

at Seatoller S : 8 m. on B 5289 – Y – ⊠ Keswick – ● 076 87 Borrowdale :

↟ **Seatoller House,** CA12 5XN, *℘* 77218, ≼ Borrowdale, *☞* – ⅍ ●
mid March-mid November – **M** (by arrangement) (communal dining) 9.00 **t.** ⅃ 5.50 – **9 rm**
⊡ (dinner included) 33.00/63.00 **t.**

at Portinscale W : 1 ½ m. by A 66 – ⊠ ● 076 87 Keswick :

🏨 **Swinside Lodge** ⅍, Newlands, CA12 5UE, S : 1 ½ m. on Grange Rd *℘* 72948, ≼
Catbells and Newlands Valley, *☞* – ⅍ ●   Y   **c**
closed mid December-mid February – **M** (unlicensed) (dinner only) 24.00 **t.** – **7 rm**
⊡ 50.00/76.00 **t.** – SB (except May-October and Bank Holidays) 85.00/110.00 **st.**

🏨 **Derwent Cottage** ⅍, CA12 5RF, *℘* 74838, *☞* – ⅍ ☑ ●, 🄰 *VISA* ✼   Y   **x**
March-November – **M** (residents only) (dinner only) 16.00 **st.** ⅃ 2.95 – **5 rm** ⊡ 21.00/
60.00 **st.** – SB 62.00/86.00 **st.**

↟ **Rooking House,** CA12 5RD, *℘* 72506 – ⅍ ☑ ● ✼   Y   **x**
March-December – **M** (by arrangement) 13.50 **st.** – **6 rm** ⊡ 27.00/44.00 **st.** – SB (except
Bank Holidays) 66.00/84.00 **st.**

at Braithwaite W : 2 m. by A 66 on B 5292 – ⊠ Keswick – ● 076 87 Braithwaite :

🏨 **Ivy House,** CA12 5SY, *℘* 78338 – ⅍ rest ☑ ☎ ●, 🄰 🄰🄴 ⊙ *VISA* *JCB* ✼   Y   **i**
closed January – **M** (dinner only) 18.95 **t.** – **12 rm** ⊡ (dinner included) 46.00/98.00 **t.**

🏨 **Middle Ruddings,** CA12 5RY, on A 66 *℘* 78436, Fax 78438, *☞* – ⅍ rest ☑ ☎ ●, 🄰
VISA ✼   Y   **v**
M *(closed dinner Monday to Friday in winter)* (bar lunch)/dinner a la carte approx. 17.50 **t.** –
13 rm ⊡ 36.00/70.00 **t.** – SB (except Bank Holidays) (weekdays only) 90.00/134.00 **st.**

🏨 **Cottage in The Wood** ⅍, Whinlatter Pass, CA12 5TW, NW : 1 ¾ m. on B 5292
℘ 78409, ≼, *☞* – ⅍ ●   Y
mid March-mid November – **M** (dinner only) 17.00 **st.** ⅃ 3.75 – **7 rm** ⊡ 43.00/60.00 **st.**

at Thornthwaite W : 3 ½ m. by A 66 – Y – ⊠ Keswick – ● 076 87 Braithwaite :

🏨 **Thwaite Howe** ⅍, CA12 5SA, *℘* 78281, ≼ Skiddaw and Derwent Valley, *☞* – ⅍ rest
☑ ● ●
4 March-29 October – **M** (dinner only) 15.00 **t.** ⅃ 4.00 – **8 rm** ⊡ 42.00/54.00 **st.** – SB (except
May, June, September and Bank Holidays) 70.00 **st.**

▇**KETTERING**▇ Northants. 🄬🄿🄰 R 26 – ● 0536.

🄱 The Coach House, Sheep St., NN16 0AN *℘* 410266/410333.

◆London 88 – ◆Birminham 54 – ◆Leicester 16 – Northampton 24.

🏨 **Kettering Park,** Kettering Parkway, NN15 6XT, S : 2 ¼ m. by A 509 (Wellingborough rd)
at junction with A 1/M 1 Link rd *℘* 416666, Fax 416171, *ⅈⅆ*, ⅀ⅇ, 🄽, *☞*, squash – 🚶
⅍ rm ☑ ☎ ●, – 🅰 200. 🄰 🄰🄴 ⊙ *VISA*
M (bar lunch Saturday) 11.95/20.00 **st.** and a la carte ⅃ 5.95 – **85 rm** ⊡ 90.00/105.00 **st.**,
3 suites – SB (weekdays only) 108.00/138.00 **st.**

🏨 **Periquito,** Market Pl., NN16 0AJ, ✆ 520732, Fax 411036 – 📺 ☎ 🅿 – 🔬 150. ⚒ 🆎 ⑩
𝗩𝗜𝗦𝗔 ⚓
M *(closed Saturday lunch)* 9.50/15.95 **st.** and a la carte ⱶ 5.00 – ⊆ 5.95 – **40 rm** 64.00 **st.**,
1 suite.

🅖 ATS Northfield Av. ✆ 512832

KETTLEWELL N. Yorks. �₄₀₂ N 21 – pop. 361 (inc. Starbotton) – ECD : Tuesday and Thursday –
✉ Skipton – 📞 0756.

◆London 237 – Bradford 33 – ◆Leeds 40.

⌂ **Cam Lodge** ⌘, BD23 5QU, ✆ 760276, ⚘ – ⌿. ⚓
March-October – **M** 10.00 **s.** – **4 rm** ⊆ 40.00 **s.**

at Starbotton NW : 1¾ m. on B 6160 – ✉ Skipton – 📞 0756 Kettlewell :

⌂ **Hilltop Country** ⌘, BD23 5HY, ✆ 760321, « 17C stone built house », ⚘ – ⌿ rm 📺
🅿. ⚓
mid March-mid November – **M** (by arrangement) 16.00 **st.** ⱶ 4.40 – **5 rm** ⊆ 42.00/56.00 **st.**

KEXBY N. Yorks. – see York.

KEYSTON Cambs. 🇄₀₄ S 26 – pop. 252 (inc. Bythorn) – ✉ Huntingdon – 📞 080 14 (3 fig.) and
0832 (6 fig.) Bythorn.

◆London 75 – ◆Cambridge 29 – Northampton 24.

✕✕ **Pheasant Inn,** Village Loop Rd, PE18 0RE, ✆ 241, Fax 340 – ⌿ rest 🅿. ⚒ 🆎 ⑩ 𝗩𝗜𝗦𝗔
M a la carte 13.15/21.50 **t.**

Prices	For full details of the prices quoted in the guide, consult the introduction.

KIDDERMINSTER Heref. and Worcs. 🇄₀₃ 🇄₀₄ N 26 – pop. 50 385 – ECD : Wednesday –
📞 0562.
🅱 Severn Valley Railway Station, Comberton Hill, DY10 1QX ✆ 829400 (summer only).
◆London 139 – ◆Birmingham 17 – Shrewsbury 34 – Worcester 15.

🏨 **Stone Manor,** DY10 4PJ, SE : 2½ m. on A 448 ✆ 777555, Fax 777834, ≤, ⌧, ⚘, park,
✕⚘ – 📺 ☎ 🅿 – 🔬 150. ⚒ 🆎 ⑩ 𝗩𝗜𝗦𝗔
M 12.50/16.50 **t.** and a la carte ⱶ 5.25 – ⊆ 10.50 – **52 rm** ⊆ 59.50 **t.** – SB (weekends only)
79.50 **st.**

at Chaddesley Corbett SE : 4½ m. by A 448 – ✉ Kidderminster – 📞 0562 Chaddesley
Corbett :

🏨 **Brockencote Hall** ⌘, DY10 4PY, on A 448 ✆ 777876, Fax 777872, ≤, « 19C mansion in
park » – 📺 ☎ 🅿. ⚒ 🆎 ⑩ 𝗩𝗜𝗦𝗔. ⚓
M *(closed Saturday lunch)* 16.50/35.50 **st.** ⱶ 5.65 – **17 rm** ⊆ 75.00/150.00 **st.** – SB (except
Christmas and New Year) 120.00/174.00 **st.**

🅖 ATS Park St. ✆ 744668/744843

KIDLINGTON Oxon. 🇄₀₃ 🇄₀₄ Q 28 – see Oxford.

KILSBY Northants. 🇄₀₃ 🇄₀₄ Q 26 – see Rugby (Warks.).

KILVE Somerset 🇄₀₃ K 30 – pop. 324 – ✉ Bridgewater – 📞 027 874 (3 fig.) and 0278
(6 fig.) Holford.
◆London 172 – ◆Bristol 49 – Minehead 13 – Taunton 23.

⌂ **Hood Arms,** TA5 1EA, ✆ 741210, ⚘ – ⌿ rest 📺 🅿. ⚒ 𝗩𝗜𝗦𝗔
closed Christmas Day – **M** 12.00/20.00 **t.** and a la carte ⱶ 3.00 – **5 rm** ⊆ 38.00/64.00 **t.** –
SB 80.00/105.00 **s.**

KINGHAM Oxon. 🇄₀₃ 🇄₀₄ P 28 – pop. 576 – ECD : Wednesday – 📞 0608.
◆London 81 – Gloucester 32 – ◆Oxford 25.

🏨 **Mill House** ⌘, OX7 6UH, ✆ 658188, Fax 658492, ⚘ – 📺 ☎ 🅿 – 🔬 30. ⚒ 🆎 ⑩ 𝗩𝗜𝗦𝗔.
⚓
M 12.95/18.95 **t.** and a la carte ⱶ 4.95 – **21 rm** ⊆ 40.00/100.00 **t.** – SB (except Bank Holidays) 100.00/130.00 **st.**

KINGSBRIDGE Devon 🇄₀₃ I 33 The West Country G. – pop. 4 164 – ECD : Thursday – 📞 0548.
See : Town★ – Boat Trip to Salcombe★★ *AC.*
Exc. : Prawle Point (≤★★★) SE : 10 m. around coast by A 379.
🇺 Thurlestone ✆ 560405.
🅱 The Quay, TQ7 1HS ✆ 853195.
◆London 236 – Exeter 36 – ◆Plymouth 20 – Torquay 21.

🏨 **Kings Arms,** Fore St., TQ7 1AB, ✆ 852071, Fax 852977, ⌧ – 📺 ☎ 🅿 – 🔬 30. ⚒ 𝗩𝗜𝗦𝗔
M (bar lunch)/dinner a la carte 8.75/16.50 **t.** ⱶ 6.00 – **11 rm** ⊆ 35.00/60.00 **t.**

at Goveton NE : 2 ½ m. by A 381 – ⊠ ⊛ 0548 Kingsbridge :

🏨 **Buckland-Tout-Saints** ⤓, TQ7 2DS, ℰ 853055, Fax 856261, ≤, « Queen Anne mansion », 🚗, park – ⅙⤢ rest 📺 ☎ 🅿. 🔼 🅰🅴 ⑩ 𝒱𝐼𝒮𝒜 ✗
M (booking essential) 17.50/28.00 **t.** ⫶ 5.55 – **12 rm** ⊑ 50.00/140.00 **t.** – SB (November-Easter) 100.00/140.00 **st.**

at Chillington E : 5 m. on A 379 – ⊠ ⊛ 0548 Kingsbridge :

🏛 **White House,** TQ7 2JX, ℰ 580580, Fax 581124, 🚗 – ⅙⤢ rest 📺 ☎ 🅿. 🔼 𝒱𝐼𝒮𝒜
April-December – **M** (dinner only) 13.25 **st.** ⫶ 4.25 – **7 rm** ⊑ 43.25/81.00 **st.**

at Torcross E : 7 m. on A 379 – ⊠ ⊛ 0548 Kingsbridge :

⌂ **The Venture,** TQ7 2TQ, ℰ 580314, ≤ – 📺. ✗
March-mid October – **M** 11.00 **s.** ⫶ 4.00 – **3 rm** ⊑ 18.00/36.00 **s.**

at Thurlestone W : 4 m. by A 381 – ⊠ ⊛ 0548 Kingsbridge :

🏩 **Thurlestone** ⤓, TQ7 3NN, ℰ 560382, Fax 561069, ≤, 🖪, 🈺, 🔽 heated, 🔼, 🏓, 🚗, ✸, squash – 🕴 ⅙⤢ rest 🖳 rest 📺 ☎ ⤶ 🅿 – 🏌 90. 🔼 𝒱𝐼𝒮𝒜
M 12.50/29.00 **st.** and lunch a la carte ⫶ 6.00 – **68 rm** ⊑ 81.00/162.00 **st.** – SB (November-March) 116.00/130.00 **st.**

at Bantham W : 5 m. by A 379 – ⊠ ⊛ 0548 Kingsbridge :

⌂ **Sloop Inn,** TQ7 3AJ, ℰ 560489 – 📺 🅿
M a la carte 9.40/13.40 **t.** – **5 rm** ⊑ 26.00/52.00 **t.** – SB 71.00/81.00 **st.**

🛢 ATS Union Rd ℰ 853247/852699

KINGSDOWN Kent 🔢 Y 30 – see Deal.

KINGSKERSWELL Devon 🔢 J 32 – pop. 3 471 – ⊠ ⊛ 0803 Torquay.

♦London 219 – Exeter 21 – ♦Plymouth 33 – Torquay 4.

XX **Pitt House,** 2 Church End Rd, TQ12 5DS, ℰ 873374, « 15C thatched dower house », 🚗 – ⅙ 🅿. 🔼 🅰🅴 𝒱𝐼𝒮𝒜
closed Saturday lunch, Sunday and Monday – **M** (lunch by arrangement)/dinner 13.40 **t.** and a la carte ⫶ 5.50.

KING'S LYNN Norfolk 🔢 🔢 V 25 Great Britain G. – pop. 37 323 – ECD : Wednesday – ⊛ 0553.

Exc. : Houghton Hall★★ *AC,* NE : 14 ½ m. by A 148 – Four Fenland Churches★ (Terrington St. Clement, Walpole St. Peter, West Walton, Walsoken) SW : by A 47.

🇹𝟵 Eagles, School Rd, Tylney All Saints ℰ 827147, W : 5 m. by A 47.

🅱 The Old Gaol House, Saturday Market Pl., PE30 5DQ ℰ 763044.

♦London 103 – ♦Cambridge 45 – ♦Leicester 75 – ♦Norwich 44.

🏨 **Duke's Head** (Forte), Tuesday Market Pl., PE30 1JS, ℰ 774996, Fax 763556 – 🕴 ⅙⤢ rm 📺 ☎ 🅿 – 🏌 230. 🔼 🅰🅴 ⑩ 𝒱𝐼𝒮𝒜 𝐽𝐶𝐵
M (bar lunch)/dinner 15.95 **t.** and a la carte ⫶ 6.45 – ⊑ 8.50 – **71 rm** 70.00/80.00 **t.** – SB 98.00 **st.**

🏨 **Knights Hill** (Best Western), Knights Hill Village, PE30 3HQ, NE : 4 ½ m. on A 148 at junction with A 149 ℰ 675566, Fax 675568, 🖪, 🈺, 🔼, 🚗, ✸ – ⅙⤢ rm 📺 ☎ 🅿 – 🏌 300. 🔼 🅰🅴 ⑩ 𝒱𝐼𝒮𝒜
M (bar lunch Monday to Saturday)/dinner 15.50 **t.** and a la carte – ⊑ 7.00 – **53 rm** 65.00/85.00 **t.** – SB (except Christmas) 108.00 **t.**

🏨 **Butterfly,** Beveridge Way, PE30 4NB, S : 2 ¼ m. by Hardwick Rd at junction of A 10 and A 47 ℰ 771707, Fax 768027 – ⅙⤢ rest 📺 ☎ 🅿 – 🏌 35. 🔼 🅰🅴 ⑩ 𝒱𝐼𝒮𝒜
M 8.75/11.95 **st.** and a la carte ⫶ 4.50 – ⊑ 6.00 – **50 rm** 49.00 **st.** – SB (weekends only) 75.00/1 72.00 **st.**

🏛 **Globe** (Chef & Brewer), Tuesday Market Pl., PE30 1EZ, ℰ 772617, Fax 761315 – 📺 ☎ ⤶ 🅿. 🔼 🅰🅴 𝒱𝐼𝒮𝒜 ✗
M 15.00/20.00 **t.** and a la carte – **39 rm** ⊑ 34.95/38.45 **t.**

⌂ **Russet House,** 53 Goodwins Rd, PE30 5PE, ℰ 773098, 🚗 – ⅙⤢ rest 📺 ☎ 🅿. 🔼 🅰🅴 ⑩ 𝒱𝐼𝒮𝒜
22 December-2 January – **M** (by arrangement) 15.00 ⫶ 4.00 – **12 rm** ⊑ 34.50/49.50 **t.**

⌂ **Fairlight Lodge** without rest., 79 Goodwins Rd, PE30 5PE, ℰ 762234, 🚗 – 📺 🅿
closed 25 and 26 December – **6 rm** ⊑ 16.00/36.00 **s.**

XX **Rococo,** 11 Saturday Market Pl., PE30 5DQ, ℰ 771483 – 🔼 𝒱𝐼𝒮𝒜
closed Monday lunch and Sunday dinner – **M** (booking essential) 12.75/23.95 **t.**

at Grimston NE : 6 ¼ m. by A 148 – ⊠ King's Lynn – ⊛ 0485 Hillington :

🏨 **Congham Hall** ⤓, Lynn Rd, PE32 1AH, ℰ 600250, Fax 601191, ≤, « Georgian manor house », 🔼 heated, 🚗, park, ✸ – ⅙⤢ rest 📺 ☎ 🅿 – 🏌 25. 🔼 🅰🅴 ⑩ 𝒱𝐼𝒮𝒜 ✗
Meals *(closed lunch Saturday and Bank Holiday Mondays)* 15.00/36.00 **t.** ⫶ 6.00 – **12 rm** ⊑ 65.00/125.00 **t.**, 2 suites – SB (except Christmas and Bank Holidays) (weekends only) 150.00/180.00 **t.**

at Tottenhill S : 5 ¼ m. on A 10 – ⊠ ✆ 0553 King's Lynn :

↑ **Oakwood House,** PE33 0RH, ✆ 810256, ☞ – 📺 🅿. 🔄 VISA ✖
M 12.75 **st.** ♦ 3.95 – **10 rm** ☑ 30.00/46.00 **st.** – SB (except Christmas and New Year) 60.00/80.00 **st.**

🔧 ATS 4 Oldmeadow Rd, Hardwick Rd Trading Est. ✆ 774035

KINGSTEIGNTON Devon 403 J 32 – pop. 6 424 – ECD : Thursday – ⊠ ✆ 0626 Newton Abbot.

♦London 223 – Exeter 17 – ♦Plymouth 33 – Torquay 7.

🏨 Passage House, Hackney Lane, TQ12 3QH, S : ½ m. ✆ 55515, Fax 63336, ≤, 🏋, ⇌, 🔄 –
🔄 📺 ☎ 🅿 – 🔬 120. ✖
37 rm, 1 suite.

KINGSTON Devon 403 I 33 – pop. 317 – ⊠ ✆ 0548 Kingsbridge.

♦London 237 – Exeter 41 – ♦Plymouth 11.

↑ **Trebles Cottage** 🔄, TQ7 4PT, ✆ 810268, ☞ – 📺 🅿. 🔄 AE VISA
M 16.00 **st.** ♦ 5.50 – **5 rm** ☑ 36.00/58.00 **st.**

KINGSTON-UPON-HULL Humbs. 402 S 22 Great Britain G. – pop. 322 144 – ECD : Monday and Thursday – ✆ 0482 Hull.

Exc. : Burton Constable★ *AC*, NE : 9 m. by A 165 and B 1238 – Z.

🏌 Springhead Park, Willerby Rd ✆ 656309, W : via Spring Bank West – Z – and A 164 –
🏌 Sutton Park, Salthouse Rd ✆ 74242, NE : 3 m. by B 1237 Z.

✈ Humberside Airport : ✆ 0652 (Barnetby) 688456, S : 19 m. by A 63 – **Terminal** : Coach Service.

⛴ to The Netherlands : Rotterdam and Belgium : Zeebrugge (North Sea Ferries).

🅱 City Information Service, Central Library, Albion St., HU1 3TF ✆ 223344 – King George Dock, Hedon Rd, HU9 5PR ✆ 702118 – 75-76 Carr Lane, HU1 3RQ ✆ 223559.

♦London 183 – ♦Leeds 61 – ♦Nottingham 94 – ♦Sheffield 68.

Plan on next page

🏨 **Forte Crest,** Castle St., HU1 2BX, ✆ 225221, Fax 213299, 🏋, ⇌, 🔄 – 🔄 ✖ rm 📺 ☎ 🔄
🅿 – 🔬 120. 🔄 AE ⓞ VISA JCB Y **n**
M 11.95/16.95 **t.** and a la carte ♦ 6.60 – ☑ 9.95 – **99 rm** 89.00/120.00 **st.** – SB (weekends only) 98.00 **st.**

🏨 **Royal** (Friendly), Ferensway, HU1 3UF, ✆ 25087, Fax 23172, 🏋, ⇌, 🔄 – 🔄 ✖ rm 🍽 rest
📺 ☎ 🔄 🅿 – 🔬 450. 🔄 AE ⓞ VISA JCB. ✖ Y **a**
M 10.00/12.50 **st.** and a la carte – ☑ 6.75 – **155 rm** 57.00/98.00 **st.** – SB (weekends only) 79.00/88.00 **st.**

🏨 **Travel Inn,** Ferriby Rd, Hessle, HU13 0JA, W : 7 m. by A 63 and A 164 ✆ 645285,
Fax 645299 – ✖ rm 📺 🔄 🅿. 🔄 AE ⓞ VISA. ✖ Z
M (grill rest.) a la carte approx. 16.00 **t.** – ☑ 4.95 – **40 rm** 33.50 **t.**

🏨 **Campanile,** Beverley Rd, Freetown Way, HU2 9AN, ✆ 25530, Fax 587578 – 📺 ☎ 🔄 🅿 –
🔬 25. 🔄 AE VISA X **a**
M 9.45 **t.** and a la carte ♦ 4.65 – ☑ 4.25 – **47 rm** 35.75 **t.**

↑ **Earlsmere,** 76-78 Sunnybank, off Spring Bank West, HU3 1LQ, ✆ 41977, Fax 473714 –
📺. 🔄 VISA Z **i**
closed Christmas – **M** (by arrangement) 12.00 **st.** ♦ 3.00 – **15 rm** ☑ 18.80/41.10 **st.** – SB (except Bank Holidays) 50.00/80.00 **st.**

🍴🍴 **Cerutti's,** 10 Nelson St., HU1 1XE, ✆ 28501, Fax 587597 – 🅿. 🔄 VISA Y **o**
closed Saturday lunch, Sunday, 1 week Christmas and Bank Holidays – **M** - Seafood 17.95 **t.** and a la carte ♦ 5.40.

at Willerby W : 5 m. by A 1079 – Z – and Willerby Rd – ⊠ Kingston-upon-Hull – ✆ 0482 Hull :

🏨 **Willerby Manor,** Well Lane, HU10 6ER, ✆ 652616, Fax 653901, ☞ – 📺 ☎ 🅿 – 🔬 400.
🔄 AE VISA. ✖
M *(closed Saturday lunch, Sunday dinner and Bank Holidays)* 12.00/15.00 **st.** and a la carte ♦ 3.95 – ☑ 7.25 – **36 rm** 59.00/82.00 **st.** – SB 111.50/184.50 **st.**

at North Ferriby W : 7 m. on A 63 – Z – ⊠ Kingston-upon-Hull – ✆ 0482 Hull :

🏨 **Forte Posthouse,** Ferriby High Rd, HU14 3LG, ✆ 645212, Fax 643332 – ✖ rm 🍽 rest 📺
☎ 🅿 – 🔬 100. 🔄 AE ⓞ VISA
M a la carte approx. 17.50 **t.** ♦ 4.65 – ☑ 6.95 – **95 rm** 53.50 **st.** – SB (weekends only) 90.00 **st.**

KINGSTON-UPON-HULL

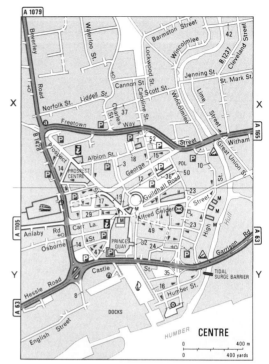

CENTRE

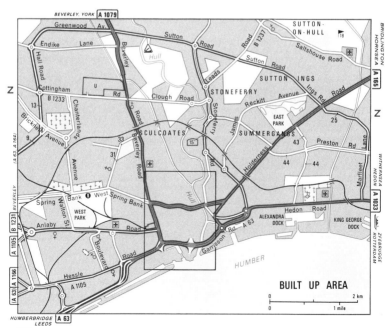

BUILT UP AREA

246

at Hedon E : 6 ½ m. by A 63 on A 1033 – Z – ⊠ Kingston-upon-Hull – 🟢 0482 Hull :

🏨 **Kingstown,** Hull Rd, HU12 9DJ, W : 1 m. on A 1033 𝒫 890461, Fax 890713 – 📺 ☎ & 🅿.
🅰 🅰🅴 🆅🅸🆂🅰. ⚒
M (in bar Sunday) 12.95 **st.** (lunch) and dinner a la carte ⅄ 4.35 – **34 rm** ☲ 45.00/85.00 **st.** –
SB (weekends only) 71.00/126.00 **st.**

◎ ATS Great Union St. 𝒫 29044   ATS Scott St. 𝒫 29370/225502

KINGSTOWN Cumbria – see Carlisle.

KINGTON Heref. and Worcs. 🔢 K 27 – pop. 2 040 – ECD : Wednesday – 🟢 0544.
🏌 Bradnor Hill 𝒫 230340, N : 1 m.

◆London 152 – ◆Birmingham 61 – Hereford 19 – Shrewsbury 54.

🏨 **Penrhos Court,** HR5 3LH, E : 1½ m. on A 44 𝒫 230720, Fax 230754, « Part 15C and 16C
house with medieval cruck hall », ☞ – ⇔ rm 📺 ☎ 🅿 – 🅰 50. 🅰 🅰🅴. ⚒
M (booking essential) (lunch by arrangement Monday to Saturday)/dinner
18.50 **t.** and a la carte ⅄ 5.00 – **11 rm** ☲ 65.00/120.00 **t.** – SB (except Easter, Whitsun and
Christmas) 88.00/196.00 **st.**

at Lyonshall E : 2½ m . by A 44 on A 480 – ⊠ Kington – 🟢 054 48 Lyonshall :

🏠 **Church House,** HR5 3HR, on A 44 𝒫 350, ☞ – ⇔ 🅿. ⚒
closed 25 December-1 January – **M** 8.50 – **3 rm** 20.00/34.00.

◎ ATS 20-22 Bridge St. 𝒫 230350

*Demandez chez votre libraire le catalogue des **publications Michelin***

KINTBURY Berks. 🔢 🔢 P 29 – pop. 2 034 – ⊠ Newbury – 🟢 0488.
◆London 73 – Newbury 6 – Reading 23.

🍴🍴 **Dundas Arms** with rm, 53 Station Rd, RG15 0UT, 𝒫 58263, Fax 58568, ≤, « Canal and
riverside setting », ☞ – 📺 ☎ 🅿. 🅰 🅰🅴 🅾 🆅🅸🆂🅰
M *(closed Sunday, Monday and Bank Holidays)* 16.50 **t.** (lunch) and dinner a la carte 20.20/
26.95 **t.** – **5 rm** ☲ 55.00/65.00 **t.**

🍴 **Bistro Roque,** Inkpen Rd, RG15 0JT, S : 1 m. 𝒫 58398 – 🅿. 🅰 🆅🅸🆂🅰
M 15.20 **t.** and a la carte.

KINVER Staffs. 🔢 🔢 N 26 – see Stourbridge (W. Mids).

KIRKBURTON W. Yorks. 🔢 🔢 O 23 ㉚ – ⊠ 🟢 0484 Huddersfield.
◆London 195 – ◆Leeds 20 – ◆Manchester 32 – ◆Sheffield 22.

🏨 **Springfield Park,** Penistone Rd, HD8 0PE, on A 629 𝒫 607788, Fax 607961 – ⇔ rm 📺
☎ 🅿 – 🅰 100. 🅰 🅰🅴 🅾 🆅🅸🆂🅰
M – **Old Mill** (dinner only and Sunday lunch)/dinner 27.00 **st.** and a la carte ⅄ 5.00 – **Topo's** -
Italian (dinner only and Sunday lunch) /dinner a la carte approx. 12.00 **st.** ⅄ 5.00 – **43 rm**
☲ 53.50/110.00 **st.** – SB (weekends only) 55.00/90.00 **st.**

KIRBY HILL N. Yorks. – see Richmond.

KIRKBY LONSDALE Cumbria 🔢 M 21 – pop. 1 557 – ECD : Wednesday – ⊠ Carnforth –
🟢 052 42.
🏌 Scaleber Lane, Barbon 𝒫 36365, N : 2 m. by Sedbergh Rd (A 683) – 🏌 Casterton, Sedbergh
Rd 𝒫 71592, NE : 3 m. by A 683.
🆔 24 Main St., LA6 2AE 𝒫 71437.

◆London 259 – ◆Carlisle 62 – Kendal 13 – Lancaster 17 – ◆Leeds 58.

🏠 **Pheasant Inn,** Casterton, LA6 2RX, NE : 1¼ m. on A 683 𝒫 71230, ☞ – ⇔ rest 📺 ☎ &
🅿. 🅰 🅾 🆅🅸🆂🅰
closed 1 week January – **M** (bar lunch)/dinner 17.50 **t.** and a la carte ⅄ 5.00 – **10 rm**
☲ 40.00/60.00 **t.**

at Cowan Bridge (Lancs) SE : 2 m. on A 65 – ⊠ Carnforth – 🟢 052 42 Kirkby Lonsdale :

🏠 **Hipping Hall,** LA6 2JJ, SE : ½ m. on A 65 𝒫 71187, Fax 72452, ☞ – 📺 🅿. 🅰 🆅🅸🆂🅰
closed January – **M** (residents only) (communal dining) (dinner only) 19.50 **st.** ⅄ 4.00 – **5 rm**
☲ 64.00/85.00 **st.**, 2 suites – SB 105.00 **st.**

🍴🍴 **Cobwebs Country House** ⚘ with rm, Leck, LA6 2HZ, NE : ¼ m. 𝒫 72141, Fax 72141,
☞ – ⇔ rest 📺 ☎ 🅿. 🅰 🆅🅸🆂🅰. ⚒
closed January and February – **M** *(closed Sunday to Tuesday to non-residents)* (booking
essential) (dinner only) 26.00 **t.** ⅄ 5.00 – **5 rm** ☲ 45.00/60.00 **t.**

at Lupton NW : 3¾ m. on A 65 – ⊠ Carnforth – 🟢 053 95 Crooklands :

🍴🍴 **Lupton Tower Vegetarian Country House** ⚘ with rm, LA6 2PR, 𝒫 67400, ≤, ☞ –
⇔ 🅿. 🅰 🆅🅸🆂🅰
closed Christmas – **M** (booking essential) (dinner only and Sunday lunch)/dinner 17.00 **t.**
⅄ 5.00 – **6 rm** ☲ 36.00/56.00 **t.**

KIRKBYMOORSIDE N. Yorks. 402 R 21 – pop. 2 227 – ECD : Thursday – ✆ 0751.

ᵢᵦ Manor Vale ✎ 31525.

◆London 244 – Scarborough 26 – York 33.

🏠 **George and Dragon,** 17 Market Pl., YO6 6AA, ✎ 31637, Fax 33334, ⟷ – 📺 ☎ Ⓟ. 🔲 VISA
    closed Christmas Day – **M** 15.00 **t.** (dinner) and a la carte 9.95/18.05 **t.** ⌀ 5.00 – **19 rm**
    ⊆ 37.50/59.00 **t.** – SB 79.00/110.00 **st.**

KIRKBY STEPHEN Cumbria 402 M 20 – pop. 1 518 – ECD : Thursday – ✆ 076 83.

🖸 Market St., CA17 4QN ✎ 71199 (summer only).

◆London 285 – ◆Carlisle 48 – Kendal 24.

🏠 **Town Head House,** High St., CA17 4SH, ✎ 71044, Fax 72128, ⟷ – ⇖⇔ 📺 ☎ Ⓟ. 🔲 VISA
    M (dinner only) a la carte 13.30/20.90 **st.** ⌀ 3.50 – **6 rm** ⊆ 40.00/73.00 **st.** – SB 91.00/
    125.00 **st.**

↑ **Ing Hill Lodge** ⌕, Mallerstang Dale, CA17 4JT, S : 4 ½ m. on B 6259 ✎ 71153,
    Fax 71153, ⟨ Mallerstang Dale, ⟷ – ⇖⇔ 📺 Ⓟ
    M 12.50 **st.** ⌀ 2.70 – **3 rm** ⊆ 25.00/50.00 **st.** – SB (September-April except Bank Holidays)
    63.70/76.50 **st.**

KIRKCAMBECK Cumbria 401 402 L 18 – see Brampton.

KIRKHAM Lancs. 402 L 22 – pop. 8 393 – ✉ Preston – ✆ 0772.

◆London 240 – ◆Blackpool 9 – Preston 7.

XX **Cromwellian,** 16 Poulton St., PR4 2AB, ✎ 685680 – 🔲 AE VISA
    closed Sunday, Monday, Easter and first 2 weeks August – **M** (dinner only) 22.95 **st.** ⌀ 5.00.

KIRKOSWALD Cumbria 401 402 L 19 – pop. 730 – ✉ Penrith – ✆ 0768 Lazonby.

◆London 300 – ◆Carlisle 23 – Kendal 41 – Lancaster 58.

🏠 Prospect Hill ⌕, CA10 1ER, N : ¾ m. ✎ 898500, ⟨, « Converted 18C farm buildings », ⟷
    – Ⓟ. ⚒
    M (dinner only and Sunday lunch)/dinner 15.00 **t.** and a la carte – **11 rm.**

KIRKWHELPINGTON Northd. 401 402 N/O 18 Great Britain G. – pop. 315 – ✉ Morpeth –
✆ 0830 Otterburn.

Envir. : Wallington House★ *AC*, E : 3½ m. by A 696 and B 6342.

◆London 305 – ◆Carlisle 46 – ◆Newcastle upon Tyne 20.

↑ **Shieldhall,** Wallington, NE61 4AQ, SE : 2½ m. by A 696 on B 6342 ✎ 40387, Fax 40387,
    ⟷ – 📺 Ⓟ. 🔲 VISA. ⚒
    M (by arrangement) 14.75 **s.** ⌀ 3.90 – **4 rm** ⊆ 35.00/52.00 **s.** – SB 69.50/109.50 **st.**

KNARESBOROUGH N. Yorks. 402 P 21 – pop. 12 910 – ECD : Thursday – ✆ 0423 Harrogate.

ᵢᵦ Boroughbridge Rd ✎ 863219, N : 1 ½ m.

🖸 35 Market Place, HG5 8AL ✎ 866886 (summer only).

◆London 217 – Bradford 21 – Harrogate 3 – ◆Leeds 18 – York 18.

🏨 **Dower House** (Best Western), Bond End, HG5 9AL, ✎ 863302, Fax 867665, ℉ₛ, ≊, 🔲,
    ⟷ – 📺 ☎ Ⓟ – 益 70. 🔲 AE Ⓞ VISA. ⚒
    M (closed Saturday lunch) 9.75/16.75 **st.** and dinner a la carte – **31 rm** ⊆ 57.00/83.00 **st.**,
    1 suite.

KNIGHTWICK Heref. and Worcs. 403 404 M 27 – pop. 82 – ECD : Wednesday – ✉ Worcester
– ✆ 0886.

◆London 132 – Hereford 20 – Leominster 18 – Worcester 8.

↑ **Talbot,** WR6 5PH, on B 4197 ✎ 21235, Fax 21060, ≊, ⌕, squash – 📺 ☎ Ⓟ. 🔲 VISA
    M (restricted dinner Sunday) a la carte 9.75/23.00 **t.** ⌀ 4.00 – **10 rm** ⊆ 26.00/58.00 **t.** –
    SB 65.00/110.00 **st.**

KNOWLE W. Mids. 403 404 O 26 – pop. 16 611 – ECD : Thursday – ✉ Solihull – ✆ 0564.

◆London 108 – ◆Birmingham 9 – Coventry 10 – Warwick 11.

🏨 **Bridgewater,** 2110 Warwick Rd, B93 0EE, S : 1 ½ m. on A 4141 ✎ 771177, Fax 770141,
    ⟷ – 🛏 rest 📺 ☎ Ⓟ. 🔲 AE Ⓞ VISA JCB
    M (Sunday dinner by arrangement) 14.95 **t.** and a la carte ⌀ 4.95 – **20 rm** ⊆ 57.50/125.00 **t.**
    – SB (weekends only) 79.95/85.90 **st.**

KNOWL HILL Berks. 404 R 29 – ✉ Twyford – ✆ 0628 Littlewick Green.

ᵢₛ Hennerton, Crazies Hill Rd, Wargrave ✎ 0734 (Wargrave) 401000, W : 2½ m.

◆London 38 – Maidenhead 5 – Reading 8.

🏨 **Bird in Hand,** Bath Rd, RG10 9UP, ✎ 826622, Fax 826748, ⟷ – 📺 ☎ & Ⓟ. 🔲 AE Ⓞ VISA.
    ⚒
    accommodation closed 23 to 30 December – **M** a la carte 10.00/20.50 **st.** ⌀ 5.50 – **15 rm**
    ⊆ 67.50/90.00 **st.** – SB (weekends only) 75.00/100.00 **st.**

🖂 Council Offices, Toft Rd, WA16 6TA ✆ 632611/632210.

◆London 187 – Chester 25 – ◆Liverpool 33 – ◆Manchester 18 – ◆Stoke-on-Trent 30.

🏨 **Cottons,** Manchester Rd, WA16 0SU, NW : 1½ m. on A 50 ✆ 650333, Fax 755351, *ℒ₅*, ≘ₛ, ☐, ☞, ※ – 🕮 ⇔ rm 📺 ☎ ৬ 🅿 – 🔬 200. 🆘 🆎 ⑩ 𝖵𝖨𝖲𝖠
M *(closed Saturday lunch)* 12.95/18.00 **st.** and a la carte ⅃ 6.45 – **73 rm** ⥮ 79.00/98.00 **st.,** 9 suites – SB (except Bank Holidays) (weekends only) 102.00/122.00 **st.**

🏨 **Royal George** (Chef & Brewer), King St., WA16 6EE, ✆ 634151, Fax 634955 – 🕮 📺 ☎ 🅿 – 🔬 80. 🆘 🆎 ⑩ 𝖵𝖨𝖲𝖠
M 15.00/20.00 **t.** and a la carte – **31 rm** ⥮ 44.95/48.45 **t.**

🏨 **Longview,** 55 Manchester Rd, WA16 0LX, ✆ 632119, Fax 652402 – 📺 ☎ 🅿. 🆘 🆎 𝖵𝖨𝖲𝖠
closed 24 December-1 January – **M** *(closed Sunday)* (lunch by arrangement)/dinner 19.50 **st.** ⅃ 7.25 – **23 rm** ⥮ 47.00/70.00 **st.** – SB (weekends only) 55.00/104.00 **st.**

🏨 **Forte Travelodge** without rest., Chester Rd, Tabley, WA16 0PP, NW : 2¾ m. by A 5033 on A 556 ✆ 652187, Reservations (Freephone) 0800 850950 – 📺 ৬ 🅿. 🆘 🆎 𝖵𝖨𝖲𝖠. ※
32 rm 31.95 **t.**

XXX **La Belle Epoque** with rm, 60 King St., WA16 6DT, ✆ 633060, Fax 634150, « Art Nouveau » – 📺. 🆘 🆎 ⑩ 𝖵𝖨𝖲𝖠. ※
closed first week January and Bank Holidays – **M** - **French** (closed Sunday) (booking essential) (dinner only) a la carte 22.50/26.50 **t.** – ⥮ 5.00 – **7 rm** ⥮ 35.00/50.00 **st.**

X **Est, Est, Est !,** 81 King St., WA16 6DX, ✆ 755487, Fax 651151 – ▤. 🆘 🆎 𝖵𝖨𝖲𝖠
closed 25-26 December and 1 January – **M** - **Italian** 9.95/12.95 **t.** and a la carte ⅃ 4.75.

at Over Peover SE : 5 m. by A 50 and Stocks Lane – 🖂 Knutsford – 🌐 0625 Chelford :

⌂ **The Dog,** Wellbank Lane, Peover Heath, WA16 8UP, ✆ 861421 – 📺 🅿. ※
M (in bar) 11.60/12.10 **t.** – **3 rm** ⥮ 35.00/55.00 **t.**

at Bucklow Hill NW : 3½ m. at junction A 556 and A 5034 – 🖂 Knutsford – 🌐 0565 Bucklow Hill :

🏨 **Swan Inn,** Bucklow Hill, Chester Rd, WA16 6RD, ✆ 830295, Fax 830614 – ⇔ rm 📺 ☎ 🅿 – 🔬 50. 🆘 🆎 ⑩ 𝖵𝖨𝖲𝖠. ※
M *(closed Saturday lunch)* 12.00 **st.** and a la carte ⅃ 5.25 – ⥮ 3.45 – **70 rm** 39.50 **st.**

⊚ ATS Malt St. ✆ 652224

See : Village★ – Lacock Abbey★ *AC* – High St.★, St. Cyriac★, Fox Talbot Museum of Photography★ *AC.*

◆London 109 – Bath 16 – ◆Bristol 30 – Chippenham 3.

⌂ **Sign of the Angel,** 6 Church St., SN15 2LA, ✆ 730230, Fax 730527, « Part 14C and 15C former wool merchant's house in National Trust village », ☞ – 📺 ☎. 🆘 🆎 𝖵𝖨𝖲𝖠
closed 1 week Christmas – **M** - **English** (closed Monday lunch except Bank Holidays and Sunday dinner to non residents) 16.00/30.00 **st.** and a la carte ⅃ 5.00 – **9 rm** ⥮ 55.00/ 93.00 **st.** – SB (except Bank Holidays) 100.00 **st.**

See : Castle★ *AC.*

🖪 Ashton Hall, Ashton-with-Stodday ✆ 752090, S : 2½ m. on A 588 – 🖪 Lansil, Caton Rd ✆ 39269, E : 2 m. by A 683 – 🖪 Robin Lane, Bentham ✆ 052 42 (Bentham) 61018, NE : by B 6480.

🖂 29 Castle Hill, LA1 1YN ✆ 32878.

◆London 252 – ◆Blackpool 26 – Bradford 62 – Burnley 44 – ◆Leeds 71 – ◆Middlesbrough 97 – Preston 26.

🏨 **Lancaster House** (Best Western), Green Lane, LA1 4GJ, S : 3¼ m. by A 6 ✆ 844822, Fax 844766, *ℒ₅*, ≘ₛ, ☐ – ⇔ rm 📺 ☎ ৬ 🅿 – 🔬 150. 🆘 🆎 𝖵𝖨𝖲𝖠 𝖩𝖢𝖡
M – **Gressingham** 10.95/18.50 **st.** and a la carte ⅃ 5.25 – **80 rm** ⥮ 57.00/114.00 **st.** – SB (except Christmas and New Year) 122.00/172.00 **st.**

🏨 **Forte Posthouse,** Waterside Park, Caton Rd, LA1 3RA, NE : 1½ m. on A 683 ✆ 65999, Fax 841265, *ℒ₅*, ≘ₛ, ☐ – 🕮 ⇔ rm 📺 ☎ ৬ 🅿 – 🔬 120. 🆘 🆎 ⑩ 𝖵𝖨𝖲𝖠
M a la carte approx. 17.50 **t.** ⅃ 4.65 – ⥮ 6.95 – **115 rm** 53.50/69.50 **st.** – SB 90.00 **st.**

⌂ **Edenbreck House** without rest., Sunnyside Lane, off Ashfield Av., LA1 5ED, via Westbourne Rd, near station ✆ 32464, ☞ – 📺 🅿. 🆘 𝖵𝖨𝖲𝖠
5 rm ⥮ 25.00/50.00.

at Carnforth N : 6¼ m. on A 6 – 🖂 🌐 0524 Lancaster :

⌂ **New Capernwray Farm** ⌂, Capernwray, LA6 1AD, NE : 3 m. by B 6254 ✆ 734284, Fax 734284, ≪, ☞ – ⇔ 📺 🅿. 🆘 𝖵𝖨𝖲𝖠
M (residents only) (communal dining) 17.50 **st.** – **3 rm** ⥮ 34.00/58.00 **s.**

at Claughton NE : 6¾ m. on A 683 – 🖂 🌐 052 42 Kirkby Lonsdale :

🏨 **Old Rectory,** LA2 9LA, on A 683 ✆ 21455, Fax 21791, ☞ – ⇔ rest 📺 ☎ 🅿. 🆘 𝖵𝖨𝖲𝖠
M *(closed Sunday)* (lunch by arrangement)/dinner 13.95 **st.** and a la carte – ⥮ 6.95 – **12 rm** 47.50/72.00 **st.** – SB (except Sunday) 78.00/99.00 **st.**

LANREATH Cornwall 403 G 32 – pop. 449 – ⊠ Looe – ✆ 0503.

♦London 269 – ♦Plymouth 26 – Truro 34.

⚲ **Punch Bowl Inn,** PL13 2NX, ✆ 220218, ☞ – 📺 🅿. 🔄 VISA
   M (bar lunch Monday to Saturday)/dinner 9.95 **t.** and a la carte – **14 rm** 🖙 18.50/59.00 **t.**

LANSALLOS Cornwall 403 G 32 – pop. 1 621 – ⊠ Fowey – ✆ 0726 St. Austell.

♦London 273 – ♦Plymouth 30.

⚭ **Carneggan House** ⫷, Lanteglos-by-Fowey, PL23 1NW, NW : 2 m. on Polruan rd
   ✆ 870327, ≤, ☞, ✾ – 📺 🅿. 🔄 AE VISA. ✾
   closed 21 to 28 December – **M** 15.00 **st.** ▯ 3.00 – **3 rm** 🖙 25.00/50.00 **st.**

LARKFIELD Kent 404 V 30 – see Maidstone.

LASTINGHAM N. Yorks. 402 R 21 – pop. 108 – ECD : Wednesday – ⊠ York – ✆ 0751.

♦London 244 – Scarborough 26 – York 32.

🏠 **Lastingham Grange** ⫷, YO6 6TH, ✆ 417345, ≤, « Country house atmosphere », ☞ –
   ✾ rest 📺 ☎ 🅿
   March-November – **M** 14.95/22.75 ▯ 4.50 – **12 rm** 🖙 56.50/110.00 **t.** – SB 126.50/144.00 **st.**

   at Hutton-le-Hole W : 2 m. – ⊠ York – ✆ 075 15 Lastingham :

⚭ **Hammer and Hand,** YO6 6UA, ✆ 417300 – ✾ 📺 ☎
   closed 1 week Christmas – **M** (by arrangement) 12.50 **st.** ▯ 5.00 – **3 rm** 🖙 27.00/44.00 **st.** –
   SB (mid October-March) 58.00/76.00 **st.**

LAUNCESTON Cornwall 403 G 32 – ✆ 0566.

♦London 273 – Exeter 50 – Plymouth 30 – Truro 33.

✗ **Randells,** Prospect House, 11 Western Rd, PL15 7AS, ✆ 776484 – 🔄 AE VISA
   closed Sunday and Monday – **M** (dinner only) a la carte 11.95/18.05 **st.** ▯ 3.80.

   Richiedete nelle librerie il catalogo delle **pubblicazioni** *Michelin.*

LAVENHAM Suffolk 404 W 27 Great Britain G. – pop. 1 658 – ECD : Wednesday – ⊠ Sudbury –
✆ 0787.

See : Town★★ – Church of SS. Peter and Paul★.

🛈 Lady St., CO10 9RA ✆ 248207 (summer only).

♦London 66 – ♦Cambridge 39 – Colchester 22 – ♦Ipswich 19.

🏨 **Swan** (Forte), High St., CO10 9QA, ✆ 247477, Fax 248286, « Part 14C timbered inn », ☞
   – ✾ 📺 ☎ 🅿 – 🔬 35. 🔄 AE ⓞ VISA JCB
   M 14.95/20.50 **t.** and a la carte ▯ 6.00 – ▯ 8.95 – **45 rm** 85.00/110.00 **t.,** 2 suites –
   SB 100.00/148.00 **st.**

⚲ **Angel,** Market Pl., CO10 9QZ, ✆ 247388, Fax 247057, « 15C inn », ☞ – 📺 ☎ 🅿. 🔄 VISA
   ✾
   M (bar lunch)/dinner a la carte 10.65/17.45 **t.** ▯ 3.50 – **7 rm** 🖙 40.00/60.00 **t.**

⚭ **Angel Corner,** 17 Market Pl., CO10 9QZ, ✆ 247168, Fax 247905, « 15C former wool-
   merchant's house », ☞ – ✾
   March-October – **M** (by arrangement) (communal dining) 13.50 **s.** – **3 rm** 🖙 21.50/37.00 **s.**

✗✗ **Great House** with rm, Market Pl., CO10 9QZ, ✆ 247431, Fax 248080, « Part 14C timbered house » – 📺 ☎. 🔄 VISA. ✾
   closed January – **M** - French (closed Sunday dinner and Monday) 7.95/14.95 **t.** and a la
   carte ▯ 6.90 – **1 rm** 🖙 50.00/80.00 **t.,** **3 suites** 68.00/80.00 **t.** – SB (except Saturday and Bank
   Holidays) 95.90/129.90 **st.**

   at Brent Eleigh SE : 2½ m. by A 1141 – ⊠ Sudbury – ✆ 0787 Lavenham :

⚭ **Street Farm** without rest., CO10 9NU, ✆ 247271, ☞ – ✾ 🅿. ✾
   closed December and January – **3 rm** 🖙 20.00/40.00 **st.**

LEA Lancs. – see Preston.

LEAMINGTON SPA Warks. 403 404 P 27 – see Royal Leamington Spa.

LEDBURY Heref. and Worcs. 403 404 M 27 – pop. 4 985 – ECD : Wednesday – ✆ 0531.

🛈 1 Church Lane, HR8 1EA ✆ 636147.

♦London 119 – Hereford 14 – Newport 46 – Worcester 16.

🏨 **Feathers,** High St., HR8 1DS, ✆ 635266, Fax 632001, « Timbered 16C inn, tasteful
   decor », squash – 📺 ☎ 🅿 – 🔬 60. 🔄 AE ⓞ VISA
   M a la carte 10.70/23.20 **st.** – **11 rm** 🖙 59.50/95.00 **st.** – SB (except Bank Holidays) 85.00/
   117.00 **st.**

   at Wellington Heath N : 2 m. by B 4214 – ⊠ ✆ 0531 Ledbury :

🏠 **Hope End** ⫷, Hope End, HR8 1JQ, N : ¾ m. ✆ 633613, Fax 636366, « 18C house,
   restored Georgian gardens », park – ✾ rest ☎ 🅿. 🔄 VISA. ✾
   closed mid December-mid February – **M** (booking essential) (dinner only) 30.00 **t.** ▯ 4.50 –
   9 rm 🖙 87.00/143.00 **st.** – SB 151.00/222.00 **st.**

LEEDS W. Yorks. **402** P 22 Great Britain G. – pop. 445 242 – ECD : Wednesday – ⊕ 0532.

See : City★ – City Art Gallery★ *AC* DZ **M**.

Envir. : Kirkstall Abbey★ *AC*, NW : 3 m. by A 65 BV – Templenewsam★ (decorative arts★) *AC*, E : 5 m. by A 64 and A 63 CX **D**.

Exc. : Harewood House★★ (The Gallery★) *AC*, N : 8 m. by A 61 CV.

🛱, 🛱 The Temple Newsam, Temple Newsam Rd, Halton ℰ 645624, E : 3 m. by A 63 CV – 🛱 Gotts Park, Armley Ridge Rd, ℰ 342019, W : 2 m. by A 647 BV – 🛱 Middleton Park, Ring Rd, Beeston Park, Middleton ℰ 709506, S : 3 m. by A 653 CX – 🛱, 🛱 Moor Allerton, Coal Rd, Wike ℰ 661154, N : 5½ m. by A 61 CV – 🛱 Howley Hall, Scotchman Lane, Morley ℰ 0924 (Morley) 472432, SW : 4 m. by A 653 BX – 🛱 Roundhay, Park Lane ℰ 662695, N : 4 m. by A 6120 CV.

✈ Leeds - Bradford Airport : ℰ 509696, NW : 8 m. by A 65 and A 658 BV.

🛈 19 Wellington St., LS1 4DG ℰ 478301/478302.

◆London 204 – ◆Liverpool 75 – ◆Manchester 43 – ◆Newcastle upon Tyne 95 – ◆Nottingham 74.

Plans on next page

🏨 **Oulton Hall** (De Vere), Rothwell Lane, Oulton, LS26 8HN, SE : 5½ m. by A 61 and A 639 ℰ 821000, Fax 828066, ≼, 🛵, ≘ₛ, 🔲, 🐾, squash – 📳 ⇆ ▤ rest 🆃 ☎ & 🄿 – 🔬 290. 🔼 AE ⓞ VISA
M – **Bronte** (closed Saturday lunch) 11.00/19.00 **st.** and a la carte 🍴 5.00 – **150 rm** 🖂 97.50/ 112.50 **st.**, 2 suites – SB 130.00 **st.**

🏨 **Leeds Marriott,** 4 Trevelyan Sq., Boar Lane, LS1 6ET, ℰ 366366, Fax 366367, 🛵, ≘ₛ, 🔲 – 📳 ⇆ rm ▤ 🆃 ☎ & 🄿 – 🔬 300. 🔼 AE ⓞ VISA JCB
M – **Dyson's** a la carte 12.70/17.95 **t.** 🍴 5.95 – 🖂 10.75 – **236 rm** 110.00/120.00 **st.**, 8 suites – SB (weekends only) 100.00/130.00 **st.**

🏨 **42 The Calls,** 42 The Calls, LS2 7EW, ℰ 440099, Fax 344100, ≼, « Converted riverside grain mill » – 📳 ⇆ rm 🆃 ☎ & 🄿 – 🔬 55. 🔼 AE ⓞ VISA. 🛠
closed 5 days at Christmas – **M** – (see **Brasserie Forty Four** below) – 🖂 10.00 – **36 rm** 76.50/130.00 **st.**, 3 suites.

🏨 **Holiday Inn,** Wellington St., LS1 4DL, ℰ 442200, Telex 557879, Fax 440460, 🛵, ≘ₛ, 🔲 – 📳 ⇆ rm ▤ 🆃 ☎ & 🄿 – 🔬 200. 🔼 AE ⓞ VISA JCB. 🛠
M (closed Saturday lunch) 14.50/18.50 **st.** and a la carte – 🖂 9.95 – **121 rm** 130.00/ 145.00 **st.**, 4 suites – SB (July, August and December) (weekends only) 100.00/120.00 **st.**

🏨 **Leeds Hilton,** Neville St., LS1 4BX, ℰ 442000, Telex 557143, Fax 433577 – 📳 ⇆ rm ▤ 🆃 ☎ & 🄿 – 🔬 400. 🔼 AE ⓞ VISA JCB
M 12.00/17.95 **t.** and a la carte 🍴 6.35 – 🖂 9.95 – **186 rm** 89.00 **st.**, 20 suites – SB (weekends only) 96.00/136.00 **st.**

🏨 **Queen's** (Forte), City Sq., LS1 1PL, ℰ 431323, Telex 55161, Fax 425154 – 📳 ⇆ rm ▤ rest 🆃 ☎ 🄿 – 🔬 600. 🔼 AE ⓞ VISA
M 15.50/17.50 **st.** and a la carte 🍴 6.50 – 🖂 9.50 – **183 rm** 90.00/100.00 **st.**, 5 suites – SB (weekends only) 116.00/119.00 **st.**

🏨 **Merrion Thistle** (Mt. Charlotte Thistle), Merrion Centre, 17 Wade Lane, LS2 8NH, ℰ 439191, Telex 55459, Fax 423527 – 📳 ⇆ rm ▤ rest 🆃 ☎ 🄿 – 🔬 80. 🔼 AE ⓞ VISA 🛠
M 14.25 **st.** and a la carte 🍴 4.95 – 🖂 7.95 – **108 rm** 75.00/85.00 **st.**, 1 suite – SB (weekends only) 87.50/194.40 **st.**

🏨 **Haley's,** Shire Oak Rd, Headingley, LS6 2DE, NW : 2 m. off Otley Rd (A 660) ℰ 784446, Fax 753342 – ⇆ 🆃 ☎ 🄿. 🔼 AE ⓞ VISA 🛠
closed 26 to 30 December – **M** (closed lunch Saturday and Monday and Sunday dinner) 16.95/23.95 **st.** and a la carte 🍴 5.50 – **22 rm** 🖂 95.00/165.00 **st.** – SB (weekends only) 100.00 **st.**

🏨 **Golden Lion** (Mt. Charlotte Thistle), 2 Lower Briggate, LS1 4AE, ℰ 436454, Fax 429327 – 📳 ⇆ rm 🆃 ☎ – 🔬 120. 🔼 AE ⓞ VISA JCB. 🛠
M (closed Sunday lunch) 5.95/15.15 **st.** and a la carte – **89 rm** 🖂 75.00/80.00 **st.** – SB 82.00/160.00 **st.**

🛏 **Aragon,** 250 Stainbeck Lane, LS7 2PS, ℰ 759306, Fax 757166, 🐾 – 🆃 ☎ 🄿. 🔼 AE ⓞ VISA
closed Christmas – **M** 9.80 **st.** – **13 rm** 🖂 25.10/46.90 **st.** – SB (weekends only) 55.60/ 98.70 **st.**

🛏 **Ash Mount** without rest., 22 Wetherby Rd, Oakwood, LS8 2QD, ℰ 658164, 🐾 – 🆃 🄿. 🔼 VISA
11 rm 🖂 20.00/42.00 **st.**

🍴🍴 **Leodis Brasserie,** Victoria Mill, Sovereign St., LS1 4BJ, ℰ 421010, Fax 430432 – 🔼 AE VISA
closed Saturday lunch and Sunday – **Meals** 10.95 **t.** and a la carte 🍴 5.50.

🍴🍴 **Brasserie Fortyfour,** 42-44 The Calls, LS2 8AQ, ℰ 343232, Fax 343332 – ▤. 🔼 AE ⓞ VISA
closed Saturday lunch, Sunday and 5 days at Christmas – **M** 7.50 **st.** and a la carte 11.85/ 21.90 **t.** 🍴 5.65.

🍴🍴 **Maxi's,** 6 Bingley St., LS3 1LX, off Kirkstall Rd ℰ 440552, Fax 343902, « Pagoda, ornate decor » – ▤. 🔼 AE ⓞ VISA
M - Chinese (Canton, Peking) 15.00/25.00 **st.** and a la carte 🍴 9.00.

CX a

DZ x

DZ z

CZ c

DZ r

DZ a

DZ e

CV s

DZ v

CV c

CV u

AZ e

DZ z

AZ a

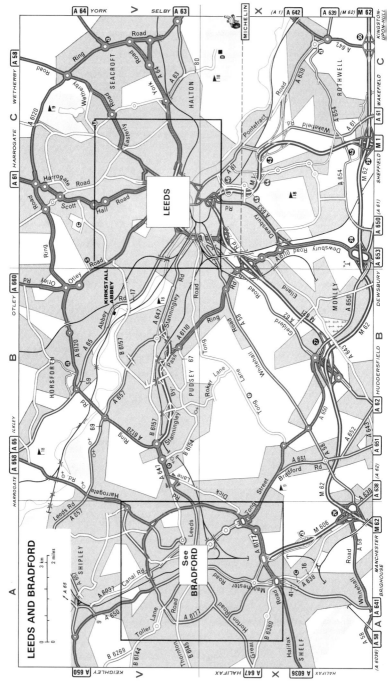

LEEDS AND BRADFORD

LEEDS

See BRADFORD

KIRKSTALL ABBEY

252

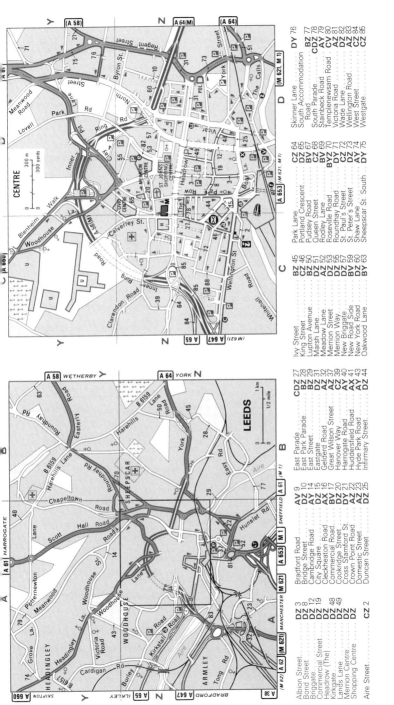

CENTRE

0   300 m
0   300 yards

A 58   A 64(M)   A 64

Regent   Street
Byron St.
Street
Meanwood Road
Lovell   Park   Rd
Ring   Rd
North   Lane
POL
York   Street
The Calls
Vicar   La.
The Headrow   Row
St Johns Shopping Centre
Merrion Centre
Calverley St.
Blenheim   Walk
Woodhouse
Clarendon   Road
Whitehall   Wellington Road
Inner   Ring
Clay   Pit   Ring   Rd

A 58(M)
A 660
A 61
A 65   A 647   (M 621)
M 621, M 1
A 653 (M 621, M 1)

A 58   WETHERBY
A 64   YORK

Roundhay   Rd
B 6159   Lane
Harehills   Lane
York   Rd
Easy   Rd
Aire

LEEDS

0   1 km
0   1/2 mile

SHEEPSCAR
Roundhay   Road
Harehills   Rd
Chapeltown   Road
Scott   Hall   Road
Woodhouse   Lane
Hunslet   Rd
Aire

HEADINGLEY
Grove   La.
Potternewton   Lane
Meanwood   La.
Victoria   Road
WOODHOUSE
Kirkstall   Road
Cardigan   Rd
Burley
Tong   Rd
ARMLEY
Aire

A 61   HARROGATE
B 6159
A 62
A 6157
B 6157
A 660   SKIPTON
A 65   ILKLEY
A 647   BRADFORD
A 38
M 621   MANCHESTER
M 621
A 653
M 1   SHEFFIELD
A 61
M 1

✗ **Sous le nez en ville,** Quebec House, Quebec St., LS1 2HA, 𝒫 440108 – ⌧ 🄰🄴 𝘝𝘐𝘚𝘈
closed Saturday lunch, Sunday and Bank Holidays except Good Friday – **M** 12.95 **st.**
(dinner) and a la carte 14.90/21.00 **st.** CZ **a**

✗ **Sang Sang,** 7 The Headrow, LS1 6PN, 𝒫 468664 – ⌧ 🄰🄴 🄾 𝘝𝘐𝘚𝘈 DZ **u**
closed Bank Holidays – **M** - **Chinese** (restricted lunch)/dinner 18.00 **t.** and a la carte ⑆ 3.30.

at Seacroft NE : 5 ½ m. at junction of A 64 and A 6120 – ✉ ۞ 0532 Leeds :

🏨 **Stakis Leeds Windmill,** Ring Rd, LS14 5QP, 𝒫 732323, Telex 55452, Fax 323018 – 🛗
⊱🛏 rm 🍴 rest 📺 ☎ 🄿 – 🛦 250. ⌧ 🄰🄴 🄾 𝘝𝘐𝘚𝘈 🄹🄲🄱 CV **a**
M 9.50/14.25 **t.** and dinner a la carte – ⌸ 8.50 – **100 rm** 69.00/85.00 **st.** – SB (weekends
only) 72.00/78.00 **st.**

at Garforth E : 6 m. at junction of A 63 and A 642 – CV – ✉ ۞ 0532 Leeds :

🏨 **Hilton National,** Wakefield Rd, LS25 1LH, 𝒫 866556, Telex 556324, Fax 868326, 🎣, 🚡,
⌧ – ⊱🛏 rm 🍴 rest 📺 ☎ 🕭 🄿 – 🛦 250. ⌧ 🄰🄴 🄾 𝘝𝘐𝘚𝘈 🎿
M (carving lunch) 15.95/17.95 **st.** and a la carte ⑆ 5.95 – ⌸ 10.25 – **144 rm** 65.00 **t.** –
SB (weekends only) 125.00/145.00 **st.**

at Pudsey W : 5 ¾ m. by A 647 – ✉ Leeds – ۞ 0274 Bradford :

✗ **Aagrah,** 483 Bradford Rd, LS28 8ED, on A 647 𝒫 668818 – 🄿. ⌧ 🄰🄴 🄾 𝘝𝘐𝘚𝘈 BV **e**
closed 25 December – **M** - **Indian** (dinner only and Sunday lunch) 7.95/12.95 **t.** and a la carte
⑆ 4.00.

at Horsforth NW : 5 m. by A 65 off A 6120 – ✉ ۞ 0532 Leeds :

✗ **Paris,** 36A Town St., LS18 4RJ, 𝒫 581885. ⌧ 🄰🄴 𝘝𝘐𝘚𝘈 BV **a**
closed 25-26 December and 1 January – **M** (dinner only) 12.95 **t.** and a la carte.

at Bramhope NW : 8 m. on A 660 – BV – ✉ ۞ 0532 Leeds :

🏨 **Forte Crest,** Leeds Rd, LS16 9JJ, 𝒫 842911, Telex 556367, Fax 843451, ≼, 🎣, 🚡, ⌧,
🌲, park – 🛗 ⊱🛏 rm 📺 ☎ 🄿 – 🛦 160. 🛦 🄾 𝘝𝘐𝘚𝘈 🄹🄲🄱
M 12.95/16.95 **t.** and dinner a la carte ⑆ 5.95 – ⌸ 9.95 – **125 rm** 89.00 **st.**, 1 suite –
SB (weekends only) 98.00/106.00 **st.**

🏨 **Parkway** (Jarvis), Otley Rd, LS16 8AG, S : 2 m. on A 660 𝒫 672551, Fax 674410, 🎣, 🚡,
⌧, 🏊, 🎿 – 🛗 ⊱🛏 rm 📺 ☎ 🕭 🄿 – 🛦 250. ⌧ 🄰🄴 🄾 𝘝𝘐𝘚𝘈
M (dinner only and Sunday lunch)/dinner 14.95 **st.** and a la carte – ⌸ 8.50 – **103 rm**
93.00/130.00 **st.** – SB 85.00 **st.**

MICHELIN Distribution Centre, Gelderd Rd, LS12 6EU, 𝒫 310548, Fax 794577 BX

◍ ATS Cross Green Lane 𝒫 459423   ATS 2 Regent St. 𝒫 430652

LEEK Staffs. 💰 💱 💲 N 24 – pop. 19 689 – ECD : Thursday – ۞ 0538.
🏌 Westwood, Newcastle Rd, Wallbridge 𝒫 398385.
🛈 Market Pl., ST13 5HH 𝒫 381000.
♦London 122 – Derby 30 – ♦Manchester 39 – ♦Stoke-on-Trent 12.

⌂ **Bank End Farm Motel** 🦢, Leek Old Rd, Longsdon, ST9 9QJ, SW : 2 ½ m. by A 53
𝒫 383608, « Working farm », ⌧ – 📺 ☎ 🄿. 𝘝𝘐𝘚𝘈
M 16.50 **st.** ⑆ 4.50 – **10 rm** ⌸ 25.00/50.00 **st.**

⌂ **Pethills Bank Cottage** 🦢 without rest., Bottom House, ST13 7PF, SE : 5 m. by A 523
𝒫 304277, Fax 304575, ≼ – ⊱🛏 📺 🄿. 🎿
March-November – **3 rm** ⌸ 31.00/42.00 **s.**

at Grindon E : 9 m. by A 523 and B 5053 on Grindon rd – ✉ ۞ 0538 Leek :

⌂ **White House** 🦢 without rest., ST13 7TP, 𝒫 304250, ≼, 🌲 – ⊱🛏 📺 🄿. 🎿
3 rm ⌸ 40.00/48.00 **s.**

LEEMING BAR N. Yorks. 💱 P 21 – pop. 1 468 – ECD : Wednesday – ✉ Northallerton –
۞ 0677 Bedale.
♦London 235 – ♦Leeds 44 – ♦Middlesbrough 30 – ♦Newcastle upon Tyne 52 – York 37.

🏨 **White Rose,** DL7 9AY, 𝒫 422707, Fax 425123 – 📺 ☎ 🄿. ⌧ 🄰🄴 🄾 𝘝𝘐𝘚𝘈
M 7.75/11.95 **st.** and a la carte – **18 rm** ⌸ 29.50/43.00 **st.**

LEE-ON-THE-SOLENT Hants. 💲 💳 Q 31 – pop. 7 068 – ECD : Thursday – ۞ 0705.
🏌 Gosport & Stokes Bay, Fort Rd, Haslar, Gosport 𝒫 851625, SE : 3 ½ m.
♦London 81 – ♦Portsmouth 13 – ♦Southampton 15 – Winchester 23.

🏨 **Belle Vue,** 39 Marine Par. East, PO13 9BW, 𝒫 550258, Fax 552624, ≼ – 📺 ☎ 🄿. ⌧ 🄰🄴
𝘝𝘐𝘚𝘈
closed 24 to 28 December – **M** a la carte 9.55/18.50 **t.** ⑆ 5.00 – ⌸ 6.50 – **27 rm** 35.00/
55.00 **t.** – SB (weekends only) 65.50/85.50 **st.**

Don't get lost, use **Michelin Maps** which are kept up to date.

See : Guildhall★ BY **B** – Museum and Art Gallery★ CY **M2** – St. Mary de Castro Church★ BY **A**.

🏌 Leicestershire, Evington Lane ℘ 736035, SE : 2 m. by A 6030 AY – 🏌 Western Park, Scudamore Rd ℘ 876158/872339, W : 4 m. by A 47 AY – 🏌 Humberstone Heights, Gypsy Lane ℘ 761905, E : 3 m. by A 47 AX – 🏌 Oadby, Leicester Road Racecourse ℘ 700215/709052, SE : 2 m. by A 6 AY.

✈ East Midlands Airport : Castle Donington ℘ 0332 (Derby) 810621, NW : 22 m. by A 50 – AX – and M1.

🚉 St. Margaret's Bus Station, LE1 3TY ℘ 511301 – 2-6 St. Martin's Walk, St. Martin's Sq., LE1 5DG ℘ 511300.

◆London 107 – ◆Birmingham 43 – ◆Coventry 24 – ◆Nottingham 26.

LEICESTER
BUILT UP AREA

Asquith Way	**AY** 2	Braunstone Way	**AY** 14	Loughborough Road	**AX** 40
Belgrave Road	**AX** 4	Checketts Road	**AX** 17	Marfitt Street	**AX** 41
Braunstone Avenue	**AY** 10	Fosse Road North	**AX** 22	Middleton Street	**AY** 43
Braunstone Lane East	**AY** 13	Fullhurst Avenue	**AY** 23	Stoughton Road	**AY** 66
		Glenfrith Way	**AX** 24	Upperton Road	**AY** 68
		Henley Road	**AX** 29	Walnut Street	**AY** 69
		Humberstone Road	**AX** 34	Wigston Lane	**AY** 75
		King Richards Road	**AY** 37	Woodville Road	**AY** 76
		Knighton Road	**AY** 38	Wyngate Drive	**AY** 78

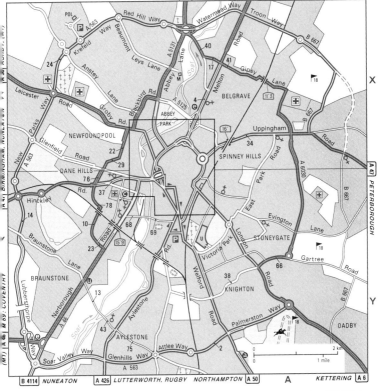

🏨 **Holiday Inn**, 129 St. Nicholas Circle, LE1 5LX, ℘ 531161, Telex 341281, Fax 513169, 🏋, ☎, 🏊 – 📶 ⚒ rm 📺 ☎ � Ꮖ – 🛗 250. 🔧 🆎 ⑩ 𝗩𝗜𝗦𝗔 𝗝𝗖𝗕   BY **c**
M 11.00/16.25 **st.** and a la carte – 🍽 9.95 – **187 rm** 84.00/94.00 **t.**, 1 suite – SB (July-August and December-January) 70.00/116.00 **st.**

🏨 **Grand** (Jarvis), 73 Granby St., LE1 6ES, ℘ 555599, Fax 544736 – 📶 ⚒ rm 📺 ☎ Ꮖ – 🛗 450. 🔧 🆎 ⑩ 𝗩𝗜𝗦𝗔   CY **o**
M (bar lunch Saturday and Bank Holidays) 11.95/18.00 **t.** 🍷 6.50 – 🍽 8.00 – **91 rm** 76.00/86.00 **t.**, 1 suite – SB (weekends only) 70.00/79.00 **st.**

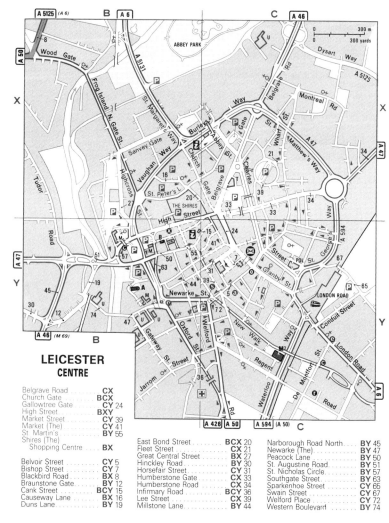

LEICESTER
CENTRE

🏨 **Belmont House** (Best Western), De Montfort St., LE1 7GR, ℰ 544773, Fax 470804 – 🛗
🚷 rm 📺 ☎ 🅿 – 🔬 100. 🔼 🄰🄴 ⓪ 𝘝𝘐𝘚𝘈 𝙅𝘾𝘉. ⋘   CY **c**
closed 24 to 28 December – **M** *(closed Saturday lunch)* 10.95/16.50 **t.** and a la carte – **65 rm**
� 68.00/88.00 **t.** – SB (weekends only) 92.00 **st.**

⌂ **Spindle Lodge,** 2 West Walk, LE1 7NA, ℰ 551380, Fax 543076 – 📺 ☎ 🅿. 🔼 𝘝𝘐𝘚𝘈
⋘
closed 24 December-1 January – **M** *(by arrangement)* approx. 11.00 – **13 rm** ⊒ 26.50/
57.50 **st.**   CY **r**

⌂ **Scotia,** 10 Westcotes Drive, LE3 0QR, ℰ 549200 – 📺   AY **c**
M *(by arrangement)* 7.95 **t.** ⬧ 3.95 – **17 rm** ⊒ 22.00/42.00 **st.**

⌂ **Seaforth** without rest., 12 Westcotes Drive, LE3 0QR, ℰ 554895 – 📺. ⋘   AY **c**
4 rm ⊒ 22.00/40.00 **s.**

%% **Welford Place,** 9 Welford Place, LE1 6ZH, ℰ 470758, Fax 471843 – 🔼 🄰🄴 ⓪ 𝘝𝘐𝘚𝘈
M 12.50/15.00 **st.** and a la carte ⬧ 4.95   CY **s**

%% **Man Ho,** 14-16 King St., LE1 6RJ, ℰ 557700, Fax 545629 – 🔼 🄰🄴 ⓪ 𝘝𝘐𝘚𝘈   CY **u**
M - Chinese 6.50 **st.** (lunch) and a la carte approx. 9.30 **t.** ⬧ 3.90.

XX **Curry House,** 64 London Rd, LE2 0QD, ℰ 550688. ◪ AE ◍ VISA CY **e**
closed lunch Bank Holiday Mondays, Sunday and 25-26 December – **M** - **Indian** a la
carte 11.25/16.45 **t.**

XX **Curry Pot,** 78-80 Belgrave Rd, LE4 5AS, ℰ 538256, Fax 625125 – ◪ AE ◍ VISA AX **e**
closed Sunday – **M** - **Indian** a la carte 13.95/23.60 **t.**

XX **Water Margin,** 76-78 High St., LE1 5YP, ℰ 516422 – ◪ AE ◍ VISA BY **x**
M - **Chinese** (Canton) 5.50/10.00 **st.** and a la carte.

X **Casa Romana,** 5 Albion St., LE1 6GD, ℰ 541174 – ◪ VISA CY **a**
closed Sunday and Bank Holidays – **M** - **Italian** (booking essential) 10.00/19.00 **st.** ⵙ 3.40.

at Rothley N : 5 m. by A 6 – AX – on B 5328 – ⊠ ⊕ 0533 Leicester :

▲▲ **Rothley Court** (Forte) ⤢, Westfield Lane, LE7 7LG, W : ½ m. on B 5328 ℰ 374141,
Fax 374483, ≼, « Part 13C house and 11C chapel », ⊅ – ⵝ⤢ rm ⓉⓋ ☎ ℗ – ⵙ 100. ◪ AE
◍ VISA JCB
M *(closed lunch Monday and Saturday)* (light lunch) 13.25/22.50 **t.** and a la carte ⵙ 6.75 –
⊆ 8.50 – **35 rm** 78.00/90.00 **st.**, 1 suite – SB 108.00/118.00 **st.**

🏠 **Limes,** 35 Mountsorrel Lane, LE7 7PS, ℰ 302531 – ▭ ⓉⓋ ☎ ℗. ◪ AE VISA. ⵘ
closed Christmas – **M** (dinner only) 12.95 **st.** and a la carte ⵙ 4.50 – **11 rm** ⊆ 42.50/65.00 **st.**

at Thrussington NE : 10 m. by A 46 – AX – ⊠ Leicester – ⊕ 0664 Melton Mowbray :

🏠 **Forte Travelodge** without rest., Green Acres Filling Station, LE7 8TF, on A 46 (southbound carriageway) ℰ 424525, Reservations (Freephone) 0800 850950 – ⓉⓋ ⅋ ℗. ◪ AE
VISA. ⵘ
32 rm 31.95 **t.**

at Oadby SE : 3½ m. on A 6 – AY – ⊠ ⊕ 0533 Leicester :

🏤 **Leicestershire Moat House** (Q.M.H.), Wigston Rd, LE2 5QE, on B 582 ℰ 719441,
Fax 720559 – ▤ ⵝ⤢ ⓉⓋ ☎ ⅋ ℗ – ⵙ 250. ◪ AE ◍ VISA
M (bar lunch Saturday) 10.60/14.50 **t.** and a la carte ⵙ 4.05 – ⊆ 6.50 – **57 rm** 66.00/77.00 **st.**
– SB (weekends only) 72.00 **st.**

at Wigston Fields SE : 3¼ m. on A 50 – ⊠ ⊕ 0533 Leicester :

🏤 **Stage,** 299 Leicester Rd, LE18 1JW, ℰ 886161, Fax 811874, �𝄄, ≘s, ▤, – ⵝ⤢ rm ⓉⓋ ☎ ⅋
℗ – ⵙ 200. ◪ AE ◍ VISA JCB. ⵘ AY **a**
M 8.95/11.95 **t.** and a la carte – **71 rm** ⊆ 39.00/75.00 **t.** – SB (weekends only) 60.00/
85.00 **st.**

at Braunstone SW : 2 m. on A 46 – ⊠ ⊕ 0533 Leicester :

▲▲ Stakis Country Court, LE3 2WQ, SW : 1¾ m. by A 46 ℰ 630066, Telex 34429, Fax 630627,
𝄄, ≘s, ▤, ⊅ – ⵝ⤢ rm ▤ rest ⓉⓋ ☎ ⅋ ℗ – ⵙ 80 AY **e**
131 rm, 10 suites.

🏤 **Forte Posthouse,** Braunstone Lane East, LE3 2FW, ℰ 630500, Fax 823623 – ▤ ⵝ⤢ rm
▤ rest ⓉⓋ ☎ ℗ – ⵙ 80. ◪ AE ◍ VISA AY **u**
M a la carte approx. 17.50 **t.** ⵙ 4.65 – ⊆ 6.95 – **170 rm** 53.50 **st.** – SB (weekends only)
90.00 **st.**

at Leicester Forest East W : 3 m. on A 47 – AY – ⊠ ⊕ 0533 Leicester :

🏤 **Leicester Forest Moat House** (Q.M.H.), Hinckley Rd, LE3 3GH, ℰ 394661, Fax 394952
– ⓉⓋ ☎ ℗ – ⵙ 100. ◪ AE ◍ VISA
accommodation closed 21 to 28 December – **M** (bar lunch Monday to Saturday)/din-
ner 13.00 **t.** and a la carte – **33 rm** ⊆ 28.60/62.00 **st.** – SB (weekends only) 72.00/76.00 **st.**

🏤 **Red Cow,** Hinckley Rd, LE3 3PG, ℰ 387878, Fax 387878 – ⵝ⤢ rm ⓉⓋ ☎ ⅋ ℗. ◪ AE ◍
VISA. ⵘ
closed 25 December – **M** (grill rest.) a la carte 9.55/15.75 **t.** – ⊆ 4.95 – **31 rm** 39.50 **t.**

🔟 ATS 16 Wanlip St. ℰ 624281 ATS 31 Woodgate ℰ 625611

LEIGH DELAMERE SERVICE AREA Wilts. – ⊠ Chippenham – ⊕ 0666 Malmesbury

🏠 **Granada Lodge** without rest., SN14 6LB, M 4 between junctions 18 and 17 (eastbound
carriageway) ℰ 837097, Fax 837112, Reservations (Freephone) 0800 555300 – ⵝ⤢ ⓉⓋ ⅋
℗. ◪ AE VISA. ⵘ
⊆ 4.00 – **35 rm** 34.95/37.95 **st.**

LEIGHTON BUZZARD Beds. 404 S 28 – pop. 29 554 – ECD : Thursday – ⊕ 0525.

🖈 Plantation Rd ℰ 373811/373812, N : 1 m. – 🖈 Aylesbury Vale, Wing ℰ 240196, W : 3 m. on
A 418.

◆London 47 – Bedford 20 – Luton 12 – Northampton 30.

🏤 **Swan** (Resort), High St., LU7 7EA, ℰ 372148, Fax 370444 – ⓉⓋ ☎ ℗ – ⵙ 40. ◪ AE ◍
VISA
M *(closed Saturday lunch)* 8.95/13.50 **t.** and a la carte – ⊆ 7.50 – **38 rm** 55.00/80.00 **t.** –
SB 80.00/120.00 **st.**

🔟 ATS Unit C, Camden Ind. Est., 83 Lake St. ℰ 376158/379238

LEOMINSTER Heref. and Worcs. 403 L 27 Great Britain G. – pop. 8 637 – ECD : Thursday – ✆ 0568.

Envir. : Berrington Hall★ *AC*, N : 3 m. by A 49.

🏌 Ford Bridge ✆ 612863, S : 3 m. on A 49.

🛈 6 School Lane, HR6 8AA ✆ 616460 (summer only).

◆London 141 – ◆Birmingham 47 – Hereford 13 – Worcester 26.

    🏨 **Talbot** (Best Western), West St., HR6 8EP, ✆ 616347, Fax 614880 – 📺 ☎ 🅿 – 🕍 120. 🖭 🖭 ⓥ *VISA* JCB

    M 10.50/15.50 **t.** and a la carte ⓵ 4.95 – **20 rm** �😐 38.00/72.00 **t.** – SB (except Christmas) 96.00/100.00 **st.**

    🏠 **Withenfield** without rest., South St., HR6 8JN, ✆ 612011, 🌼 – ⇆ 📺 ☎ 🅿. 🖭 *VISA* ⠦

    4 rm ⟺ 39.00/56.00 **st.**

    at Stoke Prior SE : 2 m. by A 44 – ✉ ✆ 0568 Leominster :

    ✗ **Wheelbarrow Castle** with rm, HR6 0NB, on Leominster rd ✆ 612219, ⟐ heated – 📺 🅿. 🖭 *VISA*

    closed 25 December – **M** (in bar) a la carte 8.90/21.10 **t.** ⓵ 4.00 – **6 rm** ⟺ 35.00/45.00 **t.**

    at Eyton NW : 2 m. by B 4361 – ✉ ✆ 0568 Leominster :

    🏠 **The Marsh** ⠦, HR6 0AG, ✆ 613952, « Part 14C timbered house », 🌼 – ⇆ 📺 ☎ 🅿. 🖭 🖭 ⓥ *VISA* ⠦

    M (booking essential) (lunch by arrangement) 20.00/30.00 **st.** ⓵ 6.50 – **5 rm** ⟺ 74.00/110.00 **st.** – SB (except Christmas and New Year) 145.00/165.00 **st.**

🔧 ATS Market Mill, Dishley St. ✆ 612679/614114

En saison, surtout dans les stations fréquentées, il est prudent de retenir à l'avance.
Cependant, si vous ne pouvez pas occuper la chambre que vous avez retenue,
prévenez immédiatement l'hôtelier.

Si vous écrivez à un hôtel à l'étranger, joignez à votre lettre
un coupon-réponse international (disponible dans les bureaux de poste).

LETCHWORTH Herts. 404 T 28 – pop. 31 146 – ECD : Wednesday – ✆ 0462.

◆London 40 – Bedford 22 – ◆Cambridge 22 – Luton 14.

    🏨 **Broadway Toby,** The Broadway, SG6 3NZ, ✆ 480111, Fax 481563 – 🛗 📺 ☎ 🅿 – 🕍 180. 🖭 🖭 ⓥ *VISA* ⠦

    M (grill rest.) a la carte approx. 18.65 **st.** ⓵ 4.95 – **35 rm** ⟺ 49.95/59.95 **st.** – SB (weekends only) 66.00/102.00 **st.**

🔧 ATS Unit 21, Jubilee Trade Centre, Works Rd ✆ 670517

LEW Oxon – ✉ Oxford – ✆ 0993 Bampton Castle

    🏠 **Farmhouse,** University Farm, OX18 2AU, ✆ 850297, Fax 850965, 🌼 – ⇆ 📺 ☎ 👤 🅿. 🖭 *VISA* ⠦

    closed Christmas and New Year – **M** *(closed Sunday)* (residents only Monday to Thursday) (dinner only) 14.25 **st.** – **6 rm** ⟺ 39.00/52.00 **st.** – SB (weekdays only) 78.50/106.50 **st.**

LEWDOWN Devon 403 H 32 The West Country G. – ✆ 056 683.

Envir. : Lydford★★ (Lydford Gorge★★) E : 4 m.

Exc. : Launceston★ - Castle★ (≼★) St. Mary Magdalene★, South Gate★, W : 8 m. by A 30 and A 388.

◆London 238 – Exeter 37 – ◆Plymouth 22.

    🏨 **Lewtrenchard Manor** ⠦, EX20 4PN, S : ¾ m. by Lewtrenchard rd ✆ 256, Fax 332, « 17C manor house and gardens », 🐾, park – ⇆ rest 📺 ☎ 🅿. 🖭 🖭 ⓥ *VISA*

    M (lunch by arrangement Monday to Saturday)/dinner 32.50 **t.** ⓵ 5.00 – **8 rm** ⟺ 75.00/130.00 **t.**

LEWES E. Sussex 404 U 31 Great Britain G. – pop. 14 499 – ECD : Wednesday – ✆ 0273.

See : Town★ (High Street★, Keere Street★) – Castle (≼★) *AC*.

Exc. : Sheffield Park Garden★ *AC*, N : 9½ m. by A 275.

🏌 Chapel Hill ✆ 473245, E : ½ m.

🛈 Lewes House, High St., BN7 2LX ✆ 483448.

◆London 53 – Brighton 8 – Hastings 29 – Maidstone 43.

    🏠 **Millers** without rest., 134 High St., BN7 1XS, ✆ 475631, 🌼 – ⇆ 📺. ⠦

    closed 20 December-3 January – **3 rm** ⟺ 34.00/45.00 **s.**

    🏠 **Hillside** without rest., Rotten Row, BN7 1TN, ✆ 473120, 🌼 – ⇆. ⠦

    3 rm ⟺ 18.00/40.00 **s.**

    ✗✗ **Pailin,** 20 Station Rd, BN7 2DB, ✆ 473906 – 🖭 🖭 ⓥ *VISA*

    closed Sunday lunch – **M** - Thai a la carte 9.45/17.65 **t.**

🔧 ATS 18 North St. ✆ 477972/3

LEYLAND Lancs. 402 L 22 – pop. 36 694 – ECD : Wednesday – ☎ 0772.

◆London 220 – ◆Liverpool 31 – ◆Manchester 32 – Preston 6.

🏨 **Leyland Resort,** Leyland Way, PR5 2JX, E : ¾ m. on B 5256 ℰ 422922, Fax 622282 – 🏷 rm 🔟 ☎ 🅿 – 🔬 200. 🖎 🆎 🔘 𝚅𝙸𝚂𝙰
M (bar lunch Saturday) 10.00/15.00 **t.** and a la carte – ⊆ 7.50 – **93 rm** 50.00/70.00 **t.** – SB 80.00/120.00 **st.**

◎ ATS Leyland Lane ℰ 431021/2

LICHFIELD Staffs. 402 403 404 O 25 Great Britain G. – pop. 25 408 – ECD : Wednesday – ☎ 0543.

See : City★ – Cathedral★★ AC.

🏇 Seedy Mill, Elmhurst ℰ 417333, N : 2 m. by A 515.

🎫 Donegal House, Bore St., WS13 6NE ℰ 252109.

◆London 128 – ◆Birmingham 16 – Derby 23 – ◆Stoke-on-Trent 30.

🏨 **Little Barrow,** Beacon St., WS13 7AR, ℰ 414500, Fax 415734 – 🔟 ☎ 🅿 – 🔬 80. 🖎 🆎 🔘 𝚅𝙸𝚂𝙰. ⚓
M 8.50/11.50 **st.** and a la carte ᐧ 4.25 – **24 rm** ⊆ 39.85/44.65 **st.** – SB (weekends only) 65.00/90.00 **st.**

🏠 **Oakleigh House,** 25 St. Chad's Rd, WS13 7LZ, ℰ 262688, ⚯ – 🍽 rest 🔟 ☎ 🅿. 🖎 𝚅𝙸𝚂𝙰. ⚓
closed 27 December-5 January – **M** (see **Conservatory** below) – **10 rm** ⊆ 37.00/60.00 **t.**

🍽🍽 **Conservatory** (at Oakleigh House H.), 25 St. Chad's Rd, WS13 7LZ, ℰ 418556, ⚯ – 🅿. 🖎 𝚅𝙸𝚂𝙰
closed Sunday dinner and Monday – **M** (dinner only and Sunday lunch)/dinner 20.50 **t.** and a la carte ᐧ 4.50.

🍽🍽 Thrales, 40-44 Tamworth St., WS13 6JJ, (corner of Backcester Lane) ℰ 255091.

◎ ATS Eastern Av. ℰ 414200

☞ Benutzen Sie für weite Fahrten in Europa die Michelin-Länderkarten :

970 Europa, 980 Griechenland, 984 Deutschland, 985 Skandinavien-Finnland,
986 Großbritannien-Irland, 987 Deutschland-Österreich-Benelux, 988 Italien,
989 Frankreich, 990 Spanien-Portugal, 991 Jugoslawien.

LIFTON Devon 403 H 32 The West Country G. – pop. 966 – ECD : Tuesday – ☎ 0566.

Envir. : Launceston★ – Castle★ (≤★) St. Mary Magdalene★, South Gate★, W : 4½ m. by A 30 and A 388.

◆London 238 – Bude 24 – Exeter 37 – Launceston 4 – ◆Plymouth 32.

🏨 **Arundell Arms** (Best Western), Fore St., PL16 0AA, on A 30 ℰ 784666, Fax 784494, ⚲, ⚯ – 🏷 rest 🔟 ☎ 🅿 – 🔬 100. 🖎 🆎 𝚅𝙸𝚂𝙰
closed 24 and 25 December – **M** 15.00/23.00 **t.** and a la carte – **29 rm** ⊆ 57.00/90.00 **t.** – SB 112.00/142.00 **st.**

🏠 **Thatched Cottage** ⚶, Sprytown, PL16 0AY, E : 1¼ m. by A 30 ℰ 784224, ⚯ – 🔟 🅿. 🖎 🆎 🔘 𝚅𝙸𝚂𝙰. ⚓
M 15.50 **t.** (dinner) and a la carte ᐧ 5.25 – **5 rm** ⊆ 35.00/90.00 **t.** – SB 120.00/170.00 **st.**

LIMPLEY STOKE Avon – see Bath.

LINCOLN Lincs. 402 404 S 24 Great Britain G. – pop. 79 980 – ECD : Wednesday – ☎ 0522.

See : City★★ – Cathedral and Precincts★★★ AC Y – High Bridge★★ Z **9** – Usher Gallery★★ AC YZ **M1** – Jew's House★ Y – Castle★ AC Y.

Envir. : Doddington Hall★ AC, W : 6 m. by B 1003 – Z – and B 1190.

Exc. : Gainsborough Old Hall★ AC, NW : 19 m. by A 57 – Z – and A 156.

🏇 Carholme ℰ 523725, W : 1 m. by A 57 Z.

✈ Humberside Airport : ℰ 0652 (Barnetby) 688456, N : 32 m. by A 15 – Y – M 180 and A 18.

🎫 9 Castle Hill, LN1 3AA ℰ 529828 – 21 The Cornhill, LN5 7HB ℰ 512971.

◆London 140 – Bradford 81 – ◆Cambridge 94 – ◆Kingston-upon-Hull 44 – ◆Leeds 73 – ◆Leicester 53 – ◆Norwich 104 – ◆Nottingham 38 – ◆Sheffield 48 – York 82.

Plan on next page

🏨 **White Hart** (Forte), Bailgate, LN1 3AR, ℰ 526222, Fax 531798, « Antique furniture » – 🖿 🏷 rm 🔟 ☎ 🅿 – 🔬 90. 🖎 🆎 🔘 𝚅𝙸𝚂𝙰 𝙹𝙲𝙱. ⚓   Y **c**
M 10.95/18.95 **st.** and a la carte ᐧ 6.45 – ⊆ 6.45 – **35 rm** 75.00/95.00 **st.**, 13 suites – SB (weekends only) 128.00/153.00 **st.**

🏨 **Courtyard by Marriott,** Brayford Side North, LN1 1YW, ℰ 544244, Fax 560805, 🗡 – 🖿
🏷 rm 🔟 ☎ 🅿 – 🔬 30. 🖎 🆎 🔘 𝚅𝙸𝚂𝙰. ⚓   Z **a**
M 11.25 **st.** and a la carte – ⊆ 7.75 – **95 rm** 58.00 **st.** – SB (weekends only) 80.00/100.00 **st.**

🏨 **Forte Posthouse,** Eastgate, LN2 1PN, ℰ 520341, Fax 510780 – 🖿 🏷 rm 🔟 ☎ 🅿 – 🔬 90. 🖎 🆎 🔘 𝚅𝙸𝚂𝙰 𝙹𝙲𝙱.   Y **z**
M a la carte approx. 17.50 **t.** ᐧ 4.65 – ⊆ 6.95 – **70 rm** 53.50 **t.** – SB 90.00 **st.**

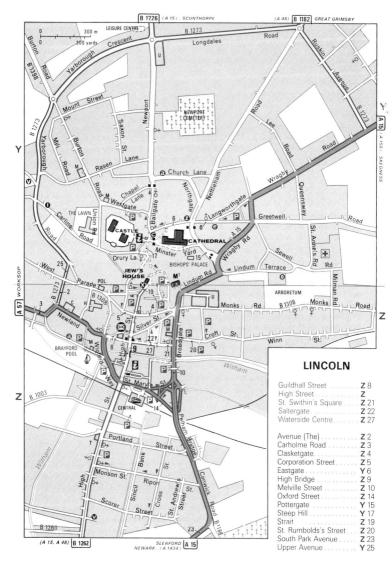

🏠 **D'Isney Place** without rest., Eastgate, LN2 4AA, ℰ 538881, Fax 511321, 🛲 – 📺 ☎. 🄰
🄰🄴 ⑩ 𝘝𝘐𝘚𝘈
Y **e**
17 rm � 41.00/72.00 **t.**

🏠 **Minster Lodge** without rest., 3 Church Lane, LN2 1QJ, ℰ 513220, Fax 513220 – 📺 ☎ 🄿.
🄰 🄰🄴 ⑩ 𝘝𝘐𝘚𝘈 ✂
Y **a**
6 rm ⊆ 42.00/49.00 **t.**

🏠 **Damons Motel** without rest., 997 Doddington Rd, LN6 3SE, SW : 4¼ m. by A 15 on B
1190 at junction with A 46 ℰ 500422, Fax 689719, 🐟 – ✂ 📺 ☎ ⅊ 🄿. 🄰 🄰🄴 ⑩ 𝘝𝘐𝘚𝘈 ✂
⊆ 3.50 – **47 rm** 34.00/42.50 **t.**
Z

🏠 **Hillcrest**, 15 Lindum Terr., LN2 5RT, ℰ 510182, Fax 510182, ≤, 🛲 – 📺 ☎ 🄿. 🄰 🄰🄴
𝘝𝘐𝘚𝘈
Y **o**
closed 21 December-2 January – **M** *(closed Sunday)* (bar lunch)/dinner a la carte 12.45/
15.50 **t.** ⓐ 4.25 – **17 rm** ⊆ 34.00/62.00 **t.** – SB 76.00/94.00 **st.**

🏠 **Carline** without rest., 3 Carline Rd, LN1 1HL, ✆ 530422 – ⇇ 📺 🅿. 🛇   **Y**   **i**
closed Christmas and New Year – **10 rm** ⊆ 18.00/38.00 **st.**

🏠 **Travel Inn,** Lincoln Rd, Canwick Hill, LN4 2RF, SE : 1 ¾ m. on B 1188 ✆ 525216,
Fax 542521 – ⇇ rm 📺 & 🅿   **Z**
M (Beefeater grill) a la carte approx. 16.00 **t.** – ⊆ 4.95 – **40 rm** 33.50 **t.**

⌂ **Fircroft,** 396-398 Newark Rd, LN6 8RX, SW : 2 m. on A 1434 ✆ 526522, Fax 543147 – 📺
☎ 🅿. 🅴 🆇 ⓞ 𝘝𝘐𝘚𝘈   by A 15   **Z**
M (by arrangement) 10.85 **st.** – **15 rm** ⊆ 22.50/43.95 **st.**

⌂ **Rowan Lodge** without rest., 58 Pennell St., LN5 7TA, ✆ 529589 – 📺 🅿. 🛇   **Z**   **v**
3 rm ⊆ 16.00/28.00.

⌂ **Tennyson,** 7 South Park Av., LN5 8EN, ✆ 521624 – 📺 🅿. 🅴 🆇 ⓞ 𝘝𝘐𝘚𝘈. 🛇
M 12.00 **st.** 🍷 4.50 – **8 rm** ⊆ 25.00/42.00 **st.** – SB (except Christmas and New Year) 58.00/
72.00 **st.**   by A 158   **Z**

⌂ **ABC** without rest., 126 Yarborough Rd, LN1 1HP, ✆ 543560, ⩽ – ⇇ 📺 🅿. 🛇   **Y**   **v**
8 rm ⊆ 18.00/40.00 **st.**

✗✗ **Jew's House,** Jew's House, 15 The Strait, LN2 1JD, ✆ 524851, « 12C town house » –
🅴 🆇 ⓞ 𝘝𝘐𝘚𝘈   **YZ**   **x**
closed Sunday, Monday and 1 week February – **M** 16.50 **t.** and a la carte 🍷 4.25.

    at Washingborough E : 3 m. by B 1188 – Z – on B 1190 – ✉ 🕿 0522 Lincoln :

🏠 **Washingborough Hall** 🦢, Church Hill, LN4 1BE, ✆ 790340, Fax 792936, ⤳ heated, ⤳
– ⇇ 📺 🅿 – 🔒 45. 🅴 🆇 ⓞ 𝘝𝘐𝘚𝘈
closed 1 week Christmas – **M** (lunch by arrangement Monday to Saturday)/dinner 21.00 **st.**
– **14 rm** ⊆ 49.00/88.00 **t.** – SB (except Christmas) 69.00/130.00 **st.**

    at Branston SE : 3 m. on B 1188 – Z – 🕿 0522 Lincoln :

🏠 **Moor Lodge,** Sleaford Rd, LN4 1HU, ✆ 791366, Fax 794389 – 📺 ☎ & 🅿 – 🔒 150. 🅴 🆇
ⓞ 𝘝𝘐𝘚𝘈
M *(closed Saturday lunch and Sunday dinner to non-residents)* 9.75/16.30 **t.** and a la carte –
25 rm ⊆ 50.00/79.50 **t.** – SB 96.00/120.00 **st.**

🔘 ATS Crofton Rd. Allenby Trading Est. ✆ 527225

LINDALE Cumbria 402 L 21 – see Grange-over-Sands.

LISKEARD Cornwall 403 G 32 The West Country G. – pop. 6 213 – ECD : Wednesday –
🕿 0579.

See : Church★.

Exc. : Lanhydrock★★, W : 11 ½ m. by A 38 and A 390 – NW : Bodmin Moor★★ – St. Endellion
Church★★ – Altarnun Church★ – St. Breward Church★ – Blisland★ (church★) – Camelford★ –
Cardinham Church★ – Michaelstow Church★ – St. Kew★ (church★) – St. Mabyn Church★ –
St. Neot★ (Parish Church★★) – St. Sidwell's, Laneast★ – St. Teath Church★ – St. Tudy★.

◆London 261 – Exeter 59 – ◆Plymouth 18 – Truro 37.

🏠 **Well House** 🦢, St. Keyne, PL14 4RN, S : 3 ½ m. on St. Keyne Well rd ✆ 342001, ⩽,
⤳ heated, ⤳, ✗ – 📺 🅿. 🅴 𝘝𝘐𝘚𝘈
Meals 19.95/29.70 **t.** 🍷 4.25 – ⊆ 7.50 – **7 rm** 60.00/105.00 **t.**

🏠 **Old Rectory** 🦢, Duloe Rd, St. Keyne, PL14 4RL, S : 3 ¼ m. on B 3254 ✆ 342617, ⤳ –
⇇ rest 📺 🅿. 🅴 𝘝𝘐𝘚𝘈
closed Christmas – **M** (residents only) (dinner only) a la carte 11.45/15.95 **st.** – **8 rm**
⊆ 25.00/60.00 **st.** – SB 65.00/94.00 **st.**

🔘 ATS 10 Dean St. ✆ 345489/345247

LITTLEBURY GREEN Essex 404 0 27 – see Saffron Walden.

LITTLE CHALFONT Bucks. 404 S 29 – pop. 4 093 – 🕿 0494.
🏌 Lodge Lane, Amersham ✆ 764877.
◆London 31 – Luton 20 – ◆Oxford 37.

✗✗ **Chalfont Dynasty,** 9 Nightingales Corner, HP7 9PZ, ✆ 764038 – 🅴 🆇 ⓞ 𝘝𝘐𝘚𝘈
closed 25 and 26 December – **M** - Chinese (Peking) 6.95/9.50 **t.** and a la carte 🍷 4.00.

LITTLEHAMPTON W. Sussex 404 S 31 – 🕿 0903.

⌂ **Amberley Court** without rest., Crookthorn Lane, Climping, BN17 5QU, W : 1 ¾ m. by
B 2187 off A 259 ✆ 725131, ⤳ – ⇇ 📺 🅿. 🛇
3 rm ⊆ 25.00/45.00 **st.**

LITTLE LANGDALE Cumbria 402 K 20 – see Ambleside.

LITTLEOVER Derbs. 402 403 404 P 25 – see Derby.

LITTLE PETHERICK Cornwall 403 F 32 – see Padstow.

LITTLEPORT Cambs 404 U 26 – see Ely.

LITTLE RISSINGTON Glos. 403 404 O 28 – see Bourton-on-the-Water.

LITTLE SINGLETON Lancs. – see Blackpool.

LITTLE SUTTON Ches. – ⊠ South Wirral – ✪ 051 Liverpool.
♦London 208 – Chester 12 – ♦Liverpool 9 – ♦Manchester 48.

  🏨 **Woodhey,** Berwick Rd, L66 4PS, at junction with A 550 ℰ 339 5121, Fax 339 3214 – ▤ rest 📺 ☎ & 🅿 – 🔏 200. 🔼 🆎 ⓪ *VISA*
    M *(closed Sunday dinner)* 12.00/14.25 **t.** and dinner a la carte ≬ 4.95 – **52 rm** � 57.00/70.00 **st.** – SB (weekends only) 90.00/94.00 **st.**

LITTLE THORNTON Lancs. 402 L 22 – see Blackpool.

LITTLE WALSINGHAM Norfolk 404 W 25 – pop. 525 – ⊠ ✪ 0328 Walsingham.
♦London 117 – ♦Cambridge 67 – Cromer 21 – ♦Norwich 32.

  ⚘ **White Horse Inn,** Fakenham Rd, East Barsham, NR21 0LH, S : 2 ¼ m. on B 1105 ℰ 820645, Fax 820645 – 📺 🅿. 🔼 *VISA*
    M 10.50 **t.** and a la carte ≬ 2.75 – **3 rm** ⊆ 32.00/60.00 **st.**

  ✗ **Old Bakehouse** with rm, 33-35 High St., NR22 6BZ, ℰ 820454 – ✂ rest 📺. 🔼 *VISA*
    ✗
    closed 3 weeks January-February, 1 week June and 1 week November – **M** *(closed Sunday and Monday except Bank Holidays)* (dinner only) a la carte 19.50/22.50 **t.** ≬ 4.65 – **3 rm** ⊆ 25.00/40.00 **t.**

LITTLE WEIGHTON Humbs. 402 S 22 – ⊠ Cottingham – ✪ 0482 Hull.
♦London 184 – ♦Kingston-upon-Hull 8 – ♦Leeds 45 – York 31.

  🏨 **Rowley Manor** ⊗, HU20 3XR, SW : ½ m. by Rowley Rd ℰ 848248, Fax 849900, ≤, « Georgian manor house », ⇙ – 📺 ☎ 🅿 – 🔏 35. 🔼 🆎 ⓪ *VISA*
    M 18.95/21.60 **st.** ≬ 5.15 – **16 rm** ⊆ 55.00/85.00 **st.** – SB (weekends only) 88.95/157.90 **st.**

LITTLEWICK GREEN Berks. 404 R 29 – see Maidenhead.

LITTLE WYMONDLEY Herts. 404 T 28 – see Hitchin.

LIVERPOOL Mersey. 402 403 L 23 Great Britain G. – pop. 538 809 – ECD : Wednesday – ✆ 051.

See : City★ – Walker Art Gallery★★ DY **M2** – Liverpool Cathedral★★ (Lady Chapel★) EZ – Metropolitan Cathedral of Christ the King★★ EY – Albert Dock★ CZ (Merseyside Maritime Museum★ *AC* **M1** – Tate Gallery Liverpool★).

Exc. : Speke Hall★ *AC*, SE : 8 m. by A 561 BX.

🏌 Allerton Park ✆ 428 1046, SE : 5 m. by B 5180 BX – 🏌 Liverpool Municipal, Ingoe Lane, Kirkby ✆ 546 5435, by B 5194 BV – 🏌 Bowring, Bowring Park, Roby Rd, Huyton ✆ 489 1901, M 62 junction 5 BX.

✈ Liverpool Airport : ✆ 486 8877, SE : 6 m. by A 561 BX – **Terminal** : Pier Head.

🚢 to Douglas (Isle of Man) (Isle of Man Steam Packet Co. Ltd) (4 h.)

🚢 to Birkenhead (Mersey Ferries) except Saturday and Sunday in summer – to Wallasey (Mersey Ferries) except Saturday and Sunday in summer.

🛈 Merseyside Welcome Centre, Clayton Square Shopping Centre, L1 1QR ✆ 709 3631.

◆London 219 – ◆Birmingham 103 – ◆Leeds 75 – ◆Manchester 35.

Town plans : Liverpool pp. 2-5

🏨 **Liverpool Moat House** (Q.M.H.), Paradise St., L1 8JD, ✆ 709 0181, Telex 627270, Fax 709 2706, *₤₅*, ≡s, 🏊, – ⋮⋮ ⅍ rm ▤ 🖂 ☎ ⅙ – ⬭ 400. ⬛ ⬛ ⑩ *VISA*   DZ **n**
M 12.00/15.00 **t.** and dinner a la carte ⅙ 5.00 – **244 rm** ⌷ 90.00/116.00 **st.**, 7 suites – SB (weekends only) 90.00/100.00 **st.**

🏨 **Atlantic Tower** (Mt. Charlotte Thistle), 30 Chapel St., L3 9RE, ✆ 227 4444, Telex 627070, Fax 236 3973, ≼ – ⋮⋮ ⅍ rm ▤ ▥ ☎ 🖂 – ⬭ 100. ⬛ ⬛ ⑩ *VISA* *JCB*   CY **r**
M *(closed Saturday lunch)* 12.95/18.25 **t.** and a la carte ⅙ 4.90 – **223 rm** ⌷ 80.00/90.00 **st.**, 3 suites – SB 84.00 **st.**

🏨 **St. George's** (Forte), St. John's Precinct, Lime St., L1 1NQ, ✆ 709 7090, Fax 709 0137, ≼ – ⋮⋮ ⅍ rm ▥ 🖂 🖂 – ⬭ 200. ⬛ ⬛ ⑩ *VISA* *JCB*   DY **v**
M *(carving rest.)* 7.95/12.95 **st.** ⅙ 5.30 – ⌷ 5.95 – **153 rm** 49.50 **st.**, 2 suites – SB 70.00 **st.**

🏨 **Gladstone**, Lord Nelson St., L3 5QB, ✆ 709 7050, Fax 709 2193 – ⋮⋮ ⅍ rm ▥ ☎ 🖂 – ⬭ 500. ⬛ ⬛ ⑩ *VISA* *JCB* ⅍   DY **i**
M a la carte 12.40/19.95 **st.** ⅙ 4.95 – ⌷ 8.95 – **149 rm** 74.00 **st.**, 1 suite – SB 86.00/90.00 **st.**

🏨 **Campanile**, Wapping and Chaloner St., L3 4AJ, ✆ 709 8104, Telex 629775, Fax 709 8725 – ⅍ rm ▥ 🖂 ☎ 🖂 – ⬭ 30. ⬛ ⬛ *VISA*   CZ **a**
M 9.45 **t.** and a la carte ⅙ 4.65 – ⌷ 4.25 – **82 rm** 35.75 **t.**

🏨 **Travel Inn**, Queens Dr., West Derby, L13 0DL, E : 4 m. on A 5058 (Ringroad) ✆ 228 4724, Fax 220 7610 – ⅍ rm ▥ ⅙ 🖂   BV **a**
M (Beefeater grill) a la carte approx. 16.00 **t.** – ⌷ 4.95 – **40 rm** 33.50 **t.**

🍴🍴🍴 **L'Oriel**, Oriel Chambers, 14 Water St., L2 8TD, ✆ 236 5025, Fax 236 2794 – ⬛ ⬛ *VISA* *JCB*   CY **o**
closed Saturday lunch, Sunday, 25-26 December and 1 January – **M** 20.00/25.00 **t.** and a la carte ⅙ 4.50.

🍴🍴🍴 **Ristorante Del Secolo**, 36-40 Stanley St., ✆ 236 4004 – ⬛ ⬛ ⑩ *VISA*   DY **e**
closed Saturday lunch and Sunday – **M** 13.95/16.95 **t.** and a la carte ⅙ 4.95.

at Bootle N : 5 m. by A 565 – AV – 📫 ✆ 051 Liverpool :

🏨 **Park**, Park Lane West, L30 3SU, on A 5036 ✆ 525 7555, Fax 525 2481 – ⋮⋮ ▥ ☎ 🖂 – ⬭ 100. ⬛ ⬛ ⑩ *VISA* *JCB* ⅍
M (bar lunch)/dinner 10.95 **st.** and a la carte – ⌷ 3.45 – **62 rm** 39.50 **st.**

at Blundellsands N : 6½ m. by A 565 – AV – 📫 Crosby – ✆ 051 Liverpool :

🏨 **Blundellsands**, The Serpentine, L23 6TN, ✆ 924 6515, Fax 931 5364 – ⋮⋮ ⅍ rm ▥ ☎ 🖂 – ⬭ 200. ⬛ ⬛ ⑩ *VISA*
M *(closed Saturday lunch)* 10.00/18.00 **t.** and a la carte – **41 rm** ⌷ 28.00/95.00 **st.** – SB (weekends only) 82.00 **st.**

at Huyton E : 7 m. by M 62 on A 5058 – BX – 📫 ✆ 051 Liverpool :

🏨 **Logwood Mill**, Fallows Way, L35 1RZ, SE : 3½ m. by A 5080 at junction with M 62 ✆ 449 2341, Fax 449 3832, *₤₅*, ≡s, – ⋮⋮ ▥ ☎ ⅙ 🖂 – ⬭ 200. ⬛ ⬛ ⑩ *VISA* ⅍
M *(closed lunch Saturday and Bank Holidays)* 12.95/15.75 **st.** and a la carte ⅙ 5.25 – **63 rm** ⌷ 59.50/119.00 **st.**

🏨 **Derby Lodge**, Roby Rd, L36 4HD, ✆ 480 4440, Fax 480 8132, ≈ – ▥ ☎ 🖂. ⬛ ⬛ ⑩ *VISA* ⅍
M *(closed lunch Saturday and Bank Holidays)* 12.25/15.75 **st.** and a la carte – **19 rm** ⌷ 63.50/110.00 **st.**

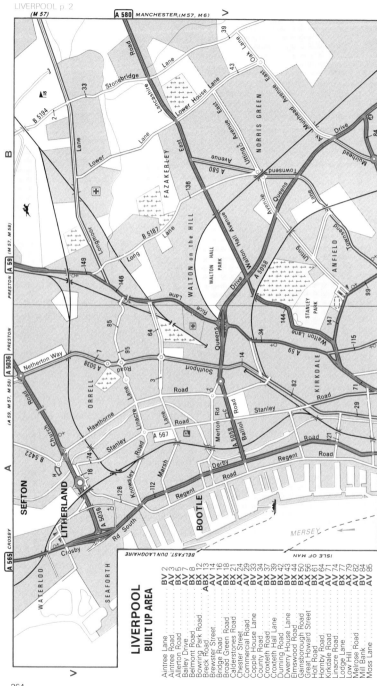

LIVERPOOL
BUILT UP AREA

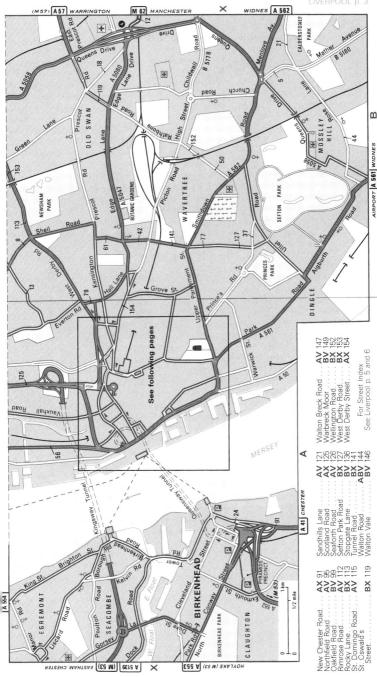

CALDERSTONES PARK

Mather   Avenue
B 5180
21

Menlove   Av
5
Lane

Queens

Childwall   Street

Church   Road

12

Queens   Drive

East Rd
Prescot   Rd

Queens Drive
18
119

B 5178

A 5058

Green   Lane

OLD SWAN
Prescot   Lane
A 5080
Edge   Lane   Drive

Rathbone

High Street
152

44

MOSSLEY   HILL   Road

Queens   Drive
B 5092

153

NEWSHAM   PARK

Prescot   Road

Edge   A 5047

BOTANIC GARDENS

Picton   Road

Smithdown   Road

50
A 562
WAVERTREE

SEFTON   PARK

B

Shell   Road
113
8

Derby   Rd

Kensington

Edge   42

61

141

77
127   37

Ullet   Road

AIRPORT A 561 WIDNES

West   Derby   Rd
13

Hall Lane
79

Grove St.

Upper   Parliament   St.

154

Prince's   Rd

PRINCES   PARK

Aigburth   Road

DINGLE

Everton Rd

Vauxhall   Road
125

See following pages

Park   A 561

Warwick   St.

A 50

56

A

MERSEY

Kingsway   Tunnel

Queensway   Tunnel

A 41 CHESTER

24

91

Tower

Birkenhead   Road

Borough   Rd

Brighton   St.

King St.
A 554

Manor   Rd

EGREMONT

Liscard   Road

Poulton   Road

SEACOMBE

Gorsey   La

Kelvin   Rd

Cleveland   Street

Conway   St.

Exmouth   St.

Duke St.

Dock   Road

North   Park Rd

BIRKENHEAD   PARK

CLAUGHTON

A 552

PYRAMIDS   PRECINCT

BIRKENHEAD

Tunnel   (M 53)

W. Float

E. Float

0   1/2 mile
0   1 km

LIVERPOOL
CENTRE

GREEN TOURIST GUIDES

Picturesque scenery, buildings

Attractive routes

Touring programmes

Plans of towns and buildings.

266

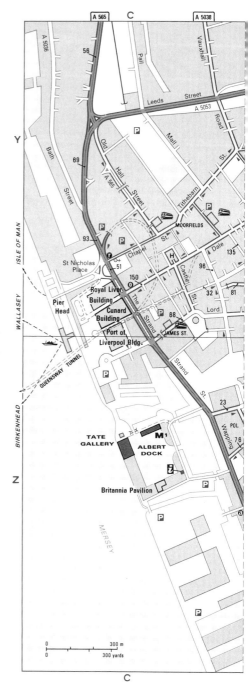

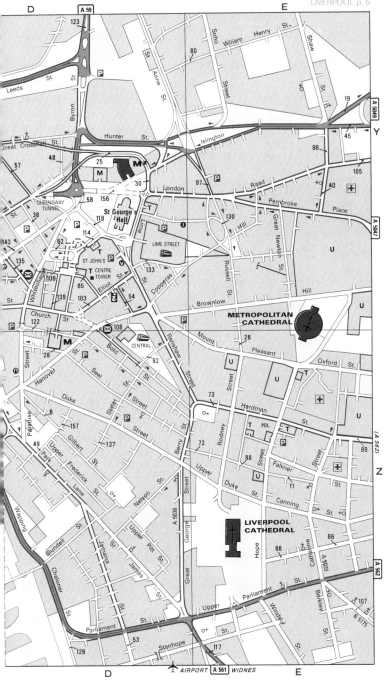

STREET INDEX TO LIVERPOOL TOWN PLANS

The names of main shopping streets are indicated in red
at the beginning of the list of streets.

at Aigburth SE : 4 m. on A 561 – BX – ⊠ 🕲 051 Liverpool :

🏠 **Grange,** 14 Holmefield Rd, L19 3PG, ☎ 427 2950, Fax 427 9055, ☞ – ⅙⅞ rest 📺 ☎ 🅿.
🔼 🎖 ⓞ 𝘝𝘐𝘚𝘈 . ⅞
M *(closed Sunday dinner to non-residents. Christmas-New Year and Bank Holidays)*
(dinner only and Sunday lunch)/dinner 14.95 **t.** and a la carte 🛆 4.60 – **25 rm** ⊡ 45.00/
85.00 **t.**

🔘 ATS 15/37 Caryl St. ☎ 709 8032
ATS Wilson Road, Huyton ☎ 489 8386/7
ATS 190-194 St. Mary's Rd, Garston
☎ 427 3665

ATS 73-77 Durning Rd, Wavertree ☎ 263 7604
ATS Musker St., Crosby ☎ 931 3166
ATS Unit E, Liver Ind. Est., Long Lane, Aintree
☎ 524 1000

LIZARD Cornwall 🔢 E 34 The West Country G. – 🕲 0326 The Lizard.

Envir. : Lizard Peninsula★ – Mullion Cove★★★ (Church★) – Kynance Cove★★★ – Cadgwith★ –
Coverack★ – Cury★ (Church★) – Gunwalloe Fishing Cove★ – St. Keverne (Church★) – Lande-
wednack★ (Church★) – Mawgan-in-Meneage (Church★) – Ruan Minor (Church★) – St. Antho-
ny-in-Meneage★.

♦London 326 – Penzance 24 – Truro 29.

🏠 **Housel Bay** ⍉, Housel Cove, TR12 7PG, ☎ 290417, Fax 290359, ≤ Housel Cove, ☞ – 🛗
⅙⅞ rest 📺 ☎ 🅿. 🔼 𝘝𝘐𝘚𝘈
closed 1 January-10 February – **M** (bar lunch Monday to Saturday)/dinner 16.00 **t.**
and a la carte 🛆 5.50 – **23 rm** ⊡ 30.00/80.00 **t.** – SB (except Christmas) 74.00/99.00 **st.**

🏠 **Penmenner House** ⍉, Penmenner Rd, TR12 7NR, ☎ 290370, ≤, ☞ – ⅙⅞ 📺 🅿. 🔼 𝘝𝘐𝘚𝘈
⅞
closed Christmas and New Year – **M** (by arrangement) 12.50 **st.** – **8 rm** ⊡ 23.50/44.00 **st.** –
SB (except June-September) 60.00/69.00 **st.**

🏠 **Parc Brawse House** ⍉, Penmenner Rd, TR12 7NR, ☎ 290466, ≤, ☞ – ⅙⅞ rest 🅿. 🔼
𝘝𝘐𝘚𝘈
March-October – **M** 10.00 **st.** – **6 rm** ⊡ 15.00/35.00 **st.** – SB (except July-September and
Bank Holidays) 40.00/50.00 **st.**

LOFTUS Cleveland 🔢 R 20 – pop. 5 626 – ECD : Wednesday – ⊠ Saltburn-by-the-Sea –
🕲 0287 Guisborough.

♦London 264 – ♦Leeds 73 – ♦Middlesbrough 17 – Scarborough 36.

🏨 **Grinkle Park** ⍉, Easington, TS13 4UB, SE : 3 ½ m. by A 174 ☎ 640515, Fax 641278, ≤,
☞, park, ⅞ – 📺 ☎ 🅿. 🔼 🎖 ⓞ 𝘝𝘐𝘚𝘈
M 6.95/15.50 **st.** and a la carte – **20 rm** ⊡ 65.00/85.00 **st.** – SB 96.00/132.00 **st.**

LOLWORTH SERVICE AREA Cambs. – see Cambridge.

Benutzen Sie auf Ihren Reisen in **EUROPA :**

– die Michelin-Länderkarten

– die Michelin-Abschnittskarten

– die Roten Michelin-Führer (Hotels und Restaurants) :

Benelux, Deutschland, España Portugal, Main Cities **Europe, France,
Great Britain and Ireland, Italia, Schweiz.**

– die Grünen Michelin-Führer
(Sehenswürdigkeiten und interessante Reisegebiete) :

Italien, Spanien

– die Grünen Regionalführer von **Frankreich**
(Sehenswürdigkeiten und interessante Reisegebiete) :

Paris, Bretagne, Côte d'Azur (Französische Riviera),
Elsaß Vogesen Champagne, Korsika, Provence, Schlösser an der Loire

London

404 folds ④ to ④ – London G. – pop. 7 566 620 – ☎ 071 or 081: see heading of each area

✈ Heathrow, ☎ (081) 759 4321, p. 8 AX – **Terminal** : Airbus (A1) from Victoria, Airbus (A2) from Paddington – Underground (Piccadilly line) frequent service daily.

✈ Gatwick, ☎ 0293 (Crawley) 535353 and ☎ 081 (London) 763 2020, p. 9 : by A 23 EZ and M 23 – **Terminal** : Coach service from Victoria Coach Station (Flightline 777, hourly service) – Railink (Gatwick Express) from Victoria (24 h service).

✈ London City Airport ☎ (071) 474 5555, p. 7 : HV.

✈ Stansted, at Bishop's Stortford, ☎ 0279 (Bishop's Stortford) 680500, Fax 662066, NE : 34 m. p. 7 : by M 11 JT and A 120.

British Airways, Victoria Air Terminal : 115 Buckingham Palace Rd, SW1, ☎ (071) 834 9411, Fax 828 7142, p. 32 BX.

🚗 Euston and Paddington ☎ 0345 090700.

🛈 British Travel Centre, 12 Regent St., Piccadilly Circus, SW1Y 4PQ ☎ (071) 971 0026.

Selfridges, basement Services, Arcade, Selfridges Store, Oxford St. WI ☎ (071) 730 3488.

Victoria Station Forecourt SWI ☎ (071) 730 3488.

Sights

Curiosités – Le curiosità
Sehenswürdigkeiten

HISTORIC BUILDINGS AND MONUMENTS

Palace of Westminster★★★ : House of Lords★★, Westminster Hall★★ (hammerbeam roof★★★), Robing Room★, Central Lobby★, House of Commons★, Big Ben★, Victoria Tower★ p. 26 LY – Tower of London★★★ (Crown Jewels★★★, White Tower or Keep★★★, St. John's Chapel★★, Beauchamp Tower★) p. 27 PVX.

Banqueting House★★ p. 26 LX – Buckingham Palace★★ (Changing of the Guard★★, Royal Mews★★) p. 32 BVX – Kensington Palace★★ p. 24 FX – Lincoln's Inn★★ p. 33 EV – London Bridge★ p. 27 PVX – Royal Hospital Chelsea★★ p. 31 FU – St. James's Palace★★ p. 29 EP – South Bank Arts Centre ★★ (Royal Festival Hall★, National Theatre★, County Hall★) p. 26 MX – The Temple★★ (Middle Temple Hall★) p. 22 MV – Tower Bridge★★ p. 27 PX.

Albert Memorial★ p. 30 CQ – Apsley House★ p. 28 BP – Burlington House★ p. 29 EM – Charter-house★ p. 23 NOU – Commonwealth Institute★ p. 24 EY – Design Centre★ p. 29 FM – George Inn★, Southwark p. 27 PX – Gray's Inn★ p. 22 MU – Guildhall★ (Lord Mayor's Show★★) p. 23 OU – Imperial College of Science and Technology★ p. 30 CR – Dr Johnson's House★ p. 23 NUV A – Lancaster House★ p. 29 EP – Leighton House★ p. 24 EY – Linley Sambourne House★ p. 24 EY – Mansion House★ (plate and insignia★★) p. 23 PV P – The Monument★ (⁂★) p. 23 PV G – Old Admiralty★ p. 26 KLX – Royal Exchange★ p. 23 PV V – Royal Opera Arcade★ (New Zealand House) p. 29 FGN – Royal Opera House★ (Covent Garden) p. 33 DX – Somerset House★ p. 33 EXY – Staple Inn★ p. 22 MU Y – Stock Exchange★ p. 23 PUV – Theatre Royal★ (Haymarket) p. 29 GM – Westminster Bridge★ p. 26 LY.

CHURCHES

The City Churches

St. Paul's Cathedral★★★ (Dome ≤★★★) p. 23 NOV.

St. Bartholomew the Great★★ (choir★) p. 23 OU K – St. Dunstan-in-the-East★★ p. 23 PV F – St. Mary-at-Hill★★ (woodwork★★, plan★) p. 23 PV B – Temple Church★★ p. 22 MV.

All Hallows-by-the-Tower (font cover★★ brasses★) p. 23 PV Y – Christ Church★ p. 23 OU E – St. Andrew Undershaft (monuments★) p. 23 PV A – St. Bride★ (steeple★★) p. 23 NV J – St. Clement Eastcheap (panelled interior★★) p. 23 PV E – St. Edmund the King and Martyr (tower and spire★) p. 23 PV D – St-Giles Cripplegate★ p. 23 OU N – St. Helen Bishopsgate★ (monuments★★) p. 23 PUV R – St. James Garlickhythe (tower and spire★, sword rests★) p. 23 OV R – St. Magnus the Martyr (tower★, sword rest★) p. 23 PV K – St. Margaret Lothbury★ (tower and spire★, woodwork★, screen★, font★) p. 23 PU S – St. Margaret Pattens (spire★, woodwork★) p. 23 PV N – St. Martin-within-Ludgate (tower and spire★, door cases★) p. 23 NOV B – St. Mary Abchurch★ (reredos★★, tower and spire★, dome★) p. 23 PV X – St. Mary-le-Bow (tower and steeple★★) p. 23 OV G – St. Michael Paternoster Royal (tower and spire★) p. 23 OV D – St. Nicholas Cole Abbey (tower and spire★) p. 23 OV F – St. Olave★ p. 23 PV S – St. Peter upon Cornhill (screen★) p. 23 PV L – St. Stephen Walbrook★ (tower and steeple★, dome★), p. 23 PV Z – St. Vedast (tower and spire★, ceiling★), p. 23 OU E.

Other Churches

Westminster Abbey★★★ (Henry VII Chapel★★★, Chapel of Edward the Confessor★★, Chapter House★★, Poets' Corner★) p. 26 LY.

Southwark Cathedral★★ p. 27 PX.

Queen's Chapel★ p. 29 EP – St. Clement Danes★ p. 33 EX – St. James's★ p. 29 EM – St. Margaret's★ p. 26 LY A – St. Martin-in-the-Fields★ p. 33 DY – St. Paul's★ (Covent Garden) p. 33 DX – Westminster Roman Catholic Cathedral★ p. 26 KY B.

PARKS

Regent's Park★★★ p. 21 HI (terraces★★), Zoo★★★.

Hyde Park★★ p. 25 GHV X – St. James's Park★★ p. 26 KXY.

Kensington Gardens★ pp. 20-21 FGX (Orangery★ A).

STREETS AND SQUARES

The City★★★ p. 23 NV.

Bedford Square★★ p. 22 KLU – Belgrave Square★★ p. 32 AVX – Burlington Arcade★★ p. 29 DM –
The Mall★★ p. 29 FP – Piccadilly★★ p. 29 EM – The Thames★★ pp. 25-27 – Trafalgar Square★★
p. 33 DY – Whitehall★★ (Horse Guards★) p. 26 LX.

Barbican★ p. 23 OU – Bond Street★ pp. 28-29 CK-DM – Canonbury Square★ p. 23 NS – Carlton
House Terrace★ p. 29 GN – Cheyne Walk★ p. 25 GHZ – Fitzroy Square★ p. 22 KU – Jermyn
Street★ p. 29 EN – Merrick Square★ p. 27 OY – Montpelier Square★ p. 31 EQ – The Piazza★
(Covent Garden) p. 33 DX – Piccadilly Arcade★ p. 29 DEN – Portman Square★ p. 28 AJ – Queen
Anne's Gate★ p. 26 KY – Regent Street★ p. 29 EM – St. James's Square★ p. 29 FN –
St. James's Street★ p. 29 EN – Sheperd Market★ p. 28 CN – Trinity Church Square★ p. 27 OY –
Victoria Embankment gardens★ p. 33 DEXY – Waterloo Place★ p. 29 FN.

MUSEUMS

British Museum★★★ p. 22 LU – National Gallery★★★ p. 29 GM – Science Museum★★★ p. 30 CR –
Tate Gallery★★★ p. 26 LZ – Victoria and Albert Museum★★★ p. 31 DR.

Courtauld Institute Galleries★★ (Somerset House) p. 33 EXY – Museum of London★★ p. 23
OU **M** – National Portrait Gallery★★ p. 29 GM – Natural History Museum★★ p. 30 CS –
Queen's Gallery★★ p. 32 BV – Wallace Collection★★ p. 28 AH.

Clock Museum★ (Guildhall) p. 22 OU – Geological Museum★ p. 30 CR – Imperial War Mu-
seum★ p. 27 NY – London Transport Museum★ p. 33 DX – Madame Tussaud's★ p. 21 IU **M** –
Museum of Mankind★ p. 29 DM – National Army Museum★ p. 31 FU – Percival David Founda-
tion of Chinese Art★ p. 22 KLT **M** – Sir John Soane's Museum★ p. 22 MU **M** – Wellington
Museum★ p. 28 BP.

OUTER LONDON

Blackheath p. 11 HX terraces and houses★, Eltham Palace★ **A** – **Brentford** p. 8 BX Syon
Park★★, gardens★ – **Bromley** p. 10 GY The Crystal Palace Park★ – **Chiswick** p. 9 CV Chiswick
Mall★★, Chiswick House★ **D**, Hogarth's House★ **E** – **Dulwich** p. 10 Picture Gallery★ FX **X** –
Greenwich pp. 10 and 11 : Cutty Sark★★ GV **F**, Footway Tunnel(≼ ★★) – National Maritime
Museum★★ (Queen's House★★) GV **M**, Royal Naval College★★ (Painted Hall★, the Chapel★) GV
G, The Park and Old Royal Observatory★ (Meridian Building : collection★★) HV **K**, Ranger's
House★ GX **N** – **Hampstead** Kenwood House★★ (Adam Library★★, paintings★★) p. 5 EU **P**,
Fenton House★, The Benton Fletcher Collection★ p. 20 ES – **Hampton Court** p. 8 BY (The
Palace★★★, gardens★★★, Fountain Court★, The Great Vine★)– **Kew** p. 9 CX Royal Botanic
Gardens★★★ : Palm House★★, Temperate House★, Kew Palace or Dutch House★★, Orangery★,
Pagoda★, Japanese Gateway★ – **Hendon★** p. 5, Royal Air Force Museum★★ CT **M** – **Houn-
slow** p. 8 BV Osterley Park★★ – **Lewisham** p. 10 GX Horniman Museum★ **M** – **Richmond** pp. 8
and 9 : Richmond Park★★, ✻★★★ CX, Richmond Hill✻★★ CX, Richmond Bridge★★ BX **R**,
Richmond Green★★ BX **S** (Maids of Honour Row★★, Trumpeter's House★), Asgill House★ BX
B, Ham House★★ BX **V** – **Shoreditch** p. 6 FU Geffrye Museum★ **M** – **Tower Hamlets** p. 6 GV
St. Katharine Dock★ **Y** – **Twickenham** p. 8 BX Marble Hill House★ **Z**, Strawberry Hill★ **A** .

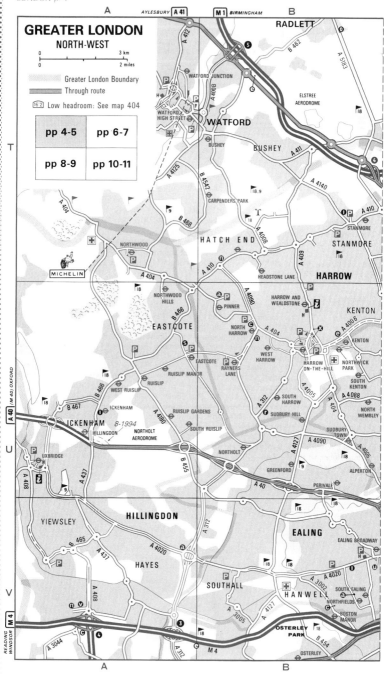

GREATER LONDON
NORTH-WEST

| 0 | | 3 km |
| 0 | | 2 miles |

Greater London Boundary
Through route

16.2 Low headroom: See map 404

| pp 4-5 | pp 6-7 |
| pp 8-9 | pp 10-11 |

MICHELIN

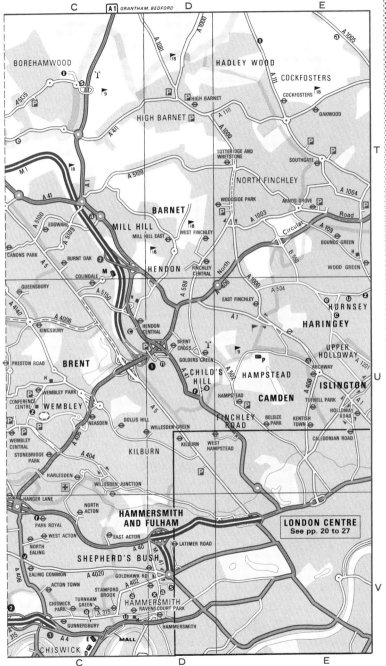

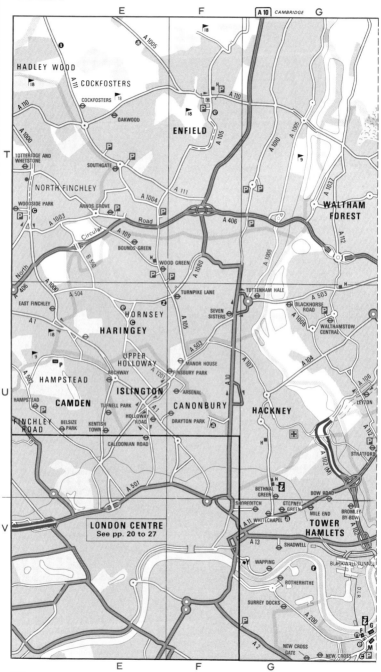

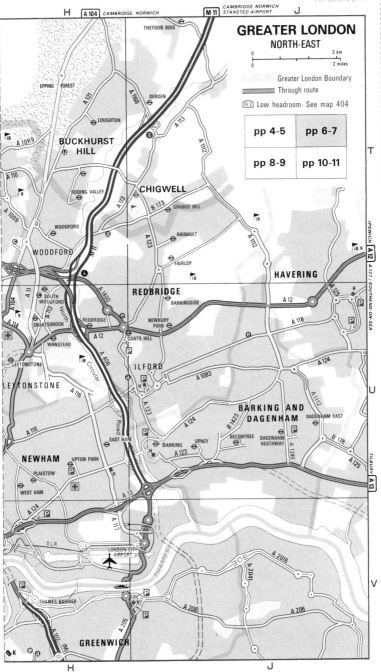

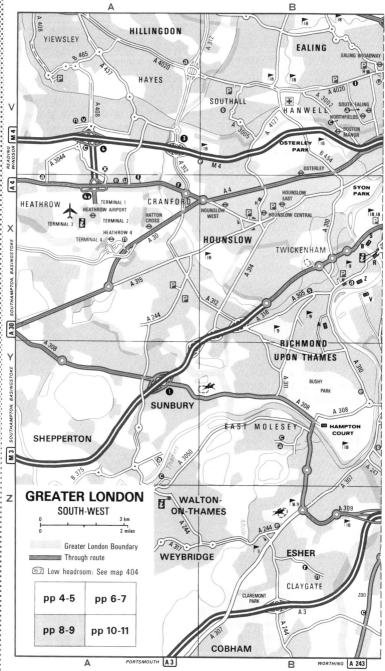

GREATER LONDON
SOUTH-WEST

0   3 km
0   2 miles

Greater London Boundary

Through route

16.2 Low headroom: See map 404

pp 4-5	pp 6-7
pp 8-9	pp 10-11

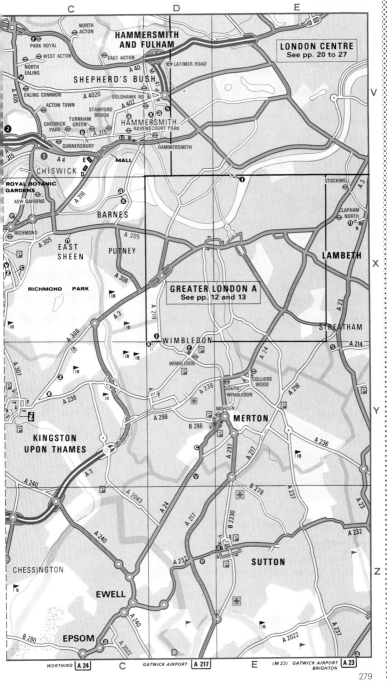

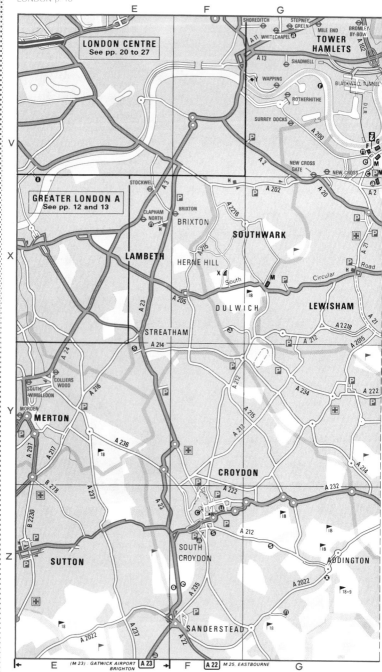

LONDON CENTRE
See pp. 20 to 27

GREATER LONDON A
See pp. 12 and 13

SHOREDITCH
STEPNEY GREEN
MILE END
BROMLEY-BY-BOW
A 11 WHITECHAPEL
TOWER HAMLETS
A 13 SHADWELL
BLACKWALL TUNNEL
WAPPING
ROTHERHITHE
SURREY DOCKS
A 200
NEW CROSS GATE
NEW CROSS
A 2
STOCKWELL
A 3
A 202
A 20
CLAPHAM NORTH
BRIXTON
A 2218
BRIXTON
SOUTHWARK
LAMBETH
A 215
HERNE HILL
Road
South
Circular
A 205
M
LEWISHAM
DULWICH
A 2218
A 21
STREATHAM
A 214
A 212
A 215
A 24
A 216
A 212
A 234
A 222
COLLIERS WOOD
SOUTH WIMBLEDON
A 215
A 213
MORDEN
MERTON
A 297
A 217
A 236
CROYDON
A 214
18
A 222
A 232
B 218
A 237
A 23
B 2230
A 212
SUTTON
SOUTH CROYDON
ADDINGTON
A 235
A 2022
18-9
SANDERSTEAD
A 2022
A 237
A 22

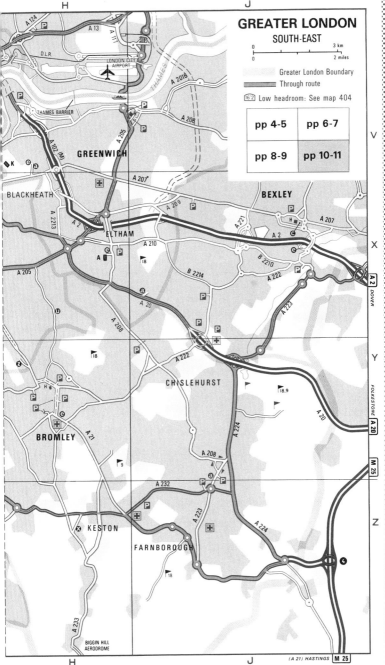

GREATER LONDON
SOUTH-EAST

| 0 | | 3 km |
| 0 | | 2 miles |

Greater London Boundary
Through route

16.2 Low headroom: See map 404

| pp 4-5 | pp 6-7 |
| pp 8-9 | pp 10-11 |

A 124
A 13
A 111
D.L.R.
LONDON CITY AIRPORT
A 2016
THAMES
A 206
THAMES BARRIER
A 205
A 1107 (M)
GREENWICH
A 207
BLACKHEATH
A 2213
A 2
ELTHAM
A 210
BEXLEY
A 221
A 2
A 207
A 209
B 2210
A 205
A 20
B 2214
A 222
A 223
A 208
A 222
CHISLEHURST
18.9
A 20
A 224
BROMLEY
A 21
A 208
9
A 232
A 223
KESTON
A 224
FARNBOROUGH
18
A 233
BIGGIN HILL AERODROME

A 2 DOVER
FOLKESTONE A 20
M 25
(A 21) HASTINGS M 25

H
J
V
X
Y
Z

281

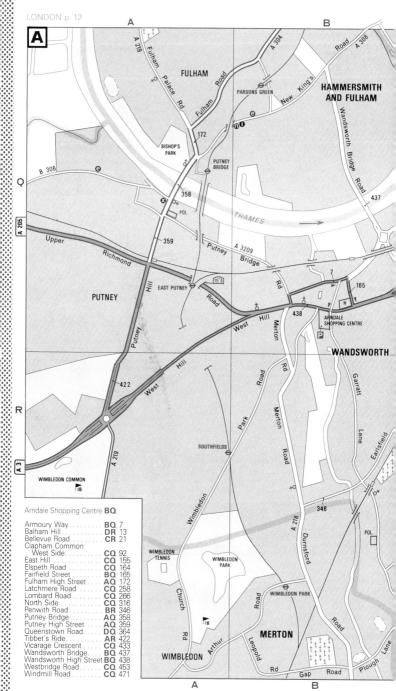

A

FULHAM

PARSONS GREEN

HAMMERSMITH AND FULHAM

BISHOP'S PARK

PUTNEY BRIDGE

THAMES

PUTNEY

EAST PUTNEY

WANDSWORTH

ARNDALE SHOPPING CENTRE

WEST HILL

SOUTHFIELDS

WIMBLEDON COMMON

WIMBLEDON TENNIS

WIMBLEDON PARK

MERTON

WIMBLEDON

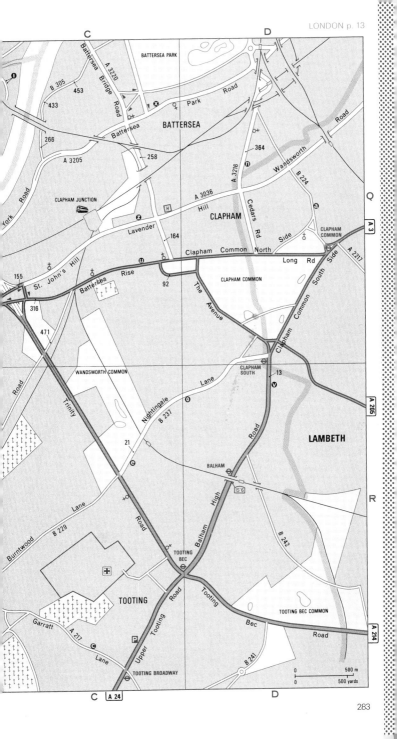

C

D

BATTERSEA PARK

B 305   453

A 3220

Battersea Bridge Road

433

Park   Road

266

Battersea

BATTERSEA

258

A 3205

364

A 3216

Wandsworth   Road

B 224

York   Road

CLAPHAM JUNCTION

A 3036

Hill

CLAPHAM

Cedars Rd

Q

A 3

Lavender

164

Clapham   Common   North

Long   Rd

CLAPHAM COMMON

Side

A 217

155

St. John's   Hill

Battersea   Rise

92

CLAPHAM COMMON

Clapham Common South Side

316

The   Avenue

471

Road

Trinity

WANDSWORTH COMMON

Lane

CLAPHAM SOUTH

13

A 205

Nightingale

B 237

Road

LAMBETH

21

BALHAM

15 6

Lane

Road

B 229

High

Burntwood

B 242

R

Balham

TOOTING BEC

TOOTING

Road

Tooting

Bec

TOOTING BEC COMMON

Garratt

A 217

Lane

Upper   Tooting   Road

Road

A 214

B 241

TOOTING BROADWAY

0   500 m
0   500 yards

C   A 24

D

283

LONDON CENTRE

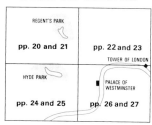

REGENT'S PARK	
pp. 20 and 21	pp. 22 and 23
	TOWER OF LONDON
HYDE PARK	PALACE OF WESTMINSTER
pp. 24 and 25	pp. 26 and 27

STREET INDEX TO LONDON CENTRE TOWN PLANS

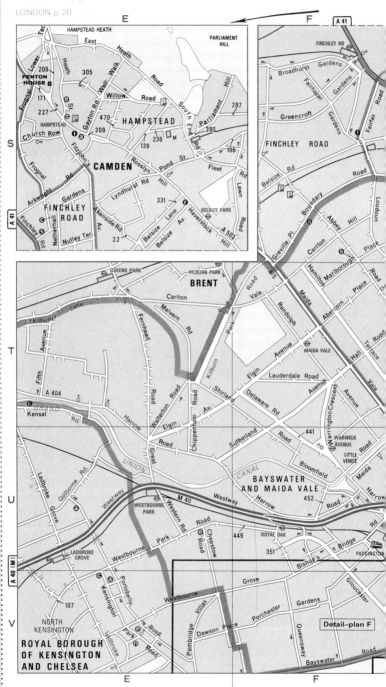

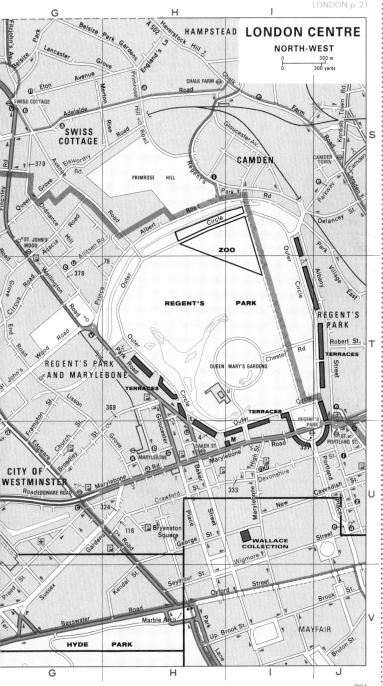

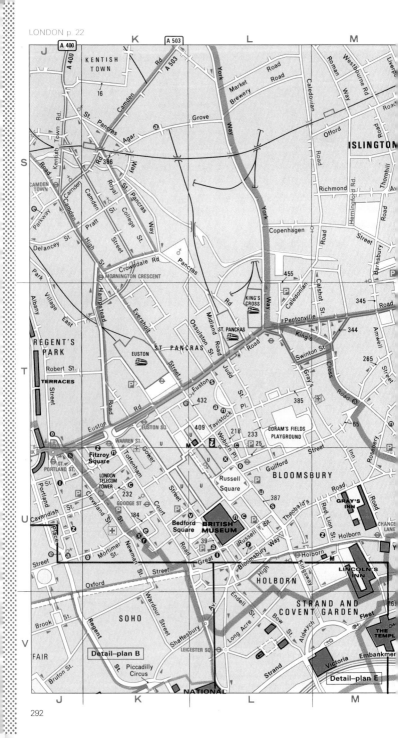

A1

N · O · P

LONDON CENTRE
NORTH-EAST

0   300 m
0   300 yards

HIGHBURY and Islington

Canonbury Square

Canonbury

St. Paul's

Road

Road

Engleﬁeld

A 10

S

Upper

Barnsbury

St. POL

ESSEX RD

Essex

Halliford St.

New North Rd.

Downham

De Beauvoir Road

Road

DALSTON

Rd.

ISLINGTON

Liverpool

Upper

Street

St.

St. Peter's St.

New North Rd.

Eagle Wharf Road

New

North

Street

Rd

343

350

235

464

Nuttall St.

Kingsland

Whiston Rd

70

78

ANGEL

St. John

City

Road

Goswell

293

City

Road

Wharf Rd

Shepherdess

Walk

East

Road

Pitﬁeld

St.

Hoxton

HACKNEY

Hackney

Rd

T

398

296

U

Percival St.

Lever

Street

St.

City

Old

St.

OLD ST.

16°

Virginia Rd

TOWER HAMLETS

FINSBURY

110

43

Street

Old

Street

Whitecross

Road

Bunhill Row

Aldersgate

141

City

Paul Street

192

126

384

32

Luke St.

Worship

St.

CHARTERHOUSE

113

Clerkenwell Rd.

166

Beech

St.

Chiswell Street

391

Wilson

Sun St.

5

St.

399

FARRINGDON

83

270

BARBICAN

Barbican Centre

BARBICAN CENTRE

Moorgate

BROADGATE

LIVERPOOL STREET

Brushfield St.

Middlesex St.

U

454

264

BARBICAN

M

MOORGATE

Liverpool St.

36

Houndsditch

London Wall

380

GUILDHALL

London Wall

71

ALDGATE EAST

A 11

178 247

Gresham St.

273

418

319 472

34

ALDGATE

45 6

A 13

168

372

168

E+

St. PAUL'S

Cheapside

352

357

BANK OF ENGLAND

417

STOCK EXCHANGE

260

145

Aldgate High St.

A

Street 376

318

304

Cannon

365

BANK

187

268

Fenchurch

St.

282

Minories

V

ST. PAUL'S CATHEDRAL

301

Queen Victoria

MANSION HOUSE

St.

250

154

197

CANNON STREET

MONUMENT

62

TOWER HILL

CITY OF LONDON

BLACKFRIARS

431

431

278

425

TOWER OF LONDON

38

THAMES

395

N · O · P

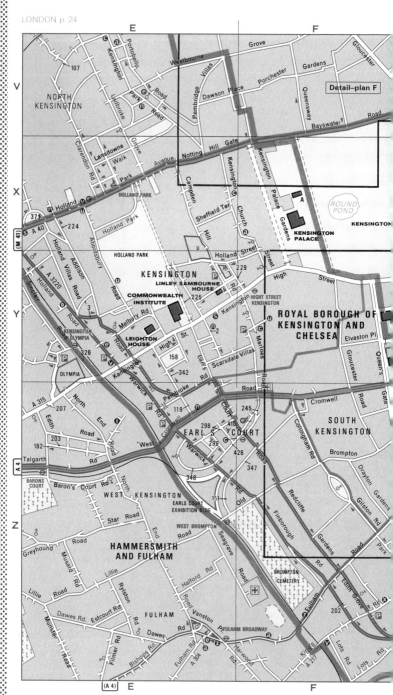

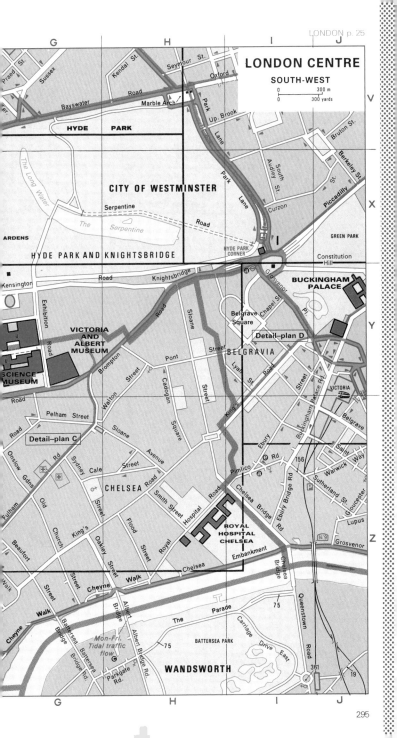

LONDON CENTRE
SOUTH-WEST

0	300 m
0	300 yards

HYDE PARK

CITY OF WESTMINSTER

The Long Water

Serpentine

The Serpentine

Road

ARDENS

GREEN PARK

HYDE PARK AND KNIGHTSBRIDGE

HYDE PARK CORNER

Constitution Hill

Kensington

Road

Knightsbridge

BUCKINGHAM PALACE

Belgrave Square

Chapel St.

Detail–plan D

VICTORIA AND ALBERT MUSEUM

BELGRAVIA

VICTORIA

SCIENCE MUSEUM

Road

Brompton

Pont

Street

Cadogan

King's

Walton

Sloane

Road

Pelham Street

Sloane

Square

Belgrave

Detail–plan C

Avenue

Onslow Gdns

Rd

Sydney

Cale

Street

Pimlico

Rd

156

Sutherland St.

Warwick Way

Fulham

Old

King's

Flood

Smith Street

Hospital

Road

Chelsea Bridge Rd

Ebury Bridge Rd

Gloucester

Lupus

CHELSEA

ROYAL HOSPITAL CHELSEA

14.9

Grosvenor

Z

Beaufort

Church

Oakley

Royal

Street

Chelsea

Embankment

Chelsea Bridge

Walk

Cheyne

Walk

Albert Bridge

Battersea Bridge

Battersea Bridge Rd.

Mon-Fri. Tidal traffic flow

The

Parade

Carriage

75

Queenstown

Road

75

BATTERSEA PARK

Drive East

Parkgate Rd.

WANDSWORTH

361

19

Praed St.

Sussex

Kendal St.

Seymour St.

Oxford

Bayswater

Road

Marble Arch

Park

Up. Brook

Lane

Bruton St.

Park

South Audley St.

Berkeley St.

Lane

Curzon

Piccadilly

Grosvenor

Belgrave

Bury

Ebury

Pl.

Buckingham Palace Rd

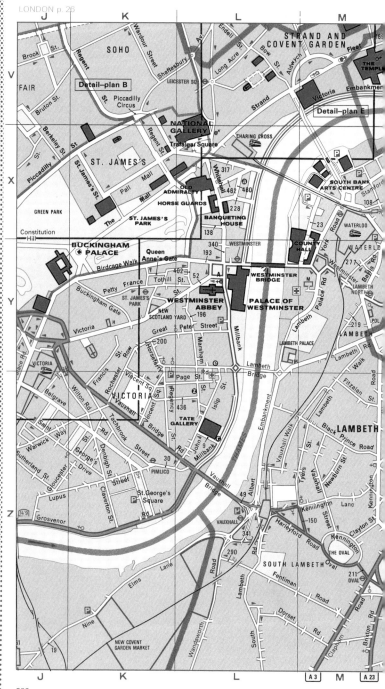

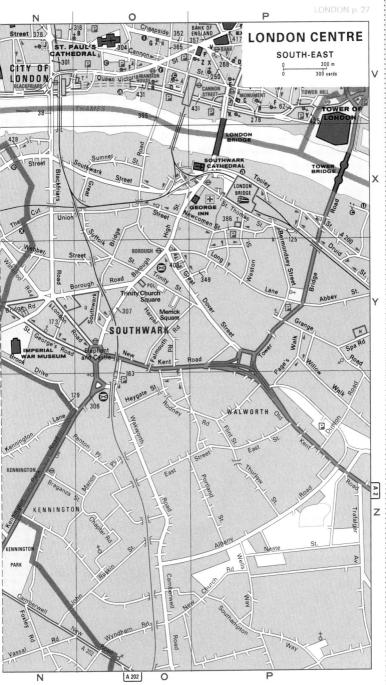

LONDON CENTRE

SOUTH-EAST

0 ___ 300 m
0 ___ 300 yards

N   O   P

Street 378
318
Cheapside 352
BANK OF ENGLAND 357

ST. PAUL'S CATHEDRAL
304 Cannon
G
365
BANK

CITY OF LONDON
301
BLACKFRIARS
Queen Victoria
MANSION HOUSE
250
268
MONUMENT
62
TOWER HILL

431
CANNON STREET
431
278
425
TOWER OF LONDON

THAMES
38
395

LONDON BRIDGE

428
Sumner
St.
SOUTHWARK CATHEDRAL
Tooley
TOWER BRIDGE

Street
Southwark
Street
LONDON BRIDGE
X

The Cut
Blackfriars
Great
Suffolk
Bridge
Street
High
St. Thomas
386
St.
Bermondsey Street
125
Road A 200
Druid St.

Union
Street
GEORGE INN
Newcomen St.

Webber
Street
BOROUGH
Long
Weston
Abbey
St.
Bridge

Waterloo Rd
Borough
Road
Borough
St.
Trinity
408
349
Great
Lane
Grange
Y

London Road
POLICE
Trinity Church Square
307
Harper
Merrick Square
Dover
Street
Spa Rd

Bridge Rd
St. George's Road
173
SOUTHWARK
Rd
Tower
Page's
Walk
Willow
Road

IMPERIAL WAR MUSEUM
Elephant and Castle
New
Kent
Road
Walk

Brook
Drive
163
Kent

129
306
Heygate St.
Rodney
WALWORTH
Old
Kent
Dunton

Kennington
Lane
Walworth
Flint St.
East
St.
Road
Road
Trafalgar

KENNINGTON
Renton Pl.
Manor
Street
East
Portland
Thurlow
St.
Av.
A 2

Braganza St.
Road
St.
Z

KENNINGTON
Chapter Rd
St.
Albany
Neate
St.

KENNINGTON PARK
Ruskin
Wells
Rd
Church

Camberwell
Foxley
John
New
Way
Southampton
Way

Vassal
Road
Rd
Wyndham
Rd
Road
Way

N   A 202   O   P

297

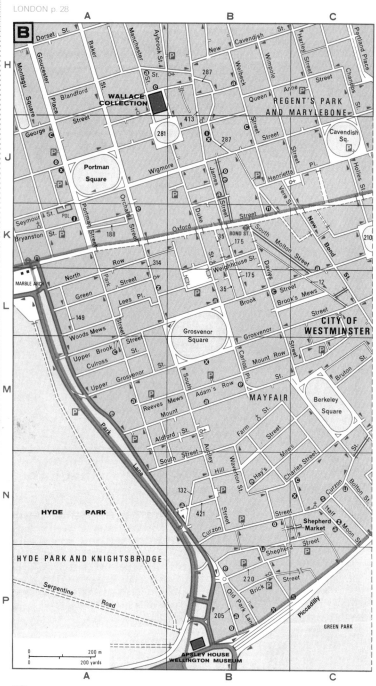

B

A   B   C

Dorset St.

Baker

Manchester

Aybrook St.

New   Cavendish   St.

Wimpole

Harley   Street

Portland Place

H

Gloucester

Montagu Square

Place

Blandford

St.

St.

287

Welbeck

Street

Chandos

Anne

Queen

St.

REGENT'S PARK AND MARYLEBONE

WALLACE COLLECTION

413

Street

Cavendish Sq.

George

Street

281

287

Street

Holles St.

J

Portman Square

Wigmore

James

Street

Henrietta

Pl.

Vere St.

New

Seymour   St.

POL

Portman Street

Orchard   Street

Oxford

Duke   Street

Street

South   Molton   Street

Bond

K

Bryanston   St.

188

BOND ST.

35   175

Street

210

Row

314

Weighhouse St.

175

Davies

12

MARBLE ARCH

North

Park

Street

35

Brook   Street

Brook's Mews

Street

L

Green

Street

Lees Pl.

CITY OF WESTMINSTER

149

Woods Mews

Street

Grosvenor Square

Grosvenor

Upper   Brook

St.

Culross

Street

M

Upper   Grosvenor

St.

South

Carlos   Pl.

Mount Row

St.

Bruton   St.

Reeves   Mews

Adam's Row

MAYFAIR

Berkeley Square

Mount

Farm   St.

Aldford   St.

Street

St.

N

Audley

South   Street

Hill

Waverton St.

Hay's   Mews

Charles Street

Curzon

Bolton St.

132

Street

421

Curzon

Street

Half

Moon St.

Shepherd Market

HYDE   PARK

Shepherd   Street

220

Brick   Street

HYDE PARK AND KNIGHTSBRIDGE

P

Serpentine   Road

Old Park Lane

Piccadilly

205

GREEN PARK

Park   Lane

0   200 m

0   200 yards

APSLEY HOUSE WELLINGTON MUSEUM

A   B   C

Oxford Street is closed to private traffic, Mondays to Saturdays : from 7 am to 7 pm between Portman Street and St. Giles Circus

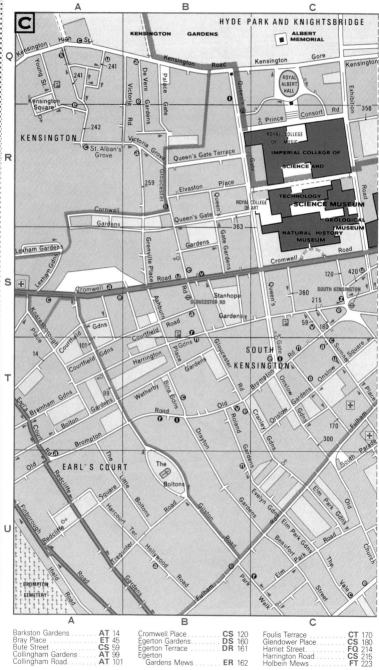

HYDE PARK AND KNIGHTSBRIDGE

KENSINGTON GARDENS

ALBERT MEMORIAL

KENSINGTON

Kensington High St.

Young Street

241

241

Kensington Square

P

242

St. Alban's Grove

Kensington Road

Kensington Gore

ROYAL ALBERT HALL

Prince Consort Rd

ROYAL COLLEGE OF MUSIC

IMPERIAL COLLEGE OF SCIENCE AND TECHNOLOGY

SCIENCE MUSEUM

NATURAL HISTORY MUSEUM

GEOLOGICAL MUSEUM

ROYAL COLLEGE OF ART

Kensington

356

De Vere Gardens

Palace Gate

Victoria Rd

Victoria Grove

Gloucester Road

Queen's Gate

259

Queen's Gate Terrace

Elvaston Place

Queen's Gate

363

Grenville Place

Gate Gardens

Gardens

Cornwall Gardens

Lexham Gardens

Lexham Gdns

Cromwell Road

Cromwell Road

Stanhope Gardens

GLOUCESTER RD.

Queen's

360

215

120

420

SOUTH KENSINGTON

Ashburn Road

Rd

Knaresborough Place

Courtfield Gdns

101

Courtfield Gdns

14

Courtfield Road

Harrington Gardens

Gloucester Rd

59

180

SOUTH KENSINGTON

Summer Square

Onslow Gardens

Onslow Place

Brompton Road

Bramham Gdns

99

Wetherby Gardens

Bina Gdns

Old Road

Roland Gardens

Cranley Gdns

Onslow Gardens

170

300

South Parade

Earl's Court Road

Bolton Gardens

Brompton Road

The Little Boltons

EARL'S COURT

The Boltons

Drayton

Gardens

Evelyn Gdns

Elm Park Gdns

Finborough Road

Redcliffe Square

Harcourt Ter

Redcliffe Road

Tregunter Road

Hollywood Road

Gilston Road

Fulham Road

Elm Park Gardens

Beaufort

Elm Park Road

Old Church Street

The Vale

BROMPTON CEMETERY

Ifield Road

Gardens

Fulham Road

Park

Walk

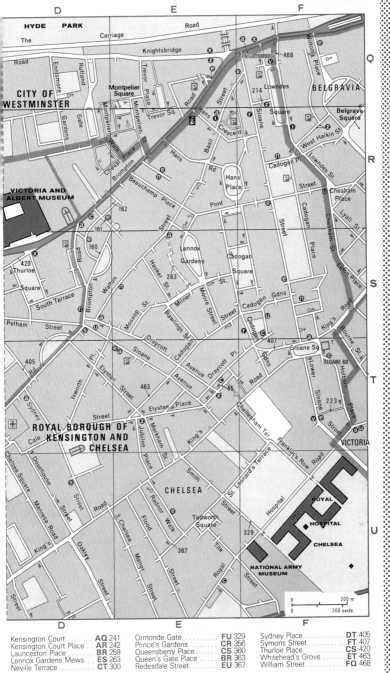

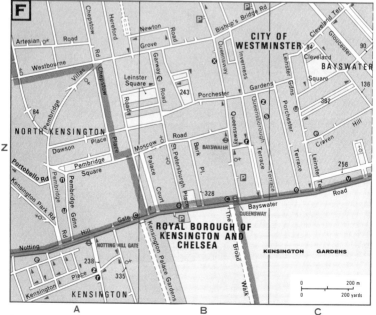

D

WELLINGTON ARCH
GREEN PARK
142
Constitution Hill
QUEEN VICTORIA MEMORIAL
The Mall
St James's Park Lake
BUCKINGHAM PALACE GARDENS
ST JAMES'S
ST. JAMES'S PARK

Grosvenor Cres.
Halkin St.
Chapel St.
Chester St.
Grosvenor
Place

BUCKINGHAM PALACE

QUEEN'S GALLERY
Birdcage Walk

V

Belgrave Square
Upper Belgrave

56 CITY OF WESTMINSTER
56
Petty
France
Palmer

BELGRAVIA
Belgrave Place
Wilton St.
ROYAL MEWS
274
Palace
Castle La.
56
Victoria

Eaton
Belgrave Place
Square
Hobart
Pl.
Grosvenor
Gdns
48
Street
H

X
Lower Belgrave St.
Victoria
Street
Howick
Pl.
8

Eaton
Square
King's
Eccleston
88
412
Ashley Pl.
416
Row

Elizabeth
Eaton
88
Palace
VICTORIA
Carlisle
WESTMINSTER CATHEDRAL
Francis

Y
389
Chester Row
Ebury
Buckingham
157
St.
Hudson's Pl.
Wilton
Vauxhall
VICTORIA
Rochester

389
Street
Gillingham
Bridge
Tachbrook
Vincent Square

201
Belgrave
Rd
Way
Road

0   200 m
0   200 yards
Eccleston Square
Hugh Street
Warwick

F

Chepstow
Newton
Road
Bishop's Bridge Rd
Cleveland Ter.
Artesian
Road
Grove
CITY OF WESTMINSTER
84
90
Cleveland
Hereford
Garway
Queensway
Inverness
Leinster Gdns
Gloucester
BAYSWATER
Westbourne
Villas
Chepstow
Leinster Square
Road
243
Porchester
Gardens
Square
136

84
Pembridge
Rd
Road
Moscow
Road
Queensway
Porchester
362

NORTH KENSINGTON
Dawson
Place
BAYSWATER
St. Petersburgh Pl.
Queensborough Terrace
Terrace
Craven
Hill
256

Z
Portobello Rd
Pembridge
Square
Palace
Court
Pl.
328
Terrace
Leinster Ter.

Kensington Park Rd
Pembridge Gdns
Gate
Bayswater
QUEENSWAY
Bayswater
Road

Notting
Hill
NOTTING HILL GATE
The Broad
Kensington Palace Gardens
Walk
ROYAL BOROUGH OF KENSINGTON AND CHELSEA
KENSINGTON GARDENS

238
335
Place
KENSINGTON

0   200 m
0   200 yards

A   B   C

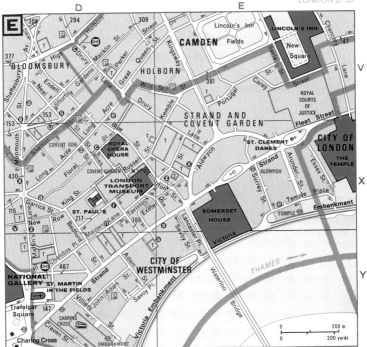

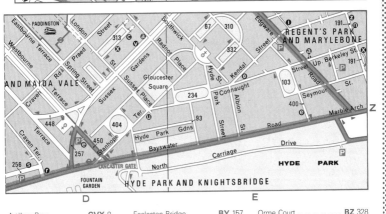

Alphabetical list of hotels and restaurants
Liste alphabétique des hôtels et restaurants
Elenco alfabetico degli alberghi e ristoranti
Alphabetisches Hotel- und Restaurantverzeichnis

Alphabetical list of areas included
Liste alphabétique des quartiers cités
Elenco alfabetico dei quartieri citati
Liste der erwähnten Bezirke

Starred establishments in London
Les établissements à étoiles de Londres
Gli esercizi con stelle a Londra
Die Stern-Restaurants Londons

		Area	Page
ⅩⅩⅩⅩ	La Tante Claire	Chelsea	59

		Area	Page
ⅩⅩⅩⅩⅩ	Chez Nico at Ninety Park Lane (at Grosvenor House H.)	Mayfair	70
ⅩⅩⅩⅩ	Le Gavroche	Mayfair	70
ⅩⅩⅩⅩ	The Restaurant (at Hyde Park H.)	Hyde Park & Knightsbridge	69

		Area	Page				Area	Page
	Connaught	Mayfair	69		ⅩⅩⅩⅩ	Oriental (at Dorchester H.)	Mayfair	70
	Capital	Chelsea	58		ⅩⅩⅩⅩ	Les Saveurs	Mayfair	71
ⅩⅩⅩⅩⅩ	Oak Room (at Le Meridien London H.)	Mayfair	70		ⅩⅩⅩ	The Canteen	Chelsea	59
ⅩⅩⅩⅩ	Four Seasons (at Four Seasons H.)	Mayfair	69		ⅩⅩⅩ	Leith's	North Kensington	62
ⅩⅩⅩⅩ	Grill Room at the Café Royal	Soho	74		ⅩⅩⅩ	Suntory	St. James's	74
					ⅩⅩ	Pied à Terre	Bloomsbury	51
					ⅩⅩ	The Square	St. James's	74

Further establishments which merit your attention
Autres tables qui méritent votre attention
Altre tavole particolarmente interessanti
Weitere empfehlenswerte Häuser

Meals

			Page					Page
ⅩⅩⅩ	Al Bustan	Belgravia	68		ⅩⅩ	Greenhouse	Mayfair	71
ⅩⅩⅩ	Bibendum	Chelsea	59		ⅩⅩ	Hilaire	South Kensington	63
ⅩⅩⅩ	Chutney Mary	Chelsea	59		ⅩⅩ	Nico Central	Regents Park and Marylebone	73
ⅩⅩⅩ	Fifth Floor (at Harvey Nichols)	Chelsea	59		ⅩⅩ	Percy's	North Harrow	56
					ⅩⅩ	Simply Nico	Victoria	77
ⅩⅩⅩ	Pont de la Tour	Southwark	66		Ⅹ	Alastair Little	Soho	75
ⅩⅩⅩ	Quaglino's	St. James's	74		Ⅹ	Bistrot Bruno	Soho	75
ⅩⅩⅩ	Zen Central	Mayfair	71		Ⅹ	Kensington Place	Kensington	61
ⅩⅩ	Le Caprice	St. James's	74					
ⅩⅩ	Clarke's	Kensington	61		Ⅹ	Malabar	Kensington	61

Restaurants classified according to type
Restaurants classés suivant leur genre
Ristoranti classificati secondo il loro genere
Restaurants nach Art und Einrichtung geordnet

Bistro

Seafood

Californian

Chinese

Chinese

English

French

French

Hungarian

Indian & Pakistan

Irish

Italian

Japanese

Lebanese

Oriental

Polish

Spanish

Swedish

Thai

Vietnamese

Restaurants open on Sunday (**L** = lunch – **D** = dinner)
and Restaurants taking last orders after 11.30 pm (•)

Restaurants ouverts le dimanche (**L** = déjeuner – **D** = dîner)
et restaurants prenant les dernières commandes après 23 h 30 (•)

Ristoranti aperti la domenica (**L** = colazione – **D** = cena)
e ristoranti che accettano ordinazioni dopo le 23.30 (•)

Restaurants, die sonntags geöffnet sind (**L** = Mittagessen – **D** = Abendessen)
BZW. Bestellungen auch nach 23.30 Uhr annehmen (•)

Boroughs and areas

Greater London is divided, for administrative purposes, into 32 boroughs plus the City : these sub-divide naturally into minor areas, usually grouped around former villages or quarters, which often maintain a distinctive character.

BARKING and DAGENHAM p. 7.

Chadwell Heath – ⊠ Essex – ☎ 081.

XX **La Scala**, 19a High Rd, RM6 6PU, ℰ 983 8818 – **℗**. ⚑ 歴 ⓞ 𝑉𝐼𝑆𝐴 𝐽𝐶𝐵   JU **e**
M - Italian a la carte approx. 15.00 **t**. ⫽ 3.80.

BARNET pp. 4 and 5.

Brent Cross – ⊠ NW2 – ☎ 081.

🏤 **Holiday Inn Garden Court**, Tilling Rd, NW2 3DS, ℰ 455 4777, Fax 455 4660 – ❄⟵ rm 📺
☎ ℗ – ⚠ 50. ⚑ 歴 ⓞ 𝑉𝐼𝑆𝐴 𝐽𝐶𝐵   DU **n**
M 11.95 **st**. and a la carte ⫽ 4.30 – 🖙 8.25 – **153 rm** 65.00 **st**.

Child's Hill – ⊠ NW2 – ☎ 071.

XX **Mezzaluna**, 424 Finchley Rd, NW2 2HY, ℰ 794 0455 – ⚑ 歴 𝑉𝐼𝑆𝐴   DU **o**
closed Saturday lunch and Monday – **M** - Italian a la carte 18.50/25.00 **t**. ⫽ 4.00.

X **Quincy's**, 675 Finchley Rd, NW2 2JP, ℰ 794 8499 – ▤. ⚑ 歴 𝑉𝐼𝑆𝐴   DU **r**
closed Sunday, Monday and 14 to 28 September – **M** (booking essential) (dinner only) 22.00 **t**. ⫽ 4.50.

X **Laurent**, 428 Finchley Rd, NW2 2HY, ℰ 794 3603 – ⚑ 歴 𝑉𝐼𝑆𝐴   DU **o**
closed Sunday, first 3 weeks August and Bank Holidays – **M** - Couscous a la carte approx. 14.40 **t**.

Hendon – ⊠ NW4 – ☎ 081.

🏌 Sanders Lane, Devonshire Rd, Hendon ℰ 346 6023, M 1 junction 2 DT.

↱ **Peacehaven** without rest., 94 Audley Rd, NW4 3HB, ℰ 202 9758, 🌲 – 📺. ⚑ 歴 ⓞ 𝑉𝐼𝑆𝐴.
❄   CU **c**
13 rm 🖙 38.00/66.00 **st**.

Mill Hill – ⊠ NW7 – ☎ 081.

🏌 100 Barnet Way, Mill Hill ℰ 959 2282 CT.

XX **Good Earth**, 143 The Broadway, NW7 4RN, ℰ 959 7011 – ▤. ⚑ 歴 ⓞ 𝑉𝐼𝑆𝐴   CT **a**
closed 24 to 27 December – **M** - Chinese 20.00/25.00 **t**. and a la carte ⫽ 4.00.

BEXLEY pp. 10 and 11.

Bexley – ⊠ Kent – ☎ 0322 Crayford

🏤 **Forte Posthouse**, Black Prince Interchange, Southwold Rd, DA5 1ND, on A 2 ℰ 526900, Fax 526113 – 📶 ❄⟵ rm ▤ rest 📺 ☎ ♿ ℗ – ⚠ 70. ⚑ 歴 ⓞ 𝑉𝐼𝑆𝐴   JX **e**
M a la carte approx. 17.50 **t**. ⫽ 4.65 – 🖙 6.95 – **100 rm** 53.50/69.50 **st**., 2 suites – SB (weekends only) 90.00 **st**.

Bexleyheath – ⊠ Kent – ☎ 081.

🏤 **Swallow**, 1 Broadway, DA6 7JZ, ℰ 298 1000, Fax 298 1234, 𝑓𝑏, ☒ – 📶 ❄⟵ rm ▤ 📺 ☎
♿ ℗ – ⚠ 240. ⚑ 歴 ⓞ 𝑉𝐼𝑆𝐴   JX **c**
M 11.95/19.50 **st**. and a la carte – **142 rm** 🖙 84.00/120.00 **st**. – SB (except Christmas and New Year) 105.00 **st**.

BRENT pp. 4 and 5.

Wembley – ⊠ Middx – ☎ 081.

🏤 **Hilton National Wembley**, Empire Way, HA9 8DS, ℰ 902 8839, Fax 900 2201 – 📶
❄⟵ rm ▤ rest 📺 ☎ ℗ – ⚠ 300. ⚑ 歴 ⓞ 𝑉𝐼𝑆𝐴 𝐽𝐶𝐵   CU **z**
M (carving rest.) (bar lunch)/dinner 19.50 **st**. and a la carte ⫽ 7.50 – 🖙 10.25 – **300 rm** 99.00/180.00 **st**. – SB 120.00/160.00 **st**.

BROMLEY pp. 10 and 11.

🏌, 🏌 Cray Valley, Sandy Lane, St. Paul's Cray ✆ 0689 (Orpington) 831927, NE : by A 224 JY.

Bromley – ✉ Kent – ✆ 081.

🏌 Magpie Hall Lane ✆ 462 7014 HY.

🏨 **Bromley Court,** Bromley Hill, BR1 4JD, ✆ 464 5011, Telex 896310, Fax 460 0899, ☞ – 🛗
🍴 rm 🔟 ☎ 🅿 – 🔬 150. 🖭 🖭 ⑩ 𝖵𝖨𝖲𝖠   HY **z**
M 9.95/14.95 **st.** and a la carte 🍴 4.60 – **120 rm** ⊆ 79.00/89.00 **st.**

XXX **Chandni,** 123-125 Mason's Hill, BR2 9HT, ✆ 290 4447 – 🗐, 🖭 🖭 ⑩ 𝖵𝖨𝖲𝖠   HY **e**
closed 25 and 26 December – **M** - **Indian** a la carte 15.95/22.10 **t.** 🍴 3.50.

XX **Peking Diner,** 71 Burnt Ash Lane, BR1 5AA, ✆ 464 7911 – 🗐. 🖭 🖭 ⑩ 𝖵𝖨𝖲𝖠   HX **u**
closed Sunday and 25-26 December – **M** - **Chinese** (Peking) a la carte 13.50/20.50 **t.** 🍴 4.50.

Keston – ✉ Kent – ✆ 0689 Farnborough.

XX **Giannino's,** 6 Commonside, BR2 6BP, ✆ 856410 – 🖭 🖭 ⑩ 𝖵𝖨𝖲𝖠   HZ **x**
closed Sunday, Monday, 2 weeks August and 2 weeks Christmas-New Year – **M** - **Italian**
12.75/14.75 **t.** and a la carte.

Orpington – ✉ Kent – ✆ 0689 Farnborough.

🏌 High Elms, High Elms Rd, Downe, Orpington ✆ 58175, off A 21 via Shire Lane JZ –
🏌 Hewitts Golf Centre, Court Rd ✆ 896266 JZ.

XX **Xian,** 324 High St., BR6 0NG, ✆ 871881 – 🗐. 🖭 🖭 ⑩ 𝖵𝖨𝖲𝖠   JZ **a**
closed Sunday lunch – **M** - **Chinese** (Peking, Szechuan) 7.50/22.00 **t.** and a la carte.

CAMDEN Except where otherwise stated see pp. 20-23.

Bloomsbury – ✉ NW1/W1/WC1 – ✆ 071.

🅱 35-36 Woburn Pl., WC1H 0JR ✆ 580 4599.

🏨🏨 Holiday Inn Kings Cross, 1 Kings Cross Rd, WC1X 9HX, ✆ 833 3900, Fax 917 6163, ≤, ℐ₅,
⩶, ℤ, squash – 🛗 🍴 rm 🗐 🔟 ☎ ₺ – 🔬 240   MT **a**
397 rm, 8 suites.

🏨🏨 **Russell** (Forte), Russell Sq., WC1B 5BE, ✆ 837 6470, Telex 24615, Fax 837 2857 – 🛗
🍴 rm 🔟 ☎ – 🔬 450. 🖭 🖭 ⑩ 𝖵𝖨𝖲𝖠 𝖩𝖢𝖡   LU **o**
M *(closed Saturday lunch)* (carving rest.) 12.95/16.50 **t.** and a la carte 🍴 6.10 – ⊆ 10.50 –
325 rm 105.00/140.00 **st.**, 3 suites – SB (weekends only) 128.00 **st.**

🏨🏨 **Mountbatten** (Edwardian), 20 Monmouth St., WC2H 9HD, ✆ 836 4300, Telex 298087,
Fax 240 3540 – 🛗 🍴 rm 🗐 rest 🔟 ☎ – 🔬 75. 🖭 🖭 ⑩ 𝖵𝖨𝖲𝖠 𝖩𝖢𝖡. ⚘
M (bar lunch Saturday and Sunday) 15.50/22.50 **st.** – ⊆ 12.00 – **121 rm** 153.00/181.00 **st.**,
6 suites – SB (weekends only) 112.00/140.00 **st.**   p.33 DV **o**

🏨🏨 **Marlborough** (Edwardian), 9-14 Bloomsbury St., WC1B 3QD, ✆ 636 5601, Telex 298274,
Fax 636 0532 – 🛗 🍴 rm 🗐 rest 🔟 ☎ ₺ – 🔬 200. 🖭 🖭 ⑩ 𝖵𝖨𝖲𝖠 𝖩𝖢𝖡. ⚘   LU **i**
M 16.95 **st.** – ⊆ 10.00 – **167 rm** 143.00/167.00 **st.**, 2 suites – SB (weekends only) 93.00/
116.00 **st.**

🏨🏨 **Grafton** (Edwardian), 130 Tottenham Court Rd, W1P 9HP, ✆ 388 4131, Telex 297234,
Fax 387 7394 – 🛗 🗐 rest 🔟 ☎ – 🔬 100. 🖭 🖭 ⑩ 𝖵𝖨𝖲𝖠 𝖩𝖢𝖡 ⚘   KU **n**
M 18.50 **st.** and a la carte – ⊆ 10.00 – **320 rm** 111.00/140.00 **st.**, 4 suites – SB (weekends
only) 79.00/99.00 **st.**

🏨🏨 **Kenilworth** (Edwardian), 97 Great Russell St., WC1B 3LB, ✆ 637 3477, Telex 25842,
Fax 631 3133 – 🛗 🍴 rm 🗐 rest 🔟 ☎ – 🔬 100. 🖭 🖭 ⑩ 𝖵𝖨𝖲𝖠 𝖩𝖢𝖡. ⚘   LU **a**
M 15.50/16.95 **st.** and a la carte – ⊆ 10.00 – **191 rm** 111.00/132.00 **st.**, 1 suite – SB 90.00/
113.00 **st.**

🏨🏨 **Montague Park,** 12-20 Montague St., WC1B 5BJ, ✆ 637 1001, Telex 23307,
Fax 637 2506 – 🛗 🗐 🔟 ☎ ₺ – 🔬 80. 🖭 🖭 ⑩ 𝖵𝖨𝖲𝖠 ⚘   LU **c**
M (bar lunch)/dinner 16.50 – **109 rm** ⊆ 80.00/170.00 **st.** – SB (weekends only) 130.00/
170.00 **st.**

🏨🏨 **Forte Crest Bloomsbury,** Coram St., WC1N 1HT, ✆ 837 1200, Telex 22113,
Fax 837 5374 – 🛗 🍴 rm 🗐 rest 🔟 ☎ ₺ – 🔬 700. 🖭 🖭 ⑩ 𝖵𝖨𝖲𝖠 𝖩𝖢𝖡   LT **c**
M (bar lunch Saturday) (carving rest.) 14.95/15.95 **st.** 🍴 5.75 – ⊆ 10.75 – **282 rm** 99.00 **st.**,
2 suites – SB (weekends only) 116.00 **st.**

🏨 **Portland,** 7 Montague St., WC1B 5BP, ✆ 323 1717, Fax 636 6498 – 🛗 🔟 ☎. 🖭 🖭 ⑩ 𝖵𝖨𝖲𝖠
𝖩𝖢𝖡. ⚘   LU **n**
M - **Italian** (closed Sunday) 14.50 **t.** and a la carte – **25 rm** ⊆ 85.00/130.00 **st.**, 1 suite –
SB (weekends only) 90.00/160.00 **st.**

🏨 **Bonnington**, 92 Southampton Row, WC1B 4BH, ✆ 242 2828, Telex 261591,
Fax 831 9170 – 🛗 🍴 rm 🗐 rest 🔟 ☎ ₺ – 🔬 250. 🖭 🖭 ⑩ 𝖵𝖨𝖲𝖠   LU **s**
M *(closed lunch Saturday and Sunday)* 9.00/15.95 **st.** and a la carte 🍴 7.50 – **215 rm**
⊆ 85.00/95.00 **st.** – SB (weekends only) 111.90/131.90 **st.**

🏦 **Kingsley** (Mt. Charlotte Thistle), Bloomsbury Way, WC1A 2SD, ℰ 242 5881, Fax 831 0225
– |≡| ⇔ rm 📺 ☎ – 🔬 100. ⚠ AE ⓞ VISA JCB   LU   **r**
M *(closed lunch Saturday, Sunday and Bank Holidays)* 8.95/15.25 **t.** and a la carte 🍷 4.80 –
� 8.95 – **98 rm** 75.00/110.00 **st.**, 2 suites.

🏦 **Bloomsbury Park** (Mt. Charlotte Thistle), 126 Southampton Row, WC1B 5AD,
ℰ 430 0434, Telex 25757, Fax 242 0665 – |≡| ⇔ rm 📺 ☎ – 🔬 30. ⚠ AE ⓞ VISA JCB.
⁒   LU   **u**
M *(closed Friday to Sunday)* (dinner only) 13.95 **st.** and a la carte 🍷 4.25 – ⊐ 8.25 – **95 rm**
75.00/120.00 **st.**

🏠 **Academy**, 17-21 Gower St., WC1E 6HG, ℰ 631 4115, Fax 636 3442 – ▤ rest 📺 ☎ –
🔬 35. ⚠ AE ⓞ VISA JCB. ⁒   KLU   **v**
M 14.95/16.95 **t.** and a la carte 🍷 5.50 – ⊐ 8.95 – **33 rm** 74.00/143.00 **s.**

↑ **Harlingford** without rest., 61-63 Cartwright Gdns, WC1H 9EL, ℰ 387 1551, Fax 387 4616
– 📺 ☎. ⚠ AE VISA. ⁒   LT   **n**
44 rm ⊐ 49.00/63.00 **st.**

↑ **Mabledon Court** without rest., 10-11 Mabledon Pl., WC1H 9BA, ℰ 388 3866,
Fax 387 5686 – |≡| 📺 ☎. ⚠ AE VISA. ⁒   LT   **s**
32 rm ⊐ 49.00/59.00 **st.**

↑ **Mentone** without rest., 54-55 Cartwright Gdns, WC1H 9EL, ℰ 387 3927, Fax 388 4671,
⁒ – 📺. ⚠ VISA. ⁒   LT   **a**
27 rm ⊐ 30.00/56.00 **t.**

XX ⁑ **Pied à Terre** (Neat), 34 Charlotte St., W1P 1HJ, ℰ 636 1178 – ▤. ⚠ AE ⓞ VISA
JCB   KU   **e**
closed Saturday lunch, Sunday, last 2 weeks August and 2 weeks December-January –
M 19.50/38.00 **st.** 🍷 8.50
Spec. Red mullet darne, pâté and fondant potato with aniseed, Roasted duck breast and confit croquette, Coconut
crème.

XX **Neal Street,** 26 Neal St., WC2H 9PS, ℰ 836 8368, Fax 497 1361 – ▤. ⚠ AE ⓞ
VISA   p. 33 DV **s**
closed Sunday, Christmas and Bank Holidays – **M** a la carte 29.50/39.50 **t.** 🍷 8.50.

XX **Mon Plaisir,** 21 Monmouth St., WC2H 9DD, ℰ 836 7243 – ⚠ AE ⓞ VISA JCB
closed Saturday lunch, Sunday and Bank Holidays – **M** - **French** 13.95 **st.** and a la carte
🍷 5.80.   p. 33 DV **a**

XX **Poons of Russell Square,** 50 Woburn Pl., WC1H 0JE, ℰ 580 1188 – ▤. ⚠ AE ⓞ VISA
JCB   LU   **x**
closed 24 to 27 December – **M** - **Chinese** 9.00/18.00 **t.** and a la carte.

XX **Bleeding Heart,** Bleeding Heart Yard, EC1N 8SJ, off Greville St., Hatton Garden
ℰ 242 2056, Fax 831 1402. ⚠ AE ⓞ VISA JCB   NU   **e**
closed Saturday, Sunday and 24 December-5 January – **M** a la carte 14.85/23.20 **t.**
🍷 3.95.

XX **Kanishka,** 161 Whitfield St., W1P 5RY, ℰ 388 0860 – ▤   KTU   **z**
M - **Indian** 22.50/27.50 **t.** and a la carte.

X **Smith's,** 25 Neal St., WC2H 9PU, ℰ 379 0310, Fax 836 4769 – ⚠ AE ⓞ VISA JCB
closed Sunday and Bank Holidays – **M** a la carte 14.50/25.00 **st.**   p. 33 DVX **u**

X **Auntie's,** 126 Cleveland St., W1P 5DN, ℰ 387 1548, Fax 387 3226 – ⚠ AE ⓞ
VISA   JU   **s**
closed Saturday lunch and Sunday – **M** - **English** 12.00/21.00 **t.** and a la carte
🍷 5.50.

X **Il Castelletto,** 17 Bury Pl., WC1A 2IB, ℰ 405 2232 – ▤. ⚠ AE ⓞ VISA   LU   **r**
closed Saturday lunch, Sunday and Bank Holidays – **M** - **Italian** 14.00 **t.** (lunch) and a la
carte 16.50/21.60 **t.** 🍷 4.75.

  Camden Town – ✉ NW1 – ☎ 071.

X **La Bougie,** 7 Murray St., NW1 9RE, ℰ 485 6400   KS   **a**
M - **Bistro** (dinner only) a la carte 13.50/15.50 **t.** 🍷 4.00.

  Euston – ✉ WC1 – ☎ 071.

🏨 **Euston Plaza,** 17/18 Upper Woburn Pl., WC1H 0HT, ℰ 383 4105, Fax 383 4106, 🛁, ☎s –
|≡| ⇔ rm ▤ 📺 ☎ – 🔬 110. ⚠ AE ⓞ VISA. ⁒   KLT   **e**
M (bar lunch)/dinner 15.00 **st.** and a la carte – ⊐ 9.50 – **149 rm** 95.00/130.00 **st.**, 1 suite –
SB 95.00/176.00 **st.**

  Finchley Road – ✉ NW3/NW6 – ☎ 071.

🏠 **Charles Bernard,** 5-7 Frognal, NW3 6AL, ℰ 794 0101, Telex 23560, Fax 794 0100 – |≡| 📺
☎ ℗. ⚠ AE ⓞ VISA. ⁒   ES   **s**
M (bar lunch)/dinner 13.50 **st.** and a la carte 🍷 4.00 – **57 rm** ⊐ 45.00/71.50 **st.** – SB (week-
ends only) 74.00/126.50 **st.**

321

Hampstead – ✉ NW3 – ☎ 071.

🏌 Winnington Rd, Hampstead 🖉 455 0203 EU.

🏨 **Swiss Cottage,** 4 Adamson Rd, NW3 3HP, 🖉 722 2281, Telex 297232, Fax 483 4588, « Antique furniture collection » – 🛗 📺 ☎ – 🔬 60. 🔼 🖭 🖭 🌠 ✦ GS **n**
M *(closed Saturday and Sunday)* (bar lunch)/dinner a la carte 12.40/19.10 **st.** ⅄ 5.95 – **74 rm** ☷ 73.00/85.00 **st.**, 6 suites.

🏨 **Forte Posthouse,** 215 Haverstock Hill, NW3 4RB, 🖉 794 8121, Fax 435 5586 – 🛗 ✦ rm
📺 ☎ 🅿 – 🔬 30. 🔼 🖭 📺 🌠 🖭 ES **r**
M a la carte approx. 17.50 **t.** ⅄ 4.65 – ☷ 6.95 – **140 rm** 53.50 **st.** – SB (weekends only) 90.00 **st.**

🏨 Clive (Hilton), Primrose Hill Rd, NW3 3NA, 🖉 586 2233, Telex 22759, Fax 586 1659 – 🛗 📺
☎ 🅿 – 🔬 300. 🌠 HS **a**
93 rm, 3 suites.

🏠 Langorf without rest., 20 Frognal, NW3 6AG, 🖉 794 4483, Fax 435 9055 – 🛗 📺 ☎. 🌠
31 rm. ES **c**

XXX **Benihana,** 100 Avenue Rd, NW3 3HF, 🖉 586 9508, Fax 586 6740 – ▤ GS **o**
M - Japanese (Teppan-Yaki) 8.50/13.95 **t.** and a la carte ⅄ 8.50.

XX **Carapace,** 118 Heath St., NW3 1DR, 🖉 435 8000, Fax 935 9582 – 🔼 🖭 🖭 ES **e**
M (dinner only and Sunday lunch)/dinner 21.85/34.50 **st.** ⅄ 4.60.

XX **Zen W3,** 83-84 Hampstead High St., NW3 1RE, 🖉 794 7863 – 🔼 🖭 🖭 ES **a**
closed Christmas Day – **M** - Chinese 10.00/15.00 **t.** and a la carte.

X **Café des Arts,** 82 Hampstead High St., NW3 1RE, 🖉 435 3608 – 🔼 🖭 🖭 ES **i**
closed 1 January lunch and 25-26 December – **M** a la carte 15.35/22.65 **t.**

Holborn – ✉ WC2 – ☎ 071.

🏨 **Drury Lane Moat House** (Q.M.H.), 10 Drury Lane, High Holborn, WC2B 5RE, 🖉 836 6666, Telex 8811395, Fax 831 1548 – 🛗 ✦ rm 📺 ☎ – 🔬 100. 🔼 🖭 🖭 🌠
M 9.50/14.85 **st.** and a la carte ⅄ 5.00 – ☷ 9.50 – **151 rm** 128.00/148.00 **st.**, 2 suites –
SB 142.00/242.00 **st.** p. 33 DV **c**

X **Imari,** 71 Red Lion St., WC1R 4NA, 🖉 405 0486, Fax 405 0473 – ▤. 🔼 🖭 🖭 🌠
🖭 MU **z**
closed Saturday, Sunday and Bank Holidays – **M** - Japanese 20.00/25.00 **st.** and a la carte.

Regent's Park – ✉ NW1 – ☎ 071.

🏨 **White House,** Albany St., NW1 3UP, 🖉 387 1200, Telex 24111, Fax 388 0091, ⅙, ≋s – 🛗
✦ rm 📺 ☎ 🕭 – 🔬 100. 🔼 🖭 🖭 🌠 🖭 🌠 JT **o**
M *(closed Saturday lunch and Sunday)* 18.50/22.50 **st.** and a la carte ⅄ 6.00 – ☷ 10.75 –
560 rm 105.00/135.00 **st.**, 15 suites.

XX **Odette's,** 130 Regent's Park Rd, NW1 8XL, 🖉 586 5486 – 🔼 🖭 🖭 🌠 HS **i**
closed Sunday dinner and 1 week Christmas – **M** 10.00 **t.** (lunch) and a la carte 16.50/23.50 **t.** ⅄ 5.00.

XX **China Jazz,** 29-31 Parkway, NW1 7PN, 🖉 482 3940 – 🔼 🖭 🖭 🌠 JS **e**
M - Chinese 22.00 **t.** (dinner) and a la carte 16.00/23.50 **t.**

X **Belgo,** 72 Chalk Farm Rd, NW1 8AN, 🖉 267 0718, Fax 267 7508 – 🔼 🖭 🖭 🌠 IS **e**
M 25.00 **t.** and a la carte.

Swiss Cottage – ✉ NW3 – ☎ 071.

🏨 **Regents Park Marriott,** 128 King Henry's Rd, NW3 3ST, 🖉 722 7711, Telex 267396, Fax 586 5822, ⅙, ≋s, ▢ – 🛗 ✦ rm ▤ 📺 ☎ 🕭 🅿 – 🔬 400. 🔼 🖭 🖭 🌠 ✦ GS **a**
M 18.50/30.00 **st.** and a la carte – ☷ 11.85 – **295 rm** 132.00/144.00 **s.**, 8 suites.

XX **Peter's,** 65 Fairfax Rd, NW3 4EE, 🖉 624 5804 – 🔼 🖭 🖭 🌠 FS **i**
closed 1-2 January and 26-27 December – **M** 10.95/13.95 **t.** and a la carte ⅄ 4.00.

X **Thai Pepper,** 115 Finchley Rd, NW3 6HY, 🖉 722 0026 – ▤. 🔼 🖭 🖭 🌠 GS **v**
closed Saturday and Sunday lunch and Bank Holidays – **M** - Thai 17.00/20.00 **t.** and a la carte ⅄ 3.90.

CITY OF LONDON – ☎ 071 Except where otherwise stated see p. 23.

XXX **Tatsuso,** 32 Broadgate Circle, EC2M 2QS, 🖉 638 5863, Fax 638 5864 – ▤. 🔼 🖭 🖭 🌠
🖭 PU **u**
closed Saturday, Sunday, 25 December and Bank Holidays – **M** - Japanese (booking essential) 60.00/65.00 **t.** and a la carte.

XX **Le Quai,** Riverside Walkway, 1 Broken Wharf, EC4V 3QQ, off High Timber St.
🖉 236 6480, Fax 236 6479 – ▤. 🔼 🖭 🖭 🌠 🖭 OV **a**
closed Saturday, Sunday and Bank Holidays – **M** (dinner booking essential) 32.50 **t.** (dinner) and a la carte.

XX **Corney and Barrow,** 109 Old Broad St., EC2N 1AP, 🖉 638 9308 – ▤. 🔼 🖭 🖭 🌠 🖭
closed Saturday and Sunday – **M** (lunch only) 21.95/26.95 **t.** PU **c**

XX **Le Poulbot** (basement), 45 Cheapside, EC2Y 6AR, 🖉 236 4379 – ▤. 🔼 🖭 🌠 🖭
closed Saturday and Sunday – **M** - French (lunch only) 31.50 **st.** OV **i**

XX **Miyama,** 17 Godliman St., EC4V 5BD, ℰ 489 1937 – ▤. 🔼 🆎 ⓞ 𝗩𝗜𝗦𝗔 🄹🄲🄱 OV **e**
closed Saturday dinner, Sunday and Bank Holidays – **M** - **Japanese** 40.00/60.00 **t.** and a la
carte ⓘ 5.00.

XX **Corney and Barrow,** 44 Cannon St., EC4N 6JJ, ℰ 248 1700 – ▤. 🔼 🆎 ⓞ 𝗩𝗜𝗦𝗔
🄹🄲🄱 OV **r**
closed Saturday, Sunday and Bank Holidays – **M** (lunch only) 21.95 **t.** ⓘ 7.50.

X **Whittington's,** 21 College Hill, EC4R 2RP, ℰ 248 5855 – ▤. 🔼 🆎 ⓞ 𝗩𝗜𝗦𝗔 🄹🄲🄱 OV **c**
closed Saturday and Sunday – **M** (lunch only) a la carte 22.10/25.95 **t.** ⓘ 4.75.

X **Bubb's,** 329 Central Market, Farringdon St., EC1A 9NB, ℰ 236 2435 – 🔼 🆎 𝗩𝗜𝗦𝗔 NU **a**
closed Saturday and Sunday – **M** - **French** (lunch only) a la carte approx. 26.00 **t.**

CROYDON pp. 10 and 11.

Addington – ✉ Surrey – ☏ 081.

▏₁₈, ▏₁₈, ▏₉ Addington Court, Featherbed Lane ℰ 657 0281/2/3, E : 3 m. GZ – ▏₈ The
Addington, Shirley Church Rd ℰ 777 1055, E : 2½ m. GZ.

XX **Willow,** 88 Selsdon Park Rd, CR2 8JT, ℰ 657 4656 – ▤ 🅿. 🔼 🆎 ⓞ 𝗩𝗜𝗦𝗔 GZ **x**
closed 25 to 27 December – **M** - **Chinese** (Peking, Szechuan) 13.50/16.50 **t.** and a la carte
ⓘ 4.50.

Coulsdon – ✉ Surrey – ☏ 081.

▏₁₈ Coulsdon Court, Coulsdon Rd ℰ 660 0468, S : 5 m. by A 23 EZ.

🏨 **Coulsdon Court** ⟨S⟩, Coulsdon Rd, via Stoats Nest Rd, CR5 2LL, ℰ 668 0414,
Fax 668 3118, ⟨park⟩, %, squash – 🛗 ⥥ rm 📺 ☎ 🅿 – 🔏 180. 🔼 🆎 𝗩𝗜𝗦𝗔. % EZ **a**
M *(closed Saturday lunch)* 13.95/14.95 **t.** and a la carte ⓘ 4.50 – ☞ 7.25 – **35 rm** 50.00/
99.00 **t.** – SB 84.00/124.00 **st.**

Croydon – ✉ Surrey – ☏ 081.

🛈 Katherine St., CR9 1ET ℰ 760 5630.

🏨🏨 **Hilton National,** Waddon Way, CR9 4HH, ℰ 680 3000, Telex 290592, Fax 681 6171, *Ⓕₛ*,
⟨≦s⟩, ⟨▢⟩ – 🛗 ⥥ rm 📺 ☎ 🅿 – 🔏 340. 🔼 🆎 ⓞ 𝗩𝗜𝗦𝗔 🄹🄲🄱 FZ **e**
M 15.00/18.00 **t.** and a la carte ⓘ 5.50 – ☞ 9.95 – **168 rm** 85.00/110.00 **t.** – SB 124.00 **st.**

🏨🏨 **Croydon Park** (Best Western), 7 Altyre Rd, CR9 5AA, ℰ 680 9200, Telex 8956268,
Fax 760 0426, ⟨≦s⟩, ⟨▢⟩, squash – 🛗 ⥥ rm ▤ ☎ 🔥 🅿 – 🔏 300. 🔼 🆎 ⓞ 𝗩𝗜𝗦𝗔 🄹🄲🄱
M 13.95/14.95 **st.** and a la carte ⓘ 4.95 – **213 rm** ☞ 87.00/97.00 **st.**, 1 suite – SB (weekends
only) 80.00 **st.** FZ **u**

🏨 **Forte Posthouse,** Purley Way, CR9 4LT, ℰ 688 5185, Fax 681 6438, ➷ – ⥥ rm 📺 ☎ 🅿
– 🔏 170. 🔼 🆎 ⓞ 𝗩𝗜𝗦𝗔 FZ **o**
M a la carte approx. 17.50 **t.** ⓘ 4.65 – ☞ 6.95 – **83 rm** 53.50 **st.** – SB (weekends only)
90.00 **st.**

🏨 **Travel Inn,** Coombe Rd, CR0 5RB, on A 212 ℰ 686 2030, Fax 686 6435 – ⥥ rm 📺 ☎ 🔥
🅿. 🔼 🆎 𝗩𝗜𝗦𝗔 % GZ **s**
M (Beefeater grill) a la carte approx. 16.00 **t.** – ☞ 4.95 – **39 rm** 33.50 **t.**

XX **Thirty Four Surrey Street,** 34 Surrey St., CR0 1RJ, ℰ 686 0586, Live jazz Friday and
Saturday evenings – 🔼 🆎 𝗩𝗜𝗦𝗔 FZ **c**
closed Saturday lunch – **M** - **Californian fish** 25.00/30.00 **t.** and a la carte ⓘ 6.95.

X **Mario,** 299 High St., CR0 1QL, ℰ 686 5624 – 🔼 🆎 𝗩𝗜𝗦𝗔 FZ **s**
closed Saturday lunch, Monday dinner, Sunday, last 2 weeks August and Bank Holidays –
M - **Italian** 12.00 **t.** and a la carte.

X **Thai Village,** 18 South End, CR0 1DN, ℰ 760 0278. 🔼 🆎 ⓞ 𝗩𝗜𝗦𝗔 FZ **a**
closed lunch Saturday and Sunday and Christmas-New Year – **M** - **Thai** 15.50 **t.** and a la
carte ⓘ 3.60.

Sanderstead – ✉ Surrey – ☏ 081.

▏₁₈ Selsdon Park Hotel, Addington Rd, Sanderstead ℰ 657 8811, S : 3 m. by A 2022 GZ.

🏨🏨 **Selsdon Park,** Addington Rd, CR2 8YA, ℰ 657 8811, Fax 651 6171, ≤, *Ⓕₛ*, ⟨≦s⟩, ⟨▢⟩ heated,
⟨▢⟩, ▏₁₈, ✐, park, %, squash – 🛗 ⥥ rm 📺 ☎ 🅿 – 🔏 150. 🔼 🆎 ⓞ 𝗩𝗜𝗦𝗔 🄹🄲🄱
M 18.50/23.50 **t.** and a la carte – ☞ 8.50 – **163 rm** 85.00/140.00 **t.**, 7 suites – SB (weekends
only and mid July-early September) 150.00/160.00 **st.** GZ **n**

EALING pp. 4 and 5.

Ealing – ✉ W5 – ☏ 081.

▏₁₈ West Middlesex, Greenford Rd ℰ 574 3450 BV – ▏₉ Horsenden Hill, Woodland Rise
ℰ 902 4555 BU.

🏨 **Carnarvon,** Ealing Common, W5 3HN, ℰ 992 5399, Fax 992 7082 – 🛗 ⥥ rm 📺 ☎ 🅿 –
🔏 220. 🔼 🆎 ⓞ 𝗩𝗜𝗦𝗔 🄹🄲🄱. % CV **v**
M 17.95 **st.** (dinner) and a la carte 12.55/19.75 **st.** ⓘ 5.50 – ☞ 9.95 – **145 rm** 87.00/110.00 **st.**
– SB (weekends only) 90.00/130.00 **st.**

XX Maxim, 153-155 Northfield Av., W13 9QT, ☎ 567 1719 – 🍽   BV **a**

XX **Laguna Tandoori,** 1-4 Culmington Par., Uxbridge Rd, W13 9BD, ☎ 579 9992 – 🍽. 🗚 🗚
ⓞ 𝗩𝗜𝗦𝗔 JCB   BV **i**
closed 25 December – **M** - **Indian** 10.55 **t.** and a la carte ⓙ 3.35.

X **Noughts 'n' Crosses,** 77 The Grove, W5 5LL, ☎ 840 7568 – 🗚 🗚 𝗩𝗜𝗦𝗔   BV **u**
closed Sunday dinner, Monday, August and 26 December-4 January – **M** (dinner only and
Sunday lunch)/dinner 18.90 **t.** ⓙ 4.60.

X **Paolo's,** 7 Hanger Green, W5 3EL, ☎ 997 8560 – 🗚 🗚 ⓞ 𝗩𝗜𝗦𝗔   CV **r**
closed Saturday lunch and Sunday – **M** - **Italian** 25.00/30.00 **t.** and a la carte ⓙ 4.00.

Hanwell – ✉ W7 – ☎ 081.

ⓘ8 Brent Valley, Church Rd, ☎ 567 1287 BV.

X New Happiness Garden, 22 Boston Par., Boston Rd, W7 2DG, ☎ 567 9314   BV **c**
M - **Chinese rest.**

ENFIELD pp. 6 and 7.

ⓘ9 Picketts Lock, Picketts Lock Lane, Edmonton ☎ 803 3611 GT.

Enfield – ✉ Middx – ☎ 081.

ⓘ8 Whitewebbs, Beggars Hollow, Clay Hill ☎ 363 4454, N : 1 m. FT.

🏨 **Royal Chase,** The Ridgeway, EN2 8AR, ☎ 366 6500, Fax 367 7191, ⌧ heated, ⇌ – 📺 ☎
ⓟ – 🗚 300. 🗚 🗚 ⓞ 𝗩𝗜𝗦𝗔. ⌘   ET **a**
closed 24 to 28 December – **M** *(closed Saturday lunch and Sunday dinner)* 14.50/17.50 **t.**
and a la carte ⓙ 4.50 – **92 rm** ⌑ 55.00/85.00 **st.**

XXX **Norfolk,** 80 London Rd, EN2 6HU, ☎ 363 0979 – 🍽. 🗚 🗚 ⓞ 𝗩𝗜𝗦𝗔   FT **e**
closed Saturday lunch, Sunday dinner, Monday, 2 weeks August and Bank Holidays –
M a la carte 16.20/25.00 ⓙ 4.25.

Hadley Wood – ✉ Herts – ☎ 081.

🏨 **West Lodge Park** ⌖, off Cockfosters Rd, ✉ Barnet, EN4 0PY, ☎ 440 8311,
Fax 449 3698, ≤, ⌧, park – 🛗 📺 ☎ ⓖ ⓟ – 🗚 70. 🗚 🗚 𝗩𝗜𝗦𝗔. ⌘   ET **i**
M 14.85 **t.** and a la carte – ⌑ 7.95 – **50 rm** 59.50/139.50 **st.** – SB (except Christmas)
(weekends only) 116.00 **st.**

GREENWICH pp. 10 and 11.

Blackheath – ✉ SE3 – ☎ 081.

🏨 **Bardon Lodge,** 15 Stratheden Rd, SE3 7TH, ☎ 853 4051, Fax 858 7387, ⌧ – 📺 ☎ ⓟ –
🗚 25. 🗚 🗚 ⓞ 𝗩𝗜𝗦𝗔   HV **a**
M – *Lamplight (closed Sunday dinner)* (bar lunch Monday to Saturday)/dinner 9.95 **t.** and a
la carte ⓙ 3.75 – ⌑ 4.95 – **34 rm** 39.00/74.00 **t.**

🏨 **Vanbrugh,** 21 St. John's Park, SE3 7TD, ☎ 853 5505 (Reservations : 853 4051),
Fax 858 7387, ⌧ – 🛗 📺 ☎ ⓟ. 🗚 🗚 ⓞ 𝗩𝗜𝗦𝗔. ⌘   HV **e**
M (see above) – ⌑ 4.95 – **32 rm** ⌑ 39.00/74.00 **t.**

Eltham – ✉ SE9 – ☎ 081.

⌂ Yardley Court without rest., 18 Court Yard, SE9 5PZ, ☎ 850 1850, ⌧ – 📺 ⓟ   HX **e**
9 rm.

⌂ **Meadow Croft Lodge** without rest., 96-98 Southwood Rd, New Eltham, SE9 3QS,
☎ 859 1488, ⌧ – 📺 ⓟ. 🗚 𝗩𝗜𝗦𝗔. ⌘   JX **a**
17 rm ⌑ 21.00/42.00 **st.**

Greenwich – ✉ SE10 – ☎ 081.

🅱 46 Greenwich Church St., SE10 9BL ☎ 858 6376.

🏨 **Hamilton,** 14 West Grove, SE10 8QT, ☎ 694 9899, Fax 694 2370 – 🍽 📺 ☎ ⓟ. 🗚 🗚 ⓞ
𝗩𝗜𝗦𝗔. ⌘   GX **a**
M (lunch by arrangement Monday to Saturday)/dinner 16.00 **st.** and a la carte ⓙ 3.00 –
12 rm ⌑ 55.00/95.00 **st.**

XX **Treasure of China,** 10-11 Nelson Rd, SE10 9JB, ☎ 858 9884 – 🍽. 🗚 🗚 ⓞ 𝗩𝗜𝗦𝗔   GV **e**
M - **Chinese** (Peking, Szechuan) 8.00/25.00 **t.** and a la carte ⓙ 3.50.

X **Spread Eagle,** 1-2 Stockwell St., SE10 9JN, ☎ 853 2333 – 🗚 🗚 ⓞ 𝗩𝗜𝗦𝗔   GV **c**
closed Sunday dinner, 25 to 30 December and Bank Holiday Mondays – **M** (lunch by
arrangement Monday to Saturday)/dinner 13.50 **t.** and a la carte ⓙ 5.00.

X **Taste of India,** 57 Greenwich Church St., SE10 9BL, ☎ 858 2668 – 🗚 🗚 ⓞ 𝗩𝗜𝗦𝗔   GV **n**
M - **Indian** 15.00/20.00 **t.** and a la carte ⓙ 3.50.

HACKNEY – p.23.

Dalston – ✉ N 1 – ☎ 071.

X **Soulard,** 113 Mortimer Rd, N1 4JY, ☎ 254 1314 – 🗚 𝗩𝗜𝗦𝗔   PS **e**
closed Saturday lunch, Sunday, Monday, 3 weeks August and Christmas – **M** - **French** a la
carte approx. 15.50 **t.**

HAMMERSMITH and FULHAM Except where otherwise stated see pp. 24-25.

Fulham – ✉ SW6 – ☎ 071.

🏛 **La Reserve**, 422-428 Fulham Rd, SW6 1DU, ℰ 385 8561, Fax 385 7662, « Contemporary decor » – 📳 ⇔ rm 📺 ☎. ✕   FZ **a**
38 rm.

XX **Blue Elephant**, 4-6 Fulham Broadway, SW6 1AA, ℰ 385 6595, Fax 386 7665 – 🗉. 🆘 🆎 ① 𝗩𝗜𝗦𝗔   EZ **z**
closed Saturday lunch and 24 to 27 December – **M** - Thai (booking essential) 25.00/28.00 **t.** and a la carte ♦ 5.95.

XX **Mao Tai**, 58 New Kings Rd., Parsons Green, SW6 4UG, ℰ 731 2520 – 🗉. 🆘 🆎 𝗩𝗜𝗦𝗔
M - Chinese (Szechuan) 17.50 **t.** and a la carte ♦ 4.00.   p. 12 BQ **e**

XX **Nayab**, 309 New Kings Rd, SW6 4RF, ℰ 731 6993 – 🗉. 🆘 🆎 𝗩𝗜𝗦𝗔   p. 12 BQ **i**
closed lunch Saturday and Bank Holidays, 25-26 December and 1 January – **M** - Indian 10.00 **t.** (lunch) and a la carte 13.60/14.95 ♦ 4.60.

XX **Chin's**, 311-313 New Kings Rd, SW6 4RF, ℰ 736 8833 – 🗉. 🆘 🆎 𝗩𝗜𝗦𝗔
closed Saturday lunch – **M** - Chinese 19.00/30.00 **t.** and a la carte.   p. 12 BQ **n**

XX **Zen Experience**, 593-599 Fulham Rd, SW6 5UA, ℰ 385 7603, Fax 610 2423 – 🗉   EZ **e**
M - Oriental (dinner only and Sunday lunch).

X **Le Midi**, 488 Fulham Rd, SW6 5NH, ℰ 386 0657 – 🆘 🆎 𝗩𝗜𝗦𝗔   EZ **a**
closed Saturday lunch and Sunday dinner – **M** 7.50/10.50 **t.** and a la carte ♦ 4.00.

Hammersmith – ✉ W6/W12/W14 – ☎ 081.

XX **Tandoori Nights**, 319-321 King St., W6 9NH, ℰ 741 4328 – 🗉. 🆘 🆎 ① 𝗩𝗜𝗦𝗔 𝗝𝗖𝗕
closed 25 and 26 December – **M** - Indian 8.95/15.00 **t.** and a la carte ♦ 5.95.   p. 9 CV **u**

X **Snows on the Green**, 166 Shepherd's Bush Rd, Brook Green, W6 7PB, ℰ (071) 603 2142 – 🆘 𝗩𝗜𝗦𝗔   p. 9 CV **x**
closed Saturday lunch, Sunday dinner, Christmas-New Year and Bank Holidays – **M** 12.50 **t.** (lunch) and a la carte 13.95/22.45 **t.** ♦ 4.25.

X **Brackenbury**, 129-131 Brackenbury Rd, W6 0BQ, ℰ 748 0107 – 🆘 🆎 𝗩𝗜𝗦𝗔
closed Saturday and Monday lunch, Sunday dinner and 23 December-2 January – **M** a la carte 10.00/17.75 **t.** ♦ 4.00.   p. 9 CV **a**

Shepherd's Bush – ✉ W12/W14 – ☎ 071.

XX **Chinon**, 23 Richmond Way, W14 0AS, ℰ 602 4082 – 🗉. 🆘 🆎 𝗩𝗜𝗦𝗔   p. 9 DV **s**
closed lunch Saturday, Sunday and Bank Holidays – **M** - Terrace a la carte 15.00/32.00 **t.**

X **Wilsons**, 236 Blythe Rd, W14 0HJ, ℰ 603 7267 – 🆘 🆎 𝗩𝗜𝗦𝗔   DV **a**
M 10.00/ **st.** and a la carte.

West Kensington – ✉ SW6/W14 – ☎ 071.

🏠 **Aston Court** without rest., 25-27 Matheson Rd, W14 8SN, ℰ 602 9954, Fax 371 1338 – 📳 📺 ☎. 🆘 🆎 ① 𝗩𝗜𝗦𝗔. ✕   p. 24 EZ **i**
29 rm ⇌ 59.50/82.50 **st.**

HARINGEY pp. 6 and 7.

Crouch End – ✉ N 8 – ☎ 081.

XX **Les Associés**, 172 Park Rd, N8 8JY, ℰ 348 8944 – 🆘 𝗩𝗜𝗦𝗔   EU **e**
closed Saturday lunch, Sunday, Monday and August – **M** - French a la carte 22.55/26.80 **st.** ♦ 5.40.

X **Florians**, 4 Topsfield Par., Middle Lane, N8 8RP, ℰ 348 8348 – 🆘 𝗩𝗜𝗦𝗔   EU **c**
closed Christmas and Bank Holidays – **M** - Italian a la carte 15.55/21.50 **t.** ♦ 5.50.

Hornsey – ✉ N8 – ☎ 081.

X **Jashan**, 19a Turnpike Lane, N8 0EP, ℰ 340 9880, Fax 347 8770 – 🗉. 🆘 🆎 ① 𝗩𝗜𝗦𝗔 EU **z**
closed Monday – **M** - Indian (dinner only) 10.95 **t.** and a la carte ♦ 6.95.

HARROW pp. 4 and 5.

Central Harrow – ✉ Middx – ☎ 081.

🅱 Civic Centre, Station Rd, HA1 2UJ ℰ 424 1103/424 1100 BU.

🏛 **Cumberland**, 1 St. John's Rd, HA1 2EF, ℰ 863 4111, Fax 861 5668, ☞s – ⇔ rm 📺 ☎ 🅿 – 🔏 50. 🆘 🆎 ① 𝗩𝗜𝗦𝗔. ✕   BU **x**
M 9.95/14.50 **st.** and a la carte ♦ 4.50 – **81 rm** ⇌ 62.00/67.00 **st.**

XX **Trattoria Sorrentina**, 6 Manor Par., Sheepcote Rd, HA1 2JA, ℰ 427 9411 – 🆘 ① 𝗩𝗜𝗦𝗔
closed Saturday lunch and Bank Holidays and Sunday – **M** - Italian a la carte 22.25/27.50 **st.** ♦ 4.50.   BU **x**

Hatch End – ✉ Middx – ☎ 081.

XX **Swan**, 322-326 Uxbridge Rd, HA5 4HR, ℰ 428 8821 – 🗉. 🆘 🆎 ① 𝗩𝗜𝗦𝗔 𝗝𝗖𝗕   BT **n**
closed 25 and 26 December – **M** - Chinese (Peking) (buffet lunch Sunday) a la carte 9.80/29.35 **st.**

Kenton – ⊠ Middx. – ✆ 081.

🏨 **Travel Inn,** Kenton Rd, HA3 8AT, ✆ 907 1671, Fax 909 1604 – ⇌ rm 📺 ⅍ 🅿. 🔼 🆎 ⑩ 𝐕𝐈𝐒𝐀. ⅍
BU **e**
M (Beefeater grill) a la carte approx. 16.00 **t.** – ⇆ 4.95 – **44 rm** 33.50 **st.**

North Harrow – ⊠ Middx. – ✆ 081.

XX **Percy's,** 66-68 Station Rd, HA2 7SJ, ✆ 427 2021, Fax 427 8134 – ⇌. 🔼 🆎 ⑩ 𝐕𝐈𝐒𝐀
BU **n**
closed Saturday lunch, Sunday and Monday – **Meals** (booking essential) 15.00/20.00 **st.**
⅃ 5.50.

X **Thai Castle,** 28 The Broadwalk, Pinner Rd, HA2 6ED, ✆ 427 4732 – 🔼 𝐕𝐈𝐒𝐀
BU **c**
closed Saturday and Sunday lunch – **M** - Thai 25.00 **t.** (dinner) and a la carte 11.50/25.75 **t.**
⅃ 3.35.

Pinner – ⊠ Middx. – ✆ 081.

X **Friends,** 11 High St., HA5 5PJ, ✆ 866 0286 – 🔼 🆎 ⑩ 𝐕𝐈𝐒𝐀
BU **a**
closed Sunday dinner, 25-26 December and Bank Holidays – **M** 13.95/16.95 **t.** and a la carte
⅃ 6.25.

South Harrow – ⊠ Middx. – ✆ 081.

X **Jaflong,** 299 Northolt Rd, HA2 8JA, ✆ 864 7345 – 🍽
BU **r**
M - Indian 12.25 **t.** (dinner) and a la carte approx. 12.50 **t.**

Stanmore – ⊠ Middx – ✆ 081.

XX **Mr Tang's Mandarin** 28 The Broadway, HA7 4DW, ✆ 954 0339 – 🍽. 🔼 🆎 ⑩ 𝐕𝐈𝐒𝐀
M - Chinese (Peking) 20.00/30.00 **t.** and a la carte ⅃ 4.00.
BT **i**

Great Britain and Ireland is now covered
by an Atlas at a scale of 1 inch to 4.75 miles.

Three easy to use versions: Paperback, Spiralbound and Hardback.

HAVERING pp. 6 and 7.

Hornchurch by A 12 – JT – on A 127 – ⊠ Essex – ✆ 0708 Romford.

🏨 **Palms,** Southend Arterial Rd (A 127), RM11 3UJ, ✆ 346789, Fax 341719 – ⇌ rm 📺 ☎ ⅍
🅿 – 🔬 200. 🔼 🆎 ⑩ 𝐕𝐈𝐒𝐀
M *(closed Saturday lunch and Bank Holidays)* 16.00 **st.** and a la carte ⅃ 5.25 – ⇆ 5.50 –
137 rm 56.00 **st.**

Romford by A 118 – JU – ⊠ Essex – ✆ 0708.

🔟₈, 🔟₉ Havering, Risebridge Chase, Lower Bedfords Rd ✆ 41429 JT.

⌂ **Coach House,** 48 Main Rd, RM1 3DB, on A 118 ✆ 751901, Fax 730290, ⤧ – 📺 🅿. 🔼 🆎
⑩ 𝐕𝐈𝐒𝐀. ⅍
M (by arrangement) 20.00 **st.** ⅃ 4.95 – **32 rm** ⇆ 29.50/49.50 **t.**

HILLINGDON pp. 4 and 8.

🔟₈ Haste Hill, The Drive ✆ 092 74 (Northwood) 22877 AU – 🔟₈ Harefield Pl., The Drive ✆ 0895 (Uxbridge) 231169, by B 467 AU.

Eastcote – ⊠ Middx – ✆ 081.

🔟₈ Ruislip, Ickenham Rd ✆ 0895 (Ruislip) 632004 AU.
🅱 Central Library, 14 High St., Uxbridge, UB8 1HD ✆ 0895 (Uxbridge) 250706.

X **Sambuca,** 113 Field End Rd, HA5 1QG, ✆ 866 7500 – 🔼 🆎 ⑩ 𝐕𝐈𝐒𝐀 𝐉𝐂𝐁
AU **s**
closed Monday and Bank Holidays – **M** - Italian (dinner only and Sunday lunch)/
dinner 10.00 **t.** and a la carte ⅃ 3.70.

Hayes – ⊠ Middx. – ✆ 081.

🏨 **Travel Inn,** 362 Uxbridge Rd, UB4 0HF, ✆ 573 7479, Fax 569 1204 – ⇌ rm 📺 ⅍ 🅿. 🔼
🆎 ⑩ 𝐕𝐈𝐒𝐀. ⅍
AV **a**
M (Beefeater grill) a la carte approx. 16.00 **t.** – ⇆ 4.95 – **40 rm** 33.50 **t.**

Heathrow Airport – ⊠ Middx – ✆ 081.

🅱 Heathrow Terminals 1,2,3, Underground Station Concourse, TW6 2JA ✆ (071) 730 3488/824 8000 AX.

🏨🏨 **Edwardian International,** Bath Rd, Hayes, UB3 5AW, ✆ 759 6311, Telex 23935, Fax 759 4559, ⅃₆, ⇌, ☒, 🔲 – ⅃ ⇌ rm 🍽 📺 ☎ 🅿 – 🔬 320. 🔼 🆎 ⑩ 𝐕𝐈𝐒𝐀 𝐉𝐂𝐁
M 25.00/30.00 **st.** and a la carte – ⇆ 11.00 – **438 rm** 153.00/184.00 **st.**, 17 suites –
SB (weekends only) 98.00 **st.**
AX **e**

🏨🏨 **Sheraton Skyline,** Bath Rd, Hayes, UB3 5BP, ✆ 759 2535, Telex 934254, Fax 750 9150, « Exotic indoor garden », 🔲 – ⅃ ⇌ rm 🍽 📺 ☎ ⅍ 🅿 – 🔬 500. 🔼 🆎 ⑩ 𝐕𝐈𝐒𝐀 𝐉𝐂𝐁. ⅍
M (dancing Friday and Saturday evenings) (light lunch Saturday and Sunday) 18.50/ 35.00 **t.** and a la carte ⅃ 7.00 – ⇆ 12.50 – **344 rm** 130.00/170.00 **st.**, 5 suites.
AX **u**

🏠🏠 **Excelsior Heathrow** (Forte), Bath Rd, West Drayton, UB7 0DU, ℰ 759 6611, Telex 24525, Fax 759 3421, ℄, ⌁, ▭ – ▯ ⇄ rm ▤ 🖵 🕿 🕹 🄿 – 🔬 700. ◪ ◭ ⑩ 𝘝𝘐𝘚𝘈 𝙅𝘾𝘽
M 15.50/16.50 **st.** and a la carte ᵶ 6.95 – **Wheelers** (closed Saturday and Sunday lunch) a la carte 18.95/31.40 **st.** ᵶ 6.95 – ⌑ 10.95 – **823 rm** 85.00/130.00 **st.**, 16 suites – SB (weekends only) 118.00/166.00 **st.**
AX **x**

🏠🏠 **London Heathrow Hilton**, Terminal 4, TW6 3AF, ℰ 759 7755, Telex 925094, Fax 759 7579, ℄, ⌁, ▭ – ▯ ⇄ rm ▤ 🖵 🕿 🕹 🄿 – 🔬 240. ◪ ◭ ⑩ 𝘝𝘐𝘚𝘈 𝙅𝘾𝘽 ⁓
M 16.95 **st.** and a la carte ᵶ 6.95 – ⌑ 10.95 – **391 rm** 135.00/145.00 **st.**, 4 suites – SB (weekends only) 106.00 **st.**
AX **n**

🏠🏠 **Holiday Inn Crowne Plaza**, Stockley Rd, West Drayton, UB7 9NA, ℰ 0895 (West Drayton) 445555, Fax 445122, ℄, ⌁, ▭, ▯⃠ – ▯ ⇄ rm ▤ 🖵 🕿 🕹 🄿 – 🔬 150. ◪ ◭ ⑩
𝘝𝘐𝘚𝘈
AV **v**
M 17.50/23.50 **st.** and a la carte – ⌑ 10.95 – **372 rm** 130.00/150.00 **st.**, 2 suites – SB (weekends only) 122.00/192.00 **st.**

🏠🏠 **Forte Crest**, Sipson Rd, West Drayton, UB7 0JU, ℰ 759 2323, Telex 934280, Fax 897 8659 – ▯ ⇄ rm ▤ 🖵 🕿 🄿 – 🔬 200. ◪ ◭ 𝘝𝘐𝘚𝘈
AV **c**
M 17.00/21.95 **st.** and a la carte ᵶ 8.00 – ⌑ 9.95 – **570 rm** 99.00 **st.**, 2 suites – SB (weekends only) 149.00/170.00 **st.**

🏠🏠 **Sheraton Heathrow**, Colnbrook by-pass, West Drayton, UB7 0HJ, ℰ 759 2424, Telex 934331, Fax 759 2091 – ▯ ⇄ rm ▤ 🖵 🕿 🄿 – 🔬 70. ◪ ◭ ⑩ 𝘝𝘐𝘚𝘈 𝙅𝘾𝘽 ⁓ AVX **a**
M 20.00/30.00 **t.** and a la carte ᵶ 6.00 – ⌑ 10.00 – **414 rm** 110.00/160.00 **st.**, 1 suite.

🏠🏠 **Novotel**, Cherry Lane, West Drayton, UB7 9HB, ℰ 0895 (West Drayton) 431431, Fax 431221, ℄, ▭ – ▯ ⇄ rm ▤ rest 🖵 🕿 🕹 🄿 – 🔬 200. ◪ ◭ ⑩ 𝘝𝘐𝘚𝘈 AV **n**
M (bar lunch Saturday and Sunday) 12.50/15.00 **st.** and a la carte ᵶ 5.95 – ⌑ 7.95 – **178 rm** 69.50/99.50 **st.**

🏠🏠 **Heathrow Park** (Mt. Charlotte Thistle), Bath Rd, Longford, West Drayton, UB7 0EQ, ℰ 759 2400, Telex 934093, Fax 759 5278 – ⇄ rm ▤ 🖵 🕿 🄿 – 🔬 650. ◪ ◭ ⑩ 𝘝𝘐𝘚𝘈 𝙅𝘾𝘽
M (carving lunch) 11.75/15.25 **st.** and a la carte ᵶ 5.50 – ⌑ 7.75 – **306 rm** 80.00/125.00 **st.** – SB (weekends only) 90.50/170.50 **st.**
off A4 AX

🏠 **Forte Posthouse**, Bath Rd, Hayes, UB3 5AJ, ℰ 759 2552, Fax 564 9265 – ▯ ⇄ rm ▤ 🖵 🕿 🄿 – 🔬 40. ◪ ◭ ⑩ 𝘝𝘐𝘚𝘈 𝙅𝘾𝘽
AX **i**
M a la carte approx. 17.50 **t.** ᵶ 4.65 – ⌑ 6.95 – **175 rm** 53.50/69.50 **st.** – SB (weekends only) 90.00 **st.**

Ickenham – ✉ Middx. – 🕿 0895 Ruislip

✗ **Roberto's**, 15 Long Lane, UB10 8TB, ℰ 632519 – ▤. ◪ ◭ ⑩ 𝘝𝘐𝘚𝘈 𝙅𝘾𝘽 AU **i**
closed Sunday – **M** - **Italian** a la carte 17.00/26.50 ᵶ 5.50.

HOUNSLOW pp. 8 and 9.

🏌 Wyke Green, Syon Lane, Isleworth ℰ (081) 560 8777, ½ m. from Gillettes Corner (A 4) BV –
🏌 Airlinks, Southall Lane ℰ 561 1418 ABV – 🏌 Hounslow Heath, Staines Rd ℰ 570 5271 BX.
🛈 24 The Treaty Centre, Hounslow High St., TW3 1ES ℰ 572 8279.

Chiswick – ✉ W4 – 🕿 081.

✗ **La Dordogne**, 5 Devonshire Rd, W4 2EU, ℰ 747 1836, Fax 994 9144 – ◪ ◭ ⑩ 𝘝𝘐𝘚𝘈
closed Saturday and Sunday lunch and Bank Holidays – **M** - **French** a la carte 17.40/26.70 **t.** ᵶ 4.60.
CV **o**

Cranford – ✉ Middx. – 🕿 081.

🏠 **Berkeley Arms** (Jarvis), Bath Rd, TW5 9QE, ℰ 897 2121, Telex 935728, Fax 897 7014, ⤢ – ▯ ⇄ rm 🖵 🕿 🄿 – 🔬 80. ◪ ◭ ⑩ 𝘝𝘐𝘚𝘈. ⁓ AX **r**
M (closed Saturday lunch) 15.95 **st.** and a la carte ᵶ 6.50 – ⌑ 8.00 – **56 rm** 79.00/104.00 **st.**

Heston Service Area – ✉ Middx. – 🕿 081.

🏠 **Granada Lodge** without rest., TW5 9NA, on M 4 (westbound carriageway) ℰ 574 5875, Fax 574 1891, Reservations (Freephone) 0800 555300 – ⇄ 🖵 🕹 🄿. ◪ ◭ 𝘝𝘐𝘚𝘈 ABV **e**
⌑ 4.00 – **46 rm** 43.95/46.95 **st.**

ISLINGTON Except where otherwise stated see pp. 20-23.

Canonbury – ✉ N1 – 🕿 071.

✗ **Anna's Place**, 90 Mildmay Park, N1 4PR, ℰ 249 9379 p. 6 FU **a**
closed Sunday, Monday, 2 weeks Easter, August and 2 weeks Christmas – **M** - **Swedish** (booking essential) a la carte 14.70/19.15 **t.**

Finsbury – ✉ WC1/EC1/EC2 – 🕿 071.

✗ **Stephen Bull's Bistro**, 71 St. John St., EC1M 4AN, ℰ 490 1750 – ▤. ◪ ◭ 𝘝𝘐𝘚𝘈 NU **r**
closed Saturday lunch, Sunday, 1 week Christmas and Bank Holidays – **M** a la carte 14.50/20.00 **t.** ᵶ 4.50.

✗ **Le Mesurier**, 113 Old St., EC1V 9JR, ℰ 251 8117 – ◪ ◭ ⑩ 𝘝𝘐𝘚𝘈 𝙅𝘾𝘽 OT **e**
closed Saturday, Sunday, 3 weeks August, 2 weeks Christmas-New Year and Bank Holidays – **M** (lunch only) (booking essential) a la carte 17.00/23.50 **t.** ᵶ 4.50.

X **Rouxl Britannia,** Triton Court, 14 Finsbury Sq., EC2A 1BR, *𝒫* 256 6997 – 🔄 ⓪ 𝗩𝗜𝗦𝗔
M – **Le Restaurant** *(closed Saturday, Sunday and Bank Holidays)* (lunch only) 19.85 **st.**
↓ 5.75 – **Le Café** *(closed Saturday, Sunday and* Bank Holidays) (lunch only) a la carte
12.40/17.35 **st.** ↓ 5.50.   PU **x**

X **Quality Chop House,** 94 Farringdon Rd, EC1R 3EA, *𝒫* 837 5093   MT **n**
closed Saturday lunch and Christmas-New Year – **M** a la carte 12.25/23.50 **t.**

Islington – ✉ N1 – ☎ 071.

X **Neshiko,** 265 Upper St., N1 2UQ, *𝒫* 359 9977, Fax 226 8863   NS **c**
M - Japanese rest.

X **Mon Plaisir du Nord,** The Mall, 359 Upper St., N1 0PD, *𝒫* 359 1932, Fax 704 2984 – 🖿
M - French rest.   NS **a**

KENSINGTON and CHELSEA (Royal Borough of).

Chelsea – ✉ SW1/SW3/SW10 – ☎ 071 – Except where otherwise stated see pp. 30
and 31.

🏨🏨 **Hyatt Carlton Tower,** 2 Cadogan Pl., SW1X 9PY, *𝒫* 235 5411, Telex 21944,
Fax 245 6570, ≼, ↓₅, ≋s, ☞, ※ – 🛗 ↳≠ rm 🖿 📺 ☎ ⇦ – 🔬 260. 🔄 🄰🄴 ⓪ 𝗩𝗜𝗦𝗔 𝗝𝗖𝗕
※   FR **u**
M – **Chelsea Room** 21.50/29.00 **t.** and a la carte ↓ 7.00 – **Rib Room** *(closed 1 to 3 January)*
21.50/29.00 **t.** and a la carte ↓ 7.00 – ⍽ 13.50 – **194 rm** 210.00/240.00 **s.**, 30 suites.

🏨🏨 **Sheraton Park Tower,** 101 Knightsbridge, SW1X 7RN, *𝒫* 235 8050, Telex 917222,
Fax 235 8231, ≼ – 🛗 ↳≠ rm 🖿 📺 ☎ ↔ 🄿 – 🔬 80. 🔄 🄰🄴 ⓪ 𝗩𝗜𝗦𝗔 𝗝𝗖𝗕 ※   FQ **v**
M 14.50 **t.** (lunch) and a la carte 16.00/28.00 **t.** ↓ 7.50 – ⍽ 14.05 – **267 rm** 195.00/290.00 **s.**,
22 suites.

🏨🏨 **Conrad Chelsea Harbour,** Chelsea Harbour, SW10 0XG, *𝒫* 823 3000, Telex 919222,
Fax 351 6525, ≼, ↓₅, ≋s, 🔳 – 🛗 ↳≠ rm 🖿 📺 ☎ ↔ 🄿 – 🔬 180   p. 13 CQ **i**
160 suites.

🏨🏨 **Durley House,** 115 Sloane St., SW1X 9PJ, *𝒫* 235 5537, Fax 259 6977, « Tastefully
furnished Georgian town house », ☞, ※ – 🛗 📺 ☎. 🔄 🄰🄴 𝗩𝗜𝗦𝗔, ※   FS **e**
M (room service only) a la carte – ⍽ 12.50 – **11 suites** 195.00/300.00 **t.**

🏨🏨 ☺ **Capital,** 22-24 Basil St., SW3 1AT, *𝒫* 589 5171, Fax 225 0011 – 🛗 🖿 📺 ☎ – 🔬 25. 🔄
🄰🄴 ⓪ 𝗩𝗜𝗦𝗔. ※   ER **a**
M 25.00/37.50 **st.** and a la carte 38.50/40.85 **st.** – ⍽ 12.50 – **48 rm** 149.00/250.00 **s.**
Spec. Sole and tomato soufflé, onion soubise, Pot roasted chicken, thyme and Riesling served with a liver risotto, Tarte
tatin of pears, cinnamon crème fraîche and Poire William sorbet.

🏨🏨 **The Franklin,** 28 Egerton Gdns., SW3 2DB, *𝒫* 584 5533, Fax 584 5449, ☞ – 🛗 🖿 📺 ☎
🄿. 🔄 🄰🄴 ⓪ 𝗩𝗜𝗦𝗔 𝗝𝗖𝗕. ※   DS **e**
M (room service only) 15.00 **st.** – ⍽ 12.50 – **36 rm** 110.00/210.00 **s.**, 1 suite.

🏨🏨 **Draycott,** 24-26 Cadogan Gdns, SW3 2RP, *𝒫* 730 6466, Fax 730 0236, ↓₅, ≋s, ☞, ※ –
🛗 📺 ☎. 🔄 🄰🄴 ⓪ 𝗩𝗜𝗦𝗔 𝗝𝗖𝗕. ※   FS **c**
M (room service only) – ⍽ 10.95 – **25 rm** 100.00/250.00 **t.**

🏨🏨 **Chelsea,** 17-25 Sloane St., SW1X 9NU, *𝒫* 235 4377, Telex 919111, Fax 235 3705 – 🛗
↳≠ rm 🖿 📺 ☎ – 🔬 120. 🔄 🄰🄴 ⓪ 𝗩𝗜𝗦𝗔 𝗝𝗖𝗕. ※   FR **r**
M 12.50 **st.** and a la carte ↓ 6.00 – ⍽ 9.50 – **219 rm** 99.00/130.00 **st.**, 6 suites – SB (weekends only) 110.00/150.00 **st.**

🏨🏨 **Cadogan,** 75 Sloane St., SW1X 9SG, *𝒫* 235 7141, Telex 267893, Fax 245 0994, ☞, ※ –
🛗 ↳≠ rm 🖿 rest 📺 ☎ – 🔬 30. 🔄 🄰🄴 ⓪ 𝗩𝗜𝗦𝗔. ※   FR **e**
M *(closed Saturday lunch)* 16.50/19.90 **t.** and dinner a la carte ↓ 6.25 – ⍽ 12.50 – **60 rm**
125.00/165.00 **st.**, 5 suites – SB 130.00/260.00 **st.**

🏨🏨 **Basil Street,** 8 Basil St., SW3 1AH, *𝒫* 581 3311, Telex 28379, Fax 581 3693 – 🛗 📺 ☎ –
🔬 55. 🔄 🄰🄴 ⓪ 𝗩𝗜𝗦𝗔   FQ **o**
M (carving lunch Saturday) 14.95/19.75 **t.** and a la carte ↓ 5.25 – ⍽ 10.60 – **91 rm**
110.50/156.50 **t.**, 1 suite.

🏨 **Egerton House,** 17-19 Egerton Terr., SW3 2BX, *𝒫* 589 2412, Fax 584 6540, ☞ – 🛗 🖿 📺
☎ 🄿. 🔄 🄰🄴 ⓪ 𝗩𝗜𝗦𝗔. ※   DR **e**
M (room service only) a la carte 19.50/37.00 **st.** ↓ 7.00 – ⍽ 12.50 – **27 rm** 95.00/160.00 **s.**,
1 suite.

🏨 **Fenja** without rest., 69 Cadogan Gdns, SW3 2RB, *𝒫* 589 7333, Fax 581 4958 – 🛗 📺 ☎. 🔄
🄰🄴 ⓪ 𝗩𝗜𝗦𝗔. ※   FS **r**
⍽ 12.15 – **13 rm** 97.75/195.00 **st.**

🏨 **Sloane,** 29 Draycott Pl., SW3 2SH, *𝒫* 581 5757, Fax 584 1348, « Victorian town house,
antiques » – 🛗 🖿 📺 ☎. 🔄 🄰🄴 ⓪ 𝗩𝗜𝗦𝗔. ※   ET **c**
M (room service only) 20.00 – ⍽ 12.50 – **12 rm** 120.00/170.00.

🏨 **Sydney House,** 9-11 Sydney St., SW3 6PU, *𝒫* 376 7711, Fax 376 4233 – 🛗 📺 ☎. 🔄 🄰🄴
⓪ 𝗩𝗜𝗦𝗔   DT **a**
M (room service only) – ⍽ 9.50 – **21 rm** 90.00/195.00 **s.**

🏨 **Beaufort** without rest., 33 Beaufort Gdns, SW3 1PP, *𝒫* 584 5252, Telex 929200,
Fax 589 2834, « English floral watercolour collection » – 🛗 🖿 📺 ☎. 🔄 🄰🄴 ⓪ 𝗩𝗜𝗦𝗔 𝗝𝗖𝗕.
※   ER **n**
closed 22 to 29 December – **28 rm** 110.00/250.00 **st.**

🏥 **Royal Court,** Sloane Sq., SW1W 8EG, ☎ 730 9191, Telex 296818, Fax 824 8381 – 📶
🍽 rest 📺 ☎ – 🔧 40. 🔼 🆎 ⓞ 𝘝𝘐𝘚𝘈   FST **a**
closed 24 to 26 December – **M** *(closed Saturday lunch)* 12.50/18.50 **t.** and a la carte 🍴 6.50 –
🍴 9.25 – **102 rm** 115.00/160.00 **st.** – SB (weekends only) 195.00/320.00 **st.**

🏥 **Eleven Cadogan Gardens,** 11 Cadogan Gdns, SW3 2RJ, ☎ 730 3426, Telex 8813318,
Fax 730 5217 – 📶 📺 ☎. 🔼 🆎 ⓞ 𝘝𝘐𝘚𝘈   FS **u**
M (room service only) – 🍴 10.00 – **57 rm** 89.00/172.00 **st.**, 5 suites.

🏥 **Claverley** without rest., 13-14 Beaufort Gdns, SW3 1PS, ☎ 589 8541, Fax 584 3410 – 📶
⛌ 📺 ☎. 🔼 🆎 𝘝𝘐𝘚𝘈. ⌘   ER **o**
31 rm 🍴 50.00/175.00 **st.**

🏥 **L'Hotel** without rest., 28 Basil St., SW3 1AT, ☎ 589 6286, Telex 919042, Fax 225 0011 – 📶
📺 ☎. 🔼 🆎 ⓞ 𝘝𝘐𝘚𝘈. ⌘   ER **i**
🍴 4.00 – **12 rm** 125.00/145.00 **st.**

🏥 **Wilbraham,** 1-5 Wilbraham Pl., Sloane St., SW1X 9AE, ☎ 730 8296, Fax 730 6815 – 📶
☎. ⌘   FS **n**
M *(closed Saturday lunch, Sunday and Bank Holidays)* (restricted menu) a la carte 8.70/
17.45 **t.** 🍴 3.50 – 🍴 5.50 – **53 rm** 36.50/78.00.

🍴🍴🍴🍴 ✿✿✿ **La Tante Claire** (Koffmann), 68-69 Royal Hospital Rd, SW3 4HP, ☎ 352 6045,
Fax 352 3257 – 🍽. 🔼 🆎 ⓞ 𝘝𝘐𝘚𝘈   EU **c**
closed Saturday, Sunday, last 2 weeks August, Christmas, New Year and Bank Holidays –
M - French (booking essential) 25.00 **st.** (lunch) and a la carte 50.00/55.00 **st.** 🍴 9.40
Spec. Coquilles St. Jacques à la planche, sauce encre. Tranche de saumon confit à la graisse d'oie, Pied de cochon
farci aux morilles et ris de veau.

🍴🍴🍴 **Waltons,** 121 Walton St., SW3 2HP, ☎ 584 0204 – 🍽. 🔼 🆎 ⓞ 𝘝𝘐𝘚𝘈 𝗝𝗖𝗕   DS **a**
M 14.75/21.00 **t.** and a la carte 🍴 4.50.

🍴🍴🍴 **Bibendum,** Michelin House, 81 Fulham Rd, SW3 6RD, ☎ 581 5817, Fax 823 7925 – 🍽. 🔼
🆎 𝘝𝘐𝘚𝘈   DS **s**
closed Easter Monday and 24 to 28 December – **Meals** 25.00 **t.** (lunch) and dinner a la
carte 22.75/45.50 **t.** 🍴 5.95.

🍴🍴🍴 ✿ **The Canteen,** Harbour Yard, Chelsea Harbour, SW10 0XL, ☎ 351 7330, Fax 351 6189
– 🍽. 🔼 𝘝𝘐𝘚𝘈   CQ **i**
M a la carte 21.95/25.50 **t.**
Spec. Roast scallops, sauce vièrge. Wood pigeon, confit of garlic and thyme sauce. Tarte tatin.

🍴🍴🍴 **Aubergine,** 11 Park walk, SW10 0AJ, ☎ 352 3449 – 🍽. 🔼 🆎 ⓞ 𝘝𝘐𝘚𝘈   CU **r**
closed Saturday lunch, Sunday, first 2 weeks August and Bank Holidays – **M** (booking
essential) 18.50 **t.**

🍴🍴🍴 **Fifth Floor** (at Harvey Nichols), Knightsbridge, SW1X 7RJ, ☎ 235 5250, Fax 235 5020 –
🍽. 🔼 🆎 𝘝𝘐𝘚𝘈 𝗝𝗖𝗕   FQ **a**
closed Sunday – **Meals** 19.50 **t.** and dinner a la carte.

🍴🍴🍴 **Turner's,** 87-89 Walton St., SW3 2HP, ☎ 584 6711, Fax 584 4441 – 🍽. 🔼 🆎 ⓞ
𝘝𝘐𝘚𝘈   ES **n**
closed Saturday lunch, 25 to 30 December and Bank Holidays – **M** 13.50/29.50 **st.** and a la
carte.

🍴🍴🍴 **Chutney Mary,** 535 King's Rd, SW10 0SZ, ☎ 351 3113, Fax 351 7694 – 🍽. 🔼 🆎 ⓞ 𝘝𝘐𝘚𝘈
𝗝𝗖𝗕   p. 24 FZ **v**
Meals - Anglo-Indian 10.00/25.00 **t.** and a la carte 17.00/24.90 **t.** 🍴 4.50.

🍴🍴🍴 **Albero and Grana,** Chelsea Cloisters, Sloane Av., SW3 3DW, ☎ 225 1048, Fax 581 3259
– 🍽. 🔼 🆎 ⓞ 𝘝𝘐𝘚𝘈 𝗝𝗖𝗕   ET **e**
M - Spanish (dinner only) a la carte 21.00/32.00 **t.** 🍴 4.25.

🍴🍴🍴 **Zen,** Chelsea Cloisters, Sloane Av., SW3 3DW, ☎ 589 1781 – 🍽. 🔼 🆎 ⓞ 𝘝𝘐𝘚𝘈   ET **a**
closed Christmas Day – **M** - Chinese a la carte 16.50/66.00 **t.**

🍴🍴 **Argyll,** 316 King's Rd, SW3 5UH, ☎ 352 0025, Fax 352 1652 – 🍽. 🔼 🆎 ⓞ 𝘝𝘐𝘚𝘈
closed Monday lunch, Sunday and Bank Holidays – **M** 10.00 **t.** (lunch) and dinner a la
carte 23.00/30.00 **t.** 🍴 6.50.   CU **e**

🍴🍴 **La Finezza,** 62-64 Lower Sloane St., SW1N 8BP, ☎ 730 8639 – 🍽. 🔼 🆎 ⓞ 𝘝𝘐𝘚𝘈
closed Sunday and Bank Holidays – **M** - Italian a la carte 21.00/41.50 🍴 7.00.   FT **v**

🍴🍴 **English Garden,** 10 Lincoln St., SW3 2TS, ☎ 584 7272 – 🍽. 🔼 🆎 ⓞ 𝘝𝘐𝘚𝘈 𝗝𝗖𝗕   ET **x**
closed 25 and 26 December – **M** - English 14.75 **t.** (lunch) and a la carte 18.50/30.75 **t.**
🍴 4.50.

🍴🍴 **Gavvers,** 61-63 Lower Sloane St., SW1W 8DH, ☎ 730 5983 – 🍽. 🔼 ⓞ 𝘝𝘐𝘚𝘈   FT **e**
closed Saturday lunch, Sunday, 2 April, 1 week Christmas and Bank Holidays – **M** - French
14.75/19.75 **st.** and a la carte 🍴 5.80.

🍴🍴 **St. Quentin,** 243 Brompton Rd, SW3 2EP, ☎ 589 8005, Fax 584 6064 – 🍽. 🔼 🆎 ⓞ 𝘝𝘐𝘚𝘈
𝗝𝗖𝗕   DR **a**
M - French 10.50/17.00 **t.** and a la carte.

🍴🍴 **Poissonnerie de l'Avenue,** 82 Sloane Av., SW3 3DZ, ☎ 589 2457, Fax 581 3360 – 🍽.
🔼 🆎 ⓞ 𝘝𝘐𝘚𝘈 𝗝𝗖𝗕   DS **u**
closed Sunday, 10 days at Christmas and Bank Holidays – **M** - French Seafood a la
carte 17.00/28.50 **t.** 🍴 5.50.

XX **Busabong Too,** 1a Langton St., SW10 0JL, ✆ 352 7517 – ☰. 🔅 AE ⑩ VISA
closed 24-25 December and 1 January – **M** - **Thai** (dinner only) 24.95 **t.** and a la carte.
p. 24 FZ **x**

XX **Toto's,** Walton House, Walton St., SW3 2JH, ✆ 589 0075 – 🔅 AE ⑩ VISA JCB ES **a**
closed 25 and 26 December – **M** - **Italian** 12.50 **st.** (lunch) and a la carte 23.00/35.00 **st.**

XX **Good Earth,** 233 Brompton Rd, SW3 2EP, ✆ 584 3658, Fax 823 8769 – ☰. 🔅 AE ⑩ VISA
JCB DR **c**
closed 24 to 27 December – **M** - **Chinese** 11.50/30.00 **t.** and a la carte ⓙ 4.00.

XX **Penang,** 294 Fulham Rd, SW10 9EW, ✆ 351 2599 – ☰. 🔅 AE ⑩ VISA BU **e**
closed Christmas – **M** - **Malaysian** (dinner only) 15.00 **t.** and a la carte ⓙ 4.00.

XX **Sandrini,** 260-262a Brompton Rd, SW3 2AS, ✆ 584 1724 – 🔅 AE ⑩ VISA DS **n**
M - **Italian** a la carte 20.00/35.40 **t.** ⓙ 6.40.

XX **Dan's,** 119 Sydney St., SW3 6NR, ✆ 352 2718, Fax 352 3265 – 🔅 AE ⑩ VISA
closed Saturday lunch, Sunday and 25 December-2 January – **M** 12.50/16.50 **t.** and a la
carte ⓙ 5.00.
p. 24 DU **s**

X **Thierry's,** 342 King's Rd, SW3 5UR, ✆ 352 3365 – ☰. 🔅 AE ⑩ VISA CU **c**
closed Christmas – **M** 15.00/25.00 **t.** and a la carte ⓙ 5.50.

X The Wilds, 356 Fulham Rd, SW10 9UH, ✆ 376 5553, Fax 376 7658 – ☰ FZ **z**

X **Monkey's,** 1 Cale St., Chelsea Green, SW3 3QT, ✆ 352 4711 – ☰. 🔅 VISA ET **z**
closed Saturday, Sunday. 2 weeks Easter and 3 weeks August – **M** 17.50/22.50 **t.** and a la
carte ⓙ 5.50.

X **Ziani,** 45-47 Radnor Walk, SW3 4BP, ✆ 351 5297, Fax 244 8387 – 🔅 AE EU **e**
closed Bank Holidays – **M** - **Italian** a la carte 10.00/25.00 **t.** ⓙ 5.45.

X Beit Eddine, 8 Harriet St., SW1 9JW, ✆ 235 3969 FQ **z**
M - Lebanese rest.

Earl's Court – ✉ SW5/SW10 – ☎ 071 – Except where otherwise stated see pp. 30
and 31.

🏨 **Comfort Inn** without rest., 22-32 West Cromwell Rd, SW5 9QJ, ✆ 373 3300,
Fax 835 2040 – ▯ ⇖⇆ ☰ 📺 ☎ – 🔏 80. 🔅 AE ⑩ VISA JCB EZ **n**
⌕ 8.50 – **126 rm** 49.50/69.50 **st.**

🏨 **Rushmore** without rest., 11 Trebovir Rd, SW5 9LS, ✆ 370 3839, Fax 370 0274 – 📺 ☎. 🔅
AE ⑩ VISA JCB p. 24 EZ **c**
22 rm 45.00/85.00 **st.**

🏨 **Amsterdam** without rest., 7 Trebovir Rd, SW5 9LS, ✆ 370 2814, Fax 244 7608 – ▯ 📺 ☎.
🔅 AE VISA JCB. ⋇ p. 24 EZ **c**
20 rm 39.00/60.00 **st.**

XX **Formula Veneta,** 14 Hollywood Rd, SW10 9HY, ✆ 352 7612 – ☰. 🔅 AE VISA BU **a**
closed Sunday dinner and Bank Holidays – **M** - **Italian** 9.95 **t.** (lunch) and a la carte 14.80/
26.60 **t.** ⓙ 4.00.

XX **Mr Wing,** 242-244 Old Brompton Rd, SW5 0DE, ✆ 370 4450 – 🔅 AE ⑩ VISA JCB AU **a**
closed 25 and 26 December – **M** - **Chinese** 20.00/35.00 **t.** and a la carte.

XX **La Primula,** 12 Kenway Rd, SW5 0RR, ✆ 370 5958 – ☰. 🔅 AE ⑩ VISA p. 24 FZ **e**
M - **Italian** 8.50/14.50 **st.** and a la carte.

Kensington – ✉ SW7/W8/W11/W14 – ☎ 071 – Except where otherwise stated see
pp. 24-27.

🏨🏨 **The Milestone,** 1-2 Kensington Court, W8 5DL, ✆ 917 1000, Telex 290404, Fax 917 1010,
ƒ₆, ⇎ – ▯ ☰ 📺 ☎. 🔅 AE ⑩ VISA JCB. ⋇ AQ **i**
M – **Chenestons** 15.50/18.50 **t.** and a la carte ⓙ 5.50 – ⌕ 13.50 – **50 rm** 180.00/210.00 **st.**,
6 suites – SB (weekends only) 204.00/314.00 **st.**

🏨🏨 **Halcyon,** 81 Holland Park, W11 3RZ, ✆ 727 7288, Telex 266721, Fax 229 8516 – ▯ ☰ 📺
☎. 🔅 AE ⑩ VISA JCB. ⋇ EX **u**
M – **The Room** (*closed Saturday lunch*) 12.95 **t.** (lunch) and a la carte 21.00/28.00 **t.** –
⌕ 12.00 – **40 rm** 165.00/235.00 **st.**, 3 suites – SB (weekends only) 310.00 **st.**

🏨🏨 **Copthorne Tara,** Scarsdale Pl., W8 5SR, ✆ 937 7211, Telex 918834, Fax 937 7100 – ▯
⇖⇆ rm ☰ 📺 ☎ ⓖ ⓟ – 🔏 500. 🔅 AE ⑩ VISA JCB. ⋇ FY **u**
M 12.50/15.00 **st.** and a la carte ⓙ 5.95 – ⌕ 10.45 – **817 rm** 105.00/140.00 **st.**, 8 suites –
SB (weekends only) 111.50/301.00 **st.**

🏨🏨 **Kensington Park** (Mt. Charlotte Thistle), 16-32 De Vere Gdns, W8 5AG, ✆ 937 8080,
Telex 929643, Fax 937 7616 – ▯ ⇖⇆ rm ☰ rest 📺 ☎ ⓖ – 🔏 120. 🔅 AE ⑩ VISA
⋇ p. 30 BQ **e**
M 15.70 **st.** and a la carte ⓙ 6.40 – ⌕ 10.25 – **325 rm** 105.00/165.00 **st.**, 7 suites –
SB 135.40/215.40 **st.**

🏨🏨 **London Kensington Hilton,** 179-199 Holland Park Av., W11 4UL, ✆ 603 3355, Telex
919763, Fax 602 9397 – ▯ ⇖⇆ rm ☰ 📺 ☎ ⓖ ⓟ – 🔏 200. 🔅 AE ⑩ VISA JCB EX **s**
M (carving lunch) 12.50/17.95 **st.** and a la carte ⓙ 7.00 – **Hiroko** - **Japanese** – ⌕ 12.50 –
596 rm 99.00/155.00 **st.**, 7 suites – SB (weekends only) 130.00/190.00 **st.**

ᐃᐃ **Kensington Palace Thistle** (Mt. Charlotte Thistle), 8 De Vere Gdns, W8 5AF, ℰ 937 8121, Telex 262422, Fax 937 2816 – |☆| ✵ rm ▤ rest ▦ ☎ – ♨ 180. ◪ ᴀᴇ ⓞ ᴠɪꜱᴀ ᴊᴄʙ
p. 30 BQ **a**
M 10.50/10.95 **st.** and a la carte ⑧ 5.60 – ⬭ 10.25 – **297 rm** 85.00/95.00 **st.**, 1 suite – SB 105.50/121.90 **st.**

ᐃᐃ **Kensington Close** (Forte), Wrights Lane, W8 5SP, ℰ 937 8170, Fax 937 8289, ⅙₅, ☎, ◪, ☞, squash – |☆| ✵ rm ▤ rest ▦ ☎ Ⓟ – ♨ 150. ◪ ᴀᴇ ⓞ ᴠɪꜱᴀ. ✻
FY **c**
M 14.95/15.95 **st.** and a la carte ⑧ 6.50 – ⬭ 8.75 – **530 rm** 99.00 **st.** – SB (weekends only) 108.00 **st.**

ᐧ **Holland Court** without rest., 31 Holland Rd, W14 8HJ, ℰ 371 1133, Fax 602 9114, ☞ – |☆|
▦ ☎. ◪ ᴀᴇ ⓞ ᴠɪꜱᴀ. ✻
EY **c**
22 rm ⬭ 65.00/100.00 **st.**

ᐧ **Russell Court** without rest., 9 Russell Rd, W14 8JA, ℰ 603 1222, Fax 371 2286 – |☆| ▦ ☎.
◪ ᴀᴇ ⓞ ᴠɪꜱᴀ. ✻
EY **v**
⬭ 4.95 – **18 rm** 49.00/69.50 **st.**

ᕽᕽᕽ **Belvedere in Holland Park**, Holland House, off Abbotsbury Rd, W8 6LU, ℰ 602 1238, « 19C orangery in park » – ▤. ◪ ᴀᴇ ⓞ ᴠɪꜱᴀ ᴊᴄʙ
EY **u**
closed Sunday dinner, 25 December and 1 January – **M** a la carte 17.50/25.50 **t.**

ᕽᕽ **Clarke's**, 124 Kensington Church St., W8 4BH, ℰ 221 9225, Fax 229 4564 – ▤. ◪ ᴠɪꜱᴀ
closed Saturday, Sunday, Easter, 2 weeks summer, Christmas-New Year and Bank Holidays
EX **c**
– Meals 26.00/37.00 **st.**

ᕽᕽ **La Pomme d'Amour**, 128 Holland Park Av., W11 4UE, ℰ 229 8532 – ▤. ◪ ᴀᴇ
closed Saturday lunch, Sunday and Bank Holidays – **M** - **French** 12.50/16.75 **t.** and a la carte
⑧ 4.50.
EX **e**

ᕽᕽ **L'Escargot Doré**, 2-4 Thackeray St., W8 5ET, ℰ 937 8508 – ▤. ◪ ᴀᴇ ⓞ ᴠɪꜱᴀ
closed Sunday, Sunday, last 2 weeks August and Bank Holidays – **M** - **French**
9.90/14.90 **t.** and a la carte ⑧ 4.80.
p. 30 AQR **e**

ᕽᕽ **La Fenice**, 148 Holland Park Av., W11 4UE, ℰ 221 6090, Fax 221 4096 – ▤. ◪ ᴀᴇ ᴠɪꜱᴀ
closed Saturday lunch, Monday and Bank Holidays – **M** - **Italian** 18.50 **t.** and a la carte
⑧ 4.75.
EX **v**

ᕽᕽ **Launceston Place**, 1a Launceston Pl., W8 5RL, ℰ 937 6912, Fax 938 2412 – ▤. ◪ ᴀᴇ
ᴠɪꜱᴀ ᴊᴄʙ
p. 30 BR **a**
closed Saturday lunch, Sunday dinner and Bank Holidays – **M** 12.50/15.50 **t.** and a la carte
⑧ 7.50.

ᕽᕽ **Boyd's**, 135 Kensington Church St., W8 7LP, ℰ 727 5452, Fax 221 0615 – ▤. ◪ ᴀᴇ ⓞ
ᴠɪꜱᴀ
p. 32 AZ **r**
closed Sunday, 2 weeks Christmas and Bank Holidays – **M** 14.00 **t.** (lunch) and a la
carte 18.70/31.45 **t.**

ᕽᕽ **Phoenicia**, 11-13 Abingdon Rd, W8 6AH, ℰ 937 0120, Fax 937 7668 – ▤. ◪ ᴀᴇ ⓞ ᴠɪꜱᴀ
ᴊᴄʙ
EY **n**
closed 24 and 25 December – **M** - **Lebanese** 15.30/28.30 **st.** and a la carte ⑧ 4.95.

ᕽᕽ **Shanghai**, 38c-d Kensington Church St., W8 4BX, ℰ 938 2501 – ▤. ◪ ᴀᴇ ⓞ ᴠɪꜱᴀ ᴊᴄʙ
closed Sunday, 24 to 26 December, 1 January and Bank Holidays – **M** - **Chinese** 24.50 **t.**
FX **a**
(dinner) and a la carte 12.60/24.50 **t.**

ᕽ **The Ark**, Kensington Court, 35 Kensington High St., W8 5BA, ℰ 937 4294 – ◪ ᴀᴇ ᴠɪꜱᴀ
closed Saturday and Sunday lunch, 3 days at Easter and 25 to 27 December – **M** 15.00 **t.**
p. 30 AQ **s**
(lunch) and a la carte 18.75/22.70 **t.**

ᕽ **Kensington Place**, 201 Kensington Church St., W8 7LX, ℰ 727 3184, Fax 229 2025 – ▤.
◪ ᴠɪꜱᴀ
p. 32 AZ **z**
closed 24 to 27 December – **Meals** 13.50 **t.** (lunch) and a la carte 17.50/28.00 **t.**

ᕽ **Cibo**, 3 Russell Gdns, W14 8EZ, ℰ 371 6271 – ◪ ᴀᴇ ⓞ ᴠɪꜱᴀ
EY **o**
M - **Italian** a la carte 19.50/31.20 ⑧ 5.50.

ᕽ **Malabar**, 27 Uxbridge St., W8 7TQ, ℰ 727 8800 – ◪ ᴠɪꜱᴀ
p. 32 AZ **e**
closed last week August and 4 days at Christmas – **Meals** - **Indian** (booking advisable)
(buffet lunch Sunday) 15.00 **st.** and a la carte ⑧ 4.60.

ᕽ **Wódka**, 12 St. Albans Grove, W8 5PN, ℰ 937 6513, Fax 937 8621 – ◪ ᴀᴇ ⓞ ᴠɪꜱᴀ
closed Saturday lunch – **M** - **Polish** a la carte 16.40/22.00 **t.** ⑧ 4.75.
p. 30 AR **c**

ᕽ **Mandarin**, 197c Kensington High St., W8 6BA, ℰ 937 1551 – ▤. ◪ ᴀᴇ ⓞ ᴠɪꜱᴀ
EY **s**
closed 25 to 27 December – **M** - **Chinese** a la carte 20.00 **st.**

North Kensington – ✉ W2/W10/W11 – ✆ 071 – Except where otherwise stated see pp. 20-23.

ᐧ **Abbey Court** without rest., 20 Pembridge Gdns, W2 4DU, ℰ 221 7518, Telex 262167, Fax 792 0858, « Tastefully furnished Victorian town house » – ▦ ☎. ◪ ᴀᴇ ⓞ ᴠɪꜱᴀ. ✻
p. 32 AZ **u**
⬭ 9.00 – **22 rm** 90.00/160.00 **t.**

ᐧ **Pembridge Court**, 34 Pembridge Gdns, W2 4DX, ℰ 229 9977, Fax 727 4982, « Collection of antique clothing » – |☆| ▤ rest ▦ ☎. ◪ ᴀᴇ ⓞ ᴠɪꜱᴀ. ✻
p. 32 AZ **n**
M *(closed Sunday and Bank Holidays)* (dinner only) a la carte 14.25/19.50 **st.** ⑧ 4.95 – **21 rm**
⬭ 90.00/150.00 **st.**

Portobello, 22 Stanley Gdns, W11 2NG, ℰ 727 2777, Fax 792 9641, « Attractive town house in Victorian terrace » – 🛗 📺 ☎. 🔼 AE ⓞ VISA EV **n**
closed 23 December-2 January – **M** (residents only) 12.95/20.95 **st.** and a la carte ⅙ 5.50 – **24 rm** ⊂⊐ 70.00/120.00 **st.**, 1 suite.

XXX ❀ **Leith's,** 92 Kensington Park Rd, W11 2PN, ℰ 229 4481 – 🖩. 🔼 AE ⓞ VISA EV **e**
closed 28-29 August and 4 days at Christmas – **M** (dinner only) 23.50/40.00 **t.** ⅙ 6.40
Spec. Feuilleté de sole and langoustine with a shellfish butter sauce, Char-grilled turbot with fettucine and a basil butter sauce, Hot blackberry soufflé with a sloe gin sorbet.

XX **Chez Moi,** 1 Addison Av., Holland Park, W11 4QS, ℰ 603 8267 – 🖩. 🔼 AE ⓞ VISA
closed Saturday, Sunday, Christmas-New Year and Bank Holidays – **M** - French 14.00 **t.** (lunch) and a la carte 21.75/27.50 **t.** ⅙ 4.50. p. 24 EX **n**

XX **Park Inn,** 6 Wellington Terr., Bayswater Rd, W2 4LW, ℰ 229 3553, Fax 229 3553 – 🖩. 🔼 AE VISA AZ **c**
M - Chinese Seafood (Peking) a la carte 13.00/35.00 **t.** ⅙ 3.90.

X **L'Altro,** 210 Kensington Park Rd, W11 1NR, ℰ 792 1066 – 🖩. 🔼 AE ⓞ VISA EV **c**
closed Sunday – **M** - Italian 20.00/35.00 **t.** and dinner a la carte ⅙ 5.95.

X **192,** 192 Kensington Park Rd, W11 2JF, ℰ 229 0482 – 🔼 AE ⓞ VISA EV **a**
closed 24 to 27 December – **M** a la carte 17.00/24.00 **t.**

X **Canal Brasserie,** Canalot Studios, 222 Kensal Rd, W10 5BN, ℰ (081) 960 2732 – 🔼 VISA ET **c**
closed Saturday and Sunday – **M** (lunch only) 17.95 **t.** and a la carte ⅙ 4.50.

X **Brasserie du Marché aux Puces,** 349 Portobello Rd, W10 5SA, ℰ (081) 968 5828 EU **a**
closed Sunday dinner and Bank Holidays – **M** a la carte 14.90/19.75 **t.** ⅙ 4.00.

X **Surinder's,** 109 Westbourne Park Rd, W2 5QL, ℰ 229 8968 – 🔼 AE VISA EU **e**
closed Sunday, Monday and 17 July-16 August – **M** (dinner only and Friday lunch)/ dinner 14.95 **st.**

South Kensington – ✉ SW5/SW7/W8 – ❀ 071 – Except where otherwise stated see pp. 30 and 31.

🏨 **Harrington Hall,** 5-25 Harrington Gdns, SW7 4JW, ℰ 396 9696, Fax 396 9090, 🔽, ≋ – 🛗 ⥼ rm 🖩 📺 ☎ ❷ – 🔬 140. 🔼 AE ⓞ VISA ⅏ BT **n**
M 12.50/14.50 **st.** and a la carte ⅙ 8.50 – ⊂⊐ 9.00 – **200 rm** 99.00/145.00 **st.**

🏨 **Pelham,** 15 Cromwell Pl., SW7 2LA, ℰ 589 8288, Fax 584 8444, « Tastefully furnished Victorian town house » – 🛗 🖩 📺 ☎ ❷. 🔼 AE VISA ⅏ CS **z**
M (room service only) – ⊂⊐ 12.50 – **34 rm** 115.00/165.00 **t.**, 3 suites.

🏨 **Blakes,** 33 Roland Gdns, SW7 3PF, ℰ 370 6701, Telex 8813500, Fax 373 0442, « Antique oriental furnishings » – 🛗 🖩 rest 📺 ☎ ❷. 🔼 AE ⓞ VISA JCB BU **n**
M 36.00 (lunch) and a la carte 33.25/55.20 **t.** ⅙ 8.00 – ⊂⊐ 16.65 – **46 rm** 130.00/295.00 **st.**, 6 suites.

🏨 **Gloucester,** 4-18 Harrington Gdns, SW7 4LH, ℰ 373 6030, Telex 917505, Fax 373 0409 – 🛗 ⥼ rm 🖩 📺 ☎ ❷ – 🔬 380. 🔼 AE ⓞ VISA ⅏ BS **r**
M 21.95 **t.** (dinner) and a la carte 10.75/32.50 **t.** ⅙ 4.95 – ⊂⊐ 11.95 – **542 rm** 140.00/155.00 **t.**, 6 suites – SB (weekends only) 110.00/250.00 **st.**

🏨 **Rembrandt,** 11 Thurloe Pl., SW7 2RS, ℰ 589 8100, Telex 295828, Fax 225 3363, 🔽, ≋, 🖼 – 🛗 ⥼ rm 🖩 rest 📺 ☎ – 🔬 250. 🔼 AE ⓞ VISA JCB ⅏ DS **x**
M 12.50/15.95 **st.** and a la carte ⅙ 5.95 – ⊂⊐ 9.25 – **195 rm** 105.00/140.00 **st.** – SB (weekends only) 131.90 **st.**

🏨 **Swallow International,** Cromwell Rd, SW5 0TH, ℰ 973 1000, Telex 27260, Fax 244 8194, 🔽, ≋, 🖼 – 🛗 ⥼ rm 🖩 rest 📺 ☎ ❷ – 🔬 200. 🔼 AE ⓞ VISA ⅏ AS **c**
closed 4 days at Christmas – **M** (carving lunch) 14.75/17.25 **st.** and a la carte ⅙ 5.00 – ⊂⊐ 9.75 – **415 rm** 95.00/120.00 **st.**, 1 suite.

🏨 **Holiday Inn,** 100 Cromwell Rd, SW7 4ER, ℰ 373 2222, Telex 911311, Fax 373 0559, 🔽, ≋, ⥦ – 🛗 ⥼ rm 🖩 📺 ☎ ⬥ – 🔬 135. 🔼 AE ⓞ VISA JCB ⅏ BS **u**
M 12.50 **st.** and a la carte ⅙ 6.50 – ⊂⊐ 10.95 – **143 rm** 90.00/105.00 **st.**, 19 suites – SB (weekends only) 220.00 **st.**

🏨 **Regency,** 100 Queen's Gate, SW7 5AG, ℰ 370 4595, Telex 267594, Fax 370 5555, 🔽, ≋ – 🛗 ⥼ rm 🖩 rest 📺 ☎ – 🔬 80. 🔼 AE VISA JCB ⅏ CT **e**
M (closed lunch Saturday and Sunday) 14.50/17.50 **st.** and a la carte ⅙ 5.00 – ⊂⊐ 12.50 – **194 rm** 80.00/115.00 **s.**, 6 suites – SB (weekends only) 118.10/213.25 **st.**

🏨 **Gore** (Best Western), 189 Queen's Gate, SW7 5EX, ℰ 584 6601, Telex 296244, Fax 589 8127, « Attractive decor » – 🛗 📺 ☎. 🔼 AE ⓞ VISA JCB BR **n**
closed 24 to 26 December – **M** – Bistrot 190 (only members and residents may book) a la carte approx. 17.00 ⅙ 4.75 – (see also **Downstairs at One Ninety** below) – **53 rm** 99.00/140.00 **st.**

🏨 **Cranley** without rest., 10-12 Bina Gardens, SW5 0LA, ℰ 373 0123, Fax 373 9497, « Tasteful decor, antiques » – 🛗 ⥼ rm 📺 ☎. 🔼 AE ⓞ VISA ⅏ BT **c**
⊂⊐ 11.45 – **32 rm** 104.00/177.00 **st.**, 4 suites.

🏨 **John Howard** (Best Western), 4 Queen's Gate, SW7 5EH, ℰ 581 3011, Telex 8813397, Fax 589 8403 – 🛗 🖩 📺 ☎. 🔼 AE ⓞ VISA. ⅏ BQ **i**
M 17.75 **st.** – **48 rm** ⊂⊐ 79.00/140.00 **st.**, 4 suites.

🏨 **Vanderbilt** (Edwardian), 168-186 Cromwell Rd, SW7 5BT, ℰ 589 2424, Telex 946944, Fax 225 2293 – 🛗 ▤ rest 📺 ☎ – 🛦 120. 🖪 🖭 🎹 ⁣⁣ **VISA** 🅹🅲🅱 ⁣⁣ ⁣⁣ ⁣ ⁣⁣ ⁣⁣⁣ BS **v**
M 12.50/14.50 st. and a la carte – � 9.50 – **223 rm** 92.00/185.00 st. – SB (weekends only) 79.00/99.00 st.

🏨 **Onslow**, 109-113 Queen's Gate, SW7 5LR, ℰ 589 6300, Telex 262180, Fax 581 1492 – 🛗
▤ rest 📺 ☎ – 🛦 80. 🖪 🖭 🎹 **VISA**. ⁣⁣ ⁣⁣ CT **i**
M 10.50/11.95 t. and a la carte – ⊠ 4.00 – **170 rm** 105.00/175.00 st.

🏨 Park International, 117-125 Cromwell Rd, SW7 4DS, ℰ 370 5711, Telex 296822, Fax 244 9211 – 🛗 📺 ☎ – 🛦 40. ⁣⁣ AS **e**
117 rm.

🏨 **Kensington Plaza**, 61 Gloucester Rd, SW7 4PE, ℰ 584 8100, Telex 8950993, Fax 823 9175 – 🛗 ▤ rest 📺 ☎ – 🛦 100. 🖪 🖭 🎹 **VISA**. ⁣⁣ BS **e**
M (dinner only) 14.50 st. ⁣⁣ 3.50 – ⊠ 4.75 – **88 rm** 69.00/85.00 st.

🏛 **Number Sixteen** without rest., 14-17 Sumner Pl., SW7 3EG, ℰ 589 5232, Telex 266638, Fax 584 8615, « Attractively furnished Victorian town houses », 🌿 – 🛗 📺 ☎. 🖪 🖭 🎹
VISA ⁣⁣ CT **c**
⊠ 8.00 – **36 rm** 60.00/155.00 t.

🏛 **Alexander** without rest., 9 Sumner Pl., SW7 3EE, ℰ 581 1591, Telex 917133, Fax 581 0824, « Attractively furnished Victorian town houses », 🌿 – 🛗 📺 ☎. 🖪 🖭 🎹
VISA ⁣⁣ CT **a**
36 rm ⊠ 90.00/168.00 t., 1 suite.

🏛 **Cranley Place** without rest., 1 Cranley Pl., SW7 3AB, ℰ 589 7704, Fax 225 3931, « Tasteful decor » – 📺 ☎. 🖪 🖭 🎹 **VISA**. ⁣⁣ CT **o**
⊠ 9.00 – **9 rm** 75.00/85.00 st.

🏛 **Five Sumner Place** without rest., 5 Sumner Pl., SW7 3EE, ℰ 584 7586, Fax 823 9962 – 🛗
📺 ☎. 🖪 🖭 **VISA** 🅹🅲🅱. ⁣⁣ DR **a**
13 rm ⊠ 70.00/98.00 st.

🏛 **Aster House** without rest., 3 Sumner Pl., SW7 3EE, ℰ 581 5888, Fax 584 4925, 🌿 – ⁣⁣⁣⁣
📺 ☎. 🖪 🖭 **VISA** 🅹🅲🅱. ⁣⁣ CT **u**
12 rm ⊠ 52.00/85.00 st.

🏛 **Cranley Gardens** without rest., 8 Cranley Gdns, SW7 3DB, ℰ 373 3232, Telex 894489, Fax 373 7944 – 🛗 📺 ☎. 🖪 🖭 🎹 **VISA**
⊠ 5.50 – **85 rm** 63.00/79.00 st. ⁣⁣ BT **e**

🏠 **Hotel 167** without rest., 167 Old Brompton Rd, SW5 0AN, ℰ 373 3221, Fax 373 3360 – 📺
☎. ⁣⁣ BT **r**
⊠ 5.50 – **19 rm** 54.00/75.00 st.

🏶🏶🏶 **Bombay Brasserie**, Courtfield Close, 140 Gloucester Rd, SW7 4UH, ℰ 370 4040, « Raj-style decor, conservatory garden » – ▤. 🖪 🎹 **VISA** ⁣⁣ BS **a**
closed 25 and 26 December – **M** - Indian (buffet lunch) 13.95 t. and dinner a la carte 18.25/23.20 t. ⁣⁣ 6.50.

🏶🏶 **Hilaire**, 68 Old Brompton Rd, SW7 3LQ, ℰ 584 8993 – ▤. 🖪 🖭 🎹 **VISA** ⁣⁣ CT **n**
closed Saturday lunch, Sunday, 1 week Christmas and Bank Holidays – **Meals** (booking essential) 13.90/25.00 t. and dinner a la carte 25.50/32.50 t. ⁣⁣ 6.50.

🏶🏶 **Downstairs at One Ninety**, 190 Queen's Gate, SW7 5EU, ℰ 581 5666, Fax 581 8172 –
▤. 🖪 🖭 🎹 **VISA** ⁣⁣ BR **n**
closed Saturday lunch, Sunday, 24 to 26 December and Bank Holidays – **M** - Seafood (booking essential) 10.00 st. (lunch) and a la carte 13.90/30.85 st. ⁣⁣ 4.95.

🏶🏶 **Khan's of Kensington**, 3 Harrington Rd, SW7 3ES, ℰ 581 2900 – ▤. 🖪 🖭 🎹
VISA ⁣⁣ CS **e**
closed 25 and 26 December – **M** - Indian 7.50/15.00 t. and a la carte ⁣⁣ 4.95.

🏶🏶 **Tui**, 19 Exhibition Rd, SW7 2HE, ℰ 584 8359, Fax 352 8343 – 🖪 🖭 🎹 **VISA** ⁣⁣ CS **u**
closed 5 days at Christmas and Bank Holidays – **M** - Thai a la carte 16.45/24.05 st. ⁣⁣ 3.95.

🏶🏶 **Delhi Brasserie**, 134 Cromwell Rd, SW7 4HA, ℰ 370 7617 – ▤. 🖪 🖭 🎹 **VISA** 🅹🅲🅱
closed 25 and 26 December – **M** - Indian 10.95/14.95 t. and a la carte. ⁣⁣ AS **a**

🏶🏶 **Memories of India**, 18 Gloucester Rd, SW7 4RB, ℰ 589 6450 – 🖪 🖭 🎹 **VISA** 🅹🅲🅱
closed 25 and 26 December – **M** - Indian 14.50/20.00 t. and a la carte. ⁣⁣ BR **s**

🏶 **Chanterelle**, 119 Old Brompton Rd, SW7 3RN, ℰ 373 5522 – 🖪 🖭 🎹 **VISA** ⁣⁣ BT **v**
closed 24 to 27 December – **M** 11.00/19.50 ⁣⁣ 5.35.

🏶 **Nam Long at Le Shaker**, 159 Old Brompton Rd, SW5 0LJ, ℰ 373 1926, Fax 373 6046 –
🖪 🖭 🎹 **VISA** ⁣⁣ BT **i**
closed Saturday lunch, Sunday and Bank Holidays – **M** - Vietnamese 16.50/21.00 t. and a la carte ⁣⁣ 5.50.

🏶 **Bangkok**, 9 Bute St., SW7 3EY, ℰ 584 8529 – ▤. 🖪 **VISA** ⁣⁣ CS **v**
closed Sunday, Christmas-New Year and Bank Holidays – **M** - Thai Bistro a la carte 14.70/19.50 t.

KINGSTON UPON THAMES pp. 8 and 9.

🏠 Home Park, Hampton Wick ℰ (081) 977 6645, by A 308 BY.

Chessington – ⊠ Surrey – ✪ 0372.

🏨 **Travel Inn,** Leatherhead Rd, KT9 2NE, on A 243 ℰ 744060, Fax 720889 – ⇟⊷ rm 📺 ♿ ❷.
🔼 🖭 ⓞ 𝘝𝘐𝘚𝘈 ❄
BZ **c**
M (Beefeater grill) a la carte approx. 16.00 **t**. – ☞ 4.95 – **42 rm** 33.50 **t**.

Hampton Wick – ⊠ Surrey – ✪ 081.

🏨 **Chase Lodge,** 10 Park Rd, KT1 4AS, ℰ 943 1862, Fax 943 9363 – ⇟⊷ rest 📺 ☎ ❷. 🔼 🖭
𝘝𝘐𝘚𝘈
BY **e**
M (lunch by arrangement Monday to Saturday)/dinner 17.00 **st**. and a la carte – **10 rm**
☞ 35.00/80.00 **st**. – SB (weekends only) 89.00/114.00 **st**.

Kingston – ⊠ Surrey – ✪ 081.

🏌 Garrison Lane ℰ 391 0948, off A 243 CZ.

🏨 **Kingston Lodge** (Forte), Kingston Hill, KT2 7NP, ℰ 541 4481, Fax 547 1013 – ⇟⊷ ▤ rest
📺 ☎ ♿ ❷ – 🔬 60. 🔼 🖭 ⓞ 𝘝𝘐𝘚𝘈 𝘑𝘊𝘉
CY **u**
M (bar lunch Monday to Saturday)/dinner 18.95 **st**. and a la carte ⓝ 5.25 – ☞ 8.50 – **62 rm**
97.50/125.00 **st**. – SB (weekends only) 108.00/118.00 **st**.

🍴🍴 **Gravier's,** 9 Station Rd, Norbiton, KT2 7AA, ℰ 549 5557 – 🔼 🖭 𝘝𝘐𝘚𝘈
CY **x**
*closed Saturday lunch, Sunday, 1 week Easter, 1 week summer, 1 week Christmas and
Bank Holidays* – **M** - French Seafood 16.50 **t**. (lunch) and a la carte 17.85/25.00 **t**. ⓝ 4.50.

🍴 **Ayudhya,** 14 Kingston Hill, KT2 7NH, ℰ 549 5984 – 🔼 🖭 ⓞ 𝘝𝘐𝘚𝘈
CY **z**
closed Monday, 1 January, 3 April and 25 December – **M** - Thai a la carte 17.80/21.55 **t**.
ⓝ 3.75.

Surbiton – ⊠ Surrey – ✪ 081.

🍴🍴 **Chez Max,** 85 Maple Rd, KT6 4AW, ℰ 399 2365 – 🔼 🖭 ⓞ 𝘝𝘐𝘚𝘈
BY **o**
closed Saturday lunch, Sunday, Monday, 1 April and 24 to 30 December – **M** (booking
essential) 15.95/16.50 **t**. ⓝ 7.00.

LAMBETH Except where otherwise stated see pp.10 and 11.

Brixton – ⊠ SW9 – ✪ 071.

🍴 **Twenty Trinity Gardens,** 20 Trinity Gdns, SW9 8DP, ℰ 733 8838 – 🔼 𝘝𝘐𝘚𝘈
EX **n**
closed Saturday lunch, Sunday dinner and 25 December – **M** 17.50 **t**. (dinner) and lunch a la
carte 12.00/14.00 **t**. ⓝ 3.75.

Clapham Common – ⊠ SW4 – ✪ 071.

🍴🍴 **The Grafton,** 45 Old Town, SW4 0JL, ℰ 627 1048 – 🔼 🖭 ⓞ 𝘝𝘐𝘚𝘈 𝘑𝘊𝘉
p. 13 DQ **a**
closed Saturday lunch, Sunday, last 3 weeks August, 1 week Christmas and Bank Holidays
– **M** - French 14.95/18.00 **t**. and a la carte ⓝ 4.50.

Streatham – ⊠ SW16 – ✪ 081.

🏠 **Barrow House** without rest., 45 Barrow Rd, SW16 5PE, ℰ 677 1925, Fax 677 1925,
« Victoriana », 🌳 – ⇟⊷ ❄
EY **s**
closed 22 December-2 January – **5 rm** ☞ 20.00/40.00 **st**.

Waterloo – ⊠ SE1 – ✪ 071.

🍴🍴 **La Rive Gauche,** 61 The Cut, SE1 8LL, ℰ 928 8645 – 🔼 🖭 ⓞ 𝘝𝘐𝘚𝘈
p. 27 NX **x**
closed Saturday lunch and Sunday – **M** - French 15.50/17.50 **st**. and a la carte ⓝ 5.50.

🍴🍴 **RSJ,** 13a Coin St., SE1 8YQ, ℰ 928 4554 – ▤. 🔼 🖭 𝘝𝘐𝘚𝘈
p. 27 NX **e**
closed Saturday lunch, Sunday, 25-26 December and Bank Holidays – **M** 15.95 **t**. and a la
carte ⓝ 5.25.

LONDON HEATHROW AIRPORT see Hillingdon, London p. 56.

MERTON pp. 8 and 9.

Morden – ⊠ Morden – ✪ 081.

🏨 **Forte Travelodge,** Epsom Rd, SM4 5PH, SW : on A 24 ℰ 640 8227, Reservations
(Freephone) 0800 850950 – 📺 ♿ ❷. 🔼 🖭 𝘝𝘐𝘚𝘈 ❄
DY **c**
M (Harvester grill) a la carte approx. 16.00 **t**. – ☞ 5.50 – **32 rm** 31.95 **t**.

Wimbledon – ⊠ SW19 – ✪ 081.

🏨🏨 **Cannizaro House** (Mt. Charlotte Thistle) ♨, West Side, Wimbledon Common, SW19
4UF, ℰ 879 1464, Telex 9413837, Fax 879 7338, ⩽, « 18C country house overlooking
Cannizaro Park », 🌳 – 📳 📺 ☎ ❷ – 🔬 45. 🔼 🖭 ⓞ 𝘝𝘐𝘚𝘈 𝘑𝘊𝘉. ❄
DXY **x**
M 16.95/25.75 **t**. and a la carte – ☞ 9.75 – **43 rm** 105.00/195.00 **t**., 2 suites.

🏠 **Worcester House** without rest., 38 Alwyne Rd, SW19 7AE, ℰ 946 1300, Fax 785 4058 –
📺 ☎. 🔼 🖭 ⓞ 𝘝𝘐𝘚𝘈. ❄
DY **r**
9 rm ☞ 45.50/62.50 **st**.

🍴🍴 **Bayee Village,** 24 High St., SW19 5DX, ℰ 947 3533, Fax 944 8392 – ▤. 🔼 🖭 ⓞ 𝘝𝘐𝘚𝘈
𝘑𝘊𝘉
DX **i**
M - Chinese (Peking, Szechuan) 15.00/21.00 **st**. and a la carte ⓝ 5.00.

REDBRIDGE pp. 6 and 7.

🛎 Town Hall, High Rd, IG1 1DD ℰ 478 3020 ext 2126.

Ilford – ✉ Essex – ☎ 081.

🏌 Wanstead Park Rd ℰ 554 5174, by A 406 HU – 🏌 Fairlop Waters, Forest Rd, Barkingside ℰ 500 9911 JT.

XX **Mandarin Palace,** 559-561 Cranbrook Rd, Gants Hill, IG2 6JZ, ℰ 550 7661 – 🍽. 🅰 🆎 ⓪ 𝘝𝘐𝘚𝘈　　　　　　　　　　　　　　　　　　　　　　　　　　　HU　e
　　M - **Chinese** (Canton, Peking) 10.50/15.00 **st.** and a la carte ⓙ 5.60.

XX **Dragon City,** 97 Cranbrook Rd, IG1 4PG, ℰ 553 0312 – 🍽. 🅰 🆎 ⓪ 𝘝𝘐𝘚𝘈　　　　HJU　a
　　M - **Chinese** (Canton, Peking) 8.00/18.50 **t.** and a la carte.

South Woodford – ✉ Essex – ☎ 081.

XX **Ho-Ho,** 20 High Rd, E18 2QL, ℰ 989 1041 – 🍽. 🅰 🆎 ⓪ 𝘝𝘐𝘚𝘈　　　　　　　HU　c
　　closed 25 to 27 December – M - **Chinese** (Peking, Szechuan) 12.00/27.00 **st.** and a la carte.

Woodford – ✉ Essex – ☎ 081.

🏌, 🏌 Hainault Forest, Chigwell Row ℰ 500 2097, NW : 5 m. JT – Chingford, 158 Station Rd ℰ 529 2107, N : 3¾ m. HT.

🏨 **Prince Regent,** Manor Rd, Woodford Bridge, IG8 8AE, ℰ 505 9966, Fax 506 0807, 🌿 –
🛗 🍽 rest 📺 ☎ ⇔ 🅿 – 🔬 350. 🅰 🆎 ⓪ 𝘝𝘐𝘚𝘈　　　　　　　　　　　　　　HT　a
　　M 8.50/11.50 **t.** and a la carte ⓙ 5.00 – **51 rm** ⇆ 75.00/125.00 **t.**

🏨 **Woodford Moat House** (Q.M.H.), 30 Oak Hill, Woodford Green, IG8 9NY, ℰ 505 4511,
Telex 264428, Fax 506 0941, 🌿 – 🛗 📺 ☎ 🅿 – 🔬 150. 🅰 🆎 ⓪ 𝘝𝘐𝘚𝘈. ❦　　HT　c
　　M (bar lunch Saturday) 14.80/16.80 **t.** and a la carte ⓙ 4.75 – **99 rm** ⇆ 58.00/68.00 **st.** –
SB (weekends only) 80.00 **st.**

RICHMOND-UPON-THAMES pp. 8 and 9.

Barnes – ✉ SW13 – ☎ 081.

XX **Sonny's,** 94 Church Rd, SW13 0DQ, ℰ 748 0393, Fax 748 2698 – 🍽. 🅰 🆎 𝘝𝘐𝘚𝘈　　CX　x
　　closed Sunday dinner – M 12.50 **t.** and a la carte ⓙ 3.75.

X **Riva,** 169 Church Rd, SW13 9HR, ℰ 748 0434 – 🆎 𝘝𝘐𝘚𝘈　　　　　　　　　　CX　a
　　closed Saturday lunch, Easter, last 2 weeks August, Christmas and Bank Holidays –
M - **Italian** a la carte 16.10/25.50 **t.** ⓙ 6.00.

East Sheen – ✉ SW14 – ☎ 081.

XX **Crowther's,** 481 Upper Richmond Rd West, SW14 7PU, ℰ 876 6372 – 🍽. 🅰 𝘝𝘐𝘚𝘈 CX　n
　　closed Saturday lunch, Sunday, Monday, 2 weeks August and 1 week Christmas –
M (booking essential) 15.50/19.00 **t.** ⓙ 4.50.

Richmond – ✉ Surrey – ☎ 081.

🏌, 🏌 Richmond Park, Roehampton Gate ℰ 876 3205/1795 CX – 🏌 Sudbrook Park ℰ 940 1463 CX.

🛎 Old Town Hall, Whittaker Av., TW9 1TP ℰ 940 9125.

🏨 **Petersham** ⑊, Nightingale Lane, Richmond Hill, TW10 6UZ, ℰ 940 7471, Telex 928556,
Fax 940 9998, ≤, 🌿 – 🛗 📺 ☎ 🅿 – 🔬 50. 🅰 🆎 ⓪ 𝘝𝘐𝘚𝘈. ❦　　　　　　CX　c
　　M - (see **Nightingales** below) – **54 rm** ⇆ 97.00/150.00 **st.** – SB 120.00/150.00 **st.**

🏨 **Richmond Gate** (Best Western), 158 Richmond Hill, TW10 6RP, ℰ 940 0061, Group
Telex 21844, Fax 332 0354, 🌿 – 📺 ☎ 🅿 – 🔬 40. 🅰 🆎 ⓪ 𝘝𝘐𝘚𝘈. ❦　　　　　CX　c
　　M (closed Saturday lunch) 15.50/18.50 **t.** and dinner a la carte ⓙ 6.50 – **61 rm** ⇆ 90.00/
125.00 **st.** – SB (weekends only) 96.00 **st.**

🏨 **Bingham,** 61-63 Petersham Rd, TW10 6UT, ℰ 940 0902, Fax 948 8737, 🌿 – 📺 ☎ –
🔬 30. 🅰 🆎 ⓪ 𝘝𝘐𝘚𝘈. ❦　　　　　　　　　　　　　　　　　　　　　　　CX　z
　　M (closed Sunday) (dinner only) 15.45 **t.** and a la carte ⓙ 5.85 – **35 rm** ⇆ 70.00/95.00 **st.**

🏨 **Richmond Park** without rest., 3 Petersham Rd, TW10 6UH, ℰ 948 4666, Fax 940 7376 –
📺 🅰 🆎 ⓪ 𝘝𝘐𝘚𝘈. ❦　　　　　　　　　　　　　　　　　　　　　　　　CX　v
　　22 rm ⇆ 69.00/84.00 **st.**

XXX **Nightingales** (at Petersham H.), Nightingale Lane, Richmond Hill, TW10 6UZ,
ℰ 940 7471, Telex 928556, Fax 940 9998, ≤, 🌿 – 🅿. 🅰 🆎 ⓪ 𝘝𝘐𝘚𝘈　　　　　　CX　c
　　M 17.50/20.00 **t.** and a la carte ⓙ 6.50.

XX **Four Regions,** 102-104 Kew Rd, TW9 2PQ, ℰ 940 9044, Fax 332 6130 – 🍽. 🅰 🆎 𝘝𝘐𝘚𝘈
　　M - **Chinese** 17.00 **t.** (dinner) and a la carte 15.00/25.50 **t.**　　　　　　　　CX　e

Twickenham – ✉ Middx. – ☎ 081.

🏌 Twickenham Park, Staines Rd ℰ 783 1698, NW : 2 m. on A 305 BX.

🛎 44 York St., TW1 3BZ ℰ 891 1411.

XX McClements, 12 The Green, TW2 5AA, ℰ 755 0176, Fax 890 1372 – ↤↦　　　　BX　s

XX **Cézanne,** 68 Richmond Rd, TW1 3BE, ℰ 892 3526 – 🅰 🆎 ⓪ 𝘝𝘐𝘚𝘈　　　　　BX　a
　　closed Saturday lunch, Sunday and Bank Holidays – M 18.25 **t.** and a la carte ⓙ 4.00.

SOUTHWARK Except where otherwise stated see pp. 10 and 11.

    Bermondsey – ⌧ SE1 – ☎ 071.

XXX **Pont de la Tour,** 36d Shad Thames, Butlers Wharf, SE1 2YE, ℰ 403 8403, Fax 403 0267, ≤, « Riverside setting » – ≣, 🝙 🝙 ⓞ 𝒱𝒮𝒜   p. 27 PX **c**
Meals *(closed Saturday lunch and 4 days at Christmas)* 25.00 **t.** (lunch) and dinner a la carte 33.25/46.00 **t.** 🍷 5.85.

X **Blue Print Café,** Design Museum, Shad Thames, Butlers Wharf, SE1 2YD, ℰ 378 7031, Fax 378 6540, ≤, « Riverside setting » – 🝙 🝙 ⓞ 𝒱𝒮𝒜   p. 27 PX **u**
closed Sunday dinner and 4 days at Christmas – **M** a la carte 15.00/25.00 **t.**

X **Cantina Del Ponte,** 36c Shad Thames, Butlers Wharf, SE1 2YE, ℰ 403 5403, Fax 403 0267, ≤, « Riverside setting » – 🝙 🝙 ⓞ 𝒱𝒮𝒜   PX **c**
closed Sunday dinner and 4 days at Christmas – **M** - **Italian-Mediterranean** a la carte 18.50/27.75 **t.** 🍷 5.95.

    Dulwich – ⌧ SE19 – ☎ 081.

XX **Luigi's,** 129 Gipsy Hill, SE19 1QS, ℰ 670 1843 – ≣. 🝙 🝙 ⓞ 𝒱𝒮𝒜   FX **a**
closed Saturday lunch, Sunday and Bank Holidays – **M** - **Italian** a la carte approx. 16.00 **t.**

    Rotherhithe – ⌧ SE16 – ☎ 071.

🏨 **Scandic Crown,** 265 Rotherhithe St., Nelson Dock, SE16 1EJ, ℰ 231 1001, Fax 231 0599, ≤, ℔, ⇌, 🗋, 🏊 – ❘❙ ⇻ rm ≣ rest 🝙 ☎ ☇ ⑫ – 🔬 350. 🝙 🝙 ⓞ 𝒱𝒮𝒜 🝙, ✺   GV **r**
M 16.50/25.00**st.** and dinner a la carte 🍷 5.00 – ⌂ 9.50 – **384 rm** 84.00/115.00 **st.**, 2 suites – SB 112.00/143.00 **st.**

    Southwark – ⌧ SE1 – ☎ 071.

XX **La Truffe Noire,** 29 Tooley St., SE1 2QF, ℰ 378 0621, Fax 403 0689 – ≣. 🝙 🝙 ⓞ 𝒱𝒮𝒜 🝙   p. 27 PX **a**
closed Saturday and Sunday – **M** - **French** 15.00/20.00 **t.** and a la carte 🍷 6.00.

SUTTON pp. 8 and 9.

    Sutton – ⌧ Surrey – ☎ 081.

🛈, ⓝ Oak Sports Centre, Woodmansterne Rd, Carshalton, ℰ 643 8363, E : 2 m. on B 278 EZ.

🏨 **Holiday Inn,** Gibson Rd, SM1 2RF, ℰ 770 1311, Telex 911319, Fax 770 1539, ℔, ⇌, 🗋 – ❘❙ ⇻ rm ≣ rest 🝙 ☎ ☇ ⑫ – 🔬 220. 🝙 🝙 ⓞ 𝒱𝒮𝒜   EZ **a**
M *(closed Saturday lunch and Bank Holidays)* 12.95/18.50 **t.** and a la carte 🍷 5.50 – ⌂ 9.50 – **115 rm** 99.50/110.00 **st.**, 1 suite – SB (weekends only) 113.00/137.00 **st.**

🏩 **Thatched House,** 135-141 Cheam Rd, SM1 2BN, ℰ 642 3131, Fax 770 0684, ☞ – 🝙 ☎ ⑫ – 🔬 40. 🝙 𝒱𝒮𝒜   DZ **e**
M *(closed Sunday)* (dinner only) 14.50 **t.** 🍷 3.95 – **27 rm** ⌂ 39.50/59.50 **st.** – SB (weekends only) 65.00/120.00 **st.**

XX **Partners Brasserie,** 23 Stonecot Hill, SM3 9HB, ℰ 644 7743 – ≣. 🝙 🝙 ⓞ 𝒱𝒮𝒜   DY **v**
closed Saturday lunch, Sunday and Monday – **M** 9.95 **t.** and a la carte 🍷 4.00.

TOWER HAMLETS – pp. 6 and 7.

🛈 Bethnal Green Library, Cambridge Heath Rd, E2 0HL ℰ 980 4831.

    Stepney – ⌧ E1 – ☎ 071.

XX Laksmi, 116 Mile End Rd, E1 4UN, ℰ 265 9403 – ≣   GV **a**
M - Indian rest.

WANDSWORTH Except where otherwise stated see pp. 12 and 13.

    Battersea – ⌧ SW8/SW11 – ☎ 071.

XX **Ransome's Dock,** 35-37 Parkgate Rd, SW11 4NP, ℰ 223 1611, Fax 924 2614 – 🝙 🝙 ⓞ 𝒱𝒮𝒜   p. 25 HZ **c**
closed Sunday dinner and Christmas – **M** 10.50 **t.** (lunch) and a la carte 14.50/20.90 **t.** 🍷 4.50.

XX **Chada,** 208-210 Battersea Park Rd, SW11 4ND, ℰ 622 2209 – ≣. 🝙 🝙 ⓞ 𝒱𝒮𝒜   CQ **x**
closed Saturday lunch, Sunday and Bank Holidays – **M** - **Thai** a la carte 17.00/25.10 **st.**

XX **Lena's,** 196 Lavender Hill, SW11 1JA, ℰ 228 3735 – ≣. 🝙 🝙 ⓞ 𝒱𝒮𝒜   CQ **z**
closed lunch Saturday and Sunday and Sunday dinner in summer – **M** - **Thai** 15.00/20.00 **t.** and a la carte 🍷 5.95.

X **Brasserie Faubourg,** 28 Queenstown Rd, SW8 3RX, ℰ 622 6245 – 🝙 🝙 ⓞ 𝒱𝒮𝒜   DQ **n**
closed Sunday and lunch Monday and Saturday – **M** 20.00 **t.** (lunch) and a la carte 18.65/22.65 **t.** 🍷 4.50.

    Clapham – ⌧ SW11 – ☎ 071.

X **Jasmin,** 50/52 Battersea Rise, SW11 1EG, ℰ 228 0336 – 🝙 🝙 ⓞ 𝒱𝒮𝒜   CQ **u**
M - **Chinese** (Canton, Peking) 20.00 **t.** (lunch) and a la carte approx. 16.00 **t.** 🍷 4.75.

Putney – ⊠ SW15 – ☎ 081.

XX **Connolly's,** 162 Lower Richmond Rd, SW15 1LY, ℰ 788 3844 – ⚞ 亜 𝑉𝐼𝑆𝐴   AQ **e**
closed Sunday dinner and Bank Holidays – **M** 9.95/15.95 **t.** ⓕ 6.75.

X **Le Cassis,** 30 Putney High St., SW15 1SQ, ℰ 788 8668 – ⚞ 亜 𝑉𝐼𝑆𝐴   AQ **x**
closed Saturday lunch, 26 December and Bank Holidays – **M** - **French** 25.00 **t.** and a la carte
ⓕ 4.50.

Tooting – ⊠ SW17 – ☎ 081.

X **Oh Boy,** 843 Garratt Lane, SW17 0PG, ℰ 947 9760 – ▤. ⚞ 亜 ⓞ 𝑉𝐼𝑆𝐴   CR **c**
closed Sunday and Christmas – **M** - **Thai** (dinner only) 15.50 **t.** and a la carte ⓕ 3.60.

Wandsworth – ⊠ SW12/SW17/SW18 – ☎ 081.

XX **Harvey's,** 2 Bellevue Rd, SW17 7EG, ℰ 672 0114 – ▤. ⚞ 亜 ⓞ 𝑉𝐼𝑆𝐴   CR **e**
closed lunch Saturday and Monday, Sunday dinner, 24 to 30 December and 1 to 4 January
– **M** 15.50 **t.** (lunch) and dinner a la carte 21.00/25.45 **t.**

XX **Tabaq,** 47 Balham Hill, SW12 9DR, ℰ 673 7820 – ▤. ⚞ 亜 ⓞ 𝑉𝐼𝑆𝐴   DR **v**
M - Indian (dinner only) a la carte 11.20/23.75 **t.** ⓕ 4.25.

X **Bombay Bicycle Club,** 95 Nightingale Lane, SW12 8NX, ℰ 673 6217 – ⚞ 亜
𝑉𝐼𝑆𝐴
closed 25 to 27 December – **M** - **Indian** (dinner only and buffet lunch Sunday) a la
carte 14.00/20.00 **t.**   DR **o**

WESTMINSTER (City of) .

Bayswater and Maida Vale – ⊠ W2/W9 – ☎ 071 – Except where otherwise stated see
pp. 32 and 33.

🏨 **Royal Lancaster,** Lancaster Terr., W2 2TY, ℰ 262 6737, Fax 724 3191, ≼ – 🛗 ⇆ rm ▤
📺 ☎ ℗ – 🔬 1 400. ⚞ 亜 ⓞ 𝑉𝐼𝑆𝐴 𝐽𝐶𝐵. ⌘   DZ **e**
M 22.50/25.75 **st.** and a la carte ⓕ 7.00 – ⌷ 13.00 – **400 rm** 125.00/140.00 **st.**,
18 suites.

🏨 **London Metropole,** Edgware Rd, W2 1JU, ℰ 402 4141, Telex 23711, Fax 724 8866, ≼,
ℐ𝓈, ≘s, ▨ – 🛗 ⇆ rm ▤ 📺 ☎ – 🔬 1 200. ⚞ 亜 ⓞ 𝑉𝐼𝑆𝐴 𝐽𝐶𝐵. ⌘   p. 21 GU **c**
M - (see **Aspects** below) – ⌷ 13.50 – **716 rm** 125.00/190.00 **st.**, 26 suites – SB (weekends
only) 132.00/360.00 **st.**

🏨 **Whites** (Mt. Charlotte Thistle), Bayswater Rd, 90-92 Lancaster Gate, W2 3NR,
ℰ 262 2711, Telex 24771, Fax 262 2147 – 🛗 ⇆ rm ▤ 📺 ☎. ⚞ 亜 ⓞ 𝑉𝐼𝑆𝐴. ⌘   CZ **v**
M *(closed Saturday lunch)* 17.50/21.50 **t.** and a la carte ⓕ 7.15 – ⌷ 10.25 – **52 rm**
135.00/225.00 **st.**, 2 suites – SB 185.00 **st.**

🏨 **Plaza on Hyde Park** (Hilton), 1-7 Lancaster Gate, W2 3NA, ℰ 262 5022, Telex 8954372,
Fax 724 8666 – 🛗 ⇆ rm 📺 ☎ – 🔬 30. ⚞ 亜 ⓞ 𝑉𝐼𝑆𝐴. ⌘   DZ **r**
M 10.75/14.75 **st.** and a la carte ⓕ 6.40 – ⌷ 9.45 – **402 rm** 74.00/108.00 **st.** – SB (weekends
only) 124.00 **st.**

🏨 **Coburg Resort,** 129 Bayswater Rd, W2 4RJ, ℰ 221 2217, Telex 268235, Fax 229 0557 –
🛗 ⇆ rm 📺 ☎ – 🔬 80. ⚞ 亜 ⓞ 𝑉𝐼𝑆𝐴 𝐽𝐶𝐵. ⌘   BZ **c**
M - (see **Spice Merchant** below) – **131 rm** ⌷ 95.00/150.00 **st.**, 1 suite – SB (weekends only)
116.00 **st.**

🏨 **Hyde Park Towers,** 41-51 Inverness Terr., W2 3JN, ℰ 221 8484, Fax 792 3201 – 🛗
▤ rest 📺 ☎ – 🔬 40. ⚞ 亜 ⓞ 𝑉𝐼𝑆𝐴 𝐽𝐶𝐵. ⌘   BZ **r**
M 9.95 **st.** and a la carte ⓕ 4.50 – ⌷ 7.50 – **115 rm** 86.00/120.00 **st.** – SB (weekends only)
103.00/226.00 **st.**

🏨 **Queen's Park,** 48 Queensborough Terr., W2 3SS, ℰ 299 8080, Telex 21723,
Fax 792 1330 – 🛗 ▤ rest 📺 ☎ – 🔬 70. ⚞ 亜 ⓞ 𝑉𝐼𝑆𝐴. ⌘   BZ **s**
M *(closed Friday and Saturday)* (dinner only) a la carte 11.20/15.75 **t.** ⓕ 4.25 – ⌷ 7.50 –
86 rm 86.00/125.00 **st.**

🏨 **London Embassy** (Jarvis), 150 Bayswater Rd, W2 4RT, ℰ 229 1212, Telex 27727,
Fax 229 2623 – 🛗 ⇆ rm ▤ rest 📺 ☎ ℗ – 🔬 60. ⚞ 亜 ⓞ 𝑉𝐼𝑆𝐴. ⌘   BZ **o**
M (carving rest.) 15.95 **t.** and a la carte ⓕ 6.75 – ⌷ 8.50 – **192 rm** 95.00/115.00 **st.**, 1 suite –
SB (weekends only) 119.00/138.90 **st.**

🏨 **Hospitality Inn** (Mt. Charlotte Thistle), 104 Bayswater Rd, W2 3HL, ℰ 262 4461, Telex
22667, Fax 706 4560, ≼ – 🛗 ⇆ rm ▤ 📺 ☎ ℗ – 🔬 40. ⚞ 亜 ⓞ 𝑉𝐼𝑆𝐴 𝐽𝐶𝐵. ⌘   CZ **o**
M (bar lunch)/dinner a la carte 12.50/20.85 **st.** – ⌷ 8.50 – **175 rm** 75.00/105.00 **st.**

🏨 **Mornington** (Best Western) without rest., 12 Lancaster Gate, W2 3LG, ℰ 262 7361,
Fax 706 1028 – 🛗 📺 ☎. ⚞ 亜 ⓞ 𝑉𝐼𝑆𝐴   DZ **s**
68 rm 75.00/108.00 **st.**

🏨 **Pavilion,** 35 Leinster Gdns, W2 3AR, ℰ 258 0269, Telex 268613, Fax 723 7295, ≘s – 🛗 📺
☎ – 🔬 70. ⚞ 亜 ⓞ 𝑉𝐼𝑆𝐴 𝐽𝐶𝐵. ⌘   CZ **u**
M *(closed 25 and 26 December)* (dinner only) 9.50 **st.** ⓕ 4.50 – **97 rm** ⌷ 79.00/97.00 **st.** –
SB (weekends only) 72.00/102.00 **st.**

🏠 **Byron** without rest., 36-38 Queensborough Terr., W2 3SH, ✆ 243 0987, Telex 263431, Fax 792 1957 – 🛗 📺 ☎. 🖪 🕮 ⓪ 💳. ⁂   BZ **z**
41 rm ⊑ 75.50/95.00 st., 1 suite.

🏠 **Century,** 18-19 Craven Hill Gdns, W2 3EE, ✆ 262 6644, Fax 262 0673 – 🛗 📺 ☎. 🖪 🕮 ⓪ 💳   CZ **e**
M 15.00/25.00 **st.** and a la carte ₰ 4.00 – ⊑ 3.00 – **60 rm** 55.00/89.00 **st.**

🏠 **Delmere,** 130 Sussex Gdns, W2 1UB, ✆ 706 3344, Telex 8953857, Fax 262 1863 – 🛗 📺 ☎. 🖪 🕮 💳   DZ **v**
M (closed Sunday and Bank Holidays) (dinner only) 16.00 **st.** and a la carte ₰ 4.50 – ⊑ 6.00 – **38 rm** 73.00/91.00 **st.**

🏠 **Gresham** without rest., 116 Sussex Gdns, W2 1UA, ✆ 402 2920, Fax 402 3137 – 🛗 📺 ☎. 🖪 🕮 ⓪ 💳 ⁂   DZ **a**
⊑ 5.00 – **38 rm** 50.00/75.00 **st.**

🏠 **Camelot** without rest., 45-47 Norfolk Sq., W2 1RX, ✆ 723 9118, Fax 402 3412 – 🛗 📺 ☎. 🖪 ⓪ 💳 ⁂   DZ **c**
44 rm ⊑ 36.50/70.00 **st.**

🏠 **Norfolk Plaza** without rest., 29-33 Norfolk Sq., W2 1RX, ✆ 723 0792, Telex 266977, Fax 224 8770 – 📺 ☎. 🖪 🕮 ⓪ 💳 💳 ⁂   DZ **x**
⊑ 6.00 – **81 rm** 69.00/98.00 **st.**, 6 suites.

🏠 **Parkwood** without rest., 4 Stanhope Pl., W2 2HB, ✆ 402 2241, Fax 402 1574 – ⇔ 📺 ☎. 🖪 💳 ⁂   EZ **e**
18 rm ⊑ 39.75/64.50 **st.**

XXX **Aspects** (at London Metropole H.), Edgware Rd, W2 1JU, ✆ 402 4141, Telex 23711, Fax 724 8866, < London – 🗐. 🖪 🕮 ⓪ 💳 💳   p. 64 GU **c**
M 21.95/29.50 **st.** and a la carte ₰ 8.50.

XX **Spice Merchant** (at Coburg H.), 130 Bayswater Rd, W2 4RJ, ✆ 221 2442, Fax 229 0557 – 🗐. 🖪 🕮 ⓪ 💳   BZ **c**
M - Indian a la carte 11.45/16.15 **st.** ₰ 5.00.

XX **Poons,** Whiteleys, Queensway, W2 4YN, ✆ 792 2884 – 🗐. 🖪 🕮 ⓪ 💳   BZ **x**
closed 3 days at Christmas – **M** - Chinese a la carte 10.00/15.60 **t.**

XX **Hsing,** 451 Edgware Rd, Little Venice, W2 1TH, ✆ 402 0904 – 🗐. 🖪 🕮 ⓪ 💳
closed Sunday and 3 days at Christmas – **M** - Chinese a la carte approx. 20.00 **st.**   p. 21 GU **a**

XX **San Marino,** 26 Sussex Pl., W2 2TH, ✆ 723 8395 – 🖪 🕮 ⓪ 💳   DZ **u**
closed Bank Holidays – **M** - Italian a la carte 18.20/29.80 **t.** ₰ 4.25.

X **Al San Vincenzo,** 30 Connaught St., W2 2AE, ✆ 262 9623 – 🖪 💳   EZ **o**
closed Saturday lunch, Sunday and 2 weeks Christmas – **M** - Italian a la carte 19.45/29.00 **t.** ₰ 5.50.

X **L'Accento,** 16 Garway Rd, W2 4NH, ✆ 243 2201, Fax 243 2201 – 🖪 💳   BZ **a**
M - Italian 10.50 **t.** and a la carte ₰ 4.00.

  Belgravia – ✉ SW1 – ☎ 071 – Except where otherwise stated see pp. 30 and 31.

🏨🏨 **Berkeley,** Wilton Pl., SW1X 7RL, ✆ 235 6000, Telex 919252, Fax 235 4330, ₰₅, ⇌s, 🔲 – 🛗 🗐 📺 ☎ ⇔ – 🕰 200. 🖪 🕮 ⓪ 💳 ⁂   FQ **e**
M - **Restaurant** (closed Saturday) 19.50/21.00 **st.** and a la carte ₰ 5.50 – **The Perroquet** (closed Sunday) 15.00/21.00 **st.** and lunch a la carte ₰ 5.50 – ⊑ 16.00 – **133 rm** 160.00/250.00 **s.**, 27 suites.

🏨🏨 **Lanesborough,** 1 Lanesborough Pl., SW1X 7TA, ✆ 259 5599, Telex 911866, Fax 259 5606 – 🛗 ⇔ rm 🗐 📺 ☎ & 🅿 – 🕰 70. 🖪 🕮 ⓪ 💳 💳 ⁂
M – **The Conservatory** 21.50/27.50 **st.** and a la carte ₰ 7.50 – (see also **The Dining Room** below) – **86 rm** 175.00/295.00 **s.**, 9 suites.   p. 25 IY **a**

🏨 **Halkin,** 5 Halkin St., SW1X 7DJ, ✆ 333 1000, Fax 333 1100, « Contemporary interior design » – 🛗 ⇔ rm 🗐 📺 ☎ – 🕰 25. 🖪 🕮 ⓪ 💳 ⁂   p. 32 AV **a**
M - Italian (closed lunch Saturday and Sunday) 25.50 **st.** (lunch) and dinner a la carte 29.50/39.50 **st.** ₰ 9.00 – ⊑ 13.50 – **36 rm** 190.00/245.00 **s.**, 5 suites.

🏨 **Sheraton Belgravia,** 20 Chesham Pl., SW1X 8HQ, ✆ 235 6040, Telex 919020, Fax 259 6243 – 🛗 ⇔ rm 🗐 📺 ☎. 🖪 🕮 ⓪ 💳 💳 ⁂   FR **u**
closed 20 December-4 January – **M** (closed lunch Saturday and Sunday) 19.95/15.00 **t.** and a la carte ₰ 5.00 – ⊑ 11.75 – **82 rm** 190.00/210.00, 7 suites.

🏨 **Lowndes** (Hyatt), 21 Lowndes St., SW1X 9ES, ✆ 823 1234, Telex 919065, Fax 235 1154 – 🛗 ⇔ rm 🗐 📺 ☎ – 🕰 25. 🖪 🕮 ⓪ 💳 ⁂   FR **i**
M a la carte 12.95/24.25 **t.** ₰ 5.25 – ⊑ 10.50 – **77 rm** 135.00/180.00 **s.**, 1 suite.

XXXX **The Dining Room** (at Lanesborough H.), 1 Lanesborough Pl., SW1X 7TA, ✆ 259 5599, Telex 911866, Fax 259 5606 – 🗐. 🖪 🕮 ⓪ 💳 💳   p. 25 IY **a**
closed Saturday and Sunday – **M** 24.00/29.00 **st.** and a la carte 29.50/48.50 **st.** ₰ 7.50.

XXX **Al Bustan,** 27 Motcomb St., SW1X 8JU, ✆ 235 8277 – 🗐. 🖪 🕮 ⓪ 💳   FR **z**
closed 25 and 26 December – **Meals** - Lebanese 15.00/20.00 **t.** and a la carte 21.50/25.50 **t.** ₰ 8.00.

XX **Motcombs,** 26 Motcomb St., SW1X 8JU, ✆ 235 6382, Fax 245 6351 – 🗐. 🖪 🕮 ⓪ 💳   FR **z**
closed Sunday dinner and Bank Holidays – **M** 14.75/25.00 **t.** and a la carte ₰ 6.50

Hyde Park and Knightsbridge – ✉ SW1/SW7 – ☎ 071 – pp. 30 and 31.

Hyde Park (Forte), 66 Knightsbridge, SW1Y 7LA, ℰ 235 2000, Telex 262057, Fax 235 4552, ≤, – 🛗 ✸ rm 🗏 📺 ☎ & – 🔬 200. 🖪 ᴁ ⓞ 𝖵𝖨𝖲𝖠 𝖩𝖢𝖡. Ꮥ   FQ x
M – Park Room - Italian 24.50/29.50 **st.** and a la carte ⓐ 6.50 – (see also **The Restaurant** below) – ☲ 14.00 – **166 rm** 195.00/215.00 **s.**, 19 suites

Knightsbridge Green without rest., 159 Knightsbridge, SW1X 7PD, ℰ 584 6274, Fax 225 1635 – 🛗 📺 ☎. 🖪 ᴁ 𝖵𝖨𝖲𝖠. ᏕᏕ   EQ z
closed 4 days at Christmas – ☲ 8.50 – **10 rm** 75.00/100.00 **st.**, **14 suites** 115.00 **st.**

The Restaurant (White), (at Hyde Park H.), 66 Knightsbridge, SW1Y 7LA, ℰ 259 5380 – 🗏. 🖪 𝖵𝖨𝖲𝖠   FQ x
closed Saturday lunch, Sunday, last week December and first week January – **M** (booking essential) 25.00/55.00 **t.** ⓐ 9.00
Spec. Terrine of pork and foie gras, sauce gribiche. Saddle of rabbit with asparagus and leeks, sauce romarin, Millefeuille of red fruits, Kirsch sabayon.

Pearl of Knightsbridge, 22 Brompton Rd, SW1X 7QN, ℰ 225 3888, Fax 225 0252 – 🖪 ᴁ ⓞ 𝖵𝖨𝖲𝖠   EQ e
M - Chinese 15.00/40.00 **t.** and a la carte.

Knightsbridge Place, 116 Knightsbridge, SW1X 7PJ, ℰ 225 3512 – 🗏   EQ x
M - Italian rest.

Mayfair – ✉ W1 – ☎ 071 – pp. 28 and 29.

Dorchester, Park Lane, W1A 2HJ, ℰ 629 8888, Telex 887704, Fax 409 0114, 𝑓₆, ☖s – 🛗 ✸ rm 🗏 📺 ☎ & ⟷ – 🔬 500. 🖪 ᴁ ⓞ 𝖵𝖨𝖲𝖠 𝖩𝖢𝖡. ᏕᏕ   BN a
M – Grill 20.00/28.00 **st.** and a la carte 25.00/38.00 **st.** ⓐ 11.00 – (see also **Oriental** and **Terrace** below) – ☲ 13.50 – **195 rm** 180.00/240.00 **s.**, 55 suites

Claridge's, Brook St., W1A 2JQ, ℰ 629 8860, Telex 21872, Fax 499 2210 – 🛗 🗏 📺 ☎ & – 🔬 60. 🖪 ᴁ ⓞ 𝖵𝖨𝖲𝖠 𝖩𝖢𝖡. ᏕᏕ   BL c
M 21.00/26.50 **st.** and a la carte 37.50/55.00 **st.** ⓐ 5.50 – **Causerie** (closed Saturday dinner and Sunday) 18.50/30.00 **st.** and a la carte 32.50/50.50 **st.** ⓐ 5.50 – ☲ 16.00 – **137 rm** 180.00/280.00 **s.**, 53 suites.

Four Seasons, Hamilton Pl., Park Lane, W1A 1AZ, ℰ 499 0888, Telex 22771, Fax 493 1895, 𝑓₆ – 🛗 ✸ rm 🗏 📺 ☎ ⟷ – 🔬 400. 🖪 ᴁ ⓞ 𝖵𝖨𝖲𝖠 𝖩𝖢𝖡. ᏕᏕ   BP a
M – Lanes 29.50 **st.** (lunch) and dinner a la carte 19.50/35.50 **st.** – (see also **Four Seasons** below) – **208 rm** 200.00/245.00 **s.**, 19 suites.

Le Meridien London, 21 Piccadilly, W1V 0BH, ℰ 734 8000, Telex 25795, Fax 437 3574, 𝑓₆, ☖s, 🔲, squash – 🛗 ✸ rm 🗏 📺 ☎ & – 🔬 250. 🖪 ᴁ ⓞ 𝖵𝖨𝖲𝖠 𝖩𝖢𝖡. ᏕᏕ   EM a
M – Terrace Garden 19.50 **st.** and a la carte 16.70/26.75 **st.** ⓐ 7.00 – (see also **Oak Room** below) – ☲ 13.25 – **237 rm** 190.00/230.00, 26 suites – SB (weekends only) 320.00 **st.**

Grosvenor House (Forte), Park Lane, W1A 3AA, ℰ 499 6363, Telex 24871, Fax 493 3341, 𝑓₆, ☖s, 🔲 – 🛗 ✸ rm 🗏 📺 ☎ ⟷ – 🔬 1 500. 🖪 ᴁ ⓞ 𝖵𝖨𝖲𝖠 𝖩𝖢𝖡. ᏕᏕ   AM a
M – Pavilion 13.50 **t.** (lunch) and a la carte 18.00/28.00 **t.** – **Pasta Vino** approx. 15.00 **t.** – (see also **Chez Nico at Ninety Park Lane** below) – ☲ 13.75 – **384 rm** 180.00/195.00 **s.**, 70 suites – SB (weekends only) 238.00 **st.**

Connaught, Carlos Pl., W1Y 6AL, ℰ 499 7070, Fax 495 3262 – 🛗 🗏 rest 📺 ☎. 🖪 ᴁ 𝖵𝖨𝖲𝖠. ᏕᏕ   BM e
M – The Restaurant and Grill Room (booking essential) 25.00/35.00 **t.** and a la carte 27.50/62.00 **t.** ⓐ 5.75 – **66 rm**, 24 suites
Spec. Galette Connaught aux 'diamants noirs', salade Aphrodite, Homard et langoustines grillés aux herbes, Crème brûlée d'un soir.

47 Park Street, 47 Park St., W1Y 4EB, ℰ 491 7282, Telex 22116, Fax 491 7281 – 🛗 🗏 📺 ☎. 🖪 ᴁ ⓞ 𝖵𝖨𝖲𝖠 𝖩𝖢𝖡. ᏕᏕ   AM c
M (room service and see also **Le Gavroche** below) – ☲ 17.00 – **52 suites** 235.00/380.00 **s.**

Brown's (Forte), 29-34 Albemarle St., W1A 4SW, ℰ 493 6020, Fax 493 9381 – 🛗 ✸ rm 🗏 📺 ☎ – 🔬 70. 🖪 ᴁ ⓞ 𝖵𝖨𝖲𝖠 𝖩𝖢𝖡. ᏕᏕ   DM e
M a la carte 21.75/38.25 **t.** ⓐ 8.50 – ☲ 13.75 – **114 rm** 165.00/245.00, 6 suites – SB (weekends only) 270.00 **st.**

London Hilton on Park Lane, 22 Park Lane, W1Y 4BE, ℰ 493 8000, Telex 24873, Fax 493 4957, « ≤ London from rooftop restaurant », ☖s – 🛗 ✸ rm 🗏 📺 ☎ & – 🔬 1 000. 🖪 ᴁ ⓞ 𝖵𝖨𝖲𝖠 𝖩𝖢𝖡. ᏕᏕ   BP e
M – Windows on the World (closed Saturday lunch, Sunday dinner and Bank Holidays) 27.95/39.00 **t.** and a la carte – **Trader Vics** a la carte approx. 30.95 **t.** – **395 rm** 195.00/245.00 **t.**, 52 suites.

Park Lane, Piccadilly, W1Y 8BX, ℰ 499 6321, Telex 21533, Fax 499 1965, 𝑓₆ – 🛗 ✸ rm 📺 ☎ ☻ – 🔬 300. ᏕᏕ   BP x
268 rm, 52 suites.

Britannia (Inter-Con), Grosvenor Sq., W1A 3AN, ℰ 629 9400, Telex 23941, Fax 629 7736 – 🛗 ✸ rm 🗏 📺 ☎ & – 🔬 80. 🖪 ᴁ ⓞ 𝖵𝖨𝖲𝖠 𝖩𝖢𝖡. ᏕᏕ   BM x
M – Adam Room (closed Saturday and Sunday) 22.00/27.00 **st.** and dinner a la carte ⓐ 5.75 – (see also **Shogun** below) – ☲ 10.75 – **305 rm** 160.00/205.00, 12 suites – SB (weekends only) 225.00/450.00 **st.**

Inter-Continental, 1 Hamilton Pl., Hyde Park Corner, W1V 0QY, $\mathscr{C}$ 409 3131, Telex 25853, Fax 409 7461, I_6, $\leqslant$s – $|\phi|$ $\Leftarrow$ rm $\equiv$ $\boxed{\text{TV}}$ $\mathbf{\widehat{a}}$ $\mathring{b}$ $\iff$ – $\underset{\text{\tiny A}}{\mathring{A}}$ 700. $\boxed{\text{N}}$ $\boxed{\text{AE}}$ $\textcircled{0}$ $\overline{\textit{VISA}}$ $\overline{\text{JCB}}$
$\mathscr{R}$ BP **o**
M 25.50/43.00 **st.** and a la carte $\mathring{\mathbb{I}}$ 8.00 – (see also **Le Soufflé** below) – $\rightleftharpoons$ 12.90 – **433 rm** 195.00/270.00, 34 suites.

May Fair Inter-Continental, Stratton St., W1A 2AN, $\mathscr{C}$ 629 7777, Telex 262526, Fax 629 1459, I_6, $\leqslant$s, $\boxed{\ }$ – $|\phi|$ $\Leftarrow$ rm $\equiv$ $\boxed{\text{TV}}$ $\mathbf{\widehat{a}}$ $\mathring{b}$ – $\underset{\text{\tiny A}}{\mathring{A}}$ 270. $\boxed{\text{N}}$ $\boxed{\text{AE}}$ $\textcircled{0}$ $\overline{\textit{VISA}}$ $\overline{\text{JCB}}$. $\mathscr{R}$
M - (see **Le Chateau** below) – $\rightleftharpoons$ 13.00 – **263 rm** 170.00/210.00 **s.**, 24 suites – SB (weekends only) 310.00/330.00 **st.** DN **z**

Marriott, Duke St., Grosvenor Sq., W1A 4AW, $\mathscr{C}$ 493 1232, Telex 268101, Fax 491 3201 – $|\phi|$ $\Leftarrow$ rm $\equiv$ $\boxed{\text{TV}}$ $\mathbf{\widehat{a}}$ $\mathring{b}$ – $\underset{\text{\tiny A}}{\mathring{A}}$ 375. $\boxed{\text{N}}$ $\boxed{\text{AE}}$ $\textcircled{0}$ $\overline{\textit{VISA}}$ $\overline{\text{JCB}}$ $\mathscr{R}$ BL **a**
M – **Diplomat** *(closed lunch Monday and Saturday)* a la carte 15.25/27.75 **st.** – $\rightleftharpoons$ 10.50 – **212 rm** 95.00/220.00 **s.**, 11 suites.

Athenaeum, 116 Piccadilly, W1V 0BJ, $\mathscr{C}$ 499 3464, Telex 261589, Fax 493 1860 – $|\phi|$ $\Leftarrow$ rm $\equiv$ $\boxed{\text{TV}}$ $\mathbf{\widehat{a}}$ – $\underset{\text{\tiny A}}{\mathring{A}}$ 55. $\boxed{\text{N}}$ $\boxed{\text{AE}}$ $\textcircled{0}$ $\overline{\textit{VISA}}$ $\overline{\text{JCB}}$. $\mathscr{R}$ CP **s**
M *(closed Saturday lunch)* 19.50 **st.** and a la carte $\mathring{\mathbb{I}}$ 9.50 – $\rightleftharpoons$ 12.50 – **106 rm** 165.00/205.00 **st.**, 6 suites – SB (weekends only) 192.00/234.00 **st.**

Westbury (Forte), Conduit St., W1A 4UH, $\mathscr{C}$ 629 7755, Telex 24378, Fax 495 1163 – $|\phi|$ $\equiv$ $\boxed{\text{TV}}$ $\mathbf{\widehat{a}}$ – $\underset{\text{\tiny A}}{\mathring{A}}$ 116. $\mathscr{R}$ DM **a**
229 rm, 14 suites.

Washington, 5-7 Curzon St., W1Y 8DT, $\mathscr{C}$ 499 7000, Telex 24540, Fax 495 6172 – $|\phi|$ $\Leftarrow$ rm $\equiv$ $\boxed{\text{TV}}$ $\mathbf{\widehat{a}}$ – $\underset{\text{\tiny A}}{\mathring{A}}$ 80. $\boxed{\text{N}}$ $\boxed{\text{AE}}$ $\textcircled{0}$ $\overline{\textit{VISA}}$ $\overline{\text{JCB}}$ $\mathscr{R}$ CN **s**
M *(closed lunch Saturday and Sunday)* a la carte 17.20/26.90 **st.** – $\rightleftharpoons$ 9.95 – **170 rm** 148.00/178.00 **st.**, 3 suites.

Holiday Inn, 3 Berkeley St., W1X 6NE, $\mathscr{C}$ 493 8282, Telex 24561, Fax 629 2827 – $|\phi|$ $\Leftarrow$ rm $\equiv$ $\boxed{\text{TV}}$ $\mathbf{\widehat{a}}$ – $\underset{\text{\tiny A}}{\mathring{A}}$ 70. $\boxed{\text{N}}$ $\boxed{\text{AE}}$ $\textcircled{0}$ $\overline{\textit{VISA}}$ $\mathscr{R}$ DN **r**
M (bar lunch Saturday) 15.75/19.50 **t.** and a la carte – $\rightleftharpoons$ 10.95 – **179 rm** 140.00/155.00 **st.**, 6 suites.

Chesterfield, 35 Charles St., W1X 8LX, $\mathscr{C}$ 491 2622, Telex 269394, Fax 491 4793 – $|\phi|$ $\Leftarrow$ rm $\boxed{\text{TV}}$ $\mathbf{\widehat{a}}$ – $\underset{\text{\tiny A}}{\mathring{A}}$ 100. $\boxed{\text{N}}$ $\boxed{\text{AE}}$ $\textcircled{0}$ $\overline{\textit{VISA}}$ $\overline{\text{JCB}}$. $\mathscr{R}$ CN **c**
M *(closed Saturday lunch)* 14.50/18.50 **t.** and a la carte $\mathring{\mathbb{I}}$ 7.95 – $\rightleftharpoons$ 9.95 – **106 rm** 115.00/170.00 **st.**, 4 suites.

Green Park, Half Moon St., W1Y 8BP, $\mathscr{C}$ 629 7522, Telex 28856, Fax 491 8971 – $|\phi|$ $\Leftarrow$ rm $\equiv$ rest $\boxed{\text{TV}}$ $\mathbf{\widehat{a}}$ – $\underset{\text{\tiny A}}{\mathring{A}}$ 70. $\boxed{\text{N}}$ $\boxed{\text{AE}}$ $\textcircled{0}$ $\overline{\textit{VISA}}$ $\overline{\text{JCB}}$. $\mathscr{R}$ CN **a**
M *(closed lunch Saturday, Sunday and Bank Holidays)* 15.00/22.50 **st.** and a la carte $\mathring{\mathbb{I}}$ 4.95 – $\rightleftharpoons$ 9.75 – **161 rm** 104.00/174.00 **st.** – SB (weekends only) 129.00/272.50 **st.**

London Mews Hilton without rest., 2 Stanhope Row, W1Y 7HE, $\mathscr{C}$ 493 7222, Telex 24665, Fax 629 9423 – $|\phi|$ $\Leftarrow$ $\equiv$ $\boxed{\text{TV}}$ $\mathbf{\widehat{a}}$ $\iff$ – $\underset{\text{\tiny A}}{\mathring{A}}$ 45. $\boxed{\text{N}}$ $\boxed{\text{AE}}$ $\textcircled{0}$ $\overline{\textit{VISA}}$ $\overline{\text{JCB}}$ BP **u**
$\rightleftharpoons$ 9.95 **71 rm** 125.00/169.00 **st.**, 1 suite.

Flemings, 7-12 Half Moon St., W1Y 7RA, $\mathscr{C}$ 499 2964, Telex 27510, Fax 629 4063 – $|\phi|$ $\equiv$ rest $\boxed{\text{TV}}$ $\mathbf{\widehat{a}}$ – $\underset{\text{\tiny A}}{\mathring{A}}$ 40. $\boxed{\text{N}}$ $\boxed{\text{AE}}$ $\textcircled{0}$ $\overline{\textit{VISA}}$ $\overline{\text{JCB}}$. $\mathscr{R}$ CN **z**
M 15.00/25.00 **st.** and a la carte $\mathring{\mathbb{I}}$ 7.50 – $\rightleftharpoons$ 10.20 – **132 rm** 104.00/196.00 **st.**, 11 suites.

XXXXX $\circledast$ **Oak Room** (at Le Meridien London H.), 21 Piccadilly, W1V 0BH, $\mathscr{C}$ 734 8000, Telex 25795, Fax 437 3574 – $\equiv$. $\boxed{\text{N}}$ $\boxed{\text{AE}}$ $\textcircled{0}$ $\overline{\textit{VISA}}$ $\overline{\text{JCB}}$ EM **a**
closed Saturday lunch and Sunday – **M** - French 25.50/47.00 **t.** and a la carte 37.50/48.00 **t.** $\mathring{\mathbb{I}}$ 10.00
Spec. Gaspacho de langoustines à la crème de courgette, Suprême de bar au beurre de truffe, Canard, sauce Arabica.

XXXXX $\circledast \circledast$ **Chez Nico at Ninety Park Lane** (Ladenis) (at Grosvenor House H.), Park Lane, W1A 3AA, $\mathscr{C}$ 409 1290, Fax 355 4877 – $\equiv$. $\boxed{\text{N}}$ $\boxed{\text{AE}}$ $\textcircled{0}$ $\overline{\textit{VISA}}$ AM **e**
closed lunch Saturday and Bank Holiday Mondays, Sunday, 4 days at Easter and 10 days at Christmas – **M** - French (booking essential) 25.00/50.00 **st.**
Spec. Bresse pigeon and artichoke salad with a truffle and mustard vinaigrette, Roast sea bass with olive oil and aromatic vinegar, Assiette gourmande.

XXXXX **Terrace** (at Dorchester H.), Park Lane, W1A 2HJ, $\mathscr{C}$ 629 8888, Telex 887704, Fax 409 0114 – $\equiv$. $\boxed{\text{N}}$ $\boxed{\text{AE}}$ $\textcircled{0}$ $\overline{\textit{VISA}}$ $\overline{\text{JCB}}$ BN **a**
closed Sunday, Monday and August – **M** - French (dinner only) 25.00/45.00 **st.** and a la carte 31.00/41.00 **st.** $\mathring{\mathbb{I}}$ 11.00.

XXXX $\circledast \circledast$ **Le Gavroche** (Roux), 43 Upper Brook St., W1Y 1PF, $\mathscr{C}$ 408 0881, Fax 409 0939 – $\equiv$. $\boxed{\text{N}}$ $\boxed{\text{AE}}$ $\textcircled{0}$ $\overline{\textit{VISA}}$ AM **c**
closed Saturday, Sunday, 24 December-4 January and Bank Holidays – **M** - French (booking essential) 37.00/60.00 **st.** and a la carte 44.50/82.30 **st.** $\mathring{\mathbb{I}}$ 10.00
Spec. Soufflé suissesse, L'Assiette du boucher, Omelette Rothschild.

XXXX $\circledast$ **Oriental** (at Dorchester H.), Park Lane, W1A 2HJ, $\mathscr{C}$ 629 8888, Telex 887704, Fax 409 0114 – $\equiv$. $\boxed{\text{N}}$ $\boxed{\text{AE}}$ $\textcircled{0}$ $\overline{\textit{VISA}}$ BN **a**
closed Saturday lunch, Sunday and August – **M** - Chinese (Canton) 20.00/28.00 **st.** and a la carte 28.00/60.50 **st.** $\mathring{\mathbb{I}}$ 11.00
Spec. Whole roasted Peking duck, Fried prawns with walnuts in a light lemon sauce, Diced beef with lemon grass and black pepper.

XXXX ❀ **Four Seasons,** Hamilton Pl., Park Lane, W1A 1AZ, ✆ 499 0888, Telex 22771, Fax 493 1895 – 🍴 🕮 ⟵. 🄰 AE ⓞ *VISA* JCB   BP **a**
M – **French** 25.00/40.00 **st.** and a la carte 30.50/47.50 **st.** ⋒ 6.40
Spec. Sautéed scallops with lemon grass and fennel in filo pastry layers, Lamb cutlets in a Stilton mousse-soufflé with lentil fricassee, Nougatine box filled with chocolate mousse, hazelnuts and caramel springs.

XXXX ❀ **Les Saveurs,** 37a Curzon St., W1Y 8EY, ✆ 491 8919, Fax 491 3658 – 🕮. 🄰 AE ⓞ *VISA*
closed Saturday, Sunday, 8 to 24 August, 24 December-10 January and Bank Holidays – **M**
- **French** 18.00/39.00 **t.**   BN **o**
Spec. Panaché de volaille et foie gras aux cèpes, Filet de rouget en salmis, Croustillant de poires rôties à la réglisse.

XXXX **Mirabelle,** 56 Curzon St., W1Y 8DL, ✆ 499 4636, Fax 499 5449 – 🕮. 🄰 AE ⓞ *VISA* JCB   CN **u**
closed Saturday lunch, Sunday and Bank Holidays – **M** 25.00/45.00 **st.** and a la carte ⋒ 7.00
– **Bon** - **Japanese** (Teppanyaki) 25.00/35.00 **st.** and a la carte ⋒ 7.00.

XXXX **Le Soufflé** (at Inter-Continental H.), 1 Hamilton Pl., Hyde Park Corner, W1V 0QY, ✆ 409 3131, Telex 25853, Fax 409 7461 – 🕮 ⟵. 🄰 AE ⓞ *VISA* JCB   BP **o**
closed Saturday lunch, Sunday dinner, Monday and August – **M** 25.50/43.00 **st.** and a la carte 32.50/50.50 **st.** ⋒ 8.00.

XXX **Princess Garden,** 8-10 North Audley St., W1Y 1WF, ✆ 493 3223, Fax 491 2655 – 🕮. 🄰 AE ⓞ *VISA* JCB   AL **z**
closed 1 week Christmas – **M** - **Chinese** (Peking, Szechuan) 33.00 **t.** (lunch) and a la carte 20.50/36.00 **t.** ⋒ 8.00.

XXX **Zen Central,** 20 Queen St., W1X 7PJ, ✆ 629 8089 – 🕮 ⓟ. 🄰 AE ⓞ *VISA*   CN **x**
Meals - **Chinese** 12.00/20.00 **t.** and a la carte.

XXX **Le Chateau** (at May Fair Inter-Continental H.), Stratton St., W1A 2AN, ✆ 629 7777, Fax 629 1459 – 🕮. 🄰 AE ⓞ *VISA* JCB   DN **z**
M 25.00/28.00 **t.** and a la carte.

XXX **Scotts,** 20 Mount St., W1Y 6HE, ✆ 629 5248, Fax 491 2477 – 🕮. 🄰 AE ⓞ *VISA* JCB   BM **a**
closed Saturday lunch, Sunday, Christmas-4 January and Bank Holidays – **M** - **Seafood** a la carte 24.65/33.60 **t.**

XX **Greenhouse,** 27a Hay's Mews, W1X 7RJ, ✆ 499 3331, Fax 225 0011 – 🕮. 🄰 AE ⓞ *VISA*   BN **e**
closed Saturday lunch, 24 December-3 January and Bank Holidays – **Meals** a la carte 17.00/29.50 **t.** ⋒ 5.95.

XX **Bentley's,** 11-15 Swallow St., W1R 7HD, ✆ 734 4756 – 🕮. 🄰 AE ⓞ *VISA* JCB   EM **i**
closed Sunday and Bank Holidays – **M** - **Seafood** 16.50/18.50 **t.** and a la carte ⋒ 5.50.

XX Langan's Brasserie, Stratton St., W1X 5FD, ✆ 491 8822 – 🕮   DN **e**
M (booking essential).

XX **Mulligans,** 13-14 Cork St., W1X 1PF, ✆ 409 1370 – 🕮. 🄰 AE ⓞ *VISA*   DM **c**
closed Saturday lunch, Sunday, 25 December-1 January and Bank Holidays – **M** - **Irish** a la carte 19.00/27.25 **t.** ⋒ 5.95.

XX **Shogun** (at Britannia H.) Adams Row, W1Y 5DE, ✆ 493 1255 – 🕮. 🄰 AE ⓞ *VISA* JCB   BM **x**
closed Monday – **M** - **Japanese** (dinner only) a la carte approx. 40.00 **t.**

X **Ikeda,** 30 Brook St., W1Y 1AG, ✆ 629 2730, Fax 628 6982 – 🕮. 🄰 AE ⓞ *VISA* JCB
closed Saturday lunch, Sunday and Bank Holidays – **M** - **Japanese** 15.00/38.00 **t.** and a la carte.   CKL **a**

Regent's Park and Marylebone – ✉ NW1/NW6/NW8/W1 – ☎ 071 – Except where otherwise stated see pp. 28 and 29.

🛈 Basement Services Arcade, Selfridges Store, Oxford St., W1 ✆ 730 3488/824 8000.

🏨🏨🏨 **Regent London,** 222 Marylebone Rd, NW1 6JQ, ✆ 631 8000, Telex 8813733, Fax 631 8080, « Victorian Gothic architecture, atrium and winter garden », ℩₅, ⇌, ▦ –
🛗 ⇔ rm 🕮 🖵 🕿 & ⓟ – 🔬 350. 🄰 AE ⓞ *VISA* JCB. ⚹   HU **u**
M – The Dining Room 27.00/32.00 **st.** and a la carte ⋒ 8.20 – ⊑ 13.25 – **307 rm** 180.00 **s.,** 2 suites.

🏨🏨🏨 Churchill Inter-Continental, 30 Portman Sq., W1A 4ZX, ✆ 486 5800, Telex 264831, Fax 486 1255, ⚹ – 🛗 ⇔ rm 🕮 🖵 🕿 – 🔬 200. 🄰 AE ⓞ *VISA* JCB. ⚹   AJ **x**
⊑ 12.50 – **406 rm** 185.00, 37 suites.

🏨🏨🏨 **SAS Portman,** 22 Portman Sq., W1H 9FL, ✆ 486 5844, Telex 261526, Fax 935 0537, ⚹ – 🛗 ⇔ rm 🕮 🖵 🕿 & ⓟ – 🔬 380. 🄰 AE ⓞ *VISA* JCB. ⚹   AJ **o**
M a la carte approx. 16.00 **st.** – ⊑ 11.50 – **259 rm** 95.00/160.00 **s.,** 13 suites.

🏨🏨🏨 **Langham Hilton,** 1c Portland Pl., W1N 3AA, ✆ 636 1000, Telex 21113, Fax 323 2340 – 🛗 ⇔ rm 🕮 🖵 🕿 & – 🔬 360. 🄰 AE ⓞ *VISA* JCB. ⚹   p. 21 JU **e**
M – Memories of the Empire 33.00 **st.** and a la carte ⋒ 8.00 – King's Room 19.95/33.00 **st.** and a la carte ⋒ 8.00 – ⊑ 13.95 – **357 rm** 180.00/240.00, 26 suites.

🏨🏨🏨 **Selfridge** (Mt. Charlotte Thistle), Orchard St., W1H 0JS, ✆ 408 2080, Telex 22361, Fax 629 8849 – 🛗 ⇔ rm 🕮 🖵 🕿 – 🔬 220. 🄰 AE ⓞ *VISA* JCB. ⚹   AK **e**
M (closed Saturday lunch and Sunday) 17.50/22.50 **st.** and a la carte ⋒ 5.75 – ⊑ 10.25 – **294 rm** 135.00/170.00 **st.,** 2 suites.

9

🖭 **Berkshire** (Edwardian), 350 Oxford St., W1N 0BY, ℰ 629 7474, Telex 22270, Fax 629 8156 – 🛗 ⇔ rm 🔟 📺 ☎ – 🔬 45. ⚞ ⚞ ⑩ 𝗩𝗜𝗦𝗔 𝗝𝗖𝗕. ⋇   BK **n**
M 17.50/23.40 **st.** and a la carte – ⌕ 13.50 – **145 rm** 80.00/204.00 **st.**, 2 suites – SB (weekends only) 138.00/172.00 **st.**

🖭 **Clifton Ford**, 47 Welbeck St., W1M 8DN, ℰ 486 6600, Telex 22569, Fax 486 7492 – 🛗
▤ rest 🔟 ☎ – 🔬 150. ⚞ ⚞ ⑩ 𝗩𝗜𝗦𝗔   BH **a**
M – Doyle's a la carte 12.75/25.00 **st.** 🍴 4.50 – ⌕ 12.95 – **197 rm** 130.00/175.00 **s.**, 3 suites.

🖭 **Berners Park Plaza**, 10 Berners St., W1A 3BE, ℰ 636 1629, Telex 25759, Fax 580 3972 –
🛗 ⇔ rm ▤ rest 🔟 ☎ ☂ – 🔬 120. ⚞ ⚞ ⑩ 𝗩𝗜𝗦𝗔 𝗝𝗖𝗕. ⋇   EJ **r**
M (closed Saturday lunch) 13.95 **st.** and a la carte 🍴 6.00 – ⌕ 9.95 – **226 rm** 110.00/150.00 **st.**, 3 suites.

🖭 **London Regent's Park Hilton**, 18 Lodge Rd, NW8 7JT, ℰ 722 7722, Telex 23101, Fax 483 2408 – 🛗 ▤ 🔟 ☎ 🐾 🅟 – 🔬 150. ⚞ ⚞ ⑩ 𝗩𝗜𝗦𝗔 𝗝𝗖𝗕. ⋇   p. 21 GT **v**
M 18.75 **t.** and a la carte 🍴 6.95 – **Kashinoki - Japanese** (closed Monday) 16.00/30.00 **t.** and a la carte – ⌕ 11.30 – **376 rm** 115.00/130.00 **st.**, 1 suite – SB (weekends only) 166.00 **st.**

🖭 **Montcalm**, Great Cumberland Pl., W1A 2LF, ℰ 402 4288, Telex 28710, Fax 724 9180, ⇌
– 🛗 ▤ 🔟 ☎ – 🔬 80. ⚞ ⚞ ⑩ 𝗩𝗜𝗦𝗔 𝗝𝗖𝗕. ⋇   p. 33 EZ **x**
M (closed Saturday lunch and Sunday) 18.50/24.00 **t.** and dinner a la carte 🍴 7.00 – ⌕ 13.50 – **101 rm** 150.00/190.00, 14 suites.

🖭 **Marble Arch Marriott**, 134 George St., W1H 6DN, ℰ 723 1277, Fax 402 0666, ⅃₆, ⇌,
⚞ – 🛗 ⇔ rm 🔟 📺 ☎ ☂ 🅟 – 🔬 120. ⚞ ⚞ ⑩ 𝗩𝗜𝗦𝗔. ⋇   p. 33 EZ **i**
M 19.95 **st.** and a la carte – ⌕ 11.85 – **237 rm** 130.00/145.00 **s.**, 2 suites – SB (except Bank Holidays) (weekends only) 136.00/272.00 **st.**

🖭 **St. George's** (Forte), Langham Pl., W1N 8QS, ℰ 580 0111, Fax 436 7997, ⪡ – 🛗 ⇔ rm
▤ rest 🔟 ☎ – 🔬 35. ⚞ ⚞ ⑩ 𝗩𝗜𝗦𝗔 𝗝𝗖𝗕   p. 21 JU **a**
M (dancing Friday and Saturday evenings) 15.95/16.95 **t.** and a la carte 🍴 7.50 – ⌕ 10.95 – **83 rm** 105.00/145.00 **st.**, 3 suites – SB (weekends only) 138.00 **st.**

🖭 **Forte Crest Regents Park**, Carburton St., W1P 8EE, ℰ 388 2300, Telex 22453, Fax 387 2806 – 🛗 ⇔ rm ▤ rest 🔟 ☎ – 🔬 600. ⚞ ⚞ ⑩ 𝗩𝗜𝗦𝗔 𝗝𝗖𝗕. ⋇   p. 21 JU **i**
M (closed lunch Saturday and Sunday) 15.95 **st.** and dinner a la carte 🍴 6.60 – ⌕ 10.95 – **315 rm** 99.00 **st.**, 2 suites – SB (weekends only) 116.00 **st.**

🖭 **Rathbone** (Best Western), Rathbone St., W1P 1AJ, ℰ 636 2001, Telex 28728, Fax 636 3882 – 🛗 ⇔ rm 🔟 📺 ☎. ⚞ ⚞ ⑩ 𝗩𝗜𝗦𝗔 𝗝𝗖𝗕. ⋇   p. 22 KU **x**
M 14.95 **st.** and a la carte 🍴 4.00 – ⌕ 9.00 – **72 rm** 115.00/140.00 **st.** – SB (except April-May and September-November) 100.00/200.00 **st.**

🏨 **Dorset Square**, 39-40 Dorset Sq., NW1 6QN, ℰ 723 7874, Fax 724 3328, « Attractively furnished Regency town houses », ⌗ – 🛗 ▤ 🔟 ☎. ⚞ ⚞ 𝗩𝗜𝗦𝗔. ⋇   p. 21 HU **s**
M (closed Sunday lunch and Saturday) 10.50 **t.** and a la carte 🍴 7.50 – ⌕ 9.50 – **37 rm** 85.00/155.00 **t.**

🏨 **25 Dorset Square** without rest., 25 Dorset Sq., NW1 3QN, ℰ 262 7505, Fax 723 0194, « Regency town houses » – 🛗 🔟 ☎. ⚞ ⚞ ⑩ 𝗩𝗜𝗦𝗔. ⋇   HU **e**
⌕ 9.00 – , **12 suites** 170.00/250.00 **st.**.

🏨 **Durrants**, 26-32 George St., W1H 6BJ, ℰ 935 8131, Fax 487 3510, « Converted Georgian houses with Regency façade » – 🛗 🔟 ☎ – 🔬 50. ⚞ ⚞ 𝗩𝗜𝗦𝗔. ⋇   AH **e**
M 19.00 **t.** and a la carte – ⌕ 8.25 – **93 rm** 85.00/99.00 **st.**, 3 suites.

🏨 Londoner, 57-59 Welbeck St., W1M 8HS, ℰ 935 4442, Telex 894630, Fax 487 3782 – 🛗
⇔ rm 🔟 ☎ – 🔬 90. ⋇   BJ **c**
144 rm.

🏨 **Langham Court**, 31-35 Langham St., W1N 5RE, ℰ 436 6622, Fax 436 2303 – 🛗 🔟 ☎ –
🔬 70. ⚞ ⚞ ⑩ 𝗩𝗜𝗦𝗔 𝗝𝗖𝗕. ⋇   p. 21 JU **z**
M (closed lunch Saturday, Sunday and Bank Holidays) 20.00/30.00 **t.** and a la carte 🍴 7.00 – ⌕ 9.50 – **60 rm** 119.00/150.00 **st.**

🏨 **Mostyn**, 4 Bryanston St., W1H 0DE, ℰ 935 2361, Telex 27656, Fax 487 2759 – 🛗 ▤ rest
🔟 ☎ – 🔬 150. ⚞ ⚞ ⑩ 𝗩𝗜𝗦𝗔. ⋇   AK **i**
M 12.50/15.50 **st.** and a la carte – **118 rm** ⌕ 98.00/124.00 **st.**, 3 suites – SB (weekends only) 148.00/250.00 **st.**

🏨 **Harewood** (Best Western), Harewood Row, NW1 6SE, ℰ 262 2707, Telex 297225, Fax 262 2975 – 🛗 ⇔ rm ▤ rest 🔟 📺 ☎. ⚞ ⚞ ⑩ 𝗩𝗜𝗦𝗔. ⋇   p. 21 HU **x**
M (closed Friday and Saturday) (dinner only) 15.00 **st.** 🍴 4.75 – ⌕ 7.75 – **92 rm** 65.00/89.00 **st.** – SB (weekends only) 105.00/110.00 **st.**

🏛 **Bryanston Court** (Best Western) without rest., 56-60 Great Cumberland Pl., W1H 7FD, ℰ 262 3141, Fax 262 7248 – 🛗 🔟 ☎. ⚞ ⚞ ⑩ 𝗩𝗜𝗦𝗔 𝗝𝗖𝗕. ⋇   p. 33 EZ **z**
⌕ 6.00 – **54 rm** 65.00/95.00 **st.**

🏛 **Concorde** without rest., 50 Great Cumberland Pl., W1H 8DD, ℰ 402 6169, Fax 724 1184 –
🛗 🔟 ☎. ⚞ ⚞ ⑩ 𝗩𝗜𝗦𝗔 𝗝𝗖𝗕.   p. 33 EZ **n**
⌕ 6.00 – **28 rm** 62.00/72.00 **st.**

⌂ **Lincoln House** without rest., 33 Gloucester Pl., W1H 3PD, ℰ 486 7630, Fax 486 0166 –
🔟 ☎. ⚞ ⚞ ⑩ 𝗩𝗜𝗦𝗔. ⋇   AJ **c**
22 rm ⌕ 35.00/65.00 **st.**

XXX Odins, 27 Devonshire St., W1N 1RJ, ℰ 935 7296 – ▤   p. 21   IU   n

XX **Walsh's,** 5 Charlotte St., W1P 1HD, ℰ 637 0222, Fax 637 0224 – ▤. **A** **AE** **①** **VISA**   KU   r
closed Saturday lunch, Sunday and Bank Holidays – **M** - **Seafood** a la carte 19.40/32.50 **st.** ▮ 4.25.

XX **Nico Central,** 35 Great Portland St., W1N 5DD, ℰ 436 8846 – ▤. **A** **AE** **①** **VISA**
closed Saturday lunch, Sunday, 4 days Easter, 10 days Christmas and Bank Holiday Mondays – **Meals** a la carte 21.20/38.90 **st.**   DJ   c

XX Masako, 6-8 St. Christopher's Pl., W1M 5HB, ℰ 935 1579   BJ   e
M - Japanese rest.

XX **Gaylord,** 79-81 Mortimer St., W1N 7TB, ℰ 580 3615 – ▤. **A** **AE** **①** **VISA** **JCB**
M - Indian 13.50 **t.** and a la carte ▮ 4.75.   p. 22   KU   o

XX **Maroush III,** 62 Seymour St., W1H 5AF, ℰ 724 5024 – ▤. **A** **AE** **①** **VISA**   EZ   r
closed Christmas Day – **M** - Lebanese 12.00/50.00 **t.** and a la carte ▮ 7.00.

XX **Stephen Bull,** 5-7 Blandford St., W1H 3AA, ℰ 486 9696 – ▤. **A** **AE** **①** **VISA**   AH   a
closed Saturday lunch, Sunday, 1 week Christmas and Bank Holidays – **M** 18.00 **t.** (lunch) and a la carte 19.75/28.00 **t.** ▮ 5.50.

XX **Asuka,** Berkeley Arcade, 209a Baker St., NW1 6AB, ℰ 486 5026, Fax 262 1456 – **A** **AE** **①** **VISA** **JCB**   p. 21   HU   u
closed Saturday lunch, Sunday and Bank Holidays – **M** - Japanese 13.50/35.00 **t.** and a la carte.

XX **La Loggia,** 68 Edgware Rd, W2 2EG, ℰ 723 0554 – ▤. **A** **AE** **①** **VISA** **JCB** p. 33 EZ a
closed Saturday lunch, Sunday and Bank Holidays – **M** - Italian a la carte 20.50/32.00 **t.** ▮ 4.80.

XX **Fontana Amorosa,** 1 Blenheim Terr., NW8 0EH, ℰ 328 5014   p. 20   FS   s
closed Monday lunch, Sunday, last 3 weeks September and Bank Holidays – **M** - Italian a la carte 17.30/26.80 **t.**

XX **Tino's Garden,** 128 Allitsen Rd, NW8 7AU, ℰ 586 6264, Fax 586 6264 – **A** **AE**
VISA   p. 21   GT   u
closed 1 January, 1 April and 25 December – **M** 13.95/25.00 **st.** and a la carte ▮ 5.25.

X **Zoe,** 3-5 Barrett St., St. Christopher's Pl., W1M 5HH, ℰ 224 1122, Fax 935 5444 – **A** **①** **VISA**   BJ   a
closed Sunday, 3 days at Easter, 4 days at Christmas and Bank Holidays – **M** a la carte 12.50/20.70 **t.** ▮ 4.50.

X **Au Bois St. Jean,** 122 St. John's Wood High St., NW8 7SG, ℰ 722 0400, Fax 586 0410 – ▤. **A** **AE** **VISA** **JCB**   p. 21   GT   e
closed 3 days at Easter and 3 days at Christmas – **M** - French 14.50/23.50 **t.** ▮ 5.50.

X **L'Aventure,** 3 Blenheim Terr., NW8 0EH, ℰ 624 6232 – **A** **AE** **①** **VISA**
closed Saturday lunch, 4 days Easter and 1 week Christmas – **M** - French 18.50/25.00 **t.** ▮ 5.25.   p. 20   FS   s

X **Nakamura,** 31 Marylebone Lane, W1M 5FH, ℰ 935 2931 – **A** **AE** **①** **VISA** **JCB**   BJ   i
closed lunch Sunday and Bank Holidays and Saturday – **M** - Japanese 11.50/37.80 **t.** and a la carte.

X Langan's Bistro, 26 Devonshire St., W1N 1RJ, ℰ 935 4531 – ▤   p. 21   IU   e

X **Chaopraya,** 22 St. Christopher's Pl., W1M 5HD, ℰ 486 0777 – **A** **AE** **①** **VISA**   BJ   o
closed Saturday lunch, Sunday and Bank Holidays – **M** - Thai 17.00 **t.** and a la carte ▮ 3.90.

St. James's – ✉ W1/SW1/WC2 – ☎ 071 – pp. 28 and 29.

🏨 **Ritz,** Piccadilly, W1V 9DG, ℰ 493 8181, Telex 267200, Fax 493 2687, « Elegant restaurant in Louis XV style » – 📶 ▤ 📺 ☎. **A** **AE** **①** **VISA** **JCB**. 🍴   DN   a
M (dancing Friday and Saturday evenings) 26.00/39.50 **st.** and a la carte 44.00/66.50 **st.** ▮ 6.50 – 🍽 14.50 – **115 rm** 190.00/280.00 **st.**, 14 suites.

🏨 **Dukes** 🍴, 35 St. James's Pl., SW1A 1NY, ℰ 491 4840, Telex 28283, Fax 493 1264 – 📶 ▤ rest 📺 ☎ – 🔏 35. **A** **AE** **①** **VISA** **JCB**. 🍴   EP   x
M (closed Saturday lunch) 19.95/28.50 **t.** and a la carte 27.00/37.50 **t.** ▮ 6.75 – 🍽 11.75 – **38 rm** 180.00/275.00 **t.**, **26 suites** 330.00/420.00 **t.**

🏨 **22 Jermyn Street,** 22 Jermyn St., SW1Y 6HL, ℰ 734 2353, Fax 734 0750 – 📶 📺 ☎. **A** **AE** **①** **VISA** **JCB**   FM   e
M (room service only) a la carte 22.00/26.50 **t.** ▮ 6.35 – 🍽 13.00 – **5 rm** 155.00 **s.**, **13 suites** 205.00/240.00 **s.**

🏨 **Stafford** 🍴, 16-18 St. James's Pl., SW1A 1NJ, ℰ 493 0111, Telex 28602, Fax 493 7121 – 📶 ▤ rest 📺 ☎ – 🔏 40. **A** **AE** **①** **VISA** **JCB**. 🍴   DN   u
M (closed Saturday lunch) 22.50/25.00 **st.** and a la carte ▮ 7.00 – 🍽 12.00 – **66 rm** 184.00/245.00 **st.**, 7 suites.

🏨 **Forte Crest St. James's,** 81 Jermyn St., SW1Y 6JF, ℰ 930 2111, Telex 263187, Fax 839 2125 – 📶 ✆ rm ▤ rest 📺 ☎ ❷ – 🔏 80. **A** **AE** **①** **VISA** **JCB**   EN   i
M 12.50/19.50 **st.** and dinner a la carte ▮ 6.60 – 🍽 10.95 – **253 rm** 119.00 **st.**, 3 suites – SB (weekends only) 138.00 **st.**

🏨 **Hospitality Inn Piccadilly** (Mt. Charlotte Thistle) without rest., 39 Coventry St., W1V 8EL, ℰ 930 4033, Telex 8950058, Fax 925 2586 – 🔄 ⇌ rm 📺 ☎. 🔊 AE ⓞ VISA JCB. ⠽ FGM **a**

⚌ 9.25 – **92 rm** 115.00/130.00.

🏨 **Royal Trafalgar Thistle** (Mt. Charlotte Thistle), Whitcomb St., WC2H 7HG, ℰ 930 4477, Telex 298564, Fax 925 2149 – 🔄 ⇌ rm 📺 ☎. 🔊 AE ⓞ VISA JCB. ⠽ GM **r**
M 15.75 **st.** and a la carte ⫶ 6.00 – ⚌ 10.25 – **108 rm** 99.00/125.00 **st.** – SB (weekends only) 141.50/229.50 **st.**

🏨 **Pastoria,** 3-6 St. Martin's St., off Leicester Sq., WC2H 7HL, ℰ 930 8641, Telex 25538, Fax 925 0551 – 🔄 📺 ☎ – 🔬 60. 🔊 AE ⓞ VISA JCB ⠽ GM **v**
M *(closed Saturday lunch, Sunday and Bank Holidays)* a la carte approx. 16.00 **t.** ⫶ 3.95 –
⚌ 9.25 – **58 rm** 99.00/119.00 **t.**

XXX ❀ **Suntory,** 72-73 St. James's St., SW1A 1PH, ℰ 409 0201, Fax 499 7993 – 🗏. 🔊 AE ⓞ VISA JCB EP **z**
closed Sunday and Bank Holidays – **M** - **Japanese** 49.80/90.00 **st.** (dinner) and a la carte 23.20/88.20 **st.** ⫶ 7.50
Spec. Kaiseki, Shabu-shabu, Teppan-yaki.

XXX **Quaglino's,** 16 Bury St., SW1Y 6AL, ℰ 930 6767, Fax 839 2866 – 🗏. 🔊 AE ⓞ VISA EN **r**
closed lunch 1 January, dinner 24 December and 25-26 December – **Meals** (booking advisable) a la carte 18.50/41.95 **t.** ⫶ 6.25.

XXX **Overton's,** 5 St. James's St., SW1A 1EF, ℰ 839 3774 – 🗏. 🔊 AE ⓞ VISA JCB EP **a**
closed Saturday lunch, Sunday dinner, 25 December-2 January and Bank Holidays –
M - **Seafood** 17.50 **t.** (lunch) and a la carte 24.75/34.45 **t.** ⫶ 5.00.

XX **Le Caprice,** Arlington House, Arlington St., SW1A 1RT, ℰ 629 2239, Fax 493 9040 – 🗏. 🔊 AE ⓞ VISA DN **c**
closed 24 December-1 January – **Meals** a la carte 20.00/34.75 **t.**

XX ❀ **The Square,** 32 King St., SW1Y 6RJ, ℰ 839 8787 – 🗏. 🔊 AE ⓞ VISA EN **v**
closed lunch Saturday, Sunday and Bank Holidays and 11 days Christmas-New Year –
M a la carte 27.00/31.00 **t.** ⫶ 10.00
Spec. Seared tuna, avocado, sauce vierge, Loin of venison, pot roasted with port sauce, Pear, blackberry and hazelnut tart.

XX **Green's,** 36 Duke St., SW1Y 6DF, ℰ 930 4566, Fax 930 1383 – 🗏 EN **n**
M - **English rest.**

XX **Matsuri,** 15 Bury St., SW1Y 6AL, ℰ 839 1101, Fax 930 7010 – 🗏. 🔊 AE ⓞ VISA JCB EN **r**
closed Sunday and Bank Holidays – **M** - **Japanese** (Teppan-Yaki, Sushi) 17.00/49.50 **t.** and a la carte ⫶ 10.00.

X **Criterion,** 224 Piccadilly, W1V 9LB, ℰ 925 0909, Fax 839 1494, « 19C Neo-Byzantine decor » – 🔊 AE ⓞ VISA FM **c**
closed dinner 24 and 31 December, Sunday and Bank Holidays – **M** - **Brasserie** a la carte 17.00/24.00 **t.**

Soho – ⊠ W1/WC2 – ✿ 071 – pp. 28 and 29.

🏨 **Hampshire** (Edwardian), Leicester Sq., WC2H 7LH, ℰ 839 9399, Telex 914848, Fax 930 8122 – 🔄 🔊 📺 ☎ – 🔬 80. 🔊 AE ⓞ VISA JCB ⠽ GM **s**
M 21.50/27.50 **st.** and a la carte – ⚌ 13.50 – **119 rm** 184.00/220.00 **st.**, 5 suites – SB (weekends only) 146.00/183.00 **st.**

🏨 **Hazlitt's** without rest., 6 Frith St., W1V 5TZ, ℰ 434 1771, Fax 439 1524 – 📺 ☎. 🔊 AE ⓞ VISA JCB. ⠽ FK **u**
closed Christmas – **22 rm** 95.00/115.00 **s.**, 1 suite.

XXXX ❀ **Grill Room at the Café Royal** (Forte), 68 Regent St., W1R 6EL, ℰ 437 9090, Fax 439 7672, « Rococo decoration » – 🗏. 🔊 AE ⓞ VISA JCB EM **e**
closed Saturday lunch, Sunday and Bank Holidays – **M** 22.50/32.00 **t.** and a la carte 29.00/65.50 **t**
Spec. Ravioli of langoustines with a tarragon butter sauce, Roasted fillet of sea bass with fennel, sun-dried tomatoes and saffron, Hot almond and apple pithivier, blackberry coulis and vanilla ice cream.

XXX ❀ **Au Jardin des Gourmets,** 5 Greek St., W1V 5LA, ℰ 437 1816, Fax 437 0043 – 🗏. AE ⓞ VISA GJ **a**
closed Saturday lunch, Sunday and Bank Holidays – **M** - **Restaurant-French** 15.00 **st.** and a la carte 19.00/27.00 **t.** ⫶ 5.50.

XX **Brasserie** - **M** 10.95 **st.** and a la carte 13.00/18.00 **t.** ⫶ 5.50.

XXX **Lindsay House,** 21 Romilly St., W1V 5TG, ℰ 439 0450, Fax 581 2848 – 🗏. 🔊 AE ⓞ VISA JCB GL **i**
closed 25 and 26 December – **M** 14.75 **t.** (lunch) and a la carte 23.50/35.50 **t.** ⫶ 5.00.

XX **L'Escargot,** 48 Greek St., W1V 5LQ, ℰ 437 2679, Fax 437 0790 – 🗏. 🔊 AE ⓞ VISA JCB GK **e**
closed Saturday lunch and Sunday – **M** a la carte 20.50/29.00 **st.**

XX **Lexington,** 45 Lexington St., W1R 3LG, ℰ 434 3401, Fax 287 2997 – 🗏. 🔊 AE ⓞ VISA EK **e**
closed Saturday lunch, Sunday and Bank Holidays – **M** a la carte 15.50/23.75 **t.**

XX **Red Fort,** 77 Dean St., W1V 5HA, ℰ 437 2115, Fax 434 0721 – 🗏. 🔊 AE ⓞ VISA FJK **r**
M - **Indian** (buffet lunch) 14.95 **t.** and dinner a la carte 17.85/33.85 **t.**

XX **Brasserie at the Café Royal** (Forte), 68 Regent St., W1R 6EL, ℰ 437 9090 – 🍽. 🔄 🖭
🔘 𝚅𝙸𝚂𝙰 𝙹𝙲𝙱 EM **e**
closed Sunday – **M** 17.75 **t.** and a la carte ⱸ 7.50.

XX **Soho Soho** (first floor), 11-13 Frith St., W1, ℰ 494 3491 – 🍽. 🔄 🖭 🔘 𝚅𝙸𝚂𝙰 FK **s**
closed Saturday lunch and Sunday – **M** a la carte 22.15/28.50 **st.** ⱸ 5.00.

XX **Ming,** 35-36 Greek St., W1V 5LN, ℰ 734 2721 – 🍽. 🔄 🖭 🔘 𝚅𝙸𝚂𝙰 𝙹𝙲𝙱 GK **c**
closed Sunday and 25-26 December – **M** - **Chinese** 12.00/19.50 **t.** and a la carte ⱸ 6.00.

XX **Gopal's,** 12 Bateman St., W1V 5TD, ℰ 434 0840 – 🍽. 🔄 🖭 🔘 𝚅𝙸𝚂𝙰 FK **e**
M - **Indian** 12.00/22.00 **t.** and a la carte.

XX **Gay Hussar,** 2 Greek St., W1V 6NB, ℰ 437 0973 – 🍽. 🔄 🖭 🔘 𝚅𝙸𝚂𝙰 GJ **c**
closed Sunday and Bank Holidays – **M** - **Hungarian** 15.50 **t.** (lunch) and dinner a la
carte 18.50/26.00 **t.** ⱸ 6.50.

XX **Gallery Rendezvous,** 53-55 Beak St., W1R 3LF, ℰ 734 0445 – 🍽. 🔄 🖭 🔘 𝚅𝙸𝚂𝙰
𝙹𝙲𝙱 EL **a**
closed Christmas and New Year – **M** - **Chinese** (Peking) 21.00/32.00 **t.** and a la carte ⱸ 8.50.

X **dell 'Ugo,** 56 Frith St., W1V 5TA, ℰ 734 8300, Fax 734 8784 – 🔄 🖭 🔘 𝚅𝙸𝚂𝙰 FK **z**
closed Sunday, 25 to 26 December, 1 January and Bank Holidays – **M** a la carte 13.65/
18.40 **t.** ⱸ 4.15.

X **Sri Siam,** 14 Old Compton St., W1V 5PE, ℰ 434 3544 – 🍽. 🔄 🖭 🔘 𝚅𝙸𝚂𝙰 GK **r**
closed Sunday lunch, 25-26 December and 1 January – **M** - **Thai** 9.00/14.95 **t.** and a la carte
ⱸ 4.60.

X **Alastair Little,** 49 Frith St., W1V 5TE, ℰ 734 5183 – 🔄 🖭 𝚅𝙸𝚂𝙰 FK **o**
closed Saturday lunch, Sunday and Bank Holidays – **Meals** (booking essential) 20.00 **t.**
(lunch) and a la carte 27.00/40.00 **t.**

X **Bistrot Bruno,** 63 Frith St., W1V 5TA, ℰ 734 4545, Fax 287 1027 – 🍽. 🔄 🖭 🔘
𝚅𝙸𝚂𝙰 FK **z**
closed Saturday lunch, Sunday and 24 to 31 December – **Meals** a la carte 15.50/21.00 **t.**
ⱸ 4.25.

X **Fung Shing,** 15 Lisle St., WC2H 7BE, ℰ 437 1539 – 🍽. 🔄 🖭 🔘 𝚅𝙸𝚂𝙰 GL **a**
closed 24 to 26 December – **M** - **Chinese** (Canton) a la carte 10.75/23.00 **t.**

X **Saigon,** 45 Frith St., W1V 5TE, ℰ 437 7109 – 🍽. 🔄 🖭 🔘 𝚅𝙸𝚂𝙰 FGK **x**
closed Sunday and Bank Holidays – **M** - **Vietnamese** 15.80/19.50 **t.** and a la carte.

Strand and Covent Garden – ✉ WC2 – ☏ 071 – Except where otherwise stated
see p. 33.

🏛🏛🏛 **Savoy,** Strand, WC2R 0EU, ℰ 836 4343, Telex 24234, Fax 240 6040 – 🛗 ⠀ rm 🍽 📺 ☎
⟸ – 🔬 500. 🔄 🖭 🔘 𝚅𝙸𝚂𝙰 𝙹𝙲𝙱 ✎ DEY **a**
M – **Grill** (*closed Saturday lunch, Sunday, August and Bank Holidays*) 29.75 **t.** (dinner)
and a la carte 33.65/48.40 **t.** ⱸ 5.50 – **River** 26.25/37.25 **st.** and a la carte 36.90/51.70 **st.**
ⱸ 5.50 – ⏤ 15.75 – **152 rm** 170.00/260.00 **s.**, 48 suites.

🏛🏛 **Howard,** 12 Temple Pl., WC2R 2PR, ℰ 836 3555, Telex 268047, Fax 379 4547 – 🛗 🍽 📺
☎ ⟸ – 🔬 100. 🔄 🖭 🔘 𝚅𝙸𝚂𝙰 ✎ EX **e**
M 25.00 **st.** and a la carte ⱸ 4.75 – ⏤ 13.85 – **133 rm** 190.00/226.00 **st.**, 2 suites.

🏛🏛 **Waldorf** (Forte), Aldwych, WC2B 4DD, ℰ 836 2400, Telex 24574, Fax 836 7244 – 🛗
⠀ rm 🍽 rm 📺 ☎ – 🔬 450. 🔄 🖭 🔘 𝚅𝙸𝚂𝙰 𝙹𝙲𝙱 ✎ EX **x**
M (in bar Sunday) 21.00/25.00 **t.** and a la carte ⱸ 7.50 – ⏤ 12.95 – **285 rm** 150.00/210.00 **st.**,
7 suites.

XXXX **Boulestin,** 1a Henrietta St., WC2E 8PS, ℰ 836 7061, Fax 836 1283 – 🍽. 🔄 🖭 🔘 𝚅𝙸𝚂𝙰
closed Saturday lunch, Sunday, last 3 weeks August and 1 week Christmas – **M** - **French**
21.50/32.50 **t.** and a la carte. DX **r**

XXX **Now and Zen,** 4a Upper St. Martin's Lane, WC2H 9EA, ℰ 497 0376, Fax 437 0641 – 🍽.
🔄 🖭 🔘 𝚅𝙸𝚂𝙰 DX **x**
closed 25 December – **M** - **Chinese** 10.50/16.80 **t.** and a la carte.

XXX **Simpson's-in-the-Strand,** 100 Strand, WC2R 0EW, ℰ 836 9112, Fax 836 1381 – 🍽. 🔄
🖭 🔘 𝚅𝙸𝚂𝙰 𝙹𝙲𝙱 EX **o**
closed 1 April and 25 to 28 December – **M** - **English** (booking essential) 10.00 **t.** and a la
carte 19.50/30.00 **t.** ⱸ 4.95.

XXX **Ivy,** 1 West St., WC2H 9NE, ℰ 836 4751, Fax 497 3644 – 🍽. 🔄 🖭 🔘 𝚅𝙸𝚂𝙰
closed Bank Holiday lunch, 24 to 27 December and 1 January – **M** 12.50 **t.** (lunch) and a la
carte 17.25/37.25 **t.** p. 29 GK **z**

XX **Kagura,** 13-15 West St., WC2H 9BL, ℰ 240 0634, Fax 240 3342 – 🍽. 🔄 🖭 🔘 𝚅𝙸𝚂𝙰
𝙹𝙲𝙱 GK **z**
closed lunch Saturday and Bank Holidays, Sunday, 25 to 27 December and 1 to 4 January –
M - **Japanese** 12.00/38.00 **t.** and a la carte.

XX **Christopher's,** 18 Wellington St., WC2E 7DD, ℰ 240 4222, Fax 240 3357 – 🔄 🖭 🔘
𝚅𝙸𝚂𝙰 EX **z**
closed Saturday, Sunday and Bank Holidays – **M** a la carte 30.00/40.00 **t.**

XX Orso, 27 Wellington St., WC2E 7DA, ℰ 240 5269, Fax 497 2148 – 🍽 EX **z**
M - **Italian** (booking essential).

XX **Rules,** 35 Maiden Lane, WC2E 7LB, ✆ 836 5314, Fax 497 1081 – ☒ 🗚 𝗩𝗜𝗦𝗔   DX **n**
closed 25 and 26 December – **M** - **English** 12.75 **t.** and a la carte ♨ 4.60.

XX **L'Estaminet,** 14 Garrick St., off Floral St., WC2 9BJ, ✆ 379 1432 – ☒ 🗚 𝗩𝗜𝗦𝗔   DX **a**
closed Sunday and Bank Holidays – **M** - **French** a la carte 20.50/25.10 **st.**

XX Sheekey's, 28-32 St. Martin's Court, WC2N 4AL, ✆ 240 2565 – ▤   DX **z**
M - Seafood rest.

X **Bertorelli's,** 44a Floral St., WC2E 9DA, ✆ 836 3969, Fax 836 1868 – ▤. ☒ 🗚 ◉ 𝗩𝗜𝗦𝗔
JCB   DX **c**
closed Sunday and 25-26 December – **M** - **Italian** a la carte 13.85/20.50 **t.**

X **Magno's Brasserie,** 65a Long Acre, WC2E 9JH, ✆ 836 6077, Fax 379 6184 – ▤. ☒ 🗚
◉ 𝗩𝗜𝗦𝗔 JCB   DV **e**
closed Saturday lunch, Sunday, Christmas and Bank Holidays – **M** - **French** 12.50/15.50 **t.**
and a la carte ♨ 6.25.

X Laguna, 50 St. Martin's Lane, WC2N 4EA, ✆ 836 0960 – ▤   DX **z**
M - Italian rest.

Victoria – ✉ SW1 – ✆ 071 – Except where otherwise stated see p. 32.

🛈 Victoria Station Forecourt, SW1V 1JU ✆ 730 3488/824 8000.

🏨 Royal Horseguards Thistle (Mt. Charlotte Thistle), 2 Whitehall Court, SW1A 2EJ,
✆ 839 3400, Telex 917096, Fax 925 2263 – 🛗 ⇔ rm ▤ rest 📺 ☎ – 🛆 60. ⋇
368 rm, 8 suites.   p. 26 LX **a**

🏨 **Stakis St. Ermin's,** 2 Caxton St., SW1H 0QW, ✆ 222 7888, Telex 917731, Fax 222 6914
– 🛗 ⇔ rm ▤ rest 📺 ☎ – 🛆 150. ☒ 🗚 ◉ 𝗩𝗜𝗦𝗔 JCB   CX **x**
M (carving rest.) 16.75 **t.** and a la carte – 🍽 9.75 – **282 rm** 112.00/179.00 **st.**, 8 suites –
SB 108.00/138.00 **st.**

🏨 **St. James Court,** Buckingham Gate, SW1E 6AF, ✆ 834 6655, Fax 630 7587, ♨, ⇌ – 🛗
⇔ rm ▤ 📺 ☎ – 🛆 180. ☒ 🗚 ◉ 𝗩𝗜𝗦𝗔 JCB. ⋇   CX **i**
M - Méditerranée a la carte approx. 15.00 **t.** – (see also **Auberge de Provence** and **Inn of
Happiness** below) – 🍽 13.25 – **375 rm** 130.00/160.00 **s.**, 18 suites – SB (weekends only)
147.25/200.50 **st.**

🏨 **Goring,** 15 Beeston Pl., Grosvenor Gdns, SW1W 0JW, ✆ 396 9000, Telex 919166,
Fax 834 4393 – 🛗 📺 ☎ – 🛆 50. ☒ 🗚 ◉ 𝗩𝗜𝗦𝗔   BX **a**
M 25.00/32.00 **t.** ♨ 7.00 – 🍽 11.00 – **73 rm** 120.00/150.00 **s.**, 5 suites.

🏨 **Royal Westminster Thistle** (Mt. Charlotte Thistle), 49 Buckingham Palace Rd, SW1W
0QT, ✆ 834 1821, Telex 916821, Fax 931 7542 – 🛗 ⇔ rm ▤ 📺 ☎ – 🛆 150. ☒ 🗚 ◉ 𝗩𝗜𝗦𝗔
JCB. ⋇   BX **z**
M *(closed Sunday)* (bar lunch)/dinner 18.75 **st.** and a la carte ♨ 5.75 – 🍽 10.25 – **134 rm**
118.00/140.00 **st.**

🏨 **Grosvenor** (Mt. Charlotte Thistle), 101 Buckingham Palace Rd, SW1W 0SJ, ✆ 834 9494,
Telex 916006, Fax 630 1978 – 🛗 ⇔ rm 📺 ☎ – 🛆 150. ☒ 🗚 ◉ 𝗩𝗜𝗦𝗔 JCB. ⋇   BX **e**
M (carving rest.) 16.35 **t.** and a la carte ♨ 6.00 – 🍽 8.75 – **363 rm** 98.00/120.00 **st.**, 3 suites –
SB 128.50/246.20 **st.**

🏨 **Rubens,** 39-41 Buckingham Palace Rd, SW1W 0PS, ✆ 834 6600, Fax 828 5401 – 🛗
⇔ rm ▤ rest 📺 ☎ – 🛆 60. ☒ 🗚 ◉ 𝗩𝗜𝗦𝗔 JCB. ⋇   BX **n**
M *(closed Saturday lunch)* (carving rest.) 14.95 **st.** and a la carte – 🍽 8.95 – **188 rm**
97.00/123.00 **st.**, 1 suite.

🏨 **Scandic Crown,** 2 Bridge Pl., SW1V 1QA, ✆ 834 8123, Telex 914973, Fax 828 1099, ♨,
⇌, ▣ – 🛗 ⇔ rm ▤ 📺 ☎ – 🛆 180. ☒ 🗚 ◉ 𝗩𝗜𝗦𝗔 JCB. ⋇   BY **i**
M 14.95/20.00 **st.** and dinner a la carte ♨ 4.95 – 🍽 9.50 – **205 rm** 85.00/145.00 **st.**, 5 suites –
SB (weekends only) 125.90/210.00 **st.**

🏨 **Rochester,** 69 Vincent Sq., SW1P 2PA, ✆ 828 6611, Telex 8813164, Fax 233 6724 – 🛗
▤ rest 📺 ☎ – 🛆 60. ☒ 🗚 ◉ 𝗩𝗜𝗦𝗔 JCB. ⋇   CY **e**
M *(closed lunch Saturday and Sunday)* 17.95 **st.** and a la carte ♨ 8.95 – 🍽 9.50 – **70 rm**
89.00/165.00 **st.** – SB 140.00/210.00 **st.**

🏨 **Tophams Ebury Court,** 24-32 Ebury St., SW1W 0LU, ✆ 730 8147, Fax 823 5966 – 🛗 📺
☎. ☒ 🗚 ◉ 𝗩𝗜𝗦𝗔 JCB   AX **i**
closed 22 December-2 January – **M** (in bar Saturday lunch and Sunday) a la carte 16.00/
24.50 **t.** ♨ 5.00 – **40 rm** 🍽 64.00/130.00 **t.** – SB 130.00/240.00 **st.**

🏨 **Hamilton House,** 60 Warwick Way, SW1V 1SA, ✆ 821 7113, Fax 630 0806 – 📺 ☎. ☒
𝗩𝗜𝗦𝗔   BY **n**
M (grill rest.) (dinner only) a la carte 8.10/16.55 **t.** ♨ 2.80 – **40 rm** 🍽 40.00/65.00 **st.**

🏠 **Winchester** without rest., 17 Belgrave Rd, SW1V 1RB, ✆ 828 2972, Fax 828 5191 – 📺.
⋇   BY **s**
18 rm.

⌂ **Collin House** without rest., 104 Ebury St., SW1W 9QD, ✆ 730 8031 – ⋇   AY **r**
closed 2 weeks Christmas – **13 rm** 🍽 36.00/58.00 **st.**

XXX **Inn of Happiness** (at St. James Court H.), Buckingham Gate, SW1E 6AF, $\mathscr{C}$ 821 1931, Telex 938075, Fax 630 7587 – ▤. ◪ ᴀᴇ ⓪ 𝗩𝗜𝗦𝗔 𝗝𝗖𝗕 CX **i**
closed Saturday lunch – **M** - **Chinese** 15.50/25.00 **t.** and a la carte ▯ 7.00.

XXX **Auberge de Provence** (at St. James Court H.), Buckingham Gate, SW1E 6AF, $\mathscr{C}$ 821 1899, Telex 938075, Fax 630 7587 – ▤. ◪ ᴀᴇ ⓪ 𝗩𝗜𝗦𝗔 𝗝𝗖𝗕 CX **i**
closed Saturday lunch and Sunday – **M** - **French** 22.50/45.00 **t.** and a la carte ▯ 6.00.

XXX **L'Incontro,** 87 Pimlico Rd, SW1W 8PH, $\mathscr{C}$ 730 6327, Fax 730 5062 – ▤. ◪ ᴀᴇ ⓪ 𝗩𝗜𝗦𝗔
closed lunch Saturday and Sunday and Bank Holidays – **M** - **Italian** 16.80 **t.** (lunch) and a la carte 24.90/43.00 **t.** p. 31 FT **u**

XXX **Santini,** 29 Ebury St., SW1W 0NZ, $\mathscr{C}$ 730 4094, Fax 730 0544 – ▤. ◪ ᴀᴇ ⓪ 𝗩𝗜𝗦𝗔
closed Saturday lunch and Sunday and Bank Holidays – **M** - **Italian** 16.50 **t.** (lunch) and a la carte 21.50/44.25 **t.** ABX **v**

XXX Shepherds, Marsham Court, Marsham St., SW1P 4LA, $\mathscr{C}$ 834 9552, Fax 233 6047 – ▤
M - **English** (booking essential). p. 26 LZ **z**

XX **Simply Nico,** 48a Rochester Row, SW1P 1JU, $\mathscr{C}$ 630 8061 – ▤. ◪ ᴀᴇ ⓪ 𝗩𝗜𝗦𝗔 CY **a**
closed Saturday lunch, Sunday, 4 days at Easter, 10 days Christmas-New Year and Bank Holidays – **Meals** (booking essential) 23.00/25.00 **st.**

XX **Mijanou,** 143 Ebury St., SW1W 9QN, $\mathscr{C}$ 730 4099, Fax 823 6402 – ╳ ▤. ◪ ᴀᴇ ⓪ 𝗩𝗜𝗦𝗔
closed Saturday, Sunday, 1 week Easter, last 3 weeks August, 2 weeks Christmas-New Year and Bank Holidays – **M** 15.00/36.00 **t.** and a la carte ▯ 6.00. AY **n**

XX **Ken Lo's Memories of China,** 67-69 Ebury St., SW1W 0NZ, $\mathscr{C}$ 730 7734, Fax 730 2992 – ▤. ◪ ᴀᴇ ⓪ 𝗩𝗜𝗦𝗔 𝗝𝗖𝗕 AY **u**
closed lunch Sunday and Bank Holidays – **M** - **Chinese** 21.00/23.20 **t.** and a la carte.

XX **L'Amico,** 44 Horseferry Rd, SW1P 2AF, $\mathscr{C}$ 222 4680 – ◪ ᴀᴇ ⓪ 𝗩𝗜𝗦𝗔
closed Saturday, Sunday and Bank Holidays – **M** - **Italian** (booking essential) 14.00/25.00 **t.** and a la carte ▯ 4.00. p. 26 LY **e**

XX **Hunan,** 51 Pimlico Rd, SW1W 8NE, $\mathscr{C}$ 730 5712 – ◪ ᴀᴇ 𝗩𝗜𝗦𝗔 p. 25 IZ **a**
closed Sunday lunch – **M** - **Chinese** (Hunan) 11.20/19.30 **t.** and a la carte ▯ 4.50.

XX **Gran Paradiso,** 52 Wilton Rd, SW1V 1DE, $\mathscr{C}$ 828 5818, Fax 828 3608 – ◪ ᴀᴇ ⓪ 𝗩𝗜𝗦𝗔 𝗝𝗖𝗕
closed Saturday lunch, Sunday, last 2 weeks August and Bank Holidays – **M** - **Italian** a la carte 18.50/20.50 **t.** ▯ 3.30. BY **a**

X **Olivo,** 21 Eccleston St., SW1W 9LX, $\mathscr{C}$ 730 2505 – ▤. ◪ ᴀᴇ 𝗩𝗜𝗦𝗔 AY **z**
closed Saturday lunch, Sunday, 3 weeks August and Bank Holidays – **M** - **Italian** 15.00 **t.** (lunch) and a la carte 17.30/23.05 **t.**

X **Tate Gallery,** Tate Gallery, Millbank, SW1P 4RG, $\mathscr{C}$ 887 8877, Fax 887 8902, « Rex Whistler murals » – ▤ p. 26 LZ **c**
closed Sunday, 1 April, 2 May, 24 to 26 December and 1 January – **M** - **English** (booking essential) (lunch only) a la carte 17.45/24.75 **t.** ▯ 6.00.

X **La Poule au Pot,** 231 Ebury St., SW1W 8UT, $\mathscr{C}$ 730 7763 – ◪ ᴀᴇ ⓪ 𝗩𝗜𝗦𝗔 IZ **e**
closed Bank Holidays – **M** - **French** 12.75 **t.** (lunch) and dinner a la carte 19.20/28.60 **t.** ▯ 5.25.

X **Mimmo d'Ischia,** 61 Elizabeth St., SW1W 9PP, $\mathscr{C}$ 730 5406 – ▤. ◪ ᴀᴇ ⓪ 𝗩𝗜𝗦𝗔 AY **o**
closed Sunday and Bank Holidays – **M** - **Italian** a la carte approx. 24.50 **t.** ▯ 5.50.

X **Villa Medici,** 35 Belgrave Rd, SW1 5AX, $\mathscr{C}$ 828 3613 – ◪ ᴀᴇ ⓪ 𝗩𝗜𝗦𝗔 𝗝𝗖𝗕 BY **c**
closed Saturday lunch, Sunday and Bank Holidays – **M** - **Italian** 12.90 **t.** and a la carte 16.40/22.00 **t.** ▯ 3.80.

X **La Fontana,** 101 Pimlico Rd, SW1W 8PH, $\mathscr{C}$ 730 6630 – ◪ ᴀᴇ ⓪ 𝗩𝗜𝗦𝗔 𝗝𝗖𝗕
M - **Italian** a la carte 22.00/34.00 **t.** ▯ 6.00. p. 31 FT **o**

When visiting London use the Green Guide **"London"**

- Detailed descriptions of places of interest
- Useful local information
- A section on the historic square-mile of the City of London with a detailed fold-out plan
- The lesser known London boroughs – their people, places and sights
- Plans of selected areas and important buildings.

LONGBRIDGE Warks. – see Warwick.

LONG CRENDON Bucks. **403** **404** R 28 – ⊠ Aylesbury – ☎ 0844 Thame.
♦ London 50 – Aylesbury 11 – ♦ Oxford 15.

   ✗   **Angel Inn,** Bicester Rd, HP18 9EE, ℰ 208268, « Part 16C inn » – ⒫, ◪ 𝗩𝗜𝗦𝗔
        closed Sunday lunch April-September and Sunday dinner – **M** a la carte 12.50/19.00 **st.**

LONG EATON Derbs. **402** **403** **404** Q 25 – see Nottingham (Notts.).

LONGFORD W. Mids. **403** **404** P 26 – see Coventry.

LONG MARSTON Warks. – see Stratford-upon-Avon.

LONG MELFORD Suffolk **404** W 27 **Great Britain G.** – pop. 2 739 – ECD : Thursday – ☎ 0787 Sudbury.
See : Melford Hall★ *AC.*
♦ London 62 – ♦ Cambridge 34 – Colchester 18 – ♦ Ipswich 24.

   🏨 **Bull** (Forte), Hall St., CO10 9JG, ℰ 378494, Fax 880307, « Part 15C coaching inn » – 🖼
       📺 ☎ ⒫ – 🔏 60. ◪ ◭ ⓞ 𝗩𝗜𝗦𝗔
       M (bar lunch Monday to Saturday)/dinner 17.95 **t.** and a la carte ⁞ 6.45 – ⊂⊐ 8.95 – **25 rm**
       70.00/120.00 **t.** – SB (except Christmas and New Year) 116.00/136.00 **st.**

   🏨 **Black Lion,** The Green, CO10 9DN, ℰ 312356, Fax 374557 – 📺 ☎ ⒫, ◪ 𝗩𝗜𝗦𝗔 𝗝𝗖𝗕
       M – **Countrymen** *(closed Sunday dinner and Monday)* 10.00/26.00 **t.** and a la carte – **8 rm**
       ⊂⊐ 45.00/85.00 **st.**, 1 suite – SB 95.00/162.00 **st.**

   ✗✗✗ **Chimneys,** Hall St., CO10 9JR, ℰ 379806, Fax 312294, « Part 16C cottage », ☞ – ◪ ◭
       ⓞ 𝗩𝗜𝗦𝗔
       closed Sunday dinner – **M** 13.95/27.50 **t.** and a la carte.

   ✗ **Scutchers Bistro,** Westgate St., CO10 9DP, on A 1092 ℰ 310200, Fax 310157, ☞ – ⒫
       ◪ ◭ 𝗩𝗜𝗦𝗔
       closed Sunday and first 2 weeks March – **M** a la carte 16.00/18.95.

   The Guide changes, so renew your Guide every year.

LONGNOR Staffs. **402** **403** **404** O 24 – pop. 381 – ⊠ Buxton – ☎ 0298.
♦ London 161 – Derby 29 – ♦ Manchester 31 – ♦ Stoke-on-Trent 22.

   ⚘ **Ye Olde Cheshire Cheese,** High St., SK17 0NS, ℰ 83218 – 📺 ⒫, ◪ 𝗩𝗜𝗦𝗔 ✖
       M *(closed Sunday dinner and Monday)* 13.00 **t.** and a la carte ⁞ 4.60 – **3 rm** ⊂⊐ 20.00/
       30.00 **t.**

LONGRIDGE Lancs. **402** M 22 – pop. 7 170 – ⊠ ☎ 0772.
♦ London 241 – Blackburn 12 – Burnley 18.

   ✗✗✗ ✿✿ **Paul Heathcote's** (Heathcote), 104-106 Higher Rd, PR3 3SY, ℰ 784969, Fax 785713
       – ◪ ◭ 𝗩𝗜𝗦𝗔
       closed lunch Tuesday to Thursday except December, Saturday lunch and Monday –
       M 20.00/32.50 **t.** and dinner a la carte 29.00/37.00 **st.** ⁞ 6.00
       Spec. Black pudding of veal sweetbreads, potatoes and thyme scented juices, Pan fried wing of skate with a leek
       compote and port wine sauce, Punch of Summer fruits with basil and peach sorbet.

LONG SUTTON Lincs. **404** U 25 – pop. 3 127 – ☎ 0406.
♦ London 100 – Lincoln 51 – ♦ Leicester 67 – ♦ Norwich 54.

   🏠 **Forte Travelodge** without rest., Wisbech Rd, PE12 9AG, SE : 1 m. at junction of A 17
       with A 1101 ℰ 362230, Reservations (Freephone) 0800 850950 – 📺 ⅃ ⒫, ◪ ◭ 𝗩𝗜𝗦𝗔 ✖
       40 rm 31.95 **t.**

LOOE Cornwall **403** G 32 **The West Country G.** – pop. 4 279 – ECD : Thursday – ☎ 0503.
See : Town★ – Monkey Sanctuary★ *AC.*
  🚲 Bin Down ℰ 050 34 (Widegates) 239, E : 3 m. – 🚲 Whitsand Bay Hotel, Portwrinkle ℰ 30276,
E : 6 m.
  🗓 The Guildhall, Fore St., PL13 1AA ℰ 262072.
♦ London 264 – ♦ Plymouth 21 – Truro 39.

   🏨 **Klymiarven** ⚘, Barbican Hill, East Looe, PL13 1BH, E : 2 m. by A 387 off B 3253 or
       access from town on foot ℰ 262333, ≤ Looe and harbour, ⅃ heated, ☞ – 🖼 rest 📺 ☎
       ⒫, ◪ 𝗩𝗜𝗦𝗔
       closed January – **M** (bar lunch)/dinner 14.00 **st.** and a la carte ⁞ 3.75 – **14 rm** ⊂⊐ 30.00/
       68.00 **st.** – SB 66.00/100.00 **st.**

   ⌂ **Harescombe Lodge** ⚘ without rest., Watergate, PL13 2NE, NW : 2 ¾ m. by A 387
       turning right opposite Waylands Farm onto single track road ℰ 263158, ☞ – ⒫, ✖
       3 rm ⊂⊐ 38.00 **s.**

   at Sandplace N : 2¼ m. on A 387 – ⊠ ☎ 0503 Polperro :

   🏠 **Polraen Country House,** PL13 1PJ, ℰ 263956, ☞ – 📺 ⒫, ◪ 𝗩𝗜𝗦𝗔
       M (bar lunch)/dinner 15.00 **st.** and a la carte ⁞ 4.75 – **5 rm** ⊂⊐ 26.50/47.00 **st.** – SB (except
       Bank Holidays) 76.90/90.00 **st.**

at Widegates NE : 3 ½ m. on B 3253 – ⊠ Looe – ✿ 050 34 Widegates :

⌂ **Coombe Farm** ⤸, PL13 1QN, on B 3253 *𝒫* 223, ≼ countryside, ⛌ heated, ✍, park –
↝ 📺 ☎ ❷. �
March-October – **M** 12.50 st. ¶ 3.50 – **10 rm** ⊇ 16.50/45.00 – SB 54.00/70.00 **st.**

at Talland Bay SW : 4 m. by A 387 – ⊠ Looe – ✿ 0503 Polperro :

🏨 **Talland Bay** ⤸, PL13 2JB, *𝒫* 72667, Fax 72940, ≼, « Country house atmosphere », ⇆,
⛌ heated, ✍ – ↝ rest 📺 ☎ ❷. ◪ ◪ ◉ VISA ✍
closed January and part February – **M** (bar lunch Monday to Saturday)/dinner 24.00 **t.** and a
la carte ¶ 3.95 – **23 rm** ⊇ (dinner included) 77.00/171.00 **t.**, 1 suite – SB 99.00/112.50 **st.**

🏠 **Allhays Country House** ⤸, PL13 2JB, *𝒫* 72434, Fax 72929, ≼, ✍ – ↝ rest 📺 ☎ ❷.
◪ ◪ VISA JCB
closed Christmas – **M** (dinner only) 13.00 **st.** ¶ 4.25 – **7 rm** ⊇ 20.00/72.00 **st.**

LOSTWITHIEL Cornwall 🔲🔲🔲 G 32 The West Country G. – pop. 1 972 – ECD : Wednesday –
✿ 0208 Bodmin.

Envir. : Lanhydrock★★, N : 4 m. by B 3268 – Restormel Castle★ *AC* (⁕★) N : 1 m. – Bodmin
(St. Petroc Church★) NW : 6 m. by B 3268.

🏌 Lower Polscoe *𝒫* 873550 – 🏌 Bodmin G. & C.C., Bodmin *𝒫* 73600, NW : 5 m.

🛈 Lostwithiel Community Centre, Liddicoat Rd, PL22 0HE *𝒫* 872207.

◆London 273 – ◆Plymouth 30 – Truro 23.

🏠 **Restormel Lodge,** 17 Castle Hill, PL22 0DD, on A 390 *𝒫* 872223, Fax 873568, ⛌ heated,
✍ – 📺 ☎ ❷. ◪ ◪ ◉ VISA
M (bar lunch)/dinner 16.50 **t.** and a la carte ¶ 4.50 – ⊇ 6.00 – **32 rm** 39.50/50.00 **t.** –
SB (except Christmas) 80.00/98.00 **st.**

LOUGHBOROUGH Leics. 🔲🔲🔲 🔲🔲🔲 Q 25 – pop. 44 895 – ECD : Wednesday – ✿ 0509.

🏌 Lingdale, Joe Moore's Lane, Woodhouse Eaves *𝒫* 890703.

🛈 John Storer House, Wards End, LE11 3HA *𝒫* 230131.

◆London 117 – ◆Birmingham 41 – ◆Leicester 11 – ◆Nottingham 15.

🏠 **Cedars,** Cedar Rd, LE11 2AB, SE : 1 m. by Leicester Rd *𝒫* 214459, Fax 233573, ⇆,
⛌ heated, ✍ – 📺 ☎ ❷. ◪ ◪ ◉ VISA
M *(closed Sunday)* (dinner only) a la carte 8.70/17.35 **t.** ¶ 4.65 – **37 rm** ⊇ 40.00/53.00 **t.** –
SB (weekends only) 65.00/69.00 **st.**

⌂ **Garendon Park,** 92 Leicester Rd, LE11 2AQ, S : ½ m. on A 6 *𝒫* 236557 – 📺. ◪ ◪ VISA
✍
M (by arrangement) 5.50 **st.** – **9 rm** ⊇ 21.50/38.00 **st.** – SB (weekends only) 53.00/76.00 **st.**

at Quorn SE : 3 m. by A 6 – ⊠ ✿ 0509 Loughborough :

🏨 **Quorn Country,** 66 Leicester Rd, LE12 8BB, *𝒫* 415050, Fax 415557, ✍ – ↝ rm ▤ rm
📺 ☎ ❷ – 🔬 50. ◪ ◪ ◉ VISA
closed 1 January – **M** *(closed Saturday lunch)* 12.35/18.45 **t.** and a la carte – ⊇ 8.75 –
16 rm 79.50/92.00 **t.**, 3 suites – SB (weekends only) 89.95/99.50 **st.**

🏨 **Quorn Grange,** 88 Wood Lane, LE12 8DB, *𝒫* 412167, Fax 415621, ✍ – 📺 ☎ & ❷ –
🔬 80. ◪ ◪ ◉ VISA
M (Saturday lunch by arrangement) 15.95 **st.** and a la carte ¶ 4.50 – ⊇ 5.85 – **17 rm**
55.00/112.00 **st.**

◎ ATS Bridge St. *𝒫* 218447/218472

LOUTH Lincs. 🔲🔲🔲 🔲🔲🔲 U 23 – ✿ 0507.

◆London 156 – Boston 34 – Great Grimsby 17 – Lincoln 26.

🏨 **Kenwick Park** ⤸, LN11 8NR, SE : 2¼ m. by B 1520 on A 157 *𝒫* 608806, Fax 608027, 🏌,
✍, park – ↝ rm 📺 ☎ ❷. 🔬 30. ◪ ◪ VISA
M 14.95 **st.** and a la carte ¶ 4.75 – **19 rm** ⊇ 59.50/95.00 **st.** – SB (weekends only) 79.50/
139.00 **st.**

🏨 **Brackenborough Arms,** Cordeaux Corner, Brackenborough, LN11 0SZ, N : 2 m. by
A 16 *𝒫* 609169, Fax 609413, ✍ – 📺 ☎ ❷. ◪ ◪ ◉ VISA. ✍
closed 25 and 26 December – **M** a la carte 15.35/21.50 **t.** ¶ 4.00 – **11 rm** ⊇ 50.00/69.00 **t.**

🏨 **Beaumont,** Victoria Rd, LN11 0BX, *𝒫* 605005, Fax 607768 – ▯ 📺 ☎ ❷ – 🔬 100. ◪ ◪
VISA JCB. ✍
M 15.50 **t.** (dinner) and a la carte 14.95/22.95 **st.** ¶ 5.25 – **17 rm** ⊇ 45.00/55.00 **t.** –
SB (weekends only) 90.00 **st.**

XX **Alfred's,** Upgate, LN11 9EY, *𝒫* 607431. ◪ ◉ VISA
closed Sunday and Monday – **M** (lunch by arrangement)/dinner a la carte 17.95/24.95 **t.**

◎ ATS 179 Newmarket *𝒫* 601975

LOWER SLAUGHTER Glos. 🔲🔲🔲 🔲🔲🔲 O 28 – see Bourton-on-the-Water.

LOWER SWELL Glos. 🔲🔲🔲 🔲🔲🔲 O 28 – see Stow-on-the-Wold.

349

LOWESTOFT Suffolk **404** Z 26 Great Britain G. – pop. 59 430 – ECD : Thursday – ✆ 0502.

Envir. : The Broads★.

📷, 🏌 Rookery Park, Carlton Colville ☎ 560380, W : 3 m. by A 146.

🛈 The Esplanade, NR33 0QF ☎ 523000 (summer only).

◆London 116 – ◆Ipswich 43 – ◆Norwich 30.

↑ **Rockville House,** 6 Pakefield Rd, NR33 0HS, ☎ 581011 – ⇔ rest 📺, ⬛ VISA. ⬚
   M 9.50 **t.** ⅃ 2.85 – **8 rm** ⊆ 21.00/43.00 **t.** – SB 53.50/83.00 **st.**

✗ **Shanghai Coolie,** 215 London Rd South, NR33 0DS, ☎ 514573 – ⬛ ▾ VISA
   closed Sunday lunch and 25-26 December – **M** - **Chinese** (Peking, Szechuan) 17.00 **t.** and a
   la carte ⅃ 3.30.

   at Oulton NW : 2 m. by B 1074 – ✉ ✆ 0502 Lowestoft :

🏨 **Parkhill,** Parkhill, NR32 5DQ, N : ½ m. on A 1117 ☎ 730322, Fax 731695, ⬚ – 📺 ☎ 🅿 –
   🏛 100. ⬛ ▾ �ⓞ VISA
   M *(closed Sunday dinner)* 15.00 **st.** and a la carte ⅃ 4.50 – **18 rm** ⊆ 30.00/75.00 **t.** –
   SB 60.00/140.00 **st.**

⬤ ATS 263 Whapload Rd ☎ 561581

LOW FELL Tyne and Wear – see Gateshead.

LOW LAITHE N. Yorks. – see Pateley Bridge.

LUCKINGTON Wilts. **403 404** N 29 – ✉ Chippenham – ✆ 0666 Malmesbury.

◆London 116 – ◆Bristol 20 – Gloucester 32 – Swindon 27.

↑ **Manor Farm** without rest , Alderton, SN14 6NL, SE : 1¼ m. by Alderton rd ☎ 840271, ⬚
   – 📺 🅿. ⬚
   3 rm ⊆ 25.00/48.00 **s.**

Prices	For full details of the prices quoted in the guide, consult the introduction.

LUDDENDEN FOOT W. Yorks. – see Halifax.

LUDLOW Shrops. **403** L 26 Great Britain G. – pop. 7 496 – ECD : Thursday – ✆ 0584.

See : Town★ – Castle★ *AC* – Feathers Hotel★ – St. Laurence's Parish Church★ (Misericords★).

Exc. : Stokesay Castle★ *AC*, NW : 6½ m. by A 49.

🛈 Castle St., SY8 1AS ☎ 875053.

◆London 162 – ◆Birmingham 39 – Hereford 24 – Shrewsbury 29.

🏨 **Feathers,** Bull Ring, SY8 1AA, ☎ 875261, Fax 876030, « Part Elizabethan house » – 📳
   ⇔ rest 📺 ☎ 🅿 – 🏛 90. ⬛ ▾ ⓞ VISA
   M 13.00/19.50 **st.** and a la carte ⅃ 4.75 – **40 rm** ⊆ 65.00/124.00 **st.** – SB (except Bank
   Holidays) 118.00/160.00 **st.**

🏨 **Dinham Hall** (Best Western), Dinham, SY8 1EJ, ☎ 876464, Fax 876019, ⨍⬩, ⇋, ⬚ – 📺
   ☎ 🅿. ⬛ ▾ VISA
   M (bar lunch Monday to Saturday)/dinner 19.95 **t.** ⅃ 4.95 – **13 rm** ⊆ 59.00/99.00 **t.** –
   SB 99.00/119.00 **st.**

🏨 **Overton Grange,** Overton Rd, SY8 4AD, S : 1¾ m. on B 431 ☎ 873500, Fax 873524, ⬚ –
   📺 ☎ 🅿 – 🏛 160. ⬛ ▾ ⓞ VISA. ⬚
   M 11.50/19.50 **t.** and a la carte ⅃ 4.95 – **16 rm** ⊆ 52.00/88.00 **st.** – SB (except Bank
   Holidays) 98.00/116.00 **t.**

🏠 **Number Eleven,** Dinham, SY8 1EJ, ☎ 878584, ≼, « Georgian town house, antique
   furnishings », ⬚ – ⇔. ⬛ VISA. ⬚
   closed February and November – **M** *(closed Sunday)* (residents only) (dinner only) 12.50 **st.**
   – **5 rm** ⊆ 25.00/56.00 **st.** – SB (December-March except Christmas and New Year) 81.00/
   85.00 **st.**

↑ **Cecil,** Sheet Rd, SY8 1LR, ☎ 872442, ⬚ – ⇔ rm 📺 🅿. ⬛ VISA
   M (by arrangement) 10.00 **st.** ⅃ 5.00 – **10 rm** ⊆ 17.00/40.00 **st.** – SB (October-April)
   (except Bank Holidays) 40.00/50.00 **st.**

⬤ ATS Weeping Cross Lane ☎ 872401

LUPTON Cumbria **402** L 21 – see Kirkby Lonsdale.

LUTON Beds. **404** S 28 Great Britain G. – pop. 163 209 – ECD : Wednesday – ✆ 0582.

See : Luton Hoo★ (Wernher Collection★★) *AC* X.

📷 Stockwood Park, London Rd ☎ 413704, S : 1 m. X – 📷, 🏌 South Beds, Warden Hill Rd,
☎ 575201, N : 3 m. by A 6 V.

🛫 Luton International Airport : ☎ 405100, E : 1½ m. X – **Terminal :** Luton Bus Station.

🛈 65-67 Bute St., LU1 2EY ☎ 401579 – Information Desk, London Luton Airport, LU2 9LY
☎ 405100.

◆London 35 – ◆Cambridge 36 – ◆Ipswich 93 – ◆Oxford 45 – Southend-on-Sea 63.

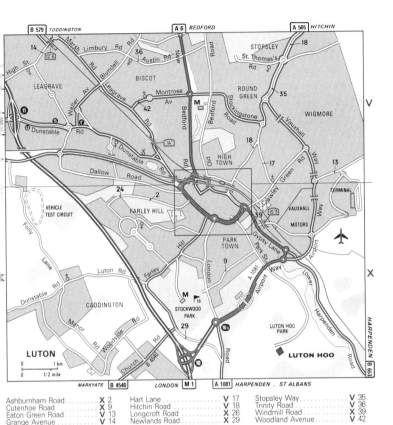

| B 579 TODDINGTON | A 6 BEDFORD | A 505 HITCHIN |

MARKYATE B 4540 | LONDON M 1 | A 1081 HARPENDEN, ST ALBANS

Ashburnham Road	**X** 2	Hart Lane	**V** 17	Stopsley Way	**V** 35
Cutenhoe Road	**X** 9	Hitchin Road	**V** 18	Trinity Road	**V** 36
Eaton Green Road	**V** 13	Longcroft Road	**X** 26	Windmill Road	**X** 39
Grange Avenue	**V** 14	Newlands Road	**X** 29	Woodland Avenue	**V** 42

Strathmore Thistle (Mt. Charlotte Thistle), Arndale Centre, LU1 2TR, ℰ 34199, Telex 825763, Fax 402528 – 🛗 🗏 rest 📺 ☎ 👶 🄿 – 🔬 200. 🔼 🄰🄴 ⓪ 𝘝𝘐𝘚𝘈 🄹🄲🄱. ⋇ Y **n**
M 12.95/17.25 **t.** and a la carte – ⌷ 8.25 – **147 rm** 75.00/105.00 **st.**, 3 suites – SB (weekends only) 84.00/181.00 **st.**

Chiltern (Forte), Waller Av., Dunstable Rd, LU4 9RU, NW : 2 m. on A 505 ℰ 575911, Fax 581859 – 🛗 ✑ rm 🗏 rest 📺 ☎ 🄿 – 🔬 250. 🔼 🄰🄴 ⓪ 𝘝𝘐𝘚𝘈 🄹🄲🄱   V **r**
M (bar lunch Saturday) a la carte 12.00/21.15 **st.** ⏶ 6.10 – ⌷ 8.95 – **91 rm** 72.00 **st.** – SB (except Christmas) 86.00 **st.**

Forte Posthouse, 641 Dunstable Rd, LU4 8RQ, NW : 2 ¾ m. on A 505 ℰ 575955, Fax 490065 – 🛗 ✑ rm 📺 ☎ 🄿 – 🔬 70. 🔼 🄰🄴 ⓪ 𝘝𝘐𝘚𝘈   V **u**
M a la carte approx. 17.50 **t.** ⏶ 4.65 – ⌷ 6.95 – **117 rm** 53.50 **st.** – SB 90.00 **st.**

Red Lion, Castle St., LU1 3AA, ℰ 413881, Fax 23864 – ✑ rm 🗏 rest 📺 ☎ 🄿 – 🔬 50. 🔼 🄰🄴 ⓪ 𝘝𝘐𝘚𝘈. ⋇   Z **e**
M (closed Saturday lunch) 7.95/12.50 **t.** and a la carte – **38 rm** ⌷ 69.50/81.00 **t.** – SB 85.00/164.00 **st.**

Leaside, 72 New Bedford Rd, LU3 1BT, ℰ 417643, Fax 34961 – 📺 ☎ 🄿. 🔼 🄰🄴 ⓪ 𝘝𝘐𝘚𝘈. ⋇   Y **a**
closed 25 and 26 December – **M** (closed Sunday dinner and Bank Holidays) 16.00 **t.** and a la carte ⏶ 4.00 – **15 rm** ⌷ 40.00/60.00 **st.** – SB (weekends only) 75.00/120.00 **st.**

🅐 ATS 67 Kingsway ℰ 597519

ATS High St./Oakley Rd, Leagrave ℰ 507020/ 592381

━ When in a hurry use the **Michelin Main Road Maps:**
970 Europe, 980 Greece, 984 Germany, 985 Scandinavia-Finland, 986 Great Britain and Ireland, 987 Germany-Austria-Benelux, 988 Italy, 989 France, 990 Spain-Portugal and 991 Yugoslavia.

LUTON

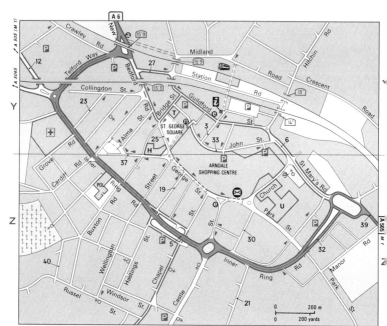

Bitte beachten Sie die Geschwindigkeitsbeschränkungen in Großbritannien

– 60 mph (= 96 km/h) außerhalb geschlossener Ortschaften
– 70 mph (= 112 km/h) auf Straßen mit getrennten Fahrbahnen und Autobahnen.

LUTTERWORTH Leics. 403 404 Q 26 – pop. 6 673 – ECD : Wednesday – ✆ 0455.

🖪 Ullesthorpe Court, Frolesworth Rd ℰ 209023, NW : 3 m.

◆London 93 – ◆Birmingham 34 – ◆Coventry 14 – ◆Leicester 16.

🏨 **Denbigh Arms** (Resort), 24 High St., LE17 4AD, ℰ 553537, Fax 556627 – 📺 ☎ 🅿 –
🔬 50. 🖼 🖭 ⓪ 𝗩𝗜𝗦𝗔
M (bar lunch Monday to Saturday)/dinner a la carte 6.95/10.95 **st.** – **31 rm** ⇌ 37.50/
65.00 **st.** – SB (weekends only) 80.00 **st.**

LYDFORD Devon 403 H 32 The West Country G. – pop. 1 762 – ⊠ Okehampton – ✆ 082 282
(3 fig.) and 0822 (6 fig.).

See : Village★★ (Lydford Gorge★★).

◆London 234 – Exeter 33 – ◆Plymouth 24.

🏕 **Castle Inn**, EX20 4BH, ℰ 242, Fax 454, « 16C inn », 🎐 – 📺 🅿 🖼 🖭 𝗩𝗜𝗦𝗔
M (bar lunch)/dinner 14.50 **t.** and a la carte ▮ 4.50 – **8 rm** ⇌ 25.00/52.50 **t.** – SB (except
Christmas and New Year) 66.50/99.00 **st.**

LYFORD Oxon – ⊠ Wantage – ✆ 0235.

◆London 70 – ◆Oxford 11 – Reading 30 – Swindon 19.

🏠 **Lyford Manor** 🐾 without rest., OX12 0EG, ℰ 868204, Fax 868266, « Part 15C farmhouse », 🎐 – 🐾 🅿 🐾
3 rm ⇌ 22.00/40.00 **s.**

See : Town★ – The Cobb★.

🏌 Timber Hill ✐ 442963.

🏢 Guildhall Cottage, Church St., DT7 3BS ✐ 442138.

♦London 160 – Dorchester 25 – Exeter 31 – Taunton 27.

🏨 **Alexandra,** Pound St., DT7 3HZ, ✐ 442010, Fax 443229, <, ⌖ – 📺 ☎ 🅿. 🖭 🖭 ⓞ 🆅🆂🅰
🃏
closed 19 December-3 February – **M** 12.50/17.50 **t.** and a la carte 🍴 4.25 – **26 rm** ⚌ 40.00/
100.00 **t.** – SB (mid October-May) 80.00/120.00 **st.**

🛖 **Red House** without rest., Sidmouth Rd, DT7 3ES, W :¾ m. on A 3052 ✐ 442055, ⌖ – 📺
🅿. 🛠
March-November – **3 rm** ⚌ 37.00/48.00 **s.**

🛖 **White House** without rest., 47 Silver St., DT7 3HR, ✐ 443420 – 📺 🅿
April-October – **7 rm** ⚌ 40.00 **st.**

at Uplyme (Devon) NW : 1¼ m. on A 3070 – ✉ 🕿 0297 Lyme Regis :

🛖 **Amherst Lodge Farm** ⌕, DT7 3XH, NW : 1 m. by A 3070, taking left turn in Yawl to
Cathole ✐ 442773, ⌕, ⌖ – ⟵ rest 📺 🅿 🛠
March-October – **M** (by arrangement) 13.00 – **3 rm** ⚌ 54.00 – SB 62.00/76.00 **st.**

⚓ to the Isle of Wight : Yarmouth (Wightlink Ltd) frequent services daily (30 mn).

🏢 The Car Park Rear of Waitrose, St. Thomas St. ✐ 672422 (summer only).

♦London 104 – Bournemouth 18 – ♦Southampton 19 – Winchester 32.

🏨 **Stanwell House,** 15 High St., SO41 9AA, ✐ 677123, Fax 677756, ⌖ – 📺 🅿 – 🅰 25. 🖭
🆅🆂🅰 🛠
M 17.50/26.00 **t.** and a la carte 🍴 5.50 – **36 rm** ⚌ 72.50/120.00 **t.** – SB (except Bank
Holidays) 98.00/130.00 **st.**

🏨 **Passford House** ⌕, Mount Pleasant Lane, Mount Pleasant, SO41 8LS, NW : 2 m. by
A 337 and Sway rd ✐ 682398, Fax 683494, <, 🛠, ⌖, 🏊 heated, 🔲, ⌖, park, ⁇ – 📺 ☎
🅿 – 🅰 60. 🖭 🖭 🆅🆂🅰
M 11.50/21.00 **t.** and a la carte 🍴 6.25 – **55 rm** ⚌ 75.00/105.00 **t.**, 1 suite – SB (October-
May) (except Bank Holidays) 112.00 **st.**

🛖 **Albany House,** Highfield, SO41 9GB, ✐ 671900, ⌖ – ⟵ rest 📺 ☎ 🅿. 🛠
M (by arrangement) 13.50 🍴 4.25 – **3 rm** ⚌ 26.00/56.00 **s.** – SB (November-April except
Bank Holidays) 58.00/98.00 **s.**

XXX **Provence at Gordleton Mill** with rm, Silver St., Hordle, SO41 6DJ, NW : 3½ m. by
A 337 and Sway Rd ✐ 682219, Fax 683073, « Part 17C mill, riverside setting », ⌖ – ⟵
▤ rest 📺 ☎ 🅿. 🖭 🖭 ⓞ 🆅🆂🅰. 🛠
Booking essential – **M** - **French** (closed Sunday dinner and Tuesday in winter) 17.50/36.00 **t.**
– **7 rm** ⚌ 50.00/80.00 **t.**

X **Limpets,** 9 Gosport St., SO41 9BG, ✐ 675595 – 🖭 🆅🆂🅰
closed December and Sunday-Monday in winter – **M** (dinner only) 22.00 **t.** and a la carte
🍴 5.25.

🔷 ATS Marsh Lane ✐ 675938/9

♦London 193 – Chester 24 – ♦Liverpool 23 – ♦Manchester 15.

🏨 **Lymm** (De Vere), Whitbarrow Rd, WA13 9AQ, via Brookfield Rd ✐ 752233, Fax 756035,
⌖ – ⟵ rm 📺 ☎ 🅿 – 🅰 100. 🖭 🖭 ⓞ 🆅🆂🅰
M *(closed Saturday lunch)* 15.00/20.00 **st.** and a la carte – **69 rm** ⚌ 55.00/75.00 **st.**

Pour voyager en **EUROPE** utilisez :

les cartes Michelin grandes routes.

les cartes Michelin détaillées.

les guides Rouges Michelin (hôtels et restaurants) :

Benelux - Deutschland - España Portugal - Main Cities Europe -
France - Great Britain and Ireland - Italia - Suisse.

les guides Verts Michelin (paysages, monuments et routes touristiques) :

Allemagne - Autriche - Belgique Grand-Duché de Luxembourg - Canada -
Espagne - France - Grande-Bretagne - Grèce - Hollande - Italie - Irlande -
Londres - Maroc - New York - Nouvelle Angleterre - Portugal - Rome - Suisse

... et la collection sur la France.

LYNDHURST Hants. [403] [404] P 31 Great Britain G. – pop. 2 828 – ECD : Wednesday – ☎ 0703.

Envir. : New Forest★★ (Bolderwood Ornamental Drive★★, Rhinefield Ornamental Drive★★).

⛳18, ⛳9 Dibden, Main Rd ☎ 845596, E : 6 m. by B 3056 – ⛳18 New Forest, Southampton Rd ☎ 282450/282752.

ℹ New Forest Museum & Visitor Centre, Main Car Park, SO43 7NY ☎ 282269.

♦London 95 – Bournemouth 20 – ♦Southampton 10 – Winchester 23.

- **Parkhill** 🔇, Beaulieu Rd, SO43 7FZ, SE : 1 ¼ m. on B 3056 ☎ 282944, Fax 283268, ≤, « Tastefully furnished country house », ♨ heated, 🌳, park – ⊁ rest 📺 ☎ P – 🎤 45. [S] [AE] [O] [VISA]
  M 15.00/23.50 **t.** and a la carte 🍷 5.95 – **17 rm** ☐ 39.00/118.00 **t.**, 3 suites – SB (except Bank Holidays) 86.00/166.00 **st.**
- **Crown** (Best Western), 9 High St., SO43 7NF, ☎ 282922, Fax 282751 – |‡| 📺 ☎ P – 🎤 40. [S] [AE] [O] [VISA] [JCB]
  M (bar lunch Monday to Thursday) 14.50 **t.** and a la carte 🍷 5.00 – **39 rm** ☐ 65.00/112.00 **t.**, 1 suite – SB 106.00/116.00 **st.**
- **Beaulieu**, Beaulieu Rd, SO42 7YQ, SE : 3 ½ m. on B 3056 ☎ 293344, Fax 292729, 🌳 – ⊁ rest 📺 ☎ P. [S] [AE] [O] [VISA]
  M (bar lunch Monday to Saturday)/dinner 15.00 **st.** and a la carte 🍷 6.50 – **17 rm** ☐ 38.00/80.00 **st.**, 1 suite.
- **Ormonde House**, Southampton Rd, SO43 7BT, ☎ 282806, Fax 283775, 🌳 – 📺 ☎ P. [S] [AE] [VISA]
  closed 25 and 26 December – **M** (by arrangement) (dinner only) 11.00 **st.** 🍷 6.00 – **15 rm** ☐ 25.00/56.00 **st.** – SB 48.00/82.00 **st.**
- **Whitemoor House** without rest., Southampton Rd, SO43 7BU, ☎ 282186 – 📺 P. [S] [VISA]. ⊁
  8 rm ☐ 25.00/46.00 **st.**

LYNMOUTH Devon [403] I 30 – see Lynton.

LYNTON Devon [403] I 30 The West Country G. – pop. 2 075 (inc. Lynmouth) – ECD : Thursday – ☎ 0598.

See : Town★ (≤★★).

Envir. : Valley of the Rocks★, W : 1 m. – Watersmeet★, E : 1 ½ m. by A 39.

Exc. : Exmoor National Park★★ – Doone Valley★, SE : 7 ½ m. by A 39 (access from Oare on foot).

ℹ Town Hall, Lee Rd, EX35 6BT ☎ 52225.

♦London 206 – Exeter 59 – Taunton 44.

- **Lynton Cottage** 🔇, North Walk Hill, EX35 6ED, ☎ 52342, Fax 52597, ≤ bay and Countisbury Hill, 🌳 – 📺 ☎ P. [S] [AE] [O] [VISA]
  closed January – **M** (bar lunch)/dinner a la carte 21.50/29.50 **st.** 🍷 6.00 – **17 rm** ☐ 48.00/117.00 **st.** – SB 107.00/134.00 **st.**
- **Hewitt's at the Hoe** 🔇, North Walk, EX35 6HJ, ☎ 52293, Fax 52489, ≤ bay and Countisbury Hill, « Victorian house in wooded cliffside setting », park – ⊁ 📺 ☎ P. [S] [VISA]. ⊁
  M 14.50/21.50 **t.** and dinner a la carte 🍷 5.75 – **9 rm** ☐ 42.00/90.00 **st.** – SB 121.00/133.00 **st.**
- **Seawood** 🔇, North Walk, EX35 6HJ, ☎ 52272, ≤ bay and headland – ⊁ rest 📺 P
  mid March-October – **M** 18.00 **st.** – **12 rm** ☐ 27.00/54.00 **st.** – SB (April, May and October) 70.00/80.00 **st.**
- **Chough's Nest** 🔇, North Walk, EX35 6HJ, ☎ 53315, ≤ bay and Countisbury Hill – ⊁ 📺 P. ⊁
  April-December – **M** (bar lunch)/dinner 12.00 **st.** 🍷 3.00 – **12 rm** ☐ 25.00/50.00 **st.**
- **Neubia House**, Lydiate Lane, EX35 6AH, ☎ 52309 – ⊁ rest 📺 ☎ P. [S] [VISA]. ⊁
  closed 2 December-6 February – **M** (dinner only) 15.00 **t.** – **12 rm** ☐ 29.00/60.00 **t.** – SB (except Bank Holidays) 72.00/80.00 **st.**
- **Crown**, Sinai Hill, EX35 6AG, ☎ 52253, Fax 53311 – 📺 ☎ P. [S] [VISA]
  closed 16 to 30 January – **M** (bar lunch Monday to Saturday)/dinner 14.00 **t.** and a la carte 🍷 4.25 – **14 rm** ☐ 34.50/90.50 **t.**
- **Victoria Lodge**, Lee Rd, EX35 6BS, ☎ 53203, 🌳 – ⊁ 📺 P. ⊁
  10 February-November – **M** 14.00 **st.** 🍷 3.00 – **10 rm** ☐ 28.00/60.00 **st.**
- **Rockvale** 🔇, Lee Rd, EX35 6HW, off Lee Rd ☎ 52279, ≤ – ⊁ rest 📺 ☎ P. [S] [VISA]
  closed 15 November-31 December – **M** (by arrangement) 12.00 **st.** 🍷 4.50 – **8 rm** ☐ 16.00/42.00 **st.** – SB (except January-mid February) 52.00/60.00 **st.**
- **Longmead House**, Longmead, EX35 6DQ, ☎ 52523, 🌳 – ⊁ P
  March-October – **M** 10.00 **st.** 🍷 3.00 – **8 rm** ☐ 16.00/40.00 **st.**

at Lynmouth – ✉ Lynmouth – ☎ 0598 Lynton :

- **Tors** 🔇, EX35 6NA, ☎ 53236, Fax 52544, ≤ Lynmouth and bay, ♨ heated, 🌳 – |‡| 📺 ☎ P. [S] [AE] [O] [VISA]
  closed 4 January-1 February – **M** 15.00/21.50 **st.** and a la carte 🍷 5.00 – **35 rm** ☐ 40.00/98.00 **st.** – SB (except May-September and Bank Holidays) 75.00/110.00 **st.**

🏠 **Rising Sun**, The Harbour, EX35 6EQ, 𝒫 53223, Fax 53480, ≼, « Part 14C inn », ⊶ – ⊱
📺 ☎. 🔼 🅰🅴 ⓞ 𝘝𝘐𝘚𝘈. ✻
M (bar lunch)/dinner 21.50 **t.** and a la carte ♨ 5.50 – **15 rm** ⊐ 39.50/89.00 **t.**, 1 suite –
SB (except July-September and Bank Holidays) 108.00/116.00 **st.**

🏠 **Beacon** ⤸ without rest., Countisbury Hill, EX35 6ND, E : ½ m. on A 39 𝒫 53268, ≼ Sea,
⊶ – 📺 🅿. ✻
April-September – **7 rm** ⊐ 22.00/44.00 **st.**

↑ **Countisbury Lodge** ⤸, Tors Park, EX35 6NB, off Countisbury Hill 𝒫 52388, ≼ – ⊱ rest
🅿. 🔼 𝘝𝘐𝘚𝘈
closed January and February – **M** 9.00 **st.** ♨ 3.50 – **6 rm** ⊐ 49.00/57.00 **st.** – SB (except
Christmas) 70.00/108.00 **st.**

↑ **Heatherville** ⤸, Tors Park, EX35 6NB, by Tors Rd 𝒫 52327 – ⊱ rest 📺 🅿
March-October – **M** 12.00 **t.** – **8 rm** ⊐ 22.50/45.00 **st.**

at Hillsford Bridges S : 4 ½ m. by A 39 – ✉ 🕸 0598 Lynton :

🏠 Combe Park ⤸, EX35 6LE, 𝒫 52356, ⊶ – ⊱ rest 🅿
9 rm.

at Woody Bay W : 3 ¼ m. on Coast road – ✉ 🕸 059 83 (3 fig.) and 0598 (6 fig.) Parracombe :

🏠 **Woody Bay** ⤸, EX31 4QX, 𝒫 264, ≼ Woody Bay – ⊱ rest 🅿. 🔼 𝘝𝘐𝘚𝘈
closed Monday to Thursday November-February – **M** (bar lunch)/dinner 16.00 **st.** and a la
carte ♨ 4.75 – **14 rm** ⊐ 48.00/96.00 **st.** – SB (except Bank Holidays) 80.00/91.00 **st.**

at Martinhoe W : 4 ¼ m. via Coast road – ✉ Barnstaple – 🕸 059 83 (3 fig.) and 0598
(6 fig.) Parracombe :

🏠 **Old Rectory** ⤸, EX31 4QT, 𝒫 368, Fax 567, ⊶ – ⊱ rest 📺 🅿. ✻
Easter-October – **M** (dinner only) 21.00 **t.** ♨ 4.50 – **8 rm** ⊐ (dinner included) 55.00/110.00 **t.**

LYONSHALL Heref. and Worcs. 🖪🖪🖪 L 27 – see Kington.

LYTHAM Lancs. 🖪🖪 L 22 – see Lytham St. Anne's.

LYTHAM ST ANNE'S Lancs. 🖪🖪 L 22 – pop. 39 599 – ECD : Wednesday – 🕸 0253 St. Anne's.
🏌 Fairhaven, Lytham Hall Park, Ansdell 𝒫 736741 – 🏌 St. Annes Old Links, Highbury Rd
𝒫 723597.
🛈 The Square, FY8 1LW 𝒫 725610.

◆London 237 – ◆Blackpool 7 – ◆Liverpool 44 – Preston 13.

🏨 **Dalmeny**, 19-33 South Promenade, FY8 1LX, 𝒫 712236, Fax 724447, ⇔, 🔲, squash – 🛗
📺 ☎ 🅿 – 🛆 180. 🔼 🅰🅴 𝘝𝘐𝘚𝘈. ✻
closed 24 to 26 December – **M** 9.50/18.50 **t.** and a la carte ♨ 5.95 – ⊐ 6.00 – **91 rm**
40.00/80.00 **st.** – SB (winter only) 91.00/138.00 **st.**

🏠 **Bedford**, 307-311 Clifton Drive South, FY8 1HN, 𝒫 724636, Fax 729244, ♬, ⇔ – 🛗 📺 ☎
🅿 – 🛆 80. 🔼 🅰🅴 ⓞ 𝘝𝘐𝘚𝘈
M (light lunch)/dinner 13.50 **st.** and a la carte ♨ 3.80 – **36 rm** ⊐ 32.00/59.00 **st.** – SB 75.00/
90.00 **st.**

at Lytham SE : 3 m. – ✉ 🕸 0253 Lytham :

🏨 Clifton Arms, West Beach, FY8 5QJ, 𝒫 739898, Telex 667463, Fax 730657, ⇔ – 🛗 ⊱ rm
📺 ☎ 🅿 – 🛆 150. ✻
39 rm, 2 suites.

🏠 County, Church Rd, FY8 5OZ, 𝒫 795128, Fax 795149 – 📺 ☎
21 rm.

MACCLESFIELD Ches. 🖪🖪 🖪🖪 🖪🖪 N 24 – pop. 47 525 – ECD : Wednesday – 🕸 0625.
🏌 The Tytherington 𝒫 434562 – 🏌 Shrigley Hall, Shrigley Park, Pott Shrigley 𝒫 575755, N :
5 m. on A 523.
🛈 Macclesfield Borough Council, Council Offices, Town Hall, SK10 1HR 𝒫 504114.

◆London 186 – Chester 38 – ◆Manchester 18 – ◆Stoke-on-Trent 21.

🏠 **Chadwick House**, 55 Beech Lane, SK10 2DS, 𝒫 615558, Fax 615558, ⇔ – ⊱ 📺 🅿. 🔼
🅰🅴 𝘝𝘐𝘚𝘈. ✻
M *(closed Friday to Sunday)* (residents only) (dinner only) 8.95 **st.** ♨ 3.00 – **12 rm** ⊐ 23.00/
55.00 **st.**

🏠 **Sutton Hall** ⤸, Bullocks Lane, Sutton, SK11 0HE, SE : 2 m. by A 523 𝒫 0260
(Sutton) 253211, Fax 252538, ⊶ – 📺 ☎ 🅿. 🔼 𝘝𝘐𝘚𝘈
M 10.95/19.95 **t.** ♨ 5.25 – **9 rm** ⊐ 68.95/85.00 **t.**

↑ **Fourways Diner Motel**, Cleulow Cross, Wincle, SK11 0QL, SE : 8 m. by A 523 on A 54
𝒫 0260 (Congleton) 227228, Fax 227228, ≼, ⊶ – 📺 🅿. 🔼 🅰🅴 ⓞ 𝘝𝘐𝘚𝘈
M (by arrangement) 12.50 **s.** ♨ 4.50 – **10 rm** ⊐ 28.00/50.00 **s.**

at Bollington N : 3 ½ m. by A 523 on B 5090 – ⊠ Macclesfield – 🐸 0625 Bollington :

✕ **Randall's,** 22 High St., Old Market Pl., SK10 5PH, ℘ 575058 – ☒ Æ ⓪ *VISA*
closed lunch except Sunday and December – **M** dinner a la carte 11.35/20.90 **t.** ⓵ 3.75.

✕ **Mauro's,** 88 Palmerston St., SK10 5PW, ℘ 573898 – ☒ Æ *VISA*
closed Sunday dinner and lunch first Sunday of month – **M** - **Italian** 8.75 **t.** (lunch) and a la
carte 12.10/23.25 **t.**

at Adlington N : 5 m. on A 523 – ⊠ 🐸 0625 Macclesfield :

🏨🏨 **Shrigley Hall** ⌇, Shrigley Park, Pott Shrigley, SK10 5SB, E : 2 m. on Pott Shrigley rd
℘ 575757, Fax 573323, « Early 19C country house in park », ₤₅, ⇌₅, ▨, ₁₈, ✕, squash –
⧗ 📺 ☎ 📵 – 🔌 300. ☒ Æ ⓪ *VISA*
M *(closed Saturday lunch)* (dancing Saturday evening) 16.50/19.50 **t.** and a la carte –
156 rm ⊏⊐ 90.00/135.00 **st.** – SB (weekends only) 260.00 **st.**

🛞 ATS 115 Hurdsfield Rd ℘ 425481/425233/424237

MACKWORTH Derbs. ₄₀₂ ₄₀₃ ₄₀₄ P 25 – see Derby.

MAGHAM DOWN E. Sussex – see Hailsham.

When visiting Scotland,
use the Michelin Green Guide **"Scotland".**

  – *Detailed descriptions of places of interest*
  – *Touring programmes*
  – *Maps and street plans*
  – *The history of the country*
  – *Photographs and drawings of monuments, beauty spots, houses...*

MAIDENBOWER W. Sussex – see Crawley.

MAIDENCOMBE Devon ₄₀₃ J 32 – see Torquay.

MAIDENHEAD Berks. ₄₀₄ R 29 – pop. 59 809 – ECD : Thursday – 🐸 0628.

₁₈ Bird Hills, Drift Rd, Hawthorn Hill ℘ 771030/75588/26035, S : 4 m. by A 330 ✕ – ₁₈
Shoppenhangers Rd ℘ 24693 ✕.

⛵ to Windsor Bridge and to Marlow via Cookham Landing Stage and Marlow Lock (Salter
Bros Ltd) (summer only).

🛈 The Library, St. Ives Rd, SL6 1QU ℘ 781110.

◆London 33 – ◆Oxford 32 – Reading 13.

Plan on next page

🏨🏨 **Holiday Inn Maidenhead,** Manor Lane, SL6 2RA, ℘ 23444, Telex 847502, Fax 770035,
₤₅, ⇌₅, ▨, ⋙, squash – ⧗ ↔ rm ▤ rest 📺 ☎ & 📵 – 🔌 400. ☒ Æ ⓪ *VISA* ᴊᴄʙ.
✕ ✕ **n**
M – **Promenade** *(closed Saturday lunch)* 15.85/17.20 **st.** and a la carte – ⊏⊐ 9.95 – **187 rm**
105.00/125.00 **st.**, 2 suites – SB (weekends only) 80.00/140.00 **st.**

🏨🏨 **Fredrick's,** Shoppenhangers Rd, SL6 2PZ, ℘ 35934, Fax 771054, ⋙ – 📺 ☎ 📵 – 🔌 50.
☒ Æ ⓪ *VISA* ✕✕
✕ **c**
closed 24 to 30 December – **M** (see below) – **36 rm** ⊏⊐ 130.00/175.00 **t.**, 1 suite.

🏨 **Thames Riviera,** at the bridge, Bridge Rd, SL6 8DW, ℘ 74057, Fax 776586, ⇐ – 📺 ☎ 📵
– 🔌 50. ☒ Æ ⓪ *VISA* ✕✕
V **e**
closed 24 to 31 December – **M** *(closed Saturday lunch in summer)* a la carte 16.20/29.20 **t.**
⓵ 4.50 – **50 rm** ⊏⊐ 75.00/115.00 **st.** – SB (weekends only) 99.00 **st.**

🏨 **Walton Cottage,** Marlow Rd, SL6 7LT, ℘ 24394, Fax 773851 – ⧗ 📺 ☎ 📵 – 🔌 30. ☒ Æ
⓪ *VISA* ✕✕
Y **e**
closed 24 December-3 January – **M** *(closed Friday to Sunday and Bank Holidays)* (dinner
only) 16.00 **t.** ⓵ 5.00 – **66 rm** ⊏⊐ 69.00/105.00 **st.**

✕✕✕ **Fredrick's,** Shoppenhangers Rd, SL6 2PZ, ℘ 24737, Fax 771054, ⋙ – ▤ 📵. ☒ Æ ⓪
VISA
✕ **c**
closed Saturday lunch and 24 to 30 December – **M** 21.50/29.50 **t.** and a la carte ⓵ 8.00.

✕✕ **Jasmine Peking,** 29 High St., SL6 1JG, ℘ 20334 – ☒ Æ *VISA*
Y **o**
M - **Chinese** a la carte 9.45/17.60 **st.**

at Littlewick Green W : 3 ¼ m. by A 4 – V – ⊠ 🐸 0628 Maidenhead :

🏨 **Freddie Starr's Crystals,** Bath Rd, SL6 3RQ, on A 4 ℘ 822085, Fax 829211 – 📺 ☎ 📵 –
🔌 30. ☒ Æ ⓪ *VISA* ✕✕
M 12.00/13.50 **t.** and a la carte ⓵ 6.50 – **19 rm** ⊏⊐ 55.00 **t.**

🛞 ATS Denmark St., Cordwallis Est. ℘ 20161

MAIDENHEAD

*For business
or tourist interest :*
MICHELIN Red Guide
Main Cities EUROPE.

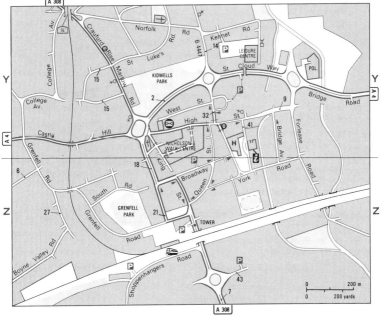

MAIDEN NEWTON Dorset 408 404 M 31 The West Country G. – pop. 777 – ECD : Thursday – ⊠ Dorchester – ✆ 0300.

Envir. : Cerne Abbas★, NE : 5½ m.

♦London 143 – Bournemouth 35 – ♦Bristol 55 – Taunton 34 – Weymouth 16.

🏠 **Maiden Newton House** ⏂, Church Rd, DT2 0AA, ☞ 320336, Fax 321021, « Attractively converted 19C medieval style manor house », ⏃, ⌗, park – ⇇ ㊊. 🖚 VISA
closed 1 to 20 December – **M** (booking essential) (communal dining) (dinner only) 25.00 **st.** ₰ 5.50 – **6 rm** ⊑ 42.00/126.00 **st.** – SB (except Christmas and New Year) 126.00/164.00 **st.**

XX **Le Petit Canard**, Dorchester Rd, DT2 0BE, ☞ 320536 – 🖚 VISA
closed Sunday and Monday – **Meals** (booking essential) (dinner only) 21.00 **t.** ₰ 5.50.

MAIDSTONE Kent 404 V 30 Great Britain G. – pop. 86 067 – ECD : Wednesday – ✆ 0622.

Envir. : Leeds Castle★ AC, SE : 4½ m. by A 20 and B 2163.

📗 Tudor Park, Ashford Rd, Bearsted ☞ 734334, E : 3 m. on A 20.

🅱 The Gatehouse, The Old Palace Gardens, Mill St., ME15 6YE ☞ 673581/602169.

♦London 36 – ♦Brighton 64 – ♦Cambridge 84 – Colchester 72 – Croydon 36 – ♦Dover 45 – Southend-on-Sea 49.

🏨 **Stakis Country Court**, Bearsted Rd, Wearvering, ME14 5AA, NE : 1 ½ m. by A 249 ☞ 734322, Telex 965689, Fax 734600, ₤₄, ⏂, 🖾 – ⇇ rm ⊟ rest 📺 ☎ & ㊊ – 🔬 90. 🖚 🔼 ⒶⒺ ⓄⒾ VISA JCB
M 16.95 **t.** (dinner) and a la carte – ⊑ 8.50 – **134 rm** 79.00/103.00 **st.** 4 suites – SB 92.00/152.00 **st.**

🏠 **Grangemoor**, 4-8 St. Michael's Rd (off Tonbridge Rd), ME16 8BS, ☞ 677623, Fax 678246, ⌗ – 📺 ☎ ㊊ – 🔬 100. 🔼 VISA
M 7.50/12.00 **st.** and a la carte ₰ 3.50 – **36 rm** ⊑ 30.00/52.00 **t.**

⌂ **Rock House** without rest., 102 Tonbridge Rd, ME16 8SL, ☞ 751616, Fax 756119 – 📺 ㊊. 🔼 VISA ⇇
closed 24 December-1 January – **12 rm** ⊑ 30.00/44.00 **st.**

at Bearsted E : 3 m. by A 249 on A 20 – ⊠ ✆ 0622 Maidstone :

🏨 **Tudor Park H. Golf & Country Club**, Ashford Rd, ME14 4NQ, E : 1 m. on A 20 ☞ 734334, Fax 735360, ⩽, ₤₄, ⏂, 🖾, 📗, ⌗, park, ⸙, squash – ⇇ rm 📺 ☎ ㊊ – 🔬 300. 🔼 ⒶⒺ ⓄⒾ VISA
M (closed Saturday lunch) (carving lunch)/dinner 16.50 **t.** and a la carte ₰ 6.50 – **119 rm** ⊑ 51.00/118.00 **st.**

XX **Soufflé**, The Green, ME14 4DN, off Yeoman Lane ☞ 737065, Fax 737065 – ㊊. 🔼 ⒶⒺ ⓄⒾ VISA
closed Saturday lunch, Sunday dinner and 1 January – **M** 18.95/28.95 **t.** and a la carte.

at Boughton Monchelsea S : 4½ m. by A 229 on B 2163 – ⊠ ✆ 0622 Maidstone :

🏠 **Tanyard** ⏂, Wierton Hill, ME17 4JT, S : 1½ m. by Park Lane ☞ 744705, Fax 741998, ⩽, « 14C tannery standing in orchards », ⌗ – 📺 ☎ ㊊. 🔼 ⒶⒺ ⓄⒾ VISA ⇇
M (residents only) (dinner only) 25.00 **t.** ₰ 5.40 – **6 rm** ⊑ 50.00/110.00 **t.**

at Wateringbury SW : 4½ m. on A 26 – ⊠ ✆ 0622 Maidstone :

🏠 **Wateringbury**, Tonbridge Rd, ME18 5NS, ☞ 812632, Telex 96265, Fax 812720, ⌗ – ⇇ rm 📺 ☎ ㊊ – 🔬 75. 🔼 ⒶⒺ ⓄⒾ VISA
M (closed Saturday lunch) 10.95/13.95 **st.** and a la carte ₰ 5.75 – ⊑ 5.50 – **40 rm** 39.50/56.00 **st.**

at Larkfield W : 3¼ m. on A 20 – ⊠ Maidstone – ✆ 0732 West Malling :

🏠 **Larkfield Priory** (Forte), 812 London Rd, ME20 6HJ, ☞ 846858, Fax 846786 – ⇇ rm ⊟ rest 📺 ☎ ㊊ – 🔬 80. 🔼 ⒶⒺ ⓄⒾ VISA JCB
M (bar lunch Monday to Saturday)/dinner 15.95 **t.** and a la carte ₰ 6.45 – ⊑ 8.50 – **52 rm** 55.00 **t.** – SB (weekends only) 86.00 **st.**

🅐🅣🅢 ATS 165 Upper Stone St. ☞ 758738/758664

MALDON Essex 404 W 28 – pop. 14 638 – ECD : Wednesday – ✆ 0621.

📗 Forrester Park, Beckingham Rd ☞ 891406, NE : 3 m. by B 1022 – 📗, 📗 Bunsay Downs, Little Baddow Rd, Woodham Walter ☞ 0245 (Chelmsford) 412648/412369, W : 4½ m. by A 414.

🅱 The Hythe, CM9 7HN ☞ 856503.

♦London 42 – Chelmsford 9 – Colchester 17.

🏠 **Blue Boar** (Forte), Silver St., CM9 7QE, ☞ 852681, Fax 856202 – ⇇ rm 📺 ☎ ㊊ – 🔬 40. 🔼 ⒶⒺ ⓄⒾ VISA
M (bar lunch Monday to Saturday)/dinner 15.95 **st.** ₰ 6.50 – ⊑ 8.50 – **28 rm** 70.00/80.00 **st.** – SB (weekends only) 86.00/169.70 **st.**

🅐🅣🅢 ATS 143-147 High St. ☞ 856541

MALMESBURY Wilts. 408 404 N 29 The West Country G. – pop. 4 220 – ECD : Thursday – ✆ 0666.

See : Town★ – Market Cross★★ – Abbey★.

🅱 Town Hall, Market Lane, SN16 9BZ ☞ 823748.

♦London 108 – ♦Bristol 28 – Gloucester 24 – Swindon 19.

358

🏰 **Whatley Manor** ⬙, Easton Grey, SN16 0RB, W : 2 ½ m. on B 4040 ℰ 822888, Fax 826120, ≼, « Part 18C manor house », ⬙s, ⬙ heated, ⬚, 🡕, park, ✗ – 📺 ☎ 🅟 – ⬙ 30. 🄽 🄰🄴 ⓞ 💳

M 15.00/28.50 **t.** ‖ 6.00 – **29 rm** ⬚ 85.00/136.00 **t.** – SB (weekends only) 137.00/160.00 **st.**

🏨 **Old Bell,** Abbey Row, SN16 0BW, ℰ 822344, Fax 825125, « Part 13C former abbots hostel », 🡕 – 📺 ☎ 🅟 – ⬙ 25. 🄽 💳 ✗

M (bar lunch Saturday in summer) 17.50/26.00 **t.** and a la carte ‖ 5.50 – **35 rm** ⬚ 72.50/98.00 **t.**, 1 suite – SB (except Bank Holidays) 98.00/118.00 **t.**

🏨 **Knoll House,** Swindon Rd, SN16 9LU, ℰ 823114, Fax 823897, ⬙, 🡕 – 📺 ☎ 🅟. 🄽 🄰🄴 💳 🄹🄲🄱

M (bar lunch Monday to Saturday)/dinner 20.50 **t.** and a la carte ‖ 5.60 – **23 rm** ⬚ 58.50/85.00 **t.** – SB (weekends only) 80.00/110.00 **st.**

at Crudwell N : 4 m. on A 429 – ✉ ☎ 0666 Malmesbury :

🏨 **Crudwell Court,** SN16 9EP, ℰ 577194, Fax 577853, « Former 17C vicarage, gardens », ⬙ heated – ⥮ rest 📺 ☎ 🅟. 🄽 🄰🄴 ⓞ 💳

M 15.50/27.95 **t.** ‖ 4.90 – **15 rm** ⬚ 55.00/120.00 **t.** – SB (except Easter, Christmas and Bank Holidays) 125.00/150.00 **st.**

🏠 **Mayfield House,** SN16 9EW, ℰ 577409, Fax 577977, 🡕 – 📺 ☎ 🅟 – ⬙ 30

M (bar lunch)/dinner 16.95 **t.** ‖ 3.65 – **20 rm** ⬚ 40.00/58.00 **t.** – SB 77.00 **st.**

MALPAS Ches. 🔢🔢 L 24 – pop. 1 522 – ☎ 0948.

◆London 177 – ◆Birmingham 60 – Chester 15 – Shrewsbury 26 – ◆Stoke-on-Trent 30.

✗✗ **Market House,** Church St., SY14 8NU, ℰ 860400, 🡕 – 🄽 💳
closed Sunday dinner, Monday to Wednesday, first week January and last 2 weeks August – **M** (booking essential) (dinner only and Sunday lunch)/dinner 11.20 **t.** and a la carte ‖ 5.75.

at Tilston NW : 3 m. on Tilston Rd – ✉ Malpas – ☎ 0829 Tilston :

🏠 **Tilston Lodge** ⬙, without rest., SY14 7DR, ℰ 250223, 🡕 – ⥮ 📺 🅟. ✗
M (by arrangement) – **3 rm** ⬚ 20.00/50.00 **st.**

En saison, surtout dans les stations fréquentées, il est prudent de retenir à l'avance.

Cependant, si vous ne pouvez pas occuper la chambre que vous avez retenue, prévenez immédiatement l'hôtelier.

Si vous écrivez à un hôtel à l'étranger, joignez à votre lettre un coupon-réponse international (disponible dans les bureaux de poste).

MALTON N. Yorks. 🔢 R 21 Great Britain G. – pop. 4 033 – ECD : Thursday – ☎ 0653.

Envir. : Castle Howard★★ (Park★★★) *AC*, W : 6 m.

🟦 Malton & Norton, Welham Park, Norton ℰ 692959.

🅱 The Old Town Hall, Market Pl., YO17 0LH ℰ 600048 (summer only).

◆London 229 – ◆Kingston-upon-Hull 36 – Scarborough 24 – York 17.

🏨 **Greenacres Country,** Amotherby, YO17 0TG, W : 2 ½ m. on B 1257 ℰ 693623, ⬙, 🡕 – ⥮ 📺 🅟. 🄽 💳 ✗
closed mid November-1 March – **M** (closed Sunday) (dinner only) 12.00 **st.** ‖ 3.50 – **9 rm** ⬚ 24.00/52.00 **st.** – SB (October-May) 71.00 **st.**

🏠 Oakdene, 29 Middlecave Rd, YO17 0NE, ℰ 693363, 🡕 – ⥮ rest 📺 🅟. ✗
6 rm.

at Wharram-Le-Street SE : 6 m. on B 1248 – ✉ Malton – ☎ 0944 North Grimston :

🏠 **Red House,** YO17 9TL, ℰ 768455, 🡕, ✗ – ⥮ rm 📺 🅟
closed 1 week Christmas – **M** (by arrangement) 12.00 **s.** ‖ 2.50 – **3 rm** ⬚ 24.00/48.00 **s.**

🔧 ATS 27 Commercial St., Norton ℰ 692567/693525

MALVERN Heref. and Worcs. 🔢🔢 N 27 – see Great Malvern.

MALVERN WELLS Heref. and Worcs. 🔢🔢 N 27 – see Great Malvern.

MANCHESTER Gtr. Manchester 🔢🔢🔢 N 23 Great Britain G. – pop. 437 612 – ☎ 061.

See : City★ – Castlefield Heritage Park★ CZ – Town Hall★ CZ – City Art Gallery★ CZ **M2** – Cathedral★ (Stalls and Canopies★) CY.

🟦 Heaton Park ℰ 798 0295, N : by A 576 ABV – 🟦 Houldsworth, Longford Rd West, Higher Levenshulme ℰ 224 5055, S : 3 ½ m. by A 57 BX – 🟦 Chorlton-cum-Hardy, Barlow Hall, Barlow Hall Rd ℰ 881 3139, SW : 4 m. by A 5103 AX – 🟦 William Wroe, Pennybridge Lane, Flixton ℰ 748 8680, SW : 6 m. by M 63 AX.

✈ Manchester International Airport ℰ 489 3000, S : 10 m. by A 5103 – AX – and M 56 – **Terminal** : Coach service from Victoria Station.

🅱 Town Hall Extension, Lloyd St., M60 2LA ℰ 234 3157/8 – Manchester Airport, International Arrivals Hall, M22 5NY ℰ 436 3344.

◆London 202 – ◆Birmingham 86 – ◆Glasgow 221 – ◆Leeds 43 – ◆Liverpool 35 – ◆Nottingham 72.

Plans on following pages

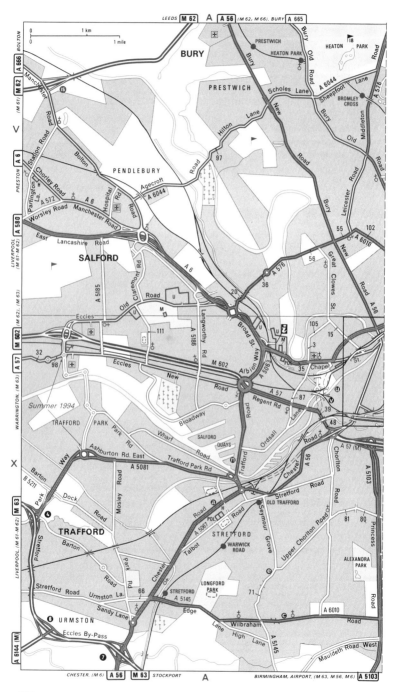

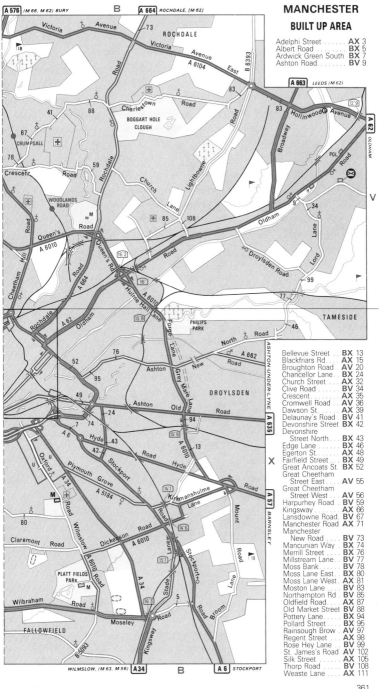

MANCHESTER
BUILT UP AREA

361

MANCHESTER
CENTRE

Arndale
  Shopping Centre......... **CY**
Deansgate................... **CYZ**
Lower Mosley Street..... **CZ**
Market Place.............. **CY**
Market Street............. **CY** 75
Mosley Street............. **CZ**
Princess Street........... **CZ**

Addington Street......... **CY** 2
Albert Square............. **CZ** 6
Aytoun Street............. **CZ** 10

Blackfriars Road......... **CY** 15
Blackfriars Street........ **CY** 17
Brazennose Street....... **CZ** 18
Cannon Street............. **CY** 21
Cateaton Street........... **CY** 22
Charlotte Street........... **CZ** 25
Cheetham Hill Road...... **CY** 27
Chepstow Street.......... **CZ** 28
Chorlton Street........... **CZ** 29
Church Street............. **CY** 31
Dale Street................ **CZ** 38
Ducie Street............... **CZ** 45
Fairfield Street............ **CZ** 49
Fennel Street.............. **CY** 50
Great Bridgewater Street . **CZ** 53
Great Ducie Street....... **CY** 57

High Street................ **CY** 62
John Dalton Street....... **CZ** 63
King Street................. **CZ** 64
Liverpool Road............ **CZ** 68
Lloyd Street............... **CZ** 69
Lower Byrom St........... **CZ** 70
Nicholas Street........... **CZ** 84
Parker Street.............. **CZ** 91
Peter Street............... **CZ** 92
St. Ann's Street.......... **CY** 101
St. Peter's Square....... **CZ** 104
Spring Gardens........... **CZ** 106
Viaduct Street............ **CY** 109
Whitworth Street West .. **CZ** 112
Withy Grove............... **CY** 113
York Street................ **CZ** 115

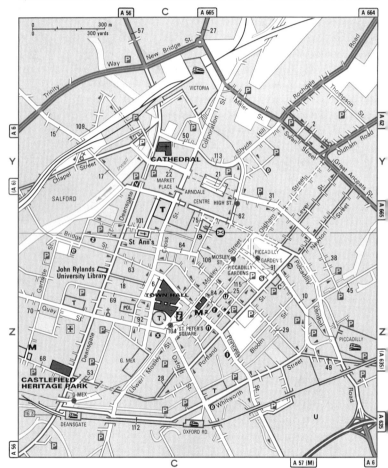

Victoria and Albert, Water St., M60 9EA, *𝒫* 832 1188, Fax 834 2484, *Ⅰ₆*, 🖘 – |✿| ⇜ rm
▤ rest 📺 ☎ ᴓ ⱷ – 🛦 250. 🖾 🖾 ⓞ 𝗩𝗜𝗦𝗔, ⅙   AX **u**
M 9.95/25.00 **st.** and a la carte ⅊ 7.60 – ⊑ 10.50 – **128 rm** 115.00/145.00 **st.**, 4 suites –
SB (weekends only) 127.50/210.00 **st.**

Holiday Inn Crowne Plaza Midland, 16 Peter St., M60 2DS, *𝒫* 236 3333, Telex
667550, Fax 228 2241, *Ⅰ₆*, 🖘, 🔲, squash – |✿| ⇜ rm ▤ 📺 ☎ ᴓ ⱷ – 🛦 500. 🖾 🖾 ⓞ
𝗩𝗜𝗦𝗔, ⅙   CZ **x**
M – French rest. (closed Sunday) (dinner only) 32.50 **t.** and a la carte ⅊ 5.95 – **Trafford Room**
(closed Saturday lunch) (carving rest.) 17.95 **t.** ⅊ 5.95 – **Wyvern** (closed Sunday)
a la carte 14.70/20.20 **t.** ⅊ 5.95 – ⊑ 10.95 – **296 rm** 118.00/136.00 **st.**, 7 suites – SB (weekends only) 99.00/158.00 **st.**

Ramada Renaissance, Blackfriars St., Deansgate, M3 2EQ, *𝒫* 835 2555, Fax 833 0731 –
|✿| ⇜ rm ▤ rest 📺 ☎ ᴓ ⱷ – 🛦 350. 🖾 🖾 ⓞ 𝗩𝗜𝗦𝗔 𝗝𝗖𝗕, ⅙   CY **v**
M (closed Saturday lunch, Sunday and Bank Holidays) 21.50 **st.** (dinner) and a la
carte 14.50/23.90 **st.** ⅊ 5.65 – ⊑ 10.90 – **200 rm** 69.00/110.00 **st.**, 5 suites.

Copthorne Manchester, Clippers Quay, Salford Quays, M5 3DL, *𝒫* 873 7321, Telex
669090, Fax 873 7318, *Ⅰ₆*, 🖘, 🔲 – |✿| ⇜ rm ▤ rest 📺 ☎ ᴓ ⱷ – 🛦 150. 🖾 🖾 ⓞ 𝗩𝗜𝗦𝗔,
⅙   AX **n**
M 14.95 **t.** and a la carte ⅊ 7.25 – ⊑ 9.50 – **166 rm** 97.00/118.00 **st.** – SB (weekends only)
106.00/125.00 **st.**

Charterhouse, Oxford St., M60 7HA, *𝒫* 236 9999, Fax 236 0674 – |✿| 📺 ☎ ᴓ – 🛦 180.
🖾 🖾 ⓞ 𝗩𝗜𝗦𝗔   CZ **o**
M (closed Saturday lunch) 10.00/17.50 **st.** and a la carte ⅊ 5.50 – ⊑ 9.75 – **45 rm**
45.00/105.00 **st.**, 13 suites – SB (weekends only) 130.00/180.00 **st.**

Portland Thistle (Mt. Charlotte Thistle), 3-5 Portland St., Piccadilly Gdns, M1 6DP,
𝒫 228 3400, Telex 669157, Fax 228 6347, 🖘 – |✿| ⇜ rm ▤ rest 📺 ☎ – 🛦 300. 🖾 🖾 ⓞ
𝗩𝗜𝗦𝗔, ⅙   CZ **a**
M (closed Sunday lunch) 14.95/16.95 **st.** and a la carte ⅊ 5.50 – ⊑ 9.85 – **204 rm** 89.00/
110.00 **st.**, 1 suite – SB (weekends only) 94.00 **st.**

Castlefield, Liverpool Rd, M3 4JR, *𝒫* 832 7073, Fax 839 0326, *Ⅰ₆*, 🖘, 🔲 – |✿| ▤ rest 📺
☎ ᴓ ⱷ – 🛦 65. 🖾 🖾 ⓞ 𝗩𝗜𝗦𝗔   AX **v**
closed 25 December and 1 January – **M** 15.00/18.00 **t.** and a la carte ⅊ 4.50 – **48 rm**
⊑ 40.00/65.00 **st.** – SB 66.00/106.00 **st.**

Chester Court, 728-730 Chester Rd, Stretford, M32 0RS, SW : 2½ m. on A 56 *𝒫* 877 5375,
Fax 877 5431 – |✿| 📺 ☎ ᴓ. ⅙   AX **a**
23 rm.

Isola Bella, Dolefield, Crown Sq., M3 3EN, *𝒫* 831 7099, Fax 839 1561 – ▤. 🖾 ⓞ
𝗩𝗜𝗦𝗔   CZ **e**
closed Sunday and Bank Holidays – **M** - Italian a la carte 13.00/21.00 **st.** ⅊ 4.60.

Quan Ju De, 44 Princess St., M1 6DE, *𝒫* 236 5236 – ▤. 🖾 🖾 𝗩𝗜𝗦𝗔   CZ **i**
closed Sunday and Bank Holidays – **M** - Chinese (Peking) 9.80/22.50 **st.** and a la carte.

Giulio's Terrazza, 14 Nicholas St., M1 4FE, *𝒫* 236 4033, Fax 236 0250 – ▤. 🖾 🖾 ⓞ 𝗩𝗜𝗦𝗔
𝗝𝗖𝗕   CZ **r**
closed Sunday and Bank Holidays – **M** - Italian 9.25/14.90 **st.** and a la carte ⅊ 5.80.

Gaylord, Amethyst House, Marriott's Court, Spring Gdns, M2 1EA, *𝒫* 832 6037 – ▤. 🖾
🖾 ⓞ 𝗩𝗜𝗦𝗔   CZ **c**
closed 25 December and 1 January – **M** - Indian 5.95/13.95 **t.** and a la carte ⅊ 5.45.

Yang Sing, 34 Princess St., M1 4JY, *𝒫* 236 2200, Fax 236 5934 – ▤. 🖾 🖾 ⓞ 𝗩𝗜𝗦𝗔   CZ **m**
closed Christmas Day – **M** - Chinese (Canton) (booking essential) 13.25 **t.** and a la carte.

Market, 104 High St., M4 1HQ, *𝒫* 834 3743 – 🖾 🖾 ⓞ 𝗩𝗜𝗦𝗔   CY **o**
closed Sunday to Tuesday, 1 week Easter, August and 1 week Christmas – **M** - Bistro
(dinner only) a la carte 15.15/22.95 **t.** ⅊ 4.50.

Little Yang Sing, 17 George St., M1 4HE, *𝒫* 228 7722, Fax 237 9257 – ▤. 🖾 🖾
𝗩𝗜𝗦𝗔   CZ **u**
closed Christmas Day – **M** - Chinese (Canton) 9.00/13.00 **t.** and a la carte.

Koreana, Kings House, 40a King St. West, M3 2WY, *𝒫* 832 4330, Fax 832 2293 – 🖾 🖾
ⓞ 𝗩𝗜𝗦𝗔   CZ **z**
closed Sunday and lunch Saturday and Bank Holiday Mondays – **M** - Korean 7.30/19.50 **t.**
and a la carte ⅊ 6.50.

at Northenden S : 5 ¼ m. by A 5103 - AX – ✉ ✆ 061 Manchester :

Forte Posthouse, Palatine Rd, M22 4FH, *𝒫* 998 7090, Fax 946 0139 – |✿| ⇜ rm 📺 ☎ ᴓ
– 🛦 150. 🖾 🖾 ⓞ 𝗩𝗜𝗦𝗔 𝗝𝗖𝗕
M a la carte approx. 17.50 **t.** ⅊ 4.65 – ⊑ 6.95 – **190 rm** 53.50 **st.** – SB (weekends only)
90.00 **st.**

at Didsbury S : 5 ½ m. by A 5103 – AX – on A 5145 – ✉ ✆ 061 Manchester :

Est, Est, Est !, 756 Wilmslow Rd, M20 0DW, *𝒫* 445 8209 – ▤. 🖾 🖾 𝗩𝗜𝗦𝗔
closed 25-26 December and 1 January – **M** - Italian 12.95 **t.** and a la carte 9.85/19.70 **t.**
⅊ 4.75.

at Manchester Airport S : 9 m. by A 5103 – AX – off M 56 – ⊠ ✆ 061 Manchester :

🏨🏨 **Manchester Airport Hilton,** Outwood Lane, Ringway, M22 5WP, ℰ 436 4404, Telex 668361, Fax 436 1521, ⇌s – |§| ⇇ rm ▦ 🅣🆅 ☎ & ℗ – 🔬 200. 🌇 🆎 ⑩ 𝗩𝗜𝗦𝗔 𝗝𝗖𝗕
M 16.00/22.00 **st.** and a la carte – ⊊ 10.95 – **223 rm** ⊊ 109.00/200.00 **st.** – SB (weekends only) 164.00/210.00 **st.**

🏨🏨 Forte Crest, Ringway Rd, Wythenshawe, M22 5NS, ℰ 437 5811, Telex 668721, Fax 436 2340, 🔓, ⇌s, 🔲 – |§| ⇇ rm ▦ 🅣🆅 ☎ ℗ – 🔬 200. 🌇 🆎 ⑩ 𝗩𝗜𝗦𝗔 𝗝𝗖𝗕
M 12.95/18.95 **t.** and a la carte 🍴 6.60 – **290 rm**, 2 suites.

🏨 **Etrop Grange,** Outwood Lane, M22 5NR, ℰ 499 0500, Fax 499 0790 – ⇇ rm 🅣🆅 ☎ & ℗
– 🔬 70. 🌇 🆎 ⑩ 𝗩𝗜𝗦𝗔 ✻
M (light lunch Saturday) 16.25/33.00 **t.** 🍴 4.95 – ⊊ 8.95 – **38 rm** 54.50/104.50 **t.**, 2 suites.

🏠 **Travel Inn,** Finney Lane, Heald Green, SK8 2QH, E : 2 m. on B 5166 ℰ 499 1944,
Fax 437 4910 – ⇇ rm 🅣🆅 & ℗   BX
M (Beefeater grill) a la carte approx. 16.00 **t.** – ⊊ 4.95 – **41 rm** 33.50 **t.**

💥💥💥 **Moss Nook,** Ringway Rd, Moss Nook, M22 5NA, ℰ 437 4778, Fax 498 8089 – ℗. 🌇 🆎
⑩ 𝗩𝗜𝗦𝗔
closed Saturday lunch, Sunday, Monday and 25 December-9 January – **M** 16.50/28.00 **t.**
and a la carte 🍴 4.75.

at Chorlton-Cum-Hardy SW : 5 m. by A 5103 on A 6010 – ⊠ ✆ 061 Manchester :

🏨 **Cornelius,** Manchester Rd, M16 0ED, ℰ 862 9565, Fax 862 9028 – 🅣🆅 ☎ ℗ – 🔬 50. 🌇
🆎 ⑩ 𝗩𝗜𝗦𝗔 𝗝𝗖𝗕   AX   **e**
M 9.00/13.00 **t.** and a la carte 🍴 4.95 – **15 rm** ⊊ 25.00/65.00 **st.** – SB (weekends only)
60.00/130.00 **st.**

🏠 **Sabre D'or,** 392 Wilbraham Rd, M21 1UH, ℰ 881 5055 – 🅣🆅 ℗   AX   **c**
M 10.00 **st.** 🍴 4.00 – **18 rm** ⊊ 25.00/40.00 **st.** – SB (weekends only) 30.00/50.00 **st.**

💥💥 **Peking Palace,** 285 Barlow Moor Rd, M21 2GH, S : 1 m. on A 5145 ℰ 881 2954 – ▣. 🌇
🆎 𝗩𝗜𝗦𝗔   AX
closed 25 December and 1 January – **M** - **Chinese** (Peking) (dinner only) 23.50 and a la carte
🍴 3.80.

at Worsley W : 7 ¼ m. by M 602 – AV – and M 62 (eastbound) on A 572 –
⊠ ✆ 061 Manchester :

🏨 **Novotel Manchester West,** Worsley Brow, M28 4YA, at junction 13 of M 62
ℰ 799 3535, Fax 703 8207, ⤳ heated – |§| ⇇ rm ▦ rest 🅣🆅 ☎ & ℗ – 🔬 200. 🌇 🆎 ⑩
𝗩𝗜𝗦𝗔
M 11.50/15.00 and a la carte 🍴 5.20 – ⊊ 7.50 – **119 rm** 59.50/64.50 – SB (weekends only)
70.00/100.00 **st.**

💥💥 **Tung Fong,** 2 Worsley Rd, M28 4NL, on A 572 ℰ 794 5331 – ▣. 🌇 🆎 𝗩𝗜𝗦𝗔
closed lunch Saturday and Sunday – **M** - **Chinese** (Peking) 25.00 **st.** and a la carte 🍴 4.50.

at Swinton NW : 4 m. by A 580 – AV – and A 572 on B 5231 – ⊠ ✆ 061 Manchester :

🏠 **New Ellesmere,** East Lancs Rd, M27 3AA, SW : ½ m. on A 580 ℰ 728 2791,
Fax 794 8222 – 🅣🆅 ☎ & ℗. 🌇 🆎 ⑩ 𝗩𝗜𝗦𝗔 ✻
M (grill rest.) a la carte 7.00/10.50 **st.** 🍴 3.75 – **27 rm** ⊊ 42.95/47.95 **st.**

🔧 ATS Chester St. ℰ 236 5505   ATS 122 Higher Rd, Urmston ℰ 748 6990/5923
ATS 98 Wilmslow Rd, Rusholme ℰ 224 6296   ATS 20/28 Waterloo Rd ℰ 832 7752
ATS Warren Rd, Trafford Park ℰ 872 7631

MANNINGTREE Essex 𝟒𝟎𝟒 X 28 – pop. 339 – ⊠ ✆ 0206 Colchester.

♦London 67 – Colchester 10 – ♦Ipswich 12.

💥 **Stour Bay Café,** 39-43 High St., CO11 1AH, ℰ 396687 – 🌇 🆎 𝗩𝗜𝗦𝗔
*closed Monday, 2 weeks January, last week September-first week October and Bank
Holidays* – **M** a la carte 12.65/22.40 **t.**

MARAZION Cornwall 𝟒𝟎𝟑 D 33 The West Country G. – pop. 1 366 – ECD : Wednesday –
⊠ ✆ 0736 Penzance.

Envir. : St. Michael's Mount★★ (≼★★) – Ludgvan★ (Church★) N : 2 m. by A 30 – Chysauster★,
N : 2 m. by A 30 – Gulval★ (Church★) W : 2½ m.

🏌 Praa Sands, Germoe Cross Rd ℰ 0736 (Penzance) 763445, SE : 4 m.

♦London 318 – Penzance 3 – Truro 26.

🏨 **Mount Haven,** Turnpike Rd, TR17 0DQ, ℰ 710249, Fax 711658, ≼ St. Michael's Mount
and Mount's Bay – ⇇ rest 🅣🆅 ☎ ℗. 🌇 🆎 𝗩𝗜𝗦𝗔
closed 1 week Christmas – **M** (bar lunch)/dinner 14.50 **st.** and a la carte 🍴 3.95 – **17 rm**
⊊ 30.00/64.00 **st.** – SB (except July-September) 70.00/94.00 **st.**

🏠 **Old Eastcliffe** without rest., Eastcliff Lane, TR17 0AZ, ℰ 710298, ≼, ☞ – ⇇ ℗. ✻
April-October – **6 rm** ⊊ 25.00/46.00 **s.**

at St. Hilary E : 2½ m. by Turnpike Rd, on B 3280 – ⊠ ✆ 0736 Penzance :

🏠 **Enny's** ≫, Trewhella Lane, TR20 9BZ, ℰ 740262, ⤳ heated, ☞, ✾ – ⇇ rm 🅣🆅 ℗. ✻
closed 25 and 26 December – **M** 15.00 **t.** – **5 rm** ⊊ 30.00/50.00 **t.** – SB (December-March)
(weekends only) 85.00/90.00 **st.**

at Perranuthnoe SE : 1 ¾ m. by A 394 – ✉ ☏ 0736 Penzance :

⌂ **Ednovean House** 🐎, TR20 9LZ, ✆ 711071, ≤ St. Michael's Mount and Mount's Bay, 🌳 – 🚭 rest [P]. [CB] [AE] [VISA]
M 12.50 **st.** 🍷 4.25 – **9 rm** ☕ 20.00/48.00 **st.**

MARCH
Cambs. [402] [404] U 26 – pop. 14 534 – ☏ 0345.

⛳ Frogs Abbey, Grange Rd ✆ 52364.

♦London 93 – ♦Cambridge 34 – ♦Norwich 63.

⌂ **Olde Griffin,** High St., PE15 9JS, ✆ 52517, Fax 50086 – [TV] ☎ [P] – 🧑‍🏫 100. [CB] [AE] [VISA]. ✗🐕
M 9.95 **st.** and a la carte 🍷 3.75 – **20 rm** ☕ 35.00/47.50 **st.**

MARDEN
Heref. and Worcs. – see Hereford.

MARKET BOSWORTH
Leics. [402] [403] [404] P 26 – pop. 2 071 – ✉ Nuneaton – ☏ 0455.

♦London 109 – ♦Birmingham 30 – ♦Coventry 23 – ♦Leicester 22.

⌂ **Softleys,** Market Pl., CV13 0JS, ✆ 290464 – 🚭 [TV] ☎. [CB] [AE] [DC] [VISA]. ✗🐕
M *(closed Monday lunch and Sunday)* (in bar) a la carte 8.45/14.70 **st.** 🍷 3.95 – **3 rm** ☕ 30.00/50.00 **st.**

MARKET DRAYTON
Shrops. [402] [403] [404] M 25 – pop. 9 003 – ECD : Thursday – ☏ 0630.

[i] 51 Cheshire St., TF9 1PH ✆ 652139.

♦London 161 – ♦Birmingham 44 – Chester 33 – Shrewsbury 19 – ♦Stoke-on-Trent 16.

🍴🍴 Jaipur, 11 Shropshire St., TF9 3BZ, ✆ 653464
M - Indian rest.

at Stoke-upon-Tern SW : 6 ¾ m. by A 53 and A 41 on Stoke-upon-Tern rd – ✉ Market Drayton – ☏ 063 084 Hodnet :

⌂ **Stoke Manor** 🐎 without rest., TF9 2DU, E : ½ m. ✆ 222, Fax 666, « Working farm, vintage tractor collection », 🌳 – 🚭 [TV] [P]. ✗🐕
closed December – **3 rm** ☕ 25.00/48.00 **st.**

◉ ATS 71-73 Shrewsbury Rd ✆ 658446/658482

Les prix — Pour toutes précisions sur les prix indiqués dans ce guide, reportez-vous à l'introduction.

MARKET HARBOROUGH
Leics. [404] R 26 – pop. 15 852 – ECD : Wednesday – ☏ 0858.

⛳ Oxendon Rd ✆ 463684, S : 1 m.

[i] Pen Lloyd Library, Adam and Eve St., LE16 7LT ✆ 462649/462699.

♦London 88 – ♦Birmingham 47 – ♦Leicester 15 – Northampton 17.

⌂ **Three Swans** (Best Western), 21 High St., LE16 7NJ, ✆ 466644, Fax 433101 – 🚭 rm [TV] ☎ ♿ [P] – 🧑‍🏫 75. [CB] [AE] [DC] [VISA] [JCB]. ✗🐕
M *(closed Sunday dinner)* (bar lunch Monday to Saturday) 12.95/18.95 **t.** 🍷 3.95 – **36 rm** ☕ 49.00/75.00 **t.**

at Glooston NE : 7 ½ m. by A 6 and B 6047 off Hallaton Rd – ✉ Market Harborough – ☏ 0858 84 (3 fig.) and 0858 (6 fig.) East Langton :

🍴 **Old Barn Inn** with rm, LE16 7ST, ✆ 215 – 🚭 rm [TV] [P]. [CB] [VISA]. ✗🐕
M *(closed Monday lunch and Sunday dinner)* 14.95 **st.** (dinner) and a la carte 8.65/17.95 **st.** 🍷 3.50 – **3 rm** ☕ 37.50/49.50 **st.** – SB (weekends only) 69.90/104.90 **st.**

at Marston Trussell (Northants.) W : 3 ½ m. by A 427 – ✉ ☏ 0858 Market Harborough :

⌂ **Sun Inn,** LE16 9TY, ✆ 465531, Fax 433155 – [TV] ☎ [P] – 🧑‍🏫 60. [CB] [AE] [VISA]
closed 25 December – **M** 17.95 **t.** and a la carte 🍷 4.75 – **20 rm** ☕ 22.50/45.00 **t.** – SB (weekends only) 99.00/149.00 **st.**

◉ ATS 47-49 Kettering Rd ✆ 464535

MARKET WEIGHTON
Humbs. [402] R-S 22 – ✉ York – ☏ 0430.

♦London 206 – ♦Kingston-upon-Hull 19 – York 20.

⌂ **Londesborough Arms,** 44 High St., YO4 3AH, ✆ 872214, Fax 872214 – [TV] ☎ [P] – 🧑‍🏫 150. [CB] [AE] [DC] [VISA]. ✗🐕
M approx. 10.50 **t.** – **16 rm** ☕ 50.00/70.00 **st.**

MARKFIELD
Leics. [402] [403] [404] Q 25 – pop. 4 140 – ☏ 0530.

♦London 113 – ♦Birmingham 45 – ♦Leicester 6 – ♦Nottingham 24.

⌂ **Field Head,** Markfield Lane, LE67 9PS, on B 5327 ✆ 245454, Fax 243740 – 🚭 rm [TV] ☎ ♿ [P] – 🧑‍🏫 50. [CB] [AE] [DC] [VISA]. ✗🐕
M 8.50/13.95 **t.** and a la carte – **28 rm** ☕ 59.50/80.00 **t.** – SB (weekends only) 80.00 **st.**

⌂ **Granada Lodge** without rest., Little Shaw Lane, LE6 0PP, NW : 1 m. on A 50, Fax 244580, Reservations (Freephone) 0800 555300 – 🚭 [TV] ♿ [P]. [CB] [AE] [VISA]. ✗🐕
☕ 4.00 – **39 rm** 34.95/37.95 **st.**

◆London 143 – Lincoln 18 – ◆Nottingham 28 – ◆Sheffield 27.

🏠 **Forte Travelodge** without rest., DN22 0QU, A 1 northbound ✎ 838091, Reservations (Freephone) 0800 850950 – 📺 🕭 🅿. 🔃 🖭 *VISA* ❄
 40 rm 31.95 **t.**

MARKINGTON N. Yorks. 402 P 21 – see Harrogate.

MARKS TEY Essex 404 W 28 – see Colchester.

MARLBOROUGH Wilts. 403 404 O 29 The West Country G. – pop. 5 330 – ECD : Wednesday – 🕲 0672.

See : Town★.

Envir. : Savernake Forest★★ (Grand Avenue★★★) SE : 2 m. by A 4 – Whitehorse (≤★) NW : 5 m. – West Kennett Long Barrow★, Silbury Hill★, W : 6 m. by A 4.

Exc. : Ridgeway Path★★ – Avebury★★ (The Stones★, Church★) W : 7 m. by A 4 – Littlecote★★ (arms and armour★, Roman mosaic floor★) *AC*, E : 10 m. by A 4 – Crofton Beam Engines★ *AC*, SE : 9 m. by A 346 – Wilton Windmill★ *AC*, SE : 10 m. by A 346 and A 338.

🔢 The Common ✎ 512147, N : 1 m. by A 345.

🅿 Car Park, George Lane, SN8 1EE ✎ 513989.

◆London 84 – ◆Bristol 47 – ◆Southampton 40 – Swindon 12.

🏠 **Ivy House,** High St., SN8 1HJ, ✎ 515333, Fax 515338 – ❄≠ rm 📺 ☎ 🅿 – 🔼 50. 🔃 🖭 *VISA*
 M – Garden 10.50/16.50 **t.** and a la carte ⅄ 4.50 – **26 rm** ⌂ 45.00/86.00 **st.** – SB 90.00/110.00 **st.**

🏠 **Castle and Ball** (Forte), High St., SN8 1LZ, ✎ 515201, Fax 515895 – ❄≠ rm 📺 ☎ 🅿 – 🔼 45. 🔃 🖭 ⓞ *VISA*
 M 13.95/17.95 **st.** and a la carte ⅄ 5.25 – ⌂ 8.50 – **36 rm** 75.00/105.00 **st.** – SB (weekends only) 118.00 **st.**

✗ **Moran's,** 2-3 London Rd, SN8 1PQ, ✎ 512405, Fax 512405 – 🔃 *VISA*
 closed Monday, Sunday and 25-26 December – **M** (booking essential) (dinner only) a la carte 19.75/24.45 **t.** ⅄ 4.50.

 at Ogbourne St. George NE : 3¾ m. by A 345 – ✉ 🕲 0672 Marlborough :

🏠 **Parklands,** SN8 1SL, ✎ 841555 – ❄≠ rm 📺 ☎ 🅿. 🔃 🖭 *VISA*
 M *(closed Sunday dinner and 25-26 December)* (lunch by arrangement)/dinner 15.00 **t.** and a la carte ⅄ 4.50 – **10 rm** ⌂ 25.00/60.00 **st.** – SB (except Christmas and New Year) (weekends only) 80.00/110.00 **st.**

↑ **Laurel Cottage,** Southend, SN8 1SG, S : ½ m. on A 345 ✎ 841288, « 16C thatched cottage », 🌳 – ❄≠ rm 📺 🅿. ❄
 early March-October – **M** (by arrangement) 12.00 **s.** – **4 rm** ⌂ 26.00/45.00 – SB 56.00/94.00 **st.**

 at Burbage SE : 5¾ m. by A 346 – ✉ 🕲 0672 Marlborough :

🏠 **Old Vicarage** 🌿, Eastcourt, SN8 3AG, (via Taskers Lane) ✎ 810495, Fax 810663, 🌳 – ❄≠ 📺 🅿. 🔃 *VISA*. ❄
 closed Christmas and New Year – **M** *(closed Thursday and Sunday dinner)* (communal dining) 25.00 **s.** – **3 rm** ⌂ 35.00/60.00 **s.**

🔧 ATS 120/121 London Rd ✎ 512274

MARLOW Bucks. 404 R 29 – pop. 18 584 – ECD : Wednesday – 🕲 0628.

🚢 to Windsor Bridge via Marlow Lock, Cookham Landing Stage, Maidenhead and Windsor Bridge (Salter Bros Ltd) (summer only) – to Henley via Hurley Lock and Hambledon Locks (Salter Bros Ltd) (summer only).

🅿 C/o Court Garden, Leisure Complex, Pound Lane, SL7 2AE ✎ 483597 (summer only).

◆London 35 – Aylesbury 22 – ◆Oxford 29 – Reading 14.

🏰 **Danesfield House** 🌿, Medmenham, SL7 2EY, SW : 2 ½ m. on A 4155 ✎ 891010, Fax 890408, « Italian Renaissance style mansion, ≤ terraced gardens and River Thames », 🔻 heated, park, ❄ – 🛗 🗐 rest 📺 ☎ 🅿 – 🔼 80. 🔃 🖭 ⓞ *VISA* *JCB* ❄
 M 19.50/29.50 **st.** and a la carte ⅄ 6.00 – **87 rm** ⌂ 125.00/150.00 **st.**, 2 suites.

🏠 **Compleat Angler** (Forte), Marlow Bridge, Bisham Rd, SL7 1RG, ✎ 484444, Telex 848644, Fax 486388, ≤ River Thames, « Riverside setting and grounds », 🦆, ❄ – 🛗 ❄≠ rm 📺 ☎ 🅿 – 🔼 120. 🔃 🖭 ⓞ *VISA* *JCB*
 M 29.50/45.00 **t.** and a la carte ⅄ 7.50 – ⌂ 11.75 – **60 rm** 125.00/175.00 **st.**, 2 suites – SB (weekends only) 198.00/213.00 **st.**

🏠 **Country House** without rest., Bisham Rd, SL7 1RP, ✎ 890606, Fax 890983, 🌳 – 📺 ☎ 🅿. 🔃 🖭 *VISA*. ❄
 9 rm ⌂ 64.00/78.00 **st.**

↑ **Holly Tree House** without rest., Burford Close, Marlow Bottom, SL7 3NF, N : 2 m. by A 4155 and Wycombe Rd, off Marlow Bottom ✎ 891110, Fax 481278, 🔻 heated, 🌳 – 📺 ☎ 🅿. 🔃 🖭 *VISA*
 5 rm ⌂ 62.50/77.50 **st.**

XX **Villa D'este,** 2 Chapel St., SL7 1DD, ✆ 472012 – 🅽 🆊 ⓞ 𝖵𝖨𝖲𝖠
closed Saturday lunch – **M** - *Italian* 11.00/18.00 **t.** and a la carte 🍷 4.00.

XX **Lillies,** 31 West St., SL7 2NL, ✆ 488155, 🍴 – 🅽 𝖵𝖨𝖲𝖠
M *(closed Saturday lunch and Sunday)* 10.00/25.00 **t.** and a la carte.

MARPLE Gtr. Manchester 𝟦𝟢𝟤 𝟦𝟢𝟥 𝟦𝟢𝟦 N 23 – pop. 18 708 – ECD : Wednesday – ☎ 061 Manchester.

♦London 190 – Chesterfield 35 – ♦Manchester 11.

🏠 **Springfield,** 99 Station Rd, SK6 6PA, ✆ 449 0721, 🍴 – 📺 ☎ ⓟ. 🅽 🆊 ⓞ 𝖵𝖨𝖲𝖠 . 🎿
M *(closed Saturday and Sunday dinner)* (lunch by arrangement)/dinner 12.50 **st.** and a la carte 🍷 4.00 – **6 rm** ⌑ 40.00/50.00 **st.** – SB 65.00/105.00 **st.**

MARSTON MORETAINE Beds. 𝟦𝟢𝟦 S 27 – see Bedford.

MARSTON TRUSSELL Northants. 𝟦𝟢𝟦 R 26 – see Market Harborough.

MARTINHOE Devon – see Lynton.

MARTOCK Somerset 𝟦𝟢𝟥 L 31 The West Country G. – pop. 3 749 – ☎ 0935.
See : Village* – All Saints**.
Envir. : Montacute House** *AC,* SE : 4 m. – Muchelney** (Parish Church**) NW : 4½ m. by B 3165.

♦London 148 – Taunton 19 – Yeovil 6.

🏛 **Hollies,** Bower Hinton, TA12 6LG, S : 1 m. on B 3165 ✆ 822232, Fax 822249, 🍴 – 📺 ☎ ⓟ. 🅽 🆊 ⓞ 𝖵𝖨𝖲𝖠
M (in bar Monday lunch and Sunday dinner) a la carte 13.45/17.95 **st.** 🍷 3.95 – **15 rm** ⌑ 45.00/60.00 **st.** – SB (weekends only) 55.00/120.00 **st.**

MARWELL ZOOLOGIAL PARK Hants. – see Winchester.

MARY TAVY Devon 𝟦𝟢𝟥 H 32 – see Tavistock.

MASHAM N. Yorks. 𝟦𝟢𝟤 P 21 – pop. 976 – ECD : Thursday – ✉ ☎ 0765 Ripon.

♦London 231 – ♦Leeds 38 – ♦Middlesbrough 37 – York 32.

🏠 **King's Head,** Market Pl., HG4 4EF, ✆ 689295 – 📺 ☎ – 🛗 35. 🅽 🆊 ⓞ 𝖵𝖨𝖲𝖠 🎿
M (bar lunch Monday to Saturday)/dinner a la carte 10.90/16.45 **st.** 🍷 3.75 – **10 rm** ⌑ 42.50/55.00 **st.**

⌂ **Bank Villa,** HG4 4DB, on A 6108 ✆ 689605, 🍴 – 🎝 rest
March-October – **M** 15.00 **st.** 🍷 3.50 – **7 rm** ⌑ 22.00/35.00 **st.**

XX **Floodlite,** 7 Silver St., HG4 4DX, ✆ 689000 – 🅽 𝖵𝖨𝖲𝖠
closed Tuesday to Thursday lunch, Monday and 3 weeks January – **M** 9.50 **t.** (lunch) and a la carte 14.00/24.95 **t.** 🍷 4.25.

at Healey W : 3 m. by A 6108 – ✉ ☎ 0765 Ripon :

⌂ **Pasture House** 🍃, Colsterdale, HG4 4LJ, W : 1½ m. ✆ 689149, ≤, 🍴, park, 🎿 – 📺 ⓟ
M (by arrangement) 8.00 – **4 rm** ⌑ 12.00/24.00 **st.**

at Jervaulx Abbey NW : 5½ m. on A 6108 – ✉ Ripon – ☎ 0677 Bedale :

🏛 **Jervaulx Hall** 🍃, HG4 4PH, ✆ 460235, Fax 460263, ≤, « Victorian manor house, country house atmosphere », 🍴, park – 🎝 rest ☎ 🕭 ⓟ
March-November – **M** (dinner only) 22.50 **t.** 🍷 4.20 – **10 rm** ⌑ (dinner included) 75.00/135.00 **t.** – SB (winter and spring only) 100.00 **st.**

MATLOCK Derbs. 𝟦𝟢𝟤 𝟦𝟢𝟥 𝟦𝟢𝟦 P 24 Great Britain G. – pop. 13 706 – ECD : Thursday – ☎ 0629.
Exc. : Hardwick Hall** *AC,* E : 12½ m. by A 615 and B 6014.
🛈 The Pavilion, DE4 3NR ✆ 55082.

♦London 153 – Derby 17 – ♦Manchester 46 – ♦Nottingham 24 – ♦Sheffield 24.

🏛 **Riber Hall** 🍃, Riber, DE4 5JU, SE : 3 m. by A 615 ✆ 582795, Fax 580475, « Part Elizabethan manor house », 🍴, 🎿 – 🎝 rm 📺 ☎ ⓟ. 🅽 🆊 ⓞ 𝖵𝖨𝖲𝖠 🎿
M 14.50 **t.** (lunch) and dinner a la carte 19.20/26.75 **t.** 🍷 5.45 – ⌑ 7.50 – **11 rm** 78.00/137.00 **t.** – SB (mid October-April except Bank Holidays) 140.00/205.00 **st.**

🏛 **New Bath** (Forte), New Bath Rd, Matlock Bath, DE4 3PX, S : 1½ m. on A 6 ✆ 583275, Fax 580268, ⚓, 🏊 heated, 🏊, 🍴, 🎿 – 🎝 rm 📺 ☎ ⓟ – 🛗 130. 🅽 🆊 ⓞ 𝖵𝖨𝖲𝖠 𝖩𝖢𝖡
M *(closed Saturday lunch)* 9.95/17.95 **st.** and a la carte 🍷 6.45 – ⌑ 8.95 – **55 rm** 70.00/180.00 **st.** – SB 128.00 **st.**

🏠 **Hodgkinson's,** 150 South Par., Matlock Bath, DE4 3NR, S : 1¼ m. on A 6 ✆ 582170, « Victoriana » – 📺 ☎ ⓟ. 🅽 🆊 𝖵𝖨𝖲𝖠
M (dinner only) 24.00 **t.** 🍷 4.95 – **6 rm** ⌑ 30.00/80.00 **t.** – SB 70.00/95.00 **st.**

at Dethick SE : 4 m. by A 615 – ✉ ☎ 0629 Matlock :

⌂ **Manor Farm** 🍃, DE4 5GG, ✆ 534246, ≤, 🍴, park – 🎝 📺 ⓟ. 🎿
closed December – **M** (by arrangement) 11.00 **st.** – **3 rm** ⌑ 25.00/36.00 **st.**

MAWNAN SMITH Cornwall 𝟦𝟢𝟥 E 33 – see Falmouth.

MAYFIELD E. Sussex 404 U 30 – pop. 1 784 – ECD : Wednesday – ✆ 0435.

◆London 46 – ◆Brighton 25 – Eastbourne 22 – Lewes 17 – Royal Tunbridge Wells 9.

☆ **Rose and Crown,** Fletching St., TN20 6TE, ℰ 872200 – 📺 ℗. ⚞ VISA. ⚜
M a la carte 10.70/15.65 **t.** – ⌑ 6.95 – **3 rm** 38.00/55.00 **t.** – SB 70.00/120.00 **st.**

☆ **Middle House,** High St., TN20 6AB, ℰ 872146, Fax 873423, ⚟ – 📺 ☎ ℗. ⚞ ﹏ VISA. ⚜
M (closed Sunday dinner and Monday except Bank Holidays) a la carte 12.95/21.50 **t.** –
7 rm ⌑ 35.00/55.00 **t.**

at Five Ashes SW : 2¾ m. on A 267 – ✉ Mayfield – ✆ 0825 Hadlow Down :

🏠 **Coles Hall,** TN20 6JH, S : ¾ m. on A 267 ℰ 830274, ≤, ⚟, park – 📺 ℗
M (by arrangement) 8.50 **s.** – **3 rm** ⌑ 17.00/32.00 **s.**

MEADOW HEAD S. Yorks. – see Sheffield.

MEALSGATE Cumbria 402 K 19 – ✉ Carlisle – ✆ 069 73 Low Ireby

🏠 **Old Rectory** ⚞, Boltongate, CA5 1DA, SE : 1½ m. by B 5299 on Ireby rd ℰ 71647, ⚟ –
℗. ⚞ VISA
March-November – **M** (by arrangement) (communal dining) 19.50 – **3 rm** ⌑ 45.00/67.00.

We suggest :

For a successful tour, that you prepare it in advance.

Michelin maps and guides will give you much useful information on route planning,
places of interest, accommodation, prices etc.

MELBOURN Cambs. 404 U 27 – pop. 3 846 – ✉ ✆ 0763 Royston (Herts.).

◆London 44 – ◆Cambridge 10.

🏛 **Melbourn Bury** ⚞, Royston Rd, SG8 6DE, SW : ¾ m. ℰ 261151, Fax 262375, ≤,
« Tastefully furnished country house of Tudor origin », ⚟, park – 📺 ℗. ⚞ ﹏ AE ① JCB
closed Easter and Christmas-New Year – **M** (booking essential) (residents only) (communal
dining) (dinner only) 15.00 **st.** ⚜ 4.00 – **3 rm** ⌑ 47.00/80.00 **st.**

🏠 **Chiswick House** without rest., 3 Chiswick End, SG8 6LZ, NW : 1 m. by Meldreth rd, off
Whitecroft Rd ℰ 260242, ⚟ – ⚞ ℗
closed Christmas – **6 rm** ⌑ 32.00/38.00 **st.**

✕✕ **Pink Geranium,** 25 Station Rd, SG8 6DX, ℰ 260215, Fax 262110, ⚟ – ⚞ ℗. ⚞ ﹏ VISA
closed Saturday lunch, Sunday dinner and Monday – **M** 17.95/24.95 **t.** and a la carte.

✕✕ **Sheen Mill** with rm, Station Rd, SG8 6DX, ℰ 261393, Fax 261376, ≤, ⚟ – 📺 ☎ ℗. ⚞
﹏ ① VISA ⚜
closed 25-26 December and Bank Holidays – **M** (closed Sunday dinner) 14.95/21.50 **t.** and a
la carte – **8 rm** ⌑ 48.00/70.00 **st.** – SB (weekends only) 98.00/123.00 **st.**

MELKSHAM Wilts. 403 404 N 29 The West Country G. – pop. 13 248 – ECD : Wednesday –
✆ 0225.

Envir. : Corsham Court★★ AC, NW : 4½ m. by A 365 and B 3353 – Lacock★ (Lacock Abbey★
AC, High Street★, St. Cyriac★, Fox Talbot Museum of Photography★ AC) N : 3½ m. by A 350.

🏛 The Roundhouse, Church St., SN12 6LS ℰ 707424.

◆London 113 – ◆Bristol 25 – Salisbury 35 – Swindon 28.

🏛 **Beechfield House,** Beanacre, SN12 7PU, N : 1 m. on A 350 ℰ 703700, Fax 790118, ≤,
« Country house and gardens », ⚞ heated, ⚜ – ﹏ rest 📺 ☎ ℗ – ⚞ 30. ⚞ ﹏ AE ① VISA
M 19.50/21.50 **t.** and a la carte ⚜ 5.75 – **20 rm** ⌑ 65.00/90.00 **t.** – SB (weekends only)
125.00/181.90 **st.**

🏛 **Shurnhold House** without rest., Shurnhold, SN12 8DG, NW : 1 m. on A 365 ℰ 790555,
« Jacobean manor house, gardens » – ﹏ 📺 ☎ ℗. ⚞ VISA. ⚜
⌑ 3.50 – **8 rm** 42.00/115.00 **s.**

🏛 **Sandridge Park** ⚞, Sandridge, SN12 7QU, E : 2 m. on A 3102 ℰ 706897, Fax 702838,
≤, « Victorian mansion », ⚟, park – ﹏ rm 📺 ℗. ⚞ VISA. ⚜
closed 25 and 26 December – **M** (booking essential) (residents only) (communal dining)
(unlicensed) (dinner only) 25.00 **s.** ⚜ 2.50 – **3 rm** ⌑ 35.00/70.00 **s.**

✕ **Toxique** with rm, 187 Woodrow Rd, SN12 7AY, NE : 1¼ m. by A 3102 ℰ 702129, ⚟ –
﹏ rest 📺 ℗. ⚞ ﹏ AE ① VISA ⚜
M (closed Saturday lunch, Sunday dinner and Monday) (booking essential) (lunch by
arrangement Tuesday to Friday)/dinner 24.00 **st.** ⚜ 5.10 – **4 rm** ⌑ 50.00/80.00 **st.** –
SB 108.00/128.00 **st.**

at Shaw NW : 1½ m. on A 365 – ✉ ✆ 0225 Melksham :

🏛 **Shaw Country,** Bath Rd, SN12 8EF, on A 365 ℰ 702836, Fax 790275, ⚟ – 📺 ☎ ℗. ⚞
﹏ VISA
M 17.00 **s.** and a la carte – **13 rm** ⌑ 38.00/79.00 **st.** – SB (except Bank Holidays) (week-
ends only) 70.00/110.00 **st.**

MELLOR Lancs. – see Blackburn.

W. Yorks. 🔲🔲 O 23 – pop. 7 098 – ✉ 📞 0484 Huddersfield.

🏠 Thick Hollins Hall *&* 850227, E : 1 m.

♦London 192 – ♦Leeds 21 – ♦Manchester 23 – ♦Sheffield 26.

🏨 **Durker Roods,** Bishops Way, HD7 3AG, *&* 851413, Fax 851843, 🚗 – 📺 📞 🅿 – 🔒 80.
🔲 🔲 🔲 🔲
M *(closed Saturday lunch)* 10.00/13.50 **t.** and a la carte 🔒 4.50 – **31 rm** ⊆ 40.00/51.00 **t.** –
SB (weekends only) 64.00 **st.**

Leics. 🔲🔲 R 25 – pop. 23 379 – ECD : Thursday – 📞 0664.

🏠 Waltham Rd, Thorpe Arnold *&* 62118, NE : 2 m. by A 607.

🏛 Melton Carnegie Museum, Thorpe End, LE13 1RB *&* 69946.

♦London 113 – ♦Leicester 15 – Northampton 45 – ♦Nottingham 18.

🏰 **Stapleford Park** 🦢, LE14 2EF, E : 5 m. by B 676 on Stapleford rd *&* 057 284 (Wymondham) 522, Fax 651, ≤, « Part 16C and 19C mansion in park », 🐎, 🚗, 🎾 – ⚽ 🛴 rest 📺
📞 🅿 – 🔒 200. 🔲 🔲 🔲 🔲 🔲
M a la carte 24.00/37.00 **t.** 🔒 8.00 – **33 rm** 125.00/195.00 **t.**, 2 suites – SB (except Bank
Holidays) 199.30 **st.**

🏨 **Quorn Lodge,** 46 Asfordby Rd, LE13 0HR, *&* 66660, Fax 480660 – 📺 📞 🅿. 🔲 🔲 🔲
🔲
M 9.50/14.50 **st.** 🔒 4.25 – **11 rm** ⊆ 39.50/54.00 **st.** – SB (weekends only) 63.00/
113.00 **st.**

🏨 **Harboro** (Forte), Burton St., LE13 1AF, *&* 60121, Fax 64296 – 🛴 rm 📺 🅿. 🔲 🔲
🔲
M (Harvester grill) a la carte approx. 16.00 **t.** – ⊆ 5.25 – **26 rm** 31.95/41.95 **t.**

at Old Dalby NW : 8 ½ m. by A 6006 on Old Dalby rd – ✉ 📞 0664 Melton Mowbray :

⌂ **Home Farm** 🦢 without rest., 9 Church Lane, LE14 3LB, *&* 822622, 🚗 – 🛴 🅿. 🔲 🔲.
🎾
5 rm ⊆ 25.00/37.50 **st.**

🛞 ATS Leicester Rd *&* 62072

Suffolk 🔲 W 27 – see Stowmarket.

Bucks. 🔲 R 28 – pop. 196 – ✉ Leighton Buzzard – 📞 0296 Cheddington.

♦London 46 – Aylesbury 10 – Luton 15.

🏨 **The Stable Yard** without rest., LU7 0QG, *&* 661488, « Attractive 19C stable and coach
yard » – 📺 🅿. 🎾
5 rm ⊆ 47.00/82.25 **st.**

Wilts. 🔲 🔲 N 30 The West Country G. – pop. 2 201 – ECD : Wednesday –
📞 0747.

Envir. : Stourhead★★★ *AC*, NW : 4 m. by B 3095 and B 3092.

Exc. : Longleat House★★★ *AC*, N : 9½ m. by A 303 and B 3092.

🏛 The Square, BA12 6JJ *&* 861211.

♦London 113 – Exeter 65 – Salisbury 26 – Taunton 40.

🏨 **Chetcombe House,** Chetcombe Rd, BA12 6AZ, *&* 860219, 🚗 – 🛴 rm 📺 🅿. 🔲 🔲
🔲
M *(closed Christmas and New Year)* (lunch by arrangement)/dinner 12.50 **st.** 🔒 2.75 – **5 rm**
⊆ 28.00/50.00 **st.** – SB (winter only) 73.00/89.00 **st.**

⌂ **Chantry** 🦢, Church St., BA12 6DS, *&* 860264, « 15C chantry priests house », ☐ heated, 🚗 – 🛴 rm 🅿. 🎾
M (booking essential) 18.00 **s.** – **3 rm** ⊆ 28.00/56.00 **s.**

Lancs. 🔲 L 23 Great Britain G. – ✉ Preston – 📞 0772 Hesketh Bank.

Envir. : Rufford Old Hall★ (Great Hall★) *AC*, SE : 4 m. by B 5246.

♦London 221 – ♦Liverpool 22 – Preston 11 – Southport 6.

✕ **Crab and Lobster,** behind the Leigh Arms, Tarleton, PR4 6LA, *&* 812734 – 🅿. 🔲
🔲
closed Christmas-January – **M** - **Seafood** (dinner only) a la carte 17.00/27.00 **t.** 🔒 4.00.

W. Mids. 🔲 🔲 P 26 – see Coventry.

Europe | Se il nome di un albergo è stampato
in carattere magro, chiedete arrivando
le condizioni che vi saranno praticate.

MEVAGISSEY Cornwall **403** F 33 The West Country G. – pop. 1 896 – ECD : Thursday – ☎ 0726.

See : Town★★.

◆London 287 – Newquay 21 – ◆Plymouth 44 – Truro 20.

⌂ **Mevagissey House** ⌖, Vicarage Hill, PL26 6SZ, ℰ 842427, ≤, ☞ – ⥄ rest ⊤⊽ **P**. **Å** **VISA**
March-October – **M** 12.00 **st.** ↟ 4.25 – **6 rm** ⊇ 32.00/46.00 **st.**

MEYSEY HAMPTON Glos. – ✉ ☎ 0285 Cirencester.

◆London 101 – ◆Bristol 44 – Gloucester 26 – ◆Oxford 29.

⌂ **Masons Arms,** 28 High St., GL7 5JT, ℰ 850164 – ⊤⊽ **P**. **Å** **VISA**
M 8.50/12.50 **t.** and a la carte ↟ 4.50 – **9 rm** ⊇ 22.00/39.00 **t.** – SB 56.00/68.00 **st.**

MICKLETON Glos. **403** **404** O 27 – see Chipping Campden.

MICKLE TRAFFORD Ches. – see Chester.

MIDDLECOMBE Somerset – see Minehead.

MIDDLEHAM N. Yorks. **402** O 21 – pop. 737 – ECD : Thursday – ☎ 0969 Wensleydale.

◆London 233 – Kendal 45 – ◆Leeds 47 – York 45.

⌂ **Miller's House,** Market Pl., DL8 4NR, ℰ 22630, Fax 23570, ☞ – ⥄ rest ⊤⊽ ☎ **P**. **Å** **VISA**
closed 2 to 31 January – **M** (dinner only) 19.50 **st.** ↟ 2.50 – **7 rm** ⊇ 34.50/85.00 **st.** – SB 105.00/124.00 **st.**

⌂ **Waterford House,** 19 Kirkgate, DL8 4PG, ℰ 22090, Fax 24020, « Part 17C house, antiques » – ⥄ rest ⊤⊽ **Å** ⑩ **VISA**
M (lunch by arrangement)/dinner 17.50 **st.** and a la carte ↟ 4.40 – **5 rm** ⊇ 35.00/60.00 **st.**

at Carlton SW : 4½ m. on Coverdale Rd – ✉ Leyburn – ☎ 0969 Wensleydale :

✗ **Foresters Arms** with rm, DL8 2BB, ℰ 40272 – ⊤⊽ **P**. **Å** **VISA**
M *(closed Sunday)* (dinner only) a la carte 10.40/25.85 **t.** ↟ 4.00 – **3 rm** ⊇ 25.00/50.00 **st.** – SB 65.00/130.00 **st.**

at West Scrafton SW : 6 m. by Coverdale Rd – ✉ Leyburn – ☎ 0969 Wensleydale :

⌂ **Coverdale Country** ⌖, Swineside, DL8 4RX, ℰ 40601, ≤, ☞ – ⥄ rest ⊤⊽ **P**. **Å** **AE** ⑩ **VISA**
M 12.00 **t.** ↟ 4.60 – **9 rm** ⊇ 31.00/64.00 **t.**

When visiting Ireland,

use the Michelin Green Guide "Ireland".

– *Detailed descriptions of places of interest*

– *Touring programmes*

– *Maps and street plans*

– *The history of the country*

– *Photographs and drawings of monuments, beauty spots, houses...*

MIDDLESBROUGH Cleveland **402** Q 20 – pop. 158 516 – ECD : Wednesday – ☎ 0642.

ㄷ Middlesbrough Municipal, Ladgate Lane ℰ 315533, S : by Acklam Rd AZ – ㄷ Brass Castle Lane ℰ 316430, S : by A 172 BZ.

✈ Teesside Airport : ℰ 0325 (Darlington) 332811, SW : 13 m. by A 66 - AZ - and A 19 on A 67.

🛈 51 Corporation Rd, TS1 1LT ℰ 243425.

◆London 246 – ◆Kingston-upon-Hull 89 – ◆Leeds 66 – ◆Newcastle upon Tyne 41.

Plan on next page

🏨 **Baltimore,** 250 Marton Rd, TS4 2EZ, ℰ 224111, Fax 226156 – ⊤⊽ ☎ **P**. **Å** **AE** ⑩ **VISA**. ⌖
M 13.75 **st.** and a la carte ↟ 4.50 – ⊇ 6.45 – **30 rm** 67.50/79.50 **st.**, 1 suite. BZ **e**

🏨 **Highfield** (Chef & Brewer), 358 Marton Rd, TS4 2PA, ℰ 817638, Fax 821219 – ⊤⊽ ☎ **P** –
🖧 60. **Å** **AE** **VISA**. ⌖ BZ **c**
M 15.00/20.00 **t.** and a la carte – **23 rm** ⊇ 34.95/38.45 **t.**

⌂ **Marton Way Toby,** Marton Rd, TS4 3BS, ℰ 817651, Fax 829409 – ⥄ rm ⊤⊽ ☎ **P** –
🖧 70. **Å** **AE** ⑩ **VISA** BZ **a**
closed 24 to 26 December – **M** (carving rest.) 7.00/9.50 **st.** and a la carte – **53 rm** ⊇ 39.00/49.00 **st.**

⌂ **Grey House,** 79 Cambridge Rd, TS5 5NL, ℰ 817485, ☞ – ⊤⊽ **P**. **Å** **VISA** AZ **n**
M (by arrangement) 8.00 – **9 rm** ⊇ 32.00/48.00 **st.** – SB (weekends only) 52.00/88.00 **st.**

 ATS Murdock Rd (off Sotherby Rd), Cargo Fleet ℰ 249245/6

MIDDLESBROUGH

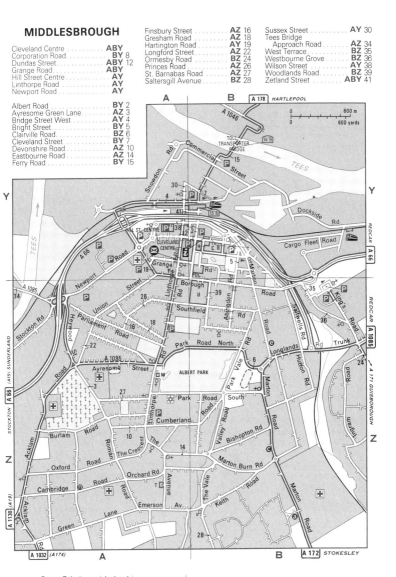

*Great Britain and Ireland is now covered
by an Atlas at a scale of 1 inch to 4.75 miles.*

Three easy to use versions: Paperback, Spiralbound and Hardback.

MIDDLETON-IN-TEESDALE Durham 401 402 N 20 – pop. 1 196 – ⊕ 0833 Teesdale.

🛈 Middleton Crafts, Courtyard of Teesdale Hotel, DL12 0QG ℰ 40400.

◆London 232 – ◆Carlisle 56 – ◆Leeds 78 – ◆Middlesbrough 35 – ◆Newcastle upon Tyne 49.

🏠 **Teesdale,** Market Sq., DL12 0QG, ℰ 40264 – 📺 ☎ 🅿. 🅐 𝗩𝗜𝗦𝗔
  M (bar lunch Monday to Saturday)/dinner 25.00 **t.** – **12 rm** � 38.50/85.00 **s.** – SB (except
  Christmas and New Year) 89.50 **st.**

MIDDLETON PRIORS Shrops. 403 404 M 26 – see Bridgnorth.

371

MIDDLETON STONEY Oxon. 📖 403 404 Q 28 – pop. 238 – ECD : Saturday – ✉ 🕿 086 989 Bicester (changing in April to 0869).

♦London 66 – Northampton 30 – ♦Oxford 12.

🏨 **Jersey Arms,** OX6 8SE, 𝒫 234 (changing in April to 343234), Fax 565 (changing in April to 343565), 🍴 – 📺 🕿 🅿. 🔼 🅰🅴 ⓞ 𝚅𝙸𝚂𝙰 🎇
M *(closed Sunday dinner)* a la carte 19.20/26.45 **t.** 🍷 4.50 – **13 rm** ⊑ 59.50/72.00 **t.**, 3 suites – SB 110.40/157.40 **st.**

MIDDLE WALLOP Hants. 📖 403 404 P 30 – ✉ Stockbridge – 🕿 0264 Andover.

♦London 80 – Salisbury 11 – ♦Southampton 21.

🏛 **Fifehead Manor,** SO20 8EG, on A 343 𝒫 781565, Fax 781400, « Converted 16C manor house », 🍴 – 📺 🕿 🕭 🅿. 🔼 🅰🅴 ⓞ 𝚅𝙸𝚂𝙰
closed 2 weeks Christmas – **M** 17.50/24.00 **t.** and a la carte – **16 rm** ⊑ 50.00/95.00 **t.** – SB (November-Easter) 110.00/130.00 **st.**

We suggest :

For a successful tour, that you prepare it in advance.

Michelin maps and guides will give you much useful information on route planning, places of interest, accommodation, prices etc.

MIDHURST W. Sussex 📖 404 R 31 – pop. 5 991 – ECD : Wednesday – 🕿 0730.

♦London 57 – ♦Brighton 38 – Chichester 12 – ♦Southampton 41.

🏛🏛 **Spread Eagle,** South St., GU29 9NH, 𝒫 816911, Fax 815668, « 15C hostelry, antique furnishings » – 📺 🕿 🅿 – 🔬 45. 🔼 🅰🅴 ⓞ 𝚅𝙸𝚂𝙰
M 16.50/25.75 **t.** 🍷 5.00 – ⊑ 3.75 – **41 rm** 59.00/130.00 **t.** – SB (except Christmas) 120.00/150.00 **st.**

🏛 **Angel,** North St., GU29 9DN, 𝒫 812421, Fax 815928, 🍴 – 🙅 rm 📺 🕿 🅿 – 🔬 60. 🔼 🅰🅴 𝚅𝙸𝚂𝙰 🎇
Meals 12.50 **t.** (lunch) and a la carte 14.45/27.25 **t.** – **17 rm** 55.00/150.00 **t.** – SB (January-Easter and weekends only) 110.00/130.00 **t.**

🏴 **Mida,** Wool Lane, GU29 9BY, 𝒫 813284
closed Sunday and Monday – **M** a la carte approx. 30.00.

🏴 **Maxine's,** Red Lion St., GU29 9PB, 𝒫 816271 – 🙅. 🔼 𝚅𝙸𝚂𝙰
closed Sunday dinner, Monday, Tuesday and first 2 weeks January – **M** 11.95 **st.** and a la carte.

at Bepton SW : 3½ m. by A 286 – ✉ 🕿 0730 Midhurst :

🏠 **Park House** 🌲, South Bepton, GU29 0JB, 𝒫 812880, Fax 815643, ⛐ heated, 🍴, 🎾 – 📺 🕿 🅿. 🔼 🅰🅴
M (by arrangement) 10.50/20.00 **t.** – **10 rm** ⊑ 47.00/110.00 **t.**

at Stedham W : 2 m. by A 272 – ✉ 🕿 0730 Midhurst :

🏴 **Nava Thai at Hamilton Arms,** School Lane, GU29 0NZ, 𝒫 812555 – 🅿. 🔼 𝚅𝙸𝚂𝙰
closed Monday except Bank Holidays and 27 to 30 December – **M** - Thai 16.75/18.00 **t.** and a la carte 🍷 4.50.

at Trotton W : 3¼ m. on A 272 – ✉ Petersfield (Hants.) – 🕿 0730 Rogate :

🏛 **Southdowns** 🌲, GU31 5JN, S : 1 m. 𝒫 821521, Fax 821790, ⚘s, 🔼, 🍴, 🎾 – 🙅 rm
▤ rest 📺 🕿 🕭 🅿 – 🔬 100. 🔼 🅰🅴 ⓞ 𝚅𝙸𝚂𝙰 🎇
M 20.00/25.00 **t.** and a la carte 🍷 5.00 – **22 rm** ⊑ 50.00/100.00 **t.** – SB 100.00/190.00 **st.**

MILFORD-ON-SEA Hants. 📖 403 404 P 31 – pop. 3 953 – ECD : Wednesday – ✉ 🕿 0590 Lymington.

♦London 109 – Bournemouth 15 – ♦Southampton 24 – Winchester 37.

🏛 **South Lawn,** Lymington Rd, SO41 0RF, 𝒫 643911, Fax 644820, 🍴 – 📺 🕿 🅿. 🔼 𝚅𝙸𝚂𝙰 🎇
closed mid December-mid January – **M** (dinner only and Sunday lunch)/dinner 21.00 **t.** 🍷 6.25 – **24 rm** ⊑ 47.50/84.00 **t.** – SB (October-May) 99.00/109.00 **st.**

🏛 **Westover Hall,** Park Lane, SO41 0PT, 𝒫 643044, Fax 644490, ≤ – 📺 🕿 🅿. 🔼 🅰🅴 ⓞ 𝚅𝙸𝚂𝙰
M 14.45/16.50 **st.** and a la carte 🍷 6.50 – **12 rm** ⊑ 35.00/80.00 **st.** – SB (weekends only) 100.00 **st.**

🏴🏴 **Rocher's,** 69-71 High St., SO41 0QG, 𝒫 642340 – 🔼 🅰🅴 𝚅𝙸𝚂𝙰
closed Monday, Tuesday, Sunday except Bank Holidays and 2 weeks June – **Meals** - French (dinner only) 22.90 **t.**

🏴 **Bridge Cottage,** 10 High St., SO41 0QD, 𝒫 642070 – 🔼 🅰🅴 ⓞ 𝚅𝙸𝚂𝙰
closed Sunday, Thursday, 17 February-9 March, 27 to 30 December and Bank Holidays – **M** (dinner only) a la carte 23.50.

MILTON DAMEREL Devon 📖 403 H 31 – pop. 454 🕿 0409.

♦London 249 – Barnstaple 21.

🏛 Woodford Bridge, EX22 7LL, N : 1 m. on A 388 𝒫 261481, Fax 261585, 𝐼ₛ, ⚘s, 🔼, 🈂, 🍴, squash – 📺 🕿 🅿 🎇
10 rm.

🏌 Abbey Hill, Monks Way, Two Mile Ash ✈ 563845 – 🏌 Windmill Hill, Tattenhoe Lane, Bletchley ✈ 378623 – 🏌, 🏌 Wavendon Golf Centre, Lower End Rd, Wavendon ✈ 281811, 1½ m. from M 1 junction 13.

🗓 536 Silbury Boulevard, NK9 3AF ✈ 232525.

◆London 56 – ◆Birmingham 72 – Bedford 16 – Northampton 18 – ◆Oxford 37.

🏨 **Forte Crest,** 500 Saxon Gate West, Milton Keynes Central, MK9 2HQ, ✈ 667722, Fax 674714, *Ⅰ₄*, ≦s, 🔲, ☒ – ☒ rm 🔲 🔲 🏧 & 🔁 – 🏧 150. 🆘 🆔 ⓪ 𝘝𝘐𝘚𝘈 𝘑𝘊𝘉
M 15.95 **st.** (dinner) and a la carte 20.70/26.95 **st.** 🍴 6.60 – ☲ 9.95 – **149 rm** 89.00 **st.**, 2 suites – SB (weekends only) 98.00 **st.**

🏨 **Milton Keynes H. & Conference Centre,** Timbold Drive, Kents Hill, MK7 6HL, SE : 4 m. by A 4146 and A 421 off Brickhill St. (V10) ✈ 694433, Fax 695533, « Contemporary interior », ≦s, 🔲, ☒ – ☒ ⊬ rm 🔲 🔲 🏧 & 🔁 – 🏧 300. 🆘 🆔 ⓪ 𝘝𝘐𝘚𝘈
M (bar lunch Saturday) 13.50/18.50 **st.** and a la carte 5.95 – ☲ 9.00 – **143 rm** 85.00 **st.**, 3 suites – SB (weekends only) 70.00/80.00 **st.**

🏨 **Shenley Church Inn** (Toby), Burchard Cres., Shenley Church End, MK5 6HQ, SW : 2 m. by A 509 and Portway (H5) off Watling St. (V4) ✈ 505467, Fax 502308 – 📶 ⊬ rm 🔲 🔲 🏧 🔁 – 🏧 85. 🆘 🆔 ⓪ 𝘝𝘐𝘚𝘈 %
M (grill rest.) a la carte 10.25/14.50 **t.** – **50 rm** ☲ 65.00/75.00 **st.**

🏨 **Peartree Bridge Inn** (Toby), Milton Keynes Marina, Waterside, Peartree Bridge, MK6 3PE, SE : 1¾ m. by A 509 off A 4146 ✈ 691515, Fax 690274, « Marina setting beside the Grand Union Canal » – 🔲 🔲 🔁 🏧 🆘 🆔 ⓪ 𝘝𝘐𝘚𝘈 %
M (grill rest.) 7.50 **st.** and a la carte 🍴 4.00 – **39 rm** ☲ 55.00/75.00 **st.**

🏨 **Friendly,** Monks Way, Two Mile Ash, MK8 8LY, NW : 2 m. by A 509 and A 5 at junction with A 422 ✈ 561666, Fax 568303, *Ⅰ₄*, ≦s – ⊬ rm 🔲 🔲 🏧 & 🔁 – 🏧 120. 🆘 🆔 ⓪ 𝘝𝘐𝘚𝘈 𝘑𝘊𝘉
M (carving rest.) (bar lunch Saturday) 10.00/12.50 **st.** and a la carte – ☲ 6.75 – **88 rm** 57.00/85.50 **st.** – SB (weekends only) 84.00/90.00 **st.**

🏨 **Caldecotte Arms,** Bletcham Way (H10), Caldecotte, MK7 8HP, SE : 5½ m. by A 509 and A 5, taking 2nd junction left signposted Milton Keynes (South and East) ✈ 366188, Fax 366603, « Windmill feature, lakeside setting » – 🔲 🔲 🏧 & 🔁. 🆘 🆔 𝘝𝘐𝘚𝘈 %
M (in bar) a la carte approx. 9.00 🍴 3.75 – **40 rm** ☲ 46.95/51.95 **t.**

🏨 **Broughton,** Broughton Village, MK10 9AA, E : 4 m. by A 509 off A 5130 ✈ 667726, Fax 604844, ⋰ – 🔲 🔲 🏧 & 🔁. 🆘 🆔 ⓪ 𝘝𝘐𝘚𝘈 %
closed 1 week Christmas – **M** (bar lunch Monday to Saturday)/dinner 13.95 **t.** and a la carte 🍴 3.50 – **30 rm** ☲ 50.00/65.50 **t.**

🏨 **Wayfarer,** Willen Lake, MK15 9HQ, E : 2 m. by A 509 off Brickhill St. (V 10) ✈ 675222, Fax 674679, ≤, « Lakeside setting » – 🔲 🔲 🔁 – 🏧 50. 🆘 🆔 ⓪ 𝘝𝘐𝘚𝘈
M (dinner only and Sunday lunch)/dinner a la carte 13.85/17.00 **st.** 🍴 4.25 – **41 rm** ☲ 39.50/70.00 **st.** – SB (weekends only) (except Christmas) 60.00/90.00 **st.**

🏨 **Travel Inn,** Secklow Gate West, Central Milton Keynes, MK9 3BZ, ✈ 663388, Fax 607481 – ⊬ rm 🔲 🔲 🏧 🔁 – 🏧 50. 🆘 🆔 ⓪ 𝘝𝘐𝘚𝘈 %
M (Beefeater grill) a la carte approx. 16.00 **t.** – ☲ 4.95 – **38 rm** 33.50 **t.**

🍴🍴 **Jaipur,** Elder House, 502 Eldergate, Station Sq., MK9 1LR, ✈ 669796 – 🔳. 🆘 🆔 ⓪ 𝘝𝘐𝘚𝘈
closed Christmas Day – **M** - Indian (buffet lunch Sunday) a la carte 14.00/21.60 **t.**

at Hanslope NW : 9 m. by A 5 and A 508 on Hanslope rd – ⊠ ☎ 0908 Milton Keynes :

🏨 **Hatton Court Resort** ⋰, Bullington End, MK19 7BQ, SE : 1½ m. on Wolverton rd ✈ 510044, Fax 510945, ⋰ – ⊬ rm 🔲 🔲 🔁 – 🏧 50. 🆘 🆔 ⓪ 𝘝𝘐𝘚𝘈
M (bar lunch Saturday) 11.95/16.95 **st.** and a la carte – ☲ 7.50 – **20 rm** 75.00/85.00 **st.** – SB 123.90/178.90 **st.**

🔧 ATS 38 Victoria Rd, Bletchley ✈ 640420

◆London 83 – ◆Birmingham 52 – Gloucester 35 – ◆Oxford 27.

🏨 **Hillborough,** The Green, OX7 6JH, ✈ 830501, Fax 830646 – 🔲 🔲 🔁. 🆘 🆔 𝘝𝘐𝘚𝘈
closed Christmas and January – **M** 11.95/20.95 **t.** and a la carte 🍴 5.25 – **10 rm** ☲ 40.00/58.00 **t.** – SB 70.00/98.00 **st.**

◆London 115 – ◆Bristol 26 – Gloucester 11 – ◆Oxford 51.

🏠 **Hunters Lodge** without rest., Dr Brown's Rd, GL6 9BT, ✈ 883588, ≤, « Cotswold stone house on Minchinhampton common », – 🔲 🔁. %
closed Christmas – **3 rm** ☲ 25.00/38.00 **s.**

🍴 **Markey's Tea & Supper Room,** The Old Ram, Market Sq., GL6 9BW, ✈ 882287 – ⊬⋈. 🆘 𝘝𝘐𝘚𝘈
closed Monday and dinner Tuesday and Sunday – **M** 5.70 **t.** (lunch) and dinner a la carte 12.00/18.80 **t.** 🍴 3.75.

EUROPE on a single sheet
Michelin map no **970**.

See : Town★ - Higher Town (Church Steps★, St. Michael's★) – West Somerset Railway★ *AC*.

Envir. : Dunster★★ - Castle★★ *AC* (upper rooms ⩽★) Water Mill★ *AC*, St. George's Church★, Dovecote★, SE : 2½ m. by A 39 – Selworthy (Church★, ⩽★★) W : 4½ m. by A 39.

Exc. : Exmoor National Park★★ – Cleeve Abbey★★ *AC*, SE : 6½ m. by A 39.

🛏 The Warren, Warren Rd ℰ 702057.

🛈 17 Friday St., TA24 5UB ℰ 702624.

◆London 187 – ◆Bristol 64 – Exeter 43 – Taunton 25.

🏨 **Northfield** (Best Western) ⬟, Northfield Rd, TA24 5PU, ℰ 705155, Fax 707715, ⩽ bay, « Gardens », 🔔, 🔲 – 🛗 🆃🆅 ☎ 🅿 – 🔬 60. 🔼 🆀🅴 ⑩ 𝗩𝗜𝗦𝗔
M 14.95 **t.** (dinner) and lunch a la carte ⌐ 3.50 – **24 rm** ⬚ 43.00/84.00 **t.** – SB 84.00/104.00 **st.**

🏨 **Benares** ⬟, Northfield Rd, TA24 5PT, ℰ 704911, Fax 706373, ⩽, « Gardens » – ⟆⟆ rest 🆃🆅 ☎ 🅿. 🔼 𝗩𝗜𝗦𝗔
26 March-2 November and Christmas – **M** (bar lunch)/dinner 16.50 **t.** ⌐ 4.30 – **19 rm** ⬚ 42.50/79.00 **t.** – SB (except Christmas) 83.00/102.00 **st.**

🏡 **Beacon Country House** ⬟, Beacon Rd, TA24 5SD, ℰ 703476, ⩽, 🔼, 🎴, park – 🆃🆅 ☎ 🅿. 🔼 𝗩𝗜𝗦𝗔. 🎴
M a la carte 20.10/23.75 **st.** ⌐ 5.00 – **8 rm** ⬚ 55.00/80.00 **st.** – SB 90.00 **st.**

🏡 **Channel House** ⬟, Church Path, TA24 5QG, off Northfield Rd ℰ 703229, ⩽, 🎴 – 🆃🆅 ☎ 🅿. 🔼 ⑩ 𝗩𝗜𝗦𝗔. 🎴
closed 8 November-20 March except Christmas – **M** (dinner only) 17.00 **t.** ⌐ 3.80 – **8 rm** ⬚ 73.50/107.00 **t.** – SB 96.00/136.00 **st.**

🏡 **Wyndcott** ⬟, Martlet Rd, TA24 5QE, ℰ 704522, ⩽, 🎴 – 🆃🆅 ☎ 🅿. 🔼 𝗩𝗜𝗦𝗔
M (lunch by arrangement)/dinner 14.95 **st.** ⌐ 2.95 – **11 rm** ⬚ 22.00/80.00 **st.** – SB 70.00/87.00 **st.**

🏡 **Beaconwood** ⬟, Church Rd, North Hill, TA24 5SB, ℰ 702032, ⩽ sea and Minehead, 🔼 heated, 🎴, 🎴 – ⟆⟆ rest 🆃🆅 ☎ 🅿. 🔼 𝗩𝗜𝗦𝗔
March-October – **M** (bar lunch)/dinner 13.00 ⌐ 4.00 – **14 rm** ⬚ 31.50/50.00 **t.**

🏡 **Remuera** ⬟, Northfield Rd, TA24 5QH, ℰ 702611, 🎴 – ⟆⟆ rest 🆃🆅 🅿. 🔼 𝗩𝗜𝗦𝗔
March-October – **M** 17.00 (dinner) and lunch a la carte ⌐ 6.00 – **7 rm** ⬚ 33.00/46.00 – SB 66.00/98.00.

✿ **York House Inn**, 48 The Avenue, TA24 5AN, ℰ 705151 – 🆃🆅 ☎ 🅿. 🔼 🆀🅴 ⑩ 𝗩𝗜𝗦𝗔. 🎴
M (bar lunch) a la carte 7.95/17.20 **st.** – **15 rm** ⬚ 25.00/50.00 **st.**

at Middlecombe W : 1½ m. by A 39 – ⊠ ☎ 0643 Minehead :

🏨 **Periton Park** ⬟, TA24 8SW, ℰ 706885, Fax 706885, ⩽, 🎴 – ⟆⟆ rest 🆃🆅 ☎ 🅿. 🔼 🆀🅴 𝗩𝗜𝗦𝗔
M (dinner only) 20.00 **st.** ⌐ 4.00 – **8 rm** ⬚ 64.00/88.00 **st.** – SB (except Bank Holidays) 110.00/128.00 **st.**

🔧 ATS Bampton St. ℰ 704808/9

When looking for a quiet hotel
use the maps found in the introductory pages
or look for establishments with the sign ⬟ *or* ⬟.

◆London 72 – Gloucester 36 – ◆Oxford 16.

🏨 **Old Swan** ⬟, Main St., Old Minster, OX8 5RN, ℰ 774441, Fax 702002, « 14C inn », ⬟, 🎴, park, 🎴 – 🆃🆅 ☎ 🅿. 🔼 🆀🅴 ⑩ 𝗩𝗜𝗦𝗔
M 10.00/30.00 **st.** and a la carte ⌐ 5.00 – **16 rm** ⬚ 60.00/125.00 **st.** – SB 110.00/190.00 **st.**

◆London 190 – ◆Kingston-upon-Hull 42 – ◆Leeds 13 – York 20.

🏨 **Monk Fryston Hall**, LS25 5DU, ℰ 682369, Fax 683544, « Italian garden », park – ⟆⟆ rest 🆃🆅 ☎ 🅿. 🔬 50. 🔼 𝗩𝗜𝗦𝗔
M 14.50/24.00 **st.** and a la carte ⌐ 5.80 – **28 rm** ⬚ 64.00/110.00 **st.** – SB (except Christmas and New Year) (weekends only) 110.00/136.00 **st.**

◆London 217 – Barnstaple 28 – Exeter 17 – Taunton 40.

↑ **Wigham** ⬟, EX17 6RJ, NE : 1 m. by Eastington rd turning right at post box after ½ m. ℰ 877350, ⩽, « 16C longhouse, working farm », 🔼 heated – ⟆⟆ 🆃🆅 🅿. 🔼 🆀🅴 𝗩𝗜𝗦𝗔. 🎴
M (communal dining) (by arrangement) ⌐ 3.95 – **5 rm** ⬚ (dinner included) 98.00.

MORECAMBE Lancs. 402 L 21 – pop. 41 432 – ECD : Wednesday – 🕿 0524.

🏊 Bare 🖉 418050, by the sea front – 🏊 Heysham, Trumacar Park, Middleton Rd 🖉 851011, S : 2 m.

🛈 Station Buildings, Central Promenade, LA4 4DB 🖉 414110.

◆London 248 – ◆Blackpool 29 – ◆Carlisle 66 – Lancaster 4.

🏨 **Strathmore** (Best Western), Marine Rd, East Promenade, LA4 5AP, 🖉 421234, Fax 414242, ← – 🛗 📺 ☎ 🅿 – 🕍 180. 🔼 🅰🅴 🕦 💳 ⋙
M 14.95 **st.** (dinner) and a la carte 12.15/21.95 **st.** 🛚 4.75 – **51 rm** ⊇ 54.00/69.00 **st.** – SB (except Christmas and New Year) 86.00/98.00 **st.**

↑ **Prospect,** 363 Marine Rd, East Promenade, LA4 5AQ, 🖉 417819, ← – 📺. 🔼 🕦 💳
M (by arrangement) – **14 rm** ⊇ 17.00/34.00 **st.** – SB 44.00 **st.**

🚗 ATS Westgate 🖉 68075/62011

MORETONHAMPSTEAD Devon 403 I 32 The West Country G. – pop. 1 420 – ECD : Thursday – ✉ Newton Abbot – 🕿 0647.

Envir. : Dartmoor National Park★★ (Brent Tor ≤★★, Haytor Rocks ≤★).

🏊 Manor House Hotel 🖉 40355.

◆London 213 – Exeter 13 – ◆Plymouth 28.

↑ **Wray Barton Manor** without rest., TQ13 8SE, SE : 1½ m. on A 382 🖉 40467, Fax 40628, ⋙ – ⋙ 📺 🅿
April-October – **5 rm** ⊇ 16.00/42.00 **st.**

↑ **Moorcote** without rest., TQ13 8LS, NW : ¼ m. on A 382 🖉 40966, ⋙ – 📺 🅿. ⋙
April-October – **6 rm** ⊇ 22.00/36.00 **st.**

✗ **Reverend Woodforde,** 11a Cross St., TQ13 8NL, 🖉 40691 – 🔼 💳
closed January and February – **M** (closed Sunday) (dinner only) 10.00/17.50 🛚 4.50.

MORETON-IN-MARSH Glos. 403 404 O 28 Great Britain G. – pop. 2 545 – ECD : Wednesday – 🕿 0608.

Envir. : Chastleton House★★, SE : 5 m. by A 44.

◆London 86 – ◆Birmingham 40 – Gloucester 31 – ◆Oxford 29.

🏨 **Manor House,** High St., GL56 0LJ, 🖉 650501, Fax 651481, « 16C manor house, gardens », 🚗, 🔟 – 🛗 ⋙ rest 📺 ☎ 🅿 – 🕍 75. 🔼 🅰🅴 🕦 💳 ⋙
M 8.50/17.50 **st.** and a la carte – **38 rm** ⊇ 69.00/108.00 **st.**, 1 suite – SB 100.00/162.00 **st.**

🏨 **Redesdale Arms,** High St., GL56 0AW, 🖉 650308, Fax 651843 – 📺 ☎ 🅿 – 🕍 100. 🔼 🅰🅴 💳 ⋙
M (bar lunch Monday to Saturday)/dinner 16.95 **st.** and a la carte 🛚 3.50 – **15 rm** ⊇ 46.95/51.95 **t.**, 2 suites.

↑ **Treetops,** London Rd, GL56 0HE, 🖉 651036, ⋙ – ⋙ 📺 🅿. 🔼 💳
M (by arrangement) 10.50 **st.** 🛚 4.50 – **6 rm** ⊇ 28.00/40.00 **st.** – SB (winter only) 59.00/73.00 **st.**

↑ **Townend Cottage and Coach House,** High St., GL56 0AD, 🖉 650846, ⋙ – ⋙ 📺. ⋙
closed February – **M** (by arrangement) 15.00 **t.** 🛚 4.00 – **4 rm** ⊇ 36.00/39.50 **t.** – SB (except summer) (weekdays only) 50.00/72.00 **st.**

✗✗✗ **Marsh Goose,** High St., GL56 0AX, 🖉 652111 – ⋙. 🔼 💳
closed Sunday dinner and Monday – **M** 21.50 **t.** (dinner) and lunch a la carte 16.50/22.50 **t.** 🛚 4.10.

✗✗ **Annies,** 3 Oxford St., GL56 0LA, 🖉 651981 – 🔼 🅰🅴 🕦 💳
closed Sunday dinner and 2 weeks January-February – **M** (dinner only and Sunday lunch)/dinner 21.00 **t.** and a la carte 🛚 4.75.

MORPETH Northd. 401 402 O 18 – pop. 14 301 – ECD : Thursday – 🕿 0670.

🏊 The Common 🖉 519980, S : 1 m. on A 197.

🛈 The Chantry, Bridge St., NE61 1PJ 🖉 511323.

◆London 301 – ◆Edinburgh 93 – ◆Newcastle upon Tyne 15.

🏨 **Linden Hall** 🐾, Longhorsley, NE65 8XF, NW : 7½ m. by A 192 on A 697 🖉 516611, Fax 88544, ←, « Country house in extensive grounds », 🏋, 😩, 🔟, 🐾, ⋙, park, ✗ – 🛗 ⋙ rest 📺 ☎ ᵹ 🅿 – 🕍 300. 🔼 🅰🅴 🕦 💳 ⋙
M 21.50/30.00 **st.** and a la carte – **52 rm** ⊇ 87.50/200.00 **st.** – SB 150.00/190.00 **st.**

🚗 ATS Coopies Lane Ind. Est. 🖉 514627

MORSTON Norfolk – see Blakeney.

MORTEHOE Devon 403 H 30 – see Woolacombe.

MORWENSTOW Cornwall 403 G 31 The West Country G. – pop. 619 – ⊠ Bude – ☎ 028 883 (3 fig.) and 0288 (6 fig.).

See : Morwenstow (Church★, cliffs★★).

Envir. : E : Tamar River★★.

◆London 259 – Exeter 58 – ◆Plymouth 51 – Truro 60.

⌂ **Old Vicarage** ⤸, EX23 9SR, ℰ 369, ≤, 🐾 – ⇗ ℗. ℘
   closed December – **M** 14.00 – **3 rm** ⊃ 19.00/38.00.

MOULSFORD Oxon. 403 404 Q 29 The West Country G. – pop. 494 – ☎ 0491 Cholsey.

Exc. : Ridgeway Path★★.

◆London 58 – ◆Oxford 17 – Reading 13 – Swindon 37.

XX **Beetle and Wedge** with rm, Ferry Lane, OX10 9JF, ℰ 651381, Fax 651376, ≤, « Thames-side setting », ⤸, 🐾 – ⇗ rm 🆃🆅 ☎ ℗. ⃠ 🆎 ⓞ 𝘝𝘐𝘚𝘈 𝘑𝘊𝘉. ℘
   closed Christmas Day – Meals (closed Sunday dinner, Monday and 2 weeks January) (booking essential) (restricted service January and February) a la carte 30.00/43.00 t. ⅃ 5.25 – **10 rm** ⊃ 70.00/125.00 **t.**

   ✗ **Boathouse** – **M** (closed Christmas Day) (booking essential) a la carte 17.25/25.75 **t.** ⅃ 5.25.

MOULTON Northants. 404 R 27 – see Northampton.

MOULTON N. Yorks. 402 P 20 – pop. 151 – ⊠ Richmond – ☎ 0325 Darlington.

◆London 243 – ◆Leeds 53 – ◆Middlesbrough 25 – ◆Newcastle upon Tyne 43.

XX **Black Bull Inn**, DL10 6QJ, ℰ 377289, Fax 377422, « Brighton Belle Pullman coach » – ℗. ⃠ 🆎 𝘝𝘐𝘚𝘈
   closed Sunday and 24 to 26 December – **M** 12.75 **t.** (lunch) and a la carte 17.00/26.25 **t.**

MOUSEHOLE Cornwall 403 D 33 The West Country G. – ECD : Wednesday except summer – ⊠ ☎ 0736 Penzance.

See : Village★ – Envir. : Penwith★★ – Lamorna (The Merry Maidens and The Pipers Standing Stone★) SW : 3 m. by B 3315.

Exc. : Land's End★ (cliff scenery★★★) W : 9 m. by B 3315.

◆London 321 – Penzance 3 – Truro 29.

🏠 Lobster Pot, TR19 6QX, ℰ 731251, Fax 731140, ≤ – ⇗ rest 🆃🆅 ☎
   M (bar lunch Monday to Saturday) – **25 rm.**

🏠 **Carn Du** ⤸, Raginnis Hill, TR19 6SS, ℰ 731233, ≤ Mounts Bay, 🐾 – ⇗ rest 🆃🆅 ℗. ⃠ 🆎 𝘝𝘐𝘚𝘈. ℘
   M (bar lunch)/dinner 14.95 ⅃ 4.00 – **7 rm** ⊃ 25.00/50.00 – SB 79.90/89.90 **st.**

MUCH BIRCH Heref. and Worcs. – see Hereford.

MUCH WENLOCK Shrops. 402 403 M26 Great Britain G. – pop. 2 486 – ☎ 074 636 Brockton.

See : Priory★ AC.

Envir. : Ironbridge Gorge Museum★★ AC (The Iron Bridge★★ – Coalport China Museum★★ – Blists Hill Open Air Museum★★ – Museum of the River and Visitor Centre★) NE : 4 ½ m. by A 4169 and B 4380.

🛈 The Museum, High St., TF13 6HR ℰ 727679 (summer only).

◆London 154 – ◆Birmingham 34 – Shrewsbury 12 – Worcester 37.

⌂ **Brockton Grange** ⤸ without rest., Brockton, TF13 6JR, SW : 5 ½ m. by B 4378 on Easthope rd ℰ 443, ⤸, 🐾, park – ⇗ 🆃🆅 ℗. ℘
   closed December – **3 rm** ⊃ 35.00/48.00.

MUDEFORD Dorset 403 404 O 31 – see Christchurch.

MULLION Cornwall 403 E 33 The West Country G. – pop. 1 958 – ECD : Wednesday – ⊠ Helston – ☎ 0326.

See : Mullion Cove★★★ (Church★) – Lizard Peninsula★.

Envir. : Kynance Cove★★★, S : 5 m.

Exc. : Helston (Flora Day Furry Dance★★) (May) N : 7 ½ m. by A 3083 – Culdrose (Flambards Village Theme Park★) AC, N : 6 m. by A 3083 – Wendron (Poldark Mine★) N : 9 ½ m. by A 3083 and B 3297.

🛈 Cury, Helston ℰ 240276.

◆London 323 – Falmouth 25 – Penzance 21 – Truro 26.

🏨 **Polurrian**, TR12 7EN, SW : ½ m. ℰ 240421, Fax 240083, ≤ Mounts Bay, Ⅰ₆, 🇪🇸, 🏊 heated, 🏊, 🐾, ℘, squash – 🆃🆅 ☎ ℗. ⃠ 🆎 ⓞ 𝘝𝘐𝘚𝘈
   April-October – **M** (bar lunch)/dinner 21.00 **st.** – **39 rm** ⊃ 76.00/172.00 **st.**, 1 suite.

MUNGRISDALE Cumbria 401 402 L 19 20 – pop. 336 – ⊠ Penrith – ☎ 076 87 Threlkeld.

◆London 301 – ◆Carlisle 33 – Keswick 8.5 – Penrith 13.

🏠 **Mill** ⤸, CA11 0XR, ℰ 79659, 🐾 – ⇗ rest 🆃🆅 ℗
   March-October – **M** (dinner only) 19.50 **t.** ⅃ 3.95 – **7 rm** ⊃ 25.00/60.00 **t.** – SB (except March) (weekdays only) 80.00/110.00 **st.**

⌂ **Mosedale House** ⤸, Mosedale, CA11 0XQ, N : 1 m. by Mosedale rd ℰ 79371 – ⇗ 🆃🆅 ⅗ ℗
   M 12.00 **st.** – **4 rm** ⊃ 19.00/52.00 **st.**

NAILSWORTH Glos. 403 404 N 28 – pop. 5 114 – ✆ 0453.

◆London 120 – ◆Bristol 30 – Swindon 41.

🏠 **Egypt Mill,** GL6 0EA, ℘ 833449, Fax 836098, ☞ – 📺 ☎ 🅿 – 🔥 100. 🌰 AE ① VISA �│
M 14.00 st. and a la carte ﹩ 4.00 – **14 rm** ⊑ 37.50/48.00 st. – SB 70.00/89.00 st.

⌂ **North Farm,** Nympsfield Rd, GL6 0ET, W : ¾ m. via Spring Hill ℘ 833598 – ⇔🍴 📺 ☎ 🅿 �│
M 12.00 st. – **3 rm** ⊑ 18.00/32.00 st. – SB 48.00/64.00 st.

⌂ **Apple Orchard House,** Orchard Close, Springhill, GL6 0LX, ℘ 832503, Fax 836213, ☞
– 📺 🅿 🌰 AE VISA
M 10.50 – **3 rm** ⊑ 20.00/34.00 s. – SB 51.00/60.00 s.

✗ **William's Bistro,** 3 Fountain St., GL6 0BL, ℘ 835507, Fax 835950 – 🌰 VISA
closed Sunday, Monday, Good Friday and Christmas – **M** - **Seafood** (dinner only) a la
carte 15.00/22.00 t. ﹩ 3.50.

✗ **Waterman's Stone Cottage,** Old Market, GL6 0BX, ℘ 832808 – 🌰 VISA
closed Sunday and Monday – **M** (dinner only) 15.00 t. and a la carte ﹩ 4.50.

Great Britain and Ireland is now covered
by an Atlas at a scale of 1 inch to 4.75 miles.

Three easy to use versions: Paperback, Spiralbound and Hardback.

NANTWICH Ches. 402 403 404 M 24 – pop. 11 867 – ECD : Wednesday – ✆ 0270.
🅱 Beam St., CW5 5LY ℘ 623914.

◆London 176 – Chester 20 – ◆Liverpool 45 – ◆Stoke-on-Trent 17.

🏨 **Rookery Hall** 🦢, Worleston, CW5 6DQ, N : 2 ½ m. by A 51 on B 5074 ℘ 610016,
Fax 626027, ≼, « Part 18C country house », 🦢, ☞, park, 🎾 – ⎹∮ ⇔🍴 📺 ☎ & 🅿 – 🔥 50.
🌰 AE ① VISA JCB. �│
M (booking essential) 16.50/25.00 st. and dinner a la carte – **42 rm** ⊑ 95.00/115.00 st.,
3 suites – SB (weekends only) 135.00/180.00 st.

🏩 **Crown** (Best Western), High St., CW5 5AS, ℘ 625283, Fax 628047, « 16C inn » – 📺 ☎ 🅿
– 🔥 120. 🌰 AE ① VISA JCB
closed 24 and 25 December – **M** 18.00 st. and a la carte ﹩ 4.20 – **18 rm** ⊑ 55.00/69.00 st. –
SB 84.00 st.

🏠 Peacock without rest., 221 Crewe Rd, CW5 6NE, E : 1 m. on A 534 ℘ 624069, Fax 610113 –
⇔🍴 📺 🅿. 🌰 🌽 & 🅿. �│
37 rm.

✗✗ **Churche's Mansion,** Hospital St., CW5 0RY, E : ¼ m. ℘ 625933, « Timbered Elizabethan house », ☞ – 🅿. 🌰 ① VISA
closed Sunday dinner, Monday and January – **M** 14.50/29.00 t. ﹩ 5.00.

at Burland W : 2½ m. on A 534 – ⊠ Nantwich – ✆ 0270 74 Burland :

⌂ **Burland Farm,** Wrexham Rd, CW5 8ND, W : ¾ m. on A 534 ℘ 210, « Working farm »,
☞ – 📺 🅿
closed Christmas and New Year – **M** (by arrangement) 15.00 – **3 rm** ⊑ 27.50/50.00.

NATIONAL EXHIBITION CENTRE W. Mids. 403 404 O 26 – see Birmingham.

NAWTON N. Yorks. – see Helmsley.

NAYLAND Essex 404 W 28 – see Colchester.

NEAR SAWREY Cumbria 402 L 20 – see Hawkshead.

NEASHAM Durham 402 P 20 – see Darlington.

NEATISHEAD Norfolk 404 Y 25 – pop. 524 – ✆ 0692 Horning.

◆London 122 – North Walsham 8.5 – ◆Norwich 11.

⌂ **Regency** without rest., The Street, NR12 8AD, ℘ 630233 – 📺. ①
5 rm ⊑ 20.00/44.00 s.

NEEDHAM MARKET Suffolk 404 X 27 – pop. 3 420 – ECD : Tuesday – ⊠ ✆ 0449.

◆London 77 – ◆Cambridge 47 – ◆Ipswich 8.5 – ◆Norwich 38.

⌂ **Pipps Ford,** Norwich Rd roundabout, IP6 8LJ, SE : 1 ¾ m. by B 1078 at junction of A 45
with A 140 ℘ 044 979 (Coddenham) 208, Fax 561, « Elizabethan farmhouse », 🛆, ☞, 🎾
– ⇔🍴 🅿. �│
closed Christmas-New Year – **M** (by arrangement) 19.00 st. ﹩ 3.50 – **6 rm** ⊑ 37.50/
66.00 st.

NESTON Ches. 402 403 K 24 – ⊠ South Wirral – ✆ 051 Liverpool.

◆London 206 – Birkenhead 10 – Chester 11 – ◆Liverpool 12.

🏠 **Elm Grove House,** 44 Parkgate Rd, L64 6QG, ℘ 336 3021, ☞ – 📺 🅿. 🌰 VISA JCB. 🌽
M (dinner only and Sunday lunch)/dinner 14.50 st. – **7 rm** ⊑ 25.00/50.00 st. – SB 62.00/
80.00 st.

NETHER WESTCOTE Oxon. – see Stow-on-the-Wold.

Oxon. 🗺️ R 29 – ✉️ Henley-on-Thames – ☎️ 0491.

◆London 44 – ◆Oxford 19 – Reading 9.

　🏠 **White Hart,** High St., RG9 5DD, 𝒫 641245, Fax 641423, « Part 15C inn », 🚗 – 📺 ☎️ 🅿️ –
　　🅰️ 40. 🔳 𝘝𝘐𝘚𝘈 🛇
　　M 11.95/17.95 **st.** and a la carte 🛠 4.00 – **6 rm** ⊃ 49.50/69.50 **st.** – SB (except first week
　　July) 87.50/135.50 **st.**

Wilts. 🗺️ 🗺️ N 29 – see Castle Combe.

Hants. 🗺️ 🗺️ Q 30 – pop. 4 117 – ✉️ ☎️ 0962 Alresford.

◆London 63 – ◆Portsmouth 40 – Reading 33 – ◆Southampton 20.

　XX **Old School House,** 60 West St., SO24 9AU, 𝒫 732134 – 🛇. 🔳 𝘝𝘐𝘚𝘈
　　closed Sunday dinner and Monday – **M** 12.95/18.95 **t.** and a la carte 🛠 5.00.

　X **Hunters** with rm, 32 Broad St., SO24 9AQ, 𝒫 732468, Fax 732468, « Former coaching
　　inn », 🚗 – 📺 🔳 🅰️ ⓪ 𝘝𝘐𝘚𝘈 🛇
　　closed 24 to 30 December – **M** *(closed Sunday dinner)* 9.95/13.95 **t.** and a la carte 🛠 4.75 –
　　3 rm ⊃ 37.50/47.50 **st.** – SB 55.00/99.00 **st.**

Notts. 🗺️ 🗺️ R 24 Great Britain G. – pop. 33 143 – ECD : Thursday –
☎️ 0636.

See : St. Mary Magdalene★.

🛏 Kelwick Coddington 𝒫 626241, E : 4 m. on A 17.

🅱️ The Gilstrap Centre, Castlegate, NG24 1BG 𝒫 78962.

◆London 127 – Lincoln 16 – ◆Nottingham 20 – ◆Sheffield 42.

　🏨 **Grange,** 73 London Rd, NG24 1RZ, S : ½ m. on A 6065 𝒫 703399, Fax 702328, 🚗, 🌮 –
　　🛇 📺 ☎️ 🅿️. 🔳 🅰️ 𝘝𝘐𝘚𝘈 🛇
　　closed Christmas and New Year – **M** (lunch by arrangement)/dinner 11.95 **t.** and a la carte
　　🛠 3.40 – **15 rm** ⊃ 39.50/59.50 **t.** – SB 76.40/111.00 **st.**

　XX **Le Gourmet,** 14 Castlegate, NG24 1BG, 𝒫 610141, Fax 612841 – 🔳 🅰️ ⓪ 𝘝𝘐𝘚𝘈
　　closed Sunday dinner and Monday – **M** - *French* 10.80/19.95 **st.** and a la carte.

　　at North Muskham N : 4 m. by A 6065 – ✉️ ☎️ 0636 Newark-on-Trent :

　🏨 **Forte Travelodge** without rest., NG23 6HT, N : ½ m. on A1 (southbound carriageway)
　　𝒫 703635, Reservations (Freephone) 0800 850950 – 📺 ♿ 🅿️. 🔳 🅰️ 𝘝𝘐𝘚𝘈 🛇
　　30 rm 31.95 **t.**

🔘 ATS 70 William St. 𝒫 77531

Berks. 🗺️ 🗺️ Q 29 The West Country G. – pop. 31 488 – ECD : Wednesday –
☎️ 0635.

Exc. : Littlecote★★ (arms and armour★, Roman mosaic floor★) *AC*, W : 10 m. by A 4.

🛏 Newbury and Crookham, Bury's Bank Road 𝒫 40035, SE : 2 m. – 🛏 Donnington Valley, Old
Oxford Rd 𝒫 32488, N : off Old Oxford rd.

🅱️ The Wharf, RG14 5AS 𝒫 30267.

◆London 67 – ◆Bristol 66 – ◆Oxford 28 – Reading 17 – ◆Southampton 38.

　🏩 **Donnington Valley H. & Golf Course,** Old Oxford Rd, Donnington, RG16 9AG, N :
　　1 ¾ m. by A 4 and B 4494 𝒫 551199, Fax 551123, 🛏, park – 📳 🛇 rm 🍽 rest 📺 ☎️ ♿ 🅿️ –
　　🅰️ 140. 🔳 🅰️ ⓪ 𝘝𝘐𝘚𝘈
　　M 8.50/30.00 **st.** and a la carte 🛠 4.95 – ⊃ 8.50 – **58 rm** 89.00/136.00 **st.** –
　　SB (weekends only) 98.00/140.00 **st.**

　🏨 **Foley Lodge,** Stockcross, RG16 8JU, NW : 2 m. by A 4 on B 4000 𝒫 528770, Fax 528398,
　　🔳, 🚗 – 🛇 rm 📺 ☎️ ♿ 🅿️ – 🅰️ 200. 🔳 🅰️ ⓪ 𝘝𝘐𝘚𝘈 🛇
　　M – **Café Jardin** *(closed Sunday lunch)* a la carte 18.00/28.00 **t.** – (see also below) – **68 rm**
　　⊃ 52.00/115.00 **t.**, 1 suite – SB (weekends only) 98.00/118.00 **st.**

　🏨 **Elcot Park Resort,** RG16 8NJ, W : 5 m. by A 4 𝒫 58100, Fax 58288, ≤, 🛠, ⛱, 🔳, 🚗,
　　park, 🌮 – 🛇 rm 🍽 rest 📺 ☎️ ♿ 🅿️ – 🅰️ 110. 🔳 🅰️ ⓪ 𝘝𝘐𝘚𝘈
　　M 15.00/16.95 **t.** and a la carte – ⊃ 7.95 – **75 rm** 75.00/100.00 **t.** – SB 96.00/176.00 **st.**

　🏨 **Hilton National,** Pinchington Lane, RG14 7HL, S : 2 m. by A 34 𝒫 529000, Telex 848247,
　　Fax 529337, 🛠, ⛱, 🔳 – 🛇 rm 🍽 rest 📺 ☎️ ♿ 🅿️ – 🅰️ 190. 🔳 🅰️ ⓪ 𝘝𝘐𝘚𝘈 𝗝𝗖𝗕
　　M (bar lunch Saturday and Bank Holidays) 20.00/30.00 **t.** and dinner a la carte – ⊃ 10.25 –
　　109 rm 85.00/150.00 **t.** – SB (weekends only) 112.00/160.00 **st.**

　🏨 **Stakis Newbury,** Oxford Rd, RG16 8XY, N : 3 ¼ m. on A 34 𝒫 247010, Telex 848694,
　　Fax 247077, 🛠, ⛱, 🔳 – 🛇 rm 🍽 rest 📺 ☎️ ♿ 🅿️ – 🅰️ 30. 🔳 🅰️ ⓪ 𝘝𝘐𝘚𝘈 𝗝𝗖𝗕
　　M 9.75/15.95 **t.** and dinner a la carte – ⊃ 8.50 – **110 rm** 81.00/101.00 **st.**, 2 suites – SB
　　82.00/116.00 **st.**

　🏨 **Chequers** (Forte), 7-8 Oxford St., RG13 1JB, 𝒫 38000, Fax 37170, 🚗 – 🛇 📺 ☎️ 🅿️ –
　　🅰️ 80. 🔳 🅰️ ⓪ 𝘝𝘐𝘚𝘈
　　M *(closed Saturday lunch)* 9.95/20.00 **t.** and a la carte 🛠 6.45 – ⊃ 8.50 – **56 rm** 80.00/
　　105.00 **st.** – SB 86.00 **st.**

🏠 **Enborne Grange,** Enborne St., Wash Common, RG14 6RP, SW : 2 ½ m. by A 343 via Essex St. ℰ 40046, Fax 580246, 🐎 – 📺 ☎ 🅿 – 🔏 40. 🔼 🖭 𝘝𝘐𝘚𝘈. 🦀
M (in bar Sunday dinner) 15.00/20.00 **t.** and a la carte 🍴 4.00 – **25 rm** ⌷ 49.50/65.00 **t.**

🏠 **Blue Boar Inn,** North Heath, RG16 8UE, N : 4 ¾ m. on B 4494 ℰ 248236, Fax 248506 – 📺 ☎ 🅿. 🔼 🖭 ⑩ 𝘝𝘐𝘚𝘈. 🦀
M (in bar Sunday) a la carte 15.40/22.40 **t.** 🍴 4.95 – **15 rm** ⌷ 37.00/57.00 **t.** – SB (weekends only) 80.00/120.00 **st.**

🏠 **Starwood** without rest., 1 Rectory Close, off Pound St., RG14 6DF, SW : ¼ m. by Enborne rd ℰ 49125 – 🗝 📺 🅿. 🦀
4 rm ⌷ 38.00/38.00 **st.**

XXX **Foley Lodge,** Stockcross, RG16 8JU, NW : 2 m. by A 4 on B 4000 ℰ 528770, Fax 528398, 🐎 – 🗝 🅿. 🔼 🖭 ⑩ 𝘝𝘐𝘚𝘈
closed Sunday – **M** a la carte 25.00/45.00 **t.**

at Woolton Hill SW : 4 ½ m. by A 34 off A 343 – ⊠ ☸ 0635 Newbury :

🏨 **Hollington House** 🦢, RG15 9XR, SW : ½ m. on East End rd ℰ 255100, Fax 255075, ≤, « Edwardian country house, gardens », ⊿ heated, park, 💥 – 📲 📺 ☎ 🅿 – 🔏 30. 🔼 🖭 𝘝𝘐𝘚𝘈. 🦀
M 21.00/25.00 **t.** and a la carte 🍴 8.50 – **19 rm** ⌷ 80.00/250.00 **t.,** 1 suite – SB 180.00/270.00 **st.**

at Hamstead Marshall SW : 5 ½ m. by A 4 – ⊠ Newbury – ☸ 0488 Kintbury :

🏠 **White Hart Inn,** Kintbury Rd, RG15 0HW, ℰ 58201, 🐎 – 📺 ☎ 🅿. 🔼 🖭 𝘝𝘐𝘚𝘈. 🦀
closed 25 and 26 December – **M** - **Italian** (closed Sunday) a la carte 12.75/23.25 **st.** 🍴 4.00 – **6 rm** ⌷ 35.00/60.00 **st.**

at Speen W : 1 ¾ m. on A 4 – ⊠ ☸ 0635 Newbury :

🏠 Hare & Hounds, Bath Rd, RG13 1QY, ℰ 521152, Fax 47708 – 📺 ☎ 🅿
29 rm, 1 suite.

🛠 ATS 30 Queens Rd ℰ 42250

*Es ist empfehlenswert, **in der Hauptsaison** und vor allem in Urlaubsorten, Hotelzimmer im voraus zu bestellen. Benachrichtigen Sie sofort das Hotel, wenn Sie ein bestelltes Zimmer nicht belegen können.*

Wenn Sie an ein Hotel im Ausland schreiben, fügen Sie Ihrem Brief einen internationalen Antwortschein bei (im Postamt erhältlich).

NEWBY BRIDGE Cumbria 𝟒𝟎𝟐 L 21 Great Britain G. – ECD : Saturday – ⊠ Ulverston – ☸ 053 95.

Envir. : Lake Windermere★★.

◆London 270 – Kendal 16 – Lancaster 27.

🏨 **Lakeside H. on Lake Windermere,** Lakeside, LA12 8AT, NE : 1 m. on Hawkshead rd ℰ 31207, Telex 65149, Fax 31699, ≤, « Lakeside setting », 🦢, 🐎 – 🗝 🗝 rest 📺 ☎ ঠ 🅿 – 🔏 100. 🔼 🖭 ⑩ 𝘝𝘐𝘚𝘈
closed 2 to 12 January – **M** (bar lunch Monday to Saturday)/dinner 25.00 – **67 rm** ⌷ 55.00/110.00 **st.,** 2 suites.

🏨 **Whitewater,** The Lakeland Village, LA12 8PX, SW : 1 ½ m. by A 590 ℰ 31133, Fax 31881, 𝑓₆, ≘, ⊿, 💥, squash – 📲 📺 ☎ 🅿 – 🔏 70. 🔼 🖭 ⑩ 𝘝𝘐𝘚𝘈
M (bar lunch Monday to Saturday)/dinner a la carte 12.15/26.40 **st.** 🍴 6.25 – **35 rm** ⌷ 60.00/95.00 **st.** – SB (weekends only) 108.00/149.00 **st.**

🏨 **Swan,** LA12 8NB, ℰ 31681, Fax 31917, ≤, 🦢, 🐎 – 📺 ☎ 🅿 – 🔏 65. 🔼 🖭 ⑩ 𝘝𝘐𝘚𝘈. 🦀
M (bar lunch Monday to Saturday)/dinner 19.50 **st.** and a la carte 🍴 5.00 – **35 rm** ⌷ 60.00/130.00 **t.,** 1 suite – SB (November-March except Bank Holidays) (weekends only) 90.00/120.00 **st.**

at Cartmell Fell NE : 3 ¼ m. by A 590 off A 592 – ⊠ Grange-over-Sands – ☸ 053 95 Newby Bridge :

🏠 **Lightwood Farmhouse** 🦢, LA11 6NP, ℰ 31454, ≤, 🐎 – 🗝 🅿. 🔼 𝘝𝘐𝘚𝘈. 🦀
February-November – **M** (by arrangement) 11.50 **t.** – **8 rm** ⌷ 26.00/45.00 **st.** – SB (winter only) 66.00/72.00 **st.**

at Bowland Bridge NE : 4 ¼ m. by A 590 off A 592 – ⊠ Grange-over-Sands – ☸ 053 95 Newby Bridge :

🏠 **Hare and Hounds,** LA11 6NN, ℰ 68333, 🐎 – 📺 ☎ 🅿. 🔼 𝘝𝘐𝘚𝘈. 🦀
M (residents only) (dinner only) 12.50 **t.** 🍴 4.50 – **16 rm** ⌷ 32.00/60.00 **t.** – SB (October-March) (except Christmas and Bank Holidays) (weekdays only) 60.00/76.00 **st.**

NEWBY WISKE N. Yorks. – see Northallerton.

NEWCASTLE AIRPORT Tyne and Wear 𝟒𝟎𝟏 𝟒𝟎𝟐 O 19 – see Newcastle upon Tyne.

Exc. : Wedgwood Visitor's Centre★ *AC*, SE : 6½ m. by A 34 Z.

📮 Newcastle Municipal, Keele Rd ✆ 627596, W : 2 m. by A 525 Z.

🅱 Ironmarket, ST5 1AT ✆ 711964.

♦London 161 – ♦Birmingham 46 – ♦Liverpool 56 – ♦Manchester 43.

Plan of Built up Area : see Stoke-on-Trent

NEWCASTLE-UNDER-LYME
CENTRE

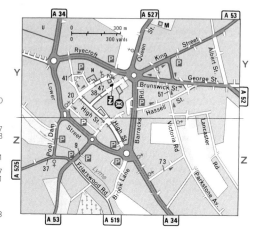

🏨 **Forte Posthouse,** Clayton Rd, Clayton, ST5 4DL, S : 2 m. on A 519 ✆ 717171, Fax 717138, *f.s.*, ⛱, 🔲, 🎱 – ⇔ rm 📺 ☎ 🅿 – 🔬 70. 🔼 ⒶⒺ ⓄⒹ 𝗩𝗜𝗦𝗔 𝗝𝗖𝗕
M a la carte approx. 17.50 **t.** ♦ 4.65 – ⊆ 6.95 – **119 rm** 53.50/69.50 **st.** – SB 90.00 **st.**
on Stoke-on-Trent town plan   V   **n**

🏨 **Clayton Lodge** (Jarvis), Clayton Rd, Clayton, ST5 4AF, S : 1¼ m. on A 519 ✆ 613093, Fax 711896 – ⇔ rm 📺 ☎ 🅿 – 🔬 270. 🔼 ⒶⒺ ⓄⒹ 𝗩𝗜𝗦𝗔 𝗝𝗖𝗕
M (lunch by arrangement)/dinner 16.45 **st.** and a la carte ♦ 5.25 – ⊆ 8.00 – **50 rm** 29.50/68.00 **st.** – SB 78.00 **st.**
on Stoke-on-Trent town plan   V   **e**

🅰 ATS Lower St. ✆ 622431

See : City★★ – Grey Street★ CZ – Quayside★ CZ : Composition★, All Saints Church★ (interior★) – Castle Keep★ *AC* CZ – Laing Art Gallery and Museum★ *AC* CY M1 – Museum of Antiquities★ CY M2.

Envir. : Hadrian's Wall★★, W : by A 69 AV.

Exc. : Beamish : North of England Open-Air Museum★★ *AC*, SW : 7 m. by A 692 and A 6076 AX – Seaton Delaval Hall★ *AC*, NE : 11 m. by A 189 - BV - and A 190.

📮 High Gosforth Park ✆ 236 4480/4867, N : 4 m. by A 189 BV – 📮 Broadway East, Gosforth ✆ 285 6710, N : 3 m. by A 189 BV – 📮 City of Newcastle, Three Mile Bridge, Gosforth ✆ 285 1775, NW : 3 m. by B 1318 AV – 📮 Wallsend, Bigges Main ✆ 262 1973, NE : by A 1058 BV – 📮 Whickham, Hollinside Park ✆ 488 7309, SW : 5 m. by A 692 AX.

🛫 Newcastle Airport : ✆ 286 0966, NW : 5 m. by A 696 AV – **Terminal** : Bus Assembly : Central Station Forecourt.

🚢 to Norway : Bergen, Haugesund and Stavanger (Color Line) 2-3 weekly – to Denmark : Esbjerg (Scandinavian Seaways) (summer only) (19 h) – to Sweden : Gothenburg (Scandinavian Seaways) (summer only) – to Germany : Hamburg (Scandinavian Seaways).

🅱 Central Library, Princess Sq., NE99 1DX ✆ 261 0691 – Main Concourse Central Station, NE1 5DL ✆ 230 0030 – Newcastle Airport, Woolsington, NE13 8BX ✆ 271 1929.

♦London 276 – ♦Edinburgh 105 – ♦Leeds 95.

Plans on following pages

🏨 **Copthorne Newcastle,** The Close, Quayside, NE1 3RT, ✆ 222 0333, Telex 53340, Fax 230 1111, ≤, *f.s.*, ⛱, 🔲, 🎱 – 🛗 ⇔ rm 🔳 rest 📺 ☎ & 🅿 – 🔬 200. 🔼 ⒶⒺ ⓄⒹ 𝗩𝗜𝗦𝗔 𝗝𝗖𝗕
M 13.95/16.95 **st.** and a la carte ♦ 5.50 – ⊆ 9.95 – **156 rm** 99.00/210.00 **st.** – SB (weekends only) 98.40 **st.**   CZ   **z**

🏨 Vermont, Castle Garth, NE1 1RQ, ✆ 233 1010, Fax 233 1234 – 🛗 📺 ☎ & 🅿 – 🔬 200
M – Blue Room *(closed Sunday and Monday)* (dinner only) – **95 rm**, 6 suites.   CZ   **s**

NEWCASTLE
UPON TYNE

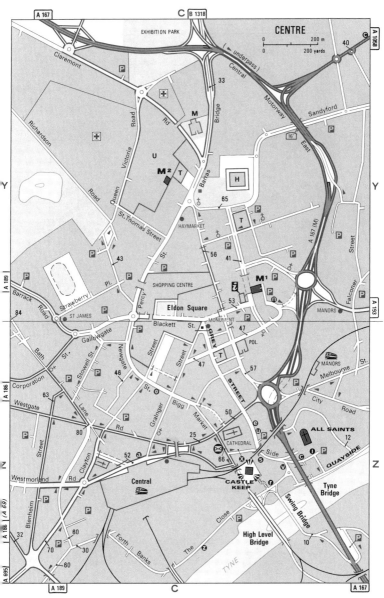

NEWCASTLE UPON TYNE

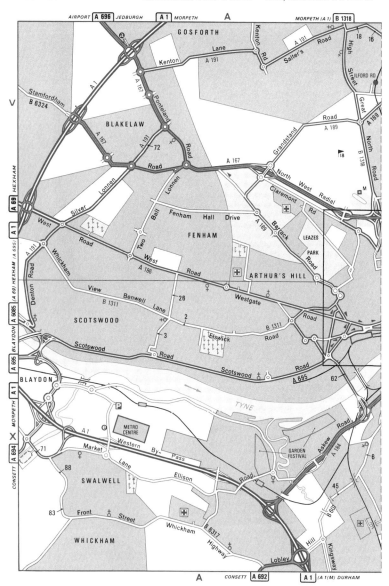

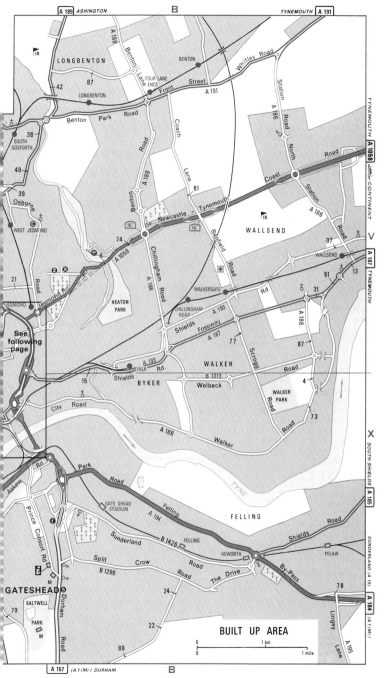

BUILT UP AREA

0   1 km
0   1 mile

🏨 **County Thistle** (Mt. Charlotte Thistle), Neville St., NE99 1AH, ℰ 232 2471, Telex 537873, Fax 232 1285 – 📶 ¾ rm 📺 ☎ – 🚗 100. 🕰 🖭 ⓪ 𝚅𝙸𝚂𝙰   CZ **a**
M (closed Saturday lunch) 10.50/16.50 **st.** and a la carte 🍷 5.75 – ⇌ 9.25 – **115 rm** 72.00/120.00 **st.** – SB (weekends only) 82.00/94.00 **st.**

🏨 **Forte Crest**, New Bridge St., NE1 8BS, ℰ 232 6191, Telex 63467, Fax 261 8529 – 📶 ¾ rm 🍽 rest 📺 ☎ & 🄿 – 🚗 400. 🕰 🖭 ⓪ 𝚅𝙸𝚂𝙰 𝙹𝙲𝙱   CY **n**
M (closed lunch Saturday and Sunday) 11.95/15.95 **st.** and a la carte – ⇌ 9.95 – **165 rm** 75.00 **st.**, 1 suite – SB (weekends only) 86.00 **st.**

🏨 **Surtees**, 12-16 Dean St., NE1 1PG, ℰ 261 7771, Fax 230 1322 – 📶 📺 ☎. 🕰 🖭 ⓪ 𝚅𝙸𝚂𝙰 ⠠⠎   CZ **u**
M (café-restaurant) 15.00/25.00 **st.** – **27 rm** ⇌ 67.50/87.50 **st.** – SB (weekends only) 65.00/130.00 **st.**

🏨 **Novotel**, Ponteland Rd, Kenton, NE3 3HZ, at junction of A1 (M) with A 696 ℰ 214 0303, Telex 53675, Fax 214 0633, 🏋, ⇌s, 🏊, – 📶 ¾ rm 🍽 rest 📺 ☎ & 🄿 – 🚗 220. 🕰 🖭 ⓪ 𝚅𝙸𝚂𝙰   AV **a**
M a la carte 13.95/19.20 **st.** 🍷 4.95 – ⇌ 7.50 – **126 rm** 60.50/65.50 **st.** – SB (weekends only) 70.00/90.00 **st.**

🏨 Bank Top Toby, Ponteland Rd., Kenton, NE3 3TY, at junction of A1 (M) with A 696 ℰ 214 0877, Fax 214 0095 – ¾ rm 📺 ☎ & 🄿 – 🚗 50   AV **a**
30 rm.

🏨 **Swallow**, 1 Newgate Arcade, Newgate St., NE1 5SX, ℰ 232 5025, Fax 232 8428 – 📶 ¾ rm 📺 ☎ 🄿 – 🚗 50. 🕰 🖭 ⓪ 𝚅𝙸𝚂𝙰   CZ **o**
M 10.25/16.75 **st.** and a la carte – **93 rm** ⇌ 78.00/90.00 **st.**

🏨 **Imperial Swallow**, Jesmond Rd, NE2 1PR, ℰ 281 5511, Fax 281 8472, 🏋, ⇌s, 🏊, – 📶 ¾ rm 📺 ☎ 🄿 – 🚗 120. 🕰 🖭 ⓪ 𝚅𝙸𝚂𝙰   CY **c**
M (closed Saturday lunch) 8.25/14.95 **st.** and a la carte 🍷 6.50 – **121 rm** ⇌ 80.00/95.00 **st.** – SB (July-August and weekends only) 95.00 **st.**

🏨 **Waterside**, 48-52 Sandhill, Quayside, NE1 3JF, ℰ 230 0111, Fax 230 1615 – 📶 📺 ☎. 🕰 🖭 ⓪ 𝚅𝙸𝚂𝙰 ⠠⠎   CZ **r**
M - (Café-restaurant) (closed Sunday lunch and 26 December) 15.00/25.00 **t.** and a la carte 🍷 3.45 – ⇌ 3.00 – **16 rm** ⇌ 40.00/73.00 **st.**, 2 suites – SB (weekends only) 61.00/140.00 **st.**

🏨 **New Kent** (Best Western), 127 Osborne Rd, Jesmond, NE2 2TB, ℰ 281 1083, Fax 281 3369 – 📺 ☎ 🄿. 🕰 🖭 ⓪ 𝚅𝙸𝚂𝙰 ⠠⠎   BV **c**
M (dinner only) 9.50 **st.** and a la carte – **32 rm** ⇌ 35.00/79.00 **st.** – SB 78.00/80.00 **st.**

🏨 **Forte Travelodge** without rest., Whitemare Pool, NE10 8YB, at junction of A 194 with A 184 ℰ 438 3333, Reservations (Freephone) 0800 850950 – 📺 & 🄿. 🕰 🖭 ⠠⠎   BX
41 rm 31.95 **t.**

🏠 **Avenue** without rest., Osborne Av., Jesmond, NE2 2LU, ℰ 281 1396 – 📺 ☎. 🕰 BV **x**
closed 23 December-10 January – **10 rm** ⇌ 18.00/42.00 **st.**

🏠 **Westland**, 27 Osborne Av., Jesmond, NE2 1JR, ℰ 281 0412, Fax 281 5005 – ¾ rest 📺   BV **z**
M (by arrangement) 8.00 **t.** 🍷 3.00 – **15 rm** ⇌ 25.00/50.00 **t.** – SB 52.00/80.00 **st.**

XXX ⚙ **21 Queen Street** (Laybourne), 21 Queen St., Princes Wharf, Quayside, NE1 3UG, ℰ 222 0755, Fax 261 9054 – 🕰 🖭 ⓪ 𝚅𝙸𝚂𝙰   CZ **a**
closed Saturday lunch, Sunday and Bank Holidays – **M** 16.00 **t.** (lunch) and a la carte 23.40/40.40 **t.** 🍷 5.50
Spec. Carpaccio of Tweed salmon with a pepper relish (spring and summer), Noisettes of Northumbrian lamb with Provençale vegetables and basil, Tarte tatin of mango with passion fruit syrup and mango sorbet.

XX **The Blackgate**, The Side, NE1 3JE, ℰ 261 7356 – 🕰 🖭 ⓪ 𝚅𝙸𝚂𝙰   CZ **x**
closed Saturday lunch, Monday dinner, Sunday and Bank Holidays – **M** 15.10/26.00 **t.** and a la carte.

XX **Vujon**, 29 Queen St., Princes Wharf, Quayside, NE1 3UG, ℰ 221 0601, Fax 221 0602 – 🖥. 🕰 🖭 ⓪ 𝚅𝙸𝚂𝙰 𝙹𝙲𝙱   CZ **i**
closed Sunday lunch and 25 December – **M** - Indian 15.00/20.00 **t.** and a la carte 🍷 4.00.

XX **Fisherman's Lodge**, Jesmond Dene, Jesmond, NE7 7BQ, ℰ 281 3281, Fax 281 6410 – ¾ 🄿. 🕰 🖭 ⓪ 𝚅𝙸𝚂𝙰   BV **e**
closed Saturday lunch, Sunday, 25 to 28 December, 1 to 3 January and Bank Holidays – **M** 19.00 **t.** (lunch) and a la carte 25.00/38.00 **t.** 🍷 5.00.

X **Courtney's**, 5-7 The Side, NE1 3JE, ℰ 232 5537 – 🕰 🖭 𝚅𝙸𝚂𝙰   CZ **v**
closed Saturday lunch, Sunday, 2 weeks May, 1 week Christmas and Bank Holidays – **M** 13.95 **t.** (lunch) and a la carte 15.95/22.85 **t.**

X **Leela's**, 20 Dean St., NE1 1PG, ℰ 230 1261 – 🕰 🖭 ⓪ 𝚅𝙸𝚂𝙰   CZ **e**
closed Sunday and Bank Holidays – **M** - South Indian 9.95/25.00 **t.** and a la carte 🍷 4.95.

at Gosforth N : 4 ¾ m. by B 1318 – AV – ✉ ⚙ 091 Tyneside :

🏨 **Swallow Gosforth Park**, High Gosforth Park, NE3 5HN, on B 1318 ℰ 236 4111, Fax 236 8192, ≤, 🏋, ⇌s, 🏊, ⛳, park, ⚒, squash – 📶 ¾ rm 📺 ☎ & 🄿 – 🚗 600. 🕰 🖭 ⓪ 𝚅𝙸𝚂𝙰
M 14.50/25.00 **st.** and a la carte 🍷 6.50 – **173 rm** ⇌ 98.00/130.00 **st.**, 5 suites – SB (weekends only) 130.00/234.00 **st.**

at Seaton Burn N : 8 m. by B 1318 – AV – ⊠ Newcastle upon Tyne – 🕿 091 Tyneside :

🏨 **Holiday Inn,** Great North Rd, NE13 6BP, N : ¾ m. at junction with A 1 ℰ 236 5432, Telex 53271, Fax 236 8091, ✿, ⊜s, ◨ – 笑 rm ▤ ㏗ 🕿 ♿ 🅿 – 🔥 300. 🔼 ﴾ⅈ ◑ 𝚅𝚂𝙰 𝙹𝙲𝙱. ✦ **M** (carving lunch) 15.85/25.00 **st.** and a la carte ⅋ 6.00 – ⌷ 9.75 – **149 rm** 95.00/120.00 **st.**, 1 suite – SB (weekends only) 76.00/98.00 **st.**

at Wallsend NE : 6 m. on A 1058 – BV – ⊠ Newcastle upon Tyne – 🕿 091 Tyneside :

🏨 Newcastle Moat House (Q.M.H.), Coast Rd, NE28 9HP, at junction with A 19 ℰ 262 8989, Telex 53583, Fax 263 4172, ✿, ⊜s – ▮𝚐▮ 笑 rm ㏗ 🕿 🅿 – 🔥 400 **146 rm.**

at Boldon E : 7 ¾ m. by A 184 - BX – 🕿 091 Tyneside

🏨 **Friendly,** Witney Way, Boldon Business Park, NE35 9PE, ℰ 519 1999, Fax 519 0655, ✿, ⊜s – 笑 rm ▤ rest ㏗ 🕿 ♿ 🅿 – 🔥 200. 🔼 ﴾ⅈ ◑ 𝚅𝚂𝙰 𝙹𝙲𝙱. ✦ **M** (closed Sunday lunch) 10.00/12.50 **st.** and dinner a la carte – ⌷ 6.75 – **82 rm** 57.00/ 85.50 **st.** – SB (weekends only) 84.00/90.00 **st.**

XX **Forsters,** 2 St. Bedes, Station Rd, East Boldon, NE36 OLE, ℰ 519 0929 – 🔼 ﴾ⅈ ◑ 𝚅𝚂𝙰 *closed Sunday, Monday and Bank Holidays* – **M** (dinner only) a la carte 17.70/23.85 **t.** ⅋ 5.00.

at Newcastle Airport NW : 6 ¾ m. by A 167 and A 696 AV – ⊠ Newcastle upon Tyne – 🕿 0661 Ponteland :

🏨 **Airport Moat House,** NE13 8DJ, ℰ 824911, Telex 537121, Fax 860157 – ▮𝚐▮ 笑 rm ㏗ 🕿 🅿 – 🔥 400. 🔼 ﴾ⅈ ◑ 𝚅𝚂𝙰 𝙹𝙲𝙱 **M** (closed Saturday lunch) 10.95/13.95 **st.** ⅋ 6.25 – **98 rm** ⌷ 69.00/79.00 **st.**, 2 suites – SB (weekends only) 80.00 **st.**

at Ponteland NW : 8 ¼ m. by A 167 on A 696 – ⊠ Newcastle upon Tyne – 🕿 0661 Ponteland :

XX **Horton Grange** with rm, NE13 6BU, NE : 3 ½ m. by Morpeth rd ℰ 860686, Fax 860308, ✿ – 笑 ㏗ 🕿 🅿 🔼 𝚅𝚂𝙰. ✦ *closed 25 and 26 December* – **Meals** (closed Sunday to non-residents) (booking essential) (dinner only) 29.90 **st.** ⅋ 4.80 – **9 rm** ⌷ 59.00/80.00 **t.** – SB 120.00 **st.**

⊕ ATS 80/90 Blenheim St. ℰ 232 3921/232 5031   ATS White St, Walker ℰ 262 0811
ATS Newton Park Garage, Newton Rd, Heaton
ℰ 281 2243

NEWENT Glos. 📖 403 404 M 28 – 🕿 0989 Ross-on-Wye.
◆London 109 – Gloucester 10 – Hereford 22 – Newport 44.

⌂ **Orchard House** ⏚, Aston Ingham Rd, Kilcot, GL18 1NP, SW : 2 ¼ m. by B 4221 on B 4222 ℰ 82417, ✿ – 笑 🅿. 🔼 𝚅𝚂𝙰. ✦ **M** 16.50 **st.** ⅋ 4.00 – **3 rm** ⌷ 29.00/55.00 **st.**

NEWHAVEN E. Sussex 404 U 31 – pop. 10 697 – ECD : Wednesday – 🕿 0273.
⌨ to France : Dieppe (Stena Sealink Line) (4 h) (4 daily).
◆London 63 – ◆Brighton 9 – Eastbourne 14 – Lewes 7.

Hotels and restaurants see : Lewes NW : 7 m. by A 26.

NEWINGTON Kent 404 V/W 29 – 🕿 0795.
◆London 40 – Canterbury 20 – Maidstone 13.

🏨 **Newington Manor,** Callaways Lane, ME9 7LU, ℰ 842053, Fax 844273, ✿ – ㏗ 🕿 🅿. 🔼 ﴾ⅈ ◑ 𝚅𝚂𝙰 *closed 26 to 31 December* – **M** (closed Saturday lunch, Sunday dinner and Bank Holiday Mondays) 14.95 **st.** and a la carte ⅋ 5.65 – ⌷ 4.00 – **12 rm** 48.00/90.00 **st.** – SB (weekends only) 61.00/102.00 **st.**

NEWLYN Cornwall 403 D 33 – see Penzance.

NEWMARKET Suffolk 404 V 27 – pop. 15 861 – ECD : Wednesday – 🕿 0638.
📐 Links, Cambridge Rd ℰ 662708, S : 1 m.
🎫 63 The Rookery, CB8 8HT ℰ 667200.
◆London 64 – ◆Cambridge 13 – ◆Ipswich 40 – ◆Norwich 48.

🏨 **Bedford Lodge** (Best Western), Bury Rd, CB8 7BX, NE : ½ m. on B 1506 ℰ 663175, Fax 667391, ✿ – 笑 ㏗ 🕿 ♿ 🅿 – 🔥 200. 🔼 ﴾ⅈ ◑ 𝚅𝚂𝙰 𝙹𝙲𝙱 **M** 15.95 **s.** and a la carte – **49 rm** ⌷ 65.00/95.00 **st.**, 7 suites – SB (except Christmas and New Year) 85.00/95.00 **st.**

🏨 **Newmarket Moat House** (Q.M.H.), Moulton Rd, CB8 8DY, ℰ 667171, Fax 666533 – ▮𝚐▮ ㏗ 🕿 🅿 – 🔥 80. 🔼 ﴾ⅈ ◑ 𝚅𝚂𝙰 **M** (bar lunch Saturday) 15.95 **t.** and a la carte ⅋ 4.75 – **47 rm** ⌷ 55.00/95.00 **st.** – SB (weekends only) 84.00 **st.**

🏨 **White Hart** (Chef & Brewer), High St., CB8 8JP, ℰ 663051, Fax 667284 – ㏗ 🕿 🅿 – 🔥 150. 🔼 ﴾ⅈ 𝚅𝚂𝙰 ✦ **M** 15.00/20.00 **t.** and a la carte – **23 rm** ⌷ 44.95/48.45 **t.**

at Six Mile Bottom (Cambs.) SW : 6 m. on A 1304 – ⊠ Newmarket – 🕲 063 870 (3 fig.) and 0638 (6 fig.) Six Mile Bottom :

🏠 **Swynford Paddocks,** CB8 0UE, 🖉 234, Fax 283, ≤, « Country house », 🐎, park, 🎾 – ⇆ rest 📺 ☎ 🅿 – 🕍 30. 🖎 🖭 ⑩ 𝘝𝘐𝘚𝘈
closed 4 days Christmas-New Year – **M** *(closed Saturday lunch)* 16.95/21.95 **st.** and a la carte ⅄ 4.50 – **15 rm** ⇌ 75.00/140.00 **st.** – SB 130.00/150.00 **st.**

🛢 ATS 2 Exeter Rd 🖉 662521

NEWMILLERDAM W. Yorks. – see Wakefield.

NEW MILTON Hants. **403 404** P 31 – ECD : Wednesday – 🕲 0425.

🏌 Barton-on-Sea, Milford Rd 🖉 615308, S : 1 m. off B 3058.

◆London 106 – Bournemouth 12 – ◆Southampton 21 – Winchester 34.

🏰 **Chewton Glen** ⌂, Christchurch Rd, BH25 6QS, W : 2 m. by A 337 and Ringwood Rd on Chewton Farm Rd 🖉 275341, Fax 272310, ≤, « Gardens », 🏌, ⓢ, 🔼 heated, 🖎, 🟥, park, 🎾 – 📺 ☎ 🅿 – 🕍 70. 🖎 🖭 ⑩ 𝘝𝘐𝘚𝘈 🛠
M 25.00/39.00 **st.** and a la carte approx. 39.00 **st.** ⅄ 6.75 – ⇌ 14.00 – **45 rm** 165.00/ 280.00 **st.**, 13 suites – SB (except Bank Holidays) 255.00/367.00 **st.**

NEWPORT Essex **404** U 28 – pop. 1 999 – ⊠ 🕲 0799 Saffron Walden.

◆London 38 – ◆Cambridge 21 – Colchester 41.

🍽 **Village House,** High St., CB11 3PF, 🖉 41560 – 🅿. 🖎 𝘝𝘐𝘚𝘈
closed Sunday, Monday and January – **M** (dinner only) a la carte 19.00/24.00 **t.** ⅄ 4.00.

NEWPORT Shrops. **402 403 404** M 25 Great Britain G. – pop. 10 339 – ECD : Thursday – 🕲 0952.

Exc. : Weston Park★★, SE : 6½ m. by A 41 and A 5.

◆London 150 – ◆Birmingham 33 – Shrewsbury 18 – ◆Stoke-on-Trent 21.

🏨 Royal Victoria, St. Mary's St., TF10 7AB, 🖉 820331, Fax 820209 – 📺 ☎ 🅿
24 rm.

NEWPORT I.O.W. **403 404** Q 31 – see Wight (Isle of).

NEWPORT PAGNELL Bucks. **404** R 27 – pop. 10 733 – ECD : Thursday – 🕲 0908.

◆London 57 – Bedford 13 – Luton 21 – Northampton 15.

🏠 **Coach House** (Lansbury), London Rd, Moulsoe, MK16 0JA, SE : 1 ½ m. by B 526 on A 509 🖉 613688, Fax 617335, ⓢ, 🐎 – ⇆ rm 📺 ☎ 🅿 – 🕍 180. 🖎 🖭 ⑩ 𝘝𝘐𝘚𝘈 🛠
M 14.95/16.95 **t.** and dinner a la carte ⅄ 5.95 – **49 rm** ⇌ 79.50/91.00 **t.** – SB (weekends only) 84.00 **st.**

🏨 **Swan Revived,** High St., MK16 8AR, 🖉 610565, Fax 210995 – ⧏| 📺 ☎ 🅿 – 🕍 50. 🖎 🖭 ⑩ 𝘝𝘐𝘚𝘈
M (bar lunch Saturday and Monday to Saturday in August) a la carte 13.00/18.10 **t.** ⅄ 5.00 – **40 rm** ⇌ 58.00/85.00 **st.** – SB (weekends only) 80.00 **st.**

NEWQUAY Cornwall **403** E 32 The West Country G. – pop. 13 905 – ECD : Wednesday – 🕲 0637.

Envir. : Penhale Point and Kelsey Head★ (≤★★) SW : by A 3075 Y – Trerice★ AC, SE : 3½ m. by A 392 - Y - and A 3058.

Exc. : St. Agnes - St. Agnes Beacon (✸★★) SW : 12½ m. by A 3075 – Y – and B 3285.

🏌 Tower Rd 🖉 872091 Z – 🏌 Treloy 🖉 878554 Y.

✈ Newquay Airport 🖉 860551 Y.

🅸 Municipal Offices, Marcus Hill, TR7 1BD 🖉 871345.

◆London 291 – Exeter 83 – Penzance 34 – ◆Plymouth 48 – Truro 14.

Plan on next page

🏠 **Bristol,** Narrowcliff, TR7 2PQ, 🖉 875181, Fax 879347, ≤, ⓢ, 🖎 – ⧏| 📺 ☎ 🅿 – 🕍 150.
🖎 🖭 ⑩ 𝘝𝘐𝘚𝘈   Z **r**
M 9.95/16.00 **st.** and a la carte ⅄ 5.00 – **73 rm** ⇌ 50.00/90.00 **st.**, 1 suite – SB (September-May except Easter and Christmas-New Year) (weekends only) 95.00 **st.**

🏨 **Trebarwith,** Trebarwith Cres., TR7 1BZ, 🖉 872288, ≤ bay and coast, ⓢ, 🖎, 🐎 –
⇆ rest 📺 ☎ 🅿 🖎 𝘝𝘐𝘚𝘈   Z **a**
April-October – **M** (bar lunch)/dinner 13.50 **st.** ⅄ 4.50 – **41 rm** ⇌ 40.00/80.00 **st.**

🏨 **Kilbirnie,** Narrowcliff, TR7 2RS, 🖉 875155, Fax 850769, ⓢ, 🔼 heated, 🖎 – ⧏| 📺 ☎ 🅿.
🖎 𝘝𝘐𝘚𝘈   Z **e**
M (bar lunch)/dinner 10.50 **t.** ⅄ 4.25 – **68 rm** ⇌ 40.00/80.00 **t.** – SB (November-May) (except Easter, Christmas and New Year) 64.00/80.00 **st.**

🏨 **Windsor,** Mount Wise, TR7 2AY, 🖉 875188, ⓢ, 🔼 heated, 🖎, 🐎, squash – ⇆ rest 📺
☎ 🅿. 🖎 🖭 ⑩ 𝘝𝘐𝘚𝘈 🛠   Z **n**
closed January-14 February – **M** (bar lunch Monday to Saturday)/dinner 15.00 **st.** and a la carte ⅄ 3.50 – **44 rm** ⇌ 25.00/88.00 **st.** – SB (September-June) 80.00/96.00 **st.**

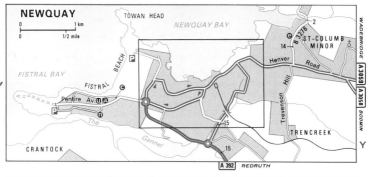

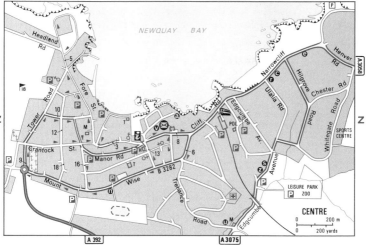

🏥 Esplanade, Esplanade Rd, Pentire, TR7 1PS, ℰ 873333, Fax 851413, ≤, ≘s, ⬜ – 🛗 ❧ rest 📺 ☎ 🅿   Y **a**
M (dinner only) – **76 rm.**

🏥 **New Garth,** Narrowcliff, TR7 2PG, ℰ 873250, Fax 850564, ≤ – 🛗 📺 ☎ 🅿. 🔼 ⒜ℰ 𝘝𝘐𝘚𝘈. ❧
closed January-March – **M** (bar lunch)/dinner 8.50 **t.** and a la carte 🍴 3.95 – **51 rm** ⬜ 30.00/60.00 **t.** – SB (except summer) 36.00/50.00 **st.**   Z **c**

🏨 **Water's Edge,** Esplanade Rd, Pentire, TR7 1QA, ℰ 872048, ≤ Fistral Bay, 🐎 – ❧ rest 📺 ☎ 🅿. 🔼 𝘝𝘐𝘚𝘈. ❧   Y **u**
May-September and Easter – **M** (residents only) (dinner only) 🍴 3.95 – **20 rm** ⬜ (dinner included) 25.00/76.00 **t.**

🏨 **Corisande Manor** ⌂, Riverside Av., Pentire, TR7 1PL, ℰ 872042, ≤ Gannel Estuary, 🐎 – 📺 🅿. 🔼   Y **n**
15 May-9 October – **M** (bar lunch)/dinner 16.00 **t.** 🍴 5.00 – **19 rm** ⬜ 20.00/52.00 **t.** – SB (except July and August) 55.00/66.00 **st.**

🏨 Philema, Esplanade Rd, Pentire, TR7 1PY, ℰ 872571, Fax 873188, ≤, ≘s, ⬜ – 📺 ☎ 🅿   Y **c**
31 rm.

🏨 **Whipsiderry,** Trevelgue Rd, Porth, TR7 3LY, NE : 2 m. by A 392 off B 3276 ℰ 874777, ≤, ≘s, ⬜ heated, 🐎 – ❧ rest 📺 🅿. 🔼   Y
Easter-October and Christmas-New Year – **M** (bar lunch)/dinner 12.75 **st.** 🍴 4.95 – **23 rm** ⬜ 28.50/56.00 **st.**

🏠 **Porth Veor Manor** 🦢, Porth Way, TR7 3LW, 🖋 873274, Fax 851690, 🖘 – 🍴 rest 📺 🅿.
🔼 *VISA*   Y **e**
M 8.95/12.85 **t.** and dinner a la carte ⏐ 4.50 – **16 rm** ⊇ 28.00/65.00 **t.** – SB (8 October-20 May) 60.00 **st.**

🏠 **Trenance Lodge,** 83 Trenance Rd, TR7 2HW, 🖋 876702, 🔥 heated, 🖘 – 🍴 📺 🅿. 🔼
VISA 🍽   Z **u**
M (dinner only) 18.00 **t.** and a la carte ⏐ 3.50 – **5 rm** ⊇ 25.00/60.00 – SB 66.00/90.00 **st.**

🏠 **Wheal Treasure,** 72 Edgcumbe Av., TR7 2NN, 🖋 874136 – 🍴 rest 📺 🅿. 🍽   Z **z**
Easter-October – **M** 8.00 **st.** – **12 rm** ⊇ 25.00/46.00 **st.**

🏠 **Copper Beech,** 70 Edgcumbe Av., TR7 2NN, 🖋 873376 – 🍴 rest 📺 🅿. 🍽   Z **s**
Easter-October – **M** approx. 8.50 – **15 rm** ⊇ 16.45/40.00 **st.**

🏠 **Towan Beach,** 7 Trebarwith Cres., TR7 1DX, 🖋 872093 – 🍴 rest 📺. 🔼 *VISA*. 🍽 Z **v**
May-September – **M** (by arrangement) 8.50 **st.** ⏐ 3.00 – **6 rm** ⊇ 20.00/44.00 **st.** – SB 48.00/58.00 **st.**

at Trerice SE : 4 ¾ m. by A 392 off A 3058 – Y – ⊠ Newquay – 🕿 0872 Mitchell :

🏠 **Trewerry Mill** 🦢, TR8 5HS, W : ½ m. 🖋 510345, 🖘 – 🍴 🅿. 🍽
April-October – **M** (by arrangement) – **6 rm** ⊇ 17.00/34.00 **st.** – SB 43.00/47.00 **st.**

at Crantock SW : 4 m. by A 3075 – Y – ⊠ Newquay – 🕿 0637 Crantock :

🏠 **Crantock Bay** 🦢, West Pentire, TR8 5SE, W : ¾ m. 🖋 830229, Fax 831111, ≤ Crantock
Bay, ⅃₅, ≋s, 🔲, 🖘, 🍽 – 🍴 rest 📺 🕿 🅿. 🔼 ᴬᴱ ⓞ *VISA*
mid March-mid November – **M** (buffet lunch)/dinner 14.95 **t.** ⏐ 4.00 – **35 rm** ⊇ 27.00/80.00 **st.**

🏠 **Crantock Plains Farmhouse,** Cubert, TR8 5PH, SE : 1 ½ m. bearing right at the fork in
the road 🖋 830253, 🖘 – 🍽
closed November and December – **M** (by arrangement) 8.00 **st.** – **7 rm** ⊇ 14.00/42.00 **st.**

NEWTON POPPLEFORD Devon 🔟🔟🔟 K 31 – pop. 1 373 – ⊠ Ottery St. Mary – 🕿 0395 Colaton
Rayleigh.

♦London 208 – Exeter 10 – Sidmouth 4.

🏠 **Coach House** 🦢, Southerton, EX11 1SE, N : 1 m. by Venn Ottery Rd 🖋 68577, 🖘 – 🍴
📺 🕿 🅿. 🔼 *VISA*. 🍽
M *(closed lunch Monday to Wednesday)* (booking essential) 7.50/17.50 **st.** ⏐ 4.20 – **6 rm**
⊇ 31.00/70.00 **st.**

NEWTON SOLNEY Derbs. 🔟🔟🔟 🔟🔟🔟 🔟🔟🔟 P 25 – see Burton-upon-Trent (Staffs.).

NITON I.O.W. 🔟🔟🔟 🔟🔟🔟 Q 32 – see Wight (Isle of).

NORMAN CROSS Cambs. 🔟🔟🔟 T 26 – see Peterborough.

NORMANTON PARK Leics. – see Stamford.

NORTHALLERTON N. Yorks. 🔟🔟🔟 P 20 – pop. 13 566 – ECD : Thursday – 🕿 0609.

🅱 Applegarth Car Park, DL7 8LZ 🖋 776864.

♦London 238 – ♦Leeds 48 – ♦Middlesbrough 24 – York 33.

🏨 **Golden Lion** (Forte), 114 High St., DL7 8PP, 🖋 777411, Fax 773250 – 🍴 rm 📺 🕿 🅿 –
🔼 100. 🔼 ᴬᴱ ⓞ *VISA* 🔤
M (bar lunch Monday to Saturday)/dinner 15.95 **t.** and a la carte ⏐ 6.45 – **24 rm** ⊇ 70.00/80.00 **t.** – SB 108.00/118.00 **st.**

🏠 **Windsor,** 56 South Par., DL7 8SL, 🖋 774100 – 📺. 🔼 *VISA*
closed 23 February-4 March – **M** 9.00 – **6 rm** ⊇ 19.00/36.00 **st.**

🍽🍽 **Pietro and Nino Romanby Court,** High St., DL7 8PG, 🖋 774918 – 🔼 ᴬᴱ ⓞ *VISA*
*closed Sunday, Monday. 16 to 31 January, 17 July-1 August and Bank Holidays except
Good Friday* – **M** - Italian a la carte 13.45/20.85 **t.** ⏐ 4.75.

at Staddlebridge NE : 7 ½ m. by A 684 on A 19 at junction with A 172 – ⊠ Northallerton
– 🕿 0609 East Harlsey :

🍽🍽 McCoys at the Tontine with rm, DL6 3JB, 🖋 882671, Fax 882660, « 1930's decor » – ▭ 📺
🕿 🅿. 🍽
6 rm.

at Newby Wiske S : 2½ m. by A 167 – ⊠ 🕿 0609 Northallerton :

🏨 **Solberge Hall** (Best Western) 🦢, DL7 9ER, NW : 1 ¼ m. on Warlaby rd 🖋 779191,
Fax 780472, ≤, 🖘, park – 📺 🕿 🅿 – 🔼 100. 🔼 ᴬᴱ ⓞ *VISA*
M 9.95/19.50 **st.** and a la carte – **24 rm** ⊇ 55.00/75.00 **st.**, 1 suite – SB (except Christmas
and New Year) 90.00/100.00 **st.**

"Short Breaks" (SB)

De nombreux hôtels proposent des conditions avantageuses

pour un séjour de deux nuits

comprenant la chambre, le dîner et le petit déjeuner.

NORTHAMPTON

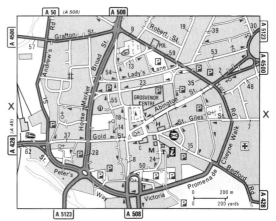

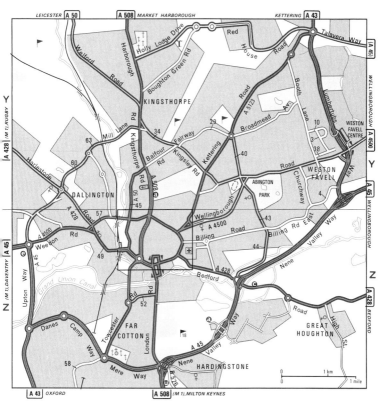

Exc. : All Saints, Brixworth★, N : 7 m. on A 508 Y.

🏌, 🏌 Delapre, Eagle Drive, Nene Valley Way ℘ 764036/763957, by A 508 Z – 🏌 Collingtree Park, Windingbrook Lane ℘ 700000, S : 2 m. by A 508 Z.

🛈 Visitor Centre, Mr Grant's House, 10 St. Giles Square, NN1 1DA ℘ 604180.

◆London 69 – ◆Cambridge 53 – ◆Coventry 34 – ◆Leicester 42 – Luton 35 – ◆Oxford 41.

Plans on preceding page

🏨 **Swallow,** Eagle Drive, NN4 7HW, SE : 2 m. by A 428 off A 45 ℘ 768700, Fax 769011, 𝕀₅,
⇌s, 🔲 – ╪ rm 🖳 rest 📺 ☎ & ℗ – 🔬 150. 🔼 🄰🄴 🄾 𝘝𝘐𝘚𝘈 . 🍴 Z **a**
M 13.50/18.00 **st.** and a la carte 🛊 6.00 – **122 rm** 89.50/125.00 **st.** – SB (except Christmas and New Year) (weekends only) 90.00/220.00 **st.**

🏨 **Stakis Country Court,** 100 Watering Lane, Collingtree, NN4 0XW, S : 3 m. on A 508 ℘ 700666, Telex 312523, Fax 702850, 𝕀₅, ⇌s, 🔲, ⟲ – ╪ rm 🖳 rest 📺 ☎ & ℗ – 🔬 300.
🔼 🄰🄴 🄾 𝘝𝘐𝘚𝘈 𝘑𝘊𝘉 Z
M 13.75/16.95 **st.** and a la carte – 🖵 8.95 – **136 rm** 89.00/109.00 **st.**, 3 suites – SB 90.00/120.00 **st.**

🏨 Northampton Moat House (Q.M.H.), Silver St., NN1 2TA, ℘ 22441, Fax 230614, 𝕀₅, ⇌s –
🕴 ╪ rm 📺 ☎ ℗ – 🔬 600 X **n**
136 rm, 4 suites.

🏨 **Courtyard by Marriott,** Bedford Rd, NN4 0YF, SE : 1 ½ m. on A 428 ℘ 22777, Fax 35454, 𝕀₅ – 🕴 ╪ rm 📺 ☎ ℗ – 🔬 30. 🔼 🄰🄴 🄾 𝘝𝘐𝘚𝘈 𝘑𝘊𝘉 Z **c**
M 12.95 **t.** and a la carte 🛊 5.45 – 🖵 7.50 – **104 rm** 39.00/62.50 **st.**

🏨 **Midway Toby,** London Rd, Wootton, NN4 0TG, S : 2 ½ m. on A 508 ℘ 769676, Fax 769523 – ╪ rm 🖳 rest 📺 ☎ & ℗ – 🔬 60. 🔼 🄰🄴 🄾 𝘝𝘐𝘚𝘈 Z
M (grill rest.) approx. 15.00 **t.** – **29 rm** 🖵 59.00/69.00 **t.**

🏨 **Queen Eleanor** (Chef & Brewer), Newport Pagnell Rd West, Wootton, NN4 0JJ, S : 1 ¾ m. by A 508 on B 526 ℘ 700220, Fax 706191, ⟲ – 📺 ☎ ℗ – 🔬 60. 🔼 🄰🄴 𝘝𝘐𝘚𝘈 . 🍴 Z **u**
M (grill rest.) 15.00/20.00 **t.** and a la carte – **19 rm** 🖵 34.95/38.45 **t.**

🏨 **Lime Trees,** 8 Langham Pl., Barrack Rd, NN2 6AA, ℘ 32188, Fax 233012 – 🖳 rest 📺 ☎ ℗. 🔼 🄰🄴 🄾 𝘝𝘐𝘚𝘈 . 🍴 Y **a**
closed 25 and 26 December – **M** *(closed Sunday and Bank Holidays)* (lunch by arrangement)/dinner 20.00 **t.** and a la carte 🛊 4.00 – **21 rm** 🖵 46.00/59.00 **t.** – SB (weekends only) 78.00/83.00 **st.**

🏠 **Travel Inn,** Harpole Turn, Weedon Rd, NN7 4DD, W : 3 ¾ m. on A 45 ℘ 832340, Fax 831807 – ╪ rm 📺 & ℗ – 🔬 60. 🔼 🄰🄴 🄾 𝘝𝘐𝘚𝘈 . 🍴 Z
M (Beefeater grill) a la carte approx. 16.00 **t.** – 🖵 4.95 – **51 rm** 33.50 **t.**

🏠 **Forte Travelodge** without rest., Upton Way (Ring Rd), NN5 6EG, SW : 1 ¾ m. by A 45 ℘ 758395, Reservations (Freephone) 0800 850950 – 📺 & ℗. 🔼 🄰🄴 𝘝𝘐𝘚𝘈 . 🍴 Z **e**
40 rm 31.95 **t.** Y

at Spratton N : 7 m. by A 508 off A 50 – Y – ✉ ⓕ 0604 Northampton :

🏠 **Broomhill** ⌂, Holdenby Rd, NN6 8LD, SW : 1 m. on Holdenby rd ℘ 845959, Fax 845834, ⪕, 🌳 heated, ⟲, park, 🎾 – 📺 ☎ ℗. 🔼 🄰🄴 🄾 𝘝𝘐𝘚𝘈 . 🍴
closed 25 and 26 December – **M** *(closed Sunday dinner)* 16.50 **t.** and a la carte 🛊 5.30 – **13 rm** 🖵 60.00/70.00 **t.** – SB (weekends only) 87.00/125.00 **st.**

at Moulton NE : 4 ½ m. by A 43 – Y – ✉ ⓕ 0604 Northampton :

⌂ **Poplars,** 33 Cross St., NN3 1RZ, ℘ 643983, ⟲ – 📺 ℗. 🔼 🄰🄴 𝘝𝘐𝘚𝘈
closed 1 week Christmas – **M** (by arrangement) 15.00 **t.** 🛊 3.50 – **21 rm** 🖵 25.00/45.00 **t.** – SB (weekends only) 55.00/95.00 **st.**

🛆 ATS Kingsthorpe Rd ℘ 713303

Envir. : Dartmoor National Park★★ (Brent Tor ⪕★★, Haytor Rocks ⪕★).

◆London 214 – Exeter 13 – ◆Plymouth 31 – Torquay 21.

⌂ **Blackaller House** ⌂, TQ13 8OY, ℘ 40322, ⪕, ⟲ – 📺 ℗
closed January – **M** (booking essential) 17.00 **st.** – **5 rm** 🖵 24.00/50.00 **st.** – SB 78.00 **st.**

See : Church of SS. Peter and Paul★ – Wool Merchants' Brasses★.

🛈 Cotswold Countryside Collection, GL54 3JH ℘ 860715 (summer only).

◆London 84 – ◆Birmingham 63 – Gloucester 21 – ◆Oxford 28 – Swindon 24.

XX **Wickens,** Market Pl., GL54 3EJ, ℰ 860421 – ⇆
closed Sunday and Monday – **M** (lunch by arrangement October-April) a la carte 16.55/
25.80 **st.** ₰ 4.25.

NORTH MUSKHAM Notts. 402 404 R 24 – see Newark-on-Trent.

NORTH NEWINGTON Oxon – see Banbury.

NORTH NIBLEY Glos. 403 404 M 29 – pop. 814 – ⊠ 🕸 0453 Dursley.

◆London 115 – ◆Bristol 21 – Gloucester 20 – Swindon 32.

🏠 **Burrows Court** 🌿, Nibley Green, GL11 6AZ, NW : 1 m. via The Street ℰ 546230, 🏊, ⇶
– ⇆ rest 📺 🅿. 🔼 🖭 VISA 🛇
M (residents only) (dinner only) 13.50 **st.** ₰ 3.50 – **10 rm** ⊑ 25.00/50.00 **st.** – SB (except
Bank Holidays) 56.00/80.00 **st.**

NORTH PERROT Somerset – see Crewkerne.

NORTH PETHERTON Somerset 403 K 30 – see Bridgwater.

NORTH STIFFORD Essex 404 ㊵ – ⊠ Grays – 🕸 0375 Grays Thurrock.

◆London 22 – Chelmsford 24 – Southend-on-Sea 20.

🏨 **Stifford Moat House** (Q.M.H.), High Rd, RM16 1UE, at junction of A 13 with A 1012
ℰ 390909, Fax 390426, ⇶, 🛇 – ▯ ⇆ rm 📺 ☎ ₰ 🅿 – 🔬 120. 🔼 🖭 ⓪ VISA
M *(closed Saturday lunch)* 17.50 **st.** and a la carte ₰ 5.95 – ⊑ 7.95 – **96 rm** 67.50/115.00 **st.**
– SB (weekends only) 70.00/76.00 **st.**

La guida cambia, cambiate la guida ogni anno.

NORTH STOKE Oxon. – see Wallingford.

NORTH WALSHAM Norfolk 403 404 Y 25 Great Britain G. – pop. 7 929 – ECD : Wednesday –
🕸 0692.

Exc. : Blicking Hall★★ *AC*, W : 8½ m. by B 1145, A 140 and B 1354.

◆London 125 – ◆Norwich 16.

↰ **Beechwood,** 20 Cromer Rd, NR28 0HD, ℰ 403231, ⇶ – ⇆ rest 🅿
closed 25 December-1 January – **M** 10.00 **t.** ₰ 3.50 – **11 rm** ⊑ 26.00/52.00 **t.** – SB 56.00/
70.00 **st.**

NORTH WALTHAM Hants. 403 404 Q 30 – pop. 692 – ⊠ 🕸 0256 Basingstoke.

◆London 59 – Reading 24 – Southampton 24 – Swindon 52.

🏨 **Wheatsheaf,** RG25 2BB, S : ¾ m. on A 30 ℰ 398282, Fax 398253 – ⇆ rm 📺 ☎ ₰ –
🔬 80. 🔼 🖭 ⓪ VISA
M (bar lunch Saturday) 11.95/13.95 **t.** and a la carte ₰ 5.95 – **28 rm** ⊑ 45.00/56.50 **t.** –
SB (except Christmas) (weekends only) 56.50/90.00 **st.**

NORTHWICH Ches. 402 403 404 M 24 – pop. 17 195 – 🕸 0606.

◆London 187 – ◆Liverpool 36 – ◆Manchester 18 – ◆Stoke-on-Trent 26.

🏠 Quincey's, London Rd, Leftwich, CW9 8EG, S : 1¼ m. on A 533 ℰ 45524, Fax 330350 – 📺
☎ ₰ – 🔬 40
33 rm.

🔩 ATS Albion Rd ℰ 48417/48418/42485

NORTON Shrops. – see Telford.

NORTON ST PHILIP Somerset 403 404 N 30 – see Bath (Avon).

NORWICH Norfolk 404 Y 26 Great Britain G. – pop. 169 814 – 🕸 0603.

See : City★★ – Cathedral★★ Y – Castle (Museum and Art Gallery★ *AC*) Z – Market Place★ Z.

Envir. : Sainsbury Centre for Visual Arts★ *AC*, W : 3 m. by B 1108 - X.

Exc. : Blicking Hall★★ *AC*, N : 11 m. by A 140 – V – and B 1354 – NE : The Broads★.

🏌 Royal Norwich, Hellesdon ℰ 425712, by A 1067 V – 🏌 Sprowston Park, Wroxham Rd
ℰ 410657, NE : 2 m. by A 1151 V – 🏌 Costessy Park ℰ 746333, W : 3 m. by A 47 V –
🏌 Bawburgh, Long Lane ℰ 746360, W : 3 m. by B 1108 X.

✈ Norwich Airport ℰ 411923, N : 3½ m. by A 140 V.

🛈 The Guildhall, Gaol Hill, NR2 1NF ℰ 666071.

◆London 109 – ◆Kingston-upon-Hull 148 – ◆Leicester 117 – ◆Nottingham 120.

Plans on following pages

🏨 **Sprowston Manor** (Best Western), Wroxham Rd, Sprowston, NR7 8RP, NE : 3¼ m. on
A 1151 ℰ 410871, Telex 975356, Fax 423911, ₰, ≋, 🏊, ⇶ – ▯ ≣ rest 📺 ☎ ₰ – 🔬 100.
🔼 🖭 ⓪ VISA 🛇   V
M 16.00/40.00 **t.** and a la carte ₰ 7.25 – ⊑ 8.25 – **96 rm** 75.00/85.00 **t.**, 1 suite – SB (except
Christmas and New Year) (weekdays only) 119.00/215.00 **st.**

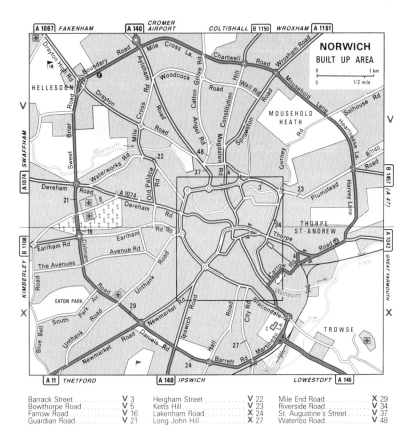

🏨 **Maid's Head** (Q.M.H.), Tombland, NR3 1LB, ℰ 761111, Fax 613688 – 🛗 📺 ☎ Ⓟ – 🕍 100
80 rm, 1 suite. **u**

🏨 **Airport Ambassador,** Norwich Airport, NR6 6JA, N : 3 m. by A 140 ℰ 410544,
Fax 789935, ₤₅, ≦ₛ, 🔲 – 🛗 ⇔ rm 🔟 rest 📺 ☎ 🕭 Ⓟ – 🕍 450. 🔼 🆎 ⓪ 𝘝𝘐𝘚𝘈   V
M 11.50/12.95 **st.** and a la carte ₳ 5.00 – **107 rm** ⇄ 63.00/89.00 **st.**

🏨 **Nelson,** Prince of Wales Rd, NR1 1DX, ℰ 760260, Fax 620008, ≤ – 🛗 🔟 rest 📺 ☎ 🕭 Ⓟ –
🕍 90. 🔼 🆎 ⓪ 𝘝𝘐𝘚𝘈 ⊗   Z **a**
M (closed lunch Saturday and Bank Holidays) 10.75/13.50 **st.** and a la carte ₳ 4.25 – **118 rm**
⇄ 71.00/100.00 **st.**, 3 suites – SB (except Christmas) 95.00/107.00 **st.**

🏨 **Friendly,** 2 Barnard Rd, Bowthorpe, NR5 9JB, W : 3 ½ m. by A 1074 on A 47 – X –
ℰ 741141, Fax 741500, ₤₅, ≦ₛ, 🔲 – ⇔ rm 📺 ☎ 🕭 Ⓟ – 🕍 180. 🔼 🆎 ⓪ 𝘝𝘐𝘚𝘈 𝗝𝗖𝗕
⊗
M (closed Saturday lunch) (carving lunch) 10.00/12.50 **st.** and a la carte – ⇄ 6.75 – **80 rm**
57.00/85.50 **st.** – SB (weekends only) 84.00/90.00 **st.**

🏨 **Forte Posthouse,** Ipswich Rd, NR4 6EP, S : 2 ¼ m. on A 140 ℰ 56431, Fax 506400, ₤₅,
≦ₛ, 🔲 – ⇔ rm 📺 ☎ Ⓟ – 🕍 65. 🔼 🆎 ⓪ 𝘝𝘐𝘚𝘈 𝗝𝗖𝗕   X
M a la carte approx. 17.50 **t.** ₳ 4.65 – ⇄ 6.95 – **116 rm** 53.50 **st.** – SB 90.00 **st.**

🏨 **Norwich** (Best Western), 121 Boundary Rd, NR3 2BA, on A 47 ℰ 787260, Fax 400466, ₤₅,
≦ₛ, 🔲 – ⇔ rm 🔟 rest 📺 ☎ 🕭 Ⓟ – 🕍 300. 🔼 🆎 ⓪ 𝘝𝘐𝘚𝘈 ⊗   V **r**
M (closed Saturday lunch) (carving lunch)/dinner 15.00 **st.** and a la carte ₳ 4.65 – **108 rm**
⇄ 56.50/66.50 **st.** – SB (except Christmas) 89.00/94.00 **st.**

🏠 **Cumberland,** 212-216 Thorpe Rd, NR1 1TJ, ℰ 34550, Fax 33355 – 📺 ☎ Ⓟ. 🔼 🆎 ⓪ 𝘝𝘐𝘚𝘈
𝗝𝗖𝗕 ⊗   X **a**
closed 25 December-4 January – **M** (by arrangement) 16.50 **st.** ₳ 3.95 – **27 rm** ⇄ 34.90/
75.00 **st.** – SB (except 10 to 20 July and 25-26 December) 64.00/84.00 **st.**

NORWICH

Castle Mall
Shopping Centre . . . . **Z**
Elm Hill . . . . **Y**
Gentleman's Walk . . . . **Z** 17
London Street . . . . **YZ** 26
St. Andrew's Street . . . . **Y** 36
St. Stephen's Street . . . . **Z**

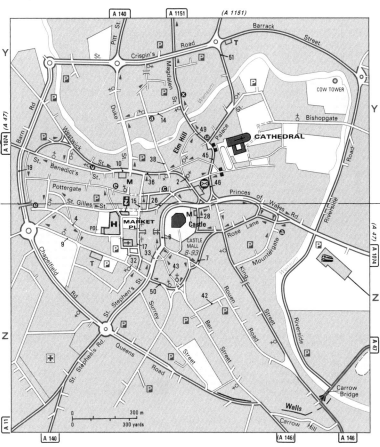

XX **Adlard's,** 79 Upper St. Giles St., NR2 1AB, ℰ 633522 – ◪ 🅰🅴 𝘝𝘐𝘚𝘈   Z **e**
closed Saturday lunch, Sunday and Monday – **M** 15.00/32.00 **t.** and dinner a la carte.

XX **Marco's,** 17 Pottergate, NR2 1DS, ℰ 624044 – 🍴. ◪ 🅰🅴 ⓪ 𝘝𝘐𝘚𝘈   Y **e**
closed Sunday, Monday, 3 weeks September-October and Bank Holidays – **M** - **Italian**
19.00 **t.** (lunch) and a la carte 23.10/30.00 **t.** ⓪ 4.25.

XX **By Appointment,** 27-29 St. Georges St., NR3 1AB, ℰ 630730 – ◪ 𝘝𝘐𝘚𝘈   Y **a**
closed Sunday – **M** (dinner only) a la carte 17.85/24.65 **t.** ⓪ 8.95.

XX **Brasted's,** 8-10 St. Andrew's Hill, NR2 1AD, ℰ 625949, Fax 766445 – ◪ 🅰🅴 ⓪ 𝘝𝘐𝘚𝘈
closed Saturday lunch, Sunday, last 2 weeks August and Bank Holidays – **M** 13.50 **t.** (lunch)
and a la carte 22.50/26.50 **t.** ⓪ 5.00.   Y **c**

X **Bombay,** 9-11 Magdalen St., NR3 1LE, ℰ 666618 – ◪ 🅰🅴 ⓪ 𝘝𝘐𝘚𝘈 🅹🅲🅱   Y **x**
closed 25 December – **M** - **Indian** a la carte 9.85/19.35 **t.**

X **St. Benedicts Grill,** 9 St. Benedict's St., NR2 4PE, ℰ 765377 – ◪ 🅰🅴 𝘝𝘐𝘚𝘈   Y **v**
closed Sunday, Monday and 25 to 31 December – **M** a la carte 12.85/18.40 **t.** ⓪ 4.95.

at Horsham St. Faith N : 4 ½ m. by A 140 – V – ⊠ ✿ 0603 Norwich :

⌂ **Elm Farm Chalet,** Norwich Rd, NR10 3HH, ℰ 898366, Fax 897129, ☞ – ⅍ 🖵 ☎ 🅿. 🄰 🄰🄴 𝚅𝚒𝚜𝚊. ✻

M (by arrangement) 12.00 **t.** ⅊ 2.80 – **18 rm** ⊐ 29.50/56.00 **t.** – SB 68.60/74.40 **st.**

at Thorpe St. Andrew E : 2 ½ m. on A 47 – X – ⊠ ✿ 0603 Norwich :

⌂ Oaklands, 89 Yarmouth Rd, NR7 0HH, on A 47 ℰ 34471, Fax 700318, ☞ – 🖵 ☎ 🅿 – ⅍ 120. ✻
38 rm.

at Hethersett SW : 6 m. by A 11 – X – ⊠ ✿ 0603 Norwich :

🏰 **Park Farm,** NR9 3DL, on B 1172 ℰ 810264, Fax 812104, ⅃ₛ, ⩲ₛ, 🄰, ☞, park, ✻ –
⅍ rest 🖵 ☎ 🅿 – ⅍ 120. 🄰 🄰🄴 ⓞ 𝚅𝚒𝚜𝚊. ✻
M 10.50/14.00 **t.** and a la carte ⅊ 5.75 – **38 rm** ⊐ 65.00/125.00 **t.** – SB 97.00/137.00 **st.**

◍ ATS Mason Rd. Mile Cross Lane ℰ 423471   ATS Aylsham Rd. Aylsham Way ℰ 426316

NOTTINGHAM Notts. 402 403 404 Q 25 Great Britain G. – pop. 273 300 – ECD : Thursday –
✿ 0602.

See : Castle Museum★ (alabasters★) *AC*, CZ **M**.
Envir. : Wollaton Hall★ *AC*, W : 3 m. by A 609 AZ **M**.
Exc. : Newstead Abbey★ *AC*, N : 9 m. by A 611 - AY - and B 683.

🔟 Bulwell Forest, Hucknall Rd ℰ 770576, NW : 4 m. by A 611 AY – 🔟 Wollaton Park ℰ 787574,
W : 2 m. by A 52 AZ – 🔟 Mapperley, Central, Av., Plains Rd ℰ 265611, NE : by B 684 BY –
🔟 Nottingham City, Lawton Drive ℰ 278021 AY – 🔟 Beeston Fields, Beeston ℰ 257062, SW :
4 m. by A 6005 AZ – 🔟 Ruddington Grange, Wilford Rd, Ruddington ℰ 846141, S : 3 m. by
B 680 BZ – 🔟, 🔟 Edwalton ℰ 234775, SE : 2 m. by A 606 BZ – 🔟 x 3 Cotgrave ℰ 334686, SE :
4 m. by A 52 BZ.

✈ East Midlands Airport : Castle Donington ℰ 0332 (Derby) 810621, SW : 15 m. by A 453 AZ.

🎫 1-4 Smithy Row, NG1 2BY ℰ 470661 – at West Bridgford : County Hall, Loughborough Rd,
NG2 7QP ℰ 773558.

◆London 135 – ◆Birmingham 50 – ◆Leeds 74 – ◆Manchester 72.

Plans on following pages

🏨 **Royal Moat House International** (Q.M.H.), Wollaton St., NG1 5RH, ℰ 414444, Telex
37101, Fax 475667, squash – ⓘ ⅍ rm ▤ 🖵 ☎ 🅿 – ⅍ 500. 🄰 🄰🄴 ⓞ 𝚅𝚒𝚜𝚊. ✻   CY **e**
closed 25 and 26 December – **M** 8.50/14.50 **t.** and a la carte ⅊ 4.70 – ⊐ 8.50 – **198 rm**
73.00/92.50 **t.**, 3 suites – SB 84.00 **st.**

🏨 **Forte Crest,** St. James's St., NG1 6BN, ℰ 470131, Telex 37211, Fax 484366 – ⓘ ⅍ rm
▤ 🖵 ☎ 🅿 – ⅍ 500. 🄰 🄰🄴 ⓞ 𝚅𝚒𝚜𝚊 𝙹𝙲𝙱. ✻   CY **a**
M 15.50 **st.** and a la carte ⅊ 6.60 – ⊐ 9.95 – **130 rm** 75.00/115.00 **st.** – SB (weekends only)
86.00 **st.**

🏨 **Gateway,** Nuthall Rd, NG8 6AZ, NW : 3¼ m. on A 610 ℰ 794949, Fax 794744 – ⓘ ⅍ rm
▤ rest 🖵 ☎ 🕭 🅿 – ⅍ 250. 🄰 🄰🄴 ⓞ 𝚅𝚒𝚜𝚊. ✻   AY **e**
M 8.30/20.00 **st.** and a la carte ⅊ 4.25 – ⊐ 6.50 – **106 rm** 23.50/85.00 **st.** – SB (except Bank
Holidays) (July-August and weekends only) 70.00/117.00 **st.**

🏨 **Rutland Square,** St. James' St., NG1 6FW, ℰ 411114, Fax 410014 – ⓘ ▤ rest 🖵 ☎ 🅿 –
⅍ 150. 🄰 🄰🄴 ⓞ 𝚅𝚒𝚜𝚊. ✻   CZ **c**
M 12.00/16.50 **st.** and lunch a la carte ⅊ 4.50 – ⊐ 6.95 – **103 rm** 52.50/58.50 **st.**, 1 suite –
SB (weekends only) 74.50/84.00 **st.**

🏨 **Strathdon Thistle** (Mt. Charlotte Thistle), 44 Derby Rd, NG1 5FT, ℰ 418501, Telex
377185, Fax 483725 – ⓘ ⅍ rm ▤ rest 🖵 ☎ 🅿 – ⅍ 70. 🄰 🄰🄴 ⓞ 𝚅𝚒𝚜𝚊. ✻   CY **c**
M *(closed lunch Saturday and Bank Holidays)* 12.95/14.70 **st.** and a la carte ⅊ 4.50 – ⊐ 8.75
– **68 rm** 64.00/110.00 **st.** – SB (except Christmas) 92.00/152.00 **st.**

🏨 **Nottingham Moat House** (Q.M.H.), Mansfield Rd, NG5 2BT, ℰ 602621, Fax 691506 – ⓘ
⅍ rm 🖵 ☎ 🕭 🅿 – ⅍ 180. 🄰 🄰🄴 ⓞ 𝚅𝚒𝚜𝚊   BY **u**
closed 24 to 26 December – **M** 12.00/15.00 **t.** – ⊐ 7.25 – **169 rm** 57.00/76.00 **st.**, 3 suites –
SB (weekends only) 90.00 **st.**

🏨 **Holiday Inn Garden Court** Castle Marina Park, off Castle Boulevard, NG7 1GX,
ℰ 500600, Fax 500433 – ⓘ ⅍ rm 🖵 ☎ 🕭 🅿 – ⅍ 40. 🄰 🄰🄴 ⓞ 𝚅𝚒𝚜𝚊 𝙹𝙲𝙱   AZ **e**
M *(closed lunch Saturday and Sunday)* (bar lunch)/dinner 12.50 **st.** and a la carte ⅊ 4.50 –
⊐ 6.95 – **100 rm** 64.50/69.50 **st.**

🏨 **Priory Toby,** Derby Rd, Wollaton Vale, NG8 2NR, W : 3 m. on A 52 ℰ 221691,
Fax 256224 – ⅍ 🖵 ☎ 🅿 – 🄰 🄰🄴 ⓞ 𝚅𝚒𝚜𝚊. ✻   AZ **s**
M 7.50 **t.** and a la carte ⅊ 4.95 – **31 rm** ⊐ 62.00/73.00 **t.**

🏨 **Friendly George,** George St., NG1 3BP, ℰ 475641, Fax 483292 – ⓘ ⅍ rm 🖵 ☎ –
⅍ 150. 🄰 🄰🄴 ⓞ 𝚅𝚒𝚜𝚊. ✻   CY **e**
M 10.00/12.50 **st.** and a la carte – ⊐ 6.75 – **69 rm** 54.00/73.00 **st.**, 1 suite – SB (weekends
only) 77.00/84.00 **st.**

🏨 Stage, Gregory Boulevard, NG7 6LB, ℰ 603261, Fax 691040 – ⅍ rm 🖵 ☎ 🅿 – ⅍ 30
52 rm.   AY **a**

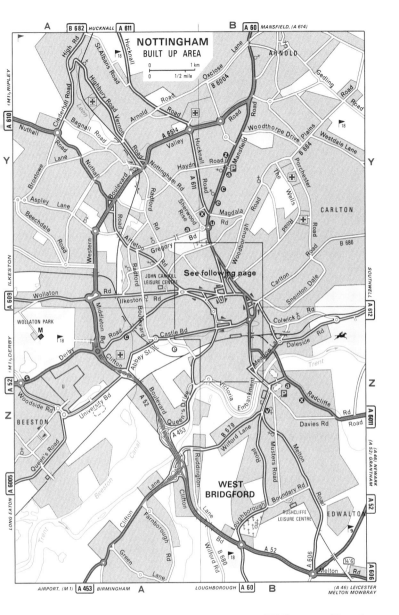

NOTTINGHAM
BUILT UP AREA

🛏 **Woodville,** 340 Mansfield Rd, NG5 2EF, ℰ 606436, Fax 856846 – 🍽 rest 📺 ☎ 🅿 –
🔬 70. 🅰 🆎 ⓘ 𝗩𝗜𝗦𝗔 ⊁   BY **c**
M *(closed Sunday dinner and Bank Holidays)* (bar lunch Monday to Saturday)/dinner 9.95/
11.95 **st.** and a la carte – ☑ 3.95 – **43 rm** 39.50/49.50 **st.**, 2 suites – SB (weekends only)
73.00/79.40 **st.**

🛏 **Lucieville St. James,** 349 Derby Rd, NG7 2DZ, ℰ 787389, Fax 790346, 🌧 – ⇄ 📺 ☎
🅿. 🅰 🆎 ⓘ 𝗩𝗜𝗦𝗔 ⊁   AZ **c**
M (residents only) 10.00/18.00 **t.** and a la carte – **8 rm** ☑ 35.00/150.00 **st.** – SB 96.00/
186.00 **st.**

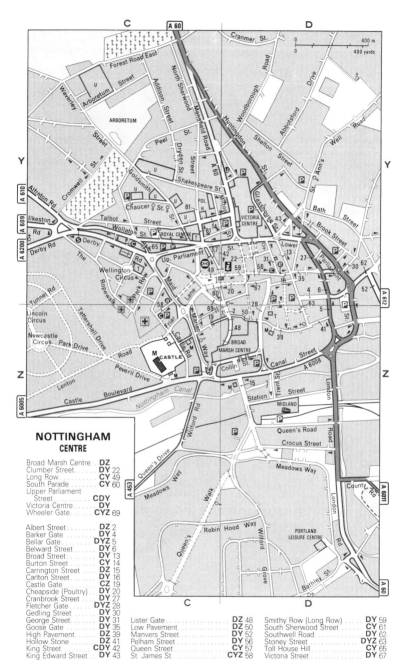

NOTTINGHAM CENTRE

*If you find you cannot take up a hotel booking you have made,
please let the hotel know immediately.*

⌂ **Claremont** without rest., 2 Hamilton Rd, Sherwood Rise, NG5 1AU, *&* 608587, Fax 608587, *☞* – 🖵 ☎ ℗. 🄰 *VISA*. *✼* BY **x**
closed 22 to 30 December – **14 rm** ⊋ 18.00/38.00 **st.**

⌂ **Royston** without rest., 326 Mansfield Rd, NG5 2EF, *&* 622947 – 🖵 ℗. 🄰 🄰🄴 🄾 *VISA*. *✼* BY **e**
14 rm ⊋ 28.50/46.00 **st.**

⌂ **Crantock** without rest., 480 Mansfield Rd, Sherwood, NG5 2GL, *&* 623294 – ▤ rest 🖵 ℗. 🄰 *VISA* BY **a**
20 rm ⊋ 20.00/45.00 **st.**

XX **Saagar,** 473 Mansfield Rd, Sherwood, NG5 2DR, *&* 622014 – ▤. 🄰 🄰🄴 *VISA* BY **z**
closed Christmas Day – **M** - Indian 6.00/13.00 **t.** and a la carte ⓘ 4.00.

XX **Ben Bowers,** 128 Derby Rd (basement), NG1 5FB, *&* 413388 – 🄰 🄰🄴 🄾 *VISA* CY **s**
closed Bank Holiday lunch and Sunday – **M** a la carte 11.75/19.85 **t.** ⓘ 4.75.

X **Sonny's,** 3 Carlton St., NG1 1NL, *&* 473041 – 🄰 🄰🄴 *VISA* DY **c**
M 9.95/12.95 **t.** and a la carte ⓘ 5.95.

at West Bridgford SE : 2 m. on A 52 – ⊠ ☏ 0602 Nottingham :

🏨 **Swans,** 84-90 Radcliffe Rd, NG2 5HH, *&* 814042, Fax 455745 – |🕿| 🖵 ☎ ℗ – 🔬 50. 🄰 BZ **a** 🄾 *VISA*. *✼*
M *(closed Saturday lunch and Sunday dinner)* 13.95 **st.** and a la carte ⓘ 4.25 – **30 rm** ⊋ 49.50/59.50 **st.**, 1 suite – SB (weekends only) 87.40/142.90 **st.**

🏨 **Windsor Lodge,** 116 Radcliffe Rd, NG2 5HG, *&* 813773, Fax 819405 – 🖵 ☎ ℗ – 🔬 30. BZ **x** 🄰 🄰🄴 🄾 *VISA*
closed 25 and 26 December – **M** *(closed Friday to Sunday)* (residents only) (dinner only) 11.75 **st.** ⓘ 3.80 – **48 rm** ⊋ 33.00/50.00 **st.**

⌂ **Cambridge,** 63-65 Loughborough Rd, NG2 7LA, on A 60 *&* 811455, Fax 455416 – 🖵 ☎ BZ **v** ℗. 🄰 🄰🄴 🄾 *VISA*. *✼*
M (by arrangement) 14.30 **st.** ⓘ 3.50 – **20 rm** ⊋ 30.00/90.00 **st.** – SB (weekends only) 60.00/100.00 **st.**

at Plumtree SE : 5 ¾ m. by A 60 - BZ - off A 606 – ⊠ ☏ 0602 Nottingham :

X **Perkins,** Old Railway Station, Station Rd, NG12 5NA, *&* 373695 – ℗. 🄰 🄰🄴 🄾 *VISA*
closed Sunday, Monday and Bank Holidays – **M** - **Bistro** a la carte 15.15/19.35 **t.**

at Toton SW : 6 ½ m. by A 52 on B 6003 – AZ – ⊠ ☏ 0602 Nottingham :

⌂ **Manor,** 350 Nottingham Rd, NG9 6EF, junction with A 6005 *&* 733487 – 🖵 ℗. 🄰 *VISA*
M (by arrangement) 10.95 **t.** ⓘ 3.25 – **13 rm** ⊋ 21.50/47.00 **t.**

at Long Eaton (Derbs.) SW : 8 m. on A 6005 – AZ – ⊠ ☏ 0602 Nottingham :

🏨 **Novotel,** Bostock Lane, NG10 4EP, NW : 1 ¾ m. by A 6005 on B 6002 *&* 720106, Fax 465900, 🏊 heated, 🈴 – |🕿| 🖵 ☎ & ℗ – 🔬 220. 🄰 🄰🄴 🄾 *JCB*
M 12.00/15.00 **st.** and dinner a la carte ⓘ 5.00 – ⊋ 7.50 – **108 rm** 49.50/54.50 **st.**

🏨 **Sleep Inn,** Bostock Lane, NG10 5NL, NW : 1 ¾ m. by A 6005 on B 6002 *&* 460000, Fax 460726 – 🕎 rm 🖵 ☎ & ℗ – 🔬 60. 🄰 🄰🄴 🄾 *VISA*. *✼*
closed 25 to 30 December – **M** a la carte 9.50/16.50 **t.** ⓘ 4.95 – ⊋ 4.95 – **101 rm** 29.95/39.50 **t.** – SB (weekends only) 59.95/79.90 **st.**

at Sandiacre (Derbs.) SW : 7 ½ m. by A 52 – AZ – on B 5010 – ⊠ ☏ 0602 Nottingham :

🏨 **Forte Posthouse,** Bostocks Lane, NG10 5NJ, SW :¾ m. at junction 25 of M 1 *&* 397800, Fax 490469 – 🕎 rm 🖵 ☎ ℗ – 🔬 50. 🄰 🄰🄴 🄾 *VISA*
M a la carte approx. 17.50 **t.** ⓘ 4.65 – ⊋ 6.95 – **91 rm** 53.50 **t.** – SB 90.00 **st.**

🖽 ATS 116 Highbury Rd, Bulwell *&* 278824 ATS 126-132 Derby Rd, Stapleford *&* 392986
ATS 66 Castle Boulevard *&* 476678 ATS Oxford St., Long Eaton. Derbs. *&* 732156

NUNEATON Warks. **403 404** P 26 – pop. 60 377 – ECD : Thursday – ☏ 0203.

🖽 Purley Chase, Pipers Lane, Ridge Lane *&* 393118, NW : 4 m. on B 4114.

🇮 Nuneaton Library, Church St., CV11 4DR *&* 384027.

♦London 107 – ♦Birmingham 25 – ♦Coventry 10 – ♦Leicester 18.

🏨 **Longshoot Toby,** Watling St., CV11 6JH, NE : 2 ½ m. on A 47 at junction with A 5 *&* 329711, Fax 344570 – 🕎 rm 🖵 ☎ ℗. 🄰 🄰🄴 🄾 *VISA*. *✼*
closed 2 weeks Christmas-New Year – **M** *(closed Saturday lunch)* (grill rest.) 5.95/15.00 and a la carte ⓘ 4.55 – **44 rm** ⊋ 38.00/48.00 **st.** – SB (weekends only) 48.00/100.00 **st.**

🏨 **Travel Inn,** Coventry Rd, CY10 7PJ, S : 2½ m. by A 444 on B 4113 *&* 343584, Fax 327156, *☞* – 🕎 rm 🖵 ☎ & ℗. 🄰 🄰🄴 🄾 *VISA*. *✼*
closed 24 to 26 December – **M** (Beefeater grill) a la carte approx. 16.00 **t.** – ⊋ 4.95 – **48 rm** 33.50 **t.**

🏨 **Forte Travelodge** without , CV12 0BN, S : 1 ½ m. on A 444 (southbound carriageway) *&* 382541, Reservations (Freephone) 0800 850950 – 🖵 & ℗. 🄰 🄰🄴 *VISA*. *✼*
40 rm 31.95 **t.**

at Sibson (Leics.) N : 7 m. on A 444 – ⊠ Nuneaton – ☏ 0827 Tamworth :

🏨 **Millers',** Main Rd, CV13 6LB, *&* 880223, Fax 880223 – 🖵 ☎ ℗. 🄰 🄰🄴 🄾 *VISA*
M *(closed Saturday lunch)* 13.95 **st.** and a la carte ⓘ 4.35 – ⊋ 5.95 – **40 rm** 34.95/45.95 **st.** – SB (weekends only) 75.00/120.00 **st.**

at Bulkington SE : 4 m. by B 4114 on B 4112 – ✉ 🕿 0203 Nuneaton :

🏨 **Weston Hall,** Weston Lane, CV12 9RU, NW : 1 ¼ m. by B 4112 🕿 312989, Fax 640846 –
📺 🕿 🅿 – 🔏 70. 🔼 🆎 ⑩ 𝗩𝗜𝗦𝗔
M 15.00 **st.** and a la carte – **25 rm** ⊑ 40.00/60.00 **st.** – SB (weekends only) 50.00/80.00 **st.**

🚗 ATS Weddington Rd 🕿 341130/341139

NUNNINGTON N. Yorks. 🖥🖥 R 21 – see Helmsley.

OADBY Leics. 🖥🖥 🖥🖥 🖥🖥 R 26 – see Leicester.

OAKHAM Leics. 🖥🖥 🖥🖥 R 25 – pop. 7 914 – ECD : Thursday – 🕿 0572.
🆔 Oakham Library, Catmose St., LE15 6HW 🕿 724329.
◆London 103 – ◆Leicester 26 – Northampton 35 – ◆Nottingham 28.

🏨 **Whipper-Inn,** Market Pl., LE15 6DT, 🕿 756971, Fax 757759 – 📺 🕿 – 🔏 60. 🔼 🆎
𝗩𝗜𝗦𝗔
M 7.95/25.00 **st.** and a la carte 🍴 6.00 – ⊑ 6.95 – **24 rm** 65.00/100.00 **st.** – SB (weekends only) 90.00/110.00 **st.**

🏨 **Barnsdale Lodge,** The Avenue, Rutland Water, LE15 8AH, E : 2 m. on A 606 🕿 724678,
Fax 724961 – ⏀ rest 📺 🕿 🅿 – 🔏 220. 🔼 🆎 ⑩ 𝗩𝗜𝗦𝗔 𝗝𝗖𝗕
M a la carte 11.80/19.95 **t.** – **17 rm** ⊑ 49.50/79.50 **t.**

🏨 **Boultons,** 4 Catmose St., LE15 6HW, 🕿 722844, Fax 724473 – 📺 🕿 🕭 🅿 – 🔏 90. 🔼 🆎
⑩ 𝗩𝗜𝗦𝗔
M (bar lunch Monday to Saturday)/dinner 14.00 **st.** and a la carte 🍴 5.50 – **25 rm** ⊑ 45.00/
70.00 **st.** – SB (except Bank Holidays) 80.00/100.00 **st.**

at Hambleton E : 3 m. by A 606 – ✉ 🕿 0572 Oakham :

🏨 🕮 **Hambleton Hall** ⧉, LE15 8TH, 🕿 756991, Fax 724721, ⇐ Rutland water, 🏊 heated,
🐎, 🎾, park, ⛾ – 📱 📺 🕿 🅿. 🔼 🆎 𝗩𝗜𝗦𝗔
M 26.50/60.00 **st.** and a la carte 42.50/52.50 **st.** 🍴 8.00 – **15 rm** 115.00/250.00 **st.**
Spec. Lasagne of brill with broad beans, tomatoes and garden herbs, Fillets of veal with a Madeira sauce and a bone marrow and morel quiche, A light crème brûlée in a nougatine shell.

OAKLEY Hants. 🖥🖥 🖥🖥 Q 30 – see Basingstoke.

OBORNE Dorset 🖥🖥 🖥🖥 M 31 – see Sherborne.

OCKHAM Surrey 🖥🖥 S 30 – pop. 408 – ✉ Ripley – 🕿 0483 Guildford.
◆London 27 – Guildford 9.

🏨 **Hautboy** ⧉, Ockham Lane, GU23 6NP, 🕿 225355, Fax 211176, ⫸ – ▤ rest 📺 🕿 🅿. 🔼
🆎 ⑩ 𝗩𝗜𝗦𝗔 ⛾
closed 26 December – **M** 11.95/22.50 **t.** and a la carte 🍴 4.95 – ⊑ 6.95 – **5 rm** 78.00/98.00 **t.**
– SB 145.00/230.00 **t.**

ODIHAM Hants. 🖥🖥 R 30 – pop. 3 002 – ECD : Wednesday – 🕿 0256.
◆London 51 – Reading 16 – Winchester 25.

🏨 **George,** 100 High St., RG25 1LP, 🕿 702081, Fax 704213, « 15C inn » – ⏀ rm 📺 🕿 🅿.
🔼 🆎 ⑩ 𝗩𝗜𝗦𝗔
M (closed dinner Sunday and Monday) (bar lunch Monday to Saturday)/dinner a la
carte 18.75/27.50 **st.** 🍴 4.50 – **18 rm** ⊑ 62.00/85.00 **st.**

OGBOURNE ST. GEORGE Wilts. 🖥🖥 🖥🖥 O 29 – see Marlborough.

OKEHAMPTON Devon 🖥🖥 H 31 The West Country G. – pop. 4 113 – ECD : Wednesday –
✉ 🕿 0837.
Exc. : S : Dartmoor National Park★★ (Brent Tor ⇐★★, Haytor Rocks ⇐★) – Lydford★★ (Lydford
Gorge★★) S : 8 m. by B 3260 and A 386.
🏌 Okehampton 🕿 52113.
🆔 3 West St., EX20 1HQ 🕿 53020 (summer only).
◆London 226 – Exeter 25 – ◆Plymouth 30.

🏨 **Forte Travelodge** without rest., Sourton Cross, EX20 4LY, SW : 4 m. by A 30 on A 386
🕿 52124, Reservations (Freephone) 0800 850950 – 📺 🕭 🅿. 🔼 🆎 𝗩𝗜𝗦𝗔 ⛾
32 rm 31.95 **t.**

at Sourton SW : 5 m. by A 30 on A 386 – ✉ Okehampton – 🕿 0837 86 Bridestowe :

🏨 **Collaven Manor** ⧉, EX20 4HH, SW : ¾ m. on A 386 🕿 522, Fax 570, « 15C manor
house, gardens » – ⏀ rest 📺 🕿 🅿. 🔼 𝗩𝗜𝗦𝗔
M 11.95/25.00 **t.** 🍴 4.50 – **7 rm** ⊑ 51.00/95.00 **t.** – SB (except Bank Holidays) 100.00/
116.00 **st.**

🚗 ATS Crediton Rd 🕿 53277/52799

Northants. – ✺ 0604 Northampton.

♦London 77 – ♦Birmingham 58 – ♦Leicester 26 – Northampton 6.

⋔ **Wold Farm** ⌂, Harrington Rd, NN6 9RJ, ℘ 781258, ☞, park – ⇟⇞ rm ❷
M (by arrangement) (communal dining) 11.00 **st.** – **6 rm** ⚏ 20.00/42.00 **st.**

Warks. – see Rugby.

Berks. 🗺 Ⓠ 29 – pop. 286 – ✉ Newbury – ✺ 0635 Burghclere.

♦London 77 – ♦Bristol 76 – Newbury 10 – Reading 27 – ♦Southampton 28.

XX **Dew Pond**, RG15 9LH, ℘ 278408, ≼ – ⇟⇞ ❷. 🄰🄽 𝑽𝑰𝑺𝑨
closed Saturday lunch, Sunday, Monday, first 2 weeks January, 2 weeks August and 24 to 26 December – **Meals** 19.50/29.00 **t.** ⌁ 4.50.

W. Mids. – see Birmingham.

Leics. 🗺 🗺 Ⓡ 25 – see Melton Mowbray.

Gtr. Manchester 🗺 🗺 Ⓝ 23 – pop. 107 095 – ECD : Tuesday – ✺ 061 Manchester.

🏌 Crompton and Royton, High Barn, Royton ℘ 624 2154, NW : 3 m. – 🏌 Lees New Rd ℘ 624 4986.

🅱 84 Union St., OL1 1DN ℘ 678 4654.

♦London 212 – ♦Leeds 36 – ♦Manchester 7 – ♦Sheffield 38.

Plan : see Manchester

🏨 **Bower** (De Vere), Hollinwood Av., Chadderton, OL9 8DE, SW : 3 ¼ m. by A 62 on A 6104
℘ 682 7254, Fax 683 4605, ☞ – 🆃🆅 ☎ ❷ – 🔬 200. 🄰🄽 🄰🄴 ⓞ 𝑽𝑰𝑺𝑨   BV **e**
M *(closed lunch Saturday and Bank Holidays)* 12.00 **st.** and a la carte ⌁ 4.95 – **63 rm** ⚏ 63.00/75.00 **st.** – SB 70.00/154.00 **st.**

🏨 **Periquito**, Manchester St., OL8 1UZ, ℘ 624 0555, Fax 627 2031 – ⫶⫶ ⇟⇞ rm 🆃🆅 ☎ ❷ –
🔬 320. 🄰🄽 🄰🄴 ⓞ 𝑽𝑰𝑺𝑨   BV
M (bar lunch Monday to Saturday)/dinner 12.50 **st.** and a la carte – ⚏ 5.50 – **130 rm** 56.00 **st.**

🏨 **Avant** (Best Western), Winsor Rd, Manchester St., OL8 4AS, ℘ 627 5500, Fax 627 5896 –
⫶⫶ ⇟⇞ rm 🔳 rest 🆃🆅 ☎ ⅋ ❷ – 🔬 250. 🄰🄽 🄰🄴 ⓞ 𝑽𝑰𝑺𝑨 . ⊗   BV
M 8.50/14.50 **t.** and a la carte ⌁ 4.50 – **101 rm** ⚏ 62.50/70.00 **t.**, 2 suites – SB 88.00/ 108.00 **st.**

🅐 ATS 169-171 Huddersfield Rd ℘ 633 1551   ATS 179-185 Hollins Rd ℘ 627 0180/665 1958

Avon 🗺 🗺 Ⓜ 29 – ECD : Thursday – ✉ Bristol – ✺ 0454 Chipping Sodbury.

🏌, 🏌 Chipping Sodbury ℘ 312024, NW : 2 m. by A 432 and B 4060.

♦London 110 – Bristol 14 – Gloucester 30 – Swindon 29.

⋔ **Dornden** ⌂, Church Lane, BS17 6NB, ℘ 313325, ≼, ☞ – 🆃🆅 ❷. ⊗
closed 3 weeks October and 2 weeks Christmas-New Year – **M** 8.50 **t.** – **9 rm** ⚏ 24.00/ 48.00 **t.**

Lancs. 🗺 Ⓛ 23 – pop. 21 939 – ECD : Wednesday – ✺ 0695.

♦London 219 – ♦Liverpool 12 – Preston 18.

🏨 **Beaufort** (Mt. Charlotte Thistle), High Lane, Burscough, L40 7SN, NE : 1 ¾ m. by B 5319 on A 59 ℘ 892655, Fax 895135 – 🆃🆅 ☎ ⅋ ❷ – 🔬 50. 🄰🄽 🄰🄴 ⓞ 𝑽𝑰𝑺𝑨 𝑱𝑪𝑩
M 10.50/17.95 **t.** and a la carte – **21 rm** ⚏ 27.00/69.00 **t.**

Shrops. 🗺 🗺 Ⓚ 25 – pop. 13 200 – ECD : Thursday – ✺ 0691.

🏌 Aston Park ℘ 069 188 (Queen's Head) 221, E : 3 m. by A 5 – 🏌 Llanymynech Pant ℘ 830542, S : 5 m. by A 483.

🅱 Mile End Services, SY11 4JA ℘ 662488 – The Heritage Centre, The Old School, Church St. ℘ 662753 (summer only).

♦London 182 – Chester 28 – Shrewsbury 18.

🏨 **Wynnstay**, Church St., SY11 2SZ, ℘ 655261, Fax 670606, ☞ – ⇟⇞ rm 🆃🆅 ☎ ❷ – 🔬 180.
🄰🄽 🄰🄴 ⓞ 𝑽𝑰𝑺𝑨
M (lunch by arrangement)/dinner 17.50 **t.** and a la carte ⌁ 4.25 – ⚏ 7.95 – **26 rm** 40.00/ 65.00 **t.**, 1 suite – SB 63.00/106.00 **st.**

🏨 **Ashfield**, Llwyn-y-Maen, Trefonen Rd, SY10 9DD, SW : 1 ½ m. ℘ 655200, ≼, ☞ –
⇟⇞ rest 🆃🆅 ☎ ❷. 🄰🄽 🄰🄴 𝑽𝑰𝑺𝑨
M (residents only) (dinner only) 20.00 **st.** and a la carte ⌁ 4.50 – **10 rm** ⚏ 45.00/60.00 **st.** – SB 80.00/100.00 **st.**

🏠 **Forte Travelodge** without rest., Mile End Service Area, SY11 4JA, SE : 1 ¼ m. at junction of A 5 with A 483 ℘ 658178, Reservations (Freephone) 0800 850950 – 🆃🆅 ⅋ ❷.
🄰🄽 🄰🄴 𝑽𝑰𝑺𝑨 . ⊗
40 rm 31.95 **t.**

XX **Starlings Castle** ⚓ with rm, Bron y Garth, SY10 7NU, NW : 7 ¼ m. by B 4579, via Selattyn ✆ 718464, Fax 718464, ≤, ⚓ – 📺 ℗, 🅰🅴 ⓄⒹ 𝗩𝗜𝗦𝗔
M (lunch by arrangement Monday to Saturday)/dinner a la carte 17.00/24.00 **t.** ⚱ 6.00 – ⌑ 3.00 – **8 rm** 20.00/40.00 **t.** – SB 80.00/94.00 **st.**

🔧 ATS Oswald Rd ✆ 653540/653256

`OTLEY` Suffolk 404 X 27 – pop. 627 – ✉ Ipswich – ☎ 0473 Helmingham.

◆London 83 – ◆Ipswich 7.5 – ◆Norwich 43.

🏠 **Otley House** ⚓, IP6 9NR, ✆ 890253, Fax 890059, ≤, « Part 17C manor house », ⚓ – ✻ 📺 ℗. ✂
March-October – **M** *(closed Sunday and Bank Holidays)* (communal dining) (dinner only) 15.00 **st.** ⚱ 4.00 – **4 rm** ⌑ 34.00/50.00 **st.** – SB 76.00/105.00 **st.**

`OTLEY` W. Yorks. 402 O 22 – pop. 14 136 – ☎ 0943.

📷 West Bust Lane ✆ 461015.

🏛 Council Offices, 8 Boroughgate, LS21 3AH ✆ 477707.

◆London 216 – Harrogate 14 – ◆Leeds 12 – York 28.

🏨 **Chevin Lodge** ⚓, Yorkgate, LS21 3NU, S : 2 m. by East Chevin Rd ✆ 467818, Fax 850335, « Pine log cabin village », ≦s, ⚓, ⚓, park, ✵ – 🔲 rest 📺 ☎ 🔌 ℗ – 🔺 100. 🅰🅴 𝗩𝗜𝗦𝗔 ✂
M 10.50/16.75 **t.** and a la carte ⚱ 4.75 – **52 rm** ⌑ 55.00/96.50 **t.** – SB (weekends only) 90.00/140.00 **st.**

`OULTON` Suffolk – see Lowestoft.

`OUNDLE` Northants. 404 S 26 – pop. 3 225 – ECD : Wednesday – ✉ Peterborough – ☎ 0832.

📷 Benefield Rd ✆ 273267, W : 1 ½ m. by A 427.

🏛 14 West St., PE8 4EF ✆ 274333.

◆London 89 – ◆Leicester 37 – Northampton 30.

🏨 **Talbot** (Forte), New St., PE8 4EA, ✆ 273621, Fax 274545, ⚓ – ✻ 📺 ☎ ℗ – 🔺 50. 🅰🅴 ⓄⒹ 𝗩𝗜𝗦𝗔
M (bar lunch Monday to Saturday)/dinner 17.95 **t.** and a la carte ⚱ 6.45 – ⌑ 8.50 – **39 rm** 70.00/80.00 **st.**, 1 suite – SB 108.00/156.00 **st.**

at Fotheringhay N : 3 ¾ m. by A 427 off A 605 – ✉ Peterborough (Cambs.) – ☎ 083 26 Cotterstock :

↑ **Castle Farm**, PE8 5HZ, ✆ 200, « Riverside garden » – ✻ rm 📺 ℗. ✂
M (by arrangement) 9.00 **st.** – **6 rm** ⌑ 22.00/46.00 **st.**

at Upper Benefield W : 5 m. on A 427 – ✉ Peterborough (Cambs.) – ☎ 083 25 Benefield :

🏠 **Wheatsheaf**, PE8 5AN, ✆ 254, Fax 245, ⚓ – 📺 ☎ ℗. 🅰🅴 ⓄⒹ 𝗩𝗜𝗦𝗔. ✂
M 9.00/14.50 **st.** ⚱ 3.50 – **9 rm** ⌑ 42.50/52.50 **st.**

`OUTLANE` W. Yorks. – see Huddersfield.

`OVER PEOVER` Ches. 402 403 404 M 24 – see Knutsford.

`OWER` Hants 403 404 P 31 – see Romsey.

`OXENHOPE` W. Yorks. 402 O 22 – ✉ ☎ 0535 Keighley.

◆London 212 – Burnley 21 – ◆Leeds 23 – ◆Manchester 33.

🏨 Leeming Wells, Leeming, BD22 9SN, E : 1 m. on B 6141 ✆ 642201, Fax 642237, ≦s, 🔲 – 📺 ☎ ℗. ✂
10 rm, 2 suites.

`OXFORD` Oxon. 403 404 O 28 Great Britain G. – pop. 113 847 – ECD : Thursday – ☎ 0865.

See : City★★★ – Christ Church★★ (Hall★★ *AC*, Tom Quad★, Tom Tower★, Cathedral★ *AC* – Choir Roof★) BZ – Merton College★★ *AC* BZ – Magdalen College★★ BZ – Ashmolean Museum★★ BY **M2** – Bodleian Library★★ (Ceiling★★, Lierne Vaulting★) *AC* BZ **F** – St. John's College★ BY – The Queen's College★ BZ – Lincoln College★ BZ – Trinity College (Chapel★) BY – New College (Chapel★) *AC*, BZ – Radcliffe Camera★ BZ **A** – Sheldonian Theatre★ *AC*, BZ **G** – University Museum★ BY **M3** – Pitt Rivers Museum★ BY **M4**.

Envir. : Iffley Church★ AZ **A**.

Exc. : Woodstock : Blenheim Palace★★★ (The Grounds★★★) *AC*, NW : 8 m. by A 4144 and A 34 AY .

⚓ to Abingdon Bridge via Iffley and Sandford-on-Thames (Salter Bros Ltd) (summer only).

🏛 St. Aldates, OX1 1DY ✆ 726871.

◆London 59 – ◆Birmingham 63 – ◆Brighton 105 – ◆Bristol 73 – ◆Cardiff 107 – ◆Coventry 54 – ◆Southampton 64.

Plans on following pages

Randolph (Forte), Beaumont St., OX1 2LN, ℰ 247481, Fax 791678 – ❘≝❘ ⇆ rm ⊡ ☎ ⇌
– ☄ 300. ◸ AE ⓞ VISA JCB **st.**   BY **n**
M 17.50/25.00 **t.** and a la carte ⅄ 8.70 – ⊆ 10.50 – **104 rm** 115.00/150.00 **st.** – 5 suites –
SB (weekends only) 178.00 **st.**

Old Parsonage, 1 Banbury Rd, OX2 6NN, ℰ 310210, Fax 311262, « Part 17C house », ⇌
– ⊡ ☎ ℗. ◸ AE ⓞ VISA ⊹   BY **e**
M (room service and meals in bar only) a la carte 20.75/25.50 **t.** ⅄ 5.50 – **30 rm** ⊆ 99.00/
190.00 **st.**

Eastgate (Forte), The High, OX1 4BE, ℰ 248244, Fax 791681 – ❘≝❘ ⇆ ☰ rest ⊡ ☎ ℗. ◸
AE ⓞ VISA   BZ **c**
M (bar lunch Monday to Saturday)/dinner 17.95 **st.** and a la carte ⅄ 6.95 – ⊆ 8.50 – **43 rm**
93.00/110.00 **st.** – SB 138.00 **st.**

Oxford Moat House (Q.M.H.), Wolvercote Roundabout, OX2 8AL, ℰ 59933, Telex
837926, Fax 310259, ⅃₆, ⇆s, ◹, squash – ⇆ rm ☰ rest ⊡ ☎ ℗ – ☄ 150. ◸ AE ⓞ
VISA   AY
closed 27 December-1 January – **M** (carving lunch) 13.50/18.50 **st.** – **155 rm** ⊆ 87.00/
170.00 **st.** – SB (weekends only) 98.00/110.00 **st.**

Linton Lodge (Hilton), Linton Rd, OX2 6UJ, ℰ 53461, Telex 837093, Fax 310365, ⇌ – ❘≝❘
⊡ ☎ ℗ – ☄ 120. ◸ AE ⓞ VISA   AY **n**
M (closed lunch Saturday and Bank Holidays) (carving lunch) 12.00/20.00 **st.** and a la carte
⅄ 6.00 – ⊆ 9.75 – **71 rm** 90.00/110.00 **st.** – SB (weekends only) 136.00/166.00 **st.**

Bath Place, 4-5 Bath Pl., OX1 3SU, ℰ 791812, Fax 791834, « 17C Flemish weavers
cottages » – ⇆ rest ☰ rest ⊡. ◸ AE VISA ⊹   BY **a**
closed first 2 weeks January and last 2 weeks August – **M** (closed Tuesday lunch, Sunday
dinner and Monday) a la carte 13.70/38.50 **t.** ⅄ 5.00 – ⊆ 7.50 – **8 rm** 70.00/100.00 **t.**
2 suites.

Pine Lodge without rest., 201 Cumnor Hill, OX2 9PJ, SW : 3 ¼ m. by A 420 off B 4044
ℰ 862217, Fax 864468 – ⇆ ⊡ ☎ ℗. ◸ VISA ⊹   AYZ
6 rm ⊆ 30.00/50.00 **st.**

Cotswold House without rest., 363 Banbury Rd, OX2 7PL, ℰ 310558, ⇌ – ⇆ ⊡ ℗.
⊹   AY **c**
closed Christmas-New Year – **7 rm** ⊆ 33.00/50.00 **st.**

Chestnuts without rest., 45 Davenant Rd, OX2 8BU, ℰ 53375 – ⇆ ⊡ ℗. ⊹   AY **s**
closed 22 December-5 January – **4 rm** ⊆ 30.00/48.00.

Marlborough House without rest., 321 Woodstock Rd, OX2 7NY, ℰ 311321, Fax 515329
– ⊡ ☎ ℗. ◸ VISA ⊹   AY **v**
closed 24 to 27 December – **12 rm** 50.00/60.00 **st.**

Mount Pleasant, 76 London Rd., Headington, OX3 9AJ, ℰ 62749, Fax 62749 – ⇆ ⊡ ☎
℗. ◸ AE ⓞ VISA JCB. ⊹   AY **a**
M 14.00 **st.** ⅄ 4.00 – **8 rm** ⊆ 37.50/65.00 **st.** – SB (except Bank Holidays) (weekends only)
70.00/115.00 **st.**

Dial House without rest., 25 London Rd, Headington, OX3 7RE, ℰ 69944, ⇌ – ⇆ ⊡
℗   AY **o**
closed Christmas and New Year – **8 rm** ⊆ 45.00/55.00 **st.**

Tilbury Lodge without rest., 5 Tilbury Lane, Botley, OX2 9NB, W : 2 m. by A 420 off
B 4044 ℰ 862138, Fax 863700, ⇌ – ⊡ ☎ ℗. ◸ VISA ⊹   AZ **e**
9 rm ⊆ 38.00/75.00 **st.**

Fifteen North Parade, 15 North Parade Av., OX2 6LX, ℰ 513773 – ◸ VISA   AY **r**
closed Sunday dinner and Bank Holidays – **M** 12.95/15.75 **t.** and dinner a la carte.

Michel's Café Français, 146 London Rd, Headington, OX3 9ED, ℰ 62587 – ◸ AE ⓞ
VISA   AY **u**
closed 25-26 December, 1 January and Bank Holidays – **M** 14.95 **t.** and a la carte ⅄ 5.95.

Gee's Brasserie, 61 Banbury Rd, OX2 6PE, ℰ 53540, « Conservatory » – ☰. ◸
VISA   AY **r**
M a la carte 14.85/19.20 **t.**

Michael's, 36 St. Michael's St., OX1 2EB, ℰ 724241 – ◸ VISA   BZ **a**
M a la carte 12.45/19.00 **t.**

at Kidlington N : 4 ½ m. on A 4260 – AY – ✉ ☎ 0865 Oxford :

Bowood House, 238 Oxford Rd, OX5 1EB, ℰ 842288, Fax 841858 – ⇆ rest ⊡ ☎ ⅊ ℗.
◸ VISA. ⊹
closed 24 December-1 January – **M** (closed Sunday) (dinner only) 15.00 **t.** and a la carte
⅄ 3.95 – **22 rm** ⊆ 34.00/62.00 **t.**

at Wheatley E : 7 m. by A 40 – AY – ✉ Oxford – ☎ 0865 Wheatley :

Forte Travelodge, London Rd, OX9 1JH, ℰ 875705, Reservations (Freephone) 0800
850950 – ⊡ ⅊ ℗. ◸ AE VISA ⊹
M (Harvester grill) a la carte approx. 16.00 **t.** – ⊆ 5.50 – **24 rm** 31.95 **t.**

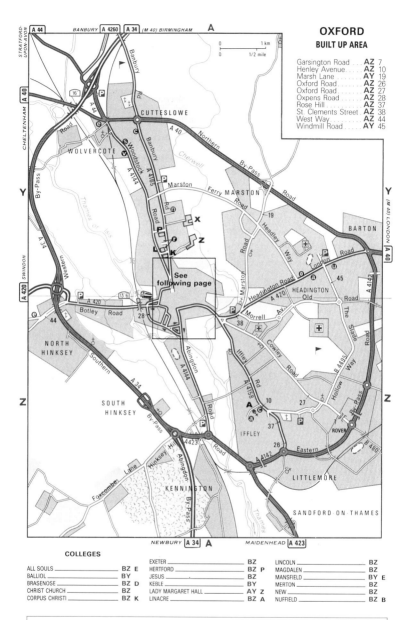

OXFORD
BUILT UP AREA

See following page

COLLEGES

When travelling for business or pleasure
in England, Wales, Scotland and Ireland:

– use the series of five maps
  (nos **401**, **402**, **403**, **404** and **405**) at a scale of 1:400 000

– they are the perfect complement to this Guide

CENTRE

at Iffley SE : 2 m. by A 4158 – ⊠ ☼ 0865 Oxford :

🏰 **Hawkwell House,** Church Way, OX4 4DZ, ℰ 749988, Fax 748525, ≈ – ⅙⅞ rest 📺 ☎ 🅿
– 🔬 150. 🄰 🄰🄴 𝐕𝐈𝐒𝐀   AZ **c**
M 14.50/22.50 **st.** and a la carte ⵠ 5.25 – **23 rm** ⊊ 70.00/95.00 **t.** – SB (weekends only)
99.00/170.00 **st.**

🏠 **The Tree,** Church Way, OX4 4EY, ℰ 775974, Fax 747554, ≈ – 📺 ☎ 🅿. 🄰 🄰🄴 𝐕𝐈𝐒𝐀. ❀
M 10.00/15.00 **t.** and dinner a la carte – **7 rm** ⊊ 50.00/75.00 **st.**   AZ **a**

at Great Milton SE : 12 m. by A 40 off A 329 – AY – ⊠ Oxford – ☎ 0844 Great Milton :

🏠 ❀❀ **Le Manoir aux Quat' Saisons** (Blanc) 🦢, Church Rd, OX44 7PD, ℰ 278881, Fax 278847, ≤, « Part 15C and 16C manor house, gardens », 🛴 heated, park, 🎾 – 🛬 rest 🔳 rest 🔟 ☎ 🅿 – 🔬 35. 🔼 🅰🅴 🆅🅸🆂🅰 ⚘
M 29.50/59.50 **st.** and a la carte 61.00/79.00 **st.** ▯ 13.00 – ⊠ 14.50 – **16 rm** 165.00/ 325.00 **st.**, 3 suites – SB (except Bank Holidays) (weekdays only) 200.00/340.00 **st.**
Spec. Trois bouchées gourmandes au Manoir (summer-autumn), Suprêmes de cailles des Dombes poêlés, sauce à l'essence de cèpes, Fondant de chocolat chaud, crème d'amandes amères et glace à la pistache.

⓪ ATS Horspath Trading Est., Pony Rd., Cowley   ATS 2 Stephen Rd, Headington ℰ 61732
ℰ 777188

OXHILL Warks. 🔲🔲 P 27 – ⊠ Stratford-upon-Avon – ☎ 0926 Warwick.
◆London 85 – ◆Birmingham 32 – ◆Oxford 25.

🏠 **Nolands Farmhouse,** CV35 0RJ, on A 422 ℰ 640309, Fax 641662, 🐾, ⌁ – 🛬 rest 🔟 🅿. 🔼 🆅🅸🆂🅰. ⚘
closed 15 December-5 January – **M** *(closed Sunday and Monday)* (dinner only) 15.00 **st.** –
9 rm ⊠ 25.00/44.00 **st.**

PADSTOW Cornwall 🔲🔲 F 32 The West Country G. – pop. 2 256 – ECD : Wednesday – ☎ 0841.
See : Town*.
Envir. : Trevone (Cornwall Coast Path**) W : 3 m. by B 3276 – Trevose Head* (≤**) W : 6 m. by B 3276.
Exc. : Bedruthan Steps*, SW : 7 m. by B 3276 – Pencarrow*, SE : 11 m. by A 389.
🏌, 🏌 Trevose, Constantine Bay ℰ 520208.
🅱 Red Brick Building, North Quay, PL28 8AF ℰ 533449 (summer only).
◆London 288 – Exeter 78 – ◆Plymouth 45 – Truro 23.

🏠 **Metropole** (Forte), Station Rd, PL28 8DB, ℰ 532486, Fax 532867, ≤ Camel Estuary, 🛴 heated, ⌁ – 📶 🛬 🔟 ☎ 🅿 – 🔬 50. 🔼 🅰🅴 ⓪ 🆅🅸🆂🅰
M (bar lunch Monday to Saturday)/dinner 16.95 **t.** and a la carte ▯ 6.45 – ⊠ 8.50 – **44 rm** 75.00/105.00 **t.** – SB 116.00/140.00 **st.**

🏠 **Old Custom House Inn,** South Quay, PL28 8ED, ℰ 532359, Fax 533372, ≤ Camel Estuary and harbour – 🔳 rest 🔟 ☎ 🅿. 🔼 🆅🅸🆂🅰
M (bar lunch)/dinner 19.00 **t.** and a la carte ▯ 4.00 – **27 rm** ⊠ 58.00/110.00 **t.** – SB (October-March) 82.00/151.00 **t.**

🏠 **St. Petroc's,** 4 New St., PL28 8EA, ℰ 532700 – 🛬 rest 🔟 ☎. 🔼 🆅🅸🆂🅰. ⚘
April-November – **M** *(closed Wednesday)* (dinner only) a la carte 11.90/20.40 **st.** – **10 rm** ⊠ 25.00/80.00 **st.**

🏠 **Woodlands,** Treator, PL28 8RU, W : 1¼ m. by A 389 on B 3276 ℰ 532426, ⌁ – 🛬 🔟 🅿
March-October – **M** 10.00 ▯ 2.50 – **9 rm** ⊠ 25.00/46.00 **st.** – SB (except summer) 60.00/ 70.00 **st.**

🍴🍴 **Seafood** with rm, Riverside, PL28 8BY, ℰ 532485, Fax 533344, ≤, « Attractively convert-ed granary on quayside » – 🔟 ☎ 🅿. 🔼 🅰🅴 🆅🅸🆂🅰
closed 18 December-1 February – **Meals** - **Seafood** (closed Sunday and 2 May) (booking essential) 19.85/26.85 **t.** and a la carte 23.20/34.90 **t.** ▯ 5.00 – **10 rm** ⊠ 34.00/107.00 **t.** – SB (except April-September) 100.00 **st.**

at Little Petherick S : 3 m. on A 389 – ⊠ Wadebridge – ☎ 0841 Rumford :

🏠 **Molesworth Manor** without rest., PL27 7QT, ℰ 540292, ≤, « Part 17C and 19C rectory », ⌁ – 🛬 🅿. ⚘
closed November and December – ⊠ 3.75 – **10 rm** 19.00/50.00.

🏠 **Old Mill Country House,** PL27 7QT, ℰ 540388, « Part 16C corn mill », ⌁ – 🛬 rest 🅿. ⚘
March-October – **M** 12.00 ▯ 3.30 – **6 rm** ⊠ 36.00/51.50.

at Constantine Bay SW : 4 m. by B 3276 – ⊠ ☎ 0841 Padstow :

🏠 **Treglos** 🦢, PL28 8JH, ℰ 520727, Fax 521163, ≤, 🔽, ⌁ – 📶 🛬 rest 🔳 rest 🔟 ☎ ⌁ 🅿. 🔼
11 March-3 November – **M** (bar lunch Monday to Saturday)/dinner 18.50 **t.** and a la carte ▯ 4.00 – **41 rm** ⊠ 54.50/140.00 **t.**, 3 suites – SB (March-April and October) 95.00/135.00 **st.**

at Treyarnon Bay SW : 4¾ m. by B 3276 – ⊠ ☎ 0841 Padstow :

🏠 **Waterbeach** 🦢, PL28 8JW, ℰ 520292, Fax 521102, ≤, ⌁, 🎾 – 🔟 ☎ 🅿. 🔼 🆅🅸🆂🅰. ⚘
April-November – **M** (bar lunch)/dinner 15.00 **t.** ▯ 3.25 – **16 rm** ⊠ 31.00/68.00 **t.**, 4 suites – SB 62.00/80.00 **st.**

PADWORTH Berks. – ⊠ ☎ 0734 Reading.
◆London 58 – Basingstoke 12 – Reading 10.

🏠 **Padworth Court** (Lansbury), Bath Rd, RG7 5HT, on A 4 ℰ 714411, Fax 714442, 🏋, 🈂 – 🛬 rm 📶 🔟 ☎ ♿ 🅿 – 🔬 180. 🔼 🅰🅴 ⓪ 🆅🅸🆂🅰 ⚘
M *(closed lunch Saturday and Bank Holidays)* 9.95/14.50 **st.** and a la carte – **50 rm** ⊠ 69.50/81.00 **st.** – SB (weekends only) 90.00/111.00 **st.**

PAIGNTON Devon 408 J 32 The West Country G. – pop. 39 565 – ECD : Wednesday – ✆ 0803.
See : Torbay★ - Kirkham House★ *AC* Y **B**.
Envir. : Paignton Zoo★★ *AC*, SW : ½ m. by A 3022 AY (see Plan of Torbay).
🛈 The Esplanade, TQ4 6BN ✆ 558383.
◆London 226 – Exeter 26 – ◆Plymouth 29.

Plan of Built up Area : see Torbay

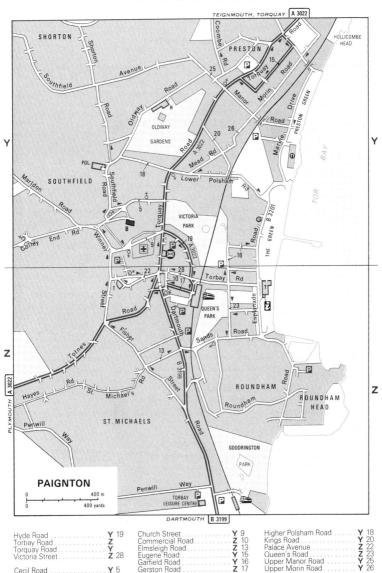

PAIGNTON

Hyde Road	**Y** 19	Church Street	**Y** 9	Higher Polsham Road	**Y** 18
Torbay Road	**Z**	Commercial Road	**Z** 10	Kings Road	**Y** 20
Torquay Road	**Y**	Elmsleigh Road	**Z** 13	Palace Avenue	**Z** 22
Victoria Street	**Z** 28	Eugene Road	**Y** 15	Queen's Road	**Z** 23
		Garfield Road	**Y** 16	Upper Manor Road	**Y** 25
Cecil Road	**Y** 5	Gerston Road	**Z** 17	Upper Morin Road	**Y** 26

🏨🏨 Palace (Forte), Esplanade Rd, TQ4 6BJ, ✆ 555121, Fax 527974, ℉₅, ⥺s, ☒ heated, ☞, ✕
– 🛗 ⇄ 📺 ☎ 🅿   Y **e**
52 rm.

🏨 **Redcliffe,** 4 Marine Drive, TQ3 2NL, ℰ 526397, Fax 528030, ⩽ Torbay, ⟂ heated, ☞ – 📶
🔲 ☎ 🅿 – 🔬 40. 🔳 _VISA_. ⋘
M (bar lunch Monday to Saturday)/dinner 14.75 **t.** and a la carte ⵗ 4.75 – **59 rm** � 45.00/
90.00 **t.** – SB (October-April) 70.00/90.00 **st.**

⊙ ATS Orient Rd ℰ 556888/558975

PAINSWICK Glos. 🔳 🔳 N 28 Great Britain G. – pop. 1 757 – ECD : Saturday – ☎ 0452.
See : Town★.
🏌 Painswick ℰ 812180, N : ½ m. on A 46.
🛈 The Library, Stroud Rd, GL6 6DT ℰ 813552 (summer only).
◆London 107 – ◆Bristol 35 – Cheltenham 10 – Gloucester 7.

🏨 **Painswick** ⌖, Kemps Lane, GL6 6YB, SE : ½ m. by Bisley St., St. Marys St. and
Tibbiwell ℰ 812160, Fax 814059, « Part 18C Palladian house », ☞ – 🔲 ☎ 🅿. 🔳 AE _VISA_
M 18.50/28.50 **st.** and a la carte ⵗ 5.50 – **19 rm** � 65.00/120.00 **st.**

⌂ **Damsell's Lodge** ⌖ without rest., The Park, GL6 6SR, N : 1 m. by A 46 on Sheep-
scombe rd ℰ 813777, ⩽, ☞ – 🔲 🅿
3 rm � 25.00/39.00 **st.**

XX **Country Elephant,** New St., GL6 6XH, ℰ 813564 – 🔳 ⓞ _VISA_
closed Sunday dinner, Monday and 25 to 30 December – **M** (dinner only and Sunday
lunch)/dinner 12.95 **st.** and a la carte ⵗ 4.50.

PAKENHAM Suffolk 🔳 W 27 – see Ixworth.

PARBOLD Lancs. 🔳 L 23 Great Britain G. – pop. 2 673 – ✉ Wigan – ☎ 0257.
Envir. : Rufford Old Hall★ (Great Hall★) _AC_, NW : 4 m. by B 5246.
◆London 212 – ◆Liverpool 25 – ◆Manchester 24 – Preston 19.

XXX **High Moor,** High Moor Lane, WN6 9QA, NE : 3 m. by B 5246 and Chorley Rd
ℰ 0257 (Appley Bridge) 252364 – 🅿. 🔳 AE ⓞ _VISA_
M (dinner only and Sunday lunch)/dinner 15.95 **st.** and a la carte ⵗ 5.00.

PARKGATE Ches. 🔳 🔳 K 24 – pop. 3 480 – ECD : Wednesday – ✉ Wirral – ☎ 051
Liverpool.
◆London 206 – Birkenhead 10 – Chester 11 – ◆Liverpool 12.

🏨 **Parkgate,** Boathouse Lane, L64 6RD, N : ½ m. on B 5135 ℰ 336 5001, Fax 336 8504, ☞ –
⅙⩟ rm 🗐 rest 🔲 ☎ 🅿 – 🔬 100. 🔳 AE ⓞ _VISA_. ⋘
M 8.75/16.95 **t.** – **27 rm** � 49.50/95.00 **t.** – SB (weekends only) 50.00/78.00 **st.**

🏨 **Ship** (Forte), The Parade, L64 6SA, ℰ 336 3931, Fax 353 0051 – 🔲 ☎ 🅿. 🔳 AE ⓞ _VISA_
M (in bar Monday to Saturday)/dinner 15.95 **t.** ⵗ 5.25 – **26 rm** � 45.00/60.00 **t.** –
SB 86.00 **st.**

PATCHWAY Avon 🔳 🔳 M 29 – see Bristol.

PATELEY BRIDGE N. Yorks. 🔳 O 21 Great Britain G. – ✉ ☎ 0423 Harrogate.
Exc. : Fountains Abbey★★★ _AC_ - Studley Royal★★ _AC_ (⩽★ from Anne Boleyn's Seat) -
Fountains Hall (Façade★), NE : 8½ m. by B 6265.
🛈 14 High St., HG3 5AW ℰ 711147 (summer only).
◆London 225 – ◆Leeds 28 – ◆Middlesbrough 46 – York 32.

🏠 **Grassfields Country House** ⌖, Ramsgill Rd, HG3 5HL, ℰ 711412, ☞ – ⅙⩟ rest 🔲 🅿
March-November – **M** (residents only) (dinner only) 12.50 **st.** ⵗ 3.00 – **9 rm** � 31.00/
50.00 **t.** – SB 62.00/87.00 **st.**

at Low Laithe SE : 2¾ m. on B 6165 – ✉ ☎ 0423 Harrogate :

XX **Dusty Miller,** Main Rd, HG3 4BU, ℰ 780837, Fax 780065 – 🅿. 🔳 AE _VISA_
closed 2 weeks August, 25 December and 1 January – **Meals** (dinner only) 24.00 **t.** and a la
carte 24.70/32.50 **t.** ⵗ 4.45.

at Wath-in-Nidderdale NW : 2¼ m. – ✉ ☎ 0423 Harrogate :

XX Sportsman's Arms ⌖ with rm, HG3 5PP, ℰ 711306, ☞ – ⅙⩟ rm 🔲 🅿
7 rm.

LES GUIDES VERTS MICHELIN

Paysages, monuments
Routes touristiques
Géographie
Histoire, Art
Itinéraires de visite
Plans de villes et de monuments

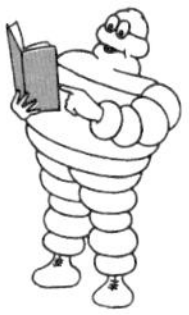

PATRICK BROMPTON N. Yorks. ⁴⁰² P 21 – pop. 145 – ⊠ ⊕ 0677 Bedale.

◆London 228 – ◆Leeds 48 – ◆Newcastle upon Tyne 33 – York 41.

⌂ **Elmfield House** ⌖, Arrathorne, DL8 1NE, NW : 2 ¼ m. by A 684 on Richmond rd
 ℰ 50558, park – ⊱⊰ rest ⊺⊽ ☎ ♿ ⊕. ⱽⁱˢᴬ. ⌖
 M 11.00 **st.** ⌗ 5.75 – **9 rm** ⊑ 25.00/44.00 **st.**

PAULERSPURY Northants. ⁴⁰³ ⁴⁰⁴ R 27 – see Towcester.

PAYHEMBURY Devon – see Honiton.

PEASMARSH E. Sussex ⁴⁰⁴ W 31 – see Rye.

PEMBURY Kent ⁴⁰⁴ U 30 – see Royal Tunbridge Wells.

PENCRAIG Heref. and Worcs. – see Ross-on-Wye.

PENDOGGETT Cornwall ⁴⁰³ F 32 – ⊠ Port Isaac – ⊕ 0208 Bodmin.

◆London 264 – Newquay 22 – Truro 30.

🏠 **Cornish Arms**, PL30 3HH, on B 3314 ℰ 880263, Fax 880335, « Retaining 16C features »
 – ⊺⊽ ☎ ⊕. ◪ ᴬᴱ ⓞ ⱽⁱˢᴬ
 M (bar lunch Monday to Saturday) 12.00/14.50 **t.** and a la carte ⌗ 4.50 – **7 rm** ⊑ 42.00/
 68.00 **t.** – SB 69.90/89.90 **st.**

I prezzi	Per ogni chiarimento sui prezzi qui riportati,
	consultate le spiegazioni alle pagine dell'introduzione.

PENRITH Cumbria ⁴⁰¹ ⁴⁰² L 19 – pop. 12 086 – ECD : Wednesday – ⊕ 0768.

🚉 Salked Rd ℰ 62217/65429, E : ½ m.

🅱 Robinson's School, Middlegate, CA11 7PT ℰ 64466.

◆London 290 – ◆Carlisle 24 – Kendal 31 – Lancaster 48.

🏨 **North Lakes**, Ullswater Rd, CA11 8QT, S : 1 m. at M 6 junction 40 ℰ 68111, Fax 68291,
 ⌗⌗, ⊜ₛ, ⊠, squash – ⌗ ⊱⊰ rm ⊺⊽ ☎ ♿ ⊕ – ⌀ 200. ◪ ᴬᴱ ⓞ ⱽⁱˢᴬ
 M (closed Saturday lunch) 12.95/18.00 **st.** and a la carte ⌗ 6.45 – **85 rm** ⊑ 89.00/128.00 **st.**
 – SB (except Bank Holidays) 128.00 **st.**

🏠 **Forte Travelodge** without rest., Redhills, CA11 0DT, SW : 1 ½ m. by A 592 on A 66
 ℰ 66958, Reservations (Freephone) 0800 850950 – ⊺⊽ ♿ ⊕. ◪ ᴬᴱ ⱽⁱˢᴬ. ⌖
 32 rm 31.95 **t.**

⌂ **Woodland House**, Wordworth St., CA11 7QY, ℰ 64177, Fax 890152 – ⊱⊰ ⊺⊽ ⊕. ⌖
 M (by arrangement) 9.50 **st.** ⌗ 4.00 – **8 rm** ⊑ 22.00/40.00 **st.**

✗ **Passepartout**, 51-52 Castlegate, CA11 7HY, ℰ 65852 – ⊱⊰. ◪ ⱽⁱˢᴬ
 closed Sunday and Monday November-Easter and first 2 weeks November – **M** (dinner
 only) 7.50 **t.** and a la carte ⌗ 3.50.

◍ ATS Gilwilly Ind. Est. ℰ 65656/7

PENSHURST Kent ⁴⁰⁴ U 30 Great Britain G. – pop. 1 749 – ⊕ 0892.

Envir. : Hever Castle★ AC, W : 6 m. by B 2176 and B 2027.

◆London 38 – Maidstone 19 – Royal Tunbridge Wells 6.

⌂ **Swale Cottage** ⌖ without rest., Old Swaylands Lane, TN11 8AH, SE : 1 m. by B 2176
 off Poundsbridge Lane ℰ 870738, ⊴, ⊸ – ⊱⊰ ⊺⊽ ⊕. ⌖
 3 rm ⊑ 32.00/54.00 **st.**

PENZANCE Cornwall ⁴⁰³ D 33 The West Country G. – pop. 18 501 – ECD : Wednesday –
⊕ 0736.

See : Town★ – Outlook★★★ – Western Promenade (⊴★★★) YZ – National Lighthouse Centre★
AC Y – Chapel St.★ Y – Maritime Museum★ AC Y **M1**.

Envir. : Penwith★★ – Trengwainton Garden★★ (⊴★★) AC, NW : 2 m. by St. Clare Street Y –
Sancreed - Church★★ (Celtic Crosses★★) W : 3½ m. by A 30 Z – St. Michael's Mount★★ (⊴★★)
E : 4 m. by B 3311 - Y – and A 30 – Lanyon Quoit★, NW : 3½ m. by St. Clare Street – Newlyn★,
SW : 1½ m. by B 3315 Z – St. Madron (St. Maddern★) NW : 1½ m. by St. Clare Street Y.

Exc. : Morvah (⊴★★) NW : 6 ½ m. by St. Clare Street Y – Zennor (Church★) NW : 6 m. by
B 3311 Y – Prussia Cove★, E : 8 m. by B 3311 - Y - and A 394 – Land's End★ (cliff scenery★★★)
SW : 10 m. by A 30 Z.

Access to the Isles of Scilly by helicopter ℰ 63871, Fax 64293.

⊆ to the Isles of Scilly : Hugh Town (Isles of Scilly Steamship Co. Ltd) (summer only).

🅱 Station Rd, TR18 2NF ℰ 62207.

◆London 319 – Exeter 113 – ◆Plymouth 77 – Taunton 155.

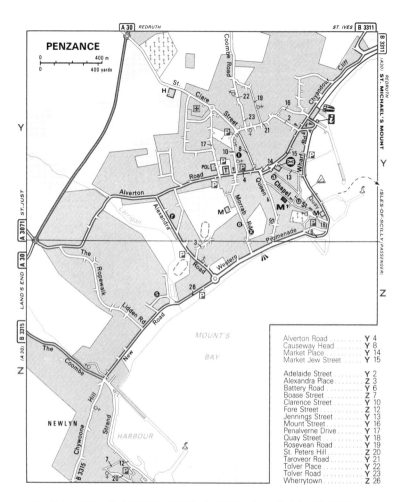

PENZANCE

Alverton Road	**Y**	4
Causeway Head	**Y**	8
Market Place	**Y**	14
Market Jew Street	**Y**	15

Adelaide Street	**Y**	2
Alexandra Place	**Z**	3
Battery Road	**Y**	6
Boase Street	**Z**	7
Clarence Street	**Y**	10
Fore Street	**Z**	12
Jennings Street	**Y**	13
Mount Street	**Y**	16
Penalverne Drive	**Y**	17
Quay Street	**Y**	18
Rosevean Road	**Y**	19
St. Peters Hill	**Z**	20
Taroveor Road	**Y**	21
Tolver Place	**Y**	22
Tolver Road	**Y**	23
Wherrytown	**Z**	26

🏠 **Abbey,** Abbey St., TR18 4AR, 🖉 66906, Fax 51163, « Attractively furnished 17C house », 🛲 – TV 🅿. 🖾 AE VISA   Y u
closed 3 days at Christmas – **M** (booking essential) (dinner only) 21.50 **t.** 🌢 4.50 – **6 rm** 🖙 60.00/120.00 **t.**, 1 suite.

🏠 **Tarbert,** 11 Clarence St., TR18 2NU, 🖉 63758, Fax 331336 – TV ☎. 🖾 AE VISA 🛠
closed 20 December-26 January – **M** (dinner only) 13.00 **t.** and a la carte 🌢 4.40 – **12 rm** 🖙 27.50/55.00 **t.** – SB 67.00/72.00 **st.**   Y i

🏠 **Sea and Horses,** 6 Alexandra Terr., TR18 4NX, 🖉 61961 – TV ☎ 🅿. 🖾 VISA 🛠   Z s
mid February-mid November – **M** (bar lunch)/dinner 9.85 **st.** – **11 rm** 🖙 22.00/48.00 **st.**

↑ **Estoril,** 46 Morrab Rd, TR18 4EX, 🖉 62468 – ⬏ rest TV ☎ 🅿. 🖾 VISA 🛠   Y o
closed December and January – **M** 11.00 **st.** 🌢 3.50 – **10 rm** 🖙 25.00/50.00 **st.** – SB (except July-September) 66.00 **st.**

↑ **Woodstock** without rest., 29 Morrab Rd, TR18 4EZ, 🖉 69049 – TV. 🖾 AE ① VISA   Y x
4 rm 🖙 14.00/34.00 **s.**

↑ **Dunedin,** Alexandra Rd, TR18 4LZ, 🖉 62652 – ⬏ rest TV   Y r
closed December – **M** 7.50 🌢 3.50 – **9 rm** 🖙 15.00/30.00 – SB (winter only) 36.00/42.00 **s.**

XX **Harris's,** 46 New St., TR18 2LZ, 🖉 64408 – 🖾 AE VISA   Y a
closed Monday lunch, Monday dinner November-May, Sunday, 2 weeks February and 2 weeks November – **M** (restricted lunch)/dinner 17.95 **t.** and a la carte 🌢 4.50.

at Newlyn SW : 1 ½ m. on B 3315 – Z – ⊠ ☻ 0736 Penzance :

🏨 **Higher Faugan** ⊗, TR18 5NS, SW : ¾ m. on B 3315 ℰ 62076, Fax 51648, *Ƅ₆*, ⌧ heated, ⌁, park, ✼ – ⇔ rest 🆃🆅 ☎ 🄿. ⚞ 🅰🅴 ⓥ *VISA*
Booking essential November-February – **M** (bar lunch)/dinner 15.00 **t.** ⌂ 3.95 – **11 rm**
⌑ 40.00/98.00 **t.** – SB 110.00/127.00 **st.**

at Drift SW : 2 ½ m. on A 30 – Z – ⊠ ☻ 0736 Penzance :

🏠 **Rose Farm** ⊗ without rest., Chyanhal, Buryas Bridge, TR19 6AN, SW : ¾ m. on
Chyanhal rd ℰ 731808, « Working farm », ⌧ – ⇔ 🆃🆅 🄿. ✼
closed Christmas – **3 rm** ⌑ 22.00/37.00 **st.**

◎ ATS Jelbert Way, Eastern Green ℰ 62768   ATS Units 25-26, Stable Hobba Ind. Est., Newlyn
                                                  ℰ 69100

◼ **PERRANUTHNOE** Cornwall 🔢 D 33 – see Marazion.

◼ **PERSHORE** Heref. and Worcs. 🔢 🔢 N 27 – pop. 6 850 – ECD : Thursday – ☻ 0386.

🅗, 🅗 The Vale, Bishampton ℰ 038 682 (Bishampton) 781.

🅱 19 High St., WR10 1AA ℰ 554262.

◆London 106 – ◆Birmingham 32 – Cheltenham 22 – Stratford-on-Avon 21 – Worcester 9.

🏨 **Avonside**, Main Rd, Wyre Piddle, WR10 2JB, NE : 2 m. by B 4082 and B 4083 on B 4084
ℰ 552654, ≼, ⌧ heated, ⌁, ⌧ – 🆃🆅 ☎ 🄿. ⚞ *VISA*. ✼
M (bar lunch Monday to Saturday)/dinner 15.95 **t.** ⌂ 3.50 – **7 rm** ⌑ 35.00/56.00 **t.** –
SB 56.00/80.00 **st.**

◎ ATS Cherry Orchard ℰ 554494

En haute saison, et surtout dans les stations, il est prudent de retenir à l'avance.

◼ **PETERBOROUGH** Cambs. 🔢 🔢 T 26 Great Britain G. – pop. 113 404 – ☻ 0733.

See : Cathedral★★ *AC* Y.

🅗 Thorpe Wood, Nene Parkway ℰ 267701, W : 3 m. by A 1179 BX – 🅗 Orton Meadows, Ham
Lane ℰ 237478, SW : 2 m. by A 605 BX.

🅱 45 Bridge St., PE1 1HA ℰ 317336.

◆London 85 – ◆Cambridge 35 – ◆Leicester 41 – Lincoln 51.

Plan on next page

🏨 **Peterborough Moat House** (Q.M.H.), Thorpe Wood, PE3 6SG, SW : 2 ¼ m. at roundabout 33 ℰ 260000, Telex 32708, Fax 262737, *Ƅ₆*, ⇐s, ⌧ – ▯ ⇔ rm ▤ rest 🆃🆅 ☎ ⌂ 🄿 –
⚠ 400. ⚞ 🅰🅴 ⓥ *VISA*   BX **s**
M (bar lunch Saturday) 15.75 **st.** and a la carte ⌂ 3.95 – ⌑ 7.45 – **121 rm** 77.00 **st.**, 4 suites
– SB (weekends only) 95.00/99.00 **st.**

🏨 **Butterfly**, Thorpe Meadows, PE3 6GA, W : 1 m. by Thorpe Rd ℰ 64240, Fax 65538 – 🆃🆅
☎ ⌂ 🄿 – ⚠ 80. ⚞ 🅰🅴 ⓥ *VISA*   BX **e**
M 9.50/12.50 **st.** and a la carte ⌂ 4.50 – ⌑ 6.00 – **70 rm** 57.50/80.00 **t.**

🏨 **Bull**, Westgate, PE1 1RB, ℰ 61364, Telex 329265, Fax 557304 – ⇔ rm 🆃🆅 ☎ 🄿 – ⚠ 160.
⚞ 🅰🅴 ⓥ *VISA*   Y **z**
closed 3 days Christmas-New Year – **M** (dancing Saturday evening) 12.50/13.95 **t.** and a la
carte ⌂ 4.80 – **103 rm** ⌑ 68.50/79.00 **t.**, 1 suite – SB (weekends only) 75.90/162.00 **st.**

🏠 **Travel Inn**, Ham Lane, Orton Meadows, PE2 0UU, SW : 3 ½ m. by Oundle Rd (A 605)
ℰ 235794, Fax 391055 – ⇔ rm 🆃🆅 ⌂ 🄿   BX **a**
M (Beefeater grill) a la carte approx. 16.00 **t.** – ⌑ 4.95 – **40 rm** 33.50 **t.**

XX **Grain Barge**, The Quayside, Embankment Rd, PE1 1EG, ℰ 311967 – ▤. ⚞ 🅰🅴 ⓥ *VISA*
M - Chinese (Peking) 13.50/19.00 **t.** and a la carte ⌂ 4.00.   Z **v**

at Norman Cross S : 5 ¾ m. on A 15 at junction with A 1 – ⊠ ☻ 0733 Peterborough :

🏨 **Forte Posthouse**, Great North Rd, PE7 3TB, ℰ 240209, Fax 244455, *Ƅ₆*, ⇐s, ⌧ – ⇔ 🆃🆅
☎ ⌂ 🄿 – ⚠ 50. ⚞ 🅰🅴 ⓥ *VISA* 🅹🅲🅱   BX **r**
M a la carte approx. 17.50 **t.** ⌂ 4.65 – ⌑ 6.95 – **93 rm** 53.50 **t.** – SB (weekends only)
90.00 **st.**

at Alwalton SW : 5 ¾ m. on Oundle Rd (A 605) – ⊠ ☻ 0733 Peterborough :

🏨 **Swallow**, Lynch Wood, PE2 6GB, (opposite East of England Showground) ℰ 371111,
Fax 236725, *Ƅ₆*, ⇐s, ⌧, ⌧ – ▯ ⇔ rm ▤ rest 🆃🆅 ☎ ⌂ 🄿 – ⚠ 275. ⚞ 🅰🅴 ⓥ *VISA*. ✼   AX **u**
M 25.00/30.00 **st.** and a la carte – **161 rm** ⌑ 88.00/105.00 **st.**, 2 suites – SB (weekends only
and July-August) 105.00 **st.**

🏠 **Forte Travelodge** without rest., Great North Rd, PE7 3UR, A 1 (southbound carriageway) ℰ 231109, Reservations (Freephone) 0800 850950 – 🆃🆅 ⌂ 🄿. ⚞ 🅰🅴 *VISA*. ✼   AX **x**
32 rm 31.95 **t.**

at Chesterton SW : 6 ¼ m. by Oundle Rd (A 605) – ⊠ ☻ 0733 Peterborough :

🏠 **Chesterton Priory**, Priory Gdns, PE7 3UB, ℰ 390678, ⌧ – ⇔ 🆃🆅 ☎ 🄿. ⚞ *VISA*. ✼
M (by arrangement) 15.00 **st.** ⌂ 3.25 – **6 rm** ⌑ 43.00/62.50 **st.**   AX **c**

409

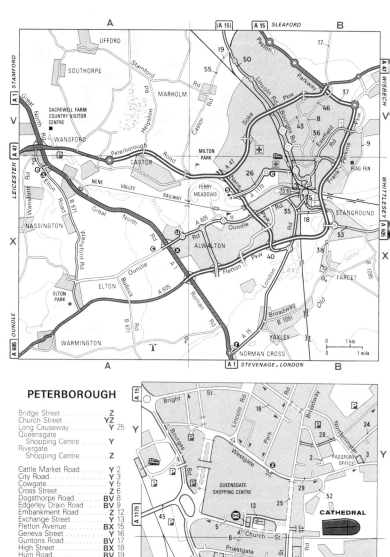

PETERBOROUGH

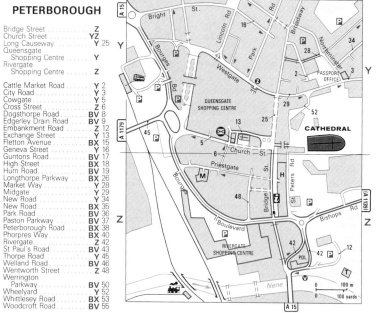

at Wansford W : 8 ½ m. by A 47 – ⊠ Peterborough – 🕓 0780 Stamford :

🏠 **Haycock,** PE8 6JA, ℘ 782223, Fax 783031, « Part 17C coaching inn », 🍽 – 📺 ☎ & 🅿 –
🏛 150. 🔼 🆎 ⓞ 𝗩𝗜𝗦𝗔 𝗝𝗖𝗕   AX **e**
M a la carte 20.00/26.90 **st.** 🍷 7.50 – **50 rm** ⊃⊂ 69.00/105.00 **st.**, 1 suite – SB 130.00 **st.**

⌃ **Stoneacre** 🦢 without rest., Elton Rd, PE8 6JT, S : ¼ m. on unmarked drive ℘ 783283,
🍽 – 🌱 📺 🅿   AX **a**
5 rm ⊃⊂ 21.00/48.00 **st.**

⊚ ATS Wareley Rd (off George St.) ℘ 67112/3

PETERSFIELD Hants. 404 R 30 – pop. 10 078 – ECD : Thursday – 🕓 0730.
🏌 Heath Rd ℘ 63725, E : ½ m.
🅱 County Library, 27 The Square, GU32 3HH ℘ 268829.
◆London 59 – ◆Brighton 45 – Guildford 25 – ◆Portsmouth 19 – ◆Southampton 32 – Winchester 19.

🏠 **Langrish House** 🦢, Langrish, GU32 1RN, W : 3 ½ m. by A 272 ℘ 266941, Fax 260543,
⪅, 🍽, park – 📺 ☎ 🅿 – 🏛 60. 🔼 🆎 𝗩𝗜𝗦𝗔. 🌸
closed 24 December-2 January – **M** *(closed Sunday and Bank Holidays)* (dinner only)
11.75 **t.** and a la carte 🍷 3.50 – **18 rm** ⊃⊂ 35.00/65.00 **t.** – SB 78.00/96.00 **st.**

⊚ ATS 15 ℘ 65151

PETERSTOW Heref. and Worcs. 403 404 M 28 – see Ross-on-Wye.

PETWORTH W. Sussex 404 S 31 Great Britain G. – pop. 2 003 – ECD : Wednesday – 🕓 0798.
See : Petworth House★★ *AC.*
🏌 Osiers Farm ℘ 0903 (Littlehampton) 713413.
◆London 54 – ◆Brighton 31 – ◆Portsmouth 33.

at Sutton S : 5 m. by A 283 – ⊠ Pulborough – 🕓 079 87 Sutton :

⌃ **White Horse Inn,** RH20 1PS, ℘ 221, Fax 291, 🍽 – 📺 ☎ 🅿. 🔼 🆎 ⓞ 𝗩𝗜𝗦𝗔. 🌸
M 12.00 **t.** and a la carte – **4 rm** ⊃⊂ 48.00/58.00 **st.** – SB 74.00/106.00 **st.**

Si vous cherchez un hôtel tranquille,

consultez d'abord les cartes de l'introduction

ou repérez dans le texte les établissements indiqués avec le signe 🦢 ou 🦢

PICKERING N. Yorks. 402 R 21 – pop. 5 316 – ECD : Wednesday – 🕓 0751.
🅱 Eastgate Car Park, YO18 7DP ℘ 73791.
◆London 237 – ◆Middlesbrough 43 – Scarborough 19 – York 25.

🏠 **Forest and Vale,** Malton Rd, YO18 7DL, ℘ 72722, Fax 72972, 🍽 – 📺 ☎ 🅿 – 🏛 100. 🔼
🆎 ⓞ 𝗩𝗜𝗦𝗔
M *(closed dinner 25 and 26 December)* 9.25/16.70 **t.** and a la carte 🍷 4.90 – **17 rm** ⊃⊂ 57.00/
88.00 **t.**

🏠 **White Swan,** Market Pl., YO18 7AA, ℘ 72288 – 🌱 rm 📺 ☎ 🅿. 🔼 𝗩𝗜𝗦𝗔
M (bar lunch Monday to Saturday) 10.50/19.50 **t.** 🍷 4.00 – **12 rm** ⊃⊂ 55.00/77.00 **t.**, 1 suite –
SB (except Bank Holidays) 99.00/143.00 **st.**

🏠 **The Lodge,** Middleton Rd, YO18 8NQ, ℘ 72976, 🍽 – 📺 ☎ 🅿. 🔼 🆎 𝗩𝗜𝗦𝗔. 🌸
M 15.95 **t.** and a la carte 🍷 3.95 – **9 rm** ⊃⊂ 29.00/58.00 **t.** – SB 75.00/85.00 **st.**

at Aislaby NW : 1 ¾ m. on A 170 – ⊠ 🕓 0751 Pickering :

✕ **Blacksmiths Arms** with rm, YO18 8PE, ℘ 72182 – 🌱 rest 📺 🅿. 🔼 𝗩𝗜𝗦𝗔
closed first 2 weeks January – **M** *(closed Monday lunch except Bank Holidays)* 11.00 **t.**
(lunch) and dinner a la carte 10.55/16.75 **t.** 🍷 3.45 – **5 rm** ⊃⊂ 21.00/42.00 **t.** – SB (November-
May) 52.00 **st.**

PICKHILL N. Yorks. 402 P 21 – pop. 300 (inc. Roxby) – ⊠ 🕓 0845 Thirsk.
◆London 229 – ◆Leeds 41 – ◆Middlesbrough 30 – York 34.

⌃ **Nags Head,** YO7 4JG, ℘ 567391, Fax 567212 – 📺 ☎ 🅿. 🔼 𝗩𝗜𝗦𝗔
M *(closed Sunday dinner)* (lunch by arrangement)/dinner 16.00 **st.** and a la carte 🍷 4.50 –
15 rm ⊃⊂ 32.00/45.00 **st.**

PILLING Lancs. 402 L 22 – pop. 1 639 – ⊠ Preston – 🕓 0253.
◆London 243 – ◆Blackpool 11 – Burnley 43 – ◆Manchester 49.

🏠 **Springfield House** 🦢, Wheel Lane, PR3 6HL, ℘ 790301, Fax 790907, 🍽 – 📺 ☎ 🅿. 🔼
𝗩𝗜𝗦𝗔. 🌸
M *(closed Monday lunch)* 8.95/14.95 **st.** 🍷 4.35 – **7 rm** ⊃⊂ 30.00/55.00 **st.** – SB 70.00/
85.00 **st.**

PIMPERNE Dorset 403 404 N 31 – see Blandford Forum.

PINHOE Devon 403 J 31 – see Exeter.

PITTON Wilts. – see Salisbury.

PLUCKLEY Kent 📘📘📘 W 30 – pop. 1 109 – ✆ 0233.

◆London 53 – Folkestone 25 – Maidstone 18.

↑ **Elvey Farm** 🦌 without rest., TN27 0SU, W : 2 m. by Smarden rd and Marley Farm rd, off Mundy Bois rd ✆ 840442, Fax 840726, ≼, 🚗 – 🕎 **℗**, 🔼 𝗩𝗜𝗦𝗔 🍳🍳🍳
  8 rm ⏖ 35.50/59.50 **t.**

PLUMTREE Notts. – see Nottingham.

PLYMOUTH Devon 📘📘📘 H 32 The West Country G. – pop. 238 583 – ECD : Wednesday – ✆ 0752.

See : Town★★ – Smeaton's Tower (≼★★) *AC* BZ – Plymouth Dome★ *AC* BZ – Royal Citadel (Ramparts ≼★★) *AC* BZ – Elizabethan House★ *AC* – City Museum and Art Gallery★ BZ **M**.

Envir. : Saltram House★★ *AC*, E : 3½ m. BY **A** – Anthony House★ *AC*, W : 5 m. by A 374 – Mount Edgcumbe (≼★) *AC*, SW : 2 m. by passenger ferry from Stonehouse AZ.

Exc. : NE : Dartmoor National Park★★ (Brent Tor ≼★★, Haytor Rocks ≼★) BY – Buckland Abbey★★ *AC*, N : 7 ½ m. by A 386 ABY – Yelverton Paperweight Centre★, N : 10 m. by A 386 ABY.

🏌 Staddon Heights, Plymstock ✆ 402475, S : 3 m. by A 379 BY – 🏌 Elfordleigh, Plympton ✆ 336428, E : 4 m. by A 38 BY.

✈ Plymouth City (Roborough) Airport ✆ 772752, N : 3½ m. by A 386 ABY.

🚢 to France : Roscoff (Brittany Ferries) (6 h) (1-2 daily) – to Spain : Santander (Brittany Ferries) (23 h).

🛈 Civic Centre, Royal Parade, PL1 2EW ✆ 264849/264851.

◆London 242 – ◆Bristol 124 – ◆Southampton 161.

🏨🏨 **Copthorne Plymouth,** Armada Centre, Armada Way, PL1 1AR, (via Western Approach southbound) ✆ 224161, Telex 45756, Fax 670688, 🏋, 🎐, 🔼 – 🕎 🌣 rm 🕎 ⤓ **℗** – 🔬 70. 🔼 🆎 ◍ 𝗩𝗜𝗦𝗔 🍳🍳🍳
  BZ **e**
  M 15.50 **st.** and a la carte ◊ 6.75 – ⏖ 8.95 – **131 rm** 85.00/98.00 **st.**, 4 suites – SB (weekends only) 91.00/135.00 **st.**

🏨🏨 **Plymouth Moat House** (Q.M.H.), Armada Way, PL1 2HJ, ✆ 662866, Telex 45637, Fax 673816, ≼ city and Plymouth Sound, 🏋, 🎐, 🔼 – 🕎 🌣 rm 🕎 ☎ ⤓ **℗** – 🔬 250. 🔼 🆎 𝗩𝗜𝗦𝗔
  BZ **s**
  M 15.50/18.50 **t.** and a la carte – ⏖ 9.00 – **210 rm** 89.00/99.00 **st.**, 1 suite – SB (except December) (weekends only) 78.00/98.00 **st.**

🏨🏨 **Grand,** Elliott St., The Hoe, PL1 2PT, ✆ 661195, Fax 600653, ≼ – 🕎 🕎 ☎ **℗** – 🔬 70. 🔼 🆎 ◍ 𝗩𝗜𝗦𝗔 🦌
  BZ **a**
  M 10.50/16.95 **st.** and a la carte – **77 rm** ⏖ 40.00/120.00 **st.** – SB (Thursday to Monday) 75.00/110.00 **st.**

🏨🏨 **Forte Posthouse,** Cliff Rd, The Hoe, PL1 3DL, ✆ 662828, Fax 660974, ≼ Plymouth Sound, 🏊 heated – 🕎 🌣 rm 🕎 ☎ **℗** – 🔬 80. 🔼 🆎 ◍ 𝗩𝗜𝗦𝗔 🍳🍳🍳
  AZ **v**
  M a la carte approx. 17.50 **t.** ◊ 4.65 – ⏖ 6.95 – **102 rm** 53.50 **st.**, 4 suites – SB (weekends only) 90.00 **st.**

🏨 **New Continental,** Millbay Rd, PL1 3LD, ✆ 220782, Fax 227013, 🏋, 🎐, 🔼 – 🕎 🕎 ☎ **℗** – 🔬 350. 🔼 🆎 𝗩𝗜𝗦𝗔
  AZ **s**
  closed 24 December-2 January – **M** (bar lunch Saturday) 9.50/14.50 **t.** and a la carte ◊ 6.50 – **99 rm** ⏖ 45.00/160.00 **t.** – SB (except Christmas) (weekends only) 74.00/85.00 **st.**

🏨 **Novotel Plymouth,** 270 Plymouth Rd., Marsh Mills Roundabout, PL6 8NH, ✆ 221422, Telex 45711, Fax 221422, 🏊 heated – 🕎 🌣 rm 🕎 ▤ rest 🕎 ☎ ⤓ **℗** – 🔬 200. 🔼 🆎 ◍ 𝗩𝗜𝗦𝗔
  BY **i**
  M 12.50 **st.** and a la carte ◊ 6.10 – ⏖ 7.50 – **100 rm** 39.50 **st.** – SB (weekends only) 69.00/89.00 **st.**

🏨 **Campanile,** Longbridge Rd, Marsh Mills, PL6 8LD, ✆ 601087, Telex 45544, Fax 223213 – 🕎 ☎ ⤓ **℗** – 🔬 25. 🔼 🆎 ◍ 𝗩𝗜𝗦𝗔
  BY **a**
  M 9.45 **st.** and a la carte ◊ 4.65 – ⏖ 4.25 – **50 rm** 35.75 **st.**

↑ **Bowling Green** without rest., 9-10 Osborne Pl., Lockyer St., The Hoe, PL1 2PU, ✆ 667485 – 🕎 ☎. 🔼 🆎 ◍ 𝗩𝗜𝗦𝗔
  BZ **r**
  closed 1 week Christmas – **12 rm** ⏖ 26.00/42.00 **st.**

↑ **Athenaeum Lodge** without rest., 4 Athenaeum St., The Hoe, PL1 2RH, ✆ 665005 – 🕎 **℗**. ◍ 🦌
  BZ **u**
  closed 24 December-2 January – **10 rm** ⏖ 16.00/34.00 **st.**

↑ **Cranbourne** without rest., 282 Citadel Rd, The Hoe, PL1 2PZ, ✆ 263858, Fax 263858 – 🕎. 🔼 🆎 𝗩𝗜𝗦𝗔
  BZ **r**
  14 rm ⏖ 15.00/40.00 **st.**

↑ **Sea Breezes,** 28 Grand Par., West Hoe, PL1 3DJ, ✆ 667205 – 🕎
  AZ **o**
  M (by arrangement) 9.50 **st.** – **7 rm** ⏖ 14.00/30.00 **st.** – SB 44.00/50.00 **st.**

↑ **Berkeley's of St. James** without rest., 4 St. James Place East, The Hoe, PL1 3AS, ✆ 221654 – 🌣 🕎. 🔼 🆎 ◍ 𝗩𝗜𝗦𝗔. 🦌
  AZ **n**
  5 rm ⏖ 15.00/30.00 **st.**

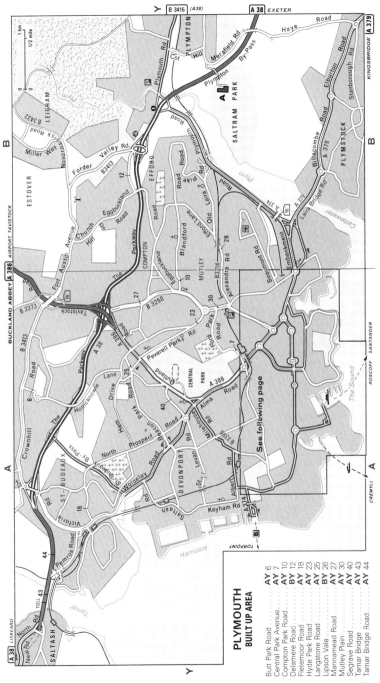

PLYMOUTH
BUILT UP AREA

413

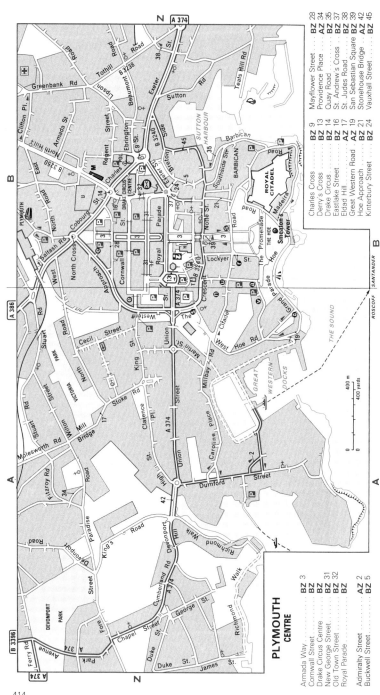

PLYMOUTH
CENTRE

414

✗ ۞ **Chez Nous** (Marchal), 13 Frankfort Gate, PL1 1QA, ℰ 266793, Fax 266793 – 🖃 🖭 ⑩ 𝖵𝖨𝖲𝖠
AZ **e**
closed Sunday, Monday, first 3 weeks February, first 3 weeks September and Bank Holidays – **M** - **French** 28.50 **t.** and a la carte 32.50/44.50 **t.** 🛦 6.50
Spec. Rillons de lapereau sauvage au cresson, Mignons de porc aux pruneaux, Treacle pudding a ma façon with clotted cream.

at Colebrook NE : 5¼ m. by A 374 and B 3416 – BY – 🖂 ۞ 0752 Plymouth :

🏰 **Boringdon Hall** ۞, Boringdon Hill, PL7 4DP, N : ½ m. ℰ 344455, Fax 346578, « Part 16C manor », 🏊, 🎾, park, 🎯 – 🖭 ☎ 🅿 – 🔬 110. 🖃 🖭 ⑩ 𝖵𝖨𝖲𝖠
M 15.95/17.95 **t.** and a la carte 🛦 4.50 – **40 rm** ⛺ 55.00/85.00 **st.** – SB (weekends only) 110.00/150.00 **st.**

🔘 ATS Teats Hill Rd ℰ 266217/227964   ATS Miller Way, Novorossisk Rd, Estover
                                              ℰ 769123

POCKLINGTON Humbs. 🔢 R 22 – pop. 5 051 – ECD : Wednesday – 🖂 York (N. Yorks.) – ۞ 0759.

♦London 213 – ♦Kingston-upon-Hull 25 – York 13.

🏠 **Feathers,** 56 Market Pl., YO4 2AH, ℰ 303155, Fax 304382 – 🖭 ☎ 🅿. 🖃 🖭 ⑩ 𝖵𝖨𝖲𝖠. 🎯
M 9.95 **t.** and a la carte – **12 rm** ⛺ 38.50/60.00 **t.** – SB (except Bank Holidays) (weekends only) 50.00 **st.**

at Barmby Moor W : 2 m. on B 1246 – 🖂 York (N. Yorks.) – ۞ 0759 Pocklington :

🏠 **Barmby Moor,** Hull Rd, YO4 5EZ, on A 1079 ℰ 302700, Fax 306459, 🏊 heated, 🎠 – 🖭 ☎ 🅿. 🖃 𝖵𝖨𝖲𝖠. 🎯
M *(closed Sunday dinner)* (dinner only and Sunday lunch)/dinner a la carte 9.65/14.95 **st.** 🛦 4.10 – ⛺ 7.00 – **10 rm** 36.00/48.00 **st.** – SB (except Sunday and Christmas) 74.00/110.00 **st.**

PODIMORE Somerset – see Yeovil.

POLPERRO Cornwall 🔢 G 33 The West Country G. – pop. 1 192 – 🖂 Looe – ۞ 0503.
See : Village★.

♦London 271 – ♦Plymouth 28.

🏠 **Claremont,** Fore St., PL13 2RG, ℰ 72241, Fax 72241 – 🖭 ☎ 🅿. 🖃 🖭 𝖵𝖨𝖲𝖠
M *(closed October-March)* (bar lunch)/dinner 16.95 **st.** and a la carte 🛦 4.85 – **11 rm** ⛺ 17.00/60.00 **st.**

🏠 **Lanhael House,** Langreek Rd, PL13 2PW, ℰ 72428, 🏊 heated, 🎠 – 🖭 🅿. 🎯
March-October – **M** (by arrangement) 9.00 **t.** – **5 rm** ⛺ 23.00/38.00 **st.**

✗ **Kitchen,** Fish Na Bridge, The Coombes, PL13 2RQ, ℰ 72780 – 🖃 𝖵𝖨𝖲𝖠
closed Sunday to Thursday November-March – **M** (dinner only) a la carte 13.50/21.80 **t.**

PONTELAND Tyne and Wear 🔢 🔢 O 19 – see Newcastle upon Tyne.

POOLE Dorset 🔢 🔢 O 31 The West Country G. – pop. 122 815 – ECD : Wednesday – ۞ 0202.
See : Town★ – Museums★ *AC* (Waterfront **M1**, Scaplen's Court **M2**).
Envir. : Compton Acres★★, (English Garden ≼★★★) *AC*, SE : 3 m. by B 3369 BX on Bournemouth town plan – Brownsea Island★ (Baden-Powell Stone 🌲★★) *AC*, by boat from Poole Quay or Sandbanks BX on Bournemouth town plan.

🚗 Parkstone, Links Rd ℰ 707138 BX on Bournemouth town plan – 🚗 Bulbury Woods, Lytchett Matravers ℰ 092 945 (Morden) 574, by a A 35 AV on Bournemouth town plan.

⛴ to France : Cherbourg (Brittany Ferries Truckline) (4 h 15 mn) (1-2 daily) – to The Channel Islands : Jersey (St. Helier) and Guernsey (St. Peter Port) (British Channel Island Ferries).

🗓 The Quay, BH15 1HE ℰ 673322 – Dolphin Shopping Centre – Passenger Ferry Terminal (summer only).

♦London 116 – Bournemouth 4 – Dorchester 23 – Weymouth 28.

Plan of Built up Area : see Bournemouth

🏰 **Haven,** Banks Rd, Sandbanks, BH13 7QL, SE : 4¼ m. on B 3369 BX ℰ 707333, Fax 708796, ≼ Ferry, Old Harry Rocks and Poole Bay, 🛁, 🏊, 🏊 heated, 🎾, squash – 🛗 🖭 ☎ 🅿 – 🔬 180. 🖃 🖭 ⑩ 𝖵𝖨𝖲𝖠 𝖩𝖢𝖡. 🎯   on Bournemouth town plan BX **c**
M 15.00/25.00 **st.** and a la carte 🛦 4.75 – (see also **La Roche** below) – **95 rm** ⛺ 65.00/160.00 **st.**, 2 suites.

🏨 **Mansion House,** 7-11 Thames St., BH15 1JN, off Poole Quay ℰ 685666, Fax 665709, « 18C town house, staircase » – 🍽 rest 🖭 ☎ 🅿 – 🔬 25. 🖃 🖭 ⑩ 𝖵𝖨𝖲𝖠. 🎯   **a**
M *(closed Saturday lunch and Sunday dinner)* 15.95/19.25 **st.** and a la carte 🛦 6.25 – **28 rm** ⛺ 50.00/130.00 **st.** – SB (weekends only) 115.00/190.00 **st.**

🏨 **Salterns** (Best Western), 38 Salterns Way, Lilliput, BH14 8JR, ℰ 707321, Fax 707488, ≼, squash – 🍽 rest 🖭 ☎ 🅿. 🖃 🖭 ⑩ 𝖵𝖨𝖲𝖠 🎯   on Bournemouth town plan BX **e**
M 15.50/22.50 **t.** 🛦 4.75 – ⛺ 8.50 – **16 rm** 66.00/86.00 **t.** – SB 132.00/172.00 **st.**

POOLE

Dolphin
  Shopping Centre

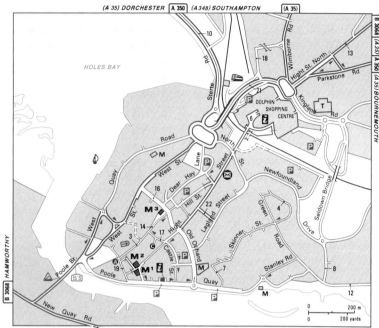

🏠 **Sea Witch,** 47 Haven Rd, Canford Cliffs, BH13 7LH, ℰ 707697 – ⤢ rm 📺 ☎ 🅿. 🄪 *VISA*
M *(residents only except Sunday lunch July and August)* (dinner only and Sunday lunch)/
dinner 10.00 **t.** ⓘ 4.00 – **10 rm** ⬚ 33.00/56.00 **t.**   on Bournemouth town plan CX **u**

XX **La Roche** (at Haven H.), Banks Rd, Sandbanks, BH13 7QL, ℰ 707333, Fax 708796 – ⤢
🅿. 🄪 🄰🄴 ① *VISA*   on Bournemouth town plan BX **c**
closed Sunday and Monday – **M** (dinner only) 21.50/35.00 **st.** and a la carte ⓘ 4.75.

X **Isabel's,** 32 Station Rd, Lower Parkstone, BH14 8UD, ℰ 747885 – 🄪 🄰🄴 ① *VISA*
closed 25 to 27 December and 1 January – **M** (dinner only) 17.00 **st.** and a la carte.
                                                          on Bournemouth town plan BX **a**

X **John B's,** 20 Old High St., BH15 1BP, ℰ 672440 – 🄪 🄰🄴 ① *VISA*   **c**
closed Sunday except Bank Holidays – **M** (dinner only) 19.50 **t.**

🚗 ATS 1 Fernside Rd ℰ 733301/733326

POOLEY BRIDGE Cumbria 🈯🈯 🈯🈯 L 20 – see Ullswater.

When visiting London use the Green Guide **"London"**

  – Detailed descriptions of places of interest

  – Useful local information

  – A section on the historic square-mile of the
    City of London with a detailed fold-out plan

  – The lesser known London boroughs – their people,
    places and sights

  – Plans of selected areas and important buildings.

Envir. : Harewood House★★ (The Gallery★) *AC*, E : 5½ m. by A 659.

♦London 204 – Bradford 10 – Harrogate 8 – ♦Leeds 10.

XXX ✿ **Pool Court** with rm, Pool Bank, LS21 1EH, ℰ 842288, Fax 843115, 🐎 – ▤ rest 📺 ☎ **②**. ⚠ 🆎 ⓪ 𝘝𝘐𝘚𝘈. ✵
closed Sunday, Monday and 2 weeks Christmas-New Year – **M** (booking essential) (dinner only) 37.50 **t.** and a la carte 19.40/29.15 **t.** ⓵ 7.35 – � 7.95 – **6 rm** 70.00/120.00 **t.** – SB (weekends only) 145.00 **t.**
Spec. Fresh Whitby crab layered with pasta, crispy fried leeks and truffle oil, Roasted calves liver with a lime sharpened sauce, White and dark chocolate terrine with pistachios.

PORLOCK Somerset 403 J 30 The West Country G. – pop. 1 453 (inc. Oare) – ECD : Wednesday – ⊠ Minehead – ✆ 0643.

See : Village★ – Porlock Hill (≤★★).

Envir. : Dunkery Beacon★★★ (≤★★★) S : 5½ m. – Luccombe★ (Church★) 3 m. by A 39 – Culbone★ (St. Beuno) W : 3½ m. by B 3225, 1½ m. on foot.

♦London 190 – ♦Bristol 67 – Exeter 46 – Taunton 28.

🏠 **Oaks,** TA24 8ES, ℰ 862265, Fax 862265, ≤ Porlock Bay, 🐎 – ↻ rest 📺 ☎ **②**. 𝘝𝘐𝘚𝘈
M (dinner only) 19.00 **st.** ⓵ 5.75 – **10 rm** ⊊ 47.50/75.00 **st.** – SB (except Easter and Christmas) 100.00/120.00 **st.**

↬ **Gable Thatch,** Doverhay, TA24 8LQ, ℰ 862552, « Part 17C thatched cottages », 🐎 – ↻ rest 📺 ☎ **②**
closed January and February – **M** 18.50 **st.** ⓵ 4.00 – **5 rm** ⊊ 29.50/63.00 **st.**

at Porlock Weir NW : 1½ m. – ⊠ Minehead – ✆ 0643 Porlock :

🏨 **Anchor and Ship Inn,** TA24 8PB, ℰ 862636, Fax 862843, ≤, 🐎 – 📺 ☎ **②**. ⚠ 🆎 𝘝𝘐𝘚𝘈
M (bar lunch Monday to Saturday)/dinner 18.50 **st.** and a la carte ⓵ 5.45 – **19 rm** ⊊ 49.75/109.50 **st.** – SB 99.50/135.50 **st.**

PORTINSCALE Cumbria – see Keswick.

PORT ISAAC Cornwall 403 F 32 – ECD : Wednesday – ✆ 0208 Bodmin.

♦London 266 – Newquay 24 – Tintagel 14 – Truro 32.

🏠 **Port Gaverne,** Port Gaverne, PL29 3SQ, S : ½ m. ℰ 880244, Fax 880151, « Retaining 17C features » – ↻ rest 📺 ☎ **②**. ⚠ 🆎 ⓪ 𝘝𝘐𝘚𝘈
closed 6 January-19 February – **M** (bar lunch)/dinner a la carte 15.50/22.50 **t.** – **18 rm** ⊊ 41.00/94.00 **t.** – SB 96.00/116.00 **st.**

🏚 **Slipway,** Slipway, PL29 3RH, ℰ 880264, « 16C inn » – ☎ **②**. ⚠ 🆎 𝘝𝘐𝘚𝘈. ✵
April-October – **M** (bar lunch)/dinner 16.50 **t.** and a la carte ⓵ 3.95 – **9 rm** ⊊ 19.00/52.00 **t.** – SB (except 11 July-August) 70.00/90.00 **st.**

↬ **Archer Farm** ⌂, Trewetha, PL29 3RU, SE : ½ m. by B 3276 ℰ 880522, ≤, 🐎 – ↻ rest 📺 ☎ **②**
May-September – **M** 14.00 ⓵ 3.75 – **6 rm** ⊊ 25.50/57.00 **t.** – SB (except mid July-mid September and Bank Holidays) 76.00/85.00 **st.**

PORTLOE Cornwall 403 F 33 – ⊠ ✆ 0872 Truro.

♦London 296 – St. Austell 15 – Truro 15.

🏠 **Lugger,** TR2 5RD, ℰ 501322, Fax 501691, ≤, ⌂ – ↻ rest 📺 ☎ **②**. ⚠ 🆎 ⓪ 𝘝𝘐𝘚𝘈. ✵
early February-late November – **M** (bar lunch Monday to Saturday)/dinner 25.00 **t.** and a la carte ⓵ 4.00 – **19 rm** ⊊ 50.00/130.00 **t.** – SB 120.00/130.00 **st.**

PORTSCATHO Cornwall 403 F 33 The West Country G. – ECD : Wednesday and Saturday – ⊠ Truro – ✆ 0872.

Envir. : St. Just-in-Roseland Church★★, W : 4 m. by A 3078 – St. Anthony-in-Roseland (≤★★) S : 3½ m.

♦London 298 – ♦Plymouth 55 – Truro 16.

🏨 **Roseland House** ⌂, Rosevine, TR2 5EW, N : 2 m. by A 3078 ℰ 580644, Fax 580801, ≤ Gerrans Bay, 🐎 – ↻ rest 📺 ☎ **②**. ⚠ 𝘝𝘐𝘚𝘈. ✵
M 9.00/18.00 **t.** and a la carte ⓵ 4.00 – **17 rm** ⊊ (dinner included) 40.00/94.00 **t.**

🏠 **Gerrans Bay,** 12 Tregassick Rd, TR2 5ED, ℰ 580338, ≤, 🐎 – **②**. ⚠ 🆎 𝘝𝘐𝘚𝘈
April-October and Christmas – **M** (bar lunch Monday to Saturday)/dinner 18.25 **t.** ⓵ 4.50 – **14 rm** ⊊ 28.00/60.00 **st.** – SB 64.00/88.00 **st.**

Wenn Sie ein ruhiges Hotel suchen,
benutzen Sie zuerst die Karte in der Einleitung
oder wählen Sie im Text ein Hotel mit dem Zeichen ⌂ oder ⌂.

417

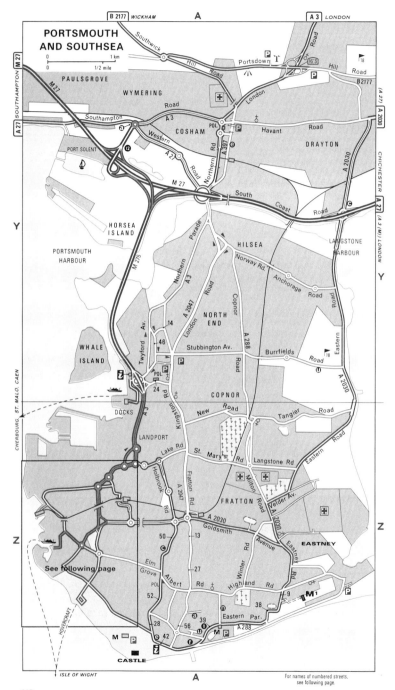

PORTSMOUTH AND SOUTHSEA

0 ___ 1 km
0 ___ 1/2 mile

For names of numbered streets,
see following page.

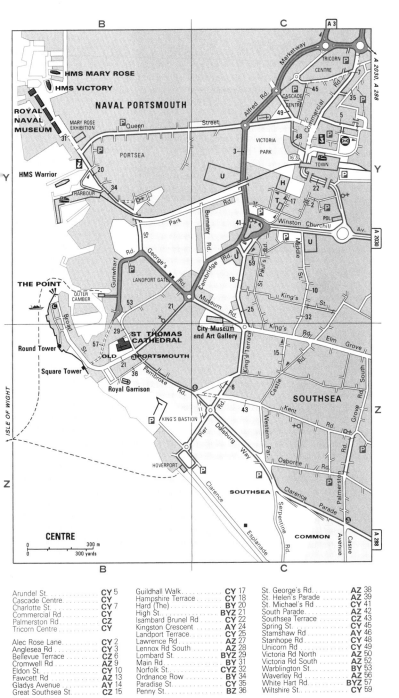

CENTRE

0   300 m
0   300 yards

See : City★ – Naval Portsmouth BY : H.M.S. Victory★★★ *AC*, The Mary Rose★★, Royal Naval Museum★★ *AC* – Old Portsmouth★ BYZ : The Point (≤★★) - St. Thomas Cathedral★ – Southsea (Castle★ *AC*) AZ – Royal Marines Museum, Eastney★ *AC*, AZ **M1.**

Envir. : Portchester Castle★ *AC*, NW : 5 1/2 m. by A 3 and A 27 AY.

🏌 Great Salterns, Burrfields Rd 🖉 664549/699519 AY – 🏌 Crookhorn Lane, Widley 🖉 372210/ 372299, NE : 7 m. by B 2177 AY – 🏌 Southwick Park, Pinsley Drive, Southwick 🖉 380131, N : 5 m. off B 2177 AY.

🚢 to France : Cherbourg (P & O European Ferries) (4 h 45 mn) (2-3 daily) – to France : Le Havre (P & O European Ferries) (5 h 45 mn) day, (7 h) night (3 daily) – to France (Brittany Ferries) : to Caen (5 h 45 mn) (2-3 daily) to St. Malo (9 h) (1 daily) – to the Isle of Wight : Fishbourne (Wightlink Ltd) (frequent services daily) (35 mn) – to Spain (Santander) (Brittany Ferries) (29 h).

🚢 to the Isle of Wight : Ryde (Wightlink Ltd) frequent services daily – from Southsea to the Isle of Wight : Ryde (Hovertravel) frequent services daily (10 mn).

🛈 The Hard, PO1 3QJ 🖉 826722 – Clarence Esplanade, PO5 3ST 🖉 832464 (summer only) – Continental Ferryport, Rudmore Roundabout, PO2 8QN 🖉 838635 (summer only) 102 Commercial Rd, PO1 1EJ 🖉 838332.

◆London 78 – ◆Brighton 48 – Salisbury 44 – ◆Southampton 21.

Plans on preceding pages

🏨 **Hilton National,** Eastern Rd, Farlington, PO6 1UN, NE : 5 m. on A 2030 🖉 219111, Telex 86598, Fax 210762, *f₆*, ⇌, 🔲, 🎾 – 🚭 rm 📺 ☎ & 🅿 – 🔬 230. 🔼 🅰🅴 🔘 📖 *VISA* **JCB**
M 11.95/14.95 **t.** and a la carte 🝐 5.50 – 🖴 9.25 – **118 rm** 55.00/120.00 **t.** – SB 85.00/ 140.00 **st.**   AY **c**

🏨 **Hospitality Inn** (Mt. Charlotte Thistle), South Par., Southsea, PO4 0RN, 🖉 731281, Telex 86719, Fax 817572, ≤ – 🔊 🚭 rm 📺 ☎ – 🔬 200. 🔼 🅰🅴 🔘 *VISA* **JCB**   AZ **r**
M (bar lunch Sunday) 9.50/14.50 **t.** and dinner a la carte 🝐 4.25 – **113 rm** 🖴 65.00/80.00 **t.**, 2 suites – SB 86.00/152.00 **t.**

🏨 **Innlodge,** Burrfields Rd, PO3 5HH, NE : 3 1/2 m. by A 2030 🖉 650510, Fax 693458, 🚗 – 🚭 rm 📺 ☎ & 🅿 – 🔬 120. 🔼 🅰🅴 🔘 *VISA* 🚗   AY **u**
M a la carte 13.50/22.70 **t.** – 🖴 5.75 – **73 rm** 42.50/65.50 **t.**

🏨 **Forte Posthouse,** Pembroke Rd, PO1 2TA, 🖉 827651, Fax 756715, *f₆*, 🔲 – 🔊 🚭 rm 📺 ☎ 🅿 – 🔬 220. 🔼 🅰🅴 🔘 *VISA*   CZ **o**
M a la carte approx. 17.50 **t.** 🝐 4.65 – 🖴 6.95 – **163 rm** 53.50 **st.** – SB (weekends only) 90.00 **st.**

🏨 **Seacrest,** 11-12 South Par., Southsea, PO5 2JB, 🖉 875666, Fax 832523, ≤ – 🔊 🚭 rest 📺 ☎ 🅿. 🔼 🅰🅴   AZ **e**
M (residents only) (dinner only) 13.95 **st.** 🝐 3.95 – **26 rm** 🖴 38.00/60.00 **t.** – SB (except June-September) 59.90/97.90 **st.**

🏨 **Sallyport,** High St., Old Portsmouth, PO1 2LU, 🖉 821860 – 📺 ☎. 🔼 🔘 *VISA* 🚗
M (bar lunch Monday to Saturday)/dinner a la carte 7.75/18.45 **t.** 🝐 4.95 – **10 rm** 🖴 39.00/ 59.00 **t.** – SB (weekends only) 69.00/98.00 **st.**   BZ **a**

🏨 **Beaufort,** 71 Festing Rd, Southsea, PO4 0NQ, 🖉 823707, Fax 870270 – 📺 ☎ 🅿. 🔼 *VISA* 🚗   AZ **n**
M (dinner only) 13.90 **st.** and a la carte 🝐 6.00 – **19 rm** 🖴 38.00/60.00 **st.** – SB (October-March) (weekends only) 70.00/114.00 **st.**

🏠 **Fortitude Cottage** without rest., 51 Broad St., Old Portsmouth, PO1 2JD, 🖉 823748 – 🚭 📺 🚗   BY **c**
closed 25 and 26 December – **3 rm** 🖴 30.00/42.00 **s.**

🏠 **St. Margaret's,** 3 Craneswater Gate, Southsea, PO4 0NZ, 🖉 820097, 🚗 – 🚭 rest 📺. 🔼 *VISA* 🚗   AZ **i**
closed 2 weeks Christmas – **M** (by arrangement) 9.00 **st.** – **13 rm** 🖴 20.00/44.00 **st.**

🏠 **Ashwood** without rest., 10 St. David's Rd, Southsea, PO5 1QN, 🖉 816228 – 📺. 🚗   AZ **c**
closed 23 December-2 January – **7 rm** 🖴 15.00/32.00 **s.**

🏠 **Cranbourne House** without rest., 6 Herbert Rd, Southsea, PO4 0QA, 🖉 824981 – 🚭 📺. 🚗   AZ **a**
4 rm 🖴 25.00/40.00 **s.**

🏠 **Glencoe** without rest., 64 Whitwell Rd, Southsea, PO4 0QS, 🖉 737413 – 📺. 🔼 🅰🅴 🔘 *VISA*   AZ **u**
7 rm 🖴 15.00/35.00 **st.**

🍴 **Bistro Montparnasse,** 103 Palmerston Rd, Southsea, PO5 3PS, 🖉 816754 – 🔼 🅰🅴 *VISA*   CZ **a**
closed Sunday, Monday except December, 1 to 14 January and Tuesday after Bank Holidays – **Meals** (dinner only) 12.50/19.90 **t.** 🝐 5.00.

at Cosham N : 4½ m. by A 3 and M 275 on A 27 – ✉ Portsmouth – ☎ 0705 Cosham :

🏨🏨 **Portsmouth Marriott,** North Harbour, PO6 4SH, ☎ 383151, Fax 388701, 🏋, ♨, 🏊, squash – 🛗 🚭 rm ▤ [TV] ☎ ♿ [P] – 👥 280. 💳 [AE] ⓓ [VISA]. 🚫🐕 AY **a**
M (bar lunch Saturday) 15.95 **st.** and a la carte 🍷 7.95 – ☕ 4.00 – **169 rm** 53.50 **st.**, 1 suite – SB (weekends only) 108.00/138.00 **st.**

🍴 **Barnard's,** 109 High St., PO6 3BB, ☎ 370226 – 💳 [VISA] AY **e**
closed Saturday lunch, Sunday, Monday, 2 weeks August and 25 December-1 January – **M** 13.50 **st.** and a la carte.

ATS 3 Margate Rd ☎ 827544

POWBURN Northd [401] [402] O 17 – ✉ Alnwick – ☎ 066 578 (3 fig.) and 0665 (6 fig.).
♦London 312 – ♦Edinburgh 73 – ♦Newcastle upon Tyne 36.

🏨 **Breamish House** 🐦, NE66 4LL, ☎ 266, Fax 500, ≤, 🌳 – 🚭 rest [TV] ☎ [P]. 💳 [VISA]
closed January-14 February – **M** (bar lunch Monday to Saturday)/dinner 21.00 **t.** 🍷 5.75 – **11 rm** ☕ 71.00/89.00 **t.** – SB (October-April) (except Bank Holidays) 103.00/130.00 **st.**

*Es ist empfehlenswert, **in der Hauptsaison** und vor allem in Urlaubsorten, Hotelzimmer im voraus zu bestellen. Benachrichtigen Sie sofort das Hotel, wenn Sie ein bestelltes Zimmer nicht belegen können.*

Wenn Sie an ein Hotel im Ausland schreiben, fügen Sie Ihrem Brief einen internationalen Antwortschein bei (im Postamt erhältlich).

POWERSTOCK Dorset [403] L 31 – see Bridport.

PRESTBURY Ches. [402] [403] [404] N 24 – pop. 2 970 – ☎ 0625.
⛳18 Wilmslow Rd, Mottram St. Andrews ☎ 828135.
♦London 184 – ♦Liverpool 43 – ♦Manchester 17 – ♦Stoke-on-Trent 25.

🏨🏨 Mottram Hall (De Vere), Wilmslow Rd, Mottram St. Andrew, SK10 4QT, NW : 2¼ m. on A 538 ☎ 828135, Fax 828950, ≤, « Part 18C mansion, gardens », 🏋, ♨, 🏊, ⛳18, park, 🎾, squash – 🛗 🚭 rm [TV] ☎ ♿ [P] – 👥 275. 🚫🐕
130 rm, 3 suites.

🏨 **White House Manor,** The Village, SK10 4HP, ☎ 829376, Fax 828627, 🌳 – [TV] ☎ [P]. 💳 [AE] ⓓ [VISA]
M (room service or see **White House** below) – ☕ 8.50 – **8 rm** 40.00/110.00 **t.**

🍴🍴 **White House,** The Village, SK10 4DG, ☎ 829376, Fax 828627 – [P]. 💳 [AE] ⓓ [VISA]
closed Monday lunch and Sunday dinner – **M** 12.90 **t.** (lunch) and a la carte 20.15/29.15 **t.** 🍷 5.00.

PRESTON Lancs. [402] L 22 – pop. 166 675 – ECD : Thursday – ☎ 0772.
⛳18 Fulwood Hall Lane, Fulwood ☎ 794234/700436, W : 1½ m. off M 6 – ⛳18 Ingol, Tanterton Hall Rd, Ingol ☎ 734556, NW : 1½ m. – ⛳18 Aston & Lea, Tudor Av., Blackpool Rd ☎ 726480, W : 3 m. by A 583 – ⛳18 Penwortham, Blundell Lane ☎ 743207, W : 1½ m. by A 59.
[i] The Guildhall, Lancaster Rd, PR1 1HT ☎ 53731.
♦London 226 – ♦Blackpool 18 – Burnley 22 – ♦Liverpool 30 – ♦Manchester 34 – ♦Stoke-on-Trent 65.

🏨 **Forte Posthouse,** The Ringway, PR1 3AU, ☎ 259411, Fax 201923 – 🛗 🚭 rm [TV] ☎ [P] – 👥 100. 💳 [AE] ⓓ [VISA]
M a la carte approx. 17.50 **t.** 🍷 4.65 – ☕ 6.95 – **121 rm** 53.50 **st.** – SB (weekends only) 90.00 **st.**

🏨 **Tulketh,** 209 Tulketh Rd, off Blackpool Rd, Ashton, PR2 1ES, NW : 1½ m. on A 5085 ☎ 728096, Fax 723743 – 🚭 rest [TV] ☎ [P]. 💳 [AE] ⓓ [VISA]. 🚫🐕
closed 24 December-2 January – **M** (dinner only) a la carte 6.75/14.50 **st.** 🍷 4.00 – **12 rm** ☕ 31.00/50.00 **st.**

🏨 **Claremont,** 516 Blackpool Rd, Ashton, PR2 1HY, NW : 1½ m. on A 5085 ☎ 729738, Fax 726274, 🌳 – [TV] ☎ [P]. 💳 [AE] ⓓ [VISA] [JCB]
M 8.75/12.95 **t.** 🍷 4.00 – **14 rm** ☕ 36.00/49.00 **t.** – SB 66.50/97.90 **st.**

at Fulwood N : 1½ m. on A 6 – ✉ ☎ 0772 Preston :

⌂ **Briarfield** without rest., 145-147 Watling Street Rd, off Garstang Rd, PR2 4AE, ☎ 700917 – [TV] [P]. 🚫🐕
closed 24 December-6 January – **10 rm** ☕ 20.00/40.00 **st.**

at Broughton N : 3 m. on A 6 – ✉ ☎ 0772 Preston :

🏨🏨 **Broughton Park,** 418 Garstang Rd, PR3 5JB, ☎ 864087, Fax 861728, 🏋, ♨, 🏊, 🌳, squash – 🛗 🚭 rm [TV] ☎ ♿ [P] – 👥 200. 💳 [AE] ⓓ [VISA]. 🚫🐕
M *(closed lunch Saturday and Bank Holidays except Christmas)* 14.00/18.50 **st.** and a la carte – **98 rm** ☕ 82.00/97.00 **st.** – SB (weekends only) 90.00/124.00 **st.**

at Samlesbury E : 2 ½ m. at junction M 6 with A 59 – ⌧ ❀ 0772 Preston :

🏨 **Swallow Trafalgar,** Preston New Rd, PR5 0UL, E : 1 m. at junction A 59 with A 677 ☝877351, Fax 877424, *£6*, ≘s, ⬜, squash – ▯ ✻⟵ rm ▤ rest ▣ ☎ ❷ – ⅍ 250. ◪ ஊ ⦿ 𝐕𝐈𝐒𝐀
M (bar lunch Saturday) 9.50/15.50 **st.** and a la carte – **78 rm** ⊐ 75.00/90.00 **st.** – SB (weekends only) 95.00 **st.**

🏨 **Tickled Trout,** Preston New Rd, PR5 0UJ, ☝877671, Fax 877463, ≼, ≘s, ⬚ – ▣ ☎ ❷ – ⅍ 100. ◪ ஊ ⦿ 𝐕𝐈𝐒𝐀
M 12.95/15.95 **t.** and dinner a la carte ⓪ 4.95 – **72 rm** ⊐ 59.50/115.00 **st.** – SB (except Christmas) 78.00/120.00 **st.**

at Bamber Bridge S : 5 m. on A 6 – ⌧ ❀ 0772 Preston :

🏨 **Novotel,** Reedfield Place, Walton Summit, PR5 6AB, SE : ¾ m. by A 6 at junction with M 6 ☝313331, Telex 677164, Fax 627868, ⬚ heated, ⊶ – ▯ ▣ ☎ ⅋ ❷ – ⅍ 160. ◪ ஊ ⦿ 𝐕𝐈𝐒𝐀
M 13.95 **st.** (dinner) and a la carte 12.75/19.90 **st.** ⓪ 5.25 – ⊐ 7.50 – **98 rm** 49.50/53.50 **st.** – SB (weekends only) 70.00/90.00 **st.**

at Lea W : 3 ½ m. on A 583 – ⌧ ❀ 0772 Preston :

🏨 **Travel Inn,** Blackpool Rd, PR4 0XL, on A 583 ☝720476, Fax 729971 – ✻⟵ rm ▣ ⅋ ❷. ◪ ஊ ⦿ 𝐕𝐈𝐒𝐀 ⊶
M (Beefeater grill) a la carte approx. 16.00 **t.** – ⊐ 4.95 – **38 rm** 33.50 **t.**

🔧 ATS 296-298 Aqueduct St. Ashton ☝57688

Stadtpläne : Die Auswahl der Straßen wurde unter Berücksichtigung

des Verkehrs und der Zufahrt zu den erwähnten Häusern getroffen.

Die weniger wichtigen Straßen wurden nur angedeutet.

PUCKERIDGE Herts. ⓸⓪⓸ U 28 – see Ware.

PUCKRUP Glos. – see Tewkesbury.

PUDDINGTON Ches. ⓸⓪⓶ ⓸⓪⓷ K 24 – pop. 318 – ⌧ South Wirral – ❀ 051 Liverpool.
♦London 204 – Birkenhead 12 – Chester 8.

🏨🏨🏨 **Craxton Wood** ⬥ with rm, Parkgate Rd, L66 9PB, on A 540 ☝339 4717, Fax 339 1740, ≼, « Gardens », park – ▣ ☎ ❷. ◪ ஊ ⦿ 𝐕𝐈𝐒𝐀 ⊶
closed first week January and last 2 weeks August – **M** *(closed Sunday and Bank Holidays)* 19.85 **st.** and a la carte ⓪ 6.95 – **13 rm** ⊐ 59.50/98.50 **st.**, 1 suite.

PUDSEY W. Yorks. ⓸⓪⓶ P 22 – see Leeds.

PULBOROUGH W. Sussex ⓸⓪⓸ S 31 – pop. 3 197 – ECD : Wednesday – ❀ 0798.
▯⬚, ▯⬚ West Chiltington, Broadford Bridge Rd ☝813574, E : 2 m.
♦London 49 – ♦Brighton 25 – Guildford 25 – ♦Portsmouth 35.

🏨 **Chequers,** Church Pl., RH20 1AD, NE : ¼ m. on A 29 ☝872486, Fax 872715, ⊶ – ▣ ☎ ❷. ◪ ஊ ⦿ 𝐕𝐈𝐒𝐀
M (bar lunch)/dinner 18.95 **st.** ⓪ 3.75 – **11 rm** ⊐ 49.50/69.00 **st.** – SB (except Christmas) 84.00/124.00 **st.**

🏨🏨 **Stane Street Hollow,** Codmore Hill, RH20 1BG, NE : 1 m. on A 29 ☝872819 – ✻⟵ ❷
closed last 2 weeks May, last 2 weeks October, 24 to 26 December and 31 December – **M** **- Swiss** (closed Saturday lunch, Sunday dinner, Monday and Tuesday) (booking essential) a la carte 16.50/23.00 **t.** ⓪ 5.00.

PURTON Wilts. ⓸⓪⓷ ⓸⓪⓸ O 29 – pop. 3 406 – ⌧ ❀ 0793 Swindon.
♦London 94 – ♦Bristol 41 – Gloucester 31 – ♦Oxford 38 – Swindon 5.

🏨 **Pear Tree at Purton,** Church End, SN5 9ED, S : ½ m. via Church St. on Lydiard Millicent rd ☝772100, Fax 772369, ≼, « Conservatory restaurant », ⊶ – ▣ ☎ ❷ – ⅍ 60. ◪ ஊ ⦿ 𝐕𝐈𝐒𝐀 𝐉𝐂𝐁
M *(closed lunch Saturday and Bank Holidays)* 17.50/27.50 **t.** ⓪ 6.00 – **16 rm** ⊐ 92.00 **t.**, 2 suites – SB (weekends only) 125.00 **st.**

QUORN Leics. – see Loughborough.

RADLETT Herts. ⓸⓪⓸ T 28 – pop. 7 749 – ECD : Wednesday – ❀ 0923.
▯⬚ Aldenham, Church Lane ☝853929, SW : 3 m. by B 462 BT.
♦London 21 – Luton 15.

Plan : see Greater London (North-West)

🏨🏨 **Tim's Table,** 335 Watling St., WD7 7LB, ☝854388 – ▤. ◪ ஊ ⦿ 𝐕𝐈𝐒𝐀   BT o
closed 25 and 26 December – **M** **- Chinese** (Peking, Szechuan) 13.50/16.50 **t.** and a la carte ⓪ 4.00.

◆London 223 – ◆Blackpool 39 – Burnley 12 – ◆Leeds 46 – ◆Manchester 13 – ◆Liverpool 39.

🏠 **Old Mill,** Springwood St., off Carr St., BL0 9DS, ℰ 822991, Fax 822291, ℩₅, �) , 🔲 – 📺 ☎ 🄿, 🖭 🄰🄴 🅾 𝗩𝗜𝗦𝗔, 🛠
M 7.50/12.50 **t.** and a la carte ⬩ 4.15 – **36 rm** ⚏ 31.50/65.00 **t.**

RAMSGATE Kent 404 Y 30 – pop. 36 678 – ECD : Thursday – ✆ 0843 Thanet.

🚢 to France : Dunkerque (Sally Ferries) (2 h 30 mn) (5 daily).

🇮 Argyle Centre, Queen St., CT11 9EE ℰ 591086.

◆London 77 – ◆Dover 19 – Maidstone 45 – Margate 4.5.

🏠 **Marina Resort,** Harbour Par., CT11 8LJ, ℰ 588276, Fax 586866, ≼, 🚪, 🔲 – 🛗 ⇄ rm
🞋 rest 📺 ☎ 🄿 – ⚜ 120. 🖭 🄰🄴 🅾 𝗩𝗜𝗦𝗔
M 9.95/12.95 **st.** and a la carte – ⚏ 7.50 – **59 rm** 55.00/65.00 **st.** – SB (except Christmas) 80.00/120.00 **st.**

at Minster W : 5½ m. by A 253 on B 2048 – ✉ Ramsgate – ✆ 0843 Thanet :

🞖 **Morton's Fork,** 42 Station Rd, CT12 4BZ, ℰ 823000 – ⇄ rest 📺 ☎. 🖭 🄰🄴 🅾 𝗩𝗜𝗦𝗔, 🛠
M *(closed Monday lunch, Sunday dinner and Bank Holidays except Good Friday)* 11.95/ 13.95 **t.** and a la carte ⬩ 4.50 – ⚏ 6.50 – **3 rm** 33.00/46.00 **st.** – SB 72.80/120.00 **st.**

⊘ ATS 82/84 Bellevue Rd ℰ 595829

RASKELF N. Yorks. – see Easingwold.

RAVENSTONEDALE Cumbria 402 M 20 – pop. 501 – ECD : Thursday – ✉ Kirkby Stephen – ✆ 053 96 Newbiggin-on-Lune.

◆London 280 – ◆Carlisle 43 – Kendal 19 – Kirkby Stephen 5.

🏠 **Black Swan,** CA17 4NG, ℰ 23204, 🞖 – ⇄ rest 📺 ☎ 🄿. 🖭 🄰🄴 🅾 𝗩𝗜𝗦𝗔 𝗝𝗖𝗕
M *(bar lunch Monday to Saturday)/dinner* 20.00 **t.** and a la carte ⬩ 4.50 – **17 rm** ⚏ 41.00/ 60.00 **t.** – SB (weekends only) 87.00/114.00 **st.**

🞖 **Fat Lamb,** Crossbank, Fell End, CA17 4LL, SE : 2 m. on A 683 ℰ 23242, ≼, 🞖 – ⇄ rest 🄿
M *(bar lunch Monday to Saturday)/dinner* 16.50 **t.** and a la carte ⬩ 3.25 – **12 rm** ⚏ 34.50/ 54.00 **t.** – SB (except Bank Holidays) 84.00/103.00 **st.**

READING Berks. 403 404 Q 29 – pop. 194 727 – ✆ 0734.

🏌 Calcot Park, Calcot ℰ 427124, W : 3 m. by A 4155 Z.

🚤 to Henley via Caversham, Sonning and Shiplake Locks (Salter Bros Ltd) (summer only).

🇮 Town Hall, Blagrave St., RG1 1QH ℰ 566226.

◆London 43 – ◆Brighton 79 – ◆Bristol 78 – Croydon 62 – ◆Luton 62 – ◆Oxford 28 – ◆Portsmouth 67 – ◆Southampton 46.

Plan on next page

🏨 **Holiday Inn** (Q.M.H.), Caversham Bridge, Richfield Av., RG1 8BD, ℰ 391818, Telex 846933, Fax 391665, ≼, « Thames-side setting », ℩₅, 🚪, 🔲 – 🛗 ⇄ rm 🞋 rest 📺 ☎ 🄖   X **e**
🄿 – ⚜ 220. 🖭 🄰🄴 🅾 𝗩𝗜𝗦𝗔 𝗝𝗖𝗕, 🛠
closed 25 to 29 December – **M** *(closed Saturday lunch)* 18.95 **t.** (dinner) and a la carte 16.30/25.80 **t.** ⬩ 6.95 – ⚏ 9.95 – **107 rm** 50.00/106.00 **t.**, 4 suites – SB (weekends only) 94.00 **st.**

🏨 **Ramada,** Oxford Rd, RG1 7RH, ℰ 586222, Telex 847785, Fax 597842, ℩₅, 🚪, 🔲 – 🛗   Z **i**
⇄ rm 🞋 📺 ☎ 🄖 🄿 – ⚜ 220. 🖭 🄰🄴 🅾 𝗩𝗜𝗦𝗔, 🛠
M *(buffet lunch)* 13.50 **st.** and dinner a la carte 12.00/18.00 **st.** ⬩ 4.50 – ⚏ 9.25 – **193 rm** 90.00/99.00 **st.**, 1 suite.

🏨 **Forte Posthouse,** 500 Basingstoke Rd, RG2 0SL, S : 2½ m. on A 33 ℰ 875485,   X **a**
Fax 311958, ℩₅, 🚪, 🔲 – ⇄ rm 🞋 📺 ☎ 🄖 🄿 – ⚜ 100. 🖭 🄰🄴 🅾 𝗩𝗜𝗦𝗔 𝗝𝗖𝗕
M a la carte approx. 17.50 **t.** ⬩ 4.65 – ⚏ 6.95 – **138 rm** 53.50/69.50 **st.** – SB (weekends only) 90.00 **st.**

🏠 **Hillingdon Prince,** 39 Christchurch Rd, RG2 7AN, ℰ 311391, Fax 756357 – 🛗 🞋 rm 📺   X **s**
☎ 🄿 – ⚜ 25. 🖭 🄰🄴 𝗩𝗜𝗦𝗔
M *(closed Sunday dinner)* 15.00/17.50 **st.** – **40 rm** ⚏ 50.00/75.00 **st.** – SB (weekends only) 80.00/150.00 **st.**

🏠 **Upcross,** Berkeley Av., RG1 6HY, ℰ 590796, Fax 576517, 🞖 – 📺 ☎ 🄿 – ⚜ 40. 🖭 🄰🄴   Y **c**
𝗩𝗜𝗦𝗔
closed 26 December-3 January – **M** *(closed Saturday lunch)* 16.00 **st.** and a la carte ⬩ 5.50 – **20 rm** ⚏ 49.00/59.00 **st.** – SB (weekends only) 60.00/80.00 **st.**

🏠 **Rainbow Corner,** 132-138 Caversham Rd, RG1 8AY, ℰ 588140, Fax 586500 – 📺 ☎ 🄿.   X **u**
🖭 🄰🄴 𝗩𝗜𝗦𝗔
M *(closed Sunday)* (dinner only) 11.95 **t.** and a la carte ⬩ 5.95 – ⚏ 4.95 – **22 rm** 54.00/ 65.00 **t.**

🏠 **Forte Travelodge,** 387 Basingstoke Rd, RG2 0JE, S : 2 m. on A 33 ℰ 750618, Reserva-   X **c**
tions (Freephone) 0800 850950 – 📺 🄖 🄿. 🖭 🄰🄴 𝗩𝗜𝗦𝗔, 🛠
M (Harvester grill) a la carte approx. 16.00 **t.** – ⚏ 5.50 – **36 rm** 31.95 **t.**

🞖 **Dittisham,** 63 Tilehurst Rd, RG3 2JL, ℰ 569483, 🞖 – ⇄ rm 📺 🄿. 🖭 𝗩𝗜𝗦𝗔   X **v**
M (by arrangement) 15.00 – **5 rm** ⚏ 18.50/40.00 **st.** – SB 53.00/66.00 **st.**

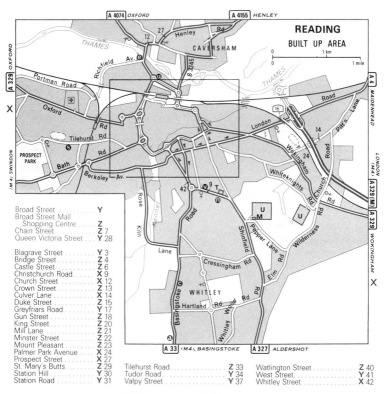

READING

BUILT UP AREA

0   1 km
0   1 mile

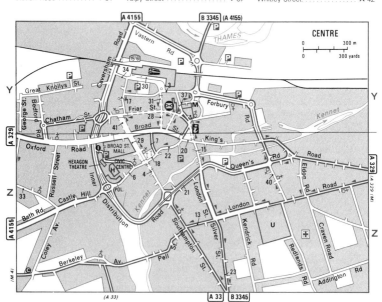

CENTRE

0   300 m
0   300 yards

XX **Café Français,** 62 Christchurch Rd, RG2 7AZ, ✐ 872823 – 🔳 🆑 ⊙ 𝘝𝘐𝘚𝘈 𝘑𝘊𝘉 🗙 n
closed 25 and 26 December – **M** - **French** 14.95 **t.** and a la carte.

at Sindlesham SE : 5 m. by A 329 on B 3030 – X – ⊠ Wokingham – 🕓 0734 Reading :

🏨 **Reading Moat House** (Q.M.H.), Mill Lane, RG11 5DF, NW : ½ m. via Mole Rd ✐ 351035,
Telex 846360, Fax 666530, *Ι₅*, ⇌ – ⅋ 🗏 rest 🔳 ☎ 🕭 ℗ – 🕭 80. 🔳 🆑 ⊙
M (bar lunch Saturday) 14.25/16.50 **st.** and dinner a la carte ⅃ 5.25 – 🖙 8.75 – **95 rm**
93.00/103.00 **st.**, 1 suite – SB (weekends only) 132.50/236.50 **st.**

at Shinfield S : 4 ¼ m. on A 327 – X – ⊠ 🕓 0734 Reading :

XXX 🕸🕸 **L'Ortolan** (Burton-Race) The Old Vicarage, Church Lane, RG2 9BY, ✐ 883783,
Fax 885391, ✐ – ℗. 🔳 🆑 ⊙ 𝘝𝘐𝘚𝘈
closed Sunday dinner, Monday, last 2 weeks February and last 2 weeks August –
M - French 29.50/55.00 **t.** ⅃ 6.95
Spec. Salade de caneton séché à l'air et pois gourmands, Filets de rouget étuvés au basilic, coulis de tomate et sauce
vierge, Chaud-froid au chocolat en deux services.

🔘 ATS Basingstoke Rd ✐ 580651

REDCAR Cleveland 🔳🔳 Q 20 – pop. 35 373 – 🕓 0642 Middlesbrough.

🏌 Wilton ✐ 465265, W : 3 m. on A 174 – 🏌 Cleveland, Queen St. ✐ 483693 – 🏌 Saltburn ✐ 0287
(Guisborough) 622812, S : 3 m.

◆London 255 – ◆Middlesbrough 9 – Scarborough 43.

🏨 **Park,** 3-5 Granville Terr., TS10 3AR, ✐ 490888, Fax 486147 – 🔳 ☎ ℗ – 🕭 40. 🔳 🆑 ⊙
𝘝𝘐𝘚𝘈
M 8.25/15.50 **t.** and a la carte ⅃ 4.75 – **33 rm** 🖙 38.00/65.00 **t.** – SB (weekends only)
50.00 **st.**

🔘 ATS Limerick Rd. Dormanstown ✐ 477100/   ATS 162 Lord St. ✐ 484013
477163

To visit a town or region : use the **Michelin Green Guides.**

REDDITCH Heref. and Worcs. 🔳🔳 🔳🔳 O 27 – pop. 61 639 – ECD : Wednesday – 🕓 0527.

🏌 Abbey Park, Dagnell End Rd ✐ 63918 – 🏌 Lower Grinsty, Green Lane, Callow Hill ✐ 543309,
SW : 3 m. by A 441 – 🏌 Pitcheroak, Plymouth Rd ✐ 541054.

🛈 Civic Square, Alcester St., B98 8AH ✐ 60806.

◆London 111 – ◆Birmingham 15 – Cheltenham 33 – Stratford-upon-Avon 15.

🏨 **Southcrest** (Best Western) 🐾, Pool Bank, Southcrest District, B97 4JG, ✐ 541511,
Fax 402600, ✐ – ⅋ 🔳 ☎ ℗ – 🕭 70. 🔳 🆑 ⊙ 𝘝𝘐𝘚𝘈
M *(closed Saturday lunch and Sunday dinner)* 10.50/12.50 **st.** and a la carte ⅃ 5.60 – **58 rm**
🖙 63.00/70.00 **st.** – SB (weekends only) 66.00 **st.**

🏠 **Old Rectory** 🐾, Ipsley Lane, Ipsley, B98 0AP, ✐ 523000, Fax 517003, ✐ – ⬱ rest ☎
℗. 🔳 🆑 ⊙ 𝘝𝘐𝘚𝘈. 🕸
M (communal dining) (dinner only) 14.95 **st.** ⅃ 3.95 – **10 rm** 🖙 39.95/77.50 **st.**

🏠 **Campanile,** Far Moore Lane, Winyates Green, B98 0SD, E : 2 ½ m. by A 4023 ✐ 510710,
Telex 339608, Fax 517269 – 🔳 ☎ 🕭 ℗. 🔳 🆑 𝘝𝘐𝘚𝘈
M 9.45 **t.** and a la carte ⅃ 4.65 – 🖙 4.25 – **47 rm** 35.75 **t.**

🔘 ATS Pipers Rd, Park Farm Ind. Est., Park Farm South ✐ 502002/502027

REDHILL Surrey 🔳🔳 T 30 – pop. 48 241 (inc. Reigate) – ECD : Wednesday – 🕓 0737.

🏌 Redhill & Reigate, Clarence Lodge, Pendleton Rd ✐ 244626/244433, S : 1 m. by A 23.

◆London 22 – ◆Brighton 31 – Guildford 20 – Maidstone 34.

🏨 **Nutfield Priory,** Nutfield, RH1 4EN, E : 2 m. on A 25 ✐ 822066, Fax 823321, ≤, *Ι₅*, ⇌,
🔲, park, squash – ⅋ 🔳 ☎ ℗ – 🕭 80. 🔳 🆑 ⊙ 𝘝𝘐𝘚𝘈
M *(closed Saturday lunch)* 17.50/19.95 **st.** and a la carte ⅃ 5.50 – 🖙 5.00 – **51 rm**
95.00/115.00 **t.**, 1 suite – SB (weekends only) 130.00/165.00 **st.**

🏨 **Lakers Toby,** 2 Redstone Hill, RH1 4BL, on A 25 ✐ 768434, Fax 768828 – 🗏 rest 🔳 ☎ 🕭
℗ – 🕭 40. 🔳 🆑 ⊙ 𝘝𝘐𝘚𝘈
M (grill rest.) 7.50 **t.** and a la carte – **37 rm** 🖙 48.50/58.50 **t.**

🏠 **Hunters Lodge,** Nutfield Rd, RH1 4ED, E : 1 ¾ m. on A 25 ✐ 773139, Fax 778190 – ⅋
🗏 rest 🔳 ☎ 🕭 ℗. 🔳 🆑 ⊙ 𝘝𝘐𝘚𝘈
M *(closed Friday to Sunday)* (dinner only) 15.00 **t.** and a la carte ⅃ 5.50 – **25 rm** 🖙 40.00/
55.00 **st.** – SB (weekends only) 69.00/119.00 **st.**

↷ **Ashleigh House** without rest., 39 Redstone Hill, RH1 4BG, on A 25 ✐ 764763,
Fax 780308, 🔲 heated, ✐ – ℗. 🔳 𝘝𝘐𝘚𝘈. 🕸
closed Christmas – **8 rm** 🖙 25.00/55.00 **st.**

at Salfords S : 2 ½ m. on A 23 – ⊠ 🕓 0737 Redhill :

🏠 Mill House, Brighton Rd, RH1 5BT, ✐ 767277, Fax 778099 – 🔳 ☎ ℗. 🕸
21 rm.

REDWORTH Durham – see Darlington.

REETH N. Yorks. 402 O 20 – pop. 534 (inc. Fremington) – ⊠ ❀ 0748 Richmond.

◆London 253 – ◆Leeds 53 – ◆Middlesbrough 36.

- ⌂ **Arkleside House,** DL11 6SG, ℰ 84200, Fax 84619, ≤, ✍ – ⇥ TV ℗, ◪ VISA
  closed January and February – **M** 15.75 st. ▯ 5.50 – **8 rm** ⊐ 40.00/75.00 st. – SB 84.50/
  108.00 **st.**

REIGATE Surrey 404 T 30 – pop. 48 241 (inc. Redhill) – ECD : Wednesday – ❀ 0737.

◆London 26 – ◆Brighton 33 – Guildford 20 – Maidstone 38.

- ⛪ **Bridge House,** Reigate Hill, RH2 9RP, N : 1¼ m. on A 217 ℰ 246801, Fax 223756 – TV ☎
  ℗ – ⩗ 40. ◪ AE ⓞ VISA. ✍
  M (dancing Tuesday to Saturday evenings) 15.75/17.50 **st.** and a la carte – ⊐ 7.50 – **37 rm**
  40.00/68.00 **st.**

- ⌂ **Cranleigh,** 41 West St., RH2 9BL, ℰ 223417, Fax 223734, ⌇ heated, ✍, ✾ – TV ☎ ℗.
  ◪ AE ⓞ VISA JCB. ✍
  M (by arrangement) 14.70 **t.** ▯ 5.00 – **10 rm** ⊐ 38.00/65.00 **t.** – SB 70.00/100.00 **st.**

- ✗ **La Barbe,** 71 Bell St., RH2 7AN, ℰ 241966, Fax 241966 – ▤, ◪ AE VISA
  closed Saturday lunch and Sunday – **M** - French 17.95/21.95 st. ▯ 5.00.

RENDCOMB Glos. 403 404 O 28 – see Cirencester.

RETFORD Notts. – see East Retford.

*Piante di città : le vie sono selezionate in funzione della loro importanza
per la circolazione e l'ubicazione degli edifici citati.*

Non indichiamo che l'inizio delle vie secondarie.

RICHMOND N. Yorks. 402 O 20 Great Britain G. – pop. 7 596 – ECD : Wednesday – ❀ 0748.

See : Castle★ *AC* – Georgian Theatre Royal and Museum★.

🗠 Bend Hagg ℰ 825319 – 🗠 Catterick Garrison, Leyburn Rd ℰ 833401, S : 3 m.

🗓 Friary Gardens, Victoria Rd, DL10 4AJ ℰ 850252/825994.

◆London 243 – ◆Leeds 53 – ◆Middlesbrough 26 – ◆Newcastle upon Tyne 44.

- ⛪ **Howe Villa** ⤢, Whitcliffe Mill, DL10 4TJ, W : ½ m. by A 6108 ℰ 850055, ≤, ✍ – ⇥ TV
  ℗.
  March-November – **M** (closed Sunday and Monday) (unlicensed) (dinner only) 20.00 **t.** –
  4 rm ⊐ 40.00/70.00 **t.**

- ⌂ **Whashton Springs Farm** ⤢, DL11 7JS, NW : 3 ½ m. by Ravensworth rd ℰ 822884,
  « Working farm », ✍, park – TV ☎ ℗. ✍
  closed mid December-February – **M** (by arrangement) 12.00 **st.** ▯ 3.00 – **8 rm** ⊐ 25.00/
  40.00 **st.** – SB (winter only) 60.00/76.00 **st.**

  at Kirby Hill NW : 4 ½ m. by Ravensworth rd – ⊠ ❀ 0748 Richmond :

- ⌂ **Shoulder of Mutton Inn,** DL11 7JH, ℰ 822772 – TV ℗. ✍
  M (closed Monday lunch) (in bar only) a la carte 7.70/12.95 **st.** ▯ 3.50 – **5 rm** ⊐ 25.00/
  39.00 **st.**

⊚ ATS Reeth Rd ℰ 824182/3

RIDGEWAY Derbs. – see Sheffield (S. Yorks.).

RINGWOOD Hants. 403 404 O 31 – pop. 10 941 – ECD : Monday and Thursday – ❀ 0425.

🗠 Ringwood ℰ 402431, NE : 4 m. – 🗠 Moors Valley, Horton Rd ℰ 479776, SW : 4 m. by A 31.

🗓 The Furlong, BH24 1AZ ℰ 470896 (summer only).

◆London 102 – Bournemouth 11 – Salisbury 17 – ◆Southampton 20.

- ⛪ **Moortown Lodge,** 244 Christchurch Rd, BH24 3AS, ℰ 471404 – ⇥ rest TV ☎ ℗. ◪
  VISA. ✍
  closed Christmas-mid January – **M** (closed Sunday to non-residents) (dinner only) 24.50 **t.**
  ▯ 4.35 – **6 rm** ⊐ 31.00/66.00 **t.** – SB 85.00/114.00 **st.**

  at Avon S : 4 m. on B 3347 – ⊠ Christchurch – ❀ 0425 Bransgore :

- ⛪ **Tyrrells Ford** ⤢, BH23 7BH, ℰ 672646, Fax 672262, ✍, park – TV ☎ ℗ – ⩗ 25. ◪ VISA.
  ✍
  M 14.95/18.95 **t.** and dinner a la carte ▯ 4.50 – **16 rm** ⊐ 50.00/90.00 **t.** – SB (except Bank
  Holidays) 70.00/140.00 **st.**

  at St Leonards (Dorset) SW : 3 m. on A 31 – ⊠ ❀ 0425 Ringwood :

- ⛪ St. Leonards, 185 Ringwood Rd, BH24 2NP, ℰ 471220, Telex 418215, Fax 480274, 🛝, ⇌
  – ⇥ rm TV ☎ ⴑ ℗ – ⩗ 50. ✍
  33 rm.

RIPLEY N. Yorks. 402 P 21 – pop. 147 – ⊠ ❀ 0423 Harrogate.

◆London 213 – Bradford 21 – ◆Leeds 18 – ◆Newcastle upon Tyne 79.

- ⛪ **Boar's Head,** HG3 3AY, ℰ 771888, Fax 771509 – TV ☎ ⴑ ℗. ◪ VISA
  M 12.95/26.50 **t.** – **25 rm** ⊐ 49.00/98.00 **t.** – SB (except Bank Holidays) 145.00/175.00 **st.**

426

RIPLEY Surrey 404 S 30 – pop. 1 903 – ECD : Wednesday – ✆ 0483 Guildford.

◆London 28 – Guildford 6.

XXX **Michels'**, 13 High St., GU23 6AQ, ℰ 224777, ☞ – ⊠ ⅍ VISA
closed Saturday lunch, Sunday dinner, Monday, 26 December and 1 January – **M** 19.00/28.00 **t.** and a la carte ᵈ 4.50.

RIPON N. Yorks. 402 P 21 Great Britain G. – pop. 13 036 – ECD : Wednesday – ✆ 0765.

See : Town★ - Cathedral★ (Saxon Crypt★★) *AC*.

Envir. : Fountains Abbey★★★ *AC* – Studley Royal★★ *AC* (≼★ from Anne Boleyn's Seat) - Fountains Hall (Façade★), SW : 2½ m. by B 6265 – Newby Hall (Tapestries★) *AC*, SE : 3½ m. by B 6265.

⌾ Ripon City, Palace Rd ℰ 603640, N : 1 m. on A 6108.

🛈 Minster Rd, HG4 1LT ℰ 604625 (summer only).

◆London 222 – ◆Leeds 26 – ◆Middlesbrough 35 – York 23.

🏨 **Ripon Spa** (Best Western), Park St., HG4 2BU, ℰ 602172, Fax 690770, ☞ – ⅋ TV ☎ ♿ ℗ – 🔬 150. ⅍ ⅍ ⓞ VISA JCB
M (lunch by arrangement Monday to Friday) 9.50/25.00 **t.** and a la carte ᵈ 6.00 – **40 rm** �☐ 56.20/98.00 **t.** – SB 104.00/116.00 **t.**

🛏 **Crescent Lodge** without rest., 42 North St., HG4 1EN, ℰ 602331 – TV ℗. ⅍
closed December and January – **10 rm** ☐ 16.00/38.00.

X **Great Wall**, 41 Market Pl. South, HG4 1BZ, ℰ 606469 – ⅍ VISA
closed Sunday to Wednesday lunch and Tuesday – **M** - Chinese a la carte 10.30/18.50 **st.**

🅜 ATS Dallamires Lane ℰ 601570

ROADE Northants. – pop. 2 703 – ✆ 0604.

◆London 66 – ◆Coventry 36 – Northampton 5.5.

XX **Roadhouse**, 16 High St., NN7 2NW, ℰ 863372 – ℗. ⅍ ⅍ VISA
closed Saturday lunch, Sunday dinner, Monday, 2 weeks summer and 1 week Christmas – **M** 16.00 **st.** (lunch) and a la carte 16.00/23.00 **st.** ᵈ 4.50.

ROCHDALE Gtr. Manchester 402 N 23 – pop. 96 359 – ✆ 0706.

⌾ Edenfield Rd, Bagslate ℰ 46024 – ⌾ Marland, Springfield Park ℰ 49801, W : m. by A 58 – ⌾ Lobden, Whitworth ℰ 343228, N : 4 m. – ⌾, ⌾, ⌾ Castle Hawk, Heywood Rd ℰ 40841.

🛈 The Clock Tower, Town Hall, OL16 1AB ℰ 356592.

◆London 224 – ◆Blackpool 40 – Burnley 11 – ◆Leeds 45 – ◆Manchester 12 – ◆Liverpool 40.

🏨 **Norton Grange**, Manchester Rd, Castleton, OL11 2XZ, SW : 3 m. by A 58 on A 644 ℰ 30788, Fax 49313, ☞ – ⅋ TV ☎ ♿ ℗ – 🔬 100. ⅍ ⅍ ⓞ VISA
M *(closed Saturday lunch)* 13.50 **t.** (dinner) and a la carte – **49 rm** ☐ 72.50/87.50 **t.**, 1 suite – SB (weekends only) 86.00/114.50 **st.**

🅜 ATS Royds St. ℰ 32411/49935   ATS Castleton Moor, Nixon St. (ASDA) ℰ 57068

ROCHESTER Kent 404 V 29 Great Britain G. – pop. 23 840 – ECD : Wednesday – ✉ Chatham – ✆ 0634 Medway.

See : Castle★ *AC* – Cathedral★ *AC*.

🛈 Eastgate Cottage, High St., ME1 1EW ℰ 843666.

◆London 30 – ◆Dover 45 – Maidstone 8 – Margate 46.

🏨 **Bridgewood Manor** (Best Western), Maidstone Rd, ME5 9AX, SE : 3 m. by A 2 on A 229 ℰ 201333, Fax 201330, ℔, ⅏, ⊑, ⅍ – ⅋ TV ☎ ♿ ℗ – 🔬 150. ⅍ ⅍ ⓞ VISA
M 10.50/15.00 **st.** and a la carte ᵈ 6.50 – **96 rm** ☐ 85.00/105.00 **st.**, 4 suites – SB (weekends only) 90.00/100.00 **t.**

🏨 **Forte Posthouse**, Maidstone Rd, ME5 9SF, SE : 2½ m. by A 2 on A 229 ℰ 687111, Telex 965933, Fax 684512, ℔, ⅏, ⊑, ☞ – ⅋ ↤ rm ⊟ rest TV ☎ ♿ ℗ – 🔬 120. ⅍ ⅍ ⓞ VISA
M a la carte approx. 17.50 **t.** ᵈ 4.65 – ☐ 6.95 – **105 rm** 53.50 **t.** – SB (weekends only) 90.00 **st.**

ROCK Cornwall 403 F 32 The West Country G. – ECD : Wednesday – ✉ Wadebridge – ✆ 0208 Bodmin.

Exc. : Pencarrow★, SE : 8½ m. by B 3314 and A 389.

◆London 288 – Newquay 22 – ◆Plymouth 45 – Truro 30.

🏨 **St. Enodoc** ⅏, PL27 6LA, ℰ 863394, Fax 863394, ≼, ℔, ⅏, ⊑ heated, ☞, squash – ↤ rest TV ☎ ℗. ⅍ ⅍ VISA
M (bar lunch)/dinner 17.95 **t.** – **13 rm** ☐ 50.00/100.00 **t.**

ROCKBOURNE Hants. 403 404 O 31 – see Fordingbridge.

ROCK FERRY Mersey. – ✉ Wirral – ✆ 051 Liverpool.

◆London 212 – Chester 15 – ◆Liverpool 5.

🛏 **Yew Tree**, 58 Rock Lane West, L42 4PA, ℰ 645 4112, Fax 645 4112 – TV ℗. ⅍ ⅍ VISA ⅍
M (by arrangement) 8.20 **st.** ᵈ 3.50 – **14 rm** ☐ 20.85/44.00 **st.**

RODBOROUGH Glos. – see Stroud.

ROGATE W. Sussex 404 R 30 – pop. 1 459 – ⊠ Petersfield (Hants.) – ✿ 0730.

🛵 Old Thorns, Longmoor Rd ℰ 724555, NE : 5 m. by A 3.

♦London 63 – ♦Brighton 42 – Guildford 29 – ♦Portsmouth 23 – ♦Southampton 36.

↷ **Mizzards Farm** 🦢 without rest., GU31 5HS, SW : 1 m. by Harting Rd ℰ 821656, ≼,
« 17C farmhouse », ⌱ heated, ☞, park – ६≯ 🆂 🆃🆅 🅿. ⌱
closed Christmas – **3 rm** ⌸ 32.00/50.00 **st.**

ROLLESTON-ON-DOVE Staffs. 402 403 404 P 25 – see Burton-upon-Trent.

ROMALDKIRK Durham 402 N 20 – see Barnard Castle.

ROMSEY Hants. 403 404 P 31 Great Britain G. – pop. 14 818 – ECD : Wednesday – ✿ 0794.

See : Abbey★ (interior★★).

Envir. : Broadlands★ *AC*, S : 1 m.

🛵 Dunwood Manor, Shootash Hill ℰ 0794 (Lockerley) 40549, 4 m. on A 27 – 🛵 Nursling ℰ 0703
(Southampton) 732218, SE : 2 m. by A 3057 – 🛵 Wellow, Ryedown Lane, East Wellow ℰ 22872,
W : 2 m.

🄳 Bus Station Car Park, Broadwater Rd, SO51 8BF ℰ 512987.

♦London 82 – Bournemouth 28 – Salisbury 16 – ♦Southampton 8 – Winchester 10.

🏨 **White Horse** (Forte), Market Pl., SO51 8ZJ, ℰ 512431, Fax 517485 – ६≯ rm 🆃🆅 ☎ 🅿. 🆔
🆎 ⓪ 🆅🆂🅰 🆁🅲🅱
M (bar lunch Monday to Saturday)/dinner 16.95 **t.** and a la carte ⌀ 5.25 – ⌸ 8.95 – **33 rm**
75.00/90.00 **st.** – SB 116.00 **st.**

↷ **Spursholt House** 🦢 without rest., Salisbury Rd, SO51 6DJ, W : 1¼ m. by A 31 on A 27
ℰ 523229, Fax 523142, « Part 17C mansion, gardens » – ६≯ 🅿. ⌱
3 rm ⌸ 24.00/40.00 **st.**

%%% **Old Manor House,** 21 Palmerston St., SO51 8GF, ℰ 517353, « Timbered 16C house » –
🅿. 🆔 🆅🆂🅰
closed Sunday dinner, Monday and 24 to 31 December – **M** 25.00/35.00 **t.** ⌀ 5.50.

at Ower SW : 3¼ m. on A 31 – ⊠ Romsey – ✿ 0703 Southampton :

🏨 **New Forest Heathlands,** Romsey Rd, SO51 6ZJ, on A 31 ℰ 814333, Fax 812123, ⌨,
⇌🅂, ☞ – 🆃🆅 ☎ 🅿 – 🔬 200. 🆔 🆎 ⓪ 🆅🆂🅰
closed 23 to 28 December – **M** *(closed Saturday lunch)* 8.00/15.75 **t.** and a la carte ⌀ 5.95 –
51 rm ⌸ 40.00/92.00 **t.** – SB 82.00/97.00 **st.**

ROSEDALE ABBEY N. Yorks. 402 R 20 Great Britain G. – pop. 273 (Rosedale) – ⊠ Pickering –
✿ 0751 Lastingham.

Envir. : ≼★ on road to Hutton-le-Hole.

♦London 247 – ♦Middlesbrough 27 – Scarborough 25 – York 36.

🏨 **Blacksmith's Arms,** Hartoft End, YO18 8EN, SE : 2½ m. on Pickering rd ℰ 417331, ≼,
☞ – 🆃🆅 ☎ 🅿. 🆔 🆎 ⓪ 🆅🆂🅰
M 14.95/25.00 **t.** and a la carte ⌀ 4.75 – **14 rm** ⌸ 46.00/72.00 **t.** – SB (except Bank Holidays)
77.00/128.00 **st.**

🏠 **Milburn Arms,** YO18 8RA, ℰ 417312, Fax 417312, ☞ – 🆃🆅 ☎ 🅿. 🆔 ⓪ 🆅🆂🅰
M (bar lunch Monday to Saturday)/dinner a la carte 18.15/23.75 **t.** ⌀ 4.25 – **11 rm** ⌸ 42.50/
70.00 **t.** – SB (except Bank Holidays) 90.00/119.00 **t.**

🏡 **White Horse Farm,** YO18 8SE, ℰ 417239, Fax 417781 – 🆃🆅 🅿. 🆔 🆎 ⓪ 🆅🆂🅰
closed 24 and 25 December – **M** (bar lunch Monday to Saturday)/dinner 18.00
t. and a la carte ⌀ 5.45 – **15 rm** ⌸ 35.00/70.00 **t.** – SB (except Bank Holidays) 75.00/
100.00 **t.**

↷ **Sevenford House** 🦢 without rest., Thorgill, YO18 8SE, NW : ¾ m. ℰ 417505, ☞ – ६≯
🆃🆅 🅿
3 rm ⌸ 20.00/32.00 **s.**

ROSSINGTON S. Yorks. 402 403 404 Q 23 – see Doncaster.

ROSS-ON-WYE Heref. and Worcs. 403 404 M 28 Great Britain G. – pop. 8 281 – ECD : Wednesday – ✿ 0989.

See : Market House★ – Yat Rock (≼★).

Envir. : SW : Wye Valley★ – Goodrich Castle★ *AC*, SW : 3½ m. by A 40.

🄳 20 Broad St., HR9 7EA ℰ 62768.

♦London 118 – Gloucester 15 – Hereford 15 – Newport 35.

🏨 **Royal** (Forte), Palace Pound, HR9 5HZ, 𝒫 65105, Fax 768058, ≤, 🐎 – ⇖ rm 📺 ☎ 🅿 –
🛕 80. 🔼 🅰🇪 ⑨ 𝗩𝗜𝗦𝗔 𝗝𝗖𝗕
M (bar lunch Monday to Saturday)/dinner 15.95 **st.** and a la carte 🛢 5.25 – ⊆ 8.50 – **40 rm**
75.00/100.00 **st.** – SB 116.00/131.00 **st.**

🏨 **Chase,** Gloucester Rd, HR9 5LH, 𝒫 763161, Fax 768330, 🐎 – 📺 ☎ 🅿 – 🛕 275. 🔼 🅰🇪
⑨ 𝗩𝗜𝗦𝗔. 🌺
M (bar lunch Saturday and Bank Holiday Mondays) 12.50/21.95 **st.** and a la carte 🛢 4.50 –
39 rm ⊆ 50.00/75.00 **st.** – SB (except Christmas and New Year) 100.00/140.00 **st.**

𝐴 **Sunnymount** 🌺, Ryefield Rd, off Gloucester Rd, HR9 5LU, 𝒫 63880 – ⇖ rest 🅿. 🔼 🅰🇪
𝗩𝗜𝗦𝗔.
closed Christmas – **M** (by arrangement) 14.00 **st.** 🛢 3.50 – **6 rm** ⊆ 29.00/48.00 **st.** –
SB 67.00/84.00 **st.**

at Weston-Under-Penyard SE : 2 m. on A 40 – ⊠ 🕙 0989 Ross-on-Wye:

🏨 Wharton Lodge, HR9 7JX, SE : 1 ½ m. on A 40 𝒫 750795, Fax 750700, 🐎, park – 📺 ☎ 🅿.
🌺
8 rm.

at Glewstone SW : 3 ¼ m. by A 40 – ⊠ Ross-on-Wye – 🕙 0989 Llangarron :

🏠 **Glewstone Court** 🌺, HR9 6AW, 𝒫 770367, Fax 770282, ≤, « Part Georgian and Victorian country house », 🐎 – 📺 ☎ 🅿. 🔼 𝗩𝗜𝗦𝗔
closed 25 to 27 December – **M** 16.00/21.00 **t.** and a la carte 🛢 4.00 – **7 rm** ⊆ 50.00/90.00 **t.**
– SB (except Bank Holidays) 100.00/140.00 **st.**

at Pencraig SW : 3 ¾ m. on A 40 – ⊠ Ross-on-Wye – 🕙 0989 Llangarron :

🏠 **Pencraig Court,** HR9 6HR, 𝒫 770306, 🐎 – 📺 ☎ 🅿. 🔼 🅰🇪 ⑨ 𝗩𝗜𝗦𝗔. 🌺
April-October – **M** (bar lunch)/dinner 13.50 **t.** 🛢 3.75 – **10 rm** ⊆ 25.00/66.00 **t.** – SB 67.00/
112.00 **st.**

at Wilton W : 1 ¼ m. on A 49 – ⊠ 🕙 0989 Ross-on-Wye :

🏠 **Castle Lodge,** HR9 6AD, 𝒫 62234, Fax 768322 – 📺 ☎ 🅿. 🔼 𝗩𝗜𝗦𝗔. 🌺
M 14.50 **t.** and a la carte 🛢 3.60 – **10 rm** ⊆ 32.50/49.50 **t.**

at Peterstow W : 2 ½ m. on A 49 – ⊠ Ross-on-Wye – 🕙 098 987 (3 fig.) and 0989
(6 fig.) Harewood End :

🏨 **Pengethley Manor** (Best Western) 🌺, HR9 6LL, NW : 1 ½ m. on A 49 𝒫 211, Fax 238,
≤, « Georgian country manor », ⤓ heated, 🐎, park – 📺 ☎ 🅿 – 🛕 35. 🔼 🅰🇪 ⑨ 𝗩𝗜𝗦𝗔
𝗝𝗖𝗕
M 16.00/24.00 **st.** and a la carte 🛢 7.25 – **20 rm** ⊆ 50.00/160.00 **st.**, 3 suites – SB 130.00/
180.00 **st.**

🏨 **Peterstow Country House** 🌺, HR9 6LB, 𝒫 62826, Fax 67264, ≤, « Converted
Georgian rectory », 🐎, park – 📺 ☎ 🅿. 🔼 🅰🇪 ⑨ 𝗩𝗜𝗦𝗔 𝗝𝗖𝗕. 🌺
M 12.50/22.50 **st.** and a la carte 🛢 9.00 – **9 rm** ⊆ 38.50/90.00 **st.** – SB 89.00/124.00 **st.**

🔧 ATS Ind. Est., Alton Rd 𝒫 64638

ROSTHWAITE Cumbria 🔢 K 20 – see Keswick.

ROTHBURY Northd 🔢 🔢 O 18 Great Britain G. – pop. 1 694 – ECD : Wednesday – ⊠
Morpeth – 🕙 0669.
See : Cragside House★ (interior★) *AC.*

🛈 National Park Information Centre, Church House, Church St., NE65 7UP 𝒫 20887 (summer
only).

◆London 311 – ◆Edinburgh 84 – ◆Newcastle upon Tyne 29.

𝐴 **Orchard,** High St., NE65 7TL, 𝒫 20684, 🐎 – ⇖ rest 📺. 🌺
April-November – **M** 13.00 **st.** 🛢 3.80 – **6 rm** ⊆ 22.00/44.00 **t.** – SB 64.00/68.00 **st.**

ROTHERHAM S. Yorks. 🔢 🔢 🔢 P 23 – pop. 122 374 – ECD : Thursday – 🕙 0709.

🏌 Thrybergh Park 𝒫 850466, E : 4 m. by A 630 – 🏌 Grange Park, Upper Wortley Rd 𝒫 559497,
W : 2 m. by A 629 – 🏌 Phoenix, Brinsworth 𝒫 382624, S : 2 m. on Bawtry rd.

🛈 Central Library, Walker Pl., S65 1JH 𝒫 823611.

◆London 166 – ◆Kingston-upon-Hull 61 – ◆Leeds 36 – ◆Sheffield 6.

🏨 **Rotherham Moat House** (Q.M.H.), 102-104 Moorgate Rd, S60 2BG, 𝒫 364902, Group
Telex 547810, Fax 368960, 𝕷, ≘s – 🛗 ⇖ rm 🍽 rest 📺 ☎ 🅿 – 🛕 100. 🔼 🅰🇪 ⑨ 𝗩𝗜𝗦𝗔. 🌺
M (bar lunch Saturday) 12.00/14.50 **st.** and a la carte 🛢 5.85 – **80 rm** ⊆ 66.00/102.00 **st.** –
SB (July-August and weekends in winter only) 84.00 **st.**

🏨 **Swallow,** West Bawtry Rd, S60 4NA, SE : 2 ¼ m. on A 630 𝒫 830630, Fax 830549, 𝕷, 🔲
– 🛗 ⇖ rm 📺 ☎ ⛴ 🅿 – 🛕 300. 🔼 🅰🇪 ⑨ 𝗩𝗜𝗦𝗔
M 11.95/15.00 **st.** and a la carte 🛢 5.95 – **98 rm** ⊆ 78.00/96.00 **st.**, 2 suites – SB (except
Christmas and New Year) 126.00/186.00 **st.**

🏠 **Travel Inn,** Bawtry Rd, S65 3JB, E : 2 m. by A 6021 on A 631 – 𝒫 543216, Fax 531546 –
⇆ rm 📺 ⅋ 🅿. 🖂 🆎 ⓞ 𝚅𝙸𝚂𝙰. 🛇
M (Beefeater grill) a la carte approx. 16.00 **t.** – ⌦ 4.95 – **37 rm** 33.50 **t.**

🏠 **Campanile,** Lowton Way, Hellaby Ind. Est., S66 8RY, E : 5 m. by A 6021 and A 631 off
Denby Way 𝒫 700255, Fax 545169 – 📺 ☎ ⅋ 🅿. 🖂 🆎 𝚅𝙸𝚂𝙰
M 9.45 **t.** and a la carte ▯ 4.65 – ⌦ 4.25 – **51 rm** 35.75 **t.**

at Bramley E : 4 m. by A 6021 off A 631 – ✉ 🅰 0709 Rotherham :

🏨 **Elton** (Best Western), Main St., S66 0SF, 𝒫 545681, Fax 549100 – ⇆ rm 📺 ☎ 🅿. 🖂 🆎
ⓞ 𝚅𝙸𝚂𝙰
M 10.50/16.95 **st.** and a la carte ▯ 5.50 – **29 rm** ⌦ 50.00/74.00 **st.** – SB (except Christmas)
(weekends only) 84.00/90.00 **st.**

◉ ATS Eastwood Works, Fitzwilliam Rd 𝒫 371556/372391

ROTHERWICK Hants – see Hook.

ROTHLEY Leics. 402 403 404 Q 25 – see Leicester.

ROTTINGDEAN E. Sussex 404 T 31 – pop. 10 888 (inc. Saltdean) – ECD : Wednesday –
✉ 🅰 0273 Brighton.

◆London 58 – ◆Brighton 4 – Lewes 9 – Newhaven 5.

⌂ **Braemar** without rest., Steyning Rd, BN2 7GA, 𝒫 304263, 🚡
15 rm ⌦ 14.00/30.00 **t.**

Pour visiter une ville ou une région : utilisez les **Guides Verts Michelin.**

ROUGHAM GREEN Suffolk – see Bury St. Edmunds.

ROWDE Wilts. 403 404 N 29 – see Devizes

ROWNHAMS SERVICE AREA Hants. 403 404 P 31 – ✉ 🅰 0703 Southampton.

🅿 M 27 Services (westbound), SO1 8AW 𝒫 730345.

🏠 **Road Chef Lodge** without rest., S01 8AW, M 27 between junctions 3 and 4 (southbound
carriageway) 𝒫 741144, Fax 740204 – ⇆ 📺 ☎ ⅋ 🅿. 🖂 🆎 ⓞ 𝚅𝙸𝚂𝙰. 🛇
closed 25 and 26 December – ⌦ 5.25 – **39 rm** 32.00/38.00 **st.**

ROWSLEY Derbs. 402 403 404 P 24 Great Britain G. – pop. 200 – ECD : Thursday – ✉ Matlock
– 🅰 0629 Matlock.
Envir. : Chatsworth★★★ (Park and Garden★★★) *AC,* N : by B 6012.

◆London 157 – Derby 23 – ◆Manchester 40 – ◆Nottingham 30.

🏨 **Peacock** (Jarvis), Bakewell Rd, DE4 2EB, 𝒫 733518, Fax 732671, « 17C stone house,
antiques », 🐟, 🚡 – 📺 ☎ 🅿. 🖂 🆎 ⓞ 𝚅𝙸𝚂𝙰
M 12.25/26.00 ▯ 7.50 – **14 rm** ⌦ 58.00/109.00 **st.** – SB 112.00/138.00 **st.**

ROWTON Ches. 402 403 L 24 – see Chester.

ROYAL LEAMINGTON SPA Warks. 403 404 P 27 – pop. 56552 – ECD : Monday and Thursday
– 🅰 0926.

🏌 Leamington and County, Golf Lane, Whitnash 𝒫 425961, S: 3 m. by Tachbrook Rd Z on plan
of Warwick.

🅱 Jephson Lodge, Jephson Gardens, The Parade, CV32 4AB 𝒫 311470.

◆London 99 – ◆Birmingham 23 – ◆Coventry 9 – Warwick 3.

Plan on next page

🏨 🅰 **Mallory Court** (Holland) 🐟, Harbury Lane, Bishop's Tachbrook, CV33 9QB, S : 2¼ m.
by B 4087 (Tachbrook Rd) 𝒫 330214, Fax 451714, ≼, « Country house in extensive
gardens », 🛥, park, 🎾, squash – 📺 ☎ 🅿. 🖂 🆎 𝚅𝙸𝚂𝙰. 🛇 plan of Warwick Z
M (booking essential) 24.50/31.50 **st.** and a la carte 40.00/63.50 **st.** – ⌦ 10.95 – **9 rm**
105.00/210.00 **st.** 1 suite – SB (weekdays only October-March) 208.00/343.00 **st.**
Spec. Lobster and wild salmon terrine with pistachios (April-October). Breast of duck with a confit of the leg. Assiette
of chocolate.

🏨 Manor House (Forte), Avenue Rd, CV31 3NJ, 𝒫 832511, Fax 425933 – 🛗 ⇆ 📺 ☎ 🅿 –
🛎 100 V i
53 rm.

🏨 **Inchfield,** 64 Upper Holly Walk, CV32 4JL, 𝒫 883777, Fax 330467, 🚡 – 📺 ☎ 🅿 – 🛎 40.
🖂 🆎 𝚅𝙸𝚂𝙰. 🛇 U o
M 15.75/28.75 **t.** and a la carte ▯ 4.50 – ⌦ 6.50 – **22 rm** 55.00/90.00 **t.** – SB (weekends only)
79.00/170.00 **st.**

🏨 **Falstaff** (Mt. Charlotte Thistle), 16-20 Warwick New Rd, CV32 5JQ, 𝒫 312044,
Fax 450574 – 🛗 rest 📺 ☎ 🅿 – 🛎 50. 🖂 🆎 ⓞ 𝚅𝙸𝚂𝙰 𝙹𝙲𝙱. 🛇 Z s
M 14.00/18.00 **t.** and a la carte ▯ 4.50 – **63 rm** ⌦ 59.00/98.00 **t.** – SB (except Christmas-
New Year) (weekends only) 78.00 **st.**

ROYAL
LEAMINGTON SPA

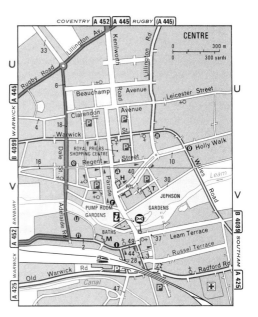

🏨 **Regent** (Best Western), 77 Parade, CV32 4AX, ℰ 427231, Telex 311715, Fax 450728 – 📶
📶 ⇔ 🍽 rest 📺 ☎ 🅿 – 🔬 100. 🖭 🖭 ⓪ 𝐕𝐈𝐒𝐀 𝐉𝐂𝐁   V a
M 11.75/16.50 **st.** and a la carte 🍷 4.75 – **80 rm** ⊊ 65.00/120.00 **st.** – SB (except Christmas
and New Year) 96.00 **st.**

🏨 **Courtyard by Marriott**, Olympus Av., Tachbrook Park, CV34 6RJ, SW : 1½ m. by A 452
ℰ 425522, Fax 881322, 🏋 – 📶 ⇔ rm 🍽 rest 📺 ☎ ♿ 🅿 – 🔬 50. 🖭 🖭 ⓪ 𝐕𝐈𝐒𝐀 𝐉𝐂𝐁. ⅌
M 13.75 **st.** and a la carte 🍷 4.00 – ⊊ 7.50 – **94 rm** 40.00/82.00 **st.** – SB (weekends only)
68.00/88.00 **st.**   plan of Warwick   Z v

🏨 **Lansdowne**, 87 Clarendon St., CV32 4PF, ℰ 450505, Fax 421313 – 📺 ☎ 🅿. 🖭 𝐕𝐈𝐒𝐀. ⅌
M (dinner only) 19.95 **t.** 🍷 4.65 – **15 rm** ⊊ 29.85/59.90 **t.** – SB 73.80/105.90 **st.**   U a

🏨 **Adams**, 22 Avenue Rd, CV31 3PQ, ℰ 450742, Fax 313110, « Regency town house », 🌿
– 📺 ☎ 🅿. 🖭 🖭 ⓪ 𝐕𝐈𝐒𝐀. ⅌   V n
M (lunch by arrangement)/dinner 18.50 and a la carte 🍷 4.30 – **14 rm** ⊊ 35.00/58.00 **t.** –
SB (weekends only) 72.95/95.00 **st.**

🏨 **Eaton Court**, 1-7 St. Marks Rd, CV32 6DL, ℰ 885848, Fax 885848, 🌿 – ⇔ 📺 ☎ 🅿 –
🔬 80. 🖭 🖭 𝐕𝐈𝐒𝐀. ⅌   plan of Warwick   Z e
closed 24 December-2 January – **M** (lunch by arrangement)/dinner 12.95 **st.** and a la carte
– **36 rm** ⊊ 22.50/75.00 **st.** – SB (weekends only) 64.90/67.95 **st.**

🏠 **York House**, 9 York Rd, CV31 3PR, ℰ 424671 – ⇔ rm 📺 ☎. 🖭 🖭 𝐕𝐈𝐒𝐀. ⅌   V u
closed 23 December-2 January – **M** (by arrangement) 10.00 **st.** – **8 rm** ⊊ 22.50/50.00 **st.**

🏠 **Flowerdale House** without rest., 58 Warwick New Rd, CV32 6AA, ℰ 426002, 🌿 – 📺
🅿. 🖭 𝐕𝐈𝐒𝐀 ⅌   plan of Warwick   Z c
6 rm ⊊ 22.00/42.00 **s.**

🏠 **Coverdale House** without rest., 8 Portland St., CV32 5HE, ℰ 330400, Fax 833388 – 📺
☎. 🖭 𝐕𝐈𝐒𝐀   U e
7 rm ⊊ 31.00/42.00 **st.**

🍴🍴 **Les Plantagenets**, 15 Dormer Pl., CV32 5AA, ℰ 451792 – 🖭 🖭 𝐕𝐈𝐒𝐀   V r
closed Saturday lunch, Sunday and Bank Holidays – **M** - French 12.50/18.50 **t.** and a la
carte.

◍ ATS 52-54 Morton St. ℰ 339643/4

See : The Pantiles★ B **26** – Calverley Park★ B

⌐₅ Langton Rd *℘* 523034 A.

🛈 Monson House, Monson Way, TN1 1LQ *℘* 515675.

◆London 36 – ◆Brighton 33 – Folkestone 46 – Hastings 27 – Maidstone 18.

ROYAL TUNBRIDGE WELLS

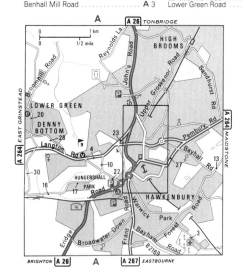

🏨🏨🏨 **Spa** (Best Western), Mount Ephraim, TN4 8XJ, *℘* 520331, Fax 510575, ≤, 𝄢, ≘s, ◪, ≋, park, ❅ – 🛗 📺 ☎ & ⑫ – 🕭 300. 🖭 🝙 ⓪ 𝓥𝓘𝓢𝓐
A v
M *(closed Saturday lunch)* 17.50/18.00 **t.** and a la carte ↥ 4.75 – ⌑ 8.50 – **72 rm** 80.00/110.00 **st.**, 4 suites – SB (weekends only) 128.00 **st.**

🏨🏨 **Russell,** 80 London Rd, TN1 1DZ, *℘* 544833, Telex 95177, Fax 515846 – ⟷ rm 📺 ☎ ⑫.
🖭 🝙 ⓪ 𝓥𝓘𝓢𝓐 JCB. ❅
B a
M 10.00/16.50 **t.** and a la carte ↥ 5.60 – **26 rm** ⌑ 50.00/88.00 **t.** – SB 96.00/116.00 **st.**

🏨🏨 **Swan,** The Pantiles, TN2 5TD, *℘* 541450, Fax 541465 – 📺 ☎ ⑫ – 🕭 55. 🖭 🝙 ⓪ 𝓥𝓘𝓢𝓐
JCB. ❅
A a
M 13.00/18.00 **t.** and a la carte ↥ 5.00 – **17 rm** ⌑ 40.00/110.00 **st.** – SB (except Christmas) 95.00/140.00 **st.**

🍴🍴 **Cheevers,** 56 High St., TN1 1XF, *℘* 545524, Fax 535956 – 🖭 🝙 𝓥𝓘𝓢𝓐
B c
closed Sunday, Monday and 1 week Christmas – Meals 22.50 **t.** (dinner) and lunch a la carte 14.75/18.00 **t.**

🍴🍴 **Eglantine,** 65 High St., TN1 1XX, *℘* 524957, Fax 527100 – 🖭 🝙 𝓥𝓘𝓢𝓐
B s
closed Tuesday and Wednesday dinner, Sunday, Monday and 23 to 27 December – **M** a la carte 11.50/14.90 **t.** ↥ 4.70.

🍴🍴 **Xian,** 54 High St., TN1 1XF, *℘* 522930 – 🖭 🝙 𝓥𝓘𝓢𝓐
B c
closed 25 and 26 December – **M** - Chinese 11.00/19.50 **t.** and a la carte ↥ 4.05.

🍴🍴 **Chi,** 26 London Rd, TN1 1DA, *℘* 513888 – 🖭 𝓥𝓘𝓢𝓐
B e
closed lunch Saturday and Sunday and 25-26 December – **M** - Chinese 17.50/22.50 **t.** and a la carte.

at Pembury NW : 4 m. by A 264 off A 21 – A – ✉ ☎ 0892 Royal Tunbridge Wells :

🏨🏨 **Pembury Resort,** 8 Tonbridge Rd, TN2 4QL, *℘* 823567, Fax 823931, 𝄢, ≘s, ◪ – 🛗
⟷ rm 📺 ☎ & ⑫ – 🕭 160. 🖭 🝙 ⓪ 𝓥𝓘𝓢𝓐
M *(closed Saturday lunch)* 10.95/16.50 **t.** and a la carte ↥ 8.75 – **74 rm** ⌑ 65.00/75.00 **t.**, 6 suites – SB 96.00/122.00 **st.**

at Frant S : 2 ½ m. on A 267 – A – ⊠ ☏ 0892 Royal Tunbridge Wells :

⌂ **Old Parsonage** without rest., Church Lane, TN3 9DX, ☏ 750773, ⊰, « Georgian rectory », 🐎 – ⥮ 📺 ❷
3 rm 🖙 38.00/54.00 **st.**

at Rusthall W : 1 ¾ m. by A 264 – ⊠ ☏ 0892 Royal Tunbridge Wells :

⌂ **Danehurst,** 41 Lower Green Rd, TN4 8TW, ☏ 527739, Fax 514804, 🐎 – ⥮ 📺 ❷. 🔊
VISA. 🦌   A ℮
M 21.50 **s. – 5 rm** 🖙 29.75/55.00 **s.** – SB (November-April) 69.50/126.90 **st.**

RUAN-HIGH-LANES Cornwall 403 F 33 – see Veryan.

RUCKHALL Heref. and Worcs. – see Hereford.

RUGBY Warks. 403 404 O 26 – pop. 59 039 – ECD : Wednesday – ☏ 0788.

🏌 Whitefields Hotel, Coventry Rd, Thurlaston ☏ 521800, SW : 3 m. by A 45.

🛈 The Library, St. Matthews St., CV21 3BZ ☏ 535348.

♦London 88 – ♦Birmingham 33 – ♦Leicester 21 – Northampton 20 – Warwick 17.

🏨 **Grosvenor,** Clifton Rd, CV21 3QQ, ☏ 535686, Fax 541297, *ℐ₅*, ≘s, ⊠ – 📺 ☏ ❷. 🔊 🈀
⓪ *VISA*. 🦌
M *(closed Saturday lunch)* 12.95/17.95 **st.** and a la carte – **20 rm** 🖙 67.50/77.50 **st.**, 1 suite
– SB (weekends only) 67.50/75.00 **st.**

✕✕ **Mr Chan's,** 3-5 Castle St., CV21 2TP, ☏ 542326, Fax 542326 – 🔊 🈀 *VISA*
closed 25 and 26 December – **M** *-* Chinese 10.00 **t.** (dinner) and a la carte 11.00/33.30 **t.**

at Old Brownsover N : 2 m. by A 426 and Brownsover Rd – ⊠ ☏ 0788 Rugby :

🏨 **Brownsover Hall,** Brownsover Lane, CV21 1HU, ☏ 546100, Fax 579241, « 18C Gothic
style hall », 🐎, 🦌 – ⥮ rm 📺 ☏ ❷ – 🔬 80. 🔊 🈀 ⓪ *VISA*
M *(closed lunch Saturday and Bank Holidays)* 9.95/16.95 **t.** and a la carte ≬ 5.00 – **31 rm**
🖙 42.50/115.00 **t.** – SB (weekends only) 78.00/98.00 **st.**

at Crick SE : 6 m. on A 428 – ⊠ ☏ 0788 Crick :

🏨 **Forte Posthouse,** NN6 7XR, W : ½ m. on A 428 ☏ 822101, Fax 823955, *ℐ₅*, ≘s, ⊠ –
⥮ rm 📺 ☏ ❷ – 🔬 200. 🔊 🈀 ⓪ *VISA* *JCB*
M a la carte approx. 17.50 **t.** ≬ 4.65 – 🖙 6.95 – **88 rm** 53.50 **st.** – SB 90.00 **st.**

at Kilsby SE : 6 ¼ m. by A 428 on A 5 – ⊠ ☏ 0788 Rugby :

✕✕ **Hunt House,** Main Rd, CV23 8XR, ☏ 823282, 🐎 – ❷. 🔊 🈀 ⓪ *VISA*
closed Sunday and Monday – **M** (dinner only) 19.50 **t.** ≬ 4.75.

at West Haddon (Northants.) SE : 10 m. on A 428 – ⊠ ☏ 0788 West Haddon :

🏠 **Pytchley,** 23 High St., NN6 7AP, ☏ 510426, Fax 510209, 🐎 – 📺 ☏ ❷. 🔊 🈀 *VISA*. 🦌
M (bar lunch Monday to Saturday)/dinner 15.95 **t.** and a la carte ≬ 4.50 – **14 rm** 🖙 28.00/
50.00 **t.**

at Stretton Under Fosse NW : 7 ½ m. by A 426 and B 4112 on A 427 – ⊠ ☏ 0788
Rugby :

🏠 **Ashton Lodge,** CV23 0PJ, N : 1 m. by A 427 on B 4112 ☏ 832278, 🐎 – 📺 ☏ ❷. 🔊 🈀
⓪ *VISA*
M *(closed Sunday dinner, Christmas-2 January and Bank Holidays)* (bar lunch)/dinner
9.50 **t.** and a la carte ≬ 3.50 – **11 rm** 🖙 30.00/57.00 **t.**

◍ ATS 73 Bath St. ☏ 574705

RUGELEY Staffs. 402 403 404 O 25 – pop. 23 751 – ECD : Wednesday – ☏ 0889.

♦London 134 – ♦Birmingham 31 – Derby 29 – ♦Stoke-on-Trent 22.

🏠 **Forte Travelodge** without rest., Western Springs Rd, WS15 2AS, at junction of A 51
with A 460 ☏ 570096, Reservations (Freephone) 0800 850950 – 📺 ⅙ ❷. 🔊 🈀 *VISA*. 🦌
32 rm 31.95 **t.**

◍ ATS Mill Lane ☏ 582500

RUNCORN Ches. 402 403 L 23 – pop. 63 995 – ECD : Wednesday – ☏ 0928.

🏌 Clifton Rd ☏ 572093.

🛈 57-61 Church St., WA7 1LG ☏ 576776.

♦London 202 – ♦Liverpool 14 – ♦Manchester 29.

🏨 **Forte Posthouse,** Wood Lane, Beechwood, WA7 3HA, SE : ½ m. off junction 12 of M 56
☏ 714000, Fax 714611, *ℐ₅*, ≘s, ⊠ – ≬ ⥮ rm 📺 ☏ ❷ – 🔬 500. 🔊 🈀 ⓪ *VISA* *JCB*
M a la carte approx. 17.50 **t.** ≬ 4.65 – 🖙 6.95 – **134 rm** 53.50 **t.** – SB (weekends only)
90.00 **st.**

🏠 **Campanile** Lowlands Rd, WA7 5TP, beside the railway station ☏ 581771, Fax 581730 –
📺 ☏ ⅙ ❷ – 🔬 30. 🔊 🈀 *VISA*
M 9.45 **t.** and a la carte ≬ 4.65 – 🖙 4.25 – **53 rm** 35.75 **t.**

◍ ATS Sandy Lane, Weston Point ☏ 567715/6

RUSHDEN Northants. 𝟜𝟘𝟜 S 27 – pop. 22 352 – ✆ 0933.

◆London 74 – ◆Cambridge 42 – Northampton 14 – Peterborough 25.

🏠 **Forte Travelodge** without rest., NN10 9EP, on A 45, (eastbound carriageway) ✆ 57008, Reservations (Freephone) 0800 850950 – 📺 ⚹ 🅿. 🔌 🇦🇪 𝖵𝖨𝖲𝖠. ✎
40 rm 31.95 **t.**

RUSHLAKE GREEN E. Sussex 𝟜𝟘𝟜 U 31 – ✉ Heathfield – ✆ 0435.

◆London 54 – ◆Brighton 26 – Eastbourne 13.

🏠 **Stone House** ⌕, TN21 9QJ, ✆ 830553, Fax 830726, « Part 14C, part Georgian country house, antiques », ⊶, ☞, park – 📺 ☎ 🅿
closed 24 December-9 January – **Meals** (residents only) (dinner only) 24.95 **st.** ⌂ 5.00 – **8 rm** ⊡ 71.25/162.50 **st.** – SB (November-March) (weekdays only) 129.90/149.90 **st.**

RUSPER W. Sussex 𝟜𝟘𝟜 T 30 – pop. 2 678 – ✆ 0293.

◆London 30 – ◆Brighton 35 – Horsham 6.

🏨 **Ghyll Manor** (Forte), High St., RH12 4PX, ✆ 871571, Fax 871419, « Part Elizabethan house », ⊟, ⎯, heated, ☞, park, ❀ – 📺 ☎ 🅿 – 🔼 80. 🔌 🇦🇪 ⓞ 𝖵𝖨𝖲𝖠 𝖩𝖢𝖡
M (bar lunch Monday to Saturday)/dinner 16.95 **st.** and a la carte – ⊡ 8.50 – **22 rm** 70.00/100.00 **st.**, 3 suites – SB 108.00 **st.**

RUSTHALL Kent – see Royal Tunbridge Wells.

When travelling through Europe
use the Michelin red-cover map series, nos 𝟿𝟪𝟶 to 𝟿𝟫𝟷.

RYARSH Kent – see West Malling.

RYE E. Sussex 𝟜𝟘𝟜 W 31 Great Britain G. – pop. 4 127 – ECD : Tuesday – ✆ 0797.

See : Old Town★★ : Mermaid Street★, St. Mary's Church (⩽★).

🔱 The Heritage Centre, Strand Quay, TN31 7AY ✆ 226696 (summer only).

◆London 61 – ◆Brighton 49 – Folkestone 27 – Maidstone 33.

🏨 **George** (Forte), High St., TN31 7JP, ✆ 222114, Fax 224065 – ✂ rm 📺 ☎ 🅿 – 🔼 60. 🔌 🇦🇪 ⓞ 𝖵𝖨𝖲𝖠 𝖩𝖢𝖡
M (bar lunch Monday to Saturday)/dinner 15.95 **st.** and a la carte ⌂ 5.25 – ⊡ 8.50 – **22 rm** 70.00/100.00 **st.** – SB 116.00/126.00 **st.**

🏨 **Mermaid Inn,** Mermaid St., TN31 7EU, ✆ 223065, Fax 225069, « 15C inn » – 📺 ☎ 🅿. 🔌 🇦🇪 ⓞ 𝖵𝖨𝖲𝖠. ✎
M 12.75/16.50 **t.** and a la carte ⌂ 4.00 – **28 rm** ⊡ 50.00/88.00 **t.**

🏠 **Green Hedges** without rest., Rye Hill, TN31 7NH, N : ½ m. off A 268 on unmarked rd ✆ 222185, ⎯ heated, ☞ – ✂ 📺. ✎
closed Christmas – **3 rm** ⊡ 35.00/55.00 **s.**

🏠 **Old Vicarage** without rest., 66 Church Sq., TN31 7HF, ✆ 222119, Fax 227466, ☞ – ✂ 📺. ✎
closed 24 to 26 December – **6 rm** ⊡ 39.00/58.00 **st.**

🏠 **Jeake's House** without rest., Mermaid St., TN31 7ET, ✆ 222828, Fax 222623 – 📺 ☎. 🔌 🇦🇪 𝖵𝖨𝖲𝖠
12 rm ⊡ 21.50/78.00 **st.**

❌❌ **Flushing Inn,** 4 Market St., TN31 7LA, ✆ 223292, « 15C inn with 16C mural » – ✂. 🔌 🇦🇪 ⓞ 𝖵𝖨𝖲𝖠
closed Monday dinner, Tuesday and first 2 weeks January – **M** - **Seafood** 13.50/23.00 **t.** and a la carte ⌂ 5.00.

❌ **Landgate Bistro,** 5-6 Landgate, TN31 7LH, ✆ 222829 – 🔌 🇦🇪 ⓞ 𝖵𝖨𝖲𝖠
closed Sunday, Monday, 1 week June, 1 week October and 1 week Christmas – **M** (dinner only) 15.00 **st.** and a la carte ⌂ 3.90.

at Rye Foreign NW : 2 m. on A 268 – ✉ ✆ 0797 Rye :

🏠 **Broomhill Lodge,** TN31 7UN, on A 268 ✆ 280421, Fax 280402, ⊟, ☞ – 📺 ☎ 🅿. 🔌 𝖵𝖨𝖲𝖠. ✎
M 14.50/18.50 **t.** ⌂ 4.50 – **12 rm** ⊡ 35.00/84.00 **st.** – SB 96.00 **st.**

at Peasmarsh NW : 4 m. on A 268 – ✉ Rye – ✆ 0797 Peasmarsh :

🏨 **Flackley Ash** (Best Western), London Rd, TN31 6YH, ✆ 230651, Telex 957210, Fax 230510, 𝑓𝑠, ⊟, 🏊, ☞ – 📺 ☎ 🅿 – 🔼 100. 🔌 🇦🇪 ⓞ 𝖵𝖨𝖲𝖠
M 15.15/25.15 **st.** – **30 rm** ⊡ 69.00/112.00 **st.**, 2 suites – SB (except Bank Holidays) 114.00/186.00 **st.**

RYE FOREIGN E. Sussex – see Rye.

RYTON ON DUNSMORE W. Mids. 𝟜𝟘𝟛 𝟜𝟘𝟜 P 28 – see Coventry.

See : Audley End★★ *AC*.

🗓 1 Market Pl., Market Sq., CB10 1HR ✆ 524282.

◆London 46 – ◆Cambridge 15 – Chelmsford 25.

🏠 **Saffron**, 10-18 High St., CB10 1AY, ✆ 522676, Fax 513979 – 📺 ☎ – 🛏 80. 🔲 🄰🄴 ⓪ 𝘝𝘐𝘚𝘈. 𝒮𝒦
   M – (see **Garden** below) – **20 rm** ⊑ 30.00/75.00 **t.** – SB 130.00 **st.**

🍴🍴 **Garden** (at Saffron H.), 10-18 High St., CB10 1AY, ✆ 522676, Fax 513979 – 🔲 🄰🄴 ⓪ 𝘝𝘐𝘚𝘈
   M 14.90 **t.** and a la carte 👌 4.50.

at Littlebury Green W : 4 ½ m. by B 1383 – ✉ Saffron Walden – ⊙ 0763 Royston :

🏠 **Elmdon Lee**, CB11 4XB, ✆ 838237, ≈ – 📺 🄿. 🔲 𝘝𝘐𝘚𝘈. 𝒮𝒦
   closed Christmas – **M** (by arrangement) (communal dining) 15.00 **s.** 👌 4.00 – **3 rm** ⊑ 25.00/50.00 **s.**

at Duddenhoe End W : 7 ½ m. by B 1052, B 1383 and B 1039 – ✉ Saffron Walden – ⊙ 0763 Royston :

🏠 **Duddenhoe End Farm** without rest., CB11 4UU, ✆ 838258, ≈ – 🄿. 𝒮𝒦
   3 rm ⊑ 20.00/40.00 **st.**

🛠 ATS Station Rd ✆ 521426

See : St. Agnes Beacon★★ (✻★★).

Envir. : Portreath★, SW : 5 ½ m.

⛳ Perranporth, Budnic Hill ✆ 572454.

◆London 302 – Newquay 12 – Penzance 26 – Truro 9.

🏠 **Rose-in-Vale** ≫, Mithian, TR5 0QD, E : 2 m. by B 3285 ✆ 552202, Fax 552700, 🏊 heated, ≈ – ⊱⊰ rest 📺 ☎ ♿ 🄿. 🔲 🄰🄴 ⓪ 𝘝𝘐𝘚𝘈
   M (bar lunch Monday to Saturday)/dinner 16.50 **st.** and a la carte 👌 3.95 – **17 rm** (dinner included) 34.50/111.00 **st.** – SB (except summer) 79.95/82.50 **st.**

See : City★ – Cathedral★ – Verulamium★ (Museum★ *AC*).

Envir. : Hatfield House★★ *AC*, E : 6 m. by A 1057.

⛳ Batchwood Drive ✆ 833349 – ⛳, ⛳ Kinsbourne Green Lane, Redbourn ✆ 793493, N : 4 m. by A 5.

🗓 Town Hall, Market Pl., AL3 5DJ ✆ 864511.

◆London 27 – ◆Cambridge 41 – Luton 10.

🏨 **Sopwell House** (Best Western) ≫, Cottonmill Lane, AL1 2HQ, SE : 1 ½ m. by A 1081 and Mile House Lane ✆ 864477, Fax 844741, 👌, ≊, 🔲, ≈, park – 🛗 📺 ☎ 🄿 – 🛏 400. 🔲 🄰🄴 ⓪ 𝘝𝘐𝘚𝘈
   M – Bejerano's Brasserie a la carte 8.95/21.20 **t.** 👌 5.00 – (see also **Magnolia Conservatory** below) – ⊑ 7.95 – **90 rm** 99.50/111.50 **t.**, 2 suites – SB (weekends only) 139.65/253.90 **st.**

🏨 **Noke Thistle** (Mt. Charlotte Thistle) Watford Rd, AL2 3DS, SW : 2 ½ m. at junction of A 405 with B 4630 ✆ 854252, Telex 893834, Fax 841906 – ⊱⊰ rm 📺 ☎ ♿ 🄿 – 🛏 50. 🔲 🄰🄴 ⓪ 𝘝𝘐𝘚𝘈 🄹🄲🄱
   M *(closed lunch Saturday and Bank Holiday Mondays)* 17.50/21.00 **t.** and a la carte 👌 5.25 – ⊑ 8.75 – **109 rm** 79.00/89.00 **t.**, 2 suites – SB (weekends only) 90.00/100.00 **st.**

🏨 **St. Michael's Manor**, Fishpool St., AL3 4RY, ✆ 864444, Telex 917647, Fax 848909, « Manor house, lake, ≼ garden », park – 📺 ☎ 🄿 – 🛏 35. 🔲 🄰🄴 ⓪ 𝘝𝘐𝘚𝘈 . 𝒮𝒦
   closed 27 to 30 December – **M** 17.00/19.50 **t.** and a la carte 👌 5.50 – **22 rm** ⊑ 50.00/100.00 **st.**

🏠 **Ardmore House**, 54 Lemsford Rd, AL1 3PR, ✆ 859313, Fax 859313, ≈ – 📺 ☎ 🄿. 🔲 🄰🄴 𝘝𝘐𝘚𝘈
   M (dinner only) a la carte 9.50/13.25 **st.** – **24 rm** ⊑ 28.00/44.00.

🏠 **Melford House** without rest., 24 Woodstock Rd North, AL1 4QQ, ✆ 853642, Fax 853642, ≈ – 🄿. 🔲 𝘝𝘐𝘚𝘈
   12 rm ⊑ 24.00/47.00 **st.**

🍴🍴🍴 **Magnolia Conservatory** (at Sopwell House H.), Cottonmill Lane, AL1 2HQ, SE : 1 ½ m. by A 1081 and Mile House Lane ✆ 864477, Fax 844741 – 🄿. 🔲 🄰🄴 ⓪ 𝘝𝘐𝘚𝘈
   closed Sunday dinner – **M** 18.50/19.50 **t.** and a la carte 👌 6.95.

🍴🍴 **Cinta**, 20-26 High St., AL3 4EN, ✆ 837606
   M - Chinese rest.

🛠 ATS Grimston Rd ✆ 835174   ATS Lyon Way, Hatfield Rd ✆ 852314

ST. AUSTELL Cornwall 🗺️ F 32 The West Country G. – pop. 20 267 – ECD : Thursday – ☎ 0726.

See : Holy Trinity Church★.

Envir. : St. Austell Bay★★ (Gribbin Head★★) E : by A 390 and A 3082 – Carthew : Wheal Martyr Museum★★ AC, N : 2 m. by A 391 – Mevagissey★★, S : 5 m. by B 3273 – Charlestown★, SE : 2 m. by A 390.

Exc. : Trewithen★★★ AC, NE : 7 m. by A 390 – Lanhydrock★★, NE : 11 m. by A 390 and B 3269 – Polkerris★, E : 7 m. by A 390 and A 3082.

🏌️ Carlyon Bay ♟️ 814250.

◆London 281 – Newquay 16 – ◆Plymouth 38 – Truro 14.

🏛️ **White Hart,** Church St., PL25 4AT, ♟️ 72100, Fax 74705 – 📺 ☎ – 🔏 50. 🔼 🖭 ⓞ 𝗩𝗜𝗦𝗔
closed 25 and 26 December – **M** 7.95/12.00 **t.** 🍷 3.75 – **18 rm** ☞ 30.00/63.50 **t.** – SB (October-May) 53.50/102.00 **st.**

at Tregrehan E : 2½ m. by A 390 – ✉ ☎ 0726 St. Austell :

🏨 **Boscundle Manor,** PL25 3RL, ♟️ 813557, Fax 814997, « Tastefully converted 18C manor gardens », ⅁ heated, park – ⛔ rest 📺 ☎ ℗. 🔼 𝗩𝗜𝗦𝗔
April-October – **M** *(closed Sunday to non-residents)* (dinner only) 22.50 **st.** 🍷 5.00 – **9 rm** ☞ 70.00/120.00 **st.**, 1 suite – SB 130.00/170.00 **se.**

at Carlyon Bay E : 2½ m. by A 3601 – ✉ ☎ 0726 St. Austell :

🏨 **Carlyon Bay,** PL25 3RD, ♟️ 812304, Fax 814938, ≼ Carlyon Bay, « Extensive gardens »
⅀, ⅁ heated, 🖭, 🏌️, ❀ – ⬦ 📺 ☎ ℗ – 🔏 50. 🔼 🖭 𝗩𝗜𝗦𝗔. 🗱
M 15.00/25.00 **t.** and a la carte 🍷 4.25 – **73 rm** ☞ 68.00/168.00 **t.** – SB (except July and August) 85.00/156.00 **st.**

🏠 **Wheal Lodge,** 91 Sea Rd, PL25 3SH, ♟️ 815543, Fax 815543, ❀ – 📺 ℗. 🗱
M 20.00 **st.** 🍷 3.50 – **6 rm** ☞ 35.00/70.00 **st.** – SB 90.00/131.00 **st.**

at Charlestown SE : 2 m. by A 390 – ✉ ☎ 0726 St. Austell :

🏛️ **Pier House,** PL25 3NJ, ♟️ 67955, Fax 69246, ≼ – 📺 ☎ ℗. 🔼 𝗩𝗜𝗦𝗔. 🗱
closed 25 December – **M** 7.25 **t.** and a la carte 🍷 3.65 – **12 rm** ☞ 28.00/58.00 **t.**

🏠 **Rashleigh Arms,** PL25 3NJ, ♟️ 73635, ❀ – 📺 ℗. 🔼 𝗩𝗜𝗦𝗔. 🗱
M 15.30/21.25 **t.** – **5 rm** ☞ 22.50/45.00 **t.**

🛢️ ATS Gover Rd ♟️ 65685/6

ST. BLAZEY Cornwall 🗺️ F 32 – pop. 8 208 – ECD : Thursday – ☎ 0726 St. Austell.

◆London 276 – Newquay 21 – ◆Plymouth 33 – Truro 19.

🏠 **Nanscawen House** ⬦, Prideaux Rd, PL24 2SR, W : ¾ m. ♟️ 814488, Fax 814488, ≼, 🛁
⅁ heated, ❀ – ⛔ ☎ ℗. 🔼 𝗩𝗜𝗦𝗔. 🗱
closed 25 and 26 December – **M** (by arrangement) 20.00 **s.** 🍷 3.50 – **3 rm** ☞ 50.00/70.00 **s.** – SB (November-February) 80.00 **st.**

ST. HELENS Mersey. 🗺️ 🗺️ L 23 – ☎ 0744.

🏌️ Sherdley Park ♟️ 813149, E : 2 m. by A 570.

◆London 207 – ◆Liverpool 12 – ◆Manchester 27.

🏨 **Chalon Court,** Chalon Way, Linkway West, WA10 1NG, ♟️ 453444, Fax 454655, 🛁, ≼⅀
🔼 – 🍴 ⛔ rm 🖭 📺 ☎ ℗ – 🔏 220. 🔼 🖭 𝗩𝗜𝗦𝗔
M 29.95 **st.** (dinner) and a la carte 18.95/29.95 **st.** 🍷 4.75 – ☞ 8.50 – **81 rm** 52.00/79.50 **st.**, 3 suites – SB (weekends only) 79.50/105.00 **st.**

🏨 **Waterside,** East Lancashire Rd, WA11 7LX, N : 1¾ m. at junction of A 580 with A 57
♟️ 23333, Fax 454231 – 📺 ☎ & ℗. 🔼 🖭 ⓞ 𝗩𝗜𝗦𝗔. 🗱
M (grill rest.) 10.00 **st.** and a la carte – ☞ 4.95 – **43 rm** 39.00 **st.**

🏛️ **The Griffin,** Church Lane, Eccleston, WA10 5AD, W : 3 m. by A 570 on B 5201 ♟️ 27907,
Fax 453475, ❀ ☎ ℗. 🔼 🖭 𝗩𝗜𝗦𝗔. 🗱
M a la carte 8.30/17.15 **t.** 🍷 3.95 – **11 rm** ☞ 42.95/47.95 **t.**

🛢️ ATS Sutton Rd ♟️ 613434   ATS Blackbrook Rd, Blackbrook ♟️ 54175/6

ST. HILARY Cornwall – see Marazion.

ST. IVES Cambs. 🗺️ T 27 – pop. 13 431 – ECD : Thursday – ✉ Huntingdon – ☎ 0480.

◆London 75 – ◆Cambridge 14 – Huntingdon 6.

🏨 **Slepe Hall,** Ramsey Rd, PE17 4RB, ♟️ 463122, Fax 300706 – 📺 ☎ ℗ – 🔏 40. 🔼 🖭 ⓞ 𝗩𝗜𝗦𝗔
M 9.95/13.95 **t.** and a la carte 🍷 4.95 – **15 rm** ☞ 49.50/65.00 **t.** – SB (weekends only) 79.00/99.00 **st.**

🏨 **Dolphin,** Bridge Foot, London Rd, PE17 4EP, ♟️ 466966, Fax 495597 – 📺 ☎ & ℗ –
🔏 100. 🔼 🖭 ⓞ 𝗩𝗜𝗦𝗔. 🗱
M 12.95/15.95 **t.** and a la carte – **47 rm** ☞ 60.00/70.00 **t.** – SB (weekends only) 80.00/92.00 **t.**

at Holywell E : 3 m. by A 1123 – ⊠ Huntingdon – ☎ 0480 St. Ives :

⚓ **Old Ferryboat Inn**, PE17 3TG, ℘ 463227, ⌂ – 📺 **ℙ**. 🅐 VISA. ⚒
accommodation closed 25 December – **M** (in bar) 9.75/19.25 **t.** – **7 rm** ⊆ 40.00/68.00 **t.** –
SB (October-February) (weekends only) 66.00/130.00 **st.**

🛞 ATS East St. ℘ 465572

ST. IVES Cornwall 403 D 33 The West Country G. – pop. 9 439 – ECD : Thursday – ☎ 0736
Penzance.

See : Town★★ – Barbara Hepworth Museum★★ *AC* Y **M1** – St. Nicholas Chapel (≼★★) Y –
St. Ia★ Y **A**.

Envir. : S : Penwith★★ Y.

Exc. : St. Michael's Mount★★ (≼★★) S : 10 m. by B 3306 Y – B 3311, B 3309 and A 30.

🐚 Tregenna Castle Hotel ℘ 795254 ext: 121 Y – 🐚 West Cornwall, Lelant ℘ 753319, SE : 2 m.
by A 3074 Z – 🐚, 🐚 Lakeside Lodge, Fen Rd, Pidley ℘ 0487 (Ramsey) 740540, N : 4 m. on
B 1040 Y.

🚩 The Guildhall, Street-an-Pol, TR26 2QS ℘ 796297.

✈London 319 – Penzance 10 – Truro 25.

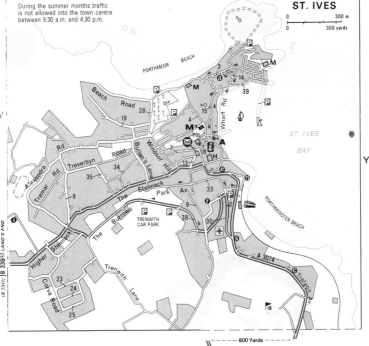

🏨 **Porthminster** (Best Western), The Terrace, TR26 2BN, ℰ 795221, Fax 797043, ≤, Ⅰₔ, ᴈˢ,
🝆 heated, 🖾, ⌀ – 🖿 🕮 ☎ 🄿. 🖾 🅰🄴 🅞 𝘝𝘐𝘚𝘈   Y s
🍽 (buffet lunch)/dinner 16.50 **st.** and a la carte ⦙ 4.45 – **48 rm** ⌸ 47.75/115.00 **st.** –
SB (October-19 May) (except Easter, Christmas and New Year) 90.00/119.00 **st.**

🏨 Pedn-Olva, The Warren, Porthminster Beach, TR26 2EA, ℰ 796222, Fax 797710, ≤ coastline – 🕮 ☎ 🄿   Y n
35 rm.

🏨 **Countryman,** Old Coach Rd, TR26 3JQ, S : 2 ½ m. by B 3306 and B 3311 on Hayle rd
ℰ 797571, ⌀ – 🕮 🄿. 🖾 🅰🄴 🅞 𝘝𝘐𝘚𝘈 𝙹𝘾𝘉. ⌀   Y
🍽 (bar lunch)/dinner a la carte 10.15/13.70 **st.** ⦙ 4.00 – **8 rm** ⌸ 25.00/42.00 **st.** – SB (September-May) 56.00/68.00 **st.**

🏨 **Skidden House,** Skidden Hill, TR26 2DU, ℰ 796899, Fax 798619 – ⇆ rest 🕮 ☎ 🄿.
🅰🄴 🅞 𝘝𝘐𝘚𝘈 𝙹𝘾𝘉   Y e
🍽 *(restricted service January, February and November)* (bar lunch)/dinner 18.50 **st.**
and a la carte ⦙ 5.00 – **7 rm** ⌸ 30.00/65.00 **st.** – SB (winter and spring) 74.00/90.00 **st.**

↑ **Old Vicarage** without rest., Parc-an-Creet, TR26 2ET, ℰ 796124, ⌀ – 🕮 🄿. 🖾 🅰🄴 𝘝𝘐𝘚𝘈
April-October – **8 rm** ⌸ 21.00/44.00.   Y i

↑ **Blue Hayes,** Trelyon Av., TR26 2AD, ℰ 797129, ≤, ⌀ – ⇆ rest 🕮 🄿. 🖾 𝘝𝘐𝘚𝘈   Y c
Easter-mid October – **M** 13.75 **st.** – **9 rm** ⌸ 30.75/70.00 **st.** – SB 75.50/79.50 **st.**

↑ **Pondarosa,** 10 Porthminster Terr., TR26 2DQ, ℰ 795875 – ⇆ 🕮 🄿. 🖾 🅰🄴 🅞 𝘝𝘐𝘚𝘈
⌀   Y r
🍽 (by arrangement) 8.00 **s.** ⦙ 2.75 – **9 rm** ⌸ 14.00/40.00 **s.** – SB 44.00/56.00 **st.**

✗ **Pig'n'Fish,** Norway Lane, TR26 1LZ, ℰ 794204 – 🖾 𝘝𝘐𝘚𝘈   Y a
closed Sunday, Monday and Christmas-mid February – **M** (dinner only) a la carte 18.50/
24.00 **t.**

at Carbis Bay S : 1 ¾ m. on A 3074 – ✉ St. Ives – ⊛ 0736 Penzance :

🏨 **Boskerris,** Boskerris Rd, TR26 2NQ, ℰ 795295, Fax 798632, ≤, 🝆 heated, ⌀ – ⇆ rest
🕮 ☎ 🄿. 🖾 🅞 𝘝𝘐𝘚𝘈   Z x
Easter-October – **M** (bar lunch)/dinner 16.00 **st.** ⦙ 4.10 – **19 rm** ⌸ 28.00/85.00 **st.** – SB (ex-
cept summer and Bank Holidays) 70.00/76.00 **st.**

ST. JOHN'S CHAPEL Durham – ✉ ⊛ 0388 Weardale.
♦London 280 – ♦Carlisle 47 – ♦Middlesbrough 52 – ♦Newcastle upon Tyne 44.

↑ **Pennine Lodge,** DL13 1QX, on A 689 ℰ 537247, ⌀ – ⇆ 🄿
   April-September – **M** 9.50 **s.** – **5 rm** ⌸ 37.00 **s.**

ST. JUST Cornwall 𝟺𝟶𝟹 C 33 The West Country G. – pop. 1 903 – ECD : Thursday – ⊛ 0736
Penzance.
See : Church★.
Envir. : Penwith★★ – Sancreed - Church★★ (Celtic Crosses★★) SE : 3 m. by A 3071 – Treng-
wainton Garden★★ (≤★★) AC, E : 4 ½ m. by A 3071 – St. Buryan★★ (Church Tower★★) SE :
5 ½ m. by B 3306 and A 30 – Land's End★ (cliff scenery★★★) S : 5 ½ m. by B 3306 and A 30 –
Cape Cornwall★ (≤★★) W : 1 ½ m. – Geevor Tin Mine★ AC, N : 3 m. by B 3306 – Carn Euny★,
SE : 3 m. by A 3071.
🖈 Cape Cornwall, St. Just, Penzance ℰ 788611, W : 1 m.
♦London 325 – Penzance 7.5 – Truro 35.

🏨 **Boscean Country** ⌆, TR19 7QP, by Boswedden Rd ℰ 788748, ≤, ⌀ – 🄿. 🖾 𝘝𝘐𝘚𝘈. ⌀
April-October – **M** (dinner only) 11.00 **t.** ⦙ 3.75 – **12 rm** ⌸ 22.50/38.00 **t.** – SB 60.00/
67.00 **s.**

ST. JUST IN ROSELAND Cornwall – see St. Mawes.

ST. KEVERNE Cornwall 𝟺𝟶𝟹 E 33 – ✉ Helston – ⊛ 0326.

✗ **Volnay,** Porthoustock, TR12 6QW, NE : 1 m. ℰ 280183 – 🄿
   closed Monday in summer and Sunday to Wednesday in winter – **M** (booking essential)
   (dinner only and Sunday lunch) a la carte 15.65/19.75 **t.** ⦙ 3.95.

ST. LEONARDS Dorset 𝟺𝟶𝟹 𝟺𝟶𝟺 O 31 – see Ringwood (Hants.).

ST. LEONARDS E. Sussex 𝟺𝟶𝟺 V 31 – see Hastings and St. Leonards.

ST. MARGARET'S AT CLIFFE Kent 𝟺𝟶𝟺 Y 30 – see Dover.

ST. MARTINS Cornwall 𝟺𝟶𝟹 ⊛ – see Scilly (Isles of).

ST. MARY'S Cornwall 𝟺𝟶𝟹 ⊛ – see Scilly (Isles of).

ST. MAWES Cornwall 𝟺𝟶𝟹 E 33 The West Country G. – – ✉ Truro – ⊛ 0326.
See : Town★ - Castle★ AC (≤★).
Envir. : St. Just in Roseland Church★★, N : 2½ m. by A 3078.
♦London 299 – ♦Plymouth 56 – Truro 18.

Tresanton, 27 Lower Castle Rd, TR2 5DR, ℰ 270544, Fax 270002, ≤ estuary, ☞ – TV
☎ 📠. ⚠ AE ① VISA
March-October and Christmas-New Year – **M** (bar lunch)/dinner a la carte 14.30/21.40 **t.** –
20 rm ⊆ (dinner included) 63.00/130.00 **t.**, 1 suite.

Idle Rocks, Tredenham Rd, TR2 5AN, ℰ 270771, Fax 270062, ≤ harbour and estuary –
TV ☎. ⚠ VISA
M 16.50 **t.** (dinner) and a la carte 18.50/22.30 **t.** – **24 rm** ⊆ 37.00/136.00 **t.** – SB (November-
March) 82.00/108.00 **st.**

Rising Sun, The Square, TR2 5DJ, ℰ 270233 – TV ☎ 📠. ⚠ AE ① VISA. ✗
M (bar lunch Monday to Saturday)/dinner 18.00 **t.** and a la carte 🛈 3.95 – **11 rm** ⊆ 27.50/
90.00 **t.** – SB 79.00/110.00 **st.**

St. Mawes, The Seafront, TR2 5DW, ℰ 270266, ≤ – TV ☎. ⚠ VISA
closed December and January – **M** 19.50/24.00 **st.** 🛈 4.50 – **7 rm** ⊆ (dinner included)
52.00/110.00 **st.**

at St. Just in Roseland N : 2½ m. on A 3078 – ⊠ Truro – 🕾 0326 St. Mawes :

Rose da Mar , TR2 5JB, N :¼ m. on B 3289 ℰ 270450, ≤, ☞ – 📠. ✗
April-September – **M** (dinner only) 14.50 **t.** 🛈 5.50 – **8 rm** ⊆ 27.00/60.00 **t.**

ST.MICHAELS-ON-WYRE Lancs. ₄₀₂ L 22 – 🕾 099 58 St. Michaels.

♦London 235 – ♦Blackpool 24 – Burnley 35 – ♦Manchester 43.

XX **Mallards,** Garstang Rd, PR3 0TE, ℰ 661 – 📠. ⚠ VISA
closed Sunday dinner, 1 week January and 2 weeks August – **M** (dinner only and Sunday
lunch)/dinner 15.50 **st.** and a la carte.

ST. NEOTS Cambs. ₄₀₄ T 27 – pop. 12 468 – 🕾 0480 Huntingdon.

Abbotsley, Eynesbury Hardwicke ℰ 474000, SE : 2 m. by B 1046 – Wyboston Lakes,
Wyboston ℰ 212501, SW : by B 1428 on A 1.

♦London 60 – Bedford 11 – ♦Cambridge 17 – Huntingdon 9.

Eaton Oak, Crosshall Rd, PE19 4AG, NW : 1 m. on B 1048 at junction with A 1 ℰ 219555,
Fax 407520 – TV ☎ 📠. ⚠ AE VISA. ✗
M 12.50 **t.** and a la carte – **9 rm** ⊆ 35.00/45.00 **t.**

XX **Chequers Inn,** St. Mary's St., Eynesbury, PE19 2TA, S :½ m. on B 1043 ℰ 472116, ☞ –
📠. ⚠ AE ① VISA
closed dinner 25 December – **M** a la carte 17.60/32.15 **t.** 🛈 3.90.

at Wyboston (Beds.) SW : 2½ m. by B 1428 on A 1 – ⊠ Bedford – 🕾 0480
Huntingdon :

Wyboston Lakes Motel without rest., Great North Rd, MK44 3AL, N :½ m. at junction
of A 45 with A 1 ℰ 219949, Fax 407349 – TV 📠. ⚠ AE VISA
closed 24 to 29 December – ⊆ 4.75 – **38 rm** 25.50/39.00 **st.**

🛒 ATS Brook St. ℰ 472920

SALCOMBE Devon ₄₀₃ I 33 The West Country G. – pop. 1 968 – ECD : Thursday – 🕾 0548.

Envir. : Sharpitor (Overbecks Museum and garden) (≤★★) *AC*, S : 2 m. by South Sands Z.

Exc. : Prawle Point (≤★★★) E : 16 m. around coast by A 381 – Y – and A 379.

🛈 Council Hall, Market St., TQ8 8DE ℰ 842736/843927 (summer only).

♦London 243 – Exeter 43 – ♦Plymouth 27 – Torquay 28.

Plan on next page

Tides Reach, South Sands, TQ8 8LJ, ℰ 843466, Fax 843954, ≤ estuary, 🛵, ☎s, ⚠, ☞,
squash – 🛗 TV ☎ 📠. ⚠ AE ① VISA   Z x
March-October – **M** (bar lunch)/dinner 24.50 **st.** and a la carte 🛈 5.25 – **38 rm** ⊆ (dinner
included) 89.50/196.00 **st.** – SB (except Easter) 120.00/164.00 **st.**

Marine, Cliff Rd, TQ8 8JH, ℰ 844444, Fax 843109, ≤ estuary, ☎s, ⚠ – 🛗 ≿ rest TV ☎
📠. ⚠ AE ① VISA   Y e
M (bar lunch Monday to Saturday)/dinner 22.00 **t.** – **50 rm** ⊆ 78.00/156.00 **t.**, 1 suite –
SB (except Bank Holidays) 160.00/220.00 **st.**

Bolt Head (Best Western) , South Sands, TQ8 8LL, ℰ 843751, Fax 843060, ≤ estuary,
🔥 heated – ▤ rest TV ☎ 📠. ⚠ AE ① VISA   Z z
10 March-7 November – **M** (buffet lunch)/dinner 37.00 **t.** 🛈 8.00 – **28 rm** ⊆ (dinner
included) 79.00/158.00 **st.** – SB (except summer) 118.00/128.00 **st.**

Grafton Towers, Moult Rd, TQ8 8LG, ℰ 842882, ≤ estuary, ☞ – ≿ rest TV 📠. ⚠ VISA
April-September – **M** (dinner only) 17.00 🛈 4.50 – **13 rm** ⊆ 38.00/75.00 **t.**   Z v

Courtenay House , Moult Hill, TQ8 8LF, ℰ 842761, Fax 842761, ≤ estuary, ☞ – ≿
TV 📠. ✗   Z a
April-October – **M** (by arrangement) (communal dining) – **3 rm** ⊆ 28.00/48.00 **s.**

The Wood , De Courcy Rd, Moult Hill, TQ8 8LQ, via Moult Rd ℰ 842778, Fax 844277,
≤ estuary, ☞ – ≿ rest TV 📠. ✗   Z e
M 15.00 **st.** 🛈 4.00 – **6 rm** ⊆ 38.00/94.00 **t.**

Bay View without rest., Bennett Rd, TQ8 8JJ, ℰ 842238, ≤ estuary – 📠. ⚠ VISA. ✗
May-September – **3 rm** ⊆ 56.00 **st.**   Z o

SALCOMBE

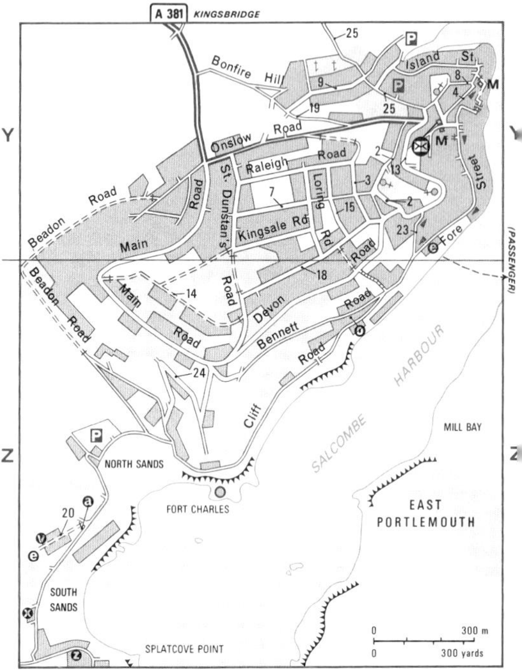

Town plans
roads most used
by traffic and those
on which guide listed
hotels and restaurants
stand are fully drawn;
the beginning only
of lesser roads
is indicated.

at Soar Mill Cove SW : 4 ¼ m. by A 381 via Malborough village – Y – ✉ Salcombe – ☎ 0548 Kingsbridge :

🏨 **Soar Mill Cove** 🌿, TQ7 3DS, ☎ 561566, Fax 561223, <, 🏊, 🏊, 🌳, 🎾 – 🚫 rest [TV] ☎ 🅿. [EN] VISA. 🚫🐕
closed November-11 February – **M** (light lunch)/dinner 37.00 **t.** and a la carte 🍷 6.00 – **15 rm** 🛏 (dinner included) 96.00/172.00 **t.** – SB (early spring and autumn) 116.00/180.00 **t.**

at Hope Cove W : 4 m. by A 381 via Malborough village - Y – ✉ ☎ 0548 Kingsbridge :

🏨 **Lantern Lodge** 🌿, TQ7 3HE, via Grand View Rd ☎ 561280, <, ≘s, 🏊, 🌳 – 🚫 rest [TV] ☎ 🅿. [EN] VISA. 🚫🐕
March-November – **M** (dinner only) 14.50 **t.** 🍷 4.10 – **14 rm** 🛏 38.50/77.00 **t.** – SB (except July-September) 73.00/85.00 **st.**

🏨 **Port Light** 🌿, Bolberry Down, TQ7 3DY, SE : 2¼ m. via Inner Hope ☎ 561384, <, 🌳 – [TV] 🅿. [EN] VISA
closed December and January – **M** *(closed Monday in low season)* 8.95/12.00 **t.** and a la carte 🍷 4.50 – **4 rm** 🛏 35.00/56.00 **t.**

SALE Gtr. Manchester [402] [403] [404] N 23 – pop. 57 993 – ECD : Wednesday – ✉ ☎ 061 Manchester.

⛳ Sale Lodge, Golf Rd ☎ 973 3404.

♦London 212 – ♦Liverpool 36 – ♦Manchester 6 – ♦Sheffield 43.

🏨 **Lennox Lea,** Irlam Rd, M33 2BH, ☎ 973 1764, Fax 969 6059, 🌳 – [TV] ☎ 🅿. [EN] [AE] [D] VISA
M *(closed Sunday)* (dinner only) a la carte 10.10/19.20 **t.** 🍷 5.65 – **30 rm** 🛏 30.00/57.75 **st.** – SB (weekends only) 57.40/145.50 **st.**

🏨 **Amblehurst,** 44 Washway Rd, M33 1QZ, on A 56 ☎ 973 8800, Group Telex 668871, Fax 905 1697, 🌳 – [TV] ☎ 🅿. [EN] [AE] VISA. 🚫🐕
M *(closed Saturday lunch and Sunday dinner)* 9.95/12.95 **t.** and a la carte 🍷 5.00 – **39 rm** 🛏 60.00/75.00 **st.** – SB (weekends only) 70.00/150.00 **st.**

🏨 **Normanhurst,** 195 Brooklands Rd, M33 3PJ, ☎ 973 1982, Fax 905 1697, 🌳 – [TV] ☎ 🅿. [EN] [AE] VISA
M *(closed dinner Friday to Sunday and Bank Holidays)* (bar lunch)/dinner 10.95 **st.** – **41 rm** 🛏 39.50/50.00 **st.** – SB (weekends only) 71.90/106.90 **st.**

↑ **Cornerstones** without rest., 230 Washway Rd, M33 4RA, ☎ 962 6909, Fax 962 6909 – ✦
📺 ☎ 🅿 ⚫ 🆅🆂🅰 . ※
closed Christmas – **8 rm** ☲ 21.50/38.00 **s.**

SALFORDS Surrey 🔢 T 30 – see Redhill.

SALISBURY Wilts. 🔢 🔢 O 30 The West Country G. – pop. 36 890 – ECD : Wednesday –
✪ 0722.

See : City★★ - Cathedral★★★ *AC* Z – Salisbury and South Wiltshire Museum★★ *AC* Z **M2** -
Close★ Z : Mompesson House★ *AC* Z A, Museum of the Duke of Edinburgh's Royal Regiment★
AC Z **M1** – Sarum St. Thomas Church★ Y **B**.

Envir. : Wilton Village (Wilton House★★★ *AC*, Royal Wilton Carpet Factory★ *AC*) W : 3 m. by
A 30 Y – Old Sarum★ *AC*, N : 2 m. by A 345 Y – Woodford (Heale House Garden★) *AC*, NW :
4½ m. by Stratford Rd Y.

Exc. : Stonehenge★★★ *AC*, NW : 10 m. by A 345 – Y - and A 303 – Wardour Castle★ *AC*, W :
15 m. by A 30 Y.

📑₈, 📑₉ Salisbury & South Wilts., Netherhampton ☎ 742645, SW : 3 m. by A 3094 Z – 📑₈ High
Post, Great Durnford ☎ 73231, N : 4 m. by A 345 Y.

🅱 Fish Row, SP1 1EJ ☎ 334956.

◆London 91 – Bournemouth 28 – ◆Bristol 53 – ◆Southampton 23.

Plans on following pages

🏨 **Milford Hall,** 206 Castle St., SP1 3TE, ☎ 417411, Fax 419444 – 📺 ☎ ♿ 🅿. 📶 🆀 ⚫ 🆅🆂🅰
🅹🅲🅱. ※   Y **a**
M 11.75/12.00 and a la carte ▮ 4.75 – **35 rm** ☲ 39.50/59.50 **t.** – SB 69.50/119.00 **st.**

🏨 **White Hart** (Forte), 1 St. John's St., SP1 2SD, ☎ 327476, Fax 412761 – ✦ rm 📺 ☎ 🅿 –
🔼 70. 📶 🆀 🆀 ⚫ 🆅🆂🅰 🅹🅲🅱   Z **s**
M *(closed Saturday lunch)* 9.95/16.95 **t.** and a la carte ▮ 5.25 – ☲ 8.50 – **68 rm** 80.00/
95.00 **t.** – SB 98.00/112.00 **st.**

🏠 **Trafalgar** (Resort), 33 Milford St., SP1 2AP, ☎ 338686, Fax 414496 – 📺 ☎ – 🔼 30. 📶 🆀
⚫ 🆅🆂🅰   Y **v**
M (grill rest.) a la carte approx. 10.25 **t.** – **18 rm** ☲ 48.00/65.00 **t.** – SB (weekends only)
70.00/116.00 **st.**

🏠 **Byways House** without rest., 31 Fowlers Rd, off Milford Hill, SP1 2QP, ☎ 328364,
Fax 322146, 🌳 – ✦ 📺 🅿. 📶 🆅🆂🅰   Z **e**
21 rm ☲ 22.00/44.00 **st.**

↑ **Cricketfield Cottage** without rest., Wilton Rd, SP2 7NS, W : 1 ¼ m. on A 36 - Y -
☎ 322595, 🌳 – ✦ 📺 🅿. ※
5 rm ☲ 20.00/38.00 **st.**

↑ Victoria Lodge, 61 Castle Rd, SP1 3RH, ☎ 320586, Fax 414507 – ✦ rest 📺 🅿   Y **e**
18 rm.

↑ **Wyndham Park Lodge** without rest., 51 Wyndham Rd, SP1 3AB, ☎ 328851, Fax 328851
– 📺 🅿   Y **u**
3 rm ☲ 15.00/36.00 **st.**

↑ **Glen Lyn** without rest., 6 Bellamy Lane, Milford Hill, SP1 2SP, ☎ 327880 – ✦ 📺 🅿.
※   YZ **x**
9 rm ☲ 20.00/40.00 **st.**

↑ **Malvern** without rest., 31 Hulse Rd, SP1 3LU, ☎ 327995, 🌳 – ✦ 📺. ※   Y **x**
3 rm ☲ 25.00/35.00 **st.**

✕ **Just Brahm's,** 68 Castle St., SP1 3TS, ☎ 328402, Fax 328593 ✦. 📶 🆀 🆀 ⚫ 🆅🆂🅰   Y **c**
closed Sunday and Bank Holiday Mondays – **M** 7.50/10.50 **st.** and a la carte ▮ 4.75.

✕ **Chef Peking,** 39 Catherine St., SP1 2DH, ☎ 326063 – 🍽. 📶 🆀 🆀 🆅🆂🅰   Z **c**
M - Chinese 17.50 **t.** and a la carte ▮ 4.20.

at Pitton E : 6 m. by A 30 – Y – ✉ Salisbury – ✪ 0722 Farley :

✕✕ **Silver Plough,** White Hill, SP5 1DZ, ☎ 72266 – 🅿. 📶 🆀 🆀 🆅🆂🅰
closed Sunday dinner, January and February – **M** 11.95/13.95 **t.** and a la carte.

at Downton S : 6 m. by A 338 – Z – on B 3080 – ✉ ✪ 0725 Downton :

↑ **Warren** without rest., 15 High St., SP5 3PG, ☎ 20263, 🌳 – 🅿
closed 15 December-10 January – **6 rm** ☲ 25.00/42.00 **st.**

at Woodfalls N : 7¾ m. by A 338 – Z – on B 3080 – ✉ Salisbury – ✪ 0725 Downton :

🏠 **Woodfalls Inn,** The Ridge, SP5 2LN, ☎ 513222, Fax 513220 – 📺 🅿. 📶 🆅🆂🅰 ※
M 14.95 **t.** and a la carte ▮ 4.95 – **7 rm** ☲ 29.95/80.00 **t.** – SB 60.00/90.00 **st.**

441

at Harnham SW : 1 ½ m. by A 3094 – ⊠ ❀ 0722 Salisbury :

🔺🔺 **Rose and Crown** (Q.M.H.), Harnham Rd, SP2 8JQ, ℰ 327908, Fax 339816, ≤, « Part 13C inn, riverside setting », 🌳 – 🆃🆅 ☎ 🄿 – 🛖 80. 🌥 🅰🅴 🅾 🆅🅸🆂🅰   Z **u**
M 15.50 **st.** and a la carte 🛈 6.00 – **28 rm** ⊇ 75.00/110.00 **st.** – SB (weekends only) 116.00 **st.**

🏠 **Grasmere,** 70 Harnham Rd, SP2 8JN, ℰ 338388, Fax 333710, ≤, 🌳 – ⇤ rm 🆃🆅 ☎ 🄿. 🌥
🆅🅸🆂🅰. 🕸   Z **a**
M 15.50/18.50 **st.** and a la carte 🛈 4.50 – **5 rm** ⊇ 40.00/65.00 **st.** – SB (except Christmas) (weekends only) 59.00/110.00 **st.**

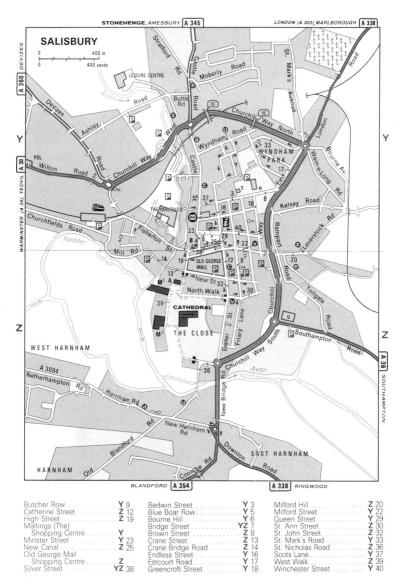

at Broad Chalke SW : 8 m. by A 354 and Broad Chalke Valley Rd – Z – ✉ ☎ 0722 Salisbury :

⚱ **Queens Head,** SP5 5EN, ✐ 780344 – 📺 ☎ 🅿. ◪ *VISA*. ✸
M 10.50/20.00 **t.** and a la carte – **4 rm** ⇨ 30.00/45.00 **t.**

↑ **Stoke Farm** ⌂, SP5 5EF, E : ¾ m. ✐ 780209, « Working farm », ⤙, ⚏, ✸ – ⇥ rm 📺
🅿.
March-October – **M** (by arrangement) 14.00 **st.** – **3 rm** ⇨ 20.00/40.00 **st.**

at Teffont W : 10¼ m. by A 36 – Z – and A 30 on B 3089 – ✉ ☎ 0722 Salisbury :

🍴🍴 **Howard's House** ⌂, with rm Teffont Evias, SP3 5RJ, on lane opposite Black Horse
✐ 716392, Fax 716820, ≤, « Part 17C former dower house », ⚏ – 📺 ☎ 🅿. ◪ AE ⓞ *VISA*.
✸
Meals (dinner only and Sunday lunch)/dinner 27.50 **t.** ⓕ 6.25 – **9 rm** ⇨ 70.00/90.00 **t.** –
SB 137.50/147.50 **st.**

◍ ATS 155 Wilton Rd ✐ 336789   ATS 28 St. Edmund's Church St. ✐ 322390/322451

SALTASH Cornwall **403** H 32 The West Country G. – pop. 12 772 – ☎ 0752.

Exc. : St. Germans Church⋆, SW : 7 m. by A 38 and B 3249.

🛆, 🛆 St. Mellion ✐ 0579 (St. Mellion) 50101 – 🛆 China Fleet C.C. ✐ 848668.

🖪 Granada Motorway Services, Carkeel Roundabout, PL12 1XX ✐ 849526.

◆London 246 – Exeter 38 – ◆Plymouth 5 – Truro 49.

🏠 **Granada Lodge** without rest., Callington Rd, Carkeel, PL12 6LF, NW : 1½ m. by A 388 on
A 38 at Saltash Service Area ✐ 848408, Reservations (Freephone) 0800 555300 – ⇥ 📺
👍 🅿. ◪ AE *VISA*. ✸
⇨ 4.00 – **31 rm** 34.95/37.95 **st.**

SALTFORD Avon **403 404** M 29 – see Bristol.

SAMLESBURY Lancs. **402** M 22 – see Preston.

SAMPFORD PEVERELL Devon **403** J 31 – ✉ ☎ 0884 Tiverton.

◆London 184 – Barnstaple 34 – Exeter 20 – Taunton 19.

🏠 **Parkway House,** EX16 7BJ, ✐ 820255, Fax 820780, ⚏ – 📺 ☎ 🅿 – 🔼 145. ◪ *VISA*
M 9.95 **st.** and a la carte – **10 rm** ⇨ 34.00/48.00 **st.**

🏠 **Old Cottage Inn,** ✉ Uffculme, EX15 3ES, E : 1¾ m. by A 361 on A 38 ✐ 0884 (Crad-
dock) 840328 – ⇥ rm 📺 🅿. ◪ ◪ *VISA*. ✸
M (in bar) approx. 8.70 **t.** – **10 rm** 31.95 **t.**

SAMPFORD PEVERELL SERVICE AREA Devon **403** J 31 – ✉ ☎ 0884 Tiverton.

◆London 184 – Barnstaple 34 – Exeter 20 – Taunton 19.

🏠 **Forte Travelodge** without rest., EX16 7HD, M 5 junction 27 ✐ 821087, Reservations
(Freephone) 0800 850950 – 📺 👍 🅿. ◪ AE *VISA*. ✸
40 rm 31.95 **t.**

SANDBACH Ches. **402 403 404** M 24 – pop. 13 753 – ECD : Tuesday – ☎ 0270 Crewe.

🛆 Malkins Bank ✐ 765931, S : 2 m. by A 534 and A 533.

🖪 Motorway Service Area, M 6 (northbound), CW11 0TD ✐ 760460.

◆London 177 – ◆Liverpool 44 – ◆Manchester 28 – ◆Stoke-on-Trent 16.

🏨 **Chimney House** (Lansbury), Congleton Rd, CW11 0ST, E : 1½ m. on A 534 ✐ 764141,
Telex 367323, Fax 768916, ⇖s, ⚏ – ⇥ rm 📺 ☎ 🅿 – 🔼 70. ✸
48 rm.

🏨 **Old Hall,** Newcastle Rd, CW11 0AL, ✐ 761221, Fax 762551, « 17C coaching inn », ⚏ –
📺 ☎ 🅿. ◪ ◪ ⓞ *VISA*
M 8.95/15.00 **t.** and a la carte – **13 rm** ⇨ 48.00/80.00 **t.** – SB (weekends only) 65.00/
110.00 **st.**

🏠 **Saxon Cross,** Holmes Chapel Rd, CW11 9SE, ✐ 763281, Fax 768723 – 📺 ☎ 🅿 – 🔼 50.
◪ ◪ *VISA*
M (closed Saturday lunch, Sunday dinner and Bank Holidays) 8.60/14.50 **st.** and a la carte
ⓕ 5.10 – ⇨ 6.50 – **52 rm** 33.00/55.00 **st.** – SB 74.00/132.00 **st.**

SANDIACRE Derbs. **402 403 404** Q 25 – see Nottingham (Notts.).

SANDIWAY Ches. – ☎ 0606.

◆London 191 – ◆Liverpool 34 – ◆Manchester 22 – ◆Stoke-on-Trent 26.

🏨🏨 **Nunsmere Hall** ⌂, Tarporley Rd, CW8 2ES, SW : 1½ m. by A 556 on A 49 ✐ 889100,
Fax 889055, ≤, « Part Victorian house on wooded peninsula », ⚏, park – ⧉ ⇥ 📺 ☎ 🅿
– 🔼 40. ◪ ◪ ⓞ *VISA* *JCB*. ✸
M 17.95/32.50 **st.** and a la carte – ⇨ 7.50 – **31 rm** 95.00/185.00 **st.**, 1 suite – SB (except
Christmas) 170.00/210.00 **st.**

SANDPLACE Cornwall – see Looe.

Norfolk 🔳 🔳 V 25 Great Britain G. – pop. 431 – ⊠ King's Lynn – ✪ 0485 Dersingham.

See : Sandringham House★ AC.

◆London 111 – King's Lynn 8 – ◆Norwich 50.

🏨 **Park House** ⤸, PE35 6EH, ✆ 543000, « Former Royal residence » Restricted to physically disabled and their companions, ⬓ heated, ⬚, park – ⬚ ⬚ rm ⬚ rest ⬚ ☎ ⬚ 🅿.
⬚ 𝖵𝖨𝖲𝖠 ⬚
closed 10 to 20 December – **M** (buffet lunch)/dinner/12.00 **st.** – **16 rm** ⬚ 58.00/98.00 **st.**

Kent 🔳 Y 30 Great Britain G. – pop. 4 184 – ECD : Wednesday – ✪ 0304.

See : Town★.

🗓 The Guildhall, Cattle Market, CT13 9AH ✆ 613565 (summer only).

◆London 72 – Canterbury 13 – ◆Dover 12 – Maidstone 41 – Margate 9.

🏨 **Bell,** The Quay, CT13 9EF, ✆ 613388, Fax 615308 – ⬚ ☎ 🅿 – ⬚ 60. ⬚ ⬚ ⬚ 𝖵𝖨𝖲𝖠
M 7.00/25.00 **st.** and a la carte – **29 rm** ⬚ 68.00/130.00 **t.** – SB 104.00/170.00 **st.**

Beds. 🔳 T 27 – pop. 7 496 – ECD : Thursday – ✪ 0767.

⬚, ⬚ John O'Gaunt, Sutton Park ✆ 260360, SE : 5 m. by B 1042 and B 1040.

◆London 49 – Bedford 8 – ◆Cambridge 24 – Peterborough 35.

🏠 **Anchor** (Chef & Brewer), Great North Rd, Tempsford, SG19 2AS, N : 3½ m. by B 1042 on A 1 ✆ 40233, Fax 41123, ⬚, ⬚, park – ⬚ ☎ 🅿. ⬚ ⬚ 𝖵𝖨𝖲𝖠 ⬚
M (carving rest.) 15.00/20.00 **t.** and a la carte – ⬚ 3.50 – **10 rm** 29.95/33.45 **t.**

🏠 **Sandy,** Gifford Bridge, London Rd, SG19 1DH, W : ¾ m. by B 1042 at junction of A 1 with A 603 ✆ 692220, Fax 680452 – ⬚ ⬚ 🅿 – ⬚ 200. ⬚ ⬚ ⬚ 𝖵𝖨𝖲𝖠
M *(closed Saturday and Sunday)* (dinner only) a la carte 10.00/20.00 **st.** ⬚ 4.00 – ⬚ 3.95 – **56 rm** 38.50/40.50 **st.**

En saison, surtout dans les stations fréquentées, il est prudent de retenir à l'avance.
Cependant, si vous ne pouvez pas occuper la chambre que vous avez retenue,
prévenez immédiatement l'hôtelier.

Si vous écrivez à un hôtel à l'étranger, joignez à votre lettre
un coupon-réponse international (disponible dans les bureaux de poste).

Devon 🔳 I 31 – see Chagford.

Hants. 🔳 🔳 Q 31 – pop. 5 682 – ⊠ Southampton – ✪ 0489 Locks Heath.

◆London 90 – ◆Portsmouth 16 – ◆Southampton 6.

🏠 **Dormy House,** 21 Barnes Lane, Sarisbury Green, SO3 6DA, S : 1 m. ✆ 572626 – ⬚ 🅿.
⬚ 𝖵𝖨𝖲𝖠 ⬚
M (by arrangement) 12.95 **st.** ⬚ 3.95 – **10 rm** ⬚ 28.50/45.00 **st.** – SB (weekends only) 58.40/92.90 **st.**

Devon 🔳 H 30 – ⊠ ✪ 0271 Braunton.

◆London 230 – Barnstaple 8 – Exeter 48.

🏨 **Preston House,** EX33 1LG, ✆ 890472, Fax 890555, ≼ Saunton Sands, ⬚, ⬓ heated, ⬚
– ⬚ ☎ 🅿. ⬚ 𝖵𝖨𝖲𝖠 ⬚
closed January – **M** (bar lunch)/dinner 17.50 **t.** and a la carte ⬚ 4.15 – **15 rm** ⬚ 30.00/85.00 **t.**

Herts. 🔳 U 28 – pop. 8 475 – ECD : Thursday and Saturday – ✪ 0279 Bishop's Stortford.

◆London 26 – ◆Cambridge 32 – Chelmsford 17.

🏨 **The Manor of Groves** ⤸, High Wych, CM21 0LA, SW : 1 ½ m. by A 1184 ✆ 600777, Fax 726972, ≼, ⬓ heated, ⬚, ⬚, park, ⬚ – ⬚ ☎ 🅿 – ⬚ 65. ⬚ ⬚ ⬚ 𝖵𝖨𝖲𝖠 ⬚
M 20.00/25.00 **t.** and a la carte – **35 rm** ⬚ 50.00/130.00 **t.** – SB (except Christmas) 80.00/140.00 **st.**

Lancs. 🔳 M 22 – pop. 179 – ✪ 0765.

◆London 242 – ◆Blackpool 39 – ◆Leeds 44 – ◆Liverpool 54.

🏨 **Spread Eagle,** BB7 4NH, ✆ 0200 (Clitheroe) 441202, Fax 441973 – ⬚ ☎ ⬚ 🅿. ⬚ ⬚ ⬚
𝖵𝖨𝖲𝖠 ⬚
M 16.95 **t.** and a la carte ⬚ 5.50 – **10 rm** ⬚ 48.00/58.00 **t.** – SB 80.00 **st.**

N. Yorks. 🔳 S 21 – see Scarborough.

N. Yorks. 🔳 S 21 – pop. 36 665 – ECD : Monday and Wednesday – ✪ 0723.

⬚ Scarborough North Cliff, North Cliff Av., Burniston Rd ✆ 360786, NW : 2 m. by A 165 Y –
⬚ Scarborough South Cliff, Deepdale Av., off Filey Rd ✆ 360522, S : 1 m. by A 165 Z.

🗓 St. Nicholas Cliff, YO11 2EP ✆ 373333.

◆London 253 – ◆Kingston-upon-Hull 47 – ◆Leeds 67 – ◆Middlesbrough 52.

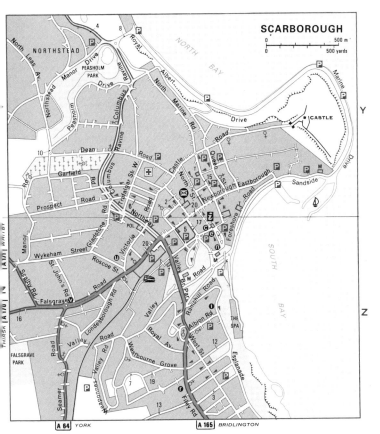

SCARBOROUGH

0   500 m
0   500 yards

Crown (Forte), 7-11 Esplanade, YO11 2AG, ℰ 373491, Fax 362271, ≤ – 🛗 ₩ rm 📺 ☎ – 🔬 200. 🖪 🖭 ⓞ 𝘝𝘐𝘚𝘈 𝐉𝐂𝐁   Z i
M (bar lunch Monday to Saturday)/dinner 16.95/25.00 **st.** and a la carte ⓜ 5.25 – ⌒ 8.95 – **77 rm** 60.00/80.00 **st.**, 1 suite – SB 108.00/116.00 **st.**

St. Nicholas, St. Nicholas Cliff, YO11 2EU, ℰ 364101, Telex 52351, Fax 500538, ≤, ⌒s, 🔲 – 🛗 📺 ☎ ⇦ – 🔬 400. 🖪 🖭 𝘝𝘐𝘚𝘈   Z n
M 12.25/20.00 **st.** ⓜ 4.95 – **135 rm** ⌒ 40.00/80.00 **st.**, 5 suites – SB 60.00/110.00 **st.**

Palm Court, St. Nicholas Cliff, YO11 2ES, ℰ 368161, Fax 371547, ⌒s, 🔲 – 🛗 📺 ☎ ⇦ – 🔬 100. 🖪 🖭 ⓞ 𝘝𝘐𝘚𝘈 ✻   Z e
M 10.00./17.50 **t.** and a la carte ⓜ 4.50 – **50 rm** ⌒ 36.00/110.00 **t.**

Bradley Court (Best Western), 7-9 Filey Rd, YO11 2SE, ℰ 360476, Fax 376661 – 🛗 📺 ☎ ℗ – 🔬 40. 🖪 🖭 ⓞ 𝘝𝘐𝘚𝘈   Z r
M 9.50/15.00 **st.** ⓜ 4.00 – **38 rm** ⌒ 37.50/60.00 **st.** – SB 79.00/90.00 **st.**

Pickwick Inn, Huntriss Row, YO11 2ED, ℰ 375787, Fax 374284 – 🛗 📺 ☎. 🖪 🖭 ⓞ 𝘝𝘐𝘚𝘈 ✻   Z c
M *(closed Monday dinner)* (bar lunch)/dinner 8.50 **t.** and a la carte ⓜ 3.75 – **11 rm** ⌒ 27.00/55.00 **t.** – SB (except Bank Holidays) 57.00/67.00 **st.**

Old Mill, Mill St., YO11 1SZ, via Victoria Rd ℰ 372735, « Restored 18C windmill » – ₩ rest 📺 ℗   Z u
14 rm.

XX **Jade Garden,** 121 Falsgrave Rd, YO12 5EG, 🖉 369099 – ▣ Æ ⓞ 𝘝𝘐𝘚𝘈　　　Z　v
M - *Chinese (closed Sunday lunch)* 15.00 **t.** (dinner) and a la carte approx. 11.20 **t.**

at Scalby NW : 3 m. by A 171 – Z – ⊠ ❀ 0723 Scarborough :

🏛 **Wrea Head** ⤜, YO13 0PB, by Barmoor Lane 🖉 378211, Fax 371780, ≤, 🛲, park – 🆃🆅 ☎
　　🄿. ▣ Æ ⓞ 𝘝𝘐𝘚𝘈. ✼
　　M 10.50/19.95 **st.** and dinner a la carte ⧍ 6.95 – **20 rm** ⊏⊐ 49.50/89.00 **t.**, 1 suite –
　　SB 105.00/145.00 **st.**

at Hackness NW : 7 m. by A 171 – Z – ⊠ ❀ 0723 Scarborough :

🏛 **Hackness Grange** (Best Western) ⤜, YO13 0JW, 🖉 882345, Fax 882391, ≤, « 18C
house », ⬛, 🛲, park, ✂ – 🆃🆅 ☎ 🄿. ▣ Æ ⓞ 𝘝𝘐𝘚𝘈 ✼
　　M 20.00/30.00 **st.** ⧍ 6.95 – **26 rm** ⊏⊐ 59.00/148.00 **st.** – SB (except Bank Holidays) 132.00 **st.**

▐ SCILLY (Isles of) ▌ Cornwall **403** ③ *The West Country G.* – pop. 2 653.

See : Islands★★ - The Archipelago (≤★★★).
Envir. : St. Agnes : Horsepoint★.

Helicopter service from St. Mary's and Tresco to Penzance : 🖉 0736 (Penzance) 63871.

✈ St. Mary's Airport : 🖉 0720 (Scillonia) 22677, E : 1½ m. from Hugh Town.

🚢 from Hugh Town to Penzance (Isles of Scilly Steamship Co. Ltd) (summer only).

🄱 Porthcressa Bank, St. Mary's, TR21 0JY 🖉 0720 (Scillonia) 22536.

　　▐ Bryher ▌ *The West Country G.* – pop. 66 – ⊠ ❀ 0720 Scillonia.
　　See : Watch Hill (≤★)̄ – Hell Bay★.

🄰 **Hell Bay** ⤜, TR23 0PR, 🖉 22947, Fax 23004, 🛲 – ✂ rest 🆃🆅. ▣ 𝘝𝘐𝘚𝘈. ✼
　　April-September – **M** (bar lunch)/dinner 20.00 **t.** ⧍ 4.00 – **9 suites** 78.50/137.00 **t.**

⋔ **Bank Cottage** ⤜, TR23 0PR, 🖉 22612, ≤, 🛲 – ✂ rest. ✼
　　April-October – **5 rm** ⊏⊐ (dinner included) 32.00/64.00 **st.**

　　▐ St. Martin's ▌ *The West Country G.* – ⊠ St. Martin's – ❀ 0720 Scillonia.
　　See : Viewpoint★★.

🏨 **St. Martin's** ⤜, TR25 0QW, 🖉 22092, Fax 22298, ≤ Tean Sound and islands, « Idyllic
island setting », ⬛, 🛲 – ✂ rest 🆃🆅 ☎. ▣ Æ ⓞ 𝘝𝘐𝘚𝘈. ✼
　　closed January and February – **M** (bar lunch)/dinner 25.00 **st.** and a la carte ⧍ 4.75 – **22 rm**
　　⊏⊐ (dinner included) 114.00/178.00 **st.**, 2 suites.

　　▐ St. Mary's ▌ *The West Country G.* – pop. 2 106 – ECD : Wednesday – ⊠ St. Mary's –
　　❀ 0720 Scillonia.
　　See : Garrison Walk★ (≤★★) – Peninnis Head★.
　　🇯 🖉 22692, N : 1½ m. from Hugh Town.

🏛 **Tregarthen's** (Best Western), Hugh Town, TR21 0PP, 🖉 22540, Fax 22089, ≤ – 🆃🆅 ☎. ▣
Æ ⓞ 𝘝𝘐𝘚𝘈. ✼
　　late March-late October – **M** (bar lunch)/dinner 18.50 **t.** ⧍ 5.50 – **29 rm** ⊏⊐ (dinner included)
　　60.00/136.00 **t.** – SB 86.00/130.00 **st.**

🏛 **Star Castle** ⤜, TR21 0JA, 🖉 22317, Fax 22343, « Elizabethan fortress », ⬛, 🛲, ✂ –
✂ rest 🆃🆅 ☎. ▣ 𝘝𝘐𝘚𝘈
　　mid March-mid September – **M** (bar lunch)/dinner 25.00 **st.** ⧍ 3.50 – **28 rm** ⊏⊐ 43.00/
　　115.00 **st.** – SB 90.00/116.00 **st.**

🏛 **Atlantic,** Hugh St., Hugh Town, TR21 0PL, 🖉 22417, Fax 23009, ≤ St. Mary's Harbour –
✂ rest 🆃🆅 ☎. ▣ 𝘝𝘐𝘚𝘈
　　closed December and January – **M** (dinner only) 16.50 **st.** and a la carte ⧍ 7.50 – **23 rm**
　　⊏⊐ (dinner included) 60.50/138.00 **st.** – SB 70.00/110.00 **st.**

⋔ **Carnwethers** ⤜, Pelistry Bay, TR21 0NX, 🖉 22415, ⥱, ⬛ heated, 🛲 – ✂ rest 🆃🆅
　　April-October – **M** 13.00 **st.** – **9 rm** ⊏⊐ 29.00/66.00 **st.**

⋔ **Tremellyn,** Church Rd, Hugh Town, TR21 0NA, 🖉 22656, 🛲 – ✂ rest 🆃🆅 🄿. ✼
　　March-October – **M** (by arrangement) 11.00 **st.** ⧍ 3.95 – **8 rm** ⊏⊐ 27.00/60.00 **st.**

　　▐ Tresco ▌ *The West Country G.* – pop. 285 – ⊠ New Grimsby – ❀ 0720 Scillonia.
　　See : Island★ - Abbey Gardens★ *AC* (Lighthouse Way ≤★★).

🏨 **Island** ⤜, Old Grimsby, TR24 0PU, 🖉 22883, Fax 23008, ≤ St. Martin's and islands,
« Idyllic island setting, sub-tropical gardens », ⬛ heated, park, ✂ – 🆃🆅 ☎. ▣ Æ 𝘝𝘐𝘚𝘈. ✼
　　closed late October-March – **M** (bar lunch)/dinner 27.50 **t.** and a la carte ⧍ 6.50 – **39 rm**
　　⊏⊐ (dinner included) 95.00/230.00 **t.**, 1 suite.

⋔ **New Inn,** TR24 0QQ, 🖉 22844, ≤, ⬛ heated, – 🆃🆅 ☎. ▣ Æ 𝘝𝘐𝘚𝘈. ✼
　　closed Christmas and New Year – **M** 15.50/21.00 **t.** and lunch a la carte ⧍ 3.70 – **12 rm**
　　⊏⊐ 35.00/112.00 **t.** – SB (September-March) 70.00/112.00 **st.**

▐ SCOLE ▌ Norfolk **404** X 26 – see Diss.

SCOTCH CORNER N. Yorks. 402 P 20 – ✉ ✆ 0748 Richmond.

ℹ Pavilion Service Area, A 1, DL10 6PQ ✆ 377677 (summer only).

♦London 235 – ♦Carlisle 70 – ♦Middlesbrough 25 – Newcastle upon Tyne 43.

🏠 **Pavilion Lodge** without rest., Middleton Tyas Lane, D10 6PQ, ✆ 0325 (Darlington) 377177, Fax 377890 – 🚭 📺 ♿ Ⓟ. EN AE ⓓ VISA JCB
☕ 4.00 – **50 rm** 31.95/35.95 **st.**

🏠 **Forte Travelodge** without rest., Skeeby, DL10 5EQ, S : 1 m. on A 1 (northbound carriageway) ✆ 823768, Reservations (Freephone) 0800 850950 – 📺 ♿ Ⓟ. EN AE VISA.
🚫
40 rm 31.95 **t.**

SCUNTHORPE Humbs. 402 S 23 – pop. 79 043 – ECD : Wednesday – ✆ 0724.

⛳18 Ashby Decoy, Burringham Rd ✆ 842913, SW : 2 m. – ⛳9 Kingsway ✆ 840945, W : ¾ m. – ⛳9 Grange Park, Butterwick Rd, Messingham ✆ 762945.

✈ Humberside Airport : ✆ 0652 (Barnetby) 688456, E : 15 m. by A 18.

♦London 167 – ♦Leeds 54 – Lincoln 30 – ♦Sheffield 45.

🏨 **Wortley House,** Rowland Rd, DN16 1SU, ✆ 842223, Fax 280646 – 📺 ☎ Ⓟ – 👥 250. EN AE ⓓ VISA
M *(closed Saturday lunch)* 10.75/12.00 **st.** and a la carte 🍷 5.00 – **38 rm** ☕ 60.00/70.00 **st.** – SB (weekends only) 100.00 **st.**

🏨 **Royal** (Forte), 74 Doncaster Rd, DN15 7DE, ✆ 282233, Fax 281826 – 🚭 rm 📺 ☎ Ⓟ – 👥 240. EN AE ⓓ VISA
M (bar lunch)/dinner 13.95 **st.** and a la carte 🍷 4.50 – **33 rm** ☕ 55.00/65.00 **st.** – SB (weekends only) 80.00 **st.**

🛞 ATS Grange Lane North ✆ 868191

SEACROFT W. Yorks. 402 ⑩ – see Leeds.

SEAFORD E. Sussex 404 U 31 – pop. 16 367 – ECD : Wednesday – ✆ 0323.

⛳18 Southdown Rd ✆ 890139.

ℹ Station Approach, BN25 2AR ✆ 897426.

♦London 65 – ♦Brighton 14 – Folkestone 64.

✕✕ **Quincy's,** 42 High St., BN25 1PL, ✆ 895490 – EN AE VISA JCB
closed Sunday dinner and Monday – **M** (dinner only and Sunday lunch)/dinner 20.45 **t.** 🍷 4.25.

at Westdean E : 3¼ m. A 259 – ✆ 0323 Alfriston :

⌂ **Old Parsonage** 🔇 without rest., BN25 4AL, ✆ 870432, ←, « 13C King John house », 🌳 – 🚭 Ⓟ. 🚫
closed Christmas and New Year – **3 rm** ☕ 30.00/60.00 **s.**

SEAHOUSES Northd 401 402 P 17 *Great Britain G.* – pop. 1 709 (inc. North Sunderland) – ECD : Wednesday – ✆ 0665.

Envir. : Farne Islands★ (by boat from harbour).

⛳18 Beadnell Rd ✆ 720794.

ℹ Car Park, Seafield Rd, NE68 7SR ✆ 720884 (summer only).

♦London 328 – ♦Edinburgh 80 – ♦Newcastle upon Tyne 46.

🏠 **Olde Ship,** 9 Main St., NE68 7RD, ✆ 720200, Fax 721383, « Nautical memorabilia » – 📺 ☎ Ⓟ. EN VISA. 🚫
closed December and January – **M** (bar lunch)/dinner 13.00 **t.** 🍷 3.45 – **15 rm** ☕ 30.00/64.00 **t.**

🏠 **Beach House,** 12a St. Aidans, Seafront, NE68 7SR, ✆ 720337, Fax 720921, ←, 🌳 – 🚭 rest 📺 ☎ ♿ Ⓟ. EN VISA
April-October – **M** (dinner only) 18.75 **t.** – **14 rm** ☕ 39.00/78.00 **t.** – SB 89.00/101.00 **st.**

🏠 **St. Aidans,** Seafront, NE68 7SR, ✆ 720355, ← – 📺 Ⓟ. EN AE ⓓ VISA
M (dinner only and Sunday lunch)/dinner 15.00 **st.** 🍷 5.50 – **9 rm** ☕ 40.00/65.00 **st.** – SB (except Bank Holidays) 70.00/100.00 **st.**

SEALE Surrey 404 R 30 – see Farnham.

SEATOLLER Cumbria – see Keswick.

SEATON BURN Tyne and Wear 402 P 18 – see Newcastle upon Tyne.

SEATON CAREW Cleveland 402 Q 20 – see Hartlepool.

SEAVIEW I.O.W. 403 404 Q 31 – see Wight (Isle of).

SEAVINGTON ST. MARY Somerset [403] L 31 The West Country G. – pop. 321 – ✉ Ilminster – ☎ 0460 South Petherton.

Envir. : Ilminster★ - St. Mary's★★, W : 2 m.

♦London 142 – Taunton 14 – Yeovil 11.

Pheasant, Water St., TA19 0QH, ☎ 40502, Fax 42388, 🌳 – 📺 ☎ Ⓟ. [VISA] [AE] [VISA]. 🐕
closed 26 December-7 January – **M** *(closed Sunday dinner)* (dinner only and Sunday lunch)/dinner a la carte 14.00/18.50 **t.** 🍷 3.50 – **8 rm** 🛏 50.00/70.00 **t.** – SB 102.30 **t.**

SEDBERGH Cumbria [402] M 21 – pop. 2 233 – ☎ 053 96.

⛳ Catholes-Abbot Holme ☎ 20993, S : 1 m. on Dent Rd.

♦London 270 – ♦Carlisle 51 – Kendal 10 – Lancaster 27.

Oakdene Country, Garsdale Rd, LA10 5JN, E : 1 ¼ m. on A 684 ☎ 20280, ≤, 🌳 – 📺 Ⓟ. [VISA] [VISA]. 🐕
closed January and February – **M** (dinner only) 15.00 **st.** and a la carte 🍷 3.50 – **6 rm** 🛏 30.00/60.00 **st.**

SEDGEFORD Norfolk [404] V 25 – pop. 468 – ✉ Hunstanton – ☎ 0485 Heacham.

♦London 122 – ♦Cambridge 59 – ♦Norwich 43.

Sedgeford Hall 🐦, PE36 5LT, SE : ¾ m. on Fring rd ☎ 70902, « Queen Anne house », 🏊, 🌳, park – 📺 Ⓟ
closed Christmas-New Year – **M** (booking essential) (communal dining) (dinner only) 26.00 **st.** 🍷 5.25 – **3 rm** 🛏 40.00/68.00 **st.** – SB 110.00/122.00 **st.**

SEDGEMOOR SERVICE AREA Somerset – ☎ 0934 Weston-Super-Mare.

[i] Somerset Visitor Centre, M 5 South, BS26 2UF ☎ 750833.

Forte Travelodge without rest., BS24 0JL, M 5 (northbound carriageway) between junctions 21 and 22 ☎ 750831, Fax 750450, Reservations (Freephone) 0800 850950 – 📺 ♿ Ⓟ. [VISA] [AE] [VISA]. 🐕
40 rm 31.95 **t.**

SEDLESCOMBE E. Sussex [404] V 31 – pop. 1 315 – ✉ Battle – ☎ 0424.

♦London 56 – Hastings 7 – Lewes 26 – Maidstone 27.

Brickwall, The Green, TN33 0QA, ☎ 870253, Fax 870785, 🏊 heated, 🌳 – 📺 ☎ Ⓟ. [VISA] [AE] [DC] [VISA]
M 13.50/16.50 **t.** 🍷 4.75 – **23 rm** 🛏 35.00/65.00 **t.** – SB 76.00/100.00 **st.**

SELBY N. Yorks. [402] Q 22 Great Britain G. – pop. 7 417 – ☎ 0757.

See : Abbey Church★.

[i] Park St., YO8 0AA ☎ 703263.

♦London 202 – ♦Kingston-upon-Hull 36 – ♦Leeds 23 – York 14.

Londesborough Arms, Market Pl., YO8 0NS, ☎ 707355, Fax 701607 – 📺 ☎ Ⓟ. [VISA] [AE] [VISA]. 🐕
M 12.00 **t.** and a la carte 🍷 4.25 – **27 rm** 🛏 40.00/55.00 **st.**

ATS Unit 1, Canal Rd, Bawtry Rd ☎ 703245/702147

SELLING Kent [404] W 30 – pop. 674 – ✉ ☎ 0795 Faversham.

♦London 56 – Canterbury 10 – ♦Dover 28 – Maidstone 25.

Parkfield House without rest., Hogben's Hill, ME13 9QU, ☎ 0227 (Canterbury) 752898, 🌳 – 🚭 Ⓟ. 🐕
closed 24 to 26 December – **4 rm** 🛏 16.50/33.00 **s.**

SELSIDE Cumbria – see Kendal.

SEMINGTON Wilts. [403] [404] N 29 – see Trowbridge.

SENNEN Cornwall [403] C 33 The West Country G. – ✉ ☎ 0736 Penzance.

See : Wayside Cross★ – Sennen Cove★ (≤★).

Envir. : Land's End★ (cliff scenery★★★) W : ½ m. – Penwith★★ – St. Buryan★★ (Church Tower★★) E : 5½ m. by B 3315 and B 3283 – Porthcurno★, SE : 3 m. by B 3315.

♦London 330 – Penzance 11 – Truro 40.

Old Success Inn, Sennen Cove, TR19 7DG, W : ¾ m. ☎ 871232, Fax 788354, ≤ – 📺 Ⓟ. [VISA] [VISA]. 🐕
M 11.50 **st.** (dinner) and a la carte 8.10/17.40 **st.** 🍷 4.25 – **12 rm** 🛏 22.50/65.00 **st.** – SB (November-March) 65.00/80.00 **st.**

SETTLE N. Yorks. [402] N 21 – pop. 3 153 – ECD : Wednesday – ☎ 0729.

⛳ Giggleswick ☎ 825288, N : 1 m. on A 65.

[i] Town Hall, Cheapside, BD24 9EJ ☎ 825192.

♦London 238 – Bradford 34 – Kendal 30 – ♦Leeds 41.

🏨 **Falcon Manor**, Skipton Rd, BD24 9BD, ℰ 823814, Fax 822087, ☞ – ↳ rest 📺 ☎ ℗. ⚐
🄌 𝗩𝗜𝗦𝗔
M (bar lunch Monday to Saturday)/dinner 17.50 **t.** and a la carte ≬ 4.35 – **19 rm** ⊐ 49.00/
88.00 **t.** – SB 88.00/118.00 **st.**

🏠 **Royal Oak**, Market Pl., BD24 9ED, ℰ 822561 – 📺 ☎ ℗. ⚒
accommodation closed 25 December – **M** (bar lunch Monday to Saturday)/dinner a la
carte 14.85/21.85 **st.** ≬ 5.00 – **6 rm** ⊐ 29.95/49.90 **st.**

✗✗ **Blue Goose**, Market Sq., BD24 9EJ, ℰ 822901 – ⚐ 𝗩𝗜𝗦𝗔
closed Sunday and January – **M** a la carte 14.20/19.95 **st.**

SEVENOAKS Kent ᪥᪥᪥ U 30 Great Britain G. – pop. 24 493 – ECD : Wednesday – ☺ 0732.

Envir. : Knole★★ *AC*, SE : ½ m. – Ightham Mote★ *AC*, E : 5 m. by A 25.

🛆 Woodlands ℰ 0959 52 (Oteford) 3805 – 🛆 Darenth Valley, Station Rd ℰ 0959 52 (Oteford)
2944, N : 3 m. by A 225.

🄯 Buckhurst Lane, TN13 1LQ ℰ 450305.

♦London 26 – Guildford 40 – Maidstone 17.

🏨 **Royal Oak**, Upper High St., TN13 1HY, ℰ 451109, Fax 740187, ⚒ – ▤ rest 📺 ☎ ℗ –
🛆 30. ⚐ 𝗔𝗘 🄌 𝗩𝗜𝗦𝗔
M 15.50/18.50 **t.** and a la carte – ⊐ 6.95 – **37 rm** 65.00/85.00 **t.** – SB (weekends only)
110.00 **t.**

at Ivy Hatch E : 4¾ m. by A 25 on Coach Rd – ⊠ ☺ 0732 Sevenoaks :

✗ **Le Chantecler** (at The Plough), TN15 0NL, ℰ 810268, ☞ – ℗. ⚐ 𝗩𝗜𝗦𝗔
closed Sunday dinner – **M** a la carte 13.20/18.70 **t.**

SHAFTESBURY Dorset ᪥᪥᪥ ᪥᪥᪥ N 30 The West Country G. – pop. 4 831 – ECD : Wednesday and
Saturday – ☺ 0747.

See : Gold Hill★ (⇐★) – Local History Museum★ *AC*.

Envir. : Wardour Castle★ *AC*, NE : 5 m.

🄯 8 Bell St., SP7 8AE ℰ (changing in 2/94 to 853514) 53514.

♦London 115 – Bournemouth 31 – ♦Bristol 47 – Dorchester 29 – Salisbury 20.

🏨 **Royal Chase** (Best Western), Royal Chase Roundabout, SP7 8DB, SE : at junction of A
30 with A 350 ℰ 53355 (changing in 2/94 to 853355), Fax 51969 (changing in 2/
94 to 851969), ⚐, ☞ – 📺 ☎ ℗ – 🛆 190. ⚐ 𝗔𝗘 🄌 𝗩𝗜𝗦𝗔
M 14.75/25.00 **t.** and a la carte ≬ 6.00 – **34 rm** ⊐ 66.00/120.00 **t.** – SB (except Bank
Holidays) 112.00/175.00 **st.**

✗✗ **La Fleur de Lys**, 25 Salisbury St., SP7 8EL, ℰ 53717 (changing in 2/94 to 853717) – ⚐
𝗔𝗘 𝗩𝗜𝗦𝗔
closed Monday lunch and Sunday dinner – **M** 18.95 **t.** and a la carte.

✗ **Jesters**, 4 Bell St., SP7 8AR, ℰ 54444 (changing in 2/94 to 854444) – ↳. ⚐ 𝗩𝗜𝗦𝗔
closed first 2 weeks January – **M** *(closed Sunday dinner and Monday)* a la carte 9.30/
17.90 **t.** ≬ 4.50.

SHALDON Devon ᪥᪥᪥ J 32 – see Teignmouth.

SHANKLIN I.O.W. ᪥᪥᪥ ᪥᪥᪥ Q 32 – see Wight (Isle of).

SHAW Wilts. ᪥᪥᪥ ᪥᪥᪥ N 29 – see Melksham.

SHAWBURY Shrops. ᪥᪥᪥ ᪥᪥᪥ ᪥᪥᪥ M 25 – pop. 2 685 – ⊠ Shrewsbury – ☺ 0939.

♦London 159 – ♦Birmingham 43 – Chester 39 – ♦Stoke-on-Trent 29 – Shrewsbury 7.

↱ **Sett Country** ⚒, Stanton-upon-Hine-Heath, SY4 4LR, NE : 2¼ m. by B 5063 ℰ 250391,
« Working farm » – ↳ ℗. ⚐ 𝗩𝗜𝗦𝗔
closed Christmas and New Year – **M** 14.00 **s.** – **3 rm** ⊐ 22.00/44.00 **s.**

SHEDFIELD Hants. ᪥᪥᪥ ᪥᪥᪥ Q 31 – pop. 3 291 – ⊠ Southampton – ☺ 0329 Wickham.

🛆, 🛆 Meon Valley Hotel G. & C.C., Sandy Lane, ℰ 833455, off A 334.

♦London 75 – ♦Portsmouth 13 – ♦Southampton 10.

🏨 **Meon Valley H. Golf & Country Club**, Sandy Lane, SO3 2HQ, off A 334 ℰ 833455,
Fax 834411, Ⓕ₄, ⛪, ⚐, 🛆, park, ⚒, squash – ↳ rm 📺 ☎ ℗ – 🛆 100. ⚐ 𝗔𝗘 🄌 𝗩𝗜𝗦𝗔 ⚒
M *(closed Saturday lunch)* (carving lunch) 21.50/40.00 **t.** ≬ 4.50 – **83 rm** ⊐ 79.00/105.00 **t.** –
SB (except Christmas and New Year) 106.00/164.00 **st.**

SHEEPWASH Devon ᪥᪥᪥ H 31 – see Hatherleigh.

SHEERNESS Kent ᪥᪥᪥ W 29 – pop. 11 087 – ECD : Wednesday – ☺ 0795.

↝ to the Netherlands : Vlissingen (Olau Line) (7 h) (2 daily).

🄯 Bridge Rd Car Park, ME12 1RH ℰ 665324.

♦London 52 – Canterbury 24 – Maidstone 20.

Hotels and Restaurants see : Sittingbourne SW : 9 m., *Maidstone* SW : 20 m.

See : Cutlers' Hall★ CZ **A** – Cathedral Church of SS. Peter and Paul CZ **B** : Shrewsbury Chapel (Tomb★).

🏌 Tinsley Park, Darnall ℰ 560237, E : by A 57 BY – 🏌 Beauchief Municipal, Abbey Lane ℰ 620648/620040, SW : by B 6068 AZ – 🏌 Birley Wood, Birley Lane ℰ 647262, SE : 4 ½ m. by A 616 BZ – 🏌 Concord Park, Shiregreen Lane ℰ 570274/570053, N : 3 ½ m. BY – 🏌 Hillsborough, Worrall Rd ℰ 343608, NW : 3 ½ m. by A 6102 AY – 🏌 Abbeydale, Twentywell Lane, Dore ℰ 360763, SW : 5 m. by A 621 AZ – 🏌 Lees Hall, Hemsworth Rd, Norton ℰ 554402, S : 3 m. AZ.

🅱 Peace Gdns, S1 2HH ℰ 734671/2 – Railway Station, Sheaf St., S1 2BP ℰ 795901.

♦London 174 – ♦Leeds 36 – ♦Liverpool 80 – ♦Manchester 41 – ♦Nottingham 44.

Plans on following pages

🏨🏨 **Holiday Inn Royal Victoria,** Victoria Station Rd, S4 7YE, ℰ 768822, Telex 547539, Fax 724519 – |‡| ⇥ rm 📺 ☎ 🅿 – 🔬 300. 🔼 🆎 ⓞ 𝒱𝒾𝒮𝒜. ⫣   DY **a**
M *(closed Saturday lunch)* 9.95/15.95 **st.** and a la carte ⫲ 7.95 – ⊐ 9.95 – **100 rm** 77.00/89.00 **st.** – SB (weekends only) 80.00/127.00 **st.**

🏨🏨 **Charnwood,** 10 Sharrow Lane, S11 8AA, ℰ 589411, Fax 555107 – |‡| 📺 ☎ 🅿 – 🔬 80. 🔼 🆎 ⓞ 𝒱𝒾𝒮𝒜. ⫣   CZ **u**
accommodation closed Christmas – **M** 11.00 **t.** and a la carte – Henfrey's *(closed Sunday and Monday)* (dinner only) 25.00/30.00 **t.** – **22 rm** ℰ 60.00/100.00 **t.** – SB (except Bank Holidays) 95.00 **st.**

🏨 **Swallow,** Kenwood Rd, S7 1NQ, ℰ 583811, Fax 500138, *Ⅰ₅,* ≘s, 🔲, ⫣, park – |‡| 📺 ☎ & 🅿 – 🔬 200. 🔼 🆎 ⓞ 𝒱𝒾𝒮𝒜   AZ **r**
M 13.25/17.00 **st.** and a la carte ⫲ 5.75 – **141 rm** ℰ 82.00/96.00 **st.** – SB (except Bank Holidays) (weekends only) 100.00 **st.**

🏨 **Beauchief** (Lansbury), 161 Abbeydale Rd South, S7 2QW, SW : 3 ½ m. ℰ 620500, Fax 350197, *Ⅰ₅,* ≘s – ⇥ rm 📺 ☎ & 🅿 – 🔬 100. 🔼 🆎 ⓞ 𝒱𝒾𝒮𝒜. ⫣
M 9.75/25.90 **t.** and a la carte ⫲ 5.50 – **41 rm** ⊐ 72.50/84.00 **t.** – SB (weekends only) 92.00/173.00 **st.**   on A 625   AZ

🏨 **Forte Crest,** Manchester Rd, Hallam, S10 5DX, ℰ 670067, Fax 682620, ≤, *Ⅰ₅,* ≘s, 🔲 – |‡| ⇥ rm 📺 ☎ & 🅿 – 🔬 300. 🔼 🆎 ⓞ 𝒱𝒾𝒮𝒜 𝒥𝒞ℬ   AZ **a**
M 11.95/15.95 **st.** and a la carte ⫲ 6.60 – ⊐ 9.95 – **133 rm** 75.00 **st.,** 2 suites – SB (weekends only) 98.00 **st.**

🏨 **Harley,** 334 Glossop Rd, S10 2HW, ℰ 752288, Fax 722383 – ⇥ rm ≣ rest 📺 ☎ – 🔬 30. 🔼 🆎 ⓞ 𝒱𝒾𝒮𝒜. ⫣   CZ **e**
M *(closed Sunday)* (dancing Friday and Saturday evenings) 9.75/11.95 **t.** and a la carte ⫲ 6.50 – **22 rm** ⊐ 50.00/80.00 **st.**

🏨 **Novotel,** Arundel Gate, S1 2PR, ℰ 781781, Telex 548261, Fax 787744, 🔲 – |‡| ⇥ rm ≣ ☎ & 🅿 – 🔬 250. 🔼 🆎 ⓞ 𝒱𝒾𝒮𝒜. ⫣   DZ **a**
M 7.50/12.50 **st.** and a la carte ⫲ 4.25 – ⊐ 7.50 – **144 rm** 55.00/60.00 **st.** – SB (weekends only) 52.00/86.00 **st.**

🏨 **Grosvenor House** (Forte), Charter Sq., S1 3EH, ℰ 720041, Fax 757199, ≤ – |‡| ⇥ rm ≣ rest 📺 ☎ 🅿 – 🔬 320 – **102 rm.** 1 suite.   CZ **n**

🏨 **Granada,** 340 Prince of Wales Rd, S2 1FF, ℰ 530935, Fax 642731 – ⇥ rm 📺 ☎ & 🅿. 🔼 🆎 ⓞ 𝒱𝒾𝒮𝒜. ⫣   BZ **a**
M *(closed 25 December)* (grill rest.) (bar lunch Saturday) 14.50 **st.** (dinner) and a la carte 14.20/22.45 **st.** ⫲ 5.75 – ⊐ 7.25 – **61 rm** 52.00 **st.** – SB (weekends only) 84.00/96.00 **st.**

🏨 **Comfort Inn** without rest., George St., S1 2PF, ℰ 739939, Fax 768332 – |‡| ⇥ rm 📺 ☎. 🔼 🆎 ⓞ 𝒱𝒾𝒮𝒜   DZ **e**
closed 24 December-1 January – ⊐ 5.95 – **50 rm** 29.95/44.95 **st.**

🏩 Westbourne House without rest., 25 Westbourne Rd, S10 2QQ, ℰ 660109, Fax 667778, ⫧ – 📺 🅿 – **9 rm.**   AZ **c**

🏠 **Millingtons** without rest., 70 Broomgrove Rd, S10 2NA, ℰ 669549 – 📺 🅿. ⫣
6 rm ⊐ 22.00/42.00 **st.**   AZ **i**

🍴🍴 **Le Neptune,** 141 West St., S1 4EW, ℰ 796677 – 🔼 🆎 𝒱𝒾𝒮𝒜   CZ **z**
M - French *(closed Sunday)* 12.25 **t.** and a la carte ⫲ 4.20.

🍴 **Zing Vaa,** 55 The Moor, S1 4PF, ℰ 722432, Fax 729213 – ≣. 🔼 🆎 ⓞ 𝒱𝒾𝒮𝒜   CZ **r**
M - Chinese *(closed 25 and 26 December)* 17.00 **t.** (dinner) and a la carte 10.40/15.90 **t.** ⫲ 3.70.

at Grenoside N : 4 ½ m. on A 61 – AY – ✉ ✆ 0742 Sheffield :

🏠 **Holme Lane Farm** without rest., 38 Halifax Rd, S30 3PB, ℰ 468858, ⫧ – 📺 🅿. 🔼 𝒱𝒾𝒮𝒜. ⫣ – **7 rm** ⊐ 26.00/45.00 **st.**

at Whitley N : 5 m. by A 6135 – AY – ✉ ✆ 0742 Sheffield :

🏨 **Whitley Hall** ⧐, Elliot Lane, Grenoside, S30 3NR, off Whitley Lane ℰ 454444, Fax 455414, ⫧, park – 📺 ☎ 🅿 – 🔬 70. 🔼 🆎 ⓞ 𝒱𝒾𝒮𝒜
closed 25-26 December and 1 January – **M** *(closed Saturday lunch and Bank Holidays)* 12.50/16.95 **t.** and a la carte – **15 rm** ⊐ 58.00/74.00 **t.** – SB (weekends only) 84.00 **st.**

at Chapeltown N : 6 m. on A 6135 – AY – ✉ ✆ 0742 Sheffield :

🏨 **Staindrop Lodge,** Lane End, S30 4UH, NW : ½ m. on High Green rd ℰ 846727, Fax 846783 – 📺 ☎ 🅿 – 🔬 80. 🔼 🆎 ⓞ 𝒱𝒾𝒮𝒜. ⫣
M *(closed lunch Saturday and Monday, Sunday dinner and Bank Holidays)* 8.10/22.00 **st.** ⫲ 4.50 – **13 rm** ⊐ 49.00/69.00 **st.** – SB (weekends only) 90.00/98.00 **st.**

Meadowhall
   Shopping Centre . . . . **BY**

Barrow Road. . . . . **BY** 4

Bawtry Road.	**BY** 5
Bradfield Road	**AY** 7
Brocco Bank	**AZ** 8
Broughton Lane	**BY** 10
Burngreave Road	**AY** 12
Handsworth Road	**BZ** 24
Holywell Road	**BY** 29
Main Road	**BZ** 32

Meadow Hall Road	**BY** 33
Middlewood Road	**AY** 34
Newhall Road	**BY** 36
Westbourne Road	**AZ** 47
Western Bank	**AZ** 48
Whitham Road	**AZ** 49
Woodbourn Road	**BYZ** 50
Woodhouse Road	**BZ** 51

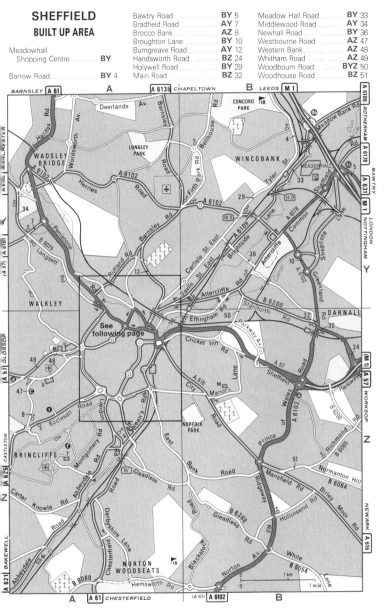

⁂⁂ **Greenhead House,** 84 Burncross Rd, S30 4SF, ✆ 469004 – ✗ **P**. 🔼 *VISA*
closed Sunday, Monday, first 2 weeks April, first 2 weeks August and 23 to 30 December –
M (booking essential) (dinner only) 29.50 **t.** ⌀ 4.75.

   at Ridgeway (Derbs.) SE : 6 ¾ m. by A 616 off B 6054 – BZ – ✉ ❀ 0742 Sheffield :

⁂⁂⁂ **Old Vicarage,** Ridgeway Moor, S12 3XW, on Marsh Lane rd ✆ 475814, Fax 477079,
« Attractively furnished », 🍽 – ✗ **P**. 🔼 AE *VISA*
closed Sunday dinner and Monday – **M** 17.50/27.50 **t.** ⌀ 6.00.

SHEFFIELD
CENTRE

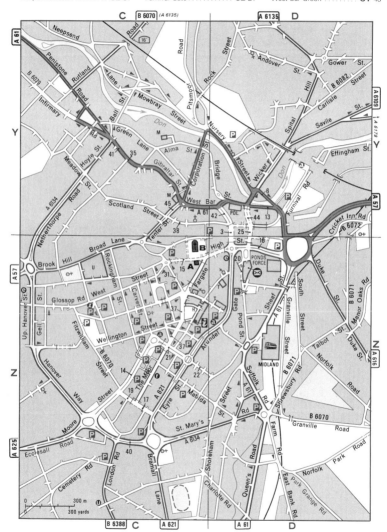

at Meadow Head S : 5¼ m. on A 61 – AZ – ⊠ – ☎ 0742 Sheffield :

🏨 **Sheffield Moat House** (Q.M.H.), Chesterfield Rd South, S8 8BW, ℰ 375376, Fax 378140, ₤₆, ≘s, ⧖ – ⧫ ⇄ ▦ rest ⊠ ☎ & **P** – 🔬 500. ⚑ ⚑ ⒶⒺ Ⓞ 𝘝𝘐𝘚𝘈
M *(closed Saturday lunch)* 11.00/15.50 **st.** and a la carte ≬ 5.75 – ⌧ 8.00 – **89 rm** 75.00/87.00 **st.**, 5 suites – SB (weekends only) 86.00 **st.**

Ⓜ ATS 87/91 Clifton St., Attercliffe ℰ 449750/449759   ATS Herries Rd ℰ 343986/7

♦London 193 – ♦Leeds 22 – ♦Manchester 30 – ♦Sheffield 20.

🏠 **Three Acres Inn,** Roydhouse, HD8 8LR, NE : 1 ½ m. by B 6116 on Flockton rd ♟ 602606, Fax 608411 – 📺 ☎ 🅿. ⋙ 🎦 VISA ❅
M *(closed Saturday lunch)* 10.95/22.15 **t.** and dinner a la carte ⋔ 4.75 – **18 rm** ⊑ 47.50/ 57.50 **t.** – SB (except Christmas) 80.00/110.00 **st.**

SHENINGTON Oxon. – see Banbury.

SHEPPERTON Surrey 404 S 29 – pop. 9 643 – ✪ 0932 Walton-on-Thames.

♦London 25.

Plan : see Greater London (South-West)

🏨 Shepperton Moat House (Q.M.H.), Felix Lane, TW17 8NP, E : 1 ¼ m. on B 375 ♟ 241404, Telex 928170, Fax 245231, ⇄s, ☞ – ⫾ 📺 ☎ 🅿 – ⩜ 300. ❅   AY   **a**
156 rm.

XX **Edwinns,** Church Sq., TW17 9JT, S : 1 m. ♟ 223543, Fax 253562 – ⋙ ⅍ ⓞ VISA   AZ
closed Saturday and Bank Holidays, Sunday dinner and 25 to 27 December –
M 9.95/12.95 **t.** and dinner a la carte ⋔ 4.95.

SHEPTON MALLET Somerset 403 404 M 30 The West Country G. – pop. 6 197 – ECD : Wednesday – ✪ 0749.

See : Town★ – SS. Peter and Paul's Church★.

Envir. : Evercreech (Church Tower★) SE : 4 m. by A 371 and B 3081 – Downside Abbey★ (Abbey Church★) N : 5 ½ m. by A 37 and A 367.

Exc. : Longleat House★★★ *AC,* E : 15 m. by A 361 and B 3092 – Wells★★ - Cathedral★★★, Vicars' Close★, Bishop's Palace★ *AC* (⩽★★) W : 6 m. by A 371 – Wookey Hole★★ (Caves★ *AC,* Papermill★, Fairground Collection★) W : 6½ m. by B 371 – Glastonbury★★ - Abbey★★★ (Abbots Kitchen★) *AC,* St. John the Baptist★★, Somerset Rural Life Museum★ *AC* – Glastonbury Tor★ (⩽★★★) SW : 9 m. by B 3136 and A 361 - Nunney★, E : 8½ m. by A 361.

🏌 Mendip, Gurney Slade ♟ 840570, N : 3 m. by A 37.

♦London 127 – ♦Bristol 20 – ♦Southampton 63 – Taunton 31.

🏨 **Charlton House,** Charlton Rd, BA4 4PR, E : 1 m. on A 361 ♟ 342008, Fax 346362, ⇄s, ☞, ❅ – 📺 ☎ 🅿. ⋙ ⅍ ⓞ VISA
accommodation closed 24 to 27 December – **M** 15.50/25.00 **t.** ⋔ 4.00 – **15 rm** ⊑ 80.00/ 110.00 **t.** – SB (except 1 week June and Christmas) 125.00/220.00 **st.**

🏠 Thatched Cottage Inn, 63-67 Charlton Rd, BA4 5QF, ♟ 342058, Fax 343265 📺 ☎ 🅿. ❅
8 rm.

↟ **Belfield** without rest., 34 Charlton Rd, BA4 5PA, ♟ 344353 – 📺 🅿. ❅
6 rm ⊑ 18.50/40.00 **st.**

XX **Bowlish House** with rm, Wells Rd, BA4 5JD, W : ½ m. on A 371 ♟ 342022, ☞ – 📺 🅿.
⋙ VISA
M (booking essential) (lunch by arrangement)/dinner 22.50 **st.** ⋔ 4.20 – ⊑ 3.50 – **3 rm** 48.00 **st.**

X **Blostin's,** 29 Waterloo Rd, BA4 5HH, ♟ 343648 – ⋙ VISA
closed Sunday, Monday, 2 weeks January, 1 week June and 1 week November – **M** (lunch by arrangement)/dinner 14.95 **t.** and a la carte ⋔ 5.95.

at Doulting E : 1 ½ m. on A 361 – ⊠ ✪ 0749 Shepton Mallet :

XX **Brottens Lodge** ⑳ with rm, BA4 4RB, S : 1 m. turning right at Abbey Barn Inn, following sign for Evercreech ♟ 880352, Fax 880601, ⩽, ☞ – 📺 ☎ 🅿. ⋙ VISA. ❅
M *(closed Sunday and lunch Monday and Saturday)* 15.50/19.50 **t.** ⋔ 4.00 – **3 rm** ⊑ 45.00/ 65.00 **st.** – SB 85.00 **st.**

at Evercreech SE : 4 m. by A 371 on B 3081 – ⊠ ✪ 0749 Shepton Mallet :

↟ **Pecking Mill,** BA4 6PG, W : 1 m. on A 371 ♟ 830336 – 📺 ☎ 🅿. ⋙ ⅍ ⓞ VISA. ❅
closed Christmas – **M** *(closed Monday lunch)* a la carte 10.25/15.60 **t.** ⋔ 3.85 – **6 rm** ⊑ 33.00/44.00 **t.** – SB (winter only) 52.00/92.00 **st.**

SHERBORNE Dorset 403 404 M 31 The West Country G. – pop. 7 405 – ECD : Wednesday – ✪ 0935.

See : Town★ - Abbey★★ – Castle★ *AC.*

Envir. : Sandford Orcas Manor House★ *AC,* NW : 4 m. by B 3148 – Purse Caundle Manor★ *AC,* NE : 5 m. by A 30.

Exc. : Cadbury Castle (⩽★★) N : 8 m. by A 30.

🏌 Clatcombe ♟ 812475, N : 1 m.

🅱 3 Tilton Court, Digby Rd, DT9 3LW ♟ 815341.

♦London 128 – Bournemouth 39 – Dorchester 19 – Salisbury 36 – Taunton 31.

🏨 **Eastbury,** Long St., DT9 3BY, ℰ 813131, Fax 817296, 🍽 – 📺 ☎ 🅿 – 🛗 60. 🔼 **VISA** ⚡
M 17.50/26.00 **t.** and a la carte 🍷 5.50 – **15 rm** ⬚ 72.50/118.00 **t.** – SB (except Bank Holidays) 98.00/118.00 **st.**

🏨 **Antelope,** Greenhill, DT9 4EP, ℰ 812077, Fax 816473 – 📺 ☎ 🕭 🅿 – 🛗 80. 🔼 🆎 ⓞ **VISA** ⚡
M 8.50/10.50 **st.** and a la carte 🍷 4.95 – **19 rm** ⬚ 35.00/55.00 **st.** – SB (weekends only) 60.00/112.00 **st.**

🏨 **Half Moon,** Half Moon St., DT9 3LN, ℰ 812017 – ⇆ rm 📺 ☎ 🅿. 🔼 🆎 ⓞ **VISA**
M a la carte 7.25/18.50 **st.** 🍷 4.45 – **15 rm** ⬚ 30.00/54.00 **st.** – SB (except Bank Holidays) (weekends only) 62.00/84.00 **st.**

⋔ **Quinns,** Marston Rd, DT9 4BL, ℰ 815008 – ⇆ 📺 🅿
M (by arrangement) (communal dining) 15.50 **s.** – **3 rm** ⬚ 25.00/50.00 – SB 42.00/50.00 **st.**

XX **Pheasants** with rm, 24 Greenhill, DT9 4EW, ℰ 815252 – 📺 🅿. 🔼 **VISA** ⚡
closed 2 weeks mid January – **M** *(closed Sunday dinner and Monday to non-residents)* 14.00/19.75 **t.** and a la carte – **5 rm** ⬚ 27.50/45.00 **t.**

at Oborne NE : 2 m. by A 30 – ✉ ❀ 0935 Sherborne :

XX **Grange** ☜, with rm, DT9 4LA, ℰ 813463, Fax 817464, ≼, 🍽 – 📺 ☎ 🅿. 🔼 🆎 **VISA** ⚡
closed 1 to 7 January and last 2 weeks August – **M** - **Italian** (closed Sunday dinner and Bank Holidays) (dinner only and Sunday lunch)/dinner 15.50 **t.** and a la carte 🍷 5.80 – **4 rm** ⬚ 40.00/60.00 **st.** – SB (weekends only) 90.00/130.00 **st.**

at Yetminster SW : 5 ½ m. by A 352 and Yetminster rd – ✉ Sherborne – ❀ 0935 Yeovil :

⋔ **Manor Farmhouse,** DT9 6LF, ℰ 872247, « 17C farmhouse », 🍽 – ⇆ 📺 🅿. 🔼 **VISA** ⚡
M (by arrangement) 15.00 **t.** – **4 rm** ⬚ 30.00/50.00 **t.**

SHERBOURNE Warks. – see Warwick.

SHERIFF HUTTON N. Yorks. 402 Q 21 – pop. 884 – ✉ York – ❀ 0347.
♦London 313 – York 10.

⋔ **Rangers House** ☜, The Park, YO6 1RH, S : 1 ¼ m. by Strensall rd ℰ 878397, Fax 878666, 🍽 – 🅿. ⚡
M 20.00 🍷 3.50 – **6 rm** ⬚ 32.00/64.00 – SB (except Bank Holidays) 90.00.

SHERINGHAM Norfolk 404 X 25 – pop. 6 861 – ECD : Wednesday – ❀ 0263.
🚇 Sheringham ℰ 822038, W : ½ m. by A 149.
🎫 Station Approach, NR26 8RA ℰ 824329 (summer only).
♦London 128 – Cromer 4 – ♦Norwich 27.

⋔ **Beacon,** 1 Nelson Rd, NR26 8BI, ℰ 822019, 🍽 – ⇆ 🅿. 🔼 **VISA** ⚡
May-September – **M** (by arrangement) – **6 rm** ⬚ 22.00/50.00 **st.** – SB 60.00/62.00 **st.**

SHIFNAL Shrops. 402 403 404 M 25 – pop. 6 094 – ECD : Thursday – ✉ ❀ 0952 Telford.
♦London 150 – ♦Birmingham 28 – Shrewsbury 16.

🏨🏨 **Park House,** Park St., TF11 9BA, ℰ 460128, Fax 461658, ⇆s, 🔲, 🍽 – 🛗 📺 ☎ 🕭 🅿 – 🛗 180. 🔼 🆎 ⓞ **VISA**
M (closed Saturday lunch) 9.00/18.50 **t.** and a la carte 🍷 5.75 – **52 rm** ⬚ 79.50/94.50 **t.**, 2 suites.

SHINFIELD Berks. 404 R 29 – see Reading.

SHIPHAM Somerset 403 L 30 The West Country G. – pop. 1 107 – ✉ Winscombe – ❀ 0934 Weston-super-Mare.
Envir. : Cheddar Gorge★★ (Gorge★★, Caves★★, Jacobs's Ladder ✳★) – St. Andrew's Church★, S : 2½ m.
🌳, 🌳 Mendip Spring, Honeyhall Lane, Congresbury, Avon ℰ 853337/852322.
♦London 135 – ♦Bristol 14 – Taunton 20.

🏨 **Daneswood House,** Cuck Hill, BS25 1RD, ℰ 843145, Fax 843824, ≼, 🍽 – 📺 ☎ 🅿. 🔼 🆎 ⓞ **VISA** ⚡
M (closed Sunday dinner to non-residents) 14.95/19.95 **st.** and a la carte 🍷 4.50 – **9 rm** ⬚ 57.50/77.50 **st.**, 3 suites – SB (except Bank Holidays) 90.00/119.00 **st.**

GRÜNE REISEFÜHRER

Landschaften, Baudenkmäler
Sehenswürdigkeiten
Fremdenverkehrsstraßen
Tourenvorschläge
Stadtpläne und Übersichtskarten

W. Yorks. 402 O 22 – pop. 28 815 – ECD : Wednesday – ✆ 0274 Bradford.

🛆 Northcliffe, High Bank Lane ✗ 584085, SW : 1 ¼ m. by A 650.

◆London 216 – Bradford 4 – ◆Leeds 12.

🏛 Hollings Hall ⤴, Hollins Hill, Baildon, BD17 7QW, NE : 2½ m. on A 6038 ✗ 530053, Telex 518363, Fax 530187, ⇄, ⤚, park – 🛗 ⇥ rm 📺 ☎ 🕭 ❷ – 🔏 200. ⚙
58 rm. 1 suite.

🍴 **Aagrah,** 27 Westgate, BD18 3QX, ✗ 594660 – 🔄 AE ① VISA
closed 25 December – **M** - Indian (booking essential) (dinner only) 12.95 **t.** and a la carte
🍷 4.00.

Warks. 403 404 P 27 – pop. 3 072 – ✆ 0608.

◆London 85 – ◆Birmingham 34 – ◆Oxford 29.

🍴🍴 **Feldon House** with rm, Lower Brailes, OX15 5HW, E : 4½ m. on B 4035 ✗ 685580, « 19C country house of 17C origins », ⤚ – 📺 ☎ ❷. 🔄 AE VISA ⚙
closed 2 weeks autumn – **M** *(closed Sunday dinner)* (booking essential) 17.95/22.95 **st.**
🍷 4.25 – **4 rm** ⤓ 30.00/60.00 **st.** – SB (except Sunday) 77.00/95.00 **st.**

Dorset – see Bridport.

☞ *Benutzen Sie für weite Fahrten in Europa die* Michelin-Länderkarten :

970 Europa, 980 Griechenland, 984 Deutschland, 985 Skandinavien-Finnland,
986 Großbritannien-Irland, 987 Deutschland-Österreich-Benelux, 988 Italien,
989 Frankreich, 990 Spanien-Portugal, 991 Jugoslawien.

Oxon. 403 404 P 28 – pop. 2 558 – ECD : Wednesday –
✆ 0993.

◆London 81 – ◆Birmingham 50 – Gloucester 37 – ◆Oxford 25.

🏠 **Lamb Inn,** High St., OX7 6DQ, ✗ 830465 – ⇥ rest 📺 ❷. 🔄 AE VISA. ⚙
M *(closed Monday except Bank Holidays)* (buffet lunch)/dinner 19.50 **t.** 🍷 4.00 – **5 rm**
⤓ 48.00/65.00 **t.**

W. Mids. 403 404 O 26 – see Solihull.

Heref. and Worcs. – pop. 347 – ✉ ✆ 0905 Worcester.

◆London 152 – ◆Birmingham 45 – Leominster 33.

🏛 **Lenchford,** WR6 6TB, SE : ½ m. on B 4196 ✗ 620229, Fax 621125, ≼, « Riverside setting », ⤴, ⤚ – 📺 ☎ ❷ – 🔏 80. 🔄 AE ① VISA ⚙
closed 24 to 26 December – **M** *(closed Sunday dinner)* (buffet lunch)/dinner a la carte 15.40/18.40 **st.** 🍷 3.95 – **16 rm** ⤓ 32.50/49.50 **st.**

Warks. 403 404 P 27 – see Warwick.

Shrops. 402 403 L 25 Great Britain G. – pop. 57 731 – ECD : Thursday –
✆ 0743.

See : Abbey★ D.

Exc. : Ironbridge Gorge Museum★★ AC (The Iron Bridge★★ - Coalport China Museum★★ - Blists Hill Open Air Museum★★ – Museum of the River and Visitor Centre★) SE : 12 m. by A 5 and B 4380.

🛆 Condover ✗ 872976, S : 4 m. by A 5191 – 🛆 Meole Brace ✗ 364050, S : 1 m. by A 5191.

🎵 The Music Hall, The Square, SY1 1LH ✗ 350761.

◆London 164 – ◆Birmingham 48 – ◆Cardiff 10 – Chester 43 – Derby 67 – Gloucester 93 – ◆Manchester 68 –
◆Stoke-on-Trent 39 – ◆Swansea 124.

Plan on next page

🏛 **Lion** (Forte), Wyle Cop, SY1 1UY, ✗ 353107, Fax 352744 – 🛗 ⇥ 📺 ☎ ❷ – 🔏 200. 🔄 AE
① VISA JCB **c**
M (bar lunch Monday to Saturday)/dinner 16.95 **st.** and a la carte 🍷 6.95 – ⤓ 8.50 – **59 rm**
70.00/95.00 **st.** – SB (except Christmas-New Year) 108.00 **st.**

🏛 **Prince Rupert** (Q.M.H.), Butcher Row, SY1 1UQ, ✗ 236000, Fax 357306 – 🛗 ▭ rest 📺
☎ ❷ – 🔏 70. 🔄 AE ① VISA ⚙ **n**
M 17.00 **t.** (dinner) and a la carte 21.80/34.50 **t.** 🍷 4.50 – **62 rm** ⤓ 70.00/85.00 **t.**, 3 suites –
SB (weekends only) 104.00/174.00 **st.**

🏠 **Fieldside** without rest., 38 London Rd, SY2 6NX, E : 1 ¼ m. via Abbey Foregate on A 5112
✗ 353143, ⤚ – ⇥ 📺 ❷. 🔄 VISA ⚙
closed 3 weeks December-January – **9 rm** ⤓ 25.00/42.00 **st.**

🍴 **Cromwells,** 11 Dogpole, SY1 1EN, ✗ 361440 – 📺. 🔄 AE VISA **x**
M *(closed Bank Holiday lunch and Sunday)* a la carte 8.50/14.75 **t.** – **7 rm** ⤓ 25.00/
40.00 **t.**

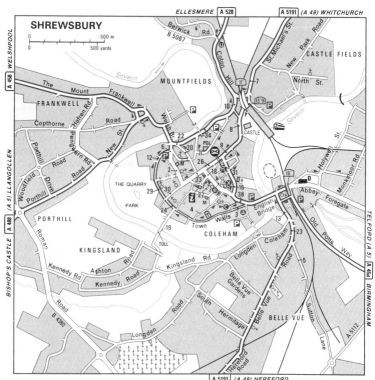

SHREWSBURY

ELLESMERE A 528   A 5191 (A 49) WHITCHURCH

WELSHPOOL A 458

BISHOP'S CASTLE A 488 (A 5) LLANGOLLEN

TELFORD (A 5) A 458 BIRMINGHAM

A 5191 (A 49) HEREFORD

↑ **Sandford House** without rest., St. Julians Friars, SY1 1XL, ℰ 343829, ﹐ – ⊡. ▦ ₩️
10 rm ⊴ 23.00/43.50 st.
a

↑ **Tudor House** without rest., 2 Fish St., SY1 1UR, ℰ 351735, « Part 15C house » – ⊡.
※
closed 24 to 26 December – **3 rm** ⊴ 27.00/44.00 st.
e

↑ **Sydney House,** Coton Cres., off Coton Hill, SY1 2LJ, ℰ 354681 – ⊡ ☎ ℗. ▦ ㏂ ₩️.
※
closed 24 to 31 December – **M** 12.00 st. ♦ 4.00 – **7 rm** ⊴ 35.00/60.00 st. – SB 60.00/
99.00 st.
u

at Albrighton N : 3 m. on A 528 – ⊠ Shrewsbury – ✆ 0939 Bomere Heath :

🏨 **Albrighton Hall,** Ellesmere Rd, SY4 3AG, ℰ 291000, Fax 291123, ♭, ⅀, ▦, ﹐, park,
squash – ⊡ ☎ ℗ – 🕰 200. ▦ ㏂ ⓞ ₩️
M (closed Saturday lunch) 10.50/16.95 st. and a la carte ♦ 6.50 – **39 rm** ⊴ 49.50/130.00 st.
– SB 98.00/118.00 st.

🏛 **Albright Hussey** ⑤, Ellesmere Rd, SY4 3AF, ℰ 290571, Fax 291143, ≤, « 16C moated
manor house », ﹐ – ⊡ ☎ ℗. ▦ ㏂ ₩️
M - Italian 12.00/16.50 t. and a la carte ♦ 5.50 – **5 rm** ⊴ 65.00/100.00 st. – SB 95.00/
150.00 st.

at Dorrington S : 7 m. on A 49 – ⊠ Shrewsbury – ✆ 0743 Dorrington :

🍴🍴 **Country Friends** with rm, SY5 7JD, ℰ 718707, ﹐ – ℗. ▦ ㏂ ₩️. ※
closed 2 weeks late July and mid October – **M** (closed Sunday, Monday and 25-
26 December) 16.90/18.90 t. and a la carte ♦ 5.50 – **3 rm** ⊴ 32.00/45.00 t.

at Hanwood SW : 4 m. on A 488 – ⊠ ❀ 0743 Shrewsbury :

⌂ **White House,** SY5 8LP, 𝒫 860414, ☞ – ⅛≈ ❶. ❄
   M (by arrangement) 15.00 **st.** – **6 rm** ⊆ 20.00/50.00 **st.** – SB 56.00/91.00 **st.**

⌂ **Old School House** without rest., SY5 8LJ, 𝒫 860694, ☞ – ▥ ❶. ❄
   3 rm ⊆ 16.00/29.00 **st.**

at Alberbury W : 7 ½ m. by A 458 – ⊠ ❀ 0743 Shrewsbury :

🏰 Rowton Castle, SY5 9EP, on A 458 𝒫 884044, Fax 884949, ≼, ☞, park – ▥ ☎ ❶ – 🏛 100
   18 rm.

🔧 ATS Lancaster Rd. Harlescott 𝒫 343954/232231

SHURDINGTON Glos. ❹❶❸ ❹❶❹ N 28 – see Cheltenham.

SIBSON Leics. – see Nuneaton (Warks.).

SIDDINGTON Ches. ❹❶❷ ❹❶❸ ❹❶❹ N 24 – pop. 400 – ⊠ Macclesfield – ❀ 0260 Congleton.

◆London 189 – ◆Liverpool 56 – ◆Manchester 19 – ◆Sheffield 40 – ◆Stoke-on-Trent 39.

⌂ **Golden Cross Farm** without rest, Pexhill Rd, SK11 9JP, 𝒫 224358, « Working farm »,
   ☞ – ⅛≈ ❶. ❄
   closed 25 December and 1 January – **4 rm** ⊆ 14.00/28.00 **s.**

SIDFORD Devon ❹❶❸ K 31 – see Sidmouth.

SIDMOUTH Devon ❹❶❸ K 31 The West Country G. – pop. 10 808 – ECD : Thursday – ❀ 0395.

Envir. : Bicton★ (Gardens★) *AC*, SW : 5 m.

🄰 Cotmaton Rd 𝒫 513023, W : ½ m.

🄱 Ham Lane, EX10 8XR 𝒫 516441.

◆London 170 – Exeter 14 – Taunton 27 – Weymouth 45.

🏰 **Victoria,** The Esplanade, Peak Hill, EX10 8RY, 𝒫 512651, Fax 579154, ≼, ≊s, ⌁ heated,
   ⊠, ☞, ❄ – ⫟ ▥ ☎ ❶. ⌸ ⌶ ⓞ 𝚅𝙸𝚂𝙰. ❄
   M (dancing Saturday evening) 10.25/20.50 **t.** and a la carte – **58 rm** ⊆ 65.00/170.00 **t.,**
   3 suites – SB (except Christmas and New Year) 84.00/154.00 **st.**

🏰 **Riviera,** The Esplanade, EX10 8AY, 𝒫 515201, Fax 577775, ≼ – ⫟ ☰ rest ▥ ☎ & ⇦ –
   🏛 85. ⌸ 𝚅𝙸𝚂𝙰. ❄
   M 11.50/18.50 **t.** and a la carte ⫶ 4.40 – **29 rm** ⊆ 61.00/144.00 **t.** – SB (October-May)
   86.00/140.00 **st.**

🏰 **Belmont,** The Esplanade, EX10 8RX, 𝒫 512555, Fax 579101, ≼, ☞ – ⫟ ▥ ☎ ❶. ⌸ ⌶
   ⓞ 𝚅𝙸𝚂𝙰. ❄
   M (dancing Saturday evening) 10.75/20.00 **t.** and a la carte ⫶ 4.95 – **51 rm** ⊆ 72.00/
   240.00 **t.** – SB (except Christmas and New Year) 90.00/174.00 **st.**

🏨 **Salcombe Hill House** ≫, Beatlands Rd, EX10 8JQ, 𝒫 514697, ⌁ heated, ☞, ❄ – ⫟
   ⅛≈ rest ▥ ☎ ❶. ⌸ ⓞ 𝚅𝙸𝚂𝙰. ❄
   March-October – **M** (bar lunch Monday to Saturday)/dinner 15.00 **t.** and a la carte ⫶ 6.50 –
   30 rm ⊆ 45.00/90.00 **t.** – SB 70.00/116.00 **st.**

🏠 **Littlecourt,** Seafield Rd, EX10 8HF, 𝒫 515279, ⌁ heated, ☞ – ⅛≈ rest ☰ rest ▥ ❶. ⌸
   ⌶ 𝚅𝙸𝚂𝙰. ❄
   19 March-October – **M** (bar lunch)/dinner 12.50 **st.** ⫶ 3.15 – **21 rm** ⊆ 23.00/70.00 **st.** –
   SB 70.00/92.00 **st.**

🏠 **Abbeydale,** Manor Rd, EX10 8RP, 𝒫 512060, ☞ – ⫟ ⅛≈ rest ▥ ☎ ❶. ❄
   April-October – **M** (bar lunch)/dinner 13.00 **t.** ⫶ 3.00 – **17 rm** ⊆ 35.00/70.00 **t.** – SB 70.00/
   96.00 **st.**

🏠 **Mount Pleasant,** Salcombe Rd, EX10 8JA, 𝒫 514694, ☞ – ⅛≈ rest ▥ ❶. ❄
   Easter-mid October – **M** (residents only) (dinner only) 13.00 **st.** ⫶ 5.00 – **16 rm** ⊆ 29.00/
   62.00 **st.**

🏠 **Woodlands,** Station Rd, Cotmaton Cross, EX10 8HG, 𝒫 513120, ☞ – ⅛≈ rest ▥ ❶. ⌸
   𝚅𝙸𝚂𝙰
   M 7.00/11.00 **t.** ⫶ 4.00 – **29 rm** ⊆ 29.00/80.00 **t.** – SB (autumn and winter only) 54.00/
   84.00 **t.**

⌂ **Broad Oak** without rest., Sid Rd, EX10 8QP, 𝒫 513713, ☞ – ⅛≈ ▥ ❶. ❄
   closed December and January – **3 rm** ⊆ 18.00/48.00.

⌂ **Salcombe Cottage,** Hillside Rd, EX10 8JF, 𝒫 516829, « 18C thatched cottage », ☞ –
   ⅛≈ ❶
   M (by arrangement) 8.00 **s.** – **4 rm** ⊆ 18.50/34.00 **s.**

at Sidford N : 2 m. – ⊠ ❀ 0395 Sidmouth :

🏠 **Salty Monk,** Church St., EX10 9QP, on A 3052 𝒫 513174, ☞ – ⅛≈ rest ▥ ❶. ⌸ 𝚅𝙸𝚂𝙰
   Restricted service in February – **M** (closed Monday lunch) 10.00/14.50 **st.** and a la carte
   ⫶ 5.25 – **7 rm** ⊆ 15.00/37.00 **st.**

🔧 ATS Vicarage Rd 𝒫 512433

SILCHESTER Hants. 403 404 Q 29 – pop. 1 072 – ✉ Reading (Berks.) – ☎ 0734.

♦London 62 – Basingstoke 8 – Reading 14 – Winchester 26.

Romans (Best Western), Little London Rd, RG7 2PN, ☎ 700421, Fax 700691, heated, , – TV ☎ P – 40. AE VISA JCB
M *(closed Saturday lunch)* 18.00/21.00 **st.** 5.50 – **24 rm** 60.00/95.00 **st.** – SB 90.00/100.00 **st.**

SILVERDALE Lancs. 402 L 21 – ✉ Carnforth – ☎ 0524 Lancaster.

♦London 257 – ♦Carlisle 60 – Kendal 12 – Lancaster 13.

Lindeth House, Lindeth Rd, LA5 0TX, via Shore rd ☎ 701238, – rest TV P.
closed January and February – **M** *(closed Friday and Saturday to non-residents)* (dinner only) 17.50 **st.** 5.00 – **3 rm** 30.00/47.00 **st.** – SB 75.00/95.00 **st.**

SIMONSBATH Somerset 403 I 30 The West Country G. – ✉ Minehead – ☎ 064 383 (3 fig.) and 0643 (6 fig.) Exford.

Envir. : Exmoor National Park★★ – Exford (Church★) E : 5½ m. by B 3223 and B 3224.

♦London 200 – Exeter 40 – Minehead 19 – Taunton 38.

Simonsbath House, TA24 7SH, ☎ 259, ≤, « 17C country house », – rest TV ☎ P. AE VISA.
closed December and January – **M** (dinner only) 20.50 **st.** 5.20 – **7 rm** 50.00/90.00 **st.** – SB 114.00/156.00 **st.**

SINDLESHAM Berks. – see Reading.

SISSINGHURST Kent 404 V 30 – see Cranbrook.

SITTINGBOURNE Kent 404 W 29 – pop. 35 893 – ECD : Wednesday – ☎ 0795.

18, 9 Upchurch River Valley, Oak Lane, Upchurch ☎ 0634 (Medway) 360626.

♦London 44 – Canterbury 16 – Maidstone 13.

Coniston, 70 London Rd, ME10 1NT, ☎ 472131, Fax 428056 – TV ☎ ♿ P – 120. AE VISA
M 8.50 **t.** and a la carte – **57 rm** 49.50/54.00 **st.** – SB (weekends only) 64.00/102.00 **st.**

ATS Crown Quay Lane ☎ 472384/472912

SIX MILE BOTTOM Cambs. – see Newmarket (Suffolk).

SKELTON N. Yorks. 402 Q 22 – see York.

SKELWITH BRIDGE Cumbria 402 K 20 – see Ambleside.

SKIPTON N. Yorks. 402 N 22 Great Britain G. – pop. 13 009 – ECD : Tuesday – ☎ 0756.

See : Castle★ *AC*.

18 off NW bypass ☎ 793722.

8 Victoria Sq., BD23 1JF ☎ 792809.

♦London 217 – Kendal 45 – ♦Leeds 26 – Preston 36 – York 43.

Randell's, Keighley Rd, BD23 2TA, S : 1¼ m. on B 6137 ☎ 700100, Fax 700107, , , , squash – TV ☎ ♿ P – 400. AE VISA
M (bar lunch Monday to Saturday)/dinner 15.95 **st.** – **60 rm** 35.00/97.50 **st.** – SB (except Christmas and New Year) 85.00 **st.**

Unicorn, Devonshire Pl., Keighley Rd, BD23 2LP, ☎ 794146 – TV ☎. AE VISA.
M (residents only) (dinner only) 11.00 **st.** 4.00 – **10 rm** 35.00/44.00 **st.**

Forte Travelodge without rest., A 65/A 59 roundabout, Gargrave Rd, BD23 1UD, W : 1¾ m. via Water St., ☎ 798091, Reservations (Freephone) 0800 850950 – TV ♿ P. AE VISA.
32 rm 31.95 **t.**

at Elslack W : 4½ m. by A 59 off A 56 – ✉ Skipton – ☎ 0282 Earby :

Tempest Arms, BD23 3AY, ☎ 842450, Fax 843331 – TV ☎ P – 80. AE VISA.
M 17.00 **st.** (dinner) and lunch a la carte 8.25/13.45 **st.** 5.00 – **10 rm** 44.00/50.00 **st.** – SB (November-April) 60.00/62.00 **st.**

ATS Carleton Rd Garage, Carleton Rd ☎ 795741/2

In alta stagione, *e soprattutto nelle stazioni turistiche, è prudente prenotare con un certo anticipo.*
Avvertite immediatamente l'albergatore se non potete più occupare la camera prenotata.

Se scrivete ad un albergo all'estero, allegate alla vostra lettera un tagliando-risposta internazionale (disponibile presso gli uffici postali).

Lancs. 402 M 22 – pop. 332 – ✉ Clitheroe – ☎ 0200.

◆London 249 – Burnley 21 – Lancaster 19 – ◆Leeds 48 – Preston 27.

🏠 **Parrock Head** ⌕, BB7 3AH, NW : 1 m. ℰ 446614, ≼ Bowland Fells, ⏤ – ᠻᚺ rest �📺 ☎ 🄿, ⚞ ℿ AE 🔢 *VISA* ※
M (bar lunch Monday to Saturday)/dinner a la carte 14.00/18.50 **t**. ♨ 5.00 – **9 rm** ⊏⊐ 40.00/65.00. – SB (except Bank Holidays) 90.00/115.00 **st**.

⌂ **Hark to Bounty,** BB7 3EP, ℰ 446246 – 📺 🄿. ⚞ ℿ AE *VISA* ※
M (bar lunch)/dinner 10.00 **st**. and a la carte – **8 rm** ⊏⊐ 19.00/45.00 **st**.

Northd. 401 402 N 19 – see Hexham.

Lincs. 402 404 S 25 – pop. 8 247 – ECD : Thursday – ☎ 0529.

🔲 South Rauceby ℰ 052 98 (South Rauceby) 273, W : 1 m. on A 153.

🄱 The Mill, Money's Yard, Carre St., NG34 7TW ℰ 414294.

◆London 119 – ◆Leicester 45 – Lincoln 17 – ◆Nottingham 39.

🏠 **Lincolnshire Oak,** East Rd, NG34 7EQ, NE : 2 m. on A 153 ℰ 413807, Fax 413710, ⏤ – ᠻᚺ rest 📺 ☎ 🄿 – ⚞ ℿ AE *VISA* ※
M a la carte approx. 14.95 **t**. ♨ 3.50 – **14 rm** ⊏⊐ 39.00/65.00 **t**. – SB (weekends only) 78.90/123.90 **st**.

🏠 **Forte Travelodge** without rest, NG34 8NP, NW : 1 m. on A 15 at junction with A 17 ℰ 414752, Reservation (Freephone) 0800 850950 – 📺 ₠ 🄿. ⚞ ℿ AE *VISA* ※
40 rm 31.95 **t**.

⌂ **Tally Ho Inn,** Aswarby, NG34 8SA, S : 4 ½ m. on A 15 ℰ 052 95 (Culverthorpe) 205, ≼, ⏤ – 📺 🄿. ⚞ ℿ *VISA* ※
closed 25 December and 1 January – **M** a la carte 11.90/17.90 **t**. ♨ 3.25 – **6 rm** ⊏⊐ 30.00/45.00 **t**. – SB 35.00/50.00 **st**.

🔘 ATS 40 Albion Terr., off Boston Rd ℰ 302908

W. Sussex – see Horsham.

En saison, surtout dans les stations fréquentées, il est prudent de retenir à l'avance.
Cependant, si vous ne pouvez pas occuper la chambre que vous avez retenue,
prévenez immédiatement l'hôtelier.

Si vous écrivez à un hôtel à l'étranger, joignez à votre lettre
un coupon-réponse international (disponible dans les bureaux de poste).

Berks. 404 S 29 – pop. 106 341 – ECD : Wednesday – ☎ 0753.

🔲 Farnham Park, Park Rd, Stoke Poges ℰ 643332, N : 2 m. – 🔲, 🔲, 🔲 Wexham Park, Wexham St., Wexham ℰ 663271, N : 2 m. – 🔲 Hollow Hill Lane, Iver ℰ 655615, E : 3 m.

◆London 29 – ◆Oxford 39 – Reading 19.

🏨 **Copthorne,** Cippenham Lane, SL1 2YE, SW : 1 ¼ m. by A 4 on A 355 ℰ 516222, Telex 220250, Fax 516237, ♣, ⩲, 🔲, – 🕸 ᠻᚺ rm ⊟ 📺 ☎ ₠ 🄿 – ⚞ 200. ℿ AE ⓞ *VISA* JCB. ※
M – **Veranda** (dancing Saturday evening) 14.10/17.90 **st**. and dinner a la carte ♨ 6.50 – **Reflections** (closed Sunday and Bank Holidays) (dinner only) 27.75 **st**. ♨ 6.50 – ⊏⊐ 9.75 – **217 rm** 110.00/135.00 **st**., 2 suites.

🏨 **Heathrow/Slough Marriott,** Ditton Rd, Langley, SL3 8PT, SE : 2 ½ m. on A 4 ℰ 544244, Fax 540272, ♣, ⩲, 🔲, ※ – 🕸 ᠻᚺ rm ⊟ 📺 ☎ ₠ 🄿 – ⚞ 300. ℿ AE ⓞ *VISA* JCB. ※
M 19.95 **t**. and dinner a la carte ♨ 6.50 – ⊏⊐ 11.85 – **349 rm** 110.00/140.00 **st**., 1 suite – SB (weekends only) 110.00/140.00 **st**.

🏠 **Courtyard by Marriott,** Church St., Chalvey, SL1 2NH, SW : 1 ¼ m. by A 4 on A 355 ℰ 551551, Fax 553333, ♣, – 🕸 ᠻᚺ rm ⊟ 📺 ☎ ₠ 🄿 – ⚞ 35. ℿ AE ⓞ *VISA* ※
M a la carte 15.95/19.45 **s**. ♨ 5.50 – ⊏⊐ 7.75 – **148 rm** 68.00 **st**. – SB (weekends only) 90.00/156.00 **st**.

🔘 ATS 1a Furnival Av. ℰ 524214

Devon – see Salcombe.

Cambs. 404 V 26 Great Britain G. – pop. 6 596 – ☎ 0353 Ely.

Envir. : Wicken Fen★, SW : 5 m. by A 142 and A 1123.

◆London 69 – ◆Cambridge 19.

⌂ Soham By-Pass Motel, CB7 5DF, NE : ½ m. on A 142 ℰ 720324, Fax 720324 – 📺 ☎ 🄿. ※
12 rm.

W. Mids. **403 404** O 26 – pop. 93 940 – ECD : Wednesday – 🏢 021 Birmingham.

🏛 Central Library, Homer Rd, B91 3RG ℰ 704 6130/704 6134.

♦London 109 – ♦Birmingham 7 – ♦Coventry 13 – Warwick 13.

🏨 **Solihull Moat House** (Q.M.H.), Homer Rd, B91 3QD, ℰ 711 4700, Telex 333355, Fax 711 2696, ℔, ⩘, 🖾 – 🛏 ⤧ rm 🖿 rest 🖵 🕾 ✚ 🕭 – 🕍 200. ◪ ◭ ⑩ 𝘝𝘐𝘚𝘈
M 10.75/14.85 **st.** and a la carte 🅰 4.25 – ⌕ 7.70 – **109 rm** 85.00/100.00 **st.**, 6 suites – SB (weekends only) 81.00/102.00 **st.**

🏨 **St. John's Swallow,** 651 Warwick Rd, B91 1AT, ℰ 711 3000, Fax 705 6629, ℔, ⩘, 🖾, ⩗ – 🛏 ⤧ rm 🖵 🕾 ✚ – 🕍 750. ◪ ◭ ⑩ 𝘝𝘐𝘚𝘈
M *(closed Saturday lunch)* 12.50/19.00 **st.** and a la carte 🅰 4.50 – **176 rm** ⌕ 85.00/98.50 **st.**, 1 suite – SB (weekends only) 100.00 **st.**

🏨 **George** (Jarvis), The Square, B91 3RF, ℰ 711 2121, Fax 711 3374 – 🛏 ⤧ rm 🖵 🕾 ✚ – 🕍 100. ◪ ◭ ⑩ 𝘝𝘐𝘚𝘈
M 13.00/15.75 **t.** and a la carte 🅰 5.50 – **127 rm** 63.50/105.00 **st.** – SB (weekends only) 78.00/88.00 **st.**

at Shirley W : 2½ m. by B 4025 – ✉ Solihull – 🏢 021 Birmingham :

🏨 **Regency,** Stratford Rd, B90 4EB, SE : 2 m. on A 34 ℰ 745 6119, Telex 334400, Fax 733 3801, ℔, ⩘, 🖾 – 🛏 ⤧ rm 🖵 🕾 ✚ – 🕍 150. ◪ ◭ ⑩ 𝘝𝘐𝘚𝘈
M 11.25/15.30 **st.** and a la carte 🅰 7.45 – **110 rm** ⌕ 89.50 **st.**, 2 suites – SB (weekends only) 85.00 **st.**

🏨 Saracen's Head, Stratford Rd, B90 3AG, ℰ 733 3888, Fax 733 2762 – 🖵 🕾 ✚ – 🕍 110. ⊗
34 rm.

🏠 **Travel Inn,** Stratford Rd, B90 4PT, SE : 2½ m. on A 34 ℰ 744 2942, Fax 733 7075 – ⤧ rm 🖵 🕭 ✚. ◪ ◭ ⑩ 𝘝𝘐𝘚𝘈. ⊗
M (Beefeater grill) a la carte approx. 16.00 **t.** – ⌕ 4.95 – **51 rm** 33.50 **t.**

XX **Chez Julien,** 1036 Stratford Rd, Monkspath, B90 4EE, SE : 2½ m. on A 34 ℰ 744 7232, Fax 745 4775 – ✚. ◪ ◭ ⑩ 𝘝𝘐𝘚𝘈
closed Saturday lunch and Sunday – **M** - French 10.00/15.00 **st.** and a la carte 🅰 4.80.

When visiting Great Britain,
use the **Michelin Green Guide** *"Great Britain".*

– *Detailed descriptions of places of interest*
– *Touring programmes*
– *Maps and street plans*
– *The history of the country*
– *Photographs and drawings of monuments, beauty spots, houses...*

Somerset **403** L 30 The West Country G. – pop. 4 339 – ECD : Wednesday – 🏢 0458.

See : Town★ - Market Place★ (cross★) – St. Michael's Church★.

Envir. : Long Sutton★ (Church★★) SW : 2½ m. by B 3165 – Huish Episcopi (St. Mary's Church Tower★★) SW : 4½ m. by B 3153 – Lytes Cary★, SE : 3½ m. by B 3151.

Exc. : Muchelney★★ (Parish Church★★) SW : 6½m. by B 3153 and A 372 – High Ham (≼★★, St. Andrew's★) NW : 6½m. by B 3153 – Midelney Manor★ *AC*, SW : 9 m. by B 3153 and A 378.

♦London 138 – ♦Bristol 32 – Taunton 17.

🏨 **Lynch Country House** without rest., 4 Behind Berry, TA11 7PD, ℰ 72316, ≼, « Attractively converted Regency house », ⩗, park – 🖵 🕾 ✚. ◪ 𝘝𝘐𝘚𝘈. ⊗
5 rm ⌕ 40.00/65.00 **t.**

🅶 ATS Bancombe Rd, Trading Est. ℰ 73467

Berks. **404** R 29 – pop. 1 469 – ECD : Wednesday – 🏢 0734 Reading.

♦London 48 – Reading 4.

🏨 **Great House at Sonning,** Thames St., RG4 0UT, ℰ 692277, Fax 441296, ⩗, ✠ – 🖵 🕾 ✚. ◪ ◭ ⑩ 𝘝𝘐𝘚𝘈
M a la carte 12.20/27.70 **st.** 🅰 5.50 – ⌕ 8.50 – **33 rm** 39.50/99.00 **st.**, 3 suites – SB (except Christmas and New Year) 89.00/119.00 **st.**

XXX **French Horn** with rm, Thames St., RG4 0TN, ℰ 692204, Fax 442210, ≼ River Thames and gardens – 🖵 🕾
closed Good Friday and 25-26 December – **M** (booking essential) 15.50/25.00 **st.** and a la carte 🅰 5.25 – **11 rm** ⌕ 75.00/85.00 **st.**, 4 suites.

Devon **403** H 31 – see Okehampton.

SOUTHAMPTON Hants. **403 404** P 31 Great Britain G. – pop. 211 321 – ✆ 0703.

See : Old Southampton AZ : Bargate★ **B** , Tudor House Museum★ **M1**.

🏌, 🏌 Southampton Municipal, Golf Course Rd, Bassett ✆ 768407, N : 2 m. by A 33 AY – 🏌 Stoneham, Bassett Green Rd, Bassett ✆ 768151, N : 2 m. AY – 🏌 Southampton Manor, Manor Farm, Botley, Chilworth ✆ 740544, by A 27 AY.

✈ Southampton/Eastleigh Airport : ✆ 629600, N : 4 m. BY.

🚢 to France : Cherbourg (Stena Sealink Line) (6 h) day, (8 h) night (1 daily) – to the Isle of Wight : East and West Cowes (Red Funnel Ferries) frequent services daily.

🚢 to America (New York) (Cunard) (5 days).

🛈 Above Bar, SO9 4XF ✆ 221106.

◆London 87 – ◆Bristol 79 – ◆Plymouth 161.

Plans on following pages

🏨 **Hilton National,** Bracken Pl., Chilworth, SO2 3UB, ✆ 702700, Telex 47594, Fax 767233, 🏋, ⇌s, 🏊 – 🔟 ⇄ rm 🗏 rest 🔟 ☎ & 🅿 – 🔬 200. 🔃 🆎 ⑩ 𝗩𝗜𝗦𝗔 🗖🆎 AY – 🏌
M *(closed Saturday lunch)* (carving lunch) 12.95/15.95 **t.** and a la carte ↓ 5.65 – ⇌ 9.25 – **133 rm** 75.00 **st.**, 2 suites.

🏨 **Southampton Park,** 12-13 Cumberland Pl., SO9 4NY, ✆ 223467, Fax 332538, 🏋, ⇌s, 🏊 – 🔟 ↦ rm 🗏 rest 🔟 ☎ – 🔬 200. 🔃 🆎 ⑩ 𝗩𝗜𝗦𝗔 AZ **u**
M (dinner only) 11.50/15.50 **st.** and a la carte ↓ 4.35 – ⇌ 7.50 – **71 rm** 55.00 **st.** – SB 89.90 **st.**

🏨 **Polygon** (Forte), Cumberland Pl., SO9 4GD, ✆ 330055, Fax 332435 – 🔟 ↦ rm 🔟 ☎ 🅿 – 🔬 500. 🔃 🆎 ⑩ 𝗩𝗜𝗦𝗔 AZ **n**
M *(closed Saturday lunch)* 9.50/16.95 **st.** and a la carte ↓ 4.75 – ⇌ 8.50 – **91 rm** 39.50/79.00 **st.**, 2 suites – SB 86.00 **st.**

🏨 **Novotel,** 1 West Quay Rd, SO1 0RA, ✆ 330550, Group Telex 477641, Fax 222158, ≤, 🏋, ⇌s, 🏊 – 🔟 ↦ rm 🗏 rest 🔟 ☎ & 🅿 – 🔬 450. 🔃 🆎 ⑩ 𝗩𝗜𝗦𝗔 AZ **x**
M 13.50 **st.** (dinner) and a la carte ↓ 6.95 – ⇌ 7.50 – **121 rm** 59.50/69.50 – SB (weekends only and July-August) 69.00/89.00 **st.**

🏨 **Southampton Moat House** (Q.M.H.), 119 Highfield Lane, Portswood, SO9 1YQ, ✆ 559555, Fax 583910, ⇌s – 🔟 ☎ 🅿 – 🔬 200. 🔃 🆎 ⑩ 𝗩𝗜𝗦𝗔 BY **e**
M *(closed Saturday lunch)* 14.00 **t.** and a la carte – **66 rm** ⇌ 53.50/63.50 **t.**

🏨 **Dolphin** (Forte), 35 High St., SO9 2DS, ✆ 339955, Fax 333650 – 🔟 ↦ rm 🔟 ☎ 🅿 – 🔬 90. 🔃 🆎 ⑩ 𝗩𝗜𝗦𝗔 𝗝𝗖𝗕 AZ **i**
M (bar lunch Monday to Saturday)/dinner 15.95 **st.** and a la carte ↓ 6.45 – **71 rm** ⇌ 60.00/70.00 **st.**, 2 suites – SB 78.00 **st.**

🏨 **Forte Posthouse,** Herbert Walker Av., SO1 0HJ, ✆ 330777, Fax 332510, ≤, 🏋, ⇌s, 🏊 – 🔟 ↦ rm 🔟 ☎ 🅿 – 🔬 150. 🔃 🆎 ⑩ 𝗩𝗜𝗦𝗔 AZ **o**
M a la carte approx. 17.50 **t.** ↓ 4.65 – ⇌ 6.95 – **128 rm** 53.50/69.50 **st.**, 2 suites – SB (weekends only) 90.00 **st.**

🏨 **Star,** 26-27 High St., SO9 4ZA, ✆ 339939, Fax 335291 – 🔟 ↦ rm 🔟 ☎ 🅿 – 🔬 70. 🔃 🆎 ⑩ 𝗩𝗜𝗦𝗔 AZ **z**
M *(closed Saturday lunch and Sunday dinner)* 7.95/20.00 **t.** and a la carte ↓ 4.95 – **45 rm** ⇌ 47.00/63.00 **st.** – SB 65.00/108.00 **st.**

🏨 **Rosida Garden,** 25-27 Hill Lane, SO1 5AB, ✆ 228501, Fax 635501, 🏊 heated, 🐎 – 🔟 ☎ & 🅿. 🔃 🆎 ⑩ 𝗩𝗜𝗦𝗔 AZ **r**
closed 24 December-2 January – **M** (dinner only) a la carte 10.00/16.00 **t.** ↓ 2.50 – **27 rm** ⇌ 40.00/60.00 **t.** – SB (except September) (weekends only) 70.00/140.00 **st.**

🏨 **Travel Inn,** Romsey Rd, Nursling, SO1 9XJ, NW : 4 m. on A 3057 ✆ 732262 – ↦ rm 🔟 & 🅿. 🔃 🆎 ⑩ 𝗩𝗜𝗦𝗔. 🐎 AY **a**
M (Beefeater grill) a la carte approx. 16.00 **t.** – ⇌ 4.95 – **32 rm** 33.50 **t.**

🏠 **Hunters Lodge,** 25 Landguard Rd, SO1 5DL, ✆ 227919, Fax 230913 – 🔟 ☎ 🅿. 🔃 🆎 𝗩𝗜𝗦𝗔. 🐎 AZ **v**
closed Christmas and New Year – **M** (by arrangement) 8.25 **st.** – **15 rm** ⇌ 24.00/54.00 **s.** – SB (weekends only) 52.50/83.00 **st.**

XX **Kuti's,** 70 London Rd, SO1 2AJ, ✆ 221585 – 🔃 🆎 𝗩𝗜𝗦𝗔 AZ **a**
M - Indian 15.00/20.00 **t.** and a la carte.

X **Brown's Brasserie,** Frobisher House, Nelson Gate, Commercial Rd, SO1 0GX, ✆ 332615 – ↦. 🔃 🆎 ⑩ 𝗩𝗜𝗦𝗔 AZ **s**
closed Sunday – **M** 14.00/24.00 **t.** and a la carte ↓ 9.95.

MICHELIN Distribution Centre, Test Lane, SO1 9JX, ✆ 872344, Fax 663617 AY

◍ ATS West Quay Rd ✆ 333231   ATS 88/94 Portswood Rd ✆ 582727

In this guide

a symbol or a character, printed in red or black, in **bold** or light type, does not have the same meaning.

Pay particular attention to the explanatory pages.

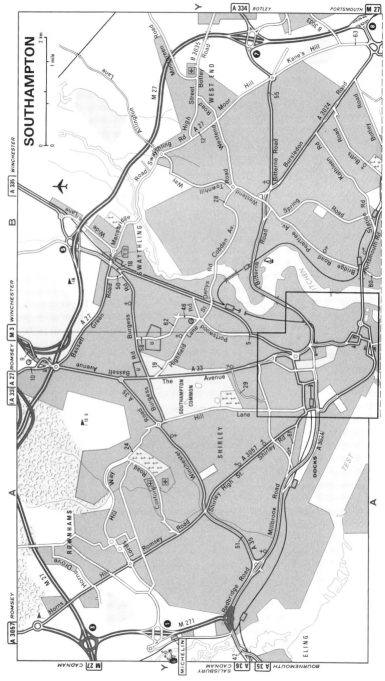

SOUTHAMPTON

462

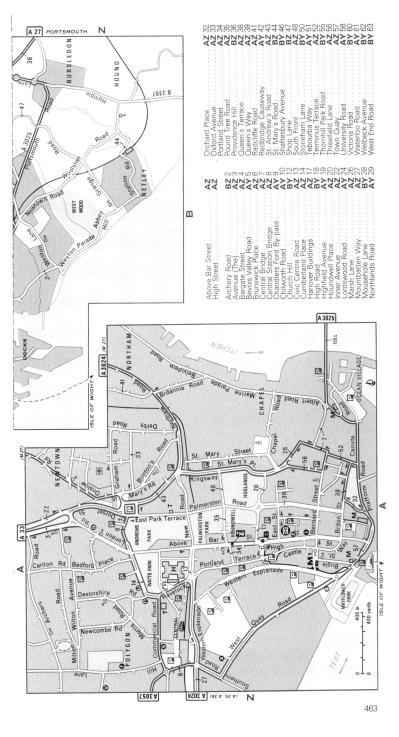

SOUTH CAVE Humbs. 402 S 22 – pop. 2 749 – ✪ 0430 Howden.

🏌 Care Castle Hotel ℰ 421286/422245.

◆London 176 – ◆Kingston-upon-Hull 12 – ◆Leeds 40 – York 30.

🏨 **Forte Travelodge** without rest., Beacon Service Area, HU15, SW : 2 ½ m. on A 63 (eastbound carriageway) ℰ 424455, Reservations (Freephone) 0800 850950 – 📺 🔥 🅿.
🔼 🗚🗛 VISA. ✸
40 rm 31.95 t.

SOUTH DALTON Humbs. 402 S 22 – see Beverley.

SOUTHEND-ON-SEA Essex 404 W 29 – pop. 155 720 – ECD : Wednesday – ✪ 0702.

🏌 Belfairs Park, Eastwood Rd North, Leigh-on-Sea ℰ 526911 – 🏌 Ballards Gore, Gore Rd, Canewdon, Rochford ℰ 258917, S : 3½ m.

✈ Southend-on-Sea ℰ 340201, N : 2 m.

🛈 High St. Precinct, SS1 1DZ ℰ 355120 – Civic Centre, Victoria Av., SS2 6ER ℰ 355122.

◆London 39 – ◆Cambridge 69 – Croydon 46 – ◆Dover 85.

🏨 **Camelia,** 178 Eastern Esplanade, SS1 3AA, ℰ 587917, Fax 585704 – ✢ 🖃 rest 📺 ☎. 🔼
🗚🗛 VISA
M (dinner only and Sunday lunch)/dinner 12.95 **st.** and a la carte – **16 rm** ⊑ 38.50/55.00 **st.**

🏨 **Balmoral,** 34-36 Valkyrie Rd, Westcliff-on-Sea, SS0 8BU, ℰ 342947, Fax 337828, ☞ –
📺 ☎ 🅿. 🔼 🗚🗛 VISA
M (closed Sunday) 9.00 **st.** and dinner a la carte – **22 rm** ⊑ 35.00/48.00 **st.**

🏠 **Pebbles,** 190 Eastern Esplanade, SS1 3AA, ℰ 582329 – 📺. ✸
M (by arrangement) 11.50 **s.** – **5 rm** ⊑ 22.00/38.00.

🏠 **Ilfracombe House,** 11-13 Wilson Rd, SS1 1HG, ℰ 351000 – 📺 ☎. 🔼 🗚🗛 ⓞ VISA. ✸
M 12.50 **st.** 👖 2.50 – **13 rm** ⊑ 28.00/40.00 **st.** – SB (except Bank Holidays) (weekends only) 58.00/84.00 **st.**

🍴🍴 **Paris,** 719 London Rd, Westcliff-on-Sea, SS0 9ST, ℰ 344077, Fax 344077 – 🔼 🗚🗛 VISA
closed Saturday lunch, Sunday dinner, Monday and Bank Holidays – **M** 14.50/25.95 **st.** and a la carte 👖 5.25.

SOUTH LOPHAM Norfolk 404 X 26 – see Diss.

When looking for a quiet hotel
use the maps found in the introductory pages
or look for establishments with the sign ⚘ or ⚘.

SOUTH MIMMS SERVICE AREA Herts. 404 T 28 – ⊠ ✪ 0707 Potters Bar.

🛈 M 25 Motorway Services, EN6 3QQ ℰ 43233.

◆London 21 – Luton 17.

🏨 **Forte Posthouse,** Bignells Corner, EN6 3NH, M 25 junction 23 at junction with A 1 (M)
ℰ 643311, Fax 646728, ⓕ₆, ➾, 🔼 – ✢ rm 🖃 rest 📺 ☎ 🅿 – 🔼 170. 🔼 🗚🗛 ⓞ VISA JCB.
✸
M a la carte approx. 17.50 **t.** 👖 4.65 – ⊑ 6.95 – **120 rm** 53.50 **st.** – SB (weekends only) 90.00 **st.**

🏨 **Forte Travelodge** without rest., Bignells Corner, EN6 3QQ, M 25 junction 23 at junction with A 1 (M) ℰ 665440, Reservations (Freephone) 0800 850950 – 📺 🔥 🅿. 🔼 🗚🗛 VISA. ✸
52 rm 31.95 **st.**

SOUTH MOLTON Devon 403 I 30 – pop. 3 552 – ECD : Wednesday – ✪ 0769.

🛈 1 East St., EX36 3BU ℰ 574122 (summer only).

◆London 210 – Exeter 35 – Taunton 39.

🏨 **Whitechapel Manor** ⚘, EX36 3EG, E : 4 m. by B 3227 and Whitechapel rd ℰ 573377, Fax 573797, ≼, « Elizabethan manor house built by Robert de Bassett », ☞, park –
✢ rest 📺 ☎ 🅿. 🔼 🗚🗛 ⓞ VISA. ✸
M (booking essential) 16.00/37.00 **st.** 👖 6.50 – **9 rm** ⊑ 65.00/160.00 **st.**, 1 suite – SB (except Easter, Christmas and New Year) 145.00/240.00 **st.**

🏨 **Park House** ⚘, EX36 3ED, N : ½ m. on North Molton rd ℰ 572610, ≼, « Victorian country house, gardens », ➾, park – ✢ rest 📺 🅿. 🔼 🗚🗛 ⓞ VISA. ✸
M (light lunch)/dinner 18.00 **t.** and a la carte 👖 4.10 – **7 rm** ⊑ 49.00/88.00 **t.** – SB 90.00/130.00 **st.**

at East Buckland NW : 6 ¼ m. by B 3226 and Filleigh rd, turning right at Stags Head – ⊠ Barnstaple – ✪ 0598 Filleigh :

🍴🍴 **Lower Pitt** ⚘, with rm, EX32 0TD, ℰ 760243, Fax 760243, ☞ – ✢ 🅿. 🔼 🗚🗛 VISA. ✸
closed 24-25 December and 1 January – **M** (closed Sunday and Monday to non residents) (booking essential) (dinner only) a la carte 14.75/19.20 **st.** 👖 4.50 – **3 rm** ⊑ 35.00/60.00 **st.** – SB (weekdays only) 95.00/120.00 **st.**

SOUTH NORMANTON Derbs. 402 403 404 Q 24 – pop. 11 607 (inc. Pinxton) – ECD : Wednesday – ☏ 0773 Ripley.
◆London 130 – Derby 17 – ◆Nottingham 15 – ◆Sheffield 31.

🏨 **Swallow,** Carter Lane East, DE55 2EH, on A 38 ℘ 812000, Fax 580032, Lɑ, ≘s, 🏊 – 🚭 rm 📺 ☎ ♿ Ⓟ – 👥 200. ▣ AE ◑ VISA
M 12.50/19.50 **st.** and a la carte 🍷 6.00 – **161 rm** ☕ 86.00/100.00 **st.** – SB 105.00 **st.**

SOUTH PETHERTON Somerset 403 L 31 The West Country G. – pop. 2 235 – ☏ 0460.
Envir. : Barrington Court Garden★ *AC*, W : 5½ m. by A 303.
◆London 138 – ◆Bristol 41 – Exeter 41 – Taunton 19 – Yeovil 7.5.

ⅩⅩ **Le Tire Bouchon at Oaklands House** with rm, 8 Palmer St., TA13 5DB, ℘ 40272, 🏊 heated, 🌳 – ☎ Ⓟ. ▣ VISA. ✗
closed 21 December-15 January – **M** - **French** (closed Sunday and Monday) (dinner only and Sunday lunch)/dinner 21.00 **st.** 🍷 4.50 – ☕ 4.00 – **5 rm** 50.00/70.00 **t.** – SB 100.00 **st.**

SOUTHPORT Mersey. 402 K 23 – pop. 88 596 – ECD : Tuesday – ☏ 0704.
⛳18 Southport Municipal, Park Rd ℘ 535286 – ⛳18 Alt, Park Rd ℘ 30435.
ℹ 112 Lord St., PR8 1NY ℘ 533333.
◆London 221 – ◆Liverpool 20 – ◆Manchester 38 – Preston 19.

🏨 Prince of Wales (Forte), Lord St., PR8 1JS, ℘ 536688, Telex 67415, Fax 543488 – ⇕ 🚭 rm 📺 ☎ Ⓟ – 👥 450
M (carving rest.) – **98 rm**, 6 suites.

🏨 **Scarisbrick,** 239 Lord St., PR8 1NZ, ℘ 543000, Fax 533335 – ⇕ 📺 ☎ – 👥 120. ▣ AE VISA
M 8.70/15.00 **t.** and a la carte 🍷 5.50 – **65 rm** ☕ 31.00/85.00 **st.** – SB (except Christmas and New Year) (weekends only) 50.00/104.00 **st.**

🏨 **Royal Clifton** (Best Western), Promenade, PR8 1RB, ℘ 533771, Telex 677191, Fax 500657, Lɑ, ≘s, 🏊 – ⇕ 📺 ☎ ♿ Ⓟ – 👥 300. ▣ AE ◑ VISA. ✗
M (bar lunch Monday to Saturday)/dinner 15.50 **t.** and a la carte – **105 rm** ☕ 65.00/80.00 **t.**, 2 suites – SB (weekends only) 98.00 **st.**

🏨 **New Bold,** 583-587 Lord St., PR9 0BE, ℘ 532578, Fax 532528 – 📺 ☎ Ⓟ. ▣ VISA. ✗
M 9.95 **t.** and a la carte 🍷 3.75 – ☕ 6.95 – **21 rm** 25.00/51.00 **t.** – SB (except Bank Holidays) 50.00/112.00 **st.**

🏨 **Stutelea,** Alexandra Rd, PR9 0NB, ℘ 544220, Fax 500232, Lɑ, ≘s, 🏊, 🌳 – ⇕ 📺 ☎ Ⓟ. ▣ AE ◑ VISA. ✗
M (light lunch)/dinner a la carte 13.00/19.40 **t.** 🍷 4.00 – **20 rm** ☕ 45.00/65.00 **t.** – SB 75.00/78.00 **st.**

⌂ **Crimond,** 28 Knowsley Rd, PR9 0HN, ℘ 536456, Fax 548643, ≘s, 🏊 – 📺 ☎ Ⓟ. ▣ AE ◑ VISA
M 15.00 **t.** 🍷 4.25 – **14 rm** ☕ 39.00/59.00 **t.** – SB (except Bank Holidays) 70.00/80.00 **st.**

⌂ **Club House,** 15 Leicester St., PR9 0ER, ℘ 533745 – 📺 Ⓟ. ▣ AE ◑ VISA. ✗
M (by arrangement) 9.50 **s.** 🍷 3.50 – **13 rm** ☕ 20.00/45.00 **s.** – SB 40.00/57.00 **st.**

⌂ **Ambassador,** 13 Bath St., PR9 0DP, ℘ 543998, Fax 536269 – 🚭 rm 📺 Ⓟ. ▣ VISA
closed 24 December-2 January – **M** 10.00 **t.** – **8 rm** ☕ 25.00/46.00 **t.**

⊛ ATS 69 Shakespeare St. ℘ 534434

SOUTHSEA Hants. 403 404 Q 31 – see Portsmouth and Southsea.

SOUTH SHIELDS Tyne and Wear 401 402 P 19 – pop. 86 488 – ECD : Wednesday – ☏ 091 Tyneside.
⛳18 Cleadon Hills ℘ 456 0475 – ⛳18 Whitburn, Lizard Lane ℘ 529 2144, SE : 2½ m.
ℹ Amphitheatre, Sea Rd, NE33 2LD ℘ 455 7411 (summer only) – Museum and Art Gallery, Ocean Rd, NE33 2HZ ℘ 454 6612.
◆London 284 – ◆Newcastle upon Tyne 9.5 – Sunderland 6.

🏨 **Sea,** Sea Rd, NE33 2LD, ℘ 427 0999, Fax 454 0500 – 📺 ☎ Ⓟ. ▣ AE ◑ VISA
M 9.95 **st.** and a la carte 🍷 4.25 – **33 rm** ☕ 58.00/73.00 **st.** – SB (weekends only) 75.00 **st.**

⊛ ATS Western Approach ℘ 454 1060/4247

SOUTHWAITE SERVICE AREA Cumbria 401 402 L 19 – ✉ Carlisle – ☏ 069 74.
ℹ M 6 Service Area, CA4 0NS ℘ 73445/73446.
◆London 300 – ◆Carlisle 14 – Lancaster 58 – Workington 48.

🏨 **Granada Lodge** without rest., CA4 0NT, on M 6 ℘ 73131, Fax 73669, Reservations (Freephone) 0800 555300 – 🚭 📺 ♿ Ⓟ. ▣ AE VISA. ✗
☕ 4.00 – **39 rm** 34.95/37.95 **st.**

SOUTH WALSHAM Norfolk 404 Y 26 Great Britain G. – pop. 543 – ✉ Norwich – ☏ 060 549 (3 and 4 fig.) and 0603 (6 fig.).
Envir. : The Broads★.
◆London 120 – Great Yarmouth 11 – ◆Norwich 9.

🏨 **South Walsham Hall H. & Country Club** 🐦, South Walsham Rd, NR13 6DQ, ℘ 378, Fax 519, <, Lɑ, ≘s, 🏊 heated, 🎣, 🌳, park, 🎾, squash – 📺 ☎ Ⓟ. ▣ AE ◑ VISA. ✗
closed first 2 weeks January – **M** 13.50/18.50 **t.** and a la carte – **17 rm** ☕ 40.00/120.00 **st.** – SB (except Christmas-New Year) (weekends only) 80.00/150.00 **st.**

SOUTHWELL Notts. 402 404 R 24 Great Britain G. – pop. 6 283 – ECD : Thursday – ✆ 0636.

See : Minster★★ *AC*.

◆London 135 – Lincoln 24 – ◆Nottingham 14 – ◆Sheffield 34.

🏨 **Saracen's Head** (Forte), Market Pl., NG25 0HE, ℰ 812701, Fax 815408 – ⇇ 🆅 ☎ 🅿 – 🔬 100. 🖪 🖻 🖾 *VISA*
  M 9.95/16.95 **st.** and a la carte ⫪ 5.25 – ☲ 8.50 – **27 rm** 70.00/80.00 **st.** – SB 98.00/138.00 **st.**

⌂ **Old Forge** without rest., 2 Burgage Lane, NG25 0ER, ℰ 812809, ⌸ – ⇇ 🆅 🅿. 🖪 *VISA*
  5 rm ☲ 30.00/44.00 **s.**

SOUTHWOLD Suffolk 404 Z 27 – pop. 3 756 – ECD : Wednesday – ✆ 0502.

🇹🇸 The Common ℰ 723234.

🅱 Town Hall, Market Pl., IP18 6EF ℰ 724729 (summer only).

◆London 108 – Great Yarmouth 24 – ◆Ipswich 35 – ◆Norwich 34.

🏨 **Swan**, Market Pl., IP18 6EG, ℰ 722186, Fax 724800, ⌸ – ⫴ ⇇ rest 🆅 ☎ 🅿 – 🔬 40. 🖪 🖻 🖻 *VISA*. 🖋
  M (bar lunch New Year-Easter) 13.95/29.50 **t.** – **43 rm** ☲ 46.00/112.00 **t.**, 2 suites – SB (winter only) (weekends only) 107.00/126.00 **st.**

🏠 **Crown**, 90 High St., IP18 6DP, ℰ 722275, Fax 724805 – 🆅 ☎ 🅿. 🖪 🖻 🖻 *VISA*. 🖋
  closed second week January – **M** 14.75/19.25 **t.** – ☲ 3.75 – **12 rm** 37.00/57.00 **t.**

SOUTH WOODHAM FERRERS Essex 404 V 29 – pop. 6 975 – ✉ ✆ 0245 Chelmsford.

◆London 36 – Chelmsford 12 – Colchester 34 – Southend-on-Sea 13.

🏠 **Oakland**, 2-6 Reeves Way, by Merchant St., CM3 5XE, ℰ 322811, Fax 329201 – 🆅 ☎. 🖪 🖻 🖻 *VISA*. 🖋
  closed 24 December-2 January – **M** (carving rest.) 15.00 **st.** and a la carte ⫪ 3.50 – **41 rm** ☲ 39.00/55.00 **st.**

SOWERBY N. Yorks. – see Thirsk.

SPALDING Lincs. 402 404 T 25 – pop. 18 020 – ✆ 0775.

🅱 Ayscoughfee Hall, Churchgate, PE11 2RA ℰ 725468/761161.

◆London 111 – Lincoln 40 – ◆Leicester 56 – ◆Norwich 65.

🍴 **Queensgate**, Westlode St., PE11 2AF, ℰ 711929, Fax 724205 – 🆅 ☎. 🖪 🖻 🖻 *VISA*
  M 6.95/10.95 **st.** and dinner a la carte ⫪ 3.50 – **11 rm** ☲ 45.00/56.00 **st.** – SB (weekends only) 80.00/100.00 **st.**

⌂ **Bedford Court**, 10 London Rd, PE11 2TA, ℰ 722377, ⌸ – ⇇ 🆅 🅿. 🖋
  M (by arrangement) – **3 rm** ☲ 25.00/35.00.

SPARK BRIDGE Cumbria – see Ulverston.

SPEEN Berks. – see Newbury.

SPEEN Bucks. – ✉ Princes Risborough – ✆ 0494 High Wycombe.

◆London 41 – Aylesbury 15 – ◆Oxford 33 – Reading 25.

🍴🍴 **Old Plow Inn** (Restaurant), Flowers Bottom, HP27 0PZ, W : ½ m. by Chapel Hill and Highwood Bottom ℰ 488300, ⌸ – 🅿. 🖪 🖻 *VISA*
  closed Sunday dinner, Monday, 5 days at Christmas and Bank Holidays – **M** 16.95/25.00 **t.**

SPORLE Norfolk – see Swaffham.

SPRATTON Northants. 404 R 27 – see Northampton.

STADDLEBRIDGE N. Yorks. – see Northallerton.

STAFFORD Staffs. 402 403 404 N 25 – pop. 60 915 – ECD : Wednesday – ✆ 0785.

🇹🇸 Brocton Hall, Brocton ℰ 662627, SE : 4 m. by A 34 – 🇹🇸 Stafford Castle, Newport Rd ℰ 223821, W : ½ m.

🅱 The Ancient High House, Greengate St., ST16 2JA ℰ 40204.

◆London 142 – ◆Birmingham 26 – Derby 32 – Shrewsbury 31 – ◆Stoke-on-Trent 17.

🏨 **Tillington Hall** (De Vere), Eccleshall Rd, ST16 1JJ, NW : 1 ½ m. on A 5013 ℰ 53531, Fax 59223, ⌸₅, ⌸, 🖳, 🖋 – ⫴ ⇇ rm 🖩 rest 🆅 ☎ 🅿 – 🔬 150. 🖪 🖻 🖻 *VISA*
  M *(closed Saturday and Bank Holidays)* 8.95/14.95 **st.** and a la carte – ☲ 6.50 – **90 rm** 25.00/102.00 **st.** – SB (except Christmas and New Year) 74.00/105.00 **st.**

🏨 **Garth**, Moss Pit, ST17 9JR, S : 2 m. on A 449 ℰ 56124, Fax 55152, ⌸ – ⇇ rm 🖩 rest 🆅 ☎ 🅿 – 🔬 120. 🖪 🖻 *VISA*
  M *(closed Saturday lunch)* a la carte 11.65/15.95 **st.** – **60 rm** ☲ 59.50 **st.** – SB (weekends only) 75.00 **st.**

🏨 **Swan** (Chef & Brewer), 46 Greengate St., ST16 2JA, ℰ 58142, Fax 223372 – 🆅 ☎ 🅿. 🖪 🖻 *VISA*. 🖋
  M (grill rest.) 15.00/20.00 **t.** and a la carte – ☲ 3.50 – **32 rm** 34.95/38.45 **t.** – SB (weekends only) 30.00 **st.**

🅰 ATS Kenworthy Rd, Astonfields Ind. Est. ℰ 223832/58118

🚢 to Windsor Bridge via Runnymede and Old Windsor Lock (Salter Bros Ltd) (summer only).

◆London 26 – Reading 25.

🏨 **Thames Lodge** (Forte), Thames St., TW18 4SF, 🖂 464433, Fax 454858, ≼ – ⅏ rm
▤ rest �📺 ☎ 🅿 – 🔬 50. 🔼 ⌶ ① 🆅🆂🅰 🆙🅲🅱. 🛇
M (bar lunch Monday to Saturday)/dinner 16.95 **st.** and a la carte ⓘ 5.25 – ⌷ 8.50 – **44 rm**
90.00/100.00 **st.** – SB (weekends only) 98.00 **st.**

See : Town★★ - St. Martin's Church★ – Lord Burghley's Hospital★ – Browne's Hospital★ *AC*.

Envir. : Burghley House★★ *AC*, SE : 1 ½ m. by B 1443.

🏌 Luffenham Heath, Ketton 🖂 720205, W : 5 m. on A 6121.

🅱 Stamford Arts Centre, 27 St. Mary's St., PE9 2DL 🖂 55611.

◆London 92 – ◆Leicester 31 – Lincoln 50 – ◆Nottingham 45.

🏨🏨 **The George of Stamford,** 71 St. Martin's, PE9 2LB, 🖂 55171, Fax 57070, « 17C coach-
ing inn with walled monastic garden » – ⅏ ☎ 🅿 – 🔬 50. 🔼 ⌶ ① 🆅🆂🅰
M 18.50 **st.** (lunch) and a la carte 26.40/31.20 **st.** – **46 rm** ⌷ 66.00/154.00 **st.**, 1 suite –
SB (except Christmas and New Year) 100.00/150.00 **st.**

🏨 **Lady Anne's,** 37-38 High St., St. Martin's Without, PE9 2LJ, 🖂 481184, Fax 65422, 🍽 –
⅏ ☎ 🅿 – 🔬 150. 🔼 ⌶ ① 🆅🆂🅰
closed 26 to 31 December – **M** 9.50/14.50 **t.** and a la carte – **29 rm** ⌷ 35.00/79.00 **t.** –
SB (weekends only) 85.00/99.00 **st.**

🏨 **Garden House,** 42 High St., St. Martin's, PE9 2LP, 🖂 63359, Fax 63339, 🍽 – ⅏ ☎ 🅿.
🔼 ⌶ 🆅🆂🅰
M (bar dinner Sunday) a la carte 17.55/26.10 **st.** ⓘ 3.90 – **20 rm** ⌷ 49.75/85.50 **st.**

🏨 **Ram Jam Inn,** Great North Rd, Stretton, LE15 7QX, NW : 8 m. by B 1081 on A 1,
🖂 Oakham (Leics.) 🖂 410776, Fax 410361, 🍽 – ⅏ ☎ 🅿 – 🔬 25. 🔼 ⌶ ① 🆅🆂🅰. 🛇
closed Christmas Day – **M** a la carte 12.20/19.15 ⓘ 5.50 – ⌷ 3.95 – **7 rm** 39.00/49.00 **t.**

✖✖ **Raj of India,** 2 All Saints St., PE9 2PA, 🖂 53556 – ▤. 🔼 ⌶ ① 🆅🆂🅰
closed Christmas Day – **M** - **Indian** a la carte 11.85/17.70 **t.** ⓘ 4.25.

✖✖ **L'Incontro,** The Old Barn Passage, St. Mary's St., PE9 2HG, 🖂 51675, « 16C barn » – 🔼
⌶ ① 🆅🆂🅰
closed Monday lunch, Sunday and Bank Holidays – **M** - **Italian** a la carte 15.20/18.15 **st.**
ⓘ 5.45.

at Collyweston (Northants.) SW : 3 ¾ m. on A 43 – 🖂 Stamford – ☎ 078 083
Duddington :

⌘ **Cavalier,** Main St., PE9 3PQ, 🖂 288 – �📺 🅿. 🔼 ① 🆅🆂🅰. 🛇
closed 25 and 26 December – **M** a la carte 12.95/17.20 **t.** ⓘ 3.40 – ⌷ 5.00 – **5 rm** 23.00/
32.00 **t.** – SB 55.00/110.00 **st.**

at Empingham (Leics.) W : 5 ¾ m. on A 606 – 🖂 Oakham – ☎ 078 086 Empingham :

🏨 **White Horse,** 2 Main St., LE15 8PR, 🖂 221, Fax 521 – �📺 ☎ 🅿 – 🔬 60. 🔼 ⌶ ① 🆅🆂🅰
M *(closed Sunday dinner)* 9.95/12.50 **t.** and dinner a la carte ⓘ 3.50 – **12 rm**
⌷ 30.00/60.00 – SB (except Christmas) 58.00/90.00 **st.**

at Normanton Park (Leics.) W : 6 ½ m. by A 606 on Edith Weston Rd – 🖂 Oakham –
☎ 0780 Stamford :

🏨 **Normanton Park** 🍽, South Shore, LE15 8RP, 🖂 720315, Fax 721086, ≼, 🐎, 🍽 – �📺 ☎
🅿 – 🔬 30. 🔼 ⌶ ① 🆅🆂🅰
M a la carte 18.15/25.15 **t.** ⓘ 3.75 – **14 rm** ⌷ 49.50/69.50 **st.** – SB (weekends only) 85.00 **st.**

◆London 210 – ◆Liverpool 22 – ◆Manchester 21 – Preston 15.

🏨 **Kilhey Court** (Best Western), Chorley Rd, Worthington, WN1 2XN, E : 1 ¾ m. by B 5239
on A 5106 🖂 472100, Fax 422401, ≊, 🔲, 🍽 – 🛗 ▤ rest �📺 ☎ ⅊ 🅿 – 🔬 150. 🔼 ⌶ ①
🆅🆂🅰. 🛇
M *(closed Saturday lunch)* 30.85 **st.** and a la carte – ⌷ 7.50 – **53 rm** 60.00/100.00 **st.** –
SB 90.00/130.00 **st.**

🏨 Almond Brook Moat House (Q.M.H.), Almond Brook Rd, WN6 0SR, W : 1 m. on A 5209
🖂 425588, Telex 677662, Fax 427327, 🛴, ≊, 🔲 – 🛗 ⅏ rm ▤ rest �📺 ☎ ⅊ 🅿 – 🔬 150
126 rm.

🏨 **Wrightington** (Mt Charlotte Thistle), Moss Lane, Wrightington (Lancs.), WN6 9PB, W :
1 ¾ m. by A 5209 on Moss Lane 🖂 425803, Fax 425830, 🛴, ≊, 🔲, squash – �📺 ☎ 🅿 –
🔬 50. 🔼 ⌶ ① 🆅🆂🅰 🆙🅲🅱
M *(closed Saturday lunch and Good Friday)* 18.00/20.00 **t.** and a la carte ⓘ 5.20 – **47 rm**
⌷ 53.00/64.00 **t.** – SB 75.90/80.00 **st.**

XX **The Beeches** with rm, School Lane, WN6 0TD, on A 5209 🖉 426432, Fax 427503 – 📺 ☎ 🅿 🔼 AE ⓪ VISA
M *(closed Sunday dinner and Monday)* a la carte 14.00/23.00 **st.** 7.75 – **11 rm** ⊂⊃ 20.00/ 50.00 **st.** – SB (weekends only) 50.00/95.00 **st.**

◎ ATS 23 Market St. 🖉 423146/423732

STANDON Herts. 404 U 28 – pop. 3 772 – ⊠ ✆ 0920 Ware.
♦London 31 – ♦Cambridge 23 – Luton 30.

XX No. 28, 28 High St., SG11 1LA, 🖉 821035, Fax 822630 – .

STANNERSBURN Northd. – ⊠ ✆ 0434 Hexham.
♦London 363 – ♦Carlisle 56 – ♦Newcastle upon Tyne 46.

☝ **Pheasant Inn** , Falstone, NE48 1DD, 🖉 240382 – 📺 🅿.
closed Mondays January-February and 25-26 December – **M** (bar lunch Monday to Saturday)/dinner a la carte 9.50/15.25 **t.** 3.75 – **8 rm** ⊂⊃ 30.00/50.00 **t.** – SB (October-April) 70.00/80.00 **t.**

STANSTEAD ABBOTS Herts. 404 U 28 – pop. 1 906 – ⊠ Ware – ✆ 0279 Roydon.
⛳ Briggens Park, Stanstead Rd 🖉 793742.
♦London 22 – ♦Cambridge 37 – Luton 32 – ♦Ipswich 66.

🏨 **Briggens** (Q.M.H.), Stanstead Rd, SG12 8LD, E : 2 m. by A 414 🖉 792416, Fax 793685, ≼, heated, , , park, – ☎ 🅿 – 100. 🔼 AE ⓪ VISA
closed 25 to 30 December – **M** 17.25/19.95 **st.** and a la carte 7.25 – ⊂⊃ 8.00 – **53 rm** 75.00/105.00 **st.**, 1 suite.

STANSTED AIRPORT Essex 404 U 28 – ⊠ Stansted Mountfitchet – ✆ 0279 Bishop's Stortford.
♦London 37 – ♦Cambridge 29 – Chelmsford 18 – Colchester 29.

🏨 **Hilton National,** Round Coppice Rd, CM24 8SE, 🖉 680800, Telex 818840, Fax 680890, , ≅, , – rest 📺 ☎ & 🅿 – 250. 🔼 AE ⓪ VISA JCB
M (carving lunch) a la carte 12.00/15.00 **t.** 6.00 – ⊂⊃ 8.75 – **238 rm** 80.00/110.00 **st.**

at Broxted NE : 3¾ m. by Broxted rd – ⊠ Great Dunmow – ✆ 0279 Bishop's Stortford :

🏨 **Whitehall,** Church End, CM6 2BZ, on B 1051 🖉 850603, Fax 850385, ≼, « Part 12C and 15C manor house, walled garden », , – 📺 ☎ 🅿 – 120. 🔼 AE ⓪ VISA
closed 26 to 31 December – **M** – (see below) – **25 rm** ⊂⊃ 75.00/155.00 **t.** – SB 142.50/ 147.50 **st.**

XXX **Whitehall,** Church End, CM6 2BZ, on B 1051 🖉 850603 – 🅿. 🔼 AE ⓪ VISA
closed 26 to 31 December – **M** 19.50/27.50 **t.** 6.50.

STANTON FITZWARREN Wilts. – see Swindon.

STANTON HARCOURT Oxon 403 404 P 28 – pop. 774 – ⊠ ✆ 0865 Oxford.
♦London 71 – Gloucester 45 – ♦Oxford 13 – Swindon 27.

X **Harcourt Arms,** OX8 1RJ, 🖉 881931 – 🅿. 🔼 AE ⓪ VISA
M 7.50/13.50 **t.** and a la carte 5.50.

STANTON WICK Avon 403 404 M 29 – see Bristol.

STARBOTTON N. Yorks. – see Kettlewell.

STAVERTON Devon 403 I 32 – pop. 643 – ⊠ ✆ 0803 Totnes.
♦London 220 – Exeter 20 – Torquay 33.

☝ **Sea Trout Inn,** TQ9 6PA, 🖉 762274, Fax 762506, – 📺 ☎ 🅿. 🔼 AE VISA
accommodation *closed 24 to 26 December* – **M** *(closed Sunday dinner)* (bar lunch Monday to Saturday)/dinner 14.95 **st.** and a la carte 4.25 – **10 rm** ⊂⊃ 38.50/54.00 **st.** – SB 68.00/ 107.00 **st.**

STAVERTON Glos. – see Cheltenham.

STEDHAM W. Sussex 404 R 31 – see Midhurst.

STEEPLE ASTON Oxon. 403 404 Q 28 – pop. 1 619 – ECD : Saturday – ⊠ Bicester – ✆ 0869.
♦London 69 – ♦Coventry 38 – ♦Oxford 10.

🏨 **Hopcrofts Holt** (Mt Charlotte Thistle), OX6 3QQ, SW : 1¼ m. at junction of A 4260 with B 4030 🖉 40259, Fax 40865, – rm 📺 ☎ 🅿 – 100. 🔼 AE ⓪ VISA
M (carving lunch Sunday) 18.00/28.00 **t.** and dinner a la carte 5.95 – **88 rm** ⊂⊃ 60.00/ 95.00 **t.** – SB 105.00/170.00 **st.**

☝ **Westfield Farm Motel,** Fenway, OX6 3SS, 🖉 40591, – 📺 ☎ 🅿. 🔼 VISA
M (by arrangement) 9.50 **st.** 3.00 – **6 rm** ⊂⊃ 32.00/46.00 **st.** – SB (weekends only) 61.00/ 83.00 **st.**

X **Red Lion,** South St., OX6 3RY, 🖉 40225 – 🅿. 🔼 VISA
closed dinner Sunday and Monday and 2 weeks September-October – **M** (bar lunch Monday to Saturday)/dinner 18.50 4.05.

STEVENAGE Herts. 404 T 28 Great Britain G. – pop. 74 757 – ECD : Monday and Wednesday – ☎ 0438.

Envir. : Knebworth House★ *AC*, S : 2½ m.

18, 9 Aston Lane ☎ 880424 – 18, 9 Chesfield Downs Family Golf Centre, Jack's Hill, Graveley ☎ 0462 (Letchworth) 482929.

Central Library, Southgate, SG1 1HD ☎ 369441.

◆London 36 – Bedford 25 – ◆Cambridge 27.

- **Stevenage Moat House** (Q.M.H.), High St., Old Town, SG1 3AZ, ☎ 359111, Fax 742169, – rm ☎ – 200. AE VISA
  M (bar lunch Saturday) 12.75 **t.** and a la carte 5.95 – **56 rm** 75.00/85.00 **t.** – SB (weekends only) 84.00 **st.**
- **Hertfordpark** (Q.M.H.), Danestrete, SG1 1EJ, ☎ 350661, Telex 825697, Fax 741880 – rm ☎ – 170. AE VISA
  closed 26 December and 31 December – **M** *(closed lunch Saturday, Sunday and Bank Holidays)* 12.50 **st.** and a la carte 5.95 – **98 rm** 53.00/68.00 **st.** – SB (except Christmas and Bank Holidays) (weekends only) 60.00 **st.**
- **Novotel Stevenage,** Knebworth Park, SG1 2AX, SW : 1½ m. by A 602 at junction with A 1 (M) ☎ 742299, Telex 826132, Fax 723872, heated – rm rest ☎ – 120. AE VISA
  M 9.50/13.50 **st.** and a la carte 4.75 – 7.50 – **100 rm** 59.50/64.50 **st.**

at Broadwater S : 1¾ m. by A 602 on B 197 – ☎ 0438 Stevenage :

- **Forte Posthouse,** Old London Rd, SG2 8DS, ☎ 365444, Fax 741308, – rm ☎ – 50. AE VISA JCB
  M a la carte approx. 17.50 **t.** 4.65 – 6.95 – **54 rm** 53.50 **st.** – SB (weekends only) 90.00 **st.**

ATS 4-8 Norton Rd ☎ 313262

STEYNING W. Sussex 404 T 31 – pop. 8 318 (inc. Upper Beeding) – ECD : Thursday – ☎ 0903.

◆London 52 – ◆Brighton 12 – Worthing 10.

- **Old Tollgate,** The Street, Bramber, BN44 3WE, SW : 1 m. ☎ 879494, Fax 813399 – ☎ . AE VISA.
  M (carving rest.) 14.45/17.25 **t.** 5.95 – 5.75 – **31 rm** 52.00/72.00 **t.** – SB (except Christmas and New Year) 91.00/141.00 **st.**
- **Springwells** without rest., 9 High St., BN44 3GG, ☎ 812446, , heated, – ☎ . AE VISA.
  closed 24 December-1 January – **10 rm** 25.00/62.00 **st.**

STILTON Cambs. 404 T 26 – pop. 1 782 – ☎ 0733 Peterbrough.

◆London 76 – ◆Cambridge 30 – Northampton 43 – Peterborough 6.

- **Bell Inn,** Great North Rd, PE7 3RA, ☎ 241066, Fax 245173, « Part 16C inn », – rm ☎ – 100. AE VISA.
  M 14.50/21.50 **st.** and a la carte 6.00 – **19 rm** 50.00/85.00 **st.** – SB (weekends only) 89.00/94.00 **st.**

STOCKBRIDGE Hants. 403 404 P 30 – pop. 524 – ECD : Wednesday – ☎ 0264 Andover.

◆London 75 – Salisbury 14 – Winchester 9.

- **Carbery,** Salisbury Hill, SO20 6EZ, on A 30 ☎ 810771, heated, – .
  closed 2 weeks Christmas – **M** 10.50 **st.** – **11 rm** 20.00/47.00 **st.**

STOCKPORT Gtr. Manchester 402 403 404 N 23 – pop. 135 489 – ECD : Thursday – ☎ 061 Manchester.

18 Heaton Moor, Mauldeth Rd, Heaton ☎ 432 2134 - 18 Romiley, Goosehouse Green ☎ 430 2392 – 18 Ladythorn Rd, Bramhall ☎ 439 4057 – 18 Davenport, Middlewood Rd, Poynton ☎ 0625 (Poynton) 877321, S : 5 m. – 18 Hazel Grove ☎ 483 3217, S : 3 m. – 18 Offerton Rd, Offerton ☎ 427 2001, SE : 4 m. on A 627.

Graylaw House, Chestergate, SK1 1NG ☎ 474 3320/1.

◆London 201 – ◆Liverpool 42 – ◆Manchester 6 – ◆Sheffield 37 – ◆Stoke-on-Trent 34.

- **Alma Lodge** (Jarvis), 149 Buxton Rd, SK2 6EL, on A 6 ☎ 483 4431, Fax 483 1983 – rm ☎ – 200. AE VISA
  M 12.50/27.50 **t.** and a la carte 6.50 – **56 rm** 65.00/99.50 **t.** – SB 91.50/155.00 **st.**
- Rudyard Toby, 271 Wellington Rd North, Heaton Chapel, SK4 5BP, ☎ 432 2753, Fax 431 0260 – rm ☎ – 120.
  21 rm.
- **Forte Travelodge** without rest., London Rd South, Adlington, SK12 4NA, ☎ 0625 (Adlington) 875292, Reservations (Freephone) 0800 850950 – . AE VISA
  32 rm 31.95 **st.**

ATS Hollingworth Rd, Bredbury ☎ 430 5221

Cleveland 402 P 20 – pop. 86 699 – ECD : Thursday – ☎ 0642.

🏌 Eaglescliffe, Yarm Rd ℰ 780098, S : 3 m. by A 135 – 🏌 Knotty Hill, Sedgefield ℰ 20320 – 🏌 Norton, Junction Rd ℰ 676385/612452/674636, E : 1 m. of A 177 on B 1274.

✈ Teesside Airport : ℰ 0325 (Darlington) 332811, SW : 6 m. by A 1027, A 135 and A 67.

🖪 Theatre Yard, off High St., TS18 1AT ℰ 615080.

♦London 251 – ♦Leeds 61 – ♦Middlesbrough 4.

🏨 **Swallow,** 10 John Walker Sq., TS18 1AQ, ℰ 679721, Fax 601714, 𝄃𝄃, ⊆ₛ, 🔲 – ▯ ✦← rm
⊟ rest 📺 ☎ ❷ – 🛦 300. 🕰 🗚 ⑩ 𝓥𝓘𝓢𝓐
M (closed Saturday lunch) 12.50/17.75 **st.** and a la carte ⅃ 5.00 – **122 rm** ⊡ 85.00/95.00 **st.**

at Eaglescliffe S : 3½ m. on A 135 – ⊠ ☎ 0642 Stockton-on-Tees :

🏨 **Parkmore** (Best Western), 636 Yarm Rd, TS16 0DH, ℰ 786815, Fax 790485, 𝄃𝄃, ⊆ₛ, 🔲,
🐎 – ✦← rm 📺 ☎ ❷ – 🛦 100. 🕰 🗚 ⑩ 𝓥𝓘𝓢𝓐 𝓙𝓒𝓑
M 13.00/18.00 **st.** and a la carte ⅃ 3.95 – **55 rm** ⊡ 54.00/90.00 **st.** – SB (weekends only) 92.00/100.00 **st.**

🔘 ATS 18 Brunswick St. ℰ 675733 ATS 112 Norton Rd ℰ 604477

Northants. 404 R 27 – pop. 345 – ⊠ Towcester – ☎ 0604 Roade.

♦London 69 – ♦Coventry 33 – Northampton 9 – ♦Oxford 33.

🍴 **Bruerne's Lock,** 5 Canalside, NN12 7SB, ℰ 863654, « Attractive canalside setting » –
🕰 🗚 𝓥𝓘𝓢𝓐
closed Saturday lunch, Sunday dinner, Monday, 2 weeks October, 1 week Christmas and
Bank Holidays – **M** 15.00 **t.** (lunch) and dinner a la carte 17.50/26.95 **t.** ⅃ 5.95.

Essex 404 W 28 – see Colchester.

Surrey 404 ⑫ – see Cobham.

Devon 403 J 33 – see Dartmouth.

Devon 403 J 32 – see Totnes.

Staffs. 402 403 404 N 24 Great Britain G. – pop. 272 446 – ECD : Thursday – ☎ 0782 – See : Museum and Art Gallery★ Y M – Gladstone Pottery Museum★ AC V.

Envir. : Wedgwood Visitor's Centre★ AC, S : 5½ m. by A 500 and A 34 V.

Exc. : Little Moreton Hall★★ AC, N : 8½ m. by A 500 on A 34 U.

🏌 Greenway Hall, Stockton Brook ℰ 503158, N : 5 m. by A 527 U – 🏌 Parkhall, Hulme Rd, Weston Coyney ℰ 599584, E : 3 m. by B 5040 V.

🖪 Potteries Shopping Centre, Quadrant Rd, Hanley, ST1 1RZ ℰ 284600.

♦London 162 – ♦Birmingham 46 – ♦Leicester 59 – ♦Liverpool 58 – ♦Manchester 41 – ♦Sheffield 53.

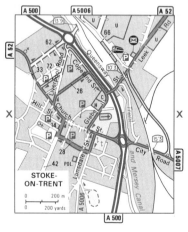

Church Street	**X**	Botteslow Street	**Y** 10	New Hall Street	**Y** 49
Old Hall Street	**Y** 52	Bucknall New Road	**Y** 13	Parliament Row	**Y** 55
Potteries		Campbell Place	**X** 14	Percy Street	**Y** 56
Shopping Centre	**Y**	Charles Street	**X** 17	Piccadilly	**Y** 58
Stafford Street	**Y** 65	Elenora Street	**X** 26	Quadrant Road	**Y** 61
		Fleming Road	**X** 28	Shelton Old Road	**X** 62
Albion Street	**Y** 2	Hartshill Road	**X** 33	Station Road	**X** 66
Bethesda Street	**Y** 6	Lichfield Street	**Y** 40	Vale Place	**Y** 70
Birch Terrace	**Y** 7	London Road	**X** 42	Vale Street	**X** 72

🏨🏨 **Stoke-on-Trent Moat House** (Q.M.H.), Etruria Hall, Festival Way, Etruria, ST1 5BQ, ℘ 219000, Telex 36304, Fax 284500, ₤₅, ≘ₛ, 🏊 – 🛏 ↤ rm 🍽 rest 📺 ☎ ♿ 🅿 – 🔬 500. 🔼 ᴁ ⓘ 𝚅𝙸𝚂𝙰 ⌔
U **n**
M (bar lunch Saturday) 10.95/15.95 **t.** and a la carte 🍴 6.50 – **143 rm** 🖵 82.00/145.00 **st.** – SB 98.00 **st.**

🏨🏨 **Stakis Stoke-on-Trent Grand,** 66 Trinity St., Hanley, ST1 5NB, ℘ 202361, Fax 286464, ₤₅, ≘ₛ, 🏊 – 🛏 ↤ rm 📺 ☎ ♿ 🅿 – 🔬 300. 🔼 ᴁ ⓘ 𝚅𝙸𝚂𝙰 𝙹𝙲𝙱
Y **c**
M 7.50/14.50 **t.** and a la carte – 🖵 8.50 – **123 rm** 73.00/94.00 **st.,** 4 suites – SB 90.00/120.00 **st.**

🏠 **White House,** 94 Stone Rd, Trent Vale, ST4 6SP, S : 2¼ m. on A 34 ℘ 642460 – 📺 ☎ 🅿.
V **a**
🔼 ᴁ ⓘ 𝚅𝙸𝚂𝙰
M (by arrangement) 8.50 **st.** 🍴 3.00 – **10 rm** 🖵 24.00/48.00 **st.**

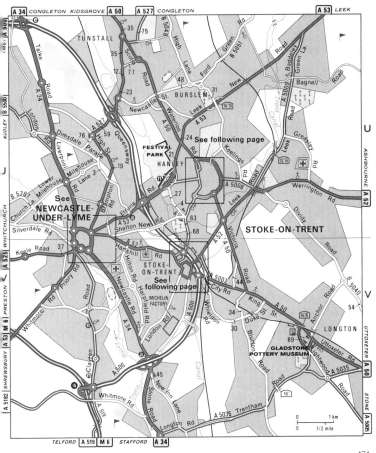

at Basford NW : 1 ¾ m. by A 500 off A 53 – ⊠ 🖲 0782 Stoke-on-Trent :

🏦 **Haydon House,** Haydon St., ST4 6JD, ✐ 711311, Fax 717470 – 🖵 ☎ 🅟 – 🔬 50. 🖭 🖭
🕥 🖾
closed first week January – **M** *(closed Sunday)* 10.50/12.90 **t.** and a la carte – � 6.00 –
24 rm 50.00/62.00 **t.**, 6 suites – SB (weekends only) 88.00/136.00 **st.**
U **a**

at Talke NW : 4 m. on A 500 at junction with A 34 – ⊠ 🖲 0782 Stoke-on-Trent :

🏦 Granada, Newcastle Rd, ST7 1UP, ✐ 777000, Fax 777162 – ⟲ rm 🖾 rest 🖵 ☎ ⅙ 🅟 –
🔬 40. 🕸
M (grill rest.) – **62 rm.**
U **e**

🕮 ATS 25 Smithpool Rd, Fenton ✐ 47081   ATS 87/89 Waterloo Rd, Burslem ✐ 838493/
836591

STOKE PRIOR Heref. and Worcs. – see Leominster.

STOKE ST. GREGORY Somerset 🆛 L 30 – ⊠ 🖲 0823 Taunton.

◆London 147 – ◆Bristol 39 – Taunton 8.

↟ **Slough Court** 🦢 without rest., Slough Lane, TA3 6JQ, ✐ 490311, « 14C moated manor
house, working farm », 🖾, 🕸 – ⟲ rest 🖵 🅟. 🕸
closed November-January – **3 rm** ⊷ 25.00/46.00 **st.**

STOKESLEY N. Yorks. 🆚 Q 20 – ⊠ 🖲 0642 Middlesbrough (Cleveland).

◆London 239 – ◆Leeds 59 – ◆Middlesbrough 8 – York 52.

🏛 **Chapter's,** 27 High St., TS9 5AD, ✐ 711888, Fax 711888, 🖾 – 🖵 ☎. 🖭 🖭 🕥 🖾
closed 25-26 December and 1 January – **M** (bar lunch and bar meals Sunday)/dinner
17.50 **t.** and a la carte ⓘ 4.95 – **13 rm** ⊷ 44.00/59.00 **t.**

STOKE-UPON-TERN Shrops. 🆚 🆛 🆜 M 25 – see Market Drayton.

STONE Glos. 🆛 🆜 M 29 – pop. 667 (inc. Ham) – ⊠ Berkeley – 🖲 0454 Falfield.

◆London 130 – ◆Bristol 17 – Gloucester 18.

🏛 **Elms at Stone,** GL13 9JX, on A 38 ✐ 260279, Fax 260279 – 🖵 ☎ 🅟. 🖭 🖾
M *(closed Sunday dinner)* 13.95 **st.** (dinner) and lunch a la carte ⓘ 4.00 – **8 rm** ⊷ 38.00/
48.00 **st.**

STONE Staffs. 🆚 🆛 🆜 N 25 – pop. 12 119 – ECD : Wednesday – 🖲 0785.

🕮 Barlaston, Meaford Rd ✐ 078 139 (Barlaston) 2795.

◆London 150 – ◆Birmingham 36 – ◆Stoke-on-Trent 9.

🏦 **Stone House** (Lansbury), ST15 0BQ, S : 1 ¼ m. by A 520 on A 34 ✐ 815531, Fax 814764,
🖚, ⇌, 🖾, 🖾, 🕸 – ⟲ rm 🖵 ☎ 🅟 – 🔬 150. 🖭 🖭 🕥 🖾
M *(closed lunch Saturday and Bank Holidays)* 9.75/15.50 **t.** and a la carte – **47 rm**
⊷ 55.00/81.00 **t.** – SB (weekends only) 90.00 **st.**

STON EASTON Somerset – ⊠ Bath (Avon) – 🖲 0761 Mendip.

◆London 131 – Bath 12 – ◆Bristol 11 – Wells 7.

🏰 **Ston Easton Park** 🦢, BA3 4DF, ✐ 241631, Fax 241377, ≼, « Palladian country house »,
🖾, park, 🕸 – ⟲ rest 🖵 ☎ 🅟. 🖭 🖭 🕥 🖾. 🕸
M 26.00/38.00 **st.** ⓘ 7.50 – ⊷ 8.50 – **19 rm** 95.00/320.00 **st.**, 2 suites – SB (November-April)
210.00/280.00 **st.**

STONOR Oxon. 🆜 R 29 – see Henley-on-Thames.

STONY STRATFORD Bucks. 🆜 R 27 – 🖲 0908.

◆London 58 – ◆Birmingham 68 – Northampton 14 – ◆Oxford 32.

🖾🖾 **Peking,** 117 High St., MK11 1AT, ✐ 563120, Fax 560084 – 🖾. 🖭 🖭 🖾
closed Sunday and 25-26 December – **M** - **Chinese** (Peking, Szechuan) 25.00 **t.** and a la
carte ⓘ 4.50.

at Cosgrove (Northants.) N : 2 ½ m. by A 508 – ⊠ 🖲 0908 Milton Keynes :

🏛 **Old Bakery,** Main St., MK19 7JL, ✐ 262255, Fax 263620 – 🖵 🅟. 🖭 🖾. 🕸
closed last 2 weeks December and first week January – **M** (dinner only) a la carte 9.95/
14.75 **st.** ⓘ 4.00 – ⊷ 6.50 – **8 rm** 42.50/50.00 **st.** – SB (October-April) (weekends only)
66.50/87.00 **st.**

at Deanshanger SW : 2 m. on A 422 – ⊠ 🖲 0908 Milton Keynes :

🏛 **Shires Motel** without rest., Open Pastures Service Area, Buckingham Rd, MK19 6AA,
SW : ½ m. on A 422 ✐ 262925, Fax 263642 – 🖵 ⅙ 🅟. 🖭 🖾. 🕸
⊷ 4.50 – **48 rm** 50.00 **t.**

♦London 54 – ♦Brighton 20 – ♦Portsmouth 36.

🏠 **Little Thakeham** ⌕, Merrywood Lane, Thakeham, RH20 3HE, N : 1 ¾ m. by B 2139 ℘ 744416, Fax 745022, ≼, « Lutyens house with gardens in the style of Gertrude Jekyll », ⊥ heated, ※ – ⊡ ☎ ❶. ◪ AE VISA ※
closed Christmas and New Year – **M** *(closed Monday lunch and Sunday dinner)* 21.50/ 32.50 **st.** ᕃ 5.50 – **7 rm** � 95.00/150.00 **st.**, 2 suites.

🏠 **Abingworth Hall** ⌕, Thakeham Rd, RH20 3EF, N : 1 ¾ m. on B 2139 ℘ 0798 (West Chiltington) 813636, Fax 813914, ⊥ heated, ⌲, ※ – ⊡ ☎ ❶ – ᕛ 50. ◪ VISA ※
M 12.50/19.50 and dinner a la carte ᕃ 3.90 – **20 rm** ⊆ 70.00/164.00 **t.** – SB (except Christmas) 124.00/160.00 **st.**

🏠 **Greenacres Farm**, Washington Rd, RH20 4AF, E : 1 m. on A 283 ℘ 742538, Fax 740017 – ⊡ ❶. ◪ VISA ※
M (by arrangement) 8.00 **st.** – **5 rm** ⊆ 20.00/70.00 **st.** – SB (June and September-March except December) 56.00/84.00 **st.**

❌❌❌ ⊛ **Manley's** (Löderer), Manley's Hill, RH20 4BT, E : ¼ m. on A 283 ℘ 742331 – ᕃ⊀ ❶. ◪ AE
closed Sunday dinner, Monday, first 2 weeks January and Bank Holidays except Good Friday and Christmas Day – **M** 18.60/25.00 **t.** and a la carte ᕃ 6.40
Spec. Gratin of crab, Breast of mallard duck with a Williams pear and port sauce, Feuilleté of caramelised apples with vanilla ice cream.

❌ **Old Forge,** 6a Church St., RH20 4LA, ℘ 743402 – ◪ AE ⓞ VISA
closed lunch Tuesday and Saturday, Sunday dinner, Monday, 1 week late spring and 3 weeks October – **Meals** 14.00/19.50 **st.** and a la carte ᕃ 4.00.

🏛 Kinver, Travellers Joy, 47 High St., DY7 6HE ℘ 872940.

♦London 147 – ♦Birmingham 14 – Wolverhampton 10 – Worcester 21.

Plan : see Birmingham p. 2

🏠 **Talbot,** High St., DY8 1DW, ℘ 394350, Fax 371318 – ⊡ ☎ ❶ – ᕛ 120. ◪ AE VISA AU **a**
M 15.00 **t.** and a la carte ᕃ 5.45 – **25 rm** ⊆ 45.00/110.00 **t.** – SB (weekends only) 70.00/ 110.00 **st.**

🏠 **Limes,** 260 Hagley Rd, Pedmore, DY9 0RW, SE : 1 ½ m. on A 491 ℘ 0562 (Hagley) 882689, ⌲ – ⊡ ☎ ❶. ◪ AE ⓞ VISA AU **z**
M (by arrangement) 6.90 **st.** – **10 rm** ⊆ 28.50/40.50 **st.**

❌ **Bon Appetit,** 38 Market St., DY8 1AG, ℘ 375372 – ❶. ◪ AE VISA AU **n**
closed Sunday lunch April-September, Sunday dinner, Monday and first 2 weeks January – **M** 11.25/21.75 **t.** ᕃ 4.50.

at Hagley S : 2½ m. by A 491 – ✉ Stourbridge – ✆ 0562 Hagley :

🏠 **Travel Inn,** Birmingham Rd, DY9 9JS, NE : 1 ½ m. on A 456 (eastbound) ℘ 883120, Fax 884416 – ᕃ⊀ rm ⊡ ♿ ❶. ◪ AE ⓞ VISA ※ AU **r**
M (Beefeater grill) a la carte 16.00 **t.** – ⊆ 4.95 – **40 rm** 33.50 **t.**

at Kinver (Staffs.) W : 5 m. by A 458 – ✉ Stourbridge – ✆ 0384 Kinver :

❌❌ **Berkley's (Piano Room),** 5-6 High St., DY7 6HG, ℘ 873679 – ◪ AE ⓞ VISA
closed Sunday, first 2 weeks February and 26 to 30 December – **M** (dinner only) a la carte 18.10/22.05 **t.** ᕃ 3.90.

♦London 137 – ♦Birmingham 21 – Worcester 12.

🏠 **Stourport Moat House** (Q.M.H.), 35 Hartlebury Rd, DY13 9LT, E : 1 ¼ m. on B 4193 ℘ 827733, Fax 878520, ᕃ₆, ⌂, ⊥, ⌲, park, ※, squash – ᕃ⊀ rm ⊡ ☎ ❶ – ᕛ 350. ◪ AE ⓞ VISA
M 13.50/14.95 **st.** and a la carte ᕃ 4.95 – **65 rm** ⊆ 52.00/65.00 **st.**, 3 suites.

❌ **Severn Tandoori,** 11 Bridge St., DY13 8UX, ℘ 823090 – ◪ AE ⓞ VISA
closed Christmas Day – **M** - **Indian** a la carte 10.80/15.30 **t.**

🏛 Wilkes Way, IP14 1DE ℘ 676800.

♦London 81 – ♦Cambridge 42 – ♦Ipswich 12 – ♦Norwich 38.

🏠 **Forte Travelodge** without rest., IP14 3PY, NW : 2 m. by A 1038 on A 45 (westbound) ℘ 615347, Reservations (Freephone) 0800 850950 – ⊡ ♿ ❶. ◪ AE VISA
40 rm 31.95 **st.**

at Mendlesham Green NE : 6 ¼ m. by B 1115, A 1120 and Mendlesham rd – ✉✆ 0449 Stowmarket :

🏠 **Cherry Tree Farm,** IP14 5RQ, ℘ 766376, ⌲ – ᕃ⊀ rm ❶. ※
closed Christmas and January – **M** (by arrangement) (communal dining) 12.50 **st.** – **3 rm** ⊆ 25.00/44.00 **st.**

at Wetherden NW : 4 ¼ m. by A 45 – ⊠ Stowmarket – ✲ 0359 Elmswell :

↑ **Old Rectory** ⑤ without rest., IP14 3RE, E : ½ m. on Bacton rd ℰ 240144, 🐎, park – ⇔
⬛ 📺 🅿 ⑤
April-November – **3 rm** ⌑ 25.00/40.00 **st.**

STOW-ON-THE-WOLD Glos. **403** **404** O 28 Great Britain G. – pop. 1 596 – ECD : Wednesday –
✲ 0451 Cotswold.

Exc. : Chastleton House★★, NE : 6 ½ m. by A 436 and A 44.

🄷 Hollis House, The Square, GI54 1AF ℰ 831082.

•London 86 – •Birmingham 44 – Gloucester 27 – •Oxford 30.

🏨 **Wyck Hill House** ⑤, GL54 1HY, S : 2 ¼ m. by A 429 on A 424 ℰ 831936, Fax 832243, ≤,
« Part Victorian country house », 🐎, park – ⇔ rest 📺 ☎ 🅿 – 🔬 50. 🔺 🆀 ⓞ 🆅🆂🅰
M 17.50 **t.** (lunch) and dinner a la carte 26.45/34.85 **t.** – **29 rm** ⌑ 70.00/130.00 **st.**, 1 suite –
SB 154.00/174.00 **st.**

🏨 **Grapevine** (Best Western), Sheep St., GL54 1AU, ℰ 830344, Fax 832278, « Mature
grapevine in restaurant » – ⇔ rest 📺 ☎ 🅿, 🔺 🆀 ⓞ 🆅🆂🅰 🅹🅲🅱 ⑤
closed 24 December-10 January – **M** (bar lunch Monday to Saturday)/dinner 15.95 **t.** –
23 rm ⌑ 69.00/138.00 **t.** – SB 88.00/188.00 **st.**

🏨 **Fosse Manor,** Fosse Way, GL54 1JX, S : 1 ¼ m. on A 429 ℰ 830354, Fax 832486, 🐎,
⇔ rest 📺 ☎ 🅿 – 🔬 40. 🔺 🆀 ⓞ 🆅🆂🅰
closed 23 to 29 December – **M** 12.95/15.95 **t.** and a la carte ⑤ 4.75 – **20 rm** ⌑ 47.50/
130.00 **t.** – SB (except Bank Holidays) 110.00/130.00 **st.**

🏨 **Unicorn** (Forte), Sheep St., GL54 1HQ, ℰ 830257, Fax 831090 – ⇔ 📺 ☎ 🅿, 🔺 🆀 ⓞ
🆅🆂🅰 🅹🅲🅱
M 12.95/16.95 **st.** and a la carte ⑤ 6.95 – ⌑ 8.50 – **20 rm** 68.00/83.00 **st.** – SB 116.00 **st.**

🏚 **Stow Lodge,** The Square, GL54 1AB, ℰ 830485, 🐎 – ⇔ rest 📺 🅿, 🆀 ⓞ, ⑤
closed Christmas and 2 to 30 January – **M** (bar lunch)/dinner 15.00 **t.** and a la carte ⑤ 6.00 –
22 rm ⌑ 49.00/90.00 **t.** – SB (except September and Bank Holidays) 80.00/150.00 **st.**

↑ **Bretton House,** Fosseway, GL54 1JU, S : ½ m. on A 429 ℰ 830388, ≤, 🐎 – ⇔ rm 📺 🅿
closed 24 and 25 December – **M** (by arrangement) 12.50 – **3 rm** ⌑ 40.00 **s.**

↑ **Wyck Hill Lodge,** Wyck Hill, GL54 1HT, S : 2 m. by A 429 on A 424 ℰ 830141, ≤, 🐎 –
⇔ 📺 🅿. ⑤
closed Christmas – **M** (by arrangement) – **3 rm** ⌑ 30.00/43.00 **st.** – SB (November-March)
63.00/68.00 **st.**

↑ **Limes** without rest., Evesham Rd, GL54 1EJ, ℰ 830034, 🐎 – 📺 🅿
closed 24 December-2 January – **3 rm** ⌑ 32.00/36.00 **s.**

↑ **Cross Keys Cottage** without rest., Park St., GL54 1AQ, ℰ 831128 – ⇔ 📺. ⑤
3 rm ⌑ 36.00/45.00 **st.**

at Broadwell NE : 1 ¾ m. by A 429 – ⊠ Moreton-in-Marsh – ✲ 0451 Cotswold :

↑ **College House,** Chapel St., GL56 0TW, ℰ 832351, « 17C house », 🐎 – ⇔ 📺 🅿. ⑤
M (by arrangement) (communal dining) 14.00 **st.** – **3 rm** ⌑ 30.00/50.00 **st.**

at Upper Oddington E : 2 ¼ m. by A 436 – ⊠ Moreton-in-Marsh – ✲ 0451 Cotswold :

🍴 **Horse and Groom Inn,** GL56 OXH, ℰ 830584, 🐎 – 📺 🅿, 🔺 🆅🆂🅰. ⑤
M (bar lunch Monday to Saturday)/dinner a la carte 11.35/18.40 **st.** ⑤ 4.90 – **7 rm** ⌑ 31.00/
46.00 **st.**

at Bledington SE : 4 m. by A 436 on B 4450 – ⊠ ✲ 0608 Kingham :

🏚 **Kings Head,** OX7 6HD, ℰ 658365, Fax 658365 – ⇔ rm 📺 ☎ 🅿. ⑤
closed Christmas Day – **M** (bar lunch)/dinner a la carte 11.90/14.75 **st.** ⑤ 3.50 – **6 rm**
⌑ 30.00/55.00 **st.** – SB (November-February) (weekends only) 65.00/84.00 **st.**

at Nether Westcote SE : 4 ¾ m. by A 429 off A 424 – ⊠ Kingham – ✲ 0993 Shipton-
under-Wychwood :

↑ **Lavender Hill,** 0X7 6SD, ℰ 831872, ≤ – 📺 🅿
M (by arrangement) 13.50 **st.** – **3 rm** ⌑ 28.00/45.00 **st.**

at Lower Swell W : 1 ¼ m. on B 4068 – ⊠ Stow-on-the-Wold – ✲ 0451 Cotswold :

🏚 **Old Farmhouse,** GL54 1LF, ℰ 830232, Fax 870962, 🐎 – ⇔ 📺 ☎ 🅿. 🔺 🆅🆂🅰
closed 2 weeks February – **M** (bar lunch Monday to Saturday)/dinner 14.50 **st.** ⑤ 3.75 –
13 rm ⌑ 22.00/64.00 **st.**, 1 suite – SB (except Bank Holidays) 62.00/67.50 **st.**

STRATFIELD TURGIS Hants. – pop. 88 – ⊠ ✲ 0256 Basingstoke.

•London 46 – Basingstoke 8 – Reading 11.

🏨 **Wellington Arms,** RG27 0AS, on A 33 ℰ 882214, Fax 882934, 🐎 – 📺 ☎ 🅿 – 🔬 60. 🔺
🆀 ⓞ 🆅🆂🅰
M *(closed Saturday lunch and Sunday dinner)* 14.50/18.50 **t.** and a la carte ⑤ 5.50 – **33 rm**
⌑ 50.00/80.00 **t.**, 2 suites – SB (July and August) 99.00/107.00 **st.**

STRATFORD-UPON-AVON Warks. [403] [404] P 27 **Great Britain G.** – pop. 20941 – ECD : Thursday – ☎ 0789.

See : Town★ - Shakespeare's Birthplace★ *AC*, AB.

Envir. : Mary Arden's House★ *AC*, NW : 4 m. by A 3400 A.

Exc. : Ragley Hall★ *AC*, W : 9 m. by A 422 A.

⛳ Tiddington Rd ☎ 297296, E : ½ m. by B 4086 B – ⛳ Welcombe Hotel, Warwick Rd ☎ 299021, NE : 1 ½ m. by A 439 B – ⛳ Stratford Oaks, Bearley Rd, Snitterfield ☎ 731571, NE : 4 m. by A 439 B.

[i] Bridgefoot, CV37 6GW ☎ 293127.

♦London 96 – ♦Birmingham 23 – ♦Coventry 18 – ♦Oxford 40.

STRATFORD-UPON-AVON

Bridge Street .... B 8
Henley Street .... A 29
High Street .... A 31
Sheep Street .... AB 35
Wood Street .... A 47

Banbury Road .... B 2
Benson Road .... B 3
Bridge Foot .... B 6
Chapel Lane .... A 13
Chapel Street .... A 14
Church Street .... A 16
Clopton Bridge .... B 18
College Lane .... A 19
Ely Street .... A 22
Evesham Place .... A 24
Great William Street .... A 25
Greenhill Street .... A 27
Guild Street .... A 28
Rother Street .... A 32
Scholars Lane .... A 33
Tiddington Road .... B 38
Trinity Street .... A 40
Warwick Road .... B 42
Waterside .... B 43
Windsor Street .... A 45

Town plans : the names of main shopping streets are indicated in red at the beginning of the list of streets.

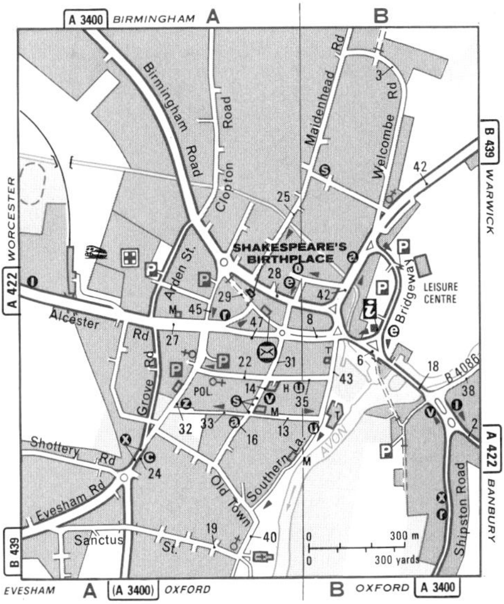

A 3400 BIRMINGHAM A
B
B 439 WARWICK
A 422 WORCESTER
A 422 BANBURY
B 439 EVESHAM A
(A 3400) OXFORD
B OXFORD A 3400
Birmingham Road
Clopton Road
Maidenhead Rd
Welcombe Rd
SHAKESPEARE'S BIRTHPLACE
LEISURE CENTRE
Bridgeway
Alcester Rd
Arden St.
Grove Rd
Shottery Rd
Evesham Rd
Sanctus St.
Old Town
Southern La.
Shipston Road
AVON
POL.
B 4086
300 m
300 yards

🏨 **Welcombe H. & Golf Course** 🐦, Warwick Rd, CV37 0NR, NE : 1 ½ m. on A 439 ☎ 295252, Telex 31347, Fax 414666, ≤, « 19C Jacobean style mansion in park », ⛳, 🌳, 🎾 – 📺 ☎ ♿ [P] – 🏛 150. [S] [AE] [O] [VISA] [JCB] B
closed 29 December-3 January – **M** 17.50/27.50 **st.** and a la carte 🍷 8.50 – **67 rm** ☕ 95.00/195.00 **st.**, 8 suites – SB 165.00/215.00 **st.**

🏨 **Ettington Park** 🐦, Alderminster, CV37 8BS, SE : 6 ¼ m. on A 3400 ☎ 450123, Fax 450472, ≤, « Victorian Gothic mansion », ♨, 🏊, 🎣, 🌳, park, 🎾 – [lift] 🚭 📺 ☎ [P] – 🏛 65. [S] [AE] [O] [VISA] 🐕 B
M 15.75/28.00 **st.** and dinner a la carte – **43 rm** ☕ 115.00/160.00 **st.**, 5 suites – SB 160.00/230.00 **st.**

🏨 **Moat House International** (Q.M.H.), Bridgefoot, CV37 6YR, ☎ 414411, Telex 311127, Fax 298589, 🏋, ♨, 🏊, 🌳 – [lift] 🚭 rm ≡ 📺 ☎ ♿ [P] – 🏛 450. [S] [AE] [O] [VISA]. 🐕 B **e**
M 11.50/14.25 **t.** and dinner a la carte – **245 rm** ☕ 95.00/125.00 **t.**, 2 suites – SB 118.00 **st.**

🏨 **Shakespeare** (Forte), Chapel St., CV37 6ER, ☎ 294771, Fax 415411, « 17C timbered inn » – [lift] 🚭 📺 ☎ [P] – 🏛 100. [S] [AE] [O] [VISA] [JCB] A **v**
M – **David Garrick** 12.95/19.95 **st.** and a la carte 🍷 6.60 – ☕ 8.50 – **62 rm** 90.00/135.00 **st.**, 1 suite – SB (except Christmas and New Year) 148.00/190.00 **st.**

🏨 **Alveston Manor** (Forte), Clopton Bridge, CV37 7HP, ☎ 204581, Telex 31324, Fax 414095, « Part Elizabethan house », 🌳 – 🚭 rm 📺 ☎ [P] – 🏛 150. [S] [AE] [O] [VISA] B **i**
M – **Manor** (bar lunch Monday to Saturday)/dinner 21.50 **st.** – ☕ 9.95 – **105 rm** 80.00/120.00 **st.**, 1 suite – SB 148.00 **st.**

🏨 **Arden Thistle** (Mt. Charlotte Thistle), 44 Waterside, CV37 6BA, ☎ 294949, Fax 415874, 🌳 – 🚭 rm 📺 ☎ [P] – 🏛 50. [S] [AE] [O] [VISA] [JCB] B **u**
M – **Bards** 9.50/15.50 **t.** and a la carte 🍷 6.50 – **63 rm** ☕ 65.00/125.00 **t.** – SB (except Christmas and New Year) 110.00/130.00 **st.**

🏨 **Windmill Park** (Best Western), Warwick Rd, CV37 0PY, NE : 3 m. on A 439 ☎ 731173, Fax 731131, 🏋, ♨, 🏊, park, 🎾 – [lift] ≡ rest 📺 ☎ ♿ [P] – 🏛 350. [S] [AE] [O] [VISA] [JCB] B
M 14.00/17.50 **st.** and a la carte – **100 rm** ☕ 82.50/115.00 **st.** – SB 110.00/180.00 **st.**

🏨 **Grosvenor** (Best Western), 12-14 Warwick Rd, CV37 6YT, 𝒫 269213, Fax 266087 – ⊱✗ rest 📺 ☎ 🅿 – ⚓ 60. 🔼 AE ⑩ VISA JCB. ✳   **B a**
M 11.50 **t.** and a la carte – **38 rm** � 62.00/95.00 **t.**, 2 suites – SB 104.00/124.00 **st.**

🏨 **Falcon** (Q.M.H.), Chapel St., CV37 6HA, 𝒫 205777, Telex 312522, Fax 414260 – |✣| ⊱✗ rm 📺 ☎ ⬥ 🅿 – ⚓ 200. 🔼 AE ⑩ VISA JCB. ✳   **A s**
M 17.00/19.00 **st.** and a la carte ⌁ 4.50 – **73 rm** ⊑ 55.00/105.00 **st.** – SB (except Christmas and New Year) 98.00/108.00 **st.**

🏨 **White Swan** (Forte), Rother St., CV37 6NH, 𝒫 297022, Fax 268773, « Part 16C inn » – ⊱✗ 📺 ☎ – ⚓ 30. 🔼 AE ⑩ VISA   **A r**
M (bar lunch)/dinner 18.95 **t.** ⌁ 5.95 – ⊑ 8.50 – **37 rm** 80.00/95.00 **st.** – SB 118.00/143.00 **st.**

🏨 **Dukes**, Payton St., CV37 6UA, 𝒫 269300, Fax 414700, ☞ – 📺 ☎ 🅿. 🔼 AE VISA JCB. ✳ *closed Christmas and New Year* – **M** *(closed Sunday)* a la carte 16.70/25.40 **t.** ⌁ 4.75 – **22 rm** ⊑ 50.00/120.00 **t.** – SB (weekends only) 60.00/110.00 **st.**   **AB o**

🏨 **Forte Posthouse**, Bridgefoot, CV37 7LT, 𝒫 266761, Fax 414547, ☞ – ⊱✗ rm 📺 ☎ 🅿. ⚓ 150. 🔼 AE ⑩ VISA JCB   **B v**
M a la carte approx. 17.50 **t.** ⌁ 4.65 – ⊑ 6.95 – **60 rm** 53.50 **st.** – SB 90.00 **st.**

🏨 **Stratford House**, 18 Sheep St., CV37 6EF, 𝒫 268288, Fax 295580 – 📺 ☎. 🔼 AE ⑩ VISA JCB. ✳   **AB u**
closed 4 days at Christmas – **M** – **Shepherd's** *(closed Monday lunch)* a la carte approx. 19.95 **t.** ⌁ 5.40 – **11 rm** ⊑ 65.00/85.00 **t.**

🏩 **Caterham House**, 58-59 Rother St., CV37 6LT, 𝒫 267309 – 🅿. 🔼 VISA. ✳   **A z**
M *(closed Saturday lunch, Sunday dinner, Monday and 15 to 29 August)* 15.00/20.00 **st.** and dinner a la carte ⌁ 6.50 – **Le Bonaparte** - **French** 10.00/15.00 **st.** and a la carte ⌁ 6.50 – **11 rm** ⊑ 33.00/56.00 **st.**

🏩 **Sequoia House** without rest., 51-53 Shipston Rd, CV37 7LN, 𝒫 268852, Fax 414559, ☞ – ⊱✗ 📺 ☎ 🅿 – ⚓ 40. 🔼 AE ⑩ VISA. ✳   **B r**
closed 20 to 27 December – **21 rm** ⊑ 29.00/39.00 **st.**

🏩 **Stratheden** without rest., 5 Chapel St., CV37 6EP, 𝒫 297119, Fax 297119 – 📺 ☎. 🔼 VISA   **A s**
closed Christmas – **9 rm** ⊑ 28.00/56.00 **t.**

🏩 **Moonraker House** without rest., 40 Alcester Rd, CV37 9DB, 𝒫 267115, Fax 295504, ☞ – ⊱✗ 📺 🅿. 🔼 VISA   **A i**
closed 24 to 26 December – **24 rm** ⊑ 28.00/60.00 **st.**

🏠 **Twelfth Night** without rest., Evesham Pl., CV37 6HT, 𝒫 414595 – ⊱✗ 📺 🅿. VISA. ✳   **A x**
7 rm ⊑ 24.00/54.00 **s.**

🏠 **Payton** without rest., 6 John St., CV37 6UB, 𝒫 266442, Fax 266442 – 📺. 🔼 AE ⑩ VISA JCB. ✳   **A e**
5 rm ⊑ 38.00/52.00 **st.**

🏠 **Virginia Lodge** without rest., 12 Evesham Pl., CV37 6HT, 𝒫 292157, ☞ – ⊱✗ 📺. ✳ *closed 23 to 29 December* – **7 rm** ⊑ 18.00/44.00 **s.**   **A x**

🏠 **Carlton** without rest., 22 Evesham Pl., CV37 6HT, 𝒫 293548 – ⊱✗ 📺 🅿. ✳   **A c**
5 rm ⊑ 22.00/50.00 **st.**

🏠 **Victoria Spa** without rest., Bishopton Lane, CV37 9QY, NW : 2 m. by A 3400 on Bishopton Lane turning left at roundabout with A 46 𝒫 267985, Fax 204728, ☞ – ⊱✗ rest 📺 🅿. 🔼 VISA   **A**
7 rm ⊑ 35.00/45.00 **t.**

🏠 **Melita** without rest., 37 Shipston Rd, CV37 7LN, 𝒫 292432, ☞ – ⊱✗ 📺 ☎ 🅿. 🔼 AE VISA   **B x**
closed Christmas – **12 rm** ⊑ 29.50/65.00 **t.**

🏠 **Hardwick House** without rest., 1 Avenue Rd, CV37 6UY, 𝒫 204307, Fax 296760 – 📺 🅿. 🔼 AE ⑩ VISA JCB. ✳   **B s**
closed Christmas – **14 rm** ⊑ 19.00/56.00 **st.**

✗✗ **Hussains**, 6a Chapel St., CV37 6EP, 𝒫 267506 – ☰. 🔼 AE ⑩ VISA   **A s**
closed Christmas Day – **M** - **Indian** 5.95/12.50 **t.** and a la carte ⌁ 3.50.

✗ **Sir Toby's**, 8 Church St., CV37 6HB, 𝒫 268822 – ☰. 🔼 AE VISA   **A a**
closed Sunday to Tuesday – **M** (dinner only) a la carte 15.00/20.00 **t.** ⌁ 4.55.

at Charlecote E : 4 ¾ m. by B 4086 on B 4088 – B – ✉ ☻ 0789 Stratford upon Avon :

🏨 **Charlecote Pheasant** (Q.M.H.), CV35 9EW, 𝒫 470333, Fax 470222, *Ⅰ₅*, ☑ heated, ☞, ✦ – ⊱✗ rm 📺 ☎ ⬥ 🅿 – ⚓ 130. 🔼 AE ⑩ VISA **M** 9.95/13.25 **t.** and dinner a la carte – **67 rm** ⊑ 69.50/135.00 **t.** – SB (weekends only) 94.00/150.00 **st.**

at Wellesbourne E : 5 ¾ m. on B 4086 – B – ✉ Warwick – ☻ 0789 Stratford-upon-Avon :

🏩 **Chadley House** ☜, Loxley Rd, CV35 9JL, SW : 1 ¼ m. by A 429 𝒫 840994, Fax 842977, ☞ – 📺 🅿. 🔼 VISA *closed 24 to 27 December* – **M** (by arrangement Sunday) (dinner only) 19.00 **t.** and a la carte – **9 rm** ⊑ 40.00/70.00 **t.** – SB (weekends only) 95.00/136.00 **st.**

🏩 Kings Head, Warwick Rd, CV35 9LX, 𝒫 840206 – 📺 ☎ 🅿. ✳
9 rm.

at Ettington SE : 6 m. on A 422 – B – ⊠ ☻ 0789 Stratford-upon-Avon :

⋔ Ettington Manor, Rodgers Lane, CV37 7SX, ✆ 740216, « Part 13C and 16C manor house », ☞ – 🍴 📺 ℗
M (by arrangement) (residents only) (communal dining) – **3 rm.**

at Long Marston SW : 7 m. by A 3400 – B – off B 4632 – ⊠ ☻ 0789 Stratford-upon-Avon :

⋔ **Kings Lodge** ⌾ without rest., CV37 8RL, ✆ 720705, ☞ – ℗. ⋇
closed December and January – **3 rm** ⌷ 18.50/48.00 **s.**

at Billesley W : 4½ m. by A 422 – A – off A 46 – ⊠ ☻ 0789 Stratford-upon-Avon :

🏛 **Billesley Manor** (Q.M.H.) ⌾, B49 6NF, ✆ 400888, Fax 764145, ≼, « Part Elizabethan manor, topiary garden », 🔲, park, ⋇ – 📺 ☎ ℗ – 🔬 90. 🅰 🄰🄴 🅞 𝗩𝗜𝗦𝗔 ⋇
M 17.00/26.00 **st.** and a la carte ⓵ 6.00 – **39 rm** ⌷ 99.00/135.00 **st.**, 2 suites – SB (weekends only) 158.00 **st.**

at Wilmcote NW : 3½ m. by A 3400 – A – ⊠ ☻ 0789 Stratford-upon-Avon :

⋔ **Pear Tree Cottage** ⌾ without rest., Church Rd, CV37 9UX, ✆ 205889, Fax 262862, ☞ – 📺 ℗
closed 24 December-2 January – **7 rm** ⌷ 28.00/40.00 **st.**

⊚ ATS Western Rd ✆ 205591

STRATTON Glos. **403 404** O 28 – see Cirencester.

STREATLEY Berks. **403 404** Q 29 Great Britain G. – pop. 1 055 – ⊠ ☻ 0491 Goring.

Envir. : Basildon Park★ *AC*, SE : 2½ m. by A 329 – Mapledurham★ *AC*, E : 6 m. by A 329, B 471 and B 4526.

Exc. : Ridgeway Path★★.

🚩 Goring & Streatley, Rectory Rd ✆ 872688.

♦London 56 – ♦Oxford 16 – Reading 11.

🏛 **Swan Diplomat,** High St., RG8 9HR, ✆ 873737, Telex 848259, Fax 872554, « ≼ Thames-side setting », 🌡, ⌾, 🔲, ☞ – 🍴 rm 📺 ☎ & ℗ – 🔬 100. 🅰 🄰🄴 🅞 𝗩𝗜𝗦𝗔
M – (see **Riverside** below) – ⌷ 9.50 – **45 rm** 86.50/126.00 **t.**, 1 suite – SB (August and weekends only) 137.50/152.00 **st.**

✕✕✕ **Riverside** (at Swan Diplomat H.), High St., RG8 9HR, ✆ 873737, Telex 848259, Fax 872554, « ≼ Thames-side setting » – ℗. 🅰 🄰🄴 🅞 𝗩𝗜𝗦𝗔
closed Saturday lunch – **M** 24.00/27.00 **t.** and a la carte ⓵ 6.95.

STREET Somerset **403** L 30 The West Country G. – pop. 9 454 – ECD : Wednesday – ☻ 0458.

See : The Shoe Museum★.

Envir. : Glastonbury★★ - Abbey★★★ (Abbots Kitchen★) *AC*, St. John the Baptist★★, Somerset Rural Life Museum★ *AC*, Glastonbury Tor★ (≼★★★) NE : 2 m. by A 39.

♦London 138 – ♦Bristol 28 – Taunton 20.

🏨 **Bear,** 53 High St., BA16 0EF, ✆ 42021, Fax 840007, ☞ – 📺 ☎ ℗ – 🔬 50. 🅰 🄰🄴 𝗩𝗜𝗦𝗔 ⋇
closed 25 to 30 December – **M** (bar lunch)/dinner a la carte 8.00/18.50 **st.** ⓵ 4.75 – **15 rm** ⌷ 30.00/90.00 **st.** – SB (weekends only) 60.00/120.00 **st.**

STRETTON Ches. **402 403 404** M 23 – see Warrington.

STRETTON Staffs. **402 403 404** P 25 – see Burton-upon-Trent.

STRETTON UNDER FOSSE Warks. **403 404** Q 26 – see Rugby.

STROUD Glos. **403 404** N 28 – pop. 37 791 – ECD : Thursday – ☻ 0453.

🚩, 🚩 Minchinhampton ✆ 832642 (old course) 833866 (new course) E : 3 m.

🅱 Subscription Rooms, George St., GL5 1AE ✆ 765768.

♦London 113 – ♦Bristol 30 – Gloucester 9.

🏨 **Stonehouse Court,** Bristol Rd, Stonehouse, GL10 3RA, W : 3¼ m. on A 419 ✆ 825155, Fax 824611, ☞ – 📺 ☎ ℗ – 🔬 120. 🅰 𝗩𝗜𝗦𝗔 ⋇
M 17.50/26.00 **t.** and a la carte ⓵ 5.50 – **35 rm** ⌷ 72.50/98.00 **t.**, 1 suite – SB (except Bank Holidays) 98.00/130.00 **st.**

🏨 **Old Nelson,** Stratford Lodge, Stratford Rd, GL5 4AF, N : ½ m. by A 46 ✆ 765821, Fax 765964 – 📺 ☎ & ℗. 🅰 🄰🄴 🅞 𝗩𝗜𝗦𝗔 ⋇
M (grill rest.) a la carte 9.00/15.00 **t.** ⓵ 3.75 – **32 rm** ⌷ 46.95/51.95 **st.** – SB (weekends only) 60.00/100.00 **st.**

🏨 **Imperial** (Chef & Brewer), Station Rd, GL5 3AP, ✆ 764077, Fax 751314 – 📺 ☎ ℗. 🅰 🄰🄴 𝗩𝗜𝗦𝗔 ⋇
M (grill rest.) 15.00/20.00 **t.** and a la carte – ⌷ 3.50 – **25 rm** 29.95/34.45 **t.** – SB (weekends only) 30.00/60.00 **st.**

🏠 **London**, 30-31 London Rd, GL5 2AJ, ☎ 759992, Fax 753363 – 📺 ☎ 🅿. ⚄ AE ⓞ VISA. ❄
M 7.95/12.95 **st.** and a la carte ⌁ 3.75 – **11 rm** ⏴ 26.00/59.00 **st.** – SB (except Bank
Holidays) 56.00/110.00 **st.**

🏠 **Old Vicarage**, 167 Slad Rd, GL5 1RD, ☎ 752315, ⟶ – ⭐⊶ 📺 ☎ 🅿. ❄
closed January – **M** *(closed Sunday)* (by arrangement) 15.00 **s.** – **3 rm** ⏴ 28.00/39.00 **s.** –
SB 59.00/98.00 **st.**

🍴🍴 ⚙ **Oakes** (Oakes), 169 Slad Rd, GL5 1RG, ☎ 759950 – 🅿. ⚄ AE VISA
closed Sunday dinner and Monday – **M** 19.00/36.00 **t.** ⌁ 5.50
Spec. Homemade Gloucestershire 'Old Spot' sausage with quails eggs and bacon, Ragout of seafood in pastry with a
tomato, mixed herb, Vermouth and cream sauce, Chocolate soufflé with a white chocolate cream.

at Brimscombe SE : 2 ¼ m. on A 419 – ✉ Stroud – ☎ 0453 Brimscombe :

🏨 **Burleigh Court** ⤵, Burleigh Lane, GL5 2PF, S : ½ m. by Burleigh rd via The Round-
abouts ☎ 883804, Fax 886870, ≤, ⬛ heated, ⟶ – ⭐⊶ rest 📺 ☎ 🅿. ⚄ AE ⓞ VISA. ❄
closed Christmas and New Year – **M** (buffet dinner Sunday) 13.95 **st.** (lunch) and dinner a la
carte 20.15/23.90 **st.** ⌁ 4.75 – **17 rm** ⏴ 59.00/96.00 **st.** – SB 108.00/128.00 **st.**

at Rodborough S : ¾ m. by A 46 – ✉ Stroud – ☎ 0453 Amberley :

🏨 **Bear of Rodborough** (Forte), Rodborough Common, GL5 5DE, SE : 1 ½ m. on Minchinhampton rd ☎ 878522, Fax 872523, ⟶ – ⭐⊶ 📺 ☎ 🅿 – ⚍ 60. ⚄ AE ⓞ VISA JCB
M (bar lunch Monday to Saturday)/dinner 25.00 **st.** and a la carte – ⏴ 8.50 – **47 rm**
65.00/78.00 **st.** – SB 108.00 **st.**

at Amberley S : 3 m. by A 46 – ✉ Stroud – ☎ 0453 Amberley :

🏠 **Amberley Inn** (Best Western), GL5 5AF, ☎ 872565, Fax 872738, ⟶ – 📺 ☎ 🅿. ⚄ AE ⓞ
VISA – **M** 14.70 **st.** (lunch) and a la carte 16.75/19.95 **st.** ⌁ 3.50 – **14 rm** ⏴ 55.00/80.00 **st.** –
SB 84.00/96.00 **st.**

◉ ATS Dudbridge Rd ☎ 758156/752191

STUCKTON Hants. – see Fordingbridge.

STUDLEY Warks. 403 404 O 27 – pop. 6 654 – ✉ Redditch – ☎ 0527.

◆London 109 – ◆Birmingham 15 – ◆ Coventry 33 – Gloucester 39.

🍴🍴 **Pepper's**, 45 High St., B80 7HN, ☎ 853183 – 🍽. ⚄ AE VISA
closed Sunday lunch and 25-26 December – **M** - **Indian** a la carte 8.70/14.90 **t.**

STURMINSTER NEWTON Dorset 403 404 N 31 The West Country G. – pop. 1 781 – ☎ 0258.

See : Mill★ *AC.*

◆London 123 – Bournemouth 30 – ◆Bristol 49 – Salisbury 28 – Taunton 41.

🏠 **Stourcastle Lodge**, Gough's Close, DT10 1BU, (off the Market Place) ☎ 472320,
Fax 473381, ⟶ – ⭐⊶ rest 📺 ☎ 🅿. ⚄ VISA. ❄
M 14.00 – **5 rm** ⏴ 19.50/64.00 **st.**

🍴🍴🍴 **Plumber Manor** ⤵ with rm, DT10 2AF, SW : 1 ¾ m. by A 357 on Hazelbury Bryan rd
☎ 472507, Fax 473370, ≤, « 18C manor house », ⟶, park, ❄ – 📺 ☎ 🅿. ⚄ AE ⓞ VISA.
❄
closed February – **M** (dinner only and Sunday lunch)/dinner 16.50/25.00 **st.** ⌁ 5.00 – **16 rm**
⏴ 60.00/110.00 **st.**

SUDBURY Suffolk 404 W 27 Great Britain G. – pop. 17 723 – ECD : Wednesday – ☎ 0787.

See : Gainsborough's House★ *AC.*

🛈 Town Hall, Market Hill, CO10 6EA ☎ 881320 (summer only).

◆London 59 – ◆Cambridge 37 – Colchester 15 – ◆Ipswich 21.

🏠 Hill Lodge, Newton Rd, CO10 6RG, on A 134 (Colchester rd) ☎ 377568 – ⭐⊶ rest 📺 🅿 –
⚍ 60. ❄
M (by arrangement) – **16 rm.**

🍴 **Mabey's Brasserie**, 47 Gainsborough St., CO10 7SS, ☎ 374298 – ⚄ AE VISA
closed Sunday and Monday – **M** a la carte 12.85/16.40 **t.** ⌁ 3.50.

at Belchamp Walter (Essex) W : 5 m. by A 131 and Belchamps rd – ✉ ☎ 0787
Sudbury :

🏠 **St. Mary Hall** ⤵, CO10 7BB, SW : 1 ½ m. on Great Yeldham rd ☎ 237202, ⟶, ❄ – 🅿.
⟶ ❄
M (by arrangement) (communal dining) 20.00 ⌁ 4.00 – **3 rm** ⏴ 26.00/56.00 **s.**

◉ ATS Edgeworth Rd ☎ 374227

SUNDERLAND Tyne and Wear 401 402 P 19 – pop. 195 064 – ECD : Wednesday –
☎ 091 Wearside.

🔹 Whitburn, Lizard Lane ☎ 529 2144, N : 2 m. by A 183 A – 🔹 Ryhope, Leechmere Way,
Hollycarrside ☎ 521 3811/523 7333, SW : 2 m. by A 1018 A.

🛈 Unit 3, Crowtree Rd, SR1 3EL ☎ 565 0960/565 0990.

◆London 272 – ◆Leeds 92 – ◆Middlesbrough 29 – ◆Newcastle upon Tyne 12.

Plans on next page

SUNDERLAND

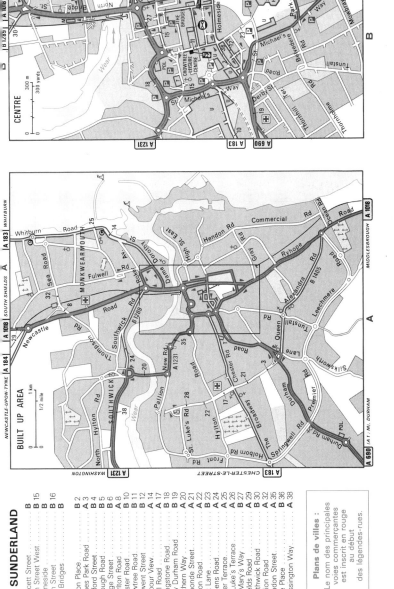

Plans de villes :
Le nom des principales
voies commerçantes
est inscrit en rouge
au début
des légendes-rues.

Swallow Sunderland, Queens Par., Seaburn, SR6 8DB, ✆ 529 2041, Telex 53168, Fax 529 4227, ⛹, ≘s, 🏊 – |‡| ⇎ rm ▤ 📺 ☎ ♿ 🅟 – 🏛 230. 🅢🅝 AE ⓓ VISA A **e**
M 13.50/20.50 **st.** and a la carte 🍷 4.50 – **65 rm** ☐ 85.00/150.00 **st.** – SB (May-August and weekends only) 115.00 **st.**

Roker (Chef & Brewer), Roker Terrace, Roker, SR6 0PH, ✆ 567 1786, Fax 510 0289, ≤ – 📺 ☎ 🅟. 🅢🅝 AE VISA. ✻ A **c**
M (grill rest.) 15.00/20.00 **t.** and a la carte – ☐ 3.50 – **45 rm** 44.95/48.45 **t.**

Gelt House, 23 St. Bedes Terr., SR2 8HS, ✆ 567 2990, Fax 510 0724 – ⇎ rest 📺 ☎ 🅟. 🅢🅝 AE ⓓ VISA. ✻ B **a**
closed 23 December-2 January – **M** *(closed Friday to Sunday)* (dinner only) a la carte approx. 8.25 **t.** 🍷 2.90 – **21 rm** ☐ 35.00/42.00 **t.**

Travel Inn, Wessington Way, SR5 3HR, ✆ 548 9384, Fax 584 4148 – ⇎ rm 📺 ♿ 🅟. 🅢🅝 AE ⓓ VISA. ✻ by A 1231 A
M (Beefeater grill) a la carte approx. 16.00 **t.** – ☐ 4.95 – **40 rm** 33.50 **t.**

ATS Monkwearmouth Bridge ✆ 565 7694

SUNNINGHILL Berks. 404 S 29 – see Ascot.

SUTTON W. Sussex – see Petworth.

SUTTON COLDFIELD W. Mids. 403 404 O 26 – pop. 101 886 – ✆ 021 Birmingham.

18 Pype Hayes, Eachelhurst Rd, Walmley ✆ 351 1014, by Chester Rd DT – 18 Boldmere, Monmouth Drive ✆ 354 3379, by A 452 DT – 18 110 Thornhill Rd ✆ 353 2014, by B 4138 DT – 18, 18 The Belfry, Wishaw ✆ 0675 (Curdworth) 470301, E : 6½ m. by A 453 on A 446 DT.

♦London 124 – ♦Birmingham 8 – ♦Coventry 29 – ♦Nottingham 47 – ♦Stoke-on-Trent 40.

Plan : see Birmingham pp. 2 and 3

Belfry (De Vere), Lichfield Rd, Wishaw, B76 9PR, E : 6 ½ m. by A 453 on A 446 ✆ 0675 (Curdworth) 470301, Fax 470178, ≤, ⛹, ≘s, 🏊, 18, 🌳, park, 🎾, squash – |‡| ⇎ rm ▤ rest 📺 ☎ ♿ 🅟 – 🏛 300. 🅢🅝 AE ⓓ VISA. ✻ by A 38 DT
M 15.95/25.50 **st.** and dinner a la carte – **209 rm** ☐ 105.00/185.00 **st.**, 10 suites – SB 130.00/190.00 **st.**

New Hall (Mt. Charlotte Thistle) 🐦, Walmley Rd, B76 8QX, SE : 1½ m. by Coleshill St., Coleshill Rd and Reddicap Hill on B 4148 ✆ 378 2442, Telex 333580, Fax 378 4637, « Part 13C moated manor house », 🌳, park, 🎾 – ⇎ rest 📺 ☎ ♿ 🅟 – 🏛 40. 🅢🅝 AE ⓓ VISA JCB. ✻ DT **i**
M *(closed Saturday lunch)* 20.00/27.30 **t.** and a la carte 🍷 5.90 – ☐ 9.65 – **55 rm** 93.00/165.00 **t.**, 5 suites – SB (weekends only) 136.00/176.00 **st.**

Penns Hall (Jarvis) 🐦, Penns Lane, Walmley, B76 8LH, SE : 2 ¾ m. by A 5127 ✆ 351 3111, Fax 313 1297, ⛹, ≘s, 🏊, 🎣, 🌳, park, squash – |‡| ⇎ rm 📺 ☎ 🅟 – 🏛 450. 🅢🅝 AE ⓓ VISA. ✻ DT **v**
M 10.50/18.50 **st.** and a la carte – ☐ 8.50 – **109 rm** 95.00/115.00 **st.**, 5 suites – SB (weekends only) 99.00 **st.**

Sutton Court, 60-66 Lichfield Rd, B74 2NA, N : ½ m. on A 5127 ✆ 355 6071, Fax 355 0083 – ⇎ rm 📺 ☎ 🅟 – 🏛 90. 🅢🅝 AE ⓓ VISA JCB DT **x**
M *(closed Bank Holidays)* 15.00/15.95 **t.** and a la carte 🍷 4.50 – ☐ 7.50 – **64 rm** 50.00/74.00 **st.** – SB 40.00/130.00 **st.**

Moor Hall (Best Western), Moor Hall Drive, B75 6LN, NE : 2 m. by A 453 and Weeford Rd ✆ 308 3751, Telex 335127, Fax 308 8974, ⛹, ≘s, 🏊, 🌳 – |‡| ⇎ rm 📺 ☎ 🅟 – 🏛 200. 🅢🅝 AE ⓓ VISA. ✻ DT **r**
M (carving lunch)/dinner 19.50 **t.** 🍷 5.00 – **75 rm** ☐ 80.00/145.00 **st.** – SB (weekends only) 99.00/106.00 **st.**

Royal, High St., B72 1UD, ✆ 355 8222, Fax 355 1837 – 📺 ☎ 🅟. 🅢🅝 AE ⓓ VISA. ✻
M (grill rest.) a la carte 9.15/14.35 **t.** – **22 rm** ☐ 44.95 **st.** DT **c**

Forte Travelodge, Boldmere Rd, B72 5UP, SW : 1¼ m. by A 5127 and A 453 on B 4142 ✆ 355 0017, Reservations (Freephone) 0800 850950 – 📺 ♿ 🅟. 🅢🅝 AE VISA. ✻
M (Harvester grill) a la carte approx. 16.00 – ☐ 5.50 – **32 rm** 31.95 **t.** DT **n**

Parson and Clerk without rest., Chester Rd North, Streetly, B73 6SP, W : 3 ½ m. by A 453 on A 452 ✆ 353 1747, Fax 352 1340 – 📺 ☎ 🅟. 🅢🅝 AE ⓓ VISA. ✻ CT **s**
☐ 5.00 – **36 rm** 33.00 **st.**

Standbridge, 138 Birmingham Rd, B72 1LY, ✆ 354 3007, 🌳 – ⇎ rest 📺 🅟. 🅢🅝 VISA
closed 30 May-5 June and 24 December-4 January – **M** (by arrangement) 7.50 **s.** 🍷 3.75 – **8 rm** ☐ 23.00/38.50 **s.** – SB 53.50/71.00 **st.** DT **a**

La Truffe, 65 Birmingham Rd, B72 1QF, ✆ 355 5836 – 🅢🅝 AE VISA DT **u**
closed Saturday lunch, Sunday, Monday, 1 week August, first 2 weeks January and Bank Holidays – **M** 14.25/18.75 **t.** and a la carte 🍷 6.10.

SUTTON COURTENAY Oxon. 403 404 Q 29 – ✉ Abingdon – ✆ 0235.

♦London 24 – ♦Oxford 12 – Reading 22 – Swindon 28.

The Fish, 4 Appleford Rd, OX14 4NQ, ✆ 848242, Fax 484242 – ⇎ 🅟. 🅢🅝 AE VISA
M a la carte 17.40/29.15 **t.** 🍷 4.50.

Michelin non applica targhe pubblicitarie agli alberghi e ristoranti segnalati in Guida.

◆London 66 – Reading 32 – Salisbury 21 – ◆Southampton 19.

🏨 **Forte Travelodge** without rest., SO21 3JY, 760779 (southside) 🖋 761016 (northside), Reservations (Freephone) 0800 850950 – 📺 ₺ 🅟. 🔃 🕮 𝓥𝓘𝓢𝓐. ✳
71 rm 31.95 **t.**

SWAFFHAM Norfolk 404 W 26 Great Britain G. – pop. 4 742 – ECD : Thursday – 🕾 0760.

Exc. : Oxburgh Hall★★ *AC*, SW : 7½ m.

┌ Granary Hotel, Little Dunham 🖋 0328 (Fakenham) 701310, NE : 4 m.

◆London 97 – ◆Cambridge 46 – King's Lynn 16 – ◆Norwich 27.

🏨 **Strattons,** Ash Close, PE37 7NH, off Market Sq. 🖋 723845, Fax 720458, « Part Queen Anne house », 🐕 – 👄 📺 🅟. 🔃 🕮 𝓥𝓘𝓢𝓐
closed Christmas – **M** (booking essential to non-residents) (dinner only) 24.00 **st.** ₺ 5.50 –
7 rm 🛏 52.00/80.00 **st.**

🏨 **George,** Station St., PE37 7LJ, 🖋 721238, Fax 725333 – 📺 🕾 🅟 – 🚲 150. 🔃 🕮 ⓞ 𝓥𝓘𝓢𝓐
M 14.50 **t.** and a la carte ₺ 4.75 – **28 rm** 🛏 45.00/59.00 **t.** – SB 84.00/119.00 **st.**

at Sporle NE : 3 m. by A 47 – ✉ King's Lynn – 🕾 0760 Swaffham :

↑ **Corfield House,** PE32 2EA, on Necton rd 🖋 723636, 🐕 – 👄 📺 🅟. 🔃 𝓥𝓘𝓢𝓐. ✳
April-December – **M** 11.50 ₺ 3.50 – **5 rm** 🛏 19.50/39.00 **st.**

⑩ ATS Unit 2a, Tower Meadow (off Station St.) 🖋 22543

Les prix	Pour toutes précisions sur les prix indiqués dans ce guide, reportez-vous à l'introduction.

SWANAGE Dorset 403 404 O 32 The West Country G. – pop. 8 411 – ECD : Thursday – 🕾 0929.

See : Town★.

Envir. : St. Aldhelm's Head★★ (≤★★★) SW : 4 m. by B 3069 – Durlston Country Park (≤★★) S : 1 m. – Studland (Old Harry Rocks★★, St. Nicholas Church★) N : 3 m. – Worth Matravers (Anvil Point Lighthouse ≤★★) S : 2 m. – Great Globe★, S : 1¼ m.

Exc. : Corfe Castle★★ (≤★★) *AC*, NW : 6 m. by A 351.

┌₁₈, ┌₉ Isle of Purbeck, Studland 🖋 44361, NW : 3 m. on B 3351.

🛈 The White House, Shore Rd, BH19 1LB 🖋 422885.

◆London 130 – Bournemouth 22 – Dorchester 26 – ◆Southampton 52.

↑ **Havenhurst,** 3 Cranborne Rd, BH19 1EA, 🖋 424224 – 👄 rest 🅟. ✳
M 10.00/12.00 **t.** ₺ 3.95 – **17 rm** 🛏 22.00/50.00 **t.** – SB (October-April except Bank Holidays) 63.00/72.00 **st.**

↑ **Crowthorne,** 24 Cluny Cres., BH19 2BT, 🖋 422108 – 👄 🅟. 🔃 𝓥𝓘𝓢𝓐. ✳
closed January – **M** 11.50 **st.** – **8 rm** 🛏 21.00/50.00 **st.** – SB (except Bank Holidays) 50.00/60.00 **st.**

SWAVESEY SERVICE AREA Cambs. 404 U 27 – see Cambridge.

SWAY Hants. 403 404 P 31 – see Brockenhurst

SWINDON Wilts. 403 404 O 29 The West Country G. – pop. 127 348 – ECD : Wednesday – 🕾 0793.

See : Great Western Railway Museum★ *AC* – Railway Village Museum★ *AC*.

Envir. : Lydiard Park (St. Mary's★) W : 4 m. by B 4534.

Exc. : Ridgeway Path★★ – Whitehorse (≤★) S : 8½ m. by A 4361.

┌₁₈, ┌₉ Broome Manor, Pipers Way 🖋 532403 – ┌₁₈ Shrivenham Park, Penny Hooks 🖋 783853, Fax 782999, E : 4 m. – ┌₁₈ Wootton Bassett 🖋 849999, S : 1 m. – ┌₁₈ Wrag Barn, Shrivenham Rd, Highworth 🖋 861327, NE : 6 m. by B 4000.

🛈 32 The Arcade, Brunel Centre, SN1 1LN 🖋 530328.

◆London 83 – Bournemouth 69 – ◆Bristol 40 – ◆Coventry 66 – ◆Oxford 29 – Reading 40 – ◆Southampton 65.

🏩 **De Vere,** Shaw Ridge Leisure Park, Whitehill Way, SN5 7DW, W : 2¾ m. by A 3102 and Tewkesbury Way (at Mannington junction) 🖋 878785, Fax 877822, ₤₅, ≦s, ☒ – ▮ 👄 rm ▤ rest 📺 ₺ 🅟 – 🚲 400. 🔃 🕮 ⓞ 𝓥𝓘𝓢𝓐
M (carving lunch) 14.25/17.50 **t.** and a la carte – **146 rm** 🛏 94.50/105.00 **t.**, 8 suites – SB (except Christmas) 114.00/120.00 **st.**

🏩 **Swindon Marriott,** Pipers Way, SN3 1SH, SE : 1½ m. by Marlborough Road off B 4006 🖋 512121, Fax 513114, ₤₅, ≦s, ☒, ✳, squash – ▮ 👄 rm ▤ 📺 🕾 ₺ 🅟 – 🚲 280. 🔃 🕮 ⓞ 𝓥𝓘𝓢𝓐. ✳
M 11.95/17.00 **st.** ₺ 8.00 – 🛏 10.25 – **153 rm** 92.00/175.00 **st.** – SB (weekends only) 100.00/130.00 **st.**

🏨 **Forte Posthouse,** Marlborough Rd, SN3 6AQ, SE : 2¾ m. on A 4259 🖋 524601, Fax 512887, ₤₅, ≦s, ☒ – 👄 rm 📺 🕾 🅟 – 🚲 80. 🔃 🕮 ⓞ 𝓥𝓘𝓢𝓐
M a la carte approx. 17.50 **t.** ₺ 4.65 – 🛏 6.95 – **98 rm** 53.50 **st.** – SB (weekends only) 90.00 **st.**

at Blunsdon N : 4 ½ m. on A 419 – ⊠ 🕙 0793 Swindon :

🏡 **Blunsdon House** (Best Western), The Ridge, SN2 4AD, 🖉 721701, Fax 721056, ≼⌁, ☜, 🔲, 🍃, 🏊, park, ❦, squash – 📲 ⇶ rm 📺 ☎ ♿ 🄿 – 🔬 300. 🅰 🄰🄴 ⑩ 𝘝𝘐𝘚𝘈 🄹🄲🄱. ❦
M 10.75/11.75 **t.** and a la carte – **87 rm** ⊏⊐ 72.50/99.50 **t.**, 1 suite – SB 118.00/125.00 **st.**

at Stanton Fitzwarren NE : 5 ¼ m. by A 4312 and A 419 off A 361 – ⊠ 🕙 0793 Swindon :

🏨 **Stanton House,** The Avenue, SN6 7SD, 🖉 861777, Fax 861857, ❦ – 📲 ▤ rest 📺 ☎ 🄿 – 🔬 120. 🅰 🄰🄴 ⑩ 𝘝𝘐𝘚𝘈 🄹🄲🄱. ❦
M - **Japanese** 12.00/26.00 **st.** and dinner a la carte ⬧ 5.00 – **86 rm** ⊏⊐ 65.00/90.00 **st.** – SB (weekends only) 105.00/180.00 **st.**

at Wroughton S : 3 ¼ m. on A 4361 – ⊠ 🕙 0793 Swindon :

🏨 **Moormead,** Moormead Rd, SN4 9BY, 🖉 814744, Fax 814119 – 📺 ☎ ♿ 🄿 – 🔬 60. 🅰 🄰🄴 ⑩ 𝘝𝘐𝘚𝘈. ❦
M (light lunch Monday to Saturday)/dinner 19.00 **st.** ⬧ 4.50 – **34 rm** ⊏⊐ 35.00/83.00 **st.** – SB (weekends only) 88.00/113.00 **st.**

at Chiseldon S : 6 ¼ m. by A 4312, A 4259 and A 345 on B 4005 – ⊠ 🕙 0793 Swindon :

🏨 **Chiseldon House** ⍟, New Rd, SN4 0NE, 🖉 741010, Fax 741059, ⬕ heated, ☞ – 📺 ☎ 🄿, 🅰 🄰🄴 ⑩ 𝘝𝘐𝘚𝘈. ❦
M – Orangery *(closed Saturday lunch)* 14.95/24.95 **t.** ⬧ 6.00 – **21 rm** ⊏⊐ 80.00/110.00 **t.**

at Wootton Bassett W : 6 ¼ m. on A 3102 – ⊠ 🕙 0793 Swindon :

🏨 **Marsh Farm,** Coped Hall, SN4 8ER, N : 1 m. by A 3102 on Purton rd 🖉 848044, Fax 851528, ☞ – 📺 ☎ 🄿 – 🔬 100. 🅰 🄰🄴 ⑩ 𝘝𝘐𝘚𝘈. ❦
M *(closed Sunday lunch)* 12.50 **st.** and a la carte ⬧ 6.75 – **28 rm** ⊏⊐ 50.00/85.00 **st.** – SB (weekends only) 75.00/110.00 **st.**

at Hook W : 6 ¼ m. by A 3102, B 4534 and Hook rd – ⊠ 🕙 0793 Swindon :

🏠 **School House,** Hook St., SN4 8EF, 🖉 851198, Fax 851025, ☞ – 📺 ☎ 🄿. 🅰 🄰🄴 ⑩ 𝘝𝘐𝘚𝘈. ❦
M *(closed Saturday lunch, Sunday and Bank Holidays to non-residents)* 17.95/19.95 **st.** and a la carte ⬧ 5.25 – **11 rm** ⊏⊐ 45.00/79.50 **st.** – SB (weekends only) 69.50/79.50 **st.**

🔧 ATS Cheney Manor Ind. Est. 🖉 521171   ATS 86 Beatrice St. 🖉 534867/431620

SWINTON Gtr.Manchester 🄴🄾🄶 🄴🄾🄷 🄴🄾🄸 N 23 – see Manchester.

SYMONDS YAT Heref. and Worcs. 🄴🄾🄷 🄴🄾🄸 M 28 Great Britain G. – ⊠ Ross-on-Wye – 🕙 0600.
See : Town★ – Yat Rock (≤★).
Envir. : S : Wye Valley★.
♦London 126 – Gloucester 23 – Hereford 17 – Newport 31.

↑ **Woodlea** ⍟, Symonds Yat (West), HR9 6BL, 🖉 890206, ☞ – ☎ 🄿. 🅰 𝘝𝘐𝘚𝘈
M 13.25 **t.** ⬧ 3.45 – **9 rm** ⊏⊐ 22.00/53.00 **t.** – SB (except Bank Holidays) (weekdays and weekends November-March) 60.00/70.00 **st.**

TALKE Staffs. 🄴🄾🄶 🄴🄾🄷 🄴🄾🄸 N 24 – see Stoke-on-Trent.

TALKIN Cumbria 🄴🄾🅁 🄴🄾🅂 L 19 – see Brampton.

TALLAND BAY Cornwall 🄴🄾🄷 G 32 – see Looe.

TAMWORTH Staffs. 🄴🄾🄶 🄴🄾🄷 🄴🄾🄸 O 26 – pop. 63 260 – ECD : Wednesday – 🕙 0827.
🏌 Eagle Drive, Amington 🖉 53850, E : 2 ½ m. by B 5000.
🅸 Town Hall, Market St., B79 7LY 🖉 59134.
♦London 128 – ♦Birmingham 12 – ♦Coventry 29 – ♦Leicester 31 – ♦Stoke-on-Trent 37.

🏨 **Castle,** Ladybank, B79 7NB, 🖉 57181, Fax 54303 – ⇶ rm 📺 ☎ – 🔬 130. 🅰 🄰🄴 ⑩ 𝘝𝘐𝘚𝘈
M (bar lunch Monday to Saturday)/dinner 14.95 **t.** and a la carte – **33 rm** ⊏⊐ 64.00/105.00 **t.** – SB (weekdays only) 78.00/120.00 **st.**

🏠 **Travel Inn,** Bitterscote, Bonehill Rd, B78 3HQ, on A 51 🖉 54414, Fax 310420 – ⇶ rm 📺 ♿ 🄿. 🅰 🄰🄴 ⑩ 𝘝𝘐𝘚𝘈. ❦
M (Beefeater grill) a la carte approx. 16.00 **t.** – ⊏⊐ 4.95 – **40 rm** 33.50 **t.**

at Bodymoor Heath S : 6 ¾ m. by A 4091 – ⊠ Sutton Coldfield – 🕙 0827 Tamworth :

🏨 **Marston Farm,** B76 9JD, 🖉 872133, Fax 875043, ⍓, park, ❦ – ⇶ rest 📺 ☎ 🄿 – 🔬 50. 🅰 🄰🄴 ⑩ 𝘝𝘐𝘚𝘈
M 12.50/15.50 **t.** and a la carte ⬧ 5.00 – **37 rm** ⊏⊐ 70.00/85.00 **t.** – SB (weekends only) 70.00/80.00 **st.**

🔧 ATS Tame Valley Ind. Est., Watling St., Wilnecote 🖉 281983

☞ *There is no paid publicity in this Guide.*

Staffs. – ⊠ ✿ 0827 Tamworth

🏠 **Granada Lodge** without rest., Green Lane, B77 6PS, A 5 / M 42 junction 10 ℰ 260120, Fax 260145, Reservations (Freephone) 0800 555300 – ✻ 🆗 ♿ ℗, 🔊 🇦🇪 𝗩𝗜𝗦𝗔. ✻
⊆ 4.00 – **63 rm** 34.95/37.95 **st.**

TAPLOW Berks. 404 R 29 – ✿ 0628 Burnham.

♦London 33 – Maidenhead 2 – Reading 12.

🏰 **Cliveden** ⬲, Cliveden, SL6 0JF, N : 2 m. by Berry Hill ℰ 668561, Telex 846562, Fax 661837, « Mid-Victorian stately home, ≼ National Trust Gardens, parterre and River Thames », 🏋, ≘, ⌁ heated, 🔲, 🐎, park, ✻, squash – 🛗 🆗 ☎ ℗ – 🔬 40. 🔊 🇴 𝗩𝗜𝗦𝗔
M – Terrace 34.00 **st.** (lunch) and a la carte 31.50/52.00 **st.** 🍴 9.00 – (see also **Waldo's** below)
– ⊆ 14.50 – **26 rm** 195.00/355.00 **st.**, 5 suites – SB (except Bank Holidays) 285.00/480.00 **st.**

✗✗✗✗ **Waldo's** (at Cliveden H.), Cliveden, SL6 0JF, N : 2 m. by Berry Hill ℰ 668561, Telex 846562, Fax 661837 – ✻ 🍽 ℗, 🔊 🇴 𝗩𝗜𝗦𝗔
closed Sunday and Monday – **M** (dinner only) 47.00/60.00 **s.** 🍴 9.00
Spec. Cornish crab with lime, pimentos, scallops and a potato and chive salad, Grilled fillet of Scotch beef with smoked foie gras, Warm caramelised apple and filo pastry tart with cinnamon ice cream.

TARPORLEY Ches. 402 403 404 M 24 – pop. 1 844 – ✿ 0829.
🏌 Portal, Cobblers Cross ℰ 733933.

♦London 186 – Chester 11 – ♦Liverpool 36 – Shrewsbury 36.

🏠 **Swan,** 50 High St., CW6 0AG, ℰ 733838, Fax 732932 – 🆗 ☎ ℗ – 🔬 100. 🔊 🇦🇪 𝗩𝗜𝗦𝗔. ✻
M a la carte 13.40/22.45 **t.** 🍴 3.75 – **14 rm** ⊆ 42.95/59.00 **t.** – SB (except Bank Holidays) 75.00/130.00 **st.**

at Willington NW : 3½ m. by A 51 – ⊠ ✿ 0829 Tarporley :

🏨 **Willington Hall** ⬲, Willington Rd, CW6 0NB, ℰ 52321, Fax 52596, ≼, ⬯, park, ✻ – 🆗 ☎ ℗, 🔊 🇴 𝗩𝗜𝗦𝗔
closed Christmas Day – **M** (in bar Sunday dinner) a la carte 12.65/22.55 **t.** 🍴 4.35 – ⊆ 6.00 – **10 rm** 38.00/68.00 **t.**

TATTENHALL Ches. 402 403 404 L 24 – pop. 1 778 – ✿ 0829.

♦London 200 – ♦Birmingham 71 – Chester 10 – ♦Manchester 38 – ♦Stoke-on-Trent 30.

🏠 **Newton Hall** ⬲ without rest., CH3 9AY, N : 1 m. by Huxley Rd ℰ 70153, « Working farm », ⬯ – ✻ ℗,
closed 24 December – **3 rm** ⊆ 20.00/35.00 **s.**

at Higher Burwardsley SE : 1 m. – ⊠ ✿ 0829 Tattenhall :

🏠 **Pheasant Inn,** CH3 9PF, ℰ 70434, Fax 71097, ≼ – 🆗 ☎ ℗, 🔊 🇦🇪 🇴 𝗩𝗜𝗦𝗔. ✻
M (bar lunch Monday to Saturday) a la carte 7.10/14.75 **st.** 🍴 3.50 – **8 rm** ⊆ 40.00/60.00 **st.** – SB (except Bank Holidays) 70.00/80.00 **st.**

TAUNTON Somerset 403 K 30 The West Country G. – pop. 47 793 – ECD : Thursday – ✿ 0823.
See : Town★ - St. Mary Magdalene★ – Somerset County Museum★ AC – St. James★ – Hammett St.★ – The Crescent★ – Bath Alley★.
Envir. : Trull (Church★) S : 2½ m. by A 38.
Exc. : Bishops Lydeard★ (Church★) NW : 6 m. – Wellington : Church★, Wellington Monument (≼★★) SW : 7½ m. by A 38 – Combe Florey★, NW : 8 m. – Gaulden Manor★ AC, NW : 10 m. by A 358 and B 3227.
🏌, 🏌 Taunton Vale, Creech Heathfield ℰ 412220, N : 3 m. by A 361 – 🏌 Vivary Park ℰ 289274 – 🏌 Taunton and Pickeridge, Corfe ℰ 42240, S : 5 m. by B 3170.
🛈 The Library, Corporation St., TA1 4AN ℰ 274785.

♦London 168 – Bournemouth 69 – ♦Bristol 50 – Exeter 37 – ♦Plymouth 78 – ♦Southampton 93 – Weymouth 50.

🏰 ✿ **Castle,** Castle Green, TA1 1NF, ℰ 272671, Fax 336066, « Part 12C castle with Norman garden » – 🛗 ✻ rest 🆗 ☎ ⬥ ℗ – 🔬 90. 🔊 🇦🇪 🇴 𝗩𝗜𝗦𝗔 𝗝𝗖𝗕
M (restricted menu Sunday dinner) 14.50/29.90 **st.** 🍴 4.50 – ⊆ 5.95 – **35 rm** 65.00/195.00 **st.** – SB 119.80/139.80 **st.**
Spec. Seared salmon with a spice crust and onion crème fraîche, Braised shoulder of lamb with thyme, garlic and spring vegetables, Baked egg custard tart with nutmeg ice cream

🏨 **Forte Posthouse,** Deane Gate Av., TA1 2UA, E : 2½ m. by A 358 at junction with M 5 ℰ 332222, Fax 332266, 🏋, ≘ – 🛗 ✻ rm 🍽 rest 🆗 ☎ ♿ ℗ – 🔬 200. 🔊 🇦🇪 🇴 𝗩𝗜𝗦𝗔
M a la carte approx. 17.50 **t.** 🍴 4.65 – ⊆ 6.95 – **97 rm** 53.50 **st.** – SB 90.00 **st.**

🏨 **County** (Forte), East St., TA1 3LT, ℰ 337651, Fax 334517 – 🛗 ✻ rm 🆗 ☎ ℗ – 🔬 300. 🔊 🇦🇪 𝗩𝗜𝗦𝗔 𝗝𝗖𝗕. ✻
M 9.95/16.95 **st.** and dinner a la carte – ⊆ 8.50 – **66 rm** 55.00/70.00 **st.** – SB 98.00 **st.**

🏠 **Travel Inn,** 81 Bridgwater Rd, TA1 2DU, E : 1¾ m. by A 358 ℰ 321112, Fax 322054 – ✻ rm 🆗 ℗, 🔊 🇦🇪 🇴 𝗩𝗜𝗦𝗔. ✻
M (Beefeater grill) a la carte approx. 16.00 **t.** – ⊆ 4.95 – **40 rm** 33.50 **t.**

🏠 **Forde House** without rest., 9 Upper High St., TA1 3PX, ℰ 279042, ⬯ – 🆗 ℗. ✻
closed Christmas-New Year – **5 rm** ⊆ 23.00/45.00 **s.**

483

at Henlade E : 3 ½ m. on A 358 – ⊠ ✆ 0823 Taunton :

🏨 **Mount Somerset** ⏚, TA3 5NB, S : ½ m. by Stoke Rd and Ash Cross rd ✎ 442500, Fax 442900, ≼, « Regency country house », ☞ – 🛉 📺 ☎ ❷ – 🏄 50. 🔺 🆎 ⓞ 🆅🆂🅰 ✖
closed 2 to 30 January – **M** 16.00/38.00 **t.** and a la carte – **9 rm** ⊡ 95.00/200.00 **t.** – SB (except Bank Holidays) 140.00/196.00 **st.**

at Hatch Beauchamp SE : 6 m. by A358 – ⊠ Taunton – ✆ 0823 Hatch Beauchamp :

🏨 **Farthings** ⏚, TA3 6SG, ✎ 480664, « Georgian country house », ☞ – 📺 ☎ ❷. 🔺 🆎 🆅🆂🅰
M (lunch by arrangement)/dinner 23.50 **st.** – **6 rm** ⊡ 70.00/100.00 **st.** – SB 115.00/ 130.00 **st.**

↑ **Frog Street Farm** ⏚, Beercrocombe, TA3 6AF, SE : 1 ¼ m. by Beercrocombe Rd ✎ 480430, « 15C farmhouse, working farm », 🐟 heated, ☞ – ✣→ rm ❷. ✖
March-October – **M** (by arrangement) (communal dining) 16.00 **st.** – **3 rm** ⊡ 27.00/ 54.00 **st.** – SB (except Bank Holidays) 46.00/50.00 **st.**

XX **Nightingales**, Bath House Farm, Lower West Hatch, TA3 5RH, W : 1 m. by A 358 ✎ 480806, ☞ – ❷. 🔺 🆅🆂🅰
closed Sunday, Monday and first 2 weeks August – **M** (booking essential) 15.95 **t.** ¶ 4.00.

at Bishop's Hull W : 1 ¾ m. by A 38 – ⊠ ✆ 0823 Taunton :

🏠 **Meryan House**, Bishop's Hull Rd, TA1 5EG, ✎ 337445, Fax 322355, ☞ – ✣→ 📺 ☎ ❷. 🔺 🆅🆂🅰
M *(closed Sunday)* (bar lunch)/dinner 14.00 **st.** – **12 rm** ⊡ 36.00/50.00 **st.** – SB (November-March) (weekends only) 40.00/50.00 **st.**

🖤 ATS 138 Bridgwater Rd, Bathpool ✎ 412826

TAUNTON DEANE SERVICE AREA Somerset 🔢 K 31 – ⊠ ✆ 0823 Taunton

🏠 **Road Chef Lodge** without rest., TA1 4BA, ✎ 332228, Fax 338131 – ✣→ 📺 ☎ ㊅ ❷. 🔺 🆎 ⓞ 🆅🆂🅰 ✖
closed 4 days at Christmas – ⊡ 5.25 – **39 rm** 32.00/38.00 **st.**

TAVISTOCK Devon 🔢 H 32 The West Country G. – pop. 8 508 – ECD : Wednesday – ✆ 0822.
Envir. : Morwellham★ *AC*, SW : 4 ½ m.
Exc. : E : Dartmoor National Park★★ (Brent Tor ≼★★, Haytor Rocks ≼★) – Buckland Abbey★★ *AC*, S : 7 m. by A 386 – Lydford★★ (Lydford Gorge★★) N : 8 ½ m. by A 386.
🖤 Down Rd ✎ 612049 – 🖤 Hurdwick, Tavistock Hamlets ✎ 612746, N : 1 m. on Brentor Church rd.
🏛 Town Hall, Bedford Sq., PL19 0AE ✎ 612938 (summer only).

◆London 239 – Exeter 38 – ◆Plymouth 15.

🏨 **Bedford** (Forte), 1 Plymouth Rd, PL19 8BB, ✎ 613221, Fax 618034 – ✣→ 📺 ☎ ❷ – 🏄 45. 🔺 🆎 ⓞ 🆅🆂🅰 ✖
M (bar lunch Monday to Saturday)/dinner 17.95 **st.** and a la carte ¶ 5.50 – ⊡ 8.75 – **31 rm** 70.00/80.00 **st.** – SB 120.00 **st.**

X **Neils**, 27 King St., PL19 0DT, ✎ 615550 – 🔺 🆎 🆅🆂🅰
closed Sunday and Monday – **M** (lunch by arrangement)/dinner 16.00 **t.** and a la carte ¶ 5.95.

at Mary Tavy N : 3 ¾ m. on A 386 – ⊠ Tavistock – ✆ 0822 Mary Tavy :

X **Stannary** with rm, PL19 9QB, ✎ 810897, Fax 810898, ☞ – ✣→ 📺 ❷. 🔺 🆅🆂🅰 ✖
M - Vegetarian (closed Sunday and Monday to non-residents) (dinner only) 24.00/35.00 **s.** ¶ 4.50 – **3 rm** ⊡ (dinner included) 70.00/120.00 **s.** – SB 120.00/140.00 **st.**

at Gulworthy W : 3 m. on A 390 – ⊠ ✆ 0822 Tavistock :

XX **Horn of Plenty** ⏚ with rm, PL19 8JD, ✎ 832528, Fax 832528, ≼ Tamar Valley and Bodmin Moor, ☞ – 📺 ☎ ❷. 🔺 🆅🆂🅰
closed 24 to 26 December – **M** (closed Monday lunch) 17.50/30.00 **t.** and a la carte ¶ 6.50 – ⊡ 5.00 – **7 rm** 62.00/90.00 **t.** – SB 122.00/191.00 **st.**

🖤 ATS 2 Parkwood Rd ✎ 612545

TEESSIDE AIRPORT Durham 🔢 P 20 – see Darlington.

TEFFONT Wilts. – see Salisbury.

When visiting Ireland,
use the Michelin Green Guide **"Ireland".**

– *Detailed descriptions of places of interest*
– *Touring programmes*
– *Maps and street plans*
– *The history of the country*
– *Photographs and drawings of monuments, beauty spots, houses...*

Happy 21st birthday to the red guide

This year, Michelin's famous Red Hotel and Restaurant Guide to Great Britain & Ireland is twenty one. It first appeared in its current form in 1974, although its origins go back to 1911.

Both early and contemporary versions share the same brevity and meticulous attention to detail. The ingenious use of symbols enables Michelin to condense potential volumes of information into one compact book, making the Guide an easy means of reference.

The care and effort which go into producing the Red Guide are immense. The results are exhaustive,

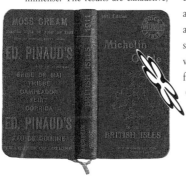

including town plans, early closing and market days, amenities and populations. This is in addition to information on the selection of hotels and restaurants, views and facilities that readers expect from the Red Guide.

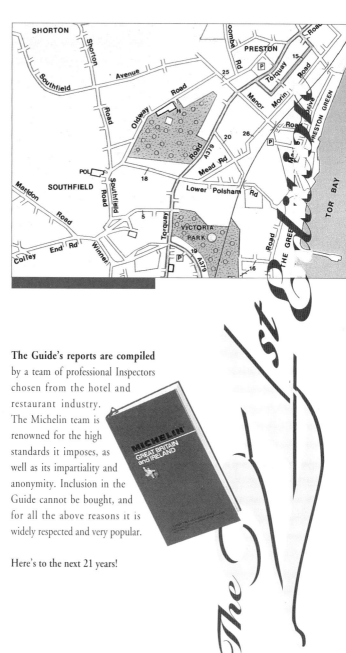

The Guide's reports are compiled
by a team of professional Inspectors
chosen from the hotel and
restaurant industry.
The Michelin team is
renowned for the high
standards it imposes, as
well as its impartiality and
anonymity. Inclusion in the
Guide cannot be bought, and
for all the above reasons it is
widely respected and very popular.

Here's to the next 21 years!

All terrain bicycle tyres

Michelin has launched an exciting new range of All Terrain Bicycle tyres designed to meet a wide variety of cycling styles and conditions. There are tyres for city riding, country rambles or competitions. Cyclists can choose tyres which perform best in the rain, on mud, on loose ground or on smooth surfaces. The range includes off-road tyres, some of which are suited to clambering over roots and rocks.

Certain tyres are intended primarily to grip, others to give extremely long life. Among the range there are matched pairs, directional tyres, and some recommended for front or rear wheel use only.

Michelin's comprehensive selection of All Terrain Bicycle tyres is proof that we understand - and can meet - different cyclists' requirements. No wonder our products are chosen by thousands of keen amateurs and professional cyclists every year.

For full details and further information on the Michelin ATB range, contact your local cycle tyre specialist.

Having developed the innovative Pilot range of high performance car tyres, Michelin seized the opportunity to show their worth. The result was Michelin Pilot Team Ford - sponsorship of two rally cars. The Ford Escort Cosworths are liveried in Michelin's distinctive yellow and blue, and cut a dash at British and international meetings throughout the season.

The Group A entrant was Malcolm Wilson, an experienced favourite and former British Rally Champion. The Group N car was driven by Robbie Head, one of the leading lights of the British rally scene - and still only in his mid-twenties.

Both drivers have been closely involved with the rally cars' development, and are familiar with the unique advantages gained by the fitment of Pilot tyres. Now road users too can choose tyres which suit their driving style. Whether the priority is speed, comfort or high mileage potential, Michelin high performance car tyres provide it. Try the new Pilot tyres and appreciate the change.

Michelin Pilot
Team Ford

The Competitive Edge

Sponsorship of the Michelin Team Pilot rally cars has generated substantial television and radio coverage and the cars' stylish livery always attracts attention. It is

specially designed to stand out in the most difficult driving conditions - in snow or mud the colours still look bright and attractive.

As well as the two main cars a third Pilot car attends shows and exhibitions and has proved a great visitor attraction. A fully equipped rally car in its own right, it has been used for races as well as promotional purposes.

Meanwhile, Michelin continues to hold a prominent position in the British Touring Car Championships, in which Renault, Peugeot and Ford vehicles are Michelin-shod.

Michelin was a major force in the World Rally Championship during 1993; Toyota, Ford, Subaru and Mitsubishi were all on Michelin tyres. Michelin was also a key player in both the Manufacturers' and Drivers' Championships for the season. Equally, the top five drivers, Kankkunen, Auriol, Delecour, Biasion and Sainz, were all on Michelin, and have increased Michelin's total of 110 international rally wins since 1974.

Comfortable...

Michelin's range of 4 x 4 tyres are specially created to complement your vehicle and suit your driving style. They are the result of close collaboration with 4 x 4 vehicle manufacturers, and all share comfort as a key design feature.

Whether you intend to drive on city roads, snowy mountain passes or sand dunes, there's a Michelin 4 x 4 tyre created to make your journey feel smooth.

Michelin's 4 x 4 tyres are fitted as original equipment to many of the most popular and exciting four wheel drive vehicles.

These currently include Landrover's Discovery, Nissan's Terrano and Ford's Maverick - and the list grows constantly.

When it comes to serious, hard terrain work, Michelin's 4 x 4 tyres are pre-eminent. Their domination of the Camel Trophy and Paris-Dakkar races continues, proving that when optimum performance is needed, top drivers rely on Michelin.

For comfort, mobility and enjoyment - even in the most demanding conditions - Michelin's 4 x 4 tyres are the obvious choice.

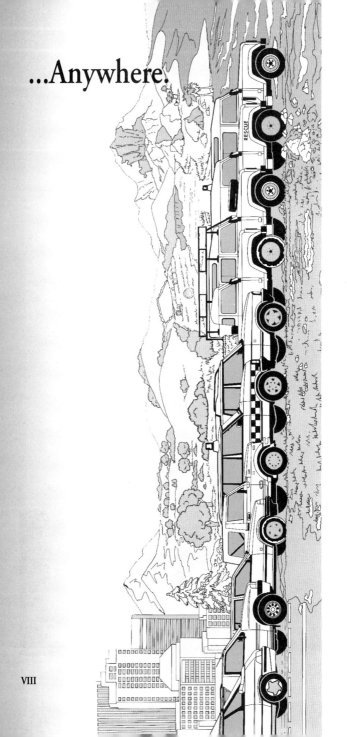

...Anywhere.

🛪 The Den, Sea Front, TQ14 8BE 🖉 779769.

◆London 216 – Exeter 16 – Torquay 8.

🏠 **London,** Bank St., TQ14 8AW, 🖉 776336, Fax 778457, 🛁, 🔟 – |♦| 🔟 ☎ – 🔬 200. 🔼 🖭 ⑩ 🎟
   M 10.25/15.00 **t.** and a la carte ♟ 4.00 – **30 rm** ⏛ 20.00/60.00 **t.** – SB (except July-August and Bank Holidays) 50.00/60.00 **st.**

🏠 **Clifden,** Dawlish Rd, TQ14 8TE, 🖉 770052, Fax 770594, ≼, Restricted to the blind and their companions, 🔟, 🛬 – ❄ rm 🔟 ☎ & 🅿. 🔼 🖭.
   M (residents only) (dinner only) ♟ 3.00 – **21 rm** ⏛ (dinner included) 40.00/65.00 **st.**

🏠 **Thomas Luny House,** Teign St., TQ14 8EG, 🖉 772976, « Georgian house built by Thomas Luny », 🛬 – ❄ rest 🔟 ☎
   closed mid December-mid January – **M** (residents only) (communal dining) (dinner only) 14.50 **st.** ♟ 6.00 – **4 rm** ⏛ 30.00/60.00 **st.** – SB 76.00.

   at Shaldon S : 1 m. on B 3199 – ✉ Teignmouth – ✿ 0626 Shaldon :

🏠 **Ness House,** Marine Par., TQ14 0HP, 🖉 873480, Fax 873486, ≼, 🛬 – 🔟 ☎ 🅿. 🔼 🖭 🎟 🛬
   M 11.50 **t.** and a la carte ♟ 4.40 – **12 rm** ⏛ 35.00/90.00 **st.** – SB (September-April) 67.00/75.00 **st.**

🏠 **Glenside,** Ringmore Rd, TQ14 0EP, W : ½ m. on B 3195 🖉 872448, 🛬 – ❄ rest 🔟 🅿.
   M 12.00 **t.** ♟ 5.00 – **10 rm** ⏛ 17.00/47.00 **t.** – SB 47.00/59.00 **st.**

Envir. : Ironbridge Gorge Museum★★ AC (The Iron Bridge★★, Coalport China Museum★★, Blists Hill Open Air Museum★★, Museum of the River and Visitor Centre★) S : 5 m. by B 4373.

Exc. : Weston Park★★ AC, E : 7 m. by A 5.

🛆, 🛆 Telford Hotel, Great Hay, Sutton Hill 🖉 585642, SE 1 m. by A 442 – 🛆 Wrekin, Wellington 🖉 244032 – 🛆, 🛆, 🛆, 🛆 The Shropshire, Muxton Grange 🖉 677866, NW : 4 m.

🛪 The Telford Centre, Management Suite, TF3 4BX 🖉 291370.

◆London 152 – ◆Birmingham 33 – Shrewsbury 12 – ◆Stoke-on-Trent 29.

🏠 **Holiday Inn,** St. Quentin Gate, TF3 4EH, SE : ½ m. 🖉 292500, Fax 291949, ₤₰, 🛁, 🔟 – |♦| ❄ rm 🗏 rest 🔟 ☎ & 🅿 – 🔬 200. 🔼 🖭 ⑩ 🎟 🛬
   M 10.95/15.95 **st.** and a la carte – ⏛ 9.50 – **100 rm** 89.00 **st.** – SB (weekends only) 108.00 **st.**

🏠 **Telford Moat House** (Q.M.H.), Forgegate, Telford Centre, TF3 4NA, 🖉 291291, Telex 35588, Fax 292012, ₤₰, 🛁, 🔟 – |♦| ❄ rm 🗏 rest 🔟 ☎ 🅿 – 🔬 400. 🔼 🖭 ⑩ 🎟
   closed 24 December-4 January – **M** (closed lunch Saturday and Bank Holidays) 14.25 **t.** and a la carte ♟ 4.75 – **144 rm** ⏛ 79.95/95.00 **t.**, 4 suites – SB (weekends only) 94.00 **st.**

🏠 **Telford H. Golf & Country Club** (Q.M.H.), Great Hay, Sutton Hill, TF7 4DT, S : 4½ m. by A 442 🖉 585642, Fax 586602, ≼, ₤₰, 🛁, 🔟, 🛆, squash – 🗏 rest 🔟 ☎ 🅿 – 🔬 400. 🔼 🖭 ⑩ 🎟
   M (closed Saturday lunch) 14.75 **st.** (dinner) and a la carte ♟ 6.50 – **Kyoto - Japanese** (closed Saturday lunch) 18.75/19.95 **st.** ♟ 6.50 – **85 rm** ⏛ 84.00/100.00 **st.**, 1 suite – SB (November-February and 2 July-5 September) 109.00/150.00 **st.**

🏠 **Madeley Court** 🛬, Castlefields Way, Madeley, TF7 5DW, S : 4½ m. by A 442 and A 4169 on B 4373 🖉 680068, Fax 684275, « Part 16C manor house », 🛬 – 🔟 ☎ 🅿 – 🔬 220. 🔼 🖭 🎟
   M (closed Sunday and Monday) (dinner only) 15.00 **t.** and a la carte – ⏛ 8.50 – **47 rm** ⏛ 78.00/120.00 **t.** – SB (except Christmas) (weekends only) 106.00 **st.**

   at Wellington W : 6 m. by M 54 on B 5061 – ✉ ✿ 0952 Telford :

🏠 **Buckatree Hall** 🛬, The Wrekin, Buckatree, TF6 5AL, SE : 2¾ m. by B 5061 🖉 641821, Fax 247540, ≼, 🛬 – ❄ rm 🔟 ☎ 🅿 – 🔬 180. 🔼 🖭 🎟 🛬
   M 16.50 **t.** and a la carte – **60 rm** ⏛ 69.00/85.00 **t.**, 2 suites – SB (weekends only) 96.00 **st.**

🏠 **White House,** Wellington Rd, Muxton, nr. Donnington, TF2 8NG, N : 4½ m. by A 518 🖉 670336, Fax 670336, 🛬 – ❄ 🔟 ☎ 🅿. 🔼 🖭 🎟 🛬
   M (bar lunch Saturday) 9.50/12.50 **st.** and a la carte ♟ 3.95 – **30 rm** ⏛ 49.50/67.50 **t.** – SB (weekends only) 70.00/90.00 **st.**

🏠 **Forte Travelodge,** Shawbirch Crossroads, Shawbirch, TF1 3QA, NW : 5¼ m. by M 54 and A 518, on A 5223 🖉 251244, Reservations (Freephone) 0800 850950 – 🔟 & 🅿. 🔼 🖭 🎟
   M (Harvester grill) a la carte approx. 16.00 **t.** – ⏛ 5.50 – **40 rm** 31.95 **t.**

   at Norton S : 7 m. on A 442 – ✉ Shifnal – ✿ 095 271 (3 fig.) and 0952 (6 fig.) Norton :

🏠 **Hundred House,** Bridgnorth Rd, TF11 9EE, 🖉 353, Fax 355, « Tastefully decorated inn, antiques », 🛬 – 🔟 ☎ 🅿. 🔼 🖭 🎟 🛬
   M a la carte 11.00/25.00 **st.** ♟ 5.50 – **9 rm** ⏛ 59.00/69.00 **st.** – SB 95.00/110.00 **st.**

⑩ ATS Queen St., Madeley 🖉 582820   ATS Kensington Way, Oakengates 🖉 613810/612198

TEMPLE SOWERBY Cumbria **401 402** M 20 – pop. 341 – ECD : Thursday – ✉ Penrith – ☎ 076 83 Kirkby Thore.

◆London 297 – ◆Carlisle 31 – Kendal 38.

🏠 **Temple Sowerby House,** CA10 1RZ, ℰ 61578, Fax 61958, ☞ – ⇔ rest ▥ ☎ ☻. ⚊ AE ◍ VISA
    M (light lunch) 10.95/21.00 **t.** ⫯ 4.50 – **12 rm** ☲ 48.00/64.00 **t.** – SB 90.00 **st.**

TENTERDEN Kent **404** W 30 – pop. 5 698 – ECD : Wednesday – ☎ 0580.

🅱 Town Hall, High St., TN30 6AN ℰ 63572 (summer only).

◆ London 57 – Folkestone 26 – Hastings 21 – Maidstone 19.

🏠 **White Lion** (Resort), 57 High St., TN30 6BD, ℰ 765077, Fax 764157 – ⇔ rm ▥ ☎ ☻ –
    ⚊ 35. ⚊ AE ◍ VISA
    M 12.95 **st.** (dinner) and a la carte 7.70/15.85 **st.** – **15 rm** ☲ 65.00/75.00 **st.** – SB 68.00/118.00 **st.**

🏠 **Little Silver Country,** Ashford Rd, St. Michaels, TN30 6SP, N : 2 m. on A 28
    ℰ 0233 (High Halden) 850321, Fax 850647, ☞ – ⇔ ▥ ☎ ☻ – ⚊ 150. ⚊ VISA. ⚘
    M (closed lunch Monday to Saturday to non-residents) (booking essential) 10.00/12.00 **st.** and a la carte ⫯ 5.20 – **10 rm** ☲ 55.00/98.00 **st.** – SB (except Christmas and Bank Holidays) 92.00/176.00 **st.**

🏡 **Brattle House,** Cranbrook Rd, TN30 6UL, W : 1 m. by A 28 ℰ 763565, ≤, ☞ – ⇔ ☻. ⚘
    closed Christmas and New Year – **M** (by arrangement) (communal dining) 15.50 – **3 rm**
    ☲ 45.00/54.00.

🏡 **Collina House,** 5 East Hill, TN30 6RL, ℰ 764852, ☞ – ▥ ☻. ⚊ VISA. ⚘
    M 20.00 **t.** ⫯ 4.50 – **11 rm** ☲ 28.00/42.00 **t.**

☛ *Keine bezahlte Reklame im Michelin-Führer.*

TETBURY Glos. **403 404** N 29 Great Britain G. – pop. 4 467 – ECD : Thursday – ☎ 0666.

Envir. : Westonbirt Arboretum★ AC, SW : 2½ m. by A 433.

🏌 Westonbirt ℰ 066 88 (Westonbirt) 242, S : 3 m. off A 433.

🅱 The Old Court House, 63 Long St., GL8 8AA ℰ 503552 (summer only).

◆London 113 – ◆Bristol 27 – Gloucester 19 – Swindon 24.

🏨 **The Close,** 8 Long St., GL8 8AQ, ℰ 502272, Fax 504401, « 16C town house with walled
    garden » – ⇔ rest ▥ ☎ ☻ – ⚊ 35. ⚊ AE ◍ VISA. ⚘
    M 19.00/20.00 **t.** and a la carte ⫯ 10.30 – **15 rm** ☲ 75.00/145.00 **t.** – SB (except Christmas and New Year) 170.00/275.00 **st.**

🏠 Snooty Fox, Market Pl., GL8 8DD, ℰ 502436, Fax 503479 – ▥ ☎. ⚘
    12 rm.

✗✗ **Number Sixty Five,** 65 Long St., GL8 8AA, ℰ 503346 – ⚊ AE ◍ VISA
    M (dinner only and Sunday lunch)/dinner 19.85 **t.** and a la carte.

at Westonbirt SW : 2½ m. on A 433 – ✉ Tetbury – ☎ 0666 Westonbirt :

🏠 **Hare and Hounds** (Best Western), GL8 8QL, ℰ 880233, Fax 880241, ☞, ⚘, squash – ▥
    ☎ ☻ – ⚊ 150. ⚊ AE ◍ VISA JCB
    M (bar lunch Saturday) 12.75/25.00 **st.** and a la carte ⫯ 3.50 – **30 rm** ☲ 55.00/85.00 **st.** – SB 92.00/112.00 **st.**

at Willesley SW : 4 m. on A 433 – ✉ ☎ 0666 Tetbury :

🏡 **Tavern House** without rest., GL8 8QU, ℰ 880444, « Part 17C former inn and staging
    post », ☞ – ⇔ ▥ ☎ ☻. ⚊ VISA. ⚘
    4 rm ☲ 37.50/59.00.

at Calcot W : 3½ m. on A 4135 – ✉ ☎ 0666 Tetbury :

🏨 ⊛ **Calcot Manor** ⚘, GL8 8YJ, ℰ 890391, Fax 890394, « Converted Cotswold farm
    buildings », ⚓ heated, ☞ – ⇔ rest ▥ ☎ ☻. ⚊ AE ◍ VISA. ⚘
    closed 2 to 7 January – **M** 17.00/26.00 **st.** ⫯ 6.25 – ☲ 5.00 – **18 rm** 85.00/135.00 **st.** – SB (except Bank Holidays) 130.00/175.00 **st.**
    Spec. Roast pigeon breast and sausage with a wild mushroom and tomato dressing, Breast of chicken stuffed with Mediterranean vegetables, light herb sauce, A strudel of bananas, prunes and apricots with a rum and raisin ice cream.

TEWKESBURY Glos. **403 404** N 28 Great Britain G. – pop. 9 454 – ECD : Thursday – ☎ 0684.

See : Town★ – Abbey★★ (Nave★★, vault★).

Envir. : St. Mary's, Deerhurst★, SW : 4 m. by A 38 and B 4213.

🏌 Tewkesbury Park Hotel, Lincoln Green Lane ℰ 295405, S : ½ m. on A 38.

🅱 64 Barton St., GL20 5PX ℰ 295027.

◆London 108 – ◆Birmingham 39 – Gloucester 11.

🏨 **Tewkesbury Park H. Golf & Country Club,** Lincoln Green Lane, GL20 7DN, S :
    1¼ m. by A 38 ℰ 295405, Fax 292386, ≤, ⅃₆, ☎s, ⚊, 🏌, park, ⚘, squash – ⇔ rest ▥ ☎
    ☻ – ⚊ 150. ⚊ AE ◍ VISA. ⚘
    M (bar lunch Saturday) 11.75/19.00 **st.** and a la carte – **78 rm** ☲ 79.00/94.00 **st.** – SB (except Christmas, New Year and Bank Holidays) (weekends only) 118.00 **st.**

🏨 **Royal Hop Pole** (Forte), Church St., GL20 5RT, ℘ 293236, Fax 296680, 🌳 – 🚭 [TV] ☎ Ⓟ. [AE] ⓓ [VISA] [JCB]
M (bar lunch Monday to Saturday)/dinner 16.95 **st.** and a la carte 🍷 5.30 – ☕ 8.50 – **29 rm** 73.00/110.00 **st.** – SB (except Christmas and New Year) 108.00 **st.**

🏨 **Bell** (Best Western), Church St., GL20 5SA, ℘ 293293, Fax 295938 – 🚭 rest [TV] ☎ Ⓟ – 👥 45. [AE] ⓓ [VISA]. 🐕
M (bar lunch Monday to Saturday)/dinner 15.95 **t.** and a la carte 🍷 4.75 – **25 rm** ☕ 58.00/110.00 **st.**

🏨 **Jessop House,** 65 Church St., GL20 5RZ, ℘ 292017, Fax 273076 – [TV] ☎ Ⓟ. [VISA]. 🐕
closed 24 to 27 December – **M** *(closed Sunday)* (bar lunch)/dinner a la carte 11.90/20.75 **st.** 🍷 3.65 – **8 rm** ☕ 49.00/65.00 **st.** – SB 78.00 **st.**

🍴 **Bistrot André,** 78 Church St., GL20 5RX, ℘ 290357, 🌳 – [VISA]
closed February – **M** - **French** (closed Sunday) (dinner only) a la carte 12.95/21.75 **st.**

at Puckrup N : 2 ½ m. on A 38 – ✉ ☎ 0684 Tewkesbury :

🏨 **Puckrup Hall** 🔇, GL20 6EL, ℘ 296200, Fax 850788, ≤, 🏋, ≘s, 🏊, 🏌18, 🌳, park – 🛗 🚭 rm [TV] ☎ Ⓟ – 👥 200. [AE] ⓓ [VISA]
M a la carte 8.00/24.50 **t.** 🍷 4.25 – ☕ 7.50 – **82 rm** 69.50/79.50 **t.**, 2 suites – SB 65.00/150.00 **st.**

at Bredons Norton NE : 4 ¾ m. by B 4080 – ✉ ☎ 0684 Tewkesbury :

🏠 Home Farm, GL20 7HA, NE : ¾ m. taking right turn at village hall ℘ 72322, « Working farm », 🌳, park – 🚭 Ⓟ
3 rm.

at Corse Lawn SW : 6 m. by A 38 and A 438 on B 4211 – ✉ ☎ 0452 Gloucester :

🏨 **Corse Lawn House** 🔇, GL19 4LZ, ℘ 780479, Fax 780840, « Queen Anne house », 🏊 heated, 🌳, 🎾 – [TV] ☎ Ⓟ – 👥 40. [AE] ⓓ [VISA]
M – (see below) – **17 rm** ☕ 70.00/90.00 **st.**, 2 suites – SB (except Christmas) 125.00/170.00 **st.**

🍴🍴🍴 **Corse Lawn House,** GL19 4LZ, ℘ 780479, Fax 780840, 🌳 – Ⓟ. [AE] ⓓ [VISA]
M 17.95/23.50 **st.** and a la carte 🍷 3.50.

ATS Oldbury Rd ℘ 292461

THAME Oxon. [404] R 28 **The West Country G.** – pop. 8 300 – ECD : Wednesday – ☎ 0844.

Exc. : Ridgeway Path★★.

ℹ Town Hall, OX9 3DP ℘ 212834.

◆London 48 – Aylesbury 9 – ◆Oxford 13.

🏨 **Spread Eagle,** 16 Cornmarket, OX9 2BW, ℘ 213661, Fax 261380 – [TV] ☎ Ⓟ – 👥 250. [AE] ⓓ [VISA] [JCB]. 🐕
closed 28 to 30 December – **M** *(closed Bank Holiday lunch except Good Friday)* 18.50/20.50 **st.** and a la carte 🍷 4.50 – ☕ 6.95 – **33 rm** 65.95/85.95 **st.**, 2 suites – SB (except Christmas) 110.00/200.70 **st.**

🏨 **Essex House,** Chinnor Rd, OX9 3LS, ℘ 217567, Fax 216420 – 🚭 [TV] ☎ Ⓟ. [AE] ⓓ [VISA]. 🐕
M *(closed Sunday)* (dinner only) a la carte 13.50 **st.** – **13 rm** ☕ 41.00/56.00 **st.** – SB (weekends only) 83.00/118.00 **st.**

🍴🍴 **Thatchers,** 29-30 Lower High St., OX9 2ED, ℘ 212146, Fax 217413 – Ⓟ. [VISA]
closed Saturday lunch and Sunday – **M** 22.95 **t.** and a la carte 🍷 3.75.

at Towersey E : 2 m. by A 4129 – ✉ ☎ 0844 Thame :

🏠 **Upper Green Farm** 🔇 without rest., Manor Rd, OX9 3QR, ℘ 212496, Fax 260399, « Part 15C and 16C thatched farmhouse, 17C barn », 🌳 – 🚭 [TV] Ⓟ. 🐕
8 rm ☕ 28.00/50.00 **st.**

THATCHAM Berks. [403] [404] Q 29 – pop. 14 779 – ✉ Newbury ☎ 0635.

◆London 69 – ◆Bristol 68 – ◆Oxford 30 – Reading 15 – ◆Southampton 40.

🏨 **Regency Park,** Bowling Green Rd, RG13 3RP, NW : 1 ¾ m. by A 4 via Northfield Rd ℘ 871555, Fax 871571, 🌳 – 🛗 ▤ rest [TV] ☎ ♿ Ⓟ – 👥 60. [AE] ⓓ [VISA]
M 13.95/19.95 **st.** and a la carte 🍷 6.95 – ☕ 8.95 – **49 rm** 75.00/85.00 **st.**, 1 suite – SB (except Christmas and New Year) (weekends only) 90.00 **st.**

When visiting Great Britain,
use the ***Michelin Green Guide* "Great Britain".**

- *Detailed descriptions of places of interest*
- *Touring programmes*
- *Maps and street plans*
- *The history of the country*
- *Photographs and drawings of monuments, beauty spots, houses...*

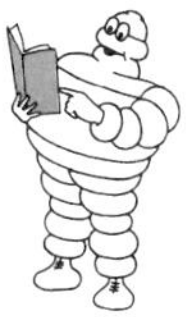

THAXTED Essex 404 V 28 – pop. 2 177 – ✪ 0371.

◆London 44 – ◆Cambridge 24 – Colchester 31 – Chelmsford 20.

🏠 **Four Seasons,** Walden Rd, CM6 2RE, NW : ½ m. on B 184 ℰ 830129, Fax 830835 – ✆
📺 ☎ 🅿. 🔌 🆎 𝗩𝗜𝗦𝗔. ✖
M *(closed dinner Sunday and Bank Holiday Mondays to non-residents)* a la carte 15.75/
23.50 **t.** 🍴 4.00 – **9 rm** ⊑ 50.00/65.00 **t.** – SB (except Christmas) 84.00/116.00 **st.**

🏠 **Farmhouse Inn,** Monk St., CM6 2NR, S : 1 ½ m. by B 184 ℰ 830864, Fax 831196 – 📺 ☎
🅿. 🔌 𝗩𝗜𝗦𝗔 ✖
M (in bar Sunday dinner and Monday to Wednesday) 12.20 **t.** and dinner a la carte 🍴 4.00 –
11 rm ⊑ 29.50/39.50 **t.** – SB (weekends only) 66.00/92.00 **st.**

↑ **Folly House,** Watling Lane, CM6 2QY, ℰ 830618, ≈ – 📺 🅿. ✖
M (by arrangement) (communal dining) 18.00 – **3 rm** ⊑ 20.00/40.00 **s.** – SB 50.00/70.00 **st.**

THELBRIDGE Devon 403 I 31 – ✉ ✪ 0884 Tiverton.

◆London 220 – Barnstaple 21 – Exeter 20 – Taunton 34.

🏠 **Thelbridge Cross Inn,** Thelbridge Cross, EX17 4SQ, on B 3042 ℰ 860316, Fax 860316,
≈ – ✆ rest 📺 ☎ 🅿. 🔌 🆔 𝗩𝗜𝗦𝗔 ✖
M *(closed 25 and 26 December)* a la carte 8.20/15.50 **st.** 🍴 4.75 – **8 rm** ⊑ 35.00/75.00 **st.**

THETFORD Norfolk 404 W 26 – pop. 19 591 – ECD : Wednesday – ✪ 0842.

◆London 83 – ◆Cambridge 32 – ◆Ipswich 33 – King's Lynn 30 – ◆Norwich 29.

🏨 **Bell** (Forte), King St., IP24 2AZ, ℰ 754455, Fax 755552 – ✆ rm 📺 ☎ 🅿 – 🔬 70. 🔌 🆎
🆔 𝗩𝗜𝗦𝗔 𝗝𝗖𝗕
M *(closed Saturday lunch)* 10.95/15.95 **st.** and a la carte 🍴 5.25 – ⊑ 8.50 – **46 rm** 70.00/
80.00 **st.**, 1 suite – SB 98.00/112.00 **st.**

🏠 **The Historical Thomas Paine** (Best Western), 33 White Hart St., IP24 1AA, ℰ 755631,
Fax 766505 – 📺 ☎ 🅿. 🔌 🆔 𝗩𝗜𝗦𝗔 𝗝𝗖𝗕 ✖
M *(closed Saturday lunch)* 10.75/15.50 and a la carte 🍴 4.75 – **13 rm** ⊑ 47.00/60.00 **t.**

↑ **Wilderness** without rest., Earls St., IP24 2AF, ℰ 764646, ≈ – ✆ 📺 🅿. ✖
4 rm ⊑ 18.00/34.00.

🔧 ATS Canterbury Way ℰ 755529

THIRSK N. Yorks. 402 P 21 – pop. 7 174 – ECD : Wednesday – ✪ 0845.

🔧 Thornton-Le-Street ℰ 522170, N : 2 m.

🔲 14 Kirkgate, YO7 1PQ ℰ 522755 (summer only).

◆London 227 – ◆Leeds 37 – ◆Middlesbrough 24 – York 24.

↑ St. James House without rest., 36 The Green, YO7 1AQ, ℰ 524120, ≈ – ✆ 📺. ✖
4 rm.

↑ **Brook House** without rest., Ingramgate, YO7 1DD, ℰ 522240, Fax 523133, ≈ – 📺 🅿.
✖
closed 2 weeks Christmas-New Year – **3 rm** ⊑ 24.00/32.00 **s.**

↑ **Thornborough House Farm,** South Kilvington, YO7 2NP, N : 2 m. by A 19 ℰ 522103,
≈ – ✆ 📺 🅿. 🔌 𝗩𝗜𝗦𝗔
M (communal dining) 7.50 **st.** – **3 rm** ⊑ 13.00/34.00 **st.** – SB (late October-mid March)
24.00/30.00 **st.**

at Asenby SW : 5¼ m. by A 19 off A 168 – ✉ ✪ 0845 Thirsk :

✗ **Crab and Lobster,** YO7 3QL, ℰ 577286, ≈ – 🅿. 🔌 🆎 𝗩𝗜𝗦𝗔
closed Sunday dinner – **M** - **Seafood** (booking essential) 12.95 **t.** (lunch) and a la
carte 14.95/24.95 **t.** 🍴 4.00.

at Sowerby S : ½ m. – ✉ ✪ 0845 Thirsk :

🏠 **Sheppard's,** Front St., YO7 1JF, ℰ 523655, Fax 524720 – ✆ rm 📺 ☎ 🅿. 🔌 𝗩𝗜𝗦𝗔 ✖
closed first week January – **M** (bar lunch) a la carte 13.45/21.50 **t.** 🍴 5.15 – **8 rm** ⊑ 55.00/
84.00 **t.**

🔧 ATS Long St. ℰ 522982/522923

THORALBY N. Yorks. 402 N/O 21 – pop. 143 – ✉ Leyburn – ✪ 0969 Wensleydale.

◆London 245 – Kendal 41 – ◆Leeds 64 – York 57.

↑ **Littleburn** ⏚, DL8 3BE, W : ½ m. via unmarked lane ℰ 663621, ≤, ≈ – ✆ 🅿
M (by arrangement) (communal dining) 17.00 **st.** 🍴 3.00 – **3 rm** ⊑ 38.00/56.00 **st.**

THORNABY-ON-TEES Cleveland 402 Q 20 – pop. 26 319 – ✉ ✪ 0642 Middlesbrough.

🔧 Tees-Side, Acklam Rd ℰ 676249.

◆London 250 – ◆Leeds 62 – ◆Middlesbrough 3 – York 49.

🏨 **Forte Posthouse,** Low Lane, Stainton Village, TS17 9LW, SE : 3 ½ m. by A 1045 on
A 1044 ℰ 591213, Fax 594989, ☞ – ✆ rm 📺 ☎ 🅿 – 🔬 100. 🔌 🆎 🆔 𝗩𝗜𝗦𝗔
M a la carte approx. 17.50 **t.** 🍴 4.65 – ⊑ 6.95 – **135 rm** 53.50 **st.** – SB 90.00 **st.**

THORNBURY Avon `403` `404` M 29 – pop. 11 948 – ECD : Thursday – ✉ Bristol – ☎ 0454.

◆London 128 – ◆Bristol 12 – Gloucester 23 – Swindon 43.

🏰 **Thornbury Castle** ⟨⟩, Castle St., BS12 1HH, ℰ 281182, Fax 416188, « 16C castle, gardens », park – ⥥ rest ☎ ☎ ℗. ⚠ AE Ⓞ VISA ⟨⟩
closed 3 days January – **M** 33.00 **t.** (dinner) and a la carte ⁙ 7.00 – �☞ 8.95 – **17 rm** 90.00/ 205.00 **t.**, 1 suite – SB (November-March) 198.00/208.00 **st.**

THORNTHWAITE Cumbria `402` K 20 – see Keswick.

THORNTON CLEVELEYS Lancs. `402` L 22 – pop. 26 615 – ☎ 0253 Blackpool.

◆London 244 – ◆Blackpool 6 – Lancaster 20 – ◆Manchester 44.

XX **Victorian House** with rm, Trunnah Rd, FY5 4HF, ℰ 860619, Fax 865350, « Victoriana », ⟨⟩ – ☎ ☎ ℗. ⚠ VISA
closed last week January-first week February – **M** *(closed Monday lunch and Sunday)* 19.95 **st.** and lunch a la carte ⁙ 6.50 – **3 rm** �☞ 49.50/70.00 **st.**

THORPE Derbs. `402` `403` `404` O 24 Great Britain G. – pop. 227 – ✉ Ashbourne – ☎ 033 529 (3 fig.) and 0335 (5 fig.) Thorpe Cloud.

See : Dovedale★★ (Ilam Rock★).

◆London 151 – Derby 16 – ◆Sheffield 33 – ◆Stoke-on-Trent 26.

🏰 **Peveril of the Peak** (Forte) ⟨⟩, DE6 2AW, ℰ 333, Fax 507, ≼, ⟨⟩, ⟨⟩ – ⥥ ☎ ☎ ℗ – ⚿ 60. ⚠ AE Ⓞ VISA
M (bar lunch Monday to Saturday)/dinner 16.95 **st.** and a la carte ⁙ 6.45 – **47 rm** ⟨⟩ 70.00/ 85.00 **st.** – SB 116.00 **st.**

Plans de ville : Les rues sont sélectionnées en fonction de leur importance pour la circulation et le repérage des établissements cités.

Les rues secondaires ne sont qu'amorcées.

THORPE MARKET Norfolk `404` X 25 – pop. 221 – ✉ North Walsham – ☎ 0263 Southrepps.

◆London 130 – ◆Norwich 21.

🏠 **Green Farm,** North Walsham Rd, NR11 8TH, ℰ 833602 – ☎ ☎ ℗. ⚠ AE Ⓞ VISA
M (bar lunch)/dinner 16.95 **st.** and a la carte ⁙ 4.25 – **7 rm** ⟨⟩ 45.00/65.00 **t.** – SB (except Christmas and New Year) 79.00/122.00 **st.**

🏠 **Elderton Lodge** ⟨⟩, Cromer Rd, NR11 8TZ, S : 1 m. on A 149 ℰ 833547, ⟨⟩ – ☎ ☎ ℗. ⚠ AE Ⓞ VISA
closed 25 and 26 December – **M** 14.50 **t.** and a la carte ⁙ 4.00 – **7 rm** ⟨⟩ 33.00/48.00 **t.**

THORPE ST. ANDREW Norfolk `404` Y 26 – see Norwich.

THRAPSTON SERVICE AREA Northants. `404` S 26 – ✉ Kettering – ☎ 0832 Thrapston

🏠 **Forte Travelodge** without rest., NN14 4UR, at junction of A 14 with A 605 ℰ 735199, Reservations (Freephone) 0800 850950 – ☎ ੬ ℗. ⚠ AE VISA
40 rm 31.95 **t.**

THREE BRIDGES W. Sussex – see Crawley.

THRELKELD Cumbria `402` K 20 – see Keswick.

THRESHFIELD N. Yorks. `402` N 21 – see Grassington.

THRUSSINGTON Leics. `402` `403` `404` Q 25 – see Leicester.

THURLESTONE Devon `403` I 33 – see Kingsbridge.

THURROCK SERVICE AREA Essex `404` V 29 – ✉ West Thurrock – ☎ 0708 Purfleet.

🛏 Belhus Park, South Ockendon ℰ 854260, N : 1 m. by A 13 at junction with M 25.

🍴 Granada Motorway Service Area (M 25), RM16 3BG ℰ 863733.

🏠 **Granada Lodge** without rest., RM16 3BG, ℰ 891111, Fax 860971, Reservations (Freephone) 0800 555300 – ☎ ⥥ ☎ ੬ ℗. ⚠ AE VISA ⟨⟩
⟨⟩ 4.00 – **44 rm** 43.95/46.95 **st.**

⦿ ATS Units 13/14, Eastern Av., Waterglade Ind. Park, Grays, West Thurrock ℰ 862237

TICEHURST E. Sussex `404` V 30 – ✉ Wadhurst – ☎ 0580.

🛏 Dale Hill, Ticehurst ℰ 200112.

🏰 **Dale Hill Golf H.,** TN5 7DQ, NE : ½ m. on A 268 ℰ 200112, Fax 201249, ⛳, ⟨⟩, ⟨⟩, 🛏, park – ☎ ☎ ੬ ℗ – ⚿ 30. ⚠ VISA
M 20.00 **t.** and a la carte ⁙ 5.00 – ⟨⟩ 3.00 – **24 rm** 40.00/80.00 **t.**, 1 suite – SB 130.00/ 180.00 **st.**

TICKTON Humbs. – see Beverley.

TILSTON Ches. `402` `403` L 24 – see Malpas.

Cornwall **403** F 32 The West Country G. – pop. 1 566 – ECD : Wednesday except summer – 🕓 0840 Camelford.

See : Arthur's Castle (site★★★) *AC* – Tintagel Church★ – Old Post Office★ *AC*.

Envir. : Delabole Quarry★ *AC*, SE : 4½ m. by B 3263.

Exc. : Camelford★, SE : 6½ m. by B 3263 and B 3266.

◆London 264 – Exeter 63 – ◆Plymouth 49 – Truro 41.

🏠 **Wootons Country**, Fore St., PL34 0DD, 🖋 770170, Fax 770978 – 📺 ☎ 🅿. 🖂 ⓞ 🆅🆂🆀. 🛠
  M (bar lunch)/dinner 10.50 **st.** and a la carte 🍴 2.50 – **11 rm** ⇌ 27.50/59.00 **st.** – SB (October-May) (except Bank Holidays) 60.00/70.00 **st.**

🏠 **Trebrea Lodge** ⚓, Trenale, PL34 0HR, SE : 1 m. by Boscastle Rd (B 3263) and Trenale Lane on Trewarmett rd 🖋 770410, ≼, « Part 18C manor house, 14C origins », 🖉 – ↜ 📺 ☎ 🅿. 🖂 🆅🆂🆀
  M (dinner only) 14.75 **t.** 🍴 3.75 – **7 rm** ⇌ 48.00/68.00 **t.** – SB 87.50/125.50 **st.**

🏠 **Bossiney House**, Bossiney Rd, PL34 0AX, NE : ½ m. on B 3263 🖋 770240, Fax 770501, ≘s, 🏊, 🖉 – ↜ 📺 ☎ 🅿. 🖂 ⓞ 🛠
  Easter-October – **M** (bar lunch)/dinner 9.00/15.00 **t.** 🍴 4.50 – **19 rm** ⇌ 29.00/48.00 **t.** – SB (except July-August and Bank Holidays) 68.00/82.00 **st.**

🕐 **Trowarmett Lodge**, Trewarmett, PL34 0ET, S : 1½ m. on B 3263 🖋 770460 – ↜ rm 🅿. 🖂 🆅🆂🆀
  15 March-24 October – **M** (bar lunch)/dinner 12.50 **st.** and a la carte 🍴 4.60 – **6 rm** ⇌ 16.00/36.00 **st.** – SB (except June-August) 52.00/58.00 **st.**

🕐 **Old Millfloor** ⚓, Trebarwith, PL34 0HA, S : 1¾ m. by B 3263 🖋 770234, « Former flour mill », 🖉, park – ↜ 📺 🅿. 🛠
  Easter-October – **M** (by arrangement) 11.00 – **3 rm** ⇌ 16.00/32.00.

🕐 **Old Borough House**, Bossiney Rd, PL34 0AY, NE : ½ m. on B 3263 🖋 770475 – ↜ rest 🅿. 🛠
  M (by arrangement) 10.00 – **5 rm** ⇌ 28.00/42.00 – SB 49.00/80.00 **st.**

Beds. **404** S 28 – pop. 4218 – ✉ Luton – 🕓 0525.

🏨 **Granada Lodge** without rest., LU5 6HR, M 1 junction 12 (southbound carriageway) 🖋 875150, Fax 878452, Reservations (Freephone) 0800 555300 – ↜ 📺 ♿ 🅿. 🖂 🆅🆂🆀. 🛠
  ⇌ 4.00 – **40 rm** 34.95/37.95 **st.**

Lancs. **402 403** N 22 – pop. 11 894 – 🕓 0706.

🅿 15 Burnley Rd, OL14 7BU 🖋 818181.

◆London 228 – Burnley 9 – ◆Leeds 29 – ◆Manchester 20.

🏨 **Scaitcliffe**, Burnley Rd, OL14 7DQ, NW : 1¼ m. on A 646 🖋 818194, Fax 818825, « Part 17C country house », 🖉, park – 📺 ☎ 🅿 – 🔬 200. 🖂 🆎 ⓞ 🆅🆂🆀
  M 14.95 **st.** and a la carte 🍴 6.95 – **13 rm** ⇌ 53.50/89.95 **st.** – SB 98.45/108.75 **st.**

S. Yorks. – pop. 1 661 – ✉ Sheffield – 🕓 0909 Worksop.

◆London 161 – ◆Nottingham 35 – ◆Sheffield 10.

🏨 Red Lion, Worksop Rd, S31 0DJ, on A 57 🖋 771654, Telex 54120, Fax 773704 – ↜ rm 📺 ☎ ♿ 🅿 – 🔬 70. 🛠
  29 rm.

Kent **404** U 30 – pop. 34 407 – ECD : Wednesday – 🕓 0732.

🖌 Poult Wood, Higham Lane 🖋 364039, N : 2 m. by A 227.

🅿 Tonbridge Castle, Castle St., TN9 1BG 🖋 770929.

◆London 33 – ◆Brighton 37 – Hastings 31 – Maidstone 14.

🏨 **Rose and Crown** (Forte), 125 High St., TN9 1DD, 🖋 357966, Fax 357194 – ↜ rm 📺 ☎ 🅿 – 🔬 80. 🖂 🆎 ⓞ 🆅🆂🆀 🅹🅲🅱
  M (bar lunch Monday to Saturday)/dinner 17.95 **t.** and a la carte 🍴 6.25 – ⇌ 9.50 – **50 rm** 65.00/100.00 **st.** – SB (weekends only) 90.00/98.00 **st.**

🍴 **The Office**, 163 High St., TN9 1BX, 🖋 353660 – 🖂 🆎 ⓞ 🆅🆂🆀 🅹🅲🅱
  closed Sunday, 3 days at Christmas and Bank Holidays – **M** a la carte 11.60/13.70 **t.**

at Golden Green NE : 4 m. by Three Elm Lane off A 26 – ✉ Tonbridge – 🕓 0732 Hadlow :

🏠 **Goldhill Mill** ⚓ without rest., TN11 0BA, 🖋 851626, Fax 851881, « Part Tudor and Georgian water mill », 🖉, park, 🎾 – ↜ 📺 ☎ 🅿. 🖂 🆅🆂🆀. 🛠
  closed 20 July-31 August and Christmas Day – **3 rm** ⇌ 55.00/70.00 **st.**

🔧 ATS 61/63 Pembury Rd 🖋 353800/352231

Devon **403** J 33 – see Kingsbridge.

☞ *When in a hurry use the Michelin Main Road Maps :*
     970 Europe, **980** Greece, **984** Germany, **985** Scandinavia-Finland,
     986 Great Britain and Ireland, **987** Germany-Austria-Benelux, **988** Italy,
     989 France, **990** Spain-Portugal and **991** Yugoslavia.

See : Torbay★ – Kent's Cavern★ *AC* CX **A**.

Envir. : Cockington★, W : 1 m. AX.

ⓝ Petitor Rd, St. Marychurch ℰ 314591, NE : 2 m. by A 379 B.

🅱 Vaughan Parade, TQ2 5JG ℰ 297428.

◆London 223 – Exeter 23 – ◆Plymouth 32.

Plans on following pages

🏩 **Imperial** (Forte), Parkhill Rd, TQ1 2DG, ℰ 294301, Telex 42849, Fax 298293, ≤ Torbay, *ƒ6*, 全s, ⊒ heated, ⊠, ☞, ✗, squash – ⫴ ⇆ rm ▤ rest ⓣⱽ ☎ ♿ ⇦ ⓟ – 🚗 350. ◩ CZ **a** ⓞ 𝚅𝙸𝚂𝙰
M 16.00/29.00 **st.** and a la carte ⬧ 6.75 – **150 rm** ☲ 85.00/160.00 **st.**, 17 suites – SB 198.00 **st.**

🏩 **Grand**, Seafront, TQ2 6NT, ℰ 296677, Fax 213462, ≤, *ƒ6*, 全s, ⊒ heated, ⊠, ✗ – ⫴ ⓣⱽ BZ **z** ☎ ⇦ – 🚗 300. ◩ 𝙰𝙴 ⓞ 𝚅𝙸𝚂𝙰
M (dancing Saturday evening) 13.50/18.50 **st.** and a la carte – **101 rm** ☲ 65.00/140.00 **st.**, 11 suites – SB 100.00/170.00 **st.**

🏩 **Palace**, Babbacombe Rd, TQ1 3TG, ℰ 200200, Fax 299899, « Extensive gardens », 全s, ⊒ heated, ⊠, ⲧ5, park, ✗, squash – ⫴ ⓣⱽ ☎ ⇦ ⓟ – 🚗 300. ◩ ⓞ 𝚅𝙸𝚂𝙰 ✗ CX **u**
M 12.50/18.50 **t.** and a la carte ⬧ 7.00 – **134 rm** ☲ 45.00/90.00 **t.**, 6 suites – SB (except Easter and Christmas-New Year) 99.00/119.00 **st.**

🏡 **Corbyn Head**, Seafront, TQ2 6RH, ℰ 213611, Fax 296152, ≤, ⊒ heated – ⓣⱽ ☎ ⓟ. ◩ 𝙰𝙴 BX **a** ⓞ 𝚅𝙸𝚂𝙰
M (bar lunch)/dinner 15.00/30.00 **t.** ⬧ 4.50 – **51 rm** ☲ 33.00/120.00 **t.** – SB 80.00/ 120.00 **st.**

🏡 **Osborne**, Hesketh Cres., Meadfoot, TQ1 2LL, ℰ 213311, Fax 296788, ≤, ⊒ heated, ⊠, ☞, ✗ – ⫴ ⓣⱽ ☎ ⓟ – 🚗 70. ◩ 𝙰𝙴 ⓞ 𝚅𝙸𝚂𝙰 ✗ CX **n**
M – **Raffles** (in bar) a la carte 11.15/18.70 **st.** ⬧ 5.25 – (see also **Langtry's** below) – **23 rm** ☲ 55.00/158.00 **st.** – SB 198.00/240.00 **st.**

🏡 **Abbey Lawn**, Scarborough Rd, TQ2 5UQ, ℰ 299199, Fax 291460, ≤, *ƒ6*, 全s, ⊒ heated, ⊠, ✗ – ⫴ ⓣⱽ ☎ ⓟ – 🚗 80. ◩ 𝙰𝙴 ⓞ 𝚅𝙸𝚂𝙰 CY **c**
M (bar lunch)/dinner 11.95 **st.** and a la carte ⬧ 4.80 – **54 rm** ☲ 35.00/70.00 **st.**, 1 suite – SB (except Bank Holidays) 79.00 **st.**

🏡 **Livermead Cliff** (Best Western), Seafront, TQ2 6RQ, ℰ 299666, Telex 42424, Fax 294496, ≤, ⊒ heated, ☞ – ⫴ ⓣⱽ ☎ ⓟ – 🚗 70. ◩ 𝙰𝙴 ⓞ 𝚅𝙸𝚂𝙰 ✗ BX **r**
M 8.50/16.75 **st.** and a la carte ⬧ 5.20 – **64 rm** ☲ 34.00/110.00 **st.** – SB (except Christmas and New Year) 72.00/89.00 **st.**

🏡 **Livermead House** (Best Western), Seafront, TQ2 6QJ, ℰ 294361, Fax 200758, ≤, 全s, ⊒ heated, ☞, ✗, squash – ⫴ ⓣⱽ ☎ ⓟ – 🚗 80. ◩ 𝙰𝙴 ⓞ 𝚅𝙸𝚂𝙰 BZ **e**
M 9.50/20.00 **st.** and a la carte ⬧ 4.95 – **64 rm** ☲ 40.00/110.00 **st.** – SB (except July-September and Bank Holidays) 70.00/84.00 **st.**

🏠 **Homers,** Warren Rd, TQ2 5TN, ℰ 213456, Fax 213458, ≤ Torbay, ☞ – ⇆ rest ⓣⱽ ☎. ◩ 𝙰𝙴 ⓞ 𝚅𝙸𝚂𝙰 CZ **n**
M (lunch by arrangement Saturday and Sunday) (bar lunch)/dinner 28.00 **st.** and a la carte ⬧ 4.50 – **13 rm** ☲ 36.00/98.00 **st.**, 1 suite – SB (except Easter and Christmas) 98.00/ 156.00 **st.**

🏠 **Albaston House**, 27 St. Marychurch Rd, TQ1 3JF, ℰ 296758 – ⓣⱽ ☎ ⓟ. ◩ ⓞ 𝚅𝙸𝚂𝙰 𝙹𝙲𝙱
closed 5 December-5 January – **M** 6.00/10.00 **st.** and a la carte ⬧ 3.00 – **13 rm** ☲ 25.00/ 50.00 **st.** CY **a**

🏠 **Fairmount House**, Herbert Rd, Chelston, TQ2 6RW, ℰ 605446, Fax 605446, ☞ – ⇆ rest ⓣⱽ ⓟ. ◩ 𝙰𝙴 𝚅𝙸𝚂𝙰 AX **a**
March-October – **M** *(closed Sunday dinner)* (bar lunch)/dinner 11.00 **t.** ⬧ 4.10 – **8 rm** ☲ 27.50/55.00 **t.** – SB (except summer and Bank Holidays) 69.00/73.00 **st.**

🛏 **Glenorleigh**, 26 Cleveland Rd, TQ2 5BE, ℰ 292135, Fax 292135, ⊒ heated, ☞ – ⇆ rest ⓟ. ◩ 𝚅𝙸𝚂𝙰 ✗ BY **n**
10 January-mid October – **M** (by arrangement) ⬧ 4.00 – **16 rm** ☲ 18.00/50.00 **st.**

🛏 **Cranborne**, 58 Belgrave Rd, TQ2 5HY, ℰ 298046 – ⇆ rest ⓣⱽ. ◩ 𝚅𝙸𝚂𝙰 ✗ BY **i**
closed Christmas-New Year – **M** (by arrangement) – **12 rm** ☲ 17.00/44.00 **t.** – SB (except Easter) 44.00/47.00 **st.**

🛏 **Belmont**, 66 Belgrave Rd, TQ2 5HY, ℰ 295028, Fax 295028 – ⓣⱽ ⓟ. ◩ 𝙰𝙴 ⓞ 𝚅𝙸𝚂𝙰 BY
M 10.00 **st.** ⬧ 3.00 – **13 rm** ☲ 14.00/50.00 **st.** – SB (October-June) 44.00/52.00 **st.**

✗✗ **Langtry's** (at Osborne H.), Hesketh Cres., Meadfoot, TQ1 2LL, ℰ 213311, Fax 296788, ≤ – ⇆ ⓟ. ◩ 𝙰𝙴 ⓞ 𝚅𝙸𝚂𝙰
M (dinner only) a la carte 20.75/27.75 **st.** ⬧ 5.25. CX **n**

✗✗ **Remy's**, 3 Croft Rd, TQ2 5UF, ℰ 292359 – ◩ 𝚅𝙸𝚂𝙰 CY **x**
closed Sunday and Monday – **M** - **French** (booking essential) (lunch by arrangement)/ dinner 15.85 **st.** ⬧ 5.00.

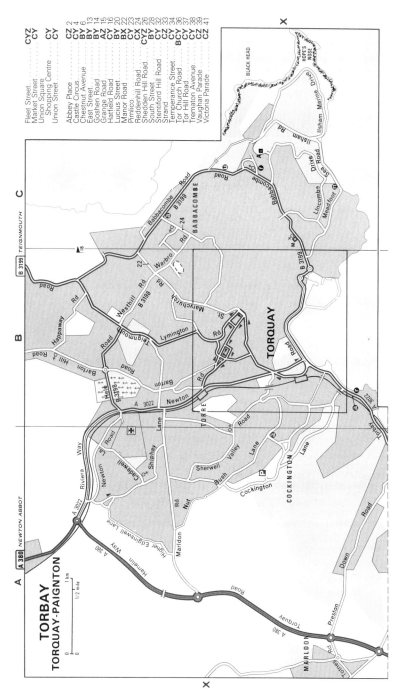

TORBAY
TORQUAY-PAIGNTON

Fleet Street	CYZ	
Market Street	CY	
Union Square Shopping Centre	CY	
Union Street	CY	
Abbey Place	CZ	2
Castle Circus	CY	4
Chestnut Avenue	BY	6
East Street	BY	13
Goshen Road	BY	14
Grange Road	AZ	15
Hatfield Road	BY	16
Lucius Street	BY	20
Manor Road	BX	22
Pimlico	CX	23
Reddenhill Road	CX	26
Sheldon Hill Road	CY	26
South Street	BY	28
Strentford Hill Road	CZ	32
Strand	CZ	33
Temperance Street	CZ	34
Tor Church Road	BCY	36
Tor Hill Road	CY	37
Trematon Avenue	CY	38
Vaughan Parade	CZ	39
Victoria Parade	CZ	41

492

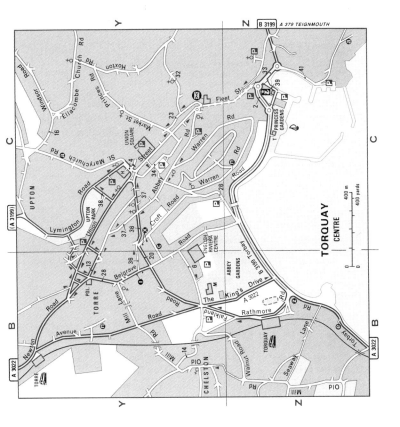

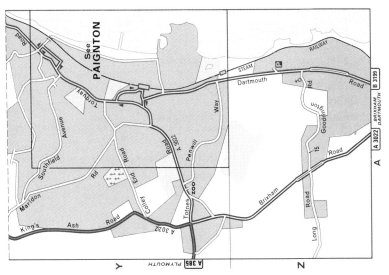

X **Mulberry Room** with rm, 1 Scarborough Rd, TQ2 5UJ, ✆ 213639 – 📺 . ❀ CY **x**
M *(closed Monday and Tuesday to non-residents)* a la carte 7.00/15.50 **st.** 🍴 5.00 – **3 rm**
� 25.00/37.00 **st.** – SB (Wednesday-Thursday and weekends only) 55.00/83.00 **st.**

X **Village Brasserie,** 5 Ilsham Rd, Wellswood, TQ1 2JG, ✆ 290855 – 🔌 🗚 🏧 CX **r**
closed Saturday lunch and Sunday except lunch November-March – **M** a la carte 9.65/
16.65 **t.** 🍴 3.75.

at Maidencombe N : 3 ½ m. by B 3199 – BX – ⊠ ✆ 0803 Torquay :

🏨 **Orestone Manor** ⪼, Rockhouse Lane, TQ1 4SX, ✆ 328098, Fax 328336, ≼, ⊒ heated,
⪼ – ≼⪼ rest 📺 ☎ 🅿. 🔌 🗚 ◉ 🗚 . ❀
closed January – **M** (dinner only and Sunday lunch)/dinner 29.50 **st.** and a la carte 🍴 4.50 –
18 rm ⊠ 110.00/190.00 **st.** – SB (November-April) 70.00/180.00 **st.**

at Babbacombe NE : 1 ½ m. – ⊠ ✆ 0803 Torquay :

XX **Table,** 135 Babbacombe Rd, TQ1 3SR, ✆ 324292 – 🔌 🗚 CX **a**
closed Monday, 1 to 18 February and 1 to 18 September – **Meals** (booking essential) (dinner
only) 26.00/28.00 **t.** 🍴 5.00.

◎ ATS 20 Tor Church Rd ✆ 293985 　　　　ATS 100 Teignmouth Rd ✆ 329495

TORVER Cumbria 402 K 20 – see Coniston.

TOTLAND BAY I.O.W. 403 404 P 31 – see Wight (Isle of).

TOTNES Devon 403 I 32 The West Country G. – pop. 6 133 – ECD : Thursday – ✆ 0803.
See : Town★ – St. Mary's★ – Butterwalk★ – Castle (≼★★★) *AC.*
Envir. : Paignton Zoo★★ *AC,* E : 4 ½ m. by A 385 and A 3022 – British Photographic Museum,
Bowden House★ *AC,* S : 1 m. by A 381.
Exc. : Dartmouth★★ (Castle ≼★★★) SE : 12 m. by A 381 and A 3122.
🏌8, 🏌9 Dartmouth Golf & C C, Blackawton ✆ 421686, NE : 4 m. by A 3122.
🛈 The Plains, TQ9 5EJ ✆ 863168.
◆London 224 – Exeter 24 – ◆Plymouth 23 – Torquay 9.

⌂ **Old Forge at Totnes** without rest., Seymour Pl., TQ9 5AY, ✆ 862174, « 14C working
forge », 🞮 – ≼⪼ 📺 🅿 🗚 . ❀
10 rm ⊠ 32.00/60.00 **st.**

at Stoke Gabriel SE : 4 m. by A 385 – ⊠ ✆ 0803 Totnes :

🏨 **Gabriel Court** ⪼, TQ9 6SF, ✆ 782206, Fax 782333, ⊒ heated, 🞮 – 📺 ☎ 🅿. 🔌 🗚 ◉
🗚
M (dinner only and Sunday lunch)/dinner 25.00 **t.** 🍴 4.85 – **20 rm** ⊠ 46.00/75.00 **st.**

at Ashprington S : 3 ½ m. by A 381 – ⊠ ✆ 0803 Totnes :

🏠 **Waterman's Arms,** Bow Bridge, TQ9 7EG, ✆ 732214, Fax 732214, « Part 15C inn », 🞮
– 📺 ☎ 🅿. 🔌 🗚
M (bar lunch Monday to Saturday)/dinner a la carte 10.65/18.20 **t.** – **10 rm** ⊠ 33.50/64.00.

at Tuckenhay S : 4 ¼ m. by A 381 – ⊠ ✆ 0803 Totnes :

XX **Floyd's Inn (sometimes)** with rm, Bow Creek, TQ9 7EQ, ✆ 732350, Fax 732651, ≼,
« Riverside setting » – 📺 ☎ 🅿. 🔌 🗚
Meals – **Restaurant** *(closed Saturday lunch Sunday dinner and Tuesday)* 28.00/42.50 **t.** –
3 rm 100.00/175.00 **t.**
X **The Canteen** – **M** (in bar) 15.50 **t.** and a la carte approx. 16.00 **t.**

◎ ATS Babbage Rd ✆ 862086

TOTON Notts. 402 403 404 Q 25 – see Nottingham.

TOTTENHILL Norfolk – see King's Lynn.

TOWCESTER Northants. 403 404 R 27 – pop. 5 010 – ✆ 0327.
🏌8, 🏌8, 🏌9 West Park G. & C.C., Whittlebury, Towcester ✆ 858092, S : 4 m. on A 413 – 🏌8
Farthingstone Hotel ✆ 36645, W : 4 m.
◆London 70 – ◆Birmingham 50 – Northampton 9 – ◆Oxford 36.

🏨 **Saracens Head,** 219 Watling St., NN12 7BX, ✆ 50414, Fax 359879 – 📺 ☎ 🅿 – 🛎 30. 🔌
🗚 ◉ 🗚 . ❀
M 5.50/14.50 **t.** and a la carte – **21 rm** ⊠ 45.00/65.00 **st.**

🏠 **Forte Travelodge** without rest., East Towcester bypass, NN12 0DD, SW : ½ m. by
Brackley rd on A 43 ✆ 359105, Reservations (Freephone) 0800 850950 – 📺 ⅊ 🅿. 🔌 🗚
🗚 . ❀
33 rm 31.95 **t.**

at Paulerspury SE : 3 ¼ m. by A 5 – ⊠ Towcester – ✆ 032 733 Paulerspury :

XX **Vine House** with rm, 100 High St., NN12 7NA, ✆ 267, Fax 309, 🞮 – 📺 ☎ 🅿. 🔌 🗚 . ❀
Meals *(closed Monday and Saturday lunch and Sunday)* a la carte 13.95/23.50 **t.** 🍴 4.40 –
6 rm ⊠ 38.80/61.10 **st.**

TOWERSEY Oxon. 404 R 28 – see Thame.

TREGONY Cornwall 🔲 F 33 The West Country G. – pop. 670 – ✉ Truro – 🕿 087 253.

Envir. : Trewithen★★★ *AC*, N : 2½ m.

◆London 291 – Newquay 18 – Plymouth 53 – Truro 10.

⌂ **Tregony House,** 15 Fore St., TR2 5RN, 🖉 671, 🍽 – ✑ rest 🅿. 🌮
March-October – **6 rm** 🖵 (dinner included) 28.75/63.50.

TREGREHAN Cornwall 🔲 F 32 – see St. Austell.

TRERICE Cornwall 🔲 E 32 – see Newquay.

TRESCO Cornwall 🔲 ⑳ – see Scilly (Isles of).

TREYARNON BAY Cornwall 🔲 E 32 – see Padstow.

TRING Herts. 🔲 S 28 – pop. 10 610 – ECD : Wednesday – 🕿 0442.

◆London 38 – Aylesbury 7 – Luton 14.

🏨 **Pendley Manor** 🌮, Cow Lane, HP23 5QY, E : 1½ m. by A 4251 and A 41 🖉 891891, Fax 890687, ≼, 🍽, park, 🎾 ⚘ ⚘ 🅿 – 🔬 200. 🔼 🄰🄴 ⓪ 𝘝𝘐𝘚𝘈
M 16.00/22.50 **st.** and a la carte ⎍ 5.50 – **71 rm** 🖵 85.00/125.00 **t.** – SB 100.00/170.00 **t.**

🏨 **Rose and Crown,** High St., HP23 5AH, 🖉 824071, Fax 890735 – ✑ rm 🕿 🅿 – 🔬 70. 🔼 🄰🄴 ⓪ 𝘝𝘐𝘚𝘈 🌮
M (bar lunch Saturday) 9.95/15.95 **t.** and a la carte ⎍ 5.00 – **27 rm** 🖵 59.50/95.00 **t.** – SB (weekends only) 90.00 **st.**

🏠 **Travel Inn,** Tring Hill, HP23 4LD, W : 1½ m. on A 41 🖉 824819, Fax 890787 – ✑ rm 🖵 ⚘ 🅿. 🔼 🄰🄴 ⓪ 𝘝𝘐𝘚𝘈 🌮
closed 24 to 26 December – **M** (Beefeater grill) a la carte approx. 16.00 **t.** – 🖵 4.95 – **30 rm** 33.50 **t.**

Se cercate un albergo tranquillo,
oltre a consultare le carte dell'introduzione,
rintracciate nell'elenco degli esercizi quelli con il simbolo 🌮 o 🌮

TROTTON W. Sussex – see Midhurst.

TROUTBECK Cumbria 🔲 L 20 – see Windermere.

TROWBRIDGE Wilts. 🔲 🔲 N 30 The West Country G. – pop. 27 299 – ECD : Wednesday – 🕿 0225.

Envir. : Westwood Manor★, NW : 3 m. by A 363 – Farleigh Hungerford Castle★ (St. Leonard's Chapel★) *AC*, W : 4 m.

Exc. : Longleat House★★★ *AC*, SW : 12 m. by A 363, A 350 and A 362 - Bratton Castle (≼★★) SE : 7½ m. by A 363 and B 3098 – Steeple Ashton★ (The Green★) E : 6 m. – Edington (St. Mary, St. Katherine and All Saints★) SE : 7½ m.

🛈 St. Stephen's Pl., BA14 8AH 🖉 777054.

◆London 115 – ◆Bristol 27 – ◆Southampton 55 – Swindon 32.

🏠 **Old Manor** 🌮, Trowle, BA14 9BL, NW : 1 m. on A 363 🖉 777393, Fax 765443, « Queen Anne house of 15C origins », 🍽 – ✑ rm 🖵 🕿 🅿. 🔼 🄰🄴 ⓪ 𝘝𝘐𝘚𝘈 𝗝𝗖𝗕. 🌮
closed 5 days at Christmas – **M** *(closed Sunday)* (residents only) (dinner only) a la carte 14.30/21.95 **t.** ⎍ 3.50 – **14 rm** 🖵 45.00/64.00 **t.** – SB 98.00/120.00 **st.**

🏠 **Hilbury Court,** Hilperton Rd, BA14 7JW, E : ¼ m. on A 361 🖉 752949, Fax 777990, 🍽 – ✑ rest 🖵 🕿 🅿. 🔼 𝘝𝘐𝘚𝘈. 🌮
closed 24 December-1 January – **M** *(closed dinner Friday to Sunday)* (residents only) (bar lunch)/dinner 12.50 **t.** ⎍ 3.80 – **13 rm** 🖵 32.00/52.00 **t.**

at Semington NE : 3 m. by A 361 on A 350 – ✉ Trowbridge – 🕿 0380 Devizes :

🍴🍴 **Highfield House,** BA14 6JN, on A 350 🖉 870554 – 🅿. 🔼 🄰🄴 ⓪ 𝘝𝘐𝘚𝘈
closed Sunday dinner and Monday – **M** 12.10/19.00 **t.** and a la carte ⎍ 4.75.

🛇 ATS Canal Rd, Ladydown Trading Est. 🖉 753469

TRURO Cornwall 🔲 E 33 The West Country G. – pop. 17 852 – ECD : Thursday – 🕿 0872.

See : Royal Cornwall Museum★ *AC*.

Envir. : Trelissick garden★★ (≼★★) *AC*, S : 4 m. by A 39 – Feock (Church★) S : 5 m. by A 39 and B 3289.

Exc. : Trewithen★★★, NE : 7½ m. by A 39 and A 390.

🏌 Treliske 🖉 72640, W : 2 m. on A 390.

🛈 Municipal Buildings, Boscawen St., TR1 2NE 🖉 74555.

◆London 295 – Exeter 87 – Penzance 26 – ◆Plymouth 52.

🏨 **Alverton Manor,** Tregolls Rd, TR1 1XQ, 🖉 76633, Fax 222989, « Mid 19C manor house, former Bishop's residence and convent », 🍽 – ⧉ ✑ rest 🖵 🕿 🅿 – 🔬 200. 🔼 🄰🄴 ⓪ 𝘝𝘐𝘚𝘈
M 16.50 **st.** (dinner) and a la carte 11.30/25.55 **st.** ⎍ 5.25 – **25 rm** 🖵 59.00/140.00 **st.** – SB (weekends only) 65.00/130.00 **st.**

⌂ **Laniley House** ⟂ without rest., Newquay Rd, nr. Trispen, TR4 9AU, NE : 3½ m. by A 39 and A 3076 on Frogmore rd ℘ 75201, ℱ – ⇄ �📺 ℗ . ⚭
closed Christmas and New Year – **3 rm** ⊆ 32.00/36.00.

⌂ **Blue Haze** without rest., The Parade, Malpas Rd, TR1 1QE, ℘ 223553, ℱ – ⇄ ⚭
3 rm ⊆ 20.00/34.00 **st.**

⌂ **Conifers** without rest., 36 Tregolls Rd, TR1 1LA, ℘ 79925 – 📺 ℗ ⚭
4 rm ⊆ 17.00/34.00 **s.**

at Blackwater W : 7 m. by A 390 – ✉ ☎ 0872 Truro :

✗ ✿ **Pennypots** (Viner), TR4 8EY, SW : ¾ m. ℘ 0209 (St. Day) 820347 – ℗ . ◪ 𝗩𝗜𝗦𝗔
closed Sunday, Monday and 3 weeks winter – **M** (dinner only) a la carte 20.50/28.40 **t.**
Spec. Twice baked cheese soufflé with cream and spring onions, Fillets of venison sautéed in hazelnut oil with spiced pears, Chocolate temptation.

🖉 ATS Tabernacle St. ℘ 74083 ⠀⠀⠀⠀⠀ ATS Newham Rd (Riverside) ℘ 40353

TUCKENHAY Devon – see Totnes.

TUNBRIDGE WELLS Kent 404 U 30 – see Royal Tunbridge Wells.

TURNERS HILL W. Sussex 404 T 30 – ☎ 0342 Copthorne.

♦London 33 – ♦Brighton 24 – Crawley 7.

🏰 **Alexander House** ⟂, RH10 4QD, E : 1 m. on B 2110 ℘ 714914, Fax 717328, ≼, « Tastefully decorated country house », ⟂, ℱ, park, ✗ – |‡| 📺 ☎ ℗ . ◪ Ⅻ ⒶⒺ ⓞ 𝗩𝗜𝗦𝗔 ⚭
M 18.50/35.00 **t.** and a la carte ‖ 7.50 – **9 rm** ⊆ 115.00/165.00 **t.**, 5 suites – SB 220.00/250.00 **st.**

TUTBURY Staffs. 402 403 404 O 25 Great Britain G. – pop. 5 099 (inc. Hatton) – ECD : Wednesday – ✉ ☎ 0283 Burton-upon-Trent.
Envir. : Sudbury Hall★★ *AC*, NW : 5½ m. by A 50.

♦London 132 – ♦Birmingham 33 – Derby 11 – ♦Stoke-on-Trent 27.

🏠 **Ye Olde Dog and Partridge,** High St., DE13 9LS, ℘ 813030, Fax 813178, « Part 15C timbered inn », ℱ – 📺 ☎ ℗ . ◪ ⒶⒺ 𝗩𝗜𝗦𝗔 ⚭
closed 25 and 26 December – **M** (carving rest.) 9.75/14.00 **t.** ‖ 4.75 – **17 rm** ⊆ 52.50/75.00 **t.**

🏠 **Mill House** without rest., Cornmill Lane, DE13 9HA, SE : ½ m. ℘ 813634, « Georgian house and watermill », ℱ – ⇄ ℗ . ⚭
closed 25 and 26 December – **3 rm** ⊆ 29.50/45.00 **st.**

TWO BRIDGES Devon 403 I 32 The West Country G. – ✉ Yelverton – ☎ 0822 Tavistock.
Envir. : Dartmoor National Park★★ (Brent Tor ≼★★, Haytor Rocks ≼★).

♦London 226 – Exeter 25 – ♦Plymouth 17.

🏠 **Prince Hall** ⟂, PL20 6SA, E : 1 m. on B 3357 ℘ 890403, Fax 890676, ≼, ℱ – ⇄ rest 📺 ☎ ℗ . ◪ ⓞ 𝗩𝗜𝗦𝗔
closed mid December-mid January – **M** (dinner only) 19.95 **t.** ‖ 3.85 – **8 rm** ⊆ (dinner included) 60.50/105.00 **t.** – SB 85.00/121.00 **st.**

TWO MILLS Ches. – see Chester.

TYNEMOUTH Tyne and Wear 401 402 P 18 – pop. 17 877 – ECD : Wednesday – ☎ 091 Tyneside.

♦London 290 – ♦Newcastle upon Tyne 8 – Sunderland 7.

🏠 **Hope House,** 47 Percy Gdns, NE30 4HH, ℘ 257 1989, Fax 257 1989, ≼, « Tastefully furnished Victorian house » – 📺 ℗ . ◪ ⒶⒺ ⓞ 𝗩𝗜𝗦𝗔 ⚭
M (communal dining) (unlicensed) (dinner only) 18.00 **s.** and a la carte ‖ 4.25 – **3 rm** ⊆ 35.00/47.50 **s.** – SB (April-October) (weekends only) 64.50/107.00 **st.**

UCKFIELD E. Sussex 404 U 31 – pop. 10 938 – ECD : Wednesday – ☎ 0825.

♦London 45 – ♦Brighton 17 – Eastbourne 20 – Maidstone 34.

🏰 **Horsted Place** ⟂, Little Horsted, TN22 5TS, S : 2½ m. by B 2102 and A 22 on A 26 ℘ 750581, Fax 750459, ≼, « Victorian Gothic country house and gardens », ◪, ⬛, park, ✗ – |‡| ⇄ rest 📺 ☎ ℗ . ◪ ⒶⒺ ⓞ 𝗩𝗜𝗦𝗔
M 18.50/32.50 **t.** and a la carte – ⊆ 7.50 – **3 rm** 115.00/140.00 **t.**, **14 suites** 160.00/225.00 **t.** – SB (except weekends) 200.00/300.00 **st.**

🏠 **Hooke Hall,** 250 High St., TN22 1EN, ℘ 761578, Fax 768025, « Queen Anne town house », ℱ – 📺 ☎ ℗ . ◪ 𝗩𝗜𝗦𝗔 ⚭
closed 24 to 31 December – **M** *(closed Sunday and Monday)* (lunch by arrangement)/dinner 25.00 **t.** and a la carte ‖ 5.00 – ⊆ 6.95 – **9 rm** 37.50/110.00 **st.** – SB 105.00/160.00 **st.**

✗ Thai Fantasy, Ringles Cross, TN22 1HV, N : 1 m. ℘ 763827, ℱ – ℗
M - Thai rest.

ULLINGSWICK Heref. and Worcs. – pop. 261 – ⊠ ✆ 0432 Hereford.

♦ London 134 – Hereford 12 – Shrewsbury 52 – Worcester 19.

↑ **Steppes Country House** ⌖, HR1 3JG, ℰ 820424, « Converted farmhouse of 14C origins », ☞ – ⇖ rest ⊤⊽ ☎ ℗. ☒ VISA
   closed 2 weeks January and 2 weeks December – **M** (bar lunch)/dinner 20.00 **st.** and a la carte – **6 rm** ⊆ 35.00/50.00 **st.** – SB (except Bank Holidays) 86.00/110.00 **st.**

ULLSWATER Cumbria 🗎🗎🗎 L 20 – ⊠ Penrith – ✆ 076 84 Pooley Bridge.

🛈 Main Car Park, Glenridding, CA11 0PA ℰ 82414 (summer only) – at Pooley Bridge, The Square, CA10 2NW ℰ 86530 (summer only).

♦ London 296 – ♦ Carlisle 25 – Kendal 31 – Penrith 6.

at Howtown SW : 4 m. of Pooley Bridge – ⊠ Penrith – ✆ 076 84 Pooley Bridge :

🏠 **Howtown** ⌖, CA10 2ND, ℰ 86514, ≤, ☞ – ℗
   April-October – **M** 8.00/11.00 **t.** ⋕ 4.00 – **14 rm** ⊆ 30.00/69.00 **t.**

at Pooley Bridge on B 5320 – ⊠ Penrith – ✆ 076 84 Pooley Bridge :

🏨 **Sharrow Bay Country House** ⌖, CA10 2LZ, S : 2 m. on Howtown rd ℰ 86301, Fax 86349, ≤ Ullswater and fells, « Lakeside setting, gardens, tasteful decor », ⌇ – ⇖ rest ⊤⊽ ☎ ℗. ℅
   closed January – **Meals** (booking essential) 29.75/39.75 **st.** and a la carte 16.50/24.50 **st.** – **22 rm** ⊆ (dinner included) 95.00/296.00 **st.**, 6 suites.

at Watermillock on A 592 – ⊠ Penrith – ✆ 076 84 Pooley Bridge :

🏨 **Leeming House** (Forte) ⌖, CA11 0JJ, on A 592 ℰ 86622, Fax 86443, ≤, « Lakeside country house and gardens », park – ⇖ ⊤⊽ ☎ ℆ ℗. ☒ AE ⊙ VISA JCB
   M 34.50 **t.** (dinner) and lunch a la carte 12.80/24.10 **t.** ⋕ 7.50 – ⊆ 9.50 – **39 rm** 75.00/155.00 **t.** – SB 148.00/193.00 **st.**

🏨 **Old Church** ⌖, CA11 0JN, ℰ 86204, Fax 86368, ≤ Ullswater and fells, « Lakeside setting », ⌇, ☞ – ⇖ rest ⊤⊽ ☎ ℗. ☒ VISA ℅
   April-October – **M** (booking essential) (dinner only) 23.50 ⋕ 7.50 – **10 rm** ⊆ 45.00/150.00 **st.**

🏨 **Rampsbeck House** ⌖, CA11 0LP, ℰ 86442, Fax 86688, ≤, ☞, park – ⇖ ⊤⊽ ☎ ℗. ☒ VISA ℅
   closed 4 January-mid February – **M** (lunch by arrangement)/dinner 25.00 **st.** ⋕ 5.95 – **19 rm** ⊆ 48.00/120.00 **st.**, 1 suite – SB (except Bank Holidays) 110.00/170.00 **st.**

↑ **Knotts Mill** ⌖, CA11 0JN, ℰ 86472, Fax 86699, ≤, ☞ – ⇖ rest ⊤⊽ ☎ ℆ ℗. ☒ VISA ℅
   closed Christmas – **M** 9.50 **st.** and a la carte ⋕ 4.25 – **9 rm** ⊆ 40.00/50.00 **st.** – SB (October-June except Bank Holidays) (weekdays only) 60.00/70.00 **st.**

ULVERSTON Cumbria 🗎🗎🗎 K 21 – pop. 11 976 – ECD : Wednesday – ✆ 0229.

🛈 Bardsea Park ℰ 52824, SW : 1 ½ m. on A 5087.

🛈 Coronation Hall, County Sq., LA12 7LZ ℰ 57120.

♦ London 278 – Kendal 25 – Lancaster 36.

🏠 **Trinity House,** 1 Princes St., LA12 7NB, off A 590 ℰ 587639, Fax 587689 – ⊤⊽ ☎ ℗. ☒ AE VISA JCB
   M *(closed Sunday to non residents)* (dinner only) 14.95 **t.** ⋕ 4.75 – **6 rm** ⊆ 40.00/60.00 **st.** – SB (except Bank Holidays) (weekends only) 90.00 **st.**

↑ **Church Walk House,** Church Walk, LA12 7EW, ℰ 582211 – ℅
   closed 2 weeks Christmas-New Year – **M** (by arrangement) 8.50/15.00 **s.** ⋕ 3.00 – **3 rm** ⊆ 16.00/38.00 **s.** – SB 60.00 **st.**

XX **Bay Horse Inn** with rm, Canal Foot, LA12 9EL, E : 2¼ m. by A 5087, Morecambe Rd and beyond Industrial area, on the coast ℰ 583972, Fax 580502, ≤ Morecambe bay – ⇖ rest ⊤⊽ ☎ ℗. ☒ VISA
   M *(closed lunch Sunday and Monday)* (booking essential) 14.50 **t.** (lunch) and a la carte 17.65/23.25 **t.** ⋕ 7.95 – **6 rm** ⊆ 80.00/140.00 **t.**

at Spark Bridge N : 5½ m. by A 590 off A 5092 – ⊠ ✆ 0229 Ulverston :

XX **Bridgefield House** ⌖ with rm, LA12 8DA, NW : 1 m. on Nibthwaite rd (first left after bridge) ℰ 885239, Fax 885379, ≤, ☞ – ⇖ rest ☎ ℗. ☒ VISA
   M (booking essential) (dinner only) 24.00 **t.** ⋕ 6.50 – **5 rm** ⊆ 35.00/70.00 **t.**

◍ ATS The Gill ℰ 53442

UMBERLEIGH Devon 🗎🗎🗎 I 31 – ✆ 0769 High Bickington.

♦ London 218 – Barnstaple 7 – Exeter 31 – Taunton 49.

🏠 **Rising Sun,** EX37 9DU, on A 377 ℰ 60447, Fax 60764, ⌇ – ⊤⊽ ☎ ℗. ☒ VISA
   M 8.95/14.95 **t.** and a la carte ⋕ 4.95 – **8 rm** 34.95/64.95 **t.**

UPLYME Devon 🗎🗎🗎 L 31 – see Lyme Regis.

UPPER BENEFIELD Northants. – see Oundle.

UPPER ODDINGTON Glos. – see Stow-on-the-Wold.

UPPER SLAUGHTER Glos. 403 404 O 28 – see Bourton-on-the-Water.

UPPINGHAM Leics. 404 R 26 – pop. 2 761 – ECD : Thursday – ✆ 0572.

◆London 101 – ◆Leicester 19 – Northampton 28 – ◆Nottingham 35.

↑ **Rutland House** without rest., 61 High St. East, LE15 9PY, ℰ 822497, Fax 822497, 🚗 – 📺
🅿. 𝘝𝘐𝘚𝘈
4 rm 🖙 28.00/38.00 **t.**

XX **Lake Isle** with rm, 16 High St. East, LE15 9PZ, ℰ 822951, Fax 822951 – 📺 ☎. 🔊 AE ◉
𝘝𝘐𝘚𝘈
M *(closed Monday lunch and Sunday to non-residents)* 12.50/24.50 **t.** and lunch a la carte
⓵ 5.90 – **10 rm** 🖙 42.00/62.00 **st.**, 2 suites – SB 85.00/118.00 **st.**

at Morcott Service Area E : 4 ¼ m. by A 6003 on A 47 – ✉ Uppingham –
✆ 0572 Morcott :

🏠 **Forte Travelodge** without rest., Glaston Rd, LE15 8SA, ℰ 87719, Reservations (Freephone) 0800 850950 – 📺 👍 🅿. 🔊 AE 𝘝𝘐𝘚𝘈. 🚿
40 rm 31.95 **t.**

UPTON ST. LEONARDS Glos. – see Gloucester.

UPTON SNODSBURY Heref. and Worcs. 403 404 N 27 – see Worcester.

UPTON-UPON-SEVERN Heref. and Worcs. 403 404 N 27 – pop. 1 537 – ECD : Thursday –
✆ 0684.

🅱 Pepperpot, Church St., WR8 0HT ℰ 594200 (summer only).

◆London 116 – Hereford 25 – Stratford-upon-Avon 29 – Worcester 11.

🏠 **White Lion,** High St., WR8 0HJ, ℰ 592551, Fax 592551 – 📺 ☎ 🅿. 🔊 AE ◉ 𝘝𝘐𝘚𝘈
closed 25 and 26 December – **M** 14.95 **t.** and a la carte ⓵ 5.00 – **10 rm** 🖙 54.50/82.50 **t.** –
SB 86.00/104.00 **st.**

🏠 **Star** (Resort), High St., WR8 0HQ, ℰ 592300, Fax 592929 – 📺 ☎ 🅿. 🔊 AE ◉ 𝘝𝘐𝘚𝘈
M 6.00 **st.** and a la carte ⓵ 9.50 – **16 rm** 🖙 45.00/60.00 **st.** – SB (weekends only) 68.00/
108.00 **t.**

↑ **Pool House** without rest., Hanley Rd, WR8 0PA, NW : ½ m. on B 4211 ℰ 592151, ⇐, ⚘,
🚗 – ⅓× 🅿. 🔊 𝘝𝘐𝘚𝘈. 🚿
closed December and January – **9 rm** 🖙 34.00/58.00 **st.**

UTTOXETER Staffs. 402 403 404 O 25 Great Britain G. – pop. 10 008 – ECD : Thursday –
✆ 0889.

Envir. : Sudbury Hall★★ *AC*, E : 5 m. by A 518 and A 50.

🅱 Wood Lane ℰ 565108.

◆London 145 – ◆Birmingham 33 – Derby 19 – Stafford 13 – ◆Stoke-on-Trent 16.

🏠 **Bank House,** Church St., ST14 8AG, ℰ 566922, Fax 567565 – 📺 ☎ 🅿. 👍 40. 🔊 AE ◉
𝘝𝘐𝘚𝘈
M a la carte 8.25/14.00 **t.** ⓵ 4.45 – **15 rm** 🖙 37.50/69.50 **t.** – SB 79.50/110.00 **st.**

🏠 **Forte Travelodge** without rest., Ashbourne Rd, ST14 5AA, junction A 50 and B 5030
ℰ 562043, Reservations (Freephone) 0800 850950 – 📺 👍 🅿. 🔊 AE 𝘝𝘐𝘚𝘈. 🚿
32 rm 31.95 **t.**

🔘 ATS Smithfield Rd ℰ 563848/565201

VENN OTTERY Devon 403 K 31 – ✉ ✆ 0404 Ottery St. Mary.

◆London 209 – Exeter 11 – Sidmouth 5.

↑ **Venn Ottery Barton** ♨, EX11 1RZ, ℰ 812733, 🚗 – ⅓× rest 🅿. 🔊 𝘝𝘐𝘚𝘈
M 15.00 **st.** ⓵ 3.50 – **16 rm** 🖙 23.50/51.00 **st.** – SB 65.00/76.00 **st.**

VENTNOR I.O.W. 403 404 Q 32 – see Wight (Isle of).

VERYAN Cornwall 403 F 33 The West Country G. – pop. 880 – ✉ ✆ 0872 Truro.

See : Village★.

◆London 291 – St. Austell 13 – Truro 13.

🏨 **Nare** ♨, Carne Beach, TR2 5PF, SW : 1 ¼ m. ℰ 501279, Fax 501856, ⇐ Carne Bay, 🗜,
⇆s, 🏊 heated, 🚗, XX – 📺 ☎ 🅿. 🔊 𝘝𝘐𝘚𝘈
closed 6 weeks January-February – **M** 13.50/26.00 **t.** and a la carte – **33 rm** 🖙 70.00/
176.00 **t.**, 2 suites.

at Ruan High Lanes W : 1 ¼ m. on A 3078 – ✉ ✆ 0872 Truro :

🏠 **Hundred House,** TR2 5JR, ℰ 501336, 🚗 – ⅓× rest 📺 ☎ 🅿. 🔊 𝘝𝘐𝘚𝘈
March-October – **M** (dinner only) 18.50 ⓵ 4.50 – **10 rm** 🖙 33.00/66.00 **t.** – SB 76.00/
92.00 **st.**

VOWCHURCH Heref. and Worcs. **403** L 27 – pop. 160 – ✉ Hereford – ✆ 0981 Peterchurch.

◆London 144 – Brecon 27 – Hereford 11.

🏠 **Croft,** HR2 0QE, E : ½ m. on B 4348 ℰ 550226, ≤, 🚗 – ⟵⟶ ▤ rest 📺 🅿. 🔼 VISA. ❄
M (dinner only and Sunday lunch)/dinner 14.95 **st.** – ⅙ 4.95 – **8 rm** ⊑ 30.00/60.00 **st.** – SB 40.00/70.00 **st.**

✗✗ **Poston Mill,** HR2 0SF, NW : ½ m. on B 4348 ℰ 550151 – 🔼 AE VISA
closed Tuesday lunch, Sunday dinner, Monday and 3 weeks Christmas-New Year –
M 15.00/20.00 **t.** ⅙ 4.40.

WADDESDON Bucks. **404** R 28 – ✆ 0296.

◆London 51 – Aylesbury 5 – Northampton 32 – ◆Oxford 31.

🏠 **Five Arrows,** High St., HP18 0JE, ℰ 651727, Fax 658596, 🚗 – ⟵⟶ rm 📺 ☎ 🅿. 🔼 VISA.
❄
M (closed Sunday and Monday dinner to non-residents) a la carte 13.40/17.85 **t.** ⅙ 6.00 –
6 rm ⊑ 45.00/65.00 **st.**

WADHURST E. Sussex **404** U 30 – pop. 3 643 – ECD : Wednesday – ✆ 0892.

◆ London 44 – Hastings 21 – Maidstone 24 – Royal Tunbridge Wells 6.

🏠 **Spindlewood** ⤵, Wallcrouch, TN5 7JG, SE : 2 ¼ m. on B 2099 ℰ 0580 (Ticehurst) 200430, Fax 201132, ≤, 🚗 – 📺 ☎ 🅿. 🔼 VISA. ❄
closed 4 days at Christmas – **M** (closed Bank Holiday lunch) 17.00/25.00 **t.** ⅙ 4.00 – **9 rm**
⊑ 47.50/77.50 **t.** – SB 89.00/112.00 **st.**

⌂ **Newbarn** ⤵ without rest., Wards Lane, TN5 6HP, E : 3 m. by B 2099 ℰ 782042, ≤ Bewl
Water and countryside, 🚗 – ⟵⟶ 🅿. ❄
3 rm ⊑ 22.00/44.00 **s.**

⌂ **Kirkstone** without rest., Mayfield Lane, TN5 6HX, ℰ 783204, 🚗 – 🅿
3 rm ⊑ 16.00/32.00 **st.**

WAKEFIELD W. Yorks. **402** P 22 Great Britain G. – pop. 74 764 – ECD : Wednesday – ✆ 0924.

Envir. : Nostell Priory★ AC, SE : 4 ½ m. by A 638.

🏌 City of Wakefield, Lupset Park, Horbury Rd ℰ 367442, W : 2 m. on A 642 – 🏌 Woodthorpe
ℰ 255104, S : 3 m. – 🏌 Low Laithes, Parkmill Lane, Flushdyke, Ossett ℰ 273275, W : 2 m. – 🏌
Normanton, Snydale Rd ℰ 892943, NE : 5 ½ m. by A 655 and B 6133 – 🏌 Painthorpe House,
Painthorpe Lane, Crigglestone ℰ 255083.

🛈 Town Hall, Wood St., WF1 2HQ ℰ 295000/295001.

◆London 188 – ◆Leeds 9 – ◆Manchester 38 – ◆Sheffield 23.

🏨 **Cedar Court,** Denby Dale Rd., Calder Grove, WF4 3QZ, SW : 3 m. on A 636 ℰ 276310,
Telex 557647, Fax 280221 – 🛗 ⟵⟶ rm ▤ 📺 ☎ 🅿 – 🔼 350. 🔼 AE ⓞ VISA
M 11.75/14.50 **st.** and a la carte ⅙ 5.75 – ⊑ 7.50 – **146 rm** 50.00/85.00 **st.**, 5 suites –
SB (weekends only) 63.00/90.00 **st.**

🏨 Swallow, Queen St., WF1 1JU, ℰ 372111, Telex 557464, Fax 383648 – ⟵⟶ rm ▤ rest 📺
☎ 🅿 – 🔼 200
64 rm.

🏨 **Forte Posthouse,** Queen's Drive, Ossett, WF5 9BE, W : 2 ½ m. on A 638 ℰ 276388,
Fax 276437 – 🛗 ⟵⟶ rm ▤ rest 📺 ☎ 🅿 – 🔼 150. 🔼 AE ⓞ VISA JCB. ❄
M a la carte approx. 17.50 **t.** ⅙ 4.65 – ⊑ 6.95 – **99 rm** 53.50 **st.** – SB 90.00 **st.**

at Newmillerdam S : 3 ½ m. on A 61 – ✉ ✆ 0924 Wakefield :

🏨 **St. Pierre,** Barnsley Rd, WF2 6QG, ℰ 255596, Fax 252746 – 🛗 ⟵⟶ rm ▤ rest 📺 ☎ ♿ 🅿 –
🔼 30. 🔼 AE ⓞ VISA
M 8.95/17.95 **t.** and a la carte ⅙ 4.95 – ⊑ 5.75 – **42 rm** 49.50 **st.**, 2 suites – SB (weekends
only) 65.00/75.00 **st.**

🅰 ATS Bethel Pl., Thornes Lane ℰ 371638

WALBERTON W. Sussex – see Arundel.

WALKINGTON Humbs. **402** S 22 – see Beverley.

WALL Northd **401** **402** N 18 – see Hexham.

WALLINGFORD Oxon. **403** **404** Q 29 The West Country G. – pop. 9 041 – ECD : Wednesday –
✆ 0491.

Exc. : Ridgeway Path★★.

🛈 9 St. Martin's St., OX10 0AL ℰ 826972.

◆London 54 – ◆Oxford 12 – Reading 16.

🏨 **George** (Mt. Charlotte Thistle), 84 High St., OX10 0BS, ℰ 836665, Fax 825359 – ⟵⟶ rm 📺
☎ 🅿 – 🔼 120. 🔼 AE ⓞ VISA JCB. ❄
M (closed lunch Saturday and Bank Holidays) 12.95/21.95 **t.** ⅙ 4.75 – ⊑ 8.50 – **39 rm**
59.00/89.00 **t.** – SB (weekends only) 92.00/139.90 **st.**

✗✗✗ **Regatta** with rm, 103 High St., OX10 0BL, ℰ 826126, Fax 826337, ≤, « Thames-side
setting » – 📺 ☎ 🅿. 🔼 AE ⓞ VISA ❄
M (closed Sunday dinner) 12.50/17.50 **t.** and a la carte ⅙ 4.50 – **3 rm** 40.00/50.00 **st.**

at North Stoke S : 2 ¾ m. by A 4130 and A 4074 on B 4009 – ✉ ✆ 0491 Wallingford :

🏨 **Springs** ⟨⟩, Wallingford Rd, OX10 6BE, ✆ 836687, Fax 836877, ≼, ⇌, ☒ heated, ⤢, park, ※ – 📺 ☎ ℗ – ⚑ 50. 🅽 AE ⓞ VISA ⤢
M 17.00/25.00 **t.** and a la carte ⓐ 6.00 – **34 rm** ⊇ 80.00/140.00 **st.**, 2 suites – SB (except Easter, Christmas and New Year) 115.00/125.00 **st.**

WALLSEND Tyne and Wear 401 402 P 18 – see Newcastle upon Tyne.

WALMERSLEY Gtr. Manchester – see Bury.

WALSALL W. Mids. 403 404 O 26 – pop. 177 923 – ECD : Thursday – ✆ 0922.

🏌 Calderfields, Aldridge Rd ✆ 640540, N : 1 m. by A 454 CT.

◆London 126 – ◆Birmingham 9 – ◆Coventry 29 – Shrewsbury 36.

Plan of enlarged area : see Birmingham pp. 2 and 3

🏨 **Forte Posthouse**, Birmingham Rd, WS5 3AB, SE : 1 ½ m. on A 34 ✆ 33555, Fax 612034 – 📶 ⤢ rm ⊟ rest 📺 ☎ ℗ – ⚑ 45. 🅽 AE ⓞ VISA JCB CT e
M a la carte approx. 17.50 **t.** ⓐ 4.65 – ⊇ 6.95 – **98 rm** 53.50 **t.** – SB (weekends only) 90.00 **st.**

🏨 **Friendly**, 20 Wolverhampton Rd, West Bentley, WS2 0BS, W : 2 ½ m. on A 454 ✆ 724444, Fax 723148, ⅃₅, ⇌, ☒ – ⤢ rm 📺 ☎ ♿ ℗ – ⚑ 150. 🅽 AE ⓞ VISA ⤢ BT a
M *(closed Saturday lunch)* (carving rest.) 10.00/12.50 **st.** and a la carte – ⊇ 6.75 – **153 rm** 57.00/98.00 **st.** – SB (weekends only) 79.00/88.00 **st.**

⓪ ATS Leamore Trading Est., Fryers Rd, Bloxwich ✆ 478631

WALSGRAVE ON SOWE W. Mids. – see Coventry.

WALTHAM ABBEY Essex 404 U 28 – pop. 16 498 – ✆ 0992 Lea Valley.

◆London 15 – ◆Cambridge 44 – ◆Ipswich 66 – Luton 30 – Southend-on-Sea 35.

🏨 **Swallow**, Old Shire Lane, EN9 3LX, SE : 1 ½ m. on A 121 ✆ 717170, Telex 916596, Fax 711841, ⅃₅, ⇌, ☒ – ⤢ rm ⊟ rest 📺 ☎ ♿ ℗ – ⚑ 200. 🅽 AE ⓞ VISA
M 14.75/21.00 **st.** and a la carte ⓐ 6.75 – **163 rm** ⊇ 70.00/150.00 **st.** – SB (weekends only) 110.00/130.00 **st.**

⓪ ATS Unit 17, Lea Rd Ind. Park, Lea Rd ✆ 88050

WALTON-ON-THAMES Surrey 404 S 29 – ECD : Wednesday – ✉ ✆ 0932.

◆London 23 – ◆Brighton 54 – ◆Portsmouth 61 – ◆Southampton 65.

🏨 **Ashley Park**, Ashley Park Rd, KT12 1JP, ✆ 220196, Fax 248721 – 📺 ☎ ℗ – ⚑ 60. 🅽 AE ⓞ VISA
M *(closed Sunday dinner)* (bar lunch Monday to Saturday)/dinner a la carte 10.55/21.15 **t.** ⓐ 5.60 – **29 rm** ⊇ 65.00/80.00 **t.**

XX **Le Pecheur** (at The Anglers), Thameside, off Manor Rd, KT12 2PG, ✆ 227423, Fax 245962, ≼ – 🅽 VISA
M *(closed Sunday dinner and Monday)* 10.45 **t.** (lunch) and a la carte 12.95/20.90 **t.** ⓐ 4.25.

WANSFORD Cambs. 404 S 26 – see Peterborough.

WARE Herts. 404 T 28 – pop. 15 344 – ECD : Thursday – ✆ 0920.

🏌 Whitehill, Dane End ✆ 438495, N : 6 m.

◆London 24 – ◆Cambridge 30 – Luton 22.

🏰 **Hanbury Manor**, Thundridge, SG12 0SD, N : 1 ¾ m. by A 1170 on A 10 ✆ 487722, Fax 487692, ≼, « Jacobean style mansion in extensive grounds, walled garden », ⅃₅, ⇌, ☒, 🏌, ※, squash – 📶 ⊟ rest 📺 ☎ ♿ ℗ – ⚑ 120. 🅽 AE ⓞ VISA JCB ⤢
M – **Conservatory** (booking essential) 19.50/30.00 **st.** and a la carte – (see also **Zodiac Room** below) – **90 rm** ⊇ 130.00/210.00 **st.**, 5 suites – SB 210.00/435.00 **st.**

🏨 **Ware Moat House** (Q.M.H.), Baldock St., SG12 9DR, N : ½ m. on A 1170 ✆ 465011, Telex 817417, Fax 468016 – ⤢ rm ⊟ rest 📺 ☎ ℗ – ⚑ 150. 🅽 AE ⓞ VISA
closed 24 December-2 January – **M** *(closed Saturday lunch)* 14.00/16.50 **t.** and a la carte ⓐ 4.75 – **49 rm** ⊇ 57.50/70.00 **t.** – SB (weekends only) 86.00 **st.**

XXXX **Zodiac Room** (at Hanbury Manor H.), Thundridge, SG12 0SD, N : 1 ¾ m. by A 1170 on A 10 ✆ 487722, Fax 487692 – ℗. 🅽 AE ⓞ VISA JCB
closed Sunday dinner – **M** (dinner only and Sunday lunch)/dinner 25.00 **st.** and a la carte.

at Puckeridge N : 5 ½ m. by A 1170 and A 10 at junction with A 120 – ✉ ✆ 0920 Ware :

🏨 **Vintage**, SG11 1SA, ✆ 822722, Fax 822877, ⤢ – 📶 📺 ☎ ℗ – ⚑ 90. 🅽 AE ⓞ VISA ⤢
M 15.65 **t.** (dinner) and a la carte 18.50/26.90 **t.** – **25 rm** ⊇ 40.00/66.45 **t.** – SB 81.30/111.30 **st.**

WAREHAM Dorset 408 404 N 31 The West Country G. – pop. 2 771 – ECD : Wednesday – ✆ 0929.

See : Town★ – St. Martin's★★.

Envir. : Blue Pool★ *AC*, S : 3 ½ m. by A 351 – Bovington★ (Bovington Camp Tank Museum★ *AC*, Woolbridge Manor★) W : 5 m. by A 352.

Exc. : Moreton Church★★, W : 9 ½ m. by A 352 – Corfe Castle★★ (≤★★) *AC*, SE : 6 m. by A 351 – Lulworth Cove★, SW : 10 m. by A 352 and B 3070.

🔟₈ Hyde ✆ 472244.

🅱 Town Hall, East St., BH20 4NG ✆ 552740.

◆London 123 – Bournemouth 13 – Weymouth 19.

🏨 **Priory** ⟋⟍, Church Green, BH20 4ND, ✆ 551666, Fax 554519, ≤, « Tastefully renovated part 16C priory, riverside gardens », ⟍ – 📺 ☎ 🅿. ◫. 🄰🄴 ⓞ 𝗩𝗜𝗦𝗔. ✵
M 16.95/26.50 **t.** and a la carte ⫶ 5.75 – **17 rm** ⊇ 70.00/150.00 **t.**, 2 suites.

🏨 **Springfield Country,** Grange Rd, Stoborough, BH20 5AL, S : 1 m. via South St. and West Lane ✆ 552177, Fax 551862, ⫷ heated, ⫸, ✵ – |✿ 📺 ☎ 🅿 – 🔬 25. 🄰🄴 𝗩𝗜𝗦𝗔
M (bar lunch Monday to Saturday)/dinner 14.95 **t.** and a la carte ⫶ 4.25 – **32 rm** ⊇ 62.00/104.00 **t.** – SB 94.00/146.00 **st.**

🏠 **Kemps Country House,** East Stoke, BH20 6AL, W : 2 ¾ m. on A 352 ✆ 0929 (Bindon Abbey) 462563, Fax 450287, ⫸ – ⫶✵ rest 📺 ☎ 🅿. 🄰🄴 ⓞ 𝗩𝗜𝗦𝗔. ✵
M *(closed Saturday lunch)* 8.95/16.95 **t.** and a la carte – **14 rm** ⊇ 55.00/78.00 **st.** – SB 79.00/119.00 **st.**

WAREN MILL Northd. – see Bamburgh.

WARMINSTER Wilts. 408 404 N 30 The West Country G. – pop. 14 826 – ECD : Wednesday – ✆ 0985.

Envir. : Longleat House★★★ *AC*, SW : 3 m.

Exc. : Stonehenge★★★ *AC*, E : 18 m. by A 36 and A 303 – Bratton Castle (≤★★) NE : 6 m. by A 350 and B 3098.

🅱 Central Car Park, BA12 9BT ✆ 218548.

◆London 111 – ◆Bristol 29 – Exeter 74 – ◆Southampton 47.

🏰 **Bishopstrow House** ⟋⟍, Boreham Rd, BA12 9HH, SE : 1 ½ m. on B 3414 (A 36) ✆ 212312, Fax 216769, ≤, ⟦s, ⫷ heated, ⟦, ⟍, ⫸, park, ✵ – 📺 ☎ 🅿 – 🔬 40. 🄰🄴 ⓞ 𝗩𝗜𝗦𝗔
M 25.00/36.00 **t.** and a la carte ⫶ 6.25 – **29 rm** ⊇ 98.00/170.00 **t.**, 3 suites – SB 162.00/184.00 **st.**

🏠 **Granada Lodge** without rest., BA12 7RU, NW : 1 ¼ m. by B 3414 on A 36 ✆ 219539, Fax 214380, Reservations (Freephone) 0800 555300 – ⫶✵ 📺 ᒼ 🅿. 🄰🄴 𝗩𝗜𝗦𝗔. ✵
⊇ 4.00 – **31 rm** 34.95/37.95 **st.**

at Crockerton S : 1 ¾ m. by A 350 – ✉ ✆ 0985 Warminster :

🛏 **Springfield,** BA12 8AU, on Polters Hill rd ✆ 213696, ⫸, ✵ – ⫶✵ rm 🅿. ✵
M (by arrangement) 18.00 **st.** – **3 rm** ⊇ 26.00/42.00 **st.** – SB 65.00/84.00 **st.**

at Horningsham SW : 5 m. by A 362 – ✉ ✆ 0985 Warminster :

🛏 **Bath Arms,** BA12 7LY, ✆ 844308, Fax 844150, ⫸ – 📺 🅿. 🄰🄴 ⓞ 𝗩𝗜𝗦𝗔
M 17.00/20.00 **t.** and a la carte ⫶ 4.00 – **6 rm** ⊇ 32.00/52.00 **t.**

WARREN STREET Kent 404 W 30 – ✉ ✆ 0622 Maidstone.

◆London 51 – Folkestone 28 – Maidstone 12.

🛏 **Harrow Inn,** ME17 2ED, ✆ 858727, Fax 850026, ⫸ – 📺 ☎ 🅿. 🄰🄴 𝗩𝗜𝗦𝗔. ✵
closed 24 and 25 December – **M** a la carte 15.45/24.70 **t.** – **15 rm** ⊇ 35.00/45.00 **t.** – SB (weekends only) 70.00 **st.**

WARRINGTON Ches. 402 408 404 M 23 – pop. 81 366 – ECD : Thursday – ✆ 0925.

🔟₈ Hill Warren, Appleton ✆ 61620, S : 3 m. – 🔟₈ Walton Hall, Warrington Rd, Higher Walton ✆ 266775, S : 2 m. – 🔟₈ Kelvin Close, Birchwood ✆ 818819 – 🔟₈ Leigh, Kenyon Hall, Culcheth ✆ 763130, NE : 5 m.

🅱 21 Rylands St., WA1 1EJ ✆ 36501/444400.

◆London 195 – Chester 20 – ◆Liverpool 18 – ◆Manchester 21 – Preston 28.

🏨 **Holiday Inn Garden Court,** Woolston Grange Av., Woolston, WA1 4PX, E : 3 ¼ m. by A 57 at junction with M 6 ✆ 838779, Fax 838859 – |✿ ⫶✵ rm 🖿 rest 📺 ☎ 🅿. 🄰🄴 ⓞ 𝗩𝗜𝗦𝗔 ᴊᴄʙ ✵
M (dinner only) 21.00 **st.** and a la carte ⫶ 4.80 – ⊇ 7.50 – **100 rm** 59.00 **st.** – SB (weekends only) 50.00/78.00 **st.**

🏨 **Fir Grove,** Knutsford Old Rd, WA4 2LD, SE : 2 m. by A 50 ✆ 267471, Fax 601092 – 📺 ☎ ⑆ 🅿 – 🔬 150. 🄰🄴 ⓞ 𝗩𝗜𝗦𝗔. ✵
M *(closed Saturday lunch and Bank Holidays)* 12.00 **t.** and a la carte ⫶ 4.95 – **40 rm** ⊇ 49.50/75.00 **t.**

🏠 **Travel Inn** without rest., Calver Rd, Winwick Quay Industrial Estate, WA2 8RN, N : 2 ¼ m. on A 49 ✆ 414417, Fax 414544 – ⫶✵ 📺 ⑆ 🅿. 🄰🄴 ⓞ 𝗩𝗜𝗦𝗔. ✵
⊇ 4.95 – **40 rm** 33.50 **t.**

at *Stretton* S : 3 ½ m. by A 49 on B 5356 – ⊠ ✆ 0925 Warrington :

🏨 **Park Royal International,** Stretton Rd, WA4 4NS, ✆ 730706, Fax 730740, ☞ – 🛏 📺 ☎
🅟 – 🛣 60. 🝣 🄰🄴 🄾 💳
M *(closed Saturday lunch)* 7.45/15.00 **st.** and a la carte 🍴 4.25 – ☑ 8.50 – **25 rm** –
SB (weekends only) 90.00/110.00 **st.**

🔘 ATS Grange Av., Latchford ✆ 32613

WARTON Lancs. 📖 L 22 – pop. 2 383 – ✆ 0772 Preston.

🖫 Silverdale, Red Bridge Lane ✆ 0524 (Carnforth) 701300, NW : 2 m.

♦London 233 – ♦Blackpool 12 – ♦Liverpool 12 – Preston 10.

🏨 Birley Arms, Bryning Lane, off Church Rd, PR4 1TN, ✆ 679988, Fax 679435 – 📺 ☎ 🅟 ⚡
16 rm.

Do not use yesterday's maps for today's journey.

WARWICK
ROYAL
LEAMINGTON SPA

High Street	**Y** 23
Jury Street	**Y**
Market Place	**Y** 29
Smith Street	**Y**
Swan Street	**Y** 46
Birmingham Road	**Z** 7
Bowling Green Street	**Y** 9
Brook Street	**Y** 12
Butts (The)	**Y** 13
Castle Hill	**Y** 15
Church Street	**Y** 17
Lakin Road	**Y** 25
Linen Street	**Y** 26
North Rock	**Y** 32
Old Square	**Y** 35
Old Warwick Road	**Z** 36
Radford Road	**Z** 39
St. John's Road	**Y** 42
St. Nicholas Church Street	**Y** 43
Theatre Street	**Y** 48
West Street	**Y** 50

*Les plans de villes
sont disposés le Nord en haut.*

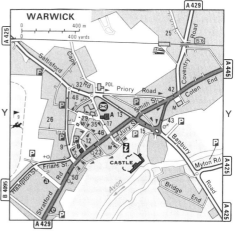

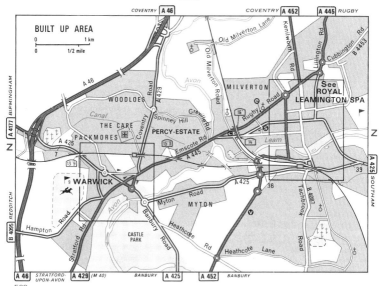

See : Town★ - Castle★★ *AC* Y – Leycester Hospital★ *AC* Y **B** – Collegiate Church of St. Mary★ (Tomb★) Y **A.**

Warwick Racecourse 🖉 494316 Y.

The Court House, Jury St., CV34 4EW 🖉 492212.

◆London 96 – ◆Birmingham 20 – ◆Coventry 11 – ◆Oxford 43.

Plans on preceding page

Old Fourpenny Shop, 27-29 Crompton St., CV34 6HJ, 🖉 491360, Fax 491360 – 🍴 📺.
🔲 🔲 🔲 🔲 –
Y **a**
M *(closed Sunday to non-residents)* 6.00/10.00 **st.**and dinner a la carte 🍷 2.75 – **7 rm**
🛏 32.50/55.00 **st.** – SB (except Bank Holidays) 63.00/100.00 **st.**

Park Cottage without rest., 113 West St., CV34 6AH, 🖉 410319, Fax 410319 – 🍴 📺 ☎
🅿. 🛀
Y **e**
closed Christmas and New Year – **4 rm** 🛏 40.00/52.00 **st.**

at Barford S : 3½ m. on A 429 – Z – ✉ 🔵 0926 Warwick :

Glebe House, Church St., CV35 8BS, on B 4462 🖉 624218, Fax 624625, 🕰, 🐝, 🔲, 🍃 –
🔲 🔲 rest 📺 ☎ 🅿 – 🔲 130. 🔲 🔲 🔲 🔲
M 16.15/23.00 **t.** and a la carte 🍷 4.95 – **39 rm** 🛏 90.00/103.00 **st.**, 2 suites – SB (August and weekends only) 100.00/120.00 **st.**

at Longbridge SW : 2 m. on A 429 – Z – ✉ 🔵 0926 Warwick :

Hilton National, Stratford Rd, CV34 6RE, junction of A 429 with M 40 🖉 499555, Telex 312468, Fax 410020, 🕰, 🐝, 🔲, – 🔲 🍴 rm 📺 ☎ 🐕 🅿 – 🔲 350. 🔲 🔲 🔲 🔲,
🐝
M *(closed Saturday lunch)* (carving lunch) 10.95/17.50 **t.** and a la carte 🍷 5.45 – 🛏 7.55 –
181 rm 90.00/120.00 **st.** – SB (weekends only) 131.95/215.00 **st.**

at Sherbourne SW : 2¾ m. by A 429– Z – ✉ 🔵 0926 Warwick :

Old Rectory, Vicarage Lane, CV35 8AB, at junction with A 46 🖉 624562, 🍃 – 📺 🅿. 🔲
🔲 🔲
closed 24 to 27 December – **M** (light meals) (dinner only) – **14 rm** 🛏 30.00/48.00 **st.**

at Hatton NW : 3½ m. by A 425 on A 4177 – Z – ✉ 🔵 0926 Warwick :

Northleigh House, Five Ways Rd, CV35 7HZ, NW : 2½ m. by A 4177, turning left at roundabout with A 4141 🖉 484203, 🍃 – 🍴 📺 🅿. 🔲 🔲
closed mid December-31 January – **M** (by arrangement) 14.50 **st.** – **6 rm** 🛏 28.00/
55.00 **st.**

at Shrewley NW : 4¾ m. by A 425 and A 4177 - Z - on B 4439 – ✉ 🔵 0926 Warwick :

Shrewley House, CV35 7AT, 🖉 842549, Fax 842216, 🍃 – 🍴 rest 📺 ☎ 🅿. 🔲
🔲
M (by arrangement) 15.00 **s.** – **3 rm** 🛏 37.00/60.00 **s.**

at Honiley NW : 6¾ by A 425 on A 4177 – Z – ✉ Warwick – 🔵 0926 Haseley Knob :

Honiley Court (Lansbury), CV8 1NP, on A 4177 🖉 484234, Fax 484474 – 🔲 🍴 rm 📺 ☎
🐕 🅿 – 🔲 150. 🔲 🔲 🔲 🐝
M 7.50/13.75 **t.** and a la carte – **62 rm** 🛏 67.50/79.00 **st.** – SB (weekends only) 76.00/
162.50 **st.**

◆London 324 – Kendal 72 – Workington 30.

Wasdale Head Inn 🐝, CA20 1EX, 🖉 26229, Fax 26334, ≤ Wasdale Head – ☎ 🅿. 🔲
🔲
closed mid January-mid February and mid November-28 December – **M** (bar lunch)/dinner a la carte 14.00/16.20 **t.** 🍷 4.25 – **10 rm** 🛏 25.00/50.00 **t.**

See : Cleeve Abbey★★ *AC*.

Envir. : Dunster★★ - Castle★★ *AC* (upper rooms ≤★) Water Mill★ *AC*, St. George's Church★,
Dovecote★, NW : 3½ m. by A 39.

◆London 178 – ◆Bristol 55 – Tauton 16.

Langtry Country House, TA23 0NT, on A 39 🖉 40484, 🍃 – 🍴 📺 🅿. 🐝
March-October – **M** (residents only) (dinner only) 13.50 **t.** 🍷 3.50 – **6 rm** 🛏 30.00/46.00 **t.** –
SB 60.00/92.00 **st.**

WASHINGTON Tyne and Wear 401 402 P 19 – pop. 48 856 – ECD : Wednesday – ✹ 091 Tyneside.

🗽 Stone Cellar Rd ☎ 417 2626.

◆London 278 – Durham 13 – ◆Middlesbrough 32 – ◆Newcastle upon Tyne 7.

🏨 **Washington Moat House** (Q.M.H.), Stone Cellar Rd, District 12, NE37 1PH, ☎ 417 2626, Telex 537143, Fax 415 1166, 𝑓₅, ≘s, ⬛, 🗽, squash – ⇥ rm 📺 ☎ 🅿 – 🛄 180. ◪ ⒶⒺ ⓞ 𝗩𝗜𝗦𝗔
M (closed Saturday lunch) 8.75/14.25 **st.** and a la carte ♦ 4.75 – ☑ 7.75 – **105 rm** 67.00/150.00 **st.** – SB (weekends only) 80.00/102.00 **st.**

🏨 **Forte Posthouse,** Emerson, District 5, NE37 1LB, at junction of A 1 (M) with A 195 ☎ 416 2264, Fax 415 3371 – 🖥 ⇥ rm 📺 ☎ 🅿 – 🛄 100. ◪ ⒶⒺ 𝗩𝗜𝗦𝗔
M a la carte approx. 17.50 **t.** ♦ 4.65 – ☑ 6.95 – **138 rm** 53.50 **st.** – SB 90.00 **st.**

🏨 **Campanile,** Emerson Rd, Emerson, District 5, NE37 1LE, at junction of A 1(M) with A 195 ☎ 416 5010, Fax 416 5023 – ⇥ rm 📺 ☎ 🅿 – 🛄 25. ◪ ⒶⒺ 𝗩𝗜𝗦𝗔
M a la carte approx. 9.95 **t.** ♦ 2.95 – **79 rm** 35.75 **t.**

WASHINGTON SERVICE AREA Tyne and Wear – ✉ Washington – ✹ 091 Tyneside

🏨 **Granada Lodge** without rest., DH3 2SJ, on A 1 (M) (southbound carriageway) ☎ 410 0076, Fax 410 0057, Reservations (Freephone) 0800 555300 – ⇥ 📺 ও 🅿. ◪ ⒶⒺ 𝗩𝗜𝗦𝗔 ※
☑ 4.00 – **35 rm** 34.95/37.95 **st.**

WATERHEAD Cumbria 402 L 20 – see Ambleside.

WATERHOUSES Staffs. 402 403 404 O 24 Great Britain G. – pop. 1 018 – ✉ Stoke-on-Trent – ✹ 0538.

Envir. : Dovedale★★ (Ilam Rock★) E : 6 m. by A 523.

◆London 115 – ◆Birmingham 63 – Derby 23 – ◆Manchester 39 – ◆Stoke-on-Trent 17.

☖ **Croft House Farm** ≫, Waterfall, ST10 3HZ, N : 1 m. by A 523 ☎ 308553, ☞ – ⇥ rest 📺 🅿 ※
M (booking) ♦ 3.00 – **6 rm** ☑ 19.50/36.00 **s.** – SB 53.00/63.00 **st.**

𝕏𝕏 ✿ **Old Beams** (Wallis) with rm, Leek Rd, ST10 3HW, ☎ 308254, Fax 308157, ☞ – ⇥ rest 📺 ☎ 🅿. ◪ ⒶⒺ ⓞ 𝗩𝗜𝗦𝗔. ※
closed 3 weeks January – **M** (closed Saturday lunch, Sunday dinner and Monday) (booking essential) 17.50/32.50 **t.** ♦ 7.95 – **6 rm** ☑ 52.50/87.00 **t.**
Spec. Ravioli of langoustines, Open tart of pigeon with wild mushrooms, Parfait of alpine strawberries (July-late September).

WATERINGBURY Kent 404 V 30 – see Maidstone.

WATERMILLOCK Cumbria 402 L 20 – see Ullswater.

WATERROW Somerset – see Wiveliscombe.

WATER YEAT Cumbria – see Coniston.

WATFORD Herts. 404 S 29 – pop. 109 503 – ECD : Wednesday – ✹ 0923.

🗽, 🗽 Bushey, High St. ☎ 081 (London) 950 2283, S : 2 m. on A 4008 BT – 🗽 Bushey Hall, Bushey Hall Drive ☎ 225802, SE : 1 m. BT – 🗽 Oxhey Park, Prestwick Rd, South Oxhey ☎ 248312, SW : 2 m. AT.

◆London 21 – Aylesbury 23.

Plan : see Greater London (North-West)

🏨 **Hilton National,** Elton Way, WD2 8HA, Watford bypass, E : 3½ m. on A 41 at junction with B 462 ☎ 235881, Telex 923422, Fax 220836, 𝑓₅, ≘s, ⬛ – 🖥 ⇥ rm 🍽 rest 📺 ☎ 🅿 – 🛄 375. ◪ ⒶⒺ ⓞ 𝗩𝗜𝗦𝗔 𝗝𝗖𝗕 ※
BT **e**
M (closed Saturday lunch) 12.95/19.50 **t.** and a la carte ♦ 5.25 – ☑ 10.25 – **194 rm** 90.00 **st.**, 1 suite – SB (August, weekends and Bank Holiday weeks only) 90.00/130.00 **st.**

WATH-IN-NIDDERDALE N. Yorks. – see Pateley Bridge.

WEAVERHAM Ches. 402 403 404 M 24 – pop. 7 561 – ✹ 0606.

◆London 191 – Chester 15 – ◆Liverpool 28 – ◆Manchester 28.

🏨 **Oaklands,** Millington Lane, Gorstage, CW8 2SU, SW : 2 m. by A 49 ☎ 853249, Fax 852419, ☞ – 📺 ☎ 🅿. ◪ 𝗩𝗜𝗦𝗔. ※
M 15.00/20.00 **st.** and a la carte ♦ 5.20 – **11 rm** ☑ 20.00/55.00 **st.** – SB (weekends only) 52.00/65.00 **st.**

WEEDON BEC Northants. 403 404 Q 27 – pop. 2 361 – ECD : Wednesday – ✉ Northampton – ✹ 0327 Weedon.

◆London 74 – ◆Coventry 18 – Northampton 8 – ◆Oxford 41.

🏨 **Heyford Manor** (Lansbury), Flore, NN7 4LP, E : 1½ m. on A 45 ☎ 349022, Fax 349017, 𝑓₅, ≘s – ⇥ rm 📺 ☎ ও 🅿 – 🛄 60. ◪ ⒶⒺ ⓞ 𝗩𝗜𝗦𝗔 ※
M (closed Saturday lunch) 9.95/16.95 **t.** and a la carte – **53 rm** ☑ 65.50/77.00 **t.** – SB 80.00/165.00 **st.**

504

WELLAND Heref. and Worcs. 🔠🔠 N 27 – see Great Malvern.

WELLESBOURNE Warks. 🔠🔠 P 27 – pop. 3 998 – see Stratford-upon-Avon.

WELLINGBOROUGH Northants. 🔠 R 27 – pop. 38 598 – ECD : Thursday – ✿ 0933.

🖭 Wellingborough Library, Pebble Lane, NN8 1AS ℰ 228101.

♦London 73 – ♦Cambridge 43 – ♦Leicester 34 – Northampton 10.

🏨 **Hind** (Q.M.H.), Sheep St., NN8 1BY, ℰ 222827, Fax 441921 – 🍽 rest 📺 ☎ 🅟 – 🔬 80. 🖪
🖃 ⓞ 𝗩𝗜𝗦𝗔
M 11.50/13.50 **st.** and a la carte 🍴 4.95 – **34 rm** ⊶ 70.00/87.00 **st.** – SB (weekends only)
80.00 **st.**

WELLINGTON Shrops. 🔠🔠🔠 M 25 – see Telford.

WELLINGTON Somerset 🔠 K 31 – ✿ 0823.

↰ **Pinksmoor Millhouse** 🐎, Pinksmoor, TA21 0HD, SW : 2¾ m. by A 38 ℰ 672361, ≼,
« Working farm », ☞ – 🖐 rm 📺 🅟 🛠
closed Christmas and New Year – **M** (by arrangement) (communal dining) 12.00 **s.** – **3 rm**
⊶ 20.50/36.00 **s.**

WELLINGTON HEATH Heref. and Worcs. 🔠🔠 M 27 – see Ledbury.

WELLS Somerset 🔠 🔠 M 30 The West Country G. – pop. 9 252 – ECD : Wednesday –
✿ 0749.

See : City★★ – Cathedral★★★ – Vicars' Close★ – Bishop's Palace★ (≼★★) AC.

Envir. : Glastonbury★★ - Abbey★★★ (Abbots Kitchen★) AC, St. John the Baptist★★, Somerset
Rural Life Museum★ AC, Glastonbury Tor★ (≼★★★) SW : 5½ m. by A 39 – Wookey Hole★★
(Caves★ AC, Papermill★, Fairground Collection★) NW : 2 m.

Exc. : Cheddar Gorge★★ (Gorge★★, Caves★★, Jacob's Ladder ❅★) St. Andrew's Church★,
NW : 7 m. by A 371 – Axbridge★★ (King John's Hunting Lodge★, St. John the Baptist Church★)
NW : 8½ m. by A 371.

🗽 East Horrington Rd ℰ 672868, E : 1½ m.

🖭 Town Hall, Market Pl., BA5 2RB ℰ 672552.

♦London 132 – ♦Bristol 20 – ♦Southampton 68 – Taunton 28.

🏨 **Swan** (Best Western), 11 Sadler St., BA5 2RX, ℰ 678877, Fax 677647, squash – 📺 ☎ 🅟
– 🔬 70. 🖪 🖃 ⓞ 𝗩𝗜𝗦𝗔
M 14.00/18.50 **t.** 🍴 5.35 – **38 rm** ⊶ 65.00/85.00 **t.** – SB 98.00/150.00 **st.**

🏨 **Star** (Resort), 18 High St., BA5 2SQ, ℰ 670500, Fax 672654 – 📺 ☎ – 🔬 75. 🖪 🖃 ⓞ
𝗩𝗜𝗦𝗔
M a la carte 7.90/12.65 **st.** 🍴 3.50 – ⊶ 5.00 – **12 rm** 40.00/50.00 **st.**

🏨 **Crown,** Market Pl., BA5 2RP, ℰ 673457, Fax 679792 – ⬩⬩ rm 📺 ☎ 🅟. 🖪 🖃 𝗩𝗜𝗦𝗔
M 10.00/15.00 **st.** and a la carte 🍴 3.75 – **15 rm** ⊶ 40.00/50.00 **st.** – SB (except Bank
Holidays) 70.00/110.00 **st.**

at Croscombe E : 3½ m. on A 371 – ✉ Wells – ✿ 0749 Shepton Mallet :

↰ **The Bull Terrier,** BA5 3QJ, ℰ 343658, ☞ – 📺 🅟. 🖪 𝗩𝗜𝗦𝗔 🛠
M (closed Sunday dinner and Monday October-March) a la carte 8.65/17.70 **st.** 🍴 5.00 –
3 rm ⊶ 21.00/50.00 **t.**

WELLS-NEXT-THE-SEA Norfolk 🔠 W 25 Great Britain G. – pop. 2 337 – ECD : Thursday –
✿ 0328 Fakenham.

Envir. : Holkham Hall★★ AC, W : 2 m. by A 149.

🖭 Staithe St., NR23 1AN ℰ 710885 (summer only).

♦London 117 – King's Lynn 31 – ♦Norwich 36.

↰ **The Cobblers,** Standard Rd, NR23 1JU, ℰ 710155, ☞ – ⬩⬩ rest 📺 🅟. 🛠
M (by arrangement) 8.95 **st.** 🍴 2.40 – **8 rm** ⊶ 18.00/37.00 **st.**

🍴 **Moorings,** 6 Freeman St., NR23 1BA, ℰ 710949 – ⬩⬩
closed Thursday lunch, Tuesday, Wednesday, 6 to 24 June and 27 November-16 December
– **M** - **Seafood** (booking essential) a la carte approx. 16.00 **t.** 🍴 3.90.

WELWYN Herts. 🔠 T 28 – ✿ 0438.

♦London 31 – Bedford 31 – ♦Cambridge 31.

🏨 **Tewin Bury Farm,** AL6 0JB, SE : 3½ m. by A 1000 on B 1000 ℰ 717793, Fax 840440, ☞
– 📺 ☎ 🅟. 🖪 🖃 𝗩𝗜𝗦𝗔 🛠
closed Christmas-New Year – **M** (closed Sunday dinner and Bank Holiday Mondays) (light
lunch)/dinner 18.95 🍴 3.95 – **16 rm** ⊶ 40.00/65.00 **st.** – SB (weekends only) 75.00/
100.00 **st.**

WELWYN GARDEN CITY Herts. 404 T 28 – pop. 40 665 – ECD : Wednesday – ✆ 0707 Welwyn Garden.

🛆 Panshanger, Old Herns Lane, ℘ 339507.

🛅 Campus West, The Campus, AL8 6BX ℘ 390653/322880.

◆London 28 – Bedford 34 – ◆Cambridge 34.

🏛 **Homestead Court** (Forte), Homestead Lane, AL7 4LX, SW : 1 ¼ m. by B 195 and Heronswood Rd off Cole Green Lane ℘ 324336, Fax 326447, ☞ – 🛗 🍴 rm 📺 ☎ 🅿 –
🔬 70. 🔼 ⒶⒺ ⓌⒾ VISA JCB
M (bar lunch Monday to Saturday)/dinner 17.50 **st.** and a la carte ⫙ 4.75 – ☲ 8.95 – **58 rm**
60.00 **st.** – SB 80.00/120.00 **st.**

🏧 ATS 17 Tewin rd ℘ 371619

WENDLING Norfolk 404 W 25 - see East Dereham.

WENTBRIDGE W. Yorks. 402 404 Q 23 – ✉ ✆ 0977 Pontefract.

◆London 183 – ◆Leeds 19 – ◆Nottingham 55 – ◆Sheffield 28.

🏛 **Wentbridge House,** Old Great North Rd, WF8 3JJ, ℘ 620444, Fax 620148, ☞ – 📺 ☎
🅿 – 🔬 90. 🔼 ⒶⒺ ⓄⒾ VISA. ⅌
closed 24 and 25 December – **M** 13.75/19.75 **t.** and a la carte ⫙ 7.50 – **12 rm** ☲ 65.00/
98.00 **st.** – SB (weekends only) 98.50/133.50 **st.**

WEOBLEY Heref. and Worcs. 403 L 27 – pop. 1 080 – ✉ Hereford – ✆ 0544.

◆London 145 – Brecon 30 – Hereford 12 – Leominster 9.

✕✕ **Ye Olde Salutation Inn** with rm, Market Pitch, HR4 8SJ, ℘ 318443, Fax 318216 – 🛗 rm
📺 🅿. 🔼 ⒶⒺ ⓄⒾ VISA. ⅌
M (closed Sunday dinner, Monday and 25 December) a la carte 15.90/22.90 **t.** ⫙ 4.75 – **4 rm**
☲ 32.00/54.50 **t.**

WEST BEXINGTON Dorset – ✉ Dorchester – ✆ 0308 Burton Bradstock.

◆London 150 – Bournemouth 43 – Bridport 6 – Weymouth 13.

🏛 **Manor,** Beach Rd, DT2 9DF, ℘ 897616, Fax 897035, ≼, ☞ – 📺 ☎ 🅿. 🔼 ⒶⒺ ⓄⒾ VISA. ⅌
M 14.50/19.95 **t.** – **13 rm** ☲ 46.00/76.00 **t.** – SB (except Christmas) 116.00/132.00 **t.**

WEST BRIDGFORD Notts. 403 404 Q 25 – see Nottingham.

WEST BROMWICH W. Mids. 403 404 O 26 – see Birmingham.

WESTBROOK Wilts – see Devizes.

WEST COKER Somerset 403 404 M 31 – see Yeovil.

WESTDEAN E. Sussex – see Seaford.

WEST DOWN Devon 403 H 30 – ✆ 0271 Barnstaple.

◆London 221 – Exeter 52 – Taunton 59.

⌂ **Long House,** The Square, EX34 8NF, ℘ 863242, ☞ – 🛗 rest 📺. 🔼 VISA. ⅌
March-October – **M** 15.00 **st.** ⫙ 3.60 – **4 rm** ☲ 28.50/50.00 **st.** – SB 72.00/79.00 **st.**

WESTERHAM Kent 404 U 30 Great Britain G. – pop. 3 392 – ECD : Wednesday – ✆ 0959.

Envir. : Chartwell★ AC, S : 2 m. by B 2026.

◆London 24 – ◆Brighton 45 – Maidstone 22.

🏛 **Kings Arms,** Market Sq., TN16 1AN, ℘ 562990, Fax 561240 – 📺 ☎ 🅿. 🔼 ⒶⒺ ⓄⒾ VISA JCB
M (closed Saturday lunch) 11.95/18.50 **s.** and a la carte ⫙ 6.05 – ☲ 7.50 – **16 rm** 63.00/
70.00 **st.** – SB (weekends only) 110.00/120.00 **st.**

WESTGATE Durham 401 402 N 19 – ✆ 0388 Weardale.

◆London 278 – ◆Carlisle 49 – ◆Middlesbrough 50 – ◆Newcastle upon Tyne 42.

⌂ **Breckon Hill** ⅊, DL13 1PD, E : ½ m. on A 689 ℘ 517228, ≼, ☞ – 🛗 📺 🅿. ⅌
M (communal dining) 10.00 **st.** ⫙ 2.90 – **5 rm** ☲ 27.00/40.00 **st.**

WEST HADDON Northants. 403 404 Q 26 – see Rugby.

WEST HUNTSPILL Somerset 403 L 30 – see Bridgwater.

WESTLETON Suffolk 404 Y 27 – pop. 493 – ECD : Wednesday – ✉ Saxmundham –
✆ 072 873 (3 fig.) and 0728 (6 fig.).

◆London 97 – ◆Cambridge 72 – ◆Ipswich 28 – ◆Norwich 31.

🏛 **Crown,** IP17 3AD, ℘ 777, Fax 239, ☞ – 📺 ☎ 🅿. 🔼 ⒶⒺ ⓄⒾ VISA
closed 25 and 26 December – **M** 16.95 **t.** and a la carte – **19 rm** ☲ 52.50/89.50 **t.** –
SB (except Bank Holidays) 73.00/153.00 **st.**

See : Lulworth Cove★.

♦London 129 – Bournemouth 21 – Dorchester 17 – Weymouth 19.

  🏠 **Cromwell House,** Main Rd, BH20 5RJ, 𝒫 253, Fax 566, ≼, ⊒ heated, ☞ – 📺 ☎ 🅟. 🅝
    AE VISA
    M (dinner only) 25.00 **t.** and a la carte ≬ 4.20 – **14 rm** ⊐ 32.50/71.00 **t.** – SB (winter only) 60.00/70.00 **st.**

  🏠 **Gatton House,** Main Rd, BH20 5RU, 𝒫 252, Fax 252, ☞ – ⤢ rest 📺 🅟. 🅝 VISA
    closed January-7 March – **M** (residents only) (dinner only) 15.50 **t.** ≬ 3.75 – **8 rm** ⊐ 37.00/ 56.00 **t.** – SB 64.00/79.00 **st.**

♦London 27 – ♦Brighton 47 – Hastings 40 – Maidstone 6.

  XX **Bombay Brasserie,** 61 High St., ME19 6NA, 𝒫 871256 – 🅝 AE VISA
    M - Indian a la carte approx. 9.10 **t.**

  at Ryarsh NW : 2½ m. by A 20 – ✉ ☎ 0732 West Malling :

  ⌂ **Heavers Farm** ⌂, Chapel St., ME19 5JU, N : ½ m. 𝒫 842074, Fax 842074, ☞ – ⤢ rest
    🅟. ⌿
    closed Christmas and New Year – **M** (by arrangement) 13.00 **st.** – **3 rm** ⊐ 20.00/32.00 **s.** – SB 28.00/40.00 **st.**

♦London 58 – Chelmsford 27 – Colchester 9.5.

  XX **Le Champenois, Blackwater H.** with rm, 20-22 Church Rd, CO5 8QH, 𝒫 383338 – 📺 🅟. 🅝 AE VISA ⌿
    closed 3 weeks January – **M** *(closed Tuesday lunch and Sunday dinner)* a la carte 17.10/ 25.75 **t.** ≬ 4.90 – **7 rm** ⊐ 31.00/68.00 **t.** – SB (except Sunday, Christmas and New Year) 74.00/104.00 **st.**

♦London 65 – ♦Birmingham 61 – Northampton 33 – ♦Oxford 8.

  🏛 **Weston Manor** (Best Western), OX6 8QL, on B 430 𝒫 50621, Fax 50901, ⊒ heated, ☞, park, squash – ⤢ rm 📺 ☎ 🅟 – 🕿 40. 🅝 AE ⓄⒹ VISA ⌿
    M 15.00/24.50 **t.** ≬ 5.50 – **36 rm** ⊐ 70.00/90.00 **st.**, 1 suite – SB 104.00/180.00 **st.**

See : Seafront (≼★★) BZ.

Exc. : Axbridge★★ (King John's Hunting Lodge★, St. John the Baptist Church★) SE : 9 m. by A 371 - BY - and A 38 – Cheddar Gorge★★ (Gorge★★, Caves★★, Jacob's Ladder ※★) - St. Andrew's Church★, SE : 10½ m. by A 371.

  🖹 Worlebury, Monks Hill 𝒫 623214, NE : 2 m. BY – 🖹 Uphill Rd North 𝒫 621360 AZ.

  🅩 Beach Lawns, BS23 1AT 𝒫 626838.

♦London 147 – ♦Bristol 24 – Taunton 32.

Plan on next page

  🏨 **Grand Atlantic** (Forte), Beach Rd, BS23 1BA, 𝒫 626543, Fax 415048, ≼, ⊒ heated, ☞, XX – 🛗 ⤢ 📺 ☎ 🅟 – 🕿 200. 🅝 AE ⓄⒹ VISA   BZ **e**
    M (bar lunch Monday to Saturday)/dinner 16.95 **st.** and a la carte ≬ 6.45 – ⊐ 8.50 – **76 rm** 68.00/120.00 **st.** – SB 108.00/123.00 **st.**

  🏛 Royal Pier (Best Western), 55-57 Birnbeck Rd, BS23 2EJ, 𝒫 626644, Fax 624169, ≼ Weston Bay and Bristol Channel – 🛗 📺 ☎ 🅟 – 🕿 65. ⌿   AY **a**
    38 rm, 2 suites.

  🏛 **Royal** (Chef & Brewer), South Par., BS23 1JN, 𝒫 623601, Fax 415135, ☞ – 🛗 📺 ☎ 🅟 – 🕿 25. 🅝 AE VISA ⌿   BZ **a**
    M 15.00/20.00 **t.** and a la carte – ⊐ 3.50 – **37 rm** 44.95/48.45 **t.**

  🏠 **Queenswood,** Victoria Park, BS23 2HZ, 𝒫 416141, Fax 621759 – ▤ rest 📺 ☎. 🅝 AE ⓄⒹ VISA   BZ **s**
    M 10.50/13.50 **st.** ≬ 4.50 – **17 rm** ⊐ 35.75/71.50 **st.** – SB (except Bank Holidays) (weekends only) 71.50 **st.**

  ⌂ **Beachlands,** 17 Uphill Rd North, BS23 4NG, 𝒫 621401, Fax 621966, ☞ – 📺 ☎ 🅟. 🅝 AE ⓄⒹ VISA   AZ **c**
    M 12.50 **t.** ≬ 4.75 – **18 rm** ⊐ 31.00/62.00 **t.** – SB (October-April) 70.00/85.00 **st.**

  X **Duets,** 103 Upper Bristol Rd, BS22 8ND, 𝒫 413428 – 🅝 VISA   BY **a**
    closed Sunday dinner, Monday, 2 weeks January and 1 week June – **M** (lunch by arrangement)/dinner 14.95 **t.** and a la carte ≬ 4.75.

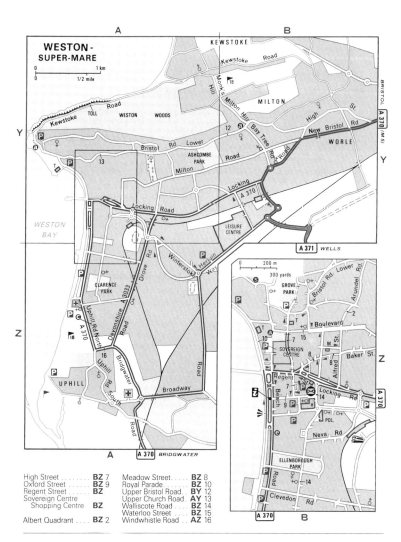

WESTON-SUPER-MARE

KEWSTOKE

1 km
1/2 mile

High Street . . . . **BZ** 7	Meadow Street . . . . . **BZ** 8
Oxford Street . . . . . . **BZ** 9	Royal Parade . . . . . . **BZ** 10
Regent Street . . . . . . **BZ**	Upper Bristol Road . . **BY** 12
Sovereign Centre	Upper Church Road . **AY** 13
Shopping Centre **BZ**	Walliscote Road . . . . **BZ** 14
	Waterloo Street . . . . **BZ** 15
Albert Quadrant . . . . **BZ** 2	Windwhistle Road . . **AZ** 16

WESTON UNDER PENYARD Heref. and Worcs. 403 404 M 28 – see Ross-on-Wye.

WEST PENNARD Somerset 403 M 30 – see Glastonbury.

WEST RUNTON Norfolk 404 X 25 – ECD : Wednesday – ⊠ Cromer – ☎ 0263.

🛐 Links Country Park Hotel, Cromer 𝒫 838383.

♦London 135 – King's Lynn 42 – ♦Norwich 24.

🏥 **Links Country Park,** Sandy Lane, NR27 9QH, 𝒫 838383, Fax 838264, ⇔s, ◱, 🛐, ⚘, ℁ – 🔄 🗏 rest 📺 ☎ ㊑ ㉿ – 🔬 150. 🔼 🔼 𝗩𝗜𝗦𝗔.
M (lunch by arrangement Monday to Saturday)/dinner 17.75 **st.** and a la carte ░ 4.95 – **40 rm** ⮐ 80.00/205.00 **st.**

🏠 **Dormy House,** Cromer Rd, NR27 9QA, on A 149 𝒫 837537, ⚘ – 🔄 ⇔ rest 📺 ☎ ㊑. 🔼 🔼 𝗩𝗜𝗦𝗔. ℁
M (dinner only and Sunday lunch)/dinner 14.50 **st.** and a la carte ░ 3.95 – **14 rm** ⮐ 39.00/ 70.00 **st.** – SB (10 October-31 March) 80.00/120.00 **st.**

℁℁ **Mirabelle,** 7 Station Rd, NR27 9QD, 𝒫 837396 – ㊑. 🔼 🔼 ⓪ 𝗩𝗜𝗦𝗔
closed Sunday dinner November-May and Monday – **M** 15.00/22.50 **t.** and a la carte ░ 3.95.

WEST SCRAFTON N. Yorks. – see Middleham.

WEST STOUR Dorset – pop. 144 – ⊠ Gillingham – ✆ 0747 East Stour.

◆London 119 – Bournemouth 35 – Salisbury 28 – Yeovil 15.

☆ **Ship Inn,** SP8 5RP, on A 30 ℰ 838640, ☞ – TV ℗. ☒ VISA. ✾
   M (in bar lunch time and Sunday to Tuesday dinner)/dinner a la carte 12.80/21.40 **t.** ₰ 4.50 –
   6 rm ☞ 28.00/42.00 **t.**

WEST WITTON N. Yorks. 402 O 21 – pop. 338 – ⊠ Leyburn – ✆ 0969 Wensleydale.

◆London 241 – Kendal 39 – ◆Leeds 60 – York 53.

🏠 **Wensleydale Heifer,** Main St., DL8 4LS, ℰ 22322, Fax 24183, ☞ – TV ☎ ℗. ☒ ☒ ⓪
   VISA
   M 11.50/22.50 **st.** ₰ 3.75 – **19 rm** ☞ 45.00/85.00 **st.** – SB (except Bank Holidays) 99.00/
   115.00 **st.**

WETHERAL Cumbria 401 402 L 19 – see Carlisle.

WETHERBY W. Yorks. 402 P 22 Great Britain G. – pop. 9 467 – ECD : Wednesday – ✆ 0937.

Envir. : Harewood House★★ (The Gallery★) *AC*, SW : 5½ m. by A 58 and A 659.

🏌 Linton Lane ℰ 580089, W : ¾ m.

🛈 Council Offices, 24 Westgate, LS22 4NL ℰ 582706.

◆London 208 – Harrogate 8 – ◆Leeds 13 – York 14.

🏨 **Wood Hall** ⟆, Trip Lane, Linton, LS22 4JA, SW : 3 m. by A 661 and Linton Rd
   ℰ 587271, Fax 584353, ≼, « Part Jacobean and Georgian country house in park », ☒,
   ☜, ☞ – TV ☎ ℗. ☒ ☒ VISA
   M lunch (Saturday) 14.95/30.00 **t.** and dinner a la carte – **43 rm** ☞ 84.00/250.00 **t.** –
   SB (except Christmas and New Year) 130.00/192.00 **st.**

🏨 **Linton Spring** ⟆, Sicklinghall Rd, LS22 4AF, W : 1 ¾ m. by A 661 ℰ 585353,
   Fax 587579, ☞ , park – TV ☎ ℗. ☒ ☒ ☒ VISA
   M 10.00/15.00 **st.** and dinner a la carte ₰ 4.00 – ☞ 7.50 – **10 rm** 60.00/80.00 **st.**, 2 suites –
   SB (weekends only) 105.00/180.00 **st.**

🏨 **Wetherby Resort,** Leeds Rd, LS22 5HE, at junction of A 58 with A 1 ℰ 583881,
   Fax 580062 – ⁙ rm TV ☎ ℗ – 🕍 120. ☒ ☒ ⓪ VISA
   M 20.00 **t.** (dinner) and a la carte 12.50/20.00 **t.** ₰ 5.25 – ☞ 7.50 – **72 rm** 55.00/80.00 **t.** –
   SB (weekends only) 76.00 **st.**

WETHERDEN Suffolk 404 W 27 – see Stowmarket.

WETHERSFIELD Essex 404 V 28 – pop. 1 165 – ⊠ Braintree – ✆ 0371 Great Dunmow.

◆London 52 – ◆Cambridge 31 – Chelmsford 19 – Colchester 22.

XX **Dicken's,** The Green, CM7 4BS, ℰ 850723, « Part 17C house » – ℗. ☒ ☒ VISA
   closed Sunday dinner, Monday and Tuesday – **M** (lunch by arrangement)/dinner 18.00 **t.**
   and a la carte ₰ 7.85.

WEYBRIDGE Surrey 404 S 29 – pop. 50 031 (inc. Walton-on-Thames) – ECD : Wednesday –
✆ 0932.

◆London 23 – Crawley 27 – Guildford 17 – Reading 33.

Plan : see Greater London (South-West)

🏨 **Oatlands Park,** Oatlands Drive, KT13 9HB, NE : ¾ m. by A 317 on A 3050 ℰ 847242,
   Telex 915123, Fax 842252, ☞ , park, ✾ – ₪ TV ☎ ℗ – 🕍 200. ☒ ☒ ☒ AY
   closed 25 to 30 December – **M** (bar lunch Saturday) 16.00 **st.** and a la carte ₰ 5.50 – **113 rm**
   ☞ 97.00/143.00 **st.**, 4 suites – SB (weekends only) 92.00/172.00 **st.**

🏨 **Ship Thistle** (Mt. Charlotte Thistle), Monument Green, High St., KT13 8BQ, ℰ 848364,
   Fax 857153 – TV ☎ ℗ – 🕍 140. ☒ ☒ ⓪ VISA JCB. ✾   by A 3050 AY
   M *(closed Saturday lunch)* 14.50/16.75 **t.** and dinner a la carte – ☞ 8.25 – **39 rm** 89.00/
   99.00 **st.** – SB (weekends only) 98.00 **st.**

XXX **Casa Romana,** 2 Temple Hall, Monument Hill, KT13 8RH, ℰ 843470 – ℗. ☒ ☒ ⓪
   VISA   by A 3050 AY
   closed Saturday lunch and 25-26 December – **M** - **Italian** 13.95/16.50 **t.** and a la carte ₰ 5.00.

XX **Colony,** 3 Balfour Rd, KT13 8HE, ℰ 842766 – ▤. ☒ ☒ ⓪ VISA   by A 317 AZ
   closed 25 and 26 December – **M** - **Chinese** (Peking) 10.00/15.00 **t.** and dinner a la carte.

X **Gaylord,** 73 Queens Rd, KT13 9UQ, E : ¾ m. on A 317 ℰ 842895 – ▤. ☒ ☒ VISA   AZ
   M - **Indian** a la carte 11.40/15.35 **t.**

Pleasant hotels and restaurants
are shown in the Guide by a red sign.   🏨🏨 ... ⋔

Please send us the names
of anywhere you have enjoyed your stay.   XXXXX ... X

Your Michelin Guide will be even better.

509

WEYMOUTH Dorset **403 404** M 32 *The West Country* G. – pop. 38 384 – ECD : Wednesday – ✆ 0305.

See : Town★ – Timewalk★ *AC* – Nothe Fort (≤★) *AC* – Boat Trip★ (Weymouth Bay and Portland Harbour) *AC*.

Envir. : Chesel Beach★★ – Portland★ - Portland Bill (❋★★) S : 2½ m. by A 354.

Exc. : Maiden Castle★★ (≤★) N : 6½ m. by A 354 – Abbotsbury★★ (Swannery★ *AC*, Sub-Tropical Gardens★ *AC*, St. Catherine's Chapel★) NW : 9 m. by B 3157.

🏌 Weymouth ✆ 784994, off Manor roundabout.

⛴ to Channel Islands : Guernsey (St. Peter Port) and Jersey (St. Helier) (Condor Ltd : hydro-foil) 2 daily.

🛈 The King's Statue, The Esplanade, DT4 7AN ✆ 765221/765223.

•London 142 – Bournemouth 35 – •Bristol 68 – Exeter 59 – Swindon 94.

🏨 **Rex,** 29 The Esplanade, DT4 8DN, ✆ 760400, Fax 760500 – 📶 📺 ☎ ⇔. 🅰 🆎 ⓪ 𝚅𝙸𝚂𝙰. ❅
M (dinner only) 12.50 **t.** and a la carte ⅛ 4.50 – **31 rm** ☷ 44.00/80.00 **t.** – SB (October-April) (weekends only) 94.00 **st.**

🏨 **Streamside,** 29 Preston Rd, Overcombe, DT3 6PX, NE : 2 m. on A 353 ✆ 833121, Fax 832043, ☞ – 📺 ☎ 🅿. 🅰 🆎 ⓪ 𝚅𝙸𝚂𝙰
closed 4 days at Christmas – **M** 9.95 **t.** (dinner) and a la carte 6.50/19.00 **t.** – **15 rm** ☷ 35.00/68.00 **t.**

🏠 **Bay Lodge,** 27 Greenhill, DT4 7SW, ✆ 782419, Fax 782828, ☞ – 📺 🅿. 🅰 🆎 ⓪ 𝚅𝙸𝚂𝙰. ❅
M 12.75 **st.** ⅛ 3.75 – **12 rm** ☷ 26.00/55.00 **st.** – SB (except May-September, Easter and Christmas) 54.00/68.00 **st.**

🏠 **Chatsworth,** 14 The Esplanade, DT4 8EB, ✆ 785012, Fax 766342 – 📺 ☎. 🅰 🆎 𝚅𝙸𝚂𝙰. ❅
M 10.00 **st.** – **8 rm** ☷ 24.00/50.00 **st.** – SB (September-April except Bank Holidays) 59.00 **st.**

🏠 **Sou'West Lodge,** Rodwell Rd, DT4 8QT, ✆ 783749 – 📺 🅿
closed 20 December-2 January – **M** (by arrangement) 6.80 **st.** – **8 rm** ☷ 20.00/43.00 **st.**

🍴 **Perry's,** The Harbourside, 4 Trinity Rd, DT4 8TJ, ✆ 785799 – 🅰 𝚅𝙸𝚂𝙰
closed lunch Monday and Saturday, Sunday dinner October-March and 25 to 28 December – **M** 10.95 **t.** (lunch) and a la carte 14.00/26.00 **t.** ⅛ 5.00.

WHALLEY Lancs. **402** M 22 – pop. 4 745 – ✉ – ✆ 0254 Blackburn.

🏌 Long Leese Barn, Clerkhill ✆ 822236.

•London 233 – •Blackpool 32 – Burnley 12 – •Manchester 28 – Preston 15.

🏨 **Foxfields,** Whalley Rd, BB6 9HY, SW : 1¼ m. ✆ 822556, Fax 824613 – 📺 ☎ ⅖ 🅿 – 🏛 150. 🅰 🆎 ⓪ 𝚅𝙸𝚂𝙰. ❅
M – (see below) – **44 rm** ☷ 60.00/85.00 **t.** – SB (weekends only) 85.00/95.00 **st.**

🏨 **Mytton Fold Farm,** Whalley Rd, Langho, BB6 8AB, SW : 1¾ m. ✆ 240662, Fax 248119, ☞ – ⅙⇔ rest 📺 ☎ ⅖ 🅿 – 🏛 300. 🅰 🆎 𝚅𝙸𝚂𝙰. ❅
M (bar lunch)/dinner 12.95 **t.** and a la carte 4.65 – **27 rm** ☷ 43.50/64.50 **t.** – SB 75.00 **st.**

🍴🍴🍴 **Foxfields,** Whalley Rd, BB6 9HY, SW : 1¼ m. ✆ 822556, Fax 824613 – ▤ 🅿. 🅰 🆎 ⓪ 𝚅𝙸𝚂𝙰
M *(closed Saturday lunch)* 11.95/16.95 **st.** and a la carte ⅛ 5.25.

🍴🍴 **Northcote Manor** with rm, Northcote Rd, Langho, BB6 8BE, SW : 2 m. on A 59 ✆ 240555, Fax 246568, ☞ – 📺 ☎ 🅿. 🅰 🆎 ⓪ 𝚅𝙸𝚂𝙰. ❅
M 15.95 **t.** (lunch) and a la carte 20.50/33.95 **t.** – **14 rm** ☷ 60.00/95.00 **t.** – SB (weekends only) 80.50/137.90 **st.**

WHAPLODE Lincs. **402 404** T 25 – pop. 1 885 – ✉ Spalding – ✆ 0406 Holbeach.

•London 106 – Lincoln 45 – •Leicester 61 – •Norwich 60.

🏠 **Guy Wells** ≫, Eastgate, PE12 6TZ, E : ½ m. by A 151 ✆ 22239, « Queen Anne house », ☞ – ⇔ 🅿. ❅
closed 20 to 27 December – **M** (by arrangement) 12.00 **st.** – **3 rm** ☷ 24.00/40.00 **st.**

WHARRAM-LE-STREET N. Yorks. – see Malton.

WHEATLEY Oxon. **403 404** Q 28 – see Oxford.

WHIMPLE Devon **403** J 31 – see Exeter.

WHITBY N. Yorks. **402** S 20 – pop. 12 982 – ECD : Wednesday – ✆ 0947.

🏌 Low Straggleton ✆ 602768, N : 2 m. by A 174 – 🛈 Langborne Rd, YO21 1YN ✆ 602674.

•London 257 – •Middlesbrough 31 – Scarborough 21 – York 45.

🏨 **Larpool Hall Country House** ≫, Larpool Lane, YO22 4ND, SE : 1 m. by A 171 ✆ 602737, Fax 602737, ≤, ☞, park – 📺 ☎ 🅿. 🅰 ⓪ 𝚅𝙸𝚂𝙰. ❅
M 12.50/18.50 **t.** and a la carte ⅛ 4.25 – **12 rm** ☷ 37.50/90.00 **t.** – SB (except Bank Holidays) 84.00/110.00 **st.**

at Dunsley W : 3¼ m. by A 171 – ✉ ✆ 0947 Whitby :

🏨 **Dunsley Hall** ≫, YO21 3TL, ✆ 83437, Fax 83505, ≤, 𝟏₆, 🅼, ☞, ✖ – 📺 🅿. 🅰 𝚅𝙸𝚂𝙰
closed 25 and 26 December – **M** (dinner only) 15.00 **st.** ⅛ 3.75 – **7 rm** ☷ 35.00/40.00 **st.** – SB (October-June) 85.00/111.00 **st.**

WHITCHURCH Shrops. 402 403 404 L 25 – pop. 7 246 – ECD : Wednesday – ✆ 0948.

🏠, 🏠 Hill Valley, Terrick Rd ✆ 663584, N : 1 m.

🅱 The Civic Centre, High St., SY13 1AX ✆ 664577.

◆London 171 – ◆Birmingham 54 – Chester 22 – ◆Manchester 43 – Shrewsbury 20.

🏨 **Dodington Lodge,** SY13 1EN, ✆ 662539, 🚗 – 📺 ☎ 🅿. 🅰 VISA
   M 7.50/12.50 **t.** and a la carte 🍴 5.00 – **10 rm** ➡ 42.50/57.50 **t.** – SB (except Christmas and New Year) 65.00/110.00 **st.**

⑩ ATS The Wharf, Mill St. ✆ 662491/662701

WHITEHAVEN Cumbria 402 J 20 – ✆ 0946.

🏠 St. Bees, Rhoda Grove, Rheda, Frizington ✆ 812105, S : 4 m.

🅱 Market Hall, Market Pl., CA28 7JG ✆ 695678.

🏨 Ennerdale, Cleator, CA23 3DT, SE : 6 m. by A 5094 and A 595 on A 5086 ✆ 813907, Fax 815260, 🚗 – 📺 ☎ 🅿
   20 rm.

⑩ ATS Meadow Rd ✆ 692576

WHITEWELL Lancs. 402 M 22 Great Britain G. – pop. 3 577 – ✉ Clitheroe – ✆ 0200 Dunsop Bridge.

Envir. : Castle Howard★★ (Park★★★) *AC*, N : 5 m. by A 64 via Welburn.

◆London 281 – Lancaster 31 – ◆Leeds 55 – ◆Manchester 41 – Preston 13.

🏨 **Inn at Whitewell,** Forest of Bowland, BB7 3AT, ✆ 448222, ≤, 🎣, 🚗 – 📺 ☎ 🅿. 🅰 🅰🅴 ⑩ VISA
   M (bar lunch)/dinner a la carte 13.20/18.00 **st.** 🍴 5.40 – **8 rm** ➡ 47.00/66.00 **st.**, 1 suite.

WHITLEY S. Yorks. – see Sheffield.

WHITLEY BAY Tyne and Wear 401 402 P 18 – ✆ 091 Tyneside.

🅱 Park Rd, NE26 1EJ ✆ 252 4494.

◆London 295 – ◆Newcastle upon Tyne 10 – Sunderland 10.

🏨 **Windsor,** South Par., NE26 2RF, ✆ 251 8888, Fax 297 0272 – ⧉ 📺 ☎ – 🔬 100. 🅰 🅰🅴 ⑩ VISA JCB. ❄
   M (closed Monday lunch) 7.00/14.75 **st.** and dinner a la carte 🍴 4.00 – **64 rm** ➡ 35.00/56.00 **st.** – SB (except Christmas) 60.00/130.00 **st.**

🏨 **Ambassador,** South Par., NE26 2RQ, ✆ 253 1218, Fax 297 0089 – 📺 ☎ 🅿. 🅰 🅰🅴 ⑩ VISA
   closed 24 to 26 December – **M** (dinner only) 9.95 **t.** and a la carte 🍴 6.95 – **27 rm** ➡ 35.00/56.00 **t.**

⑩ ATS John St., Cullercoats ✆ 253 3903

WHITTLE-LE-WOODS Lancs. 402 M 23 – see Chorley.

WICKHAM Hants. 403 404 Q 31 – pop. 3 485 – ECD : Wednesday – ✆ 0329.

◆London 74 – ◆Portsmouth 12 – ◆Southampton 11 – Winchester 16.

🏨 **Old House,** The Square, PO17 5JG, ✆ 833049, Fax 833672, « Queen Anne house », 🚗 –
   📺 ☎ 🅿. 🅰 🅰🅴 ⑩ VISA. ❄
   closed 2 weeks August and 2 weeks December – **M** (closed lunch Monday and Saturday, Sunday dinner and Bank Holidays) 28.00 **st.** 🍴 5.75 – **12 rm** ➡ 70.00/90.00 **st.** – SB 120.00/200.00 **st.**

WIDEGATES Cornwall 403 G 32 – see Looe.

WIDNES Ches. 402 403 404 L 23 – pop. 55 973 – ECD : Thursday – ✆ 051 Liverpool.

🏠 Highfield Rd ✆ 424 2440 – 🏠 Widnes Municipal, Dundalk Rd ✆ 424 6230.

🅱 Municipal Building, Kingsway, WA8 7QF ✆ 424 2061.

◆London 205 – ◆Liverpool 19 – ◆Manchester 27 – ◆Stoke-on-Trent 42.

🏨 **Everglades Park,** Derby Rd, WA8 0UJ, NE : 3 m. by A 568 on A 5080 ✆ 495 2040, Fax 424 6536 – ☰ rest 📺 ☎ 🅿 – 🔬 100. 🅰 🅰🅴 ⑩ VISA. ❄
   M 13.75 **st.** (dinner) and a la carte 6.95/26.45 **st.** 🍴 3.95 – **32 rm** ➡ 45.00/78.00 **st.** – SB 77.00/147.50 **st.**

   at Cronton NW : 2 m. by A 568 on A 5080 – ✉ Widnes – ✆ 051 Liverpool :

🏨 **Hillcrest,** Cronton Lane, WA8 9AR, ✆ 424 1616, Fax 495 1348 – 📺 ☎ 🅿 – 🔬 100. 🅰 🅰🅴 ⑩ VISA
   M (closed Saturday lunch) 9.50/12.75 **t.** and a la carte 🍴 4.50 – **51 rm** ➡ 35.00/70.00 **st.** – SB (except Bank Holidays) 70.00/100.00 **st.**

⑩ ATS Tanhouse Lane ✆ 424 3011/2945

WIGAN Lancs. 402 M 23 – ✆ 0942.

◆London 203 – ◆Liverpool 18 – ◆Manchester 24 – Preston 18.

🏨 **Oak,** Riverway, WN1 3SS, access by Orchard St. ✆ 826888, Fax 825800 – ⧉ ❄ ☰ rest 📺 ☎ 🅿 – 🔬 180. 🅰 🅰🅴 ⑩ VISA
   M 9.95/16.00 **t.** and a la carte 🍴 4.95 – ➡ 6.25 – **88 rm** 35.00/65.00 **t.**

511

WIGHT (Isle of) **403** **404** PQ 31 32 Great Britain G. – pop. **118 594**.

See : Island★★.

Envir. : Osborne House, East Cowes★★ *AC* – Carisbrooke Castle, Newport★★ *AC* (Keep ≤★) – Brading★ (Roman Villa★ *AC*, St. Mary's Church★, Nunwell House★ *AC*) – Shorwell : St. Peter's Church★ (wall paintings★).

🛥 from East to West Cowes to Southampton (Red Funnel Ferries) frequent services daily – from Yarmouth to Lymington (Wightlink Ltd) frequent services daily (30 mn) – from Fishbourne to Portsmouth (Wightlink Ltd) frequent services daily (35 mn).

🛥 from Ryde to Portsmouth (Hovertravel Ltd) frequent services daily (10 mn).

Alverstone – ⊠ ✆ 0983 Isle of Wight

⌂ **Grange** ⬙, PO36 0EZ, ℰ 403729, 🐾 – ⤙ rest ℗. ⅏
closed December and January – **M** 14.50 **st.** – **6 rm** ⊑ 21.50/48.00 **st.**

Chale – pop. 561 – ECD : Thursday – ⊠ ✆ 0983 Isle of Wight
Newport 9.

⌂ **Clarendon,** Newport Rd, PO38 2HA, ℰ 730431, Fax 730431, ≤, 🐾 – 📺 ℗. 🅰 VISA
M 10.00/17.00 **st.** and a la carte 🍴 4.50 – **12 rm** ⊑ 25.00/65.80 **st.**, 1 suite – SB (October-May except Bank Holidays) 72.00/92.00 **st.**

Cowes – pop. 16 371 – ECD : Wednesday – ⊠ ✆ 0983 Isle of Wight.
🏌 Osborne, East Cowes ℰ 295421.
🛈 The Arcade, Fountain Quay, PO31 7AR ℰ 291914.
Newport 4.

🏨 **New Holmwood,** Queens Rd, Egypt Point, PO31 8BW, ℰ 292508, Fax 295020
🏊 heated – ⤙ rm 📺 ✆ ℗ – 🔬 150. 🅰 🆎 VISA
M 15.00/17.50 **t.** and a la carte – **23 rm** ⊑ 65.00/90.00 **t.**, 1 suite – SB (except first week August) 100.00/170.00 **st.**

Freshwater – pop. 5 073 – ECD : Thursday – ⊠ ✆ 0983 Isle of Wight.
Newport 13.

⌂ **Yarlands Country House** ⬙, Victoria Rd, PO40 9PP, ℰ 752574, 🐾 – ⤙ rest 📺 ℗ ⅏
M (dinner only) 12.00 **st.** 🍴 6.75 – **6 rm** ⊑ 29.00/52.00 **st.**

⌂ **Blenheim House,** Gate Lane, Freshwater Bay, PO40 9QD, S : 1 m. ℰ 752858, 🏊 heated – 📺 ℗ ⅏
mid June-mid September – **M** (by arrangement) 8.00 **st.** – **8 rm** ⊑ 21.00/42.00 **st.**

Newport – pop. 19 758 – ECD : Thursday – ⊠ ✆ 0983 Isle of Wight.
🏌 St. George's Down, Shide ℰ 525076, SE : 1 m.
🛈 The Car Park, Church Litten, PO30 1JU ℰ 525450.

🛞 ATS 44-50 South St. ℰ 522881

Niton – ⊠ ✆ 0983 Isle of Wight
⌂ **Pine Ridge,** The Undercliff, PO38 2LY, ℰ 730802, 🐾 – 📺 ✆ ℗. 🅰 VISA ⅏
M 14.95 **t.** 🍴 3.50 – **9 rm** ⊑ 20.00/50.00 **st.** – SB (12 September-May except Bank Holidays) 59.95/69.90 **st.**

Seaview – ⊠ ✆ 0983 Isle of Wight.
⌂ **Seaview,** High St., PO34 5EX, ℰ 612711, Fax 613729 – 📺 ✆ ℗. 🅰 🆎 ① VISA
M *(closed Sunday dinner except Bank Holidays)* a la carte 16.40/22.85 **t.** 🍴 3.80 – **15 rm** ⊑ 40.00/60.00 **t.**, 1 suite – SB 90.00/110.00 **st.**

Shanklin – pop. 8 109 – ECD : Wednesday – ⊠ ✆ 0983 Isle of Wight.
🏌 Fairway Lake, Sandown ℰ 403217.
🛈 67 High St., PO37 6JJ ℰ 862942.
Newport 9.

🏨 **Brunswick,** Queens Rd, PO37 6AN, ℰ 863245, ⇆, 🏊 heated, 🔲, 🐾 – ⤙ rest 📺 ✆ ℗. 🅰 VISA
April-October and Christmas – **M** *(closed Sunday lunch)* (bar lunch)/dinner 13.00 **st.** 🍴 4.00 – **32 rm** ⊑ 25.00/50.00 **st.** – SB 50.00/80.00 **st.**

🏨 **Fern Bank,** Highfield Rd, PO37 6PP, ℰ 862790, Fax 864412, ⇆, 🔲, 🐾 – ⤙ rest 📺 ✆ ℗. 🅰 ① VISA
M (bar lunch)/dinner 13.50 **t.** and a la carte 🍴 6.95 – **23 rm** ⊑ 37.75/95.50 **t.** – SB (January-May) 60.00/70.00 **st.**

🏨 **Bourne Hall Country** ⬙, Luccombe Rd, PO37 6RR, ℰ 862820, Fax 865138, ⇆, 🏊 heated, 🔲, 🐾, ⅍ – 📺 ✆ ℗. 🅰 🆎 VISA ⅏
closed January – **M** (bar lunch)/dinner 14.00 **t.** and a la carte 🍴 4.75 – **28 rm** ⊑ 37.95/65.50 **t.** – SB (except Bank Holidays) 60.00/83.50 **st.**

🏠 **Apse Manor Country House** ⚫, Apse Manor Rd, PO37 7PN, W : 1 ½ m. by A 3020
🖋 866651, 🌳 – 🍴 rest 📺 ☎ 🅿. 🖲 *VISA*
M *(closed Sunday dinner)* (dinner only and Sunday lunch)/dinner 15.50 **st.** and a la carte
🍴 4.50 – **7 rm** ☐ 40.00/50.00 **st.**

🏠 **Queensmead,** 12 Queens Rd, PO37 6AN, 🖋 862342, ⌇ heated, 🌳 – 🍴 rest 📺 🅿. 🖲
AE VISA 🍴
March-October and Christmas – **M** (bar lunch)/dinner 15.50 **st.** 🍴 3.95 – **30 rm** ☐ 32.00/
60.00 **st.** – SB 60.00/90.00 **st.**

🏠 **Chine Lodge** ⚫, Eastcliff Rd, PO37 6AA, 🖋 862358, 🌳 – 🍴 rest 📺 🅿. 🍴
March-October – **M** (booking essential) (residents only) (dinner only) 8.00 **st.** – **7 rm**
☐ 23.50/54.00 **st.**

🏠 **Luccombe Chine Country** ⚫, Luccombe Chine, PO37 6RH, S : 2 ¼ m. by A 3055
🖋 862037, ≤, 🌳 – 📺 🅿. 🖲 *VISA*. 🍴
closed December and January – **M** (dinner only) 11.75 **st.** 🍴 4.25 – **6 rm** ☐ 50.00/90.00 **st.** –
SB (October-April) 66.00 **st.**

🛏 **Cavendish House** without rest., Eastmount Rd, PO37 6DN, 🖋 862460 – 📺 ☎ 🅿. 🖲 *VISA*
3 rm ☐ 25.00/45.00 **s.**

🛏 **Delphi Cliff,** 7 St. Boniface Cliff Rd, PO37 6ET, 🖋 862179, ≤, 🌳 – 🍴 rest 📺. 🖲 *VISA*.
🍴
April-October – **M** (by arrangement) – **10 rm** ☐ 18.00/40.00 **st.**

Totland – pop. 2 316 – ECD : Wednesday – ✉ ✆ 0983 Isle of Wight.
Newport 13.

🏠 **Sentry Mead,** Madeira Rd, PO39 0BJ, 🖋 753212, 🌳 – 🍴 rest 📺 🅿. 🖲 *AE VISA*
closed 25 and 26 December – **M** (bar lunch)/dinner 11.75 **t.** 🍴 2.50 – **14 rm** ☐ 30.00/60.00 **t.**
– SB 60.00/70.00 **st.**

🛏 **Littledene Lodge,** Granville Rd, PO39 0AX, 🖋 752411 – 🍴 rest 🅿
March-October – **M** (by arrangement) – **6 rm** ☐ 25.00/40.00 **st.** – SB 54.00/72.00 **st.**

Ventnor – pop. 7 956 – ECD : Wednesday – ✉ ✆ 0983 Isle of Wight.
🏌 Steephill Down Rd 🖋 853326.
🎫 34 High St., PO38 1RZ 🖋 853625 (summer only).
Newport 10.

🏨 **Madeira Hall** ⚫, Trinity Rd, PO38 1NS, 🖋 852624, Fax 854906, ⌇ heated, 🌳 – 🍴 📺
☎ 🅿. 🖲 *VISA*. 🍴
M (booking essential) 15.00/20.00 🍴 3.00 – **8 rm** ☐ 30.00/70.00.

at Bonchurch – ✉ ✆ 0983 Isle of Wight :

🏨 **Peacock Vane Country House** ⚫, Bonchurch Village Rd, PO38 1RJ, 🖋 852019,
Fax 854796, « Opulent Victoriana », 🌳 – 🍴 rest 📺 ☎ 🅿. 🖲 *AE* ⓞ *VISA*
closed Monday and Tuesday January-February – **M** 9.95/17.95 **t.** and dinner a la carte
🍴 5.00 – **10 rm** ☐ 50.00/85.00 **t.**, 1 suite – SB (except Christmas, New Year and Bank
Holidays) 80.00/150.00 **st.**

🏨 **Winterbourne** ⚫, PO38 1RQ, via Bonchurch Shute 🖋 852535, Fax 853056, « Country
house ≤ gardens and sea », ⌇ heated – 🍴 rest 📺 🅿. 🖲 *AE* ⓞ *VISA*
closed December and January – **M** (light lunch by arrangement)/dinner 15.50 **st.** 🍴 5.50 –
18 rm ☐ (dinner included) 43.00/132.00 **st.**

🏠 **Highfield,** 87 Leeson Rd, Upper Bonchurch, PO38 1PU, on A 3055 🖋 852800, ≤, 🌳 –
🍴 rest 📺 ☎ 🅿. 🖲 *VISA*
closed December and January – **M** 8.95/14.95 **t.** – **12 rm** ☐ 20.00/70.00 **t.** – SB (except
June-August) 60.00/80.00 **st.**

🏠 **Lake** ⚫, Shore Rd, PO38 1RF, 🖋 852613, Fax 852613, 🌳 – 🍴 rest 🅿
March-October – **M** 9.50 **t.** 🍴 3.50 – **21 rm** ☐ 28.50/59.00 **t.**

WIGSTON FIELDS Leics. 402 403 404 Q 26 – see Leicester.

WILLERBY Humbs. 402 S 22 – see Kingston-upon-Hull.

WILLERSEY Heref. and Worcs. 403 404 O 27 – see Broadway.

WILLERSEY HILL Glos. 403 404 O 27 – see Broadway (Heref. and Worcs.).

WILLESLEY Glos. 403 404 N 29 – see Tetbury.

WILLINGTON Ches. – see Tarporley.

WILLITON Somerset 403 K 30 The West Country G. – pop. 2 410 – ECD : Saturday – ✉ Taunton
– ✆ 0984.
Envir. : Cleeve Abbey★★ *AC,* W : 2 m. by A 39.
◆London 177 – Minehead 8 – Taunton 16.

🏠 **White House,** 11 Long St., TA4 4QW, 🅿 632306 – 📺 ☎ 🄿
mid May-October – **M** (dinner only) 32.00 **t.** 🍷 6.75 – **12 rm** ⬜ 34.00/85.00 **t.** – SB 112.00/
150.00 **st.**

🏠 **Fairfield House,** 51 Long St., TA4 4QY, 🅿 632636 – 🄿. 🆕 𝗩𝗜𝗦𝗔 ⚹
March-October – **M** (dinner only) 12.00 **st.** and a la carte 🍷 5.00 – **5 rm** ⬜ 25.00/48.00 **st.** –
SB 70.00/90.00 **st.**

↟ **Curdon Mill** 🌿, Lower Vellow, TA4 4LS, SE : 2 ½ m. by A 358 on Stogumber rd
🅿 56522, Fax 56197, ≤, « Converted water mill on working farm », 🔽 heated, 🦌,
park – 🛏 rm 📺 🄿. 🆕 𝗩𝗜𝗦𝗔 ⚹
M (by arrangement) 19.50 🍷 4.50 – **6 rm** ⬜ 28.00/44.00 **st.**

WILMCOTE Warks. **403** **404** O 27 – see Stratford-upon-Avon.

WILMINGTON Devon **403** K 31 – see Honiton.

WILMINGTON East Sussex **404** U 31 – see Eastbourne.

WILMSLOW Ches. **402** **403** **404** N 24 – pop. 28 827 – ECD : Wednesday – ✆ 0625.
🏌 Great Warford, Mobberley 🅿 0566 (Mobberley) 872148.
◆London 189 – ◆Liverpool 38 – ◆Manchester 12 – ◆Stoke-on-Trent 27.

🏨 **Stanneylands** 🌿, Stanneylands Rd, SK9 4EY, N : 1 m. by A 34 🅿 525225, Fax 537282,
« Gardens » – 🍽 rest 📺 ☎ ♿ 🄿 – 🔬 90. 🆕 🄰🄴 ⓞ 𝗩𝗜𝗦𝗔 ⚹
M *(closed dinner Sunday, Good Friday, 25 December and I January)* 9.50/25.00
t. and a la carte 🍷 4.00 – ⬜ 9.50 – **33 rm** 79.00/87.00 **t.** – SB (weekends only) 110.00/
150.00 **st.**

🏨 **Wilmslow Moat House** (Q.M.H.), Oversley Ford, Altrincham Rd, SK9 4LR, NW : 2¾ m.
on A 538 🅿 529201, Telex 666401, Fax 531876, 🏋, ☎, 🔽, squash – 🔆 🛏 rm 📺 ☎ 🄿 –
🔬 280. 🆕 🄰🄴 𝗩𝗜𝗦𝗔
M *(closed Saturday lunch)* 12.50/15.95 **st.** and a la carte 🍷 5.50 – ⬜ 8.00 – **125 rm**
76.00/90.00 **st.** – SB (weekends only) 90.00/96.00.

at Handforth N : 3 m. on A 34 – ✉ ✆ 0625 Wilmslow :

🏨 **Belfry,** Stanley Rd, SK9 3LD, 🅿 061 (Manchester) 437 0511, Fax 499 0597 – 🔆 📺 ☎ 🄿 –
🔬 100. 🆕 🄰🄴 ⓞ 𝗩𝗜𝗦𝗔
closed 27 and 28 December – **M** (dancing Friday evening) 21.50 **t.** and a la carte ⬜ 8.75 –
77 rm 73.50/94.00 **t.**, 3 suites.

WILTON Heref. and Worcs. **403** **404** M 28 – see Ross-on-Wye.

WIMBORNE MINSTER Dorset **403** **404** O 31 The West Country G. – pop. 14 193 – ECD :
Wednesday – ✆ 0202 Wimborne.
See : Town★ – Priest's House Museum★ *AC.*
Envir. : Kingston Lacy★★ *AC*, NW : 3 m. by B 3082.
🎫 29 High St., BH21 1HR 🅿 886116.
◆London 112 – Bournemouth 10 – Dorchester 23 – Salisbury 27 – ◆Southampton 30.

🏠 **Beechleas,** 17 Poole Rd, BH21 1QA, 🅿 841684 – 🛏 rm 📺 ☎ 🄿. 🆕 🄰🄴 𝗩𝗜𝗦𝗔 ⚹
closed 23 December-23 January – **M** (dinner only) 19.50 **t.** – ⬜ 8.50 – **7 rm** 53.00/83.00 **t.** –
SB (weekends only) 93.20/109.20 **st.**

↟ **Stour Lodge,** 21 Julians Rd, BH21 1EF, on A 31 (Dorchester rd) 🅿 888003, 🍴 – 📺 🄿
closed 20 December-5 January – **M** (by arrangement) 15.00 – **3 rm** ⬜ 25.00/45.00 **st.**

🍴🍴 **Les Bouviers,** Oakley Hill, Morley, BH21 1RJ, S : 1¼ m. on A 349 🅿 889555 – 🄿. 🆕 🄰🄴
𝗩𝗜𝗦𝗔
closed Saturday lunch and Sunday dinner – **M** 16.95/19.95 **t.** and a la carte.

at Horton N : 6 m. by B 3078 – ✉ Wimborne Minster – ✆ 0258 Witchampton :

🏠 **Northill House** 🌿, BH21 7HL, NW : ½ m. 🅿 840407, 🍴 – 🛏 rest 📺 ☎ 🄿. 🆕 🄰🄴 𝗩𝗜𝗦𝗔 ⚹
closed 20 December-15 February – **M** (bar lunch)/dinner 13.00 **st.** 🍷 4.00 – **9 rm** ⬜ 36.00/
63.00 **st.**

WINCHCOMBE Glos. **403** **404** O 28 – ✆ 0242.
◆London 100 – ◆Birmingham 43 – Gloucester 26 – ◆Oxford 43.

🏠 **White Lion,** 37 North St., GL54 5PS, 🅿 603300, Fax 221969, « Part 15C inn », 🍴 – 📺.
🆕 𝗩𝗜𝗦𝗔
M (bar lunch Monday to Saturday)/dinner a la carte 12.20/21.20 **t.** – **6 rm** ⬜ 30.00/65.00 **st.**
– SB (weekdays only) 40.00/64.00 **st.**

↟ **Sudeley Hill Farm** 🌿 without rest., GL54 5JB, E : 1 m. via Castle St. 🅿 602344, ≤,
« Part 15C house, working farm », 🦌, park – 🛏 📺 🄿
closed Christmas – **3 rm** ⬜ 25.00/40.00 **s.**

🍴🍴🍴 **Wesley House** with rm, High St., GL54 5LJ, 🅿 602366, « Part 15C house » – 🛏 rm 📺
☎. 🆕 🄰🄴 𝗩𝗜𝗦𝗔 ⚹
closed 17 January-9 February – **M** *(closed Sunday dinner except Bank Holidays and
Tuesday)* 14.00/22.50 **st.** and lunch a la carte 🍷 4.50 – **5 rm** ⬜ 35.00/65.00 **st.** – SB 75.00/
130.00 **st.**

WINCHELSEA E. Sussex 404 W 31 Great Britain G. – ✪ 0797 Rye.

See : Town★ – St. Thomas Church (effigies★).

◆London 64 – ◆Brighton 46 – Folkestone 30.

⌂ **Strand House** without rest., TN36 4JT, E : ¼ m. on A 259 ℰ 226276, « Part 14C and 15C house », ☞ – 📺 🅿. 🔃 VISA. ⚡
10 rm ⌷ 25.00/50.00 t.

WINCHESTER Hants. 403 404 P 30 Great Britain G. – pop. 34 127 – ECD : Thursday – ✪ 0962.

See : City★★ – Cathedral★★★ *AC* B – Winchester College★ *AC* B B – Castle Great Hall★ B D – God Begot House★ B A.

Envir. : St. Cross Hospital★★ *AC* A.

🛈 Guildhall, The Broadway, SO23 9LJ ℰ 840500/843180.

◆London 72 – ◆Bristol 76 – ◆Oxford 52 – ◆Southampton 12.

WINCHESTER

High Street.	**B**		
Alresford Road	**A** 2		
Andover Road	**B** 3		
Bereweeke Road	**A** 5		
Bridge Street	**B** 6		
Broadway (The)	**B** 8		
Chilbolton Avenue	**A** 9		

City Road	**B** 10	Park Road	**A** 26
Clifton Terrace	**B** 12	Quarry Road	**A** 29
East Hill	**B** 15	St. George's Street	**B** 32
Eastgate Street	**B** 16	St. Paul's Hill	**B** 33
Easton Lane	**A** 18	St. Peter's Street	**B** 34
Friarsgate	**B** 19	Southgate Street	**B** 35
Garnier Road	**A** 20	Stoney Lane	**A** 36
Kingsgate Road	**A** 22	Stockbridge Road	**B** 37
Magdalen Hill	**B** 23	Sussex Street	**B** 38
Middle Brook Street	**B** 24	Union Street	**B** 39
Morestead Road	**A** 25	Upper High Street	**B** 40

🏛 **Lainston House** ♨, Sparsholt, SO21 2LT, NW : 3½ m. by A 272 ℰ 863588, Fax 72672, ≤, « 17C manor house », ☞, park, ⚒ – 📺 ☎ 🅿 – 🔬 60
37 rm. A

🏛 **Forte Crest,** Paternoster Row, SO23 9LQ, ℰ 861611, Fax 841503, ≤ – 🛗 🕂 rm 📺 ☎ 🅿
– 🔬 100. 🔃 AE ⓞ VISA JCB B c
M 14.00/17.00 **t.** and a la carte ♦ 6.60 – ⌷ 9.95 – **93 rm** 89.00 **st.**, 1 suite – SB 128.00 **st.**

🏛 **Winchester Moat House** (Q.M.H.), Worthy Lane, SO23 7AB, ℰ 868102, Fax 840862, ₤₅, ≦s, 🔲 – 📺 ☎ ⅙ 🅿 – 🔬 200. 🔃 AE ⓞ VISA B e
M *(closed lunch Saturday, Sunday and Bank Holidays)* 13.50/17.00 **t.** and a la carte – **72 rm** ⌷ 65.00/98.00 **t.**

🏛 **Royal** (Best Western), St. Peter St., SO23 8BS, ℰ 840840, Fax 841582, ☞ – 📺 ☎ 🅿 –
🔬 80. 🔃 AE ⓞ VISA JCB B n
M 17.50 **t.** (dinner) and a la carte 22.00/27.00 **t.** ♦ 5.90 – **75 rm** ⌷ 75.00/105.00 **t.** –
SB 98.00/146.00 **st.**

⌂ **Wykeham Arms,** 75 Kingsgate St., SO23 9PE, ℰ 853834, Fax 854411, « Traditional 18C inn, memorabilia », ≦s, ☞ – ⅙ rest 📺 ☎ 🅿. 🔃 AE VISA B u
M *(closed Sunday)* (in bar) a la carte 13.15/18.15 **t.** ♦ 4.50 – **7 rm** ⌷ 62.50/75.00 **t.**

⌂ **East View** without rest., 16 Clifton Hill, SO22 5BL, ☏ 862986, ≤, 🐕 – ✗ 📺 ℗. 🅿️ 𝐕𝐈𝐒𝐀.
✗   B r
  3 rm ⊃ 30.00/40.00 **st.**

⌂ **Florum House**, 47 St. Cross Rd, SO23 9PS, ☏ 840427, 🐕 – 📺 ℗. 🅿️ 𝐕𝐈𝐒𝐀   A a
  M (by arrangement) (communal dining) 14.80 **st.** – **9 rm** ⊃ 30.00/48.00 **st.** – SB 60.00/
  96.00 **st.**

⌂ **Portland House** without rest., 63 Tower St., SO23 8TA, ☏ 865195 – 📺 ℗. ✗   B a
  4 rm ⊃ 35.00/44.00 **st.**

✗✗ **Nine The Square**, 9 Great Minster St., The Square, SO23 9HA, ☏ 864004, Fax 879586 –
🅿️ 🅰🅴 ⓓ 𝐕𝐈𝐒𝐀   B s
  closed Sunday and 1 week January – **M** 12.95 **t.** (lunch) and a la carte 22.75/30.45 **t.**

at Marwell Zoological Park SE : 7¼ m. by A 33 – B – and B 3335 on B 2177 – ✉ ✆ 0962
Winchester :

🏨 **Marwell Resort**, SO21 1JY, ☏ 777681, Fax 777625, ⊆s, 🏊, park – ✗ rm 📺 ☎ & ℗ –
🔺 130. 🅿️ 🅰🅴 ⓓ 𝐕𝐈𝐒𝐀
  M (bar lunch Monday to Saturday)/dinner 16.00 **st.** and a la carte ♨ 4.95 – ⊃ 7.50 – **67 rm**
  65.00/75.00 **st.** – SB 98.00/120.00 **st.**

⓪ ATS 61 Bar End Rd ☏ 865021

WINDERMERE Cumbria 🔢🔢🔢 L 20 Great Britain G. – pop. 6 835 – ECD : Thursday – ✆ 053 94.

Envir. : Lake Windermere★★ – Brokhole National Park Centre★ AC, NW : 2 m. by A 591.

🏌 Cleabarrow ☏ 43123, E : 1½ m. by A 5074 - Z - on B 5284.

🗓 Victoria St., LA23 1AD ☏ 46499 at Bowness, Glebe Rd, LA23 3HJ ☏ 42895 (summer only).

◆London 274 – ◆Blackpool 55 – ◆Carlisle 46 – Kendal 10.

Plan on next page

🏨 **Langdale Chase** ⌂, LA23 1LW, NW : 3 m. on A 591 ☏ 32201, Fax 32604, ≤ Lake
Windermere and mountains, « Lakeside setting », ⚲, 🐕, ✗ – ≡ rest 📺 ☎ ℗. 🅿️ 🅰🅴
ⓓ 𝐕𝐈𝐒𝐀   Y
  M 15.00/23.00 **t.** and dinner a la carte ♨ 5.25 – **31 rm** ⊃ 65.00/180.00 **t.** – SB (November-
March) 110.00/130.00 **st.**

🏨 **Holbeck Ghyll** ⌂, Holbeck Lane, LA23 1LU, NW : 3¼ m. by A 591 ☏ 32375, Fax 34743,
≤, « Former hunting lodge », 🐕, ✗ – ✗ rest 📺 ☎ ℗. 🅿️ 🅰🅴 𝐕𝐈𝐒𝐀   Y
  M (light lunch)/dinner 32.75 **t.** ♨ 5.25 – **14 rm** ⊃ (dinner included) 75.00/220.00 **t.** –
SB (November-May) 110.00/140.00 **st.**

🏨 **Merewood Country House** ⌂, Ecclerigg, LA23 1LH, NW : 2½ m. on A 591 ☏ 46484,
Fax 42128, ≤, 🐕, park – ✗ 📺 ☎ ℗ – 🔺 80. 🅿️ 🅰🅴 𝐕𝐈𝐒𝐀. ✗   Y
  M (bar lunch Monday to Saturday)/dinner a la carte 17.95 **t.** ♨ 5.00 – **20 rm** ⊃ 57.50/
131.00 **st.** – SB (low season except Christmas, New Year and Bank Holidays) (weekdays
only) 104.00/164.00 **st.**

🏠 **Quarry Garth Country House**, Troutbeck Bridge, LA23 1LF, NW : 2 m. on A 591
☏ 88282, Fax 46584, 🐕, park – ✗ rest 📺 ☎ ℗. 🅿️ 🅰🅴 ⓓ 𝐕𝐈𝐒𝐀   Y
  M (dinner only) 19.50 **st.** ♨ 6.00 – **10 rm** ⊃ 50.00/100.00 **t.** – SB (except Bank Holidays)
90.00/130.00 **st.**

🏠 **Cedar Manor**, Ambleside Rd, LA23 1AX, ☏ 43192, Fax 45970, 🐕 – ✗ rest 📺 ☎ ℗. 🅿️
𝐕𝐈𝐒𝐀   Y i
  M (dinner only) 21.00 **t.** ♨ 4.50 – **12 rm** ⊃ 34.00/64.00 **t.** – SB (winter only) 65.00/85.00 **st.**

🏠 **Glenburn**, New Rd, LA23 2EE, ☏ 42649, Fax 88998 – ✗ 📺 ☎ ℗. 🅿️ 𝐕𝐈𝐒𝐀 𝐉𝐂𝐁. ✗   Y u
  M (dinner only) 15.00 **st.** ♨ 5.50 – **16 rm** ⊃ 35.00/60.00 **st.** – SB (except Bank Holidays)
77.00/100.00 **st.**

🏠 **Woodlands**, New Rd, LA23 2EE, ☏ 43915 – ✗ 📺 ℗   Y u
  closed 2 weeks winter – **M** (residents only) (dinner only) 13.50 **st.** – **14 rm** ⊃ 25.00/
54.00 **st.**

🏠 **Hawksmoor**, Lake Rd, LA23 2EQ, ☏ 42110, Fax 42110, 🐕 – ✗ rest 📺 ℗. 🅿️ 𝐕𝐈𝐒𝐀. ✗
  closed 20 November-27 December and 11 January-12 February – **M** (dinner only) 10.50 **st.**
♨ 4.00 – **10 rm** ⊃ 25.00/59.00 **st.** – SB (November-May) (except Bank Holidays) 60.00/
77.00 **st.**   Z s

⌂ **Glencree** without rest., Lake Rd, LA23 2EQ, ☏ 45822 – 📺 ℗. 🅿️ 𝐕𝐈𝐒𝐀. ✗   Z s
  mid February-October – **5 rm** ⊃ 35.00/60.00 **st.**

⌂ **Braemount House**, Sunny Bank Rd, LA23 2EN, via Queens Drive ☏ 45967, Fax 45967 –
✗ 📺 ☎ ℗. 🅿️ 𝐕𝐈𝐒𝐀. ✗   Z u
  M (dinner only) 15.50 **st.** ♨ 5.15 – **6 rm** ⊃ 37.00/70.00 **st.** – SB (except Bank Holidays)
85.00/105.00 **st.**

⌂ **Archway**, 13 College Rd, LA23 1BU, ☏ 45613 – ✗ 📺 ☎. 🅿️ 𝐕𝐈𝐒𝐀. ✗   Y e
  closed 2 weeks January – **M** (by arrangement) 10.50 **st.** ♨ 3.50 – **5 rm** ⊃ 25.00/50.00 **st.** –
SB 60.00/72.00 **st.**

⌂ **Beaumont** without rest., Holly Rd, LA23 2AF, ☏ 47075 – ✗ 📺 ℗. 🅿️ 🅰🅴 𝐕𝐈𝐒𝐀. ✗   Y n
  February-November – **11 rm** ⊃ 30.00/54.00 **st.**

⌂ **Kirkwood** without rest., Prince's Rd, LA23 2DD, ☏ 43907 – ✗ 📺. 🅿️ 𝐉𝐂𝐁   Y r
  7 rm ⊃ 34.00/50.00 **st.**

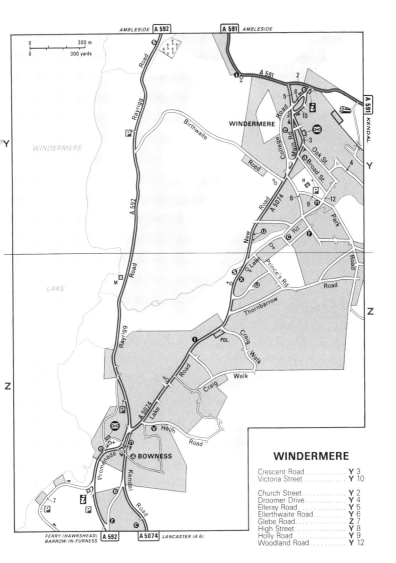

WINDERMERE

⋔ **Oldfield House** without rest., Oldfield Rd, LA23 2BY, ℰ 88445 – 🔌 📺 ☎ 🅿. 🔃 𝘝𝘐𝘚𝘈 Y **c**
JCB. ⚒
8 rm � 22.00/48.00 **st.**

⋔ **Fir Trees** without rest., Lake Rd, LA23 2EQ, ℰ 42272 – 🔌 📺 🅿. 🔃 𝘈𝘌 𝘝𝘐𝘚𝘈. ⚒ Z **x**
7 rm ⊒ 29.50/49.00 **st.**

⋔ **Kay's Cottage,** 7 Broad St., LA23 2AB, ℰ 44146 – 📺. 🔃 𝘝𝘐𝘚𝘈. ⚒ Y **a**
closed 23 to 27 December – **M** (by arrangement) – **4 rm** ⊒ 25.00/34.00 **st.**

XX **Miller Howe** with rm, Rayrigg Rd, LA23 1EY, ℰ 42536, Fax 45664, ≤ Lake Windermere
and mountains, ☞ – 🔌 rest 🍽 rest 📺 ☎ 🅿. 🔃 𝘈𝘌 ⓪ 𝘝𝘐𝘚𝘈 Y **s**
mid March-November – **M** (booking essential) (dinner only) 32.00 **t.** – **13 rm** ⊒ (dinner
included) 70.00/220.00 **t.**

XX **Roger's,** 4 High St., LA23 1AF, ℰ 44954 – 🔃 𝘈𝘌 ⓪ 𝘝𝘐𝘚𝘈 Y **o**
closed Sunday except Bank Holidays and 1 week Christmas – **M** (lunch by arrangement)/
dinner 16.50 **t.** and a la carte ♠ 5.50.

at Bowness-on-Windermere S : 1 m. – ⊠ ☻ 053 94 Windermere :

🏨 **Old England** (Forte), LA23 3DF, ℰ 42444, Fax 43432, ≤ Lake Windermere and mountains, 🔄 heated, ☞ – 🍴 🍽 📺 ☎ 🅿 – 🔬 100. 🖭 🖭 ⓞ 𝗩𝗜𝗦𝗔 𝗝𝗖𝗕   Z **e**
M (bar lunch Monday to Saturday)/dinner 12.95/17.95 **st.** – ⊑ 8.50 – **77 rm** 85.00/130.00 **st.**, 2 suites – SB 80.00/178.00 **st.**

🏨 **Linthwaite House** 🐾, Crook Rd, LA23 3JA, S : ¾ m. by A 5074 on B 5284 ℰ 88600, Fax 88601, ≤ Lake Windermere and fells, « Extensive grounds and private lake », 🗝 – 🍴 🍽 📺 ☎ 🅿. 🖭 🖭 𝗩𝗜𝗦𝗔. 🛇   Z
M (light lunch Monday to Saturday)/dinner 26.50 **st.** 🛈 6.00 – **18 rm** ⊑ 50.00/150.00 **st.** – SB (except Bank Holidays) 110.00/200.00 **st.**

🏨 **Lindeth Fell Country House** 🐾, Kendal Rd, LA23 3JP, S : 1 m. on A 5074 ℰ 43286, ≤ Lake Windermere and mountains, « Country house atmosphere, gardens », 🗝, park, 🎾 – 🍴 🍽 rest 📺 ☎ 🅿. 🖭 𝗩𝗜𝗦𝗔. 🛇
16 March-10 November – **M** (light lunch)/dinner 20.00 **t.** 🛈 3.50 – **14 rm** ⊑ (dinner included) 49.50/99.00 **t.**

🏨 **Craig Manor,** Lake Rd, LA23 3AR, ℰ 88877, Fax 88878, ≤ – 🍽 rest 📺 ☎ 🅿. 🖭 🖭 𝗩𝗜𝗦𝗔
M (bar lunch Monday to Saturday)/dinner 19.50 **st.** and a la carte 🛈 5.50 – **16 rm** ⊑ 45.00/80.00 **st.** – SB (except Bank Holidays) 104.00 **st.**   Z **i**

🏨 **Burnside,** Kendal Rd, LA23 3EP, ℰ 42211, Fax 43824, 𝟙𝟞, 🏊, 🔲, ☞, squash – 🍴 📺 ☎ 🅿 – 🔬 80. 🖭 🖭 ⓞ 𝗩𝗜𝗦𝗔 𝗝𝗖𝗕   Z **c**
M (bar lunch Monday to Saturday)/dinner 17.00 **st.** and a la carte 🛈 5.00 – **41 rm** ⊑ 50.00/90.00 **st.**, 3 suites.

🏨 **Belsfield** (Forte), Back Belsfield Rd, LA23 3EL, ℰ 42448, Fax 46397, ≤, 🏊, 🔲, ☞, 🎾 – 🍴 🍽 📺 ☎ ♿ 🅿 – 🔬 70. 🖭 🖭 ⓞ 𝗩𝗜𝗦𝗔 𝗝𝗖𝗕   Z **o**
M (bar lunch)/dinner 15.95 **st.** and a la carte 🛈 6.45 – ⊑ 8.50 – **62 rm** 80.00/95.00 **st.**, 2 suites – SB 128.00/150.00 **st.**

🏨 **Burn How,** Back Belsfield Rd, LA23 3HH, ℰ 46226, Fax 47000, ☞ – 🍽 rest 📺 ☎ 🅿. 🖭 𝗔𝗘 𝗩𝗜𝗦𝗔. 🛇   Z **r**
M (bar lunch)/dinner 17.50 **st.** and a la carte 🛈 5.00 – **26 rm** ⊑ 48.00/84.00 **st.** – SB (weekdays only) 104.00/138.00 **st.**

🏨 **Wild Boar** (Best Western), Crook Rd, LA23 3NF, SE : 4 m. by A 5074 on B 5284 ℰ 45225, Fax 42498, ☞ – 🍴 🍽 📺 ☎ 🅿. 🖭 🖭 ⓞ 𝗩𝗜𝗦𝗔 𝗝𝗖𝗕   Z
M 11.50/21.00 **t.** and a la carte – **36 rm** ⊑ 55.00/117.00 **t.** – SB 120.00/184.00 **st.**

🏠 **Crag Brow Cottage,** Helm Rd, LA23 3BU, ℰ 44080, Fax 46003, ☞ – 🍽 rest 📺 ☎ 🅿. 🖭 𝗩𝗜𝗦𝗔 𝗝𝗖𝗕. 🛇   Z **v**
M 12.95/21.95 **st.** and dinner a la carte 🛈 3.95 – **11 rm** ⊑ 45.00/75.00 **st.** – SB (except Bank Holidays) 90.00/130.00 **st.**

🏠 **Bordriggs Country House** 🐾, Longtail Hill, LA23 3LD, S : 1 m. by A 592 on B 5284 ℰ 43567, Fax 46949, 🔄 heated, ☞ – 🍽 📺 ☎ 🅿. 🖭 𝗩𝗜𝗦𝗔. 🛇   Z
M (residents only) (dinner only) 17.00 **st.** 🛈 3.00 – **10 rm** ⊑ 25.00/65.00 **st.** – SB (except Bank Holidays) (weekdays only) 75.00/104.00 **st.**

🏠 **White Foss** 🐾 without rest., Longtail Hill, LA23 3JD, S : ¾ m. by A 592 on B 5284 ℰ 46593, ≤, ☞ – 🅿. 🛇   Y
March-October – **3 rm** ⊑ 30.00/44.00 **st.**

🏠 **Laurel Cottage** without rest., St. Martins Sq., LA23 3EF, ℰ 45594 – 📺. 🛇   Z **a**
15 rm ⊑ 22.00/52.00 **st.**

🍽🍽 **Gilpin Lodge** with rm, Crook Rd, LA23 3NE, SE : 2½ m. by A 5074 on B 5284 ℰ 88818, Fax 88058, ≤, ☞ – 🍽 rest 📺 ☎ 🅿. 🖭 🖭 ⓞ 𝗩𝗜𝗦𝗔 𝗝𝗖𝗕. 🛇   Z
M (light lunch Monday to Saturday)/dinner 24.00 **st.** 🛈 5.00 – **9 rm** ⊑ 50.00/120.00 **st.** – SB (except Christmas, New Year and Bank Holidays) 90.00/150.00 **st.**

🍽 Porthole Eating House, 3 Ash St., LA23 3EB, ℰ 42793, Fax 88675   Z **n**

at Troutbeck N : 4 m. by A 592 – Y – ⊠ ☻ 053 94 Windermere :

🏠 **Mortal Man,** LA23 1PL, ℰ 33193, Fax 31261, ≤ Garburn Hill and Troutbeck Valley, ☞ – 🍽 rest 📺 ☎ 🅿
mid February-mid November – **M** (dinner only and Sunday lunch)/dinner 19.00 **st.** 🛈 5.00 – **12 rm** ⊑ (dinner included) 50.00/110.00 **st.**

WINDSOR ⊑ Berks. **404** S **29** Great Britain G. – pop. 30 832 (inc. Eton) – ECD : Wednesday – ☻ 0753.

See : Town★ – Castle★★★ : St. George's Chapel★★★ *AC* (stalls★★★), State Apartments★★ *AC*, North Terrace (≤★★) Z – Eton College★★ *AC* (College Chapel★★, Wall paintings★) Z.

Envir. : Windsor Park★ *AC* Y.

🚢 to Marlow via Maidenhead, Cookham Landing Stage and Windsor Bridge (Salter Bros Ltd) (summer only) – to Staines via Old Windsor Lock and Runnymede (Salter Bros Ltd) (summer only).

🏢 Central Station, Thames St., SL4 1PJ ℰ 852010.

♦London 28 – Reading 19 – ♦Southampton 59.

Plan on next page

WINDSOR

North is at the top
on all town plans.

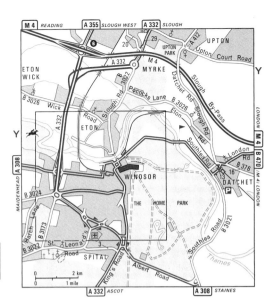

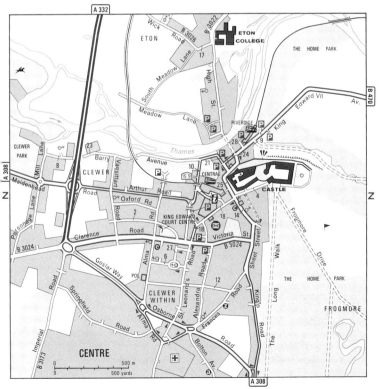

CENTRE

519

Oakley Court (Q.M.H.) 🦢, Windsor Rd, Water Oakley, SL4 5UR, W : 3 m. on A 308 *&* 0628 (Maidenhead) 74141, Telex 849958, Fax 37011, ≼, « Part Gothic mansion on banks of River Thames », 🐟, 🦢, 🛥, park – 🔄 rm 📺 ☎ ❷ – 🔼 100. 🔼 🆎 ⓞ 𝘝𝘐𝘚𝘈 𝘑𝘊𝘉. 🛥
M 19.75/29.50 **st.** and a la carte 🍷 6.70 – ⏤ 12.00 – **91 rm** 130.00/155.00 **st.**, 1 suite – SB (weekends only) 159.00/348.00 **st.**

Castle (Forte), High St., SL4 1LJ, *&* 851011, Telex 849220, Fax 830244 – 🛗 🔄 rm 📺 🛥 ❷ – 🔼 400. 🔼 🆎 ⓞ 𝘝𝘐𝘚𝘈 𝘑𝘊𝘉. 🛥
M 16.50/23.50 **st.** and a la carte 🍷 6.95 – ⏤ 10.50 – **101 rm** 95.00/125.00 **st.**, 3 suites – SB (weekends only) 138.00/158.00 **st.**

Aurora Garden, 14 Bolton Av., SL4 3JF, *&* 868686, Fax 831394, 🛥 – 📺 ☎ ❷ – 🔼 90. 🔼 🆎 ⓞ 𝘝𝘐𝘚𝘈
M 13.95/18.95 **t.** and dinner a la carte 🍷 4.95 – **15 rm** ⏤ 60.00/72.00 **st.** – SB (weekends only) 92.00/130.00 **st.**

Dorset without rest., 4 Dorset Rd, SL4 3BA, *&* 852669 – 📺 ❷. 🔼 🆎 𝘝𝘐𝘚𝘈. 🛥
5 rm ⏤ 50.00/65.00 **st.**

Fairlight Lodge, 41 Frances Rd, SL4 3AQ, *&* 861207, Fax 865963, 🛥 – 🔄 📺 ☎ ❷. 🔼 🆎 𝘝𝘐𝘚𝘈. 🛥
M a la carte 10.00/17.00 **st.** 🍷 4.50 – **10 rm** ⏤ 37.00/60.00 **st.**

WINEHAM W. Sussex 🞴🞴🞴 T 31 – see Henfield.

WINGHAM Kent 🞴🞴🞴 X 30 – pop. 1 429 – ✆ 0227 Canterbury.
♦London 66 – Canterbury 7 – ♦Dover 19 – Margate 14.

✗ **Four Seasons,** 109 High St., CT3 1BU, *&* 720286, 🛥 – 🔼 🆎 𝘝𝘐𝘚𝘈
closed 2 to 9 January – **M** (dinner only and Sunday lunch)/dinner 10.95 **t.** and a la carte 🍷 3.95.

WINSCOMBE Avon 🞴🞴🞴 L 30 – ✆ 0934 Weston-super-Mare.
♦London 137 – ♦Bristol 16 – Taunton 22.

Sidcot Arms, Bridgwater Rd, BS25 1NN, on A 38 *&* 842271, Fax 844192 – 📺 ☎ ⟁ ❷. 🔼 🆎 𝘝𝘐𝘚𝘈. 🛥
M (grill rest.) a la carte 9.35/13.75 **t.** 🍷 3.95 – **31 rm** ⏤ 46.95/51.95 **t.**, 1 suite – SB (week-ends only) 99.00 **st.**

WINSFORD Somerset 🞴🞴🞴 J 30 The West Country G. pop. 340 – ECD : Thursday – ✉ Minehead – ✆ 064 385 (3 fig.) and 0643 (6 fig.).
See : Village★.
Envir. : Exmoor National Park★★.
♦London 194 – Exeter 31 – Minehead 10 – Taunton 32.

Royal Oak Inn (Best Western), TA24 7JE, *&* 455, Fax 388, « Attractive part 12C thatched inn », 🛥 – 📺 ☎ ❷. 🔼 🆎 ⓞ
M 15.00/22.50 **t.** – **14 rm** ⏤ 75.00/95.00 **t.** – SB (except Christmas, New Year and Bank Holidays) 110.00/170.00 **st.**

Karslake House, TA24 7JE, *&* 242, 🛥 – 🔄 📺 ❷
closed 1 January-18 March, 2 weeks July and 31 October-31 December – **M** 15.50 **st.** 🍷 4.60 – **7 rm** ⏤ 40.00/59.00 **st.**

WINSLEY Wilts. 🞴🞴🞴 🞴🞴🞴 N 29 – see Bath (Avon).

WINSTER Derbs. 🞴🞴🞴 🞴🞴🞴 🞴🞴🞴 P 24 – ✆ 0629.
♦London 157 – Derby 21 – ♦Manchester 46 – ♦Nottingham 28 – ♦Sheffeild 28.

Dower House without rest., Main St., DE4 2DH, *&* 650213, Fax 650894, 🛥 – 🔄 📺 ❷
March-October – **3 rm** ⏤ 35.00/55.00 **s.**

WINTERBOURNE Avon 🞴🞴🞴 🞴🞴🞴 M 29 – see Bristol.

WINTERINGHAM Humbs. 🞴🞴🞴 S 22 – pop. 932 – ✉ ✆ 0724 Scunthorpe.
♦London 176 – ♦Kingston-upon-Hull 16 – ♦Sheffield 67.

✗✗✗ ✿ **Winteringham Fields** (Schwab) with rm, DN15 9PF, *&* 733096, Fax 733898, « Part 16C manor house », 🛥 – 🔄 📺 ☎ ❷. 🔼 𝘝𝘐𝘚𝘈. 🛥
closed first 2 weeks January, first week August and Bank Holidays – **M** *(closed lunch Monday and Saturday and Sunday)* 14.75/29.00 **st.** and a la carte 30.00/36.00 **st.** 🍷 5.25 – ⏤ 6.00 – **6 rm** 60.00/95.00 **st.**, 1 suite
Spec. Terrine of quail with rhubarb jelly, Rolled rack of Lincolnshire lamb with roast garlic, Pears presented in three ways.

WITCOMBE Glos. – see Gloucester.

♦London 42 – ♦Cambridge 46 – Chelmsford 9 – Colchester 13.

🏨 **Rivenhall Resort,** Rivenhall End, CM8 3BH, NE : 1 ½ m. by B 1389 on A 12 (southbound carriageway) 🖉 516969, Fax 513674, *Ⅰ₅*, ⭐, 🔲, squash – 🛏 rm 📺 🕿 🄿 – 🚗 185. 🖾 AE ⓞ VISA
M *(closed Saturday lunch)* 11.50/15.50 **t.** and a la carte – 🖵 7.50 – **55 rm** 55.00/65.00 **t.** – SB 80.00/150.00 **st.**

◎ ATS Unit 15, Moss Rd Ind. Est. East 🖉 518360/515671

WITHERSLACK Cumbria 🔢 L 21 – see Grange-over-Sands.

WITHINGTON Glos. 🔢 🔢 O 28 – pop. 500 – 🔘 0242.

♦London 91 – Gloucester 15 – ♦Oxford 35 – Swindon 24.

🏠 **Halewell** ⬗, GL54 4BN, 🖉 890238, Fax 890332, ≤, « Part 15C monastery, country house atmosphere », ⟁ heated, 🐾, ☞, park – 🛏 rest 📺 🄿. 🖾 AE VISA. ✿
M (booking essential) (residents only) (communal dining) (dinner only) 17.50 **st.** – **6 rm** 🖵 47.50/77.00 **st.**

WITHYPOOL Somerset 🔢 J 30 The West Country G. – pop. 231 – ECD : Thursday – ✉ Mine-head – 🔘 064 383 (3 fig.) and 0643 (6 fig.) Exford.

Envir. : Exmoor National Park★★ – Exford (Church★) NE : 4 m. by B 3223 and B 3224.

♦London 204 – Exeter 34 – Taunton 36.

🏠 **Westerclose Country House** ⬗, TA24 7QR, NW : ¼ m. 🖉 302, ≤, ☞, park – 🛏 rest 📺 🄿. 🖾 AE VISA
closed January, February and 31 December – **M** *(closed Monday to non-residents except Bank Holidays)* (bar lunch)/dinner 19.00 **t.** and a la carte ⱥ 4.50 – **10 rm** 🖵 30.00/70.00 **t.**

🏠 **Royal Oak Inn,** TA24 7QP, 🖉 506, Fax 659, « Part 17C inn », 🐾 – 📺 🕿 🄿. 🖾 AE ⓞ VISA
closed 24 to 26 December – **M** (bar lunch)/dinner 21.00 **t.** and a la carte ⱥ 4.45 – **8 rm** 🖵 32.00/70.00 **t.** – SB (except Bank Holidays) 94.00/130.00 **st.**

WITNEY Oxon 🔢 🔢 P 28 – pop. 14 090 – ECD : Tuesday – 🔘 0993.

🅱 Town Hall, Market Sq., OX8 6AG 🖉 775802.

♦London 69 – Gloucester 39 – ♦Oxford 13.

🏨 **Witney Lodge,** Ducklington Lane, OX8 7TJ, S : 1 ½ m. on A 415 🖉 779777, Fax 703467, *Ⅰ₅*, ⭐, 🔲 – 🛏 rm 📺 🕿 & 🄿 – 🚗 160. 🖾 AE VISA. ✿
M 8.75/11.50 **st.** and a la carte – 🖵 4.50 – **74 rm** 49.00/79.00 **st.** – SB (except Easter, Christmas and New Year) (weekends only) 92.00/126.00 **st.**

at Hailey N : 1 ¼ m. on B 4022 – ✉ 🔘 0993 Witney :

🏠 **Bird in Hand,** OX8 5XP, N : 1 m. on B 4022 🖉 868321, Fax 868702 – 🛏 📺 🕿 & 🄿. 🖾 VISA
M a la carte 10.95/19.90 **t.** ⱥ 4.50 – **16 rm** 🖵 43.00/60.00 **t.** – SB 78.50/105.00 **st.**

at Barnard Gate E : 3 ¼ m. by B 4022 off A 40 – ✉ 🔘 0865 Eynsham :

✗ Boot Inn, OX8 6AE, 🖉 881231, Fax 881834 – 🄿.

WIVELISCOMBE Somerset 🔢 K 30 The West Country G. – pop. 1 457 – ECD : Thursday – ✉ Taunton – 🔘 0984.

Envir. : Gaulden Manor★ *AC*, NE : 3 m. by B 3188.

♦London 185 – Barnstaple 38 – Exeter 37 – Taunton 14.

🏠 **Langley House,** Langley Marsh, TA4 2UF, NW : ½ m. 🖉 23318, Fax 24573, ☞ – 🛏 rest 📺 🕿 🄿. 🖾 AE VISA
closed February – **Meals** (booking essential) (lunch by arrangement)/dinner 28.50 **st.** ⱥ 4.50 – **8 rm** 🖵 62.00/104.00 **st.** – SB (except Christmas) 124.00/190.00 **st.**

↑ **Jews Farm House** ⬗, Huish Champflower, TA4 2HL, NW : 2 ½ m. via Langley Marsh turning opposite postbox onto unmarked rd 🖉 24218, ≤, « 13C farmhouse », ☞, park – 🛏 rm 🄿. ✿
closed December and January – **M** (by arrangement) (communal dining) 18.50 **st.** – **3 rm** 🖵 45.00/60.00 **st.**

↑ **Deepleigh** ⬗, Langley Marsh, TA4 2UU, NW : 1 m. on Whitefield rd 🖉 23379, « Converted 16C farmhouse », ☞ – 📺 🄿. ✿
M (by arrangement) 15.00 **st.** ⱥ 4.50 – **3 rm** 🖵 28.00/44.00 **st.** – SB (except Easter and Christmas) 70.00/86.00 **st.**

at Waterrow SW : 2 ½ m. on B 3227 – ✉ Taunton – 🔘 0984 Wiveliscombe :

🏠 Hurstone ⬗ without rest., TA4 2AT, E : ½ m. 🖉 23441, ≤ Tone Valley, « Converted farmhouse », ☞, park – 🛏 📺 🕿 🄿
5 rm.

♦ London 49 – Bedford 13 – Luton 13 – Northampton 24.

🏨 **Bedford Arms** (Mt. Charlotte Thistle), 1 George St., MK17 9PX, ☎ 290441, Telex 825205, Fax 290432 – ⇆ rm 📺 ☎ 🅿 – 🔬 60. 🔼 ⒶⒺ ① 𝘝𝘐𝘚𝘈
M 15.00/19.95 **st.** and a la carte ⅄ 5.75 – ⌷ 8.50 – **54 rm** 75.00/95.00 **st.**, 1 suite – SB (except Easter and Christmas) 94.00/174.00 **st.**

🏠 **Bell Inn**, 34-35 Bedford St., MK17 9QD, ☎ 290280, Fax 290017 – 📺 ☎ 🅿. 🔼 ⒶⒺ ① 𝘝𝘐𝘚𝘈 ⅄
closed 24 to 31 December – **M** - (see below) – **27 rm** ⌷ 58.00/77.00 **st.** – SB (weekends only) 105.00/170.00 **st.**

XXX **Paris House,** Woburn Park, MK17 9QP, SE : 2 ¼ m. on A 4012 ☎ 290692, Fax 290471, « Reconstructed timbered house in Park », 🌳 – 🅿. 🔼 ⒶⒺ ① 𝘝𝘐𝘚𝘈
closed Sunday dinner, Monday and February – **M** 21.50/40.00 **t.** ⅄ 5.00.

XX **Bell Inn**, 21 Bedford St., MK17 9QD, ☎ 290280, Fax 290017 – 🅿. 🔼 ⒶⒺ ① 𝘝𝘐𝘚𝘈
closed Saturday and Bank Holiday lunch, Sunday dinner and 24 to 31 December – **M** 15.95 **t.** ⅄ 5.75.

♦ London 35 – Reading 17 – ♦Southampton 57.

⌂ **Knaphill Manor** 🦢 without rest., Carthouse Lane, GU21 4XT, NW : 2 ¾ m. by Chobham Rd and Brewery Rd, via Horsell ☎ 857962, ≤, 🌳, 🎾 – 📺 🅿. 🔼 𝘝𝘐𝘚𝘈. ⅄
closed Easter and Christmas – **3 rm** ⌷ 30.00/65.00 **s.**

WOLVERHAMPTON

Darlington Street	**B**	Alfred Squire Road	**A** 2	Lichfield Street	**B** 12
Mander Centre	**B**	Birmingham New Road	**A** 3	Market Street	**B** 14
Victoria Street	**B** 24	Bridgnorth Road	**A** 6	Princess Street	**B** 15
Wulfrun Centre	**B**	Cleveland Street	**B** 7	Queen Square	**B** 17
		Garrick Street	**B** 8	Railway Drive	**B** 20
		High Street	**A** 9	Salop Street	**B** 22
		Lichfield Road	**A** 10	Thompson Avenue	**A** 23

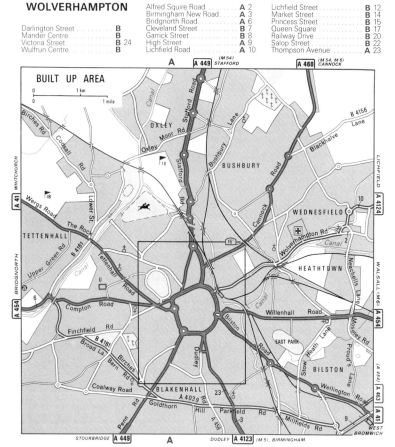

🛆 Easthampstead Park ℰ 0344 (Bracknell) 424066 – ⊺₈, ⊺₉ Sandford Lane, Hurst ℰ 345143.
◆London 43 – Reading 7 – ◆Southampton 52.

🏛 **Stakis St. Annes Manor,** London Rd, RG11 1ST, E : 1 ½ m. on A 329 ℰ 772550, Telex 847342, Fax 772526, ₭₆, ≋s, ⊠, ⨂, park, ✗ – 🕮 ⇔ rm 🔳 rest 📺 ☎ ఉ ఇ – 🔏 100. 🔼
AE ⓪ VISA JCB
M 14.95/19.75 **t.** and dinner a la carte – ⌸ 9.75 – **126 rm** 111.00/146.00 **st.**, 4 suites – SB 98.00/128.00 **st.**

🏨 Edward Court, Wellington Rd, RG11 2AN, ℰ 775886, Fax 772018 – 📺 ☎ ఇ – 🔏 40
25 rm.

⊺₈ Oxley Park, Stafford Rd, Bushbury ℰ 20506, N : 1 ½ m. by A 449 A – ⊺₈ Wergs, Keepers Lane, Tettenhall ℰ 742225, NW : 3 m. by A 41 A – ⊺₈ Perton Park, Wrottesley Park Rd ℰ 380103/ 380073, W : 6 m. by A 454 A.
🖪 18 Queen Sq., WV1 1TQ ℰ 312051.
◆London 132 – ◆Birmingham 15 – ◆Liverpool 89 – Shrewsbury 30.

Plan of Enlarged Area : see Birmingham pp. 2 and 3

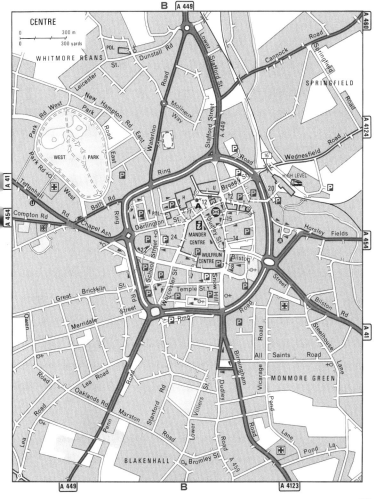

Victoria Hotel Periquito, Lichfield St., WV1 4DB, ℰ 29922, Fax 29923 – ▯ 🖵 ☎ ℗ –
🔬 210. 🌂 🖭 ⑩ 𝐕𝐈𝐒𝐀 𝐉𝐂𝐁, ❀   B e
M (dinner only and Sunday lunch)/dinner 12.50 **st.** and a la carte ⓘ 5.00 – ⟐ 6.50 – **116 rm**
49.00/59.00 **st.**, 1 suite.

Novotel, Union St., WV1 3JN, ℰ 871100, Telex 333027, Fax 870054, 🏊 heated – ▯
⟿ rm ▤ rest 🖵 ☎ ⅋ ℗ – 🔬 200. 🌂 🖭 ⑩ 𝐕𝐈𝐒𝐀   B a
M 16.00 **st.** and a la carte ⓘ 5.85 – ⟐ 7.50 – **132 rm** 55.00/60.00 **st.** – SB (weekends only)
90.00/130.00 **st.**

Mount (Jarvis) ❧, Mount Rd, Tettenhall Wood, WV6 8HL, W : 2 ½ m. by A 454
ℰ 752055, Fax 745263, ☞ – ⟿ rm 🖵 ☎ ℗ – 🔬 140. 🌂 🖭 ⑩ 𝐕𝐈𝐒𝐀   A a
M (closed lunch Saturday and Bank Holidays) 15.95 **st.** and a la carte – ⟐ 8.50 – **55 rm**
69.00/85.00 **st.**, 1 suite – SB (except Easter, Christmas and Bank Holidays) 79.00 **st.**

Ely House, 53 Tettenhall Rd, WV3 9NB, ℰ 311311, Fax 21098 – 🖵 ☎ ℗. 🌂 🖭 ⑩
𝐕𝐈𝐒𝐀   B u
closed 25 to 29 December – **M** 12.95/13.95 **t.** and a la carte – **18 rm** ⟐ 42.00/68.00 **t.**

◉ ATS 35-39 Wednesfield Rd ℰ 455055   ATS 2 Willenhall rd ℰ 871417

WOOBURN COMMON Bucks. – see Beaconsfield.

WOODBRIDGE Suffolk 𝟒𝟎𝟒 X 27 – pop. 9 697 – ECD : Wednesday – ✪ 0394.

🏌 Cretingham, Grove Farm ℰ 0728 (Cretingham) 685275 – 🏌 Seckford Hall Rd, Great Bealings
ℰ 388000, SW : by A 12.

◆London 81 – Great Yarmouth 45 – ◆Ipswich 8 – ◆Norwich 47.

Seckford Hall ❧, IP13 6NU, SW : 1 ¼ m. by A 12 ℰ 385678, Fax 380610, ≤, « Part
Tudor country house », 🗚, 🖾, 🖵, ❧, ☞, park – ⟿ rm ▤ rest 🖵 ☎ ⅋ ℗ – 🔬 100. 🌂
🖭 ⑩ 𝐕𝐈𝐒𝐀
closed 25 December – **M** 13.00 **st.** (lunch) and a la carte 22.15/33.45 **st.** ⓘ 5.00 – **26 rm**
⟐ 79.00/99.00 **st.**, 7 suites – SB 67.50/164.00 **st.**

Crown (Forte), Thoroughfare, IP12 1AD, ℰ 384242, Fax 387192 – ⟿ rm 🖵 ☎ ℗. 🌂 🖭
⑩ 𝐕𝐈𝐒𝐀
M (bar lunch Monday to Saturday)/dinner 15.95 **t.** ⓘ 6.45 – ⟐ 8.50 – **20 rm** 70.00/80.00 **st.** –
SB (except Bank Holidays) 98.00 **st.**

Grove, 39 Grove Rd, IP12 4LG, on A 12 ℰ 382202, ☞ – 🖵 ℗. 🌂 𝐕𝐈𝐒𝐀
M 11.70 **st.** ⓘ 3.65 – **9 rm** ⟐ 19.00/42.00 **st.** – SB (except Bank Holidays) 50.00/65.00 **st.**

WOODFALLS Wilts. – see Salisbury.

WOODGREEN Hants. – see Fordingbridge.

☞ Per spostarvi più rapidamente utilizzate le **carte Michelin "Grandi Strade"** :
nᵒ 𝟗𝟕𝟎 Europa, nᵒ 𝟗𝟖𝟎 Grecia, nᵒ 𝟗𝟖𝟒 Germania, nᵒ 𝟗𝟖𝟓 Scandinavia-Finlanda,
nᵒ 𝟗𝟖𝟔 Gran Bretagna-Irlanda, nᵒ 𝟗𝟖𝟕 Germania-Austria-Benelux, nᵒ 𝟗𝟖𝟖 Italia,
nᵒ 𝟗𝟖𝟗 Francia, nᵒ 𝟗𝟗𝟎 Spagna-Portogallo, nᵒ 𝟗𝟗𝟏 Jugoslavia.

WOODHALL SPA Lincs. 𝟒𝟎𝟐 𝟒𝟎𝟒 T 24 Great Britain G. – pop. 2 526 – ECD : Wednesday –
✪ 0526.

Envir. : Tattershall Castle★ AC, SE : 4 m. by B 1192 and A 153.

🏌 Woodhall Spa ℰ 352511.

🛈 The Cottage Museum, Iddlesleigh Rd, LN10 6SH ℰ 353775 (summer only).

◆London 138 – Lincoln 18.

Petwood House ❧ Stixwould Rd, LN10 6QF, ℰ 352411, Fax 353473, ≤, « Gardens »,
park – ▯ ⟿ rm 🖵 ☎ ℗ – 🔬 150. 🌂 🖭 ⑩ 𝐕𝐈𝐒𝐀, ❀
M (closed Saturday lunch) 9.85/16.95 **st.** – **46 rm** ⟐ 69.95/81.00 **st.** – SB (except Christmas
and New Year) 108.00 **st.**

Golf, The Broadway, LN10 6SG, ℰ 353535, Fax 353096, ☞ – 🖵 ☎ ℗ – 🔬 150. 🌂 🖭 ⑩
𝐕𝐈𝐒𝐀
M (bar lunch Monday to Saturday)/dinner 14.50 **t.** and a la carte ⓘ 4.25 – **50 rm** ⟐ 55.00/
85.00 **t.** – SB 79.00/119.00 **st.**

Dower House ❧, Manor Estate, via Spa Rd, LN10 6PY, ℰ 352588, ☞ – 🖵 ℗. 🌂 🖭 ⑩
𝐕𝐈𝐒𝐀
M (bar lunch)/dinner a la carte 11.70/17.65 **st.** ⓘ 3.65 – **7 rm** ⟐ 35.00/48.00 **st.** – SB 70.00/
105.30 **st.**

Oglee, 16 Stanhope Av., LN10 6SP, ℰ 353512, Fax 353512, ☞ – ⟿ rest 🖵 ℗
closed Christmas-New Year – **M** (by arrangement) – **5 rm** ⟐ 20.00/40.00 **st.**

Duns, The Broadway, LN10 6SQ, ℰ 352969 – ℗
M (by arrangement) 8.50 – **6 rm** ⟐ 17.00/45.00 **st.**

WOODSEAVES Staffs. 402 403 404 N 25 – ✿ 0785.

◆London 155 – ◆Birmingham 38 – Shrewsbury 23 – ◆Stoke-on-Trent 15.

XX **Old Parsonage Coach House** with rm, High Offley, ST20 0NE, W : 1 ¼ m. ℰ 284446, Fax 284527, ☞ – ⇆ rm 📺 ☎ 🅿. 🔄 AE ⑩ VISA
  M *(closed Monday and Bank Holidays)* 15.50/22.50 **st.** – **4 rm** � 40.00 **st.** – SB 70.00/100.00 **st.**

X **Royal Oak,** Grubb St., High Offley, ST20 0NE, W : 1¼ m. ℰ 284579 – 🅿. 🔄 ⑩ VISA
  closed Sunday dinner and Bank Holidays except Christmas – **M** (dinner only and Sunday lunch)/dinner 22.00 **t.** ░ 4.75.

WOODSTOCK Oxon. 403 404 P 28 Great Britain G. – pop. 3 057 – ECD : Wednesday – ✿ 0993.

See : Blenheim Palace★★★ (The Grounds★★★) *AC*.

🛈 Hensington Rd, OX20 1JQ. ℰ 811038 (summer only).

◆London 65 – Gloucester 47 – ◆Oxford 8.

🏩 Bear (Forte), Park St., OX20 1SZ, ℰ 811511, Fax 813380, « Part 16C inn » – ⇆ 📺 ☎ 🅿 – 🔺 70
  41 rm, 4 suites.

🏨 **Feathers,** Market St., OX20 1SX, ℰ 812291, Fax 813158, « Tastefully furnished 17C houses » – 📺 ☎. 🔄 AE ⑩ VISA
  M 15.50/23.50 **t.** and a la carte – ⊇ 7.50 – **16 rm** 75.00/138.00 **t.**, 1 suite.

WOODY BAY Devon 403 I 30 – see Lynton.

WOOLACOMBE Devon 403 H 30 The West Country G. – pop. 1 171 – ECD : Wednesday – ✿ 0271.

Envir. : Mortehoe★★ (St. Mary's Church★, Morte Point★, Vantage Point★) N : ½ m.

🛈 Hall 70, Beach Rd, EX34 7BT. ℰ 870553 (summer only).

◆London 237 – Barnstaple 15 – Exeter 55.

🏩 **Woolacombe Bay,** EX34 7BN, ℰ 870388, Fax 870613, ≤, ╟₅, ≘ₛ, ⊐ heated, 🔲, ☞, %, squash – ▐ 📺 ☎ 🅿 – 🔺 200. 🔄 AE ⑩ VISA. ※
  closed 2 January-11 February – **M** (dancing Tuesday evening) (light lunch Monday to Saturday)/dinner 17.00 **st.** and a la carte ░ 4.50 – **59 rm** ⊇ (dinner included) 83.00/166.00 **t.** – SB (weekends only) 184.00/190.00 **st.**

🏠 **Little Beach,** The Esplanade, EX34 7DJ, ℰ 870398, ≤ – ⇆ rest 📺 ☎ 🅿. 🔄 VISA
  March-October – **M** (dinner only) 12.00 **st.** ░ 3.65 – **10 rm** ⊇ 27.00/70.00 **st.** – SB (March-May and October) 60.00/72.00 **st.**

at Mortehoe N : ½ m. – ✉ ✿ 0271 Woolacombe :

🏩 **Watersmeet,** The Esplanade, EX34 7EB, ℰ 870333, Fax 870890, ≤ Morte Bay, ⊐ heated, ☞, % – ⇆ rest 📺 ☎ 🅿. 🔄 AE ⑩ VISA. ※
  closed December and January – **M** (bar lunch)/dinner 24.50 **st.** and a la carte ░ 4.75 – **24 rm** ⊇ (dinner included) 55.00/158.00 **st.** – SB (September-May) 94.00/158.00 **st.**

🏠 **Cleeve House,** EX34 7ED, ℰ 870719 – ⇆ rest 📺 🅿. 🔄. ※
  Easter-mid November – **M** (dinner only) 15.00 **st.** ░ 3.60 – **6 rm** ⊇ 35.00/72.00 **s.** – SB (except August-mid September) 72.00/94.00 **st.**

🏠 **Sunnycliffe,** Chapel Hill, EX34 7EB, ℰ 870597, ≤ Morte Bay – ⇆ rest 📺 🅿. ※
  February-mid November – **M** 15.00 **st.** – **8 rm** ⊇ 32.00/56.00 **st.** – SB 74.00/96.00 **st.**

WOOLLEY EDGE SERVICE AREA W. Yorks. – ✉ ✿ 0924 Wakefield

🏠 **Granada Lodge** without rest., WF4 4LQ, M 1 between junctions 38 and 39 ℰ 830569, Fax 830609, Reservations (Freephone) 0800 555300 – ⇆ 📺 🅿. 🔄 AE VISA. ※
  ⊇ 4.00 – **31 rm** 34.95/37.95 **st.**

WOOLSTONE Glos. – see Cheltenham.

WOOLTON HILL Berks. – see Newbury.

WOOTTON BASSETT Wilts. 403 404 O 29 – see Swindon.

WORCESTER Heref. and Worcs. 403 404 N 27 Great Britain G. – pop. 75 466 – ECD : Thursday – ✿ 0905.

See : City★ – Cathedral★★ – Royal Worcester Porcelain Works★ (Dyson Perrins Museum★) **M**.

Exc. : The Elgar Trail★.

╟₅ The Fairway, Tolladine Rd ℰ 21074 – ╟₅ Perdiswell Municipal, Bilford Rd ℰ 754668.

🛈 The Guildhall, High St., WR1 2EY ℰ 726311/723471.

◆London 124 – ◆Birmingham 26 – ◆Bristol 61 – ◆Cardiff 74.

Plan on next page

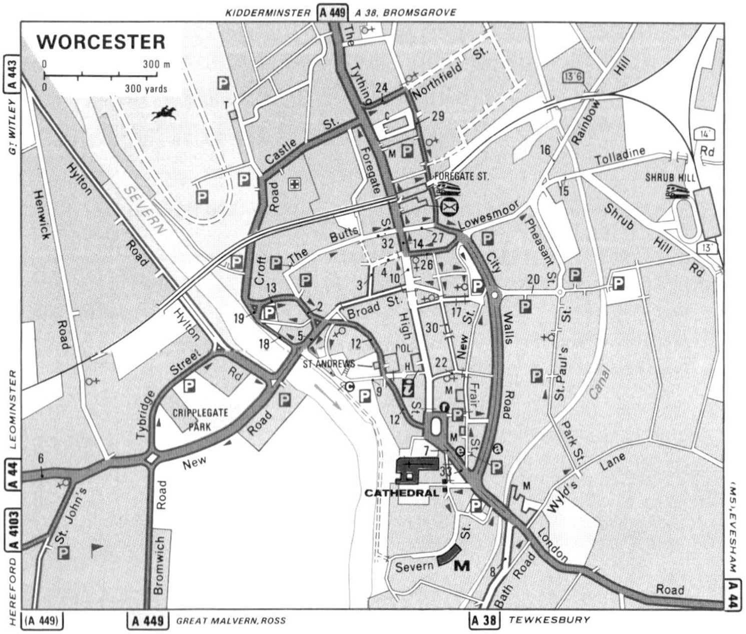

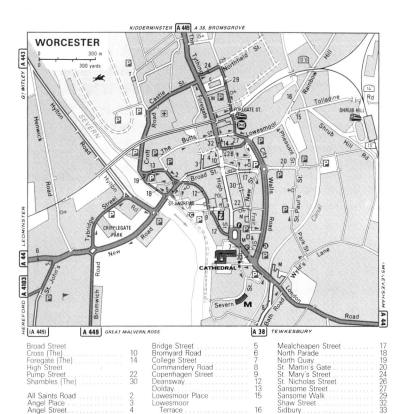

WORCESTER
0 300 m
0 300 yards
KIDDERMINSTER A 449 A 38, BROMSGROVE
A 443 G! WITLEY
LEOMINSTER A 44
HEREFORD A 4103
(A 449)
A 449 GREAT MALVERN, ROSS
A 38 TEWKESBURY
(M5), EVESHAM A 44
The Tything
Northfield St.
Castle St.
Foregate St.
FOREGATE ST.
Croft Road
The Butts
Broad St.
High St.
New St.
City Walls Road
Lowesmoor
Tolladine Rd
Rainbow Hill
SHRUB HILL
Shrub Hill Rd
Pheasant St.
St. Paul's St.
Canal
Park St.
Wyld's Lane
London Road
Bath Road
Sidbury
Severn St.
Friar St.
Deansway
ST ANDREWS
CATHEDRAL
Hylton Road
Henwick Road
SEVERN
Hylton Rd
Tybridge Street
CRIPPLEGATE PARK
New Road
Bromwich Road
St. John's

Broad Street	
Cross (The)	10
Foregate (The)	14
High Street	
Pump Street	22
Shambles (The)	30
All Saints Road	2
Angel Place	3
Angel Street	4
Bridge Street	5
Bromyard Road	6
College Street	7
Commandery Road	8
Copenhagen Street	9
Deansway	12
Dolday	13
Lowesmoor Place	15
Lowesmoor Terrace	16
Mealcheapen Street	17
North Parade	18
North Quay	19
St. Martin's Gate	20
St. Mary's Street	24
St. Nicholas Street	26
Sansome Street	27
Sansome Walk	29
Shaw Street	32
Sidbury	33

🏨 **Fownes Resort,** City Walls Rd, WR1 2AP, ✆ 613151, Fax 23742, « Converted glove factory », ≘ – ⇕ 📺 ☎ ♿ Ⓟ – 👥 120. EN AE ◑ VISA **a**
M 8.95/14.95 **st.** and a la carte 🍷 6.50 – ☕ 7.50 – **58 rm** 75.00/85.00 **st.**, 3 suites – SB 96.00/146.00 **st.**

🏨 **Giffard** (Forte), High St., WR1 2QR, ✆ 726262, Fax 723458 – ⇕ 🚭 rm 📺 ☎ Ⓟ – 👥 100. EN AE ◑ VISA JCB **r**
M (bar lunch Monday to Saturday)/dinner 13.95 **t.** and a la carte 🍷 4.50 – ☕ 6.50 – **101 rm** ☕ 45.00/54.00 **st.**, 2 suites – SB (weekends only) 84.00 **st.**

🏨 **Ye Olde Talbot,** Friar St., WR1 2NA, ✆ 23573, Telex 333315, Fax 612760 – 🚭 rm 📺 ☎ Ⓟ. EN AE ◑ VISA
M 8.95/12.95 – **29 rm** ☕ 49.50/60.50 t. – SB (weekends only) 78.00 **st.** **c**

✗✗ **Brown's,** 24 Quay St., WR1 2JJ, ✆ 26263, « Attractively converted riverside corn mill » – 🚭. EN AE ◑ VISA **c**
closed Saturday lunch, Sunday dinner, 1 week Christmas and Bank Holiday Mondays – **Meals** 15.00/30.00 **st.** 🍷 5.00.

at Upton Snodsbury E : 6 m. by A 44 on A 422 – ✉ Worcester – ☎ 0905 Upton Snodsbury :

⌂ **Upton House,** WR7 4NR, on B 4082 (beside church) ✆ 381226, « Tastefully furnished timbered house », 🌳 – 🚭 rm 📺 ☎ Ⓟ. 🐕
closed Christmas and New Year – **M** (by arrangement) (communal dining) 25.00 **st.** – **3 rm** ☕ 30.00/65.00 **st.**

⊕ ATS Little London, Barbourne ✆ 24009/28543

WORFIELD Shrops. – see Bridgnorth.

EUROPE on a single sheet
Michelin map no 970.

WORKINGTON Cumbria 402 J 20 – pop. 25 742 – ✪ 0900.

🏌️ Branthwaite Rd ✆ 603460, E : 2 m.

🏢 Central Car Park, Washington St., CA14 3AW ✆ 602923.

◆London 313 – ◆Carlisle 33 – Keswick 20.

🏨 **Washington Central,** Washington St., CA14 3AW, ✆ 65772, Fax 68770 – 🔌 📺 ☎ 🅿 – 🔬 180. 🔼 ⅅ ⑩ 𝗩𝗜𝗦𝗔. ❀
M (carving lunch Sunday) 9.00/14.95 **t.** and a la carte ⚑ 3.45 – **40 rm** ⊑ 49.50/69.50 **st.** – SB (weekends only) 100.00/130.00 **st.**

◎ ATS Annie Pit Lane, Clay Flatts Trading Est. ✆ 602352

WORKSOP Notts. 402 403 404 C 24 – pop. 34 425 – ✪ 0909.

🏌️ Kilton Forest, Blyth Rd ✆ 472488, NE : 1 m. on B 6045.

🏢 Worksop Library, Memorial Av., S80 2BP ✆ 501148.

◆London 163 – Derby 47 – Lincoln 28 – ◆Nottingham 30 – ◆Sheffield 19.

🏨 **Clumber Park** (Lansbury), Clumber Park, S80 3PA, SE : 6 ½ m. by 6040 and A 57 on A 616 ✆ 0623 (Mansfield) 835333, Fax 835525, ⇌ – 🤸 rm 📺 ✿ & 🅿 – 🔬 150. 🔼 ⅅ ⑩ 𝗩𝗜𝗦𝗔
M 11.00/15.00 **t.** and a la carte – **47 rm** ⊑ 65.50/77.00 **t.**, 1 suite – SB (weekends only) 66.00/70.00 **st.**

🏠 **Forte Travelodge** without rest., Dunkeries Mill, St. Annes Drive, S80 3QD, W : ½ m. off A 57 ✆ 501528, Reservation (Freephone) 0800 850950 – 📺 & 🅿. 🔼 ⅅ 𝗩𝗜𝗦𝗔. ❀
40 rm 31.95 **t.**

WORMINGTON Glos. 403 404 O 27 – see Broadway (Heref and Worcs.).

WORSLEY Gtr. Manchester 402 403 404 MN 23 – see Manchester.

WORSTEAD Norfolk 404 Y 25 – pop. 718 – ✪ 0692 Smallburgh.

◆London 128 – ◆Norwich 19.

🏠 **Geoffrey The Dyer House,** Church Plain, NR28 9AL, ✆ 536562 – 🤸 rm 📺 🅿
M (by arrangement) 8.50 – **3 rm** ⊑ 17.50/36.00.

WORTHING W. Sussex 404 S 31 – pop. 90 687 – ECD : Wednesday – ✪ 0903.

🏌️ Hill Barn, Hill Barn Lane ✆ 237301, by A 27 BY – 🏌️, 🏌️ Links Rd ✆ 260801, by A 24 AY.

✈ Shoreham Airport : ✆ 0273 (Shoreham-by-Sea) 452304, E : 4 m. by A 27 BY.

🏢 Chapel Rd, BN11 1HL ✆ 210022 – Marine Parade, East of Pier ✆ 210022 (summer only).

◆London 59 – ◆Brighton 11 – ◆Southampton 50.

Plan on next page

🏨 **Beach,** Marine Par., BN11 3QJ, ✆ 234001, Fax 234567, ⇐ – 🔌 📺 ☎ 🅿 – 🔬 80. 🔼 ⅅ ⑩ 𝗩𝗜𝗦𝗔 ❀ · AZ **e**
M 17.50 **t.** (dinner) and a la carte 15.50/22.50 **t.** ⚑ 3.50 – **81 rm** ⊑ 51.00/81.50 **st.**, 3 suites.

🏨 **Chatsworth,** Steyne, BN11 3DU, ✆ 236103, Fax 823726 – 🔌 📺 ☎ – 🔬 150. 🔼 ⅅ ⑩ 𝗩𝗜𝗦𝗔 ❀ · BZ **x**
M (carving lunch) 9.85/14.95 **st.** ⚑ 4.20 – **105 rm** ⊑ 49.90/77.00 **st.** – SB 77.00/90.00 **st.**

🏨 **Burlington,** Marine Par., BN11 3QL, ✆ 211222, Fax 209561 – 🔌 📺 ☎ – 🔬 80. 🔼 ⅅ 𝗩𝗜𝗦𝗔 · AZ **a**
M *(closed Sunday dinner)* 12.00 **st.** – **27 rm** ⊑ 45.00/68.00 **t.** – SB (except Easter and Christmas) (weekends only) 75.00 **st.**

🏠 **Kingsway,** 117-119 Marine Par., BN11 3QQ, ✆ 237542, Fax 204173 – 🔌 📺 ☎ 🅿. 🔼 ⅅ ⑩ 𝗩𝗜𝗦𝗔 · AZ **i**
M (carving rest.) 12.95/14.95 **t.** and a la carte ⚑ 5.30 – **28 rm** ⊑ 45.00/80.00 **t.** – SB 70.00/ 108.00 **st.**

🏠 **Cavendish,** 115/116 Marine Par., BN11 3QG, ✆ 236767, Fax 823840 – 📺 ☎ – 🔬 30. 🔼 ⅅ ⑩ 𝗩𝗜𝗦𝗔 𝗝𝗖𝗕 ❀ · AZ **u**
M *(closed Monday lunch and Sunday dinner)* 7.50/11.00 **st.** and dinner a la carte ⚑ 4.50 – **15 rm** ⊑ 26.50/72.00 **st.** – SB (except Bank Holidays) 80.00/102.00 **st.**

🏠 **Windsor House,** 14-16 Windsor Rd, BN11 2LX, ✆ 239655, Fax 210763, ≼ – 📺 ☎ 🅿 – 🔬 70. 🔼 ⅅ ⑩ 𝗩𝗜𝗦𝗔 ❀ · BY **i**
M (bar lunch)/dinner 15.50 **t.** ⚑ 4.75 – **30 rm** ⊑ 36.50/104.00 **t.** – SB (weekends only) 73.00/90.00 **st.**

🏠 Chapmans, 27 Railway Approach, BN11 1UR, ✆ 230690, Fax 204266 – 📺 ☎ · · · · · · · BZ **u**
18 rm.

🏠 **Beacons,** 18 Shelley Rd, BN11 1TU, ✆ 230948 – 📺 ☎ 🅿. 🔼 ⅅ 𝗩𝗜𝗦𝗔 · · · · · · · · · · · · BZ **e**
M 10.50 ⚑ 2.50 – **5 rm** ⊑ 22.50/43.00.

🏠 **Bonchurch House,** 1 Winchester Rd, BN11 4DJ, ✆ 202492 – 🤸 rest 📺 🅿. ❀ · · · · · AZ **v**
M (by arrangement) 10.50 **st.** ⚑ 4.00 – **6 rm** ⊑ 19.00/40.00 **st.** – SB (winter only) 53.00/ 55.00 **st.**

🏠 **Upton Farm** without rest., Upper Brighton Rd, Sompting Village, BN14 9JU, ✆ 233706, ≼ – 🤸 📺 🅿. ❀ · BY **a**
3 rm ⊑ 20.00/35.00 **st.**

WORTHING

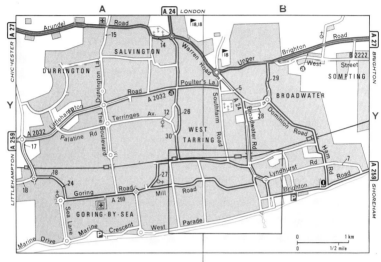

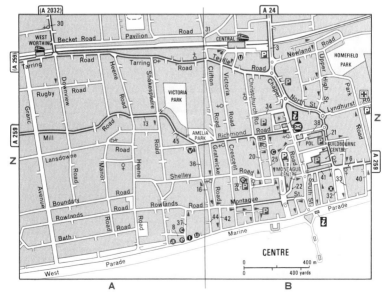

CENTRE

XX **Trenchers,** 118-120 Portland Rd, BN11 1QA, ✎ 820287 – 🔲 *VISA* BZ **c**
closed Sunday dinner – **M** 12.50 **t.** and dinner a la carte **t.** ⌀ 4.00.

XX **Paragon,** 9-10 Brunswick Rd, BN11 3NG, ✎ 233367 – 🔲 AE ⑩ *VISA* AZ **c**
closed Sunday, 24 December-10 January and Bank Holidays – **M** 14.00/18.00 **st.** and a la
carte ⌀ 4.50.

XX **Beijing,** 1 Littlehampton Rd, BN13 1PY, ✎ 694508 – 🍽. 🔲 AE ⑩ *VISA* AY **a**
Chinese (Peking, Szechuan) 10.00/20.00 **st.** and a la carte.

◉ ATS 34 Thorn Rd ✎ 237640

WRAY Lancs. 402 M 21 – pop. 401 (inc. Holton) – ✉ Lancaster – ⊙ 052 42 Kirkby Lonsdale.
◆London 258 – ◆Blackpool 44 – Kendal 24 – Lancaster 10.

⌂ **Lane Head** ⌂, Millhouses, LA2 8NF, E : 1¼ m. ✎ 21148, ⌗ – 🔲 🅿. ⌗
M *(closed Sunday to Wednesday to non-residents)* (dinner only) 10.00 **s.** and a la carte
⌀ 2.75 – **4 rm** ⌷ 30.00/50.00 **s.** – SB 55.00/94.00 **st.**

WROTHAM HEATH Kent 404 U 30 – pop. 1 669 – ✉ ⊙ 0732 Sevenoaks.
◆London 35 – Maidstone 10.

🏨 **Forte Posthouse,** London Rd, TN15 7RS, ✎ 883311, Fax 885850, ⌗, ⌗s, 🔲, ⌗ –
⌗ rm 🔲 ☎ & 🅿 – ⌂ 60. 🔲 AE ⑩
M a la carte approx. 17.50 **t.** ⌀ 4.65 – ⌷ 6.95 – **116 rm** 53.50 **st.**, 2 suites – SB (weekends
only) 90.00 **st.**

🏨 **Travel Inn,** London Rd, TN15 7RX, ✎ 884214, Fax 780368 – ⌗ rm 🔲 & 🅿. 🔲 AE ⑩
VISA. ⌗
M (Beefeater grill) a la carte approx. 16.00 **t.** – ⌷ 4.95 – **40 rm** 33.50 **t.**

WROUGHTON Wilts. 403 404 O 29 – see Swindon.

WROXHAM Norfolk 404 Y 25 *Great Britain G.* – pop. 2 954 (inc. Hoveton) – ECD : Wednesday –
✉ ⊙ 0603.
Envir. : The Broads★.
◆London 118 – Great Yarmouth 21 – ◆Norwich 7.

🏨 **Broads,** Station Rd, NR12 8UR, ✎ 782869, Fax 784066 – 🔲 ☎ 🅿. 🔲 AE ⑩ *VISA*
M (carving lunch) 8.00/9.70 **t.** and a la carte ⌀ 3.75 – **28 rm** ⌷ 34.00/55.00 **t.** – SB (October-June except Christmas and New Year) (weekends only) 61.00/94.00 **st.**

WROXTON Oxon. 403 404 P 27 – see Banbury.

WYBOSTON Beds. – see St. Neots (Cambs.).

WYCH CROSS E. Sussex 404 U 30 – see Forest Row.

WYE Kent 404 W 30 – ✉ Ashford – ⊙ 0233.
◆London 60 – Canterbury 10 – ◆Dover 28 – Hastings 34.

XX **Wife of Bath,** 4 Upper Bridge St., TN25 5AW, ✎ 812540 – 🅿. 🔲 *VISA*
closed Sunday, Monday and first 2 weeks September – **M** 11.50/19.75 **t.**
and lunch a la carte ⌀ 4.50.

WYLAM Northd. 401 402 O 19 – pop. 2 171 – ⊙ 0661.
◆London 266 – ◆Carlisle 48 – ◆Newcastle upon Tyne 10.

XX **Laburnum House,** NE41 8AJ, ✎ 852185 – 🔲 AE *VISA*
closed Sunday – **M** (dinner only) 30.00 **t.** and a la carte.

WYMONDHAM Norfolk 404 X 26 – pop. 9 088 – ECD : Wednesday – ⊙ 0953.
◆London 110 – ◆Cambridge 53 – ◆Norwich 9.

🏨 **Sinclair,** 28 Market St., NR18 0BB, ✎ 606721, Fax 601361, ⌗s – 🔲 ☎ 🅿. 🔲 AE *VISA*. ⌗
closed Christmas – **M** 12.50/15.00 **t.** and dinner a la carte ⌀ 4.75 – **20 rm** ⌷ 35.00/55.00 **t.** –
SB 64.00/80.00 **st.**

WYNDS POINT Heref. and Worcs. 403 404 M 27 – see Great Malvern.

YARLINGTON Somerset – pop. 117 – ✉ Wincanton – ⊙ 0963 North Cadbury.
◆London 127 – ◆Bristol 32 – Taunton 30 – Yeovil 12.

XX **Stags Head,** BA9 8DG, ✎ 40393 – ⌗
closed Sunday dinner and Monday – **M** (dinner only and Sunday lunch)/dinner a la
carte 17.05/20.30 **t.** ⌀ 4.10.

YARM Cleveland 402 P 20 – pop. 6 360 – ⊙ 0642 Middlesbrough.
◆London 242 – Middlesbrough 8.

🏨 **Crathorne Hall** ⌂, Crathorne, TS15 0AR, S : 3 ½ m. by A 67 ✎ 700398, Fax 700814,
« Converted Edwardian mansion », ⌗, ⌗, park – ⌗ rm 🔲 ☎ 🅿 – ⌂ 100. 🔲 AE ⑩
VISA
M 16.50/27.50 **st.** and a la carte ⌀ 5.25 – **37 rm** ⌷ 89.50/135.00 **st.** – SB (weekends only)
110.00/150.00 **st.**

YATELEY Surrey **404** R 29 – pop. 14 121 – ECD : Wednesday – ⊠ Camberley – ☎ 0252.

◆London 37 – Reading 12 – ◆Southampton 58.

🏠 **Casa Dei Cesari,** Handford Lane, Cricket Hill, GU17 7BA, ✆ 873275, Fax 870614, 🛳 – 📺 ☎ 🅿. 🔼 🅰🅴 ⑩ 𝚅𝙸𝚂𝙰. ✻
M - Italian 17.05 **t.** and a la carte ↥ 4.50 – **34 rm** ☲ 60.00/80.00 **st.**, 2 suites.

YATTENDON Berks. **403 404** Q 29 – ⊠ ☎ 0635 Newbury.

◆London 61 – ◆Oxford 23 – Reading 12.

XX **Royal Oak** with rm, The Square, RG16 0UF, ✆ 201325, Fax 201926, 🛳 – 📺 ☎ 🅿. 🔼 ⑩ 𝚅𝙸𝚂𝙰 ✻
M *(booking essential)* (closed Sunday dinner) 27.50 **t.** and a la carte ↥ 7.95 – **5 rm** ☲ 70.00/80.00 **t.**

YELVERTON Devon **403** H 32 The West Country G. – pop. 3 297 (inc. Horrabridge) – ☎ 0822.

See : Yelverton Paperweight Centre★.

Envir. : Buckland Abbey★★ *AC*, SW : 2 m.

Exc. : E : Dartmoor National Park★★ (Brent Tor ≤★★, Haytor Rocks ≤★).

🏌 Golf Links Rd ✆ 853618.

◆London 234 – Exeter 33 – ◆Plymouth 9.

🏨 **Moorland Links** 🌳, PL20 6DA, S : 2 m. on A 386 ✆ 852245, Fax 855004, ≤, 🛳, XX – ¥⤍ rm 📺 ☎ 🅿 – 🔼 50. 🔼 🅰🅴 ⑩ 𝚅𝙸𝚂𝙰
closed 24 December-2 January – **M** *(closed Saturday lunch)* 17.50 **t.** and a la carte – **29 rm** ☲ 59.95/75.90 **t.**, 1 suite – SB 91.90/105.90 **t.**

🏠 **Harrabeer Country House,** Harrowbeer Lane, PL20 6EA, ✆ 853302, 🛳 – ¥⤍ rest 📺 ☎ 🅿. 🔼 🅰🅴 𝚅𝙸𝚂𝙰
closed 22 to 31 December – **M** 13.00 **s.** ↥ 3.30 – **7 rm** ☲ 23.00/54.00 **s.** – SB (October-March) 60.00/67.00 **st.**

🏠 **Overcombe,** Horrabridge, PL20 7RN, N : 1¼ m. on A 386 ✆ 853501, ≤, 🛳 – ¥⤍ rest 📺 🔼 ♿ 🅿. 🔼 𝚅𝙸𝚂𝙰 ✻
M 11.50 **t.** ↥ 4.15 – **11 rm** ☲ 20.00/45.00 **t.** – SB (October-May) 63.00/73.00 **st.**

YEOVIL Somerset **403 404** M 31 The West Country G. – pop. 36 114 – ECD : Monday and Thursday – ☎ 0935.

See : St. John the Baptist★.

Envir. : Monacute House★★ *AC*, W : 4 m. on A 3088 – Fleet Air Arm Museum, Yeovilton★★ *AC*, NW : 5 m. by A 37 – Tintinhull House Garden★ *AC*, NW : 5½ m. – Ham Hill (≤★★) W : 5½ m. by A 3088 – Stoke sub-Hamdon (parish church★) W : 5¼ m. by A 3088.

Exc. : Muchelney★★ (Parish Church★★) NW : 14 m. by A 3088, A 303 and B 3165 – Lytes Cary★, N : 7½ m. by A 37, B 3151 and A 372 – Sandford Orcas Manor House★, NW : 8 m. by A 359 – Cadbury Castle (≤★★) NE : 10½ m. by A 359 – East Lambrook Manor★ *AC*, W : 12 m. by A 3088 and A 303.

🏌 Sherborne Rd ✆ 75949, 1 m. by A 30.

🏢 Petter's House, Petter's Way, BA20 1SH ✆ 71279 – at Podimore, Somerset Visitor Centre, Forte Services (A 303), BA22 8JG ✆ 841302 (summer only).

◆London 136 – Exeter 48 – ◆Southampton 72 – Taunton 26.

🏨 **Manor** (Forte), Hendford, BA20 1TG, ✆ 23116, Fax 706607 – ¥⤍ rm 📺 ☎ 🅿 – 🔼 60. 🔼 🅰🅴 𝚅𝙸𝚂𝙰 𝙹𝙲𝙱
M 11.95/17.95 **t.** and a la carte ↥ 3.75 – ☲ 8.50 – **41 rm** 55.50/80.00 **st.** – SB 108.00/148.00 **st.**

🏨 **Yeovil Court,** West Coker Rd., BA20 2NE, SW : 2 m. on A 30 ✆ 863746, Fax 863990 – 📺 ☎ 🅿 – 🔼 40. 🔼 🅰🅴 ⑩ 𝚅𝙸𝚂𝙰
M *(closed Saturday lunch and Sunday dinner)* a la carte 11.60/20.60 **st.** – **17 rm** ☲ 49.00/69.00 **st.**, 1 suite – SB 75.00/130.00 **st.**

at Podimore N : 9½ m. by A 37 off A 303 – ⊠ ☎ 0935 Yeovil :

🏠 **Forte Travelodge** without rest., BA22 8JG, W : ½ m. ✆ 840074, Reservations (Freephone) 0800 850950 – 📺 ♿ 🅿. 🔼 🅰🅴 𝚅𝙸𝚂𝙰 ✻
31 rm 31.95 **t.**

at Barwick S : 2 m. by A 30 off A 37 – ⊠ ☎ 0935 Yeovil :

XX **Little Barwick House** 🌳 with rm, BA22 9TD, ✆ 23902, Fax 20908, « Georgian dower house », 🛳 – ▤ rest 📺 ☎ 🅿. 🔼 🅰🅴 𝚅𝙸𝚂𝙰
closed Christmas and New Year – **M** *(closed Sunday to non-residents)* (booking essential) (dinner only) 24.90 **t.** ↥ 4.50 – **6 rm** ☲ 46.00/72.00 **st.** – SB 86.50/132.00 **st.**

at West Coker SW : 3½ m. on A 30 – ⊠ ☎ 0935 West Coker :

🏨 **Four Acres,** High St., BA22 9AJ, ✆ 862555, Telex 46666, Fax 863929, 🛳 – 📺 ☎ 🅿. 🔼 🅰🅴 ⑩ 𝚅𝙸𝚂𝙰
M 11.95 **t.** and a la carte – **25 rm** ☲ 45.00/55.00 **t.** – SB (weekends only) 75.00 **st.**

X **Skittles,** 1 Church St., BA22 9AH, ✆ 863986 – ¥⤍. 🔼 𝚅𝙸𝚂𝙰
closed Sunday dinner – **M** a la carte 9.25/21.65 **t.** ↥ 5.00.

at Montacute W : 5 ½ m. on A 3088 – ✉ 🌣 🕐 0935 Martock :

🏠 **Kings Arms,** Bishopston, TA15 6UU, 𝒫 822513, Fax 826549, 🐎 – 🍴 rest 📺 ☎ 🅿. 🔄
🄰🄴 ⓞ 𝘝𝘐𝘚𝘈
closed 25 and 26 December – **M** (buffet lunch)/dinner 21.00 **t.** and a la carte 🍴 4.10 – **11 rm**
⚏ 46.00/79.00 **t.** – SB 85.00/130.00 **st.**

🍴🍴 **Milk House** with rm, The Borough Sq., TA15 6XB, 𝒫 823823, 🐎 – 🍴 📺. 🔄 𝘝𝘐𝘚𝘈. 🍴
M *(closed Sunday dinner, Monday and Tuesday)* (dinner only and Sunday lunch)/
dinner 19.80 **st.** and a la carte 🍴 4.20 – **2 rm** ⚏ 40.00/58.00 **st.** – SB 76.00/83.00 **st.**

🛢 ATS Lyde Rd. Penmill Trading Est.. 𝒫 75580/71780

YETMINSTER Dorset **403 404** M 31 – see Sherborne.

YORK N. Yorks. **402** Q. 22 Great Britain G. – pop. 123 126 – 🌣 0904.

See : City★★★ – Minster★★★ (Stained Glass★★★, Chapter House★★, Choir Screen★★) CDY –
National Railway Museum★★★ CY – The Walls★★ CDXYZ – Castle Museum★ *AC* DZ **M2** – Jorvik
Viking Centre★ *AC* DY **M1** – Fairfax House★ *AC* DY **A** – The Shambles★ DY **54.**

🛢 Lords Moor Lane, Stronsall 𝒫 491840, NE : 6 m. by Huntington Rd BY – 🛢 Heworth,
Muncaster House, Muncastergate 𝒫 424618, by A 1036 BY.

🮮 De Grey Rooms, Exhibition Sq., YO1 2HB 𝒫 621756 – York Railway Station, Outer Concourse,
YO2 2AY 𝒫 643700 – TIC Travel Office, 6 Rougier St., YO1 1AJ 𝒫 620557.

◆London 203 – ◆Kingston-upon-Hull 38 – ◆Leeds 24 – ◆Middlesbrough 51 – ◆Nottingham 88 – ◆Sheffield 62.

Plan on next page

🏨 **Middlethorpe Hall,** Bishopthorpe Rd, YO2 1QB, S : 1 m. 𝒫 641241, Fax 620176, ≤,
« William and Mary house, gardens », park – 🛗 📺 ☎ 🅿 – 🔏 60. 🔄 🄰🄴 ⓞ 𝘝𝘐𝘚𝘈
🍴 by A 19 BZ
M 16.90/30.80 **st.** and dinner a la carte 🍴 5.50 – **Grill** *(June-September)* (dinner only Friday
and Saturday) 21.50 **st.** 🍴 5.50 – ⚏ 9.95 – **24 rm** 83.00/129.00 **st.**, 5 suites – SB (except
Bank Holidays) 172.00/232.00 **st.**

🏨 **Swallow,** Tadcaster Rd, YO2 2QQ, 𝒫 701000, Fax 702308, 🇬, ≘s, 🏊, 🐎 – 🛗 📺 ☎ 🛗
🅿 – 🔏 150. 🔄 🄰🄴 ⓞ 𝘝𝘐𝘚𝘈 AZ **a**
M 18.00/28.00 **st.** and a la carte – **111 rm** ⚏ 89.00/109.00 **st.**, 1 suite – SB 120.00/218.00 **st.**

🏨 **Viking** (Q.M.H.), North St., YO1 1JF, 𝒫 659822, Telex 57937, Fax 641793, ≤, 🇬, ≘s – 🛗
🍴 rm 🮮 rest 📺 ☎ 🛗 🅿 – 🔏 250. 🔄 🄰🄴 ⓞ 𝘝𝘐𝘚𝘈 𝘑𝘊𝘉. 🍴 CY **n**
M (carving lunch) 10.50/15.00 **t.** and a la carte 🍴 6.75 – **186 rm** ⚏ 92.50/115.00 **t.**. 1 suite –
SB 116.00/213.00 **st.**

🏨 **Mount Royale,** The Mount, YO2 2DA, 𝒫 628856, Fax 611171, « Tasteful decor and
furnishings », ≘s, 🏊 heated, 🐎 – 🮮 📺 ☎ 🅿. 🔄 🄰🄴 ⓞ 𝘝𝘐𝘚𝘈 𝘑𝘊𝘉. 🍴 AZ **s**
closed 23 to 31 December – **M** (dinner only) 35.00 **t.** 🍴 5.00 – **20 rm** ⚏ 75.00/95.00 **t.**,
1 suite – SB 110.00 **t.**

🏨 **The Grange,** Clifton, YO3 6AA, 𝒫 644744, Fax 612453, « Regency town house » – 📺 ☎
🛗 🅿 – 🔏 40. 🔄 🄰🄴 ⓞ 𝘝𝘐𝘚𝘈 𝘑𝘊𝘉 CX **u**
M 12.50/21.00 **st.** and a la carte 🍴 5.00 – **29 rm** ⚏ 86.00/120.00 **st.** – SB (except Bank
Holidays) 70.00/210.00 **st.**

🏨 **York Pavilion,** 45 Main St., Fulford, YO1 4PJ, S : 1 m. on A 19 𝒫 622099, Fax 626939, 🐎
– 📺 ☎ 🅿 – 🔏 30. 🔄 🄰🄴 ⓞ 𝘝𝘐𝘚𝘈 𝘑𝘊𝘉. 🍴 B
M 10.95/18.95 **st.** and a la carte 🍴 5.95 – **21 rm** ⚏ 75.00/110.00 **st.** – SB 112.00/166.00 **st.**

🏨 **Hudson's,** 60 Bootham, YO3 7BZ, 𝒫 621267, Fax 654719 – 🛗 📺 ☎ 🅿 – 🔏 25. 🔄 🄰🄴 ⓞ
𝘝𝘐𝘚𝘈. 🍴 CX **a**
M (lunch by arrangement)/dinner 17.50 **t.** and a la carte 🍴 5.25 – **30 rm** ⚏ 45.00/80.00 **t.**

🏨 **Ambassador,** 123-125 The Mount, YO2 2DA, 𝒫 641316, Fax 640259, 🐎 – 🛗 📺 ☎ 🅿. 🔄
🄰🄴 𝘝𝘐𝘚𝘈. 🍴 AZ **c**
M (bar lunch)/dinner 19.00 **t.** – **24 rm** ⚏ 79.00/105.00 **t.** – SB 125.00/188.00 **st.**

🏨 **Forte Posthouse,** Tadcaster Rd, YO2 2QF, 𝒫 707921, Telex 57798, Fax 702804, 🐎 – 🛗
🍴 rm 📺 ☎ 🅿 – 🔏 100. 🔄 🄰🄴 ⓞ 𝘝𝘐𝘚𝘈 AZ **r**
M a la carte approx. 17.50 **t.** 🍴 4.65 – ⚏ 6.95 – **139 rm** 53.50 **st.** – SB 90.00 **st.**

🏨 **Novotel,** Fishergate, YO1 4AD, 𝒫 611660, Telex 57556, Fax 610925, 🏊 – 🛗 🍴 rm 🮮 rest
📺 ☎ 🛗 🅿 – 🔏 200. 🔄 🄰🄴 ⓞ 𝘝𝘐𝘚𝘈 DZ **o**
M 15.00 **st.** and a la carte – ⚏ 7.50 – **124 rm** 57.50/69.50 **st.** – SB 93.00/155.00 **st.**

🏨 **Judges' Lodging,** 9 Lendal, YO1 2AQ, 𝒫 638733, Fax 679947 – 📺 ☎ 🅿. 🔄 🄰🄴 ⓞ 𝘝𝘐𝘚𝘈
M (bar lunch)/dinner 25.00 **t.** and a la carte 🍴 5.25 – **12 rm** ⚏ 60.00/130.00 **t.** – SB (November-March except Bank Holidays) 90.00/150.00 **t.** CY **x**

🏠 **Monkbar,** St. Maurice's Rd, YO3 7JA, 𝒫 638086, Fax 629195 – 📺 ☎ 🅿 – 🔏 50. 🔄
ⓞ 𝘝𝘐𝘚𝘈. 🍴 DX **a**
M 22.50/25.00 **st.** and a la carte 🍴 4.95 – **47 rm** ⚏ 69.00/119.00 **st.** – SB 85.00/150.00 **st.**

🏠 **Curzon Lodge and Stable Cottages** without rest., 23 Tadcaster Rd, YO2 2QG,
𝒫 703157, 🐎 – 📺 ☎ 🅿. 🔄 🄰🄴 AZ **a**
closed Christmas and New Year – **10 rm** ⚏ 37.00/56.00 **st.**

🏠 **Arndale** without rest., 290 Tadcaster Rd, YO2 2ET, 𝒫 702424, 🐎 – 📺 🅿. 🍴
closed Christmas and New Year – **9 rm** ⚏ 49.00/70.00 **st.** AZ **i**

YORK

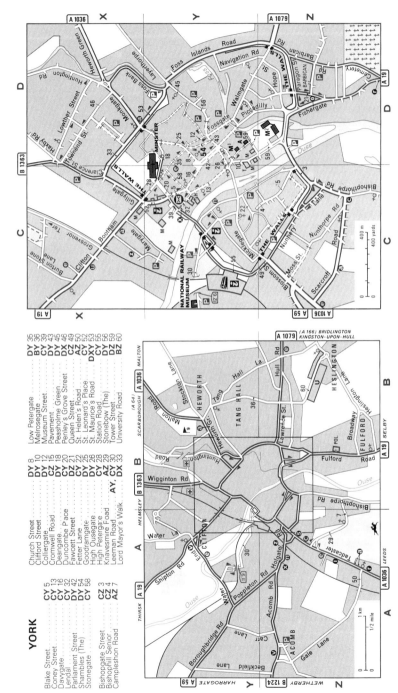

532

🏠 **Grasmead House** without rest., 1 Scarcroft Hill, YO2 1DF, ℰ 629996 – 🦶 📺. 🔼 VISA. ⋘
6 rm ⊑ 58.00 **st.**   CZ **a**

🏠 **Clifton Bridge,** Water End, YO3 6LL, ℰ 610510, Fax 640208 – 📺 ☎ 🅿. 🔼 AE VISA
closed 24 December-1 January – **M** (bar lunch)/dinner 9.00 **t.** and a la carte – **14 rm**
⊑ 38.00/60.00 **t.** – SB (except Bank Holidays) 71.00/94.00 **st.**   AY **e**

🏠 **Cottage,** 3 Clifton Green, YO3 6LH, ℰ 643711, Fax 611230 – 📺 ☎. 🔼 AE ① VISA. ⋘
closed Christmas – **M** (dinner only) 11.50 **t.** and a la carte ⱥ 4.95 – **19 rm** ⊑ 40.00/60.00 **t.** –
SB 59.00/99.00 **st.**   AY **v**

🏠 **Town House,** 98-104 Holgate Rd, YO2 4BB, ℰ 636171, Fax 623044 – 📺 ☎ 🅿. 🔼 VISA
closed 24 December-2 January – **M** (bar lunch)/dinner 12.00 **t.** and a la carte ⱥ 3.95 – **23 rm**
⊑ 26.00/65.00 **t.** – SB (except Bank Holidays) 70.00/94.00 **st.**   AZ **z**

🏠 **Priory,** 126 Fulford Rd, YO1 4BE, ℰ 625280, ⋰ – 📺 🅿. 🔼 AE ① VISA. ⋘
closed 1 week Christmas – **M** (dinner only) a la carte 11.50/17.10 **t.** ⱥ 4.25 – **19 rm** ⊑ 30.00/
50.00 **t.**   DZ **r**

🏠 **Kilima,** 129 Holgate Rd, YO2 4DE, ℰ 625787, Fax 612083, ⋰ – 🦶 rest 📺 ☎ & 🅿. 🔼 AE
① VISA
M 12.50/17.95 **st.** and a la carte ⱥ 4.95 – **15 rm** ⊑ 47.25/74.50 **st.** – SB 98.00/126.50 **st.** AZ **n**

🏠 **Field House,** 2 St. Georges Pl., YO2 2DR, ℰ 639572, ⋰ – 📺 ☎ 🅿. 🔼 AE VISA.
⋘
closed Christmas – **M** 10.00/14.00 **st.** ⱥ 4.00 – **17 rm** ⊑ 23.00/59.00 **st.** – SB 76.00/87.00 **st.** AZ **e**

🏠 Black Bull Country Lodge, Hull Rd, YO1 3LF, ℰ 411856, Fax 430667 – 🦶 rm & 🅿. ⋘
40 rm.   BZ **e**

🏠 **Heworth Court,** 76-78 Heworth Green, YO3 7TQ, ℰ 425156, Fax 415290 – 📺 ☎ 🅿. 🔼
AE ① VISA. ⋘
M 9.50/16.00 **t.** and a la carte ⱥ 4.25 – **25 rm** ⊑ 35.30/72.00 **t.** – SB 67.00/115.00 **st.**   BY **a**

🏠 **Holmwood House,** 114 Holgate Rd, YO2 4BB, ℰ 626183, Fax 670899 – 🦶 📺 ☎ 🅿. 🔼
AE VISA. ⋘   AZ **x**
closed first 2 weeks January – **M** (by arrangement) (dinner only) – **11 rm** ⊑ 45.00/70.00 **st.**

🏡 **Hobbits** without rest., 9 St. Peter's Grove, Clifton, YO3 6AQ, ℰ 624538 – 🦶 📺 🅿. 🔼
VISA   CX **e**
closed 24 to 28 December – **5 rm** ⊑ 25.00/55.00 **st.**

🏡 **Crook Lodge,** 26 St. Mary's, Bootham, YO3 7DD, ℰ 655614 – 📺 🅿. 🔼 VISA. ⋘
closed Christmas – **M** 9.45 **st.** ⱥ 3.75 – **7 rm** ⊑ 23.50/43.00 **st.** – SB (November-April)
50.00/60.00 **st.**   CX **z**

🏡 **Ashbury** without rest., 103 The Mount, YO2 2AX, ℰ 647339 – 🦶 📺. ⋘
closed 23 December-3 January – **5 rm** ⊑ 25.00/50.00 **s.**   CZ **e**

🍴🍴 **Melton's,** 7 Scarcroft Rd, YO2 1ND, ℰ 634341, Fax 629233 – 🔼 VISA
closed Sunday dinner, Monday lunch, 22 to 29 August and 24 December-13 January –
M (booking essential) 13.50 **st.** (lunch) and a la carte 17.50/23.50 **st.** ⱥ 5.20.   CZ **c**

🍴 **19 Grape Lane,** 19 Grape Lane, YO1 2HU, ℰ 636366 – 🔼 VISA   CY **e**
closed Sunday, Monday, first 2 weeks February, last 2 weeks September and Christmas –
M - **English** 18.95 **t.** (dinner) and a la carte 21.95/27.00 **t.** ⱥ 4.95.

at Kexby E : 6 ¾ m. on A 1079 - B – ✉ York – ☎ 0759 Pocklington :

🏨 **Kexby Bridge,** Hull Rd, YO4 5LD, ℰ 388223, Fax 388822, ⋱, ⋰ – 📺 ☎ 🅿 – 🛦 100. 🔼
VISA. ⋘
M 17.00 **t.** ⱥ 5.00 – **32 rm** ⊑ 50.00/75.00 **t.** – SB 80.00/110.00 **st.**

at Escrick S : 5 ¾ m. on A 19 - B – ✉ ☎ 0904 York :

🏨 **Parsonage Country House,** YO4 6LF, ℰ 728111, Fax 728151, ⋰ – 📺 ☎ 🅿 – 🛦 160.
🔼 AE ① VISA. ⋘
M 11.00/18.50 **t.** and a la carte ⱥ 4.75 – **13 rm** ⊑ 65.00/105.00 **t.** – SB (except Easter,
Christmas and New Year) 90.00/110.00 **st.**

at Bilbrough SW : 5 ½ m. by A 1036 – AZ – off A 64 – ✉ York – ☎ 0937 Tadcaster :

🏨 **Bilbrough Manor** ⋙, YO2 3PH, ℰ 834002, Fax 834724, ⋖, « Tastefully decorated
Victorian manor », ⋰, park – 📺 ☎ 🅿. 🔼 AE ① VISA. ⋘
closed 25 to 29 December – **M** 14.50/30.00 **t.** and a la carte ⱥ 6.15 – **12 rm** ⊑ 77.00/
150.00 **t.** – SB 122.50/229.00 **st.**

at Skelton NW : 3 m. on A 19 - A – ✉ ☎ 0904 York :

🏨 Fairfield Manor, Shipton Rd, YO3 6XW, ℰ 670222, Fax 670311, ⋰ – ⃒⃒ 🦶 rm ▤ rest 📺
☎ & 🅿 – 🛦 250
84 rm, 6 suites.

◉ ATS 2 James St. ℰ 412372/410375   ATS 110 Layerthorpe ℰ 628479/625884
ATS 36 Holgate Rd ℰ 654411

◆London 95 – ◆Ipswich 25 – ◆Norwich 55.

🏡 **Sans Souci** without rest., Main Rd, IP17 3EX, on A 12 ℰ 268, ⋰ – 🦶 📺 🅿. 🔼 VISA. ⋘
3 rm ⊑ 24.00/38.00.

Wales

Place with at least :

one hotel or restaurant .... ● Ruthin
a pleasant hotel or restaurant .... 🏨🏨🏨, 🛏, 🛏
one quiet, secluded hotel .... ⏏
one restaurant with ... 🕸, 🕸🕸, 🕸🕸🕸, Meals (M)
See this town for establishments
located in its vicinity .... NEATH

Localité offrant au moins :

une ressource hôtelière .... ● Ruthin
un hôtel ou restaurant agréable ..... 🏨🏨🏨, 🛏, 🛏
un hôtel très tranquille, isolé .... ⏏
une bonne table à .... 🕸, 🕸🕸, 🕸🕸🕸, Meals (M)
Localité groupant dans le texte
les ressources de ses environs .... NEATH

La località possiede come minimo :

una risorsa alberghiera .... ● Ruthin
Albergo o ristorante ameno .... 🏨🏨🏨, 🛏, 🛏
un albergo molto tranquillo, isolato .. ⏏
un'ottima tavola con .. 🕸, 🕸🕸, 🕸🕸🕸, Meals (M)
La località raggruppa nel suo testo
le risorse dei dintorni .... NEATH

Ort mit mindestens :

einem Hotel oder Restaurant .... ● Ruth n
ein angenehmes Hotel oder Restaurant 🏨🏨🏨, 🛏, 🛏
einem sehr ruhigen und abgelegenen Hotel . ⏏
einem Restaurant mit .. 🕸, 🕸🕸, 🕸🕸🕸, Meals (M)
Ort mit Angaben über Hotels und Restaurants
in seiner Umgebung .... NEATH

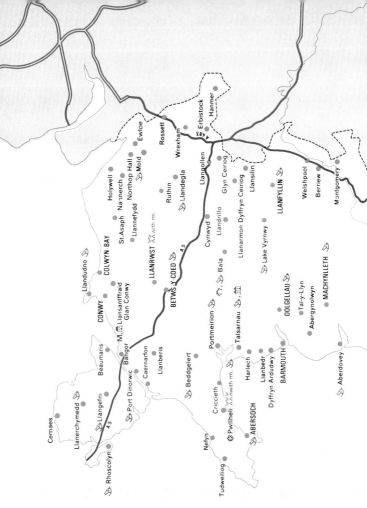

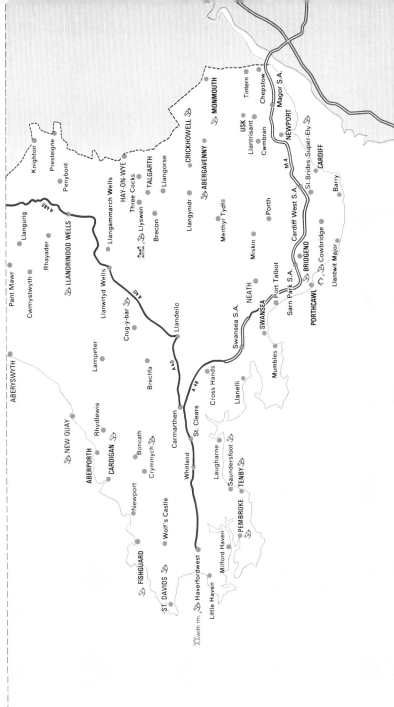

🚏 Aberdovey ✆ 767210, W : 3 m. by A 493.

◆London 230 – Dolgellau 25 – Shrewsbury 66.

🏨 **Plas Penhelig** ⌘, LL35 0NA, E : 1 m. by A 493 ✆ 767676, Fax 767783, ≼, « Terraced gardens », park, ※ – ⏹ ☎ 🅿. 🔼 VISA ⌘
mid March-December – **M** 10.50/17.00 – **11 rm** ⊂ 51.50/113.50 **t.** – SB 163.50/180.00 **st.**

🏨 **Trefeddian,** Tywyn Rd, LL35 0SB, W : 1 m. on A 493 ✆ 767213, Fax 767777, ≼ golf course and sea, 🔲, ⌘, park, ※ – 🛗 ⇄ rest ⏹ ☎ ⇆ 🅿. 🔼 VISA
mid March-28 December – **M** 9.00/15.50 **t.** ⧘ 4.70 – **46 rm** ⊂ 25.00/50.00 **t.** – SB 74.00/ 100.00 **t.**

🏨 **Penhelig Arms,** LL35 0LT, ✆ 767215, Fax 767690, ≼ – ⏹ ☎ 🅿. 🔼 VISA
closed 25 and 26 December – **M** (bar lunch Monday to Saturday)/dinner 17.50 **t.** – **10 rm** ⊂ 39.00/82.00 **t.** – SB 92.00/110.00 **st.**

🏨 **Harbour,** LL35 0EB, ✆ 767250, Fax 767418, ≼ – ⏹ ☎. 🔼 AE ⓞ VISA
M 16.50 **st.** (dinner) and a la carte 9.60/17.00 **st.** ⧘ 4.00 – **9 rm** ⊂ 52.50/90.00 **st.**

🏨 **Maybank,** LL35 0PT, E : 1 m. on A 493 ✆ 767500, ≼ – 🅿. 🔼 VISA. ⌘
closed 2 January-13 February and 8 November-22 December – **M** (booking essential) (dinner only) 18.95 **st.** – **5 rm** ⊂ 28.95/49.95 **st.** – SB (except July-September and Bank Holidays) 71.90/97.90 **st.**

🏠 **Brodawel,** Tywyn Rd, LL35 0SA, W : 1¼ m. on A 493 ✆ 767347, ≼, ⌘ – ⇄ ⏹ 🅿
closed January and February – **M** (by arrangement) 12.00 **s.** ⧘ 3.50 – **6 rm** ⊂ 25.00/36.00 **s.**

Exc. : Raglan Castle★ *AC*, SE : 9 m. by A 40.

🚏 Monmouthshire, Llanfoist ✆ 853171, S : 2 m. by B 4269.

� Swan Meadow, Cross St., NP7 5HH ✆ 857588 (summer only).

◆London 163 – Gloucester 43 – Newport 19 – ◆Swansea 49.

🏨 **Angel** (Forte), 15 Cross St., NP7 5EW, ✆ 857121, Fax 858059 – ⇄ rm ⏹ ☎ 🅿 – 🔺 60. 🔼 AE ⓞ VISA
M 10.25/15.95 **st.** and a la carte ⧘ 4.75 – ⊂ 7.95 – **29 rm** 65.00/75.00 **st.** – SB 98.00 **st.**

🏠 **Halidon House** without rest., 63 Monmouth Rd, NP7 5HR, ✆ 857855, ≼, 🔲, ⌘ – 🅿. ⌘
April-October – **4 rm** ⊂ 15.00/35.00 **st.**

🍴 Bagan Tandoori, 35 Frogmore St., NP7 5AN, ✆ 857389
M - Indian rest.

at Govilon W : 5¼ m. by A 465 on B 4246 – ✉ Abergavenny – ☎ 0873 Gilwern :

🏨 **Llanwenarth House** ⌘, NP7 9SF, N : 1 m. on B 4246 ✆ 830289, Fax 832199, ≼, « 16C manor house », ⌘ – ⇄ rest ⏹ 🅿
closed mid January-February – **M** (by arrangement) (residents only) (communal dining) (dinner only) 21.00 **s.** ⧘ 5.30 – **4 rm** ⊂ 70.00 **s.** – SB 106.00/112.00 **s.**

at Llanwenarth NW : 3 m. on A 40 – ✉ Abergavenny – ☎ 0873 Crickhowell :

🏨 **Llanwenarth Arms,** Brecon Rd, NP8 1EP, ✆ 810550, Fax 811880, ≼, ⟋ – ⏹ ☎ 🅿. 🔼 AE ⓞ VISA. ⌘
M a la carte 11.45/24.35 **st.** ⧘ 3.95 – **18 rm** ⊂ 49.00/59.00 **st.**

◍ ATS 11 Monmouth Rd ✆ 854348/855829

◆London 228 – Dolgellau 12 – Shrewsbury 63.

🏠 **Dolgoch Falls,** LL36 9UW, SW : 2½ m. on B 4405 ✆ 782258, ≼, ⌘ – ☎ 🅿. VISA
March-October – **M** 14.50 **t.** ⧘ 3.95 – **6 rm** ⊂ 21.50/50.00 **t.** – SB 58.50/65.50 **t.**

◆London 249 – Carmarthen 29 – Fishguard 26.

🏨 **Penrallt,** SA43 2BS, SW : 1 m. by B 4333 ✆ 810227, Fax 811375, ≼, Ⅰ₅, ⇌, 🔲 heated, ⌘, ※ – ⏹ ☎ 🅿. 🔼 AE ⓞ VISA. ⌘
closed 25 to 31 December – **M** (bar lunch Monday to Saturday)/dinner 15.00 **st.** and a la carte ⧘ 4.50 – **17 rm** ⊂ 48.00/95.00 **st.** – SB (except early June-early September) 170.00 **st.**

at Tresaith NE : 1¾ m. – ✉ ☎ 0239 Aberporth :

🏨 **Glandwr Manor** ⌘, SA43 2JH, ✆ 810197, ⌘ – ⇄ rest 🅿. ⌘
April-October – **M** (closed Sunday) (dinner only) 11.00 **t.** and a la carte ⧘ 3.70 – **7 rm** ⊂ 27.00/56.00 **t.**

🚏 Abersoch ✆ 712622, S : ½ m.

◆London 265 – Caernarfon 28 – Shrewsbury 101.

🏨 **Abersoch Harbour,** Lon Engan, LL53 7HR, ✆ 712406, ≼ – ⏹ 🅿. 🔼 VISA. ⌘
M (bar lunch)/dinner 15.00 **t.** and a la carte ⧘ 4.50 – **14 rm** ⊂ 32.00/140.00 **t.** – SB (except Bank Holidays) 90.00/110.00 **st.**

Riverside, LL53 7HW, ℘ 712419, Fax 712671, – TV ☎ P. VISA
mid February-mid November – **M** (bar lunch)/dinner 22.00 **st.** 5.00 – **12 rm** 30.00/80.00 **st.** – SB 100.00/160.00 **st.**

White House, LL53 7AG, ℘ 713427, Fax 713512, ≤, – TV ☎ P. VISA
M *(closed lunch October-March to non-residents)* (bar lunch)/dinner 15.50 **st.** and a la carte 4.50 – **15 rm** 26.50/59.00 **t.**

Tudor Court, Lon Sarn Bach, LL53 7EB, ℘ 713354, Fax 713354 – TV P. VISA
M 12.00/20.00 **t.** and a la carte 4.95 – **6 rm** 35.00/60.00 **t.** – SB (except Bank Holidays) 60.00/90.00 **st.**

Llwyn Du without rest., Lon Sarn Bach, LL53 7EL, ℘ 712186, – P.
3 rm 28.00/34.00 **s.**

at Bwlchtocyn S : 2 m. – ✉ Pwllheli – ☎ 0758 Abersoch :

Porth Tocyn, LL53 7BU, ℘ 713303, Fax 713538, ≤ Cardigan Bay and mountains, heated, , – TV ☎ P.
Easter-mid November – **M** (bar lunch Monday to Saturday)/dinner 23.00 **t.** 4.50 – **17 rm** 41.50/105.00 **t.** – SB 98.00/126.00 **st.**

ABERYSTWYTH Dyfed 403 H 26 Great Britain G. – pop. 8 636 – ECD : Wednesday – ☎ 0970.

See : Town★ - ≤★ from the National Library of Wales.

Exc. : Devil's Bridge (Pontarfynach)★, E : 12 m. by A 4120 – Strata Florida★ *AC*, SE : 15 m. by B 4340.

18 Bryn-y-Mor ℘ 615104, N : ½ m.

Terrace Rd, SY23 2AG ℘ 612125.

London 238 – Chester 98 – Fishguard 58 – Shrewsbury 74.

Belle Vue Royal, Marine Terrace, SY23 2BA, ℘ 617558, Fax 612190, ≤ – TV ☎ P. AE VISA.
closed 24 to 26 December – **M** 12.50/17.50 **t.** and a la carte 5.75 – **37 rm** 42.00/70.00 **t.** – SB (except Bank Holidays) 92.00/118.00 **st.**

Four Seasons, 50-54 Portland St., SY23 2DX, ℘ 612120, Fax 627458 – rest TV ☎ P. AE VISA.
closed 24 December-3 January – **M** (bar lunch Monday to Saturday)/dinner 20.00 **t.** 4.75 – **14 rm** 40.00/68.00 **t.** – SB (except Bank Holidays) 90.00/110.00 **st.**

The Groves, 44-46 North Par., SY23 2NF, ℘ 617623, Fax 627068 – TV ☎ P. AE VISA.
M (bar lunch)/dinner a la carte 16.80 **st.** 5.45 – **9 rm** 40.00/60.00 **st.** – SB (except Bank Holidays) 60.00/80.00 **st.**

Glyn-Garth without rest., South Rd, SY23 1JS, ℘ 615050 – TV.
closed Christmas and New Year – **8 rm** 17.00/44.00 **st.**

at Chancery (Rhydgaled) S : 4 m. on A 487 – ✉ ☎ 0970 Aberystwyth :

Conrah Country, SY23 4DF, ℘ 617941, Fax 624546, ≤, « 18C country house », , , park – rest TV ☎ P – 40. AE VISA.
closed 22 to 31 December – **M** 14.75/22.50 **t.** and a la carte 4.75 – **20 rm** 56.00/99.00 **t.** – SB 105.00/138.00 **st.**

ATS Glanyrafon Ind. Est., Llanbadarn ℘ 611166

ARTHOG Gwynedd 402 403 I 25 – see Dolgellau.

BALA Gwynedd 402 403 J 25 – pop. 1 852 – ECD : Wednesday – ☎ 0678.

9 Bala Lake Hotel ℘ 520344, S : 1½ m. by B 4403.

High St., LL23 7NH ℘ 520367 (summer only).

London 216 – Chester 46 – Dolgellau 18 – Shrewsbury 52.

Palé Hall, Llandderfel, LL23 7PS, E : 4¾ m. by A 494 off B 4401 ℘ 067 83 (Llandderfel) 285, Fax 220, ≤, , , park – rest TV ☎ P – 40. VISA.
M 15.00/25.00 **t.** and dinner a la carte – **15 rm** 85.00/160.00 **t.**, 2 suites – SB (except Christmas) (weekends only) 120.00/190.00 **st.**

White Lion Royal, 61 High St., LL23 7AE, ℘ 520314 – TV ☎ P. AE VISA
closed 25 December – **M** 8.95/11.50 **st.** 5.75 – **26 rm** 36.00/64.00 **st.** – SB 38.90/98.00 **st.**

Fron Feuno Hall, LL23 7YF, SW : 1 m. on A 494 ℘ 521115, ≤ Bala Lake, , , park – P.
April-October – **M** (by arrangement) (communal dining) approx. 14.00 **st.** – **3 rm** 30.00/56.00 **st.** – SB 79.00/88.00 **st.**

Dewis Cyfarfod, Llandderfel, LL23 7DR, E : 3¼ m. by A 494 on B 4401 ℘ 067 83 (Llandderfel) 243, ≤, , park – TV P. VISA.
M (by arrangement) 14.50 **st.** 4.00 – **5 rm** 28.00/48.00 **st.**

- ⌂ **Melin Meloch,** LL23 7DP, E : 1 ¾ m. by A 494 on B 4401 *𝒫* 520101, « Part 13C converted water mill », ✍ – ⇔ 📺 **◐**. ⚗
  closed January – **M** (by arrangement) (communal dining) 12.50 **s.** – **3 rm** � 18.50/36.00 **s.** – SB (weekdays only) 52.00/60.00 **s.**

- ⌂ **Llidiardau Mawr** ⌕, Llidiardau, LL23 7SG, NW : 4 ¼ m. by A 4212 *𝒫* 520555, ⩽, « 17C stone-built mill house », ✍ – **◐**. ⚗
  May-September – **M** 11.50 **st.** – **3 rm** ⊆ 20.00/36.00 **st.**

BANGOR Gwynedd 𝟜𝟘𝟚 𝟜𝟘𝟛 H 24 – pop. 12 126 – ECD : Wednesday – ✿ 0248.

🏌 St. Deiniol, Pentryn *𝒫* 353098, E : 1 m. by A 5122.

🎭 Theatr Gwynedd, Deiniol Rd, LL57 2TL *𝒫* 352786 (summer only).

♦London 247 – Birkenhead 68 – Holyhead 23 – Shrewsbury 83.

- 🏨 **Menai Court,** Craig-y-Don Rd, LL57 2BG, *𝒫* 354200, Fax 354200 – ⇔ rest 📺 ☎ **◐** –
  🔥 50. 🅰 𝑽𝑰𝑺𝑨 𝗝𝗖𝗕
  M *(closed Saturday and Sunday lunch)* 11.50 **t.** (lunch) and dinner a la carte 15.45/18.95 **t.** –
  12 rm ⊆ 40.00/68.00 – SB 79.00/90.00 **st.**

- 🏨 **Pavilion Lodge** without rest, One Stop Services, Llandegai, LL57 4BG, SE : 2 ½ m. by A 5122, at junction of A 5 with A 55 *𝒫* 370345, Fax 355959 – 📺 ⅁ **◐**. 🅰 🅰🅴 **◐** 𝑽𝑰𝑺𝑨
  ⊆ 4.00 – **34 rm** 31.95/35.95 **st.**

- 🏨 **Ty-Uchaf,** Tal-y-Bont, LL57 3UR, SE : 2 m. by A 5122 *𝒫* 352219, Fax 362913 – 📺 ☎ **◐**.
  🅰 𝑽𝑰𝑺𝑨 ⚗
  closed 24 December-2 January – **M** (in bar) 8.50 **st.** and dinner a la carte ⏹ 4.25 – **9 rm**
  ⊆ 25.00/45.00 **st.**

The Guide changes, so renew your Guide every year.

BARMOUTH (Abermaw) Gwynedd 𝟜𝟘𝟚 𝟜𝟘𝟛 H 25 – pop. 2 142 – ECD : Wednesday – ✿ 0341.

🎭 The Old Library, Station Rd, LL42 1LU *𝒫* 280787 (summer only).

♦London 231 – Chester 74 – Dolgellau 10 – Shrewsbury 67.

- 🏨 **Ty'r Graig Castle,** Llanaber Rd, LL42 1YN, on A 496 *𝒫* 280470, Fax 280470, ⩽ – ⇔ rest
  📺 ☎ **◐**. 🅰 🅰🅴 𝑽𝑰𝑺𝑨 𝗝𝗖𝗕. ⚗
  mid March-December – **M** (light lunch)/dinner 15.50 **t.** and a la carte ⏹ 5.50 – **12 rm**
  ⊆ 38.00/59.00 **t.** – SB (except Bank Holidays) 92.00 **st.**

- ⌂ **Cranbourne,** 9 Marine Par., LL42 1NA, *𝒫* 280202 – 📺. 🅰 𝑽𝑰𝑺𝑨. ⚗
  M 12.50 **st.** ⏹ 4.00 – **10 rm** ⊆ 15.00/44.00 **st.** – SB (October-March) 52.00 **st.**

  at Llanaber NW : 1 ½ m. by A 496 – ✉ ✿ 0341 Barmouth :

- ⌂ **Llwyndû Farmhouse** ⌕, LL42 1RR, N : ¾ m. on A 496 *𝒫* 280144, « Part 17C », ✍ – 📺
  ◐
  M 18.50 **t.** – **7 rm** ⊆ 46.00/50.00 **st.** – SB (November-mid March) 63.00/68.00 **st.**

BARRY (Barri) S. Glam. 𝟜𝟘𝟛 K 29 – pop. 44 443 – ECD : Wednesday – ✿ 0446.

🏌 Brynhill Port Rd, Colcot *𝒫* 735061 – 🏌 RAF, St. Athan *𝒫* 751043.

🎭 The Triangle, Paget Rd, Barry Island, CF6 8TJ *𝒫* 747171 (summer only).

♦London 167 – ♦Cardiff 10 – ♦Swansea 39.

- 🏨 **Egerton Grey,** CF62 9BZ, SW : 4 ½ m. by A 4226 and Porthkerry rd via Cardiff Airport
   𝒫 711666, Fax 711690, ⩽, « Country house atmosphere », ✍, park, ✗ – ⇔ rest 📺 ☎
  ◐. 🅰 🅰🅴 **◐** 𝑽𝑰𝑺𝑨
  M 19.50/25.00 **st.** and a la carte ⏹ 5.50 – **10 rm** ⊆ 50.00/120.00 **st.** – SB 99.00/125.00 **st.**

- 🏨 **Aberthaw House,** 28 Porthkerry Rd, CF6 8AX, *𝒫* 737314, Fax 732376 – 📺 ☎. 🅰 🅰🅴 **◐**
  𝑽𝑰𝑺𝑨. ⚗
  closed 24 December-7 January – **M** (closed Sunday) (dinner only) 14.50 **t.** and a la carte
  ⏹ 3.75 – **9 rm** ⊆ 42.50/57.50 **t.**

- 🏨 **Cwm Ciddy Toby,** Airport Rd, CF6 9BA, NW : 1 ½ m. by B 4266 *𝒫* 700075, Fax 700075 (ext. 225) – 📺 ☎ **◐**. 🅰 🅰🅴 **◐** 𝑽𝑰𝑺𝑨. ⚗
  closed 25-26 and 31 December – **M** (grill rest.) 7.50 **t.** and a la carte ⏹ 4.55 – **14 rm**
  ⊆ 48.00/58.00 **t.**

BEAUMARIS Gwynedd 𝟜𝟘𝟚 𝟜𝟘𝟛 H 24 Great Britain G. – pop. 1 413 – ECD : Wednesday –
✿ 0248.

See : Castle★★ *AC.*

Envir. : Isle of Anglesey★★.

Exc. : Plas Newydd★★ *AC*, SW : 7 m. by A 545 and A 4080.

🏌 Baron Hill *𝒫* 810231, SW : 1 m. by A 54.

♦London 253 – Birkenhead 74 – Holyhead 25.

- 🏨 **Bishopsgate House,** 54 Castle St., LL58 8BB, *𝒫* 810302, Fax 810166 – ⇔ rest 📺 ☎ **◐**.
  🅰 𝑽𝑰𝑺𝑨
  closed 20 December-January – **M** (closed lunch October-May) (bar lunch Monday to Saturday)/dinner 16.50 **st.** and a la carte ⏹ 5.00 – **10 rm** ⊆ 30.00/55.00 **st.** – SB 69.00/108.00 **st.**

XX **Ye Olde Bull's Head** with rm, Castle St., LL58 8AP, ☎ 810329, Fax 811294 – 📺 ☎ 🅿. 🗚 _VISA_ 🍴
closed 25-26 December and 1 January – **M** (bar lunch Monday to Saturday)/dinner 18.95 **t.** and a la carte ↥ 6.75 – **11 rm** ⚏ 42.00/72.00 **t.** – SB (October-April except Easter) 110.00/137.00 **st.**

BEDDGELERT Gwynedd 402 403 H 24 Great Britain G. – pop. 646 – ECD : Wednesday – ☻ 076 686 (3 fig.) and 0766 (6 fig.).
Exc. : Snowdon★★★ (🌟★★★ from summit) N : by marked footpaths or by Snowdon Mountain Railway from Llanberis.
♦London 249 – Caernarfon 13 – Chester 73.

🏤 **Royal Goat**, LL55 4YE, ☎ 224, Fax 422, ⌛ – 🔟 📺 ☎ 🅿 – 🔬 120. 🗚 🗛 ⓘ _VISA_
M 14.00/17.00 **st.** and a la carte ↥ 5.50 – **33 rm** ⚏ 42.00/66.00 **st.**, 1 suite – SB 88.00/120.00 **st.**

↑ **Sygun Fawr Country House** ⌂, LL55 4NE, NE : ¾ m. by A 498 ☎ 258, ≼ mountains and valley, « Part 16C stone built house », ☎⌛, 🍴, park – 🅿
closed January – **M** 15.00 **t.** ↥ 4.10 – **7 rm** ⚏ 28.50/48.00 **t.** – SB (November-Easter) 75.00/92.00 **st.**

BEREA Dyfed – see St. Davids.

BERRIEW (Aberriw) Powys 402 403 K 26 – pop. 1167 – ⊠ Welshpool – ☻ 0686.
♦London 190 – Chester 49 – Shrewsbury 26.

🏠 **Lion**, SY21 8PQ, ☎ 640452, Fax 640844 – 📺 ☎ 🅿. 🗚 🗛 ⓘ _VISA_. 🍴
M (booking essential) (bar lunch Monday to Saturday)/dinner 18.00 **t.** and a la carte ↥ 4.00 – **7 rm** ⚏ 52.00/85.00 **t.** – SB (except Bank Holidays) 90.00/100.00 **st.**

Great Britain and _Ireland_ is now covered
by an **Atlas** at a scale of 1 inch to 4.75 miles.

Three easy to use versions: Paperback, Spiralbound and Hardback.

BETWS-Y-COED Gwynedd 402 403 I 24 Great Britain G. – pop. 654 – ECD : Thursday – ☻ 0690.
See : Town★.
Envir. : Swallow Falls★, NW : 2 m. by A 5.
🏌 Clubhouse ☎ 710556, NE : ½ m. by A 5.
🛈 Royal Oak Stables, LL24 0AH ☎ 710426.
♦London 226 – Holyhead 44 – Shrewsbury 62.

🏤 **Royal Oak**, Holyhead Rd, LL24 0AY, ☎ 710219, Fax 710603 – 📺 ☎ 🅿. 🗚 🗛 ⓘ _VISA_. 🍴
M 10.00/18.00 **t.** and a la carte – **27 rm** ⚏ 49.00/78.00 **t.** – SB (except Bank Holidays) 98.00/150.00 **st.**

🏤 **Waterloo**, LL24 0AR, on A 5 ☎ 710411, Fax 710666, 🔥, ☎⌛, 🏊 – 📺 ☎ 🅿. 🗚 🗛 ⓘ _VISA_. 🍴
closed 24 and 25 December – **M** (bar lunch Monday to Saturday)/dinner 16.50 **t.** and a la carte ↥ 5.75 – **39 rm** ⚏ 47.50/84.00 **t.** – SB (except July, August and Bank Holidays) 91.00/112.00 **st.**

♤ **Ty Gwyn**, LL24 0SG, SE : ½ m. on A 5 ☎ 710383, « 17C inn » – 📺 🅿. 🗚 _VISA_
M (lunch by arrangement)/dinner 17.95 **t.** and a la carte ↥ 4.50 – **13 rm** ⚏ 20.00/80.00 **t.** – SB 71.90/115.90 **st.**

↑ **Park Hill**, Llanrwst Rd, LL24 0HD, NE : 1 m. by A 5 on A 470 ☎ 710540, Fax 710540, ≼ Vale of Conwy, ☎⌛, 🏊, 🍴 – 🐾 rest 📺 🅿. 🗚 🗛 ⓘ _VISA_. 🍴
M (dinner only) 14.50 **st.** ↥ 3.75 – **11 rm** ⚏ 19.50/62.00 **st.** – SB (October-March) 64.00/72.00 **st.**

at Capel Garmon E : 2 ½ m. by A 5 and A 470 on Capel Garmon rd – ⊠ ☻ 0690 Betws-y-Coed :

🏠 **Tan-y-Foel** ⌂, LL26 0RE, N : 1 m. ☎ 710507, Fax 710681, ≼ Vale of Conwy and Snowdonia, « Part 16C manor house », 🏊, park – 🐾 📺 ☎ 🅿. 🗚 🗛 _VISA_. 🍴
M (residents only) (dinner only) a la carte 23.00 **st.** – **9 rm** ⚏ 58.00/99.00 **st.** – SB (except Bank Holidays) 83.00/118.00 **st.**

at Pont-y-Pant SW : 4½ m. on A 470 – ⊠ ☻ 069 06 Dolwyddelan :

🏤 **Plas Hall** ⌂, LL25 0PJ, ☎ 206, Fax 526, ⌛, 🍴 – 📺 ☎ 👍 🅿. 🗚 _VISA_
M 6.95/14.95 **t.** and a la carte ↥ 4.50 – **17 rm** ⚏ 25.00/79.00 **st.** – SB 47.50/105.00 **st.**

BONCATH Dyfed 403 G 27 – ⊠ ☻ 0239.
♦London 247 – Carmarthen 27 – Fishguard 17.

↑ Pantyderi Mansion ⌂, SA37 0JB, W : 2 ¾ m. by B 4332 ☎ 841227, Fax 841670, ≼, « Working farm », 🏊, ⌛, 🍴, park – 📺 🅿. 🍴
8 rm.

BONTDDU Gwynedd 402 403 I 25 – see Dolgellau.

BRECHFA Dyfed 403 H 28 – ⊠ Carmarthen – ✪ 0267.

♦London 223 – Carmarthen 11 – ♦Swansea 30.

XX **Ty Mawr Country House** 🍴 with rm, Abergorlech Rd, SA32 7RA, 𝒫 202332, Fax 202437, « Part 15C and 16C house », 🐟 – ℗. 🏧 ⅭⅬⅭ VISA
closed last week January-first week February, last week November-first week December and 25-26 December – **M** (*closed Tuesday*) 10.75/18.75 **t.** 🍷 4.50 – **5 rm** ⊇ 44.00/68.00 **t.** – SB (except Bank Holidays) 96.00/108.00 **st.**

BRECON (Aberhonddu) Powys 403 J 28 Great Britain G. – pop. 7 166 – ECD : Wednesday – ✪ 0874.

Exc. : Dan-yr-Ogof Caves★★ *AC*, SW : 18 m. by A 40 and A 4067.

🏌 Penoyre Park, Cradoc 𝒫 623658, NW : 2 m. by B 4520 – 🏌 Llanfaes 𝒫 622004, W : ½ m. by A 40.

🅱 Cattle Market Car Park, LD3 9DA 𝒫 622485.

♦London 171 – ♦Cardiff 40 – Carmarthen 31 – Gloucester 65.

🏨 **Peterstone Court,** Llanhamlech, LD3 7YB, SE : 3¼ m. on A 40 𝒫 86387, Fax 86376, ≤, « Georgian manor house », 🛁, ⅀, 🏊 heated, 🐟 – ᵗᵛ ☎ ℗. 🏧 ⅭⅬⅭ ⓪ VISA
M 32.95 **st.** and a la carte – **12 rm** ⊇ 72.50/145.00 **st.** – SB (except Christmas and New Year) 90.00/180.00 **st.**

🏠 **Wellington,** The Bulwark, LD3 7AD, 𝒫 625225, Fax 623223 – ᵗᵛ ☎. 🏧 ⅭⅬⅭ VISA
M (bar lunch)/dinner 15.00 **t.** and a la carte – **20 rm** ⊇ 40.00/65.00 **t.**

🛢 ATS The Watton 𝒫 624496/624163

BRIDGEND (Pen-y-Bont) Mid Glam. 403 J 29 – pop. 31008 – ECD : Wednesday – ✪ 0656.

♦London 177 – ♦Cardiff 20 – ♦Swansea 23.

🏨 **Heronston,** Ewenny Rd, CF35 5AW, S : 2 m. on B 4265 𝒫 668811, Fax 767391, 🛁, ⅀ heated, 🐟 – 🛗 ᵗᵛ ☎ ℗ – 🔔 120. 🏧 ⅭⅬⅭ ⓪ VISA JCB
closed 26 December and 1 January – **M** 13.75/20.00 **st.** and a la carte 🍷 4.50 – **76 rm** ⊇ 60.00/120.00 **st.** – SB (weekends only) 96.50/108.00 **st.**

at Pencoed NE : 4½ m. by A 473 – ⊠ ✪ 0656 Pencoed :

🏠 **Forte Travelodge,** CF3 5HU, E : 1¼ m. by Felindre rd 𝒫 864404, Reservations (Freephone) 0800 850950 – ᵗᵛ ♿ ℗. 🏧 ⅭⅬⅭ VISA
M (Harvester grill) a la carte approx. 16.00 **st.** – ⊇ 5.50 – **40 rm** 31.95 **t.**

at Coychurch (Llangrallo) E : 2¼ m. by A 473 – ⊠ ✪ 0656 Bridgend :

🏨 **Coed-y-Mwstwr** 🍴, CF35 6AF, N : 1 m. 𝒫 860621, Fax 863122, ≤, ⅀ heated, 🐟, park, ❊ – 🛗 ᵗᵛ ☎ ℗ – 🔔 120. 🏧 ⅭⅬⅭ ⓪ VISA
M 15.50/24.00 **st.** and a la carte 🍷 3.95 – **21 rm** ⊇ 75.00/95.00 **st.**, 2 suites – SB 130.00/170.00 **st.**

at Laleston W : 2 m. on A 473 – ⊠ ✪ 0656 Bridgend :

XX **Great House** with rm, CF32 OHP, on A 473 𝒫 657644, Fax 668892 – ᵗᵛ ☎ ℗. 🏧 ⅭⅬⅭ ⓪ VISA, ❊
M (*closed Saturday lunch and Sunday dinner*) 10.75 **t.** (lunch) and dinner a la carte 19.00/26.75 **t.** 🍷 4.75 – **6 rm** ⊇ 60.00/80.00 **t.**

🛢 ATS 122 Coity Rd 𝒫 658775/6

BRONLLYS Powys 403 K 27 – see Talgarth.

BWLCHTOCYN Gwynedd 402 403 G 25 – see Abersoch.

CADOXTON W. Glam. 403 I 29 – see Neath.

CAERLEON Gwent 403 L 29 – see Newport.

CAERNARFON Gwynedd 402 403 H 24 Great Britain G. – pop. 9 271 – ECD : Thursday – ✪ 0286.

See : Town★★★ - Castle★★★ *AC*.

🏌 Llanfaglan 𝒫 3783, SW : 2½ m.

🅱 Oriel Pendeitsh, Castle St., LL55 2PB 𝒫 672232.

♦London 249 – Birkenhead 76 – Chester 68 – Holyhead 30 – Shrewsbury 85.

🏨 **Seiont Manor** 🍴, Llanrug, LL55 2AQ, E : 3 m. on A 4086 𝒫 673366, Fax 672840, 🛁, 🛁, ⅀, 🐟, park – ❊ rest ᵗᵛ ☎ ℗ – 🔔 100. 🏧 ⅭⅬⅭ ⓪ VISA
M (*closed Saturday lunch*) 11.50/30.00 **st.** and a la carte 🍷 4.75 – **28 rm** ⊇ 72.50/145.00 **st.** – SB (except Christmas and New Year) 119.00/154.00 **st.**

⌂ **Pengwern** ⤢, Saron, LL54 5UH, SW : 3 ¼ m. by A 487 on Llandwrog rd ℰ 830717, « Working farm » – ⤢ 🖂 📺 🅿. ⤢
closed December and January – **M** (by arrangement) 9.50 **st.** – **3 rm** 🖙 19.00/38.00 **st.** – SB (except June-August and Bank Holidays) 49.00/57.00 **st.**

⌂ **Isfryn** without rest., 11 Church St., LL55 1SW, ℰ 675628 – 📺
April-October – **6 rm** 🖙 16.00/35.00 **st.**

🔧 ATS Bangor Rd ℰ 673110

CAPEL GARMON Gwynedd 402 403 I 24 – see Betws-y-Coed.

☛ THE CHANNEL TUNNEL Map Guide

260 *French edition*
   with tourist sights in England

261 *English edition*
   with tourist sights on the Continent

CARDIFF **(Caerdydd)** S. Glam. 403 K 29 Great Britain G. – pop. 262 313 – ECD : Wednesday – ✆ 0222.

See : City★ – Castle★ (interiors★) AC BZ – National Museum of Wales★ (Picture Collection★) AC BY **M2** – Llandaff Cathedral★ AC AV **B**.

Envir. : Welsh Folk Museum, St. Fagan's★★ AC, by St. Fagan's Rd AV – Castell Coch★ AC, NW : 4 ½ m. by A 470 AV.

Exc. : Caerphilly Castle★★ AC, N : 7 m. by A 469 AV.

🛫 Dinas Powis ℰ 512727, SW : 3 m. by A 4055 AX.

✈ Cardiff-Wales Airport ℰ 0446 (Rhoose) 711111, SW : 8 m. by A 48 AX – **Terminal** : Central Bus Station.

🚉 Bridge St., CF1 2EE ℰ 227281.

♦London 155 – ♦Birmingham 110 – ♦Bristol 46 – ♦Coventry 124.

Plans on following pages

🏨 **Copthorne,** Copthorne Way, Culverhouse Cross, CF5 6XJ, W : 4 ¾ m. by A 4161 and A 48 at junction with A 4232 ℰ 599100, Telex 498042, Fax 599080, *Ⅰ₅*, ☎s, ⬛, ☞ – ▮⯅▮
⤢ rm 🍽 rest 📺 ☎ ᕳ 🅿 – ⚿ 250. ◪ ◪ ◉ **VISA** **JCB**   AX
M (in bar Saturday lunch and Sunday dinner) a la carte 17.50 **st.** ❙ 6.00 – 🖙 9.75 – **134 rm** 92.00/102.00 **st.**, 1 suite – SB (weekends only) 122.25/200.00 **st.**

🏨 **Cardiff Marriott,** Mill Lane, CF1 1EZ, ℰ 399944, Fax 395578, ⩣, *Ⅰ₅*, ☎s, ⬛, squash – ▮⯅▮
⤢ rm 🖂 📺 ☎ ᕳ 🅿 – ⚿ 300. ◪ ◪ ◉ **VISA** ⤢   BZ **s**
M 14.00/16.50 **st.** and a la carte ❙ 7.95 – 🖙 10.25 – **179 rm** 95.00 **st.**, 3 suites – SB (weekends only) 100.00/130.00 **st.**

🏨 **Angel** (Q.M.H.), Castle St., CF1 2QZ, ℰ 232633, Telex 498132, Fax 396212, *Ⅰ₅*, ☎s – ▮⯅▮
⤢ rm 📺 ☎ 🅿 – ⚿ 250. ◪ ◪ ◉ **VISA** **JCB**   BZ **a**
M 15.00 **st.** and a la carte ❙ 6.95 – **89 rm** 🖙 60.00/70.00 **st.**, 2 suites – SB (weekends only) 60.00 **st.**

🏨 Park (Mt. Charlotte Thistle), Park Pl., CF1 3UD, ℰ 383471, Telex 497195, Fax 399309 – ▮⯅▮
⤢ rm 📺 ☎ 🅿 – ⚿ 300. ⤢   BZ **c**
115 rm, 4 suites.

🏩 **Cardiff International** (Best Western), Mary Ann St., CF1 2EQ, ℰ 341441, Telex 498005, Fax 223742 – ▮⯅▮ ⤢ rm 🍽 rest 📺 ☎ 🅿 – ⚿ 40. ◪ ◪ ⤢   BZ **a**
M (bar lunch Monday to Saturday)/dinner 14.50 **st.** and a la carte ❙ 3.95 – 🖙 8.45 – **140 rm** 70.00/75.00 **st.**, 3 suites – SB (weekends only) 89.00/119.00 **st.**

🏩 **Cardiff Moat House** (Q.M.H.), Circle Way East, Llanedeyrn, CF3 7XF, NE : 3 m. by A 48 ℰ 732520, Telex 497582, Fax 549092, *Ⅰ₅*, ☎s, ⬛ – ▮⯅▮ ⤢ rm 📺 ☎ ᕳ 🅿 – ⚿ 180. ◪ ◪
◉ **VISA**   AV **n**
M *(closed Saturday lunch)* 14.00/16.00 **st.** and a la carte ❙ 9.00 – **133 rm** 🖙 84.00/103.00 **st.**, 2 suites – SB (weekends only) 88.00/95.00 **st.**

🏩 **Forte Crest,** Castle St., CF1 2XB, ℰ 388681, Telex 497258, Fax 371495 – ▮⯅▮ ⤢ rm 📺 ☎
🅿 – ⚿ 150. ◪ ◪ ◉ **VISA**   BZ **i**
M 12.05/17.00 **t.** and a la carte ❙ 6.60 – 🖙 9.95 – **153 rm** 75.00 **st.**, 1 suite – SB (weekends only) 98.00 **st.**

🏩 **Churchills,** Cardiff Rd, CF5 2AD, ℰ 562372, Fax 568347 – 🍽 rest 📺 ☎ ᕳ 🅿 – ⚿ 80. ◪
◪ ◉ **VISA**   AV **v**
M 8.95/25.00 **st.** and a la carte ❙ 3.80 – 🖙 6.90 – **28 rm** 60.00/70.00 **st.**, 7 suites – SB (weekends only) 72.00/150.00 **st.**

🏩 **Forte Posthouse,** Pentwyn Rd, CF2 7XA, NE : 4 m. by A 48 ℰ 731212, Fax 549147, *Ⅰ₅*,
☎s, ⬛ – ▮⯅▮ ⤢ rm 🍽 rest 📺 ☎ 🅿 – ⚿ 120. ◪ ◪ ◉ **VISA** **JCB**   AV
M a la carte 12.45/21.85 **st.** ❙ 4.65 – 🖙 6.95 – **142 rm** 53.50 **st.** – SB (weekends only) 90.00 **st.**

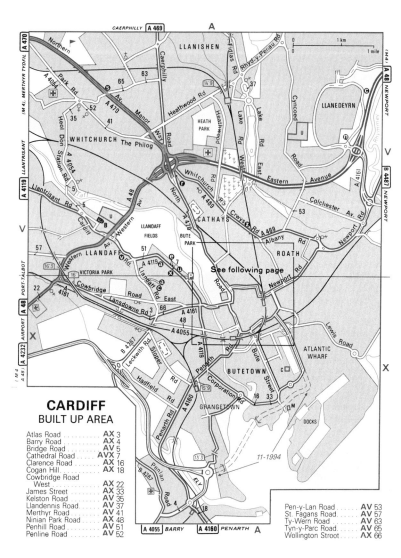

CARDIFF
BUILT UP AREA

Masons Arms (Toby), 21-23 Tyn-y-Parc Rd, CF4 6BG, NW : 3½ m. by A 470 ℰ 692554, Fax 693724 – ⇥ rm 📺 🕭 🅿 – 🔬 100. 🔼 🅰🅴 ⓞ 𝘝𝘐𝘚𝘈. ⅍   AV **s**
M (carving rest.) a la carte 9.90/15.35 **t.** – **30 rm** ⊇ 60.00/75.00 **t.**

Celtic Bay, Schooner Way, Atlantic Wharf, Cardiff Bay, CF1 5RT, ℰ 465888, Fax 481491, ⇥ – 🛊 🖿 rest 📺 🕭 🅿 – 🔬 200   BZ **x**
64 rm.

Forte Travelodge, Circle Way East, Llanedeyrn, CF3 7ND, on Coed-y-Gores rd ℰ 549564, Reservations (Freephone) 0800 850950 – 📺 ঌ 🅿. 🔼 🅰🅴 𝘝𝘐𝘚𝘈. ⅍   AV **c**
M (Harvester grill) a la carte approx. 16.00 **t.** – **32 rm** 31.95 **t.**

Willows without rest., 128 Cathedral Rd, CF1 9LQ, ℰ 340881 – 📺 🕭 🅿. 🔼 🅰🅴 𝘝𝘐𝘚𝘈. ⅍   AV **e**
13 rm 17.00/36.00 **s.**

Ferrier's without rest., 130-132 Cathedral Rd, CF1 9LQ, ℰ 383413, Fax 383413 – 📺 🕭 🅿. 🔼 🅰🅴 ⓞ 𝘝𝘐𝘚𝘈   AV **e**
closed 2 weeks Christmas-New Year – **26 rm** ⊇ 18.00/48.00 **t.**

CENTRE

↑ **Annedd Lon** without rest., 3 Dyfrig St., off Cathedral Rd, CF1 9LR, ℰ 223349, Fax 640885 – ⇌ ⊡ ⊡. ⊗
AV **u**
6 rm ⊐ 18.00/38.00 **s.**

↑ **Penrhys,** 127 Cathedral Rd, CF1 9JB, ℰ 230548, Fax 387292 – ⊡ ☎ ℗. ⚠ VISA ⊗
AV **x**
M (by arrangement) 10.95 **st.** – **18 rm** ⊐ 29.00/38.00 **st.**

↑ **Georgian** without rest., 179 Cathedral Rd, CF1 9PL, ℰ 232594, Fax 232594 – ⊡. ⚠ VISA.
⊗
AV **a**
5 rm ⊐ 20.00/35.00 **st.**

XXX **De Courcey's,** Tyla Morris Av., Pentyrch, CF4 8QN, NW : 6 m. by A 4119 on Pentyrch rd
ℰ 892232, Fax 891949 – ℗. ⚠ ⚠ ① VISA
AV
closed Saturday lunch, Sunday dinner, 25 December-4 January and Bank Holiday Mondays
– **M** 15.00/31.95 **st.**

XX **Indian Ocean,** 290 North Rd, Gabalfa, CF4 3BN, ℰ 621349 – ▤. ⚠ ⚠ ① VISA   AV **r**
closed Sunday lunch and Christmas Day – **M** - **Indian** a la carte approx. 17.90 **t.**

✗ **Le Cassoulet,** 5 Romilly Cres., Canton, CF1 9NP, ✆ 221905. ◣ AE 𝐕𝐈𝐒𝐀   AX **c**
closed Saturday lunch, Sunday, Monday, August and 2 weeks December – **M** - **French**
22.00/30.00 **t.** and a la carte ▯ 3.75.

✗ **Quayle's,** 6-8 Romilly Cres., Canton, CF1 9NR, ✆ 341264 – ◣ AE 𝐕𝐈𝐒𝐀   AX **a**
closed Sunday dinner, Tuesday and Bank Holidays – **M** - **Bistro** 11.95 **t.** (lunch) and a la
carte 12.40/20.40 **t.** ▯ 4.75.

✗ **Blas-ar-Gymru (A Taste of Wales),** 48 Crwys Rd, CF2 4NN, ✆ 382132, Fax 565062 –
🅿 ◣ AE 𝐕𝐈𝐒𝐀   AV **z**
closed Saturday lunch, Sunday, 1 to 17 January and Bank Holiday Mondays – **M** 11.95/
19.50 **t.** ▯ 4.00.

✗ **Thai House,** 23 High St., CF1 2BZ, ✆ 387404, Fax 640810 – ◣ AE ⓞ 𝐕𝐈𝐒𝐀 JCB   BZ **o**
closed Sunday and Christmas – **M** - **Thai** 16.00/26.00 **st.** and a la carte.

✗ **Armless Dragon,** 97 Wyeverne Rd, Cathays, CF2 4BG, ✆ 382357 – ◣ AE ⓞ 𝐕𝐈𝐒𝐀
closed Saturday lunch, Sunday, Monday, 25-26 December and 1 January – **M** 9.90 **t.**
(lunch) and a la carte 14.70/20.30 **t.**   BY **n**

at Thornhill N : 5 ¼ m. by A 470 on A 469 – AV – ✉ 🅣 0222 Cardiff :

🏨 **New House Country** ⤢, Caerphilly Rd, CF4 5UA, on A 469 ✆ 520280, Fax 520324, ≤,
⤴, park – 📺 ☎ 🅟 – 🔥 200. ◣ AE 𝐕𝐈𝐒𝐀
M 12.50/15.00 **t.** and a la carte ▯ 7.75 – ⬜ 5.00 – **20 rm** 58.00/80.00 **t.**

🏨 **Manor Parc,** Thornhill Rd, CF4 5UA, on A 469 ✆ 693723, Fax 614624, ⤴, ✗ – 📺 ☎ 🅟.
◣ AE 𝐕𝐈𝐒𝐀 ✑
closed 24 to 27 December – **M** 14.50 **t.** (lunch) and a la carte 20.75/29.50 **t.** ▯ 4.50 – **12 rm**
⬜ 57.50/110.00 **st.**

at Castleton (Cas-Bach) (Gwent) NE : 7 m. on A 48 – AV – ✉ Cardiff – 🅣 0633
Castleton :

🏨 **Wentloog Resort,** CF3 8UQ, ✆ 680591, Fax 681287, Ⅰ₅, ≋, ▨ – ⇔ rm ▤ rest 📺 ☎ 🅟
– 🔥 120. ◣ AE ⓞ 𝐕𝐈𝐒𝐀
M (bar lunch Monday to Friday)/dinner 13.95 **st.** and a la carte ▯ 4.25 – ⬜ 7.50 – **55 rm**
55.00/65.00 **st.** – SB 80.00/120.00 **st.**

🏠 **Travel Inn,** Newport Rd, CF3 8UQ, ✆ 680070, Fax 681143 – ⇔ rm 📺 ♿ 🅟. ◣ AE ⓞ
𝐕𝐈𝐒𝐀 ✑
M (Beefeater grill) a la carte approx. 16.00 **t.** ▯ 5.00 – ⬜ 4.95 – **48 rm** 33.50 **st.**

◍ ATS Hadfield Rd ✆ 228251/226336

S. Glam. – ✉ Pontycwn – 🅣 0222 Cardiff

🏠 **Pavilion Lodge** without rest., CF7 8SA, M 4 junction 33 ✆ 892255, Fax 892497 – ⇔ 📺
♿ 🅟 – 🔥 40. ◣ AE ⓞ 𝐕𝐈𝐒𝐀 JCB
closed 25 December – ⬜ 4.00 – **50 rm** 31.95/35.95 **st.**

(Aberteifi) Dyfed 🔟🔟🔟 G 27 – pop. 3 815 – ECD : Wednesday – 🅣 0239.

🇮🇸 Gwbert-on-Sea ✆ 612035, NW : 3 m.

🎭 Theatr Mwldan, Bath House Rd, SA43 2JY ✆ 613230.

◆London 250 – Carmarthen 30 – Fishguard 19.

🏠 **Penbontbren Farm** ⤢, Glynarthen, SA44 6PE, NE : 9 ½ m. by A 487 ✆ 810248,
Fax 811129, park – 📺 ☎ ♿ 🅟. ◣ 𝐕𝐈𝐒𝐀
closed 24 to 28 December – **M** (dinner only) a la carte 13.05/16.10 **st.** ▯ 4.10 – **10 rm**
⬜ 36.00/64.00 **st.** – SB 82.00/100.00 **st.**

at Cilgerran S : 3 m. by A 478 and Cilgerran rd – ✉ 🅣 0239 Cardigan :

↑ **Allt-y-Rheini Mansion** ⤢, SA43 2TJ, S : ½ m. on Crymmych rd ✆ 612286, ≤, ⤴ – 📺
🅟. ◣ 𝐕𝐈𝐒𝐀 ✑
M (by arrangement) 14.50 **st.** ▯ 3.75 – **5 rm** ⬜ 31.00/54.00 **t.**

at St. Dogmaels W : 1 m. by A 487 on B 4568 – ✉ 🅣 0239 Cardigan :

↑ **Berwyn** ⤢ without rest., Cardigan Rd, SA43 3HS, ≤, ⤴ – 📺 🅟. ✑
3 rm ⬜ 18.50/36.00 **st.**

at Gwbert on Sea NW : 3 m. on B 4548 – ✉ 🅣 0239 Cardigan :

🏨 **Gwbert,** SA43 1PP, on B 4548 ✆ 612638, Fax 621474, ≤ Cardigan Bay – ▐ 📺 ☎ 🅟. ◣
𝐕𝐈𝐒𝐀 ✑
M *(closed Sunday dinner)* (bar lunch Monday to Saturday)/dinner 25.00 **t.** and a la carte
▯ 3.50 – **16 rm** ⬜ 32.00/104.00 **t.** – SB (September-April except Bank Holidays) (weekends
only) 60.00/70.00 **st.**

◍ ATS 4 Bath House Rd ✆ 612917

CARMARTHEN (Caerfyrddin) Dyfed 408 G 28 – pop. 13 860 – ECD : Thursday – ☎ 0267.

🏌 Blaenycoed Rd ℘ 87214, NW : 4 m.

🛈 Lammas St., SA31 3AQ. ℘ 231557.

◆London 220 – Fishguard 45 – ◆Swansea 27.

    🏨 **Ivy Bush Royal** (Forte), 11-13 Spilman St., SA31 1LG, ℘ 235111, Fax 234914, ☎s – 🛗 🔄 📺 ☎ 🅿 – 🔬 200. 🔼 🆎 ⓞ 𝗩𝗜𝗦𝗔 𝗝𝗖𝗕
    M (bar lunch Monday to Saturday)/dinner 16.95 **st.** and a la carte ⓘ 5.25 – **74 rm** ⊇ 54.50/64.50 **st.**, 1 suite – SB (weekends only) 88.00 **st.**

⚙ ATS Pensarn Rd ℘ 236996/235456

CASTLETON (Cas-Bach) Gwent 408 K 29 – see Cardiff (South Glam.).

CEMAES Gwynedd 402 408 G 23 Great Britain G. – ☎ 0407.

Envir. : Isle of Anglesey★★.

◆London 272 – Bangor 25 – Caernarfon 32 – Holyhead 16.

    ↑ **Hafod Country House**, LL67 ODS, S : ½ m. on Llanfechell rd ℘ 710500, ⇙ – 🔄 📺 🅿. ⚘
    March-October – **M** (by arrangement) 10.00 – **3 rm** ⊇ 32.00/36.00 **st.**

CHANCERY (Rhydgaled) Dyfed 408 H 26 – see Aberystwyth.

CHEPSTOW Gwent 408 404 M 29 Great Britain G. – pop. 9 039 – ECD : Wednesday – ☎ 0291.

See : Castle★ *AC*.

Envir. : Wye Valley★ (Eagle's Nest Viewpoint, Windcliff★).

🏌, 🏌 St. Pierre ℘ 625261, SW : 3½ m. on A 48.

🛈 Bridge St., NP6 5LH ℘ 623772 (summer only).

◆London 131 – ◆Bristol 17 – ◆Cardiff 28 – Gloucester 34.

    🏨 **St. Pierre H. Golf & Country Club**, NP6 6YA, SW : 3 ½ m. on A 48 ℘ 625261, Fax 629975, ≤, Ⅰδ, ☎s, 🏊, 🏌, park, ✗, squash – 🔄 rm 📺 ☎ 🅿 – 🔬 220. 🔼 🆎 ⓞ 𝗩𝗜𝗦𝗔 ⚘
    M 12.50/15.50 **st.** and a la carte ⓘ 5.50 – **138 rm** ⊇ 85.00/110.00 **st.**, 9 suites – SB 110.00/180.00 **st.**

    🏨 **George** (Forte), Moor St., NP6 5DB, ℘ 625363, Fax 627418 – 🔄 rm 📺 ☎ 🅿 – 🔬 30. 🔼 🆎 ⓞ 𝗩𝗜𝗦𝗔
    M (bar lunch Monday to Saturday)/dinner 15.95 **st.** and a la carte ⓘ 6.45 – ⊇ 8.50 – **14 rm** 65.00/80.00 **st.** – SB 108.00 **st.**

    🏠 **Beaufort**, Beaufort Sq., NP6 5EP, ℘ 622497, Fax 627389 – 📺 ☎ 🅿. 🔼 🆎 ⓞ 𝗩𝗜𝗦𝗔
    M 5.95/9.95 **st.** and dinner a la carte ⓘ 3.45 – ⊇ 4.95 – **18 rm** 29.50/47.00 **st.** – SB (except July and August) 63.00/85.00 **st.**

    🏠 **Afon Gwy**, 28 Bridge St., NP6 5EZ, ℘ 620158, Fax 626779, ≤ – 📺. 🔼 𝗩𝗜𝗦𝗔
    M (closed dinner Sunday and Monday in winter) (bar lunch winter) a la carte 10.75/20.15 **t.** ⓘ 4.95 – **4 rm** ⊇ 30.00/41.00 **t.** – SB 64.00/82.00 **st.**

    🏠 **Castle View**, 16 Bridge St., NP6 5EZ, ℘ 620349, Fax 627397, ⇙ – 📺 ☎. 🔼 🆎 ⓞ 𝗩𝗜𝗦𝗔
    M 15.00 **st.** and a la carte ⓘ 5.50 – **11 rm** ⊇ 39.50/64.50 **st.** – SB 79.00/99.00 **st.**

    ✗✗ Beckfords, 15-16 Upper Church St., NP6 5EX, ℘ 626547.

CILGERRAN Dyfed 408 G 27 – see Cardigan.

COLWYN BAY (Bae Colwyn) Clwyd 402 408 I 24 Great Britain G. – pop. 27 002 – ECD : Wednesday – ☎ 0492.

Envir. : Bodnant Garden★★ *AC*, SW : 6 m. by A 55 and A 470.

🏌 Abergele and Pensarn, Tan-y-Goppa Rd, Abergele ℘ 0745 (Abergele) 824034, E : 6 m. –
🏌 Old Colwyn, Woodland Av. ℘ 515581, E : 2 m.

🛈 40 Station Rd, LL28 8BU ℘ 530478 – The Promenade, Rhos-on-sea ℘ 548778 (summer only).

◆London 237 – Birkenhead 50 – Chester 42 – Holyhead 41.

    🏨 **Norfolk House**, 39 Princes Drive, LL29 8PF, ℘ 531757, Fax 533781, ⇙ – 🛗 📺 ☎ 🅿 – 🔬 30. 🔼 🆎 ⓞ 𝗩𝗜𝗦𝗔
    M (bar lunch)/dinner 16.50 **st.** and a la carte ⓘ 2.80 – **25 rm** ⊇ 30.00/60.00 **st.** – SB 80.00 **st.**

    🏠 **Hopeside**, 63-67 Princes Drive, West End, LL29 8PW, ℘ 533244, Fax 532850 – 🔄 rm 📺 ☎ 🅿. 🔼 𝗩𝗜𝗦𝗔
    M 18.00/20.00 **t.** and a la carte ⓘ 5.50 – **18 rm** ⊇ 25.00/80.00 **t.** – SB (except Bank Holidays) 76.00/110.00 **st.**

    🏠 **Lyndale**, 410 Abergele Rd, Old Colwyn, LL29 9AB, E : 1 ¾ m. on A 547 ℘ 515429, Fax 518805 – 📺 ☎ 🅿. 🔼 🆎 ⓞ 𝗩𝗜𝗦𝗔
    M (bar lunch Monday to Saturday)/dinner 14.50 **st.** and a la carte – **14 rm** ⊇ 26.00/52.00 **st.** – SB (except Bank Holidays) 50.00 **st.**

    ↑ **West Point**, 102 Conway Rd, LL29 7LE, ℘ 530331, ⇙ – 🔄 rest 📺 🅿. 🔼 𝗩𝗜𝗦𝗔
    March-September – **M** 12.50 **st.** ⓘ 3.50 – **9 rm** ⊇ 15.50/37.00 **st.** – SB 43.00/49.00 **st.**

✕ **Café Niçoise,** 124 Abergele Rd, LL29 7PS, ℰ 531555 – 🔳 VISA
closed Monday lunch, Sunday, first week January and third week June – **M** 12.95 **t.** (dinner)
and a la carte 11.95/23.80 **t.** ╣ 4.85.

at Penmaenhead E : 2 ¼ m. on A 547 – ⊠ ✿ 0492 Colwyn Bay :

🏨 **Colwyn Bay,** Old Colwyn, LL29 9LD, ℰ 516555, Fax 515565, ≼ – 🔳 ☎ 🅿 – 🔏 100. 🔳
AE ① VISA JCB
M 12.00/17.00 **st.** and a la carte – ⊏ 6.50 – **43 rm** 31.95/79.90 **st.** – SB (except Christmas
and New Year) 88.50/112.50 **st.**

at Rhos-on-Sea (Llandrillo-yn-Rhos) NW : 1 m. – ⊠ ✿ 0492 Colwyn Bay :

🏡 **Ashmount,** College Av., LL28 4NT, ℰ 544582, Fax 545479 – 🔳 ☎ 🅿 . 🔳 AE ① VISA JCB
M (dinner only) 11.50 **st.** ╣ 3.95 – **18 rm** ⊏ 29.75/60.00 **st.** – SB (except Bank Holidays)
52.00/74.50 **st.**

↑ **Cabin Hill,** 12 College Av., LL28 4NT, ℰ 544568 – 🔳 . ✕
April-mid October – **M** (by arrangement) – **10 rm** ⊏ 18.00/40.00 **st.** – SB 47.00/58.00 **st.**

Prices   For full details of the prices quoted in the guide,
consult the introduction.

CONWY Gwynedd 402 403 I 24 Great Britain G. – pop. 3 649 – ECD : Wednesday –
✿ 0492 Aberconwy.

See : Town★ - Castle★★ *AC* – Town Walls★★ - Plas Mawr★★ *AC*.

Envir. : Sychnant Pass (≼★★) – Bodnant Garden★★ *AC*, S : 6 m. by A 55 and A 470.

🏌 Morfa, ℰ 593400, W : 1 ½ m. by A 55 – 🏌 Penmaenmawr ℰ 623330, W : 4 m.

🛈 Conwy Castle Visitor Centre, ℰ 592248.

◆London 241 – Caernarfon 22 – Chester 46 – Holyhead 37.

🏨 **Castle** (Forte), High St., LL32 8DB, ℰ 592324, Fax 583351 – ✚✕ 🔳 ☎ 🅿 – 🔏 30. 🔳 AE
① VISA JCB
M (bar lunch Monday to Saturday)/dinner 16.95 **st.** and a la carte – ⊏ 8.50 – **29 rm**
60.00/70.00 **st.** – SB (except Christmas and New Year) 120.00 **st.**

🏨 **Berthlwyd Hall** ⅏, Llechwedd, LL32 8DQ, SW : 2 ¼ m. by B 5106 and Sychnant rd, off
Hendre rd ℰ 592409, Fax 572290, ≼, 🔳 heated, ⊿ – 🔳 ☎ 🅿 . 🔳 AE ① VISA
M 15.50/18.50 **st.** and a la carte ╣ 4.10 – ⊏ 4.00 – **8 rm** 42.50/75.00 **st.** – SB 70.00/
122.00 **st.**

🏡 **Castle Bank,** Mount Pleasant, LL32 8NY, ℰ 593888, ≼ – ✚✕ 🔳 🅿 . 🔳 VISA . ✕
closed January-mid February – **M** (dinner only and Sunday lunch)/dinner 14.00 **t.** ╣ 4.30 –
9 rm ⊏ 25.00/53.00 **t.** – SB 78.00/86.00 **st.**

at Roewen S : 3 m. by B 5106 – ⊠ Conwy – ✿ 0492 Tynygroes :

↑ **Tir-y-Coed** ⅏, LL32 8TP, ℰ 650219, ≼, ⊿ – ✚✕ rest 🔳 🅿
March-October – **M** 10.45 **t.** ╣ 4.00 – **7 rm** ⊏ 25.25/45.90 **t.** – SB (except May-September)
58.00/61.00 **st.**

at Tal-y-Bont S : 5 ¾ m. on B 5106 – ⊠ Conwy – ✿ 0492 Dolgarrog :

🏡 **Lodge,** LL32 8YX, ℰ 660766, Fax 660534 – 🔳 ☎ 🅿 . 🔳 AE VISA
M 15.95 **st.** (dinner) and a la carte ╣ 4.95 – **10 rm** ⊏ 33.95/50.00 **st.** – SB (except Bank
Holidays) 65.00/92.40 **st.**

COWBRIDGE S. Glam. 403 J 29 – pop. 3 488 – ✿ 0656 Wick (M. Glam.).

◆London 167 – ◆Cardiff 12 – ◆Swansea 30.

↑ **Stembridge Farm** ⅏ without rest., Llandow, CF7 7NT, SW : 3 ½ m. ℰ 79389, ≼, ⊿ –
✚✕ 🔳 🅿 . ✕
closed 20 December-10 January – **3 rm** ⊏ 26.00/58.00 **st.**

COYCHURCH (Llangrallo) M. Glam. 403 J 29 – see Bridgend.

CRICCIETH Gwynedd 402 403 H 25 – pop. 1 535 – ECD : Wednesday – ✿ 0766.

🏌 Ednyfed Hill ℰ 522154.

◆London 249 – Caernarfon 17 – Shrewsbury 85.

🏡 Plas Isa, Porthmadog Rd, LL52 0HP, ℰ 522443 – 🔳 ☎ 🅿
14 rm.

↑ **Glyn-y-Coed,** Porthmadog Rd, LL52 0HL, ℰ 522870 – 🔳 🅿 . 🔳 VISA
closed Christmas and New Year – **M** 10.00 **t.** ╣ 2.75 – **9 rm** ⊏ 21.00/42.00 **t.** – SB 56.00/
62.00 **st.**

↑ **Craig-y-Mor,** West Par., LL52 0EN, ℰ 522830, ≼ – 🔳 ☎ 🅿
March-October – **M** 10.00 **st.** – **7 rm** ⊏ 19.00/38.00 **st.** – SB 51.30/55.10 **st.**

⌂ Old Rectory Hotel, Llangattock ✆ 810373.

◆London 169 – Abergavenny 6 – Brecon 14 – Newport 25.

🏨 **Gliffaes Country House** ⌂, NP8 1RH, W : 3 ¾ m. by A 40 ✆ 0874 (Bwlch) 730371, Fax 730463, ≤, « Country house and gardens on the banks of the River Usk », ⌂, park, ✂ – ☎ ℗. ⚠ ⚠ ⓞ *VISA* ❄
closed 5 January-25 February – **M** (buffet lunch Monday to Saturday)/dinner 18.25 **st.** and a la carte – **22 rm** ⌂ 32.50/96.00 **st.** – SB (weekdays only) 101.50/159.50 **st.**

🏠 **Bear,** High St., NP8 1BW, ✆ 810408, Fax 811696 – 📺 ☎ ℗. ⚠ ⚠ *VISA*
M (in bar Sunday) (lunch booking essential)/dinner a la carte 13.95/23.85 **t.** ≬ 3.95 – **30 rm** ⌂ 38.00/80.00 **t.**

at Llangattock SW : 1 ¼ m. by A 4077 and Llangynidr rd – ⊠ ⚙ 0873 Crickhowell :

🏠 **Ty Croeso** ⌂, The Dardy, NP8 1PU, ✆ 810573, Fax 810573, ≤, ⚘ – 📺 ☎ ℗. ⚠ ⚠ *VISA* JCB
M (lunch by arrangement)/dinner 13.95 and a la carte ≬ 3.75 – **8 rm** ⌂ 27.50/65.00 **t.** – SB (except Bank Holidays) 75.00/95.00 **st.**

◆London 208 – Fishguard 63 – ◆Swansea 19.

🏠 **Forte Travelodge** without rest., SA14 6NW, on A 48 ✆ 845700, Reservations (Free-phone) 0800 850950 – 📺 ⅙ ℗. ⚠ ⚠ *VISA* ❄
32 rm 31.95 **t.**

◆London 213 – Carmarthen 26 – ◆Swansea 36.

🏠 **Glanrannell Park** ⌂, SA19 8SA, SW : ½ m. by B 4302 ✆ 685230, Fax 685784, ≤, ⌂, ⚘, park – ⅙ rest ℗. ⚠ *VISA*
April-October – **M** *(closed Sunday lunch)* (bar lunch)/dinner 20.00 **t.** ≬ 3.50 – **8 rm** ⌂ 37.00/64.00 **t.** – SB 86.00/96.00 **st.**

◆London 245 – Carmarthen 25 – Fishguard 19.

⌂ **Preseli Country House** ⌂, SA34 0YP, S : 4 m. by A 478, on lane opposite disused quarry ✆ 419425, Fax 419425, ≤, ⚘, park – 📺 ℗. ⓞ ❄
M (residents only) (communal dining) 14.00 **st.** ≬ 3.95 – **5 rm** ⌂ 35.00/80.00 – SB 55.00/90.00 **st.**

◆London 149 – ◆Bristol 35 – ◆Cardiff 17 – Newport 5.

🏨 **Parkway,** Cwmbran Drive, NP44 3UW, S : 1 m. by A 4051 ✆ 871199, Telex 497887, Fax 869160, *Ⅰ₆*, ≋, ⊿ – ⅙ rm 📺 ☎ ⅙ ℗ – 🔥 550. ⚠ ⚠ ⓞ *VISA*
closed Christmas – **M** *(closed Saturday lunch)* 11.95 **st.** and a la carte ≬ 5.45 – ⌂ 8.95 – **69 rm** 47.80/78.50 **st.**, 1 suite – SB 76.00/94.00 **st.**

🟡 ATS Station Rd ✆ 484964

Envir. : Devil's Bridge (Pontarfynach)★, NW : 4 m. by B 4574.

◆London 195 – Aberystwyth 16 – Llandrindod Wells 27 – Newtown 38.

⌂ Hafod Lodge ⌂, SY23 4AD, ✆ 282247, ≤, ⚘ – ℗. ❄
3 rm.

◆London 207 – Chester 37 – Dolgellau 30 – Shrewsbury 43.

⌂ **Fron Goch,** LL21 0NA, SW : 1 m. on B 4401 ✆ 418, ≤, ⚘ – ℗
closed February and November – **M** (by arrangement) 15.00 **s.** ≬ 3.60 – **3 rm** ⌂ 16.00/45.00 **s.**

⌂ Pencefn Rd ✆ 422603, N : ½ m.

🟦 Ty Meirion, Eldon Sq., LL40 1PU ✆ 422888 (summer only).

◆London 221 – Birkenhead 72 – Chester 64 – Shrewsbury 57.

🏨 **Penmaenuchaf Hall** ⌂, Penmaenpool, LL40 1YB, W : 1 ¾ m. on A 493 ✆ 422129, Fax 422129, ≤, « Country house atmosphere », ⚘, park – ⅙ rest 📺 ☎ ℗ – 🔥 75. ⚠ ⓞ *VISA* JCB ❄
M 21.50 **st.** (dinner) and lunch a la carte 11.75/16.95 **st.** ≬ 6.00 – **14 rm** ⌂ 47.50/140.00 **st.** – SB (except Bank Holidays) (weekends only) 138.00/233.00 **st.**

🏛 **George III,** Penmaenpool, LL40 1YD, W : 2 m. by A 493 ℰ 422525, Fax 423565, ⩽ Mawddach estuary and mountains – 🔟 ☎ 🅿. ◪ ◭ *VISA* *JCB*
M (bar lunch Monday to Saturday)/dinner a la carte 15.35/22.75 **t.** – **11 rm** ⊐ 35.00/88.00 **t.**
– SB (October-April except Bank Holidays) 110.00 **st.**

at Ganllwyd N : 5 ½ m. on A 470 – ⊠ Dolgellau – ☀ 034 140 (3 fig.) and 0341 (6 fig.) Ganllwyd :

🏨 **Dolmelynllyn Hall** ⌇, LL40 2HP, ℰ 273, Fax 273, ⩽, ↩, ☞ – ⊱ 🔟 ☎ 🅿. ◪ ◭ ⦿ *VISA* ⌾
closed January, weekdays December and February and Christmas – **M** (dinner only) 22.50 **st.** ⫶ 5.50 – **11 rm** ⊐ 50.00/100.00 **st.** – SB 120.00/150.00 **st.**

at Llanfachreth NE : 3 ¾ m. – ⊠ ☀ 0341 Dolgellau :

↑ **Ty Isaf** ⌇, LL40 2EA, ℰ 423261, ⩽, « 17C longhouse », ☞ – ⊱ 🅿
M (communal dining) 10.00 **st.** ⫶ 3.00 – **3 rm** ⊐ 33.00/46.00 **st.**

at Arthog SW : 7 m. on A 493 – ⊠ Dolgellau – ☀ 0341 Fairbourne :

↑ **Cyfannedd Uchaf** ⌇ without rest., LL39 1LX, SW : 2 m. by unmarked road and 1 : 4 hill ℰ 250526, ⩽ Barmouth, Mawddach estuary and mountains – ⊱ 🅿. ⌾
March-October – **3 rm** ⊐ 16.00/32.00 **st.**

at Bontddu W : 5 m. on A 496 (Barmouth Rd) – ⊠ Dolgellau – ☀ 034 149 (3 fig.) and 0341 (6 fig.) Bontddu :

🏨 **Bontddu Hall,** LL40 2SU, ℰ 661, Fax 284, ⩽ Mawddach estuary and mountains, « Victorian mansion in extensive gardens » – ⊱ rest 🔟 ☎ 🅿. ◪ ◭ ⦿ *VISA* *JCB*
April-October – **M** 11.75/23.50 **t.** ⫶ 5.25 – **17 rm** ⊐ 52.50/90.00 **t.**, 3 suites – SB 110.00/152.00 **st.**

🏛 **Borthwnog Hall,** LL40 2TT, E : 1 m. on A 496 ℰ 271, Fax 682, ⩽ Mawddach estuary and mountains, ☞ « Part Regency house, art gallery », ☞, park – ⊱ rest 🔟 🅿. ◪ *VISA* ⌾
closed 25 to 27 December – **M** (booking essential) (dinner only) 15.50 **t.** and a la carte – **3 rm** ⊐ 120.00 **st.** – SB (except Bank Holidays) 96.00/115.00 **st.**

DRENEWYDD YN NOTAIS (Nottage) M. Glam. – see Porthcawl.

DYFFRYN ARDUDWY Gwynedd ▦ ▦ H 25 – pop. 1 122 (inc. Tal-y-bont) – ☀ 0341 Ardudwy.

♦London 237 – Dolgellau 16 – Caernarfon 44.

🏛 **Ael-Y-Bryn,** LL44 2BE, on A 496 ℰ 242701, Fax 242682, ☞, ⌾ – 🔟 🅿. ◪ *VISA*
M a la carte 7.70/15.40 **st.** ⫶ 3.00 – **8 rm** ⊐ 25.00/60.00 **st.** – SB (except Bank Holidays) 50.00/60.00 **st.**

EGLWYSFACH Dyfed ▦ I 26 – see Machynlleth (Powys).

ERBISTOCK Clwyd ▦ ▦ L 25 – pop. 329 – ⊠ ☀ 0978 Wrexham.

♦London 183 – ♦Chester 20 – Holyhead 87 – Shrewsbury 25.

✗ **Boat Inn,** LL13 0DL, ℰ 780143, Fax 780102, « 16C inn on the banks of the River Dee », ☞ – 🅿. ◪ ◭ *VISA*
M 13.95/16.95 **t.** and a la carte ⫶ 4.95.

EWLOE Clwyd – ☀ 0244 Chester.

🏧 Autolodge Site, Galeway Services, A 55 Expressway westbound, Northophall, CH7 6HE ℰ 541597.

♦London 200 – ♦Chester 8.5 – Shrewsbury 48.

🏨 **St David's Park,** St. David's Park, CH5 3YB, on B 5125 at junction with A 494 ℰ 520800, Fax 520930, *Lᴃ*, ☎s, ◪, ☞ – ⊱ rm 🔳 rest 🔟 ☎ & 🅿. – 🔏 270. ◪ ◭ ⦿ *VISA* *JCB*
M 15.50/35.00 **st.** and a la carte – ⊐ 8.95 – **120 rm** 56.00/89.00 **st.**, 1 suite.

🔘 ATS Holywell Rd (Nr. Queensferry) ℰ 520380

FISHGUARD (Abergwaun) Dyfed ▦ F 28 – pop. 2 903 – ECD : Wednesday – ☀ 0348.

⚓ to Ireland (Rosslare) (Stena Sealink Line) (3 h 30 mn) 2 daily.

🛈 4 Hamilton St., SA56 9HL ℰ 873484.

♦London 265 – ♦Cardiff 114 – Gloucester 176 – Holyhead 169 – Shrewsbury 136 – ♦Swansea 76.

🏛 **Plas Glyn-Y-Mel** ⌇ without rest., Lower Town, SA65 9LY, ℰ 872296, ⩽, ◪, ☞, park – 🔟 🅿
6 rm ⊐ 39.00/84.00 **st.**

🏛 **Manor House,** 11 Main St., SA65 9HG, ℰ 873260, ☞ – 🔟. ◪ *VISA*
closed 23 to 28 December and 2 weeks February-March – **M** (dinner only) 15.50 **st.** ⫶ 4.00 – **6 rm** ⊐ 16.00/45.00 **st.**

🏛 Cartref, 13-19 High St., SA65 9AW, ℰ 872430 – ⊱ 🔟 🅿
13 rm.

⌂ **Plain Dealings** ⌂, Tower Hill, SA65 9LA, E : 1 ½ m. ℰ 873655, ≤ – 🖵 ☎ 🅿. 🖪 ⑩ 𝘝𝘐𝘚𝘈. ⅏
M 12.00 **t.** 👗 5.00 – **3 rm** ⌷ 28.00/55.00 **t.** – SB (October-June) 68.00/80.00 **st.**

⌂ **Cefn-y-Dre** ⌂, SA65 9QS, SE : 1 ¼ m. by Hamilton St. and no through rd ℰ 874499, ⌲ – ⬞ rm 🅿. ⅏
M 12.50 **s.** 👗 2.60 – **3 rm** ⌷ 22.00/39.00 **s.**

at Pontfaen SE : 5 ½ m. by B 4313 – ✿ 0239 Newport :

🏠 **Tregynon Country Farmhouse** ⌂, Gwaun Valley, SA65 9TU, E : 6 ¼ m. ℰ 820531, Fax 820808, ⌲, park – ⬞ 🖵 ☎ 🅿 – 🔏 30. 🖪 𝘝𝘐𝘚𝘈. ⅏
closed 2 weeks winter – **M** *(closed Christmas to non-residents)* (booking essential) (dinner only) 19.75 **t.** – **8 rm** ⌷ 64.00 **t.** – SB (November-March except Christmas and New Year) 67.50/81.50 **st.**

🏠 **Gellifawr Country House** ⌂, SA65 9TX, E : 5 m. ℰ 820343, Fax 820128, ⌁ heated, ⌲, park – 🅿. 🖪 𝘝𝘐𝘚𝘈
M (bar lunch)/dinner 18.50 **t.** and a la carte – **9 rm** ⌷ 25.00/58.00 **t.** – SB 80.00/95.00 **st.**

at Llanychaer SE : 2 ¼ m. on B 4313 – ✉ ✿ 0348 Fishguard :

✗ **Penlan Oleu** ⌂ with rm, SA65 9TL, SE : 2 m. by B 4313 on Puncheston rd ℰ 881314, ≤, « Converted farmhouse », ⌲ – ⬞ rest 🅿. ⅏
closed 25 and 26 December – **M** *(closed Sunday lunch)* (booking essential) a la carte 10.00/11.90 **st.** 👗 3.50 – **5 rm** ⌷ 20.00/40.00 **st.** – SB 68.00 **st.**

at Welsh Hook SW : 7 ½ m. by A 40 – ✉ Haverfordwest – ✿ 0348 Letterston :

✗✗ **Stone Hall** ⌂ with rm, SA62 5NS, ℰ 840212, Fax 840815, « Part 14C manor house with 17C extension », ⌲ – 🖵 🅿. 🖪 🅰🅴 𝘝𝘐𝘚𝘈. ⅏
M *(closed Monday)* (dinner only) 16.00 **t.** and a la carte 👗 4.60 – **5 rm** ⌷ 46.00/63.00 **t.**

at Goodwick (Wdig) NW : 1 ½ m. – ✉ ✿ 0348 Fishguard :

🏨 **Fishguard Bay,** Quay Rd, SA64 0BT, ℰ 873571, Fax 873030, park – 📲 🖵 ☎ 🅿 – 🔏 300. 🖪 🅰🅴 ⑩ 𝘝𝘐𝘚𝘈
M (dinner only and Sunday lunch)/dinner a la carte 19.95 **st.** 👗 3.75 – **60 rm** ⌷ 38.00/80.00 **st.** – SB (except christmas-New Year) 86.00/120.00 **st.**

⌂ **Ivybridge,** Drim Mill, Dyffryn, SA64 0FT, E : ¾ m. by A 487 ℰ 872623, Fax 872623, park – 🖵 🅿
M 8.50 – **6 rm** ⌷ 21.50/43.00 **st.**

🅰 ATS Scleddau ℰ 873522

GANLLWYD Gwynedd 402 403 I 25 – see Dolgellau.

GLYN CEIRIOG Clwyd 402 403 K 25 – ✉ Llangollen – ✿ 069 172.

♦London 194 – Shrewsbury 30 – Wrexham 17.

🏨 **Golden Pheasant** ⌂, Llwynmawr, LL20 7BB, SE : 1 ¾ m. by B 4500 ℰ 281, Fax 479, ≤, ⌲ – 🖵 ☎ 🅿. 🖪 🅰🅴 ⑩ 𝘝𝘐𝘚𝘈
M 10.95/17.95 **st.** 👗 5.00 – **18 rm** ⌷ 32.00/70.00 **t.** – SB 90.00/100.00 **st.**

GOODWICK (Wdig) Dyfed 403 F 27 – see Fishguard.

GOVILON Gwent – see Abergavenny.

GWBERT ON SEA Dyfed 403 F 27 – see Cardigan.

HANMER Clwyd 402 403 L 25 – pop. 301 – ✉ Whitchurch – ✿ 094 874.

♦London 237 – Chester 26 – Shrewsbury 27 – ♦Stoke-on-Trent 28.

🏠 **Hanmer Arms,** SY13 3DE, ℰ 532, Fax 740 – 🖵 ☎ 👗 🅿 – 🔏 40. 🖪 🅰🅴 ⑩ 𝘝𝘐𝘚𝘈
M a la carte 7.95/17.30 **t.** 👗 4.30 – **11 rm** ⌷ 42.00/52.00 **t.**, 7 suites – SB (weekends only) 58.00/80.00 **st.**

HARLECH Gwynedd 402 403 H 25 Great Britain G. – pop. 1 292 – ECD : Wednesday – ✿ 0766.
See : Castle★★ *AC.*
🏩 Royal St. David's ℰ 780203.
🅱 Gwyddfor House, High St., LL46 2YA ℰ 780658 (summer only).

♦London 241 – Chester 72 – Dolgellau 21.

⌂ **Gwrach Ynys,** LL47 6TS, N : 2 ¼ m. on A 496 ℰ 780742, Fax 780742, ⌲ – ⬞ rest 🖵 ☎ 🅿
closed December and January – **M** (by arrangement) 10.00 **st.** – **7 rm** ⌷ 16.00/36.00 **st.**

✗ **The Cemlyn,** High St., LL46 2YA, ℰ 780425, ≤ Harlech Castle, Cardigan Bay and Lleyn Peninsula – 🖪 𝘝𝘐𝘚𝘈
Easter-October – **M** (dinner only) 18.50 **t.** 👗 3.50.

HAVERFORDWEST (Hwlffordd) Dyfed 403 F 28 – pop. 13 572 – ECD : Thursday – ✆ 0437.

₁₈ Arnolds Down ℰ 763565, E : 1 m. by A 40.

🖪 Old Bridge, SA61 2EZ ℰ 763110.

♦London 250 – Fishguard 15 – ♦Swansea 57.

  🏨 **Mariners,** Mariners Sq., SA61 2DU, ℰ 763353, Fax 764258 – 📺 ☎ 🅿 – 🔬 50. 🔼 🗚 ⓞ **VISA**
    closed 26-27 December and 1-2 January – **M** (bar lunch)/dinner 12.50 **t.** and a la carte
    ⚗ 4.00 – **30 rm** ⌷ 45.00/62.50 **t.** – SB (weekends only) 70.00/82.00 **t.**

  XX **Sutton Lodge** ♠ with rm, Portfield Gate, SA62 3LN, W : 3 m. by B 4327 and B 4341 off
    Sutton rd ℰ 768548, Fax 760826, ≼, ☞ – ⇥ rest 📺 🅿. ⚘
    April-December – **M** *(closed Sunday)* (booking essential) (dinner only) 22.00 **t.** ⚗ 5.60 –
    3 rm ⌷ 41.00/82.00 **st.**

◎ ATS Back Lane, Prendergast ℰ 763756/7

HAY-ON-WYE Powys 403 K 27 – pop. 1 578 – ECD : Tuesday – ✆ 0497.

₉ Rhosgoch, Builth Wells ℰ 851251, N : 5 m.

♦London 154 – Brecon 16 – Hereford 21 – Newport 62.

  🏨 **Swan** (Best Western), Church St., HR3 5DQ, ℰ 821188, Fax 821424, ⚏, ☞ – ⇥ rest 📺
    ☎ 🅿 – 🔬 100. 🔼 🗚 ⓞ **VISA** **JCB**
    M (bar lunch) Monday to Saturday)/dinner 24.50 **st.** and a la carte ⚗ 4.00 – **18 rm** ⌷ 45.00/
    80.00 **st.** – SB 96.00/116.00 **st.**

  🏠 **Kilverts Court,** Bullring, HR3 5AG, ℰ 821042, Fax 821580, ☞ – ⇥ rm 📺 ☎ 🅿. 🔼 **VISA**.
    ⚘
    M (bar lunch)/dinner a la carte 11.45/20.15 **st.** ⚗ 4.50 – **11 rm** ⌷ 27.00/70.00 **t.** – SB (No-
    vember-February) (weekdays only) 60.00/70.00 **st.**

  🏠 **Old Black Lion,** Lion St., HR3 5AD, ℰ 820841, « Part 13C and 17C inn » – 📺 ☎ 🅿. 🔼
    🗚 **VISA**. ⚘
    M (bar lunch Monday to Saturday)/dinner a la carte 11.65/18.00 **t.** ⚗ 4.95 – **10 rm** ⌷ 18.95/
    42.00 **t.** – SB 70.00/78.00 **st.**

  ⌂ **York House,** Hardwick Rd, Cusop, HR3 5QX, E : ½ m. on B 4348 ℰ 820705, ☞ – ⇥ 📺
    🅿. 🔼 **VISA**
    M (by arrangememt) 11.00 – **5 rm** ⌷ 20.00/42.00 **s.**

  ⌂ **La Fosse** without rest., Oxford Rd, HR3 5AJ, ℰ 820613 – 📺. ⚘
    5 rm ⌷ 25.00/35.00 **st.**

    at Llanigon SW : 2½ m. by B 4350 – ✉ ✆ 0497 Hay-on-Wye :

  ⌂ **Old Post Office** without rest., HR3 5QA, ℰ 820008, « 17C house » – ⇥ 🅿
    March-October – **3 rm** ⌷ 20.00/36.00 **s.**

HOLYHEAD (Caergybi) Gwynedd 402 403 G 24 – pop. 12 569 – ECD : Tuesday – ✆ 0407.

⛴ to Ireland (Dun Laoghaire) (Stena Sealink Line) 2-4 daily – to Ireland (Dublin) (B & I Line)
2 daily.

♦London 269 – Birkenhead 94 – ♦Cardiff 215 – Chester 88 – Shrewsbury 105 – ♦Swansea 190.

    Hotel see : Rhoscolyn S : 5½ m.

HOLYWELL (Treffynnon) Clwyd 402 403 K 24 – pop. 11 101 – ECD : Wednesday –
✆ 0745 Mostyn.

₉ Holywell, Brynford ℰ 710040/713937, S : 2 m. by A 5026.

♦London 217 – Chester 19 – ♦Liverpool 34.

  🏨 **Kinsale Hall** ♠, Llanerchymor, CH8 9DT, N : 3½ m. by B 5121 off A 548 ℰ 560001,
    Fax 561298, ≼, ☞, park – 📱 ⇥ rm 🔳 rest 📺 ☎ ᵫ 🅿 – 🔬 400. 🔼 🗚 **VISA**
    M 15.00/25.00 **t.** and a la carte – **28 rm** ⌷ 75.00/84.50 **st.**, 2 suites – SB 84.50/95.00 **st.**

  🏠 **Forte Travelodge** without rest., Halkyn, CH8 8RF, SE : 3½ m. on A 55 (westbound
    carriageway) ℰ 0352 (Halkyn) 780952, Reservations (Freephone) 0800 850950 – 📺 ᵫ 🅿.
    🔼 🗚 **VISA**. ⚘
    31 rm 31.95 **t.**

  🏠 **Stamford Gate,** Halkyn Rd, CH8 7SJ, ℰ 712942, Fax 713309 – 📺 ☎ 🅿. 🔼 **VISA**. ⚘
    M 10.50/17.75 **st.** and a la carte ⚗ 4.00 – **12 rm** ⌷ 38.00/48.00 **st.**

HOWEY Powys – see Llandrindod Wells.

KNIGHTON (Trefyclawdd) Powys 403 K 26 – pop. 2 687 – ✆ 0547.

₉ Little Ffrydd Wood ℰ 528646, SW : ½ m.

🖪 The Offas Dyke Centre, West St., LD7 1EW ℰ 528753.

♦London 162 – ♦Birmingham 59 – Hereford 31 – Shrewsbury 35.

  🏠 **Milebrook House,** Ludlow Rd, Milebrook, LD7 1LT, E : 2 m. on A 4113 ℰ 528632,
    Fax 520509, ⚏, ☞ – ⇥ 📺 🅿. 🔼 **VISA**. ⚘
    M *(closed Monday lunch)* (bar lunch)/dinner 18.95 **t.** ⚗ 5.60 – **6 rm** ⌷ 43.50/62.00 **t.** –
    SB (except Christmas) 93.90/118.90 **st.**

LAKE VYRNWY Powys 402 403 J 25 – ⊠ ✆ 069 173 (3 fig.) and 0691 (6 fig.) Llanwddyn.

◆London 204 – Chester 52 – Llanfyllin 10 – Shrewsbury 40.

🏨 **Lake Vyrnwy** ≫, SY10 0LY, ✆ 692, Fax 259, ≤ Lake Vyrnwy, « Country house atmosphere », ≦, ☞, park, ❊ – 📺 ☎ ⇔ ❷. ⚠ ஊ ⓞ 𝘝𝘐𝘚𝘈
M 12.75/22.50 **t.** 🛆 4.75 – **37 rm** ⊇ 60.00/95.00 **t.**, 1 suite – SB (except Bank Holidays) 100.00/210.00 **st.**

LALESTON M. Glam. 403 J 29 – see Bridgend.

LAMPETER Dyfed 403 H 27 – pop. 1 976 – ✆ 0570.

🆓 Cilgwyn, Llangybi ✆ 0570 45 (Llangybi) 286, NE : 5 m. by A 485.

◆London 223 – Carmarthen 23 – ◆Swansea 46.

↑ **Pentre Farm** ≫, Llanfair Clydogau, SA48 8LE, NE : 4 m. by A 482 and B 4343 ✆ 45313, « Working farm », ≦ – ❷. ❊
June-September – **M** (by arrangement) – **3 rm** ⊇ 17.00/34.00 **s.**

◍ ATS Mill Garage, North Rd ✆ 422040

LAMPHEY Dyfed – see Pembroke.

LANGSTONE Gwent 403 L 29 – see Newport.

☞ *Inclusion in the Michelin Guide cannot be achieved by pulling strings or by offering favours.*

LAUGHARNE Dyfed 403 G 28 – pop. 1 012 – ✆ 0994.

◆London 233 – Carmarthen 13 – Fishguard 41.

↑ **Halldown** ≫ without rest., SA33 4QS, N : 1½ m. on A 4066 ✆ 427452, ☞ – ⇔ ❷
5 rm ⊇ 16.00/32.00 **s.**

LITTLE HAVEN Dyfed 403 E 28 – ECD : Thursday – ⊠ Haverfordwest – ✆ 0437 Broad Haven.

◆London 258 – Haverfordwest 8.

🏠 **Haven Fort** ≫, Settlands Hill, SA62 3LA, ✆ 781401, ≤ St. Brides Bay, ☞ – ⇔ ❷. ❊
April-September – **M** (bar lunch)/dinner 13.95 **t.** 🛆 3.00 – **12 rm** ⊇ 27.00/47.00 **t.**

LLANABER Gwynedd 402 403 H 25 – see Barmouth.

LLANARMON DYFFRYN CEIRIOG Clwyd 402 403 K 25 – pop. 137 – ⊠ Llangollen – ✆ 069 176.

◆London 196 – Chester 33 – Shrewsbury 32.

🏨 West Arms ≫, LL20 7LD, ✆ 665, Fax 622, ≦, ☞ – ⇔ rm ❷ – 🔼 60
11 rm, 2 suites.

🏠 **Hand** ≫, LL20 7LD, ✆ 666, Fax 262, ☞, ❊ – ❷. ⚠ ஊ ⓞ 𝘝𝘐𝘚𝘈
closed February – **M** (bar lunch Monday to Friday)/dinner 16.50 **t.** – **12 rm** ⊇ 32.00/58.00 **t.** – SB (except Bank Holidays) 84.00 **st.**

LLANBEDR Gwynedd 402 403 H 25 – pop. 486 – ECD : Wednesday – ✆ 034 123.

◆London 262 – Holyhead 54 – Shrewsbury 100.

🏠 **Pensarn Hall** ≫, LL45 2HS, N : ¾ m. on A 496 ✆ 236, ≤, ☞ – 📺 ❷. ⚠ 𝘝𝘐𝘚𝘈
March-September – **M** (dinner only) 10.50 **st.** 🛆 3.00 – **7 rm** ⊇ 25.00/42.00 **st.** – SB (except Bank Holidays) 58.00/71.00 **st.**

🏠 **Ty Mawr** ≫, LL45 2NH, ✆ 440, ☞ – 📺 ❷
M (bar lunch)/dinner 15.00 **t.** and a la carte 🛆 3.50 – **10 rm** ⊇ 27.00/54.00 **t.** – SB 60.00/72.00 **st.**

⚘ **Victoria Inn**, LL45 2LD, ✆ 213, ☞ – ⇔ rest ❷. ⚠ 𝘝𝘐𝘚𝘈
M 8.50/15.50 **st.** and dinner a la carte 🛆 3.50 – **5 rm** ⊇ 25.00/47.00 **st.** – SB 63.00/101.00 **st.**

LLANBERIS Gwynedd 403 H 24 Great Britain G. – pop. 1 809 – ECD : Wednesday – ✆ 0286.

Envir. : Snowdon★★★ (✳★★★ from summit) SE : by Snowdon Mountain Railway or by marked footpaths.

🛈 Amgueddfa'r Gogledd/Museum of the North, LL55 4UR ✆ 870765 (summer only).

◆London 243 – Caernarfon 7 – Chester 65 – Shrewsbury 78.

❊❊ **Y Bistro**, 43-45 High St., LL55 4EU, ✆ 871278 – ⚠ 𝘝𝘐𝘚𝘈
closed Sunday and 3 weeks January-February – **M** (booking essential) (dinner only) 24.00 **t.**

LLANDEGLA Clwyd – pop. 458 – ⊠ Wrexham – ✆ 097 888.

◆London 203 – Chester 19 – Shrewsbury 35 – Wrexham 11.

🏨 **Bodidris Hall** ≫, LL11 3AL, NE : 1½ m. by A 5104 ✆ 434, Fax 335, ≤, « 15C manor house of 12C origins », ☞ – 📺 ☎ ❷. ❊
12 rm.

LLANDEILO Dyfed 🔲🔲 | 28 – pop. 1 598 – ECD : Thursday – ✆ 0558.

🏌 Glynhir, Llandybie, nr Ammanford ⁄ 0269 (Llandybie) 850472.

◆London 218 – Brecon 34 – Carmarthen 15 – ◆Swansea 25.

XX **Plough Inn** with rm, Rhosmaen, SA19 6NP, N : 1 m. on A 40 ⁄ 823431, Fax 823969, *Is.*, ⇌ – ▦ 👪 ⅙ 👤 – 🛏 40. 🔺 *VISA* ⁂
closed 25 and 26 December – **M** *(closed Sunday dinner)* a la carte 11.50/21.95 **t.** ⅙ 5.00 – ⊡ 4.00 – **12 rm** 40.00/60.00 **t.**

◎ ATS Towy Terr., Ffairfach ⁄ 822567

LLANDELOY Dyfed – see St. Davids.

LLANDRILLO Clwyd 🔲🔲 🔲🔲 J 25 – pop. 477 – ✉ Corwen – ✆ 049 084 (3 fig.) and 0490 (6 fig.).

◆London 210 – Chester 40 – Dolgellau 26 – Shrewsbury 46.

🏠 **Tyddyn Llan Country House** ⑊, LL21 0ST, ⁄ 264, Fax 264, « Part Georgian country house », ⑊, ⚘ – ☎ 👤. 🔺 *VISA*
M 15.00/25.00 **t.** ⅙ 7.00 – **10 rm** ⊡ 56.50/96.00 **st.** – SB (except Bank Holidays) 110.00/126.00 **st.**

LLANDRINDOD WELLS Powys 🔲🔲 J 27 Great Britain G. – pop. 4 232 – ECD : Wednesday – ✆ 0597.

Exc. : Elan Valley★★, NW : 12 m. by A 4081, A 470 and B 4518.

🏌 Llandrindod Wells ⁄ 822010/823873, E : 1 m.

🎫 Old Town Hall, Memorial Gardens, LD1 5DL ⁄ 822600.

◆London 204 – Brecon 29 – Carmarthen 60 – Shrewsbury 58.

🏠 **Metropole**, Temple St., LD1 5DY, ⁄ 823700, Fax 824828, ⇌, 🔲, ⚘ – ▯ ⅙ rm ▦ ☎
👤 – 🛏 250. 🔺 🔺 ① *VISA*
M 9.75/16.50 **t.** ⅙ 3.75 – **120 rm** ⊡ 57.00/77.00 **st.**, 2 suites – SB 98.00 **st.**

XX **Dillraj**, Emporium Building, Temple St., LD1 5DL, ⁄ 823843 – 🔺 🔺 ① *VISA*
M - Indian a la carte 7.65/16.50 **st.**

at Howey S : 1½ m. by A 483 – ✉ ✆ 0597 Llandrindod Wells :

🏠 **Three Wells Farm** ⑊, LD1 5PB, NE : ½ m. ⁄ 822484, ≤, « Working farm », ⑊, ⚘ –
⅙ rest ▦ ☎ 👤
February-October – **M** 9.00 **t.** ⅙ 4.50 – **10 rm** ⊡ 17.00/39.00 **t.**, 4 suites – SB 50.00/55.00 **st.**

🏠 **Holly Farm** ⑊, LD1 5PP, W : ½ m. ⁄ 822402, « Working farm », ⚘ – ⅙ rest 👤.
⁂
May-October – **M** 8.00 **t.** – **3 rm** ⊡ 17.00/34.00 **st.**

🏠 **Corven Hall** ⑊, LD1 5RE, S : ½ m. by A 483 on Hundred House rd ⁄ 823368, ⚘ –
⅙ rest 👤.
closed December and January – **M** 9.00 **st.** ⅙ 3.00 – **10 rm** ⊡ 20.00/34.00 **st.** – SB (except June-September) 47.00/61.00 **st.**

at Llanyre W : 1¾ m. by B 4081 – ✉ ✆ 0597 Llandrindod Wells :

🏠 **Bell Country Inn**, LD1 6DY, off B 4081 ⁄ 823959, Fax 825899 – ⅙ rm ▦ ☎ ⅙ 👤. 🔺 🔺
① *VISA* ⁂
M 13.00/14.95 **t.** and a la carte ⅙ 3.25 – **10 rm** ⊡ 32.50/57.50 **t.** – SB (except Bank Holidays) 86.40/94.90.

LLANDUDNO Gwynedd 🔲🔲 🔲🔲 | 24 Great Britain G. – pop. 13 202 – ECD : Wednesday except summer – ✆ 0492.

Exc. : Bodnant Garden★★ *AC*, S : 7 m. by A 470.

🏌 Rhos-on-Sea, Pernrhyn Bay ⁄ 549641, E : 4 m. by A 546 A – 🏌 72 Bryniau Rd, West Shore ⁄ 75325 A – 🏌 Hospital Rd ⁄ 876450 B.

🎫 1-2 Chapel St., LL30 2YU ⁄ 876413.

◆London 243 – Birkenhead 55 – Chester 47 – Holyhead 43.

Plan on next page

🏨 **Bodysgallen Hall** ⑊, LL30 1RS, SE : 2 m. on A 470 ⁄ 584466, Group Telex 837108, Fax 582519, ≤ gardens and mountains, « Part 17C and 18C hall with terraced gardens », park, ⁑ – ▦ ☎ 👤 – 🛏 50. 🔺 🔺 ① *VISA* ⁂   B
M (booking essential) 15.90/27.00 **st.** ⅙ 6.25 – ⊡ 9.95 – **19 rm** 82.00/135.00 **st.**, 9 suites – SB 164.00 **st.**

🏠 **St. Tudno**, North Parade, LL30 2LP, ⁄ 874411, Fax 860407, ≤, 🔲 – ▯ ⅙ rest ▤ rest ▦
☎ ⟿ 👤. 🔺 🔺 ① *VISA* ⁂   A **c**
M 13.50/25.00 **st.** ⅙ 5.95 – **21 rm** ⊡ 47.50/120.00 **st.** – SB (except Bank Holidays) 92.00/165.00 **st.**

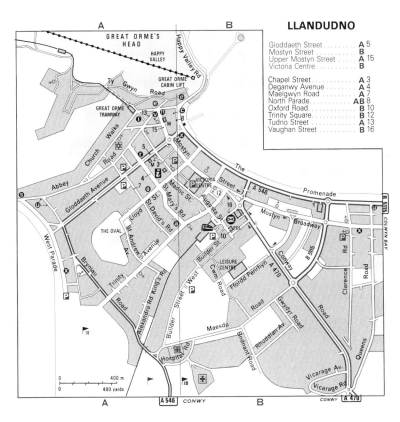

Gloddaeth Street . . . . **A** 5
Mostyn Street . . . . **B**
Upper Mostyn Street . . . . . **A** 15
Victoria Centre . . . . **B**

Chapel Street . . . . **A** 3
Deganwy Avenue . . . . **A** 4
Maelgwyn Road . . . . **A** 7
North Parade . . . . **AB** 8
Oxford Road . . . . **B** 10
Trinity Square . . . . **B** 12
Tudno Street . . . . **A** 13
Vaughan Street . . . . **B** 16

🏦 **Empire,** 73 Church Walks, LL30 2HE, ℘ 860555, Fax 860791, ⇌s, ⬛ heated, ⬛ – 🔁
▤ rest 📺 ☎ 🅿 – 🔬 30. 🔼 🅰🅴 ① 𝘝𝘐𝘚𝘈. ⬚ A **e**
closed 18 to 30 December – **M** (bar lunch Monday to Friday)/dinner 16.75 **st.** and a la carte
🍴 5.00 – **50 rm** ⥮ 45.00/95.00 **st.** – SB (except Bank Holidays) 95.00/130.00 **st.**

🏦 **Empire (No 72),** 72 Church Walks, LL30 2HE, ℘ 860555, Fax 860791, « Victoriana » –
▤ 📺 ☎ 🅿. 🔼 🅰🅴 ① 𝘝𝘐𝘚𝘈. ⬚
closed 18 to 30 December – **8 rm** ⥮ 60.00/90.00 **st.** – SB (except Bank Holidays) 115.00/
150.00 **st.**

🏦 **Gogarth Abbey,** West Shore, LL30 2QY, ℘ 876211, Fax 879881, ≤, 🛁, ⇌s, ⬛, ⚞ – 📺
☎ 🅿. 🔼 🅰🅴 𝘝𝘐𝘚𝘈 A **s**
M 11.00/17.50 **st.** 🍴 4.50 – **38 rm** ⥮ 30.00/100.00 **st.** 2 suites – SB 70.00/100.00 **st.**

🏠 **Dunoon,** Gloddaeth St., LL30 2DW, ℘ 860787, Fax 860031 – 🔁 📺 ☎ 🅿. 🔼 𝘝𝘐𝘚𝘈 A **r**
19 March-October – **M** 8.50/16.00 **st.** 🍴 4.50 – **56 rm** ⥮ 30.00/70.00 **st.** – SB 60.00/80.00 **st.**

🏠 **Belle Vue,** 26 North Par., LL30 2LP, ℘ 879547, ≤ – 🔁 📺 ☎ 🅿. 🔼 🅰🅴 ① 𝘝𝘐𝘚𝘈 B **e**
April-October and weekends March and November – **M** (bar lunch)/dinner 9.00 **t.** and
a la carte 🍴 3.50 – **17 rm** ⥮ 27.50/59.00 **t.** – SB (except July, August and Bank Holidays)
59.00/67.00 **st.**

🏠 **Bryn-y-Bia Lodge,** Bryn-y-Bia Rd, Craigside, LL30 3AS, E : 1 ½ m. by A 546 on B 5115
℘ 549644, ⚞ – ⬚ rest 📺 ☎ 🅿. 🔼 🅰🅴 ① 𝘝𝘐𝘚𝘈
M *(closed Sunday lunch to non-residents)* 17.00 **t.** (dinner) and a la carte 🍴 4.70 – **13 rm**
⥮ 30.50/58.00 **t.** – SB 63.00/80.00 **st.**

🏠 **Bromwell Court,** Promenade, 6 Craig-y-Don Par., LL30 1BG, ℘ 878416, Fax 874142 –
⬚ rest 📺 ☎. 🔼 𝘝𝘐𝘚𝘈. ⬚ B **u**
M (dinner only) 10.50 🍴 3.75 – **11 rm** ⥮ 25.00/47.00 – SB (except Bank Holidays) 52.00/
60.00 **st.**

🏠 **Rose-Tor,** 124 Upper Mostyn St., LL30 2SW, ℘ 870433 – ⬚ rest 📺 ☎. 🔼 🅰🅴 ①
𝘝𝘐𝘚𝘈 A **v**
M (bar lunch Monday to Saturday)/dinner 8.95 **t.** and a la carte 🍴 4.50 – **26 rm** ⥮ 19.80/
39.60 **t.** – SB (except Bank Holidays) 50.00/65.00 **st.**

⌂ **Craiglands,** 7 Carmen Sylva Rd, LL30 1LZ, E : 1 m. by A 546 off B 5115 📞 875090 – ☒ rest 📺   B
April-October – **M** (by arrangement) – **6 rm** ⊡ 18.50/35.00 **s.**

⌂ **Tan Lan,** Great Orme's Rd, West Shore, LL30 2AR, 📞 860221 – ☒ rest 📺 🅿. ◪ 𝖵𝖨𝖲𝖠   A u
21 March-October – **M** 11.50 **t.** 🍷 3.95 – **18 rm** ⊡ 22.00/50.00 **t.** – SB 62.00/66.00 **st.**

⌂ **Sunnymede,** West Par., West Shore, LL30 2BD, 📞 877130 – 📺 🅿. ◪ 𝖵𝖨𝖲𝖠   A x
closed January and February – **M** 11.00 **st.** 🍷 3.95 – **18 rm** ⊡ 24.00/64.00 **st.** – SB (except Bank Holidays) 60.00 **st.**

⌂ **Leamore,** 40 Lloyd St., LL30 2YG, 📞 875552 – ☒ rest 📺. ❀   A o
M 9.00 **st.** 🍷 5.00 – **12 rm** ⊡ 20.00/36.00 – SB 48.00/56.00 **st.**

⌂ **Clontarf,** 1 Great Orme's Rd, West Shore, LL30 2AR, 📞 877621 – ☒ rest 🅿. ❀ A u
March-October and 4 days at Christmas – **M** (by arrangement) 8.00 **s.** – **9 rm** ⊡ 17.50/40.00 **s.**

⌂ **Buile Hill,** 46 St. Mary's Rd, LL30 2UE, 📞 876972, ☞ – 📺 🅿   A a
March-November – **M** 10.00 **st.** 🍷 3.00 – **13 rm** ⊡ 16.00/38.00 **st.** – SB (except Bank Holidays) 46.00/54.00 **st.**

XX **Richard's Bistro,** 7 Church Walks, LL30 2HD, 📞 877924 – ☒. ◪ 🅰🅴 𝖵𝖨𝖲𝖠   A n
M (dinner only) a la carte 14.40/18.40 **st.** 🍷 3.25.

XX **Martin's,** 11 Mostyn Av., LL30 1YS, 📞 870070 – ◪ 𝖵𝖨𝖲𝖠   B x
closed Sunday dinner, Monday and first 2 weeks January – **M** a la carte 10.50/21.00 **st.** 🍷 5.50.

X **No. 1,** 1 Old Rd, LL30 2HA, 📞 875424 – ◪ 𝖵𝖨𝖲𝖠   A i
closed Monday lunch, Sunday and 10 days January-February – **M** - Bistro 9.50/12.95 **st.** and a la carte 🍷 5.95.

LLANELLI Dyfed **408** H 29 – pop. 45 336 – ECD : Tuesday – ☎ 0554.

🏌 Ashburnham, Cliffe Terr., Burry Port 📞 832466, W : 5 m. by A 484.

◆London 206 – Carmarthen 20 – ◆Swansea 11.

🏨 **Diplomat,** Felinfoel Rd, SA15 3PJ, NE : 1 m. on A 476 📞 756156, Fax 751649, *f5*, ≘s, ◪ – ☐ 📺 ☎ 🅿 – 🕙 300. ◪ 🅰🅴 ⊙ 𝖵𝖨𝖲𝖠 𝖩𝖢𝖡
M 12.95/15.95 **st.** and a la carte 🍷 4.00 – **31 rm** ⊡ 59.00/69.00 **st.** – SB 69.00/118.00 **st.**

🅐 ATS Coldstream St. (off Vauxhall) 📞 750435

LLANERCHYMEDD Gwynedd **402 403** G 24 Great Britain G. – pop. 613 – ✉ ☎ 0248.

Envir. : Isle of Anglesey★★.

◆London 262 – Bangor 18 – Caernarfon 23 – Holyhead 15.

⌂ **Llwydiarth Fawr** ⋙, LL71 8DF, N : ¾ m. on B 5111 📞 470321, ≼, « Georgian farmhouse », ☞ – ☒ 📺 🅿. ❀
closed Christmas – **M** (by arrangement) 12.50 **st.** – **4 rm** ⊡ 20.00/45.00 **st.**

⌂ **Drws-Y-Coed** ⋙, LL71 8AD, E : 2½ m. by B 5111 on Benllech rd 📞 470473, ≼ – ☒ 📺 🅿. ❀
closed December – **M** (by arrangement) 10.00 **s.** – **3 rm** ⊡ 23.00/36.00 **s.** – SB 27.00/64.00 **st.**

LLANFACHRETH Gwynedd **402 403** I 25 – see Dolgellau.

LLANFIHANGEL Powys **402 403** J 25 – see Llanfyllin.

LLANFYLLIN Powys **402 403** K 25 – pop. 1 210 – ECD : Friday – ☎ 0691.

🛈 Council Offices, High St., SY22 5DB 📞 648868 (summer only).

◆London 188 – Chester 42 – Shrewsbury 24 – Welshpool 11.

🏠 **Bodfach Hall** ⋙, SY22 5HS, NW : 1 m. on B 4391 📞 648272, Fax 648272, ≼, ☞, park – 📺 🅿. ◪ 🅰🅴 ⊙ 𝖵𝖨𝖲𝖠
March-October – **M** *(closed Sunday dinner to non-residents)* (bar lunch Monday to Saturday)/dinner 15.00 – **9 rm** ⊡ 32.50/65.00 **t.**

at LLanfihangel SW : 5 m. by A 490 and B 4393 on B 4382 – ✉ ☎ 0691 Llanfyllin :

⌂ **Cyfie Farm** ⋙, SY22 5JE, S : 1½ m. by B 4382 📞 648451, ≼ Afon Vyrnwy valley, « Working farm, restored 17C longhouse », ☞ – 📺 🅿. ❀
M 9.50 **st.** – **2 rm** ⊡ 19.50/39.00 **st.**, 1 suite – SB (except May-September) 58.00/66.00 **st.**

LLANGAMMARCH WELLS Powys **403** J 27 – ECD : Wednesday – ☎ 059 12 (3 fig.) and 0591 (6 fig.).

◆London 200 – Brecon 17 – Builth Wells 8.

🏨 **Lake** ⋙, LD4 4BS, E : ¾ m. 📞 202, Fax 457, ≼, « Country house in extensive grounds », ⤸, ☞, park, ❀ – ☒ rest 📺 ☎ 🅿. ◪ 🅰🅴 𝖵𝖨𝖲𝖠
M (lunch by arrangement) 16.50/25.50 **st.** 🍷 6.00 – **10 rm** ⊡ 78.75/103.00 **st.**, 9 suites – SB (except Christmas-New Year) 145.00/186.00 **st.**

LLANGATTOCK Powys [403] K 28 – see Crickhowell.

LLANGEFNI Gwynedd [402] [403] H 24 Great Britain G. – pop. 4100 – ECD : Tuesday – ✉ ☎ 0248.

Envir. : Isle of Anglesey★★.

⛳ Llangefni ☎ 722193, ½ m. by B 5111.

◆London 256 – Chester 75 – Caernarfon 17 – Holyhead 17.

Tre-Ysgawen Hall 🌿, Capel Coch, LL77 7UR, N : 4 ¼ m. by B 5110 and B 5111 via Tregaian ☎ 750750, Fax 750035, ≤, « Victorian mansion », 🌳, park – [TV] ☎ [P] – 🏛 120. [EN] [AE] [O] [VISA]. ✗
M 14.00/22.95 **t.** and dinner a la carte 🍷 4.90 – ☕ 8.00 – **19 rm** 71.50/148.00 **t.** – SB 141.40/222.90 **st.**

Nant Yr Odyn, Llanfawr, LL77 7YE, SW : 1 ¼ m. at junction of A 5 with A 5114 ☎ 723354, Fax 722433 – [TV] ☎ [P]. [EN] [VISA]. ✗
M *(closed Sunday)* (lunch by arrangement)/dinner 14.00 **st.** and a la carte 🍷 4.00 – **14 rm** ☕ 35.00/65.00 **st.** – SB (weekends only) 85.00/100.00 **st.**

ATS Ind. Est. ☎ 750397

LLANGOLLEN Clwyd [402] [403] K 25 Great Britain G. – pop. 2 546 – ECD : Thursday – ☎ 0978.

See : Plas Newydd★ *AC*.

Exc. : Chirk Castle★ *AC*, SE : 7 ½ m. by A 5.

⛳ Vale of Llangollen, Holyhead Rd ☎ 860040, E : 1 ½ m. by A 45.

[i] Town Hall, Castle St., LL20 5PD ☎ 860828.

◆London 194 – Chester 23 – Holyhead 76 – Shrewsbury 30.

Bryn Howel, LL20 7UW, E : 2 ¾ m. on A 539 ☎ 860331, Fax 860119, ≤, [S], 🎣, 🌳 – [lift] [TV] ☎ [P] – 🏛 250. [EN] [AE] [VISA]. ✗
closed 24 and 25 December – **M** 12.90/19.90 **t.** 🍷 7.00 – **38 rm** ☕ 65.00/105.00 **t.** – SB (weekends only) 110.00 **st.**

Wild Pheasant, Berwyn Rd, LL20 8AD, on A 5 ☎ 860629, Fax 861837, 🌳 – [TV] ☎ [P] – 🏛 100. ✗
33 rm.

Gales Wine Bar, 18 Bridge St., LL20 8PF, ☎ 860089, Fax 861313 – [TV] ☎. [EN] [VISA]. ✗
closed 25 December-4 January – **M** *(closed Sunday)* a la carte 5.55/10.45 **t.** 🍷 2.40 – **8 rm** ☕ 30.00/65.00 **t.**

Ty'n-y-Wern, LL20 7PH, E : 1 m. on A 5 ☎ 860252, ≤, 🌳 – [TV] ☎ [P]
10 rm.

LLANGORSE Powys [403] K 28 – pop. 490 – ✉ Brecon – ☎ 0874 84 (3 fig.) or 0874 (6fig.).

◆London 177 – Abergavenny 15 – Brecon 5 – Newport 33.

Red Lion, LD3 7TY, ☎ 238 – [TV] [P]. ✗
M *(closed lunch Monday to Friday November-March)* (bar lunch Monday to Saturday)/dinner 12.00 **t.** and a la carte 🍷 4.00 – **10 rm** ☕ 24.00/48.00 **t.** – SB (except Bank Holidays) 31.00/82.00 **st.**

LLANGURIG Powys [403] J 26 – pop. 620 – ECD : Thursday – ✉ Llanidloes – ☎ 055 15.

◆London 188 – Aberystwyth 25 – Carmarthen 75 – Shrewsbury 53.

Old Vicarage, SY18 6RN, ☎ 280, Fax 280 – 🚭 [TV] [P]
March-October – **M** 11.00 **st.** 🍷 3.50 – **4 rm** ☕ 28.00/40.00 **st.**

LLANGYBI Gwent – see Usk.

LLANIGON Powys [403] K 27 – see Hay-on-Wye.

LLANNEFYDD Clwyd [402] [403] J 24 – pop. 553 – ✉ Denbigh – ☎ 0745.

◆London 225 – Chester 37 – Shrewsbury 63.

Hawk and Buckle Inn, LL16 5ED, ☎ 79249, Fax 79316, ≤ – [TV] ☎ [P]. [EN] [VISA]. ✗
closed 25 December – **M** *(closed Sunday and Monday)* (bar lunch)/dinner 18.00 **t.** and a la carte – **10 rm** ☕ 38.00/50.00 **t.** – SB 68.00/96.00 **st.**

LLANRHIDIAN W. Glam. – see Swansea.

LLANRWST Gwynedd [402] [403] I 24 – pop. 2 908 – ECD : Thursday – ☎ 0492.

◆London 230 – Holyhead 50 – Shrewsbury 66.

The Priory, Maenan, LL26 0UL, N : 2 ½ m. on A 470 ☎ 660247, Fax 660734, 🎣, 🌳 – [TV] ☎ [P]. [EN] [AE] [O] [VISA]
M 9.50/14.50 **st.** and a la carte – **12 rm** ☕ 39.00/49.00 **st.** – SB (except Bank Holidays) 69.00 **st.**

Cae'r Berllan 🌿 with rm, LL26 0PP, S : 1 m. on A 470 ☎ 640027, « 16C manor house », 🌳 – 🚭 [TV] [P]. [EN] [VISA]
closed January, February and November – **M** *(closed Sunday to Tuesday to non-residents)* (booking essential) (dinner only) a la carte 12.50/21.50 **t.** 🍷 4.00 – **2 rm** ☕ 37.00/54.00 **t.** – SB (except May-September, December and Bank Holidays) 50.00/90.00 **st.**

at Trefriw NW : 2 . m. on B 5106 – ✉ ◉ 0492 Llanrwst :

🏠 **Hafod House,** LL27 0RQ, 🖉 640029, Fax 641351 – 📺 ☎ 🅿. 🔼 🅰🅴 ⓞ 𝘝𝘐𝘚𝘈. ⚞
M *(closed lunch Monday, Wednesday and Saturday)* 6.95/17.95 **t.** and a la carte ⍫ 3.95 –
7 rm ⊇ 32.00/64.00 **t.**

✗ **Chandler's Brasserie,** LL27 0JH, 🖉 640991 – ⚞✖ 🅿. 🔼 𝘝𝘐𝘚𝘈
closed Sunday, Monday, 3 weeks late January–mid February and last 2 weeks October –
M (dinner only) a la carte 16.05/18.85 **t.**

LLANSANFFRAID GLAN CONWY Gwynedd ⁴⁰²⁴⁰³ I24 Great Britain G. – pop. 1 935 –
✉ ◉ 0492 Aberconwy.

Envir. : Bodnant Garden★★ *AC*, S : 2½ m. by A 470.

♦London 241 – Colwyn Bay 4 – Holyhead 42.

🏠 **Old Rectory** ⚞, LL28 5LF, on A 470 🖉 580611, Fax 584555, ≤ Conwy estuary, « Georgian country house with antique furnishings », ⚞ – ⚞✖ 📺 ☎ 🅿. 🔼 🅰🅴 ⓞ 𝘝𝘐𝘚𝘈 ⚞
closed 20 December–1 February – Meals (dinner only) 27.50 **st.** ⍫ 5.90 – **6 rm** ⊇ 55.00/
98.00 **st.** – SB (except Bank Holidays) 99.00/139.00 **st.**

LLANSILIN Clwyd ⁴⁰²⁴⁰³ J 29 – pop. 892 – ✉ Oswestry (Shrops.) – ◉ 0691 70.

♦London 188 – Chester 36 – Shrewsbury 25.

⌂ **Bwlch Y Rhiw** ⚞ without rest., SY10 7PT, NE : 1 ½ m. on B 4580 🖉 261, ≤, « 18C
farmhouse », ⚞ – 📺 🅿. ⚞
3 rm ⊇ 25.00/34.00 **st.**

LLANTRISANT Gwent ⁴⁰³ L 28 – pop. 8 317 (inc. Pontyclun) – ✉ ◉ 0291 Usk.

♦London 148 – ♦Bristol 34 – Gloucester 43 – Newport 8.

🏠 **Greyhound Inn,** NP5 1LE, NE : ½ m. on Usk rd 🖉 672505, Fax 673255, ⚞ – 📺 ☎ ♿ 🅿.
🔼 𝘝𝘐𝘚𝘈 ⚞
M *(closed Sunday dinner)* 10.00/15.00 **t.** and a la carte ⍫ 4.20 – **10 rm** ⊇ 45.00/60.00 **t.** –
SB (weekends only) 80.00/120.00 **st.**

LLANTWIT MAJOR S. Glam. ⁴⁰³ J 29 – pop. 13 375 (inc. St. Athan) – ◉ 0446.

♦London 175 – ♦Cardiff 18 – ♦Swansea 33.

🏠 **West House,** West St., CF61 1SP, 🖉 792406, Fax 796147, ⚞ – 📺 ☎ 🅿. 🔼 🅰🅴 𝘝𝘐𝘚𝘈
M *(closed Monday lunch)* 8.95/13.50 and a la carte ⍫ 3.95 – **21 rm** ⊇ 45.00/68.00 –
SB (weekends only) 69.50/119.50 **st.**

LLANWENARTH Gwent – see Abergavenny.

LLANWRTYD WELLS Powys ⁴⁰³ J 27 – pop. 528 – ECD : Wednesday – ◉ 059 13 (3 fig.) and
0591 (6 fig.).

♦London 214 – Brecon 32 – Carmarthen 39.

⌂ **Lasswade Country House,** Station Rd, LD5 4RW, 🖉 515, ≤, ⚞ – ⚞✖ rest 📺 ☎ 🅿. 🔼
𝘝𝘐𝘚𝘈
M 14.95 **st.** ⍫ 4.95 – **8 rm** ⊇ 32.50/55.00 **st.** – SB (except Bank Holidays) 69.00/84.90 **st.**

LLANYCHAER Dyfed ⁴⁰³ F 28 – see Fishguard.

LLANYRE Powys – see Llandrindod Wells.

LLWYDAFYDD Dyfed ⁴⁰³ G 27 – see Newquay.

LLYSWEN Powys ⁴⁰³ K 27 – pop. 168 – ✉ Brecon – ◉ 0874.

♦London 188 – Brecon 8 – ♦Cardiff 48 – Worcester 53.

🏛 **Llangoed Hall** ⚞, LD3 0YP, NW : 1 ¼ m. on A 470 🖉 754525, Fax 754545, ≤,
« Edwardian mansion by Sir Clough Williams-Ellis of 17C origins », ⚞, ⚞, park, ⚞ –
⚞✖ rest 📺 ☎ 🅿. 🔼 🅰🅴 ⓞ 𝘝𝘐𝘚𝘈 ⚞
M 17.50/37.50 **t.** and a la carte 31.50/43.50 **t.** ⍫ 6.75 – **19 rm** ⊇ 95.00/185.00 **t.**, 4 suites –
SB (except weekends May–October) 170.00/370.00 **st.**

🏡 **Griffin Inn,** LD3 0UR, on A 470 🖉 754241, Fax 754592, « Part 15C inn », ⚞, ⚞ – ☎ 🅿.
🔼 🅰🅴 ⓞ 𝘝𝘐𝘚𝘈
M *(closed Sunday dinner)* (dinner only and Sunday lunch)/dinner a la carte 15.05/22.00 **t.**
⍫ 4.95 – **8 rm** ⊇ 28.50/50.00 **t.** – SB (October–March) 70.00/80.00 **st.**

MACHYNLLETH Powys ⁴⁰²⁴⁰³ I 26 – pop. 1 952 – ECD : Thursday – ◉ 0654.

🄳 Ffordd Drenewydd 🖉 702000 – 🄱 Canolfan Owain Glyndwr, SY20 8EE 🖉 702401.

♦London 220 – Shrewsbury 56 – Welshpool 37.

🏠 **Dolguog Hall** ⚞, SY20 8UJ, E : 1 ½ m. by A 489 🖉 702244, Fax 702530, ≤, « 17C
country house », ⚞, ⚞ – ⚞✖ rest 📺 ☎ 🅿. 🔼 🅰🅴 ⓞ 𝘝𝘐𝘚𝘈 ⚞
M (bar lunch Monday to Saturday)/dinner 15.00 **t.** and a la carte ⍫ 3.50 – **9 rm** ⊇ 25.00/
60.00 **t.** – SB 66.00/110.00 **st.**

↟ **Bacheiddon Farm** ⬭ without rest., Aberhosan, SY20 8SG, SE : 5¼ m. on Dylife rd, via Forge ℰ 702229, « Working farm » – ⬤ ℗. ❀
May-September – **3 rm** � 17.00/34.00 **st.**

at Eglwysfach (Dyfed) SW : 6 m. on A 487 – ✉ Machynlleth (Powys) – ✆ 0654 Glandyfi :

🏛 **Ynyshir Hall** ⬭, SY20 8TA, ℰ 781209, Fax 781366, ≼, « Georgian country house, gardens », park – ⇖ rest 📺 ☎ ℗. 🅰 AE ⓪ VISA . ❀
M (lunch by arrangement)/dinner 26.00 **st.** – **8 rm** � 65.85/130.00 **st.** – SB 120.00/ 200.00 **st.**

MAGOR SERVICE AREA Gwent – ✉ ✆ 0633 Newport

🏠 **Granada Lodge** without rest., NP6 3YL, M 4 junction 23 ℰ 880111, Fax 881896, Reservations (Freephone) 0800 555300 – ⇖ 📺 ⅙ ℗. 🅰 AE VISA . ❀
� 4.00 – **43 rm** 34.95/37.95 **st.**

MERTHYR TYDFIL M. Glam. 🔳 J 28 – pop. 52 870 – ECD : Thursday – ✆ 0685.

🅸 Morlais Castle, Pant, Dowlais ℰ 722822, N : 3 m. – 🅸 Cilsanws Mountaim, Cefn Coed ℰ 723308, NW : 2 m. by A 470.

🅱 14a Glebeland St., CF47 8AU ℰ 379884.

◆London 179 – ◆Cardiff 25 – Gloucester 59 – ◆Swansea 33.

🏠 **Tregenna,** Park Terr., CF47 8RF, ℰ 723627, Fax 721951 – 📺 ☎ ℗. 🅰 AE VISA
M 15.00 **t.** and a la carte ⬥ 4.50 – **23 rm** � 30.00/55.00 **t.** – SB 60.00/94.00 **st.**

MILFORD HAVEN (Aberdaugleddau) Dyfed 🔳 E 28 – pop. 13 927 – ECD : Thursday ✆ 0646.

🅸 Hubbertson ℰ 692368.

🅱 94 Charles St., SA73 2HL ℰ 690866 (summer only).

◆London 258 – Carmarthen 39 – Fishguard 23.

🏛 **Lord Nelson,** Hamilton Terr., SA73 3AL, ℰ 695341, Fax 694026, ⬬ – 📺 ☎ ℗. 🅰 AE ⓪ VISA . ❀
M (bar lunch)/dinner 11.50 **t.** and a la carte ⬥ 4.20 – **31 rm** � 42.00/65.00 **t.**, 1 suite – SB 50.00/106.00 **st.**

MISKIN M. Glam. – ✉ Cardiff – ✆ 0443 Pontypridd.

◆London 169 – ◆Cardiff 22 – ◆Swansea 31.

🏛 **Miskin Manor,** CF7 8ND, E : 1¾ m. by A 4119 (Groes Faen rd) ℰ 224204, Fax 237606, ≼, 🝫, ⬱, ☒, ⬬, park, squash – 📺 ☎ ℗ – 🜨 150. 🅰 AE ⓪ VISA . ❀
M 15.95/19.75 **t.** and a la carte ⬥ 5.10 – � 3.50 – **31 rm** 80.00/100.00 **t.**, 1 suite.

MOLD (Yr Wyddgrug) Clwyd 🔳 🔳 K 24 – pop. 8 487 – ECD : Thursday – ✆ 0352.

🅸 Pantmywyn ℰ 740318/741513, W : 4 m. – 🅸 Old Padeswood, Station Rd ℰ 0244 (Buckley) 547401, E : 2 m. by A 5118 – 🅸 Padeswood & Buckley, The Caia, Station Lane, Padeswood ℰ 0244 (Buckley) 550537, E : 3 m. – 🅸 Caerwys ℰ 720692.

🅱 Town Hall, Earl St., CH7 1AB ℰ 759331.

◆London 211 – Chester 12 – ◆Liverpool 29 – Shrewsbury 45.

🏛 **Soughton Hall** ⬭, CH7 6AB, N : 2½ m. by A 494 and A 5119 on Alltami rd ℰ 840811, Fax 840382, ≼, « Early 18C Italianate mansion », ⬱, ❧, ❀ – 📺 ☎ ℗. 🅰 AE ⓪ VISA . ❀
closed first 2 weeks January – **M** (closed Sunday) 24.00 **st.** (dinner) and a la carte 18.45/ 31.50 **st.** – � 6.00 – **12 rm** 80.00/119.00 **st.**

🏠 **Bryn Awel,** Denbigh Rd, CH7 1BL, on A 541 ℰ 758622, Fax 758625 – ⇖ rm 📺 ☎ ℗. 🅰 AE ⓪ VISA . ❀
M (closed Sunday dinner) 9.95 **t.** and a la carte ⬥ 3.80 – **17 rm** � 38.00/50.00 **t.** – SB 65.00/ 110.00 **st.**

◍ ATS Wrexham Rd ℰ 753682

MONMOUTH (Trefynwy) Gwent 🔳 L 28 Great Britain G. – pop. 7 379 – ECD : Thursday – ✆ 0600.

Envir. : S : Wye Valley∗ – *Exc.* : Raglan Castle∗ *AC*, SW : 8 m. by A 40.

🅸 Rolls of Monmouth, The Hendre ℰ 715353, W : 3½ m. by B 4233 – 🅸 Leasebrook Lane ℰ 712212.

🅱 Shire Hall, Agincourt Sq., NP5 3DY ℰ 713899.

◆London 147 – Gloucester 26 – Newport 24 – ◆Swansea 64.

🏠 **Riverside,** Cinderhill St., NP5 3EY, ℰ 715577 – 📺 ☎ ℗ – 🜨 150. 🅰 AE VISA . ❀
M (dinner only and Sunday lunch)/dinner 13.50 **t.** and a la carte ⬥ 2.50 – **17 rm** � 48.00/ 68.00 **t.** – SB (except Christmas) 58.00/116.00 **st.**

at Whitebrook SE : 8½ m. by A 466 – ✉ ✆ 0600 Monmouth :

✖✖ **Crown at Whitebrook** ⬭ with rm, NP5 4TX, ℰ 860524, Fax 860607, ⬬ – 📺 ☎ ℗. 🅰 AE ⓪ VISA JCB .
closed 25 and 26 December – **M** (closed Monday lunch and Sunday dinner to non-residents) 14.50/26.75 **st.** ⬥ 3.50 – **12 rm** � 50.00/80.00 **st.** – SB 112.00/120.00 **st.**

◍ ATS Wonastow Rd, Ind. Est. ℰ 6832

559

MONTGOMERY (Trefaldwyn) Powys [403] K 26 Great Britain G. – pop. 1 035 – ☎ 0686.

See : Castle★.

♦London 194 – ♦Birmingham 71 – Chester 53 – Shrewsbury 30.

🏨 **Dragon,** Town Square, SY15 6AA, ✆ 668359, Fax 668287, 🏊 – 📺 ☎ 🅿. [EC] [AE] [VISA]. 🐕
M (lunch by arrangement)/dinner 16.50 **t.** and a la carte 🍷 3.75 – **15 rm** ☕ 41.00/67.00 **t.** – SB (except Bank Holidays) 90.00/115.00 **st.**

🏠 **Little Brompton Farm** 🌿, SY15 6HY, SE : 2 m. on B 4385 ✆ 668371, « Working farm » – 🚭 🅿. 🐕
M (by arrangement) – **3 rm** ☕ 16.00/36.00 **st.** – SB 48.00/54.00 **st.**

MUMBLES W. Glam. [403] I 29 Great Britain G. – ECD : Wednesday – ✉ ☎ 0792 Swansea.

Envir. : Gower Peninsula★ : Cefn Bryn (✻★★) - Rhossili (≤★★★).

♦London 202 – ♦Swansea 6.

🏨 **Norton House,** 17 Norton Rd, SA3 5TQ, ✆ 404891, Fax 403210 – 📺 ☎ 🅿. [EC] [AE] [D] [VISA]. 🐕
M (lunch by arrangement)/dinner 19.50/23.50 **t.** 🍷 4.95 – **15 rm** ☕ 60.00/80.00 **t.** – SB (weekends only) 100.00/160.00 **st.**

🏨 **Langland Court** (Best Western), 31 Langland Court Rd, Langland Bay, SA3 4TD, W : 1 m. ✆ 361545, Fax 362302, 🌳 – 📺 ☎ 🚗 🅿 – 👥 150. [EC] [AE] [VISA] [JCB]. 🐕
closed 3 days at Christmas – **M** (bar lunch Monday to Saturday)/dinner 17.50 **t.** and a la carte 🍷 5.95 – **21 rm** ☕ 55.00/83.00 **t.** – SB 88.00/116.00 **st.**

🏨 **Osborne** (Jarvis), Rotherslade Rd, Langland Bay, SA3 4QL, W : ¾ m. ✆ 366274, Fax 363100, ≤ – 🛗 📺 ☎ 🅿 – 👥 50. [EC] [AE] [D] [VISA]
M (bar lunch Monday to Saturday)/dinner 14.95 **t.** and a la carte 🍷 4.50 – **36 rm** ☕ 72.00/85.00 **t.** – SB 84.00/110.00 **st.**

🏠 **Wittemberg,** 2 Rotherslade Rd, Langland, SA3 4QN, W : ¾ m. ✆ 369696 – 📺 🅿. [EC] [VISA]. 🐕
closed January – **M** 9.50 **st.** 🍷 3.00 – **11 rm** ☕ 30.00/52.00 **st.** – SB 56.00/80.00 **st.**

NANNERCH Clwyd [402] [403] K 24 – pop. 420 – ✉ ☎ 0352 Mold.

♦London 218 – Chester 19 – ♦Liverpool 36 – Shrewsbury 52.

🏨 **Old Mill,** Melin-y-Wern, Denbigh Rd, CH7 5RH, ✆ 741542, « Converted stables to 19C corn mill », 🌳 – 🚭 📺 ☎ 🅿. [EC] [AE] [D] [VISA] [JCB]
closed 17 to 31 December – **M** (residents only) (dinner only) 19.95 **t.** 🍷 4.95 – **7 rm** ☕ 32.50/49.50 **t.** – SB (except Christmas) 67.50/98.00 **st.**

NEATH (Castell-Ned) W. Glam. [403] I 29 – ☎ 0639.

⛳18 Swansea Bay, Jersey Marine ✆ 0792 (Swansea) 814153/812198.

♦London 188 – ♦Cardiff 40 – ♦Swansea 8.

🏨 **Castle,** The Parade, SA11 1RB, ✆ 641119, Fax 641624, 🏋 – 🚭 rm 📺 ☎ 🚗 🅿 – 👥 100. [EC] [AE] [D] [VISA]
M 6.50/17.95 **t.** 🍷 5.75 – **28 rm** ☕ 49.50/59.50 **t.** – SB (weekends only) 68.00/76.00 **st.**

at Cadoxton NW : 1½ m. by A 474 – ✉ ☎ 0639 Neath :

🏠 **Cwmbach Cottages** 🌿, Cwmbach Rd, SA10 8AH, ✆ 639825, ≤, 🌳 – 📺 🅿. 🐕
M (by arrangement) 12.00 **st.** – **5 rm** ☕ 20.00/38.00 **st.** – SB (weekends only) 43.00/56.00 **st.**

NEFYN Gwynedd [402] [403] G 25 – pop. 2 236 – ECD : Wednesday – ☎ 0758.

⛳18 Nefyn & District ✆ 720218, W : 1½ m.

♦London 265 – Caernarfon 20.

🏨 **Caeau Capel** 🌿, Rhodfar Mor, LL53 6EB, ✆ 720240, 🌳 – 🅿. [EC] [VISA]
Easter-October – **M** (bar lunch)/dinner 13.50 **t.** – **18 rm** ☕ 24.50/51.50 **t.**

NEWPORT Dyfed [403] F 27 – pop. 1 224 – ECD : Wednesday – ☎ 0239.

⛳9 Newport ✆ 820244, NW : 2½ m.

♦London 258 – Fishguard 7.

🏠 **Llysmeddyg,** East St., SA42 0SY, on A 487 ✆ 820008, 🌳 – 🚭 rm 🅿. 🐕
M (by arrangement) 12.00 **st.** 🍷 4.20 – **4 rm** ☕ 17.00/34.00 **st.**

🍴 **Cnapan** with rm, East St., SA42 0SY, on A 487 ✆ 820575, 🌳 – 🚭 rest 📺 🅿. [EC] [VISA]. 🐕
closed February and 25-26 December – **M** *(closed Monday to Saturday lunch November-January and Tuesday March-October)* (booking essential) a la carte 14.45/19.50 **t.** 🍷 4.95 – **5 rm** ☕ 29.00/48.00 **t.**

NEWPORT **(Casnewydd-Ar-Wysg)** Gwent 𝟜𝟘𝟛 L 29 Great Britain G. – pop. 115 896 – ECD : Thursday – ☎ 0633.

Envir. : Caerleon (Fortress Baths★, Roman Amphitheatre★ AC) NE : 3½ m. on B 4596.

ⓘ Tredegar Park, Bassaleg Rd ℰ 895219, NW : 2 m. by A 46 – ⓘ, ⓘ Caerleon, Broadway ℰ 420342, N : 3 m. by B 4596 – ⓘ Parc, Church Lane, Coedkenew ℰ 680933, W : 2 m. by A 48.

🛈 Museum and Art Gallery, John Frost Sq., NP9 1HZ ℰ 842962 – Ffwrrwm Art & Craft Centre, High St., NP6 1AG ℰ 430777.

◆London 145 – ◆Bristol 31 – ◆Cardiff 12 – Gloucester 48.

🏨 **Celtic Manor,** Coldra Woods, NP6 2YA, E : 3 m. on A 48 ℰ 413000, Fax 412910, ↆ₅, ⓢ, ⓢ, park – |‡| ⅙⊱ rm ▤ ⓣ ☎ ❷ – 🔬 300. 🔼 ፲፱ ⓞ ᴠ𝘐𝘚𝘈. ⅍
M (closed Saturday lunch and Sunday) 15.95/20.00 t. and a la carte ⅋ 7.00 – (see also Hedley's below) – ⌸ 8.95 – **73 rm** 85.00/150.00 t. – SB (except Christmas and New Year) (weekends only) 100.00/140.00 st.

🏨 **Hilton National,** The Coldra, NP6 2YG, E : 3 m. on A 48 ℰ 412777, Telex 497205, Fax 413087, ↆ₅, ⓢ, ⓢ – ⅙⊱ rm ⓣⓥ ☎ ❷ – 🔬 350. 🔼 ፲፱ ⓞ ᴠ𝘐𝘚𝘈 ᴶᶜᴮ
M 10.25/15.50 st. and a la carte ⅋ 5.50 – ⌸ 8.95 – **119 rm** 60.00 st. – SB 50.00/120.00 st.

🏨 **Westgate,** Commercial St., NP9 1TT, ℰ 244444, Fax 246616 – |‡| ⓣⓥ ☎ – 🔬 150. 🔼 ፲፱ ⓞ ᴠ𝘐𝘚𝘈
M 8.50/18.00 st. and dinner a la carte – ⌸ 6.50 – **69 rm** 49.50/120.00 st. – SB (except Christmas and New Year) (weekends only) 90.00/110.00 st.

🏨 Kings, High St., NP9 1QU, ℰ 842020, Fax 244667 – |‡| ⓣⓥ ☎ ❷ – 🔬 200. ⅍
47 rm.

🏠 **Newport Lodge,** 147 Bryn Bevan, Brynglas Rd, NP9 5QN, N : ¾ m. by A 4042 ℰ 821818, Fax 856360 – |‡| ⓣⓥ ☎ ❷. 🔼 ፲፱ ⓞ ᴠ𝘐𝘚𝘈
M (dinner only and Sunday lunch)/dinner 18.00 t. and a la carte ⅋ 3.50 – **27 rm** ⌸ 49.50/ 63.00 st. – SB (weekends only) 59.50/91.00 st.

⌂ **Anderley Lodge,** 216 Stow Hill, NP9 4HA, ℰ 266781, Fax 266781 – ⅙⊱ ⓣⓥ. ⅍
M (by arrangement) 10.50 – ⌸ 3.50 – **4 rm** 20.00/30.00 st. – SB 48.00/60.00 st.

⌂ **Kepe Lodge** without rest., 46a Caerau Rd, NP9 4HH, ℰ 262351, ⌾ – ⓣⓥ ❷. ⅍
closed 1 week Christmas – **8 rm** ⌸ 19.00/33.00 s.

✕✕✕ **Hedley's** (at Celtic Manor H.), Coldra Woods, NP6 2YA, E : 3 m. on A 48 ℰ 413000, Fax 412910 – ▤ ❷. 🔼 ፲፱ ⓞ ᴠ𝘐𝘚𝘈
closed Saturday lunch and Sunday – **M** 15.95/20.00 t. ⅋ 7.00.

✕✕ **Fratelli,** 173b Caerleon Rd, NP9 7FX, E : 1 m. on B 4596 ℰ 264602 – 🔼 ፲፱ ᴠ𝘐𝘚𝘈
closed Saturday lunch, Sunday, 3 weeks August and Bank Holiday Mondays – **M** - Italian a la carte 12.90/24.35 t. ⅋ 4.00.

at Caerleon NE : 3½ m. on B 4596 – ⊠ Newport – ☎ 0633 Caerleon

✕ **Bagan Tandoori,** 2 Cross St., NP6 1AF, ℰ 430086 – ▤. 🔼 ፲፱ ᴠ𝘐𝘚𝘈
M - Indian (buffet lunch Sunday) a la carte 12.30/23.65 st.

at Langstone E : 4½ m. on A 48 – ⊠ ☎ 0633 Newport :

🏨 **Stakis Country Court,** Chepstow Rd, NP6 2LX, ℰ 413737, Telex 497147, Fax 413713, ↆ₅, ⓢ, ⓢ, ⌾ – ⅙⊱ rm ▤ rest ⓣⓥ ☎ ⅋ ❷ – 🔬 80. 🔼 ፲፱ ⓞ ᴠ𝘐𝘚𝘈 ᴶᶜᴮ. ⅍
M 11.50/17.25 t. and a la carte – ⌸ 8.75 – **131 rm** 79.00/104.00 st., 10 suites – SB 83.00/ 115.00 st.

🏠 **New Inn,** Chepstow Rd, NP6 2JN, ℰ 412426, Fax 413679 – ⓣⓥ ☎ ❷. 🔼 ፲፱ ⓞ ᴠ𝘐𝘚𝘈. ⅍
M (grill rest.) a la carte 10.05/16.50 st. – ⌸ 5.00 – **34 rm** 33.00 st.

at Redwick SE : 9½ m. by M4 off B 4245 – ⊠ Magor – ☎ 0633 Newport :

⌂ **Brick House** ⌾, NP6 3DX, ℰ 880230, Fax 880230 – ⅙⊱ ❷. ⅍
M (by arrangement) 10.00 – **7 rm** ⌸ 25.00/40.00 s.

🖼 ATS 101 Corporation Rd ℰ 216115/216117

NEW QUAY **(Ceinewydd)** Dyfed 𝟜𝟘𝟛 G 27 – pop. 775 – ECD : Wednesday – ⊠ ☎ 0545.
🛈 Church St., SA45 9NZ ℰ 560865 (summer only).
◆London 234 – Aberystwyth 24 – Carmarthen 31 – Fishguard 39.

🛎 **Black Lion,** Glanmor Terr., SA45 9PT, ℰ 560209, Fax 560585, ≼, ⌾ – ⓣⓥ ❷. 🔼 ፲፱ ᴠ𝘐𝘚𝘈. ⅍
M (bar lunch Monday to Saturday)/dinner a la carte 10.50/15.00 st. ⅋ 4.00 – **7 rm** ⌸ 27.50/ 55.00 st.

561

at Llwyndafydd SW : 3 m. by A 486 on Llangrannog rd – ⊠ Llandysul – ☎ 0545 Newquay :

↑ **Park Hall** ⊗, Cwmtydu, SA44 6LG, NW : 1¾ m. ℘ 560306, ≤, ⇗ – ⇔⇔ rest ⊡ **ⓟ**. **◪ ⒜ ⓞ ⓋⒾⓈⒶ**
M (by arrangement) 17.50 **st.** ▮ 3.50 – **5 rm** ⊒ 29.50/50.00 **st.** – SB (October-April) (weekdays only) 79.00/88.00 **st.**

NORTHOP HALL Clwyd ⓐ0ⓐ ⓐ0ⓐ K 24 – pop. 4 312 (Northop) – ☎ 0244 Chester.

🅱 Autolodge Site, Gateway Services, CH7 6HE, A 55 (westbound) ℘ 541597.

◆London 220 – Chester 9 – Shrewsbury 52.

🄰 **Autolodge,** Gateway Services, CH5 6HB, A 55 (westbound carriageway) ℘ 550011, Fax 550763 – ⊡ ☎ & **ⓟ** – ⒜ 45. **◪ ⒜ ⓋⒾⓈⒶ** ⚓
M (dinner only) 12.00 **t.** and a la carte ▮ 3.75 – ⊒ 5.90 – **37 rm** 31.95/58.00 **t.**

🄰 **Forte Travelodge** without rest.,, A 55 Expressway (eastbound carriageway) ℘ 816473, Reservations (Freephone) 0800 850950 – ⊡ & **ⓟ**. **◪ ⒜ ⓋⒾⓈⒶ** ⚓
40 rm 31.95 **t.**

NOTTAGE (Drenewydd Yn Notais) M. Glam. ⓐ0ⓐ I 29 – see Porthcawl.

PANT MAWR Powys ⓐ0ⓐ I 26 – ⊠ ☎ 055 15 Llangurig.

◆London 219 – Aberystwyth 21 – Shrewsbury 55.

⇗ **Glansevern Arms,** SY18 6SY, on A 44 ℘ 240, ≤ – ⊡ **ⓟ**
closed 20 to 31 December – **M** *(closed Sunday dinner)* (booking essential) (dinner only) Sunday lunch)/dinner 17.00 **t.** ▮ 5.00 – **7 rm** ⊒ 35.00/60.00 **t.**

PEMBROKE (Penfro) Dyfed ⓐ0ⓐ F 28 Great Britain G. – pop. 15 284 – ECD : Wednesday – ☎ 0646.

See : Castle★★ *AC*.

🄵 Defensible Barracks, Pembroke Dock ℘ 683817.

⚓ to Rosslare (B & I Line) (4 h 15 mn).

🅱 The Commons Rd.

◆London 252 – Carmarthen 32 – Fishguard 26.

🄰 **Underdown Country House** ⊗, Grove Hill, SA71 5PR, ℘ 683350, Fax 621229, « Antiques and gardens » – ⊡ ☎ **ⓟ**. **◪ ⒜ ⓞ ⓋⒾⓈⒶ** ⚓
M (booking essential) (dinner only) 24.10 **t.** and a la carte ▮ 4.25 – **6 rm** ⊒ 35.00/90.00 **t.** – SB 82.50/139.00 **st.**

⇗ **Coach House,** 116 Main St., SA71 4HN, ℘ 684602, Fax 687456, ⇗ – ⊡ ☎ **ⓟ**. **◪ ⒜ ⓞ ⓋⒾⓈⒶ**
closed 1 week Christmas – **M** 15.00 **st.** (dinner) and a la carte 12.95/17.00 **st.** ▮ 6.50 – **14 rm** ⊒ 35.00/56.00 **st.** – SB 55.00/90.00 **st.**

↑ **High Noon,** Lower Lamphey Rd, SA71 4AB, ℘ 683736 – ⊡ **ⓟ**. ⚓
M 10.00 **st.** ▮ 4.00 – **9 rm** ⊒ 18.00/45.00 **st.** – SB (except Bank Holidays) 48.00/60.00 **st.**

at Lamphey E : 1¾ m. on A 4139 – ⊠ Pembroke – ☎ 0646 Lamphey :

🄷 **Court** (Best Western) ⊗, SA71 5NT, ℘ 672273, Fax 672480, 🄵₅, ⇌s, 🖳, ⇗, park – ⊡ ☎ **ⓟ** – ⒜ 80. **◪ ⒜ ⓞ ⓋⒾⓈⒶ**. ⚓
M (bar lunch)/dinner 15.95 **st.** and a la carte – **25 rm** ⊒ 59.50/99.00 **st.**, 7 suites – SB 79.00/138.00 **st.**

🄰 **Lamphey Hall,** SA71 5NR, ℘ 672394, Fax 672369, ⇗ – ⊡ ☎ **ⓟ**. **◪ ⒜ ⓞ ⓋⒾⓈⒶ**
M 8.75/15.75 **t.** and a la carte – **10 rm** ⊒ 39.00/60.00 **t.**

at Pembroke Dock NW : 2 m. on A 4139 – ⊠ ☎ 0646 Pembroke :

🄷 Cleddau Bridge, Essex Rd, SA72 6UT, NE : 1 m. by A 4139 on A 477 (at Toll Bridge) ℘ 685961, Fax 685746, 🖳 heated – ⊡ ☎ **ⓟ** – ⒜ 175
22 rm. 2 suites.

🅾 ATS Well Hill Garage, Well Hill ℘ 683217/683836

PENALLY (Penalun) Dyfed ⓐ0ⓐ F 29 – see Tenby.

PENCOED M. Glam. ⓐ0ⓐ J 29 – see Bridgend.

PENMAENHEAD Clwyd – see Colwyn Bay.

PENYBONT Powys ⓐ0ⓐ K 27 – ⊠ Llandrindod Wells – ☎ 059 787.

◆London 170 – ◆Birmingham 79 – Hereford 37 – Shrewsbury 58.

✗ **Ffaldau Country House** with rm, Llandegley, LD1 5UD, E : 1¼ m. on A 44 ℘ 421, ⇗ – **ⓟ**. **ⓋⒾⓈⒶ**. ⚓
M (residents only) (dinner only) 18.00 – **3 rm** ⊒ 22.00/45.00.

PONTFAEN Dyfed – see Fishguard.

PONT-Y-PANT Gwynedd – see Betws-y-Coed.

PORT DINORWIC (Felinheli) Gwynedd 402 403 H 24 – ✆ 0248.

◆London 249 – Caernarfon 4 – Holyhead 23.

🏠 **Ty'n Rhos Country House** ⑤, Seion, Llanddeiniolen, LL55 3AE, E : 2½ m. by A 487 off B 4547 ℰ 670489, Fax 670079, ⩽, 🐾, 🐟 – ⇤ rest 📺 ☎ ❷. 🔼 **VISA**. ⚶
closed 20 December-15 January – **M** (by arrangement) 18.50 **st.** ⚬ 5.25 – **11 rm** ⊒ 30.00/ 70.00 **st.** – SB 83.00/103.00 **st.**

PORTH M. Glam. 403 J 29 – ✆ 0443.

◆London 168 – ◆Cardiff 13 – ◆Swansea 45.

🏛 **Heritage Park**, Coed Cae Rd, CF37 2NP, on A 4058 ℰ 687057, Fax 687060 – ⇤ rm ≣ rest 📺 ☎ & ❷ – ▵ 200. 🔼 **VISA**. ⚶
M 8.95/12.00 **t.** and a la carte ⚬ 3.75 – **44 rm** ⊒ 37.00/75.00 **t.**

✕✕ **G & T's**, 64-66 Pontypridd Rd, CF39 9NL, ℰ 685775, Fax 687614 – ⇤. 🔼 **AE** ⓪ **VISA**
closed Sunday dinner – **M** a la carte 15.15/31.45 **t.**

PORTHCAWL M. Glam. 403 I 29 – pop. 15 162 – ECD : Wednesday – ✆ 0656.

🛈 The Old Police Station, John St., CF36 3DT ℰ 786639/782211.

◆London 183 – ◆Cardiff 28 – ◆Swansea 18.

🏛 **Seabank**, The Promenade, CF36 3LU, ℰ 782261, Fax 785363, ⩽, 🕿 – 🛗 ⇤ rm 📺 ☎ ❷ – ▵ 200. 🔼 **AE** ⓪ **VISA**
M 14.95 **t.** and a la carte ⚬ 5.25 – **61 rm** ⊒ 59.50/85.50 **t.**

🏠 **Atlantic**, West Drive, CF36 3LT, ℰ 785011, Fax 771877, ⩽ – 🛗 📺 ☎ ❷. 🔼 **AE** ⓪ **VISA**
M (bar lunch)/dinner 12.50 **t.** and a la carte ⚬ 4.75 – **19 rm** ⊒ 46.50/69.00 **t.** – SB (week-ends only) 70.00 **st.**

↑ **Minerva**, 52 Esplanade Av., CF36 3YU, ℰ 782428 – ⇤ rest 📺. ⚶
M 7.50 **s.** ⚬ 4.00 – **8 rm** ⊒ 14.00/38.00 **s.**

at Nottage (Drenewydd yn Notais) N : 1 m. by A 4229 – ✉ ✆ 0656 Porthcawl :

🏠 Rose and Crown (Chef & Brewer), Heol-y-Capel, CF36 3ST, ℰ 784850 – 📺 ☎ ❷. ⚶
8 rm.

PORTMEIRION Gwynedd 402 403 H 25 Great Britain G. – ✆ 0766 Porthmadog.

See : Village ⋆ AC.

◆London 245 – Caernarfon 23 – Colwyn Bay 40 – Dolgellau 24.

🏛 **Portmeirion** ⑤, LL48 6ET, ℰ 770228, Fax 771331, ⩽ village and estuary, « Private Italianate village, antiques », 🏊 heated, 🐾, park, ⚶ – ⇤ rest 📺 ☎ ❷ – ▵ 70. 🔼 **AE** ⓪ **VISA**
closed 10 January-4 February – **M** *(closed Monday lunch)* (buffet lunch)/dinner 25.00 **t.** ⚬ 5.00 – ⊒ 8.50 – **28 rm** 57.00/112.00 **st.**, 6 suites – SB 132.00/254.00 **st.**

PORT TALBOT W. Glam. 403 I 29 – pop. 47 299 – ✆ 0639.

◆London 193 – ◆Cardiff 35 – ◆Swansea 11.

🏠 **Travel Inn**, Baglan Rd, SA12 8ES, at junction of A 48 with M 4 ℰ 813017, Fax 823096 – ⇤ rm 📺 & ❷. 🔼 **AE** ⓪ **VISA**. ⚶
M (Beefeater grill) a la carte approx. 16.00 **t.** ⚬ 5.60 – ⊒ 4.95 – **40 rm** 33.50 **st.**

🏠 **Twelve Knights**, Margam Rd, SA13 2DB, ℰ 882381, Fax 897732 – 📺 ☎ ❷. 🔼 **VISA** **JCB**. ⚶
M (grill rest.) 8.00 **t.** and a la carte ⚬ 3.95 – **11 rm** ⊒ 35.00/45.00 **st.** – SB (weekends only) 57.00/110.00 **st.**

◍ ATS Afan Way ℰ 883895/885747

PRESTEIGNE Powys 403 K 27 – pop. 1 490 – ECD : Thursday – ✆ 0544.

🛈 The Old Market Hall, Broad St., LD8 2AW ℰ 260193 (summer only).

◆London 159 – Llandrindod Wells 20 – Shrewsbury 39.

🏛 **Radnorshire Arms** (Forte), High St., LD8 2BE, ℰ 267406, Fax 260418, 🐾 – ⇤ rm 📺 ☎ ❷ – ▵ 25. 🔼 **AE** ⓪ **VISA** **JCB**
M 11.95/16.95 **t.** and a la carte ⚬ 6.45 – ⊒ 8.50 – **16 rm** 65.00/75.00 **st.** – SB 108.00 **st.**

PWLLHELI Gwynedd 402 403 G 25 – pop. 4 003 – ✆ 0758.

🛝 ℰ 701644, SW : ½ m.

🛈 Y Maes, LL53 6HE ℰ 613000 (summer only).

◆London 261 – Aberystwyth 73 – Caernarfon 21.

✕✕✕ ✿ **Plas Bodegroes** (Chown) ⑤ with rm, LL53 5TH, NW : 1 ¾ m. on A 497 ℰ 612363, Fax 701247, « Georgian country house », 🐾, park – ⇤ 📺 ☎ ❷. 🔼 **VISA**
closed Monday and November-February – **M** (dinner only) 30.00 **st.** ⚬ 5.50 – **8 rm** ⊒ 40.00/ 110.00 **st.** – SB (except Monday) 110.00/170.00 **st.**
Spec. Hotpot of shellfish with lemon grass and chilli, Sea trout in Carmarthen ham with leeks and laver bread, Bara brith and butter pudding.

REDWICK Gwent 403 L 29 – see Newport.

RHAYADER (Rhaeadr) Powys 403 J 27 Great Britain G. – pop. 1 411 – ۞ 0597.

Envir. : Elan Valley★★, SW : by B 4518.

🛈 North St., LD6 ✆ 810591 (summer only) – Elan Valley Visitor Centre, LD6 5HP ✆ 81098 (summer only).

◆London 180 – Brecon 34 – Hereford 46 – Shrewsbury 60.

🏠 **Elan,** West St., LD6 5AF, ✆ 810373 – 📺 ☎ 🅿. 🔌 *VISA*

 M *(closed lunch Thursday and dinner Sunday and Monday)* 7.95/13.75 **t.** ⓘ 5.25 – **12 rm** ☞ 16.50/42.00 **t.** – SB 62.50/76.00 **st.**

RHOSCOLYN Gwynedd 402 403 G 24 Great Britain G. – pop. 543 – ✉ Holyhead – ۞ 0407 Trearddur Bay.

Envir. : Isle of Anglesey★★.

◆London 269 – Bangor 25 – Caernarfon 30 – Holyhead 5.5.

🏠 **Old Rectory** 🐾, LL65 2DQ, ✆ 860214, ≤, ☞ – ⅍ rest 📺 🅿. 🔌 *VISA*

 closed 22 to 31 December and 1-2 January – **M** (by arrangement) 15.00 – **5 rm** ☞ 29.50/ 46.00 **s.** – SB 74.00/87.00 **st.**

La guida cambia, cambiate la guida ogni anno.

RHOS-ON-SEA (Llandrillo-Yn-Rhos) Clwyd 402 403 I 24 – see Colwyn Bay.

RHYDLEWIS Dyfed 403 G 27 – ✉ Llandysul – ۞ 0239.

◆London 235 – Carmarthen 26 – Fishguard 38.

🏠 **Broniwan** 🐾, SA44 5PF, NE : ¼ m. by Plump rd, taking first turn right onto unmarked road ✆ 851261, « Working farm », ☞, park – ⅍ 🅿
 April-October – **M** 9.50 **st.** – **3 rm** ☞ 16.50/33.00 **st.**

ROEWEN Gwynedd – see Conwy.

ROSSETT (Yr Orsedd) Clwyd 402 403 L 24 – pop. 2 323 – ۞ 0244.

◆London 203 – Chester 8 – Shrewsbury 39.

🏨 **Llyndir Hall** 🐾, Llyndir Lane, LL12 0AY, N : ¾ m. by B 5445 ✆ 571648, Fax 571258, « Part Strawberry Gothic country house », ƒ₆, ≋, 🔍, ☞ – ⅍ rm 📺 ☎ ﻮ 🅿 – 🔬 120. 🔌 🅰🅴 ① *VISA* ﷼
 M (bar lunch Saturday) 14.95/17.50 **t.** and a la carte ⓘ 6.00 – ☞ 6.95 – **37 rm** 74.00/ 110.00 **t.**, 1 suite – SB (except Christmas and New Year) (weekends only) 110.00 **st.**

🏨 **Rossett Hall,** Chester Rd, LL12 0DE, ✆ 571000, Fax 571505, ☞ – ⅍ rm 📺 ☎ ﻮ 🅿 – 🔬 120. 🔌 🅰🅴 ① *VISA* 🅹🅲🅱 ﷼
 M a la carte 14.85/24.15 **t.** – **30 rm** ☞ 68.00/105.00 **t.** – SB 99.00/115.00 **st.**

RUTHIN (Rhuthun) Clwyd 402 403 K 24 – pop. 4 417 – ECD : Thursday – ۞ 0824.

🏌 Ruthin-Pwllglas ✆ 702296, S : 2½ m.

🛈 Ruthin Craft Centre, Park Rd, LL15 1BB ✆ 703992.

◆London 210 – Birkenhead 31 – Chester 23 – Shrewsbury 46.

🏨 **Ruthin Castle** (Best Western) 🐾, Corwen Rd, LL15 2NU, ✆ 702664, Fax 705978, ≤, « Reconstructed Victorian and part medieval castle », 🐾, ☞, park – 📶 📺 ☎ 🅿. 🔌 🅰🅴 ① *VISA* ﷼
 M 9.00/21.00 **st.** and dinner a la carte – **58 rm** ☞ 62.00/102.00 **st.** – SB 94.00/144.00 **st.**

🏠 **Eyarth Station** 🐾, Llanfair Dyffryn Clwyd, LL15 2EE, S : 1 ¾ m. by A 525 ✆ 703643, Fax 707464, ≤, 🔍 heated, ☞ – ⅍ rm 🅿. 🔌 *VISA*
 M 12.00 **s.** ⓘ 4.00 – **6 rm** ☞ 25.00/42.00 **s.**

ST. ASAPH (Llanelwy) Clwyd 402 403 J 24 Great Britain G. – pop. 3 156 – ECD : Thursday – ۞ 0745.

See : Cathedral★.

Envir. : Rhuddlan Castle★★, N : 2½ m. by A 525 and A 547 – Denbigh Castle★, S : 6 m. by A 525 and A 543.

◆London 225 – Chester 29 – Shrewsbury 59.

🏨 **Oriel House,** Upper Denbigh Rd, LL17 0LW, S : ¾ m. on A 525 ✆ 582716, Fax 582716, ☞ – ⅍ 📺 ☎ 🅿. 🔬 250. 🔌 🅰🅴 ① *VISA*
 M 10.00/15.95 **t.** and a la carte ⓘ 3.75 – **19 rm** ☞ 40.00/66.00 **t.** – SB (weekends only) 91.30/103.90 **st.**

🏠 **Plas Elwy,** The Roe, LL17 0LT, N : ½ m. at junction of A 525 with A 55 ✆ 582263, Fax 583864 – 📺 ☎ 🅿. 🔌 🅰🅴 ① *VISA* ﷼
 closed 26 to 31 December – **M** *(closed Sunday dinner)* (dinner only and Sunday lunch)/ dinner 12.95 **t.** and a la carte ⓘ 4.50 – **13 rm** ☞ 42.00/65.00 **t.** – SB 76.60/84.00 **st.**

S. Glam. – pop. 85 – ✪ 0446 Peterston-super-Ely.

◆London 155 – ◆Bristol 51 – ◆Cardiff 9 – Newport 22.

⌂ **Sant-Y-Nyll** ♨ without rest., CF5 6EZ, ℰ 760209, ≼, ⊶, park – 📺 🅿. 🆎. ⚶
M (by arrangement) 12.50 **st.** – **6 rm** ⚌ 25.00/45.00 **st.**

ST. CLEARS (Sancler) Dyfed 🔲🔲🔲 G 28 – pop. 2 159 – ECD : Wednesday – ✪ 0994.

◆London 229 – Carmarthen 9 – Fishguard 37.

⌂ **Forge Motel**, SA33 4NA, E : 1 m. on A 40 ℰ 230300, Fax 230300, 🝰, 🔲, ⊶ – 📺 ☎ 🅿.
🔺 𝑉𝑆𝐴
closed 25 and 26 December – **M** (grill rest.) a la carte 8.20/16.90 **t.** ◊ 3.95 – **18 rm** ⚌ 35.00/
55.00 **t.**

ST. DAVIDS (Tyddewi) Dyfed 🔲🔲🔲 E 28 Great Britain G. – pop. 1 428 – ECD : Wednesday –
✪ 0437.

See : Town★ – Cathedral★★ - Bishops Palace★ *AC.*

🇬 St. Davids City, Whitesands Bay ℰ 720312, NW : 2 m. by B 4583.

◆London 266 – Carmarthen 46 – Fishguard 16.

🏨 **Warpool Court** ♨, SA62 6BN, ℰ 720300, Fax 720676, ≼ St. Brides Bay and countryside, 🝰, 🔲, 🇬, ♘, ⊶, ⚶ – 📺 ☎ 🅿. 🔺 🆎 ⑩ 𝑉𝑆𝐴
closed 3 January-4 February – **M** 22.00/24.00 **st.** and a la carte ◊ 4.25 – **25 rm** ⚌ 72.50/
145.00 **st.** – SB (except Christmas and New Year) 98.00/172.00 **st.**

🏨 **St. Non's**, Catherine St., SA62 6RJ, ℰ 720239, Fax 721839, ⊶ – 📺 ☎ 🅿. 🔺 🆎 ⑩ 𝑉𝑆𝐴
M (bar lunch)/dinner 15.00 **t.** and a la carte ◊ 3.50 – **24 rm** ⚌ 33.00/66.00 **t.** – SB 78.00/
96.00 **st.**

⌂ Old Cross, Cross Sq., SA62 6SP, ℰ 720387, ⊶ – ≸ rm 📺 ☎ 🅿
16 rm.

⌂ **Alandale**, 43 Nun St., SA62 6NU, ℰ 720333 – ≸ rm 📺. ⚶
M 9.50 **s.** – **5 rm** ⚌ 14.50/33.00 **s.**

at Berea NE : 4 ½ m. by A 487, B 4583 and Llanrian rd – ⊠ St. Davids – ✪ 0348
Croesgoch :

⌂ **Cwmwdig Water** ♨, SA62 6DW, NE : ½ m. ℰ 831434, ≼, ⊶ – ≸ 🅿. 🔺 🆎 ⑩ 𝑉𝑆𝐴
closed Christmas – **M** (by arrangement) 13.00 **st.** ◊ 3.70 – **12 rm** ⚌ 19.00/40.00 **st.** –
SB (winter only) 54.00/60.00 **st.**

at Llandeloy E : 9 m. by A 487 and B 4330 via Treffynnon – ⊠ Haverfordwest –
✪ 0348 Croesgoch :

⌂ **Upper Vanley Farm**, SA62 6LJ, E : ¼ m. ℰ 831418, ≼, ⊶ – ≸ 📺 🅿
M *(closed Sunday)* 11.00 ◊ 6.00 – **7 rm** ⚌ 16.00/38.00.

ST.DOGMAELS Dyfed 🔲🔲🔲 G 27 – see Cardigan.

SARN PARK SERVICE AREA M. Glam. – ⊠ ✪ 0656 Bridgend.

🅱 M 4, Junction 36, CF32 9SY ℰ 654906.

◆London 174 – ◆Cardiff 17 – ◆Swansea 20.

🏠 **Forte Travelodge** without rest, CF32 9RW, M 4 junction 36 ℰ 659218, Reservations
(Freephone) 0800 850950 – 📺 㐧 🅿. 🔺 🆎 𝑉𝑆𝐴. ⚶
40 rm 31.95 **t.**

SAUNDERSFOOT Dyfed 🔲🔲🔲 F 28 – pop. 2 196 – ECD : Wednesday – ✪ 0834.

◆London 245 – Carmarthen 25 – Fishguard 34 – Tenby 3.

🏨 **St. Brides**, St. Brides Hill, SA69 9NH, ℰ 812304, Telex 48350, Fax 813303, ≼, ♨ heated,
⊶ – ≸ rm 🗖 rest 📺 ☎ 🅿 – 🔬 100. 🔺 🆎 ⑩ 𝑉𝑆𝐴
closed 1 to 17 January – **M** 15.00/21.00 **st.** and a la carte ◊ 6.50 – **43 rm** ⚌ 56.00/88.00 **st.**,
2 suites – SB (except Bank Holidays) (weekends only) 65.00/110.00 **st.**

🏠 **Glen Beach** ♨, Swallow Tree Woods, SA69 9DE, S : ½ m. by B 4316 ℰ 813430, ≼, ⊶ –
📺 ☎ 🅿.
M (dinner only) 12.50 **t.** and a la carte ◊ 3.95 – **13 rm** ⚌ 28.00/46.00 **t.** – SB (except July
and August) 60.00/76.00 **st.**

⌂ **Vine Farm**, The Ridgeway, SA69 9LA, ℰ 813543, ⊶ – 📺 🅿
April-October – **M** 10.00 – **5 rm** ⚌ 21.50/43.00 **st.**

Pleasant hotels and restaurants
are shown in the Guide by a red sign.

Please send us the names
of anywhere you have enjoyed your stay.

Your Michelin Guide will be even better.

🏯🏯 ... ⌂

✕✕✕✕✕ ... ✕

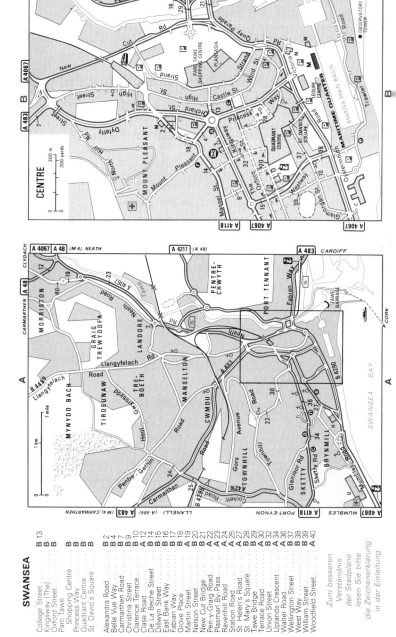

Zum besseren
Verständnis
der Stadtpläne
lesen Sie bitte
die Zeichenerklärung
in der Einleitung.

566

See : Maritime Quarter★ B – Maritime and Industrial Museum★ B **M**.

Envir. : Gower Peninsula★ :- Cefn Bryn (❄★★) - Rhossili (≤★★★) W : by A 4067 A.

🏨 Morriston, 160 Clasemont Rd 🖉 771079, N : 4 m. by A 48 A – 🏨 Clyne, 120 Owls Lodge Lane, Mayals 🖉 401989, SW : by A 4067 A – 🏨 Langland Bay 🖉 366023, SW : 6 m. by A 4067 A – 🏨 Fairwood Park, Blackhills Lane, Upper Killay 🖉 203648, W : 4 m. by A 4118 A – 🏨 Inco, Clydach 🖉 844216, NE : 6 m. by A 4067 A.

🚢 to Ireland (Cork) (Swansea Cork Car Ferries) (10 h).

🅱 PO Box 59, Singleton St., SA1 3QG 🖉 468321.

◆London 191 – ◆Birmingham 136 – ◆Bristol 82 – ◆Cardiff 40 – ◆Liverpool 187 – ◆Stoke-on-Trent 175.

Plans on preceding page

🏨 **Swansea Marriott,** Maritime Quarter, SA1 3SS, 🖉 642020, Fax 650345, ≤, *Fô*, ≘s, 🔲 – 📳 ⅙⋉ rm 🔟 ☎ 🄿 – 🔬 250. 🔼 🄰🄴 ⑨ **VISA** 🛠️ B **e**
M 13.90/15.75 **st.** and a la carte – ⊇ 10.25 – **118 rm** 58.00/122.00 **st.** – SB (weekends only) 106.00/136.00 **st.**

🏨 **Forte Crest,** 39 The Kingsway, SA1 5LS, 🖉 651074, Fax 456044, *Fô*, ≘s, 🔲 – 📳 ⅙⋉ rm 🔟 ☎ 🄿 – 🔬 250. 🔼 🄰🄴 ⑨ **VISA** B **a**
M 14.95 **st.** and a la carte – ⊇ 9.95 – **93 rm** 52.00/80.00 **st.**, 6 suites.

🏨 **Fforest,** Pontardulais Rd, Fforestfach, SA5 4BA, NW : 3 ½ m. on A 483 🖉 588711, Fax 586219, ≘s – ⅙⋉ rm 🔟 ☎ 🄿 – 🔬 200. 🔼 🄰🄴 ⑨ **VISA** 🛠️ A
M 13.95 **t.** (dinner) and a la carte 13.50/19.50 **t.** ⒤ 5.00 – **34 rm** ⊇ 59.50/71.00 **t.** – SB (weekends only) 72.00 **st.**

🏨 **Beaumont,** 72-73 Walter Rd, SA1 4QA, 🖉 643956, Fax 643044 – 🔟 ☎ 🄿. 🔼 🄰🄴 ⑨ **VISA** A **n**
M *(closed Sunday lunch)* 12.75/18.75 **t.** and a la carte ⒤ 5.50 – **17 rm** ⊇ 47.50/59.50 **t.** – SB 87.00/122.50 **st.**

🏨 **Windsor Lodge,** 15 Mount Pleasant, SA1 6EG, 🖉 642158, Fax 648996 – 🔟 ☎ 🄿. 🔼 🄰🄴 ⑨ **VISA** B **r**
closed 25 and 26 December – **M** *(closed Sunday dinner)* (booking essential) 15.00/22.00 **t.** ⒤ 3.00 – **19 rm** ⊇ 43.00/56.00 **t.** – SB (weekends only) 56.00/70.00 **st.**

🏨 **Tredilion House,** 26 Uplands Cres., Uplands, SA2 0PB, 🖉 470766, Fax 456064 – 🔟 ☎ 🄿. 🔼 🄰🄴 ⑨ **VISA**
M (by arrangement) (dinner only) 12.00 **st.** ⒤ 3.50 – **7 rm** ⊇ 34.00/48.00 **st.** – SB (except Bank Holidays) (weekends only) 63.00/100.00 **st.**

🏠 **Alexander** without rest., 3 Sketty Rd, Uplands, SA2 0EU, 🖉 470045 – 🔟 ☎. 🔼 🄰🄴 ⑨ **VISA** 🛠️ A **c**
6 rm ⊇ 20.00/45.00 **st.**

🍴🍴 **Opium Den,** 20 Castle St., SA1 1JF, 🖉 456161 B **c**
M - Chinese rest.

🍴 **Annie's,** 56 St. Helen's Rd, SA1 4BE, 🖉 655603 – 🔼 **VISA** A **o**
closed Monday except July-September and Sunday – **M** (booking essential) (dinner only) 16.80 **st.** ⒤ 5.30.

at Swansea Enterprise Park NE : 4 m. by A 4067 - A - off A 48 – ✉ 🕿 0792 Swansea :

🏨 **Hilton National,** Phoenix Way, SA7 9EG, 🖉 310330, Telex 48589, Fax 797535, *Fô*, ≘s, 🔲 – ⅙⋉ rm 📧 rest 🔟 ☎ ⅙ 🄿 – 🔬 180. 🔼 🄰🄴 ⑨ **VISA** 🛠️
M (bar lunch Saturday) 10.50/13.50 **t.** and dinner a la carte ⒤ 6.00 – ⊇ 8.95 – **119 rm** 50.00/60.00 **t.**, 1 suite – SB (weekends only) 70.00/144.90 **st.**

at Llanrhidian W : 10 ½ m. by A 4118 A and B 4271 on B 4295 – ✉ Reynoldston – 🕿 0792 Gower :

🏨 **North Gower** 🐕, SA3 1EE, 🖉 390042, Fax 584309, ☞ – 🔟 ☎ 🄿. 🔼 🄰🄴 ⑨ **VISA**
M (bar lunch)/dinner a la carte 9.00/14.50 **t.** – **17 rm** ⊇ 30.00/75.00 **t.**

🔧 ATS Neath Rd, Hafod 🖉 456379

🏨 **Pavilion Lodge** without rest., Penllergaer, SA4 1GT, M 4 : junction 47 🖉 894894, Fax 898806 – ⅙⋉ 🔟 ☎ ⅙ 🄿. 🔼 🄰🄴 ⑨ **VISA** **JCB**
⊇ 4.00 – **50 rm** 31.95/35.95 **st.**

◆London 182 – Brecon 10 – Hereford 29 – ◆Swansea 53.

🍴 **Olde Masons Arms,** LD3 0BB, 🖉 711688 – 🔟 🄿. 🔼 **VISA**
M (bar lunch)/dinner 10.50 **t.** and a la carte ⒤ 4.50 – **7 rm** ⊇ 26.50/47.00 **t.** – SB 62.00/68.00 **st.**

at Bronllys NW : 1 m. on A 438 – ✉ Brecon – 🕿 0874 Talgarth :

🍴 **Beacons Edge,** Pontithel, LD3 0RY, NE : 1 ¼ m. on A 438 🖉 711182, ≤ – 🔟 ☎ 🄿. 🔼 ⑨ **VISA**
M 10.00 **st.** ⒤ 4.20 – **11 rm** ⊇ 18.00/60.00 **st.** – SB (except Bank Holidays) 52.00/76.00 **st.**

TALSARNAU Gwynedd 402 403 H 25 – pop. 451 – ✉ ✆ 0766 Harlech.

♦London 236 – Caernafon 33 – Chester 67 – Dolgellau 25.

🏨 **Maes-y-Neuadd** ⟨⟩, LL47 6YA, S : 1 ½ m. by A 496 off B 4573 𝒫 780200, Fax 780211, ≤, « Part 14C country house », 🍽, park – ➜ rest 📺 ☎ 🅿 – 🔬 25. 🖪 🖪 ⑩ 𝒱𝐼𝑆𝐴 𝒥𝐶𝐵
M 13.50/27.00 **st.** ⸙ 4.50 – **15 rm** ⟷ 49.00/152.00 **st.**, 1 suite – SB 125.00/186.00 **st.**

↑ **Tegfan** without rest., Llandecwyn, LL47 6YG, N : 1 ¼ m. on A 496 𝒫 771354, ≤, – 🅿 ⟨⟩
2 rm ⟷ 18.00/28.00 **s.**, 1 suite.

TAL-Y-BONT Gwynedd 402 403 I 24 – see Conwy.

TAL-Y-LLYN Gwynedd 402 403 I 25 – pop. 623 (inc. Corris) – ✉ Tywyn – ✆ 0654 Abergynolwyn.

♦London 224 – Dolgellau 9 – Shrewsbury 60.

🏠 **Tynycornel,** LL36 9AJ, on B 4405 𝒫 782282, Fax 782679, ≤ lake and mountains, 🏖, 🍝 heated, 🍴, 🍽 – 📺 ☎ 🅿. 🖪 🖪 𝒱𝐼𝑆𝐴
M 10.50/16.50 **t.** ⸙ 5.15 – **15 rm** ⟷ 43.00/86.00 **t.**

🏠 **Minffordd,** LL36 9AJ, NE : 3 ¾ m. by B 4405 on A 487 𝒫 761665, Fax 761517, ≤, « Converted 18C farmhouse and inn », 🍽 – ➜ ⊛ 🅿. 🖪 ⑩ 𝒱𝐼𝑆𝐴. ⟨⟩
April-November – **M** (closed Sunday to non-residents) (dinner only) 17.00 **st.** – **6 rm** (dinner included) 59.00/98.00 **st.** – SB 98.00/118.00 **st.**

TENBY (Dinbych-Y-Pysgod) Dyfed 403 F 28 Great Britain G. – pop. 5 226 – ECD : Wednesday – ✆ 0834.

See : Town★ – Harbour and Seafront★★.

Envir. : Caldey Island★, S : by boat.

🏌 The Burrows 𝒫 842787/842978.

🛈 The Croft, SA70 8AP 𝒫 842402.

♦London 247 – Carmarthen 27 – Fishguard 36.

🏨 **Waterwynch House** ⟨⟩, Narberth Rd, SA70 8TJ, N : 1 ¾ m. on A 478 𝒫 842464, Fax 845076, ≤, 🍽, park – ➜ rest 📺 ☎ 🅿
March-October – **M** (closed Sunday dinner) (dinner only and Sunday lunch)/dinner 15.00 **t.**
14 rm ⟷ 38.00/84.00 **t.**, 3 suites – SB 72.00/108.00 **st.**

🏨 **Imperial,** The Paragon, SA70 7HR, 𝒫 843737, Fax 844342, ≤ sea and bay – 🔉 📺 ☎ ⟷ 🅿 – 🔬 40. 🖪 🖪 ⑩ 𝒱𝐼𝑆𝐴
M (bar lunch)/dinner 12.95 **st.** and a la carte ⸙ 3.95 – **46 rm** ⟷ 30.00/80.00 **st.** – SB (except Bank Holidays) 70.00/80.00 **st.**

🏠 **Fourcroft,** The Croft, SA70 8AP, 𝒫 842886, Fax 842888, ≤, 🏖, 🍝 heated, 🍽 – 🔉 ➜ rest 📺 ☎. 🖪 𝒱𝐼𝑆𝐴
closed January and February – **M** (bar lunch)/dinner 17.00 **st.** ⸙ 4.30 – **43 rm** ⟷ 38.00/ 78.00 **st.** – SB (except Christmas) 82.00/100.00 **st.**

🏠 Broadmead, Heywood Lane, SA70 8DA, NW : ¾ m. 𝒫 842641, 🍽 – 📺 🅿. ⟨⟩
20 rm.

↑ **Buckingham,** Esplanade, SA70 6DU, 𝒫 842622, ≤ – ➜ rm 📺. 🖪 𝒱𝐼𝑆𝐴
April-October – **M** 12.00 **st.** ⸙ 3.00 – **8 rm** ⟷ 18.00/44.00 **st.** – SB 56.00/74.00 **st.**

↑ **Harbour Heights** without rest., 11 The Croft, SA70 8AP, 𝒫 842132, ≤ – 📺. 🖪 𝒱𝐼𝑆𝐴
March-November – **9 rm** ⟷ 25.00/50.00 **st.**

at Penally (Penalun) SW : 2 m. by A 4139 – ✉ ✆ 0834 Tenby :

🏨 **Penally Abbey,** SA70 7PY, 𝒫 843033, Fax 844714, ≤, 🍽 📺 ☎ 🅿. 🖪 𝒱𝐼𝑆𝐴. ⟨⟩
M (dinner only) 24.00 ⸙ 5.20 – **12 rm** ⟷ (dinner included) 64.00/136.00 **st.**

THORNHILL S Glam. 403 K 29 – see Cardiff.

THREE COCKS (Aberllynfi) Powys 403 K 27 – ✉ Brecon – ✆ 0497 Glasbury.

♦London 184 – Brecon 11 – Hereford 25 – ♦Swansea 55.

XX **Three Cocks** with rm, LD3 0SL, on A 438 𝒫 847215, « Part 15C former inn », 🍽 – 🅿. 🖪 𝒱𝐼𝑆𝐴. ⟨⟩
closed December and January – **M** (closed Sunday lunch and Tuesday) 24.00 **st.** and a la carte ⸙ 3.75 – **7 rm** ⟷ 40.00/60.00 **st.** – SB (except Bank Holidays) 90.00 **st.**

TINTERN (Tyndyrn) Gwent 403 404 L 28 Great Britain G. – pop. 816 – ECD : Wednesday – ✉ Chepstow – ✆ 0291.

See : Abbey★★ AC.

Envir. : Wye Valley★.

♦London 137 – ♦Bristol 23 – Gloucester 40 – Newport 22.

🏨 **Beaufort** (Jarvis), NP6 6SF, on A 466 𝒫 689777, Fax 689727, 🍽 – 📺 ☎ 🅿 – 🔬 60. 🖪 🖪 ⑩ 𝒱𝐼𝑆𝐴
M (dinner only and Sunday lunch)/dinner 21.50 **st.** ⸙ 6.00 – **24 rm** ⟷ 60.00/92.00 **st.** – SB 79.00/92.00 **st.**

🏠 **Royal George,** NP6 6SF, on A 466 📞 689205, Fax 689448, 🍴 – 📺 ☎ 🅿. 🅽 AE ① VISA
M (bar lunch)/dinner 15.95 **t.** and a la carte – **19 rm** ⊑ 50.50/71.50 **t.** – SB 84.00/92.00 **st.**

🏠 **Parva Farmhouse,** NP6 6SQ, on A 466 📞 689411, Fax 689557 – 📺 ☎ 🅿. 🅽 VISA
M (dinner only) 16.50 **st.** and a la carte ♦ 4.80 – **9 rm** ⊑ 32.00/68.00 **st.** – SB 70.00/108.00 **st.**

TREFRIW Gwynedd 402 403 I 24 – see Llanrwst.

TRESAITH Dyfed – see Aberporth.

TUDWEILIOG Gwynedd 402 403 G 25 – pop. 882 – ✉ Pwllheli – ☎ 075 887.

♦London 267 – Caernarfon 25.

✗ **Dive Inn,** LL53 8PB, W : 2 m. by B 4417 📞 246 – 🅿. 🅽 AE VISA
closed Sunday dinner and Monday in September and Sunday to Thursday mid December-mid March – **M** - Seafood (booking essential) (bar lunch)/dinner a la carte 12.10/22.50 **st.** ♦ 6.50.

USK (Brynbuga) Gwent 403 L 28 Great Britain G. – pop. 1 783 – ECD : Wednesday – ☎ 0291.

Exc. : Raglan Castle★ *AC*, NE : 7 m. by A 472, A 449 and A 40.

🏌 Alice Springs, Bettws Newydd 📞 0873 (Nantyderry) 880772, N : 3 m. by B 45.

♦London 144 – ♦Bristol 30 – Gloucester 39 – Newport 10.

🏠 **Glen-yr-Afon House,** Pontypool Rd, NP5 1SY, 📞 672302, Fax 672597, 🍴 – 🈲 ⤫ rest
📺 ☎ 🚫 🅿 – 🔬 150. 🅽 AE VISA
M (bar lunch)/dinner 25.00 **st.** and a la carte ♦ 6.00 – **27 rm** ⊑ 35.25/58.60 **st.** – SB (weekends only) 90.00/97.50 **st.**

at Llangybi S : 2 ½ m. on Llangybi rd – ✉ Usk – ☎ 063 349 (3 fig.) and 0633 (6 fig.) Tredunnock :

🏠 **Cwrt Bleddyn,** NP5 1PG, S : 1 m. 📞 521, Fax 220, *I&*, ⇌, 🔲, 🍴, park, 🎾, squash – 📺
☎ 🅿 – 🔬 200. 🅽 AE ① VISA
M 22.50/38.00 **t.** and a la carte ♦ 6.25 – ⊑ 8.50 – **32 rm** 65.00/82.50 **t.**, 4 suites – SB 115.00/185.00 **st.**

WELSH HOOK Dyfed – see Fishguard.

WELSHPOOL (Trallwng) Powys 402 403 K 26 Great Britain G. – pop. 4 869 – ECD : Thursday – ☎ 0938.

Envir. : Powis Castle★★, S : 1 m. by A 483.

🏌 Golfa Hill 📞 093 883 (Llangadfan) 249.

🏢 The Flash Leisure Centre, SY21 📞 552043.

♦London 182 – ♦Birmingham 64 – Chester 45 – Shrewsbury 19.

🏠 **Golfa Hall,** SY21 9AF, W : 2 m. on A 458 📞 553399, Fax 554777, park – 📺 ☎ 🅿. 🅽 AE
① VISA. 🎾
M 14.50/21.50 **t.** – **12 rm** ⊑ 41.00/71.00 **t.** – SB 90.00/140.00 **st.**

🏠 **Royal Oak,** The Cross, SY21 7DG, 📞 552217, Fax 552217 – 📺 ☎ 🅿 – 🔬 150. 🅽 AE ①
VISA JCB
M 10.50/13.50 **t.** and dinner a la carte ♦ 4.00 – **24 rm** ⊑ 40.00/65.00 **t.** – SB (weekends only) 75.00 **st.**

↑ **Tynllwyn Farm** 🐷, SY21 9BW, N : 1 ½ m. on A 490 📞 553175, ≤, « Working farm » –
📺 🅿 🎾
M (by arrangement) 8.00 **st.** ♦ 3.00 – **6 rm** ⊑ 14.00/28.00 **st.** – SB (October-March) 40.00 **st.**

↑ **Moat Farm** 🐷, SY21 8SE, S : 2 ¼ m. on A 483 📞 553179, « Working farm », 🍴 – 📺 🅿.
🎾
April-October – **M** (by arrangement) (communal dining) 10.00 **st.** – **3 rm** ⊑ 20.00/36.00 **st.** – SB (except June-August) 56.00/70.00 **st.**

WHITEBROOK Gwent – see Monmouth.

WHITLAND (Hendy-Gwyn) Dyfed 403 G 28 – pop. 1 342 – ECD : Wednesday – ☎ 0994.

♦London 235 – Carmarthen 15 – Haverfordwest 17.

↑ **Cilpost Farm** 🐷, SA34 0RP, N : 1 ¼ m. by North Rd 📞 240280, ≤, « Working dairy
farm », ⇌, 🔲, – 🅿. 🎾
April-September – **M** 15.00 **st.** – **7 rm** ⊑ 17.00/40.00 **st.**

◎ ATS Emporium Garage, Market St. 📞 240587

WOLF'S CASTLE (Cas-Blaidd) Dyfed 403 F 28 – ✉ Haverfordwest – ☎ 043 787 (3 fig.) and 0437 (6 fig.) Treffgarne.

♦London 258 – Fishguard 7 – Haverfordwest 8.

🏠 **Wolfscastle Country,** SA62 5LZ, on A 40 📞 225, Fax 383, squash – 📺 ☎ 🅿. 🅽 AE VISA
M (lunch by arrangement Monday to Saturday)/dinner a la carte 13.00/20.50 **t.** ♦ 4.40 –
20 rm ⊑ 38.00/70.00 **t.** – SB (except Bank Holidays) 84.00/96.00 **st.**

WREXHAM (Wrecsam) Clwyd 402 403 L 24 Great Britain G. – pop. 39 929 – ECD : Wednesday – ✿ 0978.

See : St. Giles Church★.

Envir. : Erddig★ *AC*, SW : 2 m.

☗ Holt Rd ✆ 261033, NE : 2 m. by A 534 – ☗, ☗ Chirk G & C.C. ✆ 0691 (Chirk) 774407.

🛈 Lambpit St., LL11 1AY ✆ 292015.

◆London 192 – Chester 12 – Shrewsbury 28.

🏠 **Cross Lanes,** Marchwiel, LL13 0TF, SE : 3½ m. on A 525 ✆ 780555, Fax 780568, ☎s, ⬛, 🍽, park – 📺 ☎ 🅿 – ⚒ 100. ◪ ᴀᴇ ⓞ 𝗩𝗜𝗦𝗔 ⅏
closed 25 and 26 December – **M** *(closed Saturday lunch)* 12.95/18.95 **st.** and a la carte 🍴 4.95 – ⊐ 4.50 – **16 rm** 52.00/82.00 **st.** – SB 90.00/134.00 **st.**

🏠 **Forte Travelodge** without rest., Croes-Foel roundabout, Rhostyllen, LL14 4EJ, SW : 3½ m. on A 483 ✆ 365705, Reservations (Freephone) 0800 850950 – 📺 ♿ 🅿. ◪ ᴀᴇ 𝗩𝗜𝗦𝗔 ⅏
32 rm 31.95 **t.**

⬤ ATS Dolydd Rd, Croesnewydd ✆ 352301/352928   ATS Eagles Meadow, Clwyd (ASDA) ✆ 366510

Scotland

Place with at least :

one hotel or restaurant .... ● Tongue
a pleasant hotel or restaurant .. 🏨, ⋔, ⋇
one quiet, secluded hotel .... ⅏
one restaurant with .. ✿, ✿✿, ✿✿✿, **Meals (M)**
See this town for establishments
  located in its vicinity .... ABERDEEN

Localité offrant au moins :

une ressource hôtelière .... ● Tongue
un hôtel ou restaurant agréable 🏨, ⋔, ⋇
un hôtel très tranquille, isolé .... ⅏
une bonne table à ✿, ✿✿, ✿✿✿, **Meals (M)**
Localité groupant dans le texte
  les ressources de ses environs .. ABERDEEN

La località possiede come minimo :

una risorsa alberghiera .... ● Tongue
Albergo o ristorante ameno .... 🏨, ⋔, ⋇
un albergo molto tranquillo, isolato ...... ⅏
un'ottima tavola con . ✿, ✿✿, ✿✿✿, **Meals (M)**
La località raggruppa nel suo testo
  le risorse dei dintorni .... ABERDEEN

Ort mit mindestens :

einem Hotel oder Restaurant ..... ● Tongue
ein angenehmes Hotel oder Restaurant 🏨, ⋔, ⋇
einem sehr ruhigen und abgelegenen Hotel ⅏
einem Restaurant mit ✿, ✿✿, ✿✿✿, **Meals (M)**
Ort mit Angaben über Hotels und Restaurants
  in seiner Umgebung .... ABERDEEN

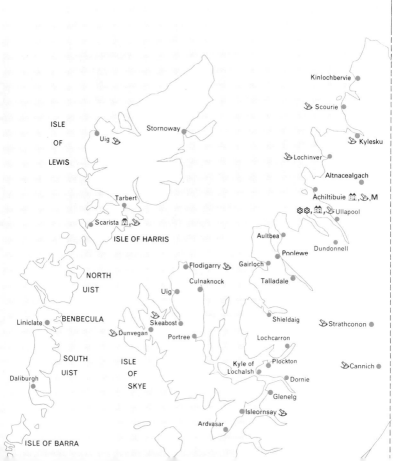

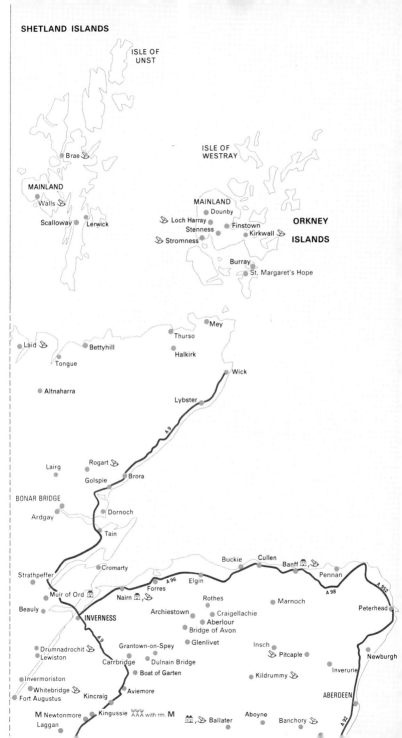

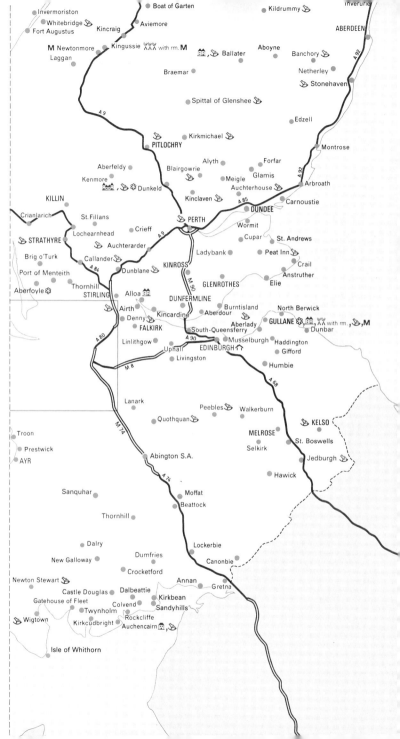

See : City★★ - Old Aberdeen★★ ˣ – St. Machar's Cathedral★★ (West Front★★★, Heraldic Ceiling★★★) ˣ **A** – Art Gallery★★ (Macdonald Collection★★) ʸ **M** – Mercat Cross★★ ʸ **B** – King's College Chapel★ (Crown Spire★★★, medieval fittings★★★) ˣ **D** – Provost Skene's House★ (painted ceilings★★) ʸ **E** – Maritime Museum★ ᶻ **M1** – Marischal College★ ʸ **U**.

Envir. : Brig o' Balgownie★, by Don St. ˣ.

Exc. : SW : Deeside★★ - Crathes Castle★★ (Gardens★★★) *AC*, SW : 16 m. by A 93 ˣ – Dunottar Castle★★ *AC* (site★★★), S : 18 m. by A 92 ˣ – Castle Fraser★ (exterior★★) *AC*, W : 16 m. by A 944 ˣ – Craigievar Castle★ *AC*, W : 27 m. by A 944 – ˣ - B 9119 and A 980.

◻, ◻ Royal Aberdeen, Balgownie, Links Rd, Bridge of Don ✆ 702571, N : 2 m. by A 92 ˣ – ◻ Auchmill, Provost Rust Drive ✆ 714577, NW : 3 m. by Provost Rust Drive ˣ – ◻ Balnagask, St. Fitticks Rd ✆ 876407 ˣ – ◻ King's Links, Golf Rd ✆ 632269 ˣ – ◻ Portlethen, Badentoy Rd ✆ 782575, S : 6 m. by A 92 ˣ – ◻, ◻ Murcar, Bridge of Don ✆ 704345, NE : 5 m. by A 92 ˣ.

✈ Aberdeen Airport ✆ 722331, NW : 7 m. by A 96 ˣ – **Terminal** : Bus Station, Guild St. (adjacent to Railway Station).

🚗 ✆ 0345 090700.

⛴ by P & O Scottish Ferries : (Orkney & Shetland Services) : to Shetland Islands : Lerwick – to Stromness, Orkney Island – by Smyril Line : to the Faroe Islands (Torshavn).

🛈 St. Nicholas House, Broad St. ✆ 632727.

◆Edinburgh 130 – ◆Dundee 67.

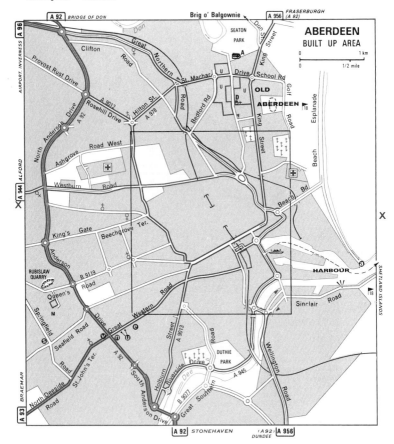

🏨 **Caledonian Thistle** (Mt. Charlotte Thistle), 10-14 Union Terr., AB9 1HE, ✆ 640233, Telex 73758, Fax 641627, ⛱ – 🛗 ⇔ rm 📺 ☎ 🄿 – 🔬 35. 🅐 🅐🅔 ⓞ 𝘝𝘐𝘚𝘈   Z **i**
M *(closed Saturday and Sunday lunch)* 12.25/19.50 **st.** and a la carte ▯ 6.95 – ⊒ 9.95 – **76 rm** 98.00/127.00 **st.**, 2 suites – SB (weekends only) 102.00 **st.**

🏨 **Stakis Aberdeen Treetops,** 161 Springfield Rd, AB9 2QH, ℰ 313377, Fax 312028, ↕5,
⇌s, 🔲, 🎨, ✗ – 🕮 ⇆ rm 📺 ☎ 🅿 – 🔬 600. 🔝 🖭 ⓞ 𝕍𝕀𝕊𝔸 𝙅𝘾𝘽   X s
M 10.50/17.50 **t.** and dinner a la carte – � 9.50 – **109 rm** 99.00/119.00 **st.**, 1 suite –
SB 84.00/92.00 **st.**

🏨 **Ardoe House** ⟡, South Deeside Rd, Blairs, AB1 5YP, SW : 5 m. on B 9077 - X -
ℰ 867355, Fax 861283, ≤, « Part 19C baronial mansion », 🎨, park – 🕮 ⇆ rest 📺 ☎ 🅿 –
🔬 120. 🔝 🖭 ⓞ 𝕍𝕀𝕊𝔸 ✾
M (closed Saturday lunch) 12.00/25.75 **t.** and a la carte ⓘ 5.50 – ⊆ 9.25 – **69 rm** 55.00/
117.00 **t.**, 2 suites – SB (weekends only) 112.00/132.00 **st.**

🏨 **Copthorne,** 122 Huntly St., AB1 1SU, ℰ 630404, Fax 640573 – 🕮 ⇆ rm 📺 ☎ – 🔬 200.
🔝 🖭 ⓞ 𝕍𝕀𝕊𝔸   Z a
M 15.25/16.25 **st.** and a la carte ⓘ 5.00 – ⊆ 9.50 – **89 rm** 110.00/135.00 **st.** – SB (weekends
only) 125.00/180.00 **st.**

ABERDEEN

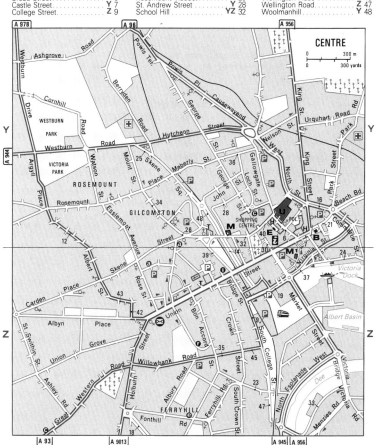

🏛 **Quality,** Bridge of Don, AB23 8BL, N : 3 m. on A 92 𝒫 706707, Fax 823923 – |≥| ⇔ rm 📺
☎ ৬ 🅿. 🔼 🅰🅴 ⓄⒹ 𝑽𝑰𝑺𝑨   X
M a la carte 9.90/22.55 **st.** – ⌂ 8.50 – **123 rm** 75.00/150.00 **st.** – SB (July-August and weekends only) 97.00/199.00 **st.**

🏛 **Amatola** (Jarvis), 448 Great Western Rd, AB1 6NP, 𝒫 318724, Fax 312716 – 📺 ☎ 🅿 –
🔬 400. 🔼 𝑽𝑰𝑺𝑨   X   v
M 14.00/22.00 **st.** and a la carte – ⌂ 8.75 – **53 rm** 79.00/95.00 **st.** – SB (weekends only) 70.00/84.00 **st.**

🏠 **Malacca,** 349 Great Western Rd, AB1 6NW, 𝒫 588901, Fax 571621 – 📺 ☎ 🅿. 🔼 🅰🅴 ⓄⒹ
𝑽𝑰𝑺𝑨   X   u
M (bar lunch Saturday) a la carte 13.00/19.95 **t.** ⓐ 3.25 – **21 rm** ⌂ 80.00/90.00 **st.**

🏠 **Craiglynn,** 36 Fonthill Rd, AB1 2UJ, 𝒫 584050, Fax 584050 – ⇔ 📺 ☎ 🅿. 🔼 🅰🅴 ⓄⒹ 𝑽𝑰𝑺𝑨
⋘   Z   s
closed Christmas – **M** (dinner only) 14.80 **t.** ⓐ 3.60 – **9 rm** ⌂ 33.00/60.00 **t.** – SB (except August and September) (weekends only) 79.10/119.60 **st.**

🏡 **Cedars** without rest., 339 Great Western Rd, AB1 6NW, 𝒫 583225, Fax 583225 – 📺 ☎
🔼 🅰🅴 𝑽𝑰𝑺𝑨 ⋘   X   e
13 rm ⌂ 38.00/52.00 **st.**

🏡 **Corner House,** 385 Great Western Rd, AB1 6NY, 𝒫 313063, Fax 313063 – ⇔ rest 📺 ☎
🅿. 🔼 𝑽𝑰𝑺𝑨 ⋘   X   u
M 12.95 **st.** – **17 rm** ⌂ 35.00/60.00 **st.** – SB (weekends only) 62.40/125.90 **st.**

🏡 **Manorville** without rest., 252 Great Western Rd, AB1 6PJ, 𝒫 594190, Fax 594190 – 📺.
     Z   c
3 rm ⌂ 22.00/36.00 **s.**

🏡 **Fourways** without rest., 435 Great Western Rd, AB1 6NJ, 𝒫 310218 – 📺 🅿. 🅰🅴.
     X   n
7 rm ⌂ 25.00/36.00 **s.**

XX **Rendez-vous,** 210-212 George St., AB1 1BS, 𝒫 633610, Fax 649389 – ▤. 🔼 🅰🅴
𝑽𝑰𝑺𝑨   Y   c
closed Sunday lunch – **M** - Chinese (Peking) and Thai rest. a la carte 10.00/20.00 **st.** ⓐ 4.50.

XX **Atlantis,** 16-17 Bon Accord Cres., AB1 2DE, 𝒫 591403 – 🔼 🅰🅴 ⓄⒹ 𝑽𝑰𝑺𝑨   Z   r
closed Saturday lunch, Sunday, 25 December and 1 January – **M** - Seafood a la carte 15.50/ 28.50 **st.** ⓐ 7.50.

XX **Nargile,** 77-79 Skene St., AB1 1QD, 𝒫 636093, Fax 636202 – 🔼 🅰🅴 ⓄⒹ 𝑽𝑰𝑺𝑨   Y   a
closed lunch Saturday and Sunday – **M** - Turkish 8.50/19.95 **t.** and a la carte.

X **Silver Darling,** Pocra Quay, North Pier Rd, AB2 1DQ, 𝒫 576229, Fax 626558 – 🔼 🅰🅴 ⓄⒹ
𝑽𝑰𝑺𝑨   X   a
closed Saturday lunch, Sunday, 2 weeks Christmas-New Year and Bank Holiday Mondays –
M - French Seafood (booking essential) a la carte 24.05/28.00 **t.**

at Murcar N : 4½ m. on A 92 – X – ✉ ☎ 0224 Aberdeen :

🏠 **Travel Inn** without rest., AB2 8BP, on B 999 𝒫 821217, Fax 706869 – ⇔ 📺 ৬ 🅿. 🔼
ⓄⒹ 𝑽𝑰𝑺𝑨. ⋘
⌂ 4.95 – **40 rm** 33.50 **t.**

at Altens S : 3 m. on A 956 – X – ✉ ☎ 0224 Aberdeen :

🏨 **Altens Skean Dhu** (Mt. Charlotte Thistle), Souterhead Rd, AB1 4LF, 𝒫 877000, Telex 739631, Fax 896964, ⧖ heated – |≥| ⇔ rm ▤ rest 📺 ☎ 🅿 – 🔬 350. 🔼 🅰🅴 ⓄⒹ 𝑽𝑰𝑺𝑨
M (closed Saturday lunch, Sunday and Bank Holidays) 15.75/18.50 **st.** and a la carte ⓐ 5.95 – ⌂ 8.50 – **220 rm** 83.00/105.00 **t.**, 1 suite – SB 92.00/196.00 **st.**

at Cults SW : 4 m. on A 93 – X – ✉ ☎ 0224 Aberdeen :

X **Faraday's,** 2 Kirk Brae, AB1 9SQ, 𝒫 869666 – 🅿. 🔼 𝑽𝑰𝑺𝑨
closed Monday lunch, Sunday and 26 December-10 January – **M** (booking essential) a la carte 9.60/18.60 **t.** ⓐ 7.10.

at Maryculter SW : 8 m. on B 9077 – X – ✉ ☎ 0224 Aberdeen :

🏛 **Maryculter House** ⧖, South Deeside Rd, AB1 0BB, 𝒫 732124, Fax 733510, « Part 13C house on River Dee », ⧖ – 📺 ☎ 🅿 – 🔬 30. 🔼 🅰🅴 ⓄⒹ 𝑽𝑰𝑺𝑨
M (closed Sunday dinner) (bar lunch Monday to Saturday)/dinner 30.00 **t.** – **23 rm** ⌂ 108.00/113.00 **t.**

at Westhill W : 6½ m. by A 944 – X – ✉ ☎ 0224 Aberdeen :

XXX **Courtyard,** Elrick, AB32 6TL, W : ½ m. by A 944 (behind Broadstraik Inn) 𝒫 742540, Fax 742796 – 🅿. 🔼 🅰🅴 𝑽𝑰𝑺𝑨
M (closed Monday and Tuesday) a la carte 9.95/23.50 **t.** ⓐ 4.50.

at Bucksburn NW : 4 m. by A 96 – X – on A 947 – ✉ ☎ 0224 Aberdeen :

🏨 **Holiday Inn Crown Plaza Aberdeen** (Q.M.H.), Oldmeldrum Rd, AB2 9LN, 𝒫 713911, Telex 73108, Fax 714020, ⓕ₆, 🔲 – |≥| ⇔ rm 📺 ☎ 🅿 – 🔬 180. 🔼 🅰🅴 ⓄⒹ 𝑽𝑰𝑺𝑨
M (closed lunch Saturday and Bank Holidays) 8.95/17.25 **st.** and a la carte ⓐ 5.95 – ⌂ 9.95 – **144 rm** 68.00/95.00 **t.**

at Dyce NW : 5 ½ m. by A 96 – X – on A 947 – ✉ ☎ 0224 Aberdeen :

🏨 **Aberdeen Marriott,** Riverview Drive, Farburn, AB2 0AZ, ✆ 770011, Fax 722347, *ₔ*, ⭲s,
⊠ – ⇌ rm ▤ ⛉ ☎ & 𝚽 – 🏛 380. 🝏 🝓 ⓪ 𝗩𝗜𝗦𝗔 ⛖
M 15.95 **st.** (lunch) and a la carte 15.65/20.45 **st.** ⅃ 7.25 – ⚏ 10.25 – **153 rm** 63.00/
125.00 **st.**, 1 suite – SB (weekends only) 80.00/280.00 **st.**

at Aberdeen Airport NW : 6 m. by A 96 – X – ✉ ☎ 0224 Aberdeen :

🏨 **Aberdeen Airport Skean Dhu** (Mt. Charlotte Thistle), Argyll Rd, AB2 0DU, ✆ 725252,
Telex 739239, Fax 723745, ⛲ heated – ⇌ rm ▣ ☎ & 𝚽 – 🏛 600. 🝏 🝓 ⓪ 𝗩𝗜𝗦𝗔 𝗝𝗖𝗕
M (bar lunch Saturday and Sunday) 13.00/20.00 **t.** and a la carte – ⚏ 8.50 – **148 rm**
87.00/109.00 **st.** – SB (weekends only) 140.00 **st.**

🏠 **Speedbird Inn,** Argyll Rd, AB2 0AF, ✆ 772884, Fax 772560 – ⇌ rm ▣ ☎ & 𝚽. 🝏 🝓
𝗩𝗜𝗦𝗔
M a la carte 8.40/16.20 **t.** ⅃ 2.75 – ⚏ 3.75 – **100 rm** 32.50/42.50 **t.** – SB (weekends only)
56.80/109.30 **st.**

🚗 ATS Beach Boulevard ✆ 592727   ATS 214 Hardgate ✆ 589461

Fife. (Fife) 𝟰𝟬𝟭 K 15 *Scotland G.* – pop. 1 460 – ECD : Wednesday – ☎ 0383.

See : Town★ - Aberdour Castle★ *AC.*

🛞 Seaside Pl. ✆ 860080.

♦Edinburgh 17 – Dunfermline 7.

🏨 **Woodside,** 80 High St., KY3 0SW, ✆ 860328, Fax 860920, ⛫s – ▣ ☎ 𝚽. 🝏 🝓 ⓪ 𝗩𝗜𝗦𝗔
M 12.50/17.50 **t.** and a la carte ⅃ 4.15 – **20 rm** ⚏ 53.00/59.50 **t.**, 1 suite.

Perth. (Tayside) 𝟰𝟬𝟭 I 14 *Scotland G.* – pop. 1 477 – ECD : Wednesday – ☎ 0887.

See : Town★.

Envir. : St. Mary's Church (painted ceiling★) NE : 2 m. by A 827.

Exc. : Loch Tay★★, SW : 6 m. by A 827 – Ben Lawers★★, SW : 16 m. by A 827 – Blair Castle★★
AC, N : 20 ½ m. by A 827 and A 9.

🛞 Taybridge Rd ✆ 820535.

🅱 The Square ✆ 820276.

♦Edinburgh 76 – ♦Glasgow 73 – ♦Oban 77 – Perth 32.

🏨 **Farleyer House** ⛇, PH15 2JE, W : 2 m. on B 846 ✆ 820332, Fax 829430, ⛰ Tay Valley,
⛳, ⛲, park – ⇌ ▣ ☎ 𝚽. 🝏 🝓 ⓪ 𝗩𝗜𝗦𝗔. ⛖
M – **Menzies** *(closed Sunday to Thursday November-March)* (dinner only) 29.00 **t.** ⅃ 5.50 –
Bistro a la carte 11.25/19.50 **t.** ⅃ 4.50 – **11 rm** ⚏ 50.00/110.00 **t.** – SB (except Christmas and
New Year) 140.00/220.00 **st.**

🏠 **Guinach House** ⛇, Urlar Rd, PH15 2ET, off Crieff Rd ✆ 820251, ⛰, ⛲ – ⇌ rest ▣ 𝚽.
🝏 𝗩𝗜𝗦𝗔
M 18.50 **t.** – **7 rm** ⚏ 35.00/70.00 **t.**

Stirling (Central) 𝟰𝟬𝟭 G 15 *Scotland G.* – pop. 546 – ECD : Wednesday –
✉ Stirling – ☎ 087 72 (3 fig.) and 0877 (6 fig.).

Envir. : The Trossachs★★★ (Loch Katherine★★) N : 5 m. by A 821 – Hilltop Viewpoint★★★
(⛰★★★) N : 2 ½ m. by A 821 – Inchmahone Priory (double effigy★) *AC*, E : 4 m. by A 81.

Exc. : Ben Lomond★★, W : 16 m. by B 829.

🛞 Braeval ✆ 493.

🅱 Main St. ✆ 352 (summer only).

♦Edinburgh 56 – ♦Glasgow 27.

🍴 ☼ **Braeval Old Mill** (Nairn), FK8 3UY, E : 1 m. by A 821 on A 81 ✆ 711 – 𝚽. 🝏 𝗩𝗜𝗦𝗔
closed Sunday dinner, Monday, 1 week February and 2 weeks November – **M** (booking
essential) (light lunch by arrangement Tuesday to Saturday)/dinner 27.50 **t.**
Spec. Salmon and cod fishcake with langoustines and a caviar butter sauce, Wild mushroom soup, Caramelised apple
tart with cinnamon sauce.

E. Lothian. (Lothian) 𝟰𝟬𝟭 L 15 – pop. 884 – ECD : Wednesday – ☎ 087 57 (3 fig.)
and 0875 (6 fig.).

♦Edinburgh 16 – Haddington 5 – North Berwick 7.5.

🏠 **Green Craig Country House** ⛇, EH32 0PY, SW : ¾ m. on A 198 ✆ 301, Fax 440, ⛰, ⛲
– ▣ ☎ 𝚽. 🝏 🝓 ⓪ 𝗩𝗜𝗦𝗔
M 23.00 **t.** and a la carte ⅃ 4.80 – **5 rm** ⚏ 60.00/90.00 **t.**, 1 suite – SB (mid October-April
except Christmas and New Year) 95.00/150.00 **st.**

🏠 **Kilspindie House,** Main St., EH32 0RE, ✆ 682, Fax 504 – ▣ ☎ 𝚽. 🝏 𝗩𝗜𝗦𝗔. ⛖
M (bar lunch Monday to Saturday)/dinner 13.50 – **26 rm** ⚏ 40.00/68.00 **t.** – SB (weekends
only) 79.00/90.00 **st.**

ABERLOUR Banff. (Grampian) 401 K 11 – ❀ 034 06 Carron (due to change to 0340).

◆Edinburgh 192 – ◆Aberdeen 60 – Elgin 15 – ◆Inverness 55.

🏛 **Dowans**, AB38 9LS, SW : ¾ m. by A 95 ☎ 871488, Fax 871038, ☞ – ☎ ℗. 🔄 𝑉𝐼𝑆𝐴
closed January-mid February – **M** (bar lunch)/dinner 18.50 **t.** ♟ 4.50 – **17 rm** 🛏 39.50/
70.00 **t.**

ABINGTON SERVICE AREA Lanark. (Strathclyde) – ✉ Biggar – ❀ 086 42 Crawford.

◆Edinburgh 43 – Dumfries 37 – ◆Glasgow 38.

🏛 **Forte Travelodge** without rest., ML12 6RG, at junction of A 74 with M 74 ☎ 782,
Reservations (Freephone) 0800 850950 – 📺 & ℗. 🔄 𝖠𝖤 𝑉𝐼𝑆𝐴. ✻
56 rm 31.95 **t.**

ABOYNE Aberdeen. (Grampian) 401 L 12 Scotland G. – pop. 1 477 – ECD : Thursday –
❀ 033 98.

Exc. : Craigievar Castle★ *AC*, NE : 12 m. by B 9094, B 9119 and A 980.

🏌 Formanston Park ☎ 86328, NE : 1½ m. by A 93.

🛈 Ballater Road Car Park ☎ 86060 (summer only).

◆Edinburgh 131 – ◆Aberdeen 30 – ◆Dundee 68.

🏛 **Birse Lodge** ⊗, Charleston Rd, AB34 5EL, ☎ 86253, ☞ – 📺 ☎ ℗. 🔄 𝖠𝖤 𝑉𝐼𝑆𝐴
M (bar lunch)/dinner 16.00 **t.** ♟ 4.30 – **16 rm** 🛏 39.00/70.00 **t.**

⌂ **Hazlehurst Lodge,** Ballater Rd, AB34 5HY, ☎ 86921, ☞ – ✺ ℗. 🔄 𝖠𝖤 ⓞ 𝑉𝐼𝑆𝐴
March-November – **M** 25.00 **t.** ♟ 7.00 – **3 rm** 🛏 30.00/54.00 **t.**

*The names of main shopping streets are indicated in red
at the beginning of the list of streets.*

ACHILTIBUIE Ross and Cromarty. (Highland) 401 D 9 – ❀ 085 482.

◆Edinburgh 243 – ◆Inverness 84 – Ullapool 25.

🏛 **Summer Isles** ⊗, IV26 2YG, ☎ 282, Fax 251, « Picturesque setting ≼ Summer Isles »,
⟍ – ✺ rest ⟍
April-mid October ℗ – Meals (booking essential) (dinner only) 31.00 **st.** – **11 rm** 🛏 41.00/
88.00 **st.**, 1 suite.

AIRTH Stirling. (Central) 401 I 15 – pop. 972 – ✉ Falkirk – ❀ 0324.

◆Edinburgh 30 – Dunfermline 14 – Falkirk 7 – Stirling 8.

🏰 **Airth Castle** ⊗, FK2 8JF, ☎ 831411, Telex 777975, Fax 831419, ≼, « Part 13C and 17C
castle and stables in extensive grounds », ♟₆, ≋, 🔲, ☞, park – 🖹 📺 ☎ & ℗ – ♟ 400.
🔄 𝖠𝖤 ⓞ 𝑉𝐼𝑆𝐴 ✻
M *(closed Saturday lunch)* 11.75/17.50 **t.** and a la carte – **75 rm** 🛏 75.00/100.00 **t.** –
SB (weekends only) 84.50/90.00 **st.**

ALLOA Stirling. (Central) 401 I 15 Scotland G. – pop. 26 362 – ❀ 0259.

Exc. : Culross★★★ (Village★★★, Palace★★ *AC*, Study★ *AC*) SE : 7 m. by A 907, A 977 and B 9037
– Castle Campbell★ (site★★★, ≼★) *AC*, NE : 8 m. by A 908 and A 91 – Stirling★★, W : 8 m.
by A 907.

🏌 Schawpark, Sauchie ☎ 722745, N : 2 m. – 🏌 Braehead, Cambus ☎ 722078, NW : 2 m.
by A 977.

◆Edinburgh 33 – ◆Dundee 48 – ◆Glasgow 35.

🏛 **Gean House** ⊗, Gean Park, Tullibody Rd, FK10 2HS, NW : 1 m. on B 9096 ☎ 219275,
Fax 213827, ≼, ☞ – ✺ rest 📺 ☎ ℗ – ♟ 50. 🔄 𝖠𝖤 ⓞ 𝑉𝐼𝑆𝐴 ✻
M (booking essential) 17.00/32.00 **t.** ♟ 6.00 – **7 rm** 🛏 70.00/140.00 **t.** – SB (weekends only)
150.00/218.00 **st.**

🔧 ATS Union St. ☎ 724253

ALLOWAY Ayr. (Strathclyde) 401 402 G 17 – see Ayr.

ALTENS Aberdeen. (Grampian) – see Aberdeen.

ALTNACEALGACH Sutherland. (Highland) 401 F 9 – ✉ Lairg – ❀ 085 486 Strathkanaird.

◆Edinburgh 235 – ◆Inverness 79 – Ullapool 20.

⛨ **Altnacealgach** ⊗, IV27 4HF, on A 837 ☎ 220, ≼, ⟍ – ℗. ✻
M (in bar) (residents only) 15.00 **t.** – **4 rm** 🛏 30.00/50.00 **t.**

ALTNAHARRA Sutherland. (Highland) 401 G 9 Scotland G. – ✉ Lairg – ❀ 054 981.

Exc. : Ben Loyal★★, N : 10 m. by A 836 – Ben Hope★ (≼★★★) NW : 14 m.

◆Edinburgh 239 – ◆Inverness 83 – Thurso 61.

🏛 **Altnaharra** ⊗, IV27 4UE, ☎ 222, Fax 222, ≼, ⟍, ☞ – ✺ rest ℗. 🔄 𝑉𝐼𝑆𝐴
March-10 October – **M** (bar lunch)/dinner 17.50 **t.** and a la carte ♟ 4.50 – **18 rm** 🛏 42.00/
84.00 **t.** – SB (except July and August) 74.00/80.00 **st.**

ALYTH Perth. (Tayside) 401 J 14 – pop. 2 256 – ✆ 082 83.

┌₈ Pitcrocknie ♗ 2268, E : 1 ½ m.

◆Edinburgh 63 – ◆Aberdeen 69 – ◆Dundee 16 – Perth 21.

🏨 **Lands of Loyal** ♧, Loyal Rd, PH11 8JQ, N : ½ m. by B 952 ♗ 3151, Fax 3313, ≼, ⚞ – 📺
☎ 🅿. ⚞ Æ ⓪ 𝘝𝘐𝘚𝘈
M 21.75 **t.** (dinner) and a la carte 10.75/18.90 **t.** 𝟆 4.95 – **14 rm** 🖙 40.00/65.00 **t.**

ANNAN Dumfries (Dumfries and Galloway) 401 402 K 19 – ✆ 0461.

◆ Edinburgh 87 – Carlisle 15 – Dumfries 16 – ◆Glasgow 84.

🏠 **Northfield House,** DG12 5LL, N : 1 m. on B 722 (Eaglesfield rd) ♗ 202851, ⚲, ⚞ – ⥥
📺 🅿
M (by arrangement) (residents only) 21.00 **t.** – **3 rm** 🖙 50.00/80.00 **t.**

ANSTRUTHER Fife. (Fife) 401 L 15 Scotland G. – pop. 2 865 – ECD : Wednesday – ✆ 0333.

See : Scottish Fisheries Museum★★ AC.

Envir. : The East Neuk★★ – Crail★★ (Old Centre★★, Upper Crail★) NE : 4 m. by A 917.

Exc. : Kellie Castle★ AC, NW : 7 m. by B 9171, B 942 and A 917.

┌₉ Marsfield Shore Rd ♗ 310956.

🎇 Scottish Fisheries Museum ♗ 311073 (summer only).

◆Edinburgh 46 – ◆Dundee 23 – Dunfermline 34.

⌂ **Spindrift,** Pittenweem Rd, KY10 3DT, ♗ 310573 – ⥥ 🅿. ⚞ 𝘝𝘐𝘚𝘈. ⚞
M (by arrangement) 18.50 **st.** 𝟆 3.60 – **5 rm** 🖙 31.00/50.00 **st.** – SB 60.00/90.00 **st.**

✗ **Cellar,** 24 East Green, KY10 3AA, ♗ 310378 – ⥥. ⚞ Æ 𝘝𝘐𝘚𝘈
closed Monday lunch, Sunday, 1 week May and 1 week November – **M** - Seafood 27.50 **t.**
(dinner) and lunch a la carte 10.95/17.95 **t.**

ARBROATH Angus. (Tayside) 401 M 14 Scotland G. – pop. 23 934 – ECD : Wednesday –
✆ 0241.

See : Town★ - Abbey★ AC.

Envir. : St. Vigeans★, N : 1 ½ m. by A 92.

┌₈ Arbroath, Elliot ♗ 72069, S : 1 m. by A 92.

🎇 Market Pl., ♗ 72609.

◆Edinburgh 72 – ◆Aberdeen 51 – ◆Dundee 16.

🏨 **Letham Grange** ♧, Colliston, DD11 4RL, NW : 4 ¾ m. by A 933 ♗ 024 189 (Gowan-
bank) 373, Fax 414, ≼, ┌₈, ⚞, park – 📺 ☎ 🅿 – 𝟆 50. ⚞ Æ ⓪ 𝘝𝘐𝘚𝘈. ⚞
M 12.50/18.75 **st.** – **19 rm** 🖙 73.00/116.00 **st.**, 1 suite – SB 154.00/191.00 **st.**

ARCHIESTOWN Moray. (Grampian) 401 K 11 – ✉ Aberlour (Banff) – ✆ 034 06 Carron (due
to change to 0340).

◆Edinburgh 194 – ◆Aberdeen 62 – ◆Inverness 49.

🏠 **Archiestown,** AB38 7QX, ♗ 218 (due to change to 810218), Fax 239 (due to change to
810239), ⚞ 📺 ☎ 🅿. ⚞ 𝘝𝘐𝘚𝘈
March-November – **M** - (see below) – **8 rm** 🖙 27.50/70.00 **st.**

✗✗ **Archiestown,** AB38 7QX, ♗ 218 (due to change to 810218), Fax 239 (due to change to
810239) – 🅿. ⚞ 𝘝𝘐𝘚𝘈
March-November – **M** (bar lunch)/dinner 22.50 **st.** and a la carte 𝟆 5.50.

ARDENTINNY Argyll. (Strathclyde) 401 F 15 – ECD : Wednesday – ✉ Dunoon – ✆ 036 981.

◆Edinburgh 107 – Dunoon 13 – ◆Glasgow 64 – ◆Oban 71.

🏠 **Ardentinny** ♧, PA23 8TR, ♗ 209, Fax 345, ≼ Loch Long, ⚞ – ⥥ rest 📺 ☎ 🅿. ⚞ Æ
⓪ 𝘝𝘐𝘚𝘈
mid March-October – **M** (bar lunch)/dinner 25.00 **t.** and a la carte 𝟆 4.00 – **11 rm** 🖙 47.00/
90.00 **st.** – SB (except June-September) 74.00/127.00 **st.**

ARDEONAIG Perth. (Central) 401 H 14 – see Killin.

ARDGAY Sutherland. (Highland) 401 G 10 – ✆ 086 32.

◆Edinburgh 205 – ◆Inverness 49 – Wick 77.

🏠 **Ardgay House,** IV24 3DH, ♗ 345, ⚞ – 📺 🅿. ⚞
March-November – **M** (residents only) (dinner only) 12.00 **st.** – **6 rm** 🖙 25.00/40.00 **st.**

ARDRISHAIG Argyll. (Strathclyde) 401 D 15 – pop. 1 283 – ✉ ✆ 0546 Lochgilpead.

◆Edinburgh 132 – ◆Glasgow 86 – ◆Oban 40.

⌂ **Allt-na-Craig,** Tarbert Rd, PA30 8EP, on A 83 ♗ 603245, ≼, ⚞ – ⥥ rest 🅿
closed Christmas and New Year – **M** (by arrangement) 15.00 **st.** 𝟆 3.25 – **6 rm** 🖙 28.00/
56.00 **st.** – SB (except Bank Holidays) 74.00/84.00 **st.**

⌂ **Fascadale House** without rest., PA30 8EP, on A 83 ♗ 603845, ≼, ⚞ – ⥥ 🅿. ⚞
March-October – **3 rm** 🖙 20.00/44.00 **st.**

Argyll. (Strathclyde) 401 D 15 Scotland G. – ECD : Wednesday – ⊠ Oban – ✆ 085 22 Kilmelford.

Exc. : Loch Awe★★, E : 12 m.ˈ by A 816 and B 840.

◆Edinburgh 142 – ◆Oban 20.

🏨 **Loch Melfort** 🦢, PA34 4XG, ℰ 233, Fax 214, ≤ Sound of Jura, ☞, park – ⇟⇟ rest 📺 ☎ 🅿. ☒ 𝘝𝘐𝘚𝘈
closed 5 January-25 February – **M** (bar lunch)/dinner 24.00 ¦ 6.95 – **26 rm** ⊑ 57.50/105.00 **t.**, 2 suites.

ARDVASAR Inverness. (Highland) 401 C 12 – see Skye (Isle of).

ARINAGOUR Argyll. (Strathclyde) 401 A 14 – see Coll (Isle of).

ARISAIG Inverness. (Highland) 401 C 13 Scotland G. – ECD : Thursday – ✆ 068 75.

See : Village★.

Envir. : Silver Sands of Morar★, N : 5½ m. by A 830.

🧭 Traigh, 5 Back of Keppoch ℰ 262.

◆Edinburgh 172 – ◆Inverness 102 – ◆Oban 88.

🏨🏨 **Arisaig House** 🦢, Beasdale, PH39 4NR, SE : 3¼ m. on A 830 ℰ 622, Fax 626, ≤ Loch nan Uamh and Roshven, « Gardens », ⇟⇟ rest 📺 ☎ 🅿. ☒ 𝘈𝘌 𝘝𝘐𝘚𝘈. ⚘
April-October – **M** (booking essential) (light lunch)/dinner 40.00 **t.** ¦ 7.00 – **11 rm** ⊑ 68.50/205.00 **t.**, 2 suites.

🏠 **Arisaig,** PH39 4NH, ℰ 210, Fax 310, ≤ – ⇟⇟ rest ☎ 🅿. ☒ 𝘝𝘐𝘚𝘈. ⚘
March-October – **M** (bar lunch)/dinner a la carte 10.15/20.95 **t.** ¦ 4.75 – ⊑ 8.50 – **15 rm** 20.00/62.50 **t.**

✗ **Old Library Lodge** with rm, High St., PH39 4NH, ℰ 651, ≤ Loch nan Ceall and Inner Hebridean Isles – 📺. ☒ 𝘝𝘐𝘚𝘈
Easter-October – **M** 19.50 **st.** (dinner) and lunch a la carte – **6 rm** ⊑ 40.00/59.00 **st.**

*Great Britain and Ireland are covered entirely
at a scale of 16 miles to 1 inch by our map « Main roads » 986.*

ARRAN (Isle of) Bute. (Strathclyde) 401 402 DE 16 17 Scotland G. – pop. 4 726.

See : Island★★ - Brodick Castle★★ AC.

⚓ by Caledonian MacBrayne : from Brodick to Ardrossan, 4-6 daily – from Lochranza to Claonaig (Kintyre Peninsula) (summer only) : frequent services daily (30 mn) – The Pier, Lochranza ℰ 320 (summer only).

Brodick – pop. 884 – ECD : Wednesday – ⊠ ✆ 0770 Brodick.

🧭 Brodick ℰ 302349 – 🧭 Machrie Bay ℰ 077 084 (Machrie Bay) 261.

🅱 The Pier ℰ 302140/302401.

🏨🏨 **Auchrannie Country House,** KA27 8BZ, ℰ 302234, Fax 302812, ₤₅, ☲s, ▨, ☞ – ⇟⇟ rest 📺 ☎ & 🅿. ☒ 𝘝𝘐𝘚𝘈 ⚘
M 22.50 **st.** (dinner) and a la carte 10.00/17.75 **st.** – **26 rm** ⊑ 58.00/96.00 **st.**, 2 suites.

🏠 **Kilmichael Country House** 🦢, Glencloy, KA27 8BY, 1 m. by Shore Rd, taking left turn opposite Golf Club ℰ 302215, ☞ – ⇟⇟ 🅿
April-October and January – **M** (dinner only) 21.00 **t.** ¦ 4.00 – **5 rm** ⊑ 38.00/75.00 **t.**, 1 suite.

🏠 **Arran,** Shore Rd, KA27 8AJ, ℰ 302265, Fax 302265, ≤, ☲s, ▨, ☞ – ⇟⇟ rest 📺 ☎ 🅿. ☒ 𝘝𝘐𝘚𝘈
M (bar lunch)/dinner 11.50 and a la carte ¦ 4.50 – **16 rm** ⊑ 29.00/65.00 **t.**

↑ **Glen Cloy Farmhouse** 🦢, KA27 8DA, ℰ 302351, ☞ – ⇟⇟ rest 🅿
March-6 November – **M** 16.50 **s.** – **5 rm** ⊑ 20.00/50.00 **s.**

↑ **Dunvegan House,** Shore Rd, KA27 8AJ, ℰ 302811, ≤, ☞ – ⇟⇟ rm 📺 🅿. ⚘
M 13.00 **s.** – **10 rm** ⊑ 19.50/52.00 **st.**

Lamlash – pop. 908 – ECD : Wednesday except summer – ⊠ Brodick – ✆ 0770 Lamlash.

🧭 Lamlash ℰ 606296.

🏠 Glenisle, Shore Rd, KA27 8LS, ℰ 600559, ≤, ☞ – 📺 ☎ 🅿
13 rm.

✗✗ **Carraig Mhor,** Shore Rd, KA27 8LS, ℰ 600453 – ⇟⇟. ☒ 𝘝𝘐𝘚𝘈
April-October – **M** *(closed Sunday)* (dinner only) a la carte 16.50/23.00 **st.**

Lochranza – ⊠ ✆ 0770 Lochranza.

🧭 Lochranza ℰ 830273.

🅱 The Pier ℰ 830320 (summer only).

↑ **Apple Lodge,** KA27 8HJ, ℰ 830229, Fax 830229, ☞ – 📺 🅿. ⚘
M 12.00 **st.** – **3 rm** ⊑ 40.00/50.00 **st.** – SB (winter only) 64.00 **st.**

↑ **Butt Lodge** 🦢, KA27 8JF, SE : ½ m. by Brodick Rd ℰ 830240, ≤, ☞ – ⇟⇟ 🅿. ☒ 𝘝𝘐𝘚𝘈. ⚘
April-October – **M** 12.50 **st.** – **5 rm** ⊑ 32.50/55.00 **st.**

Whiting Bay – ECD : Wednesday except summer – ✉ ☎ 0770 Whiting Bay.

🏇 Whiting Bay ✆ 700487.

🏠 **Royal,** Shore Rd, KA27 8PZ, ✆ 700286, ≤, 🐎 – ⇔ rest 📺 ☎ 🅿
March-October – **M** 11.00. **st.** – **6 rm** ⚏ 20.00/52.00. **st.**

ARROCHAR Dunbarton (Strathclyde) 401 F 15 Scotland G. – pop. 417 – ECD : Wednesday –
☎ 030 12.

Envir. : E : Ben Lomond★★.

Exc. : S : Loch Lomond★★.

♦Edinburgh 83 – ♦Glasgow 35 – ♦Oban 57.

🏠 **Succoth Farmhouse** 🏖 without rest., G83 7AL, N : ¾ m. on Succoth rd ✆ 591, 🐎 – ⇔
🅿. 🛇
April-September – **3 rm** ⚏ 15.00/28.00.

🏠 **Mansefield Country House,** G83 7AG, ✆ 282, ≤, 🐎 – ⇔ 📺 🅿
M (by arrangement) 15.00 **st.** – **5 rm** ⚏ 23.00/37.00 **st.**

AUCHENCAIRN Kirkcudbright. (Dumfries and Galloway) 401 402 I 19 – ✉ Castle Douglas –
☎ 055 664.

♦Edinburgh 98 – ♦Dumfries 21 – Stranraer 62.

🏛 **Collin House** 🏖, DG7 1QN, N : 1 m. by A 711 ✆ 292, « Part 18C country house,
≤ Auchencairn Bay and Cumbrian Mountains », 🐎, park – ⇔ rest 📺 ☎ 🅿. 🖭 VISA 🛇
closed 4 January-11 March – **M** (lunch residents only)/dinner 26.00 **st.** 🛇 4.80 – **6 rm**
⚏ 52.00/76.00. **st.**

🏠 **Bluehill Farm** 🏖 without rest., DG7 1QW, W : 1 m. by A 711 ✆ 228, ≤, 🐎, park – ⇔ 📺
🅿. 🛇
June-September – **3 rm** ⚏ 40.00.

AUCHTERARDER Perth. (Tayside) 401 I 15 Scotland G. – pop. 2 838 – ECD : Wednesday –
☎ 0764.

Envir. : Tullibardine Chapel★, NW : 2 m.

🏇 Ochil Rd ✆ 662804, SW : 1½ m. by A 824 – 🏇 Rollo Park, Dunning ✆ 0764 84 (Dunning) 747,
E : 4 m. by A 8062 and B 9141.

🅱 90 High St. ✆ 663450.

♦Edinburgh 55 – ♦Glasgow 45 – Perth 14.

🏨 **Gleneagles,** PH3 1NF, SW : 2 m. by A 824 on A 823 ✆ 662231, Telex 76105, Fax 662134,
≤, « Championship golf courses and extensive leisure facilities », 🏊, ⚏, 🏊, 🏇, 🏇, ⚓,
🐎, park, 🎾, squash – 🛗 ⇔ rm 🗏 rest 📺 ☎ 🖕 🅿 – 🕰 250. 🖭 🖭 ⓪ VISA JCB
M 25.00/50.00 **t.** and a la carte 🛇 9.00 – **218 rm** ⚏ 150.00/290.00 **t.,** 18 suites – SB 239.00/
299.00 **st.**

🏛 **Auchterarder House** 🏖, PH3 1DZ, N : 1½ m. on B 8062 ✆ 663646, Fax 662939, ≤,
« Scottish Jacobean house », 🐎, park – ⇔ rest 📺 ☎ 🅿. 🖭 🖭 ⓪ VISA
M (booking essential) 27.50/50.00 **t.** 🛇 7.50 – **13 rm** ⚏ 90.00/195.00 **t.,** 2 suites – SB (ex-
cept Christmas) 160.00/250.00 **st.**

🏛 **Cairn Lodge,** Tullibardine Rd, PH3 1LX, ✆ 662634, 🐎 – 📺 ☎ 🅿. 🖭 🖭 VISA
M (grill rest.) (bar lunch)/dinner a la carte 11.00/21.00 **st.** 🛇 4.50 – **6 rm** ⚏ 40.00/65.00 **st.**

🏛 **Duchally House** 🏖, PH3 1PN, S : 4 m. by A 824 off A 823 ✆ 663071, Fax 662464, ≤, 🐎,
park – 📺 ☎ 🅿 – 🕰 40. 🖭 🖭 ⓪ VISA
M 16.50/25.00 **st.** and a la carte 🛇 3.95 – **13 rm** ⚏ 50.00/90.00 **st.** – SB 85.00/160.00 **st.**

🏛 **Collearn House,** PH3 1DF, ✆ 663553, Fax 662376, 🐎 – ⇔ rm 📺 ☎ 🅿. 🖭 🖭 VISA. 🛇
M 25.00/30.00 **t.** 🛇 4.50 – **8 rm** ⚏ 55.00/80.00 **t.** – SB 95.00/135.00 **st.**

AUCHTERHOUSE Angus. (Tayside) 401 K 14 – ✉ Dundee – ☎ 082 626 (3 fig.) and 0382
(5 and 6 fig.).

♦Edinburgh 69 – ♦Dundee 7 – Perth 24.

✖✖✖ **Old Mansion House** 🏖 with rm, DD3 0QN, ✆ 366, Fax 400, ≤, « Part 15C and 17C
country house », 🏊 heated, 🐎, park, 🎾, squash – ⇔ rest 📺 ☎ 🅿. 🖭 🖭 ⓪ VISA. 🛇
closed Christmas and New Year – **M** 15.95 **s.** (lunch) and a la carte 22.50/27.95 **st.** 🛇 5.00 –
6 rm ⚏ 70.00/115.00 **st.**

AULTBEA Ross and Cromarty. (Highland) 401 D 10 Scotland G. – ECD : Wednesday – ☎ 0445.

Envir. : Inverewe Gardens★★★ AC, S : 5½ m. by A 832.

Exc. : Loch Maree★★★, S : 10 m. by A 832.

♦Edinburgh 234 – ♦Inverness 79 – Kyle of Lochalsh 80.

🏛 **Aultbea,** IV22 2HX, ✆ 731201, Fax 731214, ≤, 🐎 – 📺 ☎ 🅿. 🖭 VISA
M (bar lunch)/dinner 20.00 **t.** and a la carte 🛇 3.95 – **8 rm** ⚏ 34.00/80.00 **t.** – SB (October-
April, except Easter, Christmas and New Year) 80.00 **st.**

Les prix Pour toutes précisions sur les prix indiqués dans ce guide,
reportez-vous à l'introduction.

AVIEMORE Inverness. (Highland) 401 | 12 Scotland G. – pop. 1 510 – ECD : Wednesday - Winter sports – ✪ 0479.

See : Town★.

Exc. : The Cairngorms★★ (←★★★) - ❅★★★ from Cairn Gorm, SE : 11 m. by B 970 – Landmark Visitor Centre (The Highlander★) *AC*, N : 7 m. by A 9 – Highland Wildlife Park★ *AC*, SW : 7 m by A 9.

🛈 Grampian Rd ✆ 810363.

◆Edinburgh 129 – ◆Inverness 29 – Perth 85.

 🏨 **Stakis Aviemore Four Seasons,** Aviemore Centre, PH22 1PF, ✆ 810681, Fax 810534 ← Cairngorms, ₤₅, ⌚, 🖼 – 🔊 ⇔ rm 📺 ☎ 🅿 – 🔬 100. 🔼 🖭 ⓪ 𝘝𝘐𝘚𝘈
  M (dancing Saturday evening) (buffet lunch)/dinner 17.50 **st.** and a la carte – ⌐ 8.50
  88 rm 73.00/125.00 **st.** – SB 92.00/126.00 **st.**

 🏠 **Corrour House** ⌚, Inverdruie, PH22 1QH, SE : 1 m. on B 970 ✆ 810220, Fax 811500, ← ✎ – ⇔ rest 📺 ☎ 🅿. 🔼 𝘝𝘐𝘚𝘈
  closed November-January – **M** (dinner only) 18.00 **st.** ⅃ 3.00 – **8 rm** ⌐ 25.00/60.00 **st.**

 ↑ **Lynwilg House,** Lynwilg, PH22 1PZ, S : 2 m. by B 9152 on A 9 ✆ 811685, ←, ✎, ✎ – 📺 🅿. 🔼 𝘝𝘐𝘚𝘈. ❅
  closed November-27 December – **M** (by arrangement) 15.00 **st.** – **4 rm** ⌐ 16.00/40.00 **st.**

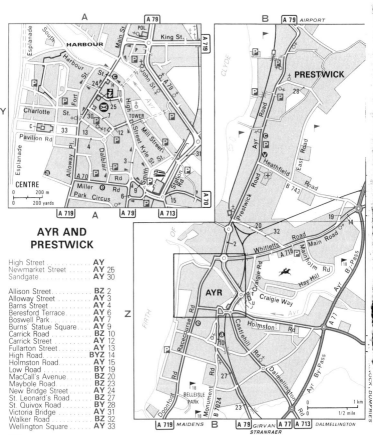

AYR AND PRESTWICK

Envir. : Alloway★ (Burns Cottage and Museum★ *AC*) S : 3 m. by B 7024 BZ.

Exc. : Culzean Castle★ *AC* (setting★★★, Oval Staircase★★) SW : 13 m. by A 719 BZ.

🔢 Belleisle *𝒫* 441258 BZ – 🔢 Dalmilling, Westwood Av., Whitletts *𝒫* 263893 BZ – 🔢 Doon Valley, Hillside, Patna *𝒫* 531607, NE : boundary by A 713 BZ.

🔢 39 Sandgate *𝒫* 284196.

◆Edinburgh 81 – ◆Glasgow 35.

Plan on preceding page

🏨 **Fairfield House,** 12 Fairfield Rd, KA7 2AR, *𝒫* 267461, Fax 261456, 🕿, 🔲, 🖙 – 📺 ☎ 🅿. 🔼 🖭 ⑩ *VISA* 🎉
AY **a**
M (dinner only and Sunday lunch)/dinner 19.50 – **30 rm** ⌷ 60.00/200.00 t., 1 suite – SB 145.00/240.00 **st.**

🏨 **Kylestrome,** 11 Miller rd, KA7 2AX, *𝒫* 262474, Fax 260863 – 📺 ☎ 🅿 – 🔼 25. 🔼 🖭 ⑩
VISA 🎉
AY **e**
M *(in bar Saturday and Sunday)* a la carte 11.00/29.50 **t.** – **12 rm** ⌷ 50.00/85.00 **t.** – SB (weekends only) 100.00/110.00 **st.**

🏨 **Pickwick,** 19 Racecourse Rd, KA7 2TD, *𝒫* 260111, Fax 285348 – 📺 ☎ 🅿. 🔼 🖭 ⑩ *VISA*
BZ **e**
M 10.75/17.50 **t.** and a la carte 🍷 5.75 – **15 rm** ⌷ 45.00/70.00 **t.**

↑ **Langley Bank** without rest., 39 Carrick rd, KA7 2RD, *𝒫* 264246 – 📺 ☎ 🅿. 🔼 🖭 🎉
BZ **a**
6 rm ⌷ 15.00/50.00 **st.**

🍴 **Fouters,** 2a Academy St., KA7 1HS, *𝒫* 261391 – 🔼 🖭 ⑩ *VISA*
AY **c**
closed Sunday lunch, Monday, 3 days at Christmas and 1 to 3 January – **M** 10.50/12.50 **t.** and a la carte 🍷 4.50.

at Alloway S : 3 m. on B 7024 – BZ – ✉ Ayr – 🕿 0292 Alloway :

🏨 **Northpark House** 🦢, 2 Alloway, KA7 4NL, *𝒫* 442336, Fax 445572 – 🖙 rest 📺 ☎ 🅿.
🔼 🖭 ⑩ *VISA*
M 18.00 **t.** (lunch) and a la carte 10.95/20.95 **t.** 🍷 4.75 – **5 rm** ⌷ 57.50/105.00 **t.** – SB (weekends only) 95.00/150.00 **st.**

🏠 Burns Monument, KA7 4PQ, *𝒫* 442466, Fax 443174, ≤, ≋, 🖙 – 📺 ☎
9 rm.

En saison, surtout dans les stations fréquentées, il est prudent de retenir à l'avance.
Cependant, si vous ne pouvez pas occuper la chambre que vous avez retenue,
prévenez immédiatement l'hôtelier.

Si vous écrivez à un hôtel à l'étranger, joignez à votre lettre
un coupon-réponse international (disponible dans les bureaux de poste).

Exc. : Glen Coe★★, E : 6 m. by A 82.

🔢 *𝒫* 296 (summer only).

◆Edinburgh 117 – ◆Inverness 80 – Kyle of Lochalsh 90 – ◆Oban 38.

🏨 **Ballachulish,** PA39 4JY, W : 2¼ m. by A 82 on A 828 *𝒫* 606, Fax 629, ≤, 🖙 – 📺 ☎ 🅿.
🔼 *VISA*
M (bar lunch)/dinner 21.50 **t.** and a la carte 🍷 4.60 – **30 rm** ⌷ 45.50/79.00 **t.** – SB 90.00 **st.**

🏨 **Isles of Glencoe,** PA39 4HL, *𝒫* 602, Fax 629, ≤ Loch Leven and the Pap of Glencoe, 🕿,
🔲, – 🖙 rest 📺 ☎ 👌 🅿. 🔼 🖭 *VISA*
M 16.00/18.50 **t.** and a la carte 🍷 4.50 – **39 rm** ⌷ 51.50/89.00 **t.**

↑ **Ballachulish House** 🦢, PA39 4JX, W : 2½ m. by A 82 on A 828 *𝒫* 266, ≤, 🖙 – 🖙 🅿.
🔼 *VISA* 🎉
closed Christmas – **M** 20.00 **st.** 🍷 4.25 – **4 rm** ⌷ 45.45/76.00 **st.**

↑ **Lyn Leven,** White St., PA39 4JP, *𝒫* 392, ≤, 🖙 – 🖙 rest 📺 🅿. 🔼 *VISA*
closed Christmas Day – **M** 9.50 – **8 rm** ⌷ 18.00/37.00 **t.**

◆Edinburgh 115 – ◆Ayr 33 – Stranraer 18.

↑ **Balkissock Lodge** 🦢, KA26 0LP, E : 4 m. by A 77 (South), taking first turning left after bridge *𝒫* 83537, Fax 83537, 🖙 – 🖙 📺 🅿. 🔼 *VISA* 🎉
closed November-mid December – **M** 19.50 **t.** – **3 rm** ⌷ 46.50/53.00 **t.**

🔢 Victoria Rd *𝒫* 55567.

🔢 Station Sq. *𝒫* 55306 (summer only).

◆Edinburgh 111 – ◆Aberdeen 41 – ◆Inverness 70 – Perth 67.

🏨 **Craigendarroch H. & Country Club,** Braemar Rd, AB35 5XA, on A 93 *𝒫* 55858, Fax 55447, ≤ Dee Valley and Grampians, 🏋, 🕿, 🔲, 🖙, 🍴, squash – 🛗 📺 ☎ 🅿 –
🔼 100. 🔼 🖭 ⑩ *VISA* 🎉
closed 5 to 7 January – **M** - Lochnagar (dinner only) 19.50 **st.** 🍷 6.75 – (see also **Oaks** below) – **49 rm** ⌷ 105.00/145.00 **t.**, 1 suite – SB (weekdays only) 110.00/216.00 **st.**

🏠 **Tullich Lodge** ⟨⟩, AB35 5SB, E : 1 ½ m. on A 93 ₰ 55406, Fax 55397, ≼ Dee Valley and Grampians, « Country house atmosphere », ⟨⟩ – ⤫ rest ☎ 🅿. ⟨⟩ 🅰🅴 ⓞ
VISA
April-November – **M** (booking essential) (bar lunch)/dinner 23.00 **st**. ◍ 6.00 – **10 rm** 🍽 (dinner included) 95.00/190.00 **st**. – SB 180.00 **st**.

🏠 **Balgonie Country House** ⟨⟩, Braemar Pl., AB35 5RQ, W : 1 m. by A 93 ₰ 55482, Fax 55482, ≼, ⟨⟩ – ⤫ rest ☎ 🅿. ⟨⟩
M (lunch by arrangement Monday to Saturday)/dinner 28.00 **t**. ◍ 6.00 – **9 rm** 🍽 (dinner included) 65.00/130.00 **t**. – SB (October-April) 110.00/150.00 **st**.

🏠 **Darroch Learg,** Braemar Rd, AB35 5UX, ₰ 55443, Fax 55443, ≼ Dee Valley and Gram-pians, ⟨⟩ – ⤫ rest 📺 ☎ 🅿. ⟨⟩ ⓞ **VISA**
closed January – **M** (light lunch Monday to Saturday)/dinner 19.75 **st**. ◍ 6.00 – **20 rm** 🍽 40.00/90.00 **st**. – SB (mid October-March) 156.00 **st**.

🏠 **Glen Lui,** 14 Invercauld Rd, AB35 5RP, ₰ 55402, Fax 55545, ≼, ⟨⟩ – ⤫ rest 📺 ☎ 🅿. ⟨⟩
🅰🅴 **VISA**
closed December and January – **M** (bar lunch)/dinner 19.50 **st**. and a la carte ◍ 4.30 – **17 rm** 🍽 30.00/70.00 **st**., 2 suites.

🏠 **Alexandra,** 12 Bridge Sq., AB35 5QJ, ₰ 55376, Fax 55466 – 📺 ☎ 🅿. ⟨⟩ 🅰🅴 ⓞ
VISA
M (bar lunch)/dinner 25.00 **t**. and a la carte ◍ 5.50 – **7 rm** 🍽 35.00/56.00 **t**. – SB (October-April) 76.00/96.00 **st**.

🏠 **Auld Kirk,** Braemar Rd, AB35 5RQ, ₰ 55762, Fax 55707, « Former 19C church » – 📺 ☎ 🅿. ⟨⟩ **VISA**
closed 25 December and 1-2 January – **M** 14.95 **t**. ◍ 3.50 – **6 rm** 🍽 25.00/40.00 **t**.

🏠 **Moorside House** without rest., 26 Braemar Rd, AB35 5RL, ₰ 55492, ⟨⟩ – 📺 🅿. ⟨⟩ **VISA**.
March-November – **9 rm** 🍽 27.00/36.00 **st**.

🏠 **Morvada** without rest., Braemar Rd, AB35 5RL, ₰ 55501, ⟨⟩ – 📺 🅿. ⟨⟩
June-October – **7 rm** 🍽 25.00/36.00 **st**.

🏠 **Highland** without rest., 12 Invercauld Rd, AB35 5RP, ₰ 55468, ⟨⟩ – ⤫ 📺 🅿. ⟨⟩
6 rm 🍽 15.00/40.00 **st**.

🏠 **Oaklands,** 30 Braemar Rd, AB35 5RL, ₰ 55013, ⟨⟩ – 📺 🅿.
May-September – **M** (by arrangement) 10.00 **st**. – **3 rm** 🍽 26.00/40.00 **st**.

🍴🍴🍴 **Oaks** (at Craigendarroch H.), Braemar Rd, AB35 5XA, on A 93 ₰ 55858, Fax 55447 – ⤫
🍽 🅿. ⟨⟩ 🅰🅴 ⓞ **VISA**
M (dinner only and Sunday lunch)/dinner 29.50 **st**. and a la carte ◍ 6.75.

🍴 **Green Inn** with rm, 9 Victoria Rd, AB35 5QQ, ₰ 55701 – 📺. ⟨⟩ **VISA**
closed 1 week January and 2 weeks October – **M** *(closed lunch Monday to Friday)* dinner a la carte 17.75/23.25 **st**. ◍ 4.75 – **3 rm** 🍽 35.00/40.00 **st**.

BALLOCH Dunbarton (Strathclyde) 🔲 G 15 Scotland G. – ✉ ⚙ 0389 Alexandria.

Envir. : N : Loch Lomond★★.

🚇 Balloch Road ₰ 53533 (summer only).

◆Edinburgh 72 – ◆Glasgow 20 – Stirling 30.

🏨 **Cameron House** ⟨⟩, Loch Lomond, G83 8QZ, NW : 1 ½ m. by A 811 and A 82 ₰ 55565, Fax 59522, ≼ Loch Lomond, « Lochside setting », ᒣ, ≋, ⟨⟩, ⟨⟩, ⟨⟩, ⟨⟩, park, ⟨⟩, squash – ㊐ ⤫ rm 🔲 ☎ ≋ 🅿. – ⟨⟩ 240. ⟨⟩ 🅰🅴 **VISA**. ⟨⟩
M - Brasserie a la carte 9.95/25.70 **t**. – (see also **Georgian Room** below) – **63 rm** 🍽 125.00/150.00 **t**., 5 suites.

🍴🍴🍴 **Georgian Room** (at Cameron House H.), Loch Lomond, G83 8QZ, ₰ 55565, Fax 59522, ≼ Loch Lomond, « Lochside setting », ⟨⟩ – ⤫ 🕭 🅿. ⟨⟩ 🅰🅴 **VISA**
closed lunch Saturday and Sunday – **M** (booking essential) 15.50/36.00 **t**. and a la carte ◍ 11.75.

BALLYGRANT Argyll. (Strathclyde) 🔲 B 16 – see Islay (Isle of).

BALQUHIDDER Perth. (Central) 🔲 G 14 – see Strathyre.

BANAVIE Inverness. (Highland) 🔲 E 13 – see Fort William.

BANCHORY Kincardine. (Grampian) 🔲 M 12 Scotland G. – pop. 4 683 – ECD : Thursday – ⚙ 0330.

Envir. : Crathes Castle★★ (Gardens★★★) *AC*, E : 3 m. by A 93.

Exc. : Dunnottar Castle★★ (site★★★) *AC*, SW : 15 ½ m. by A 93 and A 957 – Aberdeen★★, NE : 17 rm. by A 93.

ᒣ Kinneskie ₰ 822365 – ᒣ Torphins ₰ 033 98 (Lumphanan) 82115, NW : 7 m. by B 980.

🚇 Bridge St. ₰ 822000.

◆Edinburgh 118 – ◆Aberdeen 17 – ◆Dundee 55 – ◆Inverness 94.

🏨 **Raemoir House** ⟡, AB31 4ED, N : 2 ½ m. on A 980 ℰ 824884, Fax 822171, ≤, « 18C mansion with 16C Ha-House », ≦s, ☞, park, ✻ – ☑ ☎ & ℗ – 🕸 50. ☒ ㏂ ⓞ 𝑉𝐼𝑆𝐴 𝐽𝐶𝐵. ❀
closed first 2 weeks January – **M** (bar lunch Monday to Saturday)/dinner 24.50 **t.** and a la carte ♦ 6.50 – **19 rm** ⊇ 52.50/125.00 **t.**, 4 suites – SB (except Christmas and New Year) 115.00 **t.**

🏨 **Banchory Lodge** ⟡, Dee St., AB31 3HS, ℰ 822625, Fax 825019, ≤, « Part 18C house on River Dee », ≦s, ✎, ☞ – ☑ ☎ ℗. ☒ ㏂ ⓞ 𝑉𝐼𝑆𝐴
closed December and January – **M** 15.00/25.00 **st.** – **22 rm** ⊇ 60.00/120.00 **st.** – SB (October-March) 100.00/120.00 **st.**

🏨 **Tor-na-Coille,** Inchmarlo Rd, AB31 4AB, ℰ 22242, Fax 24012, ☞, squash – 🛗 ☑ ☎ ℗ – 🕸 80. ☒ ㏂ ⓞ 𝑉𝐼𝑆𝐴
closed 25 and 26 December – **M** (bar lunch Monday to Saturday)/dinner 25.00 **t.** and a la carte ♦ 7.00 – **23 rm** ⊇ 51.50/110.00 **t.** – SB (except Christmas and New Year) (weekends only) 83.00/119.00 **st.**

BANFF Banff. (Grampian) 𝟜𝟘𝟙 M 10 Scotland G. – pop. 3 843 – ECD : Wednesday – ✆ 0261.

See : Town★ - Duff House★ (baroque exterior★) *AC* – Mercat Cross★.

🏌 Royal Tarlair, Buchan St., Macduff ℰ 32548/32591, E : 2 m. by A 98 – 🏌 Duff House Royal, The Barnyards ℰ 812062, S : ½ m. by A 97.

🛈 Collie Lodge ℰ 812419 (summer only).

◆Edinburgh 177 – ◆Aberdeen 47 – Fraserburgh 26 – ◆Inverness 74.

🏠 **Eden House** ⟡, AB45 3NT, S : 5 m. by A 98 and A 947 on Scattertie Dunlugas rd ℰ 026 16 (Eden) 282, ≤, « Part 18C former shooting lodge overlooking River Deveron Valley », ✎, ☞, park, ✻ – ⇆ ℗ ❀
closed Christmas and New Year – **M** (by arrangement) (communal dining) 18.00 **st.** – **4 rm** ⊇ 32.00/64.00 **st.**

⊚ ATS Carmelite St. ℰ 812234

BARRHEAD Renfrew. (Strathclyde) 𝟜𝟘𝟙 𝟜𝟘𝟚 G 16 – ✉ ✆ 041 Glasgow.

◆Edinburgh 54 – ◆Ayr 35 – ◆Glasgow 8.

🏠 Dalmeny Park, Lochlibo Rd, G78 1LG, SW : ½ m. on A 736 ℰ 881 9211, ☞ – ☑ ☎ ℗ – 🕸 200
17 rm.

⊚ ATS Glasgow Rd, Crossmill ℰ 881 5651

BEARSDEN Dunbarton. (Strathclyde) 𝟜𝟘𝟙 G 16 – pop. 27 146 – ECD : Tuesday and Saturday – ✉ ✆ 041 Glasgow.

◆Edinburgh 51 – ◆Glasgow 5.

🍴 **La Bavarde,** 19 New Kirk Rd, G61 9JS, ℰ 942 2202 – ☒ ㏂ ⓞ 𝑉𝐼𝑆𝐴
closed Sunday, Monday, 3 weeks July and 2 weeks Christmas-New Year – **M** 7.00 **t.** (lunch) and a la carte 12.50/21.50 ♦ 4.30.

BEATTOCK Dumfries. (Dumfries and Galloway) 𝟜𝟘𝟙 𝟜𝟘𝟚 J 18 Scotland G. – ✉ Moffat – ✆ 068 33.

Exc. : Grey Mare's Tail★★, NE : 10½ m. by A 74, A 701 and A 708.

◆Edinburgh 60 – ◆Carlisle 41 – ◆Dumfries 20 – ◆Glasgow 59.

🏨 **Auchen Castle,** DG10 9SH, N : 2 m. by A 74 ℰ 407, Fax 667, ≤, ✎, ☞, park – ☑ ☎ ℗ – 🕸 30 – ☒ ㏂ ⓞ 𝑉𝐼𝑆𝐴
closed 3 weeks Christmas-New Year – **M** (bar lunch)/dinner 18.00 **st.** ♦ 4.10 – **25 rm** ⊇ 48.00/70.00 **st.** – SB 74.00/116.00 **st.**

🏠 **Broomlands Farm** without rest., DG10 9PQ, S : ½ m. by A 74 ℰ 320, « Working farm », ☞. ❀
Easter-October – **3 rm** ⊇ 18.00/32.00 **st.**

BEAULY Inverness. (Highland) 𝟜𝟘𝟙 G 11 – pop. 1 135 – ECD : Thursday – ✆ 0463.

◆Edinburgh 169 – ◆Inverness 13 – ◆Wick 125.

🏠 **Priory,** The Square, IV4 7BX, ℰ 782309, Fax 782531 – 🛗 ☑ ☎. ☒ ㏂ ⓞ 𝑉𝐼𝑆𝐴
M a la carte 8.20/19.40 **t.** ♦ 3.50 – **22 rm** ⊇ 39.50/82.50 **t.** – SB (weekends only) 59.90/69.90 **st.**

🏠 **Chrialdon,** Station Rd, IV4 7EH, ℰ 782336, ☞ – ⇆ rest ☑ ℗. ☒ 𝑉𝐼𝑆𝐴
March-October – **M** 16.50 **st.** ♦ 5.50 – **8 rm** ⊇ 18.00/54.00 **st.** – SB (winter only) 64.00/88.00 **st.**

BENBECULA Inverness. (Western Isles) 𝟜𝟘𝟙 X 11 – see Uist (Isles of).

La carta stradale Michelin è costantemente aggiornata.

BETTYHILL Sutherland. (Highland) [401] H 8 – ✉ Thurso (Caithness) – ☏ 064 12.
◆Edinburgh 262 – ◆Inverness 93 – Thurso 31.

🏠 **Tigh Na Sgoil** 🔇, Kirtomy, KW14 7TB, NE : 3 ¼ m. by A 836 on Kirtomy rd ℘ 455, Fax 457, 🐕 – 📺 🅟. ✗🐕
M (communal dining) 11.00 **st.** 🍷 2.40 – **5 rm** 26.50/53.00 **st.**

BLAIRGOWRIE Perth. (Tayside) [401] J 14 Scotland G. – pop. 7 028 – ☏ 0250.
Exc. : Scone Palace★★ *AC*, S : 12 m. by A 93.
ℹ 26 Wellmeadow ℘ 872960/873701.
◆Edinburgh 60 – ◆Dundee 19 – Perth 16.

🏨 **Kinloch House** 🔇, PH10 6SG, W : 3 m. on A 923 ℘ 884237, Fax 884333, ≤, « Country house atmosphere », 🌳, park – 🚭 rest 📺 ☎ 🅟. ✗🐕
closed 2 weeks Christmas – **M** 13.95/23.90 **st.** 🍷 5.20 – **21 rm** ☕ (dinner included) 72.95/177.45 **st.**

🏨 **Altamount House** 🔇, Coupar Angus Rd, PH10 6JN, on A 923 ℘ 873512, Fax 876200, 🌳 – 📺 ☎ 🅟. [S] VISA ✗🐕
closed 4 January-14 February – **M** (bar lunch Monday to Saturday)/dinner 23.50 **t.** 🍷 4.50 – **7 rm** ☕ 37.50/70.00 **t.** – SB (except June-August) 77.00 **st.**

🏨 **Rosemount Golf,** Golf Course Rd, PH10 6LJ, SE : 1 ¾ m. by A 923 ℘ 872604, Fax 874496, 🌳 – 📺 ☎ 🅟. [S] VISA. ✗🐕
M (bar lunch)/dinner 18.00 **st.** 🍷 4.50 – **11 rm** ☕ 39.00/58.00 **st.** – SB (mid January-April and October-mid December) 75.00/89.00 **st.**

BLAIRLOGIE Stirling. (Central) – see Stirling.

BOAT OF GARTEN Inverness. (Highland) [401] I 12 – ECD : Thursday – ☏ 047 983 (3 fig.) and 0479 (6 fig.).
⛳18 Boat-of-Garten ℘ 282.
◆Edinburgh 133 – ◆Inverness 28 – ◆Perth 89.

🏨 **The Boat,** PH24 3BH, ℘ 831258, Fax 831414, 🌳 – 📺 ☎ 🅟. [S] [AE] ⓓ VISA JCB
closed 1 November-23 December – **M** 15.00/22.50 **st.** and a la carte 🍷 5.95 – **32 rm** ☕ 35.00/90.00 **st.** – SB 100.00/120.00 **st.**

🏠 **Heathbank House,** Spey Av., PH24 3BD, ℘ 234, 🌳 – 🚭 🅟. ✗🐕
closed November-26 December – **M** 15.00 **s.** 🍷 4.30 – **7 rm** ☕ 18.00/60.00 **s.**

BONAR BRIDGE Sutherland. (Highland) [401] G 10 – pop. 480 – ECD : Wednesday – ✉ ☏ 086 32 Ardgay.
⛳9 Bonar Bridge & Ardgay ℘ 750, N : ½ m. by A 9.
ℹ ℘ 333 (summer only).
◆Edinburgh 206 – ◆Inverness 50 – ◆Wick 76.

🏠 **Kyle House,** Dornoch Rd, IV24 3EB, ℘ 360 – 🚭 rest 🅟. ✗🐕
closed January and November – **M** (by arrangement) 15.00 **s.** – **6 rm** ☕ 15.00/36.00 **s.**

at Invershin W : 3 m. on A 836 – ✉ Lairg – ☏ 054 982 Invershin :

🏠 **Gneiss House,** Balchraggan, IV27 4ET, ℘ 282, 🌳 – 🚭 🅟. [S] [AE] ⓓ VISA. ✗🐕
closed 2 weeks October, Christmas and New Year – **M** (by arrangement) – **3 rm** ☕ 21.00/32.00 **s.**

BOTHWELL Lanark. (Strathclyde) [401] [402] H 16 Scotland.G. – ✉ Glasgow – ☏ 0698.
See : Castle★ *AC*.
Envir. : Blantyre (David Livingstone Museum★) *AC*, W : 2 m. by A 724.
◆Edinburgh 39 – ◆Glasgow 8.5.

🏨 **Silvertrees,** 27-29 Silverwells Cres., G71 8DP, ℘ 852311, Fax 852311 ext : 200, 🌳 – 📺 ☎ 🅟 – 🎤 120. [S] [AE] ⓓ VISA
M *(closed Sunday dinner)* 10.00/13.00 **t.** and a la carte 🍷 5.00 – **24 rm** ☕ 35.00/70.00 **t.**

BRAE Shetland. (Shetland Islands) [401] P 2 – see Shetland Islands (Mainland).

BRAEMAR Aberdeen. (Grampian) [401] J 12 Scotland G. – ECD : Thursday except summer – ☏ 033 97.
Envir. : Lin O'Dee★, W : 5 m.
⛳18 Cluniebank Rd ℘ 41618.
ℹ Fife Mews, Mar Rd ℘ 41600.
◆Edinburgh 85 – ◆Aberdeen 58 – ◆Dundee 51 – Perth 51.

🏨 **Invercauld Arms** (Mt. Charlotte Thistle), AB35 5YR, ℘ 41605, Fax 41428 – 🛗 📺 ☎ ♿ 🅟 – 🎤 40. [S] [AE] ⓓ VISA JCB
M 9.75/20.00 **t.** and dinner a la carte 🍷 5.35 – **68 rm** ☕ 60.00/85.00 **t.** – SB 84.00/150.00 **st.**

🏨 **Braemar Lodge,** Glenshee Rd, AB35 5YQ, ℘ 41627, Fax 41627, 🌳 – 📺 🅟. [S] VISA
closed November-mid March except Christmas and New Year – **M** (dinner only) 21.00 **st.** 🍷 4.50 – **5 rm** ☕ 35.00/70.00 **st.** – SB 99.00/140.00 **st.**

BRIDGEND Argyll. (Strathclyde) [401] B 16 – see Islay (Isle of).

◆Edinburgh 157 – ◆Inverness 50.

🏠 **Delnashaugh Inn,** AB37 9AS, on A 95 ℰ 500255, Fax 500389, ≤ – 📺 ☎ 🄿. 🅰 VISA. ⋇
closed late November-mid February – **M** (bar lunch)/dinner 20.00 **t.** – **9 rm** ⊑ (dinner included) 55.00/130.00 **t.**

BRIG O'TURK Perth. (Central) 401 G 15 Scotland G. – ⊠ Callander – ✆ 0877 Trossachs.

Envir. : The Trossachs★★★ (Loch Katherine★★) W : 2 m. by A 821 – Hilltop Viewpoint★★★ (⋇★★★) SW : 3½ m. by A 821.

◆Edinburgh 58 – ◆Glasgow 36 – Perth 47.

🏠 **Dundarroch Country House** ⅏ without rest., Trossachs, FK17 8HT, ℰ 376200, Fax 376202, ≤, ⌕, park – ⋺⋸ 📺 🄿. 🅰 VISA. ⋇
closed February and November – **3 rm** ⊑ 39.95/65.50 **t.**

BRODICK Bute. (Strathclyde) 401 402 E 17 – see Arran (Isle of).

BRORA Sutherland. (Highland) 401 I 9 – pop. 1 728 – ECD : Wednesday – ✆ 0408.

🏌 Golf Rd ℰ 621417.

◆Edinburgh 234 – ◆Inverness 78 – ◆Wick 49.

🏨 **Links** (Best Western) ⅏, Golf Rd, KW9 6QS, ℰ 621225, Fax 621383, ≤, ⌕, ⌖ – 📺 ☎ 🄿. 🅰 🅰🅴 ① VISA
March-October – **M** (bar lunch)/dinner 20.00 **t.** and a la carte ⋔ 5.00 – **21 rm** ⊑ 40.00/80.00 **t.**, 1 suite – SB 100.00/120.00 **st.**

🏨 **Royal Marine** ⅏, Golf Rd, KW9 6QS, ℰ 621252, Fax 621181, ⇔, 🄽, ⌕, ⌖ – 📺 ☎ 🄿. 🅰 🅰🅴 VISA
M (bar lunch Monday to Saturday)/dinner 20.00 **t.** ⋔ 4.00 – **11 rm** ⊑ 50.00/100.00 **t.** – SB 110.00/140.00 **st.**

🏠 **Lynwood** ⅏, Golf Rd, KW9 6QS, ℰ 621226, ⌖ – ⋺⋸ rm 📺 🄿. 🅰 VISA
closed January and February – **M** (communal dining) 10.00 **st.** – **4 rm** ⊑ 18.00/37.00 **st.**

🏠 **Tigh Fada** ⅏ without rest., Golf Rd, KW9 6QS, ℰ 621332, Fax 621332, ≤, ⌖ – ⋺⋸ 🄿. ⋇
closed December – **3 rm** ⊑ 23.00/38.00 **s.**

*Great Britain and Ireland is now covered
by an Atlas at a scale of 1 inch to 4.75 miles.*

Three easy to use versions: Paperback, Spiralbound and Hardback.

BROUGHTY FERRY Angus. (Tayside) 401 L 14 – see Dundee.

BUCKIE Banff. (Grampian) 401 L 10 – pop. 7 869 – ECD : Wednesday – ✆ 0542.

🏌 Buckpool, Barhill Rd ℰ 32236 – 🏌 Strathlene ℰ 31798, E : ½ m.

🛈 Cluny Sq. ℰ 34853 (summer only).

◆Edinburgh 195 – ◆Aberdeen 66 – ◆Inverness 56.

XX **Old Monastery,** ⊠ Drybridge, AB56 2JB, SE : 3½ m. by A 942 on Deskford rd ℰ 832660, ≤, « Former chapel overlooking Spey Bay » – 🄿. 🅰 🅰🅴 VISA
closed Sunday, Monday, 2 weeks November and 3 weeks January – **M** a la carte 17.00/24.00 **t.** ⋔ 5.50.

BUCKSBURN Aberdeen. (Grampian) 401 N 12 – see Aberdeen.

BUNESSAN Argyll. (Strathclyde) 401 B 15 – see Mull (Isle of).

BURNTISLAND Fife. (Fife) 401 K 15 – pop. 6 025 – ✆ 0592.

🏌 Burntisland Golf House Club, Dodhead ℰ 873247 – 🏌 Kinghorn, McDuff Cres. ℰ 890345, NE : 2 m. by A 921.

🛈 4 Kirkgate ℰ 872667.

◆Edinburgh 20 – Dunfermline 10 – Kirkcaldy 6.

🏨 **Kingswood,** Kinghorn Rd, KY3 9LL, ℰ 872329, Fax 873123 – ⋺⋸ rm 📺 ☎ 🄿 – 🅰 60. 🅰 VISA
M (bar lunch)/dinner 14.00 **t.** and a la carte – **10 rm** ⊑ 47.00/70.00 **t.** – SB (weekends only) 87.00/120.00 **st.**

🏠 **Inchview,** 69 Kinghorn Rd, KY3 9EB, ℰ 872239, Fax 874866 – 📺 ☎ 🄿. 🅰 🅰🅴 VISA
M 8.50/17.45 **st.** and a la carte ⋔ 3.95 – **12 rm** ⊑ 39.50/60.00 **st.** – SB (weekends only) 63.00/89.00 **st.**

BURRAY Orkney. (Orkney Islands) 401 L 7 – see Orkney Islands.

BUSBY Lanark. (Strathclyde) 401 402 H 16 – see Glasgow.

BUTE (Isle of) Bute. (Strathclyde) [401] [402] E 16 – pop. 7733.

⛴ by Caledonian MacBrayne : from Rothesay to Wemyss Bay, frequent services daily (30 mn) – from Rhubodach to Colintraive, frequent services daily (5 mn).

Rothesay – ✉ ☎ 0700 Rothesay.

⛳[18] Canada Hill ☎ 502244.

🏠 **Alamein House,** 28 Battery Pl., Promenade, PA20 9DU, ☎ 502395, ⋖ – 🚭 rest [TV] [P]
closed 2 weeks October-November and Christmas-New Year – **M** 8.50 **st.** – **7 rm** ☐ 19.50/47.00 **st.** – SB 52.00/64.00 **st.**

CAIRNBAAN Argyll. (Strathclyde) [401] D 15 – see Lochgilphead.

CAIRNRYAN Wigtown (Dumfries and Galloway) [401] [402] E 19 – ✉ Stranraer – ☎ 058 12.
◆Edinburgh 149 – ◆Ayr 73 – ◆Dumfries 88 – Stranraer 20.

🏠 **Merchant's House,** Main St., DG9 8QX, ☎ 215, ⋖ – [TV]. [EN] [VISA]
closed 2 weeks March-April and 2 weeks October-November – **M** (by arrangement) 22.45 **t.** 🍷 4.50 – **3 rm** ☐ 16.00/32.00 **t.**

CALGARY Argyll. (Strathclyde) [401] C 14 – see Mull (Isle of).

CALLANDER Perth. (Central) [401] H 15 **Scotland G.** – pop. 2 286 – ECD : Wednesday except summer – ☎ 0877.

See : Town★.

Exc. : The Trossachs★★★ (Loch Katrine★★) – Hilltop Viewpoint★★★ (✱★★★) W : 10 m. by A 821.

⛳[18] Aveland Rd ☎ 30090 (changing in 94 to 330090).

[i] Rob Roy & Trossachs Visitor Centre, Ancaster Sq. ☎ 30342 (summer only) (changing in 94 to 330342).

◆Edinburgh 52 – ◆Glasgow 43 – ◆Oban 71 – Perth 41.

🏠 **Roman Camp** 🐦, Main St., FK17 8BG, ☎ 30003 (changing in 94 to 330003), Fax 31533 (changing in 94 to 331533), ⋖, « 17C hunting lodge in extensive gardens », 🐟, park – 🚭 rest [TV] ☎ ♿ [P]. [EN] [AE] [D] [VISA]. 🐕
M 17.00/35.00 **t.** and a la carte – **11 rm** ☐ 55.00/130.00 **t.**, 3 suites – SB (October-mid April except Christmas and New Year) 130.00 **st.**

🏠 **Arran Lodge,** Leny Rd, FK17 8AJ, ☎ 30976 (changing in 94 to 330976), 🐟, 🌳 – 🚭 [TV] [P]. 🐕
closed mid January-mid February and mid November-mid December – **M** (unlicensed) (residents only) (dinner only) 17.00 **s.** – **4 rm** ☐ 55.20/69.00 **s.**

🏠 **Invertrossachs Country House** 🐦 without rest., Invertrossachs, FK17 8HG, SW : 5 ½ m. by A 81 and Invertrossachs rd taking no through road after 1 ¾ m. ☎ 31126 (changing in 94 to 331126), Fax 31229 (changing in 94 to 331229), ⋖, « Edwardian hunting lodge in extensive grounds », 🐟, 🌳 – [TV] ☎ [P]. [EN] [AE] [VISA]
closed mid December-early January – **3 rm** ☐ 40.00/95.00 **st.**

🏠 **Lubnaig,** Leny Feus, FK17 8AS, ☎ 30376 (changing in 94 to 330376), 🌳 – 🚭 [TV] [P]. [EN] [VISA]. 🐕
April-October – **M** (residents only) (dinner only) 17.50 **t.** 🍷 5.95 – **10 rm** ☐ 35.00/58.00 **t.** – SB 86.00/100.00 **st.**

🏠 **Dalgair,** Main St., FK17 8BQ, ☎ 30283 (changing in 94 to 330283), Fax 31114 (changing in 94 to 331114) – [TV] ☎ [P]. [EN] [AE] [D] [VISA]. 🐕
M (bar lunch Monday to Friday)/dinner a la carte 11.55/17.20 **t.** 🍷 4.50 – **8 rm** ☐ 40.00/52.00 **st.** – SB (October-March except 23 December-4 January) 52.00/80.00 **st.**

🏠 **Priory,** Bracklinn Rd, FK17 8EH, ☎ 30001 (changing in 94 to 330001), 🌳 – 🚭 rest [TV] [P]. 🐕
April-October – **M** 9.50 **t.** – **8 rm** ☐ 25.50/51.00 **t.**

🏠 **Brook Linn** 🐦, Leny Feus, FK17 8AU, ☎ 30103 (changing in 94 to 330103), ⋖, 🌳 – 🚭 [TV] [P]
Easter-October – **M** 11.00 **st.** 🍷 4.00 – **7 rm** ☐ 16.00/48.00 **st.**

🏠 **East Mains House,** Bridgend, FK17 8AG, ☎ 30535 (changing in 94 to 330535), 🌳 – 🚭 rm [TV] [P]
M 10.00 – **5 rm** ☐ 14.00/36.00 **s.**

🏠 **Highland House,** 8 South Church St., FK17 8BN, ☎ 30269 (changing in 94 to 330269) – 🚭 [TV]. [EN] [AE] [VISA]
March-October – **M** 17.75 **st.** 🍷 3.95 – **9 rm** ☐ 22.50/45.00 **st.** – SB 65.00/94.00 **st.**

CAMPBELTOWN Argyll. (Strathclyde) [401] D 17 – see Kintyre (Peninsula).

CANNICH Inverness. (Highland) [401] F 11 – ✉ Beauly – ☎ 0456.
◆Edinburgh 184 – ◆Inverness 28 – Kyle of Lochalsh 54.

🏠 **Cozac Lodge** 🐦, IV4 7LX, W : 8 ½ m. ☎ 415263, Fax 415263, ⋖ Loch Sealbanach and Affric Hills, « Converted shooting lodge », 🐟, 🌳 – 🚭 rest [TV] [P]. [EN] [AE] [VISA]
M (residents only) (lunch by arrangement)/dinner 17.50 **t.** 🍷 5.00 – **7 rm** ☐ 41.50/65.00 **t.**

CANONBIE Dumfries. (Dumfries and Galloway) 🔢 🔢 L 18 – 🕿 038 73.

◆Edinburgh 80 – ◆Carlisle 15 – ◆Dumfries 34.

XX **Riverside Inn** with rm, DG14 0UX, 🖉 71295 – ≒⊷ rest 📺 🅿. 🔳 *VISA*. 🍴
closed last 2 weeks February and first 2 weeks November – **M** *(closed Sunday)* (booking essential) (bar lunch)/dinner a la carte 22.00 **t.** – **6 rm** 🖵 55.00/84.00 **t.** – SB (November-May) 116.00/154.00 **st.**

CARDROSS Dunbarton. (Strathclyde) 🔢 G 16 – 🕿 0389.

◆Edinburgh 63 – ◆Glasgow 17 – Helensburgh 5.

🏠 **Kirkton House** ⚶, Darleith Rd, G82 5EZ, 🖉 841951, Fax 841868, ≤, ☞ – 📺 ☎ 🅿. 🔳 *VISA*
closed 17 December-8 January – **M** 19.40 **st.** � 2.90 – **6 rm** 🖵 35.00/55.00 **st.**

CARNOUSTIE Angus. (Tayside) 🔢 L 14 – pop. 9 146 – 🕿 0241.

🏌, 🏌 Medal Starter's Box, Princes St., Monifieth 🖉 0382 (Dundee) 532767, W : 3 m. by A 930 – 🏌, 🏌 Buddon Links, Links Par. 🖉 53249 – 🏌 Panmure, Barry 🖉 53120, W : 1 m. – 🏌 Burnside, Links Par. 🖉 55344.

🛈 The Library, High St. 🖉 52258 (summer only).

◆Edinburgh 68 – ◆Aberdeen 59 – ◆Dundee 12.

XX **11 Park Avenue**, 11 Park Av., DD7 7JA, 🖉 53336 – 🔳 🆎 ⓪ *VISA*
closed Saturday lunch, Sunday, Monday and first week January – **M** 14.70/21.00 **st.** and dinner a la carte ⅄ 5.50.

CARRBRIDGE Inverness. (Highland) 🔢 I 12 – ECD : Wednesday – 🕿 0479.

🏌 Carrbridge 🖉 623.

🛈 Main St. 🖉 84630 (summer only).

◆Edinburgh 135 – ◆Aberdeen 92 – ◆Inverness 23.

🏠 **Feith Mho'r Country House** ⚶, Station Rd, PH23 3AP, W : 1 ¼ m. 🖉 841621, ≤, ☞ – ≒⊷ rest 📺 🅿
closed 10 November-22 December – **M** 11.00 – **6 rm** 🖵 20.00/44.00.

CASTLE DOUGLAS Kirkcudbright. (Dumfries and Galloway) 🔢 🔢 I 19 Scotland G. – pop. 3 546 – ECD : Thursday – 🕿 0556.

Envir. : Threave Garden★★ *AC*, SW : 2½ m. by A 75 – Threave Castle★ *AC*, W : 1 m.

🏌 Abercromby Rd 🖉 2801/2099.

🛈 Markethill Car Park 🖉 2611 (summer only).

◆Edinburgh 98 – ◆Ayr 49 – ◆Dumfries 18 – Stranraer 57.

🏠 Longacre Manor ⚶, Ernespie Rd, DG7 1LE, NE : ¾ m. on A 745 ⅄ 3886, ☞ – 📺 ☎ 🅿
🍴 – **4 rm.**

◎ ATS Station Yard 🖉 3121/2

CLACHAN SEIL Argyll. (Strathclyde) 🔢 D 15 – see Seil (Isle of).

CLEISH Fife. (Tayside) 🔢 J 15 – see Kinross.

CLYDEBANK Dunbarton. (Strathclyde) 🔢 G 16 – pop. 51 719 – 🕿 041.

🏌 Clydebank Municipal, Overtoun Rd, Dalmuir 🖉 952 8698 – 🏌 Hardgate 🖉 0389 (Dumbarton) 73289, N : 2 m.

◆Edinburgh 52 – ◆Glasgow 6.

🏨 **Patio**, 1 South Av., Clydebank Business Park, G81 2RW, 🖉 951 1133, Fax 952 3713 – 🛗 ≒⊷ rm 🍴 rest 📺 ☎ ♿ 🅿 – 🛆 150. 🔳 🆎 ⓪ *VISA*
closed 25 to 28 December and 1 to 3 January – **M** *(closed lunch Saturday and Sunday)* 14.95 **st.** and a la carte ⅄ 5.95 – **78 rm** 🖵 56.50/66.50 **st.**, 2 suites – SB 88.00/152.00 **st.**

COLL (Isle of) Argyll. (Strathclyde) 🔢 A 14 – pop. 153.

⛴ by Caledonian MacBrayne : from Arinagour to Oban – from Arinagour to Tobermory (Isle of Mull) – from Arinagour to Isle of Tiree, Armadale (Isle of Skye) and Mallaig.

Arinagour – ⌧ 🕿 087 93 Coll

🏠 **Tigh-na-Mara** ⚶ without rest., PA78 6SY, 🖉 354, ≤ Mull and Treshnish Isles, « Idyllic Hebridean setting », ⚓, ☞ – ≒⊷ 🅿
closed mid December-mid January – **8 rm** 🖵 17.00/34.00 **s.**

COLONSAY (Isle of) Argyll. (Strathclyde) 🔢 B 15 – pop. 132 – 🕿 095 12.

🏌 Isle of Colonsay 🖉 316,.

⛴ by Caledonian MacBrayne : from Scalasaig to Oban, 3 weekly (2 h 15 mn) – to Oban via Port Askaig and Kennacraig.

Scalasaig – ECD : Wednesday – ⌧ 🕿 095 12 Colonsay

🏨 **Isle of Colonsay** ⚶, PA61 7YP, 🖉 316, Fax 353, ≤, ☞ – ≒⊷ rest 📺 🅿. 🔳 🆎 ⓪ *VISA* 🆑🅱
March-early November – **M** (bar lunch)/dinner 18.50 **st.** ⅄ 5.00 – **11 rm** 🖵 50.00/100.00 **st.**

Kircudbright. (Dumfries and Galloway) Scotland G. – ✉ Dalbeattie – ✪ 055 663 Rockcliffe.

Envir. : Kippford★, NW : 2 m. by A 710.

🏌 Sandyhills, Dalbeattie ✎ 398, E : 1 ½ m. by A 710.

♦Edinburgh 99 – ♦Dumfries 19.

🏠 **Clonyard House**, D G5 4QW, NW : 1 m. on A 710 ✎ 372, Fax 422, ☞ – 📺 ☎ ᕼ 🅿. 🖭
ᴀᴇ 𝘝𝘐𝘚𝘈 ᴊᴄʙ
M (bar lunch)/dinner a la carte 8.45/16.30 **st.** ⓘ 3.70 – **15 rm** ⊐ 35.00/65.00 **st.** – SB (except
Christmas, New Year and Bank Holidays) 66.00/80.00 **st.**

CONNEL Argyll. (Strathclyde) 401 D 14 – ✉ Oban – ✪ 0631 71.

♦Edinburgh 118 – ♦Glasgow 88 – ♦Inverness 113 – ♦Oban 5.

↑ **Ards House**, PA37 1PT, ✎ 255, ≤, ☞ – ⇥ 🅿. 🖭 𝘝𝘐𝘚𝘈. ⁂
March-November – **M** 14.00 **t.** ⓘ 4.20 – **7 rm** ⊐ 30.00/57.00 **t.** – SB (except June-mid
September) 60.00/70.00 **st.**

↑ **Ronebhal** without rest., PA37 1PJ, ✎ 310, ≤, ☞ – ⇥ 🅿. 🖭 𝘝𝘐𝘚𝘈. ⁂
April-September – **6 rm** ⊐ 17.50/56.00.

CRAIGELLACHIE Banff. (Grampian) 401 K 11 Scotland G. – ✪ 0340.

Envir. : Glenfiddich Distillery★, SE : 5 m. by A 941.

♦Edinburgh 190 – ♦Aberdeen 58 – ♦Inverness 53.

🏨 **Craigellachie**, Victoria St., AB38 9SR, ✎ 881204, Fax 881253, ☎s – ⇥ rest 📺 ☎ 🅿. 🖭
ᴀᴇ ⓞ 𝘝𝘐𝘚𝘈
M (buffet lunch)/dinner 29.50 **t.** and a la carte ⓘ 5.95 – **30 rm** ⊐ 54.50/113.00 **t.** –
SB (weekends only) 142.00/208.00 **st.**

"Un atlante della Gran Bretagna e dell' Irlanda

è disponibile in tre versioni : rilegato, in brossura e a spirale."

CRAIGHOUSE Argyll. (Strathclyde) 401 C 16 – see Jura (Isle of).

CRAIL Fife. (Fife) 401 M 15 Scotland G. – pop. 1 074 – ECD : Wednesday – ✪ 0333.

See : Town★★ - Old Centre★★ - Upper Crail★.

Envir. : Scottish Fisheries Museum★★, NE : 4 m. by A 917 – The East Neuk★★, SW : 4 m. by
A 917 – Kellie Castle★ AC, NE : 5 ½ m. by B 9171 and A 917.

🏌 Crail Golfing Society, Balcomie Clubhouse ✎ 50278.

🛈 Museum & Heritage Centre, Marketgate ✎ 50869 (summer only).

♦Edinburgh 50 – ♦Dundee 23 – Dunfermline 38.

↑ **Caiplie**, 53 High St., KY10 3RA, ✎ 50564
March-October – **M** 12.50 **st.** ⓘ 3.75 – **7 rm** ⊐ 16.00/33.00 **t.**

CRIANLARICH Perth. (Central) 401 G 14 – ✪ 083 83.

♦Edinburgh 82 – ♦Glasgow 52 – Perth 53.

🏠 **Allt-Chaorain House** ⌂, FK20 8RU, NW : 1 m. on A 82 ✎ 283, Fax 238, ≤, ☞ – ⇥ 📺
☎ 🅿. 🖭 𝘝𝘐𝘚𝘈
late March-October – **M** (residents only) (communal dining) (dinner only) 17.00 **t.** – **8 rm**
⊐ 30.00/72.00 **t.** – SB 84.00/96.00 **t.**

CRIEFF Perth. (Tayside) 401 I 14 Scotland G. – pop. 5 101 – ECD : Wednesday – ✪ 0764.

See : Town★.

Envir. : Drummond Castle Gardens★ AC, S : 2 m. by A 822 – Comrie (Scottish Tartans
Museum★) W : 6 m. by A 85.

Exc. : Scone Palace ★★ AC, E : 16 m. by A 85 and A 93.

🏌, 🏌 Perth Rd ✎ 2909, NE : 1 m. by A 85 – 🏌 Muthill, Peak Rd ✎ 076 481 (Muthill) 523, S : 4 m.
by A 822.

🛈 Town Hall, High St. ✎ 652578.

♦Edinburgh 60 – ♦Glasgow 50 – ♦Oban 76 – Perth 18.

🏠 **Murraypark**, Connaught Terr., PH7 3DJ, ✎ 653731, Fax 655311, ☞ – 📺 ☎ 🅿. 🖭 ᴀᴇ ⓞ
𝘝𝘐𝘚𝘈
M (bar lunch)/dinner 25.00 and a la carte ⓘ 5.00 – **20 rm** ⊐ 48.00/70.00 **t.**, 1 suite.

↑ **Leven House**, Comrie Rd, PH7 4BA, on A 85 ✎ 652529, ≤ – ⇥ rest 📺 🅿
M 11.00 **st.** ⓘ 3.50 – **10 rm** ⊐ 18.00/40.00 **st.**

CRINAN Argyll. (Strathclyde) 401 D 15 Scotland G. – ✉ Lochgilphead – ✪ 054 683.

See : Hamlet★.

Exc. : Kilmory Knap (Macmillan's Cross★) SW : 14 m.

♦Edinburgh 137 – ♦Glasgow 91 – ♦Oban 36.

🏠 **Crinan**, PA31 8SR, ℰ 261, Fax 292, « ≤ commanding setting overlooking Loch Crinan and Sound of Jura », 🚗 – 📺 🕿 📵. 🔝 🆎 📧
closed 5 days at Christmas – **M** (bar lunch)/dinner 27.50 **t.** – (see also **Lock 16** below) –
20 rm � 85.00/200.00 **t.**

XX **Lock 16** (at Crinan H.), PA31 8SR, ℰ 261, Fax 292, « ≤ commanding setting overlooking Loch Crinan and Sound of Jura » 🚗 ≤
closed Sunday and Monday – **M** - **Seafood** (booking essential) (dinner only) 40.00 **t.**

CROCKETFORD Dumfries. (Dumfries and Galloway) 401 402 I 18 – ✉ Dumfries – 🌀 0556.
◆Edinburgh 73 – ◆Ayr 51 – Dumfries 10.

🏠 **Galloway Arms**, DG2 8RA, ℰ 690248 – 📺 📵. 🔝 📧
M (bar lunch)/dinner 15.00 **st.** and a la carte ▮ 4.25 – **13 rm** ⊐ 28.00/56.00 **st.**

CROMARTY Ross and Cromarty. (Highland) 401 H 10 Scotland G. – pop. 685 – ECD : Wednesday – 🌀 038 17.
Exc. : Fortrose (Cathedral Church setting ★) SW : 10 m. by A 832.
🏌 Fortrose & Rosemarkie, Ness Road East ℰ 0381 (Fortrose) 20529, SW : 10 m. by A 832.
◆Edinburgh 182 – ◆Inverness 26 – ◆Wick 126.

🏠 **Royal**, Marine Terr., IV11 8YN, ℰ 600217, ≤ – 📺 📵. 🔝 🆎 📧 ✂
M (closed Sunday dinner) 11.95/16.95 **st.** – **10 rm** ⊐ 30.00/53.00 **st.** – SB (October-March) 70.00/80.00 **st.**

CROSSFORD Fife. (Fife) 401 J 15 – see Dunfermline.

CULLEN Banff. (Grampian) 401 L 10 Scotland G. – pop. 1 378 – ECD : Wednesday – 🌀 0542.
See : Cullen Auld Kirk★ (Sacrament house★, panels★).
Envir. : Deskford Church (Sacrament house★) S : 4 m. by A 98 and B 9018 – Portsoy★, E : 5½ m. by A 98.
🏌 The Links ℰ 40685.
🅱 20 Seafield St. ℰ 40757 (summer only).
◆Edinburgh 189 – ◆Aberdeen 59 – Banff 12 – ◆Inverness 61.

🏠 **Bayview**, Seafield St., AB56 2SU, ℰ 841031, ≤ – 📺 🕿. 🔝 📧 ✂
M (bar lunch)/dinner a la carte 9.75/20.25 **st.** ▮ 4.00 – **6 rm** ⊐ 35.00/60.00 **st.**

CULLODEN Inverness. (Highland) 401 H 11 – see Inverness.

CULNAKNOCK Inverness. (Highland) 401 B 11 – see Skye (Isle of).

CULTS Aberdeen. (Grampian) 401 N 12 – see Aberdeen.

CUMBERNAULD Lanark. (Strathclyde) 401 I 16 – pop. 47 555 – 🌀 0236.
🏌 Palacerigg Country Park ℰ 734969, E : 3 m.
◆Edinburgh 40 – ◆Glasgow 11 – Stirling 13.

🏨 **Westerwood**, St. Andrews Drive, G68 0EW, N : 2 m. by A 8011 ℰ 457171, Fax 738478, ▮₅, 🔝, 🏌, ✂ – 📵 ✂ rm 📺 🕿 📵 – 🔟 150. 🔝 🆎 ⓪ 📧 ✂
closed 23 to 28 December – **M** Old Masters (dinner only) 18.50 **t.** and a la carte ▮ 6.75 – **41 rm** ⊐ 82.50/120.00 **t.**, 8 suites.

🏠 **Travel Inn**, 4 South Muirhead Rd, G67 1AX, off A 8011 ℰ 725339, Fax 736380 – ✂ rm 📺 🔝 📵. 🔝 🆎 ⓪ 📧 ✂
M (Beefeater grill) a la carte approx. 16.00 **t.** – ⊐ 4.95 – **37 rm** 33.50 **st.**

CUPAR Fife. (Fife) 401 K 15 – pop. 6 662 – ECD : Thursday – 🌀 0334.
🅱 Fluthers Car Park ℰ 52874 (summer only).
◆Edinburgh 45 – ◆Dundee 15 – Perth 23.

X **Ostler's Close**, Bonnygate, KY15 4BU, ℰ 55574 – 🔝 📧
closed Sunday, Monday and 2 weeks June – **M** a la carte 15.45/25.65 **t.** ▮ 4.00.

🔘 ATS St. Catherine St. ℰ 54003

DALBEATTIE Kirkcudbright. (Dumfries and Galloway) 401 402 I 19 Scotland G. – pop. 3 891 – 🌀 0556.
Envir. : Kippford★, S : 5 m. by A 710.
🏌 Dalbeattie ℰ 611421.
🅱 Town Hall ℰ 610117 (summer only).
◆Edinburgh 94 – ◆Ayr 56 – ◆Dumfries 14 – Stranraer 62.

🏠 **Auchenskeoch Lodge** ⌂, DG5 4PG, SE : 5 m. on B 793 ℰ 038 778 (Southwick) 277, 🔝, ☞, park – ✂ rest 🔝 📵. 🔝 📧
Easter-October – **M** (by arrangement) 13.50 **st.** ▮ 5.50 – **5 rm** ⊐ 32.00/49.00 **st.**

🏠 **Briardale House**, 17 Haugh Rd, DG5 4AR, ℰ 611468 – ✂ rest 📺 📵
closed November and December – **M** (by arrangement) 11.00 – **3 rm** ⊐ 20.00/38.00 – SB (January-March) 56.00 **st.**

DALCROSS Inverness. (Highland) – see Inverness.

DALIBURGH Inverness. (Western Isles) 401 X 12 – see Uist (Isles of).

DALRY (ST. JOHN'S TOWN OF) Kirkcudbright. (Dumfries and Galloway) 401 402 H 18 –
pop. 5 886 – ⊠ Castle Douglas – ✆ 064 43.

◆Edinburgh 82 – ◆Dumfries 27 – ◆Glasgow 66 – Stranraer 47.

    🏠 **Lochinvar**, 3 Main St., DG7 3UP, ✆ 210 – 📺 🅿. ⚑ AE VISA
      M (bar lunch)/dinner 12.50 **t.** and a la carte ░ 3.50 – **15 rm** ⊆ 18.00/45.00 **t.** – SB (except
      Bank Holidays) 45.00/80.00 **st.**

DENNY Stirling. (Central) 401 I 15 Scotland G. – pop. 23 172 – ✆ 0324.

Exc. : Stirling★★, N : 8 m. by A 872.

◆Edinburgh 34 – ◆Glasgow 25 – Stirling 7.

    ⌂ **Topps Farm** ⤷, Fintry Rd, FK6 5JF, W : 4 m. on B 818 ✆ 822471, ≼ – ⥵ 📺 ⅙ 🅿. ⚑
      VISA
      M (by arrangement) 13.00 **st.** ░ 4.95 – **8 rm** ⊆ 30.00/40.00 **st.** – SB 62.00/86.00 **st.**

DERVAIG Argyll. (Strathclyde) 401 B 14 – see Mull (Isle of).

DIRLETON E. Lothian. (Lothian) 401 402 L 15 – see Gullane.

DORNIE Ross and Cromarty. (Highland) 401 D 12 – ⊠ Kyle of Lochalsh – ✆ 059 985.

◆Edinburgh 212 – ◆Inverness 74 – Kyle of Lochalsh 8.

    🏠 **Loch Duich**, IV40 8DY, ✆ 213, Fax 214, ≼ Eilean Donan castle and hills, ⥵ – 🅿. ⚑ VISA
      closed 4 January-1 March and 19 to 28 December – **M** (dinner only) 17.00 **st.** and a la carte
      ░ 4.75 – **18 rm** ⊆ 23.50/44.00 **st.**

    🏠 **Castle Inn**, IV40 8DT, ✆ 205, Fax 429 – 📺 🅿. ⚑ VISA
      M (bar lunch)/dinner a la carte 9.00/17.00 **st.** ░ 3.50 – **12 rm** ⊆ 22.50/57.00 **st.**

Great Britain and Ireland is now covered
by an Atlas at a scale of 1 inch to 4.75 miles.

Three easy to use versions: Paperback, Spiralbound and Hardback.

DORNOCH Sutherland. (Highland) 401 H 10 Scotland G. – pop. 1 006 – ECD : Thursday –
✆ 0862.

See : Town★.

▸₁₈, ▸₁₈ Royal Dornoch, Golf Rd ✆ 810219.

🛈 The Square, ✆ 810400.

◆Edinburgh 219 – ◆Inverness 63 – ◆Wick 65.

    ⌂ **Highfield** without rest., Evelix Rd, IV25 3HR, ✆ 810909, ⥵ – ⥵ 📺 🅿
      3 rm ⊆ 28.00/44.00 **s.**

DOUNBY Orkney. (Orkney Islands) 401 K 6 – see Orkney Islands (Mainland).

DRUMNADROCHIT Inverness. (Highland) 401 G 11 Scotland G. – pop. 542 – ⊠ Milton –
✆ 0456.

Envir. : Loch Ness★★ – Loch Ness Monster Exhibition★ AC.

◆Edinburgh 172 – ◆Inverness 16 – Kyle of Lochalsh 66.

    🏨 **Polmaily House** ⤷, IV3 6XT, W : 2 m. on A 831 ✆ 450343, Fax 450813, « Country house
      atmosphere », ⤶ heated, ⥵, park, ⚒ – ⥵ rest 🅿. ⚑ 👁 VISA ⥵
      M 12.00/16.00 **t.** and dinner a la carte ░ 3.50 – **9 rm** ⊆ 43.00/140.00 **t.**

DRYMEN Stirling. (Central) 401 G 15 Scotland G. – pop. 771 – ECD : Wednesday – ✆ 0360.

Envir. : Loch Lomond★★, W : 3 m.

🛈 Drymen Library, The Square ✆ 60751 (summer only).

◆Edinburgh 64 – ◆Glasgow 18 – Stirling 22.

    🏨 **Buchanan Highland**, Main St., G63 0BQ, ✆ 60588, Fax 60943, ⌺, ⥱, ⚑, ⥵ , squash –
      📺 🅿 🅿 – ⅙ 120. ⚑ AE 👁 VISA
      M 9.50/18.50 **st.** and a la carte ░ 4.95 – **50 rm** ⊆ 80.00/128.00 **st.** – SB 100.00/114.00 **st.**

DULNAIN BRIDGE Inverness. (Highland) 401 J 12 – ECD : Wednesday – ⊠ Grantown-
on-Spey (Moray Highland) – ✆ 047 985.

◆Edinburgh 140 – ◆Inverness 31 – Perth 96.

    🏨 **Muckrach Lodge**, PH26 3LY, W : ½ m. on A 938 ✆ 257, Fax 325, ≼, ⥵ – 📺 ☎ ⅙ 🅿. ⚑
      AE 👁 VISA ⥵.
      closed November – **M** 12.00/22.50 **t.** and a la carte ░ 4.00 – **12 rm** ⊆ 41.00/98.00 **t.** –
      SB (January-March and October-mid December) 86.00/104.00 **st.**

    🏠 **Auchendean Lodge**, PH26 3LU, S : 1 m. on A 95 ✆ 347, ≼ Spey Valley and Cairngorms,
      ⥵ – ⥵ rest 📺 🅿. ⚑ AE 👁 VISA
      M (dinner only) 23.50 **st.** ░ 3.50 – **7 rm** ⊆ 27.00/67.00 **st.**

See : Dumbarton Castle (site*) AC.

Envir. : Loch Lomond★★, N : 5½ m. by A 82.

🏠 Vale of Leven, Northfield Rd, Bonhill ✆ 52351, N : 4 m. by A 813.

🛈 Milton, by Dumbarton A 82 (northbound) ✆ 42306 (summer only).

◆Edinburgh 64 – ◆Glasgow 12 – Greenock 17.

🏠 **Forte Travelodge** without rest., Milton, G82 2TY, E : 3 m. by A 814 on A 82 ✆ 65202, Reservations (Freephone) 0800 850950 – 📺 ⅆ 🅿. 🅐 🅐🅴 📷. ℅
32 rm 31.95 t.

When travelling for business or pleasure
*in **England, Wales, Scotland** and **Ireland** :*

– use the series of five maps
  (nos 401, 402, 403, 404 and 405) at a scale of 1:400 000

– they are the perfect complement to this Guide

DUMFRIES

High Street	**A** 18	Eastfield Rd	**B** 12
		Friars Vennel	**A** 13
Aldermanhill Road	**B** 2	Galloway Street	**A** 14
Bank Street	**A** 3	Glebe Street	**B** 15
Buccleuch Street	**A** 4	Great King Street	**A** 16
Cardoness Street	**B** 5	Hermitage Drive	**A** 17
Cassalands	**A** 6	Laurieknowe	**A** 20
Castle Street	**A** 7	Loreburn Street	**A** 21
Castle Douglas Road	**A** 8	Nith Street	**AB** 22
Catherine Street	**B** 9	Queen Street	**B** 23
Corberry Avenue	**A** 10	Queensberry Street	**A** 24
		Rae Street	**B** 26
		St. Mary's Street	**B** 27
		St. Michael Street	**B** 28

St. Michael's Bridge Road	**A** 30
Shakespeare Street	**B** 31
Union Street	**A** 32
Whitesands	**A** 34

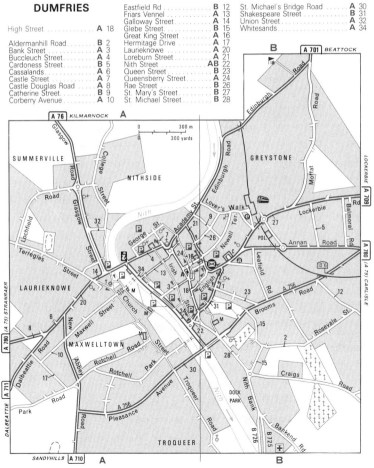

DUMFRIES Dumfries. (Dumfries and Galloway) 🖫🖫 J 18 Scotland G. – pop. 31 307 – ECD : Thursday – ✆ 0387.

See : Town★ – Midsteeple★ A **A**.

Envir. : Lincluden College (Tomb★) *AC*, N : 1 ½ m. by College St. A.

Exc. : Drumlanrig Castle★★ (cabinets★) *AC*, NW : 16 ½ m. by A 76 A – Shambellie House Museum of Costume (Costume Collection★) S : 7 ¼ m. by A 710 A - Sweetheart Abbey★ *AC*, S : 8 m. by A 710 A – Caerlaverock Castle★ (Renaissance façade★★) *AC*, SE : 9 m. by B 725 B – Glenkiln (Sculptures★) W : 9 m. by A 780 - A - and A 75 – Ruthwell Cross★, SE : 12 m. by A 780 - B - A 75 and B 724.

🚄 Dumfries & Galloway, Laurieston Av., Maxwelltown 𝒫 53582 A – 🚄 Crichton Royal, Bankend Rd 𝒫 41122, SE : 1 m. by Bankend Rd B.

🗓 Campbell House, Bankend Rd, DG1 4TH 𝒫 50434, Fax 50462 B.

◆Edinburgh 80 – ◆Ayr 59 – ◆Carlisle 34 – ◆Glasgow 79 – ◆Manchester 155 – ◆Newcastle upon Tyne 91.

Plan on preceding page

🏨 **Cairndale**, English St., DG1 2DF, 𝒫 54111, Fax 50555, 𝐼₆, ⇆, ☒ – ⬚ ↩ rm 📺 ☎ 🅿, 🗐 AE ⓞ VISA . ✄
B **a**
M 8.50/17.00 **st.** and a la carte – **76 rm** ⊂ 72.50/100.00 **st.** – SB (except Bank Holidays) 100.00/120.00 **st.**

🏨 **Station**, 49 Lovers Walk, DG1 1LT, 𝒫 54316, Fax 50388 – ⬚ 📺 ☎ 🅿 – 🔬 70. 🗐 AE ⓞ VISA
B **e**
M (bar lunch)/dinner 12.50 **st.** and a la carte ⭑ 3.80 – **32 rm** ⊂ 58.00/70.00 **st.** – SB (except Christmas and New Year) (weekends only) 75.00/110.00 **st.**

🔘 ATS Glasgow St. 𝒫 63837/8

Plans de ville : Les rues sont sélectionnées en fonction de leur importance
pour la circulation et le repérage des établissements cités.

Les rues secondaires ne sont qu'amorcées.

DUNAIN PARK Inverness. (Highland) – see Inverness.

DUNBAR E. Lothian. (Lothian) 🖫🖫 M 15 Scotland G. – pop. 5 795 – ECD : Wednesday – ✆ 0368.

See : Tolbooth★ – John Muir's Birthplace★.

Exc. : Tantallon Castle★★ (clifftop site★★★) *AC*, NW : 10 m. by A 1087, A 1 and A 198 – Preston Mill★, W : 6 m. by A 1087, A 1 and B 1407 – Tyninghame★, NW : 6 m. by A 1 and A 198 – Museum of Flight★, W : 7 m. by A 1087, A 1 and B 1377.

🚄 East Links 𝒫 62317 – 🚄 Winterfield, St. Margarets, North Rd 𝒫 62280.

🗓 143 High St. 𝒫 63353.

◆Edinburgh 28 – ◆Newcastle upon Tyne 90.

🏠 **Redheugh**, Bayswell Park, EH42 1AE, 𝒫 62793, Fax 62793 – 📺 ☎. 🗐 AE ⓞ VISA
M (dinner only) 15.50 **st.** and a la carte ⭑ 3.75 – **10 rm** ⊂ 35.00/59.00 **st.** – SB (except Christmas and New Year) 79.00/99.00 **st.**

🏠 **Courtyard**, Woodbush Brae, EH42 1HB, 𝒫 64169 – 📺 🅿. 🗐 AE ⓞ VISA
M 23.00 **st.** and a la carte ⭑ 5.50 – **7 rm** ⊂ 24.50/62.00 **st.**

↑ **St. Beys**, 2 Bayswell Rd, EH42 1AB, 𝒫 63571 – 📺. 🗐 VISA
closed December and January – **7 rm** ⊂ 17.00/38.00 **s.**

↑ **Marine** without rest., 7 Marine Rd, EH42 1AR, 𝒫 63315, ⇆
March-October – **9 rm** ⊂ 15.00/30.00 **st.**

DUNBLANE Perth. (Central) 🖫🖫 I 15 Scotland G. – pop. 6 783 – ECD : Wednesday – ✆ 0786.

See : Town★ – Cathedral★ (west front★★).

Envir. : Doune★ (castle★ *AC*) W : 4 ½ m. by A 820 – Doune Motor Museum★ *AC*, W : 5 ½ m. by A 820 and A 84.

🗓 Stirling Rd 𝒫 824428 (summer only).

◆Edinburgh 42 – ◆Glasgow 33 – Perth 29.

🏨 **Cromlix House** 🦌, Kinbuck, FK15 9JT, N : 3 ½ m. on B 8033 𝒫 822125, Fax 825450, ⇆, « Antique furnishings », 🦆, ⚲, park, ✄ – ↩ rest 📺 ☎ 🅿. 🗐 AE ⓞ VISA
closed mid January-February – **M** (booking essential) (lunch by arrangement)/dinner 34.00 **t.** ⭑ 6.00 – **6 rm** ⊂ 100.00/150.00 **t.**, **8 suites** 170.00/220.00 **t.** – SB (October-April) 140.00/200.00 **st.**

DUNDEE Angus. (Tayside) 🖫🖫 L 14 Scotland G. – pop. 172 294 – ECD : Wednesday – ✆ 0382.

See : The Frigate Unicorn★ *AC* Y A – RRS Discovery★ *AC* Y B.

🚄 Caird Park, Mains Loan Caird Park 𝒫 453606 – 🚄 Camperdown Park 𝒫 623398, NW : 2 m. by A 923.

✈ Dundee Airport : 𝒫 643242, SW : 1 ½ m. Z.

🗓 4 City Sq. 𝒫 27723.

◆Edinburgh 63 – ◆Aberdeen 67 – ◆Glasgow 83.

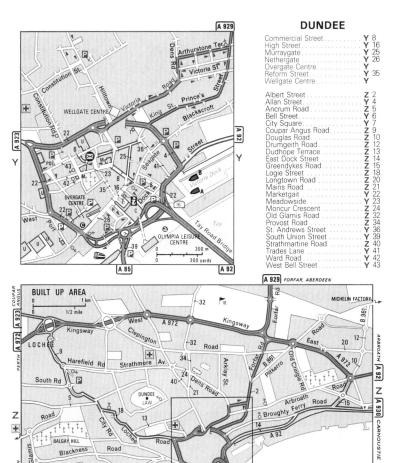

DUNDEE

🏨 **Stakis Earl Grey,** Earl Grey Pl., DD1 4DE, 𝒫 29271, Telex 76569, Fax 200072, ≼, 𝑓ₛ, ⬚s, ◻ – 📶 ⇔ rm 🗐 rest 📺 ☎ ⑂ 🕭 ⑁ – 🕸 200. ◪ 🗚 ⑪ 𝘝𝘐𝘚𝘈 𝐉𝐂𝐁   Y **a**
M 16.50 **t.** and dinner a la carte – ☑ 8.95 – **102 rm** 85.00/120.00 **st.**, 2 suites – SB 78.00/108.00 **st.**

🏨 **Angus Thistle** (Mt. Charlotte Thistle), 101 Marketgait, DD1 1QU, 𝒫 26874, Telex 76456, Fax 22564 – 📶 📺 ☎ ⑂ – 🕸 500. ◪ 🗚 ⑪ 𝘝𝘐𝘚𝘈   Y **c**
M *(closed Saturday and Sunday lunch)* 10.60/13.30 **st.** and a la carte – **53 rm** ☑ 79.00/99.00 **st.**, 5 suites – SB (weekends only) 70.00 **st.**

🏨 **Swallow,** Kingsway West (Dundee Ring Rd), DD2 5JT, W : 4 ¾ m. at junction of A 85 with A 972 𝒫 641122, Fax 568340, 𝑓ₛ, ⬚s, ◻, 𝑎 – ⇔ rm 🗐 rest 📺 ☎ ⑂ – 🕸 70. ◪ 🗚 ⑪ 𝘝𝘐𝘚𝘈   Z
M 11.75/25.00 **st.** and a la carte ⑂ 6.50 – **110 rm** ☑ 86.00/109.00 **st.** – SB (July-August and weekends only) 110.00 **st.**

🏨 **Travel Inn,** Kingsway West, Invergowerie, DD2 5JU, NW : on A 972 𝒫 561115, Fax 568431 – ⇔ rm 📺 🕭 ⑂. ◪ 🗚 ⑪ 𝘝𝘐𝘚𝘈 ⁒   Z
M (Beefeater grill) a la carte approx. 16.00 **t.** – ☑ 4.95 – **40 rm** 33.50 **t.**

597

at Broughty Ferry E : 4 ½ m. by A 930 – Z – (Dundee Rd) – ⊠ ✪ 0382 Dundee :

🏠 **Tayview** without rest., 71-73 St. Vincent St., DD5 2EZ, ℰ 79438 – ↤↦. 🖭 *VISA*. ﴾%
11 rm ⊑ 30.00/60.00 **t.**

↑ **Beach House,** 22 Esplanade, DD5 2EQ, ℰ 76614, Fax 480241 – ↤↦ rest 🖳 ☎. 🖭 *VISA*. ﴾%
M 12.00 **s.** ⌾ 3.75 – **5 rm** ⊑ 38.00/44.00 **s.**

⬤ ATS 332 Clepington Rd ℰ 88327

DUNDONNELL Ross and Cromarty. (Highland) 🟥 E 10 Scotland G. – ⊠ Garve – ✪ 085 483.

Envir. : Loch Broom★★, N : 4 ½ m. via Alt na h–Airbhe.

Exc. : Falls of Measach★★, SE : 10 m. by A 832 – Corrieshalloch Gorge★, SE : 11 ½ m. by A 832 and A 835.

◆Edinburgh 215 – ◆ Inverness 59.

🏨 **Dundonnell,** IV23 2QR, ℰ 204, Fax 366, ⇐ Dundonnell Valley – ↤↦ rest 🖳 ☎ 🅿 – ⌂ 60.
🖭 *VISA*
March-November and Christmas-New Year – **M** (bar lunch)/dinner 21.50 **st.** and a la carte –
24 rm ⊑ 35.00/85.00 **st.** – SB 90.00/130.00 **st.**

DUNFERMLINE Fife. (Fife) 🟥 J 15 Scotland G. – pop. 52 105 – ECD : Wednesday – ✪ 0383.

See : Abbey★ (Abbey Church★★) *AC*.

Envir. : Forth Bridges★★, S : 5 m. by A 823 and B 980.

Exc. : Culross★★★ (Village★★★, Palace★★ *AC*, Study★ *AC*) W : 7 m. by A 994 and B 9037.

🛆 Canmore, Venturefair ℰ 724969, N : 1 m. by A 823 – 🛆 Pitreavie, Queensferry Rd ℰ 722591,
SE : 1 ½ m. by A 823 – 🛆 Saline, Kinneddar Hill ℰ 852591, NW : 5 ½ m. by B 9155, A 907 and
B 913.

🛈 Maygate ℰ 720999 (summer only).

◆Edinburgh 16 – ◆Dundee 48 – Motherwell 39.

🏨 **King Malcolm Thistle** (Mt. Charlotte Thistle), Queensferry Rd, KY11 5DS, S : 1 m. on
A 823 ℰ 722611, Fax 730865 – ↤↦ rm ▤ rest 🖳 ☎ 🅿 – ⌂ 120. 🖭 AE ⓞ *VISA* JCB
M *(closed Saturday)* 8.50/14.95 **st.** and a la carte ⌾ 4.90 – **48 rm** ⊑ 65.00/75.00 **st.** –
SB (weekends only) 76.00/96.00 **st.**

at Crossford SW : 1 ¾ m. on A 994 – ⊠ ✪ 0383 Dunfermline :

🏨 **Keavil House** (Best Western) ⅏, Main St., KY12 8QW, ℰ 736258, Fax 621600, 🖩, ≡s,
🖭, ⅃ – ⊡ 🖳 ☎ 🅿 – ⌂ 140. 🖭 AE ⓞ *VISA*
M (bar lunch)/dinner 16.50 **st.** – **31 rm** ⊑ 50.00/85.00 **st.** – SB 110.00/150.00 **st.**

⬤ ATS 14 Dickson St., Elgin St. Est. ℰ 722802

DUNKELD Perth. (Tayside) 🟥 J 14 Scotland G. – ECD : Thursday – ✪ 0350.

See : Village★ - Cathedral Street★.

🛆 Dunkeld & Birnam, Fungarth ℰ 727524, NE : 1 m. by A 923.

🛈 The Cross ℰ 727688 (summer only).

◆Edinburgh 58 – ◆Aberdeen 88 – ◆Inverness 98 – Perth 14.

🏯 ✿ **Kinnaird** ⅏, Dalguise, PH8 0LB, NW : 6 ¾ m. by A 9 on B 898 ℰ 0796 (Pitlochry) 482440, Fax 482289, ⇐ Tay valley and hills, « Sporting estate, antique furnishings », 🖩, ✍, park, ﴾ – ⅃ ↤↦ rest 🖳 ☎ 🅿. 🖭 AE *VISA* ﴾%
closed February – **M** 24.00/38.00 **s.** ⌾ 8.30 – **8 rm** ⊑ 170.00/210.00 **t.**, 1 suite – SB (except
Bank Holidays) 225.00 **st.**
Spec. Terrine of smoked and cured salmon on a light leek cream, Sautéed best end of lamb with an onion and
coriander tartlet, Hot marzipan soufflé with amaretto ice cream.

🏨 **Stakis Dunkeld House** ⅏, PH8 0HX, ℰ 727771, Telex 76657, Fax 728924, ⇐, « Tayside
setting », 🖩, ≡s, 🖭, 🖩, ✍, park, ﴾ – ⌀ ↤↦ rm 🖳 ☎ 🖧 🅿 – ⌂ 80. 🖭 AE ⓞ *VISA* JCB
M 13.75/22.50 **st.** and dinner a la carte – ⊑ 9.75 – **89 rm** 89.00/178.00 **st.**, 3 suites –
SB 134.00/257.80 **st.**

↑ **Bheinne Mhor** without rest., Perth Rd, Birnam, PH8 0DH, S : ¾ m. by A 923 ℰ 727779,
✍ – ↤↦ 🅿. ﴾%
closed mid December-mid January – **4 rm** ⊑ 18.00/38.00 **st.**

DUNOON Argyll. (Strathclyde) 🟥 F 16 – pop. 8 797 – ECD : Wednesday – ✪ 0369.

🛆 Innellan, Knockamillie Rd ℰ 3546, S : 4 m.

⚓ by Caledonian MacBrayne : from Dunoon Pier to Gourock Railway Pier : frequent services daily (20 mn) – by Western Ferries : from Hunters Quay to McInroy's Point, Gourock :
frequent services daily (20 mn).

🛈 7 Alexandra Par. ℰ 3785.

◆Edinburgh 73 – ◆Glasgow 27 – ◆Oban 77.

🏨 **Enmore,** Marine Par., Kirn, PA23 8HH, N : 1 m. on A 815 ℰ 2230, Fax 2148, ⇐ Firth of
Clyde, ✍, squash – ↤↦ rest 🖳 ☎ 🅿. 🖭 *VISA*
M 10.00/25.00 **st.** and a la carte ⌾ 5.50 – **11 rm** ⊑ 35.00/110.00 **st.** – SB (November-May)
60.00/110.00 **st.**

⬤ ATS 247 Argyll St. ℰ 2853

DUNVEGAN Inverness. (Highland) 401 A 11 – see Skye (Isle of).

DUROR Argyll. (Strathclyde) 401 E 14 – ✉ Appin – ☎ 063 174.

♦Edinburgh 125 – Fort William 19 – ♦Oban 31.

Stewart (Best Western) ⚘, Glen Duror, PA38 4BW, ☎ 268, Fax 328, ≤, ⛱ – ⇔ rest TV ☎ P. AE VISA
April-mid October and Christmas-New Year – **M** (bar lunch Monday to Saturday)/dinner 30.00 **t.** 5.00 – **19 rm** ☐ 40.00/80.00 **t.** – SB 118.00/138.00 **st.**

DYCE Aberdeen. (Grampian) 401 N 12 – see Aberdeen.

EASDALE Argyll. (Strathclyde) 401 D 15 – see Seil (Isle of).

EAST KILBRIDE Lanark. (Strathclyde) 401 402 H 16 – pop. 70 454 – ECD : Wednesday – ☎ 035 52 (5 fig.) and 0355 (6 fig.).

18 Torrance House, Strathaven Rd ☎ 48638, S : 1½ m. by A 726.

♦Edinburgh 46 – ♦Ayr 35 – ♦Glasgow 10.

Westpoint, Stewartfield Way, G74 5LA, NW : 2¼ m. on A 726 ☎ 36300, Fax 33552, Lδ, ≘s, ☐, squash – |‡| ⇔ rm ▤ rest TV ☎ P – 150. AE VISA. ✻
M 12.50 **t.** and a la carte 9.00 – (see also **Simpsons** below) – ☐ 9.50 – **73 rm** 56.00/130.00 **t.**, 1 suite – SB (weekends only) 110.00 **st.**

Bruce Swallow, 34 Cornwall St., G74 1AF, ☎ 29771, Fax 42216 – |‡| ⇔ rm TV ☎ P – 200. AE VISA
M 9.00/20.00 **st.** and a la carte – **78 rm** ☐ 75.00/85.00 **st.**

Stuart, 1 Cornwall Way, G74 1JR, ☎ 21161, Telex 778504, Fax 64410 – |‡| TV ☎ – 200
38 rm, 1 suite.

Crutherland Country House ⚘, Strathaven Rd, G75 0QZ, SE : 2 m. on A 726 ☎ 37633, Fax 37633, ⛱, park – TV ☎ P. AE VISA
closed 1 and 2 January – **M** 17.50 **st.** (dinner) and a la carte 4.75 – **18 rm** ☐ 55.00/80.00 **st.**, 1 suite.

Travel Inn, Brunel Way, The Murray, G75 0JY, ☎ 22809, Fax 30517 – ⇔ rm TV ♿ P. AE VISA. ✻
M (Beefeater grill) a la carte approx. 16.00 **t.** – ☐ 4.95 – **40 rm** 33.50 **t.**

XXX **Simpsons** (at Westpoint H.), Stewartfield Way, G74 5LA, NW : 2¼ m. on A 726 ☎ 36300, Fax 33552 – ⇔ ▤ P. AE VISA
closed dinner Thursday and Sunday – **M** (booking essential) 18.50/24.00 **t.** and a la carte 9.00.

The Guide changes, so renew your Guide every year.

EDINBURGH Midlothian. (Lothian) 401 K 16 Scotland G. – pop. 408 822 – ☎ 031.

See : City★★★ – Edinburgh International Festival★★★ (August) – National Gallery of Scotland★★★ DY **M4** – Royal Botanic Garden★★★ AV – The Castle★★ *AC* DYZ : Site★★★ – Palace Block (Honours of Scotland★★★) – St. Margaret's Chapel (✻★★★) – Great Hall (Hammerbeam Roof★★) – ≤★★ from Argyle and Mill's Mount DZ – Abbey and Palace of Holyroodhouse★★ *AC* (Plasterwork Ceilings★★★, ✻★★ from Arthur's Seat) BV – Royal Mile★★ : St. Giles' Cathedral★★ (Crown Spire★★★) EYZ – Gladstone's Land★ *AC* EYZ **A** – Canongate Talbooth★ EY **B** – New Town★★ (Charlotte Square★★★ CY **14** – Royal Museum of Scotland (Antiquities)★★ EZ **M2** – The Georgian House★ *AC* CY **D** – National Portrait Gallery★ EY **M3** – Dundas House★ EY **E**) – Victoria Street★ EZ **84** – Scott Monument★ (≤★) *AC* EY **F** – Craigmillar Castle★ *AC* BX – Calton Hill (✻★★★ *AC* from Nelson's Monument) EY.

Envir. : Edinburgh Zoo★★ *AC* AV – Hill End Ski Centre (✻★★) *AC*, S : 5½ m. by A 702 BX – The Royal Observatory (West Tower ≤★) *AC* BX – Ingleston, Scottish Agricultural Museum★, W : 6½ m. by A 8 AV.

Exc. : Rosslyn Chapel★★ *AC* (Apprentice Pillar★★★) S : 7½ m. by A 701 - BX - and B 7006 – Forth Bridges★★, NW : 9½ m. by A 90 AV – Hopetoun House★★ *AC*, NW : 11½ m. by A 90 - AV - and A 904 – Dalmeny★ - Dalmeny House★ *AC*, St. Cuthbert's Church★ (Norman South Doorway★★) NW : 7 m. by A 90 AV – Crichton Castle (Italianate courtyard range★) *AC*, SE : 10 m. by A 7 - X - and B 6372.

18, 18 Braid Hills, Braid Hills Rd ☎ 447 6666, S : 3 m. by A 702 BX – 18 Craigmillar Park, 1 Observatory Rd ☎ 667 2837, S : 2 m. by Cluny Gdns BX – 18 Carrick Knowe, Glendevon Park ☎ 337 1096, W : 2½ m. by A 8 AX – 18 Duddingston Road West ☎ 661 1005, E : 3 m. BV – 18 Silverknowes, Parkway ☎ 336 3843, NW : 4 m. by Marine Drive AV – 18 297 Gilmerton Rd ☎ 664 8580, S : 3 m. BX - 9 Portobello Stanley St. ☎ 669 4361, E : 5 m. by Millton Road West BV – 9 Dalmahoy, Kirknewton ☎ 333 4105, SW : 7 m. by A 71 AX.

✈ Edinburgh Airport ☎ 333 1000, W : 6 m. by A 8 AV – **Terminal** : Waverley Bridge.

🚗 ☎ 0345 090700.

ℹ Edinburgh & Scotland Information Centre, 3 Princes St., ☎ 557 1700 – Edinburgh Airport, Tourist Information Desk ☎ 333 2167.

♦Glasgow 46 – ♦Newcastle upon Tyne 105.

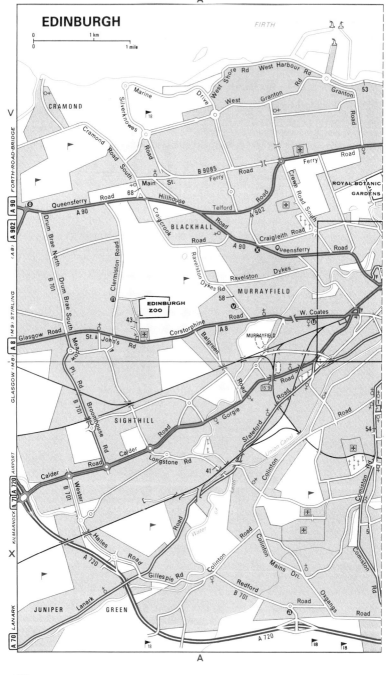

EDINBURGH

0 ____ 1 km
0 ____ 1 mile

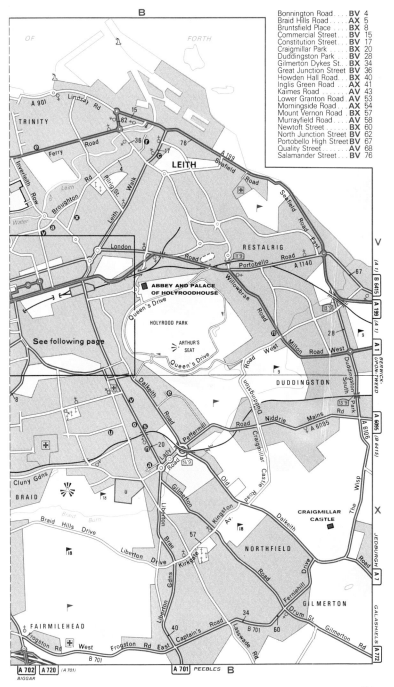

EDINBURGH
CENTRE

🏨🏨 **Caledonian** (Q.M.H.), Princes St., EH1 2AB, 𝒫 225 2433, Telex 72179, Fax 225 6632 – 🛗 ✕ rm 🖃 rest 📺 ☎ ⚿ 🅿 – 🔏 300. 🖪 ⒜🅴 ⓞ 𝓥𝓘𝓢𝓐 ✳ CY **n**
M Carriages 17.75/24.50 **t.** and a la carte ⓜ 6.50 – (see also **Pompadour** below) – ⌸ 14.50 –
228 rm 145.00/280.00 **t.**, 11 suites – SB (weekends only) 150.00/190.00 **st.**

🏨🏨 **Balmoral** (Forte), Princes St., EH2 2EQ, 𝒫 556 2414, Telex 727282, Fax 557 3747, 𝕝ऽ, ⛱,
🖪 – 🛗 ✕ rm 🖃 📺 ☎ ⚿ 🚗 – 🔏 200. 🖪 ⒜🅴 ⓞ 𝓥𝓘𝓢𝓐 ⒿⒸⒷ EY **n**
M 12.50 **t.** (lunch) and a la carte 11.75/20.50 **t.** – (see also **Grill** below) – ⌸ 11.25 – **168 rm**
120.00/215.00 **st.**, 21 suites – SB (weekends only) 189.00/198.00 **st.**

🏨🏨 **Sheraton Edinburgh,** 1 Festival Sq., EH3 9SR, 𝒫 229 9131, Telex 72398, Fax 228 4510,
𝕝ऽ, ⛱, 🖪 – 🛗 ✕ rm 🖃 📺 ☎ ⚿ – 🔏 450. 🖪 ⒜🅴 ⓞ 𝓥𝓘𝓢𝓐 ⒿⒸⒷ ✳ CDZ **v**
M 21.50 **st.** (lunch) and a la carte 20.00/51.00 **st.** ⓜ 6.00 – ⌸ 12.00 – **255 rm** 145.00/
195.00 **st.**, 6 suites – SB (weekends only) 160.00/260.00.

🏨🏨 **Carlton Highland,** 1-29 North Bridge, EH1 1SD, 𝒫 556 7277, Fax 556 2691, 𝕝ऽ, ⛱, 🖪,
squash – 🛗 ✕ rm 📺 ☎ ⚿ – 🔏 250. 🖪 ⒜🅴 ⓞ 𝓥𝓘𝓢𝓐 ✳ EY **s**
M 16.00 **t.** and a la carte ⓜ 5.00 – **193 rm** ⌸ 99.00/154.00 **t.**, 4 suites – SB (April-November)
(weekends only) 120.00/156.00 **st.**

🏨🏨 **George Inter-Continental,** 19-21 George St., EH2 2PB, 𝒫 225 1251, Telex 72570,
Fax 226 5644 – 🛗 ✕ rm 📺 ☎ ⚿ – 🔏 180. 🖪 ⒜🅴 ⓞ 𝓥𝓘𝓢𝓐 ⒿⒸⒷ ✳ DY **z**
M 15.95/23.00 **t.** and a la carte ⓜ 6.75 – **193 rm** 125.00/160.00 **st.**, 2 suites – SB (weekends
only) 137.00/306.00 **st.**

🏨🏨 **Dalmahoy H. Golf & Country Club** ⛳, Kirknewton, EH27 8EB, SW : 7 m. on A 71
𝒫 333 1845, Fax 335 3203, ≤, 𝕝ऽ, ⛱, 🖪, ⛱, ☞, park, ✳, squash – 🛗 ✕ rm 🖃 rest 📺
☎ ⚿ – 🔏 190. 🖪 ⒜🅴 ⓞ 𝓥𝓘𝓢𝓐 AX
M 18.00/25.00 **t.** and dinner a la carte – **114 rm** ⌸ 115.00/140.00 **t.**, 1 suite – SB (weekends only) 144.00/224.00 **st.**

🏨🏨 **Howard,** 32-36 Gt. King St., EH3 6QH, 𝒫 557 3500, Fax 557 6515, « Georgian town
houses » – 🛗 📺 ☎ ⚿ – 🔏 40. 🖪 ⒜🅴 ⓞ 𝓥𝓘𝓢𝓐 DY **s**
M (dinner only) 24.95 **t.** and a la carte – **16 rm** ⌸ 110.00/255.00 **st.** – SB (October-April
except Christmas-New Year) (weekends only) 150.00 **st.**

🏨🏨 **Scandic Crown,** 80 High St., EH1 1TH, 𝒫 557 9797, Telex 727298, Fax 557 9789, 𝕝ऽ, ⛱,
🛗 ✕ rm 🖃 📺 ☎ ⚿ – 🔏 200. 🖪 ⒜🅴 ⓞ 𝓥𝓘𝓢𝓐 ⒿⒸⒷ ✳ EY **z**
M 16.95/18.95 **st.** and a la carte – ⌸ 9.95 – **228 rm** 94.00/135.00 **st.**, 10 suites.

🏨🏨 **Swallow Royal Scot,** 111 Glasgow Rd, EH12 8NF, W : 4½ m. on A 8 𝒫 334 9191, Telex
727197, Fax 316 4507, 𝕝ऽ, ⛱, 🖪 – 🛗 ✕ rm 📺 ☎ ⚿ – 🔏 250. 🖪 ⒜🅴 ⓞ 𝓥𝓘𝓢𝓐 AV
M 15.50/18.75 **st.** and dinner a la carte – **255 rm** ⌸ 95.00/120.00 **st.**, 4 suites.

🏨🏨 **Hilton National,** Bells Mills, 69 Belford Rd, EH4 3DG, 𝒫 332 2545, Telex 727979,
Fax 332 3805 – 🛗 ✕ rm 📺 ☎ ⚿ – 🔏 120. 🖪 ⒜🅴 ⓞ 𝓥𝓘𝓢𝓐 ⒿⒸⒷ CY **i**
M 14.50/17.50 **t.** and dinner a la carte ⓜ 5.50 – ⌸ 10.50 – **144 rm** 98.00/190.00 **t.**

🏨🏨 **Capital Moat House** (Q.M.H.), Clermiston Rd, EH12 6UG, 𝒫 334 3391, Telex 728284,
Fax 334 9712, 𝕝ऽ, ⛱, 🖪 – 🛗 ✕ rm 📺 ☎ ⚿ – 🔏 300. 🖪 ⒜🅴 ⓞ 𝓥𝓘𝓢𝓐 AV **n**
M (buffet lunch)/dinner 15.95 **t.** and a la carte ⓜ 4.40 – ⌸ 7.95 – **110 rm** 78.00/94.00.

🏨🏨 Mount Royal (Jarvis), 53 Princes St., EH2 2DG, 𝒫 225 7161, Telex 727641, Fax 220 4671, ≤
– 🛗 📺 ☎ – 🔏 50 DY **a**
160 rm.

🏨🏨 **Royal Terrace,** 18 Royal Terrace, EH7 5AQ, 𝒫 557 3222, Telex 727182, Fax 557 5334, 𝕝ऽ,
⛱, 🖪, – 🛗 📺 ☎ – 🔏 50. 🖪 ⒜🅴 ⓞ 𝓥𝓘𝓢𝓐 ⒿⒸⒷ ✳ EY **i**
M (closed lunch Saturday and Sunday) a la carte 16.00/20.40 **t.** – ⌸ 9.00 – **94 rm** 99.00/
140.00 **st.**, 1 suite.

🏨 **King James Thistle** (Mt. Charlotte Thistle), 107 Leith St., EH1 3SW, 𝒫 556 0111, Telex
727200, Fax 557 5333 – 🛗 ✕ rm 📺 ☎ – 🔏 250. 🖪 ⒜🅴 ⓞ 𝓥𝓘𝓢𝓐 EY **u**
M (closed Sunday lunch) 18.50/20.50 **t.** and a la carte ⓜ 6.90 – ⌸ 9.75 – **142 rm** 79.00/
99.00 **st.**, 5 suites.

🏨 **Stakis Grosvenor,** Grosvenor St., EH12 5EF, 𝒫 226 6001, Telex 72445, Fax 220 2387 – 🛗
📺 ☎ ⚿ – 🔏 300. 🖪 ⒜🅴 ⓞ 𝓥𝓘𝓢𝓐 ⒿⒸⒷ CZ **a**
M (grill lunch) 9.50/14.95 **st.** and a la carte ⓜ 5.95 – ⌸ 8.50 – **135 rm** 84.00/109.00 **st.**,
1 suite – SB 74.00/124.00 **st.**

🏨 **Ellersly Country House** (Jarvis), 4 Ellersly Rd, EH12 6HZ, 𝒫 337 6888, Telex 727239,
Fax 313 2543, ☞ – 🛗 ✕ rm 📺 ☎ ⚿ – 🔏 70. 🖪 ⒜🅴 ⓞ 𝓥𝓘𝓢𝓐 AV **v**
M (bar lunch Saturday) 12.75/22.50 **t.** ⓜ 7.00 – ⌸ 8.75 – **57 rm** 79.00/104.00 **t.**

🏨 **Holiday Inn Garden Court,** 107 Queensferry Rd, EH4 3HL, 𝒫 332 2442, Telex 72541,
Fax 332 3408, ≤ – 🛗 ✕ rm 🖃 rest 📺 ☎ ⚿ – 🔏 50. 🖪 ⒜🅴 ⓞ 𝓥𝓘𝓢𝓐 ⒿⒸⒷ AV **x**
M (bar lunch)/dinner 14.90 **st.** and a la carte ⓜ 6.15 – ⌸ 8.45 – **119 rm** 84.50/150.00 **st.** –
SB 76.00/84.00 **st.**

🏨 **Barnton Thistle** (Mt. Charlotte Thistle), 562 Queensferry Rd, EH4 6AS, 𝒫 339 1144,
Fax 339 5521, ⛱ – 🛗 📺 ☎ ⚿ – 🔏 150. 🖪 ⒜🅴 ⓞ 𝓥𝓘𝓢𝓐 AV **o**
M (closed Saturday lunch) 14.00 **t.** (lunch) and a la carte 12.85/21.05 **t.** – ⌸ 8.75 – **48 rm**
75.00/85.00 **t.**, 2 suites.

🏨 **Channings,** South Learmonth Gdns, EH4 1EZ, ☎ 315 2226, Fax 332 9631 – 🛗 📺 ☎. 🔄
AE 🇻🇮 VISA ✗   CY **e**
closed 23 to 26 December – **M** (light lunch Saturday and Sunday) 7.50/16.50 and a la carte
🍴 4.80 – **48 rm** ⊡ 88.00/150.00 **t.** – SB (weekends only) 96.00 **st.**

🏨 **Bruntsfield** (Best Western), 69-74 Bruntsfield Pl., EH10 4HH, ☎ 229 1393, Telex 727897,
Fax 229 5634 – 🛗 📺 ☎ ☻. 🗛 VISA   DZ **u**
M 10.00/20.00 **st.** and a la carte 🍴 4.25 – **50 rm** ⊡ 55.00/120.00 **st.** – SB 96.00/170.00 **st.**

🏠 **Thrums,** 14-15 Minto St., EH9 1RQ, ☎ 667 5545, ☞ – 📺 ☎ ☻   BX **v**
closed 2 weeks Christmas-New Year – **M** 7.00/10.00 **t.** and a la carte 🍴 4.20 – **14 rm**
⊡ 35.00/65.00 **t.** – SB 75.00/90.00 **st.**

🏠 **Christopher North House,** 6 Gloucester Pl., EH3 6EF, ☎ 225 2720 – 📺 ☎. 🔄 AE ◉
VISA ✗   CY **s**
M *(closed Sunday lunch)* (bar lunch)/dinner a la carte approx. 13.50 **t.** – **11 rm** ⊡ 43.00/
80.00 **st.**

🏠 **Lodge,** 6 Hampton Terr., West Coates, EH12 5JD, ☎ 337 3682, Fax 313 1700 – ⇆ 📺 ℗.
🔄 VISA ✗   AV **u**
M *(closed Sunday)* (by arrangement) (dinner only) 15.50 **st.** 🍴 4.50 – **12 rm** ⊡ 45.00/
80.00 **st.** – SB (October-March) 68.00/120.00 **st.**

🏠 **Travel Inn,** 228 Willowbrae Rd, EH8 7NG, ☎ 661 3396, Fax 652 2789 – ⇆ rm 📺 ⅆ ℗.
🔄 AE VISA ✗   BV **n**
M (Beefeater grill) a la carte approx. 16.00 **t.** – ⊡ 4.95 – **39 rm** 33.50 **t.**

🏠 **Forte Travelodge** without rest., 48 Dreghorn Link, City Bypass, EH13 9QR, ☎ 441 4296,
Reservations (Freephone) 0800 850950 – 📺 ⅆ ℗. 🔄 AE VISA ✗   AX **a**
40 rm 31.95 **t.**

↑ **Sibbet House,** 26 Northumberland St., EH3 6LS, ☎ 556 1078, Fax 557 9445, « Georgian
town house » – ⇆ 📺 ☎. 🔄 VISA ✗   DY **x**
closed Christmas and New Year – **M** (by arrangement) 20.00 **st.** – **3 rm** ⊡ 50.00/65.00 **st.**

↑ **28 Northumberland Street** without rest., 28 Northumberland St., EH3 6LS, ☎ 557 8036,
Fax 558 3453, « Georgian town house » – ⇆ 📺. 🔄 ◉ VISA ✗   DY **x**
closed Christmas and New Year – **3 rm** ⊡ 30.00/60.00 **s.**

↑ **Stuart House** without rest., 12 East Claremont St., EH7 4JP, ☎ 557 9030, Fax 557 0563 –
⇆ 📺 🔄 VISA ✗   BV **x**
closed 1 week Christmas – **7 rm** ⊡ 30.00/70.00 **t.**

↑ **Dorstan,** 7 Priestfield Rd, EH16 5HJ, ☎ 667 6721, Fax 668 4644 – ⇆ rest 📺 ☎ ℗. 🔄
VISA ✗   BX **e**
M 14.00 **t.** – **14 rm** ⊡ 22.00/65.00 **t.**

↑ **International** without rest., 37 Mayfield Gdns, EH9 2BX, ☎ 667 2511, Fax 667 1109 – 📺.
✗   BX **s**
7 rm ⊡ 26.00/60.00.

↑ **Greenside** without rest., 9 Royal Terr., EH7 5AB, ☎ 557 0022, ☞ – ✗   EY **a**
closed January and February – **12 rm** ⊡ 24.50/61.00 **t.**

↑ **Teviotdale,** 53 Grange Loan, EH9 2ER, ☎ 667 4376, Fax 667 4376 – ⇆ 📺. 🔄 AE VISA
✗   BX **u**
closed 14 December-14 January – **M** (by arrangement) 18.50 **t.** – **7 rm** ⊡ 40.00/65.00 **t.**

↑ **Ravensdown** without rest., 248 Ferry Rd, EH5 3AN, ☎ 552 5438 – 📺. ✗   BV **e**
7 rm ⊡ 30.00/38.00 **s.**

↑ **Parklands** without rest., 20 Mayfield Gdns, EH9 2BZ, ☎ 667 7184. ✗   BX **o**
6 rm ⊡ 36.00/50.00.

↑ **Galloway** without rest., 22 Dean Park Cres., EH4 1PH, ☎ 332 3672 – 📺   CY **a**
10 rm ⊡ 22.00/44.00 **t.**

↑ **Glenisla,** 12 Lygon Rd, EH16 5QB, ☎ 667 4877, Fax 667 4098 – 🔄 VISA   BX **a**
M 12.50 **st.** 🍴 4.00 – **7 rm** ⊡ 21.50/52.00 **st.**

↑ **St. Margaret's** without rest., 18 Craigmillar Park, EH16 5PS, ☎ 667 2202 – 📺 ℗. 🔄 VISA
✗   BX **n**
closed January – **8 rm** ⊡ 25.00/44.00 **st.**

🍴🍴🍴🍴 **Pompadour** (at Caledonian H.), Princes St., EH1 2AB, ☎ 225 2433, Telex 72179,
Fax 225 6632 – ℗. 🔄 AE ◉ VISA   CY **n**
closed lunch Saturday and Sunday and Sunday dinner in winter – **M** 27.50/37.50 **t.** and dinner a la carte.

🍴🍴🍴🍴 **Grill** (at Balmoral H.), Princes St., EH2 2EQ, ☎ 557 6727, Telex 727282, Fax 557 3747 – 🖃
℗. 🔄 AE VISA JCB   EY **n**
closed lunch Saturday and Sunday – **M** 21.50/35.00 **st.** and a la carte.

🍴🍴 **Vintners Room,** The Vaults, 87 Giles St., Leith, EH6 6BZ, ☎ 554 6767, Fax 554 8423 – 🖃.
🔄 AE VISA   BV **r**
closed Sunday and 2 weeks Christmas-New Year – **M** a la carte 20.50/31.10 **t.** 🍴 5.00.

🍴🍴 **Martins,** 70 Rose St., North Lane, EH2 3DX, ☎ 225 3106 – ⇆. 🔄 AE ◉ VISA   DY **n**
*closed Saturday lunch, Sunday, Monday, 28 June-2 July, 24 September-1 October and
24 December-16 January* – **M** (booking essential) 16.95 **t.** (lunch) and a la carte 26.65/
32.50 **t.**

XX **L'Auberge,** 56 St. Mary's St., EH1 1SX, ☎ 556 5888, Fax 556 2588 – ▤. ⬛ AE ●
VISA EYZ **c**
closed 26 December and 1-2 January – **M** - **French** 11.00/30.00 **t.** and a la carte ⦚ 3.95.

XX **Raffaelli,** 10-11 Randolph Pl., EH3 7TA, ☎ 225 6060, Fax 225 8830 – ⬛ AE ● VISA
closed Saturday lunch, Sunday, 25-26 December and 2 January – **M** - **Italian** a la
carte 13.20/21.75 **t.** ⦚ 4.90. CY **c**

XX **Lancer's Brasserie,** 5 Hamilton Pl., Stockbridge, EH3 5BA, ☎ 332 3444 – ⬛ AE VISA
M - **North Indian** 8.95/25.00 **t.** and a la carte. CY **r**

XX **Indian Cavalry Club,** 3 Atholl Pl., EH3 8HP, ☎ 228 3282, Fax 225 1911 – ⬛ AE ● VISA
M - **Indian** 17.95 **t.** and a la carte ⦚ 6.00. CZ **o**

XX **Merchants,** 17 Merchant St., EH1 2QD, (under bridge) ☎ 225 4009, Fax 557 9318 – ⬛
AE ● VISA JCB EZ **x**
closed Sunday, 25-26 December and 1 January – **M** (booking essential) 14.50/21.50 **t.** and a
la carte ⦚ 4.70.

XX **Umberto's,** 29-33 Dublin St., EH3 6NL, ☎ 556 2231 – ⬛ AE ● VISA EY **e**
closed lunch Saturday and Sunday – **M** - **Italian** 8.95 **t.** (lunch) and a la carte 13.05/21.95 **t.**
⦚ 5.45.

XX **Denzler's 121,** 121 Constitution St., EH6 7AE, ☎ 554 3268 – ⬛ AE ● VISA JCB BV **c**
closed Saturday lunch, Sunday, Monday and 2 weeks July-August – **M** 15.00/23.50 **st.** and
a la carte ⦚ 5.35.

X **Atrium,** 10 Cambridge St., EH1 2ED, ☎ 228 8882 – ▤. ⬛ AE VISA DZ **c**
closed Sunday and 2 weeks Christmas – **M** 20.00/26.00 **t.** and a la carte ⦚ 4.50.

X **Le Marche Noir,** 2-4 Eyre Pl., EH3 5EP, ☎ 558 1608, Fax 556 0798 – ⬛ AE VISA BV **v**
closed lunch Saturday and Sunday, 25-26 December and 1-2 January – **M** (booking
essential) 16.50/22.50 **t.** ⦚ 4.25.

X **Indian Cavalry Club,** 8-10 Eyre Pl., New Town, EH3 5EP, ☎ 556 2404 – ⬛ AE ● VISA
M - **North Indian** 10.00/17.95 **t.** and a la carte. BV **a**

X **Verandah,** 17 Dalry Rd, EH11 2BQ, ☎ 337 5828, Fax 313 3853 – ⬛ AE ● VISA CZ **z**
M - North Indian a la carte 16.10/25.00 **t.** ⦚ 3.75.

X **Duncan's Land,** Gloucester St., Stockbridge, EH3 6EG, ☎ 225 1037 – ⬛ VISA CY **s**
*closed Saturday lunch, Sunday, Monday, 1 week February, 1 week June and 2 weeks
September* – **M** - **Italian** (booking essential) a la carte 14.00/20.00 **t.**

at Ingliston W : 7 ¾ m. on A 8 – AV – ✉ ✿ 031 Edinburgh :

🏨 **Norton House** ⬧, EH28 8LX, on A 8 ☎ 333 1275, Fax 333 5305, ≼, ⦙, park – 📺 ☎ &
Ⓟ – 🔆 200. ⬛ AE ● VISA
M *(closed Saturday lunch)* 15.50/21.00 **st.** and a la carte ⦚ 5.25 – **45 rm** ⬒ 100.00/
120.00 **st.**, 2 suites – SB (weekends only) 105.00 **st.**

⦿ ATS 167 Bonnington Rd, Leith ☎ 554 6617   ATS 6 Gylemuir Rd, Corstorphine ☎ 334 6174

EDZELL Angus. (Tayside) 📵 M 13 Scotland G. – pop. 751 – ECD : Thursday – ✿ 0356.

Envir. : Castle★ *AC* (The Pleasance★★★) W : 2 m.

Exc. : Glen Esk★, NW : 7 m.

▟ Trinity, Brechin ☎ 622383, S : 5 m. by B 966.

◆Edinburgh 94 – ◆Aberdeen 36 – ◆Dundee 31.

🏨 **Glenesk,** High St., DD9 7TF, ☎ 648319, Fax 647333, ⌁, ⥱, ⬚, ⦙ – 📺 ☎ Ⓟ – 🔆 80.
⬛ AE ● VISA
M 10.50/15.00 **t.** and a la carte – **24 rm** ⬒ 44.00/76.00 **t.**

ELGIN Moray. (Grampian) 📵 K 11 Scotland G. – pop. 18 702 – ECD : Wednesday – ✿ 0343.

See : Town★ - Cathedral★ (Chapter house★★) *AC.*

Exc. : Glenfiddich Distillery★, SE : 10 m. by A 941.

▟, ▟ Moray, Stotfield Rd, Lossiemouth ☎ 812018, N : 5 m. by A 941 and B 9135 –
▟ Hardhillock, Birnie Rd ☎ 542338 – ▟ Hopeman, Moray ☎ 830578, NW : 6 m. by B 9012.

🛈 17 High St. ☎ 542666.

◆Edinburgh 198 – ◆Aberdeen 68 – Fraserburgh 61 – ◆Inverness 39.

🏨 **Mansion House,** The Haugh, IV30 1AW, via Haugh Rd and Murdocks Wynd ☎ 548811,
Fax 547916, ⌁, ⥱, ⬚, ⦙ – 📺 ☎ Ⓟ. ⬛ AE ● VISA ⚸
M 12.50/30.00 **st.** and a la carte ⦚ 6.00 – **20 rm** ⬒ 75.00/140.00 **st.** – SB (weekends only)
120.00/150.00 **st.**

🏨 **Mansefield House,** 2 Mayne Rd, IV30 1NY, ☎ 540883, Fax 552491, ⥱ – ▯ ⥱ 📺 ☎ Ⓟ.
⬛ AE ● VISA ⚸
M 12.00 **t.** (lunch) and a la carte 20.15/34.70 **t.** ⦚ 5.70 – **16 rm** ⬒ 55.00/90.00 **t.** – SB (week-
ends only) 105.00/145.00 **st.**

⌂ **Lodge,** 20 Duff Av., IV30 1QS, ☎ 549981, ⦙ – ⥱ rest 📺 Ⓟ. ⚸
M (by arrangement) 12.00 **s.** – **8 rm** ⬒ 20.00/40.00 **s.**

⦿ ATS Moycroft ☎ 546333

ELIE Fife. (Fife) 401 L 15 – pop. 722 – ✆ 0333.

◆Edinburgh 41 – ◆Dundee 29 – Dunfermline 29.

XX **Bouquet Garni,** 51 High St., KY9 1BZ, ✆ 330374 – 🅴 🅰🅴 𝘝𝘐𝘚𝘈
closed Sunday dinner, first 2 weeks January and third week November – **M** a la carte 13.50/22.30 **t.** 🍷 6.40.

ERISKA (Isle of) Argyll. (Strathclyde) 401 D 14 – ⊠ Oban – ✆ 063 172 Ledaig

🏠 **Isle of Eriska** ⊗, PA37 1SD, ✆ 371, Fax 531, ⩽ Lismore and mountains, « Country house atmosphere », 🏞, 🏌, park, 🎾 – 🔟 ☎ 🕭 🄿, 🅴 𝘝𝘐𝘚𝘈
closed January and February – **M** (light lunch residents only)/dinner 35.00 **t.** 🍷 5.00 – **17 rm** 🍽 135.00/185.00 **t.**

ERSKINE Renfrew. (Strathclyde) 401 402 G 16 – ✆ 041 Glasgow.

◆Edinburgh 55 – ◆Glasgow 9.

🏨 **Forte Posthouse** ⊗, Erskine Bridge, PA8 6AN, on A 726 ✆ 812 0123, Fax 812 7642, ⩽, ⇆s, 🔲, 🏊 – 🕼 ⅙ rm 🗐 rest 🔟 ☎ 🄿 – 🔬 600. 🅴 🅰🅴 ⓄⒾ 𝘝𝘐𝘚𝘈
M a la carte approx. 17.50 **t.** 🍷 4.65 – 🍽 6.95 – **166 rm** 53.50 **st.** – SB (weekends only) 90.00 **st.**

FALKIRK Stirling. (Central) 401 I 16 – pop. 36 372 – ECD : Wednesday – ✆ 0324.

🏌 Polmonthill, Grangemouth ✆ 711500, E : 5 m. by A 803 and B 904 – 🏌 Polmont, Manuel Rigg, Maddiston ✆ 711277, SE : 4 m. by A 803 and B 805.

🎫 The Steeple, High St. ✆ 20244.

◆Edinburgh 26 – Dunfermline 18 – ◆Glasgow 25 – Motherwell 27 – Perth 43.

🏨 **Stakis Falkirk Park,** Camelon Rd, Arnothill, FK1 5RY, ✆ 28331, Telex 776502, Fax 611593 – 🕼 ⅙ rm 🔟 ☎ 🄿 – 🔬 200. 🅴 🅰🅴 ⓄⒾ 𝘝𝘐𝘚𝘈 𝘑𝘊𝘉
M (bar lunch)/dinner 13.95 **t.** and a la carte – 🍽 8.50 – **55 rm** 69.00/79.00 **st.** – SB 72.00/98.00 **st.**

at Polmont SE : 3 m. on A 803 – ⊠ ✆ 0324 Polmont :

🏨 **Inchyra Grange** (Best Western), Grange Rd, FK2 0YB, Kirk entry via Boness Rd ✆ 711911, Fax 716134, 🏋, ⇆s, 🔲, 🏊 – ⅙ rm 🔟 ☎ 🄿 – 🔬 220. 🅴 🅰🅴 ⓄⒾ 𝘝𝘐𝘚𝘈
M (bar lunch Saturday) 8.20/17.50 **t.** and a la carte – 🍽 8.00 – **43 rm** 75.00/125.00 **t.** – SB (weekends only) 70.00/98.00 **st.**

🚗 ATS Burnbank Rd ✆ 22958

FINSTOWN Orkney. (Orkney Islands) 401 K 6 – see Orkney Islands.

FIONNPHORT Argyll. (Strathclyde) 401 A 15 – Shipping Services : see Mull (Isle of).

FLODIGARRY Inverness. (Highland) - see Skye (Isle of).

FORFAR Angus. (Tayside) 401 L 14 – pop. 12 652 – ECD : Thursday – ✆ 0307.

🏌 Cunninghill ✆ 62120, E : 1 ½ m. by A 932.

🎫 The Library, West High St. ✆ 467876 (summer only).

◆Edinburgh 75 – ◆Aberdeen 55 – ◆Dundee 12 – Perth 31.

🏠 Royal, Castle St., DD8 3AE, ✆ 462691, Fax 462691, 🏋, ⇆s, 🔲 – 🔟 ☎ 🄿. 🎾 **19 rm.**

🚗 ATS Queenswell Rd ✆ 864501

FORRES Moray. (Grampian) 401 J 11 Scotland G. – pop. 8 346 – ECD : Wednesday – ✆ 0309.

See : Town★.

Envir. : Brodie Castle★ *AC*, W : 3 m. by A 96.

Exc. : Elgin★ (Cathedral★, Chapter House★★ *AC*) E : 10¼ m. by A 96.

🏌 Muiryshade ✆ 672949, S : 1 ½ m. by A 96.

🎫 Falconer Museum, Tolbooth St. ✆ 672938 (summer only).

◆Edinburgh 165 – ◆Aberdeen 80 – ◆Inverness 27.

🏠 **Ramnee,** Victoria Rd, IV36 0BN, ✆ 672410, Fax 673392, 🏞 – 🔟 ☎ 🄿 – 🔬 100. 🅴 🅰🅴 ⓄⒾ 𝘝𝘐𝘚𝘈
closed 25 December and 1 to 3 January – **M** 9.50/16.00 **t.** and a la carte 🍷 3.75 – **18 rm** 🍽 45.00/80.00 **st.** – SB (weekends only) 85.00/115.00 **st.**

🏠 **Knockomie** ⊗, Grantown Rd, IV36 0SG, S : 1 ½ m. on A 940 ✆ 673146, Fax 673290, 🏞 – ⅙ rest 🔟 ☎ 🄿 – 🔬 40. 🅴 🅰🅴 ⓄⒾ 𝘝𝘐𝘚𝘈
M 19.95/25.00 **st.** and a la carte 🍷 5.25 – **14 rm** 🍽 45.00/160.00 **st.** – SB (mid October-May except Bank Holidays) 92.00/158.00 **st.**

🏠 **Parkmount House,** St. Leonards Rd, IV36 0DW, ✆ 673312, Fax 673312, 🏞 – ⅙ rest 🔟 ☎ 🄿. 🅴 𝘝𝘐𝘚𝘈
closed 20 December-8 January – **M** (by arrangement) 15.50 **s.** – **8 rm** 🍽 35.00/60.00 **s.**

Don't get lost, use **Michelin Maps** which are kept up to date.

FORT AUGUSTUS Inverness. (Highland) 401 F 12 Scotland G. – pop. 573 – ✉ ✆ 0320.

Exc. : Loch Ness★★ – The Great Glen★.

⛳ Markethill ✆ 6460.

🅿 Car Park ✆ 6367 (summer only).

◆Edinburgh 166 – Fort William 32 – ◆Inverness 36 – Kyle of Lochalsh 57.

> 🏠 **Lovat Arms**, PH32 4DU, ✆ 6206, Fax 6677, ☞ – 📺 ☎ 🄿, 🅿 VISA
> **M** (bar lunch)/dinner 19.50 **st.** 🍷 4.30 – **21 rm** ☲ 33.50/73.00 **st.**

FORT WILLIAM Inverness. (Highland) 401 E 13 Scotland G. – pop. 10 805 – ECD : Wednesday except summer – ✆ 0397.

See : Town★.

Exc. : Road to the Isles★★ ≤★★ (Glenfinnan★ ≤★, Arisaig★, Silver Sands of Morar★, Mallaig★, Ardnamurchan Peninsula★★, Ardnamurchan Point ≤★★) NW : 46 m. by A 830 – SE : Glen Nevis★ (Ben Nevis★★ ≤★★ *AC*).

⛳ North Rd ✆ 704464.

🚗 ✆ 0345 090700.

🅿 Cameron Centre, Cameron Sq. ✆ 703781.

◆Edinburgh 133 – ◆Glasgow 104 – ◆Inverness 68 – ◆Oban 50.

> 🏰 ✿ **Inverlochy Castle** 📖, Torlundy, PH33 6SN, NE : 3 m. on A 82 ✆ 702177, Fax 702953, ≤ garden, loch and mountains, « Victorian castle in extensive grounds », 🎣, 🎾 – ≤× rest 📺 ☎ 🄿, 🅿 AE VISA 🛏
> *March-November* – **M** (booking essential) 30.00/43.00 **t.** 🍷 6.00 – **16 rm** ☲ 132.00/240.00 **t.**, 1 suite – SB (except May-October and Bank Holidays) 250.00 **st.**
> **Spec.** Loch Linnhe prawns, Roast loin of venison with celeriac, apple and walnuts, Orange soufflé.

> 🏠 **Factor's House**, Torlundy, PH33 6SN, NE : 3½ m. on A 82 ✆ 705767, Fax 702953, ☞ – 📺 ☎ 🄿, 🅿 AE VISA 🛏
> *March-October* – **M** *(closed Monday)* (dinner only) 23.00 **t.** 🍷 6.50 – **5 rm** ☲ 58.75/82.25 **t.**

> 🏠 Distillery House without rest., Nevis Bridge, North Rd, PH33 6LH, ✆ 700103, Fax 706277 – 📺 🄿
> **7 rm.**

> ↑ **Grange** without rest., Grange Rd, PH33 6JF, via Ashburn Lane ✆ 705516, ≤, ☞ – ≤× 📺 🄿
> *April-October* – **3 rm** ☲ 60.00 **st.**

> ↑ **Crolinnhe** without rest., Grange Rd, PH33 6JF, via Ashburn Lane ✆ 702709, ≤, ☞ – ≤× 📺 🄿
> *April-November* – **5 rm** ☲ 60.00 **st.**

> ↑ **Cabana House** without rest., Union Rd, PH33 6RB, ✆ 705991, ☞ – ≤× 📺 🄿, 🛏
> *closed October* – **3 rm** ☲ 25.00/42.00 **s.**

> *at Banavie* N : 3 m. by A 82 and A 830 on B 8004 – ✉ ✆ 0397 Fort William :

> 🏰 **Moorings**, PH33 7LY, ✆ 772797, Fax 772441, ≤, ☞ – ≤× rest 📺 ☎ 🄿, 🅿 AE ⓞ VISA 🛏
> *closed 24 to 26 December* – **M** – **Jacobean** (lunch by arrangement)/dinner 24.00 and a la carte 🍷 5.00 – **24 rm** ☲ 40.00/90.00 **t.** – SB (except Bank Holidays) 92.00/142.00 **st.**

GAIRLOCH Ross and Cromarty. (Highland) 401 C 10 Scotland G. – – ECD : Wednesday except summer – ✆ 0445.

Envir. : Loch Maree★★★, E : 5½ m. by A 832.

Exc. : Inverewe Gardens★★★ *AC*, NE : 8 m. by A 832 – Wester Ross★★★ – S : from Gairloch to Kyle of Lochalsh★★★ (vista★★, ≤★★★) – N : from Gairloch to Ullapool★★ (≤★★★).

⛳ Gairloch ✆ 2407, S : 1 m. by A 832.

🅿 Auchtercairn ✆ 2130.

◆Edinburgh 228 – ◆Inverness 72 – Kyle of Lochalsh 68.

> 🏠 **Shieldaig Lodge** 📖, IV21 2AW, S : 4½ m. by A 832 on B 8056 ✆ 044 583 (Badachro) 250, Fax 305, ≤ Gair Loch, « Former hunting lodge on lochside », 🎣, ☞ – ≤× rest 🄿
> *April-October* – **M** (bar lunch)/dinner 21.00 **t.** – **13 rm** ☲ 45.00/80.00 **t.**

GATEHOUSE OF FLEET Kirkcudbright. (Dumfries and Galloway) 401 402 H 19 – pop. 894 – ECD : Thursday – ✆ 0557.

⛳ Gatehouse of Fleet ✆ 814281.

🅿 Car Park ✆ 814212 (summer only).

◆Edinburgh 113 – ◆Dumfries 33 – Stranraer 42.

> 🏰 **Cally Palace** 📖, DG7 2DL, E : ½ m. on B 727 ✆ 814341, Fax 814522, ≤, ≋s, 🎱, ☞, park, 🎾 – ≤× rest 📺 ☎ 🄿, 🅿 VISA
> *closed 3 January-February* – **M** 21.00 **t.** (dinner) and a la carte 15.00/20.25 **t.** 🍷 5.80 – **50 rm** ☲ 62.00/135.00 **t.**, 6 suites – SB (except June-September and Christmas-New Year) (weekends only) 108.00/114.00 **st.**

Murray Arms, Ann St., DG7 2HY, ℰ 814207, Fax 814370, ☜, ☞ – 🖸 ☎. 🖾 ᴁ ◍ 𝗩𝗜𝗦𝗔
M (bar lunch)/dinner a la carte 7.40/21.75 **st.** ⌘ 4.50 – **13 rm** ⌑ 39.50/95.00 **st.** – SB (except Bank Holidays) 110.00/120.00 **st.**

GATTONSIDE Roxburgh. (Borders) – see Melrose.

GIFFNOCK Renfrew. (Strathclyde) 401 ⑪ 402 ⑨ – see Glasgow.

GIFFORD E. Lothian. (Lothian) 401 L 16 Scotland G. – pop. 665 – ECD : Monday and Wednesday – ✉ Haddington – ✆ 062 081 (3 fig.) and 0620 (6 fig.).

See : Village*.

Exc. : Northern foothills of the Lammermuir Hills**, S : 10½ m. by B 6355 and B 6368.

🛆 Edinburgh Rd ℰ 591.

◆Edinburgh 20 – Hawick 50.

Tweeddale Arms, High St., EH41 4QU, ℰ 240, Fax 488 – 🖸 ☎ ℗
15 rm.

GIGHA (Isle of) Argyll. (Strathclyde) 401 C 16 – ✆ 058 35 (3 fig.) and 0583 (6 fig.).

◆Edinburgh 168.

Gigha ☞, PA41 7AD, ℰ 254, Fax 254, ≼ Sound of Gigha and Kintyre Peninsula, ☞ – ℗.
🖾 𝗩𝗜𝗦𝗔
March-October – **M** (bar lunch)/dinner 18.50 **t.** ⌘ 4.50 – **13 rm** ⌑ 34.00/64.00 **t.**

GIRVAN Ayr (Strathclyde) 401 402 F 18 – ✆ 0465.

🛆 Brunston Castle, Dailly ℰ 81471, E : 4 m. – 🛆 Golf Course Rd ℰ 4272.

◆Edinburgh 100 – ◆Ayr 20 – ◆Glasgow 56 – Stranraer 31.

⌂ **Glendrissaig** without rest., KA26 0HJ, S : 1¾ m. by A 77 on A 714 ℰ 4631, ≼, ☞ – ⇥ ℗
3 rm ⌑ 20.00/40.00 **st.**

GLAMIS Angus. (Tayside) 401 K 14 Scotland G. – ✉ Forfar – ✆ 0307.

See : Village* - Castle** AC – Angus Folk Museum* AC.

Exc. : Meigle Museum** (early Christian Monuments**) AC, SW : 7 m. by A 94.

◆Edinburgh 60 – ◆Dundee 11 – Perth 25.

XX **Castleton House** with rm, Eassie, DD8 1SJ, W : 3¾ m. on A 94 ℰ 840340, Fax 840506, ☞ – ⇥ rest 🖸 ☎ ℗. 🖾 ᴁ 𝗩𝗜𝗦𝗔. ⌘
M 15.50/25.00 **t.** and a la carte – **6 rm** ⌑ 70.00/98.00 **t.** – SB 128.00/160.00 **st.**

When visiting Scotland,

use the Michelin Green Guide "Scotland".

– Detailed descriptions of places of interest

– Touring programmes

– Maps and street plans

– The history of the country

– Photographs and drawings of monuments, beauty spots, houses...

GLASGOW Lanark. (Strathclyde) 401 402 H 16 Scotland G. – pop. 754 586 – ✆ 041.

See : City*** – Cathedral*** (≼*) DZ – The Burrell Collection*** AX **M1** – Hunterian Art Gallery** (Whistler Collection***) – Mackintosh Wing***) AC CY **M4** – Museum of Transport** (Scottish Built Cars***, The Clyde Room of Ship Models***) AV **M3** – Art Gallery and Museum Kelvingrove** CY – Pollok House* (The Paintings**) AX **D** – Tolbooth Steeple* DZ **A** – Hunterian Museum (Coin and Medal Collection*) CY **M1** – City Chambers* DZ **C** – Glasgow School of Art* AC, CY **B** – Necropolis (≼* of Cathedral) DYZ.

Exc. : The Trossachs***, N : 31 m. by A 879 -BV - A 81 and A 821 – Loch Lomond**, NW : 19 m. by A 82 AV.

🛆 Littlehill, Auchinairn Rd, Bishopbriggs ℰ 772 1916, NE : by A 803 BV – 🛆 Deaconsbank, Rouken Glen Park, Stewarton Rd, Eastwood ℰ 638 7044, S : 5 m. by A 77 AX – 🛆 Linn Park, Simshill Rd ℰ 637 5871, S : 4 m. by B 766 BX – 🛆 Lethamhill, Cumbernauld Rd ℰ 770 6220, NE : 3 m. by B 765 BV – 🛆 Alexandra Park, Sannox Gdns, Alexandra Parade ℰ 556 3711, E : 2 m. by M 8 BV – 🛆 King's Park, 150a Croftpark Av., Croftfoot, S : 4 m. by B 766 BX – 🛆 Knightswood, Lincoln Av. ℰ 959 2131, NW : 4 m. by A 82 AV - 🛆 Ruchill, Brassey St. ℰ 946 7676, N : 2 m. by A 879 BV.

Access to Oban by helicopter.

✈ Glasgow Airport : ℰ 887 1111, W : 8 m. by M 8 AV – **Terminal** : Coach service from Glasgow Central and Queen Street main line Railway Stations and from Anderston Cross and Buchanan Bus Stations.

✈ see also Prestwick.

🛈 35 St. Vincent Pl. ℰ 204 4400 – Glasgow Airport, Tourist Information Desk, Paisley ℰ 848 4440.

◆Edinburgh 46 – ◆Manchester 221.

Glasgow Hilton, 1 William St., G3 8HT, ℰ 204 5555, Telex 778267, Fax 204 5004, ≤, ℐ₅, ⊜, 🗖 – 🛊 ⊱ rm ⊟ 🖵 ☎ & 🅟 – 🔏 1 000. 🖪 🖭 ⊙ 𝗩𝗜𝗦𝗔 𝗝𝗖𝗕 CZ **s**
M – **Minsky's** 16.95 **t.** and a la carte ⅛ 8.00 - (see also **Camerons** below) – ⊆ 13.50 – **317 rm** 115.00 **st.**, 4 suites – SB (weekends only) 167.90/282.90 **st.**

Glasgow Marriott, 500 Argyle St., Anderston, G3 8RR, ℰ 226 5577, Telex 776355, Fax 221 7676, ℐ₅, ⊜, 🗖, squash – 🛊 ⊱ rm ⊟ 🖵 ☎ & 🅟 – 🔏 700. 🖪 🖭 ⊙ 𝗩𝗜𝗦𝗔 ℅ CZ **a**
M 11.95/14.95 **t.** and a la carte – ⊆ 10.25 – **293 rm** 85.00/110.00 **t.**, 5 suites – SB (weekends only) 96.00/190.00 **st.**

Forte Crest, Bothwell St., G2 7EN, ℰ 248 2656, Telex 77440, Fax 221 8986, ≤ – 🛊 ⊱ rm ⊟ 🖵 ☎ 🅟 – 🔏 800. 🖭 ⊙ CZ **z**
M 13.50 **t.** and a la carte ⅛ 5.50 – ⊆ 9.50 – **248 rm** 99.00 **st.**, 3 suites – SB (except Christmas and New Year) (weekends only) 122.45/145.90 **st.**

One Devonshire Gardens, 1 Devonshire Gdns, G12 OUX, ℰ 339 2001, Fax 337 1663, « Opulent interior design » – 🖵 ☎ – 🔏 30. 🖪 🖭 ⊙ 𝗩𝗜𝗦𝗔 AV **a**
M *(closed Saturday lunch)* 19.00/35.00 **st.** ⅛ 8.00 – ⊆ 12.50 – **25 rm** 115.00/155.00 **t.**, 2 suites.

Moat House International (Q.M.H.), Congress Rd, G3 8QT, ℰ 204 0733, Telex 776244, Fax 221 2022, ≤, ℐ₅, ⊜, 🗖 – 🛊 ⊱ rm ⊟ 🖵 ☎ & 🅟 – 🔏 600. 🖪 🖭 ⊙ 𝗩𝗜𝗦𝗔 ℅ CZ **r**
M 15.95/17.95 **st.** and a la carte ⅛ 7.50 – ⊆ 10.95 – **268 rm** 97.00/107.00 **st.**, 15 suites – SB (weekends only) 99.00 **st.**

Hospitality Inn (Mt. Charlotte Thistle), 36 Cambridge St., G2 3HN, ℰ 332 3311, Telex 777334, Fax 332 4050 – 🛊 ⊱ rm 🖵 ☎ 🅟 – 🔏 1 500. 🖪 🖭 ⊙ 𝗩𝗜𝗦𝗔 𝗝𝗖𝗕 DY **z**
M *(closed Saturday lunch and Sunday)* 14.50/18.50 **st.** and a la carte – ⊆ 9.95 – **304 rm** 85.00/110.00 **st.**, 3 suites – SB (weekends only) 98.00 **st.**

Devonshire, 5 Devonshire Gdns, G12 0UX, ℰ 339 7878, Fax 339 3980 – 🖵 ☎ – 🔏 40. 🖪 🖭 𝗩𝗜𝗦𝗔 ℅ AV **a**
M (residents only) 15.00/35.00 **st.** and a la carte ⅛ 5.95 – ⊆ 9.75 – **14 rm** 80.00/200.00 **st.** – SB (weekends only) 110.00/160.00 **st.**

Copthorne Glasgow, George Sq., G2 1DS, ℰ 332 6711, Telex 778147, Fax 332 4264 – 🛊 ⊱ rm 🖵 ☎ – 🔏 100. 🖪 🖭 ⊙ 𝗩𝗜𝗦𝗔 ℅ DZ **n**
M *(closed lunch Saturday, Sunday and Bank Holidays)* (carving rest.) 12.95/15.95 **t.** and a la carte ⅛ 4.95 – ⊆ 8.95 – **136 rm** 94.00/121.00 **st.**, 4 suites – SB (weekends only) 90.00/150.00 **st.**

Swallow, 517 Paisley Rd West, G51 1RW, ℰ 427 3146, Fax 427 4059, ℐ₅, ⊜, 🗖 – 🛊 ⊱ rm ⊟ rest 🖵 ☎ 🅟 – 🔏 250. 🖪 🖭 ⊙ 𝗩𝗜𝗦𝗔 AX **a**
M *(closed Saturday)* 9.25/15.85 **st.** and dinner a la carte ⅛ 4.75 – **117 rm** ⊆ 80.00/130.00 **st.** – SB (except Christmas and New Year) (weekends only) 99.00 **st.**

Tinto Firs Thistle (Mt. Charlotte Thistle), 470 Kilmarnock Rd, G43 2BB, ℰ 637 2353, Telex 778329, Fax 633 1340 – 🖵 ☎ 🅟 – 🔏 90. 🖪 🖭 ⊙ 𝗩𝗜𝗦𝗔 AX **c**
M *(bar lunch Monday and Saturday)* 15.00/16.50 **t.** and a la carte ⅛ 4.75 – **25 rm** ⊆ 70.00/85.00 **st.**, 2 suites – SB (weekends only) 90.00 **st.**

Kelvin Park Lorne (Q.M.H.), 923 Sauchiehall St., G3 7TE, ℰ 334 4891, Telex 778935, Fax 337 1659 – 🛊 🖵 ☎ 🅟 – 🔏 175. 🖪 🖭 ⊙ 𝗩𝗜𝗦𝗔 CY **a**
closed 25-26 December and 2 January – **M** *(closed Saturday lunch)* 8.95/14.95 **t.** and a la carte ⅛ 4.50 – ⊆ 8.00 – **99 rm** 70.00/140.00 **t.** – SB (weekends only) 90.00 **st.**

Carrick, 377 Argyle St., G2 8LL, ℰ 248 2355, Fax 221 1014 – 🛊 ⊱ rm 🖵 ☎ 🅟 – 🔏 80. 🖪 🖭 ⊙ 𝗩𝗜𝗦𝗔 CZ **x**
closed 24 December-7 January – **M** *(closed lunch Saturday and Sunday)* (bar lunch)/dinner a la carte 11.30/18.40 **t.** ⅛ 6.60 – ⊆ 8.95 – **121 rm** 60.00 **st.** – SB 86.00 **st.**

Terrace House, 14 Belhaven Terr., G12 0TG, (off Great Western Rd) ℰ 337 3377, Fax 337 3377 – ⊱ rest 🖵 ☎. 🖪 🖭 ⊙ 𝗩𝗜𝗦𝗔 ℅ AV **x**
M (lunch by arrangement)/dinner a la carte 15.20/26.40 **st.** ⅛ 4.95 – **15 rm** ⊆ 52.00/68.00 **st.** – SB (weekends only) 65.00/120.00 **st.**

Manor Park, 28 Balshagray Drive, G11 7DD, ℰ 339 2143, Fax 339 5842 – 🖵 ☎. 🖪 🖭 𝗩𝗜𝗦𝗔 AV **u**
M (by arrangement) (dinner only) 16.50 **st.** and a la carte – **9 rm** ⊆ 35.00/65.00 **st.**

Albion without rest., 405-407 North Woodside Rd, G20 6NN, ℰ 339 8620, Fax 339 8159 – 🖵 ☎. 🖪 🖭 ⊙ 𝗩𝗜𝗦𝗔 ℅ CY **u**
M (dinner only) 18.00 **st.** and a la carte ⅛ 5.00 – **16 rm** ⊆ 35.00/50.00 **st.** – SB (weekends only) 45.00/70.00 **st.**

Town House, 4 Hughenden Terr., G12 9XR, ℰ 357 0862, Fax 339 9605 – ⊱ rest 🖵 ☎. 🖪 𝗩𝗜𝗦𝗔 AV **a**
M a la carte approx. 17.00 **st.** ⅛ 4.75 – **10 rm** ⊆ 48.00/59.00 **st.** – SB (October-April) (weekends only) 83.00/114.00 **st.**

Kirklee without rest., 11 Kensington Gate, G12 9LG, ℰ 334 5555, Fax 339 3828 – 🖵 ☎. 🖪 𝗩𝗜𝗦𝗔 AV **c**
9 rm ⊆ 47.00/59.00 **st.**

GLASGOW
BUILT UP AREA

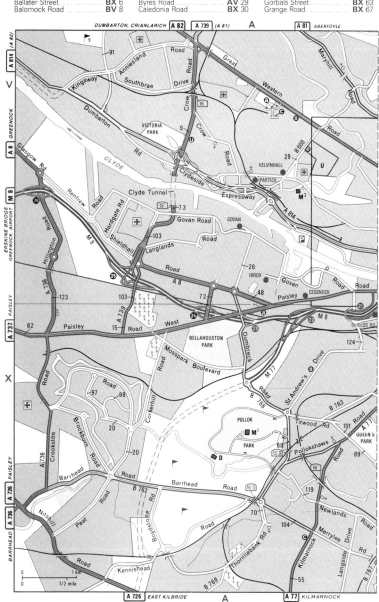

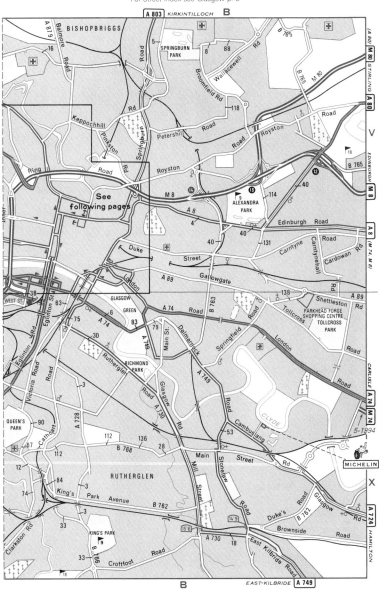

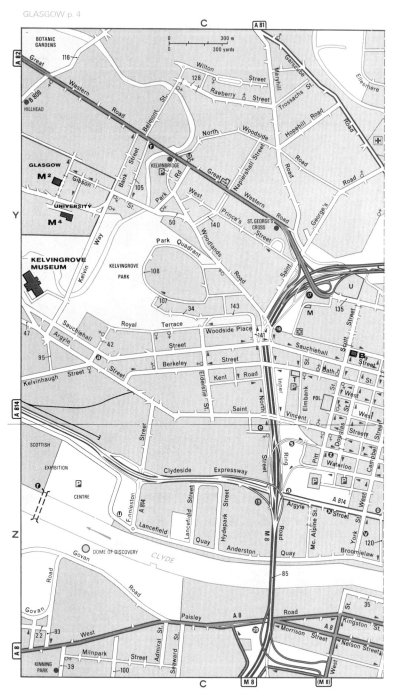

GLASGOW
CENTRE

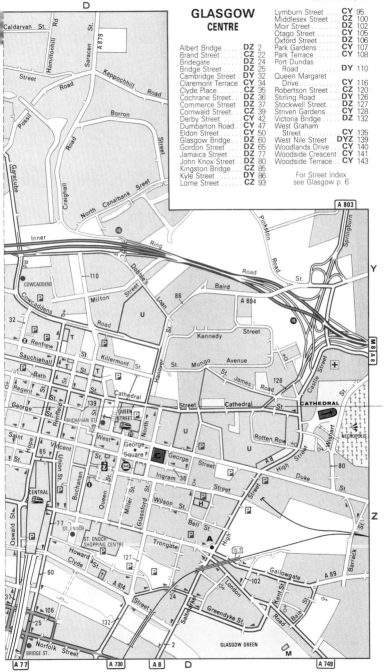

613

XXXX **Camerons** (at Glasgow Hilton H.), 1 William St., G3 8HT, ℘ 204 5555, Fax 204 5004 – 🖾
🅿   CZ **s**
closed Saturday lunch and Sunday – **M** (booking essential) 17.95/37.50 **t.** and a la carte
🍴 8.00.

XXX **North Rotunda,** 28 Tunnel St. (2nd floor), G3 8HL, ℘ 204 1238, Fax 226 4264 – 🅿. 🔼 ⒶⒺ
⓪ 𝚅𝙸𝚂𝙰   CZ **u**
closed Saturday lunch, Sunday, Monday, 26 December and 1-2 January – **M - French**
11.95/18.95 **t.** and a la carte 🍴 6.50.

XX **Buttery,** 652 Argyle St., G3 8UF, ℘ 221 8188, Fax 204 4639 – 🅿. 🔼 ⒶⒺ ⓪ 𝚅𝙸𝚂𝙰   CZ **e**
closed Saturday lunch, Sunday and Bank Holidays – **M** 14.75 **st.** (lunch) and a la
carte 19.95/27.90 **t.**

XX **Ho Wong,** 82 York St., G2 3LE, ℘ 221 3550 – 🖾. 🔼 ⒶⒺ ⓪ 𝚅𝙸𝚂𝙰   CZ **v**
closed 1 January and 1 week February – **M - Chinese** (Peking) 20.00/26.00 **t.** and a la carte
🍴 5.50.

XX **Rogano,** 11 Exchange Pl., G1 3AN, ℘ 248 4055, Fax 248 2608, « Art Deco » – 🖾. 🔼 ⒶⒺ
⓪ 𝚅𝙸𝚂𝙰   DZ **i**
closed Sunday lunch and Bank Holidays – **M - Seafood** 15.00 **t.** (lunch) and a la carte 23.50/
29.00 **t.**

XX **Sepoy Club** (at Dalmeny House H.), 62 St. Andrews Drive, Nithsdale Cross, Pol-
lokshields, G41 5EZ, ℘ 427 6288 – 🅿. 🔼 ⒶⒺ ⓪ 𝚅𝙸𝚂𝙰   AX **o**
M - Indian a la carte 8.20/12.45 **st.**

XX **Amber Royale,** 336 Argyle St., G2 8LY, ℘ 221 2550 – 🖾   CZ **o**
M - Chinese rest.

X **Ubiquitous Chip,** 12 Ashton Lane, off Byres Rd, G12 8SJ, ℘ 334 5007, Fax 337 1302 –
🔼 ⒶⒺ ⓪ 𝚅𝙸𝚂𝙰   AV **e**
closed 25 December and 1-2 January – **M** 10.00 **t.** (lunch) and a la carte 20.80/29.30 **t.**
🍴 3.95.

X **La Parmigiana,** 447 Great Western Rd, Kelvinbridge, G12 8HH, ℘ 334 0686 – 🖾. 🔼 ⒶⒺ
⓪ 𝚅𝙸𝚂𝙰   CY **r**
closed Sunday and Bank Holiday lunch – **M - Italian** 6.80 **st.** (lunch) and a la carte 13.45/
22.60 **t.** 🍴 5.35.

at Stepps NE : 5 ½ m. by M 8 on A 80 – BY – 🖂 🕲 041 Glasgow :

🏨 **Garfield House,** Cumbernauld Rd, G33 6HW, ℘ 779 2111, Fax 779 2111 – ⇤ rm 📺 ☎
🅿 – 🔬 120. 🔼 ⒶⒺ ⓪ 𝚅𝙸𝚂𝙰
M 9.00/23.00 and dinner a la carte – **46 rm** 🖛 66.00/82.50 **t.** – SB (weekends only)
106.00/174.00 **st.**

at Giffnock (Renfrew.) (Strathclyde) S : 5 ¼ m. by A 77 – AX – 🖂 🕲 041 Glasgow :

🏨 **MacDonald Thistle** (Mt. Charlotte Thistle), Eastwood Toll, G46 6RA, at junction of A 77
with A 726 ℘ 638 2225, Telex 779138, Fax 632 6231, 🖙 – 📺 ☎ 🅿 – 🔬 100. 🔼 ⒶⒺ ⓪ 𝚅𝙸𝚂𝙰
ⒿⒸⒷ
M (bar lunch Saturday and Bank Holidays) 10.50/19.50 **t.** and a la carte 🍴 4.90 – **52 rm**
🖛 70.00/85.00 **t.**, 4 suites – SB (weekends only) 70.00 **st.**

🏠 **Redhurst** (Chef & Brewer), 77 Eastwoodmains Rd, G46 6QE, ℘ 638 6465, Fax 620 0419 –
📺 ☎ 🅿. 🔼 ⒶⒺ 𝚅𝙸𝚂𝙰. ⚘
M 15.00/20.00 **t.** and a la carte – **17 rm** 🖛 34.95/38.45 **t.**

X **Turban Tandoori,** 2 Station Rd, G46 6JF, ℘ 638 6269 – 🔼 ⒶⒺ 𝚅𝙸𝚂𝙰
closed 25 December and 1 January – **M - Indian** (dinner only) 13.00 **t.** and a la carte 🍴 6.50.

at Busby S : 7 ¼ m. by A 77 – AX – on A 726 – 🖂 🕲 041 Glasgow :

🏨 **Busby,** 1 Field Rd, Clarkston, G76 8RX, ℘ 644 2661, Fax 644 4417 – 🕮 ⇤ rm 📺 ☎ 🅿 –
🔬 150. 🔼 ⒶⒺ ⓪ 𝚅𝙸𝚂𝙰. ⚘
M 6.75/15.95 **t.** and a la carte 🍴 4.95 – **32 rm** 🖛 55.00/85.00 **t.** – SB (weekends only)
70.00/100.00 **t.**

MICHELIN Distribution Centre, 60 Cunningham Rd, Rutherglen, G73 1PP, ℘ 643 2101,
Fax 647 5267 p. 3 BX
🆗 ATS 192 Finnieston St. ℘ 248 6761   ATS 1 Sawmillfield St., off Garscube Rd
ATS Rutherglen Ind. Est., Glasgow Rd, Rutherglen   ℘ 332 1945
℘ 647 9341

GLENBORRODALE Argyll. (Highland) 🗺 C 13 – 🖂 Acharacle – 🕲 097 24.
◆Edinburgh 151 – ◆Inverness 108 – ◆Oban 72.

🏰 **Glenborrodale Castle** 🔊, Ardnamurchan, PH36 4JP, ℘ 266, Fax 224, ≤ Loch Sunart
and gardens, « Victorian castle in extensive gardens », 🎣, 🖙, 🎿, park, ⚘ – ⇤ rest 📺
☎ 🅿. 🔼 ⒶⒺ 𝚅𝙸𝚂𝙰
Easter-October – **M** (booking essential) 19.50/32.50 **t.** 🍴 10.50 – 🖛 6.50 – **16 rm** 105.00/
260.00 **t.**

GLENCARSE Perth. (Tayside) 🗺 K 14 -see Perth.

GLENCRIPESDALE Argyll. (Highland) – see Strontian.

GLENELG Ross and Cromarty (Highland) **401** D 12 – ☻ 059 982.
◆Edinburgh 229 – ◆Inverness 75 – Kyle of Lochalsh 25.

　⚓ **Glenelg Inn,** IV40 8AJ, ☏ 273, Fax 373, ⇐ Glenelg Bay, ⤷, ☞ – **Ⓟ**
　　Easter-October – **M** 10.00/19.00 **t.** ⓪ 4.00 – **6 rm** ⚟ (dinner included) 70.00/150.00 **t.**

GLENFINNAN Inverness. (Highland) **401** D 13 – ✉ ☻ 0397 Fort William.
◆Edinburgh 150 – ◆Inverness 85 – ◆Oban 66.

　⚓ **Stage House,** PH37 4LT, W : ¾ m. on A 830 ☏ 722246, Fax 722307, ⇐ – ⧏✕ ⊡ **Ⓟ**. ☒ 𝐀𝐄
　　VISA
　　April-December – **M** *(closed Thursday)* (in bar) 25.95 **t.** (dinner) – **9 rm** ⚟ 44.95/69.90 **t.** –
　　SB 79.90/115.90 **st.**

GLENLIVET Banff. (Grampian) **401** J 11 – ✉ Ballindalloch – ☻ 0807.
◆Edinburgh 180 – ◆Aberdeen 59 – Elgin 27 – ◆Inverness 49.

　⚓ **Minmore House** ⤷, AB37 9DB, S : ¾ m. on Glenlivet Distillery rd ☏ 590378,
　　Fax 590472, ⇐, ☞ – ⧏✕ rest ☎ **Ⓟ**. ☒ **VISA**
　　28 April-30 October – **M** (dinner only) 22.00 **st.** ⓪ 4.00 – **10 rm** ⚟ 32.00/64.00 **st.** –
　　SB 96.00 **st.**

GLENLUCE Wigtown. **401** F 19 – ✉ Newton Stewart – ☻ 058 13.
🅱 Wigtownshire County, Mains of Park, Newton Stewart ☏ 420, W : 1 ½ m. by A 75.
◆Edinburgh 126 – ◆Ayr 62 – Dumfries 65 – Stranraer 9.

　⚓ **Kelvin House,** 53 Main St., DG8 0PP, ☏ 303 – ⊡. ⧏
　　M (bar lunch Monday to Saturday)/dinner 16.50 **t.** and a la carte ⓪ 4.25 – **5 rm** ⚟ 18.50/
　　45.00 **t.**

GLENROTHES Fife. (Fife) **401** K 15 Scotland G. – pop. 33 639 – ECD : Tuesday – ☻ 0592.
Envir. : Falkland★ (Village★, Palace of Falkland★ *AC*, Gardens★ *AC*) N : 5 ½ m. by A 92 and
A 912.
🅱 Thornton, Station Rd ☏ 771111, SE : 2 ½ m. by A 92 – 🅱 Golf Course Rd ☏ 758686/758678 –
🅱 Balbirnie Park, Markinch ☏ 752006, NE : 2 m. by A 92 – 🅱 Auchterderran, Woodend Rd,
Cardenden ☏ 721579, SW : 5 ½ m. by b 969 and B 921 – 🅱 The Myre, Falkland ☏ 0337
(Falkland) 57404, N : 5 m. – 🅱 Leslie, Balsillie Laws ☏ 620040, W : 3 m. by A 911.
🅱 Lyon Sq., Kingdom Centre, ☏ 610784.
◆Edinburgh 33 – ◆Dundee 25 – Stirling 36.

　🏨 **Albany** (Chef & Brewer), 1 North St., KY7 5NA, ☏ 752292, Fax 756451 – 🛗 ⊡ ☎ – 𝐀 200.
　　☒ 𝐀𝐄 **VISA**. ⧏
　　M 15.00/20.00 **t.** and a la carte – ⚟ 3.50 – **29 rm** 34.95/38.45 **t.**

　at Markinch NE : 1 ¾ m. by A 911 and A 92 on B 9130 – ✉ ☻ 0592 Glenrothes :

　🏨 **Balbirnie House** ⤷, Balbirnie Park, KY7 6NE, ☏ 610066, Fax 610529, « Part 18C man-
　　sion », 🎣, ☞, park – ⊡ ☎ **Ⓟ** – 𝐀 120. ☒ 𝐀𝐄 **①** **VISA**. ⧏
　　M 25.50 **t.** (dinner) and lunch a la carte ⓪ 5.40 – **29 rm** ⚟ 95.00/180.00 **t.**. 1 suite –
　　SB (weekends only) 150.00 **st.**

　at Leslie W : 3 m. by A 911 – ✉ Leslie – ☻ 0592 Glenrothes :

　⚓ **Rescobie,** 6 Valley Drive, KY6 3BQ, ☏ 742143, Fax 620231, ☞ – ⊡ ☎ **Ⓟ**. ☒ 𝐀𝐄 **①** **VISA**.
　　⧏
　　closed 25 to 27 December – **M** 16.00 **t.** (dinner) and a la carte ⓪ 4.85 – **10 rm** ⚟ 49.50/
　　70.00 **t.** – SB (weekends only) 84.00/112.00 **st.**

GOLSPIE Sutherland. (Highland) **401** I 10 – pop. 1 385 – ECD : Wednesday – ✉ ☻ 0408.
🅱 Ferry Rd ☏ 633266.
◆Edinburgh 228 – ◆Inverness 72 – ◆Wick 54.

　🏨 **Sutherland Arms,** Old Bank Rd, KW10 6RS, ☏ 633234, Fax 633234, ☞ – ⊡ ☎ **Ⓟ** –
　　𝐀 30. ☒ **VISA**
　　closed January – **M** (bar lunch)/dinner 16.95 **t.** and a la carte ⓪ 4.50 – **12 rm** ⚟ 35.00/
　　60.00 **t.** – SB (except June-August) 80.00/100.00 **st.**

GOUROCK Renfrew. (Strathclyde) **401** F 16 Scotland G. – pop. 11 087 – ECD : Wednesday –
☻ 0475.
Envir. : Greenock (⇐★★) E : 3 m. by A 770.
Exc. : The Clyde Estuary★.
🅱 Whinhill, Beith Rd, Greenock ☏ 24694, SE : 6 m. by A 770, A 78 and B 7054.
⚓ by Caledonian MacBrayne : from Railway Pier to Dunoon Pier : frequent services daily
(20 mn) – by Western Ferries : from McInroy's Point to Hunters Quay, Dunoon : frequent
services daily (20 mn).
⚓ by Caledonian MacBrayne : to Helensburgh, via Kilcreggan, 2-10 daily (except Sundays) –
from Wemyss Bay to Rothesay, frequent sevices daily (except Sundays).
🅱 Pierhead ☏ 39467 (summer only).
◆Edinburgh 71 – ◆Ayr 47 – ◆Glasgow 27.

🏠 **Stakis Gourock Gantock,** Cloch Rd, PA19 1AR, SW : 2 m. on A 770 ℰ 634671, Telex 778584, Fax 32490, ≼ Firth of Clyde, ⇌s, 🖂, ℁ – ⧉ 🛏 rm 🆅 ☎ 🄿 – 🚗 180. 🔼 🄰🄴 ⓞ 𝐕𝐈𝐒𝐀 𝐉𝐂𝐁
M 9.00/14.95 **t.** and a la carte – 🞏 7.95 – **99 rm** 72.00/92.00 **st.**, 1 suite – SB 78.00/104.00 **st.**

GRANTOWN-ON-SPEY Moray. (Highland) 𝟒𝟎𝟏 J 12 – pop. 1 800 – ECD : Thursday – 🟤 0479.
🏌 Grantown ℰ 872079 – 🏌 Abernethy, Nethy Bridge ℰ 821305, S : 3 m. by A 95 and B 970.
🄱 High St. ℰ 872773 (summer only).
♦Edinburgh 143 – ♦Inverness 34 – Perth 99.

🏠 **Ravenscourt House,** Seafield Av., PH26 3JG, ℰ 872286, Fax 873260 – ⧉ rest 🆅 🄿. 🔼 𝐕𝐈𝐒𝐀
closed December and January – **M** (dinner only) 22.50 **t.** ⑂ 3.00 – **9 rm** 🞏 39.00/70.00 **t.**

🏠 **Garth,** The Square, PH26 3HN, ℰ 872836, Fax 872116, ℛ – ⧉ rest 🆅 ☎ 🄿. 🔼 🄰🄴 ⓞ 𝐕𝐈𝐒𝐀 ℁
M (bar lunch)/dinner 24.00 **st.** and a la carte – **14 rm** 🞏 39.00/78.00 **st.** – SB 101.00/120.00 **st.**

🏠 **Culdearn House,** Woodlands Terr., PH26 3JU, ℰ 872106, Fax 873641, ℛ – ⧉ rest 🆅 🄿. 🔼 𝐕𝐈𝐒𝐀
March-October – **M** (residents only) (dinner only) ⑂ 3.65 – **9 rm** 🞏 (dinner included) 45.00/90.00 **st.** – SB 84.00 **st.**

🏠 **Ardlarig,** Woodlands Terr., PH26 3JU, ℰ 873245, ℛ – ⧉ rest 🆅 🄿
closed 1 week Christmas – **M** 10.50 **s.** ⑂ 2.40 – **7 rm** 🞏 18.50/37.00 **st.** – SB (November-April except New Year) 100.00 **st.**

🏠 **Ardconnel,** Woodlands Terr., PH26 3JU, ℰ 872104, Fax 872104, ℛ – ⧉ 🆅 🄿. 🔼 𝐕𝐈𝐒𝐀 ℁
closed January, February and November – **M** 13.50 **t.** ⑂ 3.50 – **6 rm** 🞏 28.00/50.00 **t.** – SB (March, April and October) 68.00/80.00 **st.**

"Short Breaks" (SB)

De nombreux hôtels proposent des conditions avantageuses

pour un séjour de deux nuits

comprenant la chambre, le dîner et le petit déjeuner.

GRETNA Dumfries. (Dumfries and Galloway) 𝟒𝟎𝟏 𝟒𝟎𝟐 K 19 – pop. 2 737 – ECD : Wednesday – ✉ Carlisle (Cumbria) – 🟤 0461.
🄱 The Old Headless Cross ℰ 37834 (summer only) – Gateway to Scotland, M 74 Service Area ℰ 38500.
♦Edinburgh 91 – ♦Carlisle 10 – ♦Dumfries 24.

🏠 **Garden House,** Sarkfoot Rd, CA6 5EP, on B 7076 ℰ 37621, Fax 37692, 🎿, ⇌s, 🖂 – 🆅 ☎ ⑂ 🄿. 🔼 🄰🄴 ⓞ 𝐕𝐈𝐒𝐀 𝐉𝐂𝐁. ℁
M 12.95/18.00 **t.** and a la carte ⑂ 3.30 – **21 rm** 🞏 39.00/90.00 **t.** – SB 106.00/120.00 **st.**

🏠 **Gretna Chase,** CA6 5JB, S : ¼ m. on B 7076 ℰ 37517, « Gardens » – 🆅 🄿. 🔼 🄰🄴 ⓞ 𝐕𝐈𝐒𝐀
closed 2 weeks January – **M** (closed Sunday) (bar lunch) a la carte 12.45/19.50 **t.** ⑂ 3.50 – **9 rm** 🞏 38.00/80.00 **st.**

🏠 **Forte Travelodge** without rest., CA6 5HQ, NW : 1½ m. by B 721 on A 74 (M) ℰ 37566, Fax 37752, Reservations (Freephone) 0800 850950 – 🆅 ⑂ 🄿. 🔼 🄰🄴 𝐕𝐈𝐒𝐀. ℁
64 rm 31.95 **t.**

GULLANE E. Lothian. (Lothian) 𝟒𝟎𝟏 L 15 Scotland G. – pop. 2 124 – ECD : Wednesday – 🟤 0620.
Envir. : Dirleton★ (Castle★) NE : 2 m. by A 198.
🏌 🏌, 🏌 Gullane ℰ 843115.
♦Edinburgh 19 – North Berwick 5.

🏠 **Greywalls** ⌂, Duncur Rd, Muirfield, EH31 2EG, ℰ 842144, Fax 842241, ≼ gardens and golf course, « Lutyens house, gardens by Gertrude Jekyll », ℁ – 🆅 ☎ 🄿. 🔼 🄰🄴 ⓞ 𝐕𝐈𝐒𝐀
April-October – **Meals** 33.00 **t.** (dinner) and lunch a la carte approx. 15.50 **t.** ⑂ 6.00 – **23 rm** 🞏 90.00/150.00 **t.** – SB (April and October) 170.00 **st.**

❌ ⌂ **La Potinière** (Hilary Brown), Main St., EH31 2AA, ℰ 843214 ⧉
closed 1 week June, October, 25-26 December and 1-2 January – **M** (closed lunch Friday and Saturday, dinner Sunday to Thursday and Wednesday) (booking essential) 19.50/28.50 **t.** ⑂ 4.75
Spec. Fried salmon with spicy lentils and a wild mushroom sauce. Guinea fowl leg with an apricot and mint stuffing. Warm gratin of raspberries.

at Dirleton NE : 2 m. by A 198 – ✉ 🟤 062 085 (3 fig.) and 0620 (6 fig.) Dirleton :

❌❌ **Open Arms** with rm, EH39 5EG, ℰ 241, Fax 570, « Tastefully converted stone cottages », ℛ – 🆅 ☎ 🄿. 🔼 𝐕𝐈𝐒𝐀
M (light lunch)/dinner 27.50 **st.** and a la carte ⑂ 6.75 – **7 rm** 🞏 75.00/120.00 **st.** – SB (October-May except Christmas and New Year) 120.00/220.00 **st.**

HADDINGTON E. Lothian. (Lothian) �401 L 16 Scotland G. – pop. 7 988 – ECD : Thursday – ✆ 062 082 (4 fig.) and 0620 (6 fig.).

See : Town★ - High Street★.

Envir. : Lennoxlove★ *AC*, S : 1 m.

Exc. : Tantallon Castle★★ (clifftop site★★★) *AC*, NE : 12 m. by A 1 and A 198 – Northern foothills of the Lammermuir Hills★★, S : 14 m. by A 6137 and B 6368 – Stenton★, E : 7 m.

🛆 Amisfield Park ♟ 3627.

♦Edinburgh 17 – Hawick 53 – ♦Newcastle upon Tyne 101.

🏨 **Maitlandfield House**, 24 Sidegate, EH41 4BZ, ♟ 6513, Fax 6713, ☞ – 📺 ☎ ℗ – 🔼 250. 🔝 *VISA*
M 15.00/20.00 **st.** and a la carte 🔷 3.95 – **22 rm** �y½ 37.50/57.50 **st.**

XX **Brown's** with rm, 1 West Rd, EH41 3RD, ♟ 822254, Fax 822254, ☞ – 📺 ☎ ℗. 🔝 🄰🄴 🄾 *VISA*. ✻
M (booking essential) (dinner only and Sunday lunch) dinner 24.50 **t.** – **5 rm** ⊐ 59.50/78.00 **t.**

HALKIRK Caithness. (Highland) �401 J 8 – ✆ 084 784 Westerdale.

♦Edinburgh 285 – Thurso 8 – ♦Wick 17.

⌂ **Bannochmore Farm** ⬎, (The Bungalow) Harpsdale, KW12 6UN, S : 3 ¼ m. ♟ 216, « Working farm », park – ℗ ✻
M (communal dining) 10.00 **s.** – **3 rm** ⊐ 14.00/32.00.

HAMILTON SERVICE AREA Lanark. (Strathclyde) – ✆ 0698.

🛆 Larkhall, Burnhead Rd ♟ 881113, SE : 4 m. by A 724, B 7078 and B 7019 – 🛆 Mote Hill ♟ 60155.

🄱 Road Chef Services, M 74 northbound, ♟ 285590.

♦Edinburgh 38 – ♦Glasgow 12.

🏨 **Road Chef Lodge** without rest., ML3 6JW, M 74 between junctions 6 and 5 (northbound carriageway) ♟ 891904, Fax 891682 – ⊱ 📺 ☎ ℗ ♟ – 🔼 25. 🔝 🄰🄴 🄾 *VISA*. ✻
closed 25 to 27 December – ⊐ 5.25 – **36 rm** 37.50/44.00 **st.**

HARRIS (Isle of) Inverness. (Outer Hebrides) (Western Isles) �401 Z 10 – see Lewis and Harris (Isle of).

HAWICK Roxburgh. (Borders) �401 �402 L 17 Scotland G. – pop. 16 213 – ECD : Tuesday – ✆ 0450.

Exc. : Jedburgh Abbey★★ *AC*, SW : 12½ m. by A 698 – Waterloo Monument (✳★★) NE : 12 m. by A 698, A 68 and B 6400 – Hermitage Castle★, S : 16 m. by B 6399.

🛆 Hawick, Vertish Hill ♟ 72293 (changing in May to 372293), S : 1½ m. – 🛆 Minto, Denholm ♟ 87220 (changing in May to 387220), NE : 6 m. by A 698.

🄱 Common Haugh ♟ 72547 (changing in May to 372547) (summer only).

♦Edinburgh 51 – ♦Ayr 122 – ♦Carlisle 44 – ♦Dumfries 63 – Motherwell 76 – ♦Newcastle upon Tyne 62.

🏨 **Kirklands**, West Stewart Pl., TD9 8BH, ♟ 72263 (changing in May to 372263), Fax 370404, ☞ – 📺 ☎ ℗. 🔝 🄰🄴 🄾 *VISA* 🄹🄲🄱
closed 25 and 26 December – **M** 19.50 **t.** (dinner) and a la carte 12.60/22.20 **t.** 🔷 4.25 – **12 rm** ⊐ 48.50/75.00 **t.** – SB (weekends only) 75.00/80.00 **st.**

⌂ **Rubislaw** ⬎, Newhouses, TD9 8PR, N : 3 m. by A 7 ♟ 77693 (changing in May to 377693), < Rubers law and Cheviot hills, ☞ – ⊱ 📺 ℗. 🔝 *VISA*. ✻
closed Christmas and New Year – **M** 18.00 **st.** 🔷 4.75 – **3 rm** ⊐ 34.00/56.00 **st.**

🔘 ATS Victoria Rd ♟ 73369 (changing in May to 373369)

HEITON Roxburgh. (Borders) – see Kelso.

HELENSBURGH Dunbarton. (Strathclyde) �401 F 15 Scotland G. – pop. 16 432 – ECD : Wednesday – ✆ 0436.

See : Hill House★ *AC*.

Envir. : Loch Lomond★★, NE : 4½ m. by B 832.

⛴ to Gourock via Kilcreggan (Caledonian MacBrayne) 2-10 daily (except Sunday).

🄱 The Clock Tower ♟ 72642 (summer only).

♦Edinburgh 68 – ♦Glasgow 22.

🏨 **Commodore Toby**, 112-117 West Clyde St., G84 8ER, ♟ 76924, Fax 76233, < – 📶
⊱ rm 📺 ☎ ℗ – 🔼 200. 🔝 🄰🄴 🄾 *VISA*
M (grill rest.) 12.00/15.00 **t.** 🔷 3.65 – **44 rm** ⊐ 57.00/74.00 **t.**, 1 suite – SB (weekends only) 69.95/159.90 **st.**

"Short Breaks" (SB)

Zahlreiche Hotels bieten Vorzugspreise bei einem Aufenthalt von zwei Nächten.
Diese Preise umfassen Zimmer, Abendessen und Frühstück.

HUMBIE E. Lothian (Lothian) 401 L 16 – ☎ 087 533.
◆Edinburgh 19 – Hawick 44 – ◆Newcastle upon Tyne 92.

Johnstounburn House (Mt. Charlotte Thistle) ⛰, EH36 5PL, S : 1 m. on B 6368 ☎ 696, Fax 626, ≤, « Part 17C country house in extensive gardens », ⛰, park – TV ☎ P – 🏢 30. AE VISA JCB
M 15.00/26.00 **t.** 5.30 – **20 rm** 90.00/150.00 **t.** – SB (except Easter, Christmas and New Year) 120.00/210.00 **st.**

INSCH Aberdeen (Grampian) 401 M 11 **Scotland G.** – pop. 1 247 – ECD : Thursday – ☎ 0464.
Exc. : Huntly Castle (elaborate Heraldic carvings★★★) *AC*, NW : 14½ m. by B 9002 and A 97.
Golf Terr. ☎ 20363.
◆Edinburgh 55 – ◆Aberdeen 25.

Leslie Castle ⛰, Leslie, AB52 6NX, SW : 3¾ m. by B 992 ☎ 20869, Fax 21076, « 17C fortified baronial house » – TV ☎ P. AE VISA.
M (lunch by arrangement)/dinner 25.00 **st.** 4.50 – **4 rm** 93.00/136.00 **st.**

INGLISTON Midlothian. (Lothian) 401 K 16 – see Edinburgh.

INVERCRERAN Argyll. (Strathclyde) 401 E 14 – ✉ ☎ 063 173 Appin.
◆Edinburgh 142 – Fort William 29 – ◆Oban 19.

Invercreran Country House ⛰, Glen Creran, PA38 4BJ, ☎ 414, Fax 532, ≤ Glen Creran and mountains, ≘s, ⛰, park – ⚟ rest TV ☎ P. VISA.
March-October – **M** 28.00 **t.** (dinner) and lunch a la carte 13.50/21.00 **t.** – **9 rm** 60.00/138.00 **t.** – SB 140.00/176.00 **st.**

La guida cambia, cambiate la guida ogni anno.

INVERMORISTON Inverness. (Highland) 401 G 12 **Scotland G.** – ☎ 0320 Glenmoriston.
Envir. : Loch Ness★★.
◆Edinburgh 168 – ◆Inverness 29 – Kyle of Lochalsh 56.

Glenmoriston Arms, IV3 6YA, ☎ 51206, Fax 51206, ⛰ – TV ☎ P. VISA
M (bar lunch)/dinner 18.00 **t.** and a la carte 4.95 – **8 rm** 42.00/64.00 **st.** – SB 84.00/116.00 **st.**

INVERNESS Inverness. (Highland) 401 H 11 **Scotland G.** – pop. 38 204 – ECD : Wednesday – ☎ 0463.
See : Town★ – Museum and Art Gallery★ **M.**
Envir. : Kessock Bridge (≤★) N : 1½ m. by A 82 and A 9.
Exc. : Loch Ness★★, SW : by A 82 – Clava Cairns★, E : 9 m. by Culcabock Rd, B 9006 and B 851 – Cawdor Castle★ *AC*, NE : 14 m. by A 96 and B 9090.
18 Culcabock Rd ☎ 239882, SE : 1 m. by Culcabock Rd – 18 Torvean, Glenurquhart Rd ☎ 711434, SW : 1½ m. by A 82.
✈ Dalcross Airport : ☎ 232471, NE : 8 m. by A 96.
☎ 0345 090700.
Castle Wynd ☎ 234353.
◆Edinburgh 156 – ◆Aberdeen 107 – ◆Dundee 134.

Plan on next page

Kingsmills (Swallow), Culcabock Rd, IV2 3LP, ☎ 237166, Fax 225208, Fб, ≘s, ⛰, ⛰ – ⛰ ⚟ rm TV ☎ ♿ P – 🏢 50. AE VISA **s**
M 9.95/19.50 **st.** and dinner a la carte 6.00 – **77 rm** 92.00/125.00 **st.**, 1 suite – SB (weekends only) 110.00/148.00 **st.**

Caledonian (Jarvis), 33 Church St., IV1 1DX, ☎ 235181, Fax 711206, Fб, ≘s, ⛰ – ⛰ TV ☎ ♿ P – 🏢 200. AE VISA **u**
M (bar lunch)/dinner 16.95 **st.** and a la carte – 8.00 – **103 rm** 75.00/99.00 **st.**, 3 suites – SB 84.00/200.00 **st.**

Craigmonie (Best Western), 9 Annfield Rd, IV2 3HX, ☎ 231649, Telex 94013304, Fax 233720, Fб, ≘s, ⛰ – ⛰ TV ☎ P – 🏢 120. AE VISA **e**
M 10.50 **t.** (lunch) and a la carte 17.20/29.40 **t.** 6.00 – **32 rm** 68.00/115.00 **t.**, 3 suites – SB (except Christmas and New Year) (weekends only) 92.00/116.00 **st.**

Glenmoriston, 20 Ness Bank, IV2 4SF, ☎ 223777, Fax 712378 – TV ☎ P. AE VISA.
closed 2 weeks Christmas and New Year – **M** *(closed lunch Saturday and Sunday)* 12.00/25.00 **t.** and a la carte 5.95 – **19 rm** 50.00/80.00 **t.** **x**

Glendruidh House ⛰, Old Edinburgh Rd, IV1 2AA, SW : 2 m. ☎ 226499, Fax 710745, ⛰ – ⚟ TV ☎ P. AE VISA JCB.
M (residents only) 17.50/22.00 **st.** 5.00 – **7 rm** 50.00/72.00 **st.** – SB 95.00/136.00 **st.**

Braemore without rest., 1 Victoria Drive, IV2 3QB, ☎ 243318, ⛰ – ⚟ P. **z**
3 rm 35.00/44.00 **st.**

Moyness House, 6 Bruce Gdns, IV3 5EN, ☎ 233836, Fax 233836, ⛰ – ⚟ rest TV P. VISA. **c**
closed 23 December-4 January – **M** 14.00 **st.** – **7 rm** 27.00/54.00 **st.**

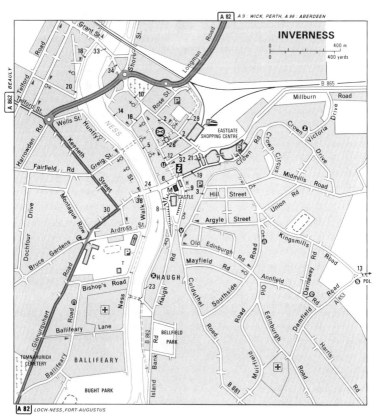

INVERNESS

A 82 — A 9 : WICK, PERTH, A 96 : ABERDEEN

A 82 — LOCH-NESS, FORT-AUGUSTUS

⌂ **Ballifeary House**, 10 Ballifeary Rd, IV3 5PJ, ℰ 235572, Fax 235572, ⋪ – ⋋⋊ ⊤⊽ 🅿. 🔊 𝗩𝗜𝗦𝗔. ⋪
Easter-mid October – **M** 14.00 st. ⅋ 4.00 – **8 rm** ⊒ 30.00/60.00 st.

⌂ **Craigside Lodge** without rest., 4 Gordon Terr., IV2 3HD, ℰ 231576, Fax 713409, ≼ – ⊤⊽ ⋪
6 rm ⊒ 15.00/36.00 st.

⌂ **Old Rectory** without rest., 9 Southside Rd, IV2 3BG, ℰ 220969, ⋪ – ⋋⋊ ⊤⊽ 🅿 ⋪
closed 21 December-10 January – **4 rm** ⊒ 16.00/36.00 st.

XX **Whitecross**, Ivy Cottage, Muirtown Locks, IV3 6LS, W : 1 ½ m. beside the Caledonian Canal ℰ 240386 – ⋋⋊. 🔊 ⓞ 𝗩𝗜𝗦𝗔
closed first 2 weeks January and first 2 weeks November – **M** *(closed Saturday lunch, Sunday dinner and Monday)* 12.00/19.75 t. and dinner a la carte ⅋ 4.00.

at Dalcross NE : 9 m. by A 96, B 9039 and Ardersier rd – ⊠ Inverness – 🕾 0667 Ardersier

⌂ **Easter Dalziel Farm**, IV1 2JL, on B 9039 ℰ 462213, « Working farm », ⋪ – 🅿
March-November – **M** (by arrangement) (communal dining) 10.00 s. – **3 rm** ⊒ 22.00/ 34.00 s. – SB 50.00/68.00 s.

at Culloden E : 3 m. by A 96 – ⊠ ✿ 0463 Inverness :

🏨 **Culloden House** ⟨⟩, IV1 2NZ, ℰ 790461, Fax 792181, ≤, « Georgian mansion », ⩲s, ⟨⟩, park, ℀ – ⥾ rm 🖵 ☎ 🄿. 🖾 🄰🄴 🄾 VISA. ℀
M 12.90/32.50 **t.** ⦚ 6.10 – **22 rm** ⊡ 120.00/165.00 **t.**, 1 suite.

at Dunain Park SW : 2 ½ m. on A 82 – ⊠ ✿ 0463 Inverness :

🏨 **Dunain Park** ⟨⟩, IV3 6JN, ℰ 230512, Fax 224532, ≤, « Country house, gardens », ⩲s, 🖾, park – ⥾ rest 🖵 ☎ 🄿. 🖾 🄰🄴 🄾 VISA JCB
closed 3 weeks January – **M** (dinner only) a la carte approx. 23.50 **t.** – **6 rm** ⊡ 35.00/130.00 **t.**, 6 suites – SB (mid October-March) 100.00/150.00 **st.**

🔘 ATS Carsegate Rd North, The Carse ℰ 236167

INVERSHIN Sutherland. (Highland) – see Bonar Bridge.

INVERURIE Aberdeen. (Grampian) 401 M 12 Scotland G. – pop. 7 701 – ECD : Wednesday – ✿ 0467.

Exc. : Castle Fraser★ (exterior★★) *AC*, SW : 6 m. by B 993 – Pitmedden Gardens★★, NE : 10 m. by B 9170 and A 920 – Haddo House★, N : 14 m. by B 9170 and B 9005 – Fyvie Castle★, N : 13 m. by B 9170 and A 947.

🏌 Blackhall Rd ℰ 20207 – 🏌 Kintore ℰ 32631, SE : 4 ½ m. by A 96 and B 977 – 🏌 Kemnay, Monymusk Rd ℰ 42225, SW : 6 m. by B 993.

🅱 Town Hall, Market Pl. ℰ 20600 (summer only).

◆Edinburgh 147 – ◆Aberdeen 17 – ◆Inverness 90.

🏨 **Thainstone House H. & Country Club** ⟨⟩, AB51 9NT, S : 2 m. by B 993 on A 96 ℰ 621643, Fax 625084, ⦚, 🖾, park – ⥾ ⥾ rest 🖵 ☎ 🄿 – 🄰 400. 🖾 🄰🄴 🄾 VISA. ℀
M 13.50/27.00 **t.** – ⊡ 7.95 – **47 rm** 54.00/99.00 **t.**, 1 suite.

🏨 **Strathburn**, Burghmuir Drive, AB51 9GY, NW : 1 ¼ by A 96 ℰ 624422, Fax 625133 – ⥾ 🖵 ☎ 🄿 – 🄰 30. 🖾 🄰🄴 VISA. ℀
M 17.75/18.75 **t.** and dinner a la carte ⦚ 4.75 – **25 rm** ⊡ 40.00/80.00 **st.** – SB (weekends only) 110.00/150.00 **st.**

During the season, particularly in resorts, it is wise to book in advance.

IRVINE Ayr. (Strathclyde) 401 402 F 17 Scotland G. – pop. 32 507 – ✿ 0294.

Envir. : Kilmarnock (Dean Castle, arms and armour★, musical instruments★) *AC*, E : 5 ½ m. by A 71 and B 7038.

🏌 Western Gailes, Gailes ℰ 311649 – 🏌 Irvine Ravenspark, Kidsneuk Lane ℰ 79550 – 🏌 Bogside ℰ 78139, N : 1 m.

◆Edinburgh 75 – Ayr 14 – ◆Glasgow 29.

🏨 **Hospitality Inn** (Mt. Charlotte Thistle), 46 Annick Rd, KA11 4LD, SE : 1 m. on B 7081 ℰ 274272, Telex 777097, Fax 277287, « Exotic indoor garden with 🖾 », 🏊 – ⥾ rm 🖵 ☎ ⦚ 🄿 – 🄰 250. 🖾 🄰🄴 🄾 VISA JCB
M (carving lunch) 14.00/18.95 **st.** and a la carte ⦚ 4.95 – ⊡ 8.50 – **127 rm** 69.00/200.00 **st.** – SB (weekends only) 112.00/158.00 **st.**

🔘 ATS 9 Kyle Rd, Ind. Est. ℰ 78727

ISLAY (Isle of) Argyll. (Strathclyde) 401 B 16 – pop. 3 997.

🏌 Port Ellen ℰ 0496 (Port Ellen) 2310.

✈ Port Ellen Airport : ℰ 0496 (Port Ellen) 2361.

⛴ by Western Ferries : from Port Askaig to Feolin (Isle of Jura) (5 mn) – by Caledonian MacBrayne : from Port Ellen to Kennacraig (Kintyre Peninsula) – from Port Askaig to Kennacraig (Kintyre Peninsula) – from Askaig to Oban – from Askaig to Colonsay (Isle of).

🅱 at Bowmore, The Square ℰ 049 681 (Bowmore) 254.

Ballygrant – ⊠ Ballygrant – ✿ 0496 84 Port Askaig

🏠 **Ballygrant Inn**, PA45 7QR, ℰ 277, ⟨⟩ – ⥾ 🄿. ℀
M (bar lunch)/dinner 17.50 **t.** – **3 rm** ⊡ 25.00/50.00 **t.**

Bridgend – ⊠ Bowmore – ✿ 049 681 Bridgend

🏨 **Bridgend**, PA44 7PJ, ℰ 212, Fax 673, ⟨⟩ – 🖵 ☎ 🄿
M (lunch by arrangement)/dinner 19.50 – **10 rm** ⊡ 37.50/75.00 **t.**

ISLE of WHITHORN Wigtown. (Dumfries and Galloway) 401 402 G 19 Scotland G. – pop. 989 – ECD : Wednesday – ⊠ Newton Stewart – ✿ 0988 Whithorn.

Envir. : Priory Museum (Early Christian Crosses★★) NW : 3 m. by A 750.

◆Edinburgh 152 – ◆Ayr 72 – ◆Dumfries 72 – Stranraer 34.

🦢 **Steam Packet**, Harbour Row, DG8 8LL, ℰ 500334, ≤ – 🖵 ☎. 🖾 VISA
closed 25 December – **M** 5.95/13.50 **t.** and a la carte ⦚ 4.50 – **5 rm** ⊡ 25.00/50.00 **t.**

ISLEORNSAY Inverness. (Highland) 401 C 12 – see Skye (Isle of).

JEDBURGH Roxburgh. (Borders) 🗺️01 🗺️02 M 17 Scotland G. – pop. 4 053 – ECD : Thursday – ✆ 0835.

See : Town★ – Abbey★★ *AC* – Mary Queen of Scots House Visitor Centre★ *AC* – The Canongate Bridge★.

Envir. : Waterloo Monument (※★★) N : 4 m. by A 68 and B 6400.

🏌 Jedburgh, Dunion Rd ✆ 63587, SW : 1 m. by B 6358.

🎦 Murray's Green ✆ 863435/863688.

◆Edinburgh 48 — ◆Carlisle 54 — ◆Newcastle upon Tyne 57.

  🏛 **Glenfriars**, The Friars, TD8 6BN, ✆ 862000, 🍽 – 📺 🅿. 🔃 🆎 *VISA*
    closed Christmas-New Year – **M** (lunch by arrangement)/dinner 15.00 **st.** ▮ 4.25 – **6 rm**
    ⚏ 35.00/58.00 **st.** – SB 76.50/90.00 **st.**

  ↑ **Hundalee House** ⌖ without rest., TD8 6PA, S : 1½ m. by A 68 ✆ 863011, ≼, ⌾, 🍽,
    park – 📺 🅿. ❀
    April-October – **4 rm** ⚏ 30.00/40.00 **st.**

  ↑ **Spinney** without rest., Langlee, TD8 6PB, S : 2 m. on A 68 ✆ 863525, 🍽 – 🅿. ❀
    March-October – **3 rm** ⚏ 36.00 **st.**

JOHN O'GROATS Caithness. (Highland) 🗺️01 K 8 – Shipping Services : see Orkney Islands.

JURA (Isle of) Argyll. (Strathclyde) 🗺️01 C 15 – pop. 239.

⛴ by Western Ferries : from Feolin to Port Askaig (Isle of Islay) (5 mn).

  Craighouse – ECD : Tuesday – ✉ ✆ 049 682 Jura

  🏛 **Jura**, PA60 7XU, ✆ 243, Fax 249, ≼ Small Isles Bay, ⌾, 🍽 – 🅿. 🔃 🆎 ① *VISA*
    closed 2 weeks Christmas-New Year – **M** (bar lunch)/dinner 16.25 **st.** ▮ 5.15 – **16 rm**
    ⚏ 27.50/68.00 **st.**, 1 suite.

KELSO Roxburgh. (Borders) 🗺️01 🗺️02 M 17 Scotland G. – pop. 5 547 – ECD : Wednesday – ✆ 0573.

See : Town★ - Market Square★★ – ≼★ from Kelso Bridge.

Envir. : Floors Castle★ *AC*, NW : 1½ m. by A 6089.

Exc. : Mellerstain★★ (Ceilings★★★, Library★★★) *AC*, NW : 6 m. by A 6089 – Waterloo Monument (※★★) SW : 7 m. by A 698 and B 6400 – Jedburgh Abbey★★ *AC*, SW : 8½ m. by A 698 – Dryburgh Abbey★★ *AC* (setting★★★) SW : 10½ m. by A 6089, B 6397 and B 6404 – Scott's View★★, W : 11 m. by A 6089, B 6397, B 6404 and B 6356 – Smailholm Tower★ (※★★) NW : 6 m. by A 6089 and B 6397 - Lady Kirk (Kirk o'Steil★) NE : 16 m. by A 698, A 697, A 6112 and B 6437.

🏌 Berrymoss Racecourse Rd ✆ 223009.

🎦 Town House, The Square ✆ 223464 (summer only).

◆Edinburgh 44 — Hawick 21 — ◆Newcastle upon Tyne 68.

  🏨 **Ednam House**, Bridge St., TD5 7HT, ✆ 224168, Fax 224316, ≼, 🍽 – 📺 ☎ 🅿. 🔃 *VISA*
    closed 24 December-10 January – **M** (bar lunch Monday to Saturday)/dinner 17.00 **st.**
    ▮ 4.00 – **32 rm** ⚏ 43.00/60.00 **t.** – SB 86.00/108.00 **st.**

  at Heiton SW : 3 m. by A 698 – ✉ Kelso – ✆ 0573 Roxburgh :

  🏨 **Sunlaws House** ⌖, TD5 8JZ, ✆ 450331, Fax 450611, ≼, « Victorian country house »,
    ⌾, 🍽, park, ❀ – 📺 ☎ 🅿. 🔃 🆎 ① *VISA* 𝐉𝐂𝐁
    M 15.00/27.00 **st.** ▮ 6.90 – **22 rm** ⚏ 85.00/165.00 **st.** – SB (except Christmas and New Year)
    156.00/230.00 **st.**

🔧 ATS The Butts ✆ 224997/8

KENMORE Perth. (Tayside) 🗺️01 I 14 Scotland G. – ECD : Thursday except summer – ✆ 0887.

See : Village★.

Envir. : Loch Tay★★.

Exc. : Ben Lawers★★, SW : 8 m. by A 827.

🏌 Taynmouth Castle ✆ 830228 – 🏌 Mains of Taynmouth ✆ 830226.

◆Edinburgh 82 — ◆Dundee 60 — ◆Oban 71 — Perth 38.

  🏨 **Kenmore**, PH15 2NU, ✆ 830205, Fax 830262, ≋s, 🏊, 🏌, ⌾, 🍽, ❀ – 🔄 ↦ rest 📺 ☎
    🅿. 🔃 🆎 *VISA* ①
    M (bar lunch)/dinner 23.00 **t.** – **38 rm** ⚏ 44.00/88.00 **t.** – SB (weekends only) 80.50/
    136.00 **st.**

When visiting Great Britain,

use the Michelin Green Guide **"Great Britain".**

  – *Detailed descriptions of places of interest*

  – *Touring programmes*

  – *Maps and street plans*

  – *The history of the country*

  – *Photographs and drawings of monuments, beauty spots, houses...*

KENTALLEN Argyll. (Highland) 401 E 14 – ⊠ Appin – ☎ 063 174 Duror.
◆Edinburgh 123 – Fort William 17 – ◆Oban 33.

🏨 **Ardsheal House** 🗞, PA38 4BX, SW : ¾ m. by A 828 𝒫 227, Fax 342, ≤, « Country house atmosphere », 🌿, park, 🎿 – ⫶✕⫶ rest ☎ 🅿. ☒ 🝿 𝖵𝖨𝖲𝖠
closed 3 weeks January – **M** 17.50/32.50 **t.** ⓙ 4.50 – **13 rm** ⊑ (dinner included) 85.00/180.00 **t.**

🏨 **Holly Tree,** Kentallen Pier, PA38 4BY, 𝒫 292, Fax 345, ≤ Loch Linnhe and mountains, 🌿 – ⫶✕⫶ rest 𝖳𝖵 ☎ & 🅿. ☒ 𝖵𝖨𝖲𝖠
closed 7 to 30 November – **M** (bar lunch)/dinner 23.50 **t.** and a la carte ⓙ 4.50 – **10 rm** ⊑ 41.50/75.00 **st.**

KILCHOAN Argyll. (Strathclyde) 401 B 13 – ⊠ Acharacle – ☎ 097 23.
◆Edinburgh 163 – ◆Inverness 120 – ◆Oban 84.

🏠 **Meall Mo Chridhe** 🗞, PH36 4LH, 𝒫 238, ≤ Sound of Mull, 🌿, park – ⫶✕⫶ 🅿
closed January, February and November – **M** *(closed Sunday to non residents)* (booking essential) (communal dining) (dinner only) 23.50 **s.** – **3 rm** ⊑ 41.50/65.00 **s.** – SB (except December) 99.00/130.00 **s.**

KILCHRENAN Argyll. (Strathclyde) 401 E 14 Scotland G. – ⊠ Taynuilt – ☎ 086 63.
Envir. : Loch Awe★★, E : 1 ¼ m.
◆Edinburgh 117 – ◆Glasgow 87 – ◆Oban 18.

🏨 **Ardanaiseig** 🗞, PA35 1HE, NE : 4 m. 𝒫 333, Fax 222, ≤ gardens and Loch Awe, « Country house in extensive informal gardens beside Loch Awe », 🌿, park, 🎿 – ⫶✕⫶ rest 𝖳𝖵 ☎ 🅿. ☒ 🝿 ⓞ 𝖵𝖨𝖲𝖠 🛠
Easter-mid October – **M** 12.50/30.00 **t.** ⓙ 5.00 – **13 rm** ⊑ (dinner included) 105.00/210.00 **t.**, 1 suite – SB 136.00/252.00 **st.**

🏨 **Taychreggan** 🗞, PA35 1HQ, SE : 1 ¼ m. 𝒫 211, Fax 244, ≤ Loch Awe and mountains, 🌿, 🌿, park – ⫶✕⫶ rest ☎ 🅿. ☒ 🝿 𝖵𝖨𝖲𝖠. 🛠
M (bar lunch)/dinner 28.00 **t.** ⓙ 3.75 – **15 rm** ⊑ (dinner only) 55.00/140.00 **t.**

KILDRUMMY Aberdeen. (Grampian) 401 L 12 Scotland G. – ⊠ Alford – ☎ 097 55.
See : Castle★ *AC.*
Exc. : Huntly Castle (Heraldic carvings★★★) N : 15 m. by A 97 – Craigievar Castle★, SE : 13 m. by A 97, A 944 and A 980.
◆Edinburgh 137 – ◆Aberdeen 35.

🏨 **Kildrummy Castle** 🗞, AB33 8RA, S : 1 ¼ m. on A 97 𝒫 71288, Fax 71345, ≤ gardens and Kildrummy castle, « 19C mansion in extensive park », 🌿 – ⫶✕⫶ rest 𝖳𝖵 ☎ 🅿. ☒ 🝿 𝖵𝖨𝖲𝖠 𝖩𝖢𝖡
closed January – **M** 16.50/26.00 **st.** and a la carte ⓙ 4.50 – **15 rm** ⊑ 65.00/130.00 **st.** – SB (October-May) 114.00/150.00 **st.**

KILFINAN Argyll. (Strathclyde) 401 E 16 – ⊠ Tighnabruaich – ☎ 070 082.
◆Edinburgh 124 – ◆Glasgow 78 – ◆Oban 78.

🏨 **Kilfinan** 🗞, PA21 2EP, 𝒫 201, Fax 205, 🌿 – ⫶✕⫶ rest 𝖳𝖵 ☎ 🅿. ☒ 🝿 𝖵𝖨𝖲𝖠. 🛠
closed February – **M** (bar lunch)/dinner 22.00 **st.** ⓙ 4.00 – **11 rm** 45.00/72.00 **st.** – SB (winter only, except Christmas and New Year) 92.00 **st.**

KILLIECRANKIE Perth. (Tayside) 401 I 13 – see Pitlochry.

KILLIN Perth. (Central) 401 H 14 Scotland G. – pop. 545 – ECD : Wednesday – ☎ 0567.
Exc. : Loch Tay★★, Ben Lawers★★, NE : 8 m. by A 827 – Loch Earn★★, SE : 7 m. by A 827 and A 85.
🏌 Killin 𝒫 820312, by A 827.
🛈 Main St. 𝒫 8202 (summer only).
◆Edinburgh 72 – ◆Dundee 65 – Perth 43 – ◆Oban 54.

🏠 **Dall Lodge Country House,** Main St., FK21 8TN, 𝒫 820217, Fax 820726, 🌿 – 𝖳𝖵 ☎ & 🅿. ☒ 𝖵𝖨𝖲𝖠
closed 25 and 26 December – **M** (dinner only) 15.00 **st.** – **10 rm** ⊑ 27.50/55.00 **st.** – SB 85.00 **st.**

🏠 **Morenish Lodge Highland House** 🗞, FK21 8TX, NE : 2 ½ m. on A 827 𝒫 820258, Fax 820258, ≤ Loch Tay and hills, 🌿, 🌿 – 🅿. ☒ 𝖵𝖨𝖲𝖠. 🛠
mid April-mid October – **M** (dinner only) 15.00 **st.** – **13 rm** ⊑ (dinner included) 35.00/78.00 **st.**

🏠 **Breadalbane House,** Main St., FK21 8UT, 𝒫 820386 – ⫶✕⫶ 𝖳𝖵 🅿
M (by arrangement) – **5 rm** ⊑ 26.00/36.00.

🏠 **Fairview House,** Main St., FK21 8UT, 𝒫 820667 – 🅿
M 8.00 **s.** – **7 rm** ⊑ 14.00/32.00 **s.**

at Ardeonaig NE : 6 ¾ m. – ⊠ ☎ 0567 Killin :

🏠 **Ardeonaig** 🗞, South Lochtayside, FK21 8SU, 𝒫 820400, Fax 820282, ≤, 🌿, 🌿 – ⫶✕⫶ rest 🅿
closed November – **M** (bar lunch)/dinner 19.50 **st.** ⓙ 4.05 – **14 rm** ⊑ 35.50/71.00 **t.**

KILMORE Argyll. (Strathclyde) [401] D 14 – see Oban.

KILNINVER Argyll. (Strathclyde) [401] D 14 – see Oban.

KINCARDINE Fife (Central) [401] I 15 Scotland G. – ☎ 0259.

Envir. : Culross*** (Village***, Palace** *AC*, Study* *AC*) E : 4 m. by B 9037.

⛳18 Tulliallan ✆ 730396.

♦Edinburgh 30 – Dunfermline 9 – ♦Glasgow 25 – Stirling 12.

- 🍴 **Unicorn Inn,** 15 Excise St., FR10 4LN, ✆ 730704 – [CB] [AE] [VISA]
closed Monday, Tuesday, 1 week June and 2 weeks October – **M** a la carte 11.95/26.25 **t.** 🍷 4.95.

KINCLAVEN Perth. (Tayside) [401] J 14 – ✉ Stanley – ☎ 0250 Meikleour.

♦Edinburgh 56 – Perth 12.

- 🏨 **Ballathie House** 🐌, PH1 4QN, ✆ 883268, Fax 883396, ≤, « Country house in extensive grounds on banks of River Tay », 🐟, 🌳, park, 🎾 – 🚭 rest [TV] ☎ 🅿. [CB] [AE] [D] [VISA]. 🐕
M 12.00/29.00 **t.** and a la carte 🍷 6.00 – **26 rm** 🛏 (dinner included) 90.00/210.00 **t.**, 1 suite – SB 132.00/142.00 **st.**

KINCRAIG Inverness. (Highland) [401] I 12 Scotland G. – ECD : Wednesday – ✉ Kingussie – ☎ 0540.

See : Highland Wildlife Park* *AC*.

Exc. : The Cairngorms** (≤***) – ✳*** from Cairn Gorm, E : 14 m. by A 9 and B 970.

♦Edinburgh 119 – ♦Inverness 37 – Perth 75.

- 🍴🍴 **Ossian** with rm, PH21 1NA, ✆ 651242, Fax 651633, ≤, 🐟, 🌳 – 🚭 rest [TV] ☎ 🅿. [CB] [VISA]
closed January and December – **M** (bar lunch)/dinner a la carte 13.70/20.90 **t.** 🍷 4.50 – **9 rm** 🛏 29.50/59.00 **t.** – SB 62.00/96.00 **st.**

KINGUSSIE Inverness. (Highland) [401] H 12 Scotland G. – pop. 1 140 – ECD : Wednesday – ☎ 0540.

Envir. : Highland Wildlife Park* *AC*, NE : 4 m. by A 9.

Exc. : Aviemore*, NE : 11 m. by A 9 – The Cairngorms** (≤***) – ✳*** from Cairn Gorm, NE : 18 m. by B 970.

⛳18 Gynack Rd ✆ 661374.

[i] King St. ✆ 661297 (summer only).

♦Edinburgh 117 – ♦Inverness 41 – Perth 73.

- 🏨 **Scot House,** Newtonmore Rd, PH21 1HE, ✆ 661351, Fax 661111 – 🚭 rest [TV] ☎ 🅿. [CB] [VISA]
M (bar lunch)/dinner 16.50 **st.** 🍷 5.50 – **9 rm** 🛏 30.00/57.00 **st.** – SB (except Easter, August, Christmas and New Year) 68.00/84.00 **st.**
- 🏨 **Columba House,** Manse Rd, PH21 1JF, ✆ 661402, 🌳 – 🚭 rest [TV] ☎ 🅿
closed November – **M** (bar lunch)/dinner 18.00 **t.** 🍷 4.10 – **7 rm** 🛏 39.00/58.00 **t.**
- 🏠 **St. Helens** without rest., Ardbroilach Rd, PH21 1JX, ✆ 661430 – 🚭 🅿. 🐕
3 rm 🛏 40.00 **s.**
- 🏠 **Homewood Lodge,** Newtonmore Rd, PH21 1HD, ✆ 661507, ≤, 🌳 – 🚭 🅿. 🐕
closed Christmas and New Year – **M** (by arrangement) 9.50 **st.** – **4 rm** 🛏 19.50/39.00 **st.**
- 🍴🍴🍴 **The Cross** 🐌 with rm, Tweed Mill Brae, Ardbroilach Rd, PH21 1TC, ✆ 661166, Fax 661080 – 🚭 [TV] ☎ 🅿. [CB] [VISA]. 🐕
March-November – **Meals** *(closed Wednesday lunch and Tuesday)* (booking essential) 15.00/35.00 **t.** 🍷 4.95 – **9 rm** 🛏 (dinner included) 65.00/170.00 **t.**

KINLOCHBERVIE Sutherland. (Highland) [401] E 8 Scotland G. – ECD : Wednesday – ✉ Lairg – ☎ 0971.

Exc. : Cape Wrath*** (≤**) *AC*, N : 28½ m. (including ferry crossing) by B 801 and A 838.

♦Edinburgh 276 – Thurso 93 – Ullapool 61.

- 🏨 **Kinlochbervie** 🐌, IV27 4RP, ✆ 521275, Fax 521438, ≤ Loch Inchard and sea – 🚭 rest [TV] ☎ 🅿. [CB] [AE] [D] [VISA]
March-October – **M** (booking essential) (bar lunch)/dinner 27.50 **t.** 🍷 4.50 – **14 rm** 🛏 52.00/104.00 **t.** – SB 136.00/176.00 **st.**
- 🏠 **Old School** 🐌, Inshegra, IV27 4RH, SE : 1½ m. ✆ 521383, ≤ – 🚭 rest [TV] ☎ 🅿. [CB] [VISA]
closed 25-26 December and 1 January – **M** a la carte approx. 11.00 **t.** – **6 rm** 🛏 25.00/48.00 **t.**

☞ *When in a hurry use the* *Michelin Main Road Maps:*
[970] Europe, [980] Greece, [984] Germany, [985] Scandinavia-Finland,
[986] Great Britain and Ireland, [987] Germany-Austria-Benelux, [988] Italy,
[989] France, [990] Spain-Portugal and [991] Yugoslavia.

KINLOCHMOIDART Inverness. (Highland) **401** C 13 – ✉ Lochailort – ☎ 0967 85 Salen

  ✗ **Kinacarra,** PH38 4ND, ✆ 238 – 🅿
    closed Monday and March – **M** (booking essential) (light lunch) a la carte 11.00/17.15 **t.**
    🍷 4.00.

KINROSS Kinross. (Tayside) **401** J 15 – pop. 3 493 – ECD : Thursday – ☎ 0577.

🛆 Green Hotel, 2 The Muirs ✆ 863467 – 🛆 Milnathort, South St. ✆ 864069, N : 1 ½ m. –
🛆 Bishopshire, Kinnesswood ✆ 0592 (Lochgelly) 780203, E : 5½ m. by a 911.

🏢 Kinross Service Area (junction 6, M 90) ✆ 863680.

♦Edinburgh 28 – Dunfermline 13 – Perth 18 – Stirling 25.

  🏨 **Windlestrae,** KY13 7AS, ✆ 863217, Fax 864733, 🏊, 🚡, 🔲, 🚿 – 📺 ☎ & 🅿 – 🔺 180.
    🔼 🆎 ⑩ 𝘝𝘐𝘚𝘈. ✻
    M 11.95/25.00 **st.** and a la carte 🍷 6.00 – **43 rm** ⊇ 65.00/95.00 **st.**, 2 suites – SB (weekends
    only) 125.00/195.00 **st.**

  🏨 **Green** (Best Western), 2 The Muirs, KY13 7AS, ✆ 863467, Fax 863180, « Gardens », 🚡,
    🔲, 🏊, ⚲, squash – 📺 ☎ 🅿 – 🔺 120. 🔼 🆎 ⑩ 𝘝𝘐𝘚𝘈
    M (bar lunch)/dinner 22.00 **st.** and a la carte 🍷 4.75 – **47 rm** ⊇ 65.00/125.00 **st.** – SB (ex-
    cept New Year) 106.00/170.00 **st.**

  🏠 **Granada Lodge** without rest., Kincardine Rd, KY13 7NQ, W : 1 m. by A 922 on A 977
    ✆ 864646, Fax 864108, Reservations (Freephone) 0800 555300 – ✄ 📺 ☎ & 🅿. 🔼 🆎
    𝘝𝘐𝘚𝘈. ✻
    ⊇ 4.00 – **35 rm** 34.95/37.95 **st.**

  at Cleish SW : 4½ m. by B 996 off B 9097 – ✉ Kinross – ☎ 0577 Cleish Hills :

  🏨 **Nivingston House** ⑤, KY13 7LS, ✆ 850216, Fax 850238, ≤, 🚿 – 📺 ☎ 🅿. 🔼 🆎 𝘝𝘐𝘚𝘈
    closed first 2 weeks January – **M** 16.50/27.50 **st.** 🍷 6.00 – **17 rm** ⊇ 70.00/120.00 **t.** –
    SB (weekends only) 110.00/140.00 **st.**

KINTYRE (Peninsula) Argyll. (Strathclyde) **401** D 16 Scotland G.

See : Carradale★ – Saddell (Collection of grave slabs★).

🛆, 🛆 Campbeltown, Machrihanish ✆ 0586 (Campbeltown) 81213.

✈ at Campbeltown (Machrihanish Airport) : ✆ 0586 (Campbeltown) 553021.

⛴ by Caledonian MacBrayne : from Claonaig to Lochranza (Isle of Arran) (summer only)
frequent services daily (30 mn) – from Kennacraig to Port Ellen (Isle of Islay) – from Kennacraig
to Port Askaig (Isle of Islay).

  Campbeltown – ECD : Wednesday – ✉ ☎ 0586 Campbeltown.
    🏢 MacKinnon House, The Pier ✆ 552056.
    ♦Edinburgh 176.

  🏠 **Seafield,** Kilkerran Rd, PA28 6JL, ✆ 554385 – 📺 ☎ 🅿. 🔼 𝘝𝘐𝘚𝘈
    M 12.50/18.95 **st.** – **9 rm** ⊇ 29.95/60.00 **t.** – SB (winter only) (weekends only) 50.00/
    76.00 **st.**

  ↑ **Rosemount,** Low Askomil, PA28 6EN, ✆ 553552, ≤, 🚿 – 📺 🅿
    M (by arrangement) 12.00 **s.** – **3 rm** ⊇ 20.00/36.00 **s.**

  ↑ **Ballegreggan House** ⑤, Ballegreggan Rd, PA28 6NN, NE : 1 m. by A 83 ✆ 552062, ≤,
    🚿 – ✄ 📺 🅿
    M 15.00 **s.** – **4 rm** ⊇ 20.00/44.00 **s.**

🔘 ATS Burnside St., Campbeltown ✆ 554404

  Machrihanish – pop. 540 – ✉ Campbeltown – ☎ 058 681 Machrihanish.
    ♦Edinburgh 182. – ♦Oban 95.

  ↑ **Ardell House** without rest., PA28 6PT, ✆ 235, ≤, 🚿 – 📺 🅿
    March-October – **10 rm** ⊇ 21.00/42.00 **st.**

  Tarbert – ✉ ☎ 0880 Tarbert.
    🛆 Kilberry Rd ✆ 820565.
    🏢 Harbour St. ✆ 820429 (summer only).

  🏠 **Columba,** East Pier Rd, PA29 6UF, E : ¾ m. ✆ 820808, Fax 820808, ≤, 🚡 – ✄ rest 📺
    🅿. 🔼 𝘝𝘐𝘚𝘈
    M (bar lunch Monday to Saturday)/dinner 16.95 **t.** 🍷 4.80 – **11 rm** ⊇ 28.95/55.90 **t.** –
    SB (except July and Bank Holidays) 65.90/91.90 **st.**

  ✗ **Anchorage,** Quayside, Harbour St., PA29 6UD, ✆ 820881 – 🔼 𝘝𝘐𝘚𝘈
    March-December – **M** - Seafood (closed Monday) (dinner only) a la carte 13.65/25.85 **t.**
    🍷 4.95.

KIRKBEAN Dumfries (Dumfries and Galloway) **401 402** J 19 – ✉ Dumfries – ☎ 038 788.

♦Edinburgh 89 – Carlisle 41 – ♦Dumfries 12.

  ↑ **Cavens House** ⑤, DG2 8AA, ✆ 234, 🚿, park – ✄ rest 📺 🅿. 🔼 𝘝𝘐𝘚𝘈. ✻
    M (by arrangement) 14.00 **st.** 🍷 4.00 – **6 rm** ⊇ 30.00/50.00 **st.** – SB (winter only) 60.00/
    100.00 **st.**

KIRKCUDBRIGHT Kirkcudbright. (Dumfries and Galloway) [401] [402] H 19 **Scotland G.** – pop. 3 352 – ECD : Thursday – ☎ 0557.

See : Town★.

Envir. : Dundrennan Abbey★ *AC*, SE : 5 m. by A 711.

⛳18 Stirling Cres. ℘ 30314.

ℹ Harbour Sq. ℘ 30494 (summer only).

♦Edinburgh 108 – ♦Dumfries 28 – Stranraer 50.

🏨 **Selkirk Arms,** Old High St., DG6 4JG, ℘ 30402, Fax 31639, 🌳 – [TV] ☎ 🅿. [S] [AE] [◑] [VISA]
M (bar lunch)/dinner 17.50 **st.** and a la carte 🍷 3.50 – **15 rm** ☕ 50.00/70.00 **st.** – SB (except Christmas and New Year) 93.00/135.00 **st.**

⌂ **Gladstone House** without rest., 48 High St., DG6 4JX, ℘ 31734, 🌳 – 🚭 [TV]. [S] [VISA]. ✗
3 rm ☕ 30.00/52.00 **st.**

KIRKMICHAEL Perth. (Tayside) [401] J 13 **Scotland G.** – ✉ Blairgowrie – ☎ 0250 Strathardle.

Envir. : Glenshee (☼★★).

♦Edinburgh 74 – Perth 30 – Pitlochry 12.

🏨 **Log Cabin** 🔇, PH10 7NB, W : 1 m. ℘ 881288, Fax 881402, <, « Scandinavian pine chalet », 🎣 – ♿ 🅿. [S] [AE] [◑] [VISA]
closed 25 and 26 December – **M** (bar lunch)/dinner 17.95 **t.** – **13 rm** ☕ 37.80/55.60 **t.**

KIRKWALL Orkney. (Orkney Islands) [401] L 7 – see Orkney Islands (Mainland).

Die Namen der wichtigsten Einkaufsstraßen sind
am Anfang des Straßenverzeichnisses in Rot *aufgeführt.*

KYLE OF LOCHALSH Ross and Cromarty. (Highland) [401] C 12 **Scotland G.** – pop. 803 – ECD : Thursday – ☎ 0599.

Exc. : N : from Kyle of Lochalsh to Gairloch★★★ (Vista★★, <★★★) – Eilean Donan Castle★ *AC*, (Site★★) E : 8 m. by A 87.

⛴ by Caledonian MacBrayne : to Kyleakin (Isle of Skye) frequent services daily (except Sunday 1 daily).

⛴ by Caledonain MacBrayne Ltd : to Mallaig (5 mn).

ℹ Car Park ℘ 4276 (summer only).

♦Edinburgh 204 – ♦Dundee 182 – ♦Inverness 82 – ♦Oban 125.

🏨 **Lochalsh,** Ferry Rd, IV40 8AF, ℘ 4202, Fax 4881, < Skye ferry and hills – [lift] [TV] ☎ 🅿. [S] [AE] [◑] [VISA]
M 12.50/28.00 **t.** and a la carte 🍷 6.50 – **38 rm** ☕ 75.00/130.00 **t.** – SB 130.00/180.00 **st.**

KYLESKU Sutherland. (Highland) – ☎ 0971 Scourie

♦Edinburgh 256 – ♦Inverness 100 – Ullapool 34.

🏨 **Newton Lodge** 🔇, IV27 4HW, S : 2 m. on A 894 ℘ 502070, < Loch Glencoul and mountains – 🚭 rest [TV] 🅿. ✗
closed Christmas and New Year – **M** (residents only) (dinner only) 12.00 **t.** – **8 rm** ☕ 20.00/50.00 **t.**

🏨 **Kylesku** 🔇, IV27 4HW, ℘ 502231, Fax 502113, < Loch Glencoul and mountains, 🎣 – [S] [VISA]
March-November – **M** (bar lunch)/dinner 11.50 **t.** 🍷 3.50 – **7 rm** ☕ 25.00/48.00 **t.** – SB 55.00/80.00 **st.**

LADYBANK Fife (fife) [401] K 15 – pop. 1 357 – ☎ 0337.

♦Edinburgh 38 – ♦Dundee 20 – Stirling 40.

⌂ **Redlands Country Lodge** 🔇, KY7 7SH, E : 1 m. on B 938 ℘ 31091, 🌳 – [TV] 🅿
closed mid February-mid March – **M** 15.00 🍷 3.00 – **4 rm** ☕ 28.00/50.00 **st.**

LAGGAN Inverness. (Highland) [401] H 12 – ✉ Newtonmore – ☎ 052 84.

♦Edinburgh 110 – ♦Inverness 52 – Perth 66.

🏨 **Gaskmore House,** PH20 1BS, E : ¾ m. on A 86 ℘ 250, Fax 350, < Grampian mountains, 🌳 – [TV] ☎ ♿ 🅿. [S] [AE] [◑] [VISA]
M - (see below) – **24 rm** ☕ 54.00/84.00 **st.** – SB (March-April and October-November) 80.00/100.00 **st.**

🍴🍴 **Gaskmore House,** PH20 1BS, E : ¾ m. on A 86 ℘ 250, Fax 350 – 🚭 🅿. [S] [AE] [◑] [VISA]
M (light lunch)/dinner a la carte 15.00/23.50 **st.** 🍷 3.80.

LAID Sutherland. (Highland) [401] F 8 – ✉ Lairg – ☎ 0971 Durness.

⛳9 Balnakeil, Durness ℘ 511364, N : 7 m. by A 838.

♦Edinburgh 242 – Thurso 59 – Ullapool 95.

⌂ **Port-na-Con House** 🔇, by Altnaharra, IV27 4UN, ℘ 511367, < Loch Eribol – 🚭. [S] [VISA]
mid March-October – **M** 10.00 **s.** 🍷 4.25 – **4 rm** ☕ 22.00/52.00 **s.**

LAIRG Sutherland. (Highland) 401 G 9 – pop. 628 – ECD : Wednesday – ✆ 0549.

◆Edinburgh 218 – ◆Inverness 61 – ◆Wick 72.

🏨 **Sutherland Arms,** IV27 4AT, ℰ 2291, Fax 2261, ≤, ⤟, 🛬 – ⵜ rest 📺 ☎ 🅿. ⚞ ⚟ ⚟⚟
April-October – **M** (bar lunch Monday to Saturday)/dinner 18.00 **t.** ⚛ 4.75 – **25 rm** ⌚ 45.00/ 95.00 **t.** – SB 94.00/124.00 **t.**

LAMLASH Bute. (Strathclyde) 401 E 17 – see Arran (Isle of).

LANARK Lanark. (Strathclyde) 401 402 I 16 – pop. 9 673 – ECD : Thursday – ✆ 0555.

🎋 Horsemarket, Ladyacre Rd ℰ 661661.

◆Edinburgh 34 – ◆Carlisle 78 – ◆ Glasgow 28.

XX **Ristorante La Vigna,** 40 Wellgate, ML11 9DT, ℰ 664320, Fax 661400 – ⚞ ⚟ ⚟ ⚟⚟
closed Sunday lunch – **M - Italian** (booking essential) a la carte 16.90/27.70 **t.** ⚛ 4.50.

LANGBANK Renfrew. (Strathclyde) 401 G 16 – ECD : Saturday – ✆ 0475.

◆Edinburgh 63 – ◆Glasgow 17 – Greenock 7.

🏨 **Gleddoch House** ⤟, PA14 6YE, SE : 1 m. by B 789 ℰ 54711, Fax 54201, ≤ Clyde and countryside, ⤢⟲, 🏇, ⌚, park, squash – 📺 ☎ 🅿. ⚞ ⚟ ⚟ ⚟ ⚟⚟
closed 2 and 3 January – **M** 18.50/29.50 **st.** and a la carte ⚛ 5.75 – **32 rm** ⌚ 90.00/ 135.00 **st.**, 1 suite – SB 140.00/150.00 **st.**

LARGS Ayr. (Strathclyde) 401 402 F 16 Scotland G. – pop. 9 619 – ECD : Wednesday – ✆ 0475.

See : Largs Old Kirk★ *AC.*

🏇 Irvine Rd ℰ 673594, S : 1 m. – 🏇 Greenock Rd ℰ 673230.

⛴ by Caledonian MacBrayne : to Cumbrae Slip (Great Cumbrae Island) frequent services daily (10 mn).

🎋 Promenade ℰ 673765.

◆Edinburgh 76 – ◆Ayr 32 – ◆Glasgow 30.

🏨 Brisbane House, 14 Greenock Rd, Esplanade, KA30 8NF, ℰ 687200, Fax 676295, ≤ – 📺 ☎ 🅿 – 🕭 50. ⌘
23 rm.

🏠 **Glen Eldon,** 2 Barr Cres., KA30 8PX, ℰ 673381, Fax 673381 – ⵜ rest 📺 ☎ 🅿. ⚞ ⚟ ⚟⚟. ⌘
closed mid January-mid March – **M** (dinner only) 13.50 **st.** – **9 rm** ⌚ 30.00/55.00 **st.**

LERWICK Shetland. (Shetland Islands) 401 Q 3 – see Shetland Islands (Mainland).

LESLIE Fife. (Fife) 401 K 15 – see Glenrothes.

LEWIS and HARRIS (Isle of) Ross and Cromarty. (Outer Hebrides) (Western Isles) 401 A 9 Scotland G.

See : Callanish Standing Stones★★ – Carloway Broch★ – St. Clement's Church, Rodel (tomb★).

⛴ by Caledonian MacBrayne : from Stornoway to Ullapool – from Kyles Scalpay to the Isle of Scalpay : 6-12 daily (10 mn) (except Sunday 1daily) – from Tarbert to Uig (Isle of Skye) 1-3 weekly (1 h 45 mn) – from Tarbert to Lochmaddy (Isle of Uist) 1-2 weekly – from Tarbert to Portavadie.

LEWIS

Stornoway – ✉ ✆ 0851 Stornoway.

🏇 Lady Lever Park ℰ 702240.

🎋 4 South Beach St. ℰ 703088.

🏨 **Cabarfeidh** (Best Western), Manor Park, PA87 2EU, N : ½ m. on A 858 ℰ 702604, Fax 705572 – ⫶ 📺 ☎ 🅿 – 🕭 300. ⚞ ⚟ ⚟ ⚟⚟
M 9.00/18.50 **st.** and dinner a la carte – **46 rm** ⌚ 68.00/90.00 **st.** – SB (October-April) 96.00/172.00 **st.**

Uig – ECD : Wednesday – ✉ Uig – ✆ 085 175 Timsgarry.

🏠 Baile-Na-Cille ⤟, Timsgarry, PA86 9JD, ℰ 242, Fax 241, ≤ Uig bay and mountains, ⤟, 🛬 – ⵜ rest 🅿
12 rm.

HARRIS

Scarista – pop. 1 247 – ECD : Thursday – ✉ ✆ 0859 Scarista.

🏠 **Scarista House** ⤟, PA85 3HX, from Tarbert, SW : 15 m. on A 859 ℰ 550238, Fax 550277, ≤ beach and mountains, 🛬 – ⵜ ☎ 🅿
mid April-mid October – **M** (booking essential) (dinner only) 25.00 **st.** ⚛ 4.50 – **7 rm** ⌚ 57.00/92.00 **st.**

Tarbert – pop. 479 – ECD : Thursday – ✉ ☎ 0859 Harris.

Harris, PA85 3DL, ✆ 2154, Fax 2281, 🌳 – ⚐ rest **P**. VISA
M 9.00/15.25 **t.** 3.50 – **24 rm** 28.85/62.40 **t.** – SB (weekends only) 74.00/93.50 **st.**

Leachin House ⛰, PA85 3AH, ✆ 502157, ≤ Loch Tarbert, 🌳 – ⚐ rest TV **P**.
closed 18 December-4 January – **M** (communal dining) 15.00 **st.** – **3 rm** 30.00/60.00 **st.**

Two Waters ⛰, PA85 3EL, S : 10 m. by A 859 on C 79 ✆ 085 983 (Manish) 246, 🐟, 🌳 – ⚐ rest **P**
May-September – **M** 13.00 **s.** – **4 rm** 34.00/48.00 **s.**

LEWISTON Inverness. (Highland) 401 G 12 **Scotland G.** – ☎ 0456 Drumnadrochit.

Envir. : Loch Ness★★.

◆Edinburgh 173 – ◆Inverness 17.

Lewiston Arms, IV3 6UN, ✆ 450225, 🌳 – TV **P**. AE VISA
M 9.00/14.75 **st.** and dinner a la carte 3.95 – **9 rm** 50.00/66.00 **st.** – SB (except Bank Holidays) (weekends only) 70.00/110.00 **st.**

LINICLATE Inverness (Weston Isles) 401 XY 11 /12 – see Usit (Isles of).

LINLITHGOW W. Lothian. (Lothian) 401 J 16 **Scotland G.** – pop. 9 524 – ☎ 0506.

See : Town★★ – Palace★★ *AC* : Courtyard (fountain★★), Great Hall (Hooded Fireplace★★), Gateway★ – Old Town★ – St. Michaels★.

Envir. : Cairnpapple Hill★ *AC*, SW : 5 m. by A 706 – House of the Binns (plasterwork ceilings★) *AC*, NE : 4½ m. by A 803 and A 904.

Exc. : Hopetoun House★★ *AC*, E : 7 m. by A 706 and A 904 – Abercorn Parish Church (Hopetoun Loft★★) NE : 7 m. by A 803 and A 904.

18 Braehead ✆ 842585 – 18 Airngath Hill ✆ 826030, N : 1 m.

Burgh Halls, The Cross ✆ 844600.

◆Edinburgh 19 – Falkirk 9 – ◆Glasgow 35.

XXX **Champany Inn,** Champany, EH49 7LU, NE : 2 m. on A 803 at junction with A 904 ✆ 834532, Fax 834302, « Converted horse mill », 🌳 – **P**. AE VISA JCB
closed Saturday lunch, Sunday and 24 to 31 December – **M** (grill rest.) 13.75/35.00 **t.** and a la carte 5.50.

LIVINGSTON Midlothian. (Lothian) 401 J 16 – pop. 38 594 – ☎ 0506.

18 Bathgate, Edinburgh Rd ✆ 52232, W : 5 m. by A 899 and A 89 – 18 Deer Park C.C., Knightsbridge ✆ 38843, N : 1½ m. by A 899.

◆Edinburgh 16 – Falkirk 23 – ◆Glasgow 32.

Hilton National, Almondview, Almondvale, EH54 6QB, ✆ 31222, Telex 727680, Fax 34666, ⚐ – ⚐ rm TV ☎ ♿ **P** – 🏛 100. AE VISA JCB
M (bar lunch)/dinner 14.95 **t.** and a la carte 5.25 – 8.75 – **120 rm** 85.00 **st.** – SB 138.00 **st.**

LOCHCARRON Ross and Cromarty. (Highland) 401 D 11 **Scotland G.** – ECD : Thursday – ☎ 052 02.

Envir. : Loch Earn★★.

9 Strathcarron ✆ 257, NE : 3 m.

Main St. ✆ 357 (summer only).

◆Edinburgh 221 – ◆Inverness 65 – Kyle of Lochalsh 23.

Lochcarron, IV54 8YS, ✆ 226, ≤ Loch Carron – TV **P**. VISA
M 6.90/15.50 **t.** and a la carte 4.80 – **10 rm** 32.00/80.00 **t.** – SB (October-April) 64.00/95.00 **st.**

LOCHEARNHEAD Perth. (Central) 401 H 14 – ECD : Wednesday – ☎ 0567.

◆Edinburgh 65 – ◆Glasgow 56 – ◆Oban 57 – Perth 36.

Mansewood Country House, FK19 8NS, S : ½ m. on A 84 ✆ 830213, 🌳 – ⚐ **P**. VISA
March-October – **M** 16.00 **st.** 4.30 – **8 rm** 20.00/46.00 **st.**

LOCHGILPHEAD Argyll. (Strathclyde) 401 D 15 **Scotland G.** – pop. 2 391 – ECD : Tuesday – ☎ 0546.

Envir. : Loch Fyne★★, E : 3½ m. by A 83.

9 Blarbuie Rd ✆ 602340, N : ½ m.

Lochnell St. ✆ 602344 (summer only).

◆Edinburgh 130 – ◆Glasgow 84 – ◆Oban 38.

🏠 **Stag,** Argyll St., PA31 8NE, ☎ 602496, Fax 603549, 🖴 – 📺 ☎ 🔌 🆚🆂🅰
M (bar lunch)/dinner 16.00 **t.** § 3.30 – **17 rm** ☲ 30.00/55.00 **t.** – SB (October-February except Christmas and New Year) (weekends only) 55.00/66.00 **st.**

🏠 **Empire Travellers Lodge** without rest., Union St., PA31 8JS, ☎ 602381 – 🖴 📺 🔌 🅿.
🔌 🆚🆂🅰 ✕
9 rm ☲ 18.50/37.00 **st.**

at Cairnbaan NW : 2 ¼ m. by A 816 on B 841 – ⊠ ✆ 0546 Lochgilphead :

🏨 **Cairnbaan,** PA31 8SJ, ☎ 603668, Fax 606045 – 🖴 rm 📺 ☎ 🅿. 🔌 🆚🆂🅰 ✕
closed mid January-mid February – **M** (bar lunch)/dinner a la carte 9.30/14.15 **t.** § 3.95 –
7 rm ☲ 40.00/90.00 **t.** – SB (winter only) 70.00/110.00 **st.**

LOCH HARRAY Orkney. (Orkney Islands) 401 K 6 – see Orkney Islands (Mainland).

LOCHINVER Sutherland. (Highland) 401 E 9 Scotland G. – – ECD : Tuesday – ⊠ Lairg – ✆ 057 14.
See : Village★.
Exc. : Loch Assynt★★, E : 6 m. by A 837.
🛈 Main St. ☎ 330 (summer only).
◆Edinburgh 251 – ◆Inverness 95 – ◆Wick 105.

🏨 **Inver Lodge** (Best Western) ☜, IV27 4LU, ☎ 496, Fax 395, ≤ Lochinver Bay, Suilven and Canisp mountains, 🖴, 🐟, 🎢, park – 📺 ☎ 🅿. 🔌 🆎 ⊙ 🆚🆂🅰 🇯🇨🇧
25 April-15 October – **M** (bar lunch Monday to Saturday)/dinner 25.00 **st.** and a la carte –
20 rm ☲ 66.00/100.00 **st.** – SB 120.00/150.00 **st.**

🏠 **Albannach** ☜, Baddidarroch, IV27 4LP, W : 1 m. by Baddidarroch rd ☎ 407, ≤, 🎢 – 🖴
🅿. 🔌 ⊙ 🆚🆂🅰
closed January and February – **M** (dinner only) 18.00 **t.** § 4.00 – **4 rm** ☲ 54.00 **t.** – SB (except May-September) 70.00/74.00 **st.**

⌂ **Veyatie** ☜ without rest., Baddidarroch, IV27 4LP, W : 1 ¼ m. by Baddidarroch rd
☎ 424, ≤ Lochinver Bay, Suilven and Canisp mountains, 🎢 – 🖴 🅿
April-October – **3 rm** ☲ 25.00/42.00 **st.**

Pour l'ensemble de la **Grande-Bretagne** *et de l'*Irlande,
procurez-vous la **carte Michelin** 986 *à 1/1 000 000.*

LOCHRANZA Bute. (Strathclyde) 401 402 E 16 – see Arran (Isle of).

LOCKERBIE Dumfries. (Dumfries and Galloway) 401 402 J 18 – pop. 3 545 – ECD : Tuesday – ✆ 0576.
🛈 Corrie Rd ☎ 203363, NE : ½ m. – 🛈 Lochmaben, Castlehill Gate ☎ 0387 (Dumfries) 810552, W : 4 m. by A 709.
◆Edinburgh 74 – ◆Carlisle 27 – ◆Dumfries 13 – ◆Glasgow 73.

🏨 **Dryfesdale,** DG11 2SF, NW : 1 m. by A 74 ☎ 202427, Fax 204187, ≤, 🎢 – 📺 ☎ 🅿. 🔌
🆎 🆚🆂🅰
M 11.00/16.00 **st.** and a la carte § 4.00 – **14 rm** ☲ 46.00/75.00 **st.** – SB (weekends only) 104.00/154.00 **st.**

LUSS Dunbarton. (Strathclyde) 401 G 15 Scotland G. – ✆ 0436.
See : Village★.
Envir. : E : Loch Lomond★★.
◆Edinburgh 89 – ◆Glasgow 26 – Oban 65.

🏠 **Lodge on Loch Lomond,** G83 8NT, ☎ 86201, Fax 86203, ≤ Loch Lomond, 🖴 – 📺 ☎
🅿. 🔌 🆚🆂🅰
M (bar lunch)/dinner 16.00 **st.** and a la carte § 4.00 – ☲ 7.00 – **10 rm** 65.00 **st.** – SB (winter only) (weekends only) 80.00/176.00 **st.**

LYBSTER Caithness. (Highland) 401 K 9 – ✆ 059 32.

🏠 **Portland Arms,** KW3 6BS, on A 9 ☎ 208, Fax 208 (ext. 200) – 📺 ☎ 🅿. 🔌 🆎 ⊙ 🆚🆂🅰
M 7.95/18.95 **st.** and lunch a la carte § 3.25 – **19 rm** ☲ 36.00/65.00 **st.** – SB 88.00/ 117.00 **st.**

MACHRIHANISH Argyll. (Strathclyde) 401 C 17 – see Kintyre (Peninsula).

MARKINCH Fife. (Fife) 401 K 15 – see Glenrothes.

MARNOCH Aberdeen. (Grampian) 401 L 11 Scotland G. – ⊠ ✆ 0466 Huntly.
Exc. : Huntly Castle (elaborate Heraldic Carvings★★★) AC, SW : 10½ m. by B 9117, B 9118 and B 9022.
◆Edinburgh 170 – ◆Aberdeen 40 – Fraserburgh 39 – ◆Inverness 77.

⌂ **Old Manse of Marnoch** ☜, AB54 5RS, on B 9117 ☎ 780873, 🎢 – 🖴 rest 🅿
closed 2 weeks November – **M** 21.00 § 6.00 – **4 rm** ☲ 60.00/80.00 – SB 105.00/140.00.

MARYCULTER Aberdeen. (Grampian) 401 N 12 – see Aberdeen.

MAYBOLE Ayr. (Strathclyde) **401** 402 F 17 Scotland G. – ✪ 065 54 Crosshill.

Envir. : Culzean Castle★ *AC* (setting★★★, Oval Staircase★★) W : 5 m. by B 7023 and A 719.

🏠 **Ladyburn** ⤷, KA19 7SG, S : 5 ½ m. by B 7023 off B 741 (Girvan rd) ℘ 585, Fax 580, ≼, ◈, park – ⇖ 🆃🆅 ☎ 🅿. 🖭 🆀🅴 *VISA*. ✻
   closed 4 weeks January-February – **M** *(closed Sunday dinner and Monday to non-resi-dents)* (booking essential) (lunch by arrangement)/dinner 26.00 **t.** and a la carte ⓘ 6.00 –
   8 rm ⌑ 95.00/150.00 **t.**

MEIGLE Perth. (Tayside) **401** K 14 Scotland G. – ✪ 082 84 (3 fig.) and 0828 (6 fig).

See : Museum★★ (early Christian Monuments★★) *AC.*

Exc. : Glamis Castle★★, NE : 7 m. by A 94.

◆Edinburgh 62 – ◆Dundee 13 – Perth 18.

🏠 **Kings of Kinloch** ⤷, Coupar Angus Rd, PH12 8QX, W : 1 m. on A 94 ℘ 273, Fax 347, ≼, ◈, park – 🆃🆅 ☎ 🅿. 🖭 *VISA*. ✻
   M 22.50 **st.** (dinner) and a la carte ⓘ 4.75 – **6 rm** ⌑ 45.00/110.00 **st.** – SB 88.50/115.00 **st.**

MELROSE Roxburgh. (Borders) **401** **402** L 17 Scotland G. – pop. 2 143 – ECD : Thursday –
✪ 089 682 (4 fig.) and 0896 (6 fig.).

See : Town★ - Abbey★★ (decorative sculptures★★★) *AC.*

Envir. : Eildon Hills (⁑★★★) – Scott's View★★ – Abbotsford★★ *AC*, W : 4 ½ m. by A 6091 and
B 6360 – Dryburgh Abbey★★ *AC* (setting★★★) SE : 4 m. by A 6091.

Exc. : Bowhill★★ *AC*, SW : 11 ½ m. by A 6091, A 7 and A 708 – Thirlestane Castle (plasterwork
ceilings★★) *AC*, NE : 21 m. by A 6091 and A 68.

🏌 Ladhope Recreation Ground, Galashiels ℘ 3724, NW : 4 m. by A 6091 and A 7 – 🏌 Melrose,
Dingleton ℘ 2855, S : 1 ½ m. by B 6359 – 🏌 Torwoodlee, Galashiels ℘ 2260, NW : 5 m. by
A 6091 and A 72.

🛈 Priorwood Gdns., ℘ 2555 (summer only).

◆Edinburgh 38 – Hawick 19 – ◆Newcastle upon Tyne 70.

🏠 **Burts**, Market Sq., TD6 9PN, ℘ 2285, Fax 2870, ☞ – 🆃🆅 ☎ 🅿. 🖭 🆀🅴 ⓪ *VISA*
   closed 24 to 27 December – **M** 16.00/24.00 **t.** and dinner a la carte ⓘ 4.60 – **21 rm**
   ⌑ 40.00/70.00 **t.** – SB (except second week April and Bank Holidays) 98.00/120.00 **st.**

⌂ **Dunfermline House** without rest., Buccleuch St., TD6 9LB, ℘ 2148 – ⇖ 🆃🆅. ✻
   5 rm ⌑ 20.00/42.00.

   at Gattonside NW : 2 ¼ m. by A 6091 on B 6360 – ✉ ✪ 089 682 (4 fig.) and 0896
   (6 fig.) Melrose :

✗ **Hoebridge Inn**, TD6 9LZ, ℘ 3082 – 🅿. 🖭 *VISA*
   closed Monday, 2 weeks April, 1 week October, 25 December and 1 January – **M** (dinner
   only) a la carte 11.85/16.00 **t.** ⓘ 4.00.

MEY Caithness. (Highland) **401** K 8 – ✪ 084 785 Barroch.

◆Edinburgh 302 – ◆Inverness 144 – Thurso 13 – ◆Wick 21.

🏠 **Castle Arms**, KW14 8XH, ℘ 244, ☞ – 🆃🆅 ☎ & 🅿. 🖭 *VISA*
   M (bar lunch Monday to Saturday and bar dinner Monday to Thursday November- March)/
   dinner 16.00 **st.** – **8 rm** ⌑ 39.00/58.00 **st.** – SB (October-May except Bank Holidays) 70.00/
   100.00 **st.**

MILNGAVIE Lanark. (Strathclyde) **401** H 16 – pop. 12 030 – ECD : Tuesday and Saturday –
✉ ✪ 041 Glasgow.

🏌, 🏌 Hilton Park, Auldmarroch Est., Stockiemuir Rd ℘ 956 5124 – 🏌 Dougalston ℘ 956 5750.

◆Edinburgh 53 – ◆Glasgow 7.

🏠 **Black Bull Thistle** (Mt.Charlotte Thistle), Main St., G62 6BH, ℘ 956 2291, Fax 956 1896 –
   🆃🆅 ☎ 🅿 – 🕭 100. 🖭 🆀🅴 ⓪ *VISA* 🅹🅲🅱
   M *(closed lunch Saturday and Bank Holiday Mondays)* 10.00/23.00 **t.** and a la carte ⓘ 4.90 –
   ⌑ 8.15 – **27 rm** 62.00/85.00 **st.** – SB (weekends only) 88.00/128.00 **st.**

MOFFAT Dumfries. (Dumfries and Galloway) **401** **402** J 17 Scotland G. – pop. 1 990 – ECD :
Wednesday – ✪ 0683.

Exc. : Grey Mare's Tail★★, NE : 9 m. by A 708.

🏌 Coatshill ℘ 20020, SW : 1 ½ m. by A 701.

🛈 Churchgate ℘ 20620 (summer only).

◆Edinburgh 61 – ◆Dumfries 22 – ◆Carlisle 43 – ◆Glasgow 60.

🏠 **Moffat House**, High St., DG10 9HL, ℘ 20039, Fax 21288, ☞ – ⇖ rest 🆃🆅 ☎ 🅿. 🖭 🆀🅴
   ⓪ *VISA*
   M (bar lunch)/dinner 22.50 **st.** and a la carte ⓘ 5.00 – **20 rm** ⌑ 45.00/72.00 **st.** – SB (except
   Bank Holidays) 98.00/130.00 **st.**

🏨 **Beechwood Country House** 🌙, Harthope Pl., by Academy Rd, DG10 9RS, ☎ 20210, Fax 20889, ≤, 🌳 – 🚭 rest [TV] ☎ [P]. [AE] [VISA]
closed 2 January-15 February – **M** *(closed lunch Monday to Wednesday)* (bar lunch Thursday to Saturday)/dinner 19.00 **t.** 🍷 5.30 – **7 rm** ☕ 48.00/68.00 **t.**

🏨 **Buccleuch Arms,** High St., DG10 9ET, ☎ 20003, Fax 21291, 🌳 – [TV] ☎. [AE] [VISA]
M a la carte 11.00/15.75 🍷 3.75 – **11 rm** ☕ 39.00/58.00 **t.** – SB 75.00/90.00 **st.**

🏠 **Hartfell House,** Hartfell Cres., DG10 9AL, via Well St. and Old Well Rd ☎ 20153, 🌳 – 🚭 rest [P]
March-November – **M** (by arrangement) 13.00 **st.** 🍷 3.50 – **9 rm** ☕ 21.50/45.00 **st.** – SB (except Easter-18 October) 57.00 **st.**

🏠 **Fernhill** without rest., Grange Rd, DG10 9HT, ☎ 20077, 🌳 – 🚭 [TV]. 🐕
May-mid September – **3 rm** ☕ 20.00/28.00 **s.**

🍴🍴 **Well View** 🌙 with rm, Ballplay Rd, DG10 9JU, E : ¾ m. by Selkirk Rd (A 708) ☎ 20184, ≤, 🌳 – 🚭 [TV] [P]. [VISA]
closed 1 week January, 2 weeks October and 1 week November – **M** *(closed Saturday lunch)* 11.00/23.00 **st.** – **5 rm** ☕ 40.00/76.00 **st.**, 1 suite.

MONTROSE Angus. (Tayside) [401] M 13 **Scotland G.** – pop. 12 127 – ECD : Wednesday – ✆ 0674.

Exc. : Edzell Castle★ (The Pleasance★★★) *AC*, NW : 17 m. by A 935 and B 966 – Cairn O'Mount Road★ (≤★★) N : 17 m. by B 966 and B 974 – Brechin (Round Tower★) W : 7 m. by A 935 – Aberlemno (Aberlemno Stones★, Pictish sculptured stones★) W : 13 m. by A 935 and B 9134.

⛳18, ⛳18 Traill Drive ☎ 72932.

[i] The Library, High St ☎ 72000 (summer only).

◆Edinburgh 92 – ◆Aberdeen 39 – ◆Dundee 29.

🏨 **Park,** 61 John St., DD10 8RJ, ☎ 73415, Fax 77091, 🌳 – [TV] ☎ [P] – 🎤 180. [AE] [VISA]
M 7.50/16.50 **t.** and a la carte 🍷 5.20 – **59 rm** ☕ 65.00/90.00 **t.** – SB 88.00/123.00 **st.**

GRÜNE REISEFÜHRER

Landschaften, Baudenkmäler
Sehenswürdigkeiten
Fremdenverkehrsstraßen
Tourenvorschläge
Stadtpläne und Übersichtskarten

MOTHERWELL Lanark. [401] I 16 – ✉ ✆ 0698.

[i] Library, Hamilton Rd ☎ 251311.

◆Edinburgh 38 – ◆Glasgow 12.

🏨 **Travel Inn** without rest., Glasgow Rd, Newhoose, ML1 5SY, NE : 4 ¼ m. by A 723 and A 73 on A 775 ☎ 860277, Fax 861353 – 🚭 rm [TV] ♿ [P] – 🎤 100. [AE] [VISA]. 🐕
☕ 4.95 – **40 rm** 33.50 **t.**

MUIR OF ORD Ross and Cromarty. (Highland) [401] G 11 – pop. 1 693 – ✆ 0463.

⛳18 Great North Rd ☎ 870825.

◆Edinburgh 173 – ◆Inverness 10 – Wick 121.

🏨 **Dower House** 🌙, Highfield, IV6 7XN, N : 1 m. on A 862 ☎ 870090, Fax 870090, « Part 17C house », 🌳 – 🚭 rest [TV] ☎ [P]. [VISA]
closed 2 weeks March, 1 week October and 25 December – **M** (lunch by arrangement)/dinner 25.00 **st.** 🍷 6.00 – **4 rm** ☕ 50.00/100.00 **st.**, 1 suite.

MULL (Isle of) Argyll. (Strathclyde) [401] C 14 **Scotland G.** – pop. 2 605.

See : Island★ - Calgary Bay★★ – Torosay Castle *AC* (Gardens★ ≤★).

Envir. : Isle of Iona★ (Madean's Cross★, St. Oran's Chapel★, St. Martin's High Cross★, Infirmary Museum★ *AC*).

⛳9 Craignure, Scallastle ☎ 068 02 (Craignure) 370.

⛴ by Caledonian MacBrayne : from Craignure to Oban : 2-6 daily – from Fishnish to Lochaline, frequent services daily (15 mn) – from Tobermory to Isle of Coll – from Tobermory to Isle of Tiree – from Tobermory to Armadale (Isle of Skye) and Mallaig – from Tobermory to Oban via Tiree - from Tobermory to Kilchoan (summer only) Monday to Saturday 4-7 daily (35 mn) – from Fionnphort to Isle of Iona frequent services daily in summer (5 mn).

[i] Main St., Tobermory ☎ 0688 (Tobermory) 2182.

Bunessan – ✉ ✆ 068 17 Fionnphort

🏠 **Ardfenaig House** 🌙, PA67 6DX, W : 3 m. by A 849 ☎ 210, Fax 210, ≤, 🌳, park – 🚭 [P]. [VISA]. 🐕
April-October – **M** (dinner only) 22.50 **st.** 🍷 4.75 – **5 rm** ☕ (dinner included) 80.00/160.00 **st.**

Calgary – ✉ Tobermory – ✆ 068 84 Dervaig

🏠 **Calgary Farmhouse,** PA75 6QW, on B 8073 ☎ 256, 🌳 – [P]. [VISA]
April-October – **M** 20.00 **t.** 🍷 4.00 – **9 rm** ☕ 31.00/54.00 **st.**

Dervaig – ⬭ Tobermory – ◉ 068 84 Dervaig

🏠 **Druimard Country House** ⬡, PA75 6QW, on Salen rd 🖉 345, ≼, 🗗 – ⭍ rest 📺 ☎
🅿. 🔼 𝘝𝘐𝘚𝘈
March-October – **M** (booking essential) (dinner only) 15.95 **t.** – **5 rm** ⬚ 54.50/85.00 **t.**,
1 suite.

🏠 **Druimnacroish Country House** ⬡, PA75 6QW, S : 2 m. by B 8073 and Salen rd
🖉 274, Fax 311, ≼ Bellart Glen, 🗗 – ⭍ 📺 ☎ 🅿. 🔼 🆎 ⓞ 𝘝𝘐𝘚𝘈
mid April-mid October – **M** (dinner only) 25.00 **st.** 🍴 3.25 – **6 rm** ⬚ 55.00/110.00 **st.**

Pennyghael – ⬭ ◉ 068 14 Pennyghael

🏠 **Pennyghael,** PA70 6HB, 🖉 288, ≼, 🗗 – 📺 ☎ 🅿. 🔼 𝘝𝘐𝘚𝘈
Easter-mid October – **M** (in bar)/dinner 18.50 🍴 4.50 – **6 rm** ⬚ 47.50/75.00 **st.**

Tiroran – ⬭ ◉ 068 15 Tiroran

🏠 **Tiroran House** ⬡, PA69 6ES, 🖉 232, Fax 232, ≼ Loch Scridain, « Country house
atmosphere », 🗗, park – ⭍ rest 🅿 ⭍
mid May-early October – **Meals** (dinner only) 28.50 **st.** 🍴 4.75 – **9 rm** ⬚ (dinner included)
125.00/220.00 **st.**

Tobermory – pop. 843 – ECD : Wednesday – ⬭ ◉ 0688 Tobermory.

🏌 Tobermory 🖉 2020.

🏠 **Western Isles,** PA75 6PR, 🖉 2012, Fax 2297, ≼ Tobermory harbour and Calve Island –
⭍ rest 📺 ☎ 🅿. 🔼 𝘝𝘐𝘚𝘈
closed 2 January-February and 1 week Christmas – **M** (bar lunch)/dinner 23.00 **t.** – **28 rm**
⬚ 35.00/150.00 **t.**

🏠 **Tobermory,** 53 Main St., PA75 6NT, 🖉 2091, ≼ ⭍ 📺 👶. 🔼 𝘝𝘐𝘚𝘈
M (dinner only) 20.00 **st.** 🍴 4.15 – **17 rm** ⬚ 35.00/78.00 **st.** – SB 103.50/114.00 **st.**

🏠 **Ulva House,** Strongarbh, PA75 6PR, 🖉 2044, ≼ Tobermory harbour and Calve Island,
🗗 – 🅿
April-September – **M** 13.95 **t.** 🍴 4.50 – **6 rm** ⬚ 25.95/51.90 **st.**

MURCAR Aberdeen. (Grampian) 🗺 N 12 – see Aberdeen.

MUSSELBURGH E. Lothian. (Lothian) 🗺 K 16 – pop. 18 573 – ◉ 031 Edinburgh.

🏌 Monktonhall 🖉 665 2005 – 🏌 Royal Musselburgh, Prestongrange House, Prestonpans
🖉 0875 (Prestonpans) 810276, E : 3 m. by B 1348 – 🏌 Musselburgh Old Course, Silver Ring
Clubhouse, Millhill 🖉 665 6981 – 🛈 Brunton Hall 🖉 665 6597 (summer only).

◆Edinburgh 6 – Berwick 54 – ◆Glasgow 53.

🏠 **Granada Lodge** without rest., Old Craighall, EH21 8RE, S : 1½ m. by B 6415 at junction
with A 1 🖉 653 6070, Fax 653 6106, Reservations (Freephone) 0800 555300 – ⭍ 📺 👶 🅿.
🔼 🆎 𝘝𝘐𝘚𝘈. ⭍
⬚ 4.00 – **44 rm** 34.95/37.95 **t.**

NAIRN Nairn. (Highland) 🗺 I 11 Scotland G. – pop. 7 366 – ECD : Wednesday – ◉ 0667.

Envir. : Forres (Sueno's Stone★★) E : 11 m. by A 96 and B 9011 – Cawdor Castle★ AC, S :
5½ m. by B 9090 – Brodie Castle★ AC, E : 6 m. by A 96.

Exc. : Fort George★, W : 7 m. by A 96, B 9092 and B 9006.

🏌 🏌 Seabank Rd 🖉 52103 – 🏌 Nairn Dunbar, Lochloy Rd 🖉 52741.

🛈 62 King St. 🖉 52753 (summer only).

◆Edinburgh 172 – ◆Aberdeen 91 – ◆Inverness 16.

🏨 **Golf View,** 63 Seabank Rd, IV12 4HD, 🖉 52301, Fax 55267, ≼, ⟃ heated, 🗗, ⁘ – ▯ 📺
☎ 🅿 – 🕰 100. 🔼 🆎 ⓞ 𝘝𝘐𝘚𝘈
M 22.00 **t.** (dinner) and lunch a la carte – **46 rm** ⬚ 69.00/116.00 **t.**, 1 suite – SB (except
Christmas and New Year) 104.00/178.00 **st.**

🏠 **Clifton House** ⬡, Viewfield St., IV12 4HW, 🖉 53119, Fax 52836, ≼, 🗗 – 🅿. 🔼 🆎 ⓞ
𝘝𝘐𝘚𝘈
closed mid December-mid January – **M** (booking essential) a la carte 17.50/25.00 **st.** 🍴 4.50
– **12 rm** ⬚ 54.00/96.00 **st.**

🏠 **Lochloy House** ⬡, Lochloy Rd, Lochloy, IV12 5LE, NE : 2½ m. 🖉 55355, Fax 54809,
≼ Moray Firth, « Country house atmosphere », ⟍, 🗗, park, ⁘ – 🅿. ⭍
April-November (booking essential) – **M** (lunch by arrangement)/dinner 20.00 **st.** 🍴 4.50 –
6 rm ⬚ 43.00/86.00 **st.** – SB 126.00 **st.**

🏠 **Links,** 1 Seafield St., IV12 4HN, 🖉 53321, Fax 53321, 🗗 – 📺 🅿. 🔼 𝘝𝘐𝘚𝘈
M (dinner only) 15.00 **st.** 🍴 5.50 – **10 rm** ⬚ 30.00/60.00 **st.**

🏠 **Claymore House,** 45 Seabank Rd, IV12 4EY, 🖉 453731, Fax 455290, 🗗 – 📺 ☎ 🅿. 🔼
🆎 𝘝𝘐𝘚𝘈
M (bar lunch Monday to Saturday)/dinner 8.75 **st.** and a la carte 🍴 3.05 – **12 rm** ⬚ 30.00/
58.00 **st.** – SB (weekdays only) 66.00/76.00 **st.**

🏠 **Sunny Brae,** Marine Rd, IV12 4EA, 🖉 52309, ≼, 🗗 – ⭍ rest 📺 🅿
April-September – **M** 8.50 **t.** – **10 rm** ⬚ 21.00/42.00 **t.**

☆ **Longhouse,** 8 Harbour St., IV12 4NU, ℘ 55532 – ⊠ Ⓐ🄴 𝗩𝗜𝗦𝗔
closed Sunday dinner, Monday, 1 week February, 1 week October and Christmas-New Year – **M** *(booking essential in winter)* (dinner only and Sunday lunch)/dinner a la carte 15.50/24.00 **t.** ♨ 3.95.

NETHERLEY Kincardine. (Grampian) 🗺️ N 12 Scotland G. – ⊠ 🅦 0569 Stonehaven.
Envir. : Muchalls Castle (plasterwork ceilings★★) *AC*, SE : 5 m. by B 979 – Deeside★★, N : 2 m. by B 979 – Aberdeen★★, NE : 3 m. by B 979 and B 9077.
Exc. : Aberdeen★★, NE : 12 m. by B 979 – Dunnottar Castle★★ (site★★★) *AC*, S : 7 m. by B 979 – Crathes Castle★★ (Gardens★★★) *AC*, NW : 13 m. by B 979, B 9077 and A 93.
♦Edinburgh 117 – ♦Aberdeen 12 – ♦Dundee 54.

XX **Lairhillock,** AB3 2QS, NE : 1 ½ m. by B 979 on Portlethan rd ℘ 30001, Fax 31175 – 🅟. ⊠ Ⓐ🄴 Ⓞ 𝗩𝗜𝗦𝗔
M (bar lunch Monday to Saturday)/dinner a la carte 19.25/24.80 **t.** ♨ 5.50.

NEWBURGH Aberdeen. (Grampian) 🗺️ N 12 Scotland G. – 🅦 035 86.
Exc. : Pitmedden Gardens★★ *AC*, W : 6 ½ m. by B 9000 – Haddo House★ *AC*, NW : 14 m. by B 900, A 92 and B 9005.
🏌 McDonald, Ellon ℘ 0358 (Ellon) 20576, N : 5 ½ m. by B 9000, A 92 and A 920 – 🏌 Newburgh-on-Ythan, Ellon ℘ 89438.
♦Edinburgh 144 – ♦Aberdeen 14 – Fraserburgh 33.

🏨 **Udny Arms,** Main St., AB41 0BL, ℘ 89444, Fax 89012, ☞ – 🆃🆅 ☎ 🅟 – 🔬 80. ⊠ 𝗩𝗜𝗦𝗔
M - (see below) – ⊡ 8.50 – **26 rm** 49.50/54.00 **t.** – SB (except Christmas) 116.00 **st.**

XX **Udny Arms,** Main St., AB41 0BL, ℘ 89444, Fax 89012 – 🅟. ⊠ 𝗩𝗜𝗦𝗔
M a la carte 15.00/24.00 **t.** ♨ 6.00.

NEW GALLOWAY Kirkcudbright. (Dumfries and Galloway) 🗺️ 🗺️ H 18 Scotland G. – pop. 290 – 🅦 064 42.
Envir. : Galloway Forest Park★, Queen's Way★ (Newton Stuart to New Galloway) SW : 19 m. by A 712.
🏌 New Galloway ℘ 737, S : by A 762.
♦Edinburgh 88 – ♦Ayr 36 – Dumfries 25.

⌂ **Leamington,** High St., DG7 3RN, ℘ 327 – ⭲ rest 🆃🆅 🅟. ⊠ 𝗩𝗜𝗦𝗔 ✕
closed November – **M** (by arrangement) 12.40 ♨ 3.20 – **9 rm** ⊡ 14.00/44.00 **t.**

NEW SCONE Perth. (Tayside) 🗺️ J 14 – see Perth.

NEWTONMORE Inverness. (Highland) 🗺️ H 12 – pop. 1 010 – ECD : Wednesday – 🅦 0540.
🏌 Newtonmore ℘ 673328.
♦Edinburgh 113 – ♦Inverness 43 – Perth 69.

🏠 **Ard-na-Coille,** Kingussie Rd, PH20 1AY, ℘ 673214, Fax 673453, ≼, ☞ – ⭲ rest ☎ 🅟. ⊠ 𝗩𝗜𝗦𝗔
closed 1 week April, 1 week September and mid November-December – **Meals** (booking essential) (dinner only) 28.50 **t.** ♨ 7.00 – **7 rm** ⊡ (dinner included) 63.00/150.00 **t.** – SB (4 January-Easter) 95.00 **st.**

⌂ **Pines** ⍦, Station Rd, PH20 1AR, ℘ 673271, ≼, ☞ – ⭲ 🅟. ✕
April-October – **M** 9.00 **s.** ♨ 2.20 – **6 rm** ⊡ 23.00/46.00 **st.**

NEWTON STEWART Wigtown. (Dumfries and Galloway) 🗺️ 🗺️ G 19 Scotland G. – pop. 3 212 – ECD : Wednesday – 🅦 0671.
Envir. : Galloway Forest Park★, Queen's Way★ (Newton Stewart to New Galloway) N : 19 m. by A 712.
🏌 Kirroughtree Av., Minnigaff ℘ 2172, by A 712.
🄱 Dashwood Sq. ℘ 2431 (summer only).
♦Edinburgh 131 – ♦Dumfries 51 – ♦Glasgow 87 – Stranraer 24.

🏨 **Kirroughtree** ⍦, DG8 6AN, NE : 1 ½ m. on A 712 ℘ 2141, Fax 2425, ≼ woodland and River Cree, « Country house, gardens », park, ❊ – 🆃🆅 ☎ 🅟. ⊠
closed January and February – **M** 25.00 **st.** (dinner) and lunch a la carte 13.20/17.00 **st.** ♨ 6.75 – **17 rm** ⊡ 70.00/136.00 **st.**, 1 suite – SB (October-April) 104.00/128.00 **st.**

🏨 **Creebridge House** ⍦, Minnigaff, DG8 6NP, ℘ 2121, Fax 3258, ☞ – ⭲ rest 🆃🆅 ☎ 🅟. ⊠ 𝗩𝗜𝗦𝗔
M (bar lunch)/dinner 18.95 **st.** and a la carte – **18 rm** ⊡ 40.00/80.00 **t.** – SB 70.00/120.00 **st.**

🏠 **Crown,** 101 Queen St., DG8 6JW, ℘ 2727 – 🆃🆅 ☎ 🅟. ⊠ 𝗩𝗜𝗦𝗔 ✕
closed November – **M** 13.50 **st.** and a la carte – **11 rm** ⊡ 23.00/50.00 **st.** – SB 74.00/79.00 **st.**

⌂ **Rowallan House** ⍦, Corsbie Rd, DG8 6JB, ℘ 2520, ☞ – ⭲ rest 🆃🆅 🅟. ✕
closed November – **M** (by arrangement) 14.00 **t.** ♨ 4.20 – **6 rm** ⊡ 27.00/54.00 **t.** – SB 80.00 **t.**

Les prix Pour toutes précisions sur les prix indiqués dans ce guide, reportez-vous à l'introduction.

NORTH BERWICK E. Lothian. (Lothian) 📖 L 15 Scotland G. – pop. 4 861 – ECD : Thursday – ✪ 0620.

Envir. : North Berwick Law (❄★★★) S : 1 m. – Tantallon Castle★★ (clifftop site★★★) *AC*, E : 3½ m. by A 198 – Dirleton★ (Castle★ *AC*) SW : 2½ m. by A 198.

Exc. : Museum of Flight★, S : 6 m. by B 1347 – Preston Mill★, S : 8½ m. by A 198 and B 1047 – Tyninghame★, S : 7 m. by A 198 – Coastal road from North Berwick to Portseton★, SW : 13 m. by A 198 and B 1348.

📒 North Berwick, Bass Rock, Tantallon, West Links, Beach Rd ✆ 2135 – 📒 Burgh Links, Glen East Links ✆ 2726.

🏛 Quality St. ✆ 2197.

◆Edinburgh 24 – ◆Newcastle upon Tyne 102.

🏨 **Marine** (Forte), 18 Cromwell Rd, EH39 4LZ, ✆ 2406, Fax 4480, ≤ golf course and Firth of Forth, 🏊, 🔥 heated, ☞, ✣, squash – 📳 ✦ rm 📺 ☎ 🅿 – 🔏 250. 🖭 🖎 ⓞ 𝑽𝑰𝑺𝑨
M 9.95/17.95 **st.** and dinner a la carte ▯ 4.95 – ⛳ 6.95 – **78 rm** 55.00/95.00 **st.** – 5 suites – SB 78.00/138.00 **st.**

🏠 **Point Garry,** 20 West Bay Rd, EH39 4AW, ✆ 2380, Fax 2848, ≤ – 📺 ☎ 🅿. 🖭 𝑽𝑰𝑺𝑨
April-October – **M** 9.95/15.95 **t.** and a la carte ▯ 4.75 – **16 rm** ⛳ 18.00/94.00 **t.** – SB (week-ends only and weekdays April, July, August and October) 64.00/114.00 **st.**

🏠 Nether Abbey, 20 Dirleton Av., EH39 4BQ, ✆ 2802, Fax 5298 – 📺 ☎ 🅿
16 rm.

↑ **Craigview** without rest., 5 Beach Rd, EH39 4AB, ✆ 2257 – ✦ 📺 ✣
2 rm ⛳ 20.00/45.00 **st.**, 1 suite.

✗ **Hardings,** 2 Station Rd, EH39 4AU, ✆ 4737 – ✦
closed Sunday to Tuesday. 2 weeks October and 3 weeks January-February – **M** 14.00/24.50 **t.** ▯ 5.35.

OBAN Argyll. (Strathclyde) 📖 D 14 Scotland G. – pop. 7 476 – ECD : Thursday – ✪ 0631.

Exc. : Loch Awe★★, SE : 17 m. by A 85 – Bonawe Furnace★, E : 12 m. by A 85 – Cruachan Power Station★ *AC*, E : 16 m. by A 85 – Sea Life Centre★ *AC*, N : 14 m. by A 828.

📒 Glencruitten Rd ✆ 62868/64115.

Access to Glasgow by helicopter.

⛴ by Caledonian MacBrayne : to Craignure (Isle of Mull) 2-6 daily – to Castlebay (Isle of Barra) via Lochboisdale (South Uist) (summer only) – to Tiree via Tobemory (Isle of Mull) and Arinagour (Isle of Coll) 3 weekly – to Port Askaig, Port Ellen and Kennacraig (summer only) – to Achnacroish (Isle of Lismore) 2-4 daily (50 mn) – to Colonsay (Isle of) via Kennacraig and Port Askaig.

🏛 Boswell House, Argyll Sq. ✆ 63122.

◆Edinburgh 123 – ◆Dundee 116 – ◆Glasgow 93 – ◆Inverness 118.

🏨 **Manor House,** Gallanach Rd, PA34 4LS, ✆ 62087, Fax 63053, ≤, ☞ – ✦ rest 📺 ☎ 🅿. 🖭 𝑽𝑰𝑺𝑨
closed 25 December-1 February – **M** (lunch by arrangement)/dinner 21.50 **st.** and a la carte ▯ 4.00 – **11 rm** ⛳ (dinner included) 80.00/150.00 **st.** – SB 110.00/156.00 **st.**

🏠 **Kilchrenan House** without rest., Corran Esplanade, PA34 5AU, ✆ 62663, ≤ – ✦ rest 📺 ☎ 🅿. 🖭 𝑽𝑰𝑺𝑨
Easter-October – **10 rm** ⛳ 25.00/48.00 **t.**

🏠 **Barriemore,** Corran Esplanade, PA34 5AQ, ✆ 66356, ≤ – ✦ rest 📺 🅿. 🖭 𝑽𝑰𝑺𝑨
21 March-November – **M** *(closed Monday)* (dinner only) 17.50 **st.** ▯ 3.75 – **13 rm** ⛳ 30.00/54.00 **st.**

at Kilmore S : 4 m. on A 816 – ⊠ Oban – ✪ 063 177 Kilmore :

🏠 **Glenfeochan House** 🦆, , PA34 4QR, S : ½ m. on A 816 ✆ 273, Fax 624, ≤, « Victorian country house in extensive gardens », 🐾, park – ✦ 📺 🅿. 🖭 𝑽𝑰𝑺𝑨 ✣
March-October – **M** (communal dining) (dinner only) 30.00 **st.** ▯ 6.00 – **3 rm** ⛳ 95.00/125.00 **st.** – SB (except May-September) 172.00/230.00 **st.**

at Kilninver SW : 8 m. by A 816 on B 844 – ⊠ Oban – ✪ 085 26 Kilninver :

🏨 **Knipoch,** PA34 4QT, NE : 1½ m. on A 816 ✆ 261, Fax 249, ≤, ☞ – ✦ rest 📺 ☎ 🅿. 🖭 🖎 ⓞ 𝑽𝑰𝑺𝑨 ✣
mid February-mid November – **M** (lunch by arrangement)/dinner 37.50 **t.** ▯ 6.90 – **17 rm** ⛳ 59.00/118.00 **t.**

When visiting Ireland,

use the Michelin Green Guide **"Ireland".**

– *Detailed descriptions of places of interest*
– *Touring programmes*
– *Maps and street plans*
– *The history of the country*
– *Photographs and drawings of monuments, beauty spots, houses...*

ONICH Inverness. (Highland) **401** E 13 – ECD : Saturday except summer – ✉ Fort William – ☎ 085 53.

◆Edinburgh 123 – ◆Glasgow 93 – ◆Inverness 79 – ◆Oban 39.

🏨 **The Lodge on the Loch,** Creag Dhu, PH33 6RY, on A 82 ℘ 237, Fax 463, ≤ Loch Linnhe and mountains, ☞ – ⇆ rest 📺 ☎ ⓺ ⓟ. ◪ *VISA*
closed 4 January-28 February and mid November-23 December – **M** 15.00/21.50 **t.** 🛇 5.00 – **20 rm** ⊑ (dinner included) 66.00/150.00 **t.** – SB (October-May except Christmas and New Year) 90.00/110.00 **st.**

🏨 **Onich,** PH33 6RY, on A 82 ℘ 214, Fax 484, ≤ Loch Linnhe and mountains, « Lochside setting », ☞ – ⇆ rest 📺 ☎ ⓟ. ◪ *AE* ⑩ *VISA*
M (bar lunch)/dinner 18.50 **st.** 🛇 4.25 – **26 rm** ⊑ 27.50/87.00 **st.** – SB 79.00/122.00 **st.**

🏨 **Allt-Nan-Ros,** PH33 6RY, on A 82 ℘ 210, Fax 462, ≤ Loch Linnhe and mountains, ☞ – ⇆ rest 📺 ☎ ⓟ. ◪ *AE* ⑩ *VISA*
April-October – **M** 19.50 **t.** (dinner) and lunch a la carte – **21 rm** ⊑ 47.50/95.00 **t.**

↑ **Cuilcheanna House** ⧖, PH33 6SD, ℘ 226, ≤, ☞, park – ⇆ rest ⓟ
April-October – **M** 12.50 **t.** 🛇 3.00 – **8 rm** ⊑ 29.00/48.00 **st.** – SB 66.00/80.00 **st.**

ORKNEY ISLANDS Orkney. (Orkney Islands) **401** KL 6 /7 Scotland G. – pop. **19 040.**

See : Islands★★.

Envir. : Old Man of Hoy★★★ – Maes Howe★★ *AC* – Skara Brae★★ *AC* – Corrigal Farm Museum★ *AC* – Brough of Birsay★ *AC* – Birsay (≤★) – Ring of Brodgar★ – Stromness★ (Pier Arts Centre, collection of abstract art★) – Unston Cairn★.

⤤ see Kirkwall.

⤥ by Orkney Islands Shipping Co. Ltd : service between Longhope (Isle of Hoy), Lyness (Isle of Hoy), Flotta (Isle of) and Houton, frequent services daily (except Sundays) – by P & O Scottish Ferries : from Stromness to Scrabster (1 h 45 mn) – from Stromness to Lerwick (Shetland Islands) via Aberdeen – by Orkney Islands Shipping Co. : to Kirkwal, Westray, Stronsay va Eday and Sanday – to Tingwall via Eglisay, Wyre and Rousay (consult operator) - to North Ronaldsay – to Shapinsay (25 mn) – to Graemsay, Houton and Lyness (Isle of Hoy) (1 weekly).

⤥ by Thomas & Bews Ferries : from Burwick (South Ronaldsay) to John O'Groats (summer only) (contact operator).

Burray – ✉ ☎ 0856 73 Burray

↑ **Ankersted,** KW17 2SS, E : ½ m. on A 961 ℘ 217, ≤ – ⇆ 📺 ⓟ. ⌀
M (by arrangement) 10.00 – **4 rm** ⊑ 16.00/32.00 **st.**

Dounby – ✉ Dounby – ☎ 085 677 Harray

🏠 **Smithfield,** KW17 2HT, ℘ 215, Fax 494 – 📺 ⓟ. ⌀
closed October-March – **M** (bar lunch)/dinner 15.00 **st.** and a la carte – **7 rm** ⊑ 23.00/46.00 **st.**

Finstown – ✉ ☎ 0856 76 Finstown

🏠 Atlantis Lodges, KW17 2EH, ℘ 581, ≤ – 📺 ☎ ⓟ
M (by arrangement) (dinner only) – **2 rm**. **8 suites.**

Kirkwall Scotland G. – pop. 5 947 – ECD : Wednesday – ✉ ☎ 0856 Kirkwall.

See : Kirkwall★★ – St. Magnus Cathedral★★ – Earl's Palace★ *AC* – Tankerness House Museum★ *AC.*

Exc. : Western Mainland★★ – Italian Chapel★ *AC.*

🏌 Grainbank ℘ 872457, W : 1 m.

⤤ Kirkwall Airport : ℘ 872421, S : 3½ m.

🛈 6 Broad St., Kirkwall ℘ 872856.

🏨 **Ayre,** Ayre Rd, KW15 1QX, ℘ 873001, Fax 876289 – 📺 ☎ ⓟ – 🛗 150. ◪ *VISA*
M 17.00 **st.** (dinner) and a la carte 🛇 4.00 – **33 rm** ⊑ 48.50/79.00 **st.**

🏠 **Foveran** ⧖, St. Ola, KW15 1SF, SW : 3 m. on A 964 ℘ 872389, Fax 876430, ≤, « Overlooking Scapa Flow », ☞ – 📺 ☎ ⓟ. ◪ *VISA*
M *(closed Sunday to non-residents)* (dinner only) a la carte 17.00/30.00 **t.** 🛇 4.50 – **8 rm** ⊑ 43.00/70.00 **t.**

🏠 **Albert,** Mounthoolie Lane, KW15 1GZ, pedestrian area off Junction Rd ℘ 876000, Fax 875397 – 📺 ☎. ◪ *AE* *VISA*
closed 25 December and 1 January – **M** (bar lunch)/dinner 15.00 **t.** and a la carte 🛇 3.45 – **19 rm** ⊑ 48.00/75.00 **t.** – SB (October-March) (weekends only) 70.00/96.00 **st.**

🏠 **Queens,** Shore St., KW15 1LG, ℘ 872200 – 📺. ◪ *VISA*. ⌀
M (in bar) 7.25 **t.** – **9 rm** ⊑ 20.00/32.00 **t.**

🏠 West End, Main St., KW15 1BU, ℘ 872368, Fax 876181 – 📺 ☎ ⓟ
16 rm.

⌂ **Polrudden,** Pickaquoy Rd, KW15 1RR, W : ¾ m. *&* 874761, Fax 874761 – ❄ rest 📺 🅟
closed 3 weeks January – **M** (by arrangement) 10.00 **st.** – **7 rm** ⌻ 25.00/40.00 **st.**

⌂ **Brekk-Ness** ⬠, Muddisdale Rd, KW15 1RS, W : 1 m. by Pickaquoy Rd *&* 874317,
Fax 874317 – ❄ rest 📺 🅟
M (by arrangement) 10.00 **t.** – **11 rm** ⌻ 26.00/42.00 **t.**

⌂ **St. Ola,** Harbour St., KW15 1LE, *&* 875090, Fax 875090 – 📺 ☎. 🔳 𝚅𝙸𝚂𝙰. ❄
M 10.00 **t.** – **6 rm** ⌻ 24.00/38.00.

🛢 ATS Junction Rd, Kirkwall *&* 872361/872158

Loch Harray – ✉ Loch Harray – ⊕ 085 677 Harray

🏛 **Merkister** ⬠, KW17 2LF, off A 986 *&* 366, Fax 515, ≤, 🖐, 🖚 – 📺 ☎ 🅟. 🔳 𝙰𝙴 ⓞ 𝚅𝙸𝚂𝙰
April-October – **M** (bar lunch)/dinner 13.50 **st.** and a la carte 🍴 4.00 – **15 rm** ⌻ 30.00/
100.00 **st.** – SB 80.00/94.00 **st.**

St. Margarets Hope – ✉ ⊕ 085 683 St. Margarets Hope

🏛 **Anchorage,** Back Rd, KW17 2SP, *&* 456 – 📺
M (communal dining) 10.00/30.00 **st.** and a la carte – **4 rm** ⌻ 17.00/30.00 **st.**

♈ **Murray Arms,** Back Rd, KW17 2SP, *&* 205 – 🅟. ❄
M (closed Monday) (in bar) 9.50/14.80 **st.** – **5 rm** ⌻ 20.00/40.00 **st.**

✕✕ **Creel** with rm, Front Rd, KW17 2SL, *&* 311, ≤ – ❄ rm 📺 🅟. 🔳 𝚅𝙸𝚂𝙰. ❄
closed Sunday to Thursday October-May and January – **M** (dinner only) a la carte 19.00/
28.00 **t.** 🍴 5.25 – **2 rm** ⌻ 25.00/50.00 **t.**

Stenness – ✉ Stenness – ⊕ 0856 Stromness

🏛 **Standing Stones,** KW16 3JX, on a 965 *&* 850449, Fax 851262, 🖚, 🖚 – ❄ rm 📺 ☎ 🅟.
🔳 𝚅𝙸𝚂𝙰 ❄
M (booking essential) (bar lunch)/dinner 15.00 **st.** and a la carte 🍴 4.30 – **17 rm** ⌻ 35.00/
64.00 **st.** – SB (except April-September) 70.00/90.00 **st.**

Stromness – ✉ ⊕ 0856 Stromness

⌂ **Thira** ⬠, Innertown, KW16 3JP, W : 1½ m. by Back Rd, Outertown rd, then first right
onto unmarked road and left turn after ½ m. *&* 851181, ≤ Hoy Island and Sound, 🖚 –
❄ 📺 🅟
closed December – **M** 8.00 **st.** – **4 rm** ⌻ 22.00/44.00 **st.**

⌂ **Stenigar,** Ness Rd, KW13 3DW, *&* 850438, ≤, 🖚 – 📺 🅟. ❄
April-September – **M** (by arrangement) (communal dining) – **5 rm** ⌻ 25.00/40.00 **s.**

✕ **Hamnovoe,** 35 Graham Pl., KW16 3BY, *&* 850606
May-October – **M** (dinner only) a la carte 11.60/16.10 **s.** 🍴 3.50.

PAISLEY Renfrew. (Strathclyde) 𝟺𝟶𝟷 𝟺𝟶𝟸 G 16 Scotland G. – pop. 84 330 – ECD : Tuesday –
⊕ 041 Glasgow.

See : Museum and Art Gallery (Paisley Shawl Section★).

🖼 Barshaw Municipal, Barshaw Park *&* 889 2908, E : 1½ m. by A 737.

🏢 Town Hall, Abbey Close, *&* 889 0711.

♦Edinburgh 53 – ♦Ayr 35 – ♦Glasgow 7.5 – Greenock 17.

🏨 **Stakis Paisley Watermill,** Lonend, PA1 1SR, *&* 889 3201, Fax 889 5938 – |🛗| ❄ rm 📺
☎ 🅟. 🔳 𝙰𝙴 ⓞ 𝚅𝙸𝚂𝙰 𝙹𝙲𝙱. ❄
M 10.95 **t.** and a la carte – **49 rm** ⌻ 53.50/95.00 **st.** – SB 70.00/100.00 **st.**

PEAT INN Fife. (Fife) 𝟺𝟶𝟷 L 15 – ✉ Cupar ⊕ 033 404 (3 fig.) and 0334 (6 fig.).

♦Edinburgh 45 – Dundee 21 – Perth 28.

✕✕✕ **The Peat Inn** ⬠ with rm, KY15 5LH, *&* 206, Fax 530, 🖚 – ❄ rest 📺 ☎ & 🅟. 🔳 𝙰𝙴 ⓞ
𝚅𝙸𝚂𝙰
M (closed Sunday, Monday. 25 December and 1 January) (booking essential) 18.50/
42.00 **st.** and a la carte 🍴 6.00 – **1 rm** ⌻ 75.00 **st.**, **7 suites** 130.00/140.00 **st.**.

PEEBLES Peebles. (Borders) 𝟺𝟶𝟷 𝟺𝟶𝟸 K 17 Scotland G. – pop. 6 404 – ECD : Wednesday –
⊕ 0721.

Exc. : Traquair House★★ *AC*, SE : 7 m. by B 7062 – Rosslyn Chapel★★ *AC*, N : 16½ m. by A 703,
A 6094, B 7026 and B 7003 – The Tweed Valley★★, SE : 11 m. by A 72.

🖼 Kirkland St. *&* 720197.

🏢 High St. *&* 720138 (summer only).

♦Edinburgh 24 – Hawick 31 – ♦Glasgow 53.

🏨 **Peebles Hydro,** Innerleithen Rd, EH45 8LX, *&* 720602, Fax 722999, ≤, 🗲 s, ≋s, 🔳, 🖚,
park, 🎾, squash – |🛗| 📺 ☎ 🅟 – 🔼 400. 🔳 𝙰𝙴 ⓞ 𝚅𝙸𝚂𝙰. ❄
M 13.50/18.75 **st.** 🍴 5.25 – **135 rm** ⌻ 60.00/112.50 **st.**, 2 suites – SB 108.50/144.50 **st.**

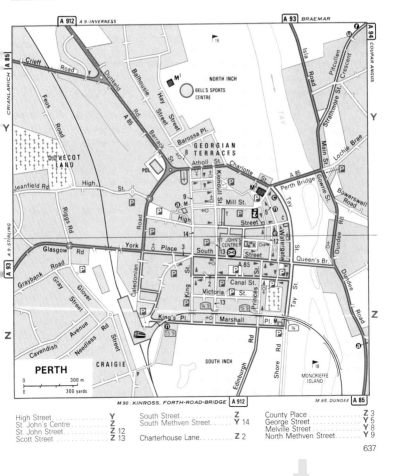

Cringletie House ⌂, EH45 8PL, N : 3 m. on A 703 ℘ 730233, Fax 730244, ≤, « Country house in extensive grounds », ☞, park, ✗ – 🔟 📺 ☎ 🅿. 🔼 *VISA*
closed 2 January-5 March – **M** 14.50/23.50 **st.** ⌂ 5.50 – **13 rm** ☲ 50.00/92.00 **st.** – SB (early March-May and late October-23 December) 107.00/134.00 **st.**

Park, Innerleithen Rd, EH45 8BA, ℘ 720451, Fax 723510, ☞ – 📺 ☎ 🅿. 🔼 🅰🅴 ⓪ *VISA*
M (bar lunch)/dinner 17.00 **t.** ⌂ 5.95 – **24 rm** ☲ 53.20/115.30 **t.** – SB (except Easter, Christmas and New Year) (weekends only) 102.50/135.00 **st.**

PENNAN Aberdeen. (Grampian) 🔢 N 10 – pop. 92 – ⌕ ✪ 034 66 New Aberdour.

◆Edinburgh 181 – ◆Aberdeen 51 – Fraserburgh 12 – ◆Inverness 85.

Pennan Inn, 17-19 Main St., AB43 4JB, ℘ 201, Fax 437 – 📺 ☎. 🔼 🅰🅴 *VISA*. ✗
M *(closed dinner Sunday and Monday)* (dinner by arrangement) (bar lunch)/dinner a la carte 15.50/25.25 **st.** – ☲ 5.00 – **6 rm** 35.00/45.00 **st.**

PENNYGHAEL Argyll (Strathclyde) – see Mull (Isle of).

Pleasant hotels and restaurants
are shown in the Guide by a red sign.

Please send us the names
of anywhere you have enjoyed your stay.

Your **Michelin Guide** will be even better.

🏨 ... 🏠

XXXXX ... ✗

PERTH

0   300 m
0   300 yards

PERTH Perth. (Tayside) **401** J 14 Scotland G. – pop. 41 916 – ECD : Wednesday – ✆ 0738.

See : City★ – Black Watch Regimental Museum★ Y **M1** – Georgian Terraces★ Y – Museum and Art Gallery★ Y **M2**.

Envir. : Scone Palace★★ *AC*, N : 2 m. by A 93 Y – Branklyn Garden★ *AC*, SE : 1 m. by A 85 Z – Kinnoull Hill (⩽★) SE : 1¼ m. by A 85 Z – Huntingtower Castle★ *AC*, NW : 3 m. by A 85 Y – Elcho Castle★ *AC*, SE : 4 m. by A 912 - Z - and Rhynd rd.

Exc. : Abernethy (11C Round Tower★), SE : 8 m. by A 912 - Z - and A 913.

🏌 Craigie Hill, Cherrybank ✆ 24377, by Needless Rd Z – 🏌 King James VI, Moncreiffe Island ✆ 25170 Z – 🏌 Murrayshall, New Scone ✆ 51171, NE : 3 m. by A 94 Y – 🏌 North Inch, c/o Perth & Kinross District Council, 3 High St. ✆ 36481 Y.

🛈 45 High Street ✆ 38353 – Caithness Glass Car Park, A 9 Western City by-pass ✆ 38481 (summer only).

♦Edinburgh 44 – ♦Aberdeen 86 – ♦Dundee 22 – Dunfermline 29 – ♦Glasgow 64 – ♦Inverness 112 – ♦Oban 94.

Plan on preceding page

🏨 **Hunting Tower** 🦢, Crieff Rd, PH1 3JT, W : 3½ m. by A 85 ✆ 83771, Fax 83777, ☞ – 📺 ☎ ❷ – 🔬 180. 🖭 🖭 ⑩ 𝖵𝖨𝖲𝖠 Y
M 12.00/18.95 **t.** and a la carte ⅄ 5.50 – **15 rm** ⊆ 62.50/79.50 **t.**. 7 suites – SB 79.00/90.00 **st.**

🏨 **Parklands,** St. Leonard's Bank, PH2 8EB, ✆ 22451, Fax 22046, ☞ – 📺 ☎ ❷. 🖭 🖭 𝖵𝖨𝖲𝖠
M 15.50/24.00 **st.** and a la carte – **14 rm** ⊆ 85.00/130.00 **st.** – SB (except Christmas and New Year) 120.00/160.00 **st.** Z **n**

🏨 **Stakis City Mills,** West Mill St., PH1 5QP, ✆ 28281, Fax 43423 – 🛌 rm 📺 ☎ ❷ – 🔬 120. 🖭 🖭 ⑩ 𝖵𝖨𝖲𝖠 𝖩𝖢𝖡 Y **a**
M 9.50/13.50 **t.** and a la carte – ⊆ 8.50 – **76 rm** 62.00/73.00 **st.** – SB 70.00/100.00 **st.**

🏨 **Royal George** (Forte), Tay St., PH1 5LD, ✆ 24455, Fax 30345 – 🛌 rm 📺 ☎ ❷ – 🔬 100. 🖭 🖭 ⑩ 𝖵𝖨𝖲𝖠 𝖩𝖢𝖡 Y **c**
M (bar lunch Monday to Saturday)/dinner 15.95 **t.** and a la carte ⅄ 8.95 – ⊆ 8.50 – **42 rm** 70.00/85.00 **t.** – SB 108.00 **st.**

🏩 **Sunbank House,** 50 Dundee Rd, PH2 7BA, ✆ 24882, Fax 24882, ☞ – 🛌 rm 📺 🕭 ❷. 🖭 𝖵𝖨𝖲𝖠 ✂ Z **a**
M (dinner only) 15.95 **t.** ⅄ 5.25 – **10 rm** ⊆ 25.00/56.00 **t.**

🏠 **Lochiel House** without rest., Pitcullen Cres., PH2 7HT, ✆ 33183 – 🛌 📺 ❷. ✂ Y **u**
3 rm ⊆ 30.00/38.00.

🏠 **Pitcullen,** 17 Pitcullen Cres., PH2 7HT, ✆ 26506 – 🛌 rest 📺 ❷. 🖭 🖭 ⑩ 𝖵𝖨𝖲𝖠 ✂ Y **r**
M (by arrangement) 12.00 **st.** – **6 rm** ⊆ 20.00/44.00 **st.**

🏠 **Ellengowan House,** Crieff Rd, Almondbank, PH1 3NG, W : 3½ m. on A 85 ✆ 83372, ☜, ☞ – 🛌 rm 📺 ☎ ❷. ✂ Y
M (communal dining) 15.00 **st.** – **3 rm** ⊆ 25.00/40.00 **st.** – SB 52.00 **st.**

🍴 **Number Thirty Three,** 33 George St., PH1 5LA, ✆ 33771 – 🖭 🖭 𝖵𝖨𝖲𝖠 Y **n**
closed Sunday, Monday and 10 days Christmas-New Year – **M** - Seafood a la carte 9.35/19.45 **t.** ⅄ 6.30.

🍴 **Timothy's,** 24 St. John St., PH1 5SP, ✆ 26641 – 🖭 𝖵𝖨𝖲𝖠 Y **e**
closed Sunday, Monday, 3 weeks July and 1 week Christmas – **M** - Smörrebrod a la carte 6.25/11.20 **t.** ⅄ 5.20.

at New Scone NE : 2½ m. on A 94 – Y – ⊠ ✆ 0738 Perth :

🏨 **Murrayshall Country House** 🦢, PH2 7PH, E : 1½ m. by A 94 ✆ 51171, Fax 52595, ⩽, 🏌, ☞, park, ✂ – 📺 ☎ ❷ – 🔬 30. 🖭 🖭 ⑩ 𝖵𝖨𝖲𝖠 ✂
closed 23 to 28 December – **M** (bar lunch Monday to Saturday)/dinner 20.00 **t.** and a la carte ⅄ 6.75 – **16 rm** ⊆ 62.50/130.00 **t.**, 3 suites – SB (November-April) 125.00/155.00 **st.**

at Glencarse E : 6¼ m. on A 85 – Y – ⊠ Perth – ✆ 073 886 Glencarse :

🏨 **Newton House,** PH2 7LX, ✆ 250, Fax 717, ☞ – 📺 ☎ ❷. 🖭 🖭 ⑩ 𝖵𝖨𝖲𝖠
M 15.50/23.50 **t.** and a la carte ⅄ 6.00 – **10 rm** ⊆ 46.00/75.00 **t.** – SB 92.00/138.00 **st.**

🅐 ATS Inveralmond Ind. Est., Ruthvenfield Rd ✆ 29481

PETERHEAD Aberdeen. (Grampian) **401** O 11 – pop. 16 804 – ECD : Wednesday – ✆ 0779.

🏌, 🏌 Cruden Bay ✆ 812285, S : 8 m. by A 952 and A 975 – 🏌, 🏌 Craigewan Links ✆ 72149, by A 952.

🛈 54 Broad St. ✆ 71904 (summer only).

♦Edinburgh 165 – ♦Aberdeen 35 – Fraserburgh 18.

🏨 **Waterside Inn,** Fraserburgh Rd, AB42 7BN, NW : 2 m. on A 952 ✆ 71121, Telex 739413, Fax 70670, 🏌, ⩳, 🏊 – 🛌 rm 📺 ☎ ❷ – 🔬 50. 🖭 🖭 ⑩ 𝖵𝖨𝖲𝖠
M 18.00/19.95 **st.** and a la carte ⅄ 4.70 – **110 rm** ⊆ 62.50/108.50 **st.** – SB 76.00/90.00 **st.**

PITCAPLE Aberdeen. (Grampian) [401] M 12 – ✆ 0467.
◆Edinburgh 51 – ◆Aberdeen 21.

- **Pittodrie House** 🐦, AB51 9HS, SW : 1 ¾ m. by Chapel of Garioch rd ✆ 681444, Fax 681648, ≤, « Country house atmosphere », 🌳, park, 🎾, squash – [TV] ☎ 🚗 [P] – 🏛 100. [S] [AE] [O] VISA
M 16.00/28.50 **t.** 🍷 7.70 – **27 rm** 🛏 89.00/110.00 **t.** – SB (except Christmas and New Year) (weekends only) 98.00/140.00 **st.**

PITLOCHRY Perth. (Tayside) [401] I 13 **Scotland G.** – pop. 2 194 – ECD : Thursday – ✆ 0796.
See : Town★.
Exc. : Blair Castle★★ *AC*, NW : 7 m. by A 9 – Queen's View★★, W : 7 m. by B 8019 – Falls of Bruar★, NW : 11 m. by A 9.
⛳18 Golf Course Rd ✆ 472792.
[i] 22 Atholl Rd ✆ 472215/472751.
◆Edinburgh 71 – ◆Inverness 85 – Perth 27.

- **Pine Trees** 🐦, Strathview Terr., PH16 5QR, ✆ 472121, Fax 472460, ≤, 🌳, park – [TV] ☎ [P]. [S] VISA. 🐕
M 12.00/21.00 **t.** 🍷 6.00 – **18 rm** 🛏 45.00/86.00 **t.**
- **Green Park** 🐦, Clunie Bridge Rd, PH16 5JY, ✆ 473248, Fax 473520, ≤, 🌳 – 🚭 rest [TV] ☎ [P]. [S] VISA. 🐕
April-October – **M** (bar lunch)/dinner 17.50 **t.** and a la carte 🍷 4.50 – **37 rm** 🛏 35.00/70.00 **t.** – SB (April and May only) 84.00 **st.**
- **Westlands,** 160 Atholl Rd, PH16 5AR, ✆ 472266, Fax 473994, 🌳 – [TV] ☎ [P]. [S] VISA
M (bar lunch)/dinner 18.50 **st.** 🍷 3.95 – **15 rm** 🛏 33.00/74.50 **st.** – SB (November-April except Christmas) 74.00/104.00 **st.**
- **Knockendarroch,** 2 Higher Oakfield, PH16 5HT, ✆ 473473, Fax 474068, ≤, 🌳 – 🚭 [TV] [P]. [S] [AE] [O] VISA
May-November – **M** (by arrangement) (dinner only) 14.00 **st.** 🍷 4.00 – **12 rm** 🛏 35.00/70.00 **st.** – SB 84.00/98.00 **st.**
- **Port-an-Eilean** 🐦, Strathtummel, PH16 5RU, NW : 10 ½ m. by A 924 on B 8019 ✆ 0882 (Tummel Bridge) 634233, ≤ Loch Tummel and mountains, « Lochside Victorian sporting lodge », 🎣, 🌳, park – [P]
May-September – **M** (dinner only) 15.00 **t.** 🍷 4.50 – **8 rm** 🛏 35.00/60.00 **t.**
- **Castlebeigh** 🐦, 10 Knockard Rd, PH16 5HJ, ✆ 472925, Fax 474068, ≤, 🌳 – 🚭 rest [TV] [P]. [S] VISA
M (dinner only) 18.00 **t.** 🍷 3.80 – **21 rm** 🛏 39.00/84.00 **t.** – SB 60.00/78.00 **st.**
- **Birchwood,** 2 East Moulin Rd, PH16 5DW, ✆ 472477, Fax 473951, 🌳 – 🚭 rest [TV] ☎ [P]. [S] VISA
March-October – **M** 17.00 **t.** (dinner) and a la carte 8.00/21.75 **t.** – **16 rm** 🛏 35.00/72.00 **t.** – SB 80.00/100.00 **st.**
- **Acarsaid,** 8 Atholl Rd, PH16 5BX, ✆ 472389 – 🚭 rest [TV] ☎ [P]. [S] VISA. 🐕
closed 2 January-11 March – **M** (light lunch)/dinner 16.50 **st.** 🍷 4.00 – **18 rm** 🛏 25.00/72.00 **st.** – SB (March and November only) 70.00/96.00 **st.**
- **Claymore,** 162 Atholl Rd, PH16 5AR, ✆ 472888, Fax 474037, 🌳 – 🚭 rest [TV] ☎ [P]. [S] VISA
closed January and February – **M** (bar lunch)/dinner 16.95 **t.** and a la carte – **11 rm** 🛏 30.00/60.00 **t.** – SB (November-April) 54.00 **st.**
- **Balrobin,** Higher Oakfield, PH16 5HT, ✆ 472901, Fax 474200, ≤, 🌳 – 🚭 rest [TV] [P]. [S] VISA
March-October – **M** (residents only) (dinner only) 16.00 **t.** – **15 rm** 🛏 20.00/74.00 **t.** – SB 63.00/84.00 **st.**
- **Dundarave,** Strathview Terr., PH16 5AT, ✆ 473109, ≤, 🌳 – [TV] [P]
closed November – **M** 13.95 **st.** – **7 rm** 🛏 28.00/56.00 **st.** – SB (October-March) (weekdays only) 64.00 **st.**
- **Torrdarach,** Golf Course Rd, PH16 5AU, ✆ 472136, 🌳 – 🚭 rest [TV] [P]. 🐕
Easter-mid October – **M** 15.00 **st.** – **7 rm** 🛏 23.00/56.00 **st.**
- 🍴🍴 **East Haugh House** with rm, East Haugh, PH16 5JS, SE : 2 m. by A 924 ✆ 473121, Fax 472473, 🌳 – [TV] ☎ [P]. [S] VISA. 🐕
M (bar lunch)/dinner 21.95 **t.** and a la carte 🍷 5.95 – **8 rm** 🛏 18.00/95.00 **t.** – SB (except Bank Holidays) 69.00/123.90 **st.**

at Killiecrankie NW : 4 m. by A 924 and B 8019 on B 8079 – ✉ ✆ 0796 Pitlochry :

- **Killiecrankie** 🐦, PH16 5LG, ✆ 473220, Fax 472451, ≤, 🌳 – 🚭 rest [TV] ☎ [P]. [S] VISA
closed January and February – **M** (bar lunch)/dinner 25.00 **t.** 🍷 6.00 – **11 rm** 🛏 48.00/92.00 **t.** – SB (March-early May and November-December) 96.00/116.00 **st.**

GREEN TOURIST GUIDES

Picturesque scenery, buildings
Attractive routes
Touring programmes
Plans of towns and buildings.

PLOCKTON Ross and Cromarty. (Highland) **401** D 11 Scotland G. – pop. 425 – 🕿 059 984.

See : Village★.

◆Edinburgh 210 – ◆Inverness 88.

🏠 **Haven,** Innes St., IV52 8TW, 🖉 223, ≼, 🚗 – 📺 🕿 🄿. 🔼 *VISA*
closed 18 December-1 February – **M** (lunch booking essential)/dinner 25.00 **t.** ♦ 3.50 –
13 rm 🖙 34.00/68.00 **t.**

POLMONT Stirling. (Central) **401 402** I 16 – see Falkirk.

POOLEWE Ross and Cromarty. (Highland) **401** D 10 – 🕿 0445 86.

◆Edinburgh 234 – ◆Inverness 78 – Kyle of Lochalsh 74.

🏠 **Pool House,** IV22 2LE, 🖉 272, Fax 403, ≼ Loch Ewe – 💱 rest 📺 🄿. 🔼 *VISA*. 🛇
M (bar lunch)/dinner 19.50 **t.** and a la carte ♦ 4.75 – **13 rm** 🖙 32.50/65.00 **t.** – SB (October-
April) 76.00/88.00 **st.**

PORT APPIN Argyll. (Strathclyde) **401** D 14 – ECD : Thursday – ✉ 🕿 063 173 Appin.

◆Edinburgh 136 – Ballachulish 20 – ◆Oban 24.

🏨 🕸 **Airds** (Allen) 🍴, PA38 4DF, 🖉 236, Fax 535, ≼ Loch Linnhe and hills of Kingairloch,
« Former ferry inn », ≼ – 💱 rest 📺 🕿 🄿. 🔼 🈺 *VISA*. 🛇
closed 7 January-7 March – **M** (light lunch)/dinner 35.00 **t.** ♦ 6.00 – **12 rm** 🖙 90.00/
190.00 **t.**
Spec. Open ravioli of wild local mushrooms with asparagus and a truffle sauce, Roast leg of marinated duckling, prune
and apple sauce and potato wafers, Millefeuille of chocolate and raspberry mousses with an orange sabayon.

En haute saison, et surtout dans les stations, il est prudent de retenir à l'avance.

PORT OF MENTEITH Perth. (Central) **401** H 15 – 🕿 087 75 (3 fig.) and 0877 (6 fig.).

◆Edinburgh 53 – ◆Glasgow 30 – Stirling 17.

🏨 **Lake** 🍴, FK8 3RA, 🖉 258, Fax 671, ≼, « Lakeside setting » – 💱 rest 📺 🕿 🄿. 🔼 *VISA*
M (bar lunch)/dinner 25.00 **t.** and a la carte ♦ 6.50 – **12 rm** 🖙 57.00/94.00 **t.** – SB (except
Bank Holidays) 74.00/156.00 **st.**

PORTPATRICK Wigtown. (Dumfries and Galloway) **401 402** E 19 – pop. 595 – ECD : Thursday
– ✉ Stranraer – 🕿 0776.

🏌, 🏌 Portpatrick Dunskey, Golf Course Rd 🖉 81273.

◆Edinburgh 141 – ◆Ayr 60 – ◆Dumfries 80 – Stranraer 9.

🏨 🕸 **Knockinaam Lodge** 🍴, DG9 9AD, SE : 5 m. by A 77 off B 7042 🖉 810471,
Fax 810435, « Country house in picturesque coastal setting », 🐟, 🚗, park – 💱 rest 📺
🕿 🄿. 🔼 🈺 🅾 *VISA*
closed 3 January-15 March – **M** (booking essential) 22.50/30.00 **t.** ♦ 5.85 – **10 rm** 🖙 68.00/
136.00 **t.**
Spec. Assiette de homard écossais aux épices parfumées (May - Sept.), Pièce de bœuf poêlée à la moelle et au vin de
Bordeaux, Croustade fine aux pommes et Drambuie son romarin grillé.

🏨 **Fernhill,** Heugh Rd, DG9 8TD, 🖉 810220, Fax 810596, ≼, 🚗 – 📺 🕿 🍴 🄿. 🔼 🈺 🅾 *VISA*
closed 25 and 26 December – **M** 7.50/16.50 **st.** and a la carte ♦ 3.95 – **21 rm** 🖙 50.00/
90.00 **st.**

🏠 **Crown,** DG9 8SX, 🖉 810261, Fax 810551, ≼ Portpatrick Harbour – 📺 🕿. 🔼 *VISA*
M a la carte 15.50/21.50 ♦ 4.80 – **12 rm** 🖙 35.00/66.00 **t.** – SB (October-April) (weekends
only) 55.00 **st.**

🏠 **Broomknowe,** School Brae, DG9 8LG, 🖉 810365, ≼, 🚗 – 💱 📺 🄿
April-September – **M** (by arrangement) 9.00 **st.** – **3 rm** 🖙 25.00/36.00 **st.**

🏠 **Blinkbonnie,** School Brae, DG9 8LG, 🖉 810282, ≼, 🚗 – 💱 📺 🄿. 🛇
M (by arrangement) 9.00 **st.** – **6 rm** 🖙 17.00/34.00 **st.**

PORTREE Inverness. (Highland) **401** B 11 – see Skye (Isle of).

PRESTWICK Ayr. (Strathclyde) **401 402** G 17 – pop. 13 355 – ECD : Wednesday – 🕿 0292.

✈ Prestwick Airport 🖉 79822 – BY – **Terminal** : Buchanan Bus Station.

✈ see also Glasgow.

🄱 Boydfield Gdns 🖉 79946 (summer only) BY.

◆Edinburgh 78 – ◆Ayr 2 – ◆Glasgow 32.

Plan of Built up Area : see Ayr

🏨 **Carlton Toby,** 187 Ayr Rd, KA9 1TP, 🖉 76811, Fax 74845 – 💱 rm 📺 🕿 🄿. 🔼 🈺 🅾 *VISA*
🛇 BY **v**
M (grill rest.) 16.00 ♦ 4.45 – **37 rm** 🖙 49.50/65.00 **st.**

🏠 **Kincraig** without rest., 39 Ayr Rd, KA9 1SY, 🖉 79480 – 📺 🄿. 🛇 BY **c**
6 rm 🖙 15.00/36.00 **st.**

640

QUOTHQUAN Lanark. (Strathclyde) **401** J 27 Scotland G. – ⊠ ۞ 0899 Biggar.

Envir. : Biggar★ (Gladstone Court Museum★ *AC* – Greenhill Covenanting Museum★ *AC*) SE : 4½ m. by B 7016.

◆Edinburgh 32 – ◆Glasgow 36.

🏨 **Shieldhill** ⊗, ML12 6NA, NE : ¾ m. ℰ 20035, Fax 21092, ≤, « Victorian country house, 12C origins », ☞ – ⍉ 🖾 ☎ ℗ – 🕍 25. 🖾 🖭 ⓪ 🗺. ✂
M (dinner only and Sunday lunch)/dinner 29.50 t. ₪ 4.75 – **11 rm** ⊊ 88.00/165.00 t.

RENFREW Renfrew. (Strathclyde) **401** G 16 – pop. 21 456 – ECD : Wednesday – ۞ 041 Glasgow.

◆Edinburgh 53 – ◆Glasgow 7.

🏨 **Glynhill,** 169 Paisley Rd, PA4 8XB, ℰ 886 5555, Telex 779536, Fax 885 2838, *₤₅*, ≘s, 🖾 – ⍉ rm 🖾 ☎ ℗ – 🕍 450. 🖾 🖭 ⓪ 🗺
M (bar lunch Saturday) 11.95/29.00 **st.** and a la carte ₪ 4.75 – **125 rm** ⊊ 69.00/164.00 **st.** – SB (except Christmas and New Year) (weekends only) 98.00/212.00 **st.**

ROCKCLIFFE Kirkcudbright. (Dumfries and Galloway) **401 402** I 19 – ⊠ Dalbeattie – ۞ 0556.

◆Edinburgh 100 – ◆Dumfries 20 – Stranraer 69.

🏠 **Millbrae,** DG5 4QG, ℰ 217 – ⍉ rest 🖾 ℗
mid February-late October and 1 week New Year – **M** (by arrangement) (communal dining) 11.00 – **5 rm** ⊊ 24.00/34.00.

🏠 **Torbay Farmhouse** ⊗, DG5 4QE, E : ¼ m. ℰ 630403, ≤, ☞ – ⍉ ℗
M (by arrangement) (communal dining) 8.00 **st.** – **3 rm** ⊊ 23.00/36.00 **st.**

ROGART Sutherland. (Highland) **401** H 9 – ۞ 0408.

◆Edinburgh 229 – ◆Inverness 73 – ◆Wick 63.

🏠 **Rovie Farm** ⊗, IV28 3TZ, W : ¾ m. by A 839 ℰ 641209, ≤, « Working farm », ☞, park – ⍉ rest ℗. ✂
Easter-November – **M** 14.00 **st.** – **6 rm** ⊊ 16.00/32.00 **st.**

ROTHES Moray. (Grampian) **401** K 11 Scotland G. – pop. 1 414 – ECD : Wednesday – ۞ 034 03.

Exc. : Glenfiddich Distillery★, SE : 7 m. by A 941.

🏌 Dufftown ℰ 0340 (Dufftown) 20325, SW : 7 m. by A 941.

◆Edinburgh 192 – ◆Aberdeen 62 – Fraserburgh 58 – ◆Inverness 49.

🏨 **Rothes Glen** ⊗, AB38 7AH, N : 3 m. on A 941 ℰ 254, Fax 566, ≤, « Country house atmosphere », ☞, park – ⍉ ℗ – 🕍. 🖾 🖭 ⓪ 🗺
closed December-February – **M** 12.50/25.00 **st.** and a la carte ₪ 4.25 – **16 rm** ⊊ 75.00/ 120.00 **st.** – SB (October-April) (weekends only) 132.00 **st.**

ROTHESAY Bute. (Strathclyde) **401 402** E 16 – see Bute (Isle of).

ST. ANDREWS Fife. (Fife) **401** L 14 Scotland G. – pop. 10 525 – ECD : Thursday – ۞ 0334.

See : City★★ - Cathedral★ (★★★) *AC* – West Port★.

Exc. : The East Neuk★★, SE : 9 m. by A 917 and B 9131 – Crail★★ (Old Centre★★, Upper Crail★) SE : 9 m. by A 917 – Kellie Castle★ *AC*, S : 9 m. by B 9131 and B 9171 – Ceres★, SW : 9 m. by B 939 - E : Inland Fife★.

🏌 (X5), 🏌 Eden, Jubilee, New, Old, Strathyrum and Balgove Courses ℰ 75757, N : 1 m. by A 91 – 🏌 St. Michael's, Leuchars ℰ 839365, NW : 6 m. by A 91 and A 919.

🛈 78 South St. ℰ 72021.

◆Edinburgh 61 – ◆Dundee 14 – Stirling 51.

🏨🏨 **St. Andrews Old Course,** Old Station Rd, KY16 9SP, ℰ 74371, Telex 76280, Fax 77668, ≤ golf courses and sea, *₤₅*, ≘s, 🖾 – 🛗 🍽 rest 🖾 ☎ ₺ ℗ – 🕍 250. 🖾 🖭 ⓪ 🗺
M 35.00 **t.** (dinner) and a la carte – **108 rm** ⊊ 150.00/235.00 **t.**, 17 suites – SB 198.00/ 352.00 **st.**

🏨 **Rusacks** (Forte), 16 Pilmour Links, KY16 9JQ, ℰ 74321, Fax 77896, ≤, ≘s – 🛗 ⍉ rm 🖾 ☎ ℗ – 🕍 100. 🖾 🖭 🗺 🅹🅲🅱
M 12.50/27.50 **t.** and a la carte ₪ 6.75 – ⊊ 12.50 – **48 rm** 95.00/155.00 **st.**, 2 suites – SB (except Christmas and New Year) 158.00/173.00 **st.**

🏨 **Rufflets,** Strathkinness Low Rd, KY16 9TX, W : 1½ m. on B 939 ℰ 72594, Fax 78703, ≤, « Country house, gardens » – ⍉ rm 🖾 ☎ ℗. 🖾 🖭 ⓪ 🗺. ✂
M 14.50/24.00 and a la carte ₪ 5.00 – **25 rm** ⊊ 65.00/150.00 **st.** – SB 110.00/198.00 **st.**

🏨 **St. Andrews Golf,** 40 The Scores, KY16 9AS, ℰ 72611, Fax 72188, ≤, ≘s – 🛗 ⍉ rest 🖾 ☎ ℗ – 🕍 200. 🖾 🖭 ⓪ 🗺 🅹🅲🅱
M 13.00/23.50 **t.** and a la carte ₪ 4.75 – **23 rm** ⊊ 70.00/139.00 **t.** – SB (except Bank Holidays) 98.00/144.00 **st.**

🏨 **The Scores** (Best Western), 76 The Scores, KY16 9BB, ℰ 72451, Fax 73947, ≤, ☞ – 🛗 ⍉ rest 🖾 ☎ ℗ – 🕍 120. 🖾 🖭 ⓪ 🗺 🅹🅲🅱. ✂
closed 3 days at Christmas – **M** (bar lunch)/dinner 21.50 **st.** ₪ 5.00 – **30 rm** ⊊ 72.00/ 134.00 **st.** – SB 79.00/136.00 **st.**

🏠 **Russell,** 26 The Scores, KY16 9AS, ℰ 73447, Fax 78279, ≤ – 🖾 ☎. 🖾 🗺. ✂
closed 24 December-9 January – **M** (bar lunch)/dinner a la carte 14.50/17.50 **t.** ₪ 4.00 – **9 rm** ⊊ 27.50/73.00 **t.** – SB (November-April) 75.00/79.00 **st.**

ST. BOSWELLS Roxburgh. (Borders) 401 402 L 17 Scotland G. – pop. 1 086 – ✆ 0835.

Envir. : Dryburgh Abbey★★ *AC* (setting★★★) NW : 4 m. by B 6404 and B 6356.

Exc. : Bowhill★★ *AC*, SW : 11½ m. by A 699 and A 708.

🛪 St. Boswells ✆ 22359, off A 68 at St. Boswells Green.

◆Edinburgh 39 – ◆Glasgow 79 – Hawick 17 – ◆Newcastle upon Tyne 66.

    🏨 **Dryburgh Abbey** ≫, TD6 0RQ, N : 3½ m. by B 6404 on B 6356 ✆ 22261, Fax 23945, ≤, ≫, ☞ – 👤 ⅓⇔ rest 📺 ☎ 🅿 – 🔬 150. 🌣 [VISA] [JCB]
        M 12.50/21.50 **st.** and lunch a la carte 🛆 6.50 – **26 rm** 🖙 45.00/90.00 **st.**, 2 suites – SB 90.00/125.00 **st.**

ST. CATHERINES Argyll. (Strathclyde) 401 E 15 Scotland G. – ✉ Cairndow – ✆ 0499 Inveraray.

Envir. : Loch Fyne★★ – Exc. : Inveraray★★ : Castle★★ (interior★★★) *AC*, NW : 12 m. by A 815 and A 83 – Auchindrain★, NW : 18 m. by A 815 and A 83.

◆Edinburgh 99 – ◆Glasgow 53 – ◆Oban 53.

    ↷ **Thistle House** without rest., PA25 8AZ, on A 815 ✆ 2209, ≤, ☞ – ⅓⇔ 🅿
        April-October – **5 rm** 🖙 40.00 **st.**

ST. FILLANS Perth. (Tayside) 401 H 14 – ECD : Wednesday – ✆ 0764.

◆Edinburgh 67 – ◆Glasgow 57 – ◆Oban 64 – Perth 30.

    🏨 **Four Seasons**, PH6 2NF, ✆ 685333, Fax 685333, ≤ Loch Earn and mountains – ⅓⇔ rest 📺 ☎ 🅿. 🌣 🌣 🗚 🐨 [VISA]
        March-November – **M** 12.95/21.50 **t.** and a la carte 🛆 4.75 – **12 rm** 🖙 50.00/80.00 **t.**

    🏠 **Achray House**, PH6 2NF, ✆ 685231, Fax 685320, ≤ Loch Earn and mountains, ☞ – ⅓⇔ rest 📺 ☎ 🅿. 🌣 [VISA] 🌣
        March-October – **M** (bar lunch Monday to Saturday)/dinner a la carte 7.20/21.30 **st.** 🛆 3.50 – **10 rm** 🖙 30.00/58.00 **st.**

ST. MARGARETS HOPE Orkney. (Orkney Islands) 401 K 6 – see Orkney Islands.

SANDYHILLS Kirkcudbright. (Dumfries and Galloway) 401 402 I 19 – ✉ Dalbeattie – ✆ 038 778 Southwick.

◆Edinburgh 99 – ◆Ayr 62 – ◆Dumfries 19 – Stranraer 68.

    🏠 **Cairngill House** ≫, DG5 4NZ, ✆ 681, ≤, ☞, 🌣 – 📺 🅿. 🌣 [VISA]
        M a la carte 7.15/13.00 **t.** 🛆 3.50 – **6 rm** 🖙 30.00/54.00 **st.** – SB (winter only) 72.00/96.00 **st.**

SANQUHAR Dumfries (Dumfries and Galloway) 401 402 I 17 – ✆ 0659.

🛪 Blackaddie Rd ✆ 50577, SW : ½ m.

🛈 Tolbooth High St. ✆ 50185.

◆Edinburgh 58 – Dumfries 27 – ◆Glasgow 24.

    🏠 **Blackaddie House**, Blackaddie Rd, DG4 6JJ, N : ¼ m. by A 76 ✆ 50270, « Riverside setting », ≫, ☞ – 📺 🅿. 🌣 [VISA]. 🌣
        M a la carte 11.05/19.15 **t.** 🛆 4.50 – **10 rm** 🖙 32.00/54.00 **t.** – SB (except September-November) 75.00/83.00 **st.**

SCALASAIG Argyll. (Strathclyde) 401 B 15 – see Colonsay (Isle of).

SCALLOWAY Shetland. (Shetland Islands) 401 Q 3 – see Shetland Islands (Mainland).

SCARISTA Inverness. (Outer Hebrides) (Western Isles) 401 Y 10 – see Lewis and Harris (Isle of).

SCOURIE Sutherland. (Highland) 401 E 8 Scotland G. – ✉ Lairg – ✆ 0971.

Exc. : Cape Wrath★★★ (≤★★) *AC*, N : 31 m. (including ferry crossing) by A 894 and A 838 – Loch Assynt★★, S : 17 m. by A 894.

◆Edinburgh 263 – ◆Inverness 107.

    🏨 **Eddrachilles** ≫, Badcall Bay, IV27 4TH, S : 2½ m. on A 894 ✆ 502080, Fax 502477, ≤ Badcall Bay and islands, ☞ – 📺 ☎ 🅿. 🌣 [VISA] 🌣
        March-October – **M** (bar lunch)/dinner 10.50 **t.** and a la carte 🛆 3.55 – **11 rm** 🖙 46.00/72.00 **t.**

    🏠 **Scourie** ≫, IV27 4SX, ✆ 502396, Fax 502423, ≤, 🌣 – ☎ 🅿. 🌣 🗚 🐨 [VISA]
        April-mid October – **M** (bar lunch)/dinner 13.50 **t.** 🛆 4.50 – **20 rm** 🖙 30.00/70.00 **t.**

SEIL (Isle of) Argyll. (Strathclyde) 401 D 15 – ✉ Oban – ✆ 085 23 Balvicar.

    Clachan Seil – ✉ Oban – ✆ 085 23 Balvicar

    🏠 **Willowburn** ≫, PA34 4TJ, ✆ 276, ≤, ☞ – 📺 🅿. 🌣 [VISA]
        April-December – **M** (bar lunch)/dinner 17.00 **t.** 🛆 4.50 – **6 rm** 🖙 (dinner included) 40.00/90.00 **t.**

    Easdale – ✉ Oban – ✆ 085 23 Balvicar

    🏠 **Inshaig Park** ≫, PA34 4RF, ✆ 256, ≤ Inner Hebridean Islands, ☞ – ⅓⇔ 📺 🅿
        Easter-October – **M** (bar lunch)/dinner 14.00 **t.** and a la carte 🛆 2.50 – **6 rm** 🖙 30.00/54.00 **st.**

SELKIRK Selkirk. (Borders) **401 402** L 17 Scotland G. – pop. 5 469 – ✿ 0750.

Envir. : Bowhill★★ *AC*, W : 3½ m. by A 708 – Abbotsbury★★ *AC*, NE : 5½ m. by A 7 and B 6360.

Exc. : Melrose Abbey★★ (decorative sculptures★★★) *AC*, NE : 8½ m. by A 7 and A 6091 – Eildon Hills (✳★★★) NE : 7½ m. by A 699 and B 6359 – The Tweed Valley★★, NW : 7½ m. by A 707 and A 72.

🏌₉ The Hill ℰ 20621, S : 1 m.

🛈 Halliwell's House ℰ 20054 (summer only).

◆Edinburgh 40 – ◆Glasgow 73 – Hawick 11 – ◆Newcastle upon Tyne 73.

🏠 **Philipburn House** 🐾, TD7 5LS, W : at junction A 707 with A 708 ℰ 20747, Fax 21690, 🛋 heated, ⇙ – ⇥ rest 🔟 ☎ 🅿. 🖭 🆎 ⓞ 𝗩𝗜𝗦𝗔
M 14.85/25.00 **t.** and a la carte ⦙ 5.95 – **16 rm** ⊒ 55.00/120.00 **t.** – SB (September-June) 139.00/172.00 **st.**

SHETLAND ISLANDS Shetland. (Shetland Islands) **401** PQ 3 Scotland G. – pop. 27 271.

See : Islands★ – Up Helly Aa★★ (last Tuesday in January) – Jarlshof★★ *AC*.

✈ Tingwall Airport ℰ 0595 (Lerwick) 84306, NW : 6½ m. of Lerwick by A 971.

✈ Unst Airport : at Baltasound ℰ 095 781 (Baltasound) 404, Fax 210.

🛳 by P & O Ferries : Orkney and Shetland Services : from Lerwick to Aberdeen via Stromness (Orkney Islands) (1 weekly) – by Shetland Islands Council : from Lerwick (Mainland) to Bressay frequent services daily (5 mn) – from Laxo (Mainland) to Symbister (Isle of Whalsay) frequent services daily (30 mn) – from Toft (Mainland) to Ulsta (Isle of Yell) frequent services daily (20 mn) – from Gutcher (Isle of Yell) to Belmont (Isle of Unst) via Oddsta (Isle of Fetlar) (booking essential) – from Fair Isle to Sumburgh (Gruntness) to Fair Isle (1-2 weekly).

MAINLAND

Brae – ✉ ✿ 080 622 (3 fig.) and 0806 (6 fig.) Brae.

🏠 **Busta House** 🐾, ZE2 9QN, SW : 1½ m. ℰ 506, Fax 588, ≼, « Part 16C and 18C country house », 🐾 – ⇥ rest 🔟 ☎ 🅿. 🖭 🆎 ⓞ 𝗩𝗜𝗦𝗔
closed 21 December-3 January – **M** (bar lunch)/dinner 21.50 **t.** – **20 rm** ⊒ 60.00/105.00 **t.**

Lerwick Scotland G. – pop. 7 223 – ECD : Wednesday – ✉ ✿ 0595 Lerwick.

Envir. : Gulber Wick (≼★) S : 2 m. by A 970.

Exc. : Mousa Broch★★★ *AC* (Mousa Island) S : 14 m. – Lerwick to Jarlshof★, S : 22 m. by A 970 – Shetland Croft House Museum★ *AC*, SW : 6 m. by A 970 and A 9073.

🏌₁₈ Lerwick ℰ 369, N : 3½ m.

🛈 Market Cross, Lerwick ℰ 3434.

🏠 **Shetland,** Holmsgarth Rd, ZE1 0PW, ℰ 5515, Fax 5828, ≼ – |☀| ⇥ rm 🔟 ☎ ♿ 🅿 – 🖾 220. 🖭 🆎 ⓞ 𝗩𝗜𝗦𝗔
M (bar lunch)/dinner 17.50 **st.** and a la carte ⦙ 3.75 – **64 rm** ⊒ 67.15/77.65 **st.**, 1 suite.

🏠 **Kveldsro House,** Greenfield Pl., ZE1 0AQ, ℰ 2195, Fax 6595 – ⇥ rest 🔟 ☎ 🅿 – 🖾 35. 🖭 🆎 ⓞ 𝗩𝗜𝗦𝗔 🦺
M (bar lunch)/dinner 26.00 **t.** ⦙ 4.90 – **17 rm** ⊒ 82.50/97.50 **t.** – SB (weekends only) 105.00/111.00 **st.**

⌂ **Whinrig** without rest., 12 Burgh Rd, ZE1 0LB, ℰ 3554, ⇙ – ⇥ 🔟 🅿. 🦺
closed Christmas and New Year – **3 rm** ⊒ 14.00/32.00 **st.**

⌂ **Breiview,** 43 Kanterstead Rd, SW : 1 m. by A 970 ℰ 5956 – 🔟 🅿. 🦺
M (communal dining) 8.00 **st.** – **6 rm** ⊒ 23.00/38.00 **st.**

◍ ATS 3 Gremista Ind. Est., Lerwick ℰ 3857

Scalloway – ✉ ✿ 0595 88 Scalloway

⌂ **Broch House** without rest., Upper Scalloway, ZE1 0UP, NE : ½ m. by A 70 taking unmarked road on left after school ℰ 767, Fax 731 – 🔟 🅿. 🦺
3 rm ⊒ 18.00/32.00 **s.**

Walls – ✉ – ✿ 059 571 Walls

⊠ **Burrastow House** 🐾 with rm, ZE2 9PB, SW : 2½ m. ℰ 307, Fax 213, ≼, « 18C house overlooking Vaila Sound », 🦤 – ⇥ 🅿. 🦺
closed mid October-mid November and 24 December-21 March – **M** *(closed Sunday dinner and Monday to non-residents)* (lunch by arrangement)/dinner 25.00 – **2 rm** ⊒ (dinner included) 56.00/112.00.

SHIELDAIG Ross and Cromarty. (Highland) **401** D 11 Scotland G. – ✉ Strachharron – ✿ 052 05.

Exc. : Wester Ross★★★.

◆Edinburgh 226 – ◆Inverness 70 – Kyle of Lochalsh 36.

🏠 **Tigh-An Eilean,** IV54 8XN, ℰ 251, Fax 321, ≼ Shieldaig Islands and Loch, « Attractively furnished inn » – 🅿. 🖭 𝗩𝗜𝗦𝗔
April-October – **M** (dinner only) 18.75 **t.** – **11 rm** ⊒ 37.50/83.50 **t.**

SKELMORLIE Ayr. (Strathclyde) ⁜⁜⁜ F 16 – pop. 1 606 – ECD : Wednesday – ✿ 0475 Wemyss Bay.

🛆 Skelmorlie ℰ 520152.

◆Edinburgh 78 – ◆Ayr 39 – ◆Glasgow 32.

🏠 **Redcliffe,** 25 Shore Rd, PA15 5EH, on A 78 ℰ 521036, Fax 521894, ≼, ☞ – 📺 ☎ 🅿. ⊠
    AE ① VISA
    M 20.00 **st.** and a la carte ⅜ 4.50 – **9 rm** ⊃ 50.00/65.00 **st.** – SB 85.00/100.00 **st.**

SKYE (Isle of) Inverness. (Highland) ⁜⁜⁜ B 11 and 12 Scotland G. – pop. 8 139.

See : Island★★ - The Cuillins★★★ – Skye of Island's Life Museum★ AC.

Envir. : N : Trotternish Peninsula★★ – W : Duirinish Peninsula★ – Portree★.

⚓ by Caledonian MacBrayne : from Kyleakin to Kyle of Lochalsh : frequent services daily – from Armadale to Mallaig (3-6 daily except Sunday) – and via Isle of Eigg, Muck (Isle of), Rhum (Isle of) and Isle of Canna – from Uig to Tarbert (Isle of Harris) 1-3 daily (1 h 45 mn) – from Uig to Lochmaddy (North Uist) via Tarbert 1-2 daily – from Sconser to Isle of Raasay ; Monday/ Saturday 5 daily – from Armadale to Tobermory (Isle of Mull), Coll (Isle of) and Tiree (Isle of).

Ardvasar – ⊠ ✿ 047 14 Ardvasar.

🏠 **Ardvasar,** IV45 8RS, ℰ 223, ☞ – 📺 🅿. ⊠ AE VISA ✻
    closed January and February – **M** a la carte 8.60/27.00 **t.** ⅜ 8.00 – **10 rm** ⊃ 35.00/65.00 **t.**

Culnaknock – ⊠ Portree – ✿ 047 062 Staffin.

🛆 Glenview Inn, IV51 9JH, ℰ 248, ≼ – 📺 🅿
    5 rm.

Dunvegan – ⊠ ✿ 047 022 Dunvegan.

🏠 **Harlosh House** ﹩, IV55 8ZG, SE : 6 m. by A 863 ℰ 367, Fax 367, ≼ Loch Bracadale and Islands – ↤↦ rest 🅿. ⊠ VISA ✻
    Easter-mid October – **M** (dinner only) a la carte 18.55/24.50 **st.** ⅜ 5.00 – **6 rm** ⊃ 43.50/ 86.00 **st.**

🏠 **Dunorin House** ﹩, Herebost, IV55 8GZ, SE : 2½ m. by A 863 on Roag rd ℰ 488, ≼ – ↤↦ 📺 🅿. ⊠ VISA ✻
    April-mid October – **M** a la carte 21.00/25.00 **t.** ⅜ 4.50 – **10 rm** ⊃ 32.00/64.00 **t.**

✕ **Three Chimneys,** Colbost, IV55 8ZT, NW : 5¾ m. by A 863 on B 884 ℰ 047 081 (Glendale) 258 – ↤↦ 🅿. ⊠ VISA
    closed November-March and Sunday except Easter and Whitsun – **M** (booking essential) (restricted lunch)/dinner a la carte 26.00/35.00 **t.**

Flodigarry – ⊠ Staffin – ✿ 047 052 Duntulm.

🏠 **Flodigarry Country House** ﹩, IV51 9HZ, ℰ 203, Fax 301, ≼ Staffin Island and coastline, ☞ – ↤↦ 🅿. ⊠ VISA ✻
    M (bar lunch Monday to Saturday)/dinner 25.00 **st.** ⅜ 4.25 – **24 rm** ⊃ 32.00/90.00 **st.**

Isleornsay – ⊠ ✿ 047 13 Isle Ornsay.

🏠 **Kinloch Lodge** ﹩, IV43 8QY, ⊠ Sleat, N : 3½ m. by A 851 ℰ 333, Fax 277, ≼ Loch Na Dal, « 17C former shooting lodge », ꙮ, ☞, park – ↤↦ 🅿. ⊠ VISA ✻
    closed 1 December-28 February – **M** (dinner only) 35.00 **t.** ⅜ 3.50 – **10 rm** ⊃ 40.00/160.00 **t.**

Portree – pop. 1 533 – ECD : Wednesday – ⊠ ✿ 0478 Portree.

🅱 Meall House, Portree ℰ 2137.

🏠 **Rosedale,** Beaumont Cres., IV51 9DB, ℰ 613131, Fax 612531, ≼ harbour – ↤↦ rest 📺 ☎ 🅿. ⊠ VISA
    May-September – **M** (dinner only) 21.00 **t.** – **23 rm** ⊃ 35.00/74.00 **t.**

↑ **Kings Haven** without rest., 11 Bosville Terr., IV51 9DJ, ℰ 612290 – 📺. ⊠ VISA ✻
    closed Christmas – **6 rm** ⊃ 35.00/52.00 **t.**

Skeabost – ECD : Wednesday – ⊠ ✿ 047 032 Skeabost Bridge.

🛆 Skeabost ℰ 202.

🏛 **Skeabost House** ﹩, IV51 9NP, ℰ 202, Fax 454, ≼ Loch Snizort Beag, « Country house atmosphere », 🛆, ☞, park – ↤↦ 🅿. ⊠ VISA
    April-October – **M** (buffet lunch)/dinner 22.50 **t.** ⅜ 5.00 – **26 rm** ⊃ 39.00/96.00 **t.**

Uig – ⊠ ✿ 047 042 Uig.

↑ **Woodbine,** Kilmiur Rd, IV51 9XP, ℰ 243 – 📺 🅿
    M 11.50 **st.** – **4 rm** ⊃ 21.00/35.00 **st.**

SOUTH QUEENSFERRY W. Lothian. (Lothian) 401 J 16 Scotland G. – pop. 7 485 – ECD : Wednesday – ☎ 031 Edinburgh.

See : Forth Bridges★★.

Envir. : Hopetoun House★★ AC, W : 2 ½ m. by A 904 – Abercorn Parish Church (Hopetoun Loft★★) W : 3 m. by A 904 – Dalmeny★ - Dalmeny House★ AC (St. Cuthberts's Church★ - Norman South Doorway★★) E : 3 m. by B 924.

Exc. : House of the Binns (plasterwork ceilings★) AC, W : 6 ½ m. by A 904.

◆Edinburgh 9 – Dunfermline 7 – ◆Glasgow 41.

Forth Bridges Moat House (Q.M.H.), EH30 9SF, at junction A 90 with Forth Bridge ✆ 331 1199, Telex 727430, Fax 319 1733, ≤ Firth of Forth and Bridges, ₣₺, ≘s, ☒, squash – |‡| ▤ rest ▣ ☎ ⓟ – 🏃 120
108 rm.

SPEAN BRIDGE Inverness. (Highland) 401 F 13 – ☎ 0397.

◆Edinburgh 143 – Fort William 10 – ◆Glasgow 94 – ◆Inverness 58 – ◆Oban 60.

Corriegour Lodge, Loch Lochy, PH34 4EB, N : 8 ¾ m. on A 82 ✆ 712685, Fax 712685, ≤, – ⅍ ▣ ⓟ. ⅁ VISA. ✻
March-October – **M** 18.00 **t.** (dinner) and a la carte 8.25/20.70 **t.** ₰ 4.45 – **8 rm** ⊏ 35.00/76.00 **t.**

Old Pines ⅏, Gairlochy Rd, PH34 4EG, NW : 1 ½ m. by A 82 on B 8004 ✆ 712324, Fax 712433, ≤, park – ⅍ ♿ ⓟ. ⅁ VISA. ✻
closed 2 weeks November – **M** (by arrangement) 17.50 **st.** – **8 rm** ⊏ 25.00/50.00 **st.** – SB (except Easter, Christmas and New Year) 75.00/85.00 **st.**

Old Station, Station Rd, PH34 4EP, ✆ 712535 – ⅍ ⓟ. ⅁ VISA
closed Wednesday, November and January – **M** (booking essential) (restricted service in winter) a la carte 11.75/15.95 **t.** ₰ 5.25.

SPITTAL OF GLENSHEE Perth. (Tayside) 401 J 13 Scotland G. – ✉ Blairgowrie – ☎ 0250 Glenshee.

Envir. : Glenshee (※★★) (chairlift AC).

◆Edinburgh 69 – ◆Aberdeen 74 – ◆Dundee 35.

Dalmunzie House ⅏, PH10 7QG, ✆ 885224, Fax 885225, ≤, ⛳9, ⅋, , park – |‡| ⓟ. ⅁ VISA
closed 7 November-27 December – **M** (bar lunch)/dinner 19.00 **t.** – **17 rm** ⊏ 51.00/83.00 **t.**

STENNESS Orkney. (Orkney Islands) 401 K 7 – see Orkney Islands.

STEPPS Lanark. (Strathclyde) 401 H 16 – see Glasgow.

STEWARTON Ayr. (Strathclyde) 401 402 G 16 Scotland G. – pop. 6 319 – ECD : Wednesday and Saturday – ☎ 0560.

Envir. : Kilmarnock (Dean Castle, arms and armour★, musical instruments★ AC) S : 5 ½ m. by A 735 and B 7038.

◆Edinburgh 68 – ◆Ayr 21 – ◆Glasgow 22.

Chapeltoun House ⅏ with rm, KA3 3ED, SW : 2 ½ m. by A 735 off B 769 ✆ 482696, Fax 485100, « Country house in extensive grounds », ⅋, , park – ⅍ rest ▣ ☎ ⓟ. ⅁ AE VISA. ✻
M 18.90/27.90 **t.** ₰ 5.20 – **8 rm** ⊏ 65.00/129.00 **t.** – SB 108.00/139.00 **st.**

STIRLING Stirling. (Central) 401 I 15 Scotland G. – pop. 36 640 – ECD : Wednesday – ☎ 0786.

See : Town★★ - Castle★★ AC (Site★★★, external elevations★★★, Stirling Heads★★, Argyll and Sutherland Highlanders Regimental Museum★) B – Argyll's Lodging★ (Renaissance decoration★) B **A** – Church of the Holy Rude★ B **B**.

Envir. : Wallace Monument (※★★) NE : 2 ½ m. by A 9 - A - and B 998.

Exc. : Dunblane★ (Cathedral★★, West Front★★), N : 6 ½ m. by A 9 A.

ℹ 41 Dumbarton Rd ✆ 475019 – Broad St. ✆ 479901 (summer only) – Motorway Service Area, M 9/M 80, junction 9 ✆ 814111 (summer only).

◆Edinburgh 37 – Dunfermline 23 – Falkirk 14 – ◆Glasgow 28 – Greenock 52 – Motherwell 30 – ◆Oban 87 – Perth 35.

Plan on next page

Stirling Highland, Spittal St., FK8 1DU, ✆ 475444, Fax 462929, ₣₺, ≘s, ☒, squash – |‡| ▣ ☎ ♿ ⓟ – 🏃 150. ⅁ AE ⓞ VISA B **e**
M 10.50/19.75 **t.** and a la carte ₰ 4.95 – **72 rm** ⊏ 98.00/128.00 **t.**, 4 suites – SB (except Christmas-New Year) (weekends only) 110.00/160.00 **st.**

Park Lodge without rest., 32 Park Terr., FK8 2JS, ✆ 474862, Fax 451291, « Tastefully decorated Georgian house, antiques », – ▣ ☎ ⓟ – 🏃 60. ⅁ VISA. ✻ B **a**
9 rm ⊏ 45.00/120.00 **st.**

Granada Lodge without rest., Pirnhall roundabout, Snabhead, FK7 8EU, S : 3 m. by A 872 ✆ 813614, Fax 815900, Reservations (Freephone) 0800 555300 – ⅍ ▣ ♿ ⓟ. ⅁ AE VISA. ✻ A
⊏ 4.00 – **37 rm** 34.95/37.95 **st.**

STIRLING

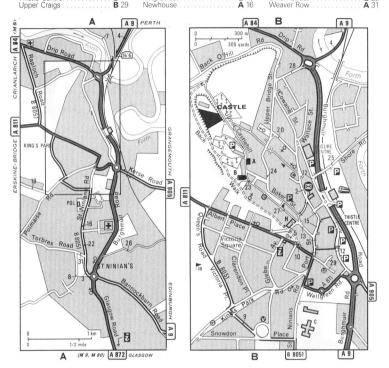

↑ **Number 10,** Gladstone Pl., FK8 2NN, ℘ 472681, ⚡ – ⇔ rm ☒ ⚶
M (by arrangement) 6.00 **st.** – **3 rm** ⇌ 16.00/36.00 **st.**   BV

↑ **Fairfield,** 14 Princes St., FK8 1HQ, ℘ 472685 – ⇔ rest ☒ ⚶
M 6.00 **st.** – **6 rm** ⇌ 18.00/36.00 **st.**   B c

XX **Regent,** 30 Upper Craigs, FK8 2DS, ℘ 472513 – ▤. 🄰 🄰🄴 ⓞ 🆅🅸🆂🅰   B u
closed 25 December and 1 January – **M** - Chinese (Canton, Peking) a la carte 13.00/27.50 **t.**
🕯 5.10.

at Blairlogie NE : 4 ½ m. by A 9 on A 91 – A – ⊠ Stirling – ☎ 0259 Alva :

🏠 **Blairlogie House,** FK9 5QE, ℘ 761441, Fax 761441, ⚡, park – ☒ ☎ ⓟ. 🄰 🆅🅸🆂🅰
closed 2 weeks Christmas-New Year – **M** (closed Sunday) 18.00 **st.** (dinner) and a la
carte 14.45/23.25 **st** 🕯 3.90 – **7 rm** ⇌ 39.50/61.50 **st** – SB (weekends only) 82.50/117.00 **st.**

🛢 ATS 45 Drip Rd ℘ 450770

STONEHAVEN Kincardine. (Grampian) 🄰🄾🄸 N 13 – ☎ 0569 Newtonhill.

♦ Edinburgh 114 – ♦ Aberdeen 16 – ♦ Dundee 51.

🏠 **Muchalls Castle** ⚘, AB3 2RS, N : 5 m. by B 979 and A 92 on Netherley rd ℘ 31170,
Fax 31480, « Early 17C laird's house, plasterwork ceilings », ⚡ – ⇔ rm ⓟ. ⚶
closed Christmas – **M** (booking essential) (communal dining) (dinner only) 25.00 **st.** 🕯 8.00 –
7 rm ⇌ 70.00/110.00 **st.**

STORNOWAY Ross and Cromarty. (Outer Hebrides) (Western Isles) 🄰🄾🄸 A 9 – see Lewis and
Harris (Isle of).

Pour visiter une ville ou une région : utilisez les Guides Verts Michelin.

STRACHUR Argyll. (Strathclyde) 401 E 15 Scotland G. – ECD : Wednesday – ⊠ Cairndow – ☼ 036 986.

Exc. : Inveraray★★ : Castle★★ (interior★★★) *AC*, NW : 17 m. by A 185 and A 83 – Loch Fyne★★.

◆Edinburgh 104 – ◆Glasgow 58 – ◆Oban 58.

🏨 **Creggans Inn**, PA27 8BX, on A 815 ✆ 279, Fax 637, ≼ Loch Fyne, ⌕, ☞ – ⚒ rest 📺 ☎ ☻ ☐ ❖ ▦ *VISA*
M (dinner only and Sunday lunch)/dinner 18.00 **t.** and a la carte ⅃ 5.75 – **21 rm** ⌸ 30.00/ 60.00 **t.** – SB (except Easter, Christmas and New Year) (weekdays only) 98.00 **st.**

STRANRAER Wigtown. (Dumfries and Galloway) 401 402 E 19 Scotland G. – pop. 10 766 – ECD : Wednesday – ☼ 0776.

Exc. : Logan Botanic Garden★ *AC*, S : 11 m. by A 77, A 716 and B 7065.

ͫ Creachmore, Leswalt ✆ 87245, NW : 2 m. by A 718.

⚓ To Northern Ireland : by Stena Sealink Line : to Larne frequent services daily (2 h 20 mn) – by Hoverspeed : to Belfast (1h 30 mn).

🛈 1 Bridge St., DG9 7JA ✆ 2595 (summer only).

◆Edinburgh 132 – ◆Ayr 51 – ◆Dumfries 75.

🏨 **North West Castle**, Portrodie, DG9 8EH, ✆ 4413, Fax 2646, ƒ₅, ☎s, ▨ – ⧅ 📺 ☎ ☻ – ⚒ 100. ❖
M 19.50 **t.** (dinner) and a la carte ⅃ 5.70 – **71 rm** ⌸ 49.00/84.00 **t.** – SB (October-April) (weekends only) 100.00/154.00 **st.**

🏠 **Kildrochet House** ⌂, DG9 9BB, S : 3¼ m. by A 77 on A 716 ✆ 0776 82 (Lochans) 216, « Former 18C dower house », ☞ – ⚒ ☻ ❖
M (by arrangement) (communal dining) 13.00 **s.** – **3 rm** ⌸ 22.00/44.00 **s.**

🛈 ATS Commerce Rd, Ind. Est. ✆ 2131

I prezzi	Per ogni chiarimento sui prezzi qui riportati, consultate le spiegazioni alle pagine dell'introduzione.

STRATHBLANE Stirling. (Central) 401 H 16 – pop. 1 933 – ECD : Wednesday – ⊠ Glasgow – ☼ 0360 Blanefield.

◆Edinburgh 52 – ◆Glasgow 11 – Stirling 26.

🏨 **Kirkhouse Inn**, G63 9AA, ✆ 70621, Fax 70896 – 📺 ☎ ☻ – ⚒ 30. ▦ ▥ ① *VISA*
M 11.50/17.50 **st.** and a la carte ⅃ 4.95 – **15 rm** ⌸ 55.25/82.00 **st.** – SB (except Christmas and New Year) (weekends only) 81.00 **st.**

STRATHCONON Ross and Cromarty. (Highland) 401 F 11 Scotland G. – ⊠ Muir of Ord – ☼ 099 77 Strathconon.

Exc. : Wester Ross★★★.

◆Edinburgh 184 – ◆Inverness 28.

🏠 **East Lodge** ⌂, IV6 7QQ, W : 11 m. from Marybank off A 832 ✆ 222, Fax 243, ≼, ⌕, ☞ – 📺 ☎ ☻ ▦ ❖
M 20.00/30.00 **t.** – **10 rm** ⌸ 32.50/85.00 **st.** – SB (October-April except Christmas and New Year) 70.00/85.00 **st.**

STRATHPEFFER Ross and Cromarty. (Highland) 401 G 11 – pop. 1 244 – ECD : Thursday – ☼ 0997.

ͫ Strathpeffer Spa ✆ 421219.

🛈 The Square ✆ 421415 (summer only).

◆Edinburgh 174 – ◆Inverness 18.

🏠 **Holly Lodge**, Golf Course Rd, IV14 9AR, ✆ 421254, ☞ – 📺 ☻ ▦ *VISA*
M 10.00/13.75 **t.** and lunch a la carte ⅃ 3.00 – **7 rm** ⌸ 27.50/55.00 **t.**

🏠 **Craigvar** without rest., The Square, IV14 9DL, ✆ 421622 – 📺 ☎ ☻ *VISA*. ❖
April-October – **3 rm** ⌸ 24.00/40.00 **st.**

STRATHYRE Perth. (Central) 401 H 15 Scotland G. – ⊠ Callander – ☼ 087 74 (3 fig.) and 0877 (6 fig.).

Exc. : The Trossacks★★★ (Loch Katherine★★) SW : 14 m. by A 84 and A 821 – Hilltop viewpoint★★★ (⚹★★★) SW : 16½ m. by A 84 and A 821.

◆Edinburgh 62 – ◆Glasgow 53 – Perth 42.

🍴 **Creagan House** with rm, FK18 8ND, on A 84 ✆ 638, Fax 638, ≼ – ⚒ ☻ ▦ *VISA*
closed February and 1 week October – **M** (booking essential) (dinner only and Sunday lunch)/dinner 21.00 **t.** ⅃ 5.10 – **5 rm** ⌸ 34.25/61.00 **t.** – SB (except Bank Holidays) 72.50/ 115.00 **st.**

at Balquhidder NW : 4 m. by A 84 – ⊠ Lochearnhead – ☼ 0877 Strathyre :

🏠 **Stronvar Country House** ⌂, FK19 8PB, ✆ 384688, Fax 384230, ≼ Loch Voil and Braes of Balquhidder, « Bygones Museum », ⌕, ☞ – ⚒ rest 📺 ☻ ▦ *VISA*. ❖
March-October – **M** (restricted lunch)/dinner 17.50 **st.** ⅃ 4.25 – **4 rm** ⌸ 39.50/59.00 **st.**

STROMNESS Orkney. (Orkney Islands) 401 K 7 – see Orkney Islands.

STRONTIAN Argyll. (Highland) 401 D 13 – ✉ ☎ 0967.
🏠 ♟ 2131 (summer only).
◆Edinburgh 139 – Fort William 23 – ◆Oban 66.

🏚 **Kilcamb Lodge** 🦢, PH36 4HY, ♟ 2257, Fax 2041, ≼, ☞, park – ⊱⇆ ℗. 🔼 𝘝𝘐𝘚𝘈
April-October – **M** (light lunch)/dinner 24.00 **st.** ⫙ 4.25 – **10 rm** ⥋ 40.00/80.00 **st.**

at Glencripesdale W : 15½ m. by A 884, Laudale rd and Forestry Commission track –
✉ Acharacle – ☎ 096 785 Salen :

🏠 **Glencripesdale House** 🦢, Loch Sunart, PH36 4JH, ♟ 263, ≼ Loch Sunart and Ben
Laga, ⟍, ☞, park – ⊱⇆ rest ℗ ♨
March-October and Christmas-New Year – **M** 17.50 **st.** ⫙ 4.25 – **4 rm** ⥋ (dinner included)
69.00/138.00 **st.**

TAIN Ross and Cromarty. (Highland) 401 H 10 – pop. 3 428 – ECD : Thursday – ☎ 0862.
🏌 Tain ♟ 892314.
◆Edinburgh 191 – ◆Inverness 35 – ◆Wick 91.

🏨 **Morangie House,** Morangie Rd, IV19 1PY, ♟ 892281, Fax 892872 – 📺 ☎ ℗. 🔼 🅰🅴 ⓞ
𝘝𝘐𝘚𝘈 ♨
M (bar lunch Monday to Saturday)/dinner 20.00 **t.** and a la carte ⫙ 4.50 – **13 rm** ⥋ 45.00/
75.00 **t.** – SB 90.00/120.00 **st.**

TALLADALE Ross and Cromarty (Highland) 401 D 10 Scotland G. – ✉ Achnasheen –
☎ 044 584 Kinlochewe.
Envir. : Loch Maree★★★ – Victoria Falls★, N : 2 m. by A 832.
Exc. : Wester Ross★★★.
◆Edinburgh 218 – ◆Inverness 62 – Kyle of Lochalsh 58.

🏚 **Loch Maree,** IV22 2HL, ♟ 288, Fax 241, ≼ – ⊱⇆ rest 📺 ☎ ⫟ ℗. 🔼 𝘝𝘐𝘚𝘈
M a la carte 13.25/20.45 **st.** ⫙ 4.35 – **18 rm** ⥋ 20.00/80.00 **st.**

🏠 **Old Mill Highland Lodge** 🦢, IV22 2HL, ♟ 271, ☞ – ⊱⇆ ℗. ♨
M 19.50 **s.** ⫙ 4.50 – **5 rm** ⥋ (dinner included) 48.50/105.00 **s.**

Prices   For full details of the prices quoted in the guide,
         consult the introduction.

TARBERT Argyll. (Strathclyde) 401 D 16 – see Kintyre (Peninsula).

TARBERT Inverness. (Outer Hebrides) (Western Isles) 401 Z 10 – see Lewis and Harris
(Isle of).

TAYVALLICH Argyll. (Strathclyde) 401 D 15 – ✉ Lochgilphead – ☎ 054 67.
◆Edinburgh 141 – ◆Glasgow 95 – ◆Oban 40.

✗ **Tayvallich Inn,** PA31 8PR, ♟ 282, ≼ – ℗. 🔼 𝘝𝘐𝘚𝘈
closed Monday November-March – **M** a la carte approx. 18.90 **t.** ⫙ 4.20.

THORNHILL Dumfries. (Dumfries and Galloway) 401 402 I 18 Scotland G. – pop. 1 449 – ECD :
Thursday – ☎ 0848.
Envir. : Drumlanrig Castle★★ (cabinets★) *AC,* NW : 2½ m. by A 76.
◆Edinburgh 64 – ◆Ayr 44 – ◆Dumfries 15 – ◆Glasgow 63.

🏚 **Trigony House,** Closeburn, DG3 5EZ, S : 1½ m. on A 76 ♟ 331211, ☞ – 📺 ☎ ℗. 🔼
𝘝𝘐𝘚𝘈 ♨
M (bar lunch)/dinner 18.45 **t.** ⫙ 5.50 – **9 rm** ⥋ 33.50/64.00 **st.** – SB (March-June) 83.00/
100.00 **st.**

THORNHILL Stirling. (Central) 401 H 15 – pop. 1 435 – ☎ 0786.
◆Edinburgh 46 – ◆Glasgow 36.

🏠 **Corshill Cottage** 🦢, FK8 3QD, E : 1 m. on A 873 ♟ 850270, ☞ – ⊱⇆ ℗
May-September – **M** (by arrangement) 12.00 – **3 rm** ⥋ 24.00/38.00 **st.**

THURSO Caithness. (Highland) 401 J 8 Scotland G. – pop. 8 828 – ECD : Thursday – ☎ 0047.
Exc. : Strathy Point★ (≼★★★) W : 22 m. by A 836.
🏌 Newlands of Geise ♟ 63807, SW : 2 m. by A 874.
⛴ by P & O Ferries : Orkney and Shetland Services : from Scrabster to Stromness (Orkney
Islands).
🏠 Riverside ♟ 62371 (summer only).
◆Edinburgh 289 – ◆Inverness 133 – ◆Wick 21.

🏨 **Forss House** 🦢, Bridge of Forss, KW14 7XY, W : 5½ m. on A 836
♟ 084 786 (Forss) 201, ≼, ☞, park – 📺 ☎ ℗. 🔼 🅰🅴 𝘝𝘐𝘚𝘈 ♨
M (dinner only) 17.50 **t.** ⫙ 4.20 – **7 rm** ⥋ 45.00/80.00 **t.**

TIRORAN Argyll. (Strathclyde) 401 B 14 – see Mull (Isle of).

TOBERMORY Argyll. (Strathclyde) 401 B 14 – see Mull (Isle of).

648

TONGUE Sutherland. (Highland) **401** G 8 Scotland G. – ECD : Saturday – ✉ Lairg – ☺ 084 755.

Exc. : Cape Wrath★★★ (≤★★) W : 44 m. (including ferry crossing) by A 838 – Ben Loyal★★, S : 8 m. by A 836 – Ben Hope★ (≤★★★) S : 15 m. by A 838 – Strathy Point★ (≤★★★) E : 22 m. by A 836 – Torrisdale Bay★ (≤★★) NE : 8 m. by A 836.

◆Edinburgh 257 – ◆Inverness 101 – Thurso 43.

Ben Loyal, Main St., IV27 4XE, ℰ 216, Fax 216, ≤ – ✄ rest 📺 ⑫. 🔼 *VISA*
closed 1 January-10 February – **M** (bar lunch)/dinner 18.50 **t.** ⑂ 5.20 – **12 rm** ⊡ 23.50/70.00 **t.** – SB 68.40/137.00 **st.**

TROON Ayr. (Strathclyde) **401 402** G 17 – pop. 14 035 – ECD : Wednesday – ☺ 0292.

⬛, ⬛, ⬛, Harling Drive ℰ 312464.

🏛 Municipal Buildings, South Beach ℰ 317696 (summer only).

◆Edinburgh 77 – ◆Ayr 7 – ◆Glasgow 31.

Marine Highland, 8 Crosbie Rd, KA10 6HE, ℰ 314444, Fax 316922, ≤, 🎣, ⛝, ⬛, squash – 📱 📺 ⑫ – 🔼 220. 🔼 🔼 ⑩ *VISA*
M a la carte 9.45/29.50 **t.** ⑂ 4.95 – **66 rm** ⊡ 88.00/140.00 **t.**, 6 suites – SB (except Christmas and New Year) 106.00/150.00 **st.**

Lochgreen House 🌿, Monktonhill Rd, Southwood, KA10 7EN, SE : 2 m. on B 749 ℰ 313343, Fax 318661, ☞, ⛝ – ✄ rest 📺 ☎ ⑫. 🔼 🔼 *VISA* *JCB*. ✦
M 16.95/23.50 **st.** ⑂ 5.95 – **6 rm** ⊡ 75.00/99.00 **st.**, 1 suite – SB 160.00/210.00 **st.**

Piersland House, 15 Craigend Rd, KA10 6HD, ℰ 314747, Fax 315613, ☞ – 📺 ☎ ⑫. 🔼 🔼 *VISA*
M 10.95/16.50 **t.** and a la carte ⑂ 7.75 – **15 rm** ⊡ 56.00/115.00 **t.**, 4 suites.

Ardneil, 51 St. Meddans St., KA10 6NU, ℰ 311611, Fax 318111 – 📺 ⑫. 🔼 🔼 *VISA*
M 12.00/15.00 **t.** and a la carte ⑂ 4.50 – **9 rm** ⊡ 25.00/50.00 **t.**

Highgrove House with rm, Old Loans Rd, Loans, KA10 7HL, E : 2 ½ m. by A 759 ℰ 312511, Fax 318228, ≤, ☞ – 📺 ☎ ⑫. 🔼 🔼 *VISA*
M 15.95 **t.** (dinner) and a la carte 9.00/23.20 **t.** ⑂ 4.95 – **9 rm** ⊡ 55.00/69.00 **st.** – SB 90.00/150.00 **st.**

TURNBERRY Ayr. (Strathclyde) **401 402** F 18 Scotland G. – ECD : Wednesday – ✉ Girvan – ☺ 0655.

Envir. : Culzean Castle★ *AC* (setting★★★, Oval Staircase★★) NE : 5 m. by A 719.

◆Edinburgh 97 – ◆Ayr 15 – ◆Glasgow 51 – Stranraer 36.

Turnberry H. & Golf Courses 🌿, KA26 9LT, on A 719 ℰ 31000, Telex 777779, Fax 31706, « Edwardian country house, ≤ golf course, bay and Ailsa Craig », 🎣, ⛝, ⬛, ⬛, ☞, ⛝, squash – 📱 📺 ☎ ⑯ ⑫ – 🔼 150. 🔼 🔼 ⑩ *VISA* *JCB*
M – Turnberry 35.00 (dinner) and lunch a la carte ⑂ 8.50 – **Bay at Turnberry** *(closed mid. October-March)* a la carte 14.70/29.75 **t.** ⑂ 8.50 – **122 rm** ⊡ 165.00/230.00 **st.**, 10 suites – SB (November-17 April except New Year) 215.00/370.00 **st.**

TWYNHOLM Kirkcudbright. (Dumfries and Galloway) **402** H 19 – ☺ 055 76.

◆Edinburgh 107 – ◆Ayr 54 – ◆Dumfries 27 – Stranraer 48.

Fresh Fields 🌿, Arden Rd, DG6 4PB, SW : ¾ m. by Burn Brae ℰ 221, Fax 221, ☞ – ✄ rest ⑫. ✦
April-October – **M** (by arrangement) – **5 rm** ⊡ (dinner included) 39.00/82.00 **st.**

UDDINGSTON Lanark. (Strathclyde) **401 402** H 16 – pop. 10 681 – ECD : Wednesday – ✉ Glasgow – ☺ 0698.

⬛ Coatbridge, Townhead Rd ℰ 0236 (Coatbridge) 28975, NE : 5 m. by B 7701, A 752 and A 89.

◆Edinburgh 41 – ◆Glasgow 10.

Redstones, 8-10 Glasgow Rd, G71 7AS, ℰ 813774, Fax 815319 – 📺 ☎ ⑫. 🔼 🔼 ⑩ *VISA*. ✦
closed 1 and 2 January – **M** *(closed Sunday dinner)* 15.95 **t.** (dinner) and a la carte 8.70/21.10 **t.** ⑂ 4.15 – **18 rm** ⊡ 52.00/74.50 **t.** – SB (weekends only) 81.00/153.90 **st.**

Il Buongustaio, 84 Main St., G71 7LR, ℰ 816000 – 🔼 🔼 ⑩ *VISA*
closed Sunday dinner and Tuesday – **M** - Italian a la carte 12.95/40.45 **t.** ⑂ 4.50.

UIG Ross and Cromarty. (Outer Hebrides) (Western Isles) **401** Y 9 – see Lewis and Harris (Isle of).

UIG Inverness. (Highland) **401** B 11 and 12 – see Skye (Isles of).

UIST (Isles of) Inverness. (Western Isles) **401** XY 11 /12 – pop. 3 677.

✈ see Liniclate.

🚢 by Caledonian MacBrayne : from Lochboisdale to Oban and Castlebay (Isle of Barra) (summer only) – from Lochmaddy to Uig (Isle of Skye) – from Lochmaddy to Tarbert (Isle of Harris).

Liniclate (Benbecula) – ☺ 0870 Benbecula.

✈ Benbecula Airport ℰ 602051.

Dark Island, PA88 5PJ, ℰ 2414, Fax 2347 – 📺 ☎ ⑫. 🔼 *VISA*
M 12.50/15.50 **t.** and a la carte ⑂ 5.50 – **42 rm** ⊡ 40.00/80.00 **t.**

Daliburgh (South Uist) – ⊠ ✪ 087 84 Lochboisdale.

🏌 Askernish ♟ 541, N : 1 m.

🏠 **Borrodale,** PA81 5SS, ♟ 444, Fax 611, ≤, 🌂 – 📺 ℗. 🏧 VISA
M 10.50/16.50 **t.** ⅄ 4.50 – **13 rm** ⊐ 32.00/52.00 **st.** – SB (weekends only) 78.00/94.00 **st.**

ULLAPOOL Ross and Cromarty. (Highland) 401 E 10 Scotland G. – pop. 1 006 – ECD : Tuesday except summer – ✪ 0854.

See : Town★.

Envir. : Loch Broom★★.

Exc. : Falls of Measach★★, S : 11 m. by A 835 and A 832 - Corrieshalloch Gorge★, SE : 10 m. by A 835 – Northwards to Lochinver★★, Morefield (≤★★ of Ullapool), ≤★ Loch Broom – S : from Ullapool to Gairloch★★ (≤★★★).

🚢 by Caledonian MacBrayne : to Stornoway (Isle of Lewis).

🏢 West Shore St. ♟ 612135 (summer only).

◆Edinburgh 215 – ◆Inverness 59.

🏨 ✿✿ **Altnaharrie Inn** (Gunn Eriksen) 🌊, IV26 2SS, SW : ½ m. via private ferry ♟ 085 483 (Dundonnell) 230, ≤ Loch Broom and Ullapool, « Idyllic setting on banks of Loch Broom », ☞ – ⇔✖. ℘
April-October – **M** (booking essential) (light lunch, residents only)/dinner 50.00/58.00 **st.** ⅄ 5.70 – **8 rm** ⊐ (dinner included) 120.00/290.00 **st.**
Spec. Warm salad of scallops and truffles with a sweet Barsac and veal jus sauce. Saddle of lamb with lamb fillet wrapped in herbs and foie gras, Ravioli of lobster and crab with ginger and a Champagne butter sauce.

🏠 **Harbour Lights,** Garve Rd, IV26 2SX, ♟ 612222, Fax 612222, ≤ Loch Broom, ☞ – 📺 ☎ ℗. 🏧 VISA
accommodation closed 23 to 27 December – **M** (bar lunch)/dinner 19.50 **t.** and a la carte ⅄ 4.50 – **22 rm** ⊐ 32.00/68.00 **t.**

🏠 **Ardvreck** 🌊 without rest., Morefield Brae, IV26 2TH, NW : 2 m. by A 835 ♟ 612561, Fax 612028, ≤ Loch Broom and mountains, ☞ – ⇔✖ 📺 ℗. ℘
10 rm ⊐ 23.00/44.00 **st.**

🏠 **Ladysmith House,** Pulteney St., IV26 2UP, ♟ 612185 – 📺. 🏧 VISA. ℘
M (dinner only) a la carte 11.75/18.65 **t.** ⅄ 4.75 – **6 rm** ⊐ 18.00/40.00 **t.**

🏠 **Sheiling** without rest., Garve Rd, IV26 2SX, ♟ 612947, ≤ Loch Broom, ☞ – ⇔✖ ℗. ℘
closed Christmas and New Year – **7 rm** ⊐ 25.00/40.00 **st.**

🏠 **Dromnan** without rest., Garve Rd, IV26 2SX, ♟ 612333, ≤ – 📺 ℗. ℘
7 rm ⊐ 25.00/40.00 **st.**

UPHALL W. Lothian. (Lothian) 401 J 16 – ECD : Wednesday – ✪ 0506 Broxburn.

🏌 Uphall ♟ 856404.

◆Edinburgh 13 – ◆Glasgow 32.

🏨 **Houstoun House,** EH52 6JS, ♟ 853831, Fax 854220, « Gardens », park – 📺 ☎ ℗. 🏧 AE ⓞ VISA
M (bar lunch Saturday) 16.50/28.50 **st.** ⅄ 5.95 – ⊐ 5.50 – **30 rm** 89.00/110.00 **st.** – SB (except Christmas and New Year) 98.00/130.00 **st.**

WALKERBURN Peebles. (Borders) 401 402 K 17 Scotland G. – pop. 713 – ✪ 089 687 (3 fig.) and 0896 (6 fig.).

Envir. : The Tweed Valley★★ – Traquair House★★, W : 4 m. by A 72 and B 709.

Exc. : Abbotsbury★★ AC, W : 10½ m. by A 72, A 6091 and B 6360.

🏌 Innerleithen, Leithen Water, Leithen Rd ♟ 830951, NW : 3 m. by A 72 and B 709.

◆Edinburgh 32 – Galashiels 10 – Peebles 8.

🏠 **Tweed Valley** 🌊, Galashiels Rd, EH43 6AA, ♟ 636, Fax 639, ≤, ⇆, 🌂, ☞ – 📺 ☎ ℗. 🏧 VISA
M 10.50/23.00 **t.** and a la carte ⅄ 5.25 – **15 rm** ⊐ 40.00/92.00 **t.** – SB (except Bank Holidays) 97.00/117.00 **st.**

WALLS Shetland. (Shetland Islands) 401 PQ 3 – see Shetland Islands (Mainland).

WESTHILL Aberdeen. (Grampian) 401 N 12 – see Aberdeen.

WHITEBRIDGE Inverness. (Highland) 401 G 12 – ✪ 045 63 (changing to 0456 in May) Gorthleck.

◆Edinburgh 171 – ◆Inverness 23 – Kyle of Lochalsh 67 – ◆Oban 92.

🏨 **Knockie Lodge** 🌊, IV1 2UP, SW : 3 ½ m. by B 862 ♟ 486276, Fax 486389, ≤ Loch Nanlann and mountains, « Tastefully converted hunting lodge », 🌂, park – ⇔✖ rest ☎ ℗. 🏧 AE ⓞ VISA
May-October – **M** (residents only) (dinner only) 30.00 **t.** ⅄ 4.00 – **10 rm** ⊐ (dinner included) 75.00/190.00 **t.**

WHITING BAY Bute. (Strathclyde) 401 402 E 17 – see Arran (Isle of).

WICK Caithness. (Highland) **401** K 8 Scotland G. – pop. 7 770 – ECD : Wednesday – ⊛ 0955.

Exc. : Duncansby Head★ (Stacks of Duncansby★★) N : 14 m. by A 9 – Grey Cairns of Camster★ (Long Cairn★★) S : 17 m. by A 9 – The Hill O'Many Stanes★, S : 10 m. by A 9.

🔟 Reiss 🖉 2726, N : 3 m. by A 9.

✈ Wick Airport 🖉 2215, N : 1 m.

🛈 Whitechapel Rd 🖉 2596.

◆Edinburgh 282 – ◆Inverness 126.

↑   **Clachan** without rest., South Rd, KW1 5NH, on A 9 🖉 5384, 📺 – ⇔ 📺. 🛇
     3 rm 😐 25.00/40.00 **st.**

WIGTOWN Wigtown. (Dumfries and Galloway) **401** G 19 Scotland G. – pop. 1 040 – ECD : Wednesday – ✉ Newton Stewart – ⊛ 098 84.

Exc. : Whithorn Museum (early Christian crosses★★) S : 10 m. by A 746.

🔟 Wigtown & Bladnoch, Lightlands Terr. 🖉 3354.

◆Edinburgh 137 – ◆Ayr 61 – ◆Dumfries 61 – Stranraer 26.

🏨   **Corsemalzie House** 🐾, DG8 9RL, SW : 6 ½ m. by A 714 on B 7005 🖉 0988
     (Mochrum) 860254, Fax 860213, 🐟, 📺, park – 📺 ☎ 🅿. 🖾 𝘝𝘐𝘚𝘈
     closed 15 January-5 March – **M** 15.75/22.75 **t.** and a la carte 🍴 3.95 – **14 rm** 😐 29.00/
     82.00 **t.** – SB 78.00/136.00 **st.**

WORMIT Fife. (Fife) **401** L 14 – ECD : Wednesday – ✉ ⊛ 0382 Newport-on-Tay.

🔟 Scotscraig, Golf Rd, Tayport 🖉 552515, NE : 4 m.

◆Edinburgh 53 – ◆Dundee 6 – St. Andrews 12.

🏨   **Sandford,** DD6 8RG, S : 2 m. at junction of A 914 with B 946 🖉 541802, Fax 542136, ≼,
     📺, 🛇 – 📺 ☎ 🅿 – 🔬 40. 🖾 🖾 ⓪ 𝘝𝘐𝘚𝘈 🛇
     M 21.95/23.95 **t.** and a la carte 🍴 5.30 – **16 rm** 😐 80.00/120.00 **t.** – SB (except 31 Decem-
     ber) 115.00/155.00 **st.**

Northern
Ireland

Place with at least :

one hotel or restaurant ...... ● Londonderry
a pleasant hotel or restaurant .. 🏨🏨, ⋔, ✗
one quiet, secluded hotel .... ⨭
one restaurant with .. ✿, ✿✿, ✿✿✿, **Meals (M)**
See this town for establishments
   located in its vicinity .... BELFAST

La località possiede come minimo :

una risorsa alberghiera ...... ● Londonderry
Albergo o ristorante ameno .... 🏨🏨, ⋔, ✗
un albergo molto tranquillo, isolato ...... ⨭
un'ottima tavola con . ✿, ✿✿, ✿✿✿, **Meals (M)**
La località raggruppa nel suo testo
   le risorse dei dintorni .... BELFAST

Localité offrant au moins :

une ressource hôtelière ...... ● Londonderry
un hôtel ou restaurant agréable 🏨🏨, ⋔, ✗
un hôtel très tranquille, isolé .... ⨭
une bonne table à ✿, ✿✿, ✿✿✿, **Meals (M)**
Localité groupant dans le texte
   les ressources de ses environs .... BELFAST

Ort mit mindestens :

einem Hotel oder Restaurant ● Londonderry
ein angenehmes Hotel oder Restaurant . 🏨🏨, ⋔, ✗
einem sehr ruhigen und abgelegenen Hotel ⨭
einem Restaurant mit ✿, ✿✿, ✿✿✿, **Meals (M)**
Ort mit Angaben über Hotels und Restaurants
   in seiner Umgebung .... BELFAST

(Áth na Long) Down 405 O 5 Ireland G. – pop. 1 823 – ✪ 039 67.

Exc. : W : Mourne Mountains** : Bryansford, Tollymore Forest Park** *AC*, Annalong Marine Park and Cornmill* *AC* – Silent Valley Reservoir* (≼*) – Spelga Pass and Dam* – Drumena Cashel and Souterrain* – Kilbroney Forest Park (viewpoint*).

♦Belfast 37 – ♦Dundalk 36.

🏠 **Glassdrumman Lodge** ⌖, 85 Mill Rd, BT34 4RH, *𝒫* 68451, Fax 67041, ≼ Irish Sea and Mourne mountains, « Working farm », ☞, park – 📺 ☎ 🅿. 🖭 *VISA* . ⌖
M (communal dining) (dinner only) 25.00 **t.** and a la carte 15.00/25.00 **t.** ⌖ 5.00 – **8 rm** ⌑ 65.00/95.00 **t.**, 1 suite – SB (winter only) (except Christmas and New Year) 60.00/100.00 **st.**

(Bealach Cláir) Antrim 405 N/O 3 – ✪ 0232.

🏌 25 Springvale Rd *𝒫* 096 03 (Carrickfergus) 42352, N : 2 m. by B 94.

♦Belfast 10 – Ballymena 14 – Larne 10.

XX **Ginger Tree**, 29 Ballyrobert Rd, BT39 9RY, S : 3¼ m. by A 57 on B 56 *𝒫* 848176 – 🅿. 🖭 AE ① *VISA* JCB
closed Saturday lunch, Sunday, 12-13 July and 24 to 26 December – **M** - **Japanese** 10.25/27.70 **t.** and dinner a la carte ⌖ 5.00.

(An Baile Meánach) Antrim 405 N 3 Ireland G. – pop. 28 166 – ✪ 0266.

Exc. : Antrim Glens*** : Murlough Bay*** (Fair Head ≼***) Glengariff Forest Park** *AC* (Waterfall**) Glengariff*, Glendun*, Rathlin Island* – Antrim (Shane's Castle Railway* *AC*, Round Tower*) S : 9½ m. by A 26.

🏌 128 Raceview Rd *𝒫* 861207, NE : 2 m. by A 42.

🄳 Ardeevin, Ballymena Council Offices, 80 Galgorm Rd, BT42 1AB *𝒫* 44111 – Morrows Shop, 17 Bridge St. *𝒫* 653663 (summer only).

♦Belfast 28 – ♦Dundalk 78 – Larne 21 – ♦Londonderry 51 – ♦Omagh 53.

🏠 **Country House** ⌖, 20 Doagh Rd, BT42 3LZ, SE : 6 m. by A 36 on B 59 *𝒫* 891663, Fax 891477, *Ⅰ₄*, ≋s, ☞ – 📺 ☎ 🅿 – ⩔ 150. 🖭 AE ① *VISA* . ⌖
closed 25 and 26 December – **M** 12.00/18.00 **t.** and dinner a la carte – **40 rm** ⌑ 70.00/125.00 **t.**

🏠 **Adair Arms**, 1-5 Ballymoney Rd, BT43 5BS, *𝒫* 653674, Fax 40436 – 📺 ☎ 🅿 – ⩔ 250. 🖭 AE ① *VISA*
closed 25 and 26 December – **M** 16.95 **st.** (dinner) and a la carte 8.25/15.00 **st.** – **39 rm** ⌑ 55.00/75.00 **st.** – SB (weekends only) 76.00/90.00 **st.**

XX **Water Margin**, 8-10 Cully Backey Rd, BT43 5DF, *𝒫* 48368 – 🅿. 🖭 AE ① *VISA*
M - Chinese 7.95/18.00 **st.** and a la carte ⌖ 5.50.

🔧 ATS Antrim Rd *𝒫* 652888

(Baile na hInse) Down 405 O 4 Ireland G. – pop. 3 721 – ✪ 0238.

Exc. : Rowallane Gardens, Saintfield* *AC*, NE : 7 m. by A 24, A 21 and A 7 – Loughinisland Churches*, SE : 7 m. by A 24 – Inch Abbey* *AC*, SE : 8 m. by A 24, B 2 and A 7 – Downpatrick (Down Cathedral*, Down County Museum*), SE : 24 m. by A 24 and A 7.

🏌 The Spa, 20 Grove Rd *𝒫* 562365, S : ½ m.

🄳 55 Windmill St., BT24 8HB *𝒫* 561950.

♦Belfast 14 – Downpatrick 10.

X **Woodlands**, 29 Spa Rd, BT24 8PT, SW : 1½ m. by A 24 on B 175 *𝒫* 562650, ☞ – 🅿. 🖭 *VISA*
closed Sunday to Wednesday – **M** (booking essential) (dinner only) 19.95 **st.** ⌖ 4.00.

See : City★ - Ulster Museum★★ (Spanish Armada Treasure★★, Shrine of St. Patrick's Hand★) AZ **M1** – City Hall★ BZ – Donegall Square★ BZ **20** – Botanic Gardens (Palm House★) AZ – St Anne's Cathedral★ BY – Crown Liquor Saloon★ BZ – Sinclair Seamen's Church★ BY – St Malachy's Church★ BZ.

Envir. : Belfast Zoological Gardens★★ *AC*, N : 5 m. by A 6 AY.

Exc. : Carrickfergus (Castle★★ *AC*, St. Nicholas' Church★) NE : 9 ½ m. by A 2 – Talnotry Cottage Bird Garden, Crumlin★ *AC*, W : 13 ½ m. by A 52.

ᵣₐ Balmoral, 518 Lisburn Rd ✆ 381514, SW : 2 m. AZ – ᵣₐ Belvoir Park, Newtonbreda ✆ 641159/692817, S : 2 ½ m. AZ – ᵣₐ Fortwilliam, Downview Av. ✆ 370770, N : 2 ½ m. AY – ᵣₐ The Knock, Summerfield, Dundonald ✆ 482249, E : 4 m. by A 20 AZ – ᵣₐ Shandon Park, 73 Shandon Park ✆ 793730, SE : 3 m. by A 55 AZ – ᵣₐ Cliftonville, Westland Rd ✆ 744158, NW : 1 ½ m. AY – ᵣₐ Ormeau, 50 Park Rd ✆ 641069, SE : 1 m. AZ.

✈ Belfast Airport ✆ 0849 (Crumlin) 422888, W : 15 ½ m. by A 52 AY Belfast City Airport, ✆ 457745 – **Terminal** : Coach service (Ulsterbus Ltd.) from Great Victoria Street Station (40 mn).

⚓ to Isle of Man : Douglas (Isle of Man Steam Packet Co.) (summer only) (4 h 30 mn) – by Hoverspeed : to Stranraer (1h 30 mn).

🛈 St. Annes Court, 59 North St., BT1 1NB ✆ 246609 – City Hall, BT1 5GS ✆ 320202 – Belfast City Airport, Sydenham Bypass, BT3 9JH ✆ 457745.

◆Dublin 103 – ◆Londonderry 70.

Plans on following pages

🏨 **Stormont,** 587 Upper Newtownards Rd, BT4 3LP, E : 4 ½ m. by A 2 on A 20 ✆ 658621, Fax 480240 – |‡| ⇆ rm 🆃🆅 ☎ 🕭 🅿 – 🔬 400. 🅧 🆀🅴 ⓞ 🆅🆂🅰 . ⁓⁓   AZ
closed Christmas Day – **M** 13.50/21.50 **st.** and a la carte ♦ 5.50 – **106 rm** 80.00/150.00 **st.** – SB (weekends only) 160.00/220.00 **st.**

🏨 **Dukes,** 65 University St., BT7 1HL, ✆ 236666, Fax 237177, ℹ, ≋s – |‡| ⇆ rm ⊟ rest 🆃🆅 ☎ 🕭 – 🔬 140. 🅧 🆀🅴 ⓞ 🆅🆂🅰 . ⁓⁓   AZ **a**
M (bar lunch Saturday) 8.50 **st.** (lunch) and a la carte 13.40/17.40 **st.** ♦ 4.00 – ☷ 6.50 – **21 rm** 69.00/79.00 **st.**

🏨 **Plaza,** 15 Brunswick St., BT2 7GE, ✆ 333555, Fax 232999 – |‡| ⇆ rm 🆃🆅 ☎ 🕭 – 🔬 75. 🅧 🆀🅴 ⓞ 🆅🆂🅰 . ⁓⁓   BZ **a**
M 9.95/15.00 **t.** and a la carte ♦ 3.95 – ☷ 3.95 – **70 rm** 35.00/79.00 **st.** – SB (weekends only) 60.00/100.00 **st.**

🏠 **Stranmillis Lodge** without rest., 14 Chlorine Gdns, BT9 5DJ, ✆ 682009, Fax 682009 – ⇆ 🆃🆅 ☎ 🅿. 🅧 🆅🆂🅰 . ⁓⁓   AZ **x**
6 rm ☷ 28.00/56.00 **st.**

⌂ **Ash Rowan** without rest., 12 Windsor Av., BT9 6EE, ✆ 661758, Fax 663227, ⚘ – 🆃🆅 ☎ 🅿. 🅧 🆅🆂🅰 . ⁓⁓   AZ **c**
closed 23 to 31 December – **4 rm** ☷ 38.00/66.00 **st.**

⌂ **Malone** without rest., 79 Malone Rd, BT9 6SH, ✆ 669565 – 🆃🆅 🅿. ⁓⁓   AZ **n**
closed mid July, Christmas and New Year – **8 rm** ☷ 22.00/45.00 **st.**

⌂ **Somerton,** 22 Lansdowne Rd, BT15 4DB, by Fortwilliam Park ✆ 370717, ⚘ – 🆃🆅   AY **i**
M (by arrangement) – **8 rm.**

XX ✿ **Roscoff** (Rankin), 7 Lesley House, Shaftesbury Sq., BT2 7DB, ✆ 331532, « Art Deco influenced interior » – ≣. 🅧 🆀🅴 🆅🆂🅰   AZ **r**
closed 11-12 July and 25-26 December – **M** 13.50/18.50 **t.** and a la carte 24.40/29.95 **t.** ♦ 5.00
Spec. Char-grilled salmon with a sun-dried tomato vinaigrette. Crisp duck confit and foie gras with savoy cabbage and a truffle butter. Warm apricot soufflé laced with Cointreau.

XX **Antica Roma,** 67/69 Botanic Av., BT7 1JL, ✆ 311121, Fax 310787 – 🅧 🆀🅴 🆅🆂🅰   AZ **z**
closed lunch Saturday and Sunday – **M** 11.15/30.00 **st.** and dinner a la carte ♦ 3.95.

X **Nick's Warehouse,** 35-39 Hill St. (1st Floor), BT1 2LB, ✆ 439690 – ≣. 🅧 ⓞ 🆅🆂🅰 BY **a**
closed Saturday lunch, Monday dinner, Sunday, 12-13 July and 25-26 December – **M** a la carte 13.70/19.85 **t.** ♦ 3.70.

X **Restaurant Forty Four,** 44 Bedford St., BT2 7FF, ✆ 244844 – ≣. 🅧 🆀🅴 ⓞ 🆅🆂🅰   BZ **e**
closed Saturday lunch, Sunday and Bank Holidays – **M** 13.95/22.00 **t.** and a la carte ♦ 4.95.

X **La Belle Epoque,** 61-63 Dublin Rd, BT2 7HE, ✆ 323244 – 🅧 🆀🅴 ⓞ 🆅🆂🅰   AZ **o**
closed Saturday lunch and Sunday – **M** a la carte 12.15/20.40 **st.** ♦ 4.00.

X **Manor House,** 43-47 Donegall Pass, BT7 1DQ, ✆ 238755 – 🅧 ⓞ 🆅🆂🅰   AZ **u**
closed 12-13 July and 25-26 December – **M** - **Chinese** (Canton) 5.50/13.50 **t.** and a la carte ♦ 3.95.

X **Strand,** 12 Stranmillis Rd, BT9 5AA, ✆ 682266 – 🅧 🆀🅴 ⓞ 🆅🆂🅰   AZ **e**
M - Bistro a la carte approx. 12.00 **st.** ♦ 3.95.

X **Saints and Scholars,** 3 University St., BT7 1FY, ✆ 325137, Fax 323240 – 🅧 🆀🅴 ⓞ 🆅🆂🅰   AZ **s**
closed 12 July and 25 December – **M** 8.95 **st.** and a la carte 9.70/15.30 **st.** ♦ 4.45.

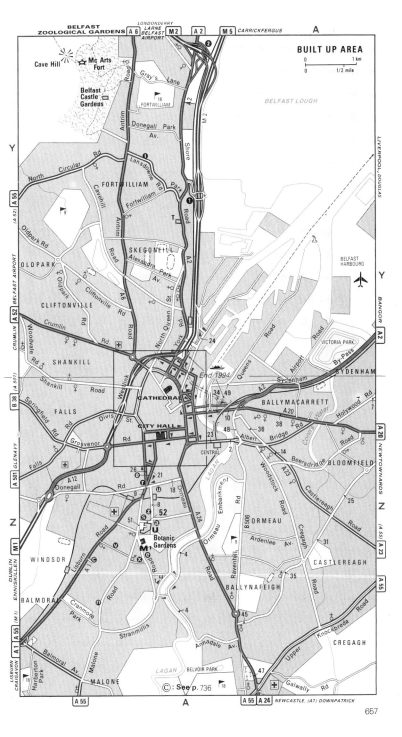

BELFAST

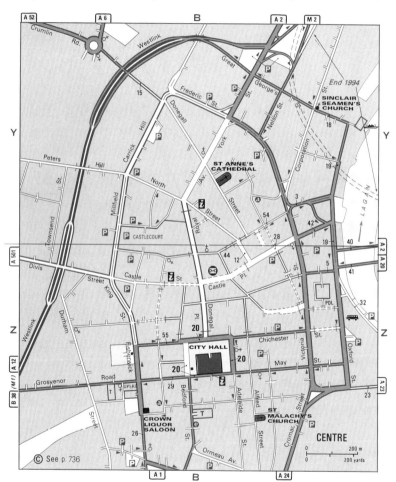

In Northern Ireland traffic and parking are controlled in the town centres. No vehicle may be left unattended in a Control Zone.

The names of main shopping streets are indicated in red at the beginning of the list of streets.

at Dundonald E : 5 ½ m. by A 2 – AZ – on A 20 – ✉ Belfast – ✆ 0247 Comber :

↑ **Cottage** without rest., 377 Comber Rd, BT16 0XB, SE : 1 ¾ m. on Comber Rd ℰ 878189, 🌫 – ✜ 🅿 . ⛝
  3 rm � 16.00/32.00 **st.**

at Dunmurry SW : 5 ½ m. on A 1 – AZ – ✉ ✆ 0232 Belfast :

🏨 **Forte Crest,** 300 Kingsway, BT17 9ES, ℰ 612101, Fax 626546, 🌫, park, squash – 📳
  ✜ rm ▤ rest 📺 ☎ 🅿 – 🔬 400. 🖪 🖽 ◍ 𝘝𝘐𝘚𝘈
  M *(closed Saturday lunch)* 12.00/18.00 **t.** and a la carte ⅄ 4.85 – � 8.95 – **80 rm** 85.00 **st.**,
  2 suites – SB (weekends only) 70.00/90.00 **st.**

MICHELIN Distribution Centre, Mallusk Park, 40 Mallusk Rd, Newtonabbey, BT36 8FS,
ℰ 842616, Fax 342732 by A6 AY

◍ ATS 4 Duncrue St. ℰ 749531   ATS 37 Boucher Rd ℰ 663623

(Aerphort Béal Feirste) Antrim 𝟺𝟶𝟻 N 4 – ✉ Aldergrove – ✆ 0849 Crumlin
🛫 Belfast Airport ℰ 422888.

◆Belfast 15 – Ballymena 20 – Larne 23.

🏨 **Novotel Belfast,** Aldergrove, BT29 4AB, ℰ 422033, Fax 423500, 🎿, ≋ – 📳 ✜ rm ▤
  📺 ♿ & 🅿 – 🔬 250. 🖪 🖽 ◍ 𝘝𝘐𝘚𝘈
  M 15.00 **st.** and a la carte ⅄ 5.00 – **108 rm** � 64.50/72.50 **st.** – SB (weekends only)
  74.50/129.00 **st.**

*Your recommendation is self-evident if you always walk into a
hotel Guide in hand.*

(Béal Leice) Fermanagh 𝟺𝟶𝟻 H 4 – ✆ 036 56.

◆Belfast 117 – ◆Londonderry 56.

↑ **Moohan's Fiddlestone** without rest., Main St., BT93 3FY, ℰ 58008 – 🖪 🖽 ◍ 𝘝𝘐𝘚𝘈. ⛝
  5 rm � 15.00/30.00 **st.**

(Muileann na Buaise) Antrim 𝟺𝟶𝟻 M 2 Ireland G. – pop. 1 381 – ✉ Bushmills –
✆ 026 57.
Exc. : Causeway Coast★★ : Giant's Causeway★★★ (Hamilton's Seat ⩽★★), Carrick-a-rede Rope
Bridge★★★, Dunluce Castle★★ *AC*, Gortmore Viewpoint★★ – Magilligan Strand★★, Downhill★
(Mussenden Temple★).
🏌 Bushfoot, Portballintrae ℰ 31317, NW : 1 m.

◆Belfast 57 – Ballycastle 12 – Coleraine 10.

🏨 **Bushmills Inn,** 25 Main St., BT57 8QA, ℰ 32339, Fax 32048 – 📺 ☎ 🅿 – 🔬 60. 🖪 𝘝𝘐𝘚𝘈
  M a la carte 9.75/17.00 **t.** ⅄ 4.95 – **11 rm** � 48.00/74.00 **st.**

(Carraig Ceasail) Londonderry – see Coleraine.

(Cúil Raithin) Londonderry 𝟺𝟶𝟻 L 2 Ireland G. – pop. 15 967 – ✆ 0265.
Exc. : Antrim Glens★★★ : Murlough Bay★★★ (Fair Head ⩽★★★), Glenariff Forest Park★★ *AC*
(Waterfall★★) – Glenariff★, Glendun★, Rathlin Island★ – Causeway Coast★★ : Giant's Cause-
way★★★ (Hamilton's Seat ⩽★★) - Carrick-a-rede Rope Bridge★★★ - Dunluce Castle★★ *AC* –
Gortmore Viewpoint★★ - Magilligan Strand★★ - Downhill★ (Mussenden Temple★).
🏌, 🏌 Castlerock, Circular Rd ℰ 828314, NW : 6 m. by A 2 – 🏌 Brown Trout, 209 Agivey Rd
ℰ 868209.
🖻 Railway Rd, BT52 1PE ℰ 44723.

◆Belfast 53 – Ballymena 25 – ◆Londonderry 31 – ◆Omagh 65.

🏨 **Blackheath House** 🌫, 112 Killeague Rd, Blackhill, BT51 4HH, S : 8 m. by A 29 on
  Macosquin rd ℰ 868433, Fax 868433, 🌫 – ✜ rest 📺 🅿 . 🖪 𝘝𝘐𝘚𝘈. ⛝
  M - **Macduffs** (closed Sunday and Monday) (booking essential) (dinner only) a la
  carte 13.50/20.00 **t.** ⅄ 4.00 – **5 rm** � 30.00/60.00 **t.**

↑ **Greenhill House** 🌫, 24 Greenhill Rd, Aghadowey, BT51 4EU, S : 9 m. by A 29 on B 66
  ℰ 868241, 🌫 – 📺 🅿 . 🖪 𝘝𝘐𝘚𝘈. ⛝
  March-October – **M** (by arrangement) 12.50 – **6 rm** � 25.00/40.00 – SB 63.00/72.00 **st.**

↑ **Camus House** 🌫 without rest., 27 Curragh Rd, BT51 3RY, SE : 3 ¾ m. on a A 54 ℰ 42982,
  🎣, 🌫, park – 🅿 . ⛝
  3 rm � 20.00/34.00 **st.**

at Castlerock NW : 6 m. by A 2 on B 119 – ✉ ✆ 0265 Castlerock :

↑ **Maritima** without rest., 43 Main St., BT51 4RA, ℰ 848388, ⩽, 🌫 – 📺 🅿 . ⛝
  3 rm � 19.00/36.00.

◍ ATS Loguestown Ind. Est., Bushmills Rd ℰ 42329

CRAWFORDSBURN (Sruth Chráfard) Down 405 O 4 Ireland G. – pop. 140 – ✪ 0247 Helen's Bay.

Envir. : Heritage Centre, Bangor★, E : 3 m. by B 20.

◆Belfast 10 – Bangor 3.

🏨 **Old Inn,** 15 Main St., BT19 1JH, ✆ 853255, Fax 852775, ☞ – 📺 ☎ **Ɒ** – 🔬 35. 🔼 AE ⑩ VISA ✾
M 11.00/16.00 t. and a la carte – **32 rm** ⇋ 59.00/85.00 t.

DUNADRY (Dún Eadradh) Antrim 405 N 3 Ireland G. – ✪ 0849 Templepatrick.

Envir. : Antrim (Round tower★, Shane's Castle Railway★ *AC*) NW : 4 m. by A 6.

Exc. : Crumlin : Talnotry Cottage Bird Garden★ *AC*, SW : 10½ m. by A 5, A 26 and A 52.

◆Belfast 15 – Larne 18 – ◆Londonderry 56.

🏨 **Dunadry Inn,** 2 Islandreagh Drive, BT41 2HA, ✆ 432474, Fax 433389, Ⅰ₆, ⬛, ❦, ☞ – 📺 ☎ **Ɒ** – 🔬 300. 🔼 AE ⑩ VISA ✾
closed 24 to 26 December – **M** (buffet lunch Saturday) 12.50/17.50 **t.** and a la carte ⓙ 4.55 – **67 rm** ⇋ 97.50/120.00 **st.** – SB (weekends only) 87.50/194.00 **st.**

DUNDONALD (Dún Dónaill) Antrim 405 O 4 – see Belfast.

DUNMURRY (Dún Muirígh) Antrim 405 N 4 – see Belfast.

ENNISKILLEN (Inis Ceithleann) Fermanagh 405 J 4 Ireland G. – pop. 10 429 – ✪ 0365.

Envir. : Castle Coole★★★ *AC*, SE : 1 m.

Exc. : NW : Lough Erne★★ :- Cliffs of Magho Viewpoint★★★ *AC* – Devenish Island★ *AC* – Castle Archdale Country Park★ – White Island★ - Janus Figure★ – Tully Castle★ *AC* – Florence Court★★ *AC*, SW : 8 m. by A 4 and A 32 – Marble Arch Caves and Forest Nature Reserve★★ *AC*, SW : 10 m. by A 4 and A 32.

🖇 Castlecoole ✆ 325250, SE : 1 m.

🅱 Lakeland Visitors Centre, Wellington Rd, BT74 7EF ✆ 323110.

◆Belfast 87 – ◆Londonderry 59.

🏨 **Killyhevlin,** Dublin Rd, BT74 4AU, SE : 1¾ m. on A 4 ✆ 323481, Fax 324726, ≼, ☞, park – 📺 ☎ **Ɒ** – 🔬 400. 🔼 AE ⑩ VISA ✾
M (carving lunch Sunday) 15.00/17.00 **t.** and a la carte ⓙ 5.00 – **21 rm** ⇋ 42.50/90.00 **st.**, 1 suite – SB 80.00/110.00 **st.**

GLENGORMLEY (Gleann Ghormlaithe) Antrim 405 O 3 – ✉ Newtownabbey – ✪ 0232.

🖇 585 Doagh Rd ✆ 848287, N : 3 m. by A 8.

◆Belfast 6 – Larne 15.

XX **Sleepy Hollow,** 15 Kiln Rd, Ballyhenry, BT36 8SU, N : 2 m. by A 8 (M) off B 56 ✆ 342042 – **Ɒ**. 🔼 AE ⑩ VISA
closed Sunday to Tuesday and 25-26 December – **M** (dinner only) 18.95 **t.** and a la carte ⓙ 3.75.

HILLSBOROUGH (Cromghlinn) Down 405 N 4 Ireland G. – ✪ 0846.

See : Town★ – Fort★.

🅱 The Square, BT26 6AH ✆ 682477.

◆Belfast 13.

🏨 **White Gables,** 14 Dromore Rd, BT26 6HU, SW : ½ m. on A 1 ✆ 682755, Fax 689532 – ✾ rm 🍴 rest 📺 ☎ ♿ **Ɒ** – 🔬 120. 🔼 AE ⑩ VISA ✾
M (closed Saturday lunch and Sunday dinner) 11.50/18.50 **t.** and a la carte ⓙ 4.95 – ⇋ 6.50 – **31 rm** 67.50/97.00 **t.**

X **Hillside,** 21 Main St., BT26 6AE, ✆ 682765 – 🔼 AE ⑩ VISA
closed Sunday dinner – **M** (bar lunch)/dinner a la carte approx. 18.00 **t.** ⓙ 4.95.

HOLYWOOD (Ard Mhic Nasca) Down 405 O 4 Ireland G. – pop. 9 462 – ✪ 0232.

Envir. : Cultra : Ulster Folk and Transport Museum★★ *AC*, NE : 1 m. by A 2.

◆Belfast 5 – Bangor 6.

🏨 **Culloden,** 142 Bangor Rd, BT18 0EX, E : 1½ m. on A 2 ✆ 425223, Fax 426777, ≼, Ⅰ₆, ⬛, ☞, park, ✾, squash – 📺 ☎ & ♿ ✾ rm **Ɒ** – 🔬 500. 🔼 AE ⑩ VISA ✾
closed 24 and 25 December – **M** (closed Saturday lunch) 17.00 **t.** and a la carte – **84 rm** ⇋ 106.00/140.00 **t.**, 7 suites – SB (weekends only) 128.00/148.00 **st.**

⌂ **Rayanne,** 60 Demesne Rd, BT18 9EX, by High St. and Downshire Rd ✆ 425859, Fax 425859, ☞ – ✾ rest 📺 **Ɒ**. 🔼 VISA ✾
M (by arrangement) approx. 20.00 – **6 rm** ⇋ 50.00/70.00 **t.** – SB (weekends only) 66.00/126.00 **st.**

IRVINESTOWN (Baile an Irbhinigh) Fermanagh 405 J 4 Ireland G. – pop. 1 827 – ۞ 036 56.

Exc. : NW : Lough Erne★★ : Cliffs of Magho Viewpoint★★★ *AC* – Devenish Island★ *AC* – Castle Archdale Country Park★ – White Island★ – Janus Figure★ – Tully Castle★ *AC*.

♦Belfast 78 – ♦Dublin 132 – Donegal 27.

🏠 **Mahon's**, 2-10 Mill St., BT94 1GS, ℰ 21656, Fax 28344 – 📺 ☎ 𝐏 – 🏠 200. ⚊ 𝘝𝘐𝘚𝘈. ⩨
M 7.50/12.00 **t.** and dinner a la carte 🍴 3.45 – **18 rm** ⇌ 29.50/55.00 **st.** – SB (weekends only) 80.00/84.00 **st.**

LARNE (Latharna) Antrim 405 O 3 Ireland G. – pop. 18 224 – ۞ 0574.

Envir. : Glenoe Waterfall★, S : 5 m. by A 2 and B 99 – SE : Island Magee (Ballylumford Dolmen★).

Exc. : NW : Antrim Glens★★★ – Murlough Bay★★★ (Fair Head⩽ ★★★), Glenariff Forest Park★★ *AC* (Waterfall★★), Glenariff★, Glendun★, Rathlin Island★.

🛳 Cairndhu, 192 Coast Rd, Ballygally ℰ 583248, N : 4 m. by A 2.

🚢 to Stranraer (Stena Sealink Line) frequent services daily – to Cairnryan (P & O European Ferries) 4-6 daily (2 h 15 mn).

🛈 Sir Thomas Dixon Buildings, Victoria Rd, BT40 1RU ℰ 272313 – Carnfunnock County Park, Coast Road ℰ 270541 – Larne Harbour, BT40 1AQ ℰ 270517 Interpretative Centre, Narrow Guage Rd ℰ 260088.

♦Belfast 23 – Ballymena 20.

🏠 **Magheramorne House** ⏩, 59 Shore Rd, Magheramorne, BT40 3HW, S : 3½ m. on A 2 ℰ 279444, Fax 260138, ⩽, ⩨, park – 🖼 📺 ☎ 𝐏 – 🏠 50. ⚊ 𝘈𝘌 ⓞ 𝘝𝘐𝘚𝘈. ⩨
M (bar lunch Monday to Saturday)/dinner 14.95 **t.** and a la carte – **22 rm** ⇌ 53.50/72.00 **t.** – SB (weekends only) 69.95/90.00 **st.**

⌂ **Derrin House** without rest., 2 Prince's Gdns, BT40 1RQ, off Glenarm Rd (A 2) ℰ 273269 – 📺 𝐏
7 rm ⇌ 17.00/32.00 **s.**

⑩ ATS Narrow Gauge Rd ℰ 274491

LONDONDERRY (Doire) Londonderry 405 K 2-3 Ireland G. – pop. 62 697 – ۞ 0504.

See : Town★ – City Walls and Gates★★ – Guildhall★ – St. Columb's Cathedral★ *AC* – Long Tower Church★.

Envir. : Grianan of Aileach★★ (⩽ ★) (Republic of Ireland) NW : 5 m. by A 2 and N 13.

Exc. : SE : by A 6 – Sperrin Mountains★ : Ulster-American Folk Park★★ – Glenshane Pass★★ (✳★★) – Sawel Mountain Drive★ (⩽★★) – Roe Valley Country Park★ – Ness Wood Country Park★ – Sperrin Heritage Centre★ *AC* – Beaghmore Stone Circles★ – Ulster History Park★ – Oak Lough Scenic Road★ – Eglinton★ – Gortin Glen Forest Park★ *AC*.

🛳, 🛳 City of Derry, 49 Victoria Rd ℰ 311610/46369.

✈ Eglinton Airport ℰ 810784, E : 6 m. by A 2.

🛈 8 Bishop St., BT48 6PW ℰ 267284 – Glenshane Road, Waterside ℰ 49331 (summer only).

♦Belfast 70 – ♦Dublin 146.

🏠 **Everglades**, Prehen Rd, BT47 2PA, S : 1½ m. by A 5 ℰ 46722, Fax 49200 – 🖼 📺 ☎ 𝐏 – 🏠 350. ⚊ 𝘈𝘌 ⓞ 𝘝𝘐𝘚𝘈. ⩨
closed 24 and 25 December – **M** *(closed Saturday lunch)* 9.95/13.95 **st.** and a la carte 🍴 6.00 – **51 rm** ⇌ 65.00/85.00 **st.**, 1 suite – SB (weekends only) 90.00/150.00 **st.**

🏠 **Beech Hill House** ⏩, 32 Ardmore Rd, BT47 3QP, SE : 3½ m. by A 6 ℰ 49279, Fax 45366, ⩯, ⩨, park – 📺 ☎ 𝐏 – 🏠 100. ⚊ 𝘈𝘌 𝘝𝘐𝘚𝘈. ⩨
closed 25 December – **M** 17.00/25.00 **t.** and a la carte 🍴 4.50 – **17 rm** ⇌ 52.50/100.00 **t.** – SB (weekends only) 95.00/110.00 **st.**

🏠 Broomhill, Limavady Rd, BT47 1LT, ℰ 47995, Fax 49304 – 📺 ☎ 𝐏 – 🏠 250
42 rm.

🏠 **White Horse**, 68 Clooney Rd, BT47 3PA, NE : 6½ m. on A 2 (Coleraine rd) ℰ 860606, Fax 860371 – 📺 ☎ 𝐏 – 🏠 500. ⚊ 𝘈𝘌 ⓞ 𝘝𝘐𝘚𝘈. ⩨
M (grill rest.) 6.95/19.95 **st.** and a la carte – ⇌ 5.25 – **43 rm** 39.00 **st.**

🏠 **Waterfoot**, 14 Clooney Rd, Caw Roundabout, BT47 1TB, NE : 3¾ m. at junction of A 39 with A 5 and A 2 ℰ 45500, Fax 311006 – 📺 ☎ 🅖 𝐏. ⚊ 𝘈𝘌 ⓞ 𝘝𝘐𝘚𝘈. ⩨
M 7.00/18.00 **st.** and a la carte – ⇌ 4.25 – **31 rm** 45.00/55.00 **st.** – SB (April-October) (weekends only) 45.00/80.00 **st.**

NEWCASTLE (An Caisleán Nua) Down 405 O 5 Ireland G. – pop. 6 246 – ۞ 039 67.

Envir. : Castlewellan Forest Park★★ *AC*, NW : 4 m. by A 50 – Dundrum Castle★ *AC*, NE : 4 m. by A 2.

Exc. : SW : Mourne Mountains★★ : Bryansford, Tollymore Forest Park★★ *AC* – Annalong Marine Park and Cornmill★ *AC* – Silent Valley Reservoir★ (⩽★) – Spelga Pass and Dam★ – Drumena Cashel and Souterrain★ – Kilbroney Forest Park (viewpoint★) – Loughinisland Churches★, NE : 10 m. by A 2 and A 24.

🛈 The Newcastle Centre, 10-14 Central Promenade, BT33 0AA ℰ 22222 (summer only).

♦Belfast 30 – ♦Londonderry 101.

🏠 **Burrendale H. & Country Club**, 51 Castlewellan Rd, BT33 0JY, N : 1 m. on A 50 ℰ 22599, Fax 22328, 🛁, ⩯, 🏊, ⩨ – 🖼 📺 ☎ 🅖 𝐏 – 🏠 150. ⚊ 𝘈𝘌 ⓞ 𝘝𝘐𝘚𝘈 𝘑𝘊𝘉. ⩨
M 10.00/16.00 **t.** and dinner a la carte 🍴 4.00 – **51 rm** ⇌ 55.00/80.00 **t.** – SB (except Easter, Christmas and New Year) 104.00/150.00 **st.**

NEWTOWNARDS (Baile Nua na hArda) Down **405** O 4 Ireland G. – pop. 20 531 – 📞 0247.

See : Priory (Cross Slabs★).

Envir. : Mount Stewart★★★ *AC*, SE : 5 m. by A 20 – Scrabo Tower (≤ ★★★) SW : 1 m. – Ballycopeland Windmill★ *AC*, E : 6 m. by B 172.

Exc. : Strangford Lough★ (Castle Espie Centre★ *AC* - Nendrum Monastery★) – Grey Abbey★ *AC*, SE : 7 m. by A 20.

🐦 Bangor 🏌 62342, N : 5 m. by A 21 – 🐦 Carnalea, Station Rd, Bangor 🏌 465004, N : 5 m. by A 21 – 🐦 Scrabo, 233 Scrabo Rd 🏌 812355, W : 2 m. – 🐦 Helen's Bay, Golf Rd, Bangor 🏌 852601, N : 6½ m. by A 21.

🏢 2 Church St., BT23 4AP 🏌 812215 – Regent Street (summer only).

♦Belfast 10 – Bangor 5.

🏨 **Strangford Arms,** 92 Church St., BT23 4AL, 🏌 814141, Fax 818846 – 🖥 rest 📺 ☎ 🅿 – ⚘ 35. 🔺 🖭 🔟 *VISA* *JCB* ✼
   M 12.00/16.00 **st.** and dinner a la carte ⓙ 2.70 – 🖙 5.75 – **40 rm** 58.00/76.00 **st.** – SB (week-ends only) 60.00 **st.**

PORTAFERRY (Port an Pheire) Down **405** P 4 Ireland G. – pop. 2 148 – 📞 024 77.

See : Aquarium★.

Envir. : Castle Ward★★ *AC*, SW : 4 m. by boat and A 25.

Exc. : SE : Lecale Peninsula★★ – Struell Wells★, Quoile Pondage★, Ardglass★, Strangford★, Audley's Castle★.

🏢 Shore St. (summer only).

♦ Belfast 29 – Bangor 24.

🏨 **Portaferry,** 10 The Strand, BT22 1PE, 🏌 28231, Fax 28999, ≤ – 📺 ☎. 🔺 🖭 🔟 *VISA*. ✼
   M 12.95/16.95 **t.** and a la carte ⓙ 4.75 – **14 rm** 🖙 45.00/80.00 **t.** – SB 49.50/125.00 **st.**

Prices   For full details of the prices quoted in the guide,
              consult the introduction.

PORT BALLINTRAE (Port Bhaile an Trá) Antrim **405** M 2 Ireland G. – pop. 586 – ✉ 📞 026 57 Bushmills.

Exc. : Causeway Coast★★ : Giant's Causeway★★★ (Hamilton's Seat ≤★★) – Carrick-a-rede Rope Bridge★★★ – Dunluce Castle★★ *AC* – Gortmore Viewpoint★★ – Magilligan Strand★★ – Downhill★ (Mussenden Temple★).

♦Belfast 68 – Coleraine 15.

🏨 **Bayview,** 2 Bayhead Rd, BT57 8RZ, 🏌 31453, Fax 32360, ≤, ≈s, 🔺 – 📺 ☎ 🅿 – ⚘ 200. 🔺 *VISA* ✼
   M 8.50/12.50 **t.** and a la carte ⓙ 3.75 – **16 rm** 🖙 40.00/70.00 **t.** – SB 80.00/120.00 **st.**

PORTRUSH (Port Rois) Antrim **405** L 2 Ireland G. – pop. 5 114 – 📞 0265.

Exc. : Causeway Coast★★ : Giant's Causeway★★★ (Hamilton's Seat ≤★★) – Carrick-a-rede Rope Bridge★★★ – Dunluce Castle★★ *AC* – Gortmore Viewpoint★★ – Magilligan Strand★★ – Downhill★ (Mussenden Temple★).

🐦, 🐦, 🐦 Royal Portrush, Dunluce Rd 🏌 822311.

🏢 Town Hall, Mark St., BT56 8BT 🏌 823333 (summer only).

♦Belfast 58 – Coleraine 4 – ♦Londonderry 35.

🏨 **Magherabuoy House,** 41 Magheraboy Rd, BT56 8NX, SW : 1 m. by A 29 🏌 823507, Fax 824687, ≤, ≈s, 🌿 – 📺 ☎ 🅿 – ⚘ 400. 🔺 🖭 🔟 *VISA*. ✼
   closed Christmas Day – **M** (bar lunch Monday to Saturday)/dinner 17.00 **st.** and a la carte –
   38 rm 🖙 50.00/75.00 **st.** – SB 100.00/130.00 **st.**

🏨 **Causeway Coast,** 36 Ballyreagh Rd, BT56 8LR, NW : 1¼ m. on A 2 (Portstewart rd) 🏌 822435, Fax 824495, ≤ – 📺 ☎ 🅿 – ⚘ 500. 🔺 🖭 🔟 *VISA*. ✼
   M 9.50/14.50 **st.** ⓙ 4.20 – **21 rm** 🖙 45.00/60.00 **st.**

↑ **Glencroft,** 95 Coleraine Rd, BT56 8HN, 🏌 822902, 🌿 – ✼ rest 📺 🅿. ✼
   closed 2 weeks November and 2 weeks Christmas – **M** (by arrangement) 14.00 **st.** – **5 rm** 🖙 32.00/36.00 **st.** – SB (except July, August and Bank Holidays) 54.00/58.00 **st.**

🍴 **Ramore,** The Harbour, BT56 8DQ, 🏌 824313, ≤ – 🖥 🅿. 🔺 *VISA*
   closed Sunday and Monday – **Meals** (booking essential) (dinner only) a la carte 11.85/21.90 **t.**

PORTSTEWART (Port Stíobhaird) Londonderry **405** L 2 Ireland G. – pop. 5 312 – 📞 0265.

Exc. : Causeway Coast★★ : Giant's Causeway★★★ (Hamilton's Seat ≤★★) – Carrick-a-rede Rope Bridge★★★ – Dunluce Castle★★ *AC* – Gortmore Viewpoint★★ – Magilligan Strand★★ – Downhill★ (Mussenden Temple★).

🏢 Town Hall, The Crescent, BT55 7AB 🏌 832286 (summer only).

♦Belfast 67 – Coleraine 6.

🏨 **Edgewater,** 88 Strand Rd, BT55 7LZ, 🏌 833314, Fax 833315, ≤, ≈s – 📺 ☎ 🅿. 🔺 🖭 🔟 *VISA* ✼
   M 10.00/15.00 **t.** and dinner a la carte – **31 rm** 🖙 39.00/76.00 **t.** – SB 66.00/92.00 **st.**

SAINTFIELD (Tamhnaigh Naomh) Down **405** O 4 – ✿ 0238.

◆Belfast 11 – Downpatrick 11.

※ **The Barn,** 120 Monlough Rd, BT24 7EU, NW : 1 ¾ m. by A 7 ✆ 510396, ☞ – **ℙ**. ◫ _VISA_
closed Sunday dinner October-May. Tuesday (June-September) and Monday – **M** (dinner only and Sunday lunch)/dinner 18.50 **t.** � 5.50.

STRABANE (An Srath Bán) Tyrone **405** J 3 Ireland G. – pop. 10 340 – ✿ 0504.

Exc. : Sperrin Mountains★ : Ulster-American Folk Park★★ – Glenshane Pass★★ (⁂★★) – Sawel Mountain Drive★ (≤★★) – Roe Valley Country Park★ – Ness Wood Country Park★ – Sperrin Heritage Centre★ AC – E : Beaghmore Stone Circles★ – Ulster History Park★ – Oak Lough Scenic Road★ – Eglinton★ – Gortin Glen Forest Park★ AC.

⛳ Ballycolman ✆ 382271/382007.

🛈 Abercorn Square ✆ 883735 (summer only) – Council Offices, 47 Derry Rd ✆ 382204.

◆Belfast 87 – Donegal 34 – ◆Dundalk 98 – ◆Londonderry 14.

🏨 **Fir Trees,** Melmount Rd, BT82 9JT, S : 1 ¼ m. on A 5 ✆ 382382, Fax 885932 – ◫ ☎ **ℙ**. ◫ ⒶⒺ ① _VISA_ ⁂
M 8.50/13.50 **st.** and dinner a la carte ⎮ 4.00 – **26 rm** ⊃ 44.00/62.00 **st.** – SB 60.00/68.00 **st.**

TEMPLEPATRICK (Teampall Phádraig) Antrim **405** N 3 – pop. 735 – ✉ Ballyclave – ✿ 084 94.

◆Belfast 12 – Ballymena 16 – ◆Dundalk 65 – Larne 16.

🏨 **Templeton,** 882 Antrim Rd, BT39 0AH, ✆ 32984, Fax 33406, ☞ – ◫ ☎ **ℙ** – ⛫ 300. ◫ ⒶⒺ ① _VISA_ ⁂
closed 24 to 26 December – **M** (bar lunch Monday to Saturday)/dinner 14.95 **st.** ⎮ 5.25 – **20 rm** ⊃ 50.00/125.00 **st.** – SB (weekends only) 90.00/130.00 **st.**

WARINGSTOWN (Baile an Bhairínigh) Armagh **405** N 4 Ireland G. – pop. 1 167 – ✿ 0762.

Exc. : The Argory★, W : 20 m. by A 26, A 76 and M 1.

◆Belfast 26 – Craigavon 4.

※※ **Grange,** Main St., BT66 7QH, ✆ 881989, ☞ – **ℙ**
closed Saturday lunch, Sunday dinner, Monday, 1 week mid July and 26 December – **M** 18.20/23.65 **t.** and a la carte ⎮ 3.90.

Channel
Islands

Place with at least :

one hotel or restaurant .... ● Catel
a pleasant hotel or restaurant .. 🏨, ⌂, ✗
one quiet, secluded hotel .... 🅢
one restaurant with .. ✿, ✿✿, ✿✿✿, **Meals (M)**
See this town for establishments
  located in its vicinity .... **GOREY**

Localité offrant au moins :

une ressource hôtelière .... ● Catel
un hôtel ou restaurant agréable 🏨, ⌂, ✗
un hôtel très tranquille, isolé .... 🅢
une bonne table à ✿, ✿✿, ✿✿✿, **Meals (M)**
Localité groupant dans le texte
  les ressources de ses environs ..... **GOREY**

La località possiede come minimo :

una risorsa alberghiera .... ● Catel
Albergo o ristorante ameno .... 🏨, ⌂, ✗
un albergo molto tranquillo, isolato ...... 🅢
un'ottima tavola con . ✿, ✿✿, ✿✿✿, **Meals (M)**
La località raggruppa nel suo testo
  le risorse dei dintorni .... **GOREY**

Ort mit mindestens :

einem Hotel oder Restaurant .... ● Catel
ein angenehmes Hotel oder Restaurant . 🏨, ⌂, ✗
einem sehr ruhigen und abgelegenen Hotel 🅢
einem Restaurant mit ✿, ✿✿, ✿✿✿, **Meals (M)**
Ort mit Angaben über Hotels und Restaurants
  in seiner Umgebung .... **GOREY**

ALDERNEY

Braye ●
St.Anne ●

ALDERNEY

GUERNSEY

Pembroke Bay — L'Ancresse
Vale
Vazon Bay
Catel — St.Peter Port
St.Saviour
St. Peter in the Wood — St.Martin
Forest — Fermain Bay

HERM

SARK

JERSEY

Greve de Lecq — Bonne Nuit Bay
Bouley Bay — Rozel Bay
St. Martin
St. Lawrence
St.Peter
St.Saviour ✿ 🏨 GOREY M
La Haule
La Pulente
St.Aubin — Grouville
St.Brelade's Bay — St.Helier
Corbiere — St. Clement

ALDERNEY 🟦🟦🟦 Q 33 and 🟦🟦🟦 ⑨ The West Country G. – pop. 2 068 – ECD : Wednesday – ✪ 0481.

See : Braye Bay★ – Mannez Garenne (≼★ from Quesnard Lighthouse) – Telegraph Bay★ – Vallee des Trois Vaux★ – Clonque Bay★.

✈ 🖉 822851 - Booking Office : Aurigny Air Services 🖉 822889, Air Ferries 🖉 822993.

🛈 States Office, Queen Elizabeth II St. 🖉 822994/823737.

St. Anne – ⬛ St. Anne – ✪ 0481 Alderney.

🚏 Route des Carrières 🖉 822835, E : 1 m.

🏠 **Inchalla** ⬙, Le Val, GY9 3UL, 🖉 823220, Fax 823551, ⇔, ≋ – 🆃🆅 ☎ 🅿. ᴎ ᴀᴇ 𝖵𝖨𝖲𝖠 ✻
closed 23 December-2 January – **M** (closed Sunday dinner) (dinner only and Sunday lunch)/dinner 12.00 and a la carte ⅃ 3.00 – ⬜ 5.50 – **10 rm** 31.00/66.00.

🏠 **Chez André**, Victoria St., 🖉 822777, Fax 822962 – 🆃🆅 ☎. ᴎ ᴀᴇ 𝖵𝖨𝖲𝖠
M 13.50 and a la carte ⅃ 4.00 – **11 rm** ⬜ 29.00/80.00 – SB (except August and Christmas) (weekdays only) 85.00/120.00.

🏠 **Rose and Crown**, Le Huret, 🖉 823414, Fax 823615, ≋ – 🆃🆅 ☎. ᴎ 𝖵𝖨𝖲𝖠 ✻
M (in bar) (closed Sunday) a la carte approx. 8.50 **s.** – **6 rm** ⬜ 35.00/70.00 **s.**

🏡 **Belle Vue**, The Butes, 🖉 822844, Fax 823601 – 🆃🆅 ☎. ᴎ ᴀᴇ ⑩ 𝖵𝖨𝖲𝖠 ✻
closed 25 and 26 December – **M** 7.50/10.00 and a la carte ⅃ 4.50 – **29 rm** ⬜ 31.00/62.00.

🍴🍴 **Nellie Gray's**, Victoria St., GY9 3TA, 🖉 823333, ≋ – ᴎ ᴀᴇ ⑩ 𝖵𝖨𝖲𝖠
April-September – **M** (closed Monday to Thursday) a la carte 11.00/21.50 ⅃ 3.80.

🍴 **Georgian House**, Victoria St., GY9 3UF, 🖉 822471, Fax 822471 – ᴎ ᴀᴇ ⑩ 𝖵𝖨𝖲𝖠
M (restricted lunch) 15.00 and a la carte 12.00/21.00 ⅃ 3.75.

Braye – ⬛ Braye – ✪ 0481 Alderney.

🍴 **First and Last**, 🖉 823162, ≼ harbour – ᴎ ᴀᴇ ⑩ 𝖵𝖨𝖲𝖠 𝖩𝖢𝖡
closed Sunday dinner, Monday and October-March – **M** a la carte 14.70/26.25 ⅃ 3.75.

GUERNSEY 🟦🟦🟦 OP 33 and 🟦🟦🟦 ⑨ ⑩ The West Country G. – pop. 53 637 – ✪ 0481.

See : Island★ – Pezeries Point★★ – Icart Point★★ – Côbo Bay★★ – St. Martins Point★★ – St. Apolline's Chapel★ – Vale Castle★ – Fort Doyle★ – La Gran'mere du Chimquiere★ – Moulin Huet Bay★ – Rocquaine Bay★ – Jerbourg Point★.

✈ La Villiaze, Forest 🖉 37766.

🛳 to France (Saint-Malo) (Emeraude Lines) summer only – to Poole (British Channel Island Ferries) – to Herm (Herm Seaways) 7 daily (25 mn).

🛳 to France (Portbail) (Service Maritime Carteret) – to France (Carteret) (Service Maritime Carteret) – to France (St. Malo) via Jersey (St. Helier) (Emeraude Lines) (summer only) – to Weymouth (Condor Ltd : hydrofoil) 2 daily – to Sark (Isle of Sark Shipping Co. Ltd) (summer only) (40 mn) – to Sark (Emeraude Lines) – to Jersey (Channiland) (50 mn) (summer only).

🛈 Crown Pier, St. Peter Port 🖉 723552 – The Airport, La Villiaze, Forest 🖉 37267.

L'Ancresse – ⬛ Vale – ✪ 0481 Guernsey.

🏠 **Lynton Park** ⬙, Hacse Lane, Clos du Valle, GY3 5DS, 🖉 45418, Fax 43581, ≋ – 🆃🆅 ☎ 🅿. ᴎ 𝖵𝖨𝖲𝖠 ✻
M (bar lunch)/dinner 18.00 and a la carte ⅃ 3.80 – **14 rm** ⬜ 28.50/34.00 **s.** – SB (spring and autumn) 50.00/68.00.

Catel – ⬛ Catel – ✪ 0481 Guernsey.

⬆ **Belvoir Farm**, Rue de la Hougue, GY5 7DY, 🖉 56004, �🇹 heated, ≋ – 🆃🆅 🅿. ✻
April-September – **M** (by arrangement) 9.00 **s.** ⅃ 3.00 – **14 rm** ⬜ (dinner included) 43.00/64.00 **s.**

Fermain Bay – ⬛ St. Peter Port – ✪ 0481 Guernsey.

🏨 **La Favorita** ⬙, Fermain Lane, GY4 6SD, 🖉 35666, Fax 35413, ≼, ⇔, ᴎ, ≋ – ↞ rest 🆃🆅 ☎ 🅿. ᴎ ᴀᴇ ⑩ 𝖵𝖨𝖲𝖠 ✻
accommodation closed December-February – **M** (closed 23 December-1 February) 19.00 **s.** (dinner) and a la carte approx. 10.50 **s.** ⅃ 3.75 – **36 rm** ⬜ 39.00/94.00 **s.**

Forest – ⬛ Forest – ✪ 0481 Guernsey.

⬆ **Tudor Lodge Deer Farm**, Forest Rd, GY8 0AG, 🖉 37849, Fax 35662, ≋, park – 🆃🆅 ☎ 🅿. 𝖵𝖨𝖲𝖠 ✻
closed November-14 January – **M** (by arrangement) 15.00 ⅃ 3.25 – **5 rm** ⬜ 30.00/50.00 – SB 61.00/85.00 **s.**

Pembroke Bay – ⬛ Vale – ✪ 0481 Guernsey.

St. Peter Port 5.

🏨 **Pembroke** ⬙, GY3 5BY, 🖉 47573 – 🆃🆅 ☎. ᴎ ᴀᴇ ⑩ 𝖵𝖨𝖲𝖠
closed January, February and November – **M** (bar lunch)/dinner 9.50 and a la carte ⅃ 3.00 – **11 rm** ⬜ 21.00/52.00 – SB 51.00/71.00 **s.**

St. Martin – pop. 5 842 – ECD : Thursday – ✉ St. Martin – ☎ 0481 Guernsey.

St. Peter Port 2.

🏨 **Green Acres** ⬅, Les Hubits, GY4 6LS, ℰ 35711, Fax 35978, ⅃ heated, ℱ – 🍽 rest 📺 ☎ 🄿. 🄰 🄰🄴 𝗩𝗜𝗦𝗔. 🦌
M (bar lunch Monday to Saturday)/dinner 12.50 **s.** and a la carte ⓘ 3.50 – **48 rm** ⊑ 47.50/75.00.

🏨 **Saints Bay** ⬅, Icart, GY4 6JG, ℰ 38888, Fax 35558, ⅃ heated, ℱ – 📺 ☎ 🄿. 🄰 🄰🄴 𝗩𝗜𝗦𝗔. 🦌
April-October – **M** (bar lunch)/dinner 13.50 and a la carte ⓘ 3.60 – **30 rm** ⊑ 53.00/86.00.

🏨 **Idlerocks** ⬅, Jerbourg Point, GY4 6BJ, ℰ 37711, Fax 35592, ≼ sea and neighbouring Channel Islands, ⅃ heated, ℱ – ⅄ rm 📺 ☎ 🄿. 🄰 🄰🄴 ⓞ 𝗩𝗜𝗦𝗔
M 15.00/25.00 and dinner a la carte ⓘ 3.95 – **28 rm** 39.00/160.00 – SB (November-March) 88.00/160.00.

🏨 **Bella Luce**, La Fosse, Moulin Huet, GY4 6EB, ℰ 38764, Fax 39561, ⇄, ⅃ heated, ℱ – 📺 ☎ 🄿. 🄰 𝗩𝗜𝗦𝗔
M (bar lunch Monday to Saturday)/dinner 28.00 and a la carte ⓘ 3.00 – **30 rm** ⊑ 43.50/84.00 – SB (winter only) 66.00/70.00.

🏨 **La Cloche** ⬅, Les Traudes, GY4 6LR, ℰ 35421, Fax 38258, ⅃ heated, ℱ – ⅄ rest 📺 ☎ 🄿. 🄰 𝗩𝗜𝗦𝗔. 🦌
April-October – **M** (residents only) (bar lunch)/dinner 10.00 **s.** ⓘ 3.10 – **10 rm** ⊑ 49.00/68.00 **s.**

🏨 **Ambassador**, Route De Sausmarez, ℰ 38356, Fax 39280, ℱ – 📺 ☎ 🄿. 🄰 𝗩𝗜𝗦𝗔. 🦌
April-October – **M** 10.95 ⓘ 3.50 – **19 rm** ⊑ 35.50/71.00 – SB 50.00/70.00 **s.**

🏨 **Wellesley** without rest., Route De Sausmarez, GY4 6SE, ℰ 38028, Fax 39501, ℱ – 📺 ☎ 🄿. 🄰
April-October – **10 rm** ⊑ 27.50/58.00.

St. Peter in The Wood – ✉ St. Peters – ☎ 0481 Guernsey.

St. Peter Port 6.

🍴 **Café Du Moulin**, Rue du Quanteraine, ℰ 65944 – 🄰 𝗩𝗜𝗦𝗔
closed Sunday dinner, Monday, last 2 weeks February, first 2 weeks March, 1 week June and 2 weeks November – **M** 14.50 (lunch) and a la carte 20.00/23.50 ⓘ 4.50.

St. Peter Port The West Country G. – pop. 15 587 – ECD : Thursday – ✉ St. Peter Port – ☎ 0481 Guernsey.

See : Town★★ - St. Peter's Church★ Z – Hauteville House (Victor Hugo's House)★ *AC* Z – Castle Cornet★ (≼★) *AC* Z.

Envir. : Saumarez Park★, W : 2 m. by road to Catel Z – Little Chapel★, SW : 2¼ m. by Mount Durand road Z.

🏌 St. Pierre Park ℰ 727039, by Grange Rd Z.

Plan on next page

🏨 **St. Pierre Park**, Rohais, GY1 1FD, ℰ 728282, Telex 4191662, Fax 712041, ≼, 🛏, ⇄, 🄽, 🏌, ℱ, park, 🦌 – 🛗 📺 ☎ 🕭 🄿. 🕿 🛎 200. 🄰 🄰🄴 ⓞ 𝗩𝗜𝗦𝗔 🦌   by Grange Rd   Z
M a la carte approx. 11.50 – (see also **Victor Hugo** below) – **131 rm** ⊑ 95.00/135.00 **s.**, 3 suites – SB (except Easter, Christmas and New Year) 152.00/214.00 **s.**

🏨 **Duke of Richmond**, Cambridge Park, GY1 1UY, ℰ 726221, Telex 4191462, Fax 728945, ⅃ heated – 🛗 🍽 rest 📺 ☎ – 🕿 60. 🄰 🄰🄴 ⓞ 𝗩𝗜𝗦𝗔   Y   c
M 10.00/14.00 and a la carte ⓘ 4.00 – **73 rm** ⊑ 45.00/90.00, 1 suite – SB (weekends only) 80.00/128.00 **s.**

🏨 **Old Government House**, Ann's Pl., GY1 4AZ, ℰ 724921, Fax 724429, ≼, ⅃ heated, ℱ – 🛗 📺 ☎ 🄿 – 🕿 100. 🄰 🄰🄴 ⓞ 𝗩𝗜𝗦𝗔 🄹🄲🄱   Y   o
M 11.95/14.75 **s.** and a la carte ⓘ 4.50 – **72 rm** ⊑ 54.00/123.00 – SB (November-March) (weekends only) 76.00/96.00 **s.**

🏨 **De Havelet**, Havelet, GY1 1BA, ℰ 722199, Fax 714057, 🄽, ℱ – 📺 ☎ 🄿. 🄰 🄰🄴 ⓞ 𝗩𝗜𝗦𝗔. 🦌   Z   u
M 12.00/15.00 and dinner a la carte ⓘ 4.00 – **34 rm** ⊑ 42.00/95.00 – SB (November-March) 61.00/102.00.

🏨 **La Collinette**, St. Jacques, GY1 1SN, ℰ 710331, Fax 713516, ⇄, ⅃ heated, ℱ – 📺 ☎ 🄿. 🄰 🄰🄴 ⓞ 𝗩𝗜𝗦𝗔   Y   a
closed January – **M** 8.95/12.50 **s.** and a la carte ⓘ 2.95 – **23 rm** ⊑ (dinner included) 41.50/83.00 **s.** – SB (October-April) 75.00 **s.**

🏨 **Moore's Central**, Le Pollet, GY1 1WH, ℰ 724452, Fax 714037 – 🛗 📺 ☎. 🄰 🄰🄴 ⓞ 𝗩𝗜𝗦𝗔. 🦌   Y   n
M 9.50/12.50 and a la carte ⓘ 4.50 – **51 rm** ⊑ 40.00/175.00 – SB (October-March) 64.00/112.00.

🏨 **Midhurst House**, Candie Rd, GY1 1UP, ℰ 724391, Fax 729451, ℱ – 📺 ☎. 🄰 𝗩𝗜𝗦𝗔. 🦌
Easter-October – **M** (residents only) (dinner only) 8.50 **s.** and a la carte ⓘ 3.20 – **8 rm** ⊑ 43.00/66.00 **s.**   Y   r

🏨 **Abbey Court**, Les Gravées, GY1 1RL, ℰ 720148, Fax 728829, ℱ – 📺 ☎ 🄿. 🄰 🄰🄴 ⓞ 𝗩𝗜𝗦𝗔 🦌   by Grange Rd   Z
Easter-October – **M** (bar lunch) ⓘ 4.00 – **25 rm** ⊑ (dinner included) 35.00/70.00.

ST. PETER PORT

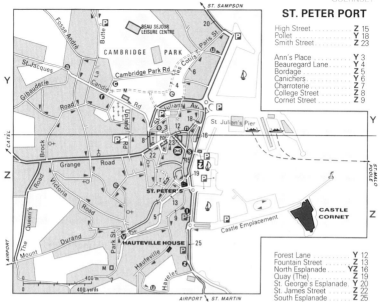

High Street	Z 15
Pollet	Y 18
Smith Street	Z 23
Ann's Place	Y 3
Beauregard Lane	Y 4
Bordage	Z 5
Canichers	Y 6
Charroterie	Z 7
College Street	Z 8
Cornet Street	Z 9

Forest Lane	Y 12
Fountain Street	Z 13
North Esplanade	YZ 16
Quay (The)	Z 19
St. George's Esplanade	Y 20
St. James Street	Z 22
South Esplanade	Z 25

↑ **Kenwood House** without rest., Allez St., GY1 1NG, ℰ 726146 – 🔺 𝘝𝘐𝘚𝘈. ⁂   Z e
   closed 15 to 31 December – **7 rm** ⊆ 27.50/43.00 **s.**

↑ Spes Bona without rest., Les Vardes, via Hauteville ℰ 725149, ⊞ – ⁂   Z
   6 rm.

↑ **Marine** without rest., Well Rd, GY1 1WS, ℰ 724978 – 🔺 𝘝𝘐𝘚𝘈. ⁂   Y u
   11 rm ⊆ 23.50/44.00 **s.**

XXXX **Victor Hugo** (at St. Pierre Park H.), Rohais, GY1 1FD, ℰ 728282, Telex 4191662,
   Fax 712041 – ▤ 🅿. 🔺 𝖠𝖤 ⓪ 𝘝𝘐𝘚𝘈   by Grange Rd   Z
   closed Sunday dinner – **M** 14.75 and a la carte approx. 26.20.

XXX **La Frégate** ⌂ with rm, Les Cotils, GY1 1UT, ℰ 724624, Fax 720443, ≤ town and
   harbour, ⊞ – 📺 ☎ 🅿. 🔺 𝖠𝖤 ⓪ 𝘝𝘐𝘚𝘈. ⁂   Y e
   M 12.50/18.00 **s.** and a la carte ⧍ 4.50 – ⊆ 8.50 – **13 rm** 55.00/95.00 **s.**

XXX **Louisiana**, South Esplanade, GY1 1BJ, ℰ 713157, Fax 712191, ≤ – ▤. 🔺 𝖠𝖤
   𝘝𝘐𝘚𝘈   Z z
   M (closed Monday except Bank Holidays) 29.00 **s.** (dinner) and a la carte 13.75/21.00 **s.**
   ⧍ 4.50.

XX **Four Seasons**, Albert House, South Esplanade, GY1 1AJ, ℰ 727444 – 🔺 𝘝𝘐𝘚𝘈   Z i
   closed Sunday and February – **M** 9.00/11.75 **s.** and a la carte ⧍ 3.75.

XX **The Absolute End**, Longstore, GY1 2BG, N :¾ m. by St. George's Esplanade ℰ 723822,
   Fax 729129 – 🔺 𝖠𝖤 ⓪ 𝘝𝘐𝘚𝘈   Y
   closed Sunday and January – **M** - Seafood 10.00 **s.** (lunch) and a la carte 12.00/26.00 **s.**
   ⧍ 4.00.

XX **La Piazza**, Trinity Sq., GY1 1LX, ℰ 725085 – 🔺 𝖠𝖤 𝘝𝘐𝘚𝘈   Z v
   closed Sunday and 24 December-23 January – **M** - Italian a la carte 13.50/21.30
   ⧍ 3.50.

XX **Le Nautique**, Quay Steps, GY1 2LE, ℰ 721714, Fax 721786, ≤ – 🔺 𝖠𝖤 ⓪ 𝘝𝘐𝘚𝘈
   𝖩𝖢𝖡   Z s
   closed Sunday and first 2 weeks January – **M** a la carte 16.00/21.00 **s.** ⧍ 4.50.

   St. Saviour – pop. 2 432 – ✉ St. Saviour – ☎ 0481 Guernsey.

   St. Peter Port 4.

🏨 **L'Atlantique**, Perelle Bay, ℰ 64056, Fax 63800, ≤, 🌊 heated, ⊞ – 📺 ☎ 🅿. 🔺 𝖠𝖤 ⓪
   𝘝𝘐𝘚𝘈. ⁂
   April-October – **M** (closed Sunday) 9.00/13.90 and dinner a la carte ⧍ 3.50 – **21 rm**
   ⊆ 25.50/76.00.

⌂ **Les Piques Farm** ♨, Rue des Piques, ℘ 64515, Fax 65857, « Part 15C farmhouse », ✍
– 🇹🇻 🄿. 🅈 𝑽𝑰𝑺𝑨. ✋
closed January and February – **M** (residents only) (dinner only) 9.95 and a la carte ╽ 3.25 –
24 rm ⊐ 33.00/72.00.

Vale – ⊠ Vale – ✆ 0481 Guernsey.

🏨 **Peninsula,** Les Dicqs, ℘ 48400, Telex 4191306, Fax 48706, ≼, ⤢ heated, ✍ – |፥| ⤦ rm
🇹🇻 ☎ ♿ 🄿 – ⚕ 180. 🅈 🄰🄴 ⓪ 𝑽𝑰𝑺𝑨 𝐉𝐂𝐁
M (bar lunch Monday to Saturday)/dinner 9.50 **s.** and a la carte ╽ 3.95 – **99 rm** ⊐ 27.50/
86.00 **s.**

Vazon Bay – ⊠ Catel – ✆ 0481 Guernsey.

⌂ Les Embruns House, Route de la Margion, ⊠ Catel, ℘ 64834, Fax 66024, ⤢ heated, ✍ –
🇹🇻 ☎ 🄿
16 rm.

HERM ISLAND 🄰🄾🄳 P 33 and 🄰🄴🄾 ⑩ The West Country G. – pop. 37 – ✆ 0481 Guernsey.
See : Le Grand Monceau★.
⤢⤢ to Guernsey, St. Peter Port (Herm Seaways) 6 daily (25 mn).
🛈 Administrative Office ℘ 722377.

Herm – ⊠ Herm – ✆ 0481 Guernsey.

🏨 **White House** ♨, GY1 3HR, ℘ 722159, Fax 710066, ≼ Belle Greve Bay and Guernsey,
⤢ heated, ✍, park, ✋ – ⤦ rest. 🅈 𝑽𝑰𝑺𝑨. ✋
April-September – **M** 15.00/16.45 **s.** ╽ 3.25 – **32 rm** ⊐ (dinner included) 50.00/100.00 **s.**

JERSEY 🄰🄾🄳 OP 33 and 🄰🄴🄾 ⑪ The West Country G. – pop. 72 970 – ✆ 0534.
See : Island★★ - Jersey Zoo★★ *AC* – St. Catherine's Bay★ (≼★★) – Grosnez Point★ – Devil's
Hole★ – St. Matthews Church, Millbrook (glasswork★) – La Hougue Bie (Neolithic tomb★ *AC*,
Chapels★, German Occupation Museum★ *AC*) – St. Catherine's Bay★ (≼★★) – Noirmont
Point★.
⤢⤢ States of Jersey Airport ℘ 46111.
⤢⤢ to France : St. Malo (Emeraude Lines) – to Poole (British Channel Island Ferries).
⤢⤢ to France : St. Quay Portrieux, Granville and St. Malo (Emeraude Lines) (summer only) –
from Gorey to France (Carteret) (Emeraude Lines) (summer only) – from Gorey to France
(Portbail) (Emeraude Lines) (summer only) – to Sark (Emeraude Lines) (summer only) – to
Guernsey (St. Peter Port) (Emeraude Lines) (summer services) – to Weymouth via Guernsey
(Condor Ltd) – by Channiland : to Guernsey (50 mn), to Sark (45 mn) (summer only), to
St. Malo and Granville (France).
🛈 Liberation Square, St. Helier, JE1 1BB ℘ 500700.

Bonne Nuit Bay – ⊠ St. John – ✆ 0534 Jersey.
St. Helier 6.

🏨 **Cheval Roc** ♨, JE3 4DJ, ℘ 862865, Fax 864611, ≼ Bonne Nuit Bay, ⤢ heated – 🇹🇻 ☎
🄿. 🅈 𝑽𝑰𝑺𝑨
May-mid October – **M** (bar lunch)/dinner 12.00 ╽ 3.00 – **42 rm** ⊐ (dinner included) 35.50/
84.00.

Bouley Bay – ⊠ Trinity – ✆ 0534 Jersey.
St. Helier 5.

🏨 **Water's Edge,** JE3 5AS, ℘ 862777, Fax 863645, ≼ Bouley Bay, ⇄s, ⤢ heated, ✍ – |፥|
🇹🇻 ☎ 🄿. 🅈 🄰🄴 ⓪ 𝑽𝑰𝑺𝑨
April-October – **M** 13.50/17.50 and a la carte – **47 rm** ⊐ 60.00/115.00, 3 suites.

Corbiere – ⊠ St. Brelade – ✆ 0534 Jersey.
St. Helier 8.

XX **Sea Crest** with rm, Petit Port, JE3 8HH, ℘ 46353, Fax 47316, ≼, ⤢, ✍ – ⊟ rest 🇹🇻 ☎ 🄿.
🅈 🄰🄴 𝑽𝑰𝑺𝑨 ✋
closed February – **M** *(closed Sunday dinner November-March and Monday)* 11.00/18.50
and a la carte ╽ 4.00 – **7 rm** ⊐ 53.00/88.50.

Gorey The West Country G. – ⊠ St. Martin – ✆ 0534 Jersey.
See : Mont Orgueil Castle★ (≼★★) *AC* – Jersey Pottery★.
St. Helier 4.

🏨 **Old Court House,** Gorey Village, JE3 9EX, ℘ 854444, Fax 853587, ⇄s, ⤢ heated, ✍ –
|፥| 🇹🇻 ☎ ♿ 🄿. 🅈 🄰🄴 ⓪ 𝑽𝑰𝑺𝑨 ✋
April-October – **M** (light lunch)/dinner 13.00 and a la carte ╽ 4.00 – **58 rm** ⊐ 44.50/96.00.

⌂ **Trafalgar Bay,** Gorey Village, JE3 9ES, ℘ 856643, Fax 856922, ⤢ heated, ✍ – 🇹🇻 🄿. 🅈
𝑽𝑰𝑺𝑨 ✋
April-October – **M** (bar lunch)/dinner 10.00 **s.** and a la carte ╽ 2.50 – **27 rm** ⊐ 35.00/90.00 **s.**

X **Jersey Pottery (Garden Restaurant),** Gorey Village, JE3 9EP, ℘ 851119, Fax 856403,
« Working Pottery », ✍ – ⤦ 🄿. 🅈 🄰🄴 ⓪ 𝑽𝑰𝑺𝑨
closed Saturday, Sunday, 1-2 January, 23 to 31 December and Bank Holidays – **Meals** -
Seafood (lunch only) a la carte 19.40/28.50 ╽ 5.50.

at Gorey Pier – ✉ St. Martin – ☎ 0534 Jersey :

Dolphin, JE3 6DR, ☎ 853370, Fax 857618 – rest TV ☎. VISA. ✱
M 14.50/28.00 **s.** and a la carte 2.85 – **16 rm** 26.50/86.00 **s.** – SB 51.00/64.00 **s.**

Moorings, JE3 6EW, ☎ 853633, Fax 857618 – rest TV ☎. AE VISA. ✱
M 12.50/17.50 and la carte 4.50 – **16 rm** 40.50/105.00 – SB (winter only) 80.00 **s.**

Grève De Lecq – ✉ St. Ouen – ☎ 0534 Jersey.

Des Pierres, JE3 2DT, on B 65 ☎ 481858, Fax 485273 – TV P. AE VISA. ✱
April-October – **M** (dinner only) 2.95 – **16 rm** (dinner included) 37.00/74.00.

Grouville – ☎ 0534 Jersey.

Lavender Villa, Rue a Don, JE3 9DA, on A 3 ☎ 854937, Fax 856147, – TV P. VISA. ✱
mid March-October – **M** (dinner only) 8.00 2.50 – **21 rm** 16.00/64.00.

Mon Desir House without rest., La Rue Des Prés, JE3 9DJ, ☎ 854718, Fax 857798, – TV P. VISA. ✱
April-mid November – **12 rm** 22.00/52.00 **s.**

La Haule – ✉ St. Brelade – ☎ 0534 Jersey.

La Place, Route du Coin, by B 25 on B 43 ☎ 44261, Telex 4192522, Fax 45164, heated – TV ☎ P
40 rm.

Au Caprice, JE3 8BA, on A 1 ☎ 22083, Fax 26199 – TV. VISA. ✱
April-October – **M** (by arrangement) 6.00 4.50 – **13 rm** 15.00/46.00 **s.**

La Pulente – ✉ St. Brelade – ☎ 0534 Jersey.

Les Mielles, The Mount, Val de la Mare, St. Ouens ☎ 81947/82787, N : 2 ½ m. by B 35.

St. Helier 7.

Atlantic, La Moye, JE3 8HE, ☎ 44101, Fax 44102, ≤, heated, – TV ☎ P – 50. AE VISA. ✱
March-October – **M** 12.00/19.50 and a la carte – **49 rm** 90.00/180.00, 1 suite.

Rozel Bay – ✉ St. Martin – ☎ 0534 Jersey.

St. Helier 6.

Chateau La Chaire, Rozel Valley, JE3 6AJ, ☎ 863354, Fax 865137, – TV ☎ P. AE VISA JCB. ✱
M (see below) – **13 rm** 100.00/130.00, 1 suite – SB (November-March) 115.00/233.00 **s.**

Le Couperon de Rozel, JE3 5BN, ☎ 865522, Fax 865332, ≤, heated – TV ☎ P. AE VISA. ✱
27 April-9 October – **M** 11.50/16.50 **s.** and a la carte 3.20 – **36 rm** 37.00/98.00 **s.**

XXX **Chateau La Chaire,** Rozel Valley, JE3 6AJ, ☎ 863354, Fax 865137 – P. AE VISA JCB
M (light lunch Monday to Saturday April-September) 14.50/23.50 and a la carte 4.50.

St. Aubin – ✉ St. Aubin – ☎ 0534 Jersey.

St. Helier 4.

Somerville, Mont du Boulevard, JE3 8AD, S : ¾ m. via harbour ☎ 41226, Telex 4192505, Fax 46621, ≤, heated, – TV ☎ P. AE VISA. ✱
April-October – **M** (dancing 4 evenings a week) 9.00/15.00 and lunch a la carte 3.25 – **59 rm** 47.00/80.00.

Panorama without rest., High St., JE3 8BR, ☎ 42429, Fax 45940, ≤ St. Aubin's Fort and Bay, – TV. AE VISA. ✱
early March-October – **17 rm** 35.00/63.00.

Bon Viveur, The Bulwarks, JE3 8AB, ☎ 41049, Fax 47540, ≤ – TV. AE VISA. ✱
March-October – **M** 8.75 and a la carte 2.75 – **19 rm** 22.00/48.00.

Sabots d'or, High St., JE3 8BR, ☎ 43732 – TV. ✱
March-October – **M** (by arrangement) – **10 rm** 18.00/40.00 **s.**

X **Old Court House Inn** with rm, St. Aubin's Harbour, ☎ 46433, Fax 45103 – TV ☎. AE VISA. ✱
M *(closed Wednesday dinner and Thursday November-March)* 14.50 (dinner) and a la carte 12.85/23.85 3.50 – **9 rm** 40.00/80.00, 1 suite.

St. Brelade's Bay The West Country G. – pop. 8 566 – ⊠ St. Brelade – ☺ 0534 Jersey.

See : Fishermen's Chapel (frescoes★).

St. Helier 6.

🏨 **L'Horizon,** JE3 8EF, ✆ 43101, Telex 4192281, Fax 46269, ≤ St. Brelade's Bay, *K₅*, ⊆s, ☒
– |≢| ▤ rest 🆃🆅 ☎ ♿ ❻ – 🔬 150. 🔌 VISA. 🛠
M 13.50/23.50 and dinner a la carte 🍴 6.75 – (see also **Star Grill** below) – **104 rm** ⊑ 75.00/
190.00, 3 suites – SB (except Bank Holidays) 150.00.

🏨 **St. Brelade's Bay,** ✆ 46141, Fax 47278, ≤ St. Brelade's Bay, ⊆s, ⤓ heated, ☞, ⚒ – |≢|
🆃🆅 ☎ ♿ . 🔌 VISA. 🛠
mid April-mid October – **M** 12.50/18.00 and a la carte – **71 rm** ⊑ 93.00/186.00, 1 suite.

🏨 **Chateau Valeuse,** Rue de la Valeuse, JE3 8EE, ✆ 46281, Fax 47110, ⤓ heated, ☞ – 🆃🆅
☎ ❻ . 🔌 VISA 🛠
M *(closed Sunday dinner to non-residents)* 11.50/14.50 and dinner a la carte 🍴 3.50 – **32 rm**
⊑ 38.00/84.00.

🏯 **Star Grill** (at L'Horizon H.), JE3 8EF, ✆ 43101, Fax 46269 – ▤ ❻ . 🔌 VISA
M 13.50 (lunch) and a la carte 24.50/40.00 🍴 6.75.

St. Clement – pop. 6 541 – ⊠ St. Clement – ☺ 0534 Jersey.

🏌 St. Clements ✆ 21938, E : 1 m.

St. Helier 2.

🏨 Shakespeare, Samares, St. Clement's Coast Rd, JE2 6SD, ✆ 51915, Fax 56269 – |≢| 🆃🆅 ☎
❻
30 rm.

🏠 **Playa D'Or,** Greve d'Azette, JE2 6PL, W : 2 m. on A 4 ✆ 22861, Fax 69668 – ⇔ 🆃🆅 ❻ .
🔌 VISA . 🛠
closed 8 December-12 January – **M** (by arrangement) 7.00 🍴 2.50 – **15 rm** ⊑ 23.00/46.00 **s.**

St. Helier The West Country G. – pop. 29 941 – ECD : Thursday and Saturday –
⊠ St. Helier – ☺ 0534 Jersey.

See : Jersey Museum★ *AC* Z – Elizabeth Castle (≤★) *AC* Z – Fort Regent (≤★ *AC*) Z.

Envir. : St. Peter's Valley (Living Legend★ *AC*) NW : 4 m. by A 1, A 11 St. Peter's Valley
rd and C 112.

Plan on next page

🏨 **Grand** (De Vere), Esplanade, JE4 8WD, ✆ 22301, Fax 37815, ≤, *K₅*, ⊆s, ☒ – |≢| ▤ rest 🆃🆅
☎ ♿ ❻ – 🔬 180. 🔌 ▲ ⦿ VISA .... Y **u**
M 16.00/21.50 and a la carte 🍴 3.50 – (see also **Victoria's** below) – **110 rm** ⊑ 60.00/
150.00 **s.**, 5 suites – SB 130.00/180.00 **s.**

🏨 **De la Plage,** Havre des Pas, JE2 4UQ, ✆ 23474, Telex 4192328, Fax 68642, ≤, *K₅* – |≢| 🆃🆅
☎ ❻ . 🔌 ▲ ☞ .... Z **g**
23 April 16 October – **M** 14.95/16.50 **s.** and a la carte 🍴 3.80 – **78 rm** ⊑ 33.00/160.00 **s.**

🏨 **Pomme d'Or,** Liberation Sq., JE2 3NR, ✆ 78644, Telex 4192309, Fax 37781 – |≢| ⇔ rm
▤ rest 🆃🆅 ☎ – 🔬 180. 🔌 ▲ ⦿ VISA 🛠 .... Z **u**
M 13.50/15.00 **s.** and a la carte 🍴 3.45 – **147 rm** ⊑ 60.00/120.00 **s.** – SB (except Christmas
and New Year) (weekends only) 109.00/150.00 **s.**

🏨 **Apollo,** 9 St. Saviour's Rd, JE2 4LA, ✆ 25441, Telex 4192086, Fax 22120, *K₅*, ⊆s, ☒ – |≢|
☎ ❻ . ▲ ▲ ⦿ VISA 🛠 .... Z **e**
M *(closed Sunday lunch)* 11.00 (dinner) and a la carte 10.00/17.50 🍴 5.00 – **85 rm** ⊑ 38.00/
98.50 **s.** – SB (winter only) (weekends only) 78.00 **s.**

🏨 **Beaufort,** Green St., JE2 4UH, ✆ 32471, Telex 4192086, Fax 20371, ☒ – |≢| 🆃🆅 ☎ ❻ . ▲
▲ ⦿ VISA 🛠 .... Z **r**
M 11.00/12.50 and a la carte 🍴 6.00 – **54 rm** ⊑ 60.00/114.00 – SB (November-March)
(weekends only) 85.00 **s.**

🏨 **Queens,** Queens Rd, JE2 3QR, ✆ 22239, Fax 21930 – 🆃🆅 ☎ ❻ . ▲ ▲ ⦿ VISA .... Y **x**
M (bar lunch)/dinner 15.00 🍴 2.50 – **37 rm** ⊑ (dinner included) 40.00/80.00 **s.**

🏨 **Mountview,** 46 New St. John's Rd, JE2 3LD, ✆ 887666, Fax 39763 – |≢| 🆃🆅 ▲ VISA Y **e**
mid March-October – **M** (bar lunch)/dinner 13.00 and a la carte 🍴 3.50 – **35 rm** ⊑ 44.00/
82.00 – SB 48.00/86.00.

🏨 **Mornington,** 60-68 Don Rd, JE2 4QD, ✆ 24452, Fax 34131 – |≢| ⇔ rest 🆃🆅 ☎ . ▲ ▲ ⦿
VISA 🛠 .... Z **c**
April-December – **M** *(closed Sunday dinner)* (dinner only and Sunday lunch)/dinner 8.00 –
31 rm ⊑ 37.00/64.00 – SB 48.00/74.00 **s.**

🏨 **Sarum,** 19-21 New St. John's Rd, JE2 3LD, ✆ 58163, Fax 31340 – |≢| 🆃🆅 ▲ VISA 🛠 Y **n**
26 March-5 November – **M** (residents only) (bar lunch)/dinner 12.50 and a la carte 🍴 3.75 –
49 rm ⊑ (dinner included) 47.50/93.00.

🏨 **Uplands,** St. John's Rd, JE2 3LE, ✆ 30151, Fax 68804, ⤓ heated – 🆃🆅 ☎ ❻ . ▲ VISA Y **a**
27 March-October – **M** (bar lunch)/dinner 8.00 **s.** 🍴 2.50 – **43 rm** ⊑ 36.75/73.50 **s.**

🏨 **Almorah,** 1 Almorah Cres., Lower Kings Cliff, JE2 3GU, ✆ 21648, Fax 68600, ☞ – 🆃🆅 ☎
❻ . ▲ VISA 🛠 .... Y **o**
February-October – **M** (dinner only) 10.00 🍴 3.50 – **14 rm** ⊑ (dinner included) 39.50/79.00 –
SB 50.00/79.00 **s.**

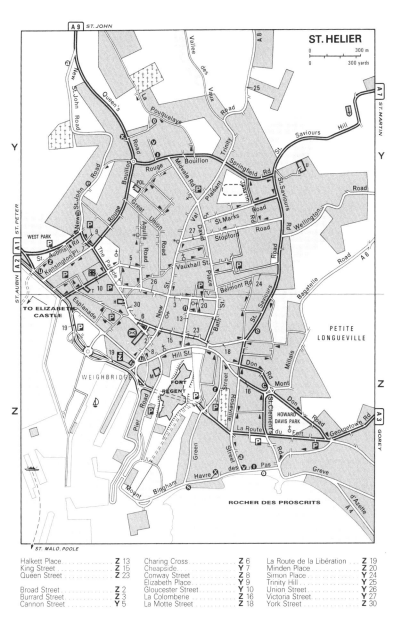

ST. HELIER

⋔ **La Bonne Vie** without rest., Roseville St., JE2 4PL, 𝒸 35955, Fax 33357 – 📺. 🔼 VISA.
⅗
Z **a**
March-November – **10 rm** ⌧ 22.00/44.00 **s.**

⋔ **Kaieteur,** 4 Ralegh Av., JE2 3ZG, 𝒸 37004, Fax 67423 – 📺. 🔼 VISA. ⅗
Y **i**
closed Christmas and New Year – **M** (by arrangement) – **10 rm** ⌧ 23.50/47.00 **s.**

⋔ **Lion d'Or,** Havre des Pas, JE2 4UQ, 𝒸 30018, Fax 32162 – 📺. 🔼 VISA. ⅗
Z **v**
13 rm ⌧ (dinner included) 56.00 **s.** – SB (low season except Bank Holidays) 72.00/90.00 **s.**

↑ **Lorraine,** 8 Havre des Pas, JE2 4UQ, ℰ 74470, Fax 23462 – 📺. 🔼 ⒶⒺ ⓞ *VISA*
⸙   Z x
March-November – **M** (by arrangement) 8.00 **s.** ⓘ 2.20 – **10 rm** ⊇ 22.00/46.00 **s.**

↑ **De L'Etang,** 33 Havre des Pas, JE2 4UQ, ℰ 21996, Fax 37829, ⇐ – 📺. *VISA*
⸙   Z i
M (by arrangement) 6.00 **s.** ⓘ 3.25 – **13 rm** ⊇ (dinner included) 27.00/54.00 **s.**

↑ **Brookfield,** 24 Ralegh Av., JE2 3ZG, ℰ 23168, Fax 21543 – 📺. 🔼 *VISA*
⸙   Y v
closed December and January – **M** (by arrangement) – **20 rm** ⊇ 28.00/56.00 **s.**

XXX **Victoria's** (at Grand H.), Peirson Rd, JE4 8WD, ℰ 22301, Fax 37815 – 🚭 ⓟ. 🔼 ⒶⒺ ⓞ
VISA   Y z
closed Sunday except lunch July-September – **M** 15.75/22.50 and a la carte ⓘ 3.50.

XX **La Capannina,** 65-67 Halkett Pl., JE2 4WG, ℰ 34602, Fax 77628 – 🔼 ⒶⒺ ⓞ *VISA*   Z n
closed Sunday – **M** - **Italian** a la carte 16.10/25.50 ⓘ 4.90.

XX **Chateau de la Mer** with rm, Havre Des Pas, JE2 4PX, ℰ 33366, Fax 36544 – 📺 ☎ ⓟ. 🔼
VISA ⸙   Z o
M 12.50 **s.** and a la carte ⓘ 4.00 – **5 rm** ⊇ 45.00/84.00 **s.**

St. Lawrence – pop. 3 845 – ✉ St. Lawrence – ☎ 0534 Jersey.
St. Helier 3.

↑ **Villa d'Oro** without rest., La Grande Route de St. Laurent, JE3 1FA, on A 10 ℰ 862262 –
📺. ⸙
April-mid October – **12 rm** ⊇ 25.00/40.00 **s.**

St. Martin – pop. 3 095 – ✉ St. Martin – ☎ 0534 Jersey.
St. Helier 4.

⛬ **Le Relais de St. Martin,** JE3 6EA, ℰ 853271, Fax 855241, ⅃, ⌗ – ↳ rest ⓟ. *VISA*
⸙
27 March-October – **M** (residents only) (dinner only) 8.25 **s.** ⓘ 3.00 – **11 rm** ⊇ 25.00/
50.00 **s.**

↑ **La Franchise Farm** ⸖ without rest., JE3 6HU, NW : ¾ m. by B 30 on C 110 ℰ 862224,
⌗ – ⓟ. ⸙
May-October – **7 rm** ⊇ 19.00/48.00 **s.**

St. Peter – pop. 3 713 – ✉ St. Peter – ☎ 0534 Jersey.
St. Helier 5.

🏨 **Mermaid,** Airport Rd, JE3 7BN, on B 36 ℰ 41255, Telex 4192086, Fax 45826, ⻏, ⇌, 🔼,
⌗, ⸖ – 📺 ⓟ – ⓐ 80. 🔼 ⒶⒺ ⓞ *VISA* ⸙
M 10.00/12.50 and a la carte ⓘ 5.00 – **68 rm** ⊇ 36.25/107.50 **s.** – SB (winter only) (weekends only) 77.00/94.00 **s.**

🏨 **Greenhill Country,** Coin Varin, Mont de l'Ecole, JE3 7EL, on C 112 ℰ 481042,
Fax 485322, ⅃ heated – 📺 ☎ ⓟ. 🔼 ⒶⒺ ⓞ *VISA* ⸙
mid February-mid December – **M** 10.50/17.00 **s.** and a la carte ⓘ 4.00 – **18 rm** ⊇ 40.00/
85.00 **s.** – SB (except June-September) 92.00/132.00 **s.**

St. Saviour – pop. 10 910 – ECD : Thursday – ✉ St. Saviour – ☎ 0534 Jersey.
St. Helier 1.

🏨 ☸ **Longueville Manor,** Longueville Rd, JE2 7SA, on A 3 ℰ 25501, Fax 31613, « Former
manor house with Jacobean panelling », ⅃ heated, ⌗, park, ⸖ – 🛗 ↳ rest 🍽 rest 📺
☎ ⓟ. 🔼 ⒶⒺ *VISA* ⸙
M 18.50/30.00 **s.** and dinner a la carte 31.50/39.50 **s.** – **30 rm** ⊇ 125.00/210.00 **s.**, 2 suites –
SB (November-March) 150.00/280.00 **s.**
Spec. Ragoût of lobster, scallops and langoustine, Roast Gressingham duck with glazed apples and confit, Blackberry
soufflé.

↑ **Champ Colin** ⸖ without rest., Rue du Champ Colin, Houge Bie, JE2 7UN, ℰ 851877, ⌗
– 📺 ⓟ. 🔼 ⒶⒺ *VISA* ⸙
3 rm ⊇ 25.00/40.00.

Per viaggiare in **EUROPA,** utilizzate :

Le carte Michelin **Le Grandi Strade ;**

Le carte Michelin dettagliate ;

Le Guide Rosse Michelin (alberghi e ristoranti) :

Benelux, Deutschland, España Portugal, Main Cities **Europe, France,
Great Britain and Ireland, Italia, Swizzera.**

Le Guide Verdi **Michelin** che descrivono
musei, monumenti, percorsi turistici interessanti.

SARK 408 P 33 and 280 ⑩ The West Country G. – pop. 560 – ✪ 0481.

See : Island★★ – La Coupee★★★ – Port du Moulin★★ – Creux Harbour★ – La Seigneurie★ AC – Pilcher Monument★ – Hog's Back★.

⇌ to France : St. Malo via St. Helier (Jersey) (Emeraude Lines) (summer only) – to Guernsey (St. Peter Port) (Isle of Sark Shipping Co. Ltd) (summer only) (40 mn) – by Channiland : to Jersey (45 mn).

🛈 Tourist Information Office ℘ 832345.

🏨 **Petit Champ** ⌂, GY9 0SF, ℘ 832046, ≼ coast, Herm, Jetou and Guernsey, « Country house atmosphere », ⊒ heated, ☞ – ⫟ rest. ☒ 쬬 ⑩ *VISA* ⌕
mid April-early October – **M** 16.50 **s.** (dinner) and a la carte 13.85/23.25 **s.** ᛯ 3.60 – **16 rm** ⌷ (dinner included) 45.00/96.00 **s.**

🏨 **Dixcart** ⌂, GY9 0SD, ℘ 832015, Fax 832164, ☞, park – ☒ *VISA* ℘1481.832015
M 14.00 ᛯ 3.00 – **16 rm** ⌷ 48.00/96.00 – SB (except August and Bank Holidays) 60.00/96.00.

🏨 **Stocks** ⌂, GY9 0SD, ℘ 832001, Fax 832130, ⊒, ☞. ☒ 쬬 ⑩ *VISA*
April-September – **M** 15.50 **s.** and a la carte ᛯ 4.50 – **23 rm** ⌷ 35.00/90.00 **s.** – SB 70.00/76.00 **s.**

🏨 **Aval du Creux**, Harbour Hill, GY9 0SB, ℘ 832036, Fax 832368, ⊒ heated, ☞ – 📺. ☒ *VISA*
May-September – **M** (booking essential) 8.95/15.95 **s.** and a la carte ᛯ 2.50 – **12 rm** ⌷ 35.00/70.00 **s.**

🗴 **La Sablonnerie** ⌂ with rm, Little Sark, ℘ 832061, Fax 832408, ☞ – ☒ 쬬 *VISA* ⌕
April-mid October – **M** 20.00/22.00 and a la carte ᛯ 4.50 – **21 rm** ⌷ 35.00/88.00, 1 suite.

675

Isle
of Man

Place with at least :

one hotel or restaurant .... ● Douglas
a pleasant hotel or restaurant ..... 🏨, ⭡, ✕
one quiet, secluded hotel .... ⅏
one restaurant with .. ✿, ✿✿, ✿✿✿, **Meals (M)**

Localité offrant au moins :

une ressource hôtelière .... ● Douglas
un hôtel ou restaurant agréable ... 🏨, ⭡, ✕
un hôtel très tranquille, isolé .... ⅏
une bonne table à ... ✿, ✿✿, ✿✿✿, **Meals (M)**

La località possiede come minimo :

una risorsa alberghiera .... ● Douglas
Albergo o ristorante ameno .... 🏨, ⭡, ✕
un albergo molto tranquillo, isolato .... ⅏
un'ottima tavola con .. ✿, ✿✿, ✿✿✿, **Meals (M)**

Ort mit mindestens :

einem Hotel oder Restaurant .... ● Douglas
ein angenehmes Hotel oder Restaurant 🏨, ⭡, ✕
einem sehr ruhigen und abgelegenen Hotel . ⅏
einem Restaurant mit . ✿, ✿✿, ✿✿✿, **Meals (M)**

ISLE OF MAN

Sulby ●
Ramsey ●
Douglas ●
● Ballasalla
Castletown ●

BALLASALLA [402] G 21 – ☎ 0624 Douglas.

ℹ Airport Information Desk, Ronaldsway ✆ 823311.

Douglas 8.

🍴🍴 **Silverburn Lodge,** ✆ 822343 – Ⓟ. [S] VISA
closed Sunday dinner, Monday and 25 December – **M** 12.50/20.00 **t.** and a la carte 🍷 5.00.

🍴 **La Rosette,** Main Rd, ✆ 822940, Fax 822702 – [S] VISA
closed Sunday, Monday and 3 weeks January – **M** 15.00/27.00 **t.** and a la carte 🍷 6.00.

CASTLETOWN [402] G 21 **Great Britain G.** – pop. 3 141 – ECD : Thursday – ☎ 0624.

Exc. : Cregneash Folk Museum★ *AC*, W : 6½ m. by A 5 and A 31.

Douglas 10.

🏨 **Castletown Golf Links** (Best Western) 🐦, Derbyhaven, E : 2 m. ✆ 822201, Fax 824633, ← sea and golf links, ♨, 🏊, 🏌18, park – 📺 ☎ ♿ Ⓟ – 👥 180. [S] [AE] ⓪ VISA
M *(closed Saturday lunch)* 12.50/18.00 **st.** and dinner a la carte 🍷 5.50 – **50 rm** ☐ 52.00/74.00 **st.**, 8 suites – SB (except Christmas and New Year) 100.00 **st.**

DOUGLAS [402] G 21 **Great Britain G.** – pop. 19 944 – ECD : Thursday – ☎ 0624.

Exc. : Snaefell★ (✳★★★) N : 8 m. by A 2 and mountain tramcar from Laxey – Laxey Wheel★★, NE : 8 m. by A 2.

🏌18 Douglas Municipal, Pulrose Park ✆ 661558, 2 m. from Douglas Pier – 🏌18 King Edward Bay, Groudle Rd, Onchan ✆ 620430/673821, N : 1 m.

✈ Ronaldsway Airport, ✆ 823311, SW : 7 m. – **Terminal** : Coach service from Lord St.

⛴ by Isle of Man Steam Packet Co. Ltd : to Belfast (summer only) (4 h 30 mn) – to Dublin : (summer only) (4 h 45 mn) – to Fleetwood : (3 h 20 mn) (summer only) – to Heysham : (3 h 45 mn) – to Liverpool : (4 h).

ℹ Sefton Tourist Information Centre, Harris Promenade ✆ 686766.

🏨 **Palace,** Central Promenade, ✆ 662662, Fax 625535, ←, 🏋, ♨, 🏊 – 🛗 ⊟ rest 📺 ☎ Ⓟ – 👥 320. [S] [AE] ⓪ VISA. 🐕
M 17.50 **st.** (dinner) and a la carte 9.00/20.00 **st.** 🍷 5.50 – **130 rm** ☐ 65.00/95.00 **st.**, 3 suites – SB (weekends only) 90.00/120.00 **st.**

🏨 **Sefton,** Harris Promenade, ✆ 626011, Fax 676004, ←, 🏋, ♨, 🏊 – 🛗 📺 ☎ Ⓟ – 👥 100. [S] [AE] ⓪ VISA JCB. 🐕
M 8.50/13.50 **st.** and dinner a la carte 🍷 3.50 – **79 rm** ☐ 37.00/68.50 **st.**, 1 suite.

🏨 **Empress,** Central Promenade, ✆ 661155, Fax 673554, 🏋, ♨ – 🛗 ⊟ rest 📺 ☎ – 👥 150. [S] VISA. 🐕
M 12.50 **t.** and a la carte – ☐ 7.50 – **99 rm** 65.00/70.00 **t.**, 3 suites – SB (weekends only) 85.00/170.00 **st.**

🏨 **Admiral House,** 12 Loch Promenade, ✆ 629551, Fax 675021 – 🛗 📺 ☎. [S] ⓪ VISA. 🐕
M *(closed Saturday lunch and Sunday)* 10.50/15.95 **t.** and a la carte 🍷 5.50 – **12 rm** ☐ 50.00/120.00 **st.** – SB (weekends only) 92.00/111.90 **st.**

🏨 **Santon Motel,** Santon, SW : 5½ m. on A 5 ✆ 822499, 🌳 – 📺 ☎ Ⓟ. [S] VISA. 🐕
M *(closed Saturday)* (dinner only) 10.50 **st.** 🍷 3.50 – ☐ 4.95 – **18 rm** 22.50/55.00 **st.** – SB (October-March) (weekends only) 54.00/99.00 **st.**

ATS Mount Vernon, Peel Rd ✆ 622661 — ATS 5-7 South Quay ✆ 676532

RAMSEY [402] G 21 **Great Britain G.** – pop. 5 778 – ☎ 0624.

Exc. : Snaefell★ (✳★★★) SW : 8 m. by A 2 and mountain tramcar from Laxey – Laxey Wheel★★, S : 8 m. by A 2.

ℹ The Library, Town Hall ✆ 812228.

Douglas 16.

🏨 **Grand Island** 🐦, Bride Rd, N : 1 m. on A 10 ✆ 812455, Fax 815291, ←, 🏋, 🎱, 🌳 – 🛗 📺 ☎ Ⓟ – 👥 200. [S] [AE] ⓪ VISA
M (bar lunch Monday to Friday)/dinner 14.95 **t.** and a la carte – **46 rm** ☐ 65.00/104.00 **t.**, 8 suites – SB (weekends only) 90.00/110.00 **st.**

🏨 **Ramsey Beach,** Ballure Promenade, ✆ 816061, Fax 816620, ←, ♨ – 🛗 📺 ☎ Ⓟ – 👥 25. [S] VISA. 🐕
M 10.00/14.00 **t.** and dinner a la carte 🍷 5.00 – **21 rm** ☐ 39.00/60.00 **t.**, 2 suites – SB (except Christmas and New Year) 80.00/98.00 **st.**

SULBY [402] G 21 – ✉ Lezayre – ☎ 0624.

Douglas 16.

🏠 **Kerrowmoar House** 🐦, E : ½ m. on Ramsey rd ✆ 897543, Fax 897927, « Part Georgian house, antiques », 🏊, 🌳, park, 🎾 – 🚭 rm 📺 ☎ Ⓟ. 🐕
M (by arrangement) 25.00 **s.** – **3 rm** ☐ 40.00/75.00 **s.**

Republic

of

Ireland

Prices quoted in this section of the guide are in « Punts »

Dans cette partie du guide, les prix sont indiqués en monnaie irlandaise « Punts »

In questa parte della guida, i prezzi sono indicati in lire irlandesi « Punts »

In diesem Teil des Führers sind die Preise in irländischer Währung « Punts » angegeben

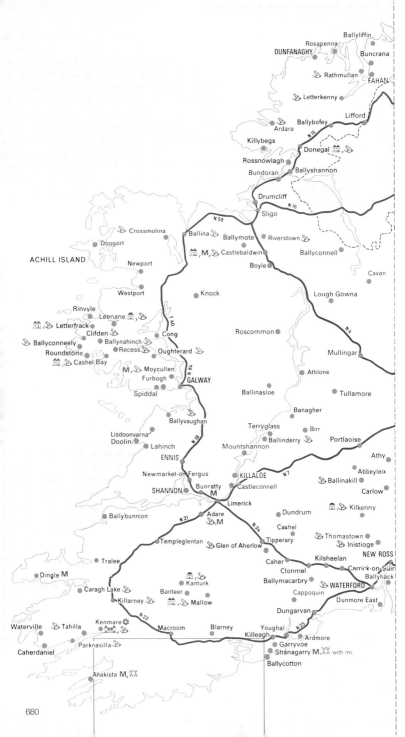

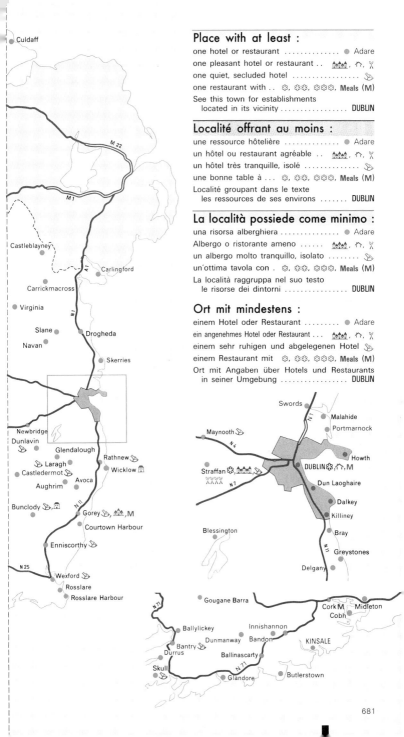

Place with at least :

one hotel or restaurant . . . . ● Adare
one pleasant hotel or restaurant . . 🏨, ⌂, ⅟
one quiet, secluded hotel . . . . ⌂
one restaurant with . . ⌂, ⌂⌂, ⌂⌂⌂, Meals (M)
See this town for establishments
located in its vicinity . . . . DUBLIN

Localité offrant au moins :

une ressource hôtelière . . . . ● Adare
un hôtel ou restaurant agréable . . 🏨, ⌂, ⅟
un hôtel très tranquille, isolé . . . . ⌂
une bonne table à . . . ⌂, ⌂⌂, ⌂⌂⌂, Meals (M)
Localité groupant dans le texte
les ressources de ses environs . . . . DUBLIN

La località possiede come minimo :

una risorsa alberghiera . . . . ● Adare
Albergo o ristorante ameno . . . . . . 🏨, ⌂, ⅟
un albergo molto tranquillo, isolato . . . . ⌂
un'ottima tavola con . ⌂, ⌂⌂, ⌂⌂⌂, Meals (M)
La località raggruppa nel suo testo
le risorse dei dintorni . . . . DUBLIN

Ort mit mindestens :

einem Hotel oder Restaurant . . . . ● Adare
ein angenehmes Hotel oder Restaurant . . . 🏨, ⌂, ⅟
einem sehr ruhigen und abgelegenen Hotel ⌂
einem Restaurant mit ⌂, ⌂⌂, ⌂⌂⌂, Meals (M)
Ort mit Angaben über Hotels und Restaurants
in seiner Umgebung . . . . DUBLIN

(Mainistir Laoise) Laois 🔲🔲🔲 J 9 – pop. 1 402 – ECD : Wednesday – 🕃 0502 Portlaoise.

◆Dublin 64 – Kilkenny 21 – ◆Limerick 65 – ◆Tullamore 30.

🏛 **Hibernian House,** Lower Main St., ℰ 31252 – ☎. 🔲 ⑩ 𝖵𝖨𝖲𝖠 . ❧
M 7.00/14.00 **st.** and dinner a la carte – **11 rm** ⌷ 18.00/32.00 **st.**

ACHILL ISLAND **(Acaill)** Mayo 🔲🔲🔲 B 5/6 Ireland G..

See : Island★.

🏛 Achill Sound ℰ 45384 (1 July-31 August).

Doogort **(Dumha Goirt)** – ✉ Achill Island – 🕃 098 Westport.
🛝 Keel ℰ 43202, S : 4 m.

↿ **Gray's** 🦢, ℰ 43244, 🖅 – 🅿. 🔲 ❧
March-October – **M** (by arrangement) 14.00 🍷 4.00 – **15 rm** ⌷ 32.00/36.00 **t.**

☛ *Inclusion in the Michelin Guide cannot be achieved by*
pulling strings or by offering favours.

ADARE **(Áth Dara)** Limerick 🔲🔲🔲 F 10 Ireland G. – pop. 785 – 🕃 061 Limerick.

See : Town★ – Adare Friary★.

Exc. : Rathkeale (Castle Matrix★ *AC*) W : 7½m. by N 21 – Newcastle West★, W : 16 m. by N 21 – Glin Castle★ *AC*, W : 29 m. by N 21, R 518 and N 69.

🏛 ℰ 396255 (mid April-30 October).

◆Dublin 131 – ◆Killarney 59 – ◆Limerick 10.

🏰 **Adare Manor** 🦢, ℰ 396566, Fax 396124, ≼, « 19C Gothic mansion in extensive parkland », 🎏, ☎, ℡, 🏊, ⚐, 🖅 – 🔋 🕿 ☎ ⇐⇒ 🅿. ⓥ 150. 🔲 🆎 ⑩ 𝖵𝖨𝖲𝖠 . ❧
M 23.00/28.00 **t.** and a la carte – ⌷ 12.50 – **64 rm** 204.00 **st.** – SB (October-April except Christmas) 246.50/310.00 **st.**

🏰 **Dunraven Arms,** Main St., ℰ 396633, Fax 396541, « Attractively furnished, antiques »,
🖅 – 🔋 🕿 🅿 – 🔬 150. 🔲 🆎 ⑩ 𝖵𝖨𝖲𝖠 . ❧
closed Good Friday and Christmas Day to non-residents – **M** – **Maigue** 13.00/25.00 **t.** and a la carte 🍷 4.25 – ⌷ 8.50 – **45 rm** 55.00/130.00 **t.**

↿ **Abbey Villa** without rest., Kildimo Rd, ℰ 396113 – 🔋 🅿. 🔲 𝖵𝖨𝖲𝖠 . ❧
6 rm ⌷ 15.00/30.00 **st.**

↿ **Village House** without rest., Main St., ℰ 396554 – 🅿. ❧
March-November – **5 rm** ⌷ 15.00/30.00 **st.**

✕✕ **Mustard Seed,** Main St., ℰ 396451 – 🔲 🆎 ⑩ 𝖵𝖨𝖲𝖠
closed Sunday, Monday and 25 January-1 March – **Meals** (dinner only) 23.00/25.00 🍷 5.00.

AHAKISTA **(Áth an Chiste)** Cork 🔲🔲🔲 D 13 – ✉ 🕃 027 Bantry.

◆Dublin 217 – ◆Cork 63 – ◆Killarney 59.

✕✕ **Shiro,** ℰ 67030, 🖅 – 🅿. 🔲 🆎 ⑩ 𝖵𝖨𝖲𝖠
closed January and February – **Meals - Japanese** (booking essential) (dinner only) 32.00 **st.**

ARAN ISLANDS **(Oileáin Árann)** 🔲🔲🔲 CD 8 Ireland G.

See : Islands★ – Inishmore (Dun Aenghus★★★).

Access by boat or aeroplane from Galway city or by boat from Kilkieran, or Fisherstreet (Clare).

🏛 ℰ 099 (Inishmore) 61263 (30 May-15 September).

Hotels see : Galway.

ARDARA **(Ard an Rátha)** Donegal 🔲🔲🔲 G 3 Ireland G. – pop. 685 – 🕃 075.

Envir. : Glengesh Pass★★★, SW : 5 m

Exc. : Gweebarra Estuary★, NE : 9 m. by R 262.

◆Dublin 188 – Donegal 24 – ◆Londonderry 58.

↿ **Woodhill House** 🦢, SE : ¼ m. by Donegal rd ℰ 41112, Fax 41516, ≼, 🖅 – 🅿. 🔲 🆎 ⑩ 𝖵𝖨𝖲𝖠 . ❧
M (by arrangement) 24.00 **t.** – **6 rm** ⌷ 16.00/48.00 **t.**

↿ **Bay View Country House** 🦢, Portnoo Rd, N : ¾ m. ℰ 41145, ≼ Loughros Bay and hills, 🖅 – 🅿. 🔲 𝖵𝖨𝖲𝖠 . ❧
March-October – **M** (by arrangement) 11.00 **st.** – **6 rm** ⌷ 14.00/28.00 **st.**

ARDMORE **(Aird Mhór)** Waterford 🔲🔲🔲 I 12 Ireland G. – pop. 318 – 🕃 024 Youghal.

See : Town★ – Round Tower★ – Church★ (arcade★).

Envir. : Whiting Bay★, W : 2 m. by the coast road.

🏛 Community Office ℰ 94444 (May-September).

◆Dublin 139 – ◆Cork 34 – ◆Waterford 43.

🏛 **Cliff House,** ℰ 94106, Fax 94496, ≼, 🖅 – ☎ 🅿. 🔲 🆎 ⑩ 𝖵𝖨𝖲𝖠 . ❧
M (bar lunch Monday to Saturday)/dinner 16.50 **st.** and a la carte 🍷 5.00 – **20 rm** ⌷ 26.00/68.00 **st.** – SB (weekends only) 85.00/91.00 **st.**

ATHLONE (Baile Átha Luain) Westmeath 405 I 7 Ireland G. – pop. 9 444 – ECD : Thursday – ✆ 0902.

Exc. : Clonmacnois★★★ (Grave Slabs★, Cross of the Scriptures★) S : 13 m. by N 6 and N 62 – N : Lough Ree (Ballykeeran Viewpoint★★, Glassan★) – Clonfinlough Stone★, S : 11 ½ m. by N 6 and N 62.

🏌 Hodson Bay ✆ 92073/92235, N : 4 m.

🗓 Tourist Office, The Castle ✆ 94630 (Easter-mid October).

◆Dublin 75 – ◆Galway 57 – ◆Limerick 75 – Roscommon 20 – ◆Tullamore 24.

🏨 **Hodson Bay,**, NW : 4¾ m. by N 61 ✆ 92444, Fax 92688, ≤, ƒ₆, ≘s, ⬛, ☞, ✗ – ⟦⟧ ⟦⟧ ☎ ₺ ₱ – ₳ 500. ⬛ ⬛ ⓞ VISA ✗
    M 13.00/35.00 **t.** and dinner a la carte ₺ 5.00 – **44 rm** ⟷ 50.00/80.00 **st.**, 2 suites – SB 87.00/115.00 **st.**

🏠 **Shelmalier House,** Retreat Rd, Cartrontroy, E : 2½ m. by Dublin rd ✆ 72245, Fax 73190, ☞ – ⟦⟧ ☎ ₱. ⬛ VISA ✗
    M (by arrangement) – **7 rm** ⟷ 18.00/28.00 **st.**

ATHY (Baile Átha Á) Kildare 405 L 9 – ✆ 0507.

◆Dublin 40 – Kilkenny 29 – Wexford 59.

🏠 **Tonlegee House,** SW : 2¼ m. by N 78 ✆ 31473, Fax 31473 – ⟦⟧ ☎ ₱. ⬛ VISA ✗
    closed first 2 weeks November and 24 to 28 December – **M** (closed Sunday to non-residents) (dinner only) 22.00 **st.** ₺ 5.00 – **5 rm** ⟷ 37.50/58.00 **st.** – SB 80.00/95.00 **st.**

AUGHRIM (Eachroim) Wicklow 405 N 9 – ✆ 0402 Arklow.

🗓 ✆ 73939 (1 May-2 October).

◆Dublin 46 – ◆Waterford 77 – Wexford 60.

🏠 **Lawless's,** ✆ 36146, Fax 36384, ☜ – ⟦⟧ ☎ ₱. ⬛ ⬛ ⓞ VISA ✗
    M (bar lunch Monday to Saturday)/dinner 18.50 **t.** and a la carte ₺ 5.25 – **10 rm** ⟷ 31.50/57.00 **t.** – SB (except July, August and Bank Holidays) 84.00/98.00 **st.**

AVOCA (Abhóca) Wicklow 405 N 9 – pop. 289 – ✆ 0402 Arklow.

◆Dublin 47 – ◆Waterford 72 – Wexford 55.

🏠 **Wooden Bridge Inn,** Vale of Avoca, SW : 2¼ m. on R 752 ✆ 35146, Fax 35573, ☞ – ⟦⟧ ☎ ₱. ⬛ ⬛ VISA ✗
    closed 24 and 25 December – **M** (bar lunch Monday to Saturday)/dinner 15.00 **st.** and a la carte ₺ 4.00 – **11 rm** ⟷ 25.00/50.00 **st.** – SB 70.00/90.00 **st.**

BALLINA (Béal an Átha) Mayo 405 E 5 Ireland G. – pop. 6 856 – ECD : Thursday – ✆ 096.

Envir. : Rosserk Abbey★, N : 4 m. by R 314.

Exc. : Moyne Abbey★, N : 7 m. by R 314 – Downpatrick Head★, N : 20 m. by R 314.

🏌 Mosgrove, Shanaghy ✆ 21050, E : 1 m.

🗓 ✆ 70848 (3 May-30 September).

◆Dublin 150 – ◆Galway 73 – Roscommon 64 – ◆Sligo 37.

🏠 **Mount Falcon Castle** ⬡, Foxford Rd, S : 4 m. on N 57 ✆ 21172, Fax 21172, ≤, « Country house atmosphere », ☜, park, ✗ – ₱. ⬛ ⬛ ⓞ VISA
    closed February, March, October and Christmas – **M** (by arrangement) (communal dining) (dinner only) 21.00 – **10 rm** ⟷ 45.00/130.00 **t.**

BALLINAKILL (Baile na Coille) Laois – pop. 357 – ✆ 0502.

◆Dublin 68 – Kilkenny 18 – ◆Limerick 69 – ◆Tullamore 34.

🏠 **Glebe House** ⬡, E : ½ m. by Carlow rd ✆ 33368, ≤, « Georgian rectory », ☜, ☞, park – ↩☜ ₱. ⬛ VISA ✗
    closed 1 week Christmas – **M** (by arrangement) 16.00 ₺ 6.00 – **4 rm** ⟷ 22.00/40.00 – SB (except Bank Holidays) (weekdays only) 72.00/76.00 **st.**

BALLINASCARTY (Béal na Scairte) Cork 405 F 12 Ireland G. – ✉ Clonakilty – ✆ 023 Bandon.

Envir. : Clonakilty (West Cork Regional Museum★ AC) S : 5 m. by N 71.

Exc. : Timoleague★ (Franciscan Friary★) SE : 7 m.

🏌 Bandon, Castlebernard ✆ 41111, NE : 6 m. by N 71.

◆Dublin 188 – ◆Cork 27.

🏠 **Árd na Gréine Farm House** ⬡, NW : 1¾ m. by N 71 ✆ 39104, Fax 39397, ☞ – ⟦⟧ ₱. ⬛ VISA
    M 14.00 **st.** ₺ 4.00 – **6 rm** ⟷ 19.00/32.00 **st.**

BALLINASLOE (Béal Átha na Sluaighe) Galway 405 H 8 Ireland G. – pop. 6 374 – ECD : Thursday – ✆ 0905 – Exc. : Turoe Stone, Bullaun★, SW : 18 m. by R 348 and R 350.

🏌 Ballinasloe ✆ 42123 – 🏌 Mount Bellew ✆ 79259.

🗓 ✆ 42131 (July and August).

◆Dublin 91 – ◆Galway 41 – ◆Limerick 66 – Roscommon 36 – ◆Tullamore 34.

🏨 **Haydens,** Dunlo St., ✆ 42347, Fax 42895, ☞ – ⇕ ☰ rest ⟦⟧ ☎ ₱ – ₳ 30. ⬛ ⬛ ⓞ VISA ✗
    closed 24 to 26 December – **M** 11.50/17.50 **t.** and dinner a la carte ₺ 4.95 – ⟷ 5.50 – **48 rm** 28.00/48.00 **t.** – SB 84.00/98.00 **st.**

Cork **405** G 12 – see Kinsale.

BALLINDERRY (Baile an Doire) Tipperary **405** H 8 Ireland G. – ⊠ ✪ 067 Nenagh.

Exc. : Portumna★ (castle★) N : 9½ m. by R 493 and N 65.

◆Dublin 111 – ◆Galway 53 – ◆Limerick 41.

⌂ **Gurthalougha House** ♨, W : 1¾ m. ℰ 22080, Fax 22154, ≤, « Country house on banks of Lough Derg », ❧, ☞, park, ※ – ☎ 🅿. ↻ Æ VISA
closed February and 1 week Christmas – **M** (dinner only) 24.00 **st.** ⅃ 5.50 – **8 rm** ⊐ 40.00/80.00 **st.** – SB (except Bank Holidays) 112.00/124.00 **st.**

BALLYBOFEY (Bealach Féich) Donegal **405** I 3 – pop. 2 928 – ECD : Wednesday – ✪ 074 Letterkenny.

🏌 Ballybofey & Stranorlar ℰ 31093.

◆Dublin 148 – ◆Londonderry 30 – ◆Sligo 58.

🏨 **Kee's**, Main St., Stranorlar, NE : ½ m. on N 15 ℰ 31018, Fax 31917, ⅃𝓈, ⇄s, ⬚ – 📺 ☎ 🅿. ↻ Æ ⓪ VISA
M 9.50/17.00 **t.** and a la carte ⅃ 5.20 – **36 rm** ⊐ 35.00/65.00 **t.** – SB (except Bank Holidays) 73.00/96.00 **st.**

BALLYBUNNION (Baile an Bhuinneánaigh) Kerry **405** D 10 Ireland G. – pop. 1 452 – ✪ 068.

Exc. : Carrigafoyle Castle★, NE : 13 m. by R 551 – Glin Castle★ AC, E : 19 m. by R 551 and N 69.

🏌, 🏌 Ballybunnion ℰ 27146, S : 1 m.

◆Dublin 176 – ◆Limerick 56 – Tralee 26.

⌂ **Marine**, Sandhill Rd, ℰ 27139, Fax 27666, ≤ – 📺 ☎ 🅿. ↻ Æ ⓪ VISA
March-October – **M** (closed lunch Monday to Saturday March, April and October) (bar lunch Monday to Saturday)/dinner 19.00 and a la carte ⅃ 6.00 – **12 rm** ⊐ 30.00/62.00 **t.** – SB 75.00/110.00 **st.**

BALLYCONNEELY (Baile Conaola) Galway **405** B 7 – ⊠ ✪ 095 Clifden.

◆Dublin 189 – ◆Galway 54.

⌂ **Erriseask House** ♨, ℰ 23553, Fax 23639, ≤ – ☎ 🅿. ↻ Æ ⓪ VISA ※
April-October – **M** (light lunch)/dinner 29.00 **t.** and a la carte ⅃ 6.00 – **8 rm** ⊐ 35.00/80.00 **st.** – SB 79.00/103.00 **st.**

BALLYCONNELL (Béal Atha Conaill) Cavan **405** J 5 – pop. 466 – ✪ 049.

◆Dublin 89 – Drogheda 76 – Enniskillen 23.

🏨 **Slieve Russell**, SE : 1¾ m. on R 200 ℰ 26444, Fax 26474, ≤, ⅃𝓈, ⇄s, ⬚, 🏌, ☞, park, ※, squash – ⋈ rest 📺 ☎ & 🅿 – 🕿 800. ↻ Æ ⓪ VISA ※
M 12.00/26.00 **st.** and a la carte ⅃ 5.25 – **145 rm** ⊐ 65.00/130.00 **st.**, 5 suites.

BALLYCOTTON (Baile Choitán) Cork **405** H 12 – ✪ 021 Cork.

◆Dublin 165 – ◆Cork 27 – ◆Waterford 66.

🏨 **Bayview**, ℰ 646746, Fax 646824, ≤, ☞ – ⋈ 📺 ☎ 🅿 – 🕿 30. ↻ Æ ⓪ VISA ※
April-October – **M** 12.00/22.00 **st.** and a la carte ⅃ 6.50 – **33 rm** ⊐ 50.00/80.00 **st.**, 2 suites – SB 120.00/140.00 **st.**

BALLYHACK (Baile Hac) Wexford **405** L 11 – pop. 221 – ⊠ New Ross – ✪ 051 Waterford.

◆Dublin 105 – ◆Waterford 8.5.

🍴 **Neptune**, Ballyhack Harbour, ℰ 89284, Fax 89284 – ↻ Æ ⓪ VISA
April-December – **M** - **Seafood** (closed dinner Monday and Sunday September-June) (dinner only and Sunday lunch)/dinner 11.90 **t.** and a la carte ⅃ 6.50.

BALLYLICKEY (Béal Átha Leice) Cork **405** D 12 Ireland G. – ⊠ ✪ 027 Bantry.

Exc. : Glengarriff★ (Garinish Island★★, access by boat) NW : 8 m. by N 71 – Healy Pass★★ (≤★★) W : 23 m. by N 71, R 572 and R 574 – Slieve Miskish Mountains (≤★★) W : 29 m. by N 71 and R 572 – Lauragh (Derreen Gardens★ AC) NW : 27½ m. by N 71, R 572 and R 574 – Allihies (copper mines★) W : 41½ m. by N 71, R 572 and R 575 – Garnish Island (≤★) W : 44 m. by N 71 and R 572.

🏌 Bantry Park, Donemark ℰ 50579, N : 1 m. by N 71.

◆Dublin 216 – ◆Cork 55 – Killarney 45.

🏨 **Ballylickey Manor House** ♨, ℰ 50071, Fax 50124, ≤, « Extensive gardens », ⬚ heated, ❧, park – ⋈ rest 📺 ☎ 🅿. ↻ Æ VISA ※
March-October – **M** (closed Wednesday) (dinner residents only) (light lunch)/dinner 32.00 **t.** ⅃ 9.00 – **7 rm** ⊐ 75.00/90.00 **t.**, 4 suites.

⌂ **Sea View House** ♨, ℰ 50462, Fax 51555, ≤, ☞ – ⋈ 📺 ☎ & 🅿. ↻ Æ ⓪ VISA
mid March-mid November – **M** (bar lunch Monday to Saturday)/dinner 22.00 **t.** ⅃ 6.00 – **16 rm** ⊐ 43.00/100.00 **st.**

⌂ **Reendesert**, ℰ 50153, Fax 50597 – 📺 ☎ 🅿. ↻ Æ ⓪ VISA
12 March-October – **M** (bar lunch Monday to Saturday)/dinner 16.00 **st.** and a la carte ⅃ 4.25 – **19 rm** ⊐ 30.00/56.00 **st.** – SB 78.00/92.00 **st.**

BALLYLIFFIN (Baile Lifín) Donegal 405 J 2 Ireland G. – pop. 260 – ✉ Carndonagh – ✆ 077 Buncrana.

Exc. : Inishowen Peninsula★★ : Malin Head★★★ (≤★★★) N : 19 m. by R 238 and R 242 – Carndonagh High Cross★, SE : 6 m. by R 238 – Gap of Mamore★, SW : 8 m. by R 238 – Lag Sand Dunes★, NE : 12 m. by R 238 and R 242.

🛅 Clonmany ✆ 76119, E : ½ m.

◆Dublin 180 – Donegal 83 – ◆Londonderry 35.

🏠 **Strand**, ✆ 76107, Fax 76486, ⊶ – 📺 ✆ ❷. 🔼 VISA ✀
   closed 24 to 26 December – **M** 8.50/16.50 **t.** ▮ 3.85 – **12 rm** ☲ 25.00/45.00 **t.** – SB (except Easter, New Year and Bank Holidays) 70.00/90.00 **st.**

BALLYMACARBRY (Baile Mhac Cairbre) Waterford 405 I 11 Ireland G. – pop. 240 – ✉ ✆ 052 Clonmel.

Exc. : W : Nier Valley Scenic Route★★.

◆Dublin 118 – ◆Cork 49 – Waterford 39.

🏠 **Clonanav Farm** ⅏, N : 1 m. by T 27 ✆ 36141, Fax 36141, ≤, ⌇, ⊶, park – ⇥ rest ✆ ❷. 🔼 VISA ✀
   February-October – **M** 12.00 **st.** ▮ 3.50 – **10 rm** ☲ 25.00/40.00 **st.**

BALLYMOTE (Baile an Mhóta) Sligo 405 G 5 – ✉ ✆ 071 Sligo.

◆Dublin 124 – Longford 48 – ◆Sligo 15.

🏠 **Mill House** without rest., Keenaghan, ✆ 83449, ⊶ – ❷. ✀
   closed 24 December-2 January – **5 rm** ☲ 13.00/26.00 **st.**

BALLYNAHINCH (Baile na hInse) Galway 405 C 7 – ✉ Recess – ✆ 095 Clifden.

◆Dublin 140 – ◆Galway 41 – Westport 49.

🏯 **Ballynahinch Castle** ⅏, Ballinafad, ✆ 31006, Fax 31085, ≤ Owenmore river and woods, ⌇, ⊶, park, ✗ – ✆ ❷. 🔼 AE ⓞ VISA ✀
   closed 1 to 26 February – **M** (bar lunch)/dinner 23.00 **t.** – **28 rm** ☲ 104.00/120.00 **t.** – SB (October-April except Bank Holidays) 104.00/154.00 **st.**

BALLYSHANNON (Béal Atha Seanaion) Donegal 405 M 4 Ireland G. – pop. 2 573 – ✆ 072.

Envir. : Rossnowlagh Strand★★, N : 6 m. by R 231.

◆Dublin 157 – Donegal 13 – ◆Sligo 27.

🏠 **Dorrian's Imperial**, Main St., ✆ 51147, Fax 51001 – 📺 ✆ ❷ – 🔬 30. 🔼 VISA ✀
   closed 23 to 31 December – **M** 9.50/16.00 **st.** and dinner a la carte ▮ 5.50 – **26 rm** ☲ 29.50/61.50 **st.** – SB (except August Bank Holiday) 70.00/85.00 **st.**

🏡 **Creevy Pier** ⅏, Creevy Pier, NW : 3½ m. by Rossnowlagh rd ✆ 51236, ≤ Donegal Bay – ❷. 🔼 VISA ✀
   mid June-mid September and Easter – **M** (bar lunch)/dinner 11.50 **st.** and a la carte – **10 rm** ☲ 28.00/45.00 **st.** – SB (except Bank Holidays) (weekends only) 62.00/76.00 **st.**

✕✕ **Danby House** ⅏ with rm, NW : ¼ m. on R 231 ✆ 51138, ≤, park – ⇥ ✆ ❷. 🔼 VISA ✀
   closed 25 and 26 December – **M** (closed Sunday) (dinner only) 19.00 **st.** ▮ 6.00 – **5 rm** ☲ 24.00/42.00 **st.** – SB (except Bank Holidays) 67.00/97.00 **st.**

BALLYVAUGHAN (Baile Uí Bheacháin) Clare 405 E 8 Ireland G. – pop. 182 – ✆ 065 Ennis.

Envir. : The Burren★★ (Cliffs of Moher★★★, Scenic Routes★★, Aillwee Cave★ AC (Waterfall★), Corcomroe Abbey★, Kilfenora Crosses★).

◆Dublin 149 – Ennis 34 – ◆Galway 29.

🏯 **Gregans Castle** ⅏, SW : 3¾ m. on N 67 ✆ 77005, Fax 77111, ≤ countryside and Galway Bay, ⊶ – ✆ ❷. 🔼 VISA JCB ✀
   April-October – **M** (bar lunch)/dinner 26.00 **t.** and a la carte ▮ 7.85 – **18 rm** ☲ 76.00/99.00 **t.**, 4 suites.

🏠 **Hyland's**, ✆ 77037, Fax 77131 – 📺 ✆ ❷. 🔼 VISA ✀
   closed 20 to 27 December and January – **M** 22.00 **s.** and a la carte ▮ 8.50 – **20 rm** ☲ 37.00/68.00 **st.** – SB 64.00/66.00 **st.**

🏡 **Rusheen Lodge** without rest., Knocknagrough, SW : ¾ m. on N 67 ✆ 77092, Fax 77152, ⊶ – ⇥ 📺 ✆ ❷. 🔼 VISA ✀
   closed 16 December-1 February – **6 rm** ☲ 25.00/36.00 **st.**

BANAGHER (Beannchar) Offaly 405 I 8 Ireland G. – pop. 1 378 – ✆ 0902.

Envir. : Clonfert Cathedral★ (West doorway★★).

◆Dublin 83 – ◆Galway 54 – Limerick 56 – ◆Tullamore 24.

🏠 **Brosna Lodge**, Main St., ✆ 51350, Fax 51521, ⊶ – ✆ ❷. 🔼 VISA
   closed February – **M** (bar lunch Monday to Friday)/dinner a la carte 5.80/15.00 **t.** – **14 rm** ☲ 25.00/48.00 **st.** – SB 70.00/80.00 **st.**

🏡 **Old Forge**, West End, ✆ 51504 – ❷. ✀
   M (by arrangement) (communal dining) – **4 rm** ☲ 15.00/30.00 **st.**

BANDON (Droichead na Bandan) Cork 405 F 12 – 🕸 023.

◆Dublin 174 – ◆Cork 19.

 🏠 **Munster Arms,** Oliver Plunkett St., ℰ 41562, Fax 41562 – 📺 ☎. 🔊 🆎 ⓞ 𝘃𝘪𝘴𝘢. ⚗️
  M 9.60/16.00 **st.** and dinner a la carte ⅊ 6.50 – ⌂ 6.00 – **29 rm** 28.00/48.00 **st.** – SB 77.00/
  88.00 **st.**

 ⌂ **St. Anne's** without rest., Clonakilty Rd, SW : ¾ m. on N 71 ℰ 44239, ⌂ – ⅘⊱ 🅿. ⚗️
  5 rm ⌂ 16.00/28.00 **st.**

BANTEER (Bántár) Cork 405 F 11 – 🕸 029.

◆Dublin 158 – ◆Cork 30 – ◆Killarney 29 – ◆Limerick 48.

 🏠 **Clonmeen Lodge** ⚗️, E : 2 m. on Mallow rd ℰ 56238, Fax 56294, ⚓, ⌂, park – 🅿. 🔊
  𝘃𝘪𝘴𝘢. ⚗️
  M (booking essential) (dinner only) a la carte 12.50/16.50 **st.** ⅊ 5.00 – **6 rm** ⌂ 30.00/
  50.00 **st.** – SB 80.00/100.00 **st.**

BANTRY (Beanntraí) Cork 405 D 12 Ireland G. – pop. 2 862 – ECD : Wednesday – 🕸 027.

See : Bantry House★ *AC*.

🛈 The Square ℰ 50229 (June-September).

◆Dublin 218 – ◆Cork 57 – ◆Killarney 48.

 🏠 **Bantry House** ⚗️, ℰ 50047, Fax 50795, ≼, « Early 18C stately home with formal
  gardens » – ☎ 🅿. 🔊 🆎 ⓞ 𝘃𝘪𝘴𝘢. ⚗️
  closed 4 days at Christmas – **M** *(closed Saturday and Sunday dinner)* (residents only)
  (dinner only) 20.00 **st.** ⅊ 6.00 – **8 rm** ⌂ 45.00/90.00 **st.**

 ⌂ **Dunauley** ⚗️ without rest., Seskin, NE : 1 m. by Vaughan's Pass rd ℰ 50290, ≼ – 🅿. ⚗️
  May-September – **5 rm** ⌂ 20.50/36.00 **s.**

 💥💥 **Larchwood House** with rm, Pearsons Bridge, NE : 4¼ m. by N 71 ℰ 66181, ≼, ⌂ – 🅿.
  🔊 🆎 ⓞ 𝘃𝘪𝘴𝘢. ⚗️
  closed 23 to 28 December – **M** *(closed Sunday)* (dinner only) 25.00 **t.** ⅊ 6.00 – **4 rm**
  ⌂ 20.00/40.00 **t.**

BAREFIELD (Gort Lomán) Clare 405 F 9 – see Ennis.

BIRR (Biorra) Offaly 405 I 8 Ireland G. – pop. 3 679 – 🕸 0509.

See : Town★ – Birr Castle Demesne★★ *AC* (Telescope★).

Exc. : Roscrea★ (Damer House★ *AC*) S : 12 m. by N 62 – Slieve Bloom Mountains★, E : 13 m.
by R 440.

🐚 The Glenns ℰ 20082, W : 2 m.

🛈 ℰ 20110 (10 May-12 September).

Athlone 28 – ◆Dublin 87 – Kilkenny 49 – ◆Limerick 49.

 🏨 **Dooly's,** Emmet Sq., ℰ 20032, Fax 21332 – 📺 ☎ – 🕍 300. 🔊 🆎 ⓞ 𝘃𝘪𝘴𝘢 𝙅𝘾𝘽. ⚗️
  closed Christmas Day – **M** 7.95/15.95 **st.** and dinner a la carte ⅊ 4.50 – **18 rm** ⌂ 29.00/
  50.00 **st.** – SB 64.00/90.00 **st.**

 🏨 **County Arms,** Station Rd, ℰ 20791, Fax 21234, ⌂, squash – 📺 ☎ 🅿 – 🕍 80. 🔊 🆎 ⓞ
  𝘃𝘪𝘴𝘢 𝙅𝘾𝘽. ⚗️
  M 11.00/17.00 **t.** and a la carte ⅊ 6.00 – **18 rm** ⌂ 25.00/67.40 **t.**

BLACKROCK (An Charraig Dhubh) Dublin 405 N 8 – see Dublin.

BLARNEY (An Bhlarna) Cork 405 G 12 Ireland G. – pop. 1 980 – ✉ 🕸 021 Cork.

See : Blarney Castle★★ *AC* – Blarney House★ *AC*.

◆Dublin 167 – ◆Cork 6.

 🏨 **Blarney Park,** ℰ 385281, Fax 381506, 🎿, ≘s, 🔲, ⌂, 💥 – 📺 ☎ 🕭 🅿 – 🕍 250. 🔊
  ⓞ 𝘃𝘪𝘴𝘢. ⚗️
  M 10.50/19.00 **st.** ⅊ 5.25 – **76 rm** ⌂ 35.00/70.00 **st.** – SB 90.00 **st.**

 at Tower W : 2 m. on R 617 – ✉ 🕸 021 Cork :

 ⌂ **Ashlee Lodge** without rest., ℰ 385346 – ⅘⊱ 🅿. ⚗️
  May-October – **5 rm** ⌂ 20.00/30.00 **st.**

BLESSINGTON (Baile Coimán) Wicklow 405 M 8 – 🕸 045.

◆Dublin 19 – Kilkenny 56 – Wexford 70.

 🏨 **Tulfarris House** ⚗️, S : 6 m. by N 81 ℰ 64574, Fax 64423, ≼, 🎿, ≘s, 🔲, 🐾, ⚓, ⌂,
  park, 💥 – 📺 ☎ 🅿. 🔊 🆎 ⓞ 𝘃𝘪𝘴𝘢
  M 13.50/24.00 **t.** and lunch a la carte ⅊ 6.00 – **21 rm** ⌂ 50.00/144.00 **st.** – SB 144.00/
  164.00 **st.**

BOYLE (Mainistir na BÍlle) Roscommon 405 H 6 Ireland G. – pop. 1 737 – ✪ 079.

See : Boyle Abbey★ *AC*.

Envir. : Lough Key Forest Park★★ *AC*, E : 2 m.

🏌 Roscommon Rd ✆ 62594, S : 1½ m.

🛈 ✆ 62145 (1 June-17 September).

◆Dublin 107 – Ballina 40 – ◆Galway 74 – Roscommon 26 – ◆Sligo 24.

   🏛 **Forest Park,** Dublin Rd, E : ½ m. on N 4 ✆ 62229, Fax 63113, ☞ – 📺 ☎ 🅿. 🖭 ᴬᴱ ⏺ 𝗩𝗜𝗦𝗔 ✁
     closed 24 to 26 December – **M** 11.50/19.50 **st.** and dinner a la carte ⵨ 5.50 – **11 rm** � 23.00/55.00 **st.** – SB 75.00/90.00 **st.**

BRAY (Bré) Wicklow 405 N 8 Ireland G. – pop. 22 853 – ECD : Wednesday – ✪ 01 Dublin.

Envir. : Powerscourt★★ (Waterfall★★★ *AC*) W : 4 m. - Killruddery House and Gardens★ *AC*, S : 2 m. by R 761.

🏌 Woodbrook, Dublin Rd ✆ 282 4799 – 162 Ferndale Rd ✆ 826055, N : 2 m. – 🏌 Ravenswell Rd ✆ 286 2484.

🛈 ✆ 2867128 (mid June-August).

◆Dublin 13 – Wicklow 20.

   ✕✕ **Tree of Idleness,** Seafront, ✆ 286 3498 – 🖭 ᴬᴱ ⏺ 𝗩𝗜𝗦𝗔
     closed Monday, first 2 weeks September and Christmas – **M** - **Greek-Cypriot** (dinner only) 19.00 **t.** and a la carte ⵨ 6.75.

BUNCLODY (Bun Clóidí) Wexford 405 M 10 Ireland G. – pop. 1 469 (inc. Carrickduff) – ✪ 054.

Envir. : Mount Leinster★, SW : 4 m.

◆Dublin 63 – Kilkenny 32 – Wexford 27.

   🏛 **Clohamon House** ⤜, Clohamon, SE : 1 ¾ m. by Carnew rd ✆ 77253, Fax 77956, ≼,
     « 18C country house », ⤸, ☞, park – ⥇ rm 🅿. 🖭 𝗩𝗜𝗦𝗔 ✁
     March-November (booking essential) – **M** *(closed Sunday except Bank Holidays)* (residents only) (communal dining) (dinner only) 20.00 **st.** ⵨ 6.50 – **4 rm** � 35.00/80.00 **st.** – SB 70.00/80.00 **st.**

BUNCRANA (Bun Cranncha) Donegal 405 J 2 – ✪ 077.

◆Dublin 160 – ◆Londonderry 15 – ◆Sligo 99.

   🏨 **Lake of Shadows,** Grianan Park, ✆ 61005 – 📺 ☎ 🅿. 🖭 ᴬᴱ 𝗩𝗜𝗦𝗔 ✁
     M 8.00/16.00 **st.** and dinner a la carte ⵨ 4.50 – **23 rm** � 25.00/46.00 **st.** – SB 74.00/78.00 **st.**

BUNDORAN (Bun Dobhráin) Donegal 405 H 4 – ✪ 072.

🛈 Main St. ✆ 41350 (June-September).

◆Dublin 161 – Donegal 17 – ◆Sligo 23.

   🏨 **Great Northern** ⤜, N : ¼ m. ✆ 41204, Fax 41114, ≼, ₲, ☎, 🖳, 🏌, ☞, ✕ – 📲 📺 ☎ ₲.
     🅿. 🖭 ᴬᴱ 𝗩𝗜𝗦𝗔
     closed 3 January-17 March – **M** (bar lunch Monday to Saturday)/dinner 21.00 **st.** ⵨ 6.00 – **94 rm** � 50.00/88.00 **st.** – SB (except Bank Holidays) 116.00/147.00 **st.**

   🏨 **Allingham Arms,** ✆ 41075, Fax 41171 – 📺 ☎ ₲ 🅿. 🖭 ᴬᴱ 𝗩𝗜𝗦𝗔 ✁
     closed Christmas Day – **M** 8.00/17.00 **st.** and dinner a la carte ⵨ 4.00 – **88 rm** � 24.00/70.00 **st.** – SB (except Bank Holidays) 77.00/82.00 **st.**

   ↑ **Bay View** without rest., Main St., ✆ 41296, Fax 41147, ≼, ☎ – 📺 ☎ 🅿. 🖭 𝗩𝗜𝗦𝗔
     19 rm � 22.00/31.00 **st.**

BUNRATTY (Bun Raite) Clare 405 F 9 Ireland G. – ✪ 061 Limerick.

See : Castle and Folk Park★★ *AC*.

🛈 ✆ 360133 (29 April-September).

◆Dublin 129 – Ennis 15 – ◆Limerick 8.

   🏨 Fitzpatrick's Shannon Shamrock, ✆ 361177, Telex 72114, Fax 471252, ☎, 🖳, ☞ –
     ⥇ rm 🍽 rest 📺 ☎ ₲ – ⚖ 200. ✁
     115 rm.

   ↑ **Shannon View** without rest., NW : 1 m. on N 18 ✆ 364056, Fax 364056, ☞ – ₲. ✁
     March-November – **4 rm** � 15.50/31.00 **st.**

   ↑ **Bunratty Lodge** without rest., N : 1½ m. ✆ 369402, ☞ – ⥇ 📺 ₲. ✁
     March-October – **6 rm** � 22.00/31.00 **st.**

   ✕✕ **MacCloskey's,** Bunratty House Mews, ✆ 364082, « Cellars of Georgian house » – ₲.
     🖭 ⏺ 𝗩𝗜𝗦𝗔
     closed Sunday, Monday and 20 December-20 January – **Meals** (dinner only) 26.00 **t.** ⵨ 6.50.

BUTLERSTOWN (Baile an Bhuitléaraigh) Cork 405 F 13 Ireland G. – ✉ ✪ 023 Bandon.

Envir. : Courtmacsherry★, N : 3 m.

◆Dublin 193 – ◆Cork 32.

   ✕ **Dunworley Cottage,** Dunworley, S : 2 m. ✆ 40314 – ₲. 🖭 ᴬᴱ ⏺ 𝗩𝗜𝗦𝗔
     closed Monday and Tuesday – **M** a la carte 13.00/24.00 **t.** ⵨ 4.00.

CAHERDANIEL (Cathair DÉnall) Kerry 405 B 12 – ✉ ☎ 0667 Waterville.

♦Dublin 238 – ♦Killarney 48.

　XX　**Loaves and Fishes,** ℰ 75273 – 🖻 VISA
　　April-September – **M** *(closed Tuesday except June-August and Monday)* (dinner only) a la carte 16.25/24.25 **t.** ⌀ 4.70.

CAHIR/CAHER (An Chathair) Tipperary 405 I 10 Ireland G. – pop. 2 120 – ECD : Thursday – ☎ 052.

See : Caher Castle★★ *AC* – Town Square★ – St. Paul's Church★.

Envir. : Swiss Cottage★ *AC*, S : 1 m. by R 670.

Exc. : Clonmel★ (County Museum★, St. Mary's Church★, Riverside★, Quay★) E : 10 m. by N 24.

🏌 Cahir Park, Kilcommon ℰ 41474, S : 1 m.

🛈 ℰ 41453 (1 May-1 October).

♦Dublin 112 – ♦Cork 49 – Kilkenny 41 – ♦Limerick 38 – ♦Waterford 39.

　🏨　**Kilcoran Lodge,** SW : 4¾ m. on N 8 ℰ 41288, Fax 41994, ♣, ⇌, 🖾, ☞, park – 📺 ☎ 🅿 – 🔬 200. 🖻 AE ⓪ VISA
　　M (carving lunch) 9.75/14.50 **t.** and dinner a la carte ⌀ 4.50 – **23 rm** ⌑ 37.50/67.50 **t.** – SB (except Christmas and New Year) 85.00/96.00 **st.**

CAPPOQUIN (Ceapach Choinn) Waterford 405 I 11 Ireland G. – pop. 950 – ☎ 058 Dungarvan.

Envir. : Lismore★ (Lismore Castle Gardens★ *AC*, St. Carthage's Cathedral★), W : 4 m. by N 72 – Mount Melleray Abbey★, N : 4 m. by R 669.

Exc. : The Gap★ (≤★) NW : 9 m. by R 669.

♦Dublin 136 – ♦Cork 31 – ♦Waterford 40.

　🏠　**Richmond House** ♠, SE : ½ m. on N 72 ℰ 54278, Fax 54988, ☞, park – ☎ 🅿. 🖻 VISA
　　closed January – **M** (dinner only) 24.00 **st.** – **10 rm** ⌑ 25.00/48.00 **st.** – SB (except Bank Holidays) (weekends only) 74.00/86.00 **st.**

CARAGH LAKE (Loch Cárthaí) Kerry 405 C 11 Ireland G. – ☎ 066 Tralee.

See : Lough Caragh★.

Exc. : Iveragh Peninsula★★★ (Ring of Kerry★★).

🏌 Dooks, Glenbeigh ℰ 68205/68200, W : 5 m.

♦Dublin 212 – ♦Killarney 22 – Tralee 25.

　🏨　**Ard-Na-Sidhe** ♠, ℰ 69105, Fax 69282, ≤, « Country house atmosphere », ♣, ☞, park – ☎ 🅿. 🖻 AE ⓪ VISA. ❄
　　May-September – **M** (dinner only) 25.00 **st.** and a la carte ⌀ 8.80 – **20 rm** ⌑ 64.00/125.00 **st.**

　🏨　**Caragh Lodge** ♠, ℰ 69115, Fax 69316, ≤, « Country house atmosphere », ⇌, ♣, ☞, ❄ – ☎ 🅿. 🖻 VISA. ❄
　　April-14 October – **M** (dinner only) 24.00 **t.** ⌀ 6.00 – **10 rm** ⌑ 60.00/90.00 **t.**

CARLINGFORD (Cairlinn) Louth 405 N 5 Ireland G. – pop. 631 – ☎ 042.

See : Town★.

Exc. : Windy Gap★, NW : 8 m. by R 173.

♦Dublin 66 – ♦Dundalk 13.

　🏠　**McKevitt's Village,** Market Sq., ℰ 73116, Fax 73144, ☞ – 📺 ☎. 🖻 AE VISA. ❄
　　M 12.50/16.50 **t.** and a la carte ⌀ 4.50 – **13 rm** ⌑ 27.50/55.00 **t.** – SB (except Bank Holidays) 80.00/85.00 **st.**

CARLOW (Ceatharlach) Carlow 405 L 9　☎ 0503.

♦Dublin 50 – Kilkenny 23 – Wexford 47.

　↑　**Barrowville Town House** without rest., Kilkenny Rd, ℰ 43324, Fax 41953, ☞ – 📺 ☎ 🅿. ❄
　　7 rm ⌑ 15.50/38.00 **st.**

　↑　**Goleen** without rest., Milford, SW : 5¼ m. on N 9 ℰ 46132, ☞ – ⇤ 📺 ☎ 🅿. 🖻 VISA. ❄
　　closed December and January – **6 rm** ⌑ 15.00/30.00 **s.**

CARRICKMACROSS (Carraig Mhachaire Rois) Monaghan 405 L 6 Ireland G. – pop. 1 815 – ☎ 042.

Envir. : Dún a' Rá Forest Park★, SW : 5 m. by R 179 – St. Mochta's House★, E : 7 m. by R 178.

🏌 Nuremore ℰ 61438, S : 1 m. by N 2.

♦Dublin 57 – Dundalk 14.

　🏨🏨　**Nuremore** ♠, S : 1 m. on N 2 ℰ 61438, Fax 61853, ≤, ♣, ⇌, 🖾, 🏌, ♣, ☞, park, ❄, squash – 🖐 📖 rest 📺 ☎ & 🅿 – 🔬 120. 🖻 AE ⓪ VISA. ❄
　　M 13.50/24.00 **st.** and a la carte – **69 rm** ⌑ 70.00/130.00 **st.** – SB (except Bank Holidays) 110.00/190.00 **st.**

(Carraig na Siúire) Tipperary 405 J 10 – pop. 5 566 – ✪ 051 Waterford.

▪ Garravone ✆ 40047, S : 1 m.

🎂 ✆ 40726 (May-7 September).

◆Dublin 95 – ◆Cork 68 – ◆Limerick 62 – ◆Waterford 16.

🏨 **Carraig,** Main St., ✆ 41455, Fax 41604 – ▤ rest 📺 ☎ 🅿 – 🔏 50. 🔼 🄰🄴 𝐕𝐈𝐒𝐀. ✍
closed Good Friday and Christmas Day – **M** 8.00/12.95 **st.** and a la carte – **11 rm** ⊏⊐ 30.00/50.00 **st.** – SB 75.90/85.90 **st.**

🏠 **Cedarfield House** ♨, Waterford Rd, E : 1 m. on N 24 ✆ 40164, ☞ – 📺 ☜ 🅿. 🔼 𝐕𝐈𝐒𝐀. ✍
closed January-March – **M** (closed Sunday to non-residents) (dinner only) 22.50 **st.** ♟ 5.50 – **6 rm** ⊏⊐ 30.00/70.00 **st.** – SB (except June-August and Bank Holidays) 85.00/100.00 **st.**

(Caiseal) Tipperary 405 I 10 Ireland G. – pop. 2 436 – ECD : Wednesday – ✪ 062.

See : Town★★★ – Rock of Cashel★★★ AC – Cormac's Chapel★★ – Round Tower★ – Museum★ – Cashel Palace Gardens★ – Cathedrals★ – GPA Bolton Library★ AC – Hore Abbey★ – Dominican Friary★.

Envir. : Holy Cross Abbey★★, N : 9 m. by R 660 – Athassel Abbey★, W : 5 m. by N 74.

🎂 Town Hall ✆ 61333 (1 April-1 October).

◆Dublin 101 – ◆Cork 60 – Kilkenny 34 – ◆Limerick 36 – ◆Waterford 44.

🏰 **Cashel Palace** ♨, Main St., ✆ 61411, Fax 61521, « Former Archbishop's palace, gardens » – 📺 ☎ 🅿 – 🔏 25. 🔼 🄰🄴 ⓞ 𝐕𝐈𝐒𝐀. ✍
closed 24 to 26 December – **M** (bar lunch)/dinner 35.00 **st.** ♟ 7.00 – ⊏⊐ 11.00 – **20 rm** 85.00/225.00 **t.** – SB 120.00/160.00 **st.**

↱ **Ros Guill House** without rest., NE : ¾ m. on R 691 ✆ 61507, ☞ – 🅿. 🔼 𝐕𝐈𝐒𝐀. ✍
April-October – **5 rm** ⊏⊐ 19.00/31.00 **st.**

✕✕ **Chez Hans,** Rockside, ✆ 61177, « Converted 19C church » – 🅿. 🔼 𝐕𝐈𝐒𝐀
closed Sunday, Monday and first 3 weeks January – **M** (dinner only) 22.50 **t.** and a la carte ♟ 6.00.

Le Guide change, changez de guide Michelin tous les ans.

(Cuan an Chaisil) Galway 405 C 7 Ireland G. – ✪ 095 Clifden.

See : Town★.

◆Dublin 173 – Galway 41.

🏨 **Cashel House** ♨, ✆ 31001, Fax 31077, ≼, « Country house atmosphere, gardens », 🐟, park, ✕ – 📺 ☎ 🅿. 🔼 🄰🄴 ⓞ 𝐕𝐈𝐒𝐀
M 19.95/29.00 **t.** and a la carte ♟ 7.00 – **32 rm** ⊏⊐ 64.00/160.00 **t.** – SB (October-April except Bank Holidays) 140.60/200.00 **st.**

🏨 **Zetland House** ♨, ✆ 31111, Fax 31117, ≼ Cashel Bay, « Country house, gardens », 🐟, ✕ – ☎ 🅿. 🔼 🄰🄴 ⓞ 𝐕𝐈𝐒𝐀
Easter-October – **M** (dinner only) 25.50 **t.** and a la carte 19.00/27.50 **t.** ♟ 8.00 – **20 rm** ⊏⊐ 70.00/140.00 **t.** – SB (except July and August) 160.00/220.00 **st.**

🏠 **Glynsk House** ♨, SW : 4½ m. on R 340 ✆ 32279, Fax 32342, ≼ – 📺 ☎ 🅿. 🔼 𝐕𝐈𝐒𝐀
March-October – **M** 10.50/18.00 **st.** and a la carte – **12 rm** ⊏⊐ 27.00/50.00 **st.** – SB 90.00/100.00 **st.**

(Béal Átha na gCarraigíní) Sligo 405 G 5 Ireland G. – ✉ Boyle (Roscommon) – ✪ 071 Sligo.

Envir. : Carrowkeel Megalithic Cemetery (≼★★) S : 3 m.

◆Dublin 118 – Longford 42 – ◆Sligo 15.

🏨 **Cromleach Lodge** ♨, Ballindoon, SE : 3½ m. ✆ 65155, Fax 65455, ≼ Lough Arrow, 🐟, ☞, park – ♿ 📺 ☎ 🅿. 🔼 🄰🄴 ⓞ 𝐕𝐈𝐒𝐀. ✍
closed 4 to 29 January and 22 to 27 December – **Meals** (dinner only) 26.50 **t.** ♟ 5.50 – **10 rm** ⊏⊐ 60.00/125.00 **t.** – SB 80.00/164.00 **st.**

(Baile na Lorgan) Monaghan 405 L 5 – pop. 2 425 – ✪ 042.

▪ Muchno Park ✆ 40197.

◆Dublin 68 – ◆Belfast 58 – ◆Drogheda 39 – ◆Dundalk 17 – ◆Londonderry 80.

🏨 **Glencarn,** Monaghan Rd, ✆ 46666, Fax 46521, ♣, 🔲 – 📺 ☎ 🅿. 🔼 🄰🄴 ⓞ 𝐕𝐈𝐒𝐀. ✍
closed 24 and 25 December – **M** (bar lunch Monday to Saturday)/dinner 14.50 **t.** and a la carte ♟ 4.95 – **27 rm** ⊏⊐ 32.00/120.00 **t.** – SB 69.00/99.00 **st.**

(Caisleán Uí Chonaill) Limerick 405 G 9 Ireland G. – pop. 1 053 – ✉ ✪ 061 Limerick.

See : Town★.

◆Dublin 111 – ◆Limerick 9.

🏨 **Castle Oaks House** ♨, ✆ 377666, Fax 377717, ≼, ♣, ≋, 🔲, 🐟, ☞, park, ✕ – 📺 ☎ 🅿. 🔼 🄰🄴 ⓞ 𝐕𝐈𝐒𝐀 𝐉𝐂𝐁. ✍
M (bar lunch Monday to Saturday)/dinner 15.50 **st.** and a la carte ♟ 4.50 – **11 rm** ⊏⊐ 54.00/100.00 **t.** – SB 95.00 **st.**

CASTLEDERMOT (Díseart Diarmada) Kildare 405 L 9 Ireland G. – pop. 792 – ✆ 0503.

Exc. : Carlow Cathedral (Marble Monument★) NE : 7 m. by N 9.

◆Dublin 44 – Kilkenny 30 – Wexford 54.

🏰 **Kilkea Castle** ⌕, Kilkea, NW : 3 ¾ m. on R 418 ℰ 45156, Fax 45187, ≼, « Part 12C castle », ⅃☆, ⅀☲, ⬚, ⍀, ⛳, park, ✗ – ⧉ ✕⊱ rm 📺 ☎ ℗ – 🔬 300. ◩ Æ ① 𝚅𝙸𝚂𝙰 𝙹𝙲𝙱. ✗ closed 21 to 27 December – **M** 14.95/25.50 **t.** ⓛ 5.50 – ⌕ 10.00 – **44 rm** 105.00/190.00 **t.**, 1 suite.

CAVAN (An Cabhán) Cavan 405 J 6 Ireland G. – pop. 3 240 – ✆ 049.

Envir. : Killykeen Forest Park★, W : 6 m. by R 198.

🛈 Farnham St. ℰ 31942 (May-September).

◆Dublin 71 – Drogheda 58 – Enniskillen 40.

🏰 **Kilmore,** Dublin Rd, E : 2 m. on N 3 ℰ 32288, Fax 32458 – 📺 ☎ ⅃ ℗ – 🔬 400. ◩ Æ ① 𝚅𝙸𝚂𝙰. ✗
M 9.50/17.50 **st.** and dinner a la carte ⓛ 4.50 – **39 rm** ⌕ 29.00/66.00 **st.**

CLIFDEN (An Clochán) Galway 405 B 7 – pop. 796 – ECD : Thursday – ✆ 095.

🛈 ℰ 21163 (3 May-30 September).

◆Dublin 181 – Ballina 77 – ◆Galway 49.

🏰 **Rock Glen Manor House** ⌕, S : 1 ¼ m. by L 102 ℰ 21035, Fax 21737, ⍀, ✗ – 📺 ☎ ℗. ◩ Æ ① 𝚅𝙸𝚂𝙰. ✗
mid March-October – **M** (bar lunch)/dinner 26.00 **t.** ⓛ 6.00 – **29 rm** ⌕ 50.00/180.00 **st.**

🏰 **Abbeyglen Castle** ⌕, Sky Rd, W : ½ m. ℰ 21201, Fax 21797, ≼, ⅀☲, ⬚ heated, ⍀, ✗ – ✕⊱ rm 📺 ☎ ℗. ◩ Æ ① 𝚅𝙸𝚂𝙰
closed 10 January-1 February – **M** (bar lunch)/dinner 19.50 **st.** ⓛ 7.00 – **38 rm** ⌕ 59.00/ 99.00 **st.**, 3 suites – SB 80.00/130.00 **st.**

🏰 **Ardagh** ⌕, Ballyconneely rd, S : 1 ¾ m. on L 102 ℰ 21384, Fax 21314, ≼ Ardbear Bay, ⍀ – 📺 ☎ ℗. ◩ Æ ① 𝚅𝙸𝚂𝙰 𝙹𝙲𝙱. ✗
April-October – **M** (bar lunch)/dinner 20.00 **t.** ⓛ 5.75 – **21 rm** ⌕ 41.50/95.00 **st.** – SB 50.00/ 140.00 **st.**

⌂ **Sunnybank House** without rest., Sunny Bank, Church Hill, ℰ 21437, ⅀☲, ⬚ heated, ⍀, ✗ – ℗ . ◩ Æ 𝚅𝙸𝚂𝙰. ✗
April-October – **11 rm** ⌕ 30.00/50.00 **t.**

⌂ **Failte** ⌕ without rest., S : 1 ¼ m. by L 102 ℰ 21159, ≼ – ℗. ◩ Æ 𝚅𝙸𝚂𝙰. ✗
April-September – **6 rm** ⌕ 13.00/30.00 **st.**

CLONEA STRAND Waterford – see Dungarvan.

CLONMEL (Cluain Meala) Tipperary 405 I 10 – pop. 12 407 – ECD : Thursday – ✆ 052.

🛈₈ Lyreanearla, Mountain Rd ℰ 21138, SE : 3 m.

🛈 Community Office, Nelson St. ℰ 22960 (17 June-7 September).

◆Dublin 108 – ◆Cork 59 – Kilkenny 31 – ◆Limerick 48 – ◆Waterford 29.

🏰 **Minella** ⌕, Coleville Rd, ℰ 22388, Fax 24381, ⍀, ✗, park – 📺 ☎ ℗ – 🔬 600. ◩ Æ ①
closed Christmas Day – **M** 16.00/20.00 **st.** and dinner a la carte ⓛ 6.50 – **45 rm** ⌕ 35.00/ 140.00 **st.** – SB 90.00/140.00 **st.**

🏰 **Clonmel Arms,** Sarsfield St., ℰ 21233, Fax 21526 – ⧉ 📺 ☎ – 🔬 300. ◩ Æ ① 𝚅𝙸𝚂𝙰
M 9.00/14.50 **t.** ⓛ 4.50 – ⌕ 5.50 – **31 rm** 46.00/72.00 **t.** – SB (weekends only) 60.00/ 70.00 **st.**

✗✗ **Jasmine Court,** 36 Gladstone St., ℰ 24888 – ◩ Æ ① 𝚅𝙸𝚂𝙰 𝙹𝙲𝙱
closed lunch Monday to Thursday, 25 December and 10 to 13 February – **M** - Chinese 7.50/13.00 **t.** and dinner a la carte.

COBH (An Cóbh) Cork 405 H 12 – ✆ 021 Cork

◆Dublin 173 – ◆Cork 13 – ◆Waterford 71.

⌂ **Tearmann** ⌕, Ballynde, N : 2 ½ m. by R 624 ℰ 813182, ⍀ – ℗. ✗
March-October – **M** (by arrangement) 11.00 **st.** – **3 rm** ⌕ 14.00/26.00 **st.**

CONG (Conga) Mayo 405 E 7 Ireland G. – pop. 213 – ✆ 092.

See : Town★ – Envir. : Lough Corrib★★.

Exc. : Ross Abbey★★ (Tower ≼★) – Joyce Country★★ (Lough Nafooey★★) W : by R 345.

◆Dublin 160 – Ballina 49 – ◆Galway 28.

🏰 **Ashford Castle** ⌕, ℰ 46003, Telex 53749, Fax 46260, ≼, « Part 13C and 18C castle, in extensive formal gardens on the shores of Lough Corrib », ⅃☆, ⍀, park, ✗ – ⧉ 📺 ☎ ℗ – 🔬 110. ◩ Æ ① 𝚅𝙸𝚂𝙰
M – George V Room (closed Christmas and New Year) 20.00/33.00 **t.** and a la carte ⓛ 8.40 – (see also **Connaught Room** below) – ⌕ 13.80 – **77 rm** 184.00/235.00 **st.**, 6 suites – SB (November-March except Christmas and New Year) 187.90/272.95 **st.**

⌂ Danagher's, ℰ 46028, Fax 46495 – 📺 ☎. ✗
11 rm.

✗✗✗✗ **Connaught Room** (at Ashford Castle H.), ℰ 46003, Telex 53749, Fax 46260, ≼ gardens, Lough Corrib and islands – ℗. ◩ Æ ① 𝚅𝙸𝚂𝙰
M (booking essential) (dinner only) a la carte 35.00/43.50 **t.** ⓛ 12.50.

CORK (Corcaigh) Cork 📖 G 12 Ireland G. – pop. 136 344 – ✆ 021.

See : City★★ – Shandon Bells★★ EY , St. Fin Barre's Cathedral★★ *AC* Z , Cork Public Museum★★ X **M** – Grand Parade★ Z , South Mall★ Z , St. Patrick Street★ Z , Crawford Art Gallery★ Y – Christ the King Church★ X **D** , Elizabethan Fort★ Z , Cork Lough★ X.

Envir. : Dunkathel House★ *AC*, E : 5¾ m. by N 8 and N 25 X.

Exc. : Fota Island★★ (Fota House★★) E : 8 m. by N 8 and N 25 X – Cobh★ (St. Colman's Cathedral★, Lusitania Memorial★) SE : 15 m. by N 8, N 25 and R 624 X.

🏌 Douglas ✆ 891086, SE : 3 m. by R 609 X – 🏌 Mahon, Cloverhill, Blackrock X – 🏌 Monkstown, Parkgarriffe ✆ 841376, SE : 7 m. by R 609 X – 🏌 Harbour Point, Clash, Little Island ✆ 353094, E : 5 m. by N 25 X.

✈ Cork Airport ✆ 313131, S : 4 m. by L 42 X – **Terminal :** Bus Station, Parnell Pl.

🚢 To France : Cherbourg and Le Harve (Irish Ferries) (summer only) - to France : Roscoff and St. Malo (Brittany Ferries) (summer only) – to Swansea (Swansea Cork Car Ferries) (10 h).

🛈 Cork City, Grand Parade ✆ 273251 – Cork Ferryport, Ringaskiddy (1 June-30 September).

◆Dublin 154.

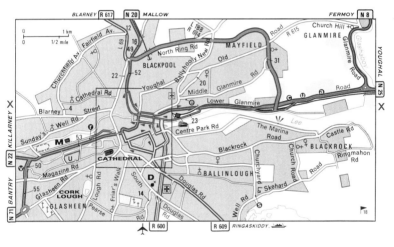

🏨 Fitzpatrick's Silver Springs, Tivoli, E : 2½ m. on N 8 ✆ 507533, Telex 76111, Fax 507641, *Lồ*, ⩵s, ◻, 🔲, ⛳, park, ⛷, squash – 🛗 🖥 rest 📺 ☎ 🅿 – 🛗 1 200. ⛷   X **c**
107 rm, 2 suites.

🏨 **Jurys,** Western Rd, by Washington St., ✆ 276622, Telex 76073, Fax 274477, *Lồ*, ⩵s, ◻, heated, ⛷, squash – 🛗 🖥 rest 📺 ☎ 🅿 – 🛗 500. 🄰 🄰🄴 ⱺ 𝘝𝘐𝘚𝘈 ⛷   Z **v**
M – Glandore 13.75/16.00 **t.** and a la carte ⋔ 5.95 – **Fastnet** (dinner only) – ⅌ 9.25 – **183 rm** 87.50/100.00 **t.**, 1 suite.

🏨 **Imperial,** South Mall, ✆ 274040, Telex 75126, Fax 274040 – 🛗 📺 ☎ 🅿 – 🛗 300. 🄰 🄰🄴 ⱺ 𝘝𝘐𝘚𝘈   Z **n**
closed 24 December-1 January – **M** 10.00/20.00 **t.** and a la carte ⋔ 5.00 – **100 rm** ⅌ 75.00/ 130.00 **t.** – SB (weekends only) 80.00 **st.**

🏨 **Morrisons Island,** Morrisons Quay, ✆ 275858, Fax 275833, ⩽ – 🛗 📺 ☎ 🅿. 🄰 🄰🄴 ⱺ 𝘝𝘐𝘚𝘈 ⛷   Z **a**
M – Riverbank (bar dinner Sunday) 9.75/23.00 **t.** and a la carte ⋔ 6.50 – ⅌ 6.50 – **8 rm** 73.00/98.00 **st.**, **32 suites** 98.00 **st.** – SB 85.00/138.00 **st.**   X

🏨 **Rochestown Park,** Rochestown Rd, SE : 3 m. by R 609 ✆ 892233, Fax 892178, *Lồ*, ⩵s, ◻, ⛷ – 🛗 📺 ☎ 🅿 – 🛗 150. 🄰 🄰🄴 ⱺ 𝘝𝘐𝘚𝘈 ⛷
M 11.00/20.00 **t.** and a la carte ⋔ 5.00 – **63 rm** ⅌ 27.00/100.00 **t.** – SB (weekends only) 110.00/149.00 **st.**

🏨 **Arbutus Lodge,** Middle Glanmire Rd, Montenotte, ✆ 501237, Fax 502893, ⛷, ⛷ – 🖥 rest 📺 ☎ 🅿. 🄰 🄰🄴 ⱺ 𝘝𝘐𝘚𝘈 ⛷   X **e**
M (see below) – **20 rm** ⅌ 42.00/110.00 **st.** – SB (weekends only) 117.00/162.00 **st.**

CORK

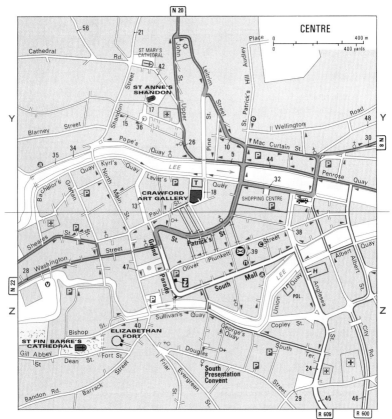

🏠 **Lotamore House** without rest., Tivoli, E : 3¼ m. on N 8 📞 822344, Fax 822219, ⌖, park
  – 📺 ☎ 🅿. 🔼 AE VISA   X **a**
  21 rm ⊇ 25.00/44.00 st.

🏠 **Victoria Lodge** without rest., Victoria Cross, 📞 542233, Fax 542572, ⌖ – 🛗 📺 ☎ 🅿. 🔼
  AE VISA   X **v**
  22 rm ⊇ 26.00/40.00 st.

🏠 **Forte Travelodge** without rest., Blackash, S : 2 ¼ m. by R 600 📞 310722, Reservations (Freephone) 0800 850950 (UK) - 1800 709709 (Eire) – 📺 ♿ 🅿. 🔼 AE ⓞ
  VISA   X
  40 rm 31.95 t.

🛏 **Seven North Mall** without rest., 7 North Mall, 📞 397191, Fax 300811 – 📺 ☎ 🅿. 🔼 VISA.
  ⌖   Y **a**
  closed 18 December-6 January – **5 rm** ⊇ 40.00/60.00 t.

🛏 **Acorn House** without rest., 14 St. Patricks Hill, 📞 502474 – 📺 🔼 VISA. ⌖   Y **e**
  closed mid December-mid January – **9 rm** ⊇ 20.00/50.00 st.

XXX **Cliffords,** 18 Dyke Par., ℰ 275333 – 🅰 🆎 ⓪ 𝗩𝗜𝗦𝗔   X **r**
closed lunch Saturday and Monday, Sunday last 2 weeks August, 1 week Christmas and Bank Holidays – **Meals** 12.75/27.00 **t.**

XXX **Arbutus Lodge,** Middle Glanmire Rd, Montenotte, ℰ 501237, Fax 502893, ⇞ – ▤ ⓟ.   X **e**
🅰 🆎 ⓪ 𝗩𝗜𝗦𝗔
closed Sunday to non-residents – **M** 12.50/22.50 **st.** and a la carte ₰ 6.75.

XXX **Flemings** with rm, Silver Grange House, Tivoli, E : 2¾ on N 8 ℰ 821621, Fax 821800, ⇞
– 📺 ☎ ⓟ. 🅰 🆎 ⓪ 𝗩𝗜𝗦𝗔 𝗝𝗖𝗕. ✄   X **u**
closed 24 to 26 December – **M** 12.50/29.00 **t.** and a la carte ₰ 6.00 – **4 rm** ⊇ 36.00/65.00 **t.**

XX **Lovett's,** Churchyard Lane, off Well Rd, Douglas, ℰ 294909 – ⓟ. 🅰 🆎 ⓪ 𝗩𝗜𝗦𝗔   X **s**
closed Saturday lunch, Sunday and 24 to 30 December – **M** 16.50/22.00 **st.** and dinner a la carte ₰ 5.50.

X **Jacques** 9 Phoenix St., ℰ 277387, Fax 270634 – ▤. 🅰 🆎 ⓪ 𝗩𝗜𝗦𝗔   Z **c**
closed Sunday, Monday, 24 December-2 January and Bank Holidays
M (dinner only) a la carte 15.00/22.90 **t.** ₰ 5.50.

COURTOWN HARBOUR **(Cuan Bhaile na Cúirte)** Wexford 405 N 10 – pop. 337 – ✉ ☏ 055 Gorey.

◆Dublin 62 – ◆Waterford 59 – Wexford 42.

🏠 **Courtown,** ℰ 25108, Fax 25304, ₭, ⩳, 🏊, – 📺 ☎ ⓟ. 🅰 🆎 ⓪ 𝗩𝗜𝗦𝗔. ✄
M 11.00/19.50 **t.** and a la carte ₰ 5.50 – **21 rm** ⊇ 35.00/79.00 **t.** – SB (April-October) 95.00/120.00 **st.**

CROOKEDWOOD **(Tigh Munna)** Westmeath 405 K 7 – ✉ Mullingar – ☏ 044.

◆Dublin 55 – ◆Drogheda 30 – Mullingar 6.

XX **Crookedwood House,** E : 1½ m. on Delvin rd ℰ 72165, Fax 72166, « 18C rectory », ⇞
– ⓟ. 🅰 🆎 ⓪ 𝗩𝗜𝗦𝗔
closed Sunday dinner, Monday and first 2 weeks November – **M** (dinner only and Sunday lunch)/dinner 17.00 **st.** and a la carte ₰ 5.45.

CROSSMOLINA **(Crois Mhaoilíona)** Mayo 405 E 5 Ireland G. – pop. 1 335 – ✉ ☏ 096 Ballina.

Envir. : Errew Abbey★, SE : 6 m. by R 315.
Exc. : Broad Haven★, NW : 27 m. by N 59 and R 313.

◆Dublin 157 – ◆Ballina 6.5.

🏠 **Enniscoe House** ✥, Castlehill, S : 2 m. on L 140 ℰ 31112, Fax 31773, ≼, « Georgian country house, antiques », ⋟, park – ⓟ. 🅰 🆎 𝗩𝗜𝗦𝗔. ✄
April-mid October and January – **M** (dinner only) 20.00 **t.** ₰ 7.00 – **6 rm** ⊇ 50.00/90.00 **t.** – SB 110.00/130.00 **st.**

CULDAFF **(Cúil Dabhcha)** Donegal 405 K 2 – ✉ Inishowen – ☏ 077 Moville.

◆Dublin 170 – ◆Londonderry 21 – ◆Sligo 115.

🏠 **Culdaff House** ✥, NW : ½ m. by Beach rd ℰ 79103, ≼, « Working farm », ⇞ – ⓟ. ✄
closed December and January – **M** (by arrangement) – **6 rm** ⊇ 17.00/28.00 **st.**

DALKEY **(Deilginis)** Dublin 405 N 8 Ireland G. – ☏ 01 Dublin.

Envir. : ≼★★ of Killiney Bay from coast road south of Sorrento Point.

◆Dublin 11.

X **Il Ristorante,** 108 Coliemore Rd, ℰ 284 0800 – 🅰 𝗩𝗜𝗦𝗔
closed Sunday, Monday, 2 weeks February, Good Friday and 1 week Christmas – **M** - **Italian** (dinner only) a la carte 22.00/25.25 **st.** ₰ 7.75.

X **Guinea Pig,** 17 Railway Rd, ℰ 285 9055 – 🅰 🆎 ⓪ 𝗩𝗜𝗦𝗔
closed Sunday, Good Friday and 25-26 December – **M** - **Seafood** (booking essential) (dinner only) 21.95 **t.** and a la carte ₰ 6.00.

DELGANY **(Deilgne)** Wicklow 405 N 8 – pop. 7 442 (inc. Greystones) – ✉ Bray – ☏ 01 Dublin.

🏌 Delganny ℰ 287 4645/287 4833.

◆Dublin 19.

🏛 **Glenview** (Best Western) ✥, Glen of the Downs, NW : 2 m. by L 164 on N 11 ℰ 287 3399, Fax 287 7511, ≼, ⇞, park – ⇲ rm 📺 ☎ ⅋ ⓟ – 🔬 160. 🅰 🆎 ⓪ 𝗩𝗜𝗦𝗔. ✄
closed 25 December – **M** 14.50/19.50 **st.** and a la carte ₰ 5.00 – **42 rm** ⊇ 50.00/150.00 **st.** – SB (except Bank Holidays) 80.00/130.00 **st.**

☞ Plan Guide **Le Tunnel sous la Manche**

    260 *Version française*
        avec les curiosités touristiques en Angleterre

    261 *Version anglaise*
        avec les curiosités touristiques sur le continent

DINGLE (An Daingean) Kerry 405 B 11 Ireland G. – pop. 1 358 – ECD : Thursday – ✆ 066 Tralee.

See : Town★ – Pier★, St. Mary's Church★.

Envir. : Gallarus Oratory★★★, NW : 5 m. by R 559 – NE : Connor Pass★★ – Kilmalkedar★, NW : 5½ m. by R 559.

Exc. : Mount Eagle (Beehive Huts★★) W : 9 m. by R 559 – Slea Head★★, W : 10½ m. by R 559 – Stradbally Strand★★, NE : 10½ m. via Connor Pass – Ballyferriter Heritage Centre★ *AC*, NW : 8 m. by R 559 – Mount Brandon★, N : 12½ m. by R 559 via Kilmalkedar – Blasket Islands★, W : 13 m. by R 559 and ferry from Dunquin.

🛈 ✆ 51188 (5 April- 31 October).

♦Dublin 216 – ♦Killarney 51 – ♦Limerick 95.

🏨 **Dingle Skellig**, SE : ½ m. by T 68 ✆ 51144, Fax 51501, ≤, 🏖, 🖾, 🐎, ✖ – 📺 ☎ 🅿. 🔼 AE ⑩ VISA ❄
mid March-mid November – **M** 9.50/19.95 **t.** and dinner a la carte – **114 rm** ⌷ 47.50/92.00 **t.**, 1 suite – SB 127.00/156.00 **st.**

🏨 **Benners**, Main St., ✆ 51638, Fax 51412, 🐎 – 📺 ☎ 🅿. 🔼 AE ⑩ VISA ❄
M (bar lunch Monday to Saturday)/dinner 18.00 **t.** and a la carte ⓘ 5.00 – **24 rm** ⌷ 28.00/80.00 **st.** – SB 60.00/76.00 **st.**

⌂ **Milltown House** 🦢, without rest., W : ¾ m. by Slea Head Drive ✆ 51372, Fax 51095, ≤, 🐎 – 📺 ☎ 🅿. 🔼 VISA ❄
closed 2 January-1 March – **7 rm** ⌷ 36.00 **st.**

⌂ **Alpine House** without rest., Mail Rd, E : on T 68 ✆ 51250, 🐎 – 📺 ☎ 🅿. 🔼 VISA ❄
closed December and January – **14 rm** ⌷ 33.00 **st.**

⌂ **Scanlons** without rest., Mail Rd, E : ½ m. on T 68 ✆ 51883, Fax 51297, ≤ – 📺 ☎ 🅿. 🔼 VISA ❄
7 rm ⌷ 35.00/40.00 **st.**

XX **Beginish**, Green St., ✆ 51588, Fax 51591, 🐎 – 🔼 AE ⑩ VISA
mid March-mid November – **M** - Seafood (closed Monday) (light lunch)/dinner a la carte 16.45/20.40 **t.** ⓘ 5.00.

X **Doyle's Seafood Bar** with rm, 4 John St., ✆ 51174, Fax 51816 – 📺 ☎. 🔼 ⑩ VISA ❄
mid March-mid November – **Meals** *(closed Sunday)* (dinner only) a la carte 17.00/22.00 **t.** ⓘ 7.00 – **8 rm** ⌷ 39.00/62.00 **st.**

DONEGAL (Dún na nGall) Donegal 405 H 4 Ireland G. – pop. 1 956 – ECD : Wednesday – ✆ 073.

See : Donegal Castle★ *AC*.

Exc. : Cliffs of Bunglass★★★, W : 30 m. by N 56 and R 263 – Glencolumbkille Folk Village★★ *AC*, W : 33 m. by N 56 and R 263 – Trabane Strand★★, W : 36 m. by N 56 and R 263 – Glenmalin Court Cairn★, W : 37 m. by N 56 and R 263 at Malin Beg.

✈ Donegal Airport ✆ (075) 48232.

🛈 The Quay ✆ 21148 (April-September).

♦Dublin 164 – ♦Londonderry 48 – ♦Sligo 40.

🏨 **St. Ernan's House** 🦢, St. Ernan's Island, SW : 2 ¼ m. by N 15 ✆ 21065, Fax 22098, « Wooded island setting ≤ Donegal Bay », park – ❄ rest 📺 ☎ 🅿. 🔼 VISA ❄
April-mid November – **M** (dinner only) 24.50 **t.** ⓘ 5.50 – **12 rm** ⌷ 100.00/130.00 **t.**

🏨 **Harvey's Point Country** 🦢, NE : 4½ m. by T 27 (Killibegs rd) ✆ 22208, Fax 22352, ≤, « Loughside setting », 🐎, park – 📺 ☎ 🅿 – 🔬 100. 🔼 AE ⑩ VISA
mid March-9 November – **M** 12.50/25.00 **t.** and a la carte ⓘ 5.80 – **20 rm** ⌷ 55.00/100.00 **t.** – SB 143.00/176.00 **st.**

⌂ **Island View House** without rest., Ballyshannon rd, SW : ¾ m. ✆ 22411, ≤ – ❄ 📺 🅿
4 rm ⌷ 22.00/28.00.

DOOLIN (Dúlainm) Clare 405 D 8 – ✆ 065 Ennis.

♦Dublin 171 – ♦Galway 43 – ♦Limerick 50.

🏠 **Aran View House** 🦢, NE : ½ m. ✆ 74061, Fax 74540, ≤, « Working farm », 🐎, park 📺 ☎ 🅿. 🔼 VISA ❄
March-October – **M** (bar lunch Monday to Friday)/dinner 20.00 **st.** and a la carte ⓘ 9.00 – **20 rm** ⌷ 30.00/50.00 **st.** – SB (except Bank Holidays) 65.00/100.00 **st.**

DROGHEDA (Droichead Átha) Louth 405 M 6 – ✆ 041.

Envir. : Monasterboice★★, N : 6 ½ m. by N 1 – Termonfeckin (Tower House★) NE : 5 m. by R 166.

♦Dublin 29 – ♦Dundalk 22.

🏨 **Boyne Valley**, on N 1 ✆ 37737, Fax 39188, 🐎, park ❄ rm 📺 ☎ 🅿 – 🔬 150. 🔼 AE ⑩ VISA
M 10.00/19.00 **st.** and a la carte ⓘ 4.50 – **38 rm** ⌷ 31.50/75.10 **st.** – SB (except Christmas) 70.00/80.00 **st.**

DRUMCLIFF (Droim Chliabh) Sligo 405 G 5 – ✆ 071 Sligo.

♦Dublin 178 – Donegal 34 – ♦Sligo 6.

⌂ **Mountain View** 🦢 without rest., Carney, NW : 1 m. ✆ 63290, ≤, « Working farm » 🐎 – 🅿 – May-October – **5 rm** ⌷ 18.00/30.00 **st.**

694

See : City★★★ – Trinity College★★★ (Library★★★ *AC*) EY – Chester Beatty Library★★★ CV –
Phoenix Park★★★ AU – Dublin Castle★★ DY – Christ Church Cathedral★★ DY – St. Patrick's
Cathedral★★ DZ – March's Library★★ DZ – National Museum★★ (Treasury★★), FZ – National
Gallery★★ FZ – Merrion Square★★ FZ – Rotunda Hospital Chapel★★ EX – Kilmainham
Hospital★★ AV – Kilmainham Gaol Museum★★ AV **M6** – National Botanic Gardens★★ BU –
No 29★ FZ **D** – Liffey Bridge★ EY – Taylors' Hall★ CV – City Hall★ DY **H** – Viking Adventure★
DY **K** – St. Audoen's Gate★ DY **B** – St. Stephen's Green★ EZ – Grafton Street★ EYZ – Powerscourt
Centre★ EY – Civic Museum★ EY **M1** – Bank of Ireland★ EY – O'ConnelStreet★ (Anna Livia
Fountain★) EX – St. Michan's Church★ DY **E** – Hush Lane Municipal Gallery of Modern Art★
EX **M4** – Pro-Cathedral★ EX – Garden of Remembrance★ EX – Custon House★ FX – Bluecoat
School★ BU **F** – Guinness Museum★ BV **M7** – Marino Casino★ CU – Zoological Gardens★ AU –
Newman House★ *AC* EZ.

Exc. : Powerscourt★★ (Waterfall★★★ *AC*), S : 14 m. by N 11 and R 117 BV – Russborough
House★★★, SW : 22 m. by N 81 BV.

🚩 Elm Park G. & S.C., Nutley House, Donnybrook ℘ 269 3438/269 3014, by R 118 CV – 🚩
Milltown, Lower Churchtown Rd ℘ 977060, S : 4 m. by R 117 BV – 🚩 Royal Dublin, Bull Island
℘ 337153, NE : 3 m. by R 105 CU – 🚩 Forrest Little ℘ 401183/401763, N : 6½ m. by N 1 BU – 🚩
Lucan, Hermitage ℘ 626 5396, W : 8 m. by N 4 AU – 🚩 Edmondstown, Rathfarnham ℘ 932461,
S : 5 m. by N 81 BV.

✈ Dublin Airport ℘ 379900, N : 5½ m. by N 1 BU – **Terminal** : Busaras (Central Bus Station)
Store St..

⛴ to Holyhead (B & I Line) 2 daily – to the Isle of Man : Douglas (Isle of Man Steam Packet
Co.) (summer only) (4 h 45 mn).

🛈 14 Upper O'Connell St. ℘ 874 7733 – Dublin Airport ℘ 844 5387.

Baggot St., Bridge ℘ 874 7733.

◆Belfast 103 – ◆Cork 154 – ◆Londonderry 146.

Plans on following pages

🏨 **Conrad Dublin**, Earlsfort Terr., D2, ℘ 676 5555, Telex 91872, Fax 676 5424 – 🛗 ⇔ rm 📺
📺 ☎ & 🅿 – 🔬 400. 🔼 📵 🕦 *VISA*. 🛠
   M – **Alexandra** *(closed Saturday lunch and Sunday)* 17.00/26.00 **t.** and a la carte 👖 6.00 –
   Plurabelle 13.50 **t.** and a la carte 👖 6.00 – ⊐ 9.95 – **182 rm** 145.00/172.00 **t.**, 9 suites –
   SB (weekends only) 135.00/250.00 **st.**
     EZ **z**

🏨 Berkeley Court, Lansdowne Rd, Ballsbridge, D4, ℘ 660 1711, Telex 30554,
   Fax 661 7238, ⇌, ▭, – 🛗 ⇔ rm 📺 rest 📺 ☎ & ⇔ 🅿 – 🔬 250. 🔼 📵 🕦 *VISA*.
   🛠
   ⊐ 8.00 – **195 rm** 120.00/140.00 **t.**, 6 suites.
     CV **c**

🏨 **Westbury**, Grafton St., D2, ℘ 679 1122, Telex 91091, Fax 679 7078 – 🛗 ⇔ rm 📺 rest 📺
   ☎ ⇔ – 🔬 200. 🔼 📵 🕦 *VISA*. 🛠
   M 14.50/18.50 **t.** and a la carte – ⊐ 7.50 – **195 rm** 132.00/147.00 **t.**, 8 suites.
     EY **z**

🏨 **Shelbourne** (Forte), 27 St. Stephen's Green, D2, ℘ 676 6471, Telex 93653, Fax 661 6006
   – 🛗 ⇔ rm 📺 ☎ ⇔ – 🔬 400. 🔼 📵 🕦 *VISA*. 🛠
   M 16.50/23.00 **st.** and a la carte 👖 5.50 – ⊐ 10.50 – **155 rm** 125.00/150.00 **t.**, 9 suites –
   SB (weekends only) 181.00/247.00 **st.**
     EZ **s**

🏨 **Gresham**, O'Connell St., D1, ℘ 874 6881, Telex 32473, Fax 878 7175 – 🛗 ▤ rest 📺 ☎
   ⇔ – 🔬 300. 🔼 📵 🕦 *VISA*. 🛠
   closed 24 and 25 December – **M** 17.00 **st.** (dinner) and a la carte 11.45/20.00 **t.** 👖 4.75 –
   ⊐ 9.55 – **194 rm** 75.00/110.00 **t.**, 6 suites.
     EX **s**

🏨 **Jurys**, Pembroke Rd, Ballsbridge, D4, ℘ 660 5000, Telex 93723, Fax 660 5540, ⌇ heated – 🛗
   ▤ rest 📺 ☎ & ⇔ 🅿 – 🔬 850. 🔼 📵 🕦 *VISA*. 🛠
   M 10.00/21.00 **t.** and a la carte 👖 7.00 – ⊐ 9.25 – **282 rm** 105.00/181.00 **t.**, 2 suites.
     CV **c**

🏨 **Towers at Jurys**, Pembroke Rd, Ballsbridge, D4, ℘ 660 5000, Telex 93723,
   Fax 660 5540 – 🛗 ⇔ rm 📺 ☎ & 🅿. 🔼 📵 🕦 *VISA*. 🛠
   M (see Jurys H. above) – ⊐ 9.25 – **96 rm** 105.00/181.00 **t.**, 4 suites.

🏨 **Burlington**, Upper Leeson St., D4, ℘ 660 5222, Telex 93815, Fax 660 8496 – 🛗 📺 ☎ &
   🅿 – 🔬 1000. 🔼 📵 🕦 *VISA*
   M 12.00/16.00 **t.** 👖 4.50 – **448 rm** 92.00/115.00 **t.**, 4 suites.
     BV **o**

🏨 **Doyle Montrose**, Stillorgan Rd, D12, SE : 4 m. by N 11 ℘ 269 3311, Telex 91207,
   Fax 269 1164 – 🛗 ▤ rest 📺 ☎ & 🅿 – 🔬 80. 🔼 📵 🕦 *VISA*. 🛠
   M 9.80/13.80 **t.** and a la carte 👖 4.75 – ⊐ 5.50 – **179 rm** 72.50/150.00 **t.**
     CV **n**

🏨 **Hibernian**, Eastmoreland Pl., Ballsbridge, D4, ℘ 668 7666, Fax 660 2655 – 🛗 📺 ☎ & 🅿.
   🔼 📵 🕦 *VISA*. 🛠
   closed Christmas – **M** *(closed Saturday lunch)* 12.95/22.95 **st.** and dinner a la carte 👖 5.95 –
   30 rm ⊐ 85.00/135.00 **st.** – SB (winter only) (weekends only) 170.00 **st.**
     BV **x**

🏨 **Central**, 1-5 Exchequer St., D2, ℘ 679 7302, Fax 679 7303 – 🛗 ⇔ rm 📺 ☎ – 🔬 80. 🔼
   📵 🕦 *VISA*. 🛠
   closed 25 and 26 December – **M** 10.00/18.50 **t.** and dinner a la carte – ⊐ 7.50 – **69 rm**
   85.00/120.00 **t.**, 1 suite – SB (weekends only) 130.00/170.00 **st.**
     EY **u**

🏨 **Stephens Hall,** Earlsfort Centre, 14-17 Lower Leeson St., D2, ℰ 661 0585, Fax 661 0606 – 📱 ↔ rm 📺 ☎ ⇔. 🄰 AE ⓞ 𝘝𝘐𝘚𝘈 ℅
    EZ **o**
M *(closed Saturday lunch and Sunday dinner)* 10.00/17.00 **t.** and a la carte 🍴 4.50 – ☲ 6.50 – **3 rm** 90.00/130.00 **st.**, **34 suites** 130.00 **st.** – SB (October-May) (weekends only) 90.00/150.00 **st.**

🏨 **Temple Bar,** Fleet St., D2, ℰ 677 3333, Fax 677 3088 – 📱 ↔ rm 📺 ☎ 🅕 – 🄰 30. 🄰 AE
    EY **e**
closed 24 to 27 December – **M** 7.50/11.00 **t.** and a la carte 🍴 5.75 – ☲ 5.50 – **108 rm** 65.00/95.00 **t.** – SB (weekends only) 80.00/110.00 **st.**

🏨 **Grafton Plaza** without rest., Johnsons Pl., D2, ℰ 475 0888, Fax 475 0908 – 📱 📺 ☎ 🅕. 🄰
AE ⓞ 𝘝𝘐𝘚𝘈 ℅
    EZ **c**
M *(closed lunch Saturday and Sunday)* a la carte 11.00/18.00 **st.** – ☲ 7.50 – **75 rm** 50.00/70.00 **st.** – SB (weekends only) 107.00/137.00 **st.**

🏨 **Doyle Tara,** Merrion Rd, D4, SE : 4 m. on T 44
ℰ 269 4666, Fax 269 1027 – 📱 ▤ rest 📺 ☎ 🅕
🄰 330. 🄰 AE ⓞ 𝘝𝘐𝘚𝘈 ℅
    CV **a**
M 9.30/13.25 **t.** and a la carte 🍴 4.20 – ☲ 6.25 –
114 rm 54.00/80.00 **t.**

🏨 **Russell Court,** 21-25 Harcourt St., D2,
ℰ 478 4066, Fax 478 1576 – 📱 📺 ☎ 🅕 – 🄰 100.
🄰 AE ⓞ 𝘝𝘐𝘚𝘈 ℅
    EZ **v**
closed 24 December-2 January – **M** (in bar
Saturday lunch and Sunday dinner) 9.95/16.00 **t.**
and dinner a la carte 🍴 6.00 – ☲ 5.25 – **42 rm**
55.00/92.00 **st.** – SB 96.00/132.00 **st.**

🏨 **Skylon,** Upper Drumcondra Rd, N : 2½ m. on N 1
ℰ 379121, Fax 372778 – 📱 ▤ rest 📺 ☎ 🅕. ℅
92 rm.
    BU **e**

🏨 **Ariel House** without rest., 52 Lansdowne Rd,
Ballsbridge, D4, ℰ 668 5512, Fax 668 5845, ☞ –
📺 ☎ 🅕. 🄰 𝘝𝘐𝘚𝘈 ℅
    CV **c**
☲ 7.50 – **28 rm** 53.00/125.00 **t.**

🏨 **Jurys Christchurch Inn,** Christchurch Pl.,
ℰ 475 0111, Fax 475 0488 – 📱 📺 ☎ &. 🄰 AE ⓞ
𝘝𝘐𝘚𝘈 ℅
    DY **e**
closed 25 and 26 December – **M** (bar lunch)/
dinner 13.80 **st.** and a la carte 🍴 5.50 – ☲ 5.00 –
183 rm 46.00 **st.**

🏠 **Longfield's,** 10 Lower Fitzwilliam St., D2,
ℰ 676 1367, Fax 676 1542 – 📱 📺 ☎. 🄰 AE ⓞ
𝘝𝘐𝘚𝘈 ℅
    FZ **i**
M *(closed lunch Saturday and Sunday)* 18.00/
22.00 **t.** and lunch a la carte 🍴 7.50 – **26 rm**
☲ 60.00/104.00 **st.** – SB (winter only) (weekends
only) 99.00/130.00 **st.**

🏠 **Leeson Court,** 26-27 Lower Leeson St.,
ℰ 676 3380, Fax 661 8273 – 📱 ▤ 📺 ℅
M (in bar) – **20 rm.**
    BV **a**

🏠 **Aberdeen Lodge,** 53-55 Park Av., D4,
ℰ 283 8155, Fax 283 7877, ☞ – 📺 ☎ 🅕. 🄰 AE
ⓞ 𝘝𝘐𝘚𝘈 ℅
    CV **e**
M (dinner only) 24.00 **t.** 🍴 8.00 – **16 rm** ☲ 35.00/
110.00 **t.** – SB 75.00/110.00 **st.**

🏠 **Lansdowne Lodge** without rest., Shelbourne
Rd, D4, ℰ 660 5755, Fax 660 5662, ☞ – 📺 🄰
🄰 𝘝𝘐𝘚𝘈 ℅
    CV **o**
12 rm ☲ 40.00/55.00 **st.**

🏠 **Georgian House,** 20-21 Lower Baggot St., D2,
ℰ 661 8832, Fax 661 8834 – 📺 ☎ 🅕. 🄰 AE ⓞ
𝘝𝘐𝘚𝘈 ℅
    FZ **a**
closed 24 and 25 December – **M** *(closed Saturday
and Sunday lunch and Bank Holidays)* (bar lunch)/
dinner 19.90 **t.** and a la carte 🍴 4.50 – **33 rm**
☲ 49.50/81.00 **st.**

🏠 **Glenogra** without rest., 64 Merrion Rd, D4,
ℰ 668 3661, Fax 668 3661 – 📺 ☎ 🅕. 🄰 𝘝𝘐𝘚𝘈 ℅
closed 22 December-10 January – **9 rm** ☲ 35.00/
65.00 **st.**
    CV **v**

🏠 **Merrion Hall** without rest., 54-56 Merrion Rd,
Ballsbridge, D4, ℰ 668 1426, Fax 668 4280, ☞ –
📺 ☎ 🅕. 🄰 𝘝𝘐𝘚𝘈 ℅
    CV **v**
closed 20 December-1 January – **15 rm** ☲ 35.00/
60.00 **st.**

DUBLIN
BUILT UP AREA

Uppercross House, 26-30 Upper Rathmines Rd, Rathmines, D6, ☏ 975486, Fax 975361 – ⇔ rm TV ☎. AE VISA BV **c**
M (dinner only) 15.00 **st.** and a la carte 4.95 – **14 rm** ☐ 30.00/50.00 **st.** – SB (winter only) 65.00/90.00 **st.**

Morehampton Townhouse without rest., 46 Morehampton Rd, Donnybrook, D4, ☏ 660 2106, Fax 660 2566 – TV ☎ P. VISA. CV **r**
closed 22 December-3 January – **6 rm** ☐ 36.00/56.00 **st.**

Raglan Lodge without rest., 10 Raglan Rd, off Pembroke Rd, Ballsbridge, D4, ☏ 660 6697, Fax 660 6781, – TV ☎ P. AE VISA. CV **z**
closed 22 to 29 December – **7 rm** ☐ 46.00/77.00 **st.**

Canal Road	**BV** 15	James' Street	**BV** 48	St. John's Road West	**AU** 78
Clanbrassil Street	**BV** 17	Leeson Street Upper	**BV** 54	Sandford Road	**BV** 81
Conyngham Road	**AU** 20	Macken Street	**BUV** 56	Shelbourne Road	**CV** 82
Denmark Street	**BU** 24	Morehampton Road	**BV** 60	Shrewsbury Road	**CV** 83
Donnybrook Road	**CV** 26	Mount Street Upper	**BV** 61	South Circular Road	**AU** 84
Dorset Street	**BU** 27	Palmerston Park	**BV** 66	Suir Road	**AV** 86
Drimnagh Road	**AV** 28	Phibsborough Road	**BU** 70	Terenure Road East	**BV** 90
Eglinton Road	**CV** 33	Rathmines Road Upper	**BV** 73	Thomas Street West	**BU** 91
Grand Parade	**BV** 40	Ringsend Road	**CV** 74	Victoria Quay	**BU** 93
Inchicore Road	**AV** 45	St. Agnes Road	**AV** 76	Western Way	**BU** 97
Infirmary Road	**AU** 46	St. Alphonsus Road	**BU** 77	Wolfe Tone Quay	**BU** 102

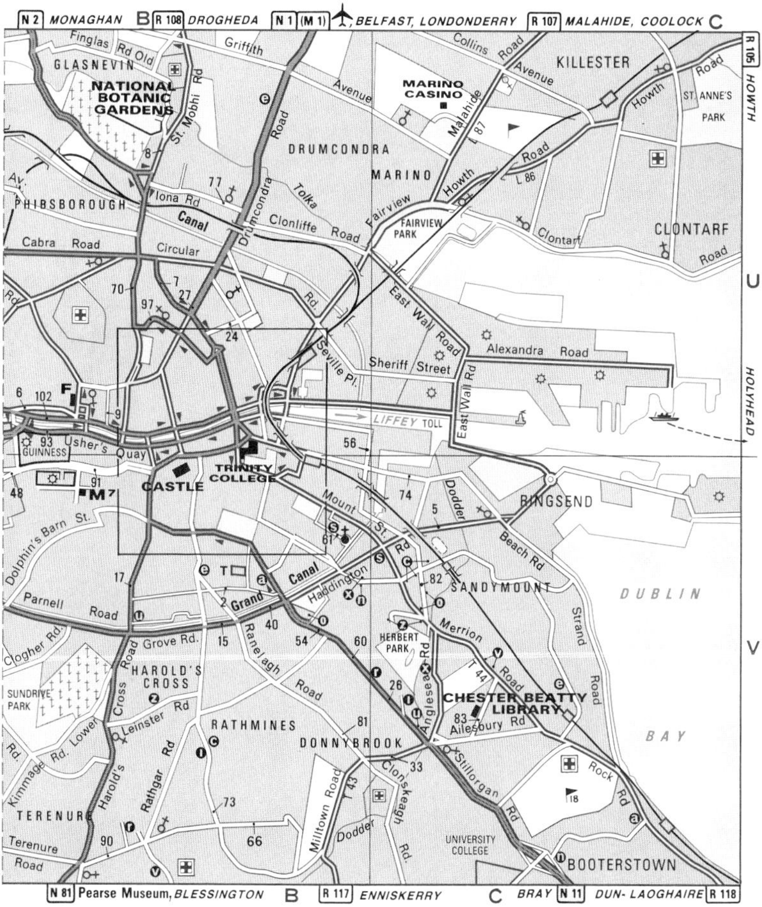

DUBLIN
CENTRE

Town plans:
roads most used by traffic
and those on which guide-
listed hotels and restaurants
stand are fully drawn;
the beginning only
of lesser roads is indicated.

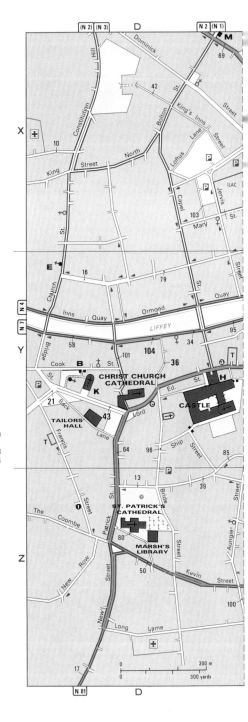

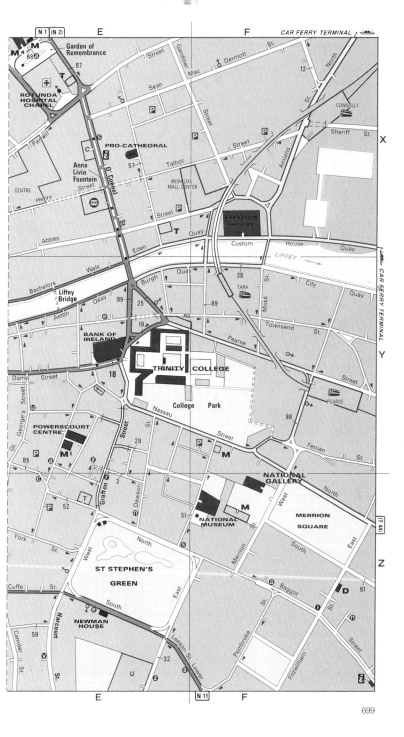

⌂ **Anglesea Town House** without rest., 63 Anglesea Rd, Ballsbridge, D4, ℰ 668 3877, Fax 668 3461 – 📺 ☎. 🔼 🟡 𝗩𝗜𝗦𝗔. ✆   CV **x**
  7 rm ⊇ 40.00/80.00.

⌂ **St. Aiden's** without rest., 32 Brighton Rd, Rathgar, D6, ℰ 906178, Fax 920234 – 📺 ☎ 🅿. 🔼 𝗩𝗜𝗦𝗔. ✆   BV **r**
  9 rm ⊇ 25.00/60.00 **st.**

⌂ **Clara House** without rest., 23 Leinster Rd, Rathmines, D6, ℰ 975904, Fax 975904 – 📺 ☎. 🔼 𝗩𝗜𝗦𝗔   BV **z**
  13 rm ⊇ 30.00/50.00 **st.**

⌂ **Glenveagh Town House** without rest., 31 Northumberland Rd, Ballsbridge, D4, ℰ 668 4612, Fax 668 4559 – 📺 ☎. 🔼 🟡 𝗩𝗜𝗦𝗔. ✆   CV **s**
  11 rm ⊇ 40.00/60.00 **t.**

⌂ **Abrae Court,** 9 Zion Rd, D6, ℰ 922242 – 📺 ☎ 🅿. 🔼 🟡 𝗩𝗜𝗦𝗔. ✆   BV **v**
  M (by arrangement) 15.00 **st.** – **14 rm** ⊇ 25.00/50.00 **st.** – SB (except Bank Holidays) 50.00/80.00 **st.**

⌂ **Wesley House** without rest., 113 Anglesea Rd, Ballsbridge, D4, ℰ 668 1201, ✇ – 📺 🅿.   CV **u**
  3 rm ⊇ 35.00/50.00 **st.**

❌❌❌ ۞ **Patrick Guilbaud,** 46 James' Pl., James' St., off Lower Baggot St., D2, ℰ 676 4192, Fax 660 1546 – 🔼 🟡 🅾️ 𝗩𝗜𝗦𝗔   FZ **n**
  closed Sunday, Monday, 17 March, Good Friday and first 2 weeks January – **M** - French 15.50/25.00 **t.** and a la carte 23.00/35.00 **t.** ⓐ 7.00
  Spec. Galette de tourteaux au confit de canard, Bouillon de langoustines et sole au laurier, Filet d'agneau pré salé, mousseline de persil et salade d'herbes.

❌❌❌ **Le Coq Hardi,** 35 Pembroke Rd, D4, ℰ 668 9070, Fax 668 9887 – 🅿. 🔼 🟡 🅾️ 𝗩𝗜𝗦𝗔 🅹🅲🅱   BV **n**
  closed Saturday lunch, Sunday and Bank Holidays – **M** 15.50/24.50 **t.** and a la carte ⓐ 7.00.

❌❌❌ ۞ **The Commons,** Newman House, 85-86 St. Stephen's Green, D2, ℰ 475 2597, Fax 478 0551, « Contemporary collection of James Joyce inspired Irish Art » – 🔼 🟡 🅾️ 𝗩𝗜𝗦𝗔 🅹🅲🅱   EZ **e**
  closed Saturday lunch, Sunday, 1 week Christmas and Bank Holidays – **M** 16.00/27.50 **t.** and a la carte ⓐ 6.00
  Spec. Foie gras and duck liver pithivier, Pan fried turbot with beetroot and sour cream, Trio of coffee desserts.

❌❌❌ **Ernie's,** Mulberry Gdns, off Morehampton Rd, Donnybrook, D4, ℰ 269 3300, « Contemporary Irish Art collection » – ▤. 🔼 🟡 🅾️ 𝗩𝗜𝗦𝗔   CV **i**
  closed Saturday lunch, Sunday, Monday and 1 week Christmas – Meals 13.95/19.95 **t.** and dinner a la carte ⓐ 6.25.

❌❌ **Locks,** 1 Windsor Terr., Portobello, ℰ 543391, Fax 538352 – 🔼 🟡 🅾️ 𝗩𝗜𝗦𝗔   BV **u**
  closed Saturday lunch, Sunday, 1 week Christmas and Bank Holidays – **M** 13.95/19.95 **t.** and a la carte ⓐ 5.15.

❌❌ **Zen,** 89 Upper Rathmines Rd, D6, ℰ 979428 – ▤. 🔼 🟡 🅾️ 𝗩𝗜𝗦𝗔   BV **i**
  closed lunch Monday, Tuesday, Wednesday and Saturday – **M** - Chinese (Szechuan) 8.00 **t.** (lunch) and a la carte 11.10/20.20 **t.** ⓐ 5.50.

❌❌ **La Stampa,** 35 Dawson St., D2, ℰ 677 8611, Fax 677 3336 – 🔼 🟡 🅾️ 𝗩𝗜𝗦𝗔   EZ **n**
  closed Sunday, lunch Bank Holiday Mondays, Easter, 25-26 December and 1 January – **M** 12.50/16.50 **t.** and a la carte ⓐ 5.00.

❌❌ **Les Frères Jacques,** 74 Dame St., D2, ℰ 679 4555, Fax 679 4725 – 🔼 🟡 𝗩𝗜𝗦𝗔   DY **a**
  closed Saturday lunch, Sunday, 2 to 8 January and Bank Holidays – **M** - French 13.00/20.00 **t.** and dinner a la carte ⓐ 5.10.

❌❌ **Chandni,** 174 Pembroke Rd, Ballsbridge, D4, ℰ 668 1458 – ▤. 🔼 🟡 🅾️ 𝗩𝗜𝗦𝗔   CV **o**
  closed Sunday lunch, Good Friday and 25-26 December – **M** - Indian 15.95 **t.** (dinner) and a la carte 10.45/18.40 **t.** ⓐ 8.50.

❌❌ **Old Dublin,** 90-91 Francis St., D8, ℰ 542028, Fax 541406 – 🔼 🟡 🅾️ 𝗩𝗜𝗦𝗔   DZ **i**
  closed Saturday lunch, Sunday and Bank Holidays – **M** - Russian-Scandinavian 11.00/24.00 **t.** ⓐ 5.00.

❌❌ **Chapter One,** 18-19 Parnell Sq., D2, ℰ 873 2266, Fax 873 2330 – ▤ 🅿   EX **a**
  M 10.50/15.00 and dinner a la carte ⓐ 6.75.

❌❌ **Kapriol,** 45 Lower Camden St., D2, ℰ 475 1235 – 🔼 🟡 🅾️ 𝗩𝗜𝗦𝗔 🅹🅲🅱   BV **e**
  closed Sunday, 3 weeks August and Bank Holidays – **M** - Italian (dinner only) 18.00 **t.** and a la carte 16.00/33.40 **t.** ⓐ 5.20.

❌❌ **Eastern Tandoori,** 34-35 South William St., D2, ℰ 671 0428, Fax 677 9232 – ▤. 🔼 🟡 🅾️ 𝗩𝗜𝗦𝗔   EY **a**
  closed Sunday lunch, Good Friday, 25-26 December and Bank Holidays – **M** - Indian 18.50 **st.** (dinner) and a la carte 11.10/15.10 **t.** ⓐ 4.95.

❌❌ **Dobbin's,** 15 Stephen's Lane, off Lower Mount St., D2, ℰ 676 4679, Fax 661 3331 – ▤. 🔼 🟡 🅾️ 𝗩𝗜𝗦𝗔   BV **s**
  closed Monday dinner, Sunday and Bank Holidays – **M** - Bistro 25.50/29.50 **st.** and a la carte ⓐ 6.25.

X **Roly's Bistro,** 7 Ballsbridge Terr., Ballsbridge, D4, ✆ 668 2611, Fax 660 8535 – ▤. ◫ ⒶⒺ
VISA CV **z**
closed Good Friday and 25-26 December – **M** 9.50 **t.** (lunch) and a la carte 13.95/20.75 **t.**
⓵ 4.50.

X **Chili Club,** 1 Anne's Lane, South Anne St., D2, ✆ 677 3721 – ◫ ⒶⒺ ⓪ *VISA* EZ **r**
closed Sunday – **M** - **Thai** (booking essential) 7.95/16.95 **t.** and dinner a la carte ⓵ 4.95.

at Blackrock SE : 4 ½ m. by T 44 – V – ✉ Blackrock – ⊛ 01 Dublin :

XX **Clarets,** 63-65 Main St., D18, ✆ 288 2008 – ◫ ⒶⒺ *VISA*
closed Saturday lunch, Sunday, Monday, 24 to 31 December and Bank Holidays –
Meals 12.95/22.95 **t.** and dinner a la carte ⓵ 6.00.

MICHELIN Distribution Centre, Spilmak Pl., Bluebell Industrial Estate, Naas Rd, Dublin 12,
✆ 509096, Fax 504302 by N7 AZ

GRÜNE REISEFÜHRER

Landschaften, Baudenkmäler
Sehenswürdigkeiten
Fremdenverkehrsstraßen
Tourenvorschläge
Stadtpläne und Übersichtskarten

DUNDRUM (Dún Droma) Tipperary 📖 H 10 – ✉ ⊛ 062 Cashel.
◆Dublin 104 – ◆Cork 66 – ◆Limerick 33.

🏨 **Dundrum House** ♦, SE : ¾ m. on R 505 ✆ 71116, Fax 71366, ┢₈, ☞, park, ❤ – ❘⧣❘ ⓣⓥ ☎
Ⓟ – ♨ 350. ◫ ⒶⒺ ⓪ *VISA*
M (bar lunch Monday to Saturday)/dinner 18.50 **t.** ⓵ 5.50 – **54 rm** ⊇ 50.00/88.00 **t.** –
SB (weekends only) 135.00/164.00 **st.**

DUNFANAGHY (Dún Fionnachaidh) Donegal 📖 I 2 Ireland G. – pop. 390 – ✉ ⊛ 074
Letterkenny.

Envir. : Horn Head Scenic Route★, N : 2 ½ m.

Exc. : Doe Castle★, SE : 7 m. by N 56 – The Rosses★, SW : 25 m. by N 56 and R 259.

┢₈ Dunfanaghy ✆ 36335, E : ½ m.

◆Dublin 172 – Donegal 54 – ◆Londonderry 43.

🏠 **Arnold's,** Main St., ✆ 36208, Fax 36352, ≤, ☞, ❤ – ⓣⓥ ☎ Ⓟ. ◫ ⒶⒺ ⓪ *VISA*. ❤
M (bar lunch Monday to Saturday)/dinner 10.00/19.00 **t.** and a la carte ⓵ 5.50 – **34 rm**
⊇ 35.00/72.00 **t.** – SB (April-November) 102.00/130.00 **st.**

🏠 **Carrig Rua,** Main St., ✆ 36133, Fax 36277, ≤ – ⓣⓥ ☎ Ⓟ. ◫ ⒶⒺ *VISA*. ❤
March-early November – **M** (bar lunch)/dinner 18.50 **st.** and a la carte – **22 rm** ⊇ 25.00/
60.00 **st.**

at Portnablahy/Portnablagh E : 1 ½ m. on T 72 – ✉ ⊛ 074 Letterkenny :

🏠 **Port-na-Blagh,** ✆ 36129, Fax 36379, ≤ Sheephaven Bay and harbour, ↘, ☞, ❤ – ⓣⓥ
☎ Ⓟ. ◫ *VISA*
Easter-October – **M** 7.50/19.50 **t.** and dinner a la carte ⓵ 5.00 – **46 rm** ⊇ (dinner
included) 29.50/92.00 **t.** – SB 76.00/92.00 **st.**

DUNGARVAN (Dún Garbháin) Waterford 📖 J 11 – ⊛ 058.
◆Dublin 118 – ◆Cork 44 – Waterford 30.

at Clonea Strand E : 3 ¾ m. by Clonea Strand rd – ✉ ⊛ 058 Dungarvan :

🏨 **Clonea Strand,** ✆ 42416, Fax 42880, ≤, ♨₅, ≊, ▣, ┢₉ – ❘⧣❘ ⓣⓥ ☎ Ⓟ – ♨ 200. ◫ *VISA*. ❤
M 9.00/17.00 **t.** and dinner a la carte ⓵ 4.45 – **58 rm** ⊇ 48.50/77.00 **t.** – SB 93.00/129.00 **st.**

DUN LAOGHAIRE (Dún Laoghaire) Dublin 📖 N 8 – pop. 54 496 – ⊛ 01 Dublin.
🛳 to Holyhead (Stena Sealink Line) 2-4 daily.
🅱 St. Michaels Wharf ✆ 280 6984.
◆Dublin 9.

Plan on next page

🏨 **Royal Marine,** Marine Rd, ✆ 280 1911, Telex 91277, Fax 280 1089, ≤, ☞ – ❘⧣❘ ▤ rest ⓣⓥ
☎ Ⓟ – ♨ 500. ◫ ⒶⒺ ⓪ *VISA*. ❤ **n**
M 12.00/17.95 **st.** and a la carte ⓵ 5.50 – ⊇ 8.00 – **104 rm** 70.00/110.00 **t.**

🏠 **Chestnut Lodge** without rest., 2 Vesey Pl., Monkstown, ✆ 280 7860, Fax 280 1466,
« Regency house, antiques », ☞ – ⓣⓥ ☎. ◫ *VISA*. ❤ **u**
4 rm ⊇ 37.50/55.00 **t.**

XXX **Na Mara,** 1 Harbour Rd, ✆ 280 6767, Fax 284 4649 – ◫ ⒶⒺ ⓪ *VISA* **i**
closed Sunday and 1 week Christmas – **M** - **Seafood** 14.25/23.00 **t.** and a la carte ⓵ 5.00.

17

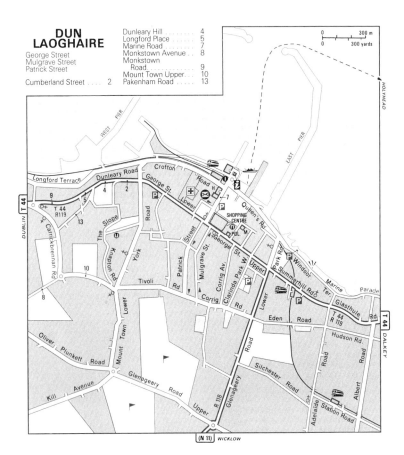

DUN LAOGHAIRE

George Street
Mulgrave Street
Patrick Street

Cumberland Street 2

Dunleary Hill 4
Longford Place 5
Marine Road 7
Monkstown Avenue .. 8
Monkstown
    Road 9
Mount Town Upper... 10
Pakenham Road 13

DUNLAVIN (Dún Luáin) Wicklow 405 L 8 – pop. 583 – ✆ 045 Naas.

♦Dublin 31 – ♦Kilkenny 44 – Wexford 61.

🏠 **Rathsallagh House** ⟩, SW : 2 m. on Grangecon Rd ℰ 53112, Fax 53343, ≤, « 18C converted stables, walled garden », ☲, ◻, park, ※ – ☎ ℗ – 🔬 25. 🖂 ⓞ 𝘝𝘐𝘚𝘈 𝗝𝗖𝗕 ※ closed 3 days at Christmas – **M** (dinner only) 25.00/35.00 **t.** ↥ 5.00 – **14 rm** ⊇ 65.00/130.00 **t.** – SB (except June-September and Bank Holidays) 160.00/220.00 **st.**

DUNMANWAY (Dún Mánmhaí) Cork 405 E 12 – pop. 1 382 – ✆ 023 Bandon.

♦Dublin 191 – ♦Cork 37 – Killarney 49.

↑ **Dun Mhuire,** W : ½ m. by T 65 ℰ 45162, ⌗ – 📺 ☎ ℗. 🖂 𝘝𝘐𝘚𝘈. ※ **M** (by arrangement) 17.00 **st.** ↥ 5.00 – **5 rm** ⊇ 26.00/40.00 **st.**

DUNMORE EAST (Dún Mór) Waterford 405 L 11 Ireland G. – pop. 734 – ✉ ✆ 051 Waterford.

See : Village★.

♦Dublin 108 – ♦Waterford 12.

✗ **Ship,** Bayview, ℰ 83141 – 🖂 𝘝𝘐𝘚𝘈 closed dinner Sunday and Monday October-April – **M** - Seafood a la carte 10.00/18.25 **t.** ↥ 5.75.

♦Dublin 17 – Drogheda 19.

⌂ **Gaulstown House** ♨, NE : 1 ½ m. by Ratoath rd ℘ 825 9147, « Working farm », ✍,
park – ⇔⇔ **℗**. ⌗
April-October – **M** (by arrangement) – **3 rm** ⌸ 16.00/28.00 – SB 50.00/54.00 **st.**

DURRUS (Dúras) Cork 405 D 13 – pop. 197 – ❸ 027.

♦Dublin 210 – ♦Cork 56 – ♦Killarney 53.

XX **Blairs Cove**, SW : 1 m. on L 56 ℘ 61127, « Converted barn », ✍ – **℗**. 🖾 🆎 ⑩
closed Sunday. Monday except summer and November-mid March – **M** (booking essential) (dinner only) 23.00 **t.** ▯ 6.00.

ENNIS (Inis) Clare 405 F 9 Ireland G. – pop. 6 223 – ECD : Thursday – ❸ 065.

See : Ennis Friary★ *AC.*

Envir. : Clare Abbey★, SE : 1 m. by R 469.

Exc. : Quin Franciscan Friary★, SE : 6 ½ m. by R 469 – Knappogue Castle★ *AC*, SE : 8 m. by
R 469 – Carrofin (Clare Heritage Centre★ *AC*), N : 8 ½ m. by N 85 and R 476 – Craggaunowen
Centre★ *AC*, SE : 11 m. by R 469 – Kilmacduagh Churches and Round Tower★, NE : 11 m. by
N 18 – Scattery Island★, SW : 27 m. by N 68 and boat from Kilrush – Bridge of Ross, Kilkee★,
SW : 35 ½ m. by N 68 and N 67.

🚇 Drumbiggle Rd ℘ 24074, SW : 1 m. by N 68.

🛈 Clare Road ℘ 28366.

♦Dublin 142 – ♦Galway 42 – ♦Limerick 22 – Roscommon 92 – ♦Tullamore 93.

🏨 **Old Ground** (Forte), O'Connell St., ℘ 28127, Fax 28112, ✍ – 🔟 ☎ **℗** – 🔬 200. 🖾 🆎 ⑩
VISA
M (dinner only) 19.00 **t.** and a la carte ▯ 5.00 – **58 rm** ⌸ 50.00/100.00 **t.** – SB 80.00/
130.00 **st.**

🏨 **Auburn Lodge,** Galway Rd, N : 1 ½ m. on N 18 ℘ 21247, Fax 21202, ✍, XX – 🔟 ☎ **℗**.
🖾 🆎 ⑩ *VISA* ⌗
M 9.00/17.00 **t.** and dinner a la carte ▯ 4.50 – **100 rm** ⌸ 30.00/75.00 **st.** – SB 70.00/
100.00 **st.**

at Barefield NE : 3 ½ m. on N 18 – ✉ ❸ 065 Ennis :

⌂ **Carraig Mhuire,** Bearnafunshin, NE : 1 ¾ m. on N 18 ℘ 27106, Fax 27375, ✍ – **℗**. ⌗
M 11.00 – **5 rm** ⌸ 11.00/26.00 **st.** – SB 36.00/40.00 **st.**

♦Dublin 76 – Kilkenny 46 – Waterford 34 – Wexford 15.

🏠 **Ballinkeele House** ♨, Ballymurn, SE : 6 ½ m. by unmarked rd and Curracloe rd
℘ 38105, Fax 38468, « 19C country house, antiques », ✍, park, XX – **℗**. 🖾 *VISA* *JCB*. ⌗
Booking essential mid November-February – **M** (communal dining) (dinner only) 18.00 **st.** –
4 rm ⌸ 34.00/70.00 **s.**

FAHAN (Fathain) Donegal 405 J 2 Ireland G. – pop. 367 – ✉ Inishowen – ❸ 077 Buncrana.

Exc. : Inishowen Peninsula★★ : (Dun Ree Fort★ *AC*), N : 11 m. by R 238.

🚇 North West, Lisfannon ℘ 61027.

♦Dublin 156 – ♦Londonderry 11 – ♦Sligo 95.

XX **St. John's,** ℘ 60289, « Loughside setting », ✍ – ⇔⇔ **℗**. 🖾 🆎 ⑩ *VISA* *JCB*
closed Good Friday and 24-25 December – **M** (dinner only) 20.00 **t.** ▯ 5.90.

FERNS (Fearna) Wexford 405 M 10 – ✉ ❸ 054 Enniscorthy.

♦Dublin 69 – Kilkenny 53 – Waterford 41 – Wexford 22.

⌂ **Clone House,**, S : 2 m. by Boolavogue rd and Monageer rd ℘ 66113, « Working farm »,
✍, park – 🔟 **℗**. ⌗
April-October – **M** (communal dining) 13.50 **s.** – **4 rm** ⌸ 22.00/34.00 **st.**

FURBOGH/FURBO (Na Forbacha) Galway 405 E 8 – ❸ 091 Galway.

♦Dublin 142 – ♦Galway 7.

🏨 **Connemara Coast,** ℘ 92108, Fax 92065, ≼, ▯ₐ, ⩳, 🔲, XX – 🔟 ☎ **℗** – 🔬 500. 🖾 ⑩
VISA ⌗
M (bar lunch)/dinner 22.00 **st.** and a la carte ▯ 6.25 – **111 rm** ⌸ 47.50/115.50 **st.**, 1 suite –
SB (except Bank Holidays) 80.00/135.00 **st.**

☞ *When in a hurry use the* Michelin Main Road Maps *:*

970 Europe, 980 Greece, 984 Germany, 985 Scandinavia-Finland,
986 Great Britain and Ireland, 987 Germany-Austria-Benelux, 988 Italy,
989 France, 990 Spain-Portugal and 991 Yugoslavia.

See : City★★ – Lynch's Castle★ – St. Nicholas' Church★ – Roman Catholic Cathedral★ – Eyre Square : Bank of Ireland Building (Mace★).

Envir. : NW : Lough Corrib★★.

Exc. : W : by boat, Aran Islands (Inishmore - Dun Aenghus★★★) – Thoor Ballylee★★, SE : 21 m. by N 6 and N 18 – Athenry★, W : 14 m. by N 6 and R 348 – Dunguaire Castle, Kinvarra★ *AC*, S : 16 m. by N 6, N 18 and N 67 – Knockmoy Abbey★, NE : 19 m. by N 17 and N 63 – Coole Park (Autograph Tree★), SE : 21 m. by N 6 and N 18 – St. Mary's Cathedral, Tuam★, NE : 21 m. by N 17 – Loughrea (St. Brendan's Cathedral★) SE : 22 m. by N 6.

🛏 Galway, Salthill *ℰ* 23038, SW : 3 m.

✈ Carnmore Airport *ℰ* 52874, NE : 4 m.

🖪 Victoria Pl., Eyre Sq. *ℰ* 63081.

◆Dublin 135 – ◆Limerick 64 – ◆Sligo 90.

🏯 **Glenlo Abbey,** Bushypark, NW : 3 ¼ m. on N 59 *ℰ* 26666, Fax 27800, « Restored part 18C house and church », 🐾, 🎣, park – |🛗| 🍴 rm 🖩 rest 📺 🕿 & 🅿 – 🛎 60. 🖎 🖭 *VISA* 🎇
closed 25 to 28 December – **M** 11.50/23.00 **t.** and dinner a la carte ¦ 7.00 – **38 rm** ☲ 75.00/120.00 **t.**, 4 suites – SB (weekends only) 95.00/150.00 **st.**

🏯 **Great Southern,** Eyre Sq., *ℰ* 64041, Telex 50164, Fax 66704, ☎, 🔲 – |🛗| 🍴 rm 📺 🕿 – 🛎 400. 🖎 🖭 ⓞ *VISA* 🎇
M (carving lunch Monday to Saturday)/dinner 19.00 **t.** and a la carte ¦ 6.00 – ☲ 7.50 – **114 rm** 68.00/102.00 **t.**

🏯 **Corrib Great Southern,** Dublin Rd, E : 1 ¾ m. on N 6 *ℰ* 755281, Telex 50044, Fax 751390, 🔲 – |🛗| 🍴 rm 🖩 rest 📺 🕿 & 🅿 – 🛎 700. 🖎 🖭 ⓞ *VISA* 🎇
M (bar lunch Saturday) 11.00/18.00 **t.** and a la carte ¦ 7.00 – **176 rm** ☲ 65.00/110.00 **t.**, 4 suites.

🏯 **Ardilaun House,** Taylor's Hill, *ℰ* 21433, Fax 21546, *I₅*, ☎, 🔲 – |🛗| 🍴 rm 📺 🕿 🅿 – 🛎 450. 🖎 🖭 *VISA*
closed 22 to 28 December – **M** 9.95/19.50 **t.** and dinner a la carte – **89 rm** ☲ 40.00/90.00 **t.**, 1 suite – SB (weekends only) 80.00/130.00 **st.**

🏨 **Jurys Galway Inn,** Quay St., *ℰ* 66444, Fax 68415, 🏊 – |🛗| 🍴 rm 📺 🕿. 🖎 🖭 ⓞ *VISA*.
closed 24 December-2 January – **M** (carving lunch Monday to Friday)/dinner 12.50 **st.** and a la carte ¦ 4.50 – ☲ 5.00 – **128 rm** 51.00 **st.**

🏨 **Brennan's Yard,** Lower Merchants Rd, *ℰ* 68166, Fax 68262 – |🛗| 🍴 rm 📺 🕿 🅿. 🖎 🖭 ⓞ *VISA* 🎇
M (booking essential) 16.50/25.00 **t.** and dinner a la carte ¦ 4.75 – **24 rm** ☲ 45.00/90.00 **t.** – SB (weekends only) 65.00/90.00 **st.**

🏨 **Galway Ryan,** Dublin Rd, E : 1 ¼ m. on N 6 *ℰ* 753181, Telex 50149, Fax 753187, 🏊 – |🛗| 📺 🕿 🅿 – 🛎 50. 🖎 🖭 ⓞ *VISA* 🎇
M (dinner only) 15.00 **t.** and a la carte 18.45/27.45 **t.** ¦ 4.50 – ☲ 8.00 – **96 rm** 60.00/98.00 **st.**

⌂ **Adare House** without rest., 9 Father Griffin Pl., Lower Salthill, *ℰ* 62638, Fax 63963 – 📺 🕿 🅿. 🖎 *VISA* 🎇
closed 23 to 27 December – **9 rm** ☲ 22.00/34.00 **st.**

XX **Casey's Westwood,** Newcastle, NW : 1 ¾ m. on N 59 *ℰ* 21442, 🏊 – 🅿. 🖎 🖭 *VISA*
closed 1 April and 23 to 27 December – **M** 11.50/19.50 **t.**

at Salthill SW : 2 m. – ✉ Salthill – ✪ 091 Galway :

🏨 **Rockbarton Park,** 5-7 Rockbarton Park, *ℰ* 22286, Fax 27692 – 📺 🕿 🅿. 🖎 🖭 ⓞ *VISA* 🎇
M (bar lunch)/dinner 15.00 **st.** and a la carte – **11 rm** ☲ 31.00/62.00 **st.** – SB (except Bank Holidays) 72.00/96.00 **st.**

⌂ **Arch Villa** without rest., Coast Rd, Gentian Hill, *ℰ* 21425, 🏊 – 🅿. 🎇
closed 23 December-5 January – **5 rm** ☲ 20.00/30.00 **st.**

◆Dublin 161 – ◆Cork 23 – Waterford 62.

🏨 **Garryvoe,** *ℰ* 646718, Fax 646824, ≤, 🏊 – 📺 🕿 🅿. 🖎 🖭 ⓞ *VISA*. 🎇
closed 25 December – **M** 12.50/19.50 **t.** and a la carte ¦ 4.50 – **20 rm** ☲ 30.00/50.00 **t.**

◆Dublin 196 – ◆Cork 44 – ◆Killarney 75.

XXX **Rectory,** *ℰ* 33072, ≤ – 🅿. 🖎 🖭 *VISA*. 🎇
closed 2 January-1 March – **M** (dinner only) 21.50 **st.** and a la carte ¦ 7.30.

◆Dublin 28 – Kilkenny 68 – Wexford 63.

🏨 **Glendalough,** *ℰ* 45135, Fax 45142, 🏊 – 📺 🕿 🅿. 🖎 🖭 ⓞ *VISA*
mid March-November – **M** 8.00/15.00 **t.** and a la carte ¦ 5.00 – **16 rm** ☲ 37.00/66.00 **t.** – SB (weekends only) 66.00/98.00 **st.**

GLEN OF AHERLOW (Gleann Eatharlaí) Tipperary 405 H 10 Ireland G. – ⊠ 🏢 062 Tipperary.

See : Glen of Aherlow★.

◆Dublin 118 – Cahir 6 – Tipperary 9.

🏨 **Aherlow House** ⊗, ℰ 56153, Fax 56212, ≤ Galty Mountains, park – 📺 ☎ & 🄿. 🔼 🄰🄴 🄾🄳 VISA 🕸
closed November-February except weekends – **M** 9.50/17.00 **st.** and dinner a la carte ▯ 4.65 – ➡ 7.00 – **10 rm** 30.00/120.00 **st.**

GOREY (Guaire) Wexford 405 N 9 Ireland G. – pop. 2 588 – ECD : Wednesday – 🏢 055.

Exc. : Ferns★, SW : 11 m. by N 11.

🏌 Courtown, Courtown Harbour ℰ 25166, SE : 4 m.

🅳 Town Centre ℰ 21248 (28 June-28 August).

◆Dublin 58 – Waterford 55 – Wexford 38.

🏨 **Marlfield House** ⊗, Courtown Rd, E : 1 m. ℰ 21124, Fax 21572, ≤, « Regency house, conservatory », ☞, 🍴, park, 💥 – 📺 ☎ 🄿. 🔼 🄰🄴 🄾🄳 VISA
closed December and January – **Meals** 18.00/29.00 **t.** ▯ 6.50 – **18 rm** ➡ 80.00/138.00 **t.**, 1 suite.

🏠 **Kia Ora Farmhouse** ⊗, Courteencurragh, ℰ 21166, « Working farm », 🍴, park – 📺 🄿. 🕸
M 15.00 – **4 rm** ➡ 18.00/30.00.

GOUGANE BARRA (Guagán Barra) Cork 405 D 12 Ireland G. – ⊠ 🏢 026 Ballingeary.

See : Gougane Barra Forest Park★★.

◆Dublin 206 – ◆Cork 45.

🏨 **Gougane Barra** ⊗, ℰ 47069, Fax 47226, ≤ lough and mountains, 🔾 – 📺 ☎ 🄿. 🔼 🄰🄴 🄾🄳 VISA 🕸
mid April-8 October – **M** 18.00 **st.** (dinner) and a la carte 10.50/19.00 **st.** – **28 rm** ➡ 37.00/54.00 **st.**

GREYSTONES (Na Clocha Liatha) Wicklow 405 N 8 – 🏢 01 Dublin

◆Dublin 22.

🍽 **Hungry Monk,** Southview Church Rd, ℰ 287 5759 – 🔼 🄰🄴 🄾🄳 VISA
closed Monday – **M** (dinner only and Sunday lunch)/dinner 14.95 **t.** and a la carte ▯ 5.50.

HOWTH (Binn Éadair) Dublin 405 N 7 Ireland G. – ⊠ 🏢 01 Dublin.

See : Town★ – The Summit★.

🏌 Deer Park ℰ 832 2624.

◆Dublin 10.

🏨 **Marine,** Sutton Cross, NW : 1½ m. ℰ 832 2613, Fax 839 0442, ≤, ☞, 🏊, 🍴 – 📺 ☎ 🄿 – 🕍 150. 🔼 🄰🄴 🄾🄳 VISA 🕸
closed 25 and 26 December – **M** 12.50/18.00 **st.** and dinner a la carte ▯ 4.50 – **27 rm** ➡ 58.00/110.00 **st.** – SB (weekends only) 89.00/100.00 **st.**

🏨 **Howth Lodge** (Best Western), ℰ 832 1010, Fax 832 2268, ≤, ☞, 🏊, – 🛗 📺 ☎ & 🄿 – 🕍 200. 🔼 🄰🄴 🄾🄳 VISA 🕸
closed 23 to 27 December – **M** *(closed Sunday dinner)* (bar lunch Monday to Saturday)/dinner 22.00 **t.** and a la carte – **46 rm** ➡ 50.00/80.00 **t.** – SB 105.00/140.00 **st.**

🏨 **Deer Park,** ℰ 832 2624, Fax 839 2405, ≤, 🏌, 🏌, park – ▤ rest 📺 ☎ & 🄿 – 🕍 140. 🔼 🄰🄴 VISA JCB 🕸
closed 25 and 26 December – **M** (bar lunch Monday to Saturday)/dinner 17.50 **t.** and a la carte ▯ 5.00 – **49 rm** ➡ 42.00/76.00 **st.** – SB 90.00/130.00 **st.**

🍽🍽🍽 **King Sitric,** Harbour Rd, East Pier, ℰ 832 5235, Fax 839 2442 – 🔼 🄰🄴 🄾🄳 VISA
closed Sunday, 1 week Easter, first week January and Bank Holidays – **M** - Seafood (light lunch Monday to Saturday May-September) (dinner only October-April)/dinner 22.00 **t.** and a la carte ▯ 6.00.

INISTIOGE (Inis Tíog) Kilkenny 405 K 10 – ⊠ 🏢 056.

◆Dublin 82 – Kilkenny 16 – ◆Waterford 19 – Wexford 33.

🏠 **Berryhill** ⊗, SE :½ m. by R 700 ℰ 58434, ≤, 🔾, 🍴, park – 🄿. 🔼. 🕸
April-November – **M** (communal dining) (dinner only) 18.00 – **3 rm** ➡ 36.00/60.00 **s.**

🍽 **Motte,** ℰ 58655 – 🔼 VISA
closed Monday and Bank Holidays – **M** (dinner only) 18.50 **t.**

INNISHANNON (Inis Eonáin) Cork 405 G 12 – pop. 286 – 🏢 021 Cork.

◆Dublin 169 – ◆Cork 15.

🏠 **Innishannon House** ⊗, S : ¾ m. on R 605 ℰ 775121, Fax 775609, « Riverside setting », 🔾, 🍴 – 📺 ☎ 🄿. 🔼 🄰🄴 🄾🄳 VISA
M 12.00/21.00 **t.** and a la carte ▯ 6.50 – **13 rm** ➡ 50.00/125.00 **st.** – SB (November-March) (except Bank Holidays) 90.00/150.00 **st.**

KANTURK (Ceann Toirc) Cork 405 F 11 Ireland G. – pop. 1 976 – ECD : Wednesday – ☻ 029.

See : Town★ - Castle★.

🗻 Fairy Hill, ℰ 50535, S : 1 ½ m. by R 579.

◆Dublin 161 – ◆Cork 33 – ◆Killarney 31 – ◆Limerick 44.

🏨 **Assolas Country House** ⬎, E : 3 ¼ m. by R 576 off R 580 ℰ 50015, Fax 50795, ≼, « Part 17C and 18C country house, gardens, riverside setting », 🦅, park, 🍴 – ☎ 🅿. 🔼 🆎 🆅🆂🅰 🛇
closed January-mid March – **M** (booking essential) (dinner only) 28.00 t. ⏶ 7.00 – **9 rm** ⚍ 55.00/140.00 t.

KENMARE (Neidín) Kerry 405 D 12 Ireland G. – pop. 1 123 – ECD : Thursday – ☻ 064 Killarney.

See : Site★.

Exc. : Iveragh Peninsula★★★ (Ring of Kerry★★) – Healy Pass★★ (≼★★), SW : 19 m. by R 571 and R 574 – Mountain Road to Glengarriff (≼★★), S : by N 71 – Slieve Miskish Mountains (≼★★) SW : 30 m. by R 571 – Lauragh (Derreen Gardens★ *AC*) SW : 14 ½ m. by R 571 – Allihies (Copper Mines★), SW : 35 ½ m. by R 571 and R 575 – Garnish Island (≼★), SW : 42 ½ m. by R 571, R 575 and R 572.

🗻 Kenmare, ℰ 41636.

🏢 The Square, ℰ 41233 (3 May-30 September).

◆Dublin 210 – ◆Cork 58 – ◆Killarney 20.

🏨 ☼ **Park** ⬎, ℰ 41200, Fax 41402, ≼ Kenmare Bay and hills, « Antiques, paintings », 🦅, park, 🍴 – 🛗 🆕 🔼 ☎ & 🅿. 🔼 🆎 🆔 🆅🆂🅰 🛇
4 April-October and 24 December-2 January – **M** 18.00/36.00 **st.** and a la carte 35.90/48.40 **t.** – **46 rm** ⚍ 84.00/206.00 **t.**, 4 suites
Spec. Nage of fresh prawns and scallops with coriander, Turbot on wild rice with a Thai style fish sauce, Millefeuille of apples.

🏨 ☼ **Sheen Falls Lodge** ⬎, SE : 1 ¼ m. by N 71 ℰ 41600, Fax 41386, « Wooded setting on banks of Sheen River and Kenmare Bay, ≼ Sheen Falls », 🅵🅳, 🆁🆂, 🦅, park, 🍴 – 🛗 🔼 rest 🆕 ☎ & 🅿 – 🔬 120. 🔼 🔼 🆎 🆔 🆅🆂🅰 🛇
closed January-4 February – **M** – **La Cascade** (bar lunch Monday to Saturday)/dinner 35.00 **t.** and a la carte 32.50/52.50 **t.** ⏶ 8.50 – **33 rm** ⚍ 175.00/220.00 **t.**, 7 suites
Spec. Saffron scented seawater consommé with shellfish, Roast breast of wood pigeon with deep fried yams and fresh truffle, Hot quark soufflé with passion fruit ice cream.

🏨 **Dromquinna Manor** ⬎, Blackwater Bridge P.O., W : 3 m. by N 71 on N 70 ℰ 41657, Fax 41791, 🦅, 🦅, park, 🍴 – 🆕 ☎ 🅿. 🔼 🆎 🆔 🆅🆂🅰
M (bar lunch Monday to Saturday)/dinner 12.50 **st.** and a la carte ⏶ 5.50 – **25 rm** ⚍ 38.50/77.00 **st.** – SB (except June-August) (weekdays only) 102.00/142.00 **st.**

🏠 **Foleys**, Henry St., ℰ 41361, Fax 41799 – 🆕. 🔼 🆅🆂🅰 🛇
M *(closed January)* (bar lunch)/dinner 16.00 **st.** and a la carte ⏶ 6.00 – **10 rm** ⚍ 18.00/40.00 **t.**

🏠 **Mylestone House** without rest., Killowen Rd, E : ¼ m. ℰ 41753, 🦅 – 🅿. 🛇
February-mid November – **5 rm** ⚍ 22.00/32.00 **st.**

🏠 **Ceann Mara** ⬎, E : 1 m. on Kilgarvan rd ℰ 41220, ≼ Kenmare Bay and hills, 🦅, 🍴 – 🅿. 🛇
June-September – **M** (by arrangement) 16.00 **s.** – **4 rm** ⚍ 32.00.

🏠 **Ard Na Mara** without rest., Pier Rd, ℰ 41399, Fax 41399, ≼ Kenmare Bay and hills, 🦅 – 🅿. 🛇
4 rm ⚍ 20.00/28.00 **t.**

🍴🍴 **Old Bank House**, Main St., ℰ 41589 – 🔼 🆅🆂🅰
closed Monday and Tuesday October-March, 24 January-10 February and 24 to 28 December – **M** (dinner only) a la carte 15.30/29.45 **st.** ⏶ 7.00.

🍴 **Lime Tree**, Shelbourne St., ℰ 41225, « Characterful former schoolhouse » – 🅿. 🔼 🆎 🆅🆂🅰
mid March-October – **M** (dinner only) a la carte 15.40/33.90 **st.** ⏶ 6.40.

🍴 **Packies**, Henry St., ℰ 41508 – 🔼 🛇
closed Sunday and November-March – **M** (dinner only) a la carte 12.50/21.50 **t.** ⏶ 4.50.

KILKEE (Cill Chaoi) Clare 405 D 9 – ☻ 065.

◆Dublin 177 – ◆Galway 77 – ◆Limerick 58.

🏨 **Halpin's**, Erin St., ℰ 56032, Fax 56317 – 🆕 ☎. 🔼 🆎 🆔 🆅🆂🅰 🛇
April-December – **M** 8.50/18.00 **t.** and dinner a la carte ⏶ 6.90 – **12 rm** ⚍ 25.00/60.00 **t.** – SB (except Bank Holidays) 60.00/84.00 **st.**

KILKENNY (Cill Chainnigh) Kilkenny 405 K 10 Ireland G. – pop. 9 466 – ECD : Thursday – ☻ 056.

See : Town★★ – St. Canice's Cathedral★★ – Kilkenny Castle and Grounds★★ *AC* – Cityscope★ *AC* – Black Abbey★.

Exc. : Dunmore Cave★ *AC*, N : 7 m. by N 77 and N 78 – Kells Priory★, S : 9 m. by R 697.

🗻 Glendine, ℰ 22125, N : 1 m.

🏢 Rose Inn St. ℰ 51500.

◆Dublin 71 – ◆Cork 86 – ◆Killarney 115 – ◆Limerick 69 – ◆Tullamore 52 – ◆Waterford 29.

🏨 **Kilkenny,** College Rd, SW : 1½ m. on N 76 ℰ 62000, Fax 65984, ƒ₆, ≘s, ☒, ☞, ℀ – ⊡ ☎ 𝐏 – ⚛ 500. ◪ 🄰🄴 ⓞ 𝘃𝘪𝘴𝘢 ⅙
M 4.95/16.00 **st.** and a la carte ⅋ 4.50 – **60 rm** ⊇ 50.00/90.00 **st.** – SB (weekends only) 110.00/130.00 **st.**

🏨 **Newpark** (Best Western), Castlecomer Rd, N : ¾ m. on N 77 ℰ 22122, Fax 61111, ƒ₆, ≘s, ☒, ☞, park, ℀ – ⊡ ☎ 𝐏 – ⚛ 600. ◪ 🄰🄴 ⓞ 𝘃𝘪𝘴𝘢 ⅙
M (in bar Sunday) 10.50/16.50 **t.** and a la carte ⅋ 5.95 – ⊇ 8.50 – **60 rm** 35.00/75.00 **t.** – SB (except Bank Holidays) 119.00/196.00 **st.**

🏠 **Blanchville House** ⌂, Dunbell, Maddoxtown, SE : 7½ m. by N 77 and N 10 ℰ 27197, ≼, « Georgian house, working farm », ☞, park – 𝐏. ◪ 𝘃𝘪𝘴𝘢
March-October – **M** (communal dining) (dinner only) 17.00 **st.** ⅋ 6.00 – **6 rm** ⊇ 30.00/ 50.00 **st.** – SB (except May-August) (weekdays only) 78.00/94.00 **st.**

🏠 **Shillogher House** without rest., Callan Rd, SW : ¾ m. on N 76 ℰ 63249, ☞ – ⛫ ⊡ ☎ 𝐏. ◪ 𝘃𝘪𝘴𝘢 ⅙
closed 20 to 27 December – **5 rm** ⊇ 20.00/40.00 **st.**

℀℀ **Lacken House** with rm, Dublin Rd, ℰ 61085, Fax 62435, ☞ – ⊡ ☎ 𝐏. ◪ 🄰🄴 ⓞ 𝘃𝘪𝘴𝘢 🄹🄲🄱 ⅙
closed 19 to 30 December – **M** *(closed Sunday and Monday)* (dinner only) 22.00 **st.** and a la carte ⅋ 6.00 – **8 rm** ⊇ 34.00/56.00 **st.**

KILLALOE (Cill Dalua) Clare ᐧᐧᐧ G 9 Ireland G. – pop. 1 022 – ECD : Wednesday – ✪ 061.

See : Town★ – St. Flannan's Cathedral★.

Envir. : Graves of the Leinstermen★, N : 4½ m. by R 494.

Exc. : Nenagh★ (Heritage Centre★★ *AC*, Castle★), NE : 12 m. by R 496 and N 7 – Holy Island★ *AC*, N : 8 m. by R 463 and boat from Tuamgraney.

🛈 ℰ 376866 (24 May-12 September).

◆Dublin 109 – ◆Limerick 13 – ◆Tullamore 58.

🏨 **Lakeside,** ℰ 376122, Fax 376431, ≼, ƒ₆, ≘s, ☒, ☜, ☞ – ⊡ ☎ 𝐏. ◪ 🄰🄴 ⓞ 𝘃𝘪𝘴𝘢 🄹🄲🄱 ⅙
closed 23 to 26 December – **M** 10.50/19.00 **st.** and a la carte ⅋ 5.00 – **32 rm** ⊇ 30.00/ 70.00 **st.** – SB 90.00/106.00 **st.**

at Ogonnelloe N : 6¼ m. on R 463 – ✉ Ogonnelloe – ✪ 061 Limerick :

🏠 **Lantern House** ⌂, ℰ 923034, Fax 923139, ≼, ☞ – ⊡ ☎ 𝐏. ◪ 🄰🄴 ⓞ 𝘃𝘪𝘴𝘢 ⅙
closed mid January-mid February and 1 November-8 December – **M** (by arrangement) 14.00 **t.** ⅋ 4.95 – **6 rm** ⊇ 24.00/36.00 **t.**

KILLARNEY (Cill Airne) Kerry ᐧᐧᐧ D 11 Ireland G. – pop. 7 693 – ECD : Thursday – ✪ 064.

See : Town★★ – Knockreer Demesne★ – St. Mary's Cathedral★.

Envir. : Killarney National Park★★★ – Muckross House★★ *AC*, S : 3 ½ m. by N 71 – Torc Waterfall★, S : 5 m. by N 71 – Gap of Dunloe★★, SW : 6 m. by R 582 – Muckross Abbey★, S : 3½ m. by N 71.

Exc. : Iveragh Peninsula★★★ (Ring of Kerry★★) – Ladies View★★, SW : 12 m. by N 71 – Moll's Gap★, SW : 15½ m. by N 71.

☍₁₈, ☍₁₈ O'Mahoney's Point ℰ 31034.

✈ Kerry (Farranfore) Airport ℰ 066 (Farranfore) 64644, N : 9½ m. by N 22.

🛈 Town Hall ℰ 31633.

◆Dublin 189 – ◆Cork 54 – ◆Limerick 69 – ◆Waterford 112.

🏨 **Europe** ⌂, Fossa, W : 3 ½ m. on T 67 ℰ 31900, Telex 73913, Fax 32118, ≼ lake and mountains, ƒ₆, ≘s, ☒, ☜, ☞, park, ℀ – ⒤ ⊡ ☎ 𝐏 – ⚛ 500. ◪ 🄰🄴 ⓞ 𝘃𝘪𝘴𝘢
April-October – **M** (bar lunch)/dinner 25.00 **st.** and a la carte ⅋ 8.80 – **197 rm** ⊇ 70.00/ 122.00 **st.**, 8 suites.

🏨 **Dunloe Castle** ⌂, Beaufort, W : 6 m. by R 562 ℰ 44111, Fax 44583, ≼ Gap of Dunloe, countryside and mountains, ≘s, ☒, ☜, ☞, park, ℀ – ⒤ ⊡ ☎ 𝐏 – ⚛ 400. ◪ 🄰🄴 ⓞ 𝘃𝘪𝘴𝘢
May-September – **M** 24.00/25.00 **st.** and a la carte ⅋ 8.80 – **119 rm** ⊇ 62.00/122.00 **st.**, 1 suite.

🏨 **Aghadoe Heights** ⌂, NW : 3 ½ m. by N 22 ℰ 31766, Telex 73942, Fax 31345, ≼ countryside, lake and Macgillycuddy's Reeks, ≘s, ☒, ☞, ℀ – ▤ rest ⊡ ☎ ⅋ 𝐏 – ⚛ 100. ◪ 🄰🄴 ⓞ 𝘃𝘪𝘴𝘢
M – Fredrick's at the Heights 17.50/29.50 **st.** and a la carte ⅋ 6.50 – **57 rm** ⊇ 100.00/ 145.00 **st.**, 3 suites.

🏨 **Great Southern,** ℰ 31262, Telex 73998, Fax 31642, ƒ₆, ≘s, ☒, ☞, park, ℀ – ⒤ ⊡ ☎ 𝐏 – ⚛ 900. ◪ 🄰🄴 ⓞ 𝘃𝘪𝘴𝘢
closed 3 January-February – **M** (bar lunch)/dinner 16.00 **t.** and a la carte ⅋ 7.00 – **Dining Room** (dinner only) – **Malton Room** (dinner only) – **178 rm** ⊇ 65.00/100.00 **t.**, 2 suites – SB 70.00/94.00 **st.**

🏨 **Muckross Park,** S : 2¾ m. on N 71 ℰ 31938, Fax 31965, ☞ – ⊡ ☎ 𝐏. ◪ 🄰🄴 ⓞ 𝘃𝘪𝘴𝘢 ⅙
closed January and February – **M** (bar lunch)/dinner 18.50 **st.** and a la carte ⅋ 6.00 – **25 rm** ⊇ 55.00/110.00 **st.**, 2 suites – SB (except Bank Holidays) 100.00/160.00 **st.**

Killarney Park, Kenmare Pl., East Avenue Rd., ℰ 35555, Fax 35266, ⬛ – |桫| ▦ rest 📺 ☎
    Ġ. ℗. ⟨⟩ ﷼ 𝓥𝓘𝓢𝓐. 𝓼𝓮
    M 12.00/20.00 **st.** and dinner a la carte ⨾ 6.00 – **55 rm** ⊐ 75.00/120.00 **st.**

Randles Court, Muckross Rd, ℰ 35333, Fax 35206 – |桫| ⟨⟩ rm 📺 ☎ ℗. ⟨⟩ ﷼ 𝓥𝓘𝓢𝓐
    closed January-March – **M** (bar lunch Monday to Saturday)/dinner 22.00 **st.** and a la carte
    ⨾ 8.00 – **37 rm** ⊐ 40.00/100.00 **t.** – SB 120.00/170.00 **st.**

Cahernane, 𝓼, Muckross Rd, S : 1 m. on N 71 ℰ 31895, Fax 34340, ≤, 𝓼, 𝓼𝓻, 𝓧𝓧 – ☎
    ℗. ⟨⟩ ﷼ ⓞ 𝓥𝓘𝓢𝓐 𝓙𝓒𝓑. 𝓼𝓮
    April-October – **M** 16.00/24.00 **st.** and dinner a la carte ⨾ 7.00 – **50 rm** ⊐ 70.00/135.00 **st.**

Torc Great Southern, Park Rd, ℰ 31611, Fax 31824, ≘, ⬛, 𝓼𝓻, 𝓧𝓧 – 📺 ☎ ℗
    M (bar lunch) – **95 rm.**

Eviston House, 97 New St., ℰ 31640, Fax 33685 – |桫| 📺 ☎. ⟨⟩ ﷼ ⓞ 𝓥𝓘𝓢𝓐. 𝓼𝓮
    M (bar lunch)/dinner 16.00 **st.** and a la carte ⨾ 5.00 – **40 rm** ⊐ 45.00/74.00 **st.** – SB (except
    Bank Holidays) 64.00/114.00 **st.**

Royal, College St., ℰ 31853, Fax 34001 – |桫| 📺 ☎. ⟨⟩ 𝓥𝓘𝓢𝓐
    closed 25 December – **M** (bar lunch Monday to Saturday)/dinner 17.00 **s.** – **49 rm** ⊐ 35.00/
    90.00 **st.**

Foley's, 23 High St., ℰ 31217, Fax 34683 – ▦ rest 📺 ☎ ℗. ⟨⟩ ﷼ 𝓥𝓘𝓢𝓐. 𝓼𝓮
    closed 22 to 27 December and 17 January-21 February – **M** (bar lunch)/dinner 35.00 **st.** and
    a la carte ⨾ 7.00 – **12 rm** ⊐ 30.00/70.00 **st.** – SB (except May-August and Bank Holidays)
    (weekdays only) 50.00/70.00 **st.**

Killeen House, Aghadoe, W : 4 m. by R 562 ℰ 31711, Fax 31811, 𝓼𝓻 – 📺 ☎ ℗. ⟨⟩ ﷼
    𝓥𝓘𝓢𝓐. 𝓼𝓮
    closed 23 December-18 March – **M** (dinner only) 25.00 **st.** and a la carte ⨾ 6.00 – **15 rm**
    ⊐ 33.00/66.00 **t.**

Whitegates, Muckross Rd, ℰ 31164, Fax 34850 – 📺 ☎ ℗. ⟨⟩ 𝓥𝓘𝓢𝓐. 𝓼𝓮
    M (bar lunch Monday to Saturday)/dinner 15.00 **st.** and a la carte ⨾ 4.50 – **20 rm** ⊐ 55.00/
    68.50 **st.**

Kathleens Country House without rest., Tralee Rd, N : 2 m. on N 22 ℰ 32810,
    Fax 32340, ≤, 𝓼𝓻 – 𝓼𝓮 📺 ☎ ℗. ⟨⟩ 𝓥𝓘𝓢𝓐. 𝓼𝓮
    17 March-6 November – **16 rm** ⊐ 35.00/60.00 **st.**

Park Lodge without rest., Cork Rd, E : ¾ m. ℰ 31539, Fax 34892, 𝓼𝓻 – 📺 ☎ ℗. 𝓼𝓮
    April-November – **20 rm** ⊐ 25.00/35.00 **st.**

Fuchsia House without rest., Muckross Rd, ℰ 33743, Fax 33743, 𝓼𝓻 – 𝓼𝓮 📺 ℗. ⟨⟩ ﷼
    ⓞ 𝓥𝓘𝓢𝓐. 𝓼𝓮
    March-November and weekends in winter – **10 rm** ⊐ 32.00/44.00 **st.**

Carriglea Farmhouse 𝓼 without rest., Muckross Rd, S : 1 ½ m. on N 71 ℰ 31116, ≤,
    𝓼𝓻 – ℗. 𝓼𝓮
    Easter-October – **9 rm** ⊐ 31.00 **st.**

Gaby's, 27 High St., ℰ 32519, Fax 32747 – ⟨⟩ ﷼ ⓞ 𝓥𝓘𝓢𝓐
    closed Monday lunch, Sunday and mid February-first week March – **M** - Seafood a la
    carte 16.10/31.90 **t.** ⨾ 6.10.

Strawberry Tree, 24 Plunkett St., ℰ 32688 – ⟨⟩ ﷼ ⓞ 𝓥𝓘𝓢𝓐
    closed January-February and Sunday-Monday October-April – **M** (dinner only) a la
    carte 20.25/24.70 **st.** ⨾ 6.25.

KILLEAGH **(Cill la)** Cork 〖405〗 H 12 – ⚫ 024 Youghal

♦Dublin 151 – ♦Cork 23 – ♦Waterford 53.

Ballymakeigh House 𝓼, N : 1 m. ℰ 95184, Fax 95370, « Working farm », 𝓼𝓻, park, 𝓧𝓧
    – ℗. 𝓼𝓮
    M 17.00 ⨾ 6.00 – **5 rm** ⊐ 22.00/40.00 **st.** – SB 70.00/74.00 **st.**

KILLYBEGS **(Na Cealla Beaga)** Donegal 〖405〗 G 4 – ⚫ 073.

♦Dublin 181 – Donegal 17 – ♦Londonderry 64 – ♦Sligo 57.

Bay View, Main St., ℰ 31950, Fax 31856, ≤, 𝓕𝓼, ≘, ⬛ – |桫| ▦ 📺 ☎ Ġ. ⟨⟩ 𝓥𝓘𝓢𝓐
    M (bar lunch Monday to Saturday)/dinner 16.00 **t.** and a la carte ⨾ 4.50 – **38 rm** ⊐ 40.00/
    73.00 **st.,** 2 suites – SB 70.00/100.00 **st.**

KILLINEY **(Cill Iníon Léinín)** Dublin 〖405〗 N 8 – ⚫ 01 Dublin.

🏌 Killiney ℰ 285 1983.

♦Dublin 8 – Bray 4.

Fitzpatrick Castle, ℰ 284 0700, Telex 30353, Fax 285 0207, ≤, 𝓕𝓼, ≘, ⬛, 𝓼𝓻, 𝓧𝓧,
    squash – |桫| 𝓼𝓮 rm 📺 ☎ ℗ – ⨺ 400. ⟨⟩ ﷼ ⓞ 𝓥𝓘𝓢𝓐 𝓙𝓒𝓑. 𝓼𝓮
    M 12.50/19.50 **t.** and dinner a la carte ⨾ 5.50 – ⊐ 8.50 – **83 rm** 83.00/114.80 **t.,** 7 suites.

Court, Killiney Bay, ℰ 285 1622, Telex 33244, Fax 285 2085, ≤, 𝓼𝓻 – |桫| 𝓼𝓮 rm ▦ rest 📺
    ☎ ℗ – ⨺ 250. ⟨⟩ ﷼ ⓞ 𝓥𝓘𝓢𝓐. 𝓼𝓮
    closed 25 and 26 December – **M** 10.95/18.95 **t.** and a la carte ⨾ 5.00 – ⊐ 7.50 – **86 rm**
    65.25/81.00 **st.** – SB (November-April) 88.00/96.00 **st.**

KILSHEELAN (Cill Síoláin) Tipperary 405 J 10 – ✉ 🕿 052 Clonmel
♦Dublin 97 – Cork 66 – ♦Limerick 53 – ♦Waterford 24.

⌂ **Highfield House** 🏞, E : 1 ¾ m. by N 24 ℰ 33192, 🐎, park – **P**. ❄
   April-September – **M** (by arrangement) (communal dining) – **3 rm** 🛏 20.00/35.00 **st.**

KINSALE (Cionn Eitigh) Cork 405 G 12 Ireland G. – pop. 1 765 – ECD : Thursday – 🕿 021 Cork.

See : Town★★ – St. Multose Church★ – Kinsale Regional Museum★ *AC*.

Envir. : Summercove★ (≤★) E : 1½ m. – Charles Fort★ *AC*, E : 1 ¾ m.

🛈 Pier Rd ℰ 774417 (March-November).
♦Dublin 178 – ♦Cork 17.

🏨 **Acton's** (Forte), Pier Rd, ℰ 772135, Fax 772231, ≤, 🖪, ≊, 🔲, 🐎 – 🛗 📺 🕿 **P** – 🔏 300.
   🔼 🗚 ⑩ *VISA*
   M (bar lunch Monday to Saturday)/dinner 19.50 **st.** ⎪ 6.25 – **57 rm** 🛏 65.00/125.00 **st.** –
   SB 120.00/160.00 **st.**

🏠 **Old Bank House,** 11 Pearse St., ℰ 774075, Fax 774296 – 📺 🕿. 🔼 🗚 *VISA*. ❄
   closed 3 days at Christmas – **M** - (see **Vintage** below) – **9 rm** 🛏 40.00/100.00 **st.**

🏠 **Blue Haven,** 3 Pearse St., ℰ 772209, Fax 774268 – 📺 🕿. 🔼 🗚 ⑩ *VISA*. ❄
   closed 25 December – **M** - (see below) – **10 rm** 🛏 35.00/84.00 **st.** – SB 80.00/140.00 **st.**

⌂ **Old Presbytery,** Cork St., ℰ 772027, « Memorabilia », 🐎 – **P**. ❄
   closed 24 to 26 December – **M** (by arrangement) 18.00 **t.** ⎪ 5.00 – **6 rm** 🛏 30.00/40.00 **st.**

⌂ **Lighthouse** without rest., The Rock, ℰ 772734 – ⇖ **P**. 🔼 *VISA*. ❄
   4 rm 🛏 33.00/39.00 **st.**

❌❌ **Vintage,** 50-51 Main St., ℰ 772502, Fax 774296 – 🔼 🗚
   closed Sunday except Bank Holidays, November-mid December and mid January-mid
   February – **M** (dinner only) 29.50 **t.** and a la carte ⎪ 8.50.

❌❌ **Chez Jean Marc,** Lower O'Connell St., ℰ 774625, Fax 774680 – **P**. 🔼 🗚 ⑩ *VISA*
   closed Monday, 15 February-8 March, 2 weeks mid November and 25-26 December –
   M (dinner only) 20.00 **t.** and a la carte.

❌❌ **Blue Haven,** 3 Pearse St., ℰ 772209, Fax 774268 – 🔼 🗚 ⑩ *VISA*
   M - Seafood (bar lunch)/dinner a la carte 16.00/24.25 **t.** ⎪ 5.25.

❌❌ **Billy Mackesy's Bawnleigh House,** N : 5½ m. on Old Cork Rd ℰ 771333 – **P**. 🔼 *VISA*
   closed Sunday, Monday, last 2 weeks October and 23 to 28 December – **M** (dinner
   only) 16.00 **t.** and a la carte ⎪ 7.00.

❌ **Max's,** Main St., ℰ 772243 – 🔼 *VISA*
   closed November and December – **M** 12.00 **t.** and a la carte ⎪ 4.80.

   at Ballinclashet E : 5 m. by R 600 – ✉ Kinsale – 🕿 021 Cork :

❌❌ **Oystercatcher,** ℰ 770822 – **P**. 🔼 *VISA*
   Booking essential November-April – **M** (dinner only) 30.95 **t.** ⎪ 6.50.

KNOCK (An Cnoc) Mayo 405 F 6 Ireland G. – pop. 332 – 🕿 094.

See : Basilica of our Lady, Queen of Ireland★.

✈ Knock (Connaught) Airport ℰ 67222, NE : 9 m. by N 17.

🛈 Knock Airport ℰ 67247.
♦Dublin 132 – Galway 46 – Wesport 32.

   Hotel and Restaurant see : **Cong** SW : 36 m. by N 17, R 331, , R 334 and R 345.

LAHINCH (An Leacht) Clare 405 D 9 Ireland G. – pop. 473 – 🕿 065.

Envir. : Cliffs of Moher★★★.

🖪, 🖪 Lahinch ℰ 81003 – ▯ Spanish Point, Miltown Malbay ℰ 84198, S : 6 m. by N 67.

🛈 ℰ 81474 (27 May-1 September).
♦Dublin 162 – ♦Galway 49 – ♦Limerick 41.

🏨 **Aberdeen Arms,** ℰ 81100, Fax 81228, 🖪, ≊, ❌ – 🛏 rest 📺 🕿 **P** – 🔏 150. 🔼 🗚 ⑩
   VISA. ❄
   M 20.00 **t.** (dinner) and a la carte 17.00/24.00 **t.** ⎪ 4.50 – **55 rm** 🛏 50.00/80.00 **t.** – SB (win-
   ter only) 103.40/147.40 **st.**

🏠 **Atlantic House,** Main St., ℰ 81049, Fax 81029 – 📺 ⊚ **P**. 🗚 *VISA*
   Easter-September – **M** 9.50/17.95 **t.** and a la carte ⎪ 5.00 – **14 rm** 🛏 20.00/38.15 **st.** –
   SB 91.75/101.30 **st.**

LARAGH (Láithreach) Wicklow 405 N 8 – ✉ 🕿 0404 Wicklow.
♦Dublin 26 – Kilkenny 70 – Wexford 61.

⌂ **Laragh Trekking Centre** 🏞, Laragh East, NW : 1 ½ m. on Sallygap rd ℰ 45282,
   Fax 45282, ≤, 🐎, 🐎 – ⇖ rest 📺 **P**. 🔼 *VISA*
   M 12.50 **st.** ⎪ 4.50 – **6 rm** 🛏 25.00/35.00 **st.** – SB 47.60/56.00 **st.**

L

LEENANE (An Lionán) Galway **405** C 7 Ireland G. – ✉ 📶 095 Clifden.

See . Killary Harbour★.

Envir. : Joyce Country★★ – Aasleagh Falls★, NE : 2 ½ m.

Exc. : Lough Nafooey★★, SE : 8 ½ m. by R 336 – Doo Lough Pass★, NW : 9 m. by N 59 and R 335.

♦Dublin 173 – Ballina 56 – ♦Galway 41.

🏠 **Delphi Lodge** ⊗, NW : 8 ¼ m. by N 59 on Louisburgh rd 🖉 42211, Fax 42296, ≤, « Georgian sporting lodge, loughside setting », 🏕, park – ☎ ℗, 🔤 VISA 🍴
January-October – **M** (residents only) (communal dining) (dinner only) 22.00 **t**. – **7 rm** ⌑ 35.00/90.00 **t**.

LETTERFRACK (Leitir Fraic) Galway **405** C 7 – 📶 095 Clifden.

♦Dublin 189 – Ballina 69 – ♦Galway 57.

🏠 **Rosleague Manor** ⊗, W : 1 ½ m. on N 59 🖉 41101, Fax 41168, ≤ Ballynakill harbour and Tully Mountain, ≋, 🌄, park, 🍴 – ↦× rest ☎ ℗, 🔤 🔤 VISA
Easter-October – **M** (bar lunch)/dinner a la carte 18.00/24.50 **t**. 🍷 6.50 – **20 rm** ⌑ 50.00/130.00 **t**. – SB (except July and August) 115.00/170.00 **st**.

LETTERKENNY (Leitir Ceanainn) Donegal **405** I 3 Ireland G. – pop. 6 444 – ECD : Monday – 📶 074.

Exc. : Glenveagh National Park★★ (Gardens★★), NW : 12 m. by R 250, R 251 and R 254 – Grianan of Aileach★★ (≤★) NE : 17 ½ m by N 13 – Church Hill (Colmcille Heritage Centre★ *AC*, Glebe House and Gallery★ *AC*) NW : 10 m. by R 250.

📇 Barnhill 🖉 21150, NE : 1 m.

🅱 Derry Rd 🖉 21160.

♦Dublin 150 – ♦Londonderry 21 – ♦Sligo 72.

🏠 **Castlegrove House** ⊗, Ramelton Rd, NE : 4 ½ m. by N 13 and R 245 🖉 51118, Fax 51384, ≤, 🏕, park – ☎ ℗, 🔤 🔤 VISA 🍴
closed 22 to 30 December – **M** *(closed Monday October-June and Sunday)* (dinner only) 30.00 **t**. and a la carte 🍷 5.00 – **8 rm** ⌑ 30.00/76.00 **t**. – SB (except July-August and Bank Holidays) 100.00/120.00 **st**.

LIFFORD (Leifear) Donegal **405** J 3 – 📶 074.

♦Dublin 133 – Donegal 32 – ♦Londonderry 14 – ♦Sligo 75.

🏠 **Daleview House** ⊗, Ballindrait, NW : 4 ½ m. by N 14 and Raphoe rd 🖉 41208, ≤, « Working farm », 🌄 – ↦× rm ℗, 🍴
mid March-September – **M** (by arrangement) 7.00 – **3 rm** ⌑ 15.00/30.00 **st**.

LIMERICK (Luimneach) Limerick **405** G 9 Ireland G. – pop. 60 736 – ECD : Thursday – 📶 061.

See : City★★ - St Mary's Cathedral★★ Y – Limerick Museum★★ Z – King John's Castle★ *AC* Y – John Square★ Z 20 – St. John's Cathedral★ Z.

Envir. : Hunt Museum, Limerick University★ *AC*, E : 2 m. by N 7 Y – Cratloe Wood (≤★) NW : 5 m. by N 18 Z.

Exc. : Lough Gur Interpretive Centre★ *AC*, S : 11 m. by R 512 and R 514 Z – Clare Glens★, E : 13 m. by N 7 and R 503 Y – Monasteranenagh Abbey★, S : 13 m. by N 20 Z.

✈ Shannon Airport : 🖉 061 (Shannon) 61444, W : 16 m. by N 18 Z – **Terminal** : Limerick Railway Station.

🅱 Arthur's Quay 🖉 317522 Y.

♦Dublin 120 – ♦Cork 58.

Plan on next page

🏨 **Castletroy Park,** Dublin Rd, E : 2 ¼ m. on N 7 🖉 335566, Fax 331117, 🏋, ≋, 🔲 – ⫯
↦× rm 📺 ☎ & ℗ – 🔬 250. 🔤 🔤 🔤 VISA 🍴   Y
closed 24 and 25 December – **M** *(closed Saturday lunch and Sunday dinner)* 15.95/21.45 **st**. and dinner a la carte 🍷 9.50 – ⌑ 9.00 – **105 rm** 91.50/140.00 **st**., 2 suites.

🏨 **Limerick Inn,** Ennis Rd, NW : 4 m. on N 18 🖉 326666, Fax 326281, 🏋, ≋, 🔲, 🌄, 🍴 –
⫯ ≣ rest 📺 ☎ & ℗ – 🔬 500. 🔤 🔤 🔤 VISA 🍴   Y
closed 24 and 25 December – **M** 11.00/21.00 **t**. and a la carte 🍷 5.00 – ⌑ 7.00 – **149 rm** 77.00/101.00 **t**., 4 suites – SB 85.00/121.00 **st**.

🏨 **Jurys,** Ennis Rd, 🖉 327777, Telex 70766, Fax 326400, 🏋, ≋, 🔲, 🌄, 🍴 – ≣ rest 📺 ☎
℗ – 🔬 200. 🔤 🔤 🔤 VISA 🍴   Y z
closed 24 and 25 December – **M** 9.50/10.90 **t**. and dinner a la carte 🍷 5.00 – ⌑ 8.00 – **94 rm** 71.00/89.00 **t**., 1 suite.

🏨 **Limerick Ryan,** Ennis Rd, NW : 1 ¼ m. on N 18 🖉 453922, Telex 70720, Fax 326333, 🌄 –
⫯ ≣ rest 📺 ☎ ℗ – 🔬 80. 🔤 🔤 🔤 VISA 🍴   Y
M 10.00/14.50 **st**. and dinner a la carte 🍷 5.00 – ⌑ 7.50 – **180 rm** 60.00/90.00 **st**., 2 suites.

🏨 Greenhills, Ennis Rd, NW : 2 ¼ m. on N 18 🖉 453033, Fax 453307, 🏋, ≋, 🔲, 🌄, 🍴 – 📺
☎ ℗ – 🔬 350. 🍴   Y
60 rm.

🍴 **De La Fontaine,** 12 Upper Gerald Griffin St., 🖉 414461 – 🔤 🔤 🔤 VISA JCB   Z a
closed Sunday and Bank Holidays – **M** - **French** (dinner only and Friday lunch)/dinner 20.00 **t**. and a la carte 🍷 5.00.

🍴 **Silver Plate,** 74 O'Connell St., 🖉 316311 – 🔤 🔤 🔤 VISA JCB   Z e
closed Sunday and Bank Holidays – **M** (dinner only) 20.00 **t**. and a la carte 🍷 4.50.

710

LIMERICK

LISDOONVARNA (Lios Dúin Bhearna) Clare 405 E 8 Ireland G. – pop. 607 – ✆ 065 Ennis.

Envir. : The Burren★★ (Cliffs of Moher★★★, Scenic Routes★★, Aillwee Cave★ AC (Waterfall★), Corcomroe Abbey★, Kilfenora Crosses★).

◆Dublin 167 – ◆Galway 39 – ◆Limerick 47.

  Sheedy's Spa View, Sulphir Hill, ℘ 74026, Fax 74026, ☞, ✗ – ☎ ☎ ℗. ☒ Æ ⓪ 𝘝𝘐𝘚𝘈. ✗
  April-September – **M** (bar lunch)/dinner 24.00 **t.** – **11 rm** ⊆ 35.00/55.00 **t.**

LOUGH GOWNA (Loch Gamhna) Cavan 405 J 6 – pop. 125 – ☎ 043 Longford.
♦Dublin 81 – ♦Tullamore 54.

🏠 Robin Hill 🐦, ☎ 83121, 🌳 – 🅿. 🚫🐕
M (by arrangement) – **5 rm.**

MACROOM (Maigh Chromtha) Cork 405 F 12 – pop. 2 495 – ECD : Wednesday – ☎ 026.
⛳9 Lackaduve ☎ 41072, SW : 4 m. by R 584.
♦Dublin 186 – ♦Cork 25 – ♦Killarney 30.

🏨 **Castle,** Main St., ☎ 41074, Fax 41505, 🏋, squash – 📺 ☎ 🅿. 💳 AE ⓓ VISA. 🚫🐕
closed 24 to 26 December – **M** 10.00/13.50 **t.** and a la carte 🍷 6.00 – **26 rm** ☕ 28.00/55.00 **t.** – SB 70.00/100.00 **st.**

🏠 **Bower,** Gortanaddan, Kilnamartyra, W : 8 m. by N 22 ☎ 40192, 🌳 – 🅿
M 11.00 **st.** – **5 rm** ☕ 13.00/29.00 **st.**

MALAHIDE (Mullach Íde) Dublin 405 N 7 Ireland G. – pop. 9 158 – ☎ 01 Dublin.
See : Castle★.
⛳18, ⛳9 Beechwood, The Grange ☎ 846 1611, S : 1½ m.
♦Dublin 9 – Drogheda 24.

🏨 **Grand,** ☎ 845 0000, Telex 31446, Fax 845 0987, ← – 🛗 🚭 rm 📺 ☎ 🅿 – 👥 600. 💳 AE ⓓ VISA. 🚫🐕
closed 25 and 26 December – **M** 10.45/18.70 **t.** and a la carte 🍷 4.50 – **97 rm** ☕ 58.00/96.00 **t.**, 3 suites.

🏠 **Liscara** without rest, Malahide Rd, Kinsealy, S : 3 m. on Dublin rd ☎ 848 3751 – 🅿. 🚫🐕
closed December and January – **6 rm** ☕ 25.00/35.00.

🍴🍴 **Chandni,** 9 Marine Court, The Green, ☎ 845 0141, ← – ❄ 🅿. 💳 AE ⓓ VISA
closed 25-26 December and Good Friday – **M** - **Indian** (dinner only) 19.95 **st.** and a la carte 🍷 4.95.

🍴🍴 **Bon Appetit,** 9 James's Terr., ☎ 8450314 – ❄. 💳 AE ⓓ VISA JCB
closed Saturday lunch, Sunday, 1 week Christmas and Bank Holidays – **M** 13.00/20.00 **t.** and a la carte 🍷 5.00.

MALLOW (Mala) Cork 405 F 11 Ireland G. – pop. 6 572 – ECD : Wednesday – ☎ 022.
See : Town★ – St. James' Church★.
Exc. : Doneraile Wildlife Park★ *AC*, NE : 6 m. by N 20 and R 581 – Buttevant Friary★, N : 7 m. by N 20.
⛳18 Balleyellis ☎ 21145, SE : 2 m.
♦Dublin 149 – ♦Cork 21 – ♦Killarney 40 – ♦Limerick 41.

🏨 **Longueville House** 🐦, W : 3½ m. by N 72 ☎ 47156, Fax 47459, ←, « Georgian mansion in extensive grounds », 🎣, 🌳 – 📺 ☎ 🅿. 💳 AE ⓓ VISA. 🚫🐕
closed 19 December-10 March – **M** – **Presidents** (booking essential) (bar lunch Monday to Saturday)/dinner 38.00 **t.** and a la carte 🍷 6.50 – **16 rm** ☕ 48.00/160.00 **t.** – SB 130.00/190.00 **st.**

MAYNOOTH (Maigh Nuad) Kildare 405 M 7 – pop. 3 388 – ECD : Wednesday – ☎ 01 Dublin.
Envir. : Castletown House★★ *AC*, SE : 4 m. by R 405.
⛳9 Kilcock ☎ 628 7283, NW : 5 m. by N 4.
♦Dublin 15.

🏨 **Moyglare Manor** 🐦, Moyglare, N : 2 m. ☎ 628 6351, Fax 628 5405, ←, « Georgian country house, antique furnishings », 🌳, park, 🎾 – ☎ 🅿 – 👥 30. 💳 AE ⓓ VISA. 🚫🐕
closed 24 to 26 December – **M** *(closed Saturday lunch to non-residents)* 15.00/20.00 **t.** and a la carte 🍷 6.95 – **17 rm** ☕ 75.00/110.00 **t.**

MIDLETON (Mainistir na Corann) Cork 405 H 12 – ☎ 021 Cork.
⛳18 East Cork, Gortacue ☎ 631687/631273.
[i] Jameson Heritage Centre ☎ 613702 (8 April-20 September).
♦Dublin 161 – ♦Cork 12 – ♦Waterford 61.

🏨 **Midleton Park,** Old Cork Rd, ☎ 631767, Fax 631605, 🌳 – ❄ rest 📺 ☎ ♿ 🅿 – 👥 300. 💳 AE ⓓ VISA
M 8.50/15.50 **t.** and a la carte 🍷 4.95 – **39 rm** ☕ 40.00/68.00 **t.**, 1 suite.

🏠 **Bailick Cottage** without rest., S : ½ m. by Broderick St. ☎ 631244, 🌳 – 🅿. 🚫🐕
6 rm ☕ 25.00/50.00.

MOYCULLEN (Maigh Cuilinn) Galway 405 E 7 – pop. 228 – ☎ 091 Galway.
♦Dublin 139 – ♦Galway 7.

🏨 **Knockferry Lodge** 🐦, Knockferry (on Lough Corrib), NE : 6½ m. ☎ 80122, Fax 80328, ←, 🎣, 🌳 – 🚭 rest 🅿. 💳 AE ⓓ VISA. 🚫🐕
May-September – **M** (dinner only) 16.00 **st.** – **10 rm** ☕ 25.00/42.00 **st.**

🏠 **Moycullen House** 🐦, SW : 1 m. on Spiddle rd ☎ 85566, Fax 85566, 🌳 – 🚭 rm 🅿. 💳 AE VISA. 🚫🐕
March-October – **M** (communal dining) 17.00 **st.** – **5 rm** ☕ 35.00/50.00 **st.**

XX **Drimcong House,** NW : 1 m. on N 59 *ℰ* 85115, « 17C estate house », ☞ – **ℙ**. **△** **AE** **◉** VISA

closed Sunday, Monday and Christmas-March – **Meals** (booking essential) (dinner only) 15.95/18.95 **t.** and a la carte 18.00/25.50 **t.** § 5.00.

MULLINAVAT (Muileann an Bhata) Kilkenny 405 K 10 – ✪ 051.

♦Dublin 88 – Kilkenny 21 – Waterford 8.

🏠 **Rising Sun,** Main St., *ℰ* 98173, Fax 98435 – 📺 ☎ **ℙ**. **△** VISA

M *(closed dinner to non-residents)* (bar lunch)/dinner 12.50 **t.** and a la carte § 3.75 – **10 rm** ☞ 24.00/40.00 **t.** – SB (except Bank Holidays) 56.00/77.00 **st.**

MULLINGAR (An Muileann gCearr) Westmeath 405 JK 7 Ireland G. – pop. 7 854 – ✪ 044.

Envir. : Belvedere House and Gardens★ *AC*, S : 3½ m. by N 52.

Exc. : Multyfarnhan Franciscan Friary★, N : 8 m. by N 4 - Tullynally Castle★ *AC*, N : 13 m. by N 4 and R 394 – Fore Abbey★, NE : 17 m. by R 394.

🏌️₁₈ Mullingar *ℰ* 48366.

🎫 Dublin Road *ℰ* 48650.

♦Dublin 49 – ♦Drogheda 36.

🏨 **Greville Arms,** Pearse St., *ℰ* 48563, Fax 48052 – 🍽 rest 📺 ☎ **ℙ** – **△** 100. **△** **AE** **◉** VISA.

closed 25 December – **M** 8.95 **st.** (lunch) and a la carte 10.90/22.15 **st.** § 5.20 – **39 rm** ☞ 28.00/70.00 **st.** – SB 76.00 **st.**

⌂ **Hilltop Country House,** Rathconnell, NE : 2½ m. off R 52 *ℰ* 48958, Fax 48013, ☞ – **ℙ**. ❀

March-October – **M** (by arrangement) – **5 rm** ☞ 19.00/30.00 **st.**

NAVAN (An Uaimh) Meath 405 L 7 – ✪ 046.

Envir. : Bective Abbey★, S : 4 m. by R 161.

Exc. : Trim★ (castle★★) SW : 8 m. by R 161.

♦Dublin 29 – Drogheda 17.

XXX **Dunderry Lodge,** SW : 6 m. by N 51 and L 23 *ℰ* 31671, « Converted farm buildings » – **ℙ**. **△** **AE** VISA

closed Sunday dinner, Monday, 1 week January and 1 week August – **M** (dinner only and Sunday lunch)/dinner 19.75 **st.** and a la carte § 5.50.

NEWBRIDGE (An Droichead Nua) Kildare 405 L 8 Ireland G. – pop. 5 780 – ECD : Tuesday – ✪ 045 Naas.

See : Town★.

Envir. : Tully★★★ (Japanese Gardens★★★ *AC*, Irish National Stud★★ *AC*) SW : 6 m. by N 7 - Kildare★ (Cathedral★★) SW : 5½ m. by N 7.

🏌️₁₈ Curragh *ℰ* 41238/41714, S : 4 m.

🎫 *ℰ* 33835 (10 June-August).

♦Dublin 28 – Kilkenny 57 – ♦Tullamore 36.

🏨 **Keadeen,** Ballymany, SW : 1 m. on N 7 *ℰ* 31666, Fax 34402, ☞ – 📺 ☎ **ℙ** – **△** 350. **△** **AE** **◉** VISA ❀

closed 23 to 28 December – **M** 15.50/32.50 **t.** and a la carte – **36 rm** ☞ 55.00/130.00 **t.**, 1 suite.

NEWMARKET-ON-FERGUS (Cora Chaitlín) Clare 405 F 7 – pop. 1 348 – ✪ 061 Shannon.

♦Dublin 136 – Ennis 8 – ♦Limerick 15.

🏰 **Dromoland Castle** ⌂, NW : 1 ½ m. on N 18 *ℰ* 368144, Telex 70654, Fax 363355, ≼, « Converted castle », 🏌️₁₈, 🎣, ☞, park, ✻ – 📺 ☎ **ℙ** – **△** 450. **△** **AE** **◉** VISA JCB. ❀

M 19.00/32.00 **t.** and a la carte § 8.50 – ☞ 12.00 – **67 rm** 194.00/235.00 **st.**, 6 suites – SB (November-March except Christmas and New Year) 210.00/330.00 **st.**

🏠 **Carrygerry House** ⌂, NW : 8 m. by N 18 *ℰ* 472339, Fax 472123, ☞, park – 📺 ☎ **ℙ**. **△** **AE** **◉** VISA. ❀

M *(closed Sunday)* (bar lunch)/dinner 17.50 **t.** and a la carte § 4.50 – **14 rm** ☞ 39.50/70.00 **t.** – SB (except Christmas) 75.00/95.00 **st.**

NEWPORT (Baile Uí Fhiacháin) Mayo 405 D 6 Ireland G. – pop. 470 – ✪ 098.

Envir. : Burrishoole Abbey★, NW : 2 m. by N 59 – Furnace Lough★, NW : 3 m. by N 59.

♦Dublin 164 – Ballina 37 – ♦Galway 60.

🏨 **Newport House** ⌂, *ℰ* 41222, Fax 41613, « Country house atmosphere, antiques », 🎣, ☞, park – ❀ rest ☎ **ℙ**. **△** **AE** **◉** VISA. ❀

19 March-2 October – **M** (dinner only) 28.00 **st.** § 5.00 – **18 rm** ☞ 61.00/122.00 **st.**

L'EUROPE en une seule feuille
Carte Michelin n° 970.

NEW ROSS (Ros Mhic Thrúlin) Wexford 405 L 10 Ireland G. – pop. 5 386 – ECD : Wednesday – ✉ Newbawn – 🕿 051.

See : St. Mary's Church★.

Exc. : Kennedy Arboretum, Campile★ *AC*, S : 7½ m. by R 733 – Dunbrody Abbey★, S : 8 m. by R 733 – Inistiage★, NW : 10 m. by N 25 and R 700 – Graiguenamanagh★ (Duiske Abbey★) N : 11 m. by N 25 and R705.

🔂 Tinneranny 🖉 21433, W : 1 m.

🖪 Town Centre 🖉 21857 (16 June-4 September).

◆Dublin 88 – Kilkenny 27 – ◆Waterford 15 – Wexford 23.

🏠 **Cedar Lodge,** Carrigbyrne, E : 8 m. on N 25 🖉 28386, Fax 28222, ☞ – 📺 🕿 🅿. 🚗 *VISA* 🛠
  closed mid December-mid January – **M** 14.00/22.00 **st.** ♨ 5.50 – **18 rm** ⊐ 45.00/80.00 **st.** – SB 80.00/85.00 **st.**

OGONNELLOE (Tuath Ó gConaíle) Clare 405 G 9 – see Killaloe.

OUGHTERARD (Uachtar Ard) Galway 405 E 7 Ireland G. – pop. 748 – 🕿 091 Galway.

See : Town★.

Envir. : Lough Corrib★★ (Shore road - NW - ≤★★) – Aughnanure Castle★ *AC*, SE : 2 m. by N 59.

🔂 Gurteeva 🖉 82131.

🖪 🖉 82808.

◆Dublin 149 – ◆Galway 17.

🏨 **Connemara Gateway,** SE : ¾ m. on N 59 🖉 82328, Fax 82332, ☎s, 🔲, ☞, 🎾 – 🍽 rest 📺 🕿 🅿. 🚗 🛈 *VISA* 🛠
  closed December-5 February except New Year – **M** (bar lunch)/dinner 21.00 **st.** and a la carte ♨ 6.00 – **62 rm** ⊐ 40.00/225.00 **st.** – SB (except Bank Holidays) 77.50/135.00 **st.**

🏠 **Currarevagh House** 🐾, NW : 4 m. 🖉 82313, Fax 82731, ≤, « Country house atmosphere », 🐾, ☞, park, 🎾 – ↔ rest 🅿. 🛠
  27 April-27 October – **M** (booking essential) (dinner only) 18.00 **t.** ♨ 4.70 – **15 rm** ⊐ 40.50/81.00 **t.**

🏠 **Ross Lake House** 🐾, Rosscahill, SE : 4½ m. by N 59 🖉 80109, Fax 80184, ☞, 🎾 – 🕿 🅿. 🚗 🗚 🛈 *VISA*
  closed November-mid March – **M** (dinner only) 19.00 **t.** ♨ 5.00 – **13 rm** ⊐ 33.00/77.00 **st.**

↑ **Cnoc na Curra** 🐾 without rest., Pier Rd, 🖉 82225, ≤, 🐾, ☞ – ↔ 🅿 🛠
  May-September – **3 rm** ⊐ 27.00/45.00 **st.**

PARKNASILLA (Páirc na Saileach) Kerry 405 C 12 Ireland G. – 🕿 064 Killarney.

Envir. : Sneem★, NW : 2½ m. by N 70.

Exc. : Iveragh Peninsula★★★ (Ring of Kerry★★) – Staigue Fort★, W : 13 m. by N 70.

◆Dublin 224 – ◆Cork 72 – ◆Killarney 34.

🏰 **Great Southern** 🐾, 🖉 45122, Telex 73899, Fax 45323, ≤ Kenmare river, bay and mountains, ☎s, 🔲, 🔂, 🐾, ☞, park, 🎾 – 🛗 📺 🕿 🅿 – 🔬 50. 🚗 🗚 🛈 *VISA*. 🛠
  closed January-March – **M** (bar lunch)/dinner 25.00 **st.** and a la carte ♨ 8.00 – **83 rm** ⊐ 97.00/160.00 **st.**, 1 suite – SB (except July and August) (weekdays only) 150.00/216.00 **st.**

PORTLAOISE (Port Laoise) Laois 405 K 8 Ireland G. – pop. 4 049 – 🕿 0502.

Envir. : Rock of Dunamase★ (≤★), E : 4 m. by N 80 – Emo Court★ *AC*, NE : 7 m. by N 7.

Exc. : Stradbally★, E : 6½ m. by N 80 – Timahoe Round Tower★, SE : 8 m. by R 426.

🔂 The Heath 🖉 46533, E : 4 m.

🖪 James Fintan Lawlor Av. 🖉 21178.

◆ Dublin 54 – Kilkenny 31 – ◆Limerick 67.

↑ **Aspen** without rest., Dunamase, E : 4½ m. by N 80 🖉 25405, Fax 25405, ☞ – ↔ 🅿. 🛠
  closed 20 to 31 December – **4 rm** ⊐ 19.00/31.00 **st.**

PORTMARNOCK (Port Mearnóg) Dublin 405 N 7 – pop. 9 055 – 🕿 01 Dublin.

◆Dublin 5 – Drogheda 28.

🏨 **Portmarnock H. & Country Club,** 🖉 846 0611, Fax 846 2442, ≤, ☞ – 📺 🕿 🅿 – 🔬 600. 🚗 🗚 🛈 *VISA* 🛠
  M (dinner only and Sunday lunch)/dinner 14.95 **st.** and a la carte – ⊐ 4.50 – **19 rm** ⊐ 42.50/125.00 **t.** – SB (weekends only) 110.00/150.00 **st.**

PORTNABLAHY/PORTNABLAGH (Port na Bláiche) Donegal 405 I 2 – see Dunfanaghy.

RATHMULLAN (Ráth Maoláin) Donegal 405 J 2 Ireland G. – pop. 584 – ✉ 🕿 074 Letterkenny.

Exc. : Knockalla Viewpoint★★, N : 8 m. by R 247 – Rathmelton★, SW : 7 m. by R 247.

🔂 Otway, Saltpans 🖉 58319, N : 3 m.

◆Dublin 165 – ◆Londonderry 36 – ◆Sligo 87.

🏠 **Rathmullan House** ⌂, N : ½ m. on R 247 *ℰ* 58188, Fax 58200, ≤ Lough Swilly and hills, « Early 19C country house, gardens », ⌂, ⊠, ⌂, park, ✗ – ↝ rest ☎ ❷. ⌛ ⌶ ⓞ *VISA*.
March-October – **M** (bar lunch)/dinner 20.00 **t.** ⌂ 8.50 – **23 rm** ⊇ 45.00/110.00 **t.** – SB 100.00/165.00 **st.**

🏠 **Fort Royal** ⌂, N : ½ m. on R 247 *ℰ* 58100, Fax 58103, ≤ Lough Swilly and hills, ⌂, park, ✗, squash – ↝ rest ☎ ❷. ⌛ ⌶ ⓞ *VISA*
closed 1 January – **M** (bar lunch Monday to Friday)/dinner 21.00 **st.** ⌂ 7.00 – **15 rm** ⊇ 35.00/90.00 **st.**

(Ráth Naoi) Wicklow 🗺 N 8 Ireland G. – pop. 1 366 – ✉ ✆ 0404 Wicklow.
Exc. : Glendalough★★★, W : 13 m. by N 11, R 763, R 755 and R 756 – W : Wicklow Mountains★★.
♦Dublin 31 – ♦Waterford 82 – Wexford 65.

🏠 **Tinakilly House** ⌂, *ℰ* 69274, Fax 67806, ≤, « Part Victorian country house », ⌂, ✗ – ⌖ ☎ ❷ – ⌂ 60. ⌛ ⌶ ⓞ *VISA* *JCB* ✗
M 16.50/27.50 **st.** and a la carte – **26 rm** ⊇ 75.00/140.00 **st.**, 3 suites – SB (except June-September and Christmas-New Year) 145.00/215.00 **st.**

🏠 **Hunter's**, Newrath Bridge, N : ¾ m. on L 29 *ℰ* 40106, Fax 40338, « Converted 18C inn, gardens » – ☎ ❷. ⌛ ⌶ ⓞ *VISA* ✗
closed Christmas Day – **M** 12.50/18.50 **t.** ⌂ 8.75 – **17 rm** ⊇ 37.50/80.00 **st.**

(Sraith Salach) Galway 🗺 C 7 – ✆ 095 Clifden.
♦Dublin 173 – Balling 72 – ♦Galway 36.

🏠 **Lough Inagh Lodge** ⌂, NW : 4 ¾ m. by N 59 *ℰ* 34706, Fax 34708, ≤ Lough Inagh and The Twelve Bens, ⌂ – ⌕ ☎ ❷. ⌛ ⌶ ⓞ *VISA* ✗
April-October – **M** (bar lunch)/dinner 23.00 **st.** ⌂ 6.00 – **12 rm** ⊇ 55.00/120.00 **st.**

(Rinn Mhaoile) Galway 🗺 C 7 – ✆ 095 Clifden.
♦Dublin 193 – Ballina 73 – ♦Galway 61.

🏠 **Renvyle House** ⌂, *ℰ* 43511, Fax 43515, ≤ Atlantic Ocean, ⌕ heated, ⌂, ⌂, ⌂, park, ✗ – ⌂ ☎ ❷. ⌛ ⌶ ⓞ *VISA* *JCB*. ✗
closed 3 January-mid March – **M** (light lunch Monday to Saturday)/dinner 19.50 **t.** ⌂ 7.50 – **59 rm** ⊇ 52.50/105.00 **t.**, 1 suite.

(Baile idir Dhá Abhainn) Sligo 🗺 G 5 – pop. 262 – ✆ 071 Sligo.
♦Dublin 123 – Sligo 13.

🏠 **Coopershill** ⌂, *ℰ* 65108, Fax 65466, ≤, ⌂, park – ↝ rm ☎ ❷. ⌛ ⌶ ⓞ *VISA* *JCB*. ✗
mid March-October – **M** (residents only) (dinner only) 21.00 ⌂ 5.00 – **7 rm** ⊇ 48.00/84.00 **st.**

(Rosapenna) Donegal 🗺 I 2 Ireland G. – ✆ 074 Letterkenny.
Envir. : N : Rosguill Peninsula Atlantic Drive★.
🏌 Golf Hotel *ℰ* 55301.
♦Dublin 216 – Donegal 52 – ♦Londonderry 47.

🏠 **Rosapenna Golf** (Best Western), Downings, *ℰ* 55301, Fax 55128, ≤, 🏌, ✗ – ⌕ ☎ ❷. ⌛ ⌶ ⓞ *VISA*
April-October – **M** (bar lunch)/dinner 20.00 **t.** ⌂ 5.50 – **46 rm** ⊇ 48.00/99.00 **t.** – SB 100.00/132.00 **st.**

(Ros Comáin) Roscommon 🗺 H 7 Ireland G. – pop. 1 363 – ✆ 0903.
See : Castle★.
Exc. : Castlestrange Stone★, SW : 7 m. by N 63 and R 362 – Strokestown Park House★ *AC*, N : 12 m. by N 61 and R 368 – Castlerea : Clonalis House★ *AC*, NW : 19 m. by N 60.
🏌 Moate Park *ℰ* 26382.
🛈 *ℰ* 26342 (1 June-31 August).
♦Dublin 94 – ♦Galway 57 – Limerick 94.

🏠 **Abbey** ⌂, on N 63 *ℰ* 26240, Fax 26021, ⌂ – ⌕ ☎ ⌂ ❷ – ⌂ 40. ⌛ ⌶ ⓞ *VISA* *JCB*. ✗
closed 25 and 26 December – **M** 12.00/19.00 **st.** and a la carte ⌂ 4.75 – **20 rm** ⊇ 35.00/60.00 **st.** – SB 94.00/120.00 **st.**

(Ros Láir) Wexford 🗺 M 11 – pop. 779 – ✆ 053 Wexford.
🏌, 🏌 Rosslare Strand *ℰ* 32113, N : 1 m.
🛥 Rosslare Terminal *ℰ* 33622.
♦Dublin 104 – ♦Waterford 50 – Wexford 12.

🏠 **Kelly's Strand**, Strand Rd, *ℰ* 32114, Fax 32222, ⌂, ⌂, ⊠, ⌂, ✗, squash – ⌂ ⌷ rest ⌕ ☎ ⌂ ❷. ⌛ ⌶ *VISA* ✗
March-4 December – **M** 11.50/20.95 **t.** ⌂ 5.50 – **99 rm** ⊇ 41.00/86.00 **st.** – SB (except summer) (weekends only) 110.00/160.00 **st.**

🏠 **Cedars**, Strand Rd, *ℰ* 32124, Fax 32243, ⌂, ⌂ – ⌷ rest ⌕ ☎ ❷. ⌛ *VISA* ✗
April-December – **M** (bar lunch Monday to Saturday)/dinner 15.95 **t.** and a la carte ⌂ 4.95 – **34 rm** ⊇ 47.00/74.00 **st.**

ROSSLARE HARBOUR (Calafort Ros Láir) Wexford [405] N 11 Ireland G. – pop. 777 – ☎ 053 Wexford.

Envir. : Lady's Island★, SW : 6 m. by N 25 and R 736 – Tacumshane Windmill★, SW : 6 m. by N 25 and R 736.

⛴ to France : – to Fishguard (Stena Sealink Line) 2 daily (3 h 30 mn) – to Pembroke (B & I Line) (4 h 15 mn).

ℹ Kilrane ✆ 33232 (1 May-mid September).

♦Dublin 105 – ♦Waterford 51 – Wexford 13.

🏨 **Great Southern,** ✆ 33233, Fax 33543, 🏋, ♨, 🏊, 🎾 – |♦| ⊁ rm 📺 ☎ ♿ 🅟 – 🎤 200. [EC] [AE] ⦿ [VISA]
mid March-October – **M** (bar lunch Monday to Saturday)/dinner a la carte 8.70/19.95 **st.** 🍷 6.50 – **100 rm** ☕ 37.50/60.80 **st.** – SB 60.80/110.00 **st.**

🏨 **Rosslare,** ✆ 33110, Fax 33386, ≤, ♨, 🏌, squash – 📺 ☎ 🅟. [EC] [AE] ⦿ [VISA]
closed 25 December – **M** 10.50/18.00 **st.** and a la carte – **25 rm** ☕ 25.00/75.00 **t.**

🏨 **Tuskar House,** St. Martins Rd, ✆ 33363, Fax 33363, ≤, 🌳 – 📺 ☎ 🅟. [EC] [AE] ⦿ [VISA]. 🚫
M (bar lunch Monday to Saturday) 11.50/17.95 **st.** and a la carte 🍷 4.95 – **22 rm** ☕ 33.00/66.00 **st.** – SB 78.00/132.00 **st.**

🏨 **Devereux,** Wexford Rd, ✆ 33216, Fax 33301, ≤ – 📺 ☎ 🅟. [EC] [AE] [VISA]. 🚫
closed 24 and 25 December – **M** (bar lunch Monday to Saturday)/dinner 11.95 and a la carte 🍷 5.00 – **16 rm** ☕ 35.00/52.00 **t.**

ROSSNOWLAGH (Ros Neamhlach) Donegal [405] H 4 – ✉ ☎ 072.

♦Dublin 153 – Donegal 14 – ♦Sligo 31.

🏨 **Sand House** 🐦, ✆ 51777, Fax 52100, ≤ bay, beach and mountains, 🐕, 🎾 – ☎ 🅟. [EC] [AE] ⦿ [VISA]. 🚫
Easter-October – **M** (bar lunch Monday to Friday) 12.50/22.50 **t.** 🍷 6.00 – **40 rm** ☕ 40.00/120.00 **t.** – SB (April-June and September except Bank Holidays) 110.00/154.00 **st.**

ROUNDSTONE (Cloch na Rón) Galway – ☎ 095 Clifden

♦Dublin 193 – ♦Galway 47.

🏨 **Eldon's,** ✆ 35933, Fax 35921, ≤, 🌳 – 📺 ☎. [EC] [AE] ⦿ [VISA]. 🚫
closed 25 December-9 March – **M** 10.00/17.50 **t.** and a la carte 🍷 4.70 – **13 rm** ☕ 30.00/70.00 **st.** – SB (except July, August and Bank Holidays) 85.00/98.50 **st.**

SALTHILL (Bóthar na Trá) Galway [405] E 8 – see Galway.

SHANAGARRY (An Seangharraí) Cork [405] H 12 Ireland G. – pop. 241 – ✉ Midleton – ☎ 021 Cork.

Envir. : Ballycotton★, SE : 2½ m. by R 629 – Cloyne Cathedral★, NW : 4 m. by R 629.

Exc. : Rostellan Wood★, W : 9 m. by R 629 and R 631 on R 630.

♦Dublin 163 – ♦Cork 25 – ♦Waterford 64.

XX **Ballymaloe House** 🐦 with rm, NW : 1 ¾ m. on L 35 ✆ 652531, Fax 652021, ≤, « Country house atmosphere », 🏊 heated, 🌳, park, 🎾 – ⊁ rest ☎ 🅟. [EC] ⦿ [VISA]. 🚫
closed 24 to 26 December – **Meals** (lunch by arrangement)/dinner 30.00 **t.** 🍷 8.00 – **29 rm** ☕ 77.00/120.00 **t.** – SB (November-26 March except Christmas-New Year) 126.00/146.00 **st.**

SHANNON (Sionainn) Clare [405] F 9 – pop. 8 005 – ☎ 061 Limerick.

✈ Shannon Airport ✆ 61444 – **Terminal** : Limerick Railway Station ✆ 42433.

🏌 Shannon ✆ 61020.

ℹ Shannon Airport ✆ 61664.

♦Dublin 136 – Ennis 16 – ♦Limerick 15.

🏨 **Oak Wood Arms,** ✆ 361500, Fax 361414 – ▤ 📺 ☎ 🅟 – 🎤 200. [EC] [AE] ⦿ [VISA]. 🚫
closed 24 and 25 December – **M** (buffet lunch)/dinner 15.50 **t.** and a la carte 🍷 5.75 – **42 rm** ☕ 50.00/80.00 **t.**, 1 suite – SB (weekdays only) 110.00/146.00 **st.**

at Shannon Airport SW : 2½ m. on N 19 – ✉ Shannon – ☎ 061 Limerick :

🏨 **Great Southern,** ✆ 471122, Telex 72078, Fax 471982 – |♦| ⊁ rm ▤ rest 📺 ☎ 🅟 – 🎤 150. [EC] [AE] ⦿ [VISA]. 🚫
April-December – **M** *(closed Saturday lunch)* (buffet lunch) 8.00/20.00 **t.** and dinner a la carte 🍷 5.00 – ☕ 6.50 – **113 rm** 58.70/85.00 **t.**, 2 suites – SB 80.00/110.00 **st.**

SKERRIES (Na Sceirí) Dublin [405] N 7 – pop. 5 793 – ☎ 01 Dublin.

🏌 Skerries ✆ 849 1204.

ℹ Community Office ✆ 8490888.

♦Dublin 19 – Drogheda 15.

XX **Red Bank,** 7 Church St., ✆ 849 1005, Fax 849 1598 – [EC] [AE] ⦿ [VISA]
closed Sunday and Monday – **M** - **Seafood** (dinner only and Sunday lunch)/dinner 21.00 **t.** and a la carte 🍷 5.75.

(An Scoil) Cork 405 D 13 – pop. 502 – ✪ 028 Skibbereen.

♦Dublin 226 – ♦Cork 65 – ♦Killarney 64.

↑ **Corthna Lodge** ⌂ without rest., W : ¾ m. by R 592 ℰ 28517, Fax 28517, ≼, 🚗 – **℗**. ⚙
April-October – **6 rm** ⊇ 25.00/40.00 **st.**

(Baile Shláine) Meath 405 M 6 – ✪ 041.

♦Dublin 29 – Drogheda 9.

🏠 **Conyngham Arms,** ℰ 24155, Fax 24205, 🚗 – 📺 rest 📺 ☎ **℗** – 🔼 120. ⚞ 🆎 ⓞ 𝘷𝘪𝘴𝘢. ⚙
closed Good Friday and 24 to 26 December – **M** (bar lunch Monday to Saturday)/dinner a la carte 13.00/20.75 **t.** ⓘ 5.45 – **16 rm** ⊇ 25.00/59.90 **t.** – SB 65.00/160.00 **st.**

(Sliabh Rua) Waterford – see Waterford.

(Sligeach) Sligo 405 G 5 Ireland G. – pop. 17 232 – ✪ 071.

See : Town★ - Abbey★.

Envir. : SE : Lough Gill★★ – Carrowmore Megalithic Cemetery★ AC, SW : 3 m. – Knocknarea★ (≼★★★) SW : 6 m. by R 292.

Exc. : Parke's Castle★★ AC, E : 9 m. by R 286 – Glencar Waterfall★, NE : 9 m. by N 16 – Creevelea Abbey, Dromahair★, SE : 11 ½ m. by N 4 and R 287 – Creevykeel Court Cairn★, N : 16 m. by N 15.

🏌 Rosses Point ℰ 77134/77186, NW : 5 m.

✈ Sligo Airport, Strandhill, ℰ 68280.

🛈 Temple St. ℰ 61201.

♦Dublin 133 – ♦Belfast 126 – ♦Dundalk 106 – ♦Londonderry 86.

🏨 **Sligo Park,** Pearse Rd, S : 1 m. on N 4 ℰ 60291, Fax 69556, ⎣₆, ⣼s, ⬛, 🚗, ⚙ – 📺 ☎ ⓑ
℗ – 🔼 500. ⚞ 🆎 ⓞ 𝘷𝘪𝘴𝘢
M (bar lunch Saturday) 11.00/22.00 **st.** and dinner a la carte ⓘ 4.75 – **88 rm** ⊇ 45.00/95.00 **st.**, 1 suite – SB (except Bank Holidays) 90.00/118.00 **st.**

↑ **Tree Tops** without rest., Cleveragh Rd, S :¼ m. off Dublin rd ℰ 60160, 🚗 – 📺 ☎ **℗**. ⚞
𝘷𝘪𝘴𝘢 ⚙
closed Christmas – **5 rm** ⊇ 16.00/30.00 **st.**

(An Spidéal) Galway 405 E 8 – ✪ 091 Galway.

♦Dublin 143 – ♦Galway 11.

🏠 **Bridge House,** Main St., ℰ 83118, 🚗 – ⚒ rest 📺 ☎ **℗**. ⚞ 🆎 𝘷𝘪𝘴𝘢. ⚙
closed mid December-mid February – **M** 14.00/20.00 **t.** and a la carte ⓘ 4.95 – **14 rm**
⊇ 40.00/65.00 **t.** – SB (except Bank Holidays) 70.00/120.00 **st.**

↑ **Ardmor Country House** without rest., W : ½ m. on L 100 ℰ 83145, Fax 83145, ≼, 🚗 –
⚒ ⚙
closed December and January – **8 rm** ⊇ 20.00/30.00 **st.**

(Teach Srafáin) Kildare 405 M 8 – pop. 303 – ✪ 01 Dublin.

🏌 Naas, Kerdiffstown ℰ 045 (Naas) 97509.

♦Dublin 15 – Mullingar 47.

🏨 **Kildare H. & Country Club** ⌂, ℰ 627 3333, Fax 627 3312, ≼, « Part early 19C country house on banks of the River Liffey », ⎣₆, ⣼s, ⬛, 🏌, 🚵, 🚗, park, ⚙, squash – 📳 📺 ☎
℗ – 🔼 45. ⚞ 🆎 ⓞ 𝘷𝘪𝘴𝘢. ⚙
M – **Legends** (in K Club) 19.00/35.00 **t.** ⓘ 7.50 – (see also **Byerley Turk** below) – **33 rm**
155.00/275.00 **t.**, 7 suites – SB 195.00/350.00 **st.**

🏨 **Barberstown Castle,** N : ½ m. ℰ 628 8157, Fax 627 7027, « Part Elizabethan, part Victorian house with 13C castle keep », 🚗 – 📺 ☎ **℗**. ⚞ 🆎 𝘷𝘪𝘴𝘢. ⚙
closed 24 to 26 December – **M** (dinner only and Sunday lunch)/dinner 22.50 **t.** ⓘ 6.50 –
10 rm ⊇ 65.00/110.00 **st.**

XXXX ✪ **Byerley Turk** (at Kildare H. & Country Club), ℰ 627 3333, Fax 627 3312, 🚗 – **℗**. ⚞ 🆎
ⓞ 𝘷𝘪𝘴𝘢
M (dinner only and Sunday lunch)/dinner 35.00 **t.** and a la carte 42.00/54.00 **t.** ⓘ 8.00
Spec. Escalope de foie gras chaud sur un lit de fèves et son consommé de légumes, Médaillon de veau et ses raviolis au lard fumé, Gratinée de framboises au beurre d'orange.

(Sord) Dublin 405 N 7 – pop. 15 312 – ✪ 01 Dublin.

🏌 Corballis, Donabate ℰ 843 6228, NW : 5 m.

♦Dublin 8 – Drogheda 22.

🏠 **Forte Travelodge,** Miltons Field, S :½ m. on N 1 ℰ 840 9233, Reservations (Freephone) 0800 850950 (UK), 1800 709709 (Eire) – 📺 ☎ **℗**. ⚞ 🆎 𝘷𝘪𝘴𝘢. ⚙
M (grill rest.) 16.00 **t.** – **40 rm** 31.95 **t.**

XX **Le Chateau,** River Mall, Main St., ℰ 840 6533, Fax 840 6533 – 📺 **℗**. ⚞ 🆎 ⓞ 𝘷𝘪𝘴𝘢
closed Sunday, 24-25 December, 1 January and Bank Holidays – **M** (lunch by arrangement)/dinner 19.50 **st.** and a la carte ⓘ 4.50.

TAHILLA (Tathuile) Kerry 405 C 12 Ireland G. – ✿ 064 Killarney.

Exc. : Iveragh Peninsula★★★ (Ring of Kerry★★).

◆Dublin 222 – ◆Cork 70 – ◆Killarney 32.

↑ **Tahilla Cove** ⌖, ℰ 45204, ≤, ↘, ☞ – ☎ ℗, ⚞⚟ AE ⓪ VISA
May-September – **M** (bar lunch)/dinner 16.00 **st.** ⏜ 4.50 – **9 rm** ⊡ 40.00/60.00 **st.**

TEMPLEGLENTAN (Teampall an Ghleanntáin) Limerick 405 E 10 Ireland G. – ✿ 069 Newcastle West.

Exc. : Newcastle West★, NE : 4½ m. by N 21.

☞ Newcastle West ℰ 62105, NE : 7½ m. by N 21.

◆Dublin 154 – ◆Killarney 36 – ◆Limerick 33.

☐ **Devon,** on N 21 ℰ 84122, Fax 84122 – �📺 ☎ ℗, ⚞⚟ AE ⓪ VISA ✼
M 8.50/13.00 **st.** and dinner a la carte ⏜ 5.00 – **18 rm** ⊡ 26.00/45.00 **st.**

TERRYGLASS (Tír Dhá Ghlas) Tipperary 405 H 8 – ✉ ✿ 067 Nenagh.

◆Dublin 114 – ◆Galway 51 – ◆Limerick 43.

↑ **Riverrun** ⌖, without rest., ℰ 22125, ↘, ✼ – ☎ ℗, ⚞⚟ AE VISA
6 rm ⊡ 25.00/40.00 **st.**

THOMASTOWN (Baile Mhic Andáin) Kilkenny 405 K 10 Ireland G. – ✉ ✿ 056 Kilkenny.

See : Ladywell Water Garden★ AC.

Envir. : Jerpoint Abbey★★, SW : 1½ m. by N9.

☞ Thomastown ℰ 24725.

◆Dublin 77 – Kilkenny 11 – ◆Waterford 30 – Wexford 38.

🏰 **Mount Juliet** ⌖, NW : 1½ m. ℰ 24455, Fax 24522, « 18C manor and sporting estate, ≤ River Nore and park », ≦s, ⚞⚟, ☞, ↘, ✼ – 📺 ☎ ⏶ ℗, ⚞⚟ AE ⓪ VISA JCB
M 33.00 **st.** and a la carte 12.25/22.50 **st.** – **30 rm** ⊡ 135.00/175.00 **st.**, 2 suites.

🏰 **Hunters Yard at Mount Juliet,** NW : 1½ m. ℰ 24725, Fax 24522, « Converted 18C stables », ≦s, ⚞⚟, ☞, ↘, park, ✼ – ☎ ℗, – ⏜ 80. ⚞⚟ AE ⓪ VISA
M 12.50/15.00 **t.** and dinner a la carte ⏜ 13.50 – **13 rm** ⊡ 98.00 **st.** – SB (weekdays only) 128.90/248.90 **st.**

Great Britain and Ireland are covered entirely
at a scale of 16 miles to 1 inch by our **map « Main roads »** 986.

TIPPERARY (Tiobraid Árann) Tipperary 405 H 10 Ireland G. – pop. 4 984 – ECD : Wednesday – ✿ 062.

Envir. : Glen of Aherlow★, S : by R 664.

Exc. : Kilmallock★★ : Abbey★, Collegiate Church★, Blossom's Gate★, Town Walls★, King's Castle★, W : 20 m. by R 515.

☞ Rathanny ℰ 51119, S : 1 m.

🛈 Community Office, James St. ℰ 51457.

◆Dublin 113 – ◆Cork 57 – ◆Limerick 24 – ◆Waterford 53.

↑ **Bansha House,** Bansha, SE : 5½ m. by N 24 ℰ 54194, ☞, park – ↔ rest ℗, ⚞⚟ VISA ✼
closed 20 to 27 December – **M** 12.50 **t.** – **7 rm** ⊡ 20.00/34.00 **t.**

TOWER Cork 405 G 12 – see Blarney.

TRALEE (Trá Lí) Kerry 405 C 11 Ireland G. – pop. 16 495 – ECD : Wednesday – ✿ 066.

Envir. : Blennerville Windmill★★ AC, SW : 2 m. by N 86 – Ardfert Cathedral★, NW : 5½ m. by R 551.

Exc. : Banna Strand★★, NW : 8 m. by R 551 - Crag Cave★★ AC, W : 13 m. by N 21 – Rattoo Round Tower★, N : 12 m. by R 556.

🛈 Ashe Memorial Hall ℰ 21288.

◆Dublin 185 – ◆Killarney 20 – ◆Limerick 64.

🏛 **Brandon,** Princes St., ℰ 23333, Group Telex 73130, Fax 25019, ⏜, ≦s, ⚞⚟, ↘ – ⏸ 📺 ☎ ℗ – ⏜ 1 000. ⚞⚟ AE ⓪ VISA
closed 24 to 26 December – **M** 9.00/16.50 **st.** ⏜ 10.50 – **159 rm** ⊡ 42.00/100.00 **st.**, 1 suite.

↑ **Kilteely House** ⌖, Ballyard, Dingle Rd, S : 1 m. ℰ 23376, Fax 25766 – ☎ ℗, ⚞⚟ VISA ✼
M (by arrangement) – **9 rm** ⊡ 17.50/56.00 **st.**

TULLAMORE (Tulach Mhór) Offaly 405 J 8 – ✿ 0506.

◆Dublin 65 – Kilkenny 52 – ◆Limerick 80.

☐ **Sea Dew House** without rest., Clonminch Rd, on N 80 ℰ 52054, Fax 52054, ☞ – ↔ 📺 ☎ ℗, ⚞⚟ VISA ✼
closed 23 December-2 January – **10 rm** ⊡ 25.00/45.00 **st.**

↑ **Pine Lodge** ⌖, Screggan, SW : 4½ m. by N 52 and Mountbolus rd ℰ 51927, Fax 51927, ≦s, ⚞⚟, ☞ – ↔ ℗ ✼
closed 15 December-15 February – **M** (booking essential) 16.50 **st.** – **4 rm** ⊡ 22.00/35.00 **st.**

♦Dublin 51 – Drogheda 39 – Enniskillen 60.

🏠 **Park** 🦅, NW : ¼ m. on Ballyjamesduff rd 🖉 47235, Fax 47203, ≤, 🚔, 📠, 🥾, park, 🍴 –
🗹 ☎ 🅿 🔥, 🖭 Æ ⓪ 🆅🆂🅰 🅹🅲🅱 🎇
mid March-October – **M** (dinner only and Sunday lunch)/dinner 22.50 **t.** and a la carte
🍸 4.50 – **19 rm** ⊇ 35.00/55.00 **t.** – SB 74.00/107.00 **st.**

See : Town★ - City Walls★ - City Hall and Theatre Royal★.

Envir. : Waterford Crystal★, SW : 1 ½ m. by N 25.

Exc. : Tramore★, S : 9 m. by R 675 – Duncannon★, E : 12 m. by R 683, ferry from Passage East
and R 374 (south) – Dunmore East★, SE : 12 m. by R 684 – Tintern Abbey★, E : 13 m. by R 683,
ferry from Passage East, R 733 and R 734 (south).

📠 Newrath 🖉 76748.

✈ Waterford Airport, Killowen, 🖉 75589.

🖪 41 The Quay 🖉 75788.

♦Dublin 96 – ♦Cork 73 – ♦Limerick 77.

🏰 **Waterford Castle** 🦅, The Island, Ballinakill, E : 2 ½ m. by R 683, Ballinakill Rd and
private ferry 🖉 78203, Telex 80332, Fax 79316, ≤, « Part 15C and 19C castle, river island
setting », 🔲, 📠, 🦅, 🥾, park, 🍴 – 🛗 🗹 ☎ 🅿. 🖭 Æ ⓪ 🆅🆂🅰 🎇
M 16.00/30.00 **t.** and a la carte 🍸 7.00 – ⊇ 10.00 – **14 rm** 135.00/185.00 **t.**, 5 suites.

🏨 **Granville** (Best Western), Meagher Quay, 🖉 55111, Fax 70307 – 🛗 🗐 rest 🗹 –
🔥 250. 🖭 Æ ⓪ 🆅🆂🅰 🅹🅲🅱 🎇
closed 25 and 26 December – **M** 9.50/16.50 **st.** and a la carte 🍸 4.95 – **Bells** 15.00/25.00 **st.**
and a la carte 🍸 4.95 – **54 rm** ⊇ 44.00/124.00 **st.** – SB (weekends only) 78.00/88.00 **st.**

🏨 **Jurys**, Ferrybank, 🖉 32111, Telex 80684, Fax 32863, ≤ City, 🏋, 🚔, 🔲, 🥾, park, 🍴 – 🛗
🍴⇌ rm 🗹 ☎ 🅿 – 🔥 700. 🖭 Æ ⓪ 🆅🆂🅰. 🎇
closed 24 and 26 December – **M** 8.80/10.00 **st.** and dinner a la carte 🍸 5.00 – ⊇ 7.25 –
98 rm 62.00/82.00 **t.**

🏨 **Tower,** The Mall, 🖉 75801, Fax 70129, 🏋, 🚔, 🔲 – 🛗 🗐 rest 🗹 ☎ ૐ – 🔥 500. 🖭 Æ ⓪
🆅🆂🅰 🅹🅲🅱 🎇
closed 24 to 27 December – **M** 12.00/18.00 **st.** and a la carte 🍸 4.75 – ⊇ 7.00 – **137 rm**
49.00/100.00 **st.**, 3 suites.

🏨 **Bridge,** The Quay, 🖉 77222, Fax 77229 – 🛗 🗹 ☎ – 🔥 50. 🖭 Æ ⓪ 🆅🆂🅰. 🎇
closed 25 December – **M** (bar lunch Monday to Saturday)/dinner 17.95 **st.** and a la carte
🍸 5.45 – **75 rm** ⊇ 55.00/90.00 **st.**

🏨 **Dooley's**, The Quay, 🖉 73531, Fax 70262 – 🍴⇌ rm 🗹 ☎. 🖭 Æ ⓪ 🆅🆂🅰 🅹🅲🅱. 🎇
closed 25 and 26 December – **M** 9.85/14.25 **st.** and a la carte 🍸 5.00 – **37 rm** ⊇ 35.20/
64.90 **st.** – SB (weekends only) 83.50/98.90 **st.**

🏠 **Foxmount Farm** 🦅, SE : 4 ½ m. by R 683, off Cheekpoint rd 🖉 74308, ≤, « Working
farm », 🥾, park – 🅿. 🎇
March-October – **M** (by arrangement) 13.50 **s.** – **6 rm** ⊇ 19.00/35.00 **st.** – SB 57.00/
70.00 **st.**

✗ **Prendiville's**, Cork Rd, SW : ¾ m. on N 25 🖉 78851 – 🅿. 🖭 Æ ⓪ 🆅🆂🅰
closed Saturday lunch and Sunday – **M** 11.00/14.00 and dinner a la carte 🍸 5.00.

at Slieverue NE : 2¼ m. by N 25 – ✉ 🕲 051 Waterford :

🏠 **Diamond Hill** without rest., 🖉 32855, Fax 32254, 🥾 – 🅿. 🖭 🆅🆂🅰. 🎇
closed 24 to 26 December – **10 rm** ⊇ 18.00/20.00 **st.**

Exc. : Iveragh Peninsula★★★ (Ring of Kerry★★) – Skellig Islands★★, W : 8 m. by N 70 , R 567
and ferry from Ballinskelligs – Derrynane National Historic Park★★ AC, S : 9 m. by N70 –
Leacanabuaile Fort (≤★★), N : 13 m. by N 70 – Cahergall Fort★, N : 12 m. by N 70.

📠 Ring of Kerry 🖉 744102/744545, NW : 1 ½ m.

♦Dublin 238 – ♦Killarney 48.

🏨 **Butler Arms,** 🖉 744144, Fax 744520, ≤, 📠, 🥾, 🍴 – 🗹 ☎ 🅿. 🖭 Æ ⓪ 🆅🆂🅰. 🎇
April-October – **M** (bar lunch)/dinner 22.50 **t.** and a la carte 🍸 4.95 – **30 rm** ⊇ 60.00/99.00 **t.**

🏠 **Klondyke House** without rest., N : ½ m. on N 70 🖉 74119, ≤ – 🅿. 🖭 🆅🆂🅰 🎇
6 rm ⊇ 18.00/30.00 **st.**

🏠 **White House,** 🖉 744233 – 🍴⇌ rest 🅿. 🆅🆂🅰. 🎇
March-October – **M** 15.00 **st.** 🍸 5.00 – **8 rm** ⊇ 18.50/29.00 **st.** – SB (except June-September) 58.00 **st.**

Gli alberghi o ristoranti ameni sono indicati nella guida
con un **simbolo rosso**.

🏰🏨 ... 🏠

Contribuite a mantenere
la guida aggiornata segnalandoci
gli alberghi ed i ristoranti dove avete soggiornato piacevolmente.

🛇🛇🛇🛇🛇 ... ✗

WESTPORT (Cathair na Mart) Mayo 405 D 6 Ireland G. – pop. 3 378 – ECD : Wednesday – ✆ 098 Newport.

See : Town★★ (Centre★) – Westport House★★ AC.

Exc. : SW : Murrisk Peninsula★★ – Silver Strand★★, SW : 21 m. by R 335 – Ballintubber Abbey★, SE : 13 m. by R 330 – Croagh Patrick★, W : 6 m. by R 335 – Bunlahinch Clapper Bridge★, W : 16 m. by R 335.

🏌 Carowholly ✆ 25113/27070, W : 2 m.

🎦 The Mall ✆ 25711.

◆Dublin 163 – ◆Galway 50 – ◆Sligo 65.

🏨 **Westport Woods,** Louisburgh Rd, W : 1 m. ✆ 25811, Fax 26212, ☞, ℅ – TV ☎ 🅿. 🄰 🄰🄴 ① VISA. ℅

    M (dinner only) 15.00 **t.** and a la carte – **56 rm** ☲ 61.00/88.00 **t.**

↑ **Wilmaur** ℅ without rest., Rosbeg, W : 2 m. on R 335 ✆ 25784, ≤, ☞ – 🅿. ℅
    April-October – **4 rm** ☲ 20.00/30.00 **s.**

WEXFORD (Loch Garman) Wexford 405 M 10 Ireland G. – pop. 11 417 – ECD : Thursday – ✆ 053.

See : Town★ - Main Street★ - Franciscan Friary★.

Envir. : Irish Agricultural Museum, Johnstown Castle★★ AC, SW : 4 ½ m. – Irish National Heritage Park, Ferrycarrig★ AC, NW : 2 ½ m. by N 11 – Curracloe★, NE : 5 m. by R 741 and R 743.

Exc. : Tacumshane Windmill★, S : 11 m. by N 25 – Lady's Island★, S : 11 m. by N 25 – Kilmore Quay★, SW : 15 m. by N 25 and R 739 (Saltee Islands★ - access by boat) – Enniscorthy Castle★ (County Museum★ AC) N : 15 m. by N 11.

🏌 Mulgannon ✆ 42238/45095, S : ½ m.

🎦 Crescent Quay ✆ 23111 – Heritage Park ✆ 41911 (March-November).

◆Dublin 88 – Kilkenny 49 – ◆Waterford 38.

🏨 **Ferrycarrig** ℅, Ferrycarrig Bridge, NW : 2¾ m. on N 11 ✆ 22999, Fax 41982, ≤, ₭₰, 🛱, ☞ – |‡| 🛏 rest TV ☎ 🅿 – 🄰 400. 🄰 🄰🄴 ① VISA. ℅
    M (bar lunch)/dinner a la carte 9.30/21.50 **st.** ♪ 5.00 – (see also **Conservatory** below) – **39 rm** 35.50/90.00 **st.** – SB (except Christmas and Bank Holidays) 70.00/90.00 **st.**

🏨 **Whitford House,** New Line Rd, W : 2¼ m. on R 733 ✆ 43444, Fax 46399, 🏊, ☞, ℅ – ⌇ rest TV ☎ 🅿. 🄰 VISA. ℅
    closed 22 December-17 January – **M** (bar lunch Monday to Saturday)/dinner 18.50 **t.** and a la carte ♪ 5.00 – **24 rm** ☲ 28.00/62.00 **t.** – SB (except Bank Holidays) 83.00/93.00 **st.**

🏨 **White's** (Best Western), George St., ✆ 22311, Telex 80630, Fax 45000, ₭₰, 🛱 – |‡| TV ☎ 🅿 – 🄰 50. 🄰 🄰🄴 ① VISA
    accommodation closed 24 and 25 December – **M** (closed Christmas Day) 11.00/20.00 **st.** and a la carte – **81 rm** ☲ 47.00/72.00 **st.**, 1 suite.

🏠 **Gateway,** Rosslare Rd, Drinagh, S : 2½ m. ✆ 43295, Fax 45827, ☞, squash – TV ☎ 🅿. 🄰 🄰🄴 ① VISA. ℅
    M (bar lunch Monday to Saturday)/dinner 20.00 **st.** and a la carte ♪ 4.50 – **11 rm** ☲ 27.00/48.00 **st.** – SB 75.00/88.00 **st.**

🏠 **Ardruadh** ℅ without rest., Spawell Rd, ✆ 23194, « Gothic style Victorian house », ☞ – TV 🅿. 🄰 VISA. ℅
    closed 20 December-1 January – **5 rm** ☲ 18.00/35.00 **s.**

🏠 **Rathaspeck Manor** ℅, Rathaspeck, SW : 4 m. by R 733 and N 25 ✆ 42661, « Georgian country house », ☞, ℅ – TV 🅿. ℅
    June-October – **M** (by arrangement) (residents only) (dinner only) 14.00 **st.** – **8 rm** ☲ 20.00/40.00 **st.**

🏠 **Newbay Country House** ℅, W : 4 m. by N 25 and Clonard rd ✆ 42779, Fax 46318, ≤, ☞, park – 🅿 VISA. ℅
    March-October – **M** (closed Sunday and Monday) (by arrangement) (residents only) (communal dining) (dinner only) 29.00 **st.** ♪ 7.00 – **6 rm** ☲ 37.00/58.00 **st.**

↑ **Clonard House** ℅, Clonard Great, SW : 2 ½ m. by R 733 ✆ 43141, ≤, « Working farm », ☞, park – ⌇ rest 🅿. ℅
    April-October – **M** 13.00 – **9 rm** ☲ 20.00/32.00 **st.**

XXX **Conservatory** (at Ferrycarrig H.), Ferrycarrig Bridge, NW : 2 ¾ m. on N 11 ✆ 22999, Fax 41982, ≤, ☞ – 🖃 🅿. 🄰 🄰🄴 ① VISA
    M a la carte approx. 23.00 **st.**

When travelling for business or pleasure

*in **England**, **Wales**, **Scotland** and **Ireland** :*

  – use the series of five maps

    (nos 401, 402, 403, 404 and 405) at a scale of 1:400 000

  – they are the perfect complement to this Guide

720

Envir. : Mount Usher Gardens, Ashford★ *AC*, NW : 4 m. by R 750 and N 11 – Devil's Glen★, NW : 8 m. by R 750 and N 11.

Exc. : Glendalough★★★ : Lower Lake★★★, Upper Lake★★, Cathedral★★, Round Tower★, St. Kevin's Church★, St. Kieran's Church★, St. Kevin's Cross★, St. Saviour's Priory★ – W : 14 m. by R 750, N 11, R 763, R 755 and R 756 – Wicklow Mountains★★ : Avondale Forest Park★★ *AC*, Wicklow Gap★★, Sally Gap★★, Meeting of the Waters★, Glenmacnass Waterfall★, Glenmalur★ – Loughs Tay and Dan★.

Blainroe ℰ 68168, S : 3½ m.

Fitzwilliam St. ℰ 69117.

◆Dublin 33 – ◆Waterford 84 – Wexford 67.

Grand, ℰ 67337, Fax 69607, ⇌ – ▤ rest ▣ ☎ ℗ – ⚿ 240. ◪ *VISA*. ⋇
M 9.45/15.75 **t.** and a la carte ⅄ 4.95 – **33 rm** �ⅎ 33.00/55.00 **t.** – SB (except Bank Holidays) 70.00/90.00 **st.**

Old Rectory, ℰ 67048, Fax 69181, ⇌ – ⅙⇌ rest ▣ ☎ ℗. ◪ ◪ ◉ *VISA*. ⋇
April-October – **M** (booking essential) (dinner only) 25.00 **st.** and a la carte ⅄ 6.50 – **5 rm** ⊊ 64.00/88.00 **st.** – SB 116.00/162.00 **st.**

See : Town★ – St. Mary's Collegiate Church★★ – Town Walls★★ – Clock Gate★ – The Red House★.

Exc. : Helvick Head★★ (≼★★), NE : 22 m. by N 25 and R 674 – Ringville (≼★★), NE : 20 m. by N 25 and R 674 – Dungarvan★ (King John's Castle★) NE : 19 m. by N 25.

Knockaverry ℰ 92787.

ℰ 92390 (1 June-mid September).

◆Dublin 146 – ◆Cork 30 – ◆Waterford 47.

Devonshire Arms, Pearse Sq., ℰ 92827, Fax 92900 – ▣ ☎ ℗. ◪ ◪ ◉ *VISA*. ⋇
closed 24 and 25 December – **M** 12.00/18.50 **t.** and a la carte ⅄ 6.50 – **10 rm** ⊊ 30.00/66.00 **st.** – SB (except Bank Holidays) 55.00/90.00 **st.**

Aherne's Seafood Bar with rm, 163 North Main St., ℰ 92424, Fax 93633 – ▣ ☎ ℗ ℗.
◪ ◪ ◉ *VISA*. ⋇
closed 5 days at Christmas – **M** 14.00/22.00 **t.** and dinner a la carte – **10 rm** ⊊ 50.00/90.00 **st.**

Major hotel groups
Abbreviations used in the Guide and central reservation telephone numbers

Principales chaînes hôtelières
Abréviations utilisées dans nos textes et centraux téléphoniques de réservation

Principali catene alberghiere
Abbreviazoni utilizzate nei nostri testi e centrali telefoniche di prenotazione

Die wichtigsten Hotelketten
Im Führer benutzte Abkürzungen der Hotelketten und ihre Zentrale für telefonische Reservierung

BEST WESTERN HOTELS	BEST WESTERN	081 (London) 541 0033
CHEF & BREWER HOTELS	CHEF & BREWER	
(No central reservations – Contact Hotels direct)		
COPTHORNE HOTELS	COPTHORNE	0800 414741 (Freephone)
DE VERE HOTELS PLC	DE VERE	0925 (Warrington) 265050
EDWARDIAN HOTELS	EDWARDIAN	081 (London) 564 8888
FORTE HOTELS	FORTE	(0345) 404040 or 0800 404040 (Freephone)
TRAVELODGES		0800 850950 (Freephone)
FRIENDLY HOTELS	FRIENDLY	0800 591910 (Freephone)
GRANADA HOTELS & LODGES	GRANADA	0800 555 300 (Freephone)
HILTON HOTELS	HILTON	071 (London) 734 6000
HOLIDAY INN WORLDWIDE	HOLIDAY INN	0800 897121 (Freephone)
HYATT HOTELS	HYATT	071 (London) 580 8197
INTERCONTINENTAL HOTELS LTD	INTER-CON	081 (London) 847 2277 or calls from outside London 0345 581444
JARVIS HOTEL	JARVIS	(0345) 581811
LANSBURY HOTELS	LANSBURY	0582 (Luton) 400158
MARRIOTT HOTELS	MARRIOTT	0800 221222 (Freephone)
MOUNT CHARLOTTE THISTLE HOTELS	MT. CHARLOTTE THISTLE	071 (London) 937 8033 0532 (Leeds) 439111
NOVOTEL	NOVOTEL	071 (London) 724 1000
QUEENS MOAT HOUSES PLC	Q.M.H.	0800 289330 (Freephone) or 0708 (Romford) 766677
RAMADA INTERNATIONAL	RAMADA	0800 181737 (Freephone)
RESORT HOTELS PLC	RESORT	(0345) 313213
SHERATON HOTELS	SHERATON	0800 353535 (Freephone)
STAKIS HOTELS	STAKIS	0800 262626 (Freephone)
SWALLOW HOTELS LTD	SWALLOW	091 (Tyneside) 529 4666
TOBY HOTELS	TOBY	
(No central reservations – Contact Hotels direct)		

Hotels d'autoroute – Alberghi autostradali
Autobahn-Rasthäuser

Hotels included in the Guide on, or near the interchanges of motorways and A (M) class roads. See appropriate town for details.

Les hôtels ci-dessous, sélectionnés dans le guide, se trouvent sur les autoroutes ou les routes principales, à proximité des échangeurs. Pour tous détails, voir le nom de la ville.

I sottoindicati alberghi, selezionati nella guida, si trovano lungo le autostrade o lungo le strade principali, in prossimità degli svincoli. Per ogni dettaglio vedere la località interessata.

Die unten aufgeführten Hotels befinden sich an Autobahnen, Hauptver-kehrsstraßen oder in der Nähe von Autobahnausfahrten. Nähere Einzelheiten unter dem Ortstext.

Location	Town	Hotel
M 1		
Junction 5 – S : 1/2 m. on A 41	**Watford**	Hilton National
Junction 6 – NE : on A 405	**St. Albans**	Noke Thistle
Junction 8 – W : 1/2 m. on A 414	**Hemel Hempstead**	Forte Posthouse
Junction 9 – NW : 1 m. on A 5	**Flamstead**	Hertfordshire Moat House
Junction 11 – E : 3/4 m. on A 505	**Luton**	Forte Crest
Junction 11 – on A 505	**Luton**	Forte Posthouse
Junction 12 – S : 1/2 m.	**Toddington Service Area**	Granada Lodge
Junction 13 – SW : 1 1/2 m. by A 507	**Aspley Guise**	Moore Place
Junction 14 – S : 1 m. by A 509 off A 5130	**Milton Keynes**	Broughton
Junction 14 – SW : 1 1/2 m. by A 509	**Milton Keynes**	Wayfarer
Junction 14 – N : 3/4 m. on A 509	**Newport Pagnell**	Coach House
Junction 15 – N : 1/4 m. on A 508	**Northampton**	Stakis Country Court
Junction 15 – NE : 3 m. by A 508 off A 45	**Northampton**	Swallow
Junction 15 – N : 1 m. on A 508	**Northampton**	Midway Toby
Junction 15 – N : 2 1/4 m. by A 508 on B 526	**Northampton**	Queen Eleanor
Junction 16 – E : 1 1/4 m. on A 45	**Northampton**	Travel Inn
Junction 16 – NW : 1 1/2 m. on A 45	**Weedon Bec**	Heyford Manor
Junction 18 – E : 1 m. on A 428	**Rugby (at Crick)**	Forte Posthouse
Junction 20 – NW : 3/4 m. by A 427 on A 426	**Lutterworth**	Denbigh Arms
Junction 21 – E : 1/2 m. on A 46	**Leicester (at Braunstone)**	Stakis Country Court
Junction 21 – NE : 2 1/2 m. by A 46	**Leicester (at Braunstone)**	Forte Posthouse
Junction 22 – SE : 1 1/4 m. by A 50	**Markfield**	Field Head
Junction 22 – NW : 1/4 m. on A 50	**Markfield**	Granada Lodge
Junction 24 – NW : 1/4 m. on A 6	**Castle Donington**	Hilton National
Junction 24 – (southbound) SW : 2 m. on A 453, (northbound) junction 23 a – W : 1 m. on A 453	**Castle Donington**	Donington Thistle
Junction 25 – N : 1/4 m.	**Nottingham (at Sandiacre)**	Forte Posthouse
Junction 25 – S : 1/2 m. on B 6002	**Nottingham (at Long Eaton)**	Novotel
Junction 25 – S : 1/2 m. on B 6002	**Nottingham (at Long Eaton)**	Sleep Inn
Junction 26 – E : 1 1/2 m. on A 610	**Nottingham**	Gateway
Junction 28 – on A 38	**South Normanton**	Swallow
Junction 28 – SW : 3 1/2 m. by A 38 on Swanwick Road	**Alfreton**	Granada

Location	Town	Hotel
Junction 30 – E : 1 3/4 m. by A 616 on A 619	Clowne	🏨 Van Dyk
Junction 31 – E : 1 m. on A 57	Todwick	🏨 Red Lion
Junction 31 – W : 1/2 m. by A 57 on A 6067	Aston	🏨 Aston Hall
Junction 33 – NE : 3/4 m. on A 630	Rotherham	🏨 Swallow
Junction 39 – W : 1/4 m. on A 636	Wakefield	🏨 Cedar Court
Junction 40 – E : 1/4 m. on A 638	Wakefield	🏨 Forte Posthouse
Woolley Edge Service Area	Woolley Edge	🏨 Granada Lodge

A 1 (M)

Location	Town	Hotel
Junction with M 25 – AI (M)	South Mimms Service Area	🏨 Forte Posthouse
Junction with M 25 – AI (M)	South Mimms Service Area	🏨 Forte Travelodge
Junction 3 – N : 1/2 m. by A 1001	Hatfield	🏨 Connet
Junction 3 – S : 1/2 m. on A 1001	Hatfield	🏨 Hazel Grove
Junction 7 – W : 1/4 m.	Stevenage	🏨 Novotel
Junction with A 630 – SW : 1/4 m.	Doncaster	🏨 Doncaster Moat House
Junction with A 167 – S : 3/4 m.	Darlington (at Coatham Mundeville)	🏨 Hall Garth Country House
Junction with A 195 – E : 1/2 m. off A 1231	Washington	🏨 Forte Posthouse
Junction with A 195 – E : 1/2 m. off A 1231	Washington	🏨 Campanile
Washington Service Area (southbound carriageway)	Washington	🏨 Granada Lodge
Junction with A 602 – W : 1 1/2 m. by A 602	Hitchin	🏨 Blackmore Thistle
Junction with A 5135 – NW : 1/4 m. on A 5135	Borehamwood	🏨 Elstree Moat House
Junction with A 5135 – NW : 3/4 m. by A 5135	Borehamwood	🏨 Oaklands

M 2

Location	Town	Hotel
Junction 3 – N : 1/2 m. on A 229	Rochester	🏨 Brigdewood Manor
Junction 3 – N : 1 m. on A 229	Rochester	🏨 Forte Crest
Farthing Corner Service Area	Farthing	🏨 Farthing Corner Lodge

M 3

Location	Town	Hotel
Junction 3 – N : 1 m. on A 30	Bagshot	🏨 Cricketers
between junctions 4 a and 5 (southbound carriageway)	Fleet Service Area	🏨 Forte Travelodge
Junction 6 – N : 1 m. at Black Dam roundabout	Basingstoke	🏨 Hilton Lodge
Junction 6 – SW : 1 1/2 m. at junction A 30 and A 339	Basingstoke	🏨 Forte Posthouse
Junction 7 – SW : 2 m. on A 30	North Waltham	🏨 Wheatsheaf

M 4

Location	Town	Hotel
Heston Service Area (westbound carriageway)	Heston (L.B. of Hounslow)	🏨 Granada Lodge
Junction 4 – N : 1/4 m. on B 379	Heathrow Airport (L.B. of Hillingdon)	🏨 Holiday Inn
Junction 4 – N : 1/4 m. by A 408	Heathrow Airport (L.B. of Hillingdon)	🏨 Novotel
Junction 4 – S : 1/2 m. on B 379	Heathrow Airport (L.B. of Hillingdon)	🏨 Forte Posthouse
Junction 5 – NW : 1/4 m. on A 4	Slough	🏨 Heathrow/ Slough Marriott
Junction 6 – N : 1/2 m. on A 355	Slough	🏨 Copthorne
Junction 6 – N : 1/2 m. on A 355	Slough	🏨 Courtyard by Marriott
Junction 9 A – NE : 1 m. by A 423 (M) on Shoppenhangers Road	Maidenhead	🏨 Frederick's
Junction 9 A – NE : 1/2 m. by A 423 (M) off Shoppenhangers Road	Maidenhead	🏨 Holiday Inn
Junction 10 – SE : 2 1/2 m. by A 329 (M)	Wokingham	🏨 Stakis St. Annes Manor
Junction 11 – N : 1/2 m. on A 33	Reading	🏨 Forte Posthouse
Junction 11 – N : 1 m. on A 33	Reading	🏨 Forte Travelodge

724

Location	Town	Hotel
Junction 13 – South at junction with A 34 (northbound carriageway)	**Newbury**	Stakis Country Court
Junction 15 – SW : 1 m. by A 345 on B 4005	**Swindon (at Chiseldon)**	Chiseldon House
Junction 15 – N : 2 m. by A 419 on A 4259	**Swindon**	Forte Posthouse
Junction 16 – NE : 1 1/2 m. by A 3102 on B 4534	**Swindon**	De Vere
between junctions 18 and 17 (eastbound carriageway)	**Leigh Delamere Service Area**	Granada Lodge
Junction 19 – SW : 2 1/2 m. by M 32 on A 4174 (this hotel also under M 32)	**Bristol (at Hambrook)**	Forte Crest
Junction 21	**Aust Service Area**	Pavilion Lodge
Junction 23	**Magor Service Area**	Granada Lodge
Junction 24 – S : 1/2 m. on A 48	**Newport (Gwent)**	Celtic Manor
Junction 24 – E : 1/4 m. on A 48	**Newport (Gwent) (at Langstone)**	Stakis Country Court
Junction 24 – E : 1 1/2 m. on A 48	**Newport (Gwent)**	Hilton National
	Newport (Gwent) (at Langstone)	New Inn
Junction 26 – S : 1/2 m. by A 4042	**Newport (Gwent)**	Newport Lodge
Junction 29 – SW : 2 m. by A 48	**Cardiff**	Forte Travelodge
Junction 32 – SE : 1 1/2 m. by A 470	**Cardiff**	Masons Arms
Junction 33 – SE : 3 1/2 m. by A 4232	**Cardiff**	Copthorne
Junction 33	**Cardiff West Service Area**	Pavilion Lodge
Junction 34 – N : 1 3/4 m. by A 4119 (Groes Faen Road)	**Miskin**	Miskin Manor
Junction 35 – N : 1 m. by A 473 off Felindre Road	**Bridgend**	Forte Travelodge
Junction 36	**Sarn Park Service Area**	Forte Travelodge
Junction 42	**Port Talbot**	Travel Inn
Junction 45 – S : 2 1/4 m. by A 4067 off A 48	**Swansea (at Swansea Enterprise Park)**	Hilton National
Junction 47 – S : 1 m. on A 483	**Swansea**	Forest
Junction 47 – N : 1/4 m. on A 483	**Swansea West Service Area**	Pavilion Lodge
M 5		
Junction 1 – W : 1 m. on A 41	**Birmingham (at West Bromwich)**	West Bromwich Moat House
Junction 2 – W : 3/4 m. on A 4123	**Birmingham (Oldbury)**	Forte Travelodge
Between junctions 3 and 4	**Frankley Service Area**	Granada Lodge
Junction 4 – S : 1 m. on A 38	**Bromsgrove**	Stakis Country Court
Junction 5 – SW : 1/2 m. on A 38	**Droitwich**	Forte Travelodge
Junction 11 – E : 1 m. on A 40	**Cheltenham (at Staverton)**	Golden Valley Thistle
Junction 11 – E : 2 m. by A 40 on Staverton Airport Rd	**Cheltenham**	White House
Junction 16 – S : 1/4 m. on A 38	**Bristol (at Almondsbury)**	Aztec
Junction 16 – S : 2 1/2 m. by A 38	**Bristol (at Patchway)**	Stakis Bristol
Junction 19	**Gordano Service Area**	Forte Travelodge
Sedgemoor Service Area (northbound carriageway)	**Sedgemoor**	Forte Travelodge
Junction 22 – N : on A 38	**Brent Knoll**	Battleborough Grange
Junction 25 – by approach road	**Taunton**	Forte Posthouse
Junction 25 – W : 1/2 m. by A 358	**Taunton**	Travel Inn
Between junction 25 and 26 southbound	**Taunton Service Area**	Road Chef Lodge
Junction 27 – NE : 1/2 m. on A 38	**Sampford Peverell**	Old Cottage Inn
Junction 27	**Sampford Peverell Service Area**	Forte Travelodge
Junction 30 – N : 1 3/4 m. via Sowton Ind. Est. and Honiton Rd off Pinn Lane	**Exeter (at Pinhoe)**	Gispy Hill

Location	Town	Hotel
Junction 30 – NW : 1 m. by Sidmouth Rd	Exeter	Exeter Arms Toby
Junction 30 – Exeter Service Area	Exeter Service Area	Granada
Junction 31 – S : 2 1/2 m. at junction of A 379 and B 3182	Exeter	Countess Wear Lodge

M 6

Location	Town	Hotel
Junction 1 – S : 1 m. by A 426	Rugby	Brownsover Hall
Junction 2 – NE : 1/4 m. on B 4065	Coventry (at Ansty)	Ansty Hall
Junction 2 – SW : 1/2 m. on A 4600	Coventry (at Walsgrave on Sowe)	Forte Crest
Junction 2 – SW : 1/2 m. by A 4600	Coventry (at Walsgrave)	Hilton National
Junction 2 – SW : 3/4 m. by 4600	Coventry (at Walsgrave)	Campanile
Junction 3 – SE : 1 m. on A 444	Coventry (at Longford)	Novotel
Junction 3 – N : 2 1/2 m. by A 444 on B 4113	Nuneaton	Travel Inn
Junction 3 – N : 3 1/2 m. on A 444	Nuneaton	Forte Travelodge
Junction 5 – N : 3 1/3 m. by A 452 on B 4148	Sutton Coldfield	New Hall
Junction 7 – N : 1/4 m. on A 34	Birmingham (at Great Barr)	Forte Posthouse
Junction 7 – NW : 2 1/2 m. on A 34	Walsall	Forte Posthouse
Junction 10 – on A 454	Walsall	Friendly
Between junctions 10 A and 11	Hilton Park Service Area	Pavilion Lodge
Junction 11 – NE : 1 1/3 m. by A 40	Cheltenham (at Staverton)	White House
Junction 12 – E : 2 m. on A 5	Cannock	Roman Way
Junction 12 – E : 2 1/4 m. on A 5	Cannock	Travel Inn
Junction 13 – N : 1 m. on A 449	Stafford	Garth
Junction 14 – SE : 1/2 m. on A 5013	Stafford	Tillington Hall
Junction 15 – N : 1/4 m. on A 519	Newcastle-under-Lyme	Forte Posthouse
Junction 15 – N : 3/4 m. on A 519	Newcastle-under-Lyme	Clayton Lodge
Junction 16 – W : 1/4 m.	Crewe (at Barthomley)	Forte Travelodge
Junction 16 – E : 3 3/4 m. on A 500 at junction with A 34	Stoke on Trent (at Talke)	Granada
Junction 17 – E : 1/2 m. on A 534	Sandbach	Chimney House
Junction 17 – SW : 1 m. by A 534	Sandbach	Old Hall
Junction 17 – NE : 1/2 m. on A 5022	Sandbach	Saxon Cross
Junction 19 – NE : 2 1/2 m. on A 556 (this hotel also under M 56)	Knutsford (at Bucklow Hill)	Swan Inn
Junction 19 – N : on A 556	Knutsford	Forte Travelodge
Junction 21	Warrington	Holiday Inn Garden Court
Junction 23 – N : 1/2 m. on A 49	Haydock	Forte Posthouse
Junction 23 – NW : 1/2 m. by A 49 on A 599	Haydock	Haydock Thistle
Junction 23 – W : 2 m. on A 580	Haydock	Forte Travelodge
Junction 27 – E : 1 m. on A 5209	Standish	Almond Brook
Junction 27 – W : 1/2 m. by A 5209	Standish	Wrightington
Junction 29 – SE : 1/4 m. hy A 6	Preston (at Bamber Bridge)	Novotel
Junction 31 – W : 1/4 m. on A 59	Preston (at Samlesbury)	Tickled Trout
Junction 31 – E : 1 1/4 m. on A 59	Preston (at Samlesbury)	Swallow Trafalgar
Junction 33 – N : 2 1/2 m. on A 6	Lancaster	Lancaster House
Junction 34 – SW : 1/4 m. on A 683	Lancaster	Forte Posthouse
Junction 40 – on A 592 Northlakes	Penrith	North Lakes
Junction 40 – W : 1/2 m. on A 66	Penrith	Forte Travelodge
Junction 44 – S : 1/4 m. on A 7	Carlisle (at Kingstown)	Forte Posthouse
Southwaite Service Area	Southwaite Service Area	Granada Lodge

M 8

Location	Town	Hotel
Junction 2 – SE : 1/2 m. on A 8	Edinburgh (at Ingliston)	Norton House
Junction 3 – SE : 2 1/2 m. by A 899	Livingston	Hilton National
Junction 6 – S : 1/2 m. by A 73	Motherwell	Travel Inn
Junction 11 – E : 1 3/4 m. by M 898 on A 726	Erskine	Forte Posthouse
Junction 27 – N : 1/4 m. on A 741	Renfrew	Glynhill

Location	Town	Hotel
M 9		
Junction 1 – SE : 1 1/2 m. on A 8	Edinburgh (at Ingliston)	Norton House
Junction 9 – at junction of M 9 and M 80	Stirling	Granada Lodge
M 10		
Junction 1 – SW : on A 405 (this hotel also under M 1)	St. Albans	Noke Thistle
M 11		
Junction 7 – NW : 1 m. on A 414	Harlow	Harlow Moat House
Junction 8 – NE : 1 m. on Airport Road	Stansted Airport	Harlequin
Junction 14 with A 604 – NW : 1 1/3 m.	Cambridge (at Bar Hill)	Cambridgeshire Moat House
M 18		
Junction 1 – E : 3/4 m. by A 361 off Denby Way	Rotherham	Campanile
Junction 1 – W : 2 m. on A 631	Rotherham	Travel Inn
M 20		
Junction 2 A – SE : 1 m. on A 20	Wrotham Heath	Forte Posthouse
Junction 3 – SE : 3 1/2 m. on A 20	Brands Hatch	Brands Hatch Thistle
Junction 3 – SE : 3 1/2 m. on A 20	Brands Hatch (at Fawkham)	Brands Hatch Place
Junction 9 – SE : 1 1/2 m. on A 28	Ashford	Forte Posthouse
Junction 9 – S : 1/2 m. on A 28	Ashford	Ashford International
M 23		
Junction 9 – in Gatwick Airport south terminal	Gatwick	London Gatwick Airport Hilton
Junction 9 – W : 1 m. on A 23	Gatwick	Gatwick Penta
Junction 9 – W : 1 m. on A 23	Gatwick	Forte Posthouse
Junction 9 A – W : 1 m. in Gatwick Airport (north terminal)	Gatwick	Forte Crest
Junction 10 – E : 1/3 m. on A 264	Crawley	Copthorne London Gatwick
Junction 10 – W : 1 1/2 m. by A 2011	Crawley	Scandic Crown
M 25		
Junction 1 A – E : 1/4 m.	Dartford	Stakis Country Court
Junction 3 – SE : 3 1/2 m. on A 20	Brands Hatch	Brands Hatch Thistle
Junction 3 – SE : 3 1/2 m. on A 20	Brands Hatch (at Fawkham)	Brands Hatch Place
Junction 8 – S : 1/2 m. on A 217	Reigate	Bridge House
Junction 10 – N : 1/4 m. by A 3 and A 245	Cobham	Hilton National
Junction 13 – S : 1 m. by A 30 and A 308	Egham	Runnymede
Junction 21 A – N : 1/2 m. on A 405	St. Albans	Noke Thistle
Junction 23 – at junction with A 1 (M)	South Mimms Service Area	Forte Posthouse
Junction 23 – at junction with A 1 (M)	South Mimms Service Area	Forte Travelodge
Junction 26 – at exit roundabout	Waltham Abbey	Swallow
Junction 28 – NE : 3/4 m. on A 1023	Brentwood	Brentwood Moat House
Junction 28 – NE : 1/4 m. on A 1023	Brentwood	Forte Posthouse
Junction 29 – E : 3 1/2 m.	East Horndon	Forte Travelodge
Junction 30 – E : 1 1/2 m. by A 13	North Stifford	Stifford Moat House
Junction 31 – E : 1/2 m. on A 1306	Thurrock Service Area	Granada Lodge
M 26		
Junction 2 on A 20	Wrotham Heath	Forte Posthouse
Junction 2 – S : 1/2 m. by A 20 on A 25	Wrotham Heath	Travel Inn

Location	Town	Hotel	

M 27

Location	Town	Hotel	
Junction 3 – SE : 1 m. by M 271 on A 3057	Southampton	🏠	Travel Inn
Junction 9 – S : 1 1/2 m. on A 27	Fareham	🏠🏠	Forte Posthouse Fareham
Junction 12 – N : at junction of A 3 and A 27	Portsmouth & Southsea (at Cosham)	🏠🏠	Portsmouth Marriott
Junction 12 – E : 1 m. on A 27 at junction with A 2030	Portsmouth & Southsea	🏠🏠	Hilton National
Junction 12 – SE : 3 m. by A 27 and A 2030	Portsmouth & Southsea	🏠	Innlodge

M 32

| Junction 1 – W : 1/2 m. on A 4174 (this hotel also under M 4) | Bristol (at Hambrook) | 🏠🏠 | Forte Crest |

M 40

Junction 2 – E : 1 3/4 m. by A 355 on A 40	Beaconsfield	🏠🏠	Bellhouse
Junction 4 – on Crest Road	High Wycombe	🏠🏠	Forte Posthouse
Junction 8 – 2 m. by A 40 and A 418 on Wheatley rd	Oxford	🏠	Forte Travelodge
Junction 15 – NE : 1/4 m. on A 429	Warwick	🏠🏠	Hilton National
Junction 15 – S : 1 1/2 m. by A 429	Warwick	🏠🏠	Glebe House
Junction 15 – SW : 1/4 m. by A 46	Warwick	🏠	Old Rectory

M 42

Junction 1 – N : 1 m. on A 38	Bromsgrove	🏠🏠	Stakis Country Court
Junction 2 – N : 1 1/4 m. on A 441	Hopwood	🏠🏠	Westmead
Junction 4 – NW : 3/4 m. on A 34	Solihull	🏠	Travel Inn
Junction 4 – NW : 1 m. on A 34	Solihull (at Shirley)	🏠🏠	Regency
Junction 5 – NW : 1 3/4 m. by A 41 on B 4025	Solihull	🏠🏠	St. Johns Swallow
Junction 5 – NW : 1 3/4 m. by A 41 and B 4025	Solihull	🏠🏠	George
Junction 6 – NW : 1 m.	Birmingham (at National Exhibition Centre)	🏠🏠🏠	Birmingham Metropole
Junction 6 – W : 1/2 m. on A 45	Birmingham (at National Exhibition Centre)	🏠🏠	Arden
Junction 9 – NE : 2 3/4 m. by A 4097	Tamworth (at Bodymoor Heath)	🏠🏠	Marston Farm
Junction 10	Tamworth Service Area	🏠	Granada Lodge

M 45

| Junction 1 – NW : 1 m. on A 45 | Dunchurch | 🏠 | Forte Travelodge |

M 50

| Junction 1 – S : 1/2 m. on A 38 | Tewkesbury (at Puckrup) | 🏠🏠 | Puckrup Hall |

M 53

| Junction 5 – N : on A 41 | Eastham | 🏠 | Forte Travelodge |
| Junction 5 – S : 1 1/4 m. by A 41 on A 550 | Little Sutton | 🏠🏠 | Woodhey |

M 54

| Junction 5 – SW : 1/2 m. | Telford | 🏠🏠 | Telford Moat House |
| Junction 7 – SE : 1 1/4 m. | Telford (at Wellington) | 🏠🏠 | Buckatree Hall |

M 55

| Junction 1 – N : 3/4 m. | Preston (at Broughton) | 🏠🏠 | Broughton Park |

M 56

| Junction 3 – N : 1/2 m. by A 5103 (this hotel also under M 63) | Manchester (at Northenden) | 🏠🏠 | Forte Posthouse |
| Junction 5 – on Airport Approach Road | Manchester (at Airport) | 🏠🏠 | Manchester Airport Hilton |

Location	Town	Hotel
Junction 5 – on Airport Approach Road	Manchester (at Airport)	Forte Crest
Junction 6 – N : 1/4 m. on A 538	Altrincham (at Halebarns)	Four Seasons
Junction 7/8 – SW : 2 m. on A 556 (this hotel also under M 6)	Knutsford (at Bucklow Hill)	Swan Inn
Junction 10 – N : 1/2 m. by A 49 on Stretton Road	Warrington (at Stretton)	Park Royal International
Junction 11 – N : 1/4 m. on A 56	Daresbury	Lord Daresbury
Junction 12 – SE : 1/2 m. by A 557	Runcorn	Forte Crest
Junction 16 – SW : 2 1/2 m. by A 5117	Chester (at Two Mills)	Tudor Rose Lodge

Location	Town	Hotel
Junction 7 – SW : 1 m. on A 5036	Liverpool	Park

Location	Town	Hotel
Junction 5 – NE : 1 m. on A 58	Bolton	Forte Posthouse
Junction 6 – 1/4 m. on A 6	Blackrod	Georgian House

Location	Town	Hotel
Junction 6 – NE : 1/4 m. on Whiston Road	Liverpool (at Huyton)	Logwood Mill
Junction 7 – S : 1 1/4 m. by A 569	Widnes (at Cronton)	Hillcrest
Junction 9 – S : 1 m. on A 49	Warrington	Travel Inn
Junction 13 – W : 1/4 m. on A 572	Manchester (at Worsley)	Novotel Manchester West
Junction 18-19	Birch Service Area	Granada Lodge
Junction 24 – SE : 1 1/2 m. on A 629	Huddersfield	Pennine Hilton
Junction 25 – N : 1/2 m. on A 644	Brighouse	Forte Crest

Location	Town	Hotel
Junction 9 – S : 1/2 m. by A 5130 (this hotel also under M 56)	Manchester (at Northenden)	Forte Posthouse

Location	Town	Hotel
Junction 7 – NW : 1/2 m. on A 678	Clayton-Le-Moors	Dunkenhalgh
Junction 10 – E : at junction of A 671 and A 679	Burnley	Forte Travelodge

Location	Town	Hotel
Junction 1 – NE : 1/4 m. on A 56	Bury (at Walmersley)	Red Hall

Location	Town	Hotel
Junction with M 1 – NE : 2 1/2 m. on A 46	Leicester (at Braunstone)	Forte Posthouse
Junction with M 6 – SW : 1/2 m. by A 4600	Coventry (at Walsgrave)	Hilton National
Junction 1 – NW : 1 m. by A 447	Hinckley	Sketchley Grange

Location	Town	Hotel
Between junctions 6 and 5 (northbound carriageway)	Hamilton Service Area	Road Chef Lodge
A 74 (M) – NW : 1 1/2 m. on A 74 (M)	Gretna	Forte Travelodge
Junction with A 74	Abington Service Area	Forte Travelodge

Location	Town	Hotel
Junction 9 – at junction of M 9 and M 80	Stirling	Granada Lodge

Location	Town	Hotel
Junction 6 – at junction with A 977	Kinross	Granada Lodge

Location	Town	Hotel
Junction 1 – E : 1/4 m.	Bradford	Novotel Bradford

Addresses of shipping companies and their principal agents

Adresses des compagnies de navigation et de leurs principales agences

Indirizzi delle compagnie di navigazione e delle loro principali agenzie

Adressen der Schiffahrtsgesellschaften und ihrer wichtigsten Agenturen

PO Box 19, B & I Ferryport, Alexandra Rd, Dublin, Eire, ℰ (01) 788 077, Telex 33303, Fax 788490
16 Westmoreland St., Dublin 2, Eire, ℰ (01) 6797977, Telex 30912, Fax 778146.
Agent : 150 New Bond St., London, W1Y 0AQ, ℰ (071) 491 86825.
Reliance House, Water St., Liverpool, L2 8TP, ℰ (051) 227 3131, Telex 627839, Fax 236 0562

BRITISH RAIL see SEALINK and HOVERSPEED

BRITISH CHANNEL ISLAND FERRIES

Corbiere House, New Quay Road, Poole, Dorset, BH15 4DU ℰ (0202) 666900, Telex 41400, Fax 666488.

BRITTANY FERRIES

BAI Brittany Ferries, Gare Maritime Port du Bloscon, 29211 Roscoff France, ℰ 98 61 22 11, Telex 940360.
Agents : Millbay Docks, Plymouth, Devon, PL1 3EW, ℰ (0752) 221321, Telex 45796, Fax 661308.
The Brittany Centre, Wharf Rd, Portsmouth, Hampshire, PO2 8RU, ℰ (0705) 827701, Telex 86878.
Tourist House, 42 Grand Parade, Cork, Eire, ℰ (021) 277801, Telex 75088.
Modesto Pineiro & Co., 27 Paseo de Pereda, Santander, Spain, ℰ (042) 214500, Telex 35913.

BRITTANY FERRIES TRUCKLINE

New Harbour Rd, Poole, Dorset BH15 4AJ, ℰ (0202) 666466, Fax 682420.

CALEDONIAN MACBRAYNE LTD.

The Ferry Terminal, Gourock, Renfrewshire, PA19 1QP, Scotland, ℰ (0475) 33755, Telex 779318, Fax 37607.

CHANNILAND

3 ter, Rue Georges Clemenceau, P.O. Box 319, 50403 Granville, France, ℰ 33 51 77 45, Fax 33 51 12 10.
Agent : Southern Ferries, 179 Piccadilly, London, WIV 9DB, ℰ (071) 491 4968, Telex 297248, Fax 491 3502.

COLOR LINE

Hjortneskaia, N-0250 Oslo 2, Norway, ℰ (02) 944400, Telex 71697, Fax 830776.
Agent : Tyne Commission Quay, North Shields, NE 29 6EA, Tyne & Wear, ℰ (091) 296 1313, Telex 537275, Fax 296 1540.

CONDOR LTD.

P.O. Box 10 Commodore House, Bulwer Av., St. Sampson, Guernsey, Channel Islands, ✆ (0481) 48771, Fax 45049.
Agents : 28 Conway St., St. Helier, Jersey, Channel Islands, ✆ (0534) 76300, Fax 365410.
Morvan Fils, 2 Place du Poids du Roi, 35402 St. Malo, France, ✆ 99 56 42 29, Telex 950486, Fax 99 40 23 66.
Condor Passenger Dept., New Jetty, White Rock, St. Peter Port, Guernsey, Channel Islands, ✆ (0481) 726121, Fax 712555.
Weymouth Quay, Weymouth, Dorset DT4 8DX, ✆ (0305) 761551, Fax 760776.

CUNARD LINE LTD.

South Western House, Canute Rd, Southampton, Hampshire, SO9 1ZA, ✆ (0703) 634166, Telex 477577, Fax 225843.
Agents : 30a Pall Mall, London SW1Y 5LS, ✆ (071) 491 3930, Telex 295483, Fax 839 1837.
555 Fifth Av., New York, NY 10017, USA, ✆ (212) 880 7500, (800) 528 6273 (freephone), Telex 220436.
Compagnie Générale de Croisières, 2/4, Rue Joseph Sansbœuf, 75008 Paris, France, ✆ 42 93 81 82, Telex 282986, Fax 42 93 71 06.

DOVER-OSTEND LINE

Channel House, Channel View Rd, Dover, Kent CT17 9TJ, ✆ (0304) 223000, Telex 96200, Fax 223223.

EMERAUDE LINES

Gare Maritime du Naye, 35400, St. Malo, France, ✆ 99 40 48 40, Telex 950271, Fax 99 81 28 73.
Agents : Channel Islands Handling Ltd., Elisabeth Harbour, St. Helier, Jersey, Channel Islands, ✆ (0534) 66566, Fax 68741.
Emeraude Lines, New Jetty, White Rock, St. Peter Port, Guernsey, ✆ (0481) 711414, Telex 4191571, Fax 715272.

FRED OLSEN LINES KDS

PO Box 1159 Sentrum, N-0107, Oslo 1, Norway, ✆ (02) 34 10 00, Fax 41 24 15.
Agent : Fred Olsen Travel, Crown House St., Ipswich, IP1 3HB, ✆ (0473) 230530, Telex 98536, Fax 230990.

HERM SEAWAY

Guernsey Bus Ltd., Picquet House, St. Peter Port, Guernsey, Channel Islands, ✆ (0481) 724677, Fax 721929.

HOVERSPEED

Maybrook House, Queens Gardens, Dover, Kent CT17 9UQ, ✆ (0304) 240241, Fax 240088.
Agents : International Hoverport, Boulogne, France, ✆ 21 30 27 26, Telex 110008.
International Hoverport, Calais, France, ✆ 21 96 67 10, Telex 810856.

HOVERTRAVEL LTD.

Quay Road, Ryde, Isle of Wight, PO33 2HB, ✆ (0983) 811000, Telex 86513, Fax 562216.
Agent : Clarence Pier, Southsea, Portsmouth, PO5 3AD, Hampshire, ✆ (0705) 829988.

IRISH FERRIES

2-4 Merrion Row, Dublin 2, Eire, ✆ (01) 610511, Telex 30355, Fax (01) 610743.
Agent : Transports et Voyages, 40 Rue Kleber, BP 244, 92307, Levallois-Perret, France, ✆ 47 59 44 21, Telex 613491, Fax 47 59 45 23.

ISLE OF MAN STEAM PACKET CO. LTD.

P.O. Box 5, Imperial Buildings, Douglas, Isle of Man, ✆ (0624) 661661, Telex 629414, Fax 661065.
Agents : W.E. Williams (N.I.) Ltd., Northern Rd, Belfast, BT3 9AL, Northern Ireland, ✆ (0232) 351009, Telex 747166, Fax 351309.
Sea Terminal, Heysham, Lancashire, LA3 2XF, ✆ (0524) 853802.
Dublin Maritime, Maritime House, North Wall, Dublin, Eire, ✆ (01) 741231, Telex 33425, Fax 725714.

ISLE OF SARK SHIPPING CO. LTD.

White Rock, St. Peter Port, Guernsey, Channel Islands, ✆ (0481) 724059, Telex 419 1549, Fax 712081.

ISLES OF SCILLY STEAMSHIP CO. LTD.

Quay St., Penzance, Cornwall, TR18 4BD, ✆ (0736) 62009, Fax 51223.
Agent : Hugh Town, St. Mary's, Isles of Scilly, TR21 OLJ, ✆ 0720 (Scillonia) 22357/8, Fax 22192.

LUNDY CO.

The Quay, Bideford, Devon, EX39 2LY, ℘ (0237) 470422.

MERSEY FERRIES

Victoria Pl., Seacombe, Wallasey, Merseyside, L44 6QY, ℘ (051) 236 7676.

NORTH SEA FERRIES LTD.

Beneluxhaven, Europoort, P.O. Box 1123, 3180 Rozenburg, Netherlands, ℘ (01819) 55500, Telex 29571, Fax 55215.
Agents : King George Dock, Hedon Rd, Hull, Humberside, HU9 5QA, ℘ (0482) 795141, Telex 592349, Fax 706438.
Leopold II Dam (Havendam) 8380, Zeebrugge, Belgium, ℘ (050) 543430, Telex 81469, Fax 546835.

OLAU-LINE (UK) LTD.

Sheerness, Kent, ME12 1SN, ℘ (0795) 666666, Telex 965605.
Agent : Olau Line Terminal, Buitenhaven, P.O. Box 231, Vlissingen, Netherlands, ℘ (01184) 88000, Telex 37817.

ORKNEY ISLANDS SHIPPING CO. LTD.

4 Ayre Road, Kirkwall, Orkney Islands, Scotland, ℘ (0856) 872044, Telex 75475, Fax 872921.

ORWELL & HARWICH NAVIGATION CO. LTD.

The Quay, Harwich, Essex, ℘ (0255) 502004.

P & O EUROPEAN FERRIES LTD.

Channel House, Channel View Rd, Dover, Kent, CT17 9TJ, ℘ (0304) 203388, Fax 223464.
Agents : The Continental Ferry Port, Mile End, Portsmouth, Hants., PO2 8QW, ℘ (0705) 827677.
European House, The Docks, Felixstowe, Suffolk, IP11 8TB, ℘ (0394) 604040.
Larne Harbour, Larne, Co. Antrim, Northern Ireland, BT40 1AQ, ℘ (0574) 274321, Telex 74528, Fax 270949.
Regie Voor Martiem Transport, Natienkaai 5, 8400 Ostend, Belgium, ℘ (059) 55 99 55.
Car Ferry Terminal, Doverlaan 7, 8380 Zeebrugge, Belgium, ℘ (050) 54 22 22, Telex 82465.
Terminal Car Ferry, 62226 Calais, France, ℘ 21 46 10 10, Telex 120878, Fax 21 46 10 10.
Gare Maritime, Quai Chanzy BP 309, 62204, Boulogne, France, ℘ 21 31 78 00, Telex 130187, Fax 21 30 12 66.
9 Place de la Madeleine, 75008 Paris, France, ℘ (1) 42 66 40 17, Telex 66 01 44, Fax 42 66 47 89.
Gare Maritime, 50101 Cherbourg, France, ℘ 33 44 20 13, Telex 170765, Fax 33 20 44 17.
Quai de Southampton, 76600 Le Havre, France, ℘ 35 21 36 50, Telex 190757, Fax 35 41 22 82.

P & O SCOTTISH FERRIES : ORKNEY & SHETLAND SERVICES

P.O. Box 5, P & O Ferries Terminal, Jamieson's Quay, Aberdeen, AB9 8DL, Scotland, ℘ (0224) 58911, Telex 73344, Fax 574411.
Agents : Terminal Building, Scrabster, Caithness, KW14 7UJ, Scotland, ℘ (0847) 62052.
Holmsgarth Terminal, Lerwick, Shetland Islands, ZE1 0PR, Scotland, ℘ (0595) 5252, Telex 75294, Fax 5496.
Terminal Building, Pier Head, Stromness, Orkney Islands, KW16 3AA, Scotland, ℘ (0856) 850655, Telex 75221, Fax 851015.
Harbour St., Kirkwall, Orkney Islands, KW15 ILE, Scotland, ℘ (0856) 87 33 30, Telex 75296.

RED FUNNEL FERRIES

12 Bugle St., Southampton, S09 4LJ, Hampshire, ℘ (0703) 330333, Fax 639438.

ST. HELENA SHIPPING CO. LTD

The shipyard, Portleven, Helston, Cornwall, TRI3 9JA, ℘ (0326) 563434, Telex 45654, Fax 564347.
Agent : La Marina 7-5, 38080, Santa Cruz, Tenerife, Spain, ℘ (922) 245860, Telex 92574, Fax 280109.

SALLY FERRIES

Argyle Centre, York St., Ramsgate, Kent, CT11 9DS, ℘ (0843) 595566, Telex 965979, Fax 589329.
Agents : 81 Piccadilly, London W1V 9HF, ℘ (071) 409 2240, Fax 493 6091.
Dunkerque Port Ouest, BP 22, 59279 Loon Plage, France, ℘ 28.21.43.44, Telex 132048, Fax 28 21 45 94.

SCANDINAVIAN SEAWAYS

Sankt Annae Plads 30, DK-1295 Copenhagen, Denmark, ☎ (33) 15 63 00, Telex 19435.
Agents : DFDS Travelbureaü, Axelborg Vesterbrogade 4A, DK-1620 Copenhagen, Denmark, ☎ (33) 15 63 41, Telex 22983, Fax 936330.
Tyne Commission Quay, North Shields, NE29 6EE, Tyne and Wear, ☎ (091) 293 6262, Telex 53201, Fax 293 6222.
15 Hanover St., London, WIR 9HG, ☎ (071) 493 6696, Telex 28257, Fax 493 46 68.
Karl Johansgate 1, Oslo 1, Norway, ☎ (02) 429350, Telex 78129, Fax 411580.
Skandiahamnen, P.O. Box 8895, S-40272 Gothenburg, Sweden, ☎ (031) 65 06 00, Telex 21724, Fax 53 23 09.
Van-der-Smissen Strasse 4, 2000 Hamburg 1, Germany, ☎ (040) 3890371, Telex 02161759. Fax : 38903120.

SERVICE MARITIME CARTERET-JERSEY

BP 15, 50270 Barneville-Carteret, France, ☎ 33 53 87 21, Telex 170477, Fax 33 04 54 61.
Gare Maritime, 50580 Port Bail, France, ☎ 33 04 86 71, Telex 170477.
Agents : CNTM Ltd., Gorey, Jersey, Channel Islands, ☎ (0534) 53737.
Nord Sud Voyages, 6 boulevard Malesherbes, 75008 Paris, ☎ (1) 47 42 25 99, Telex 660849.

SHETLAND ISLANDS COUNCIL

Grantfield, Lerwick, Shetland Islands, ZE1 ONT, ☎ (0595) 2024, Telex 75218, Fax 4544.

SMYRIL LINE

P.O. Box 370, Jonas Broncksgøta 37, FR-110 Thorshavn, Faroe Islands, ☎ 15900, Telex 81296, Fax 15707.
Agents : P & O Scottish Ferries, Orkney & Shetland Services, P.O. Box 5, P & O Ferry Terminal, Aberdeen, AB9 8DL, Scotland, ☎ (0224) 572615, Telex 73344, Fax 574411.
Norraena Ferdaskristofar, Smyril Line Iceland, Langavegur 3, 101 Reykjavik, Iceland, ☎ (91) 62 63 62, Fax (91) 29450.
Smyril Line (Norge) PO Box 4135, Dreggen, N-5023 Bergen, Noway ☎ (05) 320970, Fax 960272.

STENA SEALINK LINE

Charter House, Park St., Ashford, Kent, TN24 8EX, ☎ (0233) 64 70 47, Telex 965954, Fax 642024.
Agents : Newhaven Harbour, Newhaven, East Sussex, BN9 OBQ, ☎ (0273) 51 22 66.
Port Rodie, Stranraer, DG9 8EL, ☎ (0776) 2262, Fax 6586.
Other European Agents : SNAT, 3, rue Amboise Paré, 75010 Paris, Cedex 10, ☎ (1) 49 95 58 90, Telex 280320, Fax 48 74 79 29.
SMZ, Po Box 2, 3150 AA Hook of Holland, ☎ (01747) 3944, Telex 31272.

SWANSEA CORK CAR FERRIES

1a South Mall, Cork, Republic of Ireland, ☎ (021) 27 60 00, Fax 27 58 14.
Agent : Ferry Port, Kings Dock, Swansea, West Glam., SAI 8RU, ☎ (0792) 456116, Fax 644356.

THOMAS & BEWS FERRIES

Ferry Office, John O'Groats, Caithness, Scotland, ☎ (095 581) 353342 (summer).
Windieknap, Brough, Thurso, Caithness, Scotland, ☎ (084 785) 619 (winter), Fax (095) 58 13 01.

VEDETTES ARMORICAINES

Gare Maritime de la Bourse, B.P. 180, 35049 St. Malo, France, ☎ 99 40 17 70, Telex 950196.
Agents : Vedettes Armoricaines, Albert Pier, St. Helier, Jersey, ☎ (0534) 20361, Telex 4192131.
Boutins Travel Bureau, Library Pl., St. Helier, Jersey, ☎ (0534) 21532/3/4, Telex 4192149.
12 rue Georges-Clémenceau, B.P. 304, 50403 Granville, France, ☎ 33 50 77 45, Telex 170449.

WESTERN FERRIES (ARGYLL) LTD.

16 Woodside Crescent, Glasgow, Scotland, G3 7UT, ☎ (041) 332 9766, Telex 77203.

WHITE HORSE FERRIES LTD.

Stanley House, 65 Victoria Rd, Swindon, Wills., SWI 3BB, ☎ (0793) 618566, Fax 488428.

WIGHTLINK LTD

Gunwharf Rd, Portsmouth POI 2XB, ☎ (0705) 82 77 44, Telex 86440, Fax 855 257.

DISTANCES

All distances in this edition are quoted in miles. The distance is given from each town to other nearby towns and to the capital of each region as grouped in the guide. Towns appearing in the charts are preceded by a diamond ◆ text.

To avoid excessive repetition some distances have only been quoted once – you may therefore have to look under both town headings.

The distances in miles quoted are not necessarily the shortest but have been based on the roads which afford the best driving conditions and are therefore the most practical.

DISTANCES EN MILES

Pour chaque région traitée, vous trouverez au texte de chacune des localités sa distance par rapport à la capitale et aux villes environnantes. Lorsque ces villes sont celles des tableaux, leur nom est précédé d'un losange noir ◆.

La distance d'une localité à une autre n'est pas toujours répétée aux deux villes intéressées : voyez au texte de l'une ou de l'autre.

Ces distances ne sont pas nécessairement comptées par la route la plus courte mais par la plus pratique, c'est-à-dire celle offrant les meilleures conditions de roulage.

```
        Belfast
 250   Cork
 103  154  Dublin                                          133 Miles
  50  200   53  Dundalk
 196  122  135  153  Galway                          Dublin - Sligo
 273   54  189  223  133  Killarney
 204   58  120  154   64   69  Limerick
  70  281  146   98  176  300  231  Londonderry
  68  247  112   64  148  266  197   34  Omagh
 126  200  133  106   90  216  147   86   69  Sligo
 132  118   60   82   82  141   72  163  129   95  Tullamore
 197   73   96  147  141  112   77  242  208  176   81  Waterford
```

DISTANZE IN MIGLIA

Per ciascuna delle regioni trattate, troverete nel testo di ogni località la sua distanza dalla capitale e dalle città circostanti. Quando queste città sono comprese nelle tabelle, il loro nome è preceduto da una losanga ◆.

Le distanza da una località all'altra non è sempre ripetuta nelle due città interessate : vedere nel testo dell'una o dell'atra.

Le distanze non sono necessariamente calcolate seguendo il percorso più breve, ma vengono stabilite secondo l'itinerario più pratico, che offre cioè le migliori condizioni di viaggio.

ENTFERNUNGSANGABEN IN MEILEN

Die Entfernungen der einzelnen Orte zur Landeshauptstadt und zu den nächstgrößeren Städten in der Umgebung sind im allgemeinen Ortstext angegeben. Die Namen der Städte in der Umgebung, die auf der Tabelle zu finden sind, sind durch eine Raute ◆ gekennzeichnet.

Die Entfernung zweier Städte voneinander können Sie aus den Angaben im Ortstext der einen oder der anderen Stadt ersehen.

Die Entfernungsangaben gelten nicht immer für den kürzesten, sondern für den günstigsten Weg.

Distances between major towns
Distances entre principales villes
Distanze tra le principali città
Entfernungen zwischen den grösseren Städten

Legend / key:

442 Miles	
Example	Esempio
Exemple	Beispiel
Edinburgh – Southampton	

Triangular road-distance chart. Cities (along the diagonal, top-left to bottom-right):

Aberdeen, Ayr, Birmingham, Blackpool, Brighton, Bristol, Cambridge, Cardiff, Carlisle, Coventry, Dover, Dumfries, Dundee, Edinburgh, Glasgow, Inverness, Ipswich, Kingston upon Hull, Leeds, Leicester, Liverpool, London, Manchester, Middlesbrough, Newcastle, Norwich, Nottingham, Oban, Oxford, Plymouth, Portsmouth, Sheffield, Southampton, Stoke on Trent, Swansea, Wick.

Distance values (best reading of the mileage grid, each row gives the distances from the named town to the towns listed before it):

To town	Distances
Ayr	196
Birmingham	293 130
Blackpool	442 336 187
Brighton	616 467 180 304
Bristol	526 377 91 214 157
Cambridge	500 351 110 221 117 166
Cardiff	545 396 110 233 191 46 200
Carlisle	242 93 201 95 375 285 259 304
Coventry	461 311 18 148 158 96 88 124 219
Dover	637 488 201 325 84 199 120 233 396 179
Dumfries	221 59 234 128 408 318 292 337 34 252 154
Dundee	67 129 375 269 549 459 433 478 175 394 79 63
Edinburgh	130 81 301 195 475 385 358 403 100 319 83 79 46
Glasgow	150 35 300 194 474 384 358 403 100 318 247 134 156 172
Inverness	107 207 468 362 642 552 526 571 268 487 330 231 254 423 190
Ipswich	553 404 163 274 123 230 137 54 237 312 262 141 261 200 131 61
Kingston upon Hull	397 247 139 144 250 230 137 249 155 188 141 157 223 183 76 96 101
Leeds	366 216 119 88 262 210 147 229 124 157 99 99 216 126 75 130 107 219
Leicester	470 320 43 157 165 121 74 149 228 24 148 89 261 99 66 131 41 202 109
Liverpool	368 219 103 56 277 187 208 121 100 127 253 188 159 246 276 135 130 72 41 139
London	558 409 122 246 53 121 55 189 317 76 91 95 188 170 276 161 132 109 161 120 202
Manchester	363 214 86 51 260 170 163 205 59 100 74 74 95 117 235 130 72 26 74 41 94 189
Middlesbrough	331 182 177 123 319 267 200 286 90 178 146 74 157 168 170 235 135 168 266 365 289 141
Newcastle	235 150 206 150 349 297 230 316 59 208 157 43 91 141 223 289 92 168 179 118 93 223 116 123
Norwich	527 377 161 248 170 225 61 149 285 59 355 187 283 361 381 460 460 148 324 428 130 355 326 485 120
Nottingham	432 282 50 143 193 149 88 166 190 52 138 59 91 105 174 187 59 170 59 170 153 190 224 258 59 98
Oban	180 127 400 294 574 484 458 503 200 419 535 345 324 325 321 302 170 235 302 236 285 224 289 254 285 192 390
Oxford	509 360 69 197 105 73 107 73 268 54 667 255 324 267 265 248 182 141 170 236 242 105 256 254 264 194 98 467
Plymouth	641 492 206 329 222 287 48 222 412 161 460 324 325 171 80 78 85 161 302 385 365 44 382 412 346 599 264 562 237
Portsmouth	604 455 148 292 48 100 133 100 346 107 187 157 321 267 265 248 137 64 244 354 350 41 412 346 346 192 199 194 21 233
Sheffield	418 268 232 105 363 232 143 363 192 211 59 175 302 171 80 105 41 87 166 190 188 105 105 149 149 44 208 85 187 161
Southampton	583 434 127 271 61 79 118 79 434 67 170 251 263 166 244 80 227 320 350 350 194 177 52 53 225 161 225 137 21 64 53 208
Stoke on Trent	397 248 46 85 220 130 133 220 127 85 59 186 95 59 58 41 162 190 177 179 50 215 191 192 342 179 143 113 245 208 179 50 187
Swansea	542 392 136 227 227 82 136 40 300 149 132 275 184 187 215 275 191 312 215 312 275 342 312 295 295 192 342 143 197 225 158 342 158 295
Wick	233 333 594 488 652 697 613 768 394 678 260 282 705 515 549 126 483 520 710 705 584 549 515 483 679 584 679 679 756 793 570 483 735 679 570

442 Miles

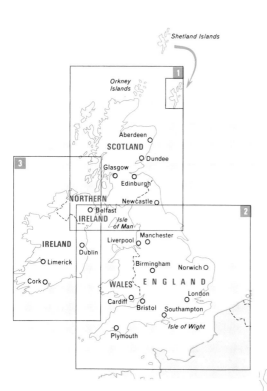

MAJOR ROADS AND PRINCIPAL SHIPPING ROUTES		**PRINCIPALES ROUTES ET LIAISONS MARITIMES**	
Motorway	═╪═	Autoroute	═╪═
Road number	A 4.T 35. N 2	N° de route	A 4.T 35. N 2
Mileage	20	Distance en miles	20

PRINCIPALI STRADE E ITINERARI MARITTIMI		**HAUPTVERKEHRSSTRASSEN UND SCHIFFSVERBINDUNGEN**	
Autostrada	═╪═	Autobahn	═╪═
Numero di strada	A 4.T 35. N 2	Straßennummer	A 4.T 35. N 2
Distanza in miglia	20	Entfernung in Meilen	20

GREAT BRITAIN : the maps and town plans in the Great Britain Section of this Guide are based upon the Ordnance Survey of Great Britain with the permission of the Controller of Her Majesty's Stationery Office, Crown Copyright reserved.

NORTHERN IRELAND : the maps and town plans in the Northern Ireland Section of this Guide are based upon the Ordnance Survey of Northern Ireland with the sanction of the Controller of H.M. Stationery Office, Permit number 616.

REPUBLIC OF IRELAND : the maps and town plans in the Republic of Ireland Section of this Guide are based upon the Ordnance Survey of Ireland by permission of the Government of the Republic, Permit number 5808.

736

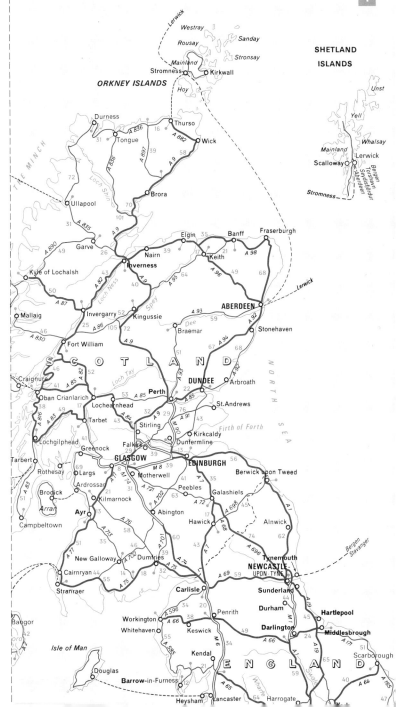

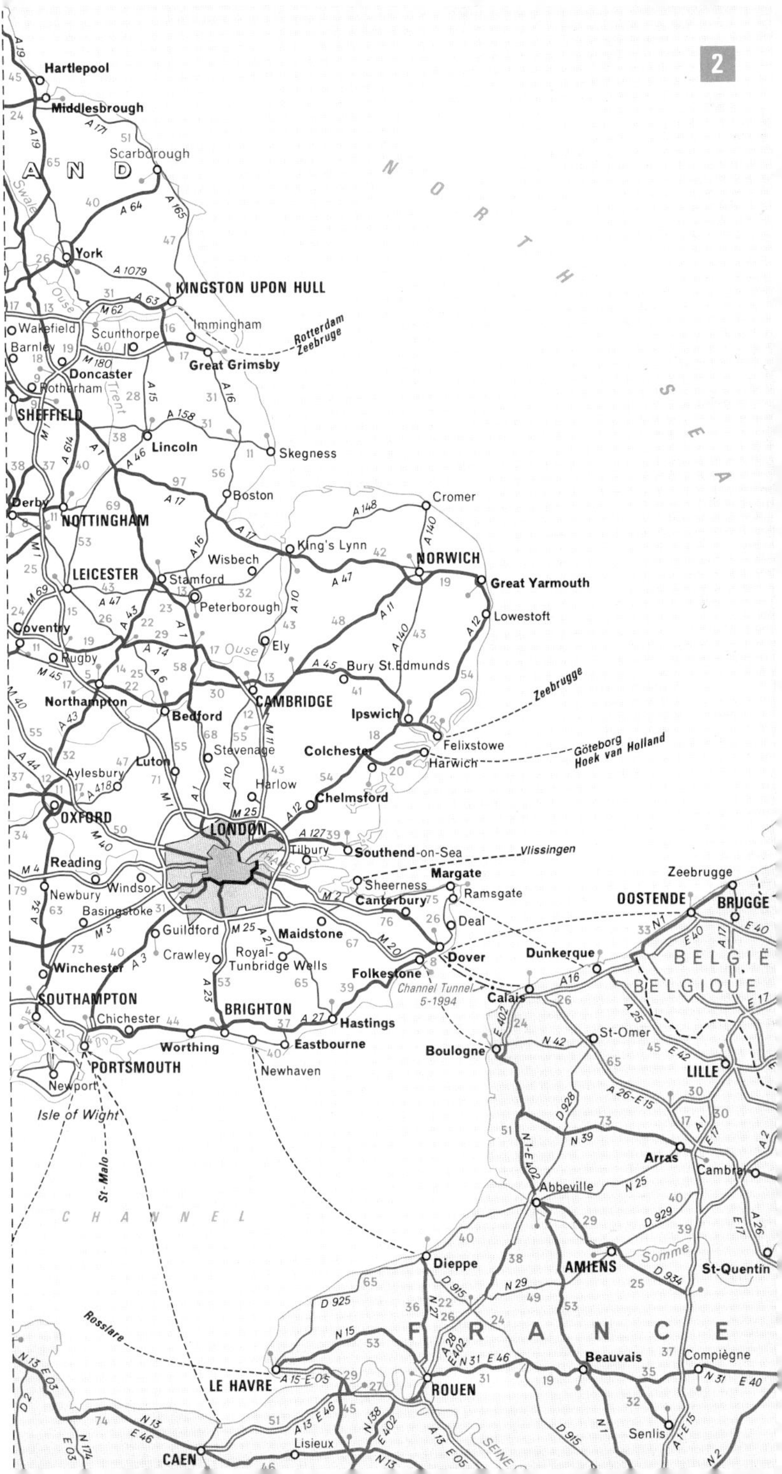

Hartlepool

Middlesbrough

Scarborough

A N D

York

KINGSTON UPON HULL

Wakefield
Barnley
Scunthorpe
Immingham
Rotterdam-Zeebrugge

Doncaster
Great Grimsby

Rotherham

SHEFFIELD

Lincoln

Skegness

Boston

Cromer

Derby

NOTTINGHAM

King's Lynn

NORWICH

Wisbech

Great Yarmouth

LEICESTER
Stamford
Peterborough
Lowestoft

Coventry

Rugby
Ely

Northampton
Bury St.Edmunds

Zeebrugge

CAMBRIDGE
Ipswich

Bedford
Felixstowe

Göteborg
Hoek van Holland

Stevenage
Colchester
Harwich

Luton
Harlow

Aylesbury

Chelmsford

OXFORD
LONDON

Reading

Southend-on-Sea

Newbury
Windsor
Tilbury

Vlissingen

Basingstoke
Sheerness
Margate

Zeebrugge

Guildford
Canterbury
Ramsgate

OOSTENDE
BRUGGE

Maidstone
Deal

Winchester
Crawley
Royal-Tunbridge Wells

Dover
Dunkerque

BELGIË

SOUTHAMPTON

Folkestone

BELGIQUE

Chichester
BRIGHTON
Hastings

Channel Tunnel
5-1994
Calais

St-Omer

Worthing
Eastbourne

Boulogne

LILLE

PORTSMOUTH
Newhaven

Newport

Isle of Wight

Arras
Cambrai

St-Malo

Abbeville

C H A N N E L

D 929

Dieppe

AMIENS
St-Quentin

Somme

Rosslare

D 925

N 15

F R A N C E

Beauvais
Compiègne

LE HAVRE
ROUEN

CAEN
Lisieux

SEINE

Senlis

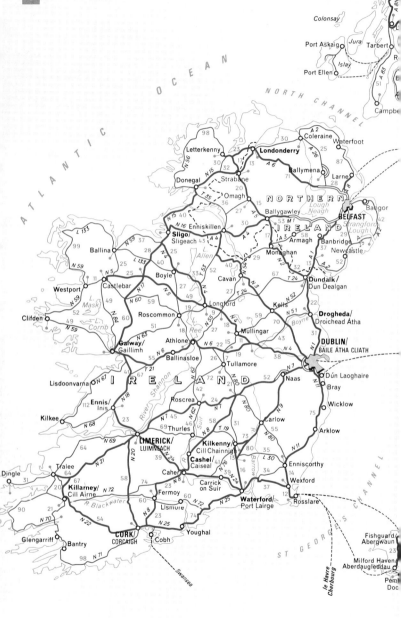

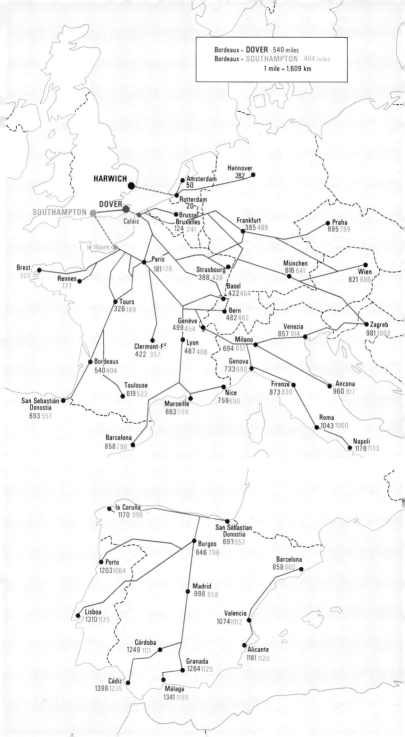

Bordeaux – **DOVER** : 540 miles
Bordeaux – SOUTHAMPTON : 404 miles
1 mile = 1,609 km

Hannover 282
Amsterdam 50
HARWICH
Rotterdam 20
DOVER
SOUTHAMPTON
Calais
Brussel
Bruxelles 124 241
Frankfurt 385 489
Praha 695 769
le Havre
Paris 181 126
Strasbourg 388 428
München 616 641
Wien 821 886
Brest 300
Rennes 177
Basel 422 464
Tours 326 189
Bern 482 462
Genève 499 454
Venezia 857 814
Zagreb 981 1002
Clermont-F.d 422 357
Lyon 467 406
Milano 694 651
Bordeaux 540 404
Genova 733 690
Firenze 873 830
Ancona 960 917
San Sebastián Donostia 693 557
Toulouse 619 522
Nice 759 698
Marseille 663 599
Roma 1043 1000
Barcelona 858 798
Napoli 1176 1133

la Coruña 1170 998
San Sebastián Donostia 693 557
Burgos 846 708
Barcelona 858 802
Porto 1203 1064
Madrid 998 858
Valencia 1074 1012
Lisboa 1310 1175
Córdoba 1249 1111
Alicante 1181 1120
Granada 1264 1125
Cádiz 1398 1235
Málaga 1341 1199

Car manufacturers' addresses

Adresses des marques automobiles
Indirizzi delle marche automobilistiche
Adressen der Automobilfirmen

Alfa Romeo (GB) Ltd
266 Bath Road, Slough, Berks, SLI 4HJ
Tel.: (0753) 690693

Aston Martin Lagonda Ltd
Tickford Street   Newport Pagnell
Bucks MK16 9AN
Tel.: (0908) 610620

BMW (GB) Ltd
Ellesfield Avenue   Bracknell
Berks RG12 8TA   Tel. (0344) 426565

Citroën UK Ltd
221 Bath Road   Slough   Berks
SL1 4BA   Tel. (0753) 812100

Colt Mitsubishi
Colt Car Co. Ltd   Watermore
Cirencester   Glos GL7 1LS
Tel.: (0285) 655777

Fiat Auto (UK) Ltd
Fiat House   266 Bath Road   Slough
Berks SL1 4HJ   Tel.: (0753) 511431

Ford Motor Company Ltd
Eagle Way   Brentwood   Essex CM13
3BW   Tel.: (0277) 253000

FSO Cars Ltd
77 Mount Ephraim   Tunbridge Wells
TN4 8BS   Tel.: (0892) 511811

Honda (UK) Ltd
Power Road   Chiswick   London W4
5YT   Tel.: 081-747 1400

Hyundai Car Distributors (UK) Ltd
Ryder Street   West Bromwich
West Midlands B70 OEJ
Tel.: 021-522 2000

Isuzu (UK) Ltd
Ryder Street   West Bromwich
West Midlands B70 OEJ
Tel.: 021-522 2000

Jaguar Cars Ltd
Browns Lane
Allesley   Coventry
West Midlands CV5 9DR
Tel.: (0203) 402121

Lada Cars
Western House   Middle Lane   Wythall
Birmingham   West Midlands B47 6LA
Tel.: (0564) 824171

Lancia UK Concessionaries
266 Bath Road   Slough   Berks
SL1 4HJ   Tel.: (0753) 690690

Land Rover Ltd
Lode Lane   Solihull   West Midlands
B92 8NW   Tel.: 021-722 2424

Leyland Daf Vans Ltd
Common Lane   Washwood Heath
Birmingham B8 2UP
Tel.: 021-322 2000

Lotus Group
Potash Lane
Hethel   Norwich   Norfolk NR14 8EZ
Tel.: (0953) 608000

Mazda Cars (UK) Ltd
77 Mount Ephraim   Tunbridge Wells
Kent TN4 8BS   Tel.: (0892) 511877

Mercedes Benz (UK) Ltd
Delaware Drive   Tongwell
Milton Keynes MK15 8BA
Tel.: (0908) 668899

Nissan (UK) Ltd
Nissan House   Columbia Drive Worthing
West Sussex BN13 3HD
Tel.: (0903) 268561

Peugeot Talbot
Motor Compagny Ltd   Aldermoor
House   PO Box 227   Aldermoor Lane
Coventry
West Midlands CV3 1LT
Tel.: (0203) 884000

Porsche Cars (GB) Ltd
Bath Road   Calcot, Reading   Berks
RG3 7SE   Tel.: (0734) 303666

Proton Cars (UK) Ltd
Pronton House
Royal Portsbury Dock
Bristol B520 ONH
Tel.: (0275) 375475

Renault (UK) Ltd
Western Avenue   London W3 ORZ
Tel.: 081-992 3481

Rolls-Royce Motors Cars Ltd
Pyms Lane   Crewe   Cheshire CW1
3PL
Tel.: (0270) 255155

Rover Group Ltd
Canley Road   Coventry   West Mid-
lands CV5 6QX
Tel.: (0203) 670111

Saab (GB) Ltd
Saab House   Globe Park   Marlow
Bucks SL7 1LY   Tel.: (0628) 486977

Seat Concessionaries (UK) Ltd
Seat House   Gatwick Road
Crawley West Sussex   RH10 2AX
Tel.: (0293) 514141

Skoda (GB) Ltd
Garamonde Drive   Great Monks Street
Wimbush   Milton Keynes MK8 8NZ
Tel.: (0908) 264000

Subaru (UK) Ltd
Ryder Street   West Bromwich
West Midlands   B70 OEJ
Tel.: 021-522 2000

Heron-Suzuki GB Cars
46-62 Gatwick Road   Crawley   West
Sussex   RH10 2XF
Tel.: (0293) 518000

Toyota (GB) Ltd
The Quadrangle Station Road   Redhill
Surrey RH1 1PX
Tel.: (0737) 768585

V.A.G. (UK) Ltd
Yeomans Drive   Blakelands   Milton
Keynes   MK14 5AN
Tel.: (0908) 679121

Vauxhall Motors Ltd
Griffin House   Osborne Road
Luton   Beds LU1 3YT
Tel.: (0582) 21122

Volvo Concessionaries Ltd
Globe Park   Marlow   Bucks
SL7 1YQ
Tel.: (0628) 477977

Yugo Cars
Worcester House   Basingstoke Road
Reading
Berks   RG2 0QB
Tel.: (0734) 866921

European dialling codes
Indicatifs téléphoniques européens
Indicativi telefonici dei paesi europei
Telefon-Vorwahlnummern europäischer Länder

	from / de / dal / von	to / en / in / nach	from / de / dal / von	to / en / in / nach
AND	Andorra ——— 1944 ———	**Great Britain**	—— 01033 ———	Andorra
A	Austria ——— 0044 ———	»	—— 01043 ———	Austria
B	Belgium ——— 0044 ———	»	—— 01032 ———	Belgium
BG	Bulgaria ——— 0044 ———	»	— 010359 ———	Bulgaria
CZ	Czech Republic — 0044 ———	»	—— 01042 ———	Czech Republic
DK	Denmark ——— 00944 ———	»	—— 01045 ———	Denmark
FIN	Finland ——— 99044 ———	»	— 010358 ———	Finland
F	France ——— 1944 ———	»	—— 01033 ———	France
D	Germany ——— 0044 ———	»	—— 01049 ———	Germany
GR	Greece ——— 0044 ———	»	—— 01030 ———	Greece
H	Hungary ——— 0044 ———	»	—— 01036 ———	Hungary
I	Italy ——— 0044 ———	»	—— 01039 ———	Italy
FL	Liechtenstein —— 0044 ———	»	—— 01041 ———	Liechtenstein
L	Luxembourg —— 0044 ———	»	— 010352 ———	Luxembourg
M	Malta ——— 0044 ———	»	— 010356 ———	Malta
MC	Monaco ——— 1944 ———	»	– 0103393 ———	Monaco
NL	Netherlands ——— 0944 ———	»	—— 01031 ———	Netherlands
N	Norway ——— 09544 ———	»	—— 01047 ———	Norway
PL	Poland ——— 0044 ———	»	—— 01048 ———	Poland
P	Portugal ——— 0044 ———	»	— 010351 ———	Portugal
IRL	Rep. of Ireland — 0044 ———	»	— 010353 ———	Rep. of Ireland
RO	Romania ——— – ———	»	—— 01040 ———	Romania
SK	Slovak Republic — 0044 ———	»	—— 01042 ———	Slovak Republic
E	Spain ——— 0744 ———	»	—— 01034 ———	Spain
S	Sweden ——— 00944 ———	»	—— 01046 ———	Sweden
CH	Switzerland ——— 0044 ———	»	—— 01041 ———	Switzerland

	from / de / dal / von	to / en / in / nach	from / de / dal / von	to / en / in / nach
AND	Andorra ——— 19353 ———	**Rep. of Ireland**	—— 0033 ———	Andorra
A	Austria ——— 00353 ———	»	—— 0043 ———	Austria
B	Belgium ——— 00353 ———	»	—— 0032 ———	Belgium
BG	Bulgaria ——— 00353 ———	»	—— 00359 ———	Bulgaria
CZ	Czech Republic – 00353 ———	»	—— 0042 ———	Czech Republic
DK	Denmark ——— 009353 ———	»	—— 0045 ———	Denmark
FIN	Finland ——— 990353 ———	»	—— 00358 ———	Finland
F	France ——— 19353 ———	»	—— 0033 ———	France
D	Germany ——— 00353 —	»	—— 0049 ———	Germany
GB	Great Britain — 010353 ———	»	—— 0044 ———	Great Britain
GR	Greece ——— 00353 ———	»	—— 0030 ———	Greece
H	Hungary ——— 00353 ———	»	—— 0036 ———	Hungary
I	Italy ——— 00353 ———	»	—— 0039 ———	Italy
FL	Liechtenstein — 00353 ———	»	—— 0041 ———	Liechtenstein
L	Luxembourg —— 00353 ———	»	—— 00352 ———	Luxembourg
M	Malta ——— 00353 ———	»	—— 00356 ———	Malta
MC	Monaco ——— 19353 ———	»	—— 0033 ———	Monaco
NL	Netherlands —— 09353 ———	»	—— 0031 ———	Netherlands
N	Norway ——— 095353 ———	»	—— 0047 ———	Norway
PL	Poland ——— 00353 ———	»	—— 0048 ———	Poland
P	Portugal ——— 00353 ———	»	—— 00351 ———	Portugal
RO	Romania ——— – ———	»	—— 0040 ———	Romania
SK	Slovak Republic - 00353 ———	»	—— 0042 ———	Slovak Republic
E	Spain ——— 07353 ———	»	—— 0034 ———	Spain
S	Sweden ——— 009353 ———	»	—— 0046 ———	Sweden
CH	Switzerland —— 00353 ———	»	—— 0041 ———	Switzerland